Goldmine

PRICE GUIDE
TO
45 RPM
RECORDS

Edited by
Tim Neely

© 1996 by
Krause Publications, Inc.

Published by

**krause
publications**

700 E. State Street • Iola, WI 54990-0001
Telephone: 715/445-2214

Please call or write for our free catalog of music publications. Our toll-free number
to place an order or obtain a free catalog is 800-258-0929 or please use our
regular business telephone 715-445-2214 for editorial comment and further information.

Library of Congress Catalog Number: 96-76685
ISBN: 0-87341-471-3
Printed in the United States of America

Table of Contents

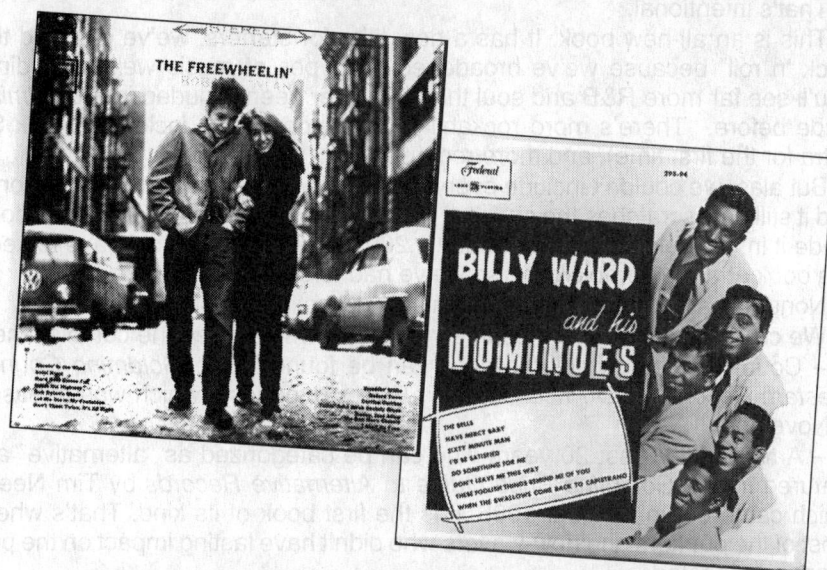

Introduction: A New Beginning

If you're a regular reader, buyer or user of the old *Goldmine Rock 'n Roll 45 RPM Price Guide*, you'll notice that this isn't the same.

That's intentional.

This is an all-new book. It has a new title, for starters; we've dropped the "rock 'n roll" because we've broadened the types of music we're including. You'll see far more R&B and soul than has ever been included in a *Goldmine* guide before. There's more rockabilly, more pop (we've included Frank Sinatra for the first time), and more recent artists.

But alas, we couldn't include everybody. This book is over 800 pages long, and it still only scratches the surface. Had everything we compiled for this book made it in, it would have been nearly 1,200 pages long! We did have to keep this book at a reasonable cost, so we've had to do a lot of paring.

Nonetheless, almost all the most highly collectible artists are inside.

We can suggest a couple sources for artists who missed the cut this time:

– Country artists not in this book can be found in the *Goldmine Country Western Record & CD Price Guide* by Fred Heggeness, which was released in November 1996.

– Artists of the past 20 years who can be categorized as "alternative" are featured in the *Goldmine Price Guide to Alternative Records* by Tim Neely, which came out in October 1996. It is the first book of its kind. That's where most of the punkers and new-wavers who didn't have lasting impact on the pop charts are located.

Otherwise, hang in there. The second edition will probably be larger, so if someone's missing this time, we probably can rectify that in the future.

So What's New?

If, as I usually do when I come upon a price guide, you've scanned the pages looking for artists and records that you know you have, you'll notice that this book's format is different than any of our prior price guides.

For starters, did you notice those cool little boxes at the beginning of each line? Yes, you can use your *Goldmine Price Guide to 45 RPM Records* as a checklist. You can keep track of what you have and don't have right here in this book.

Other than that, here's how we feel the book is an improvement.

– Within each artist, we've listed their records alphabetically by record label, and then numerically within the record label, rather than chronologically. As most records released in the United States before 1972 are not dated, you won't have to guess when a record came out to find it in the list.

In doing this, we tried to think like a beginning collector. For example, Lou Christie recorded for over a dozen different labels. Listing them alphabetically should make it easier to find the records you have, because you don't have to know if it was an early, mid-career or late-career item to find it.

For example, in the Beatles' listing, their Apple 45s are listed first, followed by Atco and Atlantic and continuing alphabetically until you get to Vee Jay. They also are listed numerically, so, under Capitol, the 2000 series is listed before the 5000 series even though the 2000 series came out after the 5000 series. At first it may seem confusing, but we think you'll get used to it.

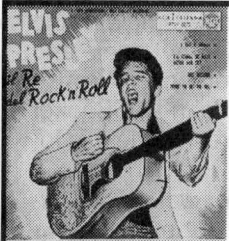

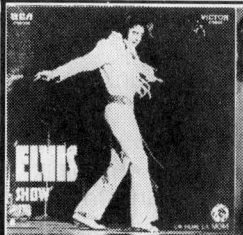

– We also have, in many cases, listed all the records by a collectible artist together, even if they recorded under other names as well. For example, in the Paul Simon section, you'll find his records as True Taylor, Jerry Landis and Paul Kane. Each of those pseudonyms, however, is cross-referenced. We also have The Wonder Who listed under the Four Seasons, and John Lee Booker and John Lee Cooker listed under John Lee Hooker. We haven't done this for all artists yet, but we're working on it.

– Also, when one or more groups share the same name, we haven't attempted to figure out which is which. A couple times, we did; for example, we separated the Motown Supremes from the other Supremes and did the same with the Temptations. It seems to us that it would be easier to find a record listed if there is only one heading for a particular group name, rather than trying to go through five or six different listings of The Chosen Few or The Dynamics to find the record you're looking for.

When we know or suspect that more than one group is contained in a listing, we'll usually say so in parentheses right below the group name.

– We've broken down extended play records into two listings, one for the record and one for the cover.

While most collectors treat EPs like LPs, most consumers of the 1950s and 1960s treated them like 45s. In other words, they kept the records and tossed the sleeves. Listing them as one item implied to me that an EP had little value without its jacket. But that is wrong. Certainly, most EPs are rare with or without a jacket. It's about time we list them the same way we list other 7-inch records: separate values for record and sleeve.

Alas, because of time constraints, most EP listings are absent from this book. They will be back, we promise. See "How You Can Help" for how you can help (duh).

– We list values of records in three grades: Very Good, Very Good Plus (which some dealers and collectors call Excellent), and Near Mint.

Demand for Mint and Near Mint records continues to increase as the supply dries up. But some collectors who want to play their records without guilt will be happy with a VG+ record or even a VG record. And in cases of certain rare items, a Near Mint copy may not even be known to exist.

One important thing we've found is that the difference in value between Very Good, the lowest grade we list, and Near Mint, the highest grade we list, isn't as great as other price guides have implied. We've found that in general, a VG+ record brings about half a NM record, and a VG record brings about half a VG+ record. For more valuable records, the percentage difference is less, as some records are almost impossible to find in *any* condition! Perhaps in the future, the difference between VG and NM will be 1:5, and some dealers who sell a lot of near-mint stuff may already see that, but in general, 1:4 is closer to reality right now. (When I started collecting, it was more like 1:2 or 1:3, so the gap is widening.)

– We've been able to document many items previously listed as unknown, and we've made some new discoveries as well.

Just before we went to press, a reader in California faxed us a copy he made of his *stock copy* of the legendary "Go Go G.T.O" by Carol & Cheryl on Colpix 767. Surf-music collectors had never seen this before; we're hoping that for the second edition of this book we can get a clean photograph of this record.

A few more items we've listed in here, as we've confirmed their existence:

– Two different label variations of Singular 711, "At the Hop"/ "Sometimes" by Danny and the Juniors, both of which are legitimate pressings.

– Stock copies of "Franklin's Tower" by the Grateful Dead and "Too Tough"/ "Miss You" by the Rolling Stones. When these were listed in the past as "unreleased" with a question mark on stock copies, it caught me by surprise, as I've had them for many years.

– Numerous records by collectible artists in the 1990s. We continue to keep a close watch on the new 45s that hit the market. In 1995 and 1996 alone, new titles by such artists as the Beach Boys, the Beatles, Neil Diamond, Elton John and Elvis Presley have been released here in America. If a 1990s record is listed in this book, you can be assured that it does exist, unless "Unreleased" is mentioned alongside of it.

And going the other direction: We've also noted when early records by collectible artists were only released on 78s at or near the time of their original issue. While we can't be certain that other 45s don't exist by artists such as Fats Domino and the Orioles, we've only listed those that are known to be out there.

Among the relatively obscure information that won't be so obscure anymore: The famous Elvis Presley "horizontal line" 45s from 1955-57 are actually *later pressings* than those that don't have the line! As a result, the values of the different pressings have equalized over the past couple years among Elvis people in the know.

So What's Happening?

The only trend that seems to be true is that nothing is true universally.

While some dealers note ever-increasing sales and demand for 45s, others can't get rid of their stocks. While some see the demand for records of the 1950s and 1960s slacking off, others say it's as strong as ever, especially in top-notch condition.

Among those who are selling 45s, it seems as if the values of the rarest items continue to increase. You'll see elsewhere that over 250 different 45s, should they ever become available, would fetch at least $1,000 in Near Mint condition! Some of these have just cracked the four-figure mark within the last several months.

The lower-tier 45s, especially 1970s and early 1980s soul music, have been inching up. Records that used to be lucky to fetch a buck are sometimes selling for $4-$5.

Original labels of national hits remain strong. For example, a copy of "Wipe Out" by the Surfaris on the DFS label, its first edition, recently sold for $1,375 in only Very Good Minus condition! It is now the most valuable surf-related record in the world.

And the demand for the hits remains strong as well. For most artists who had relatively short careers, it's the one or two hits, rather than the obscure followups or predecessors, that have the highest market price.

At first this might not make sense; after all, there's more copies of the hit out there, right? True. But fewer of them survive in even Very Good condition, much less Near Mint, than the average non-hit. And many more people are looking for them.

It is our feeling that 45s will remain an avidly collected form of music. And the trends suggest that the big-ticket items will remain that way.

Pricing Questions

We hope some of your questions already have been answered. We'd like to take on a couple more, because they've cropped up frequently.

Hey, wait a minute! I have some of these records, but when I try to sell them, they insult my intelligence. They only want to give me pennies on the dollar! What gives?

The prices in here are what these records are sold for at retail. Dealers, in order to remain dealers, have to make a profit, so they won't buy at these prices unless they need something for their own collections.

When it comes to selling your records to a dealer, at most you'll get 50 percent of book value, and more likely you'll get about 25 percent (what we list in here as the Very Good value) for a Near Mint record. If that sounds like a ripoff, well, consider the costs a dealer has to cover through sales: Rent, employees, shipping, postage, utilities, phone service (business lines cost more than residential lines), taxes, and many other sundry items, not to mention the costs of maintaining and obtaining inventory. With all that, you can see why a dealer can't buy at the same prices he or she sells!

To get prices close to what this book suggests, the best way is to sell directly to the consumer -- in essence, to become a dealer yourself, albeit temporarily. (Many dealers became dealers by starting with their own collections and finding they enjoyed the selling.)

The best way is to place an advertisement in *Goldmine* magazine. *Goldmine,* published every other week, is the world's largest marketplace for collectible music of all eras. The magazine has advertising salespeople who will help you in putting together your ad for maximum impact.

To see what *Goldmine* is about, pick up a copy. *Goldmine* magazine is available at Tower Records, Blockbuster Music and a couple other major music chains; Barnes & Noble, Borders and other larger booksellers; and many independent music shops. If you still can't find a copy, call 1-800-258-0929.

Hey, wait a minute! I'm a dealer, and I can't sell my records at these prices. If I try, they just sit until I reduce them. What gives?

Basically, how much you get for a record depends on what kind of a dealer you are.

In general, the highest prices for records are obtained by those dealers who sell mostly or entirely through mail-order to a targeted audience. These are people who sell items through auctions in *Goldmine* and sometimes through their own private auction lists. They cater to record collectors, often those from abroad (who, like it or not, often set the prices on rare items because they have to have something more than an American does). They have built reputations for sterling customer service, and their clientele is willing to pay more for the knowledge that they, indeed, are getting what they bought. They will usually get something approaching the prices in this book, and often they can get more.

But most dealers don't fit in that category.

Anyone who sells records in a store or a stand, by definition, has a larger market than a mail-order dealer (an area's entire population that might want to buy music), but a less targeted one. Therefore, it's going to be difficult for Joe's Collectible Records in Appleton, Wisconsin (a hypothetical example – there is no such store) to get the same for a record as, say, John Tefteller or Christo-

pher Chatman or Gary Hein (none of whom are hypothetical) will. The average customer at our fictional Joe's will have little or no knowledge of what collectible records sell for from an educated dealer to an educated consumer.

That's why we have price guides: to help educate average people about what their records may sell for. And after all, that's all it is: a guide. You may know from your own experience that you can't sell at these prices; adjust accordingly. You also may know that some of these prices are too low (it does happen); you know your market as well as anyone.

Finally, to anyone selling records, whether to a dealer or as a dealer: Don't overgrade! Overgrading gives the entire hobby a black mark. Trying to sell VG records at NM prices is one of our biggest problems. Admittedly, grading can be an imperfect science, but sometimes it's very obvious that someone has just put the highest price on something without being objective about the well-worn condition of the records.

A Grading Primer

The most important thing to remember is this:

Condition is (almost) everything!

That is the maxim to remember when buying (and selling) 45s. If an item is unusually rare or desirable, it may be acceptable in any condition, as you might never see it again. But even with those items with a three- and four-figure value, the better condition a record (or sleeve), the more money it will fetch.

The grading system established by *Goldmine* magazine many years ago, with the occasional refinement, has become the most widely accepted in record collecting.

Visual or Play Grading? In an ideal world, every record would be played before it is graded. But the time involved makes it impractical for most dealers, and anyway, it's rare that you get a chance to hear a record before you buy through the mail. Some advertisers play-grade everything and say so. But unless otherwise noted, records are visually graded.

How to Grade

Look at everything about a record -- its playing surface, its label, its edges -- under a strong light. Then, based on your overall impression, give it a grade based on the following criteria:

Mint (M): Absolutely perfect in every way -- certainly never played. Should be used sparingly as a grade, if at all.

Near Mint (NM or M-): A nearly perfect record. Many dealers won't give a grade higher than this, implying (perhaps correctly) that no record is ever truly perfect.

The record should show no obvious signs of wear. A 45 RPM or EP sleeve should have no more than the most minor defects, such as almost invisible ring wear or other signs of slight handling.

Near Mint is the highest price listed in this price guide. Anything that exceeds this, in the opinion of both buyer and seller, is worth significantly more than the highest value in here.

Very Good Plus (VG+): Generally worth 50 percent of the Near Mint value.

A Very Good Plus record will show some signs that it was played and otherwise handled by a previous owner who took good care of it.

Record surfaces may show some slight signs of wear and may have slight scuffs or very light scratches that don't affect one's listening experience. Slight warps that do not affect the sound are OK.

The label may have some ring wear or discoloration, but it should be barely noticeable. The center hole will not have been misshapen by repeated play.

Picture sleeves will have some slight ring wear, lightly turned-up corners, or a slight seam split.

In general, if not for a couple minor things wrong with it, this would be Near Mint. All but the most mint-crazy collectors will find a Very Good Plus record highly acceptable.

Very Good (VG): Generally worth 25 percent of the Near Mint value.

Many of the defects found in a VG+ record will be more pronounced in a VG disc.

Surface noise will be evident upon playing, especially in soft passages and during a song's intro and fade, but will not overpower the music otherwise. Groove wear will start to be noticeable, as will light scratches (deep enough to feel with a fingernail) that will affect the sound.

Labels may be marred by writing, or have tape or stickers (or their residue) attached. The same will be true of picture sleeves. However, it will not have all of these problems at the same time, only two or three of them.

Very Good is the lowest value we list in here. This, *not* the Near Mint price, should be your guide when determining how much a record is worth, as a dealer will rarely pay you more than 25 percent of its Near Mint value. (He/she has to make a profit, after all.)

Good (G), Good Plus (G+): Generally worth 10-15 percent of the Near Mint value.

Good does not mean Bad! A record in Good or Good Plus condition can be put onto a turntable and will play through without skipping. But it will have significant surface noise and scratches and visible groove wear (on a styrene record, the groove will be starting to turn white).

A sleeve will have seam splits, especially at the bottom or on the spine. Tape, writing, ring wear or other defects will start to overwhelm the object.

If it's a common item, you'll probably find another copy in better shape eventually. Pass it up. But if it's something you have been seeking for years, and the price is right, get it...and keep looking to upgrade.

Poor (P), Fair (F): Generally worth 0-5 percent of the Near Mint price.

The record is cracked, badly warped, and won't play through without skipping or repeating. The picture sleeve is water damaged, split on all three seams and heavily marred by wear and/or writing.

Except for impossibly rare records otherwise unattainable, records in this condition should be bought or sold for no more than a few cents each.

Making Sense of This Book

We've told you about most of the new features in the book. Let's break down a listing to see what a line means.

The artist's name is in bold. They are mostly alphabetized the way our computer did, so blame any things that seem out of order on it. I think we caught most of the way-out things, but if not, let us know and we'll get 'em the next time.

Underneath some artists in parentheses are cross-references or other information we feel is helpful.

Then we have grouped the discographies by record label. Under each record label are individual listings in numerical order, ignoring prefixes. The primary exception is the RCA Victor label (1949-76). We list that in order of numerical prefixes, then list the APBO series numerically, then the PB/GB series numerically (ignoring the letters).

Each line starts with a check box, which you can use to keep track of what you have. Then comes the record number. You'll also find both sides of each record listed (using chart data to try to list the A-side first), separated by a slash (or a double slash in some cases); the year of release; and the value in Very Good, Very Good-Plus and Near Mint condition.

For many listings, you'll see a letter or two before the two sides of the record. These designate something special about the listing as follows:

DJ: some sort of promotional copy, usually for radio stations, and not meant for public sale

M: mono record (for late-1950s and early-1960s records that came out in both mono and stereo)

PS: picture sleeve (this is the value for the sleeve *alone*; combine the record and sleeve value to get an estimated worth for the two together)

S: stereo record (again, when the record was pressed both in mono and stereo)

(x) where x is a number: the number of records in a set

In some cases, the VG and/or the VG+ columns are blank. That indicates that the item in question goes for under $2 in that condition. All items should have at least a Near Mint value. For those that are blank, an explanation usually follows.

Finally, some items have lines in italics following them. That defines something about the item listed above, such as who also is on the record, or a color of label or vinyl.

In a few instances, a line of italics appears above an item. That is usually a more general note about a larger group of the records appearing below it. For example, we've designated where "The Supremes" ends and "Diana Ross and the Supremes" starts, and then when "The Supremes" resumes.

Acknowledgments

This book would not have been possible without the help of a lot of people.

Most of the help with listings is in a mass of papers that would take far too long to plow through. So if I don't mention you, and you know you played a role in making this book a better product, pat yourself on the back.

Thanks to Eric Schneider, Mike Tiefenbacher, Ted Rayfer, Dave Nowlen, Sal Cuomo, Rocky Kruegel and many dealers at record shows in Austin, Texas, King of Prussia, Pennsylvania, and Milwaukee, Wisconsin for verifying the existence of some items we've never listed before. For example, dealers showed me the Del-Vikings picture sleeve on Alpine and the Phil Spector "Thank You For Giving Me the Right Time!" promo 45, not to mention the Roger Daltrey promo with his first name misspelled "Rodger."

Thanks also to Sharon Fong at Good Rockin' Tonight in Newport Beach, California. Many of the illustrations of rare items in this book came from her. Thanks also to David Hall and Gordon Wrubel at GRT. For more information on their bi-monthly auctions of "rare and important" records, call 1-800-531-1899.

A sincere debt of appreciation goes out to all the people here at Krause Publications who encouraged, cajoled and were persistent with me. Thanks first to Greg Loescher, publisher of *Goldmine*, who gave the green light to the project; Pat Klug, head of the books department, for encouragement and flexibility; and all the other people in the books department who kept an eye on what was happening. Thanks also to Michael Metzger, new editor of *Goldmine*, for his patience and understanding.

Big thanks go out to the KP proofreading department, who managed to get through the entire book in record time so it could be finished on time. Also, my appreciation to the KP art department for last-minute changes on the cover design, and to Bonnie Tetzlaff and Patsy Morrison in book production for making this look as good as it does. Finally, thanks to Maggie Thompson, editor of *Comics Buyer's Guide*, for her constant interest and even a little bit of help with the final project.

Thanks, as always, to my parents and my sisters for putting up with my inaccessibility during the final few weeks of compiling.

I also wish to thank Hurricane Fran, which belted the North Carolina coast hard enough for me to cancel a planned September 1996 vacation. Without her, this would not have been done on time.

Last but far from least, I want to thank the Spirit Fire young adult group at Nativity Parish in Green Bay, Wisconsin, who have made me feel very welcome and encouraged. During the most trying times of this book, when I wished it could be done but it wasn't, I got inspiration from Matthew 17:20 – "...If you have faith as small as a mustard seed . . . Nothing will be impossible for you." And indeed, the impossible has happened – the book is done! (Insert audible sigh of relief.) Thank you, God, for leading me.

Tim Neely
Iola, Wisconsin
November 22, 1996

The $1,000 Club

In compiling this book, we couldn't help notice that the number of truly valuable records has increased substantially over the years.

Twenty years ago, no more than about five 45s could have brought $1,000 in near-mint condition from a knowledgeable collector. And one of those was mythical – the legendary "Stormy Weather" by the Five Sharps on Jubilee 5104, which is only known to exist legitimately on 78s.

In this book, we've found 271 different 45s or picture sleeves that, in near-mint condition, would likely fetch four figures in an open auction! As we've noted elsewhere, this book is largely absent EPs; adding them would increase the length of the list significantly. And there are others in the high three figures that could crack the $1,000 barrier soon.

To be honest, the following is a dream list. The majority of the 271 precious platters and papers below have never been seen in near-mint condition. In fact, because the below are so rare and sought-after, most have been counterfeited. Some collectors, as a result, might be suspicious at a copy that looks too good to be true.

When no near-mint copy is known to exist, the value was determined based on what lesser-condition copies have brought.

As you look at the list below, you'll notice that most of them fall into highly collectible categories: vocal groups; rockabilly; Motown and so-called "Northern Soul"; the Beatles; and Elvis Presley. Most are from the 1950s and early 1960s; the oldest is from 1950. But the most recent is from 1978 – the picture sleeve from the Rolling Stones' "Beast of Burden" has cracked four figures.

Let's keep dreaming for a moment. If you were to have all 271 of these, and they were as clean as the day they were first pressed, you'd have a collection worth **$613,250!**

Remember again, these values are for near-mint stock copies (unless otherwise noted). Records in lesser conditions will bring less.

Value	Artist	Label, Number	A Side/B Side
$15,000	Hornets *Red vinyl*	States 127	I Can't Believe/Lonesome Baby
12,000	Wilson, Frank	Soul 35019	Sweeter As the Days Go By/Do I Love You
10,000	Barrix, Billy *Outrageously rare rockabilly record*	Chess 1662	Cool Off Baby/Almost
10,000	Beatles *By "Tony Sheridan and the Beat Brothers"; black label with color bars* *(all-black label with star under "Decca" should be a counterfeit)*	Decca 31382	My Bonnie/The Saints
10,000	Beatles *Value assumes that this is authentic, but it may be a clever 1970s-era bootleg*	Vee Jay Spec. DJ No. 8	Ask Me Why/Anna
10,000	Brenston, Jackie *Early rockabilly classic; obscenely rare, even though the 45s were pressed later*	Chess 1458	Rocket "88"/Come Back Where You Belong
10,000	Dells *Red vinyl*	Vee Jay 134	Tell the World/Blues at Three
10,000	Impressions *As "Jerry Butler and the Impressions"*	Vee Jay 280	For Your Precious Love/Sweet Was the Wine
10,000	Prisonaires *One of record collecting's legendary rarities, this could bring much more at open auction.*	Sun 207	There Is Love in You/What'll You Do Next
8,000	Beatles *"Ask Me Why/The Beatles" plugged on promo-only sleeve*	Vee Jay 1-903 PS	Misery/Taste of Honey//Ask Me Why/Anna
8,000	Flamingos *Red vinyl*	Parrot 811	I Really Don't Want to Know/Get With It
8,000	Hornets *Black vinyl*	States 127	I Can't Believe/Lonesome Baby
8,000	Presley, Elvis *One-sided promo with designation "For Special Academy Consideration Only"*	RCA Victor 4-834-115 DJ	I'll Be Back
8,000	Rolling Stones	London 909 PS	Street Fighting Man/No Expectations
8,000	Sof-Tones	Cee Bee 1062	Oh Why/(B-side unknown)
8,000	Windsors	Back Beat 506	My Gloria/Cool Seabreeze

Value	Artist	Label, Number	A Side/B Side
6,000	Crystals	Philles 111 DJ	(Let's Dance) The Screw -- Part 1/ (Let's Dance) The Screw -- Part 2

Light blue label. Matrix numbers are stamped in dead wax. Counterfeits have numbers hand-etched.

Value	Artist	Label, Number	A Side/B Side
6,000	Hide-A-Ways	Ronni 1000	Can't Help Lovin' That Girl of Mine/ I'm Coming Home
5,000	Larks	Apollo 1190	Stolen Love/In My Lonely Room

Red vinyl

Value	Artist	Label, Number	A Side/B Side
5,000	Presley, Elvis	RCA Victor 47-8400 DJ	Such a Night/Never Ending

An inexplicably rare regular white label promo

Value	Artist	Label, Number	A Side/B Side
5,000	Presley, Elvis	RCA Victor 37-7992 PS	Good Luck Charm/Anything That's Part of You

Special picture sleeve for Compact 33 Single record

Value	Artist	Label, Number	A Side/B Side
5,000	Velvet Underground	Verve 10427 PS	All Tomorrow's Parties/I'll Be Your Mirror
4,500	Harmonica Frank	Sun 205	Rockin' Chair Daddy/The Great Musical Menagerist
4,000	Beatles	Capitol 5150	Can't Buy Me Love/You Can't Do That

Yellow vinyl (unauthorized)

Value	Artist	Label, Number	A Side/B Side
4,000	Belltones	Grand 102	Estelle/Promise Love
4,000	Clovers	Atlantic 1083	Devil or Angel/Hey, Doll Baby

Red label, no spinner; red vinyl

Value	Artist	Label, Number	A Side/B Side
4,000	Crystals	Philles 111 DJ	(Let's Dance) The Screw -- Part 1/ (Let's Dance) The Screw -- Part 2

White label

Value	Artist	Label, Number	A Side/B Side
4,000	Five Keys	Groove 0031	I'll Follow You/Lawdy Miss Mary
4,000	Five Thrills	Parrot 800	Gloria/Wee Wee Baby

Red vinyl

Value	Artist	Label, Number	A Side/B Side
4,000	Flamingos	Chance 1145	Golden Teardrops/Carried Away

Red vinyl

Value	Artist	Label, Number	A Side/B Side
4,000	Flamingos	Parrot 811	I Really Don't Want to Know/Get With It

Black vinyl

Value	Artist	Label, Number	A Side/B Side
4,000	Larks	Apollo 1184	My Reverie/Let's Say a Prayer

Red vinyl

Value	Artist	Label, Number	A Side/B Side
4,000	Marainey, Big Memphis	Sun 184	Call Me Anything, But Call Me/Baby No, No
4,000	Nutones	Hollywood Star 798	Believe/Annie Kicked the Bucket
4,000	Orioles	Jubilee 5000	It's Too Soon to Know/Barbara Lee
4,000	Presley, Elvis	RCA Victor 37-7968 PS	Can't Help Falling in Love/Rock-a-Hula Baby

Special picture sleeve for Compact 33 Single record

Value	Artist	Label, Number	A Side/B Side
4,000	Rolling Stones	London 9641	I Wanna Be Your Man/Stoned
4,000	Shaw, John, and the Dell-Os	U-C 5002	Why Did You Leave Me/Why Does It Have to Be Her
4,000	Velveteers	Spitfire 15	Tell Me You're Mine/Boo Wacka Boo
4,000	Viceroys	Ramco 3715	My Heart/I Need Your Love So Bad
3,000	Beatles	Decca 31382 DJ	My Bonnie/The Saints

By "Tony Sheridan and the Beat Brothers"; pink label, star on label under "Decca"

Value	Artist	Label, Number	A Side/B Side
3,000	Bob and Sheri	Safari 101	The Surfer Moon/Humpty Dumpty

Light blue label (other colors and colored vinyl are reproductions or counterfeits)

Value	Artist	Label, Number	A Side/B Side
3,000	Brooks, Dusty, and His Tones	Sun 182	Heaven or Fire/Tears and Wine

with Juanita Brown

Value	Artist	Label, Number	A Side/B Side
3,000	Burnette, Johnny	Von 1006	You're Undecided/Go, Mule, Go
3,000	Cliff, Benny	Drift 1441	Shake Um Um Rock/The Breaking Point
3,000	DeBerry, Jimmy	Sun 185	Take a Little Chance/Time Has Made a Change
3,000	Jimmy and Walter	Sun 180	Before Long/Easy

The earliest known 45 on Sun

Value	Artist	Label, Number	A Side/B Side
3,000	Love, Hot Shot	Sun 196	Wolf Call Boogie/Harmonica Jam
3,000	Newlyweds	Homogenized Soul 601	Love Walked Out/The Quarrel
3,000	Orbison, Roy	Je-Wel 101	Ooby Dooby/Tryin' to Get to You

As "The Teen Kings"

Value	Artist	Label, Number	A Side/B Side
3,000	Orioles	Jubilee 5005	Tell Me So/Deacon Jones
3,000	Pejoe, Morris	Checker 766	Tired of Crying Over You/ Gonna Buy Me a Telephone

Red vinyl

Value	Artist	Label, Number	A Side/B Side
3,000	Ravens	National 9111	Count Every Star/ I'm Gonna Paper All My Walls with Your Love

The only known Ravens single on a National 45; 20 other Ravens singles exist on National 78s

Value	Artist	Label, Number	A Side/B Side
3,000	Surfaris	DFS 11/12	Wipe Out/Surfer Joe
2,500	Andantes	V.I.P. 25006	If You Were Mine//(Like a) Nightmare
2,500	Beatles	Vee Jay 581 PS	Please Please Me/From Me to You

Special "The Record That Started Beatlemania" promo-only sleeve

Value	Artist	Label, Number	A Side/B Side
2,500	Miracles	Motown TLX-2207	Bad Girl/I Love Your Baby
2,500	Miracles	Motown G 1/G 2	Bad Girl/I Love Your Baby
2,500	Presley, Elvis	RCA Victor 37-7992	Good Luck Charm/Anything That's Part of You

"Compact Single 33" (small hole, plays at LP speed)

Value	Artist	Label, Number	A Side/B Side
2,500	Presley, Elvis	Sun 215	Milkcow Blues Boogie/You're a Heartbreaker
2,400	Cotton, James	Sun 206	Cotton Crop Blues/Hold Me in Your Arms
2,250	Presley, Elvis	RCA Victor 37-7908 PS	(Marie's the Name) His Latest Flame/Little Sister

Special picture sleeve for Compact 33 Single; says "Stereo-Orthophonic" on sleeve in error

Value	Artist	Label, Number	A Side/B Side
2,000	Beatles	Apple/Americom 5715	Yellow Submarine/Eleanor Rigby

Four-inch flexi-disc sold in vending machines

Value	Artist	Label, Number	A Side/B Side
2,000	Beatles	Capitol 5112 PS	I Want to Hold Your Hand/WMCA Good Guys

Giveaway from New York radio station with photo of WMCA DJs on rear

Value	Artist	Label, Number	A Side/B Side
2,000	Beatles	Capitol 5150	Can't Buy Me Love/You Can't Do That

Yellow and black vinyl (unauthorized)

Value	Artist	Label, Number	A Side/B Side
2,000	Beatles	Vee Jay 498	Please Please Me/Ask Me Why

Correct spelling; number is "VJ 498"; brackets label

Value	Artist	Label, Number	A Side/B Side
2,000	Blue Jays	Checker 782	White Cliffs of Dover/Hey Poppa
2,000	Carpenters	Magic Lamp 704	I'll Be Yours/Looking for Love

As "Karen Carpenter", but Richard also was on this record

Two of the world's most sought-after records. At top, Jerry Butler and the Impressions' "For Your Precious Love" is not hard to find on Abner, a little tougher on Falcon, but almost impossible on Vee Jay. A Near Mint copy, which this isn't, would likely bring $10,000 or more in open auction. Below it is a stock copy of the Rolling Stones' first American single, "Stoned." Withdrawn shortly after release, it, too, is a major rarity worth up to $4,000. The song didn't re-appear in America until the release of the London Years LP/CD box set in the late 1980s.

Value	Artist	Label, Number	A Side/B Side
2,000	Charters	Mel-O-Dy 104	Trouble Lover/Show Me Some Sign
2,000	Cotton, James	Sun 199	My Baby/Straighten Up, Baby
2,000	Dr. Ross	Sun 212	The Boogie Disease/Juke Box Boogie
2,000	Five Satins	Standord 200	In the Still of the Nite/The Jones Girl
	With "Produced by Martin Kuegell" credit		
2,000	Flamingos	Chance 1133	If I Can't Have You/Someday, Somehow
	Red vinyl		
2,000	Flamingos	Chance 1140	That's My Desire/Hurry Home Baby
	Red vinyl		
2,000	Flamingos	Chance 1145	Golden Teardrops/Carried Away
	Black vinyl		
2,000	Flamingos	Parrot 808	Dream of a Lifetime/On My Merry Way
	Red vinyl		
2,000	Flamingos	Parrot 812	I'm Yours/Ko Ko Mo
	Red vinyl		
2,000	Four Lovers	Epic 9255	My Life for Your Love/Pucker Up
2,000	Gunter, Hardrock	Sun 201	Fallen Angel/Gonna Dance All Night
2,000	Haley, Bill, and His Comets	Essex 303	Rock the Joint/Icy Heart
	Red vinyl		
2,000	Mann, Carl	Jaxon 502	Gonna Rock and Roll Tonight/Rockin' Love
2,000	Martin, George	United Artists 750 PS	A Hard Day's Night/I Should Have Known Better
2,000	Matthews, Fat Man	Imperial 5211	When Boy Meets Girl/Later Baby
2,000	Mello-Harps	Do-Re-Mi 203	Love Is a Vow/Valerie
2,000	Mello-Moods	Robin 104	I Couldn't Sleep a Wink Last Night/ And You Just Can't Go Through Life Alone
2,000	Mello-Moods	Robin 105	Where Are You (Now That I Need You)/ How Could You
2,000	Moonglows	Chance 1147	Baby Please/Whistle My Love
	Red vinyl		
2,000	Moonglows	Chance 1161	My Gal/219 Train
2,000	Nazz	Very 001	Lay Down and Die, Goodbye/ Wonder Who's Loving Her Now
	Early version of Alice Cooper's group		
2,000	Orioles	Jubilee 5016	So Much/Forgive and Forget
2,000	Orioles	Jubilee 5051	I Miss You So/You Are My First Love
	Red vinyl		
2,000	Orioles	Jubilee 5065	Baby, Please Don't Go/ Don't Tell Her What's Happened to Me
	Red vinyl		
2,000	Pelicans	Parrot 793	White Cliffs of Dover/Aurelia
	Red vinyl		
2,000	Poindexter, Don, and the Starlite Wranglers	Sun 202	Now She Cares No More for Me/ My Kind of Love
2,000	Presley, Elvis	RCA Victor 37-7968	Can't Help Falling in Love/Rock-a-Hula Baby
	"Compact Single 33" (small hole, plays at LP speed)		
2,000	Presley, Elvis	RCA Victor EPA-5122	King Creole/New Orleans// As Long As I Have You/Lover Doll
	Maroon label		
2,000	Presley, Elvis	RCA Victor SPD-23 (3)	Elvis Presley
	Value is for all three discs together		
2,000	Presley, Elvis	RCA Victor SPD-23 PS	Elvis Presley
	Bonus given to buyers of a more expensive Victrola		
2,000	Presley, Elvis	RCA Victor 37-7908 PS	(Marie's the Name) His Latest Flame/Little Sister
	Special picture sleeve for Compact Single 33		
2,000	Presley, Elvis	RCA Victor SP-45-76 PS	Don't/Wear My Ring Around Your Neck
2,000	Presley, Elvis	RCA Victor 68-7850 S	Surrender/Lonely Man
	"Compact Stereo 33" in "Living Stereo"		
2,000	Presley, Elvis	Sun 209	That's All Right/Blue Moon of Kentucky
2,000	Presley, Elvis	Sun 210	Good Rockin' Tonight/ I Don't Care If the Sun Don't Shine
2,000	Royals	Federal 12064AA	Every Beat of My Heart/All Night Long
	Blue vinyl		
2,000	Royals	Federal 12088	Moonrise/Fifth Street Blues
	Blue vinyl		
2,000	Serenaders	Motown 1046	If Your Heart Says Yes/I'll Cry Tomorrow
2,000	Serratt, Howard	Sun 198	I Must Be Saved/Troublesome Waters
2,000	Sha-Wees	Aladdin 3170	No One to Love Me/Early Sunday Morning
2,000	Skyliners	Motown 1046 DJ	Since I Fell for You/I'd Die
	Record never got beyond the test pressing stage (2 known copies)		
2,000	Smith, Ray	Heart 250	Gone, Baby, Gone/(B-side unknown)
2,000	Sonics	Gaiety 114	Marlene/(B-side unknown)
2,000	Spiders	Mascot 112	Why Don't You Love Me/Hitch Hike
	Early Alice Cooper		
2,000	Strong, Barrett	Tamla 54022	Let's Rock/(B-side unknown)
2,000	Swallows	King 4501	Eternally/It Ain't the Heat
	Red vinyl		
2,000	Swallows	King 4515	Tell Me Why/Roll, Roll, Pretty Baby
2,000	Teenage Moonlighters	Mark 134	Sorry Sorry/I Want to Cry
2,000	Vel-Tones	Coy 101	Cal's Tune/Playboy
1,800	Castelles	Grand 101	My Girl Awaits Me/Sweetness
	Blue label original		
1,600	Beatles	Vee Jay 498	Please Please Me/Ask Me Why
	Misspelled "The Beattles"; number is "#498"		
1,600	Beatles	Vee Jay 498	Please Please Me/Ask Me Why
	Correct spelling; number is "#498"		

Value	Artist	Label, Number	A Side/B Side
1,500	Adams, Billy	Quincy 932	Rock Pretty Mama/(B-side unknown)
1,500	Alexander, Joe, and the Cubans	Ballad 1008	Oh Maria/I Hope These Words Will FInd You Well
	With a pre-Chess Chuck Berry in the band		
1,500	Bachelors	Aladdin 3210	Pretty Baby/Can't Help Loving You
1,500	Beatles	Capitol 5555	We Can Work It Out/Day Tripper
	Red and white "Starline" label (mispress)		
1,500	Beatles	United Artists UAEP 10029 DJ	A Hard Day's Night Open End Interview
1,500	Beatles	United ArtistsSP-2357DJ	A Hard Day's Night Theatre Lobby Spot
1,500	Beatles	Vee Jay 498	Please Please Me/Ask Me Why
	Misspelled "The Beattles"; number is "VJ 498"		
1,500	Cochran, Eddie	Liberty 55070 PS	Mean When I'm Mad/One Kiss
1,500	Cordel, Pat	Club 1011	Darling, Come Back/My My Tears
1,500	Cunningham, Buddy	Sun 208	Right or Wrong/Why Do I Care
1,500	Deacon and the Rock 'N' Rollers	Nau-Voo 804	Rockin' on the Moon/I Don't Wanna Leave
1,500	Dots	Rev 3512	Ring Chimes/Wolf Call
1,500	Eddy, Duane	Ford 500	Ramrod/Caravan
	As "Duane Eddy and His Rock-A-Billies"		
1,500	Five Echoes	Sabre 102	Baby Come Back to Me/Lonely Mood
	Red vinyl		
1,500	Five Echoes	Sabre 105	So Lonesome/Broke
	Red vinyl		
1,500	Jades	Christy 114	Look for a Lie/Blue Memories
1,500	Larks	Apollo 1184	My Reverie/Let's Say a Prayer
	Black vinyl		
1,500	Little Iva and Her Band	Miracle 2	When I Needed You/Continental Strut
1,500	Mellodots	Apollo 1192	One More Time/Just How Long
1,500	Moonglows	Chance 1150	Just a Lonely Christmas/Hey, Santa Claus
	Red vinyl (this may not exist legitimately on black vinyl)		
1,500	Moonglows	Chance 1152	Secret Love/Real Gone Mama
	Silver and blue label		
1,500	Orioles	Jubilee 5107	I Miss You So/Till Then
	Red vinyl		
1,500	Orioles	Jubilee 5092	Don't Cry Baby/See See Rider
	Red vinyl		
1,500	Orioles	Jubilee 5108	Teardrops on My Pillow/Hold Me, Thrill Me, Kiss Me
	Red vinyl		
1,500	Orioles	Jubilee 5120	I Cover the Waterfront/One More Time
	Red vinyl		
1,500	Presley, Elvis	RCA Victor 37-7908	(Marie's the Name) His Latest Flame/Little Sister
	"Compact Single 33" (small hole, plays at LP speed)		
1,500	Presley, Elvis	RCA Victor EPB-1254 (2)	Elvis Presley
	Two records have three songs on each side (12 total), as opposed to the two of the standard release		
1,500	Presley, Elvis	RCA Victor EPB-1254 PS	Elvis Presley... the most talked-about new personality in the last ten years of recorded music
1,500	Presley, Elvis	RCA Victor HO7W-0808 DJ	Blue Christmas (same on both sides)
1,500	Presley, Elvis	Sun 217	Baby Let's Play House/I'm Left, You're Right, She's Gone
1,500	Reed, Jimmy	Chance 1142	High and Lonesome/Roll and Rhumba
1,500	Rockettes	Parrot 789	I Can't Forget/Love Nobody
1,500	Satintones	Motown 1006	Angel/A Love That Can Never Be
1,500	Skelton, Eddie	Dixie 2011	Keep It Swinging/Without You
1,500	Spiders	Santa Cruz 003	Don't Blow Your Mind/No Price Tag
1,500	Spinners	Motown 1155	In My Diary/(She's Gonna Love Me) At Sundown
1,500	Supremes	Motown 1008	I Want a Guy/Never Again
1,500	Swallows	King 4458	Will You Be Mine/Dearest
1,500	Swans	Rainbow 233	No More/My True Love
	Red vinyl		
1,500	Taylor, Bill, and Smokey Jo	Flip 502	Split Personality/Lonely Sweetheart
1,500	Teen-Kings	Bee 1114/5	That's a Teen-Age Love/Tell Me If You Know
1,500	Valli, Frankie	Corona 1234	My Mother's Eyes/The Laugh's on Me
	As "Frank Valley"		
1,500	Valquins	Gaity 161/2	My Dear/Falling Star
	Red vinyl		
1,500	Vincent, Gene	Capitol F4237 PS	The Night Is So Lonely/Right Now
1,200	Beatles	United Artists ULP-42370	Let It Be Radio Spots
1,200	Buccaneers	Rama 24	In the Mission of St. Augustine/You Did Me Wrong
1,200	Castelles	Grand 103	This Silver Ring/Wonder Why
	Glossy yellow label original		
1,200	Castelles	Grand 105	Do You Remember/If You Were the Only Girl
	Glossy yellow label original		
1,200	Castelles	Grand 109	Baby Can't You See/Over a Cup of Coffee
	Blue label original		
1,200	Castelles	Grand 114	Marcella/I'm a Fool to Care
	Cream label original		
1,200	Castelles	Grand 122	My Wedding Day/Heavenly Father
	Cream label original		
1,200	Crows	Rama 10	Heartbreaker/Call a Doctor
	Red vinyl; label says "The Jewels"		
1,200	Danny and the Juniors	Singular 711	At the Hop/Sometimes
	Blue label, machine-stamped in dead wax, with "Orchestra Directed by Artie Singer" credit.		
1,200	El Rays	Checker 794	Darling I Know/Christine
	Later known as The Dells		

Value	Artist	Label, Number	A Side/B Side
1,200	Dubs	Johnson 102	Don't Ask Me (To Be Lonely)/Darling
1,200	Esquires	Epic 9024	If You Only Knew What a Three-Cent Stamp Can Do/ Now, Now, Now
	This may not exist on 45, though it certainly should.		
1,200	Esquires	Hi-Po 1003	Only the Angels Know/One Word for This
1,200	Five Keys	Aladdin 3190	These Foolish Things/Lonesome Old Story
1,200	Five Thrills	Parrot 796	My Baby's Gone/Feel So Good
1,200	Five Thrills	Parrot 800	Gloria/Wee Wee Baby
	Black vinyl		
1,200	Flamingos	Chance 1133	If I Can't Have You/Someday, Somehow
	Black vinyl		
1,200	Giordano, Lou	Brunswick 55115	Stay Close to Me/Don'Cha Know
	With Buddy Holly on guitar		
1,200	Booker, John Lee	Chance 1108	Miss Lorraine/Talkin' Boogie
	Actually John Lee Hooker		
1,200	Booker, John Lee	Chance 1110	Graveyard Blues/I Love to Boogie
	Actually John Lee Hooker		
1,200	Booker, John L.	Chance 1122	609 Boogie/Road Trouble
	Actually John Lee Hooker		
1,200	Moonglows	Champagne 7500	I Just Can't Tell No Lie/ I've Been Your Dog (Ever Since I've Been Your Man)
1,200	Presley, Elvis	RCA Victor 47-6540 PS	This Is His Life: Elvis Presley
	Promo-only sleeve issued with "I Want You, I Need You, I Love You"; no stock picture sleeve was issued		
1,200	Presley, Elvis	RCA Victor G8-MW-8705DJ	TV Guide Presents Elvis Presley
	Blue label, locked grooves (needle has to be lifted to play each of the four excerpts)		
1,200	Presley, Elvis	RCA Victor 37-7880 PS	I Feel So Bad/Wild in the Country
	Special picture sleeve for Compact Single 33		
1,200	Rolling Stones	Rolling Stones 19309 PS	Beast of Burden/Before They Make Me Run
1,200	Springsteen, Bruce	Columbia 45864	Spirit in the Night/For You
1,200	Teasers	Checker 800	I Was a Fool to Love You/ How Could You Hurt One So
	Red vinyl		
1,200	Terry, Larry	Testa 006	Hep Cat/(B-side unknown)
1,200	Ventures	Blue Horizon 101	Walk-Don't Run/Home
1,100	Beatles	Vee Jay 498 DJ	Please Please Me/Ask Me Why
	Misspelled "The Beattles"		
1,000	Beach Boys	X 301	Surfin'/Luau
1,000	Beatles	Apple/Americom 2490/M-335	Get Back/Don't Let Me Down
	Four-inch flexi-disc sold in vending machines		
1,000	Blenders	Aladdin 3449	Two Loves/Soda Shop
1,000	Bob and Sheri	Safari 101 DJ	The Surfer Moon/Humpty Dumpty
	White label; sources vary as to the legitimacy of promos of this record		
1,000	Bowen, Jimmy	Triple D 798	I'm Stickin' With You/Party Doll
	B-side by Buddy Knox		
1,000	Brenston, Jackie	Chess 1469	In My Real Gone Rocket/Tuckered Out
1,000	Brenston, Jackie	Chess 1472	Juiced/Independent Woman
1,000	Buccaneers	Rama 21	The Stars Will Remember/Come Back My Love
1,000	Buccaneers	Southern 101	Dear Ruth/Fine Brown Flame
1,000	Charmers	Central 1006	Tony, My Darling/In the Rain
1,000	Charmers	Timely 1009	I Was Wrong/The Mambo
1,000	Charmers	Timely 1011	The Church on the Hill/Battle Axe
1,000	Checkers	King 4558	Flame in My Heart/Oh, Oh, Oh Baby
1,000	Checkers	King 4581	Night's Curtains/Let Me Come Back
1,000	Classics	Ro-Ann 1002	Je Vous Aime/Burning Desire
1,000	Danny and the Juniors	Singular 711	At the Hop/Sometimes
	Blue label, machine-stamped in dead wax, no mention of Artie Singer on label		
1,000	Dells	Vee Jay 134	Tell the World/Blues at Three
1,000	Dylan, Bob	Columbia 42656	Mixed-Up Confusion/Corrine, Corrina
1,000	Dylan, Bob	Columbia 43242 PS	Subterranean Homesick Blues/She Belongs to Me
	Only issued with some promos		
1,000	Feathers, Charlie	Meteor 5032	Tongue-Tied Jill/Get With It
	Maroon label		
1,000	Flamingos	Chance 1149	Plan for Love/You Ain't Ready
	Yellow and black label		
1,000	Flamingos	Chance 1154	Cross Over the Bridge/Listen to My Plea
1,000	Flamingos	Chance 1162	Jump Children/Blues in the Letter
1,000	Flamingos	Parrot 808	Dream of a Lifetime/On My Merry Way
	Black vinyl		
1,000	Flamingos	Parrot 812	I'm Yours/Ko Ko Mo
	Black vinyl		
1,000	Hi-Liters	Vee Jay 184	Bobby Sox Baby/Hello Dear
1,000	Hooker, John Lee	Chess 1505	High Priced Woman/Union Station Blues
1,000	Hooker, John Lee	Chess 1513	Sugar Mama/Walkin' the Boogie
1,000	Hooker, John Lee	JVB 30	Boogie Rambler/No More Doggin'
1,000	Kenny and the Cadets	Randy 422	Barbie/What Is a Young Man Made Of
	Red and gold vinyl		
1,000	Larks	Apollo 429	Little Side Car/Hey Little Girl
1,000	Larks	Apollo 430	Ooh, It Feels So Good/ I Don't Believe in Tomorrow
1,000	Larks	Apollo 435	My Lost Love/How Long Must I Wait for You
1,000	Larks	Apollo 437	Darlin'/Lucy Brown
1,000	Larks	Apollo 1180	Hopefully Yours/When I Leave These Prison Walls
1,000	Larks	Apollo 1189	Shadrack/Honey in the Rock
1,000	Larks	Apollo 1190	Stolen Love/In My Lonely Room
	Black vinyl		

Value	Artist	Label, Number	A Side/B Side
1,000	Larks	Apollo 1194	I Live True to You/Hold Me
1,000	Majestics	V.I.P. 25028 DJ	Say You/All for Someone
	Promo only; stock copies credited "The Monitors"		
1,000	Mallett, Saundra, and the Vandellas	Tamla 54067	Camel Walk/It's Gonna Be Hard Times
1,000	Mason, Bonnie Jo	Annette 1000	Ringo I Love You/Beatles Blues
	Actually Cher; a Phil Spector production		
1,000	Merced Blue Notes	Soul 35007	Do the Pig/Thumping
1,000	Moonglows	Chance 1147	Baby Please/Whistle My Love
	Black vinyl		
1,000	Moonglows	Chance 1152	Secret Love/Real Gone Mama
	Yellow and black label		
1,000	Moonglows	Chance 1156	I Was Wrong/Ooh Rockin' Daddy
	Yellow and black label		
1,000	Norman, Gene, and the Rockin' Rockets	Snag 101	Snaggle Tooth Ann/Long Gone Night Train
1,000	Orioles	Jubilee 5017	What Are You Doing New Year's Eve/Lonely Christmas
1,000	Orioles	Jubilee 5017 PS	What Are You Doing New Year's Eve/Lonely Christmas
1,000	Orioles	Jubilee 5025	At Night/Every Dog-Gone Time
1,000	Parton, Dolly	Gold Band 1086	Puppy Love/Girl Left Alone
1,000	Pejoe, Morris	Checker 781	Can't Get Along/It'll Plumb Get It
	Red vinyl		
1,000	Pelicans	Imperial 5307	Chimes/Ain't Gonna Do It
1,000	Pelicans	Parrot 793	White Cliffs of Dover/Aurelia
1,000	Presley, Elvis	RCA JB-10857 DJ	Moody Blue/She Thinks I Still Care
	Colored vinyl pressings exist in five different colors -- red, white, gold, blue green. Value is for any of them.		
1,000	Presley, Elvis	RCA Victor 37-7850 PS	Surrender/Lonely Man
	Special picture sleeve for Compact Single 33		
1,000	Presley, Elvis	RCA Victor 37-7880	I Feel So Bad/Wild in the Country
	"Compact Single 33" (small hole, plays at LP speed)		
1,000	Presley, Elvis	RCA Victor 47-7506 PS	(Now and Then There's) A Fool Such As I/I Need Your Love Tonight
	Sleeve promotes the "Elvis Sails" EP		
1,000	Presley, Elvis	RCA Victor 47-7777	It's Now or Never/A Mess of Blues
	An early mispress is missing the piano part on the A-side. Has the number "L2WW-0100-3S" or "L2WW-0100-4S" in trail-off wax.		
1,000	Presley, Elvis	RCA Victor CR-15 DJ	Old Shep
	One-sided promo		
1,000	Presley, Elvis	RCA Victor EPA-747 PS	Elvis Presley
	Temporary envelope sleeve with dark blue print, "Blue Suede Shoes by Elvis Presley" in big letters		
1,000	Presley, Elvis	Sun 223	I Forgot to Remember to Forget/Mystery Train
1,000	Pretenders	Central 2605	Blue and Lonely/Daddy Needs Baby
1,000	Ravens	Columbia 39408	You Foolish Thing/Honey I Don't Want You
1,000	Rogers, Weldon	Je-Wel 103	Everybody Wants You/This Song's Just for You
1,000	Royals	Federal 12077	I Know I Love You So/Starting From Tonight
1,000	Royals	Federal 12088	Moonrise/Fifth Street Blues
1,000	Spaniels	Vee Jay 101	Baby It's You/Bounce
	Red vinyl		
1,000	Squires	V 109	The Sultan/Aurora
	Canadian release only; with a very early Neil Young		
1,000	Survivors	Capitol 5102	Pamela Jean/After the Game
	Not the Beach Boys, but Dave Nowlen, Bob Norberg and friends with help from Brian Wilson		
1,000	Swallows	King 4501	Eternally/It Ain't the Heat
1,000	Thrillers	Thriller 3530	Lessie Mae/I'm Going to Live My Life Alone
1,000	Vals	Unique Laboratories (no #)	The Song of a Lover/Compensation Blues
1,000	Vibes	After Hours 105	Stop Torturing Me/Stop Jibing, Baby
1,000	Vibes	Chariot 105	Stop Torturing Me/Stop Jibing, Baby
1,000	Vibranaires	After Hours 103	Doll Face/Ooh, I Feel So Good
1,000	Vibranaires	Chariot 103	Doll Face/Ooh, I Feel So Good

How You Can Help

Conservatively speaking, this book has 30,000 listings by thousands of artists, plus many hundreds more who missed the cut this time. All of this information is located in a growing database of records, which will make both future price guides and *Goldmine* magazine better products in the long run.

But as you look through this first 45 RPM price guide from our database, you'll see that we need help in several areas. Certain parts of this book aren't as good as they could be, and we know you can help us.

While any information is helpful, here are areas where the most help is needed:

– **Stereo and other unusual pressings of the 1958-63 era.** Record companies tried numerous 7-inch alternatives to regular mono 45s in this era. We know that many labels, including Columbia, RCA Victor, MGM, Warner Bros., ABC-Paramount, Roulette, King, and even Carlton and Big Top, released stereo singles in this period. All of these are collectible, almost without regard to artist.

Some of these are documented here, but we need more information.

– **Extended plays.** Except for the Beatles and Elvis Presley, extended play records are largely absent from this book. That's not because they aren't collectible – they most certainly are, and many fetch healthy sums. But in the limited time we had to get this book together, we simply couldn't fully document EPs. And rather than give out partial information, we figured we'd wait and get it right.

What we need is the exact contents of the EP, side 1 and side 2, plus sleeve variations. As the titles of extended plays are often not listed on the records, we feel that actually listing the songs will be of greater help to the collector.

So if you're an EP collector, you can play a big role in helping us. To see what we need, take a look at the Elvis Presley EP section.

– **Picture sleeves.** Again, we didn't list a sleeve we weren't sure about. If you have something we haven't listed, let us know.

– **B-sides.** Some records are listed as "(B-side unknown)." In many cases, it's because a record never got past the promo stage; in others, the record just hasn't crossed too many paths. If you can make some of these B-sides known, it would be appreciated.

– **Very early 45s.** We know that Capitol, MGM and Columbia, to name three, used different 45 RPM numbering systems in 1949-50 than the ones that became standard. Our information on these is somewhat sketchy. Again, if you have any of these (not to mention Columbia Microgroove 7-inch 33s from the era), let us know.

Everyone who makes a suggestion that helps the next edition will be acknowledged, unless you don't want to be. Write to:

Tim Neely
Book Editor, Goldmine
700 E. State St.
Iola, WI 54990
(715) 445-2214 or 4612, ext. 782

If you write, enclose a daytime phone number where I can call in case I have any questions. I also can be reached via fax at (715) 445-4087, but I prefer that you write or call before faxing me any large contributions.

Number		Title (A Side/B Side)	Year	VG	VG+	NM

A

ABBA
(Also see "Bjorn and Benny")
Atlantic

Number		Title (A Side/B Side)	Year	VG	VG+	NM
❏ PR 380	DJ	Happy New Year (mono/stereo)	1980	3.00	6.00	12.00
❏ PR 390	DJ	Happy New Year	1980	3.00	6.00	12.00
		One-sided promo				
❏ 3035		Waterloo/Watch Out	1974		2.50	5.00
❏ 3035	PS	Waterloo	1974	3.75	7.50	15.00
		Sleeve is promo only				
❏ 3209		Honey Honey/Dance (While the Music Still Goes On)	1974		2.50	5.00
❏ 3240		Hasta Manana/Ring Ring	1975		2.50	5.00
❏ 3265		SOS/Man in the Middle	1975		2.50	5.00
❏ 3310		I Do, I Do, I Do, I Do, I Do/Bang-a-Boomerang	1975		2.50	5.00
❏ 3315		Mamma Mia/Tropical Loveland	1976		2.50	5.00
❏ 3346		Fernando/Rock Me	1976		2.00	4.00
❏ 3346		Fernando/Tropical Loveland	1976		2.00	4.00
❏ 3372		Dancing Queen/That's Me	1976		2.00	4.00
❏ 3387		Knowing Me, Knowing You/Happy Hawaii	1977		2.00	4.00
❏ 3387	PS	Knowing Me, Knowing You/Happy Hawaii	1977		2.50	5.00
❏ 3434		Money, Money, Money/Crazy World	1977		2.00	4.00
❏ 3434	PS	Money, Money, Money/Crazy World	1977		3.00	6.00
❏ 3449		The Name of the Game/I Wonder (Departure)	1977		2.00	4.00
❏ 3457		Take a Chance on Me/I'm a Marionette	1978		2.00	4.00
❏ 3457	PS	Take a Chance on Me/I'm a Marionette	1978		3.00	6.00
❏ 3574		Does Your Mother Know/Kisses of Fire	1979		2.00	4.00
❏ 3574	PS	Does Your Mother Know/Kisses of Fire	1979		2.50	5.00
❏ 3609		Voulez-Vous/Angeleyes	1979		2.00	4.00
❏ 3609	PS	Voulez-Vous/Angeleyes	1979		2.50	5.00
❏ 3629		Chiquitita/Lovelight	1979		2.00	4.00
❏ 3630		Chiquitita (Spanish Version)/I Have a Dream (Spanish Version)	1979		2.50	5.00
❏ 3652		Gimme! Gimme! Gimme! (A Man After Midnight)/The King Has Lost His Crown	1980		2.00	4.00
❏ 3776		The Winner Takes It All/Elaine	1980		2.00	4.00
❏ 3806		Super Trouper/The Piper	1981		2.00	4.00
❏ 3806	PS	Super Trouper/The Piper	1981		2.00	4.00
❏ 3826		On and On and On/Lay All Your Love on Me	1981		2.00	4.00
❏ 3889		When All Is Said and Done/Should I Laugh or Cry	1982			3.00
❏ 3889	PS	When All Is Said and Done/Should I Laugh or Cry	1982			3.00
❏ 4031		The Visitors/Head Over Heels	1982			3.00
❏ 4031	PS	The Visitors/Head Over Heels	1982			3.00
❏ 89881		One of Us/Should I Laugh or Cry	1983			3.00
❏ 89948		The Day Before You Came/Cassandra	1982			3.00

Abstrack Reality
Sport

Number		Title (A Side/B Side)	Year	VG	VG+	NM
❏ 104		Love Burns Like a Fire/(Instrumental)	1967	50.00	100.00	200.00

Ace, Johnny
Duke

Number		Title (A Side/B Side)	Year	VG	VG+	NM
❏ 102		My Song/Follow the Rule	1952	10.00	20.00	40.00
❏ 107		Cross My Heart/Angel	1953	10.00	20.00	40.00
❏ 112		The Clock/Ace's Wild	1953	10.00	20.00	40.00
❏ 118		Saving My Love for You/Yes Baby	1953	10.00	20.00	40.00
❏ 128		Please Forgive Me/You've Been Gone So Long	1954	10.00	20.00	40.00
❏ 132		Never Let Me Go/Burley Cutie	1954	10.00	20.00	40.00
❏ 136		Pledging My Love/Anymore	1954	10.00	20.00	40.00
❏ 136		Pledging My Love/No Money	1954	10.00	20.00	40.00
❏ 144		Anymore/How Can You Be So Mean	1955	10.00	20.00	40.00
❏ 148		So Lonely/I'm Crazy	1956	7.50	15.00	30.00
❏ 154		Still Love You So/Don't You Know	1956	7.50	15.00	30.00

Ad Libs, The
AGP

Number		Title (A Side/B Side)	Year	VG	VG+	NM
❏ 101		New York in the Dark/Human	1968	25.00	50.00	100.00

Blue Cat

Number		Title (A Side/B Side)	Year	VG	VG+	NM
❏ 102		The Boy from New York City/Kicked Around	1965	3.00	6.00	12.00
❏ 114		Ask Anybody/He Ain't No Angel	1965	2.50	5.00	10.00
❏ 119		On the Corner/Oo-Wee Oh Me Oh My	1965	2.50	5.00	10.00
❏ 123		Just a Down Home Girl/Johnny My Boy	1966	2.50	5.00	10.00

Capitol

Number		Title (A Side/B Side)	Year	VG	VG+	NM
❏ 2944		Love Me/Know All About You	1970		3.00	6.00

Interphon

Number		Title (A Side/B Side)	Year	VG	VG+	NM
❏ 7717		Neighbour, Neighbour/Lovely Ladies	1965	2.00	4.00	8.00

Karen

Number		Title (A Side/B Side)	Year	VG	VG+	NM
❏ 1527		Think of Me/Every Boy and Girl	1966	5.00	10.00	20.00

Philips

Number		Title (A Side/B Side)	Year	VG	VG+	NM
❏ 40461		Don't Ever Leave Me/You're in Love	1967	2.00	4.00	8.00

Share

Number		Title (A Side/B Side)	Year	VG	VG+	NM
❏ 101		You're Just a Rolling Stone/Show a Little Appreciation	1969	2.00	4.00	8.00

Number	Title (A Side/B Side)	Year	VG	VG+	NM
❏ 104	Giving Up/Appreciation	1969	2.00	4.00	8.00
❏ 106	The Boy from New York City/	1969	2.00	4.00	8.00
	Nothing Worse Than Being Alone				

Adam's Apples
Brunswick
❏ 55330	Don't Take It Out on This World/	1967	25.00	50.00	100.00
	Don't You Want Me Home				
❏ 55367	You Are the One I Love/Stop Along the Way	1968	12.50	25.00	50.00

Adams, Art
Cherry
❏ 1004	Rock Crazy Baby/Indian Joe	1960	25.00	50.00	100.00
❏ 1018	Dancing Doll/She Don't Live Here Anymore	1960	25.00	50.00	100.00

Adams, Billy
Amy
❏ 893	You and Me/Go (Go On, Get Out of Here Now)	1963	3.00	6.00	12.00
Apt
❏ 25072	My Happiness/Big M	1962	3.00	6.00	12.00
Capitol
❏ 4308	Count Every Star/Peggy's Party	1959	6.25	12.50	25.00
❏ 4373	Can't Get Enough/The Gods Were Angry With Me	1960	6.25	12.50	25.00
Decca
❏ 30724	Baby I'm Bugged/	1958	7.50	15.00	30.00
	Short Hair and Turtle Neck Sweater				
Dot
❏ 15689	You Heard Me Knocking/	1958	7.50	15.00	30.00
	True Love Will Come Your Way				
Fern
❏ 807	Darling Take My Hand/Tender Years	1961	6.25	12.50	25.00
❏ 808	Tattle Tale/Born to Be a Loser	1961	6.25	12.50	25.00
❏ 812	Rip Van Winkle/Sleep Baby Sleep	1961	6.25	12.50	25.00
❏ 813	Comic Strip/Call Me	1961	6.25	12.50	25.00
Home of the Blues
❏ 239	Looking for My Baby/Had the Blues	1962	2.50	5.00	10.00
❏ 242	My Happiness/Big M	1962	5.00	10.00	20.00
Nau Voo
❏ 802	You've Gotta Have a Duck Tail/Walking Star	1959	25.00	50.00	100.00
❏ 805	Return of the All American Boy/That's My Baby	1959	18.75	37.50	75.00
❏ 808	Blue Eyed Ella/Fun House	1959	18.75	37.50	75.00
Quincy
❏ 932	Rock Pretty Mama/(B-side unknown)	195?	500.00	1,000	1,500
Sun
❏ 389	Got My Mojo Workin'/Betty and Dupree	1964	5.00	10.00	20.00
❏ 391	Trouble in My Mind/Lookin' for Mary Ann	1964	5.00	10.00	20.00
❏ 394	Reconsider Baby/Ruby Jane	1964	5.00	10.00	20.00
❏ 401	Open the Door, Richard/Rock Me Baby	1966	5.00	10.00	20.00

Adams, Faye
Atlantic
❏ 1007	Sweet Talk/Watch Out, I Told You	1953	12.50	25.00	50.00
Herald
❏ 416	Shake a Hand/I've Got to Leave You	1953	7.50	15.00	30.00
❏ 419	I'll Be True/Happiness to My Soul	1953	6.25	12.50	25.00
❏ 423	Say a Prayer/Every Day	1954	6.25	12.50	25.00
❏ 429	Somebody, Somewhere, Someday/	1954	6.25	12.50	25.00
	Crazy Mixed-Up World				
❏ 434	Hurts Me to My Heart/Ain't Gonna Tell	1954	6.25	12.50	25.00
❏ 439	I Owe My Heart to You/Love Ain't Nothin' to Play With	1954	6.25	12.50	25.00
❏ 444	Anything for a Friend/	1955	6.25	12.50	25.00
	Your Love Has My Heart Burning				
❏ 450	You Ain't Been True/My Greatest Desire	1955	6.25	12.50	25.00
❏ 457	Angels Tell Me/Tag Along	1955	6.25	12.50	25.00
❏ 462	No Way Out/Same Old Me	1955	6.25	12.50	25.00
❏ 470	Teen-Age Heart/Witness to the Crime	1956	6.25	12.50	25.00
❏ 480	Takin' You Back/Don't Forget to Smile	1956	6.25	12.50	25.00
❏ 489	Anytime, Anyplace, Anywhere/	1956	6.25	12.50	25.00
	The Hammer Keeps Knockin'				
❏ 512	Shake a Hand/I'll Be True	1958	5.00	10.00	20.00
Imperial
❏ 5443	Keeper of My Heart/So Much	1957	5.00	10.00	20.00
❏ 5456	Johnny Lee/You're Crazy	1957	5.00	10.00	20.00
❏ 5471	I Have a Twinkle in My Eye/Someone Like You	1957	5.00	10.00	20.00
❏ 5525	When We Kiss/Everything	1958	5.00	10.00	20.00
Lido
❏ 603	That's All Right/It Made Me Cry	1960	3.00	6.00	12.00
❏ 606	It Can't Be Wrong/I Waited So Long	1960	3.00	6.00	12.00
Savoy
❏ 1606	Cry, You Crazy Heart/Step Up and Rescue Me	1960	3.00	6.00	12.00
❏ 4357	Sinner Man/God	197?		2.50	5.00
Warwick
❏ 590	Shake a Hand/It Hurts to My Heart	1960	3.00	6.00	12.00

Number	Title (A Side/B Side)	Year	VG	VG+	NM
☐ 620	Johnny, Don't/Obey My Rules	1961	3.00	6.00	12.00
☐ 638	It Can't Be Wrong/It's Nice to Know	1961	3.00	6.00	12.00

Adams, Richie
Beltone
☐ 1001	No Mistakin' It/The Right Way	1961	3.75	7.50	15.00
☐ 1011	Two Initials (In a Heart)/What Took You So Long	1961	3.75	7.50	15.00

Congress
☐ 217	I Understand/Lookin' for the Blues	1964	3.75	7.50	15.00
☐ 226	Are You Changing/The King	1964	3.75	7.50	15.00
☐ 232	Slippin' Away/What Am I	1965	3.75	7.50	15.00
☐ 248	Every Window in the City/ I Ain't Gonna Make It Without You	1965	3.75	7.50	15.00
☐ 256	Road to Nowhere/I Can't Escape from You	1965	15.00	30.00	60.00

Imperial
☐ 5806	Something Inside of Me Died/I Got Eyes	1962	3.75	7.50	15.00
☐ 5838	My Prayer of Love/Pakistan	1962	3.75	7.50	15.00
☐ 5856	It's Worth It/Test of Love	1962	3.75	7.50	15.00

MCA
☐ 41182	The Best of the Rest of Our Lives/Warm	1980		2.00	4.00

MGM
☐ 13629	You Were Mine/Better Off Without You	1966	2.50	5.00	10.00

P.I.P.
☐ 6519	Mamacita/Lisa Lisa	1976		2.00	4.00

Ribbon
☐ 6910	Lonely One/Tell Me Baby Did You Wait	1960	3.00	6.00	12.00
☐ 6913	Back to School/Don't Go, My Love, Don't Go	1960	3.00	6.00	12.00

Addeo, Nicky
Earls
☐ 1533	Gloria/Bring Back Your Heart	19??	2.50	5.00	10.00

Melody
☐ 1417	Where There Is Love/You Can Depend on Me	1964	6.25	12.50	25.00

Revelation
☐ 7-101	Danny Boy/A Lovely Way to Spend An Evening	1964	125.00	250.00	500.00

Savoy
☐ 200	Gloria/Bring Back Your Heart *Red vinyl*	1963	100.00	200.00	400.00
☐ 200	Gloria/Bring Back Your Heart *Green vinyl*	1963	75.00	150.00	300.00
☐ 200	Gloria/Bring Back Your Heart *Black vinyl*	1963	50.00	100.00	200.00

Selsom
☐ 104	Over the Rainbow/Fool #2	1965	50.00	100.00	200.00

Addrisi Brothers, The
(Also see "Addrisi, Dick")
Bell
☐ 45,434	Somebody Found Her/Who Do You Think I Am	1974		2.00	4.00

Brad
☐ 003	I'll Be True/Everybody's Happy	1958	8.75	17.50	35.00

Buddah
☐ 566	Slow Dancin' Don't Turn Me On (Short)/ Slow Dancin' Don't Turn Me On (Long)	1977		2.50	5.00
☐ 579	Does She Do It Like She Dances/ Baby, Love Is a Two-Way Street	1977		2.00	4.00
☐ 587	Never My Love/Emergency	1977		2.00	4.00

Columbia
☐ 45521	We've Got to Get It On Again/ You Make It All Worthwhile	1972		2.50	5.00
☐ 45610	One Last Time/I Can Feel You	1972		2.50	5.00
☐ 45705	Lifetime/I Can Count on You	1972		2.50	5.00

Del-Fi
☐ 4116	Cherrystone/Lilies Grow High	1959	7.50	15.00	30.00
☐ 4120	Saving My Kisses/Un Jarro	1959	7.50	15.00	30.00
☐ 4125	It's Love/Back to the Old Salt Mine	1959	7.50	15.00	30.00
☐ 4130	Gonna See My Baby/Ven Ami	1959	6.25	12.50	25.00

Elektra
☐ 47203	Honey Come Home/Red-Eye Flight	1981		2.00	4.00

Imperial
☐ 5715	What a Night for Love/Poor Little Girls	1960	5.00	10.00	20.00

Pom Pom
☐ 4160	The Dance Is Over/Socialite	1962	6.25	12.50	25.00

Private Stock
☐ 45,012	Wait for Me/You Made All the Difference	1975		2.00	4.00

Scotti Brothers
☐ 500	Ghost Dancer/Ghost Dancer	1979		2.00	4.00
☐ 506	As Long As the Music Keeps Playing/ (B-side unknown)	1979		2.00	4.00

Number	Title (A Side/B Side)	Year	VG	VG+	NM

Valiant

☐ 720	Mr. Love/Side by Side	1965	3.00	6.00	12.00
☐ 6047	Love Me Baby/The Way You Look at Him	1964	3.00	6.00	12.00
☐ 6058	C'mon Home Baby/Little Miss Sad	1964	3.75	7.50	15.00

Warner Bros.

| ☐ 5268 | The Dance Is Over (Dance with Me)/Sleeping Beauty | 1962 | 3.75 | 7.50 | 15.00 |
| ☐ 7249 | Time to Love/Good News | 1968 | 2.50 | 5.00 | 10.00 |

Addrisi, Dick
(Of The Addrisi Brothers)

Valiant

| ☐ 742 | You're Bad/Excuse Me | 1966 | 3.00 | 6.00 | 12.00 |

Admirals, The

King

☐ 4772	Oh Yes/Left with a Broken Heart	1955	62.50	125.00	250.00
☐ 4782	Close Your Eyes/Give Me Love	1955	62.50	125.00	250.00
☐ 4792	It's a Sad, Sad Feeling/Ow	1955	12.50	25.00	50.00
	With Lucky Millinder				

Admirations, The
(Several different groups)

Atomic

| ☐ 12871 | Dear Lady/Memories Are Here to Stay | 195? | 50.00 | 100.00 | 200.00 |

Brunswick

| ☐ 55332 | Hey Mama/Lonely Street | 1967 | 5.00 | 10.00 | 20.00 |

Hull

| ☐ 1202 | Moonlight/(B-side unknown) | 1965 | 50.00 | 100.00 | 200.00 |

Kellway

| ☐ 108 | Over the Rainbow/In My Younger Days | 196? | 2.50 | 5.00 | 10.00 |

Mercury

| ☐ 71521 | The Bells of Roja Rita/Little Bo Peep | 1959 | 10.00 | 20.00 | 40.00 |
| ☐ 71883 | To the Aisle/Hey Senorita | 1962 | 50.00 | 100.00 | 200.00 |

One-derful

| ☐ 4849 | Wait Till I Get to Know You/(B-side unknown) | 1967 | 6.25 | 12.50 | 25.00 |
| ☐ 4851 | Don't Leave Me/All for You | 1967 | 6.25 | 12.50 | 25.00 |

Adorables, The

Golden World

☐ 4	Daddy Please/Deep Freeze	1964	6.25	12.50	25.00
☐ 10	School's All Over/Be	1964	6.25	12.50	25.00
☐ 25	Ooh Boy!/Devil in His Eyes	1965	10.00	20.00	40.00

Peacock

| ☐ 1924 | The Drive/Baby, Come and Get It | 1963 | 3.00 | 6.00 | 12.00 |

Adventurers, The
(Several different groups)

Blue Rock

| ☐ 4071 | Something Bad (Is Happening)/Nobody Can Save Me | 1968 | 2.00 | 4.00 | 8.00 |

Capitol

| ☐ F4292 | Rip Van Winkle/Trail Blazer | 1959 | 3.75 | 7.50 | 15.00 |

Columbia

| ☐ 42227 | Rock and Roll Uprising/My Mama Done Told Me | 1961 | 10.00 | 20.00 | 40.00 |

Compass

| ☐ 7010 | Easy Baby/(These Days) A Good Girl Is So Hard to Find | 1967 | 2.00 | 4.00 | 8.00 |

Mecca

| ☐ A-11 | 2 O'Clock Express/Shaggin' | 1960 | 10.00 | 20.00 | 40.00 |

Miracle

| ☐ 1 | 2 O'Clock Express/October Days | 1960 | 5.00 | 10.00 | 20.00 |

Aladdins, The
(Probably at least two different groups)

Aladdin

☐ 3275	Remember/Cry Baby Cry	1955	50.00	100.00	200.00
☐ 3298	I Had a Dream Last Night/Get Off My Feet	1955	50.00	100.00	200.00
☐ 3314	All My Life/So Long, Farewell, Bye Bye	1956	50.00	100.00	200.00
☐ 3358	Help Me/Lord, Show Me	1957	50.00	100.00	200.00

Frankie

| ☐ 6 | Dot, My Love/My Charlene | 1958 | 100.00 | 200.00 | 400.00 |

Witch

| ☐ 109 | Please Love Me/Munch | 1962 | 12.50 | 25.00 | 50.00 |
| ☐ 111 | Our Love Will Be/Simple Simon | 1962 | 12.50 | 25.00 | 50.00 |

Alaimo, Steve

ABC

☐ 10805	So Much Love/Truer Than True	1966	3.00	6.00	12.00
☐ 10833	Happy/On the Beach	1966	3.00	6.00	12.00
☐ 10873	Pardon Me (It's My First Day Alone)/Savin' All My Love	1966	3.00	6.00	12.00
☐ 10917	You Don't Love Me/You Don't Know Like I Know	1967	2.50	5.00	10.00

Number		Title (A Side/B Side)	Year	VG	VG+	NM

ABC-Paramount

❑ 10540		Love's Gonna Live Here/Let Her Go	1964	3.00	6.00	12.00
❑ 10553		Love Is a Many Splendored Thing/Fade Out	1964	3.00	6.00	12.00
❑ 10580		I Don't Know/That's What Love Will Do	1964	3.00	6.00	12.00
❑ 10605		Happy/Everybody Knows But Her	1964	3.00	6.00	12.00
❑ 10620		Real Live Girl/Need You	1965	3.00	6.00	12.00
❑ 10643		Laughing on the Outside/Tomorrow Is Another Day	1965	3.00	6.00	12.00
❑ 10680		Cast Your Fate to the Wind/Mais Oui	1965	3.00	6.00	12.00
❑ 10712		Blowin' in the Wind/Lady of the House	1965	3.00	6.00	12.00
❑ 10764		Bright Lights Big City/Once a Day	1966	3.00	6.00	12.00

Atco

❑ 6512		New Orleans/Ooh Poo Pah Doo	1967	2.00	4.00	8.00
❑ 6560		Cuando Yo Vuelvo Ami Tierra/Todavia	1968	2.50	5.00	10.00
❑ 6561		Denver/I Do	1968	2.00	4.00	8.00
❑ 6589		1 x 1 Ain't 2/My Friend	1968	2.00	4.00	8.00
❑ 6620		Thank You for the Sunshine Days/ Watching the Trains Go	1968	2.00	4.00	8.00
❑ 6659		I'm Thankful/After the Smoke Is Gone	1969	2.00	4.00	8.00
		With Betty Wright				
❑ 6710		One Woman/And Then I Tripped Over Your Goodbye	1969	2.00	4.00	8.00
❑ 6732		Melissa/Smilin' in My Sleep	1970		3.00	6.00
❑ 6797		Can't You See/(On the) Wild Side of Life	1971		3.00	6.00

Checker

❑ 981		Big Bad Beulah/I Cried All the Way Home	1961	3.00	6.00	12.00
❑ 989		All Night Long/I'm Thankful	1961	3.00	6.00	12.00
❑ 998		The Waiting's So Hard/You Got Me Whistling	1961	3.00	6.00	12.00
❑ 1006		Mashed Potatoes/Mashed Potatoes (Part 2)	1962	3.00	6.00	12.00
❑ 1018		My Friend/Going Back to Mary	1962	3.00	6.00	12.00
❑ 1024		Cry Myself to Sleep/One Good Reason	1962	3.00	6.00	12.00
❑ 1032		Every Day I Have to Cry/Little Girl	1962	3.00	6.00	12.00
❑ 1042		A Lifetime of Loneliness/ It's a Long, Long Way to Happiness	1963	3.00	6.00	12.00
❑ 1047		Don't Let the Sun Catch You Cryin'/I Told You So	1963	3.00	6.00	12.00
❑ 1054		Michael -- Pt. 1/Michael -- Pt. 2	1963	3.00	6.00	12.00

Dade

❑ 1800		Home by Eleven/(B-side unknown)	1959	12.50	25.00	50.00
❑ 1805		Love Letters/You Can Fall in Love	1959	12.50	25.00	50.00

Dickson

❑ 6445		My Heart Never Said Goodbye/Blue Fire	1960	5.00	10.00	20.00

Entrance

❑ 7501		When My Little Girl Is Smiling/Gemini	1971		2.50	5.00
❑ 7503		Thorn in Our Roses/Nobody's Fool	1971		2.50	5.00
❑ 7507		Amerikan Music/Nobody's Fool	1972		2.50	5.00
❑ 7513		Sand in My Pocket/Gemini	1972		2.50	5.00

Imperial

❑ 5699		My Heart Never Said Goodbye/Blue Fire	1960	3.75	7.50	15.00
❑ 5717		Unchained Melody/It Happens Ev'ry Time	1961	3.75	7.50	15.00
❑ 66003		Gotta Lotta Love/Happy Pappy	1963	3.00	6.00	12.00

Marlin

❑ 6064		I Want You to Love Me/Blue Skies	1959	7.50	15.00	30.00
❑ 6067		She's My Baby/Should I Care?	1959	6.25	12.50	25.00

Alan, Lee

Lee Alan Presents

❑ (no #)		A Trip to Miami	1964	125.00	250.00	500.00
		Interviews with the Beatles; a giveaway with Lee Alan's two-page story of his trip ($200 NM)				

Alda, Alex

(Actually Nick Massi of the Four Seasons.)

Topix

❑ 6007	DJ	Little Pony (one-sided)	1961	25.00	50.00	100.00

Alexander and the Greats

Arvee

❑ 5064		Swanee Stomp/Waterlogged	1963	10.00	20.00	40.00

Limelight

❑ 3040		Do the Mustang/Hot Dang Mustang	1964	10.00	20.00	40.00

Alexander, Arthur

Buddah

❑ 492		Every Day I Have to Cry Some/ Everybody Needs Somebody to Love	1975		2.50	5.00
❑ 522		Sharing the Night Together/ She'll Throw Stones at You	1976		2.50	5.00
❑ 602		Sharing the Night Together/ She'll Throw Stones at You	1978		2.00	4.00

Dot

❑ 16309		You Better Move On/A Shot of Rhythm and Blues	1962	5.00	10.00	20.00
❑ 16357		Soldier of Love/Where Have You Been	1962	5.00	10.00	20.00
❑ 16387		Anna/I Hang My Head and Cry	1962	5.00	10.00	20.00
❑ 16425		You're the Reason/Go Home Girl	1963	3.75	7.50	15.00
❑ 16454		I Wonder Where You Are Tonight/Dream Girl	1963	3.75	7.50	15.00
❑ 16509		Pretty Girls Everywhere/Baby Baby	1963	3.75	7.50	15.00
❑ 16554		Where Did Sally Go/Keep Her Guessin'	1963	3.75	7.50	15.00

Number	Title (A Side/B Side)	Year	VG	VG+	NM
❏ 16616	Black Knight/Ole John Amos	1964	3.00	6.00	12.00
❏ 16737	Detroit City/You Don't Care	1965	3.00	6.00	12.00

Judd

❏ 1020	Sally Sue Brown/The Girl That Radiates That Charm	1960	12.50	25.00	50.00
	As "June Alexander"				

Monument

❏ 1060	I Need You Baby/Spanish Harlem	1968	2.00	4.00	8.00

Sound Stage 7

❏ 2556	The Other Woman/(Baby) For You	1965	2.50	5.00	10.00
❏ 2572	Turn Around (And Try Me)/Show Me the Road	1966	2.50	5.00	10.00
❏ 2619	Set Me Free/Love's Where Life Begins	1968	2.00	4.00	8.00
❏ 2626	Bye Bye Love/Another	1969	2.00	4.00	8.00
❏ 2652	Glory Road/Cry Like a Baby	1970	2.00	4.00	8.00

Warner Bros.

❏ 7571	I'm Comin' Home/It Hurts to Want It So Bad	1972		3.00	6.00
❏ 7633	Mr. John/You Got Me Knockin'	1972		3.00	6.00
❏ 7658	Burning Love/It Hurts to Want It So Bad	1972		3.00	6.00

Alexander, Joe, and the Cubans
Ballad

❏ 1008	Oh Maria/I Hope These Words Will Find You Well	1954	500.00	1,000	1,500
	With a pre-Chess Chuck Berry in the band				

Alexander, June - See "Alexander, Arthur"

Alexander, Max
Caprock

❏ 116	Little Rome/Rock, Rock, Rock Everybody	1959	50.00	100.00	200.00

Alfi and Harry
Liberty

❏ 55008	The Trouble with Harry/Little Beauty	1955	6.25	12.50	25.00
❏ 55016	The Word Game Song/Persian on Excursion	1956	6.25	12.50	25.00
❏ 55066	Safari/Closing Time	1957	6.25	12.50	25.00

Alice Jean and the Mondellos - See "Mondellos, The"

Allan, Davie, and the Arrows
Cude

❏ 101	War Path/Beyond the Blue	1963	25.00	50.00	100.00

Marc

❏ 3223	War Path/Beyond the Blue	1963	12.50	25.00	50.00

MGM

❏ 14299	It's the Little Things You Do/Haven't You Heard	1971	2.00	4.00	8.00
❏ 14374	Head Over Heels/Here It Comes	1972	2.00	4.00	8.00
❏ 14432	Dawn of the 7th Cavalry/Little Big Horn	1972	2.00	4.00	8.00
❏ 14560	And Evil Did Too/Pleasure Girl	1973	2.00	4.00	8.00
❏ 14650	Apache '73/Run of the Arrow	1973	2.00	4.00	8.00

MRC

❏ 0901	Stoked on Surf/Flashback	1984		2.50	5.00

Private Stock

❏ 45,001	Touch Too Much/We Can Make It Together	1974		3.00	6.00

Sidewalk

❏ 1	Apache '65/Blue Guitar	1965	5.00	10.00	20.00

Tower

❏ 116	Apache '65/Blue Guitar	1965	3.75	7.50	15.00
❏ 133	Moon Dawg '65/Dance the Freddie	1965	3.00	6.00	12.00
❏ 142	Baby Ruth/I'm Looking Over a Four Leaf Clover	1965	3.00	6.00	12.00
❏ 158	Space Hop/Granny Goose	1965	3.00	6.00	12.00
❏ 267	Wild Angels Theme/UFO	1966	3.00	6.00	12.00
❏ 295	Blue's Theme/Bongo Party	1966	3.00	6.00	12.00
❏ 341	Devil's Angels/Cody's Theme	1967	3.00	6.00	12.00
❏ 381	Cycle-Delic/Blue Rides Again	1967	3.00	6.00	12.00
❏ 446	Wild in the Streets/Shape of Things to Come	1968	3.00	6.00	12.00

Allen, Billy
El Dorado

❏ 505	Butterfly/Oo Wee Baby	1957	5.00	10.00	20.00
	As "Bill Allen"				

Imperial

❏ 5500	Please Give Me Something/Since I Have You	1958	25.00	50.00	100.00

Allen, Jesse
Aladdin

❏ 3129	Rock This Morning/Gonna Move Away from Town	1953	50.00	100.00	200.00

Bayou

❏ 011	Dragnet/Take It Easy	1953	25.00	50.00	100.00

Coral

❏ 65078	My Suffering/Let's Party	1952	50.00	100.00	200.00

Imperial

❏ 5256	Gotta Call That Number/Gonna Tell My Mama	1953	50.00	100.00	200.00
	With Audrey Walker				
❏ 5285	Sittin' and Wonderin'/I Wonder What's the Matter	1954	62.50	125.00	250.00

Number		Title (A Side/B Side)	Year	VG	VG+	NM
❑ 5303		What a Party/The Things I'm Gonna Do	1954	50.00	100.00	200.00
❑ 5315		Rockin' and Rollin'/I Love You So	1954	50.00	100.00	200.00

Allen, Milton
RCA Victor

Number		Title (A Side/B Side)	Year	VG	VG+	NM
❑ 47-6994		Love A Love A Lover/ Just Look, Don't Touch, She's Mine	1957	7.50	15.00	30.00
❑ 47-7116		Don't Bug Me Baby/Jamboree	1957	12.50	25.00	50.00

Allen, Tony
Aladdin

Number		Title (A Side/B Side)	Year	VG	VG+	NM
❑ 3403		Time Won't Wait on You/Holy Smoke, Baby	1957	5.00	10.00	20.00

Bethlehem

Number		Title (A Side/B Side)	Year	VG	VG+	NM
❑ 3002		Come-A, Come-A Baby/Just Like Before	1961	3.00	6.00	12.00
❑ 3004		It Hurts Me So/The Trakey-Doo	1962	3.00	6.00	12.00

Dig

Number		Title (A Side/B Side)	Year	VG	VG+	NM
❑ 104		It Hurts Me So/Check Yourself	1955	5.00	10.00	20.00
❑ 109		I Found An Angel/I'm Dreaming	1956	12.50	25.00	50.00

Ebb

Number		Title (A Side/B Side)	Year	VG	VG+	NM
❑ 115		Come Back/Why in the World	1957	5.00	10.00	20.00

Imperial

Number		Title (A Side/B Side)	Year	VG	VG+	NM
❑ 5523		Strange Talk/Call My Name	1958	3.75	7.50	15.00
❑ 5547		Forgive Me/Rockin' Shoes	1958	3.75	7.50	15.00

Jamie

Number		Title (A Side/B Side)	Year	VG	VG+	NM
❑ 1143		Train of Love/God Gave Me You	1959	3.75	7.50	15.00

Kent

Number		Title (A Side/B Side)	Year	VG	VG+	NM
❑ 364		Dreaming/Be My Love, Be My Love	1961	3.00	6.00	12.00

Original Sound

Number		Title (A Side/B Side)	Year	VG	VG+	NM
❑ 13		Little Lonely Girl/I Still Love You	1960	3.00	6.00	12.00

Specialty

Number		Title (A Side/B Side)	Year	VG	VG+	NM
❑ 560		Nite Owl/I	1955	12.50	25.00	50.00
❑ 570		Check Yourself Baby/Especially	1956	7.50	15.00	30.00

Tampa

Number		Title (A Side/B Side)	Year	VG	VG+	NM
❑ 157		Be My Love, Be My Love/Tell Me As "The Wonders"	19??	7.50	15.00	30.00

Ultra

Number		Title (A Side/B Side)	Year	VG	VG+	NM
❑ 104		It Hurts Me So/Check Yourself	1955	7.50	15.00	30.00

United Artists

Number		Title (A Side/B Side)	Year	VG	VG+	NM
❑ 50190		Now Is Forever/Triple Cross	1967	2.00	4.00	8.00

Allens, Arvee - See "Valens, Ritchie"

Alley Cats, The
Epic

Number		Title (A Side/B Side)	Year	VG	VG+	NM
❑ 9778		Lily of the West/ I Should Have Stayed at Home Tonight	1965	3.00	6.00	12.00

Philles

Number		Title (A Side/B Side)	Year	VG	VG+	NM
❑ 108		Puddin N' Tain (Ask Me Again, I'll Tell You the Same)/Feel So Good	1962	6.25	12.50	25.00

Whippet

Number		Title (A Side/B Side)	Year	VG	VG+	NM
❑ 202		This Thing Called Love/Spang-a-Lang	1957	5.00	10.00	20.00
❑ 209		Snap, Crackle and Pop/Last Night	1958	5.00	10.00	20.00

Allies, The
Reprise

Number		Title (A Side/B Side)	Year	VG	VG+	NM
❑ 0674		I Would Love You/The Sound of Children	1968	5.00	10.00	20.00

Valiant

Number		Title (A Side/B Side)	Year	VG	VG+	NM
❑ 748		I'll Sell My Soul/Burning Glass	1966	10.00	20.00	40.00

Allman Joys, The
(Early Allman Brothers Band)
Dial

Number		Title (A Side/B Side)	Year	VG	VG+	NM
❑ 4046		Spoonful/You Deserve Each Other	1966	10.00	20.00	40.00

Allman, Duane and Gregg
(Of the Allman Brothers Band)
Bold

Number		Title (A Side/B Side)	Year	VG	VG+	NM
❑ 200		Morning Dew/Morning Dew	1973	2.50	5.00	10.00
❑ 200	DJ	Morning Dew/Morning Dew Promo on red vinyl	1973	5.00	10.00	20.00

Alma-Keys, The
Kiski

Number		Title (A Side/B Side)	Year	VG	VG+	NM
❑ 2056		Please Come Back to Me/Jumpin' Twist	1962	75.00	150.00	300.00

Altairs, The
(George Benson was a member)
Amy

Number		Title (A Side/B Side)	Year	VG	VG+	NM
❑ 803		If You Love Me/Groove Time	1960	5.00	10.00	20.00

Number	Title (A Side/B Side)	Year	VG	VG+	NM

Alton and Jimmy
Sun

| ☐ 323 | Have Faith in My Love/No More Crying the Blues | 1959 | 6.25 | 12.50 | 25.00 |

Alvin and Bill
Fernwood

| ☐ 124 | Typing Jive/How Long | 1960 | 15.00 | 30.00 | 60.00 |

Alvin and the Chipmunks - See "Chipmunks, The"

Ambassadors, The
(Several different groups)
Arctic

☐ 150	Ain't Got the Love of One Girl/ Music Makes You Wanna Dance	1969	2.50	5.00	10.00
☐ 153	Storm Warning/I Dig You Baby	1969	2.50	5.00	10.00
☐ 156	Can't Take My Eyes Off You/A.W.O.L.	1969	2.50	5.00	10.00

Atlantic

☐ 2442	(I've Got to Find) Happiness)/I'm So Proud of My Baby	1967	2.50	5.00	10.00
☐ 2491	Good Love Gone Bad/Happiness	1968	2.50	5.00	10.00
☐ 2547	We Got Love/Never Get Tired of Loving You	1968	2.50	5.00	10.00

Dot

| ☐ 16528 | Surfin' John Brown/Big Breaker | 1963 | 7.50 | 15.00 | 30.00 |

Sound Stage 7

| ☐ 2588 | If You Don't Know (You Better Ask Somebody)/
There's Something on My Baby's Mind | 1967 | 2.50 | 5.00 | 10.00 |

Timely

| ☐ 1001 | Darling I'm Sorry/Willa-Bea | 1954 | 100.00 | 200.00 | 400.00 |

Uptown

| ☐ 734 | I Need Someone/Bear With Me | 1965 | 6.25 | 12.50 | 25.00 |

Amboy Dukes, The
DiscReet

| ☐ 1199 | Sweet Revenge/Ain't It the Truth
As "Ted Nugent and the Amboy Dukes" | 1974 | | 3.00 | 6.00 |

Mainstream

☐ 676	Baby Please Don't Go/Psalms of Aftermath	1968	3.00	6.00	12.00
☐ 684	Journey to the Center of the Mind/ Mississippi Murderer	1968	3.75	7.50	15.00
☐ 693	You Talk Sunshine, I Breathe Fire/Scottish Tea	1968	3.00	6.00	12.00
☐ 700	Prodigal Man/Good Natured Emma	1969	3.00	6.00	12.00
☐ 704	For His Namesake/Loaded for Bear	1969	3.00	6.00	12.00
☐ 711	Flight of the Birds/(B-side unknown)	1969	3.00	6.00	12.00

Amelio, Johnny
Blue Moon

☐ 405	Jugue/Downbeat	1957	37.50	75.00	150.00
☐ 408	Jo-Ann, Jo-Ann/I'll Forever Love You	1958	25.00	50.00	100.00
☐ 410	Jugue/Jo-Ann, Jo-Ann	1958	20.00	40.00	80.00

American Beatles, The
BYP

| ☐ 1001 | She's Mine/Theme of the American Beetles
As "The American Beetles" | 1964 | 5.00 | 10.00 | 20.00 |

Roulette

| ☐ 4550 | You Did It to Me/Don't Be Unkind | 1964 | 3.75 | 7.50 | 15.00 |
| ☐ 4559 | School Days/Hey Hey Girl | 1964 | 3.75 | 7.50 | 15.00 |

American Breed, The
Acta

☐ 802	I Don't Think You Know/ Give Two Young Lovers a Chance	1967	2.00	4.00	8.00
☐ 804	Step Out of Your Mind/Same Old Thing	1967	2.50	5.00	10.00
☐ 808	Don't Forget About Me/Short Skirts	1967	2.00	4.00	8.00
☐ 811	Bend Me, Shape Me/Mindrocker	1967	3.00	6.00	12.00
☐ 821	Green Light/Don't It Make You Cry	1968	2.00	4.00	8.00
☐ 821 PS	Green Light/Don't It Make You Cry	1968	5.00	10.00	20.00
☐ 824	Ready, Willing and Able/Take Me If You Want Me	1968	2.00	4.00	8.00
☐ 827	Anyway You Want Me/Master of My Fate	1968	2.00	4.00	8.00
☐ 830	Private Zoo/Keep the Faith	1968	2.00	4.00	8.00
☐ 833	Hunky Funky/Enter Her Majesty	1969	2.00	4.00	8.00
☐ 836	Room at the Top/Walls	1969	2.00	4.00	8.00
☐ 837	Cool It/The Brain	1969	2.00	4.00	8.00

Paramount

| ☐ 0040 | When I'm With You/Can't Make It Without You | 1970 | | 3.00 | 6.00 |

American Four, The
(With Arthur Lee, future leader of Love)
Selma

| ☐ 2001 | Luci Baines/Soul Food | 1964 | 12.50 | 25.00 | 50.00 |

Number		Title (A Side/B Side)	Year	VG	VG+	NM

American Spring
(Also see "Spring")
Columbia

❑ 45834		Fallin' in Love/Shyin' Away	1973	7.50	15.00	30.00
❑ 45834	PS	Fallin' in Love/Shyin' Away	1973	15.00	30.00	60.00

Anastasia
Laurie

❑ 3066	Time Bomb/That's My Kind of Love	1960	6.25	12.50	25.00

Stasi

❑ 1000	Every Road I Walk Along/Bicycle Hop	196?	50.00	100.00	200.00
❑ 1001	Seven Days a Week/Nothing Beats My Girl	196?	37.50	75.00	150.00

Andantes, The
Dot

❑ 16495	My Baby's Gone/No Yo Ru	1963	6.25	12.50	25.00

V.I.P.

❑ 25006	If You Were Mine/((Like a) Nightmare	1964	625.00	1,250	2,500

One of the rarest of all Motown-related 45 releases

Anders, Bernie
King

❑ 4833	My Heart Believes/Too Late I Learned	1955	12.50	25.00	50.00

Anderson, Brother James
Sun

❑ 406	I'm Gonna Move in the Room with the Lord/ My Soul Needs Resting	1967	12.50	25.00	50.00

Anderson, Sonny
Imperial

❑ 5634	Yes, I'm Gonna Love You/Lonely, Lonely Train	1959	12.50	25.00	50.00
❑ 5689	Our Love Could Never Be/Fool	1960	12.50	25.00	50.00

Andrews, Lee, and the Hearts
(Also includes Lee Andrews credited alone)
Argo

❑ 1000	Tear Drops/The Girl Around the Corner	1957	12.50	25.00	50.00

Casino

❑ 110	Baby, Come Back/I Wonder	1958	7.50	15.00	30.00
❑ 452	Try the Impossible/Nobody's Home	1958	200.00	400.00	600.00

With playing cards on label

❑ 452	Try the Impossible/Nobody's Home	1958	50.00	100.00	200.00

All-black label

Chess

❑ 1665	Long Lonely Nights/The Clock	1957	6.25	12.50	25.00

Sliver-top "chess pieces" label

❑ 1665	Long Lonely Nights/The Clock	1957	3.75	7.50	15.00

All-blue label

❑ 1675	Tear Drops/The Girl Around the Corner	1957	5.00	10.00	20.00

All-blue label (if a "chess pieces" label exists, we aren't aware of it)

Crimson

❑ 1002	Oh My Love/Island of Love	1967	2.00	4.00	8.00
❑ 1009	Nevertheless/Island of Love	1967	2.00	4.00	8.00
❑ 1015	I've Had It/Little Bird	1968	2.00	4.00	8.00

Gotham

❑ 318	Bluebird of Happiness/Show Me the Meringue	1956	75.00	150.00	300.00
❑ 320	Lonely Room/Leona	1956	75.00	150.00	300.00
❑ 321	Just Suppose/It's Me!	1956	75.00	150.00	300.00

Grand

❑ 156	Teardrops/The Girl Around the Corner	1962	2.50	5.00	10.00
❑ 157	Long Lonely Nights/The Clock	1962	2.50	5.00	10.00

Main Line

❑ 102	Long Lonely Nights/The Clock	1957	75.00	150.00	300.00

Green label, no address

❑ 102	Long Lonely Nights/The Clock	1957	50.00	100.00	200.00

Black label, Philadelphia address on label

❑ 102	Long Lonely Nights/The Clock	1962	2.50	5.00	10.00

Black label, no address

❑ 105	Teardrops/The Girl Around the Corner	1962	2.50	5.00	10.00

Parkway

❑ 860	I'm Sorry, Fellow/Gee, But I'm Lonesome	1962	2.50	5.00	10.00
❑ 866	Looking Back/Operator	1963	2.50	5.00	10.00

Rainbow

❑ 252	Maybe You'll Be There/Baby Come Back	1954	200.00	400.00	800.00

Red vinyl

❑ 252	Maybe You'll Be There/Baby Come Back	1954	125.00	250.00	500.00

Black vinyl

❑ 252	Maybe You'll Be There/Baby Come Back	1962	2.50	5.00	10.00

Reissue with large print

Number	Title (A Side/B Side)	Year	VG	VG+	NM
☐ 256	White Cliffs of Dover/Much Too Much	1954	200.00	400.00	800.00
	Yellow label original				
☐ 256	White Cliffs of Dover/Much Too Much	1962	2.50	5.00	10.00
	Blue label reissue				
☐ 259	The Bells of St. Mary's/The Fairest	1954	75.00	150.00	300.00
	Yellow label original				
☐ 259	The Bells of St. Mary's/The Fairest	1962	2.50	5.00	10.00
	Blue label reissue				

RCA Victor

☐ 47-8929	Quiet As It's Kept/You're Taking a Long Time Coming Back	1966	2.50	5.00	10.00

Swan

☐ 4065	I Miss You So/I've Got to Cry	1960	25.00	50.00	100.00
☐ 4076	A Night Like This/You Gave to Me	1961	37.50	75.00	150.00
☐ 4087	P.S. I Love You/I Cried	1961	50.00	100.00	200.00

United Artists

☐ 123	Try the Impossible/Nobody's Home	1958	6.25	12.50	25.00
☐ 136	Why Do I/Glad to Be Here	1958	5.00	10.00	20.00
☐ 151	Maybe You'll Be There/All I Ask Is Love	1958	5.00	10.00	20.00
☐ 162	Boom/Just Suppose	1959	5.00	10.00	20.00
☐ 592	Try the Impossible/Nobody's Home	1963	3.75	7.50	15.00

Angel, Johnny
(May be more than one performer)

Excello

☐ 2077	I Realize/Baby I'm Confessin'	1956	6.25	12.50	25.00

Felsted

☐ 8633	Lady of Spain/Without Her Heart	1961	5.00	10.00	20.00
☐ 8646	Mashed Potatoe Stomp/One More Tomorrow	1962	5.00	10.00	20.00
☐ 8659	Looking for a Fool/Roller Motion	1962	5.00	10.00	20.00

Gardena

☐ 117	All Night Party/Baby, You've Got Soul	1961	3.75	7.50	15.00

Imperial

☐ 5673	Falling Teardrops/Doubt	1960	10.00	20.00	40.00

JAF

☐ 2024	Lonely Nights/Seven Words	1961	3.75	7.50	15.00

Liberty

☐ 55895	Summertime Blues/Biggest Part of Me	1966	2.00	4.00	8.00

Power

☐ 250	Starlight/The Story of Love	1959	30.00	60.00	120.00

Swan

☐ 4263	This Is the Night for Love/You've Been Wrong	1966	10.00	20.00	40.00

Vin

☐ 1004	Teenage Wedding/Baby, It's Love	1958	6.25	12.50	25.00

Angels, The
(Records on Gee and Grand are by a male group. The Tawny group later recorded as The Safaris.)

Ascot

☐ 2139	Irresistible/Cotton Fields	1963	3.00	6.00	12.00

Cameo

☐ 250	You Turn Me On/Raining Teardrops	1963	3.75	7.50	15.00

Caprice

☐ 107	'Til/A Moment Ago	1961	5.00	10.00	20.00
☐ 112	Cry Baby Cry/That's All I Ask of You	1962	5.00	10.00	20.00
☐ 116	Everybody Loves a Lover/Blow Joe	1962	3.75	7.50	15.00
☐ 118	You Should Have Told Me/I'd Be Good for You	1962	3.75	7.50	15.00
☐ 121	Cotton Fields/A Moment Ago	1963	3.75	7.50	15.00

Gee

☐ 1024	Glory of Love/It's You I Love Best	1956	15.00	30.00	60.00

Grand

☐ 115	Wedding Bells/Times Have Changed	1954	100.00	200.00	400.00
	With no address on label				
☐ 115	Wedding Bells/Times Have Changed	1954	12.50	25.00	50.00
	With address on label				
☐ 121	A Lovely Way to Spend An Evening/You're Still My Baby	1954	125.00	250.00	500.00
	With no address on label				
☐ 121	A Lovely Way to Spend An Evening/You're Still My Baby	1954	12.50	25.00	50.00
	With address on label				

Polydor

☐ 14222	You're All I Need to Get By/Poppa's Side of the Bed	1974		2.50	5.00

RCA Victor

☐ 47-9129	I Had a Dream I Lost You/What to Do	1967	2.50	5.00	10.00
☐ 47-9246	Go Out and Play/You'll Never Get to Heaven (If You Break My Heart)	1967	2.50	5.00	10.00
☐ 47-9404	You're the Cause of It/With Love	1967	2.50	5.00	10.00
☐ 47-9541	The Medley: Moments to Remember-Theme from A Summer Place-One Summer Night/If I Didn't Love You	1968	2.50	5.00	10.00

Number		Title (A Side/B Side)	Year	VG	VG+	NM
❑ 47-9612		But for Love/The Man with the Green Eyes	1968	2.50	5.00	10.00
❑ 47-9681		Merry Go Round/So Nice (Samba De Verao)	1968	2.50	5.00	10.00

Smash

❑ 1834		My Boyfriend's Back/(Leave Me) Now	1963	4.00	8.00	16.00
❑ 1854		I Adore Him/Thank You and Goodnight	1963	3.75	7.50	15.00
❑ 1854	PS	I Adore Him/Thank You and Goodnight	1963	10.00	20.00	40.00
❑ 1870		Wow Wow Wee (He's the Boy for Me)/ Snowflakes and Teardrops	1964	3.75	7.50	15.00
❑ 1885		Little Beatle Boy/Java	1964	5.00	10.00	20.00
❑ 1915		Jamaica Joe/Dream Boy	1964	3.75	7.50	15.00
❑ 1931		A World Without Love/The Boy from 'Cross Town	1964	3.75	7.50	15.00

Tawny

❑ 101		A Lover's Poem (To Him)/A Lover's Poem (To Her)	1959	10.00	20.00	40.00

Angie and the Chicklettes

Apt

❑ 25080		Treat Him Tender Maureen (Now That Ringo Belongs to You)/Tommy	1965	7.50	15.00	30.00

Animals, The

(Also see "Burdon, Eric, and War"; "Price, Alan")

Abkco

❑ 4025		House of the Rising Sun/Bring It On Home to Me	1973		2.50	5.00
		Contains the full-length version of A-side, its only appearance on U.S. 45				
❑ 4026		We Gotta Get Out of This Place/It's My Life	1973		2.00	4.00
❑ 4037		Don't Let Me Be Misunderstood/Talkin' About You	1973		2.00	4.00
❑ 4038		I'm Cryin'/Boom Boom	1973		2.00	4.00

I.R.S.

❑ 9920		The Night/No John No	1983		2.50	5.00
❑ 9923		Love Is For All Time/It's Too Late	1983		2.50	5.00

Jet

❑ XW1070		Fire on the Sun/Riverside County	1977		3.00	6.00

MGM

❑ 13242		Gonna Send You Back to Walker (Gonna Send You Back to Georgia)/ Baby, Let Me Take You Home	1964	3.75	7.50	15.00
❑ 13264		The House of the Rising Sun/Talkin' About You	1964	3.00	6.00	12.00
❑ 13264	PS	The House of the Rising Sun/Talkin' About You	1964	6.25	12.50	25.00
❑ 13274		I'm Crying/Take It Easy Baby	1964	3.00	6.00	12.00
❑ 13274	PS	I'm Crying/Take It Easy Baby	1964	6.25	12.50	25.00
❑ 13298		Boom Boom/Blue Feeling	1964	3.00	6.00	12.00
❑ 13298	PS	Boom Boom/Blue Feeling	1964	6.25	12.50	25.00
❑ 13311		Don't Let Me Be Misunderstood/Club A-Go-Go	1964	3.00	6.00	12.00
❑ 13339		Bring It On Home to Me/For Miss Caulker	1965	3.00	6.00	12.00
❑ 13339	PS	Bring It On Home to Me/For Miss Caulker	1965	6.25	12.50	25.00
❑ 13382		We Gotta Get Out of This Place/I Can't Believe It	1965	3.00	6.00	12.00
❑ 13414		It's My Life/I'm Going to Change the World	1965	3.00	6.00	12.00
❑ 13468		Inside-Looking Out/You're On My Mind	1966	3.00	6.00	12.00
❑ 13514		Don't Bring Me Down/Cheating	1966	3.00	6.00	12.00
		Note: Starting with the next listing, records are by "Eric Burdon and the Animals"				
❑ 13582		See See Rider/She'll Return It	1966	2.50	5.00	10.00
❑ 13636		Help Me Girl/That Ain't Where It's At	1966	2.50	5.00	10.00
❑ 13721		When I Was Young/A Girl Called Sandoz	1967	2.50	5.00	10.00
❑ 13769		San Franciscan Nights/Good Times	1967	2.50	5.00	10.00
❑ 13769	PS	San Franciscan Nights/Good Times	1967	6.25	12.50	25.00
❑ CS11-5		Celebrity Scene: The Animals	1967	20.00	40.00	80.00
		Box set of five singles. Price includes box, all 5 singles, jukebox title strips, bio. Records are sometimes found by themselves, so they are listed separately below.				
❑ 13791		Don't Bring Me Down/When I Was Young	1967	3.00	6.00	12.00
❑ 13792		See See Rider/Hey Gyp	1967	3.00	6.00	12.00
❑ 13793		Inside-Looking Out/Help Me Girl	1967	3.00	6.00	12.00
❑ 13794		San Franciscan Nights/Good Times	1967	3.00	6.00	12.00
❑ 13795		It's All Meat/The Other Side of This Life	1967	3.00	6.00	12.00
❑ 13868		Monterey/Ain't That So	1967	2.50	5.00	10.00
❑ 13868	PS	Monterey/Ain't That So	1967	6.25	12.50	25.00
❑ 13917		Anything/It's All Meat	1968	2.50	5.00	10.00
❑ 13939		Sky Pilot (Part 1)/Sky Pilot (Part 2)	1968	2.50	5.00	10.00
		First pressings have black labels				
❑ 13939		Sky Pilot (Part 1)/Sky Pilot (Part 2)	1968	2.00	4.00	8.00
		Second pressings have blue and gold labels				
❑ 14013		River Deep, Mountain High/White Houses	1968	2.00	4.00	8.00

Anka, Paul

ABC-Paramount

❑ 9831		Diana/Don't Gamble with Love	1957	5.00	10.00	20.00
❑ 9855		I Love You, Baby/Tell Me That You Love Me	1957	7.50	15.00	30.00
❑ 9880		You Are My Destiny/When I Stop Loving You	1958	5.00	10.00	20.00
❑ 9907		Crazy Love/Let the Bells Keep Ringing	1958	5.00	10.00	20.00
❑ 9937		Midnight/Verboten!	1958	5.00	10.00	20.00
❑ 9956		Just Young/So It's Goodbye	1958	5.00	10.00	20.00
❑ 9956	PS	Just Young/So It's Goodbye	1958	12.50	25.00	50.00
❑ 9987	M	(All of a Sudden) My Heart Sings/That's Love	1958	5.00	10.00	20.00
❑ S-9987	S	(All of a Sudden) My Heart Sings/That's Love	1958	12.50	25.00	50.00
❑ 10011	M	I Miss You So/Late Last Night	1959	3.75	7.50	15.00
❑ 10011	PS	I Miss You So/Late Last Night	1959	6.25	12.50	25.00

Number		Title (A Side/B Side)	Year	VG	VG+	NM
S-10011	S	I Miss You So/Late Last Night	1959	12.50	25.00	50.00
10022	M	Lonely Boy/Your Love	1959	3.75	7.50	15.00
S-10022	S	Lonely Boy/Your Love	1959	12.50	25.00	50.00
10040	M	Put Your Head on My Shoulder/Don't Ever Leave Me	1959	3.75	7.50	15.00
10040	PS	Put Your Head on My Shoulder/Don't Ever Leave Me	1959	6.25	12.50	25.00
S-10040	S	Put Your Head on My Shoulder/Don't Ever Leave Me	1959	12.50	25.00	50.00
10064	M	It's Time to Cry/Something Has Changed Me	1959	3.75	7.50	15.00
10064	PS	It's Time to Cry/Something Has Changed Me	1959	6.25	12.50	25.00
S-10064	S	It's Time to Cry/Something Has Changed Me	1959	12.50	25.00	50.00
10082	M	Puppy Love/Adam and Eve	1960	3.75	7.50	15.00
10082	PS	Puppy Love/Adam and Eve	1960	6.25	12.50	25.00
S-10082	S	Puppy Love/Adam and Eve	1960	12.50	25.00	50.00
10106	M	My Home Town/Something Happened	1960	3.75	7.50	15.00
10106	PS	My Home Town/Something Happened	1960	6.25	12.50	25.00
S-10106	S	My Home Town/Something Happened	1960	12.50	25.00	50.00
10132	M	Hello Young Lovers/I Love You in the Same Old Way	1960	3.75	7.50	15.00
10132	PS	Hello Young Lovers/I Love You in the Same Old Way	1960	6.25	12.50	25.00
S-10132	S	Hello Young Lovers/I Love You in the Same Old Way	1960	12.50	25.00	50.00
10147	M	Summer's Gone/I'd Have to Share	1960	3.75	7.50	15.00
10147	PS	Summer's Gone/I'd Have to Share	1960	5.00	10.00	20.00
S-10147	S	Summer's Gone/I'd Have to Share	1960	12.50	25.00	50.00
10163		Rudolph, the Red-Nosed Reindeer/ I Saw Mommy Kissing Santa Claus	1960	6.25	12.50	25.00
10168	M	The Story of My Love/Don't Say You're Sorry	1960	3.75	7.50	15.00
10168	PS	The Story of My Love/Don't Say You're Sorry	1960	6.25	12.50	25.00
S-10168	S	The Story of My Love/Don't Say You're Sorry	1960	12.50	25.00	50.00
10169		It's Christmas Everywhere/ Rudolph, the Red-Nosed Reindeer	1960	4.00	8.00	16.00
10169	PS	It's Christmas Everywhere/ Rudolph, the Red-Nosed Reindeer	1960	6.25	12.50	25.00
10194		Tonight My Love, Tonight/I'm Just a Fool Anyway	1961	3.00	6.00	12.00
10194	PS	Tonight My Love, Tonight/I'm Just a Fool Anyway	1961	6.25	12.50	25.00
10220		Dance On Little Girl/I Talk to You	1961	3.00	6.00	12.00
10220	PS	Dance On Little Girl/I Talk to You	1961	6.25	12.50	25.00
10239		Kissin' on the Phone/Cinderella	1961	3.00	6.00	12.00
10239	PS	Kissin' on the Phone/Cinderella	1961	6.25	12.50	25.00
10279		Loveland/The Bells at My Wedding	1961	3.00	6.00	12.00
10282		The Fools Hall of Fame/Far from the Lights of Town	1961	3.00	6.00	12.00
10311		I'll Never Find Another You/Uh Huh	1962	2.50	5.00	10.00
10338		I'm Coming Home/Why	1962	2.50	5.00	10.00

Barnaby

Number		Title (A Side/B Side)	Year	VG	VG+	NM
2027		You're Some Kind of Friend/ Why Are You Leaning on Me, Sir	1971		3.00	6.00

Buddah

Number		Title (A Side/B Side)	Year	VG	VG+	NM
252		Do I Love You/So Long City	1971		2.50	5.00
294		Everything's Been Changed/Jubilation	1972		2.50	5.00
314		Something Good Is Coming/Life Song	1972		2.50	5.00
337		While We're Still Young/This Is Your Song	1973		2.50	5.00
349		Hey Girl/You and Me Today	1973		2.50	5.00

Columbia

Number		Title (A Side/B Side)	Year	VG	VG+	NM
03897		Hold Me 'Til the Mornin' Comes/This Is the First Time	1983			3.00
03897	PS	Hold Me 'Til the Mornin' Comes/This Is the First Time	1983		2.00	4.00
04187		Gimme the Word/No Way Out	1983			3.00
		A-side: With Karla DeVito				
04407		Second Chance/Walk a Fine Line	1984			3.00
07358		No Way Out/Just for Once	1987			3.00
		A-side: Paul Anka and Julia Migenas; B-side: Migenas solo				

Epic

Number		Title (A Side/B Side)	Year	VG	VG+	NM
50298		You/Make It Up to Me in Love	1976		2.00	4.00
		With Odia Coates				

Fame

Number		Title (A Side/B Side)	Year	VG	VG+	NM
XW345		Flashback/Let Me Get to Know You	1973		2.00	4.00

RCA

Number		Title (A Side/B Side)	Year	VG	VG+	NM
PB-11351		Lovely Lady/Brought Up in New York	1978		2.00	4.00
PB-11395		This Is Love/I'm By Myself Again	1978		2.00	4.00
PB-11662		As Long As We Keep Believing/Headlines	1979		2.00	4.00
PB-11957		Rainbow/After All	1980			Unreleased
PB-12184		We Love Each Other/Think I'm in Love Again	1981			3.00
PB-12225		I've Been Waiting for You All My Life/ Think I'm in Love Again	1981			3.00
PB-12262		Lady Lay Down/You're Still a Part of Me	1981			3.00

RCA Victor

Number		Title (A Side/B Side)	Year	VG	VG+	NM
37-7977		Love Me Warm and Tender/I'd Like to Know	1962	6.25	12.50	25.00
		"Compact Single 33" (small hole, plays at LP speed)				
47-7977		Love Me Warm and Tender/I'd Like to Know	1962	2.50	5.00	10.00
47-7977	PS	Love Me Warm and Tender/I'd Like to Know	1962	5.00	10.00	20.00
47-8030		A Steel Guitar and a Glass of Wine/ I Never Knew Your Name	1962	2.50	5.00	10.00
47-8030	PS	A Steel Guitar and a Glass of Wine/ I Never Knew Your Name	1962	5.00	10.00	20.00
47-8068		Every Night (Without You)/There You Go	1962	2.50	5.00	10.00
47-8068	PS	Every Night (Without You)/There You Go	1962	5.00	10.00	20.00
47-8097		Eso Beso (That Kiss!)/Give Me Back My Heart	1962	2.50	5.00	10.00
47-8097	PS	Eso Beso (That Kiss!)/Give Me Back My Heart	1962	5.00	10.00	20.00
47-8115		Love (Makes the World Go 'Round)/ Crying in the Wind	1962	2.50	5.00	10.00

Number		Title (A Side/B Side)	Year	VG	VG+	NM
❏ 47-8115	PS	Love (Makes the World Go 'Round)/ Crying in the Wind	1962	5.00	10.00	20.00
❏ 47-8158		Think About It/At Night	1963			*Unreleased*
❏ 47-8170		Remember Diana/At Night	1963	2.50	5.00	10.00
❏ 47-8170	PS	Remember Diana/At Night	1963	5.00	10.00	20.00
❏ 47-8195		Hello Jim/You've Got the Nerve to Call This Love	1963	2.50	5.00	10.00
❏ 47-8195	PS	Hello Jim/You've Got the Nerve to Call This Love	1963	5.00	10.00	20.00
❏ 47-8237		Wondrous Are the Ways of Love/ Hurry Up and Tell Me	1963	2.50	5.00	10.00
❏ 47-8272		Did You Have a Happy Birthday/ For No Good Reason at All	1963	2.50	5.00	10.00
❏ 47-8272	PS	Did You Have a Happy Birthday/ For No Good Reason at All	1963	5.00	10.00	20.00
❏ 47-8311		From Rocking Horse to Rocking Chair/Cheer Up	1964	2.00	4.00	8.00
❏ 47-8349		My Baby's Comin' Home/No, No	1964	2.00	4.00	8.00
❏ 47-8396		In My Imagination/It's Easy to Say	1964	2.00	4.00	8.00
❏ 47-8441		Cindy Go Home/Ochi Volta	1964	2.00	4.00	8.00
❏ 47-8493		Sylvia/Behind My Smile	1965	2.00	4.00	8.00
❏ 47-8595		Dream Me Happy/The Loneliest Boy in the World	1965	2.00	4.00	8.00
❏ 47-8662		Every Day a Heart Is Broken/ As If There Were No Tomorrow	1965	2.00	4.00	8.00
❏ 47-8764		Truly Yours/Oh, Such a Stranger	1965	2.00	4.00	8.00
❏ 47-8839		I Wish/I Went to Your Wedding	1966	2.00	4.00	8.00
❏ 47-8893		I Can't Help Loving You/ Can't Get Along Very Well Without Her	1966	2.00	4.00	8.00
❏ 47-9032		Poor Old World/I'd Rather Be a Stranger	1966	2.00	4.00	8.00
❏ 47-9128		Until It's Time for You to Go/ Would You Still Be My Baby	1967	2.00	4.00	8.00
❏ 47-9228		A Woman Is a Sentimental Thing/ That's How Love Goes	1967	2.00	4.00	8.00
❏ 47-9457		Can't Get You Out of My Mind/When We Get There	1968	2.00	4.00	8.00
❏ 47-9648		Goodnight My Love/This Crazy World	1968	2.00	4.00	8.00
❏ 47-9767		Happy/Can't Get You Out of My Mind	1969	2.00	4.00	8.00
❏ 47-9846		Midnight Mistress/ Before It's Too Late-This Land Is Your Land	1970	2.00	4.00	8.00
❏ 74-0126		In the Still of the Night/Pickin' Up the Pieces	1969	2.00	4.00	8.00
❏ 74-0164		Sincerely/Next Year	1969	2.00	4.00	8.00
❏ GB-10180		Diana/Put Your Head on My Shoulders	1975	2.00	4.00	
		Gold Standard Series				
❏ GB-10181		Puppy Love/Lonely Boy	1975		2.00	4.00
		Gold Standard Series				
❏ GB-10182		You Are My Destiny/Tonight, My Love, Tonight	1975		2.00	4.00
		Gold Standard Series				

RPM

❏ 472		I Confess/Blau-Wile Deveest Fontaine	1956	15.00	30.00	60.00
❏ 499		I Confess/Blau-Wile Deveest Fontaine	1957	6.25	12.50	25.00

United Artists

❏ XW454		(You're) Having My Baby/Papa	1974		2.00	4.00
❏ XW569		One Man Woman/One Woman Man// Let Me Get to Know You	1974		2.00	4.00
		A-side: With Odia Coates				
❏ XW615		I Don't Like to Sleep Alone/ How Can Anything Be Beautiful After You	1975		2.00	4.00
❏ XW615	PS	I Don't Like to Sleep Alone/ How Can Anything Be Beautiful After You	1975		2.00	4.00
❏ XW682		(I Believe) There's Nothing Stronger Than Our Love/ Today I Became a Fool	1975		3.00	6.00
		Canada-only release				
❏ XW685		(I Believe) There's Nothing Stronger Than Our Love/ Today I Became a Fool	1975		2.00	4.00
❏ XW737		Times of Your Life/Water Runs Deep	1975		2.00	4.00
❏ XW737	PS	Times of Your Life/Water Runs Deep	1975		2.00	4.00
❏ XW789		Anytime (I'll Be There)/Something About You	1976		2.00	4.00
❏ XW896		Happier/Closing Doors	1976		3.00	6.00
		Canada-only release				
❏ XW911		Happier/Closing Doors	1976		2.00	4.00
❏ XW945		I'll Help You/ Never Gonna Fall in Love Like I Fell in Love with You	1977		2.00	4.00
❏ XW972		My Best Friend's Wife/ Never Gonna Fall in Love Like I Fell in Love with You	1977		2.00	4.00
❏ XW1018		Tonight/Everybody Ought to Be in Love	1977		2.00	4.00
❏ XW1157		(You're) Having My Baby//One Man Woman/ One Woman Man	1978			3.00
❏ XW1158		I Don't Like to Sleep Alone/Times of Your Life	1978			3.00

Anka, Paul/George Hamilton IV/Johnny Nash

ABC-Paramount

❏ 9974		The Teen Commandments/If You Learn to Pray	1958	6.25	12.50	25.00

Ann-Margret

Ariola

❏ 7511		Love Rush/For You	1979		3.00	6.00

Avco Embassy

❏ 4547		Today/Today	1970	3.75	7.50	15.00
		B-side by Lenny Stack				

Number		Title (A Side/B Side)	Year	VG	VG+	NM

LHI

❑ 1		It's a Nice World to Visit/You Turned My Head Around	1969		3.00	6.00
❑ 2		Chico/Sleep in the Grass	1969		3.00	6.00
		With Lee Hazlewood				
❑ 5		The Dark End of the Street/Victims of the Night	1969		3.00	6.00
		With Lee Hazlewood				
❑ 11		Walk Out of My Mind/Hangin' In	1970		3.00	6.00
		With Lee Hazlewood				

MCA

❑ 41186		Love Rush/For You	1980		2.50	5.00
❑ 41223		Midnight Message/For You	1980		2.50	5.00

RCA Victor

❑ 37-7857		I Ain't Got Nobody/Lost Love	1961	6.25	12.50	25.00
		"Compact Single 33" (small hole, plays at LP speed)				
❑ 37-7894		I Just Don't Understand/I Don't Hurt Anymore	1961	6.25	12.50	25.00
		"Compact Single 33" (small hole, plays at LP speed)				
❑ 37-7952		It Do Me So Good/Gimme Love	1961	6.25	12.50	25.00
		"Compact Single 33" (small hole, plays at LP speed)				
❑ 47-7857		I Ain't Got Nobody/Lost Love	1961	3.00	6.00	12.00
❑ 47-7894		I Just Don't Understand/I Don't Hurt Anymore	1961	3.75	7.50	15.00
❑ 47-7894	PS	I Just Don't Understand/I Don't Hurt Anymore	1961	6.25	12.50	25.00
❑ 47-7952		It Do Me So Good/Gimme Love	1961	2.50	5.00	10.00
❑ 47-7952	PS	It Do Me So Good/Gimme Love	1961	6.25	12.50	25.00
❑ 47-7986		What Am I Supposed to Do/	1962	2.50	5.00	10.00
		Let's Stop Kidding Each Other				
❑ 47-7986	PS	What Am I Supposed to Do/	1962	6.25	12.50	25.00
		Let's Stop Kidding Each Other				
❑ 47-8061		Jim Dandy/I Was Only Kidding	1962	2.50	5.00	10.00
❑ 47-8061	PS	Jim Dandy/I Was Only Kidding	1962	6.25	12.50	25.00
❑ 47-8130		No More/So Did I	1963	2.50	5.00	10.00
❑ 47-8168		Bye Bye Birdie/Take All the Kisses	1963	2.50	5.00	10.00
❑ 47-8168	PS	Bye Bye Birdie/Take All the Kisses	1963	6.25	12.50	25.00
❑ 47-8295		Hey Little Star/Man's Favorite Sport	1963	2.50	5.00	10.00
❑ 47-8446		He's My Man/Someday Soon	1964	2.50	5.00	10.00
❑ 47-8734		Mister Kiss Kiss Bang Bang/	1965	2.50	5.00	10.00
		What Did I Have That I Don't Have Now				
❑ 47-9013		The Swinger/	1966	2.50	5.00	10.00
		You've Come a Long Way from St. Louis				

Annette

Buena Vista

❑ 336		Jo Jo the Dog Faced Boy/Lonely Guitar	1959	5.00	10.00	20.00
❑ 336		Jo Jo the Dog Faced Boy/Love Me Forever	1959	3.75	7.50	15.00
❑ 339		Wild Willie/Lonely Guitar	1959	3.75	7.50	15.00
❑ 339	PS	Wild Willie/Lonely Guitar	1959	7.50	15.00	30.00
❑ 344		Especially for You/My Heart Became of Age	1959	3.75	7.50	15.00
❑ 349		First Name Initial/My Heart Became of Age	1959	3.75	7.50	15.00
❑ 349	PS	First Name Initial/My Heart Became of Age	1959	7.50	15.00	30.00
❑ 354		O Dio Mio/It Took Dreams	1960	3.75	7.50	15.00
❑ 354	PS	O Dio Mio/It Took Dreams	1960	7.50	15.00	30.00
❑ 359		Train of Love/Tell Me Who's the Girl	1960	3.75	7.50	15.00
❑ 359	PS	Train of Love/Tell Me Who's the Girl	1960	10.00	20.00	40.00
❑ 362		Pineapple Princess/Luau Cha Cha Cha	1960	3.75	7.50	15.00
❑ 362	PS	Pineapple Princess/Luau Cha Cha Cha	1960	7.50	15.00	30.00
❑ 369		Talk to Me Baby/I Love You Baby	1960	3.75	7.50	15.00
❑ 369	PS	Talk to Me Baby/I Love You Baby	1960	7.50	15.00	30.00
❑ 374		Dream Boy/Please, Please Signore	1961	3.75	7.50	15.00
❑ 374	PS	Dream Boy/Please, Please Signore	1961	7.50	15.00	30.00
❑ 375		Indian Giver/	1961	3.75	7.50	15.00
		Mama, Mama Rosa (Where's the Spumoni)				
❑ 375	PS	Indian Giver/	1961	7.50	15.00	30.00
		Mama, Mama Rosa (Where's the Spumoni)				
❑ 384		Hawaiian Love Talk/Blue Muu Muu	1961	3.75	7.50	15.00
❑ 384	PS	Hawaiian Love Talk/Blue Muu Muu	1961	12.50	25.00	50.00
❑ 388		Dreamin' About You/Strummin' Song	1961	3.75	7.50	15.00
❑ 388	PS	Dreamin' About You/Strummin' Song	1961	7.50	15.00	30.00
❑ 392		That Crazy Place From Outer Space/	1962	3.75	7.50	15.00
		Seven Moons (Of Batalayre)				
		B-side by Danny Saval and Tom Tryon				
❑ 392	PS	That Crazy Place From Outer Space/	1962	10.00	20.00	40.00
		Seven Moons (Of Batalayre)				
❑ 394		The Truth About Youth/I Can't Do the Sum	1962	3.75	7.50	15.00
❑ 394	PS	The Truth About Youth/I Can't Do the Sum	1962	10.00	20.00	40.00
❑ 400		My Little Grass Shack/Hukilau	1962	3.75	7.50	15.00
❑ 405		He's My Ideal/Mr. Piano Man	1962	3.75	7.50	15.00
❑ 405	PS	He's My Ideal/Mr. Piano Man	1962	7.50	15.00	30.00
❑ 407		Bella Bella Florence/Canzone d'Amoure	1962	3.75	7.50	15.00
		With Marcochi				
❑ 407	PS	Bella Bella Florence/Canzone d'Amoure	1962	37.50	75.00	150.00
❑ 414		Teenage Wedding/Walkin' and Talkin'	1962	5.00	10.00	20.00
❑ 414	PS	Teenage Wedding/Walkin' and Talkin'	1962	100.00	200.00	400.00
❑ 427		Treat Him Nicely/Promise Me Anything	1963	3.75	7.50	15.00
❑ 427	PS	Treat Him Nicely/Promise Me Anything	1963	15.00	30.00	60.00
❑ 431		Merlin Jones/The Scrambled Egghead	1964	3.00	6.00	12.00
		With Tommy Kirk				
❑ 431	PS	Merlin Jones/The Scrambled Egghead	1964	7.50	15.00	30.00

Number		Title (A Side/B Side)	Year	VG	VG+	NM
❑ 432		Custom City/Rebel Rider	1964	5.00	10.00	20.00
❑ 432	PS	Custom City/Rebel Rider	1964	20.00	40.00	60.00
❑ 433		Muscle Beach Party/I Dream About Frankie	1964	3.75	7.50	15.00
❑ 433	PS	Muscle Beach Party/I Dream About Frankie	1964	7.50	15.00	30.00
❑ 436		Bikini Beach Party/The Clyde	1964	3.75	7.50	15.00
❑ 436	PS	Bikini Beach Party/The Clyde	1964	10.00	20.00	40.00
❑ 437		The Wah-Watusi/The Clyde	1964	3.00	6.00	12.00
❑ 438		Something Borrowed, Something Blue/ How Will I Know My Love	1965	3.75	7.50	15.00
❑ 438	PS	Something Borrowed, Something Blue/ How Will I Know My Love	1965	20.00	40.00	80.00
❑ 440		The Monkey's Uncle/How Will I Know My Love	1965	3.00	6.00	12.00
		With the Beach Boys backing up				
❑ 440	PS	The Monkey's Uncle/How Will I Know My Love	1965	5.00	10.00	20.00
❑ 442		The Boy to Love/No One Else Could Be Prouder	1965	3.00	6.00	12.00
❑ 450		No Way to Go But Up/Crystal Ball	1966	3.00	6.00	12.00
❑ 475		The Computer Wore Tennis Shoes/Merlin Jones	1970	2.00	4.00	8.00

Disneyland

❑ 102		How Will I Know My Love/Don't Jump to Conclusions	1958	6.25	15.00	30.00
❑ 102	PS	How Will I Know My Love/Don't Jump to Conclusions	1958	12.50	25.00	50.00
❑ 114		That Crazy Place in Outer Space/ Gold Doubloons and Pieces of Eight	1958	10.00	20.00	40.00
		B-side: "Theme from the Hardy Boys"				
❑ 118		Tall Paul/Ma, He's Making Eyes at Me	1959	5.00	10.00	20.00
❑ 786		That Crazy Place From Outer Space/Happy Glow	196?	2.50	5.00	10.00
		No artist credit on label, but A-side is the same recording as Disneyland 114				

Epic

❑ 9829		Baby Needs Me Now/Moment of Silence	1965	6.25	12.50	25.00
		With Cecil Null				

Starview

❑ 3001		The Promised Land/In Between and Out of Love	1983	2.50	5.00	10.00
❑ 3001	PS	The Promised Land/In Between and Out of Love	1983	2.50	5.00	10.00

Tower

❑ 326		What's a Girl to Do/When You Get What You Want	1967	7.50	15.00	30.00

Annie and the Orphans

Capitol

❑ 5144		My Girl's Been Bitten by the Beatle Bug/ A Place Called Happiness	1964	5.00	10.00	20.00
❑ 5144	PS	My Girl's Been Bitten by the Beatle Bug/ A Place Called Happiness	1964	6.25	12.50	25.00

Antell, Peter

(Also see "Buchanan and Ancell")

Bounty

❑ 103		The Times They Are a-Changin'/ Yesterday and Tomorrow	1965	3.75	7.50	15.00

Cameo

❑ 234		Something About You/Night Time	1962	5.00	10.00	20.00
❑ 264		You in Disguise/Keep It Up	1963	3.75	7.50	15.00

New Voice

❑ 818		Wanting/Warm Smoke	1967	2.50	5.00	10.00

Anthony and the Sophomores

ABC

❑ 10844		Heartbreak/I'll Go Through Life Loving You	1966	5.00	10.00	20.00

ABC-Paramount

❑ 10737		Gee (But I'd Give the World)/It Depends On You	1965	5.00	10.00	20.00
❑ 10770		Get Back to You/Wild for Her	1966	5.00	10.00	20.00

Grand

❑ 163		Embraceable You/Beautiful Dreamer	1963	15.00	30.00	60.00

Jamie

❑ 1330		Serenade (From The Student Prince)/Work Out	1967	3.75	7.50	15.00
❑ 1340		One Summer Night/Work Out	1967	3.75	7.50	15.00

Mercury

❑ 72103		Play Those Oldies Mr. D.J./Clap Your Hands	1963	15.00	30.00	60.00
❑ 72168		Swingin' at the Chariot/Better Late Than Never	1963	7.50	15.00	30.00

Anthony, Lamont - See "Dozier, Lamont"

Anthony, Rayburn

Sun

❑ 333		Alice Blue Gown/St. Louis Blues	1959	5.00	10.00	20.00
❑ 339		There's No Tomorrow/ Who's Gonna Shoe Your Pretty Foot	1960	5.00	10.00	20.00
❑ 373		Big Dream/How Well I Know	1962	5.00	10.00	20.00

Antwinettes, The

RCA Victor

❑ 47-7398		Johnny/Kill It	1958	10.00	20.00	40.00

Number	Title (A Side/B Side)	Year	VG	VG+	NM

Aphrodite's Child
(Vangelis was a member.)
Philips
❑ 40536	Other People/Plastics Nevermore	1968	5.00	10.00	20.00
❑ 40587	End of the World/You Always Stand in My Way	1969	5.00	10.00	20.00

Polydor
❑ 15005	Magic Mirror/I Want to Live	1969	2.00	4.00	8.00

Vertigo
❑ 107	Babylon/Break	1973		3.00	6.00

Applejacks, The
(Dave Appell and studio musicians. Except the ones on London; those are a British Invasion group.)
B.T. Puppy
❑ 554	The Son of a Preacher Man/Girl of the Skies	1970	2.00	4.00	8.00
	As "Dave Appell"				

Cameo
❑ 110	Love in the Jungle/Chitter Chatter Baby	1957	5.00	10.00	20.00
❑ 132	Dinner with Drac/No Name Theme	1958	6.25	12.50	25.00
❑ 138	Moonlight Serenade/Walk On	1958	5.00	10.00	20.00
❑ 149	Mexican Hat Rock/Sophisticated Swing	1958	5.00	10.00	20.00
❑ 149	Mexican Hat Rock/Stop! Red Light	1958	4.00	8.00	16.00
❑ 155	Rocka-Tonga/Am I Blue	1958	5.00	10.00	20.00
	First pressing contains a typographical error on A-side				
❑ 155	Rocka-Conga/Am I Blue	1958	4.00	8.00	16.00
	Later pressings have correct A-side title				
❑ 159	Bunny Hop/Night Train Stroll	1959	4.00	8.00	16.00
❑ 170	Circle Dance/Love Scene	1959	4.00	8.00	16.00
❑ 177	The Untouchables/Memories Are Made of This	1960	4.00	8.00	16.00
❑ 184	Theme from The Young Ones/September Song	1960	3.75	7.50	15.00
	As "Dave Appell and His Orchestra"				
❑ 203	Mexican Hat Twist/Let's Continental	1961	3.75	7.50	15.00
❑ 207	Happy Jose/Noivous	1961	3.75	7.50	15.00
	As "Dave Appell and His Orchestra"				
❑ 222	Struttin' in the Summertime/Any Time	1962	3.75	7.50	15.00
❑ 248	Hippies Waltz/Back in 60 Seconds	1963	3.75	7.50	15.00
❑ 283	Hot Toddy/Dance of the Hours	1963	3.75	7.50	15.00
❑ 321	She Loves You/Bongo Beach	1964	3.75	7.50	15.00
	As "Dave Appell and His Orchestra"				

Decca
❑ 29218	Smarter/My Heart Will Wait for You	1954	5.00	10.00	20.00
❑ 29330	Sweet Patootie Pie/Reunion	1954	5.00	10.00	20.00

London
❑ 9658	Baby Jane/Tell Me When	1964	3.00	6.00	12.00
❑ 9681	Like Dreamers Do/Everybody Fall Down	1964	3.75	7.50	15.00
❑ 9709	You're the One for Me/Three Little Words	1964	3.00	6.00	12.00
❑ 9709	You're the One for Me/Send Me Love	1964	3.00	6.00	12.00

President
❑ 1005	Ring Around My Baby/Love Express	1956	5.00	10.00	20.00
❑ 1006	Teenage Meeting/Ooh Baby Ooh	1956	5.00	10.00	20.00
❑ 1011	Rock and Roll Story/Rainbow of Love	1956	5.00	10.00	20.00

Appreciations, The
Jubilee
❑ 5525	Afraid of Love/Far from Your Love	1966	3.00	6.00	12.00

Sport
❑ 108	There's a Place in My Heart/She Never Really Believed Me	1967	25.00	50.00	100.00
❑ 112	It's Better to Cry/Gimme Back My Soul	1967	50.00	100.00	200.00

Aquatones, The
Fargo
❑ 1001	You/She's the One for Me	1958	6.25	12.50	25.00
❑ 1002	Say You'll Be Mine/So Fine	1958	6.25	12.50	25.00
❑ 1003	Our First Kiss/The Drive-In	1958	6.25	12.50	25.00
❑ 1005	My Treasure/My One Desire	1959	6.25	12.50	25.00
❑ 1015	Every Time/There's a Long, Long Trail	1960	6.25	12.50	25.00
❑ 1016	Wanted/Crazy for You	1961	6.25	12.50	25.00
❑ 1022	My Treasure/Say You'll Be Mine	1961	6.25	12.50	25.00
❑ 1111	My Darling/For You, For You	196?	5.00	10.00	20.00

Arbors, The
Carney
❑ 1011	A Symphony for Susan/Love Is the Light	1966	6.25	12.50	25.00

Date
❑ 1529	A Symphony for Susan/Love Is the Light	1966	2.50	5.00	10.00
❑ 1546	Dreamer Girl/Just Let It Happen	1967	2.50	5.00	10.00
❑ 1561	Graduation Day/I Win the Whole Wide World	1967	2.50	5.00	10.00
❑ 1570	Love for All Seasons/With You Girl	1967	2.50	5.00	10.00
❑ 1581	Valley of the Dolls/You Are the Music	1967	2.50	5.00	10.00
❑ 1601	That's the Way It Is/Graduation Day	1968	2.50	5.00	10.00
❑ 1638	The Letter/Most of All	1969	3.00	6.00	12.00
❑ 1645	I Can't Quit Her/Lovin' Tonight (Maybe Tonight)	1969	2.50	5.00	10.00

Number		Title (A Side/B Side)	Year	VG	VG+	NM
❏ 1651		Touch Me/Motet	1969	2.50	5.00	10.00
❏ 1672		Julie I Tried/Okalona River Bottom Band	1970	2.50	5.00	10.00

Mercury

❏ 72456		Anybody Here for Love/ The Girl with the Heather Green Eyes	1965	3.00	6.00	12.00

Archers, The
Laurie

❏ 3207		Hey Rube/Unwind It	1963	3.75	7.50	15.00

Summer

❏ 502		Motorcycle Michael/Golden Girl	196?	7.50	15.00	30.00

Archies, The
(Also see "Dante, Ron")
Calendar

❏ 63-1006		Bang-Shang-a-Lang/Truck Driver	1968	2.00	4.00	8.00
❏ 63-1006	PS	Bang-Shang-a-Lang/Truck Driver	1968	4.00	8.00	16.00
❏ 63-1007		Feelin' So Good (S.K.O.O.B.Y.-D.O.O.)/Love Light	1968	2.00	4.00	8.00
❏ 63-1007	PS	Feelin' So Good (S.K.O.O.B.Y.-D.O.O.)/Love Light	1968	4.00	8.00	16.00
❏ 63-1008		Sugar Sugar/Melody Hill	1969	2.50	5.00	10.00

Kirshner

❏ 63-1009		Sunshine/Over and Over	1970	2.00	4.00	8.00
❏ 63-5002		Jingle Jangle/Justine	1969	2.00	4.00	8.00
❏ 63-5003		Who's Your Baby/Senorita Rita	1970	2.00	4.00	8.00
❏ 63-5009		Everything's Alright/Together We Two	1970	2.00	4.00	8.00
❏ 63-5011		Throw a Little Love My Way/This Is Love	1971	2.00	4.00	8.00
❏ 63-5014		A Summer Prayer for Peace/Maybe I'm Wrong	1971	2.00	4.00	8.00
❏ 63-5014	PS	A Summer Prayer for Peace/Maybe I'm Wrong	1971	4.00	8.00	16.00
❏ 63-5018		Love Is Living in You/Hold On to Lovin'	1972	2.00	4.00	8.00
❏ 63-5021		Strangers in the Morning/Plum Crazy	1972	2.00	4.00	8.00

Argyles, The
(Also see "Hollywood Argyles, The." The below is by a different group.)
Bally

❏ 1030		Moonbeam/Every Time You Smile	1957	10.00	20.00	40.00

Ariels, The
Brent

❏ 7060		Feels Like I'm Cryin'/I Love You	1967	15.00	30.00	60.00

Aristocrats, The
Argo

❏ 5275		Maid of the Mist/Vagabonds	1957	6.25	12.50	25.00

Essex

❏ 366		Believe Me/I'm Waiting for Ships	1954	15.00	30.00	60.00

Arlington, Bruce
King

❏ 5918		You Made Me Cry/How Could You Know	1964	7.50	15.00	30.00

Arnold, Vance, and the Avengers - See "Cocker, Joe"

Arribians, The
J.O.B.

❏ 1116		To Look at a Star/Working and Gambling	1958	200.00	400.00	800.00

Ascots, The
(Several different groups?)
Ace

❏ 650		I'm Touched/Perfect Love	1962	6.25	12.50	25.00

Arrow

❏ 736		Easier Said Than Done/Is It Really You	1958	7.50	15.00	30.00

Bethlehem

❏ 3046		Hip Talk/She Did	1962	3.75	7.50	15.00

Dual-Tone

❏ 1120		Acapulco Run/The Gladiator	1963	15.00	30.00	60.00

J&S

❏ 1628/9		What Love Can Do/Everything Will Be Alright	1958	7.50	15.00	30.00

King

❏ 5679		I Don't Care One Bit/Tonight	1962	7.50	15.00	30.00

Super

❏ 102		Monkey See, Monkey Do/You Can't Do That	1966	5.00	10.00	20.00
❏ 103		Midnight Hour/Midnight Hour (Part 2)	1966	5.00	10.00	20.00
❏ 104		Put Your Arms Around Me/Sookie Sookie	1966	5.00	10.00	20.00

Ashley, Del - See "Gates, David"

Ashley, John
Capehart

❏ 5006		Little Lou/I Need Your Lovin'	1961	12.50	25.00	50.00

Dot

❏ 15775		Born to Rock/Pickin' on the Wrong Chicken	1958	12.50	25.00	50.00
❏ 15878		My Story/Let the Good Times Roll	1958	3.75	7.50	15.00

Number		Title (A Side/B Side)	Year	VG	VG+	NM
Intro						
❑ 6097		Bermuda/Let Yourself Go Go Go	196?	7.50	15.00	30.00
Silver						
❑ 1002		I Want to Hear It from You/Seriously in Love	1959	6.25	12.50	25.00
❑ 1005		Cry of the Wild Goose/One Love	1960	6.25	12.50	25.00

Ashley, Robert
Mercury
❑ 71365		Comic Strip Rock and Roll/The Baby	1957	12.50	25.00	50.00

Ashley, Tony
Decca
❑ 32240		I'll Never Be Satisfied/All Along I've Loved You	1967	5.00	10.00	20.00
❑ 32342		We Must Have Love/I Can't Put You Down	1968	5.00	10.00	20.00
❑ 32520		I'll Go Crazy/Just a Taste	1969	15.00	30.00	60.00

Asia
(Featuring members of Yes; Emerson, Lake and Palmer; and King Crimson)
Geffen
❑ 28745		Wishing/Too Late	1986			3.00
❑ 28872		Go/After the War	1985			3.00
❑ 28872	PS	Go/After the War	1985			3.00
❑ 29475		The Smile Has Left Your Eyes/Lying to Yourself	1983		2.00	4.00
❑ 29475	PS	The Smile Has Left Your Eyes/Lying to Yourself	1983		2.00	4.00
❑ 29571		Don't Cry/Daylight	1983		2.00	4.00
❑ 29571	PS	Don't Cry/Daylight	1983		2.00	4.00
❑ 29871		Here Comes the Feelin'/Sole Survivor	1982		2.00	4.00
❑ 29970		Only Time Will Tell/Time Again	1982		2.00	4.00
❑ 29970	PS	Only Time Will Tell/Time Again	1982		2.00	4.00
❑ 50040		Heat of the Moment/Ride Easy	1982		2.00	4.00
❑ 50040	PS	Heat of the Moment/Ride Easy	1982		2.50	5.00

Association, The
Columbia
❑ 45602		Indian Wells Woman/Darling Be Home Soon	1972		2.50	5.00
❑ 45654		Come the Fall/Kicking the Gong Around	1972		2.50	5.00
Elektra						
❑ 47094		Dreamer/You Turn the Light On	1980		2.00	4.00
❑ 47146		Small Town Lovers/Across the Persian Gulf	1981		2.00	4.00
Jubilee						
❑ 5505		Babe I'm Gonna Leave You/ Baby Can't You Hear Me Call Your Name	1965	6.25	12.50	25.00
Mums						
❑ 6016		Names, Tags, Numbers & Labels/Rainbows Bent	1973		2.00	4.00
RCA Victor						
❑ PB-10217		One Sunday Morning/Life Is a Carnival	1975		2.00	4.00
Valiant						
❑ 730		Too Many Mornings/Forty Times	1965	3.75	7.50	15.00
❑ 741		Along Comes Mary/Your Own Love	1966	3.00	6.00	12.00
❑ 747		Cherish/Don't Blame It On Me	1966	3.00	6.00	12.00
❑ 755		Pandora's Golden Heebie Jeebies/Standing Still	1966	2.50	5.00	10.00
❑ 758		No Fair at All/Looking Glass	1967	2.50	5.00	10.00
Warner Bros.						
❑ 7040		Pandora's Golden Heebie Jeebies/Standing Still	1967	2.00	4.00	8.00
❑ 7041		Windy/Sometime	1967	2.50	5.00	10.00
❑ 7074		Never My Love/Requiem for the Masses	1967	2.50	5.00	10.00
❑ 7105		Along Comes Mary/Cherish	1968	2.00	4.00	8.00
		"Back to Back Hits" series on "W7" label				
❑ 7119		Windy/Never My Love	1968	2.00	4.00	8.00
		"Back to Back Hits" series on "W7" label				
❑ 7163		Everything That Touches You/We Love Us	1968	2.00	4.00	8.00
		Orange "WB" label				
❑ 7195		Time for Livin'/Birthday Morning	1968	2.00	4.00	8.00
❑ 7229		Six Man Band/Like Always	1968	2.00	4.00	8.00
❑ 7267		Goodbye Columbus/The Time It Is Today	1969	2.00	4.00	8.00
❑ 7277		Under Branches/Hear in Here	1969	2.00	4.00	8.00
❑ 7305		Yes, I Will/I Am Up for Europe	1969	2.00	4.00	8.00
❑ 7349		Are You Ready/Dubuque Blues	1969	2.00	4.00	8.00
❑ 7372		Just About the Same/Look at Me, Look at You	1970		3.00	6.00
❑ 7429		Along the Way/Traveler's Guide	1970		3.00	6.00
❑ 7471		P.F. Sloan/Traveler's Guide	1971		3.00	6.00
❑ 7515		Bring Yourself Home/It's Gotta Be Real	1971		3.00	6.00
❑ 7524		That's Racin'/Makes Me Cry (Funny Kind of Song)	1971		3.00	6.00

Astors, The
Stax
❑ 139		What Can It Be/Just Enough to Hurt Me	1963	20.00	40.00	80.00
❑ 170		Candy/I Found Out	1965	6.25	12.50	25.00
❑ 179		Mystery Woman/In the Twilight Zone	1965	6.25	12.50	25.00
❑ 232		Daddy Didn't Tell You/More Power to You	1967	3.00	6.00	12.00

Number	Title (A Side/B Side)	Year	VG	VG+	NM

Astronauts, The
(Not all are the same group)

Jan Ell

❑ 459	Geneva Twist/Take 17	1962	7.50	15.00	30.00

Luney

❑ 100	Ridge Route/Blast Off	1962	7.50	15.00	30.00

Mercury

❑ 71675	Alabama Jubilee/Gadabout	1960	3.00	6.00	12.00

Palladium

❑ 610	Come Along Baby/Trying to Get to You	1962	25.00	50.00	100.00

RCA Victor

❑ 47-8194	Baja/Kuk	1963	5.00	10.00	20.00
❑ 47-8224	Hot Doggin'/Everyone But Me	1963	5.00	10.00	20.00
❑ 47-8298	Competition Coupe/Surf Party	1963	5.00	10.00	20.00
❑ 47-8364	Go Fight for Her/Swim Little Mermaid	1964	5.00	10.00	20.00
❑ 47-8419	Main Title from Ride the Wild Surf/ Around and Around	1964	5.00	10.00	20.00
❑ 47-8463	I'm a Fool/Can't You See I Do	1964	5.00	10.00	20.00
❑ 47-8499	Almost Grown/My Sin Is Pride	1965	5.00	10.00	20.00
❑ 47-8545	Tomorrow's Gonna Be Another Day/Razza Matazz	1965	5.00	10.00	20.00
❑ 47-8628	It Doesn't Matter Anymore/The La La La Song	1965	5.00	10.00	20.00
❑ 47-8885	In My Car/Main Street	1966	3.75	7.50	15.00
❑ 47-9109	I Know You Rider/Better Things	1967	3.75	7.50	15.00

Trial

❑ 3521	Farewell/Chili Charlene	1960	50.00	100.00	200.00

Vanrus

❑ 1000	Ski Lift/Blues Beat	1962	7.50	15.00	30.00

Atlantics, The

Columbia

❑ 42877	Greensleeves/Bombera	1963	5.00	10.00	20.00
❑ 43023	War of the World/Bow Man	1964	5.00	10.00	20.00

Linda

❑ 103	Boo-Hoo-Hoo/Everything Is Gonna Be All Right	1961	6.25	12.50	25.00
❑ 107	Remember the Night/Flame of Love	1962	20.00	40.00	80.00

Rampart

❑ 614	Let Me Call You Sweetheart/Home on the Range	1964	3.00	6.00	12.00
❑ 643	Beaver Shot/Fine, Fine, Fine	1965	2.50	5.00	10.00
❑ 647	Slopp Dance/Sonny and Cher	1965	2.50	5.00	10.00

Attractions, The

Bell

❑ 659	Destination You/Find Me	1967	5.00	10.00	20.00
❑ 674	New Girl in the Neighborhood/That Girl Is Mine	1967	5.00	10.00	20.00
❑ 690	Why Shouldn't a Man Cry/Some of Your Time	1967	5.00	10.00	20.00

Atwood the Electric Iceman
(Actually the Sir Douglas Quintet with Atwood Allen)

Uni

❑ 55216	Bossier City/Michoacan	1970		3.00	6.00

Audrey

Plus

❑ 104	Dear Elvis/Dear Elvis (Part 2)	1956	15.00	30.00	60.00

August and Deneen

ABC

❑ 11082	We Go Together/Can't Get You Out of My Head	1968	15.00	30.00	60.00

Austin, Patti

ABC

❑ 11104	Music to My Heart/ Love 'Em and Leave 'Em Kind of Love	1968	3.75	7.50	15.00

Columbia

❑ 45337	Are We Ready for Love/ Now That I Know What Loneliness Is	1971		2.50	5.00
❑ 45410	Black California/All Good Gifts-Day by Day	1971		2.50	5.00
❑ 45499	God Only Knows/Can't Forget the One I Love	1971		2.50	5.00
❑ 45592	Day by Day/Didn't Say a Word	1972		2.50	5.00
❑ 45785	Come to Him/Turn On the Music	1973		2.50	5.00
❑ 45906	Being with You/Take a Closer Look	1973		2.50	5.00

Coral

❑ 62455	He's Good Enough for Me/Earl	1965	5.00	10.00	20.00
❑ 62471	I Wanna Be Loved/A Most Unusual Boy	1965	5.00	10.00	20.00
❑ 62478	Someone's Gonna Cry/ You'd Better Know What You're Getting	1966	25.00	50.00	100.00
❑ 62491	Take Your Time/Take Away the Pain Stain	1966	5.00	10.00	20.00
❑ 62500	Leave a Little Love/My Lovelight Ain't Gonna Shine	1966	5.00	10.00	20.00
❑ 62511	Got to Check You Out/What a Difference a Day Makes	1967	5.00	10.00	20.00
❑ 62518	Only All the Time/Oh How I Need You Joe	1967	5.00	10.00	20.00
❑ 62541	I'll Keep Loving You/You're Too Much a Part of Me	1967	5.00	10.00	20.00
❑ 62548	(I've Given) All My Love/Why Can't We Try It Again	1968	5.00	10.00	20.00

Number		Title (A Side/B Side)	Year	VG	VG+	NM

CTI
☐ 7		In My Life (Part 1)/In My Life (Part 2)	1973		2.50	5.00
		With Jerry Butler				
☐ 33		Say You Love Me/In My Life	1976		2.00	4.00
☐ 41		We're in Love/Golden Oldies	1977		2.00	4.00
☐ 51		Love Me by Name/You Fooled Me	1978		2.00	4.00
☐ 59		What's at the End of the Rainbow/In My Life	1978		2.00	4.00
☐ 9600		Body Language/People in Love	1980		2.00	4.00
☐ 9601		I Want You Tonight/Love Me Again	1980		2.00	4.00

Qwest
☐ 27718		Smoke Gets In Your Eyes/	1988			3.00
		How Long Has This Been Goin' On?				
☐ 28573		Only a Breath Away/	1986			3.00
		Summer Is the Coldest Time of Year				
☐ 28659		Gettin' Away with Murder/Anything Can Happen Here	1986			3.00
☐ 28788		The Heat of Heat/Hot in the Flames of Love	1986			3.00
☐ 28935		Honey for the Bees/Hot in the Flames of Love	1985			3.00
☐ 29136		All Behind Us Now/Fine Fine Fella (Got to Have You)	1984		2.00	4.00
☐ 29234		Shoot the Moon/Change Your Attitude	1984		2.00	4.00
☐ 29305		Rhythm of the Street/Solero	1984		2.00	4.00
☐ 29373		It's Gonna Be Special/Solero	1984		2.00	4.00
☐ 29618		How Do You Keep the Music Playing/	1983		2.00	4.00
		same (Long Version)				
☐ 29727		Every Home Should Have One/Solero	1983		2.00	4.00
☐ 49754		Do You Love Me/Solero	1981		2.00	4.00
☐ 49854		Every Home Should Have One/Solero	1981		2.50	5.00
☐ 50036		Baby, Come to Me/Solero	1982		2.00	4.00
		With James Ingram				

United Artists
☐ 50520		The Family Tree/Magical Boy	1969	2.00	4.00	8.00
☐ 50588		I Will Wait for You/Big Mouth	1969	2.00	4.00	8.00
☐ 50640		Your Love Made a Difference in Me/	1970	2.00	4.00	8.00
		It's Easier to Laugh Than Cry				

Avalon, Frankie
Amos
| ☐ 127 | | The Star/Woman Cryin' | 1969 | | 2.50 | 5.00 |

Bobcat
| ☐ 04103 | | Such a Miracle/You're the Miracle | 1983 | | 2.00 | 4.00 |

Chancellor
☐ 45 FX 1		Christmas Holiday/Dear Gesu Bambino	196?	5.00	10.00	20.00
☐ 1004		Cupid/Jivin' with the Saints	1957	5.00	10.00	20.00
☐ 1006		Shy Guy/Teacher's Pet	1957	5.00	10.00	20.00
☐ 1011		Dede Dinah/Ooh La La	1958	3.75	7.50	15.00
☐ 1016		You Excite Me/Darlin'	1958	3.75	7.50	15.00
☐ 1021		Ginger Bread/Blue Betty	1958	3.75	7.50	15.00
☐ 1021	PS	Ginger Bread/Blue Betty	1958	10.00	20.00	40.00
☐ 1026		I'll Wait for You/What Little Girl	1958	3.75	7.50	15.00
☐ 1026	PS	I'll Wait for You/What Little Girl	1958	10.00	20.00	40.00
☐ 1031	M	Venus/I'm Broke	1959	5.00	10.00	20.00
☐ 1031	PS	Venus/I'm Broke	1959	10.00	20.00	40.00
☐ S-1031	S	Venus/I'm Broke	1959	10.00	20.00	40.00
☐ 1036	M	Bobby Sox to Stockings/A Boy Without a Girl	1959	5.00	10.00	20.00
		Originals have pink labels				
☐ 1036	M	Bobby Sox to Stockings/A Boy Without a Girl	1959	3.00	6.00	12.00
		Reissues have black labels				
☐ 1036	PS	Bobby Sox to Stockings/A Boy Without a Girl	1959	10.00	20.00	40.00
☐ S-1036	S	Bobby Sox to Stockings/A Boy Without a Girl	1959	10.00	20.00	40.00
☐ 1040	M	Just Ask Your Heart/Two Fools	1959	3.75	7.50	15.00
☐ 1040	PS	Just Ask Your Heart/Two Fools	1959	7.50	15.00	30.00
☐ S-1040	S	Just Ask Your Heart/Two Fools	1959	10.00	20.00	40.00
☐ 1045	M	Why/Swingin' on a Rainbow	1959	3.75	7.50	15.00
☐ 1045	PS	Why/Swingin' on a Rainbow	1959	7.50	15.00	30.00
☐ S-1045	S	Why/Swingin' on a Rainbow	1959	10.00	20.00	40.00
☐ 1048		Don't Throw Away All Those Teardrops/Talk, Talk, Talk	1960	3.75	7.50	15.00
☐ 1048	PS	Don't Throw Away All Those Teardrops/Talk, Talk, Talk	1960	7.50	15.00	30.00
☐ 1052		Where Are You/Tuxedo Junction	1960	3.75	7.50	15.00
☐ 1052	PS	Where Are You/Tuxedo Junction	1960	7.50	15.00	30.00
☐ 1056		Togetherness/Don't Let Love Pass You By	1960	3.75	7.50	15.00
☐ 1056	PS	Togetherness/Don't Let Love Pass You By	1960	7.50	15.00	30.00
☐ 1065		A Perfect Love/The Puppet Song	1960	3.75	7.50	15.00
☐ 1065	PS	A Perfect Love/The Puppet Song	1960	7.50	15.00	30.00
☐ 1071		All of Everything/Call Me Anytime	1961	3.00	6.00	12.00
☐ 1071	PS	All of Everything/Call Me Anytime	1961	6.25	12.50	25.00
☐ 1077		Who Else But You/True, True Love	1961	3.00	6.00	12.00
☐ 1081		Voyage to the Bottom of the Sea/Summer of '61	1961	3.00	6.00	12.00
☐ 1081	PS	Voyage to the Bottom of the Sea/Summer of '61	1961	6.25	12.50	25.00
☐ 1087		True, True Love/Married	1961	2.50	5.00	10.00
☐ 1087	PS	True, True Love/Married	1961	5.00	10.00	20.00
☐ 1095		Sleeping Beauty/The Lonely Bit	1961	2.50	5.00	10.00
☐ 1095	PS	Sleeping Beauty/The Lonely Bit	1961	5.00	10.00	20.00
☐ 1101		After You've Gone/If You Don't Think I'm Leaving	1962	2.50	5.00	10.00
☐ 1101	PS	After You've Gone/If You Don't Think I'm Leaving	1962	5.00	10.00	20.00
☐ 1107		You Are Mine/Ponchinello	1962	2.50	5.00	10.00
☐ 1107	PS	You Are Mine/Ponchinello	1962	5.00	10.00	20.00
☐ 1114		Venus/I'm Broke	1962	2.50	5.00	10.00

Number		Title (A Side/B Side)	Year	VG	VG+	NM
❑ 1115		A Miracle/Don't Let Me Stand in Your Way	1962	2.50	5.00	10.00
❑ 1115	PS	A Miracle/Don't Let Me Stand in Your Way	1962	5.00	10.00	20.00
❑ 1125		Dance the Bossa Nova/Welcome Home	1962	2.50	5.00	10.00
❑ 1125	PS	Dance the Bossa Nova/Welcome Home	1962	5.00	10.00	20.00
❑ 1131		My Ex-Best Friend/First Love Never Dies	1963	2.50	5.00	10.00
❑ 1134		Come Fly with Me/Girl Back Home	1963	2.50	5.00	10.00
❑ 1135		Cleopatra/Heartbeats	1963	2.50	5.00	10.00
❑ 1139		Beach Party/Don't Stop Now	1963	3.75	7.50	15.00

De-Lite

Number		Title (A Side/B Side)	Year	VG	VG+	NM
❑ 907		Beauty School Dropout/Midnight Lady	1978		2.00	4.00
❑ 907	PS	Beauty School Dropout/Midnight Lady	1978		2.50	5.00
❑ 1578		Venus/Venus (Disco Version)	1976		2.00	4.00
❑ 1578	PS	Venus/Venus (Disco Version)	1976	2.00	4.00	8.00
❑ 1582		Thank You for That Extra Sunrise/It's His Game	1976		2.00	4.00
❑ 1584		It's Never Too Late/Where I Leave Off (And You Begin)	1976		2.00	4.00
❑ 1589		Midnight Lady/Does She Wonder Where I Am	1977		2.00	4.00
❑ 1591		Splish Splash/When I Said I Love You	1977		2.00	4.00
❑ 1595		Roses Grow Beyond the Wall/Midnight Lady	1977		2.00	4.00

Metromedia

Number		Title (A Side/B Side)	Year	VG	VG+	NM
❑ 181		Come On Back to Me Baby/Empty	1970		2.50	5.00
❑ 192		Heart of Everything/I Want You Near Me	1970		2.50	5.00

Regalia

Number		Title (A Side/B Side)	Year	VG	VG+	NM
❑ 5508		I'm in the Mood for Love/It's the Same Old Dream	1972		2.50	5.00

Reprise

Number		Title (A Side/B Side)	Year	VG	VG+	NM
❑ 0697		Dancing on the Stars/But I Do	1968	2.00	4.00	8.00
❑ 0796		Don't You Do It/It's Over	1968	2.00	4.00	8.00
❑ 0826		For Your Love/Why Don't They Understand	1969	2.00	4.00	8.00

United Artists

Number		Title (A Side/B Side)	Year	VG	VG+	NM
❑ 728		Again/Don't Make Fun of Me	1964	2.50	5.00	10.00
❑ 748		My Love Is Here to Stay/New-Fangled, Jingle-Jangle, Swimming Suit from Paris	1964	2.50	5.00	10.00
❑ 748	PS	My Love Is Here to Stay/New-Fangled, Jingle-Jangle, Swimming Suit from Paris	1964	5.00	10.00	20.00
❑ 800		Moon River/Every Girl Should Get Married	1964	2.50	5.00	10.00
❑ 895		There'll Be Rainbows Again/I'll Take Sweden	1965	2.50	5.00	10.00

"X"

Number		Title (A Side/B Side)	Year	VG	VG+	NM
❑ 0006		Trumpet Sorrento/The Rock	1954	12.50	25.00	50.00
❑ 0026		Trumpet Tarantella/Dormi, Dormi	1954	12.50	25.00	50.00

Avalons, The

(More than one group)

Aladdin

Number	Title (A Side/B Side)	Year	VG	VG+	NM
❑ 3336	I Miss You/Love Me	1956	7.50	15.00	30.00

Casino

Number	Title (A Side/B Side)	Year	VG	VG+	NM
❑ 108	You Do Something to Me/You Can Count on Me	1959	50.00	100.00	200.00

Groove

Number	Title (A Side/B Side)	Year	VG	VG+	NM
❑ 0141	Chains Around My Heart/Ooh-She Flew	1956	37.50	75.00	150.00
❑ 0174	It's Funny But It's True/Sugar Sugar	1956	37.50	75.00	150.00

Roulette

Number	Title (A Side/B Side)	Year	VG	VG+	NM
❑ 4568	Is It the End/Many Things from Your Window	1964	3.00	6.00	12.00

Unart

Number	Title (A Side/B Side)	Year	VG	VG+	NM
❑ 2007	Hearts Desire/Ebbtide	1958	20.00	40.00	80.00

Avantis, The

Argo

Number	Title (A Side/B Side)	Year	VG	VG+	NM
❑ 5436	Keep On Dancing/I Want to Dance	1963	3.75	7.50	15.00

Astra

Number	Title (A Side/B Side)	Year	VG	VG+	NM
❑ 1006	Gypsy Surfer/Wax 'Em Down	1963	10.00	20.00	40.00

Chancellor

Number	Title (A Side/B Side)	Year	VG	VG+	NM
❑ 1144	Gypsy Surfer/Wax 'Em Down	1963	6.25	12.50	25.00

Ikon

Number	Title (A Side/B Side)	Year	VG	VG+	NM
❑ 115	Too Much/Mid-Night Blues	196?	6.25	12.50	25.00

Pepper

Number	Title (A Side/B Side)	Year	VG	VG+	NM
❑ 435	You Got a Funny Way/One Man's Poison	196?	3.00	6.00	12.00

Regency

Number	Title (A Side/B Side)	Year	VG	VG+	NM
❑ 108	Do the Surfin' Granny/Surfin' Granny	1964	10.00	20.00	40.00
❑ 110	Phantom Surfer/Lucille	1964	10.00	20.00	40.00

Avons, The

(Probably several different groups)

Abet

Number	Title (A Side/B Side)	Year	VG	VG+	NM
❑ 9419	Talk to Me/Got to Get Used to You	1967	2.00	4.00	8.00

Astra

Number	Title (A Side/B Side)	Year	VG	VG+	NM
❑ 1023	Baby/Whisper (Softly)	1966	7.50	15.00	30.00

Excello

Number	Title (A Side/B Side)	Year	VG	VG+	NM
❑ 2296	Since I Met You Baby/He's My Hero	1968	2.00	4.00	8.00

Groove

Number	Title (A Side/B Side)	Year	VG	VG+	NM
❑ 58-0022	Oh, Gee Baby/Push a Little Harder	1963	3.75	7.50	15.00
❑ 58-0033	Words Written on Water/Rolling Stone	1964	3.00	6.00	12.00
❑ 58-0039	Whatever Happened to Our Love/Tonight Kiss Your Baby Goodbye	1964	3.00	6.00	12.00

Number	Title (A Side/B Side)	Year	VG	VG+	NM

Hull

❑ 717	Our Love Will Never End/I'm Sending S.O.S. *Black label*	1956	37.50	75.00	150.00
❑ 717	Our Love Will Never End/I'm Sending S.O.S. *Red label*	1956	7.50	15.00	30.00
❑ 722	Baby/Bonnie	1957	20.00	40.00	80.00
❑ 726	You Are So Close to Me/Gonna Catch You Nappin'	1958	12.50	25.00	50.00
❑ 728	What Will I Do/Please Come Back to Me	1958	12.50	25.00	50.00
❑ 731	What Love Can Do/On the Island	1958	12.50	25.00	50.00
❑ 744	Whisper (Softly)/If I Just (Had My Way)	1961	7.50	15.00	30.00
❑ 754	A Girl to Call My Own/ The Grass Is Greener on the Other Side	1962	10.00	20.00	40.00

Mercury

❑ 71618	We Fell in Love/Pickin' Petals	1960	3.75	7.50	15.00

Sound Stage 7

❑ 2561	Be Good to Your Baby/Just As Long As I Live	1966	2.50	5.00	10.00

Azaleas, The
Romulus

❑ 3001	Hands Off/One Drummer Can't Keep Time	1963	7.50	15.00	30.00

B

B. Bumble and the Stingers
Mercury

❑ 72614	Green Hornet Theme/Flight of the Hornet	1966	2.50	5.00	10.00
❑ 72665	Silent Movies/Twelfth Street Rag	1967	2.50	5.00	10.00

Rendezvous

❑ 140	Bumble Boogie/School Day Blues	1961	5.00	10.00	20.00
❑ 151	Boogie Woogie/Near You	1961	3.75	7.50	15.00
❑ 160	Bee Hive/Caravan	1961	3.75	7.50	15.00
❑ 166	Nut Rocker/Nautilus	1962	3.75	7.50	15.00
❑ 174	Rockin-On-And-Off/Mashed #5	1962	3.00	6.00	12.00
❑ 179	Apple Knocker/The Moon and the Sea	1962	3.00	6.00	12.00
❑ 182	Dawn Cracker/Scales	1962	3.00	6.00	12.00
❑ 186	12th Street Rag/Canadian Sunset	1962	3.00	6.00	12.00
❑ 192	Baby Mash/Night Time Madness	1962	3.00	6.00	12.00
❑ 210	In the Mood/Chicken Chow Mein	1963	3.00	6.00	12.00

B.R.A.T.T.S., The
Tollie

❑ 9024	Secret Weapon (The British Are Coming)/ Jealous Kinda Woman	1964	5.00	10.00	20.00

Babies, The
ABC Dunhill

❑ 4148	I Wanna Testify/Party Time	1968	3.00	6.00	12.00

Dunhill

❑ 4085	You Make Me Feel Like Someone/The Hand of Fate	1967	4.00	8.00	16.00
❑ 4085 PS	You Make Me Feel Like Someone/The Hand of Fate	1967	7.50	15.00	30.00
❑ 4101	I'm Not Asking for the World/ Goodbye My Love, Goodbye	1967	3.75	7.50	15.00

Baby Bugs, The
Vee Jay

❑ 594	Bingo/Bingo's Bongo Bingo Party	1964	6.25	12.50	25.00
❑ 594 PS	Bingo/Bingo's Bongo Bingo Party	1964	18.75	37.50	75.00

Baby Dolls, The
(Probably two different groups)
Boom

❑ 60002	I Will Do It ('Cause He Wants Me To)/ Now That I've Lost You	1966	2.50	5.00	10.00

Gamble

❑ 213	Please Don't Rush Me/There You Are	1968	2.00	4.00	8.00

Hollywood

❑ 1111	Got to Get You Into My Life/ Why Can't I Make Him Like You	1960	10.00	20.00	40.00

RCA Victor

❑ 47-7296	Tutti Frutti/Cause I'm in Love	1958	3.75	7.50	15.00

Warner Bros.

❑ 5086	Hey Baby/Quiet	1959	3.00	6.00	12.00

Baby Ray and the Ferns
(An early production of Frank Zappa)
Donna

❑ 1378	How's Your Bird/The World's Greatest Sinner	1963	50.00	100.00	200.00

Bachelors, The
(Several different groups. The London Bachelors are British)
Aladdin

❑ 3210	Pretty Baby/Can't Help Loving You	1953	500.00	1,000	1,500

Number		Title (A Side/B Side)	Year	VG	VG+	NM
Epic						
❑ 9369		Do the Madison/Bachelor's Club	1960	3.00	6.00	12.00
London						
❑ 9584		Charmaine/Old Bill	1963	3.00	6.00	12.00
❑ 9623		Faraway Places/Is There a Chance	1964	3.00	6.00	12.00
❑ 9632		Whispering/No Light in the Window	1964	3.00	6.00	12.00
❑ 9639		Diane/Happy Land	1964	3.00	6.00	12.00
❑ 9672		I Believe/Sweet Lullaby	1964	3.00	6.00	12.00
❑ 9672	PS	I Believe/Sweet Lullaby	1964	6.25	12.50	25.00
❑ 9693		I Wouldn't Trade You for the World/	1964	3.00	6.00	12.00
		Beneath the Willow Tree				
❑ 9693	PS	I Wouldn't Trade You for the World/	1964	6.25	12.50	25.00
		Beneath the Willow Tree				
❑ 9724		No Arms Can Ever Hold You/Oh Samuel, Don't Die	1964	3.00	6.00	12.00
❑ 9762		Marie/You Can Tell	1965	2.50	5.00	10.00
❑ 9793		Chapel in the Moonlight/The Old Wishing Well	1965	2.50	5.00	10.00
❑ 9793	PS	Chapel in the Moonlight/The Old Wishing Well	1965	5.00	10.00	20.00
❑ 9828		Love Me with All of Your Heart/	1966	2.50	5.00	10.00
		There's No Room in My Heart				
❑ 20010		Can I Trust You/My Girl	1966	2.50	5.00	10.00
❑ 20018		Walk with Faith in Your Heart/	1966	2.50	5.00	10.00
		Queen Molly Malone of Ireland				
❑ 20027		Marta/Oh How I Miss You	1967	2.00	4.00	8.00
❑ 20033		Learn to Live Without You/3 O'Clock Flamingo Street	1967	2.00	4.00	8.00
❑ 20051		Punky's Dilemma/It's a Beautiful Day	1968	2.00	4.00	8.00
❑ 20063		Love Is All/The Colours of Love	1970		3.00	6.00
❑ 20071		Diamonds Are Forever/Where There's a Heartache	1971		3.00	6.00
Mercury						
❑ 8159		Yesterday's Roses/Hereafter	1949	75.00	150.00	300.00
MGM						
❑ 12668		Sometimes/Teenage Memory	1958	5.00	10.00	20.00
National						
❑ 104		From Your Heart/A Million Teardrops	1957	6.25	12.50	25.00
❑ 115		Today, Tomorrow, Forever/I Want a Girl	1957	6.25	12.50	25.00
Poplar						
❑ 101		After/You Know, I Know (I Love You)	1957	12.50	25.00	50.00
Royal Roost						
❑ 620		I Found Love/You've Lied	1952	75.00	150.00	300.00
Smash						
❑ 1723		The Day I Met You/Hey Little Girl	1961	3.00	6.00	12.00
Badd Boys, The						
Epic						
❑ 10119		Never Going Back to Georgia/	1967	12.50	25.00	50.00
		River Deep Mountain High				
❑ 10165		Folks in a Hurry/I Told You So	1967	15.00	30.00	60.00
Badfinger						
Apple						
❑ 1803		Maybe Tomorrow/And Her Daddy's a Millionaire	1969	7.50	15.00	30.00
		By "The Iveys"; with star on label				
❑ 1803		Maybe Tomorrow/And Her Daddy's a Millionaire	1969	5.00	10.00	20.00
		By "The Iveys"				
❑ 1815		Come and Get It/Rock of All Ages	1969	2.00	4.00	8.00
		With Capitol logo on B-side bottom				
❑ 1815		Come and Get It/Rock of All Ages	1969		3.00	6.00
❑ 1822		No Matter What/Carry On Till Tomorrow	1970	5.00	10.00	20.00
		With star on A-side label				
❑ 1822		No Matter What/Carry On Till Tomorrow	1970		3.00	6.00
❑ 1841		Day After Day/Money	1971	5.00	10.00	20.00
		With star on A-side label				
❑ 1841		Day After Day/Money	1971		3.00	6.00
❑ 1841	DJ	Day After Day/Money	1971	30.00	60.00	120.00
		White label				
❑ 1844		Baby Blue/Flying	1972		3.00	6.00
❑ 1844	DJ	Baby Blue/Flying	1972	30.00	60.00	120.00
		White label				
❑ 1844	PS	Baby Blue/Flying	1972	3.75	7.50	15.00
❑ 1864		Apple of My Eye/Blind Owl	1973		3.00	6.00
❑ P-1864	DJ	Apple of My Eye (mono/stereo)	1973	6.25	12.50	25.00
Apple/Americom						
❑ 1803P/M-300		Maybe Tomorrow/And Her Daddy's a Millionaire	1969	150.00	300.00	600.00
		By "The Iveys"; four-inch flexidisc sold from vending machines				
Capitol						
❑ S7-17487		Baby Blue/Day After Day	1993		2.50	5.00
		Black vinyl				
❑ S7-17487		Baby Blue/Day After Day	1993			3.00
		Blue vinyl				
Elektra						
❑ 46022		Lost Inside Your Love/Come Down Hard	1979		2.50	5.00
❑ 46025		Love Is Gonna Come At Last/Sail Away	1979		2.50	5.00

Number	Title (A Side/B Side)	Year	VG	VG+	NM

Radio

❑ 3793	Hold On/Passin' Time	1981		2.50	5.00
❑ 3815	I Got You/Rock and Roll Contract	1981		2.50	5.00
❑ 3833	Because I Love You/Too Hung Up on You	1981		2.50	5.00

Warner Bros.

❑ 7801	I Miss You/Shine On	1974		3.00	6.00

Bagdasarian, Ross
(Real name of David Seville and the brains behind the original Chipmunks)

Coral

❑ 60544	Come On-a My House/Oh Beauty	1951	7.50	15.00	30.00
❑ 60597	The Girl with the Tambourine/He Says Mu-Humm	1951	6.25	12.50	25.00

Imperial

❑ 66379	Jone-Cone-Phone/Spanish Pizza	1969	2.50	5.00	10.00
❑ 66414	You've Got Me on a Merry-Go-Round/ You Better Open Your Eyes	1969	2.50	5.00	10.00

Liberty

❑ 55013	The Bold and the Brave/See a Teardrop Fall	1956	5.00	10.00	20.00
❑ 55193	Judy/Maria from Madrid	1959	4.00	8.00	16.00
❑ 55239	Lotta Bull/(B-side unknown)	1959	4.00	8.00	16.00
❑ 55275	Lazy Lovers/One Finger Waltz	1960	4.00	8.00	16.00
❑ 55462	Armen's Theme/Russian Roulette	1962	3.75	7.50	15.00
❑ 55557	Cecelia/Gotta Get to Your House	1963	3.75	7.50	15.00
❑ 55619	Lucy, Lucy/Scalliwags and Sinners	1963	3.75	7.50	15.00
❑ 55810	La Noche/Naval Maneuver	1965	3.00	6.00	12.00
❑ 55837	Come On-a My House/Gotta Get to Your House	1965	3.00	6.00	12.00
❑ 56004	Walking Birds of Carnaby/Red Wine	1967	3.00	6.00	12.00
❑ 56043	Yallah/Naval Maneuver	1968			Unreleased
❑ 56048	When I Look in Your Eyes/Sands of Time	1968	3.00	6.00	12.00
❑ 56165	I Treasure Thee/(B-side unknown)	1969	3.00	6.00	12.00

Mercury

❑ 70254	Let's Have a Merry, Merry Christmas/ Hey Brother, Pour the Wine	1953	6.25	12.50	25.00

Bagels, The
Warner Bros.

❑ 5420	I Wanna Hold Your Hair/Yeah, Yeah, Yeah, Yeah	1964	3.75	7.50	15.00

Baggys, The
Pipeline

❑ 501	El Surfer/El Seagull	1963	10.00	20.00	40.00

Bailey, Thomas
Federal

❑ 12559	Fran/Just Won't Move	1969	3.00	6.00	12.00
❑ 12567	Wish I Was Back/Percy's Place	1970	25.00	50.00	100.00

Baines, Vicki
Loma

❑ 2078	We Can Find True Love/Sweeter Than Sweet Things	1967	3.00	6.00	12.00

Parkway

❑ 957	Losing You/Got to Run	1965	6.25	12.50	25.00
❑ 966	Country Girl/Are You Kidding	1966	25.00	50.00	100.00

Baker, Donnie, and the Demensionals
Rainbow

❑ 219	Drinkin' Pop Sodee-Odee/Sleepy	1953	15.00	30.00	60.00

Baker, LaVern
Atlantic

❑ 1004	How Can You Leave a Man Like This/Soul on Fire	1953	12.50	25.00	50.00
❑ 1030	I Can't Hold Out Any Longer//I'm Living My Life for You	1954	10.00	20.00	40.00
❑ 1047	Tweedlee Dee/Tomorrow Night	1954	10.00	20.00	40.00
❑ 1057	Bop-Ting-a-Ling/That's All I Need	1955	10.00	20.00	40.00
❑ 1075	Play It Fair/That Lucky Old Sun	1955	10.00	20.00	40.00
❑ 1087	Get Up Get Up (You Sleepyhead)/ My Happiness Forever	1956	6.25	12.50	25.00
❑ 1093	Fee Fee Fi Fo Fum/I'll Do the Same for You	1956	6.25	12.50	25.00
❑ 1104	I Can't Love You Enough/Still	1956	6.25	12.50	25.00
❑ 1116	Jim Dandy/Tra La La	1956	7.50	15.00	30.00
❑ 1136	Jim Dandy Got Married/The Game of Love	1957	6.25	12.50	25.00
❑ 1150	Humpty Dumpty Heart/Love Me Right	1957	6.25	12.50	25.00
❑ 1163	St.Louis Blues/Miracles	1957	6.25	12.50	25.00
❑ 1176	Substitute/Learning to Love	1958	6.25	12.50	25.00
❑ 1189	Harbor Lights/Whipper Snapper	1958	6.25	12.50	25.00
❑ 2001	It's So Fine/Why Baby Why	1958	6.25	12.50	25.00
❑ 2007	I Cried a Tear/Dix-A-Billy	1958	6.25	12.50	25.00
❑ 2021	I Waited Too Long/You're Teasing Me	1959	5.00	10.00	20.00
❑ 2033	So High So Low/If You Love Me	1959	5.00	10.00	20.00
❑ 2041	Tiny Tim/For the Love of You	1959	5.00	10.00	20.00
❑ 2048	Shake a Hand/Manana	1960	5.00	10.00	20.00
❑ 2059	Wheel of Fortune/Shadows of Love	1960	3.75	7.50	15.00
❑ 2067	A Help-Each-Other Romance/How Often *With Ben E. King*	1960	3.75	7.50	15.00
❑ 2077	Bumble Bee/My Time Will Come	1960	3.75	7.50	15.00

Number		Title (A Side/B Side)	Year	VG	VG+	NM
❏ 2090		You're the Boss/I'll Never Be Free	1961	3.75	7.50	15.00
		With Jimmy Ricks				
❏ 2099		Saved/Don Juan	1961	3.75	7.50	15.00
❏ 2109		I Didn't Know I Was Crying/Hurtin' Inside	1961	3.75	7.50	15.00
❏ 2119		Hey, Memphis/Voodoo Voodoo	1961	3.75	7.50	15.00
❏ 2137		Must I Cry Again/No Love So True	1962	3.00	6.00	12.00
❏ 2167		See See Rider/The Story of My Love	1962	3.00	6.00	12.00
❏ 2186		Trouble in Mind/Half of Your Love	1963	3.00	6.00	12.00
❏ 2203		Itty Bitty Girl/Johnny, O, Johnny	1963	3.00	6.00	12.00
❏ 2234		You'd Better Find Yourself Another Fool/Go Away	1964	2.50	5.00	10.00
❏ 2267		Fly Me to the Moon/Ain't Gonna Cry No More	1965	2.50	5.00	10.00
Brunswick						
❏ 55285		Let Me Belong to You/Pledging My Love	1965	2.00	4.00	8.00
❏ 55287		Think Twice/Please Don't Hurt Me	1965	2.00	4.00	8.00
		With Jackie Wilson				
❏ 55291		One Monkey (Don't Stop the Show)/Baby	1966	2.00	4.00	8.00
❏ 55297		Batman to the Rescue/Call Me Darling	1966	2.50	5.00	10.00
❏ 55311		Nothing Like Being in Love/	1967	2.00	4.00	8.00
		Wrapped, Tied and Tangled				
❏ 55341		Born to Lose/I Need You So	1967	2.00	4.00	8.00
❏ 55408		I'm the One to Do It/Baby	1969	3.00	6.00	
King						
❏ 4556		Trying/Snuff Dipper	1952	12.50	25.00	50.00
		B-side by Todd Rhodes				
❏ 4583		Must I Cry Again/Hog Maw and Cabbage Slaw	1952	12.50	25.00	50.00
		B-side by Todd Rhodes				
❏ 4601		Lost Child/Thunderball Boogie	1953	12.50	25.00	50.00
		B-side by Todd Rhodes				

Baker, Mickey "Guitar"

(Of Mickey and Sylvia)

Atlantic

❏ 2042		Third Man Theme/Baia	1959	3.00	6.00	12.00
King						
❏ 5951		Side Show/Steam Roller	1964	2.50	5.00	10.00
❏ 5979		Do What You Do/Night Blue	1965	2.50	5.00	10.00
MGM						
❏ 12418		Spinnin' Rock Boogie/Tricky	1957	5.00	10.00	20.00
Rainbow						
❏ 288		Shake Walkin'/Greasy Spoon	1955	7.50	15.00	30.00
❏ 299		Bandstand Stomp/Rock with a Sock	1955	7.50	15.00	30.00
❏ 303		Old Devil Moon/Guitarambo	1955	7.50	15.00	30.00
Savoy						
❏ 867		Guitar Mambo/Riverboat	1952	12.50	25.00	50.00
❏ 874		Love Me Baby/Oh Happy Day	1953	12.50	25.00	50.00

Baker, Penny, and the Pillows

Witch

❏ 123		Bring Back the Beatles/Gonna Win Him	1964	5.00	10.00	20.00
❏ 123	PS	Bring Back the Beatles/Gonna Win Him	1964	5.00	10.00	20.00

Baker, Yvonne

(Of the Sensations)

Jamie

❏ 1290		What a Difference Love Makes/	1965	3.00	6.00	12.00
		Funny What Time Can Do				
Modern						
❏ 1055		A Woman Needs a Man/My Baby Needs Me	196?	2.50	5.00	10.00
Parkway						
❏ 140		You Didn't Say a Word/To Prove My Love Is True	1967	25.00	50.00	100.00

Balin, Marty

(Of Jefferson Airplane and Jefferson Starship)

Challenge

❏ 9146		Nobody But You/You Made Me Fall	1962	12.50	25.00	50.00
❏ 9156		I Specialize in Love/You're Alive with Love	1962	12.50	25.00	50.00
EMI America						
❏ 8084		Hearts/Freeway	1981		2.00	4.00
❏ 8084	PS	Hearts/Freeway	1981		2.50	5.00
❏ 8093		Atlanta Lady (Something About Your Love)/Lydia	1981		2.00	4.00
❏ 8153		What Love Is/Will You Forever	1983		2.00	4.00
❏ 8160		Do It for Love/Heart of Stone	1983		2.00	4.00

Ballard, Florence

(Of the Supremes)

ABC

❏ 11074		Goin' Out of My Head/It Doesn't Matter How I Say It	1968	7.50	15.00	30.00
❏ 11144		Love Ain't Love/Forever Faithful	1968	7.50	15.00	30.00

Ballard, Hank, and the Midnighters
(Includes Hank Ballard solo; for earlier records, see "Midnighters, The")

Number		Title (A Side/B Side)	Year	VG	VG+	NM
Chess						
❑ 2111		Love, Why Is It Taking You So Long/	1971		3.00	6.00
		I'm a Junkie for My Baby's Love				
King						
❑ 5171		Teardrops on Your Letter/The Twist	1959	7.50	15.00	30.00
❑ 5195		Kansas City/I'll Keep You Happy	1959	6.25	12.50	25.00
❑ 5215	M	Sugaree/Rain Down Tears	1959	6.25	12.50	25.00
❑ S-5213	S	Sugaree/Rain Down Tears	1959	12.50	25.00	50.00
❑ 5245		Cute Little Ways/A House with No Windows	1959	6.25	12.50	25.00
❑ 5275		I Could Love You/Never Knew	1959	6.25	12.50	25.00
❑ 5289		Look at Little Sister/I Said I Wouldn't Beg You	1959	6.25	12.50	25.00
❑ 5312		The Coffee Grind/Waiting	1960	6.25	12.50	25.00
❑ 5341		Finger Poppin' Time/I Love You, Yes I Do	1960	6.25	12.50	25.00
❑ 5400		Let's Go, Let's Go, Let's Go/If You'd Forgive Me	1960	6.25	12.50	25.00
❑ 5430		The Hoochi Coochi Coo/I'm Thinking of You	1960	5.00	10.00	20.00
❑ 5459		Let's Go Again (Where We Went Last Night)/	1961	5.00	10.00	20.00
		Deep Blue Sea				
❑ 5491		The Continental Walk/What Is This I See	1961	5.00	10.00	20.00
❑ 5491	PS	The Continental Walk/What Is This I See	1961	10.00	20.00	40.00
❑ 5510		The Switch-A-Roo/The Float	1961	3.75	7.50	15.00
❑ 5513		The Big Frog/Doin' Everything	1961	3.75	7.50	15.00
		B-side by Henry Moore				
❑ 5535		Nothing But Good/Keep On Dancing	1961	3.75	7.50	15.00
❑ 5550		Big Red Sunset/Can't You See -- I Need a Friend	1961	3.75	7.50	15.00
❑ 5578		Do You Remember/I'm Gonna Miss You	1961	3.75	7.50	15.00
❑ 5593		Do You Know How to Twist/Broadway	1962	3.75	7.50	15.00
❑ 5601		It's Twistin' Time/Autumn Breeze	1962	3.75	7.50	15.00
❑ 5635		Good Twistin' Tonight/I'm Young	1962	3.75	7.50	15.00
❑ 5655		I Want to Thank You/Excuse Me	1962	3.75	7.50	15.00
❑ 5677		Dream World/When I Need You	1962	3.75	7.50	15.00
❑ 5693		Shaky Mae/I Love and Care for You	1962	3.75	7.50	15.00
❑ 5703		Bring Me Your Love/She's the One	1962	3.75	7.50	15.00
❑ 5713		All the Things in Life That Please You/The Rising Tide	1963	3.75	7.50	15.00
❑ 5719		The House on the Hill/That Low-Down Move	1963	3.75	7.50	15.00
❑ 5729		Christmas Time for Everyone But Me/	1963	3.75	7.50	15.00
		Santa Claus Is Coming				
❑ 5746		How Could You Leave Your Man Alone/	1963	3.75	7.50	15.00
		Walkin' and Talkin'				
❑ 5798		Those Lonely, Lonely Feelings/It's Love, Baby	1963	3.75	7.50	15.00
❑ 5821		Buttin' In/I'm Leavin'	1963	3.75	7.50	15.00
❑ 5835		Don't Let Temptation Turn You Around/	1964	3.75	7.50	15.00
		Have Mercy, Have a Little Pity				
❑ 5860		Don't Fall in Love with Me/I'm So Mad with You	1964	3.75	7.50	15.00
❑ 5884		I Don't Know How to Do But One Thing/	1964	3.75	7.50	15.00
		These Young Girls				
❑ 5901		Stay Away from My Baby/	1964	3.75	7.50	15.00
		She's Got a Whole Lot of Soul				
❑ 5931		Daddy Rolling Stone/What's Your Name	1964	3.75	7.50	15.00
❑ 5954		Let's Get the Show on the Road/A Winner Never Quits	1964	3.75	7.50	15.00
❑ 5963		One Monkey Don't Stop No Show/What Can I Tell You	1964	3.75	7.50	15.00
❑ 5974		The Handwriting on the Wall/I Done It	1964	3.75	7.50	15.00
❑ 5996		Poppin' the Whip/You, Just You	1965	3.00	6.00	12.00
❑ 6001		I'm Just a Fool and Everybody Knows/Do It Zulu Style	1965	3.00	6.00	12.00
❑ 6018		Sloop and Slide/My Sun Is Going Down	1966	3.00	6.00	12.00
❑ 6031		I'm Ready/Togetherness	1966	3.00	6.00	12.00
❑ 6055		I Was Born to Move/He Came Alone	1966	3.00	6.00	12.00
❑ 6092		Here Comes the Hurt/Dance Till It Hurt Cha	1967	3.00	6.00	12.00
❑ 6119		You're in Real Good Hands/Unwind Yourself	1967	3.00	6.00	12.00
❑ 6131		Funky's Soul Train/Which Way Should I Turn	1967	3.00	6.00	12.00
❑ 6177		I'm Back to Stay/Come On Wit' It	1968	3.00	6.00	12.00
❑ 6196		How You Gonna Get Respect	1968	2.50	5.00	10.00
		(When You Haven't Cut Your Process Yet)/				
		Teardrops on Your Letter				
		As "Hank Ballard Along With The Dapps"				
❑ 6215		You're So Sexy/Thrill on the Hill	1969	2.50	5.00	10.00
		As "Hank Ballard Along With The Dapps"				
❑ 6228		Are You Lonely for Me Baby/	1969	2.50	5.00	10.00
		With Our Sweet Lovin' Self				
❑ 6244		Butter Your Popcorn/Funky Soul Train	1969	3.75	7.50	15.00
❑ 6246		Come On with It/Blackenized	1969	3.75	7.50	15.00
❑ 6332		Work With Me Annie/Sexy Ways	1970	2.50	5.00	10.00
People						
❑ 604		Teardrops on Your Letter/Annie Had a Baby	1972		2.50	5.00
❑ 606		With Your Sweet Lovin' Self/Finger Poppin' Time	1972		2.50	5.00
Polydor						
❑ 14128		Finger Poppin' Time/From the Love Side	1972		2.50	5.00
❑ 14166		Going to Get a Thrill/(B-side unknown)	1973		2.50	5.00
Silver Fox						
❑ 23		Sunday Morning Coming Down/	1970		3.00	6.00
		Love Made a Fool of Me				
Stang						
❑ 5053		Let's Go Streaking/Let's Go Streaking (Part 2)	1974		2.50	5.00
❑ 5058		Hey There Sexy Lady/(Instrumental)	1975		2.50	5.00
❑ 5061		Let's Go Skinny Dipping/Love On Love	1975		2.50	5.00

Number		Title (A Side/B Side)	Year	VG	VG+	NM

Balloon Farm, The
Laurie
❏ 3405		A Question of Tempature/Hurtin' for Your Lovin'	1967	5.00	10.00	20.00
		First pressing has misspelled A-side				
❏ 3405		A Question of Temperature/Hurtin' for Your Lovin'	1967	2.50	5.00	10.00
		Second pressing corrects A-side spelling				
❏ 3445		Hurry Up Sundown/Farmer Brown	1968	2.50	5.00	10.00

Baltineers, The
Teenage
| ❏ 1000 | | Moments Like This/New Love | 1956 | 75.00 | 150.00 | 300.00 |
| ❏ 1002 | | Tears in My Eyes/Joe's Calypso | 1956 | 75.00 | 150.00 | 300.00 |

Ban-Lons, The
Fidelity
| ❏ 4051 | | Highest Mountain/Hey Baby | 1959 | 50.00 | 100.00 | 200.00 |
| ❏ 4056 | | I Like It/(B-side unknown) | 1959 | 50.00 | 100.00 | 200.00 |

Banana Splits, The
Decca
❏ 32391		We're the Banana Splits/Wait Til Tomorrow	1968	3.00	6.00	12.00
❏ 32429		The Tra-La-La Song (One Banana, Two Banana)/	1968	3.00	6.00	12.00
		Toy Piano Melody				
❏ 32429	PS	The Tra-La-La Song (One Banana, Two Banana)/	1968	6.25	12.50	25.00
		Toy Piano Melody				
❏ 32536		Pretty Painted Carousel/Long Live Love	1969	3.00	6.00	12.00
❏ 32536	PS	Pretty Painted Carousel/Long Live Love	1969	6.25	12.50	25.00

Band Aid
(British charity group)
Columbia
| ❏ 04749 | | Do They Know It's Christmas?/Feed the World | 1984 | | 2.50 | 5.00 |
| ❏ 04749 | PS | Do They Know It's Christmas?/Feed the World | 1984 | | 2.50 | 5.00 |

Band Without a Name, The
Sidewalk
| ❏ 913 | | Theme from "Thunder Alley"/Time After Time | 1967 | 5.00 | 10.00 | 20.00 |
Tower
| ❏ 246 | | Turn On Your Love Light/Perfect Girl | 1966 | 3.75 | 7.50 | 15.00 |
| ❏ 246 | PS | Turn On Your Love Light/Perfect Girl | 1966 | 7.50 | 15.00 | 30.00 |

Bangs, The
(Early version of the Bangles)
Downkiddie
❏ 001		Getting Out of Hand/Call On Me	1981	12.50	25.00	50.00
		Yellow label (original)				
❏ 001		Getting Out of Hand/Call On Me	1981	10.00	20.00	40.00
		Blue label				
❏ 001	PS	Getting Out of Hand/Call On Me	1981	15.00	30.00	60.00

Banks, Doug
Argo
| ❏ 5483 | | I Just Keep Dancing/Baby Since You Went Away | 1964 | 15.00 | 30.00 | 60.00 |
Guyden
| ❏ 2082 | | Ain't That Just Like a Woman/Never Say Goodbye | 1963 | 15.00 | 30.00 | 60.00 |
| | | May be promo only | | | | |

Barbarians, The
Joy
| ❏ 290 | | Hey Little Bird/You've Got to Understand | 1964 | 12.50 | 25.00 | 50.00 |
Laurie
❏ 3308		Are You a Boy or Are You a Girl/Take It or Leave It	1965	5.00	10.00	20.00
❏ 3321		Susie Q/What the New Breed Say	1965	5.00	10.00	20.00
❏ 3326		Moulty/I'll Keep On Seeing You	1965	5.00	10.00	20.00

Barbees, The
Stepp
| ❏ 236 | | The Wind/Que Pasa | 1963 | 50.00 | 100.00 | 200.00 |
| | | Early version of the Velvelettes. | | | | |

Barbra and Neil
(Barbra Streisand and Neil Diamond)
Columbia
| ❏ 10840 | | You Don't Bring Me Flowers/(Instrumental) | 1978 | | 2.50 | 5.00 |

Bard, Annette
(One of the Teddy Bears)
Imperial
| ❏ 5643 | | What Difference Does It Make/Alibi | 1960 | 12.50 | 25.00 | 50.00 |

Number	Title (A Side/B Side)	Year	VG	VG+	NM

Bards, The
(At least two different groups)

Burdette

❏ 103	I Want You/Freedom Catcher	1971	2.00	4.00	8.00

Capitol

❏ 2041	The Jabberwocky/Never Too Much Love	1967	2.50	5.00	10.00
❏ 2148	The Owl and the Pussycat/The Light of Love	1968	2.50	5.00	10.00

Dawn

❏ 208	I'm a Wine Drinker/Easy Going Baby	1954	62.50	125.00	250.00
❏ 209	Gravy/Avalon	1954	62.50	125.00	250.00

Jerden

❏ 907	Good Time Charlie's Got the Blues/Tunesmith	1969	3.00	6.00	12.00

Parrot

❏ 337	Good Time Charlie's Got the Blues/Tunesmith	1969	2.50	5.00	10.00
❏ 344	Our Love/Jubilation	1970	2.50	5.00	10.00
❏ 351	Day by Day/Wadda Wadda	1970	2.50	5.00	10.00

Piccadilly

❏ 224	The Owl and the Pussycat/The Light of Love	1966	5.00	10.00	20.00
❏ 232	The Jabberwocky/My Generation	1966	3.00	6.00	12.00
❏ 242	Our Love/Jubilation	1967	3.00	6.00	12.00

Bare, Bobby
(Also see "Parsons, Bill", under which he recorded accidentally)

Capitol

❏ F3557	Down on the Corner of Love/Another Love Has Ended	1956	7.50	15.00	30.00
❏ F3686	Darling Don't/Life of a Fool	1957	7.50	15.00	30.00
❏ F3771	The Livin' End/Beggar	1957	7.50	15.00	30.00

Columbia

❏ 02577	Dropping Out of Sight/She Is Gone	1981		2.00	4.00
❏ 02690	Let Him Roll/New Cut Road	1982		2.00	4.00
❏ 02895	If You Ain't Got Nothing (You've Got Nothing To Lose)/Golden Memories	1982		2.00	4.00
❏ 03135	New Cut Road/Numbers	1982			3.00
	Reissue				
❏ 03149	(I'm Not) A Candle in the Wind/Cold Day in Hell	1982		2.00	4.00
❏ 03334	Praise the Lord and Send Me the Money/ I've Been Rained On Too	1982		2.00	4.00
❏ 03628	It's a Dirty Job/Caught in the Spotlight	1983		2.00	4.00
	A-side: With Lacy J. Dalton				
❏ 03809	Gravy Train/The Jogger	1983		2.00	4.00
❏ 04092	Diet Song/Stacy Brown Got Two	1983		2.00	4.00
❏ 10690	Too Many Nights Alone/A Yard Full of Rusty Cars	1978		2.50	5.00
❏ 10831	Sleep Tight, Good Night Man/Hot Afternoon	1978		2.50	5.00
❏ 10891	Healin'/Love Is a Cold Wind	1979		2.00	4.00
❏ 10998	Till I Gain Control Again/I'll Feel a Whole Lot Better	1979		2.00	4.00
❏ 11045	No Memories Hangin' Round/ This Has Happened Before	1979		2.00	4.00
	With Roseanne Cash				
❏ 11170	Numbers/When Hippies Get Older	1980		2.00	4.00
❏ 11259	Tequila Sheila/Quaaludes Again	1980		2.00	4.00
❏ 11365	Used Cars/Food Blues	1980		2.00	4.00
❏ 11408	Willie Jones/If That Ain't Love	1980		2.00	4.00

EMI America

❏ 8279	When I Get Home/Party of the First Part	1985			3.00
❏ 8296	Reno and Me/Party of the First Part	1985			3.00
❏ 8317	Better Not Look Down/Wait Until Tomorrow	1986			3.00
❏ 8333	Real Good/Wait Until Tomorrow	1986			3.00

Epic

❏ 10652	My God and I/In the Quiet of Your Love	1970		3.00	6.00
	B-side by Keith Barbour				

Fraternity

❏ 861	I'm Hanging Up My Rifle/That's Where I Wanna Be	1959	10.00	20.00	40.00
❏ 867	Sweet Singing Sam/More Than a Poor Boy Could Give	1960	7.50	15.00	30.00
❏ 871	No Letter from My Baby/Lynchin' Party	1960	5.00	10.00	20.00
❏ 878	Book of Love/Lorena	1961	5.00	10.00	20.00
❏ 885	Sailor Man/Island of Love	1961	5.00	10.00	20.00
❏ 890	Zigzag Twist/Brooklyn Bridge	1961	5.00	10.00	20.00
❏ 892	The Day My Rainbow Fell/That Mean Old Clock	1961	5.00	10.00	20.00

Mercury

❏ 73097	It's Freezing in El Paso/How I Got to Memphis	1970		3.00	6.00
❏ 73148	Come Sundown/ Woman You Have Been a Friend to Me	1970		3.00	6.00
❏ 73203	Please Don't Tell Me How the Story Ends/ Where Have All the Seasons Gone	1971		3.00	6.00
❏ 73236	A Million Miles to the City/Short and Sweet	1971		3.00	6.00
❏ 73279	Love Forever/What Am I Gonna Do	1972		3.00	6.00
❏ 73317	Sylvia's Mother/Music City U.S.A.	1972		3.00	6.00

RCA

❏ PB-10718	Put a Little Lovin' on Me/Those City Lights	1976		2.50	5.00
❏ PB-10790	Drop Kick Me, Jesus/Baby Wants to Boogie	1976		3.00	6.00
❏ PB-10852	Vegas/The Shelter of Your Eyes	1976		2.50	5.00
	Bobby and Jeannie Bare				

Number		Title (A Side/B Side)	Year	VG	VG+	NM
❏ PB-10902		If You Think I'm Crazy/ Look Who I'm Cheatin' On Tonight	1977		2.50	5.00
❏ PB-11037		Red Neck Hippie Romance/Bottom Dollar	1977		2.50	5.00
❏ PB-11673		Hurricane Shirley/Crazy Arms	1979		2.50	5.00
		B-side by Willie Nelson				

RCA Victor

❏ 47-8032		Shame on Me/Around and Around	1962	3.00	6.00	12.00
❏ 47-8083		I Don't Believe I'll Fall in Love Today/ To Whom It May Concern	1962	3.00	6.00	12.00
❏ 47-8146		Dear Waste Basket/I'd Fight the World	1963	3.00	6.00	12.00
❏ 47-8183		Detroit City/Heart of Ice	1963	3.75	7.50	15.00
❏ 47-8183	PS	Detroit City/Heart of Ice	1963	6.25	12.50	25.00
❏ 47-8238		500 Miles Away from Home/It All Depends On Linda	1963	3.75	7.50	15.00
❏ 47-8294		Miller's Cave/Jeannie's Last Ride	1963	3.00	6.00	12.00
❏ 47-8358		Have I Stayed Away Too Long/ More Than a Poor Boy Can Give	1964	3.00	6.00	12.00
❏ 47-8395		He Was a Friend of Mine/When I'm Gone	1964	3.00	6.00	12.00
❏ 47-8443		Four Strong Winds/Take Me Home	1964	3.00	6.00	12.00
❏ 47-8496		A Dear John Letter/Too Used to Being with You	1965	2.50	5.00	10.00
		With Skeeter Davis				
❏ 47-8509		Times Are Gettin' Hard/One Day at a Time	1965	2.50	5.00	10.00
❏ 47-8571		It's Alright/She Picked a Perfect Day	1965	2.50	5.00	10.00
❏ 47-8654		Just to Satisfy You/Memories	1965	2.50	5.00	10.00
❏ 47-8699		Talk Me Some Sense/Delia's Gone	1965	2.50	5.00	10.00
❏ 47-8758		In the Same Old Way/Long Black Veil	1965	2.50	5.00	10.00
❏ 47-8851		The Streets of Baltimore/She Took My Sunshine Away	1966	2.50	5.00	10.00
❏ 47-8963		The Game of Triangles/Bye Bye Bye	1966	2.50	5.00	10.00
		With Norma Jean and Liz Anderson				
❏ 47-8988		Homesick/Guess I'll Move On Down the Line	1966	2.50	5.00	10.00
❏ 47-9098		Charleston Railroad Tavern/Vincennes	1967	2.00	4.00	8.00
❏ 47-9191		Come Kiss Me Love/Sandy's Crying Again	1967	2.00	4.00	8.00
❏ 47-9314		The Piney Wood Hills/ They Covered Up the Old Swimmin' Hole	1967	2.00	4.00	8.00
❏ 47-9450		Find Out What's Happening/ When Am I Ever Gonna Settle Down	1968	2.00	4.00	8.00
❏ 47-9568		A Little Bit Farther On Down the Line/ Don't Do Like I Done, Son	1968	2.00	4.00	8.00
❏ 47-9643		The Town That Broke My Heart/My Baby	1968	2.00	4.00	8.00
❏ 47-9789		Your Husband, My Wife/Before the Sunshine	1969		3.00	6.00
		With Skeeter Davis				
❏ 74-0110		(Margie's At) Lincoln Park Inn/Rainy Day in Richmond	1969		3.00	6.00
❏ 74-0202		Which One Will It Be/My Frame of Mind	1969		3.00	6.00
❏ 74-0264		God Bless America Again/Baby, What Else Can I Do	1969		3.00	6.00
❏ 74-0866		Fallin' Apart/I Hate Goodbyes	1973		3.00	6.00
❏ 74-0918		Ride Me Down Easy/A Train That Never Runs	1973		3.00	6.00
❏ APBO-0063		You Know Who/Send Tomorrow to the Moon	1973		2.50	5.00
❏ AMAO-0119		Shame on Me/Above and Beyond	1973		2.50	5.00
❏ APBO-0197		Daddy What If/Restless Wind	1973		2.50	5.00
❏ APBO-0261		Marie Laveau/Mermaid	1974		2.50	5.00
❏ PB-10037		Where'd I Come From/Scarlet Ribbons	1974		2.50	5.00
❏ PB-10096		You Are/Singin' in the Kitchen	1974		2.50	5.00
		Bobby Bare and Family				
❏ GB-10166		Daddy What If/Ride Me Down Easy	1975			3.00
		Gold Standard Series issue				
❏ PB-10223		Warm and Free/Back in Huntsville Again	1975		2.50	5.00
❏ PB-10318		Alimony/Daddy's Been Around the House Too Long	1975		2.50	5.00
❏ PB-10409		Cowboys and Daddys/High Plains Jamboree	1975		2.50	5.00
❏ GB-10495		Singin' in the Kitchen/You Are	1975			3.00
		Gold Standard Series issue				
❏ GB-10496		Marie Laveau/Mermaid	1975			3.00
		Gold Standard Series issue				
❏ GB-10497		Where'd I Come From/Scarlet Ribbons	1975			3.00
		Gold Standard Series issue				
❏ PB-10556		Up Against the Wall Redneck Mother/The Winner	1976		2.50	5.00

Rice

❏ 5057		Christian Soldier/Dropping Out of Sight	1973		2.50	5.00
❏ 5060		Love Forever/A Million Miles to the City	1973		2.50	5.00
❏ 5066		I Took a Memory to Lunch/It's Freezing in St. Paul	1974		2.50	5.00

Barin, Pete

Sabina

❏ 504		So Wrong/Broken Heart	1962	12.50	25.00	50.00
❏ 512		Loneliest Guy in the World/Look Out for Cindy	1962	7.50	15.00	30.00

Baritones, The

Dore

❏ 501		After School Rock/Sentimental Baby	1958	10.00	20.00	40.00

Barker, Delbert

King

❏ 4951		That's a Sin/No Good, Robin Hood	1956	7.50	15.00	30.00
❏ 5008		Wild Heart/There Must Be a Way	1957	7.50	15.00	30.00
❏ 5031		Amanda/Broken Heart	1957	7.50	15.00	30.00
❏ 6042		It Can't Last Long/Color Me Gone	1966	2.50	5.00	10.00

Number	Title (A Side/B Side)	Year	VG	VG+	NM

Barnes, Benny

D

| ☐ 1052 | Gold Records in the Snow/Happy Little Blue Bird | 1959 | 15.00 | 30.00 | 60.00 |

Hall-Way

| ☐ 1203 | A Bar with No Beer/Headed for Heartbreak | 1964 | 2.50 | 5.00 | 10.00 |
| ☐ 1207 | It's Good to Be Home/For a Minute There | 1965 | 2.50 | 5.00 | 10.00 |

Kapp

| ☐ 859 | A Bar with No Beer/Headed for Heartbreak | 1967 | 2.00 | 4.00 | 8.00 |
| ☐ 912 | Sweet Suzannah/It's My Mind That's Broken | 1968 | 2.00 | 4.00 | 8.00 |

Mega

| ☐ 0071 | Woman, Leave My Mind Alone/
I'm Just Here to Get My Baby Off My Mind | 1972 | | 2.50 | 5.00 |

Mercury

☐ 71048	A Poor Man's Riches/Those Who Know	1957	5.00	10.00	20.00
☐ 71057	Poor Old Me/Penalty	1957	5.00	10.00	20.00
☐ 71119	Nickels Worth of Dreams/Mine All Mine	1957	5.00	10.00	20.00
☐ 71188	King for a Day/Your Old Stand By	1957	5.00	10.00	20.00
☐ 71284	Moon Over My Shoulder/Lonely Street	1958	6.25	12.50	25.00
☐ 71552	Beggar to a King/The Fastest Gun Alive	1959	3.75	7.50	15.00
☐ 71600	That-a Boy Willie/Token of Love	1960	3.75	7.50	15.00
☐ 71637	Pretty Little Girl/Message in the Wind	1960	3.75	7.50	15.00
☐ 71717	You're Still on My Mind/ I Think I'll Take a Walk and Disappear	1960	3.75	7.50	15.00
☐ 71806	Go On, Go On/Yearning	1961	3.75	7.50	15.00
☐ 71896	The World's Worst Loser/I Changed My Mind	1961	3.75	7.50	15.00

Musicor

☐ 1100	Let Me Live As Long As I Can/Tea Leaves Don't Lie	1965	2.00	4.00	8.00
☐ 1127	Have We Really Tried/Heartache's Comin'	1965	2.00	4.00	8.00
☐ 1169	Diesel Smoke/That's How I Need You	1966	2.00	4.00	8.00
☐ 1194	Stand By Your Window/You're Not There	1966	2.00	4.00	8.00
☐ 1223	What's the Matter with Me/Third Time Down	1966	2.00	4.00	8.00
☐ 1247	I'm Her Lover/Same Old Boat	1967	2.00	4.00	8.00
☐ 1277	Let One Call Do It All/Rosanna Martin	1967	2.00	4.00	8.00

Playboy

| ☐ 5808 | I've Got Some Gettin' Over You to Do/I'll Drink to That | 1977 | | 3.00 | 6.00 |

RCA Victor

| ☐ 47-9830 | An Old Memory Got in My Eye/You're Everywhere | 1970 | | 3.00 | 6.00 |
| ☐ 74-0271 | Pressure Cooker/To the Ones I Love | 1969 | | 3.00 | 6.00 |

Starday

☐ 236	Once Again/No Fault of Mine	1956	5.00	10.00	20.00
☐ 262	A Poor Man's Riches/Those Who Know	1956	5.00	10.00	20.00
☐ 401	You Gotta Pay/Heads You Win	1958	3.75	7.50	15.00

Barnes, J.J.

Buddah

| ☐ 120 | Evidence/I'll Keep Coming Back | 1969 | 3.75 | 7.50 | 15.00 |

Groovesville

☐ 1006	Baby Please Come Back Home/Chains of Love	1967	3.75	7.50	15.00
☐ 1008	Now That I Got You Back/Forgive Me	1967	3.75	7.50	15.00
☐ 1009	Easy Living/(B-side unknown)	1967	4.00	8.00	16.00

Invasion

| ☐ 1001 | My Baby/(You Still) My Baby | 1970 | 2.50 | 5.00 | 10.00 |

Kable

| ☐ 437 | Won't You Let Me Know/
My Love Came Tumbling Down | 1960 | 12.50 | 25.00 | 50.00 |

Magic Touch

| ☐ 1000 | To An Early Grave/Cloudy Days | 1970 | 2.50 | 5.00 | 10.00 |

Mickay's

| ☐ 3004 | Just One More Time/Hey Child, I Love You | 1963 | 20.00 | 40.00 | 80.00 |
| ☐ 4472 | Get a Hold of Yourself/Lonely No More | 1964 | 20.00 | 40.00 | 80.00 |

Perception

| ☐ 546 | Just a Living Doll/Touching You | 1974 | | 3.00 | 6.00 |

Revilot

☐ 216	Hold On to It/Now She's Gone	1968	3.75	7.50	15.00
☐ 218	I'll Keep Coming Back/Sad Day a-Comin'	1968	3.75	7.50	15.00
☐ 222	Our Love Is in the Pocket/All Your Goodies Are Gone	1968	20.00	40.00	80.00
☐ 225	So-Called Friends/Now She's Gone	1968	3.75	7.50	15.00

Ric-Tic

☐ 106	Please Let Me In/I Think I Found a Love	1965	3.75	7.50	15.00
☐ 110	Real Humdinger/I Ain't Gonna Do It	1966	3.75	7.50	15.00
☐ 115	Day Tripper/Don't Bring Me Bad News	1966	3.75	7.50	15.00
☐ 117	Deeper in Love/Say It	1966	3.75	7.50	15.00

Rich

| ☐ 1005 | Won't You Let Me Know/
My Love Came Tumbling Down | 1960 | 25.00 | 50.00 | 100.00 |
| ☐ 1737 | Won't You Let Me Know/
My Love Came Tumbling Down | 1962 | 6.25 | 12.50 | 25.00 |

Ring

| ☐ 101 | She Ain't Ready/Poor-Unfortunate Me | 1964 | 6.25 | 12.50 | 25.00 |

Scepter

| ☐ 1266 | Just One More Time/Hey Child, I Love You | 1964 | 7.50 | 15.00 | 30.00 |

Number		Title (A Side/B Side)	Year	VG	VG+	NM
Volt						
❏ 4027		Got to Get Rid of You/Snowflakes	1969	3.75	7.50	15.00
Barnes, Sidney						
Blue Cat						
❏ 125		I Hurt on the Other Side/Switchy Walk	1966	37.50	75.00	150.00
Chess						
❏ 2094		Baloney/Old Times	1970	2.50	5.00	10.00
Parachute						
❏ 521		Hold On I'm Coming/Your Love Is So Good to Me	1978		2.00	4.00
Red Bird						
❏ 10-039		You'll Always Be in Style/I'm So Glad	1965	10.00	20.00	40.00
❏ 10-054		I Hurt on the Other Side/Switchy Walk	1966	10.00	20.00	40.00
Barons, The						
(Several different groups)						
Bellaire						
❏ 103		The Bandit/Wanderin'	1963	5.00	10.00	20.00
Brownfield						
❏ 1035		Hope I Please You/Don't Burn It	196?	12.50	25.00	50.00
Dart						
❏ 126		Lonely Loretta/Lula Mae	1959	6.25	12.50	25.00
❏ 134		Perfect Love/Until the Thirteenth Chime	1960	6.25	12.50	25.00
Decca						
❏ 29293		Exactly Like You/Forget About Me	1954	30.00	60.00	120.00
❏ 48323		A Year and a Day/My Baby's Gone	1954	30.00	60.00	120.00
Demon						
❏ 1520		Gravel Gert/The Fight	1959	3.75	7.50	15.00
Epic						
❏ 9586		Don't Go Away (Pretty Little Girl)/Pledge of a Fool	1963	7.50	15.00	30.00
❏ 9747		Lucky Star/Remember Rita	1964	37.50	75.00	150.00
❏ 10093		Don't Go Away (Pretty Little Girl)/Pledge of a Fool	1966	3.75	7.50	15.00
Imperial						
❏ 5343		Eternally Yours/Boom Boom	1955	30.00	60.00	120.00
❏ 5343		Eternally Yours/Boom Boom	1955	75.00	150.00	300.00
		Red vinyl, probably promo only				
❏ 5359		I Know I Was Wrong/My Dream, My Love	1955	30.00	60.00	120.00
❏ 5370		Cold Kisses/Searching for You	1955	30.00	60.00	120.00
❏ 5383		So Long My Darling/Crying for You Baby	1956	30.00	60.00	120.00
❏ 5397		Don't Walk Out/Once in a Lifetime	1956	20.00	40.00	80.00
❏ 66057		Silence/I Just Go Wild Inside	1964	3.75	7.50	15.00
RCA Victor						
❏ 47-9034		Since You're Gone/	1966	6.25	12.50	25.00
		My Smile Is Bigger (Than Your Smile)				
Tender						
❏ 511		Drawbridge/(B-side unknown)	1958	3.75	7.50	15.00
Barracuda						
RCA Victor						
❏ 47-9660		The Dance of St. Francis/Lady Fingers	1968	5.00	10.00	20.00
❏ 47-9660	PS	The Dance of St. Francis/Lady Fingers	1968	10.00	20.00	40.00
❏ 47-9743		Julie (The Song I Sing Is To You)/	1969	3.00	6.00	12.00
		Sleeping Out the Storm				
Barran, Bob						
Silver Streak						
❏ 311		Tom Tom Rock/Mother Goose Hop	1960	37.50	75.00	150.00
Barrett, Richard						
Atlantic						
❏ 2142		Some Other Guy/Tricky Dicky	1962	3.75	7.50	15.00
		As "Richie Barrett"				
Crackerjack						
❏ 4012		Summer's Love/(B-side unknown)	1963	3.75	7.50	15.00
Gone						
❏ 5056		Come Softly to Me/Walking Through Dreamland	1959	7.50	15.00	30.00
		With the Chantels				
❏ 5060		Summer's Gone/All Is Forgiven	1959	7.50	15.00	30.00
		With the Chantels				
Metro						
❏ 20006		Lovable/Only One Way	1959	3.75	7.50	15.00
MGM						
❏ 12616		Smoke Gets In Your Eyes/Remember Me	1958	7.50	15.00	30.00
❏ 12659		Body and Soul/The Party	1958	7.50	15.00	30.00
Seville						
❏ 104		Dream On/I Am Yours	1960	3.75	7.50	15.00
20th Fox						
❏ 150		Lovely One/The Snake and the Bookworm	1959	3.75	7.50	15.00

Number		Title (A Side/B Side)	Year	VG	VG+	NM

Barri, Steve
Rona
❏ 1003		Down Around the Corner/Please Let It Be You	1961	10.00	20.00	40.00
❏ 1004		I Want Your Love/Story of the Ring	1961	10.00	20.00	40.00
❏ 1005		Two Different Worlds/Don't Run Away from Love	1962	10.00	20.00	40.00
❏ 1006		Never Before/Whenever You Kiss Me	1962	10.00	20.00	40.00

Barrix, Billy
Chess
❏ 1662		Cool Off Baby/Almost	1958	2,500	5,000	10,000
		Outrageously rare rockabilly record				

Barry and the Tamerlanes
(Also see "DeVorzon, Barry")
Valiant
❏ 6034		I Wonder What She's Doing Tonight/Don't Go	1963	5.00	10.00	20.00
❏ 6040		Roberta/Butterfly	1964	3.75	7.50	15.00
❏ 6046		Lucky Guy/I Don't Want to Be Your Clown	1964	3.75	7.50	15.00
❏ 6059		Gee/Don't Cry Cindy	1964	3.75	7.50	15.00
❏ 703		I Wonder What She's Doing Tonight/Roberta	1965	3.00	6.00	12.00

Barry, Jeff
A&M
❏ 1422		Walkin' in the Sun/Whatcha Wanna Do	1973		2.50	5.00
Bell
❏ 45,140		Sweet Saviour/Love Has Never Let Me Down	1971		3.00	6.00
Decca
❏ 31037		Never Never/It Won't Hurt	1959	5.00	10.00	20.00
❏ 31089		Lenore/Why Does the Feeling Go Away	1960	5.00	10.00	20.00
RCA Victor
❏ 47-7477		It's Called Rock & Roll/Hip Couples	1959	6.25	12.50	25.00
❏ 47-7797		The Face from Outer Space/Lovely Lips	1960	6.25	12.50	25.00
❏ 47-7821		All You Need Is a Quarter/Teen Quartet	1960	6.25	12.50	25.00
Red Bird
❏ 10-026		I'll Still Love You/Our Love Can Still Be Saved	1965	4.00	8.00	16.00
United Artists
❏ 440		We Got Love Money Can't Buy/Welcome Home	1962	4.00	8.00	16.00
❏ 50529		Much Too Young/Where It's At	1969	2.00	4.00	8.00

Bartholomew, Dave
Decca
❏ 48216		Tra La La/Teejim	1951	30.00	60.00	120.00
Imperial
Note: Dave Bartholomew records on Imperial before 5210 are unconfirmed on 45 rpm
❏ 5210		Who Drank the Beer While I Was in the Rear/ The Rest of My Life	1952	30.00	60.00	120.00
❏ 5249		No More Black Nights/Air Tight	1953	30.00	60.00	120.00
❏ 5273		Texas Hop/When the Saints Go Marchin' In Boogie	1954	37.50	75.00	150.00
❏ 5308		Cat Music/Jump Children	1954	30.00	60.00	120.00
❏ 5322		Another Mule/I Want to Be with Her	1955	12.50	25.00	50.00
❏ 5350		Every Night, Every Day/Four Winds	1955	12.50	25.00	50.00
❏ 5373		Shrimp and Gumbo/ An Old Cowhand from a Blues Band	1956	10.00	20.00	40.00
❏ 5390		Would You/Turn Your Lamp Down Low	1956	10.00	20.00	40.00
❏ 5408		Lovin' You/Three Time Loser	1956	7.50	15.00	30.00
❏ 5438		The Monkey/The Shuffling	1957	6.25	12.50	25.00
❏ 5460		How Could You/Barrel House	1957	6.25	12.50	25.00
❏ 5481		Hard Times (The Slop)/Cinderella	1957	6.25	12.50	25.00
❏ 5560		Button Blues/Short Subjects	1959	5.00	10.00	20.00
❏ 5702		I Cried/Somebody New	1960	5.00	10.00	20.00
❏ 5714		People Are Talking/Yeah, Yeah	1961	5.00	10.00	20.00
❏ 5803		I'm Walkin'/Going to the River	1962	3.75	7.50	15.00
❏ 5835		A Sunday Kind of Love/Honky Tonk Trumpet	1962	3.75	7.50	15.00
King
❏ 4482		Sweet Home Blues/Twins	1951	37.50	75.00	150.00
❏ 4508		In the Alley/I'll Never Be the Same	1952	50.00	100.00	200.00
❏ 4523		Lawdy, Lawdy, Lawd (Part 1)/ Lawdy, Lawdy, Lawd (Part 2)	1952	37.50	75.00	150.00
❏ 4544		My Ding-a-Ling/Bad Habit	1952	50.00	100.00	200.00
❏ 4559		The Golden Rule/Mother Knows Best	1952	25.00	50.00	100.00
❏ 4585		High Flying Woman/Stormy Weather	1953	25.00	50.00	100.00

Barton, Ernie
Phillips International
❏ 3528		Stairway of Love/Raining the Blues	1958	5.00	10.00	20.00
❏ 3541		Open the Door Richard/Shut Your Mouth	1959	37.50	75.00	150.00

Basil, Toni
A&M
❏ 791		Breakaway/I'm 28	1966	50.00	100.00	200.00
Chrysalis
❏ 2638		Mickey/Thief on the Loose	1982			3.00
❏ 2638	PS	Mickey/Thief on the Loose	1982			3.00
❏ 2665		Mickey (Spanish)/Thief on the Loose	1982		2.00	4.00
❏ 2665	PS	Mickey (Spanish)/Thief on the Loose	1982		2.00	4.00

Number		Title (A Side/B Side)	Year	VG	VG+	NM
☐ 03537		Shoppin' from A to Z/Time After Time	1983			3.00
☐ 03537	PS	Shoppin' from A to Z/Time After Time	1983			3.00
☐ 03539		Mickey/Thief on the Loose	1983			3.00
		Reissue				
☐ 42711		Street Beat/(B-side unknown)	1983			3.00
☐ 42753		Over My Head/Best Performance	1983			3.00
☐ 42753	PS	Over My Head/Best Performance	1983			3.00

Baskerville Hounds, The
Avco Embassy

☐ 4504		Hold Me/Here I Come, Miami	1968	2.50	5.00	10.00

Buddah

☐ 17		Caroline/Last Night on the Back Porch	1967	2.50	5.00	10.00

Dot

☐ 17004		Space Rock, Part 1/Space Rock, Part 2	1967	2.50	5.00	10.00
☐ 17017		Debbie/Jackie's Theme	1967	2.50	5.00	10.00
☐ 17037		Baby, Am I Losing/Never on Sunday	1967	2.50	5.00	10.00

Tema

☐ 125		Debbie/Jackie's Theme	1966	3.75	7.50	15.00
☐ 128		Space Rock, Part 1/Space Rock, Part 2	1966	3.75	7.50	15.00
☐ 131		Christmas Is Here/Make Me Your Man	1966	3.75	7.50	15.00
☐ 131	PS	Christmas Is Here/Make Me Your Man	1966	12.50	25.00	50.00
☐ 132		All You Had to Do Was Ask/Who Does She Love	1967	3.75	7.50	15.00
☐ 135		Hold Me/Here I Come, Miami	1967	3.75	7.50	15.00

Bats, The
Flame

☐ 5155		Batmobile/Batusi	1966	10.00	20.00	40.00

HBR

☐ 445		Big Bright Eyes/Nothing at All	1965	2.50	5.00	10.00

Parrot

☐ 40013		Listen to My Heart/You Look Good Together	1967	2.50	5.00	10.00

Battin, Skip
(Of Skip and Flip)
Aurora

☐ 159		The Dating Game Theme/Night Time Girl	1966	3.75		7.50	15.00

Groove

☐ 58-0055		Searchin'/She Acts Like We Never Have Met	1965	10.00	20.00	40.00
☐ 58-0065		Ten Feet Tall/What's Mine Is Mine	1965	10.00	20.00	40.00

Signpost

☐ 70010	DJ	Ballad of Dick Clark (mono/stereo)	1973		3.00	6.00
		May be promo only				

Baum, Allen
Red Robin

☐ 124		My Kinda Woman/Too Much Competition	1954	100.00	200.00	400.00

Baxter, Ronnie
Atco

☐ 6093		Drivin' Me Out of My Mind/Afraid of Love	1957	10.00	20.00	40.00

Gone

☐ 5036		Someone to Love Me/Gates of Heaven	1958	7.50	15.00	30.00
☐ 5041		Gates of Heaven/Prisoner of Love	1958	7.50	15.00	30.00
☐ 5050		Is It Because/I Finally Found You	1958	7.50	15.00	30.00
☐ 5058		Is It Because/I Finally Found You	1959	7.50	15.00	30.00
☐ 5084		It's Magic/If You Let Me	1960	6.25	12.50	25.00

Mark-X

☐ 8001		It's Magic/If You Love Me	1959	3.00	6.00	12.00

Beach Boys, The
(Also see "Campbell, Glen"; "Johnston, Bruce"; "Kenny and the Cadets"; "Wilson, Brian"; "Wilson, Brian, and Mike Love"; "Wilson, Carl"; "Wilson, Dennis")
Brother

☐ 1001		Heroes and Villains/You're Welcome	1967	3.00	6.00	12.00
☐ 1001	PS	Heroes and Villains/You're Welcome	1967	25.00	50.00	100.00
		Not to be confused with Capitol 5826, which is a completely different sleeve				

Brother/Reprise

☐ 0101		Wouldn't It Be Nice/Sloop John B	1973		2.50	5.00
		"Back to Back Hits" series				
☐ 0102		God Only Knows/Caroline, No	1973		2.50	5.00
		"Back to Back Hits" series				
☐ 0103		Good Vibrations/Heroes and Villains	1973		2.50	5.00
		"Back to Back Hits" series				
☐ 0104		Darlin'/Wild Honey	1973		2.50	5.00
		"Back to Back Hits" series				
☐ 0105		Friends/Be Here in the Morning	1973		2.50	5.00
		"Back to Back Hits" series				
☐ 0106		Do It Again/Cottonfields	1973		2.50	5.00
		"Back to Back Hits" series				
☐ 0107		I Can Hear Music/Bluebirds Over the Mountain	1973		2.50	5.00
		"Back to Back Hits" series				

Number		Title (A Side/B Side)	Year	VG	VG+	NM
❑ 0118		Rock and Roll Music/It's O.K.	1977		2.00	4.00
		"Back to Back Hits" series				
❑ 0894		Add Some Music to Your Day/Susie Cincinnati	1970	2.00	4.00	8.00
❑ 0929		Slip On Through/This Whole World	1970	2.50	5.00	10.00
❑ 0957		It's About Time/Tears in the Morning	1970	5.00	10.00	20.00
❑ 0998		Cool, Cool Water/Forever	1971	20.00	40.00	80.00
❑ 1015		Long Promised Road/Deirdre	1971	5.00	10.00	20.00
❑ 1047		Long Promised Road/'Til I Die	1971	5.00	10.00	20.00
❑ 1058		Surf's Up/Don't Go Near the Water	1971	12.50	25.00	50.00
❑ 1091		You Need a Mess of Help to Stand Alone/Cuddle Up	1972	7.50	15.00	30.00
❑ 1101		Marcella/Hold On Dear Brother	1972	7.50	15.00	30.00
❑ 1138		Sail On Sailor/Only With You	1972	2.50	5.00	10.00
❑ 1156		California Saga (On My Way to Sunny Californ-I-A)/	1973	2.50	5.00	10.00
		Funky Pretty				
❑ 1310		I Can Hear Music/Let the Wind Blow	1974	2.50	5.00	10.00
❑ 1321		Child of Winter/Susie Cincinnati	1974	12.50	25.00	50.00
❑ 1325		Sail On Sailor/Only With You	1975	2.00	4.00	8.00
❑ 1336		Wouldn't It Be Nice/Caroline, No	1975	3.00	6.00	12.00
❑ 1354		Rock and Roll Music/The T M Song	1976		2.00	4.00
❑ 1368		It's O.K./Had to Phone Ya	1976		2.00	4.00
❑ 1375		Everyone's In Love with You/Susie Cincinnati	1976		2.00	4.00
❑ 1389		Honkin' Down the Highway/Solar System	1977		2.00	4.00
❑ 1394		Peggy Sue/Hey Little Tomboy	1978		2.00	4.00

Candix

Number		Title (A Side/B Side)	Year	VG	VG+	NM
❑ 301		Surfin'/Luau	1961	75.00	150.00	300.00
		No mention of Era Records on label				
❑ 301		Surfin'/Luau	1961	50.00	100.00	200.00
		Label says "Distributed by Era Records Sales, Inc."				
❑ 331		Surfin'/Luau	1962	50.00	100.00	200.00

Capitol

Number		Title (A Side/B Side)	Year	VG	VG+	NM
❑ 2028		Wild Honey/Wind Chimes	1967	3.00	6.00	12.00
❑ 2068		Darlin'/Here Today	1967	3.00	6.00	12.00
❑ 2068	PS	Darlin'/Here Today	1967	5.00	10.00	20.00
❑ 2160		Friends/Little Bird	1968	3.00	6.00	12.00
❑ 2239		Do It Again/Wake the World	1968	3.00	6.00	12.00
❑ 2360		Bluebirds Over the Mountain/Never Learn Not to Love	1968	3.00	6.00	12.00
❑ 2432		I Can Hear Music/All I Want to Do	1969	3.00	6.00	12.00
❑ 2530		Break Away/Celebrate the News	1969	3.00	6.00	12.00
❑ 2765		Cottonfields/The Nearest Faraway Place	1970	5.00	10.00	20.00
❑ 3924		Surfin' U.S.A./The Warmth of the Sun	1974		2.50	5.00
❑ 4093		Little Honda/Hawaii	1975		2.50	5.00
❑ 4110		Barbara Ann/Little Honda	1975		2.50	5.00
❑ 4334		Be True to Your School/Graduation Day	1976		2.50	5.00
❑ 4777		Surfin' Safari/409	1962	4.00	8.00	16.00
❑ 4777	PS	Surfin' Safari/409	1962	15.00	30.00	60.00
❑ 4880		Ten Little Indians/County Fair	1962	6.25	12.50	25.00
❑ 4880	PS	Ten Little Indians/County Fair	1962	50.00	100.00	200.00
❑ 4932		Surfin' U.S.A./Shut Down	1963	4.00	8.00	16.00
		Version 1: Brian Wilson listed as composer of "Surfin' U.S.A."				
❑ 4932		Surfin' U.S.A./Shut Down	1963	3.75	7.50	15.00
		Version 2: Chuck Berry listed as composer of "Surfin' U.S.A."				
❑ 5009		Surfer Girl/Little Deuce Coupe	1963	3.75	7.50	15.00
❑ A-5030		The Beach Boys Medley/God Only Knows	1981		2.50	5.00
❑ 5069		Be True to Your School/In My Room	1963	3.75	7.50	15.00
❑ 5096		Little Saint Nick/The Lord's Prayer	1963	5.00	10.00	20.00
		Orange and yellow swirl label				
❑ 5096		Little Saint Nick/The Lord's Prayer	1969	4.50	9.00	18.00
		Red and orange "target" label				
❑ 5096		Little Saint Nick/The Lord's Prayer	1972	3.75	7.50	15.00
		Orange label with "Capitol" at bottom of label				
❑ 5096		Little Saint Nick/The Lord's Prayer	1978		2.50	5.00
		Purple label				
❑ 5096		Little Saint Nick/The Lord's Prayer	1982		2.50	5.00
		Black label with colorband				
❑ 5118		Fun, Fun, Fun/Why Do Fools Fall in Love	1964	5.00	10.00	20.00
		A-side songwriter listed as "Brian Wilson"				
❑ 5118		Fun, Fun, Fun/Why Do Fools Fall in Love	1964	4.00	8.00	16.00
		A-side songwriter listed as "Brian Wilson-Mike Love"				
❑ 5118	PS	Fun, Fun, Fun/Why Do Fools Fall in Love	1964	7.50	15.00	30.00
❑ 5174		I Get Around/Don't Worry Baby	1964	3.75	7.50	15.00
		Orange and yellow swirl label				
❑ 5174	PS	I Get Around/Don't Worry Baby	1964	7.50	15.00	30.00
❑ 5174		I Get Around/Don't Worry Baby	1969	3.00	6.00	12.00
		Red and orange "target" label				
❑ 5174		I Get Around/Don't Worry Baby	1972	2.00	4.00	8.00
		Orange label with "Capitol" at bottom				
❑ 5174		I Get Around/Don't Worry Baby	1978		2.50	5.00
		Purple label				
❑ 5174		I Get Around/Don't Worry Baby	1982		2.50	5.00
		Black label with colorband				
❑ 5245		When I Grow Up (To Be a Man)/	1964	3.75	7.50	15.00
		She Knows Me Too Well				
❑ 5245	PS	When I Grow Up (To Be a Man)/	1964	7.50	15.00	30.00
		She Knows Me Too Well				
		With blue border				

The Beach Boys are among the most collectible groups, and perhaps *the* most collectible American group, of all time. These are two of their many sought-after items: At top is an original pressing on X Records of "Surfin," their very first record. Below it is one of their rarest picture sleeves, the one for "Ten Little Indians," their second Capitol single (and pretty obscure to this day).

Number		Title (A Side/B Side)	Year	VG	VG+	NM
▓ 5245	PS	When I Grow Up (To Be a Man)/ She Knows Me Too Well	1964	8.00	16.00	32.00
		With green border				
❑ R-5267		Wendy/Don't Back Down//Little Honda/Hushabye	1964	12.50	25.00	50.00
		Better known as "4 -- By The Beach Boys"				
❑ R-5267	PS	Wendy/Don't Back Down//Little Honda/Hushabye	1964	12.50	25.00	50.00
		Better known as "4 -- By The Beach Boys"				
❑ 5306		Dance, Dance, Dance/The Warmth of the Sun	1964	3.75	7.50	15.00
❑ 5306	PS	Dance, Dance, Dance/The Warmth of the Sun	1964	20.00	40.00	80.00
▓ 5312		The Man with All the Toys/Blue Christmas	1964	5.00	10.00	20.00
❑ 5372		Do You Wanna Dance/Please Let Me Wonder	1965	3.75	7.50	15.00
❑ 5372	PS	Do You Wanna Dance/Please Let Me Wonder	1965	7.50	15.00	30.00
❑ 5395		Help Me, Rhonda/Kiss Me, Baby	1965	3.75	7.50	15.00
❑ 5395	PS	Help Me, Rhonda/Kiss Me, Baby	1965	7.50	15.00	30.00
❑ 5464		California Girls/Let Him Run Wild	1965	3.75		7.50	15.00
		Orange and yellow swirl label				
▓ 5464	PS	California Girls/Let Him Run Wild	1965	7.50	15.00	30.00
❑ 5464		California Girls/Let Him Run Wild	1969	2.50	5.00	10.00
		Red and orange "target" label				
❑ 5464		California Girls/Let Him Run Wild	1973	2.00	4.00	8.00
		Orange label with "Capitol" at bottom of label				
❑ 5464		California Girls/Let Him Run Wild	1978		2.50	5.00
		Purple label				
❑ 5540		The Little Girl I Once Knew/ There's No Other (Like My Baby)	1965	3.75	7.50	15.00
❑ 5540	PS	The Little Girl I Once Knew/ There's No Other (Like My Baby)	1965	7.50	15.00	30.00
❑ 5561		Barbara Ann/Girl Don't Tell Me	1965	3.75	7.50	15.00
❑ 5561	PS	Barbara Ann/Girl Don't Tell Me	1965	40.00	80.00	160.00
		Non-glossy finish				
❑ 5561	PS	Barbara Ann/Girl Don't Tell Me	1965	30.00	60.00	120.00
		Glossy finish				
❑ B-5595		Rock and Roll to the Rescue/ Good Vibrations (Live in London)	1986			3.00
❑ B-5595	PS	Rock and Roll to the Rescue/ Good Vibrations (Live in London)	1986		2.00	4.00
❑ 5602		Sloop John B/You're So Good to Me	1966	3.75	7.50	15.00
		Orange and yellow swirl label				
❑ 5602	PS	Sloop John B/You're So Good to Me	1966	5.00	10.00	20.00
❑ 5602		Sloop John B/You're So Good to Me	1969	2.50	5.00	10.00
		Red and orange "target" label				
❑ 5602		Sloop John B/You're So Good to Me	1973	2.00	4.00	8.00
		Orange label with "Capitol" at bottom of label				
❑ 5602		Sloop John B/You're So Good to Me	1978		2.50	5.00
		Purple label				
❑ B-5630		California Dreamin'/Lady Liberty	1986			3.00
❑ 5676		Good Vibrations/Let's Go Away for Awhile	1966	3.75	7.50	15.00
▓ 5676	PS	Good Vibrations/Let's Go Away for Awhile	1966	7.50	15.00	30.00
❑ 5706		Wouldn't It Be Nice/God Only Knows	1966	3.75	7.50	15.00
		Even though it has a higher number, this single was released before "Good Vibrations."				
❑ 5826	PS	Heroes and Villains	1967	200.00	400.00	600.00
		U.S. picture sleeve for unreleased record. This sleeve, however, was exported and used in other countries.				
❑ S7-17521		409/Punchline	1993		2.00	4.00
❑ S7-17522		Be True to Your School/Things We Did Last Summer	1993		2.00	4.00
❑ S7-17523		Do You Wanna Dance/Ruby Baby	1993		2.00	4.00
❑ S7-18205		Merry Christmas, Baby/Santa's Beard	1994		2.00	4.00
		Green vinyl				
❑ B-44297		Don't Worry Baby/Tequila Dreams	1989		2.00	4.00
		A-side: With the Everly Brothers; B-side by Dave Grusin				
❑ B-44297	PS	Don't Worry Baby/Tequila Dreams	1989	2.50	5.00	10.00
❑ S7-57886		Frosty the Snowman/Little Saint Nick	1992		2.50	5.00
		Originals on black vinyl				
❑ S7-57886		Frosty the Snowman/Little Saint Nick	1993		2.00	4.00
		Second pressing on green vinyl				
❑ 7PRO-79789	DJ	Still Cruisin' (same on both sides)	1989	15.00	30.00	60.00
		Vinyl is promo only				
❑ 7PRO-79841	DJ	Somewhere Near Japan (same on both sides)	1989	15.00	30.00	60.00
		Vinyl is promo only				

Capitol Starline

Number		Title (A Side/B Side)	Year	VG	VG+	NM
❑ 6059		Be True to Your School/In My Room	1965	3.75	7.50	15.00
		Originals have green swirl labels				
❑ 6060		Ten Little Indians/She Knows Me Too Well	1965	3.75	7.50	15.00
		Originals have green swirl labels				
❑ 6081		Help Me, Rhonda/Do You Wanna Dance?	1966	3.75	7.50	15.00
		Originals have green swirl labels				
❑ 6094		Surfin' U.S.A./Shut Down	1966	3.75	7.50	15.00
		Originals have green swirl labels				
❑ 6095		Surfin' Safari/409	1966	3.75	7.50	15.00
		Originals have green swirl labels				
❑ 6105		Dance, Dance, Dance/The Warmth of the Sun	1967	3.00	6.00	12.00
		Originals have red and white "target" labels				
❑ 6106		Fun, Fun, Fun/Why Do Fools Fall in Love	1967	3.00	6.00	12.00
		Originals have red and white "target" labels				

Number		Title (A Side/B Side)	Year	VG	VG+	NM
❑ 6107		Surfer Girl/Little Deuce Coupe	1967	3.00	6.00	12.00
		Originals have red and white "target" labels				
❑ 6132		Good Vibrations/Barbara Ann	1968	3.00	6.00	12.00
		Originals have red and white "target" labels				
❑ 6204		When I Grow Up (To Be a Man)/	197?		2.50	5.00
		She Knows Me Too Well				
		Originals have grayish labels				
❑ 6205		Wendy/Little Honda	197?		2.50	5.00
		Originals have grayish labels				
❑ 6259		Barbara Ann/Little Honda	1978		2.00	4.00
		Originals have grayish labels				
❑ 6277		Little Saint Nick/The Lord's Prayer	1981			3.00
		Originals have blue labels				
❑ 6280		I Get Around/Don't Worry Baby	1981			3.00
		Originals have blue labels				
❑ 6289		California Girls/Let Him Run Wild	1981			3.00
		Originals have blue labels				
❑ 6295		Sloop John B/You're So Good to Me	1981			3.00
		Originals have blue labels				

Caribou

❑ 02633		Come Go with Me/Don't Go Near the Water	1981			3.00
❑ 04913		Getcha Back/Male Ego	1985			3.00
❑ 04913	PS	Getcha Back/Male Ego	1985			3.00
❑ 05433		It's Gettin' Late/It's OK	1985			3.00
❑ 05433	PS	It's Gettin' Late/It's OK	1985			3.00
❑ 05624		She Believes in Love Again/It's Just a Matter of Time	1985			3.00
❑ 05624	PS	She Believes in Love Again/It's Just a Matter of Time	1985			3.00
❑ 9026		Here Comes the Night/Baby Blue	1979		2.00	4.00
❑ 9029		Good Timin'/Love Surrounds Me	1979		2.00	4.00
❑ 9030		Lady Lynda/Full Sail	1979		2.00	4.00
❑ 9031		It's a Beautiful Day/Sumahama	1979		2.00	4.00
❑ 9032		Goin' On/Endless Harmony	1980		2.00	4.00
❑ 9033		Livin' with a Heartache/Santa Ana Winds	1980		2.00	4.00
❑ 9034		School Day (Ring! Ring! Goes the Bell)/	1980			*Not known to exist*
		When Girls Get Together				
❑ 9034	DJ	School Day (Ring! Ring! Goes the Bell)	1980	50.00	125.00	250.00
		(same on both sides)				

Critique

❑ 99392		Happy Endings/California Girls	1987			3.00
		A-side: With Little Richard				

Elektra

❑ 69385		Kokomo/Tutti-Frutti	1988			3.00
		B-side by Little Richard				

FBI

❑ 7701		East Meets West/Rhapsody	1986	5.00	10.00	20.00
		With Frankie Valli and the Four Seasons				

Kapp

❑ 289		Bathing Beauty/On the Beach at Sunset	1959	6.25	12.50	25.00
		Not the ones that became famous later on.				

Ode

❑ 66016		Wouldn't It Be Nice/The Times They Are a-Changing	1971	7.50	15.00	30.00
		B-side by Merry Clayton				

Sub Pop

❑ 363		I Just Wasn't Made for These Times/	1996		2.50	5.00
		Wouldn't It Be Nice//Here Today				
		Newly released versions from the planned Pet Sounds box set				
❑ 363	PS	I Just Wasn't Made for These Times/	1996		2.50	5.00
		Wouldn't It Be Nice//Here Today				
		Not seam sealed (folded piece of cardboard)				

X

❑ 301		Surfin'/Luau	1961	250.00	500.00	1,000

Beach Bums, The

(Early Bob Seger; B-side credited to "D. Dodger")
Are You Kidding Me?

❑ 1010		Florida Time/The Ballad of the Yellow Beret	1966	15.00	30.00	60.00

Beach Girls, The

Dyno-Vox

❑ 202		Goin' Places/Skiing in the Snow	1965	6.25	12.50	25.00

Vault

❑ 905		He's My Surfin' Guy/Bobby's the Boy	1963	7.50	15.00	30.00

Beach Nuts, The

Bang

❑ 504		Out in the Sun (Hey-O)/Someday So On	1965	7.50	15.00	30.00

Coronado

❑ 131		Surf Ride '65/The Last Ride	1965	12.50	25.00	50.00
❑ 131	PS	Surf Ride '65/The Last Ride	1965	15.00	30.00	60.00

Number		Title (A Side/B Side)	Year	VG	VG+	NM

Beach, Bill
King

| □ 4940 | | Peg Pants/You're Gonna Like My Baby | 1956 | 37.50 | 75.00 | 150.00 |

Beagles, The
Era

□ 3132		Let's All Sing Like the Birdies Sing/	1964	3.75	7.50	15.00
		Deep in the Heart of Texas				
□ 3132	PS	Let's All Sing Like the Birdies Sing/	1964	6.25	12.50	25.00
		Deep in the Heart of Texas				

Hit

| □ 113 | | Can't Buy Me Love/White on White | 1964 | 3.00 | 6.00 | 12.00 |
| | | B-side by Fred York | | | | |

Bean, Young Billy - See "Burnette, Billy"

Beard, Dean
Atlantic

□ 1137		On My Mind Again/Rakin' and Scrapin'	1957	10.00	20.00	40.00
□ 1162		Party Party/Stand By Me	1957	10.00	20.00	40.00
□ 1182		Take Time to Love Me/Hold Me Close	1958	7.50	15.00	30.00

Candix

| □ 341 | | The Day That I Lost You/Villa Acuna | 1962 | 3.00 | 6.00 | 12.00 |

Challenge

| □ 59033 | | Egad, Charlie Brown/Keeper of the Key | 1958 | 6.25 | 12.50 | 25.00 |
| □ 59048 | | Holding On to a Memory/Little Lover | 1959 | 6.25 | 12.50 | 25.00 |

Edmoral

| □ 1011 | | On My Mind Again/Rakin' and Scrapin' | 1956 | 37.50 | 75.00 | 150.00 |

Joed

| □ 715 | | Coffee Break/Tropical Nights | 1962 | 6.25 | 12.50 | 25.00 |

Sims

| □ 299 | | (Are There) Honkytonks in Heaven/ | 1966 | 2.50 | 5.00 | 10.00 |
| | | Pocketful of Stardust | | | | |

Winston

□ 1063		I Don't Know How/The Red Rose	1962	3.00	6.00	12.00
□ 1073		Don't Let the Stars Get In Your Eyes/	1963	3.00	6.00	12.00
		That's How It Gets Sun Up				
□ 1075		Smile Pretty for Me Temper/To Me	1963	3.00	6.00	12.00
		With Bill Graham				

Beat Brothers, The
MGM

| □ 13201 | | Nick Nack Hully Gully/Lateren Hully Gully | 1963 | 4.00 | 8.00 | 16.00 |

Beatle-Ettes, The
Assault

| □ 1893 | | Yes, You Can Hold My Hand/ | 1964 | 5.00 | 10.00 | 20.00 |
| | | Yes, You Can Hold My Hand (Part 2) | | | | |

Jamie

| □ 1270 | | Dance, Beatle, Dance/We Were Meant to Be Married | 1964 | 5.00 | 10.00 | 20.00 |

Jubilee

| □ 5472 | | Only Seventeen/Now We're Together | 1964 | 5.00 | 10.00 | 20.00 |

Beatles, The
(Even as lengthy as the following list is, it is not complete. Please consult a Beatles price guide for even more, if you so desire. Also see "Best, Peter"; "Harrison, George"; "Lennon, John"; "McCartney, Paul"; "Starr, Ringo" for solo releases)
(Apple)

| □ MBRF-55551 | | Decade | 1974 | | | |
| | | A clever bootleg of radio spots for the Beatles' back catalog, compiled without authorization by two former Capitol employees. | | | | |

Apple

□ Promo-1970	DJ	Dialogue from the Beatles' Motion Picture "Let It Be"	1970	15.00	30.00	60.00
□ 2056		Hello Goodbye/I Am the Walrus	1971	7.50	15.00	30.00
		With star on A-side label				
□ 2056		Hello Goodbye/I Am the Walrus	1971	2.50	5.00	10.00
		Without star on A-side label				
□ 2056		Hello Goodbye/I Am the Walrus	1975	5.00	10.00	20.00
		With "All Rights Reserved" disclaimer				
□ 2138		Lady Madonna/The Inner Light	1971	7.50	15.00	30.00
		With star on A-side label				
□ 2138		Lady Madonna/The Inner Light	1971	2.50	5.00	10.00
		Without star on A-side label				
□ 2138		Lady Madonna/The Inner Light	1975	5.00	10.00	20.00
		With "All Rights Reserved" disclaimer				
□ 2276		Hey Jude/Revolution	1968	3.75	7.50	15.00
		Original: With small Capitol logo on bottom of B-side label				
□ 2276		Hey Jude/Revolution	1968	2.50	5.00	10.00
		With "Mfd. by Apple" on label				
□ 2276		Hey Jude/Revolution	1975	5.00	10.00	20.00
		With "All Rights Reserved" disclaimer				

Number	Title (A Side/B Side)	Year	VG	VG+	NM
❑ 2490	Get Back/Don't Let Me Down *Original: With small Capitol logo on bottom of B-side label*	1969	2.50	5.00	10.00
❑ 2490	Get Back/Don't Let Me Down *With "Mfd. by Apple" on label*	1969	2.50	5.00	10.00
❑ 2490	Get Back/Don't Let Me Down *With "All Rights Reserved" disclaimer*	1975	5.00	10.00	20.00
❑ 2531	The Ballad of John and Yoko/Old Brown Shoe *Original: With small Capitol logo on bottom of B-side label*	1969	2.50	5.00	10.00
❑ 2531	The Ballad of John and Yoko/Old Brown Shoe *With "Mfd. by Apple" on label*	1969	2.50	5.00	10.00
❑ 2531	PS The Ballad of John and Yoko/Old Brown Shoe	1969	20.00	40.00	80.00
❑ 2531	The Ballad of John and Yoko/Old Brown Shoe *With "All Rights Reserved" disclaimer*	1975	5.00	10.00	20.00
❑ 2654	Something/Come Together *Original: With small Capitol logo on bottom of B-side label*	1969	25.00	50.00	100.00
❑ 2654	Something/Come Together *With "Mfd. by Apple" on label*	1969	2.50	5.00	10.00
❑ 2654	Something/Come Together *With "All Rights Reserved" disclaimer*	1975	5.00	10.00	20.00
❑ 2764	Let It Be/You Know My Name (Look Up My Number) *Original: With small Capitol logo on bottom of B-side label*	1970	3.00	6.00	12.00
❑ 2764	Let It Be/You Know My Name (Look Up My Number) *With "Mfd. by Apple" on label*	1970	2.50	5.00	10.00
❑ 2764	PS Let It Be/You Know My Name (Look Up the Number)	1970	17.50	35.00	70.00
❑ 2764	Let It Be/You Know My Name (Look Up My Number) *With "All Rights Reserved" disclaimer*	1975	5.00	10.00	20.00
❑ 2832	The Long and Winding Road/For You Blue *With "Mfd. by Apple" on label*	1970	2.50	5.00	10.00
❑ 2832	The Long and Winding Road/For You Blue *Original: With small Capitol logo on bottom of B-side label*	1970	5.00	10.00	20.00
❑ 2832	PS The Long and Winding Road/For You Blue	1970	20.00	40.00	80.00
❑ 2832	The Long and Winding Road/For You Blue *With "All Rights Reserved" disclaimer*	1975	5.00	10.00	20.00
❑ 5112	I Want to Hold Your Hand/I Saw Her Standing There *With star on A-side label*	1971	7.50	15.00	30.00
❑ 5112	I Want to Hold Your Hand/I Saw Her Standing There *Without star on A-side label*	1971	2.50	5.00	10.00
❑ 5112	I Want to Hold Your Hand/I Saw Her Standing There *With "All Rights Reserved" disclaimer on label*	1975	5.00	10.00	20.00
❑ 5150	Can't Buy Me Love/You Can't Do That *With star on A-side label*	1971	7.50	15.00	30.00
❑ 5150	Can't Buy Me Love/You Can't Do That *Without star on A-side label*	1971	2.50	5.00	10.00
❑ 5150	Can't Buy Me Love/You Can't Do That *With "All Rights Reserved" disclaimer on label*	1975	3.75	7.50	15.00
❑ 5222	A Hard Day's Night/I Should Have Known Better *With star on A-side label*	1971	7.50	15.00	30.00
❑ 5222	A Hard Day's Night/I Should Have Known Better *Without star on A-side label*	1971	2.50	5.00	10.00
❑ 5222	A Hard Day's Night/I Should Have Known Better *With "All Rights Reserved" disclaimer*	1975	3.75	7.50	15.00
❑ 5234	I'll Cry Instead/I'm Happy Just to Dance with You *With star on A-side label*	1971	7.50	15.00	30.00
❑ 5234	I'll Cry Instead/I'm Happy Just to Dance with You *Without star on A-side label*	1971	2.50	5.00	10.00
❑ 5234	I'll Cry Instead/I'm Happy Just to Dance with You *With "All Rights Reserved" disclaimer*	1975	3.75	7.50	15.00
❑ 5235	And I Love Her/If I Fell *With star on A-side label*	1971	7.50	15.00	30.00
❑ 5235	And I Love Her/If I Fell *Without star on A-side label*	1971	2.50	5.00	10.00
❑ 5235	And I Love Her/If I Fell *With "All Rights Reserved" disclaimer*	1975	3.75	7.50	15.00
❑ 5255	Matchbox/Slow Down *With star on A-side label*	1971	7.50	15.00	30.00
❑ 5255	Matchbox/Slow Down *Without star on A-side label*	1971	2.50	5.00	10.00
❑ 5255	Matchbox/Slow Down *With "All Rights Reserved" disclaimer*	1975	3.75	7.50	15.00
❑ 5327	I Feel Fine/She's a Woman *With star on A-side label*	1971	7.50	15.00	30.00
❑ 5327	I Feel Fine/She's a Woman *Without star on A-side label*	1971	2.50	5.00	10.00
❑ 5327	I Feel Fine/She's a Woman *With "All Rights Reserved" disclaimer*	1975	3.75	7.50	15.00
❑ 5371	Eight Days a Week/I Don't Want to Spoil the Party *With star on A-side label*	1971	7.50	15.00	30.00
❑ 5371	Eight Days a Week/I Don't Want to Spoil the Party *Without star on A-side label*	1971	2.50	5.00	10.00
❑ 5371	Eight Days a Week/I Don't Want to Spoil the Party *With "All Rights Reserved" disclaimer*	1975	3.75	7.50	15.00

Number	Title (A Side/B Side)	Year	VG	VG+	NM
❑ 5407	Ticket to Ride/Yes It Is *With star on A-side label*	1971	7.50	15.00	30.00
❑ 5407	Ticket to Ride/Yes It Is *Without star on A-side label*	1971	2.50	5.00	10.00
❑ 5407	Ticket to Ride/Yes It Is *With "All Rights Reserved" disclaimer*	1975	3.75	7.50	15.00
❑ 5476	Help!/I'm Down *With star on A-side label*	1971	7.50	15.00	30.00
❑ 5476	Help!/I'm Down *Without star on A-side label*	1971	2.50	5.00	10.00
❑ 5476	Help!/I'm Down *With "All Rights Reserved" disclaimer*	1975	3.75	7.50	15.00
❑ 5498	Yesterday/Act Naturally *With star on A-side label*	1971	7.50	15.00	30.00
❑ 5498	Yesterday/Act Naturally *Without star on A-side label*	1971	2.50	5.00	10.00
❑ 5498	Yesterday/Act Naturally *With "All Rights Reserved" disclaimer*	1975	3.75	7.50	15.00
❑ 5555	We Can Work It Out/Day Tripper *With star on A-side label*	1971	7.50	15.00	30.00
❑ 5555	We Can Work It Out/Day Tripper *Without star on A-side label*	1971	2.50	5.00	10.00
❑ 5555	We Can Work It Out/Day Tripper *With "All Rights Reserved" disclaimer*	1975	3.75	7.50	15.00
❑ 5587	Nowhere Man/What Goes On *With star on A-side label*	1971	7.50	15.00	30.00
❑ 5587	Nowhere Man/What Goes On *Without star on A-side label*	1971	2.50	5.00	10.00
❑ 5587	Nowhere Man/What Goes On *With "All Rights Reserved" disclaimer*	1975	3.75	7.50	15.00
❑ 5651	Paperback Writer/Rain *With star on A-side label*	1971	7.50	15.00	30.00
❑ 5651	Paperback Writer/Rain *Without star on A-side label*	1971	2.50	5.00	10.00
❑ 5651	Paperback Writer/Rain *With "All Rights Reserved" disclaimer*	1975	3.75	7.50	15.00
❑ 5715	Yellow Submarine/Eleanor Rigby *With star on A-side label*	1971	7.50	15.00	30.00
❑ 5715	Yellow Submarine/Eleanor Rigby *Without star on A-side label*	1971	2.50	5.00	10.00
❑ 5715	Yellow Submarine/Eleanor Rigby *With "All Rights Reserved" disclaimer*	1975	3.75	7.50	15.00
❑ 5810	Penny Lane/Strawberry Fields Forever *With star on A-side label*	1971	7.50	15.00	30.00
❑ 5810	Penny Lane/Strawberry Fields Forever *Without star on A-side label*	1971	2.50	5.00	10.00
❑ 5810	Penny Lane/Strawberry Fields Forever *With "All Rights Reserved" disclaimer*	1975	3.75	7.50	15.00
❑ 5964	All You Need Is Love/Baby, You're a Rich Man *With star on A-side label*	1971	7.50	15.00	30.00
❑ 5964	All You Need Is Love/Baby, You're a Rich Man *Without star on A-side label*	1971	2.50	5.00	10.00
❑ 5964	All You Need Is Love/Baby, You're a Rich Man *With "All Rights Reserved" disclaimer*	1975	3.75	7.50	15.00
❑ 58348	Baby It's You/I'll Follow the Sun//Devil in Her Heart/ Boys	1995		2.00	4.00
❑ 58348	PS Baby It's You/I'll Follow the Sun//Devil in Her Heart/ Boys	1995		2.00	4.00
❑ 58497	Free as a Bird/Christmas Time (Is Here Again)	1995		2.00	4.00
	Small center hole; all with large hole were "dinked" somewhere other than when manufactured and have little, if any, value				
❑ 58497	PS Free as a Bird/Christmas Time (Is Here Again)	1995		2.00	4.00
❑ 58544	Real Love/Baby's in Black (Live)	1996			3.00
	Small center hole; all with large hole were "dinked" somewhere other than when manufactured and have little, if any, value				
❑ 58544	PS Real Love/Baby's in Black (Live)	1996			3.00

Apple/Americom

Number	Title (A Side/B Side)	Year	VG	VG+	NM
❑ 2276/M-221	Hey Jude/Revolution	1969	75.00	150.00	300.00
	Four-inch flexi-disc sold in vending machines; "Hey Jude" is edited to 3:25				
❑ 2490/M-335	Get Back/Don't Let Me Down	1969	250.00	500.00	1,000
	Four-inch flexi-disc sold in vending machines				
❑ 2531/M-382	The Ballad of John and Yoko/Old Brown Shoe	1969	200.00	400.00	800.00
	Four-inch flexi-disc sold in vending machines				
❑ 5715	Yellow Submarine/Eleanor Rigby	1969	1,000	1,500	2,000
	Four-inch flexi-disc sold in vending machines				

Atco

Number	Title (A Side/B Side)	Year	VG	VG+	NM
❑ 6302	Sweet Georgia Brown/ Take Out Some Insurance On Me Baby	1964	50.00	100.00	200.00
❑ 6308	Ain't She Sweet/Nobody's Child *With "Vocal by John Lennon" on left of label*	1964	12.50	25.00	50.00
❑ 6308	Ain't She Sweet/Nobody's Child *With "Vocal by John Lennon" under "The Beatles"*	1964	15.00	30.00	60.00

Number		Title (A Side/B Side)	Year	VG	VG+	NM
❑ 6308	PS	Ain't She Sweet/Nobody's Child	1964	125.00	250.00	500.00
		Beware! This has been counterfeited.				

Atlantic

❑ OS-13243		Ain't She Sweet/Sweet Georgia Brown	1983	2.50	5.00	10.00
		"Oldies Series"				

Backstage

❑ 1112	DJ	Like Dreamers Do/Love of the Loved	1982	6.25	12.50	25.00
		Promotional 45 from "Oui" magazine				
❑ 1122	DJ	Love of the Loved/Memphis	1983	6.25	12.50	25.00
		Promotional picture disc				
❑ 1133	DJ	Like Dreamers Do/Three Cool Cats	1983	6.25	12.50	25.00
		Promotional picture disc				
❑ 1155	DJ	Crying, Waiting, Hoping/Take Good Care of My Baby	1983	6.25	12.50	25.00

Beatles Fan Club

❑ (1964)		Season's Greetings from the Beatles	1964	75.00	150.00	300.00
		Tri-fold soundcard				
❑ (1965)		The Beatles Third Christmas Record	1965	20.00	40.00	80.00

Lyntone 948

		Flexi-disc				
❑ (1965)	PS	The Beatles Third Christmas Record	1965	25.00	50.00	100.00

Lyntone 948

❑ (1966)		Everywhere It's Christmas	1966	37.50	75.00	150.00
		Postcard				
❑ (1967)		Christmastime Is Here Again	1967	37.50	75.00	150.00
		Postcard				
❑ (1968) H-2041		The Beatles 1968 Christmas Record	1968	15.00	30.00	60.00
		Flexi-disc				
❑ (1968) H-2041	PS	The Beatles 1968 Christmas Record	1968	17.50	35.00	70.00
❑ (1969) H-2565		Happy Christmas 1969	1969	10.00	20.00	40.00
		Flexi-disc				
❑ (1969) H-2565	PS	Happy Christmas 1969	1969	15.00	30.00	60.00

Capitol

❑ 2056		Hello Goodbye/I Am the Walrus	1967	7.50	15.00	30.00
		Original: Orange and yellow swirl, without "A Subsidiary Of"... in perimeter label print; publishing credited to "Comet" (we're not sure which came first)				
❑ 2056		Hello Goodbye/I Am the Walrus	1967	7.50	15.00	30.00
		Original: Orange and yellow swirl, without "A Subsidiary Of"... in perimeter label print; publishing credited to "Maclen" (we're not sure which came first)				
❑ 2056	PS	Hello Goodbye/I Am the Walrus	1967	20.00	40.00	80.00
❑ P 2056	DJ	Hello Goodbye/I Am the Walrus	1967	62.50	125.00	250.00
		Light green label promo				
❑ 2056		Hello Goodbye/I Am the Walrus	1968	12.50	25.00	50.00
		Orange and yellow swirl label with "A Subsidiary Of" in perimeter print				
❑ 2056		Hello Goodbye/I Am the Walrus	1969	15.00	30.00	60.00
		Red and orange "target" label with Capitol dome logo				
❑ 2056		Hello Goodbye/I Am the Walrus	1969	5.00	10.00	20.00
		Red and orange "target" label with Capitol round logo				
❑ 2056		Hello Goodbye/I Am the Walrus	1976		3.00	6.00
		Orange label with "Capitol" at bottom				
❑ 2056		Hello Goodbye/I Am the Walrus	1978	2.00	4.00	8.00
		Purple label; label has reeded edge				
❑ 2056		Hello Goodbye/I Am the Walrus	1983		3.00	6.00
		Black label with colorband				
❑ 2056		Hello Goodbye/I Am the Walrus	1988		2.50	5.00
		Purple label; label has smooth edge				
❑ 2138		Lady Madonna/The Inner Light	1968	7.50	15.00	30.00
		Original: Orange and yellow swirl, without "A Subsidiary Of"... in perimeter label print				
❑ 2138		Lady Madonna/The Inner Light	1968	12.50	25.00	50.00
		Orange and yellow swirl label with "A Subsidiary Of" in perimeter print				
❑ 2138	PS	Lady Madonna/The Inner Light	1968	20.00	40.00	80.00
❑ 2138	PS	Lady Madonna/The Inner Light	1968	5.00	10.00	20.00
		"Beatles Fan Club" insert that was issued with above sleeve. Originals are glossy.				
❑ P 2138	DJ	Lady Madonna/The Inner Light	1968	50.00	100.00	200.00
		Light green label promo				
❑ 2138		Lady Madonna/The Inner Light	1969	15.00	30.00	60.00
		Red and orange "target" label with Capitol dome logo				
❑ 2138		Lady Madonna/The Inner Light	1969	5.00	10.00	20.00
		Red and orange "target" label with Capitol round logo				
❑ 2138		Lady Madonna/The Inner Light	1976		3.00	6.00
		Orange label with "Capitol" at bottom				
❑ 2138		Lady Madonna/The Inner Light	1978	2.00	4.00	8.00
		Purple label; label has reeded edge				
❑ 2138		Lady Madonna/The Inner Light	1983		3.00	6.00
		Black label with colorband				
❑ 2138		Lady Madonna/The Inner Light	1988		2.50	5.00
		Purple label; label has smooth edge				
❑ 2276		Hey Jude/Revolution	1976		3.00	6.00
		Orange label with "Capitol" at bottom				
❑ 2276		Hey Jude/Revolution	1978	2.00	4.00	8.00
		Purple label; label has reeded edge				

Number	Title (A Side/B Side)	Year	VG	VG+	NM
❑ 2276	Hey Jude/Revolution	1983		3.00	6.00
	Black label with colorband				
❑ 2276	Hey Jude/Revolution	1988		2.50	5.00
	Purple label; label has smooth edge				
❑ 2490	Get Back/Don't Let Me Down	1976		3.00	6.00
	Orange label with "Capitol" at bottom				
❑ 2490	Get Back/Don't Let Me Down	1978	2.00	4.00	8.00
	Purple label; label has reeded edge				
❑ 2490	Get Back/Don't Let Me Down	1983		3.00	6.00
	Black label with colorband; "Get Back" replaced by LP version as on Let It Be				
❑ 2490	Get Back/Don't Let Me Down	1988		2.50	5.00
	Purple label; label has smooth edge; "Get Back" replaced by LP version as on Let It Be				
❑ 2531	The Ballad of John and Yoko/Old Brown Shoe	1976			
	Orange label with "Capitol" at bottom; should exist, but not known to exist				
❑ 2531	The Ballad of John and Yoko/Old Brown Shoe	1978		3.00	6.00
	Purple label; label has reeded edge				
❑ 2531	The Ballad of John and Yoko/Old Brown Shoe	1983		3.50	7.00
	Black label with colorband				
❑ 2531	The Ballad of John and Yoko/Old Brown Shoe	1988		3.00	6.00
	Purple label; label has smooth edge				
❑ 2654	Something/Come Together	1976		3.00	6.00
	Orange label with "Capitol" at bottom				
❑ 2654	Something/Come Together	1978		3.00	6.00
	Purple label; label has reeded edge				
❑ 2654	Something/Come Together	1983		3.00	6.00
	Black label with colorband				
❑ 2654	Something/Come Together	1988		2.50	5.00
	Purple label; label has smooth edge				
❑ 2764	Let It Be/You Know My Name (Look Up My Number)	1976		3.00	6.00
	Orange label with "Capitol" at bottom				
❑ 2764	Let It Be/You Know My Name (Look Up My Number)	1978	2.00	4.00	8.00
	Purple label; label has reeded edge				
❑ 2764	Let It Be/You Know My Name (Look Up My Number)	1983		3.00	6.00
	Black label with colorband				
❑ 2764	Let It Be/You Know My Name (Look Up My Number)	1988		2.50	5.00
	Purple label; label has smooth edge				
❑ 2832	The Long and Winding Road/For You Blue	1976		3.00	6.00
	Orange label with "Capitol" at bottom				
❑ 2832	The Long and Winding Road/For You Blue	1978	2.00	4.00	8.00
	Purple label; label has reeded edge				
❑ 2832	The Long and Winding Road/For You Blue	1983		3.00	6.00
	Black label with colorband				
❑ 2832	The Long and Winding Road/For You Blue	1988		2.50	5.00
	Purple label; label has smooth edge				
❑ 4274	Got to Get You Into My Life/Helter Skelter	1976		3.00	6.00
	Original: Orange label with "Capitol" at bottom, George Martin's name not on label				
❑ 4274	Got to Get You Into My Life/Helter Skelter	1976	2.50	5.00	10.00
	Orange label with "Capitol" at bottom, George Martin's name is on label				
❑ 4274	PS Got to Get You Into My Life/Helter Skelter	1976		2.50	5.00
❑ P-4274	DJ Got to Get You Into My Life (mono/stereo)	1976	10.00	20.00	40.00
❑ P-4274	DJ Helter Skelter (mono/stereo)	1976	10.00	20.00	40.00
❑ 4274	Got to Get You Into My Life/Helter Skelter	1978		3.00	6.00
	Purple label; label has reeded edge				
❑ 4274	Got to Get You Into My Life/Helter Skelter	1983		3.00	6.00
	Black label with colorband				
❑ 4274	Got to Get You Into My Life/Helter Skelter	1988		2.50	5.00
	Purple label; label has smooth edge				
❑ 4347	Ob-La-Di, Ob-La-Da/Julia	1976	2.00	4.00	8.00
	Original: Orange label with "Capitol" at bottom				
❑ 4347	PS Ob-La-Di, Ob-La-Da/Julia	1976	2.00	4.00	8.00
	Sleeves are individually numbered; very low numbers (under 1000) can fetch premium prices				
❑ P-4347	DJ Ob-La-Di, Ob-La-Da (mono/stereo)	1976	10.00	20.00	40.00
❑ 4347	Ob-La-Di, Ob-La-Da/Julia	1978	2.00	4.00	8.00
	Purple label; label has reeded edge				
❑ 4347	Ob-La-Di, Ob-La-Da/Julia	1983		3.00	6.00
	Black label with colorband				
❑ 4347	Ob-La-Di, Ob-La-Da/Julia	1988		2.50	5.00
	Purple label; label has smooth edge				
❑ 4506	PS Girl/You're Going to Lose That Girl	1977	3.75	7.50	15.00
	Sleeve for a single that was never pressed				
❑ P-4506	DJ Girl (mono/stereo)	1977	50.00	100.00	200.00
	Promo only; all colored vinyl versions are counterfeits				
❑ 4612	Sgt. Pepper's Lonely Hearts Club Band-With a Little Help from My Friends/A Day in the Life	1978	2.00	4.00	8.00
	Original: Purple label; label has reeded edge				
❑ 4612	PS Sgt. Pepper's Lonely Hearts Club Band-With a Little Help from My Friends/A Day in the Life	1978	5.00	10.00	20.00
❑ P-4612	DJ Sgt. Pepper's Lonely Hearts Club Band-With a Little Help from My Friends (mono/stereo)	1978	10.00	20.00	40.00
❑ 4612	Sgt. Pepper's Lonely Hearts Club Band-With a Little Help from My Friends/A Day in the Life	1983		3.00	6.00
	Black label with colorband				

Number		Title (A Side/B Side)	Year	VG	VG+	NM
❑ 4612		Sgt. Pepper's Lonely Hearts Club Band-With a Little Help from My Friends/A Day in the Life	1988		2.50	5.00
		Purple label; label has smooth edge				
❑ B-5100		The Beatles' Movie Medley/Fab Four on Film	1982	12.50	25.00	50.00
		Stock copy; not officially released, but some got out by mistake				
❑ PB-5100	DJ	The Beatles' Movie Medley/Fab Four on Film	1982	6.25	12.50	25.00
❑ B-5100	PS	The Beatles' Movie Medley/Fab Four on Film	1982	5.00	10.00	20.00
❑ B-5107		The Beatles' Movie Medley/ I'm Happy Just to Dance with You	1982		2.50	5.00
❑ B-5107	PS	The Beatles' Movie Medley/ I'm Happy Just to Dance with You	1982		2.50	5.00
❑ 5112		I Want to Hold Your Hand/I Saw Her Standing There	1964	10.00	20.00	40.00
		First pressing credits "Walter Hofer" as B-side publisher				
❑ 5112		I Want to Hold Your Hand/I Saw Her Standing There	1964	8.75	17.50	35.00
		Second pressing credits "George Pincus and Sons" as B-side publisher				
❑ 5112		I Want to Hold Your Hand/I Saw Her Standing There	1964	7.50	15.00	30.00
		Third (and all later) pressings credit "Gil Music" as B-side publisher				
❑ 5112	PS	I Want to Hold Your Hand/I Saw Her Standing There	1964	20.00	40.00	80.00
		Straight cut, shows all of George Harrison's head				
❑ 5112	PS	I Want to Hold Your Hand/I Saw Her Standing There	1964	20.00	40.00	80.00
		Die-cut, crops George Harrison's head in photo				
❑ 5112	PS	I Want to Hold Your Hand/WMCA Good Guys	1964	500.00	1,000	2,000
		Giveaway from New York radio station with photo of WMCA DJs on rear				
❑ 5112		I Want to Hold Your Hand/I Saw Her Standing There	1968	15.00	30.00	60.00
		Orange and yellow swirl label with "A Subsidiary Of" in perimeter print				
❑ 5112		I Want to Hold Your Hand/I Saw Her Standing There	1969	15.00	30.00	60.00
		Red and orange "target" label, dome logo				
❑ 5112		I Want to Hold Your Hand/I Saw Her Standing There	1969	6.25	12.50	25.00
		Red and orange "target" label, round logo				
❑ 5112		I Want to Hold Your Hand/I Saw Her Standing There	1976	2.50	5.00	10.00
		Orange label, "Capitol" logo on bottom				
❑ 5112		I Want to Hold Your Hand/I Saw Her Standing There	1978	3.75	7.50	15.00
		Purple label				
❑ 5112		I Want to Hold Your Hand/I Saw Her Standing There	1984		2.50	5.00
		20th anniversary reissue; black print on perimeter of label (1964 pressings are white)				
❑ 5112	PS	I Want to Hold Your Hand/I Saw Her Standing There	1984		3.00	6.00
		Same as 1964 sleeve except has "1984" in small print, and Paul McCartney's cigarette is airbrushed out				
❑ 5112		I Want to Hold Your Hand/I Saw Her Standing There	1994		2.50	5.00
		30th anniversary reissue; has "NR-58123" engraved in record's trail-off area				
❑ 5112	PS	I Want to Hold Your Hand/I Saw Her Standing There	1994		2.00	4.00
		Same as 1964 sleeve except "Reg. U.S. Pat. Off." has periods (1964s do not). Also came with a plastic sleeve with a "30th Anniversary" and UPC stickers (add 25%)				
❑ 5150		Can't Buy Me Love/You Can't Do That	1964	7.50	15.00	30.00
		Original: Orange and yellow swirl, without "A Subsidiary Of"... in perimeter label print				
❑ 5150		Can't Buy Me Love/You Can't Do That	1964	1,000	1,500	2,000
		Yellow and black vinyl (unauthorized); value is conjecture				
❑ 5150		Can't Buy Me Love/You Can't Do That	1964	2,000	3,000	4,000
		Yellow vinyl (unauthorized); value is conjecture				
❑ 5150	PS	Can't Buy Me Love/You Can't Do That	1964	200.00	400.00	600.00
		One of the rarest Beatles picture sleeves. Numerous counterfeits exist; if in doubt, see an expert.				
❑ 5150		Can't Buy Me Love/You Can't Do That	1968	12.50	25.00	50.00
		Orange and yellow swirl label with "A Subsidiary Of" in perimeter print				
❑ 5150		Can't Buy Me Love/You Can't Do That	1969	6.25	12.50	25.00
		Red and orange "target" label, dome logo				
❑ 5150		Can't Buy Me Love/You Can't Do That	1969	15.00	30.00	60.00
		Red and orange "target" label, round logo				
❑ 5150		Can't Buy Me Love/You Can't Do That	1976		3.00	6.00
		Orange label with "Capitol" at bottom				
❑ 5150		Can't Buy Me Love/You Can't Do That	1978	3.75	7.50	15.00
		Purple label				
❑ B-5189		Love Me Do/P.S. I Love You	1982		2.50	5.00
		Original: Orange and yellow swirl label, black print				
❑ PB-5189	DJ	Love Me Do (same on both sides)	1982	3.75	7.50	15.00
❑ B-5189	PS	Love Me Do/P.S. I Love You	1982		2.50	5.00
❑ B-5189		Love Me Do/P.S. I Love You	1983		3.00	6.00
		Black label with colorband				
❑ B-5189		Love Me Do/P.S. I Love You	1988		2.00	4.00
		Purple label; label has smooth edge				
❑ 5222		A Hard Day's Night/I Should Have Known Better	1964	7.50	15.00	30.00
		Original: Orange and yellow swirl, without "A Subsidiary Of"... in perimeter label print; first version credited both "Unart" and "Maclen" as publishers				
❑ 5222		A Hard Day's Night/I Should Have Known Better	1964	7.50	15.00	30.00
		Orange and yellow swirl, without "A Subsidiary Of"... in perimeter label print; second version credited only "Maclen" as publishers				
❑ 5222	PS	A Hard Day's Night/I Should Have Known Better	1964	18.75	37.50	75.00
❑ 5222		A Hard Day's Night/I Should Have Known Better	1964	25.00	50.00	100.00
		Orange and yellow swirl with "A Subsidiary Of"... on perimeter print in black				
❑ 5222		A Hard Day's Night/I Should Have Known Better	1968	12.50	25.00	50.00
		Orange and yellow swirl with "A Subsidiary Of"... on perimeter print in white				
❑ 5222		A Hard Day's Night/I Should Have Known Better	1969	15.00	30.00	60.00
		Red and orange "target" label with Capitol dome logo				

Number	Title (A Side/B Side)	Year	VG	VG+	NM
❏ 5222	A Hard Day's Night/I Should Have Known Better *Red and orange "target" label with Capitol round logo*	1969	5.00	10.00	20.00
❏ 5222	A Hard Day's Night/I Should Have Known Better *Orange label with "Capitol" at bottom*	1976		3.00	6.00
❏ 5222	A Hard Day's Night/I Should Have Known Better *Purple label*	1978	3.75	7.50	15.00
❏ 5234	I'll Cry Instead/I'm Happy Just to Dance with You *Original: Orange and yellow swirl, without "A Subsidiary Of"... in perimeter label print*	1964	10.00	20.00	40.00
❏ 5234	PS I'll Cry Instead/I'm Happy Just to Dance with You	1964	37.50	75.00	150.00
❏ 5234	I'll Cry Instead/I'm Happy Just to Dance with You *Orange and yellow swirl label with "A Subsidiary Of" in perimeter print*	1968	15.00	30.00	60.00
❏ 5234	I'll Cry Instead/I'm Happy Just to Dance with You *Red and orange "target" label with Capitol dome logo*	1969	17.50	35.00	70.00
❏ 5234	I'll Cry Instead/I'm Happy Just to Dance with You *Red and orange "target" label with Capitol round logo*	1969	5.00	10.00	20.00
❏ 5234	I'll Cry Instead/I'm Happy Just to Dance with You *Orange label with "Capitol" at bottom*	1976		3.00	6.00
❏ 5234	I'll Cry Instead/I'm Happy Just to Dance with You *Purple label*	1978	3.75	7.50	15.00
❏ 5235	And I Love Her/If I Fell *Original: Orange and yellow swirl, without "A Subsidiary Of"... in perimeter label print; publishers listed as "Maclen" only*	1964	7.50	15.00	30.00
❏ 5235	And I Love Her/If I Fell *Original: Orange and yellow swirl, without "A Subsidiary Of"... in perimeter label print; publishers listed as "Unart" and "Maclen"*	1964	7.50	15.00	30.00
❏ 5235	PS And I Love Her/If I Fell	1964	37.50	75.00	150.00
❏ 5235	And I Love Her/If I Fell *Orange and yellow swirl with "A Subsidiary Of"... on perimeter print in black*	1968	18.75	37.50	75.00
❏ 5235	And I Love Her/If I Fell *Orange and yellow swirl with "A Subsidiary Of"... on perimeter print in white*	1968	12.50	25.00	50.00
❏ 5235	And I Love Her/If I Fell *Red and orange "target" label with Capitol round logo*	1969	15.00	30.00	60.00
❏ 5235	And I Love Her/If I Fell *Red and orange "target" label with Capitol dome logo*	1969	5.00	10.00	20.00
❏ 5235	And I Love Her/If I Fell *Orange label with "Capitol" at bottom*	1976		3.00	6.00
❏ 5235	And I Love Her/If I Fell *Purple label*	1978	3.75	7.50	15.00
❏ 5255	Matchbox/Slow Down *Original: Orange and yellow swirl, without "A Subsidiary Of"... in perimeter label print*	1964	7.50	15.00	30.00
❏ 5255	PS Matchbox/Slow Down	1964	20.00	40.00	80.00
❏ 5255	Matchbox/Slow Down *Orange and yellow swirl label with "A Subsidiary Of" in perimeter print*	1968	12.50	25.00	50.00
❏ 5255	Matchbox/Slow Down *Red and orange "target" label with Capitol dome logo*	1969	15.00	30.00	60.00
❏ 5255	Matchbox/Slow Down *Red and orange "target" label with Capitol round logo*	1969	5.00	10.00	20.00
❏ 5255	Matchbox/Slow Down *Orange label with "Capitol" at bottom*	1976		3.00	6.00
❏ 5255	Matchbox/Slow Down *Purple label*	1978	3.75	7.50	15.00
❏ 5327	I Feel Fine/She's a Woman *Original: Orange and yellow swirl, without "A Subsidiary Of"... in perimeter label print*	1964	7.50	15.00	30.00
❏ 5327	PS I Feel Fine/She's a Woman	1964	15.00	30.00	60.00
❏ 5327	I Feel Fine/She's a Woman *Orange and yellow swirl label with "A Subsidiary Of" in perimeter print*	1968	12.50	25.00	50.00
❏ 5327	I Feel Fine/She's a Woman *Red and orange "target" label with Capitol dome logo*	1969	15.00	30.00	60.00
❏ 5327	I Feel Fine/She's a Woman *Red and orange "target" label with Capitol round logo*	1969	5.00	10.00	20.00
❏ 5327	I Feel Fine/She's a Woman *Orange label with "Capitol" at bottom*	1976		3.00	6.00
❏ 5327	I Feel Fine/She's a Woman *Purple label*	1978	3.75	7.50	15.00
❏ R-5365	Honey Don't/I'm a Loser// Mr. Moonlight/Everybody's Trying to Be My Baby *Better known as "4 -- By the Beatles"*	1965	15.00	30.00	60.00
❏ R-5365	PS Honey Don't/I'm a Loser// Mr. Moonlight/Everybody's Trying to Be My Baby *Better known as "4 -- By the Beatles"; sleeve is cardboard*	1965	45.00	90.00	180.00
❏ 5371	Eight Days a Week/I Don't Want to Spoil the Party *Original: Orange and yellow swirl, without "A Subsidiary Of"... in perimeter label print*	1965	6.25	12.50	25.00
❏ 5371	PS Eight Days a Week/I Don't Want to Spoil the Party *Die-cut sleeve*	1965	5.00	10.00	20.00
❏ 5371	PS Eight Days a Week/I Don't Want to Spoil the Party *Straight-cut sleeve*	1965	12.50	25.00	50.00
❏ 5371	Eight Days a Week/I Don't Want to Spoil the Party *Orange and yellow swirl label with "A Subsidiary Of" in perimeter print*	1968	12.50	25.00	50.00
❏ 5371	Eight Days a Week/I Don't Want to Spoil the Party *Red and orange "target" label with Capitol dome logo*	1969	15.00	30.00	60.00
❏ 5371	Eight Days a Week/I Don't Want to Spoil the Party *Red and orange "target" label with Capitol round logo*	1969	5.00	10.00	20.00

Number	Title (A Side/B Side)	Year	VG	VG+	NM
❑ 5371	Eight Days a Week/I Don't Want to Spoil the Party	1976		3.00	6.00
	Orange label with "Capitol" at bottom				
❑ 5371	Eight Days a Week/I Don't Want to Spoil the Party	1978	3.75	7.50	15.00
	Purple label				
❑ 5407	Ticket to Ride/Yes It Is	1965	6.25	12.50	25.00
	Original: Orange and yellow swirl, without "A Subsidiary Of"... in perimeter label print				
❑ 5407	PS Ticket to Ride/Yes It Is	1965	25.00	50.00	100.00
❑ 5407	Ticket to Ride/Yes It Is	1968	25.00	50.00	100.00
	Orange and yellow swirl with "A Subsidiary Of"... on perimeter print in black				
❑ 5407	Ticket to Ride/Yes It Is	1968	12.50	25.00	50.00
	Orange and yellow swirl with "A Subsidiary Of"... on perimeter print in white				
❑ 5407	Ticket to Ride/Yes It Is	1969	15.00	30.00	60.00
	Red and orange "target" label with Capitol dome logo				
❑ 5407	Ticket to Ride/Yes It Is	1969	5.00	10.00	20.00
	Red and orange "target" label with Capitol round logo				
❑ 5407	Ticket to Ride/Yes It Is	1976		3.00	6.00
	Orange label with "Capitol" at bottom				
❑ 5407	Ticket to Ride/Yes It Is	1978	3.75	7.50	15.00
	Purple label				
❑ B-5439	PS Leave My Kitten Alone/Ob-La-Di, Ob-La-Da	1985	12.50	25.00	50.00
	Sleeve for a record that was never released, not even as a promo				
❑ 5476	Help!/I'm Down	1965	6.25	12.50	25.00
	Original: Orange and yellow swirl, without "A Subsidiary Of"... in perimeter label print				
❑ 5476	PS Help!/I'm Down	1965	18.75	37.50	75.00
❑ 5476	Help!/I'm Down	1968	25.00	50.00	100.00
	Orange and yellow swirl with "A Subsidiary Of"... on perimeter print in black				
❑ 5476	Help!/I'm Down	1968	12.50	25.00	50.00
	Orange and yellow swirl with "A Subsidiary Of"... on perimeter print in white				
❑ 5476	Help!/I'm Down	1969	5.00	10.00	20.00
	Red and orange "target" label with Capitol round logo				
❑ 5476	Help!/I'm Down	1969	15.00	30.00	60.00
	Red and orange "target" label with Capitol dome logo				
❑ 5476	Help!/I'm Down	1976		3.00	6.00
	Orange label with "Capitol" at bottom				
❑ 5476	Help!/I'm Down	1978	3.75	7.50	15.00
	Purple label				
❑ 5498	Yesterday/Act Naturally	1965	6.25	12.50	25.00
	Original: Orange and yellow swirl, without "A Subsidiary Of"... in perimeter label print				
❑ 5498	PS Yesterday/Act Naturally	1965	18.75	37.50	75.00
❑ 5498	Yesterday/Act Naturally	1968	25.00	50.00	100.00
	Orange and yellow swirl with "A Subsidiary Of"... on perimeter print in black				
❑ 5498	Yesterday/Act Naturally	1968	12.50	25.00	50.00
	Orange and yellow swirl with "A Subsidiary Of"... on perimeter print in white				
❑ 5498	Yesterday/Act Naturally	1969	5.00	10.00	20.00
	Red and orange "target" label with Capitol round logo				
❑ 5498	Yesterday/Act Naturally	1969	15.00	30.00	60.00
	Red and orange "target" label with Capitol dome logo				
❑ 5498	Yesterday/Act Naturally	1976		3.00	6.00
	Orange label with "Capitol" at bottom				
❑ 5498	Yesterday/Act Naturally	1978	3.75	7.50	15.00
	Purple label				
❑ 5555	We Can Work It Out/Day Tripper	1965	6.25	12.50	25.00
	Original: Orange and yellow swirl, without "A Subsidiary Of"... in perimeter label print				
❑ 5555	PS We Can Work It Out/Day Tripper	1965	18.75	37.50	75.00
❑ 5555	We Can Work It Out/Day Tripper	1968	12.50	25.00	50.00
	Orange and yellow swirl label with "A Subsidiary Of" in perimeter print				
❑ 5555	We Can Work It Out/Day Tripper	1969	15.00	30.00	60.00
	Red and orange "target" label with Capitol dome logo				
❑ 5555	We Can Work It Out/Day Tripper	1969	5.00	10.00	20.00
	Red and orange "target" label with Capitol round logo				
❑ 5555	We Can Work It Out/Day Tripper	1969	500.00	1,000	1,500
	Red and white "Starline" label (mispress)				
❑ 5555	We Can Work It Out/Day Tripper	1976		3.00	6.00
	Orange label with "Capitol" at bottom				
❑ 5555	We Can Work It Out/Day Tripper	1978	3.75	7.50	15.00
	Purple label				
❑ 5587	Nowhere Man/What Goes On	1966	6.25	12.50	25.00
	Original: Orange and yellow swirl, without "A Subsidiary Of"... in perimeter label print; composers of B-side listed as "John Lennon-Paul McCartney"				
❑ 5587	Nowhere Man/What Goes On	1966	12.50	25.00	50.00
	Orange and yellow swirl, without "A Subsidiary Of"... in perimeter label print; B-side composers listed as "Lennon-McCartney-Starkey"				
❑ 5587	PS Nowhere Man/What Goes On	1966	12.50	25.00	50.00
❑ 5587	Nowhere Man/What Goes On	1968	12.50	25.00	50.00
	Orange and yellow swirl label with "A Subsidiary Of" in perimeter print				
❑ 5587	Nowhere Man/What Goes On	1969	15.00	30.00	60.00
	Red and orange "target" label with Capitol dome logo				
❑ 5587	Nowhere Man/What Goes On	1969	5.00	10.00	20.00
	Red and orange "target" label with Capitol round logo				
❑ 5587	Nowhere Man/What Goes On	1976		3.00	6.00
	Orange label with "Capitol" at bottom				

Number		Title (A Side/B Side)	Year	VG	VG+	NM
❑ 5587		Nowhere Man/What Goes On	1978	3.75	7.50	15.00
		Purple label				
❑ B-5624		Twist and Shout/There's a Place	1986		2.50	5.00
		Black label with colorband				
❑ P-B-5624	DJ	Twist and Shout (same on both sides)	1986	3.75	7.50	15.00
❑ B-5624		Twist and Shout/There's a Place	1988		2.50	5.00
		Purple label; label has smooth edge				
▣ 5651		Paperback Writer/Rain	1966	6.25	12.50	25.00
		Original: Orange and yellow swirl, without "A Subsidiary Of"... in perimeter label print				
❑ 5651	PS	Paperback Writer/Rain	1966	18.75	37.50	75.00
❑ 5651		Paperback Writer/Rain	1968	25.00	50.00	100.00
		Orange and yellow swirl with "A Subsidiary Of"... on perimeter print in black				
❑ 5651		Paperback Writer/Rain	1968	12.50	25.00	50.00
		Orange and yellow swirl with "A Subsidiary Of"... on perimeter print in white				
❑ 5651		Paperback Writer/Rain	1969	15.00	30.00	60.00
		Red and orange "target" label with Capitol dome logo				
❑ 5651		Paperback Writer/Rain	1969	5.00	10.00	20.00
		Red and orange "target" label with Capitol round logo				
❑ 5651		Paperback Writer/Rain	1976		3.00	6.00
		Orange label with "Capitol" at bottom				
❑ 5651		Paperback Writer/Rain	1978	3.75	7.50	15.00
		Purple label				
❑ 5715		Yellow Submarine/Eleanor Rigby	1966	6.25	12.50	25.00
		Original: Orange and yellow swirl, without "A Subsidiary Of"... in perimeter label print; print on perimeter is white				
❑ 5715		Yellow Submarine/Eleanor Rigby	1966	12.50	25.00	50.00
		Orange and yellow swirl, without "A Subsidiary Of"... in perimeter label print; print on perimeter is yellow (mispress)				
❑ 5715	PS	Yellow Submarine/Eleanor Rigby	1966	25.00	50.00	100.00
❑ 5715		Yellow Submarine/Eleanor Rigby	1968	12.50	25.00	50.00
		Orange and yellow swirl label with "A Subsidiary Of" in perimeter print				
❑ 5715		Yellow Submarine/Eleanor Rigby	1969	5.00	10.00	20.00
		Red and orange "target" label with Capitol dome logo				
❑ 5715		Yellow Submarine/Eleanor Rigby	1969	15.00	30.00	60.00
		Red and orange "target" label with Capitol round logo				
❑ 5715		Yellow Submarine/Eleanor Rigby	1976		3.00	6.00
		Orange label with "Capitol" at bottom				
❑ 5715		Yellow Submarine/Eleanor Rigby	1978	3.75	7.50	15.00
		Purple label				
❑ 5810		Penny Lane/Strawberry Fields Forever	1967	6.25	12.50	25.00
		Original: Orange and yellow swirl, without "A Subsidiary Of"... in perimeter label print; "Penny Lane" time listed as 3:00				
❑ 5810		Penny Lane/Strawberry Fields Forever	1967	7.50	15.00	30.00
		Orange and yellow swirl, without "A Subsidiary Of"... in perimeter label print; "Penny Lane" time listed as 2:57				
❑ 5810	PS	Penny Lane/Strawberry Fields Forever	1967	25.00	50.00	100.00
❑ P 5810	DJ	Penny Lane/Strawberry Fields Forever	1967	75.00	150.00	300.00
		Light green promo; most copies have an extra trumpet solo at the end of "Penny Lane"				
❑ P 5810	DJ	Penny Lane/Strawberry Fields Forever	1967	150.00	300.00	600.00
		Light green promo; a few copies have no trumpet solo at the end of "Penny Lane"				
❑ 5810		Penny Lane/Strawberry Fields Forever	1968	12.50	25.00	50.00
		Orange and yellow swirl label with "A Subsidiary Of" in perimeter print				
❑ 5810		Penny Lane/Strawberry Fields Forever	1969	15.00	30.00	60.00
		Red and orange "target" label with Capitol dome logo				
❑ 5810		Penny Lane/Strawberry Fields Forever	1969	5.00	10.00	20.00
		Red and orange "target" label with Capitol round logo				
❑ 5810		Penny Lane/Strawberry Fields Forever	1976		3.00	6.00
		Orange label with "Capitol" at bottom				
❑ 5810		Penny Lane/Strawberry Fields Forever	1978	3.75	7.50	15.00
		Purple label				
❑ 5964		All You Need Is Love/Baby, You're a Rich Man	1967	6.25	12.50	25.00
		Original: Orange and yellow swirl, without "A Subsidiary Of"... in perimeter label print				
❑ 5964	PS	All You Need Is Love/Baby, You're a Rich Man	1967	12.50	25.00	50.00
❑ P 5964	DJ	All You Need Is Love/Baby, You're a Rich Man	1967	62.50	125.00	250.00
		Light green label promo				
❑ 5964		All You Need Is Love/Baby, You're a Rich Man	1968	12.50	25.00	50.00
		Orange and yellow swirl label with "A Subsidiary Of" in perimeter print				
❑ 5964		All You Need Is Love/Baby, You're a Rich Man	1969	18.75	37.50	75.00
		Red and orange "target" label with Capitol dome logo				
❑ 5964		All You Need Is Love/Baby, You're a Rich Man	1969	5.00	10.00	20.00
		Red and orange "target" label with Capitol round logo				
❑ 5964		All You Need Is Love/Baby, You're a Rich Man	1976		3.00	6.00
		Orange label with "Capitol" at bottom				
❑ 5964		All You Need Is Love/Baby, You're a Rich Man	1978	3.75	7.50	15.00
		Purple label				
❑ S7-17488		Birthday/Taxman	1994		2.00	4.00
		Green vinyl				
❑ S7-17488		Birthday/Taxman	1994	12.50	25.00	50.00
		Black vinyl "error" pressing				
❑ S7-17688		She Loves You/I'll Get You	1994		2.00	4.00
		Red vinyl				
❑ S7-17689		I Want to Hold Your Hand/This Boy	1994		2.00	4.00
		Clear vinyl				

Number	Title (A Side/B Side)	Year	VG	VG+	NM
❑ S7-17690	Can't Buy Me Love/You Can't Do That	1994		2.00	4.00
	Green vinyl				
❑ S7-17691	Help!/I'm Down	1994		2.00	4.00
	White vinyl				
❑ S7-17692	A Hard Day's Night/Things We Said Today	1994		2.00	4.00
	White vinyl				
❑ S7-17693	All You Need Is Love/Baby You're a Rich Man	1994		2.00	4.00
	Pink vinyl				
❑ S7-17694	Hey Jude/Revolution	1994		2.00	4.00
	Blue vinyl				
❑ S7-17695	Let It Be/You Know My Name (Look Up My Number)	1994		2.00	4.00
	Yellow vinyl				
❑ S7-17696	Yellow Submarine/Eleanor Rigby	1994		2.00	4.00
	Yellow vinyl				
❑ S7-17697	Strawberry Fields Forever/Penny Lane	1994		2.00	4.00
	Red vinyl				
❑ S7-17698	Something/Come Together	1994		2.00	4.00
	Blue vinyl				
❑ S7-17699	Twist and Shout/There's a Place	1994		2.00	4.00
	Pink vinyl				
❑ S7-17700	Here Comes the Sun/Octopus's Garden	1994		2.00	4.00
	Gold/orange vinyl				
❑ S7-17701	Sgt. Pepper's Lonely Hearts Club Band-With a Little Help from My Friends/A Day in the Life	1994		2.00	4.00
	Clear vinyl				
❑ S7-18888	Norwegian Wood/If I Needed Someone	1995	12.50	25.00	50.00
	Green vinyl; 1,000 pressed, given by Collectors' Choice Music to buyers of Beatles reissue LPs				
❑ S7-18889	You've Got to Hide Your Love Away/ I've Just Seen a Face	1996		2.00	4.00
	Gold/orange vinyl				
❑ S7-18890	Magical Mystery Tour/The Fool on the Hill	1996		2.00	4.00
	Yellow vinyl				
❑ S7-18891	Across the Universe/Two of Us	1996		2.00	4.00
	Clear vinyl				
❑ S7-18892	While My Guitar Gently Weeps/Blackbird	1996		2.00	4.00
	Blue vinyl				
❑ S7-18893	It's All Too Much/Only a Northern Song	1996		2.00	4.00
	Blue vinyl				
❑ S7-18894	Nowhere Man/What Goes On	1996		2.00	4.00
	Green vinyl				
❑ S7-18895	We Can Work It Out/Day Tripper	1996		2.00	4.00
	Pink vinyl				
❑ S7-18896	Lucy in the Sky with Diamonds/When I'm 64	1996		2.00	4.00
	Red vinyl				
❑ S7-18897	Here, There and Everywhere/Good Day Sunshine	1996		2.00	4.00
	Yellow vinyl				
❑ S7-18898	The Long and Winding Road/For You Blue	1996		2.00	4.00
	Blue vinyl				
❑ S7-18899	Got to Get You Into My Life/Helter Skelter	1996		2.00	4.00
	Gold/orange vinyl				
❑ S7-18900	Ob-La-Di, Ob-La-Da/Julia	1996		2.00	4.00
	Clear vinyl				
❑ S7-18901	Yesterday/Act Naturally	1996		2.00	4.00
	Pink vinyl				
❑ S7-18902	Paperback Writer/Rain	1996		2.00	4.00
	Red vinyl				
❑ S7-56785	Love Me Do/P.S. I Love You	1992		2.00	4.00
❑ S7-56785	Love Me Do/P.S. I Love You	1992	7.50	15.00	30.00
	Small pressing on red vinyl "by mistake"				
❑ 72133	Roll Over Beethoven/Please Mister Postman	1964	12.50	25.00	50.00
	Orange and yellow swirl; Canadian release that was heavily imported to the U.S.				
❑ 72144	All My Loving/This Boy	1964	12.50	25.00	50.00
	Orange and yellow swirl; Canadian release that was heavily imported to the U.S.				
❑ 72144	All My Loving/This Boy	1971	25.00	50.00	100.00
	Canadian number with U.S. labels (red and orange "target" label)				
❑ 7PRO-79551/2 DJ	Love Me Do/P.S. I Love You	1992	6.25	12.50	25.00
❑ 7PRO-79551/2 PS	Love Me Do/P.S. I Love You	1992	6.25	12.50	25.00

Capitol Starline

Number	Title (A Side/B Side)	Year	VG	VG+	NM
❑ 6061	Twist and Shout/There's a Place	1965	30.00	60.00	120.00
	Green swirl label				
❑ 6062	Love Me Do/P.S. I Love You	1965	30.00	60.00	120.00
	Green swirl label				
❑ 6063	Please Please Me/From Me to You	1965	30.00	60.00	120.00
	Green swirl label				
❑ 6064	Do You Want to Know a Secret/Thank You Girl	1965	30.00	60.00	120.00
	Green swirl label				
❑ 6065	Roll Over Beethoven/Misery	1965	30.00	60.00	120.00
	Green swirl label				
❑ 6065	Roll Over Beethoven/Misery	1971	7.50	15.00	30.00
	Red and orange "target" label				

Number	Title (A Side/B Side)	Year	VG	VG+	NM
❑ 6066	Boys/Kansas City	1965	20.00	40.00	80.00
	Green swirl label				
❑ 6066	Boys/Kansas City	1971	7.50	15.00	30.00
	Red and orange "target" label				
❑ 6278	I Want to Hold Your Hand/I Saw Her Standing There	1981	5.00	10.00	20.00
	Originals have blue labels				
❑ 6279	Can't Buy Me Love/You Can't Do That	1981	2.00	4.00	8.00
	Originals have blue labels				
❑ 6281	A Hard Day's Night/I Should Have Known Better	1981	2.00	4.00	8.00
	Originals have blue labels				
❑ 6282	I'll Cry Instead/I'm Happy Just to Dance with You	1981	2.00	4.00	8.00
	Originals have blue labels				
❑ 6283	And I Love Her/If I Fell	1981	2.00	4.00	8.00
	Originals have blue labels				
❑ 6284	Matchbox/Slow Down	1981	2.00	4.00	8.00
	Originals have blue labels				
❑ 6286	I Feel Fine/She's a Woman	1981	2.00	4.00	8.00
	Originals have blue labels				
❑ 6287	Eight Days a Week/I Don't Want to Spoil the Party	1981	2.00	4.00	8.00
	Originals have blue labels				
❑ 6288	Ticket to Ride/Yes It Is	1981	2.00	4.00	8.00
	Originals have blue labels				
❑ 6290	Help!/I'm Down	1981	2.00	4.00	8.00
	Originals have blue labels				
❑ 6291	Yesteday/Act Naturally	1981	2.00	4.00	8.00
	Originals have blue labels				
❑ 6293	We Can Work It Out/Day Tripper	1981	2.00	4.00	8.00
	Originals have blue labels				
❑ 6294	Nowhere Man/What Goes On	1981	2.00	4.00	8.00
	Originals have blue labels				
❑ 6296	Paperback Writer/Rain	1981	2.00	4.00	8.00
	Originals have blue labels				
❑ 6297	Yellow Submarine/Eleanor Rigby	1981	2.00	4.00	8.00
	Originals have blue labels				
❑ 6299	Penny Lane/Strawberry Fields Forever	1981	2.00	4.00	8.00
	Originals have blue labels				
❑ 6300	All You Need Is Love/Baby You're a Rich Man	1981	2.00	4.00	8.00
	Originals have blue labels				

Capitol/Evatone

Number	Title (A Side/B Side)	Year	VG	VG+	NM
❑ 420826cs	All My Loving/You've Got to Hide Your Love Away	1982	2.50	5.00	10.00
	Flexi-disc issued as giveaway by The Musicland Group; "Musicland" version				
❑ 420826cs	All My Loving/You've Got to Hide Your Love Away	1982	5.00	10.00	20.00
	Flexi-disc issued as giveaway by The Musicland Group; "Discount" version				
❑ 420826cs	All My Loving/You've Got to Hide Your Love Away	1982	6.25	12.50	25.00
	Flexi-disc issued as giveaway by The Musicland Group; "Sam Goody" version				
❑ 420827cs	Magical Mystery Tour/Here Comes the Sun	1982	5.00	10.00	20.00
	Flexi-disc issued as giveaway by The Musicland Group; "Discount" version				
❑ 420827cs	Magical Mystery Tour/Here Comes the Sun	1982	2.50	5.00	10.00
	Flexi-disc issued as giveaway by The Musicland Group; "Musicland" version				
❑ 420827cs	Magical Mystery Tour/Here Comes the Sun	1982	6.25	12.50	25.00
	Flexi-disc issued as giveaway by The Musicland Group; "Sam Goody" version				
❑ 420828cs	Rocky Raccoon/Why Don't We Do It in the Road?	1982	6.25	12.50	25.00
	Flexi-disc issued as giveaway by The Musicland Group; "Sam Goody" version				
❑ 420828cs	Rocky Raccoon/Why Don't We Do It in the Road?	1982	2.50	5.00	10.00
	Flexi-disc issued as giveaway by The Musicland Group; "Musicland" version				
❑ 420828cs	Rocky Raccoon/Why Don't We Do It in the Road?	1982	5.00	10.00	20.00
	Flexi-disc issued as giveaway by The Musicland Group; "Discount" version				
❑ 830771 X	Till There Was You/Three Cool Cats	1983		3.00	6.00
	Flexi-disc issued as giveaway with a book				
❑ 1214825cs	German Medley	1983	15.00	30.00	60.00
	Flexi-disc given away by House of Guitars in New York				

Cicadelic/BIOdisc

Number	Title (A Side/B Side)	Year	VG	VG+	NM
❑ 001	A Hard Day's Night Open End Interview	1990	3.75	7.50	15.00
	Limited, numbered edition of 700; lower numbers increase value substantially				
❑ 001	A Hard Day's Night Open End Interview	1990	7.50	15.00	30.00
	"Records Etc." pressing				
❑ 002	Help! Open End Interview	1990		2.50	5.00
❑ 002 PS	Help! Open End Interview	1990		2.50	5.00

Collectables

Number	Title (A Side/B Side)	Year	VG	VG+	NM
❑ 1501	I'm Gonna Sit Right Down and Cry Over You/ Roll Over Beethoven	1982			3.00
❑ 1501 PS	I'm Gonna Sit Right Down and Cry Over You/ Roll Over Beethoven	1982			3.00
❑ 1502	Hippy Hippy Shake/Sweet Little Sixteen	1982			3.00
❑ 1502 PS	Hippy Hippy Shake/Sweet Little Sixteen	1982			3.00
❑ 1503	Lend Me Your Comb/Your Feets Too Big	1982			3.00
❑ 1503 PS	Lend Me Your Comb/Your Feets Too Big	1982			3.00
❑ 1504	Where Have You Been All My Life/Mr. Moonlight	1982			3.00
❑ 1504 PS	Where Have You Been All My Life/Mr. Moonlight	1982			3.00
❑ 1505	A Taste of Honey/Besame Mucho	1982			3.00
❑ 1505 PS	A Taste of Honey/Besame Mucho	1982			3.00
❑ 1506	Till There Was You/Everybody's Trying to Be My Baby	1982			3.00

Number		Title (A Side/B Side)	Year	VG	VG+	NM
❑ 1506	PS	Till There Was You/Everybody's Trying to Be My Baby	1982			3.00
❑ 1507		Kansas City-Hey Hey Hey Hey/ Ain't Nothing Shakin Like the Leaves on a Tree	1982			3.00
❑ 1507	PS	Kansas City-Hey Hey Hey Hey/ Ain't Nothing Shakin Like the Leaves on a Tree	1982			3.00
❑ 1508		To Know Her Is To Love Her/Little Queenie	1982			3.00
❑ 1508	PS	To Know Her Is To Love Her/Little Queenie	1982			3.00
❑ 1509		Falling in Love Again/Sheila	1982			3.00
❑ 1509	PS	Falling in Love Again/Sheila	1982			3.00
❑ 1510		Be-Bop-a-Lula/Hallelujah I Love Her So	1982			3.00
❑ 1510	PS	Be-Bop-a-Lula/Hallelujah I Love Her So	1982			3.00
❑ 1511		Red Sails in the Sunset/Matchbox	1982			3.00
❑ 1511	PS	Red Sails in the Sunset/Matchbox	1982			3.00
❑ 1512		Talkin' Bout You/Shimmy Shake	1982			3.00
❑ 1512	PS	Talkin' Bout You/Shimmy Shake	1982			3.00
❑ 1513		Long Tall Sally/I Remember You	1982			3.00
❑ 1513	PS	Long Tall Sally/I Remember You	1982			3.00
❑ 1514		Ask Me Why/Twist and Shout	1982			3.00
❑ 1514	PS	Ask Me Why/Twist and Shout	1982			3.00
❑ 1515		I Saw Her Standing There/Can't Help It "Blue Angel"	1982			3.00
		B-side is actually "Reminiscing"				
❑ 1515	PS	I Saw Her Standing There/Can't Help It "Blue Angel"	1982			3.00
❑ 1516		I'll Try Anyway/I Don't Know Why I Do (I Just Do)	1987	2.50	5.00	10.00
		Despite label credit to The Beatles, both are Peter Best recordings				
❑ 1517		She's Not the Only Girl in Town/ More Than I Need Myself	1987	2.50	5.00	10.00
		Despite label credit to The Beatles, both are Peter Best recordings				
❑ 1518		I'll Have Everything Too/I'm Checking Out Now Baby	1987	2.50	5.00	10.00
		Despite label credit to The Beatles, both are Peter Best recordings				
❑ 1519		How'd You Get to Know Her Name/If You Can't Get Her	1987	2.50	5.00	10.00
		Despite label credit to The Beatles, both are Peter Best recordings				
❑ 1520		Cry for a Shadow/Rock and Roll Music	1987		2.50	5.00
		Despite label credit to The Beatles, B-side is a Peter Best recording				
❑ 1521		Let's Dance/If You Love Me Baby	1987		3.00	6.00
		Despite label credit to The Beatles, A-side is a Tony Sheridan solo recording				
❑ 1522		What'd I Say/Sweet Georgia Brown	1987		3.00	6.00
		Despite label credit to The Beatles, A-side is a Tony Sheridan solo recording				
❑ 1523		Ruby Baby/Ya Ya	1987		3.00	6.00
		Despite label credit to The Beatles, both are by Tony Sheridan without the Fab Four				
❑ 1524		Why/I'll Try Anyway	1987		3.00	6.00
		Despite label credit to The Beatles, B-side is a Peter Best recording				

Decca

❑ 31382		My Bonnie/The Saints	1962	4,000	7,000	10,000
		By "Tony Sheridan and the Beat Brothers"; black label with color bars (all-black label with star under "Decca" should be a counterfeit)				
❑ 31382	DJ	My Bonnie/The Saints	1962	1,000	2,000	3,000
		By "Tony Sheridan and the Beat Brothers"; ' pink label, star on label under "Decca"				

MGM

❑ 13213		My Bonnie (My Bonnie Lies Over the Ocean)/ The Saints (When the Saints Go Marching In)	1964	7.50	15.00	30.00
		The Beatles with Tony Sheridan; no reference to LP on label				
❑ 13213		My Bonnie (My Bonnie Lies Over the Ocean)/ The Saints (When the Saints Go Marching In)	1964	12.50	25.00	50.00
		The Beatles with Tony Sheridan; LP number on label				
❑ 13213	DJ	My Bonnie (My Bonnie Lies Over the Ocean)/ The Saints (When the Saints Go Marching In)	1964	62.50	125.00	250.00
		The Beatles with Tony Sheridan				
❑ 13213	PS	My Bonnie (My Bonnie Lies Over the Ocean)/ The Saints (When the Saints Go Marching In)	1964	25.00	50.00	100.00
		The Beatles with Tony Sheridan				
❑ 13227		Why/Cry for a Shadow	1964	30.00	60.00	120.00
		The Beatles with Tony Sheridan				
❑ 13227	DJ	Why/Cry for a Shadow	1964	62.50	125.00	250.00
		The Beatles with Tony Sheridan				
❑ 13227	PS	Why/Cry for a Shadow	1964	100.00	200.00	400.00
		The Beatles with Tony Sheridan				

Oldies 45

❑ 149		Do You Want to Know a Secret/Thank You Girl	1965	3.75	7.50	15.00
❑ 150		Please Please Me/From Me to You	1965	3.75	7.50	15.00
❑ 151		Love Me Do/P.S. I Love You	1965	3.75	7.50	15.00
❑ 152		Twist and Shout/There's a Place	1965	3.75	7.50	15.00

Swan

❑ 4152		She Loves You/I'll Get You	1963	150.00	300.00	600.00
		Semi-glossy white label/blue printing				
❑ 4152		She Loves You/I'll Get You	1963	150.00	300.00	600.00
		Semi-glossy white label/red print; "Don't Drop Out" not on label				
❑ 4152		She Loves You/I'll Get You	1963	162.50	325.00	650.00
		Flat white label/red print, "Don't Drop Out" not on label				
❑ 4152		She Loves You/I'll Get You	1963	162.50	325.00	650.00
		Semi-glossy white label/red print, "Don't Drop Out" on label				
❑ 4152	DJ	She Loves You/I'll Get You	1963	125.00	250.00	500.00
		Flat white label, no "Don't Drop Out" on label				

Number		Title (A Side/B Side)	Year	VG	VG+	NM
❑ 4152	DJ	She Loves You/I'll Get You	1963	125.00	250.00	500.00
		Thick print, no "Don't Drop Out" on label				
❑ 4152	DJ	She Loves You/I'll Get You	1963	112.50	225.00	450.00
		Thin print, "Don't Drop Out" on label				
❑ 4152		She Loves You/I'll Get You	1964	10.00	20.00	40.00
		Black label, silver print, "Don't Drop Out" not on label				
❑ 4152		She Loves You/I'll Get You	1964	7.50	15.00	30.00
		Black label, silver print, "Don't Drop Out" on label				
❑ 4152		She Loves You/I'll Get You	1964	12.50	25.00	50.00
		Black label, silver print, "Produced by George Martin" on both labels				
❑ 4152		She Loves You/I'll Get You	1964	12.50	25.00	50.00
		Black label, silver print, "Produced by George Martin" on only one label				
❑ 4152	DJ	I'll Get You (one-sided)	1964	200.00	400.00	600.00
❑ 4152	PS	She Loves You/I'll Get You	1964	30.00	60.00	120.00
❑ 4152		She Loves You/I'll Get You	196?	5.00	10.00	20.00
		Black label, silver print, "Don't Drop Out" not on label, smaller numbers in trailoff area				
❑ 4152		She Loves You/I'll Get You	196?	12.50	25.00	50.00
		White label, red or maroon print, same as above				
❑ 4182		Sie Liebt Dich (She Loves You)/I'll Get You	1964	37.50	75.00	150.00
		White label, "Sie Liebt Dich (She Loves You)" on one line				
❑ 4182		Sie Liebt Dich (She Loves You)/I'll Get You	1964	37.50	75.00	150.00
		White label, "(She Loves You)" under "Sie Liebt Dich," wide red print				
❑ 4182		Sie Liebt Dich (She Loves You)/I'll Get You	1964	37.50	75.00	150.00
		White label, "(She Loves You)" under "Sie Liebt Dich," narrow print				
❑ 4182		Sie Liebt Dich (She Loves You)/I'll Get You	1964	43.75	87.50	175.00
		White label, "(She Loves You)" under "Sie Liebt Dich," wide orange print				
❑ 4182	DJ	Sie Liebt Dich (She Loves You)/I'll Get You	1964	100.00	200.00	400.00
		White label, "(She Loves You)" under "Sie Liebt Dich"				
❑ 4182	DJ	Sie Liebt Dich (She Loves You)/I'll Get You	1964	112.50	225.00	450.00
		White label, "Sie Liebt Dich (She Loves You)" on one line				

Tollie

Number		Title (A Side/B Side)	Year	VG	VG+	NM
❑ 9001		Twist and Shout/There's a Place	1964	12.50	25.00	50.00
		Yellow label, black print, black "tollie" in box				
❑ 9001		Twist and Shout/There's a Place	1964	15.00	30.00	60.00
		Yellow label, blue print				
❑ 9001		Twist and Shout/There's a Place	1964	18.75	37.50	75.00
		Yellow label, black print, "TOLLIE" in brackets				
❑ 9001		Twist and Shout/There's a Place	1964	12.50	25.00	50.00
		Yellow label, black print, black "TOLLIE" in thin box				
❑ 9001		Twist and Shout/There's a Place	1964	12.50	25.00	50.00
		Yellow label, green print, "tollie" lowercase				
❑ 9001		Twist and Shout/There's a Place	1964	12.50	25.00	50.00
		Yellow label, black print, "TOLLIE" stands alone				
❑ 9001		Twist and Shout/There's a Place	1964	20.00	40.00	80.00
		Yellow label, green print, "TOLLIE" uppercase				
❑ 9001		Twist and Shout/There's a Place	1964	15.00	30.00	60.00
		Yellow label, black print, purple "tollie" in box				
❑ 9001		Twist and Shout/There's a Place	1964	20.00	40.00	80.00
		Yellow label, purple print				
❑ 9001		Twist and Shout/There's a Place	1964	15.00	30.00	60.00
		Black label, silver print				
❑ 9008		Love Me Do/P.S. I Love You	1964	12.50	25.00	50.00
		Yellow label, black print (any logo or print variation)				
❑ 9008		Love Me Do/P.S. I Love You	1964	12.50	25.00	50.00
		Yellow label, blue/green print				
❑ 9008		Love Me Do/P.S. I Love You	1964	15.00	30.00	60.00
		Black label, silver print				
❑ 9008	DJ	Love Me Do/P.S. I Love You	1964	100.00	200.00	400.00
❑ 9008	PS	Love Me Do/P.S. I Love You	1964	31.25	62.50	125.00

United Artists

Number		Title (A Side/B Side)	Year	VG	VG+	NM
❑ SP-2357	DJ	A Hard Day's Night Theatre Lobby Spot	1964	500.00	1,000	1,500
❑ UAEP 10029	DJ	A Hard Day's Night Open End Interview	1964	500.00	1,000	1,500
❑ ULP-42370		Let It Be Radio Spots	1970	400.00	800.00	1,200

Vee Jay

Number		Title (A Side/B Side)	Year	VG	VG+	NM
❑ (no #)	PS	We Wish You a Merry Christmas and a Happy New Year	1964	20.00	40.00	80.00
		Used with any Vee Jay or Tollie Beatles single in 1964-65 holiday season				
❑ Spec. DJ No. 8		Ask Me Why/Anna	1964?	5,000	7,500	10,000
		Value assumes that this is authentic, but it may be a clever 1970s-era bootleg				
❑ 498		Please Please Me/Ask Me Why	1963	750.00	1,125	1,500
		Misspelled "The Beatttes"; number is "VJ 498"				
❑ 498		Please Please Me/Ask Me Why	1963	800.00	1,200	1,600
		Misspelled "The Beatttes"; number is "#498"				
❑ 498	DJ	Please Please Me/Ask Me Why	1963	550.00	825.00	1,100
		Misspelled "The Beatttes"				
❑ 498		Please Please Me/Ask Me Why	1963	300.00	600.00	900.00
		Correct spelling; number is "VJ 498"; thick print				
❑ 498		Please Please Me/Ask Me Why	1963	800.00	1,200	1,600
		Correct spelling; number is "#498"				
❑ 498		Please Please Me/Ask Me Why	1963	1,000	1,500	2,000
		Correct spelling; number is "VJ 498"; brackets label				

If you were really ahead of the curve, you might have bought these two Beatles records in 1963. And today you'd have two of the most sought-after items in their catalog. At the top is "Please Please Me" on Vee Jay 498, the first record released in the United States under the name "The Beatles" (and even then, first pressings spelled it wrong). Underneath it is the follow-up, "From Me to You" on Vee Jay 522. This record actually "Bubbled Under" on the *Billboard* charts in 1963, thus implying some sales. But it's still a tough find.

Number		Title (A Side/B Side)	Year	VG	VG+	NM
❑ 522		From Me to You/Thank You Girl	1963	150.00	300.00	600.00
		Black rainbow label; "Vee Jay" in oval				
❑ 522		From Me to You/Thank You Girl	1963	300.00	600.00	900.00
		Black rainbow label; "VJ" in brackets				
❑ 522		From Me to You/Thank You Girl	1963	200.00	400.00	800.00
		Plain black label				
❑ 522	DJ	From Me to You/Thank You Girl	1963	125.00	250.00	500.00
❑ 581		Please Please Me/From Me to You	1964	12.50	25.00	50.00
		Black rainbow label, oval logo				
❑ 581		Please Please Me/From Me to You	1964	15.00	30.00	60.00
		Black rainbow label, brackets logo				
❑ 581		Please Please Me/From Me to You	1964	15.00	30.00	60.00
		Plain black label, oval logo				
❑ 581		Please Please Me/From Me to You	1964	18.75	37.50	75.00
		Plain black label, brackets logo				
❑ 581		Please Please Me/From Me to You	1964	11.25	22.50	45.00
		Plain black label with two horizontal lines				
❑ 581		Please Please Me/From Me to You	1964	15.00	30.00	60.00
		Plain black label, "VEE JAY" stands alone				
❑ 581		Please Please Me/From Me to You	1964	16.25	32.50	65.00
		Plain black label, "VJ" stands alone				
❑ 581		Please Please Me/From Me to You	1964	18.75	37.50	75.00
		Yellow label				
❑ 581		Please Please Me/From Me to You	1964	40.00	80.00	160.00
		White label				
❑ 581		Please Please Me/From Me to You	1964	62.50	125.00	250.00
		Purple label				
❑ 581	DJ	Please Please Me/From Me to You	1964	200.00	400.00	600.00
		White label, blue print; "Promotional Copy" on label				
❑ 581	DJ	Please Please Me/From Me to You	1964	300.00	600.00	900.00
		White label, blue print; no "Promotional Copy" on label				
❑ 581	PS	Please Please Me/From Me to You	1964	125.00	250.00	500.00
❑ 581	PS	Please Please Me/From Me to You	1964	1,250	1,875	2,500
		Special "The Record That Started Beatlemania" promo-only sleeve				
❑ 587		Do You Want to Know a Secret/Thank You Girl	1964	12.50	25.00	50.00
		Black rainbow label, oval logo				
❑ 587		Do You Want to Know a Secret/Thank You Girl	1964	10.00	20.00	40.00
		Black rainbow label, brackets logo				
❑ 587		Do You Want to Know a Secret/Thank You Girl	1964	16.25	32.50	65.00
		Plain black label; "Vee Jay" in oval				
❑ 587		Do You Want to Know a Secret/Thank You Girl	1964	16.25	32.50	65.00
		Plain black label; "VJ" in brackets				
❑ 587		Do You Want to Know a Secret/Thank You Girl	1964	11.25	22.50	45.00
		Plain black label with two horizontal lines; "VJ" in brackets				
❑ 587		Do You Want to Know a Secret/Thank You Girl	1964	12.50	25.00	50.00
		Plain black label; "VEE JAY" stands alone				
❑ 587		Do You Want to Know a Secret/Thank You Girl	1964	16.25	32.50	65.00
		Plain black label; "VJ" stands alone				
❑ 587		Do You Want to Know a Secret/Thank You Girl	1964	16.25	32.50	65.00
		Yellow label				
❑ 587	DJ	Do You Want to Know a Secret/Thank You Girl	1964	150.00	300.00	600.00
❑ 587	PS	Do You Want to Know a Secret/Thank You Girl	1964	30.00	60.00	120.00

EPs

Capitol

Number		Title (A Side/B Side)	Year	VG	VG+	NM
❑ EAP 1-2121		Roll Over Beethoven/This Boy//All My Loving/ Please Mr. Postman	1964	25.00	50.00	100.00
		Better known as "Four by The Beatles"				
❑ EAP 1-2121	PS	Roll Over Beethoven/This Boy//All My Loving/ Please Mr. Postman	1964	75.00	150.00	300.00
		Better known as "Four by The Beatles"; cardboard sleeve				

Vee Jay

Number		Title (A Side/B Side)	Year	VG	VG+	NM
❑ 1-903		Misery/Taste of Honey//Ask Me Why/Anna	1964	10.00	20.00	40.00
		Black rainbow label, oval logo				
❑ 1-903		Misery/Taste of Honey//Ask Me Why/Anna	1964	22.50	45.00	90.00
		Black rainbow label, brackets logo, all titles the same size				
❑ 1-903		Misery/Taste of Honey//Ask Me Why/Anna	1964	31.25	62.50	125.00
		Black rainbow label, brackets logo, "Ask Me Why" in much larger print				
❑ 1-903		Misery/Taste of Honey//Ask Me Why/Anna	1964	31.25	62.50	125.00
		Plain black label, oval logo				
❑ 1-903		Misery/Taste of Honey//Ask Me Why/Anna	1964	50.00	100.00	200.00
		Plain black label, brackets logo				
❑ 1-903		Misery/Taste of Honey//Ask Me Why/Anna	1964	37.50	75.00	150.00
		Plain black label, "VEE JAY" stands alone				
❑ 1-903	PS	Misery/Taste of Honey//Ask Me Why/Anna	1964	15.00	30.00	60.00
		"Souvenir of Their Visit to America"; cardboard sleeve				
❑ 1-903	DJ	Misery/Taste of Honey//Ask Me Why/Anna	1964	100.00	200.00	400.00
		White and blue label, all titles the same size				
❑ 1-903	DJ	Misery/Taste of Honey//Ask Me Why/Anna	1964	75.00	150.00	300.00
		White and blue label, "Ask Me Why" in much larger print				
❑ 1-903	PS	Misery/Taste of Honey//Ask Me Why/Anna	1964	4,000	6,000	8,000
		"Ask Me Why/The Beatles" plugged on promo-only sleeve				

Number		Title (A Side/B Side)	Year	VG	VG+	NM
Beau-Marks, The						
Mainstream						
❑ 688		Clap Your Hands/Daddy Said	1968	2.50	5.00	10.00
Port						
❑ 70029		Little Miss Twist/Lovely Little Lady	1962	3.75	7.50	15.00
Rust						
❑ 5035		School Is Out/Classmates	1961	5.00	10.00	20.00
❑ 5050		I'll Never Be the Same/Tender Years	1962	5.00	10.00	20.00
Shad						
❑ 5017		Clap Your Hands/Daddy Said	1960	5.00	10.00	20.00
❑ 5021		Cause We're in Love/Billy Went a-Walkin'	1960	5.00	10.00	20.00
Time						
❑ 1032		Oh Joan/Rockin' Blues	1961	7.50	15.00	30.00
Beaumont, Jimmy						
(Of the Skyliners)						
Bang						
❑ 510		Tell Me/I Feel Like I'm Falling in Love	1965	5.00	10.00	20.00
❑ 525		I Never Loved Her Anyway/	1966	7.50	15.00	30.00
		You Got Too Much Going for You				
Colpix						
❑ 607		The End of a Story/Baion Rhythms	1961	7.50	15.00	30.00
Gallant						
❑ 3007		Please Send Me Someone to Love/	196?	5.00	10.00	20.00
		There Is No Other Love				
❑ 3012		Love Is a Dangerous Game/Just a Little Closer	196?	3.00	6.00	12.00
May						
❑ 112		Ev'rybody's Cryin'/Carnera	1961	6.25	12.50	25.00
❑ 115		I Should Have Listened to Mama/Juarez	1962	6.25	12.50	25.00
❑ 120		Never Say Goodbye/I'm Gonna Try My Wings	1962	6.25	12.50	25.00
❑ 136		I'll Always Be in Love with You/Give Her My Best	1963	6.25	12.50	25.00
Beavers, The						
Capitol						
❑ F3956		Sack Dress/Rockin' at the Drive-In	1958	6.25	12.50	25.00
❑ F4015		The Road to Happiness/Low As I Can Be	1958	5.00	10.00	20.00
Beck, Bogert and Appice						
(Also see "Beck, Jeff")						
Epic						
❑ 10998		I'm So Proud/Oh to Love You	1973	2.00	4.00	8.00
❑ 11027		Lady/Oh to Love You	1973	2.00	4.00	8.00
Beck, Jeff						
(Of the Yardbirds. Also see "Beck, Bogert and Appice")						
Epic						
❑ 05595		Gets Us All in the End/You Know We Know	1985			3.00
❑ 10157		Beck's Bolero/Hi-Ho Silver Lining	1967	4.00	8.00	16.00
❑ 10218		Rock My Plimsoul/Tally Man	1967	4.00	8.00	16.00
❑ 10390		Blues De Luxe/Ol' Man River	1968	3.00	6.00	12.00
❑ 10484		Jailhouse Rock/Plynth (Water Down the Drain)	1969	3.00	6.00	12.00
❑ 10814		Got the Feeling/Situation	1971	2.50	5.00	10.00
❑ 10938		Definitely Maybe/Hi Ho Silver Lining	1973	2.50	5.00	10.00
❑ 50112		Constipated Duck/You Know What I Mean	1975		3.00	6.00
❑ 50276		Come Dancing/Head for Backstage Pass	1976		2.00	4.00
❑ 50914		Too Much to Lose/The Final Peace	1980		2.00	4.00
Bed Bugs, The						
Liberty						
❑ 55679		Yeah Yeah/Lucy Lucy	1964	6.25	12.50	25.00
Beefeaters, The						
(Group became The Byrds)						
Elektra						
❑ 45013		Please Let Me Love You/It Won't Be Long	1964	100.00	200.00	400.00
❑ 45013	DJ	Please Let Me Love You/It Won't Be Long	1964	50.00	100.00	200.00
Beehives, The						
King						
❑ 5881		I Want to Hold Your Hand/She Loves You	1964	3.75	7.50	15.00
Bees, The						
Imperial						
❑ 5314		Toy Bell/Snatchin' Back	1954	100.00	200.00	400.00
❑ 5320		I Want to Be Loved/Get Away Baby	1954	125.00	250.00	500.00
Beetles, The						
Blue Cat						
❑ 115		Ain't That Love/Welcome to My Heart	1965	3.75	7.50	15.00
Bel-Aires, The						
Crown						
❑ 126		Cherry Pie/Tick Tock	1954	12.50	25.00	50.00

Number	Title (A Side/B Side)	Year	VG	VG+	NM
Decca					
❑ 30631	Rockin' An' Strollin'/My Yearbook	1958	7.50	15.00	30.00
Flip					
❑ 303	This Paradise/Let's Party Awhile	1954	25.00	50.00	100.00
	Maroon label				
❑ 303	This Paradise/Let's Party Awhile	1954	12.50	25.00	50.00
	Blue label				
❑ 304	White Port and Lemon Juice/This Is Goodbye	1955	25.00	50.00	100.00
Nu Sound					
❑ 1022	Palmeras/Pony Rock	1962	3.00	6.00	12.00

Bell Hops, The
(More than one group)

Number	Title (A Side/B Side)	Year	VG	VG+	NM
Barb					
❑ 100	Angela/Ring Dang Doo Ting-a-Ling	1958	6.25	12.50	25.00
❑ 101/2	Teenage Years/Carmella	1958	6.25	12.50	25.00
Decca					
❑ 48208	For the Rest of My Life/It Would Take a Million Years	1951	25.00	50.00	100.00
❑ 48239	I'm All Yours/Where Is Love	1951	25.00	50.00	100.00
Tin Pan Alley					
❑ 153	Please Don't Say No to Me/Merchant Street Blues	1956	37.50	75.00	150.00

Bell Notes, The

Number	Title (A Side/B Side)	Year	VG	VG+	NM
Autograph					
❑ 204	Little Girl in Blue/Too Young or Too Old	1960	6.25	12.50	25.00
Clock					
❑ 71889	There She Goes/My Pledge to You	1961	5.00	10.00	20.00
Madison					
❑ 136	Shortnin' Bread/To Each His Own	1960	5.00	10.00	20.00
❑ 141	Real Wild Child/Friendly Star	1960	5.00	10.00	20.00
Time					
❑ 1004	I've Had It/Be Mine	1958	7.50	15.00	30.00
	First pressing on blue labels				
❑ 1004	I've Had It/Be Mine	1959	6.25	12.50	25.00
	Later pressings on red labels				
❑ 1010	Old Spanish Town/She Went Thataway	1959	6.25	12.50	25.00
❑ 1013	That's Right/Betty Dear	1959	6.25	12.50	25.00
❑ 1015	You're a Big Girl Now/Don't Ask Me Why	1959	6.25	12.50	25.00
❑ 1017	White Buckskin Sneakers and Checkerboard Socks/ No Dice	1959	6.25	12.50	25.00

Bell Tones, The

Number	Title (A Side/B Side)	Year	VG	VG+	NM
Rama					
❑ 170	Heart to Heart/The Wedding	1955	50.00	100.00	200.00

Bells, The
(Rama group is R&B; MGM and Polydor group is pop duo)

Number	Title (A Side/B Side)	Year	VG	VG+	NM
MGM					
❑ 14533	Child of Mine/He Was Me, He Was You	1973		2.00	4.00
❑ 14624	Love Once Removed/The Singer	1973		2.00	4.00
Polydor					
❑ 15016	Fly Little White Dove, Fly/Follow the Sun	1970		2.00	4.00
❑ 15023	Stay Awhile/Sing a Song of Freedom	1971		2.50	5.00
❑ 15025	Je Vais Rester/Blanc Petit Ois Eau Blanc	1970		2.00	4.00
❑ 15027	I Love You Lady Dawn/Rain	1971		2.00	4.00
❑ 15029	She's a Lady/Sweet Sounds of Music	1971		2.00	4.00
❑ 15031	To Know You Is To Love You/For Better For Worse	1971		2.00	4.00
❑ 15036	Oh My Love/You You You	1972		2.00	4.00
❑ 15039	Lord, Don't You Think It's Time/Easier Said Than Done	1972		2.00	4.00
❑ 15063	Kris Collection/Simple Song of Freedom	1973		2.00	4.00
Rama					
❑ 166	What Can I Tell Her Now/Let Me Love You, Love You	1955	125.00	250.00	500.00

Belltones, The

Number	Title (A Side/B Side)	Year	VG	VG+	NM
Grand					
❑ 102	Estelle/Promise Love	1954	2,000	3,000	4,000

Belmonts, The
(Also see "Dion and the Belmonts")

Number	Title (A Side/B Side)	Year	VG	VG+	NM
Dot					
❑ 17173	Reminiscing/She Only Wants to Do Her Thing	1968	3.75	7.50	15.00
❑ 17257	Have You Heard-The Worst That Could Happen/ Answer Me My Love	1969	3.75	7.50	15.00
Laurie					
❑ 3080	We Belong Together/Such a Long Way	1961	7.50	15.00	30.00
❑ 3631	A Brand New Song/Story Teller	1975		2.50	5.00
❑ 3698	Medley/You're the Only Girl for Me	198?		2.50	5.00
	B-side by Ernie Maresca				
Sabina					
❑ 502	I Need Some One/American Dance	1961	6.25	12.50	25.00
❑ 503	Hombre/I Confess	1962	6.25	12.50	25.00

Number	Title (A Side/B Side)	Year	VG	VG+	NM
❏ 505	Come On Little Angel/How About Me	1962	6.25	12.50	25.00
	Black label				
❏ 505	Come On Little Angel/How About Me	1962	5.00	10.00	20.00
	Greenish label				
❏ 507	Diddle-Dee-Dum	1962	5.00	10.00	20.00
	(What Happens When Your Love Has Gone)/Farewell				
❏ 509	Ann Marie/Ac-Cent-Tchu-Ate the Positive	1963	5.00	10.00	20.00
❏ 513	Let's Call It a Day/Walk On By	1963	5.00	10.00	20.00
❏ 517	More Important Things to Do/Walk On By	1963	5.00	10.00	20.00
❏ 519	C'mon Everybody/Why	1964	5.00	10.00	20.00
❏ 521	Summertime/Nothing in Return	1964	5.00	10.00	20.00

Sabrina

❏ 500	Tell Me Why/Smoke from Your Cigarette	1961	6.25	12.50	25.00
❏ 501	Searching for a New Love/	1961	6.25	12.50	25.00
	Don't Get Around Much Anymore				

Strawberry

❏ 106	Cheek to Cheek/Voyager	1976		2.50	5.00

Surprise

❏ 1000	Tell Me Why/Smoke from Your Cigarette	1961	25.00	50.00	100.00

United Artists

❏ 50007	Come with Me/You're Like a Mystery	1966	6.25	12.50	25.00
❏ 809	Wintertime/I Don't Know Why, I Just Do	1965	5.00	10.00	20.00
❏ 904	(Then) I Walked Away/Today My Love Has Gone Away	1965	5.00	10.00	20.00
❏ 966	I Got a Feeling/To Be with You	1965	5.00	10.00	20.00

Belvin, Jesse
(Also see "Cliques, The")

Aladdin

❏ 3431	Let Me Dream/Sugar Doll	1958	10.00	20.00	40.00

Cash

❏ 1056	Dry Your Tears/Beware	1957	25.00	50.00	100.00
	Black and silver label				
❏ 1056	Dry Your Tears/Beware	1957	6.25	12.50	25.00
	Orange and black label				

Class

❏ 267	I'm Confessin'/Deep in My Heart	1960	6.25	12.50	25.00

Hollywood

❏ 1059	Betty My Darling/Dear Heart	1956	100.00	200.00	400.00

Impact

❏ 23	Tonight My Love/Looking for Love	1962	3.75	7.50	15.00

Jamie

❏ 1145	Goodnight My Love (Pleasant Dreams)/My Desire	1959	5.00	10.00	20.00

Kent

❏ 326	Sentimental Reasons/Senorita	1959	6.25	12.50	25.00

Knight

❏ 2012	Little Darling/Deacon Dan Tucker	1959	10.00	20.00	40.00

Modern

❏ 1005	Goodnight My Love (Pleasant Dreams)/	1956	10.00	20.00	40.00
	I Want You With Me at Christmas				
❏ 1005	Goodnight My Love (Pleasant Dreams)/	1956	10.00	20.00	40.00
	Let Me Love You Tonight				
❏ 1013	I Need You So/Senorita	1957	7.50	15.00	30.00
❏ 1015	By My Side/Don't Close the Door	1957	7.50	15.00	30.00
❏ 1020	Sad and Lonesome/I'm Not Free	1957	7.50	15.00	30.00
❏ 1025	You Send Me/Summertime	1957	7.50	15.00	30.00
❏ 1027	My Satellite/Just to Say Hello	1957	7.50	15.00	30.00

Money

❏ 208	I'm Only a Fool/Trouble and Misery	1955	15.00	30.00	60.00

RCA Victor

❏ 47-7310	Volare/Ever Since We Met	1958	5.00	10.00	20.00
❏ 47-7387	Funny/Pledging My Love	1958	5.00	10.00	20.00
❏ 47-7469	Guess Who/My Girl Is Just Enough Woman for Me	1959	6.25	12.50	25.00
❏ 47-7543	Here's a Heart/It Could've Been Worse	1959	5.00	10.00	20.00
❏ 47-7596	Give Me Love/I'll Never Be Lonely Again	1959	5.00	10.00	20.00
❏ 47-7675	Something Happens to Me/The Door Is Always Open	1960	5.00	10.00	20.00
❏ 47-8040	Guess Who/Funny	1962	3.75	7.50	15.00
❏ 61-7469	Guess Who/My Girl Is Just Enough Woman for Me	1959	12.50	25.00	50.00
	"Living Stereo" (large hole, plays at 45 rpm)				

Recorded in Hollywood

❏ 120	Dream Girl/Hang Your Tears Out to Dry	1951	200.00	400.00	800.00
❏ 412	Love Comes Tumbling Down/(B-side unknown)	1953	150.00	300.00	600.00

Specialty

❏ 435	Confusin' Blues/Baby Don't Go	1952	20.00	40.00	80.00
❏ 550	Gone/One Little Blessing	1955	12.50	25.00	50.00
❏ 559	Where's My Girl/Love, Love of My Life	1955	12.50	25.00	50.00

Ben, La Brenda
Gordy

❏ 7009	Camel Walk/The Chaperone	1962	12.50	25.00	50.00
❏ 7021	I Can't Help It, I Gotta Dance/Just Be Yourself	1963	12.50	25.00	50.00

Number	Title (A Side/B Side)	Year	VG	VG+	NM
Motown					
❏ 1033	Camel Walk/Chaperone	1962	100.00	200.00	400.00
Bennett, Boyd					
King					
❏ 1413	Waterloo/I've Had Enough	1954	8.75	17.50	35.00
❏ 1432	Poison Ivy/You Upset Me Baby	1955	8.75	17.50	35.00
❏ 1443	Everlovin'/Boogie at Midnight	1955	8.75	17.50	35.00
❏ 1470	Seventeen/Little Old You-All	1955	8.75	17.50	35.00
	Maroon label				
❏ 1470	Seventeen/Little Old You-All	1955	6.25	12.50	25.00
	Blue label				
❏ 1475	Tennessee Rock and Roll/Oo, Oo, Oo	1955	6.25	12.50	25.00
❏ 1494	My Boy-Flat Top/Banjo Rock and Roll	1955	6.25	12.50	25.00
❏ 4853	Desperately/The Most	1955	6.25	12.50	25.00
❏ 4874	Right Around the Corner/Partners for Life	1956	6.25	12.50	25.00
❏ 4903	Blue Suede Shoes/Mumbles Blues	1956	6.25	12.50	25.00
❏ 4925	Let Me Love You/Groovy Age	1956	6.25	12.50	25.00
❏ 4953	Hit That Jive, Jack/Rabbit-Eye Pink and Charcoal Black	1956	6.25	12.50	25.00
❏ 4985	Rockin' Up a Storm/A Lock of Your Hair	1956	6.25	12.50	25.00
❏ 5021	I'm Moving On/Big Jay Shuffle	1957	6.25	12.50	25.00
❏ 5049	Big Boy/Put the Chain on the Door	1957	6.25	12.50	25.00
❏ 5097	Sentimental Journey/Boy Meets Girl	1957	6.25	12.50	25.00
❏ 5113	Signed, Sealed and Delivered/Her Momma Doesn't Think It's Right	1958	6.25	12.50	25.00
❏ 5115	Click Clack/Move	1958	6.25	12.50	25.00
❏ 5282	High School Hop/Cool Disc Jockey	1959	6.25	12.50	25.00
❏ 5374	Seventeen/My Boy Flat Top	1960	6.25	12.50	25.00
❏ 5738	Teenage Years/Hear Me Talking	1963	3.75	7.50	15.00
Mercury					
❏ 71409	Tight Tights/Tear It Up	1959	5.00	10.00	20.00
❏ 71479	Boogie Bear/A Boy Can Tell	1959	5.00	10.00	20.00
❏ 71537	Naughty Rock and Roll/Lover's Night	1959	5.00	10.00	20.00
❏ 71605	It's Wonderful/Amo, Amas, Amat	1960	5.00	10.00	20.00
❏ 71648	Seventeen/Sarasota	1960	5.00	10.00	20.00
❏ 71724	Hershey Bar/Big Junior	1960	5.00	10.00	20.00
❏ 71813	Coffee Break/The Brain	1961	5.00	10.00	20.00
Bennett, Cliff, and the Rebel Rousers					
ABC					
❏ 10842	Got to Get You Into My Life/Baby Each Day	1966	3.75	7.50	15.00
Amy					
❏ 930	If Only You'd Reply/Three Rooms with Running Water	1965	3.75	7.50	15.00
Ascot					
❏ 2146	Everybody Loves a Lover/My Old Stand By	1964	3.75	7.50	15.00
Capitol					
❏ 4621	I'm in Love with You/You've Got What I Like	1961	12.50	25.00	50.00
❏ 5309	One Way Love/I'm in Love with You	1964	3.75	7.50	15.00
Bennett, Joe, and the Sparkletones					
ABC-Paramount					
❏ 9837	Black Slacks/Boppin' Rock Boogie	1957	7.50	15.00	30.00
❏ 9867	Penny Loafers and Bobby Socks/Rocket	1957	7.50	15.00	30.00
❏ 9885	Cotton Pickin' Rocker/I Dig You Baby	1958	7.50	15.00	30.00
❏ 9929	Little Turtle/We've Had It	1958	7.50	15.00	30.00
❏ 9959	Do the Stop/Late Again	1958	7.50	15.00	30.00
Paris					
❏ 530	Bayou Rock/Beautiful One	1959	7.50	15.00	30.00
❏ 537	Boys Do Cry/What the Heck	1959	6.25	12.50	25.00
❏ 546	Softly/What the Heck	1960	6.25	12.50	25.00
Benny and the Bedbugs					
DCP					
❏ 1008	The Beatle Beat/Roll Over Beethoven	1964	3.75	7.50	15.00
❏ 1008 PS	The Beatle Beat/Roll Over Beethoven	1964	6.25	12.50	25.00
Benton, Brook					
(Also see "Benton, Brook, and Damita Jo"; "Washington, Dinah, and Brook Benton")					
All Platinum					
❏ 2364	Can't Take My Eyes Off You/Weekend with Feathers	1976		2.50	5.00
Brut					
❏ 810	Lay Lady Lay/A Touch of Class	1973		2.50	5.00
❏ 816	South Carolina/(B-side unknown)	1973		2.50	5.00
Cotillion					
❏ 44007	I Just Don't Know What to Do with Myself/Do Your Own Thing	1968	2.00	4.00	8.00
❏ 44031	She Knows What to Do with 'Em/Touch 'Em with Love	1969	2.00	4.00	8.00
❏ 44034	Nothing Can Take the Place of You/Woman Without Love	1969	2.00	4.00	8.00
❏ 44057	Rainy Night in Georgia/Where Do You Go from Here	1969	2.50	5.00	10.00
❏ 44072	My Way/A Little Bit of Soap	1970		3.00	6.00
❏ 44078	Don't It Make You Want to Go Home/I've Gotta Be Me	1970		3.00	6.00
❏ 44093	Shoes/Let Me Fix It	1970		3.00	6.00
❏ 44110	Whoever Finds This, I Love You/Heaven Help Us All	1971		3.00	6.00
❏ 44119	Take a Look at Your Hands/If You Think God Is Dead	1971		3.00	6.00

Number		Title (A Side/B Side)	Year	VG	VG+	NM
❏ 44130		Please Send Me Someone to Love/ She Even Woke Me Up to Say Goodbye	1971		3.00	6.00
❏ 44138		A Black Child Can't Smile/If You Think God Is Dead	1971		3.00	6.00
❏ 44141		Soul Santa/Let Us Get Together with the Lord	1971	2.00	4.00	8.00
❏ 44152		Movin' Day/Poor Make Believer	1972		3.00	6.00
Epic						
❏ 9177		Love Made Me Your Fool/Give Me a Sign	1956	6.25	12.50	25.00
❏ 9199		The Wall/All My Love Belongs to You	1957	6.25	12.50	25.00
Mercury						
❏ 71394		It's Just a Matter of Time/Hurtin' Inside	1959	3.75	7.50	15.00
❏ 71443		Endlessly/So Close	1959	3.75	7.50	15.00
❏ 71478		Thank You Pretty Baby/With All of My Heart	1959	3.75	7.50	15.00
❏ 71512		So Many Ways/I Want You Forever	1959	3.75	7.50	15.00
❏ 71554		This Time of the Year/Nothing in the World	1959	3.75	7.50	15.00
❏ 71558		This Time of the Year/How Many Times	1959	3.75	7.50	15.00
❏ 71566		The Ties That Bind/Hither, Thither and Yon	1960	3.00	6.00	12.00
❏ 71566	PS	The Ties That Bind/Hither, Thither and Yon	1960	5.00	10.00	20.00
❏ 71652		Kiddio/The Same One	1960	3.00	6.00	12.00
❏ 71652	PS	Kiddio/The Same One	1960	5.00	10.00	20.00
❏ 71722		Fools Rush In (Where Angels Fear to Tread)/ Someday You'll Want Me to Want You	1960	3.00	6.00	12.00
❏ 71722	PS	Fools Rush In (Where Angels Fear to Tread)/ Someday You'll Want Me to Want You	1960	5.00	10.00	20.00
❏ 71730		This Time of the Year/ Merry Christmas, Happy New Year	1960	3.00	6.00	12.00
❏ 71774		Think Twice/For My Baby	1961	3.00	6.00	12.00
❏ 71774	PS	Think Twice/For My Baby	1961	5.00	10.00	20.00
❏ 71820		The Boll Weevil Song/Your Eyes	1961	3.00	6.00	12.00
❏ 71820	PS	The Boll Weevil Song/Your Eyes	1961	5.00	10.00	20.00
❏ 71859		Frankie and Johnny/It's Just a House Without You	1961	3.00	6.00	12.00
❏ 71859	PS	Frankie and Johnny/It's Just a House Without You	1961	5.00	10.00	20.00
❏ 71903		Revenge/Really Really	1961	3.00	6.00	12.00
❏ 71903	PS	Revenge/Really Really	1961	5.00	10.00	20.00
❏ 71912		Shadrack/The Lost Penny	1961	3.00	6.00	12.00
❏ 71912	PS	Shadrack/The Lost Penny	1961	5.00	10.00	20.00
❏ 71925		Walk on the Wild Side/Somewhere in the Used to Be	1962	2.50	5.00	10.00
❏ 71925	PS	Walk on the Wild Side/Somewhere in the Used to Be	1962	5.00	10.00	20.00
❏ 71962		Hit Record/Thanks to the Fool	1962	2.50	5.00	10.00
❏ 71962	PS	Hit Record/Thanks to the Fool	1962	5.00	10.00	20.00
❏ 72009		Two Tickets to Paradise/It's Alright	1962			*Unreleased*
❏ 72024		Lie to Me/With the Touch of Your Hand	1962	2.50	5.00	10.00
❏ 72024	PS	Lie to Me/With the Touch of Your Hand	1962	5.00	10.00	20.00
❏ 72055		Hotel Happiness/Still Waters Run Deep	1962	2.50	5.00	10.00
❏ 72055	PS	Hotel Happiness/Still Waters Run Deep	1962	5.00	10.00	20.00
❏ 72099		I Got What I Wanted/Dearer Than Life	1963	2.50	5.00	10.00
❏ 72099	PS	I Got What I Wanted/Dearer Than Life	1963	5.00	10.00	20.00
❏ 72135		My True Confession/Tender Years	1963	2.50	5.00	10.00
❏ 72135	PS	My True Confession/Tender Years	1963	5.00	10.00	20.00
❏ 72177		Two Tickets to Paradise/Don't Hate Me	1963	2.50	5.00	10.00
❏ 72177	PS	Two Tickets to Paradise/Don't Hate Me	1963	5.00	10.00	20.00
❏ 72214		This Time of the Year/You're All I Want for Christmas	1963	2.50	5.00	10.00
❏ 72230		Going, Going, Gone/After Midnight	1963	2.50	5.00	10.00
❏ 72230	PS	Going, Going, Gone/After Midnight	1963	5.00	10.00	20.00
❏ 72266		Too Late to Turn Back Now/Another Cup of Coffee	1964	2.50	5.00	10.00
❏ 72266	PS	Too Late to Turn Back Now/Another Cup of Coffee	1964	5.00	10.00	20.00
❏ 72303		A House Is Not a Home/Come On Back	1964	2.50	5.00	10.00
❏ 72303	A	A House Is Not a Home/Come On Back	1964	5.00	10.00	20.00
❏ 72333		Lumberjack/Don't Do What I Did (Do What I Say)	1964	2.50	5.00	10.00
❏ 72333	PS	Lumberjack/Don't Do What I Did (Do What I Say)	1964	5.00	10.00	20.00
❏ 72365		Do It Right/Please, Please Make It Easy	1964	2.50	5.00	10.00
❏ 72365	PS	Do It Right/Please, Please Make It Easy	1964	5.00	10.00	20.00
❏ 72398		Special Years/Where There's a Will (There's a Way)	1965	2.50	5.00	10.00
❏ 72446		Love Me Now/A-Sleepin' at the End of the Bed	1965	2.50	5.00	10.00
❏ 872 796-7		It's Just a Matter of Time/Hurtin' Inside	1989		2.00	4.00
❏ 872 798-7		Endlessly/So Many Ways	1989		2.00	4.00
MGM						
❏ 14440		If You've Got the Time/You Take Me Home Honey	1972		2.50	5.00
Okeh						
❏ 7058		The Kentuckian Song/Ooh	1955	6.25	12.50	25.00
❏ 7065		Bring Me Love/Some of My Best Friends	1956	6.25	12.50	25.00
Olde World						
❏ 1100		Makin' Love Is Good for You/(B-side unknown)	1977		2.50	5.00
Polydor						
❏ 2015		I Cried for You/Love Me a Little	1979		2.00	4.00
RCA Victor						
❏ 47-7489		Only Your Love/(B-side unknown)	1959			*Unreleased?*
❏ 47-8693		Mother Nature, Father Time/You're Mine	1965	2.50	5.00	10.00
❏ 47-8693	PS	Mother Nature, Father Time/You're Mine	1965	5.00	10.00	20.00
❏ 47-8768		Where There's Life/Only a Girl Like You	1965	2.50	5.00	10.00
❏ 47-8830		Too Much Good Lovin'/A Sailor Boy's Love Song	1966	2.50	5.00	10.00
❏ 47-8879		Break Her Heart/In the Evening in the Moonlight	1966	2.50	5.00	10.00
❏ 47-8944		Where Does a Man Go to Cry/The Roach Song	1966	2.50	5.00	10.00
❏ 47-8995		So True in Life, So True in Love/If You Only Knew	1966	2.50	5.00	10.00
❏ 47-9031		Our First Christmas Together/Silent Night	1966	3.00	6.00	12.00
❏ 47-9096		Wake Up/All My Love Belongs to You	1967	2.00	4.00	8.00
❏ 47-9105		Keep the Faith Baby/Going to Soulsville	1967	2.00	4.00	8.00

Number	Title (A Side/B Side)	Year	VG	VG+	NM
Reprise					
❏ 0611	You're the Reason I'm Living/	1967	2.00	4.00	8.00
	Laura (Tell Me What He's Got That I Ain't Got)				
❏ 0649	Glory of Love/Weakness in a Man	1967	2.00	4.00	8.00
❏ 0676	Instead (Of Loving You)/Lonely Street	1968	2.00	4.00	8.00
Stax					
❏ 0231	Winds of Change/I Keep Thinking to Myself	1974		2.50	5.00
Vik					
❏ 0285	I Wanna Do Everything for You/Come On Be Nice	1957	5.00	10.00	20.00
❏ 0311	A Million Miles from Nowhere/Devoted	1957	5.00	10.00	20.00
❏ 0325	Because You Love Me/Crinoline Skirt	1958	5.00	10.00	20.00
❏ 0336	Crazy in Love with You/I'm Coming Back to You	1958	5.00	10.00	20.00

Benton, Brook, and Damita Jo

Number	Title (A Side/B Side)	Year	VG	VG+	NM
Mercury					
❏ 72196	Yaba-Taba-Do/Almost Persuaded	1963			*Unreleased*
❏ 72207	Baby You Got It Made/Stop Foolin'	1963	2.50	5.00	10.00

Bernard, Rod

Number	Title (A Side/B Side)	Year	VG	VG+	NM
Arbee					
❏ 101	Recorded in England/	1965	2.50	5.00	10.00
	Somebody Wrote That Song for My Baby				
❏ 104	Gimme Back My Cadillac/	1965	2.50	5.00	10.00
	Don't You Think I've Paid Enough				
❏ 105	Those Were Our Songs/Just Another Lie	1966	2.50	5.00	10.00
Argo					
❏ 5327	This Should Go On Forever/Pardon Mr. Gordon	1959	5.00	10.00	20.00
❏ 5338	You're On My Mind/My Life Is a Mystery	1959	5.00	10.00	20.00
Carl					
❏ (# unknown)	Linda Gail/Little Bitta Mama	1957	6.25	12.50	25.00
Crazy Cajun					
❏ 9020	Papa Thibodeaux/My Little Jollie Blonde	1978		2.50	5.00
Hallway					
❏ 1806	I Had a Girl/Wedding Bells	1963	3.75	7.50	15.00
❏ 1902	Who's Gonna Rock My Baby/Colinda	1962	3.75	7.50	15.00
❏ 1906	New Orleans Jail/Fais Do-Do	1962	3.75	7.50	15.00
❏ 1915	Forgive/I Want Somebody	1963	3.75	7.50	15.00
❏ 1917	Diggy Liggy Lo/The Clock	1963	3.75	7.50	15.00
❏ 1919	Loneliness/Boss Man's Son	1964	3.75	7.50	15.00
❏ 1922	My Own Mother-in-Law/I Might As Well	1964	3.75	7.50	15.00
Jin					
❏ 105	This Should Go On Forever/Pardon, Mr. Gordon	1958	10.00	20.00	40.00
❏ 232	Congratulations to You Darling/	1968	2.00	4.00	8.00
	You're the Reason I'm in Love				
❏ 237	To Have and Hold/Cajun Honey	1968	2.00	4.00	8.00
❏ 240	Big Mamou/New Orleans Jail	1969	2.00	4.00	8.00
❏ 307	Don't You Think I've Paid Enough/	1974		2.50	5.00
	Somebody Wrote That Song for Me				
❏ 325	Breaking Up Is Hard to Do/	1975		2.50	5.00
	Sometimes I Walk in My Sleep				
❏ 338	This Should Go On Forever/	1975		2.50	5.00
	I Spent a Week There Last Night				
❏ 350	A Winner in Love/	1975		2.50	5.00
	I Forgot I Had These Memories of You				
❏ 373	Mardi Gras in New Orleans/Oh Mother Dear	1976		2.50	5.00
❏ 376	Go On, Go On/I Never Had the One I Wanted	1976		2.50	5.00
Mercury					
❏ 71507	Shedding Teardrops Over You/One More Chance	1959	5.00	10.00	20.00
❏ 71592	One of These Days/Let's Get Together Tonight	1960	5.00	10.00	20.00
❏ 71654	Two Young Fools in Love/Dance Fool Dance	1960	5.00	10.00	20.00
❏ 71689	Strange Kisses/Just a Memory	1960	5.00	10.00	20.00
❏ 71767	Lonely Hearts Club/Who Knows	1961	4.00	8.00	16.00
❏ 71842	(Tell Me) Sometime/I'm Not Lonely Anymore	1961	4.00	8.00	16.00
Scepter					
❏ 12195	Those Were Our Songs/Recorded in England	1967	4.00	8.00	16.00
Tear Drop					
❏ 3044	Our Teenage Love/Doing the Oo-Wa-Woo	1966	2.50	5.00	10.00
❏ 3052	You're the Reason I'm in Love/My Jole Blon	1966	2.50	5.00	10.00
❏ 3060	No Money Down/Little Green Man	1967	2.50	5.00	10.00
❏ 3117	This Should Go On Forever/Recorded in England	1969	2.00	4.00	8.00

Berry Kids, The

Number	Title (A Side/B Side)	Year	VG	VG+	NM
MGM					
❏ 12379	Go, Go, Go, Right Into Town/Love Me, Love	1956	20.00	40.00	80.00
❏ 12496	Rootie Tootie/You're My Teenage Baby	1957	20.00	40.00	80.00

Berry, Chuck

(Also see "Alexander, Joe, and the Cubans")

Number	Title (A Side/B Side)	Year	VG	VG+	NM
Atco					
❏ 7203	Oh What a Thrill/California	1979		2.00	4.00
Chess					
❏ 1604	Maybellene/Wee Wee Hours	1955	12.50	25.00	50.00
❏ 1610	Thirty Days (To Come Back Home)/Together	1955	10.00	20.00	40.00
❏ 1615	No Money Down/Down Bound Train	1956	10.00	20.00	40.00

Number		Title (A Side/B Side)	Year	VG	VG+	NM
❑ 1626		Roll Over Beethoven/Drifting Heart	1956	10.00	20.00	40.00
❑ 1635		Too Much Monkey Business/ Brown Eyed Handsome Man	1956	10.00	20.00	40.00
❑ 1645		You Can't Catch Me/Havana Moon	1956	10.00	20.00	40.00
❑ 1653		School Day (Ring! Ring! Goes the Bell)/Deep Feeling	1957	10.00	20.00	40.00
❑ 1664		Oh Baby Doll/La Jaunda	1957	7.50	15.00	30.00
❑ 1671		Rock & Roll Music/Blue Feeling	1957	6.25	12.50	25.00
❑ 1683		Sweet Little Sixteen/Reelin' and Rockin'	1958	6.25	12.50	25.00
❑ 1691		Johnny B. Goode/Around and Around	1958	6.25	12.50	25.00
❑ 1697		Beautiful Delilah/Vacation Time	1958	6.25	12.50	25.00
❑ 1700		Carol/Hey Pedro	1958	6.25	12.50	25.00
❑ 1709		Sweet Little Rock and Roll/Joe Joe Gun	1958	6.25	12.50	25.00
❑ 1714		Run Rudolph Run/Merry Christmas Baby	1958	7.50	15.00	30.00
❑ 1716		Anthony Boy/That's My Desire	1959	6.25	12.50	25.00
❑ 1722		Almost Grown/Little Queenie	1959	6.25	12.50	25.00
❑ 1729		Back in the U.S.A./Memphis Tennessee	1959	6.25	12.50	25.00
❑ 1737		Broken Arrow/Childhood Sweetheart	1959	7.50	15.00	30.00
❑ 1747		Too Pooped to Pop ("Casey")/Let It Rock	1960	6.25	12.50	25.00
❑ 1754		Bye Bye Johnny/Worried Life Blues	1960	6.25	12.50	25.00
❑ 1763		I Got to Find My Baby/Mad Lad	1960	6.25	12.50	25.00
❑ 1767		Our Little Rendezvous/Jaguar and Thunderbird	1960	6.25	12.50	25.00
❑ 1779		I'm Talking About You/Little Star	1961	6.25	12.50	25.00
❑ 1799		Come On/Go-Go-Go	1961	5.00	10.00	20.00
❑ 1853		I'm Talking About You/Diploma for Two	1963	3.75	7.50	15.00
❑ 1866		Memphis/Sweet Little Sixteen	1963	3.75	7.50	15.00
❑ 1883		Nadine (Is It You?)/Orang Utang	1964	3.75	7.50	15.00
❑ 1898		No Particular Place to Go/You Too	1964	3.75	7.50	15.00
❑ 1898	PS	No Particular Place to Go/You Too	1964	12.50	25.00	50.00
❑ 1906		You Never Can Tell/Brenda Lee	1964	3.75	7.50	15.00
❑ 1906	PS	You Never Can Tell/Brenda Lee	1964	10.00	20.00	40.00
❑ 1912		Little Marie/Go Bobby Soxer	1964	3.75	7.50	15.00
❑ 1912	PS	Little Marie/Go Bobby Soxer	1964	12.50	25.00	50.00
❑ 1916		Promised Land/Things I Used to Do	1964	3.75	7.50	15.00
❑ 1916	PS	Promised Land/Things I Used to Do	1964	12.50	25.00	50.00
❑ 1926		Dear Dad/Lonely School Days	1965	3.75	7.50	15.00
❑ 1943		It Wasn't Me/Welcome Back Pretty Girl	1965	3.75	7.50	15.00
❑ 1943	PS	It Wasn't Me/Welcome Back Pretty Girl	1965	7.50	15.00	30.00
❑ 1963		Ramona Say Yes/Lonely School Days	1966	3.75	7.50	15.00
❑ 1963		Ramona Say Yes/Havana Moon	1966	3.75	7.50	15.00
❑ 2090		Tulane/Have Mercy Judge	1970		3.00	6.00
❑ 2131		My Ding-a-Ling/Johnny B. Goode	1972		2.00	4.00
		Orange and blue label				
❑ 2131		My Ding-a-Ling/Johnny B. Goode	1972		3.00	6.00
		All-blue label				
❑ 2136		Reelin' & Rockin'/Let's Boogie	1972		2.00	4.00
❑ 2140		Roll 'Em Pete/Bio	1973		2.00	4.00
❑ 2169		Baby What You Want Me to Do/Shake, Rattle and Roll	1975		2.00	4.00
Mercury						
❑ 72643		Club Nitty Gritty/Laugh and Cry	1966	2.50	5.00	10.00
❑ 72680		Back to Memphis/I Do Really Love You	1967	2.50	5.00	10.00
❑ 72748		It Hurts Me Too/Feelin' It	1967	2.50	5.00	10.00
❑ 72840		Louie to Frisco/Ma Dear	1968	2.50	5.00	10.00
❑ 72963		It's Too Dark in There/Good Looking Woman	1969	2.50	5.00	10.00
❑ 72963	PS	It's Too Dark in There/Good Looking Woman	1969	7.50	15.00	30.00
Philco						
❑ HP-34		Maybellene/Roll Over Beethoven	1969	4.00	8.00	16.00
		4-inch flexi-disc in "Philco Hip-Pocket Record" series; includes sleeve				

Berry, Jan
(Of Jan and Dean)
A&M

Number		Title (A Side/B Side)	Year	VG	VG+	NM
❑ 1957		Little Queenie/That's the Way It Is	1977	3.75	7.50	15.00
❑ 2020		Skateboard Surfin' U.S.A. (Sidewalk Surfin' with Me)/ How How I Love You	1978	3.75	7.50	15.00
Liberty						
❑ 55845		The Universal Coward/I Can't Wait to Love You	1965	5.00	10.00	20.00
❑ 55845	PS	The Universal Coward/I Can't Wait to Love You	1965	37.50	75.00	150.00
Ode						
❑ 66023		Mother Earth/Blue Moon Shuffle	1972	5.00	10.00	20.00
❑ 66034		Don't You Just Know It/Blue Moon Shuffle	1973	10.00	20.00	40.00
		With Brian Wilson on co-lead vocals on A-side				
❑ 66050		Tinsel Town/Blow Up Music	1974	5.00	10.00	20.00
		As "I Jan I"				
❑ 66120		Sing Sang a Song/ Sing Sang a Song (Singalong Version)	1976	5.00	10.00	20.00
Ripple						
❑ 6101		Tomorrow's Teardrops/My Midsummer Night's Dream	1961	25.00	50.00	100.00
		As "Jan Barry"				

Berry, Mike
Coral

Number		Title (A Side/B Side)	Year	VG	VG+	NM
❑ 62341		A Tribute to Buddy Holly/Every Little Kiss	1962	15.00	30.00	60.00
❑ 62357		Don't You Think It's Time/Loneliness	1963	7.50	15.00	30.00
❑ 62483		Gonna Fall in Love/It Comes and Goes	1966	4.00	8.00	16.00

Number		Title (A Side/B Side)	Year	VG	VG+	NM
Epic						
❑ 50748		I Am a Rocker/Boogaloo Dues	1979		2.00	4.00
❑ 50913		Stay Close to Me/One by One	1980		2.00	4.00
MCA						
❑ 40432		Don't Be Cruel/It's All Over	1975		2.50	5.00

Berry, Richard

Flair						
❑ 1016		I'm Still in Love with You/One Little Prayer	1953	20.00	40.00	80.00
❑ 1052		Bye Bye/At Last	1954	15.00	30.00	60.00
		With the Dreamers				
❑ 1055		What You Do to Me/The Big Break	1954	15.00	30.00	60.00
❑ 1058		Daddy Daddy/Baby Darling	1954	15.00	30.00	60.00
		With the Dreamers				
❑ 1064		Please Tell Me/Oh Oh Get Out of the Car	1955	12.50	25.00	50.00
❑ 1068		God Gave Me You/Doncha Go	1955	12.50	25.00	50.00
❑ 1071		Next Time/Crazy Lover	1955	12.50	25.00	50.00
❑ 1075		Together/Jelly Roll	1955	12.50	25.00	50.00
Flip						
❑ 318		Take the Key/No Kissin' and Huggin'	1956	10.00	20.00	40.00
❑ 321		Louie, Louie/You Are My Sunshine	1957	12.50	25.00	50.00
❑ 321		Louie, Louie/Rock, Rock, Rock	1957	10.00	20.00	40.00
❑ 327		Sweet Sugar You/Rock, Rock, Rock	1957	10.00	20.00	40.00
❑ 331		You're the Girl/You Look So Good	1958	10.00	20.00	40.00
❑ 336		Heaven on Wheels/The Mess Around	1958	10.00	20.00	40.00
❑ 339		Besame Mucho/Do I, Do I	1958	7.50	15.00	30.00
❑ 349		Have Love, Will Travel/No Room	1960	7.50	15.00	30.00
❑ 352		I'll Never Ever Love Again/ Somewhere There's a Rainbow	1961	7.50	15.00	30.00
❑ 360		You Look So Good/You Are My Sunshine	1962	7.50	15.00	30.00
K&G						
❑ 9001		I'm Your Fool/In a Really Big Way	1961	7.50	15.00	30.00
RPM						
❑ 448		Rockin' Man/Big John	1955	25.00	50.00	100.00
❑ 452		Pretty Brown Eyes/I Am Bewildered	1956	7.50	15.00	30.00
❑ 465		Angel of My Life/Yama Yama Pretty Mama	1956	25.00	50.00	100.00
❑ 477		Wait for Me/Good Love	1956	7.50	15.00	30.00
Smash						
❑ 1789		What Good Is a Heart/Everybody's Got a Lover But Me	1963	3.00	6.00	12.00
❑ 1811		I'm Learning/Empty Chair	1963	3.00	6.00	12.00
Warner Bros.						
❑ 5164		Walk Right In/It's All Right	1960	12.50	25.00	50.00

Best, Peter

(Also see "Beatles, The")

Cameo						
❑ 391		Boys/Kansas City	1965	20.00	40.00	80.00
❑ 391	PS	Boys/Kansas City	1965	25.00	50.00	100.00
Capitol						
❑ 2092		Carousel of Love/Want You	1968	7.50	15.00	30.00
		By the Peter Best of Australia, not the former Beatles drummer				
Happening						
❑ 405		If You Can't Get Her/Don't Play with Me	1964	45.00	90.00	180.00
❑ 1117/8		If You Can't Get Her/The Way I Feel About You	1966	37.50	75.00	150.00
		Label credit: "Best of the Beatles (Peter Best)"				
Mr. Maestro						
❑ 711		I Can't Do Without You Now/Keys to My Heart	1965	50.00	100.00	200.00
		Label credit: "Best of the Beatles"; black vinyl				
❑ 711		I Can't Do Without You Now/Keys to My Heart	1965	37.50	75.00	150.00
		Label credit: "Best of the Beatles"; blue vinyl				
❑ 712		Casting My Spell/I'm Blue	1965	50.00	100.00	200.00
		Blue vinyl				
❑ 712		Casting My Spell/I'm Blue	1965	37.50	75.00	150.00
		Black vinyl				
Original Beatles Drummer						
❑ 800		(I'll Try) Anyway/I Wanna Be There	1964	45.00	90.00	180.00

Big Beats, The

(Trini Lopez was a member)

Columbia						
❑ 41072		Clark's Expedition/Big Boy	1958	6.25	12.50	25.00
❑ 41179		Rush Me/Sentimental Journey	1958	6.25	12.50	25.00

Big Bopper

D						
❑ 1008		Chantilly Lace/ The Purple People Eater Meets the Witch Doctor	1958	50.00	100.00	200.00
Mercury						
❑ 71343		Chantilly Lace/ The Purple People Eater Meets the Witch Doctor	1958	5.00	10.00	20.00
❑ 71375		Big Bopper's Wedding/Little Red Riding Hood	1958	3.75	7.50	15.00

Number		Title (A Side/B Side)	Year	VG	VG+	NM
❑ 71416		Someone's Watching Over You/ Walking Through My Dreams	1959	3.75	7.50	15.00
❑ 71451		It's the Truth, Ruth/That's What I'm Talkin' About	1959	3.75	7.50	15.00
❑ 71482		Pink Petticoats/Time Clock	1959	3.75	7.50	15.00

Big Brother and the Holding Company
Columbia
❑ 44626		Piece of My Heart/Turtle Blues	1968	2.50	5.00	10.00
❑ 45284		Keep On/Home on the Strange	1970		3.00	6.00
❑ 45502		Black Widow Spider/Nu Boogaloo Jam	1971		3.00	6.00

Mainstream
❑ 657		All Is Loneliness/Blindman	1967	3.00	6.00	12.00
❑ 662		Down on Me/Call On Me	1967	3.00	6.00	12.00
❑ 666		Bye Bye Baby/Intruder	1968	3.00	6.00	12.00
❑ 675		Caterpillar/Women Is Losers	1968	3.00	6.00	12.00
❑ 678		Coo Coo/The Last Time	1968	3.00	6.00	12.00

Bikinis, The
Dot
❑ 15808		Fatima the Dreamer/Kitchy Koo	1958	6.25	12.50	25.00
❑ 15872		Chop Stick Rock/A'Right, A'Ready	1958	10.00	20.00	40.00

Roulette
❑ 4073		Bikini/Boogie Rock 'n' Roll	1958	6.25	12.50	25.00

Top Rank
❑ 2032		Crazy Vibrations/Spunky	1959	6.25	12.50	25.00

Billion Dollar Babies
Polydor
❑ 14394		Rock 'N' Roll Radio/Wasn't I the One	1977		2.50	5.00
❑ 14406	DJ	Too Young (stereo)/Too Young (mono)	1977	3.00	6.00	12.00

Billy and Lillie
(Also see "Ford, Billy")
ABC-Paramount
❑ 10421		Love Me Sincerely/Whip It To Me Baby	1963	7.50	15.00	30.00
❑ 10489		Carry Me Across the Threshold/Why I Love Billy (Lillie)	1963	7.50	15.00	30.00

Cameo
❑ 412		Nothing Moves (Without a Little Push)/The Two of Us	1966	2.50	5.00	10.00
❑ 435		You Got Me by the Heart/Hear You Better Hear	1966	2.50	5.00	10.00

Swan
❑ 4002		La Dee Dah/The Monster	1957	7.50	15.00	30.00
		"SWAN" in all capital letters; B-side by Billy Ford and the Thunderbirds				
❑ 4002		La Dee Dah/The Monster	1958	5.00	10.00	20.00
		Only the S in "Swan" is capitalized; B-side by Billy Ford and the Thunderbirds				
❑ 4005		Happiness/Creepin' Crawlin' Cryin'	1958	5.00	10.00	20.00
❑ 4011		The Greasy Spoon/Hanging On to You	1958	5.00	10.00	20.00
❑ 4020		Lucky Ladybug/I Promise You	1958	6.25	12.50	25.00
❑ 4030		Tumbled Down/A.H. Thomas the Cat	1959	3.75	7.50	15.00
❑ 4036		Bells, Bells, Bells/Honeymoonin'	1959	3.75	7.50	15.00
❑ 4042		Terrific Together/Swampy	1959	3.75	7.50	15.00
❑ 4051		Free for All/The Ins and Outs of Love	1960	3.75	7.50	15.00
❑ 4058		That's the Way the Cookie Crumbles (Ah-So)/ Over the Mountain, Across the Sea	1960	3.75	7.50	15.00
❑ 4069		Ain't Comin' Back (To You)/Bananas	1961	3.75	7.50	15.00

Billy and the Essentials
Cameo
❑ 344		Remember Me Baby/The Actor	1965	100.00	200.00	400.00

Jamie
❑ 1229		The Dance Is Over/Steady Girl	1962	7.50	15.00	30.00
❑ 1239		Over the Weekend/Maybe You'll Be There	1962	7.50	15.00	30.00

Landa
❑ 691		The Dance Is Over/Steady Girl	1962	12.50	25.00	50.00

Mercury
❑ 72127		Young at Heart/Lonely Weekend	1963	6.25	12.50	25.00
❑ 72210		Last Dance/Yes Sir, That's My Baby	1963	6.25	12.50	25.00

Smash
❑ 2045		Babalu's Wedding Day/My Way of Saying	1966	3.75	7.50	15.00
❑ 2071		Don't Cry (Sing Along with the Music)/Baby Go Away	1966	3.00	6.00	12.00

SSS International
❑ 706		I Wrote a Song/Oh What a Feeling	1967	3.00	6.00	12.00

Biscaynes, The
Northridge
❑ 1001		Church Key/Moment of Truth	1963	15.00	30.00	60.00
		B-side by the Surfaris				

Reprise
❑ 20,180		Church Key/Moment of Truth	1963	7.50	15.00	30.00
		B-side by the Surfaris				

Number		Title (A Side/B Side)	Year	VG	VG+	NM

Bjorn and Benny
(Early incarnation of Abba)
Playboy

❏ 50014		Merry-Go-Round/People Need Love	1972	7.50	15.00	30.00
❏ 50018		Another Town, Another Train/I Am Just a Girl	1973	7.50	15.00	30.00
❏ 50025		Rock 'N Roll Band/Another Town, Another Train	1973	7.50	15.00	30.00

Black Satin - See "Five Satins, The"

Black, Bill's, Combo
Columbia

❏ 44867		But It's Alright/Slow Action	1969		2.50	5.00
❏ 44983		California Dreamin'/Funky Train	1969		2.50	5.00
❏ 45092		Heaven Knows/One Five One Eight Chelsea	1970		2.50	5.00
❏ 45162		Keep the Customer Satisfied/ One Five One Eight Chelsea	1970		2.50	5.00

Hi

❏ 2018		Smokie (Part 2)/Smokie (Part 1)	1959	5.00	10.00	20.00
❏ 2021		White Silver Sands/The Wheel	1960	5.00	10.00	20.00
❏ 2022		Josephine/Dry Bones	1960	3.75	7.50	15.00
❏ 2022	PS	Josephine/Dry Bones	1960	6.25	12.50	25.00
❏ 2026		Don't Be Cruel/Rollin'	1960	3.75	7.50	15.00
❏ 2026	PS	Don't Be Cruel/Rollin'	1960	6.25	12.50	25.00
❏ 2027		Blue Tango/Willie	1960	3.75	7.50	15.00
❏ 2027	PS	Blue Tango/Willie	1960	6.25	12.50	25.00
❏ 2028		Hearts of Stone/Royal Blue	1961	3.00	6.00	12.00
❏ 2029		Old Time Religion/ He's Got the Whole World in His Hands *Stereo single, small hole, plays at 33 1/3 rpm*	1961	10.00	20.00	40.00
❏ 2030		Do Lord/When the Roll Is Called Up Yonder *Stereo single, small hole, plays at 33 1/3 rpm*	1961	10.00	20.00	40.00
❏ 2031		Down by the Riverside/ It Is No Secret (What God Can Do) *Stereo single, small hole, plays at 33 1/3 rpm*	1961	10.00	20.00	40.00
❏ 2032		When the Saints Go Marching In/(B-side unknown) *Stereo single, small hole, plays at 33 1/3 rpm*	1961	10.00	20.00	40.00
❏ 2033		Just a Closer Walk with Thee/This Old House *Stereo single, small hole, plays at 33 1/3 rpm*	1961	10.00	20.00	40.00
❏ 2036		Ole Buttermilk Sky/Yogi	1961	3.00	6.00	12.00
❏ 2036	PS	Ole Buttermilk Sky/Yogi	1961	6.25	12.50	25.00
❏ 2038		Movin'/Honky Train	1961	3.00	6.00	12.00
❏ 2042		Twist-Her/My Girl Josephine	1961	3.00	6.00	12.00
❏ 2045		Twist-Her/Night Train *Stereo single, small hole, plays at 33 1/3 rpm*	1962	10.00	20.00	40.00
❏ 2046		The Hucklebuck/Corrina, Corrina *Stereo single, small hole, plays at 33 1/3 rpm*	1962	10.00	20.00	40.00
❏ 2047		Johnny B. Goode/(B-side unknown) *Stereo single, small hole, plays at 33 1/3 rpm*	1962	10.00	20.00	40.00
❏ 2048		Josephine/My Girl Josephine *Stereo single, small hole, plays at 33 1/3 rpm*	1962	10.00	20.00	40.00
❏ 2049		Slippin' and Slidin'/Twist with Me, Baby *Stereo single, small hole, plays at 33 1/3 rpm*	1962	10.00	20.00	40.00
❏ 2052		Twistin' -- White Silver Sands/My Babe	1962	3.00	6.00	12.00
❏ 2052	PS	Twistin' -- White Silver Sands/My Babe	1962	6.25	12.50	25.00
❏ 2055		So What/Blues for the Red Boy	1962	3.00	6.00	12.00
❏ 2059		Joey's Song/Hot Taco	1962	3.00	6.00	12.00
❏ 2064		Do It -- Rat Now/Little Jasper	1963	3.00	6.00	12.00
❏ 2069		Monkey-Shine/Love Gone	1963	3.00	6.00	12.00
❏ 2072		Comin' On/Soft Winds	1964	3.00	6.00	12.00
❏ 2077		Tequila/Raunchy	1964	3.00	6.00	12.00
❏ 2079		Little Queenie/Boo Ray	1964	3.00	6.00	12.00
❏ 2085		Come On Home/He'll Have to Go	1964	2.50	5.00	10.00
❏ 2094		Spootin'/Crazy Feeling	1965	2.50	5.00	10.00
❏ 2106		Hey, Good Lookin'/Mountain of Love	1966	2.50	5.00	10.00
❏ 2115		Rambler/You Call Everybody Darling	1966	2.50	5.00	10.00
❏ 2124		Son of Smokie/Peg Leg	1967	2.00	4.00	8.00
❏ 2145		Turn On Your Love Life/Ribbon of Darkness	1968		3.00	6.00
❏ 2153		Red Light/Bright Lights, Big City	1968		3.00	6.00
❏ 2168		Creepin' Around/The Son of Hickory Holler's Tramp	1969		3.00	6.00
❏ 2185		No More/Closin' Time	1971		2.50	5.00
❏ 2208		Daylite/Four A.M.	1972		2.50	5.00
❏ 2234		Smokey Bourbon Street/Mighty Fine	1973		2.50	5.00
❏ 2277		Soul Serenade/Pickin'	1974		2.00	4.00
❏ 2283		Truck Stop/Boilin' Cabbage	1975		2.00	4.00
❏ 2291		Almost Persuaded/Back Up and Push	1975		2.00	4.00
❏ 2301		Fire on the Bayou/Memphis Soul	1976		2.00	4.00
❏ 2311		I Can Help/Jump Back Joe	1976		2.00	4.00
❏ 2317		Redneck Rock/Yakety Sax	1976		2.00	4.00
❏ 78508		Cashin' In (A Tribute to Luther Perkins)/L.A. Blues	1978		2.00	4.00

Mega

❏ 0036		Rings/Cotton Carnival	1971		2.50	5.00
❏ 0052		Oh Happy Day/Sugar Cured	1971		2.50	5.00
❏ 0070		Harlem Nocturne/Sassy Parts	1972		2.50	5.00
❏ 0086		Night Train/Bluff City	1972		2.50	5.00
❏ 0113		Listen to the Music/Memphis Shuffle	1973		2.50	5.00
❏ 0117		Satin Sheets/Memphis Shuffle	1973		2.50	5.00

Number		Title (A Side/B Side)	Year	VG	VG+	NM
❑ 201		Smokie Part 2/Tequila	1973		2.50	5.00
❑ 207		Oh Happy Day/Listen to the Music	1974		2.00	4.00

Black, Cilla
Bell

❑ 726		Step Inside Love/I Couldn't Take My Eyes Off You	1968	5.00	10.00	20.00

Capitol

❑ 5196		You're My World/Suffer Now I Must	1964	3.75	7.50	15.00
❑ 5258		It's for You/He Won't Ask Me	1964	3.00	6.00	12.00
❑ 5373		One Little Voice/Is It Love	1965	3.00	6.00	12.00
❑ 5414		I've Been Wrong Before/My Love Came Home	1965	3.00	6.00	12.00
❑ 5595		Love's Just a Broken Heart/Yesterday	1966	3.00	6.00	12.00
❑ 5595	PS	Love's Just a Broken Heart/Yesterday	1966	7.50	15.00	30.00
❑ 5674		Alfie/Night Time Is Here	1966	3.00	6.00	12.00
❑ 5763		Don't Answer Me/The Right One Is Left	1966	3.00	6.00	12.00
❑ 5782		A Fool Am I/For No One	1966	3.00	6.00	12.00

DJM

❑ 70007		What the World Needs Now Is Love/Only Forever Will Do	1969	2.00	4.00	8.00
❑ 70011		Without Him/It'll Never Happen Again	1969	2.00	4.00	8.00
❑ 70012		Surround Yourself with Sorrow/It'll Never Happen Again	1969	2.00	4.00	8.00
❑ 70014		Conversations/London Bridge	1969	2.00	4.00	8.00
❑ 70015		If I Thought You'd Ever Change Your Mind/It Feels So Good	1970	2.00	4.00	8.00
❑ 70016		If I Thought You'd Ever Change Your Mind/Conversations	1970	2.00	4.00	8.00
❑ 70018	DJ	Across the Universe (mono/stereo)	1970	3.00	6.00	12.00

EMI

❑ 4003		He Was a Writer/I'll Never Run Out of You	1974		3.00	6.00

Private Stock

❑ 45,040		I'll Take a Tango/To Know Him Is To Love Him	1975		2.50	5.00
❑ 45,077		Fantasy/It's Now	1976		2.50	5.00

Black, Oscar
Atlantic

❑ 956		Love, Love, Love/Troubled Man Blues	1952	37.50	75.00	150.00

Groove

❑ 0012		I'll Get By/Hold Me Baby	1954	15.00	30.00	60.00
		With Sue Allen				
❑ 0102		Be My Baby/Ain't Nobody Home But Me	1955	15.00	30.00	60.00
		With Sue Allen				
❑ 0115		Baby, Please Don't Go/I'll Live My Life Alone	1955	15.00	30.00	60.00
		With Sue Allen				
❑ 0130		Think of Tomorrow/Set a Wedding Day	1955	15.00	30.00	60.00
		With Sue Allen and the Four Students				
❑ 0168		Into Each Heart (Some Tears Must Fall)/If I Cry Tomorrow	1956	12.50	25.00	50.00
		With Sue Allen				

Savoy

❑ 1600		I Got a Feeling/I'm a Fool to Care	1961	3.75	7.50	15.00

Blackburn, Lou
Imperial

❑ 5943		Grand Prix/Jazz-a-Nova	1963	7.50	15.00	30.00
❑ 5998		Two Note Samba/17 Richmond Park	1963	5.00	10.00	20.00

Blackjack
(With Bruce Kulick, later with Kiss, and Michael Bolton. Group on 20th Century might be different)
Polydor

❑ 2026		For You/Fallin'	1979	2.50	5.00	10.00
❑ 2046		Southern Ballad (If This Means Losing You)/Without Your Love	1979	2.50	5.00	10.00
❑ 2123		My World Is Empty Without You/Airwaves	1980	2.50	5.00	10.00
❑ 14572		Heart of Mine/Love Me Tonight	1979	2.50	5.00	10.00

20th Century

❑ 2279		Inland Sea/Joyride	1976	2.00	4.00	8.00

Blackwell, Otis
Atlantic

❑ 1165		Make Ready for Love/When You're Around	1957	10.00	20.00	40.00
❑ 1178		Turtle Dove/What a Coincidence	1958	10.00	20.00	40.00

Cub

❑ 9092		Jeannie's Wedding/I'd Rather Kiss You Than Eat	1961	5.00	10.00	20.00
❑ 9107		Sister Twister/Ga Ga	1962	5.00	10.00	20.00

Date

❑ 1006		Don't Run Away/Handle with Care	1958	7.50	15.00	30.00

Epic

❑ 10654		Just Keep It Up/It's All Over Me	1970	6.25	12.50	25.00

Groove

❑ 0034		Oh, What a Babe/Here I Am	1954	10.00	20.00	40.00

Jay-Dee

❑ 784		Daddy Rolling Stone/Tears! Tears! Tears!	1953	12.50	25.00	50.00

Number	Title (A Side/B Side)	Year	VG	VG+	NM
❏ 787	You're My Love/Bartender Fill It Up Again	1954	12.50	25.00	50.00
❏ 791	On That Power Line/Don't You Know How I Love You	1954	12.50	25.00	50.00
❏ 792	I'm Standing at the Doorway/Nobody Met the Train	1954	12.50	25.00	50.00
❏ 794	My Josephine/Ain't Got No Time	1954	12.50	25.00	50.00
❏ 798	Go Away Mr. Blues/I'm Comin' Back Baby	1955	12.50	25.00	50.00
❏ 802	You Move Me Baby/My Poor Broken Heart	1955	12.50	25.00	50.00
❏ 808	Oh What a Wonderful Time/Let the Daddy Hold You	1955	12.50	25.00	50.00

MGM

❏ 13090	Kiss Away/Grandaddy of Them All	1962	5.00	10.00	20.00

RCA Victor

❏ 47-5069	Wake You Fool/Please Help Me Find	1952	12.50	25.00	50.00
❏ 47-5225	The Fool That I Be/Number 000	1953	12.50	25.00	50.00

Blades, Carol
Gee

❏ 1029	When Will I Know/What Did I Do Wrong	1957	50.00	100.00	200.00

Blaine, Hal
ABC Dunhill

❏ 4181	Beverly Drive/Midnight at Pink's	1969	3.00	6.00	12.00

Dunhill

❏ 4006	La Bamba/Topsy '65	1965	3.75	7.50	15.00
❏ 4021	Secret Agent Man/Midnight at Pink's	1966	3.75	7.50	15.00
❏ 4049	Bang Bang Rhythm/Drums A-Go-Go	1966	3.75	7.50	15.00
❏ 4074	The Swinger/Drums A-Go-Go	1967	3.75	7.50	15.00
❏ 4091	Love-In (December)/Wiggy (November)	1967	3.75	7.50	15.00
❏ 4102	The Invaders/Secret Agent Man	1967	3.75	7.50	15.00
❏ 4142	Allegro from "Mac Arthur Park"/Drums A-Go-Go	1968	3.75	7.50	15.00

Melody House

❏ 100	Slow Gate/South of Shreveport	1962	10.00	20.00	40.00

RCA Victor

❏ 47-8147	Hawaii 1963/East Side Story	1963	6.25	12.50	25.00
❏ 47-8223	Dance with the Surfin' Band/The Drummer Plays for Me	1963	6.25	12.50	25.00
❏ 47-8282	Challenger II/Gear Stripper	1963	6.25	12.50	25.00

Rock-It

❏ 1000	Alamo Rock/Alamo Rock (Part 2)	1959	12.50	25.00	50.00

Blake, Tommy
Buddy

❏ 107	I'm a Fool/Kool It	1958	7.50	15.00	30.00

Chancellor

❏ 101	I Gotta Be Somewhere/ Three Cheers for the Red, White and Blue	19??	2.50	5.00	10.00

RCA Victor

❏ 47-6925	Freedom/Mr. Hoody	1957	12.50	25.00	50.00

Sun

❏ 278	Flatfoot Sam/Lordy Hoody	1957	25.00	50.00	100.00
❏ 300	Sweetie Pie/I Dig You	1958	75.00	150.00	300.00

Bland, Bobby
(Also known as Bobby "Blue" Bland)

ABC

❏ 12105	Yolanda/When You Come to the End of Your Road	1975		2.00	4.00
❏ 12134	I Take It On Home/You've Never Been This Far Before	1975		2.00	4.00
❏ 12156	Today I Started Loving You Again/Too Far Gone	1976		2.00	4.00
❏ 12189	It Ain't the Real Thing/Who's Foolin' Who	1976		2.00	4.00
❏ 12280	The Soul of a Man/If I Weren't a Gambler	1977		2.00	4.00
❏ 12330	Sittin' on a Poor Man's Throne/ I Intend to Take Your Place	1978		2.00	4.00
❏ 12360	Love to See You Smile/I'm Just Your Man	1978		2.00	4.00
❏ 12405	Come Fly with Me/Ain't God Something	1978		2.00	4.00

ABC Dunhill

❏ 15003	Ain't No Love in the Heart of the City/ Twenty-Four Hour Blues	1974		2.50	5.00
❏ 15015	I Wouldn't Treat a Dog (The Way You Treated Me)/ I Ain't Gonna Be the First to Cry	1974		2.50	5.00
❏ 4369	This Time I'm Gone for Good/Where Baby Went	1973		2.50	5.00
❏ 4379	Goin' Down Slow/Up and Down World	1974		2.50	5.00

ABC Impulse

❏ 31006	Let the Good Times Roll/Strange Things *With B.B. King*	1976		2.00	4.00
❏ 31009	Everyday I Have the Blues/The Thrill Is Gone *With B.B. King*	1976		2.00	4.00

Duke

❏ 105	Lovin' Blues/I.O.U. Blues	1952	50.00	100.00	200.00
❏ 115	Army Blues/No Blow, No Show	1953	25.00	50.00	100.00
❏ 141	Time Out/It's My Life Baby	1955	12.50	25.00	50.00
❏ 146	You or None/Woke Up Screaming	1955	12.50	25.00	50.00
❏ 153	I Can't Put You Down/You've Got Bad Intentions	1956	10.00	20.00	40.00
❏ 160	I Learned My Lesson/Lead Us On	1956	10.00	20.00	40.00
❏ 160	I Learned My Lesson/I Don't Believe	1956	10.00	20.00	40.00
❏ 167	Don't Want No Woman/I Smell Trouble	1957	6.25	12.50	25.00
❏ 170	Farther Up the Road/Sometime Tomorrow	1957	6.25	12.50	25.00
❏ 182	Teach Me/Bobby's Blues	1957	6.25	12.50	25.00

Number	Title (A Side/B Side)	Year	VG	VG+	NM
❏ 185	You Got Me Where You Want Me/ Loan a Helping Hand	1958	6.25	12.50	25.00
❏ 196	Little Boy Blue/Last Night	1958	6.25	12.50	25.00
❏ 300	You Did Me Wrong/I Lost Sight of the World	1959	5.00	10.00	20.00
❏ 303	Wishing Well/I'm Not Ashamed	1959	5.00	10.00	20.00
❏ 310	Is It Real/Someday	1959	5.00	10.00	20.00
❏ 314	I'll Take Care of You/That's Why	1959	5.00	10.00	20.00
❏ 318	Lead Me On/Hold Me Tenderly	1960	5.00	10.00	20.00
❏ 327	Cry Cry Cry/I've Been Wrong So Long	1960	5.00	10.00	20.00
❏ 332	I Pity the Fool/Close to You	1961	3.75	7.50	15.00
❏ 336	Don't Cry No More/How Does a Cheating Woman Feel	1961	3.75	7.50	15.00
❏ 338	Ain't That Loving You/Jelly, Jelly, Jelly	1961	3.75	7.50	15.00
❏ 340	Don't Cry No More/Saint James Infirmary	1961	3.75	7.50	15.00
❏ 344	Turn On Your Love Light/You're the One (That I Need)	1961	3.75	7.50	15.00
❏ 347	Who Will the Next Fool Be/Blue Moon	1962	3.00	6.00	12.00
❏ 352	Yield Not to Temptation/ How Does a Cheating Woman Feel	1962	3.00	6.00	12.00
❏ 355	Stormy Monday Blues/Your Friends	1962	3.00	6.00	12.00
❏ 360	That's the Way Love Is/Call On Me	1962	3.00	6.00	12.00
❏ 366	Sometimes You Gotta Cry a Little/You're Worth It All	1963	3.00	6.00	12.00
❏ 369	Ain't It a Good Thing/Queen for a Day	1963	3.00	6.00	12.00
❏ 370	The Feeling Is Gone/I Can't Stop Singing	1963	3.00	6.00	12.00
❏ 375	Ain't Nothing You Can Do/Honey Child	1964	3.00	6.00	12.00
❏ 377	Share Your Love with Me/After It's Too Late	1964	2.50	5.00	10.00
❏ 383	Ain't Doing Too Bad (Part 1)/ Ain't Doing Too Bad (Part 2)	1964	2.50	5.00	10.00
❏ 385	These Hands (Small But Mighty)/Today	1965	2.50	5.00	10.00
❏ 386	Blind Man/Black Night	1965	2.50	5.00	10.00
❏ 390	Dust Got in Daddy's Eyes/Ain't No Telling	1965	2.50	5.00	10.00
❏ 393	I'm Too Far Gone (To Turn Around)/ If You Could Read My Mind	1965	2.50	5.00	10.00
❏ 402	Good Time Charlie/Good Time Charlie (Part 2)	1966	2.00	4.00	8.00
❏ 407	Poverty/Building a Fire with Hair	1966	2.00	4.00	8.00
❏ 412	Back in the Same Old Bag Again/ I Ain't Myself Anymore	1966	2.00	4.00	8.00
❏ 416	You're All I Need/Deep in My Soul	1967	2.00	4.00	8.00
❏ 421	That Did It/Getting Used to the Blues	1967	2.00	4.00	8.00
❏ 426	A Touch of the Blues/Shoes	1967	2.00	4.00	8.00
❏ 432	Driftin' Blues/You Could Read My Mind	1968	2.00	4.00	8.00
❏ 433	Honey Child/A Piece of Gold	1968	2.00	4.00	8.00
❏ 435	Save Your Love for Me/Share Your Love with Me	1968	2.00	4.00	8.00
❏ 440	Rockin' in the Same Old Boat/ Wouldn't You Rather Have Me	1968	2.00	4.00	8.00
❏ 447	Gotta Get to Know You/Baby I'm On My Way	1969	2.00	4.00	8.00
❏ 449	Chains of Love/Ask Me 'Bout Nothing (But the Blues)	1969	2.00	4.00	8.00
❏ 458	If You've Got a Heart/Sad Feeling	1970	2.00	4.00	8.00
❏ 460	Lover with a Reputation/If Love Ruled the World	1970	2.00	4.00	8.00
❏ 464	Keep On Loving Me (You'll See the Change)/ I Just Got to Forget About You	1970	2.00	4.00	8.00
❏ 466	I'm Sorry/Yum Yum Tree	1971	2.00	4.00	8.00
❏ 471	Shape Up or Ship Out/ The Love That We Share (Is True)	1971	2.00	4.00	8.00
❏ 472	Do What You Set Out to Do/Ain't Nothing You Can Do	1972	2.00	4.00	8.00
❏ 477	I'm So Tired/If You Could Read My Mind	1972	2.00	4.00	8.00
❏ 480	That's All There Is/ I Don't Want Another Mountain to Climb	1973	2.00	4.00	8.00

Kent

❏ 378	Love You Baby/Drifting *With Ike Turner*	1962	2.50	5.00	10.00

Malaco

❏ 2122	Members Only/I Just Got to Know	1985			3.00
❏ 2126	Can We Make Love Tonight/In the Ghetto	1986			3.00
❏ 2133	Angel/I Hear You Thinkin'	1986			3.00

MCA

❏ 41140	Tit for Tat/Come Fly with Me	1979		2.00	4.00
❏ 41197	Soon as the Weather Breaks/To Be Friends	1980		2.00	4.00
❏ 51068	You'd Be a Millionaire/Swat Vibrator	1981			3.00
❏ 51181	What a Difference A Day Makes/ Givin' Up the Streets for Love	1982			3.00
❏ 52085	Recess in Heaven/Exactly, Where It's At	1982			3.00
❏ 52136	Here We Go Again/You're About to Win	1982			3.00
❏ 52180	Is This the Blues/You're About to Win	1983			3.00
❏ 52270	If It Ain't One Thing/Tell Mr. Bland	1983			3.00
❏ 52436	Looking Back/You Got Me Loving You	1984			3.00
❏ 52482	Get Real Clean/It's Too Bad	1984			3.00
❏ 52508	You Are My Christmas/New Merry Christmas Baby	1984			3.00

Wand

❏ 1102	Honey, You've Been On My Mind/You've Got Time	1965	3.75	7.50	15.00

Blanders, The

Smash

❏ 2005	Jitterbug/Desert Sands	1965	12.50	25.00	50.00

Blane, Marcie

Seville

❏ 120	Bobby's Girl/Time to Dream	1962	5.00	10.00	20.00
❏ 123	What Does a Girl Do?/How Can I Tell Him	1963	4.00	8.00	16.00
❏ 126	Little Miss Fool/Rag Time Sound	1963	4.00	8.00	16.00

Number	Title (A Side/B Side)	Year	VG	VG+	NM
❏ 128	You Gave My Number to Billy/Told You So	1963	4.00	8.00	16.00
❏ 130	Why Can't I Get a Guy/ Who's Going to Take My Daddy's Place	1963	4.00	8.00	16.00
❏ 133	Bobby Did/After the Laughter	1964	4.00	8.00	16.00
❏ 137	The Hurtin' Kind/She'll Break the String	1965	4.00	8.00	16.00

Blazer Boy
Imperial
❏ 5199	Mornin'Train/Joe's Kid Sister	1952	25.00	50.00	100.00
❏ 5244	Surprise Blues/Waiting for My Baby	1953	25.00	50.00	100.00
❏ 5801	New Orleans Twist/That's Where It's At	1962	5.00	10.00	20.00

Blendells, The
Cotillion
❏ 44020	Night After Night/The Love That I Needed	1968	2.50	5.00	10.00

Rampart
❏ 641	La La La La La/Huggies Bunnies	1964	6.25	12.50	25.00

Reprise
❏ 0291	La La La La La/Huggies Bunnies	1964	5.00	10.00	20.00
❏ 0340	Dance with Me/Get Your Baby	1965	5.00	10.00	20.00

Blenders, The
(Several different groups)
AFO
❏ 305	Graveyard/It Takes Time	1962	75.00	150.00	300.00

Aladdin
❏ 3449	Two Loves/Soda Shop	1959	250.00	500.00	1,000

Class
❏ 236	My Heart's Desire/Little Rose	1958	10.00	20.00	40.00

Cortland
❏ 102	Love Is a Treasure/Fisherman	1962	3.00	6.00	12.00
❏ 103	Everybody's Got a Right/What Have You Got	1962	3.00	6.00	12.00

Decca
❏ 27403	The Masquerade Is Over/Little Small Town Girl	1951	100.00	200.00	400.00
❏ 27587	All I Gotta Do Is Think of You/The Busiest Corner	1951	75.00	150.00	300.00
❏ 28092	Just a Little Walk with Me/I'd Be a Fool Again	1952	75.00	150.00	300.00
❏ 28241	Never in a Million Years/Memories of You	1952	75.00	150.00	300.00
❏ 48156	Gone/Honeysuckle Rose	1950	75.00	150.00	300.00
❏ 48158	Count Every Star/ Would I Still Be the One in Your Heart	1950	75.00	150.00	300.00
❏ 48183	I'm So Crazy for Love/What About Tonight	1950	75.00	150.00	300.00
❏ 48244	My Heart Will Never Forget/You Do the Dreaming	1951	75.00	150.00	300.00

Jay Dee
❏ 780	Don't Play Around with You/You'll Never Smile Again	1953	50.00	100.00	200.00

Mar-V-Lus
❏ 6010	Your Love Has Got Me Down/ Love Is a Good Thing Going	1966	50.00	100.00	200.00

MGM
❏ 11488	I Don't Miss You Anymore/ If That's the Way You Want It Baby	1953	100.00	200.00	400.00
❏ 11531	Please Take Me Back/Isn't It a Shame	1953	100.00	200.00	400.00

RCA Victor
❏ 47-6591	I've Told Every Little Star/Cecilia	1956	15.00	30.00	60.00
❏ 47-6712	Wake Up to Music/New Sensations in Sound	1956	12.50	25.00	50.00
❏ 47-7009	I'm Following You/Since i Kissed My Baby Goodbye	1957	12.50	25.00	50.00

Wanger
❏ 189	Angel/Old MacDonald	1959	6.25	12.50	25.00

Witch
❏ 114	Daughter/Everybody's Got a Right	1963	4.00	8.00	16.00
❏ 117	Boys Think/Squat and Squirm	1963	3.75	7.50	15.00
❏ 123	One Time/(B-side unknown)	1964	3.75	7.50	15.00

Blessing, Michael - See "Nesmith, Michael"

Bleu Lights, The
Baysound
❏ 67003	Forever/They Don't Know My Heart	1968	10.00	20.00	40.00
❏ 67007	Bony Moronie/Lonely Man's Prayer	1968	7.50	15.00	30.00
❏ 67010	Yes I Do/The End of My Dreams	1969	7.50	15.00	30.00

Blinky
Motown
❏ 1134	I Wouldn't Change the Man He Is/I'll Always Love You	1968	2.00	4.00	8.00
❏ 1168	How You Gonna Keep It/This Time Last Summer	1970	25.00	50.00	100.00
❏ 1233	You Get a Tangle in Your Life Line/This Man of Mine	1973		3.00	6.00

Mowest
❏ 5019	For Your Precious Love/So Tired	1972		3.00	6.00
❏ 5033	T'Ain't Nobody's Bizness If I Do/What More Can I Do	1973		2.50	5.00

Soul
❏ 35089	How You Gonna Keep It/This Time Last Summer	1971		3.00	6.00

Number		Title (A Side/B Side)	Year	VG	VG+	NM

Blossoms, The
Bell
☐ 780		You've Lost That Lovin' Feeling/Something So Wrong	1969	2.00	4.00	8.00
☐ 797		(You're My) Soul and Inspiration/Stand By	1969	2.00	4.00	8.00
☐ 857		I Ain't Got to Love Nobody Else/Don't Take Your Love	1970	2.00	4.00	8.00
☐ 937		One Step Away/Break Your Promise	1970	2.00	4.00	8.00

Capitol
☐ F3822		Move On/He Promised Me	1957	7.50	15.00	30.00
☐ F3878		Little Louie/Have Faith in Me	1958	6.25	12.50	25.00
☐ F4072		Baby Daddy-O/No Other Love	1958	6.25	12.50	25.00

Challenge
☐ 9109		Son-In-Law/I'll Wait	1961	5.00	10.00	20.00
		B-side by the Coeds				
☐ 9122		Hard to Get/Write Me a Letter	1961	5.00	10.00	20.00
☐ 9138		The Search Is Over/Big Talking Jim	1962	5.00	10.00	20.00

EEOC
☐ 8172		Things Are Changing (same on both sides)	1965	37.50	75.00	150.00
☐ 8172	PS	Things Are Changing (same on both sides)	1965	37.50	75.00	150.00
		Promotional item for the Equal Employment Opportunity Commission				

Epic
| ☐ 50434 | | There's No Greater Love | 1977 | | 2.50 | 5.00 |
| | | (Than Mine for You My Love)/Walking on Air | | | | |

Lion
| ☐ 108 | | Touchdown/It's All Up to You | 1972 | | 3.00 | 6.00 |
| ☐ 125 | | Grandma's Hands/Cherish What Is Dear to You | 1972 | | 3.00 | 6.00 |

MGM
| ☐ 13964 | | Tweedlee Dee/You Got Me Hummin' | 1968 | 2.50 | 5.00 | 10.00 |

Ode
☐ 101		Stoney End/Wonderful	1967	3.00	6.00	12.00
☐ 106		Cry Like a Baby/Wonderful	1968	3.00	6.00	12.00
☐ 125		Stoney End/Wonderful	1969	3.00	6.00	12.00

Okeh
| ☐ 7162 | | I'm in Love/What Makes Love | 1963 | 5.00 | 10.00 | 20.00 |

Reprise
☐ 0436		Good, Good Lovin'/That's When the Tears Start	1965	3.75	7.50	15.00
☐ 0475		Lover Boy/My Love, Come Home	1966	3.75	7.50	15.00
☐ 0522		Let Your Love Shine on Me/Deep Into My Heart	1966	3.75	7.50	15.00
☐ 0639		Deep Into My Heart/Good, Good Lovin'	1967	3.75	7.50	15.00

Blue Belles, The
(Also see "LaBelle, Patti, and the Blue Belles"; the below is a different group)
Atlantic
| ☐ 987 | | The Story of a Fool/Cancel the Call | 1953 | 37.50 | 75.00 | 150.00 |

Blue Cheer
Mercury
| ☐ 872 804-7 | | Summertime Blues/Just a Little Bit | 1989 | | 2.00 | 4.00 |
| | | *Reissue* | | | | |

Philips
☐ 40516		Summertime Blues/Out of Focus	1968	3.00	6.00	12.00
☐ 40516	PS	Summertime Blues/Out of Focus	1968	6.25	12.50	25.00
☐ 40541		Just a Little Bit/Gypsy Ball	1968	2.50	5.00	10.00
☐ 40561		Sun Cycle/Feathers from Our Tree	1968	2.50	5.00	10.00
☐ 40561		Sun Cycle/Albert's Shuffle	1968	2.50	5.00	10.00
☐ 40602		West Coast Child of Sunshine/When It All Gets Old	1969	2.00	4.00	8.00
☐ 40651		All Night Long/Fortunes	1969	2.00	4.00	8.00
☐ 40664		Hello L.A., Bye-Bye Birmingham/Natural Man	1970	2.00	4.00	8.00
☐ 40682		Ain't That the Way/Fool	1970	2.00	4.00	8.00
☐ 40691		Babji (Twilight Raga)/Pilot	1971	2.00	4.00	8.00
☐ 40691		Babji (Twilight Raga)/Fool	1971	2.50	5.00	10.00

Blue Christie
Sun
| ☐ 1143 | | Making Love in the Summertime/The Feeling's Good | 1979 | | 2.00 | 4.00 |

Blue Diamonds, The
(With Ernie Kador, who recorded as Ernie K-Doe)
Savoy
| ☐ 1134 | | Honey Baby/No Money | 1954 | 15.00 | 30.00 | 60.00 |

Blue Jays, The
(Several different groups)
Checker
| ☐ 782 | | White Cliffs of Dover/Hey Poppa | 1953 | 1,000 | 1,500 | 2,000 |

Laurie
| ☐ 3037 | | Sweet Georgia Brown/J.J.'s Blues | 1959 | 6.25 | 12.50 | 25.00 |

Map City
☐ 300		Hang On/Hard Thing to Accept	1969		3.00	6.00
☐ 307		Freedom (Where Have You Gone)/(B-side unknown)	1971		3.00	6.00
☐ 311		Jackson/Wacka Wacka	1971		3.00	6.00

Number	Title (A Side/B Side)	Year	VG	VG+	NM
Milestone					
❑ 2008	Lover's Island/You're Gonna Cry	1961	7.50	15.00	30.00
	Dark blue label				
❑ 2008	Lover's Island/You're Gonna Cry	1961	6.25	12.50	25.00
	Light blue and white label				
❑ 2008	Lover's Island/You're Gonna Cry	1961	5.00	10.00	20.00
	Green label				
❑ 2009	Tears Are Falling/Tree Tall Men	1961	7.50	15.00	30.00
❑ 2010	Let's Make Love/Rock, Rock, Rock	1962	5.00	10.00	20.00
❑ 2012	The Right to Love/Rock, Rock, Rock	1962	5.00	10.00	20.00
❑ 2014	Venus, My Love/Tall Len	1962	15.00	30.00	60.00
Philips					
❑ 40186	Who (Will I Be Today)?/Come On Baby	1964	3.75	7.50	15.00
Roulette					
❑ 4169	Practical Joker/Barbara	1959	5.00	10.00	20.00
❑ 4264	Kum Ba Yah/Cave Man Love	1960	5.00	10.00	20.00
Warner Bros.					
❑ 7299	Edgy/I'm Only Dreaming	1969		3.00	6.00

Blue Notes, The
(Some, but not all, were the group that became Harold Melvin and the Blue Notes)

Number	Title (A Side/B Side)	Year	VG	VG+	NM
3 Sons					
❑ 103	WPLJ/(B-side unknown)	1962	7.50	15.00	30.00
Dot					
❑ 15692	My Steady Girl/Mighty Lou	1958	6.25	12.50	25.00
	B-side by Henry Wilson				
❑ 15720	Darling of Mine/I Love Her So	1958	6.25	12.50	25.00
Josie					
❑ 800	If You Love Me/	1956	25.00	50.00	100.00
	There's Something in Your Eyes, Eloise				
❑ 814	Letters/With This Pen	1957	20.00	40.00	80.00
	As "Todd Randall and the Blue Notes"				
❑ 823	The Retribution Blues/Wagon Wheels	1957	20.00	40.00	80.00
Port					
❑ 70021	If You Love Me/There's Something in Your Eyes, Eloise	1958	15.00	30.00	60.00
Rama					
❑ 25	If You'll Be Mine/Too Hot to Handle	1953	50.00	100.00	200.00
Red Top					
❑ 135	My Hero/(B-side unknown)	1963	6.25	12.50	25.00
TNT					
❑ 150	Darling of Mine/I Love Her So	1958	7.50	15.00	30.00
Uni					
❑ 55132	Got Chills and Cold Thrills/Never Gonna Leave You	1969	3.00	6.00	12.00
❑ 55201	This Time Will Be Different/Lucky Me	1970	3.00	6.00	12.00
Val-Ue					
❑ 213	My Hero/(B-side unknown)	1960	12.50	25.00	50.00
❑ 215	O Holy Night/(B-side unknown)	1960	12.50	25.00	50.00

Blue Ridge Rangers, The
(John Fogerty in disguise as a one-man band)

Number		Title (A Side/B Side)	Year	VG	VG+	NM
Fantasy						
❑ 683		Blue Ridge Mountain Blues/	1972		2.50	5.00
		Have Thine Own Way, Lord				
❑ 683	PS	Blue Ridge Mountain Blues/	1972	3.75	7.50	15.00
		Have Thine Own Way, Lord				
❑ 689		Jambalaya (On the Bayou)/Workin' on a Building	1972		2.50	5.00
❑ 700		Hearts of Stone/Somewhere Listening	1973		2.50	5.00
❑ 710		Back in the Hills/You Don't Own Me	1973		2.50	5.00

Blue Things, The

Number	Title (A Side/B Side)	Year	VG	VG+	NM
RCA Victor					
❑ 47-8692	La Do Da Da/I Must Be Doing Something Wrong	1965	6.25	12.50	25.00
❑ 47-8860	Doll House/Man on the Street	1966	6.25	12.50	25.00
❑ 47-8998	Orange Rooftop of Your Mind/One Hour Cleaners	1966	6.25	12.50	25.00
❑ 47-9203	Twist and Shout/You Can Live in Our Tree	1967	6.25	12.50	25.00
❑ 47-9308	Yes, My Friend/Somebody Help Me	1967	6.25	12.50	25.00
Ruff					
❑ 1000	Mary Lou/Your Turn to Cry	1965	10.00	20.00	40.00
❑ 1002	Pretty Thing/Just Two Days Ago	1965	10.00	20.00	40.00

Blue Tones, The

Number	Title (A Side/B Side)	Year	VG	VG+	NM
Blue Jay					
❑ 101	I'll Love You Till the End of Time/(Instrumental)	1965	37.50	75.00	150.00
	Reissued on Swan 4200 by "The Royal Teens"				

Blue, Jay

Number	Title (A Side/B Side)	Year	VG	VG+	NM
Imperial					
❑ 5587	Get Off My Back/The Coolest	1959	20.00	40.00	80.00

Blues Magoos, The

Number	Title (A Side/B Side)	Year	VG	VG+	NM
ABC					
❑ 11226	Heartbreak Hotel/I Can Feel It (Feelin' Time)	1969	2.00	4.00	8.00

Number		Title (A Side/B Side)	Year	VG	VG+	NM
☐ 11250		Never Goin' Back to Georgia/Feelin' Time	1969	2.00	4.00	8.00
☐ 11283		Gulf Coast Bound/Sea Breeze Express	1970	2.00	4.00	8.00
Ganim						
☐ 1000		Who Do You Love/Let Your Love Ride	1968	10.00	20.00	40.00
Mercury						
☐ 72590		Tobacco Road/Sometimes I Think About You	1966	3.00	6.00	12.00
☐ 72622		(We Ain't Got) Nothin' Yet/Gotta Get Away	1966	3.75	7.50	15.00
☐ 72660		Pipe Dream/There's a Chance We Can Make It	1967	3.00	6.00	12.00
☐ 72660	PS	Pipe Dream/There's a Chance We Can Make It	1967	7.50	15.00	30.00
☐ 72692		One by One/Dante's Inferno	1967	3.00	6.00	12.00
☐ 72692	PS	One by One/Dante's Inferno	1967	7.50	15.00	30.00
☐ 72707		I Wanna Be There/Summer Is the Man	1967	2.50	5.00	10.00
☐ 72729		Life Is Just a Cher O'Bowlies/There She Goes	1967	2.50	5.00	10.00
☐ 72762		Jingle Bells/Santa Claus Is Coming to Town	1967	2.50	5.00	10.00
☐ 72838		I Can Hear the Grass Grow/Yellow Rose	1968	2.50	5.00	10.00
☐ 872 806-7		(We Ain't Got) Nothin' Yet/Pipedream	1989	3.00		
		Reissue				
Verve/Folkways						
☐ 5006		People Had No Faces/So I'm Wrong and You Are Right	1966		5.00	10.00	20.00
		As "The Bloos Magoos"				
☐ 5006		People Had No Faces/So I'm Wrong and You Are Right	1966	3.75	7.50	15.00
☐ 5044		People Had No Faces/So I'm Wrong and You Are Right	1967	3.75	7.50	15.00

Blues Project, The

Capitol

Number		Title (A Side/B Side)	Year	VG	VG+	NM
☐ 3374		Crazy Girl/Easy Lady	1972	2.00	4.00	8.00
MCA						
☐ 40154		Fly Away/Louisiana Blues	1973		2.50	5.00
Verve/Folkways						
☐ 5004		Back Door Man/Violets of Dawn	1966	3.75	7.50	15.00
☐ 5013		Catch the Wind/I Want to Be Your Driver	1966	3.75	7.50	15.00
☐ 5019		Where There's Smoke There's Fire/ Goin' Down Louisiana	1966	3.75	7.50	15.00
☐ 5019	PS	Where There's Smoke There's Fire/ Goin' Down Louisiana	1966	6.25	12.50	25.00
☐ 5032		I Can't Keep from Crying Sometimes/ The Way My Baby Walks	1966	3.75	7.50	15.00
☐ 5040		No Time Like the Right Time/Steve's Song	1967	3.00	6.00	12.00
Verve/Forecast						
☐ 5063		Gentle Dreams/Lost in the Shuffle	1967	3.00	6.00	12.00

Bo Pete

(Early Harry Nilsson)
Crusader

Number		Title (A Side/B Side)	Year	VG	VG+	NM
☐ 103		Baa Baa Black Sheep/Baa Baa Black Sheep (Part 2)	1964	7.50	15.00	30.00
Try						
☐ 501		Do You Wanna/Groovy Little Suzie	1964	10.00	20.00	40.00

Bob and Lucille

Ditto

Number		Title (A Side/B Side)	Year	VG	VG+	NM
☐ 121		What's the Password/Demon Lover	1962	20.00	40.00	80.00
☐ 126		Eeny-Meeny-Miney-Moe/The Big Kiss	1962	20.00	40.00	80.00
King						
☐ 5631		Eeny-Meeny-Miney-Moe/The Big Kiss	1962	7.50	15.00	30.00

Bob and Sheri

(A very early Brian Wilson production. "Bob" is Bob Norburg, later with The Survivors)
Safari

Number		Title (A Side/B Side)	Year	VG	VG+	NM
☐ 101		The Surfer Moon/Humpty Dumpty	1962	1,500	2,250	3,000
		Light blue label (other colors and colored vinyl are reproductions or counterfeits)				
☐ 101	DJ	The Surfer Moon/Humpty Dumpty	1962	250.00	500.00	1,000
		White label				

Bob B. Soxx and the Blue Jeans

Philles

Number		Title (A Side/B Side)	Year	VG	VG+	NM
☐ 107		Zip-a-Dee-Doo-Dah/Flip and Nitty	1962	5.00	10.00	20.00
☐ 110		Why Do Lovers Break Each Other's Heart?/ Dr. Kaplan's Office	1963	5.00	10.00	20.00
☐ 113		Not Too Young to Get Married/Annette	1963	5.00	10.00	20.00

Bobbettes, The

Atlantic

Number		Title (A Side/B Side)	Year	VG	VG+	NM
☐ 1144		Mr. Lee/Look at the Stars	1957	6.25	12.50	25.00
☐ 1159		Speedy/Come-a Come-a	1957	5.00	10.00	20.00
☐ 1181		Zoomy/Rock and Ree-Ah-Zole	1958	5.00	10.00	20.00
☐ 1194		The Dream/Um Bow Bow	1958	5.00	10.00	20.00
☐ 2027		Don't Say Goodnight/You Are My Sweetheart	1959	5.00	10.00	20.00
☐ 2069		I Shot Mr. Lee/Untrue Love	1960	7.50	15.00	30.00
Diamond						
☐ 133		Row, Row, Row/Teddy	1963	3.00	6.00	12.00
☐ 142		Close Your Eyes/ Somebody Bad Stole De Wedding Bell	1963	3.00	6.00	12.00
☐ 156		My Mamma Said/Sandman	1964	3.00	6.00	12.00
☐ 166		I'm Climbing a Mountain/In Paradise	1964	3.00	6.00	12.00

Number	Title (A Side/B Side)	Year	VG	VG+	NM
❏ 181	You Ain't Seen Nothing Yet/I'm Climbing a Mountain	1965	3.00	6.00	12.00
❏ 189	Love Is Blind/Teddy	1965	3.00	6.00	12.00

End

❏ 1093	Mr. Johnny Q/Teach Me Tonight	1961	5.00	10.00	20.00
❏ 1095	I Don't Like It Like That (Part 1)/	1961	5.00	10.00	20.00
	I Don't Like It Like That (Part 2)				

Gallant

❏ 1006	Oh, My Papa/I Cried	1960	5.00	10.00	20.00

Gone

❏ 5112	I Don't Like It Like That (Part 1)/Mr. Johnny Q	1961	3.75	7.50	15.00

Jubilee

❏ 5427	Over There/Loneliness	1962	3.00	6.00	12.00
❏ 5442	The Broken Heart/Mama, Papa	1962	3.00	6.00	12.00

King

❏ 5490	Oh My Papa/Dance With Me Georgie	1961	3.75	7.50	15.00
❏ 5551	Are You Satisfied/Looking for a Lover	1961	3.75	7.50	15.00
❏ 5623	I'm Stepping Out Tonight/My Dearest	1962	3.75	7.50	15.00

RCA Victor

❏ 47-8832	I've Gotta Face the World/Having Fun	1966	3.75	7.50	15.00
❏ 47-8983	It's All Over/Happy-Go-Lucky Me	1966	3.75	7.50	15.00

Triple-X

❏ 104	I Shot Mr. Lee/Billy	1960	5.00	10.00	20.00
❏ 106	Have Mercy Baby/Dance with Me Georgie	1960	5.00	10.00	20.00

Bobbie Jean

Sun

❏ 342	You Burned the Bridges/Cheaters Never Win	1960	5.00	10.00	20.00

Bobby and the Dukes

Philips

❏ 40293	Ah, Ah, Ah/Come Go with Me	1965	5.00	10.00	20.00

Boenzee Cryque

(With Rusty Young, later of Poco)

Chicory

❏ 406	Sky Gone Gray/Still in Love with You Baby	1966	7.50	15.00	30.00

Uni

❏ 55012	Sky Gone Gray/Still in Love with You Baby	1967	5.00	10.00	20.00
❏ 55022	Watch the Time/You Won't Believe It's True	1967	5.00	10.00	20.00

Bolotin, Michael

(Changed his name to Michael Bolton)

RCA

❏ PB-10650	You Make Me Feel Like Lovin' You/	1976	2.50	5.00	10.00
	If I Had Your Lovin'				

RCA Victor

❏ PB-10283	Your Love/Dream While You Can	1975	2.50	5.00	10.00

Bon Bons, The

(Later known as the Shangri-Las)

Coral

❏ 62402	What's Wrong with Ringo/Come On Baby	1964	15.00	30.00	60.00
❏ 62435	Everybody Wants My Boyfriend/Each Time	1964	12.50	25.00	50.00

Bon-Airs, The

King

❏ 4975	Stop the World/Bermuda	1956	7.50	15.00	30.00

Bonds, Gary U.S.

Atco

❏ 6689	The Star/You Need a Personal Manager	1969		3.00	6.00

Bluff City

❏ 221	My Love Song/Blue Grass	1974		2.50	5.00

Botanic

❏ 1002	I'm Glad You're Back/Funky Lies	1968	2.00	4.00	8.00

EMI America

❏ 8079	This Little Girl/Way Back When	1981		2.00	4.00
❏ 8079 PS	This Little Girl/Way Back When	1981		2.50	5.00
❏ 8089	Jole Blon/Just Like a Child	1981		2.00	4.00
❏ 8099	Your Love/Just Like a Child	1981		2.00	4.00
❏ 8117	Out of Work/Bring Her Back	1982		2.00	4.00
❏ 8117 PS	Out of Work/Bring Her Back	1982		2.50	5.00
❏ 8133	Love's on the Line/Way Back When	1982		2.00	4.00
❏ 8145	Turn the Music Down/Way Back When	1982		2.00	4.00

Legrand

❏ 1003	New Orleans/Please Forgive Me	1960	5.00	10.00	20.00
	Original lists artist as "By-U.S. Bonds"; purple label				
❏ 1003	New Orleans/Please Forgive Me	1960	3.75	7.50	15.00
	Gold and red label				
❏ 1005	Not Me/Give Me One More Chance	1961	5.00	10.00	20.00
	Artist listed as "U.S. Bonds"; purple label				

Number	Title (A Side/B Side)	Year	VG	VG+	NM
❑ 1005	Not Me/Give Me One More Chance	1961	3.75	7.50	15.00
	Gold and red label				
❑ 1008	Quarter to Three/Time Ole Story	1961	10.00	20.00	40.00
	Artist listed as "U.S. Bonds"; purple label				
❑ 1008	Quarter to Three/Time Ole Story	1961	3.75	7.50	15.00
	Artist listed as "U.S. Bonds"; gold and red label				
❑ 1008 PS	Quarter to Three/Time Ole Story	1961	7.50	15.00	30.00
❑ 1009	School Is Out/One Million Years	1961	5.00	10.00	20.00
	Artist listed as "U.S. Bonds"				
❑ 1009	School Is Out/One Million Years	1961	3.75	7.50	15.00
	Artist listed as "Gary (U.S.) Bonds" as are all later Legrand singles				
❑ 1009 PS	School Is Out/One Million Years	1961	7.50	15.00	30.00
❑ 1012	School Is In/Trip to the Moon	1961	3.75	7.50	15.00
❑ 1015	Dear Lady/Havin' So Much Fun	1961	5.00	10.00	20.00
	Original title of A-side				
❑ 1015	Dear Lady Twist/Havin' So Much Fun	1962	3.75	7.50	15.00
❑ 1018	Twist, Twist Senora/Food of Love	1962	3.75	7.50	15.00
❑ 1019	Seven Day Weekend/Gettin' a Groove	1962	3.75	7.50	15.00
❑ 1020	Copy Cat/I'll Change That Too	1962	3.75	7.50	15.00
❑ 1022	Mixed Up Faculty/I Dig This Station	1962	3.75	7.50	15.00
❑ 1025	Do the Limbo with Me/	1962	3.75	7.50	15.00
	Where Did That Naughty Little Girl Go				
❑ 1027	I Don't Wanta Wait/What a Dream	1963	3.00	6.00	12.00
❑ 1029	No More Homework/She's Alright	1963	3.00	6.00	12.00
❑ 1030	Perdido Part 1/Perdido Part 2	1963	3.00	6.00	12.00
❑ 1031	King Kong's Monkey/My Sweet Ruby Rose	1964	3.00	6.00	12.00
❑ 1032	The Music Goes Round and Round/Ella Is Yella	1964	3.00	6.00	12.00
❑ 1034	You Little Angel You/My Little Miss America	1964	3.00	6.00	12.00
❑ 1035	Oh Yeah, Oh Yeah/Let Me Go Lover	1965	2.50	5.00	10.00
❑ 1039	Beaches U.S.A./Do the Bumpsie	1965	2.50	5.00	10.00
❑ 1040	Take Me Back to New Orleans/I'm That Kind of Guy	1966	2.50	5.00	10.00
❑ 1041	Due to Circumstances Under My Control/Slow Motion	1966	2.50	5.00	10.00
❑ 1043	Send Her Back to Me/Workin' for My Baby	1967	2.50	5.00	10.00
❑ 1045	Call Me for Christmas/Mixed Up Faculty	1967	2.50	5.00	10.00
❑ 1046	Sarah Jane/What a Crazy World	1967	2.50	5.00	10.00

MCA

Number	Title (A Side/B Side)	Year	VG	VG+	NM
❑ 52335	One More Time Around the Block, Ophelia/ Deadline U.S.A.	1984		2.00	4.00
	B-side by Shalamar				
❑ 52400	New Orleans/Rhythm of the Rain	1984		2.00	4.00
	With Neil Sedaka				

Prodigal

Number	Title (A Side/B Side)	Year	VG	VG+	NM
❑ 0612	Grandma's Washboard/Believing You	1975		2.50	5.00

Sue

Number	Title (A Side/B Side)	Year	VG	VG+	NM
❑ 17	One Broken Heart/Can't Use You in My Business	1970		3.00	6.00

Bonnevilles, The

Barry

Number	Title (A Side/B Side)	Year	VG	VG+	NM
❑ 104	Lorraine/Zu Zu	1962	7.50	15.00	30.00

Capri

Number	Title (A Side/B Side)	Year	VG	VG+	NM
❑ 102	Give Me Your Love/Until You Say We're Through	1959	12.50	25.00	50.00

Coral

Number	Title (A Side/B Side)	Year	VG	VG+	NM
❑ 62273	Johnny/Freeway U.S.A.	1961	5.00	10.00	20.00

Munich

Number	Title (A Side/B Side)	Year	VG	VG+	NM
❑ 103	Lorraine/Zu Zu	1960	75.00	150.00	300.00
	Red label				
❑ 103	Lorraine/Zu Zu	1960	25.00	50.00	100.00
	Black label				

Whitehall

Number	Title (A Side/B Side)	Year	VG	VG+	NM
❑ 30002	I Do/Make Believe Lovin'	1959	7.50	15.00	30.00

Bonnie and the Treasures

Pablo

Number	Title (A Side/B Side)	Year	VG	VG+	NM
❑ 7014	Davey, I'm So Glad It Rained/The Lonely Surfer	1964	10.00	20.00	40.00
	B-side by the Mid-Americans				

Phi-Dan

Number	Title (A Side/B Side)	Year	VG	VG+	NM
❑ 5005	Home of the Brave/Our Song	1965	10.00	20.00	40.00

Bonniwell's Music Machine - See "Music Machine, The"

Bonniwell, T.S.

(Sean Bonniwell of the Music Machine)

Capitol

Number	Title (A Side/B Side)	Year	VG	VG+	NM
❑ 2551	Sleep/Where Am I to Go	1969	2.50	5.00	10.00

Bono, Sonny - See "Sonny"

Bonzo Dog Band, The

Imperial

Number	Title (A Side/B Side)	Year	VG	VG+	NM
❑ 66345	I'm the Urban Spaceman/Canyons of Your Mind	1969	3.75	7.50	15.00
	As "The Bonzo Dog Doo-Dah Band"				
❑ 66373	Mr. Apollo/Ready Made	1969	3.75	7.50	15.00
	As "The Bonzo Dog Doo-Dah Band"				

Number		Title (A Side/B Side)	Year	VG	VG+	NM

United Artists

❏ 50809		I'm the Urban Spaceman/Caverns of Your Mind	1971	2.50	5.00	10.00
❏ 50943	DJ	Slush (Mono)/Slush (Stereo)	1972	2.50	5.00	10.00
		May be promo only				

Booker T. and Priscilla

A&M

❏ 1298		The Wedding Song/She	1971		2.50	5.00
❏ 1487		Crippled Crow/Wild Fox	1973		2.50	5.00

Booker T. and the MG's

(Includes 45s by "Booker T."; "The MG's"; and "Booker T. Jones"; also see "Booker T. and Priscilla")

A&M

	Title (A Side/B Side)	Year	VG	VG+	NM
❏ 2100	Knockin' on Heaven's Door/Let's Go Dancin'	1978		2.00	4.00
❏ 2234	The Best of You/Let's Go Dancin'	1980		2.00	4.00
❏ 2279	Will You Be the One/Cookie	1980		2.00	4.00
❏ 2374	I Want You/You're the Best	1981		2.00	4.00
❏ 2394	Don't Stop Your Love/I Came to Love You	1982		2.00	4.00

Asylum

	Title (A Side/B Side)	Year	VG	VG+	NM
❏ 45392	Sticky Stuff/The Stick	1977		2.00	4.00
❏ 45424	Grab Bag/Reincarnation	1977		2.00	4.00

Columbia

	Title (A Side/B Side)	Year	VG	VG+	NM
❏ 77526	Cruisin'/Just My Imagination	1994		2.00	4.00

Epic

	Title (A Side/B Side)	Year	VG	VG+	NM
❏ 50031	Evergreen/Song for Casey	1974		2.00	4.00
❏ 50078	Front Street Rag/Mama Stewart	1975		2.00	4.00
❏ 50149	Life Is Funny/Tennessee Voodoo	1975		2.00	4.00

Stax

	Title (A Side/B Side)	Year	VG	VG+	NM
❏ 0001	Soul-Limbo/Heads Or Tails	1968	2.00	4.00	8.00
❏ 0013	Hang 'Em High/Over Easy	1968	2.00	4.00	8.00
❏ 0028	Time Is Tight/Johnny I Love You	1969	2.00	4.00	8.00
❏ 0037	Mrs. Robinson/Soul Clap '69	1969	2.00	4.00	8.00
❏ 0049	Slum Baby/Meditation	1969	2.00	4.00	8.00
❏ 0073	Something/Sunday Sermon	1970		3.00	6.00
❏ 0082	Melting Pot/Kinda Easy Like	1970		3.00	6.00
❏ 0169	Sugarcane/Blackride	1973		2.50	5.00
❏ 0200	Breezy/Neckbone	1974		2.50	5.00
❏ 127	Green Onions/Behave Yourself	1962	5.00	10.00	20.00
	Gray label				
❏ 127	Green Onions/Behave Yourself	1962	4.00	8.00	16.00
	Blue label				
❏ 131	Jellybread/Aw' Mercy	1963	3.00	6.00	12.00
❏ 134	Big Train/Home Grown	1963	3.00	6.00	12.00
❏ 134	Big Train/Burnt Biscuits	1963	3.00	6.00	12.00
❏ 137	Chinese Checkers/Plum Nellie	1963	3.00	6.00	12.00
❏ 142	Mo' Onions/Tic Tac Toe	1963	3.00	6.00	12.00
❏ 142	Mo' Onions/Fannie Mae	1963	3.00	6.00	12.00
❏ 153	Soul Dressing/MG Party	1964	2.50	5.00	10.00
❏ 161	Can't Be Still/Terrible Thing	1964	2.50	5.00	10.00
❏ 169	Boot-Leg/Outrage	1965	2.50	5.00	10.00
❏ 182	Red Beans and Rice/Be My Lady	1965	2.50	5.00	10.00
❏ 196	Booker-Loo/My Sweet Potato	1966	2.50	5.00	10.00
❏ 203	Jingle Bells/Winter Wonderland	1966	3.00	6.00	12.00
❏ 211	Hip-Hug-Her/Summertime	1967	2.50	5.00	10.00
❏ 224	Groovin'/Slim Jenkin's Place	1967	2.50	5.00	10.00
❏ 236	Silver Bells/Winter Snow	1967	3.00	6.00	12.00

Volt

	Title (A Side/B Side)	Year	VG	VG+	NM
❏ 102	Green Onions/Behave Yourself	1962	7.50	15.00	30.00

Booker, John Lee - See "Hooker, John Lee"

Boone, Pat

Buena Vista

		Title (A Side/B Side)	Year	VG	VG+	NM
❏ 487		Little Green Tree/Sounds of Christmas	1973		2.50	5.00

Capitol

		Title (A Side/B Side)	Year	VG	VG+	NM
❏ 2763		What Are You Doing the Rest of Your Life/ Now I'm Saved	1970		2.50	5.00
❏ 2860		Picking Up Pebbles/Oh My God	1970		2.50	5.00

Dot

		Title (A Side/B Side)	Year	VG	VG+	NM
❏ S-200	S	With the Wind and the Rain in Your Hair/ Good Rockin' Tonight	1959	10.00	20.00	40.00
❏ S-203	S	For a Penny/The Wang Dang Taffy Apple Tango	1959	10.00	20.00	40.00
❏ S-207	S	Twixt Twelve and Twenty/Rock Boll Weevil	1959	10.00	20.00	40.00
❏ S-211	S	Fools Hall of Fame/The Brightest Wishing Star	1959	10.00	20.00	40.00
❏ S-218	S	Beyond the Sunset/My Faithful Heart	1959	10.00	20.00	40.00
❏ S-220	S	(Welcome) New Lovers/Words	1960	10.00	20.00	40.00
❏ S-221	S	Walking the Floor Over You/Spring Rain	1960	10.00	20.00	40.00
❏ S-228	S	Delia Gone/Candy Street	1960	10.00	20.00	40.00
❏ 15338		Two Hearts/Tra La La	1955	5.00	10.00	20.00
❏ 15377		Ain't That a Shame/Tennessee Saturday Night	1955	5.00	10.00	20.00
❏ 15422		At My Front Door/No Other Arms	1955	5.00	10.00	20.00
❏ 15435		Gee Whittakers!/Take the Time	1955	5.00	10.00	20.00
❏ 15443		Tutti Frutti/I'll Be Home	1956	5.00	10.00	20.00
❏ 15457		Long Tall Sally/Just As Long As I'm with You	1956	5.00	10.00	20.00
❏ 15472		I Almost Lost My Mind/I'm in Love with You	1956	5.00	10.00	20.00

Number		Title (A Side/B Side)	Year	VG	VG+	NM
☐ 15490		Friendly Persuasion (Thee I Love)/Chains of Love	1956	5.00	10.00	20.00
		Original on maroon label				
☐ 15490		Friendly Persuasion (Thee I Love)/Chains of Love	1956	3.75	7.50	15.00
		Second pressing on black label				
☐ 15521		Don't Forbid Me/Anastasia	1956	3.75	7.50	15.00
☐ 15545		Why Baby Why/I'm Waiting Just for You	1957	3.75	7.50	15.00
☐ 15570		Love Letters in the Sand/Bernardine	1957	3.75	7.50	15.00
☐ 15570	PS	Love Letters in the Sand/Bernardine	1957	7.50	15.00	30.00
☐ 15602		Remember You're Mine/There's a Gold Mine in the Sky	1957	3.75	7.50	15.00
☐ 15660		April Love/	1957	3.75	7.50	15.00
		When the Swallows Come Back to Capistrano				
☐ 15690		It's Too Soon to Know/A Wonderful Time Up There	1958		7.50	15.00
☐ 15750		Sugar Moon/Cherie, I Love You	1958	3.75	7.50	15.00
☐ 15750	PS	Sugar Moon/Cherie, I Love You	1958	7.50	15.00	30.00
☐ 15785		If Dreams Came True/That's How Much I Love You	1958	3.75	7.50	15.00
☐ 15825		Gee, But It's Lonely/For My Good Fortune	1958	3.75	7.50	15.00
☐ 15840		I'll Remember Tonight/The Mardi Gras March	1958	3.75	7.50	15.00
☐ 15840	PS	I'll Remember Tonight/The Mardi Gras March	1958	7.50	15.00	30.00
☐ 15888	M	With the Wind and the Rain in Your Hair/	1959	3.75	7.50	15.00
		Good Rockin' Tonight				
☐ 15914	M	For a Penny/The Wang Dang Taffy Apple Tango	1959	3.75	7.50	15.00
☐ 15955	M	Twixt Twelve and Twenty/Rock Boll Weevil	1959	3.75	7.50	15.00
☐ 15955	PS	Twixt Twelve and Twenty/Rock Boll Weevil	1959	7.50	15.00	30.00
☐ 15982	M	Fools Hall of Fame/The Brightest Wishing Star	1959	3.75	7.50	15.00
☐ 15982	PS	Fools Hall of Fame/The Brightest Wishing Star	1959	7.50	15.00	30.00
☐ 16006	M	Beyond the Sunset/My Faithful Heart	1959	3.75	7.50	15.00
☐ 16015		To the Center of the Earth Part 1/Part 2	1959	5.00	10.00	20.00
☐ 16028		Ain't That a Shame/I'll Be Home	1960	2.50	5.00	10.00
☐ 16033		I Almost Lost My Mind/Friendly Persuasion	1960	2.50	5.00	10.00
☐ 16034		Don't Forbid Me/April Love	1960	2.50	5.00	10.00
☐ 16035		Love Letters in the Sand/A Wonderful Time Up There	1960	2.50	5.00	10.00
☐ 16048		(Welcome) New Lovers/Words	1960	3.00	6.00	12.00
☐ 16048	PS	(Welcome) New Lovers/Words	1960	5.00	10.00	20.00
☐ 16073		Walking the Floor Over You/Spring Rain	1960	3.00	6.00	12.00
☐ 16073	PS	Walking the Floor Over You/Spring Rain	1960	5.00	10.00	20.00
☐ 16122		Delia Gone/Candy Street	1960	3.00	6.00	12.00
☐ 16152		Dear John/Alabam	1960	3.00	6.00	12.00
☐ 16176		The Exodus Song (This Land Is Mine)/	1961	3.00	6.00	12.00
		There's a Moon Out Tonight				
☐ 16190		Cherry Pink and Apple Blossom White/On Both Sides	1961	3.00	6.00	12.00
☐ 16209		Moody River/A Thousand Years	1961	3.75	7.50	15.00
☐ 16244		Big Cold Wind/That's My Desire	1961	3.00	6.00	12.00
☐ 16278		Louella/(B-side unknown)	1961			*Unreleased?*
☐ 16284		Johnny Will/Just Let Me Dream	1961	3.00	6.00	12.00
☐ 16312		I'll See You in My Dreams/Pictures in the Fire	1961	3.00	6.00	12.00
☐ 16349		Quando, Quando, Quando (Tell Me When)/	1962	2.50	5.00	10.00
		Willing and Eager				
☐ 16368		Speedy Gonzales/The Locket	1962	3.00	6.00	12.00
☐ 16391		The Lonely Gys/Lover's Lane	1962	2.50	5.00	10.00
☐ 16416		In the Room/Mexican Joe	1963	2.50	5.00	10.00
☐ 16439		Days of Wine and Roses/Meditation	1963	2.50	5.00	10.00
☐ 16474		Always You and Me/Main Attraction	1963	2.50	5.00	10.00
☐ 16494		Tie Me Kangaroo Down Sport/I Feel Like Crying	1963	2.50	5.00	10.00
☐ 16498		Amore Baciami/Gondoli Gondola	1963	2.50	5.00	10.00
☐ 16498		Main Attraction/Si Si Si	1963	2.50	5.00	10.00
☐ 16525		Love Me/Mr. Moon	1963	2.50	5.00	10.00
☐ 16547		Santa's Coming in a Whirleybird/Oh Holy Night	1963	2.50	5.00	10.00
☐ 16559		Some Enchanted Evening/That's Me	1963	2.50	5.00	10.00
☐ 16576		I Like What You Do/Never Put It in Writing	1964	2.00	4.00	8.00
☐ 16598		I Understand (Just How You Feel)/Rosemarie	1964	2.00	4.00	8.00
☐ 16626		Side by Side/I'll Never Be Free	1964	2.00	4.00	8.00
		By "Pat and Shirley Boone"				
☐ 16641		Sincerely/Don't You Just Know It	1964	2.00	4.00	8.00
☐ 16658		Beach Girl/Little Honda	1964	7.50	15.00	30.00
☐ 16668		Goodbye, Charlie/Love, Who Needs It	1964	2.00	4.00	8.00
☐ 16684		I'd Rather Die Young/I Want It That Way	1964	2.00	4.00	8.00
☐ 16699		Blueberry Hill/Heartaches	1965	2.00	4.00	8.00
☐ 16707		Baby Elephant Walk/Say Goodbye	1965	2.00	4.00	8.00
☐ 16728		Pearly Shells/Crazy Arms	1965	2.00	4.00	8.00
☐ 16738		Mickey Mouse/Time Marches On	1965	2.00	4.00	8.00
☐ 16738		Mickey Mouse/(Welcome) New Lovers	1965	2.00	4.00	8.00
☐ 16754		Rainy Days/With My Eyes Wide Open I'm Dreaming	1965	2.00	4.00	8.00
☐ 16785		I Love You So Much It Hurts/	1965	2.00	4.00	8.00
		Meet Me Tonight in Dreamland				
☐ 16808		A Man Alone/Run to Me, Baby	1966	2.00	4.00	8.00
☐ 16825		As Tears Go By/Judith	1966	2.00	4.00	8.00
☐ 16836		It Seems Like Yesterday/	1966	2.00	4.00	8.00
		Well Remembered, Highly Thought Of Love Affair				
☐ 16871		Five Miles from Home/	1966	2.00	4.00	8.00
		Don't Put Your Feet in the Lemonade				
☐ 16903		Wrath of Grapes/You Don't Need Me Anymore	1966	2.00	4.00	8.00
☐ 16933		Wish You Were Here, Buddy/Love for Love	1966	2.00	4.00	8.00
☐ 16998		Hurry Sundown/	1967		3.00	6.00
		What If They Gave a War and Nobody Came				
☐ 17018		Have You Heard (It's All Over)/Me	1967		3.00	6.00
☐ 17027		In the Mirror of Your Mind/Swanee Is a River	1967		3.00	6.00
☐ 17045		By the Time I Get to Phoenix/Ride Ride Ride	1967		3.00	6.00
☐ 17056		The Green Kentucky Hills of Home/	1967		3.00	6.00
		You Mean All the World to Me				

Number		Title (A Side/B Side)	Year	VG	VG+	NM
❑ 17076		It's a Happening World/Emily	1968		3.00	6.00
❑ 17098		500 Miles/I Had a Dream	1968		3.00	6.00
❑ 17122		Gonna Find Me a Bluebird/Deafening Roar of Silence	1968		3.00	6.00
❑ 17156		Beyond One Memory/September Blues	1968		3.00	6.00

Hitsville

❑ 6037		It's Gone/Texas Woman	1976		2.00	4.00
❑ 6042		Oklahoma Sunshine/Won't Be Home Tonight	1976		2.00	4.00
❑ 6047		Country Days and Country Nights/ Lovelight Comes a-Shining	1976		2.00	4.00
❑ 6054		Colorado Country Morning/ Don't Want to Fall Away from You	1977		2.00	4.00

Lion

❑ 106		Mr. Blue/Song of the Children of Israel (Exodus)	1972		2.50	5.00
		With the Boone Girls				
❑ 119		I Believe in Music/Children Learn What They Live	1972		2.50	5.00
		With the Boone Family				
❑ 126		Empty Chairs/ If You're Gonna Make a Fool of Somebody	1972		2.50	5.00

M.C.

❑ 5001		Whatever Happened to the Good Old Honky Tonk/ Ain't Going Down in the Ground Before My Time	1977		2.00	4.00

Melodyland

❑ 6001		Candy Lips/Young Girl	1974		2.00	4.00
❑ 6005		Indiana Girl/Young Girl	1975		2.00	4.00
❑ 6018		I'd Do It with You/Yester-Me, Yester-You, Yesterday	1975		2.00	4.00
❑ 6029		Glory Train/U.F.O.	1976		2.00	4.00

MGM

❑ 14242		All for the Love of Sunshine/M.I.A-P.O.W.	1971		2.50	5.00
❑ 14282		C'mon, Give a Hand/Where There's a Heartache	1971		2.50	5.00
❑ 14470		I Saw the Light/Great Speckled Bird	1972		2.50	5.00
❑ 14521		Hayden Carter/Tying the Pieces Together	1973		2.00	4.00
❑ 14601		Everything Begins and Ends with You/Golden Rocket	1973		2.00	4.00

Republic

❑ 7049		My Heart Belongs to You/Until You Tell Me So	1953	6.25	12.50	25.00
❑ 7062		Remember to Be Mine/Half Way Chance with You	1953	6.25	12.50	25.00
❑ 7084		I Need Someone/Loving You Madly	1954	6.25	12.50	25.00
❑ 7119		My Heart Belongs to You/I Need Someone	1955	5.00	10.00	20.00

Tetragrammaton

❑ 1516		July, You're a Woman/Break My Mind	1969		2.50	5.00
❑ 1529		Never Goin' Back/What's Gnawing at Me	1969		2.50	5.00
❑ 1540		You Win Again/Good Morning, Dear	1969		2.50	5.00

Warner Bros.

❑ 49097		Midnight/Can You Feel the Love	1979			3.00
		By "Pat and Shirley Boone"				
❑ 49255		Hostage Prayer/Love's Got a Way of Hanging On	1980			3.00
❑ 49596		Colorado Country Morning/ Whatever Happened to the Good Old Honky Tonk	1980			3.00
❑ 49691		Won't Be Home Tonight/Throw It Away	1981			3.00

Botkin, Perry, Jr.

A&M

❑ 1856		Nadia's Theme (The Young and the Restless)/ Down the Line	1976	2.50	5.00	10.00
		Original issue; Barry DeVorzon's name was added after he threatened legal action				
❑ 1856	PS	Nadia's Theme (The Young and the Restless)/ Down the Line	1976	2.50	5.00	10.00
		Sleeve with only Perry Botkin Jr.'s name on it (see above listing)				
❑ 1967		Looking for Home/Lovers	1977		2.00	4.00
❑ 1990		Bridges/Love Theme from Aspen	1977		2.00	4.00

Decca

❑ 30912		The Execution Theme/Waltz of the Hunter	1959	3.00	6.00	12.00

MGM

❑ 14357		Soley Soley/(B-side unknown)	1972		2.50	5.00
		As "Perry Botkin, Inc."				
❑ 14379		Bless the Beasts and Children/Lost	1972		2.50	5.00

Pride

❑ 1005		Journey to Moscow/Ellie's Theme	1972		2.50	5.00

Valiant

❑ 719		Where Does Love Go (Instrumental)/ Where Does Love Go (Vocal)	1965	2.00	4.00	8.00
		B-side by Charles Boyer				
❑ 6025		Careless Love/Wabash Cannonball	1962	2.50	5.00	10.00

Bowen, Jimmy

Capehart

❑ 5005		Teenage Dreamworld/It's Against the Law	1962	5.00	10.00	20.00
❑ 5005	PS	Teenage Dreamworld/It's Against the Law	1962	12.50	25.00	50.00

Crest

❑ 1085		Don't Drop It/Somebody to Love	1961	5.00	10.00	20.00

Reprise

❑ 0264		The Biggest Lover in Town/The Big Bus	1964	2.50	5.00	10.00
❑ 0358		The Golden Eagle/Spanish Cricket	1965	2.50	5.00	10.00

Number		Title (A Side/B Side)	Year	VG	VG+	NM
☐ 0450		Wonder Mother/Captain Gorgeous	1966	2.50	5.00	10.00
☐ 0592		Raunchy/It's Such a Pretty World Today	1967	2.50	5.00	10.00

Roulette

Number		Title (A Side/B Side)	Year	VG	VG+	NM
☐ 4001		I'm Stickin' With You/Ever Lovin' Fingers	1957	5.00	10.00	20.00
		With the Rhythm Orchids				
☐ 4010		Warm Up to Me Baby/I Trusted You	1957	5.00	10.00	20.00
☐ 4017		Ever Since That Night/Don't Tell Me Your Troubles	1957	5.00	10.00	20.00
☐ 4023		Cross Over/It's Shameful	1957	5.00	10.00	20.00
☐ 4057		Can She Kiss/Keeping You	1958	5.00	10.00	20.00
☐ 4083		By the Light of the Silvery Moon/The Two Step	1958	5.00	10.00	20.00
☐ 4102		My Kind of Woman/Blue Moon	1958	5.00	10.00	20.00
☐ 4122		Always Faithful/Wish I Were Tied to You	1958	5.00	10.00	20.00
☐ 4175		You're Just Wasting Your Time/Walkin' on Air	1959	5.00	10.00	20.00
☐ 4224		Oh Yeah! Oh Yeah! Mm Mm/Your Loving Arms	1960	5.00	10.00	20.00

Triple D

Number		Title (A Side/B Side)	Year	VG	VG+	NM
☐ 798		I'm Stickin' With You/Party Doll	1956	250.00	500.00	1,000
		B-side by Buddy Knox				

Bowie, David

Backstreet

Number		Title (A Side/B Side)	Year	VG	VG+	NM
☐ 52024		Cat People/Paul's Theme	1982			3.00
		B-side by Georgio Moroder				
☐ 52024	PS	Cat People/Paul's Theme	1982			3.00

Deram

Number		Title (A Side/B Side)	Year	VG	VG+	NM
☐ 85009		Rubber Band/There Is a Happy Land	1967	12.50	25.00	50.00
☐ 85016		Love You Till Tuesday/Did You Ever Have a Dream	1967	12.50	25.00	50.00

EMI America

Number		Title (A Side/B Side)	Year	VG	VG+	NM
☐ 43020		Time Will Crawl/Time Will Crawl	1987			3.00
☐ 43020	PS	Time Will Crawl/Time Will Crawl	1987	2.50	5.00	10.00
		Easily Bowie's scarcest EMI picture sleeve				
☐ 43031		Never Let Me Down/Never Let Me Down	1987			3.00
☐ 43031	PS	Never Let Me Down/Never Let Me Down	1987			3.00
☐ 8158		Let's Dance/Cat People (Putting Out Fire)	1983			3.00
☐ 8158	PS	Let's Dance/Cat People (Putting Out Fire)	1983			3.00
☐ 8165		China Girl/Shake It	1983			3.00
☐ 8165	PS	China Girl/Shake It	1983	2.50	5.00	
☐ 8177		Modern Love/Modern Love (Live)	1983			3.00
☐ 8177	PS	Modern Love/Modern Love (Live)	1983			3.00
☐ 8190		Without You/Criminal Law	1984			3.00
☐ 8190	PS	Without You/Criminal Law	1984			3.00
☐ 8231		Blue Jean/Dancin' with the Big Boys	1984	2.00	4.00	8.00
		First pressing on blue vinyl				
☐ 8231		Blue Jean/Dancin' with the Big Boys	1984			2.00
☐ 8231	PS	Blue Jean/Dancin' with the Big Boys	1984			2.00
		Both colors of vinyl have the same picture sleeve				
☐ 8246		Tonight/Tumble and Twirl	1984			3.00
☐ 8246	PS	Tonight/Tumble and Twirl	1984			3.00
☐ 8251		This Is Not America/(Instrumental)	1984			3.00
☐ 8251	PS	This Is Not America/(Instrumental)	1984			3.00
		With the Pat Metheny Group				
☐ 8271		Loving the Alien/Don't Look Down	1985			3.00
☐ 8271	PS	Loving the Alien/Don't Look Down	1985		2.50	5.00
		Fold-out poster sleeve				
☐ 8308		Absolute Beginners/(B-side unknown)	1986			3.00
☐ 8308	PS	Absolute Beginners/(B-side unknown)	1986			3.00
☐ 8323		Underground/(instrumental)	1986			3.00
☐ 8323	PS	Underground/(instrumental)	1986			3.00
☐ 8380		Day In Day Out/Day In Day Out	1987			3.00
☐ 8380	PS	Day In Day Out/Day In Day Out	1987			3.00

London

Number		Title (A Side/B Side)	Year	VG	VG+	NM
☐ 20079		The Laughing Gnome/ The Gospel According to Tony Day	1973	12.50	25.00	50.00

Mercury

Number		Title (A Side/B Side)	Year	VG	VG+	NM
☐ 72949		Space Oddity/Wild-Eyed Boy from Freecloud	1969	12.50	25.00	50.00
☐ 73075		Memory of a Free Festival Part 1/Part 2	1970	25.00	50.00	100.00
☐ 73173	DJ	All the Madmen (mono/stereo)	1971	25.00	50.00	100.00
		May be promo only				

RCA

Number		Title (A Side/B Side)	Year	VG	VG+	NM
☐ PB-10664		TVC 15/We Are the Dead	1976		2.50	5.00
☐ PB-10736		Stay/Word on a Wing	1976		2.50	5.00
☐ PB-10905		Sound and Vision/A New Career in a New Town	1977		2.50	5.00
☐ GB-10938		Fame/Golden Years	1977			3.00
		Gold Standard Series issue				
☐ PB-11017		Be My Wife/The Speed of Life	1977		2.50	5.00
☐ PB-11121		Heroes/V-2 Schneider	1977		2.50	5.00
☐ PB-11190		Beauty and the Beast/Sense of Doubt	1978		2.50	5.00
☐ PB-11585		Boys Keep Swinging/Fantastic Voyage	1979		2.50	5.00
☐ PB-11661		D.J./Fantastic Voyage	1979		2.50	5.00
☐ PB-11724		Look Back in Anger/Repetition	1979		2.50	5.00
☐ PB-11887		John I'm Only Dancing 1972/Golden Years	1980		2.50	5.00
☐ PB-12078		Ashes to Ashes/It's No Game	1980		2.50	5.00
☐ PB-12078	PS	Ashes to Ashes/It's No Game	1980		2.50	5.00
☐ JH-12078	PS	Ashes to Ashes/It's No Game	1980	3.75	7.50	15.00
		Promo-only sleeve of Bowie holding a shoe and looking down at it				

Number		Title (A Side/B Side)	Year	VG	VG+	NM
❏ JE-12087	DJ	Fashion/It's No Game/Teenage Wildlife	1980	100.00	200.00	400.00
❏ PB-12134		Fashion/Scream Like a Baby	1980		2.50	5.00
❏ PB-12134	PS	Fashion/Scream Like a Baby	1980		2.50	5.00
❏ PH-13400		Peace on Earth-Little Drummer Boy/Fantastic Voyage	1982		2.50	5.00
		A-side with Bing Crosby				
❏ PH-13400	PS	Peace on Earth-Little Drummer Boy/Fantastic Voyage	1982	2.50	5.00	10.00
		A-side with Bing Crosby				
❏ PB-13660		White Light-White Heat/Cracked Actor	1983		2.50	5.00
❏ PB-13769		1984/TVC 15	1984		2.50	5.00

RCA Victor

Number		Title (A Side/B Side)	Year	VG	VG+	NM
❏ 74-0605		Changes/Andy Warhol	1971	2.50	5.00	10.00
		Orange label (original)				
❏ 74-0605		Changes/Andy Warhol	1974		3.00	6.00
		Tan or gray label				
❏ 74-0719		Starman/Suffragette City	1972		3.00	6.00
❏ 74-0719	PS	Starman/Suffragette City	1972	7.50	15.00	30.00
❏ 74-0838		The Jean Genie/Hang On to Yourself	1972		3.00	6.00
❏ 74-0876		Space Oddity/The Man Who Sold the World	1973		3.00	6.00
❏ 74-0876	PS	Space Oddity/The Man Who Sold the World	1973	5.00	10.00	20.00
❏ APBO-0001		Time/The Prettiest Star	1973		3.00	6.00
❏ APBO-0001	PS	Time/The Prettiest Star	1973	150.00	300.00	600.00
❏ APBO-0028		Let's Spend the Night Together/Lady Grinning Soul	1973		3.00	6.00
❏ APBO-0160		Sorrow/Amsterdam	1973		3.00	6.00
❏ APBO-0287		Rebel Rebel/Lady Grinning Soul	1974	2.50	5.00	10.00
		All copies contain an alternate mix of "Rebel, Rebel"				
❏ APBO-0293		Diamond Dogs/Holy Holy	1974	2.50	5.00	10.00
		Part of U.S. numbering system, but released only outside the U.S.				
❏ PB-10026		1984/Queen Bitch	1974		3.00	6.00
❏ PB-10105		Rock and Roll with Me/Panic in Detroit	1974		3.00	6.00
❏ PB-10152		Young Americans/Knock on Wood	1975		3.00	6.00
❏ PB-10320		Fame/Right	1975		3.00	6.00
		John Lennon co-wrote and appears on A-side				
❏ PB-10441		Golden Years/Can You Hear Me	1975		3.00	6.00
❏ GB-10468		Changes/Andy Warhol	1975		2.00	4.00
		Gold Standard Series issue				
❏ GB-10469		Young Americans/Knock on Wood	1975		2.00	4.00
		Gold Standard Series issue				
❏ GB-10470		Space Oddity/The Man Who Sold the World	1975		2.00	4.00
		Gold Standard Series issue				

Warner Bros.

Number		Title (A Side/B Side)	Year	VG	VG+	NM
❏ 5815		Can't Stop Thinking About Me/And I Say to Myself	1966	125.00	250.00	500.00
		As "David Bowie and the Lower Third"				

EPs
RCA Victor

Number		Title (A Side/B Side)	Year	VG	VG+	NM
❏ 45-103	DJ	David Bowie	1972	5.00	10.00	20.00
❏ 45-103	PS	David Bowie	1972	5.00	10.00	20.00

Bowie, David, and Mick Jagger
(Also see individual listings)
EMI America

Number		Title (A Side/B Side)	Year	VG	VG+	NM
❏ 8288		Dancing in the Street/(instrumental)	1985			3.00
❏ 8288	PS	Dancing in the Street/(instrumental)	1985			3.00

Box Tops, The
Arista

Number		Title (A Side/B Side)	Year	VG	VG+	NM
❏ 9488		Sweet Cream Ladies/Neon Rainbow	1986			3.00
		"Flashback" oldies series				

Bell

Number		Title (A Side/B Side)	Year	VG	VG+	NM
❏ 865		Come On Home/You Keep Tightening Up on Me	1970	2.00	4.00	8.00
❏ 923		Let Me Go/Got to Hold On to You	1970	2.00	4.00	8.00
❏ 981		King's Highway/Since I've Been Gone	1971	2.00	4.00	8.00

Hi

Number		Title (A Side/B Side)	Year	VG	VG+	NM
❏ 2228		It's All Over/Sugar Creek Woman	1972		3.00	6.00
❏ 2242		Hold On Girl/Angel	1973		3.00	6.00

Mala

Number		Title (A Side/B Side)	Year	VG	VG+	NM
❏ 565		The Letter/Happy Times	1967	3.00	6.00	12.00
❏ 580		Neon Rainbow/Everything I Am	1967	2.50	5.00	10.00
❏ 593		Cry Like a Baby/The Door You Closed to Me	1968	3.00	6.00	12.00
❏ 12,005		Choo Choo Train/Fields of Clover	1968	2.50	5.00	10.00
❏ 12,017		I Met Her in Church/People Gonna Talk	1968	2.50	5.00	10.00
❏ 12,035		Sweet Cream Ladies, Forward March/I See Only Sunshine	1968	2.50	5.00	10.00
❏ 12,038		I Shall Be Released/I Must Be the Devil	1969	2.50	5.00	10.00
❏ 12,040		Soul Deep/The Happy Song	1969	2.50	5.00	10.00
❏ 12,042		Turn On a Dream/Together	1969	2.50	5.00	10.00

Philco

Number		Title (A Side/B Side)	Year	VG	VG+	NM
❏ HP-27		The Letter/Happy Times	1968	5.00	10.00	20.00
		4-inch flexi-disc in "Philco Hip-Pocket Record" series (price includes sleeve)				

Sphere Sound

Number		Title (A Side/B Side)	Year	VG	VG+	NM
❏ 77001		The Letter/Happy Times	1969	2.50	5.00	10.00
		Blue label; reissue				

Number		Title (A Side/B Side)	Year	VG	VG+	NM
❏ 77001		The Letter/Happy Times	1970	2.00	4.00	8.00
		Silver label; reissue				
❏ 77002		Cry Like a Baby/The Door You Closed to Me	1970	2.00	4.00	8.00
		Silver label; reissue				

Stax

Number		Title (A Side/B Side)	Year	VG	VG+	NM
❏ 0199		It's Gonna Be O.K./Willobee and Dale	1974		3.00	6.00

Boyce, Tommy
(Also see "Boyce, Tommy, and Bobby Hart"; "Dolenz, Jones, Boyce and Hart")

A&M

Number		Title (A Side/B Side)	Year	VG	VG+	NM
❏ 809		Sunday, The Day Before Monday/ The Green Grass (Is Turning Brown)	1966	3.75	7.50	15.00
❏ 826		In Case the Wind Should Blow/ Simon Smith and the Amazing Dancing Bear	1966	6.25	12.50	25.00

Capitol

Number		Title (A Side/B Side)	Year	VG	VG+	NM
❏ 3136		Alice My Sweet/Eve Laurain	1971		2.50	5.00

Colpix

Number		Title (A Side/B Side)	Year	VG	VG+	NM
❏ 794		Let's Go Where the Action Is/(Instrumental)	1966	5.00	10.00	20.00

Dot

Number		Title (A Side/B Side)	Year	VG	VG+	NM
❏ 16117		The Gypsy Song/Give Me the Clue	1960	5.00	10.00	20.00

MGM

Number		Title (A Side/B Side)	Year	VG	VG+	NM
❏ 13400		Pretty Thing (You Look Out of Sight Tonight)/ I Don't Have to Worry 'Bout You	1965	3.75	7.50	15.00
❏ 13429		Little Suzy Somethin'/Pee's N' Que's	1965	3.75	7.50	15.00

R-Dell

Number		Title (A Side/B Side)	Year	VG	VG+	NM
❏ 111		Betty Jean/I'm Not Sure	1960	6.25	12.50	25.00

RCA Victor

Number		Title (A Side/B Side)	Year	VG	VG+	NM
❏ 47-7975		Along Came Linda/You Look So Lonely	1961	5.00	10.00	20.00
❏ 47-8025		Come Here Joanne/The Way I Used to Do	1962	5.00	10.00	20.00
❏ 47-8074		I'll Remember Carol/Too Late for Tears	1962	5.00	10.00	20.00
❏ 47-8126		Have You Had a Change of Heart/ Sweet Little Baby, I Care	1963	5.00	10.00	20.00
❏ 47-8208		Don't Be Afraid/A Million Things to Say	1963	5.00	10.00	20.00

Wow

Number		Title (A Side/B Side)	Year	VG	VG+	NM
❏ 345		Is It True/Little One	1961	5.00	10.00	20.00

Boyce, Tommy, and Bobby Hart
(Also see "Boyce, Tommy"; "Dolenz, Jones, Boyce and Hart")

A&M

Number		Title (A Side/B Side)	Year	VG	VG+	NM
❏ 858		Out and About/My Little Chickadee	1967	2.50	5.00	10.00
❏ 858	PS	Out and About/My Little Chickadee	1967	5.00	10.00	20.00
❏ 874		Sometimes She's a Little Girl/Love Every Day	1967	2.50	5.00	10.00
❏ 893		I Wonder What She's Doing Tonight/The Ambushers	1967	3.00	6.00	12.00
❏ 893	PS	I Wonder What She's Doing Tonight/The Ambushers	1967	5.00	10.00	20.00
❏ 919		Goodbye Baby (I Don't Want to See You Cry)/ Where Angels Go, Trouble Follows	1968	2.50	5.00	10.00
❏ 919	PS	Goodbye Baby (I Don't Want to See You Cry)/ Where Angels Go, Trouble Follows	1968	5.00	10.00	20.00
❏ 948		Alice Long (You're Still My Favorite Girlfriend)/ P.O. Box 9847	1968	2.50	5.00	10.00
❏ 948	PS	Alice Long (You're Still My Favorite Girlfriend)/ P.O. Box 9847	1968	5.00	10.00	20.00
❏ 993		We're All Going to the Same Place/6 + 6	1968	2.50	5.00	10.00
❏ 1017		Maybe Somebody Heard/ It's All Happening on the Inside	1969	2.00	4.00	8.00
❏ 1031		L.U.V. (Let Us Vote)/I Wanna Be Free	1969	2.00	4.00	8.00

Aquarian

Number		Title (A Side/B Side)	Year	VG	VG+	NM
❏ 380		I'll Blow You a Kiss in the Wind/Smilin'	1970		2.00	4.00
❏ 380	PS	I'll Blow You a Kiss in the Wind/Smilin'	1970		3.00	6.00

Boyfriends, The
(Also known as the Five Discs)

Kapp

Number		Title (A Side/B Side)	Year	VG	VG+	NM
❏ 569		Let's Fall in Love/Oh Lana	1964	25.00	50.00	100.00

Boze, Calvin

Aladdin

Number		Title (A Side/B Side)	Year	VG	VG+	NM
❏ 3045		Waiting and Drinking/If You Ever Had the Blues	1950	37.50	75.00	150.00
❏ 3055		Safronia Blues/Angel City Blues	1950	37.50	75.00	150.00
❏ 3065		Lizzie Lou/Lizzie Lou (Part 2)	1950	37.50	75.00	150.00
❏ 3072		Stinkin' from Drinkin'/Look Out for Tomorrow Today	1950	25.00	50.00	100.00
❏ 3079		Beat Street on Saturday Night/ Choo Choo Ch'Boogieing My Baby Back Home	1951	25.00	50.00	100.00
❏ 3086		Slippin' and Slidin'/Baby, You're Tops with Me	1951	25.00	50.00	100.00
❏ 3100		I've Got News for You/I Can't Stop Crying	1951	20.00	40.00	80.00
❏ 3110		I'm Gonna Steam Off the Stamp/Fish Tail	1952	20.00	40.00	80.00
❏ 3122		Hey, Lawdy Miss Clawdy/My Friend Told Me	1952	20.00	40.00	80.00
❏ 3132		Good Time Sue/Keep Your Nose Out of My Business	1952	15.00	30.00	60.00
❏ 3142		The Blue Tango/The Glory of Love	1952	15.00	30.00	60.00
❏ 3143		Blue Shuffle/Popside	1952	15.00	30.00	60.00
❏ 3147		Looped/Blow Man Blow	1952	15.00	30.00	60.00
❏ 3160		Havin' a Time/Shamrock	1953	12.50	25.00	50.00
❏ 3181		That Other Woman/Shoot De Pistol	1953	12.50	25.00	50.00

Number		Title (A Side/B Side)	Year	VG	VG+	NM
Imperial						
❏ 5844		Shamrock/Safronia B	1962	3.00	6.00	12.00
Bradshaw, Tiny						
King						
❏ 4357		I Hate You/Well Oh Well	1950	15.00	30.00	60.00
❏ 4376		After You've Gone/Boogie Green	1950	15.00	30.00	60.00
❏ 4397		Butterfly/I'm Going to Have Myself a Ball	1950	15.00	30.00	60.00
❏ 4417		Breaking Up the House/ If You Don't Love Me, Tell Me So	1950	15.00	30.00	60.00
❏ 4427		Walk That Mess/One, Two, Three, Kick Blues	1951	15.00	30.00	60.00
❏ 4447		Brad's Blues/Two Dry Bones on the Pantry Shelf	1951	15.00	30.00	60.00
❏ 4457		Bradshaw Boogie/Walkin' the Chalk Line	1951	15.00	30.00	60.00
❏ 4467		I'm a High Ballin' Daddy/You Came By	1951	15.00	30.00	60.00
❏ 4487		T-99/Long Time Baby	1951	50.00	100.00	200.00
❏ 4497		The Train Kept a-Rollin'/Knockin' Blues	1951	50.00	100.00	200.00
❏ 4537		Mailman's Sack/Newspaper Boy Blues	1952	50.00	100.00	200.00
❏ 4547		Rippin' and Runnin'/Lay It on the Line	1952	50.00	100.00	200.00
❏ 4577		Strange/Soft	1952	12.50	25.00	50.00
❏ 4713		Don't Worry 'Bout Me/Overflow	1954	10.00	20.00	40.00
❏ 4727		Spider Web/The Gypsey	1954	10.00	20.00	40.00
❏ 4747		A Stack of Dollars/Cat Fruit	1954	10.00	20.00	40.00
❏ 4757		Light/Choice	1954	10.00	20.00	40.00
❏ 4777		Cat Nap/Stomping Room Only	1955	10.00	20.00	40.00
❏ 4787		Phantom Turnpike/Come On	1955	10.00	20.00	40.00
❏ 5114		Short Shorts/Bushes	1958	6.25	12.50	25.00
Brady Bunch, The						
(Also see "McCormick, Maureen"; "Chris Knight"; "Plumb, Eve"; "Williams, Barry")						
Paramount						
❏ 0062		Frosty the Snowman/Silver Bells	1971	3.00	6.00	12.00
❏ 0062	PS	Frosty the Snowman/Silver Bells	1971	5.00	10.00	20.00
❏ 0141		We Can Make the World a Whole Lot Brighter/ Time to Change	1972	3.00	6.00	12.00
❏ 0167		Time to Change/We'll Always Be Friends	1972	3.00	6.00	12.00
❏ 0205		Zuckerman's Famous Pig/Charlotte's Web	1973	3.00	6.00	12.00
❏ 0205	PS	Zuckerman's Famous Pig/Charlotte's Web	1973	5.00	10.00	20.00
❏ 0229		I'd Love You to Want Me/Everything I Do	1973	3.00	6.00	12.00
		As "The Brady Bunch Kids"				
Brass Ring, The						
ABC Dunhill						
❏ 4164		For the Love of Ivy/The Theme from The Odd Couple	1968		3.00	6.00
Dunhill						
❏ 4023		The Phoenix Love Theme (Sensa Fine)/Lightning Bug	1966		3.00	6.00
❏ 4036		Lara's Theme/Secret Love	1966		3.00	6.00
❏ 4047		California Dreamin'/Samba de Orfeu	1966		3.00	6.00
❏ 4059		Lapland/Patricia	1966		3.00	6.00
❏ 4065		The Dis-Advantages of You/The Dating Game	1967		3.00	6.00
❏ 4090		Love in the Open Air/Wait for Me	1967	5.00	10.00	20.00
❏ 4090	PS	Love in the Open Air/Wait for Me	1967	7.50	15.00	30.00
		Sleeve says this is "Paul McCartney's first non-Beatles song"				
❏ 4108		Monday, Monday/Flower Ring	1967		3.00	6.00
❏ 4132		Cherry Pink & Apple Blossom White/ Adoro (Don't Tempt Me)	1968		3.00	6.00
Breakers, The						
Amy						
❏ 938		Don't Send Me No Flowers (I Ain't Dead Yet)/ Love of My Life	1965	3.75	7.50	15.00
Brana						
❏ 1001/2		Kama-Kaze/Surf Breaker	1963	15.00	30.00	60.00
DJB						
❏ 116		Jet Stream/Beach Head	1964	12.50	25.00	50.00
❏ 116		Super Jet Rumble/Beach Head	1964	12.50	25.00	50.00
		Revised A-side title				
Impact						
❏ 14		Surfin' Tragedy/Surf Bird	1963	6.25	12.50	25.00
		Black vinyl				
❏ 14		Surfin' Tragedy/Surf Bird	1963	20.00	40.00	80.00
		Gold vinyl				
Jerden						
❏ 789		All My Nights, All My Days/Better for the Both of Us	1966	5.00	10.00	20.00
Marsh						
❏ 206		Balboa Memories/Long Way Home	1963	12.50	25.00	50.00
Riverton						
❏ 102		All My Nights, All My Days/Better for the Both of Us	1966	10.00	20.00	40.00
Brenston, Jackie						
Chess						
❏ 1458		Rocket "88"/Come Back Where You Belong	1951	5,000	7,500	10,000
		Early rockabilly classic; obscenely rare, even though these were pressed later				
❏ 1469		In My Real Gone Rocket/Tuckered Out	1951	500.00	750.00	1,000
❏ 1472		Juiced/Independent Woman	1951	500.00	750.00	1,000

Number		Title (A Side/B Side)	Year	VG	VG+	NM
❏ 1496		Leo the Louse/Hi-Ho Baby	1952	125.00	250.00	500.00
❏ 1532		Blues Got Me Again/Starvation	1953	62.50	125.00	250.00
Federal						
❏ 12283		What Can It Be/Gonna Wait for My Chance	1956	12.50	25.00	50.00
❏ 12291		Much Later/The Mistreater	1957	12.50	25.00	50.00
Sue						
❏ 736		Trouble Up the Road/You Ain't the One	1961	5.00	10.00	20.00

Briggs, Lillian
ABC-Paramount

Number		Title (A Side/B Side)	Year	VG	VG+	NM
❏ 10253		I Want You to Be My Baby/I'm Burning for You	1961	2.50	5.00	10.00
Coral						
❏ 62108		Rag Mop/Smile for the People	1959	2.50	5.00	10.00
❏ 62136		Blues in the Night/Is There a Man in the House	1959	2.50	5.00	10.00
❏ 62156		Hooray for the Rock/Diddy Boppers	1959	2.50	5.00	10.00
❏ 62193		Be Mine/Not a Soul	1960	2.50	5.00	10.00
❏ 62223		I Care for You/That's What It's Like to Be Lonesome	1960	2.50	5.00	10.00
Epic						
❏ 9115		I Want You to Be My Baby/Don't Stay Away Too Long	1955	7.50	15.00	30.00
❏ 9120		Give Me a Band and My Baby/It Could've Been Me	1955	7.50	15.00	30.00
❏ 9138		Rock and Roll-y Poly Santa Claus/Can't Stop	1955	7.50	15.00	30.00
❏ 9141		Follow the Leader/That's the Only Way to Live	1956	5.00	10.00	20.00
❏ 9151		Eddie, My Love/Teens in Jeans from New Orleans	1956	5.00	10.00	20.00
❏ 9166		The Gypsy Goofed/Too Close for Comfort	1956	5.00	10.00	20.00
❏ 9190		I'll Be Gone/Mean Words	1956	5.00	10.00	20.00
❏ 9214		Sugar Blues/Boogie Blues	1957	3.75	7.50	15.00
❏ 9249		She Sells Sea Shells/I	1957	3.75	7.50	15.00
Sunbeam						
❏ 104		Come Home/Till We Meet Again	1958	3.00	6.00	12.00
❏ 114		Hey Ba Ba Re Bop/I've Got Your Heart	1958	3.00	6.00	12.00

Brogues, The
(Two members became part of Quicksilver Messenger Service)
Challenge

Number		Title (A Side/B Side)	Year	VG	VG+	NM
❏ 59311		But Now I'm Fine/(B-side unknown)	1965	7.50	15.00	30.00
❏ 59316		I Ain't No Miracle Worker/Don't Shoot Me Down	1965	7.50	15.00	30.00
Twilight						
❏ 408		But Now I'm Fine/Early Bird	1965	10.00	20.00	40.00
❏ 408		But Now I'm Fine/Someday	1965	10.00	20.00	40.00

Brooklyn Bridge
(Featuring Johnny Maestro, ex-Crests)
Buddah

Number		Title (A Side/B Side)	Year	VG	VG+	NM
❏ 60		Little Red Boat by the Window/From My Window	1968		3.00	6.00
❏ 75		Worst That Could Happen/Your Kite, My Kite	1968	2.00	4.00	8.00
❏ 95		Welcome Me Love/Blessed Is the Rain	1969		3.00	6.00
❏ 126		Your Husband, My Wife/Upside Down	1969		3.00	6.00
❏ 139		You'll Never Walk Alone/Minstrel Sunday	1969		3.00	6.00
❏ 162		Free as the Wind/He's Not a Happy Man	1970		3.00	6.00
❏ 179		Down by the River/Look Again	1970		3.00	6.00
❏ 193		Day Is Done/Opposites	1970		3.00	6.00
❏ 193		Day Is Done/Easy Way	1970		3.00	6.00
❏ 199		Nights in White Satin/Cynthia	1971	2.00	4.00	8.00
❏ 230		Wednesday in Your Garden (mono/stereo)	1971	2.00	4.00	8.00
		Stock copy unknown				
❏ 293		Man in a Band/Bruno's Place	1972	2.00	4.00	8.00
❏ 317		I Feel Free (mono/stereo)	1972	2.50	5.00	10.00
		As "The Bridge"; stock copy unknown				

Brooks, Chuck, and the Sharpies
Dub

Number		Title (A Side/B Side)	Year	VG	VG+	NM
❏ 2844		Spinning My Wheels/You Make Me Feel Mean	1958	75.00	150.00	300.00

Brooks, Donnie
Challenge

Number		Title (A Side/B Side)	Year	VG	VG+	NM
❏ 59331		I Call Your Name/Be Fair	1966	2.00	4.00	8.00
❏ 59344		Pink Carousel/Mission Man	1966	2.00	4.00	8.00
Era						
❏ 3004		Lil' Sweetheart/If You're Lookin'	1959	5.00	10.00	20.00
❏ 3007		White Orchid/Sway and Move with the Beat	1959	5.00	10.00	20.00
❏ 3014		The Devil Ain't a Man/How Long	1960	5.00	10.00	20.00
❏ 3018		Mission Bell/Do It for Me	1960	5.00	10.00	20.00
❏ 3028		Doll House/Round Robin	1960	3.75	7.50	15.00
❏ 3028	PS	Doll House/Round Robin	1960	6.25	12.50	25.00
❏ 3042		Memphis/That's Why	1961	3.75	7.50	15.00
❏ 3042	PS	Memphis/That's Why	1961	6.25	12.50	25.00
❏ 3052		Boomerang/How Long	1961	3.75	7.50	15.00
❏ 3059		Sweet Lorraine/Up to My Ears in Tears	1961	3.75	7.50	15.00
❏ 3063		Goodnight Judy/Your Little Boy's Gone Home	1961	3.75	7.50	15.00
❏ 3071		My Favorite Kind of Face/He Stole Flo	1962	3.75	7.50	15.00
❏ 3077		Oh You Beautiful Doll/Just a Bystander	1962	3.75	7.50	15.00
❏ 3095		Cries My Heart/It's Not That Easy	1962	3.75	7.50	15.00
❏ 3194		Blue Soldier/Love Is Funny That Way	1968	2.00	4.00	8.00

Number	Title (A Side/B Side)	Year	VG	VG+	NM
Happy Tiger					
❏ 526	Abracadabra/I Know You as a Woman	1970		2.50	5.00
❏ 544	Hush/I Know You as a Woman	1970		2.50	5.00
❏ 551	My God and I/Pink Carousel	1970		2.50	5.00
❏ 566	(I Wanna) Have You for Myself/Rub-a-Dub-Dub	1971		2.50	5.00
❏ 579	I'm Gonna Make You Love Me/Pink Carousel	1971		2.50	5.00
Midsong Int'l.					
❏ 1007	Big John/Get Fame, Son	1978		2.00	4.00
Oak					
❏ 1019	The Song That I Sing Is For You/Country Dude	1971		2.50	5.00
Reprise					
❏ 0261	Gone/Girl Machine	1964	2.50	5.00	10.00
❏ 0311	Can't Help Lovin' You/Pickin' Up the Pieces	1964	2.50	5.00	10.00
❏ 0363	Hey, Little Girl/I Never Get to Love You	1965	2.50	5.00	10.00
Yardbird					
❏ 8006	Sunglasses on the Sand/ Sunshine, Summertime and Love	1968		3.00	6.00
❏ 8008	Hush/Sunshine, Summertime and Love	1968		3.00	6.00
❏ 8009	Tree Trimming Time/(Instrumental)	1968		3.00	6.00

Brooks, Dusty, and His Tones with Juanita Brown

Number	Title (A Side/B Side)	Year	VG	VG+	NM
Sun					
❏ 182	Heaven or Fire/Tears and Wine	1953	1,000	2,000	3,000

Brothers, The

Number	Title (A Side/B Side)	Year	VG	VG+	NM
Argo					
❏ 5318	Lazy Susan/Deep Sleep	1958	5.00	10.00	20.00
❏ 5329	Sioux City Sue/Deep Sleep	1959	5.00	10.00	20.00
Checker					
❏ 995	My True Love/One Lonely Heart	1961	3.75	7.50	15.00

Brown, Arthur, The Crazy World of

Number	Title (A Side/B Side)	Year	VG	VG+	NM
Atlantic					
❏ 2556	Fire/Rest Cure	1968	2.50	5.00	10.00
Mercury					
❏ 873 504-7	Fire/Rest Cure	1990			3.00
	Reissue				
Track					
❏ 2582	I Put a Spell on You/Nightmare	1968	2.00	4.00	8.00

Brown, Buster

Number	Title (A Side/B Side)	Year	VG	VG+	NM
Fire					
❏ 507	Sugar Babe/I'm Going -- But I'll Be Back	1962	5.00	10.00	20.00
❏ 516	Raise a Ruckus Tonight/Gonna Love My Baby	1962	5.00	10.00	20.00
❏ 1008	Fannie Mae/Lost in a Dream	1959	6.25	12.50	25.00
❏ 1020	The Madison Shuffle/John Henry	1960	5.00	10.00	20.00
❏ 1023	Is You Is or Is You Ain't My Baby/ Don't Dog Your Woman	1960	5.00	10.00	20.00
❏ 1032	Sincerely/Doctor Brown	1960	5.00	10.00	20.00
❏ 1040	Blues When It Rains/Good News	1961	5.00	10.00	20.00
❏ 2021	Sugar Babe/Don't Dog Your Woman	1962	3.75	7.50	15.00
White Whale					
❏ 316	The Proud One/I've Got It Made	1969	2.50	5.00	10.00

Brown, Charles

Number	Title (A Side/B Side)	Year	VG	VG+	NM
Ace					
❏ 561	Educated Fool/I Want to Go Back Home	1959	3.00	6.00	12.00
	With Amos Milburn				
Aladdin					
Note: Charles Brown records on Aladdin prior to 3076 are unconfirmed on 45 rpm					
❏ 3076	Black Night/Once There Was a Fool	1951	30.00	60.00	120.00
❏ 3091	I'll Always Be in Love with You/The Message	1951	15.00	30.00	60.00
❏ 3092	Seven Long Days/Don't Fool with My Heart	1951	15.00	30.00	60.00
❏ 3116	Hard Times/Tender Heart	1952	15.00	30.00	60.00
❏ 3120	Still Water/My Last Affair	1952	15.00	30.00	60.00
❏ 3138	See/Without Your Love	1952	15.00	30.00	60.00
❏ 3157	Rollin' Like a Pebble in the Sand/Alley Batting	1952	15.00	30.00	60.00
❏ 3163	Evening Shadows/Moonrise	1953	12.50	25.00	50.00
❏ 3176	Take Me/Rising Sun	1953	12.50	25.00	50.00
❏ 3191	Lonesome Feeling/I Lost Everything	1953	12.50	25.00	50.00
❏ 3200	All My Life/Don't Leave Me Poor	1953	12.50	25.00	50.00
❏ 3209	P.S. I Love You/Cryin' and Driftin' Blues	1953	12.50	25.00	50.00
❏ 3220	Everybody's Got Trouble/I Fool Around with You	1954	10.00	20.00	40.00
❏ 3235	Let's Walk/Crying Mercy	1954	10.00	20.00	40.00
❏ 3254	My Silent Love/Foolish	1954	10.00	20.00	40.00
❏ 3272	By the Bend of the River/Honey Slipper	1955	7.50	15.00	30.00
❏ 3284	Night After Night/Walk with Me	1955	7.50	15.00	30.00
❏ 3290	Hot Lips and Seven Kisses/Fools' Paradise	1955	7.50	15.00	30.00
❏ 3296	My Heart Is Mended/Trees, Trees	1955	7.50	15.00	30.00
❏ 3316	Please Don't Drive Me Away/One Minute to One	1956	6.25	12.50	25.00
❏ 3342	Soothe Me/I'll Always Be in Love with You	1956	6.25	12.50	25.00
❏ 3348	Merry Christmas Baby/Black Night	1956	6.25	12.50	25.00
❏ 3366	Please Believe Me/It's a Sin to Tell a Lie	1957	5.00	10.00	20.00
❏ 3423	Hard Times/Ooh, Ooh Sugar	1958	5.00	10.00	20.00

Number	Title (A Side/B Side)	Year	VG	VG+	NM
Bluesway					
❏ 61031	Merry Christmas Baby/Rainy, Rainy Day	1969		3.00	6.00
Cash					
❏ 1052	Lost in the Night/I Sold My Heart to the Junkman	1957	7.50	15.00	30.00
	B-side by the Basin Street Boys				
EastWest					
❏ 106	When Did You Leave Heaven/	1958	5.00	10.00	20.00
	We've Got a Lot in Common				
EMI					
❏ S7-18213	Please Come Home for Christmas/	1994		2.00	4.00
	Merry Christmas Baby				
	Green vinyl				
Galaxy					
❏ 762	I'm Gonna Push On/Cry No More	1968	2.50	5.00	10.00
❏ 766	Abraham, Martin, and John/(B-side unknown)	1968	2.50	5.00	10.00
Hollywood					
❏ 1006	Pleading for Your Love/The Best I Can Do	1954	10.00	20.00	40.00
❏ 1021	Merry Christmas Baby/Sleigh Ride	1954	5.00	10.00	20.00
	Charles Brown's first recording of the A-side, released on 78 on Exclusive 254 (1946); this was still in print at least into the 1960s; B-side by Lloyd Glenn				
Imperial					
❏ 5830	Fool's Paradise/Lonesome Feeling	1962	2.50	5.00	10.00
❏ 5902	Merry Christmas Baby/I Lost Everything	1962	2.50	5.00	10.00
❏ 5905	Black Night/Drifting Blues	1963	2.50	5.00	10.00
❏ 5961	I'm Savin' My Love for You/	1963	2.50	5.00	10.00
	Please Don't Drive Me Away				
Jewel					
❏ 814	Christmas in Heaven/Just a Blessing	1970		2.50	5.00
❏ 815	Merry Christmas Baby/	1970		2.50	5.00
	Please Come Home for Christmas				
❏ 830	I Don't Know/For You	1972		2.50	5.00
❏ 838	I've Got Your Love/I Just Can't Get Over You	1973		2.50	5.00
❏ 847	Please Come Home for Christmas/	1974		2.50	5.00
	Christmas in Heaven				
King					
❏ 5405	Please Come Home for Christmas/	1960	3.00	6.00	12.00
	Christmas (Comes But Once a Year)				
	B-side by Amos Milburn				
❏ 5439	Angel Baby/Baby Oh Baby	1961	3.00	6.00	12.00
❏ 5464	I Wanna Go Back Home/My Little Baby	1961	3.00	6.00	12.00
	With Amos Milburn				
❏ 5523	Butterfly/This Fool Has Learned	1961	3.00	6.00	12.00
❏ 5530	Christmas in Heaven/It's Christmas All Year 'Round	1961	3.00	6.00	12.00
❏ 5570	Without a Friend/If You Play with Cats	1961	3.00	6.00	12.00
❏ 5722	I'm Just a Drifter/I Don't Want Your Rambling Letters	1963	2.50	5.00	10.00
❏ 5726	It's Christmas Time/Christmas Finds Me Lonely	1963	2.50	5.00	10.00
❏ 5731	Christmas Questions/	1963	2.50	5.00	10.00
	Wrap Yourself in a Christmas Package				
❏ 5802	If You Don't Believe I'm Crying/I Wanna Be Close	1963	2.50	5.00	10.00
❏ 5825	Lucky Dreamer/Too Fine for Crying	1963	2.50	5.00	10.00
❏ 5852	Blow Out All the Candles/Come Home	1964	2.50	5.00	10.00
❏ 5946	Christmas Blues/My Most Miserable Christmas	1964	2.50	5.00	10.00
❏ 5947	Christmas Comes (But Once a Year)/	1964	2.50	5.00	10.00
	Bringin' In a Brand New Year				
❏ 6094	Regardless/The Plan	1967	2.00	4.00	8.00
❏ 6192	Hang On a Little Longer/Black Night	1968	2.00	4.00	8.00
❏ 6194	Merry Christmas, Baby/	1968	2.00	4.00	8.00
	Let's Make Every Day Christmas				
❏ 6420	For the Good Times/Lonesome and Driftin'	1973		2.50	5.00
Liberty					
❏ 1393	Merry Christmas Baby/Silent Night	1980		2.50	5.00
	B-side by Baby Washington				
Lilly					
❏ 506	Bon Voyage/Bye and Bye	1962	2.50	5.00	10.00
Mainstream					
❏ 607	Pledging My Love/Tomorrow Night	1965	2.00	4.00	8.00
Nola					
❏ 702	Standing on the Outside/I'll Love You (If You Let Me)	1965	2.00	4.00	8.00
Swing Time					
❏ 253	I'll Miss You/New Orleans Blues	1952	30.00	60.00	120.00
❏ 259	Be Fair with Me/Sunny Road	1952	30.00	60.00	120.00
United Artists					
❏ 0085	Drifting Blues/Black Night	1973		2.00	4.00
	Silver Spotlight Series issue				
❏ 0086	I Lost Everything/Lonesome Feeling	1973		2.00	4.00
	Silver Spotlight Series issue				
❏ XW582	Merry Christmas Baby/(B-side unknown)	1974		2.50	5.00

Brown, George Washington

(Actually Van Dyke Parks)
Warner Bros.

Number	Title (A Side/B Side)	Year	VG	VG+	NM
❏ 7026	Donovan's Colors Part 1/Part 2	1967	3.00	6.00	12.00

Number		Title (A Side/B Side)	Year	VG	VG+	NM

Brown, James

A&M

| ☐ 3022 | | I Got You (I Feel Good)/Nowhere to Run | 1988 | | | 3.00 |
| | | *B-side by Martha and the Vandellas* | | | | |

Augusta Sound

| ☐ 94023 | | Bring It On ... Bring It On/ | 1983 | | 2.00 | 4.00 |
| | | The Night Time Is the Right Time (To Be With the One That You Love) | | | | |

Backstreet

| ☐ 52215 | | King of Soul/Theme from Doctor Detroit | 1983 | | | 3.00 |
| | | *B-side by Devo* | | | | |

Bethlehem

| ☐ 3089 | | I Loves You Porgy/Yours and Mine | 1969 | 3.75 | 7.50 | 15.00 |
| ☐ 3098 | | A Man Has to Go Back to the Crossroads/The Drunk | 1969 | 3.75 | 7.50 | 15.00 |

Federal

☐ 12258		Please, Please, Please/Why Do You Do Me?	1956	6.25	12.50	25.00
☐ 12264		I Don't Know/I Feel That Old Feeling Coming On	1956	6.25	12.50	25.00
☐ 12277		No, No, No, No/Hold My Baby's Hand	1956	6.25	12.50	25.00
☐ 12289		Just Won't Do Right/Let's Make It	1957	6.25	12.50	25.00
☐ 12290		I Won't Plead No More/Chonnie On Chon	1957	6.25	12.50	25.00
☐ 12292		Gonna Try/Can't Be the Same	1957	6.25	12.50	25.00
☐ 12295		Love or a Game/Messing with the Blues	1957	6.25	12.50	25.00
☐ 12300		I Walked Alone/You're Mine, You're Mine	1957	6.25	12.50	25.00
☐ 12311		Baby Cries Over the Ocean/That Dood It	1957	6.25	12.50	25.00
☐ 12316		Begging, Begging/That's When I Lost My Heart	1958	6.25	12.50	25.00
☐ 12337		Try Me/Tell Me What I Did Wrong	1958	5.00	10.00	20.00
☐ 12348		I Want You So Bad/There Must Be a Reason	1959	5.00	10.00	20.00
☐ 12352	M	I've Got to Change/It Hurts to Tell You	1959	5.00	10.00	20.00
☐ S-12352	S	I've Got to Change/It Hurts to Tell You	1959	12.50	25.00	50.00
☐ 12361	M	Don't Let It Happen to Me/Good Good Lovin'	1959	5.00	10.00	20.00
☐ S-12361	S	Don't Let It Happen to Me/Good Good Lovin'	1959	12.50	25.00	50.00
☐ 12364		It Was You/Got to Cry	1959	5.00	10.00	20.00
☐ 12369		I'll Go Crazy/I Know It's True	1960	5.00	10.00	20.00
☐ 12370		Think/You've Got the Power	1960	5.00	10.00	20.00
☐ 12378		This Old Heart/I Wonder When You're Coming Home	1960	5.00	10.00	20.00

King

☐ 5423		The Bells/And I Do Just What I Want	1960	3.75	7.50	15.00
☐ 5438		The Scratch/Hold It	1961	3.75	7.50	15.00
☐ 5442		Bewildered/If You Want Me	1961	3.75	7.50	15.00
☐ 5466		I Don't Mind/Love Don't Love Nobody	1961	3.75	7.50	15.00
☐ 5485		Sticky/Suds	1961	3.75	7.50	15.00
☐ 5519		Night Flying/Cross Firing	1961	3.75	7.50	15.00
☐ 5524		Baby You're Right/I'll Never, Never Let You Go	1961	3.75	7.50	15.00
☐ 5547		Just You and Me, Darling/I Love You, Yes I Do	1961	3.75	7.50	15.00
☐ 5573		Lost Someone/Cross Firing	1961	3.75	7.50	15.00
☐ 5614		Night Train/Why Does Everything Happen to Me	1962	3.75	7.50	15.00
☐ 5654		Tell Me Why/Say So Long	1962	3.75	7.50	15.00
		With Yvonne Fair				
☐ 5657		Shout and Shimmy/Come Over Here	1962	3.75	7.50	15.00
☐ 5672		Mashed Potatoes U.S.A./You Don't Have to Go	1962	3.75	7.50	15.00
☐ 5687		It Hurts to Be in Love/You Can Make It If You Try	1962	3.75	7.50	15.00
		With Yvonne Fair				
☐ 5698		(Can You) Feel It Part 1/(Can You) Feel It Part 2	1962	3.75	7.50	15.00
☐ 5701		Three Hearts in a Tangle/I've Got Money	1962	3.75	7.50	15.00
☐ 5710		Like a Baby/Every Beat of My Heart	1963	3.75	7.50	15.00
☐ 5739		Prisoner of Love/Choo Choo	1963	3.75	7.50	15.00
☐ 5767		These Foolish Things/Can You Feel It -- Part 1	1963	3.75	7.50	15.00
☐ 5803		Signed, Sealed and Delivered/Waiting in Vain	1963	3.75	7.50	15.00
☐ 5829		The Bells/I've Got to Change	1963	3.75	7.50	15.00
☐ 5842		Oh Baby Don't You Weep (Part 1)/	1964	3.75	7.50	15.00
		Oh Baby Don't You Weep (Part 2)				
☐ 5842	PS	Oh Baby Don't You Weep (Part 1)/	1964	6.25	12.50	25.00
		Oh Baby Don't You Weep (Part 2)				
☐ 5853		Please, Please, Please/In the Wee Wee Hours	1964	3.75	7.50	15.00
☐ 5876		How Long Darling/Again	1964	3.75	7.50	15.00
☐ 5899		So Long/Dancin' Little Thing	1964	3.75	7.50	15.00
☐ 5922		Tell Me What You're Gonna Do/I Don't Care	1964	3.75	7.50	15.00
☐ 5952		Think/Try Me	1964	3.75	7.50	15.00
☐ 5956		Fine Old Foxy Self/Medley	1964	3.75	7.50	15.00
☐ 5968		Have Mercy Baby/Just Won't Do Right	1964	3.75	7.50	15.00
☐ 5995		This Old Heart/It Was You	1965	3.00	6.00	12.00
☐ 5999		Papa's Got a Brand New Bag Part I/	1965	3.75	7.50	15.00
		Papa's Got a Brand New Bag Part II				
☐ 6015		I Got You (I Feel Good)/	1965	3.75	7.50	15.00
		I Can't Help It (I Just Do, Do, Do)				
☐ 6020		I'll Go Crazy/Lost Someone	1966	3.00	6.00	12.00
☐ 6025		Ain't That a Groove Part I/Ain't That a Groove Part II	1966	3.00	6.00	12.00
☐ 6029		Prisoner of Love/I've Got to Change	1966	3.00	6.00	12.00
☐ 6033		Come Over Here/Tell Me What You're Gonna Do	1966	3.00	6.00	12.00
☐ 6035		It's a Man's Man's World/Is It Yes Or Is It No?	1966	3.00	6.00	12.00
☐ 6037		I've Got Money/Just Won't Do Right	1966	3.00	6.00	12.00
☐ 6040		I Don't Care/It Was You	1966	3.00	6.00	12.00
☐ 6044		This Old Heart/How Long Darling	1966	3.00	6.00	12.00
☐ 6048		Money Won't Change You Part 1/	1966	3.00	6.00	12.00
		Money Won't Change You Part 2				
☐ 6056		Don't Be a Drop-Out/Tell Me That You Love Me	1966	3.00	6.00	12.00

Number	Title (A Side/B Side)	Year	VG	VG+	NM
❏ 6064	The Christmas Song (Part 1)/ The Christmas Song (Part 2)	1966	3.00	6.00	12.00
❏ 6065	Sweet Little Baby Boy (Part 1)/ Sweet Little Baby Boy (Part 2)	1966	3.00	6.00	12.00
❏ 6071	Bring It Up/Nobody Knows	1967	3.00	6.00	12.00
❏ 6072	Let's Make Christmas Mean Something This Year (Part 1)/Let's Make Christmas Mean Something This Year (Part 2)	1967	3.00	6.00	12.00
❏ 6086	Kansas City/Stone Fox	1967	3.00	6.00	12.00
❏ 6091	Think/Nobody Cares	1967	3.00	6.00	12.00

A-side: With Vicki Anderson; B-side: Vicki Anderson solo

Number	Title (A Side/B Side)	Year	VG	VG+	NM
❏ 6100	Let Yourself Go/Good Rockin' Tonight	1967	3.00	6.00	12.00
❏ 6110	Cold Sweat -- Part 1/Cold Sweat -- Part 2	1967	3.00	6.00	12.00
❏ 6111	Mona Lisa/It Won't Be Me	1967	15.00	30.00	60.00

Evidently not released or pulled shortly after release

Number	Title (A Side/B Side)	Year	VG	VG+	NM
❏ 6112	America Is My Home -- Part 1/ America Is My Home -- Part 2	1967	3.00	6.00	12.00
❏ 6122	Get It Together (Part 1)/Get It Together (Part 2)	1967	3.00	6.00	12.00
❏ 6133	The Soul of J.B./Funky Soul #1	1967	3.00	6.00	12.00
❏ 6141	I Guess I'll Have to Cry, Cry, Cry/Just Plain Funk	1967	3.00	6.00	12.00
❏ 6144	I Can't Stand Myself (When You Touch Me)/ There Was a Time	1967	3.00	6.00	12.00
❏ 6151	You've Got to Change Your Mind/I'll Lose My Mind	1968	3.00	6.00	12.00

A-side: With Bobby Byrd; B-side: Bobby Byrd solo

Number	Title (A Side/B Side)	Year	VG	VG+	NM
❏ 6152	You've Got the Power/ What the World Needs Now Is Love	1968	3.00	6.00	12.00

A-side: With Vicki Anderson; B-side: Vicki Anderson solo

Number	Title (A Side/B Side)	Year	VG	VG+	NM
❏ 6155	I Got the Feelin'/If I Ruled the World	1968	3.00	6.00	12.00
❏ 6164	Here I Go/Shhhh	1968	3.00	6.00	12.00
❏ 6166	Licking Stick -- Licking Stick (Part 1)/ Licking Stick -- Licking Stick (Part 2)	1968	3.00	6.00	12.00
❏ 6187	Say It Loud -- I'm Black and I'm Proud (Part 1)/ Say It Loud -- I'm Black and I'm Proud (Part 2)	1968	2.50	5.00	10.00
❏ 6198	Goodbye My Love/Shades of Brown	1968	2.50	5.00	10.00
❏ 6203	Santa Claus Go Straight to the Ghetto/You Know It	1968	2.50	5.00	10.00
❏ 6204	Believers Shall Enjoy/ Tit for Tat (Ain't No Turning Back)	1968	2.50	5.00	10.00
❏ 6205	Let's Unite the World at Christmas/ In the Middle (Part 1)	1968	2.50	5.00	10.00
❏ 6206	In the Middle (Part 2)/Tit for Tat (Ain't No Turning Back)	1969	2.50	5.00	10.00

A-side: With Marva Whitney

Number	Title (A Side/B Side)	Year	VG	VG+	NM
❏ 6213	Give It Up or Turnit A Loose/I'll Lose My Mind	1969	2.50	5.00	10.00
❏ 6216	Shades of Brown (Part 2)/A Talk with the News	1969	2.50	5.00	10.00

B-side by Steve Soul

Number	Title (A Side/B Side)	Year	VG	VG+	NM
❏ 6218	You Got to Have a Job/I'm Tired, I'm Tired, I'm Tired	1969	2.50	5.00	10.00

A-side with Marva Whitney; B-side: Marva Whitney solo

Number	Title (A Side/B Side)	Year	VG	VG+	NM
❏ 6222	Soul Pride (Part 1)/Soul Pride (Part 2)	1969	2.50	5.00	10.00
❏ 6223	You've Got to Have a Mother for Me (Part 1)/ You've Got to Have a Mother for Me (Part 2)	1969	2.50	5.00	10.00
❏ 6224	I Don't Want Nobody to Give Me Nothing (Open Up the Door, I'll Get It Myself) Part 1/Part 2	1969	2.50	5.00	10.00
❏ 6235	Little Groove Maker (Part 1)/I'm Shook	1969	2.50	5.00	10.00
❏ 6235	Little Groove Maker (Part 1)/Any Day Now	1969	2.50	5.00	10.00
❏ 6240	The Popcorn/The Chicken	1969	2.50	5.00	10.00
❏ 6245	Mother Popcorn (You Got to Have a Mother for Me) Part 1/Mother Popcorn (You Got to Have a Mother for Me) Part 2	1969	2.50	5.00	10.00
❏ 6250	Lowdown Popcorn/Top of the Stack	1969	2.50	5.00	10.00
❏ 6255	Let a Man Come In and Do the Popcorn Part One/ Sometime	1969	2.50	5.00	10.00
❏ 6258	World (Part 1)/World (Part 2)	1969	2.50	5.00	10.00
❏ 6273	I'm Not Demanding (Part 1)/ I'm Not Demanding (Part 2)	1969	2.50	5.00	10.00
❏ 6275	Part Two (Let a Man Come In and Do the Popcorn)/ Get a Little Hipper	1969	2.50	5.00	10.00
❏ 6277	It's Christmas Time (Part 1)/ It's Christmas Time (Part 2)	1969	2.50	5.00	10.00
❏ 6280	Ain't It Funky Now (Part 1)/Ain't It Funky Now (Part 2)	1970	2.00	4.00	8.00
❏ 6290	Funky Drummer (Part 1)/Funky Drummer (Part 2)	1970	2.00	4.00	8.00
❏ 6292	It's a New Day (Part 1)/It's a New Day (Part 2)	1970	2.00	4.00	8.00
❏ 6293	Let It Be Me/No More Heartaches, No More Pain	1970	2.00	4.00	8.00

A-side: With Vicki Anderson; B-side: Vicki Anderson solo

Number	Title (A Side/B Side)	Year	VG	VG+	NM
❏ 6300	Talkin' Loud and Sayin' Nothing (Part 1)/ Talkin' Loud and Sayin' Nothing (Part 2)	1970	2.00	4.00	8.00
❏ 6310	Brother Rapp (Part 1)/Brother Rapp (Part 2)	1970	2.00	4.00	8.00
❏ 6318	Get Up (I Feel Like Being A) Sex Machine (Part 1)/ Get Up (I Feel Like Being A) Sex Machine (Part 2)	1970	2.00	4.00	8.00
❏ 6322	I'm Not Demanding (Part 1)/I'm Not Demanding (Part 2)	1970	2.00	4.00	8.00
❏ 6329	Call Me Super Bad (Part 1 & Part 2)/Bewitched	1970	5.00	10.00	20.00

First pressing: Note longer title

Number	Title (A Side/B Side)	Year	VG	VG+	NM
❏ 6329	Super Bad (Part 1 & Part 2)/Bewitched	1970	2.00	4.00	8.00
❏ 6339	Hey America/(Instrumental)	1970	2.00	4.00	8.00
❏ 6340	Santa Claus Is Definitely Here to Stay/Hey America	1970	2.00	4.00	8.00
❏ 6340 PS	Santa Claus Is Definitely Here to Stay/Hey America	1970	6.25	12.50	25.00
❏ 6347	Get Up, Get Into It, Get Involved Pt. 1/ Get Up, Get Into It, Get Involved Pt. 2	1971	2.00	4.00	8.00
❏ 6359	Talking Loud and Saying Nothing -- Part 1/ Talking Loud and Saying Nothing -- Part 2	1971	2.00	4.00	8.00
❏ 6363	I Cried/World (Part 2)	1971	2.00	4.00	8.00

Number		Title (A Side/B Side)	Year	VG	VG+	NM
❏ 6366		Spinning Wheel (Part 1)/Spinning Wheel (Part 2)	1971	2.00	4.00	8.00
❏ 6368		Soul Power Pt. 1/Soul Power Pt 2 & Pt. 3	1971	2.00	4.00	8.00

Mercury

❏ 885 190-7		Prisoner of Love/Please, Please, Please	1986		2.00	4.00
		Reissue				
❏ 885 194-7		Get on the Good Foot/Give It Up or Turnit A Loose	1986		2.00	4.00
		Reissue				

People

❏ 2500		Escape-ism (Part 1)/Escape-ism (Parts 2 & 3)	1971		3.00	6.00
❏ 2501		Hot Pants Pt. 1 (She Got to Use What She Got to Get What She Wants)/Hot Pants Pt. 2	1971		3.00	6.00
❏ 664		Everybody Wanna Be Funky One More Time Pt. 1/Everybody Wanna Be Funky One More Time Pt. 2	1976		2.50	5.00

Polydor

❏ 2005		Star Generation/Women Are Something Else	1979		2.50	5.00
❏ 2034		The Original Disco Man/Let the Boogie Do the Rest	1979		2.50	5.00
❏ 2054		Regrets/Stone Cold Drag	1979		2.50	5.00
❏ 2078		Let the Funk Flow/Sometimes That's All There Is	1980		2.50	5.00
❏ 2129		Get Up Offa That Thing/It's Too Funky in Here	1980		2.50	5.00
❏ 2167		Give the Bass Player Some Part 1/Part 2	1981		2.50	5.00
❏ 14088		Make It Funky Part 1/Make It Funky Part 2	1971		3.00	6.00
❏ 14098		My Part/Make It Funky, Part 3//Make It Funky, Part 4	1971		3.00	6.00
❏ 14100		I'm a Greedy Man Part 1/I'm a Greedy Man Part 2	1971		3.00	6.00
❏ 14109		Talking Loud and Saying Nothing Part 1/Part 2	1972		3.00	6.00
❏ 14110		Nothing Beats a Try But a Fail/Hot Pants Road	1972			*Unreleased*
❏ 14116		King Heroin/Theme from King Heroin	1972		3.00	6.00
❏ 14116	PS	King Heroin/Theme from King Heroin	1972	2.50	5.00	10.00
❏ 14125		There It Is Part 1/There It Is Part 2	1972		3.00	6.00
❏ 14129		Honky Tonk Part 1/Honky Tonk Part 2	1972		3.00	6.00
		Artist credit: "James Brown Soul Train"				
❏ 14139		Get On the Good Foot Part 1/Get On the Good Foot Part 2	1972		3.00	6.00
❏ 14153		I Got a Bag of My Own/Public Enemy #1	1972		3.00	6.00
❏ 14155		I Got a Bag of My Own/I Know It's True	1972	7.50	15.00	30.00
		Manufactured in U.S. for export				
❏ 14157		What My Baby Needs Now Is a Little More Lovin'/This Guy-This Girl's in Love	1972		3.00	6.00
		With Lyn Collins				
❏ 14161		Santa Goes Straight to the Ghetto/Sweet Little Baby Boy	1972		3.00	6.00
❏ 14162		I Got Ants in My Pants (and I want to dance) Part 1/Part 2	1973		2.50	5.00
❏ 14168		Down and Out in New York City/Mama's Dead	1973		2.50	5.00
❏ 14169		The Boss/Like It Is, Like It Was	1973		2.50	5.00
❏ 14177		Think/Something	1973		2.50	5.00
❏ 14185		Think/Something	1973		2.50	5.00
❏ 14193		Woman Part 1/Woman Part 2	1973		2.50	5.00
❏ 14194		Sexy, Sexy, Sexy/Slaughter Theme	1973		2.50	5.00
❏ 14199		Let It Be Me/It's All Right	1973		2.50	5.00
		With Lyn Collins				
❏ 14206		I Got a Good Thing Part 1/I Got a Good Thing Part 2	1973		2.50	5.00
❏ 14210		Stone to the Bone Part 1/Stone to the Bone Part 2	1973	2.50	5.00	10.00
❏ 14210		Stoned to the Bone Part 1/Stoned to the Bone Part 2	1973		2.50	5.00
		Notice corrected title				
❏ 14223		The Payback Part 1/The Payback Part 2	1974		2.50	5.00
❏ 14223	PS	The Payback Part 1/The Payback Part 2	1974	2.50	5.00	10.00
❏ 14244		My Thang/Public Enemy No. 1	1974		2.50	5.00
❏ 14255		Papa Don't Take No Mess Part 1/Part 2	1974		2.50	5.00
❏ 14258		Funky President (People It's Bad)/Coldblooded	1974		2.50	5.00
❏ 14268		Reality/I Need Your Love So Bad	1975		2.50	5.00
❏ 14270		Sex Machine Part 1/Sex Machine Part 2	1975		2.50	5.00
❏ 14274		Thank You For Letting Me Be Myself And... Part 1/Part 2	1975		2.50	5.00
❏ 14279		Dead On It Part 1/Dead On It Part 2	1975			*Unreleased*
❏ 14281		Hustle (Dead On It) Part 1/Hustle (Dead On It) Part 2	1975		2.50	5.00
❏ 14295		Superbad, Superslick Part 1/Superbad, Superslick Part 2	1975		2.50	5.00
❏ 14301		Hot (I Need to Be Loved, Loved, Loved, Loved)/Superbad, Superslick	1975		2.50	5.00
❏ 14302		Dooley's Junkyard Dogs Part 1/Part 2	1975		2.50	5.00
❏ 14303		(I Love You) For Sentimental Reasons/Goodnight My Love	1975		2.50	5.00
❏ 14326		Get Up Offa That Thing/Release the Pressure	1976		2.50	5.00
❏ 14354		I Refuse to Lose/Home Again	1976		2.50	5.00
❏ 14360		Bodyheat Part 1/Bodyheat Part 2	1976		2.50	5.00
❏ 14388		Kiss in 77/Woman	1977		2.50	5.00
❏ 14409		Give Me Some Skin/People Wake Up and Live	1977		2.50	5.00
		With the J.B.'s				
❏ 14433		Take Me Higher and Groove Me/Summertime	1977		2.50	5.00
		B-side by Martha and James				
❏ 14438		If You Don't Give a Doggone About It/People Who Criticize	1977		2.50	5.00
		With the New J.B.'s				
❏ 14460		Love Me Tender/Have a Happy Day	1978		2.50	5.00
		With the New J.B.'s				
❏ 14465		Eyesight/I Never Never Never Will Forget	1978		2.50	5.00

Number	Title (A Side/B Side)	Year	VG	VG+	NM
❏ 14487	The Spank/Love Me Tender	1978		2.50	5.00
❏ 14512	Nature Part 1/Nature Part 2	1978		2.50	5.00
❏ 14522	For Goodness Sakes, Look at Those Cakes Part 1/ Part 2	1979		2.50	5.00
❏ 14540	Someone to Talk To Part 1/Someone to Talk To Part 2	1979		2.50	5.00
❏ 14557	It's Too Funky in Here/Are We Really Dancing	1979		2.50	5.00
❏ 871 804-7	Think/Lost Someone	1989			3.00
	Reissue				
❏ 871 808-7	Out of Sight/Maybe the Last Time	1989			3.00
	Reissue				
❏ 887 500-7	(Get Up I Feel Like Being a) Sex Machine/ Vincent's Theme	1988			3.00
	B-side by Ethan James				

Scotti Bros.

Number	Title (A Side/B Side)	Year	VG	VG+	NM
❏ 05682	Living in America/Farewell	1985			3.00
	B-side by Vince Di Cola				
❏ 05682 PS	Living in America/Farewell	1985			3.00
❏ 06275	Gravity/Gravity (Dub Mix)	1986			3.00
❏ 06275 PS	Gravity/Gravity (Dub Mix)	1986			3.00
❏ 06568	How Do You Stop/House of Rock	1987			3.00
❏ 06568 PS	How Do You Stop/House of Rock	1987			3.00
❏ 07090	Let's Get Personal/Repeat the Bat	1987			3.00
❏ 07783	I'm Real/Gravity	1988			3.00
❏ 07783 PS	I'm Real/Gravity	1988			3.00
❏ 07975	Static/Godfather Runnin' the Joint	1988			3.00
❏ 08088	Time to Get Busy/Busy J.B.	1988			3.00
❏ 68559	It's Your Money $/You and Me	1989			3.00
❏ 75286	(So Tired of Standing Still We Got to) Move On/ You Are My Everything	1991		2.00	4.00

Smash

Number	Title (A Side/B Side)	Year	VG	VG+	NM
❏ 1898	Caledonia/Evil	1964	3.00	6.00	12.00
❏ 1898	Caldonia/Evil	1964	3.00	6.00	12.00
	Note slight spelling variation				
❏ 1898 PS	Caledonia/Evil	1964	6.25	12.50	25.00
❏ 1908	The Things That I Used to Do/Out of the Blue	1964	3.00	6.00	12.00
❏ 1908 PS	The Things That I Used to Do/Out of the Blue	1964	6.25	12.50	25.00
❏ 1919	Out of Sight/Maybe the Last Time	1964	3.00	6.00	12.00
❏ 1919 PS	Out of Sight/Maybe the Last Time	1964	6.25	12.50	25.00
❏ 1949	Who's Afraid of Virginia Woolf? Part 1/Part 2	1964			Unreleased
❏ 1975	Devil's Hideaway/Who's Afraid of Virginia Woolf?	1965	2.50	5.00	10.00
❏ 1989	I Got You/Only You	1965	12.50	25.00	50.00
	Withdrawn				
❏ 2008	Try Me/Papa's Got a Brand New Bag	1965	2.50	5.00	10.00
❏ 2028	New Breed Part 1/New Breed Part 2	1966	2.50	5.00	10.00
❏ 2042	James Brown's Boo-Ga-Loo/ Lost in the Mood of Changes	1966	2.50	5.00	10.00
❏ 2064	Let's Go Get Stoned/Our Day Will Come	1966	2.50	5.00	10.00
❏ 2093	Jimmy Mack/What Do You Like	1967	2.50	5.00	10.00

T.K.

Number	Title (A Side/B Side)	Year	VG	VG+	NM
❏ 1039	Rapp Payback (Where Iz Moses) Part 1/Part 2	1980		2.00	4.00
❏ 1042	Stay with Me/Smokin' and Drinkin'	1981		2.00	4.00

Brown, Roy

Bluesway

Number	Title (A Side/B Side)	Year	VG	VG+	NM
❏ 61002	New Orleans Women/ Standing on Broadway (Watching the Girls)	1967	2.00	4.00	8.00

DeLuxe

Note: Roy Brown singles on DeLuxe before 3318 are unconfirmed on 45 rpm

Number	Title (A Side/B Side)	Year	VG	VG+	NM
❏ 3318	Big Town/Train Time Blues	1951	50.00	100.00	200.00
	Black vinyl				
❏ 3318	Big Town/Train Time Blues	1951	100.00	200.00	400.00
	Blue vinyl				
❏ 3319	Bar Room Blues/Good Rockin' Man	1951	50.00	100.00	200.00
	Black vinyl				
❏ 3319	Bar Room Blues/Good Rockin' Man	1951	100.00	200.00	400.00
	Blue vinyl				
❏ 3323	I've Got the Last Laugh Now/Brown Angel	1951	50.00	100.00	200.00
	Black vinyl				
❏ 3323	I've Got the Last Laugh Now/Brown Angel	1951	100.00	200.00	400.00
	Blue vinyl				

Home of the Blues

Number	Title (A Side/B Side)	Year	VG	VG+	NM
❏ 107	Don't Break My Heart/A Man with the Blues	1960	6.25	12.50	25.00
❏ 110	Tired of Being Alone/Rocking All the Time	1960	6.25	12.50	25.00
❏ 115	Oh So Wonderful/Sugar Baby	1961	6.25	12.50	25.00
❏ 122	Rock and Roll Jamboree/I Need a Friend	1961	6.25	12.50	25.00

Imperial

Number	Title (A Side/B Side)	Year	VG	VG+	NM
❏ 5422	Everybody/Saturday Night	1957	7.50	15.00	30.00
❏ 5427	Party Doll/I'm Sticking with You	1957	7.50	15.00	30.00
❏ 5439	Let the Four Winds Blow/Diddy-Y-Diddy-O	1957	7.50	15.00	30.00
❏ 5455	I'm Convicted of Love/I'm Ready to Play	1957	7.50	15.00	30.00
❏ 5469	Tick of the Clock/Slow Down Little Eva	1957	7.50	15.00	30.00
❏ 5489	Ain't Gonna Do It/Sail On Little Girl	1958	7.50	15.00	30.00
❏ 5510	Hip Shakin' Baby/Be My Love Tonight	1958	7.50	15.00	30.00
❏ 5969	Let the Four Winds Blow/Diddy-Yi-Diddy-Yo	1963	5.00	10.00	20.00

Number	Title (A Side/B Side)	Year	VG	VG+	NM

King

❑ 4602	Travelin' Man/Hurry, Hurry Baby	1953	15.00	30.00	60.00
❑ 4609	Grandpa Stole My Baby/Money Can't Buy Love	1953	15.00	30.00	60.00
❑ 4704	Trouble at Midnight/Bootlegging Baby	1954	15.00	30.00	60.00
❑ 4715	Up Jumped the Devil/This Is My Last Goodbye	1954	15.00	30.00	60.00
❑ 4722	No Love at All/Don't Let It Rain	1954	15.00	30.00	60.00
❑ 4731	Ain't It a Shame/Gal from Kokomo	1954	15.00	30.00	60.00
❑ 4743	Worried Life Blues/Black Diamond	1954	15.00	30.00	60.00
❑ 4761	Fannie Brown Got Married/Queen of Diamonds	1955	12.50	25.00	50.00
❑ 4816	Shake 'Em Up Baby/Letter to Baby	1955	12.50	25.00	50.00
❑ 4834	My Little Angel Child/She's Gone Too Long	1955	12.50	25.00	50.00
❑ 5178	La-Dee-Dah-Dee/Melinda	1959	5.00	10.00	20.00
❑ 5207	I Never Had It So Good/Rinky Dinky Doo	1959	5.00	10.00	20.00
❑ 5218	Hard Luck Blues/Good Looking and Forty	1959	5.00	10.00	20.00
❑ 5247	School Bell Rock/Ain't No Rocking No More	1959	5.00	10.00	20.00
❑ 5333	Ain't Got No Blues Today/Adorable One	1960	5.00	10.00	20.00
❑ 5521	Mighty Mighty Man/Good Man Blues	1961	5.00	10.00	20.00

Mercury

❑ 73166	It's My Fault Darling/Love for Sale	1970		3.00	6.00
❑ 73219	Mail Man Blues/Hunky Funky Woman	1971		3.00	6.00

Brown, Ruth

Atlantic

Note: Ruth Brown records on Atlantic before 948 (except 919) are unconfirmed on 45 rpm

❑ 919	Teardrops from My Eyes/ Am I Making the Same Mistake	1950	100.00	200.00	400.00

This and Atlantic 914 were the label's first two 45s.

❑ 948	Shine On--Big Bright Moon Shine On/Without My Love	1951	15.00	30.00	60.00
❑ 962	5-10-15 Hours/Be Anything But Be Mine	1952	12.50	25.00	50.00
❑ 973	Daddy Daddy/Have a Good Time	1952	12.50	25.00	50.00
❑ 978	Three Letters/Good for Nothing Joe	1952	12.50	25.00	50.00
❑ 986	(Mama) He Treats Your Daughter Mean/R.B. Blues	1953	10.00	20.00	40.00
❑ 993	Wild Wild Young Men/Mend Your Ways	1953	10.00	20.00	40.00
❑ 1005	The Tears Keep Tumblin' Down/I Would If I Could	1953	7.50	15.00	30.00
❑ 1018	Love Contest/If You Don't Want Me	1954	7.50	15.00	30.00
❑ 1023	Sentimental Journey/It's All in Your Mind	1954	7.50	15.00	30.00
❑ 1027	If I Had Any Sense/Hello Little Boy	1954	7.50	15.00	30.00
❑ 1036	Oh What a Dream/Please Don't Freeze	1954	7.50	15.00	30.00
❑ 1044	Somebody Touch Me/Mambo Baby	1954	7.50	15.00	30.00
❑ 1051	Ever Since My Baby's Been Gone/Bye Bye Young Men	1955	7.50	15.00	30.00
❑ 1059	I Can See Everybody's Baby/As Long As I'm Moving	1955	7.50	15.00	30.00
❑ 1072	What'd I Say/It's Love Baby (24 Hours of the Day)	1955	7.50	15.00	30.00
❑ 1077	Love Has Joined Us Together/I Gotta Have You	1955	7.50	15.00	30.00

With Clyde McPhatter

❑ 1082	Old Man River/I Want to Do More	1956	6.25	12.50	25.00
❑ 1091	Sweet Baby of Mine/I'm Getting Right	1956	6.25	12.50	25.00
❑ 1102	I Want to Be Loved/Mom, Oh Mom	1956	6.25	12.50	25.00
❑ 1113	Smooth Operator/I Still Love You	1956	6.25	12.50	25.00
❑ 1125	Lucky Lips/My Heart Is Breaking Over You	1957	6.25	12.50	25.00
❑ 1140	When I Get You Baby/One More Time	1957	6.25	12.50	25.00
❑ 1153	Show Me/I Hope We Meet	1957	6.25	12.50	25.00
❑ 1166	A New Love/Look Me Up	1957	6.25	12.50	25.00
❑ 1177	Book of Lies/Just Too Much	1958	6.25	12.50	25.00
❑ 1197	This Little Girl's Gone/Why Me	1958	6.25	12.50	25.00
❑ 2008	Mama, He Treats Your Daughter Mean/I'll Step Aside	1958	5.00	10.00	20.00
❑ 2015	5-10-15 Hours/Itty Bitty Girl	1959	5.00	10.00	20.00
❑ 2026	Jack O'Diamonds/I Can't Hear a Word You Say	1959	5.00	10.00	20.00
❑ 2035	I Don't Know/Papa Daddy	1959	5.00	10.00	20.00
❑ 2052	Don't Deceive Me/I Burned Your Letter	1960	5.00	10.00	20.00
❑ 2064	The Door Is Still Open/What I Wouldn't Give	1960	5.00	10.00	20.00
❑ 2075	Taking Care of Business/Honey Boy	1960	5.00	10.00	20.00
❑ 2088	Sure 'Nuff/Here He Comes	1961	3.75	7.50	15.00
❑ 2104	It Tears Me All to Pieces/Anyone But You	1961	3.75	7.50	15.00

Decca

❑ 31598	What Happened to You/Yes Sir That's My Baby	1964	2.50	5.00	10.00
❑ 31640	Come a Little Closer/I Love Him and I Know It	1964	2.50	5.00	10.00

Mainstream

❑ 611	On the Good Ship Lollipop/Hurry On Down	1965	2.50	5.00	10.00

Philips

❑ 40028	Shake a Hand/Say It Again	1962	3.00	6.00	12.00
❑ 40056	Mama He Treats Your Daughter Mean/Hold My Hand	1962	3.00	6.00	12.00
❑ 40086	He Tells Me with His Eyes/If You Don't Tell Nobody	1963	3.00	6.00	12.00
❑ 40119	Satisfied/If You Don't Tell Nobody	1963	3.00	6.00	12.00

Bruce and Terry

(Bruce Johnston and Terry Melcher)

Columbia

❑ 42956	Custom Machine/Makaha at Midnight	1964	5.00	10.00	20.00
❑ 43055	Summer Means Fun/Yeah!	1964	5.00	10.00	20.00
❑ 43238	I Love You Model T/Carmen	1965	5.00	10.00	20.00
❑ 43378	Raining in My Heart/Four Strong Winds	1965	4.00	8.00	16.00
❑ 43479	Thank You Baby/Come Love	1965	4.00	8.00	16.00
❑ 43582	Don't Run Away/Girl It's All Right Now	1966	4.00	8.00	16.00

Number		Title (A Side/B Side)	Year	VG	VG+	NM

Bruce, Edwin
(Also recorded as Ed Bruce)
Sun

| ☐ 276 | | Rock Boppin' Baby/More Than Yesterday | 1957 | 7.50 | 15.00 | 30.00 |
| ☐ 292 | | Sweet Woman/Part of My Life | 1958 | 10.00 | 20.00 | 40.00 |

Bryan, Billy - See "Pitney, Gene"

Bubble Puppy, The
International Artists

☐ 128		Hot Smoke and Sasafrass/Lonely	1969	5.00	10.00	20.00
☐ 133		Beginning/If I Had a Reason	1969	6.25	12.50	25.00
☐ 136		Days of Our Time/Thinkin' About Thinkin'	1969	6.25	12.50	25.00
☐ 138		What Do You See/Hurry Sundown	1970	6.25	12.50	25.00
☐ 138	DJ	What Do You See/Hurry Sundown	1970	12.50	25.00	50.00
		Green vinyl promo				

Bubi and Bob
Sphinx

| ☐ 1201 | | The Mummy/Biscayne Beat | 1959 | 7.50 | 15.00 | 30.00 |

Buccaneers, The
Rainbow

| ☐ 211 | | Dear Ruth/Fine Brown Flame | 1953 | 125.00 | 250.00 | 500.00 |

Rama

| ☐ 21 | | The Stars Will Remember/Come Back My Love | 1954 | 250.00 | 500.00 | 1,000 |
| ☐ 24 | | In the Mission of St. Augustine/You Did Me Wrong | 1954 | 400.00 | 800.00 | 1,200 |

Southern

| ☐ 101 | | Dear Ruth/Fine Brown Flame | 1953 | 250.00 | 500.00 | 1,000 |

Buchanan and Ancell
Flying Saucer

| ☐ 501 | | The Creature/Meet the Creature | 1957 | 10.00 | 20.00 | 40.00 |

Buchanan and Cella
ABC-Paramount

| ☐ 10033 | | String Along with Pal-O-Mine/
More and More String Along with Pal-O-Mine | 1959 | 6.25 | 12.50 | 25.00 |

Buchanan and Goodman
(Also see "Buchanan, Bill"; "Goodman, Dickie")
Comic

| ☐ 500 | | Flying Saucer the Third/The Cha Cha Lesson | 1959 | 10.00 | 20.00 | 40.00 |

Luniverse

☐ 101		The Flying Saucer Part 1/The Flying Saucer Part 2	1956	12.50	25.00	50.00
☐ 101X		Back to Earth Part 1/Back to Earth Part 2	1956	50.00	100.00	200.00
☐ 102		Buchanan and Goodman On Trial/Crazy	1956	10.00	20.00	40.00
☐ 102X		Public Opinion Part 1/Public Opinion Part 2	1956		Not known to exist	
☐ 103		The Banana Boat Story/The Mystery (In Slow Motion)	1957	10.00	20.00	40.00
☐ 105		Flying Saucer The 2nd/Martian Melody	1957	10.00	20.00	40.00
☐ 107		Santa and the Satellite Part 1/ Santa and the Satellite Part 2	1957	10.00	20.00	40.00
☐ 108		The Flying Saucer Goes West/Saucer Serenade	1958	10.00	20.00	40.00

Novelty

| ☐ 301 | | Frankenstein of '59/Frankenstein Returns | 1959 | 10.00 | 20.00 | 40.00 |

Buchanan and Greenfield
Novel

☐ 711		The Invasion/What a Lovely Party	1964	7.50	15.00	30.00
		Originals have all-red labels				
☐ 711		The Invasion/What a Lovely Party	1972	2.00	4.00	8.00
		Red and white label reissue				

Buchanan, Bill
(Of Buchanan and Goodman and all the other "Buchanan and..." groups listed in here)
Gone

| ☐ 5032 | | The Thing/Happy Day | 1958 | 7.50 | 15.00 | 30.00 |

United Artists

| ☐ 531 | | The Night Before Halloween/Beware | 1962 | 3.75 | 7.50 | 15.00 |

Buckeyes, The
DeLuxe

| ☐ 6110 | | Since I Fell for You/My Only You | 1957 | 75.00 | 150.00 | 300.00 |
| ☐ 6126 | | Dottie Baby/Begging You Please | 1957 | 100.00 | 200.00 | 400.00 |

Buckingham Nicks
(Also see "Nicks, Stevie")
Polydor

☐ 14209		Don't Let Me Down Again/The Races Are Run	1973	12.50	25.00	50.00
☐ 14229		Crying in the Night/Without a Leg to Stand On	1974	12.50	25.00	50.00
☐ 14335		Don't Let Me Down Again/Crystal	1976	7.50	15.00	30.00
☐ 14428		Crying in the Night/Stephanie	1977	7.50	15.00	30.00
☐ 14428	PS	Crying in the Night/Stephanie	1977	15.00	30.00	60.00

Number		Title (A Side/B Side)	Year	VG	VG+	NM

Buckinghams, The
(The Laurie and Seg-Way Buckinghams are not the same group as the others)
Columbia

Number		Title (A Side/B Side)	Year	VG	VG+	NM
❏ 44053		Don't You Care/Why Don't You Love Me	1967	2.00	4.00	8.00
❏ 44053	PS	Don't You Care/Why Don't You Love Me	1967	3.00	6.00	12.00
❏ 44182		Mercy, Mercy, Mercy/You Are Gone	1967	2.00	4.00	8.00
❏ 44182	PS	Mercy, Mercy, Mercy/You Are Gone	1967	3.00	6.00	12.00
❏ 44254		Hey Baby (They're Playing Our Song)/And Our Love	1967	2.00	4.00	8.00
❏ 44254	PS	Hey Baby (They're Playing Our Song)/And Our Love	1967	3.00	6.00	12.00
❏ 44378		Susan/Foreign Policy	1967	2.00	4.00	8.00
❏ 44378	PS	Susan/Foreign Policy	1967	3.00	6.00	12.00
❏ 44533		Back in Love Again/You Misunderstand Me	1968	2.00	4.00	8.00
❏ 44533	PS	Back in Love Again/You Misunderstand Me	1968	3.00	6.00	12.00
❏ 44672		Where Did You Come From/Song of the Breeze	1968	2.00	4.00	8.00
❏ 44790		Can't You Find the Words/ This Is How Much I Love You	1969	2.00	4.00	8.00
❏ 44923		It's a Beautiful Day/Difference of Opinion	1969	2.00	4.00	8.00
❏ 45066		It Took Forever/I Got a Feelin'	1970	2.00	4.00	8.00

Laurie

Number		Title (A Side/B Side)	Year	VG	VG+	NM
❏ 3258		Gonna Say Goodbye/Many Times	1964	2.50	5.00	10.00

Red Label

Number		Title (A Side/B Side)	Year	VG	VG+	NM
❏ 71001		Veronica/Can We Talk About It	1985		2.00	4.00

Seg-Way

Number		Title (A Side/B Side)	Year	VG	VG+	NM
❏ 1004		Lobo Lobo/Rockin' Piper	1962	2.50	5.00	10.00

SpectraSound

Number		Title (A Side/B Side)	Year	VG	VG+	NM
❏ 4618		Sweets for My Sweet/Beginner's Love	1967	5.00	10.00	20.00

U.S.A.

Number		Title (A Side/B Side)	Year	VG	VG+	NM
❏ 844		I'll Go Crazy/I Don't Wanna Cry	1966	3.00	6.00	12.00
❏ 848		I Call Your Name/Makin' Up and Breakin' Up	1966	3.00	6.00	12.00
❏ 853		I've Been Wrong/Love Ain't Enough	1966	3.00	6.00	12.00
❏ 860		Kind of a Drag/You Make Me Feel So Good	1966	3.75	7.50	15.00
		Light blue label with all dark blue printing				
❏ 860		Kind of a Drag/You Make Me Feel So Good	1966	3.75	7.50	15.00
		Light blue label with red, white, blue and black printing				
❏ 869		Lawdy Miss Clawdy/I Call Your Name	1967	3.00	6.00	12.00
❏ 869		Lawdy Miss Clawdy/Making Up and Breaking Up	1967	3.00	6.00	12.00
❏ 873		Summertime/Don't Want to Cry	1967	3.00	6.00	12.00

Buffalo Springfield, The
(Also see "Furay, Richie"; "Stills, Stephen"; "Young, Neil")
Atco

Number		Title (A Side/B Side)	Year	VG	VG+	NM
❏ 6428		Nowadays Clancy Can't Even Sing/ Go And Say Goodbye	1966	5.00	10.00	20.00
❏ 6452		Everybody's Wrong/Burned	1966	5.00	10.00	20.00
❏ 6459		For What It's Worth/ Do I Have to Come Right Out and Say It	1967	3.00	6.00	12.00
❏ 6459		For What It's Worth (Stop, Hey, What's That Sound)/ Do I Have to Come Right Out and Say It	1967	2.50	5.00	10.00
❏ 6499		Bluebird/Mr. Soul	1967	3.75	7.50	15.00
❏ 6519		Rock 'N' Roll Woman/A Child's Claim to Fame	1967	2.00	4.00	8.00
❏ 6545		Expecting to Fly/Everydays	1968	2.00	4.00	8.00
❏ 6572		Uno Mundo/Merry-Go-Round	1968	2.00	4.00	8.00
❏ 6602		Special Care/Kind Woman	1968	2.00	4.00	8.00
❏ 6615		Four Days Gone/On the Way Home	1968	2.00	4.00	8.00

Bug Collectors, The
Catch

Number		Title (A Side/B Side)	Year	VG	VG+	NM
❏ 103		The Beatle Bug/Thief in the Night	1964	5.00	10.00	20.00

Bug Men, The
Dot

Number		Title (A Side/B Side)	Year	VG	VG+	NM
❏ 16592		Beatles, You Bug Me/Bloomin' Bird	1964	4.00	8.00	16.00

Bugaloos, The
Capitol

Number		Title (A Side/B Side)	Year	VG	VG+	NM
❏ 2946		Senses of Our World/For a Friend	1970	3.00	6.00	12.00

Buggs, The
Soma

Number		Title (A Side/B Side)	Year	VG	VG+	NM
❏ 1413		The Buggs vs. The Beatles/She Loves You	1964	6.25	12.50	25.00

Buoys, The
Polydor

Number		Title (A Side/B Side)	Year	VG	VG+	NM
❏ 14201		Liza's Last Ride/Downtown Singer	1973		3.00	6.00

Scepter

Number		Title (A Side/B Side)	Year	VG	VG+	NM
❏ 12254		These Days/Don't You Know It's Over	1969	2.00	4.00	8.00
❏ 12275		Timothy/It Feels Good	1970	2.50	5.00	10.00
❏ 12275	PS	Timothy/It Feels Good	1970	5.00	10.00	20.00
❏ 12318		Give Up Your Guns/Prince of Thieves	1971	2.00	4.00	8.00
❏ 12331		Tell Me Heaven Is Here/Bloodknot	1971	2.00	4.00	8.00

Number	Title (A Side/B Side)	Year	VG	VG+	NM

Burdon, Eric, and the Animals - See "Animals, The"

Burdon, Eric, and War

ABC

❑ 12244	Magic Mountain/Home Dream	1977		2.50	5.00

MGM

❑ 14118	Spill the Wine/Magic Mountain	1970		3.00	6.00
❑ 14118	PS Spill the Wine/Magic Mountain	1970	3.00	6.00	12.00
❑ 14196	They Can't Take Away Our Music/Home Cookin'	1970		2.50	5.00

Burgess, Dave

(Also see "Champs, The")

Challenge

❑ 1008	I'm Available/Who's Gonna Cry	1957	6.25	12.50	25.00
❑ 1018	Take This Love/Maybelle	1958	5.00	10.00	20.00

As "Dave Burgess and the Champs"

❑ 59032	Lovey Dovey Baby/I Hang My Head and Cry	1958	5.00	10.00	20.00
❑ 59037	I Don't Want to Know/Lulu	1959	5.00	10.00	20.00
❑ 59045	Everlovin'/Just for Me	1959	5.00	10.00	20.00
❑ 59101	Without You/Are You Teasing Me	1961	5.00	10.00	20.00

Okeh

❑ 7002	Don't Put a Dent in My Heart/Judalina	1953	6.25	12.50	25.00
❑ 7044	Gratefully Yours/Too Late for Tears	1954	6.25	12.50	25.00

Tampa

❑ 104	Down, Down/Don't Turn Your Back on Love	1955	6.25	12.50	25.00
❑ 105	I Love Paris/Five Foot Two, Eyes of Blue	1955	6.25	12.50	25.00

Burgess, Sonny

Phillips Int'l.

❑ 3551	Sadie's Back in Town/Kiss Goodnight	1960	7.50	15.00	30.00

Sun

❑ 247	Red Headed Woman/We Wanna Boogie	1956	37.50	75.00	150.00
❑ 263	Ain't Got a Thing/Restless	1957	20.00	40.00	80.00
❑ 285	My Bucket's Got a Hole in It/Sweet Misery	1958	12.50	25.00	50.00
❑ 304	Thunderbird/Itchy	1958	7.50	15.00	30.00

Burke, Buddy

Bullseye

❑ 1002	That Big Old Moon/Street of Sorrows	195?	37.50	75.00	150.00

Burke, Solomon

ABC Dunhill

❑ 4388	Midnight and You/I Have a Dream	1974		2.50	5.00
❑ 15009	Midnight and You/I Have a Dream	1974		2.00	4.00

Amherst

❑ 736	Please Don't You Say Goodbye to Me/See That Girl	1978		2.00	4.00

Apollo

❑ 485	Christmas Presents/When I'm All Alone	1955	7.50	15.00	30.00
❑ 487	I'm in Love/Why Do Me That Way	1956	6.25	12.50	25.00
❑ 491	I'm All Alone/To Thee	1956	6.25	12.50	25.00
❑ 500	No Man Walks Alone/Walking in a Dream	1956	6.25	12.50	25.00
❑ 505	A Picture of You/You Can Run But You Can't Hide	1957	6.25	12.50	25.00
❑ 511	I Need You Tonight/This Is It	1957	6.25	12.50	25.00
❑ 512	For You and You Alone/You Are My One Love	1957	6.25	12.50	25.00
❑ 522	They Always Say/Don't Cry	1958	6.25	12.50	25.00
❑ 527	My Heart Is a Chapel/This Is It	1958	6.25	12.50	25.00

Atlantic

❑ 2089	Keep the Magic Working/How Many Times	1961	3.75	7.50	15.00
❑ 2114	Just Out of Reach (Of My Two Open Arms)/Be-Bop Grandma	1961	3.75	7.50	15.00
❑ 2131	Cry to Me/I Almost Lost My Mind	1962	3.75	7.50	15.00
❑ 2147	Down in the Valley/I'm Hanging Up My Heart for You	1962	3.75	7.50	15.00
❑ 2157	I Really Don't Want to Know/Tonight My Heart She Is Crying (Love Is a Bird)	1962	3.75	7.50	15.00
❑ 2170	Go On Back to Him/I Said I Was Sorry	1962	3.75	7.50	15.00
❑ 2180	Words/Home in Your Heart	1963	3.75	7.50	15.00
❑ 2185	If You Need Me/You Can Make It If You Try	1963	3.75	7.50	15.00
❑ 2196	Can't Nobody Love You/Stupidity	1963	3.75	7.50	15.00
❑ 2205	You're Good for Me/Beautiful Brown Eyes	1963	3.75	7.50	15.00
❑ 2218	He'll Have to Go/Rockin' Soul	1964	3.00	6.00	12.00
❑ 2226	Goodbye Baby (Baby Goodbye)/Someone to Love Me	1964	3.00	6.00	12.00
❑ 2241	Everybody Needs Somebody to Love/Looking for My Baby	1964	3.00	6.00	12.00
❑ 2254	Yes I Do/Won't You Give Him (One More Chance)	1964	3.00	6.00	12.00
❑ 2259	The Price/More Rockin' Soul	1964	3.00	6.00	12.00
❑ 2276	Got to Get You Off My Mind/Peppin'	1965	3.00	6.00	12.00
❑ 2288	Tonight's the Night/Maggie's Farm	1965	3.00	6.00	12.00
❑ 2299	Someone Is Watching/Dance, Dance, Dance	1965	3.00	6.00	12.00
❑ 2308	Only Love (Can Save Me Now)/A Little Girl That Loves Me	1965	3.00	6.00	12.00
❑ 2314	Baby Come On Home/(No, No, No) Can't Stop Lovin' You Now	1965	3.00	6.00	12.00
❑ 2327	I Feel a Sin Coming On/Mountain of Pride	1966	2.50	5.00	10.00
❑ 2345	Lawdy Miss Clawdy/Suddenly	1966	2.50	5.00	10.00
❑ 2349	Keep Looking/Don't Want You No More	1966	2.50	5.00	10.00

Number	Title (A Side/B Side)	Year	VG	VG+	NM
❑ 2359	When She Touches Me/ Woman How Do You Make Me Love You Like I Do	1966	2.50	5.00	10.00
❑ 2369	Presents for Christmas/A Tear Fell	1966	3.00	6.00	12.00
❑ 2378	Keep a Light in the Window Till I Come Home/ Time Is a Thief	1967	2.50	5.00	10.00
❑ 2416	Take Me (Just As I Am)/Stayed Away Too Long	1967	2.50	5.00	10.00
❑ 2459	It's Been a Change/Detroit City	1967	2.50	5.00	10.00
❑ 2483	Party People/Need Your Love So Bad	1968	2.50	5.00	10.00
❑ 2507	I Wish I Knew (How It Would Feel to Be Free)/ It's Just a Matter of Time Baby	1968	2.50	5.00	10.00
❑ 2527	Save it/Meet Me in Church	1968	2.50	5.00	10.00
❑ 2566	Get Out of My Life Woman/What'd I Say	1968	2.50	5.00	10.00
Bell					
❑ 759	Up Tight Good Woman/I Can't Stop	1969	2.00	4.00	8.00
❑ 783	Proud Mary/What Am I Living For	1969	2.00	4.00	8.00
❑ 806	That Lucky Old Sun/How Big a Fool	1969	2.00	4.00	8.00
❑ 829	I'm Gonna Stay Right Here/Generation of Revelations	1969	2.00	4.00	8.00
❑ 891	God Knows I Love You/In the Ghetto	1970	3.00	6.00	
Chess					
❑ 2159	You and Your Baby Blues/ I'm Leaving on That Late, Late Train	1975		2.00	4.00
❑ 2172	Let Me Wrap My Arms Around You/Everlasting Love	1975		2.00	4.00
Infinity					
❑ 50,046	Sidewalks, Fences and Walls/ Boo-Hoo-Hoo (Cra-Cra-Craya)	1979		2.50	5.00
Mala					
❑ 420	This Little Ring/I'm Not Afraid	1960	5.00	10.00	20.00
MGM					
❑ 14185	Lookin' Out My Back Door/All for the Love of Sunshine	1970		3.00	6.00
❑ 14221	The Electronic Magnetism (That's Heavy, Baby)/ Bridge of Life	1971		3.00	6.00
❑ 14279	J.C. I Know Who You Are/ The Things Love Will Make You Do	1971		3.00	6.00
❑ 14302	The Night They Drove Old Dixie Down/PSR 1983	1971		3.00	6.00
❑ 14353	Love's Street and Fool's Road/I Got to Tell It	1972		3.00	6.00
❑ 14402	We're Almost Home/Fight Back	1972		3.00	6.00
❑ 14425	Get Up and Do Something for Yourself/ We're Almost Home	1972		3.00	6.00
❑ 14571	Shambala/Love Thy Neighbor	1973		3.00	6.00
❑ 14651	Georgia Up North/Here Comes the Train	1973		3.00	6.00
Pride					
❑ 1017	I Can't Stop Loving You (Part 1)/ I Can't Stop Loving You (Part 2)	1972		3.00	6.00
❑ 1022	All I Want for Christmas/ I Can't Stop Loving You (Part 1)	1972		3.00	6.00
❑ 1028	My Prayer/Ookie Bookie Man	1973		3.00	6.00
❑ 1038	Sentimental Journey/Vaya Con Dios *With Lady Lee*	1973		3.00	6.00

Burnette, Billy
(Son of Dorsey Burnette. Also see "Fleetwood Mac")

Number	Title (A Side/B Side)	Year	VG	VG+	NM
A&M					
❑ 743	Just Because We're Kids/Little Girl, Big Love *As "Young Billy Bean"; A-side written by Dr. Seuss!*	1964	5.00	10.00	20.00
❑ 1794	Baby/Just Another Love Song	1976		2.50	5.00
Capricorn					
❑ 18525	I Still Remember (How to Miss You)/ I Recovered, I Survived	1993			3.00
❑ 18751	Tangled Up in Texas/Into the Storm	1992			3.00
Columbia					
❑ 02527	Let the New Love Begin/I Don't Know Why	1981		2.00	4.00
❑ 02699	The Bigger the Love/I Don't Know Why	1982		2.00	4.00
Entrance					
❑ 7515	Broken Hearted/I'm Always Wondering	1972		2.50	5.00
MCA Curb					
❑ 52626	Ain't It Just Like Love/Guitar Bug	1985			3.00
❑ 52710	Who's Using Your Heart Tonight/It Ain't Over	1985			3.00
❑ 52749	It's Not Easy/Try Me	1985			3.00
❑ 52852	Soldier of Love/Guitar Bug	1986			3.00
Polydor					
❑ 2024	What's a Little Love Between Friends/Precious Times	1979		2.00	4.00
❑ 14530	Dreamin' My Way Back to You/Shoo-Be-Doo	1979		2.00	4.00
❑ 14549	Believe What You Say/Mississippi Line	1979		2.00	4.00
Warner Bros.					
❑ 7327	Frog Prince/One Extreme to the Other	1969	2.00	4.00	8.00
❑ 19042	Nothin' to Do (And All Night to Do It)/ Can't Get Over You	1992			3.00

Burnette, Dorsey
(Also see "Burnette, Dorsey, and Johnny Burnette")

Number	Title (A Side/B Side)	Year	VG	VG+	NM
Abbott					
❑ 188	Let's Fall in Love/The Devil's Queen	1956	12.50	25.00	50.00
❑ 190	At a Distance/Jungle Magic	1957	12.50	25.00	50.00

Number		Title (A Side/B Side)	Year	VG	VG+	NM
Calliope						
❏ 8012		Soon As I Touched Her/Dear Hearted Children	1977		2.50	5.00
Capitol						
❏ 3073		New Orleans Woman/After the Long Drive Home	1971		2.50	5.00
❏ 3190		Shelby County Penal Farm/Children of the Universe	1971		2.50	5.00
❏ 3307		In the Spring (The Roses Always Turn Red)/	1972		2.50	5.00
		The Same Old You, The Same Old Me				
❏ 3404		I Just Couldn't Let Her Walk Away/Church Bells	1972		2.50	5.00
❏ 3463		Cry Mama/Lonely to Be Alone	1972		2.50	5.00
❏ 3529		I Let Another Good One Get Away/	1973		2.50	5.00
		Take Your Weapons, Lay 'Em Down				
❏ 3588		Keep Out of My Dreams/Mama, Mama	1973		2.50	5.00
❏ 3678		Sweet Lovin' Woman/Darlin' (Don't Come Back)	1973		2.50	5.00
❏ 3796		It Happens Every Time/Mr. Jukebox, Sing a Lullaby	1973		2.50	5.00
❏ 3829		Bob, All the Playboys, and Me/The Bootleggers	1974		2.50	5.00
❏ 3887		Daddy Loves You Honey/True Love Means Forgiving	1974		2.50	5.00
❏ 3963		What Ladies Can Do (When They Want To)/Tangerine	1974		2.50	5.00
Cee-Jam						
❏ 16		Bertha Lou/'Til the Law Says Stop	1957	20.00	40.00	80.00
Dot						
❏ 16230		Rainin' in My Heart/A Full House	1961	4.00	8.00	16.00
❏ 16265		The Feminine Touch/Sad Boy	1961	4.00	8.00	16.00
❏ 16305		A Country Boy in the Army/A Dying Ember	1961	4.00	8.00	16.00
Elektra						
❏ 46513		Here I Go Again/What Would It Profit Me	1979		2.00	4.00
❏ 46586		B.J. Kick-a-Beaux/What Would It Profit Me	1980		2.00	4.00
Era						
❏ 3012		(There Was a)Tall Oak Tree/Juarez Town	1960	5.00	10.00	20.00
❏ 3019		Hey Little One/Big Rock Candy Mountain	1960	4.00	8.00	16.00
❏ 3025		The Ghost of Billy Malloo/Red Roses	1960	4.00	8.00	16.00
❏ 3033		The River and the Mountain/This Hotel	1960	4.00	8.00	16.00
❏ 3033	PS	The River and the Mountain/This Hotel	1960	10.00	20.00	40.00
❏ 3041		Hard Rock Mine/(It's No) Sin	1961	4.00	8.00	16.00
❏ 3045		Great Shakin' Fever/That's Me Without You	1961	4.00	8.00	16.00
Happy Tiger						
❏ 546		To Be a Man/Fly Away and Hurry Home	1970		3.00	6.00
❏ 563		One Lump Sum/Call Me Lowdown	1970		3.00	6.00
Hickory						
❏ 1458		The House That Jack Built/Ain't That Fine	1967	2.00	4.00	8.00
Imperial						
❏ 5561		Try/You Came as a Miracle	1959	6.25	12.50	25.00
❏ 5597		Lonely Train/Misery	1959	6.25	12.50	25.00
❏ 5668		Way in the Middle of the Night/Your Love	1960	6.25	12.50	25.00
❏ 5756		House with a Tin Roof Top/Circle Rock	1961	6.25	12.50	25.00
❏ 5987		House with a Tin Roof Top/Circle Rock	1963	3.75	7.50	15.00
Liberty						
❏ 56087		The Greatest Love/	1969		3.00	6.00
		Thin Little Simple Little Plain Little Girl				
Mel-O-Dy						
❏ 113		Little Acorn/Cold As Usual	1964	3.75	7.50	15.00
❏ 116		Jimmy Brown/Everybody's Angel	1964	3.75	7.50	15.00
❏ 118		Long Long Time Ago/Ever Since the World Began	1964	3.75	7.50	15.00
Melodyland						
❏ 6007		Molly (I Ain't Gettin' Any Younger)/She's Feeling Low	1975		2.50	5.00
❏ 6019		Doggone the Dogs/Lyin' in Her Arms Again	1975		2.50	5.00
❏ 6031		Ain't No Heartbreak/I Dreamed I Saw	1976		2.50	5.00
Mercury						
❏ 72546		To Remember/In the Morning	1966			*Unreleased?*
Music Factory						
❏ 417		I'll Walk Away/Son, You've Got to Make It Alone	1968	2.00	4.00	8.00
Reprise						
❏ 0246		Four for Texas/Foolish Pride	1963	3.75	7.50	15.00
❏ 0246	PS	Four for Texas/Foolish Pride	1963	10.00	20.00	40.00
❏ 20,093		Castle in the Sky/Boys Keep Hanging Around	1962	3.75	7.50	15.00
❏ 20,121		Darling Jane/I'm a Waitin' For Ya Baby	1962	3.75	7.50	15.00
❏ 20,177		Invisible Chains/Pebbles	1963	3.75	7.50	15.00
❏ 20,208		One of the Lonely/Where's the Girl	1963	3.75	7.50	15.00
Smash						
❏ 2029		To Remember/In the Morning	1966	2.50	5.00	10.00
❏ 2039		If You Want to Love Somebody/	1966	2.50	5.00	10.00
		Teach Me Little Children				
❏ 2062		Tall Oak Tree/I Just Can't Be Tamed	1966	2.50	5.00	10.00
U.S. Navy						
❏ (# unknown)		Be a Navy Man	196?	10.00	20.00	40.00
❏ (# unknown)	PS	Be a Navy Man	196?	5.00	10.00	20.00

Burnette, Dorsey, and Johnny Burnette

(Also see individual listings)

Number		Title (A Side/B Side)	Year	VG	VG+	NM
Coral						
❏ 62190		Blues Stay Away from Me/Midnight Train	1960	50.00	100.00	200.00
		As "Johnny and Dorsey Burnette"				

Number		Title (A Side/B Side)	Year	VG	VG+	NM
Imperial						
❑ 5509		Warm Love/My Honey	1958	25.00	50.00	100.00
		As "Burnette Brothers"				
Reprise						
❑ 20,153		It Don't Take Much/Hey Sue	1963	5.00	10.00	20.00
Burnette, Johnny						
(Includes the Rock & Roll Trio 45s; also see "Burnette, Dorsey, and Johnny Burnette")						
Capitol						
❑ 5023		All Week Long/It Isn't There	1963	3.75	7.50	15.00
❑ 5114		You Taught Me the Way to Love You/The Opposite	1964	3.75	7.50	15.00
❑ 5176		Walkin' Talkin' Doll/Sweet Suzie	1964	3.75	7.50	15.00
Coral						
❑ 61651		Tear It Up/You're Undecided	1956	75.00	150.00	300.00
❑ 61675		Midnight Train/Oh Baby Babe	1956	75.00	150.00	300.00
❑ 61719		The Train Kept a-Rollin'/Honey Hush	1956	75.00	150.00	300.00
❑ 61758		Lonesome Train/I Just Found Out	1956	75.00	150.00	300.00
❑ 61829		Eager Beaver Baby/Touch Me	1957	75.00	150.00	300.00
❑ 61869		Drinkin' Wine Spo-Dee-O-Dee/Butterfingers	1957	75.00	150.00	300.00
❑ 61918		Rock Billy Boogie/If You Want It Enough	1957	75.00	150.00	300.00
Freedom						
❑ 44001		I'm Restless/Kiss Me	1958	20.00	40.00	80.00
❑ 44011		Gumbo/Me and the Bear	1959	20.00	40.00	80.00
❑ 44017		Sweet Baby Doll/I'll Never Love Again	1959	20.00	40.00	80.00
Liberty						
❑ 55222		Settin' the Woods on Fire/Kentucky Waltz	1959	5.00	10.00	20.00
❑ 55243		Don't Do It/Patrick Henry	1959	5.00	10.00	20.00
❑ 55258		Dreamin'/Cincinnati Fireball	1960	3.75	7.50	15.00
❑ 55285		You're Sixteen/I Beg Your Pardon	1960	3.75	7.50	15.00
❑ 55285	PS	You're Sixteen/I Beg Your Pardon	1960	10.00	20.00	40.00
❑ 55298		Little Boy Sad/(I Go) Down to the River	1961	3.75	7.50	15.00
❑ 55298	PS	Little Boy Sad/(I Go) Down to the River	1961	10.00	20.00	40.00
❑ 55318		Big Big World/Ballad of the One Eyed Jacks	1961	3.75	7.50	15.00
❑ 55318	PS	Big Big World/Ballad of the One Eyed Jacks	1961	10.00	20.00	40.00
❑ 55345		Girls/I've Got a Lot of Things to Do	1961	3.75	7.50	15.00
❑ 55377		Honestly I Do/Fools Like Me	1961	3.75	7.50	15.00
❑ 55379		God, Country and My Baby/Honestly I Do	1961	3.75	7.50	15.00
❑ 55416		Clown Shoes/The Way I Am	1962	3.75	7.50	15.00
❑ 55448		The Fool of the Year/The Poorest Boy in Town	1962	3.75	7.50	15.00
❑ 55489		Damn the Defiant/Lonesome Waters	1962	3.75	7.50	15.00
Magic Lamp						
❑ 515		Bigger Man/Less Than a Heartache	1964	12.50	25.00	50.00
❑ 515	PS	Bigger Man/Less Than a Heartache	1964	30.00	60.00	120.00
Sahara						
❑ 512		Fountain of Love/What a Summer Day	1964	3.75	7.50	15.00
United Artists						
❑ 0018		Dreamin'/Little Boy Sad	1973		2.00	4.00
		Silver Spotlight Series issue				
❑ 0019		You're Sixteen/God, Country and My Baby	1973		2.00	4.00
		Silver Spotlight Series issue				
Von						
❑ 1006		You're Undecided/Go, Mule, Go	1954	1,500	2,250	3,000
Busters, The						
Arlen						
❑ 735		Bust Out/Astronaut's	1963	5.00	10.00	20.00
❑ 740		All American Surfer/Pine Tree Hop	1963	5.00	10.00	20.00
❑ 745		Heartaches/Torrid Zone	1964	5.00	10.00	20.00
Butler, Jerry						
(Also see "Everett, Betty, and Jerry Butler")						
Abner						
❑ 1024		Lost/One by One	1959	7.50	15.00	30.00
❑ 1028		Hold Me Darling/Rainbow Valley	1959	7.50	15.00	30.00
❑ 1030		I Was Wrong/Couldn't Go to Sleep	1959	7.50	15.00	30.00
❑ 1035		A Lonely Soldier/I Found a Love	1960	7.50	15.00	30.00
Fountain						
❑ 400		No Love Without Changes/(B-side unknown)	1982		3.00	6.00
MCA						
❑ 52177		Let's Talk It Over/Especially You	1983		2.00	4.00
		With Stix Hooper; B-side by Stix Hooper solo				
Mercury						
❑ 72592		Love (Oh How Sweet It Is)/Loneliness	1966	2.50	5.00	10.00
❑ 72625		You Make Me Feel Like Someone/ For What You Made of Me	1966	2.50	5.00	10.00
❑ 72648		I Dig You Baby/Some Kinda Magic	1966	2.50	5.00	10.00
❑ 72676		Why Do I Lose You/You Walked Into My Life	1967	2.50	5.00	10.00
❑ 72698		You Don't Know What You've Got Until You Lose It/ The Way I Love You	1967	2.50	5.00	10.00
❑ 72721		Mr. Dream Merchant/'Cause I Love You So	1967	2.50	5.00	10.00
❑ 72764		Lost/ You Don't Know What You've Got Until You Lose It	1968	2.00	4.00	8.00
❑ 72798		Never Give You Up/Beside You	1968	2.00	4.00	8.00

Number		Title (A Side/B Side)	Year	VG	VG+	NM
❏ 72850		Hey, Western Union Man/Just Can't Forget About You	1968	2.00	4.00	8.00
❏ 72876		Are You Happy/I Still Love You	1968	2.00	4.00	8.00
❏ 72898		Only the Strong Survive/ Just Because I Really Love You	1969	2.00	4.00	8.00
❏ 72929		Moody Woman/Go Away -- Find Yourself	1969	2.00	4.00	8.00
❏ 72960		What's the Use of Breaking Up/Brand New Me	1969	2.00	4.00	8.00
❏ 72991		Don't Let Love Hang You Up/ Walking Around in Teardrops	1969	2.00	4.00	8.00
❏ 73015		Got to See If I Can't Get Mommy (To Come Back Home)/I Forgot to Remember	1970	2.00	4.00	8.00
❏ 73045		I Could Write a Book/Since I Lost You, Baby	1970	2.00	4.00	8.00
❏ 73101		Where Are You Going/You Can Fly	1970	2.00	4.00	8.00
❏ 73131		How Does It Feel/Special Memory	1970	2.00	4.00	8.00
❏ 73169		If It's Real What I Feel/Why Are You Leaving Me	1971		3.00	6.00
❏ 73210		How Did We Lose It Baby/ Do You Finally Need a Friend	1971		3.00	6.00
❏ 73241		Walk Easy My Son/Let Me Be	1971		3.00	6.00
❏ 73290		I Only Have Eyes for You/A Prayer	1972		3.00	6.00
❏ 73335		One Night Affair/Life's Unfortunate Song	1972		3.00	6.00
❏ 73443		Power of Love/ What Do You Do on a Sunday Afternoon	1973		3.00	6.00
❏ 73459		That's How Heartaches Are Made/ Too Many Danger Signs	1974		3.00	6.00
❏ 73495		Take the Time to Tell Her/High Stepper	1974		3.00	6.00
❏ 73629		You and Me Against the World/Playing on You	1974		3.00	6.00
❏ 872 914-7		Only the Strong Survive/Lost	1989			3.00
	Reissue					
❏ 872 916-7		Never Give You Up/Hey, Western Union Man	1989			3.00
	Reissue					

Mistletoe

Number		Title (A Side/B Side)	Year	VG	VG+	NM
❏ 803		Silent Night/O Holy Night	1975		2.00	4.00

Motown

Number		Title (A Side/B Side)	Year	VG	VG+	NM
❏ 1403		The Devil in Mrs. Jones/Don't Wanna Be Reminded	1976		2.50	5.00
❏ 1403	PS	The Devil in Mrs. Jones/Don't Wanna Be Reminded	1976	2.50	5.00	10.00
❏ 1414		I Wanna Do It to You/I Don't Wanna Be Reminded	1977		2.50	5.00
❏ 1421		Chalk It Up/I Don't Want Nobody to Know	1977		2.50	5.00
❏ 1422		It's a Lifetime Thing/Kiss Me Now	1977		2.50	5.00
	With Thelma Houston					

Philadelphia Int'l

Number		Title (A Side/B Side)	Year	VG	VG+	NM
❏ 3113		Don't Be Ashamed/Best Love I Ever Had	1980		2.00	4.00
❏ 3117		Tell Me Girl (Why It Has to End)/ We've Got This Feeling Again	1980		2.00	4.00
❏ 3656		(I'm Just Thinking About) Cooling Out/ Are You Lonely Tonight	1978		2.00	4.00
❏ 3664		(I'm Just Thinking About) Cooling Out/ Are You Lonely Tonight	1978		2.00	4.00
❏ 3673		I'm Glad to Be Back/ Nothing Says I Love You Like I Love You	1979		2.00	4.00
❏ 3683		Let's Make Love/Dream World	1979		2.00	4.00

Vee Jay

Number		Title (A Side/B Side)	Year	VG	VG+	NM
❏ 354		He Will Break Your Heart/Thanks to You	1960	5.00	10.00	20.00
❏ 371		Silent Night/O Holy Night	1960	5.00	10.00	20.00
❏ 375		Find Another Girl/When Trouble Calls	1961	3.75	7.50	15.00
❏ 390		I See a Fool/I'm a Telling You	1961	3.75	7.50	15.00
❏ 396		For Your Precious Love/Sweet Was the Wine	1961	3.75	7.50	15.00
❏ 405		Moon River/Aware of Love	1961	3.75	7.50	15.00
❏ 426		Isle of Sirens/Chi Town	1962	3.75	7.50	15.00
❏ 451		Make It Easy on Yourself/It's Too Late	1962	3.75	7.50	15.00
❏ 463		You Can Run/I'm the One	1962	3.75	7.50	15.00
❏ 475		Theme from Taras Bulba (Wishing Star)/ You Go Right Through Me	1963	3.00	6.00	12.00
❏ 475	PS	Theme from Taras Bulba (Wishing Star)/ You Go Right Through Me	1963	10.00	20.00	40.00
❏ 486		You Won't Be Sorry/Whatever You Want	1963	3.00	6.00	12.00
❏ 526		Strawberries/I Almost Lost My Head	1963	3.00	6.00	12.00
❏ 534		Where's the Girl?/How Beautifully You Lie	1963	3.00	6.00	12.00
❏ 556		Just a Little Bit/A Woman with Soul	1963	3.00	6.00	12.00
❏ 567		Need to Belong/Give Me Your Love	1963	3.00	6.00	12.00
❏ 588		Giving Up on Love/I've Been Trying	1964	3.00	6.00	12.00
❏ 598		I Stand Accused/I Don't Want to Hear Anymore	1964	3.00	6.00	12.00
❏ 598	PS	I Stand Accused/I Don't Want to Hear Anymore	1964	7.50	15.00	30.00
❏ 651		Good Times/I've Grown Accustomed to Her Face	1965	3.00	6.00	12.00
❏ 696		I Can't Stand to See You Cry/ Nobody Needs Your Love	1965	3.00	6.00	12.00
❏ 707		Believe in Me/Just for You	1965	3.00	6.00	12.00
❏ 711		Moon River/Make It Easy on Yourself	1966	3.00	6.00	12.00
❏ 715		For Your Precious Love/Give It Up	1966	3.00	6.00	12.00

Butler, Jerry, and The Impressions - See "Impressions, The"

Butterflys, The

(Ellie Greenwich as a girl group)

Red Bird

Number	Title (A Side/B Side)	Year	VG	VG+	NM
❏ 10-009	Goodnight Baby/The Swim	1964	6.25	12.50	25.00
❏ 10-016	I Wonder/Gee, Baby, Gee	1964	6.25	12.50	25.00

Number		Title (A Side/B Side)	Year	VG	VG+	NM

Byrd, Curtis
Candix

| ❏ 340 | | Pretty Woman/Turn Some More Lights On | 1962 | 6.25 | 12.50 | 25.00 |

Byrds, The
(Also see "Beefeaters, The")
Asylum

| ❏ 11016 | | Full Circle/Long Live the King | 1973 | | 2.50 | 5.00 |
| ❏ 11019 | | Cowgirl in the Sand/Long Live the King | 1973 | | 2.50 | 5.00 |

Columbia

❏ 43271		Mr. Tambourine Man/I Knew I'd Want You	1965	3.75	7.50	15.00
❏ 43271	DJ	Mr. Tambourine Man (same on both sides)	1965	37.50	75.00	150.00
		Red vinyl promo				
❏ 43271	PS	Mr. Tambourine Man	1965	75.00	150.00	300.00
		Promo-only sleeve promoting the Byrds' appearance on the TV show Hullabaloo				
❏ 43332		All I Really Want to Do/I'll Feel a Whole Lot Better	1965	3.75	7.50	15.00
❏ 43332	DJ	I'll Feel a Whole Lot Better (same on both sides)	1965	25.00	50.00	100.00
		Red vinyl promo				
❏ 43332	DJ	All I Really Want to Do (same on both sides)	1965	18.75	37.50	75.00
		Red vinyl promo				
❏ 43424		Turn! Turn! Turn! (To Everything There Is a Season)/ She Don't Care About Time	1965	3.75	7.50	15.00
❏ 43424	DJ	Turn! Turn! Turn! (To Everything There Is a Season) (same on both sides)	1965	25.00	50.00	100.00
		Red vinyl promo				
❏ 43501		It Won't Be Wrong/Set You Free This Time	1965	3.00	6.00	12.00
❏ 43578		Eight Miles High/Why	1966	3.00	6.00	12.00
❏ 43578	PS	Eight Miles High/Why	1966	6.25	12.50	25.00
❏ 43702		5 D (Fifth Dimension)/Captain Soul	1966	3.00	6.00	12.00
❏ 43766		Mr. Spaceman/What's Happening	1966	3.00	6.00	12.00
❏ 43987		So You Want to Be a Rock 'N' Roll Star/ Everybody's Been Burned	1967	3.00	6.00	12.00
❏ 44054		My Back Pages/Renaissance Fair	1967	3.00	6.00	12.00
❏ 44157		Have You Seen Her Face/Don't Make Waves	1967	2.50	5.00	10.00
❏ 44157	PS	Have You Seen Her Face/Don't Make Waves	1967	10.00	20.00	40.00
❏ 44230		Lady Friend/Old John Robertson	1967	2.50	5.00	10.00
❏ 44362		Goin' Back/Change Is Now	1967	2.00	4.00	8.00
❏ 44499		Artificial Energy/You Ain't Going Nowhere	1968	2.00	4.00	8.00
❏ 44643		Pretty Boy Floyd/I Am a Pilgrim	1968	2.00	4.00	8.00
❏ 44746		Drug Store Truck Drivin' Man/Bad Night at the Whiskey	1969	2.00	4.00	8.00
❏ 44868		Lay Lady Lay/Old Blue	1969	2.00	4.00	8.00
❏ 44990		Wasn't Born to Follow/Ballad of Easy Rider	1969	2.00	4.00	8.00
❏ 44990		Ballad of Easy Rider/Oil in My Lamp	1969	2.50	5.00	10.00
❏ 45071		Jesus Is Just Alright/It's All Over Now, Baby Blue	1970	2.00	4.00	8.00
❏ 45259		Chestnut Mare/Just a Season	1970		3.00	6.00
❏ 45440		Glory Glory/Citizen Kane	1971		3.00	6.00
❏ 45514		America's Great National Pastime/Farther Along	1971		3.00	6.00
❏ 45761		Jesus Is Just Alright/Mr. Spaceman	1973	2.50	5.00	10.00

Byrnes, Edd
Warner Bros.

❏ 5047	M	Kookie, Kookie (Lend Me Your Comb)/You're the Top	1959	5.00	10.00	20.00
		A-side by Edward Byrnes and Connie Stevens; B-side by Edward Byrnes				
❏ 5047	PS	Kookie, Kookie (Lend Me Your Comb)/You're the Top	1959	10.00	20.00	40.00
		A-side by Edward Byrnes and Connie Stevens; B-side by Edward Byrnes				
❏ S-5047	S	Kookie, Kookie (Lend Me Your Comb)/You're the Top	1959	12.50	25.00	50.00
❏ 5087		Like I Love You/Kookie's Mad Pad	1959	4.00	8.00	16.00
		Artist credit: "Edd Byrnes and Friend"				
❏ 5087	PS	Like I Love You/Kookie's Mad Pad	1959	10.00	20.00	40.00
		Artist credit: "Edd Byrnes and Friend"				
❏ 5114		Kookie's Love Song Part 1/Kookie's Love Song Part 2	1959	4.00	8.00	16.00
		With the Mary Kay Trio				
❏ 5114	PS	Kookie's Love Song Part 1/Kookie's Love Song Part 2	1959	10.00	20.00	40.00
		With the Mary Kay Trio				
❏ 5121		Yulesville/Lonely Christmas	1959	4.00	8.00	16.00
❏ 5121	PS	Yulesville/Lonely Christmas	1959	10.00	20.00	40.00

Byron, Lord Douglas
Dot

| ❏ 16685 | | Surfin' Santa/The Drink That Makes You Shrink | 1964 | 7.50 | 15.00 | 30.00 |

Union

| ❏ 505 | | Big Bad Ho-Dad/Coffee House | 1962 | 10.00 | 20.00 | 40.00 |
| | | *B-side by the Continentals* | | | | |

C

C.A. Quintet, The
Candy Floss

| ❏ 102 | | Smooth as Silk/Dr. of Philosophy | 1968 | 20.00 | 40.00 | 80.00 |

Falcon

| ❏ 70 | | Mickey's Monkey/I Want You to Love Me Girl | 1967 | 25.00 | 50.00 | 100.00 |
| ❏ 71 | | Blow to My Soul/She's Got to Be True | 1967 | 25.00 | 50.00 | 100.00 |

Number		Title (A Side/B Side)	Year	VG	VG+	NM

C.O.D.'s, The
Kellmac

❑ 1003		Michael/Cry No More	1965	3.00	6.00	12.00
❑ 1005		Pretty Baby/I'm a Good Guy	1965	5.00	10.00	20.00
❑ 1012		Coming Back Girl/(B-side unknown)	1966	25.00	50.00	100.00

Cadets, The
(Also see "Jacks, The")
Jan-Lar

❑ 102		Don't/Car Crash	1960	15.00	30.00	60.00

Modern

❑ 956		Don't Be Angry/I Cried	1955	12.50	25.00	50.00
❑ 960		Rollin' Stone/Fine Lookin' Baby	1955	12.50	25.00	50.00
❑ 963		I Cried/Fine Lookin' Baby	1955	10.00	20.00	40.00
❑ 969		Annie Met Henry/So Will I	1955	10.00	20.00	40.00
❑ 971		Do You Wanna Rock/If It Is Wrong	1956	25.00	50.00	100.00
❑ 985		Church Bells May Ring/Heartbreak Hotel	1956	10.00	20.00	40.00
❑ 994		Stranded in the Jungle/I Want You	1956	12.50	25.00	50.00
❑ 1000		I Got Loaded/Dancin' Dan	1956	10.00	20.00	40.00
❑ 1006		Fools Rush In/I'll Be Spinning	1956	10.00	20.00	40.00
❑ 1012		Heaven Help Me/Love Bandit	1957	10.00	20.00	40.00
❑ 1017		Wiggle Waggle Woo/You Belong to Me	1957	10.00	20.00	40.00
❑ 1019		Pretty Evey/Rum, Jamaica Rum	1957	12.50	25.00	50.00
		As "Aaron Collins and the Cadets"				
❑ 1024		Hands Across the Table/Love Can Do Most Anything	1957	10.00	20.00	40.00
		As "Will Jones and the Cadets"				
❑ 1026		Ring Chimes/Baby Ya Know	1957	10.00	20.00	40.00

Sherwood

❑ 211		One More Chance/I'm Looking for a Job	1960	12.50	25.00	50.00

Cadillacs, The
Artic

❑ 101		Fool/The Right Kind of Lovin'	1964	25.00	50.00	100.00

Capitol

❑ 4825		Groovy, Groovy Love/White Gardenia	1962	5.00	10.00	20.00
❑ 4935		La Bomba/I Saw You	1963	5.00	10.00	20.00
		As "Bobby Ray and the Cadillacs"				

Josie

❑ 765		Gloria/I Wonder Why	1954	125.00	250.00	500.00
❑ 769		Wishing Well/I Want to Know About Love	1954	125.00	250.00	500.00
❑ 773		Sympathy/No Chance	1955	25.00	50.00	100.00
❑ 778		Widow Lady/Down the Road	1955	50.00	100.00	200.00
❑ 785		Speedo/Let Me Explain	1955	12.50	25.00	50.00
❑ 792		Zoom/You Are	1956	12.50	25.00	50.00
❑ 798		Woe Is Me/Betty My Love	1956	12.50	25.00	50.00
❑ 805		The Girl I Love/That's All I Need	1956	25.00	50.00	100.00
❑ 807		Rudolph the Red-Nosed Reindeer/Shack-a Doo	1956	10.00	20.00	40.00
❑ 812		Sugar Sugar/About That Girl Named Lou	1957	10.00	20.00	40.00
❑ 820		My Girl Friend/Broken Heart	1957	12.50	25.00	50.00
❑ 821		Lucy/Hurry Home	1957	10.00	20.00	40.00
		As "The Original Cadillacs"				
❑ 829		Buzz-Buzz-Buzz/Yes, Yes Baby	1957	10.00	20.00	40.00
		As "The Original Cadillacs"				
❑ 836		Speedo Is Back/A' Looka Here	1958	7.50	15.00	30.00
❑ 842		Holy Smoke Baby/I Want to Know	1958	7.50	15.00	30.00
❑ 846		Peek-a-Boo/Oh, Oh Lolita	1958	7.50	15.00	30.00
❑ 857		Copy Cat/Jay Walker	1959	7.50	15.00	30.00
❑ 861		Cool It Fool/Please Mr. Johnson	1959	7.50	15.00	30.00
❑ 866	M	Romeo/Always My Darling	1959	7.50	15.00	30.00
❑ 870		Dumbell/Bad Dan McGoon	1959	7.50	15.00	30.00
❑ 876		Tell Me Today/It's Love	1960	7.50	15.00	30.00
❑ 883		That's Why/The Boogie Man	1960	7.50	15.00	30.00
❑ 915		Wayward Wanderer/I'll Never Let You Go	1963	5.00	10.00	20.00
		As "The Original Cadillacs"				

Jubilee

❑ 8010	S	Romeo/Always My Darling	1959	15.00	30.00	60.00

Mercury

❑ 71738		I'm Willing/Thrill Me So	1961	25.00	50.00	100.00

Polydor

❑ 14031		Deep in the Heart of the Ghetto (Part 1)/ Deep in the Heart of the Ghetto (Part 2)	1969	3.75	7.50	15.00
		As "The Original Cadillacs"				

Roulette

❑ 4654		Let's Get Together/She's My Connection	1965	5.00	10.00	20.00

Smash

❑ 1712		You Are to Blame/What to Bet	1961	6.25	12.50	25.00

Caesar and Cleo - See "Sonny and Cher"

Cagle, Wade
Sun

❑ 360		Groovy Train/Highland Rock	1961	6.25	12.50	25.00

Number		Title (A Side/B Side)	Year	VG	VG+	NM

California
(Two different groups)
Laurie
❏ 3612		See You in September/Ivy Ivy	1974		2.00	4.00
❏ 3639		Song of a Thousand Voices/Abraham, Martin and John	1976		2.00	4.00
❏ 3647		Jeans On/Doo-Wop Music	1976		2.00	4.00
❏ 3651		I'm Just Thinking of You/Doo-Wop Music	1977		2.00	4.00

RCA
❏ PB-11769		Everybody Needs a Little Help/I'm a Poet	1979	2.50	5.00	10.00

RSO
❏ 901		I Can Hear Music/Love's Supposed to Be That Way	1978	2.50	5.00	10.00

Warner Bros.
❏ 8253		Happy in Hollywood/Music, Music, Music	1976	2.50	5.00	10.00
❏ 8307		(Just to Let You Know) I Love You So/Happy in Hollywood	1977	2.50	5.00	10.00

California Music
Equinox
❏ PB-10120		Don't Worry Baby/Ten Years' Harmony	1974	3.75	7.50	15.00
❏ PB-10363		Why Do Fools Fall in Love/Don't Worry Baby	1975	3.75	7.50	15.00
❏ PB-10572		Jamaica Farewell/California Music	1976	3.75	7.50	15.00

Californians, The
(With Jesse Belvin)
Federal
❏ 12231		My Angel/Heavenly Ruby	1955	75.00	150.00	300.00

Camp, The
Scepter
❏ 12159		Marching/Long Long Trail	1966	20.00	40.00	80.00

Campbell, Choker
Apt
❏ 25011		Walk Awhile/Walking on Thin-Soled Shoes	1958	15.00	30.00	60.00

Atlantic
❏ 1014		Last Call for Whiskey/How Could You Do This	1953	10.00	20.00	40.00
❏ 1038		Have You Seen My Baby/Jackie Mambo	1954	10.00	20.00	40.00

Fortune
❏ 808		Frankie and Johnny/Rocking and Jumping	1953	15.00	30.00	60.00

Motown
❏ 1072		Come See About Me/Pride and Joy	1964	6.25	12.50	25.00

Campbell, Glen
Atlantic America
❏ 99525		Call Home/Sweet 16	1986			3.00
❏ 99559		Cowpoke/Rag Doll	1986			3.00
❏ 99600		It's Just a Matter of Time/Gene Autry, My Hero	1985			3.00
❏ 99647		(Love Always) Letter to Home/An American Trilogy	1985			3.00
❏ 99691		A Lady Like You/Tennessee	1984			3.00
❏ 99768		Faithless Love/Scene of the Crime	1984			3.00
❏ 99930		I Love How You Love Me/Hang On Baby (Ease My Mind)	1983			3.00
❏ 99967		Old Home Town/Heartache #3	1982		2.00	4.00

Capehart
❏ 5008		Death Valley/Nothin' Better Than a Pretty Woman	1961	6.25	12.50	25.00

Capitol
❏ 2015		By the Time I Get to Phoenix/You've Still Got a Place in My Heart	1967		2.50	5.00
❏ 2076		Hey Little One/My Baby's Gone	1968		2.50	5.00
❏ 2076	PS	Hey Little One/My Baby's Gone	1968	2.50	5.00	10.00
❏ 2146		I Wanna Live/That's All That Matters	1968		2.50	5.00
❏ 2224		Dreams of the Everyday Housewife/Kelli Ho-Down	1968		2.50	5.00
❏ 2302		Wichita Lineman/Fate of Man	1968		2.50	5.00
❏ 2336		Christmas Is for Children/There's No Place Like Home	1968		2.50	5.00
❏ 2428		Galveston/How Come Every Time I Itch I Wind Up Scratchin' You	1969		2.50	5.00
❏ 2494		Where's the Playground Susie/Arkansas	1969		2.50	5.00
❏ 2573		True Grit/Hava Nagila	1969		2.50	5.00
❏ 2659		Try a Little Kindness/Lonely My Lonely Friend	1969		2.50	5.00
❏ 2718		Honey Come Back/Where Do You Go	1970		2.50	5.00
❏ 2787		Oh Happy Day/Someone Above	1970		2.50	5.00
❏ 2843		Everything a Man Could Ever Need/Norwood (Me and My Guitar)	1970		2.50	5.00
❏ 2905		It's Only Make Believe/Pave Your Way Into Tomorrow	1970		2.50	5.00
❏ 3062		Dream Baby (How Long Must I Dream)/Here and Now	1971		2.50	5.00
❏ 3123		The Last Time I Saw Her/Bach Talk	1971		2.50	5.00
❏ 3254		Oklahoma Sunday Morning/Everybody's Got to Go There Sometime	1972		2.00	4.00
❏ 3305		Manhattan, Kansas/Wayfaring Stranger	1972		2.00	4.00
❏ 3382		We All Pull the Load/Wherefore and Why	1972		2.00	4.00
❏ 3411		I Will Never Pass This Way Again/We All Pull the Load	1972		2.00	4.00
❏ 3483		One Last Time/All My Tomorrows	1972		2.00	4.00
❏ 3509		I Believe in Christmas/New Snow on the Roof	1972		2.00	4.00
❏ 3548		I Knew Jesus (Before He Was a Star)/On This Road	1973		2.00	4.00

Number		Title (A Side/B Side)	Year	VG	VG+	NM
❑ 3669		Bring Back My Yesterday/Beautiful Love Song	1973		2.00	4.00
❑ 3735		Wherefore and Why/	1973		2.00	4.00
		Give Me Back That Old Familiar Feeling				
❑ 3808		Houston (I'm Coming to See You)/Honestly Love	1973		2.00	4.00
❑ 3926		Bonaparte's Retreat/Too Many Mornings	1974		2.00	4.00
❑ 3988		It's a Sin When You Love Somebody/	1974		2.00	4.00
		If I Were Loving You				
❑ 4095		Rhinestone Cowboy/Lovelight	1975		2.00	4.00
❑ 4155		Country Boy (You Got Your Feet in L.A)/	1975		2.00	4.00
		Record Collector's Dream				
❑ 4245		Then You Can Tell Me Goodbye-Don't Pull Your Love/	1976		2.00	4.00
		I Miss You Tonight				
❑ 4288		See You on Sunday/Bloodline	1976		2.00	4.00
❑ 4376		Southern Nights/William Tell Overture	1976		2.00	4.00
❑ 4445		Sunflower/How High Did We Go	1977		2.00	4.00
❑ 4515		God Must Have Blessed America/Amazing Grace	1977		2.00	4.00
❑ 4584		Another Fine Mess/Can You Fool	1978		2.00	4.00
❑ 4638		Can You Fool/Let's All Sing a Song About It	1978		2.00	4.00
❑ 4682		I'm Gonna Love You/Love Takes You Higher	1979		2.00	4.00
❑ 4715		California/Never Tell You No Lies	1979		2.00	4.00
❑ 4769		Hound Dog Man/Tennessee Home	1979		2.00	4.00
❑ 4783		Too Late to Worry -- Too Blue to Cry/	1962	2.50	5.00	10.00
		How Do I Tell My Heart Not to Break				
❑ 4799		My Prayer/Don't Lose Me in the Confusion	1979		2.00	4.00
❑ 4856		Long Black Limousine/Here I Am	1962	2.50	5.00	10.00
❑ 4856	PS	Long Black Limousine/Here I Am	1962	5.00	10.00	20.00
❑ 4865		Somethin' 'Bout You Baby I Like/Late Night Confession	1980		2.00	4.00
		With Rita Coolidge				
❑ 4867		Truck Driving Man/Kentucky Means Paradise	1962	2.50	5.00	10.00
❑ 4909		Hollywood Smiles/Hooked on Love	1980		2.00	4.00
❑ 4925		Oh My Darling/Prima Donna	1963	2.50	5.00	10.00
❑ 4959		I Don't Want to Know Your Name/Daisy a Day	1981		2.00	4.00
❑ 4986		Why Don't We Just Sleep on It Tonight/It's Your World	1981		2.00	4.00
		With Tanya Tucker				
❑ 4990		Divorce Me C.O.D./Dark As a Dungeon	1963	2.50	5.00	10.00
❑ 5037		As Far As I'm Concerned/Same Old Places	1963	2.50	5.00	10.00
❑ 5172		Let Me Tell You About Mary/	1964	2.50	5.00	10.00
		Through the Eyes of a Child				
❑ 5279		Summer, Winter, Spring and Fall/	1964	2.50	5.00	10.00
		Heartaches Can Be Fun				
❑ 5360		It's a Woman's World/Tomorrow Never Comes	1965	2.50	5.00	10.00
❑ 5441		Guess I'm Dumb/That's All Right	1965	25.00	50.00	100.00
		A Brian Wilson "Pet Sounds"-like production				
❑ 5504		The Universal Soldier/Spanish Shades	1965	2.00	4.00	8.00
❑ 5545		Less of Me/Private John Q	1965	2.00	4.00	8.00
❑ 5638		Can't You See I'm Tryin'/Satisfied Mind	1966		3.00	6.00
❑ 5773		Burning Bridges/Only the Lonely	1966		3.00	6.00
❑ 5854		Just to Satisfy You/I Gotta Have My Baby Back	1967		3.00	6.00
❑ 5939		Gentle on My Mind/Just Another Man	1967		2.50	5.00
		Orange and yellow swirl, without "A Subsidiary Of"... in perimeter label print				
❑ 5939		Gentle on My Mind/Just Another Man	1968		3.00	6.00
		Orange and yellow swirl label with "A Subsidiary Of" in perimeter print				
❑ 7PRO-79107	DJ	On a Good Night (same on both sides)	1990		2.50	5.00
		Vinyl is promo only				
❑ 7PRO-79279	DJ	Somebody's Leavin' (same on both sides)	1990		2.50	5.00
		Vinyl is promo only				
❑ 7PRO-79966	DJ	Walkin' in the Sun (same on both sides)	1990		2.50	5.00
		Vinyl is promo only				

Ceneco

❑ 1324		Dreams for Sale/I've Got to Win	1961	6.25	12.50	25.00
❑ 1356		I Wonder/You, You, You	1961	5.00	10.00	20.00

Compleat

❑ 113		Letting Go/(Instrumental)	1983		2.00	4.00

Crest

❑ 1087		Turn Around, Look at Me/Brenda	1961	5.00	10.00	20.00
❑ 1096		The Miracle of Love/Once More	1962	3.75	7.50	15.00

Everest

❑ 2500		Delight, Arkansas/Walk Right In	1969		3.00	6.00

Liberty

❑ S7-18214		Blue Christmas/Feliz Navidad	1994		2.00	4.00
		B-side on EMI Latin by Jose Feliciano; red vinyl				

MCA

❑ 41323		Dream Lover/Bronco	1980		2.00	4.00
		A-side with Tanya Tucker				
❑ 52474		Slow Nights/Midnight Love	1984			3.00
		With Mel Tillis				
❑ 53108		The Hand That Rocks the Cradle/Arkansas	1987			3.00
		With Steve Wariner				
❑ 53172		Still Within the Sound of My Voice/In My Life	1987			3.00
❑ 53218		I Have You/I'm a One Woman Man	1987			3.00
❑ 53245		I Remember You/	1988			3.00
		For Sure, For Certain, Forever, For Always				
❑ 53426		Heart of the Matter/Light Years	1988			3.00
❑ 53493		More Than Enough/Our Movie	1989			3.00

Number		Title (A Side/B Side)	Year	VG	VG+	NM
Mirage						
❏ 3845		I Love My Truck/Melody's Melody	1981		2.00	4.00
Starday						
❏ 853		For the Love of a Woman/Smokey Blue Eyes	1968		3.00	6.00
Universal						
❏ 66024		She's Gone, Gone, Gone/William Tell Overture	1989			3.00
Warner Bros.						
❏ 49609		Any Which Way You Can/ Medley from Any Which Way You Can	1980		2.00	4.00
		B-side by Texas Opera Company				

Campbell, Jo Ann
ABC-Paramount

Number		Title (A Side/B Side)	Year	VG	VG+	NM
❏ 10134	M	A Kookie Little Paradise/Bobby, Bobby, Bobby	1960	6.25	12.50	25.00
❏ S-10134	S	A Kookie Little Paradise/Bobby, Bobby, Bobby	1960	12.50	25.00	50.00
❏ 10172		But Maybe This Year/Crazy Daisy	1960	5.00	10.00	20.00
❏ 10200		Motorcycle Michael/Puka Puka Pants	1961	5.00	10.00	20.00
❏ 10224		Eddie My Love/It Wasn't Right	1961	5.00	10.00	20.00
❏ 10258		Mama Don't Wait/Duane	1961	5.00	10.00	20.00
❏ 10300		I Changed My Mind Jack/You Made Me Love You	1962	5.00	10.00	20.00
❏ 10335		Amateur Night/I Wish It Would Rain All Summer	1962	5.00	10.00	20.00

Cameo

❏ 223		I'm the Girl from Wolverton Mountain/Sloppy Joe	1962	5.00	10.00	20.00
❏ 237		Let Me Do It My Way/Mr. Fix-It Man	1962	5.00	10.00	20.00
❏ 249		Mother Please/Waitin' for Love	1963	5.00	10.00	20.00

El Dorado

❏ 504		Forever Young/Come On Baby	1957	10.00	20.00	40.00
❏ 509		Funny Thing/I Can't Give You Anything But Love	1957	10.00	20.00	40.00

Gone

❏ 5014		Wait a Minute/It's True	1957	10.00	20.00	40.00
❏ 5014		Wait a Minute/I'm in Love with You	1957	7.50	15.00	30.00
❏ 5021		You're Driving Me Mad/Rock and Roll Love	1958	7.50	15.00	30.00
❏ 5027		Whassa Matter with You/You-Oo	1958	7.50	15.00	30.00
❏ 5037		I Really, Really Love You/I'm Nobody's Baby Now	1958	7.50	15.00	30.00
❏ 5049		Happy New Year Baby/Tall Boy	1958	7.50	15.00	30.00
❏ 5055		Mama/Nervous	1959	7.50	15.00	30.00
❏ 5068		Beach Comber/I Ain't Got No Steady Date	1959	7.50	15.00	30.00

Point

❏ 4		I'm Coming Home Late Tonight/Wherever You Go	1956	10.00	20.00	40.00

Rori

❏ 711		Jim Dandy/Five Minutes More	1962	5.00	10.00	20.00

Campers, The
Parkway

❏ 974		The Ballad of Batman/The Batmobile	1966	8.75	17.50	35.00
		Original label credit: "The Camps"				
❏ 974		The Ballad of Batman/The Batmobile	1966	7.50	15.00	30.00
		Includes Sonny Curtis and the Crickets				

Campi, Ray
Colpix

❏ 166		French Fries/Hear What I Wanna Hear	1960	3.75	7.50	15.00

D

❏ 1047		The Ballad of Donna and Peggy Sue/ A Man I Met (Tribute to The Big Bopper)	1959	10.00	20.00	40.00

Domino

❏ 700		My Screamin' Screamin' Meemie/With You	1958	7.50	15.00	30.00

Dot

❏ 15617		It Ain't Me/Give That Love to Me	1957	12.50	25.00	50.00

Rollin' Rock

❏ 006		Eager Boy/Dobroggie	1978		2.50	5.00
❏ 008		Tore Up/If It's All the Same to You	1978		2.50	5.00
❏ 014		Sixteen Chicks/Pan American Boogie	1979		2.50	5.00
❏ 019		My Baby Left Me/A Li'l Bit of Heartache	1979		2.50	5.00
❏ 027		Wrong, Wrong, Wrong/Booze It	1980		2.00	4.00
❏ 029		Scrumptious Baby/I Didn't Mean to Be Mean	1980		2.00	4.00
❏ 031		Merle's Boogie-Woogie-Missouri/ Sweet Temptation Guitar Rag	1980		2.00	4.00
		With Merle Travis				
❏ 038		Rockin' at the Ritz/Quit Your Triplin'	1981		2.00	4.00
❏ 044		Rattlin' Daddy/Wild One	1981		2.00	4.00
❏ 046		Texas Sands/How Long Can You Feel	1982		2.00	4.00
❏ 047		Sweet Woman Blues/The Newest Wave	1982		2.00	4.00
❏ 052		Rockabilly Man/Hollywood Cats	1983		2.00	4.00

TNT

❏ 145		Caterpillar/Play It Cool	1958	75.00	150.00	300.00

Camps, The - See "Campers, The"

Canadian Beadles, The
Tide

❏ 2203		I Think I'm Gonna Cry/I'll Show You the Way	1964	3.75	7.50	15.00

Number		Title (A Side/B Side)	Year	VG	VG+	NM
❑ 2206		I'm Coming Home/Love Walk Away	1964	3.75	7.50	15.00
		As "Vic, Paul and Bruce"				

Canned Heat

Atlantic
| ❑ 3010 | | One More River to Cross/Highway 401 | 1974 | | 2.00 | 4.00 |
| ❑ 3236 | | The Harder They Come/Rock 'N' Roll Show | 1975 | | 2.00 | 4.00 |

Capitol
❑ S7-57890		Christmas Blues/	1992		2.00	4.00
		Christmas Is the Time to Say "I Love You"				
		B-side by Billy Squier				

Liberty
❑ 55979		Rollin' and Tumblin'/Bullfrog Blues	1967	2.00	4.00	8.00
❑ 56005		Evil Woman/The World Is a Jug	1967	2.00	4.00	8.00
❑ 56038		On the Road Again/Boogie Music	1968		3.00	6.00
❑ 56077		Going Up the Country/One King Favor	1968		3.00	6.00
❑ 56077	PS	Going Up the Country/One King Favor	1968	3.75	7.50	15.00
❑ 56079		Christmas Blues/The Chipmunk Song	1968	4.00	8.00	16.00
		B-side with the Chipmunks				
❑ 56097		Time Was/Low Down	1969		3.00	6.00
❑ 56127		Sic 'Em Pigs/Poor Man	1969		3.00	6.00
❑ 56140		Change My Ways/Get Off My Back	1969		3.00	6.00
❑ 56151		Let's Work Together/I'm Her Man	1970		3.00	6.00
❑ 56180		Future Blues/Going Up the Country	1970		3.00	6.00
❑ 56217		My Time Ain't Long/Wooly Bully	1970		3.00	6.00

United Artists
❑ 0058		On the Road Again/This Was	1973		2.00	4.00
		"Silver Spotlight Series" reissue				
❑ 0059		Going Up the Country/Let's Work Together	1973		2.00	4.00
		"Silver Spotlight Series" reissue				
❑ XW167		Rock and Roll Music/Lookin' for My Rainbow	1973		2.50	5.00
❑ XW243	DJ	Harley Davidson Blues (mono/stereo)	1973		3.00	6.00
		Stock copy apparently does not exist				
❑ 50831		Long Way from L.A./Hill's Stomp	1971		2.50	5.00
❑ 50892		Rockin' with the King/I Don't Care What You Tell Me	1972		2.50	5.00
❑ 50927		Sneakin' Around/Cherokee Dance	1972		2.50	5.00

Canned Heat and John Lee Hooker

United Artists
| ❑ 50779 | | Whiskey and Wimmen/Let's Make It | 1971 | | 2.50 | 5.00 |

Cannibal and the Headhunters

Aires
| ❑ 1001 | | Mean So Much/Dance By the Light | 1968 | 3.75 | 7.50 | 15.00 |

Capitol
| ❑ 2393 | | Get It On Up (Get Up the Courage)/Mean So Much | 1969 | 3.75 | 7.50 | 15.00 |

Date
| ❑ 1516 | | La Bamba/Zulu King | 1966 | 3.75 | 7.50 | 15.00 |
| ❑ 1525 | | Land of 1,000 Dances/Love Bird | 1966 | 3.75 | 7.50 | 15.00 |

Rampart
❑ 642		Land of 1,000 Dances/I'll Show You How to Love Me	1964	5.00	10.00	20.00
❑ 644		Here Comes Love/Nau Ninny Nau	1965	3.75	7.50	15.00
❑ 646		I Need Your Loving/Follow the Music	1965	3.75	7.50	15.00
❑ 654		Out of Sight/Please Baby Please	1965	3.75	7.50	15.00

Cannon, Freddie

Amherst
| ❑ 201 | | Dance to the Bop/She's a Real Rebel Rouser | 1983 | | 2.00 | 4.00 |

Buddah
| ❑ 242 | | Rockin' Robin/Red Valley | 1971 | 2.50 | 5.00 | 10.00 |

Claridge
| ❑ 401 | | Palisades Park/Way Down Yonder in New Orleans | 1975 | | 3.00 | 6.00 |
| ❑ 416 | | Sugar/Sugar (Part 2) | 1976 | | 3.00 | 6.00 |

HQ
❑ (no #)	DJ	Kennywood Park/With a Little Love	1987		3.00	6.00
❑ (no #)	PS	Kennywood Park/With a Little Love	1987	2.00	4.00	8.00
		Promotional item for KDKA Radio, Pittsburgh, Pa.				

MCA
| ❑ 40269 | | Rock and Roll ABC's/Superman | 1974 | 3.75 | 7.50 | 15.00 |

Metromedia
| ❑ 262 | | If You've Got the Time/Take Me Back | 1972 | 2.50 | 5.00 | 10.00 |

MiaSound
❑ 1002		Let's Put the Fun Back in Rock and Roll/	1981		2.50	5.00
		Your Mama Ain't Always Right				
		With the Belmonts				

Royal American
❑ 2		Charged-Up, Turned-On Rock-N-Roll Singer/	1970	2.50	5.00	10.00
		I Ain't Much, But I'm Yours				
❑ 11		Nite Time Lady/I Ain't Much, But I'm Yours	1970	2.50	5.00	10.00
❑ 288		Strawberry Wine/Blossom Dear	1969	2.50	5.00	10.00

Sire
| ❑ 4103 | | Beautiful Downtown Burbank/If You Give Me a Title | 1969 | 2.50 | 5.00 | 10.00 |

Number		Title (A Side/B Side)	Year	VG	VG+	NM
Swan						
❏ 4031		Tallahassee Lassie/You Know	1959	5.00	10.00	20.00
❏ 4038		Okefenokee/Kookie Hat	1959	5.00	10.00	20.00
❏ 4043		Way Down Yonder in New Orleans/Fractured	1959	5.00	10.00	20.00
❏ 4043	PS	Way Down Yonder in New Orleans/Fractured	1959	10.00	20.00	40.00
❏ 4050		Chattanooga Shoe Shine Boy/Boston "My Home Town"	1960	3.75	7.50	15.00
❏ 4050	PS	Chattanooga Shoe Shine Boy/Boston "My Home Town"	1960	10.00	20.00	40.00
❏ 4053		Jump Over/The Urge	1960	3.75	7.50	15.00
❏ 4053	PS	Jump Over/The Urge	1960	10.00	20.00	40.00
❏ 4057		Happy Shades of Blue/Chattanooga Choo Choo	1960	3.75	7.50	15.00
❏ 4057	PS	Happy Shades of Blue/Chattanooga Choo Choo	1960	10.00	20.00	40.00
❏ 4061		Humdinger/My Blue Heaven	1960	3.75	7.50	15.00
❏ 4061	PS	Humdinger/My Blue Heaven	1960	10.00	20.00	40.00
❏ 4066		Muskrat Ramble/Two Thousand-88	1961	3.75	7.50	15.00
❏ 4066	PS	Muskrat Ramble/Two Thousand-88	1961	10.00	20.00	40.00
❏ 4071		Buzz Buzz A-Diddle It/Opportunity	1961	3.75	7.50	15.00
❏ 4078		Transistor Sister/Walk to the Moon	1961	3.75	7.50	15.00
❏ 4078	PS	Transistor Sister/Walk to the Moon	1961	10.00	20.00	40.00
❏ 4083		For Me and My Gal/Blue Plate Special	1961	3.75	7.50	15.00
❏ 4096		Teen Queen of the Week/Wild Guy	1962	3.75	7.50	15.00
❏ 4106		Palisades Park/June, July and August	1962	4.00	8.00	16.00
❏ 4117		What's Gonna Happen When Summer's Gone/Broadway	1962	3.75	7.50	15.00
❏ 4122		If You Were a Rock and Roll Record/The Truth, Ruth	1962	3.75	7.50	15.00
❏ 4132		Come On and Love Me/Four Letter Man	1963	3.00	6.00	12.00
❏ 4139		Patty Baby/Betty Jean	1963	3.00	6.00	12.00
❏ 4149		Everybody Monkey/Oh Gloria	1963	6.25	12.50	25.00
❏ 4155		Do What the Hippies Do/That's the Way Girls Are	1963	3.00	6.00	12.00
❏ 4168		What a Party/Sweet Georgia Brown	1964	3.00	6.00	12.00
❏ 4178		The Ups and Downs of Love/It's Been Nice	1964	6.25	12.50	25.00
Warner Bros.						
❏ 5409		Abigail Beecher/All American Girl	1964	3.00	6.00	12.00
❏ 5434		OK Wheeler, The Used Car Dealer/Odie Cologne	1964	3.00	6.00	12.00
❏ 5448		Summertime U.S.A./Gotta Good Thing Goin'	1964	3.00	6.00	12.00
❏ 5487		Little Autograph Seeker/Too Much Monkey Business	1964	3.00	6.00	12.00
❏ 5615		Little Miss A-Go-Go/In the Night	1965	3.00	6.00	12.00
❏ 5615	PS	Little Miss A-Go-Go/In the Night	1965	6.25	12.50	25.00
❏ 5645		Action/Beachwood City	1965	3.75	7.50	15.00
❏ 5666		Let Me Show You Where It's At/The Old Rag Man	1965	3.00	6.00	12.00
❏ 5673		She's Something Else/Little Bitty Corrine	1965	3.00	6.00	12.00
❏ 5693		The Dedication Song/Come On, Come On	1966	3.00	6.00	12.00
❏ 5810		The Greatest Show on Earth/Hokie Pokie Girl	1966	3.00	6.00	12.00
❏ 5832		The Laughing Song/Natalie	1966	3.00	6.00	12.00
❏ 5859		Run for the Sun/Use Your Imagination	1966	3.00	6.00	12.00
❏ 5876		A Happy Clown/In My Wildest Dreams	1966	6.25	12.50	25.00
❏ 7019		Maverick's Flat/Run to the Poet Man	1967	6.25	12.50	25.00
❏ 7075		20th Century Fox/Cincinnati Woman	1967	6.25	12.50	25.00
We Make Rock & Roll						
❏ 1601		Rock Around the Clock/Sock It to the Judge	1968		3.00	6.00
❏ 1604		Sea Cruise/She's a Friday Night Fox	1968		3.00	6.00

Capehart, Jerry
Cash

Number	Title (A Side/B Side)	Year	VG	VG+	NM
❏ 1021	Walkin' Stick Boogie/Rollin'	1956	50.00	100.00	200.00
	With Eddie and Hank Cochran				

Crest

Number	Title (A Side/B Side)	Year	VG	VG+	NM
❏ 1101	Song of New Orleans/The Young and Blue (Theme)	1962	12.50	25.00	50.00

Capitols, The
Carlton

Number	Title (A Side/B Side)	Year	VG	VG+	NM
❏ 461	I Let Her Go/(B-side unknown)	1958	125.00	250.00	500.00

Cindy

| ❏ 3002 | Rosemary/Millie | 1957 | 50.00 | 100.00 | 200.00 |

Gateway

| ❏ 721 | Day By Day/Little Things | 1964 | 50.00 | 100.00 | 200.00 |

Karen

Number	Title (A Side/B Side)	Year	VG	VG+	NM
❏ 1524	Cool Jerk/Hello Stranger	1966	2.50	5.00	10.00
❏ 1525	I Got to Handle It/Zig Zagging	1966	2.00	4.00	8.00
❏ 1526	We Got a Thing That's In the Groove/Tired Running from You	1966	2.00	4.00	8.00
❏ 1534	Patty Cake/Take a Chance on Me Baby	1967	2.00	4.00	8.00
❏ 1536	Cool Pearl/Don't Say Maybe Baby	1967	2.00	4.00	8.00
❏ 1537	Cool Jerk '68/Afro Twist	1968	2.00	4.00	8.00
❏ 1543	Soul Brother, Soul Sister/Ain't That Terrible	1968	2.00	4.00	8.00
❏ 1546	Soul Soul/When You're in Trouble	1969	2.00	4.00	8.00
❏ 1549	I Thought She Loved Me/When You're in Trouble	1969	2.00	4.00	8.00

Pet

| ❏ 807 | Angel of Love/'Cause I Love You | 1958 | 37.50 | 75.00 | 150.00 |

Triumph

| ❏ 601 | Three O'Clock Rock/Write Me a Love Letter | 1959 | 7.50 | 15.00 | 30.00 |

Capris, The
(Two different groups)
Ambient Sound

Number	Title (A Side/B Side)	Year	VG	VG+	NM
❏ 02697	There's a Moon Out Again/Morse Code of Love	1982		2.50	5.00

Number		Title (A Side/B Side)	Year	VG	VG+	NM
Candlelite						
❏ 422		Oh, My Darling/Rock Pretty Baby	196?	3.00	6.00	12.00
Gotham						
❏ 304		God Only Knows/That's What You're Doing to Me	1954	30.00	60.00	120.00
		Red label				
❏ 304		God Only Knows/That's What You're Doing to Me	1954	62.50	125.00	250.00
		Blue label				
❏ 304		God Only Knows/That's What You're Doing to Me	1956	20.00	40.00	80.00
		Yellow label				
❏ 306		It Was Moonglow/Too Poor to Love	1955	50.00	100.00	200.00
❏ 308		It's a Miracle/Let's Linger Awhile	1956	30.00	60.00	120.00
Lifetime						
❏ 1001/2		Oh My Darling/Rock Pretty Baby	1961	25.00	50.00	100.00
Lost-Nite						
❏ 101		There's a Moon Out Tonight/Indian Girl	1961	12.50	25.00	50.00
		Pink label original				
❏ 101		There's a Moon Out Tonight/Indian Girl	196?	2.00	4.00	8.00
		Yellow label reissue				
❏ 148		Little Girl/When	196?	2.00	4.00	8.00
Mr. Peeke						
❏ 118		Limbo/From the Vine Came the Grape	1963	5.00	10.00	20.00
Old Town						
❏ 1094		There's a Moon Out Tonight/Indian Girl	1961	7.50	15.00	30.00
		Light blue label				
❏ 1094		There's a Moon Out Tonight/Indian Girl	1962	5.00	10.00	20.00
		Mostly black label				
❏ 1099		Where I Fell in Love/Some People Think	1961	7.50	15.00	30.00
❏ 1103		Tears in My Eyes/Why Do I Cry	1961	7.50	15.00	30.00
❏ 1107		Girl in My Dreams/My Island in the Sun	1961	7.50	15.00	30.00
Planet						
❏ 1010		There's a Moon Out Tonight/Indian Girl	1958	300.00	600.00	900.00
Sabre						
❏ 201/2		My Promise to You/Bop! Bop! Bop!	1959	37.50	75.00	150.00
Trommers						
❏ 101		There's a Moon Out Tonight/Indian Girl	1961	6.25	12.50	25.00
20th Century						
❏ 1201		My Weakness/Yes, My Baby, Please!	1957	15.00	30.00	60.00

Captain and Tennille, The

Number		Title (A Side/B Side)	Year	VG	VG+	NM
A&M						
❏ 1624		The Way I Want to Touch You/Disney Girls	1974		3.00	6.00
❏ 1672		Love Will Keep Us Together/Gentle Stranger	1975		2.00	4.00
❏ 1672	PS	Love Will Keep Us Together/Gentle Stranger	1975		3.00	6.00
❏ 1715		Por Amor Vivremos (Love Will Keep Us Together)/	1975		2.50	5.00
		Broddy Bounce				
❏ 1725		The Way I Want to Touch You/Broddy Bounce	1975		2.00	4.00
❏ 1725	PS	The Way I Want to Touch You/Broddy Bounce	1975		3.00	6.00
❏ 1774		Como Yo Quiero Sentorte	1975		2.50	5.00
		(The Way I Want to Touch You)/El Rebote de Broddy				
❏ 1782		Lonely Night (Angel Face)/	1976		2.00	4.00
		Smile for Me One More Time				
❏ 1782	PS	Lonely Night (Angel Face)/	1976		3.00	6.00
		Smile for Me One More Time				
❏ 1817		Shop Around/Butterscotch Castle	1976		2.00	4.00
❏ 1817	PS	Shop Around/Butterscotch Castle	1976		3.00	6.00
❏ 1870		Muskrat Love/Honey Come Love Me	1976		2.00	4.00
❏ 1870	PS	Muskrat Love/Honey Come Love Me	1976		3.00	6.00
❏ 1894		Song of Joy/Wedding Song (There Is Love)	1976			Unreleased
❏ 1912		Can't Stop Dancin'/Mis Canciones (The Good Songs)	1977		2.00	4.00
❏ 1912	PS	Can't Stop Dancin'/Mis Canciones (The Good Songs)	1977		3.00	6.00
❏ 1944		Come In from the Rain/We Never Really Said Goodbye	1977		2.00	4.00
❏ 1944	PS	Come In from the Rain/We Never Really Said Goodbye	1977		3.00	6.00
❏ 1970		Circles/1954 Boogie Blues	1977		2.00	4.00
❏ 2027		I'm On My Way/We Never Really Said Goodbye	1978		2.00	4.00
❏ 2027	PS	I'm On My Way/We Never Really Said Goodbye	1978		3.00	6.00
❏ 2063		You Never Done It Like That/"D" Keyboard Blues	1978		2.00	4.00
❏ 2063	PS	You Never Done It Like That/"D" Keyboard Blues	1978		3.00	6.00
❏ 2106		You Need a Woman Tonight/Love Me Like a Baby	1978		2.00	4.00
❏ 2106	PS	You Need a Woman Tonight/Love Me Like a Baby	1978		3.00	6.00
❏ 8601		Song of Joy/Wedding Song (There Is Love)	1977		2.00	4.00
		Originals on green and yellow labels (later issues $3 NM)				
❏ 8601	PS	Song of Joy/Wedding Song (There Is Love)	1977		3.00	6.00
Butterscotch Castle						
❏ 001		The Way I Want to Touch You/Disney Girls	1974	20.00	40.00	80.00
Casablanca						
❏ 2215		Do That To Me One More Time/Deep in the Dark	1979		2.00	4.00
❏ 2243		Love on a Shoestring/How Can You Be So Cold	1980		2.00	4.00
❏ 2247		Amame Una Vez Mas	1980		2.00	4.00
		(Do That To Me One More Time)/Deep in the Dark				
❏ 2264		Baby You Still Got It/Happy Together (A Fantasy)	1980		2.00	4.00
❏ 2320		Gentle Stranger/Keep Our Love Warm	1980		2.00	4.00
❏ 2328		Don't Forget Me/Keep Our Love Warm	1981		2.00	4.00
Joyce						
❏ 101		The Way I Want to Touch You/Disney Girls	1974	10.00	20.00	40.00

Number	Title (A Side/B Side)	Year	VG	VG+	NM

Captain Beefheart
(And His Magic Band)
A&M
❑ 794	Diddy Wah Diddy/Who Do You Think You're Fooling	1966	15.00	30.00	60.00
❑ 818	Moonchild/Here I Am, Here I Always Am	1966	12.50	25.00	50.00

Buddah
❑ 9	Yellow Brick Road/Abba Zaba	1967	3.75	7.50	15.00
❑ 108	Plastic Factory/Where There's Woman	1969	3.75	7.50	15.00

Epic
❑ 03190	Ice Cream for Crow/ Light Reflected Off the Oceans of the Moon	1982		2.50	5.00

Mercury
❑ 73494	I Got Love on My Mind/Upon the My-O-My	1974	2.00	4.00	8.00

Reprise
❑ 1068	Click Clack/I'm Gonna Boogalize You Baby	1972	3.75	7.50	15.00
❑ 1133	Too Much Time/ My Head Is My Only House Unless It Rains	1972	3.75	7.50	15.00

Captain Zap and the Motortown Cut-Ups
Motown
❑ 1151	The Luney Landing/The Luney Take-Off	1969	5.00	10.00	20.00

Captivations, The
Garpax
❑ 44179	Red Hot Scrambler-Go/Speed Shift	1964	7.50	15.00	30.00
	Yes, the "s" was dropped from the A-side when issued on Garpax				

Pentacle
❑ 1635	Red Hot Scramblers-Go/Speed Shift	1964	15.00	30.00	60.00

Caravelles, The
(The Smash group is British; the Joey and Starmaker, American)
Joey
❑ 301	Falling for You/Shake Baby	1963	37.50	75.00	150.00
❑ 6208	One Little Kiss/Twistin' Marie	1962	25.00	50.00	100.00

Smash
❑ 1852	You Don't Have to Be a Baby to Cry/ The Last One to Know	1963	3.75	7.50	15.00
❑ 1869	Have You Ever Been Lonely/Don't Blow Your Cool	1964	3.00	6.00	12.00
❑ 1901	You Are Here/How Can I Be Sure	1964	3.00	6.00	12.00

Starmaker
❑ 1925	Pink Lips/Angry Angel	1961	6.25	12.50	25.00

Carbo, Chuck
(Also see "Spiders, The")
Ace
❑ 631	Tears, Tears and More Tears/I Shouldn't, But I Do	1961	3.00	6.00	12.00
❑ 666	Out on a Limb/Getting Out	1962	3.00	6.00	12.00

Imperial
❑ 5393	A-1 in My Heart/Dear Mary	1956	6.25	12.50	25.00
❑ 5405	That's the Way to Win My Heart/Goodbye	1956	6.25	12.50	25.00
❑ 5423	Honey Bee/That's My Desire	1957	5.00	10.00	20.00
❑ 5452	The Bells Are Ringing/Poor Boy	1957	5.00	10.00	20.00
❑ 5479	I Miss You/The Times	1957	5.00	10.00	20.00

Instant
❑ 3240	In the Night/Run, Henry	1962	3.00	6.00	12.00
❑ 3254	Two Tables Away/What Does It Take	1962	3.00	6.00	12.00

Rex
❑ 1003	Promises/Be My Girl	1959	3.75	7.50	15.00
❑ 1011	Lucy Brown/A Picture of You	1960	3.75	7.50	15.00
❑ 1012	Blue Velvet/It's You	1960	3.75	7.50	15.00

Cardboard Zeppelin
(Supposedly a pseudonym for the Regents)
Laurie
❑ 3433	City Lights/Ten Story Building	1968	6.25	12.50	25.00

Cardinals, The
(Two different groups?)
Atlantic
Note: Cardinals records on Atlantic before 952 are unconfirmed on 45 rpm
❑ 952	I'll Always Love You/Pretty Baby Blues	1952	75.00	150.00	300.00
❑ 958	Wheel of Fortune/Kiss Me Baby	1952	75.00	150.00	300.00
❑ 972	The Bump/She Rocks	1952	37.50	75.00	150.00
❑ 995	You Are My Only Love/Lovie Darling	1953	50.00	100.00	200.00
❑ 1025	Please Baby/Under a Blanket of Blue	1954	50.00	100.00	200.00
❑ 1054	The Door Is Still Open/Misirlou	1955	25.00	50.00	100.00
❑ 1067	Come Back My Love/Two Things I Love	1955	25.00	50.00	100.00
❑ 1079	Lovely Girl/There Goes My Heart to You	1955	25.00	50.00	100.00
❑ 1090	Choo Choo/Off Shore	1956	12.50	25.00	50.00
❑ 1103	The End of the Story/I Won't Make You Cry Anymore	1956	12.50	25.00	50.00
❑ 1126	Near You/One Love	1957	10.00	20.00	40.00

Number		Title (A Side/B Side)	Year	VG	VG+	NM
Cha Cha						
❏ 740		I Want You/Tomato Juice	1966	7.50	15.00	30.00
❏ 740	PS	I Want You/Tomato Juice	1966	12.50	25.00	50.00
❏ 741		Go Go Baby/Hatchet Face	1966	6.25	12.50	25.00
❏ 742		Saturday Night/I'm Gonna Tell on You	1966	6.25	12.50	25.00
❏ 748		When You're Away/I'm Gonna Tell on You	1966	6.25	12.50	25.00

Carefrees, The
London Int'l.

❏ 10614		We Love You Beatles/Hot Blooded Lover	1964	5.00	10.00	20.00
		Red label				
❏ 10614		We Love You Beatles/Hot Blooded Lover	1964	5.00	10.00	20.00
		Gold label				
❏ 10614	PS	We Love You Beatles/Hot Blooded Lover	1964	10.00	20.00	40.00
❏ 10615		Paddy Whack/Aren't You Glad You're You	1964	3.75	7.50	15.00

Carians, The
Indigo

❏ 136	She's Gone/Snooty Friends	1961	25.00	50.00	100.00
	Also see "Cordials, The"				

Magenta

❏ 04	Only a Dream/Girls	1961	12.50	25.00	50.00

Carla and Rufus - See "Rufus and Carla"

Carlo
Laurie

❏ 3063	Happy Time/Rockin' Rocket	1960	5.00	10.00	20.00
	As "Carlo and Jimmy"				
❏ 3151	Baby Doll/Write Me a Letter	1962	7.50	15.00	30.00
❏ 3157	Little Orphan Girl/Mairzy Doats	1963	7.50	15.00	30.00
❏ 3175	Five Minutes More/The Story of Love	1963	7.50	15.00	30.00
❏ 3227	Ring-a-Ling/Stranger in My Arms	1964	12.50	25.00	50.00

Raftis

❏ 110	Claudine/Fever	1970	3.00	6.00	12.00

Carmel Sisters, The
(Also see "Connors, Carol")
Colpix

❏ 767	Go, Go, G.T.O./Sunny Winter	1965	75.00	150.00	300.00
	As "Carol and Cheryl"				

Jubilee

❏ 5464	Joey's Comin' Home/The Rumor	1963	5.00	10.00	20.00

Carnations, The
(Several different groups)
Derby

❏ 789	Tree in the Meadow/Clown of the Masquerade	1952	100.00	200.00	400.00

Enrica

❏ 1001	Gimme, Gimme, Gimme/Love, Open My Heart	1959	6.25	12.50	25.00

Fraternity

❏ 863	Red Wing/Casual	1960	6.25	12.50	25.00

Laurie

❏ 3163	Punctuation/Funny Time	1963	6.25	12.50	25.00

Lescay

❏ 3002	Long Tall Girl/Is There Such a World	1961	25.00	50.00	100.00

Savoy

❏ 1172	Angels Sent You to Me/Night Time Is the Right Time	1955	15.00	30.00	60.00

Terry-Tone

❏ 199	Barbary Coast/Sleepy Hollow	1960	10.00	20.00	40.00

University

❏ 606	Leap Year/A Wing and a Prayer	1960	6.25	12.50	25.00

Carol and Cheryl - See "Carmel Sisters, The"

Carousels, The
ABC-Paramount

❏ 10233	Symptoms of Love/The Hush of Love	1961	6.25	12.50	25.00

Autumn

❏ 13	Beneath the Willow/Sail Away	1965	2.50	5.00	10.00

Gone

❏ 5118	You Can Come If You Want To/Pretty Little Thing	1961	12.50	25.00	50.00
❏ 5118	If You Want To/Pretty Little Thing	1961	7.50	15.00	30.00
❏ 5131	Never Let Him Go/Dirty Tricks	1962	6.25	12.50	25.00

Guyden

❏ 2102	I Wanna Fly/Something Else	1964	3.00	6.00	12.00

Jaguar

❏ 3029	Drive-In Movie/Rendezvous	1959	15.00	30.00	60.00

Spry

❏ 116	I've Cried Enough/Did I Cry Enough	1962	37.50	75.00	150.00

Number		Title (A Side/B Side)	Year	VG	VG+	NM

Carpenters
A&M

❑ 1142		Ticket to Ride/Your Wonderful Parade	1969	2.50	5.00	10.00
❑ 1183		(They Long to Be) Close to You/IKept On Loving You	1970		2.50	5.00
❑ 1217		We've Only Just Begun/All of My Life	1970		2.50	5.00
❑ 1217	PS	We've Only Just Begun/All of My Life	1970		3.00	6.00
❑ 1236		Merry Christmas Darling/Mr. Guder	1970		3.00	6.00

A-side vocal is different than later releases of this song

❑ 1236	PS	Merry Christmas Darling/Mr. Guder	1970	2.00	4.00	8.00
❑ 1243		For All We Know/Don't Be Afraid	1971		2.00	4.00
❑ 1243	PS	For All We Know/Don't Be Afraid	1971		3.00	6.00
❑ 1260		Rainy Days and Mondays/Saturday	1971		2.00	4.00
❑ 1260	PS	Rainy Days and Mondays/Saturday	1971		3.00	6.00
❑ 1289		Superstar/Bless the Beasts and Children	1971		2.00	4.00
❑ 1289	PS	Superstar/Bless the Beasts and Children	1971		3.00	6.00
❑ 1322		Hurting Each Other/Maybe It's You	1972		2.00	4.00
❑ 1322	PS	Hurting Each Other/Maybe It's You	1972		3.00	6.00
❑ 1351		It's Going to Take Some Time/Flat Baroque	1972		2.00	4.00
❑ 1351	PS	It's Going to Take Some Time/Flat Baroque	1972		3.00	6.00
❑ 1367		Goodbye to Love/Crystal Lullaby	1972		2.00	4.00
❑ 1367	PS	Goodbye to Love/Crystal Lullaby	1972		3.00	6.00
❑ 1391		Top of the World/Druscilla Penny	1972			Unreleased
❑ 1413		Sing/Druscilla Penny	1973		2.00	4.00
❑ 1413	PS	Sing/Druscilla Penny	1973		3.00	6.00
❑ 1446		Yesterday Once More/Road Ode	1973		2.00	4.00
❑ 1446	PS	Yesterday Once More/Road Ode	1973		3.00	6.00
❑ 1468		Top of the World/Heather	1973		2.00	4.00

Originals have brown labels

❑ 1468		Top of the World/Heather	1973			3.00

Second pressings have silvery labels

❑ 1468	PS	Top of the World/Heather	1973		3.00	6.00
❑ 1521		I Won't Last a Day Without You/One Love	1974		2.00	4.00
❑ 1521	PS	I Won't Last a Day Without You/One Love	1974		3.00	6.00
❑ 1646		Please Mister Postman/This Masquerade	1974		2.00	4.00
❑ 1646	PS	Please Mister Postman/This Masquerade	1974		3.00	6.00
❑ 1648		Santa Claus Is Coming to Town/Merry Christmas Darling	1974		2.50	5.00
❑ 1648	PS	Santa Claus Is Coming to Town/Merry Christmas Darling	1974	2.50	5.00	10.00
❑ 1677		Only Yesterday/Happy	1975		2.00	4.00
❑ 1677	PS	Only Yesterday/Happy	1975		3.00	6.00
❑ 1721		Solitaire/Love Me for What I Am	1975		2.00	4.00
❑ 1721	PS	Solitaire/Love Me for What I Am	1975		3.00	6.00
❑ 1800		There's a Kind of Hush (All Over the World)/(I'm Caught Between) Goodbye and I Love You	1976		2.00	4.00
❑ 1800	PS	There's a Kind of Hush (All Over the World)/(I'm Caught Between) Goodbye and I Love You	1976		3.00	6.00
❑ 1828		I Need to Be in Love/Sandy	1976		2.00	4.00
❑ 1859		Goofus/Boat to Sail	1976		2.00	4.00
❑ 1940		All You Get from Love Is a Love Song/I Have You	1977		2.00	4.00
❑ 1978		Calling Occupants of Interplanetary Craft/Can't Smile Without You	1977		2.00	4.00
❑ 1978	PS	Calling Occupants of Interplanetary Craft/Can't Smile Without You	1977		3.00	6.00
❑ 1991		The Christmas Song/Merry Christmas Darling	1977		2.50	5.00
❑ 1991	PS	The Christmas Song/Merry Christmas Darling	1977	2.00	4.00	8.00
❑ 2008		Sweet, Sweet Smile/I Have You	1978		2.00	4.00
❑ 2097		I Believe You/B'wana She No Home	1978		2.00	4.00
❑ 2344		Touch Me When We're Dancing/Because We Are in Love (The Wedding Song)	1981		2.00	4.00
❑ 2344	PS	Touch Me When We're Dancing/Because We Are in Love (The Wedding Song)	1981		2.00	4.00
❑ 2370		(Want You) Back in My Life Again/Somebody's Been Lyin'	1981		2.00	4.00
❑ 2386		Those Good Old Dreams/When It's Gone	1981		2.00	4.00
❑ 2405		Beechwood 4-5789/Two Sides	1982		2.00	4.00
❑ 2585		Make Believe It's Your First Time/Look to Your Dreams	1983		2.00	4.00
❑ 2620		Sailing on the Tide/Your Baby Doesn't Love You Anymore	1984		2.00	4.00
❑ 2700		Do You Hear What I Hear/Little Altar Boy	1984	2.50	5.00	10.00
❑ 2735		Yesterday Once More/(They Long to Be) Close to You-We've Only Just Begun	1985	5.00	10.00	20.00
❑ 2735	PS	Yesterday Once More/(They Long to Be) Close to You-We've Only Just Begun	1985	5.00	10.00	20.00

Magic Lamp

❑ 704		I'll Be Yours/Looking for Love	1967	500.00	1,000	2,000

As "Karen Carpenter", but Richard also was on this record

Carr, James
Atlantic

❑ 2803		Hold On/I'll Put It to You	1971	3.00	6.00	12.00

Goldwax

❑ 108		You Don't Want Me/Only Fools Run Away	1965	7.50	15.00	30.00
❑ 112		I Can't Make It/Lovers' Competition	1965	7.50	15.00	30.00
❑ 119		He's Better Than You/Talk Talk	1965	7.50	15.00	30.00
❑ 302		You've Got My Mind Messed Up/That's What I Want to Know	1966	5.00	10.00	20.00

Number	Title (A Side/B Side)	Year	VG	VG+	NM
❑ 309	Love Attack/Come Back to Me Baby	1966	3.75	7.50	15.00
❑ 311	Pouring Water on a Drowning Man/Forgetting You	1966	3.75	7.50	15.00
❑ 317	The Dark End of the Street/Lovable Girl	1967	4.00	8.00	16.00
❑ 323	Let It Happen/A Losing Game	1967	3.75	7.50	15.00
❑ 328	I'm a Fool for You/Gonna Send You Back to Georgia	1967	3.75	7.50	15.00
❑ 332	A Man Needs a Woman/Stronger Than Love	1968	3.75	7.50	15.00
❑ 335	Life Turned Her That Way/A Message to Young Lovers	1968	3.75	7.50	15.00
❑ 338	Freedom Train/That's the Way Love Turned Out for Me	1968	3.75	7.50	15.00
❑ 340	To Love Somebody/These Ain't Teardrops	1969	3.75	7.50	15.00
❑ 343	Everybody Needs Somebody/Row, Row Your Boat	1969	3.75	7.50	15.00

Carroll Brothers, The
Cameo
❑ 140	(My Gal Is) Red Hot/Dearly Beloved	1959	20.00	40.00	80.00
❑ 213	Don't Knock the Twist/Bo Diddley	1962	5.00	10.00	20.00
❑ 221	Sweet Georgia Brown/Boot It	1962	5.00	10.00	20.00

Felsted
❑ 8550	Movin' Day/I Found You	1959	5.00	10.00	20.00

Carroll, Andrea
Big Top
❑ 3156	It Hurts to Be Sixteen/Why Am I So Shy	1963	5.00	10.00	20.00
❑ 515	The Doolang/This Time Tomorrow	1964	10.00	20.00	40.00

Epic
❑ 9438	I've Got a Date with Frankie/Young and Lonely	1961	25.00	50.00	100.00
❑ 9450	Please Don't Talk to the Lifeguard/Room of Memories	1961	5.00	10.00	20.00
❑ 9471	Gee Dad/The Charm on My Arm	1961	5.00	10.00	20.00
❑ 9523	Miss Happiness/Fifteen Shades of Pink	1962	5.00	10.00	20.00

RCA Victor
❑ 47-8618	Mr. Music Man/Sally Fool	1965	5.00	10.00	20.00

United Artists
❑ 982	The World Isn't Big Enough/She Gets Everything She Wants	1966	5.00	10.00	20.00
❑ 50039	Hey, Beach Boy/Why Should We Take the Easy Way Out	1966	7.50	15.00	30.00

Carroll, Wayne
King
❑ 5123	Chicken Out/Cindy Lee	1958	12.50	25.00	50.00
❑ 5134	Rockin' Chair Momma/There's Been a Change in Me	1958	12.50	25.00	50.00
❑ 5146	He Cheated/Wall Around Your Heart	1958	12.50	25.00	50.00

Carter, Sonny
Carlton
❑ 481	Crying Over You/My Lonely Life	1959			Unreleased?

Dot
❑ 15921	Crying Over You/My Lonely Life	1959	7.50	15.00	30.00

King
❑ 4739	There Is No Greater Love/Oh Baby	1954	12.50	25.00	50.00
❑ 4756	It's Strange but True/I Solemnly Swear	1954	12.50	25.00	50.00

Cartey, Ric
ABC-Paramount
❑ 10415	Poor Me/Something in My Eye	1963	3.00	6.00	12.00

NRC
❑ 503	My Heart Belongs to You/Scratching on the Screen	1959	12.50	25.00	50.00

RCA Victor
❑ 47-6751	Young Love/Oooh-Eee	1956	20.00	40.00	80.00
❑ 47-6828	Heart Throb/I Wancha to Know	1957	20.00	40.00	80.00
❑ 47-6920	Let Me Tell You About Love/Born to Love One Woman	1957	30.00	60.00	120.00
❑ 47-7011	My Babe/Hello Down Easy	1957	30.00	60.00	120.00

Stars
❑ 539	Young Love/Oooh-Eee	1956	37.50	75.00	150.00

Cascades, The
Arwin
❑ 132	Cheryl's Going Home/Truly Julie's Blues	1966	2.00	4.00	8.00
❑ 134	Midnight Lace/All's Fair in Love and War	1966	2.00	4.00	8.00

Canbase
❑ 714	I Started a Joke/Sweet America	1972		2.50	5.00

Charter
❑ 1018	She Was Never Mine (To Lose)/My Best Girl	1964	3.75	7.50	15.00
❑ 1018	She Was Never Really Mine (To Lose)/My Best Girl	1964	5.00	10.00	20.00

Liberty
❑ 55822	She'll Love Again/I Bet You Won't Stay	1965	2.50	5.00	10.00

London
❑ 177	Two-Sided Man/The Woman's A Girl	1972		2.50	5.00

Probe
❑ 453	Two-Sided Man/Everyone Is Blossoming	1968	2.00	4.00	8.00

RCA Victor
❑ 47-8206	Cinderella/A Little Like Lovin'	1963	3.75	7.50	15.00
❑ 47-8268	For Your Sweet Love/Jeannie	1963	3.00	6.00	12.00

Number	Title (A Side/B Side)	Year	VG	VG+	NM
❏ 47-8321	Little Betty Falling Star/Those Were the Good Old Days	1964	3.75	7.50	15.00
❏ 47-8402	I Dare You to Cry/Awake	1964	3.00	6.00	12.00

Renee

❏ 105	Pains in My Heart/One That I Can Spare	19??	5.00	10.00	20.00

Smash

❏ 2083	Hey Little Girl of Mine/Blue Hours	1967	2.00	4.00	8.00
❏ 2101	Flying on the Ground/Main Street	1967	2.00	4.00	8.00

Uni

❏ 55152	Maybe the Rain Will Fall/Naggin' Cries	1969	2.00	4.00	8.00
❏ 55169	Indian River/Big City Country Boy	1969	2.00	4.00	8.00
❏ 55200	But For Love/Hazel Autumn Cocoa Brown	1970	2.00	4.00	8.00
❏ 55231	April, May, June and July/Big Ugly Sky	1970	2.00	4.00	8.00

Valiant

❏ 6021	There's a Reason/Second Chance	1962	6.25	12.50	25.00
❏ 6026	Rhythm of the Rain/Let Me Be	1962	4.00	8.00	16.00
❏ 6028	Shy Girl/The Last Leaf	1963	3.75	7.50	15.00
❏ 6032	I Wanna Be Your Lover/My First Day Alone	1963	3.75	7.50	15.00

Warner Bros.

❏ 7114	Rhythm of the Rain/The Last Leaf	1968			2.50
	"Back to Back Hits" series; originals on green "W7" label				

Casey, Al

(Also see "Eddy, Duane")

Blue Horizon

❏ 925	Cookin'/Hot Foot	1962	6.25	12.50	25.00

Dot

❏ 15524	A Fool's Blues/Juice	1956	7.50	15.00	30.00
❏ 15563	Guitar Man/Come What May	1957	10.00	20.00	40.00

Highland

❏ 1002	Got the Teenage Blues/(B-side unknown)	1959	10.00	20.00	40.00
❏ 1004	Night Beat/The Stinger	1960	6.25	12.50	25.00

Liberty

❏ 55117	Willa Mae/She Gotta Shake	1957	5.00	10.00	20.00

MCI

❏ 1005	Pink Panther/If I Told You	1965	3.75	7.50	15.00

Stacy

❏ 925	Cookin'/Hot Foot	1962	3.75	7.50	15.00
❏ 936	Jivin' Around/Doin' the Shotish	1962	3.75	7.50	15.00
❏ 950	Laughin'/Chicken Feathers	1962	3.75	7.50	15.00
❏ 956	Doin' It/Monte Carlo	1963	3.75	7.50	15.00
❏ 961	Full House/Indian Love Call	1963	3.75	7.50	15.00
❏ 962	Surfin' Hootenanny/Easy Pickin'	1963	10.00	20.00	40.00
	Red vinyl				
❏ 962	Surfin' Hootenanny/Easy Pickin'	1963	5.00	10.00	20.00
	Black vinyl				
❏ 964	Surfin' Blues/Guitars, Guitars, Guitars	1963	3.75	7.50	15.00
❏ 971	Cookin'/What Are We Gonna Do in '64	1964	3.75	7.50	15.00

United Artists

❏ 158	The Stinger/Keep Talking	1959	6.25	12.50	25.00
❏ 494	Jivin' Around/Doin' the Shotish	1962	6.25	12.50	25.00

Cash, Bobby

King

❏ 5844	Mona Lisa/Teen Love	1964	7.50	15.00	30.00
❏ 5864	Only Make Believe/Run, Fool, Run	1964	7.50	15.00	30.00
❏ 5894	The Answer to My Dreams/I Don't Need Your Love and Kisses	1964	7.50	15.00	30.00

Cash, Johnny

A&M

❏ 2291	The Death of Me/One More Shot	1980		2.00	4.00
	With Levon Helm				

American

❏ 18091	Drive On/Delia's Gone	1994		2.00	4.00

Cachet

❏ 4504	Wings in the Morning/What on Earth	1980		2.50	5.00

Columbia

❏ 02189	Mobile Bay/The Hard Way	1981		2.00	4.00
❏ 02669	The Reverend Mr. Black/Chattanooga City Limit Sign	1982		2.00	4.00
❏ 03058	Georgia on a Fast Train/Sing a Song	1982		2.00	4.00
❏ 03317	Fair Weather Friends/Ain't Gonna Hobo No More	1982		2.00	4.00
❏ 03524	I'll Cross Over Jordan Some Day/We Must Believe in Magic	1983		2.00	4.00
❏ 04060	I'm Ragged, But I'm Right/Brand New Dance	1983		2.00	4.00
❏ 04227	Johnny 99/New Cut Road	1983			3.00
❏ 04428	That's the Truth/Joshua Gone Barbados	1984			3.00
❏ 04513	The Chicken in Black/The Battle of Nashville	1984			3.00
❏ 04740	They Killed Him/The Three Bells	1985			3.00
	With the Carter Family				
❏ 04860	Crazy Old Soldier/It Ain't Gonna Worry My Mind	1985			3.00
	A-side: Ray Charles and Johnny Cash; B-side: Ray Charles and Mickey Gilley				

Number		Title (A Side/B Side)	Year	VG	VG+	NM
❑ 04881		Highwayman/The Human Condition	1985			3.00
		A-side: Willie Nelson/Waylon Jennings/Johnny Cash/Kris Kristofferson; B-side: Nelson, Cash				
❑ 04881	PS	Highwayman/The Human Condition	1985		2.50	5.00
		A-side: Willie Nelson/Waylon Jennings/Johnny Cash/Kris Kristofferson; B-side: Nelson, Cash				
❑ 05594		Desperadoes Waiting for a Train/	1985			3.00
		The Twentieth Century Is Almost Over				
		A-side: Willie Nelson/Waylon Jennings/Johnny Cash/Kris Kristofferson; B-side: Nelson, Cash				
❑ 05672		I'm Leaving Now/Easy Street	1985			3.00
❑ 05896		American by Birth/Even Cowgirls Get the Blues	1986			3.00
		A-side: Johnny Cash/Waylon Jennings				
❑ 08406		Highwayman/Desperadoes Waiting for a Train	1988			3.00
		Waylon Jennings/Willie Nelson/Johnny Cash/Kris Kristofferson; reissue				
❑ 10011		The Junkie and the Juicehead/	1974		2.50	5.00
		Crystal Chandeliers and Burgundy				
❑ 10048		Father and Daughter, Father and Son/	1974		2.50	5.00
		Don't Take Your Love to Town				
		With Rosey Nix				
❑ 10066		The Lady Came from Baltimore/Lonesome to the Bone	1974		2.50	5.00
❑ 10116		My Old Kentucky Home	1975		2.50	5.00
		(Turpentine and Dandelion Wine)/Hard Times Comin'				
❑ 10177		Look at Them Beans/All Around Cowboy	1975		2.50	5.00
❑ 10237		Texas -- 1947/I Hardly Ever Sing Beer Drinking Songs	1975		2.50	5.00
❑ 10279		Strawberry Cake/I Got Stripes	1975		2.50	5.00
❑ 10321		One Piece at a Time/Go On Blues	1976		2.50	5.00
❑ 10381		Sold Out of Flagpoles/Mountain Lady	1976		2.50	5.00
❑ 10424		It's All Over/Ridin' on the Cotton Belt	1976		2.50	5.00
❑ 10483		The Last Gunfighter Ballad/City Jail	1977		2.50	5.00
❑ 10587		Lady/Hit the Road and Go	1977		2.50	5.00
❑ 10623		After the Ball/Calilou	1977		2.50	5.00
❑ 10681		I Would Like to See You Again/Lately	1978		2.50	5.00
❑ 10742		There Ain't No Good Chain Gang/	1978		2.50	5.00
		I Wish I Was Crazy Again				
		With Waylon Jennings				
❑ 10817		Gone Girl/I'm Alright Now	1978		2.50	5.00
❑ 10855		It'll Be Her/It Comes and Goes	1978		2.50	5.00
❑ 10888		I Will Rock and Roll with You/A Song for the Life	1979		2.50	5.00
❑ 10961		(Ghost) Riders in the Sky/	1979		2.50	5.00
		I'm Gonna Sit on the Porch and Pick on My Guitar				
❑ 11103		I'll Say It's True/Cocaine Blues	1979		2.50	5.00
❑ 11237		Bull Rider/Lonesome to the Bone	1980		2.00	4.00
❑ 11283		Song of a Patriot/She's a Go-er	1980		2.00	4.00
❑ 11340		Cold Lonesome Morning/	1980		2.00	4.00
		The Cowboy Who Started the Fight				
❑ 11399		The Last Time/Rockabilly Blues (Texas 1965)	1980		2.00	4.00
❑ 11424		Without Love/It Ain't Nothing New Babe	1981		2.00	4.00
❑ 30843	S	titles unknown	1960	7.50	15.00	30.00
❑ 30844	S	titles unknown	1960	7.50	15.00	30.00
❑ 30845	S	titles unknown	1960	7.50	15.00	30.00
❑ 30846	S	titles unknown	1960	7.50	15.00	30.00
❑ 30847	S	titles unknown	1960	7.50	15.00	30.00
❑ 31109	S	titles unknown	1961	7.50	15.00	30.00
❑ 31110	S	titles unknown	1961	7.50	15.00	30.00
❑ 31111	S	titles unknown	1961	7.50	15.00	30.00
❑ 31112	S	titles unknown	1961	7.50	15.00	30.00
❑ 31113	S	titles unknown	1961	7.50	15.00	30.00
		Anyone who can fill in these gaps -- the above 10 all are Columbia "Stereo 7" singles -- please let us know.				
❑ 41251		All Over Again/What Do I Care	1958	3.75	7.50	15.00
❑ 41313		Don't Take Your Guns to Town/I Still Miss Someone	1959	3.75	7.50	15.00
❑ 41371		Frankie's Man, Johnny/You, Dreamer, You	1959	3.75	7.50	15.00
❑ 41427		I Got Stripes/Five Feet High and Rising	1959	3.75	7.50	15.00
❑ 41481		The Little Drummer Boy/I'll Remember You	1959	3.75	7.50	15.00
❑ 41618		Seasons of My Heart/Smiling Bill McCall	1960	3.75	7.50	15.00
❑ 41707		Second Honemoon/Honky Tonk Girl	1960	3.75	7.50	15.00
❑ 41804		Going to Memphis/Loading Coal	1960	3.75	7.50	15.00
❑ 41920		Girl in Saskatoon/Locomotive Man	1960	3.75	7.50	15.00
❑ 41995		The Rebel-Johnny Yuma/Forty Shades of Green	1961	3.00	6.00	12.00
❑ 42147		Tennessee Flat Top Box/Tall Men	1961	3.00	6.00	12.00
❑ 42301		The Big Battle/What I've Learned	1962	3.00	6.00	12.00
❑ 42425		In the Jailhouse Now/A Little at a Time	1962	3.00	6.00	12.00
❑ 42512		Bonanza!/Pick a Bale o' Cotton	1962	3.00	6.00	12.00
❑ 42615		Peace in the Valley/Were You There	1962	3.00	6.00	12.00
		With the Carter Family				
❑ 42665		Busted/Send a Picture of Mother	1963	2.50	5.00	10.00
❑ 42788		Ring of Fire/I'd Still Be There	1963	2.50	5.00	10.00
❑ 42788	DJ	Ring of Fire (same on both sides)	1963	10.00	20.00	40.00
		Red vinyl promo				
❑ 42880		The Matador/Still in Town	1963	2.50	5.00	10.00
❑ 42964		Understand Your Man/Dark as a Dungeon	1964	2.50	5.00	10.00
❑ 43058		The Ballad of Ira Hayes/Bad News	1964	2.50	5.00	10.00
❑ 43145		It Ain't Me, Babe/Time and Time Again	1964	2.50	5.00	10.00
❑ 43206		Orange Blossom Special/	1965	2.00	4.00	8.00
		All of God's Children Ain't Free				
❑ 43313		Mister Garfield/Streets of Laredo	1965	2.00	4.00	8.00
❑ 43342		The Sons of Katie Elder/A Certain Kinda Hurtin'	1965	2.00	4.00	8.00
❑ 43420		Happy to Be with You/Pickin' Time	1965	2.00	4.00	8.00
❑ 43496		The One on the Right Is On the Left/	1965	2.00	4.00	8.00
		Cotton Pickin' Hands				
❑ 43673		Everybody Loves a Nut/Austin Prison	1966		3.00	6.00

Number		Title (A Side/B Side)	Year	VG	VG+	NM
☐ 43763		Boa Constrictor/Bottom of a Mountain	1966		3.00	6.00
☐ 43921		You Beat All I Ever Saw/Put the Sugar to Bill	1966		3.00	6.00
☐ 44288		The Wind Changes/Red Velvet	1967		3.00	6.00
☐ 44373		Rosanna's Going Wild/Roll Call	1967		3.00	6.00
☐ 44373	PS	Rosanna's Going Wild/Roll Call	1967	2.50	5.00	10.00
☐ 44513		Folsom Prison Blues/The Folk Singer	1968		3.00	6.00
☐ 44513	PS	Folsom Prison Blues/The Folk Singer	1968	2.50	5.00	10.00
☐ 44689		Daddy Sang Bass/He Turned the Water Into Wine	1968		3.00	6.00
☐ 44944		A Boy Named Sue/San Quentin	1969		3.00	6.00
☐ 45020		Blistered/See Ruby Fall	1969		3.00	6.00
☐ 45134		What Is Truth/Sing a Traveling Song	1970		2.50	5.00
☐ 45211		Sunday Morning Coming Down/ I'm Gonna Try to Be That Way	1970		2.50	5.00
☐ 45269		Flesh and Blood/This Side of the Law	1970		2.50	5.00
☐ 45339		Man in Black/Little Bit of Yesterday	1971		2.50	5.00
☐ 45393		Singing in Viet Nam Talking Blues/ You've Got a New Light Shining	1971		2.50	5.00
☐ 45460		Papa Was a Good Man/I Promise You	1971		2.50	5.00
☐ 45534		A Thing Called Love/Daddy	1972		2.50	5.00
☐ 45590		Kate/Miracle Man	1972		2.50	5.00
☐ 45660		Oney/Country Trash	1972		2.50	5.00
☐ 45679		The World Needs a Melody/ A Bird with Broken Wings Can't Fly	1972		2.50	5.00
		With the Carter Family				
☐ 45740		Any Old Wind That Blows/Kentucky Straight	1972		2.50	5.00
☐ 45786		Children/Last Summer	1973		2.50	5.00
☐ 45938		Pick the Wildwood Flower/Diamonds in the Rough	1973		2.50	5.00
		With Mother Maybelle and the Carter Family				
☐ 45979		Christmas As I Knew It/That Christmasy Feeling	1973		2.50	5.00
		With Tommy Cash				
☐ 45997		Orleans Parish Prison/Jacob Green	1974		2.50	5.00
☐ 46028		Ragged Old Flag/Don't Go Near the Water	1974		2.50	5.00
☐ 60516		The Baron/I Will Dance with You	1981		2.00	4.00
☐ 69067		Ragged Old Flag/I'm Leaving Now	1989			3.00
☐ 73233		America Remains/Silver Stallion	1990			3.00
		Waylon Jennings/Willie Nelson/Johnny Cash/Kris Kristofferson				
☐ 73381		Born and Raised in Black and White/Texas	1990			3.00
		The Highwaymen (Waylon Jennings/Willie Nelson/Johnny Cash/Kris Kristofferson)				
☐ 73572		American Remains/Texas	1990			3.00
		The Highwaymen (Waylon Jennings/Willie Nelson/Johnny Cash/Kris Kristofferson)				

Epic

Number		Title (A Side/B Side)	Year	VG	VG+	NM
☐ 50778		There Ain't No Good Chain Gang/ I Wish I Was Crazy Again	1979		2.50	5.00
		Johnny Cash/Waylon Jennings				

Liberty

Number		Title (A Side/B Side)	Year	VG	VG+	NM
☐ S7-18486		It Is What It Is/The Devil's Right Hand	1995			3.00
		By The Highwaymen				

Mercury

Number		Title (A Side/B Side)	Year	VG	VG+	NM
☐ 870 010-7		W. Lee O'Daniel (And the Light Crust Dough Boys)/ Letters from Home	1987			3.00
☐ 870 237-7		Cry, Cry, Cry/Get Rhythm	1988			3.00
☐ 870 688-7		Tennessee Flat Top Box/That Old Wheel	1988			3.00
		With Hank Williams, Jr.				
☐ 872 420-7		Ballad of a Teenage Queen/Get Rhythm	1988			3.00
		With Roseanne Cash and the Everly Brothers				
☐ 874 562-7		The Last of the Drifters/(B-side unknown)	1989			3.00
		With Tom T. Hall				
☐ 875 626-7		Cat's in the Cradle/I Love You, Love You	1990			3.00
☐ 878 292-7		Goin' By the Book/Beans for Breakfast	1990			3.00
☐ 878 710-7		The Greatest Cowboy of Them All/Hey Porter	1990			3.00
☐ 878 968-7		The Mystery of Life/I'm an Easy Rider	1990			3.00
☐ 888 459-7		The Night Hank Williams Came to Town/ I'd Rather Have You	1987			3.00
☐ 888 719-7		Sixteen Tons/The Ballad of Barbara	1987			3.00
☐ 888 838-7		Let Him Roll/My Ship Will Sail	1987			3.00

Scotti Bros.

Number		Title (A Side/B Side)	Year	VG	VG+	NM
☐ 02803		The General Lee/Duelin' Dukes	1982		2.00	4.00
		Narration on B-side: Sorrell Booke				

Smash

Number		Title (A Side/B Side)	Year	VG	VG+	NM
☐ 884 934-7		Sixteen Candles/Rock & Roll (Fais-Do-Do)	1986		2.00	4.00
		With Jerry Lee Lewis, Roy Orbison and Carl Perkins				
☐ 888 142-7		We Remember the King/Class of '55	1987		2.00	4.00
		With Jerry Lee Lewis, Roy Orbison and Carl Perkins; B-side by Carl Perkins solo				

Sun

Number		Title (A Side/B Side)	Year	VG	VG+	NM
☐ 221		Hey Porter/Cry, Cry, Cry	1955	10.00	20.00	40.00
☐ 232		Folsom Prison Blues/So Doggone Lonesome	1956	7.50	15.00	30.00
☐ 241		I Walk the Line/Get Rhythm	1956	10.00	20.00	40.00
☐ 258		Train of Love/There You Go	1956	7.50	15.00	30.00
☐ 266		Next in Line/Don't Make Me Go	1957	7.50	15.00	30.00
☐ 279		Home of the Blues/Give My Love to Rose	1957	7.50	15.00	30.00
☐ 283		Ballad of a Teenage Queen/Big River	1958	6.25	12.50	25.00
☐ 295		Guess Things Happen That Way/Come In Stranger	1958	6.25	12.50	25.00
☐ 295	PS	Guess Things Happen That Way/Come In Stranger	1958	12.50	25.00	50.00

Number	Title (A Side/B Side)	Year	VG	VG+	NM
❏ 302	The Ways of a Woman in Love/ The Nearest Thing to Heaven	1958	6.25	12.50	25.00
❏ 309	It's Just About Time/Just Thought You'd Like to Know	1958	6.25	12.50	25.00
❏ 316	Luther Played the Boogie/Thanks a Lot	1959	5.00	10.00	20.00
❏ 321	Katy Too/I Forgot to Remember to Forget	1959	5.00	10.00	20.00
❏ 331	Goodbye Little Darlin'/You Tell Me	1959	5.00	10.00	20.00
❏ 334	Straight A's in Love/I Love You Because	1960	5.00	10.00	20.00
❏ 343	Story of a Broken Heart/Down the Street to 301	1960	5.00	10.00	20.00
❏ 347	Mean Eyed Cat/Port of Lonely Hearts	1960	5.00	10.00	20.00
❏ 355	Oh Lonesome Me/Life Goes On	1961	5.00	10.00	20.00
❏ 363	Sugartime/My Treasurer	1961	5.00	10.00	20.00
❏ 376	Born to Lose/Blue Train	1962	5.00	10.00	20.00
❏ 392	Wide Open Road/Belshazar	1964	5.00	10.00	20.00
❏ 1103	Get Rhythm/Hey Porter	1969		3.00	6.00
❏ 1111	Rock Island Line/Next in Line	1970		3.00	6.00
❏ 1121	Big River/Come In Stranger	1971		2.50	5.00

Warner Bros.

Number	Title (A Side/B Side)	Year	VG	VG+	NM
❏ 28979	I Will Dance with You/Too Bad for Love *With Karen Brooks*	1985			3.00

Cashmeres, The
(More than one group)
Herald

Number	Title (A Side/B Side)	Year	VG	VG+	NM
❏ 474	Little Dream Girl/Do I Upset You	1956	20.00	40.00	80.00

Josie

Number	Title (A Side/B Side)	Year	VG	VG+	NM
❏ 894	Life Line/Where Have You Been	1961	3.00	6.00	12.00

Lake

Number	Title (A Side/B Side)	Year	VG	VG+	NM
❏ 703	Everything's Gonna Be Alright/Four Lonely Nights	1960	7.50	15.00	30.00
❏ 705	Satisfied/Satisfied (Part 2)	1961	6.25	12.50	25.00

Laurie

Number	Title (A Side/B Side)	Year	VG	VG+	NM
❏ 3078	I Believe in St. Nick/A Very Special Birthday	1960	10.00	20.00	40.00
❏ 3088	I Gotta Go/Singing Waters	1961	6.25	12.50	25.00
❏ 3105	Poppa Said/Bobby Come On Home	1961	6.25	12.50	25.00

Mercury

Number	Title (A Side/B Side)	Year	VG	VG+	NM
❏ 70501	My Sentimental Heart/Yes, Yes, Yes	1954	20.00	40.00	80.00
❏ 70617	Don't Let It Happen Again/Boom Mag-Azeno-Vip Vay	1955	20.00	40.00	80.00
❏ 70679	There's a Rumor/Second Hand Heart	1955	20.00	40.00	80.00

Relic

Number	Title (A Side/B Side)	Year	VG	VG+	NM
❏ 1005	Satisfied/Satisfied (Part 2)	1970		3.00	6.00

Casinos, The
(More than one group)
Airtown

Number	Title (A Side/B Side)	Year	VG	VG+	NM
❏ 002	That's the Way/Too Good to Be True	1967	3.75	7.50	15.00

Alto

Number	Title (A Side/B Side)	Year	VG	VG+	NM
❏ 2002	I Like It Like That/Baby Don't Do It	1961	7.50	15.00	30.00

Casino

Number	Title (A Side/B Side)	Year	VG	VG+	NM
❏ 111	My Love for You/Why Am I a Fool	1960	10.00	20.00	40.00

Certron

Number	Title (A Side/B Side)	Year	VG	VG+	NM
❏ 10015	Coal River/(B-side unknown)	1970		3.00	6.00

Fraternity

Number	Title (A Side/B Side)	Year	VG	VG+	NM
❏ 944	She's Out of Sight/The Gallop	1965	2.50	5.00	10.00
❏ 949	Right There Beside You/The Gallop	1965	2.50	5.00	10.00
❏ 977	Then You Can Tell Me Goodbye/I Still Love You	1967	3.00	6.00	12.00
❏ 985	It's All Over Now/Tailor Made	1967	2.50	5.00	10.00
❏ 987	Forever and a Night/How Long Has It Been	1967	2.50	5.00	10.00
❏ 995	When I Stop Dreaming/Please Love	1967	2.50	5.00	10.00
❏ 997	Bye Bye Love/Walk Through This World with Me	1967	2.50	5.00	10.00
❏ 1020	These Are the Things We'll Share/Casinos Having Fun	1969	2.50	5.00	10.00
❏ 1028	I Wish I Were Anyone But Me/I Just Want to Stay Here	1969	2.50	5.00	10.00
❏ 1200	Father John/The Old Saloon	1970	2.50	5.00	10.00
❏ 1201	Wisdom of Love/My House	1970	2.50	5.00	10.00
❏ 1250	Loving Her Was Easier/A Restless Wind	1971	2.50	5.00	10.00

Itzy

Number	Title (A Side/B Side)	Year	VG	VG+	NM
❏ 2	Do You Recall?/The Swim	1964	7.50	15.00	30.00

Million

Number	Title (A Side/B Side)	Year	VG	VG+	NM
❏ 13	I'm Walking Behind You/Angels Were All Asleep *As "Gene Hughes and the Casinos"*	1972	2.50	5.00	10.00

Name

Number	Title (A Side/B Side)	Year	VG	VG+	NM
❏ 7739	Do You Recall?/The Swim	1959	37.50	75.00	150.00

Olimpic

Number	Title (A Side/B Side)	Year	VG	VG+	NM
❏ 251	Do You Recall?/The Swim	1963	20.00	40.00	80.00

Sims

Number	Title (A Side/B Side)	Year	VG	VG+	NM
❏ 306	Moon River/Soul Serenade	1966	3.00	6.00	12.00

Terry

Number	Title (A Side/B Side)	Year	VG	VG+	NM
❏ 115	Gee Whiz/Lovely One	1964	12.50	25.00	50.00
❏ 116	That's the Way/Too Good to Be True	1964	5.00	10.00	20.00

United Artists

Number	Title (A Side/B Side)	Year	VG	VG+	NM
❏ 50255	Here I Am/Peggy *As "Gene Hughes and the Casinos"*	1968	2.50	5.00	10.00
❏ 50313	Nobody's Child/Leaving Makes the Rain Come Down *As "Gene Hughes and the Casinos"*	1968	2.50	5.00	10.00

Number	Title (A Side/B Side)	Year	VG	VG+	NM

Castaleers, The
Donna
| ❑ 1349 | That's Why I Cry/My Baby's All Right | 1961 | 6.25 | 12.50 | 25.00 |

Felsted
❑ 8504	Come Back/Hi-Fi Baby	1958	12.50	25.00	50.00
❑ 8512	Lonely Boy/My Bull Fightin' Baby	1958	10.00	20.00	40.00
❑ 8585	You're My Dream/I'll Be Around	1959	15.00	30.00	60.00

Planet
| ❑ 44 | That's Why I Cry/My Baby's All Right | 1961 | 10.00 | 20.00 | 40.00 |

Castaways, The
(More than one group)
Bear
| ❑ 2000 | I Feel So Fine/Hit the Road Jack | 1967 | 10.00 | 20.00 | 40.00 |

Capitol
| ❑ 4340 | The Twitch/Vibrations | 1960 | 3.00 | 6.00 | 12.00 |

Excello
| ❑ 2038 | I Wish/Teasin' | 1954 | 10.00 | 20.00 | 40.00 |

Fontana
| ❑ 1615 | Walking in Different Circles/Just On High | 1968 | 2.50 | 5.00 | 10.00 |
| ❑ 1626 | Lavender Popcorn/What Kind of Face | 1968 | 2.50 | 5.00 | 10.00 |

GNP Crescendo
| ❑ 302 | Tarzan/Wild Boy | 1963 | 2.50 | 5.00 | 10.00 |
| ❑ 310 | Moritat/Pass It Around | 1964 | 2.50 | 5.00 | 10.00 |

Soma
❑ 1433	Liar, Liar/Sam	1965	3.75	7.50	15.00
❑ 1442	Goodbye Babe/A Man's Gotta Be a Man	1965	3.00	6.00	12.00
❑ 1461	Girl in Love/Should Happen to Me	1966	3.00	6.00	12.00
❑ 1469	Liar, Liar/Surfin' Bird	1966	3.00	6.00	12.00
	B-side by the Trashmen				

Witch
| ❑ 124 | Don't You Just Know It/I Go Ape | 1964 | 7.50 | 15.00 | 30.00 |

Castelles, The
Atco
| ❑ 6069 | Happy and Gay/Hey Baby Baby | 1956 | 25.00 | 50.00 | 100.00 |

Grand
❑ 101	My Girl Awaits Me/Sweetness	1954	600.00	1,200	1,800
	Blue label original				
❑ 103	This Silver Ring/Wonder Why	1954	400.00	800.00	1,200
	Glossy yellow label original				
❑ 105	Do You Remember/If You Were the Only Girl	1954	400.00	800.00	1,200
	Glossy yellow label original				
❑ 109	Baby Can't You See/Over a Cup of Coffee	1954	400.00	800.00	1,200
	Blue label original				
❑ 114	Marcella/I'm a Fool to Care	1955	400.00	800.00	1,200
	Cream label original				
❑ 122	My Wedding Day/Heavenly Father	1955	400.00	800.00	1,200
	Cream label original				

Castells, The
Decca
| ❑ 31834 | Just Walk Away/An Angel Cried | 1965 | 3.75 | 7.50 | 15.00 |
| ❑ 31967 | Life Goes On/I Thought You'd Like That | 1966 | 3.75 | 7.50 | 15.00 |

Era
❑ 3038	Little Sad Eyes/Romeo	1961	6.25	12.50	25.00
❑ 3048	Sacred/I Get Dreamy	1961	6.25	12.50	25.00
❑ 3057	My Miracle/Make Believe Wedding	1961	5.00	10.00	20.00
❑ 3064	The Vision of You/Stiki De Boom Boom	1961	5.00	10.00	20.00
❑ 3073	So This Is Love/On the Streets of Tears	1962	5.00	10.00	20.00
❑ 3083	Oh, What It Seemed to Be/Stand There, Mountain	1962	5.00	10.00	20.00
❑ 3089	Echoes in the Night/The Only One	1962	5.00	10.00	20.00
❑ 3098	Clown Prince/Eternal Spring, Eternal Love	1962	5.00	10.00	20.00
❑ 3102	Little Sad Eyes/Initials	1963	5.00	10.00	20.00
❑ 3107	Some Enchanted Evening/ What Do Little Girls Dream Of	1963	5.00	10.00	20.00

Laurie
| ❑ 3444 | I'd Like to Know/Rocky Ridges | 1968 | 2.50 | 5.00 | 10.00 |

United Artists
| ❑ 50324 | Two Lovers/Jerusalem | 1968 | 2.50 | 5.00 | 10.00 |

Warner Bros.
❑ 5421	I Do/Teardrops	1964	20.00	40.00	80.00
	A-side written and produced by Brian Wilson				
❑ 5445	Could This Be Magic/Shinny Up Your Own Side	1964	7.50	15.00	30.00
❑ 5486	Love Finds a Way/Tell Her If I Could	1964	5.00	10.00	20.00

Castle Kings, The
Atlantic
❑ 2107	You Can Get Him Frankenstein/Loch Lomond	1961	7.50	15.00	30.00
	Produced by Phil Spector				
❑ 2158	Jeanette/The Caissons Go Rolling Along	1962	3.75	7.50	15.00

Number		Title (A Side/B Side)	Year	VG	VG+	NM

Castle, Joey
Headline
| ❏ 1008 | | Rock and Roll Daddy-O/Wild Love | 1959 | 100.00 | 200.00 | 400.00 |

RCA Victor
| ❏ 47-7283 | | That Ain't Nothin' But Right/Come A Little Closer Baby | 1958 | 15.00 | 30.00 | 60.00 |

Caston, Bobby
Atlas
| ❏ 1103 | | Call Me Darling/Why Wasn't I Told | 1958 | 25.00 | 50.00 | 100.00 |

Castor, Jimmy, Bunch
(Also includes Jimmy Castor credited alone)
Atlantic
❏ 3011		Maggie (Part 1)/Maggie (Part 2)	1974		2.50	5.00
❏ 3045		Everything Man (E-Man)/Heaven Kissed	1974		2.50	5.00
❏ 3232		The Bertha Butt Boogie (Part 1)/ The Bertha Butt Boogie (Part 2)	1975		2.50	5.00
❏ 3270		Potential/Daniel	1975		2.50	5.00
❏ 3295		King Kong (Part 1)/King Kong (Part 2)	1975		2.50	5.00
❏ 3302		Merry Christmas/Christmas Song	1975		3.00	6.00
❏ 3316		Supersound/Drifting	1976		2.00	4.00
❏ 3331		Bom Bom/What's Best	1976		2.00	4.00
❏ 3362		Everything Is Beautiful to Me/The Magic Is in the Music	1976		2.00	4.00
❏ 3369	DJ	I Don't Wanna Lose You (mono/stereo)	1976		2.50	5.00
		May be promo only				
❏ 3375		Space Age/Dracula	1976		2.00	4.00
❏ 3396		I Love a Mellow Groove/I Don't Want to Lose You	1977		2.00	4.00
❏ 3424		The Return of Leroy (Part 1)/ The Return of Leroy (Part 2)	1977		2.00	4.00
❏ 3451		Magnolia/TR-7	1978		2.00	4.00
❏ 3455		Maximum Stimulation/It Was You	1978		2.00	4.00

Capitol
❏ 2358		Hey Shorty (Part 1)/Hey Shorty (Part 2)	1968	2.00	4.00	8.00
❏ 2487		Psycho Man/The Real McCoy	1969	2.00	4.00	8.00
❏ 2634		Helpless/Make Me	1969	2.00	4.00	8.00

Catawba
| ❏ 05676 | | Godzilla/(Instrumental) | 1985 | | | 3.00 |

Compass
| ❏ 7019 | | Soul Sister/Rattlesnake | 1968 | 2.00 | 4.00 | 8.00 |

Cotillion
| ❏ 44253 | | Don't Do That!/Don't Do That! (Part 2) | 1979 | | 2.00 | 4.00 |
| ❏ 45004 | | Party People/I Just Wanna Stop | 1979 | | 2.00 | 4.00 |

Decca
| ❏ 31963 | | In a Boogaloo Bag (Part 1)/In a Boogaloo Bag (Part 2) | 1966 | 2.50 | 5.00 | 10.00 |

Drive
| ❏ 6271 | | Bertha Butt Encounters Vadar/(B-side unknown) | 1978 | | 2.00 | 4.00 |
| ❏ 6276 | | You Light Up My Life/Let It Out | 1978 | | 2.00 | 4.00 |

Hull
| ❏ 758 | | Poor Loser/Oh Suzzana | 1963 | 5.00 | 10.00 | 20.00 |

Long Distance
| ❏ 702 | | Can't Help Falling in Love/ Stay with Me (Spend the Night) | 1980 | | 2.50 | 5.00 |

RCA Victor
❏ 48-1024		Say Leroy (The Creature from the Black Lagoon Is Your Father) (Parts 1 & 2)	1972		2.50	5.00
❏ 48-1029		Troglodyte (Cave Man)/I Promise to Remember	1972		3.00	6.00
❏ 74-0583		My Brightest Day/You Better Be Good	1971		2.50	5.00
❏ 74-0763		Luther the Anthropod/Party Life	1972		2.50	5.00
❏ 74-0836		Paradise/The First Time Ever I Saw Your Face	1972		2.50	5.00
❏ 74-0953		Soul Serenade/ Purple Haze-Foxey Lady (Tribute to Jimi Hendrix)	1973		2.50	5.00
❏ APBO-0047		How Beautiful You Are/I'm Not a Child Anymore	1973		2.50	5.00
❏ AMBO-0120		Troglodyte (Cave Man)/Luther the Anthropod	1973		2.00	4.00
		Gold Standard Series				

Salsoul
| ❏ 7018 | | E-Man Boogie '82/Any Way, Any Where, Any Time | 1982 | | 2.00 | 4.00 |
| ❏ 7058 | | E-Man Boogie '83/It's Just Begun | 1983 | | 2.00 | 4.00 |

Smash
❏ 2069		Hey, Leroy, Your Mama's Calling You/ Ham Hocks Espanol	1966	2.00	4.00	8.00
❏ 2085		Just You Girl/Magic Saxophone	1967	2.00	4.00	8.00
❏ 2099		Leroy Is In the Army/Dry	1967	2.00	4.00	8.00
❏ 2120		Jamaica Farewell/Mini-Sonata	1967	2.00	4.00	8.00

Wing
| ❏ 90078 | | I Promise/I Know the Meaning of Love | 1956 | 30.00 | 60.00 | 120.00 |

Casualairs, The
Autumn
| ❏ 21 | | Just For You/This Is a Mean World | 1965 | 6.25 | 12.50 | 25.00 |

Craig
| ❏ 5001 | | Bossa Nova Twist/Cruising | 1962 | 10.00 | 20.00 | 40.00 |

Number	Title (A Side/B Side)	Year	VG	VG+	NM

Mona-Lee
| ❏ 136 | At the Dance/Satisfied | 1959 | 10.00 | 20.00 | 40.00 |

Catalinas, The
(Several different groups)
Back Beat
| ❏ 513 | Speechless/Flying Formation with You | 1958 | 7.50 | 15.00 | 30.00 |

Dee Jay
| ❏ 1010 | Bail Out/Bulletin | 1963 | 10.00 | 20.00 | 40.00 |

Dial
| ❏ 3008 | Cha Cha Joe/Echo One | 1963 | 3.00 | 6.00 | 12.00 |

Glory
| ❏ 285 | Marlene/With Your Girl -- Yeah! | 1958 | 5.00 | 10.00 | 20.00 |

Little
| ❏ 811/2 | Give Me Your Love/Castle of Love | 1957 | 50.00 | 100.00 | 200.00 |

Original Sound
| ❏ 48 | Your Tender Lips/Gonna Tell | 1964 | 3.00 | 6.00 | 12.00 |

Ric
| ❏ 113 | Banzai Wipeout/Beach Walkin' | 1964 | 6.25 | 12.50 | 25.00 |
| ❏ 164 | Boss Barracuda/Surfer Boy | 1965 | 6.25 | 12.50 | 25.00 |

Rita
| ❏ 1006 | Ring of Stars/Wooly Wooly Willie | 1960 | 5.00 | 10.00 | 20.00 |

Scepter
| ❏ 12188 | Tick Tock/You Haven't the Right | 1967 | 3.75 | 7.50 | 15.00 |

Sims
| ❏ 134 | Bail Out/Bulletin | 1963 | 3.75 | 7.50 | 15.00 |

20th Fox
| ❏ 286 | Sweetheart/Unchained Melody | 1962 | 7.50 | 15.00 | 30.00 |
| ❏ 299 | Safari/Pretty Little Nashville Girl | 1962 | 7.50 | 15.00 | 30.00 |

Cates, Ronnie
Terrace
| ❏ 7501 | Ol' Man River/Long Time | 1961 | 12.50 | 25.00 | 50.00 |
| ❏ 7508 | For My Very Own/Long Time | 1962 | 12.50 | 25.00 | 50.00 |

Cathy Jean and the Roomates
(Includes Cathy Jean solo; also see "Roomates, The")
Philips
❏ 40106	My Heart Belongs to Only You/I Only Want You	1963	5.00	10.00	20.00
	By Cathy Jean				
❏ 40143	Double Trouble/Believe Me	1963	5.00	10.00	20.00
	By Cathy Jean				

Valmor
❏ 007	Please Love Me Forever/Canadian Sunset	1961	6.25	12.50	25.00
	Red label				
❏ 007	Please Love Me Forever/Canadian Sunset	1961	3.75	7.50	15.00
	Black label				
❏ 009	Make Me Smile Again/Sugar Cake	1961	6.25	12.50	25.00
❏ 011	I Only Want You/One Love	1961	5.00	10.00	20.00
❏ 016	Please Tell Me/Sugar Cake	1962	5.00	10.00	20.00

Cavaliers, The
(More than one group)
Apt
| ❏ 25004 | Dance, Dance, Dance/Play By the Rules of Love | 1958 | 10.00 | 20.00 | 40.00 |

Coral
| ❏ 62245 | Teen Fever/Funky | 1961 | 3.00 | 6.00 | 12.00 |

Decca
| ❏ 29556 | Somewhere, Sometime, Someday/Honor Bright | 1955 | 3.75 | 7.50 | 15.00 |

Galena
| ❏ 1277 | Blowin' Smoke/Ten More Miles | 1962 | 5.00 | 10.00 | 20.00 |

NRC
| ❏ 028 | Dreamy Bikini/Charm Bracelet | 1959 | 3.75 | 7.50 | 15.00 |

RCA Victor
| ❏ 47-9054 | Dance Little Girl/Hold On to My Baby | 1966 | 7.50 | 15.00 | 30.00 |
| ❏ 47-9321 | I Really Love You/I've Gotta Find Her | 1967 | 5.00 | 10.00 | 20.00 |

Celebration featuring Mike Love
(Also see "Beach Boys, The")
MCA
| ❏ 40891 | Almost Summer/Lookin' Good | 1978 | | 2.50 | 5.00 |
| ❏ 40930 | Summer in the City/Island Girl | 1978 | | 2.00 | 4.00 |

Pacific Arts
| ❏ 105 | Gettin' Hungry/Star Baby | 1979 | 2.50 | 5.00 | 10.00 |

Cellos, The
Apollo
| ❏ 510 | Rang Tang Ding Dong/You Took My Love | 1957 | 12.50 | 25.00 | 50.00 |
| ❏ 510 | Rang Tang Ding Dong (I Am the Japanese Sandman)/You Took My Love | 1957 | 6.25 | 12.50 | 25.00 |

Number		Title (A Side/B Side)	Year	VG	VG+	NM
☐ 515		Under Your Spell/The Juicy Crocodile	1957	12.50	25.00	50.00
☐ 516		The Be-Bop Mouse/Girlie That I Love	1957	12.50	25.00	50.00
☐ 524		I Beg for Your Love/What's the Matter with You	1958	15.00	30.00	60.00

Chad and Jeremy
Capitol Starline
| ☐ 6087 | | A Summer Song/Willow Weep for Me | 1966 | 2.00 | 4.00 | 8.00 |
| | | *Green and white swirl label* | | | | |

Columbia
☐ 43277		Before and After/Fare Thee Well	1965	2.50	5.00	10.00
☐ 43277	DJ	Before and After/Fare Thee Well	1965	10.00	20.00	40.00
		Red vinyl				
☐ 43339		I Don't Wanna Lose You Baby/Pennies	1965	2.00	4.00	8.00
☐ 43339	PS	I Don't Wanna Lose You Baby/Pennies	1965	5.00	10.00	20.00
☐ 43414		I Have Dreamed/Should I?	1966	2.00	4.00	8.00
☐ 43490		Teenage Failure/Early Morning Rain	1965	2.00	4.00	8.00
☐ 43682		Distant Shores/Last Night	1966	2.00	4.00	8.00
☐ 43682	PS	Distant Shores/Last Night	1966	5.00	10.00	20.00
☐ 43807		You Are She/I Won't Cry	1966	2.00	4.00	8.00
☐ 43807	PS	You Are She/I Won't Cry	1966	5.00	10.00	20.00
☐ 44131		Rest in Peace/Family Way	1967	2.00	4.00	8.00
☐ 44379		Painted Dayglow Smile/Editorial	1967	2.00	4.00	8.00
☐ 44525		Sister Marie/Rest in Peace	1968	2.00	4.00	8.00
☐ 44660		Paxton Quigley's Had the Course/You Need Feet	1968	2.00	4.00	8.00
☐ 44660	PS	Paxton Quigley's Had the Course/You Need Feet	1968	4.00	8.00	16.00

Rocshire
☐ 95046		Bite the Bullet/How Many Trains	1983		2.00	4.00
☐ 95050	DJ	Bite the Bullet/Interview	1983	3.00	6.00	12.00
☐ 95061		Dreams/Zanzibar Sunset	1983		2.00	4.00

World Artists
Note: Most World Artists singles referred to the artist as "Chad Stuart and Jeremy Clyde."
☐ 1021		Yesterday's Gone/Lemon Tree	1964	2.50	5.00	10.00
☐ 1027		A Summer Song/No Tears for Johnny	1964	2.50	5.00	10.00
☐ 1034		Willow Weep for Me/If She Was Mine	1964	2.50	5.00	10.00
☐ 1034	PS	Willow Weep for Me/If She Was Mine	1964	5.00	10.00	20.00
☐ 1041		If I Loved You/Donna, Donna	1965	2.50	5.00	10.00
☐ 1041	PS	If I Loved You/Donna, Donna	1965	5.00	10.00	20.00
☐ 1052		What Do You Want from Me/A Very Good Year	1965	2.50	5.00	10.00
☐ 1056		From a Window/My Coloring Book	1965	2.50	5.00	10.00
☐ 1060		September in the Rain/Only for the Young	1965	2.50	5.00	10.00

Chaffin, Ernie
Sun
☐ 262		Feelin' Low/Lonesome for My Baby	1957	7.50	15.00	30.00
☐ 275		Laughin' and Jokin'/I'm Lonesome	1957	7.50	15.00	30.00
☐ 307		Nothing Can Change My Love for You/Born to Lose	1958	6.25	12.50	25.00
☐ 320		Don't Ever Leave Me/Miracle of You	1959	6.25	12.50	25.00

Chain Reaction
(This Chain Reaction includes Steve Tallarico, later known as Steve Tyler [Aerosmith])
Date
| ☐ 1538 | | When I Needed You/The Sun | 1966 | 7.50 | 15.00 | 30.00 |

Chalets, The
Dart
| ☐ 1026 | | Who's Laughing-Who's Crying/Fat Fat Fat! Mom-Mi-O | 1961 | 6.25 | 12.50 | 25.00 |

Laurie
| ☐ 3348 | | She's Not the Marrying Type/
(Theme from) She's Not the Marrying Type | 1966 | 3.00 | 6.00 | 12.00 |

Musicnote
| ☐ 1001 | | Who's Laughing-Who's Crying/
Fat Fat Fat! Mom-Mi-O | 1962 | 5.00 | 10.00 | 20.00 |

Tru-Lite
| ☐ 1001 | | Who's Laughing-Who's Crying/Mom-Mia | 1961 | 12.50 | 25.00 | 50.00 |

Challengers III, The
Tri-Phi
☐ 1012		Stay/Honey, Honey, Honey	1962	7.50	15.00	30.00
		As "The Challengers"				
☐ 1012		Stay/Honey, Honey, Honey	1962	12.50	25.00	50.00
		As "The Challengers III"				
☐ 1020		Every Day/I Hear an Echo	1963	12.50	25.00	50.00

Challengers, The
(Several different groups)
Chess
| ☐ 1957 | | Tossin' and Turnin'/Don't You Know It | 1966 | 2.50 | 5.00 | 10.00 |
Cuca
| ☐ 1500 | | Hear My Message/I Wanna Hold You | 1968 | 2.00 | 4.00 | 8.00 |
GNP Crescendo
☐ 362		The Man from U.N.C.L.E./The Streets of London	1965	2.50	5.00	10.00
☐ 362		The Man from U.N.C.L.E./Summer Nights	1965	2.50	5.00	10.00
☐ 368		Walk with Me/How Could It	1966	2.50	5.00	10.00
☐ 376		Wipe Out/North Beach	1966	2.50	5.00	10.00

Number		Title (A Side/B Side)	Year	VG	VG+	NM
❑ 380		Milord/What If It Should Rain	1966	2.50	5.00	10.00
❑ 396		The Water Country/Everything to Me	1967	2.50	5.00	10.00
❑ 400		Color Me In/Before You	1968	2.50	5.00	10.00
❑ 412		Chitty Chitty Bang Bang/Lonely Little Girl	1968	2.50	5.00	10.00

Melatone

❑ 1002		I Can Tell/The Mambo Beat	1956	75.00	150.00	300.00

Members of this group later recorded as The Olympics

Night Owl

❑ 6794		I Wanna Hold You/	1967	7.50	15.00	30.00
		The Challengers Take a Ride on the Jefferson Airplane				

Triodex

❑ 102		Goofus/Lazy Twist	1960	5.00	10.00	20.00
❑ 107		Deadline/Cry of the Wild Goose	1961	5.00	10.00	20.00

Triumph

❑ 112		Pipeline/Asphalt Spinner	1966	7.50	15.00	30.00

Vault

❑ 900		Bull Dog/Torquay	1963	5.00	10.00	20.00
❑ 902		Moondawg/Tidal Wave	1963	5.00	10.00	20.00
❑ 904		Foot Tapper/On the Move	1963	5.00	10.00	20.00
❑ 910		Hot Rod Hootenanny/Maybellene	1964	7.50	15.00	30.00
❑ 913		Hot Rod Show/K-39	1964	7.50	15.00	30.00
❑ 918		Channel Nine/Can't Seem to Make You Mine	1965	5.00	10.00	20.00

Chambers Brothers, The

Avco

❑ 4632		Let's Go, Let's Go, Let's Go/Do You Believe in Magic	1974		2.00	4.00
❑ 4638		1-2-3/Looking Back	1974		2.00	4.00
❑ 4657		Miss Lady Brown/Stealin' Watermelons	1975		2.00	4.00

Columbia

❑ 43816		Time Has Come Today/Dinah	1966	3.00	6.00	12.00
❑ 43957		All Strung Out Over You/Falling in Love	1967		3.00	6.00
❑ 44080		Please Don't Leave Me/I Can't Stand It	1967		3.00	6.00
❑ 44296		Uptown/Love Me Like the Rain	1967		3.00	6.00
❑ 44414		Time Has Come Today/People Get Ready	1968	2.00	4.00	8.00
❑ 44679		I Can't Turn You Loose/Do Your Thing	1968		3.00	6.00
❑ 44679	PS	I Can't Turn You Loose/Do Your Thing	1968	2.50	5.00	10.00
❑ 44779		Are You Ready/You Got the Power to Turn Me On	1969		3.00	6.00
❑ 44890		Wake Up/Everybody Needs Someone	1969		3.00	6.00
❑ 44986		Have a Little Faith/Baby Takes Care of Business	1969		2.50	5.00
❑ 45055		Merry Christmas, Happy New Year/	1969		3.00	6.00
		Did You Stop to Pray This Morning				
❑ 45088		Love, Peace and Happiness/If You Want Me To	1970		2.50	5.00
❑ 45146		To Love Somebody/Let's Do It	1970		2.50	5.00
❑ 45277		Love, Peace and Happiness/Funky	1970		2.50	5.00
❑ 45394		When the Evening Comes/New Generation	1971		2.50	5.00
❑ 45488		Heaven/(By the Hair on) My Chinny Chin Chin	1971		3.00	6.00
❑ 45518		Merry Christmas, Happy New Year/	1971		3.00	6.00
		Did You Stop to Pray This Morning				
❑ 45837		Boogie Children/You Make the Magic	1973		3.00	6.00

Roxbury

❑ 2034		Bring It On Down Front Pretty Mama/Midnight Blue	1976		2.50	5.00

Vault

❑ 920		Call Me/Seventeen	1965	3.75	7.50	15.00
❑ 923		Pretty Girls Everywhere/Love Me Like the Rain	1966	3.00	6.00	12.00
❑ 955		Just a Closer Walk with Thee/Girls We Love You	1969		3.00	6.00
❑ 967		House of the Rising Sun/Blues Get Off My Shoulder	1970		3.00	6.00

Champ, Billy

ABC-Paramount

❑ 10518		Believe Me/Hush-A-Bye	1964	7.50	15.00	30.00

Champlains, The

(Also see "Five Satins, The")

United Artists

❑ 346		Ding Dong/Have You Changed Your Mind	1961	10.00	20.00	40.00

Champs, The

(Also see "Burgess, Dave"; "Campbell, Glen"; "Rio, Chuck"; "Seals and Crofts")

Challenge

❑ 1016		Tequila/Train to Nowhere	1958	5.00	10.00	20.00
❑ 9113		The Shoddy Shoddy/Sombrero	1961	5.00	10.00	20.00
❑ 9116		Cantina/Panic Button	1961	5.00	10.00	20.00
❑ 9131		Tequila Twist/Limbo Rock	1961	5.00	10.00	20.00
❑ 9140		Experiment in Terror/La Cucaracha	1962	3.75	7.50	15.00
❑ 9143		What a Country/I've Just Seen Her	1962	3.75	7.50	15.00
❑ 9162		Limbo Dance/Latin Limbo	1962	3.75	7.50	15.00
❑ 9174		Varsity Rock/That Did It	1962	3.75	7.50	15.00
❑ 9180		Mr. Cool//3/4 Mash	1963	3.75	7.50	15.00
❑ 9189		Nik Nak/Shades	1963	3.75	7.50	15.00
❑ 9199		Cactus Juice/Roots	1963	3.75	7.50	15.00
❑ 59007		El Rancho Rock/Midnighter	1958	5.00	10.00	20.00
❑ 59018		Chariot Rock/Subway	1958	5.00	10.00	20.00
❑ 59026		Turnpike/Rockin' Mary	1958	5.00	10.00	20.00
❑ 59035		Gone Train/Beatnik	1958	5.00	10.00	20.00
❑ 59043		Moonlight Bay/Caramba	1959	5.00	10.00	20.00

Number		Title (A Side/B Side)	Year	VG	VG+	NM
☐ 59049		Night Train/The Rattler	1959	5.00	10.00	20.00
☐ 59053		Sky High/Double Eagle Rock	1959	5.00	10.00	20.00
☐ 59063		Too Much Tequila/Twenty Thousand Leagues	1960	5.00	10.00	20.00
☐ 59076		Red Eye/The Little Matador	1960	5.00	10.00	20.00
☐ 59086		Alley Cat/Coconut Grove	1960	5.00	10.00	20.00
☐ 59097		The Face/Tough Train	1960	5.00	10.00	20.00
☐ 59103		Hokey Pokey/Jumping Bean	1961	5.00	10.00	20.00
☐ 59219		San Juan/Jalisco	1963	3.75	7.50	15.00
☐ 59236		Switzerland/Only the Young	1964	3.75	7.50	15.00
☐ 59263		Fraternity Waltz/Kahlua	1964	3.75	7.50	15.00
☐ 59276		French 75/Bright Lights, Big City	1965	3.75	7.50	15.00
☐ 59314		The Man from Durango/Red Pepper	1965	3.75	7.50	15.00
☐ 59322		Anna/Buckaroo	1965	3.75	7.50	15.00

Republic

☐ 246		Tequila '76 (Long)/Tequila '76 (Short)	1976	2.00	4.00	8.00
☐ 246	PS	Tequila '76 (Long)/Tequila '76 (Short)	1976	2.00	4.00	8.00

We're Back

☐ 1		Tequila '77/From Me to You	1977	2.00	4.00	8.00

Chandler, Gene
(Also see "Dukays, The")

Brunswick

	Title (A Side/B Side)	Year	VG	VG+	NM
☐ 55312	Girl Don't Care/My Love	1967	2.00	4.00	8.00
☐ 55339	There Goes the Lover/Tell Me What I Can Do	1967	2.00	4.00	8.00
☐ 55383	There Was a Time/Those Were the Good Old Days	1968	2.00	4.00	8.00
☐ 55394	Teacher, Teacher/Pit of Loneliness	1968	2.00	4.00	8.00
☐ 55413	Eleanor Rigby/Familiar Footsteps	1969	2.00	4.00	8.00
☐ 55425	This Bitter Earth/Suicide	1969	2.00	4.00	8.00

Checker

☐ 1155	I Fooled You This Time/Such a Pretty Thing	1966	2.00	4.00	8.00
☐ 1165	To Be a Lover/After the Laughter	1967	2.00	4.00	8.00
☐ 1190	I Won't Need You/No Peace, No Satisfaction	1967	2.00	4.00	8.00
☐ 1199	River of Tears/It's Time to Settle Down	1968	2.00	4.00	8.00
☐ 1220	Go Back Home/In My Baby's House	1969	2.00	4.00	8.00

Chi-Sound

☐ 1001	I'll Make the Living If You Make the Loving Worthwhile/ (B-side unknown)	1982		2.50	5.00
☐ 1168	Give Me the Cue/ Tomorrow We May Not Feel the Same	1978		2.00	4.00
☐ 2386	Get Down/I'm the Traveling Kind	1978		2.00	4.00
☐ 2404	Please Sunrise/Greatest Love Ever Known	1979		2.00	4.00
☐ 2411	When You're #1/I'll Remember You	1979		2.50	5.00
☐ 2451	Does She Have a Friend?/Let Me Make Love to You	1980		2.00	4.00
☐ 2468	Lay Me Gently/You've Been So Good to Me	1980		2.00	4.00
☐ 2480	Rainbow '80/I'll Be There	1980		2.00	4.00
☐ 2494	I'm Attracted to You/I've Got to Meet You	1981		2.00	4.00
☐ 2507	Love Is the Answer/Godsend	1981		2.00	4.00

Constellation

☐ 104	From Day to Day/It's So Good for Me	1963	2.50	5.00	10.00
☐ 110	Pretty Little Girl/A Little Like Lovin'	1963	2.50	5.00	10.00
☐ 112	Think Nothing About It/Wish You Were Here	1964	2.50	5.00	10.00
☐ 114	Soul Hootenanny (Part 1)/Soul Hootenanny (Part 2)	1964	2.50	5.00	10.00
☐ 124	A Song Called Soul/You Left Me	1964	2.50	5.00	10.00
☐ 130	Just Be True/A Song Called Soul	1964	2.50	5.00	10.00
☐ 136	Bless Our Love/London Town	1964	2.50	5.00	10.00
☐ 141	What Now/If You Can't Be True	1964	2.50	5.00	10.00
☐ 146	You Can't Hurt Me No More/Everybody Let's Dance	1965	2.00	4.00	8.00
☐ 149	Nothing Can Stop Me/The Big Lie	1965	2.00	4.00	8.00
☐ 158	Rainbow '65 (Part 1)/Rainbow '65 (Part 2)	1965	2.00	4.00	8.00
☐ 160	Good Times/No One Can Love You	1965	2.00	4.00	8.00
☐ 164	Here Come the Tears/Soul Hootenanny (Part 2)	1965	2.00	4.00	8.00
☐ 166	Baby That's Love/Bet You Never Thought	1966	2.00	4.00	8.00
☐ 167	(I'm Just a) Fool for You/Buddy Ain't It a Shame	1966	2.00	4.00	8.00
☐ 169	I Can Take Care of Myself/If I Can't Save It	1966	2.00	4.00	8.00
☐ 172	Mr. Big Shot/I Hate to Be the One to Say	1966	2.00	4.00	8.00

Curtom

☐ 1979	Don't Have to Be Lyin' Babe (Part 1)/ Don't Have to Be Lyin' Babe (Part 2)	1973		2.50	5.00
☐ 1986	Baby I Still Love You/I Understand	1973		2.50	5.00
☐ 1992	Without You Here/Just Be There	1973		2.50	5.00

Salsoul

☐ 7051	You're the One/I Keep Comin' Back for More With Jaime Lynn	1983		2.00	4.00

20th Century

☐ 2411	When You're #1/I'll Remember You	1979		2.00	4.00
☐ 2428	Do What Comes So Natural/That Funky Disco Rhythm	1979		2.00	4.00

Vee Jay

☐ 416	Duke of Earl/Kissin' in the Kitchen	1961	5.00	10.00	20.00
☐ 440	Walk On with the Duke/London Town As "The Duke of Earl"	1962	3.75	7.50	15.00
☐ 450	Daddy's Home/The Big Lie As "The Duke of Earl"	1962	3.75	7.50	15.00
☐ 455	I'll Follow You/You Left Me As "The Duke of Earl"	1962	3.75	7.50	15.00
☐ 461	Tear for Tear/Miracle After Miracle	1962	3.75	7.50	15.00

Number		Title (A Side/B Side)	Year	VG	VG+	NM
☐ 468		You Threw a Lucky Punch/Rainbow	1962	3.75	7.50	15.00
☐ 511		Check Yourself/Forgive Me	1963	3.75	7.50	15.00
☐ 536		Baby, That's Love/Man's Temptation	1963	3.75	7.50	15.00

Chandler, Gene, and Barbara Acklin
Brunswick

☐ 55366		Love Won't Start/Show Me the Way to Go	1968	2.00	4.00	8.00
☐ 55387		From the Teacher to the Preacher/	1968	2.00	4.00	8.00
		Anywhere But Nowhere				
☐ 55405		Little Green Apples/Will I Find You	1969	2.00	4.00	8.00

Channel, Bruce
Elektra

☐ 46587		One More Last Chance/That's the Truth, Ruth	1980		2.00	4.00

King

☐ 5294		Will I Ever Love Again/Blow Down Baby	1959	7.50	15.00	30.00
☐ 5331		Now or Never/Boy, This Stuff Kills Me	1960	7.50	15.00	30.00
☐ 5620		Now or Never/Will I Ever Love Again	1962	5.00	10.00	20.00

Le Cam

☐ 122		Going Back to Louisiana/Forget Me Not	1964	2.50	5.00	10.00
☐ 125		My Baby/Blue Monday	1964	2.50	5.00	10.00
☐ 953		Hey! Baby/Dream Girl	1961	10.00	20.00	40.00
☐ 1117		A Presley Medley/A Man Without a Woman	1977		2.50	5.00
☐ 7277		The King Is Free (Love Me)/(B-side unknown)	1977		2.50	5.00

Mala

☐ 579		Mr. Bus Driver/It's Me	1967	2.50	5.00	10.00
☐ 592		Keep On/Barbara Allen	1968	2.50	5.00	10.00
☐ 12,011		California/Water the Family Tree	1968	2.50	5.00	10.00
☐ 12,041		The Web/Mrs. P	1969	2.50	5.00	10.00
☐ 12,027		Try Me/Nobody	1968	2.50	5.00	10.00

Manco

☐ 1035		Run Romance, Run/Don't Leave Me	1962	5.00	10.00	20.00

Mel-O-Dy

☐ 112		That's What's Happenin'/Satisfied Mind	1964	3.75	7.50	15.00
☐ 114		You Make Me Happy/You Never Looked Better	1964	3.75	7.50	15.00

Smash

☐ 1731		Hey! Baby/Dream Girl	1962	5.00	10.00	20.00
☐ 1752		Number One Man/If Only I Had Known	1962	3.75	7.50	15.00
☐ 1769		Come On Baby/Mine Exclusively	1962	3.75	7.50	15.00
☐ 1780		Stand Tough/Somewhere in This Town	1962	3.75	7.50	15.00
☐ 1780	PS	Stand Tough/Somewhere in This Town	1962	7.50	15.00	30.00
☐ 1792		Oh Baby/Let's Hurt Together	1962	3.75	7.50	15.00
☐ 1826		No Other Baby/Night People	1963	3.75	7.50	15.00
☐ 1826	PS	No Other Baby/Night People	1963	7.50	15.00	30.00
☐ 1838		The Dipsy Doodle/Send Her Home	1963	3.75	7.50	15.00
☐ 1838	PS	The Dipsy Doodle/Send Her Home	1963	7.50	15.00	30.00

Teenager

☐ 601		Run Romance, Run/Don't Leave Me	1960	7.50	15.00	30.00

Chantay's
Dot

☐ 16440		Pipeline/Move It	1963	6.25	12.50	25.00
☐ 16492		Monsoon/Scotch Highs	1963	5.00	10.00	20.00

Downey

☐ 104		Pipeline/Move It	1963	10.00	20.00	40.00
☐ 108		Monsoon/Scotch Highs	1963	7.50	15.00	30.00
☐ 116		Space Probe/Continental Missile	1964	5.00	10.00	20.00
☐ 120		Only If You Care/Love Can Be Cruel	1964	5.00	10.00	20.00
☐ 126		Beyond/I'll Be Back Someday	1964	5.00	10.00	20.00
☐ 130		Three Coins in the Fountain/Greens	1965	5.00	10.00	20.00

Chanteclairs, The
Dot

☐ 1227		Baby Please/Someday Love Will Come My Way	1954	18.75	37.50	75.00
☐ 15404		Believe Me, Beloved/I've Never Been There	1955	15.00	30.00	60.00

Chantels, The
Carlton

☐ 555		Look in My Eyes/Glad to Be Back	1961	5.00	10.00	20.00
☐ 564		Still/Well, I Told You	1961	5.00	10.00	20.00
☐ 569		Summertime/Here It Comes Again	1962	5.00	10.00	20.00

End

☐ 1002		He's Gone/The Plea	1957	15.00	30.00	60.00
	Black label					
☐ 1005		Maybe/Come My Little Baby	1957	15.00	30.00	60.00
	Black label					
☐ 1005		Maybe/Come My Little Baby	1958	10.00	20.00	40.00
	Gray (white) label					
☐ 1005		Maybe/Come My Little Baby	1959	5.00	10.00	20.00
	Multicolor label					
☐ 1015		Every Night/Whoever You Are	1958	7.50	15.00	30.00
	Gray (white) label					
☐ 1015		Every Night/Whoever You Are	1959	5.00	10.00	20.00
	Multicolor label					

Number	Title (A Side/B Side)	Year	VG	VG+	NM
❑ 1020	I Love You So/How Could You Call It Off	1958	6.25	12.50	25.00
❑ 1026	Prayer/Sure of Love	1958	6.25	12.50	25.00
❑ 1030	If You Try/Congratulations	1958	6.25	12.50	25.00
❑ 1037	Never Let Go/I Can't Take It	1959	6.25	12.50	25.00
❑ 1048	I'm Confessin'/Goodbye to Love	1959	6.25	12.50	25.00
❑ 1069	Whoever You Are/How Could You Call It Off	1960	6.25	12.50	25.00
❑ 1103	Believe Me (My Angel)/I	1961	15.00	30.00	60.00
	Originally released on Princeton 102 as "The Veneers"				
❑ 1105	There's Our Song Again/I'm the Girl	1961	6.25	12.50	25.00
Ludix					
❑ 101	Eternally/Swamp Water	1963	5.00	10.00	20.00
❑ 106	That's Why I'm Happy/Some Tears Fall Dry	1963	5.00	10.00	20.00
RCA Victor					
❑ 74-0347	I'm Gonna Win Him Back/	1970	2.50	5.00	10.00
	Love Makes All the Difference in the World				
Roulette					
❑ 7064	Maybe/He's Gone	1969	2.50	5.00	10.00
TCF Hall					
❑ 123	Take Me As I Am/There's No Forgetting Me	1965	3.75	7.50	15.00
Verve					
❑ 10387	You're Welcome to My Heart/Soul of a Soldier	1966	3.75	7.50	15.00
❑ 10435	Indian Giver/It's Just Me	1966	3.75	7.50	15.00

Chantones, The
(Backing vocal group for Jack Scott)

Number	Title (A Side/B Side)	Year	VG	VG+	NM
Capitol					
❑ 4661	Stormy Weather/Sweet Georgia Brown	1961	6.25	12.50	25.00
Carlton					
❑ 485	Five Little Numbers/It's Just a Summer Love	1958	7.50	15.00	30.00
Top Rank					
❑ 2066	Don't Open That Door/Tangerock	1960	6.25	12.50	25.00

Chants, The
(Several different groups)

Number	Title (A Side/B Side)	Year	VG	VG+	NM
Cameo					
❑ 277	I Don't Care/Come Go with Me	1963	5.00	10.00	20.00
❑ 297	I Could Write a Book/A Thousand Stars	1964	5.00	10.00	20.00
Capitol					
❑ F3949	Lost and Found/Close Friends	1958	5.00	10.00	20.00
Checker					
❑ 1209	Surfside/Chicken 'N' Gravy	1968	2.00	4.00	8.00
Eko					
❑ 3567/77	Respectable/Kiss Me Goodbye	1961	7.50	15.00	30.00
Interphon					
❑ 7703	She's Mine/Then I'll Be Home	1964	3.75	7.50	15.00
MGM					
❑ 13008	Respectable/Kiss Me Goodbye	1961	5.00	10.00	20.00
Nite Owl					
❑ 40	Heaven and Paradise/When I'm With You	1960	37.50	75.00	150.00
	Maroon label original				
❑ 40	Heaven and Paradise/When I'm With You	1960	10.00	20.00	40.00
	Black label, black vinyl				
❑ 40	Heaven and Paradise/When I'm With You	196?	5.00	10.00	20.00
	Red vinyl				
❑ 40	Heaven and Paradise/When I'm With You	196?	5.00	10.00	20.00
	Blue vinyl				
❑ 40	Heaven and Paradise/When I'm With You	196?	5.00	10.00	20.00
	Yellow vinyl				
U.W.R.					
❑ 4243	Rockin' Santa/Respectable	1962	6.25	12.50	25.00

Chapel, Jean

Number	Title (A Side/B Side)	Year	VG	VG+	NM
Challenge					
❑ 59350	Tell It Like It Is/I'm Your Woman	1966	2.00	4.00	8.00
❑ 59362	You Can Take Me/Stamp Out Loneliness	1967	2.00	4.00	8.00
❑ 59370	In the Reach of Your Arms/This Waltz Is Mine	1967	2.00	4.00	8.00
❑ 59376	Hungry Eyes/Green Paper	1967	2.00	4.00	8.00
❑ 59381	Dino's TV Door/If I Never Get You	1967	2.00	4.00	8.00
❑ 59386	See and Ye Shall Find/I Really Go for You	1968	2.00	4.00	8.00
Kapp					
❑ 2034	Bluebird Ridge/I Started Loving You Again	1969		3.00	6.00
❑ 2082	I'm Your Woman/The Roll Call	1970		3.00	6.00
RCA Victor					
❑ 47-6681	I Won't Be Rockin' Tonight/Welcome to the Club	1956	10.00	20.00	40.00
❑ 47-6892	Oo-Ba La Baby/I Had a Dream	1957	6.25	12.50	25.00
Smash					
❑ 1829	Don't Let Go/Your Tender Love	1963	3.00	6.00	12.00
Sun					
❑ 244	I Won't Be Rockin' Tonight/Welcome to the Club	1956	12.50	25.00	50.00

Number		Title (A Side/B Side)	Year	VG	VG+	NM

Chaperones, The
Josie
❑ 880		Dance with Me/Cruise to the Moon	1960	37.50	75.00	150.00
		With typographical error listing group as "The Cahperones"				
❑ 880		Dance with Me/Cruise to the Moon	1960	6.25	12.50	25.00
		With correct group name on label				
❑ 885		Shining Star/My Shadow and Me	1960	6.25	12.50	25.00
❑ 891		Man from the Moon/Blueberry Sweet	1961	12.50	25.00	50.00

Chapins, The
(Harry, Tom and Steve Chapin)
Epic
| ❑ 10761 | | Workin' On My Life/ | 1971 | 3.00 | 6.00 | 12.00 |
| | | The Only Thing (You Ever Really Have to Do Is Die) | | | | |
Rock-Land
| ❑ 664 | | Old Time Movies/Not Your Kind | 1966 | 3.75 | 7.50 | 15.00 |
| ❑ 664 | PS | Old Time Movies/Not Your Kind | 1966 | 6.25 | 12.50 | 25.00 |

Chapman, Grady
Imperial
| ❑ 5591 | | Garden of Memories/Tell Me That You Care | 1959 | 3.00 | 6.00 | 12.00 |
| ❑ 5611 | | Come Away/Let's Talk About Us | 1959 | 3.00 | 6.00 | 12.00 |
Knight
| ❑ 2003 | | Say You Will Be Mine/Starlight, Starbright | 1958 | 7.50 | 15.00 | 30.00 |
Mercury
❑ 71632		Sweet Thing/I Know What I Want	1960	3.00	6.00	12.00
❑ 71698		Ambush/My Life Would Be Worth Living	1960	12.50	25.00	50.00
❑ 71771		I'll Never Question Your Love/This, That, 'N the Other	1961	3.00	6.00	12.00
Money
❑ 204		I Need You So/Don't Blooper	1955	75.00	150.00	300.00
Zephyr
❑ 016		My Love Will Never Change/Smiling	1957	7.50	15.00	30.00

Chargers, The
(Jesse Belvin was in this group)
RCA Victor
| ❑ 47-7301 | | Old MacDonald/Dandelion | 1958 | 7.50 | 15.00 | 30.00 |

Charioteers, The
Columbia
❑ 1-168		A Kiss and a Rose/A Cottage in Old Donegal	1949	150.00	300.00	600.00
		Microgroove single, small hole				
❑ 1-363		This Side of Heaven/Hawaiian Sunset	1949	150.00	300.00	600.00
		Microgroove single, small hole				
Josie
❑ 787		I've Got My Heart on My Sleeve/Don't Play No Mambo	1955	20.00	40.00	80.00
MGM
❑ 12569		The Candles/I Didn't Mean to Be Mean to You	1957	20.00	40.00	80.00

Charlatans, The
Kapp
| ❑ 779 | | The Shadow Knows/32-20 | 1967 | 12.50 | 25.00 | 50.00 |
| ❑ 779 | PS | The Shadow Knows/32-20 | 1967 | 20.00 | 40.00 | 80.00 |
Philips
❑ 40610		High Coin/When I Go Sailin' By	1969	10.00	20.00	40.00
❑ 40610	PS	High Coin/When I Go Sailin' By	1969	20.00	40.00	80.00
		Sleeve is promo only				
❑ 44824	DJ	Date: May 19, 1969	1969	15.00	30.00	60.00
		One-sided, promo only				

Charles and Carl
Red Robin
| ❑ 137 | | Lucky Star/One More Chance | 1955 | 25.00 | 50.00 | 100.00 |

Charles, Bobby
Bearsville
| ❑ 0010 | | Small Town Talk/Save Me Jesus | 1973 | | 2.00 | 4.00 |
Chess
❑ 1609		Later Alligator/On Bended Knee	1955	12.50	25.00	50.00
❑ 1617		Why Did You Leave/Don't You Know I Love You	1956	12.50	25.00	50.00
❑ 1628		Only Time Will Tell/Take It Easy, Greasy	1956	12.50	25.00	50.00
❑ 1638		Laura Lee/No Use Knocking	1956	12.50	25.00	50.00
❑ 1647		Put Your Arms Around Me/Why Can't You, Honey	1957	10.00	20.00	40.00
❑ 1658		No More/You Can Suit Yourself	1957	10.00	20.00	40.00
❑ 1670		One Eyed Jack/Yea Yea Baby	1957	10.00	20.00	40.00
Imperial
❑ 5542		Since She's Gone/At the Jamboree	1958	5.00	10.00	20.00
❑ 5557		Oh Yeah/Since I Lost You	1958	5.00	10.00	20.00
❑ 5579		The Town Is Talking/What Can I Do	1959	5.00	10.00	20.00
❑ 5642		Bye Bye Baby/Those Eyes	1960	5.00	10.00	20.00
❑ 5681		What a Party/I Just Want You	1960	5.00	10.00	20.00
❑ 5691		Four Winds/Nothing Sweet As You	1960	5.00	10.00	20.00

Number		Title (A Side/B Side)	Year	VG	VG+	NM
Jewel						
❑ 728		Everybody's Laughing/Everybody Knows	1964	2.50	5.00	10.00
❑ 729		Goodnight Irene/I Hope	1964	2.50	5.00	10.00
❑ 735		Ain't Misbehavin'/Preacher's Daughter	1964	2.50	5.00	10.00
❑ 740		Oh Lonesome Me/One More Glass of Wine	1964	2.50	5.00	10.00
Paula						
❑ 226		The Walk/Worrying Over You	1965	2.50	5.00	10.00
Charles, Ray						
ABC						
❑ 10808		Let's Go Get Stoned/At the Train	1966	2.00	4.00	8.00
❑ 10840		I Chose to Sing the Blues/Hopelessly	1966	2.00	4.00	8.00
❑ 10865		Please Say You're Fooling/I Don't Need No Doctor	1966	2.00	4.00	8.00
❑ 10901		I Want to Talk About You/Something Inside Me	1967	2.00	4.00	8.00
❑ 10938		Here We Go Again/	1967	2.00	4.00	8.00
		Somebody Ought to Write a Book About It				
❑ 10970		In the Heat of the Night/Somebody's Got to Change	1967	2.00	4.00	8.00
❑ 11009		Yesterday/Never Had Enough of Nothing Yet	1967	2.00	4.00	8.00
❑ 11045		That's a Lie/Go On Home	1968	2.00	4.00	8.00
❑ 11045	PS	That's a Lie/Go On Home	1968	3.75	7.50	15.00
❑ 11090		Eleanor Rigby/Understanding	1968	2.00	4.00	8.00
❑ 11133		Sweet Young Thing Like You/	1968	2.00	4.00	8.00
		Listen, They're Playing Our Song				
❑ 11170		If It Wasn't for Bad Luck/When I Stop Dreaming	1969	2.00	4.00	8.00
	With Jimmy Lewis					
❑ 11193		I'll Be Your Servant/I Don't Know What Time It Was	1969	2.00	4.00	8.00
❑ 11213		Let Me Love You/I'm Satisfied	1969	2.00	4.00	8.00
❑ 11239		We Can Make It/I Can't Stop Loving You Baby	1969	2.00	4.00	8.00
❑ 11251		Someone to Watch Over Me/Claudie Mae	1969	2.00	4.00	8.00
❑ 11259		Laughin' and Clownin'/That Thing Called Love	1970	2.00	4.00	8.00
❑ 11271		If You Were Mine/Till I Can't Take It Anymore	1970	2.00	4.00	8.00
❑ 11291		Don't Change on Me/Sweet Memories	1971	2.00	4.00	8.00
❑ 11308		Feel So Bad/Your Love Is So Doggone Good	1971		3.00	6.00
❑ 11317		What Am I Living For/Tired of My Tears	1971		3.00	6.00
❑ 11329		Look What They've Done to My Song, Ma/	1972		3.00	6.00
		America the Beautiful				
❑ 11337		Hey Mister/	1972		3.00	6.00
		There'll Be No Peace Without All Men as One				
❑ 11344		Every Saturday Night/Take Me Home, Country Roads	1973		3.00	6.00
❑ 11351		I Can Make It Through the Days	1973		3.00	6.00
		(But Oh Those Lonely Nights)/Ring of Fire				
ABC-Paramount						
❑ 10081		My Baby/Who You Gonna Love	1960	3.75	7.50	15.00
❑ 10118		Sticks and Stones/Worried Life Blues	1960	3.00	6.00	12.00
❑ 10135		Georgia on My Mind/Carry Me Back to Old Virginny	1960	3.00	6.00	12.00
❑ 10141		Them That Got/I Wonder	1960	2.50	5.00	10.00
❑ 10164		Ruby/Hard Hearted Woman	1960	2.50	5.00	10.00
❑ 10244		Hit the Road Jack/The Danger Zone	1961	3.00	6.00	12.00
❑ 10266		Unchain My Heart/But on the Other Hand, Baby	1961	2.50	5.00	10.00
❑ 10298		Baby It's Cold Outside/We'll Be Together Again	1962	2.50	5.00	10.00
	With Betty Carter					
❑ 10314		Hide 'Nor Hair/At the Club	1962	2.50	5.00	10.00
❑ 10330		I Can't Stop Loving You/Born to Lose	1962	3.00	6.00	12.00
❑ 10345		You Don't Know Me/Careless Love	1962	2.50	5.00	10.00
❑ 10375		You Are My Sunshine/Your Cheating Heart	1962	2.50	5.00	10.00
❑ 10405		Don't Set Me Free/The Brightest Smile in Town	1963	2.50	5.00	10.00
❑ 10435		Take These Chains from My Heart/No Letter Today	1963	2.50	5.00	10.00
❑ 10453		No One/Without Love (There Is Nothing)	1963	2.50	5.00	10.00
❑ 10481		Busted/Making Believe	1963	2.50	5.00	10.00
❑ 10509		That Lucky Old Sun/Old Man Time	1963	2.50	5.00	10.00
❑ 10530		Baby Don't You Cry/My Heart Cries for You	1964	2.50	5.00	10.00
❑ 10557		My Baby Don't Dig Me/Something's Wrong	1964	2.50	5.00	10.00
❑ 10571		No One to Cry To/A Tear Fell	1964	2.50	5.00	10.00
❑ 10588		Smack Dab in the Middle/I Wake Up Crying	1964	2.50	5.00	10.00
❑ 10609		Makin' Whoopee/(Instrumental)	1964	2.50	5.00	10.00
❑ 10615		Cry/Teardrops from My Eyes	1965	2.50	5.00	10.00
❑ 10649		I Gotta Woman (Part 1)/I Gotta Woman (Part 2)	1965	2.50	5.00	10.00
❑ 10663		Without a Song (Part 1)/Without a Song (Part 2)	1965	2.50	5.00	10.00
❑ 10700		I'm a Fool to Care/Love's Gonna Live Here	1965	2.50	5.00	10.00
❑ 10720		The Cincinnati Kid/That's All I Am to You	1965	2.50	5.00	10.00
❑ 10739		Crying Time/When My Dreamboat Comes Home	1965	2.50	5.00	10.00
❑ 10785		Together Again/You're Just About to Lose Your Clown	1966	2.50	5.00	10.00
Atlantic						
❑ 976		Roll with My Baby/The Midnight Hour	1952	37.50	75.00	150.00
❑ 984		Sun's Gonna Shine Again/Jumpin' in the Morning	1953	37.50	75.00	150.00
❑ 999		Mess Around/Funny (But I Still Love You)	1953	25.00	50.00	100.00
❑ 1008		Feelin' Sad/Heartbreaker	1953	12.50	25.00	50.00
❑ 1021		It Should've Been Me/Sinner's Prayer	1954	7.50	15.00	30.00
❑ 1037		Don't You Know/Losing Hand	1954	7.50	15.00	30.00
❑ 1050		I've Got a Woman/Come Back	1954	7.50	15.00	30.00
❑ 1063		This Little Girl of Mine/A Fool for You	1955	7.50	15.00	30.00
❑ 1076		Blackjack/Greenbacks	1955	7.50	15.00	30.00
❑ 1085		Drown in My Own Tears/Mary Ann	1956	6.25	12.50	25.00
❑ 1096		Hallelujah, I Love Her So/What Would I Do Without You	1956	6.25	12.50	25.00
❑ 1108		Lonely Avenue/Leave My Woman Alone	1956	6.25	12.50	25.00
❑ 1124		I Want to Know/Ain't That Love	1957	5.00	10.00	20.00
❑ 1143		It's All Right/Get On the Right Track Baby	1957	5.00	10.00	20.00

Number		Title (A Side/B Side)	Year	VG	VG+	NM
❏ 1154		Swanee River Rock (Talkin' 'Bout That River)/ I Want a Little Girl	1957	5.00	10.00	20.00
❏ 1172		Talkin' 'Bout You/What Kind of a Man Are You	1958	3.75	7.50	15.00
❏ 1180		Yes Indeed/I Had a Dream	1958	3.75	7.50	15.00
		With the Cookies				
❏ 1196		My Bonnie/You Be My Baby	1958	3.75	7.50	15.00
❏ 2006		Rockhouse (Part 1)/Rockhouse (Part 2)	1958	3.75	7.50	15.00
❏ 2010		(Night Time Is) The Right Time/ Tell All the World About You	1959	3.00	6.00	12.00
❏ 2022		Tell Me How Do You Feel/That's Enough	1959	3.00	6.00	12.00
❏ 2031		What'd I Say (Part I)/What'd I Say (Part II)	1959	3.75	7.50	15.00
❏ 2043		I'm Movin' On/I Believe to My Soul	1959	3.00	6.00	12.00
❏ 2047		Let the Good Times Roll/ Don't Let the Sun Catch You Cryin'	1960	3.00	6.00	12.00
❏ 2055		Heartbreaker/Just for a Thrill	1960	3.00	6.00	12.00
❏ 2068		Tell the Truth/Sweet Sixteen Bars	1960	3.00	6.00	12.00
❏ 2084		Come Rain or Come Shine/Tell Me You'll Wait for Me	1960	3.00	6.00	12.00
❏ 2094		Early in the Morning/A Bit of Soul	1961	3.00	6.00	12.00
❏ 2106		Am I Blue/It Should've Been Me	1961	3.00	6.00	12.00
❏ 2118		I Wonder Who/ Hard Times (No One Knows Better Than I)	1961	3.00	6.00	12.00
❏ 2174		Carryin' That Load/Feelin' Sad	1963	2.50	5.00	10.00
❏ 2239		Talkin' 'Bout You/In a Little Spanish Town	1964	2.50	5.00	10.00
❏ 2470		Come Rain or Come Shine/Tell Me You'll Wait for Me	1968	2.50	5.00	10.00
❏ 3443		I Can See Clearly Now/Anonymous Love	1977		2.50	5.00
❏ 3473		A Peace That We Never Could Enjoy/ Game Number Nine	1978		2.50	5.00
❏ 3527		Riding Thumb/You Forgot Your Memories	1978		2.50	5.00
❏ 3549	DJ	Christmas Time (same on both sides)	1978		3.00	6.00
		May be promo only				
❏ 3611		Some Enchanted Evening/20th Century Fox	1979		2.50	5.00
❏ 3634		Just Because/Love Me or Set Me Free	1979		2.50	5.00
❏ 3762		Compared To What/ Now That We've Found Each Other	1980		2.50	5.00
❏ 5005		Doodlin' (Part 1)/Doodlin' (Part 2)	1960	3.75	7.50	15.00
Baronet						
❏ 7111		See See Rider/I Used to be So Happy	1960	3.00	6.00	12.00
Columbia						
❏ 03429		String Bean/Born to Love Me	1982		2.00	4.00
❏ 03810		You Feel Good All Over/ 3/4 Time	1983			3.00
❏ 04083		Ain't Your Memory Got No Pride at All/ I Don't Want No Strangers Sleeping in My Bed	1983			3.00
❏ 04297		We Didn't See a Thing/I Wish You Were Here Tonight	1983			3.00
		A-side with George Jones and Chet Atkins				
❏ 04420		Do I Ever Cross Your Mind/They Call It Love	1984			3.00
❏ 04500		Woman (Sensuous Woman)/I Was On Georgia Time	1984			3.00
❏ 04531		Rock and Roll Shoes/Then I'll Be Over You	1984			3.00
		Ray Charles and B.J. Thomas				
❏ 04715		Seven Spanish Angels/Who Cares	1984			3.00
		A-side: With Willie Nelson; B-side: With Janie Frickie				
❏ 04860		It Ain't Gonna Worry My Mind/Crazy Old Soldier	1985			3.00
		A-side: With Mickey Gilley; B-side: With Johnny Cash				
❏ 05575		Two Old Cats Like Us/Little Hotel Room	1985			3.00
		A-side with Hank Williams, Jr.				
❏ 06172		Pages of My Mind/Slip Away	1986			3.00
❏ 06370		Dixie Moon/A Little Bit of Heaven	1986			3.00
❏ 06994		Baby Grand/Big Man on Mulberry Street	1987			3.00
		A-side: Billy Joel with Ray Charles; B-side: Joel solo				
❏ 06994	PS	Baby Grand/Big Man on Mulberry Street	1987			3.00
		A-side: Billy Joel with Ray Charles; B-side: Joel solo				
❏ 08393		Seven Spanish Angels/It Ain't Gonna Worry My Mind	1988			3.00
		Reissue; A-side with Willie Nelson, B-side with Mickey Gilley				
CrossOver						
❏ 973		Come Live with Me/Everybody Sing	1973		2.50	5.00
❏ 974		Louise/Somebody	1974		2.50	5.00
❏ 981		Living for the City/Then We'll Be Home	1975		2.50	5.00
❏ 985		America the Beautiful/Sunshine	1976		3.00	6.00
		A-side is a different recording than that on the B-side of ABC 11329				
Impulse!						
❏ 200		One Mint Julep/Let's Go	1961	2.50	5.00	10.00
❏ 202		I've Got News for You/ I'm Gonna Move to the Outskirts of Town	1961	2.50	5.00	10.00
RCA						
❏ PB-10800		Oh Lawd, I'm On My Way/Oh Bess, Where's My Bess	1976		2.50	5.00
Rockin'						
❏ 504		Walkin' and Talkin' (To Myself)/ I'm Wonderin' and Wonderin'	1952	75.00	150.00	300.00
Sittin' In With						
❏ 641		Baby Let Me Hear You Call My Name/Guitar Blues	1952	75.00	150.00	300.00
❏ 651		I Can't Do No More/Roly Poly	1952		Unconfirmed on 45 rpm	
Swing Time						

Note: Ray Charles records on Swing Time before 250 are unconfirmed on 45 rpm

Number		Title (A Side/B Side)	Year	VG	VG+	NM
❏ 250		Baby, Let Me Hold Your Hand/Lonely Boy	1951	75.00	150.00	300.00
❏ 274		Kissa Me Baby/I'm Glad for Your Sake	1952	75.00	150.00	300.00

Number	Title (A Side/B Side)	Year	VG	VG+	NM
❑ 297	Baby Won't You Please Come Home/Hey Now	1952	*Unconfirmed on 45 rpm*		
❑ 300	Baby Let Me Hear You Call My Name/Guitar Blues	1952	75.00	150.00	300.00
❑ 326	The Snow Is Falling/Misery in My Heart	1953	75.00	150.00	300.00

Tangerine

❑ 1015	Booty Butt/Sidewinder	1971		3.00	6.00

Time

❑ 1026	I Found My Baby/Guitar Blues	1960	3.75	7.50	15.00
❑ 1054	Why Did You Go/Back Home	1962	3.00	6.00	12.00

Warner Bros.

❑ 18611	A Song for You/I Can't Get Enough	1993			3.00
❑ 49608	Beers to You/Cotton-Eyed Clint	1980		2.50	5.00

A-side: With Clint Eastwood; B-side by Texas Opera Company

Charles, Sonny
(Also see "Checkmates Ltd., The")
Fraternity

❑ 935	Speechless/These Two Feet	1964	4.00	8.00	12.00

Highrise

❑ 2001	Put It in a Magazine/(B-side unknown)	1982		2.00	4.00
❑ 2006	Always on My Mind/(B-side unknown)	1983		2.00	4.00

RCA Victor

❑ 74-0645	It's Alright in the City/Nicasio	1972		3.00	6.00

Charmers, The
(Probably more than one group)
Aladdin

❑ 3337	All Alone/Johnny My Dear	1956	15.00	30.00	60.00
❑ 3341	He's Gone/Oh! Yes	1956	15.00	30.00	60.00

Central

❑ 1002	The Beating of My Heart/Why Does It Have to Be Me	1954	200.00	400.00	800.00
❑ 1006	Tony, My Darling/In the Rain	1954	250.00	500.00	1,000

Co-Rec

❑ 101	The Letter/Watch What You Do	1963	3.00	6.00	12.00

Imperial

❑ 5957	All Alone/Johnny My Dear	1963	5.00	10.00	20.00

Jaf

❑ 2021	Little Fool/Hard to Get	1961	5.00	10.00	20.00

Laurie

❑ 3142	My Kind of Love/Johnny	1962	5.00	10.00	20.00
❑ 3173	Shy Guy/I Cried	1963	5.00	10.00	20.00
❑ 3203	Work It Out/Sweet Talk	1963	5.00	10.00	20.00

Louis

❑ 6806	It's a Funny Way We Met/Where's the Boy	1965	3.00	6.00	12.00

Pip

❑ 8000	Looking for Trouble/After You Walk Me Home	1964	3.00	6.00	12.00

Silhouette

❑ 522	Rock, Rhythm and Blues/Letters Don't Have Arms	1957	15.00	30.00	60.00

Sure Shot

❑ 104	Lessons from the Stars/My Love	1963	75.00	150.00	300.00

Terrace

❑ 7512	Visiting Day/Whatever Happened to Baby Jane	1962	6.25	12.50	25.00

Timely

❑ 1009	I Was Wrong/The Mambo	1955	250.00	500.00	1,000
❑ 1011	The Church on the Hill/Battle Axe	1955	250.00	500.00	1,000

Charms, The
(Also see "Williams, Otis, and the Charms," a different group except for Mr. Williams and the name)
Chart

❑ 608	Love's Our Inspiration/Love, Love Stick Stov	1956	10.00	20.00	40.00
❑ 613	Heart of a Rose/I Offer You	1956	10.00	20.00	40.00
❑ 623	I'll Be True/Boom Diddy Boom Boom	1956	10.00	20.00	40.00

DeLuxe

❑ 6000	Heaven Only Knows/Loving Baby	1953	125.00	250.00	500.00
❑ 6014	Happy Are We/What Do You Know About That	1953	100.00	200.00	400.00
❑ 6034	Bye Bye Baby/Please Believe in Me	1954	100.00	200.00	400.00
❑ 6050	Quiet Please/55 Seconds	1954	100.00	200.00	400.00
❑ 6056	Come to Me Baby/My Baby, Dearest Darling	1954	50.00	100.00	200.00
❑ 6062	Hearts of Stone/Who Knows	1954	12.50	25.00	50.00
❑ 6065	Two Hearts/The First Time We Met	1954	12.50	25.00	50.00
❑ 6072	Crazy, Crazy Love/Mambo Sh-Mambo	1955	12.50	25.00	50.00
❑ 6076	Ling, Ting, Tong/Bazoom (I Need Your Lovin')	1955	12.50	25.00	50.00
❑ 6080	Ko Ko Mo (I Love You So)/Whadya Want?	1955	12.50	25.00	50.00
❑ 6082	Whadya Want?/Crazy, Crazy Love	1955	10.00	20.00	40.00
❑ 6087	When We Get Married/Let the Happenings Happen	1955	10.00	20.00	40.00
❑ 6089	One Fine Day/It's You, You, You	1955	10.00	20.00	40.00

Rockin'

❑ 516	Heaven Only Knows/Loving Baby	1953	200.00	400.00	800.00

Number		Title (A Side/B Side)	Year	VG	VG+	NM

Checker, Chubby
(Also see "Rydell, Bobby, and Chubby Checker")
Abkco

Number		Title (A Side/B Side)	Year	VG	VG+	NM
☐ 4001		The Twist/Loddy Lo	1972		2.50	5.00
☐ 4002		The Hucklebuck/Pony Time	1972		2.50	5.00
☐ 4003		Limbo Rock/Let's Limbo Some More	1972		2.50	5.00
☐ 4004		Hey Bobba Needle/Hooka Tooka	1972		2.50	5.00
☐ 4027		Slow Twistin'/Birdland	1973		2.50	5.00

Amherst

☐ 716		The Rub/Move It	1976		2.00	4.00

Buddah

☐ 100		Back in the U.S.S.R./Windy Cream	1969	3.00	6.00	12.00

MCA

☐ 51233		Running/Is Tonight the Night	1982		2.50	5.00
☐ 52015		Running/Is Tonight the Night	1982		2.00	4.00
☐ 52043		Harder Than Diamond/Your Love	1982		2.00	4.00

Parkway

☐ 006		The Jet/Ray Charles-ton	1962	7.50	15.00	30.00
☐ 105		You Got the Power/Looking at Tomorrow	1966	3.75	7.50	15.00
☐ 112		Karate Monkey/Her Heart	1966	3.75	7.50	15.00
☐ 804		The Class/Schooldays, Oh Schooldays	1959	6.25	12.50	25.00
☐ 808		Samson and Delilah/Whole Lotta Laughin'	1959	6.25	12.50	25.00
☐ 810		Dancing Dinosaur/	1960	6.25	12.50	25.00
		Those Private Eyes (Keep Watchin' Me)		?		

The existence of both Parkway 808 and 810 has been questioned.

☐ 811		The Twist/Toot	1960	7.50	15.00	30.00

First pressings have white label with blue print

☐ 811		The Twist/Toot	1960	5.00	10.00	20.00

Second pressings have orange label with black print

☐ 811		The Twist/Twistin' U.S.A.	1961	3.75	7.50	15.00
☐ 811	DJ	The Twist/Twistin' U.S.A.	1961	37.50	75.00	150.00

Promo copy on yellow vinyl

☐ 811	DJ	The Twist/Twistin' U.S.A.	1961	50.00	100.00	200.00

Promo copy on red vinyl

☐ 811	PS	The Twist/Twistin' U.S.A.	1961	7.50	15.00	30.00
☐ 813		The Hucklebuck/Whole Lotta Shakin' Goin' On	1960	3.75	7.50	15.00
☐ 818		Pony Time/Oh, Susannah	1960	3.75	7.50	15.00
☐ 822		Dance the Mess Around/Good, Good Lovin'	1961	3.75	7.50	15.00
☐ 824		Let's Twist Again/Everything's Gonna Be Alright	1961	3.75	7.50	15.00
☐ 824	PS	Let's Twist Again/Everything's Gonna Be Alright	1961	6.25	12.50	25.00
☐ 830		The Fly/That's the Way It Goes	1961	3.75	7.50	15.00
☐ 830	PS	The Fly/That's the Way It Goes	1961	6.25	12.50	25.00
☐ 835		Slow Twistin'/La Paloma Twist	1962	3.75	7.50	15.00

Features female vocal by Dee Dee Sharp

☐ 835	PS	Slow Twistin'/La Paloma Twist	1962	6.25	12.50	25.00
☐ 842		Dancin' Party/Gotta Get Myself Together	1962	3.75	7.50	15.00
☐ 842	PS	Dancin' Party/Gotta Get Myself Together	1962	6.25	12.50	25.00
☐ 849		Limbo Rock/Popeye The Hitch-Hiker	1962	3.75	7.50	15.00
☐ 849	PS	Limbo Rock/Popeye The Hitch-Hiker	1962	6.25	12.50	25.00
☐ 862		Twenty Miles/Let's Limbo Some More	1963	3.75	7.50	15.00
☐ 862	PS	Twenty Miles/Let's Limbo Some More	1963	6.25	12.50	25.00
☐ 873		Birdland/Black Cloud	1963	3.75	7.50	15.00
☐ 873	PS	Birdland/Black Cloud	1963	6.25	12.50	25.00
☐ 879		Surf Party/Twist It Up	1963	3.75	7.50	15.00
☐ 879	PS	Surf Party/Twist It Up	1963	6.25	12.50	25.00
☐ 890		Loddy Lo/Hooka Tooka	1963	3.75	7.50	15.00
☐ 890	PS	Loddy Lo/Hooka Tooka	1963	6.25	12.50	25.00
☐ 890		Loddy Lo/Everything's Gonna Be Alright	1963	4.00	8.00	16.00
☐ 890	PS	Loddy Lo/Everything's Gonna Be Alright	1963	7.00	14.00	28.00
☐ 907		Hey Bobba Needle/Spread Joy	1964	3.75	7.50	15.00
☐ 907	PS	Hey Bobba Needle/Spread Joy	1964	6.25	12.50	25.00
☐ 920		Lazy Elsie Molly/Rosie	1964	3.75	7.50	15.00
☐ 920	PS	Lazy Elsie Molly/Rosie	1964	6.25	12.50	25.00
☐ 922		She Wants T'Swim/You Better Believe It, Baby	1964	3.00	6.00	12.00
☐ 922	PS	She Wants T'Swim/You Better Believe It, Baby	1964	6.25	12.50	25.00
☐ 936		Lovely, Lovely (Loverly, Loverly)/The Weekend's Here	1964	3.00	6.00	12.00
☐ 936	PS	Lovely, Lovely (Loverly, Loverly)/The Weekend's Here	1964	6.25	12.50	25.00
☐ 949		Let's Do the Freddie/(At the) Discoteque	1965	3.00	6.00	12.00
☐ 959		Everything's Wrong/Cu Me La Be-Stay	1965	3.00	6.00	12.00
☐ 965		You Just Don't Know/Two Hearts Make One Love	1965	50.00	100.00	200.00
☐ 989		Hey You! Little Boo-Ga-Loo/Pussy Cat	1966	3.00	6.00	12.00

Sea Bright

☐ 5128		Read You Like a Book/(B-side unknown)	1986		2.00	4.00

Tin Pan Apple

☐ 887 571-7		The Twist (Yo, Twist!)/The Twist (Buffapella)	1988			3.00

"Stupid def vocals" on a Fat Boys record

☐ 887 571-7	PS	The Twist (Yo, Twist!)/The Twist (Buffapella)	1988			3.00

20th Century

☐ 2040		Reggae My Way/Gypsy	1973		2.50	5.00
☐ 2075		She's a Bad Woman/Happiness Is a Girl Like You	1974		2.50	5.00

EPs

Parkway

☐ 5001		Chubby Checker	1961	15.00	30.00	60.00

Number		Title (A Side/B Side)	Year	VG	VG+	NM
❑ 5001	PS	Chubby Checker	1961	15.00	30.00	60.00
		Paper cut-out sleeve				

Checkers, The
(More than one group)
Arvee
| ❑ 5035 | | Skooby Doo (Part 1)/Skooby Doo (Part 2) | 1961 | 5.00 | 10.00 | 20.00 |
| ❑ 5037 | | Swingin' Summer/Skooby Doo | 1961 | 5.00 | 10.00 | 20.00 |

Dottie
| ❑ 1001 | | Big Car/Buzz | 196? | 5.00 | 10.00 | 20.00 |

Federal
| ❑ 12355 | | So Fine/Sentimental Heart | 1959 | 7.50 | 15.00 | 30.00 |
| ❑ 12375 | | White Cliffs of Dover/Let Me Come Back | 1960 | 7.50 | 15.00 | 30.00 |

Jerden
| ❑ 710 | | Black Cat/Soft Blue | 1963 | 5.00 | 10.00 | 20.00 |

King
❑ 4558		Flame in My Heart/Oh, Oh, Oh Baby	1952	250.00	500.00	1,000
❑ 4581		Night's Curtains/Let Me Come Back	1952	250.00	500.00	1,000
❑ 4596		My Prayer Tonight/Love Wasn't There	1953	200.00	400.00	800.00
❑ 4626		Ghost of My Baby/I Wanna Know	1953	200.00	400.00	800.00
❑ 4673		I Promise You/You Never Had It So Good	1953	75.00	150.00	300.00
❑ 4675		White Cliffs of Dover/Without a Song	1953	75.00	150.00	300.00
❑ 4710		House with No Windows/Don't Stop Dan	1954	50.00	100.00	200.00
❑ 4719		Over the Rainbow/You've Been Fooling Around	1954	50.00	100.00	200.00
❑ 4751		I Wasn't Thinking, I Was Drinking/Mama's Daughter	1954	50.00	100.00	200.00
❑ 4764		Trying to Hold My Girl/Can't Find My Sadie	1955	62.50	125.00	250.00
❑ 5156		Heaven Only Knows/Nine More Miles	1958	37.50	75.00	150.00
❑ 5199		Teardrops Are Falling/Rock-A-Locka	1959	15.00	30.00	60.00
		Originally released as King 4781 by The Five Wings.				
❑ 5592		Over the Rainbow/Love Wasn't There	1962	5.00	10.00	20.00
		As "The Original Checkers"				

Mercury
| ❑ 72354 | | Red Ball Express/Come Back Home | 1964 | 3.00 | 6.00 | 12.00 |

Skyla
| ❑ 1120 | | Blue Saturday/Cascade | 1961 | 5.00 | 10.00 | 20.00 |

Checkmates Ltd., The
(Also see "Charles, Sonny")
A&M
❑ 1006		Spanish Harlem/Baby Don't You Get Crazy	1968	2.00	4.00	8.00
❑ 1040		Love Is All I Have to Give/Never Should Have Lied	1969	2.00	4.00	8.00
❑ 1053		Black Pearl/Lazy Susan	1969	2.50	5.00	10.00
		As "Sonny Charles and the Checkmates Ltd."				
❑ 1127		Spanish Harlem/Proud Mary	1969	2.00	4.00	8.00
		As "Sonny Charles and the Checkmates Ltd."				
❑ 1130		Proud Mary/Do You Love Your Baby	1969	2.00	4.00	8.00
		As "Sonny Charles and the Checkmates Ltd."				

Capitol
❑ 5603		Do the Walk/Glad for You	1966	5.00	10.00	20.00
❑ 5753		I Can Hear the Rain/Kissin' Her and Cryin' for You	1966	7.50	15.00	30.00
❑ 5814		Please Don't Take My World Away/ Mastered the Art of Love	1966	5.00	10.00	20.00
❑ 5922		Walk in the Sunlight/A & I	1967	5.00	10.00	20.00

Fantasy
| ❑ 800 | | Let's Do It/Take All the Time You Need | 1977 | | 2.50 | 5.00 |
| ❑ 823 | | Greedy for Your Love/ That's How It Feels (When Two People Fall in Love) | 1978 | | 2.50 | 5.00 |

Greedy
| ❑ 111 | | I'm Laying My Heart on the Line/ Make Love to Your Mind | 1977 | | 2.50 | 5.00 |

Polydor
| ❑ 14313 | | All Alone by the Telephone/Body Language | 1976 | | 2.50 | 5.00 |

Cheerios, The
Golden Oldies
| ❑ 1 | | Ding Dong Honeymoon/Where Are You Tonight | 196? | 5.00 | 10.00 | 20.00 |

Infinity
| ❑ 011 | | Ding Dong Honeymoon/Where Are You Tonight | 1961 | 100.00 | 200.00 | 400.00 |

Cheers, The
Capitol
❑ F2921		Bazoom (I Need Your Lovin')/Arrividerci	1954	6.25	12.50	25.00
❑ F3019		Whadaya Want/Bernie's Tune	1955	6.25	12.50	25.00
❑ F3075		Can't We Be More Than Friends/Blueberries	1955	6.25	12.50	25.00
❑ F3146		I Must Be Dreaming/Fancy Meeting You Here	1955	6.25	12.50	25.00
❑ F3219		Black Denim Trousers and Motorcycle Boots/ Some Night in Alaska	1955	6.25	12.50	25.00
❑ F3353		The Chicken/Don't Do Anything	1956	5.00	10.00	20.00
❑ F3409		Heaven on Earth/Que Pasa Muchacha	1956	5.00	10.00	20.00

Mercury
❑ 71083		Chug Chug Toot Toot/Big Feet	1957	3.75	7.50	15.00
❑ 71100		Two Hearts/You Never Have the Time	1957	3.75	7.50	15.00
		As "Bert Convy and the Cheers"				

Number		Title (A Side/B Side)	Year	VG	VG+	NM
NRC						
❑ 5003		Hold That Line/Blue Serenade	1958	3.75	7.50	15.00
Cher						
(Also see "Sonny and Cher")						
Atco						
❑ 6658		Yours Until Tomorrow/Thought of Loving You	1969		3.00	6.00
❑ 6684		Chastity's Song/I Walk on Gilded Splinters	1969		3.00	6.00
❑ 6704		For What It's Worth/Hangin' On	1969		3.00	6.00
❑ 6713		You've Made Me So Very Happy/First Time	1969		3.00	6.00
❑ 6793		Superstar/First Time	1971		3.00	6.00
❑ 6868		Lay Baby Lay/(Just Enough to Keep Me) Hangin' On	1972		2.50	5.00
Casablanca						
❑ 965		Take Me Home/My Song (Too Far Gone)	1979		2.00	4.00
❑ 987		It's Too Late to Love Me Now/Wasn't It Good	1979		2.00	4.00
❑ 2208		Hell on Wheels/Git Down (Guitar Groupie)	1979		2.00	4.00
❑ 2228		Boys and Girls/Holdin' Out for Love	1979		2.00	4.00
Columbia						
❑ 02850		Do I Ever Cross Your Mind/Rudy	1982		2.00	4.00
❑ 03150		Walk With Me/I Paralyze	1982		2.00	4.00
Geffen						
❑ 19023		Love and Understanding/Trail of Broken Hearts	1991		2.00	4.00
❑ 19105		Save Up All Your Tears/A World Without Heroes	1991			3.00
❑ 19659		The Shoop Shoop Song (It's In His Kiss)/ Love on a Rooftop	1990			3.00
❑ 19953		Heart of Stone/All Because of You	1990			3.00
❑ 22844		Just Like Jesse James/Starting Over	1989			3.00
❑ 22886		If I Could Turn Back Time/Some Guys	1989			3.00
❑ 22886	PS	If I Could Turn Back Time/Some Guys	1989			3.00
❑ 27529		After All (Love Theme from "Chances Are")/ Dangerous Times *With Peter Cetera*	1989			3.00
❑ 27529	PS	After All (Love Theme from "Chances Are")/ Dangerous Times	1989		2.50	5.00
❑ 27742		Main Man/((It's Been Hard Enough) Gettin' Over You	1988			3.00
❑ 27894		Skin Deep/Perfection	1988			3.00
❑ 27986		We All Sleep Alone/Working Girl	1988			3.00
❑ 27986	PS	We All Sleep Alone/Working Girl	1988			3.00
❑ 28191		I Found Someone/Dangerous Times	1987			3.00
❑ 28191	PS	I Found Someone/Dangerous Times	1987			3.00
Imperial						
❑ 66081		Dream Baby/Stan Quetzal *By "Cherilyn"*	1964	10.00	20.00	40.00
❑ 66114		All I Really Want to Do/I'm Gonna Love You	1965	3.00	6.00	12.00
❑ 66136		See See Blues/Where Do You Go	1965	3.00	6.00	12.00
❑ 66160		Bang Bang (My Baby Shot Me Down)/ Our Day Will Come	1966	3.00	6.00	12.00
❑ 66160		Bang Bang (My Baby Shot Me Down)/ Needles and Pins	1966	3.00	6.00	12.00
❑ 66192		Alfie/She's No Better Than Me	1966	2.50	5.00	10.00
❑ 66217		Behind the Door/Magic in the Air	1966	2.50	5.00	10.00
❑ 66223		Dream Baby/Mama (When My Dollies Have Babies)	1966	2.50	5.00	10.00
❑ 66252		Hey Joe/Our Day Will Come	1967	2.50	5.00	10.00
❑ 66261		You Better Sit Down Kids/ Mama (When My Dollies Have Babies)	1967	2.50	5.00	10.00
❑ 66261		You Better Sit Down Kids/Elusive Butterfly	1967	3.00	6.00	12.00
❑ 66282		But I Can't Love You More/Click Song Number One	1968	2.00	4.00	8.00
❑ 66307		Take Me for a Little While/A Song Called Children	1968	2.00	4.00	8.00
Kapp						
❑ 2134		Classified 1-A/Don't Put It on Me	1971		3.00	6.00
❑ 2146		Gypsys, Tramps and Thieves/He'll Never Know *Black label*	1971		3.00	6.00
❑ 2146		Gypsys, Tramps and Thieves/He'll Never Know *Multicolor label*	1971		2.00	4.00
❑ 2158		The Way of Love/Don't Put It on Me	1972		2.00	4.00
❑ 2171		Living in a House Divided/One Honest Man	1972		2.00	4.00
❑ 2184		Don't Hide Your Love/First Time	1972		2.00	4.00
MCA						
❑ 40039		Am I Blue/How Long Has This Been Going On	1973		2.00	4.00
❑ 40102		Half-Breed/Melody	1973		2.00	4.00
❑ 40161		Dark Lady/Two People Clinging to a Thread	1973		2.00	4.00
❑ 40245		Train of Thought/Dixie Girl	1974		2.00	4.00
❑ 40273		I Saw a Man and He Danced With His Wife/ I Hate to Sleep Alone	1974		2.00	4.00
❑ 40324		Carousel Man/ When You Find Out Where You're Going Let Me Know	1974		2.00	4.00
❑ 40375		Rescue Me/Dixie Girl	1975		2.00	4.00
Reprise						
❑ 17695		One by One/ I Wouldn't Treat a Dog (The Way You Treated Me)	1996			3.00
United Artists						
❑ 0106		All I Really Want to Do/Where Do You Go	1973		2.00	4.00
❑ 0107		Bang Bang (My Baby Shot Me Down)/ You Better Sit Down Kids	1973		2.00	4.00
		0106 and 0107 are "Silver Spotlight Series" reissues				

Number		Title (A Side/B Side)	Year	VG	VG+	NM
❑ XW511		Sunny/Alfie	1974		2.00	4.00
❑ 50864		Reason to Believe/Will You Still Love Me Tomorrow	1971		2.00	4.00
❑ 50974		Old Man River/Our Day Will Come	1972		2.00	4.00

Warner Bros.

❑ 8096		Geronimo's Cadillac/These Days	1975		2.00	4.00
❑ 8263		Borrowed Time/Long Distance Love Affair	1976		2.00	4.00
❑ 8311		Pirate/Send the Man Over	1976		2.00	4.00
❑ 8366		War Paint and Soft Feathers/Send the Man Over	1977		2.00	4.00

Warner/Spector

❑ 0400		Baby, I Love You/A Woman's Story	1974	2.50	5.00	10.00
❑ 0402		Just Enough to Keep Me Hangin' On/A Love Like Yours	1975	2.50	5.00	10.00
		With Nilsson				

Cherokees, The

(More than one group)

Challenge

❑ 9135		Cherokee Stomp/Uprisin'	1961	5.00	10.00	20.00

Grand

❑ 106		Rainbow of Love/I Had a Thrill	1954	200.00	400.00	800.00
❑ 110		Please Tell Me So/Remember When	1954	200.00	400.00	800.00

Guyden

❑ 2044		Cherokee/Harlem Nocturne	1960	3.75	7.50	15.00
❑ 2044	PS	Cherokee/Harlem Nocturne	1960	7.50	15.00	30.00

MGM

❑ 13334		Seven Daffodils/Wondrous Place	1964	3.75	7.50	15.00
❑ 13433		Dig a Little Deeper/I'l Never Turn My Back on You	1965	5.00	10.00	20.00

Peacock

❑ 1656		Drip Drip/Is She Real	1955	37.50	75.00	150.00

United Artists

❑ 367		My Heavenly Angel/Bed Bug	1961	25.00	50.00	100.00
		Fred Parris (The Five Satins) was a member of this Cherokees				

Chesterfields, The

(Each different label is probably a different group)

A&M

❑ 2041		That Is Rock and Roll/Why Do Fools Fall in Love	1978		2.50	5.00

Chess

❑ 1559		I'm in Heaven/All Messed Up	1954	100.00	200.00	400.00

Cub

❑ 9008		I Got Fired/Meet Me at the Candy Store	1958	6.25	12.50	25.00

Philips

❑ 40060		A Dream Is But a Dream/You Walked Away	1962	50.00	100.00	200.00

Chesters, The - See "Little Anthony and the Imperials"

Chi-Lites, The

Blue Rock

❑ 4007		I'm So Jealous/The Mix-Mix Song	1965	6.25	12.50	25.00
❑ 4020		Doing the Snatch/Bassology	1965	6.25	12.50	25.00
❑ 4037		Never No More/She's Mine	1965	12.50	25.00	50.00

Brunswick

❑ 55398		Give It Away/What Do I Wish For	1969	2.00	4.00	8.00
❑ 55414		Let Me Be the Man My Daddy Was/ The Twelfth of Never	1969	2.00	4.00	8.00
❑ 55422		I'm Gonna Make You Love Me/To Change My Love	1969	2.00	4.00	8.00
❑ 55426		24 Hours of Sadness/ You're No Longer Part of My Heart	1970	2.00	4.00	8.00
❑ 55438		I Like Your Lovin' (Do You Like Mine)/ You're No Longer Part of My Heart	1970	2.00	4.00	8.00
❑ 55442		Are You My Woman (Tell Me So)/Troubles A-Comin'	1970	2.00	4.00	8.00
❑ 55450		(For God's Sake) Give More Power to the People/ Troubles A-Comin'	1971	2.00	4.00	8.00
❑ 55455		We Are Neighbors/What Do I Wish For	1971	2.00	4.00	8.00
❑ 55458		I Want to Pay You Back (For Loving Me)/Love Uprising	1971	2.00	4.00	8.00
❑ 55462		Have You Seen Her/Yes I'm Ready	1971		3.00	6.00
❑ 55471		Oh Girl/Being in Love	1972		3.00	6.00
❑ 55478		The Coldest Days of My Life (Part 1)/ The Coldest Days of My Life (Part 2)	1972		3.00	6.00
❑ 55483		A Lonely Man/ The Man and the Woman (The Boy and the Girl)	1972		3.00	6.00
❑ 55489		We Need Order/Living in the Footsteps of Another Man	1972		3.00	6.00
❑ 55491		A Letter to Myself/Sally	1973		3.00	6.00
❑ 55496		My Heart Just Keeps On Breakin'/ Just Two Teenage Kids	1973		3.00	6.00
❑ 55500		Stoned Out of My Mind/Someone Else's Arms	1973		3.00	6.00
❑ 55502		I Found Someone/Marriage License	1973		3.00	6.00
❑ 55505		Homely Girl/Never Had It So Good and Felt So Bad	1974		3.00	6.00
❑ 55512		There Will Never Be Any Peace (Until God Is Seated at the Conference Table)/Too Good	1974		3.00	6.00
❑ 55514		You Got to Be the One/ Happiness Is Your Middle Name	1974		3.00	6.00
❑ 55515		Toby/That's How Long	1974		3.00	6.00
❑ 55520		It's Time for Love/Here I Am	1975		3.00	6.00
❑ 55522		Don't Burn No Bridges/(Instrumental)	1975		3.00	6.00
		With Jackie Wilson				

Number	Title (A Side/B Side)	Year	VG	VG+	NM
❏ 55525	The Devil Is Doing His Work/I'm Not a Gambler	1976		3.00	6.00
❏ 55528	You Don't Have to Go/(Instrumental)	1976		3.00	6.00
❏ 55546	First Time/Marriage License	1978		2.50	5.00

Chi-Sound

❏ 2472	Heavenly Body/Strung Out	1980		2.00	4.00
❏ 2481	Have You Seen Her/Supermad (About You Baby)	1981		2.00	4.00
❏ 2495	All I Wanna Do Is Make Love to You/Round and Round	1981		2.00	4.00
❏ 2503	Me and You/Tell Me Where It Hurts	1981		2.00	4.00
❏ 2600	Hot on a Thing (Called Love)/(B-side unknown)	1982		2.00	4.00
❏ 2604	Try My Side (Of Love)/Get Down with Me	1982		2.00	4.00

Dakar

❏ 600	Baby It's Time/Price of Love	1968	3.00	6.00	12.00

As "Marshall and the Chi-Lites"

Daran

❏ 0111	Pretty Girl/Love Bandit	1966	12.50	25.00	50.00

As "Marshall and the Chi-Lites"

❏ 222	I'm So Jealous/The Mix-Mix Song	1964	25.00	50.00	100.00

As "The Hi-Lites"

Inphasion

❏ 7205	Stay a Little Longer/Higher	1979		2.50	5.00
❏ 7208	The Only One for Me (One in a Million)/ You Won't Be Lonely Too Long	1979		2.50	5.00

Ja-Wes

❏ 0888	You Did That to Me/I Won't Care About You	1966	3.75	7.50	15.00

Larc

❏ 81015	Bottom's Up/Bottom's Up Groove	1983		2.00	4.00
❏ 81023	Bad Motor Scooter/I Just Wanna Hold You	1983		2.00	4.00

Mercury

❏ 73844	Happy Being Lonely/Love Can Be Dangerous	1976		2.50	5.00
❏ 73886	Vanishing Love/I Turn Away	1977		2.50	5.00
❏ 73934	My First Mistake/Stop Still	1977		2.50	5.00
❏ 73954	If I Had a Girl/I've Got Love on My Mind	1977		2.50	5.00

Private I

❏ 04365	Stop What You're Doin'/Little Girl	1984			3.00
❏ 04484	Let Today Come Back Tomorrow/Gimme Whatcha Got	1984			3.00

Revue

❏ 11005	Love Is Gone/Love Me	1967	3.00	6.00	12.00
❏ 11018	(Um, Um) My Baby Loves Me/That's My Baby for You	1968	3.00	6.00	12.00

Chiffons, The

B.T. Puppy

❏ 558	Secret Love/Strange, Strange Feeling	1970	2.50	5.00	10.00

Big Deal

❏ 6003	Tonight's the Night/Do You Know	1960	12.50	25.00	50.00

Buddah

❏ 171	So Much in Love/Strange, Strange Feeling	1970	2.50	5.00	10.00

Laurie

❏ 3152	He's So Fine/Oh My Lover	1963	3.75	7.50	15.00
❏ 3166	Lucy Me/Why Am I So Shy?	1963	3.75	7.50	15.00
❏ 3179	One Fine Day/Why Am I So Shy	1963	3.75	7.50	15.00
❏ 3195	A Love So Fine/Only My Friend	1963	3.00	6.00	12.00
❏ 3212	I Have a Boyfriend/I'm Gonna Dry My Eyes	1963	3.00	6.00	12.00
❏ 3224	Tonight I Met an Angel/Easy to Love	1964	3.00	6.00	12.00
❏ 3262	Sailor Boy/When the Summer Is Through	1964	3.00	6.00	12.00
❏ 3275	What Am I Gonna Do with You/ Strange, Strange Feeling	1964	3.00	6.00	12.00
❏ 3301	Nobody Knows What's Going On (In My Mind But Me)/ Did You Ever Go Steady	1965	3.00	6.00	12.00
❏ 3301	Nobody Knows What's Going On (In My Mind But Me)/The Real Thing	1965	3.00	6.00	12.00
❏ 3318	Tonight I'm Gonna Dream/Heavenly Place	1965	3.00	6.00	12.00
❏ 3340	Sweet Talkin' Guy/Did You Ever Go Steady	1966	3.00	6.00	12.00
❏ 3350	Out of This World/Just a Boy	1966	2.50	5.00	10.00
❏ 3357	Stop, Look, Listen/March	1966	2.50	5.00	10.00
❏ 3364	My Boyfriend's Back/I Got Plenty of Nuttin'	1966	2.50	5.00	10.00
❏ 3377	If I Knew Then/Keep the Boy Happy	1967	2.50	5.00	10.00
❏ 3423	Just for Tonight/Teach Me How	1968	2.50	5.00	10.00
❏ 3460	Up on the Bridge/March	1968	2.50	5.00	10.00
❏ 3497	Love Me Like You're Gonna Lose Me/ Three Dips of Ice Cream	1969	2.50	5.00	10.00
❏ 3630	My Sweet Lord/Main Nerve	1975	2.50	5.00	10.00
❏ 3648	Dream, Dream, Dream/Oh My Lover	1976	2.50	5.00	10.00

Reprise

❏ 20,103	After Last Night/Doctor of Hearts	1962	5.00	10.00	20.00

Wildcat

❏ 601	Never Never/No More Tomorrows	1961	6.25	12.50	25.00

Chimes, The

(Several different groups)

Flair

See "Flairs, The"

Number		Title (A Side/B Side)	Year	VG	VG+	NM
House of Beauty						
❏ 3		Tears from An Angel's Eyes/(B-side unknown)	1959	20.00	40.00	80.00
Laurie						
❏ 3211		Whose Heart Are You Breaking Now/ Baby's Coming Home	1963	3.00	6.00	12.00
Limelight						
❏ 3000		Cry, Baby, Cry/Angel Child	1963	6.25	12.50	25.00
❏ 3002		Du Wap/Stop, Look and Listen	1963	6.25	12.50	25.00
Metro						
❏ 1		Whose Heart Are You Breaking Now/ Baby's Coming Home	1963	5.00	10.00	20.00
Reserve						
❏ 120		When School Starts Again/Nervous Heart	1957	7.50	15.00	30.00
Royal Roost						
❏ 577		Dearest Darling/A Fool Was I	1955	37.50	75.00	150.00
Specialty						
❏ 555		Tears on My Pillow/Cindy Lou	1955	15.00	30.00	60.00
❏ 574		Chop Chop/Pretty Little Girl	1956	15.00	30.00	60.00
Tag						
❏ 444		Once in Awhile/Summer Night	1960	10.00	20.00	40.00
		Maroon label				
❏ 444		Once in Awhile/Summer Night	1960	10.00	20.00	40.00
		Light blue label				
❏ 444		Once in Awhile/Oh, How I Love You So	1960	12.50	25.00	50.00
		B-side is actually by a group called the Bi-Tones, though credited to the Chimes				
❏ 445		I'm in the Mood for Love/Only Love	1961	6.25	12.50	25.00
❏ 447		Let's Fall in Love/Dream Girl	1961	6.25	12.50	25.00
❏ 450		Paradise/My Love	1961	7.50	15.00	30.00

Chipmunks, The, David Seville and

(The originals. Some of these are credited only to The Chipmunks. Also see "Seville, David")

Number		Title (A Side/B Side)	Year	VG	VG+	NM
Dot						
❏ 16997		Apple Picker/Sorry About That, Herb	1967	3.00	6.00	12.00
EMI						
❏ S7-17645		The Chipmunk Song/Frosty the Snowman	1993		2.00	4.00
		Red vinyl				
Liberty						
❏ 55168		The Chipmunk Song/Almost Good	1958	7.50	15.00	30.00
		Black label				
❏ 55168		The Chipmunk Song/Almost Good	1958	6.25	12.50	25.00
		Blue-green label				
❏ 55178		Alvin's Harmonica/Mediocre	1959	5.00	10.00	20.00
❏ 55200		Ragtime Cowboy Joe/Flip Side	1959	5.00	10.00	20.00
❏ 55200	PS	Ragtime Cowboy Joe/Flip Side	1959	10.00	20.00	40.00
❏ 55233		Alvin's Orchestra/Copyright 1960	1960	3.75	7.50	15.00
❏ 55233	PS	Alvin's Orchestra/Copyright 1960	1960	10.00	20.00	40.00
❏ 55246		Coming 'Round the Mountain/Sing a Goofy Song	1960	3.75	7.50	15.00
❏ 55246	PS	Coming 'Round the Mountain/Sing a Goofy Song	1960	10.00	20.00	40.00
❏ 55250		The Chipmunk Song/Alvin's Harmonica	1959	3.75	7.50	15.00
❏ 55250	PS	The Chipmunk Song/Alvin's Harmonica	1959	10.00	20.00	40.00
❏ 55277		Alvin for President/Sack Time	1960	3.75	7.50	15.00
❏ 55277	PS	Alvin for President/Sack Time	1960	10.00	20.00	40.00
❏ 55289		Rudolph, the Red-Nosed Reindeer/Spain	1960	3.75	7.50	15.00
❏ 55289	PS	Rudolph, the Red-Nosed Reindeer/Spain	1960	10.00	20.00	40.00
❏ 55424		The Alvin Twist/I Wish I Could Speak French	1962	3.75	7.50	15.00
❏ 55452		America the Beautiful/My Wild Irish Rose	1962	3.75	7.50	15.00
❏ 55544		Alvin's All Star Chipmunk Band/ Old MacDonald Cha Cha Cha	1963	3.75	7.50	15.00
❏ 55544	PS	Alvin's All Star Chipmunk Band/ Old MacDonald Cha Cha Cha	1963	10.00	20.00	40.00
❏ 55632		Eefin' Alvin/Flip Side	1963	3.75	7.50	15.00
❏ 55635		The Night Before Christmas/Wonderful Day	1963	3.75	7.50	15.00
❏ 55635	PS	The Night Before Christmas/Wonderful Day	1963	7.50	15.00	30.00
❏ 55734		All My Lovin'/Do You Want to Know a Secret	1964	3.75	7.50	15.00
❏ 55773		Do-Re-Mi/Supercalifragilisticexpialidocious	1965	3.00	6.00	12.00
❏ 55832		I'm Henry VIII, I Am/What's New Pussycat	1965	3.00	6.00	12.00
❏ 56079		The Chipmunk Song/Christmas Blues	1968	4.00	8.00	16.00
		With Canned Heat				
Sunset						
❏ 61002		Talk to the Animals/My Friend the Doctor	1968	2.50	5.00	10.00
❏ 61002	PS	Talk to the Animals/My Friend the Doctor	1968	3.75	7.50	15.00
❏ 61003		Chitty Chitty Bang Bang/Hushabye Mountain	1968	2.50	5.00	10.00
❏ 61003	PS	Chitty Chitty Bang Bang/Hushabye Mountain	1968	3.75	7.50	15.00
United Artists						
❏ 0056		The Chipmunk Song/Ragtime Cowboy Joe	1973		2.00	4.00
		"Silver Spotlight Series" reissue				
❏ 0057		Alvin's Harmonica/Rudolph, the Red-Nosed Reindeer	1973		2.00	4.00
		"Silver Spotlight Series" reissue				
❏ XW576		The Chipmunk Song/Rudolph, the Red-Nosed Reindeer	1974		3.00	6.00

Number		Title (A Side/B Side)	Year	VG	VG+	NM

Chips, The
(More than one group)

Ember

❑ 1077		What a Lie/Bye, Bye, My Love	1961	5.00	10.00	20.00

Josie

❑ 803		Rubber Biscuit/Oh My Darlin'	1956	25.00	50.00	100.00

Philips

❑ 40520		Mixed Up Shook Up Girl/Break It Gently	1968	2.00	4.00	8.00

Satellite

❑ 105		As You Can See/You Make Me Feel So Good	1961	30.00	60.00	120.00

Strand

❑ 25027		Darling (I Need Your Love)/You're On My Side	1961	5.00	10.00	20.00

Tollie

❑ 9042		Party People/Long Lonely Winter	1965	2.50	5.00	10.00

Venice

❑ 101		Darling (I Need Your Love)/You're On My Side	1961	10.00	20.00	40.00

Chocolate Watch Band, The

Tower

❑ 373		Are You Gonna Be There (At the Love-In)/No Way Out	1967	12.50	25.00	50.00

Uptown

❑ 740		Baby Blue/Sweet Young Thing	1967	75.00	150.00	300.00
❑ 749		Misty Lane/She Weaves a Tender Trap	1967	12.50	25.00	50.00

Choir, The
(Featuring three future members of the Raspberries)

Canadian American

❑ 203		It's Cold Outside/I'm Goin' Home	1967	10.00	20.00	40.00

Intrepid

❑ 75020		Gonna Have a Good Time Tonight/So Much Love	1970	5.00	10.00	20.00

Roulette

❑ 4738		It's Cold Outside/I'm Goin' Home	1967	3.75	7.50	15.00
❑ 4760		No One Here to Play With/Don't You Feel a Little Sorry for Me	1967	3.75	7.50	15.00
❑ 7005		Changin' My Mind/When You Were With Me	1968	3.75	7.50	15.00

Chorals, The

Decca

❑ 29914		In My Dreams/Rock and Roll Baby	1956	20.00	40.00	80.00

Chordcats, The - See "Chords, The"

Chordettes, The

Atlantic

❑ 89310		Lollipop/Never on Sunday	1986			3.00
❑ 89310	PS	Lollipop/Never on Sunday	1986			3.00

Cadence

❑ 1239		It's You, It's You I Love/True Love Goes On and On	1954	3.75	7.50	15.00
❑ 1247		Mr. Sandman/I Don't Wanna See You Cryin'	1954	3.75	7.50	15.00
❑ 1259		Lonely Lips/The Dudelsack Song	1955	3.00	6.00	12.00
❑ 1267		Hummingbird/I Told a Lie	1955	3.00	6.00	12.00
❑ 1273		The Wedding/I Don't Know, I Don't Care	1955	3.00	6.00	12.00
❑ 1284		Eddie My Love/Whispering Willie	1956	3.00	6.00	12.00
❑ 1291		Born to Be with You/Love Never Changes	1956	3.00	6.00	12.00
❑ 1299		Lay Down Your Arms/Teenage Goodnight	1956	3.00	6.00	12.00
❑ 1307		Come Home to My Arms/(Fifi's) Walking the Poodle	1957	3.00	6.00	12.00
❑ 1310		Echo of Love/Like a Baby	1957	3.00	6.00	12.00
❑ 1330		Just Between You and Me/Soft Sands	1957	3.00	6.00	12.00
❑ 1341		Photographs/Baby of Mine	1957	3.00	6.00	12.00
❑ 1345		Lollipop/Baby Come-a Back-a	1958	3.75	7.50	15.00
❑ 1349		Zorro/Love Is a Two-Way Street	1958	3.00	6.00	12.00
❑ 1349	PS	Zorro/Love Is a Two-Way Street	1958	6.25	12.50	25.00
❑ 1361		No Other Arms, No Other Lips/We Should Be Together	1959	2.50	5.00	10.00
❑ 1366		A Girl's Work Is Never Done/No Wheels	1959	2.50	5.00	10.00
❑ 1366	PS	A Girl's Work Is Never Done/No Wheels	1959	6.25	12.50	25.00
❑ 1367		Forever/Ho Hum	1959	2.50	5.00	10.00
❑ 1382		All My Sorrows/A Broken Vow	1960	2.50	5.00	10.00
❑ 1402		Never on Sunday/A Faraway Star	1961	2.50	5.00	10.00
❑ 1412		The Exodus Song/Theme from Goodbye Again (Say No More-It's Goodbye)	1961	2.50	5.00	10.00
❑ 1417		Adios/White Rose of Athens	1962	2.50	5.00	10.00
❑ 1425		In the Deep Blue Sea/All My Sorrows	1962	2.50	5.00	10.00
❑ 1442		True Love Goes On and On/All My Sorrows	1963	2.50	5.00	10.00

Columbia

Note: Chordettes singles on Columbia before 39251 are unconfirmed on 45 rpm

❑ 39251		Runnin' Wild/Alice Blue Gown	1951	3.75	7.50	15.00
❑ 39252		Love Me and the World Is Mine/Lonesome That's All	1951	3.75	7.50	15.00
❑ 39253		Moonlight on the Ganges/Let the Rest of the World Go By	1951	3.75	7.50	15.00
❑ 39254		The World Is Waiting for the Sunrise/Love's Old Sweet Song	1951	3.75	7.50	15.00

Number	Title (A Side/B Side)	Year	VG	VG+	NM
❑ 39793	Carolina Moon//The Anniversary Waltz/ Sentimental Journey	1952	3.75	7.50	15.00
❑ 39794	A Little Street Where Old Friends Meet// Basin Street Blues + 1	1952	3.75	7.50	15.00
❑ 39795	Drifting and Dreaming + 1// I'm Drifting Back to Dreamland/Angry	1952	3.75	7.50	15.00
❑ 39796	S'posin'/The Sweetheart of Sigma Chi// Kentucky Babe/In the Sweet Long Ago	1952	3.75	7.50	15.00

Chords, The

Atco

Number	Title (A Side/B Side)	Year	VG	VG+	NM
❑ 6213	Sh-Boom/Little Maiden	1961	3.75	7.50	15.00
	As "The Sh-Booms"				

Atlantic

Number	Title (A Side/B Side)	Year	VG	VG+	NM
❑ 2074	Blue Moon/Short Skirts	1960	5.00	10.00	20.00
	As "The Sh-Booms"				

Casino

Number	Title (A Side/B Side)	Year	VG	VG+	NM
❑ 451	Tears in Your Eyes/Don't Be a Jumpin' Jack	1958	7.50	15.00	30.00

Cat

Number	Title (A Side/B Side)	Year	VG	VG+	NM
❑ 104	Sh-Boom/Cross Over the Bridge	1954	25.00	50.00	100.00
❑ 104	Sh-Boom/Little Maiden	1954	12.50	25.00	50.00
❑ 109	Zippety Zum (I'm in Love)/ Bless You (For Being an Angel)	1954	10.00	20.00	40.00
❑ 112	A Girl to Love/Hold Me Baby	1955	10.00	20.00	40.00
	As "The Chordcats"				
❑ 117	Could It Be/Pretty Wild	1955	10.00	20.00	40.00
	As "The Sh-Booms"				

Metro

Number	Title (A Side/B Side)	Year	VG	VG+	NM
❑ 20015	Elephant Walk/Pretty Face	1959	5.00	10.00	20.00

Vik

Number	Title (A Side/B Side)	Year	VG	VG+	NM
❑ 0295	I Don't Want to Set the World on Fire/Lu Lu	1957	7.50	15.00	30.00
	As "The Sh-Booms"				

Chosen Few, The
(Many different groups)

Autumn

Number	Title (A Side/B Side)	Year	VG	VG+	NM
❑ 17	Nobody But Me/I Think It's Time	1965	2.50	5.00	10.00

Canadian American

Number	Title (A Side/B Side)	Year	VG	VG+	NM
❑ 202	Cute Thing/One of Those Songs	1967	3.00	6.00	12.00

Canusa

Number	Title (A Side/B Side)	Year	VG	VG+	NM
❑ 504	Summer's Love/Hey Joe	1967	3.75	7.50	15.00

Canyon

Number	Title (A Side/B Side)	Year	VG	VG+	NM
❑ 1000	Talking All the Love I Can/Birth of a Playboy	196?	2.50	5.00	10.00

Co-Op

Number	Title (A Side/B Side)	Year	VG	VG+	NM
❑ 510	Why Can't I Love You/La La La La La	1966	3.00	6.00	12.00
❑ 511	Summer's Love/(Instrumental)	1967	3.00	6.00	12.00

Crystal

Number	Title (A Side/B Side)	Year	VG	VG+	NM
❑ 1107	You're a Big Girl Now/(B-side unknown)	196?	2.50	5.00	10.00

Dart

Number	Title (A Side/B Side)	Year	VG	VG+	NM
❑ 1080	Foolin' Around with Me/We Walk Together	1967	2.00	4.00	8.00

Denim

Number	Title (A Side/B Side)	Year	VG	VG+	NM
❑ 1092	Pink Clouds and Lemonade/Stop in the Name of Love	196?	2.00	4.00	8.00

Liberty

Number	Title (A Side/B Side)	Year	VG	VG+	NM
❑ 55919	Synthetic Man/The Last Man Alive	1966	2.50	5.00	10.00
❑ 55962	Asian Chrome/Earth Above, Sky Below	1967	2.50	5.00	10.00

North Beach

Number	Title (A Side/B Side)	Year	VG	VG+	NM
❑ 1003	Nobody But Me/I Think It's Time	1965	3.75	7.50	15.00

Playboy

Number	Title (A Side/B Side)	Year	VG	VG+	NM
❑ 106	I've Had It/Ask Me Baby	196?	2.50	5.00	10.00

Power International

Number	Title (A Side/B Side)	Year	VG	VG+	NM
❑ (# unknown)	Another Goodbye/Forget About the Past	1966	10.00	20.00	40.00

RCA Victor

Number	Title (A Side/B Side)	Year	VG	VG+	NM
❑ 74-0217	Maybe the Rain Will Fall/Deeper In	1969	2.00	4.00	8.00
❑ 74-0254	I'll Never Change You/Talk with Me	1969	2.00	4.00	8.00

Roulette

Number	Title (A Side/B Side)	Year	VG	VG+	NM
❑ 7015	Footsee/You Can Never Be Wrong	1968	2.00	4.00	8.00

Christie, Lou

Alcar

Number	Title (A Side/B Side)	Year	VG	VG+	NM
❑ 207	Close Your Eyes/Funny Thing	1963	6.25	12.50	25.00
❑ 208	You're With It/Tomorrow Will Come	1963	6.25	12.50	25.00

American Music Makers

Number	Title (A Side/B Side)	Year	VG	VG+	NM
❑ 006	The Jury/Little Did I Know	1963	7.50	15.00	30.00

Buddah

Number	Title (A Side/B Side)	Year	VG	VG+	NM
❑ 65	Genesis and the Third Verse/Rake Up the Leaves	1968	2.00	4.00	8.00
❑ 76	Canterbury Road/Saints of Aquarius	1969	2.00	4.00	8.00
❑ 116	I'm Gonna Make You Mine/I'm Gonna Get Married	1969		3.00	6.00
❑ 149	Are You Getting Any Sunshine/It'll Take Time	1970		2.50	5.00
❑ 163	Love Is Over/She Sold Me Magic	1970		2.50	5.00
❑ 192	Indian Lady/Glory River	1970		2.50	5.00

Number		Title (A Side/B Side)	Year	VG	VG+	NM
❏ 235		Waco/Lighthouse	1971		2.50	5.00
❏ 257		Mickey's Monkey/She Sold Me Magic	1971	6.25	12.50	25.00
❏ 285		Sing Me, Sing Me/Paper Song	1972		2.50	5.00
❏ 285	PS	Sing Me, Sing Me/Paper Song	1972	2.50	5.00	10.00

Sleeve appears to be promo only

❏ 312		Shuffle On Down to Pittsburgh/I'm Gonna Get Married	1972	5.00	10.00	20.00

C&C

❏ 102		The Gypsy Cried/Red Sails in the Sunset	1962	50.00	100.00	200.00

Co & Ce

❏ 235		Outside the Gates of Heaven/All That Glitters Isn't Gold	1966	2.50	5.00	10.00

Colpix

❏ 735		Merry-Go-Round/Guitars and Bongos	1964	3.00	6.00	12.00
❏ 753		Pot of Gold/Have I Sinned	1964	3.00	6.00	12.00
❏ 770		Make Summer Last Forever/Why Did You Do It Baby	1965	3.00	6.00	12.00
❏ 778		A Teenager in Love/Back Track	1965	3.00	6.00	12.00
❏ 799		Cryin' on My Knees/Big Time	1966	3.00	6.00	12.00
❏ 799	PS	Cryin' on My Knees/Big Time	1966	6.25	12.50	25.00

Columbia

❏ 44062		Shake Hands and Walk Away Cryin'/Escape	1967	3.75	7.50	15.00
❏ 44177		Self Expression/Back to the Days of the Romans	1967	3.75	7.50	15.00
❏ 44240		(I Remember) Gina/Escape	1967	3.75	7.50	15.00
❏ 44338		Back to the Days of the Romans/Don't Stop Me	1967	3.75	7.50	15.00

Epic

❏ 50244		Summer in Malibu/Ridin' in My Van	1976	3.75	7.50	15.00

MGM

✎ 13412		Lightnin' Strikes/Cryin' in the Street	1965	3.00	6.00	12.00
❏ 13473		Rhapsody in the Rain/Trapeze	1966	3.75	7.50	15.00

Original version of A-side had racy (by 1966 standards) lyrics: "We were makin' out in the rain/And in this car, our love went much too far." We're not sure how to identify this without playing it. See below listing.

❏ 13473		Rhapsody in the Rain/Trapeze	1966	3.75	7.50	15.00

Revised A-side has altered lyrics: "We fell in love in the rain/And in this car, love came like a falling star." While we're reasonably sure this exists -- we've heard it played on the radio off a 45 -- we've never found a copy of the revised version.

❏ 13473	PS	Rhapsody in the Rain/Trapeze	1966	5.00	10.00	20.00
❏ 13533		Painter/Du Ronda	1966	2.50	5.00	10.00
❏ 13533	PS	Painter/Du Ronda	1966	5.00	10.00	20.00
❏ 13576		If My Car Could Only Talk/Song of Lita	1966	2.50	5.00	10.00
❏ 13623		Since I Don't Have You/Wild Life's in Season	1966	2.50	5.00	10.00

Midland Int'l.

❏ MB-10848		You're Gonna Make Love to Me/Fantasies	1976	3.75	7.50	15.00
❏ MB-10959		Spanish Wine/Dancing in the Sand	1977	3.75	7.50	15.00

Midsong Int'l.

❏ 72013		Don't Knock My Love (Short)/Don't Knock My Love (Long)	1980	2.50	5.00	10.00

With Pia Zadora

Plateau

❏ 4551		Guardian Angels/(B-side unknown)	1981	10.00	20.00	40.00

Rhino

❏ 90105		O Holy Night (same on both sides)	1991		3.00	6.00

With the University of Pittsburgh Men's Glee Club

Roulette

❏ 4457		The Gypsy Cried/Red Sails in the Sunset	1963	5.00	10.00	20.00

White label with spokes

❏ 4457		The Gypsy Cried/Red Sails in the Sunset	1963	3.75	7.50	15.00

Pink label

❏ 4481		Two Faces Have I/All That Glitters Isn't Gold	1963	3.75	7.50	15.00
❏ 4504		How Many Teardrops/You and I (Have a Right to Cry)	1963	3.00	6.00	12.00
❏ 4527		Shy Boy/It Can Happen	1963	3.00	6.00	12.00
❏ 4545		Stay/There They Go	1964	3.75	7.50	15.00
❏ 4554		When You Dance/Maybe You'll Be There	1964	6.25	12.50	25.00

Slipped Disc

❏ 45270		Summer Days/The One and Only Original Sunshine Kid	1976	3.75	7.50	15.00

Three Brothers

❏ 400		Blue Canadian Rocky Dream/Wilma Lee and Stoney	1973	2.00	4.00	8.00
❏ 401		Beyond the Blue Horizon/Saddle the Wind	1974	2.50	5.00	
❏ 403		You Were the One/Good Morning	1974	2.00	4.00	8.00
❏ 405		Hey You Cajun/Sunbeam	1974	2.50	5.00	10.00

World

❏ 1002		The Jury/Little Did I Know	1963	7.50	15.00	30.00

Christmas Spirit

(Members of the Turtles with Linda Ronstadt)

White Whale

❏ 290		Christmas Is My Time of Year/Will You Still Believe	1968	20.00	40.00	80.00

Christy, Don - See "Sonny"

Chubby and the Turnpikes

(Some members later were in Tavares.)

Capitol

❏ 5840		I Didn't Try/I Know the Inside Story	1967	7.50	15.00	30.00

Number	Title (A Side/B Side)	Year	VG	VG+	NM

Chuck-a-Lucks, The
Bow

| ❑ 305 | Heaven Knows/Chuck-a-Luck | 1957 | 12.50 | 25.00 | 50.00 |

Candlelite

| ❑ 424 | Heaven Knows/Chuck-a-Luck | 196? | 3.00 | 6.00 | 12.00 |

Jubilee

| ❑ 5415 | Tarzan's Date/Unconditional Surrender | 1961 | 5.00 | 10.00 | 20.00 |

Lin

| ❑ 5010 | Who Am I?/The Devil's Train | 1958 | 6.25 | 12.50 | 25.00 |
| ❑ 5014 | The Magic of First Love/Disc Jockey Fever | 1958 | 12.50 | 25.00 | 50.00 |

Mel-O-Dy

| ❑ 106 | Sugar Cane Curtain/Dingbat Diller | 1963 | 6.25 | 12.50 | 25.00 |

Warner Bros.

| ❑ 5198 | Long John/Pick Up and Deliver | 1961 | 5.00 | 10.00 | 20.00 |
| ❑ 5234 | Cotton Pickin' Love/I'm Hospitalized Over You | 1961 | 5.00 | 10.00 | 20.00 |

Cinderellas, The
Columbia

| ❑ 41540 | The Trouble with Boys/Puppy Dog | 1959 | 3.75 | 7.50 | 15.00 |

Decca

| ❑ 30830 | Mr. Dee Jay/Yum Yum Yum | 1959 | 6.25 | 12.50 | 25.00 |
| ❑ 30925 | I Was Only 15/You Never Shoulda Gone Away | 1959 | 6.25 | 12.50 | 25.00 |

Dimension

| ❑ 1026 | Baby, Baby, I Still Love You/Please Don't Wake Me | 1964 | 10.00 | 20.00 | 40.00 |

Mercury

| ❑ 72394 | Fairy Tale/Mr. Happy Love | 1965 | 2.50 | 5.00 | 10.00 |

Circus Maximus
(Group features Jerry Jeff Walker.)
Vanguard

| ❑ 35063 | Lonely Man/Negative Dreamer Girl | 1968 | 5.00 | 10.00 | 20.00 |

Citations, The
(Probably more than one group)
Ballad

| ❑ 101 | I Will Stand By You/To Win the Race | 1967 | 25.00 | 50.00 | 100.00 |

Canadian American

| ❑ 136 | Mystery of Love/Magic Eyes | 1962 | 7.50 | 15.00 | 30.00 |
| | *As "Nicki North and the Citations"* | | | | |

Don-El

| ❑ 113 | It Hurts Me/Kiss in the Night | 1961 | 10.00 | 20.00 | 40.00 |

Epic

| ❑ 9603 | Moon Race/Slippin' and Slidin' | 1963 | 6.25 | 12.50 | 25.00 |

Fraternity

| ❑ 910 | The Girl Next Door/Ten Miles from Nowhere | 1963 | 5.00 | 10.00 | 20.00 |
| ❑ 992 | The Girl Next Door/Ten Miles from Nowhere | 1967 | 3.00 | 6.00 | 12.00 |

Mercury

| ❑ 72286 | Chicago/The Stomp | 1964 | 3.75 | 7.50 | 15.00 |

MGM

| ❑ 13373 | That Girl of Mine/Down Went the Curtain | 1965 | 5.00 | 10.00 | 20.00 |

Princess

| ❑ 54 | Carmen P./Everybody Philly | 1965 | 7.50 | 15.00 | 30.00 |

Roulette

| ❑ 4623 | Carmen P./Everybody Philly | 1965 | 3.75 | 7.50 | 15.00 |

Sara

| ❑ 3301 | Moon Race/Slippin' and Slidin' | 1963 | 12.50 | 25.00 | 50.00 |

Swan

| ❑ 4062 | Fiddlin' Around/Fire Ritual | 1960 | 10.00 | 20.00 | 40.00 |

Vangee

| ❑ 301 | The Girl Next Door/Ten Miles from Nowhere | 1963 | 10.00 | 20.00 | 40.00 |

City Surfers, The
Capitol

| ❑ 5002 | Beach Ball/Sun Tan Baby | 1963 | 6.25 | 12.50 | 25.00 |
| ❑ 5052 | Powder Puff/Fifty Miles to Go | 1963 | 6.25 | 12.50 | 25.00 |

City, The
(With Carole King)
Ode

❑ 113	Snow Queen/Paradise Alley	1968	3.00	6.00	12.00
❑ 117	That Old Sweet Roll/Why Are You Leaving	1968	3.00	6.00	12.00
❑ 119	(Hi-De-Ho) That Old Sweet Roll/Why Are You Leaving	1969	3.00	6.00	12.00

Clanton, Jimmy
Ace

❑ 537	I Trusted You/That's You Baby	1958	5.00	10.00	20.00
❑ 546	Just a Dream/You Aim to Please	1958	5.00	10.00	20.00
❑ 551	A Letter to An Angel/A Part of Me	1958	5.00	10.00	20.00
❑ 560	My Love Is Strong/Ship on a Stormy Sea	1959	3.75	7.50	15.00

Number		Title (A Side/B Side)	Year	VG	VG+	NM
☐ 567	M	My Own True Love/Little Boy in Love	1959	3.75	7.50	15.00
☐ 567	PS	My Own True Love/Little Boy in Love	1959	7.50	15.00	30.00
☐ 567	S	My Own True Love/Little Boy in Love	1959	7.50	15.00	30.00
☐ 575		Go, Jimmy, Go/I Trusted You	1959	6.25	12.50	25.00
		Purple label				
☐ 575		Go, Jimmy, Go/I Trusted You	1959	3.75	7.50	15.00
		Normal white label				
☐ 575	PS	Go, Jimmy, Go/I Trusted You	1959	7.50	15.00	30.00
☐ 585		Another Sleepless Night/I'm Gonna Try	1960	3.75	7.50	15.00
☐ 585	PS	Another Sleepless Night/I'm Gonna Try	1960	7.50	15.00	30.00
☐ 600		Come Back/Wait	1960	3.75	7.50	15.00
☐ 600	PS	Come Back/Wait	1960	7.50	15.00	30.00
☐ 607		What Am I Gonna Do/If I	1961	3.75	7.50	15.00
☐ 607	PS	What Am I Gonna Do/If I	1961	7.50	15.00	30.00
☐ 616		Down the Aisle/No Longer Blue	1961	3.75	7.50	15.00
☐ 616	PS	Down the Aisle/No Longer Blue	1961	7.50	15.00	30.00
		With Mary Ann Mobley				
☐ 622		I Just Wanna Make Love/Don't Look at Me	1961	3.75	7.50	15.00
☐ 622	PS	I Just Wanna Make Love/Don't Look at Me	1961	7.50	15.00	30.00
☐ 634		Lucky in Love with You/Not Like a Brother	1961	3.75	7.50	15.00
☐ 634	PS	Lucky in Love with You/Not Like a Brother	1961	7.50	15.00	30.00
☐ 641		Twist On Little Girl/Wayward Love	1962	3.75	7.50	15.00
☐ 641	PS	Twist On Little Girl/Wayward Love	1962	7.50	15.00	30.00
☐ 642		Twist On Little Girl/Wayward Love//	1962	12.50	25.00	50.00
		Green Light/Happy Times				
☐ 642	PS	Teenage Millionaire	1962	12.50	25.00	50.00
☐ 655		Just a Moment/Because I Do	1962	3.75	7.50	15.00
☐ 655	PS	Just a Moment/Because I Do	1962	7.50	15.00	30.00
☐ 664	DJ	Venus in Blue Jeans/Highway Bound	1962	6.25	12.50	25.00
		No stock copies exist with this catalog number				
☐ 668		Heart Hotel/Many Dreams	1963	3.00	6.00	12.00
☐ 8001		Venus in Blue Jeans/Highway Bound	1962	3.00	6.00	12.00
☐ 8005		Darkest Street in Town/Dreams of a Fool	1962	2.50	5.00	10.00
☐ 8006		Endless Nights/Another Day, Another Heartache	1963	2.50	5.00	10.00
☐ 8007		Cindy/I Care Enough (To Give the Very Best)	1963	2.50	5.00	10.00
Imperial						
☐ 66242		Absence of Lisa/C'mon Jim	1967	2.00	4.00	8.00
☐ 66274		Calico Junction/I'll Be Loving You	1968	2.00	4.00	8.00
Laurie						
☐ 3508		Curly/The Girl Who Cried Love (Once Too Often)	1969	2.00	4.00	8.00
☐ 3508		Curly/I'll Never Forget Your Love	1969	2.50	5.00	10.00
☐ 3534		Tell Me/I'll Never Forget Your Love	1969	2.00	4.00	8.00
Mala						
☐ 500		Hurting Each Other/Don't Keep Your Friends Away	1965	2.50	5.00	10.00
☐ 516		Everything I Touch Turns to Tears/That Special Way	1965	2.50	5.00	10.00
Philips						
☐ 40161		Red Don't Go with Blue/All the Words in the World	1963	2.50	5.00	10.00
☐ 40181		I'll Step Aside/I Won't Cry Anymore	1964	2.50	5.00	10.00
☐ 40208		If I'm a Fool for Loving You/A Million Drums	1964	2.50	5.00	10.00
☐ 40219		Follow the Sun/Lock the Windows	1964	2.50	5.00	10.00
Spiral						
☐ 3406		The Coolest Hot Pants/(Instrumental)	1971		2.50	5.00
Starcrest						
☐ 078	DJ	Old Rock 'N Roller (mono/stereo)	1978		2.50	5.00
		May be promo only				
Starfire						
☐ 104		I Wanna Go Home/You Kissed a Fool Goodbye	1976		2.50	5.00
Vin						
☐ 1028		What Am I Living For/Wedding Blues	1962	2.50	5.00	10.00

Clark, Chris

Motown

Number		Title (A Side/B Side)	Year	VG	VG+	NM
☐ 1114		From Head to Toe/The Beginning of the End	1967	3.75	7.50	15.00
☐ 1121		Whisper You Love Me Boy/The Beginning of the End	1968	3.75	7.50	15.00
V.I.P.						
☐ 25031		Do Right, Baby, Do Right/Don't Be Too Long	1965	3.75	7.50	15.00
☐ 25038		Love's Gone Mad/Put Yourself in My Place	1965	15.00	30.00	60.00
☐ 25038		Love's Gone Bad/Put Yourself in My Place	1965	5.00	10.00	20.00
		Same song as above A-side, but with corrected title				
☐ 25041		I Love You/I Want to Go Back There Again	1966	3.75	7.50	15.00

Clark, Claudine

Chancellor

Number		Title (A Side/B Side)	Year	VG	VG+	NM
☐ 1113		Party Lights/Disappointed	1962	3.75	7.50	15.00
☐ 1124		Telephone Game/Walkin' Through a Cemetery	1962	3.00	6.00	12.00
☐ 1130		Walk Me Home/Who Will You Hurt	1963	3.00	6.00	12.00
Herald						
☐ 523		Teenage Blues/Angel of Happiness	1958	10.00	20.00	40.00
Jamie						
☐ 1279		Moon Madness/(The Strength) To Be Strong	1964	2.50	5.00	10.00
☐ 1291		Buttered Popcorn/A Sometimes Thing	1964	2.50	5.00	10.00
TCF Hall						
☐ 18		Foxy/Standin' on Tip Toes	196?	2.50	5.00	10.00

Number		Title (A Side/B Side)	Year	VG	VG+	NM

Clark, Dave, Five

Congress

❏ 212		I Knew It All the Time/That's What I Said	1964	5.00	10.00	20.00
❏ 212	PS	I Knew It All the Time/That's What I Said	1964	10.00	20.00	40.00

Epic

❏ 9656		Glad All Over/I Know You	1964	3.75	7.50	15.00
❏ 9656	PS	Glad All Over/I Know You	1964	5.00	10.00	20.00
❏ 9671		Bits and Pieces/All of the Time	1964	3.00	6.00	12.00
❏ 9678		Do You Love Me/Chaquita	1964	3.00	6.00	12.00
❏ 9692		Can't You See That She's Mine/No Time to Lose	1964	3.00	6.00	12.00
❏ 9692	PS	Can't You See That She's Mine/No Time to Lose	1964	5.00	10.00	20.00
❏ 9704		Because/Theme Without a Name	1964	3.00	6.00	12.00
❏ 9704	PS	Because/Theme Without a Name	1964	5.00	10.00	20.00
❏ 9722		Everybody Knows (I Still Love You)/Ol' Sol	1964	3.00	6.00	12.00
❏ 9722	PS	Everybody Knows (I Still Love You)/Ol' Sol	1964	5.00	10.00	20.00
❏ 9739		Any Way You Want It/Crying Over You	1964	3.00	6.00	12.00
❏ 9763		Come Home/Your Turn to Cry	1965	3.00	6.00	12.00
❏ 9763	PS	Come Home/Your Turn to Cry	1965	5.00	10.00	20.00
❏ 9786		Reelin' and Rockin'/I'm Thinking	1965	3.00	6.00	12.00
❏ 9811		I Like It Like That/Hurting Inside	1965	3.00	6.00	12.00
❏ 9811	PS	I Like It Like That/Hurting Inside	1965	5.00	10.00	20.00
❏ 9833		Catch Us If You Can/On the Move	1965	3.00	6.00	12.00
❏ 9833	PS	Catch Us If You Can/On the Move	1965	5.00	10.00	20.00
❏ 9863		Over and Over/I'll Be Yours (My Love)	1965	3.00	6.00	12.00
❏ 9863	DJ	Over and Over (same on both sides)	1965	10.00	20.00	40.00
		Promo only on red vinyl				
❏ 9863	PS	Over and Over/I'll Be Yours (My Love)	1965	5.00	10.00	20.00
❏ 9882		At the Scene/I Miss You	1966	3.00	6.00	12.00
❏ 9882	PS	At the Scene/I Miss You	1966	5.00	10.00	20.00
❏ 10004		Try Too Hard/All Night Long	1966	3.00	6.00	12.00
❏ 10004	PS	Try Too Hard/All Night Long	1966	5.00	10.00	20.00
❏ 10031		Please Tell Me Why/Look Before You Leap	1966	3.00	6.00	12.00
❏ 10031	PS	Please Tell Me Why/Look Before You Leap	1966	5.00	10.00	20.00
❏ 10053		Satisfied with You/Don't Let Me Down	1966	3.00	6.00	12.00
❏ 10053	PS	Satisfied with You/Don't Let Me Down	1966	5.00	10.00	20.00
❏ 10076		Nineteen Days/Sitting Here Baby	1966	3.00	6.00	12.00
❏ 10076	PS	Nineteen Days/Sitting Here Baby	1966	5.00	10.00	20.00
❏ 10114		I've Got to Have a Reason/Good Time Woman	1966	3.00	6.00	12.00
❏ 10114	PS	I've Got to Have a Reason/Good Time Woman	1966	5.00	10.00	20.00
❏ 10144		You Got What It Takes/Doctor Rhythm	1967	3.00	6.00	12.00
❏ 10144	PS	You Got What It Takes/Doctor Rhythm	1967	5.00	10.00	20.00
❏ 10179		You Must Have Been a Beautiful Baby/ Man in the Pin Stripe Suit	1967	3.00	6.00	12.00
❏ 10179	PS	You Must Have Been a Beautiful Baby/ Man in the Pin Stripe Suit	1967	6.25	12.50	25.00
❏ 10209		A Little Bit Now/You Don't Play Me Around	1967	3.75	7.50	15.00
❏ 10209	PS	A Little Bit Now/You Don't Play Me Around	1967	5.00	10.00	20.00
❏ 10244		Red and Blue/Concentration Baby	1967	3.75	7.50	15.00
❏ 10244	PS	Red and Blue/Concentration Baby	1967	6.25	12.50	25.00
❏ 10265		Everybody Knows/Inside and Out	1967	3.75	7.50	15.00
❏ 10265	PS	Everybody Knows/Inside and Out	1967	7.50	15.00	30.00
❏ 10325		Please Stay/Forget	1968	3.75	7.50	15.00
❏ 10375		Red Balloon/Maze of Love	1968	3.75	7.50	15.00
❏ 10375	PS	Red Balloon/Maze of Love	1968	6.25	12.50	25.00
❏ 10476		Paradise (Is Half As Nice)/34-06	1969	3.75	7.50	15.00
❏ 10476	PS	Paradise (Is Half As Nice)/34-06	1969	7.50	15.00	30.00
❏ 10509		If Somebody Loves You/Best Day's Work	1969	3.75	7.50	15.00
❏ 10547		Bring It On Home to Me/Darling, I Love You	1969	3.75	7.50	15.00
❏ 10547	PS	Bring It On Home to Me/Darling, I Love You	1969	5.00	10.00	20.00
❏ 10635		Here Comes Summer/Five by Five	1970	3.75	7.50	15.00
❏ 10684		Good Old Rock and Roll (Medley)/One Night	1970	5.00	10.00	20.00
❏ 10684	PS	Good Old Rock and Roll (Medley)/One Night	1970	7.50	15.00	30.00
❏ 10704		Southern Man/If You Wanna See Me Cry	1971	10.00	20.00	40.00
❏ 10768		Won't You Be My Lady/Into Your Life	1971	5.00	10.00	20.00
❏ 10894		Rub It In/I'm Sorry Baby	1972	5.00	10.00	20.00

Epic Memory Lane

❏ 2225		Glad All Over/Bits and Pieces	1972		2.00	4.00
❏ 2230		Because/Do You Love Me	1972		2.00	4.00
❏ 2234		Any Way You Want It/Can't You See That She's Mine	1972		2.00	4.00
❏ 2239		I Like It Like That/Everybody Knows (I Still Love You)	1972		2.00	4.00
❏ 2248		Over and Over/Catch Us If You Can	1972		2.00	4.00
❏ 2294		Bring It On Home to Me/If Somebody Loves You	1972		2.00	4.00
❏ 2313		I Like It Like That/Can't You See That She's Mine	1972		2.00	4.00
❏ 2316		Come Home/You Got What It Takes	1972		2.00	4.00

Hollywood

❏ 65909		Over and Over/You Got What It Takes	1993		2.00	4.00
❏ 65909	PS	Over and Over/You Got What It Takes	1993		3.00	6.00
❏ 65910		I Like It Like That/Reelin' and Rockin'	1993		2.00	4.00
❏ 65910	PS	I Like It Like That/Reelin' and Rockin'	1993		3.00	6.00
❏ 65911		Glad All Over/Bits and Pieces	1993		2.00	4.00
❏ 65911	PS	Glad All Over/Bits and Pieces	1993		3.00	6.00
❏ 65912		Do You Love Me/Can't You See That She's Mine	1993		2.00	4.00
❏ 65912	PS	Do You Love Me/Can't You See That She's Mine	1993		3.00	6.00
❏ 65913		Catch Us If You Can/Try Too Hard	1993		2.00	4.00
❏ 65913	PS	Catch Us If You Can/Try Too Hard	1993		3.00	6.00
❏ 65914		Because/Everybody Knows (I Still Love You)	1993		2.00	4.00
❏ 65914	PS	Because/Everybody Knows (I Still Love You)	1993		3.00	6.00

Number		Title (A Side/B Side)	Year	VG	VG+	NM
❑ 65915		Any Way You Want It/Come Home	1993		2.00	4.00
❑ 65915	PS	Any Way You Want It/Come Home	1993		3.00	6.00

Jubilee

Number		Title (A Side/B Side)	Year	VG	VG+	NM
❑ 5476		Chaquita/In Your Heart	1964	7.50	15.00	30.00

Laurie

Number		Title (A Side/B Side)	Year	VG	VG+	NM
❑ 3188		I Walk the Line/First Love	1963	12.50	25.00	50.00

Rust

Number		Title (A Side/B Side)	Year	VG	VG+	NM
❑ 5078		I Walk the Line/First Love	1964	10.00	20.00	40.00

Clark, Dee

Abner

Number		Title (A Side/B Side)	Year	VG	VG+	NM
❑ 1019		Nobody But You/When I Call on You	1958	6.25	12.50	25.00
❑ 1026		Just Keep It Up/Whispering Grass	1959	6.25	12.50	25.00
❑ 1029		Hey Little Girl/If It Wasn't for Love	1959	6.25	12.50	25.00
❑ 1029	PS	Hey Little Girl/If It Wasn't for Love	1959	12.50	25.00	50.00
❑ 1032		How About That/Blues Get Off My Shoulder	1959	6.25	12.50	25.00
❑ 1037		At My Front Door/Cling-a-Ling	1960	6.25	12.50	25.00

Chelsea

Number		Title (A Side/B Side)	Year	VG	VG+	NM
❑ 3025		Ride a Wild Horse/(Instrumental)	1975		2.50	5.00

Columbia

Number		Title (A Side/B Side)	Year	VG	VG+	NM
❑ 44200		In These Very Tender Moments/Lost Girl	1967	2.00	4.00	8.00

Constellation

Number		Title (A Side/B Side)	Year	VG	VG+	NM
❑ 108		Crossfire Time/I'm Going Home	1963	3.00	6.00	12.00
❑ 113		It's Raining/That's My Girl	1964	3.00	6.00	12.00
❑ 120		Come Closer/That's My Girl	1964	3.00	6.00	12.00
❑ 132		Warm Summer Breeze/Heartbreak	1964	3.00	6.00	12.00
❑ 142		Ain't Gonna Be Your Fool/In My Apartment	1964	3.00	6.00	12.00
❑ 147		T.C.B./It's Impossible	1965	3.00	6.00	12.00
❑ 155		I Can't Run Away/She's My Baby	1965	3.00	6.00	12.00
❑ 165		I Don't Need (Nobody Like You)/Hot Potatoe	1966	3.00	6.00	12.00
❑ 173		Old Fashion Love/I'm Goin' Home	1966	3.00	6.00	12.00

Falcon

Number		Title (A Side/B Side)	Year	VG	VG+	NM
❑ 1002		Gloria/Kangaroo Hop	1957	7.50	15.00	30.00
❑ 1005		Seven Nights/24 Boy Friends	1957	10.00	20.00	40.00
❑ 1009		Oh Little Girl/Wondering	1958	10.00	20.00	40.00

Liberty

Number		Title (A Side/B Side)	Year	VG	VG+	NM
❑ 56152		24 Hours of Loneliness/ Where Did All the Good Times Go	1970		2.50	5.00

United Artists

Number		Title (A Side/B Side)	Year	VG	VG+	NM
❑ 50759		You Can Make Me Feel So Good/Old Time Religion	1971		2.50	5.00

Vee Jay

Number		Title (A Side/B Side)	Year	VG	VG+	NM
❑ 355		You're Looking Good/Gloria	1960	3.75	7.50	15.00
❑ 372		Your Friends/Because I Love You	1961	3.75	7.50	15.00
❑ 383		Raindrops/I Want to Love You	1961	5.00	10.00	20.00
❑ 394		Gotos Delluvia (Raindrops)/Livin' with Vivian	1961	3.75	7.50	15.00
		B-side by Al Smith				
❑ 409		Don't Walk Away from Me/You're Telling Our Secrets	1961	3.75	7.50	15.00
❑ 428		You Are Like the Wind/Drums in My Heart	1962	3.75	7.50	15.00
❑ 443		Dance On Little Girl/Fever	1962	3.75	7.50	15.00
❑ 462		I'm Going Back to School/Nobody But You	1962	3.75	7.50	15.00
❑ 487		I'm a Soldier Boy/Shook Up Over You	1963	3.75	7.50	15.00
❑ 532		How Is He Treating You/The Jones Boy	1963	3.75	7.50	15.00
❑ 548		Walking My Dog/Nobody But Me	1963	3.75	7.50	15.00

Wand

Number		Title (A Side/B Side)	Year	VG	VG+	NM
❑ 1177		Nobody But You (Part 1)/Nobody But You (Part 2)	1968	2.00	4.00	8.00

Warner Bros.

Number		Title (A Side/B Side)	Year	VG	VG+	NM
❑ 7720		Raindrops '73/I'm a Happy Man	1973		2.50	5.00

Clark, Doug, and the Hot Nuts

Jubilee

Number		Title (A Side/B Side)	Year	VG	VG+	NM
❑ 5536		Baby Let Me Bang Your Box Part 1/ Baby Let Me Bang Your Box Part 2	1966	5.00	10.00	20.00
❑ 5546		Milk the Cow/Go, Doug, Go	1966	3.75	7.50	15.00

Clark, Gene

(Also see "Byrds, The")

Asylum

Number		Title (A Side/B Side)	Year	VG	VG+	NM
❑ 45222		Life's Greatest Fool/From a Silver Petal	1974		2.50	5.00

Columbia

Number		Title (A Side/B Side)	Year	VG	VG+	NM
❑ 43903		Echoes/I Found You	1966	3.75	7.50	15.00
❑ 43903	PS	Echoes/I Found You	1966	75.00	150.00	300.00
❑ 44088		Is Yours Mine/So You Say You Lost Your Baby	1967	3.75	7.50	15.00

RSO

Number		Title (A Side/B Side)	Year	VG	VG+	NM
❑ 876		Home Run King/Lonely Saturday	1977		2.50	5.00

Clark, Petula

ABC Dunhill

Number		Title (A Side/B Side)	Year	VG	VG+	NM
❑ 15007		Never Been a Horse That Couldn't Be Rode/ I'm the Woman You Need	1974		2.50	5.00
❑ 15019		Loving Arms/I'm the Woman You Need	1974		2.50	5.00

Coral

Number		Title (A Side/B Side)	Year	VG	VG+	NM
❑ 60971		Song of the Mermaid/Tell Me Truly	1953	6.25	12.50	25.00
❑ 61077		Where Did My Snowman Go/Three Little Kittens	1953	6.25	12.50	25.00

Number	Title (A Side/B Side)	Year	VG	VG+	NM
Imperial					
☐ 5582	The Little Blue Man/Baby Lover	1959	5.00	10.00	20.00
☐ 5600	Where Do I Go from Here/Mama's Talkin' Soft	1959	5.00	10.00	20.00
☐ 5655	Now That I Need You/I Love a Violin	1960	5.00	10.00	20.00
King					
☐ 1371	The Little Shoemaker/Helpless	1954	6.25	12.50	25.00
Laurie					
☐ 3143	Jumble Sale/The Road	1962	3.75	7.50	15.00
☐ 3156	I Will Follow Him/Darling Cheri	1963	3.75	7.50	15.00
☐ 3236	Elle Est Finie/J'ai Tout Oublie	1964	3.75	7.50	15.00
☐ 3259	In Love/The Road	1964	3.75	7.50	15.00
☐ 3316	In Love/Darling Cheri	1965	3.00	6.00	12.00
☐ 3573	Jumble Sale/The Road	1971	3.00	6.00	
London					
☐ 10504	My Friend the Sea/With All My Love	1962	3.75	7.50	15.00
☐ 10516	Tender Love/Whistlin' for the Moon	1962	3.75	7.50	15.00
MGM					
☐ 12049	The Pendulum Song/Romance in Rome	1955	6.25	12.50	25.00
☐ 14392	My Guy/Little Bit of Lovin'	1972		2.50	5.00
☐ 14431	Wedding Song (There Is Love)/Song Without End	1972		2.50	5.00
☐ 14511	Serenade of Love/I Can't Remember	1973		2.50	5.00
☐ 14577	Gratification/I Can't Remember	1973		2.50	5.00
☐ 14673	Silver Spoon/Fixing to Live	1973		2.50	5.00
☐ 14708	Come On Home/The Old Fashioned Way	1974		2.50	5.00
Scotti Bros.					
☐ 02676	Natural Love/Because I Love Him	1982		2.00	4.00
☐ 02979	Blue Eyes Crying in the Rain/ Love Won't Always Pass You By	1982		2.00	4.00
☐ 03171	Dreamin' with My Eyes Wide Open/Afterglow	1982		2.00	4.00
Warner Bros.					
☐ 5494	Downtown/You'd Better Love Me *Originals have red labels with arrows*	1964	3.75	7.50	15.00
☐ 5494	Downtown/You'd Better Love Me *Later pressings have orange labels*	1964	2.50	5.00	10.00
☐ 5612	I Know a Place/Jack and John	1965	2.50	5.00	10.00
☐ 5643	You'd Better Come Home/Heart	1965	2.50	5.00	10.00
☐ 5661	Round Every Corner/Two Rivers	1965	2.50	5.00	10.00
☐ 5684	My Love/Where Am I Going	1965	2.50	5.00	10.00
☐ 5802	A Sign of the Times/Time for Love	1966	2.50	5.00	10.00
☐ 5835	I Couldn't Live Without Your Love/Your Way of Life	1966	2.50	5.00	10.00
☐ 5863	Who Am I/Love Is a Long Journey	1966	2.50	5.00	10.00
☐ 5882	Color My World/Take Me Home Again	1966	2.50	5.00	10.00
☐ 7002	This Is My Song/High	1967	2.50	5.00	10.00
☐ 7049	Don't Sleep in the Subway/Here Comes the Morning	1967	2.50	5.00	10.00
☐ 7073	The Cat in the Window (The Bird in the Sky)/ Fancy Dancin' Man	1967	2.50	5.00	10.00
☐ 7097	The Other Man's Grass Is Always Greener/ At the Crossroads	1967	2.50	5.00	10.00
☐ 7170	Kiss Me Goodbye/I've Got Love Going for Me *Originals have orange labels*	1968	2.50	5.00	10.00
☐ 7170	Kiss Me Goodbye/I've Got Love Going for Me *Later pressings have green labels with "W7" logo*	1968	2.00	4.00	8.00
☐ 7216	Don't Give Up/Every Time I See a Rainbow	1968	2.00	4.00	8.00
☐ 7244	American Boys/Look to the Sky	1968	2.00	4.00	8.00
☐ 7275	Happy Heart/Love Is the Only Thing	1969	2.00	4.00	8.00
☐ 7310	Look at Mine/If Somebody Loves You	1969	2.00	4.00	8.00
☐ 7343	No One Better Than You/Things Bright and Beautiful	1969	2.00	4.00	8.00
☐ 7422	Beautiful Sounds/The Song Is Love	1970	2.00	4.00	8.00
☐ 7467	The Song of My Life/Couldn't Sleep	1971	2.00	4.00	8.00
☐ 7484	I Don't Know How to Love Him (Superstar)/Maybe	1971	2.00	4.00	8.00
Warwick					
☐ 652	Romeo/Isn't It a Lovely Day	1961	5.00	10.00	20.00
Clark, Sanford					
Dot					
☐ 15481	The Fool/Lonesome for a Letter *Originals have maroon labels*	1956	12.50	25.00	50.00
☐ 15481	The Fool/Lonesome for a Letter *Second pressings have black labels*	1956	6.25	12.50	25.00
☐ 15516	A Cheat/Usta Be My Baby	1956	6.25	12.50	25.00
☐ 15534	Oooo Baby/9 Lb. Hammer	1957	6.25	12.50	25.00
☐ 15556	The Glory of Love/Darling Dear	1957	6.25	12.50	25.00
☐ 15585	Love Charms/Loo-Be-Doo	1957	6.25	12.50	25.00
☐ 15646	Swanee River Rock/The Man Who Made an Angel Cry	1957	6.25	12.50	25.00
☐ 15738	Modern Romance/Travelin' Man	1958	37.50	75.00	150.00
Jamie					
☐ 1107	Sing 'Em Some Blues/Still as the Night	1958	5.00	10.00	20.00
☐ 1120	Bad Luck/My Jealousy	1959	5.00	10.00	20.00
☐ 1129	Run Boy Run/New Kind of Fool	1959	5.00	10.00	20.00
☐ 1153	Go On Home/Pledging My Love	1960	5.00	10.00	20.00
LHI					
☐ 1203	The Son of Hickory Holler's Tramp/Black Widow Spider	1968	2.00	4.00	8.00
☐ 1213	Love Me Till Then/Farm Labor Camp No. 2	1968	2.00	4.00	8.00

Number	Title (A Side/B Side)	Year	VG	VG+	NM
MCI					
❏ 1003	The Fool/Lonesome for a Letter	1956	50.00	100.00	200.00
Ramco					
❏ 1972	The Fool '66/Step Aside	1966	3.75	7.50	15.00
❏ 1976	Shades/Once Upon a Time	1966	3.00	6.00	12.00
❏ 1979	They Call Me Country/Climbin' the Walls	1967	3.00	6.00	12.00
❏ 1987	It's Nothing to Me/Calling All Hearts	1967	3.00	6.00	12.00
❏ 1992	The Big Lie/Where's the Floor	1967	3.00	6.00	12.00
Trey					
❏ 3016	It Hurts Me Too/Guess It's Love	1961	5.00	10.00	20.00
Warner Bros.					
❏ 5473	She Taught Me/Just Blessin'	1964	3.75	7.50	15.00
❏ 5624	Houston/Hard Feelings	1965	3.75	7.50	15.00

Class-Notes, The

Number	Title (A Side/B Side)	Year	VG	VG+	NM
Dot					
❏ 15786	You Inspire Me/Goodness Gracious	1958	7.50	15.00	30.00
Hamilton					
❏ 50011	Take It Back/Bessie's House	1959	15.00	30.00	60.00

Classics IV

Number	Title (A Side/B Side)	Year	VG	VG+	NM
Arlen					
❏ 746	Don't Make Me Wait/It's Too Late	1964	5.00	10.00	20.00
Capitol					
❏ 5710	Cry Baby/Pollyanna	1966	3.75	7.50	15.00
	As "The Classics"				
❏ 5816	Little Darlin'/Nothing to Lose	1966	3.75	7.50	15.00
Imperial					
❏ 66259	Spooky/Poor People	1967	2.00	4.00	8.00
❏ 66293	Soul Train/Strange Changes	1968	2.00	4.00	8.00
❏ 66304	Mama's and Papa's/Waves	1968	2.00	4.00	8.00
❏ 66328	Stormy/Ladies' Man	1968	5.00	10.00	20.00
❏ 66328	Stormy/24 Hours of Loneliness	1968	2.00	4.00	8.00
❏ 66352	Traces/Mary, Mary Row Your Boat	1969	2.00	4.00	8.00
❏ 66378	Everyday With You Girl/Sentimental Lady	1969	2.00	4.00	8.00
Note: Starting here, records are "Dennis Yost and the Classics IV"					
❏ 66393	Change of Heart/Rainy Day	1969		3.00	6.00
❏ 66424	Midnight/The Comic	1969		3.00	6.00
❏ 66439	The Funniest Thing/Nobody Loves You But Me	1970		3.00	6.00
Liberty					
❏ 56182	God Knows I Loved Her/We Miss You	1970		3.00	6.00
❏ 56200	Where Did All the Good Times Go/Ain't It the Truth	1970		3.00	6.00
MGM					
❏ 14785	My First Day Without You/Lovin' Each Other	1975		2.00	4.00
MGM South					
❏ 7002	What Am I Crying For/All in Your Mind	1972		2.50	5.00
❏ 7012	Rosanna/One Man Show	1973		2.50	5.00
❏ 7016	Save the Sunlight/Make Me Believe It	1973		2.50	5.00
❏ 7020	I Knew It Would Happen/Love Me or Leave Me Alone	1973		2.50	5.00
❏ 7027	It's Now Winter's Day/Losing My Mind	1974		2.50	5.00
United Artists					
❏ 0125	Stormy/Spooky	1973		2.00	4.00
	"Silver Spotlight Series" reissue				
❏ 0126	Traces/Everyday with You Girl	1973		2.00	4.00
	"Silver Spotlight Series" reissue				
❏ 50777	Most of All/It's Time for Love	1971		2.50	5.00
❏ 50805	Cherry Hill Park/Pick Up the Pieces	1971		2.50	5.00

Classics, The
(Several different groups)

Number	Title (A Side/B Side)	Year	VG	VG+	NM
Bed-Stuy					
❏ 222	Again/The Way You Look Tonight	196?	2.50	5.00	10.00
Class					
❏ 219	If Only the Sky Was a Mirror/Gosh, But This Is Love	1958	5.00	10.00	20.00
Crest					
❏ 1063	Let Me Dream/You're the Prettiest One	1959	7.50	15.00	30.00
Dart					
❏ 1015	So in Love/Cinderella	1960	7.50	15.00	30.00
❏ 1024	Life Is But a Dream, Sweetheart/That's the Way	1961	50.00	100.00	200.00
❏ 1032	Angel Angela/Eenie Minie Mo	1961	12.50	25.00	50.00
Jerden					
❏ 742	Till I Met You/It Didn't Take Much	1964	2.50	5.00	10.00
Mercury					
❏ 71829	Life Is But a Dream, Sweetheart/That's the Way	1961	6.25	12.50	25.00
Musicnote					
❏ 1116	Till Then/Eenie Minie Mo	1963	6.25	12.50	25.00
	Black vinyl				
❏ 1116	Till Then/Eenie Minie Mo	1963	25.00	50.00	100.00
	Gold vinyl				

Number		Title (A Side/B Side)	Year	VG	VG+	NM
❑ 1116		Till Then/Eenie Minie Mo	1963	40.00	80.00	120.00
		Multicolor vinyl				
❑ 118		P.S. I Love You/Wrap Your Troubles in Dreams	1963	6.25	12.50	25.00
Musictone						
❑ 1114		So in Love/Cinderella	1963	5.00	10.00	20.00
❑ 6131		Too Young/Who's Laughing, Who's Crying	1964	5.00	10.00	20.00
Piccolo						
❑ 500		I Apologize/Love for Today	1965	6.25	12.50	25.00
Promo						
❑ 1010		Blue Moon/Little Boy Lost	1961	5.00	10.00	20.00
Ro-Ann						
❑ 1002		Je Vous Aime/Burning Desire	1959	250.00	500.00	1,000
Shelter						
❑ 7318		Mr. Fire Coal-Man/Flashing My Whip	1972		2.50	5.00
		B-side by Hugh Roy				
Starr						
❑ 508		Close Your Eyes/Funny Things	1960	50.00	100.00	200.00
		With Lou Christie (Also see "Christie, Lou" on Alcar)				
Stork						
❑ 2		You'll Never Know/Dancing with You	1964	6.25	12.50	25.00
Stream Line						
❑ 1028		Life Is But a Dream, Sweetheart/Nuttin' in the Noggin	1961	6.25	12.50	25.00
Top Rank						
❑ 2061		You're Everything/Burning Love	1960	3.75	7.50	15.00

Clay, Cassius
(Yes, the famous boxer later known as Muhammad Ali)
Columbia

Number		Title (A Side/B Side)	Year	VG	VG+	NM
❑ 43007		Stand By Me/I Am the Greatest	1964	6.25	12.50	25.00
❑ 43007	PS	Stand By Me/I Am the Greatest	1964	12.50	25.00	50.00
❑ ZSP 75717	DJ	Will the Real Sonny Liston Please Fall Down/ The Prediction	1964	10.00	20.00	40.00

Clay, Chris
Veltone

Number	Title (A Side/B Side)	Year	VG	VG+	NM
❑ 111	Santa Under Analysis (Part 1)/ Santa Under Analysis (Part 2)	1960	6.25	12.50	25.00

Clay, Joe
Vik

Number	Title (A Side/B Side)	Year	VG	VG+	NM
❑ 0211	Duck Tail/Sixteen Chicks	1956	25.00	50.00	100.00
❑ 0218	Get On the Right Track/Cracker Jack	1956	25.00	50.00	100.00

Clay, Tom
Big Top

Number	Title (A Side/B Side)	Year	VG	VG+	NM
❑ 3055	The Little Boy/That's All	1960	5.00	10.00	20.00

Chant

Number	Title (A Side/B Side)	Year	VG	VG+	NM
❑ 103	Marry Me/(B-side unknown)	1959	25.00	50.00	100.00

IBBB

Number	Title (A Side/B Side)	Year	VG	VG+	NM
❑ 45629	We Don't Like Them, We Love Them: Official IBBB Interview	1964	37.50	75.00	150.00

Interviews with the Beatles; the number is not on the label, but in the trail-off wax

Mowest

Number	Title (A Side/B Side)	Year	VG	VG+	NM
❑ 5002	What the World Needs Now Is Love/ Abraham, Martin and John//The Victors	1971		3.00	6.00
	Mostly orange label				
❑ 5002	What the World Needs Now Is Love/ Abraham, Martin and John//The Victors	1971		2.50	5.00
	Blue and yellow label				
❑ 5007	Whatever Happened to Love/ Baby I Need Your Loving	1971		2.00	4.00

Clayton-Thomas, David
Atco

Number	Title (A Side/B Side)	Year	VG	VG+	NM
❑ 6347	Hey Hey Hey Hey/Walk That Walk	1965	3.75	7.50	15.00

Columbia

Number	Title (A Side/B Side)	Year	VG	VG+	NM
❑ 45569	Sing a Song/We're All Meat from the Same Bone	1972		2.50	5.00
❑ 45603	North Beach Racetrack/Magnificent Sanctuary Band	1972		2.50	5.00
❑ 45675	Yesterday's Music/Falling by Degrees	1972		2.50	5.00

Decca

Number	Title (A Side/B Side)	Year	VG	VG+	NM
❑ 32556	Say Boss Man/Done Somebody Wrong	1969	2.50	5.00	10.00

Epic

Number	Title (A Side/B Side)	Year	VG	VG+	NM
❑ 03792	I Can't Blame a Broken Heart/ Some Hearts Get All the Breaks	1983		2.00	4.00

RCA Victor

Number	Title (A Side/B Side)	Year	VG	VG+	NM
❑ 74-0966	Hernando's Hideaway/Harmony Junction	1973		2.00	4.00
❑ APBO-0078	Workin' on the Railroad/Prof. Longhair	1973		2.00	4.00
❑ APBO-0216	Yolanda/Workin' on the Railroad	1974		2.00	4.00
❑ APBO-0296	Take the Money and Run/Anytime... Babe	1974		2.00	4.00

Number		Title (A Side/B Side)	Year	VG	VG+	NM
Roulette						
❏ 7048		No, No, No/Monopoly	1969	2.50	5.00	10.00
Tower						
❏ 206		Take Me Back/Out of the Sunshine	1966	3.00	6.00	12.00
❏ 263		Born with the Blues/Brainwashed	1966	3.00	6.00	12.00

Clee-Shays, The
Triumph
| ❏ 65 | | The Man from U.N.C.L.E./Dynamite | 1966 | 5.00 | 10.00 | 20.00 |

Cleftones, The
Classic Artists
❏ 121		She's So Fine/Trudy	1990		2.00	4.00
Gee						
❏ 1000		You Baby You/I Was Dreaming	1955	12.50	25.00	50.00
❏ 1011		Little Girl of Mine/You're Driving Me Mad	1956	7.50	15.00	30.00
❏ 1016		Can't We Be Sweethearts/Niki-Hoeky	1956	7.50	15.00	30.00
❏ 1025		String Around My Heart/Happy Memories	1956	7.50	15.00	30.00
❏ 1031		Why Do You Do Me Like You Do/ I Like Your Style of Making Love	1957	7.50	15.00	30.00
❏ 1038		See You Next Year/Ten Pairs of Shoes	1957	7.50	15.00	30.00
❏ 1041		Hey Babe/What Did I Do That Was Wrong	1957	7.50	15.00	30.00
❏ 1048		Lover Boy/Beginners in Love	1958	7.50	15.00	30.00
❏ 1064		Heart and Soul/How Do You Feel	1961	5.00	10.00	20.00
❏ 1067		(I Love You) For Sentimental Reasons/'Deed I Do	1961	5.00	10.00	20.00
❏ 1074		Earth Angel/Blues in the Night	1961	5.00	10.00	20.00
❏ 1077		Again/Do You	1961	5.00	10.00	20.00
❏ 1079		Lover Come Back to Me/There She Goes	1962	5.00	10.00	20.00
❏ 1080		How Deep Is the Ocean/Some Kinda Blue	1962	5.00	10.00	20.00
Roulette						
❏ 4094		Trudy/She's So Fine	1958	6.25	12.50	25.00
❏ 4161		Mish Mash Baby/Cuzin Casanova	1959	6.25	12.50	25.00
❏ 4302		She's Gone/Shadows on the Very Last Row	1960	6.25	12.50	25.00
Ware						
❏ 6001		She's Forgotten You/Right from the Git Go	1964	3.75	7.50	15.00

Clement, Jack
Sun
| ❏ 291 | | Ten Years/Your Lover Boy | 1958 | 6.25 | 12.50 | 25.00 |
| ❏ 311 | | The Black Haired Man/Wrong | 1958 | 6.25 | 12.50 | 25.00 |

Cliff, Benny
Drift
| ❏ 1441 | | Shake Um Up Rock/The Breaking Point | 1959 | 1,000 | 2,000 | 3,000 |

Clifford, Buzz
A&M
❏ 878		Just Can't Wait/On My Way	1967	2.50	5.00	10.00
Capitol						
❏ 5880		Bored to Tears/Swing in My Back Yard	1967	2.50	5.00	10.00
Columbia						
❏ 41774		Hello, Mr. Moonlight/Blue Lagoon	1960	5.00	10.00	20.00
❏ 41876		Baby Sitter Boogie/Driftwood	1960	6.25	12.50	25.00
❏ 41876		Baby Sittin' Boogie/Driftwood	1960	5.00	10.00	20.00
❏ 41876	PS	Baby Sittin' Boogie/Driftwood	1960	12.50	25.00	50.00
❏ 41979		Three Little Fishes/Just Because	1961	5.00	10.00	20.00
❏ 41979	PS	Three Little Fishes/Just Because	1961	12.50	25.00	50.00
❏ 42019		I'll Never Forget/The Awakening	1961	12.50	25.00	50.00
❏ 42019	PS	I'll Never Forget/The Awakening	1961	20.00	40.00	80.00
❏ 42177		Moving Day/Loneliness	1961	5.00	10.00	20.00
❏ 42177	PS	Moving Day/Loneliness	1961	12.50	25.00	50.00
❏ 42290		Forever/Magic Circle	1962	6.25	12.50	25.00
❏ 42290	PS	Forever/Magic Circle	1962	12.50	25.00	50.00
Dot						
❏ 17329		(Baby I Could Be) So Good At Loving You/ Children Are Crying Aloud	1970		3.00	6.00
❏ 17344		Procter and Gunther/I Am the River	1971		3.00	6.00
RCA Victor						
❏ 47-8935		Until Then/Let Her Go (It's All Right)	1966	3.00	6.00	12.00
Roulette						
❏ 4451		No One Loves Me Like You Do/More Dead Than Alive	1962	3.75	7.50	15.00

Climates, The
Holiday Inn
❏ 2206		Don't Be Cruel/Tell Him Tonite	1967	3.00	6.00	12.00
Sun						
❏ 404		No You for Me/Breaking Up Again	1967	6.25	12.50	25.00

Climbers, The
J&S
| ❏ 1652/3 | | My Darlin' Dear/Angels in Heaven Know I Love You | 1957 | 25.00 | 50.00 | 100.00 |
| ❏ 1658 | | I Love You/Train, Car, Boat or Plane | 1957 | 200.00 | 400.00 | 800.00 |

Number		Title (A Side/B Side)	Year	VG	VG+	NM

Cline, Patsy
4 Star
| ❏ 1033 | | Life's Railway to Heaven/If I Could See the World | 1978 | | 2.50 | 5.00 |

Coral
❏ 61464		A Church, a Courtroom, Then Goodbye/ Honky Tonk Merry-Go-Round	1955	7.50	15.00	30.00
❏ 61523		Turn the Cards Slowly/Hidin' Out	1955	7.50	15.00	30.00
❏ 61583		I Love You Honey/Come Right In	1956	6.25	12.50	25.00

Decca
❏ 29963		Stop, Look and Listen/I've Loved and Lost Again	1956	5.00	10.00	20.00
❏ 30221		Walkin' After Midnight/ A Poor Man's Roses (Or a Rich Man's Gold)	1957	5.00	10.00	20.00
❏ 30339		Try Again/Today, Tomorrow and Forever	1957	3.75	7.50	15.00
❏ 30406		Three Cigarettes in an Ashtray/A Stranger in My Arms	1957	3.75	7.50	15.00
❏ 30504		I Don't Wanta/Then You'll Know	1957	3.75	7.50	15.00
❏ 30542		Stop the World/Walking Dream	1958	3.75	7.50	15.00
❏ 30659		Come On In/Let the Teardrops Fall	1958	3.75	7.50	15.00
❏ 30706		Never No More/I Can See an Angel	1958	3.75	7.50	15.00
❏ 30746		Just Out of Reach (Of My Two Open Arms)/ If I Could See The World	1958	3.75	7.50	15.00
❏ 30794		Dear God/He Will Do for You	1958	3.75	7.50	15.00
❏ 30846		Yes, I Understand/Cry Not for Me	1959	3.75	7.50	15.00
❏ 30929		Got a Lot of Rhythm in My Soul/I'm Blue Again	1959	5.00	10.00	20.00
❏ 31061		Lovesick Blues/How Can I Face Tomorrow	1960	3.00	6.00	12.00
❏ 31128		There He Goes/Crazy Dream	1960	3.00	6.00	12.00
❏ 31205		I Fall to Pieces/Lovin' in Vain	1961	3.00	6.00	12.00
❏ 31317		Crazy/Who Can I Count On	1961	3.00	6.00	12.00
❏ 31354		She's Got You/Strange	1962	3.00	6.00	12.00
❏ 31377		When I Get Thru with You (You'll Love Me Too)/ Imagine That	1962	3.00	6.00	12.00
❏ 31377	PS	When I Get Thru with You (You'll Love Me Too)/ Imagine That	1962	6.25	12.50	25.00
❏ 31406		So Wrong/You're Stronger Than Me	1962	3.00	6.00	12.00
❏ 31429		Heartaches/Why Can't He Be You	1962	3.00	6.00	12.00
❏ 31455		Leavin' On Your Mind/Tra La La La La Triangle	1963	2.50	5.00	10.00
❏ 31455	PS	Leavin' On Your Mind/Tra La La La La Triangle	1963	6.25	12.50	25.00
❏ 31483		Sweet Dreams (Of You)/Back in Baby's Arms	1963	2.50	5.00	10.00
❏ 31522		Faded Love/Blue Moon of Kentucky	1963	2.50	5.00	10.00
❏ 31552		When You Need a Laugh/I'll Sail My Ship Alone	1963	2.50	5.00	10.00
❏ 31588		Your Kinda Love/ Someday You'll Want Me to Love You	1964	2.50	5.00	10.00
❏ 31616		Love Letters in the Sand/ That's How a Heartache Begins	1964	2.50	5.00	10.00
❏ 31671		He Called Me Baby/ Bill Bailey Won't You Please Come Home	1964	2.50	5.00	10.00
❏ 31754		Your Cheatin' Heart/ I Can't Help It (If I'm Still in Love with You)	1965	2.50	5.00	10.00

Everest
❏ 2011		Then You'll Know/Hungry for Love	1963	3.00	6.00	12.00
❏ 2020		Walking After Midnight/That Wonderful Someone	1963	3.00	6.00	12.00
❏ 2031		I Can See an Angel/Just Out of Reach	1963	3.00	6.00	12.00
❏ 2039		I've Loved and Lost Again/I Love You Honey	1964	2.50	5.00	10.00
❏ 2045		In Care of the Blues/ If I Could See the World (Through the Eyes of a Child)	1964	2.50	5.00	10.00
❏ 2052		Got a Lot of Rhythm (In My Soul)/ Love Me, Love Me, Honey Do	1964	2.50	5.00	10.00
❏ 2060		Crazy Dream/There He Goes	1965	2.50	5.00	10.00
❏ 20005		I Don't Wanta/I Can't Forget	1962	3.75	7.50	15.00

Kapp
| ❏ 659 | | Just a Closer Walk with Thee
One-sided release, possibly promo only | 1965 | 3.75 | 7.50 | 15.00 |

MCA
❏ 41303		Always/I Sail My Ship Alone	1980		2.00	4.00
❏ 51038		I Fall to Pieces/True Love	1980		2.00	4.00
❏ 52052		So Wrong/I Fall to Pieces *A-side with Jim Reeves (electronically created duet)*	1982			3.00
❏ 52684		Sweet Dreams/Blue Moon of Kentucky	1985			3.00

RCA
| ❏ PB-12346 | | Have You Ever Been Lonely
(Have You Ever Been Blue)/Welcome to My World
With Jim Reeves (electronically created duet) | 1981 | | | 3.00 |

Starday
| ❏ 7030 | | Walking After Midnight/Lovesick Blues | 1965 | 2.50 | 5.00 | 10.00 |
| ❏ 8024 | | Walking After Midnight/Lovesick Blues | 1971 | | 3.00 | 6.00 |

Clintonian Cubs, The
(Jimmy Castor was a member)
My Brothers
| ❏ 508 | | She's Just My Size/Confusion | 1960 | 75.00 | 150.00 | 300.00 |

Clique, The
ABC-Paramount
| ❏ 10655 | | She Ain't No Good/Time, Time, Time | 1965 | 2.50 | 5.00 | 10.00 |

Number		Title (A Side/B Side)	Year	VG	VG+	NM
Cinema						
❏ 001		Stay By Me/Splash One	1967	7.50	15.00	30.00
Laurie						
❏ 3365		Sun Come Up/Drifter's Melody	1966	2.50	5.00	10.00
Scepter						
❏ 12202		Stay By Me/Splash One	1967	5.00	10.00	20.00
❏ 12212		Gotta Get Away/Love Ain't Easy	1967	5.00	10.00	20.00
White Whale						
❏ 312		Superman/Shadow of Your Love	1969	3.00	6.00	12.00
❏ 323		Sugar on Sunday/Superman	1969	3.75	7.50	15.00
❏ 333		Soul Mate/I'll Hold Out My Hands	1969	2.50	5.00	10.00
❏ 338		I'm Alive/Sparkle and Shine	1970	2.50	5.00	10.00
❏ 361		Memphis/Southbound Wind	1970	2.50	5.00	10.00
❏ 367	DJ	Judy, Judy, Judy (same on both sides)	1970	3.00	6.00	12.00
		May be promo only				

Cliques, The
(With Jesse Belvin and Eugene Church)

Number		Title (A Side/B Side)	Year	VG	VG+	NM
Modern						
❏ 987		Girl in My Dreams/I Wanna Know Why	1956	12.50	25.00	50.00
		Blue label				
❏ 987		Girl in My Dreams/I Wanna Know Why	1956	7.50	15.00	30.00
		Black label				
❏ 995		My Desire/I'm in Love with a Gal	1956	7.50	15.00	30.00

Clovers, The

Number		Title (A Side/B Side)	Year	VG	VG+	NM
Atlantic						
❏ 934		Don't You Know I Love You/Skylark	1951	200.00	400.00	800.00
❏ 944		Fool, Fool, Fool/Needless	1951	62.50	125.00	250.00
❏ 963		One Mint Julep/Middle of the Night	1952	50.00	100.00	200.00
❏ 969		Ting-A-Ling/Wonder Where My Baby's Gone	1952	37.50	75.00	150.00
❏ 977		I Played the Fool/Hey, Miss Fannie	1952	50.00	100.00	200.00
❏ 989		Yes, It's You/Crawlin'	1953	37.50	75.00	150.00
❏ 1000		Good Lovin'/Here Goes a Fool	1953	37.50	75.00	150.00
❏ 1010		Comin' On/The Feeling Is So Good	1953	37.50	75.00	150.00
❏ 1022		Lovey Dovey/Little Mama	1954	12.50	25.00	50.00
❏ 1035		Your Cash Ain't Nothin' But Trash/ I've Got My Eyes on You	1954	12.50	25.00	50.00
❏ 1046		I Confess/Alrighty, Oh Sweetie	1954	12.50	25.00	50.00
❏ 1052		Blue Velvet/ If You Love Me (Why Don't You Tell Me So)	1955	12.50	25.00	50.00
❏ 1060		Love Big/In the Morning Time	1955	12.50	25.00	50.00
❏ 1073		Nip Sip/If I Could Be Loved By You	1955	12.50	25.00	50.00
❏ 1083		Devil or Angel/Hey, Doll Baby	1956	50.00	100.00	200.00
		Yellow label, no spinner				
❏ 1083		Devil or Angel/Hey, Doll Baby	1956	2,000	3,000	4,000
		Red label, no vinyl; red vinyl; value is conjecture				
❏ 1083		Devil or Angel/Hey, Doll Baby	1956	10.00	20.00	40.00
		Red label, no spinner				
❏ 1094		Love, Love, Love/Your Tender Lips	1956	10.00	20.00	40.00
❏ 1107		From the Bottom of My Heart/Bring Me Love	1956	7.50	15.00	30.00
❏ 1118		A Lonely Fool/Baby, Baby, Oh My Darling	1956	7.50	15.00	30.00
❏ 1129		Here Comes Romance/You Good-Looking Woman	1957	7.50	15.00	30.00
❏ 1139		I-I-I Love You/So Young	1957	7.50	15.00	30.00
❏ 1152		There's No Tomorrow/Down in the Alley	1957	7.50	15.00	30.00
❏ 1175		Wishing for Your Love/All About You	1958	7.50	15.00	30.00
❏ 2129		Drive It Home/The Bootie Green	1961	5.00	10.00	20.00
Brunswick						
❏ 55249		Love! Love! Love!/The Kickapoo	1963	3.00	6.00	12.00
Josie						
❏ 992		For Days/Too Long Without Some Loving	1968	2.50	5.00	10.00
❏ 997		Try My Lovin' On You/Sweet Side of a Soulful Woman	1968	2.50	5.00	10.00
Poplar						
❏ 110		The Gossip Wheel/Please Come On to Me	1958	6.25	12.50	25.00
❏ 111		The Good Old Summertime/Idaho	1958	6.25	12.50	25.00
Port						
❏ 3004		Poor Baby/He Sure Could Hypnotize	1965	2.50	5.00	10.00
Porwin						
❏ 1001/2		Stop Pretending/One More Time	1963	3.75	7.50	15.00
		As "Buddy Bailey and the Clovers"				
❏ 1004		It's All in the Game/That's What I Will Be	1963	3.75	7.50	15.00
		As "Buddy Bailey and the Clovers"				
Stenton						
❏ 7001		Please Mr. Sun/Gimme, Gimme, Gimme	1961	20.00	40.00	80.00
		As "Tippie and the Clovermen"				
Tiger						
❏ 201		Bossa Nova Baby/The Bossa Nova (My Heart Said)	1962	3.75	7.50	15.00
		As "Tippie and the Clovers"				
United Artists						
❏ 0133		Love Potion #9/Stay Awhile	1973		2.00	4.00
		"Silver Spotlight Series" reissue				
❏ 174		Rock and Roll Tango/That Old Black Magic	1959	6.25	12.50	25.00

Number	Title (A Side/B Side)	Year	VG	VG+	NM
☐ 180	Love Potion #9/Stay Awhile	1959	6.25	12.50	25.00
☐ 209	One Mint Julep/Lovey	1960	6.25	12.50	25.00
☐ 227	Easy Lovin'/I'm Confessin' That I Love You	1960	6.25	12.50	25.00
☐ 263	Yes It's You/Burning Fire	1960	6.25	12.50	25.00
☐ 307	The Honeydripper/Have Gun	1961	6.25	12.50	25.00

Winley

☐ 255	Let Me Hold You/Wrapped Up in a Dream	1961	3.75	7.50	15.00
☐ 265	I Need You Now/Gotta Quit You	1962	3.75	7.50	15.00
☐ 265	They're Rockin' Down the Street/Be My Baby	1962	3.75	7.50	15.00

As "The Fabulous Clovers"

Clusters, The

End

☐ 1115	Pardon My Heart/Darling Can't You Tell	1962	5.00	10.00	20.00

Epic

☐ 9330	Forecast of Our Love/Long Legged Maggie	1959	20.00	40.00	80.00

Tee Gee

☐ 102	Pardon My Heart/Darling Can't You Tell	1958	12.50	25.00	50.00

Coasters, The

(Also see "Robins, The")

American Int'l.

☐ 1122	If I Had a Hammer/If I Had a Hammer (Disco Version)	1976		2.50	5.00

As "The World Famous Coasters"

Atco

☐ 6064	Down in Mexico/Turtle Dovin'	1956	12.50	25.00	50.00
☐ 6073	One Kiss Led to Another/Brazil	1956	12.50	25.00	50.00
☐ 6087	Searchin'/Young Blood	1957	20.00	40.00	80.00

Maroon label (first pressing)

☐ 6087	Searchin'/Young Blood	1957	6.25	12.50	25.00

White and yellow label

☐ 6098	Idol with the Golden Head/(When She Wants Good Lovin') My Baby Comes to Me	1957	10.00	20.00	40.00
☐ 6104	Sweet Georgia Brown/What Is the Secret of Your Success	1957	10.00	20.00	40.00
☐ 6111	Dance!/Gee, Golly	1958	10.00	20.00	40.00
☐ 6116	Yakety Yak/Zing Went the Strings of My Heart	1958	7.50	15.00	30.00
☐ 6126	The Shadow Knows/Sorry But I'm Gonna Have to Pass	1958	7.50	15.00	30.00
☐ 6132	Charlie Brown/Three Cool Cats	1959	7.50	15.00	30.00
☐ 6141	Along Came Jones/That Is Rock and Roll	1959	6.25	12.50	25.00
☐ 6146	Poison Ivy/I'm a Hog for You	1959	6.25	12.50	25.00
☐ 6153	Run Red Run/What About Us	1959	6.25	12.50	25.00
☐ 6163	Besame Mucho (Part 1)/Besame Mucho (Part 2)	1960	6.25	12.50	25.00
☐ 6168	Wake Me, Shake Me/Stewball	1960	6.25	12.50	25.00
☐ 6178	Shoppin' for Clothes/The Snake and the Book Worm	1960	5.00	10.00	20.00
☐ 6186	Thumbin' a Ride/Wait a Minute	1961	5.00	10.00	20.00
☐ 6192	Little Egypt (Ying-Yang)/Keep On Rolling	1961	5.00	10.00	20.00
☐ 6204	Girls, Girls, Girls (Part 1)/Girls, Girls, Girls (Part 2)	1961	5.00	10.00	20.00
☐ 6210	Bad Blood/(Ain't That) Just Like Me	1961	5.00	10.00	20.00
☐ 6219	Teach Me How to Shimmy/Ridin' Hood	1962	5.00	10.00	20.00
☐ 6234	The Climb/((Instrumental)	1962	5.00	10.00	20.00
☐ 6251	The P.T.A./Bull Tick Waltz	1962	5.00	10.00	20.00
☐ 6287	Speedo's Back in Town/T'Ain't Nothin' to Me	1964	3.75	7.50	15.00
☐ 6300	Lovey Dovey/Bad Detective	1964	3.75	7.50	15.00
☐ 6321	Wild One/I Must Be Dreaming	1964	3.75	7.50	15.00
☐ 6341	Hungry/Lady Like	1965	3.75	7.50	15.00
☐ 6356	Money Honey/Let's Go Get Stoned	1965	3.75	7.50	15.00
☐ 6379	Bell Bottom Slacks and a Chinese Kimono (She's My Little Spodee-O)/Crazy Baby	1965	6.25	12.50	25.00
☐ 6407	Saturday Night Fish Fry/She's a Yum Yum	1966	3.75	7.50	15.00

Atlantic

☐ 89361	Yakety Yak/Stand By Me	1986			3.00
☐ 89361	PS Yakety Yak/Stand By Me	1986			3.00

B-side by Ben E. King. See listing of this record under "King, Ben E." for more information.

Chelan

☐ 2000	Searchin' '75/Young Blood	1975		2.50	5.00

As "The Coasters 2+2"

Date

☐ 1552	Soul Pad/Down Home Girl	1967	5.00	10.00	20.00
☐ 1607	Everybody's Woman/She Can	1968	5.00	10.00	20.00
☐ 1617	D.W. Washburn/Everybody's Woman	1968	5.00	10.00	20.00

King

☐ 6385	Love Potion #9/D.W. Washburn	1972		3.00	6.00
☐ 6389	Cool Jerk/Talkin' 'Bout a Woman	1972		3.00	6.00
☐ 6404	Soul Pad/D.W. Washburn	1972		3.00	6.00

Sal Wa

☐ 1001	Take It Easy, Greasy/You Move Me	1975		2.50	5.00

Turntable

☐ 504	Act Right/The World Is Changing	1969	2.50	5.00	10.00

Cobras, The

(Stevie Ray Vaughan was a member of this Cobras.)

Armadillo

☐ 79-1	Blow Joe Blow (Crazy 'Bout a Saxophone)/Sugaree	1980	25.00	50.00	100.00

Number		Title (A Side/B Side)	Year	VG	VG+	NM

Cochran Brothers
(Eddie Cochran and Hank Cochran, who were not brothers.)
Ekko

❑ 1003		Mr. Fiddle/Two Blue Singing Stars	1955	62.50	125.00	250.00
❑ 1005		Guilty Conscience/Your Tomorrow Never Comes	1955	62.50	125.00	250.00
❑ 3001		Tired and Sleepy/Fool's Paradise	1956	75.00	150.00	300.00

Cochran, Eddie
Capehart

❑ 5003		Rough Stuff/Our Love	1960	6.25	12.50	25.00
❑ 5003	PS	Rough Stuff/Our Love	1960	50.00	100.00	200.00

Crest

❑ 1026		Skinny Jim/Half Loved	1956	75.00	150.00	300.00

Liberty

❑ 55056		Sittin' in the Balcony/Dark Lonely Street	1957	7.50	15.00	30.00
❑ 55070		Mean When I'm Mad/One Kiss	1957	7.50	15.00	30.00
❑ 55070	PS	Mean When I'm Mad/One Kiss	1957	500.00	1,000	1,500
❑ 55087		Drive In Show/Am I Blue	1957	7.50	15.00	30.00
❑ 55112		Twenty Flight Rock/Cradle Baby	1957	25.00	50.00	100.00
❑ 55123		Jeannie, Jeannie, Jeannie/Pocketful of Hearts	1958	7.50	15.00	30.00
❑ 55138		Pretty Girl/Theresa	1958	8.75	17.50	35.00
❑ 55144		Summertime Blues/Live Again	1958	7.50	15.00	30.00
❑ 55166		C'mon Everybody/Don't Ever Let Me Go	1958	7.50	15.00	30.00
❑ 55177		Teen Age Heaven/I Remember	1959	7.50	15.00	30.00
❑ 55177		Teenage Heaven/I Remember	1959	10.00	20.00	40.00
		Note difference in title				
❑ 55203		The Boll Weevil Song/Somethin' Else	1959	7.50	15.00	30.00
❑ 55217		Hallelujah I Love Her So/Little Angel	1959	7.50	15.00	30.00
❑ 55242		Three Steps to Heaven/Cut Across Shorty	1960	10.00	20.00	40.00
❑ 55278		Lonely/Sweetie Pie	1960	6.25	12.50	25.00
❑ 55389		Weekend/Lonely	1961	7.50	15.00	30.00

United Artists

❑ 0014		Summertime Blues/Cut Across Shorty	1973		2.00	4.00
❑ 0015		C'mon Everybody/Twenty Flight Rock	1973		2.00	4.00
❑ 0016		Sittin' in the Balcony/Somethin' Else	1973		2.00	4.00
		0014, 0015, 0016 are "Silver Spotlight Series" reissues				

Cochran, Jackie Lee
ABC-Paramount

❑ 9930		Buy a Car/I Want You	1958	20.00	40.00	80.00

Decca

❑ 30206		Ruby Pearl/Mama Don't You Think I Know	1957	30.00	60.00	120.00

Jaguar

❑ 3031		Georgia Lee Brown/I Wanna See You	1959	30.00	60.00	120.00

Sims

❑ 107		Hip Shakin' Mama/Riverside Jump	1956	50.00	100.00	200.00

Spry

❑ 120		Pity Me/Endless Love	1959	62.50	125.00	250.00

Viv

❑ 988		I Want You/Buy a Car	1958	37.50	75.00	150.00

Cocker, Joe
A&M

❑ 928		Marjorine/New Age of the Lily	1968	2.50	5.00	10.00
❑ 991		With a Little Help from My Friends/ Something's Coming On	1968	2.50	5.00	10.00
❑ 1063		Feeling Alright/Sandpaper Cadillac	1969		3.00	6.00
		Reissued in 1971 with the same number				
❑ 1112		Delta Lady/She's So Good to Me	1969		2.50	5.00
❑ 1147		She Came In Through the Bathroom Window/ Change in Louise	1969		2.50	5.00
❑ 1147	PS	She Came In Through the Bathroom Window/ Change in Louise	1969		3.00	6.00
❑ 1174		The Letter/Space Captain	1970		2.50	5.00
❑ 1174	PS	The Letter/Space Captain	1970		3.00	6.00
❑ 1200		Cry Me a River/Please Give Peace a Chance	1970		2.50	5.00
❑ 1200		Cry Me a River/Give Peace a Chance	1970		2.50	5.00
❑ 1200	PS	Cry Me a River/Give Peace a Chance	1970		3.00	6.00
❑ 1258		High Time We Went/Black-Eyed Blues	1971		2.00	4.00
❑ 1258	PS	High Time We Went/Black-Eyed Blues	1971		3.00	6.00
❑ 1370		Midnight Rider/Woman to Woman	1972		2.00	4.00
❑ 1370	PS	Midnight Rider/Woman to Woman	1972		3.00	6.00
❑ 1407		Pardon Me Sir/St. James Infirmary Blues	1973		2.00	4.00
❑ 1407	PS	Pardon Me Sir/St. James Infirmary Blues	1973		3.00	6.00
❑ 1539		Put Out the Light/If I Love You	1974		2.00	4.00
❑ 1539	PS	Put Out the Light/If I Love You	1974		3.00	6.00
❑ 1626		I Can Stand a Little Rain/I Get Mad	1974		2.00	4.00
❑ 1641		You Are So Beautiful/ It's a Sin When You Love Somebody	1974		2.00	4.00
❑ 1749		I Think It's Going to Rain Today/Oh Mama	1975		2.00	4.00
❑ 1758		Jamaica Say You Will/It's All Over But the Shoutin'	1975		2.00	4.00
❑ 1805		The Man in Me (Part 1)/The Man in Me (Part 2)	1976		2.00	4.00
❑ 1830		Jealous Kind/You Came Along	1976		2.00	4.00

Number		Title (A Side/B Side)	Year	VG	VG+	NM
❏ 1855		I Broke Down/You Came Along	1976		2.00	4.00
❏ 2019		Feeling Alright/Cry Me a River	1978		2.00	4.00

Asylum

❏ 45540		Fun Time/Watching the River Flow	1978		2.00	4.00
❏ 46001		Lady Put the Light Out/Wasted Years	1978		2.00	4.00

Capitol

❏ B-5338		Civilized Man/A Girl Like You	1984			3.00
❏ B-5390		Crazy in Love/Come On In	1984			3.00
❏ B-5412		Edge of a Dream/Tempted	1984			3.00
❏ B-5412	PS	Edge of a Dream/Tempted	1984		2.00	4.00
❏ B-5557		Shelter Me/Tell Me There's a Way	1986			3.00
❏ B-5589		You Can Leave Your Hat On/	1986		2.50	5.00
		Long Drag of the Cigarette				
❏ B-5626		Don't Drink the Water/Don't You Love Me Anymore	1986			3.00
❏ S7-18124		The Simple Things/Unchain My Heart (90's Version)	1994			3.00
		White vinyl				
❏ B-44072		Unchain My Heart/Satisfied	1987			3.00
❏ B-44072	PS	Unchain My Heart/Satisfied	1987			3.00
❏ B-44101		Two Wrongs (Don't Make a Right)/Isolation	1987			3.00
❏ NR-44590		Living in the Promiseland/	1990		2.00	4.00
		She Came In Through the Bathroom Window (Live)				
❏ S7-57988		Feels Like Forever/When the Night Comes	1992			3.00
❏ 7PRO-79025	DJ	What Are You Doing with a Fool Like Me	1990		2.50	5.00
		(same on both sides)				
		Vinyl is promo only				
❏ 7PRO-79711	DJ	When the Night Comes (same on both sides)	1989		2.50	5.00
		Vinyl is promo only				

Island

❏ 99875		Throw It Away/Easy Rider	1983		2.00	4.00
❏ 99996		Up Where We Belong/Sweet Li'l Woman	1982		2.00	4.00
		A-side with Jennifer Warnes				
❏ 99996	PS	Up Where We Belong/Sweet Li'l Woman	1982		2.00	4.00

MCA

❏ 51177		I'm So Glad I'm Standing Here Today/Standing Tall	1981		2.00	4.00
		With the Crusaders				
❏ 51222		This Old World's Too Funky for Me/Standing Tall	1981		2.00	4.00
		With the Crusaders				
❏ 53077		Love Lives On/On My Way to You	1987		2.00	4.00

Philips

❏ 40255		I'll Cry Instead/Precious Words	1965	10.00	20.00	40.00
		Originally by "Vance Arnold and the Avengers"				
❏ 40255		I'll Cry Instead/Precious Words	1965	10.00	20.00	40.00
		Artist listed as "Joe Cocker"				

Coins, The

Gee

❏ 10		Cheatin' Baby/Blue, Can't Get No Place with You	1954	125.00	250.00	500.00
❏ 11		Look at Me Girl/S.R. Blues	1954	125.00	250.00	500.00
❏ 1007		Look at Me Girl/Two Loves Have I	1956	50.00	100.00	200.00
		B-side by the Colonials				

Model

❏ 2001		Loretta/Please	1955	125.00	250.00	500.00

Cole, Nat King

(Includes reissues of The King Cole Trio material)

Capitol

Note: Nat King Cole records on Capitol before F889 are unconfirmed on 45 rpm

❏ F889		I Almost Lost My Mind/	1950	3.75	7.50	15.00
		Baby Won't You Say You Love Me				
❏ F1010		Mona Lisa/The Greatest Inventor (Of Them All)	1950	3.75	7.50	15.00
❏ F1030		I Don't Know Why/You're the Cream in My Coffee	1950	3.75	7.50	15.00
❏ F1032		I'm in the Mood for Love/Don't Blame Me	1950	3.75	7.50	15.00
❏ F1033		(I Love You) For Sentimental Reasons/	1950	3.75	7.50	15.00
		I Can't See for Lookin'				
❏ F1034		Little Girl/What Can I Say	1950	3.75	7.50	15.00
❏ F1035		Portrait of Jenny/Lost April	1950	3.75	7.50	15.00
❏ F1036		Exactly Like You/That's What	1950	3.75	7.50	15.00
❏ F1037		Sweet Georgia Brown/I Know That You Know	1950	3.75	7.50	15.00
❏ F1038		This Way Out/Rex Rhumba	1950	3.75	7.50	15.00
❏ F1133		Home (When Shadows Fall)/Tunnel of Love	1950	3.75	7.50	15.00
❏ F1176		Get Out and Get Under/Hey, Not Now	1950	3.75	7.50	15.00
❏ F1184		Orange Colored Sky/Jambo	1950	3.75	7.50	15.00
❏ F1203		Frosty the Snow Man/A Little Christmas Tree	1950	7.50	15.00	30.00
❏ F1270		Time Out for Tears/Get to Gettin'	1951	3.00	6.00	12.00
❏ F1365		Jet/Magic Tree	1951	3.00	6.00	12.00
❏ F1401		Always You/Destination Moon	1951	3.00	6.00	12.00
❏ F1449		Too Young/That's My Girl	1951	3.00	6.00	12.00
❏ F1468		Red Sails in the Sunset/Little Child	1951	3.00	6.00	12.00
❏ F1501		Because of Rain/Song of Delilah	1951	3.00	6.00	12.00
❏ F1565		Early American/My Brother	1951	3.00	6.00	12.00

Note: Most of the Capitol 1600 series were reissues, some of them including material from 78s

❏ F1613		Sweet Lorraine/Kee-Mo Ky-Mo	1951	3.00	6.00	12.00
❏ F1627		Lost April/Calypso Blues	1951	3.00	6.00	12.00
❏ F1650		Embraceable You/Only a Paper Moon	1951	2.50	5.00	10.00

Number		Title (A Side/B Side)	Year	VG	VG+	NM
❏ F1663		Nature Boy/For All We Know	1951	2.50	5.00	10.00
❏ F1669		Makin' Whoopee/This Is My Night to Dream	1951	2.50	5.00	10.00
❏ F1672		Lush Life/I Miss You So	1951	2.50	5.00	10.00
❏ F1673		Mona Lisa/No Moon at All	1951	2.50	5.00	10.00
❏ F1674		Too Young/(I Love You) For Sentimental Reasons	1952	2.50	5.00	10.00
❏ F1689		Pretend/Unforgettable	1954	2.50	5.00	10.00
❏ F1747		Make Believe Land/I'll Always Remember You	1951	3.00	6.00	12.00
❏ F1808		Unforgettable/My First, My Last Love	1951	3.00	6.00	12.00
❏ F1815		I Still See Elisa/You're OK for TV	1951	3.00	6.00	12.00
❏ F1863		Walkin'/I'm Hurtin'	1951	3.00	6.00	12.00
❏ F1893		Here's to My Lady/Miss Me	1951	3.00	6.00	12.00
❏ F1925		Wine, Women and Song/A Weaver of My Dreams	1952	3.00	6.00	12.00
❏ F1968		You Weren't There/You Will Never Grow Old	1952	2.50	5.00	10.00
❏ F1994		Easter Sunday Morning/Summer Is a Comin' On	1952	2.50	5.00	10.00
❏ F2069		Somewhere Along the Way/ What Does It Take to Make You Take Me	1952	2.50	5.00	10.00
❏ 2088		Thank You, Pretty Baby/Brazilian Love Song	1968		3.00	6.00
❏ F2130		Walking My Baby Back Home/Funny (Not Much)	1952	2.50	5.00	10.00
❏ F2212		Because You're Mine/I'm Never Satisfied	1952	2.50	5.00	10.00
❏ F2230		Faith Can Move Mountains/The Ruby and the Pearl	1952	2.50	5.00	10.00
❏ F2309		Strange/How (Do I Go About It)	1952	2.50	5.00	10.00
❏ F2346		Pretend/Don't Let Your Eyes Go Shopping	1953	2.50	5.00	10.00
❏ F2389		Can't I/Blue Gardenia	1953	2.50	5.00	10.00
❏ 2451		I'm Gonna Laugh You Right Out of My Life/People	1969		3.00	6.00
❏ F2459		I Am in Love/My Flaming Heart	1953	2.50	5.00	10.00
❏ F2498		Return to Paradise/Angel Eyes	1953	2.50	5.00	10.00
❏ F2540		A Fool Was I/If Love Is Good to Me	1953	2.50	5.00	10.00
❏ F2610		Lover Come Back to Me/That's All	1953	2.50	5.00	10.00
❏ F2616		Mrs. Santa Claus/ The Little Boy That Santa Claus Forgot	1953	5.00	10.00	20.00
❏ F2687		Answer Me, My Love/Why	1953	2.50	5.00	10.00
❏ F2734		It Happens to Be Me/Alone Too Long	1954	2.50	5.00	10.00
❏ F2803		Make Her Mine/I Envy	1954	2.50	5.00	10.00
❏ F2894		Smile/It's Crazy	1954	2.50	5.00	10.00
❏ F2949		Hajji Baba (Persian Lament)/Unbelievable	1954	2.50	5.00	10.00
❏ F2955		The Christmas Song (Merry Christmas to You)/ My Two Front Teeth (All I Want for Christmas)	1954	5.00	10.00	20.00
❏ F2985		Open Up the Doghouse/Long, Long Ago	1954	3.75	7.50	15.00
With Dean Martin						
❏ F3027		Darling Je Vous Aime Beaucoup/The Sand and the Sea	1955	2.50	5.00	10.00
❏ F3095		A Blossom Fell/If I May	1955	3.75	7.50	15.00
B-side with the Four Knights						
❏ F3136		My One Sin/Blues from Kiss Me Deadly	1955	2.50	5.00	10.00
❏ F3234		Forgive My Heart/Someone You Love	1955	2.50	5.00	10.00
❏ F3305		Take Me Back to Toyland/ I'm Gonna Laugh You Right Out of My Life	1955	5.00	10.00	20.00
❏ F3328		Ask Me/Nothing Ever Changes My Love for You	1956	2.50	5.00	10.00
❏ F3390		Too Young to Go Steady/Never Let Me Go	1956	2.50	5.00	10.00
❏ F3456		That's All There Is to That/My Dream Sonata	1956	2.50	5.00	10.00
❏ F3551		Night Lights/To the Ends of the Earth	1956	2.50	5.00	10.00
❏ F3560		Mrs. Santa Claus/Take Me Back to Toyland	1956	3.75	7.50	15.00
❏ F3561		The Christmas Song (Merry Christmas to You)/ The Little Boy That Santa Claus Forgot	1956	3.75	7.50	15.00
Original with "F" prefix, Capitol logo on top						
❏ 3561		The Christmas Song (Merry Christmas to You)/ The Little Boy That Santa Claus Forgot	1960	2.00	4.00	8.00
Purple label, Capitol logo on side						
❏ 3561		The Christmas Song (Merry Christmas to You)/ The Little Boy That Santa Claus Forgot	1962	3.00	6.00	
Orange and yellow swirl label						
❏ 3561		The Christmas Song (Merry Christmas to You)/ The Little Boy That Santa Claus Forgot	1973	2.00	4.00	
Orange label with "Capitol" at bottom						
❏ F3619		Ballerina/You Are My First Love	1957	2.50	5.00	10.00
❏ F3702		When Rock and Roll Come to Trinidad/China Gate	1957	3.75	7.50	15.00
❏ F3737		Send for Me/My Personal Possession	1957	3.75	7.50	15.00
B-side with the Four Knights						
❏ F3782		With You on My Mind/The Song of Raintree County	1957	2.50	5.00	10.00
❏ F3860		Angel Smile/Back in My Arms	1957	2.50	5.00	10.00
❏ F3939		Looking Back/Do I Like It	1958	2.50	5.00	10.00
❏ F4004		Come Closer to Me/Nothing in the World	1958	2.50	5.00	10.00
❏ F4056		Non Dimenticar (Don't Forget)/Bend a Little My Way	1958	2.50	5.00	10.00
❏ F4125		Madrid/Give Me Your Love	1959	2.50	5.00	10.00
❏ F4184		You Made Me Love You/I Must Be Dreaming	1959	2.50	5.00	10.00
❏ F4248		Sweet Bird of Youth/Midnight Flyer	1959	2.50	5.00	10.00
❏ F4248	PS	Sweet Bird of Youth/Midnight Flyer	1959	7.50	15.00	30.00
❏ 4301		The Happiest Christmas Tree/Buon Natale	1959	3.00	6.00	12.00
❏ 4325		What'cha Gonna Do/Time and the River	1960	2.00	4.00	8.00
❏ 4369		Is It Better to Have Loved and Lost/That's You	1960	2.00	4.00	8.00
❏ 4393		My Love/Steady	1960	2.00	4.00	8.00
❏ 4481		If I Knew/World in My Arms	1960	2.00	4.00	8.00
❏ 4519		Illusion/When It's Summer	1961	2.00	4.00	8.00
❏ 4555		Goodnight, Little Leaguer/The First Baseball Game	1961	2.00	4.00	8.00
❏ 4582		Take a Fool's Advice/Make It Last	1961	2.00	4.00	8.00
❏ 4623		Let True Love Begin/Cappuccina	1961	2.00	4.00	8.00
❏ 4672		Magic Moment/Step Right Up	1961	2.00	4.00	8.00
❏ 4714		Look No Further/The Right Thing to Say	1962	2.00	4.00	8.00
❏ 4804		Ramblin' Rose/Good Times	1962	3.00	6.00	12.00

Number		Title (A Side/B Side)	Year	VG	VG+	NM
❏ 4804	PS	Ramblin' Rose/Good Times	1962	5.00	10.00	20.00
❏ 4870		Dear Lonely Hearts/Who's Next in Line	1962	3.00	6.00	12.00
❏ 4870	PS	Dear Lonely Hearts/Who's Next in Line	1962	5.00	10.00	20.00
❏ 4919		All Over the World/Nothing Goes Up (Without Coming Down)	1963	2.00	4.00	8.00
❏ 4965		Those Lazy-Hazy-Crazy Days of Summer/ In the Cool of Day	1963	3.00	6.00	12.00
❏ 4965	PS	Those Lazy-Hazy-Crazy Days of Summer/ In the Cool of Day	1963	5.00	10.00	20.00
❏ 5027		That Sunday, That Summer/Mr. Wishing Well	1963	3.00	6.00	12.00
❏ 5125		My True Carrie, Love/A Rag, A Bone, A Hank of Hair	1964	2.00	4.00	8.00
❏ 5155		I Don't Want to Be Hurt Anymore/People	1964	2.00	4.00	8.00
❏ 5219		Marnie/More and More of the Amore	1964	2.00	4.00	8.00
❏ 5261		L-O-V-E/I Don't Want to See Tomorrow	1964	2.00	4.00	8.00
❏ 5412		The Ballad of Cat Ballou/They Can't Make Her Cry	1965	2.00	4.00	8.00
		With Stubby Kay				
❏ 5486		Wanderlust/You'll See	1965	2.00	4.00	8.00
❏ 5549		One Sun/Looking Back	1965	2.00	4.00	8.00
❏ 5683		Let Me Tell You, Babe/For the Want of a Kiss	1966	2.00	4.00	8.00
		Note: All the Capitol 15000 series on 45 are from multi-disc box sets				
❏ F15509		Straighten Up and Fly Right/Nature Boy	1950	3.75	7.50	15.00
❏ F15510		You Call It Madness/The Frim Fram Sauce	1950	3.75	7.50	15.00
❏ F15511		(Get Your Kicks on) Route 66/ Gee Baby Ain't I Been Good to You	1950	3.75	7.50	15.00
❏ F15552		Yes Sir That's My Baby/I Used to Love You	1950	3.75	7.50	15.00
❏ F15553		For All We Know/'Tis Autumn	1950	3.75	7.50	15.00
❏ F15554		Bop Kick/Laugh Cool Clown	1950	3.75	7.50	15.00
❏ F15564		Sweet Lorraine/It's Only a Paper Moon	1950	3.75	7.50	15.00
❏ F15565		The Man I Love/Body and Soul	1950	3.75	7.50	15.00
❏ F15566		Embraceable You/What Is This Thing Called Love	1950	3.75	7.50	15.00
❏ F15643		Jumpin' at Capitol/Love for Sale	1950	3.75	7.50	15.00
		B-side by Benny Carter Orchestra				
❏ F15728		Makin' Whoopee/Honeysuckle Rose	1951	3.00	6.00	12.00
❏ F15729		I'll String Along with You/Too Marvelous for Words	1951	3.00	6.00	12.00
❏ F15730		This Is My Night to Dream/Rhumba Azul	1951	3.00	6.00	12.00
❏ F15843		Return Trip/St. Louis Blues	1952	3.00	6.00	12.00
		B-side by Freddie Slack				
❏ F15868		Penthouse Serenade/If I Should Lose You	1952	3.00	6.00	12.00
❏ F15869		Somebody Loves Me/Down by the Old Mill Stream	1952	3.00	6.00	12.00
❏ F15870		Laura/Polka Dots and Moonbeams	1952	3.00	6.00	12.00
❏ F15922		Walkin' My Baby Back Home/Kay's Lament	1952	3.00	6.00	12.00
		B-side by Kay Starr				
❏ S7-57887		The Christmas Song/O Holy Night	1992		2.00	4.00
		Originals on black vinyl				
❏ S7-57887		The Christmas Song/O Holy Night	1993			3.00
		Second pressing on red vinyl				
❏ F90036		(All I Want for Christmas Is) My Two Front Teeth/ The Christmas Song (Merry Christmas To You)	1949	5.00	10.00	20.00
		B-side is the original King Cole Trio version, possibly its only U.S. release on 45				
Tampa						
❏ 134		Vom-Vim-Veedle/All for You	1957	3.00	6.00	12.00
❏ 134	PS	Vom-Vim-Veedle/All for You	1957	6.25	12.50	25.00

Collectors, The
Valiant

Number	Title (A Side/B Side)	Year	VG	VG+	NM
❏ 760	Old Man/Looking at a Baby	1967	7.50	15.00	30.00

Warner Bros.

Number	Title (A Side/B Side)	Year	VG	VG+	NM
❏ 7059	Listen to the Words/Fisherwoman	1967	5.00	10.00	20.00
❏ 7159	Make It Easy/Fat Bird	1968	5.00	10.00	20.00
❏ 7194	Lydia Purple/I Ain't No Rich Man	1968	3.00	6.00	12.00
❏ 7194	Lydia Purple/She (Will O' the Wind)	1968	3.75	7.50	15.00
❏ 7300	Early Morning/My Love Delights Me	1969	3.00	6.00	12.00

Collegians, The
(More than one group)
Cat

Number	Title (A Side/B Side)	Year	VG	VG+	NM
❏ 110	Rickety Tickety Melody/ The Sackbut, the Psaltery and the Dulcimer	1954	6.25	12.50	25.00

Groove

Number	Title (A Side/B Side)	Year	VG	VG+	NM
❏ 0163	Blue Solitude/Please Let Me Be the One	1956	10.00	20.00	40.00

Hilltop

Number	Title (A Side/B Side)	Year	VG	VG+	NM
❏ 1866	Nomad/Fred's Boogie	1960	5.00	10.00	20.00
❏ 1867	The Saints (Part 1)/The Saints (Part 2)	1960	5.00	10.00	20.00
❏ 1868	Cookin'/Happy Parakeet	1961	5.00	10.00	20.00

Post

Number	Title (A Side/B Side)	Year	VG	VG+	NM
❏ 10002	I'm Ready/Grandma Told Me So	1962	5.00	10.00	20.00

Winley

Number	Title (A Side/B Side)	Year	VG	VG+	NM
❏ 224	Zoom, Zoom, Zoom/On Your Merry Way	1958	12.50	25.00	50.00
❏ 261	Oh I Need Your Love/Tonite, Oh Tonite	1962	7.50	15.00	30.00
❏ 263	Right Around the Corner/Teenie Weenie Little Bit	1962	7.50	15.00	30.00

Number		Title (A Side/B Side)	Year	VG	VG+	NM

X-Tra

❑ 108		Let's Go for a Ride/Heavenly Ride	1958	100.00	200.00	400.00
		Small print label (title and artist about 1/8-inch high)				
❑ 108		Let's Go for a Ride/Heavenly Ride	1961	15.00	30.00	60.00
		Large print label (title and artist about 1/4-inch high)				

Collins, Big Tom
King

❑ 4483		Heartache Blues/Real Good Feeling	1951	25.00	50.00	100.00
❑ 4568		Heart Breaking Woman/Watchin' My Stuff	1952	25.00	50.00	100.00

Colts, The
Antler

❑ 4003		Never No More/The Shiek of Araby	1959	10.00	20.00	40.00
❑ 4007		Guiding Angel/The Shiek of Araby	1959	10.00	20.00	40.00

Mambo

❑ 112		Adorable/Lips Red as Wine	1955	75.00	150.00	300.00

Plaza

❑ 505		Hey, Pretty Baby/Sweet Sixteen	1962	5.00	10.00	20.00

Vita

❑ 112		Adorable/Lips Red as Wine	1955	25.00	50.00	100.00
❑ 121		Honey Bun/Sweet Sixteen	1955	20.00	40.00	80.00
❑ 130		Never No More/Hey You Shoo-Bee-Ooh-Bee	1956	20.00	40.00	80.00

Commodores, The
(The Motown, Mowest and Polydor records are by the popular soul group; the others are not. Also see "Richie, Lionel")
Atlantic

❑ 2633		Keep On Dancing/Rise Up	1969	2.00	4.00	8.00

Brunswick

❑ 55126		Laughing with Tears/Who Dat	1959	5.00	10.00	20.00

Challenge

❑ 1004		Sweet Angel/Not a Day Goes By	1957	5.00	10.00	20.00
❑ 1007		Faith/I'll Be There	1957	5.00	10.00	20.00

Dot

❑ 15372		Uranium/Riding on a Train	1955	6.25	12.50	25.00
❑ 15425		Cream Puff/Close to My Heart	1955	6.25	12.50	25.00
❑ 15439		Speedoo/Whole Lotta Shakin' Goin' On	1956	6.25	12.50	25.00
❑ 15461		Two Loves Have I/Who Said I Said That	1956	6.25	12.50	25.00

Motown

❑ 1268		Are You Happy/There's a Song in My Heart	1973		3.00	6.00
❑ 1307		Machine Gun/There's a Song in My Heart	1974		2.50	5.00
❑ 1319		I Feel Sanctified/It Is As Good As You Make It	1974		2.50	5.00
❑ 1338		Slippery When Wet/The Bump	1975		2.50	5.00
❑ 1361		This Is Your Life/Look What You've Done to Me	1975		2.50	5.00
❑ 1366		Wide Open/(B-side unassigned)	1975			Unreleased
❑ 1381		Sweet Love/Better Never Than Forever	1976		2.00	4.00
❑ 1394		Come Inside/Time	1976			Unreleased
❑ 1399		High on Sunshine/Thumpin' Music	1976			Unreleased
❑ 1402		Just to Be Close to You/Thumpin' Music	1976		2.00	4.00
❑ 1408		Fancy Dancer/Cebu	1977		2.00	4.00
❑ 1418		Easy/Can't Let You Tease Me	1977		2.00	4.00
❑ 1425		Brick House/Captain Quickdraw	1977		2.00	4.00
❑ 1432		Too Hot Ta Trot/Funky Situation	1977		2.00	4.00
❑ 1443		Three Times a Lady/Look What You've Done to Me	1978		2.00	4.00
❑ 1452		Flying High/X-Rated Movie	1978		2.00	4.00
❑ 1457		Say Yeah/(B-side unassigned)	1978			Unreleased
❑ 1466		Sail On/Thumpin' Music	1979		2.00	4.00
❑ 1474		Still/Such a Woman	1979		2.00	4.00
❑ 1479		Wonderful/Lovin' You	1979		2.00	4.00
❑ 1489		Old Fashion Love/Sexy Lady	1980		2.00	4.00
❑ 1495		Heroes/Funky Situation	1980		2.00	4.00
❑ 1502		Jesus Is Love/Mighty Spirit	1980		3.00	6.00
❑ 1514		Lady (You Bring Me Up)/Gettin' It	1981		2.00	4.00
❑ 1527		Oh No/Lovin' You	1981		2.00	4.00
❑ 1604		Why You Wanna Try Me/X-Rated Movie	1982		2.00	4.00
❑ 1651		Painted Pictures/Reach High	1982			3.00
❑ 1661		Sexy Lady/Reach High	1983			3.00
❑ 1694		Only You/Cebu	1983			3.00
❑ 1719		Been Lovin' You/Turn Off the Lights	1984			3.00
❑ 1773		Nightshift/I Keep Running	1985			3.00
❑ 1773	PS	Nightshift/I Keep Running	1985		3.00	6.00
❑ 1788		Animal Instinct/Lightin' Up the Sky	1985			3.00
❑ 1802		Janet/I'm in Love	1985			3.00

Mowest

❑ 5009		I'm Looking for Love/At the Zoo	1972	2.00	4.00	8.00
❑ 5038		Determination/Don't You Be Worried	1973	2.00	4.00	8.00

Polydor

❑ 871 370-7		Ain't Giving Up/Grrip	1989			3.00
❑ 885 358-7		Goin' to the Bank/Serious Love	1986			3.00
❑ 885 358-7	PS	Goin' to the Bank/Serious Love	1986			3.00
❑ 885 538-7		Take It from Me/I Wanna Rock You	1987			3.00
❑ 885 538-7	PS	Take It from Me/I Wanna Rock You	1987			3.00
❑ 885 760-7		United in Love/Talk to Me	1987			3.00
❑ 887 939-7		Solitaire/Stretchhh	1988			3.00
❑ 887 939-7	PS	Solitaire/Stretchhh	1988			3.00

Number	Title (A Side/B Side)	Year	VG	VG+	NM

Companions, The
(Several different groups)
Amy
| ❏ 852 | No Fool Am I/How Could You | 1962 | 25.00 | 50.00 | 100.00 |

Arlen
| ❏ 722 | These Foolish Things/It's Too Late | 1963 | 20.00 | 40.00 | 80.00 |

Brook's
| ❏ 100 | Why, Oh Why Baby/I Didn't Know (You Got Married) | 1959 | 15.00 | 30.00 | 60.00 |

Columbia
| ❏ 42279 | I'll Always Love You/A Little Bit of Blue | 1962 | 7.50 | 15.00 | 30.00 |

Dove
| ❏ 240 | Falling/Oh, What a Feeling! | 1958 | 30.00 | 60.00 | 120.00 |

Federal
| ❏ 12397 | Why, Oh Why Baby/I Didn't Know (You Got Married) | 1960 | 7.50 | 15.00 | 30.00 |

General American
| ❏ 711 | Be Yourself/Help a Lonely Guy | 1962 | 5.00 | 10.00 | 20.00 |

Gina
| ❏ 722 | These Foolish Things/It's Too Late | 1963 | 12.50 | 25.00 | 50.00 |

Competitors, The
Dot
| ❏ 16560 | Power Shift/Little Stick Nomad | 1963 | 10.00 | 20.00 | 40.00 |

Compliments, The
Congress
| ❏ 243 | Shake It Up, Shake It Down/You Are My Sunshine | 1965 | 12.50 | 25.00 | 50.00 |
| ❏ 252 | The Time of Her Life/Everybody Loves a Lover | 1965 | 12.50 | 25.00 | 50.00 |

Midas
| ❏ 304 | Borrow 'Til Morning/Beware, Beware | 1968 | 7.50 | 15.00 | 30.00 |

Concords, The
Boom
| ❏ 60021 | Down the Aisle of Love/I Feel Love Comin' | 1966 | 10.00 | 20.00 | 40.00 |

Ember
| ❏ 1007 | I'm Satisfied with Rock 'N' Roll/I'll Always Say Please | 1956 | 15.00 | 30.00 | 60.00 |

Epic
| ❏ 9697 | Should I Cry/It's Our Wedding Day | 1964 | 12.50 | 25.00 | 50.00 |

Gramercy
| ❏ 304 | Cross My Heart/Our Last Goodbye | 1961 | 12.50 | 25.00 | 50.00 |
| ❏ 305 | My Dreams/Scarlet Ribbons | 1961 | 10.00 | 20.00 | 40.00 |

Harlem
| ❏ 2328 | Candlelight/Monticello | 1954 | 100.00 | 200.00 | 400.00 |

Herald
| ❏ 576 | Marlene/Our Love Wasn't Meant to Be | 1962 | 3.75 | 7.50 | 15.00 |
| ❏ 578 | Cold and Frosty Morning/Don't Go Now | 1963 | 7.50 | 15.00 | 30.00 |

Polydor
| ❏ 14036 | Down the Aisle of Love/I Feel a Love Comin' On | 1970 | 3.00 | 6.00 | 12.00 |

RCA Victor
| ❏ 47-7911 | Again/The Boy Most Likely | 1961 | 6.25 | 12.50 | 25.00 |

Rust
| ❏ 5048 | One Step from Heaven/Again | 1962 | 7.50 | 15.00 | 30.00 |

Confessions, The
Epic
| ❏ 9474 | Be-Bop Baby/Before You Change Your Mind | 1961 | 6.25 | 12.50 | 25.00 |

Conley, Arthur
Atco
❏ 6463	Sweet Soul Music/Let's Go Steady	1967	2.50	5.00	10.00
❏ 6494	Shake, Rattle and Roll/You Don't Have to See Me	1967	2.00	4.00	8.00
❏ 6529	Whole Lot of Woman/Love Comes and Goes	1967	2.00	4.00	8.00
❏ 6563	Funky Street/Put Our Love Together	1968	2.00	4.00	8.00
❏ 6588	People Sure Act Funny/Burning Fire	1968	2.00	4.00	8.00
❏ 6622	Is That You Love/Aunt Dora's Love Soul Shack	1968	2.00	4.00	8.00
❏ 6640	Ob-La-Di, Ob-La-Da/Otis Sleep On	1968	2.00	4.00	8.00
❏ 6661	Speak Her Name/Run On	1969		3.00	6.00
❏ 6706	Star Review/Love Sure Is a Powerful Thing	1969		3.00	6.00
❏ 6733	Hurt/They Call the Wind Maria	1970		3.00	6.00
❏ 6747	God Bless/ (Your Love Has Brought Me A) Mighty Long Way	1970		3.00	6.00
❏ 6790	Nobody's Fault But Mine/Day-O	1970		3.00	6.00

Capricorn
❏ 0001	More Sweet Soul Music/Walking on Eggs	1972	2.50	5.00	10.00
❏ 0006	Rita/More Sweet Soul Music	1972	2.00	4.00	8.00
❏ 0047	Bless You/It's So Nice	1973	2.00	4.00	8.00
❏ 8017	I'm Living Good/I'm So Glad You're Here	1971	2.50	5.00	10.00

Fame
| ❏ 1007 | I Can't Stop/In the Same Old Way | 1966 | 3.75 | 7.50 | 15.00 |
| ❏ 1009 | Take Me (Just As I Am)/I'm Gonna Forget About You | 1966 | 3.75 | 7.50 | 15.00 |

Number		Title (A Side/B Side)	Year	VG	VG+	NM
Jotis						
❑ 470		I'm a Lonely Stranger/Where Lead Me	1965	5.00	10.00	20.00
❑ 472		Who's Fooling Who/There's a Place for Us	1966	5.00	10.00	20.00

Connors, Carol
(Also see "Carmel Sisters, The"; "Teddy Bears, The")

Number		Title (A Side/B Side)	Year	VG	VG+	NM
Capitol						
❑ 5152		Never/Angel, My Angel	1964	6.25	12.50	25.00
Columbia						
❑ 41976		You Are My Answer/My Diary	1961	6.25	12.50	25.00
❑ 42155		Listen to the Beat/My Special Boy	1961	6.25	12.50	25.00
❑ 42337		That's All It Takes/What Do You See in Him	1962	6.25	12.50	25.00
Era						
❑ 3084		Two Rivers/Big, Big Love	1962	7.50	15.00	30.00
❑ 3096		Tommy Go Away/I Wanna Know	1962	7.50	15.00	30.00
Mira						
❑ 219		Lonely Little Beach Girl/ My Baby Looks, But He Don't Touch	1965	6.25	12.50	25.00
❑ 219	PS	Lonely Little Beach Girl/ My Baby Looks, But He Don't Touch	1965	12.50	25.00	50.00
N.T.C.						
❑ 3131		Yum Yum Yamaha One-sided single	1964	12.50	25.00	50.00
❑ 3131	PS	Yum Yum Yamaha	1964	25.00	50.00	100.00

Contenders, The
(More than one group)

Number		Title (A Side/B Side)	Year	VG	VG+	NM
Blue Sky						
❑ 105		Mr. Dee Jay/Yes I Do	1959	150.00	300.00	600.00
Chattahoochie						
❑ 644		The Dune Buggy/Go Ahead	1964	6.25	12.50	25.00
❑ 656		Johnny B. Goode/Rise 'N' Shine	1964	6.25	12.50	25.00
Jackpot						
❑ 48002		Tequila Song/Wild Man	1959	10.00	20.00	40.00

Contours, The

Number		Title (A Side/B Side)	Year	VG	VG+	NM
Gordy						
❑ 7005		Do You Love Me/Move Mr. Man	1962	3.75	7.50	15.00
❑ 7012		Shake Sherry/You Better Get in Line	1963	3.75	7.50	15.00
❑ 7016		Don't Let Her Be Your Baby/It Must Be Love	1963	3.00	6.00	12.00
❑ 7019		Pa I Need a Car/You Get Ugly	1963	3.00	6.00	12.00
❑ 7029		Can You Do It/I'll Stand By You	1964	3.00	6.00	12.00
❑ 7037		Can You Jerk Like Me/That Day When She Needed Me	1964	3.00	6.00	12.00
❑ 7044		First I Look at the Purse/Searching for a Girl	1965	3.00	6.00	12.00
❑ 7052		Just a Little Misunderstanding/Determination	1966	3.00	6.00	12.00
❑ 7059		It's So Hard Being a Loser/ Your Love Grows More Precious Every Day	1967	3.00	6.00	12.00
HOB						
❑ 116		I'm So Glad/Yours Is My Heart Alone	1961	30.00	60.00	120.00
Motown						
❑ 1008		Whole Lotta Woman/Come On and Be Mine	1961	125.00	250.00	500.00
❑ 1012		The Stretch/Funny	1962	200.00	400.00	800.00
Motown Yesteryear						
❑ 448		Do You Love Me/Shake Sherry	1972		2.00	4.00
❑ 448	PS	Do You Love Me/Shake Sherry "Dirty Dancing" sleeve; without cut-out hole	1988		2.50	5.00
Rocket						
❑ 41192		I'm a Winner/Makes Me Wanna Come Back	1980		2.00	4.00
Tamla						
❑ 7012		Shake Sherry/You Better Get in Line Tamla label used in error for a Gordy release	1963	37.50	75.00	150.00

Cook, Ken

Number		Title (A Side/B Side)	Year	VG	VG+	NM
Phillips Int'l.						
❑ 3534		I Was a Fool/Crazy Baby Roy Orbison appears on this record (uncredited)	1959	10.00	20.00	40.00

Cooke, Sam

Number		Title (A Side/B Side)	Year	VG	VG+	NM
Cherie						
❑ 4501		Darling I Need You Now/Win Your Love for Me	1971	2.00	4.00	8.00
Keen						
❑ 2005		Stealing Kisses/All of My Life	1958	6.25	12.50	25.00
❑ 2006		Win Your Love for Me/Almost in Your Arms	1958	6.25	12.50	25.00
❑ 2018		Everybody Likes to Cha Cha Cha/Little Things You Do	1959	6.25	12.50	25.00
❑ 2022		Only Sixteen/Let's Go Steady Again	1959	6.25	12.50	25.00
❑ 2101		Summertime (Part 1)/Summertime (Part 2)	1959	6.25	12.50	25.00
❑ 2105		There! I've Said It Again/ One Hour Ahead of the Posse	1959	6.25	12.50	25.00
❑ 2111		'T'ain't Nobody's Bizness (If I Do)/No One	1960	6.25	12.50	25.00
❑ 2112		Wonderful World/Along the Navajo Trail	1960	6.25	12.50	25.00
❑ 2117		With You/I Thank God	1960	6.25	12.50	25.00
❑ 2118		Steal Away/So Glamorous	1960	6.25	12.50	25.00
❑ 2122		Mary, Mary Lou/Eee-Yi-Ee-Yi-Oh	1960	6.25	12.50	25.00

Number		Title (A Side/B Side)	Year	VG	VG+	NM
☐ 4002		(I Love You) For Sentimental Reasons/Desire Me	1958	6.25	12.50	25.00
☐ 4009		You Were Made for Me/Lonely Island	1958	6.25	12.50	25.00
☐ 34013		You Send Me/Summertime	1957	6.25	12.50	25.00

RCA

☐ PB-14146		Bring It On Home to Me/Nothing Can Change This Love	1985	2.00	4.00	8.00

RCA Victor

☐ 47-7701		Teenage Sonata/If You Were the Only Girl	1960	5.00	10.00	20.00
☐ 47-7730		You Understand Me/I Belong to Your Heart	1960	3.75	7.50	15.00
☐ 47-7783		Chain Gang/I Fall in Love Every Day	1960	3.00	6.00	12.00
☐ 47-7783	PS	Chain Gang/I Fall in Love Every Day	1960	6.25	12.50	25.00
☐ 47-7816		Sad Mood/Love Me	1960	3.00	6.00	12.00
☐ 47-7853		That's It-I Quit-I'm Movin' On/What Do You Say	1961	3.00	6.00	12.00
☐ 47-7883		Cupid/Farewell, My Darling	1961	3.00	6.00	12.00
☐ 47-7883	PS	Cupid/Farewell, My Darling	1961	6.25	12.50	25.00
☐ 47-7927		Feel It/It's All Right	1961	3.00	6.00	12.00
☐ 47-7983		Twistin' the Night Away/One More Time	1962	3.00	6.00	12.00
☐ 47-8036		Bring It On Home to Me/Having a Party	1962	3.00	6.00	12.00
☐ 47-8088		Nothing Can Change This Love/Somebody Have Mercy	1962	3.00	6.00	12.00
☐ 47-8088	PS	Nothing Can Change This Love/Somebody Have Mercy	1962	6.25	12.50	25.00
☐ 47-8129		Send Me Some Lovin'/Baby, Baby, Baby	1963	3.00	6.00	12.00
☐ 47-8129	PS	Send Me Some Lovin'/Baby, Baby, Baby	1963	6.25	12.50	25.00
☐ 47-8164		Another Saturday Night/Love Will Find a Way	1963	3.00	6.00	12.00
☐ 47-8164	PS	Another Saturday Night/Love Will Find a Way	1963	6.25	12.50	25.00
☐ 47-8215		Frankie and Johnny/Cool Train	1963	3.00	6.00	12.00
☐ 47-8215	PS	Frankie and Johnny/Cool Train	1963	6.25	12.50	25.00
☐ 47-8247		Little Red Rooster/You Gotta Move	1963	3.00	6.00	12.00
☐ 47-8247	PS	Little Red Rooster/You Gotta Move	1963	6.25	12.50	25.00
☐ 47-8299		Good News/Basin Street Blues	1963	3.00	6.00	12.00
☐ 47-8368		Good Times/Tennessee Waltz	1964	3.00	6.00	12.00
☐ 47-8426		Cousin of Mine/That's Where It's At	1964	3.00	6.00	12.00
☐ 47-8486		Shake/A Change Is Gonna Come	1964	3.00	6.00	12.00
☐ 47-8539		It's Got the Whole World Shakin'/Ease My Troublin' Mind	1965	2.50	5.00	10.00
☐ 47-8586		When a Boy Falls in Love/The Piper	1965	2.50	5.00	10.00
☐ 47-8631		Sugar Dumpling/Bridge of Tears	1965	2.50	5.00	10.00
☐ 47-8631	PS	Sugar Dumpling/Bridge of Tears	1965	6.25	12.50	25.00
☐ 47-8751		Feel It/That's All	1965	2.50	5.00	10.00
☐ 47-8803		Let's Go Steady Again/Trouble Blues	1966	2.50	5.00	10.00
☐ 47-8934		Meet Me at Mary's Place/If I Had a Hammer	1966	2.50	5.00	10.00

Specialty

☐ 596		Forever/Lovable	1957	7.50	15.00	30.00
		As "Dale Cook"				
☐ 619		I'll Come Running Back to You/Forever	1957	7.50	15.00	30.00
☐ 627		That's All I Need to Know/I Don't Want to Cry	1958	7.50	15.00	30.00
☐ 667		Happy in Love/I Need You Now	1959	7.50	15.00	30.00
☐ 921		Must Jesus Bear the Cross Alone/The Last Mile of the Way	1970	2.50	5.00	10.00
		With the Soul Stirrers				
☐ 928		Just Another Day/Christ Is All	1973	2.50	5.00	10.00
		With the Soul Stirrers				
☐ 930		That's Heaven to Me/Lord, Remember Me	1974	2.50	5.00	10.00
		With the Soul Stirrers				

Cooker, John Lee -See "Hooker, John Lee"

Cookies, The

(At least two related, but different, groups)

Atlantic

☐ 1061		Precious Love/Later, Later	1955	7.50	15.00	30.00
☐ 1084		In Paradise/Passing Time	1956	7.50	15.00	30.00
☐ 1110		Down By the River/My Lover	1956	6.25	12.50	25.00
☐ 2079		Passing Time/In Paradise	1960	5.00	10.00	20.00

Dimension

☐ 1002		Chains/Stranger in My Arms	1962	5.00	10.00	20.00
☐ 1008		Don't Say Nothin' Bad (About My Baby)/Softly in the Night	1963	3.75	7.50	15.00
☐ 1008		Don't Say Nothin' Bad/Softly in the Night	1963	5.00	10.00	20.00
☐ 1012		I Want a Boy for My Birthday/Will Power	1963	3.75	7.50	15.00
☐ 1020		Girls Grow Up Faster Than Boys/Only to Other People	1963	3.75	7.50	15.00
☐ 1032		I Never Dreamed/The Old Crowd	1964	3.75	7.50	15.00

Josie

☐ 822		King of Hearts/Hippy-Dippy-Daddy	1957	7.50	15.00	30.00

Lamp

☐ 8008		Don't Let Go/All Night Mambo	1954	10.00	20.00	40.00

Warner Bros.

☐ 7025		All My Trials/Wounded	1967	2.50	5.00	10.00
☐ 7047		Mr. Cupid (Don't You Call on Me)/Hang My Head and Cry	1967	2.50	5.00	10.00
		B-side by the Big Guys				

Cool Heat - See "Wind"

Cooper, Alice

Atlantic

☐ 3254		Only Women/Cold Ethyl	1975		2.50	5.00

Number		Title (A Side/B Side)	Year	VG	VG+	NM
☐ 3280		Department of Youth/Some Folks	1975		2.50	5.00
☐ 3298		Welcome to My Nightmare/Cold Ethyl	1975		2.50	5.00
Epic						
☐ 08114		I Got a Line on You/Livin' on the Edge	1988			3.00
		B-side by Britney Fox				
☐ 68958		Poison/Trash	1989			3.00
☐ 73085		House of Fire/Ballad of Dwight Fry	1989			3.00
☐ 73845		Hey Stoopid/It Rained All Night	1991			3.00
☐ 73983		Love's a Loaded Gun/Fire	1991			3.00
MCA						
☐ 52904		He's Back (The Man Behind the Mask)/Billion Dollar Baby	1986			3.00
☐ 52904	PS	He's Back (The Man Behind the Mask)/Billion Dollar Baby	1986			3.00
☐ 53212		Freedom/Time to Kill	1987			3.00
☐ 53212	PS	Freedom/Time to Kill	1987			3.00
Straight						
☐ 101		Reflected/Living	1969	75.00	150.00	300.00
		Promos worth about 10% of this value				
Warner Bros.						
☐ 7141		Eighteen/Caught in a Dream	1972		2.00	4.00
		"Back to Back Hits" series (originals have green labels)				
☐ 7398		Shoe Salesman/Return of the Spiders	1970	5.00	10.00	20.00
☐ 7449		Eighteen/Body	1971		2.50	5.00
☐ 7490		Caught in a Dream/Hallowed Be My Name	1971		2.50	5.00
☐ 7529		Under My Wheels/Desperado	1971		2.50	5.00
☐ 7568		Be My Lover/Yeah, Yeah, Yeah	1972		2.50	5.00
☐ 7596		School's Out/Gutter Cat	1972		2.50	5.00
☐ 7596	PS	School's Out/Gutter Cat	1972	2.50	5.00	10.00
☐ 7631		Elected/Luney Tune	1972		2.50	5.00
☐ 7631	PS	Elected/Luney Tune	1972	2.50	5.00	10.00
☐ 7673		Hello Hurray/Generation Landslide	1972		2.50	5.00
☐ 7691		No More Mr. Nice Guy/Raped and Freezin'	1973		2.50	5.00
☐ 7724		Billion Dollar Babies/Mary Ann	1973		2.50	5.00
☐ 7762		Teenage Lament '74/Hard Hearted Alice	1973		2.50	5.00
☐ 7783		Muscle of Love/Crazy Little Child	1974		2.50	5.00
☐ 8023		I'm Eighteen/Muscle of Love	1974		2.50	5.00
☐ 8228		I Never Cry/Go to Hell	1976		2.00	4.00
☐ 8349		You and Me/It's Hot Tonight	1977		2.00	4.00
☐ 8349	PS	You and Me/It's Hot Tonight	1977	2.00	4.00	8.00
☐ 8448		(No More) Love at Your Convenience/I Never Wrote Those Songs	1977		2.50	5.00
☐ 8607		School's Out/Eighteen	1978	2.00	4.00	8.00
☐ 8695		How You Gonna See Me Now/No Tricks	1978		2.50	5.00
☐ 8760		From the Inside/Nurse Rosetta	1979		2.00	4.00
☐ 29828		I Am the Future/Tag, You're It	1982		2.00	4.00
☐ 29928		I Like Girls/Zorro's Ascent	1982		2.00	4.00
☐ 49204		Clones (We're All)/Model Citizen	1980		2.00	4.00
☐ 49204	PS	Clones (We're All)/Model Citizen	1980		2.50	5.00
☐ 49526		Dance Yourself to Death/Talk Talk	1980		2.00	4.00
☐ 49780		You Want It, You Got It/Who Do You Think We Are	1981		2.00	4.00
☐ 49848		Generation Landslide '81/Seven and Seven Is	1981		2.00	4.00

Cooper, Bo - See "Dante, Ron"

Cooper, Christine
Parkway

Number		Title (A Side/B Side)	Year	VG	VG+	NM
☐ 122		I Must Have You (Or No One)/Good Looks (They Don't Count)	1966	3.75	7.50	15.00
☐ 971		S.O.S./Say What You Feel	1966	6.25	12.50	25.00
☐ 983		(They Call Him) A Bad Boy/Heartaches Away My Boy	1966	10.00	20.00	40.00

Cooper, Dolly
Dot

Number	Title (A Side/B Side)	Year	VG	VG+	NM
☐ 15495	Big Rock Inn/I'm Looking Through Your Window	1956	3.00	6.00	12.00
☐ 15535	The Confession of a Fool/Tell Me, Tell Me	1957	3.00	6.00	12.00

Ebb

Number	Title (A Side/B Side)	Year	VG	VG+	NM
☐ 109	Wild Love/Time Brings About a Change	1957	3.00	6.00	12.00

Modern

Number	Title (A Side/B Side)	Year	VG	VG+	NM
☐ 965	My Man/Ay La Bas	1955	10.00	20.00	40.00
☐ 977	Teenage Prayer/Down So Long	1956	12.50	25.00	50.00
☐ 986	Teenage Wedding Bells/Every Day and Every Night	1956	12.50	25.00	50.00

Savoy

Number	Title (A Side/B Side)	Year	VG	VG+	NM
☐ 1121	You Gotta Be Good to Yourself/Love Can't Be Blind	1954	5.00	10.00	20.00

Copeland, Ken
Dot

Number	Title (A Side/B Side)	Year	VG	VG+	NM
☐ 15686	Where the Rio Rosa Flows/Locked in the Arms of Love	1958	3.75	7.50	15.00

Imperial

Number	Title (A Side/B Side)	Year	VG	VG+	NM
☐ 5432	Pledge of Love/Night Air	1957	5.00	10.00	20.00
	B-side by The Mints				
☐ 5453	Teenage/Bed of Lies	1957	5.00	10.00	20.00
☐ 5466	I Want to Go Steady/I Would Give My Heart	1957	5.00	10.00	20.00

Number	Title (A Side/B Side)	Year	VG	VG+	NM
Lin					
❏ 5007	Pledge of Love/Night Air	1957	10.00	20.00	40.00
	B-side by The Mints				
❏ 5017	Fanny Brown/Chaser of Hearts	1957	10.00	20.00	40.00
Cordel, Pat					
(Also see "Elegants, The")					
Club					
❏ 1011	Darling, Come Back/My My Tears	1956	500.00	1,000	1,500
	And the Crescents				
Michelle					
❏ 503	Darling, Come Back/My My Tears	1959	15.00	30.00	60.00
	And the Elegants				
Victory					
❏ 1001	Darling, Come Back/My My Tears	1963	10.00	20.00	40.00
	And the Elegants				
Cordials, The					
(At least two different groups?)					
Bethlehem					
❏ 3019	What's the Matter with Me/I'm Not Crying Anymore	1961	3.75	7.50	15.00
Cordial					
❏ 1001	I'm Ashamed/Sentimental Journey	1960	25.00	50.00	100.00
Felsted					
❏ 8653	Once in a Lifetime/What Kind of Fool Am I	1962	7.50	15.00	30.00
Liberty					
❏ 55784	Oh, How I Love Her/You Can't Believe in Love	1965	6.25	12.50	25.00
Reveille					
❏ 106	Eternal Love/The International Twist	1962	75.00	150.00	300.00
Seven Arts					
❏ 707	Dawn Is Almost Here/Keep An Eye	1961	25.00	50.00	100.00
Whip					
❏ 276	Listen My Heart/My Heart's Desire	1961	62.50	125.00	250.00
Corey, John					
Vee Jay					
❏ 466	Pollyanna/I'll Forget	1962	7.50	15.00	30.00
	Backing group: The Four Seasons				
❏ 514	Hey Little Runaround/	1963	2.50	5.00	10.00
	The Prettiest Girl I've Kissed Today				
Cornish, Gene					
(Later a member of the [Young] Rascals.)					
Dawn					
❏ 550	Let's Do the Capri/Lonely I Will Say	1964	7.50	15.00	30.00
❏ 551	I Wanna Be a Beatle/Oh Misery	1964	10.00	20.00	40.00
Vassar					
❏ 319	Since I Lost You/Winner Take All	1962	5.00	10.00	20.00
Coronets, The					
Chess					
❏ 1549	Nadine/I'm All Alone	1953	50.00	100.00	200.00
	Silver top label				
❏ 1549	Nadine/I'm All Alone	1958	3.00	6.00	12.00
	All-blue label				
❏ 1553	It Would Be Heavenly/Baby's Coming Home	1953	100.00	200.00	400.00
	Black vinyl				
❏ 1553	It Would Be Heavenly/Baby's Coming Home	1953	200.00	400.00	800.00
	Red vinyl				
Groove					
❏ 0114	I Love You More/Crime Doesn't Pay	1955	25.00	50.00	100.00
❏ 0116	The Bible Tells Me So/Hush	1955	37.50	75.00	150.00
Sterling					
❏ 903	Don't Deprive Me/Little Boy	1955	62.50	125.00	250.00
Cotton, James					
Sun					
❏ 199	My Baby/Straighten Up, Baby	1954	500.00	1,000	2,000
❏ 206	Cotton Crop Blues/Hold Me in Your Arms	1954	800.00	1,600	2,400
Count Five, The					
Double Shot					
❏ 104	Psychotic Reaction/They're Gonna Get You	1966	3.75	7.50	15.00
	First pressing, with label logo at top				
❏ 104	Psychotic Reaction/They're Gonna Get You	1966	3.00	6.00	12.00
	Later pressings, with label logo at side				
❏ 106	Peace of Mind/The Morning After	1966	3.00	6.00	12.00
❏ 110	You Must Believe Me/Teeny Bopper, Teeny Bopper	1967	3.00	6.00	12.00
❏ 115	Merry-Go-Round/Contrast	1967	3.00	6.00	12.00

Number	Title (A Side/B Side)	Year	VG	VG+	NM
☐ 125	Declaration of Independence/ Revelation in Slow Motion	1968	3.00	6.00	12.00
☐ 141	Mailman/Pretty Big Mouth	1969	3.00	6.00	12.00

Country Boys, The
(David Gates was a member)
Del-Fi

☐ 4245	The Okie Surfer/Blue Surf	1964	10.00	20.00	40.00

Country Hams, The - See "McCartney, Paul"

Counts, The
(At least two different groups)
Aware

☐ 038	Funk/Too Bad	1974		2.50	5.00
☐ 046	Sacrifice/Funk Pump	1974		2.50	5.00
☐ 049	All the Fair/On the Music	1975		2.50	5.00
☐ 054	Magic Ride/Short Cut	1975		2.50	5.00

Count

☐ 5	The Beat/After Beat	196?	5.00	10.00	20.00

Dot

☐ 1188	Darling Dear/I Need You Always	1954	10.00	20.00	40.00
☐ 1199	Hot Tamales/Baby Don't You Know	1954	10.00	20.00	40.00
☐ 1210	My Dear, My Darling/She Won't Say Yes	1954	10.00	20.00	40.00
☐ 1226	Baby I Want You/Waitin' Around for You	1954	10.00	20.00	40.00
☐ 1235	Wailin' Little Mama/Let Me Go	1955	7.50	15.00	30.00
☐ 1243	From This Day On/Love and Understanding	1955	7.50	15.00	30.00
☐ 1265	I Need You Tonight/Sally Walker	1955	7.50	15.00	30.00
☐ 1275	To Our Love/Heartbreaker	1956	6.25	12.50	25.00
☐ 16105	Darling Dear/I Need You Always	1960	5.00	10.00	20.00

Manco

☐ 1060	Surfer's Paradise/Chug-a-Lug	1964	10.00	20.00	40.00

Mercury

☐ 71318	Shake the Town/Teenage Guy and Girl	1958	3.75	7.50	15.00

Note

☐ 20000	Sweet Names/I Guess I Brought It All on Myself	1956	37.50	75.00	150.00

Panorama

☐ 9	Chitlins, Etc./Clyde, Clyde, The Cow's Outside	1965	2.50	5.00	10.00
☐ 33	Come Now/Since I Fell for You	1966	2.50	5.00	10.00

Sea Crest

☐ 6003	Turn On Song/Enchanted Sea	1964	5.00	10.00	20.00
☐ 6004	Doggin'/And Then I Cried	1964	3.75	7.50	15.00

Smash

☐ 1821	Stormy Weather/True Love's Gone	1963	2.50	5.00	10.00

Westbound

☐ 191	Thinking Single/Why Not Start All Over Again	1972		2.50	5.00

Covay, Don
Arnold

☐ 1002	Pony Time/Love Boat As "Don Covay and the Goodtimers"	1961	3.00	6.00	12.00
☐ 1002	Pony Time/Love Boat As "The Goodtimers"	1961	6.25	12.50	25.00

Atlantic

☐ 1147	Bip Bop Bip/Silver Dollar As "Pretty Boy"	1957	20.00	40.00	80.00
☐ 2280	The Boomerang/Daddy Loves Baby	1965	2.50	5.00	10.00
☐ 2286	Please Do Something/A Woman's Love	1965	2.50	5.00	10.00
☐ 2301	See Saw/I Never Get Enough of Your Love	1965	2.50	5.00	10.00
☐ 2323	Sookie Sookie/Watching the Late Late Show	1966	2.50	5.00	10.00
☐ 2340	You Put Something On Me/Iron Out the Rough Spots	1966	2.50	5.00	10.00
☐ 2357	Somebody's Got to Love You/ Temptation Was Too Strong	1966	2.50	5.00	10.00
☐ 2375	Shing-Aling '67/I Was There	1967	2.50	5.00	10.00
☐ 2407	40 Days -- 40 Nights/The Usual Place	1967	2.50	5.00	10.00
☐ 2440	You've Got Me on the Critical List/Never Had No Love	1967	2.50	5.00	10.00
☐ 2481	Chain of Fools/Prove It	1968	2.50	5.00	10.00
☐ 2494	Don't Let Go/It's In the Wind	1968	2.50	5.00	10.00
☐ 2521	Gonna Send You Back to Your Mama/ House on the Corner	1968	2.50	5.00	10.00
☐ 2565	I Stole Some Love/Snake in the Grass	1968	2.50	5.00	10.00
☐ 2609	Sweet Pea/C.C. Rider Blues	1969	2.50	5.00	10.00
☐ 2666	Ice Cream Man (The Gimmie Game)/Black Woman	1969	2.50	5.00	10.00
☐ 2725	Everything I Do Goin' Be Funky/Key to the Highway	1970	2.00	4.00	8.00
☐ 2742	Soul Stirrer/Sookie Sookie	1970	2.00	4.00	8.00

Big

☐ 617	Switchin' in the Kitchen/Rockin' the Mule As "Pretty Boy"	1958	20.00	40.00	80.00

Big Top

☐ 3060	Hey There/I'm Coming Down with the Blues	1960	3.75	7.50	15.00

Blaze

☐ 350	Standing in the Doorway/(B-side unknown)	1958	7.50	15.00	30.00

Number		Title (A Side/B Side)	Year	VG	VG+	NM
Cameo						
❑ 239		The Popeye Waddle/One Little Boy Had Money	1962	3.00	6.00	12.00
❑ 251		Wiggle Wobble/Do the Bug	1963	3.00	6.00	12.00
Columbia						
❑ 41981		Shake Wid the Snake/Every Which-a Way	1961	5.00	10.00	20.00
❑ 42058		Hand Jive Workout/See About Me	1961	5.00	10.00	20.00
❑ 42197		Now That I Need You/Teen Life Swag	1961	25.00	50.00	100.00
Epic						
❑ 9484		It's Twistin' Time/Twistin' Train	1961	3.75	7.50	15.00
		As "The Goodtimers"				
Janus						
❑ 164		Sweet Thang/Standing in the Grits Line	1971		3.00	6.00
❑ 181		Daddy Please Don't Go Out/Shoes Under My Bed	1972		3.00	6.00
Landa						
❑ 704		You're Good for Me/Truth of the Lite	1965	2.50	5.00	10.00
Mercury						
❑ 71385		I Was Checkin' Out She Was Checkin' In/Money	1973		3.00	6.00
❑ 71430		Somebody's Been Enjoying My Home/Bad Mouthing	1973		3.00	6.00
❑ 71469		It's Better to Have (And Don't Need)/Leave Him (Part 1)	1974		3.00	6.00
❑ 73311		Overtime Man/Dungeon #3	1972		3.00	6.00
❑ 73648		Rumble in the Jungle/We Can't Make It No More	1975		3.00	6.00
Newman						
❑ 500		Badd Boy/(B-side unknown)	1980		2.50	5.00
Parkway						
❑ 894		Ain't That Silly/Turn It On	1964	3.00	6.00	12.00
❑ 910		The Froog/One Little Boy Had Money	1964	3.00	6.00	12.00
Philadelphia Int'l.						
❑ 3594		Right Time for Love/No Tell Motel	1976		2.50	5.00
❑ 3602		Travelin' in Heavy Traffic/Once You Have It	1976		2.50	5.00
Rosemart						
❑ 801		Mercy Mercy/Can't Stay Away	1964	3.75	7.50	15.00
❑ 802		Take This Hurt Off Me/Please Don't Let Me Know	1964	3.00	6.00	12.00
Sue						
❑ 709		Betty Jean/Believe It or Not	1958	7.50	15.00	30.00
U-Von						
❑ 102		Back to the Roots (Part 1)/Back to the Roots (Part 2)	1977		2.50	5.00
Cowsills, The						
Gasatanka/Rockville						
❑ 6139		Christmastime (Song for Marissa)/Some Good Years	1993			3.00
		Green vinyl				
❑ 6139	PS	Christmastime (Song for Marissa)/Some Good Years	1993			3.00
Joda						
❑ 103		All I Really Wanta Be Is Me/And the Next Day, Too	1965	7.50	15.00	30.00
London						
❑ 149		On My Side/There Is No Child	1971	2.00	4.00	8.00
❑ 153		You/Crystal Claps	1971	2.00	4.00	8.00
❑ 170		Blue Road/Covered Wagon	1972	2.00	4.00	8.00
MGM						
❑ 13810		The Rain, the Park and Other Things/River Blue	1967	2.50	5.00	10.00
❑ 13810	PS	The Rain, the Park and Other Things/River Blue	1967	3.00	6.00	12.00
❑ 13886		We Can Fly/A Time for Remembrance	1967	2.00	4.00	8.00
❑ 13886	PS	We Can Fly/A Time for Remembrance	1967	3.00	6.00	12.00
❑ 13909		In Need of a Friend/Mister Flynn	1968	2.00	4.00	8.00
❑ 13909	PS	In Need of a Friend/Mister Flynn	1968	3.00	6.00	12.00
❑ 13944		Indian Lake/Newspaper Blanket	1968	2.50	5.00	10.00
		First pressings have black labels				
❑ 13944		Indian Lake/Newspaper Blanket	1968	2.00	4.00	8.00
		Second pressings have blue and gold labels				
❑ 13944	PS	Indian Lake/Newspaper Blanket	1968	3.00	6.00	12.00
❑ 13981		Poor Baby/Meet Me at the Wishing Well	1968	2.00	4.00	8.00
❑ 14011		The Impossible Years/Candy Kid	1968	2.00	4.00	8.00
❑ 14026		Hair/What Is Happy	1969	3.00	6.00	12.00
❑ 14063		The Prophecy of Daniel and John the Divine	1969	2.00	4.00	8.00
❑		(Six-Six-Six)/Gotta Get Away from It All				
❑ 14084		Silver Threads and Golden Needles/	1969	2.50	5.00	10.00
		Love, American Style				
❑ 14084	PS	Silver Threads and Golden Needles/	1969	3.00	6.00	12.00
		Love, American Style				
❑ 14106		Start to Love/Two by Two	1970	2.00	4.00	8.00
Philips						
❑ 40382		Most of All/Siamese Cat	1966	2.50	5.00	10.00
❑ 40382	PS	Most of All/Siamese Cat	1966	3.75	7.50	15.00
❑ 40406		Party Girl/What's It Gonna Be Like	1966	2.50	5.00	10.00
❑ 40437		A Most Peculiar Man/Could It Be, Let Me Know	1967	2.50	5.00	10.00
Craig, Jimmy						
Brill						
❑ 1		All for You/Gonna Love My Baby	1959	20.00	40.00	80.00
Imperial						
❑ 5592		Walking in Darkness/Oh Little Girl	1959	3.75	7.50	15.00

Number		Title (A Side/B Side)	Year	VG	VG+	NM
Warwick						
❏ 542		Drifter/Let Me Stay	1960	3.75	7.50	15.00
Craig, The						
Fontana						
❏ 1579		I Must Be Mad/Suspense	1967	6.25	12.50	25.00
Crane, Sherry						
Sun						
❏ 328		Willie Willie/Winnie the Parakeet	1959	6.25	12.50	25.00
Crawford Brothers, The						
(Bobby and Johnny Crawford; also see individual entries)						
Del-Fi						
❏ 4191		Good Buddies/You Gotta Wear Shoes	1963	3.75	7.50	15.00
❏ 4191	PS	Good Buddies/You Gotta Wear Shoes	1963	6.25	12.50	25.00
Crawford, Bobby						
(Also see "Crawford Brothers, The")						
Del-Fi						
❏ 4211		Mrs. Smith, Please Wake Up/ That Little Old Lovemaker Me	1963	3.75	7.50	15.00
❏ 4236		I Want to Be a Good Guy/(B-side unknown)	1964	3.75	7.50	15.00
Crawford, Johnny						
(Also see "Crawford Brothers, The")						
Del-Fi						
❏ 4162		Daydreams/So Goes the Story	1961	3.75	7.50	15.00
❏ 4162	PS	Daydreams/So Goes the Story	1961	6.25	12.50	25.00
❏ 4165		Your Love Is Growing Cold/Treasure	1961	3.75	7.50	15.00
❏ 4165	PS	Your Love Is Growing Cold/Treasure	1961	6.25	12.50	25.00
❏ 4172		Patti Ann/Donna	1962	3.75	7.50	15.00
❏ 4178		Cindy's Birthday/Something Special	1962	3.75	7.50	15.00
❏ 4178	PS	Cindy's Birthday/Something Special	1962	6.25	12.50	25.00
❏ 4181		Your Nose Is Gonna Grow/Mr. Blue	1962	3.75	7.50	15.00
❏ 4181	PS	Your Nose Is Gonna Grow/Mr. Blue	1962	6.25	12.50	25.00
❏ 4188		Rumors/No One Really Loves a Clown	1962	3.75	7.50	15.00
❏ 4188	PS	Rumors/No One Really Loves a Clown	1962	6.25	12.50	25.00
❏ 4193		Proud/Lonesome Town	1963	3.75	7.50	15.00
❏ 4203		Cry on My Shoulder/When I Fall in Love	1963	3.75	7.50	15.00
❏ 4215		What Happened to Janie/Petite Chanson	1963	3.75	7.50	15.00
❏ 4221		Cindy's Gonna Cry/Debbie	1963	3.75	7.50	15.00
❏ 4229		Sandy/Ol' Shorty	1963	3.75	7.50	15.00
❏ 4231		Judy Loves Me/Living in the Past	1963	3.75	7.50	15.00
❏ 4242		The Girl Next Door (Once Upon a Time)/ Sittin' and Watchin'	1964	3.75	7.50	15.00
❏ 4305		Am I Too Young/(B-side unknown)	1965	3.75	7.50	15.00
Sidewalk						
❏ 932		Angelica/Everybody Has Their Day	1968	3.00	6.00	12.00
❏ 941		Good Guys Finish Last/Everyone Should Own a Dream	1968	3.00	6.00	12.00
Wynne						
❏ 124		Dance with the Dolly (With the Hole in Her Stocking)/ Ask	1958	5.00	10.00	20.00
Cream						
Atco						
❏ 6462		I Feel Free/N.S.U.	1967	3.00	6.00	12.00
❏ 6488		Strange Brew/Tales of Brave Ulysses	1967	2.50	5.00	10.00
❏ 6522		Spoonful/Spoonful (Part 2)	1967	2.00	4.00	8.00
❏ 6544		Sunshine of Your Love/SWLABR	1968	2.00	4.00	8.00
❏ 6575		Anyone for Tennis/Pressed Rat and Warthog	1968	2.00	4.00	8.00
❏ 6617		White Room/Those Were the Days	1968	2.00	4.00	8.00
❏ 6646		Crossroads/Passing the Time	1969	2.00	4.00	8.00
❏ 6668		Badge/What a Bringdown	1969	2.00	4.00	8.00
❏ 6708		Sweet Wine/Lawdy Mama	1969	2.50	5.00	10.00
Creations, The						
(Many different groups)						
Globe						
❏ 1000		Oh Baby/Plenty of Love	1967	5.00	10.00	20.00
❏ 102		Just Remember Me/Times Are Changing	1967	5.00	10.00	20.00
❏ 103		I've Got to Find Her/Times Are Changing	1967	5.00	10.00	20.00
Jamie						
❏ 1197		The Bells/Shang Shang	1961	6.25	12.50	25.00
Lido						
❏ 501		You Are My Darling/There Goes the Girl I Love	1956	75.00	150.00	300.00
Mel-O-Dy						
❏ 101		This Is Our Night/You're My Inspiration	1962	7.50	15.00	30.00
Meridian						
❏ 7550		The Wedding/I've Got a Feeling	1962	25.00	50.00	100.00
Patti-Jo						
❏ 1703		Seventeen/You'll Always Be Mine	1962	50.00	100.00	200.00
Penny						
❏ 9022		Lady Luck/We're in Love	1962	15.00	30.00	60.00

Number		Title (A Side/B Side)	Year	VG	VG+	NM
Pine Crest						
❏ 101		Woke Up in the Morning/Strolling Through the Park	1961	100.00	200.00	400.00
Radiant						
❏ 103		Don't Listen to What Others Say/ Don't Listen to What Others Say (Part 2)	1964	6.25	12.50	25.00
Take Ten						
❏ 1501		Lady Luck/We're in Love	1963	7.50	15.00	30.00
Tip Top						
❏ 400		Every Night I Pray/Mommy and Daddy	1956	50.00	100.00	200.00
❏ 501		You Are My Darling/There Goes the Girl I Love	1956	50.00	100.00	200.00
		At least one source claims this is a bootleg.				
Top Hat						
❏ 1003		Crash/Chickie Darling	1964	10.00	20.00	40.00
❏ 1003	PS	Crash/Chickie Darling	1964	20.00	40.00	80.00
❏ 1004		Don't Be Mean/(B-side unknown)	1965	12.50	235.00	50.00
❏ 1004	PS	Don't Be Mean/(B-side unknown)	1965	25.00	50.00	100.00
Virtue						
❏ 2517		I'm So in Love with You/Save the People	1971		3.00	6.00
❏ 2518		Don't Let Me Down/The Price I Have to Pay	1971		3.00	6.00
❏ 2520		Nothing Too Good for You/You Mean So Much	1972		3.00	6.00
❏ 2521		You Make Me Feel So Good/ That's How Strong My Love Is	1972		3.00	6.00
❏ 2522		How Sweetly Simple/Lovin' Simple	1973		3.00	6.00
Zodiac						
❏ 1005		A Dream/Foot Steps	1967	2.00	4.00	8.00
Creators, The						
(May or may not all be the same group)						
Dooto						
❏ 463		I've Had You/Drafted, Volunteered, Enlisted	1961	6.25	12.50	25.00
Dore						
❏ 635		Too Far to Turn Around/ Hello There, Mister Grave Digger	1962	15.00	30.00	60.00
Epic						
❏ 9605		Crazy Love/Cross Fire	1963	3.75	7.50	15.00
Hi-Q						
❏ 5021		Wear My Ring/Booga Bear	1961	20.00	40.00	80.00
		Normal print label				
❏ 5021		Wear My Ring/Booga Bear	1961	6.25	12.50	25.00
		Bold print label				
Philips						
❏ 40058		Boy, He's Got It/Yeah, He's Got It	1962	6.25	12.50	25.00
❏ 40083		I'll Stay Home (New Year's Eve)/Shoom Ba Boom	1962	75.00	150.00	300.00
T-Kay						
❏ 110		I'll Never, Never Do It Again/Boy, He's Got It!	1962	6.25	12.50	25.00
Time						
❏ 1038		Do You Remember/There's Going to Be an Angel	1961	6.25	12.50	25.00
Creedence Clearwater Revival						
(Also see "Golliwogs, The")						
Fantasy						
❏ 616		Suzie Q (Part One)/Suzie Q (Part Two)	1968		3.00	6.00
❏ 617		I Put a Spell on You/Walk on the Water	1968	2.00	4.00	8.00
❏ 619		Proud Mary/Born on the Bayou	1969		3.00	6.00
❏ 622		Bad Moon Rising/Lodi	1969		3.00	6.00
❏ 625		Green River/Commotion	1969		3.00	6.00
❏ 634		Down on the Corner/Fortunate Son	1969		3.00	6.00
❏ 634	PS	Down on the Corner/Fortunate Son	1969	3.00	6.00	12.00
❏ 637		Travelin' Band/Who'll Stop the Rain	1970		3.00	6.00
❏ 637	PS	Travelin' Band/Who'll Stop the Rain	1970	3.00	6.00	12.00
❏ 641		Up Around the Bend/Run Through the Jungle	1970		3.00	6.00
❏ 641	PS	Up Around the Bend/Run Through the Jungle	1970	3.00	6.00	12.00
❏ 645		Lookin' Out My Back Door/Long As I Can See the Light	1970		3.00	6.00
❏ 645	PS	Lookin' Out My Back Door/Long As I Can See the Light	1970	3.00	6.00	12.00
❏ 655		Have You Ever Seen the Rain/Hey Tonight	1971		3.00	6.00
❏ 665		Sweet Hitch-Hiker/Door to Door	1971		3.00	6.00
❏ 665	PS	Sweet Hitch-Hiker/Door to Door	1971	3.00	6.00	12.00
❏ 676		Someday Never Comes/Tearin' Up the Country	1972		3.00	6.00
❏ 759		I Heard It Through the Grapevine/ Good Golly Miss Molly	1976		2.00	4.00
❏ 759	PS	I Heard It Through the Grapevine/ Good Golly Miss Molly	1976		2.50	5.00
❏ 908		Tombstone Shadow/Commotion	1981		2.00	4.00
❏ 917		Medley U.S.A./Bad Moon Rising	1981		2.00	4.00
❏ 920		Cotton Fields/Lodi	1981		2.00	4.00
❏ 957		Medley (from "I Heard It Through the Grapevine" to "Up Around the Bend")/Medley (from "Proud Mary" to "Lodi")	1985	2.50	5.00	10.00
Scorpio						
❏ 412		Porterville/Call It Pretending	1968	20.00	40.00	80.00

Number		Title (A Side/B Side)	Year	VG	VG+	NM

Crescendos, The
(More than one group?)
Atlantic
| ❏ 1109 | | Sweet Dreams/Finders Keepers | 1956 | 7.50 | 15.00 | 30.00 |
| ❏ 2014 | | I'll Be Seeing You/Sweet Dreams | 1959 | 3.75 | 7.50 | 15.00 |

Domain
| ❏ 1025 | | A Fellow Needs a Girl/Black Cat | 1964 | 3.75 | 7.50 | 15.00 |

Impro
| ❏ 5006 | | Tidal Wave/Crescendo Special | 1962 | 10.00 | 20.00 | 40.00 |

Nasco
❏ 6005		Oh Julie/My Little Girl	1957	7.50	15.00	30.00
❏ 6009		School Girl/Crazy Hop	1958	6.25	12.50	25.00
❏ 6009	PS	School Girl/Crazy Hop	1958	12.50	25.00	50.00
❏ 6021		Rainy Sunday/Young and In Love	1958	6.25	12.50	25.00
❏ 6021	PS	Rainy Sunday/Young and In Love	1958	12.50	25.00	50.00

Nu Sound
| ❏ 1007 | | Count Down/Hawk Walk | 1961 | 7.50 | 15.00 | 30.00 |
| ❏ 1014 | | Sweet Talk/Movin' Wild | 1961 | 7.50 | 15.00 | 30.00 |

Scarlet
| ❏ 4007 | | Strange Love/Let's Take a Walk | 1960 | 7.50 | 15.00 | 30.00 |
| ❏ 4009 | | Angel Face/I'm So Ashamed | 1961 | 12.50 | 25.00 | 50.00 |

Tap
| ❏ 7027 | | Oh Julie/Angel Face | 1962 | 3.75 | 7.50 | 15.00 |
| ❏ 7027 | PS | Oh Julie/Angel Face | 1962 | 6.25 | 12.50 | 25.00 |

Creschendos, The
Gone
| ❏ 5100 | | My Heart's Desire/Take My Heart | 1961 | 7.50 | 15.00 | 30.00 |

Music City
❏ 831		My Heart's Desire/Take My Heart	1960	100.00	200.00	400.00
		Green label				
❏ 831		My Heart's Desire/Take My Heart	1960	50.00	100.00	200.00
		Maroon label				
❏ 831		My Heart's Desire/Take My Heart	1961	12.50	25.00	50.00
		Black label				
❏ 839		Teenage Prayer/I Don't Mind	1961	62.50	125.00	250.00

Saturn
| ❏ 404 | | Surfing Strip/Hanging Ten | 1963 | 12.50 | 25.00 | 50.00 |

Crests, The
(Also see "Maestro, Johnny")
Coed
❏ 501		Pretty Little Angel/I Thank the Moon	1958	37.50	75.00	150.00
		"Coed" in red print				
❏ 501		Pretty Little Angel/I Thank the Moon	1958	10.00	20.00	40.00
		"Coed" in red and black print				
❏ 506		16 Candles/Beside You	1958	10.00	20.00	40.00
❏ 509		Six Nights a Week/I Do	1959	7.50	15.00	30.00
❏ 511		Flower of Love/Molly Mae	1959	7.50	15.00	30.00
❏ 515		The Angels Listened In/I Thank the Moon	1959	7.50	15.00	30.00
❏ 521		A Year Ago Tonight/Paper Clown	1959	7.50	15.00	30.00
❏ 525		Step by Step/Gee (But I'd Give the World)	1960	6.25	12.50	25.00
❏ 531		Trouble in Paradise/Always You	1960	6.25	12.50	25.00
❏ 535		Journey of Love/If My Heart Could Write a Letter	1960	6.25	12.50	25.00
❏ 537		Isn't It Amazing/Molly Mae	1960	6.25	12.50	25.00
❏ 543		I Remember (In the Still of the Night)/Good Golly Miss Molly	1961	6.25	12.50	25.00
❏ 561		Little Miracles/Baby I Gotta Know	1962	7.50	15.00	30.00

Coral
| ❏ 62403 | | You Blew Out the Candles/A Love to Last a Lifetime | 1964 | 7.50 | 15.00 | 30.00 |

Harvey
| ❏ 5002 | | Sixteen Candles/My Juanita | 1981 | 2.50 | 5.00 | 10.00 |
| | | Red vinyl | | | | |

Joyce
❏ 103		My Juanita/Sweetest One	1957	100.00	200.00	400.00
		Label name: "JoYce"				
❏ 103		My Juanita/Sweetest One	1959	12.50	25.00	50.00
		Label name: "Joyce"				
❏ 105		No One to Love/Wish She Was Mine	1957	62.50	125.00	250.00

King Tut
| ❏ 172 | | Earth Angel/Tweedlee Dee | 197? | 2.00 | 4.00 | 8.00 |

Musictone
| ❏ 1106 | | My Juanita/Sweetest One | 1961 | 5.00 | 10.00 | 20.00 |

Scepter
| ❏ 12112 | | I'm Stepping Out of the Picture/Afraid of Love | 1965 | 3.75 | 7.50 | 15.00 |

Selma
| ❏ 311 | | Guilty/Number One with Me | 1962 | 6.25 | 12.50 | 25.00 |
| | | A-side does not have spoken intro | | | | |

Number	Title (A Side/B Side)	Year	VG	VG+	NM
❑ 311	Guilty/Number One with Me	1962	18.75	37.50	75.00
	A-side has spoken intro				
❑ 4000	Did I Remember/Tears Will Fall	1963	7.50	15.00	30.00

Times Square

❑ 2	No One to Love/Wish She Was Mine	1962	5.00	10.00	20.00
	Red vinyl				
❑ 6	Baby/I Love You So	1964	3.75	7.50	15.00
❑ 97	Baby/I Love You So	1964	3.00	6.00	12.00

Trans Atlas

❑ 696	The Actor/Three Tears in a Bucket	1962	7.50	15.00	30.00

Crew Cuts, The
ABC-Paramount

❑ 10450	Hip-Huggers/You're a Star, Donna, Donna	1963	3.00	6.00	12.00

Chess

❑ 1892	Ain't That Nice/Yeah, Yeah, She Wants Me	1964	2.50	5.00	10.00

Firebird

❑ 1805	My Heart Belongs to Only You/You've Been In	1970	2.50	5.00	

4 Corners of the World

❑ 120	Don't Be Angry/Earth Angel	1962	2.50	5.00	10.00

Mercury

❑ 70341	Crazy 'Bout You Baby/Angela Mia	1954	5.00	10.00	20.00
❑ 70404	Sh-Boom/I Spoke Too Soon	1954	6.25	12.50	25.00
❑ 70404	Sh-Boom/I Spoke Too Soon	1954	12.50	25.00	50.00
	7-inch 78 rpm on vinyl				
❑ 70404 PS	Sh-Boom/I Spoke Too Soon	1954	25.00	50.00	100.00
	Sleeve accompanying the 78: "PopSi Hit Record of the Month"				
❑ 70443	Oop-Shoop/Do Me Good Baby	1954	3.75	7.50	15.00
❑ 70490	All I Wanna Do/The Barking Dog	1954	3.75	7.50	15.00
❑ 70491	Dance, Mr. Snowman, Dance/Twinkle Toes	1954	3.75	7.50	15.00
❑ 70494	The Whippenpoof Song/Varsity Drag	1954	3.75	7.50	15.00
❑ 70529	Ko Ko Mo (I Love You So)/Earth Angel	1955	3.75	7.50	15.00
❑ 70597	Don't Be Angry/Chop Chop Boom	1955	3.75	7.50	15.00
❑ 70598	Unchained Melody/Two Hearts, Two Kisses	1955	3.75	7.50	15.00
❑ 70634	A Story Untold/Carmen's Boogie	1955	3.75	7.50	15.00
❑ 70668	Gum Drop/Present Arms	1955	3.75	7.50	15.00
❑ 70710	Slam! Bam!/Are You Having Any Fun	1955	3.75	7.50	15.00
❑ 70741	Angels in the Sky/Mostly Martha	1955	3.75	7.50	15.00
❑ 70782	Seven Days/That's Your Mistake	1956	3.75	7.50	15.00
❑ 70840	Out of the Picture/Honey Hair, Sugar Lips, Eyes of Blue	1956	3.75	7.50	15.00
❑ 70890	Tell Me Why/Rebel in Town	1956	3.75	7.50	15.00
❑ 70922	Bei Mir Bist Du Shoen/Thirteen Going on Fourteen	1956	3.75	7.50	15.00
❑ 70977	Love in a Home/Keeper of the Flame	1956	3.75	7.50	15.00
❑ 71022	Young Love/Little by Little	1956	3.75	7.50	15.00
❑ 71076	The Angels/Whatever, Whenever. Whoever	1957	3.75	7.50	15.00
❑ 71125	Suzie Q/Such a Shame	1957	3.75	7.50	15.00
❑ 71168	I Sit in My Window/Hey, You Face	1957	3.75	7.50	15.00
❑ 71223	I Like It Like That/Be My Only Love	1957	3.75	7.50	15.00

RCA Victor

❑ 47-7320	Forever My Darling/Hey Stella	1958	3.00	6.00	12.00
❑ 47-7359	That's My Desire/Baby Be Mine	1958	3.00	6.00	12.00
❑ 47-7446	Fraternity Pin/Can You Hear Me	1959	3.00	6.00	12.00
❑ 47-7509	Gone, Gone, Gone/Someone in Heaven	1959	3.00	6.00	12.00
❑ 47-7577	Bermuda/Kin-Ni-Ki-Nic	1959	3.00	6.00	12.00
❑ 47-7667	It Is No Secret/No, No, Nevermore	1960	3.00	6.00	12.00
❑ 47-7734	American Beauty Rose/The Shrine on Top of the Hill	1960	3.00	6.00	12.00
❑ 47-7759	Aura Lee/Going to Church on Sunday	1960	3.00	6.00	12.00

Vee Jay

❑ 569	The Three Bells/Spanish Is the Loving Tongue	1963	3.00	6.00	12.00

Warwick

❑ 558	Over the Mountain/Searchin'	1960	3.00	6.00	12.00
❑ 585	You and the Angels/I Care for You	1960	3.00	6.00	12.00
❑ 595	Malaguena/Why Not	1960	3.00	6.00	12.00
❑ 623	The Legend of Gunga Din/Number One with Me	1961	3.00	6.00	12.00

Whale

❑ 507	Twistin' All the World/Electric Chair	1962	3.00	6.00	12.00
❑ 508	Laura Love/Little Donkey	1962	3.00	6.00	12.00
❑ 509	Hush Little Baby/Ti-Pi-Tum	1962	3.00	6.00	12.00

Crewe, Bob
(Includes The Bob Crewe Generation and other similarly-named instrumental groups)
20th Century

❑ 2271	Street Talk/Street Talk (Part 2)	1976		2.00	4.00

ABC-Paramount

❑ 10204	Swingin' Family Tree/La La Loretta	1961	3.00	6.00	12.00
❑ 10246	One More Lie/I'm Goin' Home (On My Way)	1961	3.00	6.00	12.00
❑ 10273	Another Day/Come to Me	1961	3.00	6.00	12.00

Brunswick

❑ 55021	I Can't Shake the Blues/Torn and Tattered Heart	1957	3.75	7.50	15.00

Coral

❑ 61688	Melody for Lovers/Can't Get Away from It	1956	3.75	7.50	15.00

Crewe

❑ 605	Dandylion/Day By Day & Prepare Ye	1971		2.50	5.00

Number	Title (A Side/B Side)	Year	VG	VG+	NM
Dyno Voice					
❑ 229	Music to Watch Girls By/Girls on the Rocks	1966	2.00	4.00	8.00
❑ 231	After the Ball/One More Year	1967		3.00	6.00
❑ 233	Miniskirts/Theme for a Lazy Girl	1967		3.00	6.00
❑ 237	A Lover's Concerto/You Only Live Twice	1967		3.00	6.00
❑ 902	Birds of Britain/I Will Wait for You	1968		3.00	6.00
❑ 906	Winter Warm/Song from Moulin Rouge	1968		3.00	6.00
❑ 915	To Give (The Reason I Live)/ Battle Hymn of the Republic	1968		3.00	6.00
❑ 928	Angel Is Love/Black Queen's Beads	1968		3.00	6.00
Elektra					
❑ 45346	Time for You and Me/Free (Medley)	1976		2.00	4.00
❑ 45380	Menage a Trois/I Am Free-Keep Walkin'	1976		2.00	4.00
❑ 45404	It Took a Long Time (For the First Time in My Life)/ In Another Life	1977		2.00	4.00
❑ 45425	Marriage Made in Heaven/In Another Life	1977		2.00	4.00
Jubilee					
❑ 5148	Cash Register Heart/Change of Heart	1954	5.00	10.00	20.00
❑ 5164	Punch/It's All Over	1954	5.00	10.00	20.00
Melba					
❑ 119	Guessin' Games/Don't Call Me Chicken	1957	3.75	7.50	15.00
Metromedia					
❑ 229	Mammy Blue/Better Be Gone	1972		2.50	5.00
❑ 243	Takin' Care of Each Other/(B-side unknown)	1972		2.50	5.00
Philips					
❑ 40241	Rag Doll/Ronnie	1964	2.00	4.00	8.00
Spotlight					
❑ 393	Penny Nickel Dime Quarter (On a Teenage Date)/ How Long	1956	5.00	10.00	20.00
Vik					
❑ 0307	Charm Bracelet/Do Be Do Be Do	1957	6.25	12.50	25.00
❑ 0333	Of Sun, the Sea and the Sand/Sweet Talk	1958	5.00	10.00	20.00
Warwick					
❑ 519	The Whippenpoof Song/Let's Pretend	1959	3.00	6.00	12.00
❑ 534	Cool Time/Quite a Picture	1960	3.00	6.00	12.00
❑ 553	Silhouettes/Let's Get Serious	1960	3.00	6.00	12.00
❑ 579	Little Girl of Mine/To Ev'ry Girl, To Ev'ry Boy	1960	3.00	6.00	12.00
❑ 601	Oh, How I Miss You Tonight/Ev'rytime	1960	3.00	6.00	12.00
❑ 616	She's Only Wonderful/On the Street Where You Live	1961	3.00	6.00	12.00

Crickets, The

(Also see "Curtis, Sonny"; "Holly, Buddy". The Davis, Jay Dee and MGM sides are by an R&B Crickets.)

Number	Title (A Side/B Side)	Year	VG	VG+	NM
Barnaby					
❑ 2061	Rockin' 50's Rock 'N' Roll/True Love Ways	1972	5.00	10.00	20.00
Brunswick					
❑ 55009	That'll Be the Day/I'm Looking for Someone to Love	1957	12.50	25.00	50.00
❑ 55035	Oh, Boy!/Not Fade Away	1957	12.50	25.00	50.00
❑ 55053	Maybe Baby/Tell Me How	1958	12.50	25.00	50.00
❑ 55072	Think It Over/Fool's Paradise	1958	12.50	25.00	50.00
❑ 55094	It's So Easy!/Lonesome Tears	1958	12.50	25.00	50.00
❑ 55124	Love's Made a Fool of You/Someone, Someone	1959	10.00	20.00	40.00
❑ 55153	When You Ask About Love/Deborah	1959	10.00	20.00	40.00
Coral					
❑ 62198	More Than I Can Say/Baby, My Heart	1960	10.00	20.00	40.00
❑ 62238	Peggy Sue Got Married/Don't Cha Know	1960	10.00	20.00	40.00
❑ 62407	Maybe Baby/Not Fade Away	1964	7.50	15.00	30.00
Davis					
❑ 459	I'm Going to Live My Life Alone/Man from the Moon	1958	15.00	30.00	60.00
Epic					
❑ 08028	T-Shirt/Hollywould	1988		2.50	5.00
Jay Dee					
❑ 777	Dreams and Wishes/When I Met You	1953	37.50	75.00	150.00
❑ 781	Fine As Wine/I'm Not the Same One You Love	1953	37.50	75.00	150.00
❑ 785	Changing Partners/Your Love	1954	25.00	50.00	100.00
❑ 786	Just You/My Little Baby's Shoes	1954	25.00	50.00	100.00
❑ 789	Are You Looking for a Sweetheart/Never Give Up Hope	1954	25.00	50.00	100.00
❑ 795	I'm Going to Live My Life Alone/Man from the Moon	1954	25.00	50.00	100.00
Liberty					
❑ 55392	She's Old Enough to Know Better/I'm Feeling Better	1961	6.25	12.50	25.00
❑ 55441	Don't Ever Change/I'm Not a Bad Boy	1962	6.25	12.50	25.00
❑ 55492	I Believe in You/Parisian Girl	1962	6.25	12.50	25.00
❑ 55495	Little Hollywood Girl/Parisian Girl	1962	6.25	12.50	25.00
❑ 55540	My Little Girl/Teardrops Fall Like Rain	1963	6.25	12.50	25.00
❑ 55603	Don't Say You Love Me/April Avenue	1963	6.25	12.50	25.00
❑ 55660	Lonely Avenue/You Can't Be In-Between	1964	6.25	12.50	25.00
❑ 55668	Please, Please Me/From Me to You	1964	12.50	25.00	50.00
❑ 55696	(They Call Her) La Bomba/All Over You	1964	6.25	12.50	25.00
❑ 55742	We Gotta Get Together/I Think I've Caught the Blues	1964	6.25	12.50	25.00
❑ 55767	Everybody's Got a Little Problem/Now Hear This	1965	6.25	12.50	25.00
MGM					
❑ 11428	You're Mine/Milk and Gin	1953	37.50	75.00	150.00
❑ 11507	I'll Cry No More/For You I Have Eyes	1953	37.50	75.00	150.00

Number		Title (A Side/B Side)	Year	VG	VG+	NM
❏ 14541		Hayride/Wasn't It Nice	1973	3.75	7.50	15.00
		This is the rock Crickets, not the R&B Crickets				

Music Factory

| ❏ 415 | | Million Dollar Movie/A Million Miles Apart | 1968 | 5.00 | 10.00 | 20.00 |

Critters, The
Kapp

❏ 727		He'll Make You Cry/Children & Flowers	1965	2.50	5.00	10.00
❏ 752		Younger Girl/Gone for a While	1966	3.00	6.00	12.00
❏ 769		Mr. Dieingly Sad/It Won't Be That Way	1966	3.00	6.00	12.00
❏ 769	PS	Mr. Dieingly Sad/It Won't Be That Way	1966	5.00	10.00	20.00
❏ 793		Bad Misunderstanding/Forever or No More	1966	2.50	5.00	10.00
❏ 805		Marryin' Kind of Love/New York Bound	1967	2.50	5.00	10.00
❏ 838		Don't Let the Rain Fall Down on Me/ Walk Like a Man Again	1967	2.50	5.00	10.00
❏ 858		Little Girl/Dancing in the Streets	1967	2.50	5.00	10.00

Musicor

| ❏ 1044 | | I'm Gonna Give/Georgianna | 1964 | 5.00 | 10.00 | 20.00 |

Prancer

| ❏ 6001 | | No One But You/I'm Telling Everyone | 1969 | 2.00 | 4.00 | 8.00 |

Project 3

❏ 1326		Good Morning Sunshine/A Moment of Being with You	1968	2.00	4.00	8.00
❏ 1332		Touch 'N' Go/Younger Generation	1968	2.00	4.00	8.00
❏ 1349		Cool Sunday Morning/Lisa, But Not the Same	1969	2.00	4.00	8.00
❏ 1363		She Said She Loved Him/ I Just Want to Sit Right Here and Look at You	1969	2.00	4.00	8.00

Cross, Jimmy
Chicken

| ❏ 101 | | Hey Little Girl/Hey Little Girl (Part 2) | 1966 | 3.00 | 6.00 | 12.00 |

Recordo

| ❏ 502 | | Pretty Girls Everywhere/Suntan Sally | 1961 | 3.75 | 7.50 | 15.00 |

Red Bird

| ❏ 10-042 | | Hey Little Girl/Super Duper Man | 1965 | 3.75 | 7.50 | 15.00 |

Tollie

| ❏ 9039 | | I Want My Baby Back/Play the Other Side | 1965 | 5.00 | 10.00 | 20.00 |
| ❏ 9044 | | The Ballad of James Bond/Play the Other Side Again | 1965 | 3.75 | 7.50 | 15.00 |

Crossfires, The
(The Cuca and Lucky Token records were by the band that evolved into The Turtles.)
Capco

| ❏ 104 | | Fiberglass Jungle/Dr. Jekyll and Mr. Hyde | 1963 | 20.00 | 40.00 | 80.00 |

Cuca

| ❏ 1027 | | Young Love/When My Blue Moon Turns to Gold Again | 1961 | 3.00 | 6.00 | 12.00 |

Lucky Token

| ❏ 112 | | One Potato, Two Potato/That'll Be the Day | 1965 | 12.50 | 25.00 | 50.00 |

Tower

| ❏ 278 | | Who'll Be the Next One/Making Love Is Fun | 1966 | 5.00 | 10.00 | 20.00 |

Crowns, The
(At least two different groups)
Chordette

| ❏ 1001 | | Party Time/Amazon Basin Pop | 1962 | 5.00 | 10.00 | 20.00 |

Old Town

❏ 1171		Possibility/Watch Out	1964	10.00	20.00	40.00
		Some copies were on the old blue Old Town label				
❏ 1171		Possibility/Watch Out	1964	3.75	7.50	15.00
		Black label with moon				

R&B

| ❏ 6901 | | Kiss and Make Up/I'll Forget About You | 1958 | 12.50 | 25.00 | 50.00 |
| | | *Four members of the Five Crowns plus Benjamin Nelson (Ben E. King), later to become the second Drifters.* | | | | |

Vee Jay

| ❏ 546 | | Better Luck Next Time/You Make Me Blue | 1963 | 2.50 | 5.00 | 10.00 |

Crows, The
Rama

❏ 3		Seven Lonely Days/No Help Wanted	1953	125.00	250.00	500.00
❏ 5		Gee/I Love You So	1953	125.00	250.00	500.00
		Blue label, red vinyl				
❏ 5		Gee/I Love You So	1953	18.75	37.50	75.00
		Blue label, black vinyl				
❏ 5		Gee/I Love You So	1955	7.50	15.00	30.00
		Red label, black vinyl				
❏ 10		Heartbreaker/Call a Doctor	1953	100.00	200.00	400.00
		Black vinyl				
❏ 10		Heartbreaker/Call a Doctor	1953	200.00	400.00	800.00
		Red vinyl				
❏ 10		Heartbreaker/Call a Doctor	1953	150.00	300.00	600.00
		Black vinyl, label says "The Jewels" on one side, "The Crows" on the other				
❏ 10		Heartbreaker/Call a Doctor	1953	150.00	300.00	600.00
		Black vinyl, label says "The Jewels"				

Number	Title (A Side/B Side)	Year	VG	VG+	NM
❏ 10	Heartbreaker/Call a Doctor	1953	400.00	800.00	1,200
	Red vinyl, label says "The Jewels"				
❏ 29	Baby/Untrue	1954	50.00	100.00	200.00
❏ 30	Miss You/I Really, Really Love You So	1954	100.00	200.00	400.00
	Black vinyl				
❏ 30	Miss You/I Really, Really Love You So	1954	200.00	400.00	800.00
	Red vinyl				
❏ 50	Baby Doll/Sweet Sue (It's You)	1954	100.00	200.00	400.00

Tico

❏ 1082	Mambo Shevitz/Mambo #5	1955	50.00	100.00	200.00
	B-side by Melino and Orchestra; black vinyl				
❏ 1082	Mambo Shevitz/Mambo #5	1955	75.00	150.00	300.00
	B-side by Melino and Orchestra; red vinyl				

Crudup, Arthur
(Also recorded as Big Boy Crudup)

Ace

❏ 503	I Wonder/My Baby Boogies All the Time	1955	12.50	25.00	50.00

Fire

❏ 1501	Rock Me Mama/Mean Ole Frisco	1962	3.75	7.50	15.00
❏ 1502	Katie Mae/Dig Myself a Hole	1962	3.75	7.50	15.00

Groove

❏ 0011	I Love My Baby/Fall on Your Knees and Pray	1954	10.00	20.00	40.00
❏ 0026	She's Got No Hair/If You Ever Been to Georgia	1954	10.00	20.00	40.00

RCA Victor

❏ 47-4367	Love Me Mama/Where Did You Stay Last Night	1951	25.00	50.00	100.00
❏ 47-4572	Goin' Back to Georgia/Mr. So and So	1952	20.00	40.00	80.00
❏ 47-4753	Worried 'Bout You Baby/Late in the Evening	1952	20.00	40.00	80.00
❏ 47-4933	Second Man Blues/Do It If You Want	1952	20.00	40.00	80.00
❏ 47-5070	Lookin' for My Baby/Pearly Lee	1952	20.00	40.00	80.00
❏ 47-5167	Keep On Drinkin'/Nelvina	1953	20.00	40.00	80.00
❏ 47-5563	War Is Over/My Wife and Woman	1953	20.00	40.00	80.00
❏ 50-0000	That's All Right/Crudup's After Hours	1949	75.00	150.00	300.00
	Gray label, orange vinyl; the first R&B 45 rpm record!				
❏ 50-0001	Boy Friend Blues/Katie May	1949	25.00	50.00	100.00
	Gray label, orange vinyl				
❏ 50-0013	Shout Sister Shout/Crudup's Vicksburg Blues	1949	25.00	50.00	100.00
	Gray label, orange vinyl				
❏ 50-0032	Hoodoo Lady Blues/Tired of Worry	1949	25.00	50.00	100.00
	Gray label, orange vinyl				
❏ 50-0046	Come Back Baby/Mercy Blues	1949	25.00	50.00	100.00
	Gray label, orange vinyl				
❏ 50-0074	Dust My Broom/You Know That I Love You	1950	25.00	50.00	100.00
	Gray label, orange vinyl				
❏ 50-0092	Mean Old Santa Fe/(B-side unknown)	1950	25.00	50.00	100.00
	Gray label, orange vinyl				
❏ 50-0100	Lonesome World to Me/ Hand Me Down My Walking Cane	1950	25.00	50.00	100.00
	Gray label, orange vinyl				
❏ 50-0105	She's Just Like Caldonia/(B-side unknown)	1951	25.00	50.00	100.00
	Gray label, orange vinyl				
❏ 50-0109	My Baby Left Me/Anytime Is the Right Time	1951	25.00	50.00	100.00
	Gray label, orange vinyl				
❏ 50-0117	Nobody Wants Me/Star Bootlegger	1951	25.00	50.00	100.00
	Gray label, orange vinyl				
❏ 50-0126	Roberta Blues/Behind Closed Doors	1951	25.00	50.00	100.00
	Gray label, orange vinyl				
❏ 50-0141	I'm Gonna Dig Myself a Hole/Too Much Competition	1951	25.00	50.00	100.00
	Gray label, orange vinyl				

Crusaders, The
(The ABC Blue Thumb, Blue Thumb, Chisa, MCA and Mowest sides are by the jazz group.)

ABC Blue Thumb

❏ 261	Stomp and Buck Dance/A Ballad for Joe (Louis)	1975		2.50	5.00
❏ 267	Creole/I Feel the Love	1975		2.50	5.00
❏ 269	Keep That Same Old Feeling/'Til the Sun Shines	1976		2.50	5.00
❏ 270	And Then There Was the Blues/Feeling Funky	1976		2.50	5.00
❏ 272	Feel It/The Way We Was	1977		2.50	5.00
❏ 273	Free as the Wind/The Way We Was	1977		2.50	5.00
❏ 278	Bayou Bottoms/Covert Action	1978		2.50	5.00

Blue Thumb

❏ 208	Put It Where You Want It/Mosadi	1972		2.50	5.00
❏ 217	So Far Away/That's How I Feel	1972		2.50	5.00
❏ 225	Don't Let It Get You Down/Journey from Within	1973		2.50	5.00
❏ 232	Take It or Leave It/That's How I Feel	1973		2.50	5.00
❏ 245	Lay It On the Line/Let's Boogie	1974		2.50	5.00
❏ 249	Scratch/Way Back Home	1974		2.50	5.00

Cameo

❏ 285	Boogie Woogie/At the Club	1963	3.00	6.00	12.00

Chisa

❏ 8013	Pass the Plate/Greasy Spoon	1971		3.00	6.00

Number		Title (A Side/B Side)	Year	VG	VG+	NM

DKR

| ❏ (no #) | | Seminole/Busted Surfboard | 1962 | 10.00 | 20.00 | 40.00 |

Dooto

| ❏ 472 | | Swinging Week-End/I Found Someone | 1963 | 3.75 | 7.50 | 15.00 |

MCA

❏ 41054		Street Life/Hustler	1979		2.00	4.00
❏ 41295		Sweet Gentle Love/Soul Shadows	1980		2.00	4.00
❏ 51029		Last Call/Honky Tonk Struttin'	1980		2.00	4.00
❏ 51177		I'm So Glad I'm Standing Here Today/Standing Tall	1981		2.00	4.00
		A-side with Joe Cocker				
❏ 51222		This Old World's Too Funky for Me/Standing Tall	1981		2.00	4.00
		A-side with Joe Cocker				
❏ 52098		Street Life/Overture	1982		2.00	4.00
		With B.B. King and the London Symphony Orchestra				
❏ 52365		New Move/Mr. Cool	1984		2.00	4.00
❏ 52398		Dream Street/Dead End	1984		2.00	4.00
❏ 52454		Gotta Lotta Shakalada/Zalal 'E Mini	1984		2.00	4.00
❏ 52966		The Way It Goes/Good Times	1986		2.00	4.00
❏ 53330		A.C. (Alternating Currents)/Mulholland Nights	1988			3.00

Mowest

| ❏ 5028 | | Spanish Harlem/Papa Hooper's Barrelhouse Groove | 1972 | | 3.00 | 6.00 |

Tower

| ❏ 286 | | Little Drummer Boy/Battle Hymn of the Republic | 1966 | 2.50 | 5.00 | 10.00 |
| ❏ 328 | | Make a Joyful Noise/Praise We the Lord | 1967 | 2.50 | 5.00 | 10.00 |

Cryan' Shames, The

Columbia

❏ 43836		I Wanna Meet You/We Could Be Happy	1966	2.50	5.00	10.00
❏ 44037		Mr. Unreliable/Georgia	1967	2.50	5.00	10.00
❏ 44191		It Could Be We're in Love/I Was Lonely When	1967	2.50	5.00	10.00
❏ 44191	PS	It Could Be We're in Love/I Was Lonely When	1967	5.00	10.00	20.00
❏ 44457		Up On the Roof/The Sailing Ship	1968	2.50	5.00	10.00
❏ 44545		Young Birds Fly/Sunshine Psalm	1968	2.00	4.00	8.00
❏ 44638		Greenburg, Blickstein, Charles, David Smith & Jones/The Warm	1968	2.00	4.00	8.00
❏ 44759		First Train to California/A Master's Fool	1969	2.00	4.00	8.00
❏ 45027		Rainmaker/Bits and Pieces	1969	2.00	4.00	8.00

Destination

| ❏ 624 | | Sugar and Spice/Ben Franklin's Almanac | 1966 | 3.75 | 7.50 | 15.00 |

Cryin' Shames, The

(Not the same group as the Cryan' Shames)

London

| ❏ 1001 | | What's New Pussycat/Please Stay (Don't Go) | 1966 | 2.50 | 5.00 | 10.00 |

Crystals, Ronettes and Chiffons, The

(Also see each group individually)

Geffen

| ❏ 28393 | | Little Shop of Horrors/Grow for Me | 1987 | 2.00 | 4.00 | 8.00 |
| | | *B-side by Rick Moranis* | | | | |

Crystals, The

(More than one group)

Aladdin

| ❏ 3355 | | I Love My Baby/I Do Believe | 1957 | 15.00 | 30.00 | 60.00 |

Brent

| ❏ 7011 | | Malaguena/Gypsy Ribbon | 1960 | 3.75 | 7.50 | 15.00 |

Cub

| ❏ 9064 | | Oh My You/Watching You | 1960 | 3.75 | 7.50 | 15.00 |

DeLuxe

❏ 6013		Four Women/My Dear	1953	75.00	150.00	300.00
❏ 6037		Have Faith in Me/My Love	1954	62.50	125.00	250.00
❏ 6077		God Only Knows/My Girl	1955	50.00	100.00	200.00

Felsted

| ❏ 8566 | | Mary Ellen/Blind Date | 1959 | 5.00 | 10.00 | 20.00 |

Indigo

| ❏ 114 | | Dreams and Wishes/Mr. Brush | 1961 | 5.00 | 10.00 | 20.00 |

Luna

| ❏ 100 | | Squeeze Me Baby/Come to Me, Darling | 1954 | 37.50 | 75.00 | 150.00 |
| ❏ 5001 | | Squeeze Me Baby/Come to Me, Darling | 1954 | 30.00 | 60.00 | 120.00 |

Metro

| ❏ 20026 | | Better Come Back to Me/That's Where I Belong | 1960 | 3.75 | 7.50 | 15.00 |

Michelle

| ❏ 4113 | | Ring-a-Ting-a-Ling/Should I Keep On Waiting | 1967 | 2.50 | 5.00 | 10.00 |

Pavillion

| ❏ 03333 | | Rudolph the Red-Nosed Reindeer/I Saw Mommy Kissing Santa Claus | 1982 | | 2.50 | 5.00 |
| | | *B-side by The Ronettes* | | | | |

Philles

| ❏ 100 | | There's No Other (Like My Baby)/Oh Yeah, Maybe Baby | 1961 | 6.25 | 12.50 | 25.00 |

Number		Title (A Side/B Side)	Year	VG	VG+	NM
❑ 102		Uptown/What a Nice Way to Turn Seventeen	1962	6.25	12.50	25.00
❑ 105		He Hit Me (And It Felt Like a Kiss)/	1962	12.50	25.00	50.00
		No One Ever Tells You				
❑ 106		He's a Rebel/I Love You Eddie	1962	7.50	15.00	30.00
	Orange label					
❑ 106		He's a Rebel/I Love You Eddie	1962	6.25	12.50	25.00
	Light blue label					
❑ 106		He's a Rebel/I Love You Eddie	1964	3.75	7.50	15.00
	Yellow and red label					
❑ 109		He's Sure the Boy I Love/Walkin' Along (La-La-La)	1962	6.25	12.50	25.00
❑ 111	DJ	(Let's Dance) The Screw -- Part 1/	1963	2,000	3,000	4,000
		(Let's Dance) The Screw -- Part 2				
	White label					
❑ 111	DJ	(Let's Dance) The Screw -- Part 1/	1963	3,000	4,500	6,000
		(Let's Dance) The Screw -- Part 2				
	Light blue label. Matrix numbers are stamped in dead wax. Counterfeits have numbers hand-etched.					
❑ 112		Da Do Ron Ron (When He Walked Me Home)/Git' It	1963	6.25	12.50	25.00
❑ 115		Then He Kissed Me/Brother Julius	1963	6.25	12.50	25.00
	Light blue label					
❑ 115		Then He Kissed Me/Brother Julius	1963	3.75	7.50	15.00
	Yellow and red label					
❑ 119		Little Boy/Harry (From West Virginia) and Milt	1964	6.25	12.50	25.00
❑ 119X		Little Boy/Harry (From West Virginia) and Milt	1964	5.00	10.00	20.00
❑ 122		All Grown Up/Irving (Jaggered Sixteenths)	1964	6.25	12.50	25.00
	Possible Rolling Stones involvement on instrumental B-side; "Jaggered" refers to Mick					

Regalia

❑ 17		Pony in Dixie/Espresso	1961	3.75	7.50	15.00

Rockin'

❑ 518		My Girl/Don't You Go	1953	62.50	125.00	250.00

Specialty

❑ 657		In the Deep/Love You So	1959	3.75	7.50	15.00

United Artists

❑ 927		You Can't Tie a Good Girl Down/My Place	1965	3.75	7.50	15.00
❑ 994		I Got a Man/Are You Trying to Get Rid of Me, Baby	1966	3.75	7.50	15.00

Cunningham, Buddy

Sun

❑ 208		Right or Wrong/Why Do I Care	1954	500.00	1,000	1,500

Cupids, The

(Several different groups)

Aanko

❑ 1002		Brenda/For You	1963	25.00	50.00	100.00

Aladdin

❑ 3404		Now You Tell Me/Lillie Mae	1957	15.00	30.00	60.00
	Maroon label					
❑ 3404		Now You Tell Me/Lillie Mae	1958	6.25	12.50	25.00
	Black label					

Chan

❑ 107		I Don't Know/Troubles Not At End	1956	12.50	25.00	50.00

Decca

❑ 30279		The Answer to Your Prayer/My Dog Likes Your Dog	1957	10.00	20.00	40.00

KC

❑ 115		Brenda/For You	1963	5.00	10.00	20.00

Musicnote

❑ 119		Lorraine/Little Girl of Mine	1963	3.75	7.50	15.00

Times Square

❑ 1		Pretty Baby/Let's Rock	1964	3.75	7.50	15.00

UWR

❑ 4241/2		True Love, True Love/Let's Twist	1962	5.00	10.00	20.00

Curley and the Jades

Music Makers

❑ 109		Bullfighter/Boom Stix	1962	15.00	30.00	60.00

Reprise

❑ 20,046		Bullfighter/Boom Stix	1962	7.50	15.00	30.00

Currents, The

Laurie

❑ 3205		Night Run/Riff Raff	1963	7.50	15.00	30.00

Curtis, Sonny

A&M

❑ 1359		Lights of L.A./Sunny Mornin'	1972	7.50	15.00	30.00
❑ 1408		Love Is All Around/Last Days of Childhood	1973			*Unreleased?*

Capitol

❑ 4158		Lovesick Blues/It's Only a Question of Time	1975	3.00	6.00	12.00
❑ 4227		It's Only a Question of Time/When It's Just You and Me	1976	3.00	6.00	12.00
❑ 4240		Where's Patricia Now/When It's Just You and Me	1976	3.00	6.00	12.00

Coral

❑ 60954		Someday You're Gonna Be Sorry/Forever Yours	1953	6.25	12.50	25.00

Number		Title (A Side/B Side)	Year	VG	VG+	NM
❏ 61023		No More Tears/The Best Way to Hold a Girl	1953	6.25	12.50	25.00
❏ 62207		Red Headed Stranger/Talk About My Baby	1960	10.00	20.00	40.00

Dimension

Number		Title (A Side/B Side)	Year	VG	VG+	NM
❏ 1017		So Used to Loving You/	1963	5.00	10.00	20.00
		The Last Song I'm Ever Gonna Sing				
❏ 1024		A Beatle I Want to Be/So Used to Loving You	1964	6.25	12.50	25.00

Dot

Number		Title (A Side/B Side)	Year	VG	VG+	NM
❏ 15754		Wrong Again/Laughing Stock	1958	10.00	20.00	40.00
❏ 15799		A Pretty Girl/Willa May Jones	1958	7.50	15.00	30.00

Elektra

Number		Title (A Side/B Side)	Year	VG	VG+	NM
❏ 46526		The Cowboy Singer/Cheatin' Clouds	1979		2.50	5.00
❏ 46568		Do You Remember Roll Over Beethoven/	1979		2.50	5.00
		Walk Right Back				
❏ 46616		The Real Buddy Holly Story/Ain't Nobody Honest	1980		3.00	6.00
❏ 46643		Love Is All Around/The Clone Song	1980		2.50	5.00
❏ 47048		You Made My Life a Song/	1980		2.50	5.00
		50 Ways to Leave Your Lover				
❏ 47129		Good Ol' Girls/So Used to Loving You	1981		2.50	5.00
❏ 47176		Married Woman/I Live Your Music	1981		2.50	5.00
❏ 47231	DJ	The Christmas Song/Little Drummer Boy	1981	2.00	4.00	8.00
		B-side by Hank Williams, Jr.; promo only				
❏ 69942		Together Alone/Dream Well All of You Children	1982		2.50	5.00

Liberty

Number		Title (A Side/B Side)	Year	VG	VG+	NM
❏ 55710		Bo Diddley Bach/I Pledge My Love to You	1964	5.00	10.00	20.00

Mercury

Number		Title (A Side/B Side)	Year	VG	VG+	NM
❏ 73438		Rock and Roll (I Gave You the Best Years of My Life)/	1973	3.75	7.50	15.00
❏		My Mama Sure Left Me Some Good Old Days				

Ovation

Number		Title (A Side/B Side)	Year	VG	VG+	NM
❏ 1006		Love Is All Around/Here, There and Everywhere	1970	5.00	10.00	20.00
❏ 1023		Unsaintly Judy/You Don't Belong in This Place	1970	3.75	7.50	15.00

Viva

Number		Title (A Side/B Side)	Year	VG	VG+	NM
❏ 602		My Way of Life/Last Call	1966	3.75	7.50	15.00
❏ 607		The Collection/Destiny's Child	1966	3.75	7.50	15.00
❏ 617		I'm a Gypsy Man/I Wanna Go Bummin' Around	1967	3.75	7.50	15.00
❏ 626		Day Drinker/Atlanta, Georgia Stray	1968	3.75	7.50	15.00
❏ 630		The Straight Life/How Little Men Care	1968	3.75	7.50	15.00
❏ 634		Holiday for Clowns/Day Gig	1969	3.75	7.50	15.00
❏ 636		Girl of the North/Hung Up in Your Eyes	1969	3.75	7.50	15.00

Custer and the Survivors

Ascot

Number		Title (A Side/B Side)	Year	VG	VG+	NM
❏ 2207		I Saw Her Walking/Flapjacks	1965	4.00	8.00	16.00

Golden State

Number		Title (A Side/B Side)	Year	VG	VG+	NM
❏ 1657		I Saw Her Walking/Flapjacks	1965	3.00	6.00	12.00

Vardan

Number		Title (A Side/B Side)	Year	VG	VG+	NM
❏ 202		I Saw Her Walking/Flapjacks	1965	5.00	10.00	20.00

Cute-Teens, The

Aladdin

Number		Title (A Side/B Side)	Year	VG	VG+	NM
❏ 3458		When My Teenage Days Are Over/	1959	62.50	125.00	250.00
		From This Day Forward				

Cyclone III

Philips

Number		Title (A Side/B Side)	Year	VG	VG+	NM
❏ 40258		You've Got a Bomb/Surfnanny	1965	10.00	20.00	40.00

Cymbal, Johnny

Amaret

Number		Title (A Side/B Side)	Year	VG	VG+	NM
❏ 110		Big River/Girl from Willow County	1969	2.00	4.00	8.00
❏ 111		Ode to Bubblegum/Save All Your Lovin' (Hold It for Me)	1969	2.00	4.00	8.00

Bang

Note: Bang releases as "Derek"

Number		Title (A Side/B Side)	Year	VG	VG+	NM
❏ 558		Cinnamon/This Is My Story	1968	2.00	4.00	8.00
❏ 566		Back Door Man/Tell Your Soul	1969		3.00	6.00
❏ 571		Inside Out-Outside In/Sell Your Soul	1969		3.00	6.00

Columbia

Number		Title (A Side/B Side)	Year	VG	VG+	NM
❏ 43842		Good Morning Blues/Jessica	1966	2.00	4.00	8.00

DCP

Number		Title (A Side/B Side)	Year	VG	VG+	NM
❏ 1135		Go, VW, Go/Sorrow and Pain	1965	7.50	15.00	30.00
❏ 1146		My Last Day/Summertime's Here at Last	1965	3.75	7.50	15.00

Kapp

Number		Title (A Side/B Side)	Year	VG	VG+	NM
❏ 503		Mr. Bass Man/Sacred Lovers' Vow	1963	5.00	10.00	20.00
❏ 524		Teenage Heaven/Cinderella Baby	1963	3.75	7.50	15.00
❏ 539		Surfin' at Tiajuana/Dum Dum Dee Dee	1963	3.75	7.50	15.00
❏ 556		Marshmallow/Hurdy Gurdy Man	1963	3.75	7.50	15.00
❏ 576		There Goes a Bad Girl/Refreshment Time	1964	3.75	7.50	15.00
❏ 594		Robinson Crusoe on Mars/Mitsu	1964	3.75	7.50	15.00
❏ 614		Connie/Little Miss Lonely	1964	3.75	7.50	15.00
❏ 634		Cheat, Cheat/16 Shades of Blue	1964	3.75	7.50	15.00

Kedlen

Number		Title (A Side/B Side)	Year	VG	VG+	NM
❏ 2001		Bachelor Man/Growing Up with You	1962	5.00	10.00	20.00

Number	Title (A Side/B Side)	Year	VG	VG+	NM

MGM
| ☐ 12935 | It'll Be Me/Always, Always | 1960 | 5.00 | 10.00 | 20.00 |
| ☐ 12978 | The Water Was Red/The Bunny | 1961 | 5.00 | 10.00 | 20.00 |

Musicor
| ☐ 1261 | It Looks Like Love/May I Get to Know You | 1967 | 3.00 | 6.00 | 12.00 |
| ☐ 1272 | Breaking Your Balloon/
The Marriage of Charlotte Brown | 1967 | 3.00 | 6.00 | 12.00 |

Vee Jay
| ☐ 495 | Bachelor Man/Growing Up with You | 1963 | 3.75 | 7.50 | 15.00 |

Cyrcle, The
Columbia
☐ CSM-466	Camaro/SS 396	1967	6.25	12.50	25.00
	B-side by Paul Revere and the Raiders				
☐ CSM-466	PS Camaro/SS 396	1967	12.50	25.00	50.00
	B-side by Paul Revere and the Raiders				
☐ 43589	Red Rubber Ball/How Can I Leave Her	1966	3.00	6.00	12.00
☐ 43589	DJ Red Rubber Ball (same on both sides)	1966	10.00	20.00	40.00
	Promo only on red vinyl				
☐ 43729	Turn-Down Day/Big, Little Woman	1966	2.50	5.00	10.00
☐ 43871	Please Don't Ever Leave Me/Money to Burn	1966	2.00	4.00	8.00
☐ 43965	I Wish You Could Be Here/The Visit (She Was Here)	1967	2.00	4.00	8.00
☐ 43965	PS I Wish You Could Be Here/The Visit (She Was Here)	1967	3.00	6.00	12.00
☐ 44108	We Had a Good Thing Goin'/Two Rooms	1967	2.00	4.00	8.00
☐ 44224	Penny Arcade/The Words	1967	2.00	4.00	8.00
☐ 44366	Turn of the Century/ Don't Cry, No Fears, No Tears Comin'	1967	2.00	4.00	8.00
☐ 44426	Friends/Reading Her Papers	1968	2.00	4.00	8.00
☐ 44491	Red Chair Fade Away/Where Are You Going	1968	2.00	4.00	8.00

Cyrus Erie
(Early Eric Carmen)
Epic
| ☐ 10451 | Sparrow/Get the Message | 1969 | 3.00 | 6.00 | 12.00 |

D

D-Men, The
(Early incarnation of The Fifth Estate)
Kapp
| ☐ 691 | So Little Time/Every Moment of Every Day | 1965 | 3.00 | 6.00 | 12.00 |

Veep
| ☐ 1206 | Don't You Know/No Hope for Me | 1965 | 3.75 | 7.50 | 15.00 |
| ☐ 1209 | Just Don't Care/Mousin' Around | 1965 | 3.75 | 7.50 | 15.00 |

Dache, Bertell
(Tony Orlando with Carole King on backing vocals)
Diamond
| ☐ 201 | Don't Stop the World for Me/Anchors Aweigh Girl | 1966 | 3.75 | 7.50 | 15.00 |

United Artists
| ☐ 260 | All the World Loves a Lover/You Gotta Have Chicks | 1960 | 6.25 | 12.50 | 25.00 |
| ☐ 290 | Not Just Tomorrow, But Today/Love Eyes | 1961 | 6.25 | 12.50 | 25.00 |

Daisies, The
Capitol
| ☐ 5667 | Cold Wave/Put Your Arms Around Me | 1966 | 6.25 | 12.50 | 25.00 |

Roulette
| ☐ 4571 | I Wanna Swim with Him/You Just Said You Loved Me | 1964 | 3.00 | 6.00 | 12.00 |

Dakotas, The - See "Kramer, Billy J. and the Dakotas"

Dale and Grace
Guyden
| ☐ 6002 | What's Happening to Me/Darling It's Wonderful | 1972 | | 2.50 | 5.00 |

Hanna-Barbera
| ☐ 472 | Let Them Talk/I'd Rather Be Free | 1966 | 2.00 | 4.00 | 8.00 |

Michelle
☐ 921	I'm Leaving It Up to You/That's What I Like	1963	5.00	10.00	20.00
☐ 922	Stop and Think It Over/Bad Luck	1963	3.75	7.50	15.00
☐ 928	The Loneliest Night/I'm Not Free	1964	3.75	7.50	15.00
☐ 930	Darling It's Wonderful/What's Happening to Me	1964	3.75	7.50	15.00
☐ 936	Cool Water/Rules of Love	1964	3.75	7.50	15.00

Montel
☐ 921	I'm Leaving It Up to You/That's What I Like	1963	3.00	6.00	12.00
☐ 922	Stop and Think It Over/Bad Luck	1963	3.00	6.00	12.00
☐ 928	The Loneliest Night/I'm Not Free	1964	3.00	6.00	12.00
☐ 930	Darling It's Wonderful/What's Happening to Me	1964	3.00	6.00	12.00
☐ 936	Cool Water/Rules of Love	1964	3.00	6.00	12.00
☐ 958	Make the World Go Away/Stranger	1965	3.00	6.00	12.00
☐ 989	It Keeps Right On a-Hurtin'/So Fine	1967	3.00	6.00	12.00

Montel/Michelle
| ☐ 942 | Something Special/What Am I Living For | 1964 | 3.00 | 6.00 | 12.00 |

Number		Title (A Side/B Side)	Year	VG	VG+	NM

Dale, Dick
Accent
| ❏ 1243 | | Eyes of a Child/Just a-Waitin' | 1968 | 2.00 | 4.00 | 8.00 |

Capitol
❏ 4939		Miserlou/Eight Till Midnight	1963	5.00	10.00	20.00
❏ 4940		Surf Beat/Peppermint Man	1963	5.00	10.00	20.00
❏ 4963		King of the Surf Guitar/Havah Nagilah	1963	5.00	10.00	20.00
❏ 4963	PS	King of the Surf Guitar/Havah Nagilah	1963	20.00	40.00	80.00
❏ 5010		Secret Surfin' Spot/Surfin' and a-Swingin'	1963	5.00	10.00	20.00
❏ 5048		Wild Ideas/Scavenger	1963	5.00	10.00	20.00
❏ 5098		The Wedge/Night Rider	1963	5.00	10.00	20.00
❏ 5140		The Victor/Mr. Eliminator	1964	3.75	7.50	15.00
❏ 5187		Wild, Wild Mustang/Grunge Run	1964	3.75	7.50	15.00
❏ 5225		Never on Sunday/Glory Wave	1964	3.75	7.50	15.00
❏ 5290		Oh Marie/Who Can It Be	1964	3.75	7.50	15.00
❏ 5389		Let's Go Trippin' '65/Watusi Jo	1965	3.75	7.50	15.00

Columbia
❏ 07340		Pipeline/Love Struck Baby	1987		2.00	4.00
		B-side by Stevie Ray Vaughan				
❏ 07340	PS	Pipeline/Love Struck Baby	1987		3.00	6.00

Concert Room
| ❏ 371 | | We'll Never Hear the End of It/Fairest of Them All | 1963 | 6.25 | 12.50 | 25.00 |

Cougar
| ❏ 711 | | Ramblin' Man/You're Hurtin' Now | 1967 | 3.75 | 7.50 | 15.00 |
| ❏ 712 | | Taco Wagon/Spanish Kiss | 1967 | 3.75 | 7.50 | 15.00 |

Cupid
| ❏ 106 | | We'll Never Hear the End of It/Fairest of Them All | 1960 | 7.50 | 15.00 | 30.00 |

Deltone
❏ 5012		Oh Whee Marie/Breaking Heart	1959	15.00	30.00	60.00
❏ 5013		Stop Teasin'/Without Your Love	1959	15.00	30.00	60.00
❏ 5014		Jessie Pearl/St. Louis Blues	1960	25.00	50.00	100.00
❏ 5017		Let's Go Trippin'/Del-Tone Rock	1961	6.25	12.50	25.00
❏ 5018		Shake and Stomp/Jungle Fever	1962	6.25	12.50	25.00
❏ 5019		Miserlou/Eight Till Midnight	1962	6.25	12.50	25.00
❏ 5020		Peppermint Man/Surf Beat	1962	6.25	12.50	25.00
❏ 5028		Run for Your Life/Lovin' on My Brain	1963	7.50	15.00	30.00

GNP Crescendo
| ❏ 804 | | Let's Go Trippin'/Those Memories of You | 1975 | | 3.00 | 6.00 |

Rendezvous
| ❏ 204 | | Reincarnation (Part 1)/Reincarnation (Part 2) | 1963 | 5.00 | 10.00 | 20.00 |

Saturn
| ❏ 401 | | We'll Never Hear the End of It/Fairest of Them All | 1963 | 7.50 | 15.00 | 30.00 |

U.S. Army
| ❏ 1301 | DJ | Enlistment Twist/(B-side unknown) | 1962 | 7.50 | 15.00 | 30.00 |
| ❏ 1301 | PS | Enlistment Twist/(B-side unknown) | 1962 | 7.50 | 15.00 | 30.00 |

Yes
| ❏ 7014 | | We'll Never Hear the End of It/Fairest of Them All | 1963 | 7.50 | 15.00 | 30.00 |
| ❏ 7014 | PS | We'll Never Hear the End of It/Fairest of Them All | 1963 | 10.00 | 20.00 | 40.00 |

Daley, Jimmy, and the Ding-a-Lings
Decca
❏ 30163		Rock, Pretty Baby/Can I Steal a Little Love	1956	10.00	20.00	40.00
❏ 30358		Red Lips and Green Eyes/How's About a Little Kiss?	1957	10.00	20.00	40.00
❏ 30532		Hole in the Wall/Bongo Rock	1957	10.00	20.00	40.00

Dalton Boys, The
Skyla
| ❏ 1124 | | I'm Thinkin'/It's Much More Stronger | 1962 | 7.50 | 15.00 | 30.00 |

Teen
| ❏ 505 | | Who's Gonna Hold Your Hand/Walkin' | 1959 | 12.50 | 25.00 | 50.00 |

V.I.P.
| ❏ 25025 | | I've Been Cheated/Something's Bothering You | 1965 | 12.50 | 25.00 | 50.00 |
| ❏ 25025 | | I've Been Cheated/Take My Hand | 1965 | 50.00 | 100.00 | 200.00 |

Damon's, Liz, Orient Express
Anthem
| ❏ 51005 | | Loneliness Remembers/Quiet Sound | 1971 | 2.50 | 5.00 | 10.00 |
| ❏ 51006 | | All in All/Walking Backwards Down the Road | 1971 | 2.50 | 5.00 | 10.00 |

White Whale
| ❏ 368 | | 1900 Yesterday/You're Falling in Love | 1970 | | 3.00 | 6.00 |
| ❏ 370 | | But For Love/You Make Me Feel Like Someone | 1970 | | 3.00 | 6.00 |

Dancer, Prancer, and Nervous
Capitol
❏ 4300		The Happy Reindeer/Dancer's Waltz	1959	3.00	6.00	12.00
❏ 4300	PS	The Happy Reindeer/Dancer's Waltz	1959	6.25	12.50	25.00
❏ 4353		I Wanta Be an Easter Bunny/The Happy Birthday Song	1960	3.00	6.00	12.00
		As "The Singing Reindeer"				

Daniels, Jeff
Astro
| ❏ 108 | | Foxy Dan/Someday You'll Remember | 1960 | 25.00 | 50.00 | 100.00 |

Number		Title (A Side/B Side)	Year	VG	VG+	NM

Big Howdy

❏ 777		Switch Blade Sam/You're Still on My Mind	1959	25.00	50.00	100.00
❏ 8120		Uh-Huh/Table for Two	196?	25.00	50.00	100.00
❏ 8121		Foxy Dan/Someday You'll Remember	1961	25.00	50.00	100.00

Meladee

| ❏ 117 | | Daddy-O Rock/Hey Woman | 1958 | 100.00 | 200.00 | 400.00 |

Danleers, The

Amp 3

❏ 2115		One Summer Night/Wheelin' and Dealin'	1958	15.00	30.00	60.00
		By "Dandleers"				
❏ 2115		One Summer Night/Wheelin' and Dealin'	1958	10.00	20.00	40.00
		Corrected group name on label				

Epic

| ❏ 9367 | | I Live Half a Block from an Angel/If You Don't Care | 1960 | 7.50 | 15.00 | 30.00 |
| ❏ 9421 | | I'll Always Be in Love with You/Little Lover | 1960 | 7.50 | 15.00 | 30.00 |

Everest

| ❏ 19412 | | Foolish/I'm Looking Around | 1961 | 7.50 | 15.00 | 30.00 |

LeMans

| ❏ 004 | | The Truth Hurts/Baby You've Got It | 1963 | 2.50 | 5.00 | 10.00 |
| ❏ 008 | | I'm Sorry/This Thing Called Love | 1963 | 2.50 | 5.00 | 10.00 |

Mercury

❏ 71322		One Summer Night/Wheelin' and Dealin'	1958	5.00	10.00	20.00
❏ 71356		I Really Love You/My Flaming Heart	1958	5.00	10.00	20.00
❏ 71401		A Picture of You/Prelude to Love	1959	5.00	10.00	20.00
❏ 71441		I Can't Sleep/Your Love	1959	5.00	10.00	20.00

Smash

| ❏ 1872 | | Were You There/If | 1964 | 3.00 | 6.00 | 12.00 |
| ❏ 1895 | | Where Is Love/The Angels Sent You | 1964 | 3.00 | 6.00 | 12.00 |

Danny and the Juniors

ABC-Paramount

❏ 9871		At the Hop/Sometimes (When I'm All Alone)	1957	7.50	15.00	30.00
❏ 9888		Rock and Roll Is Here to Stay/School Boy Romance	1958	7.50	15.00	30.00
❏ 9926		Dottie/In the Meantime	1958	6.25	12.50	25.00
❏ 9953		A Thief/Crazy Cave	1958	6.25	12.50	25.00
❏ 9978		Sassy Fran/I Feel So Lonely	1958	12.50	25.00	50.00
❏ 10004		Do You Love Me/Somehow I Can't Forget	1959	6.25	12.50	25.00
❏ 10052		Playing Hard to Get/Of Love	1959	6.25	12.50	25.00

Crunch

| ❏ 018001 | | At the Hop/Let the Good Times Roll | 1973 | | 2.50 | 5.00 |

Guyden

| ❏ 2076 | | Oo-La-La-Limbo/Now and Then | 1962 | 5.00 | 10.00 | 20.00 |

Luv

| ❏ 252 | | Rock and Roll Is Here to Stay/ Sometimes (When I'm All Alone) | 1968 | 2.50 | 5.00 | 10.00 |

Mercury

| ❏ 72240 | | Sad Girl/Let's Go Ski-ing | 1964 | 5.00 | 10.00 | 20.00 |

Singular

❏ 711		At the Hop/Sometimes	1957	250.00	500.00	1,000
		Blue label, machine-stamped in dead wax, no mention of Artie Singer on label				
❏ 711		At the Hop/Sometimes	1957	300.00	600.00	1,200
		Blue label, machine-stamped in dead wax, with "Orchestra Directed by Artie Singer" credit. Both versions have a "count-in" before the song starts. Singular records on black labels or without the count-in are probably reproductions.				

Swan

❏ 4060		Twistin' U.S.A./A Thousand Miles Away	1960	5.00	10.00	20.00
❏ 4064		Candy Cane. Sugary Plum/Oh Holy Night	1960	6.25	12.50	25.00
❏ 4064	PS	Candy Cane. Sugary Plum/Oh Holy Night	1960	50.00	100.00	200.00
❏ 4068		Daydreamer/Pony Express	1961	5.00	10.00	20.00
❏ 4072		Cha Cha Go Go (Chicago Cha-Cha)/Mister Whisper	1961	5.00	10.00	20.00
❏ 4082		Back to the Hop/The Charleston Fish	1961	5.00	10.00	20.00
❏ 4082	PS	Back to the Hop/The Charleston Fish	1961	25.00	50.00	100.00
❏ 4084		Just Because/Your Hair's Too Long	1961			Unreleased?
❏ 4092		Twistin' All Night Long/Some Kind of Nut	1962	5.00	10.00	20.00
❏ 4100		(Do the) Mashed Potatoes/Doin' the Continental Walk	1962	5.00	10.00	20.00
❏ 4113		We Got Soul/Funny	1962	5.00	10.00	20.00

Danny and the Memories

("Danny" is Danny Whitten, later of Crazy Horse.)

Valiant

| ❏ 6049 | | Can't Help Lovin' That Girl of Mine/Don't Go | 1964 | 6.25 | 12.50 | 25.00 |
| ❏ 705 | | Can't Help Lovin' That Girl of Mine/Don't Go | 1965 | 6.25 | 12.50 | 25.00 |

Dante

(Includes Dante and the Evergreens; Dante and His Friends)

A&M

| ❏ 788 | | Speedoo/Sweet Lover | 1966 | 2.50 | 5.00 | 10.00 |

Darrow

| ❏ 515 | | How Much I Care/Baby Baby | 1960 | 10.00 | 20.00 | 40.00 |

Decca

| ❏ 31178 | | If You Don't Know/Leave Your Tears Behind You | 1960 | 3.75 | 7.50 | 15.00 |

"At the Hop" by Danny and the Juniors was one of the most popular rock 'n' roll records of the 1950s. But the original pressing, on Singular, has become among the most desirable items in all of collecting. That's in part because the Singular pressing has one of the band members "counting into" the song, a feature deleted from all future pressings. Now, we reveal two label variations. At top is the first Singular pressing; at bottom (unfortunately, with major label damage) is the second, never-before-seen Singular pressing with "Orchestra Directed by Artie Singer" beneath Danny and the Juniors' name. Both copies have blue labels and are machine-stamped in the dead wax.

Number		Title (A Side/B Side)	Year	VG	VG+	NM
❑ 31268		Bye Bye Baby/That's Why	1961	3.75	7.50	15.00
❑ 31319		Ring or Write or Call/Say It to Me	1961	3.75	7.50	15.00
Imperial						
❑ 5798		Something Happens/Are You Just My Friend	1961	3.75	7.50	15.00
❑ 5827		Miss America/Now I've Got You	1962	3.75	7.50	15.00
❑ 5867		Magic Ring/Am I the One	1962	3.75	7.50	15.00
Madison						
❑ 130		Alley Oop/The Right Time	1960	5.00	10.00	20.00
❑ 135		Time Machine/Dream Land	1960	3.75	7.50	15.00
❑ 143		What Are You Doing New Year's Eve/Yeah Baby	1960	3.75	7.50	15.00
❑ 154		Think Sweet Thoughts/Da Doo	1961	3.75	7.50	15.00
Mercury						
❑ 71621		How Much I Care/Baby Baby	1960	5.00	10.00	20.00
Tide						
❑ 003		My Lament/Aching Heart	1960	5.00	10.00	20.00

Dante, Ron

(Of the Archies and the Cuff Links; also Barry Manilow's producer for years)

Number		Title (A Side/B Side)	Year	VG	VG+	NM
Almont						
❑ 307		Little Lollypop/(B-side unknown)	1963	3.75	7.50	15.00
Bell						
❑ 45,460		Christine/Don't Call It Love	1974		2.50	5.00
		As "Bo Cooper"				
❑ 45,610		Charmer/Yesterday Dreamin'	1974		2.00	4.00
❑ 45,619		Midnight Show/The Christian	1974	2.00	4.00	
Columbia						
❑ 43720		Think/221 East Maple	1966	2.50	5.00	10.00
❑ 43862		I Give You Things/Janie, Janie	1966	2.50	5.00	10.00
Dot						
❑ 17023		Absence of Lisa/Gypsy Be Mine	1967	2.50	5.00	10.00
Handshake						
❑ 02107		Show and Tell/God Bless Rock and Roll	1981		2.00	4.00
❑ 02552		Letter from Zowie/God Bless Rock and Roll	1981		2.00	4.00
Infinity						
Note: Infinity sides as "Dante's Inferno"						
❑ 50,008		Ain't Misbehavin' (One Never Knows, Do One?)/'Round About Midnight	1979		2.50	5.00
❑ 50,018		Fire Island/They're Playing Our Song	1979		2.50	5.00
❑ 50,038		Brand New Key/They're Playing Our Song	1979		2.50	5.00
Kirshner						
❑ 63-1010		How Do You Know/Let Me Bring You Up	1970		3.00	6.00
❑ 63-1010	PS	How Do You Know/Let Me Bring You Up	1970	2.50	5.00	10.00
❑ 63-5007		Sweet Taste of Love/C'mon Girl	1970		3.00	6.00
Mercury						
❑ 72812		Follow a Dream/He's Raining in My Sunshine	1968	2.50	5.00	10.00
Music Voice						
❑ 503		If You Love Me, Laurie/Don't Stand Up in a Canoe	1964	3.75	7.50	15.00
Musicor						
❑ 1058		Look at Me/There's Love	1965	3.00	6.00	12.00
❑ 1090		In the Rain/Poor Boys	1965	3.00	6.00	12.00
❑ 1105		If You Love Me, Laurie/Don't Stand Up in a Canoe	1965	3.00	6.00	12.00
❑ 1134		Hey Mom, Hey Pop/(Heart) Stop Calling Her Name	1965	3.00	6.00	12.00
RCA						
❑ PB-10898		How Am I to Know/Sky Rider	1977		2.00	4.00
RCA Victor						
❑ PB-10340		Sugar, Sugar/Sugar, Sugar (Disco)	1975		2.50	5.00
Scepter						
❑ 12333	DJ	That's What Life Is All About (mono/stereo)	1971		3.00	6.00
		Stock copy may not exist				

Daps, The

Number		Title (A Side/B Side)	Year	VG	VG+	NM
Marterry						
❑ 5429		When You're Alone/Down and Out	1956	15.00	30.00	60.00

Darin, Bobby

Number		Title (A Side/B Side)	Year	VG	VG+	NM
Atco						
❑ 6092		I Found a Million Dollar Baby/Talk to Me	1957	7.50	15.00	30.00
❑ 6103		Don't Call My Name/Pretty Betty	1957	7.50	15.00	30.00
❑ 6109		Just in Case You Change Your Mind/So Mean	1958	7.50	15.00	30.00
❑ 6117		Splish Splash/Judy, Don't Be Moody	1958	5.00	10.00	20.00
❑ 6121		Early in the Morning/Now We're One	1958	10.00	20.00	40.00
		As "The Rinky Dinks"				
❑ 6121		Early in the Morning/Now We're One	1958	5.00	10.00	20.00
		As "Bobby Darin with The Rinky Dinks"				
❑ 6127		Queen of the Hop/Lost Love	1958	5.00	10.00	20.00
❑ 6128		Mighty Mighty Man/You're Gone	1958	10.00	20.00	40.00
		As "The Rinky Dinks"				
❑ 6128		Mighty Mighty Man/You're Gone	1958	5.00	10.00	20.00
		As "Bobby Darin with The Rinky Dinks"				
❑ 6133	M	Plain Jane/While I'm Gone	1959	5.00	10.00	20.00
❑ 6133	PS	Plain Jane/While I'm Gone	1959	10.00	20.00	40.00

Number			Title (A Side/B Side)	Year	VG	VG+	NM
❏ SD-45-6133	S		Plain Jane/While I'm Gone	1959	10.00	20.00	40.00
❏ 6140			Dream Lover/Bullmoose	1959	5.00	10.00	20.00
❏ 6140	PS		Dream Lover/Bullmoose	1959	10.00	20.00	40.00
❏ 6147			Mack the Knife/Was There a Call for Me	1959	5.00	10.00	20.00
❏ 6147	PS		Mack the Knife/Was There a Call for Me	1959	10.00	20.00	40.00
❏ 6158			Beyond the Sea/That's the Way Love Is	1960	5.00	10.00	20.00
❏ 6158	PS		Beyond the Sea/That's the Way Love Is	1960	10.00	20.00	40.00
❏ 6161			Clementine/Tall Story	1960	5.00	10.00	20.00
❏ 6161	PS		Clementine/Tall Story	1960	10.00	20.00	40.00
❏ 6167			Won't You Come Home Bill Bailey/I'll Be There	1960	5.00	10.00	20.00
❏ 6167	PS		Won't You Come Home Bill Bailey/I'll Be There	1960	7.50	15.00	30.00
❏ 6173			Beachcomber/Autumn Blues	1960	5.00	10.00	20.00
❏ 6173	PS		Beachcomber/Autumn Blues	1960	7.50	15.00	30.00
❏ 6179			Artificial Flowers/Somebody to Love	1960	5.00	10.00	20.00
❏ 6179	PS		Artificial Flowers/Somebody to Love	1960	7.50	15.00	30.00
❏ 6183			Christmas Auld Lang Syne/Child of God	1960	6.25	12.50	25.00
❏ 6183	PS		Christmas Auld Lang Syne/Child of God	1960	10.00	20.00	40.00
❏ 6188			Lazy River/Oo-Ee Train	1961	3.00	6.00	12.00
❏ 6188	PS		Lazy River/Oo-Ee Train	1961	5.00	10.00	20.00
❏ 6196			Nature Boy/Look for My True Love	1961	3.00	6.00	12.00
❏ 6196	PS		Nature Boy/Look for My True Love	1961	5.00	10.00	20.00
❏ 6200			Come September/Walk Back to Me	1961	3.75	7.50	15.00
❏ 6206			You Must Have Been a Beautiful Baby/ Sorrow Tomorrow	1961	3.00	6.00	12.00
❏ 6206	PS		You Must Have Been a Beautiful Baby/ Sorrow Tomorrow	1961	5.00	10.00	20.00
❏ 6211			Ave Maria/O Come All Ye Faithful	1961	3.00	6.00	12.00
❏ 6211	PS		Ave Maria/O Come All Ye Faithful	1961	40.00	80.00	160.00
❏ 6214			Irresistible You/Multiplication	1961	3.00	6.00	12.00
❏ 6214	PS		Irresistible You/Multiplication	1961	5.00	10.00	20.00
❏ 6221			What'd I Say (Part 1)/What'd I Say (Part 2)	1962	3.00	6.00	12.00
❏ 6221	PS		What'd I Say (Part 1)/What'd I Say (Part 2)	1962	5.00	10.00	20.00
❏ 6229			Things/Jalier Bring Me Water	1962	3.00	6.00	12.00
❏ 6236			Baby Face/You Know How	1962	3.00	6.00	12.00
❏ 6244			I Found a New Baby/Keep a-Walkin'	1962	3.00	6.00	12.00
❏ 6297			Milord/Golden Earrings	1964	2.50	5.00	10.00
❏ 6316			Swing Low Sweet Chariot/Similau	1964	2.50	5.00	10.00
❏ 6334			Minnie the Moocher/Hard Hearted Hannah	1965	2.50	5.00	10.00

Atlantic

Number			Title (A Side/B Side)	Year	VG	VG+	NM
❏ 2305			Funny What Love Can Do/ We Didn't Ask to Be Brought Here	1965	2.00	4.00	8.00
❏ 2317			Silver Dollar/The Breaking Point	1966	2.00	4.00	8.00
❏ 2329			Mame/Walking in the Shadow of Love	1966	2.00	4.00	8.00
❏ 2341			Who's Afraid of Virginia Woolf?/Merci, Cheri	1966	2.00	4.00	8.00
❏ 2350			If I Were a Carpenter/Rainin'	1966	2.50	5.00	10.00
❏ 2367			The Girl That Stood Beside Me/Reason to Believe	1966	2.00	4.00	8.00
❏ 2376			Lovin' You/Amy	1967	2.00	4.00	8.00
❏ 2395			The Lady Came from Baltimore/I Am	1967	2.00	4.00	8.00
❏ 2420			Darlin' Be Home Soon/Hello, Sunshine	1967	2.00	4.00	8.00
❏ 2433			Talk to the Animals/After Today	1967	2.00	4.00	8.00
❏ 2433			Talk to the Animals/She Knows	1967	2.00	4.00	8.00
❏ 89166			Beyond the Sea/Mack the Knife	1987			3.00
❏ 89166	PS		Beyond the Sea/Mack the Knife	1987			3.00
			From the movie "Big Town"				

Brunswick

Number			Title (A Side/B Side)	Year	VG	VG+	NM
❏ 55073			Early in the Morning/Now We're One	1958	20.00	40.00	80.00
			As "The Ding Dongs"; also see Atco 6121				

Capitol

Number			Title (A Side/B Side)	Year	VG	VG+	NM
❏ 4837			If a Man Answers/True, True Love	1962	2.50	5.00	10.00
❏ 4837	PS		If a Man Answers/True, True Love	1962	3.75	7.50	15.00
❏ 4897			You're the Reason I'm Living/Now You're Gone	1962	2.50	5.00	10.00
❏ 4897	PS		You're the Reason I'm Living/Now You're Gone	1962	3.75	7.50	15.00
❏ 4970			18 Yellow Roses/Not for Me	1963	2.50	5.00	10.00
❏ 4970	PS		18 Yellow Roses/Not for Me	1963	3.75	7.50	15.00
❏ 5019			Treat My Baby Good/Down So Long	1963	2.50	5.00	10.00
❏ 5079			Be Mad Little Girl/Since You've Been Gone	1963	2.50	5.00	10.00
❏ 5126			I Wonder Who's Kissing Her Now/ As Long As I'm Singing	1964	2.50	5.00	10.00
❏ 5257			The Things in This House/Wait by the Water	1964	2.50	5.00	10.00
❏ 5359			Hello, Dolly!/Golden Earrings	1965	2.50	5.00	10.00
❏ 5399			A World Without You/Venice Blue	1965	2.50	5.00	10.00
❏ 5443			When I Get Home/Lonely Road	1965	2.50	5.00	10.00
❏ 5481			Gyp the Cat/That Funny Feeling	1965	2.50	5.00	10.00

Decca

Number			Title (A Side/B Side)	Year	VG	VG+	NM
❏ 29883			Rock Island Line/Timber	1956	10.00	20.00	40.00
❏ 29922			Silly Willy/Blue Eyed Mermaid	1956	12.50	25.00	50.00
❏ 30031			The Greatest Builder (Of Them All)/Hear Them Bells	1956	10.00	20.00	40.00
❏ 30225			Dealer in Dreams/Help Me	1957	10.00	20.00	40.00
❏ 30737			Silly Willy/Dealer in Dreams	1958	7.50	15.00	30.00

Direction

Number			Title (A Side/B Side)	Year	VG	VG+	NM
❏ 350			Long Line Rider/Change	1968	2.00	4.00	8.00
❏ 351			Song for a Dollar/Mr. and Mrs. Hohner	1969	2.00	4.00	8.00
❏ 352			Distractions (Part 1)/Jive	1969	2.00	4.00	8.00
❏ 4000			Sugar Man/(9 to 5) Jive's Alive	1970	2.00	4.00	8.00
❏ 4001			Baby May/Sweet Reason	1970	2.00	4.00	8.00
❏ 4002			Maybe We Can Get It Together/ Rx Pyro (Prescription: Fire)	1970	2.00	4.00	8.00

Number		Title (A Side/B Side)	Year	VG	VG+	NM

Motown

❏ 1183		Melodie/Someday We'll Be Together	1971		3.00	6.00
❏ 1193		Simple Song of Freedom/I'll Be Your Baby Tonight	1971		3.00	6.00
❏ 1203		Sail Away/Something in Her Love	1972		3.00	6.00
❏ 1212		Average People/Something in Her Love	1972		3.00	6.00
❏ 1217		Happy/Something in Her Love	1973		3.00	6.00

Darnell, Larry

Anna

❏ 1109		With Tears in My Eyes/I'll Get Along Somehow	1960	100.00	200.00	400.00

Argo

❏ 5372		With Tears in My Eyes/I'll Get Along Somehow	1960	6.25	12.50	25.00

DeLuxe

❏ 6123		Ramblin' Man/I Care	1957	7.50	15.00	30.00
❏ 6136		If You Go/Fing Fang Foy	1957	7.50	15.00	30.00
❏ 6141		Just Tell Me When/It Must Be Love	1957	7.50	15.00	30.00

Okeh

❏ 6848		Work Baby Work/Left My Baby	1952	6.25	12.50	25.00
❏ 6869		Darlin'/Boogie-Oogie	1952	6.25	12.50	25.00
❏ 6902		What's On Your Mind/Better Be on My Way	1952	6.25	12.50	25.00
❏ 6916		No Time at All/Singin' My Blues	1952	6.25	12.50	25.00
❏ 6919		I'll Get Along Somehow (Part 1)/ I'll Get Along Somehow (Part 2)	1952	6.25	12.50	25.00
❏ 6926		Christmas Blues/I Am the Sparrow	1952	6.25	12.50	25.00
❏ 6954		I'll Be Sittin', I'll Be Rockin'/Crazy She Calls Me	1953	6.25	12.50	25.00
❏ 7024		I'll Carry On/What More Do You Want Me to Do	1954	5.00	10.00	20.00
❏ 7039		I'm Gonna Change/Thank You, Darlin'	1954	5.00	10.00	20.00
❏ 7056		My Love for You/Feelin' Mighty Sad and Low	1955	5.00	10.00	20.00

Regal

Note: Larry Darnell records on Regal before 3328 are unconfirmed on 45 rpm

❏ 3328		Do You Love Me Baby/Sad and Lonesome	1951	6.25	12.50	25.00

Savoy

❏ 1151		That's All I Want from You/ Who Showed My Baby How to Love Me	1955	7.50	15.00	30.00

Warwick

❏ 506		If I Had You/Thankful	1959	5.00	10.00	20.00

Darnells, The - See "Marvelettes, The"

Darrell and the Oxfords - See "Tokens, The"

Darren, James

Buddah

❏ 177		That's My World/Wheeling, West Virginia	1970		2.50	5.00

Colpix

Colpix 102-181 by "Jimmy Darren"

❏ 102		There's No Such Thing/Mighty Pretty Territory	1959	3.75	7.50	15.00
❏ 102	PS	There's No Such Thing/Mighty Pretty Territory	1959	7.50	15.00	30.00
❏ 113		Gidget/You	1959	3.75	7.50	15.00
❏ 119	M	Angel Face/I Don't Wanna Lose Ya	1959	3.75	7.50	15.00
❏ 119	PS	Angel Face/I Don't Wanna Lose Ya	1959	7.50	15.00	30.00
❏ SCP-119	S	Angel Face/I Don't Wanna Lose Ya	1959	10.00	20.00	40.00
❏ 128		I Ain't Sharin' Sharon/Love Among the Young	1959	3.75	7.50	15.00
❏ 130		Teenage Tears/Let There Be Love	1959	3.75	7.50	15.00
❏ 138		You Are My Dream/Your Smile	1960	3.75	7.50	15.00
❏ 142		Because They're Young/Tears in My Eyes	1960	3.75	7.50	15.00
❏ 142	PS	Because They're Young/Tears in My Eyes	1960	7.50	15.00	30.00
❏ 145		P.S. I Love You/Traveling Down a Lonesome Road	1960	3.75	7.50	15.00
❏ 155		How Sweet You Are/All the Young Men	1960	3.75	7.50	15.00
❏ 168		Man About Town/Come On My Love	1960	3.75	7.50	15.00
❏ 181		Walking My Baby Back Home/Goodbye My Lady	1960	3.75	7.50	15.00
❏ 185		Fool's Paradise/Gotta Have Love	1961	3.75	7.50	15.00
❏ 189		Gidget Goes Hawaiian/Wild About the Girl	1961	3.75	7.50	15.00
❏ 194		Hand in Hand/You Are My Dream	1961	3.75	7.50	15.00
❏ 609		Goodbye Cruel World/Valerie	1961	3.75	7.50	15.00
❏ 609	PS	Goodbye Cruel World/Valerie	1961	6.25	12.50	25.00
❏ 622		Her Royal Majesty/If I Could Only Tell You	1962	3.00	6.00	12.00
❏ 629		Conscience/Dream Big	1962	3.00	6.00	12.00
❏ 644		Mary's Little Lamb/The Life of the Party	1962	3.00	6.00	12.00
❏ 655		Hail to the Conquering Hero/Too Young to Go Steady	1962	3.00	6.00	12.00
❏ 664		Hear What I Want to Hear/I'll Be Loving You	1962	3.00	6.00	12.00
❏ 672		Pin a Medal on Joey/Diamond Head	1963	3.00	6.00	12.00
❏ 685		They Should Have Given You the Oscar/ Blame It on My Youth	1963	3.00	6.00	12.00
❏ 696		Gegetta/Grande Luna, Italiana	1963	3.00	6.00	12.00
❏ 708		Under the Yum Yum Tree/Backstage	1963	3.00	6.00	12.00
❏ 758		Punch and Judy/Just Think of Tonight	1964	5.00	10.00	20.00
❏ 765		A Married Man/Baby, Talk to Me	1964	2.50	5.00	10.00

Kirshner

❏ 63-1012		I Think Somebody Loves Me/ Ain't Been Home in a Long Time	1970		2.50	5.00
❏ 63-5013		Bring Me Down Slow/More and More	1971		2.50	5.00
❏ 63-5015		Mammy Blue/As Long As You Love Me	1971		2.50	5.00
❏ 63-5025		Brian's Song/Thank Heaven for Little Girls	1973		2.50	5.00

Number		Title (A Side/B Side)	Year	VG	VG+	NM
MGM						
❑ 14558		Let the Heartaches Begin/Sad Song	1973		2.00	4.00
❑ 14667		Sad-Eyed Romany Woman/Stay	1973		2.00	4.00
Private Stock						
❑ 45,050		Love on the Screen/Losing You	1975		2.00	4.00
❑ 45,064		One Has My Name, The Other Has My Heart/ Sleepin' in a Bed of Lies	1975		2.00	4.00
❑ 45,136		You Take My Heart Away/ You Take My Heart Away (Disco)	1977		2.00	4.00
❑ 45,152	DJ	Only a Dream Away (mono/stereo) *Stock copies may not exist*	1977		2.50	5.00
RCA						
❑ PB-11316		Let Me Take You in My Arms Again/California	1978		2.00	4.00
❑ PB-11419		Next Time/Something Like Nothing Before	1978		2.00	4.00
Warner Bros.						
❑ 5648		Because You're Mine/Millions of Roses	1965	2.00	4.00	8.00
❑ 5689		I Want to Be Lonely/Tom Hawk	1966	2.00	4.00	8.00
❑ 5812		Where Did We Go Wrong/Counting the Cracks	1966	2.00	4.00	8.00
❑ 5838		Crazy Me/They Don't Know	1966	2.00	4.00	8.00
❑ 5856		Love Is Where You Find It/ (Let's Worry About) Tomorrow Tomorrow	1966	2.00	4.00	8.00
❑ 5874		All/Misty Morning Eyes	1966	2.00	4.00	8.00
❑ 7013		I Miss You So/Since I Don't Have You	1967	2.00	4.00	8.00
❑ 7053		Didn't We/Counting the Cracks	1967	2.00	4.00	8.00
❑ 7071		The House Song/They Don't Know	1967	2.00	4.00	8.00
❑ 7152		Cherie/Wait Until Dark	1967	2.00	4.00	8.00
❑ 7206		A Little Bit of Heaven/Each and Every Part of Me	1968	2.00	4.00	8.00
Dartells, The						
Arlen						
❑ 509		Hot Pastrami/Dartell Stomp	1963	6.25	12.50	25.00
❑ 513		Dance, Everybody, Dance/The Scoobie Song	1963	6.25	12.50	25.00
Dot						
❑ 16453		Hot Pastrami/Dartell Stomp	1963	5.00	10.00	20.00
❑ 16502		Dance, Everybody, Dance/The Scoobie Song	1963	5.00	10.00	20.00
❑ 16551		Convicted/Sweet Pea	1963	3.75	7.50	15.00
❑ 16646		Swiss Cheese/Dartell Stomp	1964	3.75	7.50	15.00
Hanna-Barbera						
❑ 457		Clap Your Hands/Where Do We Stand	1965	3.75	7.50	15.00
Sande						
❑ 103		The Girl Can't Help It/Stranger on the Shore	1964	7.50	15.00	30.00
Darvell, Barry						
Atlantic						
❑ 2128		Lost Love/Silver Dollar	1961	5.00	10.00	20.00
❑ 2138		Adam and Eve/A King for Tonight	1962	5.00	10.00	20.00
Colt 45						
❑ 104		Teenage Love/(B-side unknown)	1959	5.00	10.00	20.00
❑ 107		Geronimo Stomp/How Will It End	1959	15.00	30.00	60.00
❑ 110		Butterfly Baby/Send Me Some Loving	1960	6.25	12.50	25.00
❑ 301		Run Little Billy/All I Need Is You	1961	5.00	10.00	20.00
Columbia						
❑ 44197		My World of Make Believe/Beggar's Paradise	1967	2.00	4.00	8.00
Cub						
❑ 9088		Little Angel Lost/Fountain of Love	1961	5.00	10.00	20.00
Providence						
❑ 404		When You're Alone/It's Rainin', It's Pourin'	1964	3.00	6.00	12.00
World Artists						
❑ 1042		I'll Remember/Where Is the Love for Me	1965	3.00	6.00	12.00
❑ 1058		I Found a Daisy (in the City)/Kissable Lips	1965	3.00	6.00	12.00

Date with Soul, A - See "Hale and the Hushabyes"

Dave and the Marksmen
(With Dave Marks, ex-Beach Boys)

Number		Title (A Side/B Side)	Year	VG	VG+	NM
A&M						
❑ 730		Cruisin'/Kustom Kar Show	1964	12.50	25.00	50.00
Warner Bros.						
❑ 5485		I Wanna Cry/I Could Make You Mine	1964	7.50	15.00	30.00
Westco						
❑ 10		Down the Tubes/Ooh Poo Pa Doo *Black vinyl*	1963	12.50	25.00	50.00
❑ 10		Down the Tubes/Ooh Poo Pa Doo *Yellow vinyl*	1963	25.00	50.00	100.00

Dave Dee, Dozy, Beaky, Mick & Tich

Number		Title (A Side/B Side)	Year	VG	VG+	NM
Atlantic						
❑ 89757	DJ	Staying With It (same on both sides) *May be promo only*	1983		2.50	5.00
Bell						
❑ 905		Kelly/Annabella *As "Dave Dee"*	1970		3.00	6.00

Number		Title (A Side/B Side)	Year	VG	VG+	NM
❏ 942		Frisco Annie/Hey! Mr. President	1970		3.00	6.00
		As "D.B.M. & T."				

Cotillion

❏ 44061		Bad News/Tonight-Today	1970		3.00	6.00
		As "Dozy, Beaky, Mick & Tich"				

Fontana

❏ 1537		You Make It Move/No Time	1965	2.50	5.00	10.00
❏ 1545		Hold Tight/You Know What I Want	1966	2.50	5.00	10.00
❏ 1553		Hideaway/Here's a Heart	1966	2.50	5.00	10.00
❏ 1559		Bend It/She's So Good	1966	3.00	6.00	12.00
❏ 1569		Save Me/Shame	1967	2.50	5.00	10.00
❏ 1591		Okay/Master Llewellyn	1967	2.50	5.00	10.00

Imperial

❏ 66270		Zabadak/The Sun Goes Down	1968	2.50	5.00	10.00
❏ 66287		Legend of Xanadu/Please	1968	2.00	4.00	8.00
❏ 66309		Break Out/Mrs. Thursday	1968	2.00	4.00	8.00
❏ 66339		Wreck of the Antoinette/Margarita Linman	1968	2.00	4.00	8.00

Davies, Dave
(Of the Kinks)

RCA

❏ PB-12089		Wild Man/Imagination's Real	1980	2.50	5.00	10.00
❏ PB-12147		Doing the Best for You/Got No More to Lose	1981	2.50	5.00	10.00

Reprise

❏ 0614		Death of a Clown/Love Me Till the Sun Shines	1967	10.00	20.00	40.00
❏ 0660		Suzannah's Still Alive/Funny Face	1968	10.00	20.00	40.00

Warner Bros.

❏ 29425		Mean Disposition/Cold Winter	1983			*Unreleased?*
❏ 29425	DJ	Mean Disposition (same on both sides)	1983	2.50	5.00	10.00
❏ 29509		Love Gets You/One Night with You	1983	12.50	25.00	50.00
❏ 29509	DJ	Love Gets You (same on both sides)	1983	2.50	5.00	10.00

Davis, Andrea - See "Riperton, Minnie"

Davis, Bo

Crest

❏ 1027		Let's Coast Awhile/Drownin' All My Sorrows	1956	37.50	75.00	150.00
		Eddie Cochran plays guitar on this record.				

Davis, Eunice

Atlantic

❏ 992		Go to Work Pretty Daddy/My Beat Is 125th Street	1953	15.00	30.00	60.00

Coral

❏ 65075		Work Daddy Work/What Do You Want	1952	5.00	10.00	20.00

DeLuxe

❏ 6068		Get Your Enjoys/24 Hours a Day	1954	7.50	15.00	30.00

Derby

❏ 760		Evening Train/I'm a Wild West Woman	1951	7.50	15.00	30.00
❏ 768		Good News for You Baby/Tell Me I'm the Baby	1951	7.50	15.00	30.00

Grand

❏ 130		Let's Have a Party/Every Time Your Lips Meet Mine	1955	5.00	10.00	20.00

Davis, Spencer, Group
(Also see "Winwood, Steve")

Atco

❏ 6400		Keep On Running/High Time Baby	1966	3.75	7.50	15.00
❏ 6416		Somebody Help Me/Stevie's Blues	1966	3.75	7.50	15.00

Fontana

❏ 1960		I Can't Stand It/Midnight Train	1964	3.75	7.50	15.00

United Artists

❏ 0115		Gimme Some Lovin'/Keep On Running	1973		2.00	4.00
		"Silver Spotlight Series" reissue				
❏ 0116		I'm a Man/Somebody Help Me	1973		2.00	4.00
		"Silver Spotlight Series" reissue				
❏ 50108		Gimme Some Lovin'/Blues in F	1966	3.00	6.00	12.00
❏ 50144		I'm a Man/Can't Get Enough of It	1967	3.00	6.00	12.00
❏ 50162		Somebody Help Me/On the Green Light	1967	2.50	5.00	10.00
❏ 50202		Time Seller/Don't Want You No More	1967	2.50	5.00	10.00
❏ 50286		Looking Back/After Tea	1968	2.50	5.00	10.00
❏ 50922		Listen to the Rhythm/Sunday Walk in the Rain	1972		3.00	6.00
❏ 50993		Rainy Season/Tumble-Down Tenement Row	1972		3.00	6.00

Vertigo

❏ 110		Don't You Let It Bring You Down/ Today Gluggo, Tomorrow the World	1973		2.50	5.00
❏ 112		Living in a Back Street/Need a Helping Hand	1974		2.50	5.00

Dawn
(Groups, and maybe solo artists, who used this name and had nothing to do with Tony Orlando.)

ABC-Paramount

❏ 10791		Baby's Gone Away/Gotta Get Away	1966	2.00	4.00	8.00

Apt

❏ 25088		Can't Get Him Off My Mind/Two of a Kind	1965	3.75	7.50	15.00

Number	Title (A Side/B Side)	Year	VG	VG+	NM
Cadet					
❑ 5644	The Fifth Day of June/Ballad of Gene	1969		3.00	6.00
Laurie					
❑ 3388	I'm Afraid They're All Talking About Me/Lovers' Melody	1967	3.00	6.00	12.00
❑ 3417	Sandy/For the Love of Money	1968	3.00	6.00	12.00
Rust					
❑ 5128	Baby I Love You/Bring It On Home	1968	3.00	6.00	12.00
United Artists					
❑ 50096	Love Is a Magic Word/ How Can I Get Off This Merry-Go-Round	1966	3.00	6.00	12.00

Day, Bobby

Number	Title (A Side/B Side)	Year	VG	VG+	NM
Class					
❑ 207	Come Seven/So Long Baby	1957	5.00	10.00	20.00
❑ 211	Little Bitty Pretty One/ When the Swallows Come Back to Capistrano	1957	5.00	10.00	20.00
❑ 215	Beep-Beep-Beep/Darling, If I Had You	1957	5.00	10.00	20.00
❑ 225	Little Turtle Dove/Saving My Life for You	1958	5.00	10.00	20.00
❑ 229	Rock-N Robin/Over and Over	1958	5.00	10.00	20.00
❑ 241	The Bluebird, the Buzzard, and the Oriole/ Alone Too Long	1959	5.00	10.00	20.00
❑ 245	That's All I Want/Say Yes	1959	3.75	7.50	15.00
❑ 252	Mr. and Mrs. Rock & Roll/Gotta New Girl	1959	3.75	7.50	15.00
❑ 255	Ain't Gonna Cry No More/Love Is a One-Time Affair	1959	3.75	7.50	15.00
❑ 257	Unchained Melody/Three Young Rebs from Georgia	1959	3.75	7.50	15.00
❑ 263	My Blue Heaven/I Don't Want To	1960	3.75	7.50	15.00
❑ 705	Don't Leave Me Hangin' on a String/ When I Started Dancin'	1965	3.00	6.00	12.00
RCA Victor					
❑ 47-8133	Another Country, Another World/Know-It-All	1963	2.50	5.00	10.00
❑ 47-8196	Buzz Buzz Buzz/Pretty Little Girl Next Door	1963	2.50	5.00	10.00
❑ 47-8230	Down on My Knees/Jole Blon, Little Darling	1963	2.50	5.00	10.00
❑ 47-8316	When I See My Baby Smile/ On the Street Where You Live	1964	2.50	5.00	10.00
Rendezvous					
❑ 130	Teenage Philosopher/Undecided	1960	3.00	6.00	12.00
❑ 133	Rockin' Robin/Over and Over	1960	3.00	6.00	12.00
❑ 136	Gee Whiz/Over and Over	1960	3.00	6.00	12.00
❑ 146	I Need Help/Life Can Be Beautiful	1961	3.00	6.00	12.00
❑ 158	King's Highway/What Fools We Mortals Be	1961	3.00	6.00	12.00
❑ 167	Don't Worry 'Bout Me/Oop-E-Du-Pers Ball	1962	3.00	6.00	12.00
❑ 175	Undecided/Slow Pokey Joe	1962	3.00	6.00	12.00
Sure Shot					
❑ 5036	So Lonely/Spicks and Specks	1967	2.00	4.00	8.00

Day, Darlene

Number	Title (A Side/B Side)	Year	VG	VG+	NM
Music Makers					
❑ 106	I Love You So/Will	1961	25.00	50.00	100.00

Day, Terry - See "Melcher, Terry"

Daybreakers, The

Number	Title (A Side/B Side)	Year	VG	VG+	NM
Aladdin					
❑ 3434	I Wonder Why/Up, Up and Away	1958	10.00	20.00	40.00
Dial					
❑ 4066	Psychedelic Siren/Afterthoughts	1967	7.50	15.00	30.00
Lamp					
❑ 2016	I Wonder Why/Up, Up and Away	1958	15.00	30.00	60.00

Daytonas, The
(Also see "Ronny and the Daytonas")

Number	Title (A Side/B Side)	Year	VG	VG+	NM
Amy					
❑ 961	Hey Little Girl/Please Go Away	1966	5.00	10.00	20.00

De-Fenders, The

Number	Title (A Side/B Side)	Year	VG	VG+	NM
Del-Fi					
❑ 4226	Little Deuce Coupe/Hayburner *B-side by the Deuce Coupes*	1963	7.50	15.00	30.00
World Pacific					
❑ 382	(Dance to the) Yakety Sax/Wild One	1963	10.00	20.00	40.00

Deacon and the Rock 'N' Rollers

Number	Title (A Side/B Side)	Year	VG	VG+	NM
Nau-Voo					
❑ 804	Rockin' on the Moon/I Don't Wanna Leave	1959	500.00	1,000	1,500

Deal, Bill, and the Rhondels

Number	Title (A Side/B Side)	Year	VG	VG+	NM
Buddah					
❑ 318	It's Too Late/So What If It Rains	1972		3.00	6.00
❑ 330	Everybody's Got Something to Hide/I Live in the Night	1972		3.00	6.00
Heritage					
❑ 803	May I/Day By Day My Love Grows	1968	2.00	4.00	8.00
❑ 812	I've Been Hurt/I've Got My Seeds	1969	2.00	4.00	8.00
❑ 812 PS	I've Been Hurt/I've Got My Seeds	1969	3.75	7.50	15.00

Number		Title (A Side/B Side)	Year	VG	VG+	NM
❑ 817		What Kind of Fool Do You Think I Am/ Are You Ready for This	1969	2.00	4.00	8.00
❑ 818		Swingin' Tight/Tuck's Theme	1969	2.00	4.00	8.00
❑ 818	PS	Swingin' Tight/Tuck's Theme	1969	3.75	7.50	15.00
❑ 821		Nothing Succeeds Like Success/Swingin' Tight	1969	2.00	4.00	8.00
❑ 824		I'm Gonna Make You Love Me/Hey Bulldog	1970		3.00	6.00

Mala

❑ 502		Big Toe in the Wind/Don't Put Me Down	1965	7.50	15.00	30.00
		As "Bill Deal and the Big Deals"				

Polydor

❑ 14042		Do I Love You/Won't You Set Me Free	1970		3.00	6.00
❑ 14061		19 Years (Everything I Do Is Wrong)/Sea of Life	1971	3.00	6.00	
❑ 14103		Sea of Life/You Can Make It	1971		3.00	6.00

Dean and Jean
Ember

❑ 1048		We're Gonna Get Married/Too Young to Know	1958	3.00	6.00	12.00
❑ 1054		Turn It Off/Never Let Your Love Fade Away	1959	3.00	6.00	12.00

Rust

❑ TR 1		Seven Day Wonder/The Man Who Will Never Grow Old	196?	3.00	6.00	12.00
❑ 5044		Come Take a Walk with Me/Dance the Roach	1962	2.50	5.00	10.00
❑ 5046		Mack the Knife/You Can't Be Happy by Yourself	1962	2.50	5.00	10.00
❑ 5067		Tra La La La Suzy/I Love the Summertime	1963	2.50	5.00	10.00
❑ 5075		Hey Jean, Hey Dean/Please Don't Tell Me Now	1964	3.75	7.50	15.00
❑ 5081		I Wanna Be Loved/Thread Your Needle	1964	2.50	5.00	10.00
❑ 5085		Goddess of Love/The Man Who Will Never Grow Old	1964	2.50	5.00	10.00
❑ 5089		Sticks and Stones/In My Way	1964	2.50	5.00	10.00
❑ 5100		Lovingly Yours/Goddess of Love	1965	2.50	5.00	10.00
❑ 5107		She's Too Respectable/I Love the Summertime	1965	2.50	5.00	10.00

Dean, Bobby
Chess

❑ 1673		Just Go Wild Over Rock and Roll/Dime Store Pony Tail	1958	7.50	15.00	30.00
❑ 1710		I'm Ready/Go Mr. Dillon	1959	7.50	15.00	30.00

Profile

❑ 4006		Just Between Tears/It's a Fad	1959	10.00	20.00	40.00

Dean, Debbie
Motown

❑ 1007		Don't Let Him Shop Around/A New Girl	1961	10.00	20.00	40.00
❑ 1014		Itty, Bitty, Pity Love/But I'm Afraid	1961	7.50	15.00	30.00
❑ 1025		Everybody's Talking About My Baby/I Cried All Night	1962	10.00	20.00	40.00
❑ 1025	PS	Everybody's Talking About My Baby/I Cried All Night	1962	20.00	40.00	80.00

V.I.P.

❑ 25044		Why Am I Lovin' You/Stay My Love	1967	75.00	150.00	300.00

Deans, The
Laurie

❑ 3114		I Don't Want to Wait/Little White Gardenia	1961	5.00	10.00	20.00

Mohawk

❑ 114		My Heart Is Low/I'll Love You Forever	1960	6.25	12.50	25.00
❑ 119		Humpty Dumpty/La Chiam	1960	6.25	12.50	25.00
❑ 126		It's You/I Don't Wanna Wait	1960	10.00	20.00	40.00

Star Maker

❑ 1928		Oh Little Star/You Got Me Baby	1961	25.00	50.00	100.00
❑ 1931		Chills, Chills, Chills/(Lady of the) Caravan	1962	15.00	30.00	60.00

DeBerry, Jimmy
Sun

❑ 185		Take a Little Chance/Time Has Made a Change	1953	750.00	1,500	3,000

Dee, Frankie
RCA Victor

❑ 47-7276		Shake It Up Baby/After Graduation	1958	15.00	30.00	60.00

20th Fox

❑ 146		Swingin' in a Hammock/I Had the Craziest Dream	1959	7.50	15.00	30.00

Dee, Jackie - See "DeShannon, Jackie"

Dee, Jimmy
Dot

❑ 15664		Henrietta/Don't Cry No More	1957	10.00	20.00	40.00
❑ 15721		Here I Come/You're Late, Miss Kate	1958	10.00	20.00	40.00

TNT

❑ 148		Henrietta/Don't Cry No More	1957	20.00	40.00	80.00
❑ 152		Here I Come/You're Late, Miss Kate	1958	20.00	40.00	80.00
❑ 161		Feel Like Rockin'/Rock-Tick-Rock	1958	15.00	30.00	60.00

Dee, Joey, and the Starliters
Bonus

❑ 7009		Lorraine/The Girl I Walk to School	1963	12.50	25.00	50.00
❑ 7009	PS	Lorraine/The Girl I Walk to School	1963	20.00	40.00	80.00

Jubliee

❑ 5532		Feel Good About It Part 1/Feel Good About It Part 2	1966	3.75	7.50	15.00

Number		Title (A Side/B Side)	Year	VG	VG+	NM
❏ 5539		Dancing on the Beach/Good Little You	1966	3.75	7.50	15.00
❏ 5554		She's So Exceptional/It's Got You	1966	3.75	7.50	15.00
❏ 5566		Can't Sit Down/Put Your Heart In It	1967	3.75	7.50	15.00

Some doubt has been raised about the existence of these other than as promos.

Little

| ❏ 813/4 | | Lorraine/The Girl I Walk to School | 1958 | 100.00 | 200.00 | 400.00 |

Monument

| ❏ (# unknown) | DJ | Ya Ya Twist/Runaround Sue | 1962 | 6.25 | 12.50 | 25.00 |

B-side by Dion

Roulette

❏ 4401		Peppermint Twist -- Part 1/Peppermint Twist -- Part 2	1961	4.00	8.00	16.00
❏ 4408		Hey, Let's Twist/Roly Poly	1962	3.75	7.50	15.00
❏ 4408	PS	Hey, Let's Twist/Roly Poly	1962	6.25	12.50	25.00
❏ 4416		Shout -- Part 1/Shout -- Part 2	1962	3.75	7.50	15.00
❏ 4416	PS	Shout -- Part 1/Shout -- Part 2	1962	6.25	12.50	25.00
❏ 4431		Every Time (I Think About You) Part 1/Every Time (I Think About You) Part 2	1962	3.00	6.00	12.00
❏ 4438		What Kind of Love Is This/Wing Ding	1962	3.00	6.00	12.00
❏ 4438	PS	What Kind of Love Is This/Wing Ding	1962	6.25	12.50	25.00
❏ 4456		I Lost My Baby/Keep Your Mind on What You're Doing	1962	3.00	6.00	12.00
❏ 4456	PS	I Lost My Baby/Keep Your Mind on What You're Doing	1962	6.25	12.50	25.00
❏ 4467		Baby You're Driving Me Crazy/Help Me Pick Up the Pieces	1963	3.00	6.00	12.00
❏ 4488		Hot Pastrami with Mashed Potatoes -- Part 1/Hot Pastrami with Mashed Potatoes -- Part 2	1963	3.00	6.00	12.00
❏ 4503		Dance, Dance, Dance/Let's Have a Party	1963	3.00	6.00	12.00
❏ 4523		Ya Ya/Fanny Mae	1963	3.00	6.00	12.00
❏ 4539		Down by the Riverside/Getting Nearer	1963	5.00	10.00	20.00
❏ 4617		Cry a Little Sometime/Wing Ding	1965	3.00	6.00	12.00

Scepter

| ❏ 1210 | | Face of An Angel/Shimmy Baby | 1960 | 7.50 | 15.00 | 30.00 |

Originals have "Scepter" at top of label and are credited as "Joey Dee and the Starlights"

| ❏ 1210 | | Face of An Angel/Shimmy Baby | 1960 | 5.00 | 10.00 | 20.00 |

Reissues have "Scepter Records" at side of label and are credited as listed

| ❏ 1225 | | Three Memories/(Bad) Bulldog | 1961 | 7.50 | 15.00 | 30.00 |

Vaseline Hair Tonic

| ❏ (no #) | | Learn to Dance the Authentic Peppermint Twist (Parts 1 & 2) | 1962 | 3.75 | 7.50 | 15.00 |
| ❏ (no #) | PS | Learn to Dance the Authentic Peppermint Twist (Parts 1 & 2) | 1962 | 3.75 | 7.50 | 15.00 |

Dee, Johnny

Colonial

| ❏ 430 | | Sittin' in the Balcony/A-Plus in Love | 1957 | 7.50 | 15.00 | 30.00 |
| ❏ 435 | | Teenage Queen/It's Gotta Be You | 1957 | 7.50 | 15.00 | 30.00 |

Dot

| ❏ 15699 | | Somebody Sweet/They Were Right | 1958 | 7.50 | 15.00 | 30.00 |

Dee, Tommy

Challenge

| ❏ 59083 | | The Hobo and the Puppy/There's a Star Spangled Banner Waving Somewhere | 1960 | 5.00 | 10.00 | 20.00 |
| ❏ 59087 | | Ballad of a Drag Race/The Story of Susie | 1960 | 5.00 | 10.00 | 20.00 |

Crest

| ❏ 1057 | M | Three Stars/I'll Never Change | 1959 | 7.50 | 15.00 | 30.00 |

With backing group and B-side credited to "The Teen Tones and Orchestra"

| ❏ 1057 | M | Three Stars/I'll Never Change | 1959 | 6.25 | 12.50 | 25.00 |

With backing group and B-side credited to "Carol Kay and the Teen-Aires"

| ❏ 1057 | S | Three Stars/I'll Never Change | 1959 | 12.50 | 25.00 | 50.00 |

With backing group and B-side credited to "Carol Kay and the Teen-Aires"

| ❏ 1061 | | The Chair/Hello Lonesome | 1959 | 5.00 | 10.00 | 20.00 |
| ❏ 1067 | | Merry Christmas, Mary/Angel of Love | 1959 | 6.25 | 12.50 | 25.00 |

Pike

❏ 5906		Loving You (On Someone Else's Time)/Halfway to Hell	1961	5.00	10.00	20.00
❏ 5909		A Little Dog Cried/Look Homeward, Dear Angel	1961	5.00	10.00	20.00
❏ 5917		Missing on a Mountain/Look Homeward, Dear Angel	1962	5.00	10.00	20.00

Sims

| ❏ 260 | | Missing While Surfing/Goodbye High School | 1966 | 5.00 | 10.00 | 20.00 |
| ❏ 308 | | How's Your Mama Em/Goodbye High School | 1966 | 3.75 | 7.50 | 15.00 |

Deep Purple

Mercury

❏ 880 477-7		Knocking at Your Back Door/Wasted Sunset	1984		2.00	4.00
❏ 880 477-7	PS	Knocking at Your Back Door/Wasted Sunset	1984		2.50	5.00
❏ 885 617-7		Call of the Wild/Dead or Alive	1987			3.00
❏ 885 820-7		Bad Attitude/Black and White	1987			3.00

Tetragrammaton

❏ 1503		Hush/One More Rainy Day	1968	3.00	6.00	12.00
❏ 1503	PS	Hush/One More Rainy Day	1968	7.50	15.00	30.00
❏ 1508		Kentucky Woman/Hard Road	1968	3.00	6.00	12.00
❏ 1508	PS	Kentucky Woman/Hard Road	1968	3.75	7.50	15.00
❏ 1514		River Deep, Mountain High/Listen, Learn, Read On	1969	2.50	5.00	10.00
❏ 1519		The Bird Has Flown/Emmaretta	1969	2.50	5.00	10.00
❏ 1537		Hallelujah (I Am the Preacher)/April (Part 1)	1969	2.50	5.00	10.00

Number		Title (A Side/B Side)	Year	VG	VG+	NM
Warner Bros.						
❑ 7405		Black Night/Into the Fire	1970	2.00	4.00	8.00
❑ 7493		Strange Kind of Woman/I'm Alone	1971	2.00	4.00	8.00
❑ 7528		Fire Ball/I'm Alone	1971	2.00	4.00	8.00
❑ 7572		Never Before/When a Blind Man Cries	1972		3.00	6.00
❑ 7595		Lazy/When a Blind Man Cries	1972		3.00	6.00
❑ 7634		Highway Star (Part 1)/Highway Star (Part 2)	1972		3.00	6.00
❑ 7654		Hush/Kentucky Woman	1972		3.00	6.00
❑ 7672		Woman from Tokyo/Super Trouper	1972		3.00	6.00
❑ 7710		Smoke on the Water (Edited Version) Studio/ Smoke on the Water (Edited Version) Live	1973		2.50	5.00
❑ 7737		Woman from Tokyo/Super Trouper	1973		2.50	5.00
❑ 7784		Might Just Take Your Life/Coronorias Regid	1974		2.50	5.00
❑ 7809		Burn/Coronarias Regid	1974		2.50	5.00
❑ 8049		High Ball Shooter/You Can't Do It Right	1974		2.50	5.00
❑ 8069		Stormbringer/Love Don't Mean a Thing	1975		2.50	5.00
❑ 8182		Gettin' Tighter/Love Child	1976		2.50	5.00

Dekker, Desmond, and the Aces

Number		Title (A Side/B Side)	Year	VG	VG+	NM
Uni						
❑ 55129		Israelites/My Precious World	1969		3.00	6.00
❑ 55150		It Mek/Problems	1969		3.00	6.00
❑ 55261		You Can Get It If You Really Want It/Perseverance	1970		3.00	6.00

Del and the Escorts

Number		Title (A Side/B Side)	Year	VG	VG+	NM
Rome						
❑ 103		Baby Doll/Someone to Watch Over Me	1961	12.50	25.00	50.00
Symbol						
❑ 913		You Don't Love Me/Skokiian	1960			Unreleased?
Taurus						
❑ 350/1		Happy/You're for Me (And I'm for You)	1961	7.50	15.00	30.00

Del Satins

Number		Title (A Side/B Side)	Year	VG	VG+	NM
B.T. Puppy						
❑ 506		Hang Around/Candy Apple 'Vette	1965	3.75	7.50	15.00
❑ 509		Sweets for My Sweet/A Girl Named Arlene	1965	7.50	15.00	30.00
❑ 514		Relief/Throwaway Song	1966	3.75	7.50	15.00
❑ 563		I'll Do My Crying Tomorrow/A Girl Named Arlene	1970	3.00	6.00	12.00
Columbia						
❑ 42802		Feelin' No Pain/Who Cares	1963	6.25	12.50	25.00
❑ 42802	PS	Feelin' No Pain/Who Cares	1963	12.50	25.00	50.00
Diamond						
❑ 216		A Little Rain Must Fall/ Love, Hate, Revenge (If I Want You to Cry)	1967	3.75	7.50	15.00
End						
❑ 1096		I'll Pray for You/I Remember the Night	1961	50.00	100.00	200.00
Laurie						
❑ 3132		Teardrops Follow Me/ Best Wishes, Good Luck, Goodbye	1962	6.25	12.50	25.00
❑ 3149		Ballad of a Deejay/Does My Love Stand a Chance	1962	6.25	12.50	25.00
Mala						
❑ 475		Believe in Me/Two Broken Hearts	1964	5.00	10.00	20.00
Win						
❑ 702		Counting Teardrops/Remember Black label	1961	40.00	80.00	120.00
❑ 702		Counting Teardrops/Remember Orange label	1961	15.00	30.00	60.00

Del Vikings, The

(Also recorded as the Dell-Vikings)

Number		Title (A Side/B Side)	Year	VG	VG+	NM
ABC-Paramount						
❑ 10208		I'll Never Stop Crying/Bring Back Your Heart	1961	6.25	12.50	25.00
❑ 10248		I Hear Bells (Wedding Bells)/Don't Get Slick on Me	1961	12.50	25.00	50.00
❑ 10278		Kiss Me/Face the Music	1961	6.25	12.50	25.00
❑ 10304		Big Silence/One More River to Cross	1962	6.25	12.50	25.00
❑ 10341		Confession of Love/Kilimanjaro	1962	6.25	12.50	25.00
❑ 10385		An Angel Up in Heaven/Fishing Chant	1962	12.50	25.00	50.00
❑ 10425		Too Many Miles/Sorcerer's Apprentice	1963	6.25	12.50	25.00
Alpine						
❑ 66		Pistol Packin' Mama/The Sun	1960	20.00	40.00	80.00
❑ 66	PS	Pistol Packin' Mama/The Sun	1960	25.00	50.00	100.00
Bim Bam Boom						
❑ 111		Cold Feet/A Little Man Cried	1972		2.50	5.00
❑ 113		Watching the Moon/You Say You Love Me	1972		2.50	5.00
❑ 115		I'm Spinning/Girl Girl	1972		2.50	5.00
Dot						
❑ 15538		Come Go with Me/How Can I Find True Love	1957	7.50	15.00	30.00
❑ 15571		What Made Maggie Run/Little Billy Boy	1957	7.50	15.00	30.00
❑ 15592		Whispering Bells/Don't Be a Fool	1957	7.50	15.00	30.00
❑ 15636		I'm Spinning/When I Come Home As "Kripp Johnson with the Dell-Vikings"	1957	7.50	15.00	30.00
❑ 16092		Come Go with Me/How Can I Find True Love	1960	5.00	10.00	20.00
❑ 16236		Come Go with Me/Whispering Bells	1961	5.00	10.00	20.00
❑ 16248		I Hear Bells (Wedding Bells)/Don't Get Slick on Me	1961	5.00	10.00	20.00

Number		Title (A Side/B Side)	Year	VG	VG+	NM
DRC						
❑ 101		Can't You See/Oh I	196?	10.00	20.00	40.00
Fee Bee						
❑ 173		Welfare Blues/Hollywood and Vine	1977		2.50	5.00
❑ 205		Come Go with Me/How Can I Find True Love	1957	30.00	60.00	120.00
		Orange label, bee on top				
❑ 205		Come Go with Me/How Can I Find True Love	1957	20.00	40.00	80.00
		Orange label, one side has bee, the other side doesn't				
❑ 205		Come Go with Me/How Can I Find True Love	1961	7.50	15.00	30.00
		Orange label, no bee				
❑ 205		Come Go with Me/Whispering Bells	1964	5.00	10.00	20.00
❑ 206		Down in Bermuda/Maggie	1964	20.00	40.00	80.00
❑ 210		What Made Maggie Run/Uh Uh Baby	1957	20.00	40.00	80.00
❑ 210		What Made Maggie Run/When I Come Home	1957	40.00	80.00	120.00
❑ 210		What Made Maggie Run/Down by the Stream	1964	7.50	15.00	30.00
❑ 214		Whispering Bells/Don't Be a Fool	1957	30.00	60.00	120.00
❑ 218		I'm Spinning/You Say You Love Me	1957	30.00	60.00	120.00
		Bee on label				
❑ 218		I'm Spinning/You Say You Love Me	1964	7.50	15.00	30.00
		No bee on label				
❑ 221		Willette/Woke Up This Morning	1958	25.00	50.00	100.00
❑ 221		Willette/I Want to Marry You	1958	20.00	40.00	80.00
❑ 227		Tell Me/Finger Poppin' Woman	1959	20.00	40.00	80.00
❑ 902		True Love/Baby, Let Me Know	1964	7.50	15.00	30.00
		As "The Original Dell Vikings"				
Gateway						
❑ 743		We Three/I've Got to Know	1964	7.50	15.00	30.00
Jojo						
❑ 108		Keep On Walkin'/My Body, Your Shadow	1976		2.50	5.00
Luniverse						
❑ 106		Somewhere Over the Rainbow/Hey, Senorita	1957	25.00	50.00	100.00
❑ 110		Yours/Heaven and Paradise	1958			Bootleg
❑ 113		In the Still of the Night/The White Cliffs of Dover	1958			Bootleg
❑ 114		There I Go/Girl Girl	1958			Bootleg
Mercury						
❑ 71132		Cool Shake/Jitterbug Baby	1957	7.50	15.00	30.00
❑ 71180		Come Along with Me/Whatcha Gonna Lose	1957	7.50	15.00	30.00
❑ 71198		I'm Spinning/When I Come Home	1957	7.50	15.00	30.00
❑ 71241		Snowbound/Your Book of Life	1957	7.50	15.00	30.00
❑ 71266		The Voodoo Man/Can't Wait	1958	7.50	15.00	30.00
❑ 71345		You Cheated/Pretty Little Things Called Girls	1958	10.00	20.00	40.00
		Blue label				
❑ 71345		You Cheated/Pretty Little Things Called Girls	1958	7.50	15.00	30.00
		Black label				
❑ 71390		How Could You/Flat Tire	1958	7.50	15.00	30.00
Scepter						
❑ 12367		Come Go with Me/When You're Asleep	1973		2.50	5.00
Ship						
❑ 214		Sunday Kind of Love/Over the Rainbow	197?		2.00	4.00
Del-Aires, The						
Coral						
❑ 62370		Elaine/Just Wigglin' and a-Wobblin'	1963	7.50	15.00	30.00
❑ 62404		The Drag/My Funny Valentine	1964	7.50	15.00	30.00
		As "Ronnie and the Del-Aires"				
❑ 62419		Arlene/I'm Yours Baby	1964	12.50	25.00	50.00
Del-Phis, The						
(Early incarnation of Martha and the Vandellas)						
Checkmate						
❑ 1005		I'll Let You Know/It Takes Two	1961	50.00	100.00	200.00
Del-Vetts, The						
Dunwich						
❑ 125		Last Time Around/Anytime	1966	5.00	10.00	20.00
❑ 142		I Call My Baby STP/That's the Way It Is	1966	5.00	10.00	20.00
❑ 142	PS	I Call My Baby STP/That's the Way It Is	1966	7.50	15.00	30.00
		Some sleeves contain an STP decal.				
Seeberg						
❑ 3018	M	Ram Charger/Little Latin Lupe Lu	1965	7.50	15.00	30.00
❑ 3018	S	Ram Charger/Little Latin Lupe Lu	1965	10.00	20.00	40.00
		Some copies were pressed in stereo. We don't know if it's marked on the label or trail-off wax or if it must be played to identify.				
Delacardos, The						
Atlantic						
❑ 2368		Got No One/She's the One I Love	1966	2.50	5.00	10.00
❑ 2389		I Know I'm Not Much/You Don't Have to See Me	1967	2.50	5.00	10.00
❑ 2419		They Put a Spell on You/A Fool for You	1967	2.50	5.00	10.00
Dimension						
❑ 1040		Forget About the Guy/Dance, Gypsy, Dance	1964	5.00	10.00	20.00

Number	Title (A Side/B Side)	Year	VG	VG+	NM
Elgey					
❑ 1001	A Letter to a School Girl/I'll Never Let You Down	1959	12.50	25.00	50.00
Imperial					
❑ 5992	On the Beach/Everybody's Rockin'	1963	3.75	7.50	15.00
Shell					
❑ 308	Dream Girl/I Just Want to Know	1961	5.00	10.00	20.00
❑ 311	Love Is the Greatest Thing/Girl-Girl	1962	5.00	10.00	20.00
United Artists					
❑ 276	I Got It/Thing-A-Ma-Jig	1960	3.75	7.50	15.00
❑ 310	Hold Back the Tears/Mr. Dillon	1961	3.75	7.50	15.00

Delaney and Bonnie
Atco

Number	Title (A Side/B Side)	Year	VG	VG+	NM
❑ 6725	Groupie (Superstar)/Comin' Home	1969	2.00	4.00	8.00
❑ 6756	Soul Shake/Free the People	1970	2.00	4.00	8.00
❑ 6788	Miss Ann/They Call It Rock and Roll Music	1970	2.00	4.00	8.00
❑ 6804	Never Ending Song of Love/Don't Deceive Me	1971	2.00	4.00	8.00
❑ 6838	Only You Know and I Know/God Knows I Love You	1971		3.00	6.00
❑ 6866	Sing My Way Home/Move 'Em Out	1972		2.50	5.00
❑ 6883	Where There's a Will There's a Way/Lonesome and a Long Way from Home	1972		2.50	5.00
❑ 6904	Sing My Way Home/Will the Circle Be Unbroken	1972		2.50	5.00
Columbia					
❑ 45608	Country Life/Walk in the River Jordan	1972		2.50	5.00
Elektra					
❑ 45660	Soldiers of the Cross/Get Ourselves Together	1969	2.50	5.00	10.00
❑ 45662	When the Battle Is Over/Get Ourselves Together	1969	2.50	5.00	10.00
Garpax					
❑ 44184	Cherry Pie/Hey Mr. Weatherman	1964	3.75	7.50	15.00
	As "Lani & Boni"				
Independence					
❑ 78	You've Lost That Lovin' Feelin'/Don't Let It (Be the Last Time)	1967	3.00	6.00	12.00
Stax					
❑ 0003	It's Been a Long Time Coming/We've Just Been Feeling Bad	1968	2.50	5.00	10.00
❑ 0057	Hard to Say Goodbye/Just Plain Beautiful	1969	2.50	5.00	10.00

Delegates, The
(The Mainstream records are break-in novelties; the Vee Jay records are early Dee Clark)
Aura

Number	Title (A Side/B Side)	Year	VG	VG+	NM
❑ 4504	Pigmy (Part 1)/Pigmy (Part 2)	1965	3.75	7.50	15.00
❑ 4508	The Peeper/Hainty	1965	3.75	7.50	15.00
Mainstream					
❑ 5525	Convention '72/Funky Butt	1972		3.00	6.00
❑ 5525	Convention '72 (same on both sides)	1972		2.50	5.00
	Stock copy; "Funky Butt" deleted because of retailers' protests to the title				
❑ 5530	Richard M. Nixon, Face the Issues (Part 1)/Richard M. Nixon, Face the Issues (Part 2)	1972	2.00	4.00	8.00
Vee Jay					
❑ 212	The Convention/Jay's Rock	1956	15.00	30.00	60.00
	B-side by Big Jay McNeely				
❑ 243	Mother's Son/I'm Gonna Be Glad	1957	15.00	30.00	60.00
World Pacific					
❑ 4504	Pigmy (Part 1)/Pigmy (Part 2)	1965	3.00	6.00	12.00
❑ 88120	Pigmy (Part 1)/The Peeper	1966	2.50	5.00	10.00

Delfonics, The
(Also see "Harris, Major")
Arista

Number	Title (A Side/B Side)	Year	VG	VG+	NM
❑ 0308	Don't Throw It All Away/I Don't Care What People Say	1978		2.00	4.00
Cameo					
❑ 472	You've Been Untrue/I Was There	1967	3.75	7.50	15.00
Moon Shot					
❑ 6703	He Don't Really Love You/Without You	1967	3.75	7.50	15.00
Philly Groove					
❑ 150	La-La Means I Love You/Can't Get Over Losing You	1968	2.50	5.00	10.00
❑ 151	I'm Sorry/You're Gone	1968	2.50	5.00	10.00
❑ 152	Break Your Promise/Alfie	1968	2.50	5.00	10.00
❑ 154	Ready Or Not Here I Come (Can't Hide from Love)/Somebody Loves You	1968	2.50	5.00	10.00
❑ 156	Funny Feeling/My New Love	1969	2.50	5.00	10.00
❑ 157	You Got Yours and I'll Get Mine/Loving Him	1969	2.50	5.00	10.00
❑ 161	Didn't I (Blow Your Mind This Time)/Down Is Up, Up Is Down	1970	2.50	5.00	10.00
❑ 162	Trying to Make a Fool of Me/Baby I Love You	1970	2.50	5.00	10.00
❑ 163	When You Get Right Down To It/I Give to You	1970	2.50	5.00	10.00
❑ 166	Over and Over/Hey! Love	1971	2.00	4.00	8.00
❑ 169	Walk Right Up to the Sun/Round and Round	1971	2.00	4.00	8.00
❑ 172	Tell Me This Is a Dream/I'm a Man	1972	2.00	4.00	8.00
❑ 174	Think It Over/I'm a Man	1972	2.00	4.00	8.00
❑ 176	I Don't Want to Make You Wait/Baby I Miss You	1973	2.00	4.00	8.00

Number	Title (A Side/B Side)	Year	VG	VG+	NM
❑ 177	Alfie/Start All Over Again	1973	2.00	4.00	8.00
❑ 182	I Told You So/Seventeen and In Love	1973	2.00	4.00	8.00
❑ 184	Lying to Myself/Hey Baby	1974	2.00	4.00	8.00

Delicates, The
Celeste
❑ 676	My Pillow/I Played 1,2,3,4	1961	7.50	15.00	30.00

Challenge
❑ 59232	I've Been Hurt/Come On Everybody	1964	3.75	7.50	15.00
❑ 59267	I Want to Get Married/Home from Camp	1965	3.75	7.50	15.00
❑ 59304	Stop Shovin' Me Around/Comin' Down with Love	1965	3.75	7.50	15.00

Dee Dee
❑ 677	My Pillow/I Played 1,2,3,4	1961	7.50	15.00	30.00

Roulette
❑ 4321	Little Ship/Not Tomorrow	1961	5.00	10.00	20.00
❑ 4360	Little Boy of Mine/Dickie Went and Did It	1961	5.00	10.00	20.00
❑ 4387	I Don't Know Why (I Just Do)/Strange Love	1961	5.00	10.00	20.00

Unart
❑ 2017	Black and White Thunderbird/Ronnie Is My Lover	1959	6.25	12.50	25.00
❑ 2024	Ringa Ding/Meusurry	1959	6.25	12.50	25.00

United Artists
❑ 210	Flip Flip/Your Happiest Years	1960	5.00	10.00	20.00
❑ 228	The Kiss/Too Young to Date	1960	5.00	10.00	20.00

Dell, Lenny and the Demensions - See "Demensions, The"

Dell, Tony
King
❑ 5766	My Girl/Magic Wand	1963	12.50	25.00	50.00

Dells, The
ABC
❑ 12386	Super Woman/My Life Is So Wonderful	1978		2.50	5.00
❑ 12422	(I Wanna) Testify/Don't Save Me	1978		2.50	5.00
❑ 12440	(You Bring Out) The Best in Me/Wrapped Up Tight	1978		2.50	5.00

Argo
❑ 5415	God Bless the Child/I'm Going Home	1962	3.00	6.00	12.00
❑ 5428	The (Bossa Nova) Bird/Eternally	1962	3.00	6.00	12.00
❑ 5442	Hi Diddle Dee Dum Dum (It's a Good Feelin')/ If It Ain't One Thing, It's Another	1963	3.00	6.00	12.00
❑ 5456	After You/Goodbye Mary Ann	1963	3.00	6.00	12.00

Cadet
❑ 5538	Thinkin' About You/ The Change We Go Thru (For Love)	1966		3.00	6.00
❑ 5551	Over Again/Run for Cover	1967		3.00	6.00
❑ 5563	You Belong to Someone Else/Inspiration	1967		3.00	6.00
❑ 5574	O-O, I Love You/There Is	1967		3.00	6.00
❑ 5590	There Is/Show Me	1968	2.00	4.00	8.00
❑ 5599	Wear it On My Face/Please Don't Change Me Now	1968		3.00	6.00
❑ 5612	Stay in My Corner/Love Is So Simple	1969		3.00	6.00
❑ 5621	Always Together/I Want My Mama	1968		3.00	6.00
❑ 5631	Does Anybody Know I'm Here/ Make Sure (You Have Somebody to Love You)	1968		3.00	6.00
❑ 5636	I Can't Do Enough/Hallways of My Mind	1969		3.00	6.00
❑ 5641	I Can Sing a Rainbow-Love Is Blue/Hallelujah Baby	1969		3.00	6.00
❑ 5649	Oh What a Night/Believe Me	1969		3.00	6.00
❑ 5658	On the Dock of the Bay/When I'm in Your Arms	1969		3.00	6.00
❑ 5663	Oh What a Day/The Change We Go Thru (For Love)	1970		3.00	6.00
❑ 5667	Open Up My Heart/Nadine	1970		3.00	6.00
❑ 5672	Long Lonely Nights/A Little Understanding	1970		3.00	6.00
❑ 5679	The Glory of Love/A Whiter Shade of Pale	1970		3.00	6.00
❑ 5683	The Love We Had (Stays on My Mind)/Freedom Means	1971		3.00	6.00
❑ 5689	It's All Up to You/Oh, My Dear	1972		3.00	6.00
❑ 5691	Walk On By/This Guy's in Love with You	1972		3.00	6.00
❑ 5694	Just As Long As We're in Love/I'd Rather Be with You	1972		3.00	6.00
❑ 5696	Give Your Baby a Standing Ovation/Closer	1973		3.00	6.00
❑ 5698	My Pretending Days Are Over/Let's Make It Last	1973		3.00	6.00
❑ 5700	I Miss You/Don't Make Me a Storyteller	1973		3.00	6.00
❑ 5702	I Wish It Was Me You Loved/ Two Together Is Better Than One	1974		3.00	6.00
❑ 5703	Bring Back the Love of Yesterday/ Learning to Love You Was Easy (It's So Hard Trying to Get Over You)	1974		3.00	6.00
❑ 5703	Learning to Love You Was Easy (It's So Hard Trying to Get Over You)/Sweeter as the Days Go By	1974		3.00	6.00
❑ 5707	The Glory of Love/You're the Greatest	1975		3.00	6.00
❑ 5710	Love Is Missing from Our Lives/I'm in Love	1975		3.00	6.00

With the Dramatics
❑ 5711	We Got to Get Our Thing Together/The Power of Love	1975	2.00	4.00	8.00

Checker
❑ 794	Darling I Know/Christine	1954	400.00	800.00	1,200

As "The El Rays"

MCA
❑ 41051	Plastic People/What I Could	1979		2.50	5.00

Number	Title (A Side/B Side)	Year	VG	VG+	NM
Mercury					
❑ 73723	We Got to Get Our Thing Together/Reminiscing	1975		2.50	5.00
❑ 73759	The Power of Love/Gotta Get Home to My Baby	1976		2.50	5.00
❑ 73807	Slow Motion/Ain't No Black and White in Music	1976		2.50	5.00
❑ 73842	No Way Back/Too Late for Love	1976		2.50	5.00
❑ 73901	Betcha Never Been Loved (Like This Before)/Get On Down	1977		2.50	5.00
❑ 73909	Our Love/Could It Be	1977		2.50	5.00
❑ 73977	Private Property/Teaser	1977		2.50	5.00
Private I					
❑ 04343	Don't Want Nobody/You Can't Just Walk Away	1984		2.00	4.00
❑ 04448	One Step Closer/Come On Back to Me	1984		2.00	4.00
❑ 04540	Love On/Don't Want Nobody	1984		2.00	4.00
Skylark					
❑ 558	I Can't Help Myself/She's Just an Angel	198?		2.00	4.00
❑ 581	Someone to Call Me Darling/Now I Pray	198?		2.00	4.00
20th Century					
❑ 2463	I Touched a Dream/All About the Paper	1980		2.00	4.00
❑ 2475	Passionate Breezes/Your Song	1980		2.00	4.00
❑ 2504	Happy Song/Look at Us Now	1981		2.00	4.00
❑ 2602	Ain't It a Shame/Stay in My Corner	1982		2.00	4.00
Vee Jay					
❑ 134	Tell the World/Blues at Three	1955	250.00	500.00	1,000
❑ 134	Tell the World/Blues at Three — Red vinyl	1955	5,000	7,500	10,000
❑ 166	Dreams of Contentment/Zing, Zing, Zing	1955	50.00	100.00	200.00
❑ 204	Oh What a Nite/Jo-Jo	1956	25.00	50.00	100.00
❑ 230	Movin' On/I Wanna Go Home	1956	10.00	20.00	40.00
❑ 236	Why Do You Have to Go/Dance, Dance, Dance	1957	10.00	20.00	40.00
❑ 251	A Distant Love/O-Bop She-Bop	1957	10.00	20.00	40.00
❑ 258	Pain in My Heart/Time Makes You Change	1957	10.00	20.00	40.00
❑ 274	The Springer/What You Say Baby	1958	7.50	15.00	30.00
❑ 292	I'm Calling/Jeepers Creepers	1958	7.50	15.00	30.00
❑ 300	Wedding Day/My Best Girl	1958	25.00	50.00	100.00
❑ 324	Dry Your Eyes/Baby Open Up Your Heart	1959	10.00	20.00	40.00
❑ 338	Oh What a Nite/I Wanna Go Home	1960	5.00	10.00	20.00
❑ 376	Hold On to What You've Got/Swingin' Teens	1961	5.00	10.00	20.00
❑ 595	Shy Girl/What Do We Prove	1964	3.00	6.00	12.00
❑ 615	Wait Till Tomorrow/Oh What a Good Night	1964	3.00	6.00	12.00
❑ 674	Stay in My Corner/It's Not Unusual	1965	3.00	6.00	12.00
❑ 712	Poor Little Boy/Hey Sugar (Don't Get Serious)	1966	3.00	6.00	12.00
Veteran					
❑ 7-101	Thought of You Just a Little Too Much/(B-side unknown)	1989		2.50	5.00

Delmiras, The

Number	Title (A Side/B Side)	Year	VG	VG+	NM
Dade					
❑ 1821	Dry Your Eyes/The Big Sound	1961	75.00	150.00	300.00

Deltas, The

Number	Title (A Side/B Side)	Year	VG	VG+	NM
Cambridge					
❑ 124	Goodnight My Love/Give My Love a Chance	1962	10.00	20.00	40.00
Gone					
❑ 5010	Let Me Share Your Dream/Lamplight — Black label	1957	125.00	250.00	500.00
❑ 5010	Let Me Share Your Dream/Lamplight — Multicolor label	1957	15.00	30.00	60.00
Philips					
❑ 40023	My Own True Love/Work Song	1962	5.00	10.00	20.00
❑ 40023	My Own True Love/Hold Me, Thrill Me, Kiss Me	1962	3.75	7.50	15.00

Deltones, The

Number	Title (A Side/B Side)	Year	VG	VG+	NM
Jubilee					
❑ 5374	La La La/Bow-Legged Annie	1959	6.25	12.50	25.00
Vee Jay					
❑ 288	I'm Coming Home/Early Morning Rock	1958	10.00	20.00	40.00
❑ 303	A Lover's Prayer/First Man to the Moon	1958	10.00	20.00	40.00

DeMarco, Ralph

Number	Title (A Side/B Side)		Year	VG	VG+	NM
Guaranteed						
❑ 202		More Than Riches/Old Shep	1959	5.00	10.00	20.00
❑ 202	PS	More Than Riches/Old Shep	1959	10.00	20.00	40.00
Shelley						
❑ 1011		Donna/For All We Know	1960	10.00	20.00	40.00
20th Fox						
❑ 309		Keep On Walkin'/Lonely for a Girl	1962	5.00	10.00	20.00

Demensions, The

Number	Title (A Side/B Side)	Year	VG	VG+	NM
Coral					
❑ 62277	Again/Count Your Blessings Instead of Sheep	1961	6.25	12.50	25.00
❑ 62293	As Time Goes By/Seven Days a Week	1961	6.25	12.50	25.00
❑ 62323	Young at Heart/Your Cheatin' Heart	1962	5.00	10.00	20.00
❑ 62344	My Foolish Heart/Just One More Chance	1963	7.50	15.00	30.00
❑ 62359	Fly Me to the Moon/You'll Never Know	1963	6.25	12.50	25.00

Number	Title (A Side/B Side)	Year	VG	VG+	NM
❏ 62382	Just a Shoulder to Cry On/Don't Worry About Bobby	1963	6.25	12.50	25.00
❏ 62392	A Little White Gardenia/Don't Cry Pretty Baby	1964	5.00	10.00	20.00
❏ 62432	This Time Next Year/My Old Girlfriend	1964	5.00	10.00	20.00
	As "Lenny Dell and the Demensions"				
❏ 62444	Once a Day/Ting Along Ting Toy	1965	5.00	10.00	20.00
	As "Lenny Dell and the Demensions"				
❏ 65559	Over the Rainbow/Zing Went the Strings of My Heart	1962	5.00	10.00	20.00
❏ 65611	As Time Goes By/My Foolish Heart	1967	3.75	7.50	15.00

Mohawk

Number	Title (A Side/B Side)	Year	VG	VG+	NM
❏ 116	Over the Rainbow/Nursery Rhyme Rock	1960	12.50	25.00	50.00
	Maroon label				
❏ 116	Over the Rainbow/Nursery Rhyme Rock	1960	7.50	15.00	30.00
	Brown label				
❏ 116	Over the Rainbow/Nursery Rhyme Rock	1960	6.25	12.50	25.00
	Red label				
❏ 120	Zing Went the Strings of My Heart/ Don't Take Your Love from Me	1960	6.25	12.50	25.00
❏ 121	God's Christmas/Ave Maria	1960	15.00	30.00	60.00
❏ 123	A Tear Fell/Theresa	1961	15.00	30.00	60.00

DeMilles, The

Laurie

Number	Title (A Side/B Side)	Year	VG	VG+	NM
❏ 3230	Donna Lee/Um Ba Pa	1964	7.50	15.00	30.00
❏ 3247	Lazy Love/Cry and Be On Your Way	1964	12.50	25.00	50.00

Demolyrs, The

U.W.R.

Number	Title (A Side/B Side)	Year	VG	VG+	NM
❏ 900	Rain/Hey Little Rosie	1964	125.00	250.00	500.00

Demotrons, The

Atlantic

Number	Title (A Side/B Side)	Year	VG	VG+	NM
❏ 2589	I Want a Home in the Country/ I Don't Want to Play No More	1969	2.50	5.00	10.00

Cameo

| ❏ 456 | Beg, Borrow and Steal/Midnight in New York | 1967 | 2.50 | 5.00 | 10.00 |

Dorset

| ❏ 5010 | Frisky/Steel Driving Man | 196? | 5.00 | 10.00 | 20.00 |

Enrica

| ❏ 1003 | Rock-A-Way Special/Bugle Boy | 1959 | 7.50 | 15.00 | 30.00 |

Radar

❏ 2615	Hombre/Swinging Soiree	1962	5.00	10.00	20.00
❏ 2616	Pretzel Twist/Meet Mister Callaghan	1962	5.00	10.00	20.00
❏ 2621	Sticks and Stones/ Theme from "Adventures in Paradise"	1962	5.00	10.00	20.00

Rust

| ❏ 5025 | Rockin' with Mother Goose/Home on the Pad | 1960 | 5.00 | 10.00 | 20.00 |

Scepter

| ❏ 12148 | Take This Love I Have/Sleep, Sleep, Sleep | 1966 | 3.00 | 6.00 | 12.00 |
| ❏ 12174 | Brother Where Are You/Take This Love I Have | 1966 | 3.00 | 6.00 | 12.00 |

Denby, Junior

King

Number	Title (A Side/B Side)	Year	VG	VG+	NM
❏ 4717	With This Ring/I'm Still Lonesome	1954	15.00	30.00	60.00
❏ 4725	This Fool Has Learned/If You Only Have Faith in Me	1954	15.00	30.00	60.00
❏ 5217	With This Ring/I'm Still Lonesome	1959	7.50	15.00	30.00

Denson, Lee

Enterprise

Number	Title (A Side/B Side)	Year	VG	VG+	NM
❏ 9086	A Mom and Dad for Christmas/ The Miracle of the Rosary	1973		2.50	5.00

Kent

| ❏ 306 | High School Hop/Devil Doll | 1958 | 15.00 | 30.00 | 60.00 |

Vik

❏ 0251	Heart of a Fool/The Pied Piper	1957	10.00	20.00	40.00
❏ 0281	New Shoes/Climb Love Mountain	1957	20.00	40.00	80.00
	With Eddie Cochran on guitar				

Denton, Mickey

Amy

Number	Title (A Side/B Side)	Year	VG	VG+	NM
❏ 902	Top Ten/Now I'm Mr. Blue	1964	3.00	6.00	12.00

Big Top

❏ 3078	Steady Kind/Now You Can't Give Them Away	1961	6.25	12.50	25.00
❏ 3094	Nature Boy/Ain't Nobody	1962	5.00	10.00	20.00
❏ 3114	Tell Her/How Mighty Hath Fallen	1962	5.00	10.00	20.00
❏ 3142	Dance With Me Mary/The Other Side of Betty	1963	5.00	10.00	20.00

Impact

| ❏ 1002 | Ain't Love Grand/Mi Amore | 1965 | 5.00 | 10.00 | 20.00 |
| ❏ 1011 | Heartache Is My Name/King Lonely the Blue | 1966 | 5.00 | 10.00 | 20.00 |

World Artists

| ❏ 1043 | One More Time/Don't Throw My Toys Away | 1965 | 3.00 | 6.00 | 12.00 |

Number	Title (A Side/B Side)	Year	VG	VG+	NM

Denver, Boise, & Johnson
(With John Denver and Michael Johnson)
Reprise
❏ 0695	Take Me to Tomorrow/'68 Nixon (This Year's Model)	1968	3.00	6.00	12.00

Derek - See "Cymbal, Johnny"

Derek and the Dominos
Atco
❏ 6780	Tell the Truth/Roll It Over	1970	6.25	12.50	25.00
	Produced by Phil Spector; withdrawn shortly after release				
❏ 6803	Bell Bottom Blues/Keep On Growing	1971	2.50	5.00	10.00
❏ 6809	Layla (2:43)/I Am Yours	1971	2.50	5.00	10.00
❏ 6809	Layla (7:10)/I Am Yours	1972		3.00	6.00
Polydor
❏ 15040	Layla/I Am Yours	1972			*Unreleased?*
RSO
❏ 400	Presence of the Lord/ Why Does Love Got to Be So Sad	1973		3.00	6.00

DeShannon, Jackie
Amherst
❏ 725	I Don't Think I Can Wait/Don't Let the Flame Burn Out	1978	3.00	6.00	12.00
❏ 728	To Love Somebody/Just to Feel This Love from You	1978	3.00	6.00	12.00
❏ 733	You're the Only Dancer/Tonight You're Doin' It Right	1979	3.00	6.00	12.00
❏ 737	Things We Said Today/Way Above the Angels	1979	3.00	6.00	12.00
Atlantic
❏ 2871	Only Love Can Break Your Heart/Vanilla Olay	1972	2.50	5.00	10.00
❏ 2895	I Wanna Roo You/Paradise	1972	2.50	5.00	10.00
❏ 2919	Sweet Sixteen/Speak Out to Me	1972	2.50	5.00	10.00
❏ 2924	Chains on My Soul/Peaceful in My Soul	1972	2.50	5.00	10.00
❏ 2994	Your Baby Is a Lady/ (If You Never Have a Big Hit Record) You're Still Gonna Be My Star	1973	2.50	5.00	10.00
❏ 3041	You've Changed/Jimmie, Just Sing Me One More Song	1974	2.50	5.00	10.00
Capitol
❏ 3130	Salinas/Keep Me Warm	1971	2.50	5.00	10.00
❏ 3185	Stone Cold Soul/West Virginia Mine	1971	2.50	5.00	10.00
Columbia
❏ 10221	Boat to Sail/Let the Sailors Dance	1975	3.75	7.50	15.00
	With Brian Wilson on backing vocal				
❏ 10340	Fire in the City/All Night Desire	1976	2.50	5.00	10.00
Dot
❏ 15928	Cajun Blues/Just Another Lie	1959	6.25	12.50	25.00
	As "Jackie Shannon"				
❏ 15980	Trouble/Lies	1959	6.25	12.50	25.00
	As "Jackie Shannon"				
Edison International
❏ 416	I Wanna Go Home/So Warm	1960	25.00	50.00	100.00
❏ 418	Put My Baby Down/The Foolish One	1960	25.00	50.00	100.00
Gone
❏ 5008	How Wrong I Was/I'll Be True	1957	7.50	15.00	30.00
	As "Jackie Dee"				
Imperial
❏ 66110	What the World Needs Now Is Love/ I Remember the Boy	1965	2.00	4.00	8.00
❏ 66132	A Lifetime of Loneliness/Don't Turn Your Back on Me	1965		3.00	6.00
❏ 66171	Come and Get Me/Splendor in the Grass	1966		3.00	6.00
❏ 66194	Will You Love Me Tomorrow/Are You Ready for This	1966		3.00	6.00
❏ 66196	So Long Johnny/Windows and Doors	1966		3.00	6.00
❏ 66202	I Can Make It with You/To Be Myself	1966		3.00	6.00
❏ 66224	Come On Down/Find Me Love	1967		3.00	6.00
❏ 66236	Where Does the Sun Go/Wishing Doll	1967		3.00	6.00
❏ 66251	It's All in the Game/Changin' My Mind	1967		3.00	6.00
❏ 66281	Me About You/I Keep Wanting You	1968		3.00	6.00
❏ 66301	Nobody's Home to Go Home To/Nicole	1968		3.00	6.00
❏ 66312	Didn't Want to Have to Do It/Splendor in the Grass	1968		3.00	6.00
❏ 66313	The Weight/Effervescent Blue	1968		3.00	6.00
❏ 66342	Holly Would/My Heart's Been Marching	1968		3.00	6.00
❏ 66370	What Is This/Trust Me	1969		2.50	5.00
❏ 66385	Put a Little Love in Your Heart/Always Together	1969		3.00	6.00
❏ 66419	Love Will Find a Way/I Let Go Completely	1969		2.50	5.00
❏ 66430	One Christmas/ Do You Know How Christmas Trees Are Grown	1969		3.00	6.00
❏ 66438	Brighton Hill/You Can Come to Me	1970		2.50	5.00
❏ 66452	You Keep Me Hangin' On-Hurt So Bad/ What Was Your Day Like	1970		2.50	5.00
Liberty
❏ 55148	Buddy/Strolypso Dance	1958	6.25	12.50	25.00
	As "Jackie Dee"				
❏ 55288	Lonely Girl/Teach Me	1960	3.75	7.50	15.00
❏ 55342	Think About You/Heaven Is Being with You	1961	3.75	7.50	15.00
❏ 55358	I Won't Turn You Down/Wish I Could Find a Boy	1961	3.75	7.50	15.00
❏ 55387	Baby (When You Kiss Me)/Ain't That Love	1961	3.75	7.50	15.00

Number		Title (A Side/B Side)	Year	VG	VG+	NM
☐ 55425		The Prince/I'll Drown in My Own Tears	1962	3.75	7.50	15.00
☐ 55425		The Prince/That's What Boys Are Made Of	1962	3.75	7.50	15.00
☐ 55484		Guess Who/Just Like in the Movies	1962	3.75	7.50	15.00
☐ 55497		You Won't Forget Me/I Don't Think So Much of Myself	1962	3.75	7.50	15.00
☐ 55526		Faded Love/Dancing Silhouettes	1962	3.75	7.50	15.00
☐ 55563		Needles and Pins/Did He Call Today, Mama?	1963	3.75	7.50	15.00
☐ 55602		Little Yellow Roses/500 Miles	1963	3.75	7.50	15.00
☐ 55602		Little Yellow Roses/Oh Sweet Chariot	1963	3.75	7.50	15.00
☐ 55602	DJ	Little Yellow Roses	1963	20.00	40.00	80.00
		Yellow vinyl promo				
☐ 55645		When You Walk in the Room/Til You Say You're Mine	1963	3.75	7.50	15.00
☐ 55673		I'm Gonna Be Strong/Should I Cry	1964	3.75	7.50	15.00
☐ 55678		Oh Boy/I'm Looking for Someone to Love	1964	3.75	7.50	15.00
☐ 55705		Hold Your Head High/	1964	3.75	7.50	15.00
		She Don't Understand Him Like I Do				
☐ 55730		He's Got the Whole World in His Hands/It's Love Baby	1964	3.75	7.50	15.00
☐ 55735		When You Walk in the Room/Over You	1964	3.00	6.00	12.00
☐ 55787		What the World Needs Now Is Love/	1965			Unreleased
		A Lifetime of Loneliness				
☐ 56187		Mediterranean Sky/It's So Nice	1970		3.00	6.00

PJ
| ☐ 101 | | Trouble/Lies | 1959 | 10.00 | 20.00 | 40.00 |
| | | *As "Jackie Shannon"* | | | | |

RCA
| ☐ PB-11902 | | I Don't Need You Anymore/Find Love | 1980 | | 2.50 | 5.00 |

Sage and Sand
| ☐ 290 | | Just Another Lie/Cajun Blues | 1960 | 6.25 | 12.50 | 25.00 |
| ☐ 330 | | Trouble/Lies | 1960 | 6.25 | 12.50 | 25.00 |

United Artists
☐ 0033		What the World Needs Now Is Love/Needles and Pins	1973		3.00	6.00
		"Silver Spotlight Series" reissue				
☐ 0034		Put a Little Love in Your Heart/	1973		3.00	6.00
		When You Walk in the Room				
		"Silver Spotlight Series" reissue				

Desires, The

Dasa
| ☐ 102 | | Phyllis Beloved/The Girl for Me | 1962 | 7.50 | 15.00 | 30.00 |

Herald
| ☐ 532 | | Bobby You/Cold Lonely Heart | 1958 | 6.25 | 12.50 | 25.00 |

Hull
| ☐ 730 | | Hey Lena/Let It Please Be You | 1959 | 20.00 | 40.00 | 80.00 |
| ☐ 733 | | Set Me Free/Rendezvous with You | 1960 | 20.00 | 40.00 | 80.00 |

Seville
| ☐ 118 | | The Story of Love/I Ask You | 1962 | 7.50 | 15.00 | 30.00 |

Smash
| ☐ 1763 | | There I Go Again/I Never Loved Like This | 1962 | 6.25 | 12.50 | 25.00 |

20th Fox
| ☐ 195 | | I Don't Know Why/Longing | 1960 | 6.25 | 12.50 | 25.00 |

Detergents, The
(Ron Dante was a member)

Kapp
| ☐ 735 | | I Can Never Eat Home Anymore/Igor's Cellar | 1966 | 3.75 | 7.50 | 15.00 |
| ☐ 753 | | Pushin' the Panic Button/Some Sunday Morning | 1966 | 3.75 | 7.50 | 15.00 |

Roulette
☐ 4590		Leader of the Laundromat/Ulcers	1964	5.00	10.00	20.00
☐ 4590	PS	Leader of the Laundromat/Ulcers	1964	10.00	20.00	40.00
☐ 4603		Double-O-Seven/The Blue Kangaroo	1965	3.75	7.50	15.00
☐ 4616		Tea and Trumpets/Mrs. Jones (How 'Bout It)	1965	3.75	7.50	15.00
☐ 4626		Little Dum-Dum/Soldier Girl	1965	3.75	7.50	15.00
☐ 4642		Bad Girl/Here She Comes	1965	3.75	7.50	15.00

Detours, The

Atco
| ☐ 6448 | | Who Do You Love/Peace of Mind | 1966 | 6.25 | 12.50 | 25.00 |

McSherry
| ☐ 1285 | | Bring Back My Beatles to Me/Money | 1964 | 6.25 | 12.50 | 25.00 |
| ☐ 1285 | | Bring Back My Beatles/Money | 1964 | 6.25 | 12.50 | 25.00 |

Detroit Wheels, The
(Mitch Ryder's band after he went solo)

Inferno
| ☐ 5002 | | Linda Sue Dixon/Tally Ho | 1968 | 5.00 | 10.00 | 20.00 |
| ☐ 5003 | | Think (Part 1)/Think (Part 2) | 1968 | 5.00 | 10.00 | 20.00 |

Deuces of Rhythm and the Tempo Toppers, The
(With Little Richard)

Peacock
| ☐ 1616 | | Ain't That Good News/A Fool at the Wheel | 1953 | 20.00 | 40.00 | 80.00 |
| ☐ 1628 | | Always/Rice, Red Beans and Turnip Greens | 1954 | 20.00 | 40.00 | 80.00 |

Number	Title (A Side/B Side)	Year	VG	VG+	NM

Devons, The
(The Pic One group is not the same as the Decca and King group)
Decca

❏ 31777	Honda Bike/Free Fall	1965	20.00	40.00	80.00
❏ 31822	Are You Really Real/It's All Over Now, Baby Blue	1965	10.00	20.00	40.00
❏ 31899	Come On/A Little Extra Effort	1966	10.00	20.00	40.00

King

❏ 6226	Someone to Treat Me (The Way You Used To)/ Soul Party	1969	2.00	4.00	8.00

Pic One

◖ 111	Wine, Wine, Wine/Joey's Guitar	1965	20.00	40.00	80.00
	Also recorded as the Sir Douglas Quintet				

DeVorzon, Barry
(Also see "Barry and the Tamerlanes")
A&M

❏ 2129	Theme from "The Warriors"/Baseball Furies' Chase	1979		2.00	4.00

Columbia

❏ 41612	Hey Little Darlin'/Rosemary	1960	6.25	12.50	25.00
❏ 41663	Love You Baby/Can-Can Ladies	1960	6.25	12.50	25.00

RCA Victor

❏ 47-7124	Barbara Jean/Baby Doll	1957	7.50	15.00	30.00
❏ 47-7226	False Love/Raindrops at My Window	1958	7.50	15.00	30.00
❏ 47-7406	Honey Bunny/Too Soon	1958	7.50	15.00	30.00
❏ 47-7510	Cora Lee/Blue, Green and Gold	1959	7.50	15.00	30.00

Devotions, The
Delta

❏ 1001	Rip Van Winkle/I Love You for Sentimental Reasons	1961	37.50	75.00	150.00

Roulette

❏ 4406	Rip Van Winkle/I Love You for Sentimental Reasons	1962	10.00	20.00	40.00
❏ 4541	Rip Van Winkle/I Love You for Sentimental Reasons	1964	5.00	10.00	20.00
❏ 4556	A Sunday Kind of Love/Tears from a Broken Heart	1964	7.50	5.00	30.00
❏ 4580	Snow White/Zindy Lou	1964	7.50	5.00	30.00

Dewey, George and Jack
Raven

❏ 700	The Flying Saucers Have Landed (Part 1)/ The Flying Saucers Have Landed (Part 2)	195?	7.50	15.00	30.00

Dials, The
Hilltop

❏ 2009	Wondering About Your Love/Sorrento	1960	37.50	75.00	150.00
❏ 2010	School Bells Are Ringing/Ring Ting-a-Ling	1960	75.00	150.00	300.00
❏ 219	No Hard Feelings/Win Yourself a Lover	1961	12.50	25.00	50.00

Norgolde

❏ 105	Ring Ting-a Ling/All Kinds of Twistin'	1961	20.00	40.00	80.00

Philips

❏ 40040	These Foolish Things/At the Start of a New Romance	1962	10.00	20.00	40.00

Time

❏ 1068	Monkey Dance/Monkey Walk	1963	5.00	10.00	20.00

Dialtones, The
Dial

❏ 4054	Don't Let the Sun Shine on Me/ You Don't Know, You Just Don't Know	1967	5.00	10.00	20.00

Goldisc

❏ 3005	Till I Heard It from You/Jenny	1960	7.50	15.00	30.00
❏ 3020	Till I Heard It from You/Jenny	1961	5.00	10.00	20.00

Lawn

❏ 203	So Young/Chicago Bird	1963	6.25	12.50	25.00

Diamond, Neil
(Also see "Barbra and Neil")
Bang

❏ 105	Cherry, Cherry/Girl, You'll Be a Woman Soon	1973		2.00	4.00
❏ 108	Solitary Man/I'm a Believer	1973		2.00	4.00
❏ 519	Solitary Man/Do It	1966	3.75	7.50	15.00
❏ 528	Cherry, Cherry/I'll Come Running	1966	3.00	6.00	12.00
❏ 536	I Got the Feelin' (Oh No No)/The Boat That I Row	1966	3.00	6.00	12.00
❏ 540	You Got to Me/Someday Baby	1967	3.00	6.00	12.00
❏ 542	Girl, You'll Be a Woman Soon/You'll Forget	1967	3.00	6.00	12.00
❏ 547	I Thank the Lord for the Night Time/ The Long Way Home	1967	3.75	7.50	15.00
❏ 547	Thank the Lord for the Night Time/ The Long Way Home	1967	2.50	5.00	10.00
	Title altered on second pressing				
❏ 551	Kentucky Woman/The Time Is Now	1967	2.50	5.00	10.00
❏ 554	New Orleans/Hanky Panky	1968	2.50	5.00	10.00
❏ 556	Red Red Wine/Red Rubber Ball	1968	2.00	4.00	8.00
❏ 561	Shilo/La Bamba	1968	2.00	4.00	8.00
❏ 575	Shilo/La Bamba	1970		3.00	6.00
❏ 578	Solitary Man/The Time Is Now	1970		3.00	6.00

Number		Title (A Side/B Side)	Year	VG	VG+	NM
☐ 580		Do It/Hanky Panky	1970		3.00	6.00
☐ 586		I'm a Believer/Crooked Street	1971		3.00	6.00
☐ 586		I'm a Believer/Crooked Street	1971	3.75	7.50	15.00
		Rare pressing with both sides in stereo				
☐ 703		The Long Way Home/Monday, Monday	1973		2.50	5.00

Capitol

Number		Title (A Side/B Side)	Year	VG	VG+	NM
☐ 4939		Love on the Rocks/Acapulco	1980		2.00	4.00
☐ 4939	PS	Love on the Rocks/Acapulco	1980		2.00	4.00
☐ 4960		Hello Again/Amazed and Confused	1981		2.00	4.00
☐ 4960	PS	Hello Again/Amazed and Confused	1981		2.00	4.00
☐ 4994		America/Songs of Life	1981		2.00	4.00
☐ 4994	PS	America/Songs of Life	1981		2.00	4.00

Columbia

Number		Title (A Side/B Side)	Year	VG	VG+	NM
☐ 02604		Yesterday's Songs/Guitar Heaven	1981			3.00
☐ 02604	PS	Yesterday's Songs/Guitar Heaven	1981			3.00
☐ 02712		On the Way to the Sky/Save Me	1982			3.00
☐ 02712	PS	On the Way to the Sky/Save Me	1982			3.00
☐ 02928		Be Mine Tonight/Right By You	1982			3.00
☐ 03219		Heartlight/You Don't Know Me	1982			3.00
☐ 03219	PS	Heartlight/You Don't Know Me	1982		2.00	4.00
☐ 03345		Heartlight	1982		2.50	5.00
		One-sided budget release				
☐ 03503		I'm Alive/Lost Among the Stars	1983			3.00
☐ 03572		I'm Alive	1983		2.50	5.00
		One-sided budget release				
☐ 03801		Front Page Story/I'm Guilty	1983			3.00
☐ 03801	PS	Front Page Story/I'm Guilty	1983			3.00
☐ 04541		Turn Around/Brooklyn on a Saturday Night	1984			3.00
☐ 04541	PS	Turn Around/Brooklyn on a Saturday Night	1984			3.00
☐ 04646		Sleep with Me Tonight/One by One	1984			3.00
☐ 04719		You Make It Feel Like Christmas/Crazy	1984	2.00	4.00	8.00
☐ 05889		Headed for the Future/Angel	1986			3.00
☐ 05889	PS	Headed for the Future/Angel	1986			3.00
☐ 06136		The Story of My Life/Love Doesn't Live Here Anymore	1986			3.00
☐ 07614		I Dreamed a Dream/Sweet Caroline	1987			3.00
☐ 07751		Cherry, Cherry/America	1988			3.00
☐ 08514		This Time/If I Couldn't See You Again	1988			3.00
☐ 10043		Longfellow Serenade/Rosemary's Wine	1974		2.50	5.00
☐ 10084		I've Been This Way Before/Reggae Strut	1975		2.50	5.00
☐ 10138		The Last Picasso/The Gift of Song	1975		2.50	5.00
☐ 10366		If You Know What I Mean/Street Life	1976		2.50	5.00
☐ 10405		Don't Think...Feel/Home Is a Wounded Heart	1976		2.50	5.00
☐ 10452		Beautiful Noise/Signs	1976		2.50	5.00
☐ 10657		Desiree/Once in a While	1977		2.50	5.00
☐ 10897		Forever in Blue Jeans/Remember Me	1979		2.00	4.00
☐ 10945		Say Maybe/Diamond Girls	1979		2.00	4.00
☐ 11175		September Morn/I'm a Believer	1980		2.00	4.00
☐ 11232		The Good Lord Loves You/ The Sun Ain't Gonna Shine Anymore	1980		2.00	4.00
☐ 42809		Clown Town/At Night	1963	125.00	250.00	500.00
☐ 42809	DJ	Clown Town/At Night	1963	62.50	125.00	250.00
☐ 45942		Be/Flight of the Gull	1973		2.50	5.00
☐ 45998		Skybird/Lonely Looking Sky	1974		2.50	5.00
☐ 68741		The Best Years of Our Lives/Carmelita's Eyes	1989			3.00
☐ 78242		One Good Love/Kentucky Woman	1996			3.00
		A-side: Duet with Waylon Jennings				

MCA

Number		Title (A Side/B Side)	Year	VG	VG+	NM
☐ 40017		Cherry, Cherry from Hot August Night/Morningside	1973		2.50	5.00
☐ 40092		The Last Thing on My Mind/Canta Libra	1973		2.50	5.00

Philco

Number		Title (A Side/B Side)	Year	VG	VG+	NM
☐ HP-5		Girl, You'll Be a Woman Soon/Cherry, Cherry	1967	3.75	7.50	15.00
☐ HP-17		Solitary Man/You Got to Me	1967	3.75	7.50	15.00
		4-inch flexi-discs in "Philco Hip-Pocket Record" series (price includes sleeve)				

Uni

Number		Title (A Side/B Side)	Year	VG	VG+	NM
☐ 55065		Brooklyn Roads/Holiday Inn Blues	1968	2.00	4.00	8.00
☐ 55075		Two-Bit Manchild/Broad Old Woman	1968	2.00	4.00	8.00
☐ 55075	DJ	Two-Bit Manchild (same on both sides)	1968	20.00	40.00	80.00
		Red vinyl				
☐ 55075	PS	Two-Bit Manchild/Broad Old Woman	1968	6.25	12.50	25.00
☐ 55084		Sunday Sun/Honey-Drippin' Times	1968	2.00	4.00	8.00
☐ 55109		Brother Love's Travelling Salvation Show/ A Modern-Day Version of Love	1969		3.00	6.00
☐ 55136		Sweet Caroline (Good Times Never Seemed So Good)/Dig In	1969		3.00	6.00
☐ 55175		Holly Holy/Hurtin' You Don't Come Easy	1969		3.00	6.00
☐ 55204		Until It's Time for You to Go/ And the Singer Sings His Song	1970		3.00	6.00
☐ 55224		Soolaimon (African Trilogy II)/ And the Grass Won't Pay No Mind	1970		3.00	6.00
☐ 55224	PS	Soolaimon (African Trilogy II)/ And the Grass Won't Pay No Mind	1970	3.75	7.50	15.00
☐ 55250		Cracklin' Rosie/Lordy	1970		3.00	6.00
☐ 55264		He Ain't Heavy...He's My Brother/Free Life	1970		3.00	6.00
☐ 55278		I Am...I Said/Done Too Soon	1971		2.50	5.00
☐ 55310		Stones/Crunchy Granola Suite	1971		2.50	5.00
☐ 55326		Song Sung Blue/Gitchy Goomy	1972		2.50	5.00

Number		Title (A Side/B Side)	Year	VG	VG+	NM
❏ 55346		Play Me/Porcupine Pie	1972		2.50	5.00
❏ 55352		Walk on Water/High Rolling Man	1972		2.50	5.00

Diamond, Ronnie
Imperial
❏ 5554		Zig Zag/Close to My Heart	1958	3.75	7.50	15.00
❏ 5570		Candy Store/Something's Wrong with Me	1959	3.75	7.50	15.00
❏ 5588		Life Begins at 4 O'Clock/Tell Me	1959	12.50	25.00	50.00
❏ 5605		When We Kiss/Pretty Please	1959	3.75	7.50	15.00

Diamonds, The
(The Atlantic records are by a black vocal group; the Coral and Mercury by a white cover group)
Atlantic
❏ 981		A Beggar for Your Kisses/Call, Baby, Call	1952	150.00	300.00	600.00
❏ 1003		I'll Live Again/Two Loves Have I	1953	125.00	250.00	500.00
❏ 1017		Romance in the Dark/Cherry	1954	125.00	250.00	500.00

Coral
❏ 61502		Black Denim Trousers and Motorcycle Boots/Nip Sip	1955	5.00	10.00	20.00
❏ 61577		Be My Lovin' Baby/Smooch Me	1956	5.00	10.00	20.00

Mercury
❏ 70790		Why Do Fools Fall in Love/You Baby You	1956	5.00	10.00	20.00
❏ 70835		The Church Bells May Ring/Little Girl of Mine	1956	5.00	10.00	20.00
❏ 70889		Love, Love, Love/Every Night About This Time	1956	5.00	10.00	20.00
❏ 70934		Ka-Ding-Dong/Soft Summer Breeze	1956	5.00	10.00	20.00
❏ 70983		My Judge and My Jury/Put Your House in Order	1956	5.00	10.00	20.00
❏ 71021		A Thousand Miles Away/Ev'ry Minute of the Day	1956	5.00	10.00	20.00
❏ 71060		Little Darlin'/Faithful and True	1957	6.25	12.50	25.00
		The only "cover version" generally considered a significant improvement over the original (by The Gladiolas)				
❏ 71128		Words of Love/Don't Say Goodbye	1957	5.00	10.00	20.00
❏ 71165		Zip Zip/Oh How I Wish	1957	5.00	10.00	20.00
❏ 71197		Silhouettes/Daddy Cool	1957	5.00	10.00	20.00
❏ 71242		The Stroll/Land of Beauty	1957	5.00	10.00	20.00
❏ 71291		High Sign/Chick-Lets (Don't Let Me Down)	1958	3.75	7.50	15.00
❏ 71291	PS	High Sign/Chick-Lets (Don't Let Me Down)	1958	20.00	40.00	80.00
❏ 71330		Kathy-O/Happy Years	1958	3.75	7.50	15.00
❏ 71366		Walking Along/Eternal Lovers	1958	3.75	7.50	15.00
❏ 71404		She Say (Oom Dooby Doom)/ From the Bottom of My Heart	1959	5.00	10.00	20.00
❏ 71449		A Mother's Love/Gretchen	1959	3.75	7.50	15.00
❏ 71468		Sneaky Alligator/Holding Your Hand	1959	3.75	7.50	15.00
❏ 71505		Young in Years/The Twenty-Second Day	1959	3.75	7.50	15.00
❏ 71534		Walking the Stroll/ Batman, Wolfman, Frankenstein or Dracula	1959	5.00	10.00	20.00
❏ 71586		Real True Love/Tell the Truth	1960	3.75	7.50	15.00
❏ 71633		The Pencil Song/Slave Girl	1960	3.75	7.50	15.00
❏ 71734		The Crumble/You'd Be Mine	1960	3.75	7.50	15.00
❏ 71782		You Sure Changed Me/I Sure Lawd Will	1961	3.75	7.50	15.00
❏ 71818		The Munch/Woomai Ling	1961	3.75	7.50	15.00
❏ 71831		One Summer Night/It's a Doggone Shame	1961	3.75	7.50	15.00
❏ 71956		The Vanishing American/The Horizontal Lieutenant	1962	3.75	7.50	15.00

Dick and Deedee
(Also see "St. John, Dick")
Dot
❏ 17145		Escape Suite/I'm Not Gonna Get Hung-Up About It	1968	3.75	7.50	15.00
❏ 17261		We'll Sing in the Sunshine/In the Season of Our Love	1969	2.50	5.00	10.00
❏ 17305		Do I Love You/You Came Back to Haunt Me	1970	2.50	5.00	10.00

Lama
❏ 7778		The Mountain's High/I Want Someone	1961	5.00	10.00	20.00
❏ 7780		Goodbye to Love/Swing Low	1961	4.00	8.00	16.00
❏ 7783		Tell Me/Will You Always Love Me	1961	4.00	8.00	16.00

Liberty
❏ 55350		The Mountain's High/I Want Someone	1961	3.75	7.50	15.00
❏ 55382		Goodbye to Love/Swing Low	1961	3.00	6.00	12.00
❏ 55412		Tell Me/Will You Always Love Me	1962	3.00	6.00	12.00
❏ 55478		All I Want/Life's Just a Play	1962	3.00	6.00	12.00

United Artists
❏ 0036		The Mountain's High/Tell Me	1973		2.50	5.00
		"Silver Spotlight Series" reissue				

Warner Bros.
❏ 5320		The River Took My Baby/My Lonely Self	1962	2.50	5.00	10.00
❏ 5320	PS	The River Took My Baby/My Lonely Self	1962	6.25	12.50	25.00
❏ 5342		Young and In Love/Say to Me	1963	3.00	6.00	12.00
❏ 5364		Love Is a Once in a Lifetime Thing/ Chug-a Chug-a Choo Choo	1963	2.50	5.00	10.00
❏ 5383		Where Did the Good Times Go/ Guess Our Love Must Show	1963	2.50	5.00	10.00
❏ 5396		Turn Around/Don't Leave Me	1963	2.50	5.00	10.00
❏ 5411		All My Trials/Don't Think Twice, It's All Right	1964	2.50	5.00	10.00
❏ 5426		Not Fade Away/The Gift	1964	2.50	5.00	10.00
❏ 5451		You Were Mine/Remember Then	1964	2.50	5.00	10.00
❏ 5470		The Riddle Song/Without Your Love	1964	2.50	5.00	10.00
❏ 5482		Thou Shalt Not Steal/Just 'Round the River Bend	1964	3.75	7.50	15.00
		Red label with arrows				
❏ 5482		Thou Shalt Not Steal/Just 'Round the River Bend	1964	2.50	5.00	10.00
		Orange label				

Number		Title (A Side/B Side)	Year	VG	VG+	NM
❏ 5482	PS	Thou Shalt Not Steal/Just 'Round the River Bend	1964	6.25	12.50	25.00
❏ 5608		Be My Baby/Room 404	1965	2.50	5.00	10.00
❏ 5627		Blue Turns to Grey/	1965	5.00	10.00	20.00
		Some Things Just Stick in Your Mind				
		Both sides are Mick Jagger-Keith Richards songs produced by Andrew Loog Oldham				
❏ 5652		The World Is Waiting/Vini, Vini	1965	2.50	5.00	10.00
❏ 5671		P.S. 1402 (Your Local Charm School)/	1965	2.50	5.00	10.00
		Use What You've Got				
❏ 5680		New Orleans/Use What You've Got	1965	2.50	5.00	10.00
❏ 5699		Till/Sha-Ta	1966	2.50	5.00	10.00
❏ 5830		She Didn't Even Say Goodbye/	1966	2.50	5.00	10.00
		So Many Things We Didn't Know				
❏ 5860		Make Up Before We Break Up/	1966	2.50	5.00	10.00
		Can't Get Enough of Your Love				
❏ 7017		Long Lonely Nights/I'll Always Be Around	1967	2.50	5.00	10.00
❏ 7069		One in a Million/Baby, I Need You	1967	2.50	5.00	10.00
❏ 7109		Young and In Love/Thou Shalt Not Steal	1968	2.00	4.00	8.00
		"Back to Back Hits" series; originals have green labels with "W7" logo				

Dickens, The - See "NRBQ"

Dickey Doo and the Don'ts

Ascot

❏ 2178		Click Clack '65/Don't Count Me Out	1965	2.50	5.00	10.00

Casino

❏ 106		Click Clack/Lonely Hours Lady	196?	3.00	6.00	12.00
❏ 107		Flip Top Box/That's Life (That's Tough)	196?	3.00	6.00	12.00

Danna

❏ 4001		The Judge/Doo Plus Two	1967	2.50	5.00	10.00

Swan

❏ 4001		Click Clack/Did You Cry	1958	5.00	10.00	20.00
❏ 4006		Ne Ne Na Na Na Na Na Nu Nu/Flip Top Box	1959	6.25	12.50	25.00
❏ 4014		Leave Me Alone (Let Me Cry)/Wild Party	1959	5.00	10.00	20.00
❏ 4025		Teardrops Will Fall/Come with Us	1959	5.00	10.00	20.00
❏ 4033		Ballad of a Train/Dear Heart, Don't Cry	1959	5.00	10.00	20.00
❏ 4046		Wabash Cannonball/The Drums of Richard A. Doo	1960	5.00	10.00	20.00

United Artists

❏ 238		Teen Scene/Pity, Pity	1960	5.00	10.00	20.00
❏ 362		The Judge/The Little Dog Cried	1961	5.00	10.00	20.00

Dickie G. and the Don'ts - See "Goodman, Dickie"

Diddley, Bo

Checker

❏ 814		Bo Diddley/I'm a Man	1955	10.00	20.00	40.00
❏ 819		Diddley Daddy/She's Fine, She's Mine	1955	12.50	25.00	50.00
		A-side backing vocals: The Moonglows				
❏ 827		Pretty Thing/Bring It to Jerome	1955	10.00	20.00	40.00
❏ 832		Diddy Wah Diddy/I Am Looking for a Woman	1956	10.00	20.00	40.00
❏ 842		Who Do You Love?/In Bad	1956	10.00	20.00	40.00
❏ 842		Who Do You Love?/I'm Bad	1956	7.50	15.00	30.00
		Note altered B-side title				
❏ 850		Cops and Robbers/Down Home Special	1956	7.50	15.00	30.00
❏ 860		Hey! Bo Diddley/Mona	1957	7.50	15.00	30.00
		Originals of Checker 816-860 have "Checker" over a checkerboard on top of label				
❏ 878		Say! Boss Man/Before You Accuse Me	1957	6.25	12.50	25.00
❏ 896		Dearest Darling/Hush Your Mouth	1958	6.25	12.50	25.00
❏ 907		Bo Meets the Monster/Willie and Lillie	1958	7.50	15.00	30.00
❏ 914		I'm Sorry/Oh Yeah	1959	6.25	12.50	25.00
❏ 924		Crackin' Up/The Great Grandfather	1959	6.25	12.50	25.00
❏ 931		Say Man/Clock Strikes Twelve	1959	6.25	12.50	25.00
❏ 936		Say Man, Back Again/She's Alright	1959	6.25	12.50	25.00
❏ 942		Road Runner/My Story	1960	5.00	10.00	20.00
❏ 951		Walkin' and Talkin'/Crawdad	1960	5.00	10.00	20.00
❏ 965		Gun Slinger/Signifying	1960	5.00	10.00	20.00
❏ 976		Not Guilty/Aztec	1961	5.00	10.00	20.00
❏ 985		Pills/Call Me	1961	7.50	15.00	30.00
❏ 997		Bo Diddley/I'm a Man	1961	5.00	10.00	20.00
❏ 1019		You Can't Judge a Book By Its Cover/I Can Tell	1962	5.00	10.00	20.00
❏ 1045		Surfers' Love Call/Greatest Lover in the World	1963	5.00	10.00	20.00
❏ 1058		Memphis/Monkey Diddle	1963	5.00	10.00	20.00
❏ 1083		Jo Ann/Mama, Keep Your Big Mouth Shut	1964	5.00	10.00	20.00
❏ 1089		Bo's Beat/Chuck's Beat	1964	5.00	10.00	20.00
		B-side by Chuck Berry				
❏ 1098		Hey, Good Lookin'/You Ain't Bad	1965	3.75	7.50	15.00
❏ 1123		500% More Man/Let the Kids Dance	1965	3.75	7.50	15.00
❏ 1142		We're Gonna Get Married/Do the Frog	1966	3.75	7.50	15.00
❏ 1158		Ooh Baby/Back to School	1966	3.75	7.50	15.00
❏ 1168		Bo-Ga-Loo Before You Go/Wrecking My Love Life	1967	3.75	7.50	15.00
❏ 1200		Another Sugardaddy/I'm High Again	1968	3.75	7.50	15.00
❏ 1213		Bo Diddley 1969/Soul Train	1969	3.00	6.00	12.00
❏ 1238		The Shape I'm In/Pollution	1970	3.00	6.00	12.00

Chess

❏ 2117		I Love You More Than You'll Ever Know/	1971	2.50	5.00	10.00
		I Said Shut Up Woman				
❏ 2129		Bo Diddley-Itis/Infatuation	1972	2.50	5.00	10.00

Number		Title (A Side/B Side)	Year	VG	VG+	NM
❏ 2134		Bo-Jam/Husband-in-Law	1972	2.50	5.00	10.00
❏ 2142		I Don't Want No Lyin' Woman/Make a Hit Record	1973	2.50	5.00	10.00
RCA Victor						
❏ PB-10618		Not Fade Away/Drag On	1976	2.50	5.00	10.00

Dill, Danny
ABC-Paramount

Number		Title (A Side/B Side)	Year	VG	VG+	NM
❏ 9681		My Girl and His Girl/Geisha Sweetheart	1956	7.50	15.00	30.00
❏ 9734		I'm Hungry for Your Lovin'/The Stranger of Abilene	1956	12.50	25.00	50.00
Cub						
❏ 9045		He's Biding His Time/He Ain't Gonna Study War	1959	5.00	10.00	20.00

Ding Dongs, The - See "Darin, Bobby"

Dinning, Mark
Cameo

Number		Title (A Side/B Side)	Year	VG	VG+	NM
❏ 299		January/Joey	1964	2.50	5.00	10.00
❏ 313		Should We Do It/Call Her Your Sweetheart	1964	2.50	5.00	10.00
Hickory						
❏ 1293		Dial AL1-4883/I'm Glad We Fell in Love	1965	2.00	4.00	8.00
❏ 1368		Last Rose/There Stands a Lady	1966	2.00	4.00	8.00
❏ 1404		Run, Opie, Run/He Reminds Me of Me	1966	2.00	4.00	8.00
MGM						
❏ 12447		A Million Years Ago/Shameful Ways	1957	6.25	12.50	25.00
❏ 12553		School Fool/When You're Tired of Breaking Hearts	1957	6.25	12.50	25.00
❏ 12691		You Thrill Me/Do You Know	1958	6.25	12.50	25.00
❏ 12732		Blackeyed Gypsy/Secretly in Love with You	1958	6.25	12.50	25.00
❏ 12775		Cutie, Cutie/A Life of Love	1959	6.25	12.50	25.00
❏ 12845		Teen Angel/Bye Now Baby	1959	6.25	12.50	25.00
❏ 12888		A Star Is Born (A Love Has Died)/You Win Again	1960	5.00	10.00	20.00
❏ 12888	PS	A Star Is Born (A Love Has Died)/You Win Again	1960	6.25	12.50	25.00
❏ 12929		The Lovin' Touch/Come Back to Me (My Love)	1960	5.00	10.00	20.00
❏ 12929	PS	The Lovin' Touch/Come Back to Me (My Love)	1960	6.25	12.50	25.00
❏ 12958		She Cried On My Shoulder	1960	5.00	10.00	20.00
		(When She Talked About You)/(Where Can You Hide Away) The World Is Getting Smaller				
❏ 12980		Top Forty, News, Weather and Sports/	1961	3.75	7.50	15.00
		Suddenly (There's Only You)				
❏ 13007		Another Lonely Girl/Can't Forget	1961	3.75	7.50	15.00
❏ 13024		Lonely Island/Turn Me On	1961	3.75	7.50	15.00
❏ 13048		What Will My Mary Say/In a Matter of Moments	1961	3.75	7.50	15.00
❏ 13061		The Pickup/All of This for Sally	1962	3.75	7.50	15.00
❏ 13091		She's Changed/I Catch Myself Crying	1962	3.00	6.00	12.00
❏ 13150		The Twelfth of Never/Somebody Catch Me Kissin' Mary	1963	3.00	6.00	12.00
United Artists						
❏ 50169		It's Such a Pretty World Today/Atlanta, Georgia Stray	1967	2.00	4.00	8.00
❏ 50225		Hangin' On/Maggie (I Wish We'd Never Met)	1967	2.00	4.00	8.00
❏ 50305		Throw a Little Love My Way/Dissatisfied Man	1968	2.00	4.00	8.00
❏ 50540		How Little Men Care/Lemon Yellow	1969	2.00	4.00	8.00

Dino, Desi, and Billy
Columbia

Number		Title (A Side/B Side)	Year	VG	VG+	NM
❏ 44975		Hawley/Let's Talk It Over	1969	3.00	6.00	12.00
Reprise						
❏ 0324		We Know/Since You Broke My Heart	1964	2.50	5.00	10.00
❏ 0367		I'm a Fool/So Many Ways	1965	3.00	6.00	12.00
❏ 0367	PS	I'm a Fool/So Many Ways	1965	5.00	10.00	20.00
❏ 0401		Not the Lovin' Kind/Chimes of Freedom	1965	2.50	5.00	10.00
❏ 0401	PS	Not the Lovin' Kind/Chimes of Freedom	1965	5.00	10.00	20.00
❏ 0426		Please Don't Fight It/The Rebel Kind	1965	2.50	5.00	10.00
❏ 0426	PS	Please Don't Fight It/The Rebel Kind	1965	5.00	10.00	20.00
❏ 0444		Superman/I Can't Get Her Out of My Mind	1966	2.00	4.00	8.00
❏ 0462		It's Just the Way You Are/Tie Me Down	1966	2.00	4.00	8.00
❏ 0496		Look Out Girls/She's So Far Out She's In	1966	2.00	4.00	8.00
❏ 0529		I Hope She's There Tonight/Josephine	1966	2.00	4.00	8.00
❏ 0544		If You're Thinkin' What I'm Thinkin'/Pretty Flamingo	1966	2.00	4.00	8.00
❏ 0579		Two in the Afternoon/Good Luck, Best Wishes to You	1967	2.50	5.00	10.00
❏ 0619		Kitty Doyle/Without Hurtin' Some	1967	2.50	5.00	10.00
❏ 0653		My What a Shame/	1967	3.00	6.00	12.00
		The Inside Outside Caspar Milquetoast Eskimo Flash				
❏ 0698		Tell Someone You Love Them/General Outline	1968	3.00	6.00	12.00
❏ 0716		I'm a Fool/Not the Lovin' Kind	1968	2.00	4.00	8.00
		"Back to Back Hits" series; originals have both "W7" and "r:" logos				
❏ 0965		Lady Love/A Certain Sound	1970	7.50	15.00	30.00
		A-side is a Brian Wilson composition				
Uni						
❏ 55127		Someday/Thru Spray Colored Glasses	1969	3.00	6.00	12.00

Dino, Kenny
Columbia

Number		Title (A Side/B Side)	Year	VG	VG+	NM
❏ 43062		Betty Jean/Show Me	1964	5.00	10.00	20.00
Dot						
❏ 16207		Just Wait and See/A Little Bit	1961	3.00	6.00	12.00
Musicor						
❏ 1013		Your Ma Said You Cried in Your Sleep Last Night/	1962	5.00	10.00	20.00
		Dream a Girl				

Number		Title (A Side/B Side)	Year	VG	VG+	NM
❑ 1015		Rosie, Why Do You Wear My Ring/What Did I Do	1962	3.75	7.50	15.00
❑ 1021		What Good Are Dreams/What Did I Do	1962	3.75	7.50	15.00
❑ 1027		Remembering Helps Me to Forget/Heartless Moon	1962	3.75	7.50	15.00

Smash

❑ 1827		Time Will Tell/I Wanna Know	1963	3.00	6.00	12.00
❑ 1861		You Had Your Chance/Danhoff's Theme	1963	3.00	6.00	12.00

Dio, Andy
Crusade

❑ 1023		Bonnie Jean/(B-side unknown)	1961	10.00	20.00	40.00

Gone

❑ 5038		Daisy Belle/Hey Little Bluebird	1958	12.50	25.00	50.00

Johnson

❑ 114		You Are My Sunshine/Satellite	1962	5.00	10.00	20.00

Joy

❑ 283		Daisy Belle/Some of These Days	1964	10.00	20.00	40.00

Musicor

❑ 1118		Sass-Afrass/Shout	1965	2.50	5.00	10.00
❑ 1162		Dancing Bull/(B-side unknown)	1966	2.50	5.00	10.00

Dio, Ronnie
Atlantic

❑ 2145		Love Pains/Ooh-Poo-Pah-Do	1962	5.00	10.00	20.00

Kapp

❑ 697		Say You're Mine Again/Where You Gonna Run To, Girl	1965	3.75	7.50	15.00
❑ 725		Dear Darlin' (I Won't Be Comin' Home)/Smiling by Day	1965	3.75	7.50	15.00
❑ 770		The Way of Love/Walking Alone	1966	3.75	7.50	15.00

Lawn

❑ 218		Gonna Make It Alone/Swingin' Street	1963	6.25	12.50	25.00

Parkway

❑ 143		Walking in Different Circles/Ten Days with Brenda	1967	5.00	10.00	20.00

Swan

❑ 4165		Mr. Misery/Our Year	1963	5.00	10.00	20.00

Dion
(Also see "Dion and the Belmonts"; "Dion and the Timberlanes")
Arista

❑ 9797		And the Night Stood Still/Tower of Love	1989		2.00	4.00
❑ 9797	PS	And the Night Stood Still/Tower of Love	1989		2.00	4.00

Big Tree/Spector

❑ 16063		Born to Be with You/Running Close Behind You	1976	3.75	7.50	15.00
		Produced by Phil Spector				

Columbia

❑ (no #)	PS	"Dion Is Now on Columbia Records"	1962	12.50	25.00	50.00
		Promo-only sleeve issued with promos of Columbia 42662				
❑ 42662		Ruby Baby/He'll Only Hurt You	1962	3.75	7.50	15.00
❑ 42662	PS	Ruby Baby/He'll Only Hurt You	1962	7.50	15.00	30.00
❑ 42776		This Little Girl/The Loneliest Man in the World	1963	3.75	7.50	15.00
❑ 42810		Be Careful of Stones That You Throw/ I Can't Believe (That You Don't Love Me Anymore)	1963	3.75	7.50	15.00
❑ 42810	DJ	Be Careful of Stones That You Throw (same on both sides)	1963	25.00	50.00	100.00
		Colored vinyl (some sources say blue, others red)				
❑ 42852		Donna the Prima Donna/You're Mine	1963	3.75	7.50	15.00
❑ 42852	DJ	Donna the Prima Donna (same on both sides)	1963	20.00	40.00	80.00
		Promo only on red vinyl				
❑ 42917		Drip Drop/No One's Waiting for Me	1963	3.75	7.50	15.00
❑ 42977		I'm Your Hoochie Coochie Man/The Road I'm On	1964	3.75	7.50	15.00
❑ 42977	PS	I'm Your Hoochie Coochie Man/The Road I'm On	1964	7.50	15.00	30.00
❑ 43096		Johnny B. Goode/Chicago Blues	1964	3.75	7.50	15.00
❑ 43213		Sweet Sweet Baby/Unloved, Unwanted Me	1965	3.75	7.50	15.00
❑ 43293		Spoonful/Kickin' Child	1965	3.75	7.50	15.00
❑ 43423		Tomorrow Won't Bring the Rain/You Move Me Babe	1965	3.75	7.50	15.00
❑ 43423	PS	Tomorrow Won't Bring the Rain/You Move Me Babe	1965	10.00	20.00	40.00
❑ 43483		Time in My Heart for You/Wake Up Baby	1965	3.75	7.50	15.00
❑ 43692		So Much Younger/Two-Ton Feather	1966	3.75	7.50	15.00
❑ 44719		I Can't Help But Wonder Where I'm Bound/ Southern Train	1968	2.50	5.00	10.00

Laurie

❑ 3070		Lonely Teenager/Little Miss Blue	1960	5.00	10.00	20.00
❑ 3070	PS	Lonely Teenager/Little Miss Blue	1960	12.50	25.00	50.00
❑ 3081		Havin' Fun/Northeast End of the Corner	1961	5.00	10.00	20.00
❑ 3081	PS	Havin' Fun/Northeast End of the Corner	1961	12.50	25.00	50.00
❑ 3090		Kissin Game/Heaven Help Me	1961	5.00	10.00	20.00
❑ 3090	PS	Kissin Game/Heaven Help Me	1961	12.50	25.00	50.00
❑ 3101		Somebody Nobody Wants/ Could Somebody Take My Place Tonight	1961	5.00	10.00	20.00
❑ 3110		Runaround Sue/Runaway Girl	1961	3.75	7.50	15.00
❑ 3110	PS	Runaround Sue/Runaway Girl	1961	10.00	20.00	40.00
❑ 3115		The Wanderer/The Majestic	1961	3.75	7.50	15.00
❑ 3115	PS	The Wanderer/The Majestic	1961	10.00	20.00	40.00
❑ 3123		Lovers Who Wander/(I Was) Born to Cry	1962	3.75	7.50	15.00
❑ 3123	PS	Lovers Who Wander/(I Was) Born to Cry	1962	10.00	20.00	40.00

Number		Title (A Side/B Side)	Year	VG	VG+	NM
❏ 3134		Little Diane/Lost for Sure	1962	3.75	7.50	15.00
❏ 3134	PS	Little Diane/Lost for Sure	1962	10.00	20.00	40.00
❏ 3145		Love Came to Me/Little Girl	1962	3.75	7.50	15.00
❏ 3153		Sandy/Faith	1963	3.75	7.50	15.00
❏ 3171		Come Go with Me/King Without a Queen	1963	3.75	7.50	15.00
❏ 3187		Lonely World/Tag Along	1963	3.75	7.50	15.00
❏ 3225		After the Dance/Then I'll Be Loved by You	1964	5.00	10.00	20.00
❏ 3240		Shout/Little Girl	1964	5.00	10.00	20.00
❏ 3303		I Got the Blues/(I Was) Born to Cry	1965	5.00	10.00	20.00
❏ 3464		Abraham, Martin, and John/Daddy Rollin' (In Your Arms)	1968	3.00	6.00	12.00
❏ 3478		Purple Haze/The Dolphins	1969	3.00	6.00	12.00
❏ 3495		Both Sides Now/Sun Fun Song	1969	3.00	6.00	12.00
❏ 3504		Loving You Is Sweeter Than Ever/He Looks a Lot Like Me	1969	3.00	6.00	12.00

Lifesong

Number		Title (A Side/B Side)	Year	VG	VG+	NM
❏ 1765		Heart of Saturday Night/You've Awakened Something in Me	1978		3.00	6.00
❏ 1770		Midtown American Main Street Gang/Guitar Queen	1978		3.00	6.00
❏ 1785		(I Used to Be a) Brooklyn Dodger/Streetheart Theme	1979		3.00	6.00
❏ 45082		Fire in the Night/Street Mama	1980	6.25	12.50	25.00

Monument

Number		Title (A Side/B Side)	Year	VG	VG+	NM
❏ (# unknown)	DJ	Runaround Sue/Ya Ya Twist	1962	6.25	12.50	25.00
		B-side by Joey Dee and the Starliters				

The Right Stuff

Number		Title (A Side/B Side)	Year	VG	VG+	NM
❏ S7-17651		Christmas (Baby Please Come Home)/Jingle Bell Rock	1993		2.00	4.00
		Red vinyl				

Warner Bros.

Number		Title (A Side/B Side)	Year	VG	VG+	NM
❏ PRO-537	DJ	Seagull/Soft Parade	1972	3.75	7.50	15.00
❏ PRO-814	DJ	The Wanderer (same on both sides)	1979	3.75	7.50	15.00
❏ 7356		Natural Man/If We Only Have Love	1969	2.50	5.00	10.00
❏ 7401		Your Own Back Yard/Sit Down Old Friend	1970	2.50	5.00	10.00
❏ 7469		Let It Be/Close to It All	1970	2.50	5.00	10.00
❏ 7491		Josie/Sunniland	1970	2.50	5.00	10.00
❏ 7537		Sanctuary/Brand New Morning	1971	2.50	5.00	10.00
❏ 7537	PS	Sanctuary/Brand New Morning	1971	5.00	10.00	20.00
❏ 7663		Seagull/Running Close Behind You	1972	2.50	5.00	10.00
❏ 7704		Doctor Rock and Roll/Sunshine Lady	1973	2.50	5.00	10.00
❏ 7793		New York City Song/Richer Than a Rich Man	1974	2.50	5.00	10.00
❏ 8234		Hey My Love/Lover Boy Supreme	1976		3.00	6.00
❏ 8258		The Way You Do the Things You Do/Lover Boy Supreme	1976		3.00	6.00
❏ 8293		Oh the Night/Queen of '59	1976		3.00	6.00
❏ 8406		Young Virgin Eyes (I'm All Wrapped Up)/Oh the Night	1977		3.00	6.00

Warner/Spector

Number		Title (A Side/B Side)	Year	VG	VG+	NM
❏ 0403		Make the Woman Love Me/Running Close Behind You	1975	3.75	7.50	15.00
		Produced by Phil Spector				

Dion and the Belmonts

(Also see "Belmonts, The"; "Dion")

ABC

Number		Title (A Side/B Side)	Year	VG	VG+	NM
❏ 10868		My Girl the Month of May/Berimbau	1966	3.00	6.00	12.00
❏ 10896		For Bobbie/Movin' Man	1967	3.00	6.00	12.00

Laurie

Number		Title (A Side/B Side)	Year	VG	VG+	NM
❏ 3013		I Wonder Why/Teen Angel	1958	12.50	25.00	50.00
		Gray label				
❏ 3013		I Wonder Why/Teen Angel	1958	7.50	15.00	30.00
		Light blue label				
❏ 3013		I Wonder Why/Teen Angel	1958	5.00	10.00	20.00
		Black, red and white label				
❏ 3015		No One Knows/I Can't Go On (Rosalie)	1958	12.50	25.00	50.00
		Gray label				
❏ 3015		No One Knows/I Can't Go On (Rosalie)	1958	7.50	15.00	30.00
		Light blue label				
❏ 3015		No One Knows/I Can't Go On (Rosalie)	1958	5.00	10.00	20.00
		Black, red and white label				
❏ 3021		Don't Pity Me/Just You	1958	6.25	12.50	25.00
❏ 3027	M	A Teenager in Love/I've Cried Before	1959	6.25	12.50	25.00
❏ S-3027	S	A Teenager in Love/I've Cried Before	1959	12.50	25.00	50.00
❏ 3035		Every Little Thing I Do/A Lover's Prayer	1959	6.25	12.50	25.00
❏ 3035	PS	Every Little Thing I Do/A Lover's Prayer	1959	12.50	25.00	50.00
❏ 3044		Where or When/That's My Desire	1959	6.25	12.50	25.00
❏ 3044	PS	Where or When/That's My Desire	1959	12.50	25.00	50.00
❏ 3052		When You Wish Upon a Star/Wonderful Girl	1960	6.25	12.50	25.00
❏ 3052	PS	When You Wish Upon a Star/Wonderful Girl	1960	12.50	25.00	50.00
❏ 3059		In the Still of the Night/A Funny Feeling	1960	6.25	12.50	25.00
❏ 3059	PS	In the Still of the Night/A Funny Feeling	1960	12.50	25.00	50.00

Mohawk

Number		Title (A Side/B Side)	Year	VG	VG+	NM
❏ 106		Teenage Clementine/Santa Margarita	1957	15.00	30.00	60.00
		May be listed as "The Belmonts"				
❏ 107		Tag Along/We Went Away	1957	15.00	30.00	60.00

Number		Title (A Side/B Side)	Year	VG	VG+	NM

Dion and the Timberlanes
(Also see "Dion")
Jubilee

| ❑ 5294 | | The Chosen Few/Out in Colorado | 1957 | 7.50 | 15.00 | 30.00 |

Mohawk

| ❑ 105 | | The Chosen Few/Out in Colorado | 1957 | 15.00 | 30.00 | 60.00 |

Dionne and Friends
(Dionne Warwick with Elton John, Gladys Knight and Stevie Wonder)
Arista

| ❑ 9422 | | That's What Friends Are For/Two Ships Passing in the Night | 1985 | | | 3.00 |
| ❑ 9422 | PS | That's What Friends Are For/Two Ships Passing in the Night | 1985 | | | 3.00 |

DiSentri, Turner
(Actually Bob Gaudio of the Royal Teens and the Four Seasons)
Topix

| ❑ 6001 | | 10,000,000 Tears/Spanish Lace | 1961 | 25.00 | 50.00 | 100.00 |

Distants, The
Northern

| ❑ 3732 | | Come On/Always | 1960 | 150.00 | 300.00 | 600.00 |

Warwick

| ❑ 546 | | Come On/Always | 1960 | 25.00 | 50.00 | 100.00 |
| ❑ 577 | | Always/Open Up Your Heart | 1960 | 25.00 | 50.00 | 100.00 |

Dixie Cups, The
ABC

| ❑ 10855 | | Love Ain't So Bad (After All)/Daddy Said No | 1966 | 3.00 | 6.00 | 12.00 |

ABC-Paramount

❑ 10692		That's Where It's At/Two-Way-Poc-A-Way	1965	3.00	6.00	12.00
❑ 10715		I'm Not the Kind of Girl (To Marry)/What Goes Up Must Go Down	1965	3.00	6.00	12.00
❑ 10755		A-B-C Song/That's What the Kids Said	1965	3.00	6.00	12.00

Red Bird

❑ 10-001		Chapel of Love/Ain't That Nice	1964	3.75	7.50	15.00
❑ 10-006		People Say/Girls Can Tell	1964	3.75	7.50	15.00
❑ 10-012		You Should Have Seen the Way He Looked at Me/No True Love	1964	3.75	7.50	15.00
❑ 10-017		Little Bell/Another Boy Like Me	1964	3.75	7.50	15.00
❑ 10-024		Iko Iko/Gee, Baby, Gee	1965	3.75	7.50	15.00
❑ 10-024		Iko Iko/I'm Gonna Get You Yet	1965	3.75	7.50	15.00
❑ 10-032		Gee, the Moon Is Shining Bright/I'm Gonna Get You Yet	1965	3.75	7.50	15.00

Dixiebelles, The
Sound Stage 7

❑ 2507		(Down at) Papa Joe's/Rock, Rock, Rock	1963	2.50	5.00	10.00
❑ 2517		Southtown U.S.A./Why Don't You Set Me Free	1964	2.50	5.00	10.00
❑ 2521		New York Town/The Beale Street Dog	1964	2.50	5.00	10.00

Dixon, Billy, and the Topics - See "Four Seasons, The"

Dobkins, Carl, Jr.
Atco

| ❑ 6283 | | If Teardrops Were Diamonds/I'm So Sorry Little Girl | 1964 | 3.00 | 6.00 | 12.00 |

Chalet

| ❑ 1053 | | Days of Sand and Shovel/Linda the Motel Maid | 1969 | 2.50 | 5.00 | 10.00 |
| ❑ 1056 | | My Heart Is an Open Book/Pictures | 1969 | 2.50 | 5.00 | 10.00 |

Colpix

| ❑ 762 | | His Loss Is My Gain/A Little Bit Later On Down the Line | 1965 | 3.00 | 6.00 | 12.00 |

Decca

❑ 30656		Love Is Everything/If You Don't Want My Lovin'	1958	5.00	10.00	20.00
❑ 30803		My Heart Is an Open Book/My Pledge to You	1959	6.25	12.50	25.00
❑ 31020		Lucky Devil/In My Heart	1959	5.00	10.00	20.00
❑ 31020	PS	Lucky Devil/In My Heart	1959	7.50	15.00	30.00
❑ 31088		Exclusively Yours/One Little Girl	1960	3.75	7.50	15.00
❑ 31088	PS	Exclusively Yours/One Little Girl	1960	7.50	15.00	30.00
❑ 31143		Different Kind of Love/Genie	1960	3.75	7.50	15.00
❑ 31182		Lovelight/Take Time Out	1960	3.75	7.50	15.00
❑ 31260		Pretty Little Girl in the Yellow Dress/That's What I Call True Love	1961	3.75	7.50	15.00
❑ 31301		Sawdust Dolly/A Chance to Belong	1961	3.75	7.50	15.00
❑ 31353		Ask Me No Questions/Promise Me	1962	3.75	7.50	15.00

Fraternity

| ❑ 794 | | That's Why I'm Asking/Take Hold of My Hand | 1958 | 7.50 | 15.00 | 30.00 |

Dobro, Jimmy
(Actually James Burton)
Philips

| ❑ 40137 | | Swamp Surfer/Everybody Listen to the Dobro | 1963 | 10.00 | 20.00 | 40.00 |

Number		Title (A Side/B Side)	Year	VG	VG+	NM
Dobro, Lon						
4 Star						
❏ 1754		I Just Like You/All the Time	1961	15.00	30.00	60.00
Troy						
❏ 1003		Undercurrent/Mid-Night Surf	1963	12.50	25.00	50.00
Dr. John						
(Includes Dr. John, the Night Tripper; also see "Rebenack, Mac")						
Atco						
❏ 6607		I Walk on Gilded Splinters (Part 1)/	1968	3.00	6.00	12.00
		I Walk on Gilded Splinters (Part 2)				
❏ 6635		Jump Sturdy/Mama Roux	1968	3.00	6.00	12.00
❏ 6697		Patriotic Flag Waver (Long)/	1969	2.00	4.00	8.00
		Patriotic Flag Waver (Short)				
❏ 6755		Wash, Mama, Wash/Loup Gardo	1970	3.00	6.00	12.00
❏ 6882		Iko Iko/The Huey Smith Medley	1972	2.50	5.00	10.00
❏ 6898		Wang Dang Doodle/Big Chief	1972	3.00	6.00	
❏ 6900		Let the Good Times Roll/Stack-A-Lee	1972		3.00	6.00
❏ 6914		Right Place Wrong Time/I Been Hoodood	1973		3.00	6.00
❏ 6937		Such a Night/Cold, Cold, Cold	1973		3.00	6.00
❏ 6957		(Everybody Wanna Get Rich(Rite Away/Mos'Scocious	1974		3.00	6.00
❏ 6971		Let's Make a Better World/	1974		3.00	6.00
		Me Minus You Equals Loneliness				
Horizon						
❏ 117		Wild Honey/Dance the Night Away with You	1979		2.00	4.00
❏ 125		Keep That Music Simple/	1979		2.00	4.00
		I Thought I Heard New Orleans				
RCA						
❏ PB-11285		Take Me Higher/Sweet Rider	1978		2.00	4.00
Scepter						
❏ 12393		One Night Late/She's Just a Square	1974		2.50	5.00
Warner Bros.						
❏ 22976		Makin' Whoopee!/More Than You Know	1989			3.00
❏ 49703		The Sailor and the Mermaid/One Good Turn	1981		2.00	4.00
		A-side with Libby Titus; B-side by Al Jarreau				
Dr. Ross						
Sun						
❏ 193		Chicago Breakdown/Come Back Baby	1954	200.00	400.00	600.00
❏ 212		The Boogie Disease/Juke Box Boogie	1954	500.00	1,000	2,000
Dr. West's Medicine Show and Jug Band						
(With Norman Greenbaum)						
Go Go						
❏ 100		The Eggplant That Ate Chicago/	1966	3.00	6.00	12.00
		You Can't Fight City Hall Blues				
❏ 102		Gondoliers, Shakespeares, Overseers,	1967	2.50	5.00	10.00
		Playboys and Bums/Daddy, I Know				
❏ 102	PS	Gondoliers, Shakespeares, Overseers,	1967	5.00	10.00	20.00
		Playboys and Bums/Daddy, I Know				
❏ 104		You Can Fly/The Circus Left Town Today	1967	2.50	5.00	10.00
Gregar						
❏ 106		Bullets Laverne/Jigsaw	1968	2.50	5.00	10.00
❏ 71-0100		Gondoliers, Shakespeares, Overseers,	1969	2.50	5.00	10.00
		Playboys and Bums/Daddy, I Know				
Dodd, Jimmie						
ABC-Paramount						
❏ 9665		Mouseketeer Theme/Hi to You	1956	5.00	10.00	20.00
❏ 9680		Mickey Mouse Mambo/Humphrey Hop-Pussy Cat	1956	5.00	10.00	20.00
❏ 9691		Zip-A-Dee-Doo-Dah/Song of the South	1956	5.00	10.00	20.00
		B-side by Jeanne Gayle				
Dodo, Joe, and the Groovers						
RCA Victor						
❏ 47-7207		Groovy/Goin' Steady	1958	6.25	12.50	25.00
Dolenz, Jones & Tork						
(Three-fourths of The Monkees)						
Christmas						
❏ 700		Christmas Is My Time of Year/White Christmas	1976	5.00	10.00	20.00
❏ 700	PS	Christmas Is My Time of Year/White Christmas	1976	10.00	20.00	40.00
Dolenz, Jones, Boyce & Hart						
(Half of the Monkees with one of their primary writing duos)						
Capitol						
❏ 4180		You and I/I Remember the Feeling	1975	2.50	5.00	10.00
❏ 4271		Savin' My Love for You/	1976	2.50	5.00	10.00
		I Love You (And I'm Glad I Said It)				
Dolenz, Mickey						
Bell						
❏ 986		Do It in the Name of Love/Lady Jane	1971	12.50	25.00	50.00
		With Davy Jones; value is for stock copy (promos worth about 50% of this)				

Number		Title (A Side/B Side)	Year	VG	VG+	NM
Challenge						
❑ 59353		Don't Do It/Plastic Symphony III	1967	5.00	10.00	20.00
❑ 59353	PS	Don't Do It/Plastic Symphony III	1967	15.00	30.00	60.00
❑ 59372		Huff Puff/(The Obvious) Fate	1967	5.00	10.00	20.00
❑ 59372	PS	Huff Puff/(The Obvious) Fate	1967	15.00	30.00	60.00
Chrysalis						
❑ 2297		Alicia/Love Light	1979		3.00	6.00
MGM						
❑ 14309		Easy on You/Oh Someone	1971	5.00	10.00	20.00
❑ 14395		A Lover's Prayer/Unattended in the Dungeon	1972	5.00	10.00	20.00
Romar						
❑ 710		Daybreak/Love War	1973	5.00	10.00	20.00
❑ 715		Buddy Holly Tribute/Ooh, She's So Young	1974	5.00	10.00	20.00

Domino, Fats

Number	Title (A Side/B Side)	Year	VG	VG+	NM
ABC					
❑ 10902	I Don't Want to Set the World on Fire/I'm Living Right	1967	2.50	5.00	10.00
ABC-Paramount					
❑ 10444	There Goes (My Heart Again)/Can't Go On Without You	1963	2.50	5.00	10.00
❑ 10475	When I'm Walking (Let Me Walk)/I've Got a Right to Cry	1963	2.50	5.00	10.00
❑ 10484	Red Sails in the Sunset/Song for Rosemary	1963	3.00	6.00	12.00
❑ 10512	Who Cares/Just a Lonely Man	1963	2.50	5.00	10.00
❑ 10531	Lazy Lady/I Don't Want to Set the World on Fire	1964	2.50	5.00	10.00
❑ 10545	If You Don't Know What Love Is/Something You Got, Baby	1964	2.50	5.00	10.00
❑ 10567	Mary, Oh Mary/Packin' Up	1964	2.50	5.00	10.00
❑ 10584	Sally Was a Good Old Girl/For You	1964	2.50	5.00	10.00
❑ 10596	Heartbreak Hill/Kansas City	1964	2.50	5.00	10.00
❑ 10631	Why Don't You Do Right/Wigs	1965	2.50	5.00	10.00
❑ 10644	Let Me Call You Sweetheart/Goodnight Sweetheart	1965	2.50	5.00	10.00
Broadmoor					
❑ 104	The Lady in Black/Work My Way Up Steady	1967	3.75	7.50	15.00
❑ 105	Big Mouth/Wait 'Til It Happens to You	1968	5.00	10.00	20.00
Imperial					

Note: Fats Domino records on Imperial before 5167 are unconfirmed on 45 rpm, except as shown

Number	Title (A Side/B Side)	Year	VG	VG+	NM
❑ 5058	The Fat Man/Detroit City Blues	1950	125.00	250.00	500.00
	This does exist with a blue-label "script" logo, but it wasn't pressed until 1952 at the earliest				
❑ 5099	Korea Blues/Every Night About This Time	1950	200.00	400.00	800.00
	This does exist with a blue-label "script" logo, but it wasn't pressed until 1952 at the earliest				
❑ 5167	You Know I Miss You/I'll Be Gone	1952	125.00	250.00	500.00
❑ 5180	Goin' Home/Reeling and Rocking	1952	100.00	200.00	400.00
❑ 5197	Poor Poor Me/Trust in Me	1952	50.00	100.00	200.00
❑ 5209	How Long/Dreaming	1952	20.00	40.00	80.00
	Black vinyl				
❑ 5209	How Long/Dreaming	1952	75.00	150.00	300.00
	Red vinyl				
❑ 5220	Nobody Loves Me/Cheatin'	1953	20.00	40.00	80.00
	Black vinyl				
❑ 5220	Nobody Loves Me/Cheatin'	1953	75.00	150.00	300.00
	Red vinyl				
❑ 5231	Going to the River/Mardi Gras in New Orleans	1953	20.00	40.00	80.00
	Black vinyl				
❑ 5231	Going to the River/Mardi Gras in New Orleans	1953	75.00	150.00	300.00
	Red vinyl				
❑ 5240	Please Don't Leave Me/The Girl I Love	1953	15.00	30.00	60.00
	Black vinyl				
❑ 5240	Please Don't Leave Me/The Girl I Love	1953	75.00	150.00	300.00
	Red vinyl				
❑ 5251	You Said You Loved Me/Rose Mary	1953	15.00	30.00	60.00
❑ 5262	Something's Wrong/Don't Leave Me This Way	1954	12.50	25.00	50.00
	Black vinyl				
❑ 5262	Something's Wrong/Don't Leave Me This Way	1954	62.50	125.00	250.00
	Red vinyl				
❑ 5272	Little School Girl/You Done Me Wrong	1954	15.00	30.00	60.00
❑ 5283	Baby, Please/Where Did You Stay	1954	15.00	30.00	60.00
❑ 5301	You Can Pack Your Suitcase/I Lived My Life	1954	10.00	20.00	40.00
❑ 5313	Love Me/Don't You Hear Me Calling You	1954	10.00	20.00	40.00
❑ 5323	I Know/Thinking of You	1955	12.50	25.00	50.00
	Black vinyl				
❑ 5323	I Know/Thinking of You	1955	125.00	250.00	500.00
	Red vinyl				
❑ 5340	Don't You Know/Helping Hand	1955	10.00	20.00	40.00
❑ 5348	Ain't It a Shame/La La	1955	10.00	20.00	40.00
❑ 5357	All By Myself/Troubles of My Own	1955	20.00	40.00	80.00
	Red label, script logo				
❑ 5357	All By Myself/Troubles of My Own	1955	6.25	12.50	25.00
	Red or maroon label, block logo				
❑ 5369	Poor Me/I Can't Go On	1955	6.25	12.50	25.00
❑ 5375	Bo Weevil/Don't Blame It on Me	1956	6.25	12.50	25.00
❑ 5386	I'm in Love Again/My Blue Heaven	1956	6.25	12.50	25.00
❑ 5396	When My Dreamboat Comes Home/So-Long	1956	6.25	12.50	25.00
❑ 5407	Blueberry Hill/Honey Chile	1956	6.25	12.50	25.00
	Black vinyl, red label				

Number		Title (A Side/B Side)	Year	VG	VG+	NM
❏ 5407		Blueberry Hill/Honey Chile	1957	3.75	7.50	15.00
		Black vinyl, black label				
❏ 5407		Blueberry Hill/Honey Chile	1956	37.50	75.00	150.00
		Red vinyl				
❏ 5417		Blue Monday/What's the Reason I'm Not Pleasing You	1957	6.25	12.50	25.00
❏ 5428		I'm Walkin'/I'm in the Mood for Love	1957	6.25	12.50	25.00
❏ 5428	PS	I'm Walkin'/I'm in the Mood for Love	1957	12.50	25.00	50.00
❏ 5442		Valley of Tears/It's You I Love	1957	6.25	12.50	25.00
❏ 5454		When I See You/How Will I Tell My Heart	1957	6.25	12.50	25.00
❏ 5467		Wait and See/I Still Love You	1957	6.25	12.50	25.00
❏ 5477		The Big Beat/I Want You to Know	1957	6.25	12.50	25.00
❏ 5477	PS	The Big Beat/I Want You to Know	1957	6.25	12.50	25.00
❏ 5492		Yes, My Darling/Don't You Know I Love You	1958	6.25	12.50	25.00
		Black vinyl				
❏ 5492		Yes, My Darling/Don't You Know I Love You	1958	37.50	75.00	150.00
		Red vinyl				
❏ 5515		Sick and Tired/No, No	1958	6.25	12.50	25.00
❏ 5526		Little Mary/The Prisoner's Song	1958	6.25	12.50	25.00
❏ 5537		Young School Girl/It Must Be Love	1958	6.25	12.50	25.00
❏ 5553		Whole Lotta Loving/Coquette	1958	7.50	15.00	30.00
		Red label				
❏ 5553		Whole Lotta Loving/Coquette	1958	6.25	12.50	25.00
		Black label				
❏ 5553		Whole Lotta Loving/Coquette	1958	37.50	75.00	150.00
		Red vinyl (translucent)				
❏ 5569		Telling Lies/When the Saints Go Marching In	1959	3.75	7.50	15.00
❏ 5585		I'm Ready/Margie	1959	3.75	7.50	15.00
❏ 5606		I Want to Walk You Home/ I'm Gonna Be a Wheel Some Day	1959	3.75	7.50	15.00
❏ 5606	PS	I Want to Walk You Home/ I'm Gonna Be a Wheel Some Day	1959	12.50	25.00	50.00
❏ 5629		Be My Guest/I've Been Around	1959	3.75	7.50	15.00
❏ 5629	PS	Be My Guest/I've Been Around	1959	12.50	25.00	50.00
❏ 5645		Country Boy/If You Need Me	1960	3.75	7.50	15.00
❏ 5660		Tell Me That You Love Me/Before I Grow Too Old	1960	3.75	7.50	15.00
❏ 5675		Walking to New Orleans/Don't Come Knockin'	1960	3.75	7.50	15.00
❏ 5687		Three Nights a Week/Put Your Arms Around Me Honey	1960	3.75	7.50	15.00
❏ 5704		My Girl Josephine/Natural Born Lover	1960	3.75	7.50	15.00
❏ 5723		What a Price/Ain't That Just Like a Woman	1961	3.75	7.50	15.00
❏ 5734		Shu Rah/Fell in Love on Monday	1961	3.75	7.50	15.00
❏ 5753		It Keeps Rainin'/I Just Cry	1961	3.75	7.50	15.00
❏ 5764		Let the Four Winds Blow/Good Hearted Man	1961	3.75	7.50	15.00
❏ 5779		What a Party/Rockin' Bicycle	1961	3.75	7.50	15.00
❏ 5796		Jambalaya (On the Bayou)/I Hear You Knocking	1961	3.75	7.50	15.00
❏ 5816		You Win Again/Ida Jane	1962	3.75	7.50	15.00
❏ 5833		My Real Name/My Heart Is Bleeding	1962	3.75	7.50	15.00
❏ 5863		Nothing New (Same Old Thing)/ Dance with Mr. Domino	1962	3.75	7.50	15.00
❏ 5875		Did You Ever See a Dream Walking/Stop the Clock	1962	3.75	7.50	15.00
❏ 5895		Won't You Come On Back/Your Cheatin' Heart	1962	3.75	7.50	15.00
❏ 5895		Won't You Come On Back/Hands Across the Table	1962	3.75	7.50	15.00
❏ 5909		Hum Diddy Doo/Those Eyes	1963	3.75	7.50	15.00
❏ 5937		You Always Hurt the One You Love/Trouble Blues	1963	3.75	7.50	15.00
❏ 5959		Isle of Capri/True Confession	1963	3.75	7.50	15.00
❏ 5980		One Night/I Can't Go On This Way	1963	3.75	7.50	15.00
❏ 5999		Your Cheatin' Heart/Goin' Home	1963	3.75	7.50	15.00
❏ 66005		I Can't Give You Anything But Love/Goin' Home	1963	3.00	6.00	12.00
❏ 66016		When I Was Young/Your Cheatin' Heart	1964	3.00	6.00	12.00

Mercury

Number		Title (A Side/B Side)	Year	VG	VG+	NM
❏ 72463		I Left My Heart in San Francisco/I Done Got Over You	1965	2.50	5.00	10.00
❏ 72485		It's Never Too Late/What's That You Got	1965	2.50	5.00	10.00
❏ 72485	PS	It's Never Too Late/What's That You Got	1965	5.00	10.00	20.00

Reprise

Number		Title (A Side/B Side)	Year	VG	VG+	NM
❏ 0696		One for the Highway/ Honest Papas Love Their Mamas Better	1968	3.75	7.50	15.00
❏ 0763		Lady Madonna/One for the Highway	1968	3.75	7.50	15.00
❏ 0775		Lovely Rita/Wait Till It Happens to You	1968	3.75	7.50	15.00
❏ 0810		Everybody's Got Something to Hide (Except Me and My Monkey)/So Swell When You're Well	1969	3.75	7.50	15.00
❏ 0891		Have You Seen My Baby?/Make Me Belong to You	1970	3.75	7.50	15.00
❏ 0944		New Orleans Ain't the Same/Sweet Patootie	1970	3.75	7.50	15.00

The Right Stuff

Number		Title (A Side/B Side)	Year	VG	VG+	NM
❏ S7-18216		Christmas Is a Special Day/ Please Come Home for Christmas (Christmas Once Again)	1994		2.00	4.00
		Red vinyl				

Toot Toot

Number		Title (A Side/B Side)	Year	VG	VG+	NM
❏ 001		My Toot Toot/My Toot Toot (Rock)	1985		2.50	5.00
		With Doug Kershaw				
❏ 002		Don't Mess with My Popeye's/My Toot Toot	1985		2.50	5.00
		With Doug Kershaw				

United Artists

Note: 0001 through 0011 are "Silver Spotlight Series" reissues

Number		Title (A Side/B Side)	Year	VG	VG+	NM
❏ 0001		Ain't That a Shame/Goin' Home	1973		2.00	4.00
❏ 0002		Blue Monday/I'm Gonna Be a Wheel Some Day	1973		2.00	4.00
❏ 0003		I'm in Love Again/Whole Lotta Lovin'	1973		2.00	4.00

Number		Title (A Side/B Side)	Year	VG	VG+	NM
☐ 0004		Blueberry Hill/Bo Weevil	1973		2.00	4.00
☐ 0005		I'm Walkin'/One Night	1973		2.00	4.00
☐ 0006		I Hear You Knockin'/My Blue Heaven	1973		2.00	4.00
☐ 0007		Walkin' to New Orleans/Country Boy	1973		2.00	4.00
☐ 0008		I Want to Walk You Home/It's You I Love	1973		2.00	4.00
☐ 0009		I'm Ready/Wait and See	1973		2.00	4.00
☐ 0010		My Girl Josephine/When My Dreamboat Comes Home	1973		2.00	4.00
☐ 0011		Three Nights a Week/Let the Four Winds Blow	1973		2.00	4.00
☐ XW 514		The Fat Man/Valley of Tears	1974		2.50	5.00

Warner Bros.

☐ 49610		Whiskey Heaven/Beers to You	1980		2.00	4.00

B-side by Texas Opera Company

Dominoes, The - See "Ward, Billy, and the Dominoes"

Don and His Roses

Dot

☐ 15755		Since You Went Away to School/Right Now	1958	12.50	25.00	50.00
☐ 15874		Leave Those Cats Alone/Don't Try to Change Me	1958	37.50	75.00	150.00

Don and Juan

Big Top

☐ 3079		What's Your Name/Chicken Necks	1961	3.75	7.50	15.00
☐ 3106		Two Fools Are We/Pot Luck	1962	5.00	10.00	20.00
☐ 3121		Magic Wand/What I Really Meant to Say	1962	10.00	20.00	40.00
☐ 3145		True Love Never Runs Smooth/	1963	12.50	25.00	50.00
		Is It All Right If I Love You				

Mala

☐ 469		Lonely Man/Could This Be Love	1963	3.00	6.00	12.00
☐ 479		Pledging My Love/Molinda	1964	3.00	6.00	12.00
☐ 484		Sincerely/Maryana Cherie	1964	3.00	6.00	12.00
☐ 494		I Can't Help Myself/All That's Missing Is You	1964	3.00	6.00	12.00
☐ 509		The Heartbreaking Truth/Thank Goodness	1965	7.50	15.00	30.00

Twirl

☐ 2021		Because I Love You/Are You Putting Me on the Shelf	1966	7.50	15.00	30.00

Don and the Chevells

Speedway

☐ 1000		Inner Limits/The Only Girl	1964	18.75	37.50	75.00

"Don" is Don Ciccone, later of the Critters and the Four Seasons

Don and the Goodtimes

Burdette

☐ 3		Colors of Life/You Did It Before	196?	5.00	10.00	20.00

Dunhill

☐ 4008		Little Green Thing/Little Sally Tease	1965	2.50	5.00	10.00
☐ 4015		I'll Be Down Forever/	1965	2.50	5.00	10.00
		Big Big Knight (On a Big White Horse)				
☐ 4022		Sweets for My Sweet/Hey There Mary Mae	1966	2.50	5.00	10.00

Epic

☐ 10145		I Could Be So Good to You/And It's So Good	1967	2.50	5.00	10.00
☐ 10145	PS	I Could Be So Good to You/And It's So Good	1967	3.75	7.50	15.00
☐ 10199		If You Love Her, Cherish Her and Such/Happy and Me	1967	2.50	5.00	10.00
☐ 10241		Bambi/Sally (Studio A at 6 O'Clock in the Morning)	1967	2.50	5.00	10.00
☐ 10280		Ball of Fire/May My Heart Be Cast Into Stone	1968	2.50	5.00	10.00

Jerden

☐ 762		You'll Never Walk Away/Little Sally Tease	1965	3.00	6.00	12.00

Wand

☐ 165		Turn On/Make It	1964	2.50	5.00	10.00
☐ 184		Straight Scepter/There's Something on Your Mind	1965	2.50	5.00	10.00

Donays, The

Brent

☐ 7033		Devil in His Heart/Bad Boy	1962	10.00	20.00	40.00

The Beatles re-made the A-side as "Devil in Her Heart"

Donegan, Lonnie

Apt

☐ 25067		Pick a Bale of Cotton/Ramblin' Round	1962	2.50	5.00	10.00

Atlantic

☐ 2058		My Old Man's a Dustman/The Golden Vanity	1960	3.00	6.00	12.00
☐ 2063		Take This Hammer/Nobody Understands Me	1960	3.00	6.00	12.00
☐ 2081		Lorelei/Junco Partner	1960	3.00	6.00	12.00
☐ 2108		Beyond the Sunset/Have a Drink On Me	1961	3.00	6.00	12.00
☐ 2123		Wreck of the John B/	1961	3.00	6.00	12.00
		Sorry, But I'm Gonna Have to Pass				

Dot

☐ 15792		The Grand Coulee Dam/	1958	5.00	10.00	20.00
		Nobody Loves Like an Irishman				
☐ 15873		Sally Don't You Grieve/Times Are Getting Hard, Boys	1958	5.00	10.00	20.00
☐ 15911		Does Your Chewing Gum Lose Its Flavor	1959	5.00	10.00	20.00
		(On the Bedpost Overnight)/Aunt Rhody				

Reissued in 1961 with the same number

☐ 15953		Whoa, Back, Back/Fort Worth Jail	1959	5.00	10.00	20.00
☐ 16263		Whoa, Back, Back/Light from the Lighthouse	1961	3.75	7.50	15.00

Number		Title (A Side/B Side)	Year	VG	VG+	NM
Felsted						
❏ 8630		Rock Island Line/John Henry	1961	3.00	6.00	12.00
Hickory						
❏ 1247		Lemon Tree/A Very Good Year	1964	2.50	5.00	10.00
❏ 1267		Fisherman's Luck/There's a Big Wheel	1964	2.50	5.00	10.00
❏ 1274		Bad News/Interstate 40	1964	2.50	5.00	10.00
❏ 1299		Louisiana Man/Lovey Told Me Goodbye	1965	2.50	5.00	10.00
❏ 1345		Cajun Jo (Bully of the Bayou)/Nothing to Gain	1965	2.50	5.00	10.00
London						
❏ 1650		Rock Island Line/John Henry	1956	7.50	15.00	30.00
Mercury						
❏ 70872		Lost John/Stewball	1956	6.25	12.50	25.00
❏ 70949		Dead or Alive/Bring a Little Water, Sylvie	1956	6.25	12.50	25.00
❏ 71026		Don't You Rock Me Daddy-O/ How Long, How Long Blues	1957	6.25	12.50	25.00
❏ 71094		Cumberland Gap/Wabash Cannonball	1957	6.25	12.50	25.00
❏ 71181		Puttin' On the Style/Gamblin' Man	1957	6.25	12.50	25.00
❏ 71248		I'm Just a Rolling Stone/My Dixie Darling	1957	6.25	12.50	25.00
Donner, Ral						
Chicago Fire						
❏ 7402		The Wedding Song/Godfather Per Me	1974	2.00	4.00	8.00
End						
❏ GG-19		You Don't Know What You've Got (Until You Lose It)/ She's Everything (I Wanted You to Be) *An early, and sought-after, reissue*	1963	7.50	15.00	30.00
Fontana						
❏ 1503		Poison Ivy League/You Finally Said Something Good	1965	6.25	12.50	25.00
❏ 1503		Poison Ivy League/A Tear in My Eye	1965	6.25	12.50	25.00
❏ 1515		Good Lovin'/The Other Side of Me	1965	6.25	12.50	25.00
Gone						
❏ 5102		Girl of My Best Friend/It's Been a Long, Long Time *Black label*	1961	10.00	20.00	40.00
❏ 5102		Girl of My Best Friend/It's Been a Long, Long Time *Multicolor label*	1961	6.25	12.50	25.00
❏ 5108		To Love/And Then *Deleted shortly after release*	1961	10.00	20.00	40.00
❏ 5108		You Don't Know What You've Got (Until You Lose It)/ So Close to Heaven	1961	6.25	12.50	25.00
❏ 5114		Please Don't Go/I Didn't Figure on Him	1961	6.25	12.50	25.00
❏ 5119		School of Heartbreakers/Because We're Young	1961	10.00	20.00	40.00
❏ 5121		She's Everything (I Wanted You to Be)/ Because We're Young	1961	6.25	12.50	25.00
❏ 5121		She's Everything (I Wanted You to Be)/ Will You Love Me in Heaven *B-side sung by a girl group, not Ral Donner.*	1961	7.50	15.00	30.00
❏ 5125		To Love Someone/Will You Love Me in Heaven *B-side sung by Ral Donner as advertised*	1962	6.25	12.50	25.00
❏ 5129		Loveless Life/Bells of Love	1962	6.25	12.50	25.00
❏ 5133		To Love/Sweetheart	1962	6.25	12.50	25.00
Mid-Eagle						
❏ 101		(If I Had My) Life to Live Over/Lost	1968	2.50	5.00	10.00
❏ 275		The Wedding Song/So Much Lovin'	1976		3.00	6.00
MJ						
❏ 222		(All of a Sudden) My Heart Sings/Lovin' Place	1970		3.00	6.00
❏ 222	PS	(All of a Sudden) My Heart Sings/Lovin' Place	1970		3.00	6.00
Red Bird						
❏ 10-057		Love Isn't Like That/It Will Only Make You Love	1966	37.50	75.00	150.00
Reprise						
❏ 20,135		(These Are the Things That Make Up) Christmas Day/ Second Miracle	1962	10.00	20.00	40.00
❏ 20,141		I Got Burned/A Tear in My Eye	1963	10.00	20.00	40.00
❏ 20,141	PS	I Got Burned/A Tear in My Eye	1963	50.00	100.00	200.00
❏ 20,176		I Wish This Night Would Never End/ Don't Put Your Heart in His Hand	1963	12.50	25.00	50.00
❏ 20,192		Beyond the Heartbreak/Run Little Linda	1963	15.00	30.00	60.00
Rising Sons						
❏ 714		Just a Little Sunshine (In the Rain)/If I Promise	1968	2.50	5.00	10.00
Scottie						
❏ 1310		Tell Me Why/That's All Right with Me	1959	62.50	125.00	250.00
Smash						
❏ 34774/5	DJ	Good Lovin'/The Other Side of Me *A Fontana promo using Smash labels in error and omitting the Fontana number?*	1964	10.00	20.00	40.00
Starfire						
❏ 100		Don't Let It Slip Away/Wait a Minute Now	1978	2.50	5.00	10.00
❏ 103		Christmas Day/Second Miracle (Of Christmas) *Green vinyl*	1978	2.50	5.00	10.00
❏ 103	PS	Christmas Day/Second Miracle (Of Christmas)	1978	2.50	5.00	10.00
❏ 114		Rip It Up/Don't Leave Me Now	1979	2.50	5.00	10.00
❏ 114		Rip It Up/Don't Leave Me Now *Picture disc*	1979	6.25	12.50	25.00
❏ 114	PS	Rip It Up/Don't Leave Me Now	1979	2.50	5.00	10.00

Number		Title (A Side/B Side)	Year	VG	VG+	NM
Sunlight						
❏ 1006		Don't Let It Slip Away/Wait a Minute Now	1972	3.00	6.00	12.00
Tau						
❏ 105		Loneliness of a Star/And Then	1963	12.50	25.00	50.00
	Blue label					
❏ 105		Loneliness of a Star/And Then	1963	7.50	15.00	30.00
	Yellow label					
Thunder						
❏ 7801		The Day the Beat Stopped/Rock on Me	1978		3.00	6.00

Donnie and the Darlingtons
ABC-Paramount

Number		Title (A Side/B Side)	Year	VG	VG+	NM
❏ 10633		Poppin' My Clutch/Since Grandpa Got a Rail Job	1965	6.25	12.50	25.00

Donnie and the Delchords
Epic

Number		Title (A Side/B Side)	Year	VG	VG+	NM
❏ 9495		So Lonely/When You're Alone	1962	6.25	12.50	25.00
Taurus						
❏ 352		So Lonely/When You're Alone	1962	10.00	20.00	40.00
❏ 357		I Don't Care/I'll Be With You in Apple Blossom Time	1963	6.25	12.50	25.00
❏ 361		Transylvania Mist/That Old Feeling	1963	6.25	12.50	25.00
❏ 363		Be with You/I Found Heaven	1963	6.25	12.50	25.00
❏ 364		I'm in the Mood for Love/I've Got a Woman	1964	6.25	12.50	25.00

Donnie and the Dreamers
Decca

Number		Title (A Side/B Side)	Year	VG	VG+	NM
❏ 31312		Carole/Ruby My Love	1961	12.50	25.00	50.00
Whale						
❏ 500		Dorothy/Count Every Star	1961	6.25	12.50	25.00
❏ 505		Teenage Love/My Memories of You	1961	10.00	20.00	40.00

Donovan
Allegiance

Number		Title (A Side/B Side)	Year	VG	VG+	NM
❏ 3910		Lady of the Stars/(B-side unknown)	1983		2.00	4.00
Arista						
❏ 0280		Dare to Be Different/International Man	1977		2.00	4.00
Epic						
❏ 10045		Sunshine Superman/The Trip	1966	2.50	5.00	10.00
❏ 10045	PS	Sunshine Superman/The Trip	1966	3.75	7.50	15.00
❏ 10098		Mellow Yellow/Sunny South Kensington	1966	2.50	5.00	10.00
❏ 10098	PS	Mellow Yellow/Sunny South Kensington	1966	3.75	7.50	15.00
❏ 10127		Epistle to Dippy/Preachin' Love	1967	2.00	4.00	8.00
❏ 10127	PS	Epistle to Dippy/Preachin' Love	1967	3.00	6.00	12.00
❏ 10212		There Is a Mountain/Sand and Foam	1967	2.00	4.00	8.00
❏ 10253		Wear Your Love Like Heaven/Oh Gosh	1967	2.00	4.00	8.00
❏ 10253	PS	Wear Your Love Like Heaven/Oh Gosh	1967	3.00	6.00	12.00
❏ 10300		Jennifer Juniper/Poor Cow	1968	2.00	4.00	8.00
❏ 10300	PS	Jennifer Juniper/Poor Cow	1968	3.00	6.00	12.00
❏ 10345		Hurdy Gurdy Man/Teen Angel	1968	2.00	4.00	8.00
	Features John Paul Jones, Jimmy Page, and possibly John Bonham, all later of Led Zeppelin					
❏ 10345	PS	Hurdy Gurdy Man/Teen Angel	1968	3.00	6.00	12.00
❏ 10393		Lalena/Aye My Love	1968	2.00	4.00	8.00
❏ 10393	PS	Lalena/Aye My Love	1968	3.00	6.00	12.00
❏ 10434		Atlantis/To Susan on the West Coast Waiting	1969	2.00	4.00	8.00
❏ 10434	PS	Atlantis/To Susan on the West Coast Waiting	1969	3.00	6.00	12.00
❏ 10510		Goo Goo Barabajagal (Love Is Hot)/Trust	1969	2.00	4.00	8.00
❏ 10510	PS	Goo Goo Barabajagal (Love Is Hot)/Trust	1969	3.00	6.00	12.00
	With the Jeff Beck Group					
❏ 10649		Riki Tiki Tavi/Roots of Oak	1970	2.00	4.00	8.00
❏ 10649	PS	Riki Tiki Tavi/Roots of Oak	1970	3.00	6.00	12.00
❏ 10694		Celia of the Seals/Song of the Wandering Aengus	1971	2.00	4.00	8.00
❏ 10694	PS	Celia of the Seals/Song of the Wandering Aengus	1971	3.00	6.00	12.00
❏ 10983		I Like You/Earth Sign Man	1973		2.50	5.00
❏ 11023		Maria Magenta/Intergalactic Laxative	1973		2.50	5.00
❏ 11108		Yellow Star/Sailing Homeward	1974		2.50	5.00
❏ 50016		Rock and Roll with Me/ Divine Daze of Deathless Delight	1974		2.50	5.00
❏ 50077		Rock and Roll Souljer/How Silly	1975		2.50	5.00
❏ 50237		Dark Eyed Blue Jean Angel/Well Known Has-Been	1976		2.50	5.00
Hickory						
❏ 1309		Catch the Wind/Why Do You Treat Me Like You Do	1965	3.75	7.50	15.00
❏ 1324		Colours/Josie	1965	3.00	6.00	12.00
❏ 1338		Universal Soldier/Do You Hear Me Now	1965	3.00	6.00	12.00
❏ 1375		You're Gonna Need Somebody on Your Mind/ Little Tin Soldier	1966	3.00	6.00	12.00
❏ 1402		Turquoise/To Try for the Sun	1966	3.00	6.00	12.00
❏ 1417		Hey Gyp/The War Drags On	1966	3.00	6.00	12.00
❏ 1470		Sunny Goodge Street/Summer Day Reflection Song	1967	2.50	5.00	10.00
❏ 1492		Do You Hear Me Now/ Why Do You Treat Me Like You Do	1968	2.50	5.00	10.00
Janus						
❏ 138		Keep On Truckin'/Hey Gyp	1971	2.00	4.00	8.00

Number		Title (A Side/B Side)	Year	VG	VG+	NM

Dontels, The
Beltone
| ❏ 2040 | | Lover's Reunion/Make a Chance | 1963 | 62.50 | 125.00 | 250.00 |

Doors, The
Elektra
❏ 45051		Light My Fire/Love Me Two Times	1972		3.00	6.00
		"Spun Gold" series; originals have a very dark gold label				
❏ 45051		Light My Fire/Love Me Two Times	1975		2.00	4.00
		"Spun Gold" series; reissues have a lighter gold label				
❏ 45052		Touch Me/Hello, I Love You	1972		3.00	6.00
		"Spun Gold" series; originals have a very dark gold label				
❏ 45052		Touch Me/Hello, I Love You	1975		2.00	4.00
		"Spun Gold" series; reissues have a lighter gold label				
❏ 45059		Riders on the Storm/Love Her Madly	1973		3.00	6.00
		"Spun Gold" series; originals have a very dark gold label				
❏ 45059		Riders on the Storm/Love Her Madly	1975		2.00	4.00
		"Spun Gold" series; reissues have a lighter gold label				
❏ 45122		L.A. Woman/Roadhouse Blues	1983		2.00	4.00
		"Spun Gold" series; lighter gold label				
❏ 45123		People Are Strange/Break On Through	1983		2.00	4.00
		"Spun Gold" series; lighter gold label				
❏ 45611		Break On Through (To the Other Side)/End of the Night	1966	6.25	12.50	25.00
		Originals have a yellow and black label				
❏ 45611		Break On Through (To the Other Side)/End of the Night	1967	3.75	7.50	15.00
		Second pressings have a red, black and white label				
❏ 45611	PS	Break On Through (To the Other Side)/End of the Night	1966	12.50	25.00	50.00
❏ 45615		Light My Fire/The Crystal Ship	1967	6.25	12.50	25.00
		Originals have a yellow and black label				
❏ 45615		Light My Fire/The Crystal Ship	1967	3.00	6.00	12.00
		Second pressings have a red, black and white label				
❏ 45621		People Are Strange/Unhappy Girl	1967	3.00	6.00	12.00
❏ 45621	PS	People Are Strange/Unhappy Girl	1967	6.25	12.50	25.00
❏ 45624		Love Me Two Times/Moonlight Drive	1967	3.00	6.00	12.00
❏ 45628		The Unknown Soldier/We Could Be So Good Together	1968	3.00	6.00	12.00
❏ 45628	PS	The Unknown Soldier/We Could Be So Good Together	1968	7.50	15.00	30.00
❏ 45635		Hello, I Love You, Won't You Tell Me Your Name?/Love Street	1968	5.00	10.00	20.00
		Original pressings have longer title				
❏ 45635		Hello, I Love You/Love Street	1968	3.00	6.00	12.00
❏ 45646		Touch Me/Wild Child	1968	3.00	6.00	12.00
❏ 45656		Wishful Sinful/Who Scared You?	1969	2.50	5.00	10.00
❏ 45663		Tell All the People/Easy Ride	1969	2.50	5.00	10.00
❏ 45663	PS	Tell All the People/Easy Ride	1969	6.25	12.50	25.00
❏ 45675		Runnin' Blue/Do It	1969	2.50	5.00	10.00
❏ 45685		You Make Me Real/Roadhouse Blues	1970	2.50	5.00	10.00
❏ 45726		Love Her Madly/(You Need Meat) Don't Go No Further	1971	2.00	4.00	8.00
❏ 45738		Riders on the Storm/Changeling	1971	2.00	4.00	8.00
❏ 45757		Tightrope Ride/Variety Is the Spice of Life	1971	2.00	4.00	8.00
❏ 45768		Ships w/Sails/In the Eye of the Sun	1972	2.00	4.00	8.00
❏ 45793		Get Up and Dance/Treetrunk	1972	2.00	4.00	8.00
❏ 45807		The Mosquito/It Slipped My Mind	1972	2.00	4.00	8.00
❏ 45825		The Piano Bird/Good Rockin'	1972	2.00	4.00	8.00
❏ 46005		Roadhouse Blues (Live)/Albinoni/Adagio	1979		2.50	5.00
❏ 47097		People Are Strange/Not to Touch the Earth	1980		2.00	4.00
❏ 47097	PS	People Are Strange/Not to Touch the Earth	1980	2.00	4.00	8.00
		Also has an insert with photos of Doors albums				
❏ 69770		Gloria/Moonlight Drive	1983		2.00	4.00
		Contrary to prior reports, this was not issued with a picture sleeve				

Dorman, Harold
Rita
❏ 1003		Mountain of Love/To Be with You	1960	6.25	12.50	25.00
❏ 1008		I'll Come Running/River of Tears	1960	5.00	10.00	20.00
❏ 1012		Moved to Kansas City/Take a Chance on Me	1960	5.00	10.00	20.00
Santo
❏ 9005		In an Instant/There on Yonder Hill	1962	3.75	7.50	15.00
❏ 9051		Ain't Gonna Change/What Comes Next	1962	3.75	7.50	15.00
Sun
❏ 362		I'll Stick By You/There They Go	1961	5.00	10.00	20.00
❏ 370		Just One Step/Uncle Jonah's Place	1961	5.00	10.00	20.00
❏ 377		Wait 'Til Saturday Night/In the Beginning	1962	5.00	10.00	20.00

Dorn, Jerry
Arwin
| ❏ 122 | | Brother, Can You Spare a Dime/Disappointed Lover | 1959 | 3.00 | 6.00 | 12.00 |
Fling
| ❏ 711 | | Rocking Chair Rock/(B-side unknown) | 1959 | 12.50 | 25.00 | 50.00 |
King
❏ 4932		Wishing Well/Sentimental Heaven	1956	10.00	20.00	40.00
❏ 4968		I'm So in Love with You/Nightmare	1956	3.75	7.50	15.00
❏ 5029		Quicksand/The Key	1957	3.75	7.50	15.00

Number	Title (A Side/B Side)	Year	VG	VG+	NM

Dorsey, Gerry - See "Humperdinck, Engelbert"

Dorsey, Lee

ABC

☐ 12326	Night People/Can I Be the One	1978		2.00	4.00
☐ 12361	God Must Have Blessed America/Say It Again	1978		2.00	4.00

ABC-Paramount

☐ 10192	Lottie Mo/Lover of Love	1961	3.75	7.50	15.00

Amy

☐ 927	Ride Your Pony/The Kitty Cat Song	1965	2.00	4.00	8.00
☐ 939	Can You Hear Me/Work, Work, Work	1965	2.00	4.00	8.00
☐ 945	Get Out of My Life, Woman/So Long	1965	2.00	4.00	8.00
☐ 952	Confusion/The Neighbors' Daughter	1966	2.00	4.00	8.00
☐ 958	Workin' in the Coal Mine/Mexico	1966	2.50	5.00	10.00
☐ 965	Holy Cow/Operation Heartache	1966	2.00	4.00	8.00
☐ 974	Gotta Find a Job/Rain, Rain, Rain, Go Away	1967		3.00	6.00
☐ 987	My Old Car/Why Wait Until Tomorrow	1967		3.00	6.00
☐ 994	Can't Get Away/Vista Vista	1967		3.00	6.00
☐ 998	Go-Go Girl/I Can Hear You Callin'	1967		3.00	6.00
☐ 11010	I Can't Get Away/Cynthia	1968		3.00	6.00
☐ 11020	Wonder Woman/A Little Dab A Do Ya	1968		3.00	6.00
☐ 11031	Four Corners (Part 1)/Four Corners (Part 2)	1968		3.00	6.00
☐ 11048	I'm Gonna Sit Right Down/Little Ba-By	1968		3.00	6.00
☐ 11052	What Now My Love/A Lover Was Born	1969		3.00	6.00
☐ 11055	Everything I Do Gonna be Funky (From Now On)/There Should Be a Book	1969		3.00	6.00
☐ 11057	Give It Up/Candy Man	1969		3.00	6.00

Bell

☐ 908	I Can Hear You Callin'/What You Want	1970		2.50	5.00

Constellation

☐ 115	Organ Grinder's Swing/I Gotta Find a New Love	1964	5.00	10.00	20.00
☐ 135	You're Breaking Me Up/Messed Around and Fell in Love	1964	5.00	10.00	20.00

Fury

☐ 1053	Ya Ya/Give Me You	1961	3.75	7.50	15.00
☐ 1056	Do-Re-Mi/People Gonna' Talk	1961	3.00	6.00	12.00
☐ 1061	Eenie Meenie Miny Moe/Behind the 8-Ball	1962	3.00	6.00	12.00
☐ 1066	You Are My Sunshine/Give Me Your Love	1962	3.00	6.00	12.00
☐ 1074	Hoodlum Joe/When I Met My Baby	1963	3.00	6.00	12.00

Polydor

☐ 14038	Yes We Can (Part 1)/O Me O, My O	1970		2.50	5.00
☐ 14055	Sneakin' Sally Through the Alley/Tears, Tears and More Tears	1971		2.50	5.00
☐ 14106	Freedom for the Stallion/If She Won't (Find Someone Who Will)	1971		2.50	5.00
☐ 14147	When Can I Come Home/Gator Tail	1972		2.50	5.00
☐ 14181	On Your Way Down/Freedom for the Stallion	1973		2.50	5.00

Rex

☐ 1005	Rock/Lonely Evening	1959	6.25	12.50	25.00

Sansu

☐ 474	Love Lots of Lovin'/Take Care of Our Love With Betty Harris	1967	3.00	6.00	12.00

Smash

☐ 1842	Hello Good Looking/Someday	1963	2.50	5.00	10.00

Spring

☐ 114	Occapella/Tears, Tears and More Tears	1971		2.50	5.00

Valiant

☐ 1001	Lottie Mo/Lover of Love	1958	10.00	20.00	40.00

Dots, The

Caddy

☐ 101	I Confess/I Wish I Could Meet You	1956	20.00	40.00	80.00
☐ 107	I Lost You/Johnny	1957	20.00	40.00	80.00
☐ 111	Good Luck to You/Heartsick and Lonely	1957	20.00	40.00	80.00

Rev

☐ 3512	Ring Chimes/Wolf Call	1958	375.00	750.00	1,500

Douglas, Scott, and the Venture Quintet - See "Ventures, The"

Douglas, Steve

Capitol

☐ 5527	Yesterday (Part 1)/Yesterday (Part 2)	1965	3.00	6.00	12.00

Grapevine

☐ 601	Rockin' Green Sleeves/(B-side unknown)	1961	5.00	10.00	20.00

MGM

☐ 13218	Snowplows Schussing (Part 1)/Snowplows Schussing (Part 2)	1964	3.00	6.00	12.00

Philles

☐ 104	Yes Sir, That's My Baby/Lt. Col. Bogey's Parade	1962	6.25	12.50	25.00

Tandem

☐ 7000	Magic Sound/(B-side unknown)	1961	5.00	10.00	20.00

Number		Title (A Side/B Side)	Year	VG	VG+	NM

Douglas, Wayne - See "Sahm, Doug"

Dove, Ronnie

Decca

❏ 31288		Yes Darling, I'll Be Around/Party Doll	1961	5.00	10.00	20.00
❏ 32853		Just the Other Side of Nowhere/If I Cried	1971		2.50	5.00
❏ 32919		Kiss the Hurt Away/He Cries Like a Baby	1972		2.50	5.00
❏ 32997		It's No Sin/My World of Memories	1972		2.50	5.00
❏ 33038		Lilacs in Winter/Is It Wrong	1972		2.50	5.00

Diamond

❏ 163		Sweeter Than Sugar/I Believe in You	1964	2.50	5.00	10.00
❏ 167		Say You/Let Me Stay Today	1964	2.50	5.00	10.00
❏ 173		Right or Wrong/Baby Put Your Arms Around Me	1964	2.00	4.00	8.00
❏ 176		Hello Pretty Girl/Keep It a Secret	1965	2.00	4.00	8.00
❏ 179		One Kiss for Old Times' Sake/No Greater Love	1965	2.00	4.00	8.00
❏ 179		One Kiss for Old Times' Sake/Bluebird	1965	2.00	4.00	8.00
❏ 184		A Little Bit of Heaven/If I Live to Be a Hundred	1965	2.00	4.00	8.00
❏ 188		I'll Make All Your Dreams Come True/ I Had to Lose You	1965	2.00	4.00	8.00
❏ 195		When Liking Turns to Loving/ I'm Learning How to Smile Again	1965	2.00	4.00	8.00
❏ 198		Let's Start All Over Again/That Empty Feeling	1966	2.00	4.00	8.00
❏ 205		Happy Summer Days/Long After	1966	2.00	4.00	8.00
❏ 205	PS	Happy Summer Days/Long After	1966	3.75	7.50	15.00
❏ 208		I Really Don't Want to Know/Years of Tears	1966	2.00	4.00	8.00
❏ 214		Cry/Autumn Rhapsody	1966	2.00	4.00	8.00
❏ 217		One More Mountain to Climb/All	1967	2.00	4.00	8.00
❏ 221		My Babe/Put My Mind at Ease	1967	2.50	5.00	10.00
		A-side written and produced by Neil Diamond				
❏ 227		I Want to Love You for What You Are/ I Thank You for Your Love	1967	2.00	4.00	8.00
❏ 235		Dancin' Out of My Heart/Back from Baltimore	1967	2.00	4.00	8.00
❏ 240		In Some Time/Livin' for Your Lovin'	1968	2.00	4.00	8.00
❏ 244		Mountain of Love/Never Gonna Cry	1968	2.00	4.00	8.00
❏ 249		Tomboy/Tell Me Tomorrow	1968	2.00	4.00	8.00
❏ 256		What's Wrong with My World/That Empty Feeling	1969		3.00	6.00
❏ 260		I Need You Now/Bluebird	1969		3.00	6.00
❏ 271		Chains of Love/If I Live to Be a Hundred	1970		3.00	6.00

Hitsville

❏ 6038		Tragedy/Songs We Sang As Children	1976		2.00	4.00
❏ 6045		The Morning After the Night Before/Why Daddy	1976		2.00	4.00

Jalo

❏ 1406		No Greater Love/Saddest Hour	1962	6.25	12.50	25.00

M.C.

❏ 5013		The Angel in Your Eyes (Brings Out the Devil in Me)/ Songs We Sang As Children	1978		2.00	4.00

MCA

❏ 40106		So Long Dixie/Take My Love	1973		2.00	4.00

Melodyland

❏ 6004		Please Come to Nashville/Pictures on Paper	1975		2.00	4.00
❏ 6011		Here We Go Again/Things	1975		2.00	4.00
❏ 6021		Drina (Take Your Lady Off for Me)/Your Sweet Love	1975		2.00	4.00
❏ 6030		Right or Wrong/Guns	1976		2.00	4.00

Dovells, The

Abkco

❏ 4011		Bristol Stomp/You Can't Sit Down	1972		2.00	4.00
❏ 4029		Baby Workout/Hully Gully Baby	1973	2.50	5.00	10.00
❏ 4032		Bristol Twistin' Annie/Betty in Bermudas	1973		2.00	4.00

Event

❏ 216		Dancing in the Street/Back on the Road Again	1974		2.50	5.00
❏ 3310		Roll Over Beethoven/Something About You Boy	1970		2.50	5.00

Jamie

❏ 1369		Our Winter Love/Blue	1969	2.50	5.00	10.00

MGM

❏ 13628		There's a Girl/Love Is Everywhere	1966	2.50	5.00	10.00
❏ 14568		Don't Vote for Luke McCabe/Mary's Magic Show	1973		2.50	5.00

Paramount

❏ 0134		L-O-V-E Love/We're All In This Together	1971		2.50	5.00

Parkway

❏ 819		No, No, No/Letters of Love	1961	5.00	10.00	20.00
❏ 827		Bristol Stomp/Out in the Cold Again	1961	7.50	15.00	30.00
❏ 827		Bristol Stomp/Letters of Love	1961	3.75	7.50	15.00
❏ 833		Do the New Continental/Mope-Itty Mope Stomp	1962	3.75	7.50	15.00
❏ 833	PS	Do the New Continental/Mope-Itty Mope Stomp	1962	6.25	12.50	25.00
❏ 838		Bristol Twistin' Annie/The Actor	1962	3.75	7.50	15.00
❏ 838	PS	Bristol Twistin' Annie/The Actor	1962	6.25	12.50	25.00
❏ 845		Hully Gully Baby/Your Last Chance	1962	3.75	7.50	15.00
❏ 845	PS	Hully Gully Baby/Your Last Chance	1962	6.25	12.50	25.00
❏ 855		The Jitterbug/Kissin' in the Kitchen	1962	3.75	7.50	15.00
❏ 855	PS	The Jitterbug/Kissin' in the Kitchen	1962	6.25	12.50	25.00
❏ 861		Save Me Baby/You Can't Run Away from Yourself	1963	5.00	10.00	20.00
❏ 867		You Can't Sit Down/Stompin' Everywhere	1963	3.00	6.00	12.00
❏ 867		You Can't Sit Down/Wildwood Days	1963	3.75	7.50	15.00

Number		Title (A Side/B Side)	Year	VG	VG+	NM
❏ 867	PS	You Can't Sit Down/Stompin' Everywhere	1963	6.25	12.50	25.00
❏ 867	PS	You Can't Sit Down/Wildwood Days	1963	6.25	12.50	25.00
❏ 882		Betty in Bermudas/Dance the Froog	1963	3.00	6.00	12.00
❏ 882	PS	Betty in Bermudas/Dance the Froog	1963	6.25	12.50	25.00
❏ 889		Stop Monkeyin' Aroun'/No, No, No	1963	3.00	6.00	12.00
❏ 889	PS	Stop Monkeyin' Aroun'/No, No, No	1963	6.25	12.50	25.00
❏ 901		Be My Girl/Dragster on the Prowl	1964	5.00	10.00	20.00
❏ 911		One Potato/Happy Birthday Just the Same	1964	3.75	7.50	15.00
❏ 925		Watusi with Lucy/What in the World's Come Over You	1964	3.00	6.00	12.00

Swan

❏ 4231		Happy/(Hey, Hey, Hey) Alright	1965	5.00	10.00	20.00

Verve

❏ 10701		Far Away/Sometimes	1973		2.50	5.00

Dowell, Joe
Monument

❏ 952		If I Could Find Out What Is Wrong/Indian Summer Days	1966	2.00	4.00	8.00

Smash

❏ 1708		Wooden Heart/Little Bo Peep	1961	3.75	7.50	15.00
❏ 1708	PS	Wooden Heart/Little Bo Peep	1961	6.25	12.50	25.00
❏ 1717		The Bridge of Love/Just Love Me	1961	3.00	6.00	12.00
❏ 1717	PS	The Bridge of Love/Just Love Me	1961	4.00	8.00	16.00
❏ 1728		(I Wonder) Who's Spending Christmas with You/A Kiss for Christmas	1961	3.75	7.50	15.00
❏ 1730		The Sound of Sadness/The Thorn on the Rose	1962	3.00	6.00	12.00
❏ 1759		Little Red Rented Rowboat/The One I Left for You	1962	3.00	6.00	12.00
❏ 1759	PS	Little Red Rented Rowboat/The One I Left for You	1962	3.00	6.00	12.00
❏ 1786		Poor Little Cupid/No Secrets	1962	3.00	6.00	12.00
❏ 1799		Our School Days/Bringa-Branga-Brought	1963	3.00	6.00	12.00
❏ 1799	PS	Our School Days/Bringa-Branga-Brought	1963	4.00	8.00	16.00
❏ 1816		Bobby Blue Loves Linda Lou/My Darling Wears White Today	1963	3.00	6.00	12.00

Downbeats, The
(More than one group)
Gee

❏ 1019		My Girl/China Girl *Red label*	1956	75.00	150.00	300.00
❏ 1019		My Girl/China Girl *Gray label*	1958	7.50	15.00	30.00

Peacock

❏ 1689		You're So Fine/Someday She'll Come Along	1958	5.00	10.00	20.00

Sarg

❏ 168		Darling of Mine/Come On Over	1959	10.00	20.00	40.00
❏ 173		Run to Me Baby/I Need Your Love	1959	10.00	20.00	40.00
❏ 197		Falling Stars/I Just Can't Understand *As "O.S. Grant and the Downbeats"*	1960	10.00	20.00	40.00
❏ 200		You Did Me Wrong/This Woman I Love	1960	10.00	20.00	40.00
❏ 223		Greyhound (Part 1)/Greyhound (Part 2)	196?	5.00	10.00	20.00
❏ 228		Grant's Soul Blues/Sock It Uptight	196?	5.00	10.00	20.00
❏ 233		Soul Bag/Darling Dear *As "O.S. Grant and the Downbeats"*	196?	5.00	10.00	20.00

Tamla; V.I.P.
See "Elgins, The"
Wilco

❏ 9		Alfalfa/Red X	1960	5.00	10.00	20.00
❏ 16		Playin' Possum/One at a Time	1960	5.00	10.00	20.00

Dozier, Lamont
(Also see "Holland-Dozier")
ABC

❏ 11407		Trying to Hold On to My Woman/We Don't Want Nobody to Come Between Us	1973		2.00	4.00
❏ 11438		Fish Ain't Bitin'/Breaking Out All Over	1974		2.00	4.00
❏ 12012		Fish Ain't Bitin'/Breaking Out All Over	1974		2.00	4.00
❏ 12044		Let Me Start Tonite/I Wanna Be with You	1974		2.00	4.00
❏ 12076		All Cried Out/Rose	1975		2.00	4.00
❏ 12234		Out Here on My Own/Take Off Your Make-Up	1976		2.00	4.00

Anna

❏ 1125		Let's Talk It Over/Popeye *As "Lamont Anthony"*	1960	62.50	125.00	250.00
❏ 1125		Let's Talk It Over/Benny the Skinny Man *As "Lamont Anthony"*	1960	6.25	12.50	25.00

Checkmate

❏ 1001		Just to Be Loved/I Didn't Know *As "Lamont Anthony"*	1961	62.50	125.00	250.00

Columbia

❏ 02035		Cool Me Out/Starting Over (We've Made the Necessary Changes)	1981		2.00	4.00
❏ 02238		Too Little Too Long/Chained (To Your Love)	1981		2.00	4.00

M&M

❏ 502		Shout About It/(B-side unknown)	1982		2.50	5.00

Number	Title (A Side/B Side)	Year	VG	VG+	NM

Mel-O-Dy
| ❏ 102 | Dearest One/Fortune Teller Please Tell Me | 1962 | 25.00 | 50.00 | 100.00 |

Warner Bros.
| ❏ 8432 | Sight for Sore Eyes/Tear Down the Walls | 1977 | | 2.00 | 4.00 |
| ❏ 8792 | Boogie Business/True Love Is Bittersweet | 1979 | | 2.00 | 4.00 |

Dozy, Beaky, Mick & Tich - See "Dave Dee, Dozy, Beaky, Mick & Tich"

Drag Kings, The
United Artists
| ❏ 676 | Bearing Burners/Nitro | 1963 | 7.50 | 15.00 | 30.00 |

Dragons, The
(With Daryl Dragon, later of The Captain and Tennille)
Capitol
| ❏ 5278 | Elephant Stomp/Troll | 1964 | 5.00 | 10.00 | 20.00 |

Drake, Charlie
United Artists
❏ 398	My Boomerang Won't Come Back/She's My Girl	1961	7.50	15.00	30.00
	With A-side lyric "Practiced 'til I was black in the face."				
❏ 398	My Boomerang Won't Come Back/She's My Girl	1961	3.75	7.50	15.00
	With A-side lyric "Practiced 'til I was blue in the face."				
❏ 437	Tanglefoot/Drake's Progress	1962	3.00	6.00	12.00
❏ 477	Sweet Freddie Green/Zulu Drake	1962	3.00	6.00	12.00

Dramatics, The
ABC
❏ 12090	Mr. and Mrs. Jones/I Cried All the Way Home	1975		2.50	5.00
❏ 12125	(I'm Going By) The Stars in Your Eyes/ Trying to Get Over You	1975		2.50	5.00
❏ 12150	You're Fooling You/I'll Make It So Good	1975		2.50	5.00
❏ 12180	Treat Me Like a Man/I Was the Life of the Party	1976		2.50	5.00
❏ 12220	Finger Fever/Say the Word	1976		2.50	5.00
❏ 12235	Be My Girl/The Nicest Man Alive	1976		2.50	5.00
❏ 12258	I Can't Get Over You/ Sundown Is Coming (Hold Back the Night)	1977		2.50	5.00
❏ 12299	Shake It Well/That Heaven Kind of Feeling	1977		2.50	5.00
❏ 12331	Ocean of Thoughts and Dreams/Come Inside	1978		2.50	5.00
❏ 12372	Stop Your Weeping/California Sunrise	1978		2.50	5.00
❏ 12400	Do What You Want to Do/Jane	1978		2.50	5.00
❏ 12429	Why Do You Wanna Do Me Wrong/ Yo' Love (Can Only Bring Me Happiness)	1978		2.50	5.00
❏ 12460	I Just Wanna Dance with You/ I've Got a Schoolboy Crush on You	1979		2.50	5.00

Cadet
❏ 5704	Door to Your Heart/Choosing Up on You	1974		3.00	6.00
❏ 5706	Don't Make Me No Promises/Tune Up	1974		3.00	6.00
❏ 5710	Love Is Missing from Our Lives/I'm in Love	1975		3.00	6.00
	With the Dells				

Capitol
| ❏ B-5103 | Live It Up/She's My Kind of Girl | 1982 | | 2.00 | 4.00 |
| ❏ B-5140 | Treat Me Right/Night Life | 1982 | | 2.00 | 4.00 |

Crackerjack
| ❏ 4015 | Toy Soldier/Hello Summer | 1968 | 15.00 | 30.00 | 60.00 |

Fantasy
| ❏ 966 | Luv's Calling/Dream Lady | 1985 | | | 3.00 |
| ❏ 967 | One Love Ago/Dream Lady | 1986 | | | 3.00 |

Mainstream
| ❏ 5571 | No Rebate on Love/Feel It | 1976 | | 2.50 | 5.00 |

MCA
❏ 12460	I Just Wanna Dance with You/ I've Got a Schoolboy Crush on You	1979		2.00	4.00
❏ 41017	I Just Wanta Dance With You/ I've Got a Schoolboy Crush on You	1979		2.00	4.00
❏ 41056	That's My Favorite Song/Bottom Line Woman	1979		2.00	4.00
❏ 41178	Welcome Back Home/Marriage on Paper Only	1980		2.00	4.00
❏ 41241	Be With the One You Love/ If You Feel Like You Wanna Dance, Dance	1980		2.00	4.00
❏ 51004	Share Your Love with Me/Get It	1980		2.00	4.00
❏ 51041	(We Need More) Lovin' Time/ You're the Best Thing in My Life	1980		2.00	4.00

Sport
| ❏ 101 | All Because of You/If You Haven't Got Love | 1967 | 15.00 | 30.00 | 60.00 |

Volt
❏ 302	Bridge Over Troubled Water/(B-side unknown)	1989		2.00	4.00
❏ 4029	Since I've Been in Love/Your Love Was Strange	1969	2.00	4.00	8.00
❏ 4058	Whatcha See Is Whatcha Get/Thankful for Your Love	1971	2.00	4.00	8.00
❏ 4071	Get Up and Get Down/Fall in Love, Lady Love	1971	2.00	4.00	8.00
❏ 4075	In the Rain/Good Soul Music	1972	2.00	4.00	8.00
❏ 4082	Toast to the Fool/Your Love Was Strange	1972	2.00	4.00	8.00
❏ 4090	Hey You! Get Off My Mountain/The Devil Is Dope	1973	2.00	4.00	8.00
❏ 4099	Fell for You/Now You Got Me Loving You	1973	2.00	4.00	8.00

Number	Title (A Side/B Side)	Year	VG	VG+	NM
❑ 4105	And I Panicked/Beware of the Man	1974	2.00	4.00	8.00
❑ 4108	I Made Myself Lonely/Highway to Heaven	1974	2.00	4.00	8.00

Wingate

❑ 18	Somewhere/Bingo!	1966	12.50	25.00	50.00
	As "The Dynamics"				
❑ 22	Baby I Need You/Inky Dinky Wang Dang Doo	1966	12.50	25.00	50.00
	As "The Dynamics"				

Dream Girls, The
Big Top
Note: All the Big Top singles except 3059 are as "Bobbie Smith and the Dream Girls"

❑ 3059	Don't Break My Heart/I Could Write a Book	1960	5.00	10.00	20.00
❑ 3085	Wanted/Mr. Fine	1961	5.00	10.00	20.00
❑ 3100	Duchess of Earl/Mine All Mine	1962	5.00	10.00	20.00
❑ 3111	Here Comes Baby/I Got a Feeling My Love	1962	5.00	10.00	20.00
❑ 3129	Your Lovey Dovey Ways/Now He's Gone	1962	5.00	10.00	20.00

Cameo

❑ 165	Don't Break My Heart/Oh This Is Why	1959	6.25	12.50	25.00

Metro

❑ 20029	I'm in Love with You/Cryin' in the Night	1960	7.50	15.00	30.00
❑ 20034	Heartaches/Love Hen	1961	6.25	12.50	25.00

Dream Kings, The
Checker

❑ 858	M.T.Y.L.T.T./Oh What a Baby	1957	30.00	60.00	120.00

Dreamers, The
(Many different groups)
ABC-Paramount

❑ 9746	The Girl Down the Street/The Right Time for Love	1956	5.00	10.00	20.00

Aladdin

❑ 3303	My Plea/Charles My Darling	1955	37.50	75.00	150.00

Apt

❑ 25053	Mary's Little Lamb/I Sing the Song	1960	6.25	12.50	25.00

Blue Star

❑ 8001	I Really Love You/You Made Me Darling	1960	6.25	12.50	25.00

Cousins

❑ 1005	Because of You/Little Girl	1961	25.00	50.00	100.00

Event

❑ 4270	Rock 'N Roll Baby/Ding Dong	1958	7.50	15.00	30.00

Fairmount

❑ 612	Daydreamin' of You/The Promise	1963	5.00	10.00	20.00

Flip

❑ 319	Since You've Been Gone/Do Not Forget	1956	10.00	20.00	40.00
❑ 354	Since You've Been Gone/Do Not Forget	1961	5.00	10.00	20.00

Goldisc

❑ 3015	Teenage Vows of Love/Natalie	1961	7.50	15.00	30.00

Grand

❑ 131	Tears in My Eyes/535	1955	75.00	150.00	300.00

Guaranteed

❑ 219	Mary, Mary/Canadian Sunset	1961	3.75	7.50	15.00

Jubilee

❑ 5053	These Things I Miss/Can't Get You Off My Mind	1951	75.00	150.00	300.00

Manhattan

❑ 503	Lips Were Meant for Kissing/No Obligation	1956	25.00	50.00	100.00

May

❑ 133	Because of You/Little Girl	1963	10.00	20.00	40.00

Mercury

❑ 5843	I'm Gonna Hate Myself in the Morning/Ain't Gonna Worry No More	1952	37.50	75.00	150.00
❑ 70019	Please Don't Leave Me/Walkin' My Blues	1953	37.50	75.00	150.00

Nugget

❑ 1000	Don't Cry/It's Gonna Be Alright	1959	7.50	15.00	30.00

Rollin'

❑ 1001	No Man Is an Island/Melba	1954	81.25	162.50	325.00

United Artists

❑ 841	Henry, Henry, Henry/Love, Love, Love	1965	3.00	6.00	12.00

Dreamlovers, The
(These probably are all the same group)
Cameo

❑ 326	These Will Be the Good Old Days/Oh Baby Mine (I Get So Lonely)	1964	3.75	7.50	15.00

Casino

❑ 1308	Amazons and Coyotes/Together	1963	3.75	7.50	15.00

Columbia

❑ 42698	Sad, Sad Boy/If I Were a Magician	1963	5.00	10.00	20.00
❑ 42752	Sad, Sad Boy/Black Bottom	1963	3.00	6.00	12.00
❑ 42842	Pretty Little Girl/I'm Through with You	1963	12.50	25.00	50.00

Number		Title (A Side/B Side)	Year	VG	VG+	NM

End

❏ 1114		If I Should Lose You/I Miss You	1962	5.00	10.00	20.00

Heritage

❏ 102		When We Get Married/Just Because	1961	5.00	10.00	20.00
❏ 104		Welcome Home/Let Them Love (And Be Loved)	1961	3.75	7.50	15.00
❏ 107		Zoom, Zoom, Zoom/While We Were Dancing	1962	3.75	7.50	15.00

Len

❏ 1006		Take It from a Fool/For the First Time	1958	50.00	100.00	200.00

Mercury

❏ 72595		Bless Your Soul/Bad Time Make the Good Times	1966	2.50	5.00	10.00
❏ 72630		Calling Jo-Ann/You Gave Me Someone to Love	1966	2.50	5.00	10.00

Swan

❏ 4167		Amazons and Coyotes/Together	1963	5.00	10.00	20.00
		White label				
❏ 4167		Amazons and Coyotes/Together	1963	3.00	6.00	12.00
		Black label				

V-Tone

❏ 211		Annabelle Lee/Home Is Where the Heart Is	1960	5.00	10.00	20.00
❏ 229		May I Kiss the Bride/Time	1961	5.00	10.00	20.00

Warner Bros.

❏ 5619		You Gave Me Someone to Love/ Doin' Things Together with You	1965	6.25	12.50	25.00

Drifters, The

(See note after Atlantic 1187. Also see "King, Ben E."; "McPhatter, Clyde"; "Pinkney, Bill")

Atlantic

❏ 1006		Money Honey/The Way I Feel	1953	15.00	30.00	60.00
❏ 1019		Such a Night/Lucille	1954	12.50	25.00	50.00
❏ 1029		Honey Love/Warm Your Heart	1954	12.50	25.00	50.00
❏ 1043		Bip Bam/Someday You'll Want Me to Want You	1954	10.00	20.00	40.00
❏ 1048		White Christmas/The Bells of St. Mary's	1954	10.00	20.00	40.00
		Yellow label, no spinner (original)				
❏ 1048		White Christmas/The Bells of St. Mary's	1956	6.25	12.50	25.00
		Red label, no spinner				
❏ 1048		White Christmas/The Bells of St. Mary's	1962	2.00	4.00	8.00
		Red label with spinner				
❏ 1048		White Christmas/The Bells of St. Mary's	197?		2.50	5.00
		Glossy yellow label with spinner				
❏ 1055		What'Cha Gonna Do/Gone	1955	10.00	20.00	40.00
❏ 1078		Adorable/Steamboat	1955	10.00	20.00	40.00
❏ 1089		Ruby Baby/Your Promise to Be Mine	1956	7.50	15.00	30.00
❏ 1101		Soldier of Fortune/I Got to Get Myself a Woman	1956	7.50	15.00	30.00
❏ 1123		Fools Fall in Love/It Was a Tear	1957	7.50	15.00	30.00
❏ 1141		Hypnotized/Drifting Away from You	1957	7.50	15.00	30.00
❏ 1161		I Know/Yodee Yakee	1957	7.50	15.00	30.00
❏ 1187		Drip Drop/Moonlight Bay	1958	7.50	15.00	30.00

Last record by the "old" Drifters. Below are by a completely different group, although personnel changes resulted in at least one "old" Drifter (Johnny Moore) spending time with the "new" Drifters.

❏ 2025		There Goes My Baby/Oh My Love	1959	5.00	10.00	20.00
❏ 2040		Dance with Me/(If You Cry) True Love, True Love	1959	5.00	10.00	20.00
❏ 2050		This Magic Moment/Baltimore	1960	5.00	10.00	20.00
❏ 2062		Lonely Winds/Hey Senorita	1960	5.00	10.00	20.00
❏ 2071		Save the Last Dance for Me/Nobody But Me	1960	5.00	10.00	20.00
❏ 2087		I Count the Tears/Suddenly There's a Valley	1960	3.75	7.50	15.00
❏ 2096		Some Kind of Wonderful/Honey Bee	1961	3.75	7.50	15.00
❏ 2105		Please Stay/My Sweet Lovin'	1961	3.75	7.50	15.00
❏ 2117		Sweets for My Sweet/Loneliness or Happiness	1961	3.75	7.50	15.00
❏ 2127		Room Full of Tears/Somebody New Dancin' with You	1961	3.75	7.50	15.00
❏ 2134		When My Little Girl Is Smiling/Mexican Divorce	1962	3.75	7.50	15.00
❏ 2143		Stranger on the Shore/What to Do	1962	3.00	6.00	12.00
❏ 2151		Sometimes I Wonder/Jackpot	1962	3.00	6.00	12.00
❏ 2162		Up On the Roof/Another Night with the Boys	1962	3.00	6.00	12.00
❏ 2182		On Broadway/Let the Music Play	1963	3.00	6.00	12.00
❏ 2191		Rat Race/If You Don't Come Back	1963	3.00	6.00	12.00
❏ 2201		I'll Take You Home/I Feel Good All Over	1963	3.00	6.00	12.00
❏ 2216		Vaya Con Dios/In the Land of Make Believe	1964	3.00	6.00	12.00
❏ 2225		One Way Love/Didn't It	1964	3.00	6.00	12.00
❏ 2237		Under the Boardwalk/ I Don't Want to Go On Without You	1964	3.00	6.00	12.00
❏ 2253		I've Got Sand in My Shoes/He's Just a Playboy	1964	3.00	6.00	12.00
❏ 2260		Saturday Night at the Movies/Spanish Lace	1964	3.00	6.00	12.00
❏ 2260	PS	Saturday Night at the Movies/Spanish Lace	1964	6.25	12.50	25.00
❏ 2261		The Christmas Song/I Remember Christmas	1964	3.00	6.00	12.00
❏ 2268		At the Club/Answer the Phone	1965	2.50	5.00	10.00
❏ 2285		Come On Over to My Place/Chains of Love	1965	2.50	5.00	10.00
❏ 2292		Follow Me/The Outside World	1965	2.50	5.00	10.00
❏ 2298		I'll Take You Where the Music's Playing/ Far from the Maddening Crowd	1965	2.50	5.00	10.00
❏ 2310		Nylon Stockings/We Gotta Sing	1965	2.50	5.00	10.00
❏ 2325		Memories Are Made of This/My Islands in the Sun	1966	2.00	4.00	8.00
❏ 2336		Up in the Streets of Harlem/You Can't Love Them All	1966	2.00	4.00	8.00
❏ 2366		Aretha/Baby What I Mean	1966	2.00	4.00	8.00
❏ 2426		Up Jumped the Devil/Ain't It the Truth	1967	2.00	4.00	8.00
❏ 2471		I Need You Now/Still Burning in My Heart	1968	2.00	4.00	8.00
❏ 2624		Your Best Friend/Steal Away	1969	2.00	4.00	8.00

Number		Title (A Side/B Side)	Year	VG	VG+	NM
☐ 2746		You Got to Pay Your Dues/Black Silk	1970	2.50	5.00	10.00
☐ 2786		A Rose By Any Other Name/Be My Lady	1971	2.50	5.00	10.00
☐ 89189		Ruby Baby/Fever	1987		2.00	4.00
		B-side by Little Willie John				
☐ 89189	PS	Ruby Baby/Fever	1987		2.00	4.00
		From the movie "Big Town"				

Bell

☐ 45,320		You've Got Your Troubles/I'm Feelin' Sad	1973		2.50	5.00
☐ 45,387		The Songs We Used to Sing/Like Sister and Brother	1973		2.50	5.00
☐ 45,600		Kissin' in the Back Row of the Movies/I'm Feelin' Sad	1974		2.50	5.00

Capitol

See "Shadows, The"

Coral

☐ 65037		Wine Head Woman/I'm the Caring Kind	1950	75.00	150.00	300.00
☐ 65040		And I Shook/I Had to Find Out for Myself	1951	75.00	150.00	300.00

Crown

☐ 108		The World Is Changing/Sacroiliac Swing	1954	50.00	100.00	200.00

Musicor

☐ 1498		Midsummer Night in Harlem/Lonely Drifter, Don't Cry	1974		2.50	5.00
		As "Charlie Thomas and the Drifters"				

Rama

☐ 22		Besame Mucho/Summertime	1953	50.00	100.00	200.00

Steeltown

☐ 671		Peace of Mind/The Struggler	1973		2.50	5.00

Drivers, The

(At least two different groups)

Comet

☐ 2142		High Gear/Low Gear	1961	6.25	12.50	25.00

DeLuxe

☐ 6094		Women/Smooth, Slow and Easy	1956	25.00	50.00	100.00
☐ 6104		My Lonely Prayer/Midnight Hours	1957	50.00	100.00	200.00
☐ 6117		Dangerous Lips/Oh Miss Nellie	1957	20.00	40.00	80.00

King

☐ 5645		Mr. Astronaut/Dry Bones Twist	1962	3.00	6.00	12.00

Lin

☐ 1002		A Man's Glory/Teeter Totter	1954	50.00	100.00	200.00

RCA Victor

☐ 47-7023		Blue Moon/I Get Weak	1957	15.00	30.00	60.00

Du Droppers, The

Groove

☐ 0001		Speed King/Dead Broke	1954	20.00	40.00	80.00
☐ 0013		Just Whisper/How Much Longer	1954	25.00	50.00	100.00
☐ 0036		Boot 'Em Up/Let Nature Take Its Course	1955	12.50	25.00	50.00
☐ 0104		Talk That Talk/Give Me Some Consideration	1955	12.50	25.00	50.00
☐ 0120		I Wanna Love You/You're Mine Already	1955	12.50	25.00	50.00

RCA Victor

☐ 47-5229		I Wanna Know/Laughing Blues	1953	10.00	20.00	40.00
☐ 47-5321		I Found Out/Little Girl, Little Girl	1953	10.00	20.00	40.00
☐ 47-5425		Whatever You're Doin'/	1953	10.00	20.00	40.00
		Somebody Work on My Baby's Mind				
☐ 47-5504		Don't Pass Me By/Get Lost	1953	10.00	20.00	40.00
☐ 47-5543		The Note in the Bottle/Mama's Gone Goodbye	1953	10.00	20.00	40.00

Red Robin

☐ 108		Can't Do Sixty No More/	1952	37.50	75.00	150.00
		Chain Me Baby (Blues of Desire)				
		Black vinyl				
☐ 108		Can't Do Sixty No More/	1952	75.00	150.00	300.00
		Chain Me Baby (Blues of Desire)				
		Red vinyl				
☐ 116		Come On and Love Me Baby/Go Back	1953	37.50	75.00	150.00

Du'Ambra, Joey

ABC-Paramount

☐ 9917		Baby Sue/Come Back-A Little Mama	1958	7.50	15.00	30.00

Duals, The

Arc

☐ 4446		Nearest to My Heart/Bye Bye	1959	5.00	10.00	20.00

Fury

☐ 1013		Wait Up Baby/Forever and Ever	1958	10.00	20.00	40.00

Infinity

☐ 032		Oozy Groove/The Big Race	1964	6.25	12.50	25.00

Juggy

☐ 321		Oozy Groove/The Big Race	1964	12.50	25.00	50.00

Star Revue

☐ 1031		Stick Shift/Cruising	1961	200.00	400.00	800.00

Number	Title (A Side/B Side)	Year	VG	VG+	NM
Sue					
❑ 745	Stick Shift/Cruising	1961	7.50	15.00	30.00
❑ 758	Travelin' Guitar/Cha Cha Guitar	1962	6.25	12.50	25.00
United Artists					
❑ 0128	Stick Shift/Keem-O-Sabe	1973		2.00	4.00
	"Silver Spotlight Series" reissue; B-side by The Electric Indian				
Duane, Dick					
ABC-Paramount					
❑ 9656	Sobony/Now	1955	7.50	15.00	30.00
❑ 9677	To Make a Mistake/Blue Prelude	1956	7.50	15.00	30.00
❑ 9709	Fame and Fortune/Mean Don't Cry	1956	7.50	15.00	30.00
Dubs, The					
ABC-Paramount					
❑ 10056	No One/Early in the Evening	1959	6.25	12.50	25.00
❑ 10100	Don't Laugh at Me/You Never Belong to Me	1960	12.50	25.00	50.00
❑ 10150	For the First Time/Ain't That So	1960	6.25	12.50	25.00
❑ 10198	If I Only Had Magic/Joogie Boogie	1961	7.50	15.00	30.00
❑ 10269	Lullaby/Down, Down, Down I Go	1961	7.50	15.00	30.00
Clifton					
❑ 2	Where Do We Go from Here/I Only Have Eyes for You	1973		3.00	6.00
End					
❑ 1108	Now That We Broke Up/This to Me Is Love	1962	12.50	25.00	50.00
Gone					
❑ 5002	Don't Ask Me (To Be Lonely)/Darling	1957	25.00	50.00	100.00
	Black label, "shadow" logo				
❑ 5002	Don't Ask Me (To Be Lonely)/Darling	1957	15.00	30.00	60.00
	Black label, clown-face logo				
❑ 5002	Don't Ask Me (To Be Lonely)/Darling	1957	6.25	12.50	25.00
	Multicolor label				
❑ 5011	Could This Be Magic/Such Lovin'	1957	15.00	30.00	60.00
	Black label				
❑ 5011	Could This Be Magic/Such Lovin'	1957	6.25	12.50	25.00
	Multicolor label				
❑ 5020	Beside My Love/Gonna Make a Change	1957	15.00	30.00	60.00
❑ 5034	Song in My Heart/Be Sure (My Love)	1958	15.00	30.00	60.00
❑ 5046	Chapel of Dreams/Is There a Love for Me	1958	15.00	30.00	60.00
❑ 5069	Chapel of Dreams/Is There a Love for Me	1959	12.50	25.00	50.00
❑ 5138	You're Free to Go/Is There a Love for Me	1962	12.50	25.00	50.00
Johnson					
❑ 097	Connie/Home Under My Hat	1973		3.00	6.00
❑ 098	Somebody Goofed/	1973		3.00	6.00
	I Won't Have You Breaking My Heart				
❑ 102	Don't Ask Me (To Be Lonely)/Darling	1957	400.00	800.00	1,200
Josie					
❑ 911	Wisdom of a Fool/This I Swear	1963	5.00	10.00	20.00
Lana					
❑ 115	Could This Be Magic/Blue Velvet	1964	2.00	4.00	8.00
	A-side is an alternate take of the hit version				
❑ 116	Don't Ask Me (To Be Lonely)/Your Very First Love	1964	2.00	4.00	8.00
	A-side is an alternate take of the hit version				
Mark-X					
❑ 8008	Be Sure My Love/Song in My Heart	1960	5.00	10.00	20.00
Vickie					
❑ 229	I'm Downtown/Lost in the Wilderness	1971	2.50	5.00	10.00
	As "Richard Blandon and the Dubs"				
Wilshire					
❑ 201	Just You/Your Very First Love	1963	10.00	20.00	40.00
Dukays, The					
(Also see "Chandler, Gene")					
Nat					
❑ 4001	The Big Lie/The Girl's a Devil	1961	5.00	10.00	20.00
❑ 4002	Nite Owl/Festival of Love	1961	5.00	10.00	20.00
Vee Jay					
❑ 430	Nite Owl/Festival of Love	1962	3.75	7.50	15.00
❑ 442	I'm Gonna Love You So/Please Help	1962	3.75	7.50	15.00
❑ 460	I Feel Good All Over/I Never Knew	1962	3.75	7.50	15.00
❑ 491	Combination/Every Step	1963	3.75	7.50	15.00
Duke of Earl, The - See "Chandler, Gene"					
Duponts, The					
(Little Anthony was lead singer before he joined the Imperials. The Duponts are not the Imperials.)					
Roulette					
❑ 4060	Half Past Nothing/A Screamin' Ball (At Dracula Hall)	1958	6.25	12.50	25.00
Royal Roost					
❑ 627	Somebody/Prove It Tonight	1957	12.50	25.00	50.00

Number		Title (A Side/B Side)	Year	VG	VG+	NM
Savoy						
❑ 1552		Must Be Falling in Love/You	1958	6.25	12.50	25.00
		As "Little Anthony Guardine and the Duponts"				
Winley						
❑ 212		Must Be Falling in Love/You	1957	20.00	40.00	80.00
Dupree, Dave						
(Later known as Dave Burgess of the Champs)						
Challenge						
❑ 1001		Don't Cry, For You I Love/Fire in the Eyes	1957	6.25	12.50	25.00
❑ 1002		Flame of Love/Well, It Isn't Fair	1957	6.25	12.50	25.00
❑ 1005		A Job Well Done/Our Tomorrow	1957	6.25	12.50	25.00
Duprees, The						
Coed						
❑ 569		You Belong to Me/Take Me As I Am	1962	5.00	10.00	20.00
❑ 571		My Own True Love/Ginny	1962	5.00	10.00	20.00
❑ 574		I'd Rather Be Here in Your Arms/	1963	3.75	7.50	15.00
		I Wish You Could Believe Me				
❑ 576		Gone with the Wind/Let's Make Love Again	1963	3.75	7.50	15.00
❑ 580		I Gotta Tell Her Now/Take Me As I Am	1963	3.75	7.50	15.00
❑ 584		Why Don't You Believe Me/The Things I Love	1963	7.50	15.00	30.00
❑ 584		Why Don't You Believe Me/My Dearest One	1963	3.75	7.50	15.00
❑ 585		Have You Heard/Love Eyes	1963	3.75	7.50	15.00
❑ 587		(It's No) Sin/The Sand and the Sea	1964	3.75	7.50	15.00
❑ 591		Please Let Her Know/Where Are You	1964	3.75	7.50	15.00
❑ 593		Unbelievable/So Many Have Told Me	1964	3.75	7.50	15.00
❑ 595		So Little Time/It Isn't Fair	1964	3.75	7.50	15.00
❑ 596		I'm Yours/Wishing Ring	1964	3.75	7.50	15.00
Colossus						
Released as "The Italian Asphalt and Pavement Company" or "The I.A.P. Co." for short						
❑ 110		Check Yourself/The Sky's the Limit	1970		3.00	6.00
❑ 110	PS	Check Yourself/The Sky's the Limit	1970		3.00	6.00
Columbia						
❑ 43336		Around the Corner/They Said It Couldn't Be Done	1965	3.00	6.00	12.00
❑ 43464		Norma Jean/She Waits for Him	1965	3.00	6.00	12.00
❑ 43577		The Exodus Song/Let Them Talk	1966	3.00	6.00	12.00
❑ 43802		It's Not Time Now/Don't Want to Have to Do It	1966	2.50	5.00	10.00
❑ 44078		Be My Love/I Understand	1967	2.50	5.00	10.00
Heritage						
❑ 804		My Special Angel/Ring of Love	1968	2.50	5.00	10.00
❑ 805		Goodnight My Love/Ring of Love	1968	2.50	5.00	10.00
❑ 805	PS	Goodnight My Love/Ring of Love	1968	5.00	10.00	20.00
❑ 808		My Love, My Love/The Sky's the Limit	1968	2.50	5.00	10.00
❑ 808	PS	My Love, My Love/The Sky's the Limit	1968	5.00	10.00	20.00
❑ 811		Two Different Worlds/Hope	1969	2.50	5.00	10.00
❑ 811	PS	Two Different Worlds/Hope	1969	5.00	10.00	20.00
❑ 826		Have You Heard/My Love, My Love	1970	2.50	5.00	10.00
RCA Victor						
❑ PB-10407		The Sky's the Limit/Delicious	1975	2.50	5.00	10.00
Dusters, The						
ABC-Paramount						
❑ 9887		Pretty Girl/Coolation	1958	7.50	15.00	30.00
Arc						
❑ 3000		Give Me Time/Sallie Mae	1956	75.00	150.00	300.00
		Tommy Tucker was a member of the Arc group.				
Cupid						
❑ 5003		Rock at the Hop/(B-side unknown)	1958	17.50	35.00	70.00
Glory						
❑ 287		Darling Love/Teen-Age Jamboree	1958	12.50	25.00	50.00
Duvall, Huelyn						
Challenge						
❑ 1012		Teen Queen/Comin' or Goin'	1957	25.00	50.00	100.00
		Blue label				
❑ 1012		Teen Queen/Comin' or Goin'	1957	7.50	15.00	30.00
		Maroon label				
❑ 59002		Hum-Dinger/You Knock Me Out	1958	7.50	15.00	30.00
❑ 59014		Little Boy Blue/Three Months to Kill	1958	10.00	20.00	40.00
❑ 59025		Friday Night on a Dollar Bill/Juliette	1958	7.50	15.00	30.00
❑ 59069		Pucker Paint/Boom Boom Baby	1960	7.50	15.00	30.00
Dyke, Jerry						
Sun						
❑ 1109		Will the Circle Be Unbroken/A Little More, A Little Less	1970		2.50	5.00
❑ 1123		Come In Mr. Lonely/School Children	1971		2.50	5.00
Dylan, Bob						
Asylum						
❑ 11033		On a Night Like This/You Angel You	1974		3.00	6.00
❑ 11035		Something There Is About You/Going, Going, Gone	1974		3.00	6.00

Number		Title (A Side/B Side)	Year	VG	VG+	NM
❏ 11043		Most Likely You Go Your Way (And I'll Go Mine)/ Stage Fright	1974		3.00	6.00
		With The Band				
❏ 45212		All Along the Watchtower/It Ain't Me Babe	1974	3.00	6.00	12.00

Columbia

Number		Title (A Side/B Side)	Year	VG	VG+	NM
❏ 02510		Heart of Mine/The Groom's Still Waiting at the Altar	1981		2.00	4.00
❏ 02510	PS	Heart of Mine/The Groom's Still Waiting at the Altar	1981		2.50	5.00
❏ 04301		Sweetheart Like You/Union Sundown	1983		2.00	4.00
❏ 04301	PS	Sweetheart Like You/Union Sundown	1983		2.50	5.00
❏ 04425		Jokerman/Isis	1984		2.50	5.00
❏ 04933		Tight Connection to My Heart (Has Anybody Seen My Love)/We Better Talk This Over	1985		2.00	4.00
❏ 04933	PS	Tight Connection to My Heart (Has Anybody Seen My Love)/We Better Talk This Over	1985		2.00	4.00
❏ 05697		Emotionally Yours/ When the Night Comes Falling from the Sky	1985		2.00	4.00
❏ 07970		Silvio/Too Far from Home	1988		2.50	5.00
❏ 10106		Tangled Up in Blue/If You See Her Say Hello	1975		3.00	6.00
❏ 10217		Million Dollar Bash/Tears of Rage	1975	2.50	5.00	10.00
❏ 10245		Hurricane (Part 1)/Hurricane (Part 2)	1975		3.00	6.00
❏ 10245	PS	Hurricane (Part 1)/Hurricane (Part 2)	1975	3.00	6.00	12.00
❏ 10245	DJ	Hurricane (mono/stereo)	1975	5.00	10.00	20.00
		Plays at 33 1/3 rpm; does not have "Special Rush Reservice" on label				
❏ 10245	DJ	Hurricane (mono/stereo)	1975	3.75	7.50	15.00
		Plays at 33 1/3 rpm; has "Special Rush Reservice" on label				
❏ 10245	PS	Hurricane (mono/stereo)	1975	3.75	7.50	15.00
		Special sleeve for above record				
❏ 10298		Mozambique/Oh, Sister	1976		3.00	6.00
❏ 10454		Stuck Inside of Mobile with the Memphis Blues Again/ Rita Mae	1976		2.50	5.00
❏ 10454	PS	Stuck Inside of Mobile with the Memphis Blues Again/ Rita Mae	1976		3.00	6.00
❏ 10805		Baby Stop Crying/New Pony	1978		2.50	5.00
❏ 10851		Changing of the Guards/ Senor (Tales of Yankee Power)	1978		2.00	4.00
❏ 11072		Gotta Serve Somebody/Trouble in Mind	1979		2.00	4.00
❏ 11168		Man Gave Names to All the Animals/ When You Gonna Wake Up	1979		2.00	4.00
❏ 11235		Slow Train/Do Right to Me Baby (Do Unto Others)	1980		2.00	4.00
❏ 11235	PS	Slow Train/Do Right to Me Baby (Do Unto Others)	1980		2.50	5.00
❏ 11318		Solid Rock/Covenant Woman	1980		2.00	4.00
❏ 11370		Saved/Are You Ready	1980	6.25	12.50	25.00
		Scarce on stock copy (promos worth about 20%)				
❏ 42656		Mixed-Up Confusion/Corrine, Corrina	1962	500.00	750.00	1,000
❏ 42856		Blowin' in the Wind/Don't Think Twice, It's All Right	1963	125.00	250.00	500.00
❏ 42856	DJ	Blowin' in the Wind/Don't Think Twice, It's All Right	1963	100.00	200.00	400.00
		Regular promo				
❏ 42856	PS	Blowin' in the Wind/Don't Think Twice, It's All Right	1963	200.00	400.00	800.00
		"Rebel with a Cause" promotional flyer				
❏ 43242		Subterranean Homesick Blues/She Belongs to Me	1965	3.00	6.00	12.00
❏ 43242	DJ	Subterranean Homesick Blues (same on both sides)	1965	50.00	100.00	200.00
		Promo only on red vinyl				
❏ 43242	PS	Subterranean Homesick Blues/She Belongs to Me	1965	500.00	750.00	1,000
		Only issued with some promos				
❏ 43242		Subterranean Homesick Blues/She Belongs to Me	1972	7.50	15.00	30.00
		Briefly issued on gray label, which was used for about six months in 1972				
❏ 43346		Like a Rolling Stone/Gates of Eden	1965	3.00	6.00	12.00
❏ 43346	DJ	Like a Rolling Stone (same on both sides)	1965	37.50	75.00	150.00
		Promo only on red vinyl				
❏ 43389		Positively 4th Street/From a Buick 6	1965	3.00	6.00	12.00
		Standard version				
❏ 43389		Positively 4th Street/From a Buick 6	1965	50.00	100.00	200.00
		A-side contains alternate version of "Can You Please Crawl Out Your Window." Evidently must be heard to identify.				
❏ 43389	DJ	Positively 4th Street/From a Buick 6	1965	30.00	60.00	120.00
		A-side contains alternate version of "Can You Please Crawl Out Your Window." Evidently must be heard to identify.				
❏ 43389	DJ	Positively 4th Street (same on both sides)	1965	37.50	75.00	150.00
		Promo only on red vinyl				
❏ 43389	PS	Positively 4th Street/From a Buick 6	1965	12.50	25.00	50.00
❏ 43389		Positively 4th Street/From a Buick 6	1972	5.00	10.00	20.00
		Briefly issued on gray label, which was used for about six months in 1972				
❏ 43477		Can You Please Crawl Out Your Window?/ Highway 61 Revisited	1965	3.75	7.50	15.00
❏ 43541		Queen Jane Approximately/ One of Us Must Know (Sooner or Later)	1966	3.75	7.50	15.00
❏ 43592		Rainy Day Women #12 and 35/Pledging My Time	1966	2.50	5.00	10.00
❏ 43592	DJ	Rainy Day Women #12 and 35 (same on both sides)	1966	37.50	75.00	150.00
		Promo only on red vinyl				
❏ 43683		I Want You/Just Like Tom Thumb's Blues (Live)	1966	2.50	5.00	10.00
❏ 43683	DJ	I Want You (same on both sides)	1966	37.50	75.00	150.00
		Promo only on red vinyl				
❏ 43683	PS	I Want You/Just Like Tom Thumb's Blues (Live)	1966	12.50	25.00	50.00
❏ 43792		Just Like a Woman/Obviously 5 Believers	1966	2.50	5.00	10.00

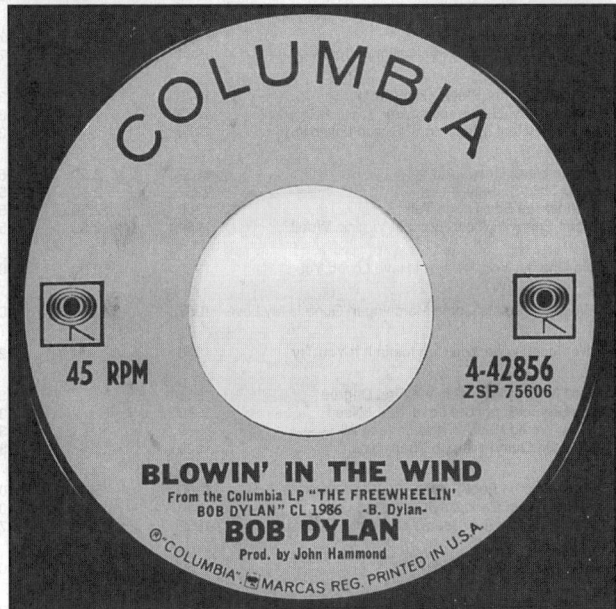

Bob Dylan, as one of the most important artists of the 1960s, remains collectible, and these are two of his most collectible. At top is his first single, "Mixed Up Confusion," a more rockin' sound than the folk-music albums he was releasing in 1962-63. Another attempt at a single, in the wake of Peter, Paul and Mary's success, was "Blowin' in the Wind." Both are three-figure items in almost any condition.

Number	Title (A Side/B Side)	Year	VG	VG+	NM
❏ 44069	Leopard-Skin Pill-Box Hat/ Most Likely You'll Go Your Way and I'll Go Mine	1967	5.00	10.00	20.00
❏ 44826	I Threw It All Away/Drifter's Escape	1969	2.00	4.00	8.00
❏ 44926	Lay Lady Lay/Peggy Day	1969	2.00	4.00	8.00
❏ 45004	Tonight I'll Be Staying Here with You/Country Pie	1969	2.50	5.00	10.00
❏ 45199	Wigwam/Copper Kettle (The Pale Moonlight)	1970		3.00	6.00
	Red label, "Columbia" repeated around outside of label				
❏ 45199	Wigwam/Copper Kettle (The Pale Moonlight)	1970		3.00	6.00
	Red label, black print				
❏ 45199	Wigwam/Copper Kettle (The Pale Moonlight)	1970		3.00	6.00
	Orange label with "Columbia" background print				
❏ 45409	Watching the River Flow/Spanish Is the Loving Tongue	1971		3.00	6.00
❏ 45516	George Jackson (Acoustic Version)/ George Jackson (Big Band Version)	1971	2.50	5.00	10.00
❏ 45913	Knockin' on Heaven's Door/Turkey Chase	1973		2.50	5.00
❏ 45982	A Fool Such As I/Lily of the West	1973		3.00	6.00
❏ 73042	Everything Is Broken/Dead Man, Dead Man	1989	2.00	4.00	8.00
❏ JZSP 75606	DJ Blowin' in the Wind/Don't Think Twice, It's All Right	1963	75.00	150.00	300.00
	"Special Album Excerpt" promo				
❏ JZSP 110939	DJ Like a Rolling Stone (Part 1)/ Like a Rolling Stone (Part 2)	1965	10.00	20.00	40.00

MCA

Number	Title (A Side/B Side)	Year	VG	VG+	NM
❏ 52811	Band of the Hand/Theme from Joe's Death	1986			3.00
	By "Bob Dylan and the Heartbreakers"				
❏ 52811	PS Band of the Hand/Theme from Joe's Death	1986			3.00

Dyna-Sores, The
Rendezvous

Number	Title (A Side/B Side)	Year	VG	VG+	NM
❏ 120	Alley-Oop/Jungle Walk	1960	6.25	12.50	25.00

Dynamics, The
(At least a dozen different groups)
Arc

Number	Title (A Side/B Side)	Year	VG	VG+	NM
❏ 4450	Enchanted Love/Happiness and Love	1959	7.50	15.00	30.00

Big Top

| ❏ 3161 | Misery/I'm the Man | 1963 | 3.75 | 7.50 | 15.00 |
| ❏ 516 | And That's a Natural Fact/I Wanna Know | 1964 | 3.75 | 7.50 | 15.00 |

Black Gold

❏ 8	What a Shame/(B-side unknown)	1973		3.00	6.00
❏ 9	Funkey Key/(B-side unknown)	1973		3.00	6.00
❏ 11	She's for Real (Bless You)/(B-side unknown)	1974		3.00	6.00

Bolo

❏ 730	At the Mardi Gras/J.A.J.	1962	2.50	5.00	10.00
❏ 735	Wild Child/Spongy	1962	2.50	5.00	10.00
❏ 740	Tennessee Boy/Tough Talk	1963	2.50	5.00	10.00
❏ 751	Knee Poppin'/Who's Afraid of Virginia Woolf?	1964	2.50	5.00	10.00

Capri

| ❏ 104 | No One but You/Always, I Have Loved You | 1959 | 50.00 | 100.00 | 200.00 |

Cindy

| ❏ 3005 | When the Saints Come Marching In/Gone Is My Love | 1957 | 20.00 | 40.00 | 80.00 |

Columbia

| ❏ 10666 | We Found Love/You Can Make It If You Try | 1978 | | 2.50 | 5.00 |

Cotillion

❏ 44004	Ain't No Sun/Murder in the First Degree	1968		3.00	6.00
❏ 44021	Ice Cream Song/The Love That I Need	1969		3.00	6.00
❏ 44038	What Would I Do/Ain't No Love at All	1969		3.00	6.00
❏ 44045	Dum-De-Dum/I Want to Thank You	1969		3.00	6.00

Decca

❏ 31046	How Should I Feel/Seems Like Only Yesterday	1960	5.00	10.00	20.00
❏ 31129	At the End of Each Day/Girl by the Gate	1960	5.00	10.00	20.00
❏ 31450	How Should I Feel/Seems Like Only Yesterday	1962	3.75	7.50	15.00

Delta

| ❏ 1002 | Blue Moon/Pigeon-Toed | 1959 | 5.00 | 10.00 | 20.00 |

Do-Kay-Lo

| ❏ 101 | I Guess You Don't Love Me (No More)/
Oh Night of Nights | 1963 | 6.25 | 12.50 | 25.00 |

Douglas

| ❏ 200 | I Love to Be Loved/You Don't Seem to Realize | 1961 | 7.50 | 15.00 | 30.00 |

Dynamic

❏ 109	Don't Be Late/Eenie Meenie	1959	6.25	12.50	25.00
❏ 504	The Girl I Met Last Night/Nobody's Going Out with Me	1959	6.25	12.50	25.00
❏ 1001	Don't Leave Me/Wasted	1959	6.25	12.50	25.00
❏ 1002	So Fine/Delsinia	1963	6.25	12.50	25.00
❏ 1008	If She Should Call/Dream Girl	1961	6.25	12.50	25.00
❏ 578/9	Christmas Plea/Dream Girl	1962	12.50	25.00	50.00

Farrall

| ❏ 964 | Later On/Departure | 196? | 7.50 | 15.00 | 30.00 |

Number	Title (A Side/B Side)	Year	VG	VG+	NM
Guaranteed					
❏ 201	Aces Up/Baby	1959	3.75	7.50	15.00
Herald					
❏ 569	Forever/Betty My Own	1962	125.00	250.00	500.00
	Later known as Anthony and the Sophomores				
Impala					
❏ 501	Moonlight/Someone	1959	12.50	25.00	50.00
Jerden					
❏ 800	I'll Be Standing There/All She Said	1966	2.50	5.00	10.00
Lavere					
❏ 186	Wrap Your Troubles in Dreams/ I Can't Give You Anything But Love	1961	6.25	12.50	25.00
Liban					
❏ 1006	If I Give My Heart to You/Blind Date	1962	10.00	20.00	40.00
Liberty					
❏ 55628	Chapel on a Hill/Conquistador	1963	10.00	20.00	40.00
Panorama					
❏ 51	Stop and Take a Look Around/(B-side unknown)	1967	2.50	5.00	10.00
Penguin					
❏ 1006	Baby/Aces Up	1959	7.50	15.00	30.00
RCA Victor					
❏ 47-9084	Love Me/I Need Your Love	1967	7.50	15.00	30.00
❏ 47-9278	Lights Out/You Make Me Feel So Good	1967	12.50	25.00	50.00
	As "Zerben R. Hicks and the Dynamics"				
Reprise					
❏ 20,183	So Fine/Delsinia	1963	3.75	7.50	15.00
Seafair					
❏ 100	Onion Salad/Lonesome Llama	1960	5.00	10.00	20.00
❏ 107	At the Mardi Gras/J.A.J.	1961	5.00	10.00	20.00
Seeco					
❏ 6008	Moonlight/Someone	1959	6.25	12.50	25.00
Top Ten					
❏ 100	Yes I Love You Baby/Soul Sloopy	1965	20.00	40.00	80.00
❏ 927	Love to a Guy/Whenever I'm Without You	196?	15.00	30.00	60.00
U.S.A.					
❏ 769	Summertime in the U.S.A./Coast to Coast	1964	6.25	12.50	25.00
Warner					
❏ 1016	A Hundred Million Lies/Ka Joom	1957	20.00	40.00	80.00
Wingate					
See "Dramatics, The"					

Dynamo, Skinny
Excello

❏ 2097	So Long, So Long/Jingle Bell	1956	7.50	15.00	30.00

E

Earls, Jack, and the Jimbos
Sun

❏ 240	Slow Down/A Fool for Loving You	1956	12.50	25.00	50.00

Earls, The
(All the same group or closely related)
ABC

Number	Title	Year	VG	VG+	NM
❏ 11109	It's Been a Long Time Coming/ My Lonely, Lonely Room	1968	3.75	7.50	15.00
Barry					
❏ 1021	I Believe/Don't Forget	1963	10.00	20.00	40.00
Clifton					
❏ 39	Lookin' for My Baby/Cross My Heart	1974		2.50	5.00
❏ 43	Lost Love/My Heart's Desire	1974		2.50	5.00
❏ 47	Dreams Come True/My Heart's Desire	1974		2.50	5.00
Columbia					
❏ 10225	Goin' Uptown/Mrs. Woman	1975	2.00	4.00	8.00
Gem					
❏ 221	Believe Me My Love/Spinnin'	1954	100.00	200.00	400.00
❏ 227	My Marie/Out of This World	197?	2.00	4.00	8.00
Gone					
❏ 5117	I'll Never Cry/My Heart's Desire	1961	12.50	52.00	50.00
Harvey					
❏ 100	A Sunday Kind of Love/Teenage Dreams	1975		3.00	6.00
Mr. G					
❏ 801	If I Could Do It Over Again/Papa	1967	3.75	7.50	15.00
Old Town					
❏ 1130	Remember Then/Let's Waddle	1963	7.50	15.00	30.00
	Blue label				

Number		Title (A Side/B Side)	Year	VG	VG+	NM
❏ 1130		Remember Then/Let's Waddle	1963	5.00	10.00	20.00
		Mostly black label with moon				
❏ 1133		Never/I Keep a-Telling You	1963	6.25	12.50	25.00
		Blue label				
❏ 1133		Never/I Keep a-Telling You	1963	4.00	8.00	16.00
		Mostly black label with moon				
❏ 1141		Eyes/Look My Way	1963	5.00	10.00	20.00
❏ 1145		Cry, Cry, Cry/Kissin'	1963	5.00	10.00	20.00
❏ 1149		I Believe/Don't Forget	1963	6.25	12.50	25.00
		Blue label				
❏ 1149		I Believe/Don't Forget	1963	4.00	8.00	16.00
		Mostly black label with moon				
❏ 1169		Oh What a Time/Ask Anybody	1964	7.50	15.00	30.00
❏ 1181	DJ	Remember Me Baby/Amor	1965	12.50	25.00	50.00
		Assigned 1181 in error; another record had been released with the number				
❏ 1182		Remember Me Baby/Amor	1965	5.00	10.00	20.00
		Error was corrected on stock copies				

Power Martin
❏ 1005		Stormy Weather/Could This Be Magic	1975		2.50	5.00
		B-side by the Pretenders				

Rome
❏ 101		Life Is But a Dream/It's You	1961	25.00	50.00	100.00
❏ 101		Life Is But a Dream/Without You	1961	7.50	15.00	30.00
❏ 102		Lookin' for My Baby/Cross My Heart	1961	7.50	15.00	30.00
❏ 111		Stormy Weather/Could This Be Magic	1976		2.50	5.00
		B-side by the Pretenders				
❏ 112/3		Little Boy and Girl/Lost Love	1976		2.00	4.00
❏ 114/5		All Through Our Teens/Whoever You Are	1976		2.00	4.00
		Black vinyl				
❏ 114/5		All Through Our Teens/Whoever You Are	1976		2.00	4.00
		Colored vinyl				

Woodbury
❏ 101		Tonight (Could Be the Night)/Meditation	1977	2.00	4.00	8.00

Easybeats, The
(Members Harry Vanda and George Young later formed Flash & The Pan)

Ascot
❏ 2214		In My Book/Make You Feel Alright (Women)	1966	3.75	7.50	15.00
❏ 2214	PS	In My Book/Make You Feel Alright (Women)	1966	10.00	20.00	40.00

Rare Earth
❏ 5009		St. Louis/Can't Find Love	1969	3.75	7.50	15.00

United Artists
❏ 0114		Friday on My Mind/Gonna Have a Good Time	1973		2.00	4.00
		"Silver Spotlight Series" reissue				
❏ 50106		Friday on My Mind/Made My Bed; Gonna Lie in It	1966	3.75	7.50	15.00
❏ 50187		Pretty Girl/Heaven and Hell	1967	2.50	5.00	10.00
❏ 50206		Falling Off the Edge of the World/Remember Sam	1967	2.50	5.00	10.00
❏ 50289		Come In, You'll Get Pneumonia/Hello, How Are You	1968	2.50	5.00	10.00
❏ 50488		Gonna Have a Good Time/Lay Me Down and Die	1969	2.50	5.00	10.00

Ebb Tides, The - See "Nino and the Ebb Tides"

Echoes, The
(Several different groups)

Andex
❏ 22102		Time/Dee Dee Di Oh	1958	7.50	15.00	30.00
		This group later recorded as The Innocents				

Ascot
❏ 2188		I Love Candy/Paper Roses	1965	12.50	25.00	50.00

Columbia
❏ 41549		Bye-Bye My Baby/Do I Love You?	1960	3.75	7.50	15.00
❏ 45709		Loving and Losing/Ecstasy	1960	3.75	7.50	15.00

Combo
❏ 128		My Little Honey/Aye Senorita	1957	10.00	20.00	40.00

Dolton
❏ 18		Born to Be With You/My Guiding Light	1960	5.00	10.00	20.00

Felsted
❏ 8614		Angel of Love/Twistin' Town	1961	12.50	25.00	50.00

Gee
❏ 1028		Ding Dong/My Heart Beats for You	1957	15.00	30.00	60.00

Hi Tide
❏ 106		Angel of Love/Twistin' Town	1961	50.00	100.00	200.00
		Black vinyl				
❏ 106		Angel of Love/Twistin' Town	1961	100.00	200.00	400.00
		Colored vinyl				

Rockin'
❏ 523		All That Wine Is Gone/Please Say You're Mine	1953	100.00	200.00	400.00

Seg-Way
❏ 1002		Angel of My Heart/Gee Oh Gee	1962	10.00	20.00	40.00
❏ 103		Baby Blue/Boomerang	1961	6.25	12.50	25.00
❏ 106		Sad Eyes (Don't You Cry)/It's Raining	1961	6.25	12.50	25.00

Number		Title (A Side/B Side)	Year	VG	VG+	NM

Smash

❑ 1766		Bluebirds Over the Mountain/	1962	3.75	7.50	15.00
		A Chicken Ain't Nothin' But a Bird				
❑ 1807		Keep an Eye on Her/A Million Miles from Nowhere	1963	3.75	7.50	15.00
❑ 1850		Annabelle Lee/If Love Is	1963	3.75	7.50	15.00

Specialty

| ❑ 601 | | Over the Rainbow/Someone | 1957 | 7.50 | 15.00 | 30.00 |

SRG

| ❑ 101 | | Baby Blue/Boomerang | 1960 | 50.00 | 100.00 | 200.00 |

Swan

| ❑ 4013 | | Scratch My Back/The Little Green Man | 1959 | 3.00 | 6.00 | 12.00 |

Ecstasies, The

Amy

| ❑ 853 | | That Lucky Old Sun/Time for Love | 1962 | 12.50 | 25.00 | 50.00 |

Eddie and the Evergreens - See "Sha Na Na"

Eddie and the Showmen

Liberty

❑ 55566		Toes on the Nose/Border Town	1963	7.50	15.00	30.00
❑ 55608		Squad Car/Scratch	1963	7.50	15.00	30.00
❑ 55659		Movin'/Mr. Rebel	1963	7.50	15.00	30.00
❑ 55695		Far Away Places/Lanky Bones	1964	7.50	15.00	30.00
❑ 55720		We Are the Young/Young and Lonely	1964	7.50	15.00	30.00

Eddie and the Starlites

Scepter

❑ 1202		To Make a Long Story Short/Pretty Little Girl	1958	7.50	15.00	30.00
		Red label				
❑ 1202		To Make a Long Story Short/Pretty Little Girl	1958	15.00	30.00	60.00
		White label				

Eddy, Duane

Big Tree

| ❑ 157 | | Renegade/Nightly News | 1972 | 2.00 | 4.00 | 8.00 |

Capitol

| ❑ B-44018 | | Spies/Rockabilly Holiday | 1987 | | 2.50 | 5.00 |
| ❑ B-44018 | PS | Spies/Rockabilly Holiday | 1987 | | 2.50 | 5.00 |

Colpix

❑ 779		Trash/South Phoenix	1965	3.75	7.50	15.00
❑ 788		Don't Think Twice, It's All Right/	1965	3.75	7.50	15.00
		House of the Rising Sun				
❑ 788	PS	Don't Think Twice, It's All Right/	1965	12.50	25.00	50.00
		House of the Rising Sun				
❑ 795		El Rancho Grande/Poppa's Movin' On	1966	3.75	7.50	15.00

Congress

| ❑ 6010 | | Freight Train/Put a Little Love in Your Heart | 1970 | 3.75 | 7.50 | 15.00 |

Elektra

| ❑ 45359 | | You Are My Sunshine/From 8 to 7 | 1977 | | 2.50 | 5.00 |

Ford

| ❑ 500 | | Ramrod/Caravan | 1957 | 500.00 | 1,000 | 1,500 |
| | | As "Duane Eddy and His Rock-A-Billies" | | | | |

Gregmark

| ❑ 5 | | Caravan (Part 1)/Caravan (Part 2) | 1961 | 3.75 | 7.50 | 15.00 |
| | | Credited to Duane Eddy, but is actually Al Casey | | | | |

Jamie

❑ JLP-71	S	Lonesome Road/I Almost Lost My Mind	1960	6.25	12.50	25.00
❑ JLP-72	S	Loving You/Anything	1960	6.25	12.50	25.00
❑ JLP-73	S	Peter Gunn/Along the Navaho Trail	1960	6.25	12.50	25.00
❑ JLP-74	S	Hard Times/Along Came Linda	1960	6.25	12.50	25.00
❑ JLP-75	S	The Battle/You Are My Sunshine	1960	6.25	12.50	25.00
		The above five are 33 1/3 rpm singles with small holes				
❑ 1101		Moovin N' Groovin'/Up and Down	1958	12.50	25.00	50.00
		Originals have pink labels				
❑ 1101		Moovin N' Groovin'/Up and Down	1958	6.25	12.50	25.00
		All-yellow label, "Jamie" at top				
❑ 1104		Rebel-'Rouser/Stalkin'	1958	6.25	12.50	25.00
❑ 1109		Ramrod/The Walker	1958	6.25	12.50	25.00
❑ 1111		Cannonball/Mason Dixon Line	1958	5.00	10.00	20.00
❑ 1117	M	The Lonely One/Detour	1959	5.00	10.00	20.00
❑ 1117	S	The Lonely One/Detour	1959	12.50	25.00	50.00
❑ 1122		Yep!/Three-30-Blues	1959	5.00	10.00	20.00
❑ 1122	PS	Yep!/Three-30-Blues	1959	10.00	20.00	40.00
❑ 1126		Forty Miles of Bad Road/The Quiet Three	1959	5.00	10.00	20.00
❑ 1126	PS	Forty Miles of Bad Road/The Quiet Three	1959	10.00	20.00	40.00
❑ 1126	S	Forty Miles of Bad Road/The Quiet Three	1959	12.50	25.00	50.00
❑ 1130	M	Some Kind-a Earthquake/First Love, First Tears	1959	5.00	10.00	20.00
❑ 1130	PS	Some Kind-a Earthquake/First Love, First Tears	1959	10.00	20.00	40.00
❑ 1130	S	Some Kind-a Earthquake/First Love, First Tears	1959	12.50	25.00	50.00
❑ 1144		Bonnie Came Back/Lost Island	1959	5.00	10.00	20.00
❑ 1144	PS	Bonnie Came Back/Lost Island	1959	10.00	20.00	40.00
❑ 1151		Shazam!/The Secret Seven	1960	3.75	7.50	15.00

Number		Title (A Side/B Side)	Year	VG	VG+	NM
❑ 1151	PS	Shazam!/The Secret Seven	1960	7.50	15.00	30.00
❑ 1156		Because They're Young/Rebel Walk	1960	3.75	7.50	15.00
❑ 1156	PS	Because They're Young/Rebel Walk	1960	7.50	15.00	30.00
❑ 1163		Kommotion/Theme from Moon Children	1960	3.75	7.50	15.00
❑ 1163	PS	Kommotion/Theme from Moon Children	1960	7.50	15.00	30.00
❑ 1168		Peter Gunn/Along the Navaho Trail	1960	3.75	7.50	15.00
❑ 1168	PS	Peter Gunn/Along the Navaho Trail	1960	7.50	15.00	30.00
❑ 1175		"Pepe"/Lost Friend	1960	3.75	7.50	15.00
❑ 1175	PS	"Pepe"/Lost Friend	1960	10.00	20.00	40.00
		Red sleeve				
❑ 1175	PS	"Pepe"/Lost Friend	1960	7.50	15.00	30.00
		Yellow sleeve				
❑ 1183		Theme from Dixie/Gidget Goes Hawaiian	1961	3.75	7.50	15.00
❑ 1183	PS	Theme from Dixie/Gidget Goes Hawaiian	1961	7.50	15.00	30.00
❑ 1187		Ring of Fire/Bobbie	1961	3.75	7.50	15.00
❑ 1187	PS	Ring of Fire/Bobbie	1961	7.50	15.00	30.00
❑ 1195		Drivin' Home/Tammy	1961	3.75	7.50	15.00
❑ 1195	PS	Drivin' Home/Tammy	1961	7.50	15.00	30.00
❑ 1200		My Blue Heaven/Along Came Linda	1961	3.75	7.50	15.00
❑ 1200	PS	My Blue Heaven/Along Came Linda	1961	7.50	15.00	30.00
❑ 1206		The Avenger/Londonderry Air	1961	3.75	7.50	15.00
❑ 1209		The Battle/Trambone	1962	3.75	7.50	15.00
❑ 1224		Runaway Pony/Just Because	1962	3.75	7.50	15.00
❑ 1303		Rebel Rouser/Movin' N' Groovin'	1965	3.00	6.00	12.00

RCA Victor

❑ 47-7999		Deep in the Heart of Texas/Saints and Sinners	1962	3.00	6.00	12.00
❑ 47-7999	PS	Deep in the Heart of Texas/Saints and Sinners	1962	6.25	12.50	25.00
❑ 47-8047		The Ballad of Paladin/The Wild Westerner	1962	3.00	6.00	12.00
❑ 47-8047	PS	The Ballad of Paladin/The Wild Westerner	1962	6.25	12.50	25.00
❑ 47-8087		(Dance with the) Guitar Man/Stretchin' Out	1962	3.75	7.50	15.00
❑ 47-8087	PS	(Dance with the) Guitar Man/Stretchin' Out	1962	7.50	15.00	30.00
❑ 47-8131		Boss Guitar/Desert Rat	1963	3.00	6.00	12.00
❑ 47-8131	PS	Boss Guitar/Desert Rat	1963	6.25	12.50	25.00
❑ 47-8180		Lonely Boy, Lonely Guitar/Joshin'	1963	3.00	6.00	12.00
❑ 47-8180	PS	Lonely Boy, Lonely Guitar/Joshin'	1963	6.25	12.50	25.00
❑ 47-8214		Your Baby's Gone Surfin'/Shuckin'	1963	3.75	7.50	15.00
❑ 47-8214	PS	Your Baby's Gone Surfin'/Shuckin'	1963	7.50	15.00	30.00
❑ 47-8276		The Son of Rebel Rouser/The Story of Three Loves	1963	3.00	6.00	12.00
❑ 47-8276	PS	The Son of Rebel Rouser/The Story of Three Loves	1963	6.25	12.50	25.00
❑ 47-8335		Guitar Child/Jerky Jalopy	1964	3.00	6.00	12.00
❑ 47-8376		Water Skiing/Theme from A Summer Place	1964	3.00	6.00	12.00
❑ 47-8442		Guitar Star/The Iguana	1964	3.00	6.00	12.00
❑ 47-8507		Moonshot/Roughneck	1965	3.00	6.00	12.00

Reprise

❑ 0504		Daydream/This Guitar Was Made for Twangin'	1966	2.50	5.00	10.00
❑ 0557		Roarin'/Monsoon	1967	2.50	5.00	10.00
❑ 0622		Guitar on My Mind/Wicked Women from Wickenborg	1967	2.50	5.00	10.00
❑ 0662		There Is a Mountain/This Town	1968	2.50	5.00	10.00
❑ 0690		Niki-Hoeky/Velvet Nights	1968	2.50	5.00	10.00

Uni

❑ 55237		The Five-Seventeen/Something	1970	3.75	7.50	15.00

Edmunds, Dave

Capitol

❑ 7PRO-79973	DJ	Closer to the Flame (same on both sides)	1990	2.50	5.00	10.00

Columbia

❑ 02960		From Small Things (Big Things One Day Come)/ Warmed Over Kisses (Left Over Love)	1982		2.00	4.00
		A-side is a Bruce Springsteen composition.				
❑ 03428		Run Rudolph Run/Deep in the Heart of Texas	1982		2.00	4.00
❑ 03428	PS	Run Rudolph Run/Deep in the Heart of Texas	1982	2.00	4.00	8.00
❑ 03877		Slipping Away/Don't Call Me Tonight	1983			3.00
❑ 04080		Information/What Have I Got to Do to Win	1983			3.00
❑ 04585		Something About You/You Can't Get Enough	1984			3.00
❑ 04700		Breaking Out/How Could I Be So Wrong	1984			3.00
❑ 04762		High School Nights/Porky's Revenge	1985			2.50
❑ 04762	PS	High School Nights/Porky's Revenge	1985			2.50
❑ 04887		Queen of the Hop/I Don't Want to Do It	1985	5.00	10.00	20.00
		B-side by George Harrison, thus accounting for this 45's value				
❑ 04923		Do You Want to Dance/Don't Call Me Tonight	1985			3.00
❑ 05487		Run Rudolph Run/ From Small Things (Big Things One Day Come)	198?			3.00
		"Golden Oldies" reissue				
❑ 06599		The Wanderer/Information	1987			3.00
❑ 07040		Paralyzed/Here Comes the Weekend	1987			3.00

MAM

❑ 3601		I Hear You Knocking/Black Bill	1970	2.00	4.00	8.00
❑ 3608		I'm Coming Home/Country Roll	1971		3.00	6.00
❑ 3611		Blue Monday/I'll Get Along	1971		3.00	6.00

MCA

❑ 53256		Gonna Move/Red River Rock	1988			2.50
		B-side by Silicon Teens				
❑ 53256	PS	Gonna Move/Red River Rock	1988			2.50
		B-side by Silicon Teens				

Number		Title (A Side/B Side)	Year	VG	VG+	NM
RCA Victor						
☐ 74-0882		Baby I Love You/Maybe	1973		3.00	6.00
☐ LPBO-5000		Born to Be with You/Pick Axe Rag	1973		3.00	6.00
☐ PB-10118		Let It Be Me/Need a Shot of Rhythm and Blues	1974		2.50	5.00
Swan Song						
☐ 70113		I Knew the Bride/Little Darlin'	1978		2.00	4.00
☐ 70116		Get Out of Denver/Work Out Suits	1978		2.00	4.00
☐ 70118		Trouble Boys/What Looks Best on You	1978		2.00	4.00
☐ 71001		Girls Talk/Creature from the Black Lagoon	1979		2.50	5.00
☐ 71002		Crawling from the Wreckage/Queen of Hearts	1979		2.50	5.00
☐ 72000		Almost Saturday Night/You'll Never Get Me Up	1981			3.00
☐ 72000	PS	Almost Saturday Night/You'll Never Get Me Up	1981			3.00
☐ 72003		The Race Is On/Singin' the Blues	1981		2.50	5.00
		Backing group: Stray Cats				

Edmunds, Dave, and Nick Lowe

Number		Title (A Side/B Side)	Year	VG	VG+	NM
Columbia						
☐ AE7-1219	DJ	Nick Lowe and Dave Edmunds Sing The Everly Brothers	1980	2.50	5.00	10.00
		Bonus EP included in the Rockpile LP Seconds of Pleasure				

Edsels, The

Number		Title (A Side/B Side)	Year	VG	VG+	NM
Capitol						
☐ 4588		Bone Shaker Joe/My Jealous One	1961	5.00	10.00	20.00
☐ 4675		If Your Pillow Could Talk/Shake Shake Sherry	1961	5.00	10.00	20.00
☐ 4836		Shaddy Daddy Dip Dip/Don't You Feel	1962	5.00	10.00	20.00
Dot						
☐ 16311		My Whispering Heart/Could It Be	1962	6.25	12.50	25.00
Dub						
☐ 2843		Lama Rama Ding Dong/Bells	1958	15.00	30.00	60.00
		Originals have the wrong title and the same recording as on Twin 700				
☐ 2843		Rama Lama Ding Dong/Bells	1958	12.50	25.00	50.00
		Repress with corrected title and the same recording as on Twin 700				
☐ 2843		Rama Lama Ding Dong/Bells	197?		2.50	5.00
		Reproduction with an alternate take of the A-side; this has confused many collectors, who believe that the original Dub and Twin records are different.				
Ember						
☐ 1078		Three Precious Words/Let's Go	1961	6.25	12.50	25.00
Musictone						
☐ 1144		Rama Lama Ding Dong/Bells	1961	3.00	6.00	12.00
Roulette						
☐ 4151		Do You Love Me/Rink-a-Dink-a-Doo	1959	6.25	12.50	25.00
Tammy						
☐ 1010		What Brought Us Together/Don't Know What to Do	1960	12.50	25.00	50.00
☐ 1014		Three Precious Words/Let's Go	1960	12.50	25.00	50.00
☐ 1023		The Girl I Love/Got to Find Out About Love	1961	10.00	20.00	40.00
☐ 1027		Count the Tears/Twenty-Four Hours	1961	10.00	20.00	40.00
Twin						
☐ 700		Rama Lama Ding Dong/Bells	1961	6.25	12.50	25.00

Edwards, J.D.

Number		Title (A Side/B Side)	Year	VG	VG+	NM
Imperial						
☐ 5245		Crying/Hobo	1953	30.00	60.00	120.00

Edwards, Johnny, and the White Caps

Number		Title (A Side/B Side)	Year	VG	VG+	NM
Northland						
☐ 7002		Rock and Roll Saddle/Why'd You Leave Me	195?	50.00	100.00	200.00

Edwards, Tommy

Number		Title (A Side/B Side)	Year	VG	VG+	NM
MGM						
☐ 10884		Once There Lived a Fool/A Friend of Johnny's	1951	5.00	10.00	20.00
☐ 10921		Gypsy Heart/Operetta	1951	5.00	10.00	20.00
☐ 10973		I'll Never Know Why/A Beggar in Love	1951	5.00	10.00	20.00
☐ 10989		The Morning Side of the Mountain/For Instance	1951	6.25	12.50	25.00
☐ 11035		It's All in the Game/All Over Again	1951	6.25	12.50	25.00
☐ 11077		Solitaire/My Concerto	1951	5.00	10.00	20.00
☐ 11097		Christmas Is for Children/Kris Kringle	1951	5.00	10.00	20.00
☐ 11134		Please Mr. Sun/I May Live with You	1952	6.25	12.50	25.00
☐ 11170		Forgive Me/The Bridge	1952	5.00	10.00	20.00
☐ 11209		My Girl/Piano, Bass and Drums	1952	5.00	10.00	20.00
☐ 11268		Easy to Say/The Greatest Sinner of Them All	1952	5.00	10.00	20.00
☐ 11326		You Win Again/Sinner and Saint	1952	5.00	10.00	20.00
☐ 11395		(Now and Then, There's) A Fool Such As I/ I Can't Love Another	1953	5.00	10.00	20.00
☐ 11465		Au Revoir/I Lived When I Met You	1953	5.00	10.00	20.00
☐ 11485		Take These Chains from My Heart/Paging Mr. Jackson	1953	5.00	10.00	20.00
☐ 11541		Lover's Waltz/Baby, Baby, Baby	1953	5.00	10.00	20.00
☐ 11582		So Little Time/Blue Bird	1953	5.00	10.00	20.00
☐ 11604		That's All/Secret Love	1953	5.00	10.00	20.00
☐ 11624		Every Day Is Christmas/It's Christmas Once Again	1953	5.00	10.00	20.00
☐ 11668		There Was a Time/Wall of Ice	1954	5.00	10.00	20.00
☐ 11718		The Joker (In the Card Game of Life)/Within My Heart	1954	5.00	10.00	20.00
☐ 11763		Linger in My Arms/If You Would Love Me Again	1954	5.00	10.00	20.00
☐ 11821		You Walk By/I Have That Kind of Heart	1954	5.00	10.00	20.00
☐ 11932		Serenade to a Fool/It Could Have Been Me	1955	5.00	10.00	20.00

Number		Title (A Side/B Side)	Year	VG	VG+	NM
☐ 11993		Welcome to My Heart/	1955	5.00	10.00	20.00
		Spring Never Came Around This Year				
☐ 12054		Teardrop on a Rose/To Those Who Wait	1955	5.00	10.00	20.00
☐ 12095		Baby, Let Me Take You Dreaming/My Sweetheart	1955	5.00	10.00	20.00
☐ 12248		Love Is a Child/There Must Be a Way to Your Heart	1956	5.00	10.00	20.00
☐ 12342		The Day That I Lost You/My Ship	1956	5.00	10.00	20.00
☐ 12514		We're Not Children Anymore/Any Place, Any Time	1957	5.00	10.00	20.00
☐ 12688		It's All in the Game/Please Love Me Forever	1958	3.75	7.50	15.00
☐ 12722		Love Is All We Need/Mr. Music Man	1958	3.75	7.50	15.00
☐ 12757		Please Mr. Sun/The Morning Side of the Mountain	1959	3.75	7.50	15.00
☐ 12794		My Melancholy Baby/It's Only the Good Times	1959	3.75	7.50	15.00
☐ 12814		I've Been There/I Looked at Heaven	1959	3.75	7.50	15.00
☐ 12837		Honestly and Truly/(New In) The Ways of Love	1959	3.75	7.50	15.00
☐ 12871		Don't Fence Me In/I'm Building Castles Again	1960	3.00	6.00	12.00
☐ 12890		I Really Don't Want to Know/Unloved	1960	3.00	6.00	12.00
☐ 12890	PS	I Really Don't Want to Know/Unloved	1960	7.50	15.00	30.00
☐ 12916		It's Not the End of Everything/Blue Heartaches	1960	3.00	6.00	12.00
☐ 12959		Suzie Wong/As You Desire Me	1960	3.00	6.00	12.00
☐ 12981		Vaya Con Dios/One and Twenty	1961	3.00	6.00	12.00
☐ 13002		The Golden Chain/That's the Way with Love	1961	3.00	6.00	12.00
☐ 13032		I'm So Lonesome I Could Cry/My Heart Would Know	1961	3.00	6.00	12.00
☐ 13057		I'll Cry You Out of My Heart/Tables Are Turning	1962	3.00	6.00	12.00
☐ 13100		Please Don't Tell Me/Tonight I Won't Be There	1962	3.00	6.00	12.00
☐ 13128		May I/Sometimes You Win, Sometimes You Lose	1963	2.50	5.00	10.00
☐ 13172		Country Boy/Love Is Best of All	1963	2.50	5.00	10.00
☐ 13317		Take These Chains from My Heart/You WIn Again	1965	2.50	5.00	10.00

Musicor

☐ 1046		Left-Over Dreams/9 Chances Out of 10	1964	2.50	5.00	10.00
☐ 1159		I Must Be Doing Something Wrong/I Cried, I Cried	1966	2.50	5.00	10.00

Edwards, Vern
Probe

☐ 100		Cool Baby, Cool/Glenda	1959	50.00	100.00	200.00

El Dorados
Paula

☐ 347		Looking In from the Outside/	1971	2.50	5.00	10.00
		Since You Came Into My Life				
☐ 369		Loose Booty (Part 1)/Loose Booty (Part 2)	1971	2.50	5.00	10.00

Torrid

☐ 100		In Over My Head/You Make My Heart Sing	1970	3.75	7.50	15.00

Vee Jay

☐ 115		Baby I Need You/My Loving Baby	1954	100.00	200.00	400.00
		Red vinyl				
☐ 115		Baby I Need You/My Loving Baby	1954	20.00	40.00	80.00
☐ 118		Annie's Answer/Living with Vivian	1954	75.00	150.00	300.00
		Red vinyl				
☐ 118		Annie's Answer/Living with Vivian	1954	20.00	40.00	80.00
☐ 127		One More Chance/Little Miss Love	1954	50.00	100.00	200.00
☐ 147		At My Front Door/What's Buggin' You Baby	1955	12.50	25.00	50.00
☐ 165		I'll Be Forever Lovin' You/I Began to Realize	1955	10.00	20.00	40.00
☐ 180		Now That You've Gone/Rock 'N' Roll's for Me	1956	10.00	20.00	40.00
☐ 197		Fallen Tear/Chop Ling Soon	1956	12.50	25.00	50.00
☐ 211		Bim Bam Boom/There in the Night	1956	20.00	40.00	80.00
☐ 250		Tears on My Pillow/A Rose for My Darling	1957	7.50	15.00	30.00
☐ 263		Three Reasons Why/Boom Diddle Boom	1958	37.50	75.00	150.00
☐ 302		Oh What a Girl/The Lights Are Low	1958	37.50	75.00	150.00

El Rays, The - See "Dells, The"

Elbert, Donnie
All Platinum

☐ 2330		Where Did Our Love Go/That's If You Love Me	1971		3.00	6.00
☐ 2333		Sweet Baby/Can't Get Over Losing You	1971		3.00	6.00
☐ 2336		If I Can't Have You/Can't Get Over Losing You	1972		3.00	6.00
☐ 2337		Little Piece of Leather/Sweet Baby	1972		3.00	6.00
☐ 2338		That's If You Love Me/Can't Get Over Losing You	1972		3.00	6.00
☐ 2346		This Feeling of Losing You/	1973		3.00	6.00
		Can't Stand These Lonely Nights				
☐ 2351		Love Is Strange/(Instrumental)	1973		3.00	6.00
☐ 2367		What Do You Do/Will You Love Me Tomorrow	1974		2.50	5.00
☐ 2374		You Should Be Dancing/What Do You Do	1974		2.50	5.00

Atco

☐ 6550		Too Far Gone/In Between the Heartaches	1968	2.00	4.00	8.00

Avco

☐ 4587		I Can't Help Myself/Love Is Here and Now You're Gone	1972		3.00	6.00
☐ 4598		Ooh, Baby Baby/Tell Her for Me	1972		3.00	6.00

Cub

☐ 9125		Don't Cry My Love/Love Stew	1963	3.00	6.00	12.00

DeLuxe

☐ 6125		What Can I Do/Hear My Plea	1957	5.00	10.00	20.00
☐ 6143		Believe It or Not/Tell Me So	1957	5.00	10.00	20.00
☐ 6148		Leona/Have I Sinned	1957	5.00	10.00	20.00
☐ 6156		Wild Child/Let's Do the Stroll	1958	5.00	10.00	20.00
☐ 6161		My Confession of Love/Peek-a-Boo	1958	5.00	10.00	20.00

Number		Title (A Side/B Side)	Year	VG	VG+	NM
❏ 6168		I Want to Be Near You/Come On Sugar	1958	5.00	10.00	20.00
❏ 6175		Just a Little Bit of Lovin'/When You're Near Me	1958	5.00	10.00	20.00

Deram

| ❏ 7526 | | Without You/Baby Please Come Home | 1969 | 2.00 | 4.00 | 8.00 |

Parkway

| ❏ 844 | | Set My Heart at Ease/Baby Cares | 1962 | 3.75 | 7.50 | 15.00 |

Vee Jay

❏ 336		Hey Baby/Will You Ever Be Mine	1960	3.75	7.50	15.00
❏ 353		Baby Let Me Love You Tonight/Half as Old	1960	3.75	7.50	15.00
❏ 370		I've Loved You Baby/I Beg of You	1960	3.75	7.50	15.00

Electric Flag, The

Atlantic

| ❏ 3222 | | Sweet Soul Music/Every Now and Then | 1974 | | 2.00 | 4.00 |
| ❏ 3237 | | Doctor Oh Doctor/The Band Kept Playing | 1975 | | 2.00 | 4.00 |

Columbia

❏ 44307		Groovin' Is Easy/Over-Lovin' You	1967	2.00	4.00	8.00
❏ 44307	PS	Groovin' Is Easy/Over-Lovin' You	1967	3.75	7.50	15.00
❏ 44376		Soul Searchin'/Sunny	1967	2.00	4.00	8.00
❏ 44765		Soul Searchin'/Sunny	1969		3.00	6.00

Sidewalk

| ❏ 929 | | Green and Gold/Peter's Trip | 1967 | 3.75 | 7.50 | 15.00 |

Electric Light Orchestra

(Also see "Wood, Roy")

CBS Associated

❏ 05766		Calling America/Caught in a Trap	1986			3.00
❏ 05766	PS	Calling America/Caught in a Trap	1986			3.00
❏ 05892		So Serious/Endless Lies	1986			3.00
❏ 05892	PS	So Serious/Endless Lies	1986			3.00

Jet

❏ XW1099		Turn to Stone/Mister Kingdom	1977		2.00	4.00
❏ XW1099	PS	Turn to Stone/Mister Kingdom	1977	2.00	4.00	8.00
❏ XW1145		Sweet Talkin' Woman/Fire on High	1978		2.00	4.00
❏ XW1145		Sweet Talkin' Woman/Fire on High	1978		2.50	5.00
		Purple vinyl				
❏ XW1145	PS	Sweet Talkin' Woman/Fire on High	1978		2.50	5.00
❏ 02408		Hold On Tight/When Time Stood Still	1981		2.00	4.00
❏ 02559		Twilight/Julie Don't Live Here	1981		2.00	4.00
❏ 02693		Rain Is Falling/Another Heart Broke	1982		2.00	4.00
❏ 03086		Hold On Tight/Mr. Blue Sky	1982			3.00
		Reissue				
❏ 03694		Rock and Roll Is King/After All	1983		2.00	4.00
❏ 04130		Four Little Diamonds/Letter from Spain	1983		2.00	4.00
❏ 04208		Stranger/Train of Gold	1983		2.00	4.00
❏ 5050		Mr. Blue Sky/One Summer Dream	1978		2.00	4.00
❏ 5052		It's Over/The Whale	1978		2.00	4.00
❏ 5057		Shine a Little Love/Jungle	1979		2.00	4.00
❏ 5057	PS	Shine a Little Love/Jungle	1979	2.00	4.00	8.00
❏ 5060		Don't Bring Me Down/Dreaming of 4000	1979		2.00	4.00
❏ 5060	PS	Don't Bring Me Down/Dreaming of 4000	1979	25.00	50.00	100.00
		Indications are that this is one of the rarest 1970s picture sleeves				
❏ 5064		Confusion/Poker	1979		2.00	4.00
❏ 5067		Last Train to London/Down Home Town	1979		2.00	4.00

MCA

❏ 41246		I'm Alive/Drum Dreams	1980		2.00	4.00
❏ 41246	PS	I'm Alive/Drum Dreams	1980		2.50	5.00
❏ 41285		Xanadu/Whenever You're Away from Me	1980		2.00	4.00
		A-side: Olivia Newton-John/Electric Light Orchestra				
❏ 41289		All Over the World/Drum Dreams	1980		2.00	4.00
❏ 41289	PS	All Over the World/Drum Dreams	1980		2.50	5.00

United Artists

❏ XW173		Roll Over Beethoven/Queen of the Hours	1973		3.00	6.00
❏ XW337		Showdown/In Old England Town	1973		3.00	6.00
❏ XW405		Daybreaker/Ma-Ma-Ma-Belle	1974		3.00	6.00
❏ XW513		Roll Over Beethoven/Showdown	1974		2.00	4.00
		Reissue				
❏ XW573		Can't Get It Out of My Head/Illusions in G Major	1974		2.00	4.00
❏ XW573	PS	Can't Get It Out of My Head/Illusions in G Major	1974		3.00	6.00
❏ XW634		Boy Blue/Eldorado	1975		2.50	5.00
❏ XW729		Evil Woman/10538 Overture (Live)	1975		2.00	4.00
❏ XW770		Strange Magic/New World Rising	1976		2.00	4.00
❏ XW770	PS	Strange Magic/New World Rising	1976		3.00	6.00
❏ XW842		Showdown/Daybreaker (Live)	1976		2.50	5.00
❏ XW888		Livin' Thing/Ma-Ma-Ma-Belle	1976		2.00	4.00
❏ XW939		Do Ya/Nightrider	1977		2.00	4.00
❏ XW1000		Telephone Line/Poorboy (The Greenwood)	1977		2.50	5.00
		Green vinyl				
❏ XW1000		Telephone Line/Poorboy (The Greenwood)	1977		2.00	4.00
❏ XW1000	PS	Telephone Line/Poorboy (The Greenwood)	1977		2.50	5.00
		Picture sleeves were not issued with black vinyl versions				
❏ XW1176		Can't Get It Out of My Head/Strange Magic	1978		2.00	4.00
❏ XW1177		Evil Woman/Livin' Thing	1978		2.00	4.00
❏ XW1178		Do Ya/Nightrider	1978		2.00	4.00

Number		Title (A Side/B Side)	Year	VG	VG+	NM
☐ XW1179		Boy Blue/Telephone Line	1978		2.00	4.00
☐ XW1180		Ma-Ma-Ma-Belle/10538 Overture	1978		2.00	4.00
		1176 through 1180, all reissues, were available for a very short time just before ELO's rights transfered from UA to CBS.				
☐ 50914		10538 Overture/(Battle of) Marston Moor	1972	2.00	4.00	8.00

Electric Prunes, The
Reprise
☐ PRO-277	DJ	Sanctus/Credo	1968	12.50	25.00	50.00
☐ PRO-305	DJ	Help Us (Our Father, Our King)/The Adoration	1968	10.00	20.00	40.00
☐ 0473		Ain't It Hard/Little Olive	1966	10.00	20.00	40.00
☐ 0532		I Had Too Much to Dream (Last Night)/Lovin	1966	5.00	10.00	20.00
☐ 0564		Get Me to the World on Time/Are You Lovin' Me	1967	6.25	12.50	25.00
☐ 0594		Hideaway/Dr. Do-Good	1967	6.25	12.50	25.00
☐ 0607		The Great Banana Hoax/Wind-Up Toys	1967	6.25	12.50	25.00
☐ 0652		You Never Had It So Good/Everybody Knows You're Not in Love	1967	10.00	20.00	40.00
☐ 0704		I Had Too Much to Dream (Last Night)/Get Me to the World On Time	1968		2.50	5.00
		"Back to Back Hits" series -- originals have "W7" and "r:" logos				
☐ 0805		Hey, Mr. President/Flowing Smoothly	1969	6.25	12.50	25.00
☐ 0833		Violent Rose/Sell	1969	10.00	20.00	40.00
☐ 0858		Love Grows/Finders Keepers, Losers Weepers	1969	6.25	12.50	25.00

Elegants, The
ABC-Paramount
☐ 10219		I've Seen Everything/Tiny Cloud	1961	10.00	20.00	40.00

Apt
☐ 25005		Little Star/Getting Dizzy	1958	12.50	25.00	50.00
		All-black label				
☐ 25005		Little Star/Getting Dizzy	1958	7.50	15.00	30.00
		Black label with rainbow				
☐ 25017		Goodnight/Please Believe Me	1958	7.50	15.00	30.00
☐ 25029		Pay Day/True Love Affair	1959	7.50	15.00	30.00

Bangar
☐ 613		Minor Chaos/Lost Souls	1964	7.50	15.00	30.00

Bim Bam Boom
☐ 121		It's Just a Matter of Time/Lonesome Weekends	1974		3.00	6.00
		Colored vinyl				
☐ 121		It's Just a Matter of Time/Lonesome Weekends	1974		2.00	4.00
		Black vinyl				

Crystal Ball
☐ 139		Maybe/Woo Woo Train	197?		2.50	5.00

Hull
☐ 732		Little Boy Blue/Get Well Soon	1960	25.00	50.00	100.00

Laurie
☐ 3283		A Letter from Viet Nam/Barbara Beware	1965	7.50	15.00	30.00
☐ 3298		Wake Up/Bring Back Wendy	1965	12.50	25.00	50.00
☐ 3324		Belinda/Lazy Love	1965	6.25	12.50	25.00
		As "Vito and the Elegants"				

Photo
☐ 2662		Dressin' Up/A Dream Can Come True	1963	12.50	25.00	50.00
☐ 2662	PS	Dressin' Up/A Dream Can Come True	1963	25.00	50.00	100.00

United Artists
☐ 230		Speak Low/Let My Prayers Be With You	1960	10.00	20.00	40.00
☐ 295		Happiness/Spiritual	1961	12.50	25.00	50.00

Elephants Memory
Apple
☐ 1854		Liberation Special/Madness	1972	2.00	4.00	8.00
☐ 1854		Liberation Special/Power Boogie	1972	100.00	200.00	400.00
☐ 1854	PS	Liberation Special/Madness	1972	2.50	5.00	10.00

Atlantic
☐ 3257		Shakedown/Brother Can You Spare Me a Dime	1975		2.50	5.00

Buddah
☐ 98		Cross Roads of the Stepping Stones/Jungle Gym at the Zoo	1969	2.00	4.00	8.00

Metromedia
☐ 182		Mongoose/I Couldn't Dream	1970		3.00	6.00
☐ 182	PS	Mongoose/I Couldn't Dream	1970		3.00	6.00
☐ 210		Skyscraper Commando/Power	1971		3.00	6.00

RCA Victor
☐ APBO-0268		Rock and Roll Streaker/Angels Forever	1974		2.50	5.00

Elgins, The
(At least three different groups)
A.B.S.
☐ 113		Pretending/Lonesome	196?	25.00	50.00	100.00

Congress
☐ 214		The Times We've Wasted/Rita Mae	1964	5.00	10.00	20.00
☐ 225		Here in Your Arms/We're Gonna Have a Good Time	1964	10.00	20.00	40.00

Number		Title (A Side/B Side)	Year	VG	VG+	NM
Dot						
❑ 16563		Cheryl/Tell Gina	1963	15.00	30.00	60.00
Flip						
❑ 353		Uncle Sam's Man/Casey Cop	1961	7.50	15.00	30.00
Joed						
❑ 716		Once Upon a Time/The Huddle	1964	150.00	300.00	600.00
Lummtone						
❑ 109		A Winner Never Quits/Johnny I'm Sorry	1962	6.25	12.50	25.00
❑ 110		You Got Your Magnet on Me Baby/Johnny I'm Sorry	1962	6.25	12.50	25.00
❑ 112		Finally/I Lost My Love in the Big City	1963	6.25	12.50	25.00
❑ 113		Your Lovely Ways/Finding a Sweetheart	1963	6.25	12.50	25.00
MGM						
❑ 12670		A Picture of You/Mademoiselle	1958	15.00	30.00	60.00
Tamla						
❑ 54056		Request of a Fool/Your Baby's Back	1962	75.00	150.00	300.00
		As "The Downbeats"; with "Tamla" circling globe at top of label				
❑ 54056		Request of a Fool/Your Baby's Back	1962	7.50	15.00	30.00
		As "The Downbeats"; with "Tamla" in globe at top of label				
Titan						
❑ 1724		My Illness/Extra, Extra	1962	62.50	125.00	250.00
❑ 1724		My Illness/Heartache Heartbreak	1962	50.00	100.00	200.00
V.I.P.						
❑ 25029		Darling Baby/Put Yourself in My Place	1965	50.00	100.00	200.00
		First pressings credited "The Downbeats"				
❑ 25029		Darling Baby/Put Yourself in My Place	1965	5.00	10.00	20.00
❑ 25037		Heaven Must Have Sent You/Stay in My Lonely Arms	1965	5.00	10.00	20.00
❑ 25043		It's Been a Long, Long Time/I Understand My Man	1966	5.00	10.00	20.00
❑ 25065		Heaven Must Have Sent You/Stay in My Lonely Arms	1970	2.50	5.00	10.00
Valiant						
❑ 712		Street Scene/You Found Yourself Another Fool	1965	5.00	10.00	20.00

Elliott, Bill, and the Elastic Oz Band
(With John Lennon and Yoko Ono)

Number		Title (A Side/B Side)	Year	VG	VG+	NM
Apple						
❑ 1835		God Save Us/Do the Oz	1971	2.00	4.00	8.00
❑ 1835	PS	God Save Us/Do the Oz	1971	2.50	5.00	10.00
❑ P-1835	DJ	God Save Us/Do the Oz	1971	6.25	12.50	25.00
		Has black star on A-side and unsliced apple on both sides				

Ellis, Jimmy
(Also see "Orion")

Number		Title (A Side/B Side)	Year	VG	VG+	NM
Atlantic						
❑ 2572		I Don't Mind/Take the Lord With You	1968	2.00	4.00	8.00
Boblo						
❑ 526		Tupelo Woman/The Closer He Gets	1976		2.00	4.00
❑ 531		There You Go/Here Comes That Wonderful Feeling	1977		2.00	4.00
❑ 532		Movin' On/My Baby's Out of Sight	1977		2.00	4.00
❑ 536		I'm Not Trying to Be Like Elvis/ Games You've Been Playing	1978		2.00	4.00
❑ 536	PS	I'm Not Trying to Be Like Elvis/ Games You've Been Playing	1978	2.50	5.00	10.00
Dradco						
❑ 1892		Don't Count Your Chickens/Love Is But Love	1964	3.75	7.50	15.00
Goldband						
❑ 1191		Woman in the Picture/What Swinging Doors Did to Me	196?	2.50	5.00	10.00
MCA						
❑ 40060		There Ya Go/Here Comes That Feeling Again	1973		2.00	4.00
Sun						
❑ 1129		That's All Right/Blue Moon of Kentucky	1973		2.50	5.00
		Originals have no artist on label in an attempt to make people believe these were outtakes from Elvis Presley's Sun sessions.				
❑ 1129		That's All Right/Blue Moon of Kentucky	1973		2.00	4.00
		Second pressings credit Jimmy Ellis				
❑ 1131		I Use Her to Remind Me of You/Changing	1974		2.00	4.00
❑ 1136		D.O.A./Misty/That's All Right/Blue Moon of Kentucky	1977		2.00	4.00

Ellis, Shirley

Number		Title (A Side/B Side)	Year	VG	VG+	NM
Columbia						
❑ 43829		Truly, Truly, Truly/Birds, Bees, Cupids and Bows	1966	2.00	4.00	8.00
❑ 44021		Soul Time/Waitin'	1967	2.00	4.00	8.00
❑ 44137		Sugar Let's Shing-a-Ling/How Lonely Is Lonely	1967	2.00	4.00	8.00
Congress						
❑ 202		The Nitty Gritty/Give Me a List	1963	2.50	5.00	10.00
❑ 208		(That's) What the Nitty Gritty Is/Get Out	1964	2.50	5.00	10.00
❑ 210		Shy One/Takin' Care of Business	1964	2.50	5.00	10.00
❑ 221		Such a Night/Bring It On Home to Me	1964	2.50	5.00	10.00
❑ 230		The Name Game/Whisper to the Wind	1964	2.50	5.00	10.00
❑ 230	PS	The Name Game/Whisper to the Wind	1964	5.00	10.00	20.00
❑ 234		The Clapping Song (Clap Pat Clap Slap)/	1965	2.50	5.00	10.00
❑ 234	PS	The Clapping Song (Clap Pat Clap Slap)/ This Is Beautiful	1965	5.00	10.00	20.00

Number	Title (A Side/B Side)	Year	VG	VG+	NM
❑ 238	The Puzzle Song (A Puzzle in Song)/ I See It, I Like It, I Want It	1965	2.50	5.00	10.00
❑ 246	I Never Will Forget/I Told You So	1965	2.50	5.00	10.00
❑ 251	One Sour Note/You Better Be Good, World	1965	2.50	5.00	10.00
❑ 260	Ever See a Diver Kiss His Wife While the Bubbles Bounce About Above the Water/Stardust	1965	2.50	5.00	10.00

Emanons, The
ABC-Paramount
| ❑ 9913 | Dear One/We Teenagers (Know What We Want) | 1958 | 5.00 | 10.00 | 20.00 |

Winley
| ❑ 226 | Dear One/We Teenagers (Know What We Want) | 1958 | 10.00 | 20.00 | 40.00 |

Emerson, Billy
Chess
❑ 1711	Give Me a Little Love/Woodchuck	1959	5.00	10.00	20.00
❑ 1728	Holy Mackerel Baby/Believe Me	1959	5.00	10.00	20.00
❑ 1740	Uh Huh, My Baby/I'll Get to You	1959	5.00	10.00	20.00

Constellation
| ❑ 148 | Aunt Molly (Part 1)/Aunt Molly (Part 2) | 1965 | 3.75 | 7.50 | 15.00 |

Sun
❑ 195	No Teasin' Around/If Lovin' Is Believin'	1954	100.00	200.00	400.00
❑ 203	I'm Not Going Home/The Woodchuck	1954	200.00	400.00	600.00
❑ 214	Move, Baby, Move/When It Rains, It Pours	1955	12.50	25.00	50.00
❑ 219	Red Hot/No Greater Love	1955	18.75	37.50	75.00
❑ 233	Something for Nothing/Little Fine Healthy Thing	1956	12.50	25.00	50.00

Vee Jay
❑ 219	Every Woman I Know/Tomorrow Never Comes	1956	10.00	20.00	40.00
❑ 247	Somebody Show Me/The Pleasure Is All Mine	1957	10.00	20.00	40.00
❑ 261	You Never Miss the Water/Do Yourself a Favor Billy	1957	10.00	20.00	40.00

Emotions, The
(Male groups)
Brainstorm
| ❑ 125 | Can't Stand No More Heartaches/ You'd Better Get Used to It | 1968 | 2.00 | 4.00 | 8.00 |

Calla
| ❑ 122 | Baby I Need Your Lovin'/ She's My Baby (I Just Can't Let Her Go) | 1966 | 3.75 | 7.50 | 15.00 |

Card
| ❑ 600 | (By the Light of the) Silvery Moon/ Do You Love Me | 1962 | 37.50 | 75.00 | 150.00 |

Flip
| ❑ 356 | I Ran to You/Keep Lookin' Your Way | 1961 | 7.50 | 15.00 | 30.00 |

Fury
| ❑ 1010 | Candlelight/It's Love | 1958 | 10.00 | 20.00 | 40.00 |

Kapp
| ❑ 490 | Echo/Come Dance Baby | 1962 | 5.00 | 10.00 | 20.00 |
| ❑ 513 | L-O-V-E/A Million Reasons | 1963 | 5.00 | 10.00 | 20.00 |

Karate
| ❑ 506 | Hey Baby/I Wonder | 1964 | 5.00 | 10.00 | 20.00 |

Laurie
| ❑ 3167 | Fool's Paradise/Starlit Night | 1963 | 5.00 | 10.00 | 20.00 |

20th Fox
❑ 430	A Story Untold/One Life, One Love, One You	1963	3.75	7.50	15.00
❑ 452	Rainbow/Little Miss Blue	1963	3.75	7.50	15.00
❑ 478	Boomerang/I Love You Madly	1964	3.75	7.50	15.00
❑ 6623	Heart Strings/Every Time	1966	3.75	7.50	15.00

Vardan
| ❑ 201 | Love of a Girl/Do This for Me | 1965 | 5.00 | 10.00 | 20.00 |

Empires, The
(Several different groups)
Amp 3
| ❑ 132 | If I'm a Fool/Zippety Zip | 1957 | 25.00 | 50.00 | 100.00 |

Calico
| ❑ 121 | Definition of Love/Only in My Dreams | 1960 | 5.00 | 10.00 | 20.00 |

Candi
| ❑ 1026 | Love You So Bad/Come Back Girl | 1962 | 6.25 | 12.50 | 25.00 |
| ❑ 1033 | You're on Top, Girl/(B-side unknown) | 1963 | 6.25 | 12.50 | 25.00 |

Chavis
| ❑ 1026 | Love You So Bad/Come Back Girl | 1962 | 3.00 | 6.00 | 12.00 |

Colpix
| ❑ 680 | Everyone Knew But Me/Three Little Fishes | 1963 | 5.00 | 10.00 | 20.00 |

DCP
| ❑ 1116 | Have Mercy/Love Is Strange | 1964 | 3.00 | 6.00 | 12.00 |

Epic
| ❑ 9527 | A Time and a Place/Punch Your Nose | 1962 | 6.25 | 12.50 | 25.00 |

Featuring David Blatt, later Jay Black (of Jay and the Americans)

Number	Title (A Side/B Side)	Year	VG	VG+	NM

Harlem
| ❑ 2325 | Corn Whiskey/My Baby, My Baby | 1954 | 100.00 | 200.00 | 400.00 |
| ❑ 2333 | Magic Mirror/Make Me or Break Me | 1955 | 100.00 | 200.00 | 400.00 |

Lake
| ❑ 711 | Over the Summer Vacation/You're So Popular | 1961 | 3.75 | 7.50 | 15.00 |

Whirlin' Disc
| ❑ 104 | Linda/Whispering Heart | 1957 | 15.00 | 30.00 | 60.00 |

Wing
❑ 90023	I Want to Know/Shirley	1955	12.50	25.00	50.00
❑ 90050	By the Riverside/Tell Me Pretty Baby	1956	10.00	20.00	40.00
❑ 90080	Don't Touch My Gal/My First Discovery	1956	10.00	20.00	40.00

Enchanters, The
(More than one group)

Bald Eagle
| ❑ 3001 | Come On Baby, Let's Do the Stroll/Rock Around | 1958 | 7.50 | 15.00 | 30.00 |

Bamboo
| ❑ 513 | Touch of Love/Cafe Bohemian | 1961 | 6.25 | 12.50 | 25.00 |

Candelite
| ❑ 432 | Oh Rose Marie/Bewildered | 1964 | 2.50 | 5.00 | 10.00 |

Coral
❑ 61756	True Love Gone/Wait a Minute Baby	1956	6.25	12.50	25.00
❑ 61832	There Goes (A Pretty Girl)/Fan Me Baby	1957	12.50	25.00	50.00
	Full-length version of A-side; matrix number is "100,974"				
❑ 61832	There Goes (A Pretty Girl)/Fan Me Baby	1957	5.00	10.00	20.00
	Edited version of A-side; matrix number is "102,966"				
❑ 61916	Mambo Santa Mambo/Bottle Up and Go	1957	5.00	10.00	20.00
❑ 62373	True Love Gone/The Day	1963	5.00	10.00	20.00
❑ 65610	True Love Gone/Today Is Your Birthday	1963	2.50	5.00	10.00

Ep-Som
| ❑ 103 | I Need Your Love/Goddess of Love | 1962 | 75.00 | 150.00 | 300.00 |

J.J. & M.
| ❑ 1562 | Oh Rose Marie/Bewildered | 1962 | 37.50 | 75.00 | 150.00 |

Jubilee
| ❑ 5072 | Today Is Your Birthday/How Could You | 1952 | 62.50 | 125.00 | 250.00 |
| ❑ 5080 | I've Lost/Housewife Blues | 1952 | 50.00 | 100.00 | 200.00 |

Loma
❑ 2012	I Want to Be Loved/I Paid for the Party	1965	2.50	5.00	10.00
❑ 2035	You Were Meant to Be My Baby/	1966	2.50	5.00	10.00
	God Bless the Girl, and Me				
❑ 2054	We Got Love/I've Lost All Communications	1966	2.50	5.00	10.00

Mercer
| ❑ 992 | True Love Gone/Wait a Minute Baby | 1956 | 100.00 | 200.00 | 400.00 |

Musitron
| ❑ 1072 | I Lied to My Heart/Talk While You Walk | 1961 | 10.00 | 20.00 | 40.00 |

Orbit
| ❑ 532 | Touch of Love/Cafe Bohemian | 1959 | 12.50 | 25.00 | 50.00 |

Sharp
| ❑ 105 | We Make Mistakes/The Decision | 1960 | 6.25 | 12.50 | 25.00 |

Stardust
| ❑ 102 | Spellbound by the Moon/Know It All | 1956 | 125.00 | 250.00 | 500.00 |

Tom Tom
| ❑ 301 | Surf Blast/Tom Tiki | 1963 | 15.00 | 30.00 | 60.00 |

Warner Bros.
| ❑ 5460 | I Wanna Thank You/I'm a Good Man | 1964 | 3.00 | 6.00 | 12.00 |

Enchords, The

Laurie
| ❑ 3089 | Zoom Zoom Zoom/I Need You Baby | 1961 | 12.50 | 25.00 | 50.00 |

Enemys, The
(With Cory Wells, later of Three Dog Night)

MGM
❑ 13485	Glitter and Gold/Too Much Monkey Business	1966	3.75	7.50	15.00
❑ 13525	Hey Joe/My Dues Have Been Paid	1966	3.75	7.50	15.00
❑ 13573	Mo-Jo Woman/My Dues Have Been Paid	1966	3.75	7.50	15.00

Valiant
| ❑ 714 | Say Goodbye to Donna/Sinner Man | 1965 | 6.25 | 12.50 | 25.00 |
| | *As "Corey Wells and the Enemys"* | | | | |

Engel, Scott
(Later one of the Walker Brothers)

Challenge
| ❑ 9206 | Devil Surfer/Your Guess | 1963 | 5.00 | 10.00 | 20.00 |

Liberty
| ❑ 55312 | Mr. Jones/Anything Will Do | 1961 | 5.00 | 10.00 | 20.00 |
| ❑ 55428 | Anything Will Do/Forever More | 1962 | 5.00 | 10.00 | 20.00 |

Martay
| ❑ 2004 | Devil Surfer/Your Guess | 1963 | 10.00 | 20.00 | 40.00 |

Number		Title (A Side/B Side)	Year	VG	VG+	NM

Orbit
☐ 506		The Livin' End/Good for Nothin'	1958	5.00	10.00	20.00
☐ 506	PS	The Livin' End/Good for Nothin'	1958	12.50	25.00	50.00
☐ 511		Charley Bop/All I Do Is Dream	1958	7.50	15.00	30.00
☐ 511	PS	Charley Bop/All I Do Is Dream	1958	15.00	30.00	60.00
☐ 512		Blue Bell/Paper Doll	1958	5.00	10.00	20.00
☐ 512	PS	Blue Bell/Paper Doll	1958	12.50	25.00	50.00
☐ 537		Golden Rule of Love/Sunday	1959	5.00	10.00	20.00
☐ 537	PS	Golden Rule of Love/Sunday	1959	12.50	25.00	50.00
☐ 545		Comin' Home/I Don't Wanna Know	1959	5.00	10.00	20.00

RKO Unique
| ☐ 386 | | Steady As a Rock/When Is a Boy a Man | 1957 | 6.25 | 12.50 | 25.00 |

Engler, Jerry, and the Four Ekkos
Brunswick
| ☐ 55037 | | Sputnik (Satellite Girl)/Unfaithful One | 1957 | 12.50 | 25.00 | 50.00 |
| | | *Buddy Holly may appear on this record* | | | | |

English, Barbara
Alithia
All on Alithia as "Barbara Jean English"
☐ 6040		I'm Living a Lie/All This	1972		3.00	6.00
☐ 6041		So Many Ways to Die/(B-side unknown)	1972		3.00	6.00
☐ 6042		I'm Sorry/Lil' Baby	1972		3.00	6.00
☐ 6046		Baby I'm-a Want You/Don't Make Me Over	1973		3.00	6.00
☐ 6053		You're Gonna Need Somebody to Love (While You're Looking for Someone to Love)/All This	1973		3.00	6.00
☐ 6059		Comin' or Goin'/Love's Arrangement	1973		3.00	6.00
☐ 6064		Breakin' Up a Happy Home/Guess Who	1974		3.00	6.00

Aurora
| ☐ 155 | | Standin' on Tip-Toe/(You Got Me) Sittin' in the Corner | 1965 | 20.00 | 40.00 | 80.00 |

Mala
| ☐ 488 | | Easy Come, Easy Go/I Don't Deserve a Boy Like You | 1964 | 6.25 | 12.50 | 25.00 |

Reprise
| ☐ 0290 | | I've Gotta Date/Shoo Fly | 1964 | 6.25 | 12.50 | 25.00 |
| ☐ 0349 | | Small Town Girl/Tell It Like It Is | 1965 | 6.25 | 12.50 | 25.00 |

Roulette
| ☐ 4428 | | We Need Them/La-Ta-Tee-Ta-Ta | 1962 | 7.50 | 15.00 | 30.00 |

Warner Bros.
| ☐ 5685 | | All Because I Love Somebody/All the Good Times Are Gone | 1965 | 5.00 | 10.00 | 20.00 |

English, Scott
Dot
| ☐ 16099 | | White Cliffs of Dover/4000 Miles Away | 1960 | 7.50 | 15.00 | 30.00 |

Janus
☐ 171		Brandy/Lead Me Back	1971	3.00	6.00	12.00
		A-side later recorded by Barry Manilow as "Mandy"				
☐ 192		Woman in My Life/Ballad of the Unloved	1972		2.50	5.00

Joker
| ☐ 777 | | Ugly Pills (You're Takin')/When | 1962 | 12.50 | 25.00 | 50.00 |

Spokane
| ☐ 4003 | | High on a Hill/When | 1964 | 6.25 | 12.50 | 25.00 |
| ☐ 4007 | | Here Comes the Pain/All I Want Is You | 1964 | 10.00 | 20.00 | 40.00 |

Sultan
| ☐ 1003 | | High on a Hill/When | 1963 | 12.50 | 25.00 | 50.00 |

Eno, Brian
(Also see "Roxy Music")
Island
| ☐ 036 | | The Lion Sleeps Tonight/I'll Come Running (To Tie Your Shoes) | 1975 | 6.25 | 12.50 | 25.00 |
| ☐ 036 | DJ | The Lion Sleeps Tonight (mono/stereo) | 1975 | 3.75 | 7.50 | 15.00 |

Entwistle, John
(Of The Who)
Atco
| ☐ 7337 | | Too Late the Hero/Dancin' Master | 1981 | | 2.00 | 4.00 |
| ☐ 7344 | | Talk Dirty/Try Me | 1982 | | 2.00 | 4.00 |

Decca
| ☐ 32896 | | I Believe in Everything/My Size | 1971 | | 3.00 | 6.00 |
| ☐ 33052 | | I Wonder/Who Cares | 1973 | | 3.00 | 6.00 |

Track
| ☐ 40066 | | Made in Japan/Roller Skate Kate | 1973 | | 2.50 | 5.00 |

Epps, Preston
Admiral
| ☐ 901 | | Bongo Express/Flamenco Bongo | 1963 | 3.75 | 7.50 | 15.00 |

Donna
| ☐ 1367 | | Mister Bongo/B'Wana Bongo | 1962 | 3.75 | 7.50 | 15.00 |

Embassy
| ☐ 203 | | Rockin' in the Congo/Sing Donna Go | 1961 | 3.75 | 7.50 | 15.00 |

Number		Title (A Side/B Side)	Year	VG	VG+	NM
Majesty						
❑ 1300		Bongo Boogie/Flamenco Bongo	1962	3.75	7.50	15.00
Original Sound						
❑ 4	M	Bongo Rock/Bongo Party	1959	5.00	10.00	20.00
❑ 4	S	Bongo Rock/Bongo Party	1959	12.50	25.00	50.00
❑ 9		Bongo, Bongo, Bongo/Hully Gully Bongo	1960	5.00	10.00	20.00
❑ 14		Bongo Shuffle/Bongo in the Congo	1960	3.75	7.50	15.00
❑ 17		Bongo Rocket/Jungle Drums	1961	3.75	7.50	15.00
Polo						
❑ 218		Bongo Rock 1965/Bongo Waltz	1965	3.00	6.00	12.00
Top Rank						
❑ 2067		Blue Bongo/Bongola	1960	3.75	7.50	15.00
❑ 2091		Bongo Hop/Caravan	1960	3.75	7.50	15.00
Equadors, The						
Argo						
❑ 5353		Say You'll Be Mine/Let Me Sleep, Woman	1959	15.00	30.00	60.00
Miracle						
❑ 7		You're My Desire/Someone to Call My Own	1961	37.50	75.00	150.00
Equals, The						
Bang						
❑ 582		Ain't Got Nothing to Give You/Black Skin, Blue Eyed Boys	1971	2.50	5.00	10.00
President						
❑ 103		Fire/I Won't Be There	1967	3.00	6.00	12.00
❑ 105		My Life Ain't Easy/You Got Too Many Boyfriends	1967	3.00	6.00	12.00
❑ 108		Giddy Up a Ding-Dong/I Get So Excited	1968	3.00	6.00	12.00
❑ 109		Lovely Rita/Softly, Softly	1968	3.00	6.00	12.00
❑ 110		Honey Gun/Michael and the Slipper Tree	1968	3.00	6.00	12.00
❑ 111		I Can't Let You Go/Viva Bobby Joe	1969	3.00	6.00	12.00
RCA Victor						
❑ 47-9186		Baby Come Back/Hold Me Closer	1967	3.75	7.50	15.00
❑ 47-9583		Baby Come Back/Hold Me Closer	1968	2.50	5.00	10.00
Shout						
❑ 247		Ain't Got Nothing to Give You/Black Skin, Blue Eyed Boys	1970	3.00	6.00	12.00
Equipe 84						
Imperial						
❑ 66266		The Twenty-Ninth of September/Auschwitz	1967	5.00	10.00	20.00
Ernie and the Emperors						
Reprise						
❑ 0414		Got a Lot I Want to Say/Meet Me at the Corner	1965	7.50	15.00	30.00
Escorts, The						
(Several different groups)						
Alithia						
❑ 6048		All We Need (Is Another Chance) (Short)/All We Need (Is Another Chance) (Long)	1973		3.00	6.00
❑ 6052		Look Over Your Shoulder/By the Time I Get to Phoenix	1973		2.50	5.00
❑ 6055		I'll Be Sweeter Tomorrow/I'm So Glad I Found You	1973		2.50	5.00
❑ 6062		Disrespect Can Wreck/All We Need	1974		2.50	5.00
❑ 6066		Let's Make Love (At Home Sometime)/Within Without	1974		2.50	5.00
Boomerang						
❑ 621		Little Big Horn/Wiped Out	1962	10.00	20.00	40.00
Coral						
❑ 62302		Gloria/Seven Wonders of the World	1961	10.00	20.00	40.00
❑ 62317		As I Love You/Gaudeamus	1962	7.50	15.00	30.00
❑ 62336		Somewhere/Submarine Race Watching	1962	6.25	12.50	25.00
❑ 62349		One Hand, One Heart/I Can't Be Free	1963	6.25	12.50	25.00
❑ 62372		Back Home Again/Something Has Changed Him	1963	6.25	12.50	25.00
		As "Goldie and the Escorts"				
❑ 62385		Give Me Tomorrow/My Heart Cries for You	1963	6.25	12.50	25.00
Fontana						
❑ 1512		Come On Home Baby/She Gets No Loving	1965	3.75	7.50	15.00
❑ 1912		Dizzy Miss Lizzy/All I Want Is You	1964	3.75	7.50	15.00
Judd						
❑ 1014		My First Year/Clap Happy	1959	3.75	7.50	15.00
RCA Victor						
❑ 47-6834		Bad Boy/Tore Up Over You	1957	3.75	7.50	15.00
❑ 47-6963		So Hard to Laugh, So Easy to Cry/Lonely Man	1957	3.75	7.50	15.00
❑ 47-8228		You Can't Even Be My Friend/Itchy Coo	1963	3.00	6.00	12.00
❑ 47-8327		The Hurt/No City Folks Allowed	1964	3.00	6.00	12.00
Scarlet						
❑ 4005		I Will Be Home Again/Leaky Heart and His Red Go-Kart	1960	15.00	30.00	60.00
Scepter						
❑ 1201		Why Why Why/Ugly Duckling	1958	10.00	20.00	40.00
		With Don Crawford				

Number		Title (A Side/B Side)	Year	VG	VG+	NM

Soma

❑ 1144		Main Drag/Judy or Jo Ann	1961	6.25	12.50	25.00

Esquerita

Capitol

❑ F4007		Please Come On Home/Oh Baby	1958	7.50	15.00	30.00
❑ F4058		Rockin' the Joint/Esquerita and the Voola	1958	7.50	15.00	30.00
❑ F4145		Laid Off/Just Another Lie	1959	7.50	15.00	30.00

Esquires, The

(More than one group)

Argo

❑ 5435		Boat of Love/With a Feeling	1963	5.00	10.00	20.00

Bunky

❑ 7750		Get On Up/Listen to Me	1967	2.50	5.00	10.00
❑ 7752		And Get Away/Everybody's Laughin'	1967	2.50	5.00	10.00
❑ 7753		You Say/State Fair	1968	2.50	5.00	10.00
❑ 7755		Why Can't I Stop/The Feeling's Gone	1968	2.50	5.00	10.00
❑ 7756		How Could It Be/I Know I Can	1968	2.50	5.00	10.00

Capitol

❑ 2650		Reach Out/Listen to Me	1969	2.00	4.00	8.00

Columbia

❑ 43815		It's a Dirty Shame/Love Hides a Multitude of Sins	1966	5.00	10.00	20.00

Dot

❑ 16954		Misfortune/She's My Woman	1966	3.00	6.00	12.00

Durco

❑ 1001		Flashin' Red/What a Burn	1964	10.00	20.00	40.00

Epic

❑ 9024		If You Only Knew What a Three-Cent Stamp Can Do/ Now, Now, Now *This may not exist on 45, though it certainly should.*	1954	400.00	800.00	1,200.

Hi-Po

❑ 1003		Only the Angels Know/One Word for This	1955	400.00	800.00	1,200

Ju Par

❑ 104		Get On Up '76/(B-side unknown)	1976		3.00	6.00

Lamarr

❑ 1001		Girls in the City/(B-side unknown)	1971	2.00	4.00	8.00

Scepter

❑ 12232		You've Got the Power/No Doubt About It *(Possibly reassigned to Wand?)*	1968			Unreleased?

Tower

❑ 174		Love's Made a Fool of You/Summertime	1965	3.75	7.50	15.00

Wand

❑ 11201		Whip It On Me/It Was Yesterday	1969	2.00	4.00	8.00
❑ 1193		You've Got the Power/No Doubt About It	1968	2.00	4.00	8.00
❑ 1195		I Don't Know/Part Angel	1969	2.00	4.00	8.00

Essex, David

Columbia

❑ 10005		America/Dance Little Girl	1974		2.50	5.00
❑ 10039		Gonna Make You a Star/Window	1974		2.50	5.00
❑ 10183		Coconut Ice/Rolling Stone	1975		2.50	5.00
❑ 10256		Good Ol' Rock 'N' Roll/Hold Me Close	1975		2.50	5.00
❑ 45940		Rock On/On and On	1973		2.50	5.00
❑ 45940	PS	Rock On/On and On	1973	2.50	5.00	10.00
❑ 46041		Lamplight/We're All Insane	1974		2.50	5.00
❑ 46041	PS	Lamplight/We're All Insane	1974	2.50	5.00	10.00

RSO

❑ 1006		Oh What a Circus (From Evita)/ Ships That Pass in the Night	1979		2.00	4.00

Uni

❑ 55020		She's Leaving Home/He's a Better Man Than Me	1967	2.50	5.00	10.00

Essex, The

Bang

❑ 537		The Eagle/Moonlight, Music, and You	1966	2.00	4.00	8.00

Roulette

❑ 4494		Easier Said Than Done/Are You Going My Way	1963	3.00	6.00	12.00
❑ 4515		A Walkin' Miracle/What I Don't Know Won't Hurt Me	1963	2.50	5.00	10.00
❑ 4530		She's Got Everything/Out of Sight, Out of Mind	1964	2.50	5.00	10.00
❑ 4542		What Did I Do/Curfew Lover	1964	2.50	5.00	10.00

Estrada, Roy, and the Rocketeers

(Roy Estrada was one of the original Mothers of Invention. See "Zappa, Frank")

King

❑ 5368		Jungle Dream (Part 1)/Jungle Dream (Part 2)	1960	12.50	25.00	50.00

Evans, Paul

Atco

❑ 6138		At My Party/Beat Generation	1959	3.75	7.50	15.00
❑ 6170		Long Gone/Mickey, My Love	1960	3.75	7.50	15.00

Number	Title (A Side/B Side)	Year	VG	VG+	NM
Big Tree					
❑ 16050	Happy Birthday, America/You Made Me Over	1975		2.50	5.00
Carlton					
❑ 539	Show Folk/I Love to Make Love to You	1961	3.75	7.50	15.00
❑ 543	After the Hurricane/Not Me	1961	3.75	7.50	15.00
❑ 554	Just Because I Love You/This Pullover	1961	3.75	7.50	15.00
❑ 558	Over the Mountain, Across the Sea/Sisal Twine	1961	3.75	7.50	15.00
Columbia					
❑ 44472	One Red Rose/Bound to Silence	1968		3.00	6.00
Decca					
❑ 30680	I Think About You All the Time/Oh No	1958	5.00	10.00	20.00
Dot					
❑ 17463	That's What Loving You Is All About/Do You Remember	1973		2.50	5.00
Epic					
❑ 9726	Bewitched/I Think I'm Gonna Kill Myself	1964	2.50	5.00	10.00
	By Paul & Mimi Evans				
❑ 9751	Little Miss Tease/Gina Marina Petunia	1964	2.50	5.00	10.00
❑ 9842	I Wonder What to Do/Always Thinking of the Roses	1965	2.50	5.00	10.00
Guaranteed					
❑ 200	Seven Little Girls Sitting in the Back Seat/Worshipping an Idol	1959	5.00	10.00	20.00
❑ 205	Midnite Special/Since I Met You Baby	1960	3.75	7.50	15.00
❑ 208	Happy-Go-Lucky Me/Fish in the Ocean	1960	3.75	7.50	15.00
❑ 210	The Brigade of Broken Hearts/Twins	1960	3.75	7.50	15.00
❑ 213	Hushabye Little Guitar/Blind Boy	1960	3.75	7.50	15.00
Kapp					
❑ 473	A Picture of You/Feelin' No Pain	1962	3.00	6.00	12.00
❑ 486	D-Darling/Gonna Build a Mountain	1962	3.00	6.00	12.00
❑ 499	The Bell That Couldn't Jingle/Gilding the Lily	1962	3.00	6.00	12.00
❑ 520	(Mama and Papa) We've Got Something On You/What Are the Lips of Janet	1963	3.00	6.00	12.00
❑ 527	Ten Thousand Years/Even Tan	1963	3.00	6.00	12.00
Laurie					
❑ 3571	Think Summer/For Old Times Sake	1971		3.00	6.00
❑ 3581	The Man in a Row Boat/Here We Go Around Again	1971		3.00	6.00
Mercury					
❑ 73499	But I Was Born in New York City/Just As Long As You Are There	1974		2.50	5.00
❑ 73650	All My Children/Move In with Me	1975		2.50	5.00
Musicor					
❑ 6305	Roses Are Red Medley/If I Had My Life to Live Over	1977		2.00	4.00
Ranwood					
❑ 928	Try It, You'll Like It/We Liked It	1972		3.00	6.00
RCA Victor					
❑ 47-6806	What Do You Know/Dorothy	1957	5.00	10.00	20.00
❑ 47-6924	Looking for a Sweetie/Any Little Thing	1957	5.00	10.00	20.00
❑ 47-6992	Caught/Poor Broken Heart	1957	5.00	10.00	20.00
Spring					
❑ 183	Hello, This Is Joanie (The Telephone Answering Machine Song)/Lullabye Tissue Paper Company	1978		2.00	4.00
❑ 187	Down at the Bluebird/I'm Givin' Up My Baby	1978		2.00	4.00
❑ 193	Disneyland Daddy/Build An Ark	1979		2.00	4.00
Everett, Betty					
ABC					
❑ 10829	In Your Arms/Nothing I Wouldn't Do	1966	2.00	4.00	8.00
❑ 10861	Bye, Bye Baby/Your Love Is Important to Me	1966	2.00	4.00	8.00
❑ 10919	Love Comes Tumbling Down/People Around Me	1967	2.00	4.00	8.00
❑ 10978	I Can't Say/My Baby Loving My Best Friend	1967	2.00	4.00	8.00
CJ					
❑ 611	Why Did You Have to Go/Please Come Back	1961	5.00	10.00	20.00
❑ 619	Your Lovin' Arms/Happy I Long to Be	1961	5.00	10.00	20.00
❑ 674	Days Gone By/Her New Love	1964	3.75	7.50	15.00
Cobra					
❑ 5019	My Love/My Life Depends on You	1957	7.50	15.00	30.00
❑ 5024	Ain't Gonna Cry/Killer Diller	1958	6.25	12.50	25.00
❑ 5031	Weep No More/Tell Me Darling	1959	6.25	12.50	25.00
Fantasy					
❑ 652	I Got to Tell Somebody/Why Are You Leaving Me	1970		2.50	5.00
❑ 658	Ain't Nothing Gonna Change Me/What Is It?	1971		2.50	5.00
❑ 667	I'm a Woman/Prove It	1971		2.50	5.00
❑ 687	Black Girl/Innocent Bystanders	1972		2.50	5.00
❑ 687	Black Girl/What Is It?	1972		2.50	5.00
❑ 696	Danger/Just a Matter of Time Till You're Gone	1973		2.50	5.00
❑ 714	Sweet Dan/Who Will Your Next Fool Be	1973		2.50	5.00
❑ 725	Try It, You'll Like It/Wondering	1974		2.50	5.00
❑ 738	Happy Endings/Keep It Up	1974		2.50	5.00
One-derful					
❑ 4806	I've Got a Claim on You/Your Love Is Important to Me	1962	3.75	7.50	15.00
❑ 4823	I'll Be There/Please Love Me	1964	3.00	6.00	12.00

Number		Title (A Side/B Side)	Year	VG	VG+	NM

Uni

❑ 55100		Take Me/There'll Come a Time	1968		3.00	6.00
❑ 55122		I Can't Say No to You/Better Tomorrow Than Today	1969		3.00	6.00
❑ 55141		1900 Yesterday/Maybe	1969		3.00	6.00
❑ 55174		Just a Man's Way/Been a Long Time	1969		3.00	6.00
❑ 55189		Sugar/Just Another Winter	1969		3.00	6.00
❑ 55219		Unlucky Girl/Better Tomorrow Than Today	1970		3.00	6.00

United Artists

❑ XW1200		True Love (You Took My Heart)/You Can Do It	1978		2.00	4.00

Vee Jay

❑ 513		By My Side/Prince of Players	1963	3.75	7.50	15.00
❑ 566		You're No Good/Chained to Your Love	1963	3.75	7.50	15.00
❑ 585		The Shoop Shoop Song (It's In His Kiss)/Hands Off	1964	3.75	7.50	15.00
❑ 599		I Can't Hear You/Can I Get to Know You	1964	3.00	6.00	12.00
❑ 610		It Hurts to Be in Love/Until You Were Gone	1964	3.00	6.00	12.00
❑ 628		Getting Mighty Crowded/Chained to a Memory	1964	3.00	6.00	12.00
❑ 683		The Real Thing/Gonna Be Ready	1965	3.00	6.00	12.00
❑ 699		I Don't Hurt Anymore/Too Hot to Hold	1965	3.00	6.00	12.00
❑ 716		Trouble Over the Weekend/My Shoe Won't Fly	1966	3.00	6.00	12.00

Everett, Betty, and Jerry Butler
(Also see individual listings)

Vee Jay

❑ 613		Let It Be Me/Ain't That Loving You Baby	1964	3.00	6.00	12.00
❑ 633		Smile/Love Is Strange	1964	3.00	6.00	12.00
❑ 676		Since I Don't Have You/Just Be True	1965	3.00	6.00	12.00
❑ 691		Fever/The Way You Do the Things You Do	1965	3.00	6.00	12.00

Everett, Vince

ABC-Paramount

❑ 10313		Such a Night/Don't Go	1962	15.00	30.00	60.00
❑ 10360		I Ain't Gonna Be Your Low Down Dog No More/ Sugaree	1962	12.50	25.00	50.00
❑ 10472		Baby, Let's Play House/Livin' High	1963	20.00	40.00	80.00
❑ 10538		Sweet Flavors/Box Candy	1964	10.00	20.00	40.00
❑ 10624		Big Brother/To Have, to Hold and Let Go	1965	10.00	20.00	40.00

Town

❑ 1964		Buttercup/Land of No Return	1960	10.00	20.00	40.00

Everly Brothers, The
(Also see "Everly, Don"; "Everly, Phil"; "Kimberly, Adrian")

Barnaby

❑ 500		('Til) I Kissed You/Oh, What a Feeling	197?		2.50	5.00
❑ 501		Wake Up Little Susie/Maybe Tomorrow	197?		2.50	5.00
❑ 502		Bye, Bye Love/I Wonder If I Care As Much	197?		2.50	5.00
❑ 503		This Little Girl of Mine/Should We Tell Him?	197?		2.50	5.00
❑ 504		Problems/Love of My Life	197?		2.50	5.00
❑ 505		Take a Message to Mary/Poor Jenny	197?		2.50	5.00
❑ 506		Let It Be Me/Since You Broke My Heart	197?		2.50	5.00
❑ 507		When Will I Be Loved/Be Bop-A-Lula	197?		2.50	5.00
❑ 508		Like Strangers/Brand New Heartache	197?		2.50	5.00
❑ 509		All I Have to Do Is Dream/Claudette	197?		2.50	5.00
❑ 510		Bird Dog/Devoted to You	197?		2.50	5.00
❑ 511		I'm Here to Get My Baby Out of Jail/Lightning Express	197?		2.50	5.00
		All Barnaby records are reissues of original Cadence recordings				

Cadence

❑ 1315		Bye, Bye Love/I Wonder If I Care As Much	1957	6.25	12.50	25.00
❑ 1337		Wake Up Little Susie/Maybe Tomorrow	1957	6.25	12.50	25.00
❑ 1337	PS	Wake Up Little Susie/Maybe Tomorrow	1957	50.00	100.00	200.00
❑ 1342		This Little Girl of Mine/Should We Tell Him?	1958	6.25	12.50	25.00
❑ 1348		All I Have to Do Is Dream/Claudette	1958	6.25	12.50	25.00
❑ 1348		All I Have to Do Is Dream/Claudette	1961	5.00	10.00	20.00
		Reissue with red and black label; scarcer than original				
❑ 1350		Bird Dog/Devoted to You	1958	6.25	12.50	25.00
❑ 1355		Problems/Love of My Life	1958	6.25	12.50	25.00
❑ 1355	PS	Problems/Love of My Life	1958	12.50	25.00	50.00
❑ 1364		Take a Message to Mary/Poor Jenny	1959	6.25	12.50	25.00
❑ 1369		('Til) I Kissed You/Oh, What a Feeling	1959	6.25	12.50	25.00
❑ 1369	PS	('Til) I Kissed You/Oh, What a Feeling	1959	12.50	25.00	50.00
❑ 1376		Let It Be Me/Since You Broke My Heart	1959	6.25	12.50	25.00
❑ 1376	PS	Let It Be Me/Since You Broke My Heart	1959	12.50	25.00	50.00
❑ 1380		When Will I Be Loved/Be Bop A-Lula	1960	6.25	12.50	25.00
❑ 1388		Like Strangers/Brand New Heartache	1960	6.25	12.50	25.00
❑ 1429		I'm Here to Get My Baby Out of Jail/Lightning Express	1962	5.00	10.00	20.00
❑ 1429	PS	I'm Here to Get My Baby Out of Jail/Lightning Express	1962	10.00	20.00	40.00

Capitol

❑ B-44297		Don't Worry Baby/Tequila Dreams	1989		2.00	4.00
		A-side: With the Beach Boys; B-side by Dave Grusin				
❑ B-44297	PS	Don't Worry Baby/Tequila Dreams	1989		2.50	5.00	10.00

Columbia

❑ 21496		Keep A Lovin' Me/The Sun Keeps Shining	1956	125.00	250.00	500.00
❑ 21496	DJ	Keep A Lovin' Me/The Sun Keeps Shining	1956	50.00	100.00	200.00

Mercury

❑ 872 098-7		Ride the Wind/Don't Worry Baby	1988			3.00

Number		Title (A Side/B Side)	Year	VG	VG+	NM
❑ 872 420-7		Ballad of a Teenage Queen/Get Rhythm	1988			3.00
		With Johnny Cash and Roseanne Cash				
❑ 880 213-7		On the Wings of a Nightingale/Asleep	1984		2.50	5.00
		A-side written and produced by Paul McCartney				
❑ 880 423-7		The Story of Me/First in Line	1984		2.00	4.00
❑ 884 428-7		Don't Say Goodnight/Born Yesterday	1986		2.00	4.00
❑ 884 694-7		I Know Love/These Shoes	1986		2.00	4.00
❑ 884 694-7	PS	I Know Love/These Shoes	1986		2.00	4.00
RCA Victor						
❑ SP45-409	DJ	Pass the Chicken and Listen	1971	7.50	15.00	30.00
		Promo-only interview record				
❑ 74-0717		Stories We Could Tell/Ridin' High	1972	2.50	5.00	10.00
❑ 74-0849		Lay It Down/Paradise	1972	2.50	5.00	10.00
❑ 74-0901		Not Fade Away/Ladies Love Outlaws	1973	2.50	5.00	10.00
Warner Bros.						
❑ GWB 0311		That's Old Fashioned/Bowling Green	197?		2.00	4.00
		"Back to Back Hits" series; originals have palm-tree labels				
❑ GWB 0314		Ebony Eyes/Walk Right Back	197?		2.00	4.00
		"Back to Back Hits" series; originals have palm-tree labels				
❑ 5151	DJ	Cathy's Clown/Always It's You	1960	25.00	50.00	100.00
		Promo-only gold vinyl pressing				
❑ 5151	M	Cathy's Clown/Always It's You	1960	5.00	10.00	20.00
		Original stock copies have pink labels				
❑ 5151	M	Cathy's Clown/Always It's You	1960	3.75	7.50	15.00
		Second-pressing stock copies have red labels with arrows				
❑ 5151	PS	Cathy's Clown/Always It's You	1960	7.50	15.00	30.00
❑ S-5151	S	Cathy's Clown/Always It's You	1960	12.50	25.00	50.00
❑ 5163		So Sad (To Watch Good Love Go Bad)/Lucille	1960	3.75	7.50	15.00
❑ 5163	DJ	So Sad (To Watch Good Love Go Bad)/Lucille	1960	25.00	50.00	100.00
		Promo-only gold vinyl pressing				
❑ 5163	PS	So Sad (To Watch Good Love Go Bad)/Lucille	1960	5.00	10.00	20.00
❑ 5199		Ebony Eyes/Walk Right Back	1961	3.75	7.50	15.00
❑ 5199	DJ	Ebony Eyes/Walk Right Back	1961	25.00	50.00	100.00
		Promo-only gold vinyl pressing				
❑ 5199	PS	Ebony Eyes/Walk Right Back	1961	5.00	10.00	20.00
❑ 5220		Temptation/Stick With Me, Baby	1961	3.75	7.50	15.00
❑ 5220	PS	Temptation/Stick With Me, Baby	1961	7.50	15.00	30.00
❑ 5250		Crying in the Rain/I'm Not Angry	1961	3.75	7.50	15.00
❑ 5250	PS	Crying in the Rain/I'm Not Angry	1961	5.00	10.00	20.00
❑ 5273		That's Old Fashioned	1962	3.75	7.50	15.00
		(That's the Way Love Should Be)/How Can I Meet Her?				
❑ 5273	PS	That's Old Fashioned	1962	7.50	15.00	30.00
		(That's the Way Love Should Be)/How Can I Meet Her?				
❑ 5297		Don't Ask Me to Be Friends/	1962	5.00	10.00	20.00
		No One Can Make My Sunshine Smile				
❑ 5297	PS	Don't Ask Me to Be Friends/	1962	7.50	15.00	30.00
		No One Can Make My Sunshine Smile				
❑ 5346		(So It Was...So It Is...) So It Always Will Be/	1963	3.75	7.50	15.00
		Nancy's Minuet				
❑ 5362		I'm Afraid/It's Been Nice	1963	3.75	7.50	15.00
❑ 5389		Love Her/The Girl Sang the Blues	1963	3.75	7.50	15.00
❑ 5422		Hello, Amy/Ain't That Loving You, Baby	1964	3.75	7.50	15.00
❑ 5441		The Ferris Wheel/Don't Forget to Cry	1964	3.75	7.50	15.00
❑ 5466		You're the One I Love/Ring Around My Rosie	1964	3.75	7.50	15.00
❑ 5478		Gone, Gone, Gone/Torture	1964	3.75	7.50	15.00
❑ 5501		Don't Blame Me/Walk Right Back//Muskrat/Lucille	1961	5.00	10.00	20.00
❑ 5501	PS	Don't Blame Me/Walk Right Back//Muskrat/Lucille	1961	10.00	20.00	40.00
		Part of Warner Bros. "+2" series, with two new songs and excerpts of two prior hits				
❑ 5600		You're My Girl/Don't Let the World Know	1965	3.00	6.00	12.00
❑ 5611		That'll Be the Day/Give Me a Sweetheart	1965	3.00	6.00	12.00
❑ 5628		The Price of Love/It Only Costs a Dime	1965	3.00	6.00	12.00
❑ 5635		I'll Never Get Over You/Follow Me	1965	3.00	6.00	12.00
❑ 5649		Love Is Strange/A Man with Money	1965	3.00	6.00	12.00
❑ 5649	PS	Love Is Strange/A Man with Money	1965	7.50	15.00	30.00
❑ 5682		It's All Over/I Used to Love You	1965	3.00	6.00	12.00
❑ 5698		The Doll House Is Empty/Lovey Kravezit	1966	3.00	6.00	12.00
❑ 5808		The Power of Love/Leave My Girl Alone	1966	3.00	6.00	12.00
❑ 5833		Somebody Help Me/Hard, Hard Year	1966	3.00	6.00	12.00
❑ 5857		Fifi the Flea/Like Every Time Before	1966	3.00	6.00	12.00
❑ 5901		She Never Smiles Anymore/Devil Child	1967	3.00	6.00	12.00
❑ 7020		Bowling Green/I Don't Want to Love You	1967	3.00	6.00	12.00
❑ 7062		Mary Jane/Talking to the Flowers	1967	3.00	6.00	12.00
❑ 7088		Love of the Common People/The Voice Within	1967	3.00	6.00	12.00
❑ 7110		Cathy's Clown/So Sad	1968	2.00	4.00	8.00
		"Back to Back Hits" series; originals have green "W7" label				
❑ 7111		Crying in the Rain/Lucille	1968	2.00	4.00	8.00
		"Back to Back Hits" series; originals have green "W7" label				
❑ 7120		Wake Up Little Susie/Bird Dog	1969	2.00	4.00	8.00
		"Back to Back Hits" series; originals have green "W7" label; re-recordings				
❑ 7121		Bye Bye Love/All I Have to Do Is Dream	1969	2.00	4.00	8.00
		"Back to Back Hits" series; originals have green "W7" label; re-recordings				
❑ 7192		Empty Boxes/It's My Time	1968	3.00	6.00	12.00
❑ 7226		Lord of the Manor/Milk Train	1968	3.00	6.00	12.00
❑ 7262		T for Texas/I Wonder If I Care As Much	1969	3.00	6.00	12.00
❑ 7290		I'm On My Way Home Again/Cuckoo Bird	1969	3.00	6.00	12.00

Number	Title (A Side/B Side)	Year	VG	VG+	NM
❑ 7326	Carolina on My Mind/My Little Yellow Bird	1969	3.75	7.50	15.00
❑ 7425	Yves/The Human Race	1970	3.75	7.50	15.00

Everly, Don
(Of the Everly Brothers)
ABC Hickory

❑ 54002	Love at Last Sight/Oh I'd Like to Go Away	1976		3.00	6.00
❑ 54005	Deep Water/Since You Broke My Heart	1977		3.00	6.00
❑ 54012	Brother Juke-Box/Oh, What a Feeling	1977		3.00	6.00

Hickory/MGM

❑ 368	Never Like This/ Yesterday Just Passed My Way Again	1976		3.00	6.00

Ode

❑ 66009	Only Me/Tumbling Tumbleweeds	1970	2.00	4.00	8.00
❑ 66046	Warming Up the Band/Evelyn Swing	1974	2.00	4.00	8.00

Everly, Phil
(Of the Everly Brothers)
Capitol

❑ B-5197	One Way Love/Who's Gonna Keep Me Warm	1983	2.50	5.00	10.00

Curb

❑ 02116	Sweet Southern Love/In Your Eyes	1981	2.50	5.00	10.00
❑ 5401	Dare to Dream Again/Lonely Days, Lonely Nights	1980	2.50	5.00	10.00

Elektra

❑ 46007	Don't Say You Don't Love Me No More/ I Seek the Night	1979		2.50	5.00
	A-side: With Sondra Locke; B-side: Sondra Locke solo				
❑ 46519	Living Alone/I Just Don't Feel Like Dancing	1979		2.50	5.00
❑ 46556	Buy Me a Beer/You Broke It	1979		2.50	5.00

Pye

❑ 71014	Old Kentucky River/Summershine	1975	2.00	4.00	8.00
❑ 71036	New Old Song/Better Than Now	1975	2.00	4.00	8.00
❑ 71050	You and I Are a Song/Better Than Now	1975	2.00	4.00	8.00
❑ 71055	Words in Your Eyes/ Back When the Bands Played in Rag Time	1976	2.00	4.00	8.00
❑ 71056	God Bless Older Ladies/Sweet Grass Country	1976		3.00	6.00

RCA Victor

❑ APBO-0064	God Bless Older Ladies/Sweet Grass Country	1973	2.00		8.00

Every Mother's Son
MGM

❑ 13733	Come On Down to My Boat/I Believe in You	1967	2.50	5.00	10.00
❑ 13788	Put Your Mind at Ease/Proper Four Leaf Clover	1967	2.00	4.00	8.00
❑ 13788 PS	Put Your Mind at Ease/Proper Four Leaf Clover	1967	3.00	6.00	12.00
❑ 13844	Pony with the Golden Mane/Dolls in the Clock	1967	2.00	4.00	8.00
❑ 13887	No One Knows/What Became of Mary	1968	2.00	4.00	8.00
❑ 13987	Rainflowers/For Brandy	1968	2.00	4.00	8.00

Evil Encorporated
Scene

❑ 101	Hey You/The Thing Is...	1967	7.50	15.00	30.00
❑ 102	Baby It's You/All I Really Want to Do	1967	7.50	15.00	30.00

Excels, The
Carla

❑ 1901	Little Innocent Girl/Some Kind of Fun	1968	5.00	10.00	20.00
❑ 2529	Gonna Make You Mine Girl/Goodbye Poor Boy	1966	5.00	10.00	20.00
❑ 2534	I Wanna Be Free/Too Much Too Soon	1967	5.00	10.00	20.00
❑ 2536	California on My Mind/Arrival of Mary	1967	5.00	10.00	20.00

Central

❑ 2601	You're Mine Forever/Baby Doll	1957	12.50	25.00	50.00

Gone

❑ 5094	My Foolish Heart/Just You and I Together	1960	6.25	12.50	25.00

Relic

❑ 1007	You're Mine Forever/Baby Doll	1965	2.50	5.00	10.00

RSVP

❑ 111	Can't Help Lovin' That Girl of Mine/Till You	1961	7.50	15.00	30.00

Exception, The
(Peter Cetera, later of Chicago, was a member of this group)
Capitol

❑ 2046	Business As Usual/My Mind Goes Traveling	1967	3.00	6.00	12.00
❑ 2120	You Always Hurt Me/You Don't Know Like I Know	1968	3.00	6.00	12.00
❑ 5982	The Girl from New York City/As Far As I Can See	1967	3.00	6.00	12.00

Exciters, The
Bang

❑ 515	A Little Bit of Soap/I'm Gonna Get Him Someday	1966	3.00	6.00	12.00
❑ 518	You Better Come Home/Weddings Make Me Cry	1966	7.50	15.00	30.00

RCA Victor

❑ 47-9633	Take One Step (I'll Take Two)/If You Want My Love	1968	7.50	15.00	30.00
❑ 47-9723	You Don't Know What You're Missing ('Til It's Gone!)/ Blowing Up My Mind	1969	7.50	15.00	30.00

Number		Title (A Side/B Side)	Year	VG	VG+	NM
❏ 48-1035		You Don't Know What You're Missing ('Til It's Gone!)/ Blowing Up My Mind	1972	3.75	7.50	15.00

Roulette

❏ 4591		I Want You to Be My Boy/Tonight, Tonight	1965	3.00	6.00	12.00
❏ 4594		Are You Satisfied/Just Not Ready	1965	3.00	6.00	12.00
❏ 4614		My Father/Run Mascara	1965	3.00	6.00	12.00
❏ 4632		I Knew You Would/There They Go	1965	3.00	6.00	12.00

Shout

❏ 205		Number One/You Got Love	1966	2.50	5.00	10.00
❏ 214		Soulmotion/You Know It Ain't Right	1967	2.50	5.00	10.00

Today

❏ 1002		Learning How to Fly/Life, Love and Peace	1970	2.00	4.00	8.00

United Artists

❏ 0029		Tell Him/Do-Wah-Diddy	1973		2.00	4.00
		"Silver Spotlight Series" reissue				
❏ 544		Tell Him/Hard Way to Go	1963	3.75	7.50	15.00
❏ 572		Drama of Love/He's Got the Power	1963	3.00	6.00	12.00
❏ 604		Get Him/It's So Exciting	1963	3.00	6.00	12.00
❏ 662		Do-Wah-Diddy/If Love Came Your Way	1963	3.00	6.00	12.00
❏ 721		Having My Fun/ We Were Lovers (When the Party Began)	1964	3.00	6.00	12.00
❏ 830		Having My Fun/ We Were Lovers (When the Party Began)	1965	2.50	5.00	10.00

Exodus
Wand

❏ 11248		M&M/Silhouettes-You Cheated	1972	25.00	50.00	100.00
		Black and white label				
❏ 11248		M&M/Silhouettes-You Cheated	1972	7.50	15.00	30.00
		Multicolored label				

Exports, The
King

❏ 5917		Car Hop/Seat Belts Please	1964	6.25	12.50	25.00
❏ 5985		Mustang '65/Always It's You	1965	6.25	12.50	25.00

Expressions, The
Arliss

❏ 1012		My Love, My Love/The Sign of Happiness	1962	12.50	25.00	50.00

Federal

❏ 12533		You Better Know It/Out of My Life	1964	2.50	5.00	10.00

Guyden

❏ 2122		Be-Bop-a-Lula/Skinnie Minnie	1965	3.75	7.50	15.00
		As "J-D and the Expressions"				

Parkway

❏ 892		On the Corner/To Cry	1963	3.75	7.50	15.00

Reprise

❏ 0360		Playboy/One Plus One	1965	5.00	10.00	20.00

Smash

❏ 1848		Karen/Thrill	1963	3.75	7.50	15.00

Teen

❏ 101		Now That You've Gone/Crazy	1957	50.00	100.00	200.00

Exterminators, The
Chancellor

❏ 1143		The Beetle Bomb/Stomp 'Em Out	1963	6.25	12.50	25.00
❏ 1148		Beatle Stomp/Stomp 'Em Out	1964	3.75	7.50	15.00
		A-sides are the same song with different titles				

Golden West

❏ 1002		Beatle Stomp/Stomp 'Em Out	1964	5.00	10.00	20.00

F

Fabares, Shelley
Colpix

❏ 621		Johnny Angel/Where's It Gonna Get Me	1962	5.00	10.00	20.00
❏ 621	PS	Johnny Angel/Where's It Gonna Get Me	1962	50.00	100.00	200.00
❏ 631		What Did They Do Before Rock and Roll/Very Unlikely	1962	5.00	10.00	20.00
❏ 631	PS	What Did They Do Before Rock and Roll/Very Unlikely	1962	20.00	40.00	80.00
		With Paul Petersen				
❏ 636		Johnny Loves Me/I'm Growing Up	1962	5.00	10.00	20.00
❏ 636	PS	Johnny Loves Me/I'm Growing Up	1962	37.50	75.00	150.00
❏ 654		The Things We Did Last Summer/ Breaking Up Is Hard to Do	1962	5.00	10.00	20.00
❏ 667		Big Star/Telephone (Don't You Ring)	1962	5.00	10.00	20.00
❏ 682		Ronnie, Call Me When You Get a Chance/ I Left a Note to Say Goodbye	1963	5.00	10.00	20.00
❏ 705		Welcome Home/Billy Boy	1963	5.00	10.00	20.00
❏ 721		Football Season's Over/He Don't Love Me	1963	25.00	50.00	100.00
		Produced by Jan Berry of Jan and Dean				

Number		Title (A Side/B Side)	Year	VG	VG+	NM
Dunhill						
❏ 4001		My Prayer/Pretty Please	1965	7.50	15.00	30.00
❏ 4041		See Ya 'Round on the Rebound/Pretty Please	1966	7.50	15.00	30.00
Vee Jay						
❏ 632		I Know You'll Be There/Lost Summer Love	1964	10.00	20.00	40.00
Fabian						
Chancellor						
❏ 1020		I'm in Love/Shivers	1958	6.25	12.50	25.00
❏ 1024		Be My Steady Date/Lilly Lou	1958	6.25	12.50	25.00
❏ 1029	M	I'm a Man/Hypnotized	1959	5.00	10.00	20.00
❏ 1029	PS	I'm a Man/Hypnotized	1959	10.00	20.00	40.00
❏ S-1029	S	I'm a Man/Hypnotized	1959	12.50	25.00	50.00
❏ 1033	M	Turn Me Loose/Stop Thief!	1959	5.00	10.00	20.00
❏ 1033	PS	Turn Me Loose/Stop Thief!	1959	10.00	20.00	40.00
❏ S-1033	S	Turn Me Loose/Stop Thief!	1959	12.50	25.00	50.00
❏ 1037	M	Tiger/Mighty Cold (To a Warm, Warm Heart)	1959	5.00	10.00	20.00
❏ 1037	PS	Tiger/Mighty Cold (To a Warm, Warm Heart)	1959	10.00	20.00	40.00
❏ S-1037	S	Tiger/Mighty Cold (To a Warm, Warm Heart)	1959	12.50	25.00	50.00
❏ 1041	M	Come On and Get Me/Got the Feeling	1959	5.00	10.00	20.00
❏ 1041	PS	Come On and Get Me/Got the Feeling	1959	10.00	20.00	40.00
❏ S-1041	S	Come On and Get Me/Got the Feeling	1959	12.50	25.00	50.00
❏ 1044		Hound Dog Man/Friendly World	1959	6.25	12.50	25.00
❏ 1044	M	Hound Dog Man/This Friendly World	1959	5.00	10.00	20.00
		Note difference in B-side title				
❏ 1044	PS	Hound Dog Man/This Friendly World	1959	10.00	20.00	40.00
❏ S-1044	S	Hound Dog Man/This Friendly World	1959	12.50	25.00	50.00
❏ 1047	M	About This Thing Called Love/String Along	1960	3.00	6.00	12.00
❏ 1047	PS	About This Thing Called Love/String Along	1960	7.50	15.00	30.00
❏ S-1047	S	About This Thing Called Love/String Along	1960	12.50	25.00	50.00
❏ 1051		I'm Gonna Sit Right Down and Write Myself a Letter/ Strollin' in the Springtime	1960	3.00	6.00	12.00
❏ 1051	PS	I'm Gonna Sit Right Down and Write Myself a Letter/ Strollin' in the Springtime	1960	7.50	15.00	30.00
❏ 1055		Tomorrow/King of Love	1960	3.00	6.00	12.00
❏ 1055	PS	Tomorrow/King of Love	1960	7.50	15.00	30.00
❏ 1061		Kissin' and Twistin'/Long Before	1960	3.00	6.00	12.00
❏ 1061	PS	Kissin' and Twistin'/Long Before	1960	7.50	15.00	30.00
❏ 1067		You Know You Belong to Someone Else/Hold On	1961	3.00	6.00	12.00
❏ 1067	PS	You Know You Belong to Someone Else/Hold On	1961	7.50	15.00	30.00
❏ 1072		Grapevine/David and Goliath	1961	3.00	6.00	12.00
❏ 1079		The Love That I'm Giving to You/ You're Only Young Once	1961	3.75	7.50	15.00
❏ 1079	PS	The Love That I'm Giving to You/ You're Only Young Once	1961	10.00	20.00	40.00
❏ 1084		A Girl Like You/Dream Factory	1961	3.00	6.00	12.00
❏ 1084	PS	A Girl Like You/Dream Factory	1961	7.50	15.00	30.00
❏ 1086		Tongue-Tied/Kansas City	1961	5.00	10.00	20.00
❏ 1092		Wild Party/Made You	1961	5.00	10.00	20.00
❏ 1092	PS	Wild Party/Made You	1961	10.00	20.00	40.00
Cream						
❏ 7717		The American East/Ease On Into My Life	1977		2.50	5.00
❏ 7717	PS	The American East/Ease On Into My Life	1977		2.50	5.00
Dot						
❏ 16413		Break Down and Cry/She's Staying Inside with Me	1963	2.50	5.00	10.00
Fabs, The						
Cotton Ball						
❏ 1005		That's the Bag I'm In/Dinah Wants Religion	1966	37.50	75.00	150.00
Fabulons, The						
Ember						
❏ 1069		Smoke From Your Cigarette/Give Me Back My Ring White label	1960	12.50	25.00	50.00
❏ 1069		Smoke From Your Cigarette/Give Me Back My Ring Black label	1960	6.25	12.50	25.00
Tower						
❏ 259		Since You've Been Gone/Don't Ask Me	1966	3.75	7.50	15.00
Fabulous Four, The						
Brass						
❏ 311		Now You Cry/Got to Get Her Back	1964	5.00	10.00	20.00
❏ 314		Who Could It Be/Happy	1964	5.00	10.00	20.00
❏ 316		I'm Always Doing Something Wrong/Young Blood	1964	5.00	10.00	20.00
Chancellor						
❏ 1062		In the Chapel in the Moonlight/Mr. Twist	1960	6.25	12.50	25.00
❏ 1068		Let's Try Again/Precious Moments	1961	6.25	12.50	25.00
❏ 1078		Why Do Fools Fall in Love/Sounds of Summer	1961	10.00	20.00	40.00
❏ 1085		Prisoner of Love/Betty Ann	1961	20.00	40.00	80.00
❏ 1090		Everybody Knows/I'm Coming Home	1961	5.00	10.00	20.00
❏ 1098		Mr. Twist/Everybody Knows	1961	5.00	10.00	20.00
❏ 1102		Forever/(It's No) Sin	1962	6.25	12.50	25.00
Coral						
❏ 62479		Now You Cry/Got to Get Her Back	1966	3.75	7.50	15.00

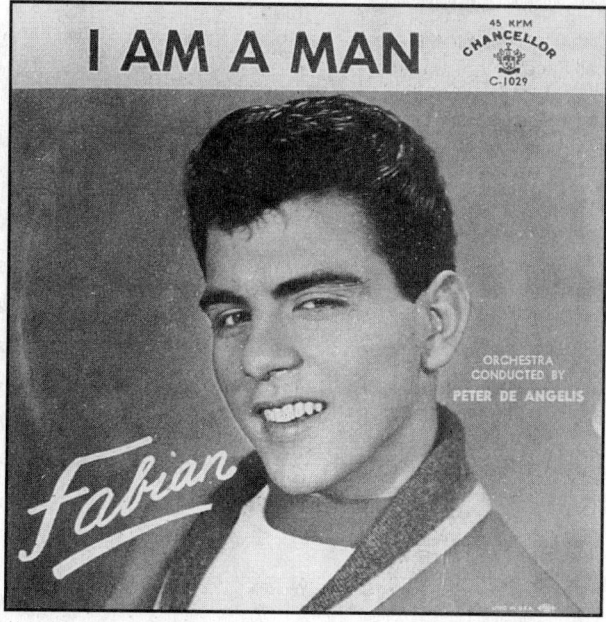

Two cases of titles changing: First, an original pressing of the Doors' second No. 1 hit, "Hello, I Love You," featuring the little-known full-length original title, "Hello, I Love You, Won't You Tell Me Your Name?" Below it is a picture sleeve from an early Fabian single with the incorrect title "I Am a Man." (The record is actually called "I'm a Man.")

Number	Title (A Side/B Side)	Year	VG	VG+	NM
Melic					
❑ 4114	Welcome Me Home/Oop Shoobee Doop	1962	12.50	25.00	50.00
Facenda, Tommy					
Atlantic					
❑ 45-51	High School U.S.A.-Virginia/Plea of Love	1959	10.00	20.00	40.00
❑ 45-52	High School U.S.A.-New York City/Plea of Love	1959	10.00	20.00	40.00
❑ 45-53	High School U.S.A.-North & South Carolina/Plea of Love	1959	10.00	20.00	40.00
❑ 45-54	High School U.S.A.-Washington, D.C./Plea of Love	1959	10.00	20.00	40.00
❑ 45-55	High School U.S.A.-Philadelphia/Plea of Love	1959	10.00	20.00	40.00
❑ 45-56	High School U.S.A.-Detroit/Plea of Love	1959	10.00	20.00	40.00
❑ 45-57	High School U.S.A.-Pittsburgh/Plea of Love	1959	10.00	20.00	40.00
❑ 45-58	High School U.S.A.-Minneapolis-St. Paul/Plea of Love	1959	10.00	20.00	40.00
❑ 45-59	High School U.S.A.-Florida/Plea of Love	1959	10.00	20.00	40.00
❑ 45-60	High School U.S.A.-Newark, N.J./Plea of Love	1959	10.00	20.00	40.00
❑ 45-61	High School U.S.A.-Boston/Plea of Love	1959	10.00	20.00	40.00
❑ 45-62	High School U.S.A.-Cleveland/Plea of Love	1959	10.00	20.00	40.00
❑ 45-63	High School U.S.A.-Buffalo/Plea of Love	1959	10.00	20.00	40.00
❑ 45-64	High School U.S.A.-Hartford, Conn./Plea of Love	1959	10.00	20.00	40.00
❑ 45-65	High School U.S.A.-Nashville/Plea of Love	1959	10.00	20.00	40.00
❑ 45-66	High School U.S.A.-Indianapolis/Plea of Love	1959	10.00	20.00	40.00
❑ 45-67	High School U.S.A.-Chicago/Plea of Love	1959	10.00	20.00	40.00
❑ 45-68	High School U.S.A.-New Orleans/Plea of Love	1959	10.00	20.00	40.00
❑ 45-69	High School U.S.A.-St. Louis & Kansas City/Plea of Love	1959	10.00	20.00	40.00
❑ 45-70	High School U.S.A.-Georgia, Alabama/Plea of Love	1959	10.00	20.00	40.00
❑ 45-71	High School U.S.A.-Cincinnati/Plea of Love	1959	10.00	20.00	40.00
❑ 45-72	High School U.S.A.-Memphis/Plea of Love	1959	10.00	20.00	40.00
❑ 45-73	High School U.S.A.-Los Angeles/Plea of Love	1959	10.00	20.00	40.00
❑ 45-74	High School U.S.A.-San Francisco/Plea of Love	1959	10.00	20.00	40.00
❑ 45-75	High School U.S.A.-Texas/Plea of Love	1959	10.00	20.00	40.00
❑ 45-76	High School U.S.A.-Seattle, Portland/Plea of Love	1959	10.00	20.00	40.00
❑ 45-77	High School U.S.A.-Denver/Plea of Love	1959	10.00	20.00	40.00
❑ 45-78	High School U.S.A.-Oklahoma/Plea of Love	1959	10.00	20.00	40.00
❑ 2057	Bubba Ditty/I Don't Know	1960	5.00	10.00	20.00
Legrand					
❑ 1001	High School U.S.A./Give Me Another Chance	1959	6.25	12.50	25.00
	Original pressings have purple labels				
Nasco					
❑ 6018	Little Baby/You Are My Everything	1958	6.25	12.50	25.00
Faces - See "Small Faces"					
Factory, The					
(Lowell George was in this group before Little Feat)					
Uni					
❑ 55005	Smile, Let Your Life Begin/When I Was An Apple	1967	3.00	6.00	12.00
Fairlanes, The					
Argo					
❑ 5357	Little Girl, Little Girl/Comin' After You	1960	7.50	15.00	30.00
Continental					
❑ 1001	Writing This Letter/Playboy	1961	75.00	150.00	300.00
Dart					
❑ 109	Just for Me/Bullseye	1959	12.50	25.00	50.00
Lucky Seven					
❑ 102	Seventeen Steps/Johnny Rhythm	1959	12.50	25.00	50.00
Minaret					
❑ 103	The Dagwood/I'm Not the Kind of Guy	1962	5.00	10.00	20.00
Radiant					
❑ 101	Baby Baby/Tell Me	1964	50.00	100.00	200.00
Reprise					
❑ 20,213	Surf Train/Lonely Weekends	1963	7.50	15.00	30.00
Faith, Adam					
Amy					
❑ 895	So Long Baby/The First Time	1964	3.75	7.50	15.00
❑ 899	We Are in Love/What Now	1964	3.75	7.50	15.00
❑ 913	It's Alright/I Just Don't Know	1964	3.75	7.50	15.00
❑ 922	Talk About Love/Stop Feeling Sorry for Yourself	1965	3.75	7.50	15.00
❑ 936	Don't You Know/Someone's Taken Marie Away	1965	3.75	7.50	15.00
Capitol					
❑ 5543	I'm Used to Losing You/I Don't Need That Kind of Lovin'	1965	2.50	5.00	10.00
❑ 5699	To Make a Big Man Cry/Here's Another Day	1966	2.50	5.00	10.00
Cub					
❑ 9061	What Do You Want/From Now Until September	1960	5.00	10.00	20.00
❑ 9068	Poor Me/The Reason	1960	5.00	10.00	20.00
❑ 9074	I Did What You Told Me/When Johnny Comes Marching Home	1960	5.00	10.00	20.00
Dot					
❑ 16405	Don't That Beat All/Mix Me a Person	1962	3.75	7.50	15.00

Number		Title (A Side/B Side)	Year	VG	VG+	NM

Laurie

| ❑ 3455 | | Daddy, What'll Happen to Me/
Cowman, Milk Your Cow | 1968 | 2.00 | 4.00 | 8.00 |

Faithfull, Marianne
Collectables

❑ 2605		Broken English/Why D'Ya Do It	199?			3.00
		Reissue				
❑ 4238		As Tears Go By/Gloria	199?			3.00
		Reissue; B-side by Them				

Island

❑ 49121		Broken English/Brain Drain	1979		2.50	5.00
❑ 49873		Sweetheart/For Beauty's Sake	1981		2.00	4.00
❑ 94997		Broken English/Why D'Ya Do It?	198?		2.00	4.00
		Gold label "Revival of the Fittest" series				
❑ 99888		Running for Our Lives/(B-side unknown)	1983		2.00	4.00

London

❑ 1022		Sister Morphine/Something Better	1969	25.00	50.00	100.00
		Promo worth about 50% of these values.				
❑ 9697		As Tears Go By/Greensleeves	1964	3.00	6.00	12.00
❑ 9731		Come and Stay with Me/What Have I Done Wrong	1965	2.50	5.00	10.00
❑ 9759		This Little Bird/Morning Sun	1965	2.50	5.00	10.00
❑ 9780		Summer Nights/The Sha-La-La Song	1965	2.50	5.00	10.00
❑ 9802		Go Away from My World/Oh Look Around You	1965	2.50	5.00	10.00
❑ 9802	PS	Go Away from My World/Oh Look Around You	1965	5.00	10.00	20.00
❑ 20012		Counting/Tomorrow's Calling	1966	2.50	5.00	10.00
❑ 20012	PS	Counting/Tomorrow's Calling	1966	5.00	10.00	20.00
❑ 20020		Is This What I Get for Loving You/Tomorrow's Calling	1966	2.50	5.00	10.00

Falcons, The
(More than one group)

Anna

| ❑ 1110 | | Just for Your Love/This Heart of Mine | 1959 | 25.00 | 50.00 | 100.00 |

Atlantic

❑ 2153		Darling/Lah-Tee-Lah-Tah	1962	5.00	10.00	20.00
❑ 2179		Let's Kiss and Make Up/Take This Love I've Got	1963	5.00	10.00	20.00
❑ 2207		Oh Baby/Fine, Fine, Fine	1963	5.00	10.00	20.00

Big Wheel

| ❑ 1967 | | Standing On Guard/I Can't Help It | 1966 | 5.00 | 10.00 | 20.00 |
| ❑ 321 | | I Must Love You/Love, Love, Love | 1966 | 5.00 | 10.00 | 20.00 |

Cash

| ❑ 1002 | | Tell Me Why/I Miss You Darling | 1955 | 100.00 | 200.00 | 400.00 |

Chess

| ❑ 1743 | | Just for Your Love/This Heart of Mine | 1959 | 6.25 | 12.50 | 25.00 |

Falcon

| ❑ 1006 | | Now That It's Over/My Only Love | 1957 | 37.50 | 75.00 | 150.00 |

Flick

| ❑ 001 | | You're So Fine/Goddess of Angels | 1959 | 75.00 | 150.00 | 300.00 |
| ❑ 008 | | You Must Know I Love You/That's What I Aim to Do | 1960 | 15.00 | 30.00 | 60.00 |

Flip

| ❑ 301 | | Stay Mine/Du-Bi-A-Do | 1954 | 50.00 | 100.00 | 200.00 |
| ❑ 302 | | You Are the Only One/Mambo Baby Tonight | 1954 | 50.00 | 100.00 | 200.00 |

Kudo

| ❑ 661 | | This Heart of Mine/Romanita | 1958 | 100.00 | 200.00 | 400.00 |

LuPine

❑ 103		I Found a Love/Swim	1962	12.50	25.00	50.00
❑ 124		Lonely Nights/Has It Happened to You	1962	25.00	50.00	100.00
❑ 1003		I Found a Love/Swim	1962	5.00	10.00	20.00
❑ 1024		Lonely Nights/Has It Happened to You	1962	10.00	20.00	40.00

Mercury

| ❑ 70940 | | Baby That's It/This Day | 1956 | 12.50 | 25.00 | 50.00 |

Silhouette

| ❑ 522 | | Can This Be Christmas/Sent Up | 1957 | 75.00 | 150.00 | 300.00 |

Unart

❑ 2013	M	You're So Fine/Goddess of Angels	1959	7.50	15.00	30.00
❑ 2013-S	S	You're So Fine/Goddess of Angels	1959	20.00	40.00	80.00
		Actually rechanneled stereo				
❑ 2022		You're Mine/Country Shack	1959	6.25	12.50	25.00

United Artists

❑ 0108		You're So Fine/Showtime	1973		2.00	4.00
		"Silver Spotlight Series" reissue				
❑ 229		The Teacher/Waiting for You	1960	5.00	10.00	20.00
❑ 255		I Plus Love Plus You/Wonderful Love	1960	5.00	10.00	20.00
❑ 289		Pow! You're in Love/Workin' Man's Song	1961	5.00	10.00	20.00
❑ 420		You're So Fine/Goddess of Angels	1962	5.00	10.00	20.00

Fallen Angels, The
Laurie

| ❑ 3343 | | Everytime I Fall in Love/I Have Found | 1966 | 6.25 | 12.50 | 25.00 |
| ❑ 3369 | | Have You Ever Lost a Love/
A Little Love from You Will Do | 1966 | 6.25 | 12.50 | 25.00 |

Number	Title (A Side/B Side)	Year	VG	VG+	NM

Philco

| ❏ HP-23 | Room at the Top/Most Children Do | 1968 | 3.75 | 7.50 | 15.00 |
| | *4-inch flexi-disc in "Philco Hip-Pocket Record" series (price includes sleeve)* | | | | |

Roulette

| ❏ 4770 | Room at the Top/Your Friends Here in Dunderville | 1967 | 5.00 | 10.00 | 20.00 |
| ❏ 4785 | Most Children Do/Hello Girl | 1967 | 5.00 | 10.00 | 20.00 |

Tollie

| ❏ 9049 | Up on the Mountain/So Young, So Fine | 1965 | 6.25 | 12.50 | 25.00 |

Falling Pebbles, The
(Early version of the Buckinghams)

Alley Cat

| ❏ 201 | Lawdy Miss Clawdy/Virginia Wolf | 1964 | 6.25 | 12.50 | 25.00 |

Fame, Georgie

Epic

❏ 10166	Because I Love You/Bidin' My Time ('Cos I Love You)	1967	2.00	4.00	8.00
❏ 10283	The Ballad of Bonnie and Clyde/Beware of the Dog	1968	2.50	5.00	10.00
❏ 10347	Hideaway/Runaway Child	1968		3.00	6.00
❏ 10402	Someone to Watch Over Me/For Your Pleasure	1968		3.00	6.00
❏ 10477	I'll Be Your Baby Tonight/Down Along the Cove	1969		3.00	6.00
❏ 10546	Peaceful/Hideaway	1969		3.00	6.00
❏ 10640	Fire and Rain/The Movie Star Song	1970		3.00	6.00

Imperial

❏ 66086	Yeh, Yeh/Preach and Teach	1965	3.00	6.00	12.00
❏ 66104	Let the Sunshine In/In the Meantime	1965	2.50	5.00	10.00
❏ 66125	Blue Monday/Like We Used to Be	1965	2.50	5.00	10.00
❏ 66189	El Bandido/Get Away	1966	2.50	5.00	10.00
❏ 66220	Last Night/Sitting in the Park	1966	2.50	5.00	10.00
❏ 66299	Funny How Time Slips Away/Last Night	1968	2.00	4.00	8.00

Island

| ❏ 035 | Everlovin' Woman/Ozone | 1975 | | 2.50 | 5.00 |

Fans, The

Dot

| ❏ 16688 | I Want a Beatle for Christmas/
How Far Should I Let My Heart Go Tonight | 1964 | 3.75 | 7.50 | 15.00 |

Fantastic Baggys, The
(Steve Barri and P.F. Sloan)

Imperial

❏ 66047	Tell 'Em I'm Surfin'/Surfer Boy's Dream	1964	10.00	20.00	40.00
❏ 66072	Anywhere the Girls Are/Debbie Be True	1964	10.00	20.00	40.00
❏ 66092	Alone on the Beach/It Was I	1965	12.50	25.00	50.00

Fantastic Four, The

Eastbound

| ❏ 609 | I Had the Whole World to Choose From/
If You Need Me | 1973 | | 3.00 | 6.00 |
| ❏ 620 | I'm Falling in Love (I Feel Good All Over)/
I Believe in Miracles | 1974 | | 3.00 | 6.00 |

Ric-Tic

❏ 113	Can't Stop Looking for My Baby/ Can't Stop Looking for My Baby (Part 2)	1966	50.00	100.00	200.00
❏ 119	Girl Have Pity/Live Up to What She Thinks	1967	3.75	7.50	15.00
❏ 121	Can't Stop Looking for My Baby/Just the Lonely	1967	25.00	50.00	100.00
❏ 122	The Whole World Is a Stage/Ain't Love Wonderful	1967	3.75	7.50	15.00
❏ 128	You Gave Me Something (And Everything's Alright)/ I Don't Wanna Live Without You	1967	3.75	7.50	15.00
❏ 130	To Share Your Love/As Long As I Live (I Live for You)	1967	3.75	7.50	15.00
❏ 134	Goddess of Love/As Long As the Feeling Is There	1968	3.75	7.50	15.00
❏ 136	Love Is a Many-Splendored Thing/Goddess of Love	1968	3.75	7.50	15.00
❏ 137	No Love Like Your Love/A Man in Love	1968	3.75	7.50	15.00
❏ 139	I've Got to Have You/Win or Lose	1968	3.75	7.50	15.00
❏ 144	I Love You Madly/(Instrumental)	1968	5.00	10.00	20.00

Soul

❏ 35052	I Love You Madly/(Instrumental)	1968	3.00	6.00	12.00
❏ 35058	I Feel Like I'm Falling in Love/Pin Point It Out	1969	3.75	7.50	15.00
❏ 35065	Just Another Lonely Night/ I Don't Care Why You Want Me	1969	3.75	7.50	15.00
❏ 35072	On the Brighter Side of a Blue World/ I'm Gonna Hurry On	1970	3.00	6.00	12.00

Westbound

❏ 5009	Alvin Stone (The Birth & Death of a Gangster)/ I Believe in Miracles, I Believe in You	1975		2.50	5.00
❏ 5017	Have a Little Mercy/County Line	1975		2.50	5.00
❏ 5030	Don't Risk Your Happiness On Foolish Things/ They Took the Show on the Road	1976		2.50	5.00
❏ 5032	Hideaway/They Took the Show on the Road	1976		2.50	5.00
❏ 55403	I Got to Have Your Love/Ain't I Been Good to You	1977		2.50	5.00
❏ 55408	Mixed Up Moods and Attitudes/Disco Fool Blues	1978		2.50	5.00
❏ 55417	Sexy Lady/If This Is Love	1979		2.50	5.00
❏ 55419	B.Y.O.F. (Bring Your Own Funk)/If This Is Love	1979		2.50	5.00

Number	Title (A Side/B Side)	Year	VG	VG+	NM

Fantastics, The
(More than one group)
Bell

❏ 977	Something Old, Something New/High and Dry	1971	5.00	10.00	20.00
❏ 45,157	(Love Me) Love the Life I Lead/Old Rags and Tatters	1971	3.75	7.50	15.00

Deram

❏ 7528	Face to Face with Heartache/ This Must Be My Rainy Day	1970	3.75	7.50	15.00

RCA Victor

❏ 47-7572	There Goes My Love/I Wanna Be a Millionaire Hobo	1959	10.00	20.00	40.00
❏ 47-7572	There Goes My Love/I Wanna Be a Millionaire Hobo	1965	3.75	7.50	15.00

Evidently, a reissue with the same number, but the dog on side of label rather than on top, exists

❏ 47-7664	This Is My Wedding Day/I Got a Zero	1960	10.00	20.00	40.00

Scorpio

❏ 407	Malaguena/Dance for an Unnamed Gypsy Queen	1966	6.25	12.50	25.00

Sound Stage 7

❏ 2565	Have a Little You/Me and You	1966	3.00	6.00	12.00

United Artists

❏ 309	Dancing Dolls/I Told You Once	1961	12.50	25.00	50.00

Farlowe, Chris
Immediate

❏ 5002	Paint It Black/You're So Good to Me	1967	2.50	5.00	10.00
❏ 5005	Handbags and Gladrags/Everyone Makes a Mistake	1968	2.50	5.00	10.00
❏ 5011	What Have I Been Doing/Paint It Black	1968	2.50	5.00	10.00

MGM

❏ 13567	Out of Time/Baby Make It Soon	1966	5.00	10.00	20.00

A-side is a Mick Jagger-Keith Richards composition only later recorded by the Rolling Stones.

Polydor

❏ 14008	Circles 'Round the Sun/Save Your Tears	1969	2.00	4.00	8.00
❏ 14013	Medicated Goo/Betty Lou	1970	2.00	4.00	8.00

Farner, Mark
(Of Grand Funk Railroad)
Atlantic

❏ 3448	You and Me Baby/Second Chance to Dance	1977		2.00	4.00
❏ 3510	When a Man Loves a Woman/If It Took All Day	1978		2.00	4.00
❏ 3529	Just One Look/Crystal Eyes	1978		2.00	4.00

Lucky Eleven

❏ 352	Down in the Dumps/I Got News for You	1968	2.50	5.00	10.00

Farner, Mark, and Don Brewer
(Both later of Grand Funk Railroad)
Lucky Eleven

❏ 366	Does It Matter to You Girl/We Gotta Have Love	1968	3.00	6.00	12.00

Fascinations, The
(More than one group)
A&G

❏ 101	I'm Gonna Cry/Since You Went Away	1972	2.50	5.00	10.00

ABC-Paramount
Note: Some of the ABC-Paramount pressings are misspelled "Fasinations"

❏ 10387	Mama Didn't Lie/Someone Like You	1962	5.00	10.00	20.00
❏ 10443	Tears In My Eyes/You're Gonna Be Sorry	1963	6.25	12.50	25.00

Dore

❏ 593	If I Had Your Love/Why	1961	12.50	25.00	50.00

Paxley

❏ 750	If I Had Your Love/Why	1960	37.50	75.00	150.00

Sure

❏ 106	Midnight/Boom Bada Boom	1960	30.00	60.00	120.00
❏ 106	It's Midnight/Boom Bada Boom	1960	20.00	40.00	80.00

Fascinators, The
(Probably more than one group)
Bim Bam Boom

❏ 110	Oh, Rose Marie/Forgive Me, My Darling	1974	2.50	5.00	10.00

Blue Lake

❏ 112	Can't Stop/Don't Give My Love Away	1953	125.00	250.00	500.00

Burn

❏ 845	I'll Be Gone/Can't You See I'm Lonely	1965	3.00	6.00	12.00

Capitol

❏ F4053	Chapel Bells/I Wonder Who	1958	37.50	75.00	150.00
❏ F4137	Come to Paradise/Who Do You Think You Are	1959	25.00	50.00	100.00
❏ F4247	Oh Rose Marie/Fried Chicken and Macaroni	1959	50.00	100.00	200.00
❏ 4544	Chapel Bells/I Wonder Who	1961	20.00	40.00	80.00

Dooto

❏ 441	Teardrop Eyes/Shivers and Shakes	1958	15.00	30.00	60.00

King

❏ 5119	Cuddle Up with Carolyn/Tee Hee	1958	12.50	25.00	50.00

Number	Title (A Side/B Side)	Year	VG	VG+	NM
Trans Atlas					
❑ 688	You're to Blame/Revived	196?	7.50	15.00	30.00
Your Copy					
❑ 1135	The Bells of My Heart/Sweet Baby	1954	150.00	300.00	600.00
	Black vinyl				
❑ 1135	The Bells of My Heart/Sweet Baby	1954	200.00	400.00	800.00
	Colored vinyl				
❑ 1136	My Beauty, My Own/Don't Give It Away	1954	150.00	300.00	600.00

Fastest Group Alive, The
Teen

❑ 100	The Bears/Beside	1966	7.50	15.00	30.00
Valiant					
❑ 754	The Bears/Beside	1966	5.00	10.00	20.00
❑ 759	Lullabye/5:15 Sports	1967	5.00	10.00	20.00

Featherbed
(Barry Manilow was a member)
Bell

❑ 971	Amy/Morning	1971	15.00	30.00	60.00
❑ 45,133	DJ Could It Be Magic (mono/stereo)	1971	15.00	30.00	60.00
	Stock copy may not exist				

Feathers, Charlie
Flip

❑ 503	I've Been Deceived/Peeping Eyes	1955	125.00	250.00	500.00
Holiday Inn					
❑ 114	Deep Elm Blues/Nobody's Darling	1962	50.00	100.00	200.00
Kay					
❑ 1001	Jungle Fever/Why Don't You	1960	50.00	100.00	200.00
King					
❑ 4971	Can't Hardly Stand It/Everybody's Lovin' My Baby	1956	75.00	150.00	300.00
❑ 4997	One Hand Loose/Bottle to the Baby	1956	62.50	125.00	250.00
❑ 5022	Nobody's Woman/When You Decide	1957	50.00	100.00	200.00
❑ 5043	When You Come Around/Too Much Alike	1957	50.00	100.00	200.00
Memphis					
❑ 103	Wild, Wild Party/Today and Tomorrow	1961	25.00	50.00	100.00
Meteor					
❑ 5032	Tongue-Tied Jill/Get With It	1956	75.00	150.00	300.00
	Black label				
❑ 5032	Tongue-Tied Jill/Get With It	1956	500.00	750.00	1,000
	Maroon label				
Philwood					
❑ 223	Tear It Up/Stutterin' Cindy	197?	2.00	4.00	8.00
Pompadour					
❑ 231	Uh-Huh Honey/A Wedding Gown of White	1974	2.00	4.00	8.00
Rollin' Rock					
❑ 45-025	That Certain Female/She Set Me Free	1978	2.00	4.00	8.00
Sun					
❑ 231	Defrost Your Heart/Wedding Gown of White	1956	200.00	400.00	600.00
❑ 503	I've Been Deceived/Peeping Eyes	1956	200.00	400.00	600.00
Wal-May					
❑ 101	Dinky John/South of Chicago	1960	50.00	100.00	200.00

Felicity
(Either Don Henley or Glenn Frey was a member of this group -- sources differ as to which one)
Wilson

❑ 101	Hurtin'/I'll Try It	1965	7.50	15.00	30.00

Felix and the Escorts
(An early version of the [Young] Rascals. "Felix" is Felix Cavaliere)
Jag

❑ 685	The Syracuse/Save	1964	37.50	75.00	150.00

Female Beatles, The
20th Fox

❑ 531	I Don't Want to Cry/I Want You	1964	5.00	10.00	20.00

Fender IV
Imperial

❑ 66061	Mar-Gaya/You Better Tell Me Now	1964	12.50	25.00	50.00
❑ 66098	Malibu Run/Everybody Up	1965	12.50	25.00	50.00

Fender, Freddy
ABC

❑ 12339	Louisiana Woman/If You're Looking for a Fool	1978		2.00	4.00
❑ 12370	Talk to Me/Please Mr. Sun	1978		2.00	4.00
❑ 12415	I'm Leaving It All Up to You/	1978		2.00	4.00
	When It Rains It Really Pours				
❑ 12453	Sweet Summer Day/Walking Piece of Heaven	1979		2.00	4.00

Number	Title (A Side/B Side)	Year	VG	VG+	NM

ABC/Dot

❏ 17540	Before the Next Teardrop Falls/Waiting for Your Love	1974		2.50	5.00
❏ 17558	Wasted Days and Wasted Nights/	1975		2.50	5.00
	I Love My Rancho Grande				
❏ 17585	Secret Love/Loving Cajun Style	1975		2.00	4.00
❏ 17607	You'll Lose a Good Thing/I'm to Blame	1976		2.00	4.00
❏ 17627	Vaya Con Dios/My Happiness	1976		2.00	4.00
❏ 17652	Living It Down/Take Her a Message, I'm Lonely	1976		2.00	4.00
❏ 17686	The Rains Came/Sugar Coated Love	1977		2.00	4.00
❏ 17713	If You Don't Love Me	1977		2.00	4.00
	(Why Don't You Just Leave Me Alone)/				
	Thank You, My Love				
❏ 17730	Think About Me/If That's the Way You Want It	1977		2.00	4.00
❏ 17734	Christmas Time in the Valley/	1977		2.00	4.00
	Please Come Home for Christmas				

Argo

❏ 5375	A Man Can Cry/You're Something Else for Me	1960	3.75	7.50	15.00

ARV International

❏ 5083	Crazy Arms/She Thinks I Still Care	196?	2.50	5.00	10.00
❏ 5102	Un Dia de Sol/La Costumbre	196?	2.50	5.00	10.00
❏ 5146	El Rock de la Carcel/No Seasa Cruel	196?	2.50	5.00	10.00
❏ 5216	Crazy Arms/She Thinks I Still Care	198?		2.50	5.00

Crazy Cajun

❏ 2002	Before the Next Teardrop Falls/Crazy, Crazy Baby	198?		2.50	5.00
❏ 2002	Before the Next Teardrop Falls/Waiting for Your Love	198?		2.50	5.00
❏ 2006	Esta Noche Mia Sera/(B-side unknown)	198?		2.50	5.00
❏ 2014	No Toquen Ya/I Love My Rancho Grande	198?		2.50	5.00
❏ 2019	Vaya Con Dios/No Say El Mismo	198?		2.50	5.00
❏ 2037	Fannie Mae/Going Out with the Tide	198?		2.50	5.00
	With Tommy McLain				
❏ 2060	My Confession/Goin' Honky Tonkin'	198?		2.00	4.00

Duncan

❏ 1000	Mean Woman/Holy One	1959	10.00	20.00	40.00
❏ 1001	Wasted Days and Wasted Nights/San Antonio Walk	1959	6.25	12.50	25.00
❏ 1002	Wild Side of Life/Crazy Baby	1959	6.25	12.50	25.00
❏ 1004	Since I Met You Baby/Little Mama	1959	6.25	12.50	25.00

Goldband

❏ 1214	My Tears of Love/Carmelia	1969	2.50	5.00	10.00
❏ 1264	Bye, Bye, Little Angel/Oh My Love	1975		2.50	5.00
❏ 1272	Three Wishes/Me and My Bottle of Rum	1975		2.50	5.00

GRT

❏ 031	Since I Met You Baby/Little Mama	1975		2.50	5.00
❏ 039	Wild Side of Life/Go On Baby	1975		2.50	5.00

Imperial

❏ 5659	Mean Woman/Holy One	1960	5.00	10.00	20.00
❏ 5670	Wasted Days and Wasted Nights/	1960	5.00	10.00	20.00
	I Can't Remember When I Didn't Love You				

Instant

❏ 3332	Some People Say/Today's Your Wedding Day	1972	2.00	4.00	8.00

MCA

❏ 12453	Sweet Summer Day/Walking Piece of Heaven	1979		2.00	4.00
❏ 52003	Across the Borderline/Before the Next Teardrop Falls	1982		2.00	4.00

Norco

❏ 100	Love's Light Is an Ember/The New Stroll	1963	2.50	5.00	10.00
❏ 102	You Made Me Cry/Never Trust a Cheating Woman	1963	2.50	5.00	10.00
❏ 103	Coming Home Soon/Going Out with the Tide	1964	2.50	5.00	10.00
❏ 104	Just a Little Bit/You Made Me a Fool	1964	2.50	5.00	10.00
❏ 106	Ooh Poo Pah Doo/Three Wishes	1964	2.50	5.00	10.00
❏ 107	Magic of Love/Bony Moronie	1965	2.50	5.00	10.00
	With Noel Vill				
❏ 108	In the Still of the Night/You Don't Have to Go	1965	2.50	5.00	10.00
❏ 111	Donna/Lover's Quarrel	1965	2.50	5.00	10.00

Pa-Go-Go

❏ 115	Cool Mary Lou/You Are My Sunshine	1967	2.50	5.00	10.00

Pacemaker

❏ 1973	Wasted Days and Wasted Nights/Bidin' My Time	197?		2.50	5.00

Reprise

❏ 19143	It's All in the Game/Before the Next Teardrop Falls	1992			3.00

Starflite

❏ 4900	Yours/Rock Down in My Shoe	1979		2.00	4.00
❏ 4904	Squeeze Box/Turn Around	1979		2.00	4.00
❏ 4906	My Special Prayer/(B-side unknown)	1979		2.00	4.00
❏ 4908	Please Talk to My Heart/(B-side unknown)	1980		2.00	4.00

Warner Bros.

❏ 29794	Chokin' Kind/I Might As Well Forget You	1983		2.00	4.00

Fendermen, The

Cuca

❏ 1003	Mule Skinner Blues/Torture	1960	37.50	75.00	150.00

Soma

❏ 1137	Mule Skinner Blues/Torture	1960	6.25	12.50	25.00
❏ 1142	Don't You Just Know It/Beach Party	1960	5.00	10.00	20.00
❏ 1155	Heartbreakin' Special/Can't You Wait	1960	5.00	10.00	20.00

Number		Title (A Side/B Side)	Year	VG	VG+	NM
Ferris and the Wheels						
Bambi						
❑ 801		I Want to Dance (Every Night)/Chop Chop	1961	6.25	12.50	25.00
United Artists						
❑ 458		Moments Like This/He Was a Fortune Teller	1962	25.00	50.00	100.00
Ferry Aid						
(Charity group assembled by Paul McCartney)						
Profile						
❑ 5147		Let It Be/Let It Be (Gospel Jam Mix)	1987	2.50	5.00	10.00
❑ 5147	PS	Let It Be/Let It Be (Gospel Jam Mix)	1987	2.50	5.00	10.00
Fever Tree						
Ampex						
❑ 11013		She Comes in Colors/You're Not the Same Baby	1970	3.75	7.50	15.00
❑ 11028		I Put a Spell on You/Hey Joe, Where You Gonna Go	1970	3.75	7.50	15.00
Mainstream						
❑ 661		Hey Mister/I Can Beat Your Drum	1967	3.00	6.00	12.00
❑ 665		Girl, Oh Girl (Don't Push Me)/Steve Lenore	1967	3.00	6.00	12.00
Uni						
❑ 55060		San Fransisco Girls (Return of the Native)/Come with Me	1968	3.00	6.00	12.00
❑ 55060	DJ	San Fransisco Girls (Return of the Native) (same on both sides)	1968	10.00	20.00	40.00
		Promo only on blue vinyl				
❑ 55095		What Time Did You Say It Is in Salt Lake City/Where Do You Go	1968	3.75	7.50	15.00
❑ 55146		Love Makes the Sun Rise/Filigree and Shadow	1969	3.75	7.50	15.00
❑ 55172		The Sun Also Rises/Clancey	1969	3.75	7.50	15.00
❑ 55201		Catcher in the Rye/What Time Did You Say It Is in Salt Lake City?	1970	5.00	10.00	20.00
❑ 55228		I Am/Grand Candy Young Sweet	1970	5.00	10.00	20.00
Fi-Dells, The						
Imperial						
❑ 5780		What Is Love/Don't Let Me Love You	1961	6.25	12.50	25.00
Warner						
❑ 1014		No Other Love/Come Back to Me	1957	5.00	10.00	20.00
Field, Jerry, and the Lawyers						
Parkway						
❑ 801		The Trial/Easy Steppin'	1958	7.50	15.00	30.00
		Blue label				
❑ 801		The Trial/Easy Steppin'	1958	5.00	10.00	20.00
		White label. This is actually a cover of a break-in record! (For the original, see "Herb B. Lou and the Legal Eagles".)				
Fiestas, The						
Chimneyville						
❑ 10216		Tina, the Disco Queen/I'm No Better Than You	1977	3.00	6.00	12.00
❑ 10221		Is That Long Enough for You/I'm Gonna Make Myself	1977	3.00	6.00	12.00
Cotillion						
❑ 44117		So Fine/Broken Heart	1971	6.25	12.50	25.00
Old Town						
❑ 1062		So Fine/Last Night I Dreamed	1958	12.50	25.00	50.00
		Versions pressed by Columbia have a piano intro not available elsewhere. Look for "ZTSP" on label				
❑ 1062		So Fine/Last Night I Dreamed	1958	6.25	12.50	25.00
		Standard version; no "ZTSP" on label				
❑ 1067		Grandma Gave a Party/I'm Your Slave	1959	6.25	12.50	25.00
❑ 1069		Our Anniversary/I'm Your Slave	1959	6.25	12.50	25.00
❑ 1074		Good News/That Was Me	1959	6.25	12.50	25.00
❑ 1080		Dollar Bill/It Don't Make Sense	1960	6.25	12.50	25.00
❑ 1090		So Nice/You Could Be My Girlfriend	1960	6.25	12.50	25.00
❑ 1104		Look at That Girl/Mr. Dillon, Mr. Dillon	1961	6.25	12.50	25.00
❑ 1111		Hobo's Prayer/She's Mine	1961	10.00	20.00	40.00
❑ 1122		Broken Heart/Railroad Song	1962	5.00	10.00	20.00
❑ 1127		I Feel Good All Over/Look at That Girl	1962	5.00	10.00	20.00
❑ 1134		The Gypsy Said/Mama Put the Law Down	1963	5.00	10.00	20.00
❑ 1140		The Party's Over/Try It One More Time	1963	5.00	10.00	20.00
❑ 1148		Foolish Dreamer/Rock-a-By Baby	1963	5.00	10.00	20.00
❑ 1166		All That's Good/Rock-a-By Baby	1964	5.00	10.00	20.00
❑ 1178		Think Smart/Anna	1965	20.00	40.00	80.00
❑ 1187		Love Is Strange/Love Is Good to Me	1965	3.75	7.50	15.00
❑ 1189		Ain't She Sweet/I Gotta Have Your Lovin'	1965	3.75	7.50	15.00
Respect						
❑ 2509		I Can't Shake Your Love (Can't Shake You Loose)/A Sometimes Storm	1972	2.00	4.00	8.00
Strand						
❑ 25046		Come On Everybody/Julia	1961	10.00	20.00	40.00
Vigor						
❑ 712		So Fine/Darling You've Changed	1974	2.00	4.00	8.00

Number		Title (A Side/B Side)	Year	VG	VG+	NM

Fifth Dimension, The
ABC
❑ 12136		Magic in My Life/Lean On Me Always	1975		2.00	4.00
❑ 12168		Walk Your Feet in the Sunshine/ Speaking with My Heart	1976		2.00	4.00
❑ 12181		Love Hangover/Will You Be There	1976		2.00	4.00

Arista
❑ 0101		No Love in the Room/ I Don't Know How to Look for Love	1975		2.00	4.00

Bell
❑ 860		Medley: A Change Is Gonna Come & People Gotta Be Free/The Declaration	1970		2.50	5.00
❑ 880		Puppet Man/A Love Like Ours	1970		2.50	5.00
❑ 895		Save the Country/Dimension 5	1970		2.50	5.00
❑ 913		On the Beach (In the Summertime)/This Is Your Life	1970		2.50	5.00
❑ 940		One Less Bell to Answer/Feelin' Alright?	1970		2.50	5.00
❑ 965		Love's Lines, Angles and Rhymes/The Singer	1971		2.50	5.00
❑ 999		Light Sings/Viva Tirado	1971		2.50	5.00
❑ 45,134		Never My Love/A Love Like Ours	1971		2.50	5.00
❑ 45,170		Together Let's Find Love/I Just Wanta Be Your Friend	1972		2.50	5.00
❑ 45,195		(Last Night) I Didn't Get to Sleep at All/The River Witch	1972		2.50	5.00
❑ 45,261		If I Could Reach You/ Tomorrow Belongs to the Children	1972		2.50	5.00
❑ 45,310		Living Together, Growing Together/ What Do I Need to Be Me	1973		2.00	4.00
❑ 45,338		Everything's Been Changed/There Never Was a Day	1973		2.00	4.00
❑ 45,380		Ashes to Ashes/The Singer	1973		2.00	4.00
❑ 45,425		Flashback/Diggin' for a Livin'	1973		2.00	4.00
❑ 45,612		Harlem/My Song	1974		2.00	4.00

Motown
❑ 1437		You Are the Reason (I Feel Like Dancing)/ Slipping Into Something New	1978		2.00	4.00
❑ 1453		Everybody's Got to Give It Up/You're My Star	1978		2.00	4.00

Soul City
❑ 752		I'll Be Loving You Forever/Train, Keep On Moving	1966	3.75	7.50	15.00
❑ 753		Go Where You Wanna Go/Too Poor to Die	1967	2.00	4.00	8.00
❑ 753	PS	Go Where You Wanna Go/Too Poor to Die	1967	5.00	10.00	20.00
❑ 755		Another Day, Another Heartache/Rosecrans Blvd.	1967	2.50	5.00	10.00
❑ 755	PS	Another Day, Another Heartache/Rosecrans Blvd.	1967	5.00	10.00	20.00
❑ 756		Up-Up and Away/Which Way to Nowhere	1967	2.00	4.00	8.00
❑ 760		Paper Cup/Poor Side of Town	1967	2.00	4.00	8.00
❑ 762		Carpet Man/Magic Garden	1968	2.00	4.00	8.00
❑ 766		Stoned Soul Picnic/The Sailooat Song	1968	2.00	4.00	8.00
❑ 766	PS	Stoned Soul Picnic/The Sailboat Song	1968	3.75	7.50	15.00
❑ 768		Sweet Blindness/Bobby's Blues	1968	2.00	4.00	8.00
❑ 768	PS	Sweet Blindness/Bobby's Blues	1968	3.75	7.50	15.00
❑ 770		California Soul/It'll Never Be the Same	1968	2.00	4.00	8.00
❑ 772		Aquarius/Let the Sunshine In (The Flesh Failures)// Don'tcha Hear Me Callin' To Ya	1969	2.00	4.00	8.00
❑ 772	PS	Aquarius/Let the Sunshine In (The Flesh Failures)// Don'tcha Hear Me Callin' To Ya	1969	3.75	7.50	15.00
❑ 776		Workin' on a Groovy Thing/Broken Wing Bird	1969	2.00	4.00	8.00
❑ 779		Wedding Bell Blues/Lovin' Stew	1969	2.00	4.00	8.00
❑ 780		Blowing Away/Skinny Man	1970		3.00	6.00
❑ 781		The Girls' Song/It'll Never Be the Same Again	1970		3.00	6.00

Sutra
❑ 122		Surrender/Fantasy	1983		2.00	4.00

Fifth Estate, The
(Also see "D-Men, The")
Jubilee
❑ 5573		Ding! Dong! The Witch Is Dead/The Rub-a-Dub	1967	3.00	6.00	12.00
❑ 5588		Lost Generation/The Goofin' Song	1967	2.00	4.00	8.00
❑ 5595		Heigh-Ho/It's Waiting There for You	1967	2.00	4.00	8.00
❑ 5607		Morning, Morning/Tomorrow Is My Turn	1967	2.00	4.00	8.00
❑ 5617		Do Drop Inn/That's Love	1968	2.00	4.00	8.00
❑ 5627		Coney Island Sally/Tomorrow Is My Turn	1968	2.00	4.00	8.00
❑ 5655		Mickey Mouse Club March/ I Knew You Before I Met You	1969	2.00	4.00	8.00
❑ 5683	DJ	Parade of the Wooden Soldiers (mono/stereo)	1969	2.50	5.00	10.00
		Stock copies may not exist ("I Knew You Before I Met You" was listed as B-side)				

Red Bird
❑ 10-064		Love Is All a Game/Like I Love You	1966	3.75	7.50	15.00

Fireballs, The
(With and without Jimmy Gilmer. Dot records are The Fireballs unless indicated)
Astra
❑ 1021		Torquay/Sweet Walk	1966	2.50	5.00	10.00

Atco
❑ 6491		Bottle of Wine/Can't You See I'm Tryin'	1967	2.50	5.00	10.00
❑ 6569		Goin' Away/Groovy Motions	1968	2.00	4.00	8.00
❑ 6595		Chicken Little/Three Minutes' Time	1968	2.00	4.00	8.00
❑ 6614		Come On, React!/Woman Help Me	1968	2.00	4.00	8.00
❑ 6651		Long Green/Light in the Window	1969	2.00	4.00	8.00
❑ 6678		Watch Her Walk/Good Morning Shame	1969	2.00	4.00	8.00

Number		Title (A Side/B Side)	Year	VG	VG+	NM
Dot						
❏ 16487		Sugar Shack/My Heart Is Free	1963	3.75	7.50	15.00
		Jimmy Gilmer and the Fireballs				
❏ 16493		Torquay Two/Peg Leg	1963	3.75	7.50	15.00
❏ 16539		Daisy Petal Pickin'/When My Tears Have Dried	1963	3.00	6.00	12.00
		Jimmy Gilmer and the Fireballs				
❏ 16583		Ain't Gonna Tell Anybody/Young Am I	1964	3.00	6.00	12.00
		Jimmy Gilmer and the Fireballs				
❏ 16591		Daytona Drag/Gently, Gently	1964	3.75	7.50	15.00
❏ 16609		I'll Send for You/Look at Me	1964	2.50	5.00	10.00
		Jimmy Gilmer and the Fireballs				
❏ 16642		Wishing/What Kinda Love	1964	2.50	5.00	10.00
		Jimmy Gilmer and the Fireballs				
❏ 16661		Dumbo/Mr. Reed	1964	3.75	7.50	15.00
❏ 16666		Cry Baby/Thunder 'N' Lightnin'	1964	2.50	5.00	10.00
		Jimmy Gilmer and the Fireballs				
❏ 16687		Break His Heart for Me/Cinnamon Cindy	1965	2.50	5.00	10.00
		Jimmy Gilmer and the Fireballs				
❏ 16692		Yummie Yama Papa/Baby, What's Wrong	1965	3.75	7.50	15.00
❏ 16714		Born to Be with You/Lonesome Tears	1965	2.50	5.00	10.00
		Jimmy Gilmer and the Fireballs				
❏ 16715		More Than I Can Say/Beating of My Heart	1965	3.75	7.50	15.00
❏ 16743		The Fool/Somebody Stole My Watermelon	1965	2.50	5.00	10.00
		Jimmy Gilmer and the Fireballs				
❏ 16745		Ahhh, Soul/Campusology	1965	3.75	7.50	15.00
❏ 16768		Codine/Come to Me	1965	2.50	5.00	10.00
		Jimmy Gilmer and the Fireballs				
❏ 16786		She Belongs to Me/Rambler's Blues	1965	2.50	5.00	10.00
		Jimmy Gilmer and the Fireballs				
❏ 16833		Hungry, Hungry, Hungry/Wild Roses	1966	2.50	5.00	10.00
		Jimmy Gilmer and the Fireballs				
❏ 16834		Jada/What I Am	1966	3.75	7.50	15.00
❏ 16881		All I Do Is Dream of You/Ain't That Rain	1966	2.50	5.00	10.00
		Jimmy Gilmer and the Fireballs				
❏ 16918		Torquay Two/Say I Am	1966	3.75	7.50	15.00
❏ 16979		Sugar Shack/Daisy Petal Pickin'	1966	2.50	5.00	10.00
		Jimmy Gilmer and the Fireballs				
❏ 16992		Shy Girl/I Think I'll Catch a Bus	1967	2.50	5.00	10.00
		Jimmy Gilmer and the Fireballs				
Hamilton						
❏ 50036		Blacksmith Blues/Tuff-a-Nuff	1960	5.00	10.00	20.00
Jaro						
❏ 77029		Long, Long Ponytail/Let There Be Love	1960	20.00	40.00	80.00
		Chuck Tharp and the Fireballs				
Kapp						
❏ 248		Fireball/I Don't Know	1958	25.00	50.00	100.00
		Chuck Tharp and the Fireballs				
Seven Arts						
❏ 714		Callin' the Sheriff/Don't Stop	1961	3.75	7.50	15.00
		Jimmy Gilmer and the Fireballs				
❏ 714	PS	Callin' the Sheriff/Don't Stop	1961	12.50	25.00	50.00
Top Rank						
❏ 2008		Torquay/Cry Baby	1959	5.00	10.00	20.00
❏ 2026	M	Bulldog/Nearly Sunrise	1959	5.00	10.00	20.00
❏ 2026ST	S	Bulldog/Nearly Sunrise	1959	12.50	25.00	50.00
❏ 2038	M	Foot Patter/Kissin'	1959	5.00	10.00	20.00
❏ 2038ST	S	Foot Patter/Kissin'	1959	12.50	25.00	50.00
❏ 2054		Vaquero/Chief Whoopin'-Koff	1960	5.00	10.00	20.00
❏ 2081		Almost Paradise/Sweet Talk	1960	5.00	10.00	20.00
❏ 3003		Rick-a-Tic/Tacky Doo	1961	5.00	10.00	20.00
Warwick						
❏ 630		Rik-A-Tik/Yackey-Doo	1961	4.00	8.00	16.00
❏ 644		Quite a Party/Gunshot	1961	4.00	8.00	16.00

Fireflies, The

(Also see "Rogers, Kenny")

Number		Title (A Side/B Side)	Year	VG	VG+	NM
Canadian American						
❏ 117		Marianne/Give All Your Love to Me	1960	5.00	10.00	20.00
Ribbon						
❏ 6901		You Were Mine/Stella Got a Fella	1959	6.25	12.50	25.00
❏ 6904		I Can't Say Goodbye/What Did I Do Wrong	1959	5.00	10.00	20.00
❏ 6906		My Girl/Because of My Pride	1960	5.00	10.00	20.00
Taurus						
❏ 355		One O'Clock Twist/You Were Mine for Awhile	1962	5.00	10.00	20.00
❏ 366		Good Friends/My Prayer for You	1964	5.00	10.00	20.00
❏ 376		Runaround/Could You Mean More	1965	5.00	10.00	20.00
❏ 380		Tonight/A Time for Us	1965	5.00	10.00	20.00

First Edition, The

(Also see "Rogers, Kenny")

Number		Title (A Side/B Side)	Year	VG	VG+	NM
Reprise						
❏ 0628		Ticket to Nowhere/I Found a Reason	1967	2.00	4.00	8.00

Number		Title (A Side/B Side)	Year	VG	VG+	NM
❏ 0655		Just Dropped In (To See What Condition	1967	3.00	6.00	12.00
		My Condition Was In)/Shadow in the Corner of Your Mind				
		Original pressing has orange and brown label				
❏ 0655		Just Dropped In (To See What Condition	1967	2.50	5.00	10.00
		My Condition Was In)/Shadow in the Corner of Your Mind				
		Second pressing has lighter orange "steamboat" Reprise/W7 label				
❏ 0683		Dream On/Only Me	1968		3.00	6.00
❏ 0693		Look Around, I'll Be There/Charlie the Fer-De-Lance	1968		3.00	6.00
❏ 0737		Just Dropped In (To See What Condition	1971		2.00	4.00
		My Condition Was In)/But You Know I Love You				
		As Kenny Rogers and the First Edition; "Back to Back Hits" series				
❏ 0738		Ruby, Don't Take Your Love to Town/Reuben James	1971		2.00	4.00
		As Kenny Rogers and the First Edition; "Back to Back Hits" series				
❏ 0747		Something's Burning/Someone Who Cares	1972		2.00	4.00
		As Kenny Rogers and the First Edition; "Back to Back Hits" series				
❏ 0748		Tell It All Brother/Heed the Call	1972		2.00	4.00
		As Kenny Rogers and the First Edition; "Back to Back Hits" series				
❏ 0773		If I Could Only Change Your Mind/	1968		3.00	6.00
		Are My Thoughts With You				
❏ 0799		But You Know I Love You/Homemade Lies	1968		3.00	6.00
		Note: Starting with 0822, all are by "Kenny Rogers and the First Edition"				
❏ 0822		Good Time Liberator/Once Again She's All Alone	1969		2.50	5.00
❏ 0829		Ruby, Don't Take Your Love to Town/	1969		2.50	5.00
		Girl Get a Hold of Yourself				
❏ 0854		Ruben James/Sunshine	1969		2.50	5.00
❏ 0854		Reuben James/Sunshine	1969		2.50	5.00
❏ 0888		Something's Burning/Mama's Waiting	1970		2.50	5.00
❏ 0923		Tell It All Brother/Just Remember You're My Sunshine	1970		2.50	5.00
❏ 0953		Heed the Call/A Stranger in My Place	1970		2.50	5.00
❏ 0999		Someone Who Cares/Mission of San Mohera	1971		2.50	5.00
❏ 1018		Take My Hand/All God's Lonely Children	1971		2.50	5.00
❏ 1053		Where Does Rosie Go/What Am I Gonna Do	1971		2.50	5.00
❏ 1069		School Teacher/Trigger Happy Kid	1972		2.50	5.00

Fisher, Toni
(Some identify her as "Miss Toni Fisher")

Big Top
| ❏ 3097 | | West of the Wall/What Did I Do | 1962 | 3.00 | 6.00 | 12.00 |

Capitol
| ❏ 5901 | | Train of Love/A Million Heartbeats from Now | 1967 | 2.00 | 4.00 | 8.00 |

Columbia
| ❏ 42066 | | If I Loved You/Love Big | 1961 | 3.00 | 6.00 | 12.00 |

Signet
❏ 275		The Big Hurt/Memphis Belle	1959	3.75	7.50	15.00
❏ 276		How Deep Is the Ocean/Blue, Blue, Blue	1960	3.00	6.00	12.00
❏ 279		Everlasting Love/The Red Sea of Mars	1960	3.00	6.00	12.00
❏ 364		You Never Told Me/Toot Toot Amore	1964	2.00	4.00	8.00
❏ 400		A Man That's Steady/You Never Told Me	196?	2.00	4.00	8.00
❏ 664		Springtime of Love/Train of Love	1964	2.00	4.00	8.00

Smash
❏ 1797		Hold Me/Laugh or Cry	1963	2.50	5.00	10.00
❏ 1820		Cry a Little for Me/365 Disappointments	1963	2.50	5.00	10.00
❏ 1832		Lovers, Dreamers, Fools/You Won't Forget Me	1963	2.50	5.00	10.00
❏ 1847		Your Royal Majesty/Billy, Marry Me	1963	2.50	5.00	10.00

Five Americans, The

ABC-Paramount
| ❏ 10686 | | Show Me/Love, Love, Love | 1965 | 3.00 | 6.00 | 12.00 |

Abnak
❏ 106		Say That You Love Me/Without You	1965	2.50	5.00	10.00
❏ 106	DJ	Say That You Love Me/Without You	1965	6.25	12.50	25.00
		Promo only on yellow vinyl				
❏ 109		I See the Light/The Outcast	1965	5.00	10.00	20.00
❏ 109	DJ	I See the Light/The Outcast	1965	6.25	12.50	25.00
		Promo only on yellow vinyl				
❏ 114		Reality/Sympathy	1966	2.50	5.00	10.00
❏ 114	DJ	Reality/Sympathy	1966	6.25	12.50	25.00
		Promo only on yellow vinyl				
❏ 116		If I Could/Now That It's Over	1966	2.50	5.00	10.00
❏ 116	DJ	If I Could/Now That It's Over	1966	6.25	12.50	25.00
		Promo only on yellow vinyl				
❏ 118		Western Union/Now That It's Over	1967	3.00	6.00	12.00
❏ 118	DJ	Western Union/Now That It's Over	1967	6.25	12.50	25.00
		Promo only on yellow vinyl				
❏ 120		Sound of Love/Sympathy	1967	2.00	4.00	8.00
❏ 120	DJ	Sound of Love/Sympathy	1967	6.25	12.50	25.00
		Promo only on yellow vinyl				
❏ 123		Zip Code/Sweet Bird of Youth	1967	2.00	4.00	8.00
❏ 123	DJ	Zip Code/Sweet Bird of Youth	1967	6.25	12.50	25.00
		Promo only on yellow vinyl				
❏ 125		Stop Light/Tell Ann I Love Her	1967	2.00	4.00	8.00
❏ 125	DJ	Stop Light/Tell Ann I Love Her	1967	6.25	12.50	25.00
		Promo only on yellow vinyl				
❏ 125	PS	Stop Light/Tell Ann I Love Her	1967	3.75	7.50	15.00

Number		Title (A Side/B Side)	Year	VG	VG+	NM
☐ 126		7:30 Guided Tour/See Saw Baby	1967	2.00	4.00	8.00
☐ 126	DJ	7:30 Guided Tour/See Saw Baby	1967	6.25	12.50	25.00
		Promo only on yellow vinyl				
☐ 126	PS	7:30 Guided Tour/See Saw Baby	1967	3.75	7.50	15.00
☐ 128		The Rain Maker/No Communication	1968	2.00	4.00	8.00
☐ 128	DJ	The Rain Maker/No Communication	1968	6.25	12.50	25.00
		Promo only on yellow vinyl				
☐ 131		Con Man/Lovin' Is Lovin'	1968	2.00	4.00	8.00
☐ 131	DJ	Con Man/Lovin' Is Lovin'	1968	6.25	12.50	25.00
		Promo only on yellow vinyl				
☐ 132		Generation Gap/The Source	1968	2.00	4.00	8.00
☐ 132	DJ	Generation Gap/The Source	1968	6.25	12.50	25.00
		Promo only on yellow vinyl				
☐ 134		Virginia Girl/Call on Me	1969	2.00	4.00	8.00
☐ 134	DJ	Virginia Girl/Call on Me	1969	6.25	12.50	25.00
		Promo only on yellow vinyl				
☐ 137		Scrooge/Ignert Woman	1969	2.00	4.00	8.00
☐ 137	DJ	Scrooge/Ignert Woman	1969	6.25	12.50	25.00
		Promo only on yellow vinyl				
☐ 142		She's Too Good to Me/Molly Black	1969	2.00	4.00	8.00
☐ 142	DJ	She's Too Good to Me/Molly Black	1969	6.25	12.50	25.00
		Promo only on yellow vinyl				

Hanna-Barbera

Number		Title (A Side/B Side)	Year	VG	VG+	NM
☐ 454		I See the Light/The Outcast	1965	3.00	6.00	12.00
☐ 468		Evol-Not Love/Don't Blame Me	1966	3.00	6.00	12.00
☐ 468	PS	Evol-Not Love/Don't Blame Me	1966	3.75	7.50	15.00

Jetstar

Number	Title (A Side/B Side)	Year	VG	VG+	NM
☐ 104	It's You Girl/I'm Gonna Leave You	1966	6.25	12.50	25.00
☐ 105	I'm Feeling OK/Slippin' and Slidin'	1966	7.50	15.00	30.00

Philco

Number	Title (A Side/B Side)	Year	VG	VG+	NM
☐ HP-10	Western Union/Power of Love	1968	5.00	10.00	20.00
	4-inch flexi-disc in "Philco Hip-Pocket Record" series (price includes sleeve)				

Five Blobs, The

Columbia

Number	Title (A Side/B Side)	Year	VG	VG+	NM
☐ 41250	The Blob/Saturday Night in Tijuana	1958	6.25	12.50	25.00

Joy

Number	Title (A Side/B Side)	Year	VG	VG+	NM
☐ 226	Rockin' Pow Wow/From the Top of Your Guggle	1959	5.00	10.00	20.00
☐ 230	Juliet/Young and Wild	1959	5.00	10.00	20.00

Five Crowns, The

(More than one group?)

Caravan

Number	Title (A Side/B Side)	Year	VG	VG+	NM
☐ 15609	I Can't Pretend/Popcorn Willie	1955	12.50	25.00	50.00

De'Besth

Number	Title (A Side/B Side)	Year	VG	VG+	NM
☐ 1121/2	A Surprise from Outer Space/Memories of Yesterday	1959	100.00	200.00	400.00
☐ 1123	I Want You/Hillum Boy	1959	100.00	200.00	400.00

Gee

Number	Title (A Side/B Side)	Year	VG	VG+	NM
☐ 1001	Do You Remember/God Bless You	1956	50.00	100.00	200.00

Old Town

Number	Title (A Side/B Side)	Year	VG	VG+	NM
☐ 790	Good Luck Darling/You Could Be My Love	1952	100.00	200.00	400.00
	Black vinyl				
☐ 790	Good Luck Darling/You Could Be My Love	1952	200.00	400.00	800.00
	Red vinyl				
☐ 792	Lullaby of the Bells/Later, Later Baby	1952			
	Unconfirmed on 45 rpm				

Rainbow

Number	Title (A Side/B Side)	Year	VG	VG+	NM
☐ 179	A Star/You're My Inspiration	1952	125.00	250.00	500.00
	Black vinyl				
☐ 179	A Star/You're My Inspiration	1952	200.00	400.00	800.00
	Colored vinyl				
☐ 184	Who Can Be True/$19.50 Due	1952		*Unconfirmed on 45 rpm*	
☐ 202	Keep It a Secret/Why Don't You Believe Me	1953	125.00	250.00	500.00
☐ 206	Alone Again/Don't Have to Hunt No More	1953		*Unconfirmed on 45 rpm*	
☐ 281	I Was Wrong/Hug Me Baby	1954	125.00	250.00	500.00
☐ 335	You Came to Me/Ooh Wee Baby	1956	50.00	100.00	200.00
	Reissued by "The Duvals"				

Riviera

Number	Title (A Side/B Side)	Year	VG	VG+	NM
☐ 990	You Came to Me/Ooh Wee Baby	1955	200.00	400.00	800.00

Trans World

Number	Title (A Side/B Side)	Year	VG	VG+	NM
☐ 717	I Can't Pretend/Popcorn Willie	1956	20.00	40.00	80.00

Five Debonaires, The

Herald

Number	Title (A Side/B Side)	Year	VG	VG+	NM
☐ 509	Darlin'/Whispering Blues	1957	50.00	100.00	200.00

Five Delights, The

Abel

Number	Title (A Side/B Side)	Year	VG	VG+	NM
☐ 228	The Thought of Losing You/That Love Affair	1959	75.00	150.00	300.00

Newport

Number	Title (A Side/B Side)	Year	VG	VG+	NM
☐ 7002	There'll Be No Goodbye/Okey Dokey Mama	1958	37.50	75.00	150.00

Number	Title (A Side/B Side)	Year	VG	VG+	NM

Unart
| ❏ 2003 | There'll Be No Goodbye/Okey Dokey Mama | 1958 | 7.50 | 15.00 | 30.00 |

Five Discs, The
(Probably more than one group)
Calo
❏ 202	Adios/My Baby Loves Me	1961	37.50	75.00	150.00
	Green label				
❏ 202	Adios/My Baby Loves Me	1962	25.00	50.00	100.00
	White label				

Cheer
❏ 1000	Never Let You Go/That Was the Time	1962	25.00	50.00	100.00
	Black label				
❏ 1000	Never Let You Go/That Was the Time	1962	12.50	25.00	50.00
	Red label				
❏ 1000	DJ Never Let You Go/That Was the Time	1962	75.00	150.00	300.00
	White label, promo only				

Crystal Ball
❏ 114	Mirror Mirror/Most of All I Wonder Why	1978	2.50	5.00	10.00
❏ 120	Unchained Melody/The Shrine of St. Cecelia	1978	2.50	5.00	10.00
❏ 136	Playing a Game of Love/Bells	1979	2.00	4.00	8.00
❏ 141	This Love of Ours/To the Fair	1979	2.00	4.00	8.00

Dwain
❏ 6072	My Chinese Girl/Roses	1959	100.00	200.00	400.00
❏ 803	My Chinese Girl/Roses	1959	50.00	100.00	200.00
	As "Mario and the Five Discs"				
❏ 803	My Chinese Girl/Roses	1959	37.50	75.00	150.00

Emge
| ❏ 1004 | I Remember/The World Is a Beautiful Place | 1958 | 100.00 | 200.00 | 400.00 |

Laurie
| ❏ 3601 | Rock and Roll Revival/Gypsy Women | 1973 | 3.75 | 7.50 | 15.00 |

Mello Mood
| ❏ 1002 | My Chinese Girl/Roses | 1964 | 3.75 | 7.50 | 15.00 |

Pyramid
| ❏ 166 | Let's Fall in Love/That Was the Time | 197? | | 3.00 | 6.00 |

Rust
| ❏ 5027 | I Remember/The World Is a Beautiful Place | 1961 | 5.00 | 10.00 | 20.00 |

Vik
| ❏ 0327 | I Remember/The World Is a Beautiful Place | 1958 | 20.00 | 40.00 | 80.00 |

Yale
| ❏ 240 | When Love Comes Knocking/Go-Go | 1961 | 100.00 | 200.00 | 400.00 |
| ❏ 243/4 | Come On Baby/I Don't Know What to Do | 1961 | 100.00 | 200.00 | 400.00 |

Five Echoes, The
Sabre
❏ 102	Baby Come Back to Me/Lonely Mood	1953	150.00	300.00	600.00
	Black vinyl				
❏ 102	Baby Come Back to Me/Lonely Mood	1953	750.00	1,125	1,500
	Red vinyl				
❏ 105	So Lonesome/Broke	1954	150.00	300.00	600.00
	Black vinyl				
❏ 105	So Lonesome/Broke	1954	750.00	1,125	1,500
	Red vinyl				

Vee Jay
❏ 129	I Really Do/Tell Me Baby	1954	75.00	150.00	300.00
❏ 156	Fool's Prayer/Tastee Freeze	1955	62.50	125.00	250.00
❏ 190	Soldier Boy/Pledging to You	1956	50.00	100.00	200.00

Five Keys, The
Aladdin
❏ 3085	With a Broken Heart/Too Late	1951		*Unconfirmed on 45 rpm*	
❏ 3099	The Glory of Love/Hucklebuck with Jimmy	1951	150.00	300.00	600.00
❏ 3113	It's Christmas Time/Old Mac Donald	1951	200.00	400.00	800.00
❏ 3118	Yes Sir That's My Baby/Old Mac Donald	1952	175.00	350.00	700.00
❏ 3119	Darling/Goin' Downtown	1952	175.00	350.00	700.00
❏ 3127	Red Sails in the Sunset/Be Anything, But Be Mine	1952	225.00	450.00	900.00
❏ 3131	How Long/Mistakes	1952	200.00	400.00	800.00
❏ 3136	Hold Me/I Hadn't Anyone Till You	1952	200.00	400.00	800.00
❏ 3158	I Cried for You/Serve Another Round	1953	175.00	350.00	700.00
❏ 3167	Can't Keep From Crying/Come Go My Bail, Louise	1953	150.00	300.00	600.00
❏ 3175	There Ought to Be a Law/Mama (Your Daughter Told a Lie on Me)	1953	150.00	300.00	600.00
❏ 3182	I'll Always Be in Love with You/Rocking and Crying Blues	1953	150.00	300.00	600.00
❏ 3190	These Foolish Things/Lonesome Old Story	1953	400.00	800.00	1,200
❏ 3204	Teardrops in Your Eyes/I'm So High	1953	150.00	300.00	600.00
❏ 3214	My Saddest Hour/Oh! Babe!	1953	125.00	250.00	500.00
❏ 3228	Someday Sweetheart/Love My Loving	1954	150.00	300.00	600.00
❏ 3245	Deep in My Heart/How Do You Expect Me to Get It	1954	150.00	300.00	600.00
❏ 3263	My Love/Why, Oh Why	1954	75.00	150.00	300.00
❏ 3312	Story of Love/Serve Another Round	1956	75.00	150.00	300.00

Number	Title (A Side/B Side)	Year	VG	VG+	NM
Bangar					
❑ 661	Run-Around/I Tell My Heart	1965	3.75	7.50	15.00
Capitol					
❑ F2945	Ling, Ting, Tong/I'm Alone	1954	12.50	25.00	50.00
❑ F3032	Close Your Eyes/Doggone It, You Did It	1955	12.50	25.00	50.00
❑ F3127	The Verdict/Me Make Um Pow Wow	1955	12.50	25.00	50.00
❑ F3185	Don't You Know I Love You/ I Wish I'd Never Learned to Read	1955	12.50	25.00	50.00
❑ F3267	'Cause You're My Lover/Gee Whittakers	1955	12.50	25.00	50.00
❑ F3318	You Broke the Rules of Love/What Goes On	1956	12.50	25.00	50.00
❑ F3392	She's the Most/I Dreamt I Dwelt in Heaven	1956	12.50	25.00	50.00
	Regular large hole				
❑ F3392	She's the Most/I Dreamt I Dwelt in Heaven	1956	17.50	35.00	70.00
	Small hole				
❑ F3455	My Pigeon's Gone/Peace and Love	1956	10.00	20.00	40.00
❑ F3502	Out of Sight, Out of Mind/That's Right	1956	10.00	20.00	40.00
❑ F3597	Wisdom of a Fool/Now Don't That Prove I Love You	1956	10.00	20.00	40.00
❑ F3660	Tiger Lily/Let There Be You	1957	10.00	20.00	40.00
❑ F3710	Four Walls/It's a Groove	1957	10.00	20.00	40.00
❑ F3738	This I Promise You/The Blues Don't Care	1957	10.00	20.00	40.00
❑ F3786	Boom Boom/Face of An Angel	1957	7.50	15.00	30.00
❑ F3830	Do Anything/It's a Cryin' Shame	1957	7.50	15.00	30.00
❑ F3861	From Me to You/Whippety Whirl	1957	7.50	15.00	30.00
❑ F3948	You're for Me/With All My Love	1958	6.25	12.50	25.00
❑ F4009	Emily Please/Handy Andy	1958	6.25	12.50	25.00
❑ F4092	One Great Love/Really-O, Truly-O	1958	6.25	12.50	25.00
❑ 4828	Out of Sight, Out of Mind/From the Bottom of My Heart	1962	5.00	10.00	20.00
Groove					
❑ 0031	I'll Follow You/Lawdy Miss Mary	1954	2,000	3,000	4,000
Inferno					
❑ 4500	Hey Girl/No Matter	1967	5.00	10.00	20.00
King					
❑ 5251	I Took Your Love for a Toy/Ziggus	1959	7.50	15.00	30.00
❑ 5273	Dancing Senorita/Dream On	1959	5.00	10.00	20.00
❑ 5302	How Can I Forget You/I Burned Your Letter	1960	5.00	10.00	20.00
❑ 5330	Gonna Be Too Late/Rosetta	1960	5.00	10.00	20.00
❑ 5358	I Didn't Know/No, Says My Heart	1960	5.00	10.00	20.00
❑ 5398	Bimbo/Valley of Love	1960	5.00	10.00	20.00
❑ 5446	You Broke the Only Heart/ That's What You're Doing to Me	1961	5.00	10.00	20.00
❑ 5496	Do Something for Me/Stop Your Crying	1961	5.00	10.00	20.00
❑ 5877	I'll Never Stop Loving You/I Can't Escape from You	1964	3.00	6.00	12.00
Liberty					
❑ 1394	It's Christmas Time/It's Christmas	1980	2.00	4.00	8.00
	B-side by Robert and Johnny				
Owl					
❑ 321	A Dreamer/Your Teeth and Your Tongue	1973	2.00	4.00	8.00
Seg-Way					
❑ 1008	Out of Sight, Out of Mind/You're the One	1962	3.75	7.50	15.00
United Artists					
❑ 0150	The Glory of Love/My Saddest Hour	1973		2.00	4.00
	"Silver Spotlight Series" reissue				

Five Playboys, The

Number	Title (A Side/B Side)	Year	VG	VG+	NM
Dot					
❑ 15605	When We Were Young/Pages of My Scrapbook	1957	6.25	12.50	25.00
Fee Bee					
❑ 213	When We Were Young/Pages of My Scrapbook	1958	12.50	25.00	50.00
❑ 232	Angel Mine/She's My Baby	1959	25.00	50.00	100.00
Mercury					
❑ 71269	Time Will Allow/Why Be a Fool	1958	6.25	12.50	25.00
Petite					
❑ 504	She's My Baby/Mr. Echo	1959	10.00	20.00	40.00

Five Royales, The

(Also known as The Five Royals and The "5" Royales)

Number	Title (A Side/B Side)	Year	VG	VG+	NM
ABC-Paramount					
❑ 10348	Catch That Teardrop/Goof Ball	1962	2.50	5.00	10.00
❑ 10368	What's In Your Heart/I Want It Like That	1962	2.50	5.00	10.00
Apollo					
❑ 441	Courage to Love/You Know I Know	1952	37.50	75.00	150.00
	Black vinyl				
❑ 441	Courage to Love/You Know I Know	1952	75.00	150.00	300.00
	Red vinyl				
❑ 443	Baby Don't Do It/Take All of Me	1952	25.00	50.00	100.00
❑ 446	Help Me, Somebody/Crazy, Crazy, Crazy	1953	25.00	50.00	100.00
❑ 448	Too Much Lovin' (Much Too Much)/Laundromat Blues	1953	25.00	50.00	100.00
❑ 449	I Want to Thank You/All Righty	1953	20.00	40.00	80.00
❑ 452	I Do/Good Things	1954	12.50	25.00	50.00
❑ 454	Cry Some More/I Like It Like That	1954	12.50	25.00	50.00
❑ 458	What's That/Let Me Come Back Home	1954	10.00	20.00	40.00
❑ 467	With All Your Heart/6 O'Clock in the Morning	1955	10.00	20.00	40.00

Number	Title (A Side/B Side)	Year	VG	VG+	NM
Home of the Blues					
❏ 112	Please, Please, Please/I Got to Know	1960	3.75	7.50	15.00
❏ 218	If You Don't Need Me/I'm Gonna Tell Them	1961	3.75	7.50	15.00
❏ 232	Take Me With You Baby/Not Going to Cry	1961	3.75	7.50	15.00
❏ 234	Much in Need/They Don't Know	1962	3.00	6.00	12.00
❏ 243	Catch That Teardrop/Goof Ball	1962	3.00	6.00	12.00
King					
❏ 4740	I'm Gonna Run It Down/Behave Yourself	1954	10.00	20.00	40.00
❏ 4744	Monkey Hips and Rice/Devil with the Rest	1954	10.00	20.00	40.00
❏ 4762	School Girl/One Mistake	1955	10.00	20.00	40.00
❏ 4770	Every Dog Has His Day/You Didn't Learn It at Home	1955	10.00	20.00	40.00
❏ 4785	How I Wonder/Mohawk Squaw	1955	10.00	20.00	40.00
❏ 4806	I Need Your Lovin'/When I Get Like This	1955	7.50	15.00	30.00
❏ 4819	Women About to Make Me Go Crazy/Do Unto You	1955	7.50	15.00	30.00
❏ 4830	I Ain't Gettin' Caught/Someone Made You for Me	1955	7.50	15.00	30.00
❏ 4869	When You Walked Through the Door/ Right Around the Corner	1956	7.50	15.00	30.00
❏ 4901	I Could Love You/My Wants for Love	1956	7.50	15.00	30.00
❏ 4952	Get Something Out of It/Come On and Save Me	1956	7.50	15.00	30.00
❏ 4973	Just As I Am/Mine Forevermore	1956	7.50	15.00	30.00
❏ 5032	Tears of Joy/Thirty Second Lover	1957	6.25	12.50	25.00
❏ 5053	Think/I'd Better Make a Move	1957	6.25	12.50	25.00
❏ 5082	Messin' Up/Say It	1957	6.25	12.50	25.00
❏ 5098	Dedicated to the One I Love/Don't Be Ashamed	1958	6.25	12.50	25.00
❏ 5131	Do the Cha Cha Cherry/The Feeling Is Real	1958	6.25	12.50	25.00
❏ 5141	Tell the Truth/Double or Nothing	1958	6.25	12.50	25.00
❏ 5153	The Slummer the Slum/Don't Let It Be in Vain	1958	6.25	12.50	25.00
❏ 5162	Your Only Love/The Real Thing	1958	6.25	12.50	25.00
❏ 5191	Miracle of Love/I Know It's Hard, But It's Fair	1959	6.25	12.50	25.00
❏ 5237	Tell Me You Care/Wonder Where Your Love Has Gone	1959	6.25	12.50	25.00
❏ 5266	My Sugar Sugar/It Hurts Inside	1959	6.25	12.50	25.00
❏ 5329	Don't Give No More Than You Can Take/I'm with You	1960	6.25	12.50	25.00
❏ 5357	Why/Within My Heart	1960	6.25	12.50	25.00
❏ 5453	Dedicated to the One I Love/Miracle of Love	1961	3.75	7.50	15.00
❏ 5756	Dedicated to the One I Love/Tears of Joy	1963	3.75	7.50	15.00
❏ 5892	I Wonder Where Your Love Has Gone/ I Need Your Lovin' Baby	1964	3.75	7.50	15.00
Smash					
❏ 1936	Baby Don't Do It/I Like It Like That	1964	2.50	5.00	10.00
❏ 1963	Never Turn Your Back/Faith	1965	2.50	5.00	10.00
Todd					
❏ 1086	I'm Standing in the Shadows/Doin' Everything	1963	2.50	5.00	10.00
❏ 1088	Baby Don't Do It/There's Somebody Over There	1963	2.50	5.00	10.00
Vee Jay					
❏ 412	Much in Need/They Don't Know	1961	3.75	7.50	15.00
❏ 431	Help Me Somebody/Talk About My Woman	1962	3.75	7.50	15.00

Five Satins, The

(Also see "Parris, Fred")

Number	Title (A Side/B Side)	Year	VG	VG+	NM
Buddah					
❏ 477	Everybody Stand and Clap Your Hands/ Hey There Pretty Lady	1975		2.50	5.00
	As "Black Satin"				
Candelite					
❏ 411	She's Gone (With the Wind)/ Somewhere a Voice Is Calling	1974		3.00	6.00
Chancellor					
❏ 1110	The Masquerade Is Over/Raining in My Heart	1962	5.00	10.00	20.00
❏ 1121	Do You Remember/Downtown	1962	5.00	10.00	20.00
Cub					
❏ 9077	These Foolish Things/A Beggar with a Dream	1960	6.25	12.50	25.00
❏ 9090	Golden Earrings/Can I Come Over Tonight	1961	6.25	12.50	25.00
Elektra					
❏ 47411	Memories of Days Gone By Medley/ Loving You (Would Be the Sweetest Thing)	1982	5.00	10.00	20.00
	As "Fred Parris and the Five Satins"				
❏ 69888	Didn't I (Blow Your Mind)/ Loving You (Would Be the Sweetest Thing)	1982		2.50	5.00
❏ 69938	Breaking Up/ Loving You (Would Be the Sweetest Thing)	1982		2.50	5.00
❏ 69984	I'll Be Seeing You/ Loving You (Would Be the Sweetest Thing)	1982		2.50	5.00
Ember					
❏ 1005	In the Still of the Nite/The Jones Girl *Red label; has "6106A" in the trail-off vinyl*	1956	50.00	100.00	200.00
❏ 1005	In the Still of the Nite/The Jones Girl *Red label; has "E-2105-45" in the trail-off vinyl*	1956	12.50	25.00	50.00
❏ 1005	In the Still of the Nite/The Jones Girl *Red label; has "E-1005" in the trail-off vinyl*	1956	7.50	15.00	30.00
❏ 1005	I'll Remember (In the Still of the Nite)/The Jones Girl *Red label*	1956	7.50	15.00	30.00
❏ 1005	I'll Remember (In the Still of the Nite)/The Jones Girl *Multicolor "logs" label; reads "Special Demand Release"*	1959	12.50	25.00	50.00

Number	Title (A Side/B Side)	Year	VG	VG+	NM
❑ 1005	I'll Remember (In the Still of the Nite)/The Jones Girl *Multicolor "logs" label; no "Special Demand Release"*	1959	7.50	15.00	30.00
❑ 1005	I'll Remember (In the Still of the Nite)/The Jones Girl *Black label*	1961	7.50	15.00	30.00
❑ 1008	Weeping Willow/Wonderful Girl	1956	10.00	20.00	40.00
❑ 1014	Our Love Is Forever/Oh Happy Day	1957	10.00	20.00	40.00
❑ 1019	To the Aisle/Wish I Had My Baby *Red label*	1957	10.00	20.00	40.00
❑ 1019	To the Aisle/Wish I Had My Baby *Black label*	1961	5.00	10.00	20.00
❑ 1025	Our Anniversary/Pretty Baby *Red label*	1957	10.00	20.00	40.00
❑ 1025	Our Anniversary/Pretty Baby *Black label*	1957	5.00	10.00	20.00
❑ 1028	A Million to One/Love with No Love in Return	1957	10.00	20.00	40.00
❑ 1038	A Night to Remember/Senorita Lolita *As "Fred Parris and the Satins"*	1958	7.50	15.00	30.00
❑ 1056	Shadows/Toni My Love	1959	7.50	15.00	30.00
❑ 1061	I'll Be Seeing You/A Night Like This	1960	7.50	15.00	30.00
❑ 1066	Candlelight/The Time	1960	6.25	12.50	25.00
❑ 1070	Wishing Ring/Tell Me Dear	1961	6.25	12.50	25.00
First					
❑ 104	When Your Love Comes Along/Skippity Doo *Green label*	1959	6.25	12.50	25.00
❑ 104	When Your Love Comes Along/Skippity Doo *Orange label*	1959	10.00	20.00	40.00
Kirshner					
❑ 4251	Very Precious Oldies/You Are Love	1974	2.50	5.00	10.00
❑ 4252	Two Different Worlds/Love Is Such a Beautiful Thing	1974	2.50	5.00	10.00
Klik					
❑ 1020	I Love You So/Story to You	1973	2.50	5.00	10.00
Mama Sadie					
❑ 1001	In the Still of the Night "67"/Heck No (Instrumental)	1967	3.00	6.00	12.00
Musictone					
❑ 1108	To the Aisle/Just to Be Near You	1961	6.25	12.50	25.00
Nightrain					
❑ 901	All Mine/The Voice	1970	2.50	5.00	10.00
RCA					
❑ 6989-7-R	In the Still of the Night/Yes *B-side by Merry Clayton*	1988			3.00
RCA Victor					
❑ 74-0478	Summer in New York/Dark at the Top of My Heart	1971	2.50	5.00	10.00
Roulette					
❑ 4563	Ain't Gonna Cry/You Can Count on Me	1964	2.50	5.00	10.00
Sammy					
❑ 103	No One Knows/Musical Chairs	196?	7.50	15.00	30.00
Signature					
❑ 001	Everybody's Got a Home But Me/Heartache	1990		2.50	5.00
Standord					
❑ 100	All Mine/Rose Mary *Red label*	1956	150.00	300.00	600.00
❑ 100	All Mine/Rose Mary *Maroon label*	1962	50.00	100.00	200.00
❑ 200	In the Still of the Nite/The Jones Girl	1956	300.00	600.00	900.00
❑ 200	In the Still of the Nite/The Jones Girl *With "Produced by Martin Kuegell" credit*	1956	1,000	1,500	2,000
Time Machine					
❑ 570	Wonder Why/No One Knows	1962	2.00	4.00	8.00
❑ 571	The Masquerade Is Over/Lonely Hearts	1962	2.00	4.00	8.00
Times Square					
❑ 4	All Mine/Rose Mary *Blue vinyl*	1962	5.00	10.00	20.00
❑ 21	Paradise on Earth/Monkey Business	1963	5.00	10.00	20.00
❑ 94	Paradise on Earth/Monkey Business	1964	3.75	7.50	15.00
United Artists					
❑ 368	On a Lover's Island/Till the End	1961	6.25	12.50	25.00
Warner Bros.					
❑ 5367	Remember Me/Kangaroo	1963	3.00	6.00	12.00
X-Bat					
❑ 1000	When the Swallows Come Back to Capistrano/ Dance Girl Dance *Red vinyl*	1995		2.50	5.00
❑ 1000	PS When the Swallows Come Back to Capistrano/ Dance Girl Dance	1995		2.50	5.00

Five Secrets, The

Decca

❑ 30350	See You Next Year/Queen Bee *As "The Secrets"*	1957	10.00	20.00	40.00
❑ 30350	See You Next Year/Queen Bee	1957	20.00	40.00	80.00

Number		Title (A Side/B Side)	Year	VG	VG+	NM

Five Sharks, The
Amber

| ❏ 852 | | The Lion Sleeps Tonight/Land of 1000 Dances | 1966 | 2.50 | 5.00 | 10.00 |

Old Timer

❏ 604		Gloria/Flames	1964	5.00	10.00	20.00
❏ 605		Stand By Me/I'll Never Let You Go	1964	4.00	8.00	16.00
		Blue vinyl				
❏ 605		Stand By Me/I'll Never Let You Go	1964	5.00	10.00	20.00
		Gold vinyl				
❏ 611		Gloria/Flames	1965	3.75	7.50	15.00
		Black vinyl				
❏ 611		Gloria/Flames	1965	5.00	10.00	20.00
		Red vinyl				

Relic

| ❏ 525 | | Stormy Weather (2:45)/If You Love Me | 1965 | 2.50 | 5.00 | 10.00 |

Siamese

| ❏ 404 | | Gloria/Flames | 1965 | 3.00 | 6.00 | 12.00 |

Times Square

❏ 35		Stormy Weather (2:45)/If You Love Me	1964	7.50	15.00	30.00
❏ 35		Stormy Weather (3:45)/If You Love Me	1964	10.00	20.00	40.00
		Black vinyl				
❏ 35		Stormy Weather (3:45)/If You Love Me	1964	15.00	30.00	60.00
		Blue vinyl				

Five Sharps, The
Bim Bam Boom

| ❏ 103 | | Stormy Weather/Sleepy Cowboy | 1972 | 2.00 | 4.00 | 8.00 |
| | | *Reissue mastered off the cracked Jubilee 78 (see below); the original master is long since lost* | | | | |

Jubilee

❏ 5104		Stormy Weather/Sleepy Cowboy	1952			
		Only released on 78 RPM (2 or 3 known copies, one of which is cracked); all known 45s are counterfeits. Even the cracked 78 would likely sell for $10,000; if a legitimate 45 would be confirmed, it could sell for more than any record ever made!				
❏ 5478		Stormy Weather/Mammy Jammy	1964	3.00	6.00	12.00
		Not the same group or the same recordings as above				

Five Stairsteps, The
Buddah

❏ 20		Something's Missing/Tell Me Who	1967	2.00	4.00	8.00
❏ 20	PS	Something's Missing/Tell Me Who	1967	3.75	7.50	15.00
❏ 26		A Million to One/You Make Me So Mad	1968	2.00	4.00	8.00
❏ 26	PS	A Million to One/You Make Me So Mad	1968	3.75	7.50	15.00
		Buddah 20 and 26 as "Five Stairsteps and Cubie"				
❏ 35		The Shadow of Your Love/Bad News	1968	2.00	4.00	8.00
❏ 165		Dear Prudence/O-o-h Child	1970	2.00	4.00	8.00
❏ 165		O-o-h Child/Who Do You Belong To	1970		3.00	6.00
❏ 188		Because I Love You/America Standing	1970		2.50	5.00
		Starting with 213, as "Stairsteps"				
❏ 213		Didn't It Look So Easy/Peace Is Gonna Come	1971		2.50	5.00
❏ 222		Snow/Look Out	1971		2.50	5.00
❏ 277		I Love You-Stop/I Feel a Song (In My Heart Again)	1972		2.50	5.00
❏ 291		Hush Child/The Easy Way	1972		2.50	5.00
❏ 320		Every Single Way/Two Weeks' Notice	1972		2.50	5.00

Curtom

❏ 1931		Don't Change Your Love/New Dance Craze	1968		3.00	6.00
❏ 1933		I Made a Mistake/Stay Close to Me	1968		3.00	6.00
❏ 1936		Baby Make Me Feel So Good/Little Young Lover	1969		3.00	6.00
❏ 1944		Madame Mary/Little Boy Blue	1969		3.00	6.00
❏ 1945		We Must Be in Love/Little Young Lover	1969		3.00	6.00
		All Curtom releases as "Five Stairsteps and Cubie"				

Dark Horse

❏ 10005		From Us to You/Time	1975		2.50	5.00
❏ 10009		Tell Me Why/Salaam	1976		2.50	5.00
		Both Dark Horse releases as "Stairsteps"				

Windy "C"

❏ 601		You Waited Too Long/Don't Waste Your Time	1966	2.50	5.00	10.00
❏ 602		World of Fantasy/Playgirl's Love	1966	2.50	5.00	10.00
❏ 603		Come Back/You Don't Love Me	1966	2.50	5.00	10.00
❏ 604		Danger, She's a Stranger/Behind Curtains	1967	2.50	5.00	10.00
❏ 605		Ain't Gonna Rest (Till I Get You)/You Can't See	1967	2.50	5.00	10.00
❏ 607		Oooh, Baby Baby/The Girl I Love	1967	2.50	5.00	10.00
❏ 608		The Touch of You/Change of Face	1967	2.50	5.00	10.00

Five Stars, The
(Several different groups)
ABC-Paramount

| ❏ 9911 | | Pickin' on the Wrong Chicken/Dreaming | 1958 | 6.25 | 12.50 | 25.00 |

Atco

| ❏ 6065 | | Take Five/Humpty Dump | 1956 | 7.50 | 15.00 | 30.00 |

Blues Boys Kingdom

| ❏ 106 | | So Lonely, Baby/Hey Juanita | 1957 | 37.50 | 75.00 | 150.00 |

Number	Title (A Side/B Side)	Year	VG	VG+	NM

Columbia
| ❑ 42056 | Baby Baby/Blabber Mouth | 1961 | 15.00 | 30.00 | 60.00 |

Dot
| ❑ 15579 | Atom Bomb Baby/You Sweet Little Thing | 1957 | 6.25 | 12.50 | 25.00 |

End
| ❑ 1028 | Baby Baby/Blabber Mouth | 1958 | 20.00 | 40.00 | 80.00 |

Hunt
| ❑ 318 | Pickin' on the Wrong Chicken/Dreaming | 1959 | 5.00 | 10.00 | 20.00 |

Kernel
| ❑ 3195 | Atom Bomb Baby/You Sweet Little Thing | 1957 | 10.00 | 20.00 | 40.00 |

Mark-X
| ❑ 7006 | Dead Wrong/Ooh Shucks | 1957 | 25.00 | 50.00 | 100.00 |

Note
❑ 10011	Pickin' on the Wrong Chicken/Dreaming	1958	7.50	15.00	30.00
❑ 10016	My Paradise/Friction	1958	10.00	20.00	40.00
❑ 10031	Am I Wasting My Time/Gamblin' Man	1959	7.50	15.00	30.00

Show Time
| ❑ 1102 | Where Did Caledonia Go?/Walkin' An' Talkin' | 1954 | 31.25 | 62.50 | 125.00 |

Treat
| ❑ 505 | Let's Fall in Love/We Danced in the Moonlight | 1955 | 150.00 | 300.00 | 600.00 |

Five Supremes, The
Garpax
| ❑ 44170 | There's a Fool Born Every Day/Big Shot | 1962 | 20.00 | 40.00 | 80.00 |

Five Thrills, The
Parrot
❑ 796	My Baby's Gone/Feel So Good	1954	400.00	800.00	1,200
❑ 800	Gloria/Wee Wee Baby	1954	400.00	800.00	1,200
	Black vinyl				
❑ 800	Gloria/Wee Wee Baby	1954	2,000	3,000	4,000
	Red vinyl				

Five Tinos, The
Sun
| ❑ 222 | Sitting By My Window/Don't Do That | 1955 | 200.00 | 400.00 | 600.00 |

Five Willows, The
Allen
❑ 1000	My Dear, Dearest Darling/Rock, Little Francis	1953	150.00	300.00	600.00
❑ 1002	Delores/All Night Long	1953	150.00	300.00	600.00
❑ 1003	White Cliffs of Dover/With These Hands	1953	175.00	350.00	700.00

Herald
| ❑ 433 | Baby Come a Little Closer/Lay Your Head on My Shoulder | 1954 | 50.00 | 100.00 | 200.00 |
| ❑ 442 | Look Me in the Eyes/So Help Me | 1954 | 50.00 | 100.00 | 200.00 |

Pee Dee
| ❑ 290 | Love Bells/Please, Baby | 1953 | 150.00 | 300.00 | 600.00 |

Five Wings, The
King
❑ 4778	Johnny Has Gone/Johnny's Still Singing	1955	50.00	100.00	200.00
❑ 4781	Teardrops Are Falling/Rock-A-Locka	1955	62.50	125.00	250.00
	Later released on King 5199 as The Checkers.				

Flairs, The
(More than one group)
ABC-Paramount
| ❑ 9740 | Aladdin's Lamp/Steppin' Out | 1956 | 7.50 | 15.00 | 30.00 |

Epic
| ❑ 9447 | Shake, Shake Sherry/The Memory Lingers On | 1961 | 10.00 | 20.00 | 40.00 |
| | *Reissued shortly after release as "The Redwoods"* | | | | |

Flair
❑ 1012	I Had a Love/She Wants to Rock	1953	100.00	200.00	400.00
❑ 1019	Tell Me You Love Me/You Should Care for Me	1953	100.00	200.00	400.00
❑ 1028	Love Me Girl/Gettin' High	1954	100.00	200.00	400.00
❑ 1041	Baby Wants/You Were Untrue	1954	100.00	200.00	400.00
❑ 1044	This Is the Night for Love/Let's Make with Some Love	1954	100.00	200.00	400.00
❑ 1051	Love Me, Love Me, Love Me/My Heart's Crying for You	1954	100.00	200.00	400.00
	As "The Chimes"				
❑ 1056	I'll Never Let You Go/Hold Me, Thrill Me, Chill Me	1955	75.00	150.00	300.00
❑ 1067	She Loves to Dance/My Darling, My Sweet	1955	75.00	150.00	300.00

Palms
| ❑ 726 | Roll Over Beethoven/Brazil | 1961 | 12.50 | 25.00 | 50.00 |
| | *Reissued on Jamie as "The Velaires"* | | | | |

Flame, The
(With Rikki Fataar and Blondie Chaplin, future Beach Boys. Fataar also was with The Rutles)
Brother
| ❑ 3501 | See the Light/Got Your Mind Made Up | 1970 | 3.75 | 7.50 | 15.00 |
| ❑ 3502 | Another Day Like Heaven/I'm So Happy | 1970 | 3.75 | 7.50 | 15.00 |

Number		Title (A Side/B Side)	Year	VG	VG+	NM
Flamingos, The						
Chance						
❑ 1133		If I Can't Have You/Someday, Somehow	1953	400.00	800.00	1,200
		Black vinyl				
❑ 1133		If I Can't Have You/Someday, Somehow	1953	1,000	1,500	2,000
		Red vinyl				
❑ 1140		That's My Desire/Hurry Home Baby	1953	125.00	250.00	500.00
		Black vinyl				
❑ 1140		That's My Desire/Hurry Home Baby	1953	1,000	1,500	2,000
		Red vinyl				
❑ 1145		Golden Teardrops/Carried Away	1953	1,000	1,500	2,000
		Black vinyl				
❑ 1145		Golden Teardrops/Carried Away	1953	2,000	3,000	4,000
		Red vinyl				
❑ 1149		Plan for Love/You Ain't Ready	1953	250.00	500.00	1,000
		Yellow and black label				
❑ 1149		Plan for Love/You Ain't Ready	1953	200.00	400.00	800.00
		Blue and silver label				
❑ 1154		Cross Over the Bridge/Listen to My Plea	1954	250.00	500.00	1,000
❑ 1162		Jump Children/Blues in the Letter	1954	250.00	500.00	1,000
Checker						
❑ 815		That's My Baby (Chick-a-Boom)/When	1955	20.00	40.00	80.00
❑ 821		I Want to Love You/Please Come Back Home	1955	20.00	40.00	80.00
❑ 830		I'll Be Home/Need Your Love	1956	20.00	40.00	80.00
❑ 837		A Kiss from Your Lips/Get With It	1956	20.00	40.00	80.00
❑ 846		The Vow/Shilly Dilly	1956	20.00	40.00	80.00
❑ 853		Just for a Kick/Would I Be Crying	1957	20.00	40.00	80.00
		Originals of above Checker singles are maroon with a checkerboard at top of label				
❑ 915		Whispering Stars/Dream of a Lifetime	1959	12.50	25.00	50.00
❑ 1084		Lover Come Back to Me/Your Little Guy	1964	3.75	7.50	15.00
❑ 1091		Goodnight Sweetheart/Does It Really Matter	1964	3.75	7.50	15.00
Decca						
❑ 30335		The Ladder of Love/Let's Make Up	1957	7.50	15.00	30.00
❑ 30454		Helpless/My Faith in You	1957	7.50	15.00	30.00
❑ 30687		Rock and Roll March/Where Mary Go	1958	7.50	15.00	30.00
❑ 30880		Kiss-A Me/Ever Since I Met Lucy	1959	7.50	15.00	30.00
❑ 30948		Jerri-Lee/Hey Now	1959	7.50	15.00	30.00
End						
❑ 1035		Please Wait for Me/That Love Is You	1958	12.50	25.00	50.00
❑ 1035		Lovers Never Say Goodbye/That Love Is You	1958	6.25	12.50	25.00
		A-sides of End 1035 are the same song, the titles were changed				
❑ 1040		I Shed a Tear at Your Wedding/But Not for Me	1959	7.50	15.00	30.00
❑ 1044		At the Prom/Love Walked In	1959	10.00	20.00	40.00
❑ 1046	M	I Only Have Eyes for You/Goodnight Sweetheart	1959	7.50	15.00	30.00
❑ 1046	M	I Only Have Eyes for You/At the Prom	1959	6.25	12.50	25.00
❑ 1046	M	I Only Have Eyes for You/Love Walked In	1959	6.25	12.50	25.00
❑ 1046	S	I Only Have Eyes for You/(B-side unknown)	1959	12.50	25.00	50.00
		We're not sure which flip the stereo version had on its B-side				
❑ 1055	M	Yours/Love Walked In	1959	6.25	12.50	25.00
❑ 1055	S	Yours/Love Walked In	1959	12.50	25.00	50.00
❑ 1062		I Was Such a Fool/Heavenly Angel	1959	6.25	12.50	25.00
❑ 1065		Mio Amore/You, Me and the Sea	1960	6.25	12.50	25.00
❑ 1068		Nobody Loves Me Like You/Besame Mucho	1960	7.50	15.00	30.00
❑ 1068		Nobody Loves Me Like You/You, Me and the Sea	1960	6.25	12.50	25.00
❑ 1070		Besame Mucho/You, Me and the Sea	1960	6.25	12.50	25.00
❑ 1073		Mio Amore/At Night	1960	5.00	10.00	20.00
❑ 1079		Beside You/When I Fall in Love	1960	5.00	10.00	20.00
❑ 1081		Your Other Love/Lovers Gotta Cry	1960	5.00	10.00	20.00
❑ 1085		That's Why I Love You/Ko Ko Mo	1961	5.00	10.00	20.00
❑ 1092		Time Was/Dream Girl	1961	5.00	10.00	20.00
❑ 1099		My Memories of You/I Want to Love You	1961	5.00	10.00	20.00
❑ 1111		It Must Be Love/I'm No Fool Anymore	1962	5.00	10.00	20.00
❑ 1116		For All We Know/Near You	1962	5.00	10.00	20.00
❑ 1121		I Know Better/Flame of Love	1963	5.00	10.00	20.00
❑ 1124		(Talk About) True Love/Come to My Party	1963	5.00	10.00	20.00
Julmar						
❑ 506		Dealin' (Groovin' with Feelin')/Dealin' All the Way	1969	2.50	5.00	10.00
Mercury						
❑ 72455		Temptation/Call Her on the Phone	1965			Cancelled
Parrot						
❑ 808		Dream of a Lifetime/On My Merry Way	1954	250.00	500.00	1,000
		Black vinyl				
❑ 808		Dream of a Lifetime/On My Merry Way	1954	1,000	1,500	2,000
		Red vinyl				
❑ 811		I Really Don't Want to Know/Get With It	1955	2,000	3,000	4,000
		Black vinyl				
❑ 811		I Really Don't Want to Know/Get With It	1955	4,000	6,000	8,000
		Red vinyl				
❑ 812		I'm Yours/Ko Ko Mo	1955	250.00	500.00	1,000
		Black vinyl				
❑ 812		I'm Yours/Ko Ko Mo	1955	1,000	1,500	2,000
		Red vinyl				

Number		Title (A Side/B Side)	Year	VG	VG+	NM

Philips

❑ 40308		Temptation/Call Her on the Phone	1965	3.75	7.50	15.00
❑ 40347		The Boogaloo Party/The Nearness of You	1965	3.75	7.50	15.00
❑ 40378		Brooklyn Boogaloo/Since My Baby Put Me Down	1966	3.75	7.50	15.00
❑ 40413		Itty Bitty Baby/She Shook My World	1966	3.75	7.50	15.00
❑ 40452		Koo Koo/It Keeps the Doctor Away	1967	3.75	7.50	15.00
❑ 40496		Oh Mary Don't You Worry/Do It, Do It	1967	3.75	7.50	15.00

Polydor

❑ 14019		Buffalo Soldier (Long)/Buffalo Soldier (Short)	1970	2.50	5.00	10.00
❑ 14044		Straighten It Up (Get It Together)/ Lover Come Back to Me	1970	2.50	5.00	10.00

Ronze

❑ 111		Welcome Home/Gotta Have All Your Lovin'	1971		2.50	5.00
❑ 115		Someone to Watch Over Me/Heavy Hips	1972		2.50	5.00
❑ 116		Love Keeps the Doctor Away (Long)/ Love Keeps the Doctor Away (Short)	1972		2.50	5.00

Roulette

❑ 4524		Ol' Man River (Part 1)/Ol' Man River (Part 2)	1963	5.00	10.00	20.00

Skylark

❑ 541		If I Could Love You/I Found a New Baby	197?		2.50	5.00

Times Square

❑ 102		A Lovely Way to Spend an Evening/ Walking My Baby Back Home	1964	3.75	7.50	15.00

Vee Jay

❑ 384		Golden Teardrops/Carried Away	1961	6.25	12.50	25.00

Worlds

❑ 103		Think About Me/(Instrumental)	1974		2.50	5.00

Fleetwood Mac

(Also see "Kirwan, Danny"; "Nicks, Stevie"; "Spencer, Jeremy"; "Welch, Bob")

Blue Horizon

❑ 304		Hungry Country Woman/Walkin'	1970	3.00	6.00	12.00
		A-side by Otis Spann with Fleetwood Mac; B-side by Otis Spann				

DJM

❑ 1007		Man of the World/Best Girl in the World	1976		3.00	6.00
		B-side by Danny Kirwan				

Epic

❑ 10351		Black Magic Woman/Long Grey Mare	1968	3.00	6.00	12.00
❑ 10368		Stop Messin' Around/Need Your Love So Bad	1968	3.00	6.00	12.00
❑ 10436		Albatross/Jigsaw Puzzle Blues	1969	2.50	5.00	10.00
❑ 11029		Albatross/Black Magic Woman	1973	2.00	4.00	8.00

Reprise

❑ 0860		Rattlesnake Shake/Coming Your Way	1969	5.00	10.00	20.00
❑ 0860	DJ	Rattlesnake Shake/Coming Your Way	1969	2.50	5.00	10.00
❑ 0883		Oh Well, Part 1/Oh Well, Part 2	1970	4.00	8.00	16.00
❑ 0883	DJ	Oh Well, Part 1/Oh Well, Part 2	1970	2.50	5.00	10.00
❑ 0925		The Green Manalishi (With the Two-Prong Crown)/ World In Harmony	1970	5.00	10.00	20.00
❑ 0925	DJ	The Green Manalishi (With the Two-Prong Crown)/ World In Harmony	1970	2.50	5.00	10.00
❑ 0984		Jewel-Eyed Judy/Station Man	1971	5.00	10.00	20.00
❑ 0984	DJ	Jewel-Eyed Judy/Station Man	1971	2.50	5.00	10.00
❑ 1057		Sands of Time/Lay It All Down	1971	2.00	4.00	8.00
❑ 1077		Oh Well, Part 1/ The Green Manalishi (With the Two-Prong Crown) *"Back to Back Hits" reissue*	1971		2.50	5.00
❑ 1093		Sentimental Lady/Sunny Side of Heaven	1972	2.00	4.00	8.00
❑ 1159		Remember Me/Dissatisfied	1973		3.00	6.00
❑ 1172		Did You Ever Love Me/Revelation	1973		3.00	6.00
❑ 1188		For Your Love/Hypnotized	1973		3.00	6.00
❑ 1188	DJ	For Your Love (Long)/For Your Love (Short)	1973	2.50	5.00	10.00
❑ 1317		Heroes Are Hard to Find/Born Enchanter	1974		3.00	6.00
❑ 1339		Over My Head/I'm So Afraid	1975		2.00	4.00
❑ 1345		Rhiannon (Will You Ever Win)/Sugar Daddy	1976		2.00	4.00
❑ 1356		Say You Love Me (Edited)/Monday Morning	1976		2.00	4.00
		The A-sides of Reprise 1339, 1345 and 1356 feature significantly different mixes than those on their parent album, "Fleetwood Mac."				

Warner Bros.

❑ 8354		Go Your Own Way/Silver Springs	1976		2.50	5.00
❑ 8371		Dreams/Songbird	1977		2.00	4.00
❑ 8413		Don't Stop/Never Going Back Again	1977		2.00	4.00
❑ 8413	PS	Don't Stop/Never Going Back Again	1977		2.50	5.00
❑ 8483		You Make Loving Fun/Gold Dust Woman	1977		2.00	4.00
❑ 18661		Paper Doll/The Chain	1993			3.00
❑ 19866		Save Me/Another Woman	1990			3.00
❑ 19867		Skies the Limit/The Second Time	1990			3.00
❑ 27644		As Long As You Follow/Oh Well (Live)	1988			3.00
❑ 27644	PS	As Long As You Follow/Oh Well (Live)	1988			3.00
❑ 28114		Family Man/Down Endless Street	1988			3.00
❑ 28114	PS	Family Man/Down Endless Street	1988			3.00
❑ 28143		Everywhere/When I See You Again	1987			3.00
❑ 28143	PS	Everywhere/When I See You Again	1987			3.00
❑ 28291		Little Lies/Ricky	1987			3.00
❑ 28291	PS	Little Lies/Ricky	1987			3.00

Number		Title (A Side/B Side)	Year	VG	VG+	NM
☐ 28317		Seven Wonders/Book of Miracles	1987			3.00
☐ 28317	PS	Seven Wonders/Book of Miracles	1987			3.00
☐ 28398		Big Love/You and I, Part 1	1987			3.00
☐ 28398	PS	Big Love/You and I, Part 1	1987			3.00
☐ 29698		Oh Diane/That's Alright	1983			3.00
☐ 29848		Love in Store/Can't Go Back	1983			3.00
☐ 29918		Gypsy/Cool Water	1982			3.00
☐ 29918	PS	Gypsy/Cool Water	1982			3.00
☐ 29966		Hold Me/Eyes of the World	1982			3.00
☐ 29966	PS	Hold Me/Eyes of the World	1982			3.00
☐ 49077		Tusk/Never Make Me Cry	1979		2.00	4.00
☐ 49077	PS	Tusk/Never Make Me Cry	1979		2.50	5.00
		Version 1: Brown print, small dog photo				
☐ 49077	PS	Tusk/Never Make Me Cry	1979		2.00	4.00
		Version 2: Black print, large dog photo				
☐ 49150		Sara/That's Enough for Me	1979		2.00	4.00
☐ 49150	PS	Sara/That's Enough for Me	1979		3.00	6.00
☐ 49196		Think About Me/Save Me a Place	1980		2.00	4.00
☐ 49196	PS	Think About Me/Save Me a Place	1980		3.00	6.00
☐ 49500		Sisters of the Moon/Walk a Thin Line	1980	2.50	5.00	10.00
		Scarce on stock copy; A-side also is a different mix than the LP version				
☐ 49660		Fireflies/Over My Head (Live)	1981		2.00	4.00
☐ 49660	PS	Fireflies/Over My Head (Live)	1981		2.00	4.00
☐ 49700		The Farmer's Daughter/Monday Morning (Live)	1982		2.50	5.00
☐ 49700	PS	The Farmer's Daughter/Monday Morning (Live)	1982		2.50	5.00

Fleetwoods, The
Dolphin
☐ 1		Come Softly to Me/I Care So Much	1959	5.00	10.00	20.00

Dolton
☐ 3	M	Graduation's Here/Oh Lord, Let It Be	1959	5.00	10.00	20.00
☐ S-3	S	Graduation's Here/Oh Lord, Let It Be	1959	12.50	25.00	50.00
☐ 5		Mr. Blue/You Mean Everything to Me	1959	5.00	10.00	20.00
☐ 15		Outside My Window/Magic Star	1960	5.00	10.00	20.00
☐ 22		Runaround/Truly Do	1960	5.00	10.00	20.00
☐ 22	PS	Runaround/Truly Do	1960	10.00	20.00	40.00
☐ 27		The Last One to Know/Dormilona	1960	3.75	7.50	15.00
☐ 30		Confidential/I Love You So	1960	3.75	7.50	15.00
☐ 40		Tragedy/Little Miss Sad One	1961	3.75	7.50	15.00
☐ 45		(He's) The Great Impostor/Poor Little Girl	1961	3.75	7.50	15.00
☐ 49		Billy Old Buddy/Trouble	1962	3.75	7.50	15.00
☐ 62		Lovers by Night, Strangers by Day/ They Tell Me It's Summer	1962	3.75	7.50	15.00
☐ 74		You Should Have Been There/ Sure Is Lonesome Downtown	1963	3.75	7.50	15.00
☐ 75		Goodnight My Love/Jimmy Beware	1963	3.75	7.50	15.00
☐ 86		Baby Bye-O/What'll I Do	1963	2.50	5.00	10.00
☐ 93		Lonesome Town/Ruby Red Baby Blue	1964	2.50	5.00	10.00
☐ 97		Ten Times Blue/Ska Light Ska Bright	1964	2.50	5.00	10.00
☐ 98		Mr. Sandman/This Is My Prayer	1964	2.50	5.00	10.00
☐ 302		Before and After (Losing You)/ Lonely Is As Lonely Does	1964	2.50	5.00	10.00
☐ 307		Come Softly to Me/I'm Not Jimmy	1965	2.50	5.00	10.00
☐ 310		Rainbow/Just As I Need You	1965	2.50	5.00	10.00
☐ 315		For Lovin' Me/This Is Where I See Her	1965	2.50	5.00	10.00

Liberty
☐ 55188	M	Come Softly to Me/I Care So Much	1959	6.25	12.50	25.00
☐ 77188	S	Come Softly to Me/I Care So Much	1959	12.50	25.00	50.00

United Artists
☐ 0038		Come Softly to Me/Runaround	1973		2.00	4.00
☐ 0039		Mr. Blue/Tragedy	1973		2.00	4.00
☐ 0040		He's the Great Impostor/Goodnight My Love	1973		2.00	4.00
		0038, 0039 and 0040 are "Silver Spotlight Series" reissues				
☐ XW515		(He's) The Great Impostor/Goodnight My Love	1974		2.00	4.00
		Reissue				

Flemons, Wade
Vee Jay
☐ 295		Here I Stand/My Baby Likes to Rock	1958	7.50	15.00	30.00
☐ 309		Hold Me Close/You'll Remain Forever	1959	7.50	15.00	30.00
☐ 321		Slow Motion/Wailing by the River	1959	7.50	15.00	30.00
☐ 335		Goodnite, It's Time To Go/What's Happening	1959	7.50	15.00	30.00
☐ 344		Easy Lovin'/Woops Now	1960	7.50	15.00	30.00
☐ 368		Ain't That Lovin' You Baby/I'll Come Runnin'	1960	5.00	10.00	20.00
☐ 377		At the Party/Devil in Your Soul	1961	5.00	10.00	20.00
☐ 389		Please Send Me Someone to Love/Keep On Loving Me	1961	5.00	10.00	20.00
☐ 427		Half a Love/Welcome Stranger	1962	5.00	10.00	20.00
☐ 471		Ain't These Tears/I Hope, I Think, I Wish	1962	5.00	10.00	20.00
☐ 533		That Time of the Year/I Came Running	1963	3.75	7.50	15.00
☐ 578		When It Rains, It Pours/Watch Over Her	1964	3.75	7.50	15.00
☐ 614		I Knew You When/That Other Place	1964	3.75	7.50	15.00
☐ 668		Where Did You Go Last Night/Empty Balcony	1965	3.00	6.00	12.00

Floridians, The
ABC-Paramount
☐ 10185		That Lucky Old Sun/I Love Marie	1961	12.50	25.00	50.00

Number		Title (A Side/B Side)	Year	VG	VG+	NM

Floyd, Eddie
Atlantic

❑ 2275		Hush Hush/Drive On	1965	3.00	6.00	12.00

LuPine

❑ 115		Set My Soul on Fire/Will I Be the One	1963	3.75	7.50	15.00

Malaco

❑ 1032		Somebody Touch Me/Never Too Old	1976		2.50	5.00
❑ 1035		Chi-Town Hustler/In Paradise	1976		2.50	5.00
❑ 1039		Special Christmas Day/Mother, My Dear Mother	1976		2.50	5.00
❑ 1040		We Should Really Be in Love/I'll Never Be Loved	1977		2.50	5.00
		With Dorothy Moore				
❑ 1043		You're Gonna Walk Out on Me/Prove It to Me	1977		2.50	5.00

Mercury

❑ 73964		If You Really Love Me/It's Me	1977		2.00	4.00
❑ 74003		Disco Summer/Do It in the Water	1978		2.00	4.00

Stax

❑ 0002		I've Never Found a Girl (To Love Me Like You Do)/ I'm Just the Kind of Fool	1968		3.00	6.00
❑ 0012		Bring It On Home to Me/The Sweet Things You Do	1968		3.00	6.00
❑ 0025		I've Got to Have Your Love/Girl I Love You	1969		3.00	6.00
❑ 0036		Don't Tell Your Mama (Where You've Been)/ Consider Me	1969		3.00	6.00
❑ 0041		Never Never Let You Go/Ain't That Good	1969		3.00	6.00
		With Mavis Staples				
❑ 0051		Why Is the Wine Sweeter (On the Other Side)/ People Get It Together	1969		3.00	6.00
❑ 0060		California Glrl/The Woodman	1970		3.00	6.00
❑ 0072		My Girl/Laurie	1970		3.00	6.00
❑ 0077		The Best Years of My Life/My Little Girl	1970		3.00	6.00
❑ 0087		Oh How It Rained/When My Baby Said Goodbye	1971		3.00	6.00
❑ 0095		Blood Is Thicker Than Water/ Have You Heard the Word	1971		3.00	6.00
❑ 0109		Yum Yum Yum (I Want Some)/Tears of Joy	1971		3.00	6.00
❑ 0134		You're Good Enough (To Be My Baby)/ Spend All You Have on Love	1972		3.00	6.00
❑ 0158		Knock on Wood/Lay Your Loving on Me	1973		3.00	6.00
❑ 0171		Baby Lay Your Head Down (Gently on My Bed)/ Check Me Out	1973		3.00	6.00
❑ 0188		I Wanna Do Things for You/ We've Been Through Too Much Together	1973		3.00	6.00
❑ 0209		Guess Who/Something to Write Home About	1974		3.00	6.00
❑ 0216		Soul Street/Highway Man	1974		3.00	6.00
❑ 0232		Stealing Love/I Got a Reason to Smile	1974		3.00	6.00
❑ 0239		Talk to the Man/I Got a Reason to Smile	1975		3.00	6.00
❑ 0251		I'm So Glad I Met You/I'm So Grateful	1975		3.00	6.00
❑ 187		Things Get Better/Good Love, Bad Love	1966	2.50	5.00	10.00
❑ 194		Knock on Wood/Got to Make a Comeback	1966	2.50	5.00	10.00
❑ 208		Raise Your Hand/I've Just Been Feeling Bad	1967	2.00	4.00	8.00
❑ 219		Don't Rock the Boat/This House	1967	2.00	4.00	8.00
❑ 223		Love Is a Doggone Good Thing/Hey Now	1967	2.00	4.00	8.00
❑ 233		On a Saturday Night/Under My Nose	1967	2.00	4.00	8.00
❑ 246		Holding On with Both Hands/Big Bird	1968	2.00	4.00	8.00

Flyers, The
Atco

❑ 6088		On Bended Knee/My Only Desire	1957	10.00	20.00	40.00

Fogerty, Tommy, and the Blue Velvets
(Early Creedence Clearwater Revival)
Orchestra

❑ (# unknown)		Yes, You Did/Now You're Not Mine	1962	20.00	40.00	80.00
❑ 1010		Have You Ever Been Lonely/Bonita	1961	20.00	40.00	80.00
❑ 6177		Come On Baby/Oh! My Love	1961	20.00	40.00	80.00

Foghat
Bearsville

❑ 0008		I Just Want to Make Love to You/Hole to Hide In	1973		2.50	5.00
❑ 0014		What a Shame/Helping Hand	1973		2.50	5.00
❑ 0019		That'll Be the Day/Wild Cherry	1974		2.50	5.00
❑ 0021		Maybelline/Step Outside	1974		2.50	5.00
❑ 0306		Slow Ride/Save Your Loving	1975		2.50	5.00
❑ 0307		Fool for the City/Take It or Leave It	1976		2.50	5.00
❑ 0313		Drivin' Wheel/Night Shift	1976		2.00	4.00
❑ 0315		I'll Be Standing By/Take Me to the River	1977		2.00	4.00
❑ 0319		I Just Want to Make Love to You (Live)/ Fool for the City (Live)	1977		2.00	4.00
❑ 0325		Stone Blue/Chevrolet	1978		2.00	4.00
❑ 0329		High on Love/Sweet Home Chicago	1978		2.00	4.00
❑ 29612		Seven Day Weekend/That's What Love Can Do	1983		2.00	4.00
❑ 29860		Slipped, Tripped, Fell in Love/ And I Do Just What I Want	1982		2.00	4.00
❑ 49125		Third Time Lucky (First Time I Was a Fool)/ Love in Motion	1979		2.00	4.00
❑ 49125	PS	Third Time Lucky (First Time I Was a Fool)/ Love in Motion	1979		2.50	5.00

Number		Title (A Side/B Side)	Year	VG	VG+	NM
❑ 49510		Stranger in My Home Town/Be My Woman	1980		2.00	4.00
❑ 49779		Love Zone/Wide Boy	1981		2.00	4.00

Fontaine, Eddie
"X"

❑ 0096		Rock Love/All My Love Belongs to You	1955	7.50	15.00	30.00
❑ 0108		On Bended Knees/I Miss You So	1955	7.50	15.00	30.00
❑ 0128		Rollin' Stone/I'm Through Chasin' After You	1955	7.50	15.00	30.00
❑ 0151		Poor Little Monday/The Rain Song	1955	7.50	15.00	30.00
❑ 0184		Turn the Light On/Boom-De-De-Boom	1955	7.50	15.00	30.00
❑ 0193		Here 'Tis/I Look at You	1956	7.50	15.00	30.00
❑ 0203		Stand On That Rock/Baby You Did This to Me	1956	7.50	15.00	30.00

Argo

❑ 5309		Nothin' Shakin'/Don't Ya Know	1958	6.25	12.50	25.00

Chancellor

❑ 1018		Goodness, It's Gladys/Middle of the Road	1958	5.00	10.00	20.00

Decca

❑ 30042		Cool It Baby/Into Each Life Some Rain Must Fall	1956	6.25	12.50	25.00
❑ 30108		A Rose and a Baby Ruth/The Years Before	1956	6.25	12.50	25.00
❑ 30121		As Far As I'm Concerned/'Til Tonight	1956	6.25	12.50	25.00
		With Karen Chandler				
❑ 30202		I'll Be There/East of Mississippi	1957	6.25	12.50	25.00
❑ 30256		Money/Homesick Blues	1957	6.25	12.50	25.00
❑ 30338		Hey Marie, Rock with Me/The One and Only	1957	6.25	12.50	25.00
❑ 30446		Fun Lovin'/Honky Tonk Man	1957	6.25	12.50	25.00

Jalo

❑ 102		Where Is Da Woman/(B-side unknown)	1956	20.00	40.00	80.00

Liberty

❑ 55776		Blue Roses/Way Down Home	1965	2.50	5.00	10.00
❑ 55823		I Need You/It Can Happen to You	1965	2.50	5.00	10.00

Sunbeam

❑ 105		Nothin' Shakin'/Oh, Wonderful Night	1958	10.00	20.00	40.00
❑ 112		Nobody Can Handle This Job/I'm Ready As I'll Ever Be	1958	6.25	12.50	25.00
		B-side by Gerry Granahan				
❑ 118		Love Eyes/Something Cha Cha	1958	6.25	12.50	25.00

Vik

❑ 0184		Turn the Light On/Boom-De-De-Boom	1955	6.25	12.50	25.00
❑ 0193		Here 'Tis/I Look at You	1956	6.25	12.50	25.00
❑ 0203		Stand On That Rock/Baby You Did This to Me	1956	6.25	12.50	25.00

Warner Bros.

❑ 5313		My Heart Belongs to You/I'm Gonna Settle Down	1962	3.75	7.50	15.00
❑ 5345		(It's No) Sin/All I Want Is You	1963	3.75	7.50	15.00

Fontaine, Frank
MGM

❑ 12129		Everybody Rocks/Livin' It Up	1955	15.00	30.00	60.00

Fontana, Wayne
(Also see "Fontana, Wayne, and the Mindbenders")
Brut

❑ 812		Sweet America/Interested	1973		2.50	5.00

Metromedia

❑ 133		Say Goodbye to Yesterday/Dayton, Ohio	1969		3.00	6.00

MGM

❑ 13456		It Was Easier to Hurt Her/ You Made Me What I Am Today	1966	2.00	4.00	8.00
❑ 13516		Come On Home/My Eyes	1966	2.00	4.00	8.00
❑ 13661		Pamela, Pamela/Something Keeps Calling Me Back	1967		3.00	6.00
❑ 13762		From a Boy to a Girl/24 Sycamore	1967		3.00	6.00

Fontana, Wayne, and the Mindbenders
(Also see "Fontana, Wayne"; "Mindbenders, The")
A&M

❑ 3010		Game of Love/What a Wonderful World	1988		2.00	4.00
		B-side by Louis Armstrong				
❑ 3010	PS	Game of Love/What a Wonderful World	1988		2.00	4.00

Fontana

❑ 1503		Game of Love/Since You've Been Gone	1965	3.75	7.50	15.00
❑ 1509		Game of Love/One More Time	1965	3.00	6.00	12.00
❑ 1514		It's Just a Little Bit Too Late/Long Time Comin'	1965	2.50	5.00	10.00
❑ 1524		She Needs Love/Like I Do	1965	2.50	5.00	10.00
❑ 1917		Stop, Look, Listen/Road Runner	1964	3.00	6.00	12.00
❑ 1945		Um, Um, Um, Um, Um, Um/First Taste of Love	1964	3.00	6.00	12.00

Force Five, The
Ascot

❑ 2206		Gee Too Tiger/I Want You Babe	1966	12.50	25.00	50.00

Ford, Billy
(Of Billy and Lillie)
Josie

❑ 775		String of Pearls/Stop Lyin' on Me	1955	10.00	20.00	40.00

Number		Title (A Side/B Side)	Year	VG	VG+	NM
Reprise						
❑ 0265		This Is Worth Fighting For/My Girl	1964	3.00	6.00	12.00
United						
❑ 142		Smooth Rocking/You Foxie Thing	1954	7.50	15.00	30.00
❑ 167		Confessing/Old Age	1955	7.50	15.00	30.00
Vik						
❑ 0263		How Can I Be Sure/Billy Boy Blow	1957	6.25	12.50	25.00

Ford, Dee Dee
(Of Don Gardner and Dee Dee Ford)

Number		Title (A Side/B Side)	Year	VG	VG+	NM
ABC-Paramount						
❑ 10503		Just Like a Fool (I Keep Hopin')/Shoo-Fly Pie	1963	3.00	6.00	12.00
Todd						
❑ 1049		Good Morning Blues/I Just Can't Believe	1959	3.75	7.50	15.00

Ford, Frankie

Number		Title (A Side/B Side)	Year	VG	VG+	NM
ABC						
❑ 11431		All Alone Am I/Blue Monday	1974		2.50	5.00
Ace						
❑ 549		The Last One to Cry/Cheatin' Woman	1958	6.25	12.50	25.00
❑ 554		Sea Cruise/Roberta	1959	10.00	20.00	40.00
❑ 566		Alimony/Can't Tell My Heart (What to Do)	1959	6.25	12.50	25.00
❑ 580		Time After Time/Want to Be Your Man	1960	6.25	12.50	25.00
❑ 592		Chinatown/What's Goin' On	1960	6.25	12.50	25.00
❑ 592	PS	Chinatown/What's Goin' On	1960	8.75	17.50	35.00
❑ 8009		Ocean Full of Tears/Hour of Need	1963	3.75	7.50	15.00
Briarmeade						
❑ 7600		I've Found Someone of My Own/Battle Hymn of the Republic	1976		2.50	5.00
❑ 7701		Desperado/Mardi Gras in New Orleans	1977		2.50	5.00
❑ 7901		Halfway to Paradise/I'm Proud of What I Am	1979		2.50	5.00
Cinnamon						
❑ 752		When I Stop Dreamin'/I'm Proud of What I Am	1972		2.50	5.00
❑ 767		Talk to a Carpenter/When I Stop Dreamin'	1973		2.50	5.00
Constellation						
❑ 101		Chinatown/Ocean Full of Tears	1963	3.75	7.50	15.00
Doubloon						
❑ 101		Half a Crown/I Can't Face Tomorrow	1967	2.50	5.00	10.00
Imperial						
❑ 5686		You Talk Too Much/If You've Got Troubles	1960	3.75	7.50	15.00
❑ 5706		My Southern Belle/The Groom	1960	3.75	7.50	15.00
❑ 5735		Seventeen/Doghouse	1961	3.75	7.50	15.00
❑ 5749		Saturday Night Fish Fry/Love Don't Love Nobody	1961	3.75	7.50	15.00
❑ 5776		Let 'Em Talk/What Happened to You	1961	3.75	7.50	15.00
❑ 5819		They Said It Couldn't Be Done/A Man Only Does	1962	3.75	7.50	15.00
Paula						
❑ 351		Peace of Mind/I'm Proud of What I Am	1971	2.00	4.00	8.00
SYC						
❑ 1227		Growing Pains/Ups and Downs	1982		2.00	4.00
❑ 1228		My Prayer/Gospel Ship	1983		2.00	4.00

Formations, The

Number		Title (A Side/B Side)	Year	VG	VG+	NM
Bank						
❑ 1007		At the Top of the Stairs/Magic Melody	1968	7.50	15.00	30.00
MGM						
❑ 13899		At the Top of the Stairs/Magic Melody	1968	2.50	5.00	10.00
❑ 13963		Love's Not Only for the Heart/Lonely Voice of Love	1968	5.00	10.00	20.00
❑ 14009		Don't Get Close/There's No Room	1968	3.00	6.00	12.00

Fortune, Johnny

Number		Title (A Side/B Side)	Year	VG	VG+	NM
Arena						
❑ 102		I'm a Fool for You/Gee But I Miss You	1963	5.00	10.00	20.00
Arhaven						
❑ 1001		I'm a Fool for You/Gee But I Miss You	1962	6.25	12.50	25.00
Beaver						
❑ 111		I'm Requesting a Love Song/Stay Just One More Day	1966	3.75	7.50	15.00
Crusader						
❑ 104		If You Love Me/Gee But I Miss You	1964	3.75	7.50	15.00
Current						
❑ 101		Say You Will/Come On and Love Me	1965	3.75	7.50	15.00
❑ 104		Dan Stole My Girl/You Want Me to Be Your Baby	1965	3.75	7.50	15.00
❑ 105		I Am Lonely for You/I'll Never Let You Go	1965	3.75	7.50	15.00
Emmy						
❑ 1001		If You Love Me/Alone and Crying	1960	7.50	15.00	30.00
❑ 1002		I'm in Heaven (When You Kiss Me)/Gee But I Miss You	1960	7.50	15.00	30.00
Park Avenue						
❑ 104		Need You/One Less Angel	1963	3.75	7.50	15.00
❑ 110		Midnight Surf/Soul Surfer	1963	3.75	7.50	15.00
❑ 126		Surfer's Trip/Soul Traveler	1963	3.75	7.50	15.00
❑ 130		Dragster/Siboney	1963	3.75	7.50	15.00
❑ 4905		I'm Talkin' About You/My Wandering Love	1963	3.75	7.50	15.00

Number	Title (A Side/B Side)	Year	VG	VG+	NM

United Artists

❏ 720	Juarez/It Ain't Necessarily So	1964	3.75	7.50	15.00
❏ 780	Don't You Lie to Me/Don't Stay Out After Midnight	1964	3.75	7.50	15.00

Vault

❏ 954	Your True Love/Tell Me You Love Me	1969	2.50	5.00	10.00

Fortunes, The
(The Capitol, Press, United Artists and World Pacific records are a British Invasion group)

Argo

❏ 5364	Congratulations/Look at Me, Look at You	1960	15.00	30.00	60.00

Capitol

❏ 3086	Here Comes That Rainy Day Feeling Again/ I Gotta Dream	1971		3.00	6.00
❏ 3179	There's a Man/Freedom Comes, Freedom Goes	1971		2.00	4.00
❏ 3248	Storm in a Teacup/I'm Not Following You	1971		2.00	4.00
❏ 3445	Wait Until September/Don't Sing to Me	1972		2.00	4.00
❏ 3514	I Can't Remember When the Sun Went In/Secret Love	1973		2.00	4.00
❏ 3626	Give Me Some Room/Whenever It's a Sunday	1973		2.00	4.00

Checker

❏ 818	Believe in Me/My Baby Is Fine	1955	15.00	30.00	60.00

Cub

❏ 9123	The Ghoul in School/ You Don't Know (What I've Been Through)	1963	3.75	7.50	15.00

Decca

❏ 30541	Tarnished Angel/Who Cares?	1958	15.00	30.00	60.00
❏ 30688	How Clever of You/Trees	1958	12.50	25.00	50.00

DRA

❏ 320	Tell Me/Running Away from Love	1962	50.00	100.00	200.00

Press

❏ 60001	Gone with My Mind/Silent Street	1966	2.50	5.00	10.00
❏ 9773	You've Got Your Troubles/I've Gotta Go	1965	4.00	8.00	16.00
	White label stock copy				
❏ 9773	You've Got Your Troubles/I've Gotta Go	1965	3.00	6.00	12.00
	Purple label				
❏ 9798	Here It Comes Again/Things I Should Have Known	1965	3.75	7.50	15.00
	White label stock copy				
❏ 9798	Here It Comes Again/Things I Should Have Known	1965	2.50	5.00	10.00
	Purple label				
❏ 9811	This Golden Ring/Someone to Care	1966	2.50	5.00	10.00

Queen

❏ 24010	Nothing Matters Anymore/Ugly Duckling	1962	6.25	12.50	25.00

Top Rank

❏ 2019	Steady Vows/In the Night	1959	10.00	20.00	40.00

United Artists

❏ 50211	The Idol/His Smile Was a Lie	1967	2.50	5.00	10.00
❏ 50280	Painting a Shadow/Fire Brigade	1968	2.50	5.00	10.00

World Pacific

❏ 77937	That Same Old Feeling/Lifetime of Love	1970	2.00	4.00	8.00

Yucca

❏ 168	Laugh of the Train/Chi Wawa	1964	7.50	15.00	30.00
❏ 170	Lonely Teardrops/This Is Love	1964	10.00	20.00	40.00

Foster, John, and Sons Black Dyke Mills Band

Apple

❏ 1800	Thingumybob/Yellow Submarine	1968	30.00	60.00	120.00
	With black star on uncut apple side				
❏ 1800	Thingumybob/Yellow Submarine	1968	25.00	50.00	100.00
	With "Yellow Submarine" on uncut apple side				
❏ 1800	Thingumybob/Yellow Submarine	1968	25.00	50.00	100.00
	With "Thingumybob" on uncut apple side				

Foto-Fi Four, The

Foto-Fi

❏ 107	Stand Up and Holler!/Ismael	1964	6.25	12.50	25.00
	Some sources say Harry Nilsson is on this recording				
❏ 107	PS Stand Up and Holler!/Ismael	1964	12.50	25.00	50.00
	Sleeve states: "The Beatles arrive in America! Have fun running the film with this specially scored recording." Price does not include film.				

Four Aims, The - See "Four Tops"

Four Buddies, The
(More than one group)

Coral

❏ 62217	Hurt/Moonglow & Theme from Picnic	1960	5.00	10.00	20.00
❏ 62325	The Light/Cin Cin (Che Bell)	1962	5.00	10.00	20.00

Imperial

❏ 66018	I Want to Be the Boy You Love/ Just Enough of Your Love	1964	10.00	20.00	40.00

Philips

❏ 40122	Lonely Summer/Slow Locomotion	1963	5.00	10.00	20.00

Number	Title (A Side/B Side)	Year	VG	VG+	NM

Savoy

❏ 769	I Will Wait/Just to See You Smile Again	1951	100.00	200.00	400.00
❏ 779	Don't Leave Me Now/Sweet Slumber	1951	75.00	150.00	300.00
❏ 789	My Summer's Gone/Why at a Time Like This	1951	62.50	125.00	250.00
❏ 817	Heart and Soul/Sin	1951	62.50	125.00	250.00
❏ 823	Window Eyes/Simply Say Goodbye	1951	62.50	125.00	250.00
❏ 845	You're Part of Me/Story Blues	1952	50.00	100.00	200.00
❏ 866	What's the Matter with Me/Sweet Tooth for My Baby	1952	50.00	100.00	200.00
❏ 888	My Mother's Eyes/Ooh Ow	1953	50.00	100.00	200.00
❏ 891	I'd Climb the Highest Mountain/I Wanna Know	1953	50.00	100.00	200.00
	B-side by Dolly Cooper				

Four Cal-Quettes, The

Capitol

❏ 4534	Sparkle and Shine/In This World	1961	7.50	15.00	30.00
	As "The Four Coquettes"				
❏ 4574	Billy, My Billy/Star Bright	1961	7.50	15.00	30.00
❏ 4657	Most of All/I'm Gonna Love Him Anyway	1961	7.50	15.00	30.00
❏ 4725	I'll Never Come Back (Silly Boy)/Again	1962	7.50	15.00	30.00

Liberty

❏ 55540	I Cried/Movie Magazines	1963	3.75	7.50	15.00

Four Cheers, The

End

❏ 1034	Fatal Charms of Love/Periwinkle Blue	1958	37.50	75.00	150.00

Four Chevelles, The

Band Box

❏ 357	This Is Our Wedding Day/Darling Forever	1957	5.00	10.00	20.00
❏ 358	I Can't Believe/I Know	1957	5.00	10.00	20.00

Delft

❏ 357	This Is Our Wedding Day/Darling Forever	1957	100.00	200.00	400.00

Four Dates, The

Chancellor

❏ 1014	I'm Happy/Eloise	1958	5.00	10.00	20.00
❏ 1019	I Say Babe/Hey Roly Poly	1958	5.00	10.00	20.00
❏ 1027	Feel Good/Teenage Neighbor	1958	6.25	12.50	25.00

Four Directions, The

Coral

❏ 62456	(Doin' the) Arthur/Tonight We Love	1965	7.50	15.00	30.00

Four Dukes, The

Duke

❏ 116	Crying in the Chapel/I Done Done It	1953	150.00	250.00	400.00

Imperial

❏ 5653	Baby Won't You Please Come Home/John Henry	1960	7.50	15.00	30.00

Four Epics, The

Heritage

❏ 109	I'm On My Way to Love/When the Music Ends	1962	25.00	50.00	100.00

Laurie

❏ 3155	Again/I Love You Diane	1963	6.25	12.50	25.00
❏ 3183	How I Wish I Was Single Again/Dance Joanne	1963	6.25	12.50	25.00

Four Esquires, The

Cadence

❏ 1260	Three Things/The Sphinx Won't Tell	1955	5.00	10.00	20.00
❏ 1277	Adorable/Thunderbolt	1955	5.00	10.00	20.00

Paris

❏ 501	Song of April/Everyone's Sweet on My Sugar	1957	5.00	10.00	20.00
❏ 505	The Chopstick Rock/Never Look for Love	1957	5.00	10.00	20.00
❏ 509	Love Me Forever/I Ain't Been Right Since You Left	1957	5.00	10.00	20.00
❏ 512	Always and Forever/I Walk Down the Street	1958	5.00	10.00	20.00
❏ 515	All Around the Clock/The Big Dance	1958	5.00	10.00	20.00
❏ 520	Hideaway/Repeat After Me	1958	5.00	10.00	20.00
	With Rosemary June				
❏ 526	Follow Me/The Land of You and Me	1958	5.00	10.00	20.00
❏ 531	Lucky Old Sun/Non E Cosi	1959	5.00	10.00	20.00
❏ 535	Act Your Age/So Ends the Night	1959	5.00	10.00	20.00
❏ 539	Wonderful One/Wouldn't It Be Wonderful	1959	5.00	10.00	20.00
❏ 544	Make Them Mine/Peg O' My Heart	1960	5.00	10.00	20.00
❏ 549	Sweet Sixteen She'll Never Be/The Chopstick Rock	1960	5.00	10.00	20.00

Pilgrim

❏ 717	Follow Me/Summer Vacation	1956	6.25	12.50	25.00
❏ 718	Click-I-Dee/Maybe Someday	1956	6.25	12.50	25.00

Terrace

❏ 7502	Can't Help Falling in Love/Merry-Go-Round of Love	1961	3.75	7.50	15.00
❏ 7516	The James Bond Theme (Double-O-Seven)/Summer Vacation	1963	6.25	12.50	25.00
	Betcha didn't know this had lyrics...				

Number	Title (A Side/B Side)	Year	VG	VG+	NM

Four Exceptions, The
Parkway
| ❏ 986 | You Got the Power/A Sad Goodbye | 1966 | 12.50 | 25.00 | 50.00 |

Four Fifths, The
Columbia
| ❏ 43913 | If You Still Want Me/Have You Ever Loved a Girl | 1966 | 3.00 | 6.00 | 12.00 |

Hudson
❏ 8101	After Graduation/Come On Girl	1963	37.50	75.00	150.00
	Black vinyl				
❏ 8101	After Graduation/Come On Girl	1963	100.00	200.00	400.00
	Blue vinyl				

Four Graduates, The
Crystal Ball
| ❏ 116 | May I Have This Dance/Caught in a Lie | 1978 | | 2.00 | 4.00 |
| ❏ 119 | Your Initials/Every Year About This Time | 1978 | | 2.00 | 4.00 |

Rust
❏ 5062	Picture of An Angel/	1963	25.00	50.00	100.00
	A Lovely Way to Spend An Evening				
❏ 5084	Candy Queen/A Girl in Love	1964	45.00	90.00	180.00

Four Horsemen, The
United Artists
| ❏ 134 | A Long Long Time/My Heartbeat | 1958 | 50.00 | 100.00 | 200.00 |

Four Hues, The
Coral
| ❏ 61617 | Ivory Tower/Sister Jenny | 1956 | 7.50 | 15.00 | 30.00 |

Four Imperials, The
Chant
| ❏ 10067 | My Girl/Teen Age Fool | 1958 | 12.50 | 25.00 | 50.00 |

Dial
| ❏ 101 | Valley of Tears/Time Out | 1959 | 37.50 | 75.00 | 150.00 |

Dot
| ❏ 15737 | Lazy Bonnie/Let's Make a Scene | 1958 | 6.25 | 12.50 | 25.00 |

Fox
| ❏ 102 | Give Me One More Chance/Look Up and Live | 1958 | 20.00 | 40.00 | 80.00 |

Lorelei
| ❏ 4444 | Lazy Bonnie/Let's Make a Scene | 1958 | 25.00 | 50.00 | 100.00 |

Twirl
| ❏ 2005 | Santa's Got a Coupe de Ville/Seven Lonely Days | 1960 | 6.25 | 12.50 | 25.00 |

Four J's, The
Congress
| ❏ 6003 | Dreamin'/Love My Life | 1969 | 2.50 | 5.00 | 10.00 |

4-J
| ❏ 506 | Will You Be My Love/Nursery | 1963 | 3.75 | 7.50 | 15.00 |

Herald
| ❏ 528 | Kissin' at the Drive-In/Dreams Are a Dime a Dozen | 1958 | 7.50 | 15.00 | 30.00 |

Jamie
❏ 1267	Here I Am Broken-Hearted/	1964	6.25	12.50	25.00
	She Said That She Loved Me				
❏ 1274	By Love Possessed/My Love, My Love	1964	6.25	12.50	25.00

United Artists
| ❏ 125 | Rock and Roll Age/Be Nice, Don't Fight | 1958 | 10.00 | 20.00 | 40.00 |

Four Jets, The - See "Shadows, The"

Four Jokers, The
(More than one group)
Amy
| ❏ 832 | She's a Flirt/Boo-Ga-Loo | 1961 | 5.00 | 10.00 | 20.00 |

Crystallette
| ❏ 730 | Your Decision/We Met in Catalina | 1959 | 3.75 | 7.50 | 15.00 |
| ❏ 733 | Beyond the Reef/That's the Way | 1959 | 3.75 | 7.50 | 15.00 |

Diamond
| ❏ 3004 | Transfusion/You Did | 1956 | 7.50 | 15.00 | 30.00 |
| | _Nervous Norvus (Jimmy Drake) was in this group_ | | | | |

MGM
| ❏ 11815 | Tell Me Now/Caring | 1954 | 7.50 | 15.00 | 30.00 |

Sue
| ❏ 703 | Written in the Stars/The Run-Around | 1958 | 15.00 | 30.00 | 60.00 |

Four Knights, The
Capitol
❏ F1587	I Love the Sunshine of Your Smile/Sentimental Fool	1951	12.50	25.00	50.00
❏ F1707	Walkin' Whistlin' Blues/Who Am I	1951	10.00	20.00	40.00
❏ F1787	I Go Crazy/Get Her Off My Hands	1951	10.00	20.00	40.00
❏ F1806	It's No Sin/The Glory of Love	1951	10.00	20.00	40.00

Number	Title (A Side/B Side)	Year	VG	VG+	NM
❑ F1875	Cry/Charmaine	1951	10.00	20.00	40.00
❑ F1914	Marshmallow Moon/Five Foot Two, Eyes of Blue	1951	7.50	15.00	30.00
❑ F1930	The Way I Feel/I Wish I Had a Girl	1952	7.50	15.00	30.00
❑ F1971	There Are Two Sides to Every Heartache/ Walkin' in Sunshine	1952	7.50	15.00	30.00
❑ F1998	The More I Go Out with Somebody Else/ The Doll with the Sawdust Heart	1952	7.50	15.00	30.00
❑ F2087	I'm the World's Biggest Fool/It's a Sin to Tell a Lie	1952	7.50	15.00	30.00
❑ F2127	Win or Lose/Do-Wacka-Do	1952	7.50	15.00	30.00
❑ F2195	Say No More/That's the Way It's Gonna Be	1952	7.50	15.00	30.00
❑ F2234	Lies/One Way Kisses	1952	7.50	15.00	30.00
❑ F2315	Oh Happy Day/A Million Tears	1953	6.25	12.50	25.00
❑ F2403	Anniversary Song/A Few Kind Words	1953	6.25	12.50	25.00
❑ F2517	Baby Doll/Tennessee Train	1953	6.25	12.50	25.00
❑ F2654	I Get So Lonely (When I Dream About You)/ I Couldn't Stay Away from You	1953	5.00	10.00	20.00
❑ F2654	Oh Baby Mine/I Couldn't Stay Away from You	1953	10.00	20.00	40.00
❑ F2782	I Was Meant for You/They Tell Me	1954	5.00	10.00	20.00
❑ F2847	How Wrong Can You Be/Period	1954	5.00	10.00	20.00
❑ F2894	In the Chapel in the Moonlight/Easy Street	1954	5.00	10.00	20.00
❑ F2938	I Don't Wanna See You Cryin'/Saw Your Eyes	1954	5.00	10.00	20.00
❑ F3024	Write Me Baby/Honey Bunch	1955	5.00	10.00	20.00
❑ F3093	Foolishly Yours/Inside You	1955	5.00	10.00	20.00
❑ F3155	Gratefully Yours/Me	1955	5.00	10.00	20.00
❑ F3192	Don't Sit Under the Apple Tree/Believing You	1955	5.00	10.00	20.00
❑ F3250	Perdido/After	1955	5.00	10.00	20.00
❑ F3279	Guilty/You	1955	5.00	10.00	20.00
❑ F3339	I Love You Still/Happy Birthday Baby	1956	3.75	7.50	15.00
❑ F3386	Bottle Up the Moonlight/Mistaken	1956	3.75	7.50	15.00
❑ F3494	Don't Depend on Me/You're a Honey	1956	3.75	7.50	15.00
❑ F3689	It Doesn't Cost Money/How Can You Not Believe	1957	3.75	7.50	15.00
❑ F3730	Walkin' and Whistlin' Blues/I Love That Song	1957	3.75	7.50	15.00
❑ F15895	I Ain't Got Nobody/When My Baby Smiles at Me	1952	7.50	15.00	30.00
❑ F15896	Easy Street/Ida, Sweet As Apple Cider	1952	7.50	15.00	30.00
❑ F15897	Georgia on My Mind/Sentimental Journey	1952	7.50	15.00	30.00
Coral					
❑ 61936	The Four Minute Mile/When Your Lover Has Gone	1958	3.00	6.00	12.00
❑ 61981	Yes I Do/If You Ever Change Your Mind	1958	3.00	6.00	12.00
❑ 62045	O Falling Star/Foolish Tears	1959	3.00	6.00	12.00
❑ 62110	Where Is the Love/Things to Do Today	1959	3.00	6.00	12.00
Decca					
❑ 48018	He'll Understand and Say Well Done/ Lead Me to That Rock	1952	25.00	50.00	100.00

Reissue of original 78 from 1947. (Decca 48014 and 48026 are known to exist only on 78s.)

Four Larks, The
Tower

❑ 364	Rain/Another Chance	1967	7.50	15.00	30.00
❑ 402	I Still Love You (From the Bottom of My Heart)/ Groovin' at the Go-Go	1968	10.00	20.00	40.00
❑ 450	Can I Have Another Helping, Please/I've Got Plenty	1968	2.50	5.00	10.00

Uptown

❑ 748	You and Me/That's All That Counts	1967	10.00	20.00	40.00

Four Lovers, The
(Frankie Valli was in this group, a precursor to the Four Seasons)
Epic

❑ 9255	My Life for Your Love/Pucker Up	1957	500.00	1,000	2,000

RCA Victor

❑ 47-6518	You're the Apple of My Eye/The Girl of My Dreams	1956	10.00	20.00	40.00
❑ 47-6519	Honey Love/Please Don't Leave Me	1956	10.00	20.00	40.00
❑ 47-6646	Be Lovey Dovey/Jambalaya	1956	7.50	15.00	30.00
❑ 47-6768	Happy Am I/Never Never	1956	7.50	15.00	30.00
❑ 47-6812	Shake a Hand/The Stranger	1957	10.00	20.00	40.00
❑ 47-6819	Night Train/The Stranger	1957	10.00	20.00	40.00

Four Naturals, The
Red Top

❑ 113	How Strange/Blue Moon	1958	12.50	25.00	50.00
	As "The Naturals"				
❑ 119	I Hear a Rhapsody/When I'm In Your Arms	1959	12.50	25.00	50.00
❑ 125	The Thought of You Darling/Long Long Ago	1959	20.00	40.00	80.00

Four Pearls, The
Dolton

❑ 26	Look at Me/It's Almost Tomorrow	1960	37.50	75.00	150.00

Four Pennies, The
(The group on Rust also recorded as The Chiffons)
Brunswick

❑ 55304	You Have No Time to Lose/ You're a Gas with Your Trash	1966	2.50	5.00	10.00
❑ 55324	Shake a Hand/'Tis the Season	1967	5.00	10.00	20.00

Philips

❑ 40202	Tell Me Girl, What Are You Gonna Do/Juliet	1964	3.75	7.50	15.00
❑ 40333	Till Another Day/Until It's Time to Go	1965	3.75	7.50	15.00

Number		Title (A Side/B Side)	Year	VG	VG+	NM
Rust						
❑ 5070		When the Boy's Happy (The Girl's Happy Too)/ Hockaday (Part 1)	1963	6.25	12.50	25.00
❑ 5071		Dry Your Eyes/My Block	1963	6.25	12.50	25.00
Four Preps, The						
Capitol						
❑ F3576		Dreamy Eyes/Fools Will Be Fools	1956	5.00	10.00	20.00
❑ F3621		Moonstruck in Madrid/I Cried a Million Tears	1957	5.00	10.00	20.00
❑ F3699		Falling Star/Where Wuzz You	1957	5.00	10.00	20.00
❑ F3761		Promise Me Baby/Again 'N Again 'N Again	1957	5.00	10.00	20.00
❑ F3775		Band of Angels/How About That	1957	5.00	10.00	20.00
❑ F3845		26 Miles (Santa Catalina)/It's You	1957	5.00	10.00	20.00
❑ F3960		Big Man/Stop Baby	1958	5.00	10.00	20.00
❑ F4023		Lazy Summer Night/Summertime Lies	1958	5.00	10.00	20.00
❑ F4078		Cinderella/Gidget	1958	5.00	10.00	20.00
❑ F4126		She Was Five and He Was Ten/Riddle of Love	1959	5.00	10.00	20.00
❑ F4218		Big Surprise/Try My Arms	1959	5.00	10.00	20.00
❑ F4256		I Ain't Never/Memories, Memories	1959	5.00	10.00	20.00
❑ 4312		Down by the Station/Listen Honey	1959	3.00	6.00	12.00
❑ 4362		Got a Girl/Wait Till You Hear It from Me	1960	3.00	6.00	12.00
❑ 4400		Sentimental Kid/Madelina	1960	3.00	6.00	12.00
❑ 4435		The Sand and the Sea/Kaw-Liga	1960	3.00	6.00	12.00
❑ 4478		Balboa/I've Already Started In	1960	3.00	6.00	12.00
❑ 4508		Calcutta/Gone Are the Days	1961	3.00	6.00	12.00
❑ 4568		Dream, Boy, Dream/Grounded	1961	7.50	15.00	30.00
❑ 4599		More Money for You and Me/Swing Down Chariot	1961	3.75	7.50	15.00
		With full-length version of A-side				
❑ 4599		More Money for You and Me/Swing Down Chariot	1961	3.00	6.00	12.00
		With edited version of A-side				
❑ 4599	PS	More Money for You and Me/Swing Down Chariot	1961	5.00	10.00	20.00
❑ 4641		Smoke Gets In Your Eyes/Swing Down Chariot	1961	3.00	6.00	12.00
❑ 4659		Once Around the Block/The Seine	1961	3.00	6.00	12.00
❑ 4716		The Big Draft/Suzy Cockroach	1962	2.50	5.00	10.00
❑ 4716	PS	The Big Draft/Suzy Cockroach	1962	2.50	5.00	10.00
❑ 4792		Alice/Goodnight Sweetheart	1962	2.50	5.00	10.00
❑ 4974		Charmaine/Hi-Ho Anybody Home	1963	2.50	5.00	10.00
❑ 5020		Oh Where, Oh Where/Demons and Witches	1963	2.50	5.00	10.00
❑ 5074		The Greatest Surfer Couple/ I'm Falling in Love with a Girl	1963	2.50	5.00	10.00
❑ 5143		A Letter to the Beatles/College Cannonball	1964	6.25	12.50	25.00
❑ 5178		I've Known You All My Life/What Kind of Bird Is That	1964	2.00	4.00	8.00
❑ 5236		A Girl Without a Top/Two Wrongs Don't Make a Right	1964	2.00	4.00	8.00
❑ 5274		How to Succeed in Love/My Love, My Love	1964	2.00	4.00	8.00
❑ 5351		Everlasting/I'll Set My Love to Music	1965	2.00	4.00	8.00
❑ 5450		Now I'll Never Be the Same/Our First American Dance	1965	2.00	4.00	8.00
❑ 5609		Annie in Her Granny/Something to Remember You By	1966	2.00	4.00	8.00
❑ 5687		Let's Call It a Day, Girl/ The Girl in the Shade of a Striped Umbrella	1966	2.00	4.00	8.00
❑ 5819		Love of the Common People/ What I Don't Know Won't Hurt Me	1967	2.00	4.00	8.00
❑ 5921		Draft Dodger Rag/The Hitchhiker	1967	2.00	4.00	8.00
Four Seasons						
(Not the Frankie Valli group)						
Alanna						
❑ 555		I'm Still in Love with You, Baby/ That's the Way the Ball Bounces	1959	6.25	12.50	25.00
❑ 555		Don't Sweat It Baby/That's the Way the Ball Bounces	1959	5.00	10.00	20.00
❑ 558		Love Knows No Season/Hot Water Bottle	1959	5.00	10.00	20.00
Robbee						
❑ 106		Mirage/Nancy's Trampoline	1960	12.50	25.00	50.00
Four Seasons, The						
(Also see "Valli, Frankie"; "Four Lovers, The")						
Columbia						
❑ (# unknown)		Big Man's World	1964	7.50	15.00	30.00
		One-sided cardboard soundsheet, a promo for the Columbia Record Club. Number has been reported as both 6675 and 6724.				
Crewe						
❑ 333		And That Reminds Me (My Heart Reminds Me)/ The Singles Game	1969	2.00	4.00	8.00
❑ 333	PS	And That Reminds Me (My Heart Reminds Me)/ The Singles Game	1969	2.50	5.00	10.00
FBI						
❑ 7701		East Meets West/Rhapsody	1986	5.00	10.00	20.00
		With the Beach Boys				
Gone						
❑ 5122		Bermuda/Spanish Lace	1961	20.00	40.00	80.00
❑ 5122	DJ	Bermuda/Spanish Lace	1961	15.00	30.00	60.00
MCA/Curb						
❑ 52618		Streetfighter/Deep Blue Sea	1985		2.00	4.00
❑ 52724		Moonlight Memories/What About Tomorrow	1985		2.00	4.00
❑ 52871		Book of Love/What About Tomorrow	1986		2.00	4.00

Number		Title (A Side/B Side)	Year	VG	VG+	NM
❏ 53440		Big Girls Don't Cry (Enhanced Original Mix)/ Big Girls Don't Cry (Dirty Dancing Rap)	1988		2.00	4.00
Motown						
❏ 1255		How Come/Life and Breath	1973	2.50	5.00	10.00
❏ 1288		Hickory/Charisma	1973	2.50	5.00	10.00
Mowest						
❏ 5026		Walk On, Don't Look Back/Sun Country	1972	2.50	5.00	10.00
Oldies 45						
❏ 18		Sherry/I've Cried Before	1964	2.00	4.00	8.00
❏ 47		Big Girls Don't Cry/Connie-O	1964	2.00	4.00	8.00
❏ 60		Walk Like a Man/Lucky Ladybug	1964	2.00	4.00	8.00
❏ 116		Candy Girl/Marlena	1964	2.00	4.00	8.00
❏ 319		Stay/Goodnight My Love	1965	2.00	4.00	8.00
Philips						
❏ 40166		Dawn (Go Away)/No Surfin' Today	1964	3.00	6.00	12.00
❏ 40185		Ronnie/Born to Wander	1964	2.50	5.00	10.00
❏ 40185	PS	Ronnie/Born to Wander	1964	6.25	12.50	25.00
❏ 40211		Rag Doll/Silence Is Golden	1964	2.50	5.00	10.00
❏ 40211	PS	Rag Doll/Silence Is Golden *Yellow sleeve*	1964	6.25	12.50	25.00
❏ 40211	PS	Rag Doll/Silence Is Golden *Green sleeve*	1964	6.25	12.50	25.00
❏ 40225		Save It for Me/Funny Face	1964	2.50	5.00	10.00
❏ 40238		Big Man in Town/Little Angel	1964	2.50	5.00	10.00
❏ 40238	PS	Big Man in Town/Little Angel	1964	6.25	12.50	25.00
❏ 40260		Bye, Bye Baby (Baby Goodbye)/Searching Wind	1965	2.50	5.00	10.00
❏ 40260	PS	Bye, Bye Baby (Baby Goodbye)/Searching Wind	1965	6.25	12.50	25.00
❏ 40278		Toy Soldier/Betrayed	1965	2.50	5.00	10.00
❏ 40278	PS	Toy Soldier/Betrayed	1965	6.25	12.50	25.00
❏ 40305		Girl Come Running/Cry Myself to Sleep	1965	2.50	5.00	10.00
❏ 40305	PS	Girl Come Running/Cry Myself to Sleep	1965	6.25	12.50	25.00
❏ 40317		Let's Hang On!/On Broadway Tonight	1965	2.50	5.00	10.00
❏ 40324		Don't Think Twice/Sassy	1965	2.50	5.00	10.00
❏ 40324	PS	Don't Think Twice/Sassy *Philips 40324 by "The Wonder Who?"*	1965	6.25	12.50	25.00
❏ 40350		Working My Way Back to You/Too Many Memories	1966	2.50	5.00	10.00
❏ 40370		Opus 17 (Don't You Worry 'Bout Me)/ Beggar's Paradise	1966	2.50	5.00	10.00
❏ 40370	PS	Opus 17 (Don't You Worry 'Bout Me)/ Beggar's Paradise	1966	6.25	12.50	25.00
❏ 40380		On the Good Ship Lollipop/ You're Nobody Until Somebody Loves You	1966	2.50	5.00	10.00
❏ 40380	PS	On the Good Ship Lollipop/ You're Nobody Until Somebody Loves You *Philips 40380 by "The Wonder Who?"*	1966	6.25	12.50	25.00
❏ 40393		I've Got You Under My Skin/Huggin' My Pillow	1966	2.50	5.00	10.00
❏ 40393	PS	I've Got You Under My Skin/Huggin' My Pillow	1966	6.25	12.50	25.00
❏ 40412		Tell It to the Rain/Snow Girl	1966	2.50	5.00	10.00
❏ 40412	PS	Tell It to the Rain/Snow Girl	1966	6.25	12.50	25.00
❏ 40433		Beggin'/Dody	1967	2.50	5.00	10.00
❏ 40433	PS	Beggin'/Dody	1967	6.25	12.50	25.00
❏ 40460		C'mon Marianne/Let's Ride Again *Black label*	1967	2.50	5.00	10.00
❏ 40460		C'mon Marianne/Let's Ride Again *Blue label; contains a noticeably different, slowed-down mix of A-side*	1967	3.00	6.00	12.00
❏ 40460	PS	C'mon Marianne/Let's Ride Again	1967	6.25	12.50	25.00
❏ 40471		Lonesome Road/Around and Around	1967	2.50	5.00	10.00
❏ 40471	PS	Lonesome Road/Around and Around *Philips 40471 by "The Wonder Who?"*	1967	6.25	12.50	25.00
❏ 40490		Watch the Flowers Grow/Raven	1967	2.50	5.00	10.00
❏ 40490	PS	Watch the Flowers Grow/Raven	1967	6.25	12.50	25.00
❏ 40500		Donneybrook/Around and Around *Only released in Canada*	1968	5.00	10.00	20.00
❏ 40523		Will You Love Me Tomorrow/Around and Around *Black label*	1968	3.00	6.00	12.00
❏ 40523		Will You Love Me Tomorrow/Around and Around *Blue label*	1968	2.50	5.00	10.00
❏ 40542		Saturday's Father/Good-Bye Girl	1968	3.00	6.00	
❏ 40542	PS	Saturday's Father/Good-Bye Girl *Standard sleeve*	1968	2.50	5.00	10.00
❏ 40542	PS	Saturday's Father/Good-Bye Girl *Fold-open sleeve*	1968	3.75	7.50	15.00
❏ 40577		Electric Stories/Pity	1968		3.00	6.00
❏ 40597		Something's On Her Mind/Idaho	1969		3.00	6.00
❏ 40597	PS	Something's On Her Mind/Idaho	1969	2.50	5.00	10.00
❏ 40662		Patch of Blue/She Gives Me Light *As "Frankie Valli & The 4 Seasons"*	1970	2.00	4.00	8.00
❏ 40662	PS	Patch of Blue/She Gives Me Light	1970	2.50	5.00	10.00
❏ 40688		Lay Me Down (Wake Me Up)/ Heartaches and Rainbows	1970	6.25	12.50	25.00
❏ 40688	DJ	Lay Me Down (Wake Me Up) (mono/stereo)	1970	3.75	7.50	15.00
❏ 40694		Where Are My Dreams?/Any Day Now-Oh Happy Day	1971	6.25	12.50	25.00
❏ 40694	DJ	Where Are My Dreams? (mono/stereo)	1971	3.75	7.50	15.00

Number		Title (A Side/B Side)	Year	VG	VG+	NM

Seasons 4-Ever

❑ 777		Trance/I Am All Alone	1971	3.75	7.50	15.00
		Colored vinyl				
❑ 777		Trance/I Am All Alone	1971	2.00	4.00	8.00

Topix

❑ 6000		Too Young to Start/Red Lips	1960	25.00	50.00	100.00
		As "The Village Voices"; yellow, black and white label				
❑ 6000		Too Young to Start/Red Lips	1960	37.50	75.00	150.00
		As "The Village Voices"; yellow and black label				
❑ 6002		I Am All Alone/Trance	1961	37.50	75.00	150.00
		As "Billy Dixon and the Topics"				
❑ 6008		Lost Lullaby/Trance	1961	50.00	100.00	200.00
		As "Billy Dixon and the Topics"				

Vee Jay

❑ 456		Sherry/I've Cried Before	1962	3.75	7.50	15.00
		First pressings have black rainbow labels with oval logo				
❑ 456		Sherry/I've Cried Before	1962	6.25	12.50	25.00
		A later pressing has an all-black label				
❑ 465		Big Girls Don't Cry/Connie-O	1962	3.75	7.50	15.00
		First pressings have black rainbow labels with oval logo				
❑ 465		Big Girls Don't Cry/Connie-O	1962	6.25	12.50	25.00
		A later pressing has an all-black label				
❑ 476		Santa Claus Is Coming to Town/Christmas Tears	1962	6.25	12.50	25.00
❑ 485		Walk Like a Man/Lucky Ladybug	1963	3.75	7.50	15.00
❑ 512		Ain't That a Shame!/Soon (I'll Be Home Again)	1963	5.00	10.00	20.00
❑ 539		Candy Girl/Marlena	1963	3.75	7.50	15.00
❑ 539	PS	Candy Girl/Marlena	1963	18.75	37.50	75.00
❑ 562		New Mexican Rose/That's the Only Way	1963	3.75	7.50	15.00
❑ 562	DJ	New Mexican Rose/That's the Way It Is	1963	7.50	15.00	30.00
		Wrong title on B-side; evidently only exists on promos				
❑ 576		Peanuts/Stay	1963	25.00	50.00	100.00
❑ 576	DJ	Peanuts/Stay	1963	15.00	30.00	60.00
❑ 582		Stay/Goodnight My Love	1964	3.75	7.50	15.00
❑ 597		Alone/Long, Lonely Nights	1964	3.75	7.50	15.00
		Black rainbow label				
❑ 597		Alone/Long, Lonely Nights	1964	6.25	12.50	25.00
		Plain black label				
❑ 597		Alone/Long, Lonely Nights	1964	7.50	15.00	30.00
		Yellow label				
❑ 597	PS	Alone/Long, Lonely Nights	1964	12.50	25.00	50.00
❑ 608		Sincerely/One Song	1964	5.00	10.00	20.00
❑ 618		Happy, Happy Birthday Baby/	1964	5.00	10.00	20.00
		You're the Apple of My Eye				
❑ 626		I Saw Mommy Kissing Santa Claus/Christmas Tears	1964	12.50	25.00	50.00
❑ 626		I Saw Mommy Kissing Santa Claus/Christmas Tears	1964	5.00	10.00	20.00
❑ 639		Never on Sunday/Connie-O	1965	5.00	10.00	20.00
❑ 664		Since I Don't Have You/Tonite, Tonite	1965	7.50	15.00	30.00
❑ 713		Little Boy (In Grown Up Clothes)/Silver Wings	1965	7.50	15.00	30.00
		Black label				
❑ 713		Little Boy (In Grown Up Clothes)/Silver Wings	1965	5.00	10.00	20.00
		Maroon label				
❑ 717		Peanuts/My Sugar	1966	7.50	15.00	30.00
		As "The Wonder Who"				
❑ 719		My Mother's Eyes/Stay	1966	3.75	7.50	15.00
❑ 901	DJ	Peanuts	1963	25.00	50.00	100.00
		One-sided promo from E.P.				

WABC Radio

❑ 77		Cousin Brucie Go Go	1964	37.50	75.00	150.00
		One-sided yellow vinyl; theme song for Cousin Brucie's radio show				

Warner Bros.

❑ 8122		Who Loves You/Who Loves You (Disco Version)	1975		2.50	5.00
❑ 8168		December, 1963 (Oh, What a Night)/Slip Away	1975		2.50	5.00
❑ 8203		Silver Star/Mystic Mr. Sam	1976		2.50	5.00
❑ 8407		Down the Hall/I Believe in You	1977	2.00	4.00	8.00
❑ 49585		Heaven Must Have Sent You (Here in the Night)/	1981	2.00	4.00	8.00
		Silver Star				
❑ 49597		Spend the Night in Love/Slip Away	1980	2.00	4.00	8.00

Wibbage

❑ WIBG		Jody Reynolds Theme/Rats in My Room	1965	25.00	50.00	100.00
		Custom pressing for Philadelphia radio station				

WXYZ Detroit

❑ 121003		Jody Reynolds Theme (same on both sides)	1965	25.00	50.00	100.00
		Custom pressing for Detroit radio station				

Four Speeds, The

Challenge

❑ 9187		R.P.M./My Sting Ray	1963	10.00	20.00	40.00
❑ 9202		Four on the Floor/Cheater Slicks	1963	10.00	20.00	40.00

Four Teens, The

Challenge

❑ 59021		Go Little Go Cat/Spark Plug	1958	15.00	30.00	60.00

Number		Title (A Side/B Side)	Year	VG	VG+	NM

Four Temptations, The
ABC-Paramount
| ☐ 9920 | | Cathy/Rock and Roll Baby | 1958 | 7.50 | 15.00 | 30.00 |

Four Tops, The
ABC
☐ 12096		Seven Lonely Nights/I Can't Hold Out Much Longer	1975		2.00	4.00
☐ 12123		We All Gotta Stick Together/	1975		2.00	4.00
		(It Would Almost) Drive Me Out of My Mind				
☐ 12155		I'm Glad You Walked Into My Life/	1975		2.00	4.00
		Mama, You're All Right with Me				
☐ 12214		Catfish/Look at My Baby	1976		2.00	4.00
☐ 12223		Look at My Baby/Catfish	1976		2.00	4.00
☐ 12236		Feel Free/I Know You Like It	1976		2.00	4.00
☐ 12267		Strung Out for Your Love/You Can't Hold Back on Love	1977		2.00	4.00
☐ 12315		Runnin' From Your Love/The Show Must Go On	1977		2.00	4.00
☐ 12427		Inside a Brokenhearted Man/H.E.L.P.	1978		2.00	4.00
☐ 12457		Just in Time/This House	1978		2.00	4.00

ABC Dunhill
☐ 4330		Keeper of the Castle/Jubilee with Soul	1972		2.50	5.00
☐ 4334		Guardian De Tu Castle/Jubilee with Soul	1972		2.50	5.00
☐ 4339		Ain't No Woman (Like the One I've Got)/	1973		2.50	5.00
		The Good Lord Knows				
☐ 4354		Are You Man Enough/Peace of Mind	1973		2.50	5.00
☐ 4366		Sweet Understanding Love/Main Street People	1973		2.50	5.00
☐ 4377		I Just Can't Get You Out of My Mind/	1973		2.50	5.00
		Am I My Brother's Keeper?				
☐ 4386		One Chain Don't Make No Prison/Light of Your Love	1974		2.50	5.00
☐ 15005		Midnight Flower/All My Love	1974		2.50	5.00

Arista
☐ 9706		Indestructible/Are You With Me	1988			3.00
☐ 9706	PS	Indestructible/Are You With Me	1988			3.00
☐ 9766		If Ever a Love There Was/Let's Jam	1988			3.00
		A-side with Aretha Franklin				
☐ 9766	PS	If Ever a Love There Was/Let's Jam	1988			3.00
☐ 9801		Change of Heart/Loco in Acapulco	1989			3.00
☐ 9850		If Ever a Love There Was/	1989			3.00
		It Wasn't, It Isn't, It Ain't Never Gonna Be				
		A-side: With Aretha Franklin; B-side: Aretha Franklin and Whitney Houston				
☐ 9850	PS	If Ever a Love There Was/	1989			3.00
		It Wasn't, It Isn't, It Ain't Never Gonna Be				

Casablanca
☐ 2338		When She Was My Girl/Something to Remember	1981		2.00	4.00
☐ 2344		Let Me Set You Free/From a Distance	1981		2.00	4.00
☐ 2345		Tonight I'm Gonna Love You All Over/	1981		2.00	4.00
		I'll Never Leave Again				
☐ 2353		Sad Hearts/I Believe in You and Me	1982		2.00	4.00

Chess
| ☐ 1623 | | Could It Be You?/Kiss Me, Baby | 1956 | 50.00 | 100.00 | 200.00 |

Columbia
| ☐ 41755 | | Ain't That Love/Lonely Summer | 1960 | 15.00 | 30.00 | 60.00 |
| ☐ 43356 | | Ain't That Love/Lonely Summer | 1965 | 6.25 | 12.50 | 25.00 |

Grady
| ☐ 012 | | If Only I Had Known/(B-side unknown) | 1956 | 150.00 | 300.00 | 600.00 |
| | | As "The Four Aims" | | | | |

Motown
☐ 1062		Baby I Need Your Loving/Call On Me	1964	2.50	5.00	10.00
☐ 1069		Without the One You Love (Life's Not Worth While)/	1964	2.50	5.00	10.00
		Love Has Gone				
☐ 1073		Ask the Lonely/Where Did You Go	1965	2.50	5.00	10.00
☐ 1073	PS	Ask the Lonely/Where Did You Go	1965	20.00	40.00	80.00
☐ 1076		I Can't Help Myself/Sad Souvenirs	1965	2.50	5.00	10.00
☐ 1081		It's the Same Old Song/Your Love Is Amazing	1965	2.50	5.00	10.00
☐ 1084		Something About You/Darling, I Hum Our Song	1965	2.50	5.00	10.00
☐ 1090		Shake Me, Wake Me (When It's Over)/	1966	2.50	5.00	10.00
		Just As Long As You Need Me				
☐ 1096		Loving You Is Sweeter Than Ever/	1966	2.50		10.00
		I Like Everything About You				
☐ 1098		Reach Out I'll Be There/Until You Love Someone	1966	2.50	5.00	10.00
☐ 1098	PS	Reach Out I'll Be There/Until You Love Someone	1966	10.00	20.00	40.00
☐ 1102		Standing in the Shadows of Love/	1966	2.50	5.00	10.00
		Since You've Been Gone				
☐ 1104		Bernadette/I Got a Feeling	1967	2.50	5.00	10.00
☐ 1110		7-Rooms of Gloom/I'll Turn to Stone	1967	2.50	5.00	10.00
☐ 1113		You Keep Running Away/If You Don't Want My Love	1967	2.50	5.00	10.00
☐ 1119		Walk Away Renee/Your Love Is Wonderful	1968	2.50	5.00	10.00
☐ 1124		If I Were a Carpenter/Wonderful Baby	1968	2.50	5.00	10.00
☐ 1127		Yesterday's Dreams/For Once in My Life	1968	2.00	4.00	8.00
☐ 1132		I'm in a Different World/Remember When	1968	2.00	4.00	8.00
☐ 1147		What Is a Man/Don't Bring Back Memories	1969	2.00	4.00	8.00
☐ 1159		Don't Let Him Take Your Love from Me/The Key	1969	2.00	4.00	8.00
☐ 1164		It's All in the Game/Love (Is the Answer)	1970	2.00	4.00	8.00
☐ 1164	PS	It's All in the Game/Love (Is the Answer)	1970	5.00	10.00	20.00
☐ 1170		Still Water (Love)/Still Water (Peace)	1970		3.00	6.00

Number		Title (A Side/B Side)	Year	VG	VG+	NM
❑ 1175		Just Seven Numbers (Can Straighten Out My Life)/ I Wish I Were Your Mirror	1971		3.00	6.00
❑ 1175	PS	Just Seven Numbers (Can Straighten Out My Life)/ I Wish I Were Your Mirror	1971	5.00	10.00	20.00
❑ 1185		In These Changing Times/Right Before My Eyes	1971		3.00	6.00
❑ 1189		MacArthur Park (Part 2)/MacArthur Park (Part 1)	1971		3.00	6.00
❑ 1196		A Simple Game/L.A. My Town	1972		3.00	6.00
❑ 1198		I Can't Quit Your Love/Happy (Is a Bumpy Road)	1972		3.00	6.00
❑ 1210		(It's the Way) Nature Planned It/I'll Never Change	1972		3.00	6.00
❑ 1254		Hey Man-We Gotta Get You a Woman/ How Can I Forget You	1973			Unreleased
❑ 1706		I Just Can't Walk Away/Hang	1983			3.00
❑ 1718		Make Yourself Right at Home/ Sing a Song of Yesterday	1984			3.00
❑ 1790		Sexy Ways/Body and Soul	1985			3.00
❑ 1811		Don't Tell Me That It's Over/I'm Ready for Love	1985			3.00
❑ 1854		Hot Nights/Again	1986			3.00

Reliant

❑ 1691		I'm Here Again/(Instrumental)	198?		2.00	4.00

Riverside

❑ 4534		Pennies from Heaven/Where Are You?	1962	18.75	37.50	75.00

RSO

❑ 1069		Back to School Again/Rock-a-Hula Luau	1982			3.00
❑ 1069	PS	Back to School Again/Rock-a-Hula Luau B-side by The Cast (from the movie Grease 2)	1982			3.00

Topps/Motown

❑ 5		I Can't Help Myself	1967	18.75	37.50	75.00
❑ 9		Baby I Need Your Loving These are cardboard discs	1967	18.75	37.50	75.00

Four Tunes, The

Jubilee

❑ 5128		Marie/I Gambled with Love	1953	10.00	20.00	40.00
❑ 5132		I Understand Just How You Feel/Sugar Lump	1953	7.50	15.00	30.00
❑ 5135		My Wild Irish Rose/Do-Do-Do It Again	1954	7.50	15.00	30.00
❑ 5152		Lonesome/The Greatest Feeling in the World	1954	7.50	15.00	30.00
❑ 5165		Don't Cry Darling/L'Amour Toujours, L'Amour	1954	7.50	15.00	30.00
❑ 5174		I Sold My Heart to the Junkman/Let Me Go Lover	1954	7.50	15.00	30.00
❑ 5174		I Sold My Heart to the Junkman/Good News	1954	7.50	15.00	30.00
❑ 5183		I Hope/I Close My Eyes	1955	6.25	12.50	25.00
❑ 5200		Tired of Waitin'/Time Out for Texas	1955	6.25	12.50	25.00
❑ 5212		Brooklyn Bridge/Three Little Chickens	1955	6.25	12.50	25.00
❑ 5218		You Are My Love/At the Steamboat River Ball	1955	6.25	12.50	25.00
❑ 5232		Rock and Roll Call/Our Love	1956	5.00	10.00	20.00
❑ 5239		I Gotta Go/Hold Me Closer	1956	5.00	10.00	20.00
❑ 5245		Far Away Places/Dancing with Tears in My Eyes	1956	5.00	10.00	20.00
❑ 5255		The Ballad of James Dean/Japanese Farewell	1956	5.00	10.00	20.00
❑ 5276		Cool Water/A Little on the Lonely Side	1957	5.00	10.00	20.00
❑ 6000		I Understand/Marie	196?	2.50	5.00	10.00

Kay-Ron

❑ 1000		I Want to Be Loved/Savannah Sings the Blues	1953	10.00	20.00	40.00
❑ 1005		I Understand/Just in Case You Change Your Mind	1953	10.00	20.00	40.00

RCA Victor

❑ 47-3881		Say When/Do I Worry?	1950	12.50	25.00	50.00
❑ 47-3967		How Can You Say That I Don't Care/Cool Water	1950	10.00	20.00	40.00
❑ 47-4102		Wishing You Were Here Tonight/The Last Roundup	1951	10.00	20.00	40.00
❑ 47-4198		Cool Water/Carry Me Back to the Lone Prairie	1951	10.00	20.00	40.00
❑ 47-4241		The Prisoner's Song/I Married An Angel	1951	7.50	15.00	30.00
❑ 47-4305		My Buddy/Early in the Morning	1951	7.50	15.00	30.00
❑ 47-4427		Tell Me Why/I'll See You in My Dreams	1951	10.00	20.00	40.00
❑ 47-4489		Greatest Song I Ever Heard/Come What May	1952	6.25	12.50	25.00
❑ 47-4663		I Wonder/Can I Say Any More?	1952	6.25	12.50	25.00
❑ 47-4828		They Don't Understand/Why Did You Do This	1952	6.25	12.50	25.00
❑ 47-4968		I Don't Want to Set the World On Fire/ Let's Give Love Another Chance	1952	10.00	20.00	40.00
❑ 47-5532		Don't Get Around Much Anymore/Water Boy	1953	7.50	15.00	30.00
❑ 50-0008		You're Heartless/Careless Love Gray label, orange vinyl	1949	50.00	100.00	200.00
❑ 50-0016		My Last Affair/I'm the Guy Gray label, orange vinyl	1949	50.00	100.00	200.00
❑ 50-0042		I'm Just a Fool in Love/The Lonesome Road Gray label, orange vinyl	1949	50.00	100.00	200.00
❑ 50-0072		There Goes My Heart/Am I Blue Gray label, orange vinyl	1950	37.50	75.00	150.00
❑ 50-0085		Old Fashioned Love/Kentucky Babe Gray label, orange vinyl	1950	37.50	75.00	150.00
❑ 50-0131		May That Day Never Come/ Carry Me Back to the Lone Prairie Gray label, orange vinyl	1951	37.50	75.00	150.00

Four Upsetters, The

Sun

❑ 381		Crazy Arms/Midnight Soiree	1962	5.00	10.00	20.00
❑ 386		Surfin' Calliope/Wabash Cannonball	1963	7.50	15.00	30.00

Number	Title (A Side/B Side)	Year	VG	VG+	NM

Four Winds, The
(The B.T. Puppy and Swing, and possibly the Crystal Ball, records are the same group, also known as The Tokens)

B.T. Puppy

❏ 555	Let It Ride/One Face in the Crowd	1970	2.50	5.00	10.00

Chattahoochie

❏ 655	Down and Out/To Love or Not to Love	1964	3.75	7.50	15.00

Crystal Ball

❏ 102	Come Softly to Me/Judy	1978		2.50	5.00
❏ 105	Arlene/Goodbye, Maureen	1978		2.50	5.00
❏ 105	Arlene/Goodbye, Maureen	1978	2.50	5.00	10.00
	Colored vinyl				

Decor

❏ 175	Short Shorts/Five Minutes More	1961	3.75	7.50	15.00

Derby

❏ 10022	Playgirl/Jennifer	1964	7.50	15.00	30.00

Dial

❏ 3006	Woe Is Me/Promised Land	1962	3.75	7.50	15.00

Felsted

❏ 8703	Playgirl/Jennifer	1964	5.00	10.00	20.00

Hide-a-Way

❏ 101	Mission by the Sea/These Hearts Were Mine	1958	5.00	10.00	20.00

Swing

❏ 100	Remember Last Summer/Strange, Strange Feeling	1964	5.00	10.00	20.00

Vik

❏ 0221	Colorado Moon/Find Someone New	1956	5.00	10.00	20.00

Warwick

❏ 633	Daddy's Home/Bull-Moose Stomp	1961	10.00	20.00	40.00

Four-Evers, The
Chattahoochie

❏ 630	Colors/Come Up in the World	1963	3.75	7.50	15.00

Columbia

❏ 42303	You Belong to Me/Such a Good Night for Dreaming	1962	15.00	30.00	60.00
❏ 43886	A Lovely Way to Spend An Evening/The Girl I Want	1966	5.00	10.00	20.00

Constellation

❏ 151	Stormy/Out of the Crowd	1965	7.50	15.00	30.00

Jamie

❏ 1247	Everybody South Street/One More Time	1963	3.75	7.50	15.00

Red Bird

❏ 10-078	You Never Had It So Good/What a Scene	1966	6.25	12.50	25.00

Smash

❏ 1853	Lover Come Back to Me/It's Love	1963	3.75	7.50	15.00
❏ 1887	Please Be Mine/If I Were a Magician	1964	7.50	15.00	30.00
❏ 1887	Be My Girl/If I Were a Magician	1964	3.75	7.50	15.00
	Same A-side, different title				
❏ 1921	(Say I Love You) Do Be Dum/Everlasting	1964	3.75	7.50	15.00

Fourmost, The
Atco

❏ 6280	Hello Little Girl/Just in Case	1963	5.00	10.00	20.00
❏ 6285	I'm in Love/Respectable	1964	3.75	7.50	15.00
❏ 6307	If You Cry/Little Bit of Loving	1964	3.75	7.50	15.00
❏ 6317	How Can I Tell Her/You Got That Way	1964	3.75	7.50	15.00

Capitol

❏ 5591	Girls, Girls, Girls/Why Do Fools Fall in Love	1966	3.00	6.00	12.00
❏ 5738	Here, There and Everywhere/You've Changed	1966	5.00	10.00	20.00
❏					

Fox, Norman, and the Rob Roys
Back Beat

❏ 499	Lover Doll/Little Star	197?		2.00	4.00
	Bootleg				
❏ 501	Tell Me Why/Audrey	1957	10.00	20.00	40.00
	Red label				
❏ 501	Tell Me Why/Audrey	1957	20.00	40.00	80.00
	White label				
❏ 508	Dance Girl Dance/My Dearest One	1958	20.00	40.00	80.00

Capitol

❏ 4128	Dream Girl/Pizza Pie	1959	100.00	200.00	400.00

Francis, Connie
GSF

❏ 6901	The Answer (Should I Tie a Yellow Ribbon Round the Ole Oak Tree?)/Paint the Rain	1973		2.50	5.00

Ivanhoe

❏ 508	I Don't Wanna Walk Without You/Don't Turn Around	197?		2.50	5.00

Number			Title (A Side/B Side)	Year	VG	VG+	NM
MGM							
☐ SB-9	S		Rock-A-Bye Your Baby with a Dixie Melody/	1960	12.50	25.00	50.00
			Ciao Ciao Bambino				
☐ SB-10	S		I Almost Lost My Mind/Come Back to Sorrento	1960	12.50	25.00	50.00
☐ 126			Stupid Cupid/I'm Sorry I Made You Cry	196?	2.00	4.00	8.00
☐ 129			Who's Sorry Now/You Were Only Fooling	196?	2.00	4.00	8.00
☐ 135			Mama/You're Gonna Miss Me	196?	2.00	4.00	8.00
☐ 136			Among My Souvenirs/God Bless America	196?	2.00	4.00	8.00
☐ 139			Lipstick on Your Collar/Frankie	196?	2.00	4.00	8.00
☐ 141			My Happiness/If I Didn't Care	196?	2.00	4.00	8.00
☐ 148			My Heart Has a Mind of Its Own/Malaguena	196?	2.00	4.00	8.00
☐ 150			Where the Boys Are/No One	196?	2.00	4.00	8.00
☐ 153			Breakin' In a Brand New Broken Heart/	196?	2.00	4.00	8.00
			Somebody Else's Boy				
☐ 155			Together/Too Many Rules	196?	2.00	4.00	8.00
☐ 156			Many Tears Ago/Senza Mama E Numerata	196?	2.00	4.00	8.00
☐ 157			Don't Break the Heart That Loves You/	196?	2.00	4.00	8.00
			Second Hand Love				
☐ 165			Everybody's Somebody's Fool/Al Di La	196?	2.00	4.00	8.00
☐ 169			Jealous Heart/Forget Domani	196?	2.00	4.00	8.00
			MGM 126-169 are 1960s reissues				
☐ 511			Who's Sorry Now/Stupid Cupid	197?		2.50	5.00
☐ 512			Lipstick on Your Collar/Mama	197?		2.50	5.00
☐ 513			Everybody's Somebody's Fool/Al Di La	197?		2.50	5.00
☐ 524			My Happiness/If I Didn't Care	197?		2.50	5.00
			MGM 511-524 are 1970s reissues				
☐ 12015			Freddy/Didn't I Love You Enough	1955	12.50	25.00	50.00
☐ 12056			Oh Please Make Him Jealous/Goody Goodbye	1955	12.50	25.00	50.00
☐ 12122			Are You Satisfied/My Treasure	1956	6.25	12.50	25.00
☐ 12191			My First Real Love/Believe in Me	1956	15.00	30.00	60.00
☐ 12251			Send for My Baby/Forgetting	1956	6.25	12.50	25.00
☐ 12335			My Sailor Boy/Everyone Needs Someone	1956	6.25	12.50	25.00
☐ 12375			I Never Had a Sweetheart/Little Blue Wren	1957	6.25	12.50	25.00
☐ 12440			No Other One/I Leaned on a Man	1957	6.25	12.50	25.00
☐ 12490			Eighteen/Faded Orchid	1957	6.25	12.50	25.00
☐ 12555			You, My Darlin', You/The Majesty of Love	1957	6.25	12.50	25.00
			Connie Francis and Marvin Rainwater				
☐ 12588			Who's Sorry Now?/You Were Only Fooling	1958	5.00	10.00	20.00
☐ 12647			I'm Sorry I Made You Cry/Lock Up Your Heart	1958	5.00	10.00	20.00
☐ 12669			Heartaches/I Miss You So	1958	12.50	25.00	50.00
☐ 12683			Stupid Cupid/Carolina Moon	1958	5.00	10.00	20.00
☐ 12713			Fallin'/Happy Days and Lonely Nights	1958	5.00	10.00	20.00
☐ 12738	M		My Happiness/Never Before	1958	5.00	10.00	20.00
☐ 12738	PS		My Happiness/Never Before	1958	7.50	15.00	30.00
			Pink sleeve				
☐ 12738	PS		My Happiness/Never Before	1958	10.00	20.00	40.00
			White sleeve				
☐ 12769			If I Didn't Care/Toward the End of the Day	1959	5.00	10.00	20.00
☐ 12769	PS		If I Didn't Care/Toward the End of the Day	1959	7.50	15.00	30.00
☐ 12793	M		Lipstick on Your Collar/Frankie	1959	5.00	10.00	20.00
☐ 12824	M		You're Gonna Miss Me/Plenty Good Lovin'	1959	5.00	10.00	20.00
☐ 12841	M		Among My Souvenirs/God Bless America	1959	5.00	10.00	20.00
			Second pressing has a black label				
☐ 12841	M		Among My Souvenirs/God Bless America	1959	7.50	15.00	30.00
			First pressing has a yellow label				
☐ 12878			Mama/Teddy	1960	3.75	7.50	15.00
☐ 12899			Everybody's Somebody's Fool/Jealous of You	1960	3.75	7.50	15.00
☐ 12899	PS		Everybody's Somebody's Fool/Jealous of You	1960	5.00	10.00	20.00
☐ 12923			My Heart Has a Mind of Its Own/Malaguena	1960	3.75	7.50	15.00
☐ 12923	PS		My Heart Has a Mind of Its Own/Malaguena	1960	5.00	10.00	20.00
☐ 12964			Many Tears Ago/Senza Mama (With No One)	1960	3.75	7.50	15.00
☐ 12964	PS		Many Tears Ago/Senza Mama (With No One)	1960	5.00	10.00	20.00
☐ 12971			Where the Boys Are/No One	1961	3.75	7.50	15.00
☐ 12971	PS		Where the Boys Are/No One	1961	5.00	10.00	20.00
☐ 12995			Breakin' In a Brand New Broken Heart/	1961	3.75	7.50	15.00
			Someone Else's Boy				
☐ 12995	PS		Breakin' In a Brand New Broken Heart/	1961	5.00	10.00	20.00
			Someone Else's Boy				
☐ 13005			Atashi-No/Swanee	1961	7.50	15.00	30.00
☐ 13019			Together/Too Many Rules	1961	3.75	7.50	15.00
☐ 13019	PS		Together/Too Many Rules	1961	5.00	10.00	20.00
☐ 13039			(He's My) Dreamboat/Hollywood	1961	3.75	7.50	15.00
☐ 13039	PS		(He's My) Dreamboat/Hollywood	1961	5.00	10.00	20.00
☐ 13051			When the Boy in Your Arms (Is the Boy in Your Heart)/	1961	3.75	7.50	15.00
			Baby's First Christmas				
☐ 13051	PS		When the Boy in Your Arms (Is the Boy in Your Heart)/	1961	5.00	10.00	20.00
			Baby's First Christmas				
☐ 13059			Don't Break the Heart That Loves You/Drop It, Joe	1962	3.75	7.50	15.00
☐ 13059	PS		Don't Break the Heart That Loves You/Drop It, Joe	1962	5.00	10.00	20.00
☐ 13074			Second Hand Love/Gonna Git That Man	1962	5.00	10.00	20.00
			A-side produced by Phil Spector				
☐ 13074	PS		Second Hand Love/Gonna Git That Man	1962	6.25	12.50	25.00
☐ 13087			Vacation/The Biggest Sin of All	1962	3.75	7.50	15.00
☐ 13087	PS		Vacation/The Biggest Sin of All	1962	5.00	10.00	20.00
☐ 13096			I Was Such a Fool (To Fall in Love with You)/	1962	3.00	6.00	12.00
			He Thinks I Still Care				
☐ 13096	PS		I Was Such a Fool (To Fall in Love with You)/	1962	4.00	8.00	16.00
			He Thinks I Still Care				

Number		Title (A Side/B Side)	Year	VG	VG+	NM
❏ 13116		I'm Gonna' Be Warm This Winter/Al Di La	1962	3.00	6.00	12.00
❏ 13116	PS	I'm Gonna' Be Warm This Winter/Al Di La	1962	4.00	8.00	16.00
❏ 13127		Follow the Boys/Waiting for Billy	1962	3.00	6.00	12.00
❏ 13127	PS	Follow the Boys/Waiting for Billy	1962	4.00	8.00	16.00
❏ 13143		If My Pillow Could Talk/	1963	3.00	6.00	12.00
		You're the Only One Who Can Hurt Me				
❏ 13143	PS	If My Pillow Could Talk/	1963	4.00	8.00	16.00
		You're the Only One Who Can Hurt Me				
❏ 13160		Drownin' My Sorrows/Mala Femmena	1963	3.00	6.00	12.00
❏ 13160	PS	Drownin' My Sorrows/Mala Femmena	1963	4.00	8.00	16.00
❏ 13176		Your Other Love/Whatever Happened to Rosemarie?	1963	3.00	6.00	12.00
❏ 13176	PS	Your Other Love/Whatever Happened to Rosemarie?	1963	4.00	8.00	16.00
❏ 13203		In the Summer of His Years/My Buddy	1963	3.00	6.00	12.00
❏ 13203	PS	In the Summer of His Years/My Buddy	1963	4.00	8.00	16.00
❏ 13214		Blue Winter/	1964	3.00	6.00	12.00
		You Know You Don't Want Me (So Why Don't You Leave Me Alone)				
❏ 13214	PS	Blue Winter/	1964	4.00	8.00	16.00
		You Know You Don't Want Me (So Why Don't You Leave Me Alone)				
❏ 13237		Be Anything (But Be Mine)/Tommy	1964	3.00	6.00	12.00
❏ 13237	PS	Be Anything (But Be Mine)/Tommy	1964	4.00	8.00	16.00
❏ 13256		Looking for Love/This Is My Happiest Moment	1964	3.00	6.00	12.00
❏ 13256	PS	Looking for Love/This Is My Happiest Moment	1964	4.00	8.00	16.00
❏ 13287		Don't Ever Leave Me/	1964	3.00	6.00	12.00
		We Have Something More (Than a Summer Love)				
❏ 13287	PS	Don't Ever Leave Me/	1964	4.00	8.00	16.00
		We Have Something More (Than a Summer Love)				
❏ 13303		Whose Heart Are You Breaking Tonight/C'mon, Jerry	1965	2.50	5.00	10.00
❏ 13303	PS	Whose Heart Are You Breaking Tonight/C'mon, Jerry	1965	3.00	6.00	12.00
❏ 13325		For Mama (La Mamma)/	1965	3.00	6.00	12.00
		She'll Be Coming 'Round the Mountain				
❏ 13331		Wishing It Was You/	1965	2.50	5.00	10.00
		You're Mine (Just When You're Lonely)				
❏ 13331	PS	Wishing It Was You/	1965	3.00	6.00	12.00
		You're Mine (Just When You're Lonely)				
❏ 13363		Forget Domani/No One Sends Me Roses	1965	2.50	5.00	10.00
❏ 13389		Roundabout/Bossa Nova Hand Dance	1965	2.50	5.00	10.00
❏ 13420		Jealous Heart/Can I Rely on You	1965	2.50	5.00	10.00
❏ 13470		Love Is Me, Love Is You/	1966	2.50	5.00	10.00
		I'd Let You Break My Heart All Over Again				
❏ 13470	PS	Love Is Me, Love Is You/	1966	3.00	6.00	12.00
		I'd Let You Break My Heart All Over Again				
❏ 13505		It's a Different World/Empty Chapel	1966	2.50	5.00	10.00
❏ 13505	PS	It's a Different World/Empty Chapel	1966	5.00	10.00	20.00
❏ 13545		A Letter from a Soldier (Dear Mama)/	1966	2.50	5.00	10.00
		Somewhere, My Love				
❏ 13550	DJ	A Nurse in the U.S. Army (same on both sides)	1966	7.50	15.00	30.00
		Promotional item for the U.S. Army				
❏ 13578		All the Love in the World/So Nice	1966	2.50	5.00	10.00
❏ 13610		Spanish Nights and You/Games That Lovers Play	1966	2.50	5.00	10.00
❏ 13610	PS	Spanish Nights and You/Games That Lovers Play	1966	5.00	10.00	20.00
❏ 13665		Another Page/Souvenir d'Italie	1967	2.50	5.00	10.00
❏ CS6-5		Celebrity Scene: Connie Francis	1967	15.00	30.00	60.00
		Box set of five singles. Price includes box, all 5 singles, jukebox title strips, bio. Records are sometimes found by themselves, so they are listed separately below.				
❏ 13708	DJ	Mama/Never on Sunday	1967	2.50	5.00	10.00
❏ 13709	DJ	My Happiness/Al Di La	1967	2.50	5.00	10.00
❏ 13710	DJ	Malaguena/I Love You Much Too Much	1967	2.50	5.00	10.00
❏ 13711	DJ	Once in a Lifetime/Oh Lonesome Me	1967	2.50	5.00	10.00
❏ 13712	DJ	Jealous Heart/Will You Still Be Mine	1967	2.50	5.00	10.00
❏ 13718		Time Alone Will Tell/Born Free	1967	2.50	5.00	10.00
❏ 13773		My Heart Cries for You/	1967	2.50	5.00	10.00
		Someone Took the Sweetness Out of Sweetheart				
❏ 13773	PS	My Heart Cries for You/	1967	5.00	10.00	20.00
		Someone Took the Sweetness Out of Sweetheart				
❏ 13814		Lonely Again/When You Care a Lot for Someone	1967	2.50	5.00	10.00
❏ 13876		My World Is Slipping Away/Till We're Together	1967	2.50	5.00	10.00
❏ 13923		Why Say Goodbye/Adios, Me Amore	1968	2.00	4.00	8.00
❏ 13948		Somebody Else Is Taking My Place/	1968	2.00	4.00	8.00
		Brother, Can You Spare a Dime?				
❏ 14004		I Don't Wanna Play House/The Welfare Check	1968	2.00	4.00	8.00
❏ 14034		The Wedding Cake/Over Hill, Under Ground	1969	2.00	4.00	8.00
❏ 14058		Gone Like the Wind/Am I Blue?	1969	2.00	4.00	8.00
❏ 14058	PS	Gone Like the Wind/Am I Blue?	1969	5.00	10.00	20.00
❏ 14089		Invierno Trieste/Noches Espanolas Y Tu	1969		Not known to exist	
❏ 14091		Mr. Love/Zingara	1969	2.00	4.00	8.00
❏ 14091	PS	Mr. Love/Zingara	1969	5.00	10.00	20.00
❏ 14853		I'm Me Again/Comme Si, Comme Sa	1976		3.00	6.00
❏ SK-50117	S	My Happiness/Never Before	1958	12.50	25.00	50.00
❏ SK-50121	S	Lipstick on Your Collar/Frankie	1959	15.00	30.00	60.00
❏ SK-50129	S	You're Gonna Miss Me/Plenty Good Lovin'	1959	12.50	25.00	50.00
❏ SK-50133	S	Among My Souvenirs/God Bless America	1959	12.50	25.00	50.00

Polydor

Number		Title (A Side/B Side)	Year	VG	VG+	NM
❏ 2143		I'm Me Again/Comme Si, Comme Sa	1981		2.50	5.00
❏ 810 087-1		There's Still a Few Good Love Songs Left in Me/	1983		2.50	5.00
		Let's Make It Love Tonight				

Frankie and the C-Notes

Richie

Number		Title (A Side/B Side)	Year	VG	VG+	NM
❏ 2		Forever and Ever/Fade Out	1959	100.00	200.00	400.00

Number		Title (A Side/B Side)	Year	VG	VG+	NM

Franklin, Aretha

Arista

Number		Title (A Side/B Side)	Year	VG	VG+	NM
❏ SP-103	DJ	What a Fool Believes (Long)/	1980	2.00	4.00	8.00
		What a Fool Believes (Short)				
❏ 0569		United Together/Take Me With You	1980		2.00	4.00
❏ 0591		What a Fool Believes/Love Me Forever	1980		2.00	4.00
❏ 0600		Come to Me/School Days	1981		2.00	4.00
❏ 0624		Love All the Hurt Away/Whole Lotta Me	1981		2.00	4.00
		Aretha Franklin and George Benson				
❏ 0646		It's My Turn/Kind of Man	1981		2.00	4.00
❏ 0665		Livin' in the Streets/There's a Star for Everyone	1982		2.00	4.00
❏ 0699		Jump To It/Just My Daydream	1982		2.00	4.00
❏ 1023		Love Me Right/(It's Just) Your Love	1982		2.00	4.00
❏ 1043		This Is for Real/I Just Want to Make It Up to You	1983		2.00	4.00
❏ 2239		Everyday People/You Can't Take Me for Granted	1991		2.50	5.00
❏ 9034		Get It Right/Giving In	1983		2.00	4.00
❏ 9095		Every Girl (Wants My Guy)/I Got Your Love	1983		2.00	4.00
❏ 9354		Freeway of Love/Until You Say You Love Me	1985			3.00
❏ 9354	PS	Freeway of Love/Until You Say You Love Me	1985			3.00
❏ 9410		Who's Zoomin' Who/Bittersweet Love	1985			3.00
❏ 9410	PS	Who's Zoomin' Who/Bittersweet Love	1985			3.00
❏ 9453		Another Night/Kind of Man	1986			3.00
❏ 9474		Ain't Nobody Ever Loved You/Push	1986			3.00
		B-side with Peter Wolf				
❏ 9528		Jumpin' Jack Flash/Integrity	1986		2.50	5.00
		Original pressings on clear vinyl				
❏ 9528	PS	Jumpin' Jack Flash/Integrity	1986		2.50	5.00
		Picture sleeve with clear vinyl pressing lists catalog number as ALC-9528				
❏ 9528		Jumpin' Jack Flash/Integrity	1986			3.00
		Second pressing on black vinyl				
❏ 9528	PS	Jumpin' Jack Flash/Integrity	1986			3.00
		Picture sleeve with black vinyl pressing lists catalog number as AL-9528				
❏ 9546		Jimmy Lee/If You Need My Love Tonight	1986			3.00
❏ 9546	PS	Jimmy Lee/If You Need My Love Tonight	1986			3.00
❏ 9557		Jimmy Lee/An Angel Cries	1987			Unreleased?
❏ 9559		I Knew You Were Waiting (For Me)/(Instrumental)	1987			3.00
❏ 9559	PS	I Knew You Were Waiting (For Me)/(Instrumental)	1987			3.00
		Aretha Franklin and George Michael				
❏ 9574		Rock-A-Lott/Look to the Rainbow	1987			3.00
❏ 9574	PS	Rock-A-Lott/Look to the Rainbow	1987			3.00
❏ 9623		If You Need My Love Tonight/He'll Come Along	1987			3.00
		A-side with Larry Graham				
❏ 9672		Oh Happy Day/The Lord's Prayer	1988		2.00	4.00
❏ 9766		If Ever a Love There Was/Let's Jam	1988			3.00
		A-side: With the Four Tops; B-side: Four Tops solo				
❏ 9809		Through the Storm/Come to Me	1989			3.00
		A-side: Aretha Franklin and Elton John				
❏ 9809	PS	Through the Storm/Come to Me	1989			3.00
❏ 9850		It Isn't, It Wasn't, It Ain't Never Gonna Be/	1989			3.00
		If Ever a Love There Was				
		A-side: With Whitney Houston; B-side: With the Four Tops				
❏ 9850	PS	It Isn't, It Wasn't, It Ain't Never Gonna Be/	1989			3.00
		If Ever a Love There Was				
		A-side: With Whitney Houston; B-side: With the Four Tops				
❏ 9884		Gimme Your Love/Think	1989			3.00
		B-side with James Brown				

Atlantic

Number	Title (A Side/B Side)	Year	VG	VG+	NM
❏ 2386	I Never Loved a Man (The Way I Love You)/	1967	2.50	5.00	10.00
	Do Right Woman, Do Right Man				
❏ 2403	Respect/Dr. Feelgood	1967	2.50	5.00	10.00
❏ 2427	Baby I Love You/Going Down Now	1967	2.50	5.00	10.00
❏ 2441	(You Make Me Feel Like) A Natural Woman/	1967	2.50	5.00	10.00
	Baby, Baby, Baby				
❏ 2464	Chain of Fools/Prove It	1967	2.50	5.00	10.00
❏ 2486	(Sweet Sweet Baby) Since You've Been Gone/	1968	2.50	5.00	10.00
	Ain't No Way				
❏ 2518	Think/You Send Me	1968	2.50	5.00	10.00
❏ 2546	I Say a Little Prayer/The House That Jack Built	1968	2.50	5.00	10.00
❏ 2574	See Saw/My Song	1968	2.00	4.00	8.00
❏ 2603	The Weight/Tracks of My Tears	1969	2.00	4.00	8.00
❏ 2619	I Can't See Myself Leaving You/Gentle On My Mind	1969	2.00	4.00	8.00
❏ 2650	Share Your Love with Me/Pledging My Love-The Clock	1969	2.00	4.00	8.00
❏ 2683	Eleanor Rigby/It Ain't Fair	1969	2.00	4.00	8.00
❏ 2706	Call Me/Son of a Preacher Man	1970	2.00	4.00	8.00
❏ 2731	Spirit in the Dark/The Thrill Is Gone	1970	2.00	4.00	8.00
❏ 2751	Don't Play That Song/Let It Be	1970	2.00	4.00	8.00
❏ 2772	Border Song (Holy Moses)/You and Me	1970	2.00	4.00	8.00
❏ 2787	You're All I Need to Get By/Pullin'	1971		3.00	6.00
❏ 2796	Bridge Over Troubled Water/Brand New Me	1971		3.00	6.00
❏ 2817	Spanish Harlem/Lean On Me	1971		3.00	6.00
❏ 2838	Rock Steady/Oh Me Oh My (I'm a Fool for You Baby)	1971		3.00	6.00
❏ 2866	Day Dreaming/I've Been Loving You Too Long	1972		3.00	6.00
❏ 2883	All the King's Horses/April Fools	1972		3.00	6.00
❏ 2901	Wholy Holy/Give Yourself to Jesus	1972		3.00	6.00
❏ 2941	Master of Eyes (The Deepness of Your Eyes)/	1973		3.00	6.00
	Moody's Mood for You				

Number		Title (A Side/B Side)	Year	VG	VG+	NM
❏ 2969		Angel/Hey Hey Now (Sister from Texas)	1973		3.00	6.00
❏ 2995		Until You Come Back to Me	1973		3.00	6.00
		(That's What I'm Gonna Do)/If You Don't Think				
❏ 2999		I'm in Love/Oh Baby	1974		3.00	6.00
❏ 3200		Ain't Nothing Like the Real Thing/Eight Days a Week	1974		3.00	6.00
❏ 3224		Without Love/Don't Go Breaking My Heart	1974		3.00	6.00
❏ 3249		With Everything I Feel in Me/Sing It Again, Say It Again	1975		3.00	6.00
❏ 3289		Mr. D.J. (5 for the D.J.)/As Long As You Are There	1975		3.00	6.00
❏ 3311		You/Without You	1975		3.00	6.00
❏ 3326		Something He Can Feel/Loving You, Baby	1976		3.00	6.00
❏ 3358		Jump/Hooked on Your Love	1976		3.00	6.00
❏ 3373		Look Into Your Heart/Rock with Me	1977		3.00	6.00
❏ 3393		Break It To Me Gently/Meadows of Springtime	1977		3.00	6.00
❏ 3468		Almighty Fire/I'm Your Speed	1978		3.00	6.00
❏ 3495		More Than Just a Joy/This You Can Believe	1979		3.00	6.00

Checker

❏ 861		Never Grow Old/You Grow Closer	1957	5.00	10.00	20.00
❏ 941		Precious Lord (Part 1)/Precious Lord (Part 2)	1960	3.75	7.50	15.00

Columbia

❏ 31202	S	titles unknown	1961	3.00	6.00	12.00
❏ 31203	S	titles unknown	1961	3.00	6.00	12.00
❏ 31204	S	titles unknown	1961	3.00	6.00	12.00
❏ 31205	S	titles unknown	1961	3.00	6.00	12.00
❏ 31206	S	titles unknown	1961	3.00	6.00	12.00

Anyone who can fill in these gaps -- the above five all are Columbia "Stereo 7" singles -- please let us know.

❏ 41793		Today I Sing the Blues/Love Is the Only Thing	1960	3.00	6.00	12.00
❏ 41923		Won't Be Long/Right Now	1961	3.00	6.00	12.00
❏ 41965		Are You Sure/Maybe I'm a Fool	1961	3.00	6.00	12.00
❏ 42157		Rock-A-Bye Your Baby with a Dixie Melody/	1961	3.00	6.00	12.00
		Operation Heartbreak				
❏ 42266		I Surrender, Dear/Rough Lover	1962	2.50	5.00	10.00
❏ 42266	PS	I Surrender, Dear/Rough Lover	1962	7.50	15.00	30.00
❏ 42456		Don't Cry, Baby/Without the One You Love	1962	2.50	5.00	10.00
❏ 42456	PS	Don't Cry, Baby/Without the One You Love	1962	7.50	15.00	30.00
❏ 42520		Try a Little Tenderness/Just for a Thrill	1962	2.50	5.00	10.00
❏ 42625		Trouble in Mind/God Bless the Child	1962	2.50	5.00	10.00
❏ 42796		Here's Where I Came In/Say It Isn't So	1963	2.50	5.00	10.00
❏ 42796	PS	Here's Where I Came In/Say It Isn't So	1963	7.50	15.00	30.00
❏ 42874		Skylark/You've Got Her	1963	2.50	5.00	10.00
❏ 42933		Johnny/Kissin' by the Mistletoe	1963	2.50	5.00	10.00
❏ 43009		Soulville/Evil Gal Blues	1964	2.50	5.00	10.00
❏ 43113		Runnin' Out of Fools/It's Just a Matter of Time	1964	2.50	5.00	10.00
❏ 43177		Winter Wonderland/	1964	2.50	5.00	10.00
		The Christmas Song (Chestnuts Roasting on an Open Fire)				
❏ 43203		Can't You Just See Me/Little Miss Raggedy Ann	1965	2.50	5.00	10.00
❏ 43241		One Step Ahead/	1965	2.50	5.00	10.00
		I Can't Wait Until I See My Baby's Face				
❏ 43333		(No, No) I'm Losing You/Sweet Bitter Love	1965	2.50	5.00	10.00
❏ 43442		You Made Me Love You/There Is No Greater Love	1966	2.50	5.00	10.00
❏ 43515		Hands Off/Tighten Up Your Tie, Button Up Your Jacket	1966	2.50	5.00	10.00
❏ 43637		Until You Were Gone/Swanee	1966	2.50	5.00	10.00
❏ 43827		Cry Like a Baby/Swanee	1966	2.50	5.00	10.00
❏ 44181		Until You Were Gone/Lee Cross	1967	2.50	5.00	10.00
❏ 44270		Take a Look/Follow Your Heart	1967	2.50	5.00	10.00
❏ 44381		Mockingbird/A Mother's Love	1967	2.00	4.00	8.00
❏ 44441		Soulville/If Ever I Would Leave You	1968	2.00	4.00	8.00
❏ 44851		Friendly Persuasion/Jim	1969	2.00	4.00	8.00
❏ 44951		Today I Sing the Blues/People	1969	2.00	4.00	8.00

JVB

❏ 47		Never Grow Old/You Grow Closer	1957	7.50	15.00	30.00
❏ 75		Precious Lord (Part 1)/Precious Lord (Part 2)	1959	7.50	15.00	30.00

Franklin, Erma

(Aretha's sister)

Brunswick

❏ 55403		Change My Thoughts from You/Gotta Find Me a Lover	1969	2.00	4.00	8.00
❏ 55415		Saving My Love/You've Been Cancelled	1969	2.00	4.00	8.00
❏ 55424		I Just Don't Need You (At All)/It Could've Been Me	1969	2.00	4.00	8.00
❏ 55430		Whispers (Gettin' Louder)/(I Get the) Sweetest Feeling	1970	2.00	4.00	8.00

Epic

❏ 9488		Hello Again/It's Over	1962	5.00	10.00	20.00
❏ 9511		Each Night I Cry/Time After Time	1962	5.00	10.00	20.00
❏ 9516		Dear Mama/Never Again	1962	5.00	10.00	20.00
❏ 9559		Don't Wait Too Long/Time After Time	1962	5.00	10.00	20.00
❏ 9594		Have You Ever Had the Blues/	1963	3.75	7.50	15.00
		I Don't Want No Mama's Boy				
❏ 9610		Abracadabra/Love Is Blind	1963	3.75	7.50	15.00

Shout

❏ 218		Big Boss Man/Didn't Catch the Dog's Bone	1967	2.50	5.00	10.00
❏ 221		Piece of My Heart/Baby What You Want Me to Do	1967	3.00	6.00	12.00
❏ 230		Open Up Your Soul/I'm Just Not Ready for Love	1967	2.50	5.00	10.00
❏ 234		Right to Cry/I'm Just Not Ready for Love	1968	2.50	5.00	10.00

Frantics, The

Bolo

❏ 728		Pony Moronie/Meet Me in Seattle Twist	1962	2.50	5.00	10.00
❏ 736		Oh Yeah/Let Our Love Roll On	1962	2.50	5.00	10.00

Number		Title (A Side/B Side)	Year	VG	VG+	NM
Dolton						
❑ 2		Straight Flush/Young Blues	1959	5.00	10.00	20.00
❑ 6		Rug Cutter/Black Sapphire	1959	5.00	10.00	20.00
❑ 13		Checkerboard/Werewolf	1959	5.00	10.00	20.00
❑ 16		Werewolf/No Werewolf	1960	3.75	7.50	15.00
❑ 24		The Whip/Delilah	1960	3.75	7.50	15.00
❑ 31		Yankee Doodlin'/One Minute of Flamenco	1961	3.75	7.50	15.00
❑ 33		San Antonio Rose/Trees	1961	3.75	7.50	15.00
Seafair						
❑ 111		San Francisco Swim/Blue Day	1964	2.50	5.00	10.00

Freberg, Stan

Number		Title (A Side/B Side)	Year	VG	VG+	NM
Capitol						
❑ F1356		John & Marsha/Ragtime Dan	1951	7.50	15.00	30.00
❑ F1697		St. George and the Dragonet/Little Blue Riding Hood	1954	5.00	10.00	20.00
		Reissue (despite the lower number)				
❑ F1711		That's My Boy/I've Got You Under My Skin	1951	7.50	15.00	30.00
❑ F1962		Maggie/Tele-Vee-Shun	1951	7.50	15.00	30.00
❑ F2029		Try/Pass the Udder Udder	1952	7.50	15.00	30.00
❑ F2125		Abe Snake for President/Ba Ba Ball and Chain	1952	12.50	25.00	50.00
❑ F2279		The World Is Waiting for the Sunrise/ Boogie Woogie Banjo Man from Birmingham	1952	6.25	12.50	25.00
❑ F2596		St. George and the Dragonet/Little Blue Riding Hood	1953	7.50	15.00	30.00
❑ F2671		Christmas Dragnet (Part 1)/Christmas Dragnet (Part 2)	1953	7.50	15.00	30.00
❑ F2677		C'est Si Bon (It's So Good)/ A Dear John & Marsha Letter	1953	6.25	12.50	25.00
❑ F2838		Point of Order/Person to Person	1954	6.25	12.50	25.00
❑ F2929		Sh-Boom/Widescreen Mama Blues	1954	6.25	12.50	25.00
❑ F2986		Yulenet (Part 1)/Yulenet (Part 2)	1954	6.25	12.50	25.00
		Same recording as "Christmas Dragnet" (Capitol F2671)				
❑ F3138		The Honey Earthers/The Lone Psychiatrist	1955	7.50	15.00	30.00
❑ F3249		The Yellow Rose of Texas/ Rock Around Stephen Foster	1955	6.25	12.50	25.00
❑ F3280		Nuttin' for Christmas/The Night Before Christmas	1955	6.25	12.50	25.00
❑ 3355		Try/John and Marsha	1972	2.50	5.00	10.00
❑ F3396		The Great Pretender/ The Quest for Bridey Hammerschlaugen	1956	6.25	12.50	25.00
❑ F3480		Heartbreak Hotel/Rock Island Line	1956	6.25	12.50	25.00
❑ 3503		Green Chritma (Part 1)/Green Chritma (Part 2)	1972	2.50	5.00	10.00
❑ F3687		Banana Boat (Day-O)/Tele-Vee-Shun	1957	6.25	12.50	25.00
❑ F3815		Wun'erful, Wun'erful! (Part uh-one)/ Wun'erful, Wun'erful! (Part uh-two)	1957	6.25	12.50	25.00
❑ F3892		Ya Got Trouble/Gary Indiana	1958	5.00	10.00	20.00
❑ F4097		Green Chritma/The Meaning of Christmas	1958	5.00	10.00	20.00
❑ F4097	PS	Green Chritma/The Meaning of Christmas	1958	7.50	15.00	30.00
❑ 4329		The Old Payola Roll Blues (Part 1)/ The Old Payola Roll Blues (Part 2)	1960	5.00	10.00	20.00
❑ 4329	PS	The Old Payola Roll Blues (Part 1)/ The Old Payola Roll Blues (Part 2)	1960	7.50	15.00	30.00
❑ 4433		Comments for Our Time (Part 1)/ Comments for Our Time (Part 2)	1960	5.00	10.00	20.00
❑ 5726		Flackman and Reagan (Part 1)/ Flackman and Reagan (Part 2)	1966	5.00	10.00	20.00
❑ 5726	PS	Flackman and Reagan (Part 1)/ Flackman and Reagan (Part 2)	1966	7.50	15.00	30.00
❑ S7-57891		Nuttin' for Christmas/I Yust Go Nuts at Christmas	1992		2.00	4.00
		B-side by Yogi Yorgesson				

Fred, John, and His Playboy Band

(Also includes John Fred listed alone)

Number		Title (A Side/B Side)	Year	VG	VG+	NM
Bell						
❑ 45,382		I'm in Love Again/In the Mood	1973		2.50	5.00
		As "John Fred and the Creepers"				
Jewel						
❑ 730		The Fool/There'll Be No Teardrops Tonight	1964	2.50	5.00	10.00
❑ 736		Lenne/You're Mad at Me	1964	2.50	5.00	10.00
❑ 737		Boogie Children/My First Love	1964	2.50	5.00	10.00
		As "The Playboys"				
❑ 743		Wrong to Me/How Can I Prove	1965	2.50	5.00	10.00
Montel						
❑ 904		Down in New Orleans/I Love You	1959	3.75	7.50	15.00
❑ 1002		Shirley/My Love for You	1959	3.75	7.50	15.00
❑ 1007		Good Lovin'/You Know You Made Me Cry	1961	2.50	5.00	10.00
❑ 2000		Mirror Mirror (On the Wall)/To Have and to Hold	1962	2.50	5.00	10.00
N-Joy						
❑ 1005		Boogie Children/My First Love	1965	2.50	5.00	10.00
Paula						
❑ 225		Fortune Teller/Making Love to You	1965	2.00	4.00	8.00
❑ 234		Can't I Get a Word In/Sun City	1966	2.00	4.00	8.00
❑ 244		Doin' the Best I Can/Leave Her Never	1966	2.00	4.00	8.00
❑ 247		Outta My Head/Love Comes in Time	1966	2.00	4.00	8.00
❑ 259		Up and Down/Wind-Up Doll	1967	2.00	4.00	8.00
❑ 273		Agnes English/Sad Story	1967	2.00	4.00	8.00
❑ 282		Judy in Disguise (With Glasses)/ When the Lights Go Out	1967	3.00	6.00	12.00
		White label				

Number		Title (A Side/B Side)	Year	VG	VG+	NM
❑ 282		Judy in Disguise (With Glasses)/ When the Lights Go Out Yellow label	1967	2.50	5.00	10.00
❑ 282		Judy in Disguise (With Glasses)/ When the Lights Go Out Pink label	1967	2.00	4.00	8.00
❑ 294		Hey Hey Bunny/No Letter Today	1968	2.00	4.00	8.00
❑ 303		Lonely Are the Lonely/We Played Games	1968	2.00	4.00	8.00
❑ 310		Tissue Paper/Little Dum Dum	1968	2.00	4.00	8.00
❑ 315		What Is Happiness/Sometimes You Just Can't Win	1968	2.00	4.00	8.00

Sugarcane

Number		Title (A Side/B Side)	Year	VG	VG+	NM
❑ 1001		Keep It Hid/You Had to Be a Woman	1975		2.00	4.00
❑ 1002		Jukebox Shirley/Hey, Good Lookin'	1975		2.00	4.00

Uni

Number		Title (A Side/B Side)	Year	VG	VG+	NM
❑ 55135		Back in the U.S.S.R./Silly Sarah Carter	1969		3.00	6.00
❑ 55160		Open Doors/Three Deep Is a Feeling	1969		3.00	6.00
❑ 55187		Love My Soul/Julia Julia	1969		3.00	6.00
❑ 55220		Come with Me/Where's Everybody Going	1970		3.00	6.00

Freddie and the Dreamers

Capitol

Number		Title (A Side/B Side)	Year	VG	VG+	NM
❑ 5053		I'm Telling You Now/What Have I Done to You	1963	5.00	10.00	20.00
❑ 5137		You Were Made for Me/Send a Letter to Me	1964	5.00	10.00	20.00

Mercury

Number		Title (A Side/B Side)	Year	VG	VG+	NM
❑ 72285		I Love You Baby/Don't Make Me Cry	1965	2.50	5.00	10.00
❑ 72285	PS	I Love You Baby/Don't Make Me Cry	1965	5.00	10.00	20.00
❑ 72327		Don't Do That to Me/Just for You	1965	2.50	5.00	10.00
❑ 72377		I Understand (Just How You Feel)/I Will	1965	2.50	5.00	10.00
❑ 72428		Do the Freddie/Tell Me When	1965	2.50	5.00	10.00
❑ 72462		A Little You/Things I'd Like to Say	1965	2.50	5.00	10.00
❑ 72487		I Don't Know/Windmill in Old Amsterdam	1965	2.50	5.00	10.00
❑ 72487	PS	I Don't Know/Windmill in Old Amsterdam	1965	5.00	10.00	20.00
❑ 72604		Some Day/Short Shorts	1966	2.50	5.00	10.00

Super K

Number		Title (A Side/B Side)	Year	VG	VG+	NM
❑ 146		She Needs Me/Susan's Tuba	1970	2.00	4.00	8.00

Tower

Number		Title (A Side/B Side)	Year	VG	VG+	NM
❑ 125		I'm Telling You Now/What Have I Done to You	1964	3.75	7.50	15.00
❑ 127		You Were Made for Me/Send a Letter to Me	1965	5.00	10.00	20.00
❑ 127		You Were Made for Me/So Fine B-side: "Introducing the Beat Merchants"	1965	3.75	7.50	15.00
❑ 163		Send a Letter to Me/There's Not One Thing B-side by 4 Just Men	1965	3.75	7.50	15.00

United Artists

Number		Title (A Side/B Side)	Year	VG	VG+	NM
❑ 50239		Come Back When You Grow Up/ Oh What a Lovely Day	1967			Unreleased

Freddie and the Parliaments
(May be a pseudonym for Johnny and the Hurricanes)

Twirl

Number		Title (A Side/B Side)	Year	VG	VG+	NM
❑ 1003		Darlene/That Girl	1959	25.00	50.00	100.00

Freed, Alan

Coral

Number		Title (A Side/B Side)	Year	VG	VG+	NM
❑ 61626		Right Now, Right Now/Tina's Cantine	1956	7.50	15.00	30.00
❑ 61660		The Camel Rock/I Don't Need Lotsa Money	1956	7.50	15.00	30.00
❑ 61693		The Space Man/Jazzbo's Theory With Al "Jazzbo" Collins and the Modernaires	1956	7.50	15.00	30.00
❑ 61749		Rock 'N' Roll Boogie/The Grey Bear	1956	10.00	20.00	40.00
❑ 61818		Sentimental Journey/Stop! Look! and Run!	1957	10.00	20.00	40.00

Freeman Brothers, The

Mala

Number		Title (A Side/B Side)	Year	VG	VG+	NM
❑ 553		I'm Counting on You/Everyday It's You	1966	6.25	12.50	25.00

Soul

Number		Title (A Side/B Side)	Year	VG	VG+	NM
❑ 35011		My Baby/Beautiful Brown Eyes	1965	10.00	20.00	40.00

Freeman, Bobby

Autumn

Number		Title (A Side/B Side)	Year	VG	VG+	NM
❑ 1		Come to Me/Let's Surf Again	1964	5.00	10.00	20.00
❑ 2		C'mon and Swim/C'mon and Swim -- Part 2 White label, red print	1964	3.00	6.00	12.00
❑ 2		C'mon and Swim/C'mon and Swim -- Part 2 Tan label	1964	2.50	5.00	10.00
❑ 5		S-W-I-M/That Little Old Heartbreaker	1964	2.50	5.00	10.00
❑ 9		I'll Never Fall in Love Again/Friends	1965	2.50	5.00	10.00
❑ 25		Cross My Heart/The Duck	1965	2.50	5.00	10.00

Double Shot

Number		Title (A Side/B Side)	Year	VG	VG+	NM
❑ 139		There Oughta Be a Law/Everybody's Got a Hang-Up	1969		3.00	6.00
❑ 144		Susie Sunshine/ Four Piece Funky Nitty Gritty Junky Band	1969		3.00	6.00
❑ 148		Can You Stand the Pressure/ Put Another Dime in the Parking Meter	1970		3.00	6.00
❑ 152		Do You Wanna Dance 1970/ Society for the Prevention of Cruelty to People	1970		3.00	6.00

Number	Title (A Side/B Side)	Year	VG	VG+	NM

Josie

❏ 835	Do You Want to Dance/Big Fat Woman	1958	3.75	7.50	15.00
❏ 841	Betty Lou Got a New Pair of Shoes/Starlight	1958	3.75	7.50	15.00
❏ 844	Need Your Love/Shame On You, Miss Johnson	1958	3.75	7.50	15.00
❏ 855	A Love to Last a Lifetime/When You're Smiling	1959	3.75	7.50	15.00
❏ 863	Love Me/Mary Ann Thomas	1959	3.75	7.50	15.00
❏ 867	My Guardian Angel/Where Did My Baby Go	1959	3.75	7.50	15.00
❏ 872	Ebb Tide/Sinbad	1959	3.75	7.50	15.00
❏ 879	I Need Someone/First Day of Spring	1960	3.00	6.00	12.00
❏ 886	Miss You So/Baby What Would You Do	1961	3.00	6.00	12.00
❏ 887	The Mess Around/So Much to Do	1961	3.00	6.00	12.00
❏ 889	Put You Down/She Said She Wants to Dance	1961	3.00	6.00	12.00
❏ 896	Love Me/Little Girl Don't You Understand	1962	3.00	6.00	12.00
❏ 928	The Mess Around/Little Girl Don't You Understand	1965	2.50	5.00	10.00

King

❏ 5373	Shimmy Shimmy/You Don't Understand	1960	3.00	6.00	12.00
❏ 5953	Fever/What Can I Do	1964	2.50	5.00	10.00
❏ 5962	Somebody, Somewhere/Be My Little Chick-A-Dee	1964	2.50	5.00	10.00
❏ 5975	Come to Me/There's Gonna Be a Change	1965	2.50	5.00	10.00

Loma

❏ 2056	Shadow of Your Love/Soulful Sound of Music	1966	2.00	4.00	8.00
❏ 2080	I Got a Good Thing/Lies	1967	2.00	4.00	8.00

Parkway

❏ 875	She's a Hippy/Whip It Up Baby	1963	3.00	6.00	12.00

Freewheelers, The

Epic

❏ 9664	Walk, Walk/The Best of It	1964	5.00	10.00	20.00
❏ 9700	San Francisco Bay Blues/Susu	1964	5.00	10.00	20.00
❏ 9725	Beach Boy/Annie	1964	3.75	7.50	15.00

Frogmen, The

Astra

❏ 1009	Underwater/The Mad Rush	1961	12.50	25.00	50.00
❏ 1010	Beware Below/Tioga	1961	12.50	25.00	50.00

Candix

❏ 314	Underwater/The Mad Rush	1961	6.25	12.50	25.00
❏ 326	Beware Below/Tioga	1961	6.25	12.50	25.00

Scott

❏ 101	Seahorse Flats/Tioga	1964	12.50	25.00	50.00
❏ 102	Underwater/Beware Below	1964	12.50	25.00	50.00

Tee Jay

❏ 131	Sea Haunt/Diamond Back	1964	20.00	40.00	80.00
	Blue vinyl				

Front Page News

Dial

❏ 4052	Thoughts/You Better Behave	1967	6.25	12.50	25.00

Frost, Max, and the Troopers

(Davie Allan was a member)

Sidewalk

❏ 938	There Is a Party Going On/Stomper's Ride	1968	3.75	7.50	15.00

Tower

❏ 419	Shape of Things to Come/Free Lovin'	1968	3.75	7.50	15.00
❏ 452	52%/Max Frost Theme	1968	3.75	7.50	15.00
❏ 478	Paxton Quigley's Had the Course/Sittin' in Circles	1969	3.75	7.50	15.00

Fuller, Bobby, Four

(Also includes Bobby Fuller solo)

Capitol

❏ 3038	The Only God I Know/A Name Like Watermelon	1971	5.00	10.00	20.00

Donna

❏ 1403	Those Memories of You/Our Favorite Martian	1965	50.00	100.00	200.00
	As "Bobby Fuller and the Fantastics"				

Eastwood

❏ 345	Not Fade Away/Nervous Breakdown	1962	25.00	50.00	100.00

Exeter

❏ 122	King of the Beach/Wine, Wine, Wine	1964	50.00	100.00	200.00
❏ 124	I Fought the Law/She's My Girl	1964	87.50	175.00	350.00
❏ 126	Fool of Love/Shakedown	1964	30.00	60.00	120.00

Liberty

❏ 55812	Let Her Dance/Another Sad and Lonely Night	1965	7.50	15.00	30.00

Mustang

❏ 3004	She's My Girl/Take My Hand	1965	6.25	12.50	25.00
❏ 3006	Let Her Dance/Another Sad and Lonely Night	1965	3.75	7.50	15.00
❏ 3011	Never to Be Forgotten/You Kissed Me	1965	6.25	12.50	25.00
❏ 3012	Let Her Dance/Another Sad and Lonely Night	1965	3.75	7.50	15.00
❏ 3014	I Fought the Law/Little Annie Lou	1966	3.75	7.50	15.00
❏ 3016	Love's Made a Fool of You/Don't Ever Let Me Know	1966	3.00	6.00	12.00
❏ 3018	Magic Touch/My True Love	1966	3.00	6.00	12.00

Todd

❏ 1090	Saturday Night/The Stinger	1963	25.00	50.00	100.00

Number		Title (A Side/B Side)	Year	VG	VG+	NM
Yucca						
❏ 140		You're in Love/Guess We'll Fall in Love	1961	20.00	40.00	80.00
		Slow version				
❏ 140		You're in Love/Guess We'll Fall in Love	1961	10.00	20.00	40.00
		Fast version				
❏ 144		My Heart Jumped/Gently My Love	1961	20.00	40.00	80.00

Funkadelic
(Also see "Parliament"; "Parliaments, The"; "P-Funk All Stars, The")

Number		Title (A Side/B Side)	Year	VG	VG+	NM
LAX						
❏ 70055		Connections and Disconnections/The Witch	1981		2.00	4.00
MCA						
❏ 53654		By Way of the Drum/(Instrumental)	1989			3.00
Warner Bros.						
❏ 8618		One Nation Under a Groove (Part 1)/	1978		2.50	5.00
		One Nation Under a Groove (Part 2)				
❏ 8618	PS	One Nation Under a Groove (Part 1)/	1978		2.50	5.00
		One Nation Under a Groove (Part 2)				
❏ 8735		Cholly (Funk Getting Ready to Roll)/Into You	1979		2.50	5.00
❏ 49040		(Not Just) Knee Deep -- Part 1/	1979		2.50	5.00
		(Not Just) Knee Deep -- Part 2				
❏ 49117		Uncle Jam (Part 1)/Uncle Jam (Part 2)	1979		2.50	5.00
❏ 49667		The Electric Spanking of War Babies/	1981		2.00	4.00
		The Electric Spanking of War Babies (Part 2)				
❏ 49667	PS	The Electric Spanking of War Babies/	1981		2.50	5.00
		The Electric Spanking of War Babies (Part 2)				
❏ 49807		Shockwaves/Bullino's Bounce	1981		2.00	4.00
Westbound						
❏ 148		Music for My Mother/(Instrumental)	1969	2.50	5.00	10.00
❏ 150		I'll Bet You/Open Your Eyes	1969	2.50	5.00	10.00
❏ 158		I Got a Thing, You Got a Thing,	1970	2.50	5.00	10.00
		Everybody's Got a Thing/Fish, Chips and Sweat				
❏ 167		I Wanna Know If It's Good to You?/	1970	2.50	5.00	10.00
		I Wanna Know If It's Good to You? (Part 2)				
❏ 175		You and Your Folks, Me and My Folks/	1971	2.50	5.00	10.00
		Funky Dollar Bill				
❏ 185		Can You Get to That/Back in Our Minds	1971	2.50	5.00	10.00
❏ 197		I Miss My Baby/Baby I Owe You Something Good	1972	2.50	5.00	10.00
		As "U.S. Music with Funkadelic"				
❏ 198		Hit It and Quit It/A Whole Lot of B.S.	1972	2.50	5.00	10.00
❏ 205		A Joyful Process/Loose Booty	1972	2.50	5.00	10.00
❏ 218		Cosmic Slop/	1973	2.50	5.00	10.00
		If You Don't Like the Effects, Don't Produce the Cause				
❏ 224		Standing on the Verge of Getting It On/	1974	2.50	5.00	10.00
		Jimmy's Got a Little Bit of Bitch in Him				
❏ 5000		Red Hot Momma/Vital Juices	1975	2.00	4.00	8.00
❏ 5014		Better by the Pound/Stuffs and Things	1975	2.00	4.00	8.00
❏ 5026		Let's Take It to the Stage/Biological Speculation	1976	2.00	4.00	8.00
❏ 5029		Undisco Kidd/How Do Yeau View You	1976	2.00	4.00	8.00

Fury, Billy

Number		Title (A Side/B Side)	Year	VG	VG+	NM
London						
❏ 1857		Maybe Tomorrow/Gonna Type a Letter	1959	5.00	10.00	20.00
❏ 1925		Colette/Baby How I Cried	1960	5.00	10.00	20.00
❏ 2004		Stick Around/Coming Up in the World	1961	5.00	10.00	20.00
❏ 9548		Once Upon a Dream/Running Around	1962	3.75	7.50	15.00
❏ 9594		Because of Love/Like I've Never Loved Before	1963	3.75	7.50	15.00
❏ 9615		Don't Walk Away/When Will I Say I Love You	1963	3.75	7.50	15.00
❏ 9662		The Hippy Hippy Shake/(B-side unknown)	1964	3.75	7.50	15.00
❏ 9675		What Am I Living For/I Will	1964	3.75	7.50	15.00
❏ 9692		Baby, What Do You Want Me to Do/	1964	3.75	7.50	15.00
		It's Only Make Believe				
❏ 9704		Go Ahead and Ask Her/I'm Lost Without You	1964	3.75	7.50	15.00
❏ 9740		I'm Lost Without You/Go Ahead and Ask Her	1965	3.75	7.50	15.00
Mala						
❏ 569		Loving You/I'll Go Along With It	1967	2.50	5.00	10.00
❏ 583		Suzanne in the Mirror/It Just Don't Matter Now	1968	2.50	5.00	10.00
❏ 595		Beyond the Shadow of a Doubt/Baby Do You Love Me	1968	2.50	5.00	10.00
❏ 12,018		Silly Boy Blue/One Minute Woman	1968	2.50	5.00	10.00
United Artists						
❏ 968		Away from You/In Thoughts of You	1966	3.00	6.00	12.00
❏ 50061		She's So Far Out She's In/Give Me Your Word	1966	3.00	6.00	12.00

Fuse
(Group evolved into Cheap Trick)

Number		Title (A Side/B Side)	Year	VG	VG+	NM
Epic						
❏ 10514		Cruisin' for Burgers/Hound Dog	1969	6.25	12.50	25.00

Fut, The
(Maurice Gibb was in this group, which often was bootlegged as a "lost" Beatles record. It has no Beatles involvement whatsoever)

Number		Title (A Side/B Side)	Year	VG	VG+	NM
Beacon						
❏ 160		Have You Heard the Word/Futting	1970	2.50	5.00	10.00
Fut						
❏ 160		Have You Heard the Word/Futting	1976		2.50	5.00

Number	Title (A Side/B Side)	Year	VG	VG+	NM

G

G-Clefs, The
Loma

Number	Title (A Side/B Side)	Year	VG	VG+	NM
❑ 2034	Party '66/Little Lonely Boy	1966	2.50	5.00	10.00
❑ 2048	I Can't Stand It/Whirlwind	1966	2.50	5.00	10.00

Paris

❑ 502	Symbol of Love/Love Her in the Mornin'	1957	7.50	15.00	30.00
❑ 506	Zing Zang Zoo/Is This the Way	1957	6.25	12.50	25.00

Pilgrim

❑ 715	Ka-Ding-Dong/Darla My Darlin'	1956	7.50	15.00	30.00
	Purple label				
❑ 715	Ka-Ding-Dong/Darla My Darlin'	1956	5.00	10.00	20.00
	Red label				
❑ 720	'Cause You're Mine/Please Write While I'm Away	1956	7.50	15.00	30.00

Regina

❑ 1314	To the Winner Goes the Prize/I Believe in All I Feel	1964	3.75	7.50	15.00
❑ 1319	Angel Listen to Me/Nobody But Betty	1964	5.00	10.00	20.00

Terrace

❑ 7500	I Understand (Just How You Feel)/Little Girl I Love You	1961	5.00	10.00	20.00
❑ 7503	Girl Has to Know/ Lad (There Never Was a Dog Like You)	1962	5.00	10.00	20.00
❑ 7507	Make Up Your Mind/They'll Call Me Away	1962	5.00	10.00	20.00
❑ 7510	A Lover's Prayer/Sitting in the Moonlight	1962	6.25	12.50	25.00
❑ 7514	All My Trials/Big Train	1963	6.25	12.50	25.00

Veep

❑ 1218	I Have/On the Other Side of Town	1965	3.75	7.50	15.00
❑ 1226	This Time/On the Other Side of Town	1965	3.75	7.50	15.00

G.T.O.'s
Claridge

❑ 312	She Rides with Me/Rudy Vahoo	1966	5.00	10.00	20.00
	Reissue of Claridge 304 by "Joey and the Continentals"				

Parkway

❑ 108	Girl from New York City/Missing Out on the Fun	1966	3.75	7.50	15.00

Gabriel and the Angels
Amy

❑ 802	Chumba/Hey	1960	5.00	10.00	20.00
❑ 823	Zing Went the Strings of My Heart/The Rooster	1961	10.00	20.00	40.00

Norman

❑ 506	I'm Gabriel/Ginza	1961	3.75	7.50	15.00
❑ 510	Gabriel, Blow Your Horn (Part 1)/ Gabriel, Blow Your Horn (Part 2)	1961	3.75	7.50	15.00
❑ 514	Miss You So/See See Rider	1962	3.75	7.50	15.00
	As "Gabriel and His Trumpet"				

Swan

❑ 4118	That's Life (That's Tough)/Don't Wanna Twist No More	1962	3.00	6.00	12.00
❑ 4133	The Peanut Butter Song/All Work and No Play	1963	3.00	6.00	12.00

Gadabouts, The
Jaro

❑ 77022	Caress Me/Deep Are the Roots of a Happy Home	1960	3.75	7.50	15.00

Mercury

❑ 70495	By the Waters of the Minnetonka/Giuseppe Mandolino	1954	6.25	12.50	25.00
❑ 70581	Go Boom Boom/Oochi Pachi	1955	6.25	12.50	25.00
❑ 70823	Busy Body Rock/All My Love Belongs to You	1956	6.25	12.50	25.00
❑ 70898	Stranded in the Jungle/Blues Train	1956	6.25	12.50	25.00

Wing

❑ 90008	Two Things I Love/Glass Heart	1955	6.25	12.50	25.00
❑ 90043	Teenage Rock/If You Only Had a Heart	1955	6.25	12.50	25.00
❑ 90062	Busy Body Rock/All My Love Belongs to You	1956	5.00	10.00	20.00

Gailtones, The
Decca

❑ 30726	Lover Boy/Please Don't Go	1958	10.00	20.00	40.00

Gaines, Roy
Chart

❑ 606	Loud Mouth Lucy/I'm Setting You Free	1955	15.00	30.00	60.00

Del-Fi

❑ 4169	What Is This Thing Called Love/Lizzie	1961	3.75	7.50	15.00

DeLuxe

❑ 6119	Isabella/Gainesville	1957	6.25	12.50	25.00
❑ 6132	You're Right, I'm Left/Stolen Moments	1957	6.25	12.50	25.00
❑ 6147	Annabelle/Night Beat	1957	6.25	12.50	25.00

Groove

❑ 0146	Right Now Baby/De Dat De Dum Dum	1956	7.50	15.00	30.00
❑ 0161	Worried 'Bout You Baby/All My Life	1956	7.50	15.00	30.00

RCA Victor

❑ 47-7243	Skippy Is a Sissy/Weeping Willow	1958	15.00	30.00	60.00

Number	Title (A Side/B Side)	Year	VG	VG+	NM

Galaxies, The
Capitol
| ❏ 4427 | Big Triangle/Until the Next Time | 1960 | 3.75 | 7.50 | 15.00 |

Chess
| ❏ 1757 | This Rock and Roll/6:15 | 1960 | 5.00 | 10.00 | 20.00 |

Dot
| ❏ 16212 | My Blue Heaven/Tremble | 1961 | 6.25 | 12.50 | 25.00 |

Etiquette
❏ 17	I'm a Worker/Make Love to Me Baby	1965	5.00	10.00	20.00
❏ 20	On the Beach/She Said I Do	1965	5.00	10.00	20.00
❏ 25	I (Who Have Nothing)/I Am Yours	1966	5.00	10.00	20.00

Guaranteed
| ❏ 216 | My Tattle Tale/Love Has Its Way | 1960 | 12.50 | 25.00 | 50.00 |

Eddie Cochran plays guitar on this record

Panorama
| ❏ 54 | Along Comes the Man/She Said I Do | 1966 | 2.50 | 5.00 | 10.00 |

Richie
| ❏ 458 | Dear Someone/The Leopard | 1961 | 18.75 | 37.50 | 75.00 |

Ronnie
| ❏ 201 | Just Another Date/Little Man | 1976 | | 3.00 | 6.00 |

Seafair
| ❏ 110 | Shaken/Tacoma | 1964 | 3.75 | 7.50 | 15.00 |

Galaxys, The
Carthay
| ❏ 103 | A Lover's Prayer/Jelly Bean | 1959 | 100.00 | 200.00 | 400.00 |

Gales, The
Debra
| ❏ 1002 | Tommy/Around the Clock with You | 1963 | 10.00 | 20.00 | 40.00 |

J.O.B.
| ❏ 3001 | Darling Patricia/All Is Well, All Is Well | 1956 | 50.00 | 100.00 | 200.00 |

JVB
| ❏ 34 | His Eyes Keep Me in Trouble/Don't Let the Sun Catch You Cryin' | 1955 | 100.00 | 200.00 | 400.00 |
| ❏ 35 | Darling Patricia/All Is Well, All Is Well | 1955 | 100.00 | 200.00 | 400.00 |

Mel-O
| ❏ 111 | Guiding Angel/Boy Come Home | 1958 | 62.50 | 125.00 | 250.00 |
| ❏ 113 | Josephine/If I Could Forget | 1958 | 62.50 | 125.00 | 250.00 |

Winn
| ❏ 916 | I Love You/Squeeze Me | 1960 | 125.00 | 250.00 | 500.00 |

Gallahads, The
Beechwood
| ❏ 3001 | Keeper of Dreams/Sad Girl | 1960 | 25.00 | 50.00 | 100.00 |

Capitol
| ❏ F3060 | Ooh Ah/Careless | 1955 | 6.25 | 12.50 | 25.00 |
| ❏ F3175 | Do You Believe Me/If It Wasn't for You | 1955 | 6.25 | 12.50 | 25.00 |

Del-Fi
❏ 4137	Lonely Guy/Jo Jo the Big Wheel	1960	10.00	20.00	40.00
	Green label				
❏ 4137	Lonely Guy/Jo Jo the Big Wheel	1960	5.00	10.00	20.00
	Black label				
❏ 4148	Be Fair/I'm Without a Girl Friend	1960	10.00	20.00	40.00
	Green label				
❏ 4148	Be Fair/I'm Without a Girl Friend	1960	5.00	10.00	20.00
	Black label				

Donna
| ❏ 1322 | Lonely Guy/Jo Jo the Big Wheel | 1960 | 10.00 | 20.00 | 40.00 |
| ❏ 1361 | This Letter to You/The Answer to Love | 1962 | 12.50 | 25.00 | 50.00 |

Jubilee
| ❏ 5252 | The Fool/The Morning Mail | 1956 | 6.25 | 12.50 | 25.00 |
| ❏ 5259 | Take My Love/I Give You My Word | 1956 | 6.25 | 12.50 | 25.00 |

Nite Owl
| ❏ 20 | Gone/So Long | 1961 | 15.00 | 30.00 | 60.00 |

Rendezvous
| ❏ 153 | Gone/Why Do Fools Fall in Love | 1961 | 10.00 | 20.00 | 40.00 |

Sea Crest
| ❏ 6005 | Have Love, Will Travel/My Offering | 1964 | 10.00 | 20.00 | 40.00 |

Starla
| ❏ 15 | Keeper of Dreams/Sad Girl | 1960 | 5.00 | 10.00 | 20.00 |

Vik
❏ 0291	Take Back My Ring/One Love Alone	1957	6.25	12.50	25.00
❏ 0316	Best Wishes/Steady Man	1958	6.25	12.50	25.00
❏ 0332	Silently/Barracuda	1958	6.25	12.50	25.00

Number		Title (A Side/B Side)	Year	VG	VG+	NM

Gamble, Kenny
(Legendary Philly-soul producer)
Arctic
☐ 107		Down by the Seashore (Part 1)/Down by the Seashore (Part 2)	1965	50.00	100.00	200.00
☐ 114		Ain't It Baby (Part 1)/Ain't It Baby (Part 2)	1965	50.00	100.00	200.00
☐ 123		The Joke's on You/Don't Stop Loving Me	1966	50.00	100.00	200.00

Columbia
| ☐ 43132 | | Our Love/You Don't Know What You Got Until You Lose It | 1964 | 7.50 | 15.00 | 30.00 |

Epic
| ☐ 9636 | | Standing in the Shadows/No Mail on Monday | 1963 | 7.50 | 15.00 | 30.00 |

Gamblers, The
(Bruce Johnston and Sandy Nelson were in this group)
Last Chance
| ☐ 2 | | Teen Machine/Tonky | 1961 | 7.50 | 15.00 | 30.00 |
| ☐ 108 | | Teen Machine/Tonky | 1962 | 5.00 | 10.00 | 20.00 |

World Pacific
| ☐ 615 | | Moon Dawg/LSD-25 | 1960 | 12.50 | 25.00 | 50.00 |

Gandalf
Capitol
| ☐ 2400 | | Golden Earrings/Never Too Far | 1969 | 6.25 | 12.50 | 25.00 |

Gants, The
Aladdin
| ☐ 3387 | | My Unfaithful Love/Happening After School | 1957 | 15.00 | 30.00 | 60.00 |

Liberty
☐ 55829		Road Runner/My Baby Don't Care	1965	3.75	7.50	15.00
☐ 55853		Smoke Rings/Little Boy Sad	1966	2.50	5.00	10.00
☐ 55884		Dr. Feelgood/Crackin' Up	1966	2.50	5.00	10.00
☐ 55903		I Want Your Lovin'/A Spoonful of Sugar	1966	2.50	5.00	10.00
☐ 55940		Greener Days/I Wonder	1967	2.50	5.00	10.00
☐ 55965		Drifter's Sunrise/Just a Good Show	1967	2.50	5.00	10.00

Statue
☐ 605		Road Runner/My Baby Don't Care	1965	12.50	25.00	50.00
☐ 608		What's Happening/Careless Hands	1965	6.25	12.50	25.00
		B-side by the Niteliters				

Garcia, Jerry
(Of the Grateful Dead)
Round
| ☐ 4504 | | Let It Rock/Midnight Town | 1974 | | 3.00 | 6.00 |

Warner Bros.
| ☐ 7551 | | Deal/The Wheel | 1972 | | 3.00 | 6.00 |
| ☐ 7569 | | Deep Hour/Sugaree | 1972 | | 3.00 | 6.00 |

Gardner, Don
(Also see "Gardner, Don, and Dee Dee Ford")
Bruce
☐ 105		How Do You Speak to an Angel/Sonotone Bounce	1954	15.00	30.00	60.00
☐ 108		I'll Walk Alone/Going Down Mary	1954	12.50	25.00	50.00
☐ 127		It's a Sin to Tell a Lie/I Hear a Rhapsody	1955	12.50	25.00	50.00

DeLuxe
| ☐ 6133 | | This Nearly Was Mine/A Dagger in My Chest | 1957 | 6.25 | 12.50 | 25.00 |
| ☐ 6155 | | There! I've Said It Again/I Don't Want to Go Home | 1958 | 6.25 | 12.50 | 25.00 |

Jubilee
☐ 5482		I Really Love You Baby/Talking About You	1964	2.50	5.00	10.00
☐ 5484		The Bitter with the Sweet/I Don't Know What I'm Gonna Do	1964	2.50	5.00	10.00
☐ 5493		Little Girl Blue/I'm In Such Misery	1964	2.50	5.00	10.00

Gardner, Don, and Dee Dee Ford
(Also see individual entries)
Fire
☐ 508		I Need Your Loving/Tell Me	1962	5.00	10.00	20.00
		Red label				
☐ 508		I Need Your Loving/Tell Me	1962	3.75	7.50	15.00
		Multicolor label				
☐ 513		Don't You Worry/I'm Coming Home to Stay	1962	3.75	7.50	15.00
☐ 517		Lead Me On/TCB (Taking Care of Business)	1962	3.75	7.50	15.00

KC
| ☐ 196 | | Glory of Love/'Deed I Do | 1963 | 3.00 | 6.00 | 12.00 |

Ludix
| ☐ 104 | | You Upset My Soul/Son My Son | 1963 | 3.00 | 6.00 | 12.00 |

Garfunkel, Art
(Of Simon and Garfunkel)
Columbia
| ☐ 02307 | | A Heart in New York/Is This Love | 1981 | | 2.00 | 4.00 |
| ☐ 02307 | PS | A Heart in New York/Is This Love | 1981 | | 2.00 | 4.00 |

Number		Title (A Side/B Side)	Year	VG	VG+	NM
❏ 02627		Bright Eyes/The Romance	1981		2.00	4.00
❏ 06590		Carol of the Birds/The Decree	1986			3.00
		With Amy Grant				
❏ 06590	PS	Carol of the Birds/The Decree	1986			3.00
❏ 07711		So Much in Love/King of Tonga	1988			3.00
❏ 07949		This Is the Moment/Slow Breakup	1988			3.00
❏ 08511		When a Man Loves a Woman/I Have a Love	1988			3.00
❏ 10020		Second Avenue/Woyaya	1974		2.50	5.00
		As "Garfunkel"				
❏ 10190		I Only Have Eyes for You/Looking for the Right One	1975		2.50	5.00
❏ 10274		Breakaway/Disney Girls	1975		2.50	5.00
❏ 10608		Crying in My Sleep/Mr. Shuck 'N' Jive	1977		2.50	5.00
❏ 10676		(What a) Wonderful World/Wooden Planes	1978		3.00	6.00
		A-side: Art Garfunkel with Paul Simon and James Taylor				
❏ 10933		In a Little While (I'll Be On My Way)/And I Know	1979		2.00	4.00
❏ 10999		Since I Don't Have You/	1979		2.00	4.00
		When Someone Doesn't Want You				
❏ 11050		Bright Eyes/Sail on a Rainbow	1979		2.00	4.00
❏ 45926		All I Know/Mary Was An Only Child	1973		2.50	5.00
		As "Garfunkel"				
❏ 45926		All I Know/Mary Was An Only Child	1973		2.50	5.00
		As "Art Garfunkel"				
❏ 45926	DJ	All I Know/Mary Was An Only Child	1973	2.50	5.00	10.00
		As "Art Garfunkel"; promo-only quadraphonic pressing with "SQ/Quad" on label				
❏ 45983		I Shall Sing/	1973		2.50	5.00
		Feuilles-Oh: Do Space Men Pass Dead Souls on Their Way to the Moon				
		As "Garfunkel"				
❏ 46030		Traveling Boy/Old Men	1974		2.50	5.00
		As "Garfunkel"				
Octavia						
❏ 8002		Forgive Me/Private World	1960	10.00	20.00	40.00
		As "Artie Garr"				
Warwick						
❏ 515		Beat Love/Dream Alone	1959	10.00	20.00	40.00
		As "Artie Garr"				

Garr, Artie - See "Garfunkel, Art"

Garrett, Scott
Laurie

❏ 3023		House of Love/So Far So Good	1959	5.00	10.00	20.00
❏ 3029		Love Story/Graduation Souvenir	1959	12.50	25.00	50.00
		With vocal backing by the Mystics				
❏ 3034		Where Are You/Jumpin' Blue Blazes	1959	5.00	10.00	20.00
Okeh						
❏ 7104		In My Heart/The Day I Died	1960	5.00	10.00	20.00

Garrison, Glen
Crest

❏ 1047	Lovin' Lorene/You're My Darling	1958	15.00	30.00	60.00
Imperial					
❏ 66191	Green to Blue/You Can't Win 'Em All	1966	2.50	5.00	10.00
❏ 66215	Where Do I Go from Here/	1966	2.50	5.00	10.00
	Strong and Handsome, Sweet and Simple Side				
❏ 66230	Listen, They're Playing My Song/My New Creation	1967	2.50	5.00	10.00
❏ 66257	Goodbye Swingers/Hello Mama	1967	2.50	5.00	10.00
❏ 66279	Your Side of Me/If I Lived Here (I'd Be Home Now)	1968	2.00	4.00	8.00
❏ 66300	I'll Be Your Baby Tonight/You Know I Love You	1968	2.00	4.00	8.00
❏ 66333	That Lucky Old Sun/She Thinks I Still Care	1968	2.00	4.00	8.00
❏ 66401	Goodnight Irene/Change Me	1969	2.00	4.00	8.00
Lode					
❏ 106	Pony Tail Girl/Ballad of Hank Gordon	1959	15.00	30.00	60.00

Gary and Clyde - See "Skip and Flip"

Gary and the Casuals
Vandan

❏ 609	My Own Desire/Someone Like You	1959	15.00	30.00	60.00

Gary and the Knight-Lites
(Later became The American Breed)
Bell

❏ 643	Lonely Soldier's Pledge/So Far Away from Home	1966	3.75	7.50	15.00
Nike					
❏ 1020	I'm Glad She's Mine/How Can I Forget Her	1963	10.00	20.00	40.00
Prima					
❏ 1016	I Can't Love You Anymore/Will You Go Steady	1963	25.00	50.00	100.00
Seeburg					
❏ 3016	Sweet Little Sixteen/Take Me Back	1965	6.25	12.50	25.00
❏ 3017	Bony Moronie/Glad You're Mine	1965	6.25	12.50	25.00
U.S.A.					
❏ 833	Big Bad Wolf/I Don't Need Your Help	1966	5.00	10.00	20.00

Number		Title (A Side/B Side)	Year	VG	VG+	NM

Gates, David
(Was in Bread, 1969-73 and again 1976-77. Also see "Manchesters, The")
Arista
| ❏ 0615 | | Take Me Now/It's What You Say | 1981 | | 2.00 | 4.00 |
| ❏ 0653 | | Come Home for Christmas/Lady Valentine | 1981 | | 2.50 | 5.00 |

Del-Fi
| ❏ 4206 | | No One Really Loves a Clown/ You Had It Comin' To Ya | 1963 | 6.25 | 12.50 | 25.00 |

EastWest
| ❏ 123 | | Walkin' and Talkin'/Swingin' Baby Doll | 1959 | 37.50 | 75.00 | 150.00 |

Elektra
❏ 45223		Never Let Her Go/Watch Out	1974		2.00	4.00
❏ 45245		Part-Time Love/Chain Me	1975		2.00	4.00
❏ 45450		Goodbye Girl/Sunday Rider	1977		2.00	4.00
❏ 45450	PS	Goodbye Girl/Sunday Rider	1977		2.50	5.00
		Version 1: Titles on both sides, no photo				
❏ 45450	PS	Goodbye Girl/Sunday Rider	1977		2.50	5.00
		Version 2: Titles on one side, photo on other side				
❏ 45500		Took the Last Train/Ann	1978		2.00	4.00
❏ 45857		Clouds/I Use the Soap	1973		2.00	4.00
❏ 45868		Sail Around the World/Help Is On the Way	1973		2.00	4.00
❏ 46588		Where Does the Lovin' Go/Starship Ride	1980		2.00	4.00
❏ 46646		Can I Call You/Chingo	1980		2.00	4.00
❏ 47011		Falling in Love Again/Sweet Desire	1980		2.00	4.00

Mala
❏ 413		You'll Be My Baby/What's This I Hear	1960	12.50	25.00	50.00
❏ 418		The Happiest Man Alive/A Road That Leads to Love	1960	12.50	25.00	50.00
❏ 427		Jo-Baby/Teardrops in My Heart	1961	12.50	25.00	50.00

Manchester
| ❏ 101 | | There's a Heaven/She Don't Cry | 196? | 10.00 | 20.00 | 40.00 |
| | | *As "Del Ashley"* | | | | |

Perspective
| ❏ (no #) | | Jo-Baby/Lovin' at Night | 1961 | 37.50 | 75.00 | 150.00 |

Planetary
❏ 103		Little Miss Stuck-Up/The Brighter Side	1965	6.25	12.50	25.00
		As "Del Ashley"				
❏ 108		Let You Go/Once Upon a Time	1965	5.00	10.00	20.00

Robbins
| ❏ 1008 | | Jo-Baby/Lovin' at Night | 1961 | 25.00 | 50.00 | 100.00 |

Gaye, Marvin
(His duets with Tammi Terrell, Mary Wells and Kim Weston are listed separately next. His duets with Diana Ross are listed after her section)
Columbia
❏ 03302		Sexual Healing/(Instrumental)	1982		2.00	4.00
❏ 03344		Sexual Healing	1982		3.00	6.00
		One-sided budget release				
❏ 03585		Sexual Healing/(Instrumental)	1983			3.00
		Reissue				
❏ 03589		'Til Tomorrow/Rockin' After Midnight	1983		2.00	4.00
❏ 03860		Joy/(Instrumental)	1983		2.00	4.00
❏ 03870		Star Spangled Banner/Turn On Some Music	1983			Unreleased?
❏ 03935		Joy/Turn On Some Music	1983		2.00	4.00
❏ 04861		Sanctified Lady/(Instrumental)	1985		2.00	4.00
❏ 05442		It's Madness/Ain't It Funny (How Things Turn Around)	1985		2.00	4.00
❏ 05791		Just Like/More	1986		2.00	4.00

Detroit Free Press
| ❏ (no #) | DJ | The Teen Beat Song/ Loraine Alterman Interviews Marvin Gaye | 1966 | 37.50 | 75.00 | 150.00 |

Tamla
❏ (no #)	DJ	Masquerade (Is Over)/Witchcraft	1962	150.00	300.00	600.00
		As "Marvin Gay"; label states "Single Not Available extracted from Album (TM-221)"				
❏ S4KM 0741/2	DJ	This Is the Life/My Way	1965	12.50	25.00	50.00
❏ 54041		Let Your Conscience Be Your Guide/Never Let You Go	1961	25.00	50.00	100.00
❏ 54055		Sandman/I'm Yours, You're Mine	1962	15.00	30.00	60.00
❏ 54062		Masquerade (Is Over)/Witchcraft	1962			Unreleased
❏ 54063		Soldier's Plea/Taking My Time	1962	12.50	25.00	50.00
		With label credit "Marvin Gaye"				
❏ 54063		Soldier's Plea/Taking My Time	1962	10.00	20.00	40.00
		With label credit "Marvin Gaye Love Tones"				
❏ 54068		Stubborn Kind of Fellow/It Hurts Me Too	1962	7.50	15.00	30.00
❏ 54075		Hitch Hike/Hello There Angel	1963	3.75	7.50	15.00
❏ 54079		Pride and Joy/One of These Days	1963	3.75	7.50	15.00
❏ 54087		Can I Get a Witness/I'm Crazy 'Bout My Baby	1963	3.75	7.50	15.00
❏ 54093		You're a Wonderful One/When I'm Alone I Cry	1964	3.75	7.50	15.00
❏ 54095		Try It Baby/If My Heart Could Sing	1964	3.75	7.50	15.00
❏ 54095	PS	Try It Baby/If My Heart Could Sing	1964	10.00	20.00	40.00
❏ 54101		Baby Don't You Do It/Walk on the Wild Side	1964	3.75	7.50	15.00
❏ 54101	PS	Baby Don't You Do It/Walk on the Wild Side	1964	10.00	20.00	40.00
❏ 54107		How Sweet It Is To Be Loved By You/Forever	1964	3.75	7.50	15.00
❏ 54112		I'll Be Doggone/You've Been a Long Time Coming	1965	3.75	7.50	15.00
❏ 54117		Pretty Little Baby/Now That You've Won Me	1965	3.75	7.50	15.00

Number		Title (A Side/B Side)	Year	VG	VG+	NM
☐ 54122		Ain't That Peculiar/She's Got to Be Real	1965	3.75	7.50	15.00
☐ 54129		One More Heartache/When I Had Your Love	1966	3.00	6.00	12.00
☐ 54132		Take This Heart of Mine/	1966	3.00	6.00	12.00
		Need Your Lovin' (Want You Back)				
☐ 54138		Little Darling, I Need You/Hey Diddle Diddle	1966	3.00	6.00	12.00
☐ 54153		Your Unchanging Love/I'll Take Care of You	1967	2.50	5.00	10.00
☐ 54160		You/Change What You Can	1967	2.50	5.00	10.00
☐ 54170		Chained/At Last I Found a Love	1968	2.50	5.00	10.00
☐ 54176		I Heard It Through the Grapevine/	1968	2.50	5.00	10.00
		You're What's Happening (In the World Today)				
☐ 54181		Too Busy Thinking About My Baby/	1969	2.00	4.00	8.00
		Wherever I Lay My Hat (That's My Home)				
☐ 54185		That's the Way Love Is/	1969	2.00	4.00	8.00
		Gonna Keep On Tryin' Till I Win Your Love				
☐ 54190		Gonna Give Her All the Love I've Got/	1970	2.00	4.00	8.00
		How Can I Forget You				
☐ 54195		The End of Our Road/Me and My Lonely Room	1970	2.00	4.00	8.00
☐ 54201		What's Going On/God Is Love	1971		3.00	6.00
☐ 54207		Mercy Mercy Me (The Ecology)/Sad Tomorrows	1971		3.00	6.00
☐ 54209		Inner City Blues (Make Me Wanna Holler)/Wholly Holy	1971		3.00	6.00
☐ 54221		You're the Man (Part 1)/You're the Man (Part 2)	1972		3.00	6.00
☐ 54228		Trouble Man/Don't Mess With Mister "T"	1972		3.00	6.00
☐ 54229		Christmas in the City/I Want to Go Home	1972			Unreleased
☐ 54234		Let's Get It On/I Wish It Would Rain	1973		2.00	4.00
☐ 54241		Come Get to This/Distant Lover	1973		2.00	4.00
☐ 54244		You Sure Love to Ball/Just to Keep You Satisfied	1974		2.00	4.00
☐ 54253		Distant Lover/Trouble Man	1974		2.00	4.00
☐ 54264		I Want You/I Want You (Instrumental)	1975		2.00	4.00
☐ 54273		After the Dance/Feel All My Love Inside	1976		2.00	4.00
☐ 54280		Got to Give It Up -- Pt. 1/Got to Give It Up -- Pt. 2	1977		2.00	4.00
☐ 54280	PS	Got to Give It Up -- Pt. 1/Got to Give It Up -- Pt. 2	1977	2.50	5.00	10.00
☐ 54298		Funky Space Reincarnation -- Pt. 1/	1979		2.00	4.00
		Funky Space Reincarnation -- Pt. 2				
☐ 54300		Time to Get It Together/Anger	1979	2.50	5.00	10.00
		Only released in Canada				
☐ 54305		Ego Tripping Out/(Instrumental)	1979		2.00	4.00
☐ 54322		Funk Me/Praise	1981		2.00	4.00
☐ 54326		Heavy Love Affair/Far Cry	1981		2.00	4.00

Topps/Motown

☐ 6		How Sweet It Is	1967	18.75	37.50	75.00
		Cardboard record				

Gaye, Marvin, and Tammi Terrell

Tamla

☐ 54149		Ain't No Mountain High Enough/Give a Little Love	1967	2.00	4.00	8.00
☐ 54156		Your Precious Love/Hold Me Oh My Darling	1967	2.00	4.00	8.00
☐ 54161		If I Could Build My Whole World Around You/	1967	2.00	4.00	8.00
		If This World Were Mine				
☐ 54163		Ain't Nothing Like the Real Thing/	1968	2.00	4.00	8.00
		Little Ole Boy, Little Ole Girl				
☐ 54169		You're All I Need to Get By/Two Can Have a Party	1968	2.00	4.00	8.00
☐ 54173		You Ain't Livin' Till You're Lovin'/	1968		3.00	6.00
		Keep On Lovin' Me Honey				
☐ 54179		Good Lovin' Ain't Easy to Come By/Satisfied Feelin'	1969		3.00	6.00
☐ 54187		What You Gave Me/How You Gonna Keep It	1969		3.00	6.00
☐ 54192		The Onion Song/California Soul	1970		3.00	6.00

Gaye, Marvin, and Mary Wells

Motown

☐ 1057		Once Upon a Time/What's the Matter with You Baby	1964	3.75	7.50	15.00
☐ 1057	PS	Once Upon a Time/What's the Matter with You Baby	1964	10.00	20.00	40.00

Gaye, Marvin, and Kim Weston

Tamla

☐ 54104		What Good Am I Without You/I Want You 'Round	1964	3.75	7.50	15.00
☐ 54141		It Takes Two/It's Got to Be a Miracle	1966	3.00	6.00	12.00

Gayles, The

ABC-Paramount

☐ 9707		Shortnin' Bread Rock/You Fool	1956	6.25	12.50	25.00

King

☐ 4846		My Boy, Flat Top/I Get So Happy	1955	5.00	10.00	20.00
☐ 4860		I Had to Love You/Too Late I Learned	1955	5.00	10.00	20.00

Gee Cees, The

Crest

☐ 1088		Buzz Saw/Annie Had a Party	1961	10.00	20.00	40.00
		Glen Campbell is on A-side; Eddie Cochran is on B-side. Also see "Kelly Four, The"				
☐ 1088		Buzz Saw Twist/Annie Had a Party	1962	7.50	15.00	30.00

Gene and Eunice

Aladdin

☐ 3276		Ko Ko Mo (I Need You So)/You and Me	1954	6.25	12.50	25.00
☐ 3282		This Is My Story/Move It Over Baby	1954	6.25	12.50	25.00
☐ 3292		Flim Flam/Can We Forget It	1954	6.25	12.50	25.00
☐ 3305		I Gotta Go Home/Have You Changed Your Mind	1954	6.25	12.50	25.00
☐ 3315		Hootchy Kootchy/I'll Never Believe in You	1955	5.00	10.00	20.00

Number		Title (A Side/B Side)	Year	VG	VG+	NM
❑ 3321		Let's Get Together/I'm So in Love with You	1955	5.00	10.00	20.00
❑ 3351		Bom Bom Lulu/Hi Diddle Diddle	1956	5.00	10.00	20.00
❑ 3374		The Vow/Strange World	1957	5.00	10.00	20.00
❑ 3376		Doodle Doodle Doo/Don't Treat Me This Way	1957	5.00	10.00	20.00
❑ 3414		I Mean Love/The Angels Gave You to Me	1958	5.00	10.00	20.00

Combo

Number		Title (A Side/B Side)	Year	VG	VG+	NM
❑ 64		Ko Ko Mo (I Need You So)/You and Me	1954	7.50	15.00	30.00

Lilly

| ❑ 512 | | Everlovin' Baby/Got a Right to Know | 1962 | 3.75 | 7.50 | 15.00 |

United Artists

| ❑ 0151 | | Ko Ko Mo (I Love You So)/This Is My Story | 1973 | | 2.00 | 4.00 |
| | | *"Silver Spotlight Series" reissue* | | | | |

Genesis

(Also see "Rutherford, Mike." Records on Mercury, Ripchord, Scepter and probably Buddah are different groups)

Atco

Number		Title (A Side/B Side)	Year	VG	VG+	NM
❑ 7013		The Lamb Lies Down on Broadway/Counting Out Time	1975	5.00	10.00	20.00
❑ 7050		Entangled/Ripples	1976	2.50	5.00	10.00
❑ 7076		Your Own Special Way/In That Quiet Earth	1977	2.50	5.00	10.00

Atlantic

❑ 3474		Follow You Follow Me/Inside and Out	1978		2.00	4.00
		A radically different mix than the LP version of A-side				
❑ 3511		Go West Young Man (In the Motherlode)/Scene from a Night's Dream	1978		2.00	4.00
❑ 3662		Misunderstanding/Behind the Lines	1980		2.00	4.00
❑ 3662	PS	Misunderstanding/Behind the Lines	1980		2.50	5.00
❑ 3751		Turn It On Again/Evidence of Autumn	1980		2.00	4.00
❑ 3858		No Reply At All/Heaven Love My Life	1981		2.00	4.00
❑ 3891		Abacab/Who Dunnit?	1982		2.00	4.00
❑ 3891	PS	Abacab/Who Dunnit?	1982		2.00	4.00
❑ 4025		Man on the Corner/Submarine	1982		2.00	4.00
❑ 4025	PS	Man on the Corner/Submarine	1982		2.00	4.00
❑ 4053		Paperlate/You Might Recall	1982		2.00	4.00
❑ 4053	PS	Paperlate/You Might Recall	1982		2.50	5.00
❑ 87481		Hold On My Heart/Way of the World	1992		2.00	4.00
❑ 87532		I Can't Dance/On the Shoreline	1992		2.00	4.00
❑ 87571		No Son of Mine/Living Forever	1991		2.00	4.00
❑ 89290		Tonight, Tonight, Tonight/In the Glow of the Night	1987			3.00
❑ 89290	PS	Tonight, Tonight, Tonight/In the Glow of the Night	1987		2.00	4.00
		Color sleeve				
❑ 89290	PS	Tonight, Tonight, Tonight/In the Glow of the Night	1987		2.50	5.00
		Black and white sleeve				
❑ 89316		In Too Deep/I'd Rather Be You	1987			3.00
❑ 89316	PS	In Too Deep/I'd Rather Be You	1987		2.00	4.00
❑ 89336		Land of Confusion/Feeding the Fire	1986			3.00
		Regular Atlantic red and black label				
❑ 89336		Land of Confusion/Feeding the Fire	1986	2.50	5.00	10.00
		Black label with different Atlantic logo				
❑ 89336	PS	Land of Confusion/Feeding the Fire	1986	2.50	5.00	10.00
		Sleeve came only with black-label versions				
❑ 89372		Throwing It All Away/Do the Neurotic	1986			3.00
❑ 89372	PS	Throwing It All Away/Do the Neurotic	1986			3.00
❑ 89407		Invisible Touch/The Last Domino	1986			3.00
❑ 89407	PS	Invisible Touch/The Last Domino	1986			3.00
❑ 89656		Taking It All Too Hard/Silver Rainbow	1984			3.00
❑ 89656	PS	Taking It All Too Hard/Silver Rainbow	1984			3.00
❑ 89698		Illegal Alien/Turn It On Again (Live in Philadelphia)	1984			3.00
❑ 89698	PS	Illegal Alien/Turn It On Again (Live in Philadelphia)	1984			3.00
❑ 89724		That's All/Second Home by the Sea	1983			3.00
❑ 89724	PS	That's All/Second Home by the Sea	1983		2.50	5.00
		Brown title sleeve with no center cut-out				
❑ 89724	PS	That's All/Second Home by the Sea	1983		2.00	4.00
		Brown title sleeve with center cut-out				
❑ 89770		Mama/It's Gonna Get Better	1983			3.00

Buddah

| ❑ 132 | | Journey to the Moon (Part 1)/Journey to the Moon (Part 2) | 1969 | 2.50 | 5.00 | 10.00 |

Charisma

| ❑ 103 | | Watcher of the Skies/Willow Farm | 1973 | 12.50 | 25.00 | 50.00 |
| ❑ 26002 | | I Know What I Like/Twilight Ale House | 1973 | 10.00 | 20.00 | 40.00 |

Mercury

| ❑ 72806 | | Angeline/Suzanne | 1968 | 2.50 | 5.00 | 10.00 |
| ❑ 72869 | | Gloomy Sunday/What's It All About | 1968 | 2.50 | 5.00 | 10.00 |

Parrot

| ❑ 3018 | DJ | Silent Sun/That's Me | 1968 | 25.00 | 50.00 | 100.00 |
| | | *May be promo only* | | | | |

Ripchord

| ❑ 004 | | Window of Sand/Would You Like To | 1967 | 2.50 | 5.00 | 10.00 |

Scepter

| ❑ 12341 | | Second Coming/Double Bubble | 1972 | | 2.50 | 5.00 |

Number		Title (A Side/B Side)	Year	VG	VG+	NM

Genteels, The
Capitol
| ❏ 4798 | | Take It Off/Hitchhiker | 1962 | 6.25 | 12.50 | 25.00 |

Stag
| ❏ 2930/1 | | Take It Off/Hitch Hiker | 1962 | 12.50 | 25.00 | 50.00 |
| ❏ 4949/ | 50 | The Force of Gravity/Springboard | 1962 | 12.50 | 25.00 | 50.00 |

Gentry, Ray
Maverick
| ❏ 614 | | Willie Was a Bad Boy/Do the Fly | 1958 | 100.00 | 200.00 | 400.00 |

Gentrys, The
Bell
❏ 720		You Better Come Home/I Can't Go Back to Denver	1968		3.00	6.00
❏ 740		Thinking Like a Child/Silky	1968		3.00	6.00
❏ 753		Midnight Train/You Tell Me You Care	1968		3.00	6.00

Capitol
| ❏ 3459 | | Changin'/Let Me Put This Ring Upon Your Finger | 1972 | | 2.50 | 5.00 |

Hit
| ❏ 229 | | Keep On Dancing/A Lover's Concerto | 1965 | 5.00 | 10.00 | 20.00 |
| | | B-side by Alpha Zoe | | | | |

MGM
❏ 13379		Keep On Dancing/Make Up Your Mind	1965	3.75	7.50	15.00
❏ 13432		Spread It On Thick/Brown Paper Bag	1965	3.00	6.00	12.00
❏ 13432	PS	Spread It On Thick/Brown Paper Bag	1965	4.00	8.00	16.00
❏ 13495		Everyday I Have to Cry/Don't Let It Be (This Time)	1966	3.00	6.00	12.00
❏ 13561		There Are Two Sides to Every Story/ Woman of the World	1966	3.00	6.00	12.00
❏ 13690		There's a Love/You Make Me Feel So Good	1967	6.25	12.50	25.00
❏ 13749		I Can See/90 Pound Weakling	1967	2.50	5.00	10.00

Stax
| ❏ 0223 | | All Hung Up on You/Little Gold Band | 1974 | | 2.00 | 4.00 |
| ❏ 0242 | | High Flyer/Little Gold Band | 1975 | | 2.00 | 4.00 |

Sun
❏ 1108		I Need Love/Why Should I Cry	1969		2.50	5.00
❏ 1114		Cinnamon Girl/I Just Got the News	1970		2.50	5.00
❏ 1114	DJ	Cinnamon Girl/I Just Got the News	1970	2.50	5.00	10.00
		Promo only on blue vinyl				
❏ 1118		I Hate to See You Go/He'll Never Love Me	1970		2.50	5.00
❏ 1120		Friends/Goddess of Love	1970		2.50	5.00
❏ 1122		Wild World/Sunshine	1971		2.50	5.00
❏ 1126		God Save Our Country/Love You All My Life	1971		2.50	5.00

Youngstown
| ❏ 600 | | Sometimes/Little Drops of Water | 1965 | 6.25 | 12.50 | 25.00 |
| ❏ 601 | | Keep On Dancing/Make Up Your Mind | 1965 | 7.50 | 15.00 | 30.00 |

George and Louis
Sun
❏ 301		The Return of Jerry Lee/Lewis Boogie	1958	7.50	15.00	30.00
		B-side by Jerry Lee Lewis				
❏ 301		The Return of Jerry Lee/The Return of Jerry Lee, Part 2	1958	6.25	12.50	25.00

George, Barbara
A.F.O.
| ❏ 302 | | I Know (You Don't Love Me No More)/Love | 1961 | 3.00 | 6.00 | 12.00 |
| ❏ 304 | | You Talk About Love/Whip-O-Will | 1962 | 2.50 | 5.00 | 10.00 |

Sue
❏ 763		If You Think/If When You've Done the Best You Can	1962	2.00	4.00	8.00
❏ 766		Send for Me (If You Need Some Lovin')/Bless You	1962	2.00	4.00	8.00
❏ 773		Recipe (For Perfect Fools)/Try Again	1962	2.00	4.00	8.00
❏ 796		Something's Definitely Wrong/(B-side unknown)	1963	2.50	5.00	10.00

United Artists
| ❏ XW516 | | I Know (You Don't Love Me No More)/Mockingbird | 1974 | | 2.00 | 4.00 |
| | | Reissue; B-side by Charles and Inez Foxx | | | | |

George, Lowell
(Of Little Feat)
Warner Bros.
| ❏ 8847 | | What Do You Want the Girl to Do/A Million Things | 1979 | | 2.50 | 5.00 |

Gerry and the Pacemakers
(Also see "Marsden, Gerry")
Laurie
❏ 3162		How Do You Do It/Away From You	1963	5.00	10.00	20.00
❏ 3196		I Like It/It Happened to Me	1963	5.00	10.00	20.00
❏ 3218		You'll Never Walk Alone/It's All Right	1964	5.00	10.00	20.00
❏ 3233		I'm the One/You've Got What I Like	1964	5.00	10.00	20.00
❏ 3233		I'm the One/It's All Right	1964	3.75	7.50	15.00
❏ 3251		Don't Let the Sun Catch You Crying/Away from You	1964	3.75	7.50	15.00
❏ 3261		How Do You Do It/You'll Never Walk Alone	1964	3.00	6.00	12.00
❏ 3271		I Like It/Jambalaya	1964	3.00	6.00	12.00
❏ 3279		I'll Be There/You, You, You	1964	3.00	6.00	12.00
❏ 3284		Ferry Cross the Mersey/Pretend	1965	3.00	6.00	12.00

Number	Title (A Side/B Side)	Year	VG	VG+	NM
❏ 3293	It's Gonna Be Alright/Skinny Minnie	1965	2.50	5.00	10.00
❏ 3302	You'll Never Walk Alone/Away from You	1965	2.50	5.00	10.00
❏ 3313	Give All Your Love to Me/You're the Reason	1965	2.50	5.00	10.00
❏ 3323	Dreams/Walk Hand in Hand	1965	2.50	5.00	10.00
❏ 3337	La La La/Without You	1966	2.50	5.00	10.00
❏ 3354	Girl on a Swing/The Way You Look Tonight	1966	2.50	5.00	10.00
❏ 3370	The Big Bright Green Pleasure Machine/Looking for My Life	1966	3.00	6.00	12.00

Gibson, Bobby, and the Voyagers
Gibson

❏ 6003	B-52/Samoa	1959	12.50	25.00	50.00

Gibson, Jill
Imperial

❏ 66068	It's as Easy as 1,2,3/Jilly's Flip Side	1964	15.00	30.00	60.00
	Produced by Jan Berry				

Gigolos, The
Broadway

❏ 1000	Movin' Out/Black and Blue	1961	7.50	15.00	30.00

Chess

❏ 1715	Luna Rock/La Companola	1959	7.50	15.00	30.00

Daynite

❏ 1	Swingin' Saints/Night Crawlers	1960	12.50	25.00	50.00

Enterprise

❏ 5000	Don't You Just Know It/Movin' Out	1965	3.75	7.50	15.00

Gilmer, Jimmy
(Also see "Fireballs, The")
Atco

❏ 6583	Three Squares (And a Place to Lay Your Head)/Baby	1968	2.00	4.00	8.00
❏ 6716	Sugar in the Woods/Model Child	1969	2.00	4.00	8.00

Decca

❏ 30942	Look Alive/Because I Need You	1959	6.25	12.50	25.00

Hamilton

❏ 50037	Won't Be Long/I'm Gonna Go Walkin'	1960	3.75	7.50	15.00

Warwick

❏ 592	Good Good Lovin'/Do You Think	1960	5.00	10.00	20.00

Gilmer, Jimmy, and the Fireballs - See "Fireballs, The"

Ginger
(Also see "Ginger and the Snaps"; "Honeys, The")
Titan

❏ 1717	Dry Tears/Spare Time	1961	25.00	50.00	100.00

Ginger and the Chiffons
Groove

❏ 58-0003	She/Where Were You Last Night	1963	7.50	15.00	30.00

Ginger and the Snaps
(Also see "Honeys, The")
MGM

❏ 13413	Growing Up Is Hard to Do/Seven Days in September	1965	37.50	75.00	150.00

Tore

❏ 1008	Love Me the Way That I Love You/Truly	1961	18.75	37.50	75.00

Gino and the Dells
Golden Crest

❏ 567	Altar of Dreams/Baby Don't Go Now	1962	75.00	150.00	300.00
❏ 576	We'll Make It Someday/I'm a Boy in Love	1963	10.00	20.00	40.00
❏ 581	It's Only a Paper Moon/Home Sweet Home	1963	10.00	20.00	40.00

Giordano, Lou
Brunswick

❏ 55115	Stay Close to Me/Don'Cha Know	1959	400.00	800.00	1,200
	With Buddy Holly on guitar				

Glad, The
(Timothy B. Schmit, later of Poco and the Eagles, was in this group)
ABC

❏ 11163	Johnny Silver's Ride/Love Needs the World	1969	3.00	6.00	12.00

Equinox

❏ 70004	See What You Mean/(B-side unknown)	1968	5.00	10.00	20.00
❏ 70006	A New Tomorrow/Pickin' Up the Pieces	1968	5.00	10.00	20.00

Gladiolas, The
(Maurice Williams was a member of this group)
Excello

❏ 2101	Little Darlin'/Sweetheart, Please Don't Go	1957	15.00	30.00	60.00
❏ 2110	Run, Run, Little Joe/Comin' Home to You	1957	12.50	25.00	50.00

Number		Title (A Side/B Side)	Year	VG	VG+	NM
☐ 2120		Hey Little Girl/I Wanta Know	1957	12.50	25.00	50.00
☐ 2136		Shoop Shoop/Say You'll Be Mine	1958	12.50	25.00	50.00

Glitter, Gary
Arista
| ☐ 0173 | | I Love You Love Me Love/Hands Up! It's a Stick-Up | 1976 | | 2.50 | 5.00 |

Bell
☐ 45,237		Rock and Roll, Part 2/Rock and Roll, Part 1	1972		3.00	6.00
☐ 45,276		I Didn't Know I Loved You (Till I Saw You Rock and Roll)/Shakey Sue	1972		2.50	5.00
☐ 45,326		Do You Wanna Touch Me (Oh Yeah)/ I Would If I Could But I Can't	1973		2.50	5.00
☐ 45,345		Baby Please Don't Go/I.O.U.	1973		2.50	5.00
☐ 45,375		Come On, Come In/Happy Birthday	1973		2.50	5.00
☐ 45,398		(I'm the) Leader of the Gang (I Am)/(B-side unknown)	1973		2.50	5.00
☐ 45,438		I Love You Love Me Love/(B-side unknown)	1974		2.50	5.00

Decca
| ☐ 32714 | | Goodbye Seattle/Wait for Me | 1970 | 3.75 | 7.50 | 15.00 |
| | | *As "Paul Raven"* | | | | |

Tommy Boy
| ☐ 639 | | Rock 'N' Roll Part 2...The Hey Song (same on both sides) | 1995 | | | 3.00 |
| | | *Original recording with overdubbed crowd sounds* | | | | |

Globetrotters
Kirshner
☐ 63-5006		Cheer Me Up/Gravy	1970	3.00	6.00	12.00
☐ 63-5006	PS	Cheer Me Up/Gravy	1970	3.75	7.50	15.00
☐ 63-5008		Rainy Day Bells/Meadowlark	1970	3.75	7.50	15.00
☐ 63-5012		Duke of Earl/Everybody's Got Hot Pants	1971	3.00	6.00	12.00
☐ 63-5016		Everybody Needs Love/ESP	1971	3.00	6.00	12.00

Glorytones, The
Epic
| ☐ 9243 | | You Only Came Back to Hurt Me/ Was That the Right Thing to Do | 1957 | 10.00 | 20.00 | 40.00 |

Glowtones, The
Atlantic
| ☐ 1156 | | The Girl I Love/Ping Pong | 1957 | | | |
| | | *Only known on 78 rpm; 45 rpm release was on EastWest 101* | | | | |

EastWest
| ☐ 101 | | The Girl I Love/Ping Pong | 1957 | 7.50 | 15.00 | 30.00 |

Go-Go's, The
(No relation to the 1980s girl group)
RCA Victor
| ☐ 47-8370 | | Lonely Girl/Chicken of the Sea | 1964 | 3.75 | 7.50 | 15.00 |
| ☐ 47-8435 | | The Wild One/Saturday's Hero | 1964 | 7.50 | 15.00 | 30.00 |

Gold Bugs, The
Coral
| ☐ 62453 | | Stop That Wedding/It's So Nice | 1965 | 10.00 | 20.00 | 40.00 |

Goldberg-Miller Blues Band
("Miller" is Steve Miller)
Epic
☐ 9865		More Soul Than Soulful/Mother Song	1965	3.75	7.50	15.00
☐ 9865	DJ	More Soul Than Soulful/Mother Song	1965	6.25	12.50	25.00
		Promo only on blue vinyl				
☐ 9865	PS	More Soul Than Soulful/Mother Song	1965	12.50	25.00	50.00
		Promo only				
☐ 10033		Ginger Man/Whole Lotta Shakin' Goin' On	1966	3.75	7.50	15.00

Golden Nuggets, The
Futura
| ☐ 1691 | | I Was a Fool/Teenage Josephine | 1959 | 150.00 | 300.00 | 600.00 |

Hawk
| ☐ 107/8 | | Surf Everybody/Everybody Bird | 1963 | 10.00 | 20.00 | 40.00 |

Goldenrods, The
Vee Jay
| ☐ 307 | | Wish I Was Back in School/Color Cartoons | 1959 | 62.50 | 125.00 | 250.00 |

Goldie, Dan
Teardrop
| ☐ 3070 | | Take Our Last Walk Tonight/Walking the Streets | 1966 | 6.25 | 12.50 | 25.00 |
| | | *The Sir Douglas Quintet is the backing band* | | | | |

Goldtones, The
A&R
| ☐ 714 | | Strike/Gutterball | 1963 | 7.50 | 15.00 | 30.00 |
| ☐ 714 | PS | Strike/Gutterball | 1963 | 12.50 | 25.00 | 50.00 |

Number		Title (A Side/B Side)	Year	VG	VG+	NM

Golliwogs, The
(Early Creedence Clearwater Revival)
Fantasy
❏ 590		Don't Tell Me No Lies/	1964	15.00	30.00	60.00
		Little Girl, Does Your Mama Know				
❏ 597		Where You Been/You Came Walking	1965	15.00	30.00	60.00
❏ 599		You Got Nothin' on Me/You Can't Be True	1965	12.50	25.00	50.00

Scorpio
❏ 404		Brown Eyed Girl/You Better Be Careful	1967	12.50	25.00	50.00
❏ 405		Fragile Child/Fight Fire	1967	12.50	25.00	50.00
❏ 408		Walking on the Water/	1967	12.50	25.00	50.00
		You Better Get It Before It Gets You				
❏ 412	DJ	Porterville/Call It Pretending	1968	15.00	30.00	60.00

Only promos credit the Golliwogs; all known stock copies credit "Creedence Clearwater Revival"

Gone All Stars
Gone
| ❏ 5016 | | 7-11/Down Yonder Rock | 1957 | 6.25 | 12.50 | 25.00 |

Gonn
Emir
| ❏ 9217 | | Blackout of Gretley/Pain in My Heart | 1966 | 100.00 | 200.00 | 400.00 |

Emir/MCCM
❏ 88-9217		Blackout of Gretley/Pain in My Heart	1988	3.75	7.50	15.00
		Colored vinyl				
❏ 88-9217		Blackout of Gretley/Pain in My Heart	1988		2.50	5.00
		Black vinyl				

Merry Jaine
| ❏ 2318 | | You're Looking Fine/Come with Me | 1967 | 25.00 | 50.00 | 100.00 |

Goobers, The
Surf
| ❏ 1001 | | Hawaiian Holiday/Buyer Beware | 1963 | 12.50 | 25.00 | 50.00 |

Good, Tommy
Gordy
| ❏ 7034 | | Baby I Miss You/Leaving Here | 1964 | 10.00 | 20.00 | 40.00 |

Goodman, Dickie
(King of break-in records. Also see "Buchanan and Goodman")
ASI
| ❏ 1013 | | Rocky and the Angel/Pug Rock | 1977 | | 3.00 | 6.00 |
| | | *As "Dickie G. and the Don'ts"* | | | | |

Audio Spectrum
| ❏ 75 | | Presidential Interview (Flying Saucer '64)/ | 1964 | 10.00 | 20.00 | 40.00 |
| | | Paul Revere | | | | |

Cash
| ❏ 451 | | Mr. Jaws/Irv's Theme | 1975 | | 2.50 | 5.00 |

Cotique
❏ 158		On Campus/Mombo Suzie	1969		3.00	6.00
		B-side by Johnny Colo				
❏ 173		Luna Trip/My Victrola	1969		3.00	6.00
		B-side by Joey Pastrana				

Davy Jones
| ❏ 663 | | White House Happening/President Johnson | 1967 | 6.25 | 12.50 | 25.00 |
| ❏ 663 | PS | White House Happening/President Johnson | 1967 | 10.00 | 20.00 | 40.00 |

Diamond
| ❏ 119 | | Ben Crazy/Flip Side | 1962 | 3.75 | 7.50 | 15.00 |

Extran
| ❏ 601 | | Hey, E.T./Get a Job | 1982 | | 2.50 | 5.00 |

Goodname
| ❏ 7100 | | Safe Sex Report/Safety First | 1987 | 3.75 | 7.50 | 15.00 |
| | | *His last record* | | | | |

Hot Line
| ❏ 1017 | | Energy Crisis '79/Pain | 1979 | | 3.00 | 6.00 |

J.M.D.
| ❏ 001 | | Ben Crazy/Flip Side | 1962 | 6.25 | 12.50 | 25.00 |

Janus
| ❏ 271 | | Star Warts/The Boys Tune | 1977 | | 2.50 | 5.00 |

M.D.
| ❏ 101 | | Schmonanza/Backwards Theme | 1961 | 5.00 | 10.00 | 20.00 |

Mark-X
❏ 8009		The Touchables/Martian Melody	1961	7.50	15.00	30.00
		Yellow label				
❏ 8009		The Touchables/Martian Melody	1961	5.00	10.00	20.00
		Black label				
❏ 8010		The Touchables in Brooklyn/Mystery	1961	5.00	10.00	20.00

Number		Title (A Side/B Side)	Year	VG	VG+	NM
Montage						
❑ 1220		Hey, E.T./The Ride of Paul Revere	1982	3.75	7.50	15.00
❑ 1220	DJ	Hey, E.T. (same on both sides)	1982		2.50	5.00
Prelude						
❑ 8018		Election '80 (same on both sides)	1980		2.50	5.00
Rainy Wednesday						
❑ 202		Watergate/Friends	1973		3.00	6.00
❑ 204		Purple People Eater/Ruthie's Socks	1973		3.00	6.00
❑ 205		The Constitution/The End	1973		3.00	6.00
❑ 206		Energy Crisis '74/Ruthie's Theme	1974	2.00	4.00	8.00
❑ 206		Energy Crisis '74/The Mistake	1974		3.00	6.00
❑ 207		Mr. President/Popularity	1974		3.00	6.00
❑ 208		Gerry Ford, A Special Report/Robert	1974		3.00	6.00
❑ 209		Inflation in the Nation/Jon and Jed's Theme	1975		3.00	6.00
Ramgo						
❑ 501		Speaking of Ecology/Dayton's Theme	1970	6.25	12.50	25.00
Red Bird						
❑ 10-058		Batman & His Grandmother/Suspense	1966	5.00	10.00	20.00
Rhino						
❑ 019		Radio Russia/Washington Inside Out	1984		2.00	4.00
Rori						
❑ 601		Horror Movies/Whoa, Mule	1961	6.25	12.50	25.00
❑ 602		The Berlin Top Ten/Little Tiger	1961	6.25	12.50	25.00
❑ 701		Santa and the Touchables/North Pole Rock	1961	6.25	12.50	25.00
Scepter						
❑ 12339		Speaking of Ecology/Dayton's Theme	1971	3.00	6.00	12.00
Shark						
❑ 1001		Mrs. Jaws/(B-side unknown)	1979	5.00	10.00	20.00
❑ 1002		Super Superman/(B-side unknown)	1979	3.75	7.50	15.00
Shell						
❑ 711		Election '84/Herb's Theme	1984		2.00	4.00
Shock						
❑ 6		Kong/Ed's Tune	1977		2.50	5.00
20th Fox						
❑ 443		Senate Hearing/Lock-Up	1963	3.75	7.50	15.00
Twirl						
❑ 2015		James Bomb/Seventh Theme	1966	3.75	7.50	15.00
Wacko						
❑ 1001		Mr. President/Dancin' U.S.A.	1981		2.50	5.00
❑ 1002		Super-Duper Man/Robert's Tune	1981		2.50	5.00
❑ 1381		America '81/(B-side unknown)	1981	2.00	4.00	8.00
Z-100						
❑ 100	DJ	Attack of the Z Monster/Mystery	1984	2.50	5.00	10.00
		Promo item for New York radio station				

Goodman, Shirley
(Of Shirley and Lee; also of Shirley [and Company])

Imperial						
❑ 5944		When a Boy Meets a Girl/Don't Marry Too Soon	1963	3.00	6.00	12.00

Goodtimers, The - See "Covay, Don"

Gordon, Mike, and the Agates

Dore						
❑ 681		Rumble at Newport Beach/Last Call for Dinner	1963	7.50	15.00	30.00
❑ 780		Curfew on the Strip/Last Call for Dinner	1966	3.75	7.50	15.00

Gordon, Mike, and the El Tempos

Cat						
❑ 101		Why Don't You Do Right/You Got to Give	1954	12.50	25.00	50.00

Gordon, Roscoe

ABC-Paramount						
❑ 10351		A Girl to Love/As You Walk Away	1962	3.00	6.00	12.00
❑ 10407		A Little Bit of Magic/I Want Revenge	1963	3.00	6.00	12.00
❑ 10501		I Don't Stand a Chance/That's What You Did	1963	3.00	6.00	12.00
		As "Barbara & Roscoe Gordon"				
Calla						
❑ 145		Just a Little Bit/I Really Love You	1968	2.00	4.00	8.00
Chess						
❑ 1487		Booted/I Love You Till the Day I Die	1951	75.00	150.00	300.00
Duke						
❑ 101		Tell Daddy/Hey Fat Girl	1952	25.00	50.00	100.00
❑ 106		T-Model Boogie/New Orleans Woman	1953	12.50	25.00	50.00
❑ 109		Too Many Women/Wise to You, Baby	1953	12.50	25.00	50.00
❑ 114		Ain't No Use/Roscoe's Mambo	1953	12.50	25.00	50.00
❑ 129		Three Can't Love/You Figure It Out	1954	12.50	25.00	50.00
❑ 165		Keep On Doggin'/Bad Dream	1957	7.50	15.00	30.00
❑ 173		I've Loved and Lost/Tummer Tee	1957	7.50	15.00	30.00
❑ 320		Dilly Bop/You'll Never Know	1960	3.75	7.50	15.00

Number		Title (A Side/B Side)	Year	VG	VG+	NM
Flip						
❑ 227		Weeping Blues/Just Love Me, Baby	1956	75.00	150.00	300.00
❑ 237		The Chicken (Dance with You)/Love for You Baby	1956	12.50	25.00	50.00
Old Town						
❑ 1167		Gotta Keep Rollin'/Just a Little at a Time	1964	2.50	5.00	10.00
❑ 1175		It Ain't Right/Could This Be Love	1965	2.50	5.00	10.00
		As "Roscoe and Barbara"				
RPM						
❑ 324		Saddled the Cow/Ouch, Pretty Baby	1951	100.00	200.00	400.00
❑ 336		Dime a Dozen/A New Remedy for Love	1951	62.50	125.00	250.00
❑ 344		Booted/Cold, Cold Winter	1952	25.00	50.00	100.00
❑ 350		No More Doggin'/Maria	1952	20.00	40.00	80.00
❑ 358		New Orleans Woman/I Remember Your Kisses	1952	20.00	40.00	80.00
❑ 365		What You Got on Your Mind/Two Kinds of Women	1952	20.00	40.00	80.00
❑ 369		Trying/Dream Baby	1952	15.00	30.00	60.00
❑ 373		Lucille/Blues for My Baby	1953	15.00	30.00	60.00
❑ 379		I'm in Love/Just In from Texas	1953	15.00	30.00	60.00
❑ 384		We're All Loaded/Tomorrow May Be Too Late	1953	15.00	30.00	60.00
Sun						
❑ 227		Weeping Blues/Just Love Me, Baby	1956	125.00	250.00	500.00
❑ 237		The Chicken (Dance with You)/Love for You Baby	1956	50.00	100.00	200.00
❑ 257		Shoobie Oobie/Cheese and Crackers	1956	12.50	25.00	50.00
❑ 305		Sally Jo/Torro	1958	6.25	12.50	25.00
Vee Jay						
❑ 316		A Fool in Love/No More Doggin'	1959	3.75	7.50	15.00
❑ 332		Just a Little Bit/Goin' Home	1959	3.75	7.50	15.00
❑ 348		Surely I Love You/What You Do to Me	1960	3.75	7.50	15.00
❑ 385		What I Wouldn't Do/Let 'Em Try	1961	3.00	6.00	12.00

Gore, Lesley

Number		Title (A Side/B Side)	Year	VG	VG+	NM
A&M						
❑ 1710		Give It to Me, Sweet Thing/Immortality	1975		2.50	5.00
❑ 1710	PS	Give It to Me, Sweet Thing/Immortality	1975		3.00	6.00
❑ 1830		Sometimes/Give It To Me, Sweet Thing	1976		2.50	5.00
Crewe						
❑ 338		Why Doesn't Love Make Me Happy/ Tomorrow's Children	1970	2.50	5.00	10.00
❑ 344		When Yesterday Was Tomorrow/Why Me, Why You	1970	2.50	5.00	10.00
❑ 601		Back Together/Quiet Love	1971	2.50	5.00	10.00
Manhattan						
❑ 50039		Since I Don't Have You-It's Only Make Believe/ Our Love Was Meant to Be	1986	2.00	4.00	8.00
		With Lou Christie				
Mercury						
❑ 72119		It's My Party/Danny	1963	3.00	6.00	12.00
❑ 72119	PS	It's My Party/Danny	1963	5.00	10.00	20.00
❑ 72143		Judy's Turn to Cry/Just Let Me Cry	1963	3.00	6.00	12.00
❑ 72143	PS	Judy's Turn to Cry/Just Let Me Cry	1963	5.00	10.00	20.00
❑ 72180		She's a Fool/The Old Crowd	1963	3.00	6.00	12.00
❑ 72180	PS	She's a Fool/The Old Crowd	1963	5.00	10.00	20.00
❑ 72206		You Don't Own Me/Run, Bobby, Run	1963	3.00	6.00	12.00
❑ 72206	PS	You Don't Own Me/Run, Bobby, Run	1963	5.00	10.00	20.00
❑ 72245		Je Ne Sais Plus/Je N'ose Pas	1964	5.00	10.00	20.00
❑ 72259		That's the Way Boys Are/ That's the Way the Ball Bounces	1964	2.50	5.00	10.00
❑ 72259	PS	That's the Way Boys Are/ That's the Way the Ball Bounces	1964	5.00	10.00	20.00
❑ 72270		I Don't Wanna Be a Loser/It's Gotta Be You	1964	2.50	5.00	10.00
❑ 72270	PS	I Don't Wanna Be a Loser/It's Gotta Be You	1964	5.00	10.00	20.00
❑ 72309		Maybe I Know/Wonder Boy	1964	2.50	5.00	10.00
❑ 72309	PS	Maybe I Know/Wonder Boy	1964	5.00	10.00	20.00
❑ 72352		Hey Now/Sometimes I Wish I Were a Boy	1964	2.50	5.00	10.00
❑ 72352	PS	Hey Now/Sometimes I Wish I Were a Boy	1964	5.00	10.00	20.00
❑ 72372		Look of Love/Little Girl Gone Home	1964	2.50	5.00	10.00
❑ 72372	PS	Look of Love/Little Girl Gone Home	1964	5.00	10.00	20.00
❑ 72412		All of My Life/I Cannot Hope for Anything	1965	2.50	5.00	10.00
❑ 72412	PS	All of My Life/I Cannot Hope for Anything	1965	5.00	10.00	20.00
❑ 72433		Sunshine, Lollipops and Rainbows/ You've Come Back	1965	2.50	5.00	10.00
❑ 72433	PS	Sunshine, Lollipops and Rainbows/ You've Come Back	1965	5.00	10.00	20.00
❑ 72475		My Town, My Guy and Me/Girl in Love	1965	2.50	5.00	10.00
❑ 72475	PS	My Town, My Guy and Me/Girl in Love	1965	5.00	10.00	20.00
❑ 72513		I Won't Love You Anymore (Sorry)/ No Matter What You Do	1966	2.50	5.00	10.00
❑ 72513	PS	I Won't Love You Anymore (Sorry)/ No Matter What You Do	1966	5.00	10.00	20.00
❑ 72530		We Know We're in Love/That's What We'll Do	1966	2.50	5.00	10.00
❑ 72553		Young Love/I Just Don't Know If I Can	1966	2.50	5.00	10.00
❑ 72580		Off and Running/I Don't Care	1966	2.50	5.00	10.00
❑ 72611		Maybe Now/Treat Me Like a Lady	1966	2.50	5.00	10.00
❑ 72649		California Nights/I'm Goin' Out	1967	2.50	5.00	10.00
❑ 72649	PS	California Nights/I'm Goin' Out	1967	5.00	10.00	20.00
❑ 72683		Summer and Sandy/I'm Fallin' Down	1967	2.50	5.00	10.00
❑ 72683	PS	Summer and Sandy/I'm Fallin' Down	1967	5.00	10.00	20.00
❑ 72726		Brink of Disaster/On a Day Like This	1967	2.50	5.00	10.00

Number	Title (A Side/B Side)	Year	VG	VG+	NM
❏ 72759	It's a Happening/Magic Colors	1967	2.50	5.00	10.00
❏ 72787	Small Talk/Say What You See	1968	3.00	6.00	12.00
❏ 72819	He Gives Me Love (La, La, La)/Brand New Me	1968	3.00	6.00	12.00
❏ 72842	Where Can I Go/I Can't Make It Without You	1968	3.00	6.00	12.00
❏ 72867	Look the Other Way/I'll Be Standing By	1968	3.00	6.00	12.00
❏ 72892	Take Good Care (Of My Heart)/ I Can't Make It Without You	1969	3.00	6.00	12.00
❏ 72892	Take Good Care (Of My Heart)/ You Sent Me Silver Bells	1969	3.00	6.00	12.00
❏ 72931	Summer Symphony/98.6-Lazy Day	1969	3.75	7.50	15.00
❏ 72969	Wedding Bell Blues/One by One	1969	3.75	7.50	15.00
Mowest					
❏ 5029	The Road I Walk/She Said That	1972	2.50	5.00	10.00
❏ 5042	Give It to Me, Sweet Thing/Don't Want to Be One	1973			*Unreleased*

Gospel Stars, The
Tamla
❏ 54037	He Lifted Me/Behold the Saints of God	1961	15.00	30.00	60.00
	Globe logo				
❏ 54037	He Lifted Me/Behold the Saints of God	1961	37.50	75.00	150.00
	Horizontal lines logo				

Gotham City Crime Fighters, The
Batwing
❏ 1001	Who Stole the Batmobile/That's Life	1966	7.50	15.00	30.00

Gouldman, Graham
(Member of 10CC)
A&M
❏ 2251	Away from It All/Bionic Boar	1980		2.00	4.00
RCA Victor
❏ 47-9453	Impossible Years/No Milk Today	1968	3.00	6.00	12.00
❏ 47-9584	For Your Love/Pamela, Pamela	1968	3.00	6.00	12.00

Gowens, Sammy
United Artists
❏ 114	Kissin' at the Drive-In/Rockin' By Myself	1958	25.00	50.00	100.00

Gracie, Charlie
Cameo
❏ 105	Butterfly/Ninety-Nine Ways	1957	6.25	12.50	25.00
❏ 107	Fabulous/Just Lookin'	1957	5.00	10.00	20.00
❏ 111	I Love You So Much It Hurts/Wandering Eyes	1957	5.00	10.00	20.00
❏ 118	Cool Baby/You've Got a Heart Like a Rock	1957	5.00	10.00	20.00
❏ 127	Crazy Girl/Dressin' Up	1958	5.00	10.00	20.00
❏ 141	Love Bird/Trying	1958	5.00	10.00	20.00
Coral
❏ 62073	Hurry Up Buttercup/Doodlebug	1959	3.75	7.50	15.00
❏ 62115	Angel of Love/I'm a Fool, That's Why	1959	3.75	7.50	15.00
❏ 62141	Oh-Well-a/Because I Love You So	1959	3.75	7.50	15.00
Diamond
| ❏ 178 | He'll Never Love You Like I Do/
Keep My Love Next to Your Heart | 1965 | 6.25 | 12.50 | 25.00 |
Felsted
| ❏ 8629 | W-Wow/Makin' Whoopee | 1961 | 3.75 | 7.50 | 15.00 |
President
| ❏ 825 | Pretty Baby/Night and Day U.S.A. | 1962 | 3.75 | 7.50 | 15.00 |
| ❏ 828 | Count to Three/Just Like Us | 1963 | 3.75 | 7.50 | 15.00 |
Roulette
| ❏ 4255 | I Look for You/The Race | 1960 | 3.75 | 7.50 | 15.00 |
| ❏ 4312 | Sorry for You/Scenery | 1960 | 3.75 | 7.50 | 15.00 |
20th Century
| ❏ 5033 | Head Home, Honey/My Baby Loves Me | 1955 | 12.50 | 25.00 | 50.00 |
| ❏ 5035 | Honey Honey/Wildwood Boogie | 1955 | 15.00 | 30.00 | 60.00 |

Graduates, The
Corsican
❏ 0058	What Good Is Graduation/Lonely	1959	10.00	20.00	40.00
GNP Crescendo
| ❏ 404 | (The Shape of) Things to Come/Listen to the Music | 1968 | 2.50 | 5.00 | 10.00 |
Lawn
| ❏ 208 | Ballad of a Girl and Boy/Goodbye My Love | 1963 | 5.00 | 10.00 | 20.00 |
Rising Sons
| ❏ 712 | If Ever I Get Out of This Mess I'm In/
Seventh Generation Breakthrough | 1968 | 7.50 | 15.00 | 30.00 |
Shan-Todd
| ❏ 0055 | Ballad of a Girl and Boy/Care | 1959 | 7.50 | 15.00 | 30.00 |

Granahan, Gerry
(Also see "Dickey Doo and the Don'ts")
Atco
❏ 6122	Sweet Affection/Confess It to Your Heart	1958	7.50	15.00	30.00

Number		Title (A Side/B Side)	Year	VG	VG+	NM

Canadian American

❑ 116		When Irish Eyes Are Smiling/In My Heart	1960	5.00	10.00	20.00
❑ 119		You'll Never Walk Alone/Where's the Girl	1960	5.00	10.00	20.00
❑ 121		Short Skirts/I'm Afraid You'll Never Know	1960	5.00	10.00	20.00

Caprice

❑ 106		Unchained Melody/Dancing Man	1961	5.00	10.00	20.00
❑ 108		Too Big for Her Bikini/Dance, Girl, Dance	1961	25.00	50.00	100.00

With backing by the Belmonts or the Five Satins (sources disagree)

Gone

❑ 5065		Let the Rumors Fly/Put Me Anywhere	1959	5.00	10.00	20.00
❑ 5081		It Hurts/Look for Me	1959	5.00	10.00	20.00

Mark

❑ 121		Love's Young Dream/Oh Well-A Watch-A Gonna Do	1957	8.75	17.50	35.00

Sunbeam

❑ 102		No Chemise, Please/Girl of My Dreams	1958	7.50	15.00	30.00
❑ 108		Baby Wait/Completely	1958	6.25	12.50	25.00
❑ 112		I'm Ready As I'll Ever Be/Nobody Can Handle This Job	1958	6.25	12.50	25.00

B-side by Eddie Fontaine

❑ 122		King Size/I'm Afraid You'll Never Know	1958	6.25	12.50	25.00
❑ 127		A Ring, a Bracelet, a Heart/You're Adorable	1959	6.25	12.50	25.00

20th Fox

❑ 425		Hang Up the Phone/Too Weak to Win	1963	3.75	7.50	15.00
❑ 541		Racing Fever: Title/Racing Fever: Mainstream	1964	3.75	7.50	15.00

B-side by Arnold Goland and His Orchestra

Veep

❑ 1205		All the Live-Long Day/Sophia	1965	3.00	6.00	12.00

Grant, Janie

Caprice

❑ 104		Triangle/She's Going Steady with You	1961	3.75	7.50	15.00
❑ 109		Romeo/Roller Coaster	1961	3.75	7.50	15.00
❑ 111		I Wonder Who's Kissing You Now/Unhappy	1961	3.75	7.50	15.00
❑ 113		Oh Johnny/Oh My Love	1962	3.75	7.50	15.00
❑ 115		That Greasy Kid Stuff/Trying to Forget You	1962	3.75	7.50	15.00
❑ 119		Peggy Got Engaged/	1962	3.75	7.50	15.00
		Two Is Company and Three's a Crowd				

Parkway

❑ 982		My Heart, Your Heart/And That Reminds Me of You	1966	7.50	15.00	30.00

United Artists

❑ 616		Tell Me Mama/Whose Heart Are You Breaking Now	1963	3.00	6.00	12.00
❑ 649		That Kind of Boy/Priceless Persuasion	1963	3.00	6.00	12.00
❑ 731		Ribbons and Roses/Too Young for Me	1964	3.00	6.00	12.00
❑ 775		After Last Night/All I Did Was Fall in Love	1964	3.00	6.00	12.00
❑ 843		I Shouldn't Care (If You're Using Me)/	1965	3.00	6.00	12.00
		There Ain't No Party Tonight				

Grass Roots, The

(Early records on Dunhill were by P.F. Sloan and Steve Barri. Starting with 4084, a real group called The Grass Roots recorded these. Also see "Grill, Rob.")

ABC Dunhill

❑ 4144		Midnight Confessions/Who Will You Be Tomorrow	1968	2.00	4.00	8.00
❑ 4162		Della Linda/Hot Bright Blues	1968	3.00	6.00	12.00
		Some labels have A-side typographical error as shown				
❑ 4162		Bella Linda/Hot Bright Blues	1968	2.00	4.00	8.00
❑ 4180		Lovin' Things/You and Love Are the Same	1969	2.00	4.00	8.00
❑ 4187		The River Is Wide/(You Gotta) Live for Love	1969	2.00	4.00	8.00
❑ 4198		I'd Wait a Million Years/Fly Me to Havana	1969		3.00	6.00
❑ 4217		Heaven Knows/Don't Remind Me	1969		3.00	6.00
❑ 4227		Walking Through the Country/Truck Drivin' Man	1970		3.00	6.00
❑ 4237		Baby Hold On/Get It Together	1970		3.00	6.00
❑ 4237	PS	Baby Hold On/Get It Together	1970	2.50	5.00	10.00
❑ 4249		Come On and Say It/Something's Comin' Over Me	1970		3.00	6.00
❑ 4249	PS	Come On and Say It/Something's Comin' Over Me	1970	2.50	5.00	10.00
❑ 4263		Temptation Eyes/Keepin' Me Down	1971		2.50	5.00
❑ 4279		Sooner or Later/I Can Turn Off the Rain	1971		2.50	5.00
❑ 4289		Two Divided by Love/Let It Go	1971		2.50	5.00
❑ 4302		Glory Bound/The Only One	1972		2.50	5.00
❑ 4316		The Runway/Move Along	1972		2.50	5.00
❑ 4325		Any Way the Wind Blows/Monday Love	1972		2.50	5.00
❑ 4335		Love Is What You Make It/Someone to Love	1973		3.00	6.00
❑ 4345		Where There's Smoke There's Fire/	1973	2.50	5.00	10.00
		Look but Don't Touch				
❑ 4371		We Can't Dance to Your Music/Look but Don't Touch	1973	2.50	5.00	10.00
❑ 15006		Stealin' Love (In the Night)/	1974	3.75	7.50	15.00
		We Almost Made It Together				

Dunhill

❑ 4013		Mr. Jones (A Ballad of a Thin Man)/You're a Lonely Girl	1965	5.00	10.00	20.00
❑ 4029		Where Were You When I Needed You/	1966	3.75	7.50	15.00
		(These Are) Bad Times				
❑ 4043		Only When You're Lonely/	1966	5.00	10.00	20.00
		This Is What I Was Made For				
❑ 4053		Tip of My Tongue/Look Out, Girl	1966	6.25	12.50	25.00
❑ 4084		Let's Live for Today/Depressed Feeling	1967	3.00	6.00	12.00
❑ 4094		Things I Should Have Said/Tip of My Tongue	1967	2.50	5.00	10.00

Number		Title (A Side/B Side)	Year	VG	VG+	NM
❑ 4094	PS	Things I Should Have Said/Tip of My Tongue	1967	3.75	7.50	15.00
❑ 4105		Wake Up, Wake Up/No Exit	1967	2.50	5.00	10.00
❑ 4122		A Melody for You/Hey Friend	1968	2.50	5.00	10.00
❑ 4129		Feelings/Here's Where You Belong	1968	2.50	5.00	10.00
❑ 4144		Midnight Confessions/Who Will You Be Tomorrow	1968	7.50	15.00	30.00
		Original label has no "ABC" logo next to "Dunhill"				

Haven

❑ 802		Out in the Open/Optical Illusion	1976	2.00	4.00	8.00
❑ 7015		Mamacita/Last Time Around	1975		2.50	5.00
❑ 7021		Naked Man/Nothing Good Comes Easy	1975		2.50	5.00

MCA

❑ 52058		Here Comes That Feeling Again/Temptation Eyes	1982	2.50	5.00	10.00
❑ 52104		She Don't Know Me/Keep On Burning	1982	2.50	5.00	10.00

Grateful Dead, The
(Also see "Garcia, Jerry")

Arista

❑ 0276		Dancin' in the Streets/Terrapin Station	1977		3.00	6.00
❑ 0291		Passenger/Terrapin Station	1977		3.00	6.00
❑ 0383		Good Lovin'/Stagger Lee	1978		3.00	6.00
❑ 0410		France/Shakedown Street	1979		3.00	6.00
❑ 0519		Alabama Getaway/Far from Me	1980		2.50	5.00
❑ 0519	PS	Alabama Getaway/Far from Me	1980		2.50	5.00
❑ 0546		Don't Ease Me In/Far from Me	1980		2.50	5.00
❑ 9606		Touch of Grey/My Brother Esau	1987			3.00
		Black vinyl (not issued with picture sleeve)				
❑ 9606		Touch of Grey/My Brother Esau	1987		2.50	5.00
		Gray vinyl				
❑ 9606	PS	Touch of Grey/My Brother Esau	1987		2.50	5.00
		Fold-open poster sleeve (add $2 for sticker attached to original shrink wrap)				
❑ 9643		Throwing Stones (Ashes Ashes) Edit/ Throwing Stones (Ashes Ashes) LP Version	1987			3.00
❑ 9643	PS	Throwing Stones (Ashes Ashes) Edit/ Throwing Stones (Ashes Ashes) LP Version	1987			3.00
❑ 9899		Foolish Heart/We Can Run	1989		2.00	4.00
❑ 9899	PS	Foolish Heart/We Can Run	1989		2.00	4.00

Grateful Dead

❑ 01		Here Comes Sunshine/Let Me Sing Your Blues Away	1973	2.50	5.00	10.00
❑ 02		Eyes of the World/Weather Report (Part 1)	1974	2.50	5.00	10.00
❑ 03		U.S. Blues/Loose Lucy	1974	2.50	5.00	10.00
❑ 03	PS	U.S. Blues/Loose Lucy	1974	5.00	10.00	20.00
❑ XW718		The Music Never Stopped/Help on the Way	1975	3.00	6.00	12.00
❑ XW762		Franklin's Tower/Help on the Way	1976	5.00	10.00	20.00

Scorpio

❑ 201		Stealin'/Don't Ease Me In	1966	150.00	300.00	600.00

Warner Bros.

❑ 7016		The Golden Road (To Unlimited Devotion)/ Cream Puff War	1967	6.25	12.50	25.00
❑ 7186		Dark Star/Born Cross-Eyed	1968	6.25	12.50	25.00
❑ 7186	PS	Dark Star/Born Cross-Eyed	1968	75.00	150.00	300.00
❑ 7324		Dupree's Diamond Blues/Cosmic Charlie	1969	6.25	12.50	25.00
❑ 7410		Uncle John's Band/New Speedway Boogie	1970	3.00	6.00	12.00
❑ 7464		Truckin'/Ripple	1971	3.00	6.00	12.00
❑ 7627		Johnny B. Goode/So Fine	1972	5.00	10.00	20.00
		B-side by Elvin Bishop Group				
❑ 7653		Truckin'/Johnny B. Goode	1973	2.00	4.00	8.00
		"Back to Back Hits" series				
❑ 7667		Sugar Magnolia/Mr. Charlie	1972	3.00	6.00	12.00

Gray, Dobie

Arista

❑ 1047		One Can Fake It/(B-side unknown)	1983		2.00	4.00

Capitol

❑ 2241		We the People/Funny and Groovy	1968	2.50	5.00	10.00
❑ 5853		River Deep, Mountain High/Tennessee Waltz	1967	3.75	7.50	15.00
❑ B-5562		Gonna Be a Long Night/That's One to Grown On	1986			3.00
❑ B-5596		The Dark Side of Life/ A Night in the Life of a Country Boy	1986			3.00
❑ B-5647		From Where I Stand/So Far So Good	1986			3.00
❑ B-44087		Take It Real Easy/ You Must Have Been Reading My Heart	1987			3.00
❑ B-44126		Love Letters/Steady As She Goes	1988			3.00

Capricorn

❑ 0249		If Love Must Go/Lover's Sweat	1975		2.00	4.00
❑ 0259		Find 'Em, Fool 'Em and Forget 'Em/Mellow Man	1976		2.00	4.00
❑ 0267		Let Go/Mellow Man	1976		2.00	4.00

Charger

❑ 105		The "In" Crowd/To Be a Man	1964	3.00	6.00	12.00
❑ 107		See You at the "Go-Go"/Walk with Love	1965	2.50	5.00	10.00
❑ 109		In Hollywood/Mr. Engineer	1965	2.50	5.00	10.00
❑ 113		Monkey Jerk/My Baby	1965	2.50	5.00	10.00
❑ 115		No Room to Cry/Out on the Floor	1966	2.50	5.00	10.00

Cordak

❑ 1602		Look at Me/(B-side unknown)	1962	3.75	7.50	15.00

Number	Title (A Side/B Side)	Year	VG	VG+	NM
Decca					
❏ 33057	Drift Away/City Stars	1973		2.50	5.00
Infinity					
❏ 50,003	You Can Do It/Sharing the Night Together	1978		2.00	4.00
❏ 50,010	Who's Lovin' You/Thank You for Tonight	1979		2.00	4.00
❏ 50,020	Spending Time, Making Love, and Going Crazy/	1979		2.00	4.00
	Let This Man Take Hold of Your Life				
❏ 50,043	The In Crowd/Let This Man Take Hold of Your Life	1979		2.00	4.00
MCA					
❏ 40100	Loving Arms/Now That I'm Without You	1973		2.00	4.00
❏ 40153	Good Old Song/Reachin' for the Feelin'	1973		2.00	4.00
❏ 40188	Rose/Lovin' the Easy Way	1974		2.00	4.00
❏ 40201	There's a Honky Tonk Angel (Who'll Take Me Back In)/	1974		2.00	4.00
	Lovin' the Easy Way				
❏ 40268	Watch Out for Lucy/Turning On You	1974		2.00	4.00
❏ 40315	The Music's Real/Roll On Sweet Mississippi	1974		2.00	4.00
White Whale					
❏ 300	Rose Garden/Where's the Girl Gone	1969	2.50	5.00	10.00
❏ 330	What a Way to Go/Do You Really Have a Heart	1969	50.00	100.00	200.00
❏ 342	Honey, You Can't Take It Back	1970	15.00	30.00	60.00

Gray, Gene, and the Stingrays

Dot					
❏ 16478	Surf Bunny/Surfer's Mood	1963	5.00	10.00	20.00
Linda					
❏ 110	Surf Bunny/Surfer's Mood	1963	10.00	20.00	40.00

Grayzell, Rudy

Sun					
❏ 290	Judy/I Think of You	1958	12.50	25.00	50.00

Great Society, The

(Grace Slick was in this group before she joined Jefferson Airplane)

Columbia					
❏ 44583	Sally Go 'Round the Roses/Didn't Think So	1968	5.00	10.00	20.00
North Beach					
❏ 1001	Someone to Love/Free Advice	1966	50.00	100.00	200.00
	As "The Great!! Society!!"				

Greats, The

Ebb					
❏ 145	Marching Elvis/Fiddler's Rock	1958	12.50	25.00	50.00

Green, Lil

Atlantic					
❏ 951	Every Time/I've Got That Feeling	1952	25.00	50.00	100.00

Greenbaum, Norman

(Also see "Dr. West's Medicine Show and Jug Band")

Gregar					
❏ 71-0107	Nancy Whiskey/Twentieth Century Fox	1969	2.50	5.00	10.00
Reprise					
❏ 0739	Spirit in the Sky/Canned Ham	1971		2.00	4.00
	"Back to Back Hits" series				
❏ 0752	Children of Paradise/School for Sweet Talk	1968	2.50	5.00	10.00
❏ 0818	Marcy/Children of Paradise	1969	2.50	5.00	10.00
❏ 0846	Jubilee/Skyline	1969	2.50	5.00	10.00
❏ 0885	Spirit in the Sky/Milk Cow	1969	2.00	4.00	8.00
❏ 0919	Canned Ham/Junior Cadillac	1970		3.00	6.00
❏ 0956	Rhode Island Red/I.J. Foxx	1970		3.00	6.00
❏ 1008	California Earthquake/Rhode Island Red	1971		3.00	6.00
❏ 1134	Dairy Queen/Petaluma	1972		3.00	6.00

Greenwich, Ellie

(Also see "Raindrops, The")

Bell					
❏ 855	Ain't That Peculiar/I Don't Want to Be Left Outside	1970	2.50	5.00	10.00
❏ 933	That Certain Someone/	1970	2.50	5.00	10.00
	It's Like a Sad Old Kind of Movie				
Red Bird					
❏ 10-034	You Don't Know/Baby	1965	10.00	20.00	40.00
United Artists					
❏ 50151	I Want You to Be My Baby/Goodnight, Goodnight	1967	3.75	7.50	15.00
❏ 50278	A Long Time Comin'/Niki-Hoeky	1968	3.75	7.50	15.00
Verve					
❏ 10719	Today I Met the Boy I'm Gonna Marry/Maybe I Know	1973	2.50	5.00	10.00
❏ 10724	Chapel of Love/River Deep, Mountain High	1973	2.50	5.00	10.00

Gregory, Ivan, and the Blue Notes

G&G					
❏ 110	Elvis Presley Blues/Kathy	1956	62.50	125.00	250.00

Number		Title (A Side/B Side)	Year	VG	VG+	NM

Grier, Frankie, Quartet
Swan

❑ 4019		Oh, Gloria/Lonesome for You	1958	100.00	200.00	400.00

Griffin, Jimmy
(Of Bread. Some were credited to "James Griffin.")
Imperial

❑ 66108		These Are the Times/Walking to New Orleans	1965	3.00	6.00	12.00
❑ 66152		He Will Break Your Heart/Hard Row to Hoe	1965	3.00	6.00	12.00

Polydor

❑ 14213		Breakin' Up Is Easy/Melody Maker	1973		2.50	5.00
❑ 14236		She Knows/Beachwood Band	1974		2.50	5.00
❑ 14282		Treat Her Right/How Do You Say Goodbye	1975		2.50	5.00

Reprise

❑ 0268		All My Loving/My Baby Made Me Cry	1964	3.75	7.50	15.00
❑ 0280		Gotta Lotta Love/Running to You	1964	3.75	7.50	15.00
❑ 0304		You're Nobody Till Somebody Loves You/Try	1964	3.75	7.50	15.00
❑ 20,114		Girls Grow Up Faster Than Boys/It's a Free Country	1962	5.00	10.00	20.00
❑ 20,161		What Kind of Girl Are You/A Little Like Lovin' You	1963	5.00	10.00	20.00
❑ 20,178		Love Letters in the Sand/Summer Holiday	1963	5.00	10.00	20.00
❑ 20,221		Little Miss Cool/Marie Is Moving	1963	5.00	10.00	20.00

Viva

❑ 611		Miracle Worker/Looking So Much Better	1967	2.50	5.00	10.00
❑ 627		Thank You Love/Light of Your Mind	1968	2.50	5.00	10.00
❑ 642		Miracle Worker/Thank You Love	1970	2.50	5.00	10.00

Griner, Linda
Motown

❑ 1037		Good-By Cruel World/Envious	1963	87.50	175.00	350.00
		With incorrect A-side title				
❑ 1037		Good-By Cruel Love/Envious	1963	50.00	100.00	200.00
		With corrected A-side title				

Groovie Goolies, The
RCA Victor

❑ 74-0383		The First Annual Semi-Formal Combination	1970	2.50	5.00	10.00
		Celebration Meet-the-Monster Population Party/Save Your Good Lovin' for Me				

Groundspeed
Decca

❑ 32344		In a Dream/L-12 East	1968	6.25	12.50	25.00

Group "B"
(An early incarnation of Blue Cheer)
Scorpio

❑ 402		Stop Calling Me/She's Gone	1967	6.25	12.50	25.00
❑ 406		I Know Your Name Girl/I Never Really Knew	1967	6.25	12.50	25.00

Grunion Hunters, The
Highland

❑ 1035		The Four-Eyed, Tongue-Tied, Swimmin' Surfer Biter/	1963	10.00	20.00	40.00
		Sing Along to the Swimmin' Surfer Biter				

Grunions, The
Jocko

❑ 505		Surfin' Psycho/Big Noise from Winnetka	1963	12.50	25.00	50.00

Guard, Dave, and the Whiskeyhill Singers
(Dave Guard had been with the Kingston Trio)
Capitol

❑ 4787		Plane Wreck at Los Gatos/Ride On, Railroad Bill	1962	2.50	5.00	10.00

Guess Who, The
Amy

❑ 967		And She's Mine/All Right	1966	5.00	10.00	20.00
		The existence of stock copies of this record has been questioned				
❑ 976		His Girl/It's My Pride	1967	5.00	10.00	20.00
		The existence of stock copies of this record has been questioned				

Fontana

❑ 1597		This Time Long Ago/There's No Getting Away from It	1967	7.50	15.00	30.00

Hilltak

❑ 7803		C'mon Little Mama/Moon Wave Maker	1979		3.00	6.00
❑ 7807		Sweet Young Thing/It's Getting Pretty Bad	1979		3.00	6.00

RCA Victor

❑ 74-0102		These Eyes/Lightfoot	1969		3.00	6.00
❑ 74-0195		Laughing/Undun	1969		3.00	6.00
❑ 74-0300		No Time/Proper Stranger	1969		3.00	6.00
❑ 74-0325		American Woman/No Sugar Tonight	1970		2.50	5.00
❑ 74-0367		Hand Me Down World/Runnin' Down the Street	1970		2.50	5.00
❑ 74-0388		Share the Land/Bus Rider	1970		2.50	5.00
❑ 74-0388	PS	Share the Land/Bus Rider	1970	2.50	5.00	10.00
❑ 74-0414		Hang On to Your Life/Do You Miss Me, Darlin'?	1970		2.50	5.00
❑ 74-0458		Albert Flasher/Broker	1971		2.50	5.00

Number	Title (A Side/B Side)	Year	VG	VG+	NM
☐ 74-0522	Rain Dance/One Divided	1971		2.50	5.00
☐ 74-0578	Sour Suite/Life in the Bloodstream	1971		2.50	5.00
☐ 74-0659	Heartbroken Bopper/Arrividerci Girl	1972		2.50	5.00
☐ 74-0708	Guns, Guns, Guns/	1972		2.50	5.00
	Heaven Only Moved Just Once Yesterday				
☐ 74-0803	Runnin' Back to Saskatoon/New Mother Nature	1972		2.50	5.00
☐ 74-0880	Follow Your Daughter Home/Bye Bye Babe	1973		2.50	5.00
☐ 74-0926	The Watcher/Orly	1973		2.50	5.00
☐ 74-0977	Lie Down/Glamour Boy	1973		2.50	5.00
☐ APBO-0217	Star Baby/Musicione	1974		2.50	5.00
☐ APBO-0324	Clap for the Wolfman/Road Food	1974		2.50	5.00
☐ PB-10075	Dancin' Fool/	1974		2.50	5.00
	Seems Like I Can't Live With You, But I Can't Live Without You				
☐ GB-10161	Clap for the Wolfman/Star Baby	1975		2.00	4.00
	Gold Standard Series				
☐ PB-10216	Loves Me Like a Brother/Hoe Down Time	1975		2.50	5.00
☐ PB-10360	Dreams/Rosanne	1975		2.50	5.00
☐ PB-10410	When the Band Was Singin' (Shakin' All Over)/Women	1975		3.00	6.00
☐ PB-10716	Silver Bird/Runnin' Down the Street	1976	3.00	6.00	12.00

Scepter

☐ 1295	Shakin' All Over/Till We Kissed	1965	3.75	7.50	15.00
☐ 12108	Hey Ho What You Do to Me/Goodnight Goodnight	1965	3.75	7.50	15.00
☐ 12118	Hurting Each Other/Baby's Birthday	1965	5.00	10.00	20.00
☐ 12131	Believe Me/Baby Feelin'	1966	5.00	10.00	20.00
☐ 12144	One Day/Clock on the Wall	1966	5.00	10.00	20.00

Guitar Slim

Atco

☐ 6072	Oh Yeah/Down Through the Years	1956	10.00	20.00	40.00
☐ 6097	It Hurts to Love Someone/If I Should Lose You	1957	7.50	15.00	30.00
☐ 6108	I Won't Mind at All/Hello, How Ya' Been, Goodbye	1958	7.50	15.00	30.00
☐ 6120	If I Had My Life to Live Over/	1958	7.50	15.00	30.00
	When There's No Way Out				

Imperial

☐ 5278	Woman Troubles/Cryin' in the Mornin'	1954	15.00	30.00	60.00
☐ 5310	New Arrival/Standing at the Station	1954	15.00	30.00	60.00

Specialty

☐ 482	The Things That I Used to Do/Well, I Done Get Over It	1954	7.50	15.00	30.00
☐ 490	Story of My Life/A Letter to My Girl Friend	1954	7.50	15.00	30.00
☐ 527	Later for You Baby/Troubles Don't Last	1954	6.25	12.50	25.00
☐ 536	Sufferin' Mind/Twenty-Five Lies	1955	6.25	12.50	25.00
☐ 542	Stand By Me/Our Only Child	1955	6.25	12.50	25.00
☐ 551	You're Gonna Miss Me/I Got Sumpin' for You	1955	6.25	12.50	25.00
☐ 557	Think It Over/Quicksand	1955	6.25	12.50	25.00
☐ 569	Sumthin' to Remember Me By/	1956	6.25	12.50	25.00
	You Give Me Nothin' But the Blues				

Guitar, Bonnie

Columbia

☐ 45643	Just As Soon As I Get Over Loving You/	1972		2.50	5.00
	Happy Everything				

Dolton

☐ 10	Candy Apple Red/Come to Me, I Love You	1959	3.00	6.00	12.00
☐ 19	Candy Apple Red/Come to Me, I Love You	1960	2.50	5.00	10.00

Dot

☐ 15550	Dark Moon/Big Mile	1957	3.75	7.50	15.00
☐ 15587	Half Your Heart/If You See My Love Dancing	1957	3.00	6.00	12.00
☐ 15612	There's a New Moon Over My Shoulder/	1957	3.00	6.00	12.00
	Mister Fire Eyes				
☐ 15678	Making Believe/I Saw Your Face in the Moon	1957	3.00	6.00	12.00
☐ 15708	A Very Precious Love/Johnny Vagabond	1958	3.00	6.00	12.00
☐ 15776	I Found You Out/If You'll Be the Teacher	1958	3.00	6.00	12.00
☐ 15862	Rocky Mountain Moon/Whispering Hope	1958	3.00	6.00	12.00
☐ 15894	Baby Moon/Solitude	1959	3.00	6.00	12.00
☐ 16811	I'm Living in Two Worlds/Goodtime Charlie	1965		3.00	6.00
☐ 16872	Would You Believe/Get Your Life the Way You Want It	1966		3.00	6.00
☐ 16919	Are You Sincere/The Tallest Tree	1966		3.00	6.00
☐ 16968	I'll Be Missing You (Under the Mistletoe)/	1966		3.00	6.00
	Blue Christmas				
☐ 16987	The Kickin' Tree/Only I	1967		3.00	6.00
☐ 17007	You Can Steal Me/Ramblin' Man	1967		3.00	6.00
☐ 17029	I Want My Baby/Woman in Love	1967		3.00	6.00
☐ 17057	Wings of a Dove/Stop the Sun	1967		3.00	6.00
☐ 17097	Faded Love/I Believe in Love	1968		2.50	5.00
☐ 17150	Almost Like Being with You/	1968		2.50	5.00
	Leaves Are the Tears of Autumn				
☐ 17249	Perfect Strangers/I'll Meet You in Denver	1969		2.50	5.00
☐ 17276	I'll Pick Up My Heart/That See Me Later Look	1969		2.50	5.00

Fabor

☐ 138	Ra Ta Ta Ta/Leave Weeping to the Willow Tree	1964	2.00	4.00	8.00
☐ 4013	If You See My Love Dancing/	1956	5.00	10.00	20.00
	Hello, Hello, Please Answer				
☐ 4017	Clinging Vine/Dream Dreamers	1956	5.00	10.00	20.00
☐ 4018	Dark Moon/Big Mile	1957	10.00	20.00	40.00

Number	Title (A Side/B Side)	Year	VG	VG+	NM

4 Star
❑ 1006	I Wanna Spend My Life with You/Maggie	1975		2.00	4.00
❑ 1041	Honey on the Moon/Lonely Eyes	1980		2.00	4.00
	Number also listed as 1003. Which is correct? Or are both?				

Jerden
❑ 707	There'll Be No Teardrops Tonight/The Fool	1963	2.50	5.00	10.00

MCA
❑ 40192	The Bed I Love In/Wishing Star	1974		2.00	4.00
❑ 40306	From This Moment On/Shine	1974		2.00	4.00

Paramount
❑ 0004	A Truer Love You'll Never Find (Than Mine)/ That's When	1969		2.50	5.00
	As "Bonnie and Buddy" (Buddy is Buddy Killen)				
❑ 0045	Allegheny/Red Checkered Blazer	1970		2.50	5.00

Playback
❑ 75714	Still the Same/(B-side unknown)	1989		2.00	4.00

Radio
❑ 101	Please, My Love/Love Is Over, Love Is Done	1958	3.00	6.00	12.00
❑ 110	Shanty Boat/Only the Moon Man Knows	1958	3.00	6.00	12.00

RCA Victor
❑ 47-7951	I'll Step Down/Tell Her Bye	1961	2.50	5.00	10.00
❑ 47-8063	Broken Hearted Girl/Who Is She	1962	2.50	5.00	10.00

Guitars, Inc.
(Pseudonym for "The Fireballs")

Hamilton
❑ 50035	Little Toy/Holiday Love	1960	6.25	12.50	25.00

Gulliver
(With Daryl Hall. John Oates joined later, but is not on these records)

Elektra
❑ 45689	Angelina/Every Day's a Lovely Day	1970	2.00	4.00	8.00
❑ 45698	A Truly Good Song/Every Day's a Lovely Day	1970	2.00	4.00	8.00

Gum Drops, The

Coral
❑ 62003	My Own True Love/On the Wings of the Wind	1958	3.75	7.50	15.00
❑ 62102	I Spoke Too Soon/Sie Tu (It's You, It's You)	1959	3.75	7.50	15.00
❑ 62138	It Happens Every Day/They Wake Me	1959	3.75	7.50	15.00

Decca
❑ 30584	You're the One/Gum Drop Shoes and Bells in Her Hair	1958	5.00	10.00	20.00

King
❑ 1496	Gum Drop/Don't Take It So Hard	1955	5.00	10.00	20.00
❑ 1499	I'll Wait for One More Train/Don't Take It So Hard	1955	5.00	10.00	20.00
❑ 4913	I Wonder and Wonder/I'll Follow You	1956	6.25	12.50	25.00
❑ 4963	Natural Born Lover/Chapel of Hearts	1956	6.25	12.50	25.00
❑ 5051	Ba-Bee Da Boat Is Leaving/Pigeon	1957	5.00	10.00	20.00

Gunter, Cornel
(Also see "Flairs, The")

ABC-Paramount
❑ 9698	She Loves to Rock/In Self Defense	1956	6.25	12.50	25.00

Challenge
❑ 59281	If I Had the Key to Your Heart/Wishful	1965	2.50	5.00	10.00

Dot
❑ 15654	You Send Me/Call Me a Fool	1957	5.00	10.00	20.00

Eagle
❑ 301	Baby Come Home/I Want You Madly	1957	7.50	15.00	30.00

Liberty
❑ 55096	If We Should Meet Again/Neighborhood Dance	1957	5.00	10.00	20.00

Loma
Note: The Loma singles credit "The Ermines," and may or may not mention Gunter.
❑ 701	True Love/Peek, Peek-a-Boo	1955	25.00	50.00	100.00
❑ 703	You Broke My Heart/ (Pretty Baby) I'm Used to You Now	1956	25.00	50.00	100.00
❑ 704	Keep Me Alive/Muchacha, Muchacha	1956	20.00	40.00	80.00
❑ 705	I'm Sad/One Thing	1956	25.00	50.00	100.00

Warner Bros.
❑ 5266	Lift Me Up Angel/Hope of Sand	1962	3.00	6.00	12.00
❑ 5292	It Ain't No Use/In a Dream of Love	1962	3.00	6.00	12.00

Gunter, Hardrock

Decca
❑ 46300	Boogie Woogie on a Saturday Night/Honky Tonk	1951	10.00	20.00	40.00
❑ 46350	I've Done Gone Hog Wild/ I Believe That Mountain Music	1951	6.25	12.50	25.00
❑ 46363	Sixty Minute Man/Tennessee Blues	1951	6.25	12.50	25.00
❑ 46383	Hesitation Boogie/Don't You Agree	1951	6.25	12.50	25.00
❑ 46401	Silver and Gold/Senator from Tennessee	1952	6.25	12.50	25.00

King
❑ 4858	Turn the Other Cheek/Before My Time	1955	5.00	10.00	20.00

Number		Title (A Side/B Side)	Year	VG	VG+	NM
MGM						
❏ 11520		Like the Lovers Do/Naptown, Indiana	1953	6.25	12.50	25.00
❏ 11596		Sunday Angel/Where Have You Been	1953	6.25	12.50	25.00
Sun						
❏ 201		Fallen Angel/Gonna Dance All Night	1954	500.00	1,000	2,000

Gunter, Shirley
(Also see "Flairs, The")
Flair

Number		Title (A Side/B Side)	Year	VG	VG+	NM
❏ 1020		Send Him Back/Since I Fell for You	1953	10.00	20.00	40.00
❏ 1027		Found Some Good Lovin'/Strange Romance	1954	7.50	15.00	30.00
❏ 1050		Oop Shoop/It's You	1955	7.50	15.00	30.00
❏ 1060		You're Mine/Why	1955	7.50	15.00	30.00
❏ 1065		What Difference Does It Make/Baby I Love You So	1955	7.50	15.00	30.00
❏ 1070		That's the Way I Like It/Gimme, Gimme, Gimme	1955	7.50	15.00	30.00
❏ 1076		How Can I Tell You/Ipsy Gypsy Ooh	1955	15.00	30.00	60.00
		With the Flairs				
Modern						
❏ 979		Please Tell Me/Come On	1956	6.25	12.50	25.00
❏ 1001		Fortune in Love/Just Got Rid of a Heartache	1956	6.25	12.50	25.00
		With the Flairs				
❏ 1011		I'm So Sorry/I've Been Searching	1956	6.25	12.50	25.00
Tangerine						
❏ 949		Stuck Up/You Let My Love Grow Cold	1965	2.50	5.00	10.00

H

Hackert, Valine
Brunswick

Number	Title (A Side/B Side)	Year	VG	VG+	NM
❏ 55151	Billy Boy/Show Me How	1959	50.00	100.00	200.00

Hagan, Sammy, and the Viscounts
Capitol

Number	Title (A Side/B Side)	Year	VG	VG+	NM
❏ F3772	Out of Your Heart/Shoochie Poochie	1957	10.00	20.00	40.00
❏ F3818	Wild Bird/Don't Cry	1957	10.00	20.00	40.00
❏ F3885	Tail Light/Snuggle Bunny	1958	7.50	15.00	30.00

Haggett, Jimmy
Caprock

Number	Title (A Side/B Side)	Year	VG	VG+	NM
❏ 107	All I Have Is You/Without You	1958	10.00	20.00	40.00
Meteor					
❏ 5043	Gonna Shut You Off Baby/Tell Her True	1957	50.00	100.00	200.00
Sun					
❏ 236	No More/They Call Our Love a Sin	1956	150.00	300.00	600.00

Haig, Ronnie
ABC-Paramount

Number	Title (A Side/B Side)	Year	VG	VG+	NM
❏ 10209	Don't You Hear Me Calling, Baby/Traveler of Love	1961	20.00	40.00	80.00
❏ 9912	Don't You Hear Me Calling, Baby/Traveler of Love	1958	7.50	15.00	30.00
Note					
❏ 10010	Don't You Hear Me Calling, Baby/Traveler of Love	1958	7.50	15.00	30.00
❏ 10014	Rockin' with Rhythm and Blues/ Money Is a Thing of the Past	1958	25.00	50.00	100.00

Haircuts, The
Parkway

Number		Title (A Side/B Side)	Year	VG	VG+	NM
❏ 899		She Loves You/Love Me Do	1964	5.00	10.00	20.00
❏ 899	PS	She Loves You/Love Me Do	1964	10.00	20.00	40.00

Hale and the Hushabyes
(All-star group including Brian Wilson, Jackie DeShannon, and Sonny and Cher)
Apogee

Number	Title (A Side/B Side)	Year	VG	VG+	NM
❏ 104	Yes Sir, That's My Baby/900 Quetzals	1964	75.00	150.00	300.00
Reprise					
❏ 0299	Yes Sir, That's My Baby/Jack's Theme	1964	50.00	100.00	200.00
	Reissued in 1967 by "A Date With Soul"				
York					
❏ 408	Yes Sir, That's My Baby/Bee Side Soul	1967	12.50	25.00	50.00
	As "A Date with Soul"				

Halee's Comet
(Roy Halee, later producer for Simon and Garfunkel)
Epic

Number	Title (A Side/B Side)	Year	VG	VG+	NM
❏ 10207	All I Want Is What's Real/From a Parachute	1967	3.00	6.00	12.00

Haley, Bill, and His Comets
Apt

Number	Title (A Side/B Side)	Year	VG	VG+	NM
❏ 25081	Stop, Look, and Listen/Burn That Candle	1965	5.00	10.00	20.00
❏ 25087	Haley A-Go-Go/Tongue Tied Tony	1965	6.25	12.50	25.00

Number		Title (A Side/B Side)	Year	VG	VG+	NM
Arzee						
❑ 4677		Yodel Your Blues Away/ Within This Broken Heart of Mine	1978	6.25	12.50	25.00
❑ 4677	PS	Yodel Your Blues Away/ Within This Broken Heart of Mine	1978	6.25	12.50	25.00
Buddah						
❑ 169		Rock Around the Clock/Framed	1970	3.75	7.50	15.00
Decca						
❑ 29124		(We're Gonna) Rock Around the Clock/ Thirteen Women (And Only One Man in Town)	1954	6.25	12.50	25.00
		With lines on either side of "Decca"				
❑ 29124		(We're Gonna) Rock Around the Clock/ Thirteen Women (And Only One Man in Town)	1955	10.00	20.00	40.00
		With star under "Decca"				
❑ 29204		Shake, Rattle and Roll/A.B.C. Boogie	1954	5.00	10.00	20.00
		With lines on either side of "Decca"				
❑ 29204		Shake, Rattle and Roll/A.B.C. Boogie	1954	7.50	15.00	30.00
		With star under "Decca"				
❑ 29317		Dim, Dim the Lights (I Want Some Atmosphere)/ Happy Baby	1954	5.00	10.00	20.00
		With lines on either side of "Decca"				
❑ 29317		Dim, Dim the Lights (I Want Some Atmosphere)/ Happy Baby	1954	7.50	15.00	30.00
		With star under "Decca"				
❑ 29418		Mambo Rock/Birth of the Boogie	1955	6.25	12.50	25.00
❑ 29552		Razzle-Dazzle/Two Hound Dogs	1955	6.25	12.50	25.00
❑ 29713		Burn That Candle/Rock-a-Beatin' Boogie	1955	6.25	12.50	25.00
❑ 29791		See You Later, Alligator/ The Paper Boy (On Main Street, U.S.A.)	1956	6.25	12.50	25.00
❑ 29870		R-O-C-K/The Saints Rock 'N' Roll	1956	6.25	12.50	25.00
❑ 29948		Hot Dog Buddy Buddy/Rockin' Through the Rye	1956	6.25	12.50	25.00
❑ 30028		Rip It Up/Teenager's Mother (Are You Right?)	1956	6.25	12.50	25.00
❑ 30085		Rudy's Rock/Blue Comet Blues	1956	6.25	12.50	25.00
❑ 30148		Don't Knock the Rock/Choo Choo Ch'Boogie	1956	6.25	12.50	25.00
❑ 30214		Forty Cups of Coffee/Hook, Line and Sinker	1957	6.25	12.50	25.00
❑ 30314		(You Hit the Wrong Note) Billy Goat/ Rockin' Rollin' Rover	1957	6.25	12.50	25.00
❑ 30314	PS	(You Hit the Wrong Note) Billy Goat/ Rockin' Rollin' Rover	1957	25.00	50.00	100.00
❑ 30394		The Dipsy Doodle/Miss You	1957	6.25	12.50	25.00
❑ 30461		Rock the Joint/How Many	1957	6.25	12.50	25.00
❑ 30530		It's a Sin/Mary, Mary Lou	1957	6.25	12.50	25.00
❑ 30530	PS	It's a Sin/Mary, Mary Lou	1957	12.50	25.00	50.00
❑ 30592		Skinny Minnie/Stay with Me	1958	7.50	15.00	30.00
❑ 30681		Lean Jean/Don't Nobody Move	1958	6.25	12.50	25.00
❑ 30741		Chiquita Linda/Whoa Mabel	1958	6.25	12.50	25.00
❑ 30781		Corrine, Corrina/B.B. Betty	1958	6.25	12.50	25.00
❑ 30844		Charmaine/I Got a Woman	1959	6.25	12.50	25.00
❑ 30873		(Now and Then, There's) A Fool Such As I/ Where Did You Go Last Night	1959	6.25	12.50	25.00
❑ 30926		Caldonia/Shakey	1959	6.25	12.50	25.00
❑ 30956		Joey's Song/Ooh, Look-a-There, Ain't She Pretty	1959	6.25	12.50	25.00
❑ 31030		Skokiaan (South African Song)/Puerto Rican Peddler	1959	6.25	12.50	25.00
❑ 31080		Music, Music, Music/Strictly Instrumental	1960	6.25	12.50	25.00
❑ 31649		The Green Door/Yeah, She's Evil	1964	3.00	6.00	12.00
Essex						
❑ 102		Rock Around the Clock/Crazy Man, Crazy	1955	12.50	25.00	50.00
		Actually a bootleg, but highly sought-after nonetheless				
❑ 303		Rock the Joint/Icy Heart	1952	20.00	40.00	80.00
		Black vinyl, block logo ("ESSEX" in all caps)				
❑ 303		Rock the Joint/Icy Heart	1952	15.00	30.00	60.00
		Black vinyl, script logo ("Essex" not in all caps)				
❑ 303		Rock the Joint/Icy Heart	1952	1,000	1,500	2,000
		Red vinyl				
❑ 305		Rocking Chair on the Moon/ Dance with a Dolly (With a Hole in Her Stocking)	1952	25.00	50.00	100.00
		Essex 303 and 305 credit "Bill Haley and the Saddlemen"				
❑ 310		Real Rock Drive/Stop Beatin' Round the Mulberry Bush	1952	30.00	60.00	120.00
		Blue label				
❑ 310		Real Rock Drive/Stop Beatin' Round the Mulberry Bush	1952	20.00	40.00	80.00
		Orange label				
❑ 321		Crazy Man, Crazy/Whatcha Gonna Do	1953	12.50	25.00	50.00
❑ 327		Pat-a-Cake/Fractured	1953	10.00	20.00	40.00
❑ 332		Live It Up/Farewell, So Long, Goodbye	1953	10.00	20.00	40.00
❑ 340		Ten Little Indians/I'll Be True	1953	10.00	20.00	40.00
❑ 348		Chattanooga Choo Choo/Straight Jacket	1954	10.00	20.00	40.00
❑ 374		Sundown Boogie/Jukebox Cannonball	1954	18.75	37.50	75.00
❑ 381		Rocket 88/Green Tree Boogie	1955	31.25	62.50	125.00
❑ 399		Rock the Joint/Farewell, So Long, Goodbye	1955	18.75	37.50	75.00
GNP Crescendo						
❑ 475		I'm Walkin'/Crazy Man, Crazy	1974	3.00	6.00	12.00
Gone						
❑ 5111		Spanish Twist/My Kind of Woman	1961	6.25	12.50	25.00
❑ 5116		Riviera/War Paint	1961	6.25	12.50	25.00

Number		Title (A Side/B Side)	Year	VG	VG+	NM
Holiday						
❑ 113		Sundown Boogie/Jukebox Cannonball	1951	125.00	250.00	500.00
		The only Holiday single known to exist on a 45. Earlier Holiday singles only eixst on 78s.				
Janus						
❑ 162		Travelin' Band/A Little Piece at a Time	1971	3.00	6.00	12.00
Kama Sutra						
❑ 508		Rock Around the Clock/Framed	1970	5.00	10.00	20.00
Kasey						
❑ 7006		A.B.C. Boogie/Rock Around the Clock	1961	5.00	10.00	20.00
		B-side by Phil Flowers				
Newtown						
❑ 5013		Tenor Man/Up Goes My Love	1962	5.00	10.00	20.00
❑ 5024		Dance Around the Clock/	1963	5.00	10.00	20.00
		What Can I Say After I Say I'm Sorry				
Nicetown						
❑ 5025		You Call Everybody Darling/Tandy	1963	5.00	10.00	20.00
Trans World						
❑ 718		Real Rock Drive/Yes, Indeed	1954	50.00	100.00	200.00
United Artists						
❑ 50483		Ain't Love Funny, Ha Ha Ha/	1969	2.50	5.00	10.00
		That's How I Got to Memphis				
Warner Bros.						
❑ 5145		Candy Kisses/Tamiami	1960	6.25	12.50	25.00
❑ 5145	DJ	Candy Kisses/Tamiami	1960	12.50	25.00	50.00
		Promo only on yellow vinyl				
❑ 5154		Hawk/Chick Safari	1960	6.25	12.50	25.00
❑ 5171		Let the Good Times Roll, Creole/So Right Tonight	1960	6.25	12.50	25.00
❑ 5228		Flip, Flop and Fly/Honky Tonk	1961	6.25	12.50	25.00
❑ 7124		Rock Around the Clock/Shake, Rattle and Roll	1969	3.75	7.50	15.00
Hall, Larry						
Hot						
❑ 1		Sandy/Lovin' Tree	1959	12.50	25.00	50.00
Strand						
❑ 25007		Sandy/Lovin' Tree	1959	6.25	12.50	25.00
❑ 25013		A Girl Like You/Rosemary	1960	5.00	10.00	20.00
❑ 25016		For Every Boy/I'll Stay Single	1960	5.00	10.00	20.00
❑ 25025		The Girl I Left Behind/Kool Love	1961	5.00	10.00	20.00
❑ 25029		Lips of Wine/Rebel Heart	1961	5.00	10.00	20.00
❑ 25048		Ladder of Love/The One You Left Behind	1961	5.00	10.00	20.00
Hall, Roy						
Decca						
❑ 29697		Whole Lotta Shakin' Goin' On/All By Myself	1955	12.50	25.00	50.00
❑ 29786		See You Later, Alligator/Don't Stop Now	1956	12.50	25.00	50.00
❑ 29880		Blue Suede Shoes/Luscious	1956	12.50	25.00	50.00
❑ 30060		Three Alley Cats/Diggin' the Boogie	1956	12.50	25.00	50.00
Fortune						
❑ 170		Going Down the Road/Jealous Love	1952	10.00	20.00	40.00
		B-side by the Davis Sisters				
❑ 521		Corrine, Corrina/Don't Ask Me No Questions	1956	12.50	25.00	50.00
Hi-Q						
❑ 5045		Three Alley Cats/Bedspring Motel	196?	15.00	30.00	60.00
❑ 5050		Go Go Little Queenie/Everybody Dig That Boogie	196?	15.00	30.00	60.00
Halloway, Larry						
Parkway						
❑ 903		Beatle Teen Beat/Going Up	1964	5.00	10.00	20.00
Hamilton, George, IV						
ABC						
❑ 12342	DJ	Only the Best (mono/stereo)	1978		2.50	5.00
		May be promo only				
❑ 12376		One Day at a Time/Take This Heart	1978		2.00	4.00
ABC-Paramount						
❑ 9765		A Rose and a Baby Ruth/If You Don't Know	1956	7.50	15.00	30.00
❑ 9782		Only One Love/If I Possessed a Printing Press	1957	7.50	15.00	30.00
❑ 9838		High School Romance/Everybody's Baby	1957	7.50	15.00	30.00
❑ 9862		Why Don't They Understand/Even Tho'	1957	7.50	15.00	30.00
❑ 9898		Now and For Always/One Heart	1958	6.25	12.50	25.00
❑ 9924		I Know Where I'm Goin'/	1958	6.25	12.50	25.00
		Who's Taking You to the Prom				
❑ 9946		When Will I Know/Your Cheatin' Heart	1958	6.25	12.50	25.00
❑ 9966		Lucy, Lucy/The Two of Us	1958	6.25	12.50	25.00
❑ 10009		The Steady Game/Can You Blame Us	1959	5.00	10.00	20.00
❑ 10028		Gee/I Know Your Sweetheart	1959	5.00	10.00	20.00
❑ 10059		One Little Acre/Little Tom	1959	5.00	10.00	20.00
❑ 10090		Why I'm Walkin'/Tremble	1960	5.00	10.00	20.00
❑ 10125		Before This Day Ends/Loneliness All Around Me	1960	5.00	10.00	20.00
❑ 10167		A Walk on the Wild Side of Life/It's Just the Idea	1960	5.00	10.00	20.00

Number	Title (A Side/B Side)	Year	VG	VG+	NM
ABC/Dot					
❏ 17687	I Wonder Who's Kissing Her Now/ In the Palm of Her Hand	1977		2.00	4.00
❏ 17708	Cornbread, Beans and Sweet Potato Pie/ May the Wind Be Always at Your Back	1977		2.00	4.00
❏ 17723	Everlasting (Everlasting Love)/In the Palm of Your Hand	1977		2.00	4.00
Colonial					
❏ 420	A Rose and a Baby Ruth/If You Don't Know	1956	20.00	40.00	80.00
❏ 451	I've Got a Secret/Sam	1956	10.00	20.00	40.00
GRT					
❏ 063	Blue Jeans, Ice Cream and Saturday Shoes/ Bad Romancer	1976		2.50	5.00
MCA					
❏ 41149	Forever Young/'Rangement Blues	1979		2.00	4.00
❏ 41215	I'll Be Here in the Morning/Spin Spin	1980		2.00	4.00
❏ 41282	Catfish Bates/Mose Rankin	1980		2.00	4.00
RCA					
❏ 2722-7-R	Abilene/Oh So Many Tears	1990		2.00	4.00
RCA Victor					
❏ 47-7881	Three Steps to the Picnic/The Ballad of Widder Jones	1961	3.75	7.50	15.00
❏ 47-7934	To You and Yours (From Me and Mine)/I Want a Girl	1961	3.75	7.50	15.00
❏ 47-8001	China Doll/Commerce Street and Sixth Avenue North	1962	3.75	7.50	15.00
❏ 47-8062	If You Don't Know, I Ain't Gonna Tell You/ Where Nobody Knows Me	1962	3.75	7.50	15.00
❏ 47-8118	In This Very Same Room/If You Want Me To	1962	3.75	7.50	15.00
❏ 47-8181	Abilene/Oh So Many Years	1963	3.00	6.00	12.00
❏ 47-8250	There's More Pretty Girls Than One/ If You Don't, Somebody Else Will	1963	3.00	6.00	12.00
❏ 47-8304	Linda with the Lonely Eyes/Fair and Tender Ladies	1963	3.00	6.00	12.00
❏ 47-8392	Fort Worth, Dallas or Houston/Life's Railway to Heaven	1964	3.00	6.00	12.00
❏ 47-8462	Truck Driving Man/The Little Grave	1964	3.00	6.00	12.00
❏ 47-8537	The Last Mister Jones/Anymore	1965	2.50	5.00	10.00
❏ 47-8608	Walking the Floor Over You/Driftwood on the River	1965	2.50	5.00	10.00
❏ 47-8690	Write Me a Picture/Twist of the Wrist	1965	2.50	5.00	10.00
❏ 47-8797	Steel Rail Blues/Tobacco	1966	2.50	5.00	10.00
❏ 47-8924	Early Morning Rain/Slightly Used	1966	2.50	5.00	10.00
❏ 47-9059	Urge for Going/Changes	1966	2.50	5.00	10.00
❏ 47-9239	Break My Mind/Something Special to Me	1967	2.00	4.00	8.00
❏ 47-9385	Little World Girl/Song for a Winter's Night	1967	2.00	4.00	8.00
❏ 47-9519	It's My Time/Canadian Railroad Trilogy	1968	2.00	4.00	8.00
❏ 47-9637	Take My Hand for Awhile/ Wonderful World of My Dreams	1968	2.00	4.00	8.00
❏ 47-9775	Natividad/Little Grave	1969	2.00	4.00	8.00
❏ 47-9829	She's a Little Bit Country/My Nova Scotia Home	1970		3.00	6.00
❏ 47-9886	Back Where It's At/Then I Miss You	1970		3.00	6.00
❏ 47-9893	Let's Get Together/Everything Is Beautiful	1970		3.00	6.00
	With Skeeter Davis				
❏ 47-9937	Natividad/Little Grave	1970		3.00	6.00
❏ 47-9945	Anyway/The Best That I Can Do	1971		3.00	6.00
❏ 74-0100	Back to Denver/Suzanne	1969	2.00	4.00	8.00
❏ 74-0171	Canadian Pacific/Sisters of Mercy	1969	2.00	4.00	8.00
❏ 74-0256	Carolina in My Mind/ I'm Gonna Be a Country Boy Again	1969	2.00	4.00	8.00
❏ 74-0469	Countryfied/My North Country Home	1971		3.00	6.00
❏ 74-0531	West Texas Highway/ There's No Room in This Rat Race	1971		3.00	6.00
❏ 74-0622	10 Degrees and Getting Colder/Tumbleweed	1971		3.00	6.00
❏ 74-0697	Country Music in My Soul/Child's Song	1972		2.50	5.00
❏ 74-0776	Travelin' Light/Alberta Bound	1972		2.50	5.00
❏ 74-0854	Blue Train (Of the Heartbreak Line)/Maritime Farewell	1972		2.50	5.00
❏ 74-0948	Dirty Old Man/Abilene	1973		2.50	5.00
❏ APBO-0084	Second Cup of Coffee/Farmer's Song	1973		2.00	4.00
❏ APBO-0203	Claim on Me/Early Mornin' Rain	1973		2.00	4.00
❏ APBO-0314	The Ways of a Country Girl/Pictou County Jail	1974		2.00	4.00

Hamilton, Judd

Number	Title (A Side/B Side)	Year	VG	VG+	NM
Dolton					
❏ 80	Dream/Your Only Boy	1963	7.50	15.00	30.00

Hamilton, Roy

Number	Title (A Side/B Side)	Year	VG	VG+	NM
AGP					
❏ 113	The Dark End of the Street/100 Years	1969	2.00	4.00	8.00
❏ 116	Angelica/Hang Ups	1969	2.00	4.00	8.00
❏ 125	It's Only Make Believe/100 Years	1969	2.00	4.00	8.00
Capitol					
❏ 2057	Let This World Be Free/Wait Until Dark	1967	2.00	4.00	8.00
Epic					
❏ 9015	You'll Never Walk Alone/ I'm Gonna Sit Right Down and Cry	1954	6.25	12.50	25.00
❏ 9047	So Let There Be Love/If You Loved Me	1954	6.25	12.50	25.00
❏ 9068	Ebb Tide/Beware	1954	6.25	12.50	25.00
❏ 9086	Hurt/Star of Love	1954	6.25	12.50	25.00
❏ 9092	I Believe/If You Are But a Dream	1955	5.00	10.00	20.00
❏ 9102	Unchained Melody/From Here to Eternity	1955	6.25	12.50	25.00
❏ 9111	Forgive This Fool/You Wanted to Change Me	1955	5.00	10.00	20.00
❏ 9118	A Little Voice/All This Is Mine	1955	5.00	10.00	20.00

Number		Title (A Side/B Side)	Year	VG	VG+	NM
☐ 9125		Without a Song/Cuban Love Song	1955	5.00	10.00	20.00
☐ 9132		Everybody's Got a Home/Take Me with You	1955	5.00	10.00	20.00
☐ 9147		There Goes My Heart/Walk Along with Kings	1956	5.00	10.00	20.00
☐ 9160		Somebody, Somewhere/Since I Fell for You	1956	5.00	10.00	20.00
☐ 9180		I Took My Grief to Him/Chained	1956	5.00	10.00	20.00
☐ 9203		The Simple Prayer/A Mother's Love	1957	5.00	10.00	20.00
☐ 9212		My Faith, My Hope, My Love/So Long	1957	5.00	10.00	20.00
☐ 9224		The Aisle/That Old Feeling	1957	5.00	10.00	20.00
☐ 9232		(All of a Sudden) My Heart Sings/ I'm Gonna Lock You in My Heart	1957	5.00	10.00	20.00
☐ 9257		Don't Let Go/The Night to Love	1957	5.00	10.00	20.00
☐ 9268		Crazy Feelin'/In a Dream	1958	3.75	7.50	15.00
☐ 9274		Lips/Jungle Fever	1958	3.75	7.50	15.00
☐ 9282		Wait for Me/Everything	1958	3.75	7.50	15.00
☐ 9294		Pledging My Love/My One and Only Love	1958	3.75	7.50	15.00
☐ 9301		It's Never Too Late/Somewhere Along the Way	1959	3.75	7.50	15.00
☐ 9307		I Need Your Lovin'/Blue Prelude	1959	3.75	7.50	15.00
☐ 9323		Time Marches On/Take It Easy, Joe	1959	3.75	7.50	15.00
☐ 9342		Great Romance/On My Way Back Home	1959	3.75	7.50	15.00
☐ 9354		The Ten Commandments/ Nobody Knows the Trouble I've Seen	1959	5.00	10.00	20.00
☐ 9354		The Ten Commandments/Down by the Riverside	1959	3.75	7.50	15.00
☐ 9372		Down by the Riverside/ Nobody Knows the Trouble I've Seen	1960	3.75	7.50	15.00
☐ 9373		I Let a Song Go Out of My Heart/ I Get the Blues When It Rains	1960	3.75	7.50	15.00
☐ 9374		My Story/Please Send Me Someone to Love	1960	3.75	7.50	15.00
☐ 9375		Something's Gotta Give/Cheek to Cheek	1960			Unreleased?
☐ 9376		Sing You Sinners/Blow, Gabriel, Blow	1960	3.75	7.50	15.00
☐ 9386		Having Myself a Ball/Slowly	1960	3.75	7.50	15.00
		B-side by Bobby Sykes				
☐ 9388		Never Let Me Go/I Get the Blues When It Rains	1960			Unreleased?
☐ 9390		The Clock/I Get the Blues When It Rains	1960	3.75	7.50	15.00
☐ 9398		A Lover's Prayer/Never Let Me Go	1960	3.75	7.50	15.00
☐ 9407		Lonely Hands/Your Love	1960	3.75	7.50	15.00
☐ 9434		You Can Have Her/Abide With Me	1961	3.75	7.50	15.00
☐ 9434	PS	You Can Have Her/Abide With Me	1961	7.50	15.00	30.00
☐ 9443		You're Gonna Need Magic/To the One I Love	1961	3.75	7.50	15.00
☐ 9443	PS	You're Gonna Need Magic/To the One I Love	1961	7.50	15.00	30.00
☐ 9449		No Substitute for Love/Please Louise	1961	3.75	7.50	15.00
☐ 9460		Excerpts from "You Can Have Her"	1961	3.75	7.50	15.00
☐ 9461		Excerpts from "You Can Have Her"	1961	3.75	7.50	15.00
☐ 9462		Excerpts from "You Can Have Her"	1961	3.75	7.50	15.00
☐ 9463		Excerpts from "You Can Have Her"	1961	3.75	7.50	15.00
☐ 9464		Excerpts from "You Can Have Her"	1961	3.75	7.50	15.00
☐ 9466		There We Were/If	1961	3.00	6.00	12.00
☐ 9492		Don't Come Cryin' to Me/If Only I Had Known	1962	3.00	6.00	12.00
☐ 9520		Climb Ev'ry Mountain/I'll Come Running Back to You	1962	3.00	6.00	12.00
☐ 9538		I Am/Earthquake	1962	3.00	6.00	12.00
☐ 10559		You'll Never Walk Alone/The Golden Boy	1969	2.00	4.00	8.00

MGM

☐ 13138		Let Go/You Still Love Him	1963	2.50	5.00	10.00
☐ 13157		Midnight Town-Daybreak City/Intermezzo	1963	2.50	5.00	10.00
☐ 13175		Theme from "The V.I.P.'s" (The Willow)/The Sinner	1963	2.50	5.00	10.00
☐ 13217		The Panic Is On/There She Is	1964	6.25	12.50	25.00
☐ 13247		Answer Me, My Love/Unchained Melody	1964	2.50	5.00	10.00
☐ 13291		You Can Count on Me/She Makes Me Wanna Dance	1964	6.25	12.50	25.00
☐ 13315		Sweet Violets/A Thousand Years Ago	1965	2.50	5.00	10.00

RCA Victor

☐ 47-8641		Heartache/Ain't It the Truth	1965	2.50	5.00	10.00
☐ 47-8705		And I Love Her/Tore Up Over You	1965	2.50	5.00	10.00
☐ 47-8813		The Impossible Dream/She's Got a Heart	1966	2.50	5.00	10.00
☐ 47-8960		Walk Hand in Hand/Crackin' Up Over You	1966	6.25	12.50	25.00
☐ 47-9061		I Taught Her Everything She Knows/Lament	1967	2.50	5.00	10.00
☐ 47-9171		So High My Love/You Shook Me Up	1967	12.50	25.00	50.00
☐ 48-1034		Walk Hand in Hand/Crackin' Up Over You	1972	2.50	5.00	10.00

Hammer, MC

Bustin'

☐ 1987-7		Let's Get It Started/(Instrumental)	1987	5.00	10.00	20.00

Capitol

☐ B-44229		Let's Get It Started/(Instrumental)	1988			3.00
☐ B-44266		Pump It Up/(Instrumental)	1988			3.00
☐ B-44290		Turn This Mutha Out/Ring 'Em	1989			3.00
☐ B-44353		(Hammer Hammer) They Put Me in the Mix/ Cold Go M.C. Hammer	1989			Unreleased?
☐ B-44497		Help the Children/(Instrumental)	1989			3.00
☐ NR-44794		Addams Groove/(Instrumental)	1991		2.00	4.00
☐ S7-57700		2 Legit to Quit (Long)/2 Legit to Quit (Short)	1992		2.00	4.00
☐ S7-57730		Do Not Pass Me By/Gaining Momentum	1992		2.00	4.00
☐ S7-57740		Good to Go/Count It Off	1992		2.00	4.00
☐ 7PRO-79072	DJ	U Can't Touch This (same on both sides)	1990	5.00	10.00	20.00
☐ 7PRO-79150	DJ	Have You Seen Her (same on both sides)	1990	2.50	5.00	10.00
☐ 7PRO-79284/95 DJ		Pray (Radio Edit)/Pray (LP Version)	1990	2.50	5.00	10.00
☐ 7PRO-79667	DJ	(Hammer Hammer) They Put Me in the Mix (same on both sides)	1989		3.00	6.00
☐ 7PRO-79893	DJ	Dancin' Machine (same on both sides)	1990		3.00	6.00

Number		Title (A Side/B Side)	Year	VG	VG+	NM
Giant						
❏ 18218		Pumps & a Bump (Radio Edit)/Pumps & a Bump (Album Version)	1994			3.00
❏ 18271		It's All Good/(Instrumental)	1994			3.00
Hammond-Hazlewood						
Capitol						
❏ 2616		Wendy, Wendy/Broken Hearts Brigade	1969	2.50	5.00	10.00
Haney, Jack, and Nikiter Armstrong						
Mel-O-Dy						
❏ 107		The Interview/Peaceful	1963	5.00	10.00	20.00
Happenings, The						
B.T. Puppy						
❏ 181	DJ	Have Yourself a Merry Little Christmas (same on both sides)	1966	7.50	15.00	30.00
		Stock copies do not exist				
❏ 517		Girls on the Go/Go-Go	1966	2.50	5.00	10.00
❏ 520		See You in September/He Thinks He's a Hero	1966	2.50	5.00	10.00
❏ 522		Go Away Little Girl/Tea Time	1966	2.00	4.00	8.00
❏ 523		Goodnight My Love/Lillies By Money	1966	2.00	4.00	8.00
❏ 527		I Got Rhythm/You're in a Bad Way	1967	2.00	4.00	8.00
❏ 530		My Mammy/I Believe in Nothing	1967	2.00	4.00	8.00
❏ 532		Why Do Fools Fall in Love/When the Summer Is Through	1967	2.00	4.00	8.00
❏ 538		Music, Music, Music/When I Lock My Door	1968	2.00	4.00	8.00
❏ 540		Randy/Love Song of Mommy and Daddy	1968	2.00	4.00	8.00
❏ 542		Sealed with a Kiss/Anyway	1968	2.00	4.00	8.00
❏ 543		Breaking Up Is Hard to Do/Anyway	1968	2.00	4.00	8.00
❏ 545		Crazy Rhythm/Love Song of Mommy and Daddy	1968	2.00	4.00	8.00
❏ 549		That's All I Want from You/He Thinks He's a Hero	1968	2.00	4.00	8.00
Big Tree						
❏ 146		Strawberry Morning/Workin' My Way Back to You	1972		2.00	4.00
❏ 153		Me Without You/God Bless Joanna	1972		2.00	4.00
Jubilee						
❏ 5666		Where Do I Go and Be In/New Day Comin'	1969		3.00	6.00
❏ 5677		El Paso County Jail/Won't Anybody Listen	1969		3.00	6.00
❏ 5686		Answer Me, My Love/I Need a Woman	1970		3.00	6.00
❏ 5698		Tomorrow, Today Will Be Yesterday/Chain of Hands	1970		3.00	6.00
❏ 5702		Crazy Love/Chain of Hands	1970		3.00	6.00
❏ 5703		Condition Red/Sweet September	1970	2.50	5.00	10.00
		As "The Honor Society"				
❏ 5712		Lullaby in the Rain/I Wish You Could Know Me (Naomi)	1971		3.00	6.00
❏ 5721	DJ	Make Your Own Kind of Music (mono/stereo)	1971		3.00	6.00
		Stock copies may not exist				
Midland Int'l.						
❏ MB-10897		That's Why I Love You/Beyond the Hurt	1977		2.00	4.00
❏ MB-11127		Let Me Stay/Someone Special	1977		2.00	4.00
Harbor Lights, The						
(Early Jay and the Americans)						
Jaro						
❏ 77020		Is That Too Much to Ask/What Would I Do Without You	1960	10.00	20.00	40.00
Mala						
❏ 422		Angel of Love/Tick-a-Tick-a-Tock	1960	12.50	25.00	50.00
Harmonica Frank						
Sun						
❏ 205		Rockin' Chair Daddy/The Great Musical Menagerist	1954	1,500	3,000	4,500
Harmony Grits, The						
(Members of the original Drifters formed this group after their firing)						
End						
❏ 1051		Am I to Be the One/I Could Have Told You	1959	6.25	12.50	25.00
❏ 1063		Gee/I Could Have Told You	1959	6.25	12.50	25.00
Harper, Chuck						
(As Chuck Fassert, he recorded with the Regents)						
Felsted						
❏ 8658		Summer Is Thru/Call on Me	1962	7.50	15.00	30.00
Harpo, Slim						
Excello						
❏ 2113		I'm a King Bee/I Got Love If You Want It	1957	15.00	30.00	60.00
❏ 2138		Wonderin' and Worryin'/Strange Love	1958	7.50	15.00	30.00
❏ 2162		One More Day/You'll Be Sorry One Day	1959	7.50	15.00	30.00
❏ 2171		Buzz Me Babe/Late Last Night	1960	7.50	15.00	30.00
❏ 2184		Blues Hangover/What a Dream	1960	7.50	15.00	30.00
❏ 2194		Rainin' in My Heart/Don't Start Cryin' Now	1961	5.00	10.00	20.00
❏ 2239		Buzzin'/I Love the Life I'm Livin'	1963	3.75	7.50	15.00
❏ 2246		Little Queen Bee (Got a Brand New King)/I Need Money (Keep Your Alibis)	1964	3.00	6.00	12.00
❏ 2253		Still Rainin' in My Heart/We're Two of a Kind	1964	3.00	6.00	12.00

Number	Title (A Side/B Side)	Year	VG	VG+	NM
☐ 2261	Sittin' Here Wondering/What's Goin' On Baby	1964	3.00	6.00	12.00
☐ 2265	Please Don't Turn Me Down/Harpo's Blues	1965	3.00	6.00	12.00
☐ 2273	Baby Scratch My Back/I'm Gonna Miss You (Like the Devil)	1965	3.00	6.00	12.00
☐ 2276	Goin' Away Blues/Just a Lonely Stranger	1966	2.50	5.00	10.00
☐ 2278	Midnight Blues/Shake Your Hips	1966	2.50	5.00	10.00
☐ 2282	I'm Your Bread-Maker, Baby/Loving You (The Way I Do)	1966	2.50	5.00	10.00
☐ 2285	Tip On In (Part 1)/Tip On In (Part 2)	1967	2.50	5.00	10.00
☐ 2289	I'm Gonna Keep What I've Got/ I've Got to Be with You Tonight	1967	2.50	5.00	10.00
☐ 2294	Te-Ni-Lee-Ni-Nu/Mailbox Blues	1968	2.50	5.00	10.00
☐ 2301	Mohair Sam/I Just Can't Leave You	1969	2.00	4.00	8.00
☐ 2305	Just for You/That's Why I Love You	1969	2.00	4.00	8.00
☐ 2306	Folsom Prison Blues/Mutual Friend	1969	2.00	4.00	8.00
☐ 2309	I've Got My Finger on Your Trigger/ The Price Is Too High	1969	2.00	4.00	8.00
☐ 2316	Rainin' in My Heart/Jody Man	1970	2.00	4.00	8.00

Harptones, The
Ambient Sound

☐ 02807	Love Needs a Heart/It's You	1982		3.00	6.00

Andrea

☐ 100	What Is Your Decision/Gimme Some	1956	10.00	20.00	40.00

Bruce

☐ 101	A Sunday Kind of Love/I'll Never Tell *"Bruce" in script lettering*	1953	150.00	300.00	600.00
☐ 101	A Sunday Kind of Love/I'll Never Tell *"Bruce" in block lettering*	1953	15.00	30.00	60.00
☐ 102	My Memories of You/It Was Just for Laughs	1954	15.00	30.00	60.00
☐ 102	My Memories of You/The Laughs on You *Same B-side with different title (and missing the apostrophe)*	1954	25.00	50.00	100.00
☐ 104	I Depended on You/Mambo Boogie	1954	15.00	30.00	60.00
☐ 109	Forever Mine/Why Should I Love You	1954	15.00	30.00	60.00
☐ 113	Since I Fell for You/Oobidee-Oobidee-Oo	1954	12.50	25.00	50.00
☐ 123	High Flying Baby/Losing a Girl Like You	1955	12.50	25.00	50.00
☐ 128	I Almost Lost My Mind/Oh Wee Baby	1955	12.50	25.00	50.00

Coed

☐ 540	Answer Me My Love/Rain Down Kisses	1960	5.00	10.00	20.00

Companion

☐ 102	All in Your Mind/The Last Dance	1961	7.50	15.00	30.00
☐ 103	What Will I Tell My Heart/Foolish Me	1961	20.00	40.00	80.00

Cub

☐ 9097	Devil in Velvet/Your Love Is a Good Love	1961	5.00	10.00	20.00

Gee

☐ 1045	Cry Like I Cried/So Good, So Fine, You're Mine	1957	7.50	15.00	30.00

KT

☐ 201	Sunset/I Gotta Have Your Love	1963	12.50	25.00	50.00

Paradise

☐ 101	Life Is But a Dream/You Know You're Doing Me Wrong *Maroon label*	1954	20.00	40.00	80.00
☐ 101	Life Is But a Dream/You Know You're Doing Me Wrong *Purple label*	1954	7.50	15.00	30.00
☐ 103	My Success/I've Got a Notion	1955	20.00	40.00	80.00
☐ 105	It All Depends on You/Guitar Shuffle *Maroon label*	1955	20.00	40.00	80.00
☐ 105	It All Depends on You/Guitar Shuffle *Purple label*	1955	7.50	15.00	30.00

Rama

☐ 203	Three Wishes/That's the Way It Goes	1956	7.50	15.00	30.00
☐ 214	The Masquerade Is Over/On Sunday Afternoon	1956	7.50	15.00	30.00
☐ 221	The Shrine of St. Cecelia/Oo Wee Baby	1957	7.50	15.00	30.00

Raven

☐ 8001	A Sunday Kind of Love/Mambo Boogie	1962	3.75	7.50	15.00

Tip Top

☐ 401	My Memories of You/High Flyin' Baby	1956	10.00	20.00	40.00

Warwick

☐ 500	I Remember/Laughing on the Outside	1959	6.25	12.50	25.00
☐ 512	Love Me Completely/Hep Teenager	1959	6.25	12.50	25.00
☐ 551	No Greater Miracle/What Kind of a Fool	1960	6.25	12.50	25.00

Harris, Genee
ABC-Paramount

☐ 9900	Bye Bye Elvis/You're Like a Jumping Jack	1958	12.50	25.00	50.00

Harris, Major
(Member of the Delfonics)
Atlantic

☐ 3217	Each Morning I Wake Up/Just a Thing I Do	1974		2.50	5.00
☐ 3248	Love Won't Let Me Wait/After Loving You	1975		2.00	4.00
☐ 3299	DJ Loving You Is Mellow (mono/stereo) *May be promo only*	1975		2.50	5.00

Number		Title (A Side/B Side)	Year	VG	VG+	NM
❏ 3303		I Got Over Love/Loving You Is Mellow	1975		2.00	4.00
❏ 3321		Jealousy/Tynisa (What's Your Hurry)	1976		2.00	4.00
❏ 3336		It's Got to Be Magic/Just a Thing That I Do	1976		2.00	4.00

Okeh

❏ 7314		Just Love Me/Loving You More	1968	7.50	15.00	30.00
❏ 7327		Like a Rolling Stone/Call Me Tomorrow	1969	15.00	30.00	60.00

WMOT

❏ 02091		Here We Are/Living's Easy Now	1981		2.00	4.00
❏ 4002		Laid Back Love/(B-side unknown)	1976		2.00	4.00

Harris, Ray
Sun

❏ 254		Come On Little Mama/Where'd You Stay Last Night	1956	37.50	75.00	150.00
❏ 272		Greenback Dollar Watch and Chain/Foolish Hearts	1957	25.00	50.00	100.00

Harris, Rolf
Epic

❏ 9567		Sun Arise/Someone's Pinched My Winkles	1963	3.00	6.00	12.00
❏ 9596		Tie Me Kangaroo Down, Sport/The Big Black Hat	1963	3.75	7.50	15.00
❏ 9596	PS	Tie Me Kangaroo Down, Sport/The Big Black Hat	1963	5.00	10.00	20.00
❏ 9615		Nick Teen & Al K. Hall/I Know a Man	1963	3.00	6.00	12.00
❏ 9615	PS	Nick Teen & Al K. Hall/I Know a Man	1963	5.00	10.00	20.00
❏ 9641		Lost Little Boy/Six White Boomers	1963	2.50	5.00	10.00
❏ 9641	PS	Lost Little Boy/Six White Boomers	1963	5.00	10.00	20.00
❏ 9682		The Court of King Caractacus/Two Buffalos	1964	2.50	5.00	10.00
❏ 9721		Ringo for President/Click Go the Shears	1964	3.75	7.50	15.00
❏ 9756		The Thing/Wild Colonial Boy	1965	2.50	5.00	10.00
❏ 9780		Tie My Hunting Dog Down, Jed/ Five Young Apprentices	1965	2.50	5.00	10.00
❏ 10037		Jake the Pig/Big Dog	1966	2.50	5.00	10.00

MGM

❏ 14103		Two Little Boys/I Love My Love	1970	2.50	5.00	10.00

20th Fox

❏ 207		Tie Me Kangaroo Down, Sport/Nick Teen & Al K. Hall	1960	5.00	10.00	20.00
		Different versions than the Epic recordings				
❏ 230		Lost Little Boy/Big Black Hat	1960	3.75	7.50	15.00

Harris, Thurston
Aladdin

❏ 3398		Little Bitty Pretty One/ I Hope You Won't Hold It Against Me	1957	5.00	10.00	20.00
❏ 3399		Do What You Did/I'm Asking Forgiveness	1957	3.75	7.50	15.00
❏ 3415		Be Baby Leba/I'm Out to Getcha	1958	3.75	7.50	15.00
❏ 3428		Only One Love Is Blessed/Smokey Joe's	1958	3.75	7.50	15.00
❏ 3430		Over and Over/You're Gonna Miss Me	1958	3.75	7.50	15.00
❏ 3435		Over Someone Else's Shoulder/Tears from My Heart	1958	3.75	7.50	15.00
❏ 3440		Purple Stew/I Heard a Rhapsody	1958	3.75	7.50	15.00
❏ 3447		From the Bottom of My Heart/ You Don't Know How Much I Love You	1959	3.75	7.50	15.00
❏ 3448		Don't You Know/From the Bottom of My Heart	1959	3.75	7.50	15.00
❏ 3450		Hey Little Girl/My Love Will Last	1959	3.75	7.50	15.00
❏ 3452		Runk Bunk/Bless Your Heart	1959	3.75	7.50	15.00
❏ 3456		Slip Slop/Paradise Hill	1959	3.75	7.50	15.00
❏ 3462		Moonlight Cocktail/Recess in Heaven	1960	3.75	7.50	15.00
❏ 3468		One Scotch, One Bourbon, One Beer/ Send Me Some Loving	1960	3.75	7.50	15.00

Cub

❏ 9108		I'd Like to Start Over Again/Mr. Satan	1962	3.00	6.00	12.00

Dot

❏ 16415		Quiet As It's Kept/Goddess of Angels	1963	2.50	5.00	10.00
❏ 16427		Poop-A-Loop/She's the One	1963	2.50	5.00	10.00

Imperial

❏ 5928		Got You on My Mind/Tears from My Heart	1963	2.50	5.00	10.00
❏ 5971		You're Gonna Need Me/I'm Asking Forgiveness	1963	2.50	5.00	10.00

Reprise

❏ 0255		Dance On Little Girl/Dancing Silhouettes	1964	2.50	5.00	10.00

United Artists

❏ 0152		Little Bitty Pretty One/Over and Over	1973		2.00	4.00
		"Silver Spotlight Series" reissue				

Harris, Tony
Dee Gee

❏ 3014		Super Man/How Much Do I Love You	1966	4.00	8.00	16.00

Triumph

❏ 60		Go, Go, Little Scrambler/Poor Boy	1964	7.50	15.00	30.00

Harris, Wynonie
Atco

❏ 6081		Destination Love/Tell a Whale of a Tale	1956	7.50	15.00	30.00

King

❏ 4210		Good Rockin' Tonight/Good Morning Mister Blues	1952	30.00	60.00	120.00
		78 originally released in 1948; the only known Wynonie Harris 45 on King before 4461				
❏ 4461		Bloodshot Eyes/Confessin' the Blues	1951	30.00	60.00	120.00
❏ 4468		I'll Never Give Up/Man Have I Got Troubles	1951	30.00	60.00	120.00

Number		Title (A Side/B Side)	Year	VG	VG+	NM
☐ 4485		Lovin' Machine/Luscious Woman	1951	30.00	60.00	120.00
		Black vinyl				
☐ 4485		Lovin' Machine/Luscious Woman	1951	100.00	200.00	400.00
		Red vinyl				
☐ 4507		My Playful Baby's Gone/Here Comes the Night	1952	25.00	50.00	100.00
☐ 4526		Keep On Churnin'/Married Women Stay Married	1952	25.00	50.00	100.00
☐ 4555		Do it Again Please/Night Train	1952	25.00	50.00	100.00
☐ 4565		Drinking Blues/Adam Come and Get Your Rib	1952	25.00	50.00	100.00
☐ 4592		Greyhound/Rot Gut	1953	25.00	50.00	100.00
☐ 4593		Bad News Baby (There'll Be Rockin' Tonight)/	1953	25.00	50.00	100.00
		Bring It Back				
☐ 4620		Mama Your Daughter Done Lied on Me/	1953	25.00	50.00	100.00
		Wasn't That Good				
☐ 4635		Song of the Bayou/The Deacon Doesn't Like It	1953	25.00	50.00	100.00
☐ 4662		Tremblin'/Rot Gut	1953	20.00	40.00	80.00
☐ 4668		Please Louise/Nearer My Love to Thee	1953	20.00	40.00	80.00
☐ 4685		Down Boy Down/Quiet Whiskey	1953	20.00	40.00	80.00
☐ 4716		Shake That Thing/Keep A-Talking	1954	20.00	40.00	80.00
☐ 4724		I Get a Thrill/Don't Take My Whiskey Away from Me	1954	20.00	40.00	80.00
☐ 4763		All She Wants to Do Is Mambo/Christina	1955	15.00	30.00	60.00
☐ 4774		Good Mambo Tonight/Git to Gittin' Baby	1955	15.00	30.00	60.00
☐ 4789		Fishtail Blues/Mr. Dollar	1955	15.00	30.00	60.00
☐ 4814		Drinkin' Sherry Wine/Get With the Guts	1955	12.50	25.00	50.00
☐ 4826		Wine, Wine, Sweet Wine/Man's Best Friend	1955	12.50	25.00	50.00
☐ 4839		Shot Gun Wedding/I Don't Know Where to Go	1955	12.50	25.00	50.00
☐ 4852		Good Morning Judge/Bloodshot Eyes	1955	12.50	25.00	50.00
☐ 5050		Big Ole Country Fool/That's Me Right Now	1957	7.50	15.00	30.00
☐ 5073		There's No Substitute for Love/A Tale of Woe	1957	7.50	15.00	30.00
☐ 5416		Good Rockin' Tonight/Bloodshot Eyes	1960	3.75	7.50	15.00
☐ 6011		Big Old Country Fool/Bloodshot Eyes	1965	2.50	5.00	10.00
☐ 6304		Good Rockin' Tonight/Good Morning Judge	1970		3.00	6.00
Roulette						
☐ 4291		Bloodshot Eyes/Sweet Lucy Brown	1960	3.00	6.00	12.00

Harrison, George

(Also see "Beatles, The"; "Traveling Wilburys")

Apple

Number		Title (A Side/B Side)	Year	VG	VG+	NM
☐ 1828		What Is Life/Apple Scruffs	1971	3.75	7.50	15.00
		With star on A-side label				
☐ 1828		What Is Life/Apple Scruffs	1971	2.00	4.00	8.00
		Without star on A-side label				
☐ 1828	PS	What Is Life/Apple Scruffs	1971	10.00	20.00	40.00
☐ 1836		Bangla-Desh/Deep Blue	1971	2.00	4.00	8.00
		With star on A-side label				
▉ 1836		Bangla-Desh/Deep Blue	1971	6.25	12.50	25.00
		Without star on A-side label				
☐ 1836	PS	Bangla-Desh/Deep Blue	1971	5.00	10.00	20.00
☐ 1862		Give Me Love (Give Me Peace on Earth)/	1973	2.00	4.00	8.00
		Miss O'Dell (2:30)				
		With incorrect time for B-side listed				
☐ 1862		Give Me Love (Give Me Peace on Earth)/	1973	2.00	4.00	8.00
		Miss O'Dell (2:20)				
		B-side playing time corrected				
☐ P-1862	DJ	Give Me Love (Give Me Peace on Earth) (mono/stereo)	1973	12.50	25.00	50.00
☐ 1877		Dark Horse/I Don't Care Anymore	1974	2.50	5.00	10.00
		White label; NOT a promo				
☐ 1877		Dark Horse/I Don't Care Anymore	1974	2.00	4.00	8.00
		Light blue and white custom photo label				
☐ 1877	PS	Dark Horse/I Don't Care Anymore	1974	20.00	40.00	80.00
☐ P-1877	DJ	Dark Horse (full length mono/stereo)	1974	10.00	20.00	40.00
☐ P-1877	DJ	Dark Horse (edited mono/stereo)	1974	15.00	30.00	60.00
☐ 1879		Ding Dong, Ding Dong/Hari's on Tour (Express)	1974	62.50	125.00	250.00
		Blue and white custom photo label				
☐ 1879		Ding Dong, Ding Dong/Hari's on Tour (Express)	1974	5.00	10.00	20.00
		Black and white custom photo label				
☐ 1879	PS	Ding Dong, Ding Dong/Hari's on Tour (Express)	1974	5.00	10.00	20.00
☐ P-1879	DJ	Ding Dong, Ding Dong (remixed mono/edited stereo)	1974	10.00	20.00	40.00
☐ 1884		You/World of Stone	1975		3.00	6.00
☐ 1884	PS	You/World of Stone	1975	3.75	7.50	15.00
☐ P-1884	DJ	You (mono/stereo)	1975	10.00	20.00	40.00
☐ 1885		This Guitar (Can't Keep from Crying)/Maya Love	1975	6.25	12.50	25.00
☐ P-1885	DJ	This Guitar (Can't Keep from Crying) (mono/stereo)	1975	12.50	25.00	50.00
☐ 2995		My Sweet Lord/Isn't It a Pity	1970	10.00	20.00	40.00
		With black star on label				
☐ 2995		My Sweet Lord/Isn't It a Pity	1970	2.00	4.00	8.00
		With "Mfd. by Apple" on label				
☐ 2995	PS	My Sweet Lord/Isn't It a Pity	1970	10.00	20.00	40.00
☐ 2995		My Sweet Lord/Isn't It a Pity	1975	6.25	12.50	25.00
		With "All Rights Reserved" disclaimer				

Capitol

Number		Title (A Side/B Side)	Year	VG	VG+	NM
☐ 1828		What Is Life/Apple Scruffs	1976	7.50	15.00	30.00
		Orange label				
☐ 1828		What Is Life/Apple Scruffs	1978		3.00	6.00
		Purple late-1970s label				

Number		Title (A Side/B Side)	Year	VG	VG+	NM
❑ 1836		Bangla-Desh/Deep Blue	1976	7.50	15.00	30.00
		Orange label				
❑ 1836		Bangla-Desh/Deep Blue	1978		3.00	6.00
		Purple late-1970s label				
❑ 1836		Bangla-Desh/Deep Blue	1983	3.75	7.50	15.00
		Black colorband label				
❑ 1862		Give Me Love (Give Me Peace on Earth)/Miss O'Dell	1978	2.00	4.00	8.00
		Purple late-1970s label				
❑ 1862		Give Me Love (Give Me Peace on Earth)/Miss O'Dell	1978	3.75	7.50	15.00
		Black colorband label				
❑ 1879		Ding Dong, Ding Dong/Hari's on Tour (Express)	1978	2.00	4.00	8.00
		Purple late-1970s label				
❑ 2995		My Sweet Lord/Isn't It a Pity	1976	5.00	10.00	20.00
		Orange label with "Capitol" at bottom				
❑ 2995		My Sweet Lord/Isn't It a Pity	1978		3.00	6.00
		Purple label; label has reeded edge				
❑ 2995		My Sweet Lord/Isn't It a Pity	1983		3.00	6.00
		Black label with colorband				
❑ 2995		My Sweet Lord/Isn't It a Pity	1988		2.50	5.00
		Purple label; label has smooth edge				

Columbia

❑ 04887		I Don't Want to Do It/Queen of the Hop	1985	6.25	12.50	25.00
		B-side by Dave Edmunds				

Dark Horse

❑ 27913		This Is Love/Breath Away from Heaven	1988		2.50	5.00
❑ 27913	PS	This Is Love/Breath Away from Heaven	1988		2.50	5.00
❑ 28131		When We Was Fab/Zig Zag	1988		2.50	5.00
❑ 28131	PS	When We Was Fab/Zig Zag	1988		2.50	5.00
❑ 28178		Got My Mind Set on You/Lay His Head	1987		2.00	4.00
❑ 28178	PS	Got My Mind Set on You/Lay His Head	1987		2.00	4.00
❑ 29744		I Really Love You/Circles	1983	6.25	12.50	25.00
❑ 29864		Wake Up My Love/Greece	1982	2.50	5.00	10.00
❑ 49725		All Those Years Ago/Writing's on the Wall	1981		2.50	5.00
❑ 49725	PS	All Those Years Ago/Writing's on the Wall	1981		2.50	5.00
❑ 49785		Teardrops/Save the World	1981	2.50	5.00	10.00
❑ 8294		This Song/Learning How to Love You	1976	2.00	4.00	8.00
		White label, NOT a promo				
❑ 8294		This Song/Learning How to Love You	1976	2.50	5.00	10.00
		Tan label				
❑ 8294	DJ	This Song (mono/stereo)	1976	6.25	12.50	25.00
❑ 8294	PS	This Song (mono/stereo)	1976	10.00	20.00	40.00
		Promotional only sleeve, different from stock sleeve				
❑ 8294	PS	This Song (mono/stereo)	1976	10.00	20.00	40.00
		Flyer with "The Story Behind This Song"				
❑ 8294	PS	This Song/Learning How to Love You	1976	7.50	15.00	30.00
❑ 8313		Crackerbox Palace/Learning How to Love You	1977	2.50	5.00	
❑ 8763		Blow Away/Soft-Hearted Hana	1979	5.00	10.00	20.00
		Without "RE-1" on label (no "Loka Productions S.A." on label)				
❑ 8763		Blow Away/Soft-Hearted Hana	1979		2.50	5.00
		With "RE-1" on label				
❑ 8763	PS	Blow Away/Soft-Hearted Hana	1979		2.50	5.00
❑ 8844		Love Comes to Everyone/Soft Touch	1979	2.50	5.00	10.00
❑ 8844	PS	Love Comes to Everyone/Soft Touch	1979	250.00	500.00	750.00

Warner Bros.

❑ 22807		Cheer Down/That's What It Takes	1989	3.75	7.50	15.00
❑ 22807	DJ	Cheer Down (same on both sides)	1989	50.00	100.00	200.00
❑ 22807	PS	Cheer Down/That's What It Takes	1989	3.75	7.50	15.00

Harrison, Jerry
(Of Talking Heads)

Sire

❑ 27977		Rev It Up/Bobby (Aboriginal Mix)	1988			3.00

Harrison, Wilbert

Bell

❑ 869		C.C. Rider/Since I Fell for You	1970		3.00	6.00

Brunswick

❑ 55511		Lovin' Operator/Love You	1974		3.00	6.00
❑ 55519		I'm Going to the River/I Need Some (Honey Honey)	1975		3.00	6.00

Chart

❑ 626		Cool Water/Calypso Man	1956	6.25	12.50	25.00

Constellation

❑ 122		New York World's Fair/Mama, Mama, Mama	1964	2.50	5.00	10.00

DeLuxe

❑ 6002		This Woman of Mine/The Letter	1953	15.00	30.00	60.00
❑ 6031		Nobody Knows My Trouble/Gin and Coconut Milk	1954	15.00	30.00	60.00

Fury

❑ 1023		Kansas City/Listen, My Darling	1959	3.75	7.50	15.00
❑ 1027		Cheating Baby/Don't Wreck My Life	1959	3.00	6.00	12.00
❑ 1028		Goodbye Kansas City/1960	1960	3.00	6.00	12.00
❑ 1031		C.C. Rider/Why Did You Leave	1960	3.00	6.00	12.00
❑ 1037		Since I Fell for You/Little School Girl	1960	3.00	6.00	12.00

Number		Title (A Side/B Side)	Year	VG	VG+	NM
❏ 1041		The Horse/Da-De-Ya-Da (I'd Do Anything for You)	1961	3.00	6.00	12.00
❏ 1047		Happy in Love/Calypso Dance	1961	3.00	6.00	12.00
❏ 1055		Drafted/My Heart Is Yours	1961	3.00	6.00	12.00
❏ 1059		Let's Stick Together/Kansas City Twist	1962	3.75	7.50	15.00
❏ 1063		Let's Stick Together/My Heart Is Yours	1962	3.00	6.00	12.00

Glades

❏ 603		Gonna Tell You a Story/Letter Edged in Black	1959	3.00	6.00	12.00

Port

❏ 3003		Baby Move On/You're Still My Baby	1965	2.00	4.00	8.00
❏ 3009		Don't Take It So Hard/Sugar Lump	1965	2.00	4.00	8.00

Rockin'

❏ 526		This Woman of Mine/The Letter	1952	25.00	50.00	100.00

Roulette

❏ 4752		No One's Love But Yours/Mini-Parade	1967	2.00	4.00	8.00

Savoy

❏ 1138		Don't Drop It/The Ways of a Woman	1954	10.00	20.00	40.00
❏ 1149		Women and Whiskey/Da-De-Ya-Da (I'd Do Anything for You)	1955	7.50	15.00	30.00
❏ 1164		Florida Special/Darling, Listen to This Song	1955	7.50	15.00	30.00
❏ 1198		Confessin' My Dream/The Way I Feel	1956	7.50	15.00	30.00
❏ 1517		My Love Is True/I Know My Baby Loves Me	1957	6.25	12.50	25.00
❏ 1531		Baby Don't You Know/My Love for You Lingers On	1958	5.00	10.00	20.00
❏ 1571		Don't Drop It/Baby Don't You Know	1959	3.75	7.50	15.00

SSS International

❏ 830		My Heart Is Yours/Pretty Little Woman	1971		3.00	6.00

Sue

❏ 11		Let's Work Together (Part 1)/ Let's Work Together (Part 2)	1969		3.00	6.00

Wet Soul

❏ 4		My Heart Is Yours/Pretty Little Woman	1970	2.00	4.00	8.00

Harshman, Robert Luke – See "Hart, Bobby"

Hart, Bobby
(Also see "Boyce, Tommy, and Bobby Hart"; "Dolenz, Jones, Boyce and Hart")
Ariola America

❏ 809		Lovers for the Night/You Get Smoke in Your Eyes	1980		2.50	5.00

Bamboo

❏ 507		The Girl I Used to Know/The Spider and the Fly	1961	7.50	15.00	30.00

Chelsea

❏ BCBO-0026		Easy Evil/California	1973		2.50	5.00

DCP

❏ 1113		That'll Be the Day/Turn On Your Lovelight	1964	5.00	10.00	20.00
❏ 1142		Baby Let Your Hair Down/Jealous Feeling	1965	6.25	12.50	25.00
❏ 1152		Around the Corner/Cry My Eyes Out	1966	5.00	10.00	20.00

Era

❏ 3039		Girl in the Window/Journey of Love	1961	5.00	10.00	20.00

Guyden

❏ 2022		Is You Is Or Is You Ain't My Baby/Girl of My Dreams	1959	7.50	15.00	30.00
		As "Robert Luke Harshman"				

Infinity

❏ 017		Too Many Teardrops/The People Next Door	1963	5.00	10.00	20.00
❏ 022		Lovesick Blues/I Think It's Called a Heartache	1963	5.00	10.00	20.00

Radio

❏ 122		Stop Talkin', Start Lovin'/Love Whatcha Doin' to Me	1959	10.00	20.00	40.00
		As "Robert Luke Harshman"				

Reel

❏ 100		Girl in the Window/Journey of Love	1961		20.00	40.00

Warner Bros.

❏ 8058		Hard Core Man/To Keep from Crying	1974		2.50	5.00
❏ 8058	PS	Hard Core Man/To Keep from Crying	1974	2.00	4.00	8.00
❏ 49079		The Loneliest Night/Sometimes Love	1979		2.50	5.00

Hart, Mickey
(Of the Grateful Dead)
Warner Bros.

❏ 7644		Blind John/Pump Man	1972	2.50	5.00	10.00

Hart, Rocky
Big Top

❏ 3069		Crying/(B-side unknown)	1961	7.50	15.00	30.00

Cub

❏ 9052		Every Day/Come with Me	1959	7.50	15.00	30.00

Glo

❏ 216		I Play the Part of a Fool/ Someone Stole My Baby While Doing the Twist	1961	50.00	100.00	200.00

Hartford, Ken
Southern Sound

❏ 119		Jay Walker/Little Joe, Go Lightly	1963	6.25	12.50	25.00
		With Frankie Valli				

Number		Title (A Side/B Side)	Year	VG	VG+	NM

Harvey
(Also see "Moonglows, The")
Chess
❑ 1713		I Want Somebody/Da Da Goo Goo	1959	10.00	20.00	40.00
❑ 1725		Twelve Months of the Year/Don't Be Afraid of Love	1959	10.00	20.00	40.00
❑ 1749		Blue Skies/Ooh, Ouch, Stop!	1960	6.25	12.50	25.00
❑ 1760		If I Can't Have You/My Heart Cries	1960	6.25	12.50	25.00
		As "Etta and Harvey" (Etta is Etta James)				
❑ 1771		Spoonful/It's a Crying Shame	1960	6.25	12.50	25.00
		As "Etta and Harvey" (Etta is Etta James)				
❑ 1781		The First Time/Mama	1961	6.25	12.50	25.00
		As "Harvey Fuqua"				

Harvey
❑ 121		What Can You Do Now/Will I Do	1962	10.00	20.00	40.00
		As "Harvey and Ann"				

Tri-Phi
❑ 1017		She Loves Me So/Any Way You Wanta	1962	10.00	20.00	40.00
❑ 1024		Memories of You/Come On and Answer Me	1963	15.00	30.00	60.00

Harvey and Doc with the Dwellers
Annette
❑ 1002		Oh, Baby/Uncle Kev	1964	62.50	125.00	250.00
		Phil Spector appeared on and produced this				

Harvey and the Moonglows – See "Moonglows, The"

Harvey, Phil
(Actually Phil Spector)
Imperial
❑ 5583		Willy Boy/Bumbershoot	1959	37.50	75.00	150.00

Hassan, Ali
Philles
❑ 103		Malaguena/Chop Sticks	1962	7.50	15.00	30.00

Hassles, The
(Billy Joel was in this group)
United Artists
❑ 50215		You've Got Me Hummin'/I'm Thinkin'	1967	3.00	6.00	12.00
❑ 50215	PS	You've Got Me Hummin'/I'm Thinkin'	1967	5.00	10.00	20.00
❑ 50258		I Hear Voices/Every Step I Take	1968	3.00	6.00	12.00
❑ 50450		4 O'Clock in the Morning/	1968	3.00	6.00	12.00
		Let Me Bring You to the Sunshine				
❑ 50513		Night After Day/Country Boy	1969	3.00	6.00	12.00
❑ 50586		Traveling Band/Great Balls of Fire	1969	3.00	6.00	12.00

Hatfield, Bobby
(Of the Righteous Brothers)
Moonglow
❑ 220		I Need a Girl/Hot Tamale	1963	6.25	12.50	25.00

Verve
❑ 10598		Hang-Ups/Soul Cafe	1968	2.00	4.00	8.00
❑ 10621		Brothers/What's the Matter Baby	1968	2.00	4.00	8.00
❑ 10634		Only You/The Wonder of You	1969	2.00	4.00	8.00
❑ 10639		My Prayer/I Wish I Didn't Love You So	1969	2.00	4.00	8.00
❑ 10641		Answer Me My Love/I Only Have Eyes for You	1969	2.00	4.00	8.00

Warner Bros.
❑ 7566		Rock 'N Roll Woman/Oo Wee Baby, I Love You	1972		2.50	5.00
❑ 7649		Stay with Me/Rock 'N Roll Woman	1972		2.50	5.00

Hawk, The
(Actually Jerry Lee Lewis)
Phillips Int'l.
❑ 3559		In the Mood/I Get the Blues When It Rains	1960	12.50	25.00	50.00

Hawkins, Dale
ABC-Paramount
❑ 10668		I'll Fly High/La La Song	1965	2.50	5.00	10.00

Abnak
❑ 110		The Flag/And I Believed You	1965	3.00	6.00	12.00

Atlantic
❑ 2126		Stay at Home, Lulu/I Can't Erase You	1961	5.00	10.00	20.00
❑ 2150		What a Feeling/Women, That's What's Happening	1962	5.00	10.00	20.00

Bell
❑ 807		Back Street/Little Rain Cloud	1969	2.00	4.00	8.00
❑ 827		Heavy on My Mind/Joe	1969	2.00	4.00	8.00

Checker
❑ 843		See You Soon, Baboon/Four Letter Word	1956	7.50	15.00	30.00
❑ 863		Susie-Q/Don't Treat Me This Way	1957	10.00	20.00	40.00
❑ 876		Baby, Baby/Mrs. Merguitory's Daughter	1957	7.50	15.00	30.00
❑ 892		Little Pig/Tornado	1958	6.25	12.50	25.00
❑ 900		La-Do-Dada/Cross Ties	1958	6.25	12.50	25.00

Number		Title (A Side/B Side)	Year	VG	VG+	NM
❑ 906		My Babe/A House, a Car, and a Wedding Ring	1958	6.25	12.50	25.00
❑ 913		Someday, One Day/Take My Heart	1959	6.25	12.50	25.00
❑ 916		Class Cutter (Yeah Yeah)/Lonely Nights	1959	6.25	12.50	25.00
❑ 923		Ain't That Lovin' You Baby/My Dream	1959	6.25	12.50	25.00
❑ 929		Our Turn/Lifeguard Man	1959	6.25	12.50	25.00
❑ 934		Liza Jane/Back to School Blues	1959	6.25	12.50	25.00
❑ 940		Hot Dog/Don't Break Your Promise to Me	1960	5.00	10.00	20.00
❑ 944		Poor Little Rhode Island/Every Little Girl	1960	5.00	10.00	20.00
❑ 944	PS	Poor Little Rhode Island/Every Little Girl	1960	37.50	75.00	150.00
❑ 962		Linda/Who	1960	5.00	10.00	20.00
❑ 970		Grandma's House/I Want to Love You	1961	5.00	10.00	20.00

Lincoln

❑ 002		Johnny B. Goode/Baby We Had It	196?	2.00	4.00	8.00

Paula

❑ 424		First Cut Is the Deepest/ Nothing Left to Do But Say Goodbye	1977		2.50	5.00

Tilt

❑ 781		Money Honey/The Same Old Way	1962	5.00	10.00	20.00
❑ 783		Forbidden Love/Wish I Hadn't Called Home	1962	5.00	10.00	20.00
❑ 785		Hawk Blows, Band Plays (Part 1)/ Hawk Blows, Band Plays (Part 2)	1962	5.00	10.00	20.00

Zonk

❑ 1002		Gotta Dance/Peaches	1973		2.50	5.00

Hawkins, Jalacy – See "Hawkins, Screamin' Jay"

Hawkins, Ronnie
(And the Hawks on Roulette, who later recorded as "Levon and the Hawks" and "The Band")

Cotillion

❑ 44060		Matchbox/Down in the Alley	1970		3.00	6.00
❑ 44067		Forty Days/Bitter Green	1970		3.00	6.00
❑ 44076		Little Bird/One More Night	1970		3.00	6.00

Monument

❑ 8548		Lawdy Miss Clawdy/Cora Mae	1972		2.50	5.00
❑ 8561		Lonesome Town/Kinky	1973		2.50	5.00
❑ 8573		Diddley Daddy/Cora Mae	1973		2.50	5.00
❑ 8583		Bo Diddley/Lonely Hours	1973		2.50	5.00

Roulette

❑ 4154	M	Forty Days/One of These Days	1959	6.25	12.50	25.00
❑ SSR-4154	S	Forty Days/One of These Days	1959	15.00	30.00	60.00
❑ 4177	M	Mary Lou/Need Your Lovin'	1959	6.25	12.50	25.00
❑ SSR-4177	S	Mary Lou/Need Your Lovin'	1959	15.00	30.00	60.00
❑ 4209		Southern Love/Love Me Like You Can	1959	5.00	10.00	20.00
❑ 4228		Lonely Hours/Clara	1960	5.00	10.00	20.00
❑ 4231		The Ballad of Caryl Chessman/ The Tale of Floyd Collins	1960	5.00	10.00	20.00
❑ 4249		Ruby Baby/Hayride	1960	5.00	10.00	20.00
❑ 4267		Summertime/Mister and Mississippi	1960	5.00	10.00	20.00
❑ 4311		Cold, Cold Heart/Nobody's Lonesome for Me	1960	5.00	10.00	20.00
❑ 4400		Come Love/I Feel Good	1961	5.00	10.00	20.00
❑ 4483		Bo Diddley/Who Do You Love	1963	5.00	10.00	20.00
❑ 4502		High Blood Pressure/There's a Screw Loose	1963	5.00	10.00	20.00

Hawkins, Screamin' Jay

Apollo

❑ 506		Please Try to Understand/Not Anymore	1957	6.25	12.50	25.00
❑ 528		Baptize Me in Wine/Not Anymore	1958	6.25	12.50	25.00

Chancellor

❑ 1117		Ashes/Nitty Gritty	1962	3.75	7.50	15.00

Decca

❑ 32019		All Night/I'm Not Made of Clay	1966	3.75	7.50	15.00
❑ 32100		I Put a Spell On You/You're an Exception to the Rule	1967	10.00	20.00	40.00

Enrica

❑ 1010		I Hear Voices/I Just Don't Care	1962	3.75	7.50	15.00

Grand

❑ 135		Take Me Back/I Is	1957	6.25	12.50	25.00

Mercury

❑ 70549		This Is All/She Put the Whammee on Me	1955	20.00	40.00	80.00

Okeh

❑ 7072		I Put a Spell On You/Little Demon	1956	10.00	20.00	40.00
❑ 7084		You Made Me Love You/Darling, Please Forgive Me	1957	7.50	15.00	30.00
❑ 7087		Person to Person/Frenzy	1957	7.50	15.00	30.00
❑ 7101		Alligator Wine/There's Something Wrong with You	1958	7.50	15.00	30.00

Philips

❑ 40606		Stone Crazy/I'm Lonely	1969		3.00	6.00
❑ 40636		Too Many Teardrops/Makaka Ways	1969		3.00	6.00
❑ 40645		Constipation Blues/Do You Really Love Me	1969		3.00	6.00
❑ 40668		Moanin'/Do You Really Love Me	1970		3.00	6.00
❑ 40674		Our Love Is Not for Three/Take Me Back	1970		3.00	6.00

Providence

❑ 411		My Kind of Love/Po' Folks	1965	3.00	6.00	12.00

RCA Victor

❑ PB-10127		You Put the Spell on Me/Voodoo	1974		2.50	5.00

Number	Title (A Side/B Side)	Year	VG	VG+	NM
Timely					
❑ 1004	Baptize Me in Wine/Not Anymore	1954	20.00	40.00	80.00
❑ 1005	I Found My Way to Wine/Please Try to Understand	1954	20.00	40.00	80.00
Wing					
❑ 90005	Well, I Tried/You're All of Life to Me	1955	10.00	20.00	40.00
❑ 90055	Even Though/Talk About Me	1956	7.50	15.00	30.00

Hawks, The
(More than one group, none of them the band that became "The Band")
ABC-Paramount

❑ 10116	Grasshopper/The Grissle	1960	5.00	10.00	20.00
Del-Fi					
❑ 4108	A Little More Wine, My Dear?/Fussy	1958	10.00	20.00	40.00
Imperial					
❑ 5266	Joe the Grinder/Candy Girl	1954	30.00	60.00	120.00
❑ 5281	She's All Right/Good News	1954	25.00	50.00	100.00
❑ 5292	It Ain't That Way/I-Yi	1954	15.00	30.00	60.00
❑ 5306	Nobody But You/Give It Up	1954	15.00	30.00	60.00
❑ 5317	All Women Are the Same/That's What You Are	1954	15.00	30.00	60.00
❑ 5332	It's Too Late Now/I Can't See for Lookin'	1955	15.00	30.00	60.00
Mala					
❑ 401	Cupcake/Lupp!!	1959	5.00	10.00	20.00
Modern					
❑ 990	It's All Over/Ever Since You Been Gone	1956	20.00	40.00	80.00
Post					
❑ 2004	These Blues/Why Oh Why	1955	75.00	150.00	300.00

Hawley, Deane
Dore

❑ 524	New Fad/Pretty Little Mary	1959	3.75	7.50	15.00
❑ 536	Good Morning, Mr. Sun/Bossman	1959	3.75	7.50	15.00
❑ 543	Where Is My Angel/I'll Never Be a Fool Again	1960	3.75	7.50	15.00
❑ 554	Look for a Star/Bossman	1960	3.75	7.50	15.00
❑ 569	Like a Fool/Stay at Home Blues	1960	3.75	7.50	15.00
❑ 577	Hey There/Rainbow	1960	3.75	7.50	15.00
Liberty					
❑ 55359	Pocketful of Rainbows/That Dream Could Never Be	1961	5.00	10.00	20.00
❑ 55446	Queen of the Angels/You Conquered Me	1962	6.25	12.50	25.00
Sundown					
❑ 111	I Hate to See Me Go/Love of the Common People	196?	2.50	5.00	10.00
❑ 113	That's the Name of the Game/Canterbury Station	196?	2.50	5.00	10.00
Valor					
❑ 2003	Mummy's Bracelet/Don't Keep Me Guessin'	1961	7.50	15.00	30.00
Warner Bros.					
❑ 5484	I Know She'll Be There/You'll Never Have to Cry Again	1964	3.00	6.00	12.00

Hayes, Jimmy, and the Soul Surfers
Imperial

❑ 5986	Summer Surfin'/Down on the Beach	1963	6.25	12.50	25.00

Hayes, Linda
Antler

❑ 4000	I Had a Dream/You Ain't Movin' Me	1956	7.50	15.00	30.00
Decca					
❑ 29644	Our Love's Forever Blessed/You're the Only One for Me	1955	7.50	15.00	30.00
Hollywood					
❑ 1003	Take Me Back/Yours for the Asking	1953	12.50	25.00	50.00
❑ 1009	No Next Time/Don't Do Nothin' Baby	1954	10.00	20.00	40.00
❑ 1016	Play It Right/Your Back's Out	1954	10.00	20.00	40.00
❑ 1019	Non-Cooperation/Grrr! Mambo	1954	10.00	20.00	40.00
❑ 1027	Change of Heart/Darling Angel	1954	10.00	20.00	40.00
❑ 1031	Johnny Ace's Last Letter/Why Johnny Why	1955	12.50	25.00	50.00
	With Johnny Moore				
❑ 1032	Our Love's Forever Blessed/You're the Only One for Me	1955	15.00	30.00	60.00
King					
❑ 4752	My Name Ain't Annie/Let's Babalu	1954	18.75	37.50	75.00
❑ 4773	Please Have Mercy/Oochi Poochi	1955	12.50	25.00	50.00
Recorded in Hollywood					
❑ 244	Yes! I Know (What You're Putting Down)/Sister Ann	1953	12.50	25.00	50.00
❑ 246	Big City (Part 1)/Big City (Part 2)	1953	12.50	25.00	50.00

Hayes, Tommy
Philips

❑ 40259	Trance/Glistening Lights	1965	7.50	15.00	30.00
	The Four Seasons sing backup				

Heartbeats, The
(Lead singer James Sheppard later formed "Shep and the Limelites")
Gee

❑ 1043	When I Found You/Hands Off My Baby	1957	12.50	25.00	50.00

Number	Title (A Side/B Side)	Year	VG	VG+	NM
❏ 1047	500 Miles to Go/After New Year's Eve	1958	10.00	20.00	40.00
	Red label				
❏ 1047	500 Miles to Go/After New Year's Eve	1958	5.00	10.00	20.00
	Gray label				
❏ 1061	People Are Talking/Your Way	1960	5.00	10.00	20.00
❏ 1062	Darling How Long/Hurry Home Baby	1960	5.00	10.00	20.00

Guyden

❏ 2011	One Million Years/Let's Get Married	1959	10.00	20.00	40.00
	Yellow label				
❏ 2011	One Million Years/Let's Get Married	1959	7.50	15.00	30.00
	Purple label				

Hull

❏ 711	Crazy for You/Rockin-N-Rollin-N-Rhythm-N-Blues-N	1955	75.00	150.00	300.00
	Pink label, "Sheppard-Miller" as A-side composers				
❏ 711	Crazy for You/Rockin-N-Rollin-N-Rhythm-N-Blues-N	1955	37.50	75.00	150.00
	Pink label, "Miller" as A-side composer				
❏ 711	Crazy for You/Rockin-N-Rollin-N-Rhythm-N-Blues-N	1955	12.50	25.00	50.00
	Black label				
❏ 711	DJ Crazy for You/Rockin-N-Rollin-N-Rhythm-N-Blues-N	1955	150.00	300.00	600.00
	White label				
❏ 713	Darling How Long/Hurry Home Baby	1956	37.50	75.00	150.00
❏ 716	People Are Talking/Your Way	1956	37.50	75.00	150.00
❏ 720	A Thousand Miles Away/Oh Baby Don't	1957	50.00	100.00	200.00
	Black label				
❏ 720	A Thousand Miles Away/Oh Baby Don't	1957	15.00	30.00	60.00
	Red label				

Jubilee

❏ 5202	Finally/Boil and Bubble	1955	7.50	15.00	30.00

Network

❏ 71200	Tormented/After Everybody's Gone	1955	75.00	150.00	300.00
	Cream label, black vinyl				
❏ 71200	Tormented/After Everybody's Gone	195?	15.00	30.00	60.00
	Yellow label, black vinyl				
❏ 71200	Tormented/After Everybody's Gone	195?	6.25	12.50	25.00
	Red vinyl; all the above on Network as "The Heart Beats Quintet"				

Rama

❏ 216	A Thousand Miles Away/Oh Baby Don't	1956	7.50	15.00	30.00
❏ 222	Wedding Bells/I Won't Be the Fool Anymore	1957	10.00	20.00	40.00
❏ 231	I Want to Know/Everybody's Somebody's Fool	1957	10.00	20.00	40.00

Roulette

❏ 4054	I Found a Job/Down on My Knees	1958	7.50	15.00	30.00
❏ 4091	One Day Next Year/Sometimes I Wonder	1958	7.50	15.00	30.00
❏ 4194	Crazy for You/Down on My Knees	1959	7.50	15.00	30.00

Heartbreakers, The

(Several different groups, none of which have anything to do with Johnny Thunders or Tom Petty)

Atco

❏ 6258	The Willow Wept/You Had Time	1963	5.00	10.00	20.00

Brent

❏ 7037	I'm Leaving It All Up to You/Corrido Mash	1962	7.50	15.00	30.00

Donna

❏ 1381	Everytime I See You/Cradle Rock	1963	30.00	60.00	120.00
	Frank Zappa plays guitar on this record				

Linda

❏ 114	Please Answer/She Is My Baby	1964	3.75	7.50	15.00

Markay

❏ 106	Since You've Been Gone/John Law	1962	20.00	40.00	80.00

MGM

❏ 13129	It's Hard Being a Girl/Special Occasions	1963	3.75	7.50	15.00

RCA Victor

❏ 47-4327	Heartbreaker/Wanda	1951	150.00	300.00	600.00
❏ 47-4508	You're So Necessary to Me/	1952	150.00	300.00	600.00
	I'm Only Following My Heart				
❏ 47-4662	Why Don't I/Rockin' Daddy-O	1952	125.00	250.00	500.00
❏ 47-4849	There Is Time/It's OK With Me	1952	125.00	250.00	500.00

Swan

❏ 4242	Baby Baby/I Told You So	1966	3.75	7.50	15.00

Vik

❏ 0261	Without a Cause/One, Two, I Love You	1957	37.50	75.00	150.00
❏ 0299	My Love/Love You Till the Day I Die	1957	62.50	125.00	250.00

Hedgehoppers Anonymous

Parrot

❏ 3002	Remember/Baby (You're My Everything)	1966	2.50	5.00	10.00
❏ 9800	It's Good News Week/Afraid of Love	1965	3.00	6.00	12.00
❏ 9817	Don't Push Me/Please Don't Hurt Your Heart for Me	1966	2.50	5.00	10.00

Heinz

London

❏ 9619	Don't You Knock on My Door/Just Like Eddie	1963	3.75	7.50	15.00

Number		Title (A Side/B Side)	Year	VG	VG+	NM
Tower						
❏ 110		Questions I Can't Answer/The Beating of My Heart	1964	5.00	10.00	20.00
❏ 172		Digging My Potatoes/Don't Think Twice, It's All Right	1965	5.00	10.00	20.00
❏ 195		Don't Worry Baby/Heart Full of Sorrow	1966	7.50	15.00	30.00
❏ 253		I'm Not a Bad Boy/Movin' In	1966	5.00	10.00	20.00

Hendrix, Al
ABC-Paramount

❏ 9901		Rhonda Lee/Go, Daddy, Rock	1958	6.25	12.50	25.00
Legree						
❏ 701		Young and Wild/(B-side unknown)	1960	30.00	60.00	120.00
Tally						
❏ 119		Rhonda Lee/Go, Daddy, Rock	1957	20.00	40.00	80.00

Hendrix, Jimi
Audio Fidelity

❏ 167		No Such Animal (Part 1)/No Such Animal (Part 2)	1970	3.75	7.50	15.00
❏ 167	PS	No Such Animal (Part 1)/No Such Animal (Part 2)	1970	10.00	20.00	40.00
Reprise						
❏ 0572		Hey Joe/51st Anniversary	1967	25.00	50.00	100.00
❏ 0572	PS	Hey Joe/51st Anniversary	1967	150.00	300.00	600.00
❏ PRO 595	DJ	Little Drummer Boy-Silent Night/Auld Lang Syne	1974	25.00	50.00	100.00
❏ PRO 595	PS	...And a Happy New Year	1974	25.00	50.00	100.00
❏ 0597		Purple Haze/The Wind Cries Mary	1967	3.75	7.50	15.00
❏ 0641		Foxey Lady/Hey Joe	1967	3.75	7.50	15.00
❏ 0665		Up from the Skies/One Rainy Wish	1968	5.00	10.00	20.00
❏ 0728		Purple Haze/Foxey Lady	1968	3.00	6.00	12.00
		"Back to Back Hits" series -- originals have both "r:" and "W7" logos				
❏ 0742		All Along the Watchtower/Crosstown Traffic	1971		3.00	6.00
		"Back to Back Hits" series				
❏ 0767		All Along the Watchtower/Burning of the Midnight Lamp	1968	3.75	7.50	15.00
❏ 0792		Crosstown Traffic/Gypsy Eyes	1968	3.75	7.50	15.00
❏ 0853		If 6 Was 9/Stone Free	1969	3.75	7.50	15.00
❏ 0905		Stepping Stone/Izabella	1970	25.00	50.00	100.00
❏ 1000		Freedom/Angel	1971	3.75	7.50	15.00
❏ 1044		Star Spangled Banner/Dolly Dagger	1971	3.75	7.50	15.00
❏ 1082		Johnny B. Goode/Lover Man	1972	3.75	7.50	15.00
❏ 1118		The Wind Cries Mary/Little Wing	1972	3.75	7.50	15.00
❏ 29845		Fire/Little Wing	1982		3.00	6.00

Henhouse Five Plus Too – See "Stevens, Ray"

Henry, Clarence
(Also known as Clarence "Frogman" Henry)
Argo

❏ 5259		Ain't Got No Home/Troubles, Troubles	1956	5.00	10.00	20.00
❏ 5266		I'm a Country Boy/Lonely Tramp	1957	4.00	8.00	16.00
❏ 5273		Found a Home/It Won't Be Long	1957	4.00	8.00	16.00
❏ 5305		I'm in Love/Baby Baby Please	1958	4.00	8.00	16.00
❏ 5378		I Don't Know Why/Just Baby and Me	1960	5.00	10.00	20.00
❏ 5378		But I Do/Just Baby and Me	1960	4.00	8.00	16.00
		A-side: Same song, new title				
❏ 5388		You Always Hurt the One You Love/Hello, Hello	1961	3.75	7.50	15.00
❏ 5395		Lonely Street/Why Can't You	1961	3.75	7.50	15.00
❏ 5401		On Bended Knees/Standing in the Need of Love	1961	3.75	7.50	15.00
❏ 5408		A Little Too Much/I Wish That I Could Stay the Same	1962	3.00	6.00	12.00
❏ 5414		Dream Myself a Sweetheart/Lost Without You	1962	3.00	6.00	12.00
❏ 5426		Jealous Kind/Come On and Dance	1962	3.00	6.00	12.00
❏ 5448		If I Didn't Care/It Takes Two to Tango	1963	3.00	6.00	12.00
❏ 5480		Looking Back/Long Lost and Worried	1964	2.50	5.00	10.00
Cadet						
❏ 5259		Ain't Got No Home/Troubles, Troubles	1966	2.00	4.00	8.00
Dial						
❏ 4057		This Time/Hummin' a Heartache	1967		3.00	6.00
❏ 4072		Shake Your Money Maker/That's When I Guessed	1968		3.00	6.00
Parrot						
❏ 45004		Have You Ever Been Lonely/Little Green Frog	1964	2.50	5.00	10.00
❏ 45009		I Told My Pillow/Can't Hide My Tear	1964	2.50	5.00	10.00
❏ 45015		I Might As Well/Tore Up Over You	1965	2.50	5.00	10.00

Henry, Earl
Dot

❏ 15756		Whatcha Gonna Do?/I Am the Man	1958	12.50	25.00	50.00
❏ 15875		My Suzanne/Believe a Traveler	1958	7.50	15.00	30.00

Hep Stars, The
(With Benny Andersson, later of Bjorn & Benny as well ABBA)
Chartmaker

❏ 414		It's Now Winter's Day/Musty Dusty	1969	5.00	10.00	20.00
Dunhill						
❏ 4040		Sunny Girl/No Response	1966	6.25	12.50	25.00

Number		Title (A Side/B Side)	Year	VG	VG+	NM

Heralds, The
Herald

| ❏ 435 | | Eternal Love/Gonna Love You | 1954 | 62.50 | 125.00 | 250.00 |

Herd, The
(Peter Frampton was in this group)
Fontana

❏ 1588		I Can Fly/Understand Me	1967	2.50	5.00	10.00
❏ 1602		Sweet William/From the Underworld	1967	2.50	5.00	10.00
❏ 1610		Paradise Lost/Come On, Believe Me	1968	2.50	5.00	10.00
❏ 1618		Our Fairy Tale/I Don't Want Our Loving to Die	1968	2.50	5.00	10.00
❏ 1646		The Game/Beauty Queen	1969	2.50	5.00	10.00

Herman's Hermits
(Also see "Noone, Peter")
Abkco

❏ 4021		Mrs. Brown You've Got a Lovely Daughter/ I'm Henry VIII, I Am	1972		2.50	5.00
❏ 4022		I'm Into Something Good/ Can't You Hear My Heartbeat	1972		2.50	5.00
❏ 4023		There's a Kind of Hush (All Over the World)/ Wonderful World	1972		2.50	5.00
❏ 4024		Listen People/Dandy	1972		2.50	5.00
❏ 4042		Silhouettes/Just a Little Bit Better	1973		2.50	5.00
❏ 4043		A Must to Avoid/Leaning on the Lamp Post	1973		2.50	5.00

Buddah

| ❏ 516 | | Lonely Situation (Love Is All I Need)/ Blond Haired, Blue Eyed Boy | 1976 | 2.00 | 4.00 | 8.00 |

MGM

❏ 13280		I'm Into Something Good/Your Hand in Mine	1964	2.50	5.00	10.00
❏ 13310		Can't You Hear My Heartbeat/I Know Why	1964	2.50	5.00	10.00
❏ 13310	PS	Can't You Hear My Heartbeat/I Know Why	1964	3.75	7.50	15.00
❏ 13332		Silhouettes/Walkin' With My Angel	1965	2.50	5.00	10.00
❏ 13341		Mrs. Brown You've Got a Lovely Daughter/ I Gotta Dream On	1965	2.50	5.00	10.00
❏ 13341	PS	Mrs. Brown You've Got a Lovely Daughter/ I Gotta Dream On	1965	3.75	7.50	15.00
❏ 13354		Wonderful World/Traveling Light	1965	2.50	5.00	10.00
❏ 13354	PS	Wonderful World/Traveling Light	1965	3.75	7.50	15.00
❏ 13367		I'm Henry VIII, I Am/The End of the World	1965	2.50	5.00	10.00
❏ 13367	PS	I'm Henry VIII, I Am/The End of the World	1965	5.00	10.00	20.00
❏ 13398		Just a Little Bit Better/Sea Cruise	1965	2.50	5.00	10.00
❏ 13398	PS	Just a Little Bit Better/Sea Cruise	1965	3.75	7.50	15.00
❏ 13437		A Must to Avoid/The Man with the Cigar	1966	2.00	4.00	8.00
❏ 13462		Listen People/Got a Feeling	1966	2.00	4.00	8.00
❏ 13500		Leaning on the Lamp Post/Hold On	1966	2.00	4.00	8.00
❏ 13548		This Door Swings Both Ways/For Love	1966	2.00	4.00	8.00
❏ 13603		Dandy/My Reservation's Been Confirmed	1966	2.00	4.00	8.00
❏ 13603	PS	Dandy/My Reservation's Been Confirmed	1966	3.75	7.50	15.00
❏ 13639		East West/What Is Wrong What Is Right	1966	2.00	4.00	8.00
❏ 13681		There's a Kind of Hush/No Milk Today	1967	2.00	4.00	8.00
❏ 13681	PS	There's a Kind of Hush/No Milk Today	1967	3.75	7.50	15.00
❏ 13761		Don't Go Out Into the Rain (You're Going to Melt)/ Moonshine Man	1967	2.00	4.00	8.00
❏ 13761	PS	Don't Go Out Into the Rain (You're Going to Melt)/ Moonshine Man	1967	3.75	7.50	15.00
❏ 13787		Museum/Last Bus Home	1967	2.00	4.00	8.00
❏ 13787	PS	Museum/Last Bus Home	1967	3.75	7.50	15.00
❏ 13885		I Can Take or Leave Your Loving/Marcel's	1967	2.00	4.00	8.00
❏ 13934		Sleepy Joe/Just One Girl	1968	2.50	5.00	10.00
❏ 13973		Sunshine Girl/Nobody Needs to Know	1968	2.50	5.00	10.00
❏ 13994		Ooh, She's Done It Again/ The Most Beautiful Thing in My Life	1968	2.50	5.00	10.00
❏ 14035		Something's Happening/ Little Miss Sorrow, Child of Tomorrow	1969	2.50	5.00	10.00
❏ 14060		My Lady/My Sentimental Friend	1969	2.50	5.00	10.00
❏ 14100		It's Alright Now/(Here Comes) The Star	1969	2.50	5.00	10.00

Private Stock

| ❏ 45,019 | | Ginny Go Softly/Blond Haired, Blue Eyed Boy | 1975 | 2.00 | 4.00 | 8.00 |

Roulette

| ❏ 7213 | | Truck Stop Mama/Heart Get Ready for Love | 1977 | 3.75 | 7.50 | 15.00 |

Herrold, Dennis
Imperial

| ❏ 5482 | | Hip Hip Baby/Make with the Lovin' | 1957 | 20.00 | 40.00 | 80.00 |

Hi-Fives, The
(Two different groups?)
Bell

| ❏ 634 | | Julie/Son of Raunchy | 1965 | 10.00 | 20.00 | 40.00 |

Bingo

| ❏ 1006 | | Felicia/Windy City Special | 1960 | 7.50 | 15.00 | 30.00 |

Decca

| ❏ 30576 | | My Friend/How Can I Win? | 1958 | 10.00 | 20.00 | 40.00 |

Number		Title (A Side/B Side)	Year	VG	VG+	NM
❑ 30657		Dorothy/Just a Shoulder to Cry On	1958	12.50	25.00	50.00
❑ 30744		Lonely/What's New	1958	10.00	20.00	40.00
Jerden						
❑ 730		Goin' Away/Tort	1964	3.75	7.50	15.00

Hi-Liters, The

Hico

❑ 2432		Let Me Be True to You/In the Night	1958	25.00	50.00	100.00
❑ 2433		Over the Rainbow/(B-side unknown)	1958	37.50	75.00	150.00
		Hico sides with King Bassie and His Three Aces...Ben Vereen was a member				

Vee Jay

❑ 184		Bobby Sox Baby/Hello Dear	1956	250.00	500.00	1,000

Wen-Dee

❑ 1927		Baby Don't Treat Me This Way/Route 66	1955	15.00	30.00	60.00

Hi-Lites, The – See "Chi-Lites, The"

Hickey, Ersel

Epic

❑ 9263		Bluebirds Over the Mountain/Hangin' Around	1958	7.50	15.00	30.00
❑ 9278		Goin' Down That Road/Lovers' Land	1958	6.25	12.50	25.00
❑ 9298		You Never Can Tell/Wedding Day	1958	6.25	12.50	25.00
❑ 9309		Don't Be Afraid of Love/You Threw a Dart	1959	6.25	12.50	25.00
❑ 9320		I Can't Love Another/People Gotta Talk	1959	6.25	12.50	25.00
❑ 9357		Love in Bloom/What Do You Want	1960	6.25	12.50	25.00
❑ 9395		Another Wasted Day/Money Brought Me You	1960	6.25	12.50	25.00
Janus						
❑ 151		Bluebirds Over the Mountain/Self Made Man	1971		2.50	5.00
Kapp						
❑ 372		Teardrops at Dawn/I Guess You Can Call It Love	1961	5.00	10.00	20.00
Laurie						
❑ 3165		Some Enchanted Evening/Put Your Mind at Ease	1963	5.00	10.00	20.00
Toot						
❑ 602		Tryin' to Get to You/Blue Skies	196?	2.50	5.00	10.00

Hide-A-Ways, The

MGM

❑ 55004		Cherie/Me Makem Powwow	1955	125.00	250.00	500.00

Ronni

❑ 1000		Can't Help Lovin' That Girl of Mine/I'm Coming Home	1954	3,000	4,500	6,000

High Numbers, The – See "Who, The"

Highwaymen, The (Country group) – See either "Nelson, Willie" or "Cash, Johnny"

Hildebrand, Ray

(Of Paul and Paula)
Philips

❑ 40174		It's All Over, Paula/Snow Girl	1964	2.50	5.00	10.00
		As "Paul"				
❑ 40318		Hey Little Julie/The Way of the DJ	1965	2.00	4.00	8.00
❑ 40339		Hello Viet Nam (Goodbye My Love)/ You, Wonderful You	1965	2.00	4.00	8.00

Hill Sisters, The

Anna

❑ 103		Hit and Run Away Love/Advertising for Love	1959	125.00	250.00	500.00
❑ 1103		Hit and Run Away Love/Advertising for Love	1959	12.50	25.00	50.00

Hill, Bunker

Mala

❑ 451		Hide and Go Seek (Part 1)/Hide and Go Seek (Part 2)	1962	5.00	10.00	20.00
❑ 457		Red Ridin' Hood and the Wolf/Nobody Knows	1962	5.00	10.00	20.00
❑ 464		The Girl Can't Dance/ You Can't Make Me Doubt My Baby	1963	6.25	12.50	25.00

Hill, Raymond

Sun

❑ 204		Bourbon Street Jump/The Snuggle	1954	250.00	500.00	750.00

Him – See "Sahm, Doug"

Hindu Love Gods

(Side project from members of R.E.M.)
I.R.S.

❑ 52867		Gonna Have a Good Time Tonight/Narrator	1986	2.00	4.00	8.00
❑ 52867	PS	Gonna Have a Good Time Tonight/Narrator	1986	2.00	4.00	8.00

Hinton, Joe

Arvee

❑ 5028		My Love Is Real/I Won't Be Your Fool	1961	3.00	6.00	12.00
❑ 5029		Your Kind of Love/Let's Start a Romance	1961	3.00	6.00	12.00
		Arvee titles as "Little Joe Hinton"				

Number		Title (A Side/B Side)	Year	VG	VG+	NM

Back Beat
☐ 519		I Know/Ladder of Prayer	1958	3.75	7.50	15.00
☐ 526		Pretty Little Mama/Will You	1959	3.75	7.50	15.00
☐ 532		If You Love Me/A Thousand Cups of Happiness	1960	3.75	7.50	15.00
☐ 535		The Girls in My Life/Come On Baby	1961	3.75	7.50	15.00
☐ 537		You Know It Ain't Right/Love Sick Blues	1963	3.00	6.00	12.00
☐ 539		Better to Give Than Receive/There Is No In Between	1963	3.00	6.00	12.00
☐ 540		There Oughta Be a Law/You're My Girl	1964	3.00	6.00	12.00
☐ 541		Funny/You Gotta Have Love	1964	3.75	7.50	15.00
☐ 545		I Want a Little Girl/True Love	1965	3.00	6.00	12.00
☐ 547		Darling Come and Talk to Me/Everything	1965	3.00	6.00	12.00
☐ 550		Pledging My Love/Just a Kid Named Joe	1965	3.00	6.00	12.00
☐ 565		I'm Waiting/How Long Can I Last	1966	2.50	5.00	10.00
☐ 574		If I Had Only Known/Lots of Love	1966	2.50	5.00	10.00
☐ 581		Close to MyHeart/You've Been Good to Me	1967	2.50	5.00	10.00
☐ 589		I'm Satisfied/Be Ever Wonderful	1968	2.50	5.00	10.00
☐ 594		Got You on My Mind/Please	1968	2.50	5.00	10.00

Soul
| ☐ 35080 | | Let's Save the Children/You Are Blue | 1971 | 6.25 | 12.50 | 25.00 |

Hippies, The
Parkway
| ☐ 863 | | Memory Lane/A Lonely Piano | 1963 | 5.00 | 10.00 | 20.00 |
| | | *Originally released as "The Tams"* | | | | |

Hit Pack, The
Soul
| ☐ 35010 | | Never Say No to Your Baby/Let's Dance | 1965 | 12.50 | 25.00 | 50.00 |

Ho-Dads, The
Imperial
| ☐ 66001 | | Legends/Honey | 1963 | 7.50 | 15.00 | 30.00 |
| ☐ 66023 | | After Dark/Space Race | 1964 | 7.50 | 15.00 | 30.00 |

Hodges, Eddie
Aurora
☐ 150		Across the Street (Is a Million Miles Away)/ She Doesn't Love Me	1965	2.50	5.00	10.00
☐ 153		New Orleans/Hard Times for Young Lovers	1965	2.50	5.00	10.00
☐ 156		Love Minus Zero (No Limit)/ The Water Is Over My Head	1965	2.50	5.00	10.00
☐ 161		Hitch Hike/Old Man Rag	1966	2.50	5.00	10.00

Cadence
☐ 1397		I'm Gonna Knock on Your Door/ Ain't Gonna Wash for a Week	1961	3.75	7.50	15.00
☐ 1397	PS	I'm Gonna Knock on Your Door/ Ain't Gonna Wash for a Week	1961	6.25	12.50	25.00
☐ 1410		Bandit of My Dreams/Mugmates	1962	5.00	10.00	20.00
☐ 1421		(Girls, Girls, Girls) Made to Love/ I Make Believe It's You	1962	3.75	7.50	15.00

Columbia
☐ 42649		Seein' Is Believin'/Secret	1962	3.00	6.00	12.00
☐ 42649	PS	Seein' Is Believin'/Secret	1962	4.00	8.00	16.00
☐ 42811		Rainin' in My Heart/Halfway	1963	3.00	6.00	12.00

Decca
| ☐ 30675 | | That Funny Little Dog/What Would It Be Like in Heaven | 1958 | 3.75 | 7.50 | 15.00 |
| ☐ 30903 | | High Hopes/Don't Dance on Momma's Rug | 1959 | 3.75 | 7.50 | 15.00 |

MGM
| ☐ 13219 | | Avalanche/Just a Kid in Love | 1964 | 2.50 | 5.00 | 10.00 |

Hog Heaven
(The Shondells after Tommy James went solo)
Roulette
☐ 7091		Theme from a Thought/(B-side unknown)	1970	2.00	4.00	8.00
☐ 7101		Happy/Prayer	1971	2.00	4.00	8.00
☐ 7106		If It Feels Good/(B-side unknown)	1971	2.00	4.00	8.00

Hogs, The
(Later recorded as The Chocolate Watch Band)
Hanna-Barbera
| ☐ 511 | | Loose Lip Sync Ships/Blues Theme | 1967 | 37.50 | 75.00 | 150.00 |
| | | *A-side produced by Frank Zappa* | | | | |

Holden, Ron
Challenge
| ☐ 59360 | | I Tried/I'll Forgive and Forget | 1967 | 10.00 | 20.00 | 40.00 |

Donna
☐ 1315		Love You So/My Babe	1959	7.50	15.00	30.00
☐ 1324		Gee, But I'm Lonesome/Susie Jane	1960	6.25	12.50	25.00
☐ 1331		Who Says There Ain't No Santa Claus/ Your Line Is Busy	1960	6.25	12.50	25.00
☐ 1335		The Big Shoe/Rock and Roll Call	1961	5.00	10.00	20.00

Eldo
| ☐ 117 | | I'll Be Happy/I'll Always Have You | 1961 | 5.00 | 10.00 | 20.00 |

Number		Title (A Side/B Side)	Year	VG	VG+	NM

Nite Owl
| ❑ 10 | | Love You So/My Babe | 1959 | 20.00 | 40.00 | 80.00 |

Rampart
| ❑ 645 | | Girl I Love You/Nothing I Wouldn't Do | 1965 | 3.00 | 6.00 | 12.00 |

Holiday, John E.
Atlantic
| ❑ 2091 | | Yes I Will Love You Tomorrow/Till the End of Time | 1961 | 5.00 | 10.00 | 20.00 |

Holland, Brian
(Also see "Holland-Dozier")
Invictus
| ❑ 1265 | | I'm So Glad (Part 1)/I'm So Glad (Part 2) | 1974 | | 2.50 | 5.00 |
| ❑ 1272 | | Super Woman/Let's Get Together | 1974 | | 2.50 | 5.00 |

Kudo
| ❑ 667 | | (Where's the Joy?) In Nature Boy/Shock | 1958 | 150.00 | 300.00 | 600.00 |
| | | *First name as "Briant"* | | | | |

Holland, Eddie
Mercury
| ❑ 71290 | | You/Little Miss Ruby | 1958 | 25.00 | 50.00 | 100.00 |

Motown
❑ 1021		Jamie/Take a Chance on Me	1961	6.25	12.50	25.00
❑ 1026		You Deserve What You Got/Last Night I Had a Vision	1962	6.25	12.50	25.00
❑ 1030		If Cleopatra Took a Chance/What About Me	1962	6.25	12.50	25.00
❑ 1030	PS	If Cleopatra Took a Chance/What About Me	1962	12.50	25.00	50.00
❑ 1031		If It's Love (It's All Right)/It's Not Too Late	1962	6.25	12.50	25.00
❑ 1036		Darling I Hum Our Song/Just a Few Memories	1963	6.25	12.50	25.00
❑ 1043		Brenda/Baby Shake	1963	6.25	12.50	25.00
❑ 1049		I'm On the Outside Looking In/ I Couldn't Cry If I Wanted To	1963	37.50	75.00	150.00
❑ 1052		Leaving Here/Brenda	1964	3.75	7.50	15.00
❑ 1058		Just Ain't Enough Love/Last Night I Had a Vision	1964	3.75	7.50	15.00
❑ 1063		Candy to Me/If You Don't Want My Love	1964	3.75	7.50	15.00

Tamla
| ❑ 102 | | Merry-Go-Round/It Moves Me | 1959 | 62.50 | 125.00 | 250.00 |

United Artists
❑ 172		Merry-Go-Round/It Moves Me	1959	7.50	15.00	30.00
❑ 191		Because I Love Her/Everybody's Going	1959	7.50	15.00	30.00
❑ 207		Magic Mirror/Will You Love Me	1960	7.50	15.00	30.00
❑ 280		The Last Laugh/Why Do You Want to Let Me Go	1960	7.50	15.00	30.00

Holland-Dozier
(Also see "Dozier, Lamont"; "Holland, Brian")
Invictus
❑ 1253		Slipping Away/Can't Get Enough	1973		2.50	5.00
❑ 1254		If You Don't Wanta Be in My Life/ New Breed Kinda Woman	1973		2.50	5.00
❑ 1258		You Took Me from a World Outside/ I'm Gonna Hijack Ya, Kidnap Ya, Take What I Want	1973		2.50	5.00
❑ 9110		Don't Leave Me (Part 1)/Don't Leave Me (Part 2)	1972		2.50	5.00
❑ 9133		Don't Leave Me Starvin' for Your Love (Part 1)/ Don't Leave Me Starvin' for Your Love (Part 2)	1972		2.50	5.00

Motown
| ❑ 1045 | | What Goes Up Must Come Down/Come On Home | 1963 | 6.25 | 12.50 | 25.00 |

Hollies, The
Atlantic
❑ 89784		Someone Else's Eyes/If the Lights Go Out	1983			3.00
❑ 89819		Stop in the Name of Love/Musical Pictures	1983			3.00
❑ 89819	PS	Stop in the Name of Love/Musical Pictures	1983			2.50	5.00

Epic
❑ 10180		Carrie-Anne/Signs That Will Never Change	1967	2.00	4.00	8.00
❑ 10180	PS	Carrie-Anne/Signs That Will Never Change	1967	3.75	7.50	15.00
❑ 10234		King Midas in Reverse/Water on the Brain	1967	2.00	4.00	8.00
❑ 10234	PS	King Midas in Reverse/Water on the Brain	1967	3.75	7.50	15.00
❑ 10251		Dear Eloise/When Your Light's Turned On	1967	2.00	4.00	8.00
❑ 10298		Jennifer Eccles/Try It	1968	2.00	4.00	8.00
❑ 10361		Do the Best You Can/Elevated Observations	1968	2.00	4.00	8.00
❑ 10400		Listen to Me/Everything Is Sunshine	1968	2.00	4.00	8.00
❑ 10454		Sorry Suzanne/Not That Way at All	1969	2.00	4.00	8.00
❑ 10532		He Ain't Heavy, He's My Brother/ Cos You Like to Love Me	1969		3.00	6.00
		A-side: Elton John on piano				
❑ 10613		I Can't Tell the Bottom from the Top/ Mad Professor Blythe	1970		3.00	6.00
❑ 10677		Gasoline Alley Bred/Dandelion Wine	1970	2.50	5.00	10.00
❑ 10716		Survival of the Fittest/Man Without a Heart	1971	3.00	6.00	12.00
❑ 10754		Hey Willy/Row the Boat Together	1971	2.50	5.00	10.00
❑ 10842		The Baby/Oh Granny	1972	2.50	5.00	10.00
❑ 10842	PS	The Baby/Oh Granny	1972	12.50	25.00	50.00
❑ 10871		Long Cool Woman (In a Black Dress)/ Look What We've Got	1972			2.50	5.00
❑ 10920		Long Dark Road/Indian Girl	1972		2.50	5.00
❑ 10951		Magic Woman Touch/Blue in the Morning	1973		2.50	5.00

Number		Title (A Side/B Side)	Year	VG	VG+	NM
❑ 10989		Jesus Was a Crossmaker/I Had a Dream	1973		2.50	5.00
❑ 11025		Won't We Feel Good/Slow Down	1973		2.50	5.00
❑ 11051		The Day That Curley Billy Shot Down Crazy Sam McGee/Born a Man	1973		2.50	5.00
❑ 11100		The Air That I Breathe/No More Riders	1974		2.50	5.00
❑ 50029		Don't Let Me Down/Layin' to the Music	1974		2.50	5.00
❑ 50086		Sandy/Second Hand Hangups	1975		2.50	5.00
❑ 50110		Another Night/Time Machine Jive	1975		2.00	4.00
❑ 50144		Look Out Johnny/I'm Down	1975		2.00	4.00
❑ 50204		Crocodile Woman (She Bites)/Write On	1976		2.00	4.00
❑ 50359		Sandy/Second Hand Hangups	1977		2.00	4.00
❑ 50422		Draggin' My Heels/I Won't Move Over	1977		2.00	4.00
❑ 50522		Burn Out/Writing on the Wall	1978		2.00	4.00

Imperial

Number		Title (A Side/B Side)	Year	VG	VG+	NM
❑ 66026		Just One Look/Keep Off That Friend of Mine	1964	5.00	10.00	20.00
❑ 66044		Here I Go Again/Lucille	1964	3.75	7.50	15.00
❑ 66070		Come On Back/We're Through	1964	3.75	7.50	15.00
❑ 66099		Yes I Will/Nobody	1965	10.00	20.00	40.00
❑ 66119		I'm Alive/You Know He Did	1965	3.75	7.50	15.00
❑ 66134		Look Through Any Window/So Lonely	1965	3.00	6.00	12.00
❑ 66158		I Can't Let Go/I've Got a Way of My Own	1966	3.75	7.50	15.00
❑ 66186		Bus Stop/Don't Run and Hide	1966	3.00	6.00	12.00
❑ 66214		Stop Stop Stop/It's You	1966	3.00	6.00	12.00
❑ 66231		On a Carousel/All the World Is Love	1967	3.00	6.00	12.00
❑ 66231	PS	On a Carousel/All the World Is Love	1967	7.50	15.00	30.00
❑ 66240		Pay You Back With Interest/Whatcha Gonna Do 'Bout It	1967	3.00	6.00	12.00
❑ 66258		Just One Look/Running Through the Night	1967	3.00	6.00	12.00
❑ 66271		If I Needed Someone/I'll Be True to You (Yes I Will)	1968	10.00	20.00	40.00

Liberty

Number		Title (A Side/B Side)	Year	VG	VG+	NM
❑ 55674		Stay/Now's the Time	1964	15.00	30.00	60.00

United Artists

Number		Title (A Side/B Side)	Year	VG	VG+	NM
❑ 50079		After the Fox/The Fox Trot	1966	5.00	10.00	20.00
		With Peter Sellers				

Holloway, Brenda

Donna

Number		Title (A Side/B Side)	Year	VG	VG+	NM
❑ 1358		Echo/Hey Fool	1962	10.00	20.00	40.00
❑ 1366		Game of Love/Echo-Echo-Echo	1962	12.50	25.00	50.00
❑ 1370		I'll Give My Life/More Echo	1962	12.50	25.00	50.00

Tamla

Number		Title (A Side/B Side)	Year	VG	VG+	NM
❑ 54094		Every Little Bit Hurts/Land of 1,000 Boys	1964	3.00	6.00	12.00
❑ 54099		I'll Always Love You/Sad Song	1964	3.75	7.50	15.00
❑ 54111		When I'm Gone/I've Been Good to You	1965	3.75	7.50	15.00
❑ 54111	PS	When I'm Gone/I've Been Good to You	1965	12.50	25.00	50.00
❑ 54115		Operator/I'll Be Available	1965	3.75	7.50	15.00
❑ 54121		You Can Cry on My Shoulder/How Many Times Did You Mean It	1965	5.00	10.00	20.00
❑ 54125		Sad Song/Together 'Til the End of Time	1965	5.00	10.00	20.00
❑ 54137		Hurt a Little Every Day/Where Were You	1966	7.50	15.00	30.00
❑ 54144		'Til Johnny Comes/Where Were You	1967	50.00	100.00	200.00
❑ 54148		Just Look What You've Done/Starting the Hurt All Over Again	1967	6.25	12.50	25.00
❑ 54155		You've Made Me So Very Happy/I've Got to Find It	1967	5.00	10.00	20.00
❑ 206312	DJ	Play It Cool, Stay in School	1966	150.00	300.00	600.00
		Promo for Women's Ad Club of Detroit				

Holloway, Patrice

(Later sang with Josie and the Pussycats)

Capitol

Number		Title (A Side/B Side)	Year	VG	VG+	NM
❑ 5680		Stolen Hours/Lucky My Boy	1966	20.00	40.00	80.00
❑ 5778		Love and Desire/Ecstasy	1967	15.00	30.00	60.00
❑ 5985		Stay with Your Own Kind/That's All You Got to Do	1967	12.50	25.00	50.00

Taste

Number		Title (A Side/B Side)	Year	VG	VG+	NM
❑ 125		Do the Del Viking/(B-side unknown)	1963	7.50	15.00	30.00

Holly Twins, The

Liberty

Number		Title (A Side/B Side)	Year	VG	VG+	NM
❑ 55015		Take Me Back/It's Easy	1956	6.25	12.50	25.00
❑ 55048		I Want Elvis for Christmas/The Tender Age	1956	12.50	25.00	50.00

Rendezvous

Number		Title (A Side/B Side)	Year	VG	VG+	NM
❑ 180		Okee-Feenokee/Potato Chips	1962	3.00	6.00	12.00

Holly, Buddy

(Also see "Crickets, The")

Coral

Note: Promos for any Coral title valued at $50 or under Near Mint are worth 2-4 times the stock copy value.

Number		Title (A Side/B Side)	Year	VG	VG+	NM
❑ 61852		Words of Love/Mailman, Bring Me No More Blues	1957	150.00	250.00	400.00
❑ 61885		Peggy Sue/Everyday	1957	12.50	25.00	50.00
❑ 61947		I'm Gonna Love You Too/Listen to Me	1958	12.50	25.00	50.00
❑ 61985		Rave On/Take Your Time	1958	12.50	25.00	50.00
❑ 62006		Early in the Morning/Now We're One	1958	12.50	25.00	50.00
❑ 62051		Heartbeat/Well...All Right	1958	12.50	25.00	50.00
❑ 62074		It Doesn't Matter Anymore/Raining in My Heart	1959	10.00	20.00	40.00
❑ 62134		Peggy Sue Got Married/Crying, Waiting, Hoping	1959	15.00	30.00	60.00
❑ 62210		True Love Ways/That Makes It Tough	1960	12.50	25.00	50.00

Number		Title (A Side/B Side)	Year	VG	VG+	NM
❑ 62283		You're So Square (Baby I Don't Care)/Valley of Tears	1961	40.00	80.00	160.00
		Evidently only released in Canada				
❑ 62329		Reminiscing/Wait Till the Sun Shines, Nellie	1962	7.50	15.00	30.00
❑ 62352		True Love Ways/Bo Diddley	1963	15.00	30.00	60.00
❑ 62369		Brown Eyed Handsome Man/Wishing	1963	10.00	20.00	40.00
❑ 62390		Rock Around with Ollie Vee/I'm Gonna Love You Too	1963	10.00	20.00	40.00
❑ 62448		Slippin' and Slidin'/What to Do	1965	25.00	50.00	100.00
❑ 62554		Rave On/Early in the Morning	1968	7.50	15.00	30.00
❑ 62558		Love Is Strange/You're the One	1969	5.00	10.00	20.00
❑ 62558	PS	Love Is Strange/You're the One	1969	7.50	15.00	30.00
Decca						
❑ 29854		Blue Days, Black Nights/Love Me	1956	125.00	250.00	500.00
		With lines on either side of "Decca"				
❑ 29854		Blue Days, Black Nights/Love Me	1956	62.50	125.00	250.00
		With star under "Decca"				
❑ 29854	DJ	Blue Days, Black Nights/Love Me	1956	75.00	150.00	300.00
		Promos have blue labels				
❑ 30166		Modern Don Juan/You Are My One Desire	1956	100.00	200.00	400.00
		With lines on either side of "Decca"				
❑ 30166		Modern Don Juan/You Are My One Desire	1956	62.50	125.00	250.00
		With star under "Decca"				
❑ 30166	DJ	Modern Don Juan/You Are My One Desire	1956	75.00	150.00	300.00
		Promos have blue labels				
❑ 30434		That'll Be the Day/Rock Around with Ollie Vee	1957	75.00	150.00	300.00
		With lines on either side of "Decca"				
❑ 30434		That'll Be the Day/Rock Around with Ollie Vee	1957	50.00	100.00	200.00
		With star under "Decca"				
❑ 30434	DJ	That'll Be the Day/Rock Around with Ollie Vee	1957	50.00	100.00	200.00
		Promos have blue labels				
❑ 30543		Love Me/You Are My One Desire	1958	62.50	125.00	250.00
❑ 30543	DJ	Love Me/You Are My One Desire	1958	50.00	100.00	200.00
		Blue label promos				
❑ 30543	DJ	Love Me/You Are My One Desire	1958	75.00	150.00	300.00
		Green label promos				
❑ 30650		Ting-a-Ling/Girl on My Mind	1958	62.50	125.00	250.00
❑ 30650	DJ	Ting-a-Ling/Girl on My Mind	1958	50.00	100.00	200.00
		Promos have blue labels				
MCA						
❑ 40905		It Doesn't Matter Anymore/Peggy Sue	1978		2.50	5.00
❑ 40905	PS	It Doesn't Matter Anymore/Peggy Sue	1978		2.50	5.00

Hollyhawks, The
(With Niki Sullivan, ex-Crickets)
Jubilee

❑ 5441		I Cry All the Time/When Came the Fall	1962	20.00	40.00	80.00

Hollywood Argyles, The
(Gary Paxton was in this group; so, some say, was Kim Fowley)
Brent

❑ 7004		Vacation Days Are Over/It Takes Time	1959	7.50	15.00	30.00
		As "The Argyles"				
Chattahoochie						
❑ 691		Long Hair, Unsquare Dude Called Jack/Ole	1965	3.75	7.50	15.00
Felsted						
❑ 8674		Bossy Nover/Find Another Way	1963	5.00	10.00	20.00
Finer Arts						
❑ 1002		The Morning After/See You in the Morning	1961	5.00	10.00	20.00
Kammy						
❑ 105		Alley-Oop '65/Do the Funky Foot	1965	5.00	10.00	20.00
		As "The New Hollywood Argyles"				
Lute						
❑ 5905		Alley Oop/Sho' Know a Lot About Love	1960	6.25	12.50	25.00
❑ 5908		Gun Totin' Critter Called Jack/Bug Eyed Man	1960	5.00	10.00	20.00
❑ 6002		Hully Gully/So Fine	1960	5.00	10.00	20.00
Paxley						
❑ 752		You've Been Torturing Me/The Grubble	1960	5.00	10.00	20.00

Hollywood Flames, The
Atco

❑ 6155		Every Day, Every Way/If I Thought I Needed You	1959	3.75	7.50	15.00
❑ 6164		Ball and Chain/I Found a Boy	1960	3.75	7.50	15.00
❑ 6171		Devil or Angel/Do You Ever Think of Me	1960	3.75	7.50	15.00
❑ 6180		Money Honey/My Heart's On Fire	1960	3.75	7.50	15.00
Chess						
❑ 1787		Gee/Yes They Do	1961	3.00	6.00	12.00
Decca						
❑ 29285		Peggy/Ooh La La	1954	18.75	37.50	75.00
❑ 48331		Let's Talk It Over/I Know	1955	18.75	37.50	75.00
Ebb						
❑ 119		Buzz-Buzz-Buzz/Crazy	1957	7.50	15.00	30.00
❑ 131		Give Me Back My Heart/A Little Bird	1958	6.25	12.50	25.00

Number	Title (A Side/B Side)	Year	VG	VG+	NM
❏ 144	Frankenstein's Den/Strollin' on the Beach	1958	6.25	12.50	25.00
❏ 146	Chains of Love/Let's Talk It Over	1958	6.25	12.50	25.00
❏ 149	A Star Fell/I'll Get By	1958	6.25	12.50	25.00
❏ 153	I'll Be Seeing You/Just for You	1959	7.50	15.00	30.00
❏ 158	So Good/There Is Something on Your Mind	1959	6.25	12.50	25.00
❏ 162	Now That You're Gone/Hawaiian Dream	1959	6.25	12.50	25.00
❏ 163	Much Too Much/In the Dark	1959	6.25	12.50	25.00
Lucky					
❏ 001	One Night with a Fool/Ride, Helen, Ride	1954	100.00	200.00	400.00
❏ 006	Peggy/Ooh-La-La	1954	100.00	200.00	400.00
❏ 009	Let's Talk It Over/I Know	1954	62.50	125.00	250.00
Mona-Lee					
❏ 135	Buzz-Buzz-Buzz/Crazy	1958	6.25	12.50	25.00
Money					
❏ 202	Fare Thee Well/I'm Leaving	1954	100.00	200.00	400.00
Swing Time					
❏ 345	Let's Talk It Over/I Know	1953	125.00	250.00	500.00
❏ 346	Go and Get Some More/Another Soldier Gone	1953	125.00	250.00	500.00
	B-side by the Question Marks				
Symbol					
❏ 211	Dance Senorita/Annie Don't Love Me Anymore	1965	3.00	6.00	12.00
❏ 215	I'm Coming Home/I'm Gonna Stand By You	1966	3.00	6.00	12.00
Vee Jay					
❏ 515	Drop Me a Line/Letter to My Love	1963	3.75	7.50	15.00

Hollywood Persuaders, The

Original Sound

❏ 39	Tijuana/Grunion Run	1964	12.50	25.00	50.00
❏ 39	Tijuana Surf/Grunion Run	1964	12.50	25.00	50.00
❏ 44	Persuasion/Juarez	1964	6.25	12.50	25.00
❏ 50	Drums-A-Go-Go/Agua Caliente	1965	6.25	12.50	25.00
❏ 58	Hollywood A-Go-Go/Eve of Destruction	1965	6.25	12.50	25.00

Hollywood Playboys, The

(With Nick Massi, later of the Four Seasons)
Sure

❏ 105	Ding Dong School Is Out/Talk to Audrey	1960	7.50	15.00	30.00

Hollywood Producers, The

Parkway

❏ 993	White Silk Glove/You're Not Welcome	1966	7.50	15.00	30.00

Holman, Eddie

ABC

❏ 11149	I Love You/I Surrender	1968	2.50	5.00	10.00
❏ 11240	Hey There Lonely Girl/It's All in the Game	1969		3.00	6.00
❏ 11261	Don't Stop Now/Since I Don't Have You	1970		3.00	6.00
❏ 11265	I'll Be There/Cause You're Mine Little Girl	1970		3.00	6.00
❏ 11276	Cathy Called/I Need Somebody	1970		3.00	6.00
❏ 11292	Love Story/Four Walls	1971		3.00	6.00
Ascot					
❏ 2142	Go Get Your Own/Laughing at Me	1963	3.75	7.50	15.00
Bell					
❏ 712	I'm Not Gonna Give Up/I'll Cry 1,000 Tears	1968	5.00	10.00	20.00
GSF					
❏ 6873	My Mind Keeps Telling Me	1972		3.00	6.00
	(That I Really Love You, Girl)/Stranded in a Dream				
❏ 6885	Young Girl/I'll Call You Joy	1972		3.00	6.00
Parkway					
❏ 106	Am I a Loser/You Know That I Will	1966	5.00	10.00	20.00
❏ 133	Somewhere Waits a Lonely Girl/	1967	5.00	10.00	20.00
	Stay Mine for Heaven's Sake				
❏ 157	Why Do Fools Fall in Love/Never Let Me Go	1967	5.00	10.00	20.00
❏ 960	This Can't Be True/A Free Country	1965	5.00	10.00	20.00
❏ 981	Don't Stop Now/Eddie's My Name	1966	5.00	10.00	20.00
❏ 994	Return to Me/Stay Mine for Heaven's Sake	1966	5.00	10.00	20.00
Salsoul					
❏ 2026	This Will Be a Night to Remember/Time Will Tell	1977		2.50	5.00
❏ 2043	You Make My Life Complete/	1977		2.50	5.00
	Somehow You Make Me Feel				
Silver Blue					
❏ 807	You're My Lady (Right Or Wrong)/(Instrumental)	1974		2.50	5.00
❏ 815	Just Say I Love Her/Darling Take Me Back	1974		2.50	5.00
United Artists					
❏ 609	Go Get Your Own/Laughing at Me	1963			Unreleased

Hombres, The

Sun

❏ 1104	If This Ain't Loving You Baby/You Made Me What I Am	1969	2.50	5.00	10.00
Verve Forecast					
❏ 5058	Let It All Hang Out/Go Girl, Go	1967	3.75	7.50	15.00
❏ 5058	Let It Out (Let It All Hang Out)/Go Girl, Go	1967	3.00	6.00	12.00

Number		Title (A Side/B Side)	Year	VG	VG+	NM
☐ 5076		It's a Gas/Am I High	1967	2.50	5.00	10.00
☐ 5083		The Prodigal/Mau, Mau, Mau	1968	2.50	5.00	10.00
☐ 5093		Pumpkin Man/Take My Overwhelming Love	1968	2.50	5.00	10.00

Hondells, The
Amos
☐ 131		Follow the Bouncing Ball/ The Legend of Frankie and Johnny	1969	3.00	6.00	12.00
☐ 150		Shine On Ruby Mountain/The Legend of Frankie and Johnny	1970	3.00	6.00	12.00

Columbia
☐ 44361		Just One More Chance/Yes to You	1967	5.00	10.00	20.00
☐ 44557		Another Woman/Atlanta Georgia Stray	1968	5.00	10.00	20.00

Mercury
☐ 72324		Little Honda/Hot Rod High	1964	5.00	10.00	20.00
☐ 72366		My Buddy Seat/You're Gonna Ride with Me	1964	5.00	10.00	20.00
☐ 72366	PS	My Buddy Seat/You're Gonna Ride with Me	1964	6.25	12.50	25.00
☐ 72405		Little Sidewalk Surfer Girl/Come On Baby (Pack It In)	1965	5.00	10.00	20.00
☐ 72443		Sea of Love/Do As I Say	1965	5.00	10.00	20.00
☐ 72479		You Meet the Nicest People on a Honda/Sea Cruise	1965	5.00	10.00	20.00
☐ 72479	PS	You Meet the Nicest People on a Honda/Sea Cruise	1965	7.50	15.00	30.00
☐ 72523		Endless Sleep/Follow Your Heart	1966	3.75	7.50	15.00
☐ 72563		Younger Girl/All American Girl	1966	3.75	7.50	15.00
☐ 72605		Country Love/Kissin' My Life Away	1966	3.75	7.50	15.00
☐ 72626		Cheryl's Goin' Home/Show Me	1966	3.75	7.50	15.00
☐ 7212		Ace in the Hole/Ooo Baby Baby	1972		3.00	6.00
☐ 7301		If I Can't Fly/Woman Can't Live by Bread Alone	1973		3.00	6.00
☐ 9255		The Truth Will Come Out/ Somebody Is Always Messing Up a Good Thing	1974		3.00	6.00

Honeycombs, The
Interphon
☐ 7707		Have I the Right?/Please Don't Pretend Again	1964	3.00	6.00	12.00
☐ 7713		I Can't Stop/I'll Cry Tomorrow	1964	2.50	5.00	10.00
☐ 7713	PS	I Can't Stop/I'll Cry Tomorrow	1964	6.25	12.50	25.00
☐ 7716		Color Slide/That's the Way	1965	2.50	5.00	10.00
☐ 7716	PS	Color Slide/That's the Way	1965	6.25	12.50	25.00

Warner Bros.
☐ 5634		I'll See You Tomorrow/Something Better Beginning	1965	2.50	5.00	10.00
☐ 5655		I Can't Get Through to You/That's the Way	1965	2.50	5.00	10.00
☐ 5803		How Will I Know/Who Is Sylvia	1966	2.50	5.00	10.00

Honeycones, The
Ember
☐ 1033		Betty Moretti/Cool It Baby	1958	5.00	10.00	20.00
☐ 1036		Op/Vision of You	1958	6.25	12.50	25.00
☐ 1042		Gee Whiz/Rockin' in the Knees	1958	5.00	10.00	20.00
☐ 1049		Tell Me Baby/Your Face	1959	5.00	10.00	20.00

Honeycutt, Glenn
Fernwood
☐ 142		Campus Love/Tombigbee Queen	1964	25.00	50.00	100.00

Sun
☐ 264		I'll Be Around/I'll Wait Forever	1957	7.50	15.00	30.00

Honeys, The
(Girl group with heavy Brian Wilson involvement)
Capitol
☐ 2454		Goodnight My Love/Tonight You Belong to Me	1969	20.00	40.00	80.00
☐ 4952		Surfin' Down the Swanee River/Shoot the Curl	1963	37.50	75.00	150.00
☐ 4952	PS	Surfin' Down the Swanee River/Shoot the Curl	1963	150.00	300.00	600.00
☐ 5034		Hide Go Seek/Pray for Surf	1963	50.00	100.00	200.00
☐ 5093		The One You Can't Have/From Jimmy With Tears	1963	50.00	100.00	200.00

Warner Bros.
☐ 5430		He's a Doll/The Love of a Boy and Girl	1964	150.00	300.00	600.00

Honor Society, The – See "Happenings, The"

Hooker, John Lee
ABC
☐ 11298		Doin' the Shout/Kick Hit 4 Hit Kix U	1971		3.00	6.00
☐ 11320		Never Get Out of These Blues Alive/ Boogie with the Hook	1972		3.00	6.00

Battle
☐ 45901		No More Doggin'/I Need Some Money	1962	2.50	5.00	10.00

Bluesway
☐ 61010		Motor City Is Burning/Want Ad Blues	1967	2.00	4.00	8.00
☐ 61014		Mr. Lucky/Cry Before I Go	1968		3.00	6.00
☐ 61017		Back Biters and Syndicators/ Think Twice Before You Go	1968		3.00	6.00
☐ 61023		I Don't Wanna Go to Vietnam/Simply the Truth	1969		3.00	6.00

Chance
☐ 1108		Miss Lorraine/Talkin' Boogie	1951	400.00	800.00	1,200
		As "John Lee Booker"				

Two records rarely seen in stock copies: At top, the Grateful Dead's "Franklin's Tower" from the *Blues for Allah* album, which was generally believed to exist only as a promo. Below it is the Honeys' "He's a Doll," of which a promo copy was pictured in the third edition of the *Goldmine Rock 'n Roll 45 RPM Price Guide* with the theory that stock copies were rarely, if ever, seen.

Number	Title (A Side/B Side)	Year	VG	VG+	NM
❏ 1110	Graveyard Blues/I Love to Boogie	1952	400.00	800.00	1,200
	As "John Lee Booker"				
❏ 1122	609 Boogie/Road Trouble	1952	400.00	800.00	1,200
	As "John L. Booker"				

Chart
❏ 609	Going South/Wobbling Baby	1955	12.50	25.00	50.00

Chess
❏ 1505	High Priced Woman/Union Station Blues	1952	250.00	500.00	1,000
❏ 1513	Sugar Mama/Walkin' the Boogie	1952	250.00	500.00	1,000
❏ 1562	It's My Own Fault/Women and Honey	1954	25.00	50.00	100.00
❏ 1965	Let's Go Out Tonight/In the Mood	1966	2.50	5.00	10.00

DeLuxe
❏ 6004	Blue Monday/Lovin' Guitar Man	1953	100.00	200.00	400.00
	As "John Lee Booker"				
❏ 6032	Stuttering Blues/Pouring Down Rain	1954	50.00	100.00	200.00
	As "John Lee Booker"				
❏ 6046	My Baby Don't Love Me/Real, Real Gone	1954	50.00	100.00	200.00
	As "John Lee Booker"				

Elmor
❏ 303	Blues for Christmas/Big Fine Woman	1959	5.00	10.00	20.00

Federal
❏ 12377	Late Last Night/Don't You Remember Me	1960	3.75	7.50	15.00

Fortune
❏ 853	Cry Baby/Love You Baby	1960	5.00	10.00	20.00
❏ 855	Crazy About That Walk/We're All God's Chillun	1960	5.00	10.00	20.00

Galaxy
❏ 716	I Lost My Job/You Gotta Shake It Up and Go	1963	2.50	5.00	10.00

Hi-Q
❏ 5018	Blues for Christmas/Big Fine Woman	1960	5.00	10.00	20.00

Impulse
❏ 242	Honey/Bottle Up and Go	1966	2.50	5.00	10.00

Jewel
❏ 824	I Feel Good (Part 1)/I Feel Good (Part 2)	1971		2.50	5.00
❏ 852	Stand By (Part 1)/Stand By (Part 2)	1977		2.00	4.00

JVB
❏ 30	Boogie Rambler/No More Doggin'	1953	250.00	500.00	1,000

King
❏ 4504	Moaning Blues/Stomp Boogie	1952	125.00	250.00	500.00
	As "John Lee Cooker"				
❏ 6298	Don't Go Baby/Moanin' and Stompin' Blues	1970		3.00	6.00

Lauren
❏ 361	Ballad to Abraham Lincoln (He Got Assassinated)/Mojo Hand (Louisiana Voodoo)	1961	5.00	10.00	20.00
❏ 362	I Lost My Job/You Gotta Shake It Up and Go	1961	5.00	10.00	20.00

Modern
❏ 835	How Can You Do It/I'm in the Mood	1951	50.00	100.00	200.00
❏ 847	Anybody Seen My Baby? (Johnny Says Come Back)/Turn Over a New Leaf	1951	50.00	100.00	200.00
❏ 852	Ground Hog Blues/Louise	1951	25.00	50.00	100.00
❏ 862	Cold Chills All Over Me/Rock Me, Mama	1952	20.00	40.00	80.00
❏ 876	It Hurts Me So/I Got Eyes for You	1952	20.00	40.00	80.00
	With Little Eddie Kirkland				
❏ 886	Key to the Highway/Bluebird Blues	1952	20.00	40.00	80.00
❏ 893	New Boogie Chillen/I Tried	1952	20.00	40.00	80.00
❏ 897	It's Been a Long Time Baby/Rock House Boogie	1952	20.00	40.00	80.00
❏ 901	Ride Till I Die/It's Stormin' and Rainin'	1953	15.00	30.00	60.00
❏ 908	Please Take Me Back/Love Money Can't Buy	1953	15.00	30.00	60.00
❏ 916	Too Much Boogie/Need Somebody	1953	15.00	30.00	60.00
❏ 923	Gotta Boogie/Down Child	1953	15.00	30.00	60.00
❏ 931	Jump Me/I Wonder Little Darling	1954	15.00	30.00	60.00
❏ 935	I Tried Hard/Let's Talk It Over	1954	12.50	25.00	50.00
❏ 942	Cool Little Car/Bad Boy	1954	12.50	25.00	50.00
❏ 948	Half a Stranger/Shake, Holler and Run	1954	12.50	25.00	50.00
❏ 958	Taxi Driver/You Receive Me	1955	12.50	25.00	50.00
❏ 966	Hug and Squeeze/The Syndicator	1955	12.50	25.00	50.00
❏ 978	Looking for a Woman/I'm Ready	1955	15.00	30.00	60.00

Riverside
❏ 438	I Need Some Money/No More Doggin'	1960	3.75	7.50	15.00

Rockin'
❏ 524	Blue Monday/Lovin' Guitar Man	1953	100.00	200.00	400.00
	As "John Lee Booker"				
❏ 525	Stuttering Blues/Pouring Down Rain	1953	100.00	200.00	400.00
	As "John Lee Booker"				

Specialty
❏ 528	Everybody's Blues/I'm Mad	1954	10.00	20.00	40.00

Stax
❏ 0053	Slow and Easy/Grinder Man	1969		3.00	6.00

Vee Jay
❏ 164	Mambo Chillen/Time Is Marching	1955	7.50	15.00	30.00
❏ 188	Every Night/Trouble Blues	1956	7.50	15.00	30.00
❏ 205	Dimples/Baby Lee	1956	7.50	15.00	30.00

Number		Title (A Side/B Side)	Year	VG	VG+	NM
☐ 233		The Road Is So Rough/I'm So Worried Baby	1957	6.25	12.50	25.00
☐ 245		I'm So Excited/I See You When You're Weak	1957	6.25	12.50	25.00
☐ 255		Little Wheel/Rosie Mae	1957	6.25	12.50	25.00
☐ 265		You Can Lead Me, Baby/Unfriendly Baby	1958	6.25	12.50	25.00
☐ 293		I Love You Honey/You've Taken My Woman	1958	6.25	12.50	25.00
☐ 308		Maudie/I'm In the Mood	1959	6.25	12.50	25.00
☐ 319		Tennessee Blues/Boogie Chillun	1959	6.25	12.50	25.00
☐ 331		Hobo Blues/Crawlin' King Snake	1959	6.25	12.50	25.00
☐ 349		No Shoes/Solid Sender	1960	6.25	12.50	25.00
☐ 366		Dusty Road/Tupelo	1960	6.25	12.50	25.00
☐ 379		I'm Mad Again/I'm Going Upstairs	1961	6.25	12.50	25.00
☐ 397		Want Ad Blues/Take Me As I Am	1961	6.25	12.50	25.00
☐ 438		Boom Boom/Drug Store Woman	1962	5.00	10.00	20.00
☐ 453		She's Mine/A New Leaf	1962	5.00	10.00	20.00
☐ 493		Take a Look at Yourself/I Love Her	1963	12.50	25.00	50.00
☐ 493		Take a Look at Yourself/Frisco Blues	1963	5.00	10.00	20.00
☐ 538		I'm Leaving/Birmingham Blues	1963	3.75	7.50	15.00
☐ 575		Send Me Your Pillow/Don't Look Back	1964	3.75	7.50	15.00
☐ 670		Big Legs, Tight Skirt/Your Baby Ain't Sweet Like Mine	1965	3.00	6.00	12.00
☐ 708		It Serves Me Right/Flowers on the Hour	1966	2.50	5.00	10.00

Hopkin, Mary
Apple

Number		Title (A Side/B Side)	Year	VG	VG+	NM
☐ 1801		Those Were the Days/Turn, Turn, Turn	1968	2.50	5.00	10.00
☐ 1806		Goodbye/Sparrow	1969	2.00	4.00	8.00
☐ 1806	PS	Goodbye/Sparrow	1969	3.00	6.00	12.00
☐ 1816		Temma Harbour/Lantano Dagli Occhi	1970	2.00	4.00	8.00
☐ 1816	PS	Temma Harbour/Lantano Dagli Occhi	1970	3.00	6.00	12.00
☐ 1823		Que Sera, Sera (Whatever Will Be, Will Be)/ Fields of St. Etienne	1970	2.00	4.00	8.00
☐ 1825		Think About Your Children/Heritage _With star on A-side label_	1970	3.00	6.00	12.00
☐ 1825		Think About Your Children/Heritage	1970	2.00	4.00	8.00
☐ 1825	PS	Think About Your Children/Heritage	1970	3.00	6.00	12.00
☐ 1843		Water, Paper and Clay/Streets of London _With star on A-side label_	1972	3.00	6.00	12.00
☐ 1843		Water, Paper and Clay/Streets of London	1972	2.00	4.00	8.00
☐ 1855		Knock Knock Who's There/International	1972	2.00	4.00	8.00

Apple/Americom

Number	Title (A Side/B Side)	Year	VG	VG+	NM
☐ 1801P/M-238	Those Were the Days/Turn, Turn, Turn _Four-inch flexi-disc sold from vending machines_	1969	150.00	300.00	600.00

RCA Victor

Number	Title (A Side/B Side)	Year	VG	VG+	NM
☐ PB-10694	Tell Me Now/If You Love Me	1976		2.00	4.00

Hopkins, Nicky
(Prominent keyboardist who played on Beatles and Rolling Stones sessions, among dozens of others)
Columbia

Number	Title (A Side/B Side)	Year	VG	VG+	NM
☐ 45869	Speed On/Sundown in Mexico	1973		2.50	5.00

Decca

Number	Title (A Side/B Side)	Year	VG	VG+	NM
☐ 32139	Mister Pleasant/Nothing As Yet	1967	3.00	6.00	12.00

Hornets, The
(Several different groups)
Columbia

Number	Title (A Side/B Side)	Year	VG	VG+	NM
☐ 42999	Fruit Cake/Seven Days to Tahiti	1964	15.00	30.00	60.00

Emerald

Number	Title (A Side/B Side)	Year	VG	VG+	NM
☐ 501	Runt/Breakfast in Bed	196?	7.50	15.00	30.00

Flash

Number	Title (A Side/B Side)	Year	VG	VG+	NM
☐ 125	Crying Over You/Tango Moon	1957	50.00	100.00	200.00

Liberty

Number	Title (A Side/B Side)	Year	VG	VG+	NM
☐ 55688	Motorcycle U.S.A./On the Track	1964	7.50	15.00	30.00

Rev

Number	Title (A Side/B Side)	Year	VG	VG+	NM
☐ 3515	Slow Dance/Strollin'	1958	6.25	12.50	25.00

States

Number	Title (A Side/B Side)	Year	VG	VG+	NM
☐ 127	I Can't Believe/Lonesome Baby _Black vinyl_	1953	4,000	6,000	8,000
☐ 127	I Can't Believe/Lonesome Baby _Red vinyl_	1953	7,500	10,000	15,000

V.I.P.

Number	Title (A Side/B Side)	Year	VG	VG+	NM
☐ 25004	She's My Baby/Give Me a Kiss	1964	15.00	30.00	60.00

Horton, Jay
Mustang

Number	Title (A Side/B Side)	Year	VG	VG+	NM
☐ 3010	I Trip on You Girl/(B-side unknown)	1965	7.50	15.00	30.00
☐ 3021	It's Love/Come What May	1966	7.50	15.00	30.00

Horton, Johnny
Abbott

Number	Title (A Side/B Side)	Year	VG	VG+	NM
☐ 100	Candy Jones/Devilish Lovelight	1951	10.00	20.00	40.00
☐ 101	Happy Millionaire/Mean Mean Son of a Gun	1951	10.00	20.00	40.00
☐ 102	Plaid and Calico/Done Roving _B-side by Bill Thompson's Westerners_	1951	10.00	20.00	40.00
☐ 103	Birds and Butterflies/Coal Smoke, Valve Oil and Steam	1951	10.00	20.00	40.00

Number		Title (A Side/B Side)	Year	VG	VG+	NM
❏ 104		Go and Wash (Those Dirty Feet)/ In My Home in Shelby County	1951	10.00	20.00	40.00
❏ 105		Shadows on the Old Bayou/Talk Gobbler Talk	1951	10.00	20.00	40.00
❏ 106		Smokey Joe's Barbeque/Words	1951	10.00	20.00	40.00
❏ 107		Long Rocky Road/On the Banks of the Beautiful Nile	1952	10.00	20.00	40.00
❏ 108		Somebody Rocking in My Broken Chair/Betty Lorraine	1952	10.00	20.00	40.00
		With Hillbilly Barton				
❏ 109		Rhythm in My Baby's Walk/Bowlin' Baby	1952	10.00	20.00	40.00
❏ 135		Plaid and Calico/Shadows on the Old Bayou	1953	7.50	15.00	30.00

Columbia

Number		Title (A Side/B Side)	Year	VG	VG+	NM
❏ 21504		Honky Tonk Man/I'm Ready If You're Willing	1956	7.50	15.00	30.00
❏ 21538		I'm a One Woman Man/I Don't Like I Did	1956	6.25	12.50	25.00
❏ 31104	S	titles unknown	1961	5.00	10.00	20.00
❏ 31105	S	titles unknown	1961	5.00	10.00	20.00
❏ 31106	S	titles unknown	1961	5.00	10.00	20.00
❏ 31107	S	titles unknown	1961	5.00	10.00	20.00
❏ 31108	S	titles unknown	1961	5.00	10.00	20.00

Anyone who can fill in these gaps -- the above five all are Columbia "Stereo 7" singles -- please let us know.

Number		Title (A Side/B Side)	Year	VG	VG+	NM
❏ 40813		I'm Coming Home/I Got a Hole in My Picture	1957	7.50	15.00	30.00
❏ 40919		She Knows Why/The Woman I Need	1957	5.00	10.00	20.00
❏ 40986		I'll Do It Every Time/Let's Take the Long Way Home	1957	5.00	10.00	20.00
❏ 41043		You're My Baby/Lover's Rock	1957	7.50	15.00	30.00
❏ 41110		Honky Tonk Hardwood Floor/The Wild One	1958	15.00	30.00	60.00
❏ 41210		All Grown Up/Counterfeit Love	1958	5.00	10.00	20.00
❏ 41308		When It's Springtime in Alaska (It's Forty Below)/ Whispering Pines	1958	3.75	7.50	15.00
❏ 41308	PS	When It's Springtime in Alaska (It's Forty Below)/ Whispering Pines	1958	7.50	15.00	30.00
		Promo-only black and white sleeve				
❏ 41339		The Battle of New Orleans/All for the Love of a Girl	1959	3.75	7.50	15.00
❏ 41339	PS	The Battle of New Orleans/All for the Love of a Girl	1959	5.00	10.00	20.00
❏ 41437		Johnny Reb/Sal's Got a Sugar Lip	1959	3.75	7.50	15.00
❏ 41502		I'm Ready If You're Willing/Take Me Like I Am	1959	3.75	7.50	15.00
❏ 41522		They Shined Up Rudolph's Nose/ The Electrified Donkey	1959	3.75	7.50	15.00
❏ 41568		Sink the Bismarck/ The Same Old Tale the Crow Told Me	1960	3.00	6.00	12.00
❏ 41568	PS	Sink the Bismarck/ The Same Old Tale the Crow Told Me	1960	5.00	10.00	20.00
❏ 41685		Johnny Freedom/Comanche	1960	3.00	6.00	12.00
❏ 41685	PS	Johnny Freedom/Comanche	1960	5.00	10.00	20.00
❏ 41782		North to Alaska/The Mansion You Stole	1960	3.00	6.00	12.00
❏ 41782	PS	North to Alaska/The Mansion You Stole	1960	5.00	10.00	20.00
❏ 41963		Sleepy Eyed John/They'll Never Take Her Home	1961	3.00	6.00	12.00
❏ 41963	PS	Sleepy Eyed John/They'll Never Take Her Home	1961	5.00	10.00	20.00
❏ 42063		Ole Slewfoot/Miss Marcy	1961	3.00	6.00	12.00
❏ 42302		Honky Tonk Man/Words	1962	3.75	7.50	15.00
❏ 42302	PS	Honky Tonk Man/Words	1962	5.00	10.00	20.00
❏ 42653		All Grown Up/I'm a One Woman Man	1962	3.00	6.00	12.00
❏ 42774		Sugar Coated Baby/When It's Springtime in Alaska (It's Forty Below)	1963	2.50	5.00	10.00
❏ 42993		Hooray for That Little Difference/ Tell My Baby I Love Her	1964	2.50	5.00	10.00
❏ 43143		Lost Highway/The Same Old Tale the Crow Told Me	1964	2.50	5.00	10.00
❏ 43719		Sam Magee/All for the Love of a Girl	1966	2.00	4.00	8.00
❏ 44156		The Battle of New Orleans/All for the Love of a Girl	1967		3.00	6.00

Cormac

Number	Title (A Side/B Side)	Year	VG	VG+	NM
❏ 1193	Plaid and Calico/Done Roving	1951	30.00	60.00	120.00
❏ 1197	Birds and Butterflies/Coal Smoke, Valve Oil and Steam	1951	30.00	60.00	120.00

Dot

Number	Title (A Side/B Side)	Year	VG	VG+	NM
❏ 15966	Plaid and Calico/Shadows on the Old Bayou	1959	3.00	6.00	12.00

Mercury

Number	Title (A Side/B Side)	Year	VG	VG+	NM
❏ 6412	The Devil Sent Me You/First Train Headin' South	1952	7.50	15.00	30.00
❏ 6418	The Rest of Your Life/This Won't Be the First Time	1952	7.50	15.00	30.00
❏ 70014	I Won't Forget/The Child's Side of Life	1952	7.50	15.00	30.00
❏ 70100	Tennessee Jive/The Mansion You Stole	1953	7.50	15.00	30.00
❏ 70156	S.S. Loveline/I Won't Get Dreamy-Eyed	1953	7.50	15.00	30.00
❏ 70198	You, You, You/Red Lips and Warm Red Wine	1953	7.50	15.00	30.00
❏ 70227	All for the Love of a Girl/Broken Hearted	1953	7.50	15.00	30.00
❏ 70325	Move On Down the Line/Train with the Rhumba Beat	1954	7.50	15.00	30.00
❏ 70399	The Door of Your Mansion/Ha Ha and Moonface	1954	7.50	15.00	30.00
❏ 70462	No True Love/There'll Never Be Another Mary	1954	7.50	15.00	30.00
❏ 70636	Journey with No End/Ridin' the Sunshine Special	1955	7.50	15.00	30.00
❏ 70707	Big Wheels Rollin'/Hey Sweet, Sweet Thing	1955	7.50	15.00	30.00

Hosea, Don

Sun

Number	Title (A Side/B Side)	Year	VG	VG+	NM
❏ 368	Since I Met You/Uh Huh Huh	1961	5.00	10.00	20.00

Hotlegs

(Evolved into 10CC)

Capitol

Number	Title (A Side/B Side)	Year	VG	VG+	NM
❏ 2886	Neanderthal Man/ You Didn't Like It, Because You Didn't Think of It	1970	2.50	5.00	10.00
❏ 3043	Run Baby Run/How Many Times	1971	3.75	7.50	15.00

Number		Title (A Side/B Side)	Year	VG	VG+	NM

Hound Dog Clowns
Uni
| ☐ 55047 | | Superfox/Wicked Witch | 1968 | 5.00 | 10.00 | 20.00 |

Hour Glass, The
(With Duane and Gregg Allman)
Liberty
☐ 56002		Heartbeat/Nothing But Tears	1967	3.00	6.00	12.00
☐ 56029		Power of Love/I Still Want Your Love	1968	3.00	6.00	12.00
☐ 56053		D-I-V-O-R-C-E/Changing of the Guard	1968	3.00	6.00	12.00
☐ 56065		She Is My Woman/Going Nowhere	1968	3.00	6.00	12.00
☐ 56072		Now Is the Time/She Is My Woman	1968	3.00	6.00	12.00
☐ 56091		I've Been Trying/Silently	1969	3.00	6.00	12.00

Houston, Cissy
(Whitney's mom)
Columbia
| ☐ 11058 | | Warning-Danger (This Love Affair May Be Hazardous to You)/An Umbrella Song | 1979 | | 2.00 | 4.00 |
| ☐ 11208 | | Break It To Me Gently/Gonna Take the Easy Way Out | 1980 | | 2.00 | 4.00 |
Commonwealth United
| ☐ 3010 | | I'll Be There/So I Believe | 1970 | | 3.00 | 6.00 |
Congress
| ☐ 268 | | Bring Him Back/World of Broken Hearts | 1966 | 15.00 | 30.00 | 60.00 |
| | | As "Susie Houston" | | | | |
Janus
☐ 131		I Just Don't Know What to Do with Myself/Empty Place	1970		3.00	6.00
☐ 145		Be My Baby/I'll Be There	1971		3.00	6.00
☐ 159		Hang On to a Dream/Darling Take Me Back	1971		3.00	6.00
☐ 177		I Love You/Making Love	1971		3.00	6.00
☐ 190		Didn't We/It's Not Easy	1972		3.00	6.00
☐ 206		Midnight Train to Georgia/Will You Still Love Me Tomorrow	1972		3.00	6.00
☐ 230		I'm So Glad I Can Love Again/One Time You Say You Love Me	1973		3.00	6.00
☐ 255		I Believe/Nothing Can Stop Me	1975		3.00	6.00
Kapp
| ☐ 814 | | Don't Come Running to Me/One Broken Heart for Sale | 1967 | 7.50 | 15.00 | 30.00 |
| | | As "Sissie Houston" | | | | |
Private Stock
☐ 45,137		Love Is Something That Leads You/If I Ever Lose This Heaven	1977		2.50	5.00
☐ 45,153		Tomorrow/Love Is Holding On	1977		2.50	5.00
☐ 45,171		Things to Do/It Never Really Ended	1977		2.50	5.00
☐ 45,204		Think It Over/The Umbrella Song	1978		2.50	5.00

Houston, David
(For his other records, see the Goldmine Country Western price guide)
Sun
| ☐ 403 | | Sherry's Lips/Miss Brown | 1966 | 5.00 | 10.00 | 20.00 |
| ☐ 1127 | | Sherry's Lips/Miss Brown | 1972 | | 2.50 | 5.00 |

Houston, Soldier Boy
Atlantic
| ☐ 971 | | Western Rider Blues/Hug Me Baby | 1952 | 62.50 | 125.00 | 250.00 |

Houston, Thelma
ABC Dunhill
☐ 11	DJ	Everybody Gets to Go to the Moon (same on both sides)	1969	3.75	7.50	15.00
		Special Apollo 11 promotional item				
☐ 4197		Sunshower/If This Was the Last Song	1969	2.50	5.00	10.00
☐ 4212		Jumpin' Jack Flash/This Is Your Life	1969	2.50	5.00	10.00
☐ 4222		Save the Country/I Just Can't Stay Away	1970	2.00	4.00	8.00
☐ 4260		The Good Earth/Ride, Louie, Ride	1970	2.00	4.00	8.00
Capitol
| ☐ 5767 | | Baby Mine/Woman Behind Her Man | 1966 | 12.50 | 25.00 | 50.00 |
| ☐ 5882 | | Don't Cry, My Soldier Boy/Let's Try to Make It | 1967 | 12.50 | 25.00 | 50.00 |
MCA
☐ 52196		Working Girl/Running in Circles	1983			3.00
☐ 52239		Make It Last/Just Like All the Rest	1983			3.00
☐ 52489		(I Guess) It Must Be Love/Running in Circles	1984			3.00
☐ 52491		Love Is a Dangerous Game/You Used to Hold Me So Tight	1984			3.00
☐ 52574		Keep It Light/My Lucille	1985			3.00
		B-side by B.B. King				
☐ 52582		What a Woman Feels Inside/Fantasy and Heartbreak	1985			3.00
Motown
☐ 1245		I'm Just a Part of Yesterday/Piano Man	1973		2.50	5.00
☐ 1260		Do You Know Where You're Going/Together	1973		2.50	5.00
☐ 1316		You've Been Doing Wrong for So Long/Pick Up the Week	1974		2.50	5.00
☐ 1385		The Bingo Long Song/Razzle Dazzle	1976		2.50	5.00
		B-side by William Goldstein				

Number		Title (A Side/B Side)	Year	VG	VG+	NM
☐ 1422		It's a Lifetime Thing/Kiss Me Now	1977		2.50	5.00
		With Jerry Butler				
Mowest						
☐ 5008		I Want to Go Back There Again/Pick Up the Week	1972		3.00	6.00
☐ 5013		Me and Bobby McGee/	1972		3.00	6.00
		No One's Gonna Be a Fool Forever				
☐ 5023		Piano Man/Me and Bobby McGee	1972		3.00	6.00
☐ 5027		What If/There Is a Fool	1972		3.00	6.00
☐ 5046		If It's the Last Thing I Do/And I Never Did	1973			Unreleased
☐ 5050		I'm Just a Part of Yesterday/Piano Man	1973		3.00	6.00
RCA						
☐ PB-11913		Suspicious Minds/Gone	1980		2.50	5.00
☐ PB-12215		If You Feel It/Hollywood	1981		2.00	4.00
☐ PB-12285		96 Tears/There's No Runnin' Away from Love	1981		2.00	4.00
Tamla						
☐ 54275		One Out of Every Six	1976			Unreleased?
☐ 54278		Don't Leave Me This Way (Short Version)/	1977		2.00	4.00
		Today Will Soon Be Yesterday				
☐ 54278	DJ	Don't Leave Me This Way (Long Version)/	1977		3.00	6.00
		Don't Leave Me This Way (Short Version)				
☐ 54283		If It's the Last Thing I Do/	1977		2.00	4.00
		If You Won't Let Me Walk on the Water				
☐ 54287		I'm Here Again/Sharin' Something Perfect	1977		2.00	4.00
☐ 54292		Any Way You Like It/Take My Love	1978		2.00	4.00
☐ 54295		I'm Not Strong Enough to Love You/Triplin'	1978		2.00	4.00
☐ 54297		Saturday Night, Sunday Morning/Come to Me	1979		2.00	4.00

Hubcaps, The
(Ernie Maresca is in this group)
Laurie

☐ 3219		Hot Rod City (Vocal)/Hot Rod City (Instrumental)	1964	3.75	7.50	15.00

Huddle, Jack
Kapp

☐ 207		Starlight/Believe Me	1959	50.00	100.00	200.00
		Buddy Holly plays guitar on these tracks				

Petsy

☐ 1002		Starlight/Believe Me	1958	125.00	250.00	500.00

Hughes, Jimmy
Atlantic

☐ 2454		Uncle Sam/It Ain't What You've Got	1967	2.00	4.00	8.00

Fame

☐ 1000		Midnight Affair/When It Comes to Dancing	1965	2.50	5.00	10.00
☐ 1003		Neighbor, Neighbor/It's a Good Thing	1966	2.00	4.00	8.00
☐ 1006		I Worship the Ground You Walk On/	1966	2.00	4.00	8.00
		A Shot of Rhythm and Blues				
☐ 1011		Why Not Tonight/I'm a Man of Action	1967	2.00	4.00	8.00
☐ 1014		Don't Lose Your Good Thing/	1967	2.00	4.00	8.00
		You Can't Believe Everything That You Hear				
☐ 1015		Hi-Heel Sneakers/Time Will Bring You Back	1967	2.00	4.00	8.00
☐ 6401		Steal Away/Lollipops, Lace and Lipstick	1964	5.00	10.00	20.00
		Black label				
☐ 6401		Steal Away/Lollipops, Lace and Lipstick	1964	3.00	6.00	12.00
		Red label				
☐ 6403		Try Me/Lovely Ladies	1964	2.50	5.00	10.00
☐ 6404		I Want Justice/I'm Getting Better	1964	2.50	5.00	10.00
☐ 6407		Goodbye My Lover, Goodbye/It Was Nice	1965	2.50	5.00	10.00
☐ 6410		You Really Know How to Hurt a Guy/	1965	2.50	5.00	10.00
		The Loving Physician				

Guyden

☐ 2075		I'm Qualified/My Loving Time	1962	5.00	10.00	20.00

Jamie

☐ 1280		I'm Qualified/My Loving Time	1964	3.75	7.50	15.00

Volt

☐ 4002		I Like Everything About You/What Side of the Door	1968	2.00	4.00	8.00
☐ 4008		Let 'Em Down Baby/The Sweet Things You Do	1969	2.00	4.00	8.00
☐ 4017		Chains of Love/I'm Not Ashamed to Beg or Plead	1969	2.00	4.00	8.00
☐ 4024		I'm So Glad/Lay It on the Line	1969	2.00	4.00	8.00

Hullabaloos, The
Roulette

☐ 4587		I'm Gonna Love You Too/Party Doll	1964	5.00	10.00	20.00
☐ 4587	PS	I'm Gonna Love You Too/Party Doll	1964	10.00	20.00	40.00
☐ 4593		Beware/Did You Ever	1965	5.00	10.00	20.00
☐ 4593	PS	Beware/Did You Ever	1965	10.00	20.00	40.00
☐ 4612		Learning the Game/Don't Stop	1965	5.00	10.00	20.00
☐ 4612	PS	Learning the Game/Don't Stop	1965	10.00	20.00	40.00
☐ 4622		I Won't Turn Around Now/My Heart Keeps Telling Me	1965	5.00	10.00	20.00
☐ 4622	PS	I Won't Turn Around Now/My Heart Keeps Telling Me	1965	10.00	20.00	40.00

Number		Title (A Side/B Side)	Year	VG	VG+	NM

Human Beinz, The
Capitol
☐ 2119		Turn On Your Love Light/It's Fun to Be Clean	1968	2.50	5.00	10.00
☐ 2119	PS	Turn On Your Love Light/It's Fun to Be Clean	1968	5.00	10.00	20.00
☐ 2198		Every Time Woman/The Face	1968	2.50	5.00	10.00
☐ 2431		I've Got to Keep On Pushin'/This Little Girl of Mine	1969	2.50	5.00	10.00
☐ 5990		Nobody But Me/Sueno	1967	3.75	7.50	15.00

Gateway
☐ 828		Gloria/The Times They Are a-Changin'	1967	3.75	7.50	15.00
☐ 838		You Can't Make Me Cry/The Pied Piper	1967	3.75	7.50	15.00

Human Expression, The
Accent
☐ 1214		Every Night/Love at Psychedelic Velocity	1967	50.00	100.00	200.00
☐ 1226		Calm Me Down/Optical Sound	1967	25.00	50.00	100.00
☐ 1252		I Don't Need Nobody/Sweet Child of Nothingness	1967	25.00	50.00	100.00

Humperdinck, Engelbert
Epic
☐ 02060		Don't You Love Me Anymore/Till I Get It Right	1981			3.00
☐ 02245		Maybe This Time/When the Night Ends	1981			3.00
☐ 03817		Till You and Your Lover Are Lovers Again/What Will I Write	1983			3.00
☐ 50270		After the Lovin'/Let's Remember the Good Times	1976		2.50	5.00
☐ 50365		I Believe in Miracles/Goodbye My Friend	1977		2.00	4.00
☐ 50447		A Lover's Holiday/Look at Me	1977		2.00	4.00
☐ 50488		A Night to Remember/Silent Night	1977		2.00	4.00
☐ 50526		The Last of the Romantics/I Have Paid the Toll	1978		2.00	4.00
☐ 50566		Love Me Tender/This Time One Year Ago	1978		2.00	4.00
☐ 50579		Love's In Need of Love Today/Sweet Marjorene	1978		2.00	4.00
☐ 50632		This Moment in Time/And the Day Begins	1978		2.00	4.00
☐ 50692		Can't Help Falling in Love/You Know Me	1979		2.00	4.00
☐ 50732		Lovin' Too Well/Much, Much Greater Love	1979		2.00	4.00
☐ 50844		Love's Only Love/Burning Ember	1980			3.00
☐ 50899		A Chance to Be a Hero/Any Kind of Love at All	1980			3.00
☐ 50933		Don't Cry Out Loud/Don't Touch That Dial	1980			3.00
☐ 50958		It's Not Easy to Live Together/Royal Affair	1980			3.00

Hickory
☐ 1337		Baby Turn Around/If I Could Do the Things I Want to Do	1965	4.00	8.00	16.00
		As "Gerry Dorsey"				

Parrot
☐ 40011	M	Release Me (And Let Me Love Again)/Ten Guitars	1967	2.00	4.00	8.00
☐ 40011	S	Release Me (And Let Me Love Again)/Ten Guitars	1967	5.00	10.00	20.00
		Both sides in true stereo. Letters "XDR" are stamped in run-off area before the matrix number				
☐ 40015		There Goes My Everything/You Love	1967	2.00	4.00	8.00
☐ 40019		The Last Waltz/That Promise	1967	2.00	4.00	8.00
☐ 40019	PS	The Last Waltz/That Promise	1967	3.00	6.00	12.00
☐ 40023		Am I That Easy to Forget/Pretty Ribbons	1967	2.00	4.00	8.00
☐ 40023	PS	Am I That Easy to Forget/Pretty Ribbons	1967	3.00	6.00	12.00
☐ 40027		A Man Without Love/Call on Me	1968	2.00	4.00	8.00
☐ 40032		Les Bicyclettes De Belsize/Three Little Words	1968	2.00	4.00	8.00
☐ 40032	PS	Les Bicyclettes De Belsize/Three Little Words	1968	3.00	6.00	12.00
☐ 40036		The Way It Used to Be/A Good Thing Going	1969		3.00	6.00
☐ 40036	PS	The Way It Used to Be/A Good Thing Going	1969	2.50	5.00	10.00
☐ 40040		I'm a Better Man/Cafe	1969		3.00	6.00
☐ 40044		Winter World of Love/Take My Heart	1969		3.00	6.00
☐ 40044	PS	Winter World of Love/Take My Heart	1969	2.50	5.00	10.00
☐ 40049		My Marie/Sweetheart	1970		3.00	6.00
☐ 40049	PS	My Marie/Sweetheart	1970	2.00	4.00	8.00
☐ 40054		Sweetheart/Born to Be Wanted	1970		3.00	6.00
☐ 40054	PS	Sweetheart/Born to Be Wanted	1970	2.00	4.00	8.00
☐ 40059		When There's No You/Stranger, Step In My World	1971		3.00	6.00
☐ 40059	PS	When There's No You/Stranger, Step In My World	1971	2.00	4.00	8.00
☐ 40065		Another Time, Another Place/You're the Window of My World	1971		3.00	6.00
☐ 40069		Too Beautiful to Last/A Hundred Times a Day	1972		2.50	5.00
☐ 40071		In Time/How Does It Feel	1972		2.50	5.00
☐ 40072		I Never Said Goodbye/Time After Time	1972		2.50	5.00
☐ 40073		I'm Leavin' You/My Summer Song	1973		2.00	4.00
☐ 40076		Love Is All/Lady of the Night	1973		2.00	4.00
☐ 40077		Free as the Wind/My Friend the Wind	1974		2.00	4.00
☐ 40079		Catch Me I'm Falling/Love, Oh Precious Love	1974		2.00	4.00
☐ 40082		Forever and Ever/Precious Love	1974		2.00	4.00
☐ 40085		This Is What You Mean to Me/A World Without Music	1975		2.00	4.00

Hunt, D.A.
Sun
☐ 183		Lonesome Ol' Jail/Greyhound Blues	1953			
		Unknown on 45 rpm, although both Sun 182 and 184 exist on 45s.				

Hunter, Ivory Joe
Atlantic
☐ 1049		It May Sound Silly/I Got to Learn to Do the Mambo	1954	6.25	12.50	25.00
☐ 1066		I Want Somebody/Heaven Came Down to Earth	1955	6.25	12.50	25.00
☐ 1086		A Tear Fell/I Need You By My Side	1956	6.25	12.50	25.00

Number	Title (A Side/B Side)	Year	VG	VG+	NM
❑ 1095	You Mean Everything to Me/That's Why I Dream	1956	6.25	12.50	25.00
❑ 1111	Since I Met You Baby/ You Can't Stop This Rocking and Rolling	1956	6.25	12.50	25.00
❑ 1128	Empty Arms/Love's a Hurting Game	1957	5.00	10.00	20.00
❑ 1151	She's Gone/Everytime I Hear That Song	1957	5.00	10.00	20.00
❑ 1164	All About the Blues/If Only You Were Here with Me	1957	5.00	10.00	20.00
❑ 1173	You're On My Mind/Baby, Baby, Count on Me	1958	5.00	10.00	20.00
❑ 1183	I'm So Glad I Found You/Shooty Booty	1958	5.00	10.00	20.00
❑ 1191	You Flip Me Baby/Yes, I Want You	1958	5.00	10.00	20.00
❑ 2020	I Just Want to Love You/Now I Don't Worry No More	1959	3.75	7.50	15.00

Capitol

Number	Title (A Side/B Side)	Year	VG	VG+	NM
❑ 4587	I'm Hooked/Because I Love You	1961	3.00	6.00	12.00
❑ 4648	May the Best Man Win/You Better Believe It Baby	1961	3.00	6.00	12.00
❑ 4688	The Life I Live/A Great Big Heart Full of Love	1962	3.00	6.00	12.00

Dot

Number	Title (A Side/B Side)	Year	VG	VG+	NM
❑ 15880	City Lights/Stolen Moments	1958	3.75	7.50	15.00
❑ 15930	Old Fashioned Love/Cottage for Sale	1959	3.75	7.50	15.00
❑ 15957	I Love You So Much It Hurts/Welcome Home Baby	1959	3.75	7.50	15.00
❑ 15986	My Search Was Ended/Did You Mean It	1959	3.75	7.50	15.00

Epic

Number	Title (A Side/B Side)	Year	VG	VG+	NM
❑ 10725	Heartbreak and Misery/ I'm Coming Down with the Blues	1971		3.00	6.00
❑ 10725	Heartbreak and Misery/ We All Like That Groovy Feeling	1971		3.00	6.00

Goldisc

Number	Title (A Side/B Side)	Year	VG	VG+	NM
❑ 3010	It's Love, It's Love, It's Love/You Satisfy Me Baby	1960	3.75	7.50	15.00

Goldwax

Number	Title (A Side/B Side)	Year	VG	VG+	NM
❑ 307	Every Little Bit Helped Me/I Can Make You Happy	1966	5.00	10.00	20.00

King

Note: Ivory Joe Hunter records on King before 4422 are unconfirmed on 45 rpm

Number	Title (A Side/B Side)	Year	VG	VG+	NM
❑ 4424	False Friend Blues/Send Me Pretty Mama	1951	10.00	20.00	40.00
❑ 4443	She's Gone Blues/Stop Rockin' That Train	1951	10.00	20.00	40.00
❑ 4455	Old Gal and New Gal Blues/Woo Wee Blues	1951	10.00	20.00	40.00
❑ 5166	Jealous Heart/I Like It	1958	3.75	7.50	15.00
❑ 5271	Guess Who/Don't Fall in Love with Me	1959			Unreleased
❑ 5280	Guess Who/Don't Fall in Love with Me	1959	3.75	7.50	15.00

MGM

Number	Title (A Side/B Side)	Year	VG	VG+	NM
❑ 8011	I Almost Lost My Mind/If I Give You My Love *Original 45 issue of this record*	1949	12.50	25.00	50.00
❑ 10578	I Almost Lost My Mind/If I Give You My Love	1949	10.00	20.00	40.00
❑ 10618	S.P. Blues/Why Fool Yourself	1950	7.50	15.00	30.00
❑ 10663	I Need You So/Leave Her Alone	1950	7.50	15.00	30.00
❑ 10733	Let Me Dream/Gimme a Pound of Round Ground	1950	7.50	15.00	30.00
❑ 10761	Old Man's Boogie/Living a Lie	1950	7.50	15.00	30.00
❑ 10818	It's A Sin/Don't You Believe Me	1950	7.50	15.00	30.00
❑ 10899	I Found My Baby/I Ain't Got No Gal	1951	7.50	15.00	30.00
❑ 10951	I Can't Get You Off My Mind/I Can't Resist You	1951	7.50	15.00	30.00
❑ 10995	You Lied/When I Lost You	1951	7.50	15.00	30.00
❑ 11052	I'm Yours/Wrong Woman Blues	1951	7.50	15.00	30.00
❑ 11132	Blue Moon/U Name It	1952	7.50	15.00	30.00
❑ 11165	Laugh/Where Shall I Go	1952	7.50	15.00	30.00
❑ 11195	I'm Sorry for You My Friend/I Will Be	1952	7.50	15.00	30.00
❑ 11263	I Get That Lonesome Feeling/I Thought I Had Loved	1952	7.50	15.00	30.00
❑ 11325	Big Bounce/Tell Her for Me	1952	7.50	15.00	30.00
❑ 11378	Rockin' Chair Boogie/Music Before Dawn	1952	7.50	15.00	30.00
❑ 11459	I Had a Girl/If You See My Baby	1953	7.50	15.00	30.00
❑ 11549	I'm Afraid/Don't Make Me Cry	1953	7.50	15.00	30.00
❑ 11599	I Must Be Talking to Myself/My Best Wishes	1953	7.50	15.00	30.00
❑ 11702	I Have a Secret/I Feel So Good	1954	6.25	12.50	25.00
❑ 11818	Do You Miss Me/Whose Arms Are You Missing	1954	6.25	12.50	25.00

Paramount

Number	Title (A Side/B Side)	Year	VG	VG+	NM
❑ 0253	He'll Never Love You/San Antonio Rose	1973		3.00	6.00

Smash

Number	Title (A Side/B Side)	Year	VG	VG+	NM
❑ 1825	My Arms Are Waiting/Congratulations	1963	3.00	6.00	12.00
❑ 1860	There's No Forgetting You/My Lover's Prayer	1963	3.00	6.00	12.00

Sound Stage 7

Number	Title (A Side/B Side)	Year	VG	VG+	NM
❑ 2623	Ivory Tower/I'll Give You All Night to Stop	1968	2.00	4.00	8.00
❑ 2635	Until the Day I Die/I Built a Wall Around Me	1969	2.00	4.00	8.00
❑ 2643	Straighten Up Baby/Baby Me Baby	1969	2.00	4.00	8.00

Stax

Number	Title (A Side/B Side)	Year	VG	VG+	NM
❑ 155	This Kind of Woman/Can't Explain Why It Happened	1964	3.00	6.00	12.00

Vee Jay

Number	Title (A Side/B Side)	Year	VG	VG+	NM
❑ 452	Somebody's Stealing My Love/ You Only Want Me When You Need Me	1962	3.00	6.00	12.00

Veep

Number	Title (A Side/B Side)	Year	VG	VG+	NM
❑ 1258	What's the Matter Baby/Don't You Believe Me	1967	2.00	4.00	8.00
❑ 1270	Did She Ask About Me/From the First Time We Met	1967	2.00	4.00	8.00

Hurricanes, The

King

Number	Title (A Side/B Side)	Year	VG	VG+	NM
❑ 4817	Poor Little Dancin' Girl/Pistol Packin' Mama	1955	30.00	60.00	120.00
❑ 4867	Maybe It's All for the Best/Yours	1956	25.00	50.00	100.00
❑ 4898	Raining in My Heart/Tell Me Baby	1956	25.00	50.00	100.00
❑ 4926	Little Girl of Mine/Your Promise to Me	1956	25.00	50.00	100.00

Number		Title (A Side/B Side)	Year	VG	VG+	NM
❑ 4947		Dear Mother/You May Not Know	1956	20.00	40.00	80.00
❑ 5018		Fallen Angel/I'll Always Be in Love with You	1957	15.00	30.00	60.00
❑ 5042		Priceless/Now That I Need You	1957	15.00	30.00	60.00

Hutton, Danny
(Later of Three Dog Night)
Almo

❑ 213		Why Don't You Love Me Anymore/Home in Pasadena	1964	5.00	10.00	20.00
		As "Daring Dan Hutton"				

Hanna-Barbera

❑ 447		Roses and Rainbows/Monster Shindig	1965	3.75	7.50	15.00
❑ 447	PS	Roses and Rainbows/Monster Shindig	1965	7.50	15.00	30.00
❑ 453		Big Bright Eyes/Monster Shindig (Part 2)	1965	3.75	7.50	15.00

MGM

❑ 13502		Funny How Love Can Be/Dreamin' Isn't Good for You	1966	2.50	5.00	10.00
❑ 13502	PS	Funny How Love Can Be/Dreamin' Isn't Good for You	1966	5.00	10.00	20.00
❑ 13613		Hang On to a Dream/Hit the Wall	1966	2.50	5.00	10.00

Hyland, Brian
ABC-Paramount

❑ 10236		Let Me Belong to You/Let It Die	1961	2.50	5.00	10.00
❑ 10262		I'll Never Stop Wanting You/The Night I Cried	1961	2.50	5.00	10.00
❑ 10262	PS	I'll Never Stop Wanting You/The Night I Cried	1961	5.00	10.00	20.00
❑ 10294		Ginny Come Lately/I Should Be Gettin' Better	1962	2.50	5.00	10.00
❑ 10294	PS	Ginny Come Lately/I Should Be Gettin' Better	1962	5.00	10.00	20.00
❑ 10336		Sealed with a Kiss/Summer Job	1962	3.00	6.00	12.00
❑ 10336	PS	Sealed with a Kiss/Summer Job	1962	5.00	10.00	20.00
❑ 10359		Warmed Over Kisses (Left Over Love)/ Walk a Lonely Mile	1962	2.50	5.00	10.00
❑ 10359	PS	Warmed Over Kisses (Left Over Love)/ Walk a Lonely Mile	1962	5.00	10.00	20.00
❑ 10374		I May Not Live to See Tomorrow/It Ain't That Way at All	1962	2.50	5.00	10.00
❑ 10374	PS	I May Not Live to See Tomorrow/It Ain't That Way at All	1962	5.00	10.00	20.00
❑ 10400		If Mary's There/Remember Me	1963	2.50	5.00	10.00
❑ 10400	PS	If Mary's There/Remember Me	1963	5.00	10.00	20.00
❑ 10427		Somewhere in the Night/I Wish Today Was Yesterday	1963	2.50	5.00	10.00
❑ 10452		I'm Afraid to Go Home/Save Your Heart for Me	1963	2.50	5.00	10.00
❑ 10494		Nothing Matters But You/Let Us Make Our Mistakes	1963	2.50	5.00	10.00
❑ 10549		Act Naturally/Out of Sight, Out of Mind	1964	2.50	5.00	10.00

Dot

❑ 17050		Apologize/Words on Paper	1967		3.00	6.00
❑ 17061		It's Christmas Time Once Again/Words on Paper	1967		3.00	6.00
❑ 17078		Come with Me/Delilah	1968		3.00	6.00
❑ 17109		The Lover/Springfield, Illinois	1968		3.00	6.00
❑ 17176		Tragedy/You'd Better Stop and Think It Over	1968		3.00	6.00
❑ 17222		A Million to One/It Could All Begin Again	1969		3.00	6.00
❑ 17258		Early April Morning/Stay and Love Me All Summer	1969		3.00	6.00
❑ 17291		Dreamy Eyes/Gonna Make a Woman Out of You	1970		3.00	6.00

Kapp

❑ 342		Itsy Bitsy Teeny Weeny Yellow Polka Dot Bikini/ Don't Dilly Dally, Sally	1960	3.75	7.50	15.00
❑ 342	PS	Itsy Bitsy Teeny Weeny Yellow Polka Dot Bikini/ Don't Dilly Dally, Sally	1960	7.50	15.00	30.00
❑ 352		Four Little Heels (The Clickety Clack Song)/ That's How Much	1960	3.00	6.00	12.00
❑ 352	PS	Four Little Heels (The Clickety Clack Song)/ That's How Much	1960	6.25	12.50	25.00
❑ 363		I Gotta Go/Lopsided, Over Loaded	1960	3.00	6.00	12.00
❑ 363	PS	I Gotta Go/Lopsided, Over Loaded	1960	6.25	12.50	25.00
❑ 401		Lipstick on Your Lips/When Will I Know	1961	3.00	6.00	12.00

Leader

❑ 801		Library Love Affair/Rosemary	1960	5.00	10.00	20.00
❑ 805		Itsy Bitsy Teeny Weeny Yellow Polka Dot Bikini/ Don't Dilly Dally, Sally	1960	7.50	15.00	30.00

Philips

❑ 40179		Here's to Our Love/Two Kinds of Girls	1964	2.00	4.00	8.00
❑ 40179	PS	Here's to Our Love/Two Kinds of Girls	1964	3.00	6.00	12.00
❑ 40203		Devoted to You/Pledging My Love	1964	2.00	4.00	8.00
❑ 40203	PS	Devoted to You/Pledging My Love	1964	3.00	6.00	12.00
❑ 40221		Now I Belong to You/ One Step Forward, Two Steps Back	1964	2.00	4.00	8.00
❑ 40263		He Don't Understand You/Love Will Find a Way	1965	2.00	4.00	8.00
❑ 40263	PS	He Don't Understand You/Love Will Find a Way	1965	3.00	6.00	12.00
❑ 40306		Stay Away from Her/I Can't Keep a Secret	1965	2.00	4.00	8.00
❑ 40354		3000 Miles/ Sometimes They Do, Sometimes They Don't	1966	2.00	4.00	8.00
❑ 40377		The Joker Went Wild/I Can Hear the Rain	1966	2.50	5.00	10.00
❑ 40405		Why Did You Do It/Run, Run, Look and See	1966	2.00	4.00	8.00
❑ 40424		Hung Up in Your Eyes/Why Mine	1967	2.00	4.00	8.00
❑ 40424	PS	Hung Up in Your Eyes/Why Mine	1967	3.00	6.00	12.00
❑ 40444		Holiday for Clowns/Yesterday I Had a Girl	1967	2.00	4.00	8.00
❑ 40472		Get the Message/Kinda Groovy	1967		3.00	6.00

Uni

❑ 55193		You and Me/Could You Dig It	1970		3.00	6.00
❑ 55240		Gypsy Woman/You and Me (#2)	1970		3.00	6.00
❑ 55272		Lonely Teardrops/Lorraine	1971		2.50	5.00

Number		Title (A Side/B Side)	Year	VG	VG+	NM
❏ 55287		So Long, Marianne/No Place to Run	1971		2.50	5.00
❏ 55306		Out of the Blue/If You Came Back	1971		2.50	5.00
❏ 55323		I Love Every Little Thing About You/	1972		2.50	5.00
		With My Eyes Wide Open				
❏ 55334		Only Wanna Make You Happy/	1972		2.50	5.00
		When You're Lovin' Me				

I

I.V. Leaguers, The
Dot
❏ 15677		Ring Chimes/The Story	1957	5.00	10.00	20.00

Nau-Voo
❏ 803		Told by the Stars/Jim Jam	1959	100.00	200.00	400.00

Porter
❏ 1004		Ring Chimes/The Story	1957	12.50	25.00	50.00

Ian and the Zodiacs
Philips
❏ 40244		The Cryin' Game/Livin' Lovin' Wreck	1964	2.50	5.00	10.00
❏ 40277		Good Morning Little Schoolgirl/Message to Martha	1965	2.50	5.00	10.00
❏ 40291		So Much in Love with You/This Empty Place	1965	2.50	5.00	10.00
❏ 40291	PS	So Much in Love with You/This Empty Place	1965	6.25	12.50	25.00
❏ 40343		Why Can't It Be Me/Leave It to Me	1965	2.50	5.00	10.00
❏ 40369		No Money, No Honey/Where Were You	1966	2.50	5.00	10.00

Ideals, The
Checker
❏ 920		Knee Socks/Mary's Lamb	1959	6.25	12.50	25.00
❏ 979		Knee Socks/Mary's Lamb	1961	3.75	7.50	15.00
		As "Johnny Brantley and the Ideals"				

Cool
❏ 108		Do I Have the Right/You Won't Like It	1958	75.00	150.00	300.00

Cortland
❏ 110		Don Juan/Gorilla	1963	5.00	10.00	20.00
❏ 113		Mo Joe Hanna/Simple Simon	1964	3.75	7.50	15.00
❏ 115		Feeling of a Kiss/You Came a Long Way from St. Louis	1964	3.75	7.50	15.00
❏ 117		Local Boy/L.A.	1964	3.75	7.50	15.00

Decca
❏ 30720		Annie Has a Stroller/My Girl	1959	10.00	20.00	40.00
❏ 30800		Ivy League Lover/Don't Be a Baby, Baby	1959	6.25	12.50	25.00

Fargo
❏ 1024		The Duchess/Trans Zizstor	1962	5.00	10.00	20.00

Paso
❏ 6401		Together/What's the Matter with You Sam	1961	12.50	25.00	50.00
❏ 6402		Magic/Teens	1961	12.50	25.00	50.00

Satellite
❏ 2007		You Lost and I Won/You Hurt Me	1965	6.25	12.50	25.00
❏ 2009		Kissing/I Had a Dream	1966	6.25	12.50	25.00
❏ 2011		Go Go Gorilla/Kissing Won't Go Out of Style	1966	6.25	12.50	25.00

St. Lawrence
❏ 1001		Cathy's Clown/Go Get a Wig	1965	3.00	6.00	12.00
❏ 1020		I Got Lucky (When I Found You)/Tell Her I Apologize	1966	3.75	7.50	15.00

Stars of Hollywood
❏ 1001		Please, Jan/Always Yours	1959	10.00	20.00	40.00

Idle Race, The
(Jeff Lynne of Electric Light Orchestra was in this group)
Liberty
❏ 55997		Here We Go 'Round the Lemon Tree/My Father's Son	1967	5.00	10.00	20.00
❏ 56064		The End of the Road/The Morning Sunshine	1968	6.25	12.50	25.00

Idols, The
Dot
❏ 16210		Just a Little Bit More/Why Must I Cry	1961	3.75	7.50	15.00
		B-side by the Swans				

E-Z
❏ 1		Jeannine/Can't Tag Along	1961	10.00	20.00	40.00

RCA Victor
❏ 47-7339		30 Days/The Prowler	1958	5.00	10.00	20.00
❏ 47-7417		Here in My Heart/The Counterfeiter	1958	5.00	10.00	20.00

Reveille
❏ 1002		Just a Little Bit More/Why Must I Cry	1961	7.50	15.00	30.00
		B-side by the Swans				

Iggy and the Stooges
Bomp!
❏ 139		I Got a Right/Gimme Some Skin	1991			2.00
❏ 139	PS	I Got a Right/Gimme Some Skin	1991			2.00

Columbia
❏ 45877		Search and Destroy/Penetration	1973	2.50	5.00	10.00

Number		Title (A Side/B Side)	Year	VG	VG+	NM
Elektra						
❑ 45664		I Wanna Be Your Dog (Part 1)/ I Wanna Be Your Dog (Part 2) *As "The Stooges"*	1970	7.50	15.00	30.00
❑ 45695		Down on the Street/I Feel Alright *As "The Stooges"*	1970	7.50	15.00	30.00
Siamese						
❑ 001		I Got a Right/Gimme Some Skin	1977	6.25	12.50	25.00
❑ 001		I Got a Right/Gimme Some Skin *Second pressing: "Siamese" in fake Asian lettering with iguana logo*	1977	2.50	5.00	10.00
❑ 001	PS	I Got a Right/Gimme Some Skin *Only issued with Bomp!-distributed copies; has "Iggy & & The Stooges" on cover*	1977		3.00	6.00
EPs						
Bomp!						
❑ 114		Jesus Loves the Stooges	1977		3.75	7.50
❑ 114	PS	Jesus Loves the Stooges	1977		3.75	7.50

III Wind, The
ABC

Number	Title (A Side/B Side)	Year	VG	VG+	NM
❑ 11107	In My Dark World/Walkin' and Singin'	1968	6.25	12.50	25.00

III Winds, The
(Later incarnation of the "Chantay's")
Reprise

Number	Title (A Side/B Side)	Year	VG	VG+	NM
❑ 0423	So Be On Your Way (I Won't Cry)/Fear of the Rain	1965	3.75	7.50	15.00
❑ 0492	I Idolize You/A Letter	1966	3.75	7.50	15.00

Illusions, The
(Many different groups)
Columbia

Number	Title (A Side/B Side)	Year	VG	VG+	NM
❑ 43700	I Know/Take My Heart	1966	2.50	5.00	10.00
Coral					
❑ 62173	The Letter/Henry and Henrietta	1960	10.00	20.00	40.00
Dial					
❑ 4004	I Don't Believe It/The World Outside	1965	2.50	5.00	10.00
Dot					
❑ 16752	Secrets of Love/Don't Put Me Down	1965	5.00	10.00	20.00
Ember					
❑ 1071	How High Is the Mountain/Can't We Fall in Love	1961	7.50	15.00	30.00
Kape					
❑ 1001	The Closer You Are/For Sentimental Reasons	196?	2.50	5.00	10.00
Laurie					
❑ 3245	Maybe/In the Beginning	1964	5.00	10.00	20.00
Little Debbie					
❑ 105	Story of My Life/Walking Boy	1964	37.50	75.00	150.00
Mali					
❑ 104	Hey Boy/Lonely Soldier	1962	12.50	25.00	50.00
Northeast					
❑ 801	Hey Boy/Lonely Soldier	1962	3.75	7.50	15.00
Relic					
❑ 512	Hey Boy/Lonely Soldier	1964	2.50	5.00	10.00
Round					
❑ 1018	Jezebel/Nightmare	1963	20.00	40.00	80.00
Sheraton					
❑ 104	Hey Boy/Lonely Soldier	1962	6.25	12.50	25.00

Imaginations, The
(Several different groups)
Ballad

Number	Title (A Side/B Side)	Year	VG	VG+	NM
❑ 500	Wait a Little Longer Son/Mama's Little Baby	1962	3.75	7.50	15.00
Bo Marc					
❑ 301	Guardian Angel/Hey You	1961	10.00	20.00	40.00
Duel					
❑ 507	Guardian Angel/Hey You	1961	5.00	10.00	20.00
Dunhill					
❑ 4092	I Love You When You're Mad/Summer in New York *With P.F. Sloan and Steve Barri*	1967	5.00	10.00	20.00
Fraternity					
❑ 1001	I Just Can't Get Over Losing You/ Strange Neighborhood	1967	7.50	15.00	30.00
❑ 1006	No One Ever Lost More/Strange Voice	1968	6.25	12.50	25.00
Music Makers					
❑ 103	Goodnight Baby/The Search Is Over	1961	12.50	25.00	50.00
❑ 108	Guardian Angel/Hey You	1961	12.50	25.00	50.00

Number	Title (A Side/B Side)	Year	VG	VG+	NM

Impacts, The
(More than one group)
Anderson
| ❏ 104 | Summer/Linda | 1964 | 12.50 | 25.00 | 50.00 |

Carlton
❏ 548	Darling, No You're Mine/Help Me Somebody	1961	12.50	25.00	50.00
	With incorrect A-side title				
❏ 548	Darling, Now You're Mine/Help Me Somebody	1961	7.50	15.00	30.00

DCP
❏ 1147	Wishing Well/Heartaches	1965	12.50	25.00	50.00
	As "Kenny and the Impacts"				
❏ 1150	Just Because/Pigtails	1965	10.00	20.00	40.00

Kip
| ❏ 1890 | Burnt Valves/Chrome Reverse | 1963 | 12.50 | 25.00 | 50.00 |

RCA Victor
| ❏ 47-7583 | Bobby Sox Squaw/Croc-O-Doll | 1959 | 5.00 | 10.00 | 20.00 |
| ❏ 47-7609 | Canadian Sunset/They Say | 1959 | 12.50 | 25.00 | 50.00 |

Watts
| ❏ 5599 | Now Is the Time/Soup | 1959 | 20.00 | 40.00 | 80.00 |

Impalas, The
(More than one group)
Bunky
| ❏ 7760 | What Should He Do/I Still Love You | 1969 | 2.00 | 4.00 | 8.00 |
| ❏ 7762 | Whip it On Me/I Still Love You | 1969 | 2.00 | 4.00 | 8.00 |

Capitol
| ❏ 2709 | Speed Up/Soul | 1969 | 2.00 | 4.00 | 8.00 |

Checker
| ❏ 999 | For the Love of Mike/I Need You So Much | 1961 | 3.00 | 6.00 | 12.00 |

Cub
❏ 9022	I Ran All the Way Home/Fool, Fool, Fool	1959	12.50	25.00	50.00
	Original A-side title				
❏ 9022	Sorry (I Ran All the Way Home)/Fool, Fool, Fool	1959	3.75	7.50	15.00
❏ 9033	Oh What a Fool/Sandy Went Away	1959	5.00	10.00	20.00
❏ 9053	Peggy Darling/Bye Everybody	1959	5.00	10.00	20.00

Hamilton
| ❏ 50026 | I Was a Fool/First Date | 1960 | 5.00 | 10.00 | 20.00 |

Red Boy
| ❏ 113 | When You Dance/I Can't See Me Without You | 1966 | 6.25 | 12.50 | 25.00 |

Rite-On
| ❏ 101 | I Can't See Me Without You/Old Man Mose | 196? | 5.00 | 10.00 | 20.00 |

Steady
| ❏ 044 | When You Dance/I Can't See Me Without You | 1967 | 5.00 | 10.00 | 20.00 |

Sundown
| ❏ 115 | The Lonely One/Lost Boogie | 1959 | 3.75 | 7.50 | 15.00 |

20th Fox
| ❏ 428 | Last Night I Saw a Girl/There Is Nothin' Like a Dame | 1963 | 3.00 | 6.00 | 12.00 |

Imperials, The
(Also see "Little Anthony and the Imperials")
Capitol
| ❏ 4921 | I'm Still Dancing/Bermuda Wonderful | 1963 | 3.75 | 7.50 | 15.00 |

Carlton
| ❏ 566 | Faithfully Yours/Vut Vut | 1961 | 5.00 | 10.00 | 20.00 |

Newtime
| ❏ 503 | A Short Prayer/Where Will You Be | 1962 | 3.75 | 7.50 | 15.00 |
| ❏ 505 | The Letter/Go and Get Your Heart Broken | 1962 | 3.75 | 7.50 | 15.00 |

Omni
| ❏ 5501 | Who's Gonna Love Me/Better Take Time to Love | 1978 | | 2.50 | 5.00 |

Impossibles, The
(Probably more than one group)
Blanche
| ❏ 029 | Chapel Bells/Little by Little | 1960 | 100.00 | 200.00 | 400.00 |

Reprise
| ❏ 0305 | Lonely Bluebird/Paint Me a Pretty Picture | 1964 | 6.25 | 12.50 | 25.00 |

RMP
| ❏ 1030 | Mr. Maestro/Well, It's Alright | 1964 | 6.25 | 12.50 | 25.00 |
| ❏ 501 | Everywhere I Go/Well, It's Alright | 1966 | 6.25 | 12.50 | 25.00 |

Roulette
| ❏ 4745 | I Wanna Know/It's All Right | 1967 | 5.00 | 10.00 | 20.00 |

Impressions, The
(Also see "Butler, Jerry"; "Mayfield, Curtis". These could be more than one group)
ABC
❏ 10831	Can't Satisfy/This Must End	1966	2.00	4.00	8.00
❏ 10869	Love's a-Comin'/Wade in the Water	1966	2.00	4.00	8.00
❏ 10900	You Always Hurt Me/Little Girl	1967	2.00	4.00	8.00
❏ 10932	It's Hard to Believe/You've Got Me Runnin'	1967	2.00	4.00	8.00

Number		Title (A Side/B Side)	Year	VG	VG+	NM
❑ 10964		I Can't Stay Away from You/ You Ought to Be in Heaven	1967	2.00	4.00	8.00
❑ 11022		We're a Winner/It's All Over	1967	2.00	4.00	8.00
❑ 11071		We're Rolling On (Part 1)/We're Rolling On (Part 2)	1968	2.00	4.00	8.00
❑ 11103		I Loved and I Lost/Up, Up and Away	1968	2.00	4.00	8.00
❑ 11135		Don't Cry My Love/Sometimes I Wonder	1968	2.00	4.00	8.00
❑ 11188		East of Java/Just Before Sunrise	1969	2.00	4.00	8.00

ABC-Paramount

Number		Title (A Side/B Side)	Year	VG	VG+	NM
❑ 10241		Gypsy Woman/As Long As You Love Me	1961	3.75	7.50	15.00
❑ 10289		Grow Closer Together/Can't You See	1962	3.75	7.50	15.00
❑ 10328		Little Young Lover/Never Let Me Go	1962	3.75	7.50	15.00
❑ 10357		You've Come Home/Minstrel and Queen	1962	3.75	7.50	15.00
❑ 10386		I'm the One Who Loves You/I Need Your Love	1962	3.75	7.50	15.00
❑ 10431		Sad, Sad Girl and Boy/Twist and Limbo	1963	3.75	7.50	15.00
❑ 10487		It's All Right/You'll Want Me Back	1963	3.00	6.00	12.00
❑ 10511		Talking About My Baby/Never Too Much Love	1963	3.00	6.00	12.00
❑ 10537		Girl You Don't Know Me/A Woman Who Loves Me	1964	3.00	6.00	12.00
❑ 10544		I'm So Proud/I Made a Mistake	1964	3.00	6.00	12.00
❑ 10554		Keep On Pushing/I Love You (Yeah)	1964	3.00	6.00	12.00
❑ 10581		You Must Believe Me/See the Real Me	1964	3.00	6.00	12.00
❑ 10602		Amen/Long, Long Winter	1964	3.00	6.00	12.00
❑ 10622		People Get Ready/I've Been Trying	1965	2.50	5.00	10.00
❑ 10647		Woman's Got Soul/Get Up and Move	1965	2.50	5.00	10.00
❑ 10670		Meeting Over Yonder/I've Found That I've Lost	1965	2.50	5.00	10.00
❑ 10710		I Need You/Never Could You Be	1965	2.50	5.00	10.00
❑ 10725		Just One Kiss from You/Twilight Time	1965	2.50	5.00	10.00
❑ 10750		You've Been Cheatin'/Man, Oh Man	1965	2.50	5.00	10.00
❑ 10761		Since I Lost the One I Love/Falling in Love with You	1966	2.50	5.00	10.00
❑ 10789		Too Slow/No One Else	1966	2.50	5.00	10.00

Abner

Number		Title (A Side/B Side)	Year	VG	VG+	NM
❑ 1013		For Your Precious Love/Sweet Was the Wine	1958	7.50	15.00	30.00
		As "Jerry Butler and the Impressions"				
❑ 1017		Come Back My Love/Love Me	1958	7.50	15.00	30.00
❑ 1023		The Gift of Love/At the County Fair	1959	7.50	15.00	30.00
❑ 1025		Lonely One/Senorita I Love You	1959	7.50	15.00	30.00
❑ 1034		Say That You Love Me/A New Love	1960	7.50	15.00	30.00

Bandera

Number		Title (A Side/B Side)	Year	VG	VG+	NM
❑ 2504		Listen/Shorty's Got to Go	1959	12.50	25.00	50.00

Chi-Sound

Number		Title (A Side/B Side)	Year	VG	VG+	NM
❑ 2418		Sorry/All I Wanna Do Is Make Love to You	1979		2.50	5.00
❑ 2438		Maybe I'm Mistaken/ All I Wanna Do Is Make Love to You	1980		2.50	5.00
❑ 2491		For Your Precious Love/You're Mine	1981		2.50	5.00
❑ 2499		Love, Love, Love/Fan the Fire	1981		2.50	5.00

Cotillion

Number		Title (A Side/B Side)	Year	VG	VG+	NM
❑ 44210		This Time/I'm a Fool for Love	1976		2.50	5.00
❑ 44211		Silent Night/I Saw Mommy Kissing Santa Claus	1976		3.00	6.00
❑ 44214		You'll Never Find/Stardust	1977		2.50	5.00
❑ 44222		Can't Get Along/You're So Right for Me	1977		2.50	5.00

Curtom

Number		Title (A Side/B Side)	Year	VG	VG+	NM
❑ 0103		Sooner or Later/Miracle Woman	1975		2.50	5.00
❑ 0106		Same Thing It Took/I'm So Glad	1975		2.50	5.00
❑ 0110		Loving Power/First Impressions	1975		2.50	5.00
❑ 0116		Sunshine/I Wish I'd Stayed in Bed	1976		2.50	5.00
❑ 1932		Fool for You/I'm Loving Nothing	1968		3.00	6.00
❑ 1932	PS	Fool for You/I'm Loving Nothing	1968	3.75	7.50	15.00
❑ 1934		This Is My Country/My Woman's Love	1968		3.00	6.00
❑ 1937		My Deceiving Heart/You Want Somebody Else	1969		3.00	6.00
❑ 1940		Seven Years/The Girl I Find	1969		3.00	6.00
❑ 1943		Choice of Colors/Mighty Mighty Spade and Whitey	1969		3.00	6.00
❑ 1946		Say You Love Me/You'll Be Always Mine	1969		3.00	6.00
❑ 1948		Wherever She Leadeth Me/Amen (1970)	1970		3.00	6.00
❑ 1951		Check Out Your Mind/Can't You See	1970		3.00	6.00
❑ 1954		(Baby) Turn On to Me/Soulful Love	1970		3.00	6.00
❑ 1957		Ain't Got Time/I'm So Proud	1971		3.00	6.00
❑ 1959		Love Me/Do You Wanna Win	1971		3.00	6.00
❑ 1966		Inner City Blues/We Must Be in Love	1971		3.00	6.00
❑ 1970		This Loves for Real/Times Have Changed	1972		3.00	6.00
❑ 1973		I Need to Belong to Someone/Love Me	1972		3.00	6.00
❑ 1982		Preacher Man/Times Have Changed	1973		3.00	6.00
❑ 1985		Thin Line/I'm Loving You	1973		3.00	6.00
❑ 1994		If It's In You to Do Wrong/Times Have Changed	1973		3.00	6.00
❑ 1997		Finally Got Myself Together (I'm a Changed Man)/ I'll Always Be Here	1974		3.00	6.00
❑ 2003		Something's Mighty, Mighty Wrong/ Three the Hard Way	1974		3.00	6.00

Falcon

Number		Title (A Side/B Side)	Year	VG	VG+	NM
❑ 1013		For Your Precious Love/Sweet Was the Wine	1958	12.50	25.00	50.00
		As "Jerry Butler and the Impressions"				

MCA

Number		Title (A Side/B Side)	Year	VG	VG+	NM
❑ 52995		Can't Wait 'Til Tomorrow/Love Workin' On Me	1987			3.00

Port

Number		Title (A Side/B Side)	Year	VG	VG+	NM
❑ 70031		Listen/Shorty's Got to Go	1962	3.75	7.50	15.00

Swirl

Number		Title (A Side/B Side)	Year	VG	VG+	NM
❑ 107		I Need Your Love/Don't Leave Me	1962	5.00	10.00	20.00

Number	Title (A Side/B Side)	Year	VG	VG+	NM
20th Fox					
❑ 172	All Through the Night/Meanwhile, Back in My Heart	1959	10.00	20.00	40.00
Vee Jay					
❑ 280	For Your Precious Love/Sweet Was the Wine	1958	2,500	5,000	10,000
	As "Jerry Butler and the Impressions"				
❑ 424	Say That You Love Me/Senorita I Love You	1962	5.00	10.00	20.00
❑ 574	The Gift of Love/At the County Fair	1963	3.75	7.50	15.00
❑ 621	Say That You Love Me/Senorita I Love You	1964	3.75	7.50	15.00

In-Betweens, The
(At least one source says this is early Slade)

Number	Title (A Side/B Side)	Year	VG	VG+	NM
Highland					
❑ 1173	Girl Child, I Am An Evil Witchman/Security	1966	75.00	150.00	300.00

Indigo Girls

Number	Title (A Side/B Side)	Year	VG	VG+	NM
Epic					
❑ 68912	Closer to Fine/Cold As Ice	1989	2.50	5.00	10.00
❑ 73003	Land of Canaan/Never Stop	1989	2.50	5.00	10.00

Ingram, Luther

Number	Title (A Side/B Side)	Year	VG	VG+	NM
Decca					
❑ 31794	Ain't That Nice/You Never Miss Your Water	1965	3.00		6.00	12.00
Hib					
❑ 698	If It's All the Same To You Babe/(B-side unknown)	1967	20.00	40.00	80.00
KoKo					
❑ 101	I Can't Stop/You Got to Give Love to Get Love	1968	2.50	5.00	10.00
❑ 103	Missing You/Since You Don't Want Me	1968	2.50	5.00	10.00
❑ 721	Ain't Good for Nothing/These Are the Things	1976		3.00	6.00
❑ 724	Let's Steal Away to the Hideaway/I've Got Your Love in My Life	1977		3.00	6.00
❑ 725	I Like the Feeling/Gonna Be the Next Time	1977		3.00	6.00
❑ 728	Do You Love Somebody/How I Miss My Baby	1977		3.00	6.00
❑ 731	Get to Me/Trying to Find My Love	1978		3.00	6.00
❑ 2101	You Can Depend on Me/Looking for a New Love	1969	2.00	4.00	8.00
❑ 2102	Pity for the Lonely/Looking for a New Love	1969	2.00	4.00	8.00
❑ 2103	Puttin' Game Down/Since You Don't Want Me	1969	2.00	4.00	8.00
❑ 2104	My Honey and Me/I Can't Stop	1969	2.00	4.00	8.00
❑ 2105	Ain't That Loving You (For More Reasons Than One)/Home Don't Seem Like Home	1970	2.00	4.00	8.00
❑ 2106	To the Other Man/I'll Just Call You Honey	1970	2.00	4.00	8.00
❑ 2107	Be Good to Me Baby/Since You Don't Want Me	1971	2.00	4.00	8.00
❑ 2108	I'll Love You Until the End/Ghetto Train	1971	2.00	4.00	8.00
❑ 2110	You Were Made for Me/Missing You	1972	2.00	4.00	8.00
❑ 2111	(If Loving You Is Wrong) I Don't Want to Be Right/Puttin' Game Down	1972	2.00	4.00	8.00
❑ 2113	I'll Be Your Shelter (In Time of Storm)/I Can't Stop	1972	2.00	4.00	8.00
❑ 2115	Always/Help Me Love	1973	2.00	4.00	8.00
❑ 2116	Love Ain't Gonna Run Me Away/To the Other Man	1973	2.00	4.00	8.00
Profile					
❑ 5125	Baby Don't Go Too Far/How Sweet It Would Be	1986			3.00
❑ 5132	Don't Turn Around/(B-side unknown)	1987			3.00
❑ 5143	Gotta Serve Somebody/All in the Name of Love	1987			3.00
Smash					
❑ 2019	(I Spy) For the F.B.I./Foxey Devil	1966	5.00	10.00	20.00

Initials, The
(The Congress group is probably not the same as the Dee and Sherry group)

Number	Title (A Side/B Side)	Year	VG	VG+	NM
Congress					
❑ 207	School Day/The Song Is Number One	1964	3.00	6.00	12.00
❑ 219	Dancing on the Sand/Seventeen Guys on a Blanket at the Beach	1964	3.00	6.00	12.00
❑ 229	Someday She'll Love Me/I Should Have Listened	1964	3.00	6.00	12.00
	As "Angelo and the Initials"				
Dee					
❑ 1001	Bells of Joy/You	1959	50.00	100.00	200.00
Sherry					
❑ 667	Bells of Joy/You	1959	12.50	25.00	50.00

Inner Circle, The
(Another P.F. Sloan and Steve Barri creation)

Number	Title (A Side/B Side)	Year	VG	VG+	NM
Dunhill					
❑ 4128	So Long Mary Ann/Goes to Show	1968	5.00	10.00	20.00
Impact					
❑ 1019	Sally Go Round the Roses/Sugar	1967	5.00	10.00	20.00

Innocents, The

Number	Title (A Side/B Side)	Year	VG	VG+	NM
Decca					
❑ 31519	Don't Cry/Come On Lover	1963	5.00	10.00	20.00
Indigo					
❑ 105	Honest I Do/My Baby Hully Gullys	1960	5.00	10.00	20.00
❑ 111	Gee Whiz/Please Mr. Sun	1960	5.00	10.00	20.00
❑ 116	Kathy/In the Beginning	1961	5.00	10.00	20.00
❑ 124	Beware/Because I Love You So	1961	5.00	10.00	20.00

Number		Title (A Side/B Side)	Year	VG	VG+	NM
❏ 128		Donna/You Got Me Goin'	1961	5.00	10.00	20.00
❏ 132		Pains in My Heart/When I Become a Man	1961	5.00	10.00	20.00
Port						
❏ 3026		Gee Whiz/Please Mr. Sun	196?	2.00	4.00	8.00
Reprise						
❏ 20,112		Be Mine/Oh How I Miss My Baby	1962	6.25	12.50	25.00
❏ 20,122		Be Mine/Oh How I Miss My Baby	1962			*Unreleased*
❏ 20,125		You're Never Satisfied/Oh How I Miss My Baby	1962	5.00	10.00	20.00
Warner Bros.						
❏ 5450		My Heart Stood Still/Don't Call Me Lonely Anymore	1964	7.50	15.00	30.00

Insects, The
Applause

Number		Title (A Side/B Side)	Year	VG	VG+	NM
❏ 1002		Let's Bug the Beatles/Dear Beatles	1964	6.25	12.50	25.00
		B-side by the Little Lady Beatles				

Inspirations, The
Al-Brite

Number		Title (A Side/B Side)	Year	VG	VG+	NM
❏ 1651		Angel in Disguise/Stool Pigeon	1960	20.00	40.00	80.00
Beltone						
❏ 2037		The Girl By My Side/Neckin'	1963	15.00	30.00	60.00
Gone						
❏ 5097		Angel in Disguise/Stool Pigeon	1961	6.25	12.50	25.00
Jamie						
❏ 1034		Dry Your Eyes/Good-Bye	1956	18.75	37.50	75.00
❏ 1212		Dry Your Eyes/Good-Bye	1962	5.00	10.00	20.00
Rondak						
❏ 9787		Ring Those Bells/The Cumberland and the Merrimac	1961	75.00	150.00	300.00
Sparkle						
❏ 102		Angel in Disguise/Stool Pigeon	1960	37.50	75.00	150.00
Sultan						
❏ 1		The Genie/The Feeling of Her Kiss	1959	7.50	15.00	30.00
❏ 1	PS	The Genie/The Feeling of Her Kiss	1959	12.50	25.00	50.00

International Submarine Band, The
(Gram Parsons, later of the Byrds and the Flying Burrito Brothers, was in this group)
Ascot

Number		Title (A Side/B Side)	Year	VG	VG+	NM
❏ 2218		The Russians Are Coming/Truck Driving Man	1966	3.75	7.50	15.00
❏ 2218	PS	The Russians Are Coming/Truck Driving Man	1966	10.00	20.00	40.00
Columbia						
❏ 43935		Sum Up Broke/One Day Week	1966	7.50	15.00	30.00
LHI						
❏ 1205		Luxury Liner/Blue Eyes	1968	3.75	7.50	15.00
❏ 1217		Miller's Cave/I Must Be Somebody Else	1968	3.75	7.50	15.00

Intruders, The
(The Beltone and Fame records may not be by the same group as the others)
Beltone

Number		Title (A Side/B Side)	Year	VG	VG+	NM
❏ 1009		Camptown Rock/Morse Code	1961	3.75	7.50	15.00
Fame						
❏ 101		Fried Eggs/Jeffrie's Rock	1959	6.25	12.50	25.00
❏ 313		Creepin'/Frankfurters and Sauerkraut	1959	6.25	12.50	25.00
❏ 616		Rock-A-Ma-Roll/Era-Rock-A	1959	6.25	12.50	25.00
Gamble						
❏ 201		(We'll Be) United/Up and Down the Ladder	1966	2.50	5.00	10.00
❏ 203		Devil with an Angel's Smile/	1966	2.50	5.00	10.00
		A Book for the Broken Hearted				
❏ 203	PS	Devil with an Angel's Smile/	1966	3.75	7.50	15.00
		A Book for the Broken Hearted				
❏ 204		It Must Be Love/Check Yourself	1966	2.50	5.00	10.00
❏ 205		Together/Up and Down the Ladder	1967	2.50	5.00	10.00
❏ 209		Baby I'm Lonely/A Love That's Real	1967	2.50	5.00	10.00
❏ 214		Cowboys to Girls/Turn the Hands of Time	1968	2.50	5.00	10.00
❏ 217		(Love Is Like a) Baseball Game/Friends No More	1968	2.50	5.00	10.00
❏ 221		Slow Drag/So Glad I'm Yours	1968	2.50	5.00	10.00
❏ 223		Give Her a Transplant/Girls, Girls, Girls	1969	2.50	5.00	10.00
❏ 225		Me Tarzan, You Jane/Favorite Candidate	1969	2.50	5.00	10.00
❏ 231		Lollipop (I Like You)/Don't Give It Away	1969	2.50	5.00	10.00
❏ 235		Sad Girl/Let's Go Downtown	1969	2.50	5.00	10.00
❏ 240		Old Love/Every Day Is a Holiday	1969	2.50	5.00	10.00
❏ 2501		(Win, Place or Show) She's a Winner/	1972	2.00	4.00	8.00
		Memories Are Here to Stay				
❏ 2506		I'll Always Love My Mama (Part 1)/	1973	2.00	4.00	8.00
		I'll Always Love My Mama (Part 2)				
❏ 2508		I Wanna Know Your Name/Hang On In There	1973	2.00	4.00	8.00
❏ 4001		Tender (Was the Love We Knew)/	1970	2.00	4.00	8.00
		By the Time I Get to Phoenix				
❏ 4004		When We Get Married/Doctor Doctor	1970	2.00	4.00	8.00
❏ 4007		This Is My Love Song/Let Me in Your Mind	1970	2.00	4.00	8.00
❏ 4009		I'm Girl Scoutin'/Wonder What Kind of Bag She's In	1971	2.00	4.00	8.00
❏ 4014		Pray for Me/Best Days of My Life	1971	2.00	4.00	8.00

Number	Title (A Side/B Side)	Year	VG	VG+	NM
❑ 4016	I Bet He Don't Love You (Like I Love You)/ Do You Remember Yesterday	1971	2.00	4.00	8.00
❑ 4019	(Win, Place or Show) She's a Winner/ Memories Are Here to Stay	1972	2.50	5.00	10.00

Gowen
❑ 1401	I'm Sold on You/Come Home Soon	1961	6.25	12.50	25.00

Philadelphia Int'l.
❑ 3624	I'll Always Love My Mama (Part 1)/ I'll Always Love My Mama (Part 2)	1977		2.50	5.00
❑ 3689	I'll Always Love My Mama/Save the Children	1979		2.50	5.00

TSOP
❑ 4758	A Nice Girl Like You/To Be Happy Is the Real Thing	1974		3.00	6.00
❑ 4766	Rainy Days and Mondays/Be on Time	1975		3.00	6.00
❑ 4771	Plain Old Fashioned Girl/Energy of Love	1975		3.00	6.00

Invitations, The
(Probably all the same group)

Diamond
❑ 253	Got to Have It Now/Swingin' on the Love Vine	1968	3.00	6.00	12.00

Dyno Voice
❑ 206	Written on the Wall/Hallelujah	1965	7.50	15.00	30.00
❑ 210	What's Wrong with Me Baby/ Why Did My Baby Turn Bad	1965	7.50	15.00	30.00
❑ 215	Skiing in the Snow/Why Did My Baby Turn Bad	1966	15.00	30.00	60.00

MGM
❑ 13574	The Skate/Girl I'm Leavin' You	1966	3.75	7.50	15.00
❑ 13666	Watch Out Little Girl/You're Like a Mystery	1967	3.75	7.50	15.00

Silver Blue
❑ 801	They Say the Girl's Crazy/For Your Precious Love	1973	2.00	4.00	8.00
❑ 804	Let's Love/Love Has to Grow	1973	2.00	4.00	8.00
❑ 809	Living Together Is Keeping Us Apart/I Didn't Know	1974	2.00	4.00	8.00
❑ 818	Look on the Good Side/Look on the Good Side (Part 2)	1974	2.00	4.00	8.00

Iridescents, The

Hudson
❑ 8102	Three Coins in the Fountain/Strong Love	1963	6.25	12.50	25.00
❑ 8102	Three Coins in the Fountain/Strong Love *Blue vinyl*	1963	25.00	50.00	100.00

Ultrasonic
❑ 109	I Know/The Angels Sang	1960	100.00	200.00	400.00

Irish Rovers, The
(Also see "Rovers, The")

Decca
❑ 32254	The Unicorn/Black Velvet Band	1968	2.00	5.00	10.00
❑ 32333	(The Puppet Song) Whiskey on a Sunday/ The Orange and the Green	1968	2.00	4.00	8.00
❑ 32371	Liverpool Lou/The Bi-Plane, Ever More	1968	2.00	4.00	8.00
❑ 32444	Lily the Pink/Mrs. Crandall's Boardinghouse	1969	2.00	4.00	8.00
❑ 32529	Peter Knight/Did She Mention My Name	1969	2.00	4.00	8.00
❑ 32575	Fifi O'Toole/Winkin', Blinkin', and Nod	1969	2.00	4.00	8.00
❑ 32616	Rhymes and Reasons/Penny Whistler Peddlers	1970		3.00	6.00
❑ 32723	Two Little Boys/Years May Come, Years May Go	1970		3.00	6.00
❑ 32775	The Marvelous Toy/Marika's Lullaby	1970		3.00	6.00

Irridescents, The

Hawk
❑ 4001	Bali Ha'i/Swamp Surfer	1963	12.50	25.00	50.00

Infinity
❑ 037	Bali Ha'i/Swamp Surfer	1963	6.25	12.50	25.00

Oldies 45
❑ 183	Bali Ha'i/Swamp Surfer	1964	3.00	6.00	12.00

Isle, Jimmy

Bally
❑ 1034	Baby-O/Hassle	1957	6.25	12.50	25.00

Everest
❑ 19320	Oh Judy/Billy Boy	1959	6.25	12.50	25.00

Mala
❑ 459	Our Town/Everybody Gotta Little Girl But Me	1963	5.00	10.00	20.00

Roulette
❑ 4065	Goin' Wild/You and Johnny Smith	1958	7.50	15.00	30.00

Sun
❑ 306	Diamond Ring/I've Been Waiting	1958	6.25	12.50	25.00
❑ 318	Time Will Tell/Without a Love	1959	6.25	12.50	25.00
❑ 332	What a Life/Together	1959	6.25	12.50	25.00

Isley Brothers, The

Atlantic
❑ 2092	Jeepers Creepers/Teach Me How to Shimmy	1961	3.75	7.50	15.00
❑ 2100	Shine On Harvest Moon/Standing on the Dance Floor	1961	3.75	7.50	15.00
❑ 2110	Your Old Lady/Write to Me	1961	3.75	7.50	15.00
❑ 2122	A Fool for You/Just One More Time	1961	3.75	7.50	15.00

Number	Title (A Side/B Side)	Year	VG	VG+	NM
❏ 2263	Looking for a Love/The Last Girl	1964	2.50	5.00	10.00
❏ 2277	Simon Says/Wild As a Tiger	1965	2.50	5.00	10.00
❏ 2303	Move Over and Let Me Dance/	1965	3.75	7.50	15.00
	Have You Ever Been Disappointed				

Cindy

❏ 3009	Don't Be Jealous/This Is the End	1958	18.75	37.50	75.00
"Cindy" in regular print					
❏ 3009	Don't Be Jealous/This Is the End	1958	37.50	75.00	150.00
"Cindy" in shadow print					

Gone

❏ 5022	I Wanna Know/Everybody's Gonna Rock and Roll	1958	20.00	40.00	80.00
❏ 5048	My Love/The Drag	1958	20.00	40.00	80.00

Mark-X

❏ 7003	The Drag/Rockin' MacDonald	1957	25.00	50.00	100.00
❏ 8000	The Drag/Rockin' MacDonald	1959	7.50	15.00	30.00

RCA

❏ 447-0589	Shout (Part 1)/Shout (Part 2)	1976		2.00	4.00
Gold Standard Series; black label, dog near top					

RCA Victor

❏ 447-0589	Shout (Part 1)/Shout (Part 2)	1962	3.00	6.00	12.00
Gold Standard Series; black label, dog on top (this charted with this number in 1962)					
❏ 447-0589	Shout (Part 1)/Shout (Part 2)	1965	2.00	4.00	8.00
Gold Standard Series; black label, dog on side					
❏ 447-0589	Shout (Part 1)/Shout (Part 2)	1969		2.50	5.00
Gold Standard Series; red label					
❏ 47-7537	I'm Gonna Knock on Your Door/Turn to Me	1959	6.25	12.50	25.00
❏ 47-7588	Shout (Part 1)/Shout (Part 2)	1959	7.50	15.00	30.00
❏ 47-7657	Respectable/Without a Song	1959	6.25	12.50	25.00
❏ 47-7718	He's Got the Whole World in His Hands/	1960	6.25	12.50	25.00
	How Deep Is the Ocean				
❏ 47-7746	Gypsy Love Song/Open Up Your Heart	1960	6.25	12.50	25.00
❏ 47-7787	Say You Love Me Too/Tell Me Who	1960	6.25	12.50	25.00
❏ 61-7588	Shout (Part 1)/Shout (Part 2)	1959	15.00	30.00	60.00
"Living Stereo" (large hole, plays at 45 rpm)					

T-Neck

❏ 501	Testify (Part 1)/Testify (Part 2)	1964	3.75	7.50	15.00
❏ 901	It's Your Thing/Don't Give It Away	1969		3.00	6.00
❏ 902	I Turned You On/I Know Who You Been Socking It To	1969		3.00	6.00
❏ 906	Black Berries -- Pt. 1/Black Berries -- Pt. 2	1969		3.00	6.00
❏ 908	Was It Good to You/I Got to Get Myself Together	1969		3.00	6.00
❏ 912	Bless Your Heart/Give the Women What They Want	1969		3.00	6.00
❏ 914	Keep On Doin'/Save Me	1970		3.00	6.00
❏ 919	If He Can, You Can/Holdin' On	1970		3.00	6.00
❏ 921	Girls Will Be Girls, Boys Will Be Boys/	1970		3.00	6.00
	Get Down Off of the Train				
❏ 924	Get Into Something/Get Into Something (Part 2)	1970		3.00	6.00
❏ 927	Freedom/I Need You So	1970		3.00	6.00
❏ 929	Warpath/I Got to Find Me One	1971		3.00	6.00
❏ 930	Love the One You're With/He's Got Your Love	1971		3.00	6.00
❏ 932	Spill the Wine/Take Inventory	1971		3.00	6.00
❏ 933	Lay Lady Lay/Vacuum Cleaner	1971		3.00	6.00
❏ 934	Lay-Away/Feel Like the World	1972		3.00	6.00
❏ 935	Pop That Thang/I Got to Find Me One	1972		3.00	6.00
❏ 936	Work to Do/Beautiful	1972		3.00	6.00
❏ 937	It's Too Late/Nothing to Do But Today	1973		3.00	6.00
❏ 2251	That Lady (Part 1)/That Lady (Part 2)	1973		2.50	5.00
❏ 2252	What It Comes Down To/Highways of My Life	1973		2.50	5.00
❏ 2253	Summer Breeze (Part 1)/Summer Breeze (Part 2)	1974		2.50	5.00
❏ 2254	Live It Up (Part 1)/Live It Up (Part 2)	1974		2.50	5.00
❏ 2255	Midnight Sky (Part 1)/Midnight Sky (Part 2)	1974		2.50	5.00
❏ 2256	Fight the Power Part 1/Fight the Power Part 2	1975		2.50	5.00
❏ 2259	For the Love of You (Part 1&2)/You Walk Your Way	1975		2.50	5.00
❏ 2260	Who Loves You Better-Part 1/	1976		2.50	5.00
	Who Loves You Better-Part 2				
❏ 2261	Harvest for the World/Harvest for the World (Part 2)	1976		2.50	5.00
❏ 2262	The Pride (Part 1)/The Pride (Part 2)	1977		2.50	5.00
❏ 2264	Livin' in the Life/Go for Your Guns	1977		2.50	5.00
❏ 2270	Voyage to Atlantis/Do You Wanna Stay Down	1977		2.50	5.00
❏ 2272	Take Me to the Next Phase (Part 1)/	1978		2.50	5.00
	Take Me to the Next Phase (Part 2)				
❏ 2277	Groove with You/Footsteps in the Dark	1978		2.50	5.00
❏ 2278	Showdown (Part 1)/Showdown (Part 2)	1978		2.50	5.00
❏ 2279	I Wanna Be with You (Part 1)/	1979		2.50	5.00
	I Wanna Be with You (Part 2)				
❏ 2284	Winner Takes All/Fun and Games	1979		2.50	5.00
❏ 2287	It's a Disco Night (Rock Don't Stop)/	1979		2.50	5.00
	Ain't Givin' Up on Love				
❏ 2290	Don't Say Goodnight (It's Time for Love) (Part 1)/	1980		2.50	5.00
	Don't Say Goodnight (It's Time for Love) (Part 2)				
❏ 2291	Here We Go Again (Part 1)/Here We Go Again (Part 2)	1980		2.50	5.00
❏ 2292	Say You Will (Part 1)/Say You Will (Part 2)	1980		2.50	5.00
❏ 2293	Who Said?/(Can't You See) What You've Done to Me	1980		2.50	5.00
❏ 02033	Hurry Up and Wait/(Instrumental)	1981		2.50	5.00
❏ 02151	Don't Say Goodnight (It's Time for Love) (Parts 1 & 2)	1981		2.00	4.00
Reissue					

Number		Title (A Side/B Side)	Year	VG	VG+	NM
❑ 02179		I Once Had Your Love (And I Can't Let Go)/ (Instrumental)	1981		2.50	5.00
❑ 02270		Voyage to Atlantis/Do You Wanna Stay Down	1981		2.00	4.00
	Reissue					
❑ 02293		Who Said?/(Can't You See) What You Do to Me	1981		2.00	4.00
	Reissue					
❑ 02531		Inside You (Part 1)/Inside You (Part 2)	1981		2.50	5.00
❑ 02705		Party Night/Welcome Into My Night	1982		2.50	5.00
❑ 02985		The Real Deal/(Instrumental)	1982		2.50	5.00
❑ 03281		It's Alright with Me/(Instrumental)	1982		2.50	5.00
❑ 03797		Between the Sheets/(Instrumental)	1983		2.50	5.00
❑ 03994		Choosey Lover/(Instrumental)	1983		2.50	5.00
❑ 04320		Let's Make Love Tonight/(Instrumental)	1984		2.50	5.00

Tamla

❑ 54128		This Old Heart of Mine (Is Weak for You)/ There's No Love Left	1966	3.75	7.50	15.00
❑ 54133		Take Some Time Out for Love/ Who Could Ever Doubt My Love	1966	3.00	6.00	12.00
❑ 54135		I Guess I'll Always Love You/I Hear a Symphony	1966	3.00	6.00	12.00
❑ 54146		Got to Have You Back/Just Ain't Enough Love	1967	3.00	6.00	12.00
❑ 54154		One Too Many Heartaches/That's the Way Love Is	1967	3.00	6.00	12.00
❑ 54164		Take Me in Your Arms (Rock Me a Little While)/ Why When Love Is Gone	1968	3.00	6.00	12.00
❑ 54175		Behind a Painted Smile/All Because I Love You	1968	3.00	6.00	12.00
❑ 54182		Take Some Time Out for Love/Just Ain't Enough Love	1969	3.00	6.00	12.00

Teenage

| ❑ 1004 | | Angels Cried/The Cow Jumped Over the Moon | 1957 | 200.00 | 400.00 | 800.00 |

United Artists

❑ 605		She's Gone/Tango	1963	5.00	10.00	20.00
❑ 638		Surf and Shout/Whatcha Gonna Do	1963	5.00	10.00	20.00
❑ 659		Please, Please, Please/You'll Never Leave Him	1963	5.00	10.00	20.00
❑ 714		Who's That Lady/My Little Girl	1964	5.00	10.00	20.00
❑ 798		Love Is a Wonderful Thing/Open Up Her Eyes	1964			Unreleased
❑ 923		Love Is a Wonderful Thing/Open Up Her Eyes	1965			Unreleased

V.I.P.

| ❑ 25020 | | I Hear a Symphony/Who Could Ever Doubt My Love | 1965 | 200.00 | 400.00 | 800.00 |

Veep

| ❑ 1230 | | Love Is a Wonderful Thing/Open Up Her Eyes | 1966 | 2.50 | 5.00 | 10.00 |

Wand

❑ 118		Right Now/The Snake	1962	3.00	6.00	12.00
❑ 124		Twist and Shout/Spanish Twist	1962	3.75	7.50	15.00
❑ 127		Twistin' with Linda/You Better Come Home	1962	3.00	6.00	12.00
❑ 131		Nobody But Me/I'm Laughing to Keep from Crying	1963	3.00	6.00	12.00
❑ 137		I Say Love/Hold On Baby	1963	3.00	6.00	12.00

Warner Bros.

❑ 22748		One of a Kind/You'll Never Walk Alone	1989			3.00
❑ 22900		Spend the Night (Ce Soir)/(Instrumental)	1989			3.00
❑ 22900	PS	Spend the Night (Ce Soir)/(Instrumental)	1989			3.00
❑ 27954		It Takes a Good Woman/(Instrumental)	1988		2.00	4.00
❑ 28129		I Wish/(Instrumental)	1988		2.00	4.00
❑ 28129	PS	I Wish/(Instrumental)	1988		2.00	4.00
❑ 28241		Come My Way/(Instrumental)	1987		2.00	4.00
❑ 28385		Smooth Sailin' Tonight/(Instrumental)	1987		2.00	4.00
❑ 28385	PS	Smooth Sailin' Tonight/(Instrumental)	1987		2.00	4.00
❑ 28764		May I?/(Instrumental)	1986		2.00	4.00
❑ 28860		Colder Are My Nights/(Instrumental)	1985		2.00	4.00

Italian Asphalt and Pavement Company, The – See "Duprees, The"

Ivan

Coral

❑ 62017		Real Wild Child/Oh You Beautiful Doll	1958	50.00	100.00	200.00
	With Buddy Holly on guitar					
❑ 62081		That'll Be Alright/Frankie Frankenstein	1959	100.00	200.00	400.00
❑ 65607		Real Wild Child/That'll Be Alright	1967	12.50	25.00	50.00

Iveys, The – See "Badfinger"

Ivoleers, The

Buzz

| ❑ 101 | | Lover's Quarrel/Come with Me | 1959 | 100.00 | 200.00 | 400.00 |

Ivorys, The

Darla

| ❑ 1000 | | Wishing Well/Deep Freeze | 1962 | 100.00 | 200.00 | 400.00 |

Sparta

| ❑ 001 | | Why Don't You Write Me/Deep Freeze | 1962 | 20.00 | 40.00 | 80.00 |

Ivy League, The

Cameo

❑ 343		Wait a Minute/What More Do You Want	1965	3.75	7.50	15.00
❑ 356		Lonely Room/Funny How Love Can Be	1965	3.75	7.50	15.00
❑ 365		A Girl Like You/That's Why I'm Crying	1965	3.75	7.50	15.00
❑ 377		Tossing & Turning/Graduation Day	1965	3.75	7.50	15.00

Number		Title (A Side/B Side)	Year	VG	VG+	NM
❑ 388		Our Love Is Slipping Away/ I Could Make You Fall in Love	1966	3.75	7.50	15.00
❑ 388	PS	Our Love Is Slipping Away/ I Could Make You Fall in Love	1966	6.25	12.50	25.00
❑ 402		Rain Rain Go Away/Running Around in Circles	1966	3.75	7.50	15.00
❑ 449		When You're Young/My World Fell Down	1966	3.75	7.50	15.00

Ivy Three, The
Shell

❑ 302		Nine Out of Ten/I've Cried Enough for Two	1961	7.50	15.00	30.00
		Gold label				
❑ 302		Nine Out of Ten/I've Cried Enough for Two	1961	5.00	10.00	20.00
		Multicolored label				
❑ 306		Bagoo/Suicide	1961	3.75	7.50	15.00
❑ 720		Yogi/Was Judy There	1960	5.00	10.00	20.00
		Originals have blue labels				
❑ 720		Yogi/Was Judy There	1961	3.75	7.50	15.00
		Reissues have multicolored labels				
❑ 723		Alone in the Chapel/Hush Little Baby	1960	6.25	12.50	25.00

J

J.B.'s, The
(James Brown's backing group, it also recorded with Fred Wesley)
King

❑ 6317		The Grunt (Part 1)/The Grunt (Part 2)	1970	2.50	5.00	10.00
❑ 6333		These Are the J.B.'s (Part 1)/ These Are the J.B.'s (Part 2)	1970	2.50	5.00	10.00

Jackie and Jill
U.S.A.

❑ 791		I Want a Beatle for Christmas/Jingle Bells	1964	5.00	10.00	20.00

Jacks, The
(Also see "Cadets, The")
Kent

❑ 344		Why Don't You Write Me/This Empty Heart	1960	3.75	7.50	15.00

RPM

❑ 428		Why Don't You Write Me/Smack Dab in the Middle	1955	30.00	60.00	120.00
❑ 428		Why Don't You Write Me/My Darling	1955	15.00	30.00	60.00
❑ 433		I'm Confessin'/Since My Baby's Been Gone	1955	15.00	30.00	60.00
❑ 444		This Empty Heart/My Clumsy Heart	1955	12.50	25.00	50.00
❑ 454		So Wrong/How Soon	1956	12.50	25.00	50.00
❑ 458		Sugar Baby/Why Did I Fall in Love	1956	15.00	30.00	60.00
❑ 467		Let's Make Up/Dream a Little Longer	1956	15.00	30.00	60.00

Jackson Five, The - See "Jacksons, The"

Jackson, Bull Moose
King

❑ 4181		I Love You Yes I Do/Sneaky Pete	1951	15.00	30.00	60.00
		78 originally released in 1947				
❑ 4189		I Want a Bowlegged Woman/ All My Love Belongs to You	1951	30.00	60.00	120.00
		78 originally released in 1948 -- 4181 and 4189 are his only legitimate 45s known before 4451				
❑ 4451		Trust in Me/Wonder When My Baby's Coming Home	1951	15.00	30.00	60.00
❑ 4462		Unless/End This Misery	1951	15.00	30.00	60.00
❑ 4472		Cherokee Boogie/I'm Lucky I Have You	1951	15.00	30.00	60.00
❑ 4493		I'll Be Home for Christmas/ I Never Loved Anyone But You	1951	15.00	30.00	60.00
❑ 4524		Nosey Joe/Sad	1952	20.00	40.00	80.00
❑ 4535		(Let Me Love You) All Night Long/Bootsie	1952	15.00	30.00	60.00
❑ 4551		Bearcat Blues/There Is No Greater Love	1952	15.00	30.00	60.00
❑ 4580		Big Ten Inch Record/I Needed You	1952	62.50	125.00	250.00
❑ 4634		Meet Me with Your Black Dress On/Try to Forget Him	1953	10.00	20.00	40.00
❑ 4655		If You'll Let Me/Hodge Podge	1953	10.00	20.00	40.00
❑ 4775		If You Ain't Lovin'/I Wanna Hug Ya, Kiss Ya	1955	6.25	12.50	25.00
❑ 4802		I'm Glad for Your Sake/Must You Keep On Pretending	1955	6.25	12.50	25.00

Seven Arts

❑ 705		I Love You Yes I Do/Aw Shucks Baby	1961	5.00	10.00	20.00

Warwick

❑ 575		I Found My Love/More of the Same	1960	5.00	10.00	20.00

Jackson, Chuck
ABC

❑ 11368		I Only Get This Feeling/Slowly But Surely	1973		3.00	6.00
❑ 11398		I Can't Break Away/Just a Little Tear	1973		3.00	6.00
❑ 11423		If Only You Believe/Maybe This Will be the Morning	1974		3.00	6.00
❑ 12024		Take Off Your Make-Up/Talk a Little Less	1974		3.00	6.00

All Platinum

❑ 2357		Love Lights/(Instrumental)	1975		2.50	5.00
❑ 2360		I'm Needing You, Wanting You/ We Can't Hide It Anymore	1975		2.50	5.00

Number		Title (A Side/B Side)	Year	VG	VG+	NM
☐ 2363		If You Were My Woman (Part 1)/ If You Were My Woman (Part 2)	1976		2.50	5.00
☐ 2370		One of Those Yesterdays/Love Lights	1976		2.50	5.00
☐ 2373		I Fell Asleep/One of Those Yesterdays	1976		2.50	5.00

Amy

Number		Title (A Side/B Side)	Year	VG	VG+	NM
☐ 849		Come On and Love Me/Ooh Baby	1962	3.75	7.50	15.00
☐ 868		I'm Yours/Hula Lula	1962	3.75	7.50	15.00

Atco

☐ 6197		Never Let Me Go/Baby I Want to Marry You	1961	3.00	6.00	12.00

Beltone

☐ 1005		Mr. Price/Hula Lula	1961	5.00	10.00	20.00

Clock

Note: Clock sides as "Charles Jackson"

☐ 1015		Come On and Love Me/Ooh Baby	1959	6.25	12.50	25.00
☐ 1022		Hula Hula/I'm Yours	1960	6.25	12.50	25.00
☐ 1027		This Is It/Mr. Pride	1960	6.25	12.50	25.00

Dakar

☐ 4512		I Forgot to Tell You/The Man and the Woman	1972		3.00	6.00

Dot

☐ 15673		Woke Up This Morning/Wilette	1957	7.50	15.00	30.00

With Kripp Johnson

EMI America

☐ 8042		I Wanna Give You Some Love/Waiting in Vain	1980		2.00	4.00
☐ 8056		After You/Let's Get Together	1980		2.00	4.00

Motown

☐ 1118		(Don't Let the Boy Overpower) The Man in You/ Girls, Girls, Girls	1968	2.50	5.00	10.00
☐ 1144		Are You Lonely for Me Baby/Your Wonderful Love	1969	2.50	5.00	10.00
☐ 1152		Honey Come Back/What Am I Gonna Do Without You	1969	2.50	5.00	10.00
☐ 1160		The Day My World Stood Still/Baby, I'll Get It	1970	125.00	250.00	500.00

Sugarhill

☐ 764		Sometimes When We Touch/(B-side unknown)	1981		2.00	4.00

V.I.P.

☐ 25052		The Day My World Stood Still/Baby, I'll Get It	1970	2.50	5.00	10.00
☐ 25056		Let Somebody Love Me/Two Feet from Happiness	1970	2.50	5.00	10.00
☐ 25059		Is There Anything Love Can't Do/Pet Names	1971	2.50	5.00	10.00
☐ 25067		Who You Gonna Run To/Forgive My Jealousy	1971	100.00	200.00	400.00

Vibration

☐ 569		We Can't Hide It Anymore/ I'm Needing You, Wanting You	1977		2.50	5.00

With Sylvia

Wand

☐ 106		I Don't Want to Cry/Just Once	1961	2.50	5.00	10.00
☐ 108		(It Never Happens) In Real Life/The Same Old Story	1961	2.50	5.00	10.00
☐ 110		I Wake Up Crying/Everybody Needs Love	1961	2.50	5.00	10.00
☐ 115		The Breaking Point/My Willow Tree	1961	2.50	5.00	10.00
☐ 119		What'cha Gonna Say Tomorrow/Angel of Angels	1962	2.50	5.00	10.00
☐ 122		Any Day Now (My Wild Beautiful Bird)/The Prophet	1962	2.50	5.00	10.00
☐ 126		I Keep Forgetting/Who's Gonna Pick Up the Pieces	1962	2.50	5.00	10.00
☐ 128		Gettin' Ready for the Heartbreak/In Between Tears	1962	2.50	5.00	10.00
☐ 132		Tell Him I'm Not Home/Lonely Am I	1963	2.50	5.00	10.00
☐ 132	PS	Tell Him I'm Not Home/Lonely Am I	1963	6.25	12.50	25.00
☐ 138		I Will Never Turn My Back on You/Tears of Joy	1963	2.50	5.00	10.00
☐ 141		Any Other Way/Big New York	1963	2.50	5.00	10.00
☐ 149		Hand It Over/Look Over Your Shoulder	1964	2.00	4.00	8.00
☐ 154		Beg Me/This Broken Heart	1964	2.00	4.00	8.00
☐ 161		Somebody New/Stand By Me	1964	2.00	4.00	8.00
☐ 169		Since I Don't Have You/Hand It Over	1964	2.00	4.00	8.00
☐ 179		I Need You/Soul Brother Twist	1965	2.00	4.00	8.00
☐ 188		If I Didn't Love You/Just a Little Bit of Your Soul	1965	2.00	4.00	8.00
☐ 1105		Good Things Come to Those Who Wait/Yah	1965	2.00	4.00	8.00
☐ 1119		All in My Mind/And That's Saying a Lot	1966	2.00	4.00	8.00
☐ 1129		These Chains of Love/Theme to the Blues	1966	2.00	4.00	8.00
☐ 1142		I've Got to Be Strong/Where Did She Stay	1967	2.00	4.00	8.00
☐ 1151		Every Man Needs a Down Home Girl/Need You There	1967	2.00	4.00	8.00
☐ 1159		Hound Dog/Love Me Tender	1967	2.00	4.00	8.00
☐ 1166		Shame on Me/Candy	1967	2.00	4.00	8.00
☐ 1178		My Child's Child/Theme to the Blues	1968	2.00	4.00	8.00

Jackson, Earl

ABC

☐ 11142		Self Soul Satisfaction/ Looking Through the Eyes of Love	1968	7.50	15.00	30.00

Jackson, Jill

("Paula" of Paul and Paula)

Reprise

☐ 0297		Hey Handsome Boy/All Over Again	1964	3.75	7.50	15.00
☐ 0323		Pixie Girl/I Just Don't Know What to Do With Myself	1964	3.75	7.50	15.00
☐ 0362		Born Too Late/Here Comes the Night	1965	3.75	7.50	15.00
☐ 0411		Treasure of Love/I'll Love You for a While	1965	3.75	7.50	15.00

Number		Title (A Side/B Side)	Year	VG	VG+	NM

Jackson, June

Bell

| ❏ 45,173 | | Little Dog Heaven/Tenderly with Feeling | 1972 | 5.00 | 10.00 | 20.00 |

Imperial

| ❏ 66185 | | It's What's Up Front That Counts/Fifty Percent Won't Do | 1966 | 7.50 | 15.00 | 30.00 |

Jackson, Lil' Son

Imperial

Note: Lil' Son Jackson records on Imperial before 5204 are unconfirmed on 45 rpm

❏ 5204		Journey Back Home/Rockin' and Rollin' #2	1952	25.00	50.00	100.00
❏ 5218		Black and Brown/Sad Letter Blues	1953	25.00	50.00	100.00
❏ 5229		Lonely Blues/Freight Train Blues	1953	25.00	50.00	100.00
❏ 5237		Spending Money Blues/All Alone	1953	25.00	50.00	100.00
❏ 5248		Movin' to the Country/Confession	1953	25.00	50.00	100.00
❏ 5259		Dirty Work/Little Girl	1953	25.00	50.00	100.00
❏ 5267		Thrill Me, Baby/Doctor, Doctor	1954	20.00	40.00	80.00
❏ 5276		Big Rat/Piggly Wiggly	1954	20.00	40.00	80.00
❏ 5286		Trouble Don't Last Always/Blues by the Hour	1954	20.00	40.00	80.00
❏ 5300		Get High Everybody/Let Me Down Easy	1954	20.00	40.00	80.00
❏ 5312		How Long/Good Ole Wagon	1954	20.00	40.00	80.00
❏ 5319		My Younger Days/I Wish to Go Home	1954	20.00	40.00	80.00
❏ 5339		Sugar Mama/Messin' Up	1955	20.00	40.00	80.00
❏ 5703		Rockin' and Rollin'/Peace Breaking People	1960	3.75	7.50	15.00
❏ 5851		Everybody's Blues/Travelin' Woman	1962	3.75	7.50	15.00
❏ 5963		Prison Bound/Rolling Mill	1963	3.00	6.00	12.00

Post

| ❏ 2014 | | No Money/Lonely Blues | 1955 | 10.00 | 20.00 | 40.00 |

Jackson, Michael

(One of the Jacksons and self-proclaimed King of Pop)

Columbia

❏ 04168		Say, Say, Say/Ode to a Koala Bear	1983		2.00	4.00
		A-side: Paul McCartney/Michael Jackson; B-side: Paul McCartney				
❏ 04168	PS	Say, Say, Say/Ode to a Koala Bear	1983		2.00	4.00
		A-side: Paul McCartney/Michael Jackson; B-side: Paul McCartney				

Epic

❏ 02156		Rock with You/Off the Wall	1981			3.00
		Reissue				
❏ 02157		She's Out of My Life/Lovely One	1981			3.00
		Reissue; B-side by The Jacksons				
❏ 03288		The Girl Is Mine/Can't Get Outta the Rain	1982		2.50	5.00
		A-side: Michael Jackson/Paul McCartney				
❏ 03288	PS	The Girl Is Mine/Can't Get Outta the Rain	1982		2.50	5.00
		A-side: Michael Jackson/Paul McCartney				
❏ 03372		The Girl Is Mine	1982	2.50	5.00	10.00
		Michael Jackson/Paul McCartney; one-sided budget release				
❏ 03509		Billie Jean/Can't Get Outta the Rain	1983		2.00	4.00
❏ 03575		Billie Jean	1983	3.00	6.00	12.00
		One-sided budget release				
❏ 03759		Beat It/Get On the Floor	1983		2.00	4.00
❏ 03914		Wanna Be Startin' Somethin'/(Instrumental)	1983		2.00	4.00
❏ 03914	PS	Wanna Be Startin' Somethin'/(Instrumental)	1983		2.50	5.00
❏ 04026		Human Nature/Baby Be Mine	1983		2.00	4.00
❏ 04026	PS	Human Nature/Baby Be Mine	1983		2.50	5.00
❏ 04165		P.Y.T. (Pretty Young Thing)/Working Day and Night	1983		2.00	4.00
❏ 04165	PS	P.Y.T. (Pretty Young Thing)/Working Day and Night	1983		2.50	5.00
❏ 04364		Thriller/Can't Get Outta the Rain	1984		2.00	4.00
❏ 07253		I Just Can't Stop Loving You/Baby Be Mine	1987			3.00
❏ 07253	PS	I Just Can't Stop Loving You/Baby Be Mine	1987			3.00
❏ 07418		Bad/I Can't Help It	1987			3.00
❏ 07418	PS	Bad/I Can't Help It	1987			3.00
❏ 07645		The Way You Make Me Feel/(Instrumental)	1987			3.00
❏ 07645	PS	The Way You Make Me Feel/(Instrumental)	1987			3.00
❏ 07668		Man in the Mirror/(Instrumental)	1988			3.00
❏ 07668	PS	Man in the Mirror/(Instrumental)	1988			3.00
❏ 07739		Dirty Diana/(Instrumental)	1988			3.00
❏ 07739	PS	Dirty Diana/(Instrumental)	1988			3.00
❏ 07962		Another Part of Me/(Instrumental)	1988			3.00
❏ 07962	PS	Another Part of Me/(Instrumental)	1988			3.00
❏ 08044		Smooth Criminal/(Instrumental)	1988			3.00
❏ 08044	PS	Smooth Criminal/(Instrumental)	1988			3.00
❏ 50654		You Can't Win (Part 1)/You Can't Win (Part 2)	1979		3.00	6.00
❏ 50742		Don't Stop 'Til You Get Enough/I Can't Help It	1979		2.00	4.00
❏ 50797		Rock with You/Working Day and Night	1979		2.00	4.00
❏ 50838		Off the Wall/Get On the Floor	1980		2.00	4.00
❏ 50871		She's Out of My Life/Get On the Floor	1980		2.00	4.00
❏ 74100		Black or White/(Instrumental)	1991			3.00
❏ 74200		Remember the Time/	1992			3.00
		Black or White (The Underground Club Mix)				
❏ 74266		In the Closet (7" Edit)/	1992			3.00
		In the Closet (The Mission Radio Edit)				
❏ 74333		Jam/Rock with You (Masters At Work Remix)	1992			3.00
❏ 74406		Who Is It/Wanna Be Startin' Somethin'	1992			3.00
❏ 74708		Heal the World/She Drives Me Wild	1992			3.00

Number		Title (A Side/B Side)	Year	VG	VG+	NM
☐ 77060		Will You Be There/(Instrumental)	1993			3.00
☐ 77312		Gone Too Soon/(Instrumental)	1993			3.00
☐ 78000		Scream/Childhood	1995			3.00
		A-side with Janet Jackson				
☐ 78002		You Are Not Alone/Scream Louder	1995			3.00
☐ 78264		They Don't Care About Us/	1996			3.00
		Rock with You (Frankie Knuckles Mix)				

MCA

☐ S45-1786	DJ	Someone in the Dark (same on both sides)	1982	12.50	25.00	50.00
☐ S45-1786	PS	Someone in the Dark (same on both sides)	1982	12.50	25.00	50.00
☐ 40947		Ease On Down the Road/Poppy Girls	1978		2.50	5.00
☐ 40947	PS	Ease On Down the Road/Poppy Girls	1978		2.50	5.00
		With Diana Ross				

Motown

☐ 1191		Got to Be There/Maria (You Were the Only One)	1971		2.50	5.00
☐ 1197		Rockin' Robin/Love Is Here and Now You're Gone	1972		2.50	5.00
☐ 1202		I Wanna Be Where You Are/	1972		2.50	5.00
		We Got a Good Thing Going				
☐ 1202	PS	I Wanna Be Where You Are/	1972	2.50	5.00	10.00
		We Got a Good Thing Going				
☐ 1207		Ben/You Can Cry on My Shoulder	1972		2.50	5.00
☐ 1218		With a Child's Heart/Morning Glow	1973		2.50	5.00
☐ 1270		Doggin' Around/Up Again	1974			Unreleased
☐ 1341		We're Almost There/Take Me Back	1975		2.50	5.00
☐ 1349		Just a Little Bit of You/Dear Michael	1975		2.50	5.00
☐ 1512		One Day in Your Life/Take Me Back	1981		2.00	4.00
☐ 1739		Farewell My Summer Love/Call On Me	1984		2.00	4.00
☐ 1739	PS	Farewell My Summer Love/Call On Me	1984		2.50	5.00
☐ 1757		Girl You're So Together/Touch the One You Love	1984		2.00	4.00
☐ 1914		Twenty-Five Miles/Up on the House Top	1987	2.00	4.00	8.00
☐ 1914	PS	Twenty-Five Miles/Up on the House Top	1987	2.00	4.00	8.00
☐ 1930		Get it/(Instrumental)	1988			3.00
☐ 1930	PS	Get it/(Instrumental)	1988			3.00
		With Stevie Wonder				

Jackson, Wanda

ABC

☐ 12116		Take a Look/I Can't Stand to Hear You Say Goodbye	1975		2.50	5.00

Capitol

☐ 2021		A Girl Don't Have to Drink to Have Fun/	1967	2.50	5.00	10.00
		My Days Are Darker Than Your Nights				
☐ 2085		By the Time You Get to Phoenix/Wishing Well	1968	2.00	4.00	8.00
☐ 2151		My Baby Walked Right Out on Me/	1968	2.00	4.00	8.00
		No Place to Go But Home				
☐ 2245		Little Boy Soldier/I Talk a Pretty Story	1968	2.00	4.00	8.00
☐ 2315		I Wish I Was Your Friend/Poor Old Me	1968	2.00	4.00	8.00
☐ 2379		If I Had a Hammer/The Pain of It All	1969	2.00	4.00	8.00
☐ 2472		Your Tender Love/As the Day Wears On	1969	2.00	4.00	8.00
☐ 2524		Everything's Leaving/You Cheated Me	1969	2.00	4.00	8.00
☐ 2614		My Big Iron Skillet/The Hunter	1969	2.00	4.00	8.00
☐ 2693		Two Separate Bar Stools/	1969	2.00	4.00	8.00
		Two Wrongs Don't Make a Right				
☐ 2761		A Woman Lives for Love/What Have We Done	1970		3.00	6.00
☐ 2872		Who Shot John/Stop the World	1970		3.00	6.00
☐ 2986		Fancy Satin Pillows/	1970		3.00	6.00
		Why Don't We Love Like That Anymore				
☐ 3070		People Gotta Be Loving/Glory Hallelujah	1971		3.00	6.00
☐ 3143		Back Then/I'm Gonna Walk Out of Your Life	1971		3.00	6.00
☐ 3218		I Already Know (What I'm Gettin' for My Birthday)/	1971		3.00	6.00
		The Man You Could Have Been				
☐ 3293		I'll Be Whatever You Say/The More You See Me Less	1972		3.00	6.00
☐ 3385		I Wouldn't Want You Any Other Way/Song of the Wind	1972		3.00	6.00
☐ 3498		Roll with the Tide/Tennessee Women's Prison	1972		3.00	6.00
☐ F3575		The Hot Dog That Made Him Mad/	1956	10.00	20.00	40.00
		Silver Threads and Golden Needles				
☐ 3599		I Don't Know How to Tell Him/	1973		3.00	6.00
		Your Memory Comes and Gets Me				
☐ F3637		Cryin' Through the Night/Baby Loves Him	1957	12.50	25.00	50.00
☐ F3485		I Gotta Know/Half As Good a Girl	1956	10.00	20.00	40.00
☐ F3683		Don'a Wana/Let Me Explain	1957	7.50	15.00	30.00
☐ F3764		Cool Love/Did You Miss Me	1957	7.50	15.00	30.00
☐ F3843		Fujiyama Mama/No Wedding Bells for Joe	1957	7.50	15.00	30.00
☐ F3941		Just a Queen for a Day/Honey Bop	1958	7.50	15.00	30.00
☐ F4026		(Every Time They Play) Our Song/Mean, Mean Man	1958	7.50	15.00	30.00
☐ F4081		Sinful Heart/Rock Your Baby	1958	7.50	15.00	30.00
☐ F4142		Savin' My Love/I Wanna Waltz	1959	6.25	12.50	25.00
☐ F4207		A Date with Jerry/You're the One for Me	1959	6.25	12.50	25.00
☐ F4286		Reaching/I'd Rather Have You	1959	6.25	12.50	25.00
☐ 4354		My Destiny/Please Call Today	1960	5.00	10.00	20.00
☐ 4397		Let's Have a Party/Journey of Love	1960	6.25	12.50	25.00
☐ 4469		Mean, Mean Man/Happy, Happy Birthday	1960	5.00	10.00	20.00
☐ 4520		Riot in Cell Block #9/Little Charm Bracelet	1961	5.00	10.00	20.00
☐ 4553		Right or Wrong/Funnel of Love	1961	5.00	10.00	20.00
☐ 4635		In the Middle of a Heartache/I'd Be Ashamed	1961	5.00	10.00	20.00
☐ 4681		A Little Bitty Tear/I Don't Wanta Go	1962	5.00	10.00	20.00
☐ 4723		If I Cried Every Time You Hurt Me/Let My Love Walk In	1962	5.00	10.00	20.00
☐ 4723	PS	If I Cried Every Time You Hurt Me/Let My Love Walk In	1962	7.50	15.00	30.00
☐ 4785		I Misunderstood/Between the Window and the Phone	1962	3.75	7.50	15.00

Number	Title (A Side/B Side)	Year	VG	VG+	NM
❑ 4833	The Greatest Actor/You Bug Me Bad	1962	3.75	7.50	15.00
❑ 4884	Whirlpool/One Teardrop at a Time	1962	3.75	7.50	15.00
❑ 4917	But I Was Lying/Sympathy	1963	3.75	7.50	15.00
❑ 4973	This Should Go On Forever/	1963	3.75	7.50	15.00
	We Haven't a Moment to Lose				
❑ 5015	Memory Mountain/Let Me Talk to You	1963	3.75	7.50	15.00
❑ 5072	Slippin'/Just for You	1963	3.75	7.50	15.00
❑ 5142	The Violet and a Rose/To Tell You the Truth	1964	3.00	6.00	12.00
❑ 5228	Leave My Baby Alone/I'm Mad at Me	1964	3.00	6.00	12.00
❑ 5287	Candy Man/Weary Blues From Waitin'	1964	3.00	6.00	12.00
❑ 5364	My Baby's Gone/If I Were You	1965	3.00	6.00	12.00
❑ 5433	Have I Grown Used to Missing You/Take Me Home	1965	3.00	6.00	12.00
❑ 5491	My First Day Without You/Send Me No Roses	1965	3.00	6.00	12.00
❑ 5559	The Box It Came In/Look Out Heart	1965	3.00	6.00	12.00
❑ 5645	Because It's You/Long As I Have You	1966	2.50	5.00	10.00
❑ 5712	This Gun Don't Care/I Wonder If She Knows	1966	2.50	5.00	10.00
❑ 5789	Tears Will Be the Chaser for Your Wine/	1967	2.50	5.00	10.00
	Reckless Love Affair				
❑ 5863	Both Sides of the Line/Famous Last Words	1967	2.50	5.00	10.00
❑ 5960	My Heart Gets All the Breaks/	1967	2.50	5.00	10.00
	You'll Always Have My Love				

Decca

Number	Title (A Side/B Side)	Year	VG	VG+	NM
❑ 29140	You Can't Have My Love/Lovin' Country Style	1954	15.00	30.00	60.00
	With Billy Gray				
❑ 29253	The Right to Love/If You Knew What I Know	1954	15.00	30.00	60.00
❑ 29267	If You Don't, Somebody Else Will/	1954	12.50	25.00	50.00
	You'd Be the First One to Know				
	With Billy Gray				
❑ 29514	Tears at the Grand Ole Opry/Nobody's Darlin' But Mine	1955	12.50	25.00	50.00
❑ 29677	Don't Do the Things He'd Do/It's the Same World	1955	7.50	15.00	30.00
❑ 29803	Wasted/I Cried Again	1956	12.50	25.00	50.00
❑ 30153	You Won't Forget (About Me)/	1956	7.50	15.00	30.00
	A Heart You Could Have Had				

Jin

Number	Title (A Side/B Side)	Year	VG	VG+	NM
❑ 300	Lonely Days, Lonely Nights/My Memories	197?		2.50	5.00

Myrrh

Number	Title (A Side/B Side)	Year	VG	VG+	NM
❑ 122	When It's Time to Fall in Love Again/Say "I Do"	1973		2.50	5.00
❑ 126	Come On Home (To This Lonely Heart)/	1973		2.50	5.00
	It's a Long, Long Time to Cry				
❑ 143	Jesus Put a Yodel in My Soul/(B-side unknown)	1974		2.50	5.00
❑ 152	Where Do I Put His Memory/Take a Look	1975		2.50	5.00

Jacksons, The

(The Dynamo, Motown and Steeltown releases credit The Jackson Five, except as noted. Also see "Jackson, Michael")

Dynamo

Number	Title (A Side/B Side)	Year	VG	VG+	NM
❑ 146	You Don't Have to Be Over Twenty-One to Fall in Love/	1971	10.00	20.00	40.00
	Some Girls Want Me for Their Love				

Epic

Number	Title (A Side/B Side)	Year	VG	VG+	NM
❑ 01032	Can You Feel It/Everybody	1981		2.00	4.00
❑ 02132	Walk Right Now/Your Ways	1981		2.00	4.00
❑ 02157	Lovely One/She's Out of My Life	1981			3.00
	Reissue; B-side by Michael Jackson				
❑ 02720	The Things I Do for You/Working Day and Night	1982		2.00	4.00
❑ 04503	State of Shock/Your Ways	1984		2.00	4.00
	A-side with Mick Jagger				
❑ 04503	PS State of Shock/Your Ways	1984		2.00	4.00
❑ 04575	Torture/(Instrumental)	1984		2.00	4.00
❑ 04575	PS Torture/(Instrumental)	1984		2.00	4.00
❑ 04673	Body/(Instrumental)	1984		2.00	4.00
❑ 04673	PS Body/(Instrumental)	1984		2.00	4.00
❑ 50595	Blame It on the Boogie/Ease On Down the Road	1978		2.00	4.00
❑ 50656	Shake Your Body (Down to the Ground)/	1979		2.50	5.00
	That's What You Get (For Being Polite)				
	Original issue has orange label				
❑ 50656	Shake Your Body (Down to the Ground)/	1979		2.00	4.00
	That's What You Get (For Being Polite)				
	Second issue has dark blue label				
❑ 50938	Lovely One/Bless His Soul	1980		2.00	4.00
❑ 50959	Heartbreak Hotel/The Things I Do for You	1980		2.00	4.00
❑ 68688	Nothing (That Compares 2 U)/Alright with Me	1989			3.00
❑ 69022	2300 Jackson Street/When I Look at You	1989			3.00

Epic/Phila. Int'l.

Number	Title (A Side/B Side)	Year	VG	VG+	NM
❑ 50289	Enjoy Yourself/Style of Life	1976		2.50	5.00
❑ 50350	Show You the Way to Go/Blues Away	1977		2.50	5.00
❑ 50454	Goin' Places/Do What You Wanna	1977		2.50	5.00
❑ 50496	Find Me a Girl/Different Kind of Lady	1977		2.50	5.00

MCA

Number	Title (A Side/B Side)	Year	VG	VG+	NM
❑ 53032	Time Out for the Burglar/News at Eleven	1987			3.00
	B-side by the Distants				
❑ 53032	PS Time Out for the Burglar/News at Eleven	1987			3.00

Motown

Number	Title (A Side/B Side)	Year	VG	VG+	NM
❑ 1157	I Want You Back/Who's Lovin' You	1969	2.00	4.00	8.00
❑ 1163	ABC/The Young Folks	1970	2.00	4.00	8.00
❑ 1166	The Love You Save/I Found That Girl	1970	2.00	4.00	8.00

Number		Title (A Side/B Side)	Year	VG	VG+	NM
❑ 1166	DJ	The Love You Save	1970	7.50	15.00	30.00
		Blank back promo				
❑ 1166	DJ	I Found That Girl (same on both sides)	1970	5.00	10.00	20.00
		Red vinyl				
❑ 1171		I'll Be There/One More Chance	1970	2.00	4.00	8.00
❑ 1174		Santa Claus Is Coming to Town/	1970	3.00	6.00	12.00
		Christmas Won't Be the Same This Year				
❑ 1177		Mama's Pearl/Darling Dear	1971		3.00	6.00
❑ 1177	PS	Mama's Pearl/Darling Dear	1971	3.75	7.50	15.00
❑ 1179		Never Can Say Goodbye/She's Good	1971		3.00	6.00
❑ 1186		Maybe Tomorrow/I Will Find a Way	1971		3.00	6.00
❑ 1194		Sugar Daddy/I'm So Happy	1971		3.00	6.00
❑ 1199		Little Bitty Pretty One/If I Had to Move a Mountain	1972		3.00	6.00
❑ 1205		Looking Through the Windows/Love Song	1972		3.00	6.00
❑ 1214		Corner of the Sky/To Know	1972		3.00	6.00
❑ 1224		Hallelujah Day/You Made Me What I Am	1973		3.00	6.00
❑ 1230		Boogie Man/Don't Let Your Baby Catch You	1973			Unreleased
❑ 1277		Get It Together/Touch	1973		3.00	6.00
❑ 1286		Dancing Machine/It's Too Late to Change the Time	1974		3.00	6.00
❑ 1308		Whatever You Got, I Want/I Can't Quit Your Love	1974		3.00	6.00
❑ 1310		I Am Love (Parts 1 & 2)/I Am Love (Part 2)	1975		3.00	6.00
❑ 1310		I Am Love (Part 1)/I Am Love (Part 2)	1975	2.00	4.00	8.00
❑ 1356		Forever Came Today/All I Do Is Think of You	1975		3.00	6.00
❑ 1365		Body Language/Call of the Wild	1975			Unreleased
❑ 2193		Who's Lovin' You/	1992		2.00	4.00
		In the Still of the Night (I'll Remember)				
		B-side by Boyz II Men				

Steeltown

❑ 681		Big Boy/You've Changed	1968	25.00	50.00	100.00
❑ 684		You Don't Have to Be Over Twenty-One to Fall in Love/	1968	25.00	50.00	100.00
		Some Girls Want Me for Their Love				
❑ 689		Let Me Carry Your School Books/I Never Had a Girl	1969	20.00	40.00	80.00
		By "The Ripples and Waves plus Michael"				

Jades, The
(More than one group)
Adona

❑ 1445		Hey Senorita/(B-side unknown)	1962	7.50	15.00	30.00

Capitol

❑ 2281		Ain't It Funny What Love Can Do/	1968		3.00	6.00
		Baby I Need Your Love				

Christy

❑ 110		Oh Why/Big Beach Party	1959	125.00	250.00	500.00
❑ 111		Tell Me Pretty Baby/Applesauce	1959	62.50	125.00	250.00
❑ 113		Don't Be a Fool/Friday Night with My Baby	1959	125.00	250.00	500.00
❑ 114		Look for a Lie/Blue Memories	1959	375.00	750.00	1,500

Dore

❑ 687		Hold Back the Dawn/When They Ask About You	1963	5.00	10.00	20.00

Dot

❑ 15822		I'm Pretending/Beverly	1958	20.00	40.00	80.00

Gaity

❑ 2-23-64		Surfin' Crow/Blue Black Hair	1964	45.00	90.00	180.00

Imperial

❑ 66383		Wheel of Fortune/Gotta Find Somebody to Love	1969		3.00	6.00
❑ 66425		L-O-V-E I Love You/Don't Give What's Mine Away	1969		3.00	6.00

Liberty

❑ 56192		All's Quiet on West 23rd/Love of a Woman	1970		2.50	5.00

MGM

❑ 13399		There's a Kinder Way to Say Goodbye/	1965	3.00	6.00	12.00
		You're So Right for Me				

Nau Voo

❑ 807		Walking All Alone/Hey Little Girl	1959	37.50	75.00	150.00

Oxboro

❑ 2002		Surfin' Crow/Blue Black Hair	1964	30.00	60.00	120.00
❑ 2005		Little Marlene/Shake Baby Shake	1965	30.00	60.00	120.00

Port

❑ 70042		He's My Guy/There Will Come a Day	1964	6.25	12.50	25.00

Time

❑ 1002		Leave Her For Me/So Blue	1957	50.00	100.00	200.00
		Lou Reed is alleged to have been in this group, but he would have been 15 at the time.				

Uni

❑ 55019		The Glide/Flower Power	1967	2.00	4.00	8.00
❑ 55032	DJ	Privilege (same on both sides)	1967	2.00	4.00	8.00

Verve

❑ 10385		For Just Another Day/I'm By Your Side (Baby)	1966	3.00	6.00	12.00

James, Etta
Argo

❑ 5359		All I Could Do Was Cry/Girl of My Dreams	1960	2.50	5.00	10.00
❑ 5368		My Dearest Darling/Tough Mary	1960	2.50	5.00	10.00
❑ 5380		At Last/I Just Want to Make Love to You	1961	2.50	5.00	10.00
❑ 5385		Trust in Me/Anything to Say You're Mine	1961	2.50	5.00	10.00

Number	Title (A Side/B Side)	Year	VG	VG+	NM
❑ 5390	Dream/Fool That I Am	1961	2.50	5.00	10.00
❑ 5393	Sunday Kind of Love/Don't Cry, Baby	1961	2.50	5.00	10.00
❑ 5402	It's Too Soon to Know/Seven Day Fool	1961	2.50	5.00	10.00
❑ 5409	Something's Got a Hold on Me/ Waiting for Charlie to Come Home	1962	2.50	5.00	10.00
❑ 5418	Stop the Wedding/Street of Texas	1962	2.50	5.00	10.00
❑ 5424	Next Door to An Angel/Fools Rush In	1962	2.50	5.00	10.00
❑ 5430	How Do You Speak to An Angel/ Would It Make Any Difference to You	1962	2.50	5.00	10.00
❑ 5437	Pushover/Can't Hold It In Anymore	1963	2.50	5.00	10.00
❑ 5445	Be Honest with Me/Pay Back	1963	2.50	5.00	10.00
❑ 5452	Two Sides (To Every Story)/I Worry 'Bout You	1963	2.50	5.00	10.00
❑ 5459	Baby What You Want Me to Do/What'd I Say	1964	2.50	5.00	10.00
❑ 5465	Look Who's Blue/Loving You More Every Day	1964	2.50	5.00	10.00
❑ 5477	Breaking Point/That Man Belongs Back Here with Me	1964	2.50	5.00	10.00
❑ 5485	Mellow Fellow/Bobby Is His Name	1964	2.50	5.00	10.00

Cadet

❑ 5519	Somewhere Down the Line/Do I Make Myself Clear	1966	2.00	4.00	8.00
	With Sugar Pie DeSanto				
❑ 5526	Only Time Will Tell/I'm Sorry for You	1966	2.00	4.00	8.00
❑ 5539	In the Basement -- Part 1/In the Basement -- Part 2	1966	2.00	4.00	8.00
	With Sugar Pie DeSanto				
❑ 5552	I Prefer You/I'm So Glad	1966	2.00	4.00	8.00
❑ 5564	Don't Take Me for Your Fool/It Must Be Your Love	1967	2.00	4.00	8.00
❑ 5568	Happiness/842-3089 (Call My Name)	1967	2.00	4.00	8.00
❑ 5578	Tell Mama/I'd Rather Go Blind	1967	2.00	4.00	8.00
❑ 5594	Security/I'm Gonna Take What He's Got	1968	2.00	4.00	8.00
❑ 5606	I Got You Babe/I Worship the Ground You Walk On	1968	2.00	4.00	8.00
❑ 5620	Fire/You Got It	1968	2.00	4.00	8.00
❑ 5630	Almost Persuaded/Steal Away	1968	2.00	4.00	8.00
❑ 5655	Miss Pitiful/Bobby Is His Name	1969	2.00	4.00	8.00
❑ 5664	Tighten Up Your Own Thing/What Fools We Mortals Be	1970	2.00	4.00	8.00
❑ 5671	The Sound of Love/When I Stop Dreaming	1970	2.00	4.00	8.00
❑ 5676	Losers Weepers -- Part 1/Losers Weepers -- Part 2	1970	2.00	4.00	8.00

Capitol

❑ B-44333	Avenue D/My Head Is a City	1989		2.00	4.00
	With David A. Stewart				

Chess

❑ 1760	If I Can't Have You/My Heart Cries	1960	6.25	12.50	25.00
	As "Etta and Harvey"				
❑ 1771	Spoonful/It's a Crying Shame	1960	6.25	12.50	25.00
	As "Etta and Harvey"				
❑ 2100	The Love of My Man/ Nothing from Nothing Leaves Nothing	1971		3.00	6.00
❑ 2112	I Think It's You/Take Out Some Insurance	1971		3.00	6.00
❑ 2125	I Found a Love/Nothing from Nothing Leaves Nothing	1972		3.00	6.00
❑ 2144	All the Way Down/Lay Back Daddy	1973		3.00	6.00
❑ 2148	Leave Your Hat On/Only a Fool	1974		3.00	6.00
❑ 2153	Out on the Street Again/Feeling Uneasy	1974		3.00	6.00
❑ 2171	Lovin' Arms/Take Out Some Insurance	1975		3.00	6.00
❑ 31001	Jump Into Love/(B-side unknown)	1976		2.50	5.00

Epic

❑ 68593	Baby What You Want Me to Do/ Max's Theme (Instrumental)	1989		2.00	4.00

Kent

❑ 304	Baby, Baby, Every Night/Sunshine of Love	1958	7.50	15.00	30.00
❑ 345	Roll with Me Henry/Good Rockin' Daddy	1960	6.25	12.50	25.00
❑ 352	How Big a Fool/Good Rockin' Daddy	1961	6.25	12.50	25.00
❑ 370	Do Something Crazy/Good Rockin' Daddy	1962	6.25	12.50	25.00

Modern

❑ 947	The Wallflower (Roll With Me Henry)/ Hold Me, Squeeze Me	1955	10.00	20.00	40.00
❑ 947	The Wallflower (Dance With Me Henry)/ Hold Me, Squeeze Me	1955	6.25	12.50	25.00
❑ 957	Hey Henry (Doin' Fine, Henry)/Be Mine	1955	6.25	12.50	25.00
❑ 962	Good Rockin' Daddy/Crazy Feeling	1955	7.50	15.00	30.00
❑ 972	That's All/W-O-M-A-N	1955	6.25	12.50	25.00
❑ 984	I'm a Fool/Number One (My One and Only)	1956	6.25	12.50	25.00
❑ 988	Shortnin' Bread Rock/Tears of Joy	1956	6.25	12.50	25.00
❑ 998	Fools We Mortals Be/Tough Lover	1956	7.50	15.00	30.00
❑ 1007	Good Lookin'/Then I'll Care	1957	6.25	12.50	25.00
❑ 1016	The Pick-Up/Market Place	1957	6.25	12.50	25.00
❑ 1022	By the Light of the Silvery Moon/Come What May	1957	6.25	12.50	25.00

T-Electric

❑ 41264	It Takes Love to Keep a Woman/Mean Mother	1980		2.50	5.00

Warner Bros.

❑ 8545	Piece of My Heart/Lovesick Blues	1978		2.50	5.00
❑ 8611	Sugar on the Floor/Lovesick Blues	1978		2.50	5.00

James, Joni

MGM

❑ 11223	Let There Be Love/My Baby Just Cares for Me	1952	6.25	12.50	25.00
❑ 11295	You Belong to Me/Yes, Yes, Yes	1952	6.25	12.50	25.00
❑ 11333	Why Don't You Believe Me/Purple Shades	1952	7.50	15.00	30.00
❑ 11390	Have You Heard/Wishing Ring	1953	5.00	10.00	20.00

Number		Title (A Side/B Side)	Year	VG	VG+	NM
❏ 11426		Your Cheatin' Heart/I'll Be Waiting for You	1953	5.00	10.00	20.00
❏ 11470		Is It Any Wonder/Almost Always	1953	5.00	10.00	20.00
❏ 11543		My Love, My Love/You're Fooling Someone	1953	5.00	10.00	20.00
❏ 11606		I'll Never Stand in Your Way/Why Can't I	1953	5.00	10.00	20.00
❏ 11637		Christmas and You/Nina-Non	1953	5.00	10.00	20.00
❏ 11696		Am I in Love/Maybe Next Time	1954	5.00	10.00	20.00
❏ 11753		In a Garden of Roses/Every Day	1954	5.00	10.00	20.00
❏ 11802		Mama, Don't Cry at My Wedding/Pa Pa Pa	1954	5.00	10.00	20.00
❏ 11865		Everytime You Tell Me You Love Me/	1954	5.00	10.00	20.00
		When We Come of Age				
❏ 11919		How Important Can It Be?/This Is My Confession	1955	5.00	10.00	20.00
❏ 11960		When You Wish Upon a Star/	1955	5.00	10.00	20.00
		Is This the End of the Line				
❏ 12020		The Moment I Saw You/	1955	5.00	10.00	20.00
		Where Is That Someone for Me				
❏ 12066		You Are My Love/I Lay Me Down to Sleep	1955	5.00	10.00	20.00
❏ 12091		The Christmas Song/	1955	6.25	12.50	25.00
		Have Yourself a Merry Little Christmas				
❏ 12126		My Believing Heart/You Never Fall in Love Again	1955	5.00	10.00	20.00
❏ 12175		Don't Tell Me Not to Love You/	1956	3.75	7.50	15.00
		Somewhere Someone Is Lonely				
❏ 12213		I Woke Up Crying/The Maverick Queen	1956	3.75	7.50	15.00
❏ 12288		Give Us This Day/How Lucky You Are	1956	3.75	7.50	15.00
❏ 12353		Love Letters/Don't Take Your Love from Me	1956	3.75	7.50	15.00
❏ 12368		White Christmas/I'll Be Home for Christmas	1956	5.00	10.00	20.00
❏ 12369		Danny Boy/To You I Give My Heart	1956	3.75	7.50	15.00
❏ 12450		I Need You So/Only Trust Your Heart	1957	3.75	7.50	15.00
❏ 12480		Summer Love/I'm Sorry for You, My Friend	1957	3.75	7.50	15.00
❏ 12531		Crying in the Shadows/Day Dreaming	1957	3.75	7.50	15.00
❏ 12565		Never 'Til Now/I Give You My Heart	1957	3.75	7.50	15.00
❏ 12565	PS	Never 'Til Now/I Give You My Heart	1957	6.25	12.50	25.00
❏ 12607		Dansero/Love Works Miracles	1958	3.75	7.50	15.00
❏ 12627		Nothing Will Ever Change/Does It Show	1958	3.75	7.50	15.00
❏ 12639		Arrividerci Roma/Non Dimenticar	1958	3.75	7.50	15.00
❏ 12660		Coming from You/Junior Prom	1958	3.75	7.50	15.00
❏ 12706		There Goes My Heart/Funny	1958	3.75	7.50	15.00
❏ 12706	PS	There Goes My Heart/Funny	1958	12.50	25.00	50.00
❏ SK-12706	S	There Goes My Heart/Funny	1958	10.00	20.00	40.00
		Note different prefix. Also, label will say "Stereo."				
❏ 12746		There Must Be a Way/Sorry for Myself	1959	3.75	7.50	15.00
❏ 12779		I Still Get a Thrill (Thinking of You)/Perhaps	1959	3.75	7.50	15.00
❏ 12779	PS	I Still Get a Thrill (Thinking of You)/Perhaps	1959	6.25	12.50	25.00
❏ 12807		I Still Get Jealous/My Prayer of Love	1959	3.75	7.50	15.00
❏ 12828		Are You Sorry/What I Don't Know Won't Hurt Me	1959	3.75	7.50	15.00
❏ 12849		Little Things Mean a Lot/I Laughed at Love	1959	3.75	7.50	15.00
❏ 12885		I Need You Now/You Belong to Me	1960	3.00	6.00	12.00
❏ 12895		They Really Don't Know You/We Know	1960	3.00	6.00	12.00
❏ 12933		My Last Date (With You)/	1960	3.00	6.00	12.00
		I Can't Give You Anything But Love				
❏ 12933	PS	My Last Date (With You)/	1960	3.00	6.00	12.00
		I Can't Give You Anything But Love				
❏ 12948		Be My Love/Tall As a Tree	1960	3.00	6.00	12.00
❏ 12990		Theme from "Carnival"/Can You Imagine That	1961	3.00	6.00	12.00
❏ 13016		Go Away (Bother Me No More)/I Gave My Love	1961	3.00	6.00	12.00
❏ 13037		Somebody Else Is Taking My Place/You Were Wrong	1961	3.00	6.00	12.00
❏ 13080		It's Magic/Tender and True	1962	3.00	6.00	12.00
❏ 13092		You Are My Sunshine/Lend Me Your Handkerchief	1962	3.75	7.50	15.00
❏ 13117		Anyone But Her/Forgive a Fool	1962	3.75	7.50	15.00
❏ 13159		Hey, Good Lookin'/He Says the Same Things to Me	1963	3.75	7.50	15.00
❏ 13180		Red Sails in the Sunset/Every Time I Meet You	1963	3.75	7.50	15.00
❏ 13206		Teach Me to Forget You/Un Cafe	1964	5.00	10.00	20.00
❏ 13243		Break, My Heart, Break/Don't Let the Neighbors Know	1964	5.00	10.00	20.00
❏ 13267		Pearly Shells/Hawaiian War Chant	1964	5.00	10.00	20.00
❏ 13288		Sentimental Me/You're Nearer	1964	20.00	40.00	80.00
❏ 13304		Dondi/Once I Loved	1964	5.00	10.00	20.00
❏ 13365		There Goes My Heart/I Still Get Jealous	1965	5.00	10.00	20.00
❏ SK-50111	S	There Must Be a Way/Sorry for Myself	1959	7.50	15.00	30.00

Sharp

Number		Title (A Side/B Side)	Year	VG	VG+	NM
❏ 46		Let There Be Love/My Baby Just Cares for Me	1952	75.00	150.00	300.00
❏ 50		You Belong to Me/Yes, Yes, Yes	1952	62.50	125.00	250.00

James, Tommy, and the Shondells
(Also see "Hog Heaven")

Red Fox

Number		Title (A Side/B Side)	Year	VG	VG+	NM
❏ 110		Hanky Panky/Thunderbolt	1966	10.00	20.00	40.00
		As "The Shondells"				

Roulette

Number		Title (A Side/B Side)	Year	VG	VG+	NM
❏ 4686		Hanky Panky/Thunderbolt	1966	2.50	5.00	10.00
❏ 4695		Say I Am (What I Am)/Lots of Pretty Girls	1966	2.00	4.00	8.00
❏ 4695	PS	Say I Am (What I Am)/Lots of Pretty Girls	1966	3.75	7.50	15.00
❏ 4710		It's Only Love/Don't Let My Love Pass You By	1966	2.00	4.00	8.00
❏ 4710		It's Only Love/Ya Ya	1966	3.00	6.00	12.00
❏ 4720		I Think We're Alone Now/Gone, Gone, Gone	1967	2.50	5.00	10.00
❏ 4720	PS	I Think We're Alone Now/Gone, Gone, Gone	1967	3.75	7.50	15.00
❏ 4736		Mirage/Run, Run, Baby, Run	1967	2.00	4.00	8.00
❏ 4736	PS	Mirage/Run, Run, Baby, Run	1967	3.75	7.50	15.00
❏ 4756		I Like the Way/(Baby) Baby I Can't Take It No More	1967	2.00	4.00	8.00
❏ 4762		Gettin' Together/Real Girl	1967	2.00	4.00	8.00

Number		Title (A Side/B Side)	Year	VG	VG+	NM
❏ 4762	PS	Gettin' Together/Real Girl	1967	3.75	7.50	15.00
❏ 4775		Out of the Blue/Love's Closin' In on Me	1967	2.00	4.00	8.00
❏ 7000		Get Out Now/Wish It Were True	1968	2.00	4.00	8.00
❏ 7008		Mony Mony/One, Two, Three and I Fell	1968	2.50	5.00	10.00
❏ 7016		Somebody Cares/Do Unto Me	1968	2.00	4.00	8.00
❏ 7024		Do Something to Me/Ginger Bread Man	1968	2.00	4.00	8.00
❏ 7028		Crimson and Clover/(I'm) Taken	1968	3.75	7.50	15.00
❏ 7028		Crimson and Clover/Some Kind of Love	1968	2.50	5.00	10.00
❏ 7039		Sweet Cherry Wine/Breakaway	1969	2.00	4.00	8.00
❏ 7050		Crystal Blue Persuasion/I'm Alive	1969	2.50	5.00	10.00
❏ 7060		Ball of Fire/Makin' Good Time	1969	2.00	4.00	8.00
❏ 7066		She/Loved One	1969	2.00	4.00	8.00
❏ 7071		Gotta Get Back to You/Red Rover	1970	2.00	4.00	8.00
❏ 7076		Come to Me/Talkin' and Signifyin'	1970	2.00	4.00	8.00

Snap

❏ 102		Hanky Panky/Thunderbolt	1963	20.00	40.00	80.00
		As "The Shondells"; no mention of Red Fox Records on label				
❏ 102		Hanky Panky/Thunderbolt	1966	7.50	15.00	30.00
		As "The Shondells"; with "Dist. by Red Fox Records, Pgh, Pa." on label				

Jamie and Jane
("Jamie" is Gene Pitney)
Decca

❏ 30862		Snuggle Up Baby/Strollin' Thru the Park	1959	7.50	15.00	30.00
❏ 30934		Faithful Our Love/Classical Rock and Roll	1959	7.50	15.00	30.00

Jamies, The
Epic

❏ 9281		Summertime, Summertime/Searching for You	1958	3.00	6.00	12.00
		Reissued in 1962 with the same catalog number and label design				
❏ 9281	PS	Summertime, Summertime/Searching for You	1958	5.00	10.00	20.00
❏ 9299		When the Sun Goes Down/Snow Train	1958	5.00	10.00	20.00
❏ 9565		When the Sun Goes Down/Snow Train	1963	3.00	6.00	12.00
❏ 11129		Summertime, Summertime/Searching for You	1974	2.50	5.00	

United Artists

❏ 193		The Evening Star/Don't Darken My Door	1959	5.00	10.00	20.00

Jan and Arnie
(Jan Berry and Arnie Ginsburg)
Arwin

❏ 108		Jennie Lee/Gotta Getta Date	1958	12.50	25.00	50.00
❏ 111		Gas Money/Bonnie Lou	1958	12.50	25.00	50.00
❏ 113		I Love Linda/The Beat That Can't Be Beat	1958	15.00	30.00	60.00

Dore

❏ 522		Baby Talk/Jeannette Get Your Hair Done	1959	100.00	200.00	400.00
		Actually by Jan and Dean, but incorrectly credited				

Dot

❏ 16116		Gas Money/Gotta Getta Date	1960	12.50	25.00	50.00

Jan and Dean
(Jan Berry and Dean Torrence. Also see "Berry, Jan")
Challenge

❏ 9111		Heart and Soul/A Midsummer Night's Dream	1961	5.00	10.00	20.00
❏ 9111		Heart and Soul/Those Words	1961	10.00	20.00	40.00
❏ 9120		Wanted: One Girl/Something a Little Bit Different	1961	7.50	15.00	30.00

Columbia

❏ 44036		Yellow Balloon/Taste of Rain	1967	7.50	15.00	30.00

Dore

❏ 522		Baby Talk/Jeannette Get Your Hair Done	1959	7.50	15.00	30.00
❏ 531		There's a Girl/My Heart Sings	1959	6.25	12.50	25.00
❏ 539		Clementine/You're On My Mind	1960	6.25	12.50	25.00
❏ 548		Cindy/Whiter Tennis Sneakers	1960	6.25	12.50	25.00
❏ 555		We Go Together/Rosilane	1960	6.25	12.50	25.00
❏ 555	PS	We Go Together/Rosilane	1960	20.00	40.00	80.00
❏ 555		We Go Together/Rosie Lane	1960	6.25	12.50	25.00
		B-side title was altered after the record no longer was issued with picture sleeve				
❏ 576		Gee/Such a Good Night to Be Together	1960	6.25	12.50	25.00
❏ 576	PS	Gee/Such a Good Night to Be Together	1960	50.00	100.00	200.00
❏ 583		Baggy Pants/Judy's an Angel	1961	7.50	15.00	30.00
❏ 610		Julie/Don't Fly Away	1961	7.50	15.00	30.00

J&D

❏ 001		California Lullabye/Summertime	1966	7.50	15.00	30.00
❏ 002		Like a Summer Rain/Louisiana Man	1966	7.50	15.00	30.00

Jan & Dean

❏ 10		Hawaii/Tijuana	1966	18.75	37.50	75.00
❏ 11		Fan Tan/Love and Hate	1966	30.00	60.00	120.00

Liberty

❏ 55397		A Sunday Kind of Love/Poor Little Puppet	1961	6.25	12.50	25.00
❏ 55454		Tennessee/Your Heart Has Changed Its Mind	1962	6.25	12.50	25.00
❏ 55496		Who Put the Bomp/My Favorite Dream	1962	12.50	25.00	50.00
❏ 55522		Frosty the Snowman/She's Still Talkin' Baby Talk	1962	37.50	75.00	150.00
		Promos worth about half this value				
❏ 55531		Linda/When I Learn How to Cry	1963	6.25	12.50	25.00
❏ 55580		Surf City/She's My Summer Girl	1963	5.00	10.00	20.00

Number		Title (A Side/B Side)	Year	VG	VG+	NM
☐ 55580	PS	Surf City/She's My Summer Girl	1963	7.50	15.00	30.00
☐ 55613		Honolulu Lulu/Someday	1963	3.75	7.50	15.00
☐ 55613	PS	Honolulu Lulu/Someday	1963	6.25	12.50	25.00
☐ 55641		Drag City/Schlock Rod (Part 1)	1963	3.75	7.50	15.00
☐ 55641	PS	Drag City/Schlock Rod (Part 1)	1963	6.25	12.50	25.00
☐ 55672		Dead Man's Curve/The New Girl in School	1964	3.75	7.50	15.00
☐ 55672	PS	Dead Man's Curve/The New Girl in School	1964	6.25	12.50	25.00
☐ 55704		The Little Old Lady (From Pasadena)/My Mighty G.T.O.	1964	3.75	7.50	15.00
☐ 55704	PS	The Little Old Lady (From Pasadena)/My Mighty G.T.O.	1964	6.25	12.50	25.00
☐ 55724		Ride the Wild Surf/ The Anaheim, Azusa and Cucamonga Sewing Circle, Book Review and Timing Association	1964	3.75	7.50	15.00
☐ 55724	PS	Ride the Wild Surf/ The Anaheim, Azusa and Cucamonga Sewing Circle, Book Review and Timing Association	1964	6.25	12.50	25.00
☐ 55727		Sidewalk Surfin'/When It's Over	1964	3.75	7.50	15.00
☐ 55727	PS	Sidewalk Surfin'/When It's Over	1964	6.25	12.50	25.00
☐ 55766		(Here They Come) From All Over the World/ Freeway Flyer	1965	3.00	6.00	12.00
☐ 55766	PS	(Here They Come) From All Over the World/ Freeway Flyer	1965	5.00	10.00	20.00
☐ 55792		You Really Know How to Hurt a Guy/ It's As Easy As 1-2-3	1965	3.00	6.00	12.00
☐ 55792	PS	You Really Know How to Hurt a Guy/ It's As Easy As 1-2-3	1965	5.00	10.00	20.00
☐ 55816		It's a Shame to Say Goodbye/The Submarine Races	1965		Unreleased	
☐ 55833		I Found a Girl/It's a Shame to Say Goodbye	1965	3.00	6.00	12.00
☐ 55849		Folk City/A Beginning from an End	1965	3.00	6.00	12.00
☐ 55849	PS	Folk City/A Beginning from an End	1965	5.00	10.00	20.00
☐ 55856		Norwegian Wood/I Can't Wait to Love You	1966		Unreleased	
☐ 55860		Batman/Bucket "T"	1966	6.25	12.50	25.00
☐ 55886		Popsicle/Norwegian Wood	1966	3.00	6.00	12.00
☐ 55905		Fiddle Around/Surfer's Dream	1966	3.00	6.00	12.00
☐ 55923		The New Girl in School/School Days	1966	3.00	6.00	12.00

Magic Lamp

☐ 401		California Lullabye/Summertime	1966	7.50	15.00	30.00

Ode

☐ 66111		Fun City/Totally Wild	1975	6.25	12.50	25.00

United Artists

☐ 0089		Jennie Lee/Baby Talk	1973	3.75	7.50	15.00
☐ 0090		Linda/The New Girl in School	1973	3.75	7.50	15.00
☐ 0091		Surf City/Ride the Wild Surf	1973	3.75	7.50	15.00
☐ 0092		Dead Man's Curve/Drag City	1973	3.75	7.50	15.00
☐ 0093		Honolulu Lulu/Sidewalk Surfin'	1973	3.75	7.50	15.00
☐ 0094		The Little Old Lady (From Pasadena)/Popsicle	1973	3.75	7.50	15.00
		0089 through 0094 are "Silver Spotlight Series" reissues				
☐ 50859		Jennie Lee/Vegetables	1971	3.75	7.50	15.00
☐ 50859	PS	Jennie Lee/Vegetables	1971	6.25	12.50	25.00
☐ XW670		Sidewalk Surfin'/Gonna Hustle You	1975	3.75	7.50	15.00

Warner Bros.

☐ 7151		Only a Boy/Love and Hate	1967	10.00	20.00	40.00
☐ 7219		Laurel and Hardy/I Know My Mind	1968	12.50	25.00	50.00
☐ 7240	DJ	In the Still of the Night/Girl, You're Blowing My Mind	1968	20.00	40.00	80.00
		Stock copy may not exist				

Japanese Beatles, The
Golden Crest

☐ 584		The Beatle Song (Japanese Style) (Part 1)/ The Beatle Song (Japanese Style) (Part 2)	1964	5.00	10.00	20.00

Jarmels, The
Laurie

☐ 3085		Little Lonely One/She Loves to Dance	1961	3.75	7.50	15.00
☐ 3098		A Little Bit of Soap/The Way You Look Tonight	1961	5.00	10.00	20.00
☐ 3116		I'll Follow You/Gee Oh Gosh	1962	3.75	7.50	15.00
☐ 3124		Red Sails in the Sunset/Loneliness	1962	3.75	7.50	15.00
☐ 3142		Little Bug/One By One	1962	3.75	7.50	15.00
☐ 3174		Come On Girl/Keep Your Mind on Me	1963	3.75	7.50	15.00

Jarvis, Felton
ABC-Paramount

☐ 10570		Be-I-Bye/Ski King	1964	3.75	7.50	15.00
☐ 10610		Honky Tonk Song/Everybody's Going to the Party	1964	3.75	7.50	15.00
☐ 10641		Too Many Tigers/Knuckie, Knuckie	1965	3.75	7.50	15.00

MGM

☐ 12982		Indian Love Call/Goin' Downtown	1961	5.00	10.00	20.00

Thunder Int'l.

☐ 1023		Swingin' Cat/(B-side unknown)	1960	25.00	50.00	100.00

Viva

☐ 1001		Don't Knock Elvis/Honest John	1959	10.00	20.00	40.00

Jay and the Americans
EEOC

☐ 1140		Things Are Changing/Things Are Changing	1965	37.50	75.00	150.00
☐ 1140	PS	Things Are Changing/Things Are Changing	1965	37.50	75.00	150.00
		Promotional item for the Equal Employment Opportunity Commission				

Number		Title (A Side/B Side)	Year	VG	VG+	NM

United Artists

☐ 0026		She Cried/Come a Little Bit Closer	1973		2.50	5.00
☐ 0027		Cara Mia/Let's Lock the Door (And Throw Away the Key)	1973		2.50	5.00
☐ 0028		This Magic Moment/Walking in the Rain	1973		2.50	5.00
		0026, 0027, 0028 are "Silver Spotlight Series" reissues				
☐ 353		Tonight/The Other Girls	1961	3.00	6.00	12.00
☐ 415		She Cried/Dawning	1962	3.75	7.50	15.00
☐ 479		It's My Turn to Cry/This Is It	1962	3.00	6.00	12.00
☐ 504		Tomorrow/Yes	1962	3.00	6.00	12.00
☐ 566		What's the Use/Strangers Tomorrow	1963	2.50	5.00	10.00
☐ 626		Only in America/My Clair De Lune	1963	2.50	5.00	10.00
☐ 669		Come Dance with Me/Look in My Eyes Maria	1963	2.50	5.00	10.00
☐ 693		To Wait for Love/Friday	1964	2.50	5.00	10.00
☐ 759		Come a Little Bit Closer/Goodbye Boys, Goodbye	1964	2.50	5.00	10.00
☐ 805		Let's Lock the Door (And Throw Away the Key)/ I'll Remember You	1965	2.50	5.00	10.00
☐ 845		Think of the Good Times/If You Were Mine, Girl	1965	2.50	5.00	10.00
☐ 881		Cara Mia/When It's All Over	1965	2.50	5.00	10.00
☐ 919		Some Enchanted Evening/Girl	1965	2.50	5.00	10.00
☐ 919	PS	Some Enchanted Evening/Girl	1965	3.75	7.50	15.00
☐ 948		Sunday and Me/Through This Doorway	1965	2.50	5.00	10.00
☐ 992		Why Can't You Bring Me Home/Baby Stop Your Cryin'	1966	2.00	4.00	8.00
☐ 50016		Crying/I Don't Need a Friend	1966	2.00	4.00	8.00
☐ 50016	PS	Crying/I Don't Need a Friend	1966	3.00	6.00	12.00
☐ 50046		Livin' Above Your Head/Look at Me, What Do You See	1966	2.00	4.00	8.00
☐ 50046	PS	Livin' Above Your Head/Look at Me, What Do You See	1966	3.00	6.00	12.00
☐ 50086		Baby Come Home/Stop the Clock	1966	2.00	4.00	8.00
☐ 50094		(He's) Raining in My Sunshine/ The Reason for Living (For You My Darling)	1966	2.00	4.00	8.00
☐ 50139		Nature Boy/You Ain't As Hip As All That, Baby	1967	2.00	4.00	8.00
☐ 50196		(We'll Meet in the) Yellow Forest/ Got Hung Up Along the Way	1967	2.00	4.00	8.00
☐ 50222		Shanghai Noodle Factory/French Provincial	1967	2.00	4.00	8.00
☐ 50282		No Other Love/No, I Don't Know Her	1968	2.00	4.00	8.00
☐ 50448		You Ain't Gonna Wake Up Cryin'/Gemini	1968	2.00	4.00	8.00
☐ 50475		This Magic Moment/Since I Don't Have You	1969	3.00	6.00	12.00
☐ 50510		When You Dance/No, I Don't Know Her	1969		3.00	6.00
☐ 50535		Hushabye/Gypsy Woman	1969		3.00	6.00
☐ 50567		(I'd Kill) For the Love of a Lady/Learnin' How to Fly	1969		3.00	6.00
☐ 50605		Walkin' in the Rain/(I'd Kill) For the Love of a Lady	1969	2.00	4.00	8.00
☐ 50654		Do You Ever Think of Me/Capture the Moment	1970		3.00	6.00
☐ 50683		Do I Love You?/Tricia (Tell Your Daddy)	1970		3.00	6.00
☐ 50858		There Goes My Baby/Solitary Man	1971		3.00	6.00

Jay and the Deltas
Warner Bros.

☐ 5404		Bells Are Ringing/Super Hawk	1964	12.50	25.00	50.00

Jay, Ira
Sun

☐ 351		You Don't Love Me/More Than Anything	1960	5.00	10.00	20.00

Jay, Jerry
(California DJ, better known as Jerry Osborne)
Quality

☐ 201		The King's Country/Merry Christmas To You	1966	25.00	50.00	100.00

Jayhawks, The
(Later recorded as The Vibrations)
Aladdin

☐ 3393		Everyone Should Know/The Creature	1957	20.00	40.00	80.00

Argyle

☐ 1005		Lonely Highway/La Macerena	1961	6.25	12.50	25.00

Eastman

☐ 792		Start the Fire/I Wish the World Owed Me a Living	1958	37.50	75.00	150.00
☐ 798		New Love/Betty Brown	1958	37.50	75.00	150.00

Flash

☐ 105		Counting Teardrops/The Devil's Cousin	1955	50.00	100.00	200.00
☐ 109		Stranded in the Jungle/My Only Darling	1956	7.50	15.00	30.00
☐ 111		Love Train/Don't Mind Dyin'	1956	7.50	15.00	30.00

Jaynetts, The
J&S

☐ 1177		Out Behind the Daisies/Is It My Imagination	196?	2.00	4.00	8.00
☐ 1468/9		Chicken, Chicken, Crane or Crow/Winky Dinky	196?	2.00	4.00	8.00
☐ 1473		Peepin' In and Out the Window/ Extra, Extra, Read All About It	196?	2.00	4.00	8.00
☐ 1477		Who Stole the Cookie/That's My Boy	196?	2.00	4.00	8.00
☐ 4418/9		Vangie Don't You Cry/My Guy Is As Sweet As Can Be	196?	2.00	4.00	8.00

Tuff

☐ 369		Sally, Go 'Round the Roses/(Instrumental)	1963	3.00	6.00	12.00
☐ 371		Keep an Eye on Her/(Instrumental)	1963	2.00	4.00	8.00
☐ 374		Snowman/(Instrumental)	1963	2.50	5.00	10.00
☐ 377		No Love at All/Tonight You Belong to Me	1964	2.00	4.00	8.00

Number		Title (A Side/B Side)	Year	VG	VG+	NM

Jaytones, The
Brunswick
| ❏ 55087 | | The Clock/Gasoline | 1958 | 15.00 | 30.00 | 60.00 |
Cub
| ❏ 9057 | | My Only Love/Absolutely Right | 1960 | 10.00 | 20.00 | 40.00 |
Timely
| ❏ 1003/4 | | My Darling/The Bells | 1958 | 125.00 | 250.00 | 500.00 |

Jefferson Airplane
(Also see "Balin, Marty"; "Starship")
Epic
| ❏ 73044 | | Summer of Love/Panda | 1989 | | 2.50 | 5.00 |
Grunt
❏ 65-0500		Pretty As You Feel/Wild Turkey	1971		2.50	5.00
❏ 65-0500	PS	Pretty As You Feel/Wild Turkey	1971	2.50	5.00	10.00
❏ 65-0506		Long John Silver/Milk Train	1972		2.50	5.00
❏ 65-0506	PS	Long John Silver/Milk Train	1972	3.75	7.50	15.00
❏ 65-0511		Trial by Fire/Twilight Double Header	1972		2.50	5.00
❏ JB-10988	DJ	White Rabbit (mono/stereo)	1978	7.50	15.00	30.00
		White vinyl				
RCA
❏ 5156-7-R		White Rabbit/Plastic Fantastic Lover	1987		2.50	5.00
		White vinyl				
❏ 5156-7-R	PS	White Rabbit/Plastic Fantastic Lover	1987		2.50	5.00
RCA Victor
❏ 47-8769		It's No Secret/Runnin' 'Round This World	1966	3.75	7.50	15.00
❏ 47-8848		Come Up the Years/Blues from an Airplane	1966	3.75	7.50	15.00
❏ 47-8967		Bringing Me Down/Let Me In	1966	3.75	7.50	15.00
❏ 47-9063		My Best Friend/How Do You Feel	1967	3.75	7.50	15.00
❏ 47-9140		Somebody to Love/She Has Funny Cars	1967	3.00	6.00	12.00
❏ 47-9248		White Rabbit/Plastic Fantastic Lover	1967	3.00	6.00	12.00
❏ 47-9297		Ballad of You & Me & Pooneil/Two Heads	1967	2.50	5.00	10.00
❏ 47-9389		Watch Her Ride/Martha	1967	2.50	5.00	10.00
❏ 47-9496		Greasy Heart/Share a Little Joke (With the World)	1968	2.00	4.00	8.00
❏ 47-9644		Crown of Creation/Lather	1968	2.00	4.00	8.00
❏ 47-9644	PS	Crown of Creation/Lather	1968	5.00	10.00	20.00
❏ 74-0150		Plastic Fantastic Lover/Other Side of This Life	1969	3.00	6.00	
❏ 74-0150	PS	Plastic Fantastic Lover/Other Side of This Life	1969	5.00	10.00	20.00
❏ 74-0245		Volunteers/We Can Be Together	1969	3.00	6.00	
❏ 74-0245	PS	Volunteers/We Can Be Together	1969	3.75	7.50	15.00
❏ 74-0343		Have You Seen the Saucers/Mexico	1970	3.00	6.00	
❏ 74-0343	PS	Have You Seen the Saucers/Mexico	1970	3.75	7.50	15.00

Jelly Beans, The
Eskee
| ❏ 001 | | I'm Hip to You/You Don't Mean No Good to Me | 1965 | 3.75 | 7.50 | 15.00 |
Red Bird
| ❏ 10-003 | | I Wanna Love Him So Bad/So Long | 1964 | 5.00 | 10.00 | 20.00 |
| ❏ 10-011 | | The Kind of Boy You Can't Forget/Baby Be Mine | 1964 | 5.00 | 10.00 | 20.00 |

Jesse and Marvin
("Jesse" is Jesse Belvin)
Specialty
❏ 447		Dream Girl/Daddy Loves Baby	1952	18.75	37.50	75.00
		Black vinyl				
❏ 447		Dream Girl/Daddy Loves Baby	1952	50.00	100.00	200.00
		Red vinyl				

Jesters, The
(More than one group)
Amy
| ❏ 859 | | Alexander Graham Bell/Buffalo | 1962 | 2.00 | 4.00 | 8.00 |
Cyclone
| ❏ 5011 | | I Laughed/Now That You're Gone | 1958 | 12.50 | 25.00 | 50.00 |
Feature
| ❏ 101 | | Panther Pounce/Tiger Tail | 1964 | 12.50 | 25.00 | 50.00 |
Sidewalk
| ❏ 910 | | Leave Me Alone/Don't Try to Crawl Back | 1967 | 2.50 | 5.00 | 10.00 |
| ❏ 916 | | Hands of Time/If You Love Her, Tell Her So | 1967 | 2.50 | 5.00 | 10.00 |
Sun
| ❏ 400 | | Cadillac Man/My Babe | 1966 | 7.50 | 15.00 | 30.00 |
Ultima
| ❏ 705 | | Drag Like Boogie/A-Rab | 1964 | 7.50 | 15.00 | 30.00 |
Winley
❏ 218		So Strange/Love No One But You	1957	12.50	25.00	50.00
❏ 221		I'm Falling in Love/Please Let Me Love You	1957	12.50	25.00	50.00
❏ 225		The Plea/Oh Baby	1958	10.00	20.00	40.00

Number	Title (A Side/B Side)	Year	VG	VG+	NM
❑ 242	The Wind/Sally Green	1959	10.00	20.00	40.00
❑ 248	That's How It Goes/Tutti Frutti	1961	7.50	15.00	30.00
	Black vinyl				
❑ 248	That's How It Goes/Tutti Frutti	1961	12.50	25.00	50.00
	Red vinyl				
❑ 252	Come Let Me Show You/Uncle Henry's Basement	1961	7.50	15.00	30.00

Jet Set, The
Capitol

❑ 5358	True to You/You Got Me Hooked	1965	6.25	12.50	25.00
❑ 5421	How Can I Know/Dancing Yet	1965	6.25	12.50	25.00
	As "Liza and the Jet Set"				

Jewel and Eddie
(Jewel Akens and Eddie Daniels; Eddie Cochran plays guitar)
Silver

❑ 1004	Opportunity/Doin' the Hully Gully	1960	10.00	20.00	40.00
❑ 1004	Opportunity/Strollin' Guitar	1960	7.50	15.00	30.00
❑ 1008	My Eyes Are Cryin' for You/Sixteen Tons	1960	7.50	15.00	30.00

Jewels, The
(More than one group)
Antler

❑ 1102	The Wind/Pearlie Mae	1959	7.50	15.00	30.00

Dimension

❑ 1034	Opportunity/Gotta Find a Way	1964	3.75	7.50	15.00
❑ 1048	Smokey Joe/But I Do	1965	3.00	6.00	12.00

Federal

❑ 12541	My Song/This Is My Story	1966	3.00	6.00	12.00

Fern

❑ 806	Jewel Rock/Space Guitar	1961	3.75	7.50	15.00

Imperial

❑ 5351	Angel in My Life/Hearts Can Be Broken	1955	15.00	30.00	60.00
❑ 5362	Natural, Natural Ditty/Please Return	1955	12.50	25.00	50.00
❑ 5377	How/Rickety Rock	1956	10.00	20.00	40.00
❑ 5387	My Baby/Goin', Goin', Goin'	1956	10.00	20.00	40.00

King

❑ 6068	Smokie Joe's/Lookie Lookie	1967	3.00	6.00	12.00

MGM

❑ 13577	We Got Togetherness/I'm Forever Blowing Bubbles	1966	5.00	10.00	20.00

Olimpic

❑ 244	Jimmy Lee/The Hash	1964	6.25	12.50	25.00

Original Sound

❑ 38	Hearts of Stone/Oh Yes I Know	1964	3.00	6.00	12.00

R&B

❑ 1301	Hearts of Stone/Runnin'	1954	25.00	50.00	100.00
❑ 1303	Oh Yes I Know/A Fool in Paradise	1954	20.00	40.00	80.00

Rama
See "Crows, The"

RPM

❑ 474	She's a Flirt/Be-Bomp Baby	1956	12.50	25.00	50.00

Shasta

❑ 115	I Worry 'Bout You/Are You Coming to the Party	1959	5.00	10.00	20.00

Jill and Ray – See "Paul and Paula"

Jimmy and Duane
("Duane" is Duane Eddy)
Eb X. Preston

❑ 213	Soda Fountain Girl/(B-side unknown)	1955	50.00	100.00	200.00

Jimmy and Walter
Sun

❑ 180	Before Long/Easy	1953	1,000	2,000	3,000
	The earliest known 45 on Sun				

Jive Five, The
Ambient Sound

❑ 02742	Magic Maker, Music Maker/Oh Baby	1982		2.50	5.00
❑ 03053	Hey Sam/Don't Believe Him Donna	1982		2.50	5.00

Avco

❑ 4568	Come Down in Time/Love Is Pain	1971		3.00	6.00
❑ 4589	Follow the Lamb/Let the Feeling Belong	1972		3.00	6.00
❑ 4589	Follow the Lamb/Lay Lady Lay	1972		3.00	6.00

Beltone

❑ 1006	My True Story/When I Was Single	1961	6.25	12.50	25.00
❑ 1014	Never, Never/People from Another World	1961	5.00	10.00	20.00
❑ 2019	Hully Gully Calling Time/No, Not Again	1962	5.00	10.00	20.00
❑ 2024	What Time Is It?/Beggin' You Please	1962	5.00	10.00	20.00
❑ 2029	These Golden Rings/Do You Hear Wedding Bells	1962	5.00	10.00	20.00
❑ 2030	Lily Marlene/Johnny Never Knew	1963	5.00	10.00	20.00
❑ 2034	She's My Girl/Rain	1963	5.00	10.00	20.00

Number		Title (A Side/B Side)	Year	VG	VG+	NM

Brut

| ❏ 814 | | All I Ever Do Is Dream About You/
Super Woman (Part 2) | 1973 | | 3.00 | 6.00 |

Decca

| ❏ 32671 | | (If You Let Me Make Love to You)
Why Can't I Touch You/
You Showed Me the Light of Love | 1970 | 2.00 | 4.00 | 8.00 |
| ❏ 32736 | | I Want You to Be My Baby/Give Me Just a Chance | 1970 | 2.00 | 4.00 | 8.00 |

Musicor

❏ 1250		Crying Like a Baby/You'll Fall in Love	1967	3.00	6.00	12.00
❏ 1270		No More Tears/You'll Fall in Love	1967	3.00	6.00	12.00
❏ 1305		Sugar (Don't Take Away My Candy)/ Blues in the Ghetto	1968	3.00	6.00	12.00

Sketch

| ❏ 219 | | United/Prove Every Word You Say | 1964 | 3.75 | 7.50 | 15.00 |

United Artists

❏ 0100		I'm a Happy Man/It Will Stand	1973		2.50	5.00
		"Silver Spotlight Series" reissue; B-side by The Showmen				
❏ 807		United/Prove Every Word You Say	1965	5.00	10.00	20.00
❏ 853		I'm a Happy Man/Kiss Kiss Kiss	1965	5.00	10.00	20.00
❏ 936		Please Baby Please/A Bench in the Park	1965	5.00	10.00	20.00
❏ 50004		Goin' Wild/Main Street	1966	3.75	7.50	15.00
❏ 50033		In My Neighborhood/Then Came Heartbreak	1966	3.75	7.50	15.00
❏ 50069		You're a Puzzle/Ha Ha	1966	3.75	7.50	15.00
❏ 50107		You/You Promised Me Great Things	1966	3.75	7.50	15.00

Jodimars, The
(Members of Bill Haley's Comets)

Capitol

❏ F3285		Well Now -- Dig This/Let's All Rock Together	1955	6.25	12.50	25.00
❏ F3360		Dancin' the Bop/Boom Boom My Bayou Baby	1956	6.25	12.50	25.00
❏ F3436		Lotsa Love/Rattle My Bones	1956	6.25	12.50	25.00
❏ F3512		Rattle Shakin' Daddy/Eat Your Heart Out, Annie	1956	6.25	12.50	25.00
❏ F3588		Clarabella/Midnight	1956	6.25	12.50	25.00
❏ F3633		Cloud 99/Later	1957	6.25	12.50	25.00

President

| ❏ 1017 | | Shoo-Sue/Story-Telling Baby | 1957 | 5.00 | 10.00 | 20.00 |

Joey and the Continentals

Claridge

| ❏ 304 | | She Rides with Me/Rudy Vahoo | 1966 | 6.25 | 12.50 | 25.00 |
| | | Reissued on Claridge 312 as "The G.T.O.'s" | | | | |

Komet

| ❏ 1001 | | Linda/Will Love Ever Come My Way | 196? | 3.75 | 7.50 | 15.00 |

Laurie

| ❏ 3294 | | Sad Girl/Baby | 1965 | 6.25 | 12.50 | 25.00 |

Joey and the Lexingtons

Comet

| ❏ 2154 | | Heaven/The Girl I Love | 1962 | 37.50 | 75.00 | 150.00 |

Dunes

| ❏ 2029 | | Bobbie/Tears from My Eyes | 1963 | 25.00 | 50.00 | 100.00 |

Joey and the Teenagers

Columbia

| ❏ 42054 | | What's On Your Mind/The Draw | 1961 | 20.00 | 40.00 | 80.00 |

John and Ernest

Rainy Wednesday

❏ 201		Super Fly Meets Shaft/Part Two	1973		2.50	5.00
❏ 201		Super Fly Meets Shaft/Problems	1973		2.50	5.00
❏ 203		Soul President Number One/Crossover	1973		2.50	5.00

John's Children

White Whale

| ❏ 239 | | Strange Affair/Smashed, Blocked | 1966 | 5.00 | 10.00 | 20.00 |

John, Elton

Congress

❏ 6017		Lady Samantha/It's Me That You Need	1970	12.50	25.00	50.00
❏ 6017	DJ	Lady Samantha/It's Me That You Need	1970	7.50	15.00	30.00
❏ 6022		Border Song/Bad Side of the Moon	1970	12.50	25.00	50.00
❏ 6022	DJ	Border Song/Bad Side of the Moon	1970	7.50	125.00	30.00

DJM

| ❏ 70,008 | | Lady Samantha/All Across the Havens | 1969 | 75.00 | 150.00 | 300.00 |
| ❏ 70,008 | DJ | Lady Samantha/All Across the Havens | 1969 | 20.00 | 40.00 | 80.00 |

Geffen

❏ 28578		Heartache All Over the World/Highlander	1986			3.00
❏ 28578	PS	Heartache All Over the World/Highlander	1986			3.00
❏ 28800		Nikita/Restless	1985			3.00
❏ 28800	PS	Nikita/Restless	1985			3.00

Number		Title (A Side/B Side)	Year	VG	VG+	NM
❏ 28873		Wrap Her Up/The Man Who Never Died	1985			3.00
❏ 28873	PS	Wrap Her Up/The Man Who Never Died	1985			3.00
❏ 28956		Act of War, Part 1/Act of War, Part 2	1985		2.00	4.00
		By Elton John and Millie Jackson				
❏ 28956	PS	Act of War, Part 1/Act of War, Part 2	1985		2.00	4.00
		By Elton John and Millie Jackson				
❏ 29111		In Neon/Tactics	1984			3.00
❏ 29189		Who Wears These Shoes?/Lonely Boy	1984			3.00
❏ 29189	PS	Who Wears These Shoes?/Lonely Boy	1984			3.00
❏ 29292		Sad Songs (Say So Much)/A Simple Man	1984			3.00
❏ 29292	DJ	Sad Songs (Say So Much) (2 mixes)	1984	2.50	5.00	10.00
		One side features a 4:05 mix unavailable elsewhere				
❏ 29402		Cold As Christmas (In the Middle of the Year)/ (B-side unassigned)	1983			Unreleased
❏ 29460		I Guess That's Why They Call It the Blues/The Retreat	1983			3.00
❏ 29460	PS	I Guess That's Why They Call It the Blues/The Retreat	1983			3.00
❏ 29568		Kiss the Bride/Choc Ice Goes Mental	1983			3.00
❏ 29568	PS	Kiss the Bride/Choc Ice Goes Mental	1983			3.00
❏ 29639		I'm Still Standing/Love So Cold	1983			3.00
❏ 29639	PS	I'm Still Standing/Love So Cold	1983			3.00
❏ 29846		Ball & Chain/Where Have All the Good Times Gone?	1982		2.00	4.00
❏ 29954		Blue Eyes/Hey Papa Legba	1982		2.00	4.00
❏ 29954	PS	Blue Eyes/Hey Papa Legba	1982		2.50	5.00
❏ 49722		Nobody Wins/Fools in Fashion	1981		2.00	4.00
❏ 49722	PS	Nobody Wins/Fools in Fashion	1981		2.50	5.00
❏ 49788		Chloe/Tortured	1981		2.00	4.00
❏ 49788	DJ	Chloe//Fanfare/Chloe	1981	2.00	4.00	8.00
		B-side of this promo-only single is full-length version				
❏ 50049		Empty Garden (Hey Hey Johnny)/ Take Me Down to the Ocean	1982		2.00	4.00
❏ 50049	DJ	Empty Garden (LP version)/Empty Garden (Edit)	1982	2.00	4.00	8.00
❏ 50049	PS	Empty Garden (Hey Hey Johnny)/ Take Me Down to the Ocean	1982		2.50	5.00

MCA

Number		Title (A Side/B Side)	Year	VG	VG+	NM
❏ L45-1938	DJ	Love Song (Long)/Love Song (Short)	1976	5.00	10.00	20.00
		Promo-only release from the Here And There live album				
❏ 40000		Crocodile Rock/Elderberry Wine	1972		3.00	6.00
		Original pressings have a solid black label				
❏ 40046		Daniel/Skyline Pigeon	1973		2.50	5.00
❏ 40105		Saturday Night's Alright for Fighting// Jack Rabbit/Whenever You're Ready	1973		2.50	5.00
❏ 40148		Goodbye Yellow Brick Road/Young Man's Blues	1973		2.50	5.00
❏ 40198		Bennie and the Jets/Harmony	1974		2.50	5.00
❏ 40259		Don't Let the Sun Go Down on Me/Sick City	1974		2.50	5.00
❏ 40297		The Bitch Is Back/Cold Highway	1974		2.50	5.00
❏ 40344		Lucy in the Sky with Diamonds/One Day at a Time	1974		2.50	5.00
		Both sides feature "Dr. Winston O'Boogie" (John Lennon)				
❏ 40344	PS	Lucy in the Sky with Diamonds/One Day at a Time	1974	2.50	5.00	10.00
❏ 40364		Philadelphia Freedom/I Saw Her Standing There	1975		2.50	5.00
		B-side features John Lennon				
❏ 40364	PS	Philadelphia Freedom/I Saw Her Standing There	1975		3.00	6.00
❏ 40364	PS	Philadelphia Freedom/I Saw Her Standing There	1975	10.00	20.00	40.00
		Promo-only sleeve from WFIL radio in Philadelphia				
❏ 40421		Someone Saved My Life Tonight/House of Cards	1975		2.50	5.00
		Original copies have "Captain Fantastic" label				
❏ 40421		Someone Saved My Life Tonight/House of Cards	1975		2.00	4.00
		With MCA black/rainbow label				
❏ 40461		Island Girl/Sugar on the Floor	1975		2.00	4.00
❏ 40505		Grow Some Funk of Your Own/I Feel Like a Bullet (in the Gun of Robert Ford)	1976		2.00	4.00
❏ 40892		Ego/Flinstone Boy	1978		2.00	4.00
❏ 40892	PS	Ego/Flinstone Boy	1978	2.50	5.00	10.00
❏ 40973		Part-Time Love/I Cry at Night	1978		2.00	4.00
❏ 40993		Song for Guy/Lovesick	1979	2.50	5.00	10.00
		The stock copy is much scarcer than the promo, the only Elton John MCA single where this is the case.				
❏ 40993	DJ	Take Me Down to the Ocean/Song for Guy/Lovesick	1979		2.50	5.00
❏ 40993	PS	Song for Guy/Lovesick	1979		2.50	5.00
❏ 41042		Mama Can't Buy You Love/Three Way Love Affair	1979		2.00	4.00
❏ 41042	PS	Mama Can't Buy You Love/Three Way Love Affair	1979		2.00	4.00
❏ 41126		Victim of Love/Strangers	1979	2.00	4.00	8.00
		Label incorrectly says "From the MCA LP...'Thunder in the Night'"				
❏ 41126		Victim of Love/Strangers	1979		2.00	4.00
		Label correctly says "From the MCA LP...'Victim of Love'"				
❏ 41159		Johnny B. Goode/Georgia	1980		2.50	5.00
❏ 41236		Little Jeannie/Conquer the Sun	1980		2.00	4.00
		Originals have a colorful custom label				
❏ 41236	PS	Little Jeannie/Conquer the Sun	1980		2.50	5.00
❏ 41293		(Sartorial Eloquence) Don't Ya Wanna Play This Game No More?// Cartier/White Man Danger	1980		2.00	4.00
		A picture sleeve is rumored to exist, but we've never seen one				
❏ 53196		Candle in the Wind/ Sorry Seems to Be the Hardest Word	1987			3.00
❏ 53196	PS	Candle in the Wind/	1987		2.00	4.00

Number		Title (A Side/B Side)	Year	VG	VG+	NM
		Sorry Seems to Be the Hardest Word				
		White sleeve				
❏ 53196	PS	Candle in the Wind/	1987			3.00
		Sorry Seems to Be the Hardest Word				
		Yellow sleeve with album jackets pictured on back				
❏ 53260		Take Me to the Pilot/Tonight	1988		2.00	4.00
❏ 53260	PS	Take Me to the Pilot/Tonight	1988		2.00	4.00
❏ 53345		I Don't Wanna Go On with You Like That/	1988			3.00
		Rope Around a Fool				
❏ 53345	PS	I Don't Wanna Go On with You Like That/	1988			3.00
		Rope Around a Fool				
❏ 53408		A Word in Spanish/Heavy Traffic	1988			3.00
❏ 53408	PS	A Word in Spanish/Heavy Traffic	1988			3.00
❏ 53692		Healing Hands/Dancing in the End Zone	1989			3.00
❏ 53750		Sacrifice/Love Is a Cannibal	1989			3.00
❏ 54423		The One/Suit of Wolves	1992			3.00
❏ 54452		Runaway Train/Understanding Women	1992			3.00
		A-side: Elton John and Eric Clapton				
❏ 54581		Simple Life/The North	1993			3.00
❏ 54762		True Love/Runaway Train	1993			3.00
		A-side: Elton John and Kiki Dee; B-side: Elton John and Eric Clapton				
❏ 65018		Step Into Christmas/	1973		2.50	5.00
		Ho Ho Ho (Who'd Be a Turkey at Christmas)				
		Originals have black labels with rainbow				
❏ 79026		Club at the End of the Street/Sacrifice	1990			3.00

Polydor

❏ PRO-002		Pinball Wizard/Acid Queen	1975	10.00	20.00	40.00
		Promo-only release; B-side by Tina Turner				

Rocket

❏ 40585		Don't Go Breakin' My Heart/Snow Queen	1976		2.00	4.00
		By "Elton John and Kiki Dee"				
❏ 40585	PS	Don't Go Breakin' My Heart/Snow Queen	1976		2.50	5.00
		By "Elton John and Kiki Dee"				
❏ 40645		Sorry Seems to Be the Hardest Word/Shoulder Holster	1976		2.00	4.00
❏ 40677		Bite Your Lip (Get up and dance!)/Chameleon	1977		2.00	4.00
❏ 852 172-7		Made in England/Lucy in the Sky with Diamonds	1995		2.00	4.00
		B-side recorded live at Madison Square Garden in 1974 with John Lennon				
❏ 852 394-7		Blessed/Latitude	1995		2.00	4.00
❏ 856 014-7		Believe/The One (Live)	1995			3.00
❏ 856 014-7	PS	Believe/The One (Live)	1995			3.00

Uni

❏ 55246		Border Song/Bad Side of the Moon	1970		3.00	6.00
❏ 55265		Your Song/Take Me to the Pilot	1970		3.00	6.00
❏ 55277		Friends/Honey Roll	1971		3.00	6.00
❏ 55314		Levon/Goodbye	1971		3.00	6.00
❏ 55318		Tiny Dancer/Razor Face	1971		3.00	6.00
		Stock copies have full-length version of A-side				
❏ 55318	DJ	Tiny Dancer/Razor Face	1971	2.50	5.00	10.00
		With a severely truncated version of the A-side				
❏ 55328		Rocket Man/Suzie (Dramas)	1972		3.00	6.00
❏ 55343		Honky Cat/Slave	1972		3.00	6.00

Viking

❏ 1010		From Denver to L.A./Warm Summer Rain	1970	15.00	30.00	60.00
		B-side by The Barbara Moore Singers				
❏ 1010	DJ	From Denver to L.A. (same on both sides)	1970	6.25	12.50	25.00
		The promo version of this has been counterfeited; some say all are counterfeits.				

John, Little Willie

Atlantic

❏ 89189		Fever/Ruby Baby	1987			3.00
		B-side by the Drifters				
❏ 89189	PS	Fever/Ruby Baby	1987			3.00

King

❏ 4818		All Around the World/Don't Leave Me Dear	1955	6.25	12.50	25.00
❏ 4841		Need Your Love So Bad/Home at Last	1955	6.25	12.50	25.00
❏ 4893		Are You Ever Coming Back/I'm Stickin' with You Baby	1956	6.25	12.50	25.00
❏ 4935		Fever/Letter from My Darling	1956	7.50	15.00	30.00
❏ 4960		Do Something for Me/My Nerves	1956	6.25	12.50	25.00
❏ 4989		I've Been Around/Suffering with the Blues	1956	6.25	12.50	25.00
❏ 5003		Will the Sun Shine Tomorrow/A Little Bit of Loving	1956	6.25	12.50	25.00
❏ 5023		Love, Life and Money/	1957	6.25	12.50	25.00
		You Got to Get Up Early in the Morning				
❏ 5045		I've Got to Go Cry/Look What You've Done to Me	1957	6.25	12.50	25.00
❏ 5066		Young Girl/If I Thought You Needed Me	1957	6.25	12.50	25.00
❏ 5083		Uh Uh Baby/Summer Date	1957	6.25	12.50	25.00
❏ 5091		Person to Person/Until You Do	1957	6.25	12.50	25.00
❏ 5108		Talk to Me, Talk to Me/Spasms	1958	7.50	15.00	30.00
❏ 5142		Let's Rock While the Rockin's Good/	1958	6.25	12.50	25.00
		You're a Sweetheart				
❏ 5147		Tell It Like It Is/Don't Be Ashamed to Call My Name	1958	6.25	12.50	25.00
❏ 5154		All My Love Belongs to You/	1958	6.25	12.50	25.00
		Why Don't You Haul Off and Love Me				
❏ 5170		No Regrets/I'll Carry Your Love Wherever I Go	1959	5.00	10.00	20.00
❏ 5179		Made for Me/Do More in Life	1959	5.00	10.00	20.00
❏ 5219		Leave My Kitten Alone/Let Nobody Love You	1959	5.00	10.00	20.00

Number	Title (A Side/B Side)	Year	VG	VG+	NM
❑ 5274	Let Them Talk/Right There	1959	5.00	10.00	20.00
❑ 5318	Loving Care/My Love Is	1960	5.00	10.00	20.00
❑ 5342	I'm Shakin'/Cottage for Sale	1960	5.00	10.00	20.00
❑ 5356	Heartbreak (It's Hurtin' Me)/Do You Love Me	1960	5.00	10.00	20.00
❑ 5394	Sleep/There's a Difference	1960	5.00	10.00	20.00
❑ 5428	Walk Slow/You Hurt Me	1960	3.75	7.50	15.00
❑ 5452	Leave My Kitten Alone/I'll Never Go Back on My Word	1961	3.75	7.50	15.00
❑ 5458	I'm Sorry/The Very Thought of You	1961	3.75	7.50	15.00
❑ 5503	(I've Got) Spring Fever/Flamingo	1961	3.75	7.50	15.00
❑ 5516	Take My Love (I Want to Give It All to You)/ Now You Know	1961	3.75	7.50	15.00
❑ 5539	Need Your Love So Bad/Drive Me Home	1961	3.75	7.50	15.00
❑ 5577	There Is Someone in This World for Me/ Autumn Leaves	1961	3.75	7.50	15.00
❑ 5591	Fever/Bo-Da-Ley Dino-Ley	1962	3.75	7.50	15.00
❑ 5602	The Masquerade Is Over/Katanga	1962	3.75	7.50	15.00
❑ 5628	Until Again My Love/Mister Glenn	1962	3.75	7.50	15.00
❑ 5641	Every Beat of My Heart/I Wish I Could Cry	1962	3.75	7.50	15.00
❑ 5667	She Thinks I Still Care/Come Back to Me	1962	3.75	7.50	15.00
❑ 5681	Doll Face/Big Blue Diamonds	1962	3.75	7.50	15.00
❑ 5694	Without a Friend/Half a Love	1962	3.75	7.50	15.00
❑ 5717	Don't Play with Love/Heaven All Around Me	1963	3.00	6.00	12.00
❑ 5744	My Baby's in Love with Another Guy/Come On Sugar	1963	3.00	6.00	12.00
❑ 5799	Let Them Talk/Talk to Me	1963	3.00	6.00	12.00
❑ 5818	So Lovely/Inside Information	1963	3.00	6.00	12.00
❑ 5823	Person to Person/I'm Shakin'	1963	3.00	6.00	12.00
❑ 5850	Bill Bailey/My Love Will Never Change	1964	3.00	6.00	12.00
❑ 5870	Rock Love/It Only Hurts for a Little While	1964	3.00	6.00	12.00
❑ 5886	All Around the World/All My Love Belongs to You	1964	3.00	6.00	12.00
❑ 5949	Do Something for Me/Don't You Know I'm in Love	1964	3.00	6.00	12.00
❑ 6003	Talk to Me/Take My Love	1965	2.50	5.00	10.00
❑ 6170	Fever/Let Them Talk	1968	2.50	5.00	10.00
❑ 6302	All Around the World/Need Your Love So Bad	1970	2.00	4.00	8.00

John, Mable
Motown

| ❑ 54031 | Who Wouldn't Love a Man Like That/ You Made a Fool Out of Me | 1960 | 125.00 | 250.00 | 500.00 |

Mispress with wrong label; may have been promo only

Stax

❑ 0016	Running Out/Shouldn't I Love Him	1968	5.00	10.00	20.00
❑ 192	Your Good Thing (Is About to End)/It's Catching	1966	5.00	10.00	20.00
❑ 205	If You Give Up What You Got/ You're Taking Up Another Man's Place	1967	5.00	10.00	20.00
❑ 215	Same Time, Same Place/Bigger and Better	1967	5.00	10.00	20.00
❑ 225	I'm a Big Girl Now/Wait You Dog	1967	5.00	10.00	20.00
❑ 234	Don't Hit Me No More/Left Over Love	1967	5.00	10.00	20.00
❑ 249	Don't Get Caught/Able Mable	1968	5.00	10.00	20.00

Tamla

| ❑ 54031 | Who Wouldn't Love a Man Like That/ You Made a Fool Out of Me | 1960 | 37.50 | 75.00 | 150.00 |
| ❑ 54040 | No Love/Looking for a Love | 1961 | 30.00 | 60.00 | 120.00 |

Version with long intro

| ❑ 54040 | No Love/Looking for a Love | 1961 | 25.00 | 50.00 | 100.00 |

Version with no intro

| ❑ 54050 | Take Me/Action Speaks Louder Than Words | 1962 | 20.00 | 40.00 | 80.00 |
| ❑ 54081 | Who Wouldn't Love a Man Like That/ Say You'll Never Let Me Go | 1963 | 30.00 | 60.00 | 120.00 |

Johnnie and Joe
ABC-Paramount

| ❑ 10079 | I Adore You/I Want You Here Beside Me | 1960 | 3.75 | 7.50 | 15.00 |
| ❑ 10117 | Your Love/Why Do You Hurt Me So | 1960 | 3.75 | 7.50 | 15.00 |

Ambient Sound

| ❑ 03410 | Kingdom of Love/Tossin' Turnin' (Yearnin' Burnin' For Your Love) | 1982 | | 2.50 | 5.00 |

Chess

| ❑ 1641 | I'll Be Spinning/Feel Alright | 1956 | 5.00 | 10.00 | 20.00 |
| ❑ 1654 | Over the Mountain; Across the Sea/ My Baby's Gone, On, On | 1957 | 6.25 | 12.50 | 25.00 |

Originals with blue and silver "chess pieces" label

| ❑ 1654 | Over the Mountain; Across the Sea/ My Baby's Gone, On, On | 1958 | 3.00 | 6.00 | 12.00 |

Reissues on blue labels

| ❑ 1654 | Over the Mountain; Across the Sea/ My Baby's Gone, On, On | 1963 | 2.50 | 5.00 | 10.00 |

Reissues on other labels (multicolor, black)

| ❑ 1677 | I Was So Lonely/If You Tell Me You're Mine | 1957 | 5.00 | 10.00 | 20.00 |
| ❑ 1693 | Why Oh Why/Why Did She Go | 1958 | 5.00 | 10.00 | 20.00 |

Number		Title (A Side/B Side)	Year	VG	VG+	NM
❏ 1706		My Baby's Gone/Darling	1958	5.00	10.00	20.00
❏ 1769		Across the Sea/You Said It, And Don't Forget It	1960	3.75	7.50	15.00
Gone						
❏ 5024		Who Do You Love/Trust in Me	1958	7.50	15.00	30.00
J&S						
❏ 1008		Over the Mountain (Part 2)/	1959	6.25	12.50	25.00
		Won't You Come Back to Me				
❏ 1603		I Was So Lonely/If You Tell Me You're Mine	1957	6.25	12.50	25.00
❏ 1605/6		Who Do You Love/Trust in Me	1958	6.25	12.50	25.00
❏ 1630/1		Warm, Soft and Lovely/False Love Has Got to Go	1958	6.25	12.50	25.00
❏ 1659		It Was There/There Goes My Heart	1957	6.25	12.50	25.00
❏ 1664		Over the Mountain; Across the Sea/	1957	12.50	25.00	50.00
		My Baby's Gone, On, On				
		With horizontal lines on label				
❏ 1664		Over the Mountain; Across the Sea/	1962	5.00	10.00	20.00
		My Baby's Gone, On, On				
		Without horizontal lines on label				
❏ 1701		Where Did She Go/Red Sails in the Sunset	1959	6.25	12.50	25.00
❏ 4420		The Devil Said No, Gone With You Bad Self/	196?	3.75	7.50	15.00
		You Can Always Count on Me				
❏ 8719		Tell Me/Sincere Love	196?	3.75	7.50	15.00
❏ 42832		You're the Loveliest Song/	196?	3.75	7.50	15.00
		Let Your Mind Do the Walking				
❏ 87187		False Love Has Got to Go/Jamaica -- Our Thing	196?	3.75	7.50	15.00
Tuff						
❏ 379		Here We Go Baby/That's the Way You Go	1964	3.00	6.00	12.00

Johnny and the Dreams
Richie
Number		Title (A Side/B Side)	Year	VG	VG+	NM
❏ 457		You're Too Young/Are You for Me	1961	125.00	250.00	500.00
		Red vinyl				
❏ 457		You're Too Young/Are You for Me	1961	62.50	125.00	250.00
		Black vinyl				

Johnny and the Hurricanes
Atila
Number		Title (A Side/B Side)	Year	VG	VG+	NM
❏ 211		Saga of the Beatles/Rene	1967	2.50	5.00	10.00
❏ 214		Judy's Moody/I Love You	1967	2.50	5.00	10.00
❏ 215		Because I Love You/Wisdom's 5th Take	1967	2.50	5.00	10.00
❏ 216		Red River Rock '67/The Psychedelic Woman	1967	2.50	5.00	10.00
Big Top						
❏ 3036		Down Yonder/Sheba	1960	5.00	10.00	20.00
❏ 3036	PS	Down Yonder/Sheba	1960	10.00	20.00	40.00
❏ 3051		Revival/Rocking Goose	1960	5.00	10.00	20.00
❏ 3051	PS	Revival/Rocking Goose	1960	10.00	20.00	40.00
❏ 3056		You Are My Sunshine/Molly-O	1960	5.00	10.00	20.00
❏ 3056	PS	You Are My Sunshine/Molly-O	1960	10.00	20.00	40.00
❏ 3063		Ja-Da/Mr. Lonely	1961	5.00	10.00	20.00
❏ 3063	PS	Ja-Da/Mr. Lonely	1961	10.00	20.00	40.00
❏ 3076		Old Smokey/High Voltage	1961	5.00	10.00	20.00
❏ 3090		Traffic Jam/Farewell, Farewell	1961	5.00	10.00	20.00
❏ 3103		Miserlou/Salvation	1962	5.00	10.00	20.00
❏ 3113		San Antonio Rose/Come On Train	1962	5.00	10.00	20.00
❏ 3125		Shiek of Araby/Minnesota Fats	1962	5.00	10.00	20.00
❏ 3132		Whatever Happened to Baby Jane?/	1963	5.00	10.00	20.00
		The Greenest Beans				
❏ 3146		James Bond Theme/Hungry Eye	1963	5.00	10.00	20.00
❏ 3159		Rough Road/Kaw-Liga	1963	5.00	10.00	20.00
Jeff						
❏ 211		Saga of the Beatles/Rene	1964	3.75	7.50	15.00
Mala						
❏ 470		It's a Mad, Mad, Mad, Mad World/Shadows	1963	2.50	5.00	10.00
❏ 483		That's All/Honey, Honey	1964	2.50	5.00	10.00
Twirl						
❏ 1001		Crossfire/Lazy	1958	12.50	25.00	50.00
Warwick						
❏ 502		Crossfire/Lazy	1959	7.50	15.00	30.00
❏ 509	M	Red River Rock/Buckeye	1959	7.50	15.00	30.00
❏ 509 ST	S	Red River Rock/Buckeye	1959	15.00	30.00	60.00
❏ 513	M	Reveille Rock/Time Bomb	1959	7.50	15.00	30.00
❏ 513 ST	S	Reveille Rock/Time Bomb	1959	15.00	30.00	60.00
❏ 520		Beatnik Fly/Sand Storm	1960	6.25	12.50	25.00
❏ 520	PS	Beatnik Fly/Sand Storm	1960	12.50	25.00	50.00

Johnny and the Tokens
Warwick
Number		Title (A Side/B Side)	Year	VG	VG+	NM
❏ 658		The Taste of a Tear/Never Till Now	1961	5.00	10.00	20.00

Johnson, Bill
Sun
Number		Title (A Side/B Side)	Year	VG	VG+	NM
❏ 340		Bobaloo/Bad Times Ahead	1960	5.00	10.00	20.00

Johnson, Cliff
Columbia
Number		Title (A Side/B Side)	Year	VG	VG+	NM
❏ 40865		Go 'Way Hound Dog/Twenty Four Hours a Day	1957	20.00	40.00	80.00

Number		Title (A Side/B Side)	Year	VG	VG+	NM

Johnson, Marv
Gordy
❑ 7042		Why Do You Want to Let Me Go/I'm Not a Plaything	1965	3.75	7.50	15.00
❑ 7051		Just the Way You Are/Miss You Baby	1966	3.75	7.50	15.00
❑ 7077		I'll Pick a Rose for My Rose/You Got the Love I Love	1968	3.75	7.50	15.00

Kudo
| ❑ 663 | | My Baby-O/Once Upon a Time | 1958 | 150.00 | 300.00 | 600.00 |

Tamla
❑ 101		Come to Me/Whisper	1959	75.00	150.00	300.00
		No address on label				
❑ 101		Come to Me/Whisper	1959	62.50	125.00	250.00
		With Gladstone St., Detroit, address on label				

United Artists
❑ 0030		You've Got What It Takes/I Love the Way You Love	1973		2.50	5.00
		"Silver Spotlight Series" reissue				
❑ 0031		Move Two Mountains/Come to Me	1973		2.50	5.00
		"Silver Spotlight Series" reissue				
❑ 160		Come to Me/Whisper	1959	6.25	12.50	25.00
❑ 175		River of Tears/I'm Coming Home	1959	5.00	10.00	20.00
❑ 185		You Got What It Takes/Don't Leave Me	1959	5.00	10.00	20.00
❑ 208		I Love the Way You Love/Let Me Love You	1960	5.00	10.00	20.00
❑ 226		Ain't Gonna Be That Way/All the Love I've Got	1960	5.00	10.00	20.00
❑ 241		(You've Got to) Move Two Mountains/I Need You	1960	3.75	7.50	15.00
❑ 273		Happy Days/Baby, Baby	1960	3.75	7.50	15.00
❑ 294		Merry-Go-Round/Tell Me That You Love Me	1961	3.75	7.50	15.00
❑ 322		How Can We Tell Him/I've Got a Notion	1961	5.00	10.00	20.00
❑ 359		Show Me/Oh Mary	1961	5.00	10.00	20.00
❑ 386		Easier Said Than Done/Johnny One Stop	1961	5.00	10.00	20.00
❑ 423		Magic Mirror/With All That's In Me	1962	5.00	10.00	20.00
❑ 454		He Gave Me You/That's How Bad	1962	5.00	10.00	20.00
❑ 483		Let Yourself Go/That's Where I Lost My Baby	1962	5.00	10.00	20.00
❑ 556		Keep Tellin' Yourself/ Everyone Who's Been in Love with You	1963	5.00	10.00	20.00
❑ 590		He's Got the Whole World In His Hands/ Another Tear Falls	1963	5.00	10.00	20.00
❑ 617		Come On and Stop/Not Available	1963	5.00	10.00	20.00
❑ 643		Congratulations, You've Hurt Me Again/ Crying on My Pillow	1963	5.00	10.00	20.00
❑ 691		Unbreakable Love/A Man Who Don't Believe in Love	1964	6.25	12.50	25.00

Johnston, Bruce
(Of the Beach Boys)
Columbia
| ❑ 10568 | | Pipeline/Disney Girls | 1977 | | 2.50 | 5.00 | 10.00 |
| | | *Promos (with "Pipeline" on both sides) worth 50% less* | | | | |

Del-Fi
❑ 4202		The Original Surfer Stomp/Pajama Party	1963	15.00	30.00	60.00
		Originals credit "The Surf Stompers"				
❑ 4202		The Original Surfer Stomp/Pajama Party	1963	7.50	15.00	30.00

Donna
❑ 1354		Do the Surfer Stomp (Part 1)/ Do the Surfer Stomp (Part 2)	1962	12.50	25.00	50.00
		Originals credit "The Surf Stompers"				
❑ 1354		Do the Surfer Stomp (Part 1)/ Do the Surfer Stomp (Part 2)	1962	7.50	15.00	30.00
❑ 1354	PS	Do the Surfer Stomp (Part 1)/ Do the Surfer Stomp (Part 2)	1962	15.00	30.00	60.00
❑ 1364		Soupy Shuffle Stomp (SSS)/Moon Shot	1962	7.50	15.00	30.00
❑ 1374		The Original Surfer Stomp (Part 1)/ The Original Surfer Stomp (Part 2)	1962	7.50	15.00	30.00

Ronda
| ❑ 1003 | | Do the Surfer Stomp (Part 1)/ Do the Surfer Stomp (Part 2) | 1962 | 10.00 | 20.00 | 40.00 |

Johnston, Bruce, and Terry Melcher
(Also see individual entries)
Equinox
| ❑ PB-10238 | | Rebecca/Take It to Mexico | 1975 | | 2.50 | 5.00 | 10.00 |

Jones Brothers, The
Sun
| ❑ 213 | | Every Night/Look to Jesus | 1954 | 200.00 | 400.00 | 800.00 |

Jones, Davy
(Of the Monkees)
Bell
| ❑ 45,111 | | Rainy Jane/Welcome to My Love | 1971 | | 2.50 | 5.00 | 10.00 |
| ❑ 45,136 | | I Really Love You/Sitting in the Apple Tree | 1971 | | 2.50 | 5.00 | 10.00 |

Number		Title (A Side/B Side)	Year	VG	VG+	NM
❑ 45,159		Girl/Take My Love	1971	12.50	25.00	50.00
❑ 45,178		I'll Believe in You/The Road to Love	1972	5.00	10.00	20.00

Colpix

Note: Colpix sides as "David Jones"

❑ 764		Dream Girl/Take Me to Paradise	1965	5.00	10.00	20.00
❑ 764	PS	Dream Girl/Take Me to Paradise	1965	7.50	15.00	30.00
❑ 784		What Are We Going to Do/This Bouquet	1965	5.00	10.00	20.00
❑ 784	PS	What Are We Going to Do/This Bouquet	1965	7.50	15.00	30.00
❑ 789		The Girl from Chelsea/Theme for a New Love	1965	5.00	10.00	20.00
❑ 789	PS	The Girl from Chelsea/Theme for a New Love	1965	10.00	20.00	40.00

MGM

❑ 14458		You're a Lady/Who Was It	1972	7.50	15.00	30.00
❑ 14524		Rubberene/Who Was It	1973	7.50	15.00	30.00

Jones, Jimmy

ABC-Paramount

❑ 10094		Blue and Lonely/Daddy Needs Baby	1960	3.75	7.50	15.00
		As "Jimmy Jones and the Pretenders"				

Arrow

❑ 717		Heaven in Your Eyes/The Whistlin' Man	1957	45.00	90.00	180.00
		As "Jimmy Jones and the Jones Boys"				

Bell

❑ 682		Personal Property/39-21-40	1967	2.00	4.00	8.00
❑ 689		True Love Ways/Snap My Fingers	1967	2.00	4.00	8.00

Capitol

❑ 3849		If I Knew Then (What I Know Now)/	1974		2.50	5.00
		Everything's Gonna Be All Right				

Cub

❑ 9049		Handy Man/The Search Is Over	1959	5.00	10.00	20.00
❑ 9067		Good Timin'/My Precious Angel	1960	5.00	10.00	20.00
❑ 9072		That's When I Cried/I Just Go for You	1960	5.00	10.00	20.00
❑ 9072	PS	That's When I Cried/I Just Go for You	1960	12.50	25.00	50.00
❑ 9076		Itchin'/Ee-I-Ee-I-Oh	1960	3.75	7.50	15.00
❑ 9082		Ready for Love/For You	1960	3.75	7.50	15.00
❑ 9085		I Told You So/You Got It	1961	3.75	7.50	15.00
❑ 9093		Dear One/I Say Love	1961	3.75	7.50	15.00
❑ 9102		Mr. Music Man/Holler Hey	1961	3.75	7.50	15.00
❑ 9110		You're Much Too Young/Nights of Mexico	1962	3.75	7.50	15.00

Epic

❑ 9339		Whenever You Need Me/You for Me to Love	1959	30.00	60.00	120.00

Parkway

❑ 988		Don't You Just Know It/Dynamite	1966	2.50	5.00	10.00

Rama

❑ 210		Lover/Plain Old Love	1956	30.00	60.00	120.00
		As "Jimmy Jones and the Pretenders"				

Roulette

❑ 4232		Lover/Plain Old Love	1960	7.50	15.00	30.00
		As "Jimmy 'Handyman' Jones"				

Vee Jay

❑ 505		No Insurance (For a Broken Heart)/Mr. Fix-It	1963	3.75	7.50	15.00

Jones, Joe

Capitol

❑ F2951		Adam Bit the Apple/Will Call	1954	10.00	20.00	40.00

Herald

❑ 488		You Done Me Wrong/	1956	10.00	20.00	40.00
		When Your Hair Has Turned to Silver				

Ric

❑ 972		You Talk Too Much/I Love You Still	1960	6.25	12.50	25.00

Roulette

❑ 4304		You Talk Too Much/I Love You Still	1960	3.75	7.50	15.00
❑ 4316		One Big Mouth/Here's What You Gotta Do	1960	3.00	6.00	12.00
❑ 4344		California Sun/	1961	3.00	6.00	12.00
		Please Don't Talk About Me When I'm Gone				
❑ 4377		The Big Mule/I've Got a Uh Uh Wife	1961	3.00	6.00	12.00

Jones, John Paul

(In Led Zeppelin 1968-80)

Cotillion

❑ 44102		Got to Get Together Now/Man from Nazareth	1971	6.25	12.50	25.00

Parkway

❑ 915		Baja/A Foggy Day in Vietnam	1964	10.00	20.00	40.00

Jones, Little Johnny

Atlantic

❑ 1045		Hoy, Hoy/Doin' the Best I Can	1954	20.00	40.00	80.00

Number		Title (A Side/B Side)	Year	VG	VG+	NM

Jones, Ronnie, and the Classmates
End
☐ 1002		Teenage Rock/Little Girl Next Door	1957	30.00	60.00	120.00
☐ 1014		Lonely Boy/Baby Cries	1958	30.00	60.00	120.00
☐ 1125		Teenage Rock/Little Girl Next Door	1963	6.25	12.50	25.00

Josie and the Pussycats
(Also see "Holloway, Patrice")
Capitol
☐ CP 58-1		Letter to Mama/Inside, Outside, Upside Down	1970	5.00	10.00	20.00
☐ CP 58-1	PS	Letter to Mama/Inside, Outside, Upside Down	1970	7.50	15.00	30.00
☐ CP 59-2		With Every Beat of My Heart/Josie	1970	5.00	10.00	20.00
☐ CP 59-2	PS	With Every Beat of My Heart/Josie	1970	7.50	15.00	30.00
☐ CP 60-3		Voodoo/If That Isn't Love	1970	5.00	10.00	20.00
☐ CP 60-3	PS	Voodoo/If That Isn't Love	1970	7.50	15.00	30.00
☐ CP 61-4		I Wanna Make You Happy/It's Gotta Be Him	1970	5.00	10.00	20.00
☐ CP 61-4	PS	I Wanna Make You Happy/It's Gotta Be Him	1970	7.50	15.00	30.00
☐ 2967		Every Beat of My Heart/It's All Right with Me	1970	5.00	10.00	20.00
		Same song as CP 59, but a slightly different title and a mono mix				
☐ 3045		Stop, Look and Listen/You've Come a Long Way, Baby	1971	5.00	10.00	20.00

Journeymen, The
(The Iona group is not the same as the Amy and Capitol. Also see "McKenzie, Scott"; "Phillips, John")
Amy
| ☐ 821 | | Cup-E-Co/Hush Storm | 1961 | 3.00 | 6.00 | 12.00 |
Capitol
☐ 4625		500 Miles/The River She Comes Down	1961	2.50	5.00	10.00
☐ 4678		Soft Blow the Summer Winds/Kumbaya	1962	2.50	5.00	10.00
☐ 4737		Don't Turn Around/Hush Now Sally	1962	2.50	5.00	10.00
☐ 4829		What'll I Do/Loadin' Coal	1962	2.50	5.00	10.00
☐ 4943		Rag Mama/I Never Will Marry	1963	2.50	5.00	10.00
☐ 4943	PS	Rag Mama/I Never Will Marry	1963	10.00	20.00	40.00
☐ 5031		Kumbaya/Ja Da	1963	2.50	5.00	10.00
Iona
☐ 1111		Work Out/Bag's Groove	1961	12.50	25.00	50.00
☐ 1115		Surfer's Blues/Surfer's Rule	1963	12.50	25.00	50.00
☐ 1115		Surfer's Blues/Surfer's Rule	1963	10.00	20.00	40.00
		Re-release as "The Baylanders"				

Joy, Roddie
Parkway
☐ 101		Something Strange Is Going On/Stop	1966	3.00	6.00	12.00
☐ 134		Every Breath I Take/Walkin' Back	1967	3.00	6.00	12.00
☐ 151		I Want You Back/Let's Start All Over	1967	3.00	6.00	12.00
☐ 991		A Boy Is Just a Toy/Stop	1966	3.75	7.50	15.00
Red Bird
☐ 10-021		Love Hit Me with a Wallop/Come Back Baby	1965	5.00	10.00	20.00
☐ 10-031		The La La Song/He's So Easy to Love	1965	6.25	12.50	25.00
☐ 10-037		If There's Anything Else You Want (Let Me Know)/Stop	1965	10.00	20.00	40.00

Julian, Don, and the Meadowlarks
Classic Artists
| ☐ 101 | | Quickie Wedding/Our Love | 1988 | | 2.00 | 4.00 |
| ☐ 105 | | White Christmas/Merry Christmas, Baby | 1988 | | 2.00 | 4.00 |
Dooto
| ☐ 424 | | Blue Moon/Big Mama Wants to Rock | 1957 | 12.50 | 25.00 | 50.00 |
Dootone
☐ 359		Heaven and Paradise/Embarrassing Moments	1955	25.00	50.00	100.00
☐ 367		Always and Always/I Got Tore Up	1955	18.75	37.50	75.00
		Red label				
☐ 367		Always and Always/I Got Tore Up	1955	12.50	25.00	50.00
		Maroon label				
☐ 372		This Must Be Paradise/Mine All Mine	1955	15.00	30.00	60.00
☐ 394		Please Love a Fool/Oop Boopy Oop	1956	12.50	25.00	50.00
☐ 405		I Am a Believer/Boogie Woogie Teenager	1956	20.00	40.00	80.00
Dynamite
| ☐ 1112 | | Heaven Only Knows/Popeye | 1962 | 7.50 | 15.00 | 30.00 |
Original Sound
| ☐ 3 | | Please Say You Want Me/Doin' the Cha Cha Cha | 1959 | 10.00 | 20.00 | 40.00 |
| ☐ 12 | | There's a Girl/Blue Moon | 1960 | 7.50 | 15.00 | 30.00 |
RPM
☐ 399		Love Only You/Real Pretty Mama	1954	62.50	125.00	250.00
		As "The Meadow Larks"				
☐ 406		LSMFT Blues (Lord Find My Sweet Theresa)/Pass the Gin	1954	62.50	125.00	250.00
		As "The Meadow Larks"				

Juliana
RCA Victor
| ☐ 47-7906 | | You Can Have Any Boy/You're Saying Goodnight | 1961 | 15.00 | 30.00 | 60.00 |

Number		Title (A Side/B Side)	Year	VG	VG+	NM
Jumpin' Jacks, The						
Decca						
☐ 29973		You'll Wonder Where the Yellow Went/A Frantic Antic	1956	7.50	15.00	30.00
☐ 29973	PS	You'll Wonder Where the Yellow Went/A Frantic Antic	1956	10.00	20.00	40.00
Junior and His Friends						
ABC-Paramount						
☐ 10089		Who's Our Pet, Annette!/A.B.C. Love	1960	7.50	15.00	30.00
Justis, Bill						
Bell						
☐ 921		Electric Dreams/Dark Continent Contribution	1970		2.50	5.00
MCA						
☐ 40810		Foxy Lady/Orange Blossom Special	1977			
Monument						
☐ 8699		Sea Dream/Touching, Feeling, Dreaming	1976		2.50	5.00
☐ 956		Yellow Summer/So Until I See You	1966	2.50	5.00	10.00
NRC						
☐ 1119		Blowing Rock/Boogie Woogie Rock	1959	5.00	10.00	20.00
Phillips Int'l.						
☐ 3519		Raunchy/Midnight Man	1957	6.25	12.50	25.00
☐ 3522		College Man/The Stranger	1958	5.00	10.00	20.00
☐ 3525		Wild Ride/Scroungie	1958	5.00	10.00	20.00
☐ 3529		Cattywampus/Summer Holiday	1958	5.00	10.00	20.00
☐ 3535		Bop Train/String of Pearls	1958	5.00	10.00	20.00
☐ 3544		Flea Circus/Cloud Nine	1959	5.00	10.00	20.00
Smash						
☐ 1812		I'm Gonna Learn to Dance/Tamoure	1963	2.50	5.00	10.00
☐ 1812	PS	I'm Gonna Learn to Dance/Tamoure	1963	4.00	8.00	16.00
☐ 1851		Sunday in Madrid/Satin and Velvet	1963	2.50	5.00	10.00
☐ 1902		Lavender Sax/Fia, Fia	1964	2.50	5.00	10.00
☐ 1955		How Soon/Ska-Ha	1964	2.50	5.00	10.00
☐ 1977		Late Game/Last Farewell	1965	2.50	5.00	10.00

K

Number		Title (A Side/B Side)	Year	VG	VG+	NM
K-Doe, Ernie						
Duke						
☐ 378		My Mother-in-Law (Is In My Hair Again)/Looking Into the Future	1964	2.00	4.00	8.00
☐ 387		Little Bit of Everything/Someone	1965	2.00	4.00	8.00
☐ 400		Please Don't Stop/Boomerang	1966	2.00	4.00	8.00
☐ 404		Little Marie/Somebody Told Me	1966	2.00	4.00	8.00
☐ 411		Later for Tomorrow/Dancin' Man	1966	2.00	4.00	8.00
☐ 420		Love Me Like I Wanna/Don't Kill My Groove	1967	2.00	4.00	8.00
☐ 423		(It Will Have to Do) Until the Real Thing Comes Along/Little Marie	1967	2.00	4.00	8.00
☐ 437		Gotta Pack My Bag/How Sweet You Are	1968	2.00	4.00	8.00
☐ 450		I'm Sorry/Trying to Make You Love Me	1969	2.00	4.00	8.00
☐ 456		I'll Make Everything Be Alright/Wishing in Vain	1969	2.00	4.00	8.00
Ember						
☐ 1050		My Love for You/Tuff-Enuff	1959	6.25	12.50	25.00
☐ 1075		My Love for You/Shirley's Tuff	1961	3.75	7.50	15.00
Instant						
☐ 3260		Baby, SInce I Met You/Sufferin' So	1963	2.50	5.00	10.00
☐ 3264		Reaping What I Sow/Talking Out of My Head	1964	2.50	5.00	10.00
Island						
☐ 031		Let Me Love You/(B-side unknown)	1975		3.00	6.00
Janus						
☐ 167		Here Come the Girls/Long Way Home	1971		3.00	6.00
Minit						
☐ 604		Make You Love Me/There's a Will, There's a Way	1959	7.50	15.00	30.00
☐ 614		'Tain't It the Truth/Hello My Lover	1960	5.00	10.00	20.00
☐ 623		Mother-in-Law/Wanted, $10,000 Reward	1961	5.00	10.00	20.00
☐ 627		Te Ta Te Ta Ta/Real Man	1961	3.75	7.50	15.00
☐ 634		A Certain Girl/I Cried My Last Tear	1961	3.75	7.50	15.00
☐ 641		Popeye Joe/Come On Home	1962	3.75	7.50	15.00
☐ 645		Hey Hey Hey/Love You the Best	1962	3.75	7.50	15.00
☐ 651		Beating Like a Tom-Tom/I Got to Find Somebody	1962	3.75	7.50	15.00
☐ 656		Loving You/Get Out of My House	1962	3.75	7.50	15.00
☐ 661		Easier Said Than Done/Be Sweet	1963	3.75	7.50	15.00
☐ 665		I'm the Boss/Pennies Worth o' Happiness	1963	3.75	7.50	15.00
Sansu						
☐ 1006		Stoop Down/(B-side unknown)	197?	5.00	10.00	20.00
☐ 1016		Hotcha Mama/She Gave It All to Me	197?	5.00	10.00	20.00
Specialty						
☐ 563		Eternity/Do Baby Do	1955	10.00	20.00	40.00
		As "Ernest Kador"				
United Artists						
☐ 0110		Mother-in-Law/A Wonderful Dream	1973		2.50	5.00
		"Silver Spotlight Series" reissue; B-side by the Majors				

Number		Title (A Side/B Side)	Year	VG	VG+	NM

Kact-Ties, The
Atco
| ❏ 6299 | | Oh What a Night/Let Me In Your Life | 1964 | 3.75 | 7.50 | 15.00 |
| | | As "The Kac-Ties" | | | | |

Kape
Note: All on Kape as "The Kac-Ties"
❏ 501		Happy Birthday/Girl in My Heart	1965	3.75	7.50	15.00
❏ 502		Walkin' in the Rain/Smile	1965	3.75	7.50	15.00
❏ 503		Let Your Love Light Shine/Were-Wolf	1965	3.75	7.50	15.00

Shelley
| ❏ 163 | | Let Your Love Light Shine/Were-Wolf | 1963 | 6.25 | 12.50 | 25.00 |
| ❏ 165 | | Oh What a Night/Let Me In Your Life | 1963 | 6.25 | 12.50 | 25.00 |

Trans Atlas
❏ 695		Walkin' in the Rain/Smile	1962	75.00	150.00	300.00
		With thunderstorm sound effects				
❏ 695		Walkin' in the Rain/Smile	1962	37.50	75.00	150.00
		Without thunderstorm sound effects				

Kak
(Gary Yoder, later of Blue Cheer, was in this group)
Epic
❏ 10383	DJ	Everything's Changing (Long Version)/	1968	5.00	10.00	20.00
		Everything's Changing (Edited Version)				
		May be promo only				
❏ 10446		I've Got Time/Disbelievin'	1969	5.00	10.00	20.00

Kaleidoscope
Epic
❏ 10117		Elevator Man/Please	1967	7.50	15.00	30.00
❏ 10219		Little Orphan Annie/Why Try	1967	7.50	15.00	30.00
❏ 10239		I Found Out/Rampe Rampe	1967	7.50	15.00	30.00
❏ 10332		Just a Taste/Hello Trouble	1968	7.50	15.00	30.00
❏ 10481		Lie to Me/Let the Good Love Flow	1969	7.50	15.00	30.00
❏ 10500		Killing Floor/Lie to Me	1969	7.50	15.00	30.00

Fontana
| ❏ 1633 | | Jimmy Artichoke/Just How Much You Are | 1968 | | Unreleased | |

Kalin Twins, The
Amy
| ❏ 969 | | Thinkin' About You Baby/Sometimes It Comes | 1966 | 2.00 | 4.00 | 8.00 |

Decca
❏ 30552		Jumpin' Jack/Walkin' to School	1958	5.00	10.00	20.00
❏ 30642		When/Three O'Clock Thrill	1958	6.25	12.50	25.00
❏ 30745		Forget Me Not/Dream of Me	1958	6.25	12.50	25.00
❏ 30807		It's Only the Beginning/Oh My Goodness	1959	5.00	10.00	20.00
❏ 30868		Cool/When I Look in the Mirror	1959	5.00	10.00	20.00
❏ 30911		Sweet Sugar Lips/Moody	1959	5.00	10.00	20.00
❏ 30977		Why Don't You Believe Me/The Meaning of the Blues	1959	5.00	10.00	20.00
❏ 30977	PS	Why Don't You Believe Me/The Meaning of the Blues	1959	7.50	15.00	30.00
❏ 31064		Loneliness/Chicken Thief	1960	3.75	7.50	15.00
❏ 31111		True to You/Blue, Blue Town	1960	3.75	7.50	15.00
❏ 31169		Zing! Went the Strings of My Heart/No Money Can Buy	1960	3.75	7.50	15.00
❏ 31220		Momma-Poppa/You Mean the World to Me	1961	3.75	7.50	15.00
❏ 31286		Bubbles (I'm Forever Blowing Bubbles)/One More Time	1961	3.75	7.50	15.00
❏ 31410		Trouble/A Picture of You	1962	3.75	7.50	15.00

Kane, Paul – See "Simon, Paul"

Kartunes, The
MGM
| ❏ 12598 | | Raindrops/Will You Marry Me | 1957 | 7.50 | 15.00 | 30.00 |
| ❏ 12680 | | Dedicated to Love/Willie the Weeper | 1958 | 6.25 | 12.50 | 25.00 |

Kayli, Bob
Anna
| ❏ 1104 | | Never More/Peppermint (You Know What to Do) | 1959 | 10.00 | 20.00 | 40.00 |

Carlton
| ❏ 482 | | Everyone Was There/I Took a Dare | 1958 | 7.50 | 15.00 | 30.00 |

Gordy
| ❏ 7004 | | Toodle Loo/Everyone Was There | 1962 | 20.00 | 40.00 | 80.00 |
| ❏ 7008 | | Toodle Loo/Hold On Pearl | 1962 | 7.50 | 15.00 | 30.00 |

Tamla
| ❏ 54051 | | Small Sad Sam/Tie Me Tight | 1962 | 7.50 | 15.00 | 30.00 |

Keith
Columbia
| ❏ 43268 | | Dream/Caravan of Lonely Men | 1965 | 3.75 | 7.50 | 15.00 |
| | | As "Keith and the Admirations" | | | | |

DiscReet
| ❏ 1193 | | What Did You Do in the Revolution, Dad/ | 1974 | | 2.50 | 5.00 |
| | | In and Out of Love | | | | |

Number		Title (A Side/B Side)	Year	VG	VG+	NM
Mercury						
❏ 72596		Ain't Gonna Lie/Our Love Started All Over Again	1966	2.00	4.00	8.00
❏ 72639		98.6/The Teenie Bopper Song	1966	2.50	5.00	10.00
❏ 72639	PS	98.6/The Teenie Bopper Song	1966	3.75	7.50	15.00
❏ 72652		Tell Me To My Face/Pretty Little Shy One	1967	2.00	4.00	8.00
❏ 72652	PS	Tell Me To My Face/Pretty Little Shy One	1967	3.75	7.50	15.00
❏ 72695		Daylight Savin' Time/Happy Walking Around	1967	2.00	4.00	8.00
❏ 72695	PS	Daylight Savin' Time/Happy Walking Around	1967	3.00	6.00	12.00
❏ 72715		Easy-As-Pie/Sugar Man	1967	2.00	4.00	8.00
❏ 72746		I'm So Proud/Candy Candy	1967	2.00	4.00	8.00
❏ 72794		Hurry/Pleasure of Your Company	1968	2.00	4.00	8.00
❏ 72824		Always Tomorrow/I Can't Go Wrong	1968	2.00	4.00	8.00
RCA Victor						
❏ 74-0140		Marstrand/The Problem	1969		3.00	6.00
❏ 74-0222		Trixin's Election/A Fairy Tale or Two	1969		3.00	6.00

Keller, Jerry

Number		Title (A Side/B Side)	Year	VG	VG+	NM
Capitol						
❏ 4630		Never Wake Up/ Be Careful How You Drive, Young Joey	1961	3.00	6.00	12.00
❏ 4668		I'll Get By/My Year of Love	1961	3.00	6.00	12.00
Coral						
❏ 62348		It's Too Late/What Will I Tell My Darling	1963	2.50	5.00	10.00
❏ 62361		Sume-Summer/Goodnight Pretty Girl	1963	2.50	5.00	10.00
❏ 62378		Sea Shell Sherry/ What Happens When He Comes Home	1963	2.50	5.00	10.00
❏ 62409		Small Wonder/The Tears Keep Falling Down	1964	2.50	5.00	10.00
Kapp						
❏ 277	M	Here Comes Summer/Time Has a Way	1959	3.75	7.50	15.00
❏ KS-277	S	Here Comes Summer/Time Has a Way	1959	7.50	15.00	30.00
❏ 295		If I Had a Girl/Lovable	1959	3.00	6.00	12.00
❏ 310		Now, Now, Now/There Are Such Things	1959	3.00	6.00	12.00
❏ 322		American Beauty Rose/Lonesome Lullaby	1960	3.00	6.00	12.00
❏ 337		My Name Ain't Joe/White for You and Bless for Me	1960	3.00	6.00	12.00
❏ 353		What More Can I Say/Whole-Heartedly	1960	3.00	6.00	12.00
RCA Victor						
❏ 47-9221		You're Leanin' On My Mind/ My Heart Loves the Samba (Best of All)	1967	2.00	4.00	8.00
Reprise						
❏ 0351		Fickle Finger of Fate/Glory of Love	1965	2.00	4.00	8.00
❏ 0397		Ma (She's Such a Quiet Girl)/The Mack	1965	2.00	4.00	8.00

Kelly Four, The
(Eddie Cochran played guitar)

Number	Title (A Side/B Side)	Year	VG	VG+	NM
Candix					
❏ 325	Annie Had a Party/Sweet Angelina *A-side is an alternate take of Silver 1006*	1961	6.25	12.50	25.00
❏ 325	Annie Had a Party/Sweet Angelina *As "Big Daddy Greenfield"; same recordings as above*	1961	6.25	12.50	25.00
Silver					
❏ 1001	Strollin' Guitar/Guybo *A-side was reissued on Silver 1004 by "Jewel and Eddie"*	1959	10.00	20.00	40.00
❏ 1006	Annie Had a Party/So Fine, Be Mine *A-side was reissued on Crest 1088 by "The Gee Cees"*	1960	10.00	20.00	40.00

Kemper, Jimmy, and the Tiers

Number	Title (A Side/B Side)	Year	VG	VG+	NM
Le Mans					
❏ 002	Lonely for Kathy/I'm Free to Choose	1964	37.50	75.00	150.00

Kendrick, Nat, and the Swans
(James Brown's backing band, later known as the J.B.'s)

Number	Title (A Side/B Side)	Year	VG	VG+	NM
Dade					
❏ 1804	(Do the) Mashed Potatoes (Part 1)/ (Do the) Mashed Potatoes (Part 2)	1960	3.75	7.50	15.00
❏ 1808	Dish Rag (Part 1)/Dish Rag (Part 2)	1960	3.75	7.50	15.00
❏ 1812	Hot Chili/Slow Down	1960	3.75	7.50	15.00
❏ 5003	Wobble Wobble (Part 1)/Wobble Wobble (Part 2)	1961	3.75	7.50	15.00
❏ 5004	(Do the) Mashed Potatoes (Part 1)/(Do the) Mashed Potatoes (Part 2)	1961	3.00	6.00	12.00

Kenner, Chris

Number	Title (A Side/B Side)	Year	VG	VG+	NM
Baton					
❏ 220	Grandma's House/Don't Let Her Pin That Charge	1956	10.00	20.00	40.00
Imperial					
❏ 5448	Sick and Tired/Nothing Will Keep Me from You	1957	6.25	12.50	25.00
❏ 5488	Will You Be Mine/I Have News for You	1958	6.25	12.50	25.00
❏ 5767	Sick and Tired/Nothing Will Keep Me from You	1961	3.00	6.00	12.00
Instant					
❏ 3229	I Like It Like That, Part 1/I Like It Like That, Part 2	1961	3.75	7.50	15.00
❏ 3234	A Very True Story/Packin' Up	1961	3.00	6.00	12.00
❏ 3237	Something You Got/Come See About Me	1961	3.00	6.00	12.00
❏ 3244	How Far/Time	1962	3.00	6.00	12.00
❏ 3247	Let Me Show You How (To Twist)/Johnny Little	1962	3.00	6.00	12.00

Number	Title (A Side/B Side)	Year	VG	VG+	NM
☐ 3252	Land of 1000 Dances/That's My Girl	1962	3.00	6.00	12.00
☐ 3257	Come Back and See/Go Thru Life	1963	3.00	6.00	12.00
☐ 3263	What's Wrong with Life/Never Reach Perfection	1963	3.00	6.00	12.00
☐ 3265	She Can Dance/Anybody Here See My Baby	1964	3.00	6.00	12.00
☐ 3277	I'm Lonely, Take Me/Cinderella	1966	2.50	5.00	10.00
☐ 3280	All Night Rambler, Part 1/All Night Rambler, Part 2	1966	2.50	5.00	10.00
☐ 3283	Shoo Rah/Stretch My Hands to You	1967	2.50	5.00	10.00
☐ 3286	Fumigate Funky Broadway/Wind the Clock	1967	2.50	5.00	10.00
☐ 3290	Memories of a King (Let Freedom Ring), Part 1/Memories of a King (Let Freedom Ring), Part 2	1968	3.00	6.00	12.00
☐ 3293	Mini-Skirts and Soul/Sad Mistake	1968	2.50	5.00	10.00

Ron
| ☐ 335 | Rocket to the Moon/Life's Just a Struggle | 1961 | 3.00 | 6.00 | 12.00 |

Uptown
| ☐ 708 | Life of My Baby/They Took My Money | 1965 | 2.50 | 5.00 | 10.00 |
| ☐ 716 | I'm the Greatest/Get On This Train | 1965 | 2.50 | 5.00 | 10.00 |

Valiant
| ☐ 3229 | I Like It Like That, Part 1/I Like It Like That, Part 2 | 1960 | 10.00 | 20.00 | 40.00 |

Kenny and the Cadets
Randy
☐ 422	Barbie/What Is a Young Man Made Of	1962	100.00	200.00	400.00
	Pink label original (white labels are counterfeits)				
☐ 422	Barbie/What Is a Young Man Made Of	1962	250.00	500.00	1,000
	Red and gold vinyl				

Kenny and the Fiends
Dot
| ☐ 16568 | House on Haunted Hill (Part 1)/House on Haunted Hill (Part 2) | 1963 | 5.00 | 10.00 | 20.00 |
| ☐ 16596 | Moon Shot/One-Two-Three-Four | 1964 | 5.00 | 10.00 | 20.00 |

Posea
☐ 80	The Raven (Part 1)/The Raven (Part 2)	1963	7.50	15.00	30.00
☐ 87	House on Haunted Hill/Green Door	1963	10.00	20.00	40.00
	As "Kenny and the Beach Fiends"				

Princess
| ☐ 51 | House on Haunted Hill (Part 1)/House on Haunted Hill (Part 2) | 1963 | 7.50 | 15.00 | 30.00 |

Kenny and the Kasuals
Mark IV
☐ 911	Nothin' Better to Do/Floatin'	1965	7.50	15.00	30.00
☐ 1002	Don't Let Your Baby Go/(B-side unknown)	1966	7.50	15.00	30.00
☐ 1003	It's All Right/You Make Me Feel So Good	1966	7.50	15.00	30.00
☐ 1004	Strings of Time/(B-side unknown)	1966	7.50	15.00	30.00
☐ 1006	I'm Gonna Make It/Journey to Tyme	1966	10.00	20.00	40.00
☐ 1008	See-Saw Ride/(B-side unknown)	1967	7.50	15.00	30.00

United Artists
| ☐ 50085 | I'm Gonna Make It/Journey to Tyme | 1966 | 5.00 | 10.00 | 20.00 |

Kenny and the Socialites
Crosstown
| ☐ 001 | I'll Have to Decide/King Tut Rock | 1958 | 37.50 | 75.00 | 150.00 |

Kent, Al
Baritone
| ☐ 942 | Hold Me/Tell Me Why | 1960 | 37.50 | 75.00 | 150.00 |

Checker
| ☐ 881 | Dat's Why (I Love You So)/Am I the Man | 1958 | 15.00 | 30.00 | 60.00 |

Ric-Tic
☐ 123	The Way You Been Acting Lately/(Instrumental)	1967	5.00	10.00	20.00
☐ 127	You've Got to Pay the Price/Where Do I Go from Here	1967	5.00	10.00	20.00
☐ 133	Finders Keepers/Ooh! Pretty Lady	1967	5.00	10.00	20.00
☐ 140	Bless You (My Love)/(Instrumental)	1968	3.75	7.50	15.00

Wingate
| ☐ 004 | You Know I Love You/Country Boy | 1965 | 6.25 | 12.50 | 25.00 |

Wizard
| ☐ 100 | Hold Me/You Know Me | 1959 | 25.00 | 50.00 | 100.00 |

Kent, Billy, and the Andantes
Mah's
☐ 000.2	Your Love/Take All of Me	1960	30.00	60.00	120.00
	First pressing, with Detroit address on label				
☐ 000.2	Your Love/Take All of Me	1960	15.00	30.00	60.00
	Second pressing, without address and with Roulette distribution mentioned on label				

Kents, The
Argo
| ☐ 5299 | I Found My Girl/With All My Heart and Soul | 1958 | 7.50 | 15.00 | 30.00 |

Dome
| ☐ 501 | I Love You So/Happy Beat | 1958 | 125.00 | 250.00 | 500.00 |

Number	Title (A Side/B Side)	Year	VG	VG+	NM

Kid, The
Rumble
| ❑ 1347 | Sleep Tight/True Love | 1959 | 45.00 | 90.00 | 180.00 |

Kidd, Johnny, and the Pirates
Apt
| ❑ 25040 | Shakin' All Over/Yes Sir, That's My Baby | 1960 | 6.25 | 12.50 | 25.00 |
Capitol
| ❑ 5065 | I'll Never Get Over You/Then I Got Everything | 1963 | 3.75 | 7.50 | 15.00 |

Kidds, The
Imperial
| ❑ 5335 | Are You Forgetting Me/Drunk, Drunk, Drunk | 1955 | 125.00 | 250.00 | 500.00 |
Post
| ❑ 2003 | You Broke My Heart/I Won't Be Back | 1955 | 75.00 | 150.00 | 300.00 |

Kimberly, Adrian
(Actually Don Everly)
Calliope
❑ 6501	The Graduation Song...Pomp and Circumstance/Black Mountain Stomp	1961	10.00	20.00	40.00
❑ 6503	Greensleeves/God Bless America	1961	10.00	20.00	40.00
❑ 6504	When You Wish Upon a Star/Draggin' Dragon	1961	10.00	20.00	40.00

King Curtis
ABC-Paramount
| ❑ 10133 | Beatnick Hoedown/King Neptune's Guitar | 1960 | 3.75 | 7.50 | 15.00 |
Alcor
| ❑ 1016 | Jay Walk/The Lone Prairie | 1961 | 5.00 | 10.00 | 20.00 |
Apollo
| ❑ 507 | King's Rock/Dynamite at Midnight | 1957 | 7.50 | 15.00 | 30.00 |
Atco
❑ 6114	The Birth of the Blues/Just Smoochin'	1958	5.00	10.00	20.00
❑ 6124	You Made Me Love You/Ific	1958	5.00	10.00	20.00
❑ 6135	Castle Rock/Chili	1959	5.00	10.00	20.00
❑ 6143	Honey Dripper (Part 1)/Honey Dripper (Part 2)	1959	5.00	10.00	20.00
❑ 6152	Heavenly Blues/Restless Guitar	1959	5.00	10.00	20.00
❑ 6387	Spanish Harlem/The Boss	1965	2.50	5.00	10.00
❑ 6406	On Broadway/Quicksand	1966	2.00	4.00	8.00
❑ 6419	Make the World Go Away/You've Lost That Lovin' Feeling	1966	2.00	4.00	8.00
❑ 6429	Dancing in the Streets/He'll Have to Go	1966	2.00	4.00	8.00
❑ 6447	Pots and Pans (Part 1)/Pots and Pans (Part 2)	1966	2.00	4.00	8.00
❑ 6457	Something on Your Mind/Soul Theme	1966	2.00	4.00	8.00
❑ 6476	Jump Back/When Something Is Wrong with My Baby	1967	2.00	4.00	8.00
❑ 6496	You Don't Miss Your Water/Green Onions	1967	2.00	4.00	8.00
❑ 6511	Memphis Soul Stew/Blue Nocturne	1967	2.00	4.00	8.00
❑ 6516	Ode to Billie Joe/In the Pocket	1967	2.00	4.00	8.00
	As "The Kingpins"				
❑ 6534	For What It's Worth/Cook Out	1968	2.00	4.00	8.00
❑ 6547	I Never Loved a Man (The Way I Love You)/I Was Made to Love Her	1968	2.00	4.00	8.00
❑ 6562	(Sittin' On) The Dock of the Bay/This Is Soul	1968	2.00	4.00	8.00
❑ 6582	(Theme from) Valley of the Dolls/Eighth Wonder	1968	2.00	4.00	8.00
❑ 6598	I Heard It Through the Grapevine/Whiter Shade of Pale	1968	2.00	4.00	8.00
❑ 6613	Harper Valley P.T.A./Makin' Hey	1968	2.00	4.00	8.00
❑ 6630	The Christmas Song/What Are You Doing New Year's Eve?	1968	2.00	4.00	8.00
❑ 6664	Games People Play/Foot Pattin' (Part 2)	1969	2.00	4.00	8.00
❑ 6680	Instant Groove/Sweet Inspiration	1969	2.00	4.00	8.00
❑ 6695	Little Green Apples/La Jeanne	1969	2.00	4.00	8.00
❑ 6711	C.C. Rider/Rocky Roll	1969	2.00	4.00	8.00
❑ 6720	Pop Corn Willie/Patty Cake	1969		3.00	6.00
❑ 6738	Soulin'/Teasin'	1970		3.00	6.00
❑ 6762	Get Ready/Bridge Over Troubled Water	1970		3.00	6.00
❑ 6779	Whole Lotta Love/Floatin'	1970		3.00	6.00
❑ 6785	Changes (Part 1)/Changes (Part 2)	1970		3.00	6.00
❑ 6834	Changes (Part 1)/Changes (Part 2)	1971		3.00	6.00
❑ 6908	Ridin' Thumb (Part 1)/Ridin' Thumb (Part 2)	1972		3.00	6.00
Capitol
❑ 4788	Beach Party/Turn 'Em On	1962	2.50	5.00	10.00
❑ 4841	Beautiful Brown Eyes/Your Cheatin' Heart	1962	2.50	5.00	10.00
❑ 4891	Strollin' Home/Mess Around	1962	2.50	5.00	10.00
❑ 4998	Do the Monkey/Feel All Right	1963	2.50	5.00	10.00
❑ 5061	Theme from "Lilies of the Field" (Part 1)/Theme from "Lilies of the Field" (Part 2)	1963	2.50	5.00	10.00
❑ 5109	Soul Serenade/More Soul	1964	2.50	5.00	10.00
❑ 5212	Summer Dream/Melancholy Serenade	1964	2.50	5.00	10.00
❑ 5270	Stranger on the Shore/Hide Away	1964	2.50	5.00	10.00
❑ 5324	Sister Sadie/Tanya	1964	2.50	5.00	10.00
❑ 5377	Bill Bailey/Soul Twine	1965	2.50	5.00	10.00
❑ 5490	The Prance/Slow Drag	1965	2.50	5.00	10.00
DeLuxe
| ❑ 6142 | The Stranger/Steel Guitar Rag | 1957 | 6.25 | 12.50 | 25.00 |
| ❑ 6157 | Wicky Wacky (Part 1)/Wicky Wacky (Part 2) | 1958 | 6.25 | 12.50 | 25.00 |

Number	Title (A Side/B Side)	Year	VG	VG+	NM
Enjoy					
❑ 1000	Soul Twist/Twisting Time	1962	3.75	7.50	15.00
❑ 1001	Twisting with the King/Wobble Twist	1962	3.75	7.50	15.00
Everest					
❑ 19406	Jay Walk/The Lone Prairie	1961	3.75	7.50	15.00
Everlast					
❑ 5030	Soul Twist/Twisting Time	1965	2.50	5.00	10.00
Gem					
❑ 208	Tenor in the Sky/No More Crying on My Pillow	1954	10.00	20.00	40.00
Groove					
❑ 1060	Movin' On/Rockabye Baby	1956	6.25	12.50	25.00
King					
❑ 5647	King Curtis Stomp/Steel Guitar Rag	1962	3.00	6.00	12.00
Monarch					
❑ 702	Wine Head/I've Got News for You Baby	1953	15.00	30.00	60.00
New Jazz					
❑ 45-510	Soul Meeting/All the Way	1961	3.75	7.50	15.00
Seg-Way					
❑ 1006	Hot Rod/Bonaparte's Retreat	1962	3.75	7.50	15.00
Sky Rocket					
❑ 106	Madisonville (Part 1)/Madisonville (Part 2)	1960	5.00	10.00	20.00
Tru Sound					
❑ 401	Trouble in Mind/But That's Alright	1961	3.75	7.50	15.00
❑ 406	Twistin' and Jivin'/I Have to Worry	1961	3.75	7.50	15.00
❑ 412	So Rare/Hucklebuck Twist	1961	3.75	7.50	15.00
❑ 415	Free for All/When the Saints Go Marching In	1962	3.75	7.50	15.00
❑ 422	Low Down/I'll Wait for You	1962	3.75	7.50	15.00

King Pins, The

Number	Title (A Side/B Side)	Year	VG	VG+	NM
Larse					
❑ 101	94 Second Turf/Rod Hot Rod	1966	10.00	20.00	40.00
MGM					
❑ 13535	Rod Hot Rod/Door Banger	1966	7.50	15.00	30.00

King, B.B.

Number	Title (A Side/B Side)	Year	VG	VG+	NM
ABC					
❑ 10856	Don't Answer the Door (Part 1)/Don't Answer the Door (Part 2)	1966	2.00	4.00	8.00
❑ 10889	Waitin' on You/Night Life	1966	2.00	4.00	8.00
❑ 11268	Hummingbird/Ask Me No Questions	1970		2.50	5.00
❑ 11280	Chains and Things/King's Special	1970		2.50	5.00
❑ 11290	Ask Me No Questions/Nobody Loves Me But My Mother	1971		2.50	5.00
❑ 11302	Help the Poor/Lucille's Granny	1971		2.50	5.00
❑ 11310	Ghetto Woman/Seven Minutes	1971		2.50	5.00
❑ 11316	Ain't Nobody Home/Alexi's Boogie	1971		2.50	5.00
❑ 11319	Sweet Sixteen/I've Been Blue Too Long	1972		2.50	5.00
❑ 11321	I Got Some Help I Don't Need/Lucille's Granny	1972		2.50	5.00
❑ 11330	Guess Who/Better Lovin' Man	1972		2.50	5.00
❑ 11339	Summer in the City/Five Long Years	1972		2.50	5.00
❑ 11373	To Know You Is to Love You/I Can't Leave	1973		2.50	5.00
❑ 11406	I Like to Live the Love/Love	1973		2.50	5.00
❑ 11433	Who Are You/On to Me	1974		2.50	5.00
❑ 12029	Philadelphia/Up at 5 A.M.	1974		2.50	5.00
❑ 12053	Friends/My Song	1974		2.50	5.00
❑ 12158	When I'm Wrong/Have Faith	1976		2.50	5.00
❑ 12247	Slow and Easy/I Wonder Why	1977		2.00	4.00
❑ 12380	Never Make a Move Too Soon/Let Me Make You Cry a Little Longer	1978		2.00	4.00
❑ 12412	I Just Can't Leave Your Love Alone/Midnight Believer	1978		2.00	4.00
ABC Impulse					
❑ 31006	Let the Good Times Roll/Strange Things	1976		2.00	4.00
❑ 31009	Everyday I Have the Blues/The Thrill Is Gone	1976		2.00	4.00
Both ABC Impulse singles are with Bobby Bland					
ABC-Paramount					
❑ 10316	I'm Gonna Sit In Till You Give In/You Ask Me	1962	2.50	5.00	10.00
❑ 10334	Blues at Midnight/My Baby's Coming Home	1962	2.50	5.00	10.00
❑ 10361	Chains of Love/Sneakin' Around	1962	2.50	5.00	10.00
❑ 10367	Tomorrow Night/Mother's Love	1962	2.50	5.00	10.00
❑ 10390	Guess Who/By Myself	1962	2.50	5.00	10.00
❑ 10455	On My Word of Honor/Young Dreamers	1963	2.50	5.00	10.00
❑ 10486	How Do I Love You/Slowly Losing My Mind	1963	2.50	5.00	10.00
❑ 10527	How Blue Can You Get/Please Accept My Love	1964	2.00	4.00	8.00
❑ 10552	Help the Poor/I Wouldn't Have It Any Other Way	1964	2.00	4.00	8.00
❑ 10576	Whole Lotta Lovin'/The Hurt	1964	2.00	4.00	8.00
❑ 10597	Never Trust a Woman/Worryin' Blues	1964	2.00	4.00	8.00
❑ 10616	Please Send Me Someone to Love/The Worst Thing in My Life	1965	2.00	4.00	8.00
❑ 10634	Everyday I Have the Blues/It's My Own Fault	1965	2.00	4.00	8.00
❑ 10675	Tired of Your Jive/Night Owl	1965	2.00	4.00	8.00
❑ 10724	All Over Again/The Things You Put Me Through	1965	2.00	4.00	8.00
❑ 10754	Goin' to Chicago Blues/I'd Rather Drink Muddy Water	1965	2.00	4.00	8.00
❑ 10766	Tormented/You're Still a Square	1966	2.00	4.00	8.00

Number		Title (A Side/B Side)	Year	VG	VG+	NM
Bluesway						
☐ 61004		Think It Over/I Don't Want You Cutting Off Your Hair	1967		3.00	6.00
☐ 61007		Worried Dream/That's Wrong, Little Mama	1967		3.00	6.00
☐ 61011		Raining in My Heart/Heartbreaker	1967		3.00	6.00
☐ 61012		Sweet Sixteen (Part 1)/Sweet Sixteen (Part 2)	1968		3.00	6.00
☐ 61015		Paying the Cost to Be the Boss/Having My Say	1968		3.00	6.00
☐ 61018		I'm Gonna Do What They Do to Me/Losing Faith in You	1968		3.00	6.00
☐ 61019		You Put It On Me/B.B. Jones	1968		3.00	6.00
☐ 61021		Dance with Me/Please Send Me Someone to Love	1968		3.00	6.00
☐ 61022		Don't Waste My Time/Get Myself Somebody	1969		3.00	6.00
☐ 61024		Why I Sing the Blues/Friends	1969		3.00	6.00
☐ 61026		Get Off My Back Woman/I Want You So Bad	1969		3.00	6.00
☐ 61029		Just a Little Love/My Mood	1969		3.00	6.00
☐ 61032		The Thrill Is Gone/You're Mean	1969	2.00	4.00	8.00
☐ 61032	PS	The Thrill Is Gone/You're Mean	1969	3.00	6.00	12.00
☐ 61035		So Excited/Confessin' the Blues	1970		3.00	6.00
Kent						
☐ 301		You Know I Go for You/ Why Do Everything Happen to Me	1958	5.00	10.00	20.00
☐ 307		Days of Old/Don't Look Now, But You Got the Blues	1958	5.00	10.00	20.00
☐ 315		Please Accept My Love/You've Been an Angel	1958	6.25	12.50	25.00
		With the Vocal Chords				
☐ 317		Worry Worry/I Am	1959	5.00	10.00	20.00
☐ 319		The Fool/Come By Here	1959	5.00	10.00	20.00
☐ 325		A Lonely Lover's Plea/Woman in Love	1959	5.00	10.00	20.00
☐ 327		Everyday I Have the Blues/Time to Say Goodbye	1959	5.00	10.00	20.00
☐ 329		Sugar Mama/Mean Old Friend	1959	5.00	10.00	20.00
☐ 330		Sweet Sixteen, Pt. 1/Sweet Sixteen, Pt. 2	1960	3.75	7.50	15.00
☐ 333		Got a Right to Love My Baby/My Own Fault	1960	3.75	7.50	15.00
☐ 336		Please Love Me/Crying Won't Help You	1960	3.75	7.50	15.00
☐ 337		Blind Love/You Upset Me Baby	1960	3.75	7.50	15.00
☐ 338		Ten Long Years/Everyday I Have the Blues	1960	3.75	7.50	15.00
☐ 339		Did You Ever Love a Woman/Three O'Clock Blues	1960	3.75	7.50	15.00
☐ 340		Sweet Little Angel/ You Done Lost Your Good Thing Now	1960	3.75	7.50	15.00
☐ 346		Partin' Time/Good Man Gone Bad	1960	3.75	7.50	15.00
☐ 350		Waking Dr. Bill/You Done Lost Your Good Thing Now	1960	3.75	7.50	15.00
☐ 351		Things Are Not the Same/Fishin' After Me	1961	3.75	7.50	15.00
☐ 353		Bad Luck Soul/Get Out of Here	1961	3.75	7.50	15.00
☐ 358		Hold That Train/Understand	1961	3.75	7.50	15.00
☐ 360		Peace of Mind/Someday	1961	3.75	7.50	15.00
☐ 362		You're Breaking My Heart/Bad Case of Love	1961	3.75	7.50	15.00
☐ 365		My Sometime Baby/Lonely	1962	3.00	6.00	12.00
☐ 372		Gonna Miss You Around Here/Hully Gully Twist	1962	3.00	6.00	12.00
☐ 373		3 O'Clock Stomp/Mashed Potato Twist	1962	3.00	6.00	12.00
☐ 381		Tell Me Baby/Mashing the Popeye	1962	3.00	6.00	12.00
☐ 383		Going Down Slow/ When My Heart Beats Like a Hammer	1962	3.00	6.00	12.00
☐ 386		Your Letter/Blues for Me	1962	3.00	6.00	12.00
☐ 387		Christmas Celebration/Easy Listening	1962	3.00	6.00	12.00
☐ 388		Whole Lot of Loving/Down Now	1963	2.50	5.00	10.00
☐ 389		Trouble in Mind/Long Nights	1963	2.50	5.00	10.00
☐ 390		My Reward/The Road I Travel	1963	2.50	5.00	10.00
☐ 391		The Letter/You Never Know	1963	2.50	5.00	10.00
☐ 392		Army of the Lord/Precious Lord	1964	3.75	7.50	15.00
☐ 393		Rock Me Baby/I Can't Lose	1964	2.50	5.00	10.00
☐ 396		Let Me Love You/You're Gonna Miss Me	1964	2.50	5.00	10.00
☐ 403		Beautician Blues/I Can Hear My Name	1964	2.50	5.00	10.00
☐ 412		Christmas Celebration/Easy Listening	1964	2.50	5.00	10.00
☐ 415		Got 'Em Bad/The Worst Thing in My Life	1965	2.50	5.00	10.00
☐ 421		Please Love Me/Baby Look at You	1965	2.50	5.00	10.00
☐ 426		Blue Shadows/And Like That	1965	2.00	4.00	8.00
☐ 429		Just a Dream/Why Do Everything Happen to Me	1965	2.00	4.00	8.00
☐ 435		Mercy, Mercy, Mercy/Broken Promise	1965	2.00	4.00	8.00
☐ 441		Eyesight to the Blind/Just Like a Woman	1966	2.00	4.00	8.00
☐ 445		Five Long Years/Love, Honor and Obey	1966	2.00	4.00	8.00
☐ 447		Ain't Nobody's Business/I Wonder Why	1966	2.00	4.00	8.00
☐ 450		I Stay in the Mood/Early Every Morning	1966	2.00	4.00	8.00
☐ 458		It's a Mean World/Blues Stay Away	1966	2.00	4.00	8.00
☐ 462		The Jungle/Long Gone Baby	1967	2.00	4.00	8.00
☐ 467		Treat Me Right/Who Can Your Good Man Be	1967	2.00	4.00	8.00
☐ 470		Bad Breaks/Growing Old	1967	2.00	4.00	8.00
☐ 475		Sweet Thing/Soul Beat	1967	2.00	4.00	8.00
☐ 484		Worry, Worry, Worry/Why Do Everything Happen to Me	1968		3.00	6.00
☐ 492		The Woman I Love/Blues for Me	1968		3.00	6.00
☐ 499		Slow Burn/3 O'Clock Blues	1968		3.00	6.00
☐ 510		Your Fool/Shoutin' the Blues	1969		3.00	6.00
☐ 4513		I'm Cracking Up Over You/Powerhouse	1969		3.00	6.00
☐ 4515		Dreams/House Rocker	1970		3.00	6.00
☐ 4526		Worried Life/Walkin' Dr. Bill	1970		3.00	6.00
☐ 4542		That Evil Child/Tell Me Baby	1971		3.00	6.00
☐ 4549		I'll Survive/Long Nights	1971		3.00	6.00
☐ 4562		Precious Lord/Swing Low, Sweet Chariot	1972		3.00	6.00
☐ 4566		Don't Get Around Much Anymore/Poontanging	1972		3.00	6.00
☐ 4572		Recession Blues/Walkin' Dr. Bill	1972		3.00	6.00
MCA						
☐ 41062		Happy Birthday Blues/Better Not Look Down	1979		2.00	4.00

Number	Title (A Side/B Side)	Year	VG	VG+	NM
❑ 51101	There Must Be a Better World Somewhere/	1981		2.00	4.00
	You're Going with Me				
❑ 52057	Since I Met You Baby/One of Those Nights	1982			3.00
❑ 52098	Street Life/Overture	1982			3.00
	With the Crusaders and the London Symphony Orchestra				
❑ 52125	Love Me Tender/The World I Never Made	1982			3.00
❑ 52218	Sell My Monkey/Inflation Blues	1983			3.00
❑ 52530	Into the Night/Century City Chase of J.B. in Teheran	1985			3.00
❑ 52574	My Lucille/Keep It Light	1985			3.00
	B-side by Thelma Houston				
❑ 52675	Big Boss Man/My Guitar Sings the Blues	1985			3.00
❑ 52751	Memory Lane/Six Silver Strings	1985			3.00
❑ 53269	(You've Become a) Habit to Me/	1988			3.00
	(You've Become a) Habit to Me (Long)				
❑ 53644	Lay Another Log on the Fire/Go On	1989			3.00
❑ 54339	The Blues Come Over Me	1992		2.00	4.00
	(Wild & Bluesy Club Mix Edit)/The Blues Come Over Me (Integrity Mix)				

RPM

Note: B.B. King singles on RPM before 339 are unconfirmed on 45 rpm

Number	Title (A Side/B Side)	Year	VG	VG+	NM
❑ 339	3 O'Clock Blues/That Ain't the Way to Do It	1951	75.00	150.00	300.00
❑ 348	Fine Lookin' Woman/She Don't Move Me No More	1952	25.00	50.00	100.00
❑ 355	Shake It Up and Go/My Own Fault, Darling	1952	25.00	50.00	100.00
❑ 360	Gotta Find My Baby/Someday Somewhere	1952	20.00	40.00	80.00
❑ 363	You Know I Love You/You Didn't Want Me	1952	20.00	40.00	80.00
❑ 374	Story from My Heart and Soul/Boogie Woogie Woman	1952	20.00	40.00	80.00
❑ 380	Woke Up This Morning (My Baby She Was Gone)/	1953	10.00	20.00	40.00
	Don't Have to Cry				
❑ 386	Please Love Me/Highway Bound	1953	10.00	20.00	40.00
❑ 391	Please Hurry Home/Neighborhood Affair	1953	10.00	20.00	40.00
❑ 395	Why Did You Leave Me/Blind Love	1953	10.00	20.00	40.00
❑ 403	Praying to the Lord/Please Help Me	1954	7.50	15.00	30.00
❑ 408	Love Me Baby/The Woman I Love	1954	7.50	15.00	30.00
❑ 411	Everything I Do Is Wrong/	1954	7.50	15.00	30.00
	Don't You Want a Man Like Me				
❑ 412	When My Heart Beats Like a Hammer/Bye Bye Baby	1954	7.50	15.00	30.00
❑ 416	You Upset Me Baby/Whole Lotta' Love	1954	7.50	15.00	30.00
❑ 421	Every Day I Have the Blues/Sneakin' Around	1955	7.50	15.00	30.00
❑ 425	Lonely and Blue/Jump with You Baby	1955	7.50	15.00	30.00
❑ 430	I'm in Love/Shut Your Mouth	1955	7.50	15.00	30.00
❑ 435	Talkin' the Blues/Boogie Rock	1955	7.50	15.00	30.00
❑ 437	Ten Long Years/What Can I Do	1955	7.50	15.00	30.00
❑ 450	I'm Cracking Up Over You/Ruby Lee	1956	6.25	12.50	25.00
❑ 451	Crying Won't Help You/Sixteen Tons	1956	6.25	12.50	25.00
❑ 451	Crying Won't Help You/Can't We Talk It Over	1956	6.25	12.50	25.00
❑ 457	Did You Ever Love a Woman/Let's Do the Boogie	1956	6.25	12.50	25.00
❑ 459	Dark Is the Night (Part 1)/Dark Is the Night (Part 2)	1956	6.25	12.50	25.00
❑ 468	Bad Luck/Sweet Little Angel	1956	6.25	12.50	25.00
❑ 479	On My Word of Honor/Bim Bam	1956	6.25	12.50	25.00
❑ 486	You Don't Know/Early in the Morning	1957	6.25	12.50	25.00
❑ 490	How Do I Love You/You Can't Fool My Heart	1957	6.25	12.50	25.00
❑ 492	Troubles, Troubles, Troubles/I Want to Get Married	1957	6.25	12.50	25.00
❑ 494	Quit My Baby/Be Careful with a Fool	1957	6.25	12.50	25.00
❑ 498	I Wonder/I Need You So Bad	1957	6.25	12.50	25.00
❑ 501	The Key to My Kingdom/My Heart Belongs to Only You	1957	6.25	12.50	25.00

King, Ben E.
(Of the second version of The Drifters)

Atco

Number	Title (A Side/B Side)	Year	VG	VG+	NM
❑ 6166	Show Me the Way/Brace Yourself	1960	4.00	8.00	16.00
❑ 6185	Spanish Harlem/First Taste of Love	1960	5.00	10.00	20.00
❑ 6194	Stand By Me/On the Horizon	1961	5.00	10.00	20.00
❑ 6203	Amor/Souvenir of Mexico	1961	4.00	8.00	16.00
❑ 6207	Young Boy Blues/Here Comes the Night	1961	4.00	8.00	16.00
❑ 6215	Ecstasy/Yes	1962	4.00	8.00	16.00
❑ 6222	Don't Play That Song (You Lied)/	1962	4.00	8.00	16.00
	Hermit of Misty Mountain				
❑ 6231	Too Bad/My Heart Cries for You	1962	3.00	6.00	12.00
❑ 6237	I'm Standing By/Walking in the Footsteps of a Fool	1962	3.00	6.00	12.00
❑ 6246	Tell Daddy/Auf Wiedersehn	1962	3.00	6.00	12.00
❑ 6256	How Can I Forget/Gloria Gloria	1963	3.00	6.00	12.00
❑ 6267	I (Who Have Nothing)/The Beginning of Time	1963	3.00	6.00	12.00
❑ 6275	I Could Have Danced All Night/Gypsy	1963	3.00	6.00	12.00
❑ 6284	What Now My Love/Groovin'	1964	2.50	5.00	10.00
❑ 6288	That's When It Hurts/Around the Corner	1964	2.50	5.00	10.00
❑ 6303	What Can a Man Do/Si, Senor	1964	2.50	5.00	10.00
❑ 6315	It's All Over/Let the Water Run Down	1964	2.50	5.00	10.00
❑ 6328	Seven Letters/River of Tears	1964	2.50	5.00	10.00
❑ 6343	The Record (Baby I Love You)/The Way You Shake It	1965	2.50	5.00	10.00
❑ 6357	She's Gone Again/Not Now (I'll Tell You When)	1965	2.50	5.00	10.00
❑ 6371	Cry No More/There's No Place to Hide	1965	2.50	5.00	10.00
❑ 6390	Goodnight My Love/I Can't Break the News to Myself	1965	2.50	5.00	10.00
❑ 6413	So Much Love/Don't Drive Me Away	1966	2.00	4.00	8.00
❑ 6431	Get in a Hurry/I Swear by the Stars Above	1966	2.00	4.00	8.00
❑ 6454	They Don't Give Medals to Yesterday's Heroes/	1966	2.00	4.00	8.00
	What Is Soul				
❑ 6472	A Man Without a Dream/Tears, Tears, Tears	1967	2.00	4.00	8.00
❑ 6493	Katherine/Teeny Weeny Little Bit	1967	2.00	4.00	8.00

Number		Title (A Side/B Side)	Year	VG	VG+	NM
❏ 6527		Don't Take Your Sweet Love Away/ She Knows What to Do for Me	1967	2.50	5.00	10.00
❏ 6557		We Got a Thing Goin' On/What 'Cha Gonna Do About It With Dee Dee Sharp	1968	2.00	4.00	8.00
❏ 6571		Don't Take Your Love from Me/Forgive This Soul	1968	2.00	4.00	8.00
❏ 6596		Where's the Girl/It's Amazing	1968	2.00	4.00	8.00
❏ 6637		It Ain't Fair/Till I Can't Take It Anymore	1968	2.00	4.00	8.00
❏ 6666		Hey Little One/When You Love Someone	1969	2.50	5.00	10.00

Atlantic

❏ 3241		Supernatural Thing -- Part 1/ Supernatural Thing -- Part 2	1975		2.50	5.00
❏ 3274		Do It in the Name of Love/Imagination	1975		2.50	5.00
❏ 3308		We Got Love/I Had a Love	1975		2.50	5.00
❏ 3337		I Betch'a You Didn't Know/Smooth Sailing	1976		2.50	5.00
❏ 3359		One More Time/Somebody's Knocking	1976		2.50	5.00
❏ 3402		Get It Up/Keepin' It To Myself With the Average White Band	1977		2.50	5.00
❏ 3427		A Star in the Ghetto/What Is Soul? With the Average White Band	1977		2.50	5.00
❏ 3444		Fool for You Anyway/The Message With the Average White Band	1977		2.50	5.00
❏ 3494		I See the Light/Tippin'	1978		2.50	5.00
❏ 3535		Fly Away to My Wonderland/Spoiled	1978		2.50	5.00
❏ 3635		Music Trance/And This Is Love	1979		2.00	4.00
❏ 3808		Street Tough/Why Is the Question	1981		2.00	4.00
❏ 3839		You Made the Difference in My Life/Souvenirs of Love	1981		2.00	4.00
❏ 89234		Spanish Harlem/First Taste of Love	1987			3.00
❏ 89361	DJ	Stand By Me Medley (same on both sides)	1986	2.00	4.00	8.00

Contains excerpts from all 10 songs on the "Stand By Me" soundtrack album. It is listed here because it uses the same number as the stock release of "Stand By Me."

❏ 89361	PS	Stand By Me Medley	1986	2.00	4.00	8.00

Promo-only sleeve accompanying above medley. Stock and promo sleeves are identical in front but different on back.

❏ 89361		Stand By Me/Yakety Yak	1986			3.00

B-side by the Coasters

❏ 89361	PS	Stand By Me/Yakety Yak	1986			3.00

Ichiban

❏ 254		You've Got All of Me/It's All Right	1992			3.00
❏ 257		You Still Move Me/I'm Gonna Be Somebody	1992			3.00

Mandala

❏ 2512		Take Me to the Pilot/I Guess It's Goodbye	1972		2.50	5.00
❏ 2513		Into the Mystic/White Moon	1972		2.50	5.00
❏ 2518		Spread Myself Around/Travellin' Woman	1973		2.50	5.00

Maxwell

❏ 800		I Can't Take It Like a Man/(B-side unknown)	1969	2.00	4.00	8.00

King, Carole
(Also see "City, The"; "Dache, Bertell")

ABC-Paramount

❏ 9921		Goin' Wild/The Right Girl	1958	37.50	75.00	150.00
❏ 9986		Baby Sittin'/Under the Stars	1958	37.50	75.00	150.00

Alpine

❏ 57		Oh, Neil/A Very Special Boy	1959	100.00	200.00	400.00

Atlantic

❏ 4026		One to One/(B-side unknown)	1982		2.00	4.00
❏ 4026	PS	One to One/(B-side unknown)	1982		2.50	5.00
❏ 4062		Read Between the Lines/Life Without Love	1982		2.00	4.00
❏ 89694	DJ	Spending Time (same on both sides) May be promo only	1984		2.00	4.00
❏ 89756		Crying in the Rain/Sacred Heart of Stone	1983		2.00	4.00

Capitol

❏ 4455		Hard Rock Cafe/To Know That I Love You	1977		2.00	4.00
❏ 4455	PS	Hard Rock Cafe/To Know That I Love You	1977		2.50	5.00
❏ 4497		Simple Things/Hold On	1977		2.00	4.00
❏ 4593		Main Street Saturday Night/Changes	1978		2.00	4.00
❏ 4649		Sunbird/Morning Sun	1978		2.00	4.00
❏ 4718		Move Lightly/Whiskey	1979		2.00	4.00
❏ 4766		Time Gone By/Dreamlike I Wander	1979		2.00	4.00
❏ 4864		One Fine Day/Rulers of This World	1980		2.00	4.00
❏ 4864	PS	One Fine Day/Recipients of History	1980	2.00	4.00	8.00

First pressing sleeves list the wrong title for the B-side (no records are known to exist with this title)

❏ 4864	PS	One Fine Day/Rulers of This World	1980		2.00	4.00

Second pressing sleeves don't list a B-side at all

❏ 4911		The Locomotion/Oh No Not My Baby	1980		2.00	4.00
❏ 4941		Chains/Bad Girl	1980		2.00	4.00
❏ B-44336		City Streets/Time Heals All Wounds	1989			3.00
❏ B-44336	PS	City Streets/Time Heals All Wounds	1989			3.00
❏ 7PRO-79520	DJ	City Streets (same on both sides)	1989		2.00	4.00
❏ 7PRO-79520	PS	City Streets (same on both sides)	1989		2.00	4.00

Companion

❏ 2000		It Might As Well Rain Until September/ Nobody's Perfect	1962	37.50	75.00	150.00

Number		Title (A Side/B Side)	Year	VG	VG+	NM
Dimension						
❑ 1004		School Bells Are Ringing/I Didn't Have Any	1962	5.00	10.00	20.00
❑ 1009		He's a Bad Boy/We Grew Up Together	1963	5.00	10.00	20.00
❑ 2000		It Might As Well Rain Until September/Nobody's Perfect	1962	3.00	6.00	12.00
Ode						
❑ 66006		Eventually/Up On the Roof	1970	2.00	4.00	8.00
❑ 66015		It's Too Late/I Feel the Earth Move	1971		2.00	4.00
❑ 66015	PS	It's Too Late/I Feel the Earth Move	1971		2.50	5.00
❑ 66019		So Far Away/Smackwater Jack	1971		2.00	4.00
❑ 66019	PS	So Far Away/Smackwater Jack	1971		2.50	5.00
❑ 66022		Sweet Seasons/Pocket Money	1971		2.00	4.00
❑ 66022	PS	Sweet Seasons/Pocket Money	1971		2.50	5.00
❑ 66026		It's Going to Take Some Time/Brother Brother	1972		3.00	6.00
❑ 66031		Been to Canaan/Bitter with the Sweet	1972		2.00	4.00
❑ 66031	PS	Been to Canaan/Bitter with the Sweet	1972		2.50	5.00
❑ 66035		Believe in Humanity/You Light Up My Life	1973		2.00	4.00
❑ 66035	PS	Believe in Humanity/You Light Up My Life	1973		2.50	5.00
❑ 66039		Corazon/That's How Things Go Down	1973		2.00	4.00
❑ 66047		Jazzman/You Go Your Way, I'll Go Mine	1974		2.50	5.00
❑ 66047	PS	Jazzman/You Go Your Way, I'll Go Mine	1974		3.00	6.00
❑ 66101		Jazzman/You Go Your Way, I'll Go Mine	1974		2.00	4.00
❑ 66101	PS	Jazzman/You Go Your Way, I'll Go Mine	1974		2.50	5.00
❑ 66106		Nightingale/You're Something New	1975		2.00	4.00
❑ 66112 SP		Chicken Soup with Rice/Pierre	1975	2.00	4.00	8.00
33 1/3 rpm 7-inch record						
❑ 66112 SP	PS	Chicken Soup with Rice/Pierre	1975	2.50	5.00	10.00
❑ 66119		Only Love Is Real/Still Here Thinking of You	1976		2.00	4.00
❑ 66123		High Out of Time/I'd Like to Know You Better	1976		2.00	4.00
RCA Victor						
❑ 47-7560		Short Mort/Queen of the Beach	1959	20.00	40.00	80.00
Tomorrow						
❑ 7502		A Road to Nowhere/Some of Your Lovin'	1966	10.00	20.00	40.00

King, Curtis
(No, not King Curtis...)

Number		Title (A Side/B Side)	Year	VG	VG+	NM
Columbia						
❑ 44096		Bad Habits/So Nice While It Lasted	1967	5.00	10.00	20.00

Kingsmen, The
(At least two different groups. The EastWest band comprises some of Bill Haley's Comets)

Number		Title (A Side/B Side)	Year	VG	VG+	NM
All Star						
❑ 500		Guardian Angel/I'm Your Lover Man	1957	20.00	40.00	80.00
Arnold						
❑ 2106		Goodnight Sweetheart/Humpty Dumpty	196?	30.00	60.00	120.00
Capitol						
❑ 3576		You Better Do Right/Today	1973		2.50	5.00
EastWest						
❑ 115		Week End/Better Believe It	1958	10.00	20.00	40.00
❑ 120		Conga Rock/The Cat Walk	1958	10.00	20.00	40.00
Jalynne						
❑ 108		Ladies Choice/Dig This	1960	5.00	10.00	20.00
Jerden						
❑ 712		Louie Louie/Haunted Castle	1963	15.00	30.00	60.00
Neil						
❑ 102		One Foolish Mistake/Stranded Love	1956	15.00	30.00	60.00
Wand						
❑ 143		Louie, Louie/Haunted Castle	1963	5.00	10.00	20.00
❑ 143		Louie Louie 64-65-66.../Haunted Castle	1966	3.75	7.50	15.00
❑ 150		Money/Bent Scepter	1964	3.00	6.00	12.00
❑ 157		Little Latin Lupe Lu/David's Mood	1964	2.50	5.00	10.00
❑ 164		Death of an Angel/Searchin' for Love	1964	2.50	5.00	10.00
❑ 172		The Jolly Green Giant/Long Green	1965	3.00	6.00	12.00
❑ 183		The Climb/I'm Waiting	1965	2.50	5.00	10.00
❑ 189		Annie Fanny/Give Her Lovin'	1965	2.50	5.00	10.00
❑ 1107		(You Got) Gamma Goochie/It's Only the Dog	1965	3.75	7.50	15.00
❑ 1115		Killer Joe/Little Green Thing	1966	3.75	7.50	15.00
❑ 1118		The Krunch/The Climb	1966	3.75	7.50	15.00
❑ 1118	PS	The Krunch/The Climb	1966	6.25	12.50	25.00
❑ 1127		My Wife Can't Dance/Little Sally Tease	1966	2.50	5.00	10.00
❑ 1137		If I Need Someone/The Grass Is Green	1966	2.50	5.00	10.00
❑ 1147		Trouble/Daytime Shadows	1967	2.00	4.00	8.00
❑ 1154		The Wolf of Manhattan/Children's Caretaker	1967	2.00	4.00	8.00
❑ 1157		(I Have Found) Another Girl/Don't Say No	1967	2.00	4.00	8.00
❑ 1164		Bo Diddley Bach/Just Before the Break of Day	1968	2.00	4.00	8.00
❑ 1174		Get Out of My Life Woman/Since You've Been Gone	1968	2.00	4.00	8.00
❑ 1180		I Guess I Was Dreamin'/Oh Love	1968	2.00	4.00	8.00

Kingston Trio, The
(Also see "Guard, Dave")

Number		Title (A Side/B Side)	Year	VG	VG+	NM
Capitol						
❑ PRO 856	DJ	The Merry Minuet/Tick, Tick, Tick	1959	10.00	20.00	40.00
❑ 2006/7	DJ	Farewell Adelita/Corey, Corey	1960	3.75	7.50	15.00

Number			Title (A Side/B Side)	Year	VG	VG+	NM
❏ 2006/7		PS	Farewell Adelita/Corey, Corey	1960	6.25	12.50	25.00
			Promo item for Welgrume Sportswear				
❏ 2782/3		DJ	Molly Dee/Haul Away	1959	3.75	7.50	15.00
❏ 2782/3		PS	Molly Dee/Haul Away	1959	6.25	12.50	25.00
			Promo item for "The New March of Dimes"				
❏ 3149			Tell the Riverboat Captain/Windy Wakefield	1971	2.50	5.00	10.00
			As "The New Kingston Trio"				
❏ F3970			Scarlet Ribbons (For Her Hair)/Three Jolly Coachmen	1958	5.00	10.00	20.00
❏ F4049			Tom Dooley/Ruby Red	1958	6.25	12.50	25.00
❏ F4114			Raspberries, Strawberries/Sally	1959	5.00	10.00	20.00
❏ F4167	M		The Tijuana Jail/Oh Cindy	1959	5.00	10.00	20.00
❏ SF4167	S		The Tijuana Jail/Oh Cindy	1959	12.50	25.00	50.00
❏ F4221			M.T.A./All My Sorrows	1959	5.00	10.00	20.00
❏ F4271			A Worried Man/San Miguel	1959	5.00	10.00	20.00
❏ 4303			Coo Coo-U/Green Grasses	1959	3.75	7.50	15.00
❏ 4338			El Matador/Home from the Hill	1960	3.75	7.50	15.00
❏ 4338		PS	El Matador/Home from the Hill	1960	7.50	15.00	30.00
❏ 4379			Bad Man Blunder/Escape of Old John Webb	1960	3.75	7.50	15.00
❏ 4441			Everglades/This Mornin', This Evenin', So Soon	1960	3.75	7.50	15.00
❏ 4475			Somerset Gloucestershire Wassail/Goodnight My Baby	1960	3.75	7.50	15.00
❏ 4536			You're Gonna Miss Me/En El Aqua	1961	3.75	7.50	15.00
❏ 4642			Coming from the Mountains/ Nothing More to Look Forward To	1961	3.75	7.50	15.00
❏ 4671			Where Have All the Flowers Gone/O Ken Karanga	1961	3.75	7.50	15.00
❏ 4740			Scotch and Soda/Jane, Jane, Jane	1962	2.50	5.00	10.00
❏ 4740		PS	Scotch and Soda/Jane, Jane, Jane	1962	7.50	15.00	30.00
❏ 4808			Old Joe Clark/C'mon Betty Home	1962	2.50	5.00	10.00
❏ 4842			One More Town/She Was Too Good to Me	1962	2.50	5.00	10.00
❏ 4842		PS	One More Town/She Was Too Good to Me	1962	7.50	15.00	30.00
❏ 4898			Greenback Dollar/New Frontier	1963	2.50	5.00	10.00
❏ 4951			Reverend Mr. Black/One More Round	1963	2.50	5.00	10.00
❏ 5005			Desert Pete/Ballad of the Thresher	1963	2.50	5.00	10.00
❏ 5078			Ally Ally Oxen Free/Marcelle Vanine	1963	2.50	5.00	10.00
❏ 5132			Last Night I Had the Strangest Dream/Patriot Game	1964	2.50	5.00	10.00
❏ 5166			Seasons in the Sun/If You Don't Look Around	1964	2.50	5.00	10.00

Decca

Number			Title (A Side/B Side)	Year	VG	VG+	NM
❏ 31702			My Ramblin' Boy/Hope You Understand	1964	3.75	7.50	15.00
❏ 31702		PS	My Ramblin' Boy/Hope You Understand	1964	6.25	12.50	25.00
❏ 31730			Little Play Soldiers/I'm Going Home	1965	2.50	5.00	10.00
❏ 31790			Stay Awhile/Yes I Can Feel It	1965	2.50	5.00	10.00
❏ 31790		PS	Stay Awhile/Yes I Can Feel It	1965	6.25	12.50	25.00
❏ 31860			The Runaway Song/Parchment Farm (Blues)	1965	2.50	5.00	10.00
❏ 31922			Norwegian Wood/Put Your Money Away	1966	2.50	5.00	10.00
❏ 31961			The Spinnin' of the World/A Little Soul Is Born	1966	2.50	5.00	10.00
❏ 32010			Lock All the Windows/Hit and Run	1966	2.50	5.00	10.00
❏ 32040			Babe, You've Been On My Mind/ Texas Across the River	1966	2.50	5.00	10.00

Mountain Creek

Number		Title (A Side/B Side)	Year	VG	VG+	NM
❏ 301/2		Big Ship Glory/Johnson Party of Four	1977	6.25	12.50	25.00

Nautilus

Number		Title (A Side/B Side)	Year	VG	VG+	NM
❏ NR2-45		Aspen Gold/Longest Beer of the Night	1979		2.50	5.00

Tetragrammaton

Number		Title (A Side/B Side)	Year	VG	VG+	NM
❏ 1526		One Too Many Mornings/Scotch and Soda	1969	2.50	5.00	10.00

Xeres

Number			Title (A Side/B Side)	Year	VG	VG+	NM
❏ 10004			Looking for the Sunshine/Reverend Mr. Black	1982		2.00	4.00
❏ 10004		PS	Looking for the Sunshine/Reverend Mr. Black	1982		2.00	4.00

Kinks, The
(Also see "Davies, Dave")

Arista

Number			Title (A Side/B Side)	Year	VG	VG+	NM
❏ 0240			Sleepwalker/Full Moon	1977		2.00	4.00
❏ 0247			Life Goes On/Juke Box Music	1977		2.00	4.00
❏ 0296			Father Christmas/Prince of the Punks	1977		2.50	5.00
❏ 0296		PS	Father Christmas/Prince of the Punks	1977		2.50	5.00
❏ 0342			A Rock and Roll Fantasy/Permanent Wave	1978		2.00	4.00
❏ 0342			A Rock and Roll Fantasy/Artificial Light	1978		2.00	4.00
❏ 0342			A Rock and Roll Fantasy/Get Up	1978		2.00	4.00
			We're not sure in what order these B-sides were released. Please advise.				
❏ 0372			Black Messiah/Live Life	1978		2.00	4.00
❏ 0409			Superman/Party Line	1979		2.50	5.00
			Originals do not have subtitle on A-side				
❏ 0409			(Wish I Could Fly Like) Superman/Party Line	1979		2.00	4.00
			Second pressings add subtitle on A-side				
❏ 0448			Low Budget/A Gallon of Gas	1979		2.00	4.00
❏ 0458			Catch Me Now I'm Falling/Low Budget	1979		2.00	4.00
❏ 0541			Lola/Celluloid Heroes	1980		2.00	4.00
❏ 0541		PS	Lola/Celluloid Heroes	1980		2.50	5.00
❏ 0577			You Really Got Me/Attitude	1980		2.00	4.00
❏ 0619			Destroyer/Back to Back	1981		2.00	4.00
❏ 0649			Better Things/Yo-Yo	1981		2.00	4.00
❏ 1054			Come Dancing/Noise	1983		2.00	4.00
❏ 1054		PS	Come Dancing/Noise	1983		2.00	4.00
❏ 9016			Come Dancing/Noise	1983			3.00
❏ 9016		PS	Come Dancing/Noise	1983			3.00

Number		Title (A Side/B Side)	Year	VG	VG+	NM
❑ 9075		Don't Forget to Dance/Young Conservatives	1983			3.00
❑ 9309		Do It Again/Guilty	1984			3.00
❑ 9309	PS	Do It Again/Guilty	1984			3.00
❑ 9334		Summer's Gone/Going Solo	1985			3.00

Cameo

Number		Title (A Side/B Side)	Year	VG	VG+	NM
❑ 308		Long Tall Sally/I Took My Baby Home	1964	100.00	200.00	400.00
❑ 345		Long Tall Sally/I Took My Baby Home	1965	50.00	100.00	200.00
❑ 348		You Still Want Me/You Do Something to Me	1965			

Can someone truly confirm or deny that this exists, either as a stock or promo? Debates have raged for over 20 years!

MCA

Number		Title (A Side/B Side)	Year	VG	VG+	NM
❑ 52960		Rock 'N' Roll Cities/Sleazy Town	1986			3.00
❑ 52960	PS	Rock 'N' Roll Cities/Sleazy Town	1986			3.00
❑ 53015		Lost and Found/Killing Time	1987			3.00
❑ 53015	PS	Lost and Found/Killing Time	1987			3.00
❑ 53093		Working at the Factory/How Are You	1987	2.50	5.00	10.00
❑ 53699		How Do I Get Close/War Is Over	1989	2.50	5.00	10.00

RCA Victor

Number		Title (A Side/B Side)	Year	VG	VG+	NM
❑ 74-0620		20th Century Man/Skin and Bones	1971	2.00	4.00	8.00
❑ 74-0807		Supersonic Rocket Ship/You Don't Know My Name	1972	2.00	4.00	8.00
❑ 74-0852		Celluloid Heroes/Hot Potatoes	1972	2.00	4.00	8.00
❑ 74-0940		One of the Survivors/Scrap Heap City	1973	50.00	100.00	200.00

Released with acoustic versions of the two songs rather than the LP versions and quickly deleted

Number		Title (A Side/B Side)	Year	VG	VG+	NM
❑ APBO-0275		Money Talks/Here Comes Flash	1974	2.50	5.00	10.00
❑ LPBO-5001		Sitting in the Midday Sun/Sweet Lady Genevieve	1973	2.50	5.00	10.00
❑ PB-10019		Mirror of Love/It's Evil	1974		3.00	6.00
❑ PB-10121		Preservation/Salvation Road	1974		3.00	6.00
❑ PB-10251		Starmaker/Ordinary People	1975		3.00	6.00
❑ PB-10551		I'm in Disgrace/The Hard Way	1976		3.00	6.00

Reprise

Number		Title (A Side/B Side)	Year	VG	VG+	NM
❑ 0306		You Really Got Me/It's All Right	1964	6.25	12.50	25.00

Originals have peach labels

Number		Title (A Side/B Side)	Year	VG	VG+	NM
❑ 0306		You Really Got Me/It's All Right	1964	3.75	7.50	15.00

Second pressings have orange and brown labels

Number		Title (A Side/B Side)	Year	VG	VG+	NM
❑ 0334		All Day and All of the Night/I Gotta Move	1964	3.75	7.50	15.00
❑ 0347		Tired of Waiting for You/Come On Now	1965	3.75	7.50	15.00
❑ 0366		Who'll Be the Next in Line/Everybody's Gonna Be Happy	1965	3.75	7.50	15.00
❑ 0379		Set Me Free/I Need You	1965	3.75	7.50	15.00
❑ 0409		See My Friends/Never Met a Girl Like You Before	1965	3.75	7.50	15.00
❑ 0420		A Well Repected Man/Such a Shame	1965	3.75	7.50	15.00
❑ 0454		Till the End of the Day/Where Have All the Good Times Gone	1966	3.75	7.50	15.00
❑ 0471		Dedicated Follower of Fashion/Sittin' on My Sofa	1966	3.75	7.50	15.00
❑ 0497		Sunny Afternoon/I'm Not Like Everybody Else	1966	3.75	7.50	15.00
❑ 0540		Dead End Street/Big Black Smoke	1966	10.00	20.00	40.00
❑ 0587		Mr. Pleasant/Harry Rag	1967	10.00	20.00	40.00
❑ 0612		Waterloo Sunset/Two Sisters	1967	10.00	20.00	40.00
❑ 0647		Autumn Almanac/David Watts	1967	10.00	20.00	40.00
❑ 0691		Wonderboy/Polly	1968	10.00	20.00	40.00
❑ 0708		Sunny Afternoon/Dead End Street	1968	2.50	5.00	10.00
❑ 0712		Dedicated Follower of Fashion/Who'll Be the Next in Line	1968	2.50	5.00	10.00
❑ 0715		A Well Respected Man/Set Me Free	1968	2.50	5.00	10.00
❑ 0719		Tired of Waiting for You/All Day and All of the Night	1968	2.50	5.00	10.00
❑ 0722		You Really Got Me/It's All Right	1968	2.50	5.00	10.00

0708 through 0722 are "Back to Back Hits" series -- originals have both "r:" and "W7" on label

Number		Title (A Side/B Side)	Year	VG	VG+	NM
❑ 0743		Lola/Apeman	1972		2.50	5.00

"Back to Back Hits" series

Number		Title (A Side/B Side)	Year	VG	VG+	NM
❑ 0762		Days/She's Got Everything	1968	10.00	20.00	40.00
❑ 0806		Starstruck/Picture Book	1969	10.00	20.00	40.00
❑ 0847		The Village Green Preservation Society/Do You Remember Walter	1969	10.00	20.00	40.00
❑ 0863		Victoria/Brainwashed	1969	3.75	7.50	15.00
❑ 0930		Lola/Mindless Child of Motherhood	1970	2.50	5.00	10.00
❑ 0979		Apeman/Rats	1970	2.50	5.00	10.00
❑ 1017		God's Children/The Way Love Used to Be	1971	5.00	10.00	20.00
❑ 1094		King Kong/Waterloo Sunset	1972	3.75	7.50	15.00

Kippington Lodge
(With Nick Lowe)

Capitol

Number		Title (A Side/B Side)	Year	VG	VG+	NM
❑ 2236		And She Cried/Rumors	1968	7.50	15.00	30.00

Kiss
(Also see "Simmons, Gene"; "Stanley, Paul")

Casablanca

Number		Title (A Side/B Side)	Year	VG	VG+	NM
❑ 0004		Love Theme from Kiss/Nothin' to Lose	1974	3.00	6.00	12.00
❑ 0011		Kissin' Time/Nothin' to Lose	1974	3.00	6.00	12.00
❑ 0015		Strutter/100,000 Years	1974	3.00	6.00	12.00
❑ 823		Let Me Go, Rock and Roll/Hotter Than Hell	1975	3.00	6.00	12.00
❑ 829		Rock and Roll All Nite/Getaway	1975	3.00	6.00	12.00
❑ 841		C'mon and Love Me/Getaway	1975	3.00	6.00	12.00
❑ 850		Rock and Roll All Nite (Live)/Rock and Roll All Night (Studio)	1975	2.50	5.00	10.00

Number		Title (A Side/B Side)	Year	VG	VG+	NM
❑ 854		Shout It Out Loud/Sweet Pain	1976	2.50	5.00	10.00
❑ 858		Flaming Youth/God of Thunder	1976	2.50	5.00	10.00
❑ 858	PS	Flaming Youth/God of Thunder	1976	15.00	30.00	60.00
❑ 863		Detroit Rock City/Beth	1976	2.50	5.00	10.00
		With "Detroit Rock City" listed as "Side A"				
❑ 863		Beth/Detroit Rock City	1976		2.50	5.00
		With "Beth" listed as "Side A"				
❑ 873		Hard Luck Woman/Mr. Speed	1976		3.00	6.00
❑ 880		Calling Dr. Love/Take Me	1977		3.00	6.00
❑ 889		Christine Sixteen/Shock Me	1977		3.00	6.00
❑ 895		Love Gun/Hooligan	1977		3.00	6.00
❑ 906		Shout It Out Loud (Live)/Nothin' to Lose	1977		3.00	6.00
❑ 915		Rocket Ride/Tomorrow and Tonight	1978		3.00	6.00
❑ 928		Strutter '78/Shock Me	1978		3.00	6.00
❑ 983		I Was Made for Lovin' You/Hard Times	1979		2.50	5.00
❑ 2205		Sure Know Something/Dirty Livin'	1979		2.50	5.00
❑ 2282		Shandi/She's So European	1980		2.50	5.00
❑ 2299		Tomorrow/Naked City	1980		2.50	5.00
❑ 2343		A World Without Heroes/Dark Light	1981		2.50	5.00
❑ 2365		I Love It Loud/Danger	1982		2.50	5.00
❑ 2365	PS	I Love It Loud/Danger	1982	5.00	10.00	20.00
Mercury						
❑ 814 671-7		Lick It Up/Dance All Over Your Face	1983		2.00	4.00
❑ 818 214-7		Young and Wasted/All Hell Is Breaking Loose	1984		2.00	4.00
❑ 858 894-7		Detroit Rock City/Detroit Rock City	1994		2.00	4.00
		B-side by Mighty Mighty Bosstones; small center hole; green vinyl				
❑ 858 894-7	PS	Detroit Rock City/Detroit Rock City	1994		2.00	4.00
❑ 870 022-7		Reason to Live/Thief in the Night	1987		2.00	4.00
❑ 870 022-7	PS	Reason to Live/Thief in the Night	1987		2.50	5.00
❑ 870 215-7		Turn On the Night/Hell or High Water	1988		2.00	4.00
❑ 870 215-7	PS	Turn On the Night/Hell or High Water	1988		2.50	5.00
❑ 872 244-7		Let's Put the X in Sex/Calling Dr. Love	1989		2.50	5.00
❑ 872 244-7	PS	Let's Put the X in Sex/Calling Dr. Love	1989		3.00	6.00
❑ 876 146-7		Hide Your Heart/Betrayed	1989		2.50	5.00
❑ 876 716-7		Forever/The Street Giveth and the Street Taketh Away	1990		2.50	5.00
❑ 880 205-7		Heaven's on Fire/Lonely Is the Hunter	1984		2.00	4.00
❑ 880 535-7		Thrills in the Night/Burn Bitch Burn	1985		2.00	4.00
❑ 884 141-7		Tears Are Falling/Any Way You Slice It	1985		2.00	4.00
❑ 884 141-7	PS	Tears Are Falling/Any Way You Slice It	1985		2.50	5.00
❑ 888 796-7		Crazy Crazy Nights/No, No, No	1987		2.00	4.00
❑ 888 796-7	PS	Crazy Crazy Nights/No, No, No	1987		2.50	5.00

Klein, George
Sun

Number		Title (A Side/B Side)	Year	VG	VG+	NM
❑ 358		U.T. Party (Part 1)/U.T. Party (Part 2)	1961	5.00	10.00	20.00

Knickerbockers, The
Challenge

Number		Title (A Side/B Side)	Year	VG	VG+	NM
❑ 59268		All I Need Is You/Bite, Bite Barracuda	1965	10.00	20.00	40.00
❑ 59293		Jerktown/Room for One More	1965	3.75	7.50	15.00
❑ 59321		Lies/The Coming Generation	1965	4.00	8.00	16.00
❑ 59326		One Track Mind/I Must Be Doing Something Right	1966	3.75	7.50	15.00
❑ 59332		High on Love/Stick with Me	1966	3.75	7.50	15.00
❑ 59335		Just One Girl/Chapel in the Fields	1966	3.75	7.50	15.00
❑ 59341		Love Is a Bird/Rumors, Gossip, Words Untrue	1966	3.75	7.50	15.00
❑ 59348		Can You Help Me/Please Don't Love Him	1966	3.75	7.50	15.00
❑ 59359		What Does That Make You/Sweet Green Fields	1967	3.75	7.50	15.00
❑ 59366		Come and Get It/Wishful Thinking	1967	3.75	7.50	15.00
❑ 59380		You'll Never Walk Alone/I Can Do It Better	1967	3.75	7.50	15.00
❑ 59384		As a Matter of Fact/They Ran for Their Lives	1968	3.75	7.50	15.00

Knight, Chris
(Peter Brady of The Brady Bunch)
Paramount

Number		Title (A Side/B Side)	Year	VG	VG+	NM
❑ 0177		Good for Each Other/Over and Over	1972	3.75	7.50	15.00
❑ 0177	PS	Good for Each Other/Over and Over	1972	3.75	7.50	15.00

Knight, Gladys, and the Pips
(Includes Gladys Knight solo and The Pips without her. Also see "Dionne and Friends")
Brunswick

Number		Title (A Side/B Side)	Year	VG	VG+	NM
❑ 55048		Whistle My Love/Ching Ching	1958	30.00	60.00	120.00
Buddah						
❑ 363		Where Peaceful Waters Flow/Perfect Love	1973		2.50	5.00
❑ 363	PS	Where Peaceful Waters Flow/Perfect Love	1973	2.00	4.00	8.00
❑ 383		Midnight Train to Georgia/(Instrumental)	1973		3.00	6.00
❑ 383		Midnight Train to Georgia/Window Raising Granny	1973		2.50	5.00
❑ 393		I've Got to Use My Imagination/I Can See Clearly Now	1973		2.50	5.00
❑ 403		Best Thing That Ever Happened to Me/	1974		2.50	5.00
		Once in a Lifetime				
❑ 423		On and On/The Makings of You	1974		2.50	5.00
❑ 423	PS	On and On/The Makings of You	1974	2.00	4.00	8.00
❑ 432		I Feel a Song (In My Heart)/	1974		2.50	5.00
		Don't Burn Down the Bridge				
❑ 453		Love Finds It's Own Way/Better You Go Your Way	1975		2.50	5.00
❑ 463		The Way We Were-Try to Remember/The Need to Be	1975		2.50	5.00
❑ 487		Money/Street Brothers	1975		2.50	5.00

Number		Title (A Side/B Side)	Year	VG	VG+	NM
☐ 513		Part Time Love/Where Did I Put His Memory	1975		2.50	5.00
☐ 523		Make Yours a Happy Home/	1976		2.50	5.00
		The Going Up and the Coming Down				
☐ 544		So Sad the Song/(Instrumental)	1976		2.50	5.00
☐ 569		Baby Don't Change Your Mind/	1977		2.50	5.00
		I Love to Feel That Feelin'				
☐ 584		Sorry Doesn't Always Make It Right/	1977		2.50	5.00
		You Put a New Life in My Body				
☐ 592		The One and Only/Pipe Dreams	1978		2.50	5.00
☐ 598		It's a Better Than Good Time/	1978		2.50	5.00
		Everybody's Got to Find a Way				
☐ 601		I'm Coming Home Again/Love Gives You the Power	1978		2.50	5.00
☐ 605		Sail Away/I'm Still Caught Up with You	1979		2.50	5.00
☐ 1974	DJ	Do You Hear What I Hear/Silent Night	1974		3.00	6.00

Casablanca

☐ 912		If I Could Bring Back Yesterday/Since I Found Love	1978		2.00	4.00
☐ 949		Baby I'm Your Fool/Lights of the City	1978		2.00	4.00

Columbia

☐ 02113		Forever Yesterday (For the Children)/(Instrumental)	1981		2.00	4.00
☐ 02113	PS	Forever Yesterday (For the Children)/(Instrumental)	1981		2.50	5.00
☐ 02413		If That'll Make You Happy/Love Was Made for Two	1981		2.00	4.00
☐ 02549		I Will Fight/God Is	1981		2.00	4.00
☐ 02706		Friend of Mine/Reach High	1982		2.00	4.00
☐ 03418		That Special Time of Year/	1982		2.00	4.00
		Santa Claus Is Comin' to Town				
☐ 03761		Save the Overtime (For Me)/Ain't No Greater Love	1983		2.00	4.00
☐ 04033		You're Number 1 in My Book/Oh La De Dah	1983		2.00	4.00
☐ 04219		Hero (The Wind Beneath My Wings)/Seconds	1983		2.50	5.00
☐ 04333		Here's That Sunny Day/Oh La De Da	1984		2.00	4.00
☐ 04369		When You're Far Away/Seconds	1984		2.00	4.00
☐ 04761		My Time/(Instrumental)	1985		2.00	4.00
☐ 04761	PS	My Time/(Instrumental)	1985		2.50	5.00
☐ 04873		Keep Givin' Me Love/Do You Wanna Have Some Fun	1985		2.00	4.00
☐ 05679		Till I See You Again/Strivin'	1985		2.00	4.00
☐ 10922		Am I Too Late/(B-side unknown)	1979		2.00	4.00
☐ 10996		You Bring Out the Best in Me/You Loved Away the Pain	1979		2.00	4.00
☐ 11088		The Best Thing We Can Do Is Say Goodbye/	1979		2.00	4.00
		You Don't Have to Say I Love You				
☐ 11239		Landlord/We Need Hearts	1980		2.00	4.00
☐ 11330		Taste of Bitter Love/Add It Up	1980		2.00	4.00
☐ 11375		Bourgie', Bourgie'/Get the Love	1980		2.00	4.00
☐ 11409		When a Child Is Born/The Lord's Prayer	1980		2.00	4.00
		With Johnny Mathis				

Enjoy

☐ 2012		What Shall I Do/Love Call	1964	3.75	7.50	15.00

Everlast

☐ 5025		Happiness/I Had a Dream Last Night	1963	6.25	12.50	25.00
		As "The Pips"				

Fury

☐ 1050		Every Beat of My Heart/Room in Your Heart	1961	6.25	12.50	25.00
		Re-recordings of the same songs on Huntom and Vee Jay				
☐ 1052		Guess Who/Stop Running Around	1961	3.75	7.50	15.00
☐ 1054		Letter Full of Tears/You Broke Your Promise	1961	3.75	7.50	15.00
☐ 1064		Operator/I'll Trust in You	1962	3.75	7.50	15.00
☐ 1067		Darling/Linda	1962	5.00	10.00	20.00
		As "The Pips"				
☐ 1073		Come See About Me/I Want That Kind of Love	1963	7.50	15.00	30.00

Huntom

☐ 2510		Every Beat of My Heart/Room in Your Heart	1961	125.00	250.00	500.00
		As "The Pips"				

Maxx

☐ 326		Giving Up/Maybe, Maybe Baby	1964	3.75	7.50	15.00
☐ 329		Lovers Always Forget/Another Love	1964	3.75	7.50	15.00
☐ 331		Either Way I Lose/Go Away, Stay Away	1964	3.75	7.50	15.00
☐ 334		Who Knows/Stop and Get a Hold of Myself	1965	3.75	7.50	15.00
☐ 335		Tell Her You're Mine/If I Should Ever Be in Love	1965	3.75	7.50	15.00

MCA

☐ 53002		Send It to Me/	1987			3.00
		When You Love Somebody (It's Christmas Every Day)				
☐ 53210		Love Overboard/(Instrumental)	1987			3.00
☐ 53210	PS	Love Overboard/(Instrumental)	1987			3.00
☐ 53211		Lovin' on Next to Nothin'/(Instrumental)	1988			3.00
☐ 53211	PS	Lovin' on Next to Nothin'/(Instrumental)	1988			3.00
☐ 53351		It's Gonna Take All Our Love/(Instrumental)	1988			3.00
☐ 53657		Licence to Kill/You	1989			3.00
☐ 53676		Licence to Kill/Pam	1989			3.00
		B-side by National Philharmonic Orchestra				
☐ 54117		Men/(Instrumental)	1991			3.00

Scotti Bros.

☐ 06267		Loving on Borrowed Time (Love Theme from Cobra)/	1986			3.00
		Angel of the City				
		A-side: Gladys Knight and Bill Medley; b-side: Robert Tepper				

Soul

☐ 35023		Just Walk in My Shoes/Stepping Closer to Your Heart	1966	2.00	4.00	8.00

Number		Title (A Side/B Side)	Year	VG	VG+	NM
❏ 35033		Take Me in Your Arms and Love Me/ Do You Love Me Just a Little More?	1967	2.00	4.00	8.00
❏ 35034		Everybody Needs Love/Since I've Lost You	1967	2.00	4.00	8.00
❏ 35039		I Heard It Through the Grapevine/It's Time to Go Now	1967	2.50	5.00	10.00
❏ 35042		The End of Our Road/ Don't Let Her Take Your Love from Me	1968	2.00	4.00	8.00
❏ 35045		It Should Have Been Me/You Don't Love No More	1968	2.00	4.00	8.00
❏ 35047		I Wish It Would Rain/It's Summer	1968	2.00	4.00	8.00
❏ 35057		Didn't You Know (You'd Have to Cry Sometime)/ Keep an Eye	1969	2.00	4.00	8.00
❏ 35063		The Nitty Gritty/Got Myself a Good Man	1969	2.00	4.00	8.00
❏ 35068		Friendship Train/Cloud Nine	1969	2.00	4.00	8.00
❏ 35071		You Need Love Like I Do (Don't You)/ You're My Everything	1970	2.00	4.00	8.00
❏ 35078		If I Were Your Woman/The Tracks of My Tears	1970		3.50	7.00
❏ 35083		I Don't Want to Do Wrong/ Is There a Place In His Heart for Me	1971		3.00	6.00
❏ 35091		Make Me the Woman You Come Home To/ If You're Gonna Leave (Just Leave)	1972		3.00	6.00
❏ 35094		Help Me Make It Through the Night/ If You're Gonna Leave (Just Leave)	1972		3.00	6.00
❏ 35098		Neither One of Us (Wants to Be the First to Say Goodbye)/ Can't Give It Up No More	1972		3.00	6.00
❏ 35105		Daddy Could Swear I Declare/For Once in My Life	1973		3.00	6.00
❏ 35107		All I Need Is Time/ The Only Time You Love Me (Is When You're Losing Me)	1973		3.00	6.00
❏ 35111		Between Her Goodbye and My Hello/ This Child Needs Its Father	1974		3.00	6.00

Vee Jay

❏ 386		Every Beat of My Heart/Room in Your Heart By "The Pips"	1961	5.00	10.00	20.00
❏ 386		Every Beat of My Heart/ Ain'tcha Got Some Room (In Your Heart for Me) By "The Pips"; same B-side, different title	1961	5.00	10.00	20.00
❏ 545		A Love Like Mine/Queen of Tears	1963	5.00	10.00	20.00

Knight, Sonny
A&M

❏ 718		Evil Minded Woman/Georgia Town	1963	2.50	5.00	10.00
❏ 728		Be True to Your Dog/State Street	1964	2.50	5.00	10.00

Aladdin

❏ 3357		But Officer/Dear Wonderful God	1957	7.50	15.00	30.00

Aura

❏ 403		If You Want This Love/I Just Called to Say Hello	1964	2.00	4.00	8.00
❏ 4505		Love Me As Though There Were No Tomorrow/ Fool Like Me	1964	2.00	4.00	8.00
❏ 4505	PS	Love Me As Though There Were No Tomorrow/ Fool Like Me	1964	5.00	10.00	20.00
❏ 4508		Rose Mary/(B-side unknown)	1965	2.00	4.00	8.00

Dot

❏ 15507		Confidential/Jailbird Originals have maroon labels	1956	5.00	10.00	20.00
❏ 15507		Confidential/Jailbird Second pressings have black labels	1956	3.75	7.50	15.00
❏ 15542		End of a Dream/Worthless and Lowdown	1957	3.75	7.50	15.00
❏ 15597		Lovesick Blues/Insha Allot	1957	3.75	7.50	15.00
❏ 15635		Dedicated to You/Short Walk	1957	3.75	7.50	15.00

Mercury

❏ 72033		Just One More Chance/Lost Child	1962	2.50	5.00	10.00

Original Sound

❏ 2		Once in Awhile/School's Out	1959	5.00	10.00	20.00
❏ 18		Those Oldies But Goodies Are Dedicated to You/ She Had Me Reelin'	1961	3.75	7.50	15.00

Specialty

❏ 594		Keep a-Walkin'/My Baby Don't Want Me	1957	3.75	7.50	15.00

Vita

❏ 137		Confidential/Jailbird	1956	10.00	20.00	40.00

World Pacific

❏ 403		If You Want This Love/I Just Called to Say Hello	1964	3.00	6.00	12.00
❏ 77811		If I May/Need Your Love So Bad	1966	2.00	4.00	8.00
❏ 77832		Angel Love/If I Ruled the World	1966	2.00	4.00	8.00
❏ 77858		The Quiet Man/I Can't Let You Go	1966			Unreleased

Knight, Terry, and the Pack
(Don Brewer and Mark Farner of this group later were part of Grand Funk Railroad)
A&M

❏ 769		Kids Will Be the Same/You Lie	1965	3.75	7.50	15.00

Cameo

❏ 482		Forever and a Day/Lizbeth Peach	1967	2.50	5.00	10.00
❏ 495		Come Home Baby/Lively Lady	1967	2.50	5.00	10.00

Number		Title (A Side/B Side)	Year	VG	VG+	NM
Capitol						
❏ 2174		Without a Woman/Let Me Stand Next to Your Fire	1968	3.00	6.00	12.00
		As "The Pack"				
❏ 2409		Such a Lonely Life/Lullaby	1969	2.50	5.00	10.00
❏ 2506		St. Paul/(Legend of) William and Mary	1969	2.50	5.00	10.00
❏ 2737		I'll Keep Waiting Patiently/Lullaby	1970	2.50	5.00	10.00
Lucky Eleven						
❏ 003		Harlem Shuffle/I've Got News for You	1965	4.00	8.00	16.00
		As "The Pack"				
❏ 007		Does It Matter to You Girl/Wide Trackin'	1965	4.00	8.00	16.00
		As "The Fabulous Pack"				
❏ 007	PS	Does It Matter to You Girl/Wide Trackin'	1965	6.25	12.50	25.00
		As "The Fabulous Pack"				
❏ 225		How Much More/I've Been Told	1966	3.75	7.50	15.00
❏ 226		I Got Love/Better Man Than I	1966	3.75	7.50	15.00
❏ 228		Lady Jane/Lovin' Kind	1966	3.75	7.50	15.00
❏ 229		What's On Your Mind/A Change on the Way	1966	3.75	7.50	15.00
❏ 230		I (Who Have Nothing)/Numbers	1966	3.75	7.50	15.00
❏ 235		This Precious Time/Love, Love, Love, Love, Love	1967	3.75	7.50	15.00
❏ 236		One Monkey Don't Stop No Show/The Train	1967	3.75	7.50	15.00
Wingate						
❏ 007		The Tears Come Rollin'/The Colour of My Love	1965	6.25	12.50	25.00
		As "The Pack"				

Knights, The
Capitol

Number		Title (A Side/B Side)	Year	VG	VG+	NM
❏ 5302		Hot Rod High/Theme for Teen Love	1964	12.50	25.00	50.00

Knockouts, The
MGM

Number		Title (A Side/B Side)	Year	VG	VG+	NM
❏ 13010		Fever/You Can Take My Girl	1961	5.00	10.00	20.00
Scepter						
❏ 1269		Got My Mojo Workin'/Every Day of the Week	1964	3.00	6.00	12.00
Shad						
❏ 5013		Darling Lorraine/Riot in Room 3C	1959	12.50	25.00	50.00
		With long ending on A-side				
❏ 5013		Darling Lorraine/Riot in Room 3C	1959	6.25	12.50	25.00
		With short ending on A-side				
❏ 5018		Please Be Mine/Rich Boy, Poor Boy	1960	6.25	12.50	25.00
Tribute						
❏ 199		Got My Mojo Working (Part 1)/Got My Mojo Working (Part 2)	1964	3.75	7.50	15.00
❏ 201		Tweet-Tweet/What's On Your Mind	1964	4.00	8.00	16.00

Knox, Buddy
Liberty

Number		Title (A Side/B Side)	Year	VG	VG+	NM
❏ 55290		Lovey Dovey/I Got You	1960	3.00	6.00	12.00
❏ 55305		Ling, Ting, Tong/The Kisses	1961	3.00	6.00	12.00
❏ 55305	PS	Ling, Ting, Tong/The Kisses	1961	7.50	15.00	30.00
❏ 55366		All By Myself/Three Eyed Man	1961	3.00	6.00	12.00
❏ 55411		Cha-Hua-Hua/Open	1962	3.00	6.00	12.00
❏ 55473		She's Gone/There's Only Me	1962	3.00	6.00	12.00
❏ 55503		Dear Abby/Three Way Love Affair	1962	3.00	6.00	12.00
❏ 55592		Shadaroom/Tomorrow Is a-Comin'	1963	2.50	5.00	10.00
❏ 55650		Thanks a Lot/Hitchhike Back to Georgia	1963	2.50	5.00	10.00
❏ 55694		Good Lovin'/All Time Loser	1964	2.50	5.00	10.00
Reprise						
❏ 0395		Livin' in a House Full of Love/Good Time Girl	1965	2.50	5.00	10.00
❏ 0431		A Lover's Question/You Said Goodbye	1965	2.50	5.00	10.00
❏ 0463		A White Sport Coat/That Don't Do Me No Good	1966	2.50	5.00	10.00
❏ 0501		Love Has Many Ways/Sixteen Feet of Patio	1966	2.50	5.00	10.00
Roulette						
❏ 4002		Party Doll/My Baby's Gone	1957	12.50	25.00	50.00
		Maroon label with roulette wheel around outside				
❏ 4002		Party Doll/My Baby's Gone	1957	7.50	15.00	30.00
		Red label, roulette wheel on top half of label				
❏ 4002		Party Doll/My Baby's Gone	1957	6.25	12.50	25.00
		Red label, no roulette wheel				
❏ 4009		Rock Your Little Baby to Sleep/Don't Make Me Cry	1957	10.00	20.00	40.00
		Maroon label with roulette wheel around outside				
❏ 4009		Rock Your Little Baby to Sleep/Don't Make Me Cry	1957	6.25	12.50	25.00
		Red label, roulette wheel on top half of label				
❏ 4009		Rock Your Little Baby to Sleep/Don't Make Me Cry	1957	5.00	10.00	20.00
		Red label, no roulette wheel				
❏ 4018		Hula Love/Devil Woman	1957	6.25	12.50	25.00
❏ 4042		Swingin' Daddy/Whenever I'm Lonely	1958	6.25	12.50	25.00
❏ 4082		Somebody Touched Me/C'mon Baby	1958	6.25	12.50	25.00
❏ 4120		That's Why I Cry/Teaseable, Pleaseable You	1958	6.25	12.50	25.00
❏ 4140		I Think I'm Gonna Kill Myself/To Be with You	1959	6.25	12.50	25.00
❏ 4179		Taste of the Blues/I Ain't Sharin' Sharon	1959	6.25	12.50	25.00
❏ 4262		Long Lonely Nights/Storm Clouds	1960	6.25	12.50	25.00

Number		Title (A Side/B Side)	Year	VG	VG+	NM
Ruff						
❑ 1001		Jo-Ann/Don't Make a Ripple	1965	2.50	5.00	10.00
Triple D						
❑ 798		Party Doll/I'm Stickin' With You	1956	250.00	500.00	1,000
		B-side by Jimmy Bowen				
United Artists						
❑ 50301		This Time Tomorrow/Gypsy Man	1968	2.00	4.00	8.00
❑ 50463		Today My Sleepless Nights Came Back to Town/	1968	2.00	4.00	8.00
		A Million Years or So				
❑ 50526		God Knows I Love You/Night Runners	1969	2.00	4.00	8.00
❑ 50596		Salt Lake City/I'm Only Rockin'	1969	2.00	4.00	8.00
❑ 50644		Yesterday Is Gone/Back to New Orleans	1970		3.00	6.00
❑ 50722		White Dove/Glory Train	1970		3.00	6.00
❑ 50789		Come Softly to Me/Travelin' Light	1971		3.00	6.00

Kool Gents
(Dee Clark was a member of this group)

Vee Jay						
❑ 173		This Is the Night/Do Ya Do	1956	50.00	100.00	200.00
❑ 207		You Know/I Can't Help Myself	1956	50.00	100.00	200.00

Kramer, Billy J., and the Dakotas

Epic						
❑ 10331		1941/His Love Is Just a Lie	1968	2.50	5.00	10.00
Imperial						
❑ 66027		Little Children/Bad to Me	1964	3.00	6.00	12.00
❑ 66048		I'll Keep You Satisfied/I Know	1964	3.00	6.00	12.00
❑ 66051		From a Window/I'll Be On My Way	1964	3.00	6.00	12.00
❑ 66051	PS	From a Window/I'll Be On My Way	1964	6.25	12.50	25.00
❑ 66085		It's Gotta Last Forever/They Remind Me of You	1965	3.00	6.00	12.00
❑ 66115		Trains and Boats and Planes/I'll Be On My Way	1965	3.00	6.00	12.00
❑ 66135		Irresistible You/Twilight Time	1965	2.50	5.00	10.00
❑ 66143		I'll Be Doggone/Neon City	1965	2.50	5.00	10.00
❑ 66210		You Make Me Feel Like Someone/Take My Hand	1966	2.50	5.00	10.00
Liberty						
❑ 55586		Do You Want to Know a Secret/I'll Be On My Way	1963	7.50	15.00	30.00
❑ 55618		The Cruel Surf/The Millionaire	1963	10.00	20.00	40.00
		As "The Dakotas"				
❑ 55626		Bad to Me/I Call Your Name	1963	7.50	15.00	30.00
❑ 55643		I'll Keep You Satisfied/I Know	1963	7.50	15.00	30.00
❑ 55667		Bad to Me/Do You Want to Know a Secret	1964	6.25	12.50	25.00
❑ 55687		Little Children/They Remind Me of You	1964			*Unreleased*

Kuban, Bob, and the In-Men

Musicland U.S.A.						
❑ 20,001		The Cheater/Try Me Baby	1966	3.00	6.00	12.00
		With "Vocal by Walter Scott" on only B-side label				
❑ 20,001		The Cheater/Try Me Baby	1966	2.50	5.00	10.00
		With no mention of "Vocal by Walter Scott"				
❑ 20,001		The Cheater/Try Me Baby	1966	5.00	10.00	20.00
		With "Vocal by Walter Scott" on both sides' labels				
❑ 20,006		The Teaser/All I Want	1966	2.50	5.00	10.00
❑ 20,007		Drive My Car/The Pretzel	1966	2.50	5.00	10.00
❑ 20,013		Harlem Shuffle/Theme from "Virginia Wolff"	1967	2.00	4.00	8.00
❑ 20,017		Batman Theme/You Better Run, You Better Hide	1967	2.00	4.00	8.00
Norman						
❑ 558		Jerkin' Time/Turn On Your Lovelight	1965	3.00	6.00	12.00
❑ 567		Little Girl/I Don't Want to Know	1965	3.00	6.00	12.00
Reprise						
❑ 0937		Soul Man/Hard to Handle	1970	2.00	4.00	8.00

Kuf-Linx, The

Challenge						
❑ 1013		So Tough/What'cha Gonna Do	1957	5.00	10.00	20.00
		Original pressings have blue or white labels				
❑ 1013		So Tough/What'cha Gonna Do	1958	3.75	7.50	15.00
		Reissues have maroon labels				
❑ 59004		Eyeballin'/Service with a Smile	1958	3.75	7.50	15.00
		B-side by John Jennings				
❑ 59015		Climb Love Mountain/All That's Good	1958	3.75	7.50	15.00
❑ 59102		So Tough/What'cha Gonna Do	1961	3.00	6.00	12.00

Kustom Kings, The
(Bruce Johnston sings on this record)

Smash						
❑ 1883		In My '40 Ford/Clutch Rider	1964	12.50	25.00	50.00

Number		Title (A Side/B Side)	Year	VG	VG+	NM

L

LaBeef, Sleepy
Columbia

☐ 44068		Sure Beats the Heck Out of Settlin' Down/Schneider	1967	2.50	5.00	10.00
☐ 44261		Completely Destroyed/Go Ahead On Baby	1967	2.50	5.00	10.00
☐ 44455		Every Day/If I'm Right I'm Wrong	1968	2.50	5.00	10.00

Crescent

☐ 102		Turn Me Loose/(B-side unknown)	195?	50.00	100.00	200.00

Mercury

☐ 71112		I'm Through/All Alone	1957	25.00	50.00	100.00
☐ 71179		All the Time/Lonely	1957	25.00	50.00	100.00

Picture

☐ 1937		Ride On Josephine/(B-side unknown)	1959	37.50	75.00	150.00

Plantation

☐ 55		Too Much Monkey Business/Got You on My Mind	1970	6.25	12.50	25.00
☐ 66		Asphalt Cowboy/Got You on My Mind	1971	2.50	5.00	10.00
☐ 74		Blackland Farmer/Got You on My Mind	1971	2.50	5.00	10.00

Starday

☐ 292		I'm Through/All Alone	1957	37.50	75.00	150.00

Sun

☐ 1132		Thunder Road/A Hundred Pounds of Lovin'	1974		2.00	4.00
☐ 1133	DJ	Ghost Riders in the Sky (same on both sides)	1975		2.00	4.00
☐ 1134		There Ain't Much After Taxes/ A Hundred Pounds of Lovin'	1976		2.00	4.00
☐ 1137		Good Rockin' Boogie (Part 1)/ Good Rockin' Boogie (Part 2)	1978		2.00	4.00
☐ 1145		Flying Saucers Rock and Roll/ Boogie Woogie Country Girl	1979		2.00	4.00

Wayside

Wayside titles as "Tommy LaBeef"

☐ 1651		Ride On Josephine/(B-side unknown)	1959	50.00	100.00	200.00
☐ 1652		Walkin' Slowly/(B-side unknown)	1959	62.50	125.00	250.00
☐ 1654		Tore Up/Lonely	1959	75.00	150.00	300.00

LaBelle, Patti, and the Blue Belles
Atlantic

☐ 2311		All or Nothing/You Forgot How to Love	1965	3.00	6.00	12.00
☐ 2318		A Groovy Kind of Love/Over the Rainbow	1966	2.50	5.00	10.00
☐ 2333		Ebb Tide/Patti's Prayer	1966	2.50	5.00	10.00
☐ 2347		I'm Still Waiting/Family Man	1966	2.50	5.00	10.00
☐ 2373		Take Me for a Little While/ I Don't Want to Go On Without You	1967	2.50	5.00	10.00
☐ 2390		(There's) Always Something There to Remind Me/ Tender Words	1967	2.50	5.00	10.00
☐ 2408		Unchained Melody/Dreamer	1967	2.50	5.00	10.00
☐ 2446		Oh My Love/I Need Your Love	1967	2.50	5.00	10.00
☐ 2548		He's My Man/Wonderful	1968	2.50	5.00	10.00
☐ 2610		Dance to the Rhythm of Love/He's Gone	1969	2.50	5.00	10.00
☐ 2629		Loving Blues/Pride's No Match for Love	1969	2.50	5.00	10.00
☐ 2712		Suffer/Trustin' in You	1970	2.50	5.00	10.00

King

☐ 5777		Down the Aisle (Wedding Song)/C'est La Vie	1963	3.75	7.50	15.00

Newtime

☐ 510		Love Me Just a Little/The Joke's On You	1962	5.00	10.00	20.00

Newtown

Most of the Newtown sides credit "The Blue-Belles"

☐ 5000		I Sold My Heart to the Junkman/Itty Bitty Twist	1962	6.25	12.50	25.00
		Credited to "The Blue-Belles" but actually recorded by The Starlets				
☐ 5006		I Found a New Love/Pitter Patter	1962	5.00	10.00	20.00
☐ 5007		Tear After Tear/Go On, This Is Goodbye	1962	5.00	10.00	20.00
☐ 5009		Cool Water/When Johnny Comes Marching Home	1962	5.00	10.00	20.00
☐ 5019		Academy Award/Decatur Street	1963	5.00	10.00	20.00
☐ 5777		Down the Aisle (Wedding Song)/C'est La Vie	1963	3.75	7.50	15.00

Nicetown

☐ 5020		You'll Never Walk Alone/Where Are You	1963	3.75	7.50	15.00

Parkway

☐ 896		You'll Never Walk Alone/Decatur Street	1964	3.00	6.00	12.00
☐ 896	PS	You'll Never Walk Alone/Decatur Street	1964	10.00	20.00	40.00
☐ 913		One Phone Call/You Will Fill My Eyes No More	1964	3.00	6.00	12.00
☐ 935		Danny Boy/I Believe	1964	3.00	6.00	12.00

Lady Bugs, The
(May be three different groups!)
Chattahoochie

☐ 637		How Do You Do It/Liverpool	1964	3.75	7.50	15.00

Del-Fi

☐ 4233		Sooner or Later/It's the Last Time	1964	5.00	10.00	20.00

Legrand

☐ 1033		Who Sends the Love Note/Fraternity U.S.A.	1964	5.00	10.00	20.00

Number		Title (A Side/B Side)	Year	VG	VG+	NM

Lake, Karen
ABC-Paramount
☐ 10050		Nine O'Clock/Will I Know	1959	5.00	10.00	20.00
☐ 10087		Kiss Me Quick and Go/	1960	5.00	10.00	20.00
		When I'm Not Teen Age Anymore				

Big Top
☐ 3077		Air Mail Special Delivery/	1961	7.50	15.00	30.00
		I'd Like to Miss My Graduation				
		Produced by Phil Spector				

LaMarr, Gene
Spry
☐ 113		Crazy Little House on the Hill/	1959	37.50	75.00	150.00
		You Don't Love Me Anymore				
☐ 114		You Can Count on Me/Just a Little Bit Longer	1959	37.50	75.00	150.00
☐ 115		Close to Me/Moon Eyes	1959	25.00	50.00	100.00

Lambert, Rudy – See "Mondellos, The"

Lamplighters, The
Federal
☐ 12149		Part of Me/Turn Me Loose	1953	50.00	100.00	200.00
☐ 12152		Give Me/Be-Bop Wino	1953	25.00	50.00	100.00
☐ 12166		Smootchie/I Can't Stand It	1954	25.00	50.00	100.00
☐ 12176		Tell Me You Came/I Used to Cry Mercy, Mercy	1954	25.00	50.00	100.00
☐ 12182		Salty Dog/Ride, Jockey, Ride	1954	20.00	40.00	80.00
☐ 12192		Five Minutes Longer/You Hear	1954	20.00	40.00	80.00
☐ 12197		Yum! Yum!/Goody Good Times	1954	15.00	30.00	60.00
☐ 12206		I Wanna Know/Believe in Me	1955	15.00	30.00	60.00
☐ 12212		Roll On/Love, Rock and Thrill	1955	15.00	30.00	60.00
☐ 12242		Don't Make It So Good/Hug a Little, Kiss a Little	1955	12.50	25.00	50.00
☐ 12255		You Were Sent Down from Heaven/Bo-Peep	1956	10.00	20.00	40.00
☐ 12261		It Ain't Right/Everything's All Right	1956	10.00	20.00	40.00

King
| ☐ 5890 | | Be-Bop Wino/Thunderbird | 1964 | 3.75 | 7.50 | 15.00 |
| | | *B-side by Dossie Terry* | | | | |

Lance, Major
Columbia
| ☐ 10488 | | Come On, Have Yourself a Good Time/ | 1977 | | 2.50 | 5.00 |
| | | Come What May | | | | |

Curtom
☐ 1953		Stay Away from Me (I Love You Too Much)/	1970		3.00	6.00
		Gypsy Woman				
☐ 1956		Must Be Love Coming Down/Little Young Lover	1970		3.00	6.00

Dakar
| ☐ 608 | | Follow the Leader/Since You've Been Gone | 1969 | 2.00 | 4.00 | 8.00 |
| ☐ 612 | | Shadows of a Memory/Sweeter As the Days Go By | 1969 | 2.00 | 4.00 | 8.00 |

Kat Family
| ☐ 03024 | | I Wanna Go Home/(Instrumental) | 1982 | | 2.00 | 4.00 |
| ☐ 04185 | | Are You Leaving Me/I Wanna Go Home | 1983 | | 2.00 | 4.00 |

Mercury
| ☐ 71582 | | I've Got a Girl/Phyllis | 1960 | 7.50 | 15.00 | 30.00 |

Okeh
☐ 7175		The Monkey Time/Mama Didn't Know	1963	3.00	6.00	12.00
☐ 7180		Hey Little Girl/Crying in the Rain	1963	2.50	5.00	10.00
☐ 7187		Um, Um, Um, Um, Um, Um/Sweet Music	1964	3.00	6.00	12.00
☐ 7187	PS	Um, Um, Um, Um, Um, Um/Sweet Music	1964	5.00	10.00	20.00
☐ 7191		The Matador/Gonna Get Married	1964	2.50	5.00	10.00
☐ 7197		It Ain't No Use/Girls	1964	2.50	5.00	10.00
☐ 7200		Think Nothing About It/It's Alright	1964	12.50	25.00	50.00
☐ 7203		Rhythm/Please Don't Say No More	1964	2.50	5.00	10.00
☐ 7203	PS	Rhythm/Please Don't Say No More	1964	3.75	7.50	15.00
☐ 7209		Sometimes I Wonder/I'm So Lost	1965	2.50	5.00	10.00
☐ 7216		Come See/You Belong to Me My Love	1965	2.50	5.00	10.00
☐ 7216	PS	Come See/You Belong to Me My Love	1965	3.75	7.50	15.00
☐ 7223		Ain't It a Shame/Gotta Get Away	1965	2.50	5.00	10.00
☐ 7226		Too Hot to Hold/Dark and Lovely	1965	2.50	5.00	10.00
☐ 7233		Everybody Loves a Good Time/I Just Can't Help It	1965	3.75	7.50	15.00
☐ 7250		Little Young Lover/Investigate	1966	3.75	7.50	15.00
☐ 7255		It's the Beat/You'll Want Me Back	1966	2.50	5.00	10.00
☐ 7266		Ain't No Soul (In These Shoes)/I	1966	3.75	7.50	15.00
☐ 7284		You Don't Want Me No More/	1967	12.50	25.00	50.00
		Wait Till I Get You in Your Arms				
☐ 7298		Without a Doubt/Forever	1967	2.50	5.00	10.00

Osiris
| ☐ 001 | | You're Everything I Need/(B-side unknown) | 1975 | | 2.50 | 5.00 |

Playboy
| ☐ 6017 | | Um, Um, Um, Um, Um, Um/Last of the Red Hot Lovers | 1974 | | 2.50 | 5.00 |
| ☐ 6020 | | Sweeter/Wild and Free | 1975 | | 2.50 | 5.00 |

Soul
| ☐ 35123 | | I Never Thought I'd Be Losing You/Chicago Disco | 1977 | | 2.50 | 5.00 |

Volt
| ☐ 4079 | | I Wanna Make Up/That's the Story of My Life | 1972 | | 3.00 | 6.00 |
| ☐ 4085 | | Ain't No Sweat/Since I Lost My Baby's Love | 1972 | | 3.00 | 6.00 |

Number	Title (A Side/B Side)	Year	VG	VG+	NM

Landis, Jerry – See "Simon, Paul"

Lands, Liz

Gordy
☐ 7023	We Shall Overcome/I Have a Dream	1963	6.25	12.50	25.00
	B-side by Rev. Martin Luther King				
☐ 7026	May What He Lived For Live/	1963	7.50	15.00	30.00
	He's Got the Whole World in His Hands				
☐ 7030	Midnight Journey/Keep Me	1964	12.50	25.00	50.00
	The Temptations sing backup				

One-derful
| ☐ 4847 | One Man's Poison/Don't Shut Me Out | 1967 | 3.75 | 7.50 | 15.00 |

Lane, Billy

Taba
| ☐ 201 | Beginner in Love/Space Ship Blues | 196? | 40.00 | 80.00 | 160.00 |

Lani & Boni – See "Delaney and Bonnie"

Larados, The
(Members of this group were later in The Reflections)

Fox
| ☐ 962/3 | Now the Parting Begins/Bad Guitar Man | 1958 | 50.00 | 100.00 | 200.00 |

Madog
| ☐ 801 | Will You Love Me Tomorrow/You Didn't Care | 1980 | 3.75 | 7.50 | 15.00 |

Larks, The
(The Apollo and Lloyds are by one group, the others are by the ex-Don Julian and the Meadowlarks)

Apollo
☐ 429	Little Side Car/Hey Little Girl	1951	250.00	500.00	1,000
☐ 430	Ooh, It Feels So Good/I Don't Believe in Tomorrow	1951	250.00	500.00	1,000
☐ 435	My Lost Love/How Long Must I Wait for You	1952	250.00	500.00	1,000
☐ 437	Darlin'/Lucy Brown	1952	250.00	500.00	1,000
☐ 475	No Mama No/Honey from the Bee	1955	100.00	200.00	400.00
☐ 1180	Hopefully Yours/When I Leave These Prison Walls	1951	250.00	500.00	1,000
☐ 1184	My Reverie/Let's Say a Prayer	1951	375.00	750.00	1,500
	Black vinyl				
☐ 1184	My Reverie/Let's Say a Prayer	1951	2,000	3,000	4,000
	Red vinyl				
☐ 1189	Shadrack/Honey in the Rock	1952	250.00	500.00	1,000
☐ 1190	Stolen Love/In My Lonely Room	1952	2,500	3,750	5,000
	Red vinyl				
☐ 1190	Stolen Love/In My Lonely Room	1952	250.00	500.00	1,000
	Black vinyl				
☐ 1194	I Live True to You/Hold Me	1952	250.00	500.00	1,000

Cross Fire
| ☐ 74-49/50 | Fabulous Cars and Diamond Rings/Life Is Sweeter Now | 1961 | 5.00 | 10.00 | 20.00 |

Guyden
| ☐ 2098 | I Want Her to Love Me/(Instrumental) | 1963 | 3.00 | 6.00 | 12.00 |
| ☐ 2103 | Fabulous Cars and Diamond Rings/Life Is Sweeter Now | 1964 | 3.00 | 6.00 | 12.00 |

Jett
| ☐ 3001 | Love You So/Love Me True | 1965 | 15.00 | 30.00 | 60.00 |

Lloyds
☐ 108	Margie/Rockin' in the Rockin' Room	1954	200.00	400.00	800.00
☐ 110	Tippin' In/If It's a Crime	1954	200.00	400.00	800.00
☐ 112	No Other Girl/The World Is Waiting for the Sunrise	1954	200.00	400.00	800.00
☐ 114	Forget It/I Live True to You	1954	150.00	300.00	600.00

Money
☐ 104	The Jerk/Forget Me	1964	3.00	6.00	12.00
☐ 109	Mickey's East Coast Jerk/Soul Jerk	1965	2.50	5.00	10.00
☐ 110	The Slauson Shuffle/Soul Jerk	1965	2.50	5.00	10.00
☐ 112	The Roman/Heavenly Father	1965	2.50	5.00	10.00
☐ 115	Can You Do the Duck/Sad Sad Boy	1965	2.50	5.00	10.00
☐ 119	Lost My Love Yesterday/The Answer Came Too Late	1966	2.50	5.00	10.00
☐ 122	Philly Dog/Heaven Only Knows	1966	2.50	5.00	10.00
☐ 127	The Skate/Come Back Baby	1967	2.50	5.00	10.00
☐ 601	I Love You/I Want You Back	1973		3.00	6.00
☐ 604	My Favorite Beer Joint/(Instrumental)	1973		3.00	6.00
☐ 607	Shorty the Pimp (Part 1)/Shorty the Pimp (Part 2)	1974		3.00	6.00
	Money 604 and 607 as "Don Julian and the Larks"				

Nasco
| ☐ 028 | I Love You/I Want You Back | 1972 | 2.00 | 4.00 | 8.00 |

Sheryl
| ☐ 334 | It's Unbelievable/I Can't Believe It | 1961 | 6.25 | 12.50 | 25.00 |
| ☐ 338 | There Is a Girl/Let's Drink a Toast | 1961 | 6.25 | 12.50 | 25.00 |

Stacy
| ☐ 969 | Food Sticks/Scavenger | 1963 | 3.00 | 6.00 | 12.00 |

Violet
| ☐ 1051 | I Want Her to Love Me/(Instrumental) | 1962 | 5.00 | 10.00 | 20.00 |

Number		Title (A Side/B Side)	Year	VG	VG+	NM

Larktones, The
ABC-Paramount

| ❑ 9909 | | The Letter/Rockin' Swingin' Man | 1958 | 7.50 | 15.00 | 30.00 |

Riki

| ❑ 140 | | Why Are You Tearing Us Apart/Nosy Neighbor | 1960 | 15.00 | 30.00 | 60.00 |

Larry and the Crossfires
Searcy

| ❑ 711 | | Torquay '65/Wee Wee Hours | 1965 | 12.50 | 25.00 | 50.00 |

Larry and the Legends
Atlantic

| ❑ 2220 | | Don't Pick On My Baby/The Creep | 1964 | 6.25 | 12.50 | 25.00 |
| | | *With the Four Seasons* | | | | |

Laughing Gravy
(Dean Torrence with the Esquires, singing to a salvaged backing track from the Beach Boys' Smile LP)
White Whale

| ❑ 261 | | Vegetables/ | 1968 | 50.00 | 100.00 | 200.00 |
| | | Snow Flakes on Laughing Gravy's Whiskers | | | | |

Laurels, The
"X"

| ❑ 0143 | | Truly, Truly/'Tis Night | 1955 | 62.50 | 125.00 | 250.00 |

ABC-Paramount

| ❑ 10048 | | Hand in Hand/Picture of Love | 1959 | 12.50 | 25.00 | 50.00 |

Spring

| ❑ 1112 | | Baby Talk/You Left Me | 1959 | 15.00 | 30.00 | 60.00 |

Lawrence, Syd
Cosmic

| ❑ 1001 | | The Answer to the Flying Saucer/Haunted Guitar | 1956 | 10.00 | 20.00 | 40.00 |
| | | *B-side by Billy Mure* | | | | |

Lawrence, Walt
Hollywood Int'l.

| ❑ 2 | | Cascade/Twilight Adrift | 195? | 10.00 | 20.00 | 40.00 |

Leaping Ferns, The
(Also recorded as the "Chantay's")
X-Panded Sound

| ❑ 103 | | It Never Works Out for Me/Maybe Baby | 1964 | 7.50 | 15.00 | 30.00 |

Leary, Dr. Timothy
Mercury

| ❑ 72713 | | Turn On, Tune In, Drop Out (Part 1)/ | 1967 | 7.50 | 15.00 | 30.00 |
| | | Turn On, Tune In, Drop Out (Part 2) | | | | |

Leather Boy
Flower

| ❑ 100 | | My Prayer/You Gotta Have Soul | 1968 | 7.50 | 15.00 | 30.00 |

MGM

❑ 13724		I'm a Leather Boy/Shadows	1967	7.50	15.00	30.00
❑ 13724	PS	I'm a Leather Boy/Shadows	1967	15.00	30.00	60.00
❑ 13790		On the Go/Soulin'	1967	7.50	15.00	30.00

Parkway

| ❑ 125 | | Jersey Thursday/Black Friday | 1966 | 7.50 | 15.00 | 30.00 |

Led Zeppelin
(Also see "Jones, John Paul"; "Page, Jimmy"; "Plant, Robert")
Atlantic

❑ PR 157	DJ	Gallows Pole (mono/stereo)	1971	37.50	75.00	150.00
❑ PR 175	DJ	Stairway to Heaven (mono/stereo)	1972	20.00	40.00	80.00
❑ PR 175	PS	Stairway to Heaven (mono/stereo)	1972	30.00	60.00	120.00
❑ PR 269	DJ	Stairway to Heaven (mono/stereo)	1973	12.50	25.00	50.00
❑ 2613		Communication Breakdown/Good Times Bad Times	1969	6.25	12.50	25.00
❑ 2690		Whole Lotta Love/	1969	2.50	5.00	10.00
		Living Loving Maid (She's Just a Woman)				
		With A-side time of 5:33				
❑ 2690		Whole Lotta Love/	1969	2.00	4.00	8.00
		Living Loving Maid (She's Just a Woman)				
		With A-side time of 3:12				
❑ 2777		Immigrant Song/Hey, Hey, What Can I Do	1970	6.25	12.50	25.00
		First pressings with "Do What Thou Wilt Shalt Be the Whole of the Law" in trail-off				
❑ 2777		Immigrant Song/Hey, Hey, What Can I Do	1970	3.75	7.50	15.00
		Second pressings without "Do What Thou Wilt Shalt Be the Whole of the Law" in trail-off				
❑ 2777		Immigrant Song/Hey, Hey, What Can I Do	1970		2.50	5.00
		Third pressings with smaller, bolder type; in print well into the late 1980s				
❑ 2777	DJ	Immigrant Song	1970	37.50	75.00	150.00
		One-sided promo				
❑ 2849		Black Dog/Misty Mountain Hop	1971	2.50	5.00	10.00
❑ 2865		Rock and Roll/Four Sticks	1972	2.50	5.00	10.00

Number		Title (A Side/B Side)	Year	VG	VG+	NM
2970		Over the Hills & Far Away/Dancing Days	1973	2.50	5.00	10.00
2986		D'yer Mak'er/The Crunge	1973	2.50	5.00	10.00
		Normal pressing in true stereo throughout.				
2986		D'yer Mak'er/The Crunge	1973		3.00	6.00
		Defective pressing -- the left channel starts to fade out midway through the A-side, making it sound like rechan-neled stereo. The number "3" follows the matrix number in the trail-off wax of those copies we've encountered.				

Swan Song

Number		Title (A Side/B Side)	Year	VG	VG+	NM
70102		Trampled Under Foot/Black Country Woman	1975		3.00	6.00
70110		Candy Store Rock/Royal Orleans	1976		3.00	6.00
71003		Fool in the Rain/Hot Dog	1979		3.00	6.00

Lee – See "Mareno, Lee"

Lee and the Leopards
Fortune

Number		Title (A Side/B Side)	Year	VG	VG+	NM
867		What About Me/Don't Press Your Luck	1964	12.50	25.00	50.00

Gordy

7002		Come Into My Palace/Trying to Make It	1962	15.00	30.00	60.00

Laurie

3197		Come Into My Palace/Trying to Make It	1963	6.25	12.50	25.00

Lee, Billy, and the Rivieras
(Early version of Mitch Ryder and the Detroit Wheels)
Hyland

3016		Won't You Dance with Me/You Know	1964	6.25	12.50	25.00

Lee, Brenda
Apollo

Number		Title (A Side/B Side)	Year	VG	VG+	NM
490		I Ain't Gonna Give Nobody None/ I'll Never Get Rich Again	1956	7.50	15.00	30.00
		Not the same Brenda Lee; this one's real name is Brenda Lee Jones				

Decca

Number		Title (A Side/B Side)	Year	VG	VG+	NM
30050		Jambalaya (On the Bayou)/Bigelow 6-2000	1956	7.50	15.00	30.00
30107		Christy Christmas/I'm Gonna Lasso Santa Claus	1956	6.25	12.50	25.00
30198		One Step at a Time/Fairyland	1957	6.25	12.50	25.00
30333		Dynamite/Love You 'Til I Die	1957	6.25	12.50	25.00
30411		Ain't That Love/One Teenager to Another	1957	6.25	12.50	25.00
30535		Rock-a-Bye Baby Blues/Rock the Bop	1958	6.25	12.50	25.00
30673		Ring-a My Phone/Little Jonah	1958	7.50	15.00	30.00
30776		Rockin' Around the Christmas Tree/Papa Noel	1958	6.25	12.50	25.00
		Originals have black labels with star under "Decca"				
30776		Rockin' Around the Christmas Tree/Papa Noel	1960	3.75	7.50	15.00
		Reissues have black labels with color bars				
30776	PS	Rockin' Around the Christmas Tree/Papa Noel	1960	7.50	15.00	30.00
30806		Bill Bailey Won't You Please Come Home/ Hummin' the Blues	1959	6.25	12.50	25.00
30885		Let's Jump the Broomstick/One of These Days	1959	7.50	15.00	30.00
30967		Sweet Nothin's/Weep No More My Baby	1959	3.75	7.50	15.00
30967	PS	Sweet Nothin's/Weep No More My Baby	1959	20.00	40.00	80.00
31093		I'm Sorry/That's All You Gotta Do	1960	3.75	7.50	15.00
31093	PS	I'm Sorry/That's All You Gotta Do	1960	6.25	12.50	25.00
31149		I Want to Be Wanted/Just a Little	1960	3.75	7.50	15.00
31149	PS	I Want to Be Wanted/Just a Little	1960	6.25	12.50	25.00
31195		Emotions/I'm Learning About Love	1961	3.75	7.50	15.00
31195	PS	Emotions/I'm Learning About Love	1961	6.25	12.50	25.00
31231		You Can Depend on Me/It's Never Too Late	1961	3.75	7.50	15.00
31231	PS	You Can Depend on Me/It's Never Too Late	1961	6.25	12.50	25.00
31272		Dum Dum/Eventually	1961	3.75	7.50	15.00
31272	PS	Dum Dum/Eventually	1961	6.25	12.50	25.00
31309		Fool #1/Anybody But Me	1961	3.75	7.50	15.00
31309	PS	Fool #1/Anybody But Me	1961	6.25	12.50	25.00
31348		Break It To Me Gently/So Deep	1962	3.75	7.50	15.00
31348	PS	Break It To Me Gently/So Deep	1962	6.25	12.50	25.00
31379		Everybody Loves Me But You/ Here Comes That Feelin'	1962	3.75	7.50	15.00
31407		Heart in Hand/It Started All Over Again	1962	3.75	7.50	15.00
31424		All Alone Am I/Save All Your Lovin' for Me	1962	3.75	7.50	15.00
31424	PS	All Alone Am I/Save All Your Lovin' for Me	1962	6.25	12.50	25.00
31454		Your Used to Be/She'll Never Know	1963	3.75	7.50	15.00
31454	PS	Your Used to Be/She'll Never Know	1963	6.25	12.50	25.00
31510		My Whole World Is Falling Down/I Wonder	1963	3.75	7.50	15.00
31510	PS	My Whole World Is Falling Down/I Wonder	1963	6.25	12.50	25.00
31539		The Grass Is Greener/Sweet Impossible You	1963	3.75	7.50	15.00
31539	PS	The Grass Is Greener/Sweet Impossible You	1963	6.25	12.50	25.00
31570		As Usual/Lonely Lonely Lonely Me	1963	3.75	7.50	15.00
31599		Think/The Waiting Game	1964	2.50	5.00	10.00
31599	PS	Think/The Waiting Game	1964	3.75	7.50	15.00
31628		Alone with You/My Dreams	1964	2.50	5.00	10.00
31628	PS	Alone with You/My Dreams	1964	3.75	7.50	15.00
31654		When You Loved Me/Be Sure to Remember Me	1964	2.50	5.00	10.00
31654	PS	When You Loved Me/Be Sure to Remember Me	1964	3.75	7.50	15.00
31687		Jingle Bell Rock/Winter Wonderland	1964	3.00	6.00	12.00
31687	PS	Jingle Bell Rock/Winter Wonderland	1964	4.00	8.00	16.00
31688		This Time of the Year/ Christmas Will Be Just Another Lonely Day	1964	3.00	6.00	12.00

Number		Title (A Side/B Side)	Year	VG	VG+	NM
❑ 31688	PS	This Time of the Year/	1964	4.00	8.00	16.00
		Christmas Will Be Just Another Lonely Day				
❑ 31690		Is It True/Just Behind the Rainbow	1964	2.50	5.00	10.00
❑ 31690	PS	Is It True/Just Behind the Rainbow	1964	3.75	7.50	15.00
❑ 31728		Thanks a Lot/The Crying Game	1965	2.50	5.00	10.00
❑ 31762		Truly, Truly, True/I Still Miss Someone	1965	2.50	5.00	10.00
❑ 31762	PS	Truly, Truly, True/I Still Miss Someone	1965	3.75	7.50	15.00
❑ 31792		Too Many Rivers/No One	1965	2.50	5.00	10.00
❑ 31849		Rusty Bells/If You Don't (Not Like You)	1965	2.50	5.00	10.00
❑ 31917		Too Little Time/Time and Time Again	1966	2.00	4.00	8.00
❑ 31970		Ain't Gonna Cry No More/It Takes One to Know One	1966	2.00	4.00	8.00
❑ 32018		Coming On Strong/You Keep Coming Back to Me	1966	2.00	4.00	8.00
❑ 32079		Ride, Ride, Ride/Lonely People Do Foolish Things	1967	2.00	4.00	8.00
❑ 32119		Born to Be By Your Side/Take Me	1967	2.00	4.00	8.00
❑ 32161		My Heart Keeps Hangin' On/Where Love Is	1967	2.00	4.00	8.00
❑ 32213		Save Me for a Rainy Day/Where's the Melody	1967	2.00	4.00	8.00
❑ 32248		That's All Right/Fantasy	1967	2.00	4.00	8.00
❑ 32299		Cabaret/Mood Indigo	1968	2.00	4.00	8.00
		With Pete Fountain				
❑ 32330		Kansas City/Each Day Is a Rainbow	1968	2.00	4.00	8.00
❑ 32428		Johnny One Time/I Must Have Been Out of My Mind	1968	2.00	4.00	8.00
❑ 32428	PS	Johnny One Time/I Must Have Been Out of My Mind	1968	3.75	7.50	15.00
❑ 32491		You Don't Need Me for Anything Anymore/	1969		3.00	6.00
		Bring Me Sunshine				
❑ 32560		Let It Be Me/You Better Move On	1969		3.00	6.00
❑ 32675		I Think I Love You Again/Hello Love	1970		3.00	6.00
❑ 32734		Do Right Woman, Do Right Man/Sisters in Sorrow	1970		3.00	6.00
❑ 32848		If This Is Our Last Time/	1971		3.00	6.00
		Everybody's Reaching Out for Someone				
❑ 32918		I'm a Memory/Misty Memories	1972		3.00	6.00
❑ 32975		Always on My Mind/That Ain't Right	1972		3.00	6.00
❑ 88215		Christy Christmas/I'm Gonna Lasso Santa Claus	1956	12.50	25.00	50.00
		As "Little Brenda Lee" on Decca's Children's Series				
❑ 88215	PS	Christy Christmas/I'm Gonna Lasso Santa Claus	1956	15.00	30.00	60.00
Elektra						
❑ 45492		Left-Over Love/Could It Be I Found Love Tonight	1978		2.50	5.00
Epic						
❑ 04723		Hallelujah I Love Her So/(What Love Can Do)	1984		2.00	4.00
		The Second Time Around				
		George Jones and Brenda Lee				
MCA						
❑ 40003		Nobody Wins/We Had a Good Thing Goin'	1973		2.50	5.00
❑ 40107		Sunday Sunrise/Must I Believe	1973		2.50	5.00
❑ 40171		Wrong Ideas/Something For A Rainy Day	1973		2.50	5.00
❑ 40262		Big Four Poster Bed/Castles In The Sand	1974		2.50	5.00
❑ 40318		Rock On Baby/More Than A Memory	1974		2.50	5.00
❑ 40385		He's My Rock/Feel Free	1975		2.50	5.00
❑ 40442		Bringing It Back/Papa's Knee	1975		2.50	5.00
❑ 40511		Find Yourself Another Puppet/What I Had With You	1976		2.50	5.00
❑ 40584		Brother Shelton/Now He's Coming Home	1976		2.50	5.00
❑ 40640		Takin' What I Can Get/	1976		2.50	5.00
		Your Favorite Wornout Nightmare's Coming Home				
❑ 40683		Ruby's Lounge/Oklahoma Superstar	1977		2.50	5.00
❑ 41130		Tell Me What It's Like/Let Your Love Fall Back On Me	1979		2.50	5.00
❑ 41187		The Cowgirl And The Dandy/	1980		2.50	5.00
		Do You Wanna Spend The Night				
❑ 41262		Keeping Me Warm For You/At The Moonlight	1980		2.50	5.00
❑ 41270		Don't Promise Me Anything (Do It)/	1980		2.50	5.00
		You Only Broke My Heart				
❑ 41322		Broken Trust/Right Behind The Rain	1980		2.50	5.00
		With the Oak Ridge Boys				
❑ 51047		Every Now And Then/He'll Play The Music	1981		2.00	4.00
❑ 51113		Fool, Fool/Right Behind The Rain	1981		2.00	4.00
❑ 51154		Enough For You/What Am I Gonna Do	1981		2.00	4.00
❑ 51195		Only When I Laugh/Too Many Nights Alone	1981		2.00	4.00
❑ 51230		From Levis To Calvin Klein Jeans/	1982		2.00	4.00
		I Know A Lot About Love				
❑ 52060		Keeping Me Warm For You/	1982		2.00	4.00
		There's More To Me Than You Can See				
❑ 52124		Just For The Moment/Love Letters	1982		2.00	4.00
		With the Oak Ridge Boys				
❑ 52268		Didn't We Do It Good/We're So Close	1983		2.00	4.00
❑ 52394		A Sweeter Love (I'll Never Know)/A Woman's Mind	1984		2.00	4.00
❑ 52654		I'm Takin' My Time/That's The Way It Was Then	1985		2.00	4.00
❑ 52720		Why You Been Gone So Long/?	1985		2.00	4.00
❑ 52804		Two Hearts/Loving Arms	1986		2.00	4.00
Monument						
❑ 03781		You're Gonna Love Yourself (In the Morning)/	1983		2.00	4.00
		What Do You Think About Lovin'				
		A-side: With Willie Nelson; B-side: With Dolly Parton				
Warner Bros.						
❑ 19303		A Little Unfair/Some of These Days	1991			3.00
❑ 19397		Your One and Only/You Better Do Better	1991			3.00

Number		Title (A Side/B Side)	Year	VG	VG+	NM

Lee, Curtis

Dunes
☐ 801		California GH-903/Then I'll Know	1960	5.00	10.00	20.00
☐ 2001		Special Love/"D" in Love	1960	5.00	10.00	20.00
☐ 2003		Pledge of Love/Then I'll Know	1961	5.00	10.00	20.00
☐ 2007		Pretty Little Angel Eyes/Gee, How I Wish	1961	6.25	12.50	25.00
☐ 2008		Under the Moon of Love/Beverly Jean	1961	6.25	12.50	25.00
		2007 and 2008 were Phil Spector productions				
☐ 2012		Just Another Fool/A Night at Daddy G's	1962	5.00	10.00	20.00
☐ 2015		Does He Mean That Much to You/The Wobble	1962	5.00	10.00	20.00
☐ 2020		Lonely Weekends/Better Him Than Me	1963	5.00	10.00	20.00
☐ 2021		Pickin' Up the Pieces of My Heart/Mr. Mistaker	1963	5.00	10.00	20.00

Hot
☐ 7		I Never Knew What Love Could Do/Gotta Have You	1960	18.75	37.50	75.00

Mira
☐ 240		Sweet Baby/Is She In Your Town	1967	5.00	10.00	20.00

Rojac
☐ 114		Get In My Bag/Everybody's Going Wild	1967	3.00	6.00	12.00

Sabra
☐ 517		Let's Take a Ride/I'm Asking Forgiveness	1960	6.25	12.50	25.00

Warrior
☐ 1555		With All My Heart/Pure Love	1959	7.50	15.00	30.00

Left Banke, The

Camerica
☐ 005		Queen of Paradise/And One Day	1978		2.50	5.00

Smash
☐ 2041		Walk Away Renee/I Haven't Got the Nerve	1966	3.75	7.50	15.00
☐ 2074		Pretty Ballerina/Lazy Day	1966	3.75	7.50	15.00
☐ 2089		Ivy, Ivy/And Suddenly	1967	3.00	6.00	12.00
☐ 2097		She May Call You Up Tonight/ Barterers and Their Wives	1967	3.00	6.00	12.00
☐ 2119		Desiree/I've Got Something on My Mind	1967	3.00	6.00	12.00
☐ 2119	PS	Desiree/I've Got Something on My Mind	1967	6.25	12.50	25.00
☐ 2165		Dark Is the Bark/My Friend Today	1968	3.00	6.00	12.00
☐ 2198		Goodbye Holly/Sing, Little Bird, Sing	1968	3.00	6.00	12.00
☐ 2209		Bryant Hotel/Give the Man a Hand	1969	3.00	6.00	12.00
☐ 2243		Myrah/Pedestal	1969	10.00	20.00	40.00
		Picture sleeves for 2243 are bootlegs				

Legendary Masked Surfers, The

(Primary members: Dean Torrence, Bruce Johnston, Terry Melcher)

United Artists
☐ 50958		Summertime, Summertime/Gonna Hustle You	1972	7.50	15.00	30.00
☐ XW270		Summer Means Fun/Gonna Hustle You	1973	5.00	10.00	20.00
		Original pressings have a Jan & Dean recording on them by mistake				
☐ XW270		Summer Means Fun/Gonna Hustle You	1973	30.00	60.00	120.00
		With the intended recording, a newly-recorded vocal track				
☐ XW270	PS	Summer Means Fun/Gonna Hustle You	1973	7.50	15.00	30.00

Legendary Stardust Cowboy, The

Mercury
☐ 72862		Paralyzed/Who's Knocking on My Door	1968	5.00	10.00	20.00
☐ 72891		Down in the Wrecking Yard/ I Took a Trip on a Gemini Spaceship	1969	5.00	10.00	20.00
☐ 72912		Everything's Getting Bigger But Our Love/Kiss and Run	1969	5.00	10.00	20.00

Norton
☐ 012		I Hate CD's/Linda	199?			2.00
☐ 012	PS	I Hate CD's/Linda	199?			2.00

Psycho-Suave
☐ 1033		Paralyzed/Who's Knocking on My Door	1968	7.50	15.00	30.00

Legends, The

(Numerous different groups)

Bridge Society
☐ 2204		Keep On Running/Cheating	1968	10.00	20.00	40.00

Caldwell
☐ 410		Go Away with Me/Jungle Lullaby	1962	6.25	12.50	25.00

Capitol
☐ 5014		Summertime Blues/Run to the Movies	1963	5.00	10.00	20.00

Columbia
☐ 41949		Theme from "Exodus"/Later	1961	3.00	6.00	12.00

Doc Holliday
☐ 107		Surf's Up/Dance with the Drummer Man	1963	10.00	20.00	40.00
☐ 107	PS	Surf's Up/Dance with the Drummer Man	1963	12.50	25.00	50.00

Epic
☐ 10937		Rock and Roll Woman/Problems	1973	2.00	4.00	8.00

Ermine
☐ 39		My Love for You/Say Mama	1962	12.50	25.00	50.00
☐ 41		Lariat/Late Train	1962	10.00	20.00	40.00

Number		Title (A Side/B Side)	Year	VG	VG+	NM
❑ 43		Bop-A-Lena/I Wish I Knew	1962	12.50	25.00	50.00
❑ 45		Temptation/Marionette	1962	10.00	20.00	40.00

Hart-Van

❑ 18003		Traction/(B-side unknown)	1962	7.50	15.00	30.00

Heart

❑ 7672		Rock and Roll Woman/Problems	1972	5.00	10.00	20.00

Hull

❑ 727		The Legend of Love/Now I'm Telling You	1958	25.00	50.00	100.00
		Red label				
❑ 727		The Legend of Love/Now I'm Telling You	1962	7.50	15.00	30.00
		Multicolor label				

Jamie

❑ 1228		Tell the Truth/You'll Never See the Forest	1962	5.00	10.00	20.00

Key

❑ 1002		Lariat/Late Train	1961	10.00	20.00	40.00
❑ 1002		Lariat/Gail	1961	10.00	20.00	40.00

Melba

❑ 109		I'll Never Fall in Love Again/Eyes of an Angel	1957	37.50	75.00	150.00
		Label with double horizontal lines				
❑ 109		I'll Never Fall in Love Again/Eyes of an Angel	1961	10.00	20.00	40.00
		Label with no horizontal lines				

Parrot

❑ 45010		Just in Case/If I Only Had Her Back	1965	3.00	6.00	12.00
❑ 45011		Alright/How Can I Find Her	1965	3.00	6.00	12.00

Railroad House

❑ 12003		High Towers/Fever Games	1969	5.00	10.00	20.00
❑ 12003	PS	High Towers/Fever Games	1969	7.50	15.00	30.00

Thames

❑ 104		Raining in My Heart/(B-side unknown)	1964	7.50	15.00	30.00

Up

❑ 2202		Baby, Get Your Head Screwed On/Why	1968	12.50	25.00	50.00

Warner Bros.

❑ 5457		Here Comes the Rain/Don't Be Ashamed	1964	3.75	7.50	15.00

Leigh, Linda

American Int'l.

❑ 540		I Promise You/My Guy	1959	6.25	12.50	25.00
❑ 543		Beri-Beri/The Plan	1959	12.50	25.00	50.00
❑ 546		Foolish Dreams/The Scent	1960	5.00	10.00	20.00

Kash

❑ 1028		Heart/Here I Go Out of Your Life	1965	3.00	6.00	12.00

Rendezvous

❑ 103		Move Out/It's Real	1958	5.00	10.00	20.00
❑ 106		Please Please (Let Me Go Steady)/Teardrops	1959	5.00	10.00	20.00

Reprise

❑ 20,060		Someone Special/Please	1962	3.00	6.00	12.00
❑ 20,078		Lover's Beach/A Thousand Violins	1962	3.00	6.00	12.00

Lemon Pipers, The

Buddah

❑ 11		Turn Around and Take a Look/Danger	1967	2.50	5.00	10.00
❑ 23		Green Tambourine/No Help from Me	1967	3.00	6.00	12.00
❑ 31		Rice Is Nice/Blueberry Blue	1968	2.50	5.00	10.00
❑ 31	PS	Rice Is Nice/Blueberry Blue	1968	3.75	7.50	15.00
❑ 41		Jelly Jungle (Of Orange Marmalade)/Shoe Shine Boy	1968	2.50	5.00	10.00
❑ 63		Wine and Violet/Lonely Atmosphere	1968	2.50	5.00	10.00
❑ 136		I Was Not Born to Follow/Rainbow Tree	1969	2.00	4.00	8.00

Carol

❑ 107		Quiet Please/Monaural 78	1966	3.75	7.50	15.00

Lennon, Freddie

(John Lennon's father)

Jerden

❑ 792		That's My Life (My Love and My Home)/Next Time You Feel Important	1966	20.00	40.00	80.00

Lennon, John

(Also see "Beatles, The")

Apple

❑ 1809		Give Peace a Chance/Remember Love	1969		2.50	5.00
		As "Plastic Ono Band"				
❑ 1809	PS	Give Peace a Chance/Remember Love	1969	3.00	6.00	12.00
❑ 1813		Cold Turkey/	1969	2.50	5.00	
		Don't Worry Kyoko (Mummy's Only Looking for a Hand in the Snow)				
		As "Plastic Ono Band"; most copies skip on A-side on the third chorus because of a pressing defect				
❑ 1813		Cold Turkey/	1969	2.50	5.00	10.00
		Don't Worry Kyoko (Mummy's Only Looking for a Hand in the Snow)				
		As "Plastic Ono Band"; some copies don't skip on A-side. They tend to have wider, bolder print than those that do.				
❑ 1813	PS	Cold Turkey/	1969	18.75	37.50	75.00
		Don't Worry Kyoko (Mummy's Only Looking for a Hand in the Snow)				

Number	Title (A Side/B Side)	Year	VG	VG+	NM
❑ 1818	Instant Karma! (We All Shine On)/ Who Has Seen the Wind?	1970		2.00	4.00
	As "John Ono Lennon"; B-side by "Yoko Ono Lennon"				
❑ 1818	DJ Instant Karma! (We All Shine On)	1970	50.00	100.00	200.00
	As "John Ono Lennon"; one-sided promo				
❑ 1818	PS Instant Karma! (We All Shine On)/ Who Has Seen the Wind?	1970	3.00	6.00	12.00
❑ 1827	Mother/Why	1970	3.00	6.00	12.00
	As "John Lennon/Plastic Ono Band"; star on A-side label				
❑ 1827	Mother/Why	1970	2.00	4.00	8.00
	As "John Lennon/Plastic Ono Band"; B-side by "Yoko Ono/Plastic Ono Band"				
❑ 1827	Mother/Why	1970	10.00	20.00	40.00
	As "John Lennon/Plastic Ono Band"; "MONO" on A-side label				
❑ 1827	PS Mother/Why	1970	25.00	50.00	100.00
❑ 1830	Power to the People/Touch Me	1971	2.00	4.00	8.00
	As "John Lennon/Plastic Ono Band"; B-side by "Yoko Ono/Plastic Ono Band"				
❑ 1830	Power to the People/Touch Me	1971	2.00	4.00	8.00
	As "John Lennon/Plastic Ono Band"; with star on A-side label				
❑ 1830	PS Power to the People/Touch Me	1971	7.50	15.00	30.00
❑ 1840	Imagine/It's So Hard	1971	2.00	4.00	8.00
	As "John Lennon Plastic Ono Band"; tan label				
❑ 1840	Imagine/It's So Hard	1975	3.00	6.00	12.00
	As "John Lennon Plastic Ono Band"; green label with "All Rights Reserved"				
❑ 1842	Happy Xmas (War Is Over)/Listen, the Snow Is Falling	1971	3.75	7.50	15.00
	As "John & Yoko/Plastic Ono Band with the Harlem Community Choir"; green vinyl, faces label				
❑ 1842	Happy Xmas (War Is Over)/Listen, the Snow Is Falling	1971	2.50	5.00	10.00
	As "John & Yoko/Plastic Ono Band with the Harlem Community Choir"; green vinyl, Apple label				
❑ 1842	PS Happy Xmas (War Is Over)/Listen, the Snow Is Falling	1971	5.00	10.00	20.00
❑ 1848	Woman Is the Nigger of the World/Sisters O Sisters	1972	2.00	4.00	8.00
	As "John Lennon/Plastic Ono Band..."; B-side by "Yoko Ono/Plastic Ono Band..."				
❑ 1848	PS Woman Is the Nigger of the World/Sisters O Sisters	1972	6.25	12.50	25.00
❑ 1868	Mind Games/Meat City	1973	3.00	6.00	
❑ 1868	PS Mind Games/Meat City	1973	3.75	7.50	15.00
❑ P-1868	DJ Mind Games (mono/stereo)	1973	12.50	25.00	50.00
❑ 1874	Whatever Gets You Thru the Night/Beef Jerky	1974	3.00	6.00	
	As "John Lennon and the Plastic Ono Nuclear Band"				
❑ P-1874	DJ Whatever Gets You Thru the Night (mono/stereo)	1974	12.50	25.00	50.00
	As "John Lennon and the Plastic Ono Nuclear Band"				
❑ 1878	#9 Dream/What You Got	1974	2.00	4.00	8.00
❑ P-1878	DJ #9 Dream (edited mono/stereo)	1974	12.50	25.00	50.00
❑ P-1878	DJ What You Got (mono/stereo)	1974	25.00	50.00	100.00
❑ 1881	Stand By Me/Move Over Ms. L.	1975	2.00	4.00	8.00
❑ P-1881	DJ Stand By Me (mono/stereo)	1975	12.50	25.00	50.00
❑ P-1883	DJ Slippin' and Slidin' (mono/stereo)	1975	50.00	100.00	200.00
	No stock copies issued				
❑ P-1883	DJ Ain't That a Shame (mono/stereo)	1975	50.00	100.00	200.00
	No stock copies issued				
❑ S45X-47663/4	DJ Happy Xmas (War Is Over)/Listen, the Snow Is Falling	1971	187.50	375.00	750.00
	As "John & Yoko/Plastic Ono Band with the Harlem Community Choir"; white label on styrene				

Apple/Americom

❑ 1809P/M-435	Give Peace a Chance/Remember Love	1969	187.50	375.00	750.00
	As "Plastic Ono Band"; four-inch flexi-disc sold in vending machines				

Atlantic

❑ PR-104/5	DJ John Lennon on Ronnie Hawkins: The Short Rap/ The Long Rap	1970	25.00	50.00	100.00

Capitol

❑ 1840	Imagine/It's So Hard	1978		3.00	6.00
	As "John Lennon Plastic Ono Band"; purple late 1970s label				
❑ 1840	Imagine/It's So Hard	1983		3.00	6.00
	As "John Lennon Plastic Ono Band"; black colorband label				
❑ 1840	Imagine/It's So Hard	1988		2.50	5.00
	As "John Lennon Plastic Ono Band"; purple late-1980s label (wider)				
❑ 1842	Happy Xmas (War Is Over)/Listen, the Snow Is Falling	1976	12.50	25.00	50.00
	As "John & Yoko/Plastic Ono Band with the Harlem Community Choir"; orange label				
❑ 1842	Happy Xmas (War Is Over)/Listen, the Snow Is Falling	1978		3.00	6.00
	As "John & Yoko/Plastic Ono Band with the Harlem Community Choir"; purple late-1970s label				
❑ 1842	Happy Xmas (War Is Over)/Listen, the Snow Is Falling	1983		3.00	6.00
	As "John & Yoko/Plastic Ono Band with the Harlem Community Choir"; black colorband label				
❑ 1842	Happy Xmas (War Is Over)/Listen, the Snow Is Falling	1988	5.00	10.00	20.00
	As "John & Yoko/Plastic Ono Band with the Harlem Community Choir"; purple late-1980s label (wider)				
❑ 1868	Mind Games/Meat City	1978		3.00	6.00
	Purple late-1970s label				
❑ 1868	Mind Games/Meat City	1983	3.00	6.00	12.00
	Black colorband label				
❑ 1874	Whatever Gets You Thru the Night/Beef Jerky	1978		3.00	6.00
	Purple late-1970s label				
❑ 1874	Whatever Gets You Thru the Night/Beef Jerky	1983		3.00	6.00
	Black colorband label				
❑ 1874	Whatever Gets You Thru the Night/Beef Jerky	1988		3.00	6.00
	Purple late-1980s label				

Number		Title (A Side/B Side)	Year	VG	VG+	NM
❑ 1878		#9 Dream/What You Got	1976	10.00	20.00	40.00
		Orange label				
❑ 1878		#9 Dream/What You Got	1978		3.00	6.00
		Purple late-1970s label				
❑ 1878		#9 Dream/What You Got	1983		2.50	5.00	10.00
		Black colorband label				
❑ S7-17644		Happy Xmas (War Is Over)/Listen, the Snow Is Falling	1993		2.00	4.00
		John & Yoko/The Plastic Ono Band; green vinyl				
❑ S7-17783		Give Peace a Chance/Remember Love	1994	25.00	50.00	100.00
		CEMA Special Markets issue; meant for gold-plating in a special plaque. About 100 were not.				
❑ B-44230		Jealous Guy/Give Peace a Chance	1988		2.50	5.00
❑ B-44230	PS	Jealous Guy/Give Peace a Chance	1988		2.50	5.00
❑ S7-57849		Imagine/It's So Hard	1992	12.50	25.00	50.00
		CEMA Special Markets issue; meant for gold-plating in a special plaque. About 1,000 were not.				

Cotillion

❑ PR-104/5	DJ	John Lennon on Ronnie Hawkins: The Short Rap/The Long Rap	1970	22.50	45.00	90.00
		No promo markings on white label				
❑ PR-104/5	DJ	John Lennon on Ronnie Hawkins: The Short Rap/The Long Rap	1970	20.00	40.00	80.00
		White label with promo markings				

Geffen

❑ 29855		Happy Xmas (War Is Over)/Beautiful Boy (Darling Boy)	1982		2.50	5.00
❑ 29855	PS	Happy Xmas (War Is Over)/Beautiful Boy (Darling Boy)	1982		2.50	5.00
❑ 49604		(Just Like) Starting Over/Kiss Kiss Kiss	1980		2.00	4.00
		B-side by Yoko Ono				
❑ 49604	PS	(Just Like) Starting Over/Kiss Kiss Kiss	1980		2.00	4.00
❑ 49644		Woman/Beautiful Boys	1980		2.00	4.00
		B-side by Yoko Ono				
❑ 49644	PS	Woman/Beautiful Boys	1980		2.00	4.00
❑ 49695		Watching the Wheels/Yes, I'm Your Angel	1981		2.00	4.00
		B-side by Yoko Ono				
❑ 49695	PS	Watching the Wheels/Yes, I'm Your Angel	1981		2.00	4.00

KYA

❑ 1260	DJ	The KYA 1969 Peace Talk	1969	50.00	100.00	200.00

Polydor

❑ 817 254-7		Nobody Told Me/O' Sanity	1983		2.50	5.00
		With "Manufactured and Marketed by Polygram..." on label; B-side by Yoko Ono				
❑ 817 254-7		Nobody Told Me/O' Sanity	1983	2.50	5.00	10.00
		With "Manufactured by Polydor Incorporated..." on label; B-side by Yoko Ono				
❑ 817 254-7	PS	Nobody Told Me/O' Sanity	1983		2.50	5.00
❑ 821 107-7		I'm Stepping Out/Sleepless Night	1984		2.00	4.00
		B-side by Yoko Ono				
❑ 821 107-7	PS	I'm Stepping Out/Sleepless Night	1984		2.00	4.00
❑ 821 204-7		Borrowed Time/Your Hands	1984		2.50	5.00
		B-side by Yoko Ono				
❑ 821 204-7	PS	Borrowed Time/Your Hands	1984		2.50	5.00
❑ 881 378-7		Every Man Has a Woman Who Loves Him/It's Alright	1984	2.00	4.00	8.00
		B-side by Sean Ono Lennon				
❑ 881 378-7	PS	Every Man Has a Woman Who Loves Him/It's Alright	1984	2.00	4.00	8.00

Quaker Granola Dipps

❑ (no #)		A Tribute to John Lennon	1986	3.75	7.50	15.00
		Cardboard record included in specially marked boxes of Quaker Granola Dipps				

Quaye/Trident

❑ SK 3419	DJ	Rock 'N' Roll	1975	125.00	250.00	500.00
		Radio spot to promote the album Rock 'N' Roll				

Lester, Bobby, and the Moonlighters
(The Moonlighters are the Moonglows)

Checker

❑ 806		So All Alone/Shoo Doo-Be Do (My Loving Baby)	1954	25.00	50.00	100.00
		Maroon label with checkerboard top				
❑ 806		So All Alone/Shoo Doo-Be Do (My Loving Baby)	1958	10.00	20.00	40.00
		Maroon label, vertical logo				
❑ 813		New Gal/The Hug and a Kiss	1955	20.00	40.00	80.00

Levon and the Hawks
(Later became The Band)

Atco

❑ 6383		He Don't Love You (And He'll Break Your Heart)/Stones I Throw	1965	7.50	15.00	30.00
❑ 6625		He Don't Love You (And He'll Break Your Heart)/Go Go Lisa Jane	1968	7.50	15.00	30.00

Lewis, Barbara

Atlantic

❑ 2141		My Heart Went Do Dat Da/The Longest Night of the Year	1962	3.00	6.00	12.00
❑ 2159		My Mama Told Me/Gonna Love You Till the Day I Die	1962	3.00	6.00	12.00
❑ 2184		Hello Stranger/Think a Little Sugar	1963	3.75	7.50	15.00
❑ 2200		Straighten Up Your Heart/If You Love Her	1963	3.00	6.00	12.00

Number			Title (A Side/B Side)	Year	VG	VG+	NM
☐ 2214			Puppy Love/Snap Your Fingers	1963	3.00	6.00	12.00
☐ 2227			Someday We're Gonna Love Again/Spend a Little Time	1964	2.50	5.00	10.00
☐ 2255			Come Home/Pushin' a Good Thing Too Far	1964	2.50	5.00	10.00
☐ 2283			Baby, I'm Yours/I Say Love	1965	3.00	6.00	12.00
☐ 2300			Make Me Your Baby/Love to Be Loved	1965	3.00	6.00	12.00
☐ 2316			Don't Forget About Me/It's Magic	1965	2.50	5.00	10.00
☐ 2346			Make Me Belong to You/Girls Need Loving Care	1966	2.00	4.00	8.00
☐ 2361			I Remember the Feeling/	1966	2.00	4.00	8.00
			Baby What You Want Me to Do				
☐ 2400			Love Makes the World Go Round/	1967	2.00	4.00	8.00
			I'll Make Him Love Me				
☐ 2413			Fool, Fool, Fool/Only All the Time	1967	2.00	4.00	8.00
☐ 2482			Thankful for What I Got/Sho Nuff	1968	2.00	4.00	8.00
☐ 2514			On Bended Knees/I'll Keep Believing	1968	2.00	4.00	8.00
☐ 2550			I'm All You've Got/You're a Dream Maker	1968	2.00	4.00	8.00
Enterprise							
☐ 9012			You Made Me a Woman/Just the Way You Are Today	1970		3.00	6.00
☐ 9027			Ask the Lonely/Why Did It Take You So Long	1970		3.00	6.00
☐ 9029			Anyway/That's the Way I Like It	1970		3.00	6.00
Karen							
☐ 313			My Heart Went Do Dat Da/	1961	7.50	15.00	30.00
			The Longest Night of the Year				
Reprise							
☐ 1146			Rock and Roll Lullaby/I'm So Thankful	1972		2.50	5.00

Lewis, Bobby

(These are the R&B Bobby Lewis. Not included are records by the country Bobby Lewis)

Number			Title (A Side/B Side)	Year	VG	VG+	NM
ABC-Paramount							
☐ 10565			That's Right/Fannie Lewis	1964	3.00	6.00	12.00
☐ 10592			Jealous Love/Stark Raving Wild	1964	3.00	6.00	12.00
Beltone							
☐ 1002			Tossin' and Turnin'/Oh Yes I Love You	1961	5.00	10.00	20.00
☐ 1012			One Track Mind/Are You Ready	1961	5.00	10.00	20.00
☐ 1015			What a Walk/Cry No More	1961	3.75	7.50	15.00
☐ 1016			Yes, Oh Yes, It Did/Mamie in the Afternoon	1962	3.75	7.50	15.00
☐ 2018			A Man's Gotta Be a Man/Day by Day I Need Your Love	1962	3.75	7.50	15.00
☐ 2023			I'm Tossin' and Turnin' Again/Nothin' But the Blues	1962	3.75	7.50	15.00
☐ 2026			Lonely Teardrops/Boom-a-Chick-Chick	1962	3.75	7.50	15.00
☐ 2035			Nothin' But the Blues/Intermission	1963	3.75	7.50	15.00
Mercury							
☐ 71245			Mumbles Blues/Oh Baby	1957	6.25	12.50	25.00
Philips							
☐ 40519			Soul Seekin'/Give Me Your Yesterdays	1968	5.00	10.00	20.00
Roulette							
☐ 4182			You Better Stop/Fire of Love	1959	3.75	7.50	15.00
Spotlight							
☐ 394			Mumbles Blues/Oh Baby	1957	7.50	15.00	30.00

Lewis, Clarence

Number			Title (A Side/B Side)	Year	VG	VG+	NM
Fury							
☐ 1032			Cupid's Little Helper/Half a Heart	1960	3.75	7.50	15.00
Red Robin							
☐ 136			Lost Everything/Your Heart Must Be Made of Stone	1955	20.00	40.00	80.00

Lewis, Gary, and the Playboys

Number			Title (A Side/B Side)	Year	VG	VG+	NM
Epic							
☐ 50068			One Good Woman/Ooh Baby	1975	2.00	4.00	8.00
			Gary Lewis solo				
Liberty							
☐ (no #)	DJ		Way Way Out (same on both sides)	1967	125.00	250.00	500.00
☐ 55756			This Diamond Ring/Hard to Find	1964	3.00	6.00	12.00
☐ 55756			This Diamond Ring/Tijuana Wedding	1964	2.50	5.00	10.00
☐ 55778			Count Me In/Little Miss Go-Go	1965	2.50	5.00	10.00
☐ 55809			Save Your Heart for Me/Without a Word of Warning	1965	2.50	5.00	10.00
☐ 55818			Everybody Loves a Clown/Time Stands Still	1965	2.50	5.00	10.00
☐ 55818	PS		Everybody Loves a Clown/Time Stands Still	1965	3.75	7.50	15.00
☐ 55846			She's Just My Style/I Won't Make That Mistake Again	1965	2.50	5.00	10.00
☐ 55846	PS		She's Just My Style/I Won't Make That Mistake Again	1965	3.75	7.50	15.00
☐ 55865			Sure Gonna Miss Her/I Don't Wanna Say Goodnight	1966	2.50	5.00	10.00
☐ 55865	PS		Sure Gonna Miss Her/I Don't Wanna Say Goodnight	1966	3.75	7.50	15.00
☐ 55880			Green Grass/I Can Read Between the Lines	1966	2.50	5.00	10.00
☐ 55880	PS		Green Grass/I Can Read Between the Lines	1966	3.75	7.50	15.00
☐ 55898			My Heart's Symphony/Tina	1966	2.50	5.00	10.00
☐ 55898	PS		My Heart's Symphony/Tina	1966	3.75	7.50	15.00
☐ 55914			(You Don't Have to) Paint Me a Picture/	1966	2.50	5.00	10.00
			Looking for the Stars				
☐ 55914	PS		(You Don't Have to) Paint Me a Picture/	1966	3.75	7.50	15.00
			Looking for the Stars				
☐ 55932			Down on the Sloop John B/Ice Melts in the Sun	1966		*Unreleased*	
☐ 55933			Where Will the Words Come From/	1966	2.50	5.00	10.00
			May the Best Man Win				
☐ 55949			The Loser (With a Broken Heart)/Ice Melts in the Sun	1967	2.50	5.00	10.00
☐ 55949	PS		The Loser (With a Broken Heart)/Ice Melts in the Sun	1967	3.75	7.50	15.00
☐ 55971			Girls in Love/Let's Be More Than Friends	1967	2.00	4.00	8.00
☐ 55985			Jill/New in Town	1967	2.00	4.00	8.00

Number		Title (A Side/B Side)	Year	VG	VG+	NM
☐ 56011		Has She Got the Nicest Eyes/Happiness	1967	2.00	4.00	8.00
☐ 56037		Sealed with a Kiss/Sara Jane	1968	2.00	4.00	8.00
☐ 56075		C.C. Rider/Main Street	1968		3.00	6.00
☐ 56093		Rhythm of the Rain/Mister Memory	1969		3.00	6.00
☐ 56093		Every Day I Have to Cry Some/Mister Memory	1969		3.00	6.00
☐ 56121		Hayride/Gary's Groove	1969		3.00	6.00
☐ 56144		I Saw Elvis Presley Last Night/Something Is Wrong	1969	3.00	6.00	12.00
☐ 56158		Great Balls of Fire/I'm On the Road Right Now	1970		3.00	6.00
☐ 65-227	DJ	Doin' the Flake//This Diamond Ring/Little Miss Go-Go	1965	6.25	12.50	25.00
☐ 65-227	PS	Doin' the Flake//This Diamond Ring/Little Miss Go-Go	1965	12.50	25.00	50.00
		Kellogg's Corn Flakes giveaway				

Scepter

☐ 12359		Peace of Mind/Then Again Maybe	1972	2.00	4.00	8.00
		Gary Lewis solo				

United Artists

Note: 0064 through 0067 are "Silver Spotlight Series" reissues

☐ 0064		This Diamond Ring/My Heart's Symphony	1973		2.00	4.00
☐ 0065		Count Me In/Save Your Heart for Me	1973		2.00	4.00
☐ 0066		Everybody Loves a Clown/Sure Gonna Miss Her	1973		2.00	4.00
☐ 0067		She's Just My Style/Green Grass	1973		2.00	4.00

Lewis, Jerry Lee

Elektra

☐ 46030		Rockin' My Life Away/I Wish I Was Eighteen Again	1979		2.00	4.00
☐ 46067		Who Will the Next Fool Be/Rita May	1979		2.00	4.00
☐ 46591		When Two Worlds Collide/Good News Travels Fast	1980		2.00	4.00
☐ 46642		Honky Tonk Stuff/Rockin' Jerry Lee	1980		2.00	4.00
☐ 47026		Over the Rainbow/Folsom Prison Blues	1980		2.00	4.00
☐ 47095		Thirty-Nine and Holding/Change Places with Me	1980		2.00	4.00
☐ 69962		I'd Do It All Again/Who Will Buy the Wine	1982		2.00	4.00

MCA

☐ 52151		My Fingers Do the Talkin'/Forever Forgiving	1983			3.00
☐ 52188		Come As You Were/Circumstantial Evidence	1983			3.00
☐ 52233		She Sings Amazing Grace/ Why You Been Gone So Long	1983			3.00
☐ 52369		I Am What I Am/That Was the Way It Was Then	1984			3.00

Mercury

☐ 55011		Middle Age Crazy/Georgia on My Mind	1977		2.00	4.00
☐ 55021		Come On In/Who's Sorry Now	1977		2.00	4.00
☐ 55028		I'll Find It Where I Can/ Don't Let the Stars Get In Your Eyes	1977		2.00	4.00
☐ 73099		There Must Be More to Love Than This/ Home Away from Home	1970		3.00	6.00
☐ 73155		I Can't Have a Merry Christmas, Mary (Without You)/ In Loving Memories	1970		3.00	6.00
☐ 73192		Touching Home/Woman, Woman	1971		3.00	6.00
☐ 73227		When He Walks on You (Like You Have Walked on Me)/ Foolish Kind of Man	1971		3.00	6.00
☐ 73248		Would You Take Another Chance on Me/ Me and Bobby McGee	1971		3.00	6.00
☐ 73273		Chantilly Lace/Think About It Darlin'	1972		2.50	5.00
☐ 73296		Lonely Weekends/Turn On Your Love Light	1972		2.50	5.00
☐ 73303		Writing on the Wall/Me and Jesus	1972		2.50	5.00
		With Linda Gail Lewis				
☐ 73328		Who's Gonna Play This Old Piano/ No Honky Tonks in Heaven	1972		2.50	5.00
☐ 73361		No More Hanging On/Mercy of a Letter	1973		2.50	5.00
☐ 73374		Drinking Wine Spo-Dee O'Dee/Rock and Roll Medley	1973		2.50	5.00
☐ 73402		No Headstone on My Grave/Jack Daniels	1973		2.50	5.00
☐ 73423		Sometimes a Memory Ain't Enough/ I Think I Need to Pray	1973		2.50	5.00
☐ 73452		I'm Left, You're Right, She's Gone/ I've Fallen to the Bottom	1974		2.50	5.00
☐ 73491		Tell Tale Signs/Cold, Cold Morning Light	1974		2.50	5.00
☐ 73618		He Can't Fill My Shoes/Tomorrow's Taking Baby Away	1974		2.50	5.00
☐ 73661		I Can Still Hear the Music in the Restroom/ Remember Me	1975		2.00	4.00
☐ 73685		Boogie Woogie Country Man/I'm Still Jealous of You	1975		2.00	4.00
☐ 73729		A Damn Good Country Song/ When I Take My Vacation in Heaven	1975		2.00	4.00
☐ 73763		Don't Boogie Woogie/That Kind of Fool	1976		2.00	4.00
☐ 73822		Let's Put It Back Together Again/ Jerry Lee's Rock and Roll Revival Show	1976		2.00	4.00
☐ 73872		The Closest Thing to You/You Belong to Me	1976		2.00	4.00
☐ 76148		I'm So Lonesome I Could Cry/(B-side unknown)	1982		2.00	4.00

Polydor

☐ 889 312-7		Breathless/Great Balls of Fire	1989		2.00	4.00
☐ 889 798-7		Crazy Arms/Great Balls of Fire	1989		2.00	4.00

SCR

☐ 386		Get Out Your Big Roll, Daddy/ Honky Tonkin' Rock 'N' Roll Piano Man	1985		2.50	5.00

Sire

☐ 19809		It Was the Whiskey Talkin' (Not Me)/ same (Rock and Roll Version)	1990			3.00

Two really cool, and rarely seen, picture sleeves: At top is Jerry Lee Lewis making small talk with a pretty woman in "Great Balls of Fire," a scarce Sun sleeve. Below it is the promo-only picture sleeve for the Mamas and the Papas' semi-autobiographical hit "Creeque Alley."

Number		Title (A Side/B Side)	Year	VG	VG+	NM
Smash						
❑ 1857		Pen and Paper/Hit the Road Jack	1963	3.75	7.50	15.00
❑ 1886		I'm on Fire/Bread and Butter Man	1964	10.00	20.00	40.00
❑ 1906		She Was My Baby (He Was My Friend)/ The Hole He Said He'd Dig for Me	1964	3.75	7.50	15.00
❑ 1930		High Heel Sneakers/You Went Back on Your Word	1964	3.75	7.50	15.00
❑ 1969		Baby Hold Me Close/I Believe in You	1965	3.75	7.50	15.00
❑ 1992		This Must Be the Place/ Rocking Pneumonia and the Boogie Woogie Flu	1965	3.75	7.50	15.00
❑ 2006		Green, Green Grass of Home/ You've Got What It Takes	1965	3.75	7.50	15.00
❑ 2027		Sticks and Stones/What a Heck of a Mess	1966	3.00	6.00	12.00
❑ 2053		If I Had It All to Do Over/Memphis Beat	1966	3.00	6.00	12.00
❑ 2103		Holding On/It's a Hang-Up, Baby	1967	3.00	6.00	12.00
❑ 2122		Turn On Your Love Light/Shotgun Man	1967	3.00	6.00	12.00
❑ 2146		Another Place, Another Time/ Walking the Floor Over You	1968	2.50	5.00	10.00
❑ 2164		What's Made Milwaukee Famous (Has Made a Loser Out of Me)/ All the Good Is Gone	1968	2.50	5.00	10.00
❑ 2186		She Still Comes Around (To Love What's Left of Me)/ Slipping Around	1968	2.50	5.00	10.00
❑ 2202		To Make Love Sweeter for You/Let's Talk About Us	1968	2.50	5.00	10.00
❑ 2220		Don't Let Me Cross Over/ We Live in Two Different Worlds *With Linda Gail Lewis*	1969	2.00	4.00	8.00
❑ 2224		One Has My Name (The Other Has My Heart)/ I Can't Stop Loving You	1969	2.00	4.00	8.00
❑ 2244		She Even Woke Me Up to Say Goodbye/Echoes	1969	2.00	4.00	8.00
❑ 2254		Roll Over Beethoven/Secret Places *With Linda Gail Lewis*	1969	2.00	4.00	8.00
❑ 2257		Once More with Feeling/ You Went Out of Your Way (To Walk on Me)	1970	2.00	4.00	8.00
❑ 884 934-7		Sixteen Candles/Rock and Roll (Fais-Do-Do) *B-side with Roy Orbison, Carl Perkins and Johnny Cash*	1986		2.00	4.00
❑ 888 142-7		We Remember the King/Class of '55 *With Johnny Cash, Roy Orbison and Carl Perkins; B-side by Carl Perkins solo*	1987		2.00	4.00
Sun						
❑ 259		Crazy Arms/End of the Road *As "Jerry Lee Lewis"*	1957	25.00	50.00	100.00
❑ 259		Crazy Arms/End of the Road *As "Jerry Lee Lewis and His Pumping Piano"*	1957	12.50	25.00	50.00
❑ 267		Whole Lot of Shakin' Going On/It'll Be Me	1957	7.50	15.00	30.00
❑ 281		Great Balls of Fire/You Win Again	1957	7.50	15.00	30.00
❑ 281	PS	Great Balls of Fire/You Win Again	1957	15.00	30.00	60.00
❑ 288		Breathless/Down the Line	1958	6.25	12.50	25.00
❑ 296		High School Confidential/Fools Like Me	1958	6.25	12.50	25.00
❑ 296	PS	High School Confidential/Fools Like Me	1958	15.00	30.00	60.00
❑ 301		Lewis Boogie/The Return of Jerry Lee *B-side by George and Louis*	1958	7.50	15.00	30.00
❑ 303		I'll Make It All Up to You/Break-Up	1958	6.25	12.50	30.00
❑ 312		I'll Sail My Ship Alone/It Hurt Me So	1958	6.25	12.50	25.00
❑ 317		Lovin' Up a Storm/Big Blond Baby	1959	6.25	12.50	25.00
❑ 324		Let's Talk About Us/Ballad of Billy Joe	1959	6.25	12.50	25.00
❑ 330		Little Queenie/I Could Never Be Ashamed of You	1959	6.25	12.50	25.00
❑ 337		Old Black Joe/Baby Baby, Bye Bye	1960	5.00	10.00	20.00
❑ 344		Hang Up My Rock and Roll Shoes/John Henry	1960	5.00	10.00	20.00
❑ 352		Love Made a Fool of Me/When I Get Paid	1960	5.00	10.00	20.00
❑ 356		What'd I Say/Livin' Lovin' Wreck	1961	5.00	10.00	20.00
❑ 364		Cold, Cold Heart/It Won't Happen with Me	1961	5.00	10.00	20.00
❑ 367		Save the Last Dance for Me/As Long As I Live	1961	5.00	10.00	20.00
❑ 371		Money/Bonnie B	1961	5.00	10.00	20.00
❑ 374		I've Been Twistin'/Ramblin' Rose	1962	5.00	10.00	20.00
❑ 379		Sweet Little Sixteen/How's My Ex Treating You	1962	5.00	10.00	20.00
❑ 382		Good Golly Miss Molly/I Can't Trust Me	1962	5.00	10.00	20.00
❑ 384		Teenage Letter/Seasons of My Heart	1963	5.00	10.00	20.00
❑ 396		Carry Me Back to Old Virginny/I Know What It Means	1965	5.00	10.00	20.00
❑ 1101		Invitation to Your Party/ I Could Never Be Ashamed of You	1969		3.00	6.00
❑ 1107		One Minute Past Eternity/Frankie and Johnny	1969		3.00	6.00
❑ 1115		I Can't Seem to Say Goodbye/Goodnight Irene	1970		2.50	5.00
❑ 1119		Waiting for the Train (All Around the Watertank)/ Big Legged Woman	1970		2.50	5.00
❑ 1125		Love on Broadway/Matchbox	1971		2.50	5.00
❑ 1128		Your Loving Ways/ I Can't Trust Me in Your Arms Anymore	1972		2.50	5.00
❑ 1130		Good Rockin' Tonight/ I Can't Trust Me in Your Arms Anymore	1973		2.50	5.00
❑ 1138		Matchbox/Am I to Be the One	1978		2.00	4.00
❑ 1139		Save the Last Dance for Me/Am I to Be the One *With uncredited "duet" partner, actually Orion (Jimmy Ellis); a shameless attempt to concoct a "lost Elvis Presley duet"*	1978		2.00	4.00
❑ 1141		Cold, Cold Heart/Hello Josephine	1979		2.00	4.00
❑ 1151		Be-Bop-a-Lula/The Breakup *B-side by Charlie Rich; both sides are duets with Orion*	1980		2.00	4.00

Number	Title (A Side/B Side)	Year	VG	VG+	NM

Lewis, Rudy
(Ex-Drifters)
Atlantic

| ☐ 2193 | I've Loved You So Long/Baby I Dig Love | 1963 | 3.00 | 6.00 | 12.00 |

RCA Victor

| ☐ 47-7792 | Moonbeam/Beer, Beer and More Beer | 1960 | 5.00 | 10.00 | 20.00 |
| | *With the Sputnicks* | | | | |

Lewis, Sabby
ABC-Paramount

| ☐ 9685 | Ding-a-Ling/Kenny's Blues | 1956 | 10.00 | 20.00 | 40.00 |
| ☐ 9687 | Forgive Me, My Love/Regretting | 1956 | 10.00 | 20.00 | 40.00 |

Gone

| ☐ 5074 | Swana/Sabby | 1959 | 6.25 | 12.50 | 25.00 |
| | *With the Uniques* | | | | |

Lewis, Sammie
Sun

| ☐ 218 | So Long Baby Goodbye/I Feel So Worried | 1955 | 25.00 | 50.00 | 100.00 |

Lewis, Smiley
Dot

| ☐ 16674 | I Wonder/Lookin' for My Woman | 1964 | 2.50 | 5.00 | 10.00 |

Imperial

Note: Smiley Lewis records on Imperial before 5194 are unconfirmed on 45 rpm

☐ 5194	The Bells Are Ringing/Lillie Mae	1952	30.00	60.00	120.00
☐ 5208	Gumbo Blues/It's So Peaceful	1952	25.00	50.00	100.00
☐ 5224	Gypsy Blues/You're Not the One	1953	25.00	50.00	100.00
☐ 5234	Play Girl/Big Mamou	1953	20.00	40.00	80.00
☐ 5234	Play Girl/Big Mamou	1953	62.50	125.00	250.00
	Red vinyl				
☐ 5241	Caldonia's Party/Oh Baby	1953	20.00	40.00	80.00
☐ 5252	Little Fernandez/It's Music	1953	20.00	40.00	80.00
☐ 5268	Down the Road/Blue Monday	1954	20.00	40.00	80.00
☐ 5279	I Love You for Sentimental Reasons/The Rocks	1954	20.00	40.00	80.00
☐ 5296	Can't Stop Loving You/That Certain Door	1954	20.00	40.00	80.00
☐ 5316	Too Many Drivers/Ooh La La	1954	20.00	40.00	80.00
☐ 5325	Jailbird/Farewell	1955	20.00	40.00	80.00
☐ 5349	Real Gone Lover/Nobody Knows	1955	20.00	40.00	80.00
☐ 5356	I Hear You Knocking/Bumpity Bump	1955	25.00	50.00	100.00
☐ 5372	Queen of Hearts/Come On	1956	20.00	40.00	80.00
☐ 5380	One Night/Ain't Gonna Do It	1956	20.00	40.00	80.00
☐ 5389	She's Got Me (Hook, Line and Sinker)/ Please Listen to Me	1956	20.00	40.00	80.00
☐ 5404	Down Yonder We Go Ballin'/Someday You'll Want Me	1956	20.00	40.00	80.00
☐ 5418	Shame, Shame, Shame/No No	1957	15.00	30.00	60.00
☐ 5431	You Are My Sunshine/ Sweeter Words Have Never Been Spoken	1957	10.00	20.00	40.00
☐ 5450	Go On Fool/Goin' to Jump and Shout	1957	7.50	15.00	30.00
☐ 5470	Rootin' and Tootin'/I Can't Believe	1957	7.50	15.00	30.00
☐ 5478	Bad Luck Blues/School Days Are Back Again	1957	7.50	15.00	30.00
☐ 5531	Lil' Liza Jane/My Love Is Gone	1958	6.25	12.50	25.00
☐ 5662	Oh Red!/I Want to Be with Her	1960	3.75	7.50	15.00
☐ 5676	Last Night/Ain't Goin' There No More	1960	3.75	7.50	15.00
☐ 5719	Stormy Monday Blues/Tell Me Who	1961	3.75	7.50	15.00
☐ 5820	Gumbo Blues/Tee Nah Nah	1962	3.75	7.50	15.00

Knight

| ☐ 2007 | Baby Please/I Shall Not Be Moved | 1959 | 3.75 | 7.50 | 15.00 |
| ☐ 2011 | Lost Weekend/By the Water | 1959 | 3.75 | 7.50 | 15.00 |

Loma

| ☐ 2024 | Bells Are Ringing/Walkin' the Girl | 1965 | 2.50 | 5.00 | 10.00 |

Okeh

| ☐ 7146 | I'm Coming Down with the Blues/Tune-Up | 1962 | 3.00 | 6.00 | 12.00 |

Lifeguards, The
(More than one group)
ABC-Paramount

| ☐ 10021 | Everybody Out'a the Pool/Teenage Tango | 1959 | 10.00 | 20.00 | 40.00 |

Casa Blanca

| ☐ 5535 | Everybody Out'a the Pool/Teenage Tango | 1959 | 12.50 | 25.00 | 50.00 |

Catch

| ☐ 104 | State Beach/(B-side unknown) | 1964 | 7.50 | 15.00 | 30.00 |

DR

| ☐ 69 | Everybody Out'a the Pool/Teenage Tango | 1965 | 3.75 | 7.50 | 15.00 |

Reprise

| ☐ 0277 | Swim Party/Swimtime U.S.A. | 1964 | 6.25 | 12.50 | 25.00 |
| | *P.F. Sloan and Steve Barri* | | | | |

Lightfoot, Gordon
ABC-Paramount

| ☐ 10352 | Daisy-Doo/I'm the One (Remember Me) | 1962 | 6.25 | 12.50 | 25.00 |
| ☐ 10373 | It's Too Late, He Wins/Negotiations | 1962 | 6.25 | 12.50 | 25.00 |

Number		Title (A Side/B Side)	Year	VG	VG+	NM

Chateau

☐ 142		Daisy-Doo/I'm the One (Remember Me)	1962	12.50	25.00	50.00
☐ 148		It's Too Late, He Wins/Negotiations	1962	12.50	25.00	50.00
☐ 152		I'll Meet You in Michigan/Is My Baby Blue Tonight	1962	10.00	20.00	40.00

Reprise

☐ 0744		If You Could Read My Mind/Me and Bobby McGee	1972		2.00	4.00
		"Back to Back Hits" series				
☐ 0745		Talking in Your Sleep/Summer Side of Life	1972		2.00	4.00
		"Back to Back Hits" series				
☐ 0926		Me and Bobby McGee/Pony Man	1970		2.50	5.00
☐ 0974		If You Could Read My Mind/Poor Little Allison	1970		3.00	6.00
☐ 1020		Talking in Your Sleep/Nous Vivons Ensemble	1971		2.50	5.00
☐ 1035		Summer Side of Life/Love and Maple Syrup	1971		2.50	5.00
☐ 1088		Beautiful/Don Quixote	1972		2.50	5.00
☐ 1128		You Are What I Am/The Same Old Obsession	1972		2.50	5.00
☐ 1145		Can't Depend on You/It's Worth Believin'	1972		2.50	5.00
☐ 1194		Sundown/Too Late for Prayin'	1974		2.00	4.00
☐ 1309		Carefree Highway/Seven Island Suite	1974		2.00	4.00
☐ 1328		Rainy Day People/Cherokee Bend	1975		2.00	4.00
☐ 1369		The Wreck of the Edmund Fitzgerald/ The House You Live In	1976		2.00	4.00
☐ 1380		Race Among the Ruins/Protocol	1976		2.00	4.00

United Artists

☐ 929		Just Like Tom Thumb's Blues/Ribbon of Darkness	1965	2.50	5.00	10.00
☐ 50055		For Lovin' Me/Spin, Spin	1966	2.00	4.00	8.00
☐ 50114		I'll Be Alright/Go Go Round	1967	2.00	4.00	8.00
☐ 50152		The Way I Feel/Peaceful Waters	1967	2.00	4.00	8.00
☐ 50281		Pussywillows, Cat-Tails/Black Day in July	1968	2.00	4.00	8.00
☐ 50447		Does Your Mother Know/Bitter Green	1968	2.00	4.00	8.00
☐ 50765		If I Could/Softly	1971		2.50	5.00

Warner Bros.

☐ 5621		For Lovin' Me/I'm Not Sayin'	1965	3.75	7.50	15.00
☐ 8518		The Circle Is Small/Sweet Guinevere	1978		2.50	5.00
		Without A-side subtitle				
☐ 8518		The Circle Is Small (I Can See It In Your Eyes)/ Sweet Guinevere	1978		2.00	4.00
		Subtitle added to later pressings				
☐ 8579		Daylight Katy/Hangdog Hotel Room	1978		2.00	4.00
☐ 8644		Dreamland/Songs the Minstrel Sang	1978		2.00	4.00
☐ 28222		Ecstasy Made Easy/Morning Glory	1987			3.00
☐ 28422		East of Midnight/I'll Tag Along	1987			3.00
☐ 28553		Stay Loose/Morning Glory	1986			3.00
☐ 28655		Anything for Love/Let It Ride	1986			3.00
☐ 29466		Someone to Believe In/Without You	1983		2.00	4.00
☐ 29511		Knotty Pine/Salute	1983		2.00	4.00
☐ 29859		Shadows/In My Fashion	1982		2.00	4.00
☐ 29963		Blackberry Wine/(B-side unknown)	1982		2.00	4.00
☐ 49516		If You Need Me/Mister Rock of Ages	1980		2.00	4.00
☐ 50012		Baby Step Back/Thank You for the Promises	1982		2.00	4.00

Listen

(With Robert Plant, later of Led Zeppelin)

Columbia

☐ 43967		You Better Run/Everybody's Gonna Say	1967	50.00	100.00	150.00

Litter

Probe

☐ 461		Silly People/Feeling	1968	6.25	12.50	25.00
☐ 467		Blue Ice/On Our Minds	1969	6.25	12.50	25.00

Scotty

☐ 6710		Action Woman/A Legal Matter	1967	25.00	50.00	100.00

Warick

☐ 6711		Somebody Help Me/I'm a Man	1967	50.00	100.00	200.00
☐ 6712		Action Woman/Whatcha Gonna Do About It	1967	37.50	75.00	150.00

Little Anthony and the Imperials

(Also see "Imperials, The"; some of these are as "Anthony and the Imperials")

Apollo

☐ 521		The Fires Burn No More/Lift Up Your Hands	1957	15.00	30.00	60.00
		As "The Chesters"				

Avco

☐ 4635		I'm Falling in Love with You/ What Good Am I Without You	1974		2.50	5.00
☐ 4645		I Don't Have to Worry/Loneliest House on the Block	1974		2.50	5.00
☐ 4651		Hold On (Just a Little Bit Longer)/ I've Got to Let You Go (Part 1)	1975		2.50	5.00
☐ 4655		I'll Be Loving You Sooner or Later/Young Girl	1975		2.50	5.00

DCP

☐ 1104		I'm On the Outside (Looking In)/Please Go	1964	2.50	5.00	10.00
☐ 1119		Goin' Out of My Head/Make It Easy on Yourself	1964	2.50	5.00	10.00
☐ 1128		Hurt So Bad/Reputation	1965	2.50	5.00	10.00
☐ 1128	PS	Hurt So Bad/Reputation	1965	3.75	7.50	15.00
☐ 1136		Take Me Back/Our Song	1965	2.00	4.00	8.00

Number		Title (A Side/B Side)	Year	VG	VG+	NM
❏ 1149		I Miss You So/Get Out of My Life	1965	2.00	4.00	8.00
❏ 1154		Hurt/Never Again	1966	2.00	4.00	8.00

End

❏ 1027		Tears on My Pillow/Two People in the World	1958	10.00	20.00	40.00
		As "The Imperials"				
❏ 1027		Tears on My Pillow/Two People in the World	1958	6.25	12.50	25.00
		As "Little Anthony and the Imperials"				
❏ 1036		So Much/Oh Yeah	1958	5.00	10.00	20.00
❏ 1038		The Diary/Cha Cha Henry	1959	6.25	12.50	25.00
❏ 1039		When You Wish Upon a Star/Wishful Thinking	1959	5.00	10.00	20.00
❏ 1047		A Prayer and a Juke Box/River Path	1959	5.00	10.00	20.00
❏ 1053		So Near and Yet So Far/I'm Alright	1959	5.00	10.00	20.00
❏ 1060		Shimmy, Shimmy, Ko-Ko Bop/I'm Still in Love with You	1959	5.00	10.00	20.00
❏ 1067		My Empty Room/Bayou, Bayou, Baby	1960	3.75	7.50	15.00
❏ 1074		I'm Taking a Vacation from Love/Only Sympathy	1960	3.75	7.50	15.00
❏ 1080		Limbo (Part 1)/Limbo (Part 2)	1960	3.75	7.50	15.00
❏ 1083		Formula of Love/Dream	1961	3.75	7.50	15.00
❏ 1086		Please Say You Want Me/So Near and Yet So Far	1961	3.75	7.50	15.00
❏ 1091		Traveling Stranger/Say Yea	1961	3.75	7.50	15.00
❏ 1104		Dream/A Lovely Way to Spend an Evening	1961	3.75	7.50	15.00

Janus

❏ 160		Father, Father/Each One, Teach One	1971		3.00	6.00
❏ 166		Madeline/Universe	1971		3.00	6.00
❏ 178		(Where Do I Begin) Love Story/There's an Island	1972		3.00	6.00

Liberty

❏ 55119		The Glory of Love/C'mon Tiger (Gimme a Growl)	1958	7.50	15.00	30.00
		As "The Imperials"				

MCA

❏ 41258		Daylight/Your Love	1980		2.00	4.00
		Little Anthony solo				

PCM

❏ 202		This Time We're Winning/Your Love	1983		2.00	4.00

Pure Gold

❏ 101		Nothing from Nothing/Running with the Wrong Crowd	1976		2.50	5.00

Roulette

❏ 4379		That Lil' Ole Lovemaker Me/It Just Ain't Fair	1961	3.00	6.00	12.00
		Little Anthony solo				
❏ 4477		Lonesome Romeo/I've Got a Lot to Offer Darling	1963	3.00	6.00	12.00
		Little Anthony solo				

United Artists

❏ 0117		Goin' Out of My Head/I'm On the Outside (Looking In)	1973		2.00	4.00
		"Silver Spotlight Series" reissue				
❏ 0118		Hurt So Bad/Take Me Back	1973		2.00	4.00
		"Silver Spotlight Series" reissue				
❏ 50552		Out of Sight, Out of Mind/Summer's Comin'	1969		3.00	6.00
❏ 50598		The Ten Commandments of Love/Let the Sunshine In	1969		3.00	6.00
❏ 50625		It'll Never Be the Same Again/Don't Get Close	1970		3.00	6.00
❏ 50677		World of Darkness/The Change	1970		3.00	6.00
❏ 50720		Help Me Find a Way (To Say I Love You)/If I Love You	1970		3.00	6.00

Veep

❏ 1228		Better Use Your Head/The Wonder of It All	1966	2.00	4.00	8.00
❏ 1228	PS	Better Use Your Head/The Wonder of It All	1966	3.75	7.50	15.00
❏ 1233		You Better Take It Easy Baby/	1966	2.00	4.00	8.00
		Gonna Fix You Good (Every Time You're Bad)				
❏ 1239		Tears on My Pillow/Who's Sorry Now	1966		3.00	6.00
❏ 1240		I'm On the Outside (Looking In)/Please Go	1966		3.00	6.00
❏ 1241		Goin' Out of My Head/Shing-a-Ling	1966		3.00	6.00
❏ 1242		Hurt So Bad/Reputation	1966		3.00	6.00
❏ 1243		Take Me Back/Our Song	1966		3.00	6.00
❏ 1244		I Miss You So/Get Out of My Life	1966		3.00	6.00
❏ 1245		Hurt/Never Again	1966		3.00	6.00
❏ 1248		It's Not the Same/Down on Love	1966	2.00	4.00	8.00
❏ 1255		Don't Tie Me Down/	1967	2.00	4.00	8.00
		Where There's a Will There's a Way				
❏ 1262		Hold On to Someone/Lost in Love	1967	2.00	4.00	8.00
❏ 1269		You Only Live Twice/Hungry Heart	1967	2.00	4.00	8.00
❏ 1275		Beautiful People/If I Remember to Forget	1967	2.00	4.00	8.00
❏ 1278		I'm Hypnotized/Hungry Heart	1968	2.00	4.00	8.00
❏ 1283		What Greater Love/In the Back of My Heart	1968	2.00	4.00	8.00
❏ 1285		Yesterday Has Gone/My Love Is a Rainbow	1968	2.00	4.00	8.00
❏ 1293		The Flesh Failures (Let the Sunshine In)/Gentle Rain	1969	2.00	4.00	8.00
❏ 1303		Anthem (Revelation)/Goodbye Good Times	1969	2.00	4.00	8.00

Little Bubber

Imperial

❏ 5225		High Class Woman/Come Back Baby	1953	20.00	40.00	80.00
❏ 5238		Runnin' Around/Never Trust a Woman	1953	20.00	40.00	80.00

Little Cheryl

Cameo

❏ 270		Heaven Only Knows/Can't We Just Be Friends	1963	10.00	20.00	40.00
❏ 276		Mama Let the Phone Bell Ring/	1963	3.00	6.00	12.00
		Can't We Just Be Friends				

Number	Title (A Side/B Side)	Year	VG	VG+	NM
❑ 292	Come On Home/I Love You Conrad	1964	3.00	6.00	12.00
❑ 307	Yeh Yeh We Love 'Em All/Nick and Joe Callin'	1964	4.00	8.00	16.00

Reprise

❑ 20,109	Jim/Pocketful of Money	1962	3.75	7.50	15.00

Little Doug – See "Sahm, Doug"

Little Eva

Amy

❑ 943	Stand By Me/That's My Man	1965	2.00	4.00	8.00

Bell

❑ 45,264	The Loco-Motion/Will You Love Me Tomorrow	1972		2.50	5.00

Dimension

❑ 1000	The Loco-Motion/He Is the Boy	1962	3.75	7.50	15.00
❑ 1003	Keep Your Hands Off/Where Do I Go	1962	3.75	7.50	15.00
	Some copies have this shortened title				
❑ 1003	Keep Your Hands Off My Baby/Where Do I Go	1962	3.00	6.00	12.00
	Most copies have longer, and correct, title				
❑ 1006	Let's Turkey Trot/Down Home	1963	3.00	6.00	12.00
❑ 1011	Old Smokey Locomotion/Just a Little Girl	1963	3.00	6.00	12.00
❑ 1013	The Trouble with Boys/What I Gotta Do	1963	3.00	6.00	12.00
❑ 1019	Let's Start the Party Again/Please Hurt Me	1963	3.00	6.00	12.00
❑ 1035	Makin' with the Magilla/Conga	1964	2.50	5.00	10.00
❑ 1035	Makin' with the Magilla/Run to Her	1964	2.50	5.00	10.00
❑ 1042	Wake Up John/Takin' Back What I Said	1964	2.50	5.00	10.00

Spring

❑ 101	Mama Said/Something About You Boy	1970		3.00	6.00
❑ 107	Night After Night/Something About You Boy	1970		3.00	6.00

Verve

❑ 10459	Bend It/Just One Word Isn't Enough	1966	2.00	4.00	8.00
❑ 10529	Everything Is Beautiful About You Boy/Take a Step in My Direction	1967	2.00	4.00	8.00

Little Feat

Warner Bros.

❑ 7431	Strawberry Flats/Hamburger Midnight	1970	2.00	4.00	8.00
❑ 7689	Dixie Chicken/Lafayette Railroad	1973		3.00	6.00
❑ 8054	Oh Atlanta/Down the Road	1974		2.50	5.00
❑ 8174	Long Distance Love/Romance Dance	1975		2.50	5.00
❑ 8219	All That You Dream/One Love Stand	1976		2.50	5.00
❑ 8420	Time Loves a Hero/Sailin' Shoes	1977		2.50	5.00
❑ 8566	Oh Atlanta/Willin'	1978		2.50	5.00
❑ 27684	On a Clear Moment/Changin' Luck	1988			3.00
❑ 27728	Hate to Lose Your Lovin'/Cajun Girl	1988			3.00
❑ 49801	Front Page News/Easy to Sleep	1981		2.50	5.00
❑ 49841	Strawberry Flats/Gringo	1981		2.50	5.00

Little Guy and the Giants

Lawn

❑ 103	It's You/So Young	1960	50.00	100.00	200.00

Little Iva and Her Band

Miracle

❑ 2	When I Needed You/Continental Strut	1960	500.00	1,000	1,500

Little Junior's Blue Flames – See "Parker, Junior"

Little Lady Beatles, The – See "Insects, The"

Little Milton

Sun

❑ 194	Beggin' My Baby/Somebody Told Me	1954	50.00	100.00	200.00
❑ 200	If You Love Me/Alone and Blue	1954	125.00	250.00	500.00
❑ 220	Looking for My Baby/Lonesome for My Baby	1955	200.00	400.00	600.00
	He has had numerous other 45s on other labels, which we plan to chronicle in a future edition				

Little Otis

Tamla

❑ 54058	I Out-Duked the Duke/Baby I Need You	1962	7.50	15.00	30.00

Little Richard

(Also see "Deuces of Rhythm and the Tempo Toppers,The")

Atlantic

❑ 2181	Crying in the Chapel/Hole in the Wall	1963	3.00	6.00	12.00
❑ 2192	It Is No Secret (What God Can Do)/Travelin' Shoes	1963	3.00	6.00	12.00

Bell

❑ 45,385	Good Golly Miss Molly/Good Golly Miss Molly (Part 2)	1973		2.50	5.00

Brunswick

❑ 55362	She's Together/Try Some of Mine	1968	2.00	4.00	8.00
❑ 55377	Stingy Jenny/Baby Don't You Tear My Clothes	1968	2.00	4.00	8.00
❑ 55386	Soul Train/Can I Count on You	1968	2.00	4.00	8.00

Coral

❑ 62366	Milky White Way/Need Him	1963	2.50	5.00	10.00

Number	Title (A Side/B Side)	Year	VG	VG+	NM
Critique					
❑ 99392	Happy Endings/California Girls	1987			3.00
	A-side: With the Beach Boys; B-side: The Beach Boys without Little Richard				
Elektra					
❑ 69370	Tutti Frutti/Rave On	1988			3.00
	B-side by John Cougar Mellencamp				
❑ 69384	Tutti Frutti/Powerful Stuff	1988			3.00
	B-side by the Fabulous Thunderbirds				
❑ 69385	Tutti Frutti/Kokomo	1988			3.00
	B-side by the Beach Boys				
End					
❑ 1057	Troubles of the World/Save Me Lord	1959	3.75	7.50	15.00
❑ 1058	Milky White Way/I've Just Come From the Fountain	1959	3.75	7.50	15.00
Green Mountain					
❑ 413	In the Middle of the Night/	1973		2.50	5.00
	Where Will I Find a Place to Sleep This Evening				
Kent					
4567	*Mississippi/In the Name* 1972 *Unreleased*				
❑ 4568	Don't You Know I/In the Name	1972		2.50	5.00
Mainstream					
❑ 5572	Try to Help Your Brother/Funk Proof	1975		2.50	5.00
Manticore					
❑ 7007	Call My Name/Steal Miss Liza (Miss Liza Jane)	1975		2.00	4.00
MCA					
❑ 52780	Great Gosh A-Mighty! (It's a Matter of Time)/The Ride	1986			3.00
	B-side by Charlie Midnight				
❑ 52780 PS	Great Gosh A-Mighty! (It's a Matter of Time)/The Ride	1986			3.00
Mercury					
❑ 71884	He's Not Just a Soldier/Joy, Joy, Joy	1962	3.75	7.50	15.00
❑ 71911	Do You Care/Ride On King Jesus	1962	3.75	7.50	15.00
❑ 71965	Why Don't You Change Your Ways/	1962	3.75	7.50	15.00
	He Got What He Wanted				
Modern					
❑ 1018	Holy Mackerel/Baby, Don't You Want a Man Like Me	1966	3.00	6.00	12.00
❑ 1018 PS	Holy Mackerel/Baby, Don't You Want a Man Like Me	1966	5.00	10.00	20.00
❑ 1019	Do You Feel It (Part 1)/Do You Feel It (Part 2)	1966	3.00	6.00	12.00
❑ 1022	Directly from My Heart to You/I'm Back	1966	3.00	6.00	12.00
❑ 1030	Slippin' and Slidin'/Bring It Back Home to Me	1967	3.00	6.00	12.00
❑ 1043	Baby What You Want Me to Do (Part 1)/	1967	3.00	6.00	12.00
	Baby What You Want Me to Do (Part 2)				
Okeh					
❑ 7251	Poor Dog (Who Can't Wag His Own Tail)/Well	1966	3.75	7.50	15.00
❑ 7251 PS	Poor Dog (Who Can't Wag His Own Tail)/Well	1966	6.25	12.50	25.00
❑ 7262	I Need Love/Commandments of Love	1966	3.00	6.00	12.00
❑ 7271	Hurry Sundown/I Don't Want to Discuss It	1967	3.00	6.00	12.00
❑ 7278	Don't Deceive Me (Please Don't Go)/	1967	3.00	6.00	12.00
	Never Gonna Let You Go				
❑ 7286	Money/Little Bit of Something	1967	3.00	6.00	12.00
❑ 7325	Lucille/Whole Lotta Shakin' Goin' On	1969	2.50	5.00	10.00
Peacock					
❑ 1658	Little Richard's Boogie/Directly from My Heart to You	1956	25.00	50.00	100.00
❑ 1673	Maybe I'm Right/I Love My Baby	1957	12.50	25.00	50.00
RCA Victor					
❑ 47-4392	Taxi Blues/Every Hour	1951	125.00	250.00	500.00
❑ 47-4582	Get Rich Quick/Thinkin' 'Bout My Mother	1952	125.00	250.00	500.00
❑ 47-4772	Why Did You Leave Me?/Ain't Nothin' Happenin'	1952	75.00	150.00	300.00
❑ 47-5025	Please Have Mercy on Me/I Brought It All on Myself	1952	125.00	250.00	500.00
Reprise					
❑ 0907	Freedom Blues/Dew Drop Inn	1970	2.50	5.00	10.00
❑ 0942	Greenwood Mississippi/I Saw Her Standing There	1970	2.50	5.00	10.00
❑ 1005	Shake a Hand (If You Can)/Somebody Saw You	1971	2.00	4.00	8.00
❑ 1043	Green Power/Dancing in the Street	1971	2.00	4.00	8.00
❑ 1062	Money Is/Money Runner	1972	2.00	4.00	8.00
	B-side by Quincy Jones				
❑ 1130	Mockingbird Sally/Nuki Suki	1972	2.00	4.00	8.00
Specialty					
❑ 561	Tutti-Frutti/I'm Just a Lonely Guy	1955	7.50	15.00	30.00
❑ 572	Long Tall Sally/Slippin' and Slidin' (Peepin' and Hidin')	1956	7.50	15.00	30.00
❑ 579	Rip It Up/Ready Teddy	1956	7.50	15.00	30.00
❑ 584	Heebie-Jeebies/She's Got it	1956	7.50	15.00	30.00
❑ 591	The Girl Can't Help It/All Around the World	1956	7.50	15.00	30.00
❑ 598	Lucille/Send Me Some Lovin'	1957	7.50	15.00	30.00
❑ 606	Jenny, Jenny/Miss Ann	1957	7.50	15.00	30.00
❑ 606 PS	Jenny, Jenny/Miss Ann	1957	12.50	25.00	50.00
❑ 611	Keep a Knockin'/Can't Believe You Wanna Leave	1957	7.50	15.00	30.00
❑ 611 PS	Keep a Knockin'/Can't Believe You Wanna Leave	1957	12.50	25.00	50.00
❑ 624	Good Golly, Miss Molly/Hey-Hey-Hey-Hey!	1958	7.50	15.00	30.00
❑ 624 PS	Good Golly, Miss Molly/Hey-Hey-Hey-Hey!	1958	12.50	25.00	50.00
❑ 633	Ooh! My Soul/True, Fine Mama	1958	7.50	15.00	30.00
❑ 633 PS	Ooh! My Soul/True, Fine Mama	1958	12.50	25.00	50.00
❑ 645	Baby Face/I'll Never Let You Go	1958	6.25	12.50	25.00
❑ 652	She Knows How to Rock/Early One Morning	1958	6.25	12.50	25.00

Number	Title (A Side/B Side)	Year	VG	VG+	NM
❏ 660	By the Light of the Silvery Moon/Wonderin'	1959	6.25	12.50	25.00
❏ 664	Kansas City/Lonesome and Blue	1959	6.25	12.50	25.00
❏ 670	Shake a Hand/All Night Long	1959	6.25	12.50	25.00
❏ 680	Whole Lotta Shakin' Goin' On/Maybe I'm Right	1959	6.25	12.50	25.00
❏ 681	I Got It/Baby	1960	6.25	12.50	25.00
❏ 686	The Most I Can Offer/Directly from My Heart	1964	3.75	7.50	15.00
❏ 692	Bama Lama Bama Loo/Annie's Back	1964	3.75	7.50	15.00
❏ 697	Keep a Knockin'/Bama Lama Bama Loo	1964	3.75	7.50	15.00
❏ 699	Poor Boy Paul/Wonderin'	1964	3.75	7.50	15.00
❏ 734	Chicken Little Baby/Oh Why	1974	3.00	6.00	

Vee Jay

❏ 612	Whole Lotta Shakin' Goin' On/Goodnight Irene	1964	2.50	5.00	10.00
❏ 625	Blueberry Hill/Cherry Red	1964	2.50	5.00	10.00
❏ 652	It Ain't Whatcha Do/Cross Over	1965	2.50	5.00	10.00
❏ 665	Without Love/Dance What You Wanna	1965	2.50	5.00	10.00
❏ 698	I Don't Know What You've Got But It's Got Me -- Part I/ I Don't Know What You've Got But It's Got Me -- Part II	1965	2.50	5.00	10.00

Warner Bros.

❏ 28491	Big House Reunion/Somebody's Comin'	1987		2.00	4.00

WTG

❏ 08492	Twins (Long)/Twins (Short)	1988		2.00	4.00
	With Philip Bailey				

Little Sammy and the Tones
Jaclyn

❏ 1761	Christine/Over the Rainbow	1962	12.50	25.00	50.00

Little Sylvia – See "Sylvia"

Little Wheels, The
(With Ray Hildebrand and Jill Jackson, better known as "Paul and Paula")
Dot

❏ 16676	Four Wheeled, Ball Bearing Surfing Board/The Bumper	1964	7.50	15.00	30.00

Littles, Hattie
Gordy

❏ 7004	Back in My Arms Again/(B-side unknown)	1962	200.00	400.00	800.00
❏ 7007	Here You Come/Your Love Is Wonderful	1962	20.00	40.00	80.00

Lively Ones, The
Del-Fi

❏ 4184	Guitarget/Crying Guitar	1962	7.50	15.00	30.00
❏ 4189	Misirlou/Blue Tears	1962	7.50	15.00	30.00
❏ 4189	Misirlou/Livin'	1962	7.50	15.00	30.00
❏ 4196	Surf Rider/Surfer's Lament	1963	6.25	12.50	25.00
❏ 4205	Surfer Boogie/Ric-a-Tic	1963	6.25	12.50	25.00
❏ 4210	High Tide/Goofy Foot	1963	6.25	12.50	25.00
❏ 4217	Surf City/Telstar Surf	1963	6.25	12.50	25.00

MGM

❏ 13691	Bugalu Movement/Take It While You Can	1967	3.75	7.50	15.00

Smash

❏ 1880	Night and Day/Hey Scrounge	1964	6.25	12.50	25.00

Livers, The
Constellation

❏ 118	Beatle Time/This Is the Night	1964	3.75	7.50	15.00

Load of Mischief
Holiday Inn

❏ 2205	I'm a Lover/Back in My Arms Again	1967	5.00	10.00	20.00

Sun

❏ 407	I'm a Lover/Back in My Arms Again	1967	20.00	40.00	80.00
	The last of the Sam Phillips Sun 45s				

Lollipops, The
Atco

❏ 6787	Nothing's Gonna Stop Our Love/I Believe in Love	1970		3.00	6.00

Gordy

❏ 7089	Cheating Is Telling On You/Need Your Love	1969	200.00	400.00	800.00

Impact

❏ 1021	Lovin' Good Feelin'/Step Aside Baby	1967	7.50	15.00	30.00

RCA Victor

❏ 47-8344	Peggy Got Engaged/I'll Set My Love to Music	1964	5.00	10.00	20.00
❏ 47-8390	Don't Monkey With Me/Love Is the Only Answer	1964	5.00	10.00	20.00
❏ 47-8430	Billy, Billy Baby/Big Brother	1964	5.00	10.00	20.00
❏ 47-8494	Busy Signal/I Want You Back Again	1965	3.75	7.50	15.00

Smash

❏ 2057	He's the Boy/Gee Whiz Baby	1966	3.00	6.00	12.00

SSS International

❏ 777	You Don't Know/Feel So Comfortable	1969	2.00	4.00	8.00

V.I.P.

❏ 25051	Cheating Is Telling On You/Need Your Love	1968	6.25	12.50	25.00

Number		Title (A Side/B Side)	Year	VG	VG+	NM

Lomax, Jackie
Apple

☐ 1802		Sour Milk Sea/The Eagle Laughs at You	1968	5.00	10.00	20.00
		With B-side author listed as "(Jackie Lomax)"				
☐ 1802		Sour Milk Sea/The Eagle Laughs at You	1968	5.00	10.00	20.00
		With B-side author listed as "(George Harrison)"				
☐ 1807		New Day/Thumbin' a Ride	1969	18.75	37.50	75.00
		With star on A-side label				
☐ 1807		New Day/Thumbin' a Ride	1969	15.00	30.00	60.00
		Without star on A-side label				
☐ 1819		How the Web Was Woven/I Fall Inside Your Eyes	1970	2.00	4.00	8.00
☐ 1819	PS	How the Web Was Woven/I Fall Inside Your Eyes	1970	2.50	5.00	10.00
☐ 1834		Sour Milk Sea/(I) Fall Inside Your Eyes	1971	2.00	4.00	8.00
☐ PRO-6240/1	DJ	Sour Milk Sea/(I) Fall Inside Your Eyes	1971	7.50	15.00	30.00

Capitol

☐ 4384		More (Livin' for Lovin')/I Remember (Memorabilia)	1976		2.50	5.00

Epic

☐ 10270		One Minute Woman/Genuine Imitation of Life	1967	3.00	6.00	12.00

Warner Bros.

☐ 7503		Helluva Woman/Higher Ground	1971		3.00	6.00
☐ 7564		Lavender Dream/Lost	1972		3.00	6.00
☐ 7589		Roll On/Hellfire, Night Crier	1972		3.00	6.00

Long, Huey
Fidelity

☐ 4054		How to Tell My Heart/Waiting for a Letter	1962	5.00	10.00	20.00
☐ 4055		Elvis Stole My Gal/Ballad of John Glenn	1962	12.50	25.00	50.00

Long, Shorty
(This does not knowingly include the country Shorty Long)

King

☐ 5605		Take Me to the Happy Land/Mary, Oh Mary	1962	6.25	12.50	25.00

RCA Victor

☐ 47-6472		Hey, Doll Baby/Luscious	1956	25.00	50.00	100.00
☐ 47-6572		Vacation Rock/Burnt Toast and Black Coffee	1956	25.00	50.00	100.00
☐ 47-6804		Another Love Has Ended/Little White Horse	1957	25.00	50.00	100.00
☐ 47-6873		You Don't Have to Be a Baby to Cry/I'd Crawl Back	1957	25.00	50.00	100.00

Soul

☐ 35001		Devil with the Blue Dress/Wind It Up	1964	6.25	12.50	25.00
☐ 35005		It's a Crying Shame/Out to Get You	1964	6.25	12.50	25.00
☐ 35021		Function at the Junction/Call On Me	1966	3.75	7.50	15.00
☐ 35031		Chantilly Lace/Your Love Is Amazing	1966	3.75	7.50	15.00
☐ 35040		Night Fo' Last/(Instrumental)	1968	2.50	5.00	10.00
☐ 35044		Here Comes the Judge/Sing What You Wanna	1968	2.50	5.00	10.00
☐ 35054		I Had a Dream/Ain't No Justice	1969	2.50	5.00	10.00
☐ 35064		A Whiter Shade of Pale/When You Are Available	1969	2.50	5.00	10.00

Tri-Phi

☐ 1006		I'll Be There/Bad Willie	1962	12.50	25.00	50.00
☐ 1015		Too Smart/I'll Be There	1962	17.50	35.00	70.00
☐ 1021		What's the Matter/Going Away	1963	15.00	30.00	60.00

Longbranch Pennywhistle
(Glenn Frey, J.D. Souther and Ry Cooder all were members of this group)

Amos

☐ 121		Don't Talk Now/Jubilee Anne	1969	3.75	7.50	15.00
☐ 129		Lucky Love/Rebecca	1969	3.75	7.50	15.00
☐ 148		Star Spangled Bus/Bring Back Funky Women	1970	3.75	7.50	15.00

Lonnie and the Carollons
Mohawk

☐ 108		Chapel of Tears/My Heart	1958	37.50	75.00	150.00
		Green label				
☐ 108		Chapel of Tears/My Heart	1961	7.50	15.00	30.00
		Red label				
☐ 108		Chapel of Tears/My Heart	1965	5.00	10.00	20.00
		White label				
☐ 111		Hold Me Close/Trudy	1958	12.50	25.00	50.00
☐ 112		Back Yard Rock/You Say	1958	12.50	25.00	50.00
☐ 113		The Gang All Knows/Ike Hammer	1959	15.00	30.00	60.00
☐ 122		Need Your Lovin'/Beeline	1960	6.25	12.50	25.00
		As "Lonnie"				

Lonnie and the Crisis
Universal

☐ 103		Bells in the Chapel/Santa Town USA	1961	50.00	100.00	200.00

Lookinland, Mike
("Bobby Brady" of the Brady Bunch)

Capitol

☐ 3914		Gum Drop/Love Doesn't Care Who's In It	1974	2.50	5.00	10.00
☐ 3914	PS	Gum Drop/Love Doesn't Care Who's In It	1974	3.75	7.50	15.00

Number		Title (A Side/B Side)	Year	VG	VG+	NM
Lopez, Trini						
Capitol						
❏ 3195		Some Kind of a Summer/Poor Old Billy	1971		2.50	5.00
❏ 3312		Ruby Mountain/Y Volvere	1972		2.50	5.00
❏ 3402		Mammy Blue/Viva	1972		2.50	5.00
D.R.A.						
❏ 7008		Rosita/Only in My Dreams	1962	3.75	7.50	15.00
Griffin						
❏ 504		Butterfly/Don't Burn Your Bridges Behind You	1973		2.50	5.00
❏ 508		Bring Back the Sunshine/We Gotta Make It Together	1974		2.50	5.00
King						
❏ 5173		Rosalia/Nola	1959	5.00	10.00	20.00
❏ 5187		Since I Don't Have You/Rock On	1959	6.25	12.50	25.00
❏ 5198		Love Me Tonight/Here Comes Sally	1959	5.00	10.00	20.00
❏ 5234		Don't Let Your Sweet Love Die/I'm Grateful	1959	5.00	10.00	20.00
❏ 5284		Nobody Loves Me/ Nobody Listens to Our Teenage Problems	1959	5.00	10.00	20.00
❏ 5304		Chain of Love/Sweet Thing	1960	5.00	10.00	20.00
❏ 5324		Schemes/Jeannie Marie	1960	5.00	10.00	20.00
❏ 5344		It Hurts to Be in Love/The Search Goes On	1960	5.00	10.00	20.00
❏ 5418		Don't Treat Me That Way/Then You Know	1960	5.00	10.00	20.00
❏ 5487		One Heart, One Life, One Love/ You Broke the Only Heart	1961	5.00	10.00	20.00
❏ 5801		Jeannie Marie/Love Me Tonight	1963	3.00	6.00	12.00
❏ 5820		Don't Go/It Seems	1963	3.00	6.00	12.00
❏ 5824		Nobody Loves Me/The Club for Broken Hearts	1963	3.00	6.00	12.00
❏ 5849		Yes You Do/Won't You Be	1964	3.00	6.00	12.00
❏ 6000		Jeannie Marie/Nobody Listens, Nobody Cares	1965	2.00	4.00	8.00
❏ 6021		The Search Goes On/Chain of Love	1966	2.00	4.00	8.00
Private Stock						
❏ 45,024		Somethin' 'Bout You Baby I Like/Sweet Life	1975		2.50	5.00
❏ 45,035		Seco Sulto Y Tonton/(B-side unknown)	1975		2.50	5.00
❏ 45,044		Heavy Makes You Happy (Sha-La-Boom-Boom-Yeah)/ Satisfaction	1975		2.50	5.00
Reprise						
❏ 0239		La Bamba/Granada *Released only in Latin America*	1963	3.75	7.50	15.00
❏ 0260		Jailer, Bring Me Water/You Can't Say Goodbye	1964	2.00	4.00	8.00
❏ 0276		Ya Ya/What Have I Got of My Own	1964	2.00	4.00	8.00
❏ 0300		Michael/San Francisco De Assisi	1964	2.00	4.00	8.00
❏ 0328		Sad Tomorrows/I've Lost My Love for You	1964	2.00	4.00	8.00
❏ 0328	PS	Sad Tomorrows/I've Lost My Love for You	1964	3.75	7.50	15.00
❏ 0336		Lemon Tree/Pretty Eyes	1965	2.50	5.00	10.00
❏ 0336	PS	Lemon Tree/Pretty Eyes	1965	3.75	7.50	15.00
❏ 0376		Are You Sincere/You'll Be Sorry	1965	2.00	4.00	8.00
❏ 0405		Sinner Man/Double Trouble	1965	2.00	4.00	8.00
❏ 0405	PS	Sinner Man/Double Trouble	1965	3.75	7.50	15.00
❏ 0421		Regressa A Mi/Mi Felicidad	1965	2.00	4.00	8.00
❏ 0435		Pretty Little Girl/Made in Paris	1965	2.00	4.00	8.00
❏ 0455		The 32nd of May/I'm Coming Home, Cindy	1966	2.00	4.00	8.00
❏ 0480		La Bamba -- Part 1/Trini's Tune	1966	2.00	4.00	8.00
❏ 0508		Hall of Fame/Pancho Lopez	1966	2.00	4.00	8.00
❏ 0536		Your Ever Changin' Mind/Takin' the Back Roads	1966	2.00	4.00	8.00
❏ 0547		Gonna Get Along Without Ya' Now/Love Letters	1967		3.00	6.00
❏ 0574		In the Land of Plenty/Up To Now	1967		3.00	6.00
❏ 0596		Ballad of the Dirty Dozen/The Bramble Bush	1967		3.00	6.00
❏ 0618		I Wanna Be Free/Together	1967		3.00	6.00
❏ 0648		It's a Great Life/Let's Take a Walk	1967		3.00	6.00
❏ 0659		Sally Was a Good Old Girl/It's a Great Life	1968		3.00	6.00
❏ 0687		Good Old Mountain Dew/Mental Journey	1968		3.00	6.00
❏ 0700		If I Had a Hammer/Lemon Tree *"Back to Back Hits" series*	1968		2.50	5.00
❏ 0725		La Bamba/Kansas City *"Back to Back Hits" series*	1968		2.50	5.00
❏ 0770		Something Tells Me/Malaguena Salerosa	1968		3.00	6.00
❏ 0801	DJ	El Nino Del Tambor/ Nocho De Paz (Let There Be Peace) *Stock copy may not exist*	1968	2.00	4.00	8.00
❏ 0814		Come a Little Bit Closer/My Baby Loves Sad Songs	1969		3.00	6.00
❏ 0825		Don't Let the Sun Catch You Cryin'/ My Baby Loves Sad Songs	1969		3.00	6.00
❏ 0879		Games People Play/Love Story	1969		3.00	6.00
❏ 0912		5 O'Clock World/You Make My Day	1970		2.50	5.00
❏ 0933		Mexican Medicine Man/Time to Get It Together	1970		2.50	5.00
❏ 0947		Su-Kal-De-Don/Mexican Medicine Man	1970		2.50	5.00
❏ 0975		Let's Think About Living/There Was a Crooked Man	1970		2.50	5.00
❏ 20,168		A-M-E-R-I-C-A/Let It Be Known	1963	2.50	5.00	10.00
❏ 20,190		La Bamba (Part 1)/La Bamba (Part 2)	1963	2.50	5.00	10.00
❏ 20,198		If I Had a Hammer/Unchain My Heart	1963	3.00	6.00	12.00
❏ 20,218		If I Had a Hammer/La Bamba *Released only in Italy*	1963	3.75	7.50	15.00
❏ 20,223		This Land Is Your Land/Cielito Lindo *Released only in Holland*	1963	3.75	7.50	15.00
❏ 20,224		Bye Bye Blackbird/Medley *Released only in Holland*	1963	3.75	7.50	15.00

Number	Title (A Side/B Side)	Year	VG	VG+	NM
❑ 20,234	This Land Is Your Land/La Bamba	1963	3.75	7.50	15.00
	Released only in West Germany				
❑ 20,236	Kansas City/Lonesome Traveler	1963	2.00	4.00	8.00
Roulette					
❑ 7214	Beautiful People/Helplessly	1977		2.50	5.00
Volk					
❑ 101	The Right to Rock/(B-side unknown)	1958	7.50	15.00	30.00

Lord Sitar
(Not George Harrison, as often rumored)
Capitol

❑ 5972	Black Is Black/	1967	5.00	10.00	20.00
	Have You Seen Your Mother, Baby, Standing in the Shadow				

Lord, Brian, and the Midnighters
(Frank Zappa was a member of this group)
Capitol

❑ 4981	Big Surfer/Not Another One	1963	37.50	75.00	150.00
Vigah					
❑ 001	Big Surfer/Not Another One	1963	75.00	150.00	300.00

Los Bravos
Parrot

❑ 3020	Bring a Little Lovin'/Make It Last	1968	3.00	6.00	12.00
❑ 3023	Dirty Street/Two People in Me	1968	2.50	5.00	10.00
Press					
❑ 60002	Black Is Black/I Want a Name	1966	3.75	7.50	15.00
❑ 60003	Going Nowhere/Brand New Baby	1966	2.50	5.00	10.00
❑ 60004	You'll Never Get the Chance Again/I'm All Ears	1967	2.50	5.00	10.00

Lothar and the Hand People
Capitol

❑ 2008	Have Mercy (Mercy, Mercy, Mercy)/	1967	2.50	5.00	10.00
	Let the Boy Pretend				
❑ 2376	Machines/Milkweed Love	1969	2.00	4.00	8.00
❑ 2556	Midnight Ranger/Yes, I Love You	1969	2.00	4.00	8.00
❑ 5874	L-O-V-E/Rose Colored Glasses	1967	2.50	5.00	10.00
❑ 5945	Comic Strip/Every Single Word	1967	2.50	5.00	10.00

Lou, Herb B., and the Legal Eagles
Arch

❑ 1607	The Trial/(B-side unknown)	1958	10.00	20.00	40.00
	Break-in record with Herb Alpert involvement; a cover version was done by "Field, Jerry, and the Lawyers"				

Love
Blue Thumb

❑ 106	Stand Out/I'll Pray for You	1970		3.00	6.00
❑ 7116	Keep On Shining/Everlasting First	1970		3.00	6.00
Elektra					
❑ 45603	My Little Red Book/Message to Pretty	1966	2.50	5.00	10.00
❑ 45605	7 and 7 Is/No. Fourteen	1966	2.50	5.00	10.00
❑ 45608	Stephanie Knows Who/Orange Sky	1966	7.50	15.00	30.00
❑ 45608	She Comes in Colors/Orange Sky	1966	2.50	5.00	10.00
❑ 45613	Que Vida/Hey Joe	1967	12.50	25.00	50.00
❑ 45629	Alone Again Or/A House Is Not a Motel	1968	2.50	5.00	10.00
❑ 45633	Laughing Stock/You're Mine and We Belong Together	1968	3.75	7.50	15.00
❑ 45700	Alone Again Or/Good Times	1970	2.00	4.00	8.00
RSO					
❑ 502	Time Is Like a River/With a Little Energy	1974		2.50	5.00
❑ 506	Good Old Fashioned Dream/You Said You Would	1975		2.50	5.00

Love Notes, The
(Two different groups)
Holiday

❑ 2605	United/Tonight	1957	15.00	30.00	60.00
	Glossy label				
❑ 2605	United/Tonight	1957	5.00	10.00	20.00
	Flat (matte) label				
❑ 2607	If I Could Make You Mine/Don't Go	1957	10.00	20.00	40.00
Imperial					
❑ 5254	Surrender Your Heart/Get On My Train	1953	150.00	300.00	600.00
Rainbow					
❑ 266	I'm Sorry/Sweet Lulu	1954	75.00	150.00	300.00
Riviera					
❑ 970	I'm Sorry/Sweet Lulu	1954	150.00	300.00	600.00
❑ 975	Since I Fell for You/Don't Be No Fool	1954	150.00	300.00	600.00
Wilshire					
❑ 200	Nancy/Our Songs of Love	1963	7.50	15.00	30.00
❑ 203	Gloria/The Mathematics of Love	1963	25.00	50.00	100.00

Number		Title (A Side/B Side)	Year	VG	VG+	NM

Love Sculpture
(Dave Edmunds was in this group)
Parrot

❏ 335		Sabre Dance/Think of Love	1969	3.75	7.50	15.00
❏ 362		In the Land of the Few/Farandole	1970	3.75	7.50	15.00

Love, Darlene
Columbia

❏ 07984		He's Sure the Man I Love/Everybody Needs	1988		2.50	5.00

Passport

❏ 7926		Christmas (Baby Please Come Home)/ Playing for Keeps	1983	3.00	6.00	12.00

Philles

❏ 111		(Today I Met) The Boy I'm Gonna Marry/ My Heart Beat a Little Faster	1963	6.25	12.50	25.00
❏ 111		(Today I Met) The Boy I'm Gonna Marry/ Playing for Keeps	1963	5.00	10.00	20.00
❏ 114		Wait 'Til My Bobby Gets Home/Take It From Me	1963	5.00	10.00	20.00
❏ 117		A Fine Fine Boy/Nino & Sonny (Big Trouble)	1963	5.00	10.00	20.00
❏ 119		Christmas (Baby Please Come Home)/ Harry and Milt Meet Hal B.	1963	10.00	20.00	40.00
❏ 123	DJ	Stumble and Fall/(He's a) Quiet Guy	1964	37.50	75.00	150.00

White label. Stock copy is unknown.

❏ 125		Christmas (Baby Please Come Home)/X-Mas Blues	1964	100.00	200.00	400.00
❏ 125X		Christmas (Baby Please Come Home)/ Winter Wonderland	1965	6.25	12.50	25.00

Reprise

❏ 0534		Too Late to Say You're Sorry/If	1966	2.50	5.00	10.00

Warner/Spector

❏ 0401		Christmas (Baby Please Come Home)/ Winter Wonderland	1974	2.50	5.00	10.00
❏ 0410		Lord, If You're a Woman/Stumble and Fall	1975	2.50	5.00	10.00

Love, Hot Shot
Sun

❏ 196		Wolf Call Boogie/Harmonica Jam	1954	1,000	2,000	3,000

Love, Mike
(Also see "Beach Boys, The")
Boardwalk

❏ NB7-11-128		Looking Back with Love/One Good Reason	1981		2.00	4.00

Lovers, The
(Several different groups)
Agon

❏ 1011		Caravan of Lonely Men/In My Tenement	1965	6.25	12.50	25.00

Aladdin

❏ 3419		Tell Me/Love Bug Bit Me	1958	7.50	15.00	30.00

Casino

❏ 103		Let's/Big Axe	1958	5.00	10.00	20.00

Checker

❏ 1100		It's Too Late/Security	1965	2.50	5.00	10.00

Decca

❏ 29862		Don't Touch Me/Let Me Be the First to Know	1956	7.50	15.00	30.00

Gate

❏ 501		Someone/Do This For Me	1965	10.00	20.00	40.00

Imperial

❏ 5845		Darling It's Wonderful/I Want to Be Loved	1962	3.75	7.50	15.00
❏ 5960		Tell Me/Let's Elope	1963	3.75	7.50	15.00
❏ 66055		Darling It's Wonderful/I Want to Be Loved	1964	3.75	7.50	15.00

Keller

❏ 101		Party Line/Strange As It Seems	1961	10.00	20.00	40.00

Lamp

❏ 2005		Darling It's Wonderful/Gotta Whole Lot of Livin' to Do	1957	6.25	12.50	25.00
❏ 2013		I Wanna Be Loved/Let's Elope	1957	7.50	15.00	30.00
❏ 2018		Tell Me/Love Bug Bit Me	1958	7.50	15.00	30.00

Marlin

❏ 3313		Discomania (Part 1)/Discomania (Part 2)	1977		2.00	4.00

Philips

❏ 40353		Someone/Do This for Me	1966	2.50	5.00	10.00

Post

❏ 10007		Darling It's Wonderful/Gotta Whole Lot of Livin' to Do	1963	3.75	7.50	15.00

Lovin' Spoonful, The
(Also see "Sebastian, John"; "Yanovsky, Zalman")
Kama Sutra

❏ 201		Do You Believe in Magic/On the Road Again	1965	3.00	6.00	12.00

Originals have a mostly red-orange label.

❏ 201		Do You Believe in Magic/On the Road Again	1965	2.00	4.00	8.00

Second pressings have a mostly yellow label with "Kama Sutra" in red

Number		Title (A Side/B Side)	Year	VG	VG+	NM
❏ 201		Do You Believe in Magic/On the Road Again	1965	2.50	5.00	10.00
		Third pressings have a mostly yellow label with "Kama Sutra" in black				
❏ 205		You Didn't Have to Be So Nice/My Gal	1965	3.00	6.00	12.00
		Originals have a mostly red-orange label				
❏ 205		You Didn't Have to Be So Nice/My Gal	1965	2.50	5.00	10.00
		Second pressings have a mostly yellow label with "Kama Sutra" in red				
❏ 205		You Didn't Have to Be So Nice/My Gal	1965	2.00	4.00	8.00
		Third pressings have a mostly yellow label with "Kama Sutra" in black				
❏ 205	PS	You Didn't Have to Be So Nice/My Gal	1965	3.75	7.50	15.00
❏ 208		Daydream/Night Owl Blues	1966	3.00	6.00	12.00
		Originals have a mostly yellow label with "Kama Sutra" in red				
❏ 208		Daydream/Night Owl Blues	1966	2.50	5.00	10.00
		Second pressings have a mostly yellow label with "Kama Sutra" in black				
❏ 208	PS	Daydream/Night Owl Blues	1966	3.75	7.50	15.00
❏ 209		Did You Ever Have to Make Up Your Mind/ Didn't Want to Have to Do It	1966	2.50	5.00	10.00
❏ 209	PS	Did You Ever Have to Make Up Your Mind/ Didn't Want to Have to Do It	1966	3.75	7.50	15.00
❏ 211		Summer in the City/Butchie's Tune	1966	2.50	5.00	10.00
❏ 211	PS	Summer in the City/Butchie's Tune	1966	3.75	7.50	15.00
❏ 216		Rain on the Roof/Pow	1966	2.50	5.00	10.00
❏ 216	PS	Rain on the Roof/Pow	1966	3.75	7.50	15.00
❏ 219		Nashville Cats/Full Measure	1966	2.50	5.00	10.00
❏ 219	PS	Nashville Cats/Full Measure	1966	3.75	7.50	15.00
❏ 220		Darling Be Home Soon/Darlin' Companion	1967	2.50	5.00	10.00
❏ 220	PS	Darling Be Home Soon/Darlin' Companion	1967	3.75	7.50	15.00
❏ 225		Six O'Clock/The Finale	1967	2.50	5.00	10.00
❏ 225	PS	Six O'Clock/The Finale	1967	3.75	7.50	15.00
❏ 231		Lonely (Amy's Theme)/You're a Big Boy Now	1967	3.75	7.50	15.00
❏ 239		She Is Still a Mystery/Only Pretty, What a Pity	1967	2.50	5.00	10.00
❏ 239	PS	She Is Still a Mystery/Only Pretty, What a Pity	1967	3.75	7.50	15.00
❏ 241		Money/Close Your Eyes	1967	2.00	4.00	8.00
❏ 250		Never Going Back/Forever	1968	2.00	4.00	8.00
❏ 251		Revelation Revolution '69/Run with You	1968	2.00	4.00	8.00
❏ 255		Me About You/Amazing Air	1968	2.00	4.00	8.00
❏ 551		Summer in the City/You and Me and Rain on the Roof	1972		3.00	6.00
❏ 608	DJ	Daydream (mono/stereo)	1976		3.00	6.00
		Stock copy not known to exist				

Lowe, Virginia
Melba

Number		Title (A Side/B Side)	Year	VG	VG+	NM
❏ 107		I'm in Love with Elvis Presley/Empty Feeling	1956	12.50	25.00	50.00

Luke, Robin
Dot

Number		Title (A Side/B Side)	Year	VG	VG+	NM
❏ 15781		Susie Darlin'/Living's Loving You	1958	6.25	12.50	25.00
❏ 15839		My Girl/Chicka Chicka Honey	1958	5.00	10.00	20.00
❏ 15899		Strollin' Blues/You Can't Stop Me from Dreaming	1959	5.00	10.00	20.00
❏ 15959		Five Minutes More/Who's Gonna Hold Your Hand	1959	5.00	10.00	20.00
❏ 16001		Make Me a Dreamer/Walkin' in the Moonlight	1959	5.00	10.00	20.00
❏ 16040		Bad Boy/School Bus Love Affair	1960	5.00	10.00	20.00
❏ 16096		Everlovin'/Well Oh Well Oh	1960	5.00	10.00	20.00
❏ 16096	PS	Everlovin'/Well Oh Well Oh	1960	12.50	25.00	50.00
❏ 16170		So Alone/All Because of You	1960	5.00	10.00	20.00
❏ 16229		Part of a Fool/Poor Little Rich Boy	1961	3.75	7.50	15.00
❏ 16366		Foggin' Up the Windows/Time	1962	3.75	7.50	15.00
		With Roberta Shore				

International

Number		Title (A Side/B Side)	Year	VG	VG+	NM
❏ 206		Susie Darlin'/Living's Loving You	1958	12.50	25.00	50.00
❏ 206	PS	Susie Darlin'/Living's Loving You	1958	25.00	50.00	100.00
❏ 208		My Girl/Chicka Chicka Honey	1958	7.50	15.00	30.00
❏ 210		Strollin' Blues/You Can't Stop Me from Dreaming	1959	7.50	15.00	30.00
❏ 212		Five Minutes More/Who's Gonna Hold Your Hand	1959	7.50	15.00	30.00

Lulu
Alfa

Number		Title (A Side/B Side)	Year	VG	VG+	NM
❏ 7006		I Could Never Miss You (More Than I Do)/ Dance to the Feeling	1981		2.00	4.00
❏ 7006	PS	I Could Never Miss You (More Than I Do)/ Dance to the Feeling	1981		3.00	6.00
		With Lulu not wearing a headband (original)				
❏ 7006	PS	I Could Never Miss You (More Than I Do)/ Dance to the Feeling	1981		2.50	5.00
		With Lulu wearing a spotted headband				
❏ 7011		If I Were You/You Win, I Lose	1981		2.00	4.00
❏ 7011	PS	If I Were You/You Win, I Lose	1981		2.50	5.00
❏ 7021		Who's Foolin' Who/You Win, I Lose	1982		2.00	4.00

Atco

Number		Title (A Side/B Side)	Year	VG	VG+	NM
❏ 6722		Oh Me Oh My (I'm a Fool for You Baby)/ Sweep Around Your Own Back Door	1969	2.00	4.00	8.00
❏ 6749		Hum a Song (From Your Heart)/Where's Eddie	1970		3.00	6.00
❏ 6761		Good Day Sunshine/After the Feeling Is Gone	1970		3.00	6.00
❏ 6774		Melody Fair/To the Other Woman	1970		3.00	6.00
❏ 6819		Goodbye My Love, Goodbye/Everybody's Got to Clap	1971		3.00	6.00
❏ 6885		It Takes a Real Man/ You Ain't Wrong, You Just Ain't Right	1972		3.00	6.00

Number		Title (A Side/B Side)	Year	VG	VG+	NM

Chelsea

❑ 78-0121		Make Believe World/Help Me Help You	1973	2.00	4.00	8.00
❑ 3001		The Man Who Sold the World/Watch That Man	1974	7.50	15.00	30.00
		A David Bowie song on the A-side...and produced by Bowie, too				
❑ 3009		The Man with a Golden Gun/Baby I Don't Care	1974	5.00	10.00	20.00
❑ 3011		Take Your Mama for a Ride (Long)/	1975	2.50	5.00	10.00
		Take Your Mama for a Ride (Short)				
❑ 3019		Boy Meets Girl//(B-side unknown)	1975	2.50	5.00	10.00
❑ 3038		Heaven and Earth and the Stars/(B-side unknown)	1976	5.00	10.00	20.00

Epic

❑ 10187		To Sir with Love/The Boat That I Row	1967	2.50	5.00	10.00
❑ 10210		Dreamy Nights and Days/Let's Pretend	1967	2.00	4.00	8.00
❑ 10260		Best of Both Worlds/Love Loves to Love Love	1967	2.00	4.00	8.00
❑ 10260	PS	Best of Both Worlds/Love Loves to Love Love	1967	5.00	10.00	20.00
❑ 10302		Me, the Peaceful Heart/Look Out	1968	2.00	4.00	8.00
❑ 10302	PS	Me, the Peaceful Heart/Look Out	1968	5.00	10.00	20.00
❑ 10346		Sad Memories/Boy	1968	2.00	4.00	8.00
❑ 10367		Morning Dew/You and I	1968	2.00	4.00	8.00
❑ 10403		Without Him/This Time	1968	2.00	4.00	8.00
❑ 10420		Rattler/I'm a Tiger	1968	2.00	4.00	8.00

Parrot

❑ 9678		Shout/Forget Me Baby	1964	5.00	10.00	20.00
❑ 9714		Here Comes the Night/I'll Come Running	1964	5.00	10.00	20.00
❑ 9778		Leave a Little Love/He Don't Want Your Love Anymore	1965	5.00	10.00	20.00
❑ 9791		Try to Understand/Not in This Whole World	1965	5.00	10.00	20.00
❑ 40021		Shout/When He Touches Me	1967	2.50	5.00	10.00

Rocket

❑ RB-11355		Don't Take Love for Granted/	1978		2.50	5.00
		Love Is the Sweetest Mistake				

Luman, Bob

Capitol

❑ F3972		Try Me/I Know My Baby Cares	1958	7.50	15.00	30.00
❑ F4059		Precious/Svengali	1958	7.50	15.00	30.00

Epic

❑ 10312		Pretty Girls (In Mini Skirts)/	1968		3.00	6.00
		Where the Chilly Winds Don't Blow				
❑ 10381		I Like Trains/A World of Unhappiness	1968		3.00	6.00
❑ 10416		I'm In This Town for Good/A Woman Without Love	1968		3.00	6.00
❑ 10439		Big, Big World/	1969		3.00	6.00
		Come On Home and Sing the Blues to Daddy				
❑ 10480		Every Day I Have to Cry Some/	1969		3.00	6.00
		Livin' in a House Full of Love				
❑ 10535		Cleanin' Up the Streets of Memphis/The Gun	1969		3.00	6.00
❑ 10581		Maybelline/Gettin' Back to Norma	1970		3.00	6.00
❑ 10631		Honky Tonk Man/I Ain't Built That Way	1970		3.00	6.00
❑ 10667		The Time to Remember/What About the Hurt	1970		3.00	6.00
❑ 10699		Is It Any Wonder That I Love You?/	1971		2.50	5.00
		Give Us One More Chance				
❑ 10755		I Got a Woman/One Hundred Songs on the Jukebox	1971		2.50	5.00
❑ 10786		Don't Let Love Pass You By/Chain Don't Take to Me	1971		2.50	5.00
❑ 10823		When You Say Love/Have a Little Faith	1972		2.50	5.00
❑ 10869		Let's Think About Livin'/It Takes You	1972		2.50	5.00
❑ 10905		Love Ought to Be a Happy Thing/	1972		2.50	5.00
		Lonely Women Make Good Lovers				
❑ 10943		Neither One of Us/Anything But Lonesome	1973		2.00	4.00
❑ 10994		Have I Ever Said "I Love You" to a Lady/	1973		2.00	4.00
		Good Love Is Like a Good Song				
❑ 11039		Still Loving You/I'm Gonna Write a Song	1973		2.00	4.00
❑ 11087		Baby Make It Good/Just Enough to Make It Stay	1974		2.00	4.00
❑ 11138		Let Me Make the Bright Lights Shine/	1974		2.00	4.00
		The Closest Thing to Heaven That I Love				
❑ 50065		Proud of You Baby/Tonight Your Baby's Coming Home	1975		2.00	4.00
❑ 50136		How Do You Start Over/Shame on Me	1975		2.00	4.00
❑ 50183		Satisfied Mind/Cleanin' Up the Streets of Memphis	1975		2.00	4.00
❑ 50216		It's Only Make Believe/The Man from Bowling Green	1976		2.00	4.00
❑ 50247		How Do You Start Over/	1976		2.00	4.00
		Red Cadillac and Black Mustache				
❑ 50297		Blond Haired Woman/Labor of Love	1976		2.00	4.00
❑ 50323		He's Got a Way with Women/	1976		2.00	4.00
		Here We Are Making Love Again				

Hickory

❑ 1201		You're Welcome/Interstate 40	1963	3.00	6.00	12.00
❑ 1219		Can't Take the Country from the Boy/	1963	3.00	6.00	12.00
		I'm Gonna Write a Song of Love				
❑ 1221		Too Hot to Dance/I Like Your Kind of Love	1963	3.00	6.00	12.00
		With Sue Thompson				
❑ 1238		The File/Bigger Men Than I (Have Cried)	1964	3.00	6.00	12.00
❑ 1266		Lonely Room (Empty Walls)/	1964	3.00	6.00	12.00
		Run On Home Baby Brother				
❑ 1277		Fire Engine Red/Old George Dickel	1964	3.00	6.00	12.00
❑ 1289		Bad, Bad Day/Tears from Out of Nowhere	1965	2.50	5.00	10.00
❑ 1307		Jealous Heart/Go On Home Boy	1965	2.50	5.00	10.00
❑ 1333		I Love You Because/Love Worked a Miracle	1965	2.50	5.00	10.00
❑ 1355		Five Miles from Home (Soon I'll See Mary)/	1965	2.50	5.00	10.00
		(I Get So) Sentimental				
❑ 1382		Poor Boy Blues/(Can't Get You) Off My Mind	1966	2.50	5.00	10.00

Number		Title (A Side/B Side)	Year	VG	VG+	NM
☐ 1410		Come On and Sing/It's a Sin	1966	2.50	5.00	10.00
☐ 1430		Hardly Anymore/Freedom of Living	1967	2.00	4.00	8.00
☐ 1460		If You Don't Love Me	1967	2.00	4.00	8.00
		(Then Why Don't You Leave Me Alone)/Throwin' Kisses				
☐ 1481		Running Scared/The Best Years of My Wife	1967	2.00	4.00	8.00
☐ 1536		It's All Over (But the Shouting)/Still Loving You	1969		3.00	6.00
☐ 1564		Still Loving You/Meet Mr. Mud	1970		3.00	6.00

Imperial

☐ 5705		A Red Cadillac and a Black Moustache/All Night Long	1960	6.25	12.50	25.00
☐ 8311		A Red Cadillac and a Black Moustache/All Night Long	1957	20.00	40.00	80.00
☐ 8313		Red Hot/Whenever You're Ready	1957	20.00	40.00	80.00
☐ 8315		Make Up Your Mind, Baby/Your Love	1958	15.00	30.00	60.00

The same coupling was slated for Imperial 8314 but not released.

Polydor

☐ 14408		I'm a Honky-Tonk Woman's Man/	1977		2.00	4.00
		Lonely Women Make Good Lovers				
☐ 14431		The Pay Phone/He'll Be the One	1977		2.00	4.00
☐ 14444		A Christmas Tribute/	1977		2.00	4.00
		Give Someone You Love (A Little Bit of Love This Year)				
☐ 14454		Proud Lady/Let Me Love Him Out of You	1978		2.00	4.00

Rollin' Rock

☐ 028		Stranger Than Fiction/You're the Cause of It All	1978		2.00	4.00

Warner Bros.

☐ 5081		My Baby Walks All Over Me/Class of '59	1959	6.25	12.50	25.00
☐ 5105		Dreamy Doll/Buttercup	1959	6.25	12.50	25.00
☐ 5172		Let's Think About Living/You've Got Everything	1960	5.00	10.00	20.00
☐ 5172	PS	Let's Think About Living/You've Got Everything	1960	10.00	20.00	40.00
☐ 5184		Why, Why, Bye, Bye/Oh Lonesome Me	1960	5.00	10.00	20.00
☐ 5204		The Great Snow Man/The Pig Latin Song	1961	5.00	10.00	20.00
☐ 5204	PS	The Great Snow Man/The Pig Latin Song	1961	10.00	20.00	40.00
☐ 5233		Private Eyes/You've Turned Down the Lights	1961	5.00	10.00	20.00
☐ 5255		Louisiana Man/Rocks of Reno	1962	5.00	10.00	20.00
☐ 5272		Big River Rose/Belonging to You	1962	5.00	10.00	20.00
☐ 5299		Hey Joe/The Fool	1962	5.00	10.00	20.00
☐ 5321		You're Everything/Envy	1962	5.00	10.00	20.00
☐ 5506		Boston Rocker/Old Friends//Bad Bad Day/	1960	25.00	50.00	100.00
		Let's Think About Living				

Part of Warner Bros. "+2" series, with two new songs and excerpts of two prior hits

☐ 5506	PS	Boston Rocker/Old Friends//Bad Bad Day/	1960	25.00	50.00	100.00
		Let's Think About Living				

Lurex, Larry – See "Mercury, Freddie"

Ly-Dells, The

Master

☐ 111		Genie of the Lamp/Teenage Tears	1961	62.50	125.00	250.00
☐ 251		Wizard of Love/Let This Night Last	1961	15.00	30.00	60.00

Pam

☐ 103		There Goes the Boy/Talking to Myself	1959	50.00	100.00	200.00

Parkway

☐ 897		There Goes the Boy/Talking to Myself	1964	5.00	10.00	20.00

Roulette

☐ 4493		Karen/Doing the Wiggle Wobble	1963	6.25	12.50	25.00

SCA

☐ 18001		Book of Songs/Hear That Train	1962	10.00	20.00	40.00

Southern Sound

☐ 122		Three Little Monkeys/Playing Hide and Seek	1965	15.00	30.00	60.00

Lyman, Joni

Reprise

☐ 0378		Happy Birthday Blue/	1965	10.00	20.00	40.00
		I Just Don't Know What to Do with Myself				

Lymon, Frankie

(Also see "Lymon, Frankie, and the Teenagers")

Big Kat

☐ 7008		I Want You to Be My Girl/Portable on My Shoulder	1968	2.50	5.00	10.00
☐ 7008	PS	I Want You to Be My Girl/Portable on My Shoulder	1968	3.00	6.00	12.00

Columbia

☐ 43094		Somewhere/Sweet and Lovely	1964	12.50	25.00	50.00

Gee

☐ 1039		Goody Goody/Creation of Love	1957	6.25	12.50	25.00
☐ 1052		I'm Not Too Young to Dream/Goody Good Girl	1959	6.25	12.50	25.00

Roulette

☐ 4026		So Goes My Love/My Girl	1957	6.25	12.50	25.00
☐ 4035		It's Christmas Once Again/Little Girl	1957	6.25	12.50	25.00
☐ 4044		Footsteps/Thumb Thumb	1958	5.00	10.00	20.00
☐ 4068		Mama Don't Allow It/Portable on My Shoulder	1958	5.00	10.00	20.00
☐ 4093		Melinda/The Only Way to Love	1958	5.00	10.00	20.00
☐ 4128		No Matter What You've Done/Up Jumped a Rabbit	1959	5.00	10.00	20.00
☐ 4150		Before I Fall Asleep/What a Little Moonlight Can Do	1959	5.00	10.00	20.00
☐ 4257		Little Bitty Pretty One/Creation of Love	1960	5.00	10.00	20.00
☐ 4283		Buzz, Buzz, Buzz/Waitin' in School	1960	5.00	10.00	20.00
☐ 4310		Jailhouse Rock/Silhouettes	1961	5.00	10.00	20.00

Number	Title (A Side/B Side)	Year	VG	VG+	NM
❏ 4348	Change Partners/So Young	1961	5.00	10.00	20.00
❏ 4391	I Put the Bomp/So Young	1962	5.00	10.00	20.00

TCF

❏ 11	Teacher Teacher/To Each His Own	1964	3.75	7.50	15.00

Lymon, Frankie, and the Teenagers
(Also see "Lymon, Frankie"; "Teenagers, The")

Gee

❏ 1002	Why Do Fools Fall in Love/Please Be Mine	1956	20.00	40.00	80.00
	Red and gold label				
❏ 1002	Why Do Fools Fall in Love/Please Be Mine	1956	12.50	25.00	50.00
	Red and black label; vocal duet on B-side				
❏ 1002	Why Do Fools Fall in Love/Please Be Mine	1956	7.50	15.00	30.00
	Red and black label; vocal solo on B-side. All of the above credit "The Teenagers featuring Frankie Lymon"				
❏ 1012	I Want You to Be My Girl/I'm Not a Know-It-All	1956	12.50	25.00	50.00
	As "The Teenagers featuring Frankie Lymon"				
❏ 1012	I Want You to Be My Girl/I'm Not a Know-It-All	1956	7.50	15.00	30.00
	As "Frankie Lymon and the Teenagers"				
❏ 1018	I Promise to Remember/Who Can Explain	1956	7.50	15.00	30.00
❏ 1022	The ABC's of Love/Share	1956	7.50	15.00	30.00
❏ 1026	I'm Not a Juvenile Delinquent/Baby Baby	1957	7.50	15.00	30.00
❏ 1032	Teenage Love/Paper Castles	1957	7.50	15.00	30.00
❏ 1035	Am I Fooling Myself Again/Love Is a Clown	197?			
	Evidently a 1970s bootleg to fill in a gap in the Gee Records discography				
❏ 1036	Miracle of Love/Out in the Cold Again	1957	7.50	15.00	30.00
❏ 1039	Goody Goody/Creation of Love	1957	10.00	20.00	40.00
	Actually a Frankie Lymon solo recording; the first pressing credited the entire group				

Lynn, Donna

Capitol

❏ 5087	Ronnie/That's Me, I'm the Brother	1963	3.75	7.50	15.00
❏ 5127	My Boyfriend Got a Beatle Haircut/That Winter Weekend	1964	5.00	10.00	20.00
❏ 5156	Java Jones/Things That I Feel	1964	3.75	7.50	15.00
❏ 5213	Silly Girl/There Goes the Boy I Love with Mary	1964	3.75	7.50	15.00
❏ 5378	I'd Much Rather Be with the Girls/I'm Sorry More Than You Know	1965	3.00	6.00	12.00
❏ 5456	True Blue/When Your Heart Rings, Answer	1965	3.00	6.00	12.00

Palmer

❏ 5016	Don't You Dare/It Was Raining	1967	6.25	12.50	25.00

Lynyrd Skynyrd
(Also see "Rossington-Collins Band")

Atina

❏ 129	Need All My Friends/Michelle	1978	3.75	7.50	15.00

Columbia

❏ 78284	White Knuckle Ride/Tearin' It Up	1996			3.00
	B-side by Joe Diffie				

MCA

❏ L45-1966 DJ	Gimme Back My Bullets (same on both sides)	1976	6.25	12.50	25.00
❏ 40258	Sweet Home Alabama/Take Your Time	1974		2.50	5.00
❏ 40328	Free Bird/Down South Jukin'	1974		2.50	5.00
❏ 40416	Saturday Night Special/Made in the Shade	1975		2.50	5.00
❏ 40532	Double Trouble/Roll Gypsy Roll	1975		2.50	5.00
❏ 40565	Gimme Back My Bullets/All I Can Do Is Write About It	1976		2.50	5.00
❏ 40647	Gimme Three Steps/Travelin' Man	1976		2.50	5.00
❏ 40665	Free Bird/Searching	1976		2.50	5.00
❏ 40819	What's Your Name/I Know a Little	1977		2.50	5.00
	"What's Your Name" is a different mix than that on the Street Survivors LP.				
❏ 40888	You Got That Right/Ain't No Good Life	1978		2.50	5.00
❏ 40957	Down South Jukin'/Wino	1978		2.50	5.00
❏ 53206	When You Got Good Friends/Truck Drivin' Man	1987		2.00	4.00
❏ 60191	Sweet Home Alabama/Saturday Night Special	1976		2.00	4.00
	Reissue				

Shade Tree

❏ 101	Need All My Friends/Michelle	1971	125.00	250.00	500.00
	As "Lynard Skynard"; approximately 300 copies pressed; value is conjecture				

Sounds of the South

❏ 40158	Gimme Three Steps/Mr. Banker	1973	2.00	4.00	8.00
❏ 40231	Don't Ask Me No Questions/Take Your Time	1974	2.00	4.00	8.00
❏ 40258	Sweet Home Alabama/Take Your Time	1974	2.00	4.00	8.00

M

M.C. Hammer – See "Hammer, MC"

Mach, Leon

Lavender

❏ 1554	You Hurt Me So/It's You I Love	1960	25.00	50.00	100.00

Number		Title (A Side/B Side)	Year	VG	VG+	NM

Mad Milo
Combo
☐ 131   Elvis on Trial/A Date with Elvis   1957   12.50   25.00   50.00
Million
☐ 20018   Elvis for Christmas/New Year   1957   12.50   25.00   50.00
     B-side by Ron Tan and Combo

Madonna
Geffen
☐ GGEF 0540   Gambler/Crazy for You   198?   3.00
     "Back to Back Hits" series; first issue of A-side on U.S. 45
☐ 29051   Crazy for You/No More Words   1985   3.00
     B-side by Berlin
☐ 29051   PS   Crazy for You/No More Words   1985   3.00
Maverick
☐ 17714   Love Don't Live Here Anymore1996   3.00
     (Soulpower Radio Remix)/
     Love Don't Live Here Anymore (Album Remix)
☐ 17719   You'll See/Live to Tell (Live Edit)   1995   3.00
☐ 17882   Human Nature/Sanctuary   1995   3.00
☐ 17926   Bedtime Story/Survival   1995   3.00
☐ 18000   Take a Bow/Take a Bow (In Da Soul Mix)   1994   3.00
☐ 18035   Secret/Secret (instrumental)   1994   3.00
☐ 18247   I'll Remember/Secret Garden   1994   3.00
☐ 18505   Rain/Waiting   1993   3.00
☐ 18639   Deeper and Deeper/(Instrumental)   1992   3.00
☐ 18650   Bad Girl/Fever   1993   3.00
☐ 18782   Erotica/Erotica (instrumental)   1992   3.00
Sire
☐ GSRE 0494   Borderline/Holiday   198?   3.00
     "Back to Back Hits" reissue
☐ GSRE 0506   Like a Virgin/Lucky Star   198?   3.00
     "Back to Back Hits" reissue
☐ GSRE 0507   Material Girl/Angel   198?   3.00
     "Back to Back Hits" reissue
☐ GSRE 0539   Into the Groove/Dress You Up   198?   3.00
     "Back to Back Hits" series; first issue of A-side on U.S. 45
☐ PRO-S-2023   DJ   Physical Attraction/Physical Attraction   1983   2.50   5.00   10.00
☐ 18822   This Used to Be My Playground/   1992   3.00
     This Used to Be My Playground (Long Version)
☐ 19485   Justify My Love/Express Yourself 1990   1990   3.00
☐ 19490   Rescue Me/Rescue Me (Alternate Single Mix)   1990   3.00
☐ 19789   Hanky Panky/More   1990   3.00
☐ 19863   Vogue (Single Version)/Vogue (Bette Davis Dub)   1990   3.00
☐ 19986   Keep It Together/Keep It Together (instrumental)   1990   3.00
☐ 19986   PS   Keep It Together/Keep It Together (instrumental)   1990   3.75   7.50   15.00
☐ 21860   Express Yourself/Cherish   199?   3.00
     "Back to Back Hits" reissue
☐ 21861   Like a Prayer/Oh Father   199?   3.00
     "Back to Back Hits" reissue
☐ 21940   Who's That Girl/Causing a Commotion   198?   3.00
     "Back to Back Hits" reissue
☐ 21941   La Isla Bonita/Open Your Heart   198?   3.00
     "Back to Back Hits" reissue
☐ 21985   Live to Tell/True Blue   198?   3.00
     "Back to Back Hits" reissue
☐ 21986   Papa Don't Preach/Everybody   198?   3.00
     "Back to Back Hits" reissue
☐ 22723   Oh Father/Pray for Spanish Eyes   1989   3.00
☐ 22883   Cherish/Supernatural   1989   3.00
☐ 22883   PS   Cherish/Supernatural   1989   3.00
☐ 22948   Express Yourself/The Look of Love   1989   3.00
☐ 22948   PS   Express Yourself/The Look of Love   1989   3.00
☐ 27539   Like a Prayer/Act of Contrition   1989   3.00
☐ 27539   DJ   Like a Prayer (7" Remix Edit)/   1989   2.50   5.00   10.00
     Like a Prayer (7" Version with Fade)
☐ 27539   PS   Like a Prayer/Act of Contrition   1989   3.00
☐ 28224   Causing a Commotion/Jimmy, Jimmy   1987   3.00
☐ 28224   PS   Causing a Commotion/Jimmy, Jimmy   1987   3.00
☐ 28341   Who's That Girl?/White Heat   1987   3.00
☐ 28341   PS   Who's That Girl?/White Heat   1987   3.00
☐ 28425   La Isla Bonita/La Isla Bonita (instrumental)   1987   3.00
☐ 28425   PS   La Isla Bonita/La Isla Bonita (instrumental)   1987   3.00
☐ 28508   Open Your Heart/White Heat   1986   3.00
☐ 28508   PS   Open Your Heart/White Heat   1986   3.00
☐ 28591   True Blue/Ain't No Big Deal   1986   2.50   5.00
     Blue vinyl
☐ 28591   PS   True Blue/Ain't No Big Deal   1986   2.50   5.00
     "Limited edition blue vinyl pressing" on sleeve
☐ 28591   True Blue/Ain't No Big Deal   1986   3.00
☐ 28591   PS   True Blue/Ain't No Big Deal   1986   3.00
☐ 28660   Papa Don't Preach/Pretender   1986   3.00
☐ 28660   PS   Papa Don't Preach/Pretender   1986   3.00

Number		Title (A Side/B Side)	Year	VG	VG+	NM
❏ 28717		Live to Tell/Live to Tell (instrumental)	1986			3.00
❏ 28717	PS	Live to Tell/Live to Tell (instrumental)	1986			3.00
❏ 28919		Dress You Up/Shoo-Be-Doo	1985			3.00
❏ 28919	PS	Dress You Up/Shoo-Be-Doo	1985	12.50	25.00	50.00
❏ 29008		Angel/Angel (12" Remix Edit)	1985			3.00
❏ 29008	PS	Angel/Angel (12" Remix Edit)	1985			3.00
❏ 29083		Material Girl/Pretender	1985			3.00
❏ 29083	PS	Material Girl/Pretender	1985			3.00
❏ 29177		Lucky Star/I Know It	1984		2.00	4.00
❏ 29210		Like a Virgin/Stay	1984			3.00
❏ 29210	PS	Like a Virgin/Stay	1984			3.00
❏ 29354		Borderline/Think of Me	1984		2.00	4.00
❏ 29354	PS	Borderline/Think of Me	1984	12.50	25.00	50.00
		Fold-out poster sleeve				
❏ 29478		Holiday/Holiday (instrumental)	1983		2.00	4.00
❏ 29841		Everybody/Everybody (instrumental)	1982	2.50	5.00	10.00

Maestro, Johnny
(Of The Crests and The Brooklyn Bridge)
Apt
❏ 25075		Phone Booth on the Highway/She's All Mine Alone	1965	12.50	25.00	50.00

Buddah
❏ 201		The Rains Came/Never Knew This Kind of Hurt Before	1971	2.50	5.00	10.00
❏ 236		Yours Until Tomorrow/Man in a Band	1971	2.50	5.00	10.00
❏ 289	DJ	Snow (mono/stereo)	1971	2.50	5.00	10.00
		May be promo only				

Cameo
❏ 256		Over the Weekend/I'll Be There	1963	7.50	15.00	30.00
❏ 305		Lean on Me/(It's Harder to) Make Up My Mind	1964	5.00	10.00	20.00

Coed
❏ 527		Say It Isn't So/The Great Physician	1960	6.25	12.50	25.00
		As "Johnny Masters"				
❏ 545		Model Girl/We've Got to Tell Them	1961	6.25	12.50	25.00
		As "Johnny Mastro"				
❏ 549		What a Surprise/Warning Voice	1961	6.25	12.50	25.00
❏ 552		Mr. Happiness/Test of Love	1961	6.25	12.50	25.00
❏ 557		I.O.U./The Way You Look Tonight	1961	7.50	15.00	30.00
❏ 562		Besame Baby/It Must Be Love	1962	100.00	200.00	400.00

Parkway
❏ 118		My Times/Is It You	1966	5.00	10.00	20.00
❏ 987		Heartburn/Try Me	1966	3.75	7.50	15.00
❏ 987	DJ	Heartburn	1966	15.00	30.00	60.00
		One-sided white label promo				
❏ 999		I Care About You/Come See Me (I'm Your Man)	1966	3.75	7.50	15.00

United Artists
❏ 474		Before I Loved Her/Fifty Million Heartbeats	1962	10.00	20.00	40.00

Magic Christians, The
(Trevor Burton of The Move was in this studio group)
Commonwealth United
❏ 3006		Come and Get It/Nats	1970	3.00	6.00	12.00

Magic Lanterns
(Contrary to some opinions, Ozzy Osbourne was never in this group. But Albert Hammond was)
Atlantic
❏ 2560		Shame, Shame/Baby, I Gotta Go Now	1968	2.50	5.00	10.00
❏ 2600		Give Me Love/Biding My Time	1969	2.00	4.00	8.00
❏ 2626		Melt All Your Troubles Away/	1969	2.00	4.00	8.00
		Bossa Nova 1940-Hello You Lovers				
❏ 2715		One Night Stand/Frisco Annie	1970	2.00	4.00	8.00

Big Tree
❏ 109		One Night Stand/Frisco Annie	1970		3.00	6.00
❏ 113		Let the Sunshine In/(B-side unknown)	1971		3.00	6.00
		May be promo only				

Charisma
❏ 100		Country Woman/(B-side unknown)	1972		2.50	5.00

Epic
❏ 10062		Excuse Me Baby/Greedy Girl	1966	2.00	4.00	8.00
❏ 10062	PS	Excuse Me Baby/Greedy Girl	1966	5.00	10.00	20.00
❏ 10111		Knight in Rusty Armour/Simple Things	1966	2.00	4.00	8.00

Magistrates, The
MGM
❏ 13946		Here Comes the Judge/Girl	1968	3.00	6.00	12.00
❏ 13980		After the Fox/Tear Down the Walls	1968	3.00	6.00	12.00

Magnets, The
Groove
❏ 58-0058		Surprise/You Just Say the Word	1965	10.00	20.00	40.00

London Int'l.
❏ 10036		Drag Race/Joker	1963	6.25	12.50	25.00

Number	Title (A Side/B Side)	Year	VG	VG+	NM

RCA Victor
☐ 47-7391 — When the School Bells Ring/Don't Tarry, Little Mary — 1958 — 6.25 — 12.50 — 25.00

Magnificents, The
Checker
☐ 1016 — The Dribble Twist/Do You Mind — 1962 — 3.75 — 7.50 — 15.00
Kansoma
☐ 03 — The Dribble Twist/Do You Mind — 1962 — 7.50 — 15.00 — 30.00
Vee Jay
☐ 183 — Up On the Mountain/Why Did She Go — 1956 — 18.75 — 37.50 — 75.00
☐ 208 — Hiccup/Caddy Bo — 1956 — 25.00 — 50.00 — 100.00
☐ 235 — Off the Mountain/Lost Lovers — 1957 — 18.75 — 37.50 — 75.00
☐ 281 — Don't Leave Me/Ozeta — 1958 — 25.00 — 50.00 — 100.00
☐ 367 — Up On the Mountain/Let's Do the Cha Cha — 1960 — 5.00 — 10.00 — 20.00

Majestics, The
(Several different groups)
Chess
☐ 1802 — Oasis (Part 1)/Oasis (Part 2) — 1961 — 5.00 — 10.00 — 20.00
Chex
☐ 1000 — Give Me a Cigarette/Shoppin' and Hoppin' — 1962 — 25.00 — 50.00 — 100.00
☐ 1004 — Unhappy and Blue/Treat Me Like You Want — 1962 — 12.50 — 25.00 — 50.00
☐ 1004 — Give Me a Cigarette/So I Can Forget — 1962 — 10.00 — 20.00 — 40.00
☐ 1006 — Lonely Heart/Gwendolyn — 1962 — 7.50 — 15.00 — 30.00
☐ 1009 — Baby/Teach Me How to Limbo — 1963 — 6.25 — 12.50 — 25.00
Contour
☐ 501 — Teen Age Gossip/Hard Times — 1960 — 20.00 — 40.00 — 80.00
Dunes
☐ 2014 — The Boss Walk (Part 1)/The Boss Walk (Part 2) — 1962 — 10.00 — 20.00 — 40.00
Faro
☐ 592 — TV Cowboys/So You Want to Rock — 1959 — 6.25 — 12.50 — 25.00
Foxie
☐ 7004 — The Lone Stranger/Sweet One — 1960 — 5.00 — 10.00 — 20.00
Jordan
☐ 1057 — Angel of Love/Searching for a New Love — 1961 — 75.00 — 150.00 — 300.00
Yellow vinyl
☐ 1057 — Angel of Love/Searching for a New Love — 1961 — 12.50 — 25.00 — 50.00
Linda
☐ 111 — Strange World/Everything Is Gonna Be All Right — 1963 — 12.50 — 25.00 — 50.00
☐ 121 — Girl of My Dreams/It Hurts Me — 1963 — 5.00 — 10.00 — 20.00
Marlin
☐ 802 — Nitey Nite/Cave Man Rock — 1956 — 150.00 — 300.00 — 600.00
Sam Moore of Sam and Dave was in this group
MGM
☐ 13488 — Love Has Forgotten Me/Smile Through My Tears — 1966 — 3.00 — 6.00 — 12.00
NRC
☐ 502 — Please Don't Say No/Divided Heart — 1958 — 18.75 — 37.50 — 75.00
Nu-Tone
☐ 123 — Angel of Love/Searching for a New Love — 1961 — 6.25 — 12.50 — 25.00
Pixie
☐ 6901 — Angel of Love/Searching for a New Love — 1961 — 5.00 — 10.00 — 20.00
Sam
☐ 112 — Jaguar/Blue Feeling — 1962 — 12.50 — 25.00 — 50.00
☐ 117 — Riptide/Big Noise from Makaba — 1962 — 12.50 — 25.00 — 50.00
☐ 123 — XL-3/My Little Baby — 1963 — 12.50 — 25.00 — 50.00
Sioux
☐ 91459 — The Lone Stranger/Sweet One — 1959 — 12.50 — 25.00 — 50.00
20th Fox
☐ 171 — The Lone Stranger/Sweet One — 1959 — 6.25 — 12.50 — 25.00
V.I.P.
☐ 25028 — DJ Say You/All for Someone — 1965 — 250.00 — 500.00 — 1,000
Promo only; stock copies credited "The Monitors"

Major Lance – See "Lance, Major"

Majors, The
(More than one group)
Derby
☐ 763 — At Last/You Ran Away from My Heart — 1951 — 200.00 — 400.00 — 800.00
☐ 779 — Laughing on the Outside/Come On Up to My Room — 1951 — 150.00 — 300.00 — 600.00
Felsted
☐ 8501 — Blue Sunset/Rockin' the Boogie — 1958 — 7.50 — 15.00 — 30.00
☐ 8576 — Come Go with Me/Les Qua — 1959 — 6.25 — 12.50 — 25.00
☐ 8707 — Come Go with Me/Les Qua — 1964 — 3.75 — 7.50 — 15.00
Imperial
☐ 5855 — A Wonderful Dream/Time Will Tell — 1962 — 3.75 — 7.50 — 15.00
☐ 5879 — She's a Troublemaker/A Little Bit Now, A Little Bit Later — 1962 — 3.00 — 6.00 — 12.00
☐ 5914 — What in the World/Anything You Can Do — 1963 — 3.00 — 6.00 — 12.00
☐ 5936 — Tra La La/What Have You Been Doin' — 1963 — 3.00 — 6.00 — 12.00
☐ 5968 — One Happy Ending/Get Up Now — 1963 — 3.00 — 6.00 — 12.00

Number		Title (A Side/B Side)	Year	VG	VG+	NM
☐ 5991		Which Way Did She Go/Your Life Begins (Sweet 16)	1963	3.00	6.00	12.00
☐ 66009		I'll Be There/Ooh Wee Baby	1963	3.00	6.00	12.00

Original

| ☐ 1003 | | Big Eyes/Go 'Way | 1954 | 100.00 | 200.00 | 400.00 |

United Artists

| ☐ 0110 | | A Wonderful Dream/Mother-in-Law | 1973 | | 2.50 | 5.00 |
| | | *"Silver Spotlight Series" reissue; B-side by Ernie K-Doe* | | | | |

Mallett, Saundra, and the Vandellas

Tamla

| ☐ 54067 | | Camel Walk/It's Gonna Be Hard Times | 1962 | 250.00 | 500.00 | 1,000 |

Mamas and the Papas, The

(Also see "Phillips, John"; "Phillips, Michelle")

ABC Dunhill

☐ 4125		Safe in My Garden/Too Late	1968	2.00	4.00	8.00
☐ 4150		For the Love of Ivy/Strange Young Girls	1968	2.00	4.00	8.00
☐ 4171		Do You Wanna Dance/My Girl	1968	2.00	4.00	8.00
☐ 4301		Step Out/Shooting Star	1972		3.00	6.00

Dunhill

Note: Most of the 1966 Dunhill singles credited "The Mama's and the Papa's"

☐ 4018	DJ	Go Where You Wanna Go/Somebody Groovy	1966	5.00	10.00	20.00
		Withdrawn before stock copies were released				
☐ 4020		California Dreamin'/Somebody Groovy	1966	2.50	5.00	10.00
☐ 4020	PS	California Dreamin'/Somebody Groovy	1966	25.00	50.00	100.00
		Sleeve is promo only				
☐ 4026		Monday, Monday/Got a Feeling	1966	2.50	5.00	10.00
☐ 4031		I Saw Her Again/Even If I Could	1966	2.50	5.00	10.00
☐ 4050		Look Through My Window/ Once Was a Time I Thought	1966	2.50	5.00	10.00
☐ 4057		Words of Love/Dancing in the Street	1966	2.50	5.00	10.00
☐ 4077		Dedicated to the One I Love/Free Advice	1967	2.50	5.00	10.00
☐ 4083		Creeque Alley/Did You Ever Want to Cry	1967	2.50	5.00	10.00
☐ 4083	PS	Creeque Alley/Did You Ever Want to Cry	1967	10.00	20.00	40.00
		Sleeve is promo only				
☐ 4099		Twelve Thirty (Young Girls Are Coming to the Canyon)/ Straight Shooter	1967	2.50	5.00	10.00
☐ 4107		Glad to Be Unhappy/Hey Girl	1967	2.50	5.00	10.00
☐ 4115		Dancing Bear/John's Music Box	1967	2.50	5.00	10.00
☐ 4115	PS	Dancing Bear/John's Music Box	1967	3.00	6.00	12.00
☐ 4125		Safe in My Garden/Too Late	1968	6.25	12.50	25.00
		Without the "ABC" logo at top of label				

Manchesters, The

(Featuring David Gates)

Vee Jay

| ☐ 700 | | I Don't Come from England/Dragonfly | 1965 | 6.25 | 12.50 | 25.00 |

Manfred Mann

Ascot

☐ 2151		Hubble Bubble (Toil and Trouble)/I'm Your Kingpin	1964	7.50	15.00	30.00
☐ 2157		Do Wah Diddy Diddy/What You Gonna Do?	1964	3.00	6.00	12.00
☐ 2165		Sha La La/John Hardy	1964	2.50	5.00	10.00
☐ 2165	PS	Sha La La/John Hardy	1964	6.25	12.50	25.00
☐ 2170		Come Tomorrow/What Did I Do Wrong	1965	2.50	5.00	10.00
☐ 2170	PS	Come Tomorrow/What Did I Do Wrong	1965	6.25	12.50	25.00
☐ 2181		Poison Ivy/I Can't Believe What You Say	1965		Unreleased?	
☐ 2184		My Little Red Book/What Am I Doing Wrong	1965	2.50	5.00	10.00
☐ 2194		If You Gotta Go, Go Now/The One in the Middle	1965	2.50	5.00	10.00
☐ 2210		She Needs Company/Hi Lili, Hi Lo	1966	2.50	5.00	10.00
☐ 2241		My Little Red Book/I Can't Believe What You Say	1967	2.50	5.00	10.00

Mercury

☐ 72607		Just Like a Woman/I Wanna Be Rich	1966	2.50	5.00	10.00
☐ 72607	PS	Just Like a Woman/I Wanna Be Rich	1966	6.25	12.50	25.00
☐ 72629		Semi-Detached Suburban Mr. Jones/ Each and Every Day	1966	2.50	5.00	10.00
☐ 72675		Ha, Ha, Said the Clown/Feeling So Good	1967	2.50	5.00	10.00
☐ 72770		The Mighty Quinn (Quinn the Eskimo)/ By Request -- Edwin Garvey	1968	3.00	6.00	12.00
		Red label with "Mercury" in all capital letters				
☐ 72770		The Mighty Quinn (Quinn the Eskimo)/ By Request -- Edwin Garvey	1968	2.50	5.00	10.00
		Orange and red swirl label				
☐ 72770		The Mighty Quinn (Quinn the Eskimo)/ By Request -- Edwin Garvey	1968	2.00	4.00	8.00
		Red label with white "Mercury" in a circle				
☐ 72770		Quinn the Eskimo/By Request -- Edwin Garvey	1968	3.00	6.00	12.00
		Orange and red swirl label				
☐ 72770		Quinn the Eskimo/By Request -- Edwin Garvey	1968	2.50	5.00	10.00
		Red label with white "Mercury" in a circle				
☐ 72822		My Name Is Jack/There Is a Man	1968	2.00	4.00	8.00
☐ 72822	PS	My Name Is Jack/There Is a Man	1968	3.75	7.50	15.00

Number	Title (A Side/B Side)	Year	VG	VG+	NM
☐ 72879	Fox on the Run/Too Many People	1968	2.00	4.00	8.00
☐ 72921	Ragamuffin Man/A B-Side	1969	2.00	4.00	8.00
Polydor					
☐ 14026	Sometimes/Snakeskin Garter	1970		3.00	6.00
☐ 14074	California Coastline/Part Time	1971			Unreleased
☐ 14097	Please Mrs. Henry/Prayers	1971		2.50	5.00
Prestige					
☐ 312	5-4-3-2-1/Without You	1964	25.00	50.00	100.00
☐ 314	Blue Brave/Brother Jack	1964	25.00	50.00	100.00
	Either unreleased or withdrawn immediately after release				
United Artists					
☐ 0048	Do Wah Diddy Diddy/Sha La La	1973		2.50	5.00
	"Silver Spotlight Series" reissue				
☐ 0049	Pretty Flamingo/Come Tomorrow	1973		2.50	5.00
	"Silver Spotlight Series" reissue				
☐ 50040	Pretty Flamingo/You're Standing By	1966	2.50	5.00	10.00
☐ 50066	When Will I Be Loved/Do You Have to Do That	1966	2.50	5.00	10.00

Manhattans, The
(More than one group)

Number	Title (A Side/B Side)	Year	VG	VG+	NM
Atlantic					
☐ 1142	Wowie/A Basketful of Blueberries	1957	5.00	10.00	20.00
Avanti					
☐ 1401	What Should I Do/Later for You	1963	5.00	10.00	20.00
Big Mack					
☐ 3911	Why Should I Cry/The Feeling Is Mutual	196?	50.00	100.00	200.00
Capitol					
☐ 4591	Molly Brown Medley/I Ain't Down Yet	1961	5.00	10.00	20.00
☐ 4730	La La La/Sing All the Day	1962	5.00	10.00	20.00
Carnival					
☐ 504	I've Got Everything But You/For the Very First Time	1964	3.75	7.50	15.00
☐ 506	There Goes a Fool/Call Somebody Please	1964	7.50	15.00	30.00
☐ 507	I Wanna Be (Your Everything)/What's It Gonna Be	1965	3.00	6.00	12.00
☐ 509	Searchin' for My Baby/I'm the One That Love Forgot	1965	3.75	7.50	15.00
☐ 512	Follow Your Heart/The Boston Money	1965	3.00	6.00	12.00
☐ 514	Baby I Need You/Teach Me the Philly Dog	1966	3.00	6.00	12.00
☐ 517	Can I/That New Girl	1966	3.00	6.00	12.00
☐ 522	I Betcha (Couldn't Love Me)/Sweet Little Girl	1966	3.75	7.50	15.00
☐ 524	It's That Time of the Year/Alone on New Year's Eve	1966	3.00	6.00	12.00
☐ 526	All I Need Is Your Love/Our Love Will Never Die	1967	3.00	6.00	12.00
☐ 529	When We're Made As One/Baby I'm Sorry	1967	3.00	6.00	12.00
☐ 533	I Call It Love/Manhattan Stomp	1967	3.00	6.00	12.00
☐ 542	I Don't Wanna Go/Love Is Breaking Out	1968	3.00	6.00	12.00
☐ 545	Til You Come Back to Me/Call Somebody Please	1968	3.00	6.00	12.00
Colpix					
☐ 115	Big Wheel Express/Powder Blue	1959	7.50	15.00	30.00
Columbia					
☐ 02164	Shining Star/Summertime in the City	1981			3.00
	Reissue				
	Just One Moment Away/When I Leave Tomorrow	1981		2.00	4.00
☐ 02191	Let Your Love Come Down/I Gotta Thank You	1981		2.00	4.00
☐ 02548	Money, Money/I Wanta Thank You	1982		2.00	4.00
☐ 02666	Crazy/Gonna Find You	1983		2.00	4.00
☐ 03939	Forever By Your Side/Locked Up in Your Love	1983		2.00	4.00
☐ 04110	You Send Me/You're Gonna Love Being Loved By Me	1985		2.00	4.00
☐ 04754	You Send Me/You're Gonna Love Being Loved By Me	1985		2.00	4.00
☐ 04754 PS	Don't Say No/Dreamin'	1985		2.00	4.00
☐ 04930	Where Did We Go Wrong/Maybe Tomorrow	1986			3.00
☐ 06376					
	With Regina Belle				
☐ 07010	Mr. D.J./All I Need	1987			3.00
☐ 10045	Don't Take Your Love/The Day the Robins Sang to Me	1974		2.50	5.00
☐ 10140	Hurt/Nursery Rhymes	1975		2.50	5.00
☐ 10410	Kiss and Say Goodbye/Wonderful World of Love	1976		2.50	5.00
☐ 10430	I Kinda Miss You/Gypsy Man	1976		2.50	5.00
☐ 10495	It Feels So Good to Be Loved By You/On the Street (Where I Live)	1977		2.50	5.00
☐ 10586	We Never Danced to a Love Song/Let's Start It All Over Again	1977		2.50	5.00
☐ 10674	Am I Losing You/Movin'	1978		2.50	5.00
☐ 10766	Everybody Has a Dream/Happiness	1978		2.50	5.00
☐ 10921	Here Comes the Hurt Again/Don't Say Goodbye	1979		2.50	5.00
☐ 11024	The Way We Were-Memories/New York City	1979		2.50	5.00
☐ 11222	Shining Star/I'll Never Run Away from Love Again	1980		2.00	4.00
☐ 11321	Girl of My Dreams/The Closer You Are	1980		2.00	4.00
☐ 11398	I'll Never Find Another (Another Just Like You)/Rendezvous	1980		2.00	4.00
☐ 45838	There's No Me Without You/I'm Not a Run-Around	1973		2.50	5.00
☐ 45927	You'd Better Believe It/Soul Train	1973		2.50	5.00
☐ 45971	Wish That You Were Mine/It's So Hard Loving You	1973		2.50	5.00
☐ 46081	Summertime in the City/The Other Side of Me	1974		2.50	5.00
☐ 60511	Do You Really Mean Goodbye/Rendezvous	1981		2.00	4.00
DeLuxe					
☐ 109	The Picture Became Quite Clear/Oh Lord, How I Wish I Could Sleep	1969	2.00	4.00	8.00

Number		Title (A Side/B Side)	Year	VG	VG+	NM
☐ 115		It's Gonna Take a Lot to Bring Me Back/Give Him Up	1970	2.00	4.00	8.00
☐ 122		If My Heart Could Speak/Loneliness	1970	2.00	4.00	8.00
☐ 129		From Atlanta to Goodbye/Fantastic Journey	1970	2.00	4.00	8.00
☐ 132		Let Them Talk/Straight to My Heart	1970	2.00	4.00	8.00
☐ 136		Do You Ever/I Can't Stand for You to Leave Me	1971	2.00	4.00	8.00
☐ 137		A Million to One/Cry If You Wanna Cry	1971	2.00	4.00	8.00
☐ 139		One Life to Live/It's the Only One	1972	2.00	4.00	8.00
☐ 144		Back Up/Fever	1972	2.00	4.00	8.00
☐ 146		Rainbow Week/Loneliness	1973	2.00	4.00	8.00
☐ 152		Do You Ever/If My Heart Could Speak	1973	2.00	4.00	8.00
Enjoy						
☐ 2008		Come On Back/Long Time No See	1964	5.00	10.00	20.00
		As "Ronnie and the Manhattans"				
Golden World						
☐ 14		Just a Little Loving/Beautiful Brown Eyes	1964	7.50	15.00	30.00
King						
☐ 5228		Ebb Tide (Part 1)/Ebb Tide (Part 2)	1959	3.75	7.50	15.00
☐ 5259		Sugar Tooth/Like Saying Something	1959	3.75	7.50	15.00
Piney						
☐ 107		Live It Up/Go Baby Go	1962	6.25	12.50	25.00
☐ 108		Crazy Love/The Hawk and the Crow	1962	6.25	12.50	25.00
Valley Vue						
☐ 75723		Sweet Talk/(B-side unknown)	1989			3.00
☐ 75749		Why You Wanna Love Me Like That/(B-side unknown)	1989			3.00
Warner						
☐ 1015		How Do I Say I'm Sorry/Love Is Where You Find It	1958	30.00	60.00	120.00

Mann, Barry

Number		Title (A Side/B Side)	Year	VG	VG+	NM
ABC-Paramount						
☐ 10143		War Paint/Counting Teardrops	1960	5.00	10.00	20.00
☐ 10180		Happy Birthday, Broken Heart/Millionaire	1961	5.00	10.00	20.00
☐ 10237		Who Put the Bomp (In the Bomp, Bomp, Bomp)/Love, True Love	1961	6.25	12.50	25.00
☐ 10263		Little Miss U.S.A./Find Another Fool	1961	5.00	10.00	20.00
☐ 10356		Hey Baby I'm Dancin'/Like I Don't Love You	1962	5.00	10.00	20.00
☐ 10380		Teenage Has-Been/Bless You	1962	5.00	10.00	20.00
Arista						
☐ 0194		The Princess and the Punk/Jennifer	1976		2.00	4.00
Capitol						
☐ 2082		Young Electric Psychedelic Hippy Flippy Folk & Funky Philosophic Turned On Groovy Twelve-String Band/Take Your Love	1968	3.75	7.50	15.00
☐ 2217		I Just Can't Help Believin'/Where Do I Go from Here	1968	2.50	5.00	10.00
☐ 5695		Looking at Tomorrow/Angelica	1966	2.50	5.00	10.00
☐ 5894		Where Do I Go from Here/She Is Today	1967	2.50	5.00	10.00
Casablanca						
☐ 2287		Brown-Eyed Woman/In My Own Way	1980		2.00	4.00
Colpix						
☐ 691		Graduation Time/Johnny Surfboard	1963	5.00	10.00	20.00
JDS						
☐ 5002		I Love to Last a Lifetime/All the Things You Are	1959	7.50	15.00	30.00
New Design						
☐ 1000		Carry Me Home/Sundown	1971		2.50	5.00
☐ 1005		When You Get Right Down to It/Don't Give Up on Me	1972		2.50	5.00
☐ 1006		Too Many Mornings/Lay It All Out	1972		2.50	5.00
☐ 1006		Too Many Mornings/On Broadway	1972		2.50	5.00
RCA Victor						
☐ PB-10104		Nobody But You/Woman, Woman, Woman	1974		2.50	5.00
☐ PB-10230		Nothing Good Comes Easy/Woman, Woman, Woman	1975		2.50	5.00
☐ PB-10319		Don't Seem Right/I'm a Survivor	1975		2.50	5.00
Red Bird						
☐ 10-015		Talk to Me Baby/Amy	1964	3.75	7.50	15.00
Scepter						
☐ 12281		Feelings/Let Me Stay with You	1970		3.00	6.00
United Artists						
☐ XW1021		Best That I Know How/Lettin' Good Times Get Away	1977		2.00	4.00
Warner Bros.						
☐ 8752		For No Reason at All/Almost Gone	1979		2.00	4.00
☐ 8752	PS	For No Reason at All/Almost Gone	1979		2.50	5.00

Mann, Carl

Number		Title (A Side/B Side)	Year	VG	VG+	NM
ABC						
☐ 12071		Neon Lights/Just About Out	1975		2.50	5.00
☐ 12092		It's Not the Coffee/Cheatin' Time	1975		2.50	5.00
ABC/Dot						
☐ 17596		Back Loving/Annie Over Time	1975		2.50	5.00
☐ 17621		Twilight Time/Belly-Rubbin' Country Soul	1976		2.50	5.00
Jaxon						
☐ 502		Gonna Rock and Roll Tonight/Rockin' Love	1957	500.00	1,000	2,000
Phillips Int'l.						
☐ 3539		Mona Lisa/Foolish One	1959	7.50	15.00	30.00

Number	Title (A Side/B Side)	Year	VG	VG+	NM
❑ 3546	Pretend/Rockin' Love	1959	6.25	12.50	25.00
❑ 3550	Some Enchanted Evening/I Can't Forget	1960	6.25	12.50	25.00
❑ 3555	South of the Border/I'm Comin' Home	1960	6.25	12.50	25.00
❑ 3564	The Wayward Wind/Born to Be Bad	1961	6.25	12.50	25.00
❑ 3569	I Ain't Got No Home/If I Could Change You	1961	6.25	12.50	25.00
❑ 3579	When I Grow Too Old to Dream/Mountain Dew	1962	6.25	12.50	25.00

Mann, Rev. Columbus
Cye
❑ 1001	Soon Very Soon (He's Coming Back)/(B-side unknown)	196?	10.00	20.00	40.00

Tamla
❑ 54047	Jesus Loves/They Shall Be Mine	1961	12.50	25.00	50.00

Manzarek, Ray
(Ex-Doors)
Mercury
❑ 73477	Solar Boat/Moorish Idol	1974		2.50	5.00
❑ 73601	Downbound Train/Choose Up and Choose Off	1974		2.50	5.00
❑ 73644	The Whole Thing Started with Rock and Roll (And Now It's Out of Control)/Art Deco Fandango	1974		2.50	5.00

Mar-Keys
Satellite
❑ 107	Last Night/Night Before	1960	5.00	10.00	20.00

Stax
❑ 112	Morning After/Diana	1961	3.00	6.00	12.00
❑ 114	About Noon/Sack-O-Woe	1961	3.00	6.00	12.00
❑ 115	Foxy/One Degree North	1961	3.00	6.00	12.00
❑ 121	Pop-Eye Stroll/Po-Dunk	1962	3.00	6.00	12.00
❑ 124	What's Happening/You Got It	1962	3.00	6.00	12.00
❑ 129	Sailor Man Waltz/Sack-O-Woe	1963	3.00	6.00	12.00
❑ 133	The Dribble/Bo Time	1963	3.00	6.00	12.00
❑ 156	Beach Bash/Bush Bash	1964	2.50	5.00	10.00
❑ 166	The Shovel/Banana Juice	1965	2.50	5.00	10.00
❑ 181	Grab This Thing (Part 1)/Grab This Thing (Part 2)	1965	2.50	5.00	10.00
❑ 185	Philly Dog/Honey Pot	1966	2.50	5.00	10.00

Mar-Vels, The
Butane
❑ 778	Go On and Have Yourself a Ball/How Do I Keep the Girls Away	1963	3.75	7.50	15.00

In
❑ 102	Surfing at Makeha/Endless Nights	1964	12.50	25.00	50.00

Love
❑ 5011/2	Cherry Lips/Could Be You	1958	7.50	15.00	30.00

Tammy
❑ 1016	Somewhere in Life/Voo Doo Hurt	1961	75.00	150.00	300.00
❑ 1019	My Guardian Angel/Marble Stomp	1961	75.00	150.00	300.00

Marainey, Big Memphis
Sun
❑ 184	Call Me Anything, But Call Me/Baby No, No	1953	2,000	3,000	4,000

Marathons, The
(Also see "Vibrations, The")
Argo
❑ 5389	Peanut Butter/Down in New Orleans	1961	3.75	7.50	15.00
	As "Vibrations Named By Others As MARATHONS"				

Arvee
❑ 5027	Peanut Butter/Talkin' Trash	1961	5.00	10.00	20.00
	Actually the Vibrations in disguise. All the others on Arvee are by a different group.				
❑ 5038	Tight Sweater/C. Percy Mercy of Scotland	1961	3.00	6.00	12.00
❑ 5048	Chicken Spaceman/You Bug Me Baby	1962	3.00	6.00	12.00

Chess
❑ 1790	Peanut Butter/Down in New Orleans	1961	4.00	8.00	16.00

Plaza
❑ 507	Mashed Potatoes One More Time/Little Pancho	1962	3.00	6.00	12.00

Marauders, The
Almo
❑ 221	Like You/Slippin' and Slidin'	1965	3.75	7.50	15.00

Hawk
❑ 4002	Sand Flea/Stomp Watch	1962	12.50	25.00	50.00

Laurie
❑ 3356	Out of Sight, Out of Mind/Jug Band Music	1966	5.00	10.00	20.00

Lee
❑ 9449	Nightmare/Lovin'	1965	7.50	15.00	30.00

Skyview
❑ 001	Since I Met You/I Don't Know How	1966	5.00	10.00	20.00

Number		Title (A Side/B Side)	Year	VG	VG+	NM

Marcels, The

All Ears

☐ 810085		Blue Moon/Clap Your Hands (When I Clap My Hands)	1981		3.00	6.00

Baron

☐ 109		Betty Lou/Take Me Back	197?	2.00	4.00	8.00

Chartbound

☐ 009		Letter Full of Tears/Tell Me	197?	2.00	4.00	8.00

Colpix

☐ 186		Blue Moon/Goodbye to Love	1961	6.25	12.50	25.00
☐ 186	PS	Blue Moon/Goodbye to Love	1961	12.50	25.00	50.00
☐ 196		Summertime/Teeter-Totter Love	1961	5.00	10.00	20.00
☐ 606		You Are My Sunshine/Find Another Fool	1961	5.00	10.00	20.00
☐ 612		Heartaches/My Love for You	1961	5.00	10.00	20.00
☐ 612	PS	Heartaches/My Love for You	1961	20.00	40.00	80.00
☐ 617		Merry Twist-Mas/Don't Cry for Me This Christmas	1961	6.25	12.50	25.00
☐ 617	PS	Merry Twist-Mas/Don't Cry for Me This Christmas	1961	15.00	30.00	60.00
☐ 624		My Melancholy Baby/Really Need Your Love	1962	5.00	10.00	20.00
☐ 629		Footprints in the Sand/Twistin' Fever	1962	12.50	25.00	50.00
☐ 640		Flowerpot/Hold On	1962	7.50	15.00	30.00
☐ 651		Loved Her the Whole Week Through/Friendly Loans	1962	6.25	12.50	25.00
☐ 665		Alright, Okay, You Win/Lollipop Baby	1962	6.25	12.50	25.00
☐ 683		That Old Black Magic/Don't Turn Your Back on Me	1963	6.25	12.50	25.00
☐ 687		Give Me Back Your Love/I Wanna Be the Leader	1963	7.50	15.00	30.00
☐ 694		One Last Kiss/You Got to Be Sincere	1963	50.00	100.00	200.00
☐ 694		One Last Kiss/Teeter-Totter Love	1963	25.00	50.00	100.00

888 Records

☐ 101		How Deep Is the Ocean/Lonely Boy	1964	3.75	7.50	15.00

Kyra

☐ 100		Comes Love/Your Red Wagon	1964	12.50	25.00	50.00
☐ 100		Comes Love/Your Red Wagon	1964	25.00	50.00	100.00
	Red vinyl					

Monogram

☐ 112		I'll Be Forever Loving You/A Fallen Tear	1974	3.00	6.00	12.00
☐ 113		Sweet Was the Wine/Over the Rainbow	1974	3.00	6.00	12.00
☐ 115		Two People in the World/Most of All	1974	3.00	6.00	12.00

Owl

☐ 324		(You Gave Me) Peace of Mind/Crazy Bells	197?	2.00	4.00	8.00

Queen Bee

☐ 47001		In the Still of the Night/High on a Hill	1973	3.75	7.50	15.00

Rocky

☐ 13711		(You Gave Me) Peace of Mind/That Lucky Old Sun	1975	2.00	4.00	8.00
	As "The Fabulous Marcels"					

St. Clair

☐ 13711		(You Gave Me) Peace of Mind/That Lucky Old Sun	1975	2.50	5.00	10.00
	As "The Fabulous Marcels"					

March, Little Peggy

Olde World

☐ 1105		Average People/Isn't This the Way We Are	1975	2.00	4.00	8.00

RCA Victor

☐ 47-8107		Little Me/Pagan Love Song	1962	3.75	7.50	15.00
☐ 47-8139		I Will Follow Him/Wind-Up Doll	1963	5.00	10.00	20.00
☐ 47-8189		I Wish I Were a Princess/My Teenage Castle	1963	3.75	7.50	15.00
☐ 47-8189	PS	I Wish I Were a Princess/My Teenage Castle	1963	7.50	15.00	30.00
☐ 47-8221		Hello Heartache, Goodbye Love/Boy Crazy	1963	3.75	7.50	15.00
☐ 47-8221	PS	Hello Heartache, Goodbye Love/Boy Crazy	1963	7.50	15.00	30.00
☐ 47-8267		The Impossible Happened/Waterfall	1963	3.00	6.00	12.00
☐ 47-8291		My Heart Keeps Telling Me/His	1963			Unreleased
☐ 47-8302		(I'm Watching) Every Little Move You Make/After You	1963	3.00	6.00	12.00
	Note: All records from 47-8357 on are as "Peggy March."					
☐ 47-8357		Takin' the Long Way Home/Leave Me Alone	1964	2.50	5.00	10.00
☐ 47-8418		Oh My, What a Guy/	1964	2.50	5.00	10.00
☐ 47-8460		Only You Could Do That to My Heart	1964	2.50	5.00	10.00
		Watch What You Do With My Baby/				
		Can't Stop Thinking About Him				
☐ 47-8534		Why Can't He Be You/Losin' My Touch	1965	2.50	5.00	10.00
☐ 47-8605		Let Her Go/Your Girl	1965	2.50	5.00	10.00
☐ 47-8710		He Couldn't Care Less/Heaven for Lovers	1965	2.50	5.00	10.00
☐ 47-8840		Ein Boy Wie Du (A Boy Like You)/	1966	5.00	10.00	20.00
		Sechs Tage Lang (Six Long Days)				
☐ 47-8877		Play a Simple Melody/Old Fashioned Wedding	1966	2.50	5.00	10.00
	With Gary Marshall					
☐ 47-8903		He's Back Again/Running Scared	1966	2.50	5.00	10.00
☐ 47-9033		Fool, Fool, Fool (Look in the Mirror)/	1966	2.50	5.00	10.00
		Try to See It My Way				
☐ 47-9143		January First/How Can I Tell Him	1967	2.50	5.00	10.00
☐ 47-9223		Mama Dear, Papa Dear/	1967	2.50	5.00	10.00
		Your Good Girl's Gonna Go Bad				
☐ 47-9283		This Heart Wasn't Made to Kick Around/Foolin' Around	1967	2.50	5.00	10.00
☐ 47-9359		Have a Good Time/Let Me Down Hard	1967	2.50	5.00	10.00
☐ 47-9494		If You Would Love Me/Thinking Through My Tears	1968	2.50	5.00	10.00
☐ 47-9566		Roses on the Sea/Time and Time Again	1968	2.50	5.00	10.00
☐ 47-9627		I've Been Here Before/Aren't You Glad	1968	2.50	5.00	10.00

Number	Title (A Side/B Side)	Year	VG	VG+	NM
☐ 47-9718	Purple Hat/Try to See It My Way	1969	2.50	5.00	10.00
☐ 74-0136	Boom Bang-a Bang/Lilac Skies	1969	2.50	5.00	10.00

Mareno, Lee
New Art
☐ 103	Goddess of Love/He's Gone	1961	30.00	60.00	120.00

Scepter
☐ 1222	Goddess of Love/He's Gone	1961	7.50	15.00	30.00
☐ 12222	Goddess of Love/Lonely Summer	1968	3.00	6.00	12.00
	As "Lee"				

Maresca, Ernie
Laurie
☐ 3345	The Good Life/A Bum Can't Cry	1966	2.50	5.00	10.00
☐ 3371	My Son/My Shadow and Me	1967	2.50	5.00	10.00
☐ 3447	What Is a Marine/The Night My Papa Died	1968	2.00	4.00	8.00
☐ 3496	Blind Date/People Get Jealous	1969	2.00	4.00	8.00
☐ 3519	The Spirit of Woodstock/Web of Love	1969	2.00	4.00	8.00
☐ 3671	The Night My Poppa Died/ Please Don't Play Me a Seven	1978		3.00	6.00
☐ 3698	You're the Only Girl for Me/Medley	1980		3.00	6.00
	B-side by the Belmonts				

Providence
☐ 417	Rockin' Blvd. St./Am I Better Off Than Them	1965	12.50	25.00	50.00

Rust
☐ 5076	The Beetle Dance/Theme from Lilly, Lilly	1964	3.75	7.50	15.00

Seville
☐ 107	Lonesome Blues/I Don't Know Why	1960	3.75	7.50	15.00
☐ 117	Shout! Shout! (Knock Yourself Out)/Crying Like a Baby	1962	5.00	10.00	20.00
☐ 119	Down on the Beach/Mary Jane	1962	3.75	7.50	15.00
☐ 122	Something to Shout About/How Many Times	1962	3.75	7.50	15.00
☐ 125	Love Express/Lorelei	1963	12.50	25.00	50.00
☐ 129	The Rovin' Kind/Please Be Fair	1963	3.75	7.50	15.00
☐ 138	I Can't Dance/It's Their World	1965	3.75	7.50	15.00

Margo, Margo, Medress and Siegel – See "Tokens, The"

Marketts, The
Arvee
☐ 5063	Beach Bum/Sweet Potatoes	1962	5.00	10.00	20.00

Calliope
☐ 8003	Mary Hartman, Mary Hartman/(B-side unknown)	1977		2.50	5.00
	As "The New Marketts"				
☐ 8009	City Nights/Soul Coaxing	1977		2.50	5.00
	As "The New Marketts"				

Farr
☐ 007	Song from M.A.S.H./ Song from M.A.S.H. (Disco Version)	1976		2.50	5.00
	As "The New Marketts"				
☐ 019	The Hustle/Song from M.A.S.H.	1977		2.50	5.00
	As "The New Marketts"				
☐ 021	Looking for Mr. Goodbar (Terry's Theme)/Black	1977		2.50	5.00
	As "Danny Welton and the New Marketts"				

Liberty
☐ 55401	Surfer's Stomp/Start	1962	5.00	10.00	20.00
	As "The Mar-Kets"				
☐ 55443	Balboa Blue/Stompede	1962	5.00	10.00	20.00
	As "The Mar-Kets"				
☐ 55506	Stomping Room Only/Canadian Sunset	1962	5.00	10.00	20.00
	As "The Mar-Kets"				

Mercury
☐ 73433	Mystery Movie Theme/Sister Candy	1973	2.00	4.00	8.00

Seminole
☐ 501	Song from M.A.S.H./ Song from M.A.S.H. (Disco Version)	1976	2.00	4.00	8.00
	As "The New Marketts"				

Uni
☐ 55173	The Undefeated/They Call the Wind Maria	1969	2.00	4.00	8.00

Union
☐ 501	Surfer's Stomp/Start	1961	7.50	15.00	30.00
☐ 504	Balboa Blue/Stompede	1962	7.50	15.00	30.00
☐ 507	Stomping Room Only/Canadian Sunset	1962	7.50	15.00	30.00

United Artists
☐ 0043	Surfer's Stomp/Balboa Blue	1973		2.50	5.00
	"Silver Spotlight Series" reissue				

Warner Bros.
☐ 5365	Woody Wagon/Cobra	1963	3.75	7.50	15.00
☐ 5391	Outer Limits/Bella Dalena	1963	7.50	15.00	30.00
	Original title of A-side				
☐ 5391	Out of Limits/Bella Dalena	1963	5.00	10.00	20.00
☐ 5423	Vanishing Point/Borealis	1964	3.00	6.00	12.00

Number	Title (A Side/B Side)	Year	VG	VG+	NM
❑ 5468	Come See, Come Ska/Look for a Star	1964	3.00	6.00	12.00
❑ 5641	Miami's Blue/Napoleon's Solo	1965	2.50	5.00	10.00
❑ 5670	Ready Steady Go/Lady in the Cage	1965	2.50	5.00	10.00
❑ 5696	Batman Theme/Richie's Theme	1966	3.00	6.00	12.00
❑ 5814	Theme from "The Avengers"/	1966	5.00	10.00	20.00
	A Touch of Velvet, a Sting of Brass				
❑ 5847	Tarzan/Stirrin' Up Some Soul	1966	2.50	5.00	10.00
❑ 7116	Out of Limits/Batman Theme	1968		3.00	6.00
	"Back to Back Hits" series -- originals have green labels with "W7" logo				

World Pacific

❑ 77874	Sunshine Girl/Sun Power	1967	2.50	5.00	10.00
❑ 77899	California Summer (People Moving West)/	1968	2.50	5.00	10.00
	Groovin' Time				

Markeys, The
Gone

❑ 5028	Special Delivery/Along Came Love	1958	7.50	15.00	30.00
	Not the Mar-Keys of Stax fame				

RCA Victor

❑ 47-7256	Hot Rod/Yakkaty Yal	1958	6.25	12.50	25.00
❑ 47-7412	Time to Love/Make a Record Man	1958	6.25	12.50	25.00

20th Century

❑ 1210	Eternal Love/You've Got Me on a String	1956	12.50	25.00	50.00

Marksmen, The
(With Don Wilson of the Ventures)
Blue Horizon

❑ 6052	Night Run/Scratch	1960	37.50	75.00	150.00

Marlo, Micki
ABC-Paramount

❑ 9762	Little By Little/It All Started With Your Kiss	1956	6.25	12.50	25.00
❑ 9807	Ain't That Love/The Beginning of Love	1957	3.75	7.50	15.00
❑ 9841	What You've Done to Me/That's Right	1957	7.50	15.00	30.00
	With "Vocal assist by Paul Anka"				
❑ 9841	What You've Done to Me/That's Right	1957	3.75	7.50	15.00
	New mix, without "Vocal assist by Paul Anka"				

Marquees, The
(Marvin Gaye was in this group)
Okeh

❑ 7096	Hey Little School Girl/Wyatt Earp	1957	30.00	60.00	120.00

Marsden, Gerry
(Of Gerry and the Pacemakers)
Columbia

❑ 44309	Gilbert Green/Please Let Them Be	1967	2.50	5.00	10.00

Marsh, Richie
(Also known as Dick Marsh, he later recorded as Sky Saxon in the Seeds)
Acama

❑ 125	Baby, Baby, Baby/Half Angel	1960	7.50	15.00	30.00

Ava

❑ 122	Goodbye/Crying Inside My Heart	1963	5.00	10.00	20.00

Rosco

❑ 412	There's Only One Girl/What Chance Have I	1960	5.00	10.00	20.00

Shepherd

❑ 2203	They Say Darling/I Swear That It's True	1962	6.25	12.50	25.00

Martells, The
Bella

❑ 20	Rockin' Santa Claus/Carol Lee	1959	10.00	20.00	40.00
	As "Eulis Mason and the Martells"				
❑ 45	Forgotten Spring/Va Va Voom	1961	12.50	25.00	50.00

Cessna

❑ 477	Forgotten Spring/Va Va Voom	1961	20.00	40.00	80.00

Relic

❑ 517	Forgotten Spring/Va Va Voom	1964	2.50	5.00	10.00

Martha and the Vandellas
A&M

❑ 3022	Nowhere to Run/I Got You (I Feel Good)	1988		2.00	4.00
	B-side by James Brown				
❑ 3022 PS	Nowhere to Run/I Got You (I Feel Good)	1988		2.00	4.00

Gordy

❑ 7011	I'll Have to Let Him Go/My Baby Won't Come Back	1962	6.25	12.50	25.00
❑ 7014	Come and Get These Memories/Jealous Love	1963	5.00	10.00	20.00
❑ 7022	Heat Wave/A Love Like Yours	1963	3.75	7.50	15.00
❑ 7025	Quicksand/Darling, I Hum Our Song	1963	3.75	7.50	15.00
❑ 7027	Live Wire/Old Love	1964	3.75	7.50	15.00
❑ 7031	In My Lonely Room/A Tear for the Girl	1964	3.75	7.50	15.00
❑ 7033	Dancing in the Street/There He Is (At My Door)	1964	3.75	7.50	15.00

Number		Title (A Side/B Side)	Year	VG	VG+	NM
☐ 7033	PS	Dancing in the Street/There He Is (At My Door)	1964	12.50	25.00	50.00
☐ 7036		Wild One/Dancing Slow	1964	3.00	6.00	12.00
☐ 7039		Nowhere to Run/Motoring	1965	3.00	6.00	12.00
☐ 7045		You've Been in Love Too Long/ Love (Makes You Do Foolish Things)	1965	3.00	6.00	12.00
☐ 7048		My Baby Loves Me/Never Leave Your Baby's Side	1965	3.00	6.00	12.00
☐ 7053		What Am I Gonna Do Without Your Love/ Go Ahead and Laugh	1966	3.00	6.00	12.00
☐ 7056		I'm Ready for Love/He Doesn't Love Her Anymore	1966	3.00	6.00	12.00
☐ 7058		Jimmy Mack/Third Finger, Left Hand	1967	2.50	5.00	10.00
☐ 7062		Love Bug Leave My Heart Alone/One Way Out	1967	2.50	5.00	10.00
☐ 7067		Honey Chile/Show Me the Way	1967	2.50	5.00	10.00
		Starting with 7067, as "Martha Reeves and the Vandellas"				
☐ 7070		I Promise to Wait My Love/Forget Me Not	1968	2.50	5.00	10.00
☐ 7075		I Can't Dance to That Music You're Playin'/I Tried	1968	2.50	5.00	10.00
☐ 7080		Sweet Darlin'/Without You	1968	2.50	5.00	10.00
☐ 7085		(We've Got) Honey Love/In Love (And I Know It)	1969	2.00	4.00	8.00
☐ 7094		Taking My Love (And Leaving Me)/Heartless	1969	2.00	4.00	8.00
☐ 7098		I Should Be Proud/Love, Guess Who	1970	2.00	4.00	8.00
☐ 7103		I Gotta Let You Go/You're the Loser Now	1970	2.00	4.00	8.00
☐ 7110		Bless You/Hope I Don't Get My Heart Broke	1971	2.00	4.00	8.00
☐ 7113		In and Out of My Life/ Your Love Makes It All Worthwhile	1972	2.00	4.00	8.00
☐ 7118		Tear It On Down/I Want You Back	1972	2.00	4.00	8.00
☐ 7127		Baby Don't Leave Me/I Won't Be the Fool I've Been Again	1973	2.00	4.00	8.00

Topps/Motown

☐ 7		Dancing in the Street	1967	18.75	37.50	75.00
		Cardboard record				
☐ 14		Love Is Like a Heat Wave	1967	18.75	37.50	75.00
		Cardboard record				

Martin, Dean
Capitol
Note: Dean Martin singles on Capitol before 691 are unconfirmed on 45 rpm

Number		Title (A Side/B Side)	Year	VG	VG+	NM
☐ 54-691		Just for Fun/My One, My Only, My All	1949	5.00	10.00	20.00
☐ 54-726		That Lucky Old Sun/Vieni Su	1949	5.00	10.00	20.00
☐ F937		Rain/Zing-a, Zing-a, Boom	1950	3.75	7.50	15.00
☐ F948		Muskrat Ramble/ I'm Gonna Paper All My Walls with Love Letters	1950	3.75	7.50	15.00
☐ F981		Choo'n Gum/I Don't Care If the Sun Don't Shine	1950	3.75	7.50	15.00
☐ F1002		I Still Get a Thrill/Be Honest with Me	1950	3.75	7.50	15.00
☐ F1028		I'll Always Love You/Baby Obey Me	1950	3.75	7.50	15.00
☐ F1052		Bye Bye Blackbird/Happy Feet	1950	3.75	7.50	15.00
☐ F1139		Peddler's Serenade/Wham, Bam, Thank You, Ma'am	1950	3.75	7.50	15.00
☐ F1160		Don't Rock the Boat/I'm in Love with You	1950	3.75	7.50	15.00
		With Margaret Whiting				
☐ F1342		If/I Love the Way	1950	3.75	7.50	15.00
☐ F1358		You and Your Beautiful Eyes/Tonda Wanda Hoy	1951	3.75	7.50	15.00
☐ F1458		Beside You/Who's Sorry Now	1951	3.75	7.50	15.00
☐ F1682		Oh Marie/I'll Always Love You	1951	3.00	6.00	12.00
☐ F1703		In the Cool, Cool, Cool of the Evening/Bonne Nuit	1951	3.75	7.50	15.00
☐ F1797		Hanging Around with You/Aw C'mon	1951	3.75	7.50	15.00
☐ F1811		Meanderin'/Bella Bimba	1951	3.75	7.50	15.00
☐ F1885		Night Train to Memphis/Blue Smoke	1951	3.75	7.50	15.00
☐ F1901		Never Before/Sailors Polka	1951	3.75	7.50	15.00
☐ F1921		As You Are/Oh Boy	1952	3.75	7.50	15.00
☐ F1938		Until/My Heart Found Home	1952	3.75	7.50	15.00
☐ F1975		All I Have to Give/When You're Smiling	1952	3.75	7.50	15.00
☐ F2001		Pretty as a Picture/Won't You Surrender	1952	3.75	7.50	15.00
☐ F2071		Bet-i-Cha/I Passed Your House Tonight	1952	3.75	7.50	15.00
☐ F2140		Oh Marie/Come Back to Sorrento	1952	3.75	7.50	15.00
☐ F2165		You Belong to Me/Hominy Grits	1952	3.75	7.50	15.00
☐ F2240		I Know a Dream When I See One/Second Chance	1952	3.75	7.50	15.00
☐ F2319		What Could Be More Beautiful/The Kiss	1953	3.00	6.00	12.00
☐ F2378		Little Did We Know/There's My Lover	1953	3.00	6.00	12.00
☐ F2485		Love Me, Love Me/Till I Find You	1953	3.00	6.00	12.00
☐ F2555		If I Could Sing Like Bing/Don't You Remember	1953	3.75	7.50	15.00
☐ F2589		That's Amore/You're the Right One	1953	3.00	6.00	12.00
☐ F2640		Christmas Blues/If I Should Love Again	1953	3.00	6.00	12.00
☐ F2749		Hey Brother Pass the Wine/I'd Cry Like a Baby	1954	3.00	6.00	12.00
☐ F2818		Money Burns a Hole in My Pocket/Sway	1954	3.00	6.00	12.00
☐ F2870		That's What I Like/Peddler Man	1954	3.00	6.00	12.00
☐ F2911		Try Again/One More Time	1954	3.00	6.00	12.00
☐ F2985		Open Up the Doghouse/Long, Long Ago	1954	3.75	7.50	15.00
		With Nat King Cole				
☐ F3011		Confused/Belle from Barcelona	1955	2.50	5.00	10.00
☐ F3036		Young and Foolish/Under the Bridges of Paris	1955	2.50	5.00	10.00
☐ F3133		Chee Chee Oo-Chee/Ridin' Into Love	1955	2.50	5.00	10.00
☐ F3153		Simpatico/Love Is All That Matters	1955	2.50	5.00	10.00
☐ F3196		Two Sleepy People/Relax Ay Voo	1955	2.50	5.00	10.00
		With Line Renaud				
☐ F3238		I Like Them All/In Napoli	1955	2.50	5.00	10.00
☐ F3295		Memories Are Made of This/Change of Heart	1955	3.00	6.00	12.00
☐ F3352		Innamorata/Lady with a Big Umbrella	1956	2.50	5.00	10.00
☐ F3414		Standing on the Corner/Watching the World Go By	1956	2.50	5.00	10.00
☐ F3468		Street of Love/I'm Gonna Steal You Away	1956	2.50	5.00	10.00

Number		Title (A Side/B Side)	Year	VG	VG+	NM
☐ F3521		Mississippi Dreamboat/Test of Time	1956	2.50	5.00	10.00
☐ F3577		The Look/Give Me a Sign	1956	2.50	5.00	10.00
☐ F3604		Just Kiss Me/I Know I Can't Forget	1956	2.50	5.00	10.00
☐ F3648		Captured/The Man Who Plays the Mandolino	1957	2.50	5.00	10.00
☐ F3680		Bamboozled/Only Trust Your Heart	1957	2.50	5.00	10.00
☐ F3718		I Can't Give You Anything But Love/	1957	2.50	5.00	10.00
		I Never Had a Chance				
☐ F3752		Write to Me from Naples/Beau James	1957	2.50	5.00	10.00
☐ F3787		Promise Her Anything/Triche Trache	1957	2.50	5.00	10.00
☐ F3842		Makin' Love Ukulele Style/Good Morning Life	1957	2.50	5.00	10.00
☐ F3894		Return to Me/Forgetting You	1958	2.00	4.00	8.00
☐ F3988		Angel Baby/I'll Gladly Make the Same Mistake Again	1958	2.00	4.00	8.00
☐ F4028		Volare (Nel Blu Dipinto Di Blu)/Outa My Mind	1958	2.00	4.00	8.00
☐ F4028	PS	Volare (Nel Blu Dipinto Di Blu)/Outa My Mind	1958	6.25	12.50	25.00
☐ F4065		Once Upon a Time/The Magician	1958	2.00	4.00	8.00
☐ F4124		It Takes So Long/You Were Made for Love	1959	2.00	4.00	8.00
☐ F4174		Rio Bravo/My Rifle, My Pony and Me	1959	2.00	4.00	8.00
☐ F4222		On an Evening in Roma/You Can't Love 'Em All	1959	2.00	4.00	8.00
☐ F4222	PS	On an Evening in Roma/You Can't Love 'Em All	1959	6.25	12.50	25.00
☐ F4287		I Ain't Gonna Lead This Life No More/Career	1959	2.00	4.00	8.00
☐ 4328		Love Me, My Love/Who Was That Lady	1960	2.00	4.00	8.00
☐ 4361		Napoli/Professor, Professor	1960	2.00	4.00	8.00
☐ 4391		Just in Time/Buttercup a Golden Hair	1960	2.00	4.00	8.00
☐ 4420		Ain't That a Kick in the Head/Humdinger	1960	2.00	4.00	8.00
☐ 4472		How Sweet It Is/Sogni D'Oro	1960	2.00	4.00	8.00
☐ 4518		Sparklin' Eyes/Tu Sei Bella Signorina	1961	2.00	4.00	8.00
☐ 4551		Bella, Bella Bambina/All in a Night's Work	1961	2.00	4.00	8.00
☐ 4570		The Story of Life/Giuggiola	1961	2.00	4.00	8.00
☐ B-44153		That's Amore/(B-side unknown)	1988		2.00	4.00
☐ S7-57889		Rudolph, the Red-Nosed Reindeer/White Christmas	1992		2.50	5.00

MCA

Number	Title (A Side/B Side)	Year	VG	VG+	NM
☐ 52662	L.A. Is My Home/Drinking Champagne	1985		2.00	4.00

Reprise

Number	Title (A Side/B Side)	Year	VG	VG+	NM
☐ 0252	La Giostra (Merry-Go-Round)/Grazie, Prego, Scusi	1964	2.00	4.00	8.00
☐ 0281	Everybody Loves Somebody/A Little Voice	1964	2.50	5.00	10.00
☐ 0307	The Door Is Still Open to My Heart/	1964	2.00	4.00	8.00
	Every Minute, Every Hour				
☐ 0333	You're Nobody Till Somebody Loves You/	1964	2.00	4.00	8.00
	You'll Always Be the One I Love				
☐ 0344	Send Me the Pillow You Dream On/I'll Be Seeing You	1965	2.00	4.00	8.00
☐ 0369	(Remember Me) I'm the One Who Loves You/	1965	2.00	4.00	8.00
	Born to Lose				
☐ 0393	Houston/Bumming Around	1965	2.00	4.00	8.00
☐ 0415	I Will/You're the Reason I'm in Love	1965	2.00	4.00	8.00
☐ 0443	Somewhere There's a Someone/	1965	2.00	4.00	8.00
	That Old Clock on the Wall				
☐ 0466	Come Running Back/Bouquet of Roses	1966		3.00	6.00
☐ 0500	A Million and One/Shades	1966		3.00	6.00
☐ 0516	Nobody's Baby Again/It Just Happened That Way	1966		3.00	6.00
☐ 0538	(Open Up the Door) Let the Good Times In/	1966		3.00	6.00
	I'm Not the Marrying Kind				
☐ 0542	Blue Christmas/A Marshmallow World	1966		3.00	6.00
☐ 0571	Lay Some Happiness on Me/Think About Me	1967		3.00	6.00
☐ 0601	In the Chapel in the Moonlight/Welcome to My World	1967		3.00	6.00
☐ 0608	Little Ole Wine Drinker, Me/I	1967		3.00	6.00
	Can't Help Remembering You				
☐ 0640	In the Misty Moonlight/Wallpaper Roses	1967		3.00	6.00
☐ 0640	In the Misty Moonlight/The Glory of Love	1967		3.00	6.00
☐ 0672	You've Still Got a Place in My Heart/Old Yellow Line	1968		2.50	5.00
☐ 0703	Lay Some Happiness on Me/	1968		2.50	5.00
	(Open Up the Door) Let the Good Times In				
☐ 0709	Everybody Loves Somebody/A Million and One	1968		2.50	5.00
☐ 0711	Somewhere There's a Someone/Come Running Back	1968		2.50	5.00
☐ 0714	Houston/I Will	1968		2.50	5.00
☐ 0717	You're Nobody Till Somebody Loves You/	1968		2.50	5.00
	(Remember Me) I'm the One Who Loves You				
☐ 0718	Send Me the Pillow You Dream On/	1968		2.50	5.00
	The Door Is Still Open to My Heart				
☐ 0730	In the Chapel in the Moonlight/	1968		2.50	5.00
	Little Ole Wine Drinker, Me				
☐ 0735	In the Misty Moonlight/Not Enough Indians	1970		2.00	4.00

0703 through 0735 are "Back to Back Hits" series

Number	Title (A Side/B Side)	Year	VG	VG+	NM
☐ 0761	April Again/That Old Time Feelin'	1968		2.50	5.00
☐ 0765	Five Card Stud/One Lonely Boy	1968		2.50	5.00
☐ 0780	Not Enough Indians/Rainbows Are Back in Style	1968		2.50	5.00
☐ 0812	Gentle on My Mind/That's When I See the Blues	1969		2.50	5.00
☐ 0841	I Take a Lot of Pride in What I Am/	1969		2.50	5.00
	Drowning in My Tears				
☐ 0857	Crying Time/One Cup of Happiness	1969		2.50	5.00
☐ 0893	Down Home/Come On Down	1970		2.50	5.00
☐ 0915	For the Love of a Woman/The Tracks of My Tears	1970		2.50	5.00
☐ 0934	My Woman, My Woman, My Wife/Here We Go Again	1970		2.50	5.00
☐ 0955	Detroit City/Turn the World Around	1970		2.50	5.00
☐ 0973	For the Good Times/Georgia Sunshine	1970		2.50	5.00
☐ 1004	She's a Little Bit Country/Raining in My Heart	1971		2.50	5.00
☐ 1060	What's Yesterday/The Right Kind of Woman	1971		2.50	5.00
☐ 1085	I Can Give You What You Want Now/Guess Who	1972		2.50	5.00
☐ 1141	Amor Mio/You Made Me Love You	1972		2.50	5.00
☐ 1166	Smile/Get On With Your Livin'	1973		2.50	5.00

Number		Title (A Side/B Side)	Year	VG	VG+	NM
❑ 1178		You're the Best Thing That Ever Happened to Me/	1973		2.50	5.00
		Free to Carry On				
❑ 20,058		Just Close Your Eyes/Tik-A-Tee Tik-A-Tay	1962	3.00	6.00	12.00
❑ 20,076		C'est Si Bon/The Poor People of Paris	1962	6.25	12.50	25.00
		Released only in Italy				
❑ 20,082		Baby-O/Dame Su Amor	1962	2.50	5.00	10.00
❑ 20,116		From the Bottom of My Heart (Dammi, Dammi, Dammi)/	1962	2.50	5.00	10.00
		Who's Got the Action				
❑ 20,116	PS	From the Bottom of My Heart (Dammi, Dammi, Dammi)/	1962	5.00	10.00	20.00
		Who's Got the Action				
❑ 20,128		Sam's Song/Me and My Shadow	1962	3.75	7.50	15.00
		A-side: With Sammy Davis, Jr.; B-side: Sammy Davis, Jr. and Frank Sinatra				
❑ 20,140		Who's Got the Action/Send a Fine	1963	2.50	5.00	10.00
❑ 20,150		Ain't Gonna Try Anymore/A Face in the Crowd	1963	2.50	5.00	10.00
❑ 20,194		Corrine, Corrina/My Sugar's Gone	1963	2.50	5.00	10.00
❑ 20,215		Via Veneto/Mama Roma	1963	2.50	5.00	10.00
❑ 20,217		Fugue for Tinhorns/	1963	3.75	7.50	15.00
		The Oldest Established (Permanent Floating Crap Game in New York)				
		By Frank Sinatra/Bing Crosby/Dean Martin				
❑ 20,217	PS	Fugue for Tinhorns/	1963	20.00	40.00	80.00
		The Oldest Established (Permanent Floating Crap Game in New York)				
		By Frank Sinatra/Bing Crosby/Dean Martin				

Warner Bros.

❑ 29480		Drinking Champagne/Since I Met You Baby	1983		2.00	4.00
❑ 29584		Hangin' Around/My First Country Song	1983		2.00	4.00

Martin, George
United Artists

❑ 745		Ringo's Theme (This Boy)/And I Love Her	1964	6.25	12.50	25.00
❑ 745	PS	Ringo's Theme (This Boy)/And I Love Her	1964	75.00	150.00	300.00
❑ 750		A Hard Day's Night/I Should Have Known Better	1964	25.00	50.00	100.00
❑ 750	PS	A Hard Day's Night/I Should Have Known Better	1964	500.00	1,000	2,000
❑ 831		All Quiet on the Mersey Front/	1965	3.75	7.50	15.00
		Cast Your Fate to the Wind				
❑ 873		I Feel Fine/Downtown	1965	3.75	7.50	15.00
❑ 50148		Love in the Open Air/Bahama Sound	1967	7.50	15.00	30.00

Martin, Janis
Palette

❑ 5058		Hard Times Ahead/Here Today and Gone Tomorrow	1960	6.25	12.50	25.00
❑ 5071		Teen Street/Cry Guitar	1961	6.25	12.50	25.00

RCA Victor

❑ 47-6491		Drugstore Rock and Roll/Will You, Willyum	1956	10.00	20.00	40.00
❑ 47-6560		Ooby-Dooby/One More Year to Go	1956	10.00	20.00	40.00
❑ 47-6652		My Boy Elvis/Little Bit	1956	15.00	30.00	60.00
❑ 47-6744		Let's Elope, Baby/Barefoot Baby	1956	7.50	15.00	30.00
❑ 47-6832		Love Me to Pieces/Two Long Years	1957	7.50	15.00	30.00
❑ 47-6983		Love and Kisses/I'll Never Be Free	1957	7.50	15.00	30.00
❑ 47-7104		All Right Baby/Billy Boy, Billy Boy	1957	7.50	15.00	30.00
❑ 47-7184		Cracker Jack/Good Love	1958	7.50	15.00	30.00

Marty
Novelty

❑ 101		Marty on Planet Mars (Part 1)/	1956	10.00	20.00	40.00
		Marty on Planet Mars (Part 2)				

Marty and the Symbols
Graphic Arts

❑ 1000		You're the One/Rip Van Winkle	1963	20.00	40.00	80.00

Marvelettes, The
A&M

❑ 1201		Danger Heartbreak Dead Ahead/	1988		2.00	4.00
		Baby Please Don't Go				
		B-side by Them				
❑ 1201	PS	Danger Heartbreak Dead Ahead/	1988		2.00	4.00
		Baby Please Don't Go				
		"Good Morning Vietnam" sleeve				

Gordy

❑ 7024		Too Hurt to Cry, Too Much in Love to Say Goodbye/	1963	20.00	40.00	80.00
		Come On Home				
		As "The Darnells"				

Tamla

❑ 54046		Please Mr. Postman/So Long Baby	1961	5.00	10.00	20.00
❑ 54046	PS	Please Mr. Postman/So Long Baby	1961	25.00	50.00	100.00
❑ 54054		Twistin' Postman/I Want a Guy	1962	3.75	7.50	15.00
❑ 54054	PS	Twistin' Postman/I Want a Guy	1962	25.00	50.00	100.00
❑ 54060		Playboy/All the Love I Got	1962	3.75	7.50	15.00
❑ 54065		Beechwood 4-5789/Someday, Someway	1962	3.75	7.50	15.00
❑ 54072		Strange I Know/Too Strung Out to Be Strung Along	1962	3.75	7.50	15.00
❑ 54077		Forever/Locking Up My Heart	1963	3.75	7.50	15.00
❑ 54082		Tie a String Around My Finger/My Daddy Knows Best	1963	5.00	10.00	20.00
❑ 54088		As Long As I Know He's Mine/Little Girl Blue	1963	3.00	6.00	12.00
❑ 54091		He's a Good Guy (Yes He Is)/Goddess of Love	1964	3.00	6.00	12.00

Number		Title (A Side/B Side)	Year	VG	VG+	NM
❏ 54091	DJ	Yes He Is	1964	18.75	37.50	75.00
		One-sided promo with different title than stock copy				
❏ 54097		You're My Remedy/	1964	2.50	5.00	10.00
		A Little Bit of Sympathy, A Little Bit of Love				
❏ 54097	PS	You're My Remedy/A	1964	12.50	25.00	50.00
		Little Bit of Sympathy, A Little Bit of Love				
❏ 54105		Too Many Fish in the Sea/A Need for Love	1964	2.50	5.00	10.00
❏ 54116		I'll Keep Holding On/No Time for Tears	1965	2.50	5.00	10.00
❏ 54120		Danger, Heartbreak Dead Ahead/Your Cheating Ways	1965	2.50	5.00	10.00
❏ 54126		Don't Mess with Bill/Anything You Wanna Do	1965	2.50	5.00	10.00
❏ 54131		You're the One/Paper Boy	1966	2.50	5.00	10.00
❏ 54143		The Hunter Gets Captured by the Game/	1967	2.50	5.00	10.00
		I Think I Can Change You				
❏ 54150		When You're Young and In Love/	1967	2.50	5.00	10.00
		The Day You Take One, You Have to Take the Other				
❏ 54158		My Baby Must Be a Magician/I Need Someone	1967	2.50	5.00	10.00
❏ 54166		Here I Am Baby/Keep Off, No Trespassing	1968	2.50	5.00	10.00
❏ 54171		Destination: Anywhere/	1968	2.50	5.00	10.00
		What's So Easy for Two Is So Hard for One				
❏ 54177		I'm Gonna Hold On Long As I Can/	1968	2.50	5.00	10.00
		Don't Make Hurting Me a Habit				
❏ 54186		That's How Heartaches Are Made/Rainy Morning	1969	2.50	5.00	10.00
❏ 54198		Marionette/After All	1970	2.00	4.00	8.00
❏ 54213		A Breath Taking Guy/You're the One for Me Baby	1972	2.00	4.00	8.00

Topps/Motown

Number		Title (A Side/B Side)	Year	VG	VG+	NM
❏ 12		Please Mr. Postman	1967	18.75	37.50	75.00
		Cardboard record				

Marvellos, The
(More than one group)

Cha Cha

Number	Title (A Side/B Side)	Year	VG	VG+	NM
❏ 756	Come Back My Love/Boyee Yoing	1963	6.25	12.50	25.00

Exodus

Number	Title (A Side/B Side)	Year	VG	VG+	NM
❏ 6214	Salty Sam/She Told Me Lies	1962	15.00	30.00	60.00
❏ 6216	I Ask of You/Hip Enough	1962	20.00	40.00	80.00

Loma

Number	Title (A Side/B Side)	Year	VG	VG+	NM
❏ 2045	Something's Burning/We Go Together	1966	3.00	6.00	12.00
❏ 2061	You're Such a Sweet Thing/	1966	3.00	6.00	12.00
	Why Do You Want to Hurt the One You Love				

Marvello

Number	Title (A Side/B Side)	Year	VG	VG+	NM
❏ 5005	Red Hot Momma/I Need a Girl	1955	75.00	150.00	300.00

Modern

Number	Title (A Side/B Side)	Year	VG	VG+	NM
❏ 1054	Down in the City/In the Sunshine	1967	2.50	5.00	10.00

Reprise

Number	Title (A Side/B Side)	Year	VG	VG+	NM
❏ 20,088	Salty Sam/She Told Me Lies	1962	6.25	12.50	25.00

Stepheny

Number	Title (A Side/B Side)	Year	VG	VG+	NM
❏ 1818	Come Back My Love/Boyee Yoing	1958	15.00	30.00	60.00

Theron

Number	Title (A Side/B Side)	Year	VG	VG+	NM
❏ 117	You're the Dream/Calypso Mama	1957	100.00	200.00	400.00

Warner Bros.

Number	Title (A Side/B Side)	Year	VG	VG+	NM
❏ 7011	Don't Play with My Heart/Let Me Keep You Satisfied	1967	2.50	5.00	10.00
❏ 7054	Piece of Silk/Yes I Do	1967	2.50	5.00	10.00

Marvelows, The

ABC

Number	Title (A Side/B Side)	Year	VG	VG+	NM
❏ 10820	Fade Away/You've Been Going to Sally	1966	2.50	5.00	10.00
❏ 11011	In the Morning/Talkin' 'Bout Ya, Baby	1967	2.00	4.00	8.00
	As "The Mighty Marvelows"				
❏ 11073	I'm So Confused/I'm Without a Girl	1968	2.00	4.00	8.00
	As "The Mighty Marvelows"				
❏ 11139	Hey, Hey Girl/Wait, Be Cool	1968	2.00	4.00	8.00
	As "The Mighty Marvelows"				
❏ 11189	You're Breaking My Heart/This Town's Too Much	1969	2.00	4.00	8.00
	As "The Mighty Marvelows"				

ABC-Paramount

Number	Title (A Side/B Side)	Year	VG	VG+	NM
❏ 10613	A Friend/Hey, Hey Baby	1965	2.50	5.00	10.00
❏ 10629	I Do/My Heart	1965	3.75	7.50	15.00
❏ 10708	Shim Sham/Your Little Sister	1965	2.50	5.00	10.00
❏ 10756	Do It/I've Got My Eyes on You	1965	2.50	5.00	10.00

Marvels, The
(More than one group)

ABC-Paramount

Number	Title (A Side/B Side)	Year	VG	VG+	NM
❏ 9771	I Won't Have You Breaking My Heart/	1956	100.00	200.00	400.00
	Jump Rock and Roll				
	Also recorded as The Dubs				

Laurie

Number	Title (A Side/B Side)	Year	VG	VG+	NM
❏ 3106	I Shed So Many Tears/So Young, So Sweet	1958	10.00	20.00	40.00
	Also released as "The Marvells"				

Mun-Rab

Number	Title (A Side/B Side)	Year	VG	VG+	NM
❏ 1008	Just Another Fool/You Crack Me Up	1959	100.00	200.00	400.00

Number	Title (A Side/B Side)	Year	VG	VG+	NM

Winn
| ❑ 1916 | For Sentimental Reasons/Come Back | 1961 | 50.00 | 100.00 | 200.00 |

Marvin and Johnny
Aladdin
❑ 3371	Yak Yak/Pretty Eyes	1957	7.50	15.00	30.00
❑ 3408	You're in My Heart/Smack Smack	1958	7.50	15.00	30.00
❑ 3439	It's Christmas Time/The Valley of Love	1958	7.50	15.00	30.00

Felsted
| ❑ 8681 | Hot Biscuits and Gravy/Tired of Being Alone | 1963 | 3.00 | 6.00 | 12.00 |

Jamie
| ❑ 1188 | Once Upon a Time/Tick Tock | 1961 | 3.00 | 6.00 | 12.00 |

Modern
❑ 933	Tick Tock/Cherry Pie	1954	15.00	30.00	60.00
❑ 941	Sugar/Kiss Me	1954	12.50	25.00	50.00
❑ 946	Little Honey/Honey Girl	1955	12.50	25.00	50.00
❑ 949	Ko Ko Mo/Sometimes I Wonder	1955	10.00	20.00	40.00
❑ 952	I Love You, Yes I Do/Baby Won't You Marry Me	1955	10.00	20.00	40.00
❑ 959	Butler Ball/Sugar Mama	1955	10.00	20.00	40.00
❑ 968	Will You Love Me/Sweet Dreams	1956	7.50	15.00	30.00
❑ 974	Ain't That Right/Let Me Know	1956	7.50	15.00	30.00

Specialty
❑ 479	Baby Doll/I'm Not a Fool	1953	15.00	30.00	60.00
❑ 479	Baby Doll/I'm Not a Fool	1953	25.00	50.00	100.00
	Red vinyl				
❑ 488	Jo Jo/How Long Has She Been Gone	1954	15.00	30.00	60.00
❑ 498	School of Love/Boy Loves Girl	1954	15.00	30.00	60.00

Swingin'
| ❑ 641 | I'm Tired of Being Alone/Baby You Don't Know | 1962 | 3.00 | 6.00 | 12.00 |
| ❑ 645 | Pretty One/Second Helping of Cherry Pie | 1963 | 3.00 | 6.00 | 12.00 |

Marx, The
Chante
| ❑ 1002 | One Minute More/You Are My Love | 19?? | 50.00 | 100.00 | 200.00 |

Dahlia
| ❑ 1002 | One Minute More/You Are My Love | 19?? | 25.00 | 50.00 | 100.00 |

Marylanders, The
Jubilee
❑ 5079	I'm a Sentimental Fool/Sittin' By the River	1952	100.00	200.00	400.00
❑ 5091	Make Me Thrill Again/Please Love Me	1952	100.00	200.00	400.00
❑ 5114	Fried Chicken/Good Old 99	1953	100.00	200.00	400.00
	Red vinyl				
❑ 5114	Fried Chicken/Good Old 99	1953	75.00	150.00	300.00

Mascots, The
ABC
| ❑ 11152 | Baby, You're So Wrong/Moreen | 1968 | 2.00 | 4.00 | 8.00 |

Blast
❑ 206	Once Upon a Love/Hey Little Angel	1963	10.00	20.00	40.00
	Red label				
❑ 206	Once Upon a Love/Hey Little Angel	1963	5.00	10.00	20.00
	White label				

King
❑ 5377	The Story of My Heart/Do the Wiggle	1960	15.00	30.00	60.00
❑ 5435	Lonely Rain/That's the Way I Feel	1960	10.00	20.00	40.00
	The King group later recorded as The O'Jays				

Mermaid
| ❑ 107 | Bluebirds Over the Mountain/Timberlands | 1962 | 15.00 | 30.00 | 60.00 |

MGM
❑ 12027	Relax-Ay-Voo/The Others I Like	1955	5.00	10.00	20.00
❑ 12107	Nobody's Arms/Little Mustard Seed	1955	5.00	10.00	20.00
❑ 12236	Who Put the Devil in Evelyn's Eyes/Java Jive	1956	5.00	10.00	20.00

Masked Marauders, The
(Legendary non-group. This is actually the Cleanliness and Godliness Skiffle Band)
Deity
| ❑ 0870 | I Can't Get No Nookie/Cow Pie | 1969 | 3.75 | 7.50 | 15.00 |

Mason, Bonnie Jo
(Actually Cher)
Annette
| ❑ 1000 | Ringo I Love You/Beatles Blues | 1964 | 250.00 | 500.00 | 1,000 |
| | *A Phil Spector production* | | | | |

Masters, Johnny; Mastro, Johnny – See "Maestro, Johnny"

Matadors, The
(More than one group)
Chart Maker
| ❑ 404 | Let Me Dream/Wiggle Wobble | 1966 | 7.50 | 15.00 | 30.00 |

Number		Title (A Side/B Side)	Year	VG	VG+	NM
Colpix						
❏ 698		Ace of Hearts/Perfidia	1963	6.25	12.50	25.00
❏ 718		I've Gotta Drive/La Corrida	1963	12.50	25.00	50.00
		A-side is a Jan and Dean track with a new spoken introduction				
❏ 741		C'mon, Let Yourself Go (Part 1)/	1964	6.25	12.50	25.00
		C'mon, Let Yourself Go (Part 2)				
Forbes						
❏ 230		Let Me Dream/Wiggle Wobble	1966	5.00	10.00	20.00
Jamie						
❏ 1226		Listen/So Near	1962	5.00	10.00	20.00
Keith						
❏ 6502		If You Left Me Today/It Ain't Nothin' But Rock 'N' Roll	1962	5.00	10.00	20.00
❏ 6504		You'd Be Crying, Too/My Foolish Heart	1963	5.00	10.00	20.00
Sue						
❏ 700		Pennies from Heaven/Vengeance	1957	25.00	50.00	100.00
❏ 701		Be Good to Me/Have Mercy Baby	1957	15.00	30.00	60.00

Mathis, Bobby, and the Sevilles

Number		Title (A Side/B Side)	Year	VG	VG+	NM
Sioux						
❏ 51860		Girl in the Drugstore/Going to the City	1960	37.50	75.00	150.00

Matthews, Fat Man

Number		Title (A Side/B Side)	Year	VG	VG+	NM
Bayou						
❏ 016		I'm Thankful/Goin' Down	1952	37.50	75.00	150.00
Imperial						
❏ 5211		When Boy Meets Girl/Later Baby	1952	1,000	1,500	2,000
❏ 5235		Down the Line/You Know It	1953	25.00	50.00	100.00

Maximillian

(Del Shannon's organist/keyboardist)

Number		Title (A Side/B Side)	Year	VG	VG+	NM
Big Top						
❏ 3068		The Wanderer/The Snake	1961	5.00	10.00	20.00
❏ 3095		The Twistin' Ghost/	1961	5.00	10.00	20.00
		The Breeze and I-Peter Gunn Theme				
Cub						
❏ 9046		Gee Baby, You're the Utmost/	1959	6.25	12.50	25.00
		Blowing My Brains Out (Over You)				

MC5

Number		Title (A Side/B Side)	Year	VG	VG+	NM
A-Square						
❏ 333		Looking at You/Borderline	1967	20.00	40.00	80.00
		500 copies of this record were pressed				
❏ 333	PS	Looking at You/Borderline	1967	10.00	20.00	40.00
AMG						
❏ 1000	DJ	I Can Only Give You Everything (same on both sides)	1966	12.50	25.00	50.00
❏ 1001		I Can Only Give You Everything/One of the Guys	1969	12.50	25.00	50.00
		Yellow label				
❏ 1001		I Can Only Give You Everything/I Just Don't Know	1969	12.50	25.00	50.00
		Black label				
Atlantic						
❏ 2678		Tonight/Looking at You	1969	3.75	7.50	15.00
❏ 2724		The American Ruse/Shakin' Street	1970	3.75	7.50	15.00
Elektra						
❏ MC5-1	DJ	Kick Out the Jams/Motor City Is Burning	1968	10.00	20.00	40.00
		Distributed free at Fillmore East concert 12/12/68; A-side is an alternate take				
❏ 45648		Kick Out the Jams/Motor City Is Burning	1969	5.00	10.00	20.00

McCartney, Linda – See "McCartney, Paul"; "Suzy and the Red Stripes"

McCartney, Paul

(Also includes Wings; label credits, if not to "Paul McCartney", are noted. Also see "Beatles, The")

Number		Title (A Side/B Side)	Year	VG	VG+	NM
Apple						
❏ 1829		Another Day/Oh Woman, Oh Why	1971	2.00	4.00	8.00
❏ 1829		Another Day/Oh Woman, Oh Why	1971	3.00	6.00	12.00
		With star on A-side label				
❏ 1837		Uncle Albert/Admiral Halsey//Too Many People	1971	3.75	7.50	15.00
		Paul and Linda McCartney; with "Pual" misspelling on producer credit				
❏ 1837		Uncle Albert/Admiral Halsey//Too Many People	1971	2.00	4.00	8.00
		Paul and Linda McCartney; with no misspelling				
❏ 1837		Uncle Albert/Admiral Halsey//Too Many People	1971	12.50	25.00	50.00
		Paul and Linda McCartney; with unsliced apple on B-side label				
❏ 1837		Uncle Albert/Admiral Halsey//Too Many People	1975	7.50	15.00	30.00
		Paul and Linda McCartney; with "All rights reserved" on label				
❏ 1847		Give Ireland Back to the Irish/	1972	2.50	5.00	10.00
		Give Ireland Back to the Irish (Version)				
		Wings				
❏ 1847	PS	Give Ireland Back to the Irish/	1972	7.50	15.00	30.00
		Give Ireland Back to the Irish (Version)				
		Wings; title sleeve with large center hole				

Number	Title (A Side/B Side)	Year	VG	VG+	NM
❏ 1851	Mary Had a Little Lamb/Little Woman Love Wings	1972	2.50	5.00	10.00
❏ 1851	DJ Mary Had a Little Lamb/Little Woman Love White label promo, lists artist as Paul McCartney	1972	75.00	150.00	300.00
❏ 1851	PS Mary Had a Little Lamb/Little Woman Love Wings; without "Little Woman Love" on sleeve	1972	6.25	12.50	25.00
❏ 1851	PS Mary Had a Little Lamb/Little Woman Love Wings; with "Little Woman Love" on sleeve	1972	10.00	20.00	40.00
❏ 1857	Hi Hi Hi/C Moon Wings; red label	1972	2.50	5.00	10.00
❏ 1861	My Love/The Mess Paul McCartney and Wings; custom "Red Rose Speedway" label	1973	2.00	4.00	8.00
❏ 1861	DJ My Love/The Mess Paul McCartney and Wings; white label	1973	50.00	100.00	200.00
❏ 1863	Live and Let Die/I Lie Around Wings	1973	2.00	4.00	8.00
❏ 1869	Helen Wheels/Country Dreamer Paul McCartney and Wings	1973	2.00	4.00	8.00
❏ 1871	Jet/Mamunia Paul McCartney and Wings; A-side incorrectly listed as playing for 2:49	1974	25.00	50.00	100.00
❏ 1871	Jet/Mamunia Paul McCartney and Wings	1974	2.50	5.00	10.00
❏ 1871	Jet/Let Me Roll It Paul McCartney and Wings	1974	2.00	4.00	8.00
❏ P-1871	DJ Jet (Edited Mono)/Jet (Stereo) Paul McCartney and Wings	1974	12.50	25.00	50.00
❏ 1873	Band on the Run/Nineteen Hundred and Eighty-Five Paul McCartney and Wings	1974	2.00	4.00	8.00
❏ P-1873	DJ Band on the Run (mono/stereo, both edits) Paul McCartney and Wings	1974	25.00	50.00	100.00
❏ P-1873	DJ Band on the Run (Edited Mono)/ Band on the Run (Full-length Stereo) Paul McCartney and Wings	1974	10.00	20.00	40.00
❏ 1875	Junior's Farm/Sally G Paul McCartney and Wings	1974	2.00	4.00	8.00
❏ 1875	Junior's Farm/Sally G Paul McCartney and Wings; with "All Rights Reserved" on label	1975	20.00	40.00	80.00
❏ P-1875	DJ Junior's Farm (Edited Mono)/ Junior's Farm (Full-length Stereo) Paul McCartney and Wings	1974	12.50	25.00	50.00
❏ P-1875	DJ Sally G (mono/stereo) Paul McCartney and Wings	1974	20.00	40.00	80.00
❏ PRO-6193/4	DJ Another Day/Oh Woman, Oh Why	1971	20.00	40.00	80.00
❏ PRO-6786	DJ Helen Wheels (mono/stereo) Paul McCartney and Wings	1973	12.50	25.00	50.00
❏ PRO-6787	DJ Country Dreamer (mono/stereo) Paul McCartney and Wings	1973	100.00	200.00	400.00

Capitol

Number	Title (A Side/B Side)	Year	VG	VG+	NM
❏ (no #)	DJ Figure of Eight (same on both sides) Test pressings with blank label; most known copies come in a Capitol sleeve	1989	25.00	50.00	100.00
❏ 1829	Another Day/Oh Woman, Oh Why Black label	1976	3.75	7.50	15.00
❏ 1837	Uncle Albert/Admiral Halsey//Too Many People Black label	1976	3.75	7.50	15.00
❏ 1847	Give Ireland Back to the Irish/ Give Ireland Back to the Irish Wings; black label; no "(Version)" on label	1976	5.00	10.00	20.00
❏ 1851	Mary Had a Little Lamb/Little Woman Love Wings; black label	1976	3.00	6.00	12.00
❏ 1857	Hi Hi Hi/C Moon Wings; black label	1976	3.75	7.50	15.00
❏ 1861	My Love/The Mess Paul McCartney and Wings; black label; "The Mess" plays normally	1976	5.00	10.00	20.00
❏ 1861	My Love/The Mess Paul McCartney and Wings; black label; "The Mess" plays too fast	1976	5.00	10.00	20.00
❏ 1863	Live and Let Die/I Lie Around Wings; black label	1976	3.00	6.00	12.00
❏ 1869	Helen Wheels/Country Dreamer Paul McCartney and Wings; black label	1976	3.75	7.50	15.00
❏ 1871	Jet/Let Me Roll It Paul McCartney and Wings; black label	1976	3.75	7.50	15.00
❏ 1873	Band on the Run/Nineteen Hundred and Eighty-Five Paul McCartney and Wings; black label	1976	3.75	7.50	15.00
❏ 1875	Junior's Farm/Sally G Paul McCartney and Wings; black label	1976	3.75	7.50	15.00
❏ 4091	Listen to What the Man Said/Love in Song	1975		2.50	5.00
❏ 4091	PS Listen to What the Man Said/Love in Song Wings	1975	3.00	6.00	12.00

Number		Title (A Side/B Side)	Year	VG	VG+	NM
❏ 4145		Letting Go/You Gave Me the Answer	1975		2.50	5.00
		Wings				
❏ 4175		Venus and Mars Rock Show/	1975		2.50	5.00
		Magneto and Titanium Man				
		Wings				
❏ 4256		Silly Love Songs/Cook of the House	1976		2.00	4.00
		Wings; "Speed of Sound" label (more common version)				
❏ 4256		Silly Love Songs/Cook of the House	1976	2.00	4.00	8.00
		Wings; black label				
❏ 4293		Let 'Em In/Beware My Love	1976		2.00	4.00
		Wings; "Speed of Sound" label				
❏ 4293		Let 'Em In/Beware My Love	1976		3.00	6.00
		Wings; black label (more common version)				
❏ 4385		Maybe I'm Amazed/Soily	1976		2.00	4.00
		Wings; custom label (more common version)				
❏ 4385		Maybe I'm Amazed/Soily	1976	5.00	10.00	20.00
		Wings; black label				
❏ 4504		Girls' School/Mull of Kintyre	1977		2.50	5.00
		Wings; black label (more common version)				
❏ 4504	PS	Girls' School/Mull of Kintyre	1977	3.00	6.00	12.00
		Wings				
❏ 4504		Girls' School/Mull of Kintyre	1978	30.00	60.00	120.00
		Wings; purple label, label has reeded edge				
❏ 4559		With a Little Luck/Backwards Traveller-Cuff Link	1978		2.00	4.00
		Wings				
❏ 4594		I've Had Enough/Deliver Your Children	1978		2.00	4.00
		Wings				
❏ 4625		London Town/I'm Carrying	1978		2.00	4.00
		Wings				
❏ B-5537		Spies Like Us/My Carnival	1985			3.00
❏ B-5537	PS	Spies Like Us/My Carnival	1985			6.00
❏ B-5597		Press/It's Not True	1986		2.50	5.00
❏ B-5597	PS	Press/It's Not True	1986		2.50	5.00
❏ B-5636		Stranglehold/Angry	1986		2.50	5.00
❏ B-5636	PS	Stranglehold/Angry	1986		2.50	5.00
❏ B-5672		Only Love Remains/Tough on a Tightrope	1987		2.50	5.00
❏ B-5672	PS	Only Love Remains/Tough on a Tightrope	1987		2.50	5.00
❏ S7-17318		Off the Ground/Cosmically Conscious	1993		3.00	6.00
		White vinyl standard issue				
❏ S7-17318		Off the Ground/Cosmically Conscious	1993		3.00	6.00
		Black vinyl "error" issue				
❏ S7-17319		Biker Like an Icon/Things We Said Today	1993		3.00	6.00
		White vinyl standard issue				
❏ S7-17319		Biker Like an Icon/Things We Said Today	1993		3.00	6.00
		Black vinyl "error" issue				
❏ S7-17489		C'mon People/Down to the River	1993	2.00	4.00	8.00
		All copies on white vinyl				
❏ S7-17643		Wonderful Christmastime/	1993		3.00	6.00
		Rudolph, the Red-Nosed Reggae				
		Paul McCartney & Wings; red vinyl				
❏ B-44367		My Brave Face/Flying to My Home	1989	2.50	5.00	10.00
		Version 1: Both title and artist in block print, time of A-side is "3:17"				
❏ B-44367		My Brave Face/Flying to My Home	1989	2.00	4.00	8.00
		Version 2: Artist in custom print, title in block print, time of A-side is "3:17"				
❏ B-44367		My Brave Face/Flying to My Home	1989		2.50	5.00
		Version 3: Same as Version 2, time of A-side is "3:16"				
❏ B-44367	PS	My Brave Face/Flying to My Home	1989		2.50	5.00
❏ S7-56946		Hope of Deliverance/Long Leather Coat	1993		3.00	6.00
❏ 7PRO-79700	DJ	This One (same on both sides)	1989	100.00	200.00	400.00
		Vinyl is promo only				

Columbia

❏ 02171		Silly Love Songs/Cook of the House	1981	6.25	12.50	25.00
		Wings; despite label information, this has an edited version of A-side				
❏ 02860		Ebony and Ivory/Rainclouds	1982		2.00	4.00
		A-side: With Stevie Wonder				
❏ 02860	PS	Ebony and Ivory/Rainclouds	1982		2.00	4.00
		A-side: With Stevie Wonder				
❏ 03018		Take It Away/I'll Give You a Ring	1982			3.00
❏ 03018	PS	Take It Away/I'll Give You a Ring	1982			3.00
❏ 03235		Tug of War/Get It	1982	3.00	6.00	12.00
❏ 04127		Wonderful Christmastime/	1983	7.50	15.00	30.00
		Rudolph the Red-Nosed Reggae				
		Scarce reissue with B-side in stereo				
❏ 04168		Say, Say, Say/Ode to a Koala Bear	1983		2.00	4.00
		A-side: Paul McCartney/Michael Jackson				
❏ 04168	PS	Say, Say, Say/Ode to a Koala Bear	1983		2.00	4.00
		A-side: Paul McCartney/Michael Jackson				
❏ 04296		So Bad/Pipes of Peace	1983		2.50	5.00
❏ 04296	PS	So Bad/Pipes of Peace	1983		2.50	5.00

Number		Title (A Side/B Side)	Year	VG	VG+	NM
❏ 04581		No More Lonely Nights/ No More Lonely Nights (playout version)	1984		2.00	4.00
❏ 04581	PS	No More Lonely Nights/ No More Lonely Nights (playout version) *Title print in white, credit print in gray*	1984		2.50	5.00
❏ 04581	PS	No More Lonely Nights/ No More Lonely Nights (playout version) *Title print in gray, credit print in white*	1984	7.50	15.00	30.00
❏ 04581		No More Lonely Nights/ No More Lonely Nights (Special Dance Version)	1984	10.00	20.00	40.00
❏ 10939		Goodnight Tonight/Daytime Nighttime Suffering *Wings*	1979		3.00	6.00
❏ 11020		Getting Closer/Spin It On *Wings*	1979		3.00	6.00
❏ 11020	PS	Getting Closer/Spin It On *Title sleeve with large center hole*	1979	7.50	15.00	30.00
❏ 11070		Arrow Through Me/Old Siam, Sir *Wings*	1979		3.00	6.00
❏ 11162		Wonderful Christmastime/ Rudolph the Red-Nosed Reggae	1979	2.50	5.00	10.00
❏ 11162	PS	Wonderful Christmastime/ Rudolph the Red-Nosed Reggae	1979	3.75	7.50	15.00
❏ 11263		Coming Up//Coming Up (Live at Glasgow)/ Lunch Box-Odd Sox	1980		2.00	4.00
❏ 11263	PS	Coming Up//Coming Up (Live at Glasgow)/ Lunch Box-Odd Sox	1980		2.50	5.00
❏ 11335		Waterfalls/Check My Machine	1980		3.00	6.00
❏ 11335	PS	Waterfalls/Check My Machine	1980	5.00	10.00	20.00

EMI

❏ 3977		Walking in the Park with Eloise/ Bridge on the River Suite	1974	15.00	30.00	60.00
❏ 3977	PS	Walking in the Park with Eloise/ Bridge on the River Suite *As "The Country Hams"*	1974	20.00	40.00	80.00

Epic

❏ 03288		The Girl Is Mine/Can't Get Outta the Rain *A-side: Michael Jackson/Paul McCartney; B-side: Michael Jackson*	1982		2.50	5.00
❏ 03288	PS	The Girl Is Mine/Can't Get Outta the Rain *A-side: Michael Jackson/Paul McCartney; B-side: Michael Jackson*	1982		2.50	5.00
❏ 03372		The Girl Is Mine *Michael Jackson/Paul McCartney; one-sided budget release*	1982	2.50	5.00	10.00

McClay, Yul, and the Mondellos – See "Mondellos, The"

McCormick, Maureen
(Marcia Brady of The Brady Bunch)
Paramount

❏ 0246		Little Bird/Just a-Singin' Along *With Chris Knight*	1973	3.75	7.50	15.00
❏ 0292		Love's in the Roses/Harmonize	1974	3.75	7.50	15.00

McCoys, The
(The RCA Victor group is not the same as the one on Bang and Mercury.)
Bang

❏ 506	Hang On Sloopy/I Can't Explain It	1965	3.75	7.50	15.00
❏ 511	Fever/Sorrow	1965	2.50	5.00	10.00
❏ 516	Up and Down/If You Tell a Lie	1966	2.50	5.00	10.00
❏ 522	Come On Let's Go/Little People	1966	2.50	5.00	10.00
❏ 527	(You Make Me Feel) So Good/Runaway	1966	2.50	5.00	10.00
❏ 532	Don't Worry Mother, Your Son's Heart Is Pure/Ko-Ko	1966	2.50	5.00	10.00
❏ 538	I Got to Go Back (And Watch That Little Girl Dance)/ Dynamite	1966	2.50	5.00	10.00
❏ 543	Beat the Clock/Like You Do to Me	1967	2.50	5.00	10.00
❏ 549	I Wonder If She Remembers Me/ Say Those Magic Words	1967	2.50	5.00	10.00

Mercury

❏ 72843	Jesse Brady/Resurrection	1968	2.00	4.00	8.00
❏ 72897	Daybreak/Epilogue	1969	2.00	4.00	8.00
❏ 72967	Don't Fight It/Rosa Rodriguez	1969	3.75	7.50	15.00

RCA Victor

❏ 47-7204	Daddy's Geisha Girl/Our Love Goes On and On	1958	5.00	10.00	20.00
❏ 47-7354	Full Grown Cat/Throwing Kisses	1958	6.25	12.50	25.00

McCracken, Hugh
Congress

❏ 257	Buzz in My Head/You Blow My Mind	1965	6.25	12.50	25.00
❏ 261	Runnin', Runnin'	1966	6.25	12.50	25.00

McCullers, Mickey
Tamla

❏ 54064	Same Old Story/I'll Cry a Million Tears	1962	10.00	20.00	40.00

V.I.P.

❏ 25009	Same Old Story/Who You Gonna Run To	1964	12.50	25.00	50.00

Number	Title (A Side/B Side)	Year	VG	VG+	NM

McDaniels, Gene
Atlantic
| ☐ 2805 | The Lord Is Back/Tell Me Mr. President | 1971 | | 3.00 | 6.00 |
| | *As "Eugene McDaniels"* | | | | |

Columbia
| ☐ 43800 | Something Blue/Cause I Love You So | 1966 | 2.50 | 5.00 | 10.00 |
| ☐ 44010 | Touch of Your Lips/Sweet Lover No More | 1967 | 2.50 | 5.00 | 10.00 |

Liberty
☐ 55231	In Times Like These/Once Before	1959	3.75	7.50	15.00
☐ 55265	The Green Door/Facts of Life	1960	3.75	7.50	15.00
☐ 55308	A Hundred Pounds of Clay/Take a Chance on Love	1961	4.00	8.00	16.00
☐ 55344	A Tear/She's Come Back	1961	3.75	7.50	15.00
☐ 55371	Tower of Strength/The Secret	1961	4.00	8.00	16.00
☐ 55405	Chip Chip/Another Tear Falls	1962	3.75	7.50	15.00
☐ 55444	Funny/Chapel of Tears	1962	3.75	7.50	15.00
☐ 55480	Point of No Return/Warmer Than a Whisper	1962	3.75	7.50	15.00
☐ 55510	Spanish Lace/Somebody's Waiting	1962	3.75	7.50	15.00
☐ 55541	The Puzzle/Cry Baby Cry	1963	3.00	6.00	12.00
☐ 55597	It's a Lonely Town/False Friends	1963	3.00	6.00	12.00
☐ 55637	Old Country/Anyone Else	1963	3.00	6.00	12.00
☐ 55723	Make Me a Present of You/In Times Like These	1964	3.00	6.00	12.00
☐ 55752	Emily/Forgotten Man	1964	3.00	6.00	12.00
☐ 55805	A Miracle/Walk with a Winner	1965	2.50	5.00	10.00
☐ 55834	Hang On/Will It Last Forever	1965	2.50	5.00	10.00

MGM
| ☐ 14613 | Ol' Heartbreak Top Ten/River | 1973 | | 2.50 | 5.00 |

Ode
| ☐ 66107 | Lady Fair/Natural Juices | 1975 | | 2.00 | 4.00 |

United Artists
☐ 0053	A Hundred Pounds of Clay/Tower of Strength	1973		2.00	4.00
	"Silver Spotlight Series" reissue				
☐ 0054	Chip Chip/Point of No Return	1973		2.00	4.00
	"Silver Spotlight Series" reissue				

McGhee, Brownie
Dot
| ☐ 1184 | Cheatin' and Lyin'/Need Someone to Love | 1954 | 62.50 | 125.00 | 250.00 |

Harlem
☐ 2323	Worrying Over You/Christina	1954	15.00	30.00	60.00
☐ 2329	My Confession (I Want to Thank You)/	1954	15.00	30.00	60.00
	Bluebird, Bluebird				

Jax
☐ 302	Smiling and Crying Blues/A Letter to Lightnin' Hopkins	1951	30.00	60.00	120.00
☐ 304	I Feel So Good/Key to the Highway	1952	30.00	60.00	120.00
☐ 307	Meet You in the Morning/Brownie's Blues	1952	30.00	60.00	120.00
☐ 310	Guitar Strangers Blues/Dissatisfied Woman	1952	30.00	60.00	120.00
☐ 312	I'm 10,000 Years Old/Cherry Red	1952	30.00	60.00	120.00
☐ 322	New Bad Blood Blues/Pawnshop Blues	1953	30.00	60.00	120.00

Red Robin
| ☐ 111 | Don't Dog Your Woman/Daisy | 1953 | 62.50 | 125.00 | 250.00 |

Savoy
☐ 835	Diamond Ring/So Much Trouble	1952	7.50	15.00	30.00
☐ 872	Tell Me Baby/Bad Nerves	1952	7.50	15.00	30.00
☐ 899	Sweet Baby Blues/4 O'Clock in the Morning	1953	7.50	15.00	30.00
☐ 1177	I'd Love to Love You/Anna Mae	1955	5.00	10.00	20.00
☐ 1185	When It's Love Time/My Fault	1956	5.00	10.00	20.00
☐ 1564	Living with the Blues/Be My Friend	1959	3.75	7.50	15.00

McGhee, Stick(s)
Atlantic
Note: Stick McGhee records on Atlantic before 955 are unconfirmed on 45 rpm
| ☐ 955 | Wee Wee Hours (Part 1)/Wee Wee Hours (Part 2) | 1952 | 25.00 | 50.00 | 100.00 |
| ☐ 991 | New Found Love/Meet You in the Morning | 1953 | 20.00 | 40.00 | 80.00 |

Atlantic Classics
| ☐ 873 | Drinkin' Wine Spo-Dee-O-Dee/ | 1971 | 5.00 | 10.00 | 20.00 |
| | Blues Mixture (I'd Rather Drink Muddy Water) | | | | |

Herald
| ☐ 553 | Money Fever/Sleep-In Job | 1960 | 3.75 | 7.50 | 15.00 |

King
☐ 4610	Little Things We Used to Do/Head Happy with Wine	1953	25.00	50.00	100.00
☐ 4628	Whiskey, Women and Loaded Dice/	1953	25.00	50.00	100.00
	Blues in My Heart and Tears in My Eyes				
☐ 4672	Jungle Juice/Dealing from the Bottom	1953	25.00	50.00	100.00
☐ 4700	I'm Doin' All This Time/Wiggle Waggin' Woo	1954	25.00	50.00	100.00
☐ 4783	Double Crossin' Liquor/Six to Eight	1955	30.00	60.00	120.00
☐ 4800	Get Your Mind Out the Gutter/Sad, Bad, Glad	1955	25.00	50.00	100.00

London
| ☐ 978 | You Gotta Have Something on the Ball/ | 1951 | 62.50 | 125.00 | 250.00 |
| | (B-side unknown) | | | | |

Savoy
| ☐ 1148 | Things Have Changed/Help Me Baby | 1955 | 7.50 | 15.00 | 30.00 |

Number		Title (A Side/B Side)	Year	VG	VG+	NM

McGill, Jerry
Sun
| ☐ 326 | | Love Struck/I Wanna Make Sweet Love | 1959 | 7.50 | 15.00 | 30.00 |

McGuire, Barry
Dunhill
☐ 4009		Eve of Destruction/What Exactly's the Matter with Me	1965	3.00	6.00	12.00
☐ 4014		Child of Our Times/Upon a Painted Ocean	1965	2.50	5.00	10.00
☐ 4014	PS	Child of Our Times/Upon a Painted Ocean	1965	3.75	7.50	15.00
☐ 4019		This Precious Time/Don't You Wonder Where It's At	1966	3.00	6.00	12.00

A-side backing group: The Mamas and The Papas

☐ 4028		Cloudy Summer Afternoon (Raindrops)/ I'd Have to Be Outta My Mind	1966	2.50	5.00	10.00
☐ 4048		There's Nothing Else on My Mind/ Why Not Stop and Dig It	1966	2.50	5.00	10.00
☐ 4098		Masters of War/Stop Now and Dig It While You Can	1967	2.00	4.00	8.00
☐ 4116		Lollipop Train/Inner-Manipulations	1968	2.00	4.00	8.00
☐ 4124		Grasshopper Song/Top o' the Hill	1968	2.50	5.00	10.00
☐ 4124	PS	Grasshopper Song/Top o' the Hill	1968	3.75	7.50	15.00

Horizon
☐ 4		One by One/Town and Country	1963	3.00	6.00	12.00
☐ 8		Oh, Miss Mary/So Long, Stay Well	1963	3.00	6.00	12.00
☐ 354		Another Man/Bull 'Gine Run	1962	3.00	6.00	12.00

With Barry Kane

Mira
| ☐ 205 | | Greenback Dollar/Oh, Miss Mary | 1965 | 2.50 | 5.00 | 10.00 |

Mosaic
| ☐ 1001 | | The Three/Theme from The Tree | 1961 | 3.00 | 6.00 | 12.00 |
| ☐ 1004 | | I've Got a Secret/Cindy and Johnny | 1962 | 3.00 | 6.00 | 12.00 |

Myrrh
| ☐ 119 | | Love Is/David and Goliath | 1973 | | 2.50 | 5.00 |

Ode
| ☐ 66010 | | Old Farm/South of the Border | 1970 | | 3.00 | 6.00 |

McKenzie, Scott
Capitol
☐ 5348		All I Want Is You/Look in Your Eyes	1965	2.50	5.00	10.00
☐ 5500		There Stands the Glass/ Wipe the Tears (From Your Face)	1965	2.50	5.00	10.00
☐ 5961		All I Want Is You/Look in Your Eyes	1967		3.00	6.00

Epic
| ☐ 10124 | | No, No, No, No, No/I Want to Be Alone | 1967 | 2.00 | 4.00 | 8.00 |

Ode
| ☐ 103 | | San Francisco "Wear Some Flowers in Your Hair"/
What's the Difference | 1967 | 3.75 | 7.50 | 15.00 |

Original title; also has a different mix (echoey bass drum in bridge) than the later, more common version

| ☐ 103 | | San Francisco (Be Sure to Wear Flowers in Your Hair)/
What's the Difference | 1967 | 2.00 | 4.00 | 8.00 |

Revised title

☐ 105		Like an Old Time Movie/ What's the Difference, Chapter II	1967		3.00	6.00
☐ 107		Holy Man/What's the Difference, Chapter III	1968		3.00	6.00
☐ 66012		Going Home Again/Take a Moment	1970		2.50	5.00

McLawler, Sarah
King
| ☐ 4549 | | Please Try to Love Me/Ready, Willing, and Able | 1952 | 25.00 | 50.00 | 100.00 |
| ☐ 4561 | | Romance in the Dark/I'm Just Another One | 1952 | 25.00 | 50.00 | 100.00 |

Vee Jay
| ☐ 199 | | Babe in the Woods/Flamingo | 1956 | 7.50 | 15.00 | 30.00 |
| ☐ 239 | | Snowfall/Relax Miss Frisky | 1957 | 7.50 | 15.00 | 30.00 |

With Richard Otto

McNabb, Cecil
King
| ☐ 5116 | | Clock Tickin' Rhythm/Nothing Like This | 1958 | 62.50 | 125.00 | 250.00 |

McNair, Barbara
Audio Fidelity
| ☐ 153 | | Love Has a Way/(B-side unknown) | 1969 | 2.50 | 5.00 | 10.00 |
| ☐ 162 | | After St. Francis/I Can Tell | 1969 | 2.50 | 5.00 | 10.00 |

Coral
☐ 61923		Till There Was You/Bobby	1958	6.25	12.50	25.00
☐ 61972		He's Got the Whole World in His Hands/ Flipped Over You	1958	7.50	15.00	30.00
☐ 61996		Indiscreet/Waltz Me Around	1958	6.25	12.50	25.00
☐ 62020		Too Late This Spring/See If I Care	1958	6.25	12.50	25.00
☐ 62071		Goin' Steady with the Moon/I Feel a Feeling	1959	6.25	12.50	25.00
☐ 62116		Lover's Prayer/Old Devil Moon	1959	6.25	12.50	25.00

KC
| ☐ 109 | | Cross Over the Bridge/Gloryland | 1962 | 12.50 | 25.00 | 50.00 |
| ☐ 112 | | A Little Bird Told Me/Nobody Rings My Bell | 1963 | 10.00 | 20.00 | 40.00 |

Number		Title (A Side/B Side)	Year	VG	VG+	NM

Motown

☐ 1087		Touch of Time/You're Gonna Love My Baby	1965	6.25	12.50	25.00
☐ 1099		What a Day/Everything Is Good About You	1966	6.25	12.50	25.00
☐ 1106		Here I Am Baby/My World Is Empty Without You	1966	6.25	12.50	25.00
☐ 1112		Steal Away Tonight/For Once in My Life	1967	125.00	250.00	500.00
☐ 1123		Where Would I Be Without You/For Once in My Life	1968	6.25	12.50	25.00
☐ 1133		You Could Never Love Him/Fancy Passes	1968	6.25	12.50	25.00

Signature

☐ 12024		He's a King/Murray, What's Your Hurry	1960	5.00	10.00	20.00
☐ 12033		All About Love/You Done Me Wrong	1960	5.00	10.00	20.00
☐ 12049		Kansas City/Love Talk	1960	5.00	10.00	20.00

Warner Bros.

☐ 5633		Wanted Me/It Was Never Like This	1965	7.50	15.00	30.00

McPhatter, Clyde

(Original lead singer of the first version of the Drifters; also was with the Dominoes)

Amy

☐ 941		Everybody's Somebody's Fool/I Belong to You	1965	3.75	7.50	15.00
☐ 950		Little Bit of Sunshine/Everybody Loves a Good Time	1966	3.00	6.00	12.00
☐ 968		A Shot of Rhythm and Blues/ I'm Not Going to Work Today	1966	3.00	6.00	12.00
☐ 975		Sweet and Innocent/Lavender Lace	1967	3.00	6.00	12.00
☐ 993		I Dreamt I Died/Lonely People Can't Afford to Cry	1967	3.00	6.00	12.00

Atlantic

☐ 1070		Everybody's Laughing/Hot Ziggity	1955	7.50	15.00	30.00
☐ 1077		Love Has Joined Us Together/I Gotta Have You	1955	7.50	15.00	30.00
	With Ruth Brown					
☐ 1081		Seven Days/I'm Not Worthy	1956	7.50	15.00	30.00
☐ 1092		Treasure of Love/When You're Sincere	1956	7.50	15.00	30.00
☐ 1106		Thirty Days/I'm Lonely Tonight	1956	7.50	15.00	30.00
☐ 1117		Without Love (There Is Nothing)/I Make Believe	1956	7.50	15.00	30.00
☐ 1133		No Matter What/Just to Hold My Hand	1957	6.25	12.50	25.00
☐ 1149		Long Lonely Nights/Heartaches	1957	6.25	12.50	25.00
☐ 1158		You'll Be There/Rock and Cry	1957	6.25	12.50	25.00
☐ 1170		That's Enough for Me/No Love Like Her Love	1958	6.25	12.50	25.00
☐ 1185		Come What May/Let Me Know	1958	6.25	12.50	25.00
☐ 1199		A Lover's Question/I Can't Stand Up Long	1958	6.25	12.50	25.00
☐ 2018		Lovey Dovey/My Island of Dreams	1959	5.00	10.00	20.00
☐ 2028		Since You've Been Gone/Try, Try Baby	1959	5.00	10.00	20.00
	B-side actually the "old" Drifters (uncredited)					
☐ 2038		You Went Back on Your Word/There You Go	1959	5.00	10.00	20.00
	B-side actually the "old" Drifters (uncredited)					
☐ 2049		Just Give Me a Ring/Don't Dog Me	1960	5.00	10.00	20.00
	B-side actually the "old" Drifters (uncredited)					
☐ 2060		Deep Sea Ball/Let the Boogie-Woogie Roll	1960	5.00	10.00	20.00
	B-side actually the "old" Drifters (uncredited)					
☐ 2082		If I Didn't Love You Like I Do/Go! Yes Go!	1960	5.00	10.00	20.00
	B-side actually the "old" Drifters (uncredited)					

Decca

☐ 32719		Book of Memories/I'll Belong to You	1970	2.00	4.00	8.00
☐ 32753		Why Can't We Get Together/Mixed-Up Cup	1970	2.00	4.00	8.00

Deram

☐ 85032		Thank You Love/Only a Fool	1968	2.50	5.00	10.00
☐ 85039		Baby You've Got It/ Baby I Could Be So Good at Loving You	1969	2.50	5.00	10.00

Mercury

☐ 71660		Ta Ta/I Ain't Giving Up Nothing	1960	3.75	7.50	15.00
☐ 71692		I Just Want to Love You/You're for Me	1960	3.75	7.50	15.00
☐ 71692	PS	I Just Want to Love You/You're for Me	1960	6.25	12.50	25.00
☐ 71740		One More Chance/Before I Fall in Love Again	1960	3.75	7.50	15.00
☐ 71740	PS	One More Chance/Before I Fall in Love Again	1960	6.25	12.50	25.00
☐ 71783		Tomorrow Is a-Comin'/ I'll Love You Till the Cows Come Home	1961	3.75	7.50	15.00
☐ 71783	PS	Tomorrow Is a-Comin'/ I'll Love You Till the Cows Come Home	1961	6.25	12.50	25.00
☐ 71809		A Whole Heap o'Love/You're Movin' Me	1961	3.75	7.50	15.00
☐ 71809	PS	A Whole Heap o'Love/You're Movin' Me	1961	6.25	12.50	25.00
☐ 71841		I Never Knew/Happiness	1961	3.75	7.50	15.00
☐ 71841	PS	I Never Knew/Happiness	1961	6.25	12.50	25.00
☐ 71868		Same Time, Same Place/Your Second Choice	1961	3.75	7.50	15.00
☐ 71868	PS	Same Time, Same Place/Your Second Choice	1961	6.25	12.50	25.00
☐ 71941		Lover Please/Let's Forget About the Past	1962	3.75	7.50	15.00
☐ 71941	PS	Lover Please/Let's Forget About the Past	1962	6.25	12.50	25.00
☐ 71987		Little Bitty Pretty One/Next to Me	1962	3.75	7.50	15.00
☐ 71987	PS	Little Bitty Pretty One/Next to Me	1962	6.25	12.50	25.00
☐ 72025		Maybe/I Do Believe	1962	3.75	7.50	15.00
☐ 72025	PS	Maybe/I Do Believe	1962	6.25	12.50	25.00
☐ 72051		The Best Man Cried/Stop	1962	3.75	7.50	15.00
☐ 72051	PS	The Best Man Cried/Stop	1962	6.25	12.50	25.00
☐ 72166		So Close to Being in Love/From One to One	1963	3.75	7.50	15.00
☐ 72166	PS	So Close to Being in Love/From One to One	1963	6.25	12.50	25.00
☐ 72220		Deep in the Heart of Harlem/Happy Good Times	1963	3.75	7.50	15.00
☐ 72220	PS	Deep in the Heart of Harlem/Happy Good Times	1963	6.25	12.50	25.00
☐ 72253		Second Window, Second Floor/In My Tenement	1964	3.75	7.50	15.00

Number		Title (A Side/B Side)	Year	VG	VG+	NM
❏ 72317		Lucille/Baby, Baby	1964	3.75	7.50	15.00
❏ 72407		Crying Won't Help You Now/I Found My Love	1965	3.75	7.50	15.00
❏ 72407	PS	Crying Won't Help You Now/I Found My Love	1965	6.25	12.50	25.00

MGM

❏ 12780		I Told Myself a Lie/The Masquerade Is Over	1959	5.00	10.00	20.00
❏ 12816		Twice As Nice/Where Did I Make My Mistake	1959	5.00	10.00	20.00
❏ 12843	M	Let's Try Again/Bless You	1959	5.00	10.00	20.00
❏ 12877		Think Me a Kiss/When the Right Time Comes Along	1960	5.00	10.00	20.00
❏ 12949		One Right After Another/This Is Not Goodbye	1960	5.00	10.00	20.00
❏ 12988		The Glory of Love/Take a Step	1961	5.00	10.00	20.00
❏ SK-50134	S	Let's Try Again/Bless You	1959	10.00	20.00	40.00

Medallions, The
Dooto
All as "Vernon Green and the Medallions"

❏ 419		For Better or For Worse/I Wonder, Wonder, Wonder	1957	7.50	15.00	30.00
❏ 425		A Lover's Prayer/Unseen	1957	7.50	15.00	30.00
❏ 446		Magic Mountain/59 Volvo	1959	6.25	12.50	25.00
❏ 454		Behind the Door/Rocket Ship	1959	6.25	12.50	25.00

Dootone

❏ 347		The Letter/Buick 59 *Red label*	1955	17.50	35.00	70.00
❏ 347		The Letter/Buick 59 *Black label*	1955	10.00	20.00	40.00
❏ 357		The Telegram/Coupe de Ville Baby *Maroon label*	1955	15.00	30.00	60.00
❏ 357		The Telegram/Coupe de Ville Baby *Blue label*	1955	10.00	20.00	40.00
❏ 364		Edna/Speeding	1955	12.50	25.00	50.00
❏ 373		My Pretty Baby/I'll Never Love Again	1955	15.00	30.00	60.00

As "Johnny Twovoice and the Medallions"

❏ 379		Dear Darling/Don't Shoot Baby	1955	17.50	35.00	70.00
❏ 393		I Want a Love/Dance and Swing	1956	12.50	25.00	50.00
❏ 400		Shedding Tears for You/Push Button Automobile	1956	15.00	30.00	60.00

As "Vernon Green and the Medallions"

❏ 407		My Mary Lou/Did You Have Fun	1956	15.00	30.00	60.00

As "Vernon Green and the Medallions"

❏ 479		Can You Talk/You Don't Know	1964	3.75	7.50	15.00

Essex

❏ 901		I Know/Laki-Lani	1955	100.00	200.00	400.00

Lenox

❏ 5556		You Are Irresistible/Why Do You Look at Me	1962	5.00	10.00	20.00

Minit

❏ 32034		Look at Me, Look at Me/Am I Ever Gonna See My Baby	1968	5.00	10.00	20.00

As "Vernon Green and the Medallions"

Pan World

❏ 71		Dear Ann/Shimmy Shimmy Shake	1962	12.50	25.00	50.00

As "Vernon Green and the Medallions"

Sarg

❏ 191		I Love You True/My Baby's Gone	1961	10.00	20.00	40.00
❏ 194		Lovin' Time/Home Town	1961	10.00	20.00	40.00

Singular

❏ 1002		A Broken Heart/Lolo Baby	1957	10.00	20.00	40.00

Sultan

❏ 4004		Love That Girl/Carachi	1959	7.50	15.00	30.00

Meek, Joe
London

❏ 9634		Kennedy March/Theme of Freedom	1964	5.00	10.00	20.00

Megadeth
Capitol

❏ S7-57798		Symphony of Destruction/Breakpoint	1992	2.00	4.00	8.00

Label misspells band's name as "Megadeath"

Melcher, Terry
Columbia

❏ 42427		I Waited Too Long/That's All I Want	1962	5.00	10.00	20.00

As "Terry Day"

❏ 42678		Be a Soldier/I Love You Betty	1963	5.00	10.00	20.00

As "Terry Day"

❏ 42678	PS	Be a Soldier/I Love You Betty	1963	10.00	20.00	40.00

RCA Victor

❏ PB-10587		Fire in a Rainstorm/So Right Tonight	1976	2.50	5.00	10.00

Mello-Harps, The
Casino

❏ 104		Gumma Gumma/No Good	1959	15.00	30.00	60.00

Number	Title (A Side/B Side)	Year	VG	VG+	NM
Do-Re-Mi					
☐ 203	Love Is a Vow/Valerie	1956	1,000	1,500	2,000
Tin Pan Alley					
☐ 145/6	I Love Only You/Ain't Got the Money	1955	100.00	200.00	400.00
☐ 157/8	What Good Are My Dreams/Gone	1956	150.00	300.00	600.00
☐ 159	I Couldn't Believe/My Bleeding Heart	1956	150.00	300.00	600.00

Mello-Kings, The

Number	Title (A Side/B Side)	Year	VG	VG+	NM
Herald					
☐ 502	Tonite Tonite/Do Baby Do	1957	100.00	200.00	400.00
	First pressing credits "The Mellotones"				
☐ 502	Tonite Tonite/Do Baby Do	1957	12.50	25.00	50.00
	Label corrected to "The Mello-Kings"; script print inside flag				
☐ 502	Tonite Tonite/Do Baby Do	1961	6.50	12.50	25.00
	Reissue; block print inside flag				
☐ 507	Chapel on the Hill/Sassafras	1957	7.50	15.00	30.00
☐ 511	Baby Tell Me Why Why Why/	1958	7.50	15.00	30.00
	The Only Girl I'll Ever Know				
☐ 518	Valerie/She's Real Cool	1958	7.50	15.00	30.00
☐ 536	Chip Chip/Running to You	1959	7.50	15.00	30.00
	Both sides play as labeled				
☐ 536	Chip Chip/Running to You	1959	37.50	75.00	150.00
	Mispressing; plays "Rockin' at the Bandstand"/"Down in Cuba" by the Royal Holidays				
☐ 548	Our Love Is Beautiful/Dear Mr. Jock	1960	6.25	12.50	25.00
☐ 554	Kid Stuff/I Promise	1960	6.25	12.50	25.00
☐ 561	Penny/Till There Were None	1961	6.25	12.50	25.00
☐ 567	Love at First Sight/She's Real Cool	1961	6.25	12.50	25.00
Lescay					
☐ 3009	Walk Softly/But You Lied	1962	7.50	15.00	30.00

Mello-Moods, The

Number	Title (A Side/B Side)	Year	VG	VG+	NM
Gamble					
☐ 2512	Stop Taking My Love for Granted/	1972	2.50	5.00	10.00
	Inspirational Pleasure				
Hamilton					
☐ 143	I'm Lost/I Woke Up This Morning	1953	25.00	50.00	100.00
Prestige					
☐ 799	Call on Me/I Tried and Tried and Tried	1953	175.00	350.00	700.00
☐ 856	I'm Lost/I Woke Up This Morning	1953	175.00	350.00	700.00
Robin					
☐ 104	I Couldn't Sleep a Wink Last Night/	1952	1,000	1,500	2,000
	And You Just Can't Go Through Life Alone				
☐ 105	Where Are You (Now That I Need You)/	1952	1,000	1,500	2,000
	How Could You				

Mello-Tones, The

Number	Title (A Side/B Side)	Year	VG	VG+	NM
Columbia					
☐ 6-90?	When The Rain Gates Unfold/	1950	100.00	200.00	400.00
	What Are They Doing in Heaven				
	Probably originally released on Columbia's short-lived special numbering system for 7-inch records				
☐ 39051	When The Rain Gates Unfold/	1950	75.00	150.00	300.00
	What Are They Doing in Heaven				
☐ 39215	Looking for a City/Flying Saucers	1951	75.00	150.00	300.00
Decca					
☐ 48318	Winos on Parade/Man Loves Woman	1954	100.00	200.00	400.00
☐ 48319	I'm Just Another One in Love with You/I'm Gonna Get	1954	100.00	200.00	400.00
Fascination					
☐ 1001	Rosie Lee/I'll Never Fall in Love Again	1957	37.50	75.00	150.00
Gee					
☐ 1037	Rosie Lee/I'll Never Fall in Love Again	1957	10.00	20.00	40.00
☐ 1040	Ca-Sandra/Rattle Shake Roll	1957	10.00	20.00	40.00
Okeh					
☐ 6828	Rough and Rocky Road/Cool by the River Banks	1951	75.00	150.00	300.00

Mellodots, The

Number	Title (A Side/B Side)	Year	VG	VG+	NM
Apollo					
☐ 1192	One More Time/Just How Long	1952	750.00	1,125	1,500

Mellow Drops, The

Number	Title (A Side/B Side)	Year	VG	VG+	NM
Imperial					
☐ 5324	When I Grow Too Old to Dream/The Crazy Song	1955	50.00	100.00	200.00

Melo Gents, The

Number	Title (A Side/B Side)	Year	VG	VG+	NM
Warner Bros.					
☐ 5056	Baby Be Mine/Get Off My Back	1959	12.50	25.00	50.00

Melody Makers, The

Number	Title (A Side/B Side)	Year	VG	VG+	NM
Hollis					
☐ 1001	Carolina Moon/Let's Make Love Worthwhile	1957	25.00	50.00	100.00
☐ 1002	The Nearness of You/Gotta Go	1957	37.50	75.00	150.00

Number		Title (A Side/B Side)	Year	VG	VG+	NM
Memories, The						
Way-Lin						
❑ 101		Love Bells/I Promise	1959	100.00	200.00	400.00
Merced Blue Notes, The						
Accent						
❑ 1069		Rufus/Your Tender Lips	1961	10.00	20.00	40.00
Galaxy						
❑ 738		Rufus Jr./Thumping	1965	7.50	15.00	30.00
❑ 744		Mama Rufus/Bad Bad Whiskey	1965	7.50	15.00	30.00
Soul						
❑ 35007		Do the Pig/Thumping	1965	250.00	500.00	1,000
Tri-Phi						
❑ 1011		Midnight Sessions (Part 1)/Midnight Sessions (Part 2)	1962	12.50	25.00	50.00
❑ 1023		Whole Lotta Nothin'/Fragile	1963	10.00	20.00	40.00
Mercer, Will						
Constellation						
❑ 109		Penny Candy/Willowy Billowy Land	1963	3.75	7.50	15.00
Sun						
❑ 329		You're Just My Kind/Ballad of St. Mark's	1959	6.25	12.50	25.00
Mercury, Freddie						
(Of Queen)						
Anthem						
❑ 104		I Can Hear Music/Going Back	1973	37.50	75.00	150.00
		As "Larry Lurex"; A-side matrix number on label is "A-0009"				
❑ 104		I Can Hear Music/Going Back	1973	25.00	50.00	100.00
		As "Larry Lurex"; A-side matrix number on label is "A-0009-REMIX"				
Capitol						
❑ B-5696		The Great Pretender/Exercises in Free Love	1987			3.00
Columbia						
❑ 04606		Love Kills/Rotwang's Party (Robot Dance)	1984		2.00	4.00
		Lead singer of Queen				
❑ 04606	PS	Love Kills/Rotwang's Party (Robot Dance)	1984		2.00	4.00
❑ 04869		I Was Born to Love You/Stop All the Fighting	1985		2.00	4.00
❑ 04869	PS	I Was Born to Love You/Stop All the Fighting	1985		2.00	4.00
❑ 05455		Living on My Own/She Blows Hot and Cold	1985		2.00	4.00
Mercy						
Sundi						
❑ 6811		Love (Can Make You Happy)/Fire Ball	1969	2.00	4.00	8.00
Warner Bros.						
❑ 7291		Love Can Make You Happy/	1969	3.75	7.50	15.00
		Happy As Can Be, La La La				
		Pressed in U.S. for export only; A-side is a re-recording of the hit on Sundi				
❑ 7297		Forever/The Morning's Come	1969		3.00	6.00
❑ 7331		Hello Baby/Heard You Went Away	1969		3.00	6.00
Merri-Men, The						
(Members of Bill Haley's Comets)						
Apt						
❑ 25051		Big Daddy/St. Louis Blues	1960	6.25	12.50	25.00
Mersey Lads, The						
MGM						
❑ 13481		Johnny No Love/What 'Cha Gonna Do Baby	1966	3.75	7.50	15.00
Merseybeats, The						
Fontana						
❑ 1513		It Would Take a Long Time/Don't Let It Happen to Us	1965	3.75	7.50	15.00
❑ 1532		I Love You, Yes I Do/See Me Back	1965	3.75	7.50	15.00
❑ 1882		Mr. Moonlight/I Think of You	1964	3.75	7.50	15.00
❑ 1905		Don't Turn Around/Really Mystified	1964	3.75	7.50	15.00
❑ 1950		See Me Back/Last Night	1964	3.75	7.50	15.00
Merseys, The						
Mercury						
❑ 72582		Sorrow/Some Other Day	1966	5.00	10.00	20.00
Metallica						
Elektra						
❑ 69329		One/The Prince	1988		2.50	5.00
❑ 69329	PS	One/The Prince	1988		2.50	5.00
❑ 69357		Eye of the Beholder/Breadfan	1988	2.50	5.00	10.00
Metros, The						
Just						
❑ 1502		All of My Life/Lookin'	1959	62.50	125.00	250.00
1-2-3						
❑ 1720		If You Can Feel/The Dampness from Your Kiss	1969	2.50	5.00	10.00

Number	Title (A Side/B Side)	Year	VG	VG+	NM

RCA Victor

☐ 47-8994	Time Changes Things/Sweetest One	1966	2.50	5.00	10.00
☐ 47-9159	Since I Found My Baby/No Baby	1967	7.50	15.00	30.00
☐ 47-9331	Let's Groove/The Replacer	1967	5.00	10.00	20.00

Metrotones, The
Reserve

| ☐ 116 | Please Come Back/Skitter Skatter | 1957 | 62.50 | 125.00 | 250.00 |

Michaels, Marilyn
RCA Victor

| ☐ 47-7771 | Tell Tommy I Miss Him/Everyone Was There But You | 1960 | 5.00 | 10.00 | 20.00 |
| ☐ 47-7831 | Past the Age of Innocence/Danny | 1961 | 3.75 | 7.50 | 15.00 |

Mickey and Kitty
(Mickey Baker of Mickey and Sylvia with Kitty Noble)
Atlantic

☐ 2024	Ooh-Sha-Lala/The Kid Brother	1959	3.75	7.50	15.00
☐ 2036	First Love/St. Louis Blues	1959	3.75	7.50	15.00
☐ 2046	My Reverie/Buttercup	1959	3.75	7.50	15.00

Mickey and Sylvia
(Also see "Baker, Mickey"; "Sylvia")
All Platinum

| ☐ 2307 | Lovedrops/Because You Do It to Me | 1969 | | 3.00 | 6.00 |
| ☐ 2310 | Anytime/Souling with Mickey and Sylvia | 1969 | | 3.00 | 6.00 |

Cat

| ☐ 102 | Fine Love/Speedy Life | 1954 | 10.00 | 20.00 | 40.00 |
| | *As "Little" Sylvia Vanderpool and Mickey Baker* | | | | |

Groove

| ☐ 0164 | No Good Lover/Walkin' in the Rain | 1956 | 10.00 | 20.00 | 40.00 |
| ☐ 0175 | Love Is Strange/I'm Going Home | 1956 | 10.00 | 20.00 | 40.00 |

King

| ☐ 5737 | Baby, Let's Dance/Oh Yea, Ah Ah | 1963 | 3.00 | 6.00 | 12.00 |
| ☐ 6006 | Love Is Strange/Darling | 1965 | 2.50 | 5.00 | 10.00 |

Rainbow

| ☐ 316 | I'm So Glad/Se De Boom Run Dun | 1955 | 7.50 | 15.00 | 30.00 |
| ☐ 318 | Forever and a Day/Ride, Sally, Ride | 1955 | 7.50 | 15.00 | 30.00 |

RCA

| ☐ 5224-7-RX | Love Is Strange/(I've Had) The Time of My Life | 1987 | | | 3.00 |
| | *B-side by Bill Medley and Jennifer Warnes* | | | | |

RCA Victor

☐ 37-7877	Love Is the Only Thing/Love Lesson	1961	12.50	25.00	50.00
	"Compact Single 33" (small hole, plays at LP speed)				
☐ 47-7403	To the Valley/Oh Yeah! Uh-Huh	1958	5.00	10.00	20.00
☐ 47-7774	Sweeter As the Days Go By/Mommy Out De Light	1960	3.75	7.50	15.00
☐ 47-7811	What Would I Do/This Is My Story	1960	5.00	10.00	20.00
☐ 47-7877	Love Is the Only Thing/Love Lesson	1961	3.75	7.50	15.00
☐ 47-8517	Let's Shake Some More/Gypsy	1965	3.00	6.00	12.00
☐ 47-8582	Fallin' in Love/From the Beginning of Time	1965	3.00	6.00	12.00
☐ 61-7774	Sweeter As the Days Go By/Mommy Out De Light	1960	10.00	20.00	40.00
	"Living Stereo" (large hole, plays at 45 rpm)				
☐ 61-7811	What Would I Do/This Is My Story	1960	10.00	20.00	40.00
	"Living Stereo" (large hole, plays at 45 rpm)				
☐ APAO-0080	Love Is Strange/(B-side unknown)	1973		3.00	6.00

Stang

| ☐ 5004 | Rocky Raccoon/Souling with Mickey and Sylvia | 1969 | 2.00 | 4.00 | 8.00 |
| ☐ 5047 | Baby You're So Fine/Anytime You Want To | 1973 | | 3.00 | 6.00 |

Vik

☐ 0252	Love Is Strange/I'm Going Home	1957	7.50	15.00	30.00
☐ 0267	There Oughta Be a Law/Dearest	1957	6.25	12.50	25.00
☐ 0280	Two Shadows on Your Window/ Love Will Make You Fail in School	1957	6.25	12.50	25.00
☐ 0290	Love Is a Treasure/Let's Have a Picnic	1957	6.25	12.50	25.00
☐ 0297	There'll Be No Backin' Out/Where Is My Honey	1957	6.25	12.50	25.00
☐ 0324	Rock and Stroll Room/Bewildered	1958	5.00	10.00	20.00
☐ 0334	It's You I Love/True, True Love	1958	5.00	10.00	20.00

Willow

☐ 23000	Baby, You're So Fine/Lovedrops	1961	3.75	7.50	15.00
☐ 23002	Darling (I Miss You So)/I'm Guilty	1961	3.75	7.50	15.00
☐ 23004	Since I Fell for You/He Gave Me Everything	1962	3.75	7.50	15.00
☐ 23006	Love Is Strange/Walking in the Rain	1962	3.75	7.50	15.00

Middleton, Tony
(Of the Willows)
A&M

| ☐ 1084 | Angela/Keep On Dancing | 1969 | 5.00 | 10.00 | 20.00 |
| ☐ 1124 | Harlem Lady/Sound of Goodbye | 1969 | 3.75 | 7.50 | 15.00 |

ABC-Paramount

| ☐ 10695 | You Spoiled My Reputation/If I Could Write a Song | 1965 | 7.50 | 15.00 | 30.00 |

Alfa

| ☐ 113 | My Home Town/Please Take Me | 1962 | 3.00 | 6.00 | 12.00 |

Number		Title (A Side/B Side)	Year	VG	VG+	NM
Alto						
❏ 2001		Untouchable/I Need You	1960	3.00	6.00	12.00
Big Top						
❏ 3037		Unchained Melody/Sweet Baby of Mine	1960	7.50	15.00	30.00
Eldorado						
❏ 508		First Taste of Love/Only My Heart	1957	7.50	15.00	30.00
Gone						
❏ 5015		Let's Fall in Love/Say Yeah	1957	15.00	30.00	60.00
Mala						
❏ 544		Out of This World/My Baby Likes to Boogaloo	1966	6.25	12.50	25.00
MGM						
❏ 13493		Don't Ever Leave Me/To the Ends of the Earth	1966	10.00	20.00	40.00
Mr. G						
❏ 811		Let Me Down Easy (Part 1)/Let Me Down Easy (Part 2)	1968	3.00	6.00	12.00
❏ 815		Good Morning World/(B-side unknown)	1968	3.00	6.00	12.00
Philips						
❏ 40151		I Need You Tonight/Send Me Away	1963	3.00	6.00	12.00
❏ 40184		Too Hot to Handle/I Just Couldn't Help Myself	1964	3.00	6.00	12.00
Roulette						
❏ 4345		Is It This or Is It That/ I'm Gonna Try Love One More Time	1961	6.25	12.50	25.00
Saxony						
❏ 104		I'm On My Way/(B-side unknown)	1958	12.50	25.00	50.00
Scepter						
❏ 12290		Border Song (Holy Moses)/Silliest People	1970	2.50	5.00	10.00
Toy						
❏ 3803		Rock and Roll Lullaby/Sittin' in the Sunshine	1972	2.00	4.00	8.00
Triumph						
❏ 600		Count Your Blessings (See What Love Has Done)/ I Just Want Somebody	1959	6.25	12.50	25.00
❏ 605		The Universe/Blackjack	1959	6.25	12.50	25.00
United Artists						
❏ 410		Drifting/Memories Are Made of This	1962	3.75	7.50	15.00

Midnight Angels, The

Apex						
❏ 77073		I'm Sufferin'/In the Moonlight	1967	7.50	15.00	30.00
❏ 77073	PS	I'm Sufferin'/In the Moonlight	1967	10.00	20.00	40.00

Midnighters, The

(Also see "Ballard, Hank, and the Midnighters"; "Royals, The")

Federal						
❏ 12169		Work With Me Annie/Until I Die	1954	25.00	50.00	100.00
		Silver top label; as " The Midnighters (Formerly Known As the Royals)"; see "Royals, The" for original				
❏ 12169		Work With Me Annie/Until I Die	1954	10.00	20.00	40.00
		All-green label; as "The Midnighters (Formerly Known As the Royals)"				
❏ 12177		Give It Up/That Woman	1954	20.00	40.00	80.00
		As "The Midnighters Formerly the Royals"				
❏ 12185		Sexy Ways/Don't Say Your Last Goodbye	1954	12.50	25.00	50.00
		As "The Midnighters Formerly the Royals"				
❏ 12195		Annie Had a Baby/She's the One	1954	10.00	20.00	40.00
❏ 12200		Annie's Aunt Fanny/Crazy Loving	1954	10.00	20.00	40.00
❏ 12202		Tell Them/Stingy Little Thing	1954	10.00	20.00	40.00
❏ 12205		She's the One/Moonrise	1955	10.00	20.00	40.00
❏ 12210		Ashamed of Myself/Ring-a-Ling-Ling	1955	10.00	20.00	40.00
❏ 12220		Why Are We Apart/Switchie, Witchie, Titchie	1955	10.00	20.00	40.00
❏ 12224		Henry's Got Flat Feet (Can't Dance No More)/ Whatsoever You Do	1955	10.00	20.00	40.00
❏ 12227		It's Love Baby (24 Hours a Day)/Looka Here	1955	10.00	20.00	40.00
❏ 12230		Give It Up/That Woman	1955	10.00	20.00	40.00
❏ 12240		Rock and Roll Wedding/That House on the Hill	1955	10.00	20.00	40.00
❏ 12243		Don't Change Your Pretty Ways/ We'll Never Meet Again	1955	10.00	20.00	40.00
❏ 12251		Partners for Life/Sweet Mama, Do Right	1956	7.50	15.00	30.00
❏ 12260		Rock Granny Roll/Open Up the Back Door	1956	7.50	15.00	30.00
❏ 12270		Tore Up Over You/Early One Morning	1956	7.50	15.00	30.00
❏ 12285		I'll Be Home Some Day/Come On and Get It	1957	7.50	15.00	30.00
❏ 12288		Let Me Hold Your Hand/Oh Bah Baby	1957	7.50	15.00	30.00
❏ 12293		E Basta Cosi/In the Doorway Crying	1957	7.50	15.00	30.00
❏ 12299		Oh, So Happy/Is Your Love for Real	1957	7.50	15.00	30.00
❏ 12305		Let 'Em Roll/What Made You Change Your Mind	1957	7.50	15.00	30.00
❏ 12317		Stay By My Side/Daddy's Little Baby	1958	7.50	15.00	30.00
❏ 12339		Baby Please/Ow-Wow-Oo-Wee	1958	7.50	15.00	30.00

Mighty Marvelows, The – See "Marvelows, The"

Mike and the Jays

Doyl						
❏ 1001		My Only Girl/Dingle Dangle Doll	1960	20.00	40.00	80.00

Number		Title (A Side/B Side)	Year	VG	VG+	NM

Mike and the Modifiers
Gordy
- [ ] 7006   I Found Myself a Brand New Baby/It's Too Bad   1962   15.00   30.00   60.00

Mike and the Utopians
Cee Jay
- [ ] 574   Erlene/I Found a Penny   1958   37.50   75.00   150.00
- [ ] 574   Erlene/I Wish   1958   75.00   150.00   300.00

Mike, John and Bill
("Mike" is Michael Nesmith, later of the Monkees)
Omnibus
- [ ] 239   How Can You Kiss Me/Just a Little Love   1963   12.50   25.00   50.00

Milburn, Amos
Aladdin
- [ ] 3014   Chicken Shack Boogie/It Took a Long, Long Time   1950   50.00   100.00   200.00
  78 originally released in 1948
- [ ] 3018   Bewildered/A and M Blues   1950   30.00   60.00   120.00
  78 originally released in 1948

Note: Amos Milburn singles on Aladdin before 3068 are unconfirmed on 45 rpm except those listed above

- [ ] 3068   Bad, Bad Whiskey/I'm Going to Tell My Mama   1950   20.00   40.00   80.00
- [ ] 3080   Let's Rock a While/Tears, Tears, Tears   1951   20.00   40.00   80.00
- [ ] 3090   Everybody Clap Hands/That Was Your Last Mistake   1951   20.00   40.00   80.00
- [ ] 3093   Ain't Nothin' Shaking/Just One More Drink   1951   20.00   40.00   80.00
- [ ] 3105   She's Gone Again/Boogie Woogie   1951   20.00   40.00   80.00
- [ ] 3124   Thinking and Drinking/Trouble in Mind   1952   15.00   30.00   60.00
- [ ] 3125   Flying Home/Put Something in My Hand   1952   15.00   30.00   60.00
- [ ] 3133   I Won't Be Your Fool Anymore/Roll Mr. Jelly   1952   15.00   30.00   60.00
- [ ] 3146   Button Your Lip/Everything I Do Is Wrong   1952   15.00   30.00   60.00
- [ ] 3150   Kiss Me Again/Greyhound   1952   15.00   30.00   60.00
- [ ] 3159   Rock, Rock, Rock/Boo Hoo   1953   15.00   30.00   60.00
- [ ] 3164   Let Me Go Home, Whiskey/Three Times a Fool   1953   12.50   25.00   50.00
- [ ] 3168   Long, Long Day/Please Mr. Johnson   1953   12.50   25.00   50.00
- [ ] 3197   One Scotch, One Bourbon, One Beer/What Can I Do   1953   12.50   25.00   50.00
- [ ] 3218   Good, Good Whiskey/Let's Have a Party   1954   12.50   25.00   50.00
- [ ] 3226   How Could You Hurt Me So/Rocky Mountain   1954   12.50   25.00   50.00
- [ ] 3240   Milk and Water/I'm Still a Fool for You   1954   12.50   25.00   50.00
- [ ] 3248   Glory of Love/Baby, Baby All the Time   1954   12.50   25.00   50.00
- [ ] 3253   Vicious, Vicious Vodka/I Done Done It   1954   12.50   25.00   50.00
- [ ] 3269   That's It/One, Two, Three Everybody   1954   12.50   25.00   50.00
- [ ] 3281   Why Don't You Do Right/I Love You Anyway   1955   10.00   20.00   40.00
- [ ] 3293   All Is Well/My Happiness Depends on You   1955   10.00   20.00   40.00
- [ ] 3306   House Party/I Guess I'll Go   1955   10.00   20.00   40.00
- [ ] 3320   French Fried Potatoes and Ketchup/I Need Someone   1956   10.00   20.00   40.00
- [ ] 3332   Chicken Shack Boogie/Juice, Juice, Juice   1956   10.00   20.00   40.00
- [ ] 3340   Girl of My Dreams/Everyday of the Week   1956   10.00   20.00   40.00
- [ ] 3363   Rum and Coca-Cola/Soft Pillow   1957   7.50   15.00   30.00
- [ ] 3370   Greyhound/Dear Angel   1957   7.50   15.00   30.00
- [ ] 3383   Thinking of You Baby/If I Could Be with You   1957   7.50   15.00   30.00

Imperial
- [ ] 5831   I'm Still a Fool for You/Rocky Mountain   1962   3.00   6.00   12.00

King
- [ ] 5405   Christmas (Comes But Once a Year)/Please Come Home for Christmas   1960   3.00   6.00   12.00
  B-side by Charles Brown
- [ ] 5464   I Wanna Go Back Home/My Little Baby   1961   3.00   6.00   12.00
  With Charles Brown
- [ ] 5483   My Sweet Baby's Love/Heartaches That Make You Cry   1961   3.00   6.00   12.00
- [ ] 5529   Movin' Time/The Hammer   1961   3.00   6.00   12.00
- [ ] 6095   Whiz O Shoo Pepi/Same Old Thing   1967   3.00   6.00   12.00

Motown
- [ ] 1038   I'll Make It Up to You Somehow/My Baby Gave Me Another Chance   1963   7.50   15.00   30.00
- [ ] 1046   My Daily Prayer/(B-side unknown)   1963   7.50   15.00   30.00

United Artists
- [ ] 0149   Chicken Shack Boogie/Revitalized   1973   2.50   5.00
  "Silver Spotlight Series" reissue

Miles, Garry
Liberty
- [ ] 55261   Look for a Star/Afraid of Love   1960   3.75   7.50   15.00
- [ ] 55261   PS   Look for a Star/Afraid of Love   1960   7.50   15.00   30.00
- [ ] 55279   Wishing Well/Dream Girl   1960   3.00   6.00   12.00
- [ ] 55596   Candy/Do the Bug   1963   3.00   6.00   12.00
- [ ] 55685   What Kind of Girl Are You/What's New   1964   2.50   5.00   10.00
- [ ] 55714   Here Goes a Fool/Ecstasy   1964   2.50   5.00   10.00
- [ ] 55738   How Are Things in Paradise/Please Take the Time   1964   2.50   5.00   10.00

United Artists
- [ ] 0099   Look for a Star/Look for a Star   1973   2.50   5.00
  "Silver Spotlight Series" reissue; B-side by Garry Mills

Number	Title (A Side/B Side)	Year	VG	VG+	NM

Miller Sisters, The

Acme
☐ 111	Let's Start Anew/The Flip Skip	1957	12.50	25.00	50.00
☐ 717	You Made Me a Promise/Crazy Billboard Song	1957	10.00	20.00	40.00
☐ 721	Let's Start Anew/The Flip Skip	1958	10.00	20.00	40.00

Ember
☐ 1004	Guess Who/How Am I to Know	1956	7.50	15.00	30.00

Flip
☐ 504	Someday You Will Pay/I Knew You Would	1955	50.00	100.00	200.00

Glodis
☐ 1003	Pop Your Finger/You Got to Reap What You Sow	1961	3.75	7.50	15.00

GMC
☐ 10006	I'm Telling It Like It Is/ Until You Come Home I'll Walk Alone	1967	2.50	5.00	10.00

Herald
☐ 455	Hippity Ha/Until You're Mine	1955	12.50	25.00	50.00
☐ 527	Hippity Ha/Until You're Mine	1958	5.00	10.00	20.00

Hull
☐ 718	Please Don't Leave/Do You Wanna Go	1956	10.00	20.00	40.00
☐ 736	Just Wait and See/Black Pepper	1960	6.25	12.50	25.00
	B-side by Leo Price and Band				
☐ 750	Roll Back the Rug (And Twist)/Don't You Forget	1962	6.25	12.50	25.00
☐ 752	I Cried All Night/Hully Gully Reel	1962	5.00	10.00	20.00

Miller
☐ 1140	Oh Lover/Remember That	1960	5.00	10.00	20.00
☐ 1141	Pony Dance/Give Me Some Old Fashioned Love	1960	5.00	10.00	20.00
☐ 1143	Please Mr. D.J./(B-side unknown)	1960	5.00	10.00	20.00

Onyx
☐ 507	Sugar Candy/My Own	1957	12.50	25.00	50.00

Rayna
☐ 5001	I Miss You So/Dance Little Sister	1962	3.75	7.50	15.00
☐ 5004	Oh Why/Walk On	1962	3.75	7.50	15.00

Riverside
☐ 4535	Dance Close/Tell Him	1962	5.00	10.00	20.00

Roulette
☐ 4491	Baby Your Baby/Silly Girl	1963	3.00	6.00	12.00

Stardust
☐ 3001	Feel Good/Cooncha	1964	2.50	5.00	10.00

Sun
☐ 230	There's No Right Way to Do Me Wrong/ You Can Tell Me	1956	12.50	25.00	50.00
☐ 255	Finders Keepers/Ten Cats Down	1956	12.50	25.00	50.00
☐ 504	Someday You Will Pay/I Knew You Would	1955	37.50	75.00	150.00

Yorktown
☐ 75	Looking Over My Life/Si Senor	1965	2.50	5.00	10.00

Miller, Hal, and the Rays
("The Rays" actually, in this case, are the Four Seasons-to-be)

Amy
☐ 909	I Still Care/On My Own Two Feet	1964	25.00	50.00	100.00
☐ 920	A Blessing in Disguise/Cry Like the Rain	1965	20.00	40.00	80.00

Topix
☐ 6003	An Angel Cried/Faith, Hope, Dreams	1961	10.00	20.00	40.00

Miller, Ned

Capitol
☐ 2074	Endless/Only a Fool	1968		3.00	6.00
☐ 4607	My Heart Waits at the Door/Cold Gray Bars	1961	3.00	6.00	12.00
☐ 4652	Dark Moon/Go On Back, You Fool	1961	3.00	6.00	12.00
☐ 5431	Whistle Walkin'/ Two Voices, Two Shadows, Two Faces	1965	2.00	4.00	8.00
☐ 5502	Fall of the King/Down the Street	1965	2.00	4.00	8.00
☐ 5568	Lovin' Pains/If the World Turned Into Ashes	1965	2.00	4.00	8.00
☐ 5661	Right Behind These Lips/Summer Roses	1966	2.00	4.00	8.00
☐ 5742	Lorraine/Teardrop Lane	1966	2.00	4.00	8.00
☐ 5868	The Hobo/Echo of the Pines	1967	2.00	4.00	8.00

Dot
☐ 15601	From a Jack to a King/Parade of Broken Hearts	1957	10.00	20.00	40.00
☐ 15651	Turn Back/Lights in the Street	1957	3.75	7.50	15.00

Fabor
☐ 114	From a Jack to a King/Parade of Broken Hearts	1962	3.00	6.00	12.00
☐ 116	One Among the Many/Man Behind the Gun	1963	2.50	5.00	10.00
☐ 121	Another Fool Like Me/Magic Moon	1963	2.50	5.00	10.00
☐ 125	Big Love/Sunday Morning Tears	1964	2.50	5.00	10.00
☐ 128	Invisible Tears/Old Restless Ocean	1964	2.50	5.00	10.00
☐ 137	Do What You Do Do Well/Dusty Guitar	1964	2.00	4.00	8.00
☐ 139	What I Know/Lights in the Street	1965	2.00	4.00	8.00

Jackpot
☐ 48020	Girl from the Second World/Ring the Bell for Johnny	1960	3.00	6.00	12.00
	With Jan Howard				

Number		Title (A Side/B Side)	Year	VG	VG+	NM
Republic						
☐ 1404		Autumn Winds/My Last Go-Round	1969		2.50	5.00
☐ 1410		Breakin'/Just Walkin' in the Rain	1970		2.50	5.00
☐ 1411		The Lover's Song/Cold Gray Bars	1970		2.50	5.00
☐ 1416		Back to Oklahoma/I Hang My Head and Cry	1970		2.50	5.00

Miller, Roger

Number		Title (A Side/B Side)	Year	VG	VG+	NM
Buena Vista						
☐ 493		Whistle Stop/Not in Nottingham	1973		2.50	5.00
☐ 493	PS	Whistle Stop/Not in Nottingham	1973		2.50	5.00
Columbia						
☐ 02681		Old Friends/When a House Is Not a Home	1982		2.00	4.00
		Roger Miller/Willie Nelson/Ray Price				
☐ 10052		Our Love/Yester Waltz	1974		2.50	5.00
☐ 10107		I Love a Rodeo/Lovin' You Is Always on My Mind	1975		2.50	5.00
☐ 45873		Open Up Your Heart/Qua La Linta	1973		2.50	5.00
☐ 45948		I Believe in the Sunrise/Shannon's Song	1973		2.50	5.00
☐ 46000		Whistle Stop/The 4th of July	1974		2.50	5.00
Decca						
☐ 30763		On This Mountaintop/	1958	3.75	7.50	15.00
		It's Been a Long, Long Time for Me				
		A-side: Donna Young and Roger Miller; B-side: Donna Young				
☐ 30838		Wrong Kind of Girl/A Man Like Me	1959	3.75	7.50	15.00
☐ 30953		Sweet Ramona/Jason Fleming	1959	3.75	7.50	15.00
Elektra						
☐ 47192		Everyone Gets Crazy Now and Then/Aladam Bama	1981		2.00	4.00
MCA						
☐ 52663		River in the Rain/Hand for the Hog	1985			3.00
☐ 52855		Some Hearts Get All the Breaks/Arkansas	1986			3.00
Mercury						
☐ 73102		South/Don't We All Have the Right	1970		2.50	5.00
☐ 73190		Tomorrow Night in Baltimore/A Million Years or So	1971		2.50	5.00
☐ 73230		Loving Her Was Easier	1971		2.50	5.00
		(Than Anything I'll Ever Do Again)/Que La Linta				
☐ 73268		We Found It in Each Other's Arms/	1972		2.50	5.00
		Sunny Side of My Life				
☐ 73321		Rings for Sale/Conversations	1972		2.50	5.00
☐ 73354		Hoppy's Gone/I Jumped from Uncle Harvey's Plane	1972		2.50	5.00
Musicor						
☐ 1102		Can't Stop Loving You/You're Forgetting Me	1965	2.50	5.00	10.00
RCA Victor						
☐ 47-7776		Footprints in the Snow/You Don't Want My Love	1960	3.75	7.50	15.00
☐ 47-7878		When Two Worlds Collide/Every Which-A-Way	1961	3.75	7.50	15.00
☐ 47-7958		Burma Shave/Fair Swiss Maiden	1961	3.75	7.50	15.00
☐ 47-8028		Sorry, Willie/Hitch-Hiker	1962	3.00	6.00	12.00
☐ 47-8091		Trouble on the Turnpike/Hey Little Star	1962	3.00	6.00	12.00
☐ 47-8175		Lock, Stock and Teardrop/I Know Who It Is	1963	3.00	6.00	12.00
☐ 47-8651		If You Want Me To/Hey Little Star	1965	2.50	5.00	10.00
Smash						
☐ 1876		Less and Less/Got Two Again	1964	3.00	6.00	12.00
☐ 1881		Dang Me/Got Two Again	1964	2.50	5.00	10.00
☐ 1881	PS	Dang Me/Got Two Again	1964	3.75	7.50	15.00
☐ 1926		Chug-a-Lug/Reincarnation	1964	2.50	5.00	10.00
☐ 1947		Do-Wacka-Do/Love Is Not for Me	1964	2.50	5.00	10.00
☐ 1947	PS	Do-Wacka-Do/Love Is Not for Me	1964	3.75	7.50	15.00
☐ 1965		King of the Road/Atta Boy Girl	1965	3.00	6.00	12.00
☐ 1983		Engine, Engine #9/The Last Word in Lonesome Is Me	1965	2.00	4.00	8.00
☐ 1994		One Dyin' and a-Buryin'/It Happened Just That Way	1965	2.00	4.00	8.00
☐ 1994	PS	One Dyin' and a-Buryin'/It Happened Just That Way	1965	3.75	7.50	15.00
☐ 1998		Kansas City Star/	1965	2.00	4.00	8.00
		Guess I'll Pick Up My Heart (And Go Home)				
☐ 2010		England Swings/Good Old Days	1965	2.00	4.00	8.00
☐ 2024		Husbands and Wives/I've Been a Long Time Leavin'	1966	2.00	4.00	8.00
☐ 2043		You Can't Roller Skate in a Buffalo Herd/Train of Life	1966	2.00	4.00	8.00
☐ 2055		My Uncle Used to Love Me But She Died/	1966	2.00	4.00	8.00
		You're My Kingdom				
☐ 2066		Heartbreak Hotel/Less and Less	1966	2.00	4.00	8.00
☐ 2081		Walkin' in the Sunshine/Home	1967	2.00	4.00	8.00
☐ 2121		The Ballad of Waterhole #3 (Code of the West)/	1967	2.00	4.00	8.00
		Rainbow Valley				
☐ 2130		Old Toy Trains/Silent Night	1967	2.50	5.00	10.00
☐ 2148		Little Green Apples/Our Little Love	1968	2.00	4.00	8.00
☐ 2148	PS	Little Green Apples/Our Little Love	1968	3.00	6.00	12.00
☐ 2183		What I'd Give (To Be the Wind)/Toliver	1968	2.00	4.00	8.00
☐ 2197		Vance/Little Children Run and Play	1968	2.00	4.00	8.00
☐ 2230		Me and Bobby McGee/	1969		3.00	6.00
		I'm Gonna Teach My Heart to Bend (Instead of Break)				
☐ 2246		Where Have All the Average People Gone/	1969		3.00	6.00
		Boeing Boeing 707				
☐ 2258		The Tom Green County Fair/I Know Who It Is	1970		3.00	6.00
Starday						
☐ 356		Can't Stop Loving You/You're Forgetting Me	1958	5.00	10.00	20.00
☐ 718		Playboy/Poor Little John	1965	2.50	5.00	10.00
☐ 7029		Under Your Spell Again/I Ain't Never	197?		2.50	5.00

Number		Title (A Side/B Side)	Year	VG	VG+	NM
☐ 7032		Country Girl/Jimmy Brown, The Newsboy	197?		2.50	5.00
☐ 7038		Tip of My Fingers/I Wish I Could Fall in Love Today	197?		2.50	5.00

20th Century

☐ 2421		The Hat/Pleasing the Crowd	1979		2.00	4.00

Windsong

☐ CB-11072		Baby Me Baby/Dark Side of the Moon	1977		2.00	4.00
☐ CB-11166		Oklahoma Woman/There's Nobody Like You	1977		2.00	4.00

Mills, Garry

Imperial

☐ 5674		Look for a Star -- Part 1/Look for a Star -- Part 2	1960	3.75	7.50	15.00

United Artists

☐ 0099		Look for a Star/Look for a Star	1973		2.50	5.00
		"Silver Spotlight Series" reissue; B-side by Gary Miles				

Mills, Hayley

Buena Vista

☐ 385		Let's Get Together/Cobbler, Cobbler	1961	3.00	6.00	12.00
☐ 385	PS	Let's Get Together/Cobbler, Cobbler	1961	6.25	12.50	25.00
☐ 395		Johnny Jingo/Jeepers Creepers	1962	2.50	5.00	10.00
☐ 395	PS	Johnny Jingo/Jeepers Creepers	1962	6.25	12.50	25.00
☐ 401		Side by Side/Ching Ching and a Ring Ding Ding	1962	2.50	5.00	10.00
☐ 401	PS	Side by Side/Ching Ching and a Ring Ding Ding	1962	6.25	12.50	25.00
☐ 408		Castaway/Sweet River	1962	2.50	5.00	10.00
☐ 408	PS	Castaway/Sweet River	1962	6.25	12.50	25.00
☐ 409		Let's Climb/Enjoy It	1962	2.50	5.00	10.00
		With Maurice Chevalier				
☐ 409	PS	Let's Climb/Enjoy It	1962	6.25	12.50	25.00
☐ 420		Flitterin'/Beautiful Beulah	1963	2.50	5.00	10.00
		With Eddie Hodges				
☐ 420	PS	Flitterin'/Beautiful Beulah	1963	6.25	12.50	25.00

Mainstream

☐ 656		Gypsy Girl/Younger Than Seventeen	1966	2.00	4.00	8.00

Mimms, Garnet, and the Enchanters

(Many of these are Garnet Mimms solo)

Arista

☐ 0239		What It Is (Part 1)/What It Is (Part 2)	1977		2.00	4.00
☐ 0289		Johnny Perter/Tail Snatcher	1977		2.00	4.00
☐ 0332		Right Here in the Palm of My Hand/Tail Snatcher	1978		2.00	4.00

GSF

☐ 6874		Another Place/Stop and Check Yourself	1972		3.00	6.00
☐ 6887		I'll Keep On Loving/Somebody, Someplace	1972		3.00	6.00

United Artists

☐ 0109		Cry Baby/For Your Precious Love	1973		2.00	4.00
		"Silver Spotlight Series" reissue				
☐ 629		Cry Baby/Don't Change Your Heart	1963	3.75	7.50	15.00
☐ 658		Baby Don't You Weep/For Your Precious Love	1963	3.00	6.00	12.00
☐ 694		Tell Me Baby/Anytime You Want Me	1964	3.00	6.00	12.00
☐ 715		One Girl/A Quiet Place	1964	3.00	6.00	12.00
☐ 773		One Woman Man/Look Away	1964	3.00	6.00	12.00
☐ 796		A Little Bit of Soap/I'll Make It Up to You	1964	3.00	6.00	12.00
☐ 848		So Close/It Was Easier to Hurt Her	1965	3.00	6.00	12.00
☐ 868		Welcome Home/The Adventures of Moll Flanders	1965	3.00	6.00	12.00
☐ 887		Everytime/That Goes to Show You	1965	3.00	6.00	12.00
☐ 951		Looking for You/More Than a Miracle	1965	3.00	6.00	12.00
☐ 995		Prove It to Me/I'll Take Good Care of You	1966	3.00	6.00	12.00
☐ 50058		My Baby/Keep On Smilin'	1966			*Unreleased*

Veep

☐ 1232		Thinkin'/It's Been Such a Long Time Comin'	1966	2.00	4.00	8.00
☐ 1234		My Baby/Keep On Smilin'	1966	2.00	4.00	8.00
☐ 1252		All About Love/The Truth Hurts	1967	2.00	4.00	8.00

Verve

☐ 10596		Stop and Think It Over/I Can Hear My Baby Crying	1968	2.00	4.00	8.00
☐ 10624		Can You Top This/We Can Find That Love	1968	2.00	4.00	8.00
☐ 10642		Take Me/Happy Landing	1969	2.00	4.00	8.00
☐ 10650		Sad Song/Get It While You Can	1970	2.00	4.00	8.00

Mindbenders, The

(Also see "Fontana, Wayne, and the Mindbenders")

Fontana

☐ 1541		A Groovy Kind of Love/Love Is Good	1966	3.00	6.00	12.00
☐ 1555		Ashes to Ashes/Don't Know About Love	1966	2.00	4.00	8.00
☐ 1571		I Want Her, She Wants Me/Morning After	1967	2.00	4.00	8.00
☐ 1595		It's Getting Harder All the Time/Off and Running	1967	2.00	4.00	8.00
☐ 1620		Yellow Brick Road/Blessed Are the Lonely	1968	2.00	4.00	8.00
☐ 1628		Uncle Joe the Ice Cream Man/ The Man Who Loved Trees	1968	2.00	4.00	8.00

Mineo, Sal

Decca

☐ 31692		Why Don't You Love Me/A Girl Across the Way	1964	3.00	6.00	12.00

Number		Title (A Side/B Side)	Year	VG	VG+	NM
Epic						
☐ 9216		Start Movin' (In My Direction)/Love Affair	1957	6.25	12.50	25.00
☐ 9216	PS	Start Movin' (In My Direction)/Love Affair	1957	10.00	20.00	40.00
☐ 9227		Lasting Love/You Shouldn't Do That	1957	5.00	10.00	20.00
☐ 9227	PS	Lasting Love/You Shouldn't Do That	1957	7.50	15.00	30.00
☐ 9246		Party Time/The Words That I Whisper	1957	5.00	10.00	20.00
☐ 9246	PS	Party Time/The Words That I Whisper	1957	7.50	15.00	30.00
☐ 9260		Little Pigeon/Cuttin' In	1958	5.00	10.00	20.00
☐ 9260	PS	Little Pigeon/Cuttin' In	1958	7.50	15.00	30.00
☐ 9271		Seven Steps to Love/A Couple of Crazy Kids	1958	5.00	10.00	20.00
☐ 9287		Baby Face/Souvenirs of Summertime	1958	5.00	10.00	20.00
☐ 9327		Young As We Are/Make Believe Baby	1959	5.00	10.00	20.00
☐ 9327	PS	Young As We Are/Make Believe Baby	1959	7.50	15.00	30.00
☐ 9345		I'll Never Be Myself Again/ The Words That I Whisper	1959	5.00	10.00	20.00
Fontana						
☐ 1504		Save the Last Dance for Me/Take Me Back	1965	3.00	6.00	12.00

Minorbops, The

Number		Title (A Side/B Side)	Year	VG	VG+	NM
Lamp						
☐ 2012		Need You Tonight/Want You for My Own	1957	75.00	150.00	300.00

Mint Juleps, The

Number		Title (A Side/B Side)	Year	VG	VG+	NM
Herald						
☐ 481		Bells of Love/Vip-a-Dip	1956	25.00	50.00	100.00
		With script logo inside flag				
☐ 481		Bells of Love/Vip-a-Dip	1956	6.25	12.50	25.00
		With block logo inside flag				

Mints, The – See "Copeland, Ken"

Minute Men, The

Number		Title (A Side/B Side)	Year	VG	VG+	NM
Argo						
☐ 5469		Please Keep the Beatles in England/ My Love Is Gone	1964	3.75	7.50	15.00

Miracles, The

(Also see "Robinson, Smokey")

Number		Title (A Side/B Side)	Year	VG	VG+	NM
Baton						
☐ 210		A Lover's Chant/Come Home with Me	1955	37.50	75.00	150.00
		Not the Smokey Robinson-related group				
Cash						
☐ 1008		You're An Angel/A Gal Named Jo	1955	50.00	100.00	200.00
		Not the Smokey Robinson-related group				
Chess						
☐ 1734		Bad Girl/I Love Your Baby	1959	15.00	30.00	60.00
		Blue label with vertical Chess logo (original)				
☐ 1734		Bad Girl/I Love Your Baby	1963	6.25	12.50	25.00
		Black label				
☐ 1734		Bad Girl/I Love Your Baby	1966	5.00	10.00	20.00
		Blue label with "Chess" at top				
☐ 1768		I Need a Change/All I Want (Is You)	1960	10.00	20.00	40.00
Columbia						
☐ 10464		Spy for Brotherhood/The Bird Must Fly Away	1976		2.50	5.00
☐ 10517		Women (Make the World Go 'Round)/ I Can Touch the Sky	1977		2.50	5.00
☐ 10706		Mean Machine/The Magic of Your Eyes (Laura's Eyes)	1978		2.50	5.00
End						
☐ 1017		Got a Job/My Mama Done Told Me	1958	15.00	30.00	60.00
☐ 1029		Money/I Cry	1958	12.50	25.00	50.00
		Mostly gray-white label, no mention of Roulette Records				
☐ 1029		Money/I Cry	1958	10.00	20.00	40.00
		Multicolor label with "A Division of Roulette Records Inc." on label				
☐ 1084		Money/I Cry	1961	6.25	12.50	25.00
Motown						
☐ G 1/G 2		Bad Girl/I Love Your Baby	1959	1,250	1,875	2,500
☐ TLX-2207		Bad Girl/I Love Your Baby	1959	1,250	1,875	2,500
Standard Groove						
☐ 13090	DJ	I Care About Detroit	1968	50.00	100.00	200.00
		With Tamla globe logo on label				
☐ 13090	DJ	I Care About Detroit	1968	37.50	75.00	150.00
		With no Tamla logo on label				
Tamla						
☐ EX-009	DJ	The Christmas Song/Christmas Everybody	1963	50.00	100.00	200.00
☐ 54028		The Feeling Is So Fine/You Can Depend On Me	1960	100.00	200.00	400.00
☐ 54028		The Feeling Is So Fine/You Can Depend On Me	1960	125.00	250.00	500.00
		With alternate take of B-side; matrix number followed by "A" in trail-off wax				
☐ 54028		Way Over There/Depend on Me	1960	37.50	75.00	150.00
		No strings on A-side recording				
☐ 54028		Way Over There/Depend On Me	1960	15.00	30.00	60.00
		With overdubbed strings on A-side				

Number		Title (A Side/B Side)	Year	VG	VG+	NM
❏ 54034		Shop Around/Who's Lovin' You	1960	25.00	50.00	100.00
		Original take, withdrawn shortly after release. In trail-off wax is "H55518A."				
❏ 54034		Shop Around/Who's Lovin' You	1960	6.25	12.50	25.00
		Hit take. In trail-off wax is "L-1." Horizontal lines label.				
❏ 54034		Shop Around/Who's Lovin' You	1960	3.00	6.00	12.00
		Hit take. In trail-off wax is "L-1." Globe label.				
❏ 54036		Ain't It Baby/The Only One I Love	1961	37.50	75.00	150.00
❏ 54044		Mighty Good Lovin'/Broken Hearted	1961	12.50	25.00	50.00
❏ 54044	PS	Mighty Good Lovin'/Broken Hearted	1961	37.50	75.00	150.00
❏ 54048		Everybody's Gotta Pay Some Dues/I Can't Believe	1961	12.50	25.00	50.00
❏ 54048		You Gotta Pay Some Dues/I Can't Believe	1961	25.00	50.00	100.00
		Alternate A-side title				
❏ 54048	PS	Everybody's Gotta Pay Some Dues/I Can't Believe	1961	15.00	30.00	60.00
❏ 54053		What's So Good About Good-By/	1962	7.50	15.00	30.00
		I've Been Good to You				
❏ 54053	PS	What's So Good About Good-By/	1962	25.00	50.00	100.00
		I've Been Good to You				
❏ 54059		I'll Try Something New/You Never Miss a Good Thing	1962	5.00	10.00	20.00
❏ 54059	PS	I'll Try Something New/You Never Miss a Good Thing	1962	25.00	50.00	100.00
❏ 54069		Way Over There/If Your Mother Only Knew	1962	5.00	10.00	20.00
❏ 54073		You've Really Got a Hold on Me/Happy Landing	1962	3.75	7.50	15.00
❏ 54078		A Love She Can Count On/I Can Take a Hint	1963	3.75	7.50	15.00
❏ 54083		Mickey's Monkey/Whatever Makes You Happy	1963	3.75	7.50	15.00
❏ 54089		I Gotta Dance to Keep from Crying/	1963	3.75	7.50	15.00
		Such Is Love, Such Is Life				
❏ 54092		(You Can't Let the Boy Overpower) The Man in You/	1964	3.75	7.50	15.00
		Heartbreak Road				
❏ 54098		I Like It Like That/You're So Fine and Sweet	1964	3.75	7.50	15.00
❏ 54098	PS	I Like It Like That/You're So Fine and Sweet	1964	25.00	50.00	100.00
❏ 54102		That's What Love Is Made Of/Would I Love You	1964	3.00	6.00	12.00
❏ 54109		Come On Do the Jerk/Baby Don't You Go	1964	3.00	6.00	12.00
❏ 54113		Ooo Baby Baby/All That's Good	1965	2.50	5.00	10.00
❏ 54118		The Tracks of My Tears/A Fork in the Road	1965	2.50	5.00	10.00
❏ 54123		My Girl Has Gone/Since You Won My Heart	1965	2.50	5.00	10.00
❏ 54127		Going to A-Go-Go/Choosey Beggar	1965	2.50	5.00	10.00
❏ 54127	PS	Going to A-Go-Go/Choosey Beggar	1965	25.00	50.00	100.00
❏ 54134		Whole Lot of Shakin' in My Heart (Since I Met You)/	1966	2.00	4.00	8.00
		Oh Be My Lover				
❏ 54140		Come 'Round Here -- I'm the One You Need/Save Me	1966	2.00	4.00	8.00
❏ 54140	PS	Come 'Round Here -- I'm the One You Need/Save Me	1966	20.00	40.00	80.00
		Starting below, through Tamla 54225, as "Smokey Robinson and the Miracles"				
❏ 54145		The Love I Saw in You Was Just a Mirage/	1967	2.00	4.00	8.00
		Come Spy with Me				
❏ 54152		More Love/Swept for You Baby	1967	2.00	4.00	8.00
❏ 54159		I Second That Emotion/You Must Be Love	1967	2.00	4.00	8.00
❏ 54162		If You Can Want/	1968	2.00	4.00	8.00
		When the Words from Your Heart Get Caught Up in Your Throat				
❏ 54167		Yester Love/Much Better Off	1968	2.00	4.00	8.00
❏ 54172		Special Occasion/Give Her Up	1968	2.00	4.00	8.00
❏ 54178		Baby, Baby Don't Cry/Your Mother's Only Daughter	1968	2.00	4.00	8.00
❏ 54183		Here I Go Again/Doggone Right	1969	2.00	4.00	8.00
❏ 54184		Abraham, Martin, and John/Much Better Off	1969	2.00	4.00	8.00
❏ 54189		Point It Out/Darling Dear	1969	2.00	4.00	8.00
❏ 54194		Who's Gonna Take the Blame/I Gotta Thing For You	1970	2.00	4.00	8.00
❏ 54199		The Tears of a Clown/Promise Me	1970		3.00	6.00
❏ 54205		I Don't Blame You at All/That Girl	1971		3.00	6.00
❏ 54206		Crazy About the La La La/Oh Baby Baby I Love You	1971		3.00	6.00
❏ 54211		Satisfaction/Flower Girl	1971		3.00	6.00
❏ 54220		We've Come Too Far to End It Now/	1972		3.00	6.00
		When Sundown Comes				
❏ 54225		I Can't Stand to See You Cry/With Your Love Came	1972		3.00	6.00
		Starting below, name reverts to The Miracles				
❏ 54237		Don't Let It End (Til You Let It Begin)/Wigs and Lashes	1973		2.50	5.00
❏ 54240		Give Me Just Another Day/I Wanna Be with You	1973		2.50	5.00
❏ 54248		Do It Baby/I Wanna Be with You	1974		2.50	5.00
❏ 54256		Don't Cha Love It/Up Again	1974		2.50	5.00
❏ 54259		You Are Love/Gemini	1975		2.50	5.00
❏ 54262		Love Machine (Part 1)/Love Machine (Part 2)	1975		2.50	5.00
❏ 54268		Night Life/Smog	1976		2.50	5.00

Topps/Motown

❏ 11		Shop Around	1967	18.75	37.50	75.00
		Cardboard record				

Misfits, The
(More than one group)

Aries

❏ 3		Midnight Star/I Don't Know	1961	37.50	75.00	150.00

Hush

❏ 105		Give Me Your Heart/My Mother-in-Law	1960	100.00	200.00	400.00

Imperial

❏ 66054		This Little Piggy (I'm a Hog for You)/Lost Love	1964	6.25	12.50	25.00

Joey

❏ 117		Naughty Rooster/Chicago Confidential	1961	3.00	6.00	12.00

Sound Stage 7

❏ 2538		It's Up to You/Skiing Time	1965	6.25	12.50	25.00

Number		Title (A Side/B Side)	Year	VG	VG+	NM

Troy
| ❑ 227 | | The Uncle Willie/Big Bad Wolf | 196? | 6.25 | 12.50 | 25.00 |

Mr. Clean
Original Sound
| ❑ 40 | | Mr. Clean/Jessie Lee | 1964 | 37.50 | 75.00 | 150.00 |
| | | *Written, produced and performed on by Frank Zappa* | | | | |

Mitchell, Chad, Trio
Colpix
❑ 133		Sally Ann/Vaya Con Dios	1959	3.00	6.00	12.00
❑ 136		Up On the Mountain/Walkin' on the Green Grasses	1959	3.00	6.00	12.00
❑ 144		I Do Adore Her/The Gallows Tree	1960	3.00	6.00	12.00
❑ 154		The Ballad of Herbie Spear/(B-side unknown)	1960	3.00	6.00	12.00
❑ 157		Devil Road/Paddy West	1960	3.00	6.00	12.00
❑ 610		Six Men/I'm Going Home	1961	2.50	5.00	10.00
		B-side by Eugene Lamarr				

Kapp
❑ 439		Lizzie Borden/Super Skier	1961	3.00	6.00	12.00
❑ 439	PS	Lizzie Borden/Super Skier	1961	5.00	10.00	20.00
❑ 457		John Birch Society/Golden Vanity	1962	2.50	5.00	10.00
❑ 481		Alberta/Come Along Home	1962	2.50	5.00	10.00
❑ 485		You Can Tell the World/Hello, Susan Brown	1962	2.50	5.00	10.00
❑ 510		Blowing in the Wind/Adios, Mi Corazon	1963	2.50	5.00	10.00
❑ 518		Green Grow the Lilacs/Leave Me If You Want To	1963	2.50	5.00	10.00

May
| ❑ 116 | | The Ballad of Herbie Spear/Sally Ann | 1962 | 2.50 | 5.00 | 10.00 |

Mercury
❑ 72197		The Marvelous Toy/Bonny Streets of Fyve-10	1963	2.50	5.00	10.00
❑ 72197	PS	The Marvelous Toy/Bonny Streets of Fyve-10	1963	3.75	7.50	15.00
❑ 72234		Tarrier's Song/Tell Old Billy	1964	2.00	4.00	8.00
❑ 72257		What Did You Learn in School Today/Barry's Boys	1964	2.00	4.00	8.00
❑ 72340		I Can't Help But Wonder/Stewball and Griselda	1964	2.00	4.00	8.00
❑ 72340	PS	I Can't Help But Wonder/Stewball and Griselda	1964	3.75	7.50	15.00
Starting below, as "The Mitchell Trio"						
❑ 72400		You Were On My Mind/My Name Is Morgan	1965	2.00	4.00	8.00
❑ 72518		That's the Way It's Gonna Be/Violets of Dawn	1966	2.00	4.00	8.00
❑ 72544		Your Friendly, Liberal, Neighborhood Ku Klux Klan/Violets of Dawn	1966	2.00	4.00	8.00
❑ 72591		Dark Shadows and Empty Hallways/Stay with Me	1966	2.00	4.00	8.00

Reprise
Reprise records as "The Mitchell Trio"						
❑ 0588		Leaving on a Jet Plane/Baby, That's Where It Is	1967		3.00	6.00
❑ 0630		She Loves You/Like to Deal with the Ladies	1967		3.00	6.00

Mitchell, Lee
Phillips Int'l.
| ❑ 3530 | | The Frog/A Little Bird Told Me | 1958 | 3.75 | 7.50 | 15.00 |
Sharp
| ❑ 0862 | | Rootie Tootie Baby/Who's That Big Man | 1959 | 75.00 | 150.00 | 300.00 |

Mitchell, Marlon
Vena
| ❑ 100 | | Ice Cold Baby/Bermuda Shorts | 1957 | 30.00 | 60.00 | 120.00 |

Mitchell, Rose
Imperial
| ❑ 5243 | | Slipping In/I'm Searching | 1953 | 15.00 | 30.00 | 60.00 |
| ❑ 5260 | | Live My Life/Baby Please Don't Go | 1954 | 15.00 | 30.00 | 60.00 |

Mitchell, Stan
Gone
| ❑ 5106 | | Devil in Disguise/Lovin' Man | 1961 | 7.50 | 15.00 | 30.00 |

Mizell, Hank
Amazon
| ❑ 711 | | Jungle Rock/Then I'm In Your Arms | 1963 | 12.50 | 25.00 | 50.00 |
Eko
| ❑ 506 | | Jungle Rock/Then I'm In Your Arms | 1958 | 150.00 | 300.00 | 600.00 |
King
| ❑ 5236 | | Jungle Rock/Then I'm In Your Arms | 1959 | 75.00 | 150.00 | 300.00 |

Moby Grape
Columbia
❑ 44170		Changes/Fall on You	1967	2.00	4.00	8.00
❑ 44170	PS	Changes/Fall on You	1967	5.00	10.00	20.00
❑ 44171		Sitting by the Window/Indifference	1967	2.00	4.00	8.00
❑ 44171	PS	Sitting by the Window/Indifference	1967	5.00	10.00	20.00
❑ 44172		8:05/Mister Blues	1967	2.00	4.00	8.00
❑ 44172	PS	8:05/Mister Blues	1967	5.00	10.00	20.00
❑ 44173		Omaha/Someday	1967	2.00	4.00	8.00
❑ 44173	PS	Omaha/Someday	1967	5.00	10.00	20.00
❑ 44174		Hey Grandma/Come in the Morning	1967	2.00	4.00	8.00

Number		Title (A Side/B Side)	Year	VG	VG+	NM
44174	PS	Hey Grandma/Come in the Morning	1967	5.00	10.00	20.00
44567		Can't Be So Bad/Bitter Wind	1968		3.00	6.00
44789		If You Can't Learn From My Mistakes/Trucking Man	1969		3.00	6.00
44885		Ooh Mama Ooh/It's a Beautiful Day Today	1969		3.00	6.00

Reprise

1040		Gypsy Wedding/Apocalypse	1971		2.50	5.00
1055		Goin' Down to Texas/About Time	1971		2.50	5.00
1096		Gone Fishin'/Gypsy Wedding	1972		2.50	5.00

Mockingbirds, The
(With Graham Gouldman and Kevin Godley, later of 10CC)

ABC-Paramount

10653		That's How/I Never Should Have Kissed You	1965	3.75	7.50	15.00

Mojo Men, The
(Some of these as "Mojo")

Autumn

11		Mama's Little Baby/Off the Hook	1965	3.75	7.50	15.00
19		Dance with Me/The Loneliest Boy in Town	1965	3.75	7.50	15.00
27		She's My Baby/Fire in My Heart	1966	3.75	7.50	15.00

GRT

5		Flower of Love/I Can't Let Go	1969	2.50	5.00	10.00
8		Candle to Burn/Make You at Home	1969	2.50	5.00	10.00
16		Everyday Love/There Goes My Mind	1969	2.50	5.00	10.00

Reprise

0486		She's My Baby/Do the Hanky Panky	1966	5.00	10.00	20.00
0539		Sit Down, I Think I Love You/ Don't Leave Me Crying Like Before	1966	2.50	5.00	10.00
0580		Me About You/When You're in Love	1967	2.50	5.00	10.00
0617		Whatever Happened to Happy/Make You at Home	1967	2.50	5.00	10.00
0661		Not Too Old to Start Crying/New York City	1968	2.50	5.00	10.00
0689		Should I Cry/You to Me	1968	2.50	5.00	10.00
0707		Sit Down, I Think I Love You/Me About You "Back to Back Hits" series	1968		3.00	6.00
0759		Don't Be Cruel/Let It Be Him	1968	2.50	5.00	10.00

Tide

2000		Surfin' Fat Man/Paula	1964	10.00	20.00	40.00

Mollern, Ronnie

King

5365		Rockin' Up/Fat Mama	1960	37.50	75.00	150.00

Monarchs, The
(More than one group)

Dot

15228		Gravy/Caravan Mambo	1954	10.00	20.00	40.00

Melba

101		Pretty Little Girl/In My Younger Days	1956	15.00	30.00	60.00

Monument

03484		Look Homeward, Angel/This Old Heart	1983		2.50	5.00

Neil

101		Pretty Little Girl/In My Younger Days	1956	17.50	35.00	70.00
103		Always Be Faithful/How Are You	1956	17.50	35.00	70.00

Sound Stage 7

2502		This Old Heart/'Til I Hear It From You	1963	3.00	6.00	12.00
2516		Look Homeward, Angel/ What Made You Change Your Mind	1964	3.00	6.00	12.00
2530		Climb Every Mountain/Take Me Home	1964	3.00	6.00	12.00

Wing

90040		Angels in the Sky/Wanna Go Home	1955	20.00	40.00	80.00

Yucca

172		Forever Lost/Cuckoo	1964	12.50	25.00	50.00

Zone

1067		Friday Night/El Bandito	1963	3.75	7.50	15.00

Mondellos, The

Rhythm

102		Come Back Home/100 Years from Today *As "Alice Jean and the Mondellos"*	1956	50.00	100.00	200.00
105		Over the Rainbow/Never Leave Me Alone *As "Yul McClay and the Mondellos"*	1956	37.50	75.00	150.00
106		That's What I Call Love/Daylight Saving Time	1956	37.50	75.00	150.00
109		Hard to Please/Happiness Street	1957	37.50	75.00	150.00
114		My Heart/That's What I Call Love *As "Rudy Lambert and the Mondellos"*	1957	37.50	75.00	150.00
128		That Old Feeling/Sunday Kind of Love *As "Rudy Lambert and the Mondellos"*	1957	37.50	75.00	150.00

Monitors, The
(More than one group)

Aladdin

3309		Tonight's the Night/Candy Coated Kisses	1955	25.00	50.00	100.00

Number		Title (A Side/B Side)	Year	VG	VG+	NM
Buddah						
❏ 278		Fence Around Your Heart/Have You Seen Her	1972		2.50	5.00
Circus						
❏ 219		A Boyfriend's Prayer/Nita	1957	30.00	60.00	120.00
Soul						
❏ 35049		Step by Step (Hand in Hand)/Time Is Passing By	1968	3.75	7.50	15.00
Specialty						
❏ 595		Our Schooldays/I've Got a Dream	1957	15.00	30.00	60.00
❏ 622		Closer to Heaven/Rock 'N' Roll Forever	1957	15.00	30.00	60.00
❏ 636		Mamma Linda/Hop Scotch	1958	15.00	30.00	60.00
V.I.P.						
❏ 25028		Say You/All for Someone	1965	5.00	10.00	20.00
❏ 25032		Greetings (From Uncle Sam)/No. 1 in Your Heart	1965	5.00	10.00	20.00
❏ 25039		Since I Lost You Girl/	1966	5.00	10.00	20.00
		Don't Put Off Till Tomorrow What You Can Do Today				
❏ 25046		Bring Back the Love/	1967	5.00	10.00	20.00
		The Further You Look, The Less You See				
❏ 25049		Step by Step (Hand in Hand)/Time Is Passing By	1968	12.50	25.00	50.00

Monkees, The

(Also see "Dolenz, Mickey"; "Jones, Davy"; "Nesmith, Michael")

Number		Title (A Side/B Side)	Year	VG	VG+	NM
Arista						
❏ 0201		Daydream Believer/Monkee's Theme	1976	2.50	5.00	10.00
❏ 9505		That Was Then, This Is Now/	1986	2.50	5.00	10.00
		(Theme from) The Monkees				
		First pressings list both sides' artist as "The Monkees"				
❏ 9505	PS	That Was Then, This Is Now/	1986	2.50	5.00	10.00
		(Theme from) The Monkees				
		Without "By Mickey Dolenz and Peter Tork (of the Monkees)" on sleeve				
❏ 9505		That Was Then, This Is Now/	1986			3.00
		(Theme from) The Monkees				
		With A-side artist listed as " Mickey Dolenz and Peter Tork (of the Monkees)"				
❏ 9505	PS	That Was Then, This Is Now/	1986			3.00
		(Theme from) The Monkees				
		With "By Mickey Dolenz and Peter Tork (of the Monkees)" on sleeve				
❏ 9532		Daydream Believer/Randy Scouse Git	1986		2.00	4.00
❏ 9532	PS	Daydream Believer/Randy Scouse Git	1986		2.00	4.00
Colgems						
❏ 66-1001		Last Train to Clarksville/Take a Giant Step	1966	3.75	7.50	15.00
❏ 66-1001	PS	Last Train to Clarksville/Take a Giant Step	1966	7.50	15.00	30.00
		With no mention of the Monkees' fan club				
❏ 66-1001	PS	Last Train to Clarksville/Take a Giant Step	1966	5.00	10.00	20.00
		With "Write The Monkees" on sleeve				
❏ 66-1002		I'm a Believer/(I'm Not Your) Steppin' Stone	1966	3.75	7.50	15.00
❏ 66-1002	PS	I'm a Believer/(I'm Not Your) Steppin' Stone	1966	7.50	15.00	30.00
❏ 66-1003		A Little Bit Me, A Little Bit You/She Hangs Out	1967			Unreleased
❏ 66-1004		A Little Bit Me, A Little Bit You/	1967	3.75	7.50	15.00
		The Girl I Knew Somewhere				
❏ 66-1007		Pleasant Valley Sunday/Words	1967	3.75	7.50	15.00
❏ 66-1007	PS	Pleasant Valley Sunday/Words	1967	7.50	15.00	30.00
❏ 66-1012		Daydream Believer/Goin' Down	1967	3.75	7.50	15.00
❏ 66-1012	PS	Daydream Believer/Goin' Down	1967	7.50	15.00	30.00
❏ 66-1019		Valleri/Tapioca Tundra	1968	2.50	5.00	10.00
❏ 66-1023		D.W. Washburn/It's Nice to Be with You	1968	2.50	5.00	10.00
❏ 66-1023	PS	D.W. Washburn/It's Nice to Be with You	1968	7.50	15.00	30.00
❏ 66-1031		Porpoise Song/As We Go Along	1968	2.50	5.00	10.00
❏ 66-1031	PS	Porpoise Song/As We Go Along	1968	5.00	10.00	20.00
❏ 66-5000		Tear Drop City/A Man Without a Dream	1969	2.50	5.00	10.00
❏ 66-5000	PS	Tear Drop City/A Man Without a Dream	1969	6.25	12.50	25.00
❏ 66-5004		Listen to the Band/Someday Man	1969	2.50	5.00	10.00
❏ 66-5004	PS	Listen to the Band/Someday Man	1969	6.25	12.50	25.00
		"Listen to the Band" listed first				
❏ 66-5004	PS	Someday Man/Listen to the Band	1969	5.00	10.00	20.00
		"Someday Man" listed first				
❏ 66-5005		Good Clean Fun/Mommy and Daddy	1969	3.75	7.50	15.00
❏ 66-5005	PS	Good Clean Fun/Mommy and Daddy	1969	6.25	12.50	25.00
❏ 66-5011		Oh My My/I Love You Better	1970	3.75	7.50	15.00
❏ 66-5011	PS	Oh My My/I Love You Better	1970	7.50	15.00	30.00
Rhino						
❏ 74408		Heart and Soul/M.G.B.G.T.	1987			3.00
❏ 74408	PS	Heart and Soul/M.G.B.G.T.	1987		2.00	4.00
❏ 74410		Every Step of the Way/(I'll) Love You Forever	1987			3.00

Monorays, The

Number		Title (A Side/B Side)	Year	VG	VG+	NM
20th Fox						
❏ 594		You're No Good/Love	1965	12.50	25.00	50.00
Red Rocket						
❏ 476		Guardian Angel/Five Minutes to Love You	1959	10.00	20.00	40.00
Tammy						
❏ 1005		Guardian Angel/Five Minutes to Love You	1959	50.00	100.00	200.00

The Monkees' "reunion" single of 1986, "That Was Then, This Is Now," generated an interesting, but little-known, variation. At top is the original pressing, which credits "The Monkees," even though neither Michael Nesmith nor Davy Jones appeared on the record. In the interests of accuracy, the second, more common, pressing changed the label credit to "Micky Dolenz and Peter Tork (of the Monkees)." This also was released with a picture sleeve, which was altered on second pressings as well.

Number		Title (A Side/B Side)	Year	VG	VG+	NM
Monotones, The						
ABC-Paramount						
❏ 10796		Crystal Ball/A Thousand Faces	1966	5.00	10.00	20.00
Argo						
❏ 5290		Book of Love/You Never Loved Me	1958	7.50	15.00	30.00
❏ 5301		Tom Foolery/Zombi	1958	7.50	15.00	30.00
❏ 5321		The Legend of Sleepy Hollow/Soft Shadows	1958	7.50	15.00	30.00
❏ 5339		Tell It to the Judge/Fools Will Be Fools	1959	12.50	25.00	50.00
Hickory						
❏ 1250		Is It Right/What Would You Do	1964	5.00	10.00	20.00
❏ 1306		When Will I Be Loved/If You Can't Give Me All	1965	5.00	10.00	20.00
Hull						
❏ 735		Reading the Book of Love/Dream	1960	12.50	25.00	50.00
❏ 743		Daddy's Home, But Momma's Gone/Tattle Tale	1961	12.50	25.00	50.00
Mascot						
❏ 124		Book of Love/You Never Loved Me	1957	150.00	300.00	600.00
Monroe, Marilyn						
RCA Victor						
❏ 47-5745		River of No Return/I'm Gonna File My Claim	1954	12.50	25.00	50.00
❏ 47-5745	DJ	River of No Return/I'm Gonna File My Claim	1954	30.00	60.00	120.00
		Promo only with Marilyn Monroe's picture on label				
❏ 47-5745	PS	River of No Return/I'm Gonna File My Claim	1954	30.00	60.00	120.00
❏ 47-6033		Heat Wave/After You Get What You Want	1955	7.50	15.00	30.00
❏ 47-6033	PS	Heat Wave/After You Get What You Want	1955	30.00	60.00	120.00
20th Fox						
❏ 311		River of No Return/One Silver Dollar	1962	5.00	10.00	20.00
❏ 311	PS	River of No Return/One Silver Dollar	1962	20.00	40.00	80.00
United Artists						
❏ 161		I Wanna Be Loved By You/I'm Through with Love	1959	5.00	10.00	20.00
Montclairs, The						
(Several different groups)						
ABC-Paramount						
❏ 10463		I Believe (In Your Love)/No Baby	1963	3.75	7.50	15.00
Audicon						
❏ 111		Goodnight, Well, It's Time to Go/A Broken Promise	1961	7.50	15.00	30.00
Hi-Q						
❏ 5001		Golden Angel/Don Juan	1957	75.00	150.00	300.00
Paula						
❏ 345		Is This for Real/All I Really Care About Is You	1971		2.50	5.00
❏ 363		Dreaming Out of Season/I Just Can't Get Away	1972		2.50	5.00
❏ 375		Beggin' Is Hard to Do/Unwanted Love	1973		2.50	5.00
❏ 381		Make Up for Lost Time/How Can One Man Live	1973		2.50	5.00
❏ 382		I Need You More Than Ever/Prelude to a Heartbreak	1973		2.50	5.00
❏ 390		I'm Calling You/Hung Up on Your Love	1973		2.50	5.00
❏ 409		Baby, You Know I'm Gonna Miss You (Part 1)/ Baby, You Know I'm Gonna Miss You (Part 2)	1974		2.50	5.00
Premium						
❏ 404		Give Me a Chance/My Every Dream	1956	100.00	200.00	400.00
Sonic						
❏ 104		All I Want Is Love/I've Heard About You	1956	100.00	200.00	400.00
Sunburst						
❏ 106		Wait for Me/Happy Feet Time	1965	3.00	6.00	12.00
❏ 115		Poopsie/Sore Feet	1965	3.00	6.00	12.00
United Int'l.						
❏ 1007		Lisa/Tap Tap Daisy	1963	6.25	12.50	25.00
❏ 1013		Young Wings Can Fly/Come On and Hold Me	1964	5.00	10.00	20.00
Montereys, The						
(Probably several different groups)						
Arwin						
❏ 130		Goodbye My Love/It Hurts Me So	1961	10.00	20.00	40.00
Blast						
❏ 219		Face in the Crowd/Step Right Up	1965	100.00	200.00	400.00
Dominion						
❏ 1019		First Kiss/Just One More Kiss	1964	10.00	20.00	40.00
EastWest						
❏ 121		I'll Love You Again/The American Teens	1958	6.25	12.50	25.00
GNP Crescendo						
❏ 314		For Sentimental Reasons/I Still Love You	1964	6.25	12.50	25.00
Impala						
❏ 213		Without a Girl/So Deep	1959	30.00	60.00	120.00
Major						
❏ 1009		A Crowded Room/You Said That You Loved Me	1959	17.50	35.00	70.00
Prince						
❏ 5060		Rita/Billy Bud	1960	3.75	7.50	15.00
Rose						
❏ 109		You're the Girl for Me/Ape Shape	1958	25.00	50.00	100.00

Number	Title (A Side/B Side)	Year	VG	VG+	NM
Saturn					
❑ 1002	My Girl/With You	1956	10.00	20.00	40.00
Trans American					
❑ 1000/1	Darlin' Send Me a Letter/Late Darlin'	1960	150.00	300.00	600.00
Montez, Chris					
A&M					
❑ 780	Call Me/Go Head On	1965	2.00	4.00	8.00
❑ 796	The More I See You/You, I Love You	1966	2.50	5.00	10.00
❑ 810	There Will Never Be Another You/ You Can Hurt the One You Love	1966	2.00	4.00	8.00
❑ 822	Keep Talkin'/Time After Time	1966	2.00	4.00	8.00
❑ 839	Because of You/Elena	1967	2.00	4.00	8.00
❑ 852	Just Friends/Twiggy	1967		3.00	6.00
❑ 855	Foolin' Around (Jin-Jee)	1967		3.00	6.00
❑ 906	Once in a While/The Face I Love	1968		3.00	6.00
❑ 958	Love Is Here to Stay/Nothing to Hide	1968		3.00	6.00
❑ 985	Where Are You Now/Watch What Happens	1968		3.00	6.00
Jamie					
❑ 1410	Let's Dance/Somebody Loves You	1973		2.50	5.00
Monogram					
❑ 500	All You Had to Do (Was Tell Me)/Love Me	1962	3.00	6.00	12.00
❑ 505	Let's Dance/You're the One	1962	5.00	10.00	20.00
❑ 507	Some Kinda Fun/Tell Me	1962	3.00	6.00	12.00
❑ 508	Rovkin' Blues/(Let's Do the) Limbo	1963	3.75	7.50	15.00
❑ 513	In An English Towne/My Baby Loves to Dance	1963	3.00	6.00	12.00
❑ 516	No, No, No/Monkey Fever	1963	3.00	6.00	12.00
❑ 517	You're the One/All You Had to Do Was Tell Me *With Kathy Young*	1964	3.00	6.00	12.00
❑ 520	It Takes Two/To Shoot the Curl *With Kathy Young*	1964	3.00	6.00	12.00
❑ 522	(It's Not) Puppy Love/He's Been Leading You On	1964	3.00	6.00	12.00
Paramount					
❑ 0109	We Can Make the World a Whole Lot Brighter/ The End of the Line	1971		2.50	5.00
Montgomery, Bob					
Brunswick					
❑ 55157	Because I Love You/Taste of the Blues	1959	10.00	20.00	40.00
Montgomery, Christopher					
Dolton					
❑ 84	My Paradise/Giants of Bombora	1963	7.50	15.00	30.00
Montgomery, Tammy					
(Later known as Tammi Terrell)					
Checker					
❑ 1072	If I Would Marry You/This Time Tomorrow *Maroon label*	1964	10.00	20.00	40.00
❑ 1072	If I Would Marry You/This Time Tomorrow *Mostly blue label with red and black checkers*	1964	6.25	12.50	25.00
Scepter					
❑ 1224	If You See Bill/It's Mine	1961	15.00	30.00	60.00
Try Me					
❑ 28001	I Cried/If You Don't Think *As "Tana Montgomery"*	1962	7.50	15.00	30.00
Wand					
❑ 123	Voice of Experience/Wancha To Be Sure	1962	7.50	15.00	30.00
Montgomerys, The					
Amy					
❑ 883	Promise of Love/Gotta Make a Hit Record	1963	62.50	125.00	250.00
Moody Blues, The					
Deram					
❑ 85023	Nights in White Satin/Cities *Composer of "Nights in White Satin" listed as "Redwave"*	1968	2.50	5.00	10.00
❑ 85023	Nights in White Satin/Cities *Composer of "Nights in White Satin" listed as "Justin Hayward"*	1968	2.00	4.00	8.00
❑ 85028	Tuesday Afternoon (Forever Afternoon)/ Another Morning	1968	2.00	4.00	8.00
❑ 85033	Ride My See-Saw/Voices in the Sky	1968	2.00	4.00	8.00
❑ 85044	Never Comes the Day/So Deep Within You	1969	2.00	4.00	8.00
London					
❑ 270	Steppin' in a Slide Zone/I'll Be Level with You	1978		2.00	4.00
❑ 273	Driftwood/I'm Your Man	1978		2.50	5.00
❑ 1005	This Is My House (But Nobody Calls)/ Boulevard de la Madelaine	1967	3.00	6.00	12.00
❑ 9726	Go Now!/Lose Your Money *Blue swirl label, "London" in black*	1965	2.00	4.00	8.00
❑ 9726	Go Now!/Lose Your Money *Blue swirl label, "London" in white*	1965	3.00	6.00	12.00

Number		Title (A Side/B Side)	Year	VG	VG+	NM
❑ 9726		Go Now!/Lose Your Money	1965	6.25	12.50	25.00
		White, purple and blue label				
❑ 9764		From the Bottom of My Heart (I Love You)/	1965	3.75	7.50	15.00
		And My Baby's Gone				
❑ 9799		Ev'ry Day/You Don't	1965	3.75	7.50	15.00
❑ 9810		Stop!/Bye Bye Bird	1966	3.75	7.50	15.00
❑ 20030		Fly Me High/I Really Haven't Got the Time	1967	3.00	6.00	12.00

Polydor

Number		Title (A Side/B Side)	Year	VG	VG+	NM
❑ 870 990-7		No More Lies/River of Endless Love	1988			3.00
❑ 870 990-7	PS	No More Lies/River of Endless Love	1988			3.00
❑ 871 270-7		Al Fin Voy a Encontrarte/	1989		2.50	5.00
		I Know You're Out There Somewhere				
❑ 883 906-7		Your Wildest Dreams/Talkin' Talkin'	1986			3.00
❑ 883 906-7	PS	Your Wildest Dreams/Talkin' Talkin'	1986			3.00
❑ 885 201-7		The Other Side of Life/The Spirit	1986		2.50	5.00
		Blue vinyl				
❑ 885 201-7	PS	The Other Side of Life/The Spirit	1986		2.50	5.00
		Special sleeve for blue vinyl version				
❑ 885 212-7		The Other Side of Life/The Spirit	1986			3.00
❑ 885 212-7	PS	The Other Side of Life/The Spirit	1986			3.00
❑ 887 600-7		I Know You're Out There Somewhere/Miracle	1988			3.00
❑ 887 600-7	PS	I Know You're Out There Somewhere/Miracle	1988			3.00
❑ 887 815-7		Here Comes the Weekend/River of Endless Love	1988			3.00

Threshold

Number		Title (A Side/B Side)	Year	VG	VG+	NM
❑ 601		Gemini Dream/Painted Smile	1981		2.00	4.00
❑ 602		The Voice/22,000 Days	1981		2.00	4.00
❑ 602	PS	The Voice/22,000 Days	1981		3.00	6.00
❑ 603		Talking Out of Turn/Veteran Cosmic Rocker	1981		2.00	4.00
❑ 604		Sitting at the Wheel/Going Nowhere	1983		2.00	4.00
❑ 604	PS	Sitting at the Wheel/Going Nowhere	1983		3.00	6.00
❑ 605		Blue World/Sorry	1983		2.00	4.00
❑ 606		Running Water/Under My Feet	1983		2.00	4.00
❑ 67004		Question/Candle of Life	1970		3.00	6.00
❑ 67006		The Story in Your Eyes/Melancholy Man	1971		3.00	6.00
❑ 67006	PS	The Story in Your Eyes/Melancholy Man	1971	3.00	6.00	12.00
❑ 67009		Isn't Life Strange/After You Came	1972		2.50	5.00
❑ 67012		I'm Just a Singer (In a Rock and Roll Band)/	1973		2.50	5.00
		For My Lady				

Moon Beams, The

Grate

Number		Title (A Side/B Side)	Year	VG	VG+	NM
❑ 100		A Lover's Plea/Don't Go Away	1959	37.50	75.00	150.00

Moon, Keith

(Of The Who)

Track

Number		Title (A Side/B Side)	Year	VG	VG+	NM
❑ 40316		Teenage Idol/Don't Worry Baby	1974	3.75	7.50	15.00
❑ 40387		Solid Gold/Move Over Ms. L.	1975	3.75	7.50	15.00
❑ 40435		In My Life/Crazy Like a Fox	1975	3.75	7.50	15.00

Moon, The

(With David Marks, ex-Beach Boys)

Imperial

Number		Title (A Side/B Side)	Year	VG	VG+	NM
❑ 66285		Mothers and Fathers/Someday Girl	1968	7.50	15.00	30.00
❑ 66330		Faces/John Automaton	1968	6.25	12.50	25.00
❑ 66415		Not to Know/Pirate	1969	6.25	12.50	25.00

Moonglows, The

(Also see "Harvey" — also, Marvin Gaye was briefly a member around 1959)

Big P

Number		Title (A Side/B Side)	Year	VG	VG+	NM
❑ 101		Sincerely '72/You've Chosen Me	1972	2.50	5.00	10.00

Champagne

Number		Title (A Side/B Side)	Year	VG	VG+	NM
❑ 7500		I Just Can't Tell No Lie/	1952	300.00	600.00	1,200.
		I've Been Your Dog (Ever Since I've Been Your Man)				

Chance

Number		Title (A Side/B Side)	Year	VG	VG+	NM
❑ 1147		Baby Please/Whistle My Love	1953	250.00	500.00	1,000
		Black vinyl				
❑ 1147		Baby Please/Whistle My Love	1953	500.00	1,000	2,000
		Red vinyl				
❑ 1150		Just a Lonely Christmas/Hey, Santa Claus	1953	375.00	750.00	1,500
		Red vinyl (this may not exist legitimately on black vinyl)				
❑ 1152		Secret Love/Real Gone Mama	1954	375.00	750.00	1,500
		Silver and blue label				
❑ 1152		Secret Love/Real Gone Mama	1954	250.00	500.00	1,000
		Yellow and black label				
❑ 1156		I Was Wrong/Ooh Rockin' Daddy	1954	250.00	500.00	1,000
		Yellow and black label				
❑ 1156		I Was Wrong/Ooh Rockin' Daddy	1954	150.00	300.00	600.00
		Black and white label				
❑ 1161		My Gal/219 Train	1954	500.00	1,000	2,000

Number	Title (A Side/B Side)	Year	VG	VG+	NM

Chess
Values for Chess 1581-1669 are for blue label, silver top originals

❑ 1581	Sincerely/Tempting	1954	15.00	30.00	60.00
❑ 1589	Most of All/She's Gone	1955	15.00	30.00	60.00
❑ 1598	Foolish Me/Slow Down	1955	15.00	30.00	60.00
❑ 1605	Starlite/In Love	1955	15.00	30.00	60.00
❑ 1611	In My Diary/Lover, Love Me	1955	15.00	30.00	60.00
❑ 1619	We Go Together/Chickie Um Bah	1956	12.50	25.00	50.00
❑ 1629	See Saw/When I'm With You	1956	12.50	25.00	50.00
❑ 1646	Over and Over Again/I Knew from the Start	1957	15.00	30.00	60.00

With slower version of A-side; "8189A" is in the run-off area

❑ 1646	Over and Over Again/I Knew from the Start	1957	12.50	25.00	50.00

With normal version of A-side

❑ 1651	I'm Afraid the Masquerade Is Over/Don't Say Goodbye	1957	12.50	25.00	50.00
❑ 1661	Please Send Me Someone to Love/ Mr. Engineer (Bring Her Back to Me)	1957	12.50	25.00	50.00
❑ 1669	The Beating of My Heart/Confess It to Your Heart	1957	12.50	25.00	50.00

In general, for the above singles, the blue label with vertical "Chess" versions are 60% of the above values; yellow early-1960s label versions are 40% of above; and black mid-1960s versions are 40% of above; and blue late-1960s versions, with "Chess" on top, are about 20%.

❑ 1681	Too Late/Here I Am	1958	7.50	15.00	30.00
❑ 1689	In the Middle of the Night/Soda Pop	1958	7.50	15.00	30.00
❑ 1701	This Love/Sweeter Than Words	1958	7.50	15.00	30.00
❑ 1705	Ten Commandments of Love/Mean Old Blues	1958	7.50	15.00	30.00

As "Harvey and the Moonglows"

❑ 1717	Love Is a River/I'll Never Stop Wanting You	1959	6.25	12.50	25.00
❑ 1738	Mama Loocie/Unemployment	1959	6.25	12.50	25.00

As "Harvey and the Moonglows"

❑ 1770	Beatnick/Junior	1960	6.25	12.50	25.00
❑ 1811	Blue Velvet/Penny Arcade	1962	6.25	12.50	25.00

As "Bobby Lester and the Moonglows"

Crimson

❑ 1003	My Imagination/Gee	1964	5.00	10.00	20.00

RCA Victor

❑ 74-0759	Sincerely/I Was Wrong	1972		2.50	5.00
❑ 74-0839	When I'm With You/You've Chosen Me	1972		2.50	5.00

Vee Jay

❑ 423	Secret Love/Real Gone Mama	1962	6.25	12.50	25.00

Moore, Harv
American Arts

❑ 20	Interview of the Fab Four/(B-side unknown)	1964	75.00	150.00	300.00

Moore, Melvin
King

❑ 4539	Possessed/Hold Me, Kiss Me, Squeeze Me	1952	25.00	50.00	100.00

Moore, Scotty
(Of Elvis Presley, Scotty and Bill)
Fernwood

❑ 107	Have Guitar Will Travel/Rest	1958	7.50	15.00	30.00

Morgan, Loumell
Atlantic

❑ 953	Charmaine/Jock-O-Mo	1952	50.00	100.00	200.00

Morissette, Alanis
Maverick

❑ 17644	You Learn/You Oughta Know	1996			3.00

B-side is "Live Grammy Version"

❑ 17698	Ironic/Forgiven (Live)	1996			3.00

Morris, Joe
Atlantic

❑ 914	Any Time, Any Place, Any Where/ Come Back Daddy Daddy	1950	125.00	250.00	500.00

With Laura Tate...Atlantic's earliest number on 45. Morris had numerous 78s on Atlantic before 914, which are not listed here.

❑ 985	I'm Goin' to Leave You/ That's What Makes My Baby Fat	1953	25.00	50.00	100.00
❑ 1160	Going, Going, Gone/Sinner Woman	1957	5.00	10.00	20.00

Herald

❑ 420	Travelin' Man/No, It Can't Be Done	1954	10.00	20.00	40.00

Black vinyl

❑ 420	Travelin' Man/No, It Can't Be Done	1954	20.00	40.00	80.00

Red vinyl

❑ 446	Be Careful/Way Down Yonder	1955	7.50	15.00	30.00

Moses, Johnny
Imperial

❑ 5329	You're Torturing Me/Do You Love Me? Do You?	1955	10.00	20.00	40.00

Number		Title (A Side/B Side)	Year	VG	VG+	NM

Moss, Roy
Fascination
| ☐ 1002 | | Wiggle Walkin' Baby/(B-side unknown) | 1957 | 50.00 | 100.00 | 200.00 |

Mercury
| ☐ 70770 | | You're My Big Baby Now/You Nearly Lost Your Mind | 1955 | 50.00 | 100.00 | 200.00 |
| ☐ 70858 | | Corinne, Corinna/You Don't Know My Mind | 1956 | 50.00 | 100.00 | 200.00 |

Mothers of Invention, The – See "Zappa, Frank"

Motions, The
(Probably more than one group)
ABC-Paramount
| ☐ 10529 | | Big Chief/Where Is Your Heart | 1964 | 3.00 | 6.00 | 12.00 |

Congress
| ☐ 237 | | It's Gone/I've Got Money | 1965 | 3.00 | 6.00 | 12.00 |

Laurie
| ☐ 3112 | | Make Me a Love/Mr. Night | 1961 | 30.00 | 60.00 | 120.00 |

Mercury
☐ 72297		Beatle Drums/Long Hair	1964	6.25	12.50	25.00
☐ 72368		I Can Dance/Land Beyond the Moon	1964	5.00	10.00	20.00
☐ 72413		Bumble Bee '65/Motions	1965	5.00	10.00	20.00

Motley Crue
Elektra
☐ 64985		Without You/Slice of Your Pie	1990			3.00
☐ 69248		Kickstart My Heart/She Goes Down	1990			3.00
☐ 69271		Dr. Feelgood/Sticky Sweet	1989			3.00
☐ 69271	PS	Dr. Feelgood/Sticky Sweet	1989			3.00
☐ 69429		You're All I Need/All in the Name	1987			3.00
☐ 69449		Wild Side/Five Years Dead	1987			3.00
☐ 69449	PS	Wild Side/Five Years Dead	1987			3.00
☐ 69465		Girls, Girls, Girls/Sumthin' for Nuthin'	1987			3.00
☐ 69465	PS	Girls, Girls, Girls/Sumthin' for Nuthin'	1987			3.00
☐ 69591		Home Sweet Home/Red Hot	1985		2.00	4.00
☐ 69625		Smokin' in the Boys' Room/Use It or Lose It	1985		2.00	4.00
☐ 69625	PS	Smokin' in the Boys' Room/Use It or Lose It	1985		2.00	4.00
☐ 69732		Too Young to Fall in Love/Take Me to the Top	1984		2.50	5.00
☐ 69732	PS	Too Young to Fall in Love/Take Me to the Top	1984		2.50	5.00
☐ 69756		Looks That Kill/Piece of Your Action	1984		2.50	5.00
☐ 69756	PS	Looks That Kill/Piece of Your Action	1984		2.50	5.00

Leathur
| ☐ 001 | | Stick to Your Guns/Toast of the Town | 1981 | 20.00 | 40.00 | 80.00 |
| ☐ 001 | PS | Stick to Your Guns/Toast of the Town | 1981 | 37.50 | 75.00 | 150.00 |

Mourning Reign, The
Contour
| ☐ 601 | | Evil Hearted You/Get Out of My Life, Woman | 1967 | 6.25 | 12.50 | 25.00 |

Link
☐ 1		Satisfaction Guaranteed/Our Fate	1966	7.50	15.00	30.00
☐ 1	PS	Satisfaction Guaranteed/Our Fate	1966	150.00	300.00	600.00
☐ 2		Evil Hearted You/Get Out of My Life, Woman	1966	7.50	15.00	30.00

Mouse and the Traps
Capitol
| ☐ 2460 | | Streets of a Dusty Town/Mouse | 1969 | 2.50 | 5.00 | 10.00 |

Fraternity
☐ 956		A Public Execution/All for You	1966	5.00	10.00	20.00
☐ 966		Mad of Sugar/I Am the One	1966	3.75	7.50	15.00
☐ 971		Would You Believe/Like I Know You Do	1966	3.75	7.50	15.00
☐ 973		Promises, Promises/Do the Best You Can	1966	3.75	7.50	15.00
☐ 989		Ya Ya/Cryin' Inside	1967	3.75	7.50	15.00
☐ 1000		Beg, Borrow, and Steal/L.O.V.E. Love	1967	3.75	7.50	15.00
☐ 1005		Sometimes You Just Can't Win/Cryin' Inside	1968	3.75	7.50	15.00
☐ 1005	PS	Sometimes You Just Can't Win/Cryin' Inside	1968	20.00	40.00	80.00
☐ 1011		I Satisfy/Good Times	1968	3.75	7.50	15.00
☐ 1015		Look at the Sun/Requiem for Sarah	1968	3.75	7.50	15.00

Move, The
(Evolved into Electric Light Orchestra. Also see "Wood, Roy")
A&M
☐ 884		Flowers in the Rain/(Here We Go Round the) Lemon Tree	1967	3.00	6.00	12.00
☐ 914		Walk Upon the Water/Fire Brigade	1968	3.75	7.50	15.00
☐ 966		Yellow Rainbow/Something	1968	3.00	6.00	12.00
☐ 1020		Blackberry Way/Something	1969	3.00	6.00	12.00
☐ 1119		This Time Tomorrow/Curly	1969	3.00	6.00	12.00
☐ 1197		Brontosaurus/Lightning Never Strikes Twice	1970	3.00	6.00	12.00
☐ 1239		When Alice Comes Back to the Farm/What?	1971	3.00	6.00	12.00
☐ 1546		Zing Went the Strings of My Heart/Wild Tiger Woman	1974	2.50	5.00	10.00

Capitol
| ☐ 3126 | | Tonight/Don't Mess Me Up | 1971 | 5.00 | 10.00 | 20.00 |

Deram
| ☐ 7504 | | The Disturbance/Night of Fear | 1967 | 3.75 | 7.50 | 15.00 |

Number		Title (A Side/B Side)	Year	VG	VG+	NM
❏ 7506		I Can Hear the Grass Grow/ Wave the Flag and Stop the Train	1967	3.75	7.50	15.00

MGM

| ❏ 14332 | DJ | Chinatown/Down by the Bay
Evidently not released as stock copy | 1971 | 5.00 | 10.00 | 20.00 |

United Artists

❏ XW202		Tonight/My Marge	1973		3.00	6.00
❏ 50876		Chinatown/Down on the Bay	1972	2.00	4.00	8.00
❏ 50928		Do Ya/California Man	1972	2.00	4.00	8.00

Moving Sidewalks, The
(With Billy Gibbons, later of ZZ Top)

Tantara

❏ 3101		99th Floor/What Are You Going to Do	1967	10.00	20.00	40.00
❏ 3103		I Want to Hold Your Hand/Joe Blues	1968	10.00	20.00	40.00
❏ 3113		Flashback/(B-side unknown)	1969	7.50	15.00	30.00

Wand

| ❏ 1156 | | 99th Floor/What Are You Going to Do | 1967 | 6.25 | 12.50 | 25.00 |
| ❏ 1167 | | Need Me/Every Night a New Surprise | 1968 | 6.25 | 12.50 | 25.00 |

Mudcrutch
(Early Tom Petty and the Heartbreakers)

Pepper

| ❏ 9449 | | Up in Mississippi/Cause Is Understood | 1971 | 100.00 | 200.00 | 400.00 |

Shelter

| ❏ 40357 | | Depot Street/Wild Eyes | 1975 | 7.50 | 15.00 | 30.00 |

Mudslinger, Roger

Red Bird

| ❏ 10-013 | | The Election Year 1964 (Part 1)/
The Election Year 1964 (Part 2) | 1964 | 5.00 | 10.00 | 20.00 |

Mugwumps, The
(Denny Doherty, Cass Elliott, John Sebastian and Zal Yanovsky all were in this group)

Sidewalk

| ❏ 900 | | Bald Headed Woman/Jug Band Music | 1966 | 6.25 | 12.50 | 25.00 |
| ❏ 909 | | Season of the Witch/My Gal | 1967 | 5.00 | 10.00 | 20.00 |

Warner Bros.

| ❏ 5471 | | I'll Remember Tonight/I Don't Wanna Know | 1964 | 3.75 | 7.50 | 15.00 |
| ❏ 7018 | | Searchin'/Here It Is, Another Day | 1967 | 2.50 | 5.00 | 10.00 |

Mulberry Fruit Band, The

Buddah

| ❏ 1 | | Yes, We Have No Bananas/The Audition | 1967 | 3.00 | 6.00 | 12.00 |

Multiplication Rock (Soundtrack)

Capitol

| ❏ 3693 | | Naughty Number Nine/I Got Six | 1973 | 3.75 | 7.50 | 15.00 |

Murmaids, The

Chattahoochie

❏ 628		Popsicles and Icicles/Blue Dress	1963	5.00	10.00	20.00
❏ 628		Popsicles and Icicles/Huntington Flats	1963	3.75	7.50	15.00
❏ 628		Popsicles and Icicles/Bunny Stomp	1963	3.75	7.50	15.00
❏ 628		Popsicles and Icicles/Comedy and Tragedy	1963	3.75	7.50	15.00
❏ 636		Heartbreak Ahead/He's Good to Me	1964	2.50	5.00	10.00
❏ 641		Wild and Wonderful/Bull Talk	1964	2.50	5.00	10.00
❏ 668		Stuffed Animals/Little White Lies	1965	2.50	5.00	10.00
❏ 711		Little Boys/Go Away	1966	2.50	5.00	10.00

Liberty

| ❏ 56069 | | Paper Sun/Song Through Perception | 1968 | | | *Unreleased* |
| ❏ 56078 | | Paper Sun/Song Through Perception | 1968 | 2.50 | 5.00 | 10.00 |

Murphy, Keith, and the Daze

King

| ❏ 6171 | | Dirty Ol' Sam/Slightly Reminiscent of Her | 1968 | 25.00 | 50.00 | 100.00 |

Murray The "K"

BRS

| ❏ 1/2 | | Murray the "K" and The Beatles As It Happened | 1964 | 10.00 | 20.00 | 40.00 |
| ❏ 1/2 | PS | Murray the "K" and The Beatles As It Happened | 1964 | 30.00 | 60.00 | 120.00 |

IBC

| ❏ F4KM-0082/3 | | Murray the "K" and The Beatles As It Happened | 1976 | 2.50 | 5.00 | 10.00 |
| ❏ F4KM-0082/3 | PS | Murray the "K" and The Beatles As It Happened | 1976 | 2.50 | 5.00 | 10.00 |

Red Bird

| ❏ 10-045 | | It's What's Happening, Baby/Sins of a Family | 1966 | 3.75 | 7.50 | 15.00 |

Murray, Ray, and the Dynamics

Arbo

| ❏ 222 | | With All My Love/Baby, What You Want Me to Do | 1960 | 25.00 | 50.00 | 100.00 |

Number		Title (A Side/B Side)	Year	VG	VG+	NM

Music Explosion, The
Attack
| ☐ 1404 | | The Little Black Egg/Stay By My Side | 1966 | 6.25 | 12.50 | 25.00 |

Laurie
☐ 3380		Little Bit O'Soul/I See the Light	1967	3.00	6.00	12.00
☐ 3400		Can't Stop Now/Sunshine Games	1967	2.00	4.00	8.00
☐ 3414		We Gotta Go Home/Hearts and Flowers	1967	2.00	4.00	8.00
☐ 3429		What You Want/Road Runner	1968	2.00	4.00	8.00
☐ 3440		Where Are We Going/Flash	1968	2.00	4.00	8.00
☐ 3454		Yes Sir/Dazzling	1968	2.00	4.00	8.00
☐ 3466		Jack in the Box/Rewind	1968	2.00	4.00	8.00
☐ 3479		What's Your Name/Call Me Anything	1969	2.00	4.00	8.00
☐ 3500		The Little Black Egg/Stay By My Side	1969	2.00	4.00	8.00

Music Machine, The
Bell
| ☐ 764 | | Mother Nature--Father Earth/Advise and Consent | 1969 | 2.00 | 4.00 | 8.00 |

Original Sound
☐ 61		Talk Talk/Come On In	1966	3.00	6.00	12.00
☐ 67		The People in Me/Masculine Institution	1967	2.50	5.00	10.00
☐ 71		Double Yellow Line/Absolutely Positive	1967	2.50	5.00	10.00
☐ 75		I've Loved You/The Eagle Never Hunts the Fly	1967	2.50	5.00	10.00
☐ 82		Hey Joe/Wrong	1968	2.50	5.00	10.00

Warner Bros.
☐ 7093		Bottom of the Soul/Astrologically Incompatible	1968	2.00	4.00	8.00
☐ 7093	PS	Bottom of the Soul/Astrologically Incompatible	1968	3.75	7.50	15.00
☐ 7199		To the Light/You'll Love Me Again	1968	2.00	4.00	8.00

Myddle Class, The
Buddah
| ☐ 150 | | I Happen to Love You/Don't Let Me Sleep Too Long | 1969 | 2.50 | 5.00 | 10.00 |

Tomorrow
☐ 7501		Gates of Eden/Free As the Wind	1966	5.00	10.00	20.00
☐ 7503		I Happen to Love You/Don't Let Me Sleep Too Long	1966	6.25	12.50	25.00
☐ 912		Don't Look Back/Wind Chimes Laughter	1966	5.00	10.00	20.00

Myles, Billy
Dot
| ☐ 15809 | | King of Clowns/So In Need of You | 1958 | 5.00 | 10.00 | 20.00 |

Ember
☐ 1026		The Joker (That's What They Call Me)/Honey Bee	1957	7.50	15.00	30.00
☐ 1040		Price of Your Love/I'm Too Sentimental	1958	6.25	12.50	25.00
☐ 1046		I'm Gonna Walk/Price of Your Love	1958	6.25	12.50	25.00

King
| ☐ 5395 | | Dance Little Girlie/Two Empty Arms | 1960 | 3.75 | 7.50 | 15.00 |

Mystery Tour, The
MGM
| ☐ 14097 | | The Ballad of Paul/The Ballad of Paul (Follow the Bouncing Ball) | 1969 | 6.25 | 12.50 | 25.00 |

Mystics, The
(More than one group)
Ambient Sound
| ☐ 02871 | | Now That Summer Is Here/Prayer to An Angel | 1982 | | 2.50 | 5.00 |

Black Cat
| ☐ 101 | | Snoopy/Ooh Poo Pah Doo | 1966 | 10.00 | 20.00 | 40.00 |

Constellation
| ☐ 138 | | She's Got Everything/Just a Loser | 1964 | 3.00 | 6.00 | 12.00 |

Dot
| ☐ 16862 | | Now and For Always/Didn't We Have a Good Time | 1966 | 2.50 | 5.00 | 10.00 |

King
| ☐ 5678 | | Mashed Potatoes With Me/The Hoppy Hop | 1962 | 3.75 | 7.50 | 15.00 |
| ☐ 5735 | | The Jumpin' Bean/Just For Your Love | 1963 | 3.75 | 7.50 | 15.00 |

Laurie
☐ 3028	M	Hushabye/Adam and Eve	1959	7.50	15.00	30.00
☐ S-3028	S	Hushabye/Adam and Eve	1959	37.50	75.00	150.00
☐ 3038		Don't Take the Stars/So Tenderly	1959	6.25	12.50	25.00
☐ 3047		All Through the Night/To Think of You Again	1960	6.25	12.50	25.00
☐ 3058		White Cliffs of Dover/Blue Star	1960	6.25	12.50	25.00
☐ 3086		Star Crossed Lovers/Goodbye Mr. Blue	1961	6.25	12.50	25.00
☐ 3104		Sunday Kind of Love/Darling I Know How	1961	7.50	15.00	30.00

Nolta
| ☐ 353 | | The Fox/Dan | 1963 | 3.75 | 7.50 | 15.00 |

N

Nabay
Impact
| ☐ 1032 | | Believe It or Not/(Instrumental) | 1967 | 100.00 | 200.00 | 400.00 |

Number		Title (A Side/B Side)	Year	VG	VG+	NM

Napoleon XIV
Warner Bros.

❏ 5831		They're Coming to Take Me Away, Ha-Haaa!/	1966	3.00	6.00	12.00
		!Aaah-Ah, Yawa Em Ekat ot Gnimoc Er'yeht				
❏ 5853		I'm in Love with My Little Red Tricycle/	1966	2.50	5.00	10.00
		Doin' the Napoleon				
❏ 7726		They're Coming to Take Me Away, Ha-Haaa!/	1973	2.00	4.00	8.00
		!Aaah-Ah, Yawa Em Ekat ot Gnimoc Er'yeht				

Nash, Johnny
(Also see "Anka, Paul-George Hamilton IV-Johnny Nash")
ABC-Paramount

❏ 9743		Out of Town/A Teenager Sings the Blues	1956	5.00	10.00	20.00
❏ 9844		The Ladder of Love/I'll Walk Alone	1957	5.00	10.00	20.00
❏ 9874		A Very Special Love/	1957	5.00	10.00	20.00
		Won't You Let Me Share My Love with You				
❏ 9894		My Pledge to You/It's So Easy to Say	1958	5.00	10.00	20.00
❏ 9927		Please Don't Go/I Lost My Love Last Night	1958	5.00	10.00	20.00
❏ 9942		Truly Love/You're Looking at Me	1958	5.00	10.00	20.00
❏ 9960		Almost in Your Arms/Midnight Moonlight	1958	5.00	10.00	20.00
❏ 9989		Roots of Heaven/Walk with Faith in Your Heart	1958	5.00	10.00	20.00
❏ 9996		As Time Goes By/The Voice of Love	1959	5.00	10.00	20.00
❏ 9996	PS	As Time Goes By/The Voice of Love	1959	10.00	20.00	40.00
❏ 10026		And the Angels Sing/Baby, Baby, Baby	1959	5.00	10.00	20.00
❏ 10046		Take a Giant Step/But Not for Me	1959	5.00	10.00	20.00
❏ 10060		The Wish/Too Proud	1959	5.00	10.00	20.00
❏ 10076		A Place in the Sun/Goodbye	1960	3.75	7.50	15.00
❏ 10095		Never My Love/(You've Got the) Love I Love	1960	3.75	7.50	15.00
❏ 10112		Let the Rest of the World Go By/Music of Love	1960	3.75	7.50	15.00
❏ 10137		(Looks Like) The End of the World/We Kissed	1960	3.75	7.50	15.00
❏ 10160		Kisses/Somebody	1960	3.75	7.50	15.00
❏ 10181		World of Tears/Some of Your Lovin'	1961	3.00	6.00	12.00
❏ 10205		I Need Someone to Stand By/A House on the Hill	1961	3.00	6.00	12.00
❏ 10212		A Thousand Miles Away/	1961	3.00	6.00	12.00
		I Need Someone to Stand By Me				
❏ 10230		I'm Counting on You/I Lost My Baby	1961	3.00	6.00	12.00
❏ 10251		Too Much Love/Love's Young Dream	1961	3.00	6.00	12.00

Argo

❏ 5471		Talk to Me/Love Ain't Nothin'	1964	2.00	4.00	8.00
❏ 5479		Then You Can Tell Me Goodbye/Always	1964	2.00	4.00	8.00
❏ 5492		Spring Is Here/Strange Feeling	1965	2.00	4.00	8.00
❏ 5501		Teardrops in the Rain/I Know What I Want	1965	2.00	4.00	8.00

Atlantic

❏ 2344		Big City/Somewhere	1966	2.00	4.00	8.00

Cadet

❏ 5528		Teardrops in the Rain/Get Myself Together	1966	5.00	10.00	20.00

Epic

❏ 10873		Stir It Up/Cream Puff	1972		3.50	7.00
❏ 10902		I Can See Clearly Now/How Good It Is	1972		3.00	6.00
❏ 10949		Stir It Up/Ooh Baby You've Been Good to Me	1973		3.00	6.00
❏ 11003		My Merry-Go-Round/	1973		2.50	5.00
		We're Trying to Get Back to You				
❏ 11034		Ooh What a Feeling/Yellow House	1973		2.50	5.00
❏ 11070		Loving You/Gonna Open Up My Heart Again	1973		2.50	5.00
❏ 50021		You Can't Go Halfway/The Very First Time	1974		2.50	5.00
❏ 50051		Beautiful Baby/Celebrate Life	1974		2.50	5.00
❏ 50091		Good Vibrations/The Very First Time	1975		2.50	5.00
❏ 50138		Tears on My Pillow (I Can't Take It)/Beautiful Baby	1975		2.50	5.00
❏ 50219		(What a) Wonderful World/	1976		2.50	5.00
		Rock It Baby (We've Got a Date)				
❏ 50386		Back in Time/That Woman	1977		2.00	4.00
❏ 50737		Closer/Mr. Sea	1979		2.00	4.00
❏ 50821		You're the One/Don't Forget	1980		2.00	4.00

Groove

❏ 58-0018		Helpless/I've Got a Lot to Offer, Darling	1963	2.50	5.00	10.00
❏ 58-0021		Deep in the Heart of Harlem/What Kind of Love Is This	1963	10.00	20.00	40.00
❏ 58-0026		It's No Good for Me/Town of Lonely Hearts	1963	2.50	5.00	10.00
❏ 58-0030		I'm Leaving/Oh Mary Don't You Weep	1964	2.50	5.00	10.00

Jad

❏ 207		Hold Me Tight/Cupid	1968	2.00	4.00	8.00
❏ 209		You Got Soul/Don't Cry	1968	2.00	4.00	8.00
❏ 214		Lovey Dovey/You Got Soul	1969		3.00	6.00
❏ 215		Sweet Charity/People in Love	1969		3.00	6.00
❏ 218		Love and Peace/People in Love	1969		3.00	6.00
❏ 220		Cupid/Hold Me Tight	1969		3.00	6.00
❏ 223		What a Groovy Feeling/You Got Soul (Part 1)	1970		3.00	6.00

Janus

❏ 136		Falling In and Out of Love/	1970		3.00	6.00
		You've Got to Change Your Ways				

JoDa

❏ 102		Let's Move and Groove (Together)/Understanding	1965	2.50	5.00	10.00
❏ 105		One More Time/Got to Find Her	1965	2.50	5.00	10.00
❏ 106		Somewhere/Big City	1966	2.50	5.00	10.00

MGM

❏ 13637		Amen/Perfumed Flower	1966	2.00	4.00	8.00

Number		Title (A Side/B Side)	Year	VG	VG+	NM
☐ 13683		Good Goodness/You Never Know	1967	2.00	4.00	8.00
☐ 13805		Stormy/(I'm So) Glad You're My Baby	1967	2.00	4.00	8.00

Warner Bros.

☐ 5270		Don't Take Your Love Away/Moment of Weakness	1962	3.00	6.00	12.00
☐ 5301		Ol' Man River/My Dear Little Sweetheart	1962	3.00	6.00	12.00
☐ 5336		Cigarettes, Whiskey and Wild, Wild Women/ I'm Movin' On	1963	3.00	6.00	12.00

Nashville Teens, The
London

☐ 9689		Tobacco Road/I Like It Like That	1964	3.75	7.50	15.00
☐ 9712		T.N.T./Google Eyes	1964	3.00	6.00	12.00
☐ 9736		Devil-in-Law/Find My Way Back Home	1965	3.00	6.00	12.00

MGM

☐ 13357		Little Bird/Whatcha Gonna Do	1965	2.50	5.00	10.00
☐ 13406		I Know How It Feels to Be Loved/Soon Forgotten	1965	2.50	5.00	10.00
☐ 13483		The Hard Way/Upside Down	1966	2.50	5.00	10.00
☐ 13678		That's My Woman/Words	1967	2.50	5.00	10.00

United Artists

☐ 50880		Tennessee/Ella James	1972	5.00	10.00	20.00

Nature Boy & Friends
Bertram Int'l.

☐ 255		Surfer John/John John	1964	10.00	20.00	40.00

Nazz, The
(The SCG group features Todd Rundgren; the Very group features Alice Cooper)
SGC

☐ 001		Hello It's Me/Open My Eyes	1969	5.00	10.00	20.00
		First pressing: Light yellow label, no horizontal lines on label				
☐ 001		Hello It's Me/Open My Eyes	1969	3.00	6.00	12.00
		Second pressing: Darker yellow label with horizontal lines				
☐ 001		Hello It's Me/Open My Eyes	1969	2.00	4.00	8.00
		Third printing: Mostly green label with some yellow. Red vinyl copies on any label are bootlegs.				
☐ 001	PS	Hello It's Me/Open My Eyes	1969	5.00	10.00	20.00
		Legitimate sleeves are paper, not cardboard				
☐ 006		Not Wrong Long/Under the Ice	1969	3.00	6.00	12.00
☐ 006	PS	Not Wrong Long/Under the Ice	1969	5.00	10.00	20.00
☐ 009		Magic Me/Kicks	1970	6.25	12.50	25.00
☐ 009		Magic Me/Some People	1970	3.00	6.00	12.00

Very

☐ 001		Lay Down and Die, Goodbye/ Wonder Who's Loving Her Now	1967	1,000	1,500	2,000

Neal, Jerry
Dot

☐ 15810		I Hates Rabbits/Scratchin'	1958	20.00	40.00	80.00
		With Eddie Cochran on guitar on B-side				

Ned and Gary
Liberty

☐ 55160		Lovin'/I Bust My Seams	1958	15.00	30.00	60.00

Ned and Nelda
(Frank Zappa and Ray Collins)
Vigah

☐ 002		Hey Nelda/Surf Along	1963	37.50	75.00	150.00

Neil and Jack
(Neil Diamond and Jack Parker)
Duel

☐ 508		What Will I Do/You Are My Love at Last	1962	100.00	200.00	400.00
☐ 517		I'm Afraid/Till You've Tried Love	1962	100.00	200.00	400.00

Nelson, Ricky
Capitol

☐ 4962		Almost Saturday Night/The Loser Babe Is You	1981		2.50	5.00
☐ 4974		Call It What You Want/It Hasn't Happened Yet	1981		2.50	5.00
☐ 4988		Believe What You Say/The Loser Babe Is You	1981		2.50	5.00
☐ B-5178		No Fair Falling in Love/Give 'Em My Number	1982		2.50	5.00

Decca

☐ 31475		You Don't Love Me Anymore (And I Can Tell)/ I Got a Woman	1963	3.75	7.50	15.00
☐ 31475	PS	You Don't Love Me Anymore (And I Can Tell)/ I Got a Woman	1963	7.50	15.00	30.00
☐ 31495		String Along/Gypsy Woman	1963	3.75	7.50	15.00
☐ 31495	PS	String Along/Gypsy Woman	1963	7.50	15.00	30.00
☐ 31533		Fools Rush In/Down Home	1963	3.75	7.50	15.00
☐ 31533	PS	Fools Rush In/Down Home	1963	7.50	15.00	30.00
☐ 31574		For You/That's All She Wrote	1963	3.75	7.50	15.00
☐ 31574	PS	For You/That's All She Wrote	1963	7.50	15.00	30.00
☐ 31612		The Very Thought of You/ I Wonder (If Your Love Will Ever Belong to Me)	1964	3.00	6.00	12.00

Number		Title (A Side/B Side)	Year	VG	VG+	NM
❑ 31612	PS	The Very Thought of You/	1964	7.50	15.00	30.00
		I Wonder (If Your Love Will Ever Belong to Me)				
❑ 31656		There's Nothing I Can Say/Lonely Corner	1964	3.00	6.00	12.00
❑ 31656	PS	There's Nothing I Can Say/Lonely Corner	1964	7.50	15.00	30.00
❑ 31703		A Happy Guy/Don't Breathe a Word	1964	3.00	6.00	12.00
❑ 31703	PS	A Happy Guy/Don't Breathe a Word	1964	7.50	15.00	30.00
❑ 31756		Mean Old World/When the Chips Are Down	1965	3.00	6.00	12.00
❑ 31756	PS	Mean Old World/When the Chips Are Down	1965	7.50	15.00	30.00
❑ 31800		Yesterday's Love/Come Out Dancin'	1965	3.00	6.00	12.00
❑ 31845		Love and Kisses/Say You Love Me	1965	3.00	6.00	12.00
❑ 31900		Your Kind of Lovin'/Fire Breathin' Dragon	1966	3.00	6.00	12.00
❑ 31956		Louisiana Man/You Just Can't Quit	1966	3.00	6.00	12.00
❑ 32026		Alone/The Things You Gave Me	1966	3.00	6.00	12.00
❑ 32055		They Don't Give Medals (To Yesterday's Heroes)/	1966	3.00	6.00	12.00
		Take a Broken Heart				
❑ 32120		I'm Called Lonely/Take a City Bride	1967	2.50	5.00	10.00
❑ 32176		Moonshine/Suzanne on a Sunday Morning	1967	2.50	5.00	10.00
❑ 32222		Dream Weaver/Baby Close Your Eyes	1967	2.50	5.00	10.00
❑ 32284		Don't Blame It on Your Wife/Promenade in Green	1968	2.50	5.00	10.00
❑ 32298		Barefoot Boy/Don't Make Promises	1968	2.50	5.00	10.00
❑ 32550		She Belongs to Me/Promises	1969	2.00	4.00	8.00
❑ 32635		Easy to Be Free/Come On In	1970	2.00	4.00	8.00
❑ 32635	PS	Easy to Be Free/Come On In	1970	3.75	7.50	15.00
❑ 32676		If You Gotta Go, Go Now/I Shall Be Released	1970	2.00	4.00	8.00
❑ 32711		Look at Mary/We Got Such a Long Way to Go	1970	2.00	4.00	8.00
❑ 32739		How Long/Down Along the Bayou Country	1970	2.00	4.00	8.00
❑ 32779		California/Life	1971		3.00	6.00
❑ 32860		Thank You Lord/Sing Me a Song	1971		3.00	6.00
❑ 32906		Love Minus Zero-No Limit/Gypsy Pilot	1971		3.00	6.00
❑ 32980		Garden Party/So Long Mama	1972		3.00	6.00
❑ 34193	S	titles unknown	1963	25.00	50.00	100.00
❑ 34194	S	Pick Up the Pieces/Every Time I See You Smilin'	1963	25.00	50.00	100.00
❑ 34195	S	titles unknown	1963	25.00	50.00	100.00
❑ 34196	S	Let's Talk the Whole Thing Over/I Got a Woman	1963	25.00	50.00	100.00
❑ 34197	S	I Will Follow You/What Comes Next	1963	25.00	50.00	100.00

The above five singles play at 33 1/3 rpm and were intended for jukebox use. The set came with the below packaging:

Number		Title (A Side/B Side)	Year	VG	VG+	NM
❑ 34193/7	PS	Envelope, bonus photo and intact jukebox title strips	1963	25.00	50.00	100.00
		for above 5 singles				

Epic

Number		Title (A Side/B Side)	Year	VG	VG+	NM
❑ 06066		Dream Lover/Rave On	1986		2.00	4.00
❑ 06066	PS	Dream Lover/Rave On	1986		2.00	4.00
❑ 50458		It's Another Day/You Can't Dance	1977		2.50	5.00
❑ 50501		Gimme A Little Sign/Something You Can't Buy	1978		2.50	5.00
❑ 50674		Dream Lover/	1979		2.50	5.00
		That Ain't the Way Love's Supposed to Be				

Imperial

Number		Title (A Side/B Side)	Year	VG	VG+	NM
❑ 5463		Be-Bop Baby/Have I Told You Lately That I Love You	1957	10.00	20.00	40.00
		Red label				
❑ 5463		Be-Bop Baby/Have I Told You Lately That I Love You	1957	6.25	12.50	25.00
		Black label				
❑ 5463	PS	Be-Bop Baby/Have I Told You Lately That I Love You	1957	12.50	25.00	50.00
❑ 5483		Stood Up/Waitin' in School	1957	10.00	20.00	40.00
		Red label				
❑ 5483		Stood Up/Waitin' in School	1957	6.25	12.50	25.00
		Black label				
❑ 5483	PS	Stood Up/Waitin' in School	1957	10.00	20.00	40.00
❑ 5503		Believe What You Say/My Bucket's Got a Hole in It	1958	6.25	12.50	25.00
❑ 5503	PS	Believe What You Say/My Bucket's Got a Hole in It	1958	10.00	20.00	40.00
❑ 5528		Poor Little Fool/Don't Leave Me This Way	1958	6.25	12.50	25.00
❑ 5545		Lonesome Town/I Got a Feeling	1958	150.00	300.00	600.00
		Red vinyl				
❑ 5545		Lonesome Town/I Got a Feeling	1958	6.25	12.50	25.00
❑ 5545	PS	Lonesome Town/I Got a Feeling	1958	10.00	20.00	40.00
❑ 5565		Never Be Anyone Else But You/It's Late	1959	6.25	12.50	25.00
❑ 5565	PS	Never Be Anyone Else But You/It's Late	1959	12.50	25.00	50.00
❑ 5595		Just a Little Too Much/Sweeter Than You	1959	6.25	12.50	25.00
❑ 5595	PS	Just a Little Too Much/Sweeter Than You	1959	10.00	20.00	40.00
❑ 5614		I Wanna Be Loved/Mighty Good	1959	5.00	10.00	20.00
❑ 5614	PS	I Wanna Be Loved/Mighty Good	1959	10.00	20.00	40.00
❑ 5663		Young Emotions/Right By My Side	1960	5.00	10.00	20.00
❑ 5663	PS	Young Emotions/Right By My Side	1960	10.00	20.00	40.00
❑ 5685		I'm Not Afraid/Yes Sir, That's My Baby	1960	5.00	10.00	20.00
❑ 5685	PS	I'm Not Afraid/Yes Sir, That's My Baby	1960	10.00	20.00	40.00
❑ 5707		You Are the Only One/Milk Cow Blues	1960	5.00	10.00	20.00
❑ 5707	PS	You Are the Only One/Milk Cow Blues	1960	10.00	20.00	40.00
❑ 5741		Travelin' Man/Hello Mary Lou	1961	150.00	300.00	600.00
		Red vinyl				
❑ 5741		Travelin' Man/Hello Mary Lou	1961	5.00	10.00	20.00
❑ 5741	PS	Travelin' Man/Hello Mary Lou	1961	7.50	15.00	30.00

Starting with 5770, Imperial singles by "Rick Nelson"

Number		Title (A Side/B Side)	Year	VG	VG+	NM
❑ 5770		A Wonder Like You/Everlovin'	1961	5.00	10.00	20.00
❑ 5770	PS	A Wonder Like You/Everlovin'	1961	7.50	15.00	30.00
❑ 5805		Young World/Summertime	1962	5.00	10.00	20.00
❑ 5805	PS	Young World/Summertime	1962	7.50	15.00	30.00

Number		Title (A Side/B Side)	Year	VG	VG+	NM
☐ 5864		Teen Age Idol/I've Got My Eyes on You	1962	5.00	10.00	20.00
☐ 5864	PS	Teen Age Idol/I've Got My Eyes on You	1962	7.50	15.00	30.00
☐ 5901		It's Up to You/I Need You	1962	5.00	10.00	20.00
☐ 5901	PS	It's Up to You/I Need You	1962	7.50	15.00	30.00
☐ 5910		That's All/I'm in Love Again	1963	6.25	12.50	25.00
☐ 5935		Old Enough to Love/If You Can't Rock Me	1963	5.00	10.00	20.00
☐ 5935	PS	Old Enough to Love/If You Can't Rock Me	1963	7.50	15.00	30.00
☐ 5958		A Long Vacation/Mad Mad World	1963	75.00	150.00	300.00
		Red vinyl				
☐ 5958		A Long Vacation/Mad Mad World	1963	5.00	10.00	20.00
☐ 5985		Time After Time/There's Not a Minute	1963	5.00	10.00	20.00
☐ 66004		Today's Teardrops/Thank You Darlin'	1963	3.75	7.50	15.00
☐ 66004	PS	Today's Teardrops/Thank You Darlin'	1963	7.50	15.00	30.00
☐ 66017		Congratulations/One Minute to One	1964	3.75	7.50	15.00
☐ 66039		Everybody But Me/Lucky Star	1964	3.75	7.50	15.00

MCA

Number		Title (A Side/B Side)	Year	VG	VG+	NM
☐ 40001		Palace Guard/A Flower Opens Gently By	1973		3.00	6.00
☐ 40130		Evil Woman Child/Lifestream	1973		3.00	6.00
☐ 40187		Windfall/Legacy	1974		3.00	6.00
☐ 40214		One Night Stand/Lifestream	1974		3.00	6.00
☐ 40392		Louisiana Belle/Try (Try to Fall in Love)	1975		3.00	6.00
☐ 40458		Rock and Roll Lady/Fadeaway	1975		3.00	6.00
☐ 52781		You Know What I Mean/Don't Leave Me This Way	1986		2.50	5.00
☐ 52781	PS	You Know What I Mean/Don't Leave Me This Way	1986		2.50	5.00

United Artists

0071 through 0080 are "Silver Spotlight Series" reissues

Number		Title (A Side/B Side)	Year	VG	VG+	NM
☐ 0071		Be-Bop Baby/Stood Up	1973		2.50	5.00
☐ 0072		Lonesome Town/It's Up to You	1973		2.50	5.00
☐ 0073		Poor Little Fool/My Bucket's Got a Hole in It	1973		2.50	5.00
☐ 0074		Travelin' Man/Believe What You Say	1973		2.50	5.00
☐ 0075		Teen Age Idol/Young Emotions	1973		2.50	5.00
☐ 0076		Never Be Anyone Else But You/That's All	1973		2.50	5.00
☐ 0077		Young World/It's Late	1973		2.50	5.00
☐ 0078		Just a Little Too Much/Waitin' in School	1973		2.50	5.00
☐ 0079		Hello Mary Lou/Sweeter Than You	1973		2.50	5.00
☐ 0080		A Wonder Like You/Everlovin'	1973		2.50	5.00

Verve

Number		Title (A Side/B Side)	Year	VG	VG+	NM
☐ 10047		I'm Walkin'/A Teenager's Romance	1957	12.50	25.00	50.00
		Orange and yellow label				
☐ 10047		I'm Walkin'/A Teenager's Romance	1957	10.00	20.00	40.00
		Black and white label				
☐ 10070		You're My One and Only Love/Honey Rock	1957	10.00	20.00	40.00
		B-side by Barney Kessel				

Nelson, Sandy

Imperial

Number	Title (A Side/B Side)	Year	VG	VG+	NM
☐ 5630	Drum Party/Big Noise from Winnetka	1959	3.00	6.00	12.00
☐ 5648	Party Time/The Wiggle	1960	3.00	6.00	12.00
☐ 5672	Bouncy/Lost Dreams	1960	3.00	6.00	12.00
☐ 5708	Cool Operator/Jive Talk	1960	3.00	6.00	12.00
☐ 5745	Big Noise from the Jungle/Get With It	1961	3.00	6.00	12.00
☐ 5775	Let There Be Drums/Quite a Beat	1961	3.75	7.50	15.00
☐ 5809	Drums Are My Beat/The Birth of the Beat	1962	3.00	6.00	12.00
☐ 5829	Drummin' Up a Storm/Drum Stomp	1962	3.00	6.00	12.00
☐ 5860	All Night Long/Rompin' and Stompin'	1962	3.00	6.00	12.00
☐ 5870	And Then There Were Drums/Live It Up	1962	3.00	6.00	12.00
☐ 5884	Teenage House Party/Day Train	1962	3.00	6.00	12.00
☐ 5904	Be-Bop Baby/Let the Four Winds Blow	1962	3.00	6.00	12.00
☐ 5932	Ooh Poo Pa Doo/Feel So Good	1963	3.00	6.00	12.00
☐ 5940	You Name It/Alexis	1963	3.00	6.00	12.00
☐ 5965	Here We Go Again/Just Bill	1963	3.00	6.00	12.00
☐ 5988	Caravan/Sandy	1963	3.00	6.00	12.00
☐ 66019	Drum Shack/Kitty's Theme	1964	2.50	5.00	10.00
☐ 66034	Castle Rock/You Don't Say	1964	2.50	5.00	10.00
☐ 66060	Teen Beat '65/Kitty's Theme	1964	3.00	6.00	12.00
☐ 66093	Chop Chop/Reach for a Star	1965	2.50	5.00	10.00
☐ 66107	Land of 1000 Dances/Let There Be Drums	1965	2.50	5.00	10.00
☐ 66127	Drums A-Go-Go/Caesar	1965	2.50	5.00	10.00
☐ 66146	A Lover's Concerto/Treat Her Right	1965	2.50	5.00	10.00
☐ 66193	Rock It To 'Em J.B./The Charge	1966	2.50	5.00	10.00
☐ 66209	Let's Go Trippin'/Pipeline	1966	3.00	6.00	12.00
☐ 66246	The Drums Go On/Lawdy Miss Clawdy	1967	2.50	5.00	10.00
☐ 66253	Peter Gunn/You Got Me Hummin'	1967	2.50	5.00	10.00
☐ 66284	Alligator Boogaloo/Midnight Magic	1968	2.50	5.00	10.00
☐ 66350	Rebirth of the Beat/Lion in Winter	1969	2.50	5.00	10.00
☐ 66375	Manhattan Spiritual/The Stripper	1969	2.50	5.00	10.00
☐ 66402	Let There Be Drums and Brass/Leap Frog	1969	2.50	5.00	10.00

Original Sound

Number	Title (A Side/B Side)	Year	VG	VG+	NM
☐ 5	Teen Beat/Big Jump	1959	6.25	12.50	25.00

United Artists

Number	Title (A Side/B Side)	Year	VG	VG+	NM
☐ 0082	Teen Beat/Let There Be Drums	1973		2.50	5.00
	"Silver Spotlight Series" reissue				
☐ XW383	You Are the Sunshine of My Life/	1974	2.50	5.00	10.00
	Dance with the Devil				
☐ 50830	Sapporo '72	1971			Unreleased

Number		Title (A Side/B Side)	Year	VG	VG+	NM
Veebletronics						
❑ 1		Drum Tunnel/Boogie #5	198?		2.50	5.00
❑ 2		Hunk of Drums/Witch Hunt	198?		2.50	5.00
❑ 3		A Drum Is a Woman/Boogie #5	198?		2.50	5.00
Nelson, Willie						
(Also see "Waylon and Willie")						
American Gold						
❑ 7601		Night Life/Rainy Day Blues	1976		2.50	5.00
Atlantic						
❑ 2968		Shotgun Willie/Sad Songs and Waltzes	1973		2.50	5.00
❑ 2979		Devil in a Sleepin' Bag/Stay All Night	1973		2.50	5.00
❑ 3008		Heaven and Hell/I Still Can't Believe You're Gone	1974		2.50	5.00
❑ 3020		Phases and Stages/Bloody Mary Morning	1974		2.50	5.00
❑ 3228		Sister's Coming Home/Pick Up the Tempo	1974		2.50	5.00
❑ 3334		Heaven and Hell/I Still Can't Believe You're Gone	1976		2.50	5.00
❑ 4028		After the Fire Is Gone/Whiskey River	1976		2.50	5.00
		By "Tracy and Willie Nelson"				
Bellaire						
❑ 107		Night Life/Rainy Day Blues	1963	15.00	30.00	60.00
		Colored vinyl				
❑ 107		Night Life/Rainy Day Blues	1963	7.50	15.00	30.00
❑ 5000		Night Life '76/Man with the Blues	1976		2.50	5.00
Betty						
❑ 5702		What a Way to Love/Misery Mansion	1964	5.00	10.00	20.00
❑ 5703		Man with the Blues/The Storm Has Just Begun	1964	5.00	10.00	20.00
Capitol						
❑ 4635		Ain't Life Hell/I'm Going With You This Time	1978		2.50	5.00
		With Hank Cochran				
Challenge						
❑ 59280		I'm Talking About Love/	1965	3.75	7.50	15.00
		I'm in Love with a Dancing Girl Working at Metropole				
Columbia						
❑ AE7 1182	DJ	White Christmas/Blue Christmas	1979	6.25	12.50	25.00
		Green vinyl				
❑ AE7 1183	DJ	Pretty Paper/Rudolph the Red-Nosed Reindeer	1979	6.25	12.50	25.00
		Red vinyl				
❑ 02000		Mona Lisa/Twinkle, Twinkle Little Star	1981		2.00	4.00
❑ 02166		On the Road Again/September Song	1981			3.00
		Reissue				
❑ 02187		I'm Gonna Sit Right Down and Write Myself a Letter/	1981		2.00	4.00
		Over the Rainbow				
❑ 02558		Heartaches of a Fool/Uncloudy Day	1981		2.00	4.00
❑ 02681		Old Friends/When a House Is Not a Home	1982		2.00	4.00
		Roger Miller/Willie Nelson/Ray Price				
❑ 02741		Always on My Mind/The Party's Over	1982		2.00	4.00
❑ 03073		Let It Be Me/Permanently Lonely	1982		2.00	4.00
❑ 03123		Angel Flying Too Close to the Ground/Mona Lisa	1982			3.00
		Reissue				
❑ 03124		Heartache of a Fool/Midnight Rider	1982			3.00
		Reissue				
❑ 03231		In the Jailhouse Now/Back Street Affair	1982		2.00	4.00
		Willie Nelson and Webb Pierce				
❑ 03385		Last Thing I Needed First Thing This Morning/	1982		2.00	4.00
		Old Fords and a Natural Stone				
❑ 03476		White Christmas/Pretty Paper	1982		2.50	5.00
❑ 03674		Beer Barrel Polka/Little Old Fashioned Karma	1983		2.00	4.00
❑ 03965		Why Do I Have to Choose/	1983		2.00	4.00
		Would You Lay with Me (In a Field of Stone)				
❑ 04131		Take It to the Limit/Till I Gain Control Again	1983		2.00	4.00
		Willie Nelson and Waylon Jennings				
❑ 04217		To All the Girls I've Loved Before/	1984			3.00
		I Don't Want to Wake You				
		Julio Iglesias & Willie Nelson; B-side by Julio Iglesias solo				
❑ 04217	PS	To All the Girls I've Loved Before/	1984		2.50	5.00
		I Don't Want to Wake You				
		Julio Iglesias & Willie Nelson; first sleeve has artists' names in both capital and small letters				
❑ 04217	PS	To All the Girls I've Loved Before/	1984		2.00	4.00
		I Don't Want to Wake You				
		Julio Iglesias & Willie Nelson; second sleeve has artists' names in all capital letters				
❑ 04263		Without a Song/I Can't Begin to Tell You	1983			3.00
❑ 04495		As Time Goes By/You'll Never Know	1984	6.25	12.50	25.00
		Willie Nelson and Julio Iglesias; withdrawn immediately upon release				
❑ 04568		City of New Orleans/Why Are You Pickin' On Me	1984			3.00
❑ 04568	PS	City of New Orleans/Why Are You Pickin' On Me	1984		2.00	4.00
❑ 04652		How Do You Feel About Foolin' Around/	1984			3.00
		Eye of the Storm				
		Willie Nelson and Kris Kristofferson				
❑ 04715		Seven Spanish Angels/Who Cares	1984			3.00
		A-side: Ray Charles and Willie Nelson; B-side: Ray Charles and Janie Frickie				

Number	Title (A Side/B Side)	Year	VG	VG+	NM
❑ 04847	Forgiving You Was Easy/ You Wouldn't Cross the Street (To Say Goodbye)	1985			3.00
❑ 04881	Highwayman/The Human Condition	1985			3.00

A-side: Willie Nelson/Waylon Jennings/Johnny Cash/Kris Kristofferson; B-side: Nelson, Cash

❑ 04881	PS Highwayman/The Human Condition	1985		2.00	
❑ 05594	Desperadoes Waiting for a Train/ The Twentieth Century Is Almost Over	1985			3.00

A-side: Willie Nelson/Waylon Jennings/Johnny Cash/Kris Kristofferson; B-side: Nelson, Cash

❑ 05597	Me and Paul/I Let My Mind Wander	1985			3.00
❑ 05677	Slow Movin' Outlaw/They All Went to Mexico	1985			3.00

A-side: With Lacy J. Dalton; B-side: With Carlos Santana

❑ 05749	I Told a Lie to My Heart/Slow Movin' Outlaw	1986			3.00

A-side: With Hank Williams, Jr.; B-side: With Lacy J. Dalton

❑ 05834	Living in the Promiseland/Bach Minuet in G	1986			3.00
❑ 06227	I've Already Cheated on You/Take My Advice	1986			3.00

A-side: With David Allan Coe; B-side: Coe solo

❑ 06246	I'm Not Trying to Forget You/ I've Got the Craziest Feeling	1986			3.00
❑ 06530	Partners After All/Home Away from Home	1986			3.00
❑ 07007	Heart of Gold/So Much Like My Dad	1987			3.00
❑ 07202	Island in the Sun/ There Is No Easy Way (But There Is a Way)	1987			3.00
❑ 07636	Nobody There But Me/Wake Me When It's Over	1987			3.00
❑ 08044	Spanish Eyes/Ole Buttermilk Sky	1988			3.00

With Julio Iglesias

❑ 08395	Living in the Promiseland/Forgiving You Was Easy	1988			3.00

Reissue

❑ 08406	Highwayman/Desperadoes Waiting for a Train	1988			3.00

Waylon Jennings/Willie Nelson/Johnny Cash/Kris Kristofferson; reissue

❑ 10176	Blue Eyes Cryin' in the Rain/Bandera	1975		2.50	5.00
❑ 10275	Remember Me/Time of the Preacher	1975		2.50	5.00
❑ 10327	I'd Have to Be Crazy/Amazing Grace	1976		2.50	5.00
❑ 10383	If You've Got the Money, I've Got the Time/ The Sound in Your Mind	1976		2.50	5.00
❑ 10453	Uncloudy Day/Precious Memories	1976		2.50	5.00
❑ 10480	Lily Dale/Please Don't Leave Me	1976		2.50	5.00

With Darrell McCall

❑ 10588	I Love You a Thousand Ways/Mom and Dad's Waltz	1977		2.50	5.00
❑ 10644	Something to Brag About/ Anybody's Darlin' (Anybody But Mine)	1977		2.50	5.00

With Mary Kay Place

❑ 10704	Georgia on My Mind/On the Sunny Side of the Street	1978		2.50	5.00
❑ 10784	Blue Skies/Moonlight in Vermont	1978		2.50	5.00
❑ 10834	All of Me/Unchained Melody	1978		2.50	5.00
❑ 10877	Whiskey River/Under the Double Eagle	1978		2.50	5.00
❑ 10929	September Song/Don't Get Around Much Anymore	1979		2.00	4.00
❑ 11023	Heartbreak Hotel/Sioux City Sue	1979		2.00	4.00

With Leon Russell

❑ 11119	Trouble in Mind/ One for My Baby (And One More for the Road)	1979		2.00	4.00

With Leon Russell

❑ 11126	Help Me Make It Through the Night/ The Pilgrim: Chapter 33	1979		2.00	4.00
❑ 11186	My Heroes Have Always Been Cowboys/ Rising Star (Love Theme)	1980		2.00	4.00
❑ 11257	Midnight Rider/Do You Think You're a Cowboy	1980		2.00	4.00
❑ 11329	Faded Love/This Cold World with You	1980		2.00	4.00

With Ray Price

❑ 11351	On the Road Again/Jumpin' Cotton-Eyed Joe	1980		2.00	4.00

B-side by Johnny Gimble

❑ 11405	Don't You Ever Get Tired (Of Loving Me)/ Funny How Time Slips Away	1980		2.00	4.00

With Ray Price

❑ 11418	Angel Flying Too Close to the Ground/ I Guess I've Come to Live Here in Your Eyes	1981		2.00	4.00
❑ 68541	Twilight Time/Ac-Cent-Tchu-Ate the Positive	1989			3.00
❑ 68923	Nothing I Can Do About It Now/If I Were a Painting	1989			3.00
❑ 73015	There You Are/Spirit	1989			3.00
❑ 73233	America Remains/Silver Stallion	1990			3.00

Waylon Jennings/Willie Nelson/Johnny Cash/Kris Kristofferson

❑ 73249	The Highway/Spirit	1990			3.00
❑ 73374	Is the Better Part Over/Mr. Record Man	1990			3.00
❑ 73381	Born and Raised in Black and White/Texas	1990			3.00

The Highwaymen (Waylon Jennings/Willie Nelson/Johnny Cash/Kris Kristofferson)

❑ 73518	It Ain't Necessarily So/I Never Cared for You	1990			3.00
❑ 73572	American Remains/Texas	1990			3.00

The Highwaymen (Waylon Jennings/Willie Nelson/Johnny Cash/Kris Kristofferson)

❑ 73655	The Piper Came Today/ (I Don't Have a Reason) To Go to California Anymore	1991			3.00
❑ 73749	Ten with a Two/You Decide	1991			3.00
❑ 77184	Still Is Still Moving to Me/Valentine	1993			3.00

D

❑ 1084	Man with the Blues/The Storm Has Just Begun	1959	7.50	15.00	30.00
❑ 1131	What a Way to Love/Misery Mansion	1960	7.50	15.00	30.00

Number	Title (A Side/B Side)	Year	VG	VG+	NM

Epic

❏ 03494	Reasons to Quit/Half a Man	1983		2.00	4.00
	Willie Nelson and Merle Haggard				
❏ 03495	Reasons to Quit	1983	2.00	4.00	8.00
	Willie Nelson and Merle Haggard; one-sided budget release				
❏ 03842	Pancho and Lefty/Opportunity to Cry	1983		2.00	4.00
	Willie Nelson and Merle Haggard				
❏ 73832	If I Can Find a Clean Shirt/	1991			3.00
	Put Me on a Train Back to Texas				
	Waylon Jennings and Willie Nelson				
❏ 74024	Tryin' to Outrun the Wind/The Makin's of a Song	1991			3.00
	Waylon Jennings and Willie Nelson				

Liberty

❏ S7-18486	It Is What It Is/The Devil's Right Hand	1995			3.00
	By The Highwaymen				
❏ S7-18584	One After 909/Yesterday	1995			3.00
	B-side by Billy Dean				
❏ 55155	Susie/No Dough	1958	6.25	12.50	25.00
❏ 55386	Mr. Record Man/The Part Where I Cry	1961	5.00	10.00	20.00
❏ 55403	Willingly/Chain of Love	1962	3.75	7.50	15.00
	A-side: With Shirley Collie				
❏ 55439	Touch Me/Where My House Lives	1962	3.75	7.50	15.00
❏ 55468	You Dream About Me/Is This My Destiny	1962	3.75	7.50	15.00
	A-side: With Shirley Collie				
❏ 55494	Wake Me When It's Over/	1962	3.75	7.50	15.00
	There's Gonna Be Love in My House				
❏ 55532	Half a Man/The Last Letter	1963	3.00	6.00	12.00
❏ 55591	Take My Word/Feed It a Memory	1963	3.00	6.00	12.00
❏ 55638	How Long Is Forever/You Took My Happy Away	1963	3.00	6.00	12.00
❏ 55661	Am I Blue/There'll Be No Teardrops Tonight	1964	2.50	5.00	10.00
❏ 55697	River Boy/Opportunity to Cry	1964	2.50	5.00	10.00
❏ 56143	Right or Wrong/I Hope So	1969		3.00	6.00

Lone Star

| ❏ 703 | The End of Understanding/Will You Remember Mine | 1978 | | 2.50 | 5.00 |

Monument

❏ 855	I Never Cared for You/You Left Me	1964	3.75	7.50	15.00
❏ 03408	Everything Is Beautiful (In Its Own Way)/	1982		2.00	4.00
	Put It Off Until Tomorrow				
	A-side: Willie Nelson and Dolly Parton; B-side: Dolly Parton and Kris Kristofferson				
❏ 03781	You're Gonna Love Yourself (In the Morning)/	1983		2.00	4.00
	What Do You Think About Lovin'				
	A-side: Willie Nelson and Brenda Lee; B-side: Dolly Parton and Brenda Lee				

Paradise

| ❏ 629 | Wabash Cannonball/Tennessee Waltz | 1984 | | 2.00 | 4.00 |
| | *A-side with Hank Wilson; B-side by Wilson solo* | | | | |

RCA

❏ PB-10969	I'm a Memory/It Should Be Easier Now	1977		2.50	5.00
	With Darrell McCall				
❏ PB-11061	You Ought to Hear Me Cry/One in a Row	1977		2.50	5.00
❏ PB-11235	If You Can Touch Her at All/Rainy Day Blues	1978		2.50	5.00
❏ PB-11465	Sweet Memories/Little Things	1979		2.50	5.00
❏ PB-11673	Crazy Arms/Hurricane Shirley	1979		2.50	5.00
	B-side by Bobby Bare				
❏ GB-11995	Sweet Memories/If You Can Touch Her At All	1980			3.00
	Gold Standard Series				
❏ PB-12254	Good Times/Where Do You Stand	1981		2.00	4.00
❏ PB-12328	Mountain Dew/Laying My Burdens Down	1981		2.00	4.00

RCA Victor

❏ 47-8484	Pretty Paper/What a Merry Christmas This Could Be	1964	3.75	7.50	15.00
❏ 47-8519	She's Not for You/Permanently Lonely	1965	3.00	6.00	12.00
❏ 47-8594	Healing Hands of Time/One Day at a Time	1965	3.00	6.00	12.00
❏ 47-8682	I Just Can't Let You Say Goodbye/	1965	3.00	6.00	12.00
	And So Will You, My Love				
❏ 47-8801	Columbus Stockade Blues/He Sits at My Table	1966	3.00	6.00	12.00
❏ 47-8852	I'm Still Not Over You/I Love You Because	1966	3.00	6.00	12.00
❏ 47-8933	One in a Row/San Antonio Rose	1966	3.00	6.00	12.00
❏ 47-9029	Pretty Paper/What a Merry Christmas This Could Be	1966	3.00	6.00	12.00
❏ 47-9100	The Party's Over/Make Way for a Better Man	1967	2.50	5.00	10.00
❏ 47-9202	Blackjack County Chain/Some Other World	1967	2.50	5.00	10.00
❏ 47-9324	San Antonio/To Make a Long Story Short	1967	2.50	5.00	10.00
❏ 47-9427	Little Things/I'll Stay Around	1968	2.50	5.00	10.00
❏ 47-9536	Good Times/Don't You Ever Get Tired	1968	2.50	5.00	10.00
❏ 47-9605	Johnny One Time/She's Still Gone	1968	2.50	5.00	10.00
❏ 47-9684	Bring Me Sunshine/Don't Say Love or Nothing	1968	2.50	5.00	10.00
❏ 47-9778	Pretty Paper/What a Merry Christmas This Could Be	1969			Unreleased
❏ 47-9798	Who Do I Know in Dallas/Once More with Feeling	1969	2.00	4.00	8.00
❏ 47-9903	Laying My Burdens Down/Truth Number One	1970	2.00	4.00	8.00
❏ 47-9931	Pretty Paper/What a Merry Christmas This Could Be	1970	2.00	4.00	8.00
❏ 47-9951	I'm a Memory/I'm So Lonesome I Could Cry	1971		3.00	6.00
❏ 47-9984	Kneel at the Feet of Jesus/	1971		3.00	6.00
	What Can You Do to Me Now				
❏ 74-0162	Jimmy's Road/Natural to Be Gone	1969	2.00	4.00	8.00
❏ 74-0542	Yesterday's Wine/Me and Paul	1971		3.00	6.00

Number	Title (A Side/B Side)	Year	VG	VG+	NM
❑ 74-0635	A Moment Isn't Very Long/Words Don't Fit the Picture	1972		3.00	6.00
❑ 74-0816	Mountain Dew/	1972		3.00	6.00
	Phases, Stages, Circles, Cycles, and Scenes				
❑ PB-10429	I'm a Memory/Fire and Rain	1975		2.50	5.00
❑ PB-10461	Pretty Paper/What a Merry Christmas This Could Be	1975		2.50	5.00
❑ PB-10591	Summer of Roses/I Gotta Get Drunk	1976		2.50	5.00

Sarg

❑ 260	A Storm Has Just Begun/	196?	12.50	25.00	50.00
	When I Sang My Last Hillbilly Song				
	Some sources say this came out in 1955, but that doesn't coincide with this label's numbering system				

Songbird

❑ 41313	Family Bible/In God's Eyes	1980		2.00	4.00

United Artists

❑ 641	Night Life/Rainy Day Blues	1963	3.75	7.50	15.00
❑ XW771	The Last Letter/There Goes a Man	1976		2.50	5.00
❑ XW1165	Hello Walls/The Last Letter	1978		2.50	5.00
❑ XW1254	There'll Be Teardrops Tonight/	1978		2.50	5.00
	Blue Must Be the Color of the Blues				

Willie Nelson

❑ 628	No Place for Me/(B-side unknown)	1957	75.00	150.00	300.00

Neons, The
(More than one group)

Challenge

❑ 9147	Magic Moment/Fat Girls	1962	12.50	25.00	50.00

Gone

❑ 5090	Angel Face/Golden Dreams	1960	10.00	20.00	40.00

Tetra

❑ 4444	Angel Face/Kiss Me Quickly	1956	12.50	25.00	50.00
❑ 4449	Road of Romance/My Chickadee	1957	12.50	25.00	50.00

Vintage

❑ 1016	Honey Bun/Golden Dreams	1974		2.50	5.00

Waldon

❑ 1001	My Lover/Tucson	1961	50.00	100.00	200.00

Nero, Frances

Soul

❑ 35020	Keep On Lovin' Me/Fight Off Fire with Fire	1966	12.50	25.00	50.00

Nervous Norvus
(Also see "Four Jokers, The")

Dot

❑ 15470	Transfusion/Dig	1956	12.50	25.00	50.00
	Originals have maroon labels				
❑ 15470	Transfusion/Dig	1956	7.50	15.00	30.00
	Second pressings have black labels				
❑ 15485	Ape Call/Wild Dog of Kentucky	1956	7.50	15.00	30.00
	Originals have maroon labels				
❑ 15485	Ape Call/Wild Dog of Kentucky	1956	5.00	10.00	20.00
	Second pressings have black labels				
❑ 15500	The Fang/The Bullfrog	1956	7.50	15.00	30.00
	Originals have maroon labels				
❑ 15500	The Fang/The Bullfrog	1956	5.00	10.00	20.00
	Second pressings have black labels				
❑ 16765	Transfusion/Ape Call	1965	3.00	6.00	12.00

Embee

❑ 117	I Like Girls/Stone Age Woo	1959	5.00	10.00	20.00

Nesmith, Michael
(Ex-Monkees)

Colpix

❑ 787	The New Recruit/A Journey	1965	37.50	75.00	150.00
❑ 792	Until It's Time for You to Go/What's the Trouble, Officer	1965	37.50	75.00	150.00
	Both Colpix records as "Michael Blessing"				

Edan

❑ 1001	Just a Little Love/Curson Terrace	1965	30.00	60.00	120.00

Pacific Arts

❑ 084		Life, the Unsuspecting Captive/Rio	1977	2.00	4.00	8.00
❑ 101		Roll with the Flow/I've Just Begun to Care	1978	3.00	6.00	
❑ 104		Casablanca Moonlight/Rio	1978		3.00	6.00
❑ 104	PS	Casablanca Moonlight/Rio	1978	3.00	6.00	12.00
❑ 106		Magic (This Night Is Magic)/Dance	1979		3.00	6.00
❑ 108		Cruisin'/Horserace	1979		3.00	6.00
❑ 6373		Life, the Unsuspecting Captive/Rio	1976	2.50	5.00	10.00
❑ 6398		Navajo Trail/Love's First Kiss	1976	2.50	5.00	10.00

RCA Victor

❑ 47-9853		Rose City Chimes/Little Red Rider	1970	2.50	5.00	10.00
❑ 74-0368		Joanne/One Rose	1970	3.00	6.00	12.00
❑ 74-0399		Silver Moon/Lady of the Valley	1970	2.50	5.00	10.00
❑ 74-0453		Nevada Fighter/Here I Am	1971	2.00	4.00	8.00
❑ 74-0453	PS	Nevada Fighter/Here I Am	1971	5.00	10.00	20.00

Number			Title (A Side/B Side)	Year	VG	VG+	NM
❏ 74-0491			Tumbling Tumbleweeds/Texas Morning	1971	2.00	4.00	8.00
❏ 74-0540			Only Bound/Propinquity	1971	2.00	4.00	8.00
❏ 74-0629			Lazy Lady/Mama Rocker	1971	2.00	4.00	8.00
❏ 74-0804			Roll with the Flow/Keep On	1972	2.00	4.00	8.00

Neuman, Alfred E., and the Furshlugginer Five
ABC-Paramount
❏ 10013			What -- Me Worry?/Potrzebie	1959	10.00	20.00	40.00

New Colony Six, The
Centaur
❏ 1201			I Confess/Dawn Is Breaking	1966	3.75	7.50	15.00
❏ 1202			I Lie Awake/At the River's Edge	1966	3.75	7.50	15.00
MCA
❏ 40215			Never Be Lonely/Long Time to Be Alone	1974		3.00	6.00
❏ 40288			I Really Don't Want to Go/Run	1974		3.00	6.00
Mercury
❏ 72737			Rap-a-Tap/Treat Her Groovy	1967	2.50	5.00	10.00
❏ 72737	PS		Rap-a-Tap/Treat Her Groovy	1967	3.75	7.50	15.00
❏ 72775			I Will Always Think About You/Hold Me with Your Eyes	1968	3.00	6.00	12.00
			Red label with "Mercury" logo in all capital letters				
❏ 72775			I Will Always Think About You/Hold Me with Your Eyes	1968	2.50	5.00	10.00
			Orange and red swirl label				
❏ 72817			Can't You See Me Cry/	1968	2.00	4.00	8.00
			Summertime's Another Name for Love				
❏ 72817	PS		Can't You See Me Cry/	1968	3.75	7.50	15.00
			Summertime's Another Name for Love				
❏ 72858			Things I'd Like to Say/Come and Give Your Love to Me	1968	2.50	5.00	10.00
❏ 72920			I Could Never Lie to You/Just Feel Worse	1969	2.00	4.00	8.00
❏ 72961			I Want You to Know/Free	1969	2.00	4.00	8.00
❏ 73004			Barbara, I Love You/Prairie Grey	1970	2.00	4.00	8.00
❏ 73063			People and Me/Ride the Wicked Wind	1970	3.75	7.50	15.00
❏ 73093			Close Your Eyes Little Girl/	1970	3.75	7.50	15.00
			Love, That's the Best I Can Do				
Sentar
❏ 1203			Sunshine/Cadillac	1966	3.75	7.50	15.00
❏ 1204			Power of Love/(Ballad of the) Wingbat Marmaduke	1966	3.75	7.50	15.00
❏ 1205			Love You So Much/Let Me Love You	1967	3.75	7.50	15.00
❏ 1206			You're Gonna Be Mine/Woman	1967	3.75	7.50	15.00
❏ 1207			Hello Lonely/	1967	3.75	7.50	15.00
			I'm Just Waiting Anticipating for Her to Show Up				
Sunlight
❏ 1001			Roll On/If You Could See	1971		3.00	6.00
❏ 1004			Long Time to Be Alone/Never Be Lonely	1971		3.00	6.00
❏ 1005			Come On Down/Someone, Sometime	1972		2.50	5.00
Twilight
❏ 1004			Long Time to Be Alone/Never Be Lonely	1973		2.50	5.00

New Kingston Trio, The – See "Kingston Trio, The"

New Marketts, The – See "Marketts, The"

New Things, The
Accent
❏ 1228			Dumbo/I Want You Back	1967	10.00	20.00	40.00

New York Dolls
Mercury
❏ DJ-378	DJ		Trash (mono/stereo)	1973	3.75	7.50	15.00
❏ DJ-378	PS		Trash (mono/stereo)	1973	18.75	37.50	75.00
			Promo-only numbered sleeve				
❏ DJ-387	DJ		Personality Crisis (mono/stereo)	1973	3.75	7.50	15.00
❏ 73414			Trash/Personality Crisis	1973	15.00	30.00	60.00
❏ 73414	PS		Trash/Personality Crisis	1973	3.75	7.50	15.00
❏ 73478			Stranded in the Jungle/Who Are the Mystery Girls	1974	3.75	7.50	15.00
❏ 73615			Puss 'N' Boots/Showmen	1974	5.00	10.00	20.00

New Yorkers, The
(Several different groups)
Decca
❏ 32569			I Guess the Lord Must Be in New York City/	1969	2.50	5.00	10.00
			Do Wah Diddy				
Jerden
❏ 906			Adrienne/Ice Cream World	1968	3.00	6.00	12.00
❏ 908			Land of Ur/Michael Glover	1969	3.00	6.00	12.00
Scepter
			This group was later known as The Hudson Brothers				
❏ 12190			You're Not My Girl/When I'm Gone	1967	3.75	7.50	15.00
❏ 12199			Mr. Kirby/Seeds of Spring	1967	3.75	7.50	15.00
❏ 12207			Again/Show Me the Way to Love	1968	3.00	6.00	12.00
Tac-Ful
❏ 101			You Should Have Told Me/Don't Want to Be Your Fool	1964	3.00	6.00	12.00
Wall
This group featured Fred Parris of the Five Satins

Number		Title (A Side/B Side)	Year	VG	VG+	NM
❑ 547		Dream a Little Dream/Miss Fine	1961	6.25	12.50	25.00
❑ 548		Tears in My Eyes/A Little Bit	1961	7.50	15.00	30.00

Warner Bros.

Number		Title (A Side/B Side)	Year	VG	VG+	NM
❑ 7318		Lonely/There'll Come a Time	1969	2.50	5.00	10.00

Newlyweds, The
Homogenized Soul

Number		Title (A Side/B Side)	Year	VG	VG+	NM
❑ 601		Love Walked Out/The Quarrel	1961	1,500	2,250	3,000

Newman, Randy
Dot

Number		Title (A Side/B Side)	Year	VG	VG+	NM
❑ 16411		Golden Gridiron Boy/Country Boy	1962	12.50	25.00	50.00
		May be promo only				

Reprise

Number		Title (A Side/B Side)	Year	VG	VG+	NM
❑ 0692		I Think It's Going to Rain Today/The Beehive State	1968	3.75	7.50	15.00
❑ 0771		Last Night I Had a Dream/I Think He's Hiding	1968	6.25	12.50	25.00
		May be promo only				
❑ 0917		Have You Seen My Baby/Hold On	1970	3.75	7.50	15.00
❑ 0945		Gone Dead Train/Harry Flowers	1970	3.75	7.50	15.00
❑ 1102		Sail Away/Political Science	1972		3.00	6.00
❑ 1123		You Can Leave Your Hat On/Memo to My Son	1972		3.00	6.00
❑ 1324		Guilty/Naked Man	1975		2.50	5.00
❑ 1387		Louisiana 1927/Marie	1977		2.50	5.00
❑ 22798		I'd Love to See You Smile/	1989			3.00
		End Title (I'd Love to See You Smile)				
❑ 27709		It's Money That Matters/Roll with the Punches	1988			3.00
❑ 27709	PS	It's Money That Matters/Roll with the Punches	1988			3.00
❑ 27856		Falling in Love/Bad News from Home	1989			3.00

Warner Bros.

Number		Title (A Side/B Side)	Year	VG	VG+	NM
❑ 8492		Short People/Old Man on the Farm	1977		2.50	5.00
❑ 8550		Baltimore/You Can't Fool the Fat Man	1978		2.00	4.00
❑ 8630		Rider in the Rain/	1978		2.00	4.00
		Sigmund Freud's Impersonation of Albert Einstein in America				
❑ 29241		The Natural/The Natural (Final Game)	1984		2.00	4.00
❑ 29687		I Love L.A./Song for the Dead	1983		2.00	4.00
❑ 29803		The Blues/The Same Girl	1983		2.00	4.00
		A-side: With Paul Simon				
❑ 29803	PS	The Blues/The Same Girl	1983		2.00	4.00
❑ 49088		It's Money That I Love/Ghosts	1979		2.00	4.00
❑ 49149		Half a Man/The Story of a Rock and Roll Band	1979		2.00	4.00
❑ 49223		Spies/Political Science (Let's Drop the Big One)	1980		2.00	4.00

Newton Brothers, The
(With Wayne Newton)
Capitol

Number		Title (A Side/B Side)	Year	VG	VG+	NM
❑ F4236		The Real Thing/I Spy	1959	20.00	40.00	80.00

Nice, The
(Keith Emerson was in this group)
Immediate

Number		Title (A Side/B Side)	Year	VG	VG+	NM
❑ 5004		Azrial (Angel of Death)/Thoughts of Emerlist Davjack	1968	3.00	6.00	12.00
❑ 5008		America/Diamond Hard Apples of the Moon	1968	3.00	6.00	12.00

Mercury

Number		Title (A Side/B Side)	Year	VG	VG+	NM
❑ 73114		Country Pie/(B-side unknown)	1970	2.00	4.00	8.00
❑ 73272		Country Pie-Brandenburg Concerto No. 6 (Part 1)/	1972		3.00	6.00
		Finale-5th Bridge				

Nick and the Jaguars
Tamla

Number		Title (A Side/B Side)	Year	VG	VG+	NM
❑ 5501F		Ich-I-Bon #1/Cool and Crazy	1960	75.00	150.00	300.00

Nick and the Nacks
Barry

Number		Title (A Side/B Side)	Year	VG	VG+	NM
❑ 108		The Night/That Old Black Magic	1964	100.00	200.00	400.00

Nick and the Stingrays
Mill-Mont

Number		Title (A Side/B Side)	Year	VG	VG+	NM
❑ 1628		You Are So Beautiful/Broken Hearted Baby	196?	50.00	100.00	200.00

Nickie and the Nitelites
(With Nick Massi, later of the Four Seasons)
Brunswick

Number		Title (A Side/B Side)	Year	VG	VG+	NM
❑ 55155		I'm Lonely/Tell Me You Care	1959	25.00	50.00	100.00

Nicks, Stevie
(Also see "Buckingham Nicks"; "Fleetwood Mac")
Modern

Number		Title (A Side/B Side)	Year	VG	VG+	NM
❑ 3836		Stop Draggin' My Heart Around/Kind of Woman	1981			*Unreleased?*
❑ 7336		Stop Draggin' My Heart Around/Kind of Woman	1981		2.00	4.00
		With Tom Petty and the Heartbreakers				
❑ 7336	PS	Stop Draggin' My Heart Around/Kind of Woman	1981		3.00	6.00
❑ 7341		Leather and Lace/Bella Donna	1981		2.50	5.00
		With Don Henley; first pressing states "Written for Waylon Jennings and Jessi Colter"				

Number		Title (A Side/B Side)	Year	VG	VG+	NM
❑ 7341		Leather and Lace/Bella Donna	1981		2.00	4.00
		With Don Henley; with no reference to Waylon Jennings and Jessi Colter on label				
❑ 7341	PS	Leather and Lace/Bella Donna	1981	2.50	5.00	10.00
❑ 7401		Edge of Seventeen (Just Like the White Winged Dove)/	1982		2.00	4.00
		Edge of Seventeen (Live)				
❑ 7401	PS	Edge of Seventeen (Just Like the White Winged Dove)/	1982		3.00	6.00
		Edge of Seventeen (Live)				
❑ 7405		After the Glitter Fades/Think About It	1982		2.00	4.00
❑ 7405	PS	After the Glitter Fades/Think About It	1982		3.00	6.00
❑ 99150		Whole Lotta Trouble/Ghosts	1989			3.00
❑ 99179		Two Kinds of Love/Real Tears	1989			3.00
❑ 99216		Rooms on Fire/Slice	1989			3.00
❑ 99216	PS	Rooms on Fire/Slice	1989			3.00
❑ 99532		Has Anyone Ever Written Anything for You/	1986			3.00
		Imperial Hotel				
❑ 99532	PS	Has Anyone Ever Written Anything for You/	1986			3.00
		Imperial Hotel				
❑ 99565		I Can't Wait/The Nightmare	1986			3.00
❑ 99565	PS	I Can't Wait/The Nightmare	1986			3.00
❑ 99565	DJ	I Can't Wait (Remix)/I Can't Wait (Soft Intro)	1986	2.00	4.00	8.00
❑ 99565	PS	I Can't Wait (Remix)/I Can't Wait (Soft Intro)	1986	3.00	6.00	12.00
❑ 99582		Talk to Me/One More Big Time Rock and Roll Star	1985			3.00
❑ 99582	PS	Talk to Me/One More Big Time Rock and Roll Star	1985			3.00
❑ 99799		Nightbird/Gate and Garden	1984			3.00
❑ 99799	PS	Nightbird/Gate and Garden	1984	12.50	25.00	50.00
❑ 99832		If Anyone Falls/Wild Heart	1983		2.00	4.00
❑ 99832	PS	If Anyone Falls/Wild Heart	1983		2.00	4.00
❑ 99863		Stand Back/Garbo	1983			3.00
❑ 99863	PS	Stand Back/Garbo	1983		2.00	4.00

Nicky and the Nobles

End

❑ 1021		Schoolhouse Rock/A Way to Tell Her	1958	12.50	25.00	50.00
❑ 1098		School Bells/School Day Crush	1961	6.25	12.50	25.00

Gone

❑ 5039		School Bells/School Days	1958	25.00	50.00	100.00
		With B-side title variation				
❑ 5039		School Bells/School Day Crush	1958	15.00	30.00	60.00
		Black label				
❑ 5039		School Bells/School Day Crush	1958	6.25	12.50	25.00
		Multicolor label				

Nicol, Jimmy

(His 15 minutes of fame were from his brief stint filling in for an ailing Ringo on a 1964 Beatles tour)

Argo

❑ 5464		Night Train/Humpty Dumpty	1964			Unreleased

Mar Mar

❑ 313		Night Train/Humpty Dumpty	1965	37.50	75.00	150.00

Parrot

❑ 9752		Sweet Clementine/Roaring Blue	1965	6.25	12.50	25.00

Nightcrawlers, The

Kapp

❑ 709		The Little Black Egg/You're Running Wild	1965	3.75	7.50	15.00
❑ 746		A Basket of Flowers/Washboard	1966	3.75	7.50	15.00
❑ 826		My Butterfly/Today I'm Happy	1967	7.50	15.00	30.00

Lee

❑ 1012		The Little Black Egg/You're Running Wild	1965	12.50	25.00	50.00

Marlin

❑ 1904		A Basket of Flowers/Washboard	1966	5.00	10.00	20.00

Nilsson

(Also see "Bo Pete")

Musicor

❑ 6308		Please Mr. Music Man/Foolish Clock	1977		2.00	4.00

Polydor

❑ 881 177-7		Silver Horse/Loneliness	1984		2.00	4.00

RCA

❑ PB-10759		Just One Look-Baby I'm Yours/That Is All	1976		2.00	4.00
		With Lynda Lawrence				
❑ PB-11059		Perfect Day/Who Done It	1977		2.00	4.00
❑ PB-11144		All I Think About Is You/	1977		2.00	4.00
		I Never Thought I'd Get This Lonely				
❑ PB-11193		Ain't It Kinda Wonderful/I'm Bringing a Red, Red Rose	1978		2.00	4.00
❑ PB-11318		Spaceman/Me and My Arrow	1978		2.00	4.00

RCA Victor

❑ 47-9206		Without Her/Freckles	1967	2.00	4.00	8.00
❑ 47-9298		You Can't Do That/Ten Little Indians	1967	2.50	5.00	10.00
❑ 47-9383		River Deep Mountain High/	1967	2.00	4.00	8.00
		She Sang Hymns Out of Tune				
❑ 47-9442		One/Sister Marie	1968	2.00	4.00	8.00
❑ 47-9544		Everybody's Talkin'/Don't Leave Me	1968	3.00	6.00	12.00
❑ 47-9675		Rainmaker/I Will Take You There	1968	2.00	4.00	8.00

Number		Title (A Side/B Side)	Year	VG	VG+	NM
❑ 74-0161		Everybody's Talkin'/Rainmaker	1969	2.50	5.00	10.00
❑ 74-0207		Maybe/Marchin' Down Broadway	1969	2.00	4.00	8.00
❑ 74-0261		I Guess the Lord Must Be in New York City/Maybe	1969	2.00	4.00	8.00
❑ 74-0310		I'll Be Home/Waiting	1970		3.00	6.00
❑ 74-0336		Caroline/Yellow Man	1970		3.00	6.00
❑ 74-0362		Down to the Valley/Buy My Album	1970		3.00	6.00
❑ 74-0443		Me and My Arrow/Are You Sleeping	1971		3.00	6.00
❑ 74-0524		Without Her/Good Old Desk	1971		3.00	6.00
❑ 74-0604		Without You/Gotta Get Up	1971		2.50	5.00
❑ 74-0673		The Moonbeam Song/Jump Into the Fire	1972		2.50	5.00
❑ 74-0718		Coconut/Down	1972		2.50	5.00
❑ 74-0788		Spaceman/Turn On Your Radio	1972		2.50	5.00
❑ 74-0855		Remember (Christmas)/The Lottery Song	1972		2.50	5.00
❑ APBO-0039		As Time Goes By/Lullabye in Ragtime	1973		3.00	6.00
❑ APBO-0246		Daybreak/Down	1974		2.00	4.00
❑ APBO-0246	PS	Daybreak/Down	1974		3.00	6.00
❑ PB-10001		Many Rivers to Cross/Don't Forget Me	1974	2.00	4.00	8.00
❑ PB-10078		Subterranean Homesick Blues/Mucho Mungo	1974	2.00	4.00	8.00
❑ PB-10130		Remember (Christmas)/The Lottery Song	1974		2.00	4.00
❑ PB-10139		Loop De Loop/Don't Forget Me	1974		2.00	4.00
❑ PB-10183		Kojak Columbo/Turn Out the Light	1975		2.00	4.00
❑ PB-10634		Sail Away/Moonshine Bandit	1976		2.00	4.00

Tower

❑ 103		Sixteen Tons/I'm Gonna Lose My Mind	1964	3.75	7.50	15.00
❑ 136		You Can't Take Your Love Away from Me/ Born in Grenada	1965	3.75	7.50	15.00
❑ 244		She's Yours/Growing Up	1966	3.75	7.50	15.00
❑ 518		Good Time/Growin' Up	1969	3.75	7.50	15.00

Nimble, Jack B. and the Quicks
Del Rio

❑ 2303/4		Like Keyed/Babes in Toyland	1962	6.25	12.50	25.00
❑ 2305		Nut Rocker/Never on Sunday	1962	7.50	15.00	30.00

Dot

❑ 16319		Nut Rocker/Never on Sunday	1962	3.75	7.50	15.00

94 East
(Prince and Andre Cymone in the early days)
Hot Pink

❑ 3223		Just Another Sucker/(B-side unknown)	1986		3.00	6.00

Polydor

❑ 14414		Be My Fortune Teller/I Just Wanna Be	1977			
		Record not known to exist, even as a promo.				

1910 Fruitgum Company
Attack

❑ 10293		Lawdy, Lawdy/The Clock	1970	3.00	6.00	12.00

Buddah

❑ 24		Simon Says/Reflections from the Looking Glass	1968	2.50	5.00	10.00
❑ 39		May I Take a Giant Step (Into Your Heart)/ (Poor Old) Mr. Jensen	1968	2.00	4.00	8.00
❑ 54		1,2,3, Red Light/Sticky, Sticky	1968	2.50	5.00	10.00
❑ 71		Goody Goody Gumdrops/Candy Kisses	1968	2.00	4.00	8.00
❑ 91		Indian Giver/Pow Wow	1969	2.50	5.00	10.00
❑ 114		Special Delivery/No Good Annie	1969	2.00	4.00	8.00
❑ 130		The Train/Eternal Light	1969	2.00	4.00	8.00
❑ 146		When We Get Married/Baby Sweet	1969	2.00	4.00	8.00

Super K

❑ 115		Go Away/The Track	1970	3.00	6.00	12.00

Nino and the Ebb Tides
Acme

❑ 720		Franny Franny/Darling I'll Love Only You	1958	75.00	150.00	300.00

Madison

❑ 162		Those Oldies But Goodies (Remind Me of You)/ Don't Run Away	1961	10.00	20.00	40.00
❑ 166		Juke Box Saturday Night/(Someday) I'll Fall in Love	1961	7.50	15.00	30.00

Mala

❑ 480		Automatic Reaction/Linda Lou Garrett Like 24 Karat	1964	5.00	10.00	20.00

Marco

❑ 105		Little Miss Blue/Someday	1961	12.50	25.00	50.00

Mr. Peacock

❑ 102		Wished I Was Home/Happy Guy	1961	6.25	12.50	25.00
❑ 117		Lovin' Time/Stamps, Baby, Stamps	1962	6.25	12.50	25.00

Mr. Peeke

❑ 123		Tonight I'll Be Lonely/Nursery Rhymes	1963	6.25	12.50	25.00

Recorte

❑ 405		Puppy Love/You Make Me Rock 'N' Roll	1958	12.50	25.00	50.00
❑ 408		The Real Meaning of Christmas/ Two Purple Shadows in the Snow	1958	75.00	150.00	300.00
❑ 409		I'm Confessin'/Tell the World I Do	1959	12.50	25.00	50.00
❑ 413		Don't Look Around/I Love Girls	1959	25.00	50.00	100.00

Number		Title (A Side/B Side)	Year	VG	VG+	NM

Nirvana
(The group on Bell is not the same as the others)
Bell
☐ 715		We Can Help You/Pentecost Hotel	1968	2.50	5.00	10.00
☐ 730		You Are Just the One/Girl in the Park	1968	2.50	5.00	10.00
☐ 739		Trapeze/The Touchables	1968	2.50	5.00	10.00

Communion
☐ 23		Here She Comes Now/Venus in Furs	1991	3.00	6.25	12.50
		B-side by The Melvins; green vinyl				
☐ 23		Here She Comes Now/Venus in Furs	1991	3.00	6.25	12.50
		B-side by The Melvins; blue vinyl				
☐ 23	PS	Here She Comes Now/Venus in Furs	1991	3.00	6.25	12.50
		B-side by The Melvins				

DGC
☐ 19050		Smells Like Teen Spirit/Even In His Youth	1991	2.00	4.00	8.00
☐ 19120		Come As You Are/Drain You	1992	2.00	4.00	8.00

Sub Pop
☐ 23		Love Buzz/Big Cheese	1988	18.75	37.50	75.00
		#1 in Sub Pop Singles Club series				
☐ 23	PS	Love Buzz/Big Cheese	1988	18.75	37.50	75.00
		Hand-numbered edition of 1,000				
☐ 73		Sliver/Dive	1990	10.00	20.00	40.00
		First 3,000 on blue vinyl				
☐ 73		Sliver/Dive	1990	12.50	25.00	50.00
		Clear pink/lavender vinyl				
☐ 73		Sliver/Dive	1990	2.50	5.00	10.00
		Black vinyl, no California address on label				
☐ 73		Sliver/Dive	1990		3.50	7.00
		Later issues on pale yellow vinyl with California address on label				
☐ 73		Sliver/Dive	1990			3.00
		Still later issues on black vinyl with California address on label				
☐ 73	PS	Sliver/Dive	1990	2.50	5.00	10.00
		Original picture sleeves were fold-over, not seam sealed				
☐ 73	PS	Sliver/Dive	1990			3.00
		Later picture sleeves were seam sealed				
☐ 97		Molly's Lips (Live)/Candy	1991	8.75	17.50	35.00
		B-side by Fluid; green vinyl				
☐ 97		Molly's Lips (Live)/Candy	1991	2.50	5.00	10.00
		B-side by Fluid; black vinyl				
☐ 97	PS	Molly's Lips (Live)/Candy	1991	2.50	5.00	10.00
		B-side by Fluid; #27 in Sub Pop Singles Club series				

Nitzsche, Jack
Fantasy
☐ 760		One Flew Over the Cuckoo's Nest/The Last Dance	1976		3.00	6.00

MCA
☐ 40897		Coke Machine/Hard Workin' Man	1978		2.00	4.00

Reprise
☐ 0262		The Last Race/Man with the Golden Arm	1964	5.00	10.00	20.00
☐ 0285		Theme from The Long Ships/Zapata	1964	5.00	10.00	20.00
☐ 0337		The Green Grass of Texas/Night Walker	1965	5.00	10.00	20.00
☐ 0364		Senorita from Detroit/Puerto Vallarta	1965	5.00	10.00	20.00
☐ 20,202		The Lonely Surfer/Song for a Summer Night	1963	7.50	15.00	30.00
☐ 20,202	PS	The Lonely Surfer/Song for a Summer Night	1963	25.00	50.00	100.00
☐ 20,225		Rumble/Theme for a Broken Heart	1963	5.00	10.00	20.00

No Names, The
Guyden
☐ 2114		Love/Jam	1964	12.50	25.00	50.00

Nobells, The
Mar
☐ 101		Searchin' for My Love/Crying Over You	1962	25.00	50.00	100.00

Nobles, The
(More than one group)
ABC-Paramount
☐ 10012		Just for Me/To Me	1959	3.75	7.50	15.00
☐ 9984		Till the End of Time/Standing Loose	1958	3.75	7.50	15.00

Columbia
☐ 10642		Nobody But You/We Can Make the Difference	1977		2.50	5.00

Klik
☐ 305		Poor Rock and Roll/Ting-a-Ling	1958	50.00	100.00	200.00

Selbon
☐ 1005		Black Widow/Jaguar	1963	10.00	20.00	40.00

Stacy
☐ 926		Serenade/You Ain't Right	1962	5.00	10.00	20.00

Tee Gee
☐ 101		Oops Oh Lawdy/Stop Crying	1958	12.50	25.00	50.00

Number	Title (A Side/B Side)	Year	VG	VG+	NM

Times Square

☐ 1	Poor Rock and Roll/Ting-a-Ling	1963	6.25	12.50	25.00
	Green vinyl				
☐ 1	Poor Rock and Roll/Ting-a-Ling	1963	7.50	15.00	30.00
	Blue vinyl				
☐ 12	Crime Doesn't Pay/Darkness	1963	5.00	10.00	20.00
	All copies on blue vinyl				
☐ 33	Why Be a Fool/The Search	1964	5.00	10.00	20.00

U.S.A.

| ☐ 788 | Marlene/That Special One | 1965 | 6.25 | 12.50 | 25.00 |

Nodaens, The
(With Dave Nowlen, formerly of the Survivors)

Gold

| ☐ 1001 | Beach Girl/Gypsy | 196? | 20.00 | 40.00 | 80.00 |

Noel, Sid

Aladdin

☐ 3331	The Flying Saucer (Part 1)/	1956	10.00	20.00	40.00
	The Flying Saucer (Part 2)				
	Cover version of the Buchanan and Goodman break-in record				

Nolan, Frankie

ABC-Paramount

| ☐ 10231 | I Still Care/(I Wish It Were) Summer All Year Round | 1961 | 10.00 | 20.00 | 40.00 |
| | *Frankie Valli also appears on this record* | | | | |

Noland, Terry

Apt

| ☐ 25065 | There Goes a Girl/Long Gone Baby | 1962 | 3.75 | 7.50 | 15.00 |

Brunswick

☐ 55010	Hypnotized/Ten Little Women	1957	7.50	15.00	30.00
☐ 55036	Patti Baby/Don't Do Me This Way	1957	7.50	15.00	30.00
☐ 55054	Puppy Love/Oh Baby, Look at Me	1958	7.50	15.00	30.00
☐ 55069	Crazy Dream/Everyone But One	1958	7.50	15.00	30.00
☐ 55092	There Was a Fungus Among Us/Sugar Drop	1958	10.00	20.00	40.00
☐ 55122	Guess I'm Gonna Fall/Teenage Teardrops	1959	7.50	15.00	30.00

Coral

| ☐ 62274 | There Was a Fungus Among Us/Sugar Drop | 1961 | 5.00 | 10.00 | 20.00 |

Non-Conformists, The

Scepter

| ☐ 12184 | Two-Legged Big Eyed Yellow Haired Crying Canary/ | 1967 | 7.50 | 15.00 | 30.00 |
| | Bird Walk | | | | |

Noone, Peter
(Ex-Herman's Hermits)

Bell

☐ 45,131	Oh You Pretty Thing/Because You're There	1971	12.50	25.00	50.00
	Allegedly features David Bowie on A-side piano				
☐ 45,266	Should I/(B-side unknown)	1972	2.00	4.00	8.00

Casablanca

☐ 0017	Meet Me at the Corner Down at Joe's Cafe/	1974		2.50	5.00
	(Blame It)On the Pony Express				
☐ 0106	Meet Me at the Corner Down at Joe's Cafe/	1974		2.00	4.00
	(Blame It)On the Pony Express				
☐ 802	Meet Me at the Corner Down at Joe's Cafe/	1974		2.00	4.00
	(Blame It)On the Pony Express				
☐ 823	Something Old, Something New//(B-side unknown)	1975		2.00	4.00

Johnston

| ☐ 02838 | (I Don't Wanna Love You But) You Got Me Anyway/ | 1982 | | 2.00 | 4.00 |
| | I'm One of the Glory Boys | | | | |

Philips

| ☐ 40730 | All SIng Together/Getting Over You | 1974 | | 2.50 | 5.00 |

Norman, Gene, and the Rockin' Rockets

Snag

| ☐ 101 | Snaggle Tooth Ann/Long Gone Night Train | 1958 | 250.00 | 500.00 | 1,000 |

Normanaires, The

MGM

| ☐ 11622 | My Greatest Sin/Wrap It Up | 1953 | 20.00 | 40.00 | 80.00 |

Norris, Charles

Atlantic

| ☐ 994 | Messin' Up/Let Me Know | 1953 | 15.00 | 30.00 | 60.00 |

Northern Lights, The
(With Bjorn Ulvaeus, later of ABBA)

United Artists

| ☐ 991 | Time to Move Along/No Time | 1966 | 5.00 | 10.00 | 20.00 |

Number		Title (A Side/B Side)	Year	VG	VG+	NM

Note-Torials, The
Impala
| ❑ 201 | | Valerie/Loved and Lost | 1958 | 100.00 | 200.00 | 400.00 |

Sunbeam
| ❑ 119 | | Valerie/Loved and Lost | 1958 | 50.00 | 100.00 | 200.00 |

Notes, The
Capitol
| ❑ F3332 | | Don't Leave Me Now/Cha Jezebel | 1956 | 75.00 | 150.00 | 300.00 |

MGM
| ❑ 12338 | | Trust in Me/Round and Round | 1956 | 50.00 | 100.00 | 200.00 |

Sarg
| ❑ 177 | | Little Girl/G.I. Blues | 1959 | 12.50 | 25.00 | 50.00 |

Novas, The
Parrot
| ❑ 45005 | | The Crusher/Take 7 | 1964 | 20.00 | 40.00 | 80.00 |

Twin Town
| ❑ 713 | | Novas Coaster/On the Road Again | 1965 | 10.00 | 20.00 | 40.00 |

NRBQ
Bearsville
| ❑ 29588 | | Rain at the Drive-In/Shackaroo | 1983 | | 2.50 | 5.00 |

Button
| ❑ 037 | | Froggy Went a-Courtin'/Bless Your Beautiful Hide | 1975 | 12.50 | 25.00 | 50.00 |

Columbia
❑ 44865		Stomp/I Didn't Know Myself	1969		3.00	6.00
❑ 44937		C'mon Everybody/Rocket No. 9	1969		3.00	6.00
❑ 45019		Sure to Fall (In Love With You)/Down in My Heart	1969		3.00	6.00

Kama Sutra
❑ 544		Howard Johnson's Got His Hojo Workin'/Do You Feel It	1972		3.00	6.00
❑ 549		Only You/Magnet	1972		3.00	6.00
❑ 575		C'mon If You're Comin'/RC Cola and a Moon Pie	1973		3.00	6.00
❑ 586		Get That Gasoline Blues/Mona	1974		3.00	6.00

Mercury
| ❑ 73991 | | Green Lights/I Love Her, She Loves Me | 1978 | | 2.50 | 5.00 |

Red Rooster
❑ 1001		Ridin' in My Car/Do the Bump	1977	2.50	5.00	10.00
❑ 1002		I Got a Rocket in My Pocket/Tapdancin' Bats	1977	3.00	6.00	
❑ 1002	PS	I Got a Rocket in My Pocket/Tapdancin' Bats	1977	2.50	5.00	10.00

Rounder
❑ 1010		Captain Lou!/Boardin' House Pie	1982		2.00	4.00
❑ 1010	PS	Captain Lou!/Boardin' House Pie	1982		2.00	4.00
❑ 4521		Hot Biscuits and Sweet Marie/She Don't Look Good	1979		2.50	5.00
❑ 4522		Get That Gasoline Blues/Wacky Tobacky	1979		2.50	5.00
❑ 4525		Christmas Wish/Jolly Old St. Nicholas	1979		2.50	5.00
❑ 4525	PS	Christmas Wish/Jolly Old St. Nicholas	1979		3.00	6.00
❑ 4531		Me and the Boys/People	1980		2.50	5.00
❑ 4531	PS	Me and the Boys/People	1980	2.50	5.00	10.00
❑ 4539		Never Take the Place of You/ Captain Lou Albano for Tiddlywinks	1980		2.50	5.00
❑ 4556		Things to Do/I Can't Stop Loving You Now	1985		2.00	4.00
		With Skeeter Davis				

Scepter
| ❑ 12322 | | Sho' Need Love/Don't Talk About My Music | 1971 | 12.50 | 25.00 | 50.00 |
| | | *As "The Dickens"* | | | | |

Select-O-Hit
| ❑ 022 | | Sourpuss/Rumors | 1974 | 12.50 | 25.00 | 50.00 |

Virgin
| ❑ 99130 | | If I Don't Have You/Boozoo, That's Who | 1989 | | 2.00 | 4.00 |
| ❑ 99161 | DJ | Wild Weekend/This Love Is True | 1989 | | 2.00 | 4.00 |

Nu Tornados, The
Carlton
| ❑ 492 | | Philadelphia, U.S.A./Magic Record | 1959 | 6.25 | 12.50 | 25.00 |
| ❑ 497 | | The "Ole Mummers" Strut/Let's Have a Party | 1959 | 5.00 | 10.00 | 20.00 |

Felsted
| ❑ 8577 | | Cry Baby Cry/Keep a Flower Growing in Your Heart | 1959 | 5.00 | 10.00 | 20.00 |

Numbers, The
Bonneville
| ❑ 101 | | Big Red/My Pillow | 1962 | 50.00 | 100.00 | 200.00 |

Dore
| ❑ 641 | | Big Red/My Pillow | 1962 | 12.50 | 25.00 | 50.00 |

Nutmegs, The
Baby Grand
| ❑ 800 | | Story Untold '72/Tell Me | 1972 | 2.00 | 4.00 | 8.00 |

Herald
| ❑ 452 | | Story Untold/Make Me Lose My Mind | 1955 | 12.50 | 25.00 | 50.00 |

Number		Title (A Side/B Side)	Year	VG	VG+	NM
❑ 459		Ship of Love/Rock Me	1955	7.50	15.00	30.00
❑ 466		Whispering Sorrows/Betty Lou	1955	10.00	20.00	40.00
❑ 475		Key to the Kingdom (Of Your Heart)/	1956	10.00	20.00	40.00
		Gift O' Gabbin' Woman				
❑ 492		Love So True/Comin' Home	1956	7.50	15.00	30.00
❑ 538		My Sweet Dream/My Story	1959	10.00	20.00	40.00
❑ 574		Rip Van Winkle/Crazy 'Bout You	1962	6.25	12.50	25.00

Nightrain

Number		Title (A Side/B Side)	Year	VG	VG+	NM
❑ 905		Shifting Sands/Take Me and Make Me	1973	2.00	4.00	8.00

Tel

Number		Title (A Side/B Side)	Year	VG	VG+	NM
❑ 1014		A Dream of Love/Someone, Somewhere (Help Me)	1960	25.00	50.00	100.00

Times Square

Number		Title (A Side/B Side)	Year	VG	VG+	NM
❑ 6		Let Me Tell You/Hello	1963	6.25	12.50	25.00
	Blue vinyl					
❑ 14		The Way Love Should Be/Wide Hoop Skirts	1963	5.00	10.00	20.00
❑ 19		Down to Earth/Coo Coo Cuddle Coo	1963	5.00	10.00	20.00
	B-side by the Admirations					
❑ 22		Why Must We Go to School/	1963	5.00	10.00	20.00
		Ink Dries Quicker Than Tears				
	B-side by the Volumes					
❑ 27		Down in Mexico/My Sweet Dreams	1964	5.00	10.00	20.00
❑ 103		You're Crying/Wa-Do-Wa	1964	5.00	10.00	20.00

Nutones, The
Combo

Number		Title (A Side/B Side)	Year	VG	VG+	NM
❑ 127		At Midnight/Beans 'N' Greens	1957	37.50	75.00	150.00

Hollywood Star

Number		Title (A Side/B Side)	Year	VG	VG+	NM
❑ 798		Believe/Annie Kicked the Bucket	1955	2,000	3,000	4,000
❑ 798		Believe/You're No Barking Dog	1955	150.00	300.00	600.00

Nutty Squirrels, The
Columbia

Number		Title (A Side/B Side)	Year	VG	VG+	NM
❑ 41818		Please Don't Take Our Tree for Christmas/Nutty Noel	1960	5.00	10.00	20.00
❑ 41818	PS	Please Don't Take Our Tree for Christmas/Nutty Noel	1960	10.00	20.00	40.00

Hanover

Number		Title (A Side/B Side)	Year	VG	VG+	NM
❑ 4540		Uh! Oh! (Part 1)/Uh! Oh! (Part 2)	1959	6.25	12.50	25.00
❑ 4540	PS	Uh! Oh! (Part 1)/Uh! Oh! (Part 2)	1959	12.50	25.00	50.00
❑ 4551		Eager Beaver/Zowee	1960	5.00	10.00	20.00

RCA Victor

Number		Title (A Side/B Side)	Year	VG	VG+	NM
❑ 47-8287		Hello Again/Bluesette	1963	3.75	7.50	15.00

O

O'Jays, The
Apollo

Number		Title (A Side/B Side)	Year	VG	VG+	NM
❑ 759		Miracles/Can't Take It	1961	7.50	15.00	30.00

Astroscope

Number		Title (A Side/B Side)	Year	VG	VG+	NM
❑ 106		Wisdom of a Child/Peace	1974	2.00	4.00	8.00
❑ 110		Peace/	1974	2.00	4.00	8.00
		Don't You Know a True Love (When You See Her)				

Bell

Number		Title (A Side/B Side)	Year	VG	VG+	NM
❑ 45,378		Look Over Your Shoulder/Four for the Price of One	1973		2.50	5.00
❑ 691		I'll Be Sweeter Tomorrow (Than I Was Today)/	1967	2.50	5.00	10.00
		I Dig Your Act				
❑ 704		Look Over Your Shoulder/I'm So Glad I Found You	1968	2.50	5.00	10.00
❑ 737		The Choice/Going, Going, Gone	1968	2.50	5.00	10.00
❑ 749		I Miss You/Now That I Found You	1968	2.50	5.00	10.00
❑ 770		Don't You Know a True Love/That's All Right	1969	2.00	4.00	8.00

EMI

Number		Title (A Side/B Side)	Year	VG	VG+	NM
❑ S7-17491		Somebody Else Will/Decisions	1993		2.00	4.00
❑ S7-18914		Have Yourself a Merry Little Christmas/	1995			3.00
		I Can Hardly Wait 'Til Christmas				
❑ 50180		Have You Had Your Love Today/	1989			3.00
		The Pot Can't Call the Kettle Black				
❑ 50212		Out of My Mind (Radio Mix)/	1989			3.00
		Out of My Mind (Soul 2 Mix)				

Imperial

Number		Title (A Side/B Side)	Year	VG	VG+	NM
❑ 5942		How Does It Feel/Crack Up Laughing	1963	3.75	7.50	15.00
❑ 5976		Lonely Drifter/That's Enough	1963	2.50	5.00	10.00
❑ 66007		Stand Tall/The Storm Is Over	1963	2.50	5.00	10.00
❑ 66025		I'll Never Stop Loving You/My Dearest Beloved	1964	2.50	5.00	10.00
❑ 66037		You're on Top/Lovely Dee	1964	2.50	5.00	10.00
❑ 66076		Girl Machine/Oh How You Hurt Me	1964	2.50	5.00	10.00
❑ 66102		Lipstick Traces/Think It Over, Baby	1965	2.50	5.00	10.00
❑ 66121		Whip It On Me Baby/I've Cried My Last Tear	1965	2.50	5.00	10.00
❑ 66131		You're the One (You're the Only One)/	1965	2.50	5.00	10.00
		Let It All Come Out				
❑ 66145		I'll Never Let You Go/It Won't Hurt	1965	2.50	5.00	10.00
❑ 66162		I'll Never Forget You/Pretty Words	1966	10.00	20.00	40.00
❑ 66177		No Time for You/It's a Blowin' Wind	1966	2.50	5.00	10.00
❑ 66197		Friday Night/Stand In for Love	1966	2.50	5.00	10.00
❑ 66200		Lonely Drifter/That's Enough	1966	2.50	5.00	10.00

Number	Title (A Side/B Side)	Year	VG	VG+	NM
Little Star					
❑ 124	How Does It Feel/Crack Up Laughing	1963	6.25	12.50	25.00
❑ 125	Dream Girl/Joey St. Vincent	1963	6.25	12.50	25.00
❑ 1401	Now He's Home/Just to Be with You	1962	6.25	12.50	25.00
Minit					
❑ 32015	Hold On/Working on Your Case	1967	2.50	5.00	10.00
Neptune					
❑ 12	One Night Affair/ There's Someone (Waiting Back Home)	1969	2.00	4.00	8.00
❑ 18	Branded Bad/You're the Best Thing Since Candy	1969	2.00	4.00	8.00
❑ 20	Christmas Ain't Christmas New Year's Ain't New Year's Without the One You Love/There's Someone Waiting	1969	2.50	5.00	10.00
❑ 22	Deeper (In Love with You)/I've Got the Groove	1970	2.00	4.00	8.00
❑ 31	Looky Looky (Look at Me Girl)/Let Me in Your World	1970	2.00	4.00	8.00
❑ 33	Christmas Ain't Christmas New Year's Ain't New Year's Without the One You Love/Just Can't Get Enough	1970	2.00	4.00	8.00
Philadelphia Int'l.					
❑ 02096	Forever Mine/Girl, Don't Let It Get You Down	1981			3.00
	Reissue				
❑ 02834	Don't Walk Away Mad/I Just Want to Satisfy	1982		2.00	4.00
❑ 02982	One by One/My Favorite Person	1982		2.00	4.00
❑ 03009	Out in the Real World/Your Body's Here with Me	1982		2.00	4.00
❑ 3517	Back Stabbers/Sunshine	1972		2.50	5.00
❑ 3522	992 Arguments/Listen to the Clock on the Wall	1972		2.50	5.00
❑ 3524	Love Train/Who Am I	1973		2.50	5.00
❑ 3531	Time to Get Down/ Shiftless, Shady, Jealous Kind of People	1973		2.50	5.00
❑ 3535	Put Your Hands Together/You Got Your Hooks in Me	1973		2.50	5.00
❑ 3537	Christmas Ain't Christmas New Year's Ain't New Year's Without the One You Love/Just Can't Get Enough	1973		3.00	6.00
❑ 3544	For the Love of Money/People Keep Tellin' Me	1974		2.50	5.00
❑ 3558	Sunshine (Part 1)/Sunshine (Part 2)	1974		2.50	5.00
❑ 3565	Give the People What They Want/ What Am I Waiting For	1975		2.50	5.00
❑ 3573	Let Me Make Love to You/Survival	1975		2.50	5.00
❑ 3577	I Love Music (Part 1)/I Love Music (Part 2)	1975		2.50	5.00
❑ 3581	Christmas Ain't Christmas New Year's Ain't New Year's Without the One You Love/Just Can't Get Enough	1975		2.50	5.00
❑ 3587	Livin' for the Weekend/Stairway to Heaven	1976		2.50	5.00
❑ 3594	Family Reunion/Unity	1976		2.50	5.00
❑ 3601	Message in Our Music/She's Only a Woman	1976		2.50	5.00
❑ 3610	Darlin' Darlin' Baby (Sweet, Tender, Love)/A Prayer	1976		2.50	5.00
❑ 3631	Work On Me/Let's Spend Some Time Together	1977		2.50	5.00
❑ 3642	Use Ta Be My Girl/This Time Baby	1978		2.50	5.00
❑ 3652	Brandy/Take Me to the Stars	1978		2.50	5.00
❑ 3666	Cry Together/Strokety Stroke	1978		2.50	5.00
❑ 3707	Sing a Happy Song/One in a Million (Girl)	1979		2.50	5.00
❑ 3726	I Want You Here with Me/Get On Out and Party	1979		2.50	5.00
❑ 3727	Forever Mine/Get On Out and Party	1979		2.50	5.00
❑ 03892	A Letter to My Friends/I Can't Stand the Pain	1983		2.00	4.00
❑ 04069	Put Our Heads Together/Nice and Easy	1983		2.00	4.00
❑ 04437	I Really Need You Now/Extraordinary Girl	1984		2.00	4.00
❑ 04535	Let Me Show You (How Much I Really Love You)/ Love You Direct	1984		2.00	4.00
❑ 50013	Just Another Lonely Night/ What Good Are These Arms of Mine	1985			3.00
❑ 50021	What a Woman/I Love America	1985			3.00
❑ 50067	Don't Take Your Love Away/ I Just Want Somebody to Love Me	1987			3.00
❑ 50084	Lovin' You/Don't Let the Dream Get Along	1987			3.00
❑ 50104	Let Me Touch You/Undercover Lover	1987			3.00
❑ 50122	I Just Want Someone to Love Me/Lovin' You	1988			3.00
Saru					
❑ 1220	Shattered Man/La De Da (Means I'm Out to Get You)	1971		3.00	6.00
TSOP					
❑ 4790	Girl, Don't Let It Get You Down/ You're the Girl of My Dreams	1980		2.00	4.00
❑ 4791	Once Is Not Enough/To Prove I Love You	1980		2.00	4.00
❑ 70050	You Won't Fall/ You'll Never Know (All There Is to Know 'Bout Love)	1981		2.00	4.00

Obsessions, The
Accent

❑ 1182	Love Always/A Fool	1964	50.00	100.00	200.00

Octaves, The
Val

❑ 1001	You're Too Young/Mambo Carolyn	1958	18.75	37.50	75.00

Oddis, Ray
V.I.P.

❑ 25012	Happy Ghoul Tide/Ray the Newspaper Boy	1964	5.00	10.00	20.00

Off Keys, The
Rowe

❑ 003	Our Wedding Day/Singing Bells	1962	25.00	50.00	100.00

Number	Title (A Side/B Side)	Year	VG	VG+	NM

Technichord

❑ 1001	Our Wedding Day/Singing Bells	1962	12.50	25.00	50.00
	Glossy red label				
❑ 1001	Our Wedding Day/Singing Bells	1962	6.25	12.50	25.00
	Flat maroon label				

Ohio Express, The

Buddah

❑ 38	Yummy Yummy Yummy/Zig Zag	1968	2.50	5.00	10.00
❑ 56	Down at Lulu's/She's Not Coming Home	1968	2.00	4.00	8.00
❑ 70	Chewy Chewy/Firebird	1968	2.50	5.00	10.00
❑ 92	Sweeter Than Sugar/Bitter Than Lemon	1969	2.00	4.00	8.00
❑ 102	Mercy/Roll It Up	1969	2.00	4.00	8.00
❑ 117	Pinch Me (Baby, Convince Me)/Peanuts	1969	2.00	4.00	8.00
❑ 129	Sausalito (Is the Place to Go)/Make Love Not War	1969	2.00	4.00	8.00
	With Graham Gouldman, later of 10CC, on lead vocal				
❑ 147	Cowboy Convention/The Race (That Took Place)	1970	2.00	4.00	8.00
❑ 160	Love Equals Love/Peanuts	1970	2.00	4.00	8.00
❑ 386	Wham Bam/Slow and Steady	1973	3.75	7.50	15.00
	As "Ohio Ltd."				

Cameo

❑ 483	Beg, Borrow and Steal/Maybe	1967	3.00	6.00	12.00
❑ 2001	Try It/Soul Struttin'	1967	3.00	6.00	12.00

Super K

❑ 114	Hot Dog/Ooh La La	1970	2.50	5.00	10.00

Ohio Untouchables, The

(Early version of the Ohio Players)

LuPine

❑ 109	She's My Heart's Desire/What to Do	1962	12.50	25.00	50.00
❑ 110	Love Is Amazing/Forgive Me Darling	1962	12.50	25.00	50.00
❑ 116/7	I'm Tired/Uptown	1962	10.00	20.00	40.00
❑ 1009	She's My Heart's Desire/What to Do	1964	5.00	10.00	20.00
❑ 1010	Love Is Amazing/Forgive Me Darling	1964	5.00	10.00	20.00
❑ 1011	I'm Tired/Uptown	1964	3.75	7.50	15.00

Oldham, Andrew

(Producer of the Rolling Stones 1963-67)

Parrot

❑ 9684	Theme from The Dick Van Dyke Show/	1964	7.50	15.00	30.00
	I'd Like to See Me on the "B" Side				
❑ 9745	I Get Around/Save It For Me	1965	7.50	15.00	30.00

Olivers, The

Phalanx

❑ 1022	Bleecker Street/I Saw What You Did	1967	15.00	30.00	60.00

RCA Victor

❑ 47-9113	Bleecker Street/I Saw What You Did	1967	5.00	10.00	20.00

Olympics, The

Arvee

❑ 562	(Baby) Hully Gully/Private Eye	1959	6.25	12.50	25.00
❑ 595	Big Boy Pete/The Slop	1960	6.25	12.50	25.00
❑ 5006	Shimmy Like Kate/Workin' Hard	1960	5.00	10.00	20.00
❑ 5020	Dance by the Light of the Moon/Dodge City	1960	5.00	10.00	20.00
❑ 5023	Little Pedro/The Bullfight	1961	5.00	10.00	20.00
❑ 5031	Stay Where You Are/Dooley	1961	10.00	20.00	40.00
❑ 5044	Mash Them 'Taters/The Stomp	1961	5.00	10.00	20.00
❑ 5051	Everybody Likes to Cha Cha Cha/The Twist	1962	3.75	7.50	15.00
❑ 5056	Baby It's Hot/The Scotch	1962	3.75	7.50	15.00
❑ 5073	What'd I Say (Part 1)/What'd I Say (Part 2)	1963	3.75	7.50	15.00
❑ 6501	Big Boy Pete '65/Stay Where You Are	1965	3.00	6.00	12.00

Demon

❑ 1508	Western Movies/Well!	1958	7.50	15.00	30.00
❑ 1512	Dance with the Teacher/Everybody Needs Love	1958	6.25	12.50	25.00
❑ 1514	Your Love/The Chicken	1959	6.25	12.50	25.00

Duo Disc

❑ 104	The Boogler (Part 1)/The Boogler (Part 2)	1964	3.00	6.00	12.00
❑ 105	Return of Big Boy Pete/Return of the Watusi	1964	3.00	6.00	12.00

Jubilee

❑ 5674	The Cartoon Song/Things That Make Me Laugh	1969	2.00	4.00	8.00

Loma

❑ 2010	I'm Comin' Home/Rainin' in My Heart	1965	2.50	5.00	10.00
❑ 2013	Good Lovin'/Olympic Shuffle	1965	2.50	5.00	10.00
❑ 2017	Baby I'm Yours/No More Will I Cry	1965	2.50	5.00	10.00

MGM

❑ 14505	Worm in Your Wheatgerm/The Apartment	1973		2.50	5.00

Mirwood

❑ 5504	We Go Together (Pretty Baby)/Secret Agents	1966	2.00	4.00	8.00
❑ 5513	Mine Exclusively/Secret Agents	1966	2.00	4.00	8.00
❑ 5523	Baby Do the Philly Dog/Western Movies	1966	2.00	4.00	8.00
❑ 5525	The Bounce/The Duck	1966	2.00	4.00	8.00

Number		Title (A Side/B Side)	Year	VG	VG+	NM
☐ 5529		The Same Old Thing/I'll Do a Little Bit More	1967	2.00	4.00	8.00
☐ 5533		Big Boy Pete/(Baby) Hully Gully	1967	2.00	4.00	8.00

Parkway

☐ 6003		Lookin' for a Love/Good Things	1968	2.00	4.00	8.00

Titan

☐ 1718		The Chicken/Cool Short	1961	6.25	12.50	25.00

Tower

☐ 137		Que Sera Sera/I Really Do	1965	2.00	4.00	8.00

As "Earl Royce and the Olympics" (may not be the same group as the others)

Tri Disc

☐ 105		Return of Big Boy Pete/Return of the Watusi	1962	3.75	7.50	15.00
☐ 106		The Bounce/Fireworks	1963	3.75	7.50	15.00
☐ 107		Dancin' Holiday/Do the Slauson Shuffle	1963	3.75	7.50	15.00
☐ 110		Bounce Again/A New Dancin' Partner	1963	3.75	7.50	15.00
☐ 112		The Broken Hip/So Goodbye	1963	3.75	7.50	15.00

Warner Bros.

☐ 7369		Girl, You're My Kind of People/Please, Please, Please	1970		3.00	6.00

Ono, Yoko

(Also see "Lennon, John"; all her B-sides of his singles can be found there)

Apple

☐ GM/OYB-1	DJ	Greenfield Morning/Open Your Box	1971	200.00	400.00	800.00

Exactly six copies made for the personal use of Yoko Ono.

☐ 1839		Mrs. Lennon/Midsummer New York	1971		3.50	7.00

As "Yoko Ono/Plastic Ono Band"

☐ 1853		Now or Never/Move On Fast	1972		3.50	7.00
☐ 1853	PS	Now or Never/Move On Fast	1972	2.00	4.00	8.00
☐ 1859		Death of Samantha/Yang Yang	1973		3.50	7.00
☐ 1867		Woman Power/Men, Men, Men	1973		3.50	7.00

Capitol

☐ S7-18550		Never Say Goodbye/We're All Water	1995			3.00

Geffen

☐ PRO-S-935	DJ	Walking on Thin Ice (3:23)/Walking on Thin Ice (5:58)	1981	2.50	5.00	10.00
☐ 49683		Walking on Thin Ice/It Happened	1981		2.00	4.00
☐ 49683	PS	Walking on Thin Ice/It Happened	1981		2.00	4.00

Includes picture sleeve and lyric insert

☐ 49802		No, No, No/Will You Touch Me	1981		2.00	4.00
☐ 49802	PS	No, No, No/Will You Touch Me	1981		2.00	4.00
☐ 49849		Goodbye Sadness/I Don't Know Why	1981		2.00	4.00

Polydor

☐ 2224		My Man/Let the Tears Dry	1982			3.00
☐ 2224	PS	My Man/Let the Tears Dry	1982			3.00
☐ 883 455-7		Hell in Paradise/(B-side unknown)	1985			3.00
☐ 883 455-7	PS	Hell in Paradise/(B-side unknown)	1985			3.00

Orbison, Roy

(Also see "Traveling Wilburys")

Asylum

☐ 46048		Tears/Easy Way Out	1979		2.50	5.00
☐ 46541		Poor Baby/Lay It Down	1979		2.50	5.00

Je-Wel

☐ 101		Ooby Dooby/Tryin' to Get to You	1956	1,000	2,000	3,000

As "The Teen Kings"

Mercury

☐ 73610		Sweet Mama Blue/Heartache	1974	2.00	4.00	8.00
☐ 73652		Hung Up on You/Spanish Nights	1975		3.00	6.00
☐ 73705		It's So Lonely/Still	1975		3.00	6.00

MGM

☐ 13386		Ride Away/Wonderin'	1965	2.50	5.00	10.00
☐ 13386	PS	Ride Away/Wonderin'	1965	5.00	10.00	20.00
☐ 13410		Crawling Back/If You Can't Say Something Nice	1965	2.50	5.00	10.00
☐ 13410	PS	Crawling Back/If You Can't Say Something Nice	1965	5.00	10.00	20.00
☐ 13446		Breakin' Up Is Breakin' My Heart/Wait	1966	2.50	5.00	10.00
☐ 13446	PS	Breakin' Up Is Breakin' My Heart/Wait	1966	5.00	10.00	20.00
☐ 13498		Twinkle Toes/Where Is Tomorrow	1966	2.50	5.00	10.00
☐ 13498	PS	Twinkle Toes/Where Is Tomorrow	1966	5.00	10.00	20.00
☐ 13549		Too Soon to Know/You'll Never Be Sixteen Again	1966	2.50	5.00	10.00
☐ 13549	PS	Too Soon to Know/You'll Never Be Sixteen Again	1966	5.00	10.00	20.00
☐ 13634		Communication Breakdown/Going Back to Gloria	1966	2.50	5.00	10.00
☐ 13685		So Good/Memories	1967	2.50	5.00	10.00
☐ CS9-5		Celebrity Scene: Roy Orbison	1967	25.00	50.00	100.00

Box set of five singles. Price includes box, all 5 singles, jukebox title strips, bio. Records are sometimes found by themselves, so they are listed separately below.

☐ 13756		Ride Away/Crawlin' Back	1967	3.75	7.50	15.00
☐ 13757		Breakin' Up Is Breakin' My Heart/Too Soon to Know	1967	3.75	7.50	15.00
☐ 13758		Twinkle Toes/Where Is Tomorrow?	1967	3.75	7.50	15.00
☐ 13759		Sweet Dreams/Going Back to Gloria	1967	3.75	7.50	15.00
☐ 13760		You'll Never Be Sixteen Again/There Won't Be Many Coming Home	1967	3.75	7.50	15.00
☐ 13764		Cry Softly Lonely One/Pistolero	1967	2.50	5.00	10.00
☐ 13764	PS	Cry Softly Lonely One/Pistolero	1967	5.00	10.00	20.00
☐ 13817		She/Here Comes the Rain Baby	1967	2.50	5.00	10.00

Number		Title (A Side/B Side)	Year	VG	VG+	NM
☐ 13889		Shy Away/Born to Be Loved by You	1968	2.50	5.00	10.00
☐ 13950		Flowers/Walk On	1968	2.50	5.00	10.00
☐ 13991		Heartache/Sugar Man	1968	2.50	5.00	10.00
☐ 14039		Southbound Jericho Parkway/My Friend	1969	2.50	5.00	10.00
☐ 14079		Penny Arcade/Tennessee Own My Soul	1969	2.50	5.00	10.00
☐ 14105		How Do You Start Over/She Cheats on Me	1970	2.50	5.00	10.00
☐ 14121		So Young/If I Had a Woman Like You	1970	2.50	5.00	10.00
☐ 14293		Close Again/Last Night	1971	2.50	5.00	10.00
☐ 14358		Changes/God Loves You	1972	2.50	5.00	10.00
☐ 14413		Remember the Good/Harlem Woman	1972	2.50	5.00	10.00
☐ 14441		I Can Read Between the Lines/Memphis, Tennessee	1972	2.50	5.00	10.00
☐ 14552		Rain Rain (Coming Down)/Sooner or Later	1973	2.50	5.00	10.00
☐ 14626		I Wanna Live/You Lay So Easy on My Mind	1973	2.50	5.00	10.00

Monument

Number		Title (A Side/B Side)	Year	VG	VG+	NM
☐ 409		Paper Boy/With the Bug	1959	10.00	20.00	40.00
☐ 412		Uptown/Pretty One	1959	7.50	15.00	30.00
☐ 421		Only the Lonely (Know How I Feel)/Here Comes That Song Again	1960	5.00	10.00	20.00
☐ 425		Blue Angel/Today's Teardrops	1960	3.75	7.50	15.00
☐ 433		I'm Hurtin'/I Can't Stop Loving You	1960	3.75	7.50	15.00
☐ 433	PS	I'm Hurtin'/I Can't Stop Loving You	1960	7.50	15.00	30.00
☐ 438		Running Scared/Love Hurts	1961	3.75	7.50	15.00
☐ 438	PS	Running Scared/Love Hurts	1961	7.50	15.00	30.00
☐ 447		Crying/Candy Man	1961	3.75	7.50	15.00
☐ 447	PS	Crying/Candy Man	1961	7.50	15.00	30.00
☐ 456		Dream Baby (How Long Must I Dream)/The Actress	1962	3.75	7.50	15.00
☐ 456	PS	Dream Baby (How Long Must I Dream)/The Actress	1962	7.50	15.00	30.00
☐ 461		The Crowd/Mama	1962	3.75	7.50	15.00
☐ 461	PS	The Crowd/Mama	1962	7.50	15.00	30.00
☐ 467		Leah/Workin' for the Man	1962	3.75	7.50	15.00
☐ 467	PS	Leah/Workin' for the Man	1962	7.50	15.00	30.00
☐ 806		In Dreams/Shahdaroba	1963	3.75	7.50	15.00
☐ 806	PS	In Dreams/Shahdaroba	1963	7.50	15.00	30.00
☐ 824		Mean Woman Blues/Blue Bayou	1963	3.75	7.50	15.00
☐ 830		Pretty Paper/Beautiful Dreamer	1963	3.75	7.50	15.00
☐ 837		It's Over/Indian Wedding	1964	3.75	7.50	15.00
☐ 837	PS	It's Over/Indian Wedding	1964	7.50	15.00	30.00
☐ 851		Pretty Woman/Yo Te Amo Maria	1964	6.25	12.50	25.00
		Original title				
☐ 851		Oh Pretty Woman/Yo Te Amo Maria	1964	3.75	7.50	15.00
		Revised title				
☐ 873		Goodnight/Only with You	1965	3.75	7.50	15.00
☐ 891		(Say) You're My Girl/Sleepy Hollow	1965	3.75	7.50	15.00
☐ 906		Let the Good Times Roll/Distant Drums	1965	3.75	7.50	15.00
☐ 939		Lana/Our Summer Song	1966	3.75	7.50	15.00
☐ 8690		Belinda/All These Chains	1976		2.50	5.00
☐ 45200		(I'm a) Southern Man/Born to Love Me	1976		2.50	5.00
☐ 45215		Drifting Away/Under Suspicion	1977		2.50	5.00

RCA Victor

Number		Title (A Side/B Side)	Year	VG	VG+	NM
☐ 47-7381		Sweet and Innocent/Seems to Me	1958	10.00	20.00	40.00
☐ 47-7447		Almost Eighteen/Julie	1959	10.00	20.00	40.00

Sun

Number		Title (A Side/B Side)	Year	VG	VG+	NM
☐ 242		Ooby Dooby/Go! Go! Go!	1956	25.00	50.00	100.00
☐ 251		Rockhouse/You're My Baby	1956	12.50	25.00	50.00
☐ 265		Devil Doll/Sweet and Easy to Love	1957	12.50	25.00	50.00
☐ 284		Chicken Hearted/I Like Love	1958	10.00	20.00	40.00
☐ 353		Devil Doll/Sweet and Easy to Love	1960	50.00	100.00	200.00

Virgin

Number		Title (A Side/B Side)	Year	VG	VG+	NM
☐ 99159		Oh Pretty Woman/Claudette	1989			3.00
☐ 99159	PS	Oh Pretty Woman/Claudette	1989			3.00
☐ 99202		California Blue/In Dreams	1989			3.00
☐ 99202	PS	California Blue/In Dreams	1989			3.00
☐ 99227		She's a Mystery to Me/Dream Baby	1989			3.00
☐ 99227	PS	She's a Mystery to Me/Dream Baby	1989			3.00
☐ 99245		You Got It/The Only One	1989			3.00
☐ 99245	PS	You Got It/The Only One	1989			3.00
☐ 99388		Crying/Falling	1988			3.00
		A-side: With k.d. lang				
☐ 99388	PS	Crying/Falling	1988			3.00
☐ 99434		In Dreams/Leah	1987			3.00
☐ 99434	PS	In Dreams/Leah	1987		2.00	4.00

Warner Bros.

Number		Title (A Side/B Side)	Year	VG	VG+	NM
☐ 49262		That Lovin' Feeling Again/Lola	1980		2.50	5.00
		A-side: With Emmylou Harris; B-side by Craig Hundley				

Orbits, The

(More than one group)

Argo

Number		Title (A Side/B Side)	Year	VG	VG+	NM
☐ 5286		Who Are You/Mr. Bad Luck	1958	10.00	20.00	40.00

Dooto

Number		Title (A Side/B Side)	Year	VG	VG+	NM
☐ 601		Tell Me Baby/Two Crazy Scientists	196?	5.00	10.00	20.00

Flair-X

Number		Title (A Side/B Side)	Year	VG	VG+	NM
☐ 5000		Message of Love/I Really Do	1956	7.50	15.00	30.00

Number	Title (A Side/B Side)	Year	VG	VG+	NM

Nu-Kat
☐ 116/7 — Knock Her Down/My Love — 1959 — 7.50 — 15.00 — 30.00

Orchids, The
(Several different groups)
Columbia
☐ 42913 — That Boy Is Messin' Up My Mind/Harlem Tango — 1963 — 5.00 — 10.00 — 20.00
☐ 43066 — Tell Me a Story/From Bad to Worse — 1964 — 5.00 — 10.00 — 20.00
☐ 43175 — Christmas Is the Time to Be With Your Baby/It Doesn't Matter — 1964 — 5.00 — 10.00 — 20.00
Harlow
☐ 101 — I Don't Think You Missed Me/(B-side unknown) — 1962 — 5.00 — 10.00 — 20.00
King
☐ 4661 — Oh Why/All Night Baby — 1953 — 100.00 — 200.00 — 400.00
☐ 4663 — I've Been a Fool from the Start/Beginning to Miss You — 1953 — 100.00 — 200.00 — 400.00
Parrot
☐ 815 — Newly Wed/You're Everything to Me — 1955 — 75.00 — 150.00 — 300.00
☐ 819 — I Can't Refuse/You Said You Loved Me — 1955 — 75.00 — 150.00 — 300.00
Roulette
☐ 4412 — Pony Walk/Good Time Stomp — 1962 — 5.00 — 10.00 — 20.00
☐ 4633 — Good Good Time/Love Is What You Make It — 1965 — 3.00 — 6.00 — 12.00
United Artists
☐ 375 — You'll Never Know/Say Yes — 1961 — 5.00 — 10.00 — 20.00
Wall
☐ 549 — Soft Shadows/Good Gully — 1961 — 5.00 — 10.00 — 20.00

Orients, The
Laurie
☐ 3232 — Queen of the Angels/Shouldn't I — 1964 — 10.00 — 20.00 — 40.00

Original Cadillacs, The – See "Cadillacs, The"

Original Casuals, The
Back Beat
☐ 503 — So Tough/I Love My Darling — 1958 — 10.00 — 20.00 — 40.00
Original pressings by "The Casuals"
☐ 503 — So Tough/I Love My Darling — 1958 — 6.25 — 12.50 — 25.00
☐ 510 — Ju-Judy/Don't Pass Me By — 1958 — 6.25 — 12.50 — 25.00
☐ 514 — Three Kisses Past Midnight/It's Been a Long Time — 1958 — 6.25 — 12.50 — 25.00

Originals, The
(More than one group)
Diamond
☐ 102 — At Times Like These/Gimme a Little Kiss, Will Ya, Huh? — 1961 — 10.00 — 20.00 — 40.00
☐ 116 — Summer School/You and I — 1962 — 10.00 — 20.00 — 40.00
Jackpot
☐ 48007 — The Whip/The Blue Kat — 1959 — 7.50 — 15.00 — 30.00
☐ 48012 — Anna/Sleepless Nights — 1959 — 7.50 — 15.00 — 30.00
Chuck Rio was in this group
Motown
☐ PR-1 DJ — Young Train (same on both sides?) — 1973 — 50.00 — 100.00 — 200.00
☐ 1355 — Good Lovin' Is Just a Dime Away/Nothing Can Take the Place (Of Your Love) — 1975 — — 3.00 — 6.00
☐ 1370 — 50 Years/Financial Affair — 1975 — — 3.00 — 6.00
☐ 1379 — Everybody's Got to Do Something/(Instrumental) — 1975 — — 3.00 — 6.00
Original Sound
☐ 10 — Wishing Star/Let Me Hear You Say Yeah — 1960 — 7.50 — 15.00 — 30.00
Tony Allen was in this group
Phase II
☐ 02061 — Baby I'm for Real/Share Your Love with Me — 1981 — — 2.00 — 4.00
☐ 02147 — The Magic Is You/Let Me Dance — 1981 — — 2.00 — 4.00
☐ 02724 — Baby I'm for Real/The Magic Is You — 1982 — — 2.00 — 4.00
As "Hank Dixon and the Originals"
☐ 5653 — Waitin' on a Letter-Mr. Postman/(B-side unknown) — 1981 — — 2.50 — 5.00
Soul
☐ 35029 — Goodnight Irene/Need Your Loving (Want It Back) — 1967 — 3.00 — 6.00 — 12.00
☐ 35056 — We've Got a Way Out Love/You're the One — 1969 — 3.00 — 6.00 — 12.00
☐ 35061 — Green Grow the Lilacs/You're the One — 1969 — 3.00 — 6.00 — 12.00
☐ 35066 — Baby I'm for Real/The Moment of Truth — 1969 — 2.00 — 4.00 — 8.00
☐ 35069 — The Bells/I'll Wait for You — 1970 — 2.00 — 4.00 — 8.00
☐ 35074 — We Can Make It Baby/I Like Your Style — 1970 — 2.00 — 4.00 — 8.00
☐ 35079 — God Bless Whoever Sent You/Desperate Young Man — 1970 — 2.00 — 4.00 — 8.00
☐ 35085 — Keep Me/A Man Without Love — 1971 — — 3.00 — 6.00
☐ 35093 — I'm Someone Who Cares/Once I Have You — 1972 — — 3.00 — 6.00
☐ 35102 — Be My Love/Endlessly Love — 1973 — — 3.00 — 6.00
☐ 35109 — First Lady (Sweet Mother's Love)/There's a Chance When You Love, You Love — 1973 — — 3.00 — 6.00
☐ 35112 — Supernatural Voodoo Woman (Part 1)/Supernatural Voodoo Woman (Part 2) — 1974 — — 3.00 — 6.00
☐ 35113 — Game Called Love/Ooh You Put a Spell on Me — 1974 — — 3.00 — 6.00
☐ 35115 — You're My Only World/So Near (And Yet So Far) — 1974 — — 3.00 — 6.00

Number		Title (A Side/B Side)	Year	VG	VG+	NM
❑ 35117		Touch/Ooh You Put a Spell on Me	1975		3.00	6.00
❑ 35119		Down to Love Town/Just to Be Closer to You	1976		3.00	6.00
❑ 35121	DJ	Call On Your Six Million Dollar Man (mono/stereo)	1977		3.00	6.00

Orioles, The
(Also see "Til, Sonny")

Abner

❑ 1016		Sugar Girl/Didn't I Say	1958	15.00	30.00	60.00

Charlie Parker

❑ 211		Secret Love/The Wobble	1962	5.00	10.00	20.00
❑ 212		In the Chapel in the Moonlight/Hey! Little Woman	1962	5.00	10.00	20.00
❑ 213		Back to the Chapel Again/	1962	5.00	10.00	20.00
		(It's Gonna Be a) Lonely Christmas				
❑ 214		What Are You Doing New Year's Eve/	1962	5.00	10.00	20.00
		Don't Mess Around with My Love				
❑ 215		It's Too Soon to Know/I Miss You So	1963	3.75	7.50	15.00
❑ 216		Write and Tell Me Why/	1963	3.75	7.50	15.00
		Don't Tell Her What Happens to Me				
❑ 219		I Miss You So/Hey! Little Woman	1963	3.75	7.50	15.00

Jubilee

❑ 5000		It's Too Soon to Know/Barbara Lee	1951	2,000	3,000	4,000
Note: Jubilee 5001 and 5002 known to exist only on 78 rpm						
❑ 5005		Tell Me So/Deacon Jones	1951	1,500	2,250	3,000
Note: Jubilee 5008 and 5009 known to exist only on 78 rpm						
❑ 5016		So Much/Forgive and Forget	1951	500.00	1,000	2,000
❑ 5017		What Are You Doing New Year's Eve/Lonely Christmas	1951	250.00	500.00	1,000
❑ 5017	PS	What Are You Doing New Year's Eve/Lonely Christmas	1954	250.00	500.00	1,000
Note: Jubilee 5018 known to exist only on 78 rpm						
❑ 5025		At Night/Every Dog-Gone Time	1951	250.00	500.00	1,000
Note: Jubilee 5026, 5028, 5031 and 5037 known to exist only on 78 rpm						
❑ 5040		I Cross My Fingers/Can't Seem to Laugh Anymore	1951	200.00	400.00	800.00
❑ 5045		Oh Holy Night/The Lord's Prayer	1951	150.00	300.00	600.00
❑ 5045	PS	Oh Holy Night/The Lord's Prayer	1954	200.00	400.00	800.00
❑ 5051		I Miss You So/You Are My First Love	1951	1,000	1,500	2,000
		Red vinyl				
❑ 5051		I Miss You So/You Are My First Love	1951	200.00	400.00	800.00
❑ 5055		Pal of Mine/Happy Go Lucky Local Blues	1951	200.00	400.00	800.00
Note: Jubilee 5057 known to exist only on 78 rpm						
❑ 5061		I'm Just a Fool in Love/Hold Me, Squeeze Me	1951	200.00	400.00	800.00
❑ 5065		Baby, Please Don't Go/	1951	1,000	1,500	2,000
		Don't Tell Her What's Happened to Me				
		Red vinyl				
❑ 5065		Baby, Please Don't Go/Don	1951	150.00	300.00	600.00
		't Tell Her What's Happened to Me				
❑ 5071		When You're Not Around/How Blind Can You Be	1952	150.00	300.00	600.00
❑ 5074		Trust in Me/Shrimp Boats	1952	125.00	250.00	500.00
❑ 5076		Proud of You/You Never Cared for Me	1952	125.00	250.00	500.00
❑ 5082		It's All Over Because We're Through/Waiting	1952	125.00	250.00	500.00
❑ 5084		Barfly/Getting Tired, Tired, Tired	1952	100.00	200.00	400.00
❑ 5092		Don't Cry Baby/See See Rider	1952	100.00	200.00	400.00
❑ 5092		Don't Cry Baby/See See Rider	1952	375.00	750.00	1,500
		Red vinyl				
❑ 5102		You Belong to Me/I Don't Want to Take a Chance	1952	100.00	200.00	400.00
❑ 5107		I Miss You So/Till Then	1952	375.00	750.00	1,500
		Red vinyl				
❑ 5107		I Miss You So/Till Then	1952	100.00	200.00	400.00
❑ 5107		I Miss You So/Till Then	1963	6.25	12.50	25.00
		Reissue, credited to "Sonny Til and the Orioles"				
❑ 5108		Teardrops on My Pillow/Hold Me, Thrill Me, Kiss Me	1953	100.00	200.00	400.00
❑ 5108		Teardrops on My Pillow/Hold Me, Thrill Me, Kiss Me	1953	375.00	750.00	1,500
		Red vinyl				
❑ 5115		Bad Little Girl/Dem Days	1953	75.00	150.00	300.00
❑ 5120		I Cover the Waterfront/One More Time	1953	75.00	150.00	300.00
❑ 5120		I Cover the Waterfront/One More Time	1953	375.00	750.00	1,500
		Red vinyl				
❑ 5122		Crying in the Chapel/Don't You Think I Ought to Know	1953	15.00	30.00	60.00
❑ 5127		In the Mission of St. Augustine/Write and Tell Me Why	1953	12.50	25.00	50.00
❑ 5134		There's No One But You/Rose of Calvary	1954	12.50	25.00	50.00
❑ 5137		Secret Love/Don't Go to Strangers	1954	12.50	25.00	50.00
❑ 5143		Maybe You'll Be There/	1954	20.00	40.00	80.00
		Drowning Every Hope I Ever Had				
❑ 5154		In the Chapel in the Moonlight/	1954	12.50	25.00	50.00
		Thank the Lord, Thank the Lord				
❑ 5161		If You Believe/Longing	1954	12.50	25.00	50.00
❑ 5172		Runaround/Count Your Blessings Instead of Sheep	1954	12.50	25.00	50.00
❑ 5177		I Love You Mostly/Fair Exchange	1955	10.00	20.00	40.00
❑ 5189		I Need You Baby/The Good Lord Will Smile	1955	10.00	20.00	40.00
❑ 5221		Please Sing My Blues Tonight/Moody Over You	1955	10.00	20.00	40.00
❑ 5231		Angel/Don't Go to Strangers	1956	15.00	30.00	60.00
❑ 5363		Tell Me So/At Night	1959	3.75	7.50	15.00
		As "Sonny Til and the Orioles"				
❑ 5384		Come On Home/The First of Summer	1960	3.75	7.50	15.00
		As "Sonny Til and the Orioles"				
❑ 6001		Crying in the Chapel/(B-side unknown)	196?	3.75	7.50	15.00

Number		Title (A Side/B Side)	Year	VG	VG+	NM

Vee Jay
❑ 196		I Just Got Lucky/Happy 'Til the Letter	1956	7.50	15.00	30.00
❑ 228		For All We Know/Never Leave Me Baby	1956	7.50	15.00	30.00
❑ 244		Sugar Girl/Didn't I Say	1957	10.00	20.00	40.00

Orion
(Also see "Ellis, Jimmy")
Kristal
| ❑ 2292 | | I'm Saving Up My Pennies/Starting Over | 1985 | | 2.00 | 4.00 |

Sun
❑ 1142		Honey/Ebony Eyes	1979		2.00	4.00
❑ 1147		Before the Next Teardrop Falls/Washing Machine	1979		2.00	4.00
❑ 1148		Remember Bethlehem/Silent Night	1979		2.00	4.00
❑ 1148	DJ	Remember Bethlehem (same on both sides)	1979	2.50	5.00	10.00
		Yellow vinyl promo				
❑ 1151		Be-Bop-a-Lula/The Breakup	1980		2.00	4.00
		A-side with Jerry Lee Lewis; B-side with Charlie Rich				
❑ 1152		It Ain't No Mystery/Stranger in My Place	1980		2.00	4.00
❑ 1152	DJ	It Ain't No Mystery (same on both sides)	1980	2.50	5.00	10.00
		Yellow vinyl promo				
❑ 1153		Texas Tea/Faded Love	1980		2.00	4.00
❑ 1153	DJ	Texas Tea (same on both sides)	1980	2.50	5.00	10.00
		Yellow vinyl promo				
❑ 1156		Am I That Easy to Forget/Crazy Arms	1980		2.00	4.00
❑ 1156	DJ	Am I That Easy to Forget (same on both sides)	1980	2.50	5.00	10.00
		Yellow vinyl promo				
❑ 1159		Rockabilly Rebel/Memphis Sun	1980		2.00	4.00
❑ 1159	DJ	Rockabilly Rebel (same on both sides)	1980	2.50	5.00	10.00
		Yellow vinyl promo				
❑ 1162		Crazy Little Thing Called Love/Matchbox	1981		2.00	4.00
❑ 1165		Born/If I Can't Have You	1981		2.00	4.00
❑ 1165	DJ	Born (same on both sides)	1981	2.50	5.00	10.00
		Yellow vinyl promo				
❑ 1170		Some You Win, Some You Lose/Ain't No Good	1981		2.00	4.00
❑ 1170	DJ	Some You Win, Some You Lose (same on both sides)	1981	2.50	5.00	10.00
		Yellow vinyl promo				
❑ 1172		Baby Please Say Yes/Mathilda	1982		2.00	4.00
❑ 1175		Honky Tonk Heaven/Morning, Noon and Night	1982		2.00	4.00
❑ 1175	DJ	Honky Tonk Heaven (same on both sides)	1982	2.50	5.00	10.00
		Yellow vinyl promo				
❑ 1178		That Old-Time Feelin'/Morning, Noon and Night	1982		2.00	4.00

Orlando, Tony
Atco
| ❑ 6376 | | Think Before You Act/She Loves Me (For What I Am) | 1965 | 2.50 | 5.00 | 10.00 |

Cameo
| ❑ 471 | | Sweet Sweet/Manuelito (Little Manuel) | 1967 | 2.50 | 5.00 | 10.00 |

Casablanca
❑ 967		They're Playing Our Song (Medley)/Moonlight	1979		2.00	4.00
❑ 991		Sweets for My Sweet/High Steppin'	1979		2.00	4.00
❑ 2229		San Pedros Children/High Steppin'	1979		2.00	4.00
❑ 2249		Pullin' Together/She Always Knew	1980		2.00	4.00

Epic
❑ 9441		Halfway to Paradise/Lonely Tomorrows	1961	3.75	7.50	15.00
❑ 9441	PS	Halfway to Paradise/Lonely Tomorrows	1961	6.25	12.50	25.00
❑ 9452		Bless You/Am I the Guy	1961	3.75	7.50	15.00
❑ 9452	PS	Bless You/Am I the Guy	1961	6.25	12.50	25.00
❑ 9476		Happy Times (Are Here to Stay)/Lonely Am I	1961	3.00	6.00	12.00
❑ 9476	PS	Happy Times (Are Here to Stay)/Lonely Am I	1961	6.25	12.50	25.00
❑ 9491		My Baby's a Stranger/Talkin' About You	1962	3.00	6.00	12.00
❑ 9491	PS	My Baby's a Stranger/Talkin' About You	1962	6.25	12.50	25.00
❑ 9502		I'd Never Find Another You/Love on Your Lips	1962	3.00	6.00	12.00
❑ 9519		At the Edge of Tears/Chills	1962	3.00	6.00	12.00
❑ 9519	PS	At the Edge of Tears/Chills	1962	6.25	12.50	25.00
❑ 9562		Beautiful Dreamer/The Loneliest	1962	2.50	5.00	10.00
❑ 9570		Joanie/Shirley	1963	2.50	5.00	10.00
❑ 9622		I'll Be There/What Am I Gonna Do	1963	2.50	5.00	10.00
❑ 9668		She Doesn't Know It/Tell Me What I Can Do	1964	2.50	5.00	10.00
❑ 9715		To Wait for Love/Accept It	1964	2.50	5.00	10.00

Milo
| ❑ 101 | | Ding Dong/You and Only You | 1959 | 25.00 | 50.00 | 100.00 |
| | | *Not the same Tony Orlando* | | | | |

Orlons, The
ABC
| ❑ 10894 | | Everything/Keep Your Hands Off My Baby | 1967 | 2.50 | 5.00 | 10.00 |
| ❑ 10948 | | Kissin' Time/Once Upon a Time | 1967 | 2.50 | 5.00 | 10.00 |

Calla
| ❑ 113 | | Spinnin' Top/Anyone Who Had a Heart | 1966 | 2.50 | 5.00 | 10.00 |

Cameo
❑ 198		I'll Be True/Heart Darling Angel	1961	12.50	25.00	50.00
❑ 211		Mr. 21/Please Let It Be Me	1961	12.50	25.00	50.00
❑ 218		The Wah-Watusi/Holiday Hill	1962	3.75	7.50	15.00

Number		Title (A Side/B Side)	Year	VG	VG+	NM
☐ 231		Don't Hang Up/The Conservative	1962	3.75	7.50	15.00
☐ 231	PS	Don't Hang Up/The Conservative	1962	6.25	12.50	25.00
☐ 243		South Street/Those Terrible Boots	1963	3.75	7.50	15.00
☐ 243	PS	South Street/Those Terrible Boots	1963	6.25	12.50	25.00
☐ 257		Not Me/My Best Friend	1963	3.75	7.50	15.00
☐ 257	PS	Not Me/My Best Friend	1963	6.25	12.50	25.00
☐ 273		Cross Fire!/It's No Big Thing	1963	3.75	7.50	15.00
☐ 273	PS	Cross Fire!/It's No Big Thing	1963	6.25	12.50	25.00
☐ 287		Bon-Doo-Wah/Don't Throw Your Love Away	1963	3.75	7.50	15.00
☐ 287	PS	Bon-Doo-Wah/Don't Throw Your Love Away	1963	6.25	12.50	25.00
☐ 295		Shimmy Shimmy/Everyone Nice	1964	3.75	7.50	15.00
☐ 295	PS	Shimmy Shimmy/Everyone Nice	1964	6.25	12.50	25.00
☐ 319		Rules of Love/Heartbreak Hotel	1964	3.75	7.50	15.00
☐ 319	PS	Rules of Love/Heartbreak Hotel	1964	6.25	12.50	25.00
☐ 332		Knock! Knock! (Who's There)/Goin' Places	1964	3.75	7.50	15.00
☐ 332	PS	Knock! Knock! (Who's There)/Goin' Places	1964	6.25	12.50	25.00
☐ 346		I Ain't Coming Back/Envy (In My Eyes)	1965	3.00	6.00	12.00
☐ 352		Come On Down Baby/I Ain't Coming Back	1965	3.00	6.00	12.00
☐ 372		Don't You Want My Lovin'/I Can't Take It	1965	3.00	6.00	12.00
☐ 384		No Love But Your Love/Envy (In My Eyes)	1965	10.00	20.00	40.00

Orr, J.D.
Summit

☐ 105		Hula-Hoop Boogie/Lonesome Hearted Blues	1958	100.00	200.00	400.00

Orrell, David
Felsted

☐ 8515		Be My Baby/You're the One	1958	20.00	40.00	80.00

Orsi, Phil, and the Little Kings
Lucky

☐ 1009		Come On Everybody/Oh My Darling	1963	18.75	37.50	75.00
☐ 1015		Don't You Just Know It/(B-side unknown)	1964	6.25	12.50	25.00

U.S.A.

☐ 837		Stay/Whoever He May Be	1965	6.25	12.50	25.00
☐ 841		Sorry (I Ran All the Way Home)/Whoever He May Be	1965	6.25	12.50	25.00

Osborne, Arthur
Brunswick

☐ 55068		Hey Ruby/Don't Give Me Heartaches	1958	15.00	30.00	60.00

Osborne, Kell, and the Chicks
Class

☐ 302		Little Chick-A-Dee/Do You Mind	1962	3.75	7.50	15.00

Loma

☐ 2023		That's What's Happening/You Can't Outsmart a Woman	1965	2.50	5.00	10.00

Titanic

☐ 5008		Quicksand/(B-side unknown)	1963	25.00	50.00	100.00

Trey

☐ 3006		The Bells of St. Mary's/That's Alright, Baby	1960	6.25	12.50	25.00

Oshins, Milt
Pelvis

☐ 169		All About Elvis/All About Elvis (Part 2)	1956	18.75	37.50	75.00

Osmonds, The
(Many of these credit "The Osmond Brothers")

Barnaby

☐ 2002		Mary Elizabeth/Speak Like a Child	1968	2.50	5.00	10.00
☐ 2004		I've Got Loving on My Mind/Mollie-"A"	1968	2.50	5.00	10.00
☐ 2005		Taking a Chance on Love/Groove With What You Got	1969	2.50	5.00	10.00

Elektra

☐ 47438		I Think About Your Lovin'/Working Man's Blues	1982		2.00	4.00
☐ 69883		Never Ending Song of Love/You'll Be Seeing Me	1982		2.00	4.00
☐ 69969		It's Like Falling in Love/Your Leaving Was the Last Thing on My Mind	1982		2.00	4.00

EMI America

☐ 8298		Baby When Your Heart Breaks Down/(B-side unknown)	1985			3.00
☐ 8313		Baby Wants/(B-side unknown)	1986			3.00
☐ 8325		You Look Like the One I Love/(B-side unknown)	1986			3.00
☐ 8360		Looking for Suzanne/(B-side unknown)	1986			3.00

Mercury

☐ 74079		Emily/Rainin'	1979		2.00	4.00

MGM

☐ 13162		Be My Little Baby Bumble Bee/I Wouldn't Trade the Silver in My Mother's Hair	1963	3.75	7.50	15.00
☐ 13174		Theme from "The Travels of Jamie McPheeters"/Aura Lee	1963	3.75	7.50	15.00
☐ 13281		Mister Sandman/My Mom	1964	5.00	10.00	20.00
☐ 14159		Movin' Along/Open Up Your Heart	1970	2.00	4.00	8.00
☐ 14193		One Bad Apple/He Ain't Heavy, He's My Brother	1970		3.00	6.00
☐ 14259		Double Lovin'/Chilly Winds	1971		3.00	6.00
☐ 14295		Yo-Yo/Keep on My Side	1971		3.00	6.00

Number		Title (A Side/B Side)	Year	VG	VG+	NM
☐ 14324		Down by the Lazy River/He's the Light of the World	1971		3.00	6.00
☐ 14405		Hold Her Tight/Love Is	1972		2.50	5.00
☐ 14450		Crazy Horses/That's My Girl	1972		2.50	5.00
☐ 14562		Goin' Home/Are You Up There	1973		2.50	5.00
☐ 14617		Let Me In/One Way Ticket to Anywhere	1973		2.50	5.00
☐ 14617	PS	Let Me In/One Way Ticket to Anywhere	1973	2.00	4.00	8.00
☐ 14623		"Having a Party" Medley/Just Too Good to Be True	1973		2.50	5.00
☐ 14746		Love Me for a Reason/Fever	1974		2.50	5.00
☐ 14791		The Proud One/The Last Day Is Coming	1975		2.50	5.00
☐ 14831		Thank You/I'm Still Gonna Need You	1975		2.50	5.00

Polydor

Number		Title (A Side/B Side)	Year	VG	VG+	NM
☐ 14348		Check It Out/I Can't Live a Dream	1976		2.00	4.00

Uni

Number		Title (A Side/B Side)	Year	VG	VG+	NM
☐ 55015		I Can't Stop/Flower Music	1967	2.50	5.00	10.00
☐ 55276		I Can't Stop/Flower Music	1971		3.00	6.00

Warner Bros.

Number		Title (A Side/B Side)	Year	VG	VG+	NM
☐ 28982		Any Time/(B-side unknown)	1985			3.00
☐ 29312		If Every Man Had a Woman Like You/Come Back to Me	1984		2.00	4.00
☐ 29387		Where Does An Angel Go When She Cries/One More for Lovers	1984		2.00	4.00
☐ 29594		She's Ready for Someone to Love Her/You Make the Long Road Shorter with Your Love	1983		2.00	4.00

Other Tikis, The – See "Tikis, The"

Otis and Carla
(Otis Redding and Carla Thomas, each also listed individually)

Atco

Number	Title (A Side/B Side)	Year	VG	VG+	NM
☐ 6665	When Something Is Wrong with My Baby/Ooh Carla, Ooh Otis	1968	2.50	5.00	10.00

Stax

Number	Title (A Side/B Side)	Year	VG	VG+	NM
☐ 216	Tramp/Tell It Like It Is	1967	2.50	5.00	10.00
☐ 228	Knock on Wood/Let Me Be Good to You	1967	2.50	5.00	10.00
☐ 244	Lovey Dovey/New Year's Resolution	1968	2.50	5.00	10.00

Otis, Johnny
Atlantic

Number		Title (A Side/B Side)	Year	VG	VG+	NM
☐ 2409		Keep the Faith -- Part I/Keep the Faith -- Part II	1967	3.00	6.00	12.00

Capitol

Number		Title (A Side/B Side)	Year	VG	VG+	NM
☐ F3799/3802		The Johnny Otis Show	1957	100.00	200.00	400.00

Four-record set with four-pocket cover. Price is for entire set. Records alone are valued separately below.

Number		Title (A Side/B Side)	Year	VG	VG+	NM
☐ F3799		Can't You Hear Me Callin'/My Ding-a-Ling	1957	12.50	25.00	50.00
☐ F3800		Ma, He's Makin' Eyes at Me/In the Dark	1957	12.50	25.00	50.00
☐ F3801		Stay with Me/Tell Me So	1957	12.50	25.00	50.00
☐ F3802		It's Too Soon to Know/Star of Love	1957	12.50	25.00	50.00
☐ F3852		Bye Bye Baby/Good Golly	1957	6.25	12.50	25.00
☐ F3889		Well, Well, Well/You Just Kissed Me Goodbye	1958	6.25	12.50	25.00
☐ F3966		Willie and the Hand Jive/Ring-a-Ling	1958	6.25	12.50	25.00
☐ F4060		Willie Did the Cha Cha/Crazy Country Hop	1958	6.25	12.50	25.00
☐ F4156		My Dear/You	1959	5.00	10.00	20.00
☐ F4168	M	Castin' My Spell/Telephone Baby	1959	5.00	10.00	20.00
☐ S-F4168	S	Castin' My Spell/Telephone Baby	1959	12.50	25.00	50.00
☐ F4226		Three Girls Named Molly (Doin' the Hully Gully)/I'll Do the Same for You	1959	5.00	10.00	20.00
☐ F4260		Let the Sun Shine in My Life/Baby, Just You	1959	5.00	10.00	20.00
☐ 4326		Mumblin' Mosie/Hey Baby, Don't You Know	1960	3.75	7.50	15.00

Dig

Number	Title (A Side/B Side)	Year	VG	VG+	NM
☐ 119	Hey! Hey! Hey! Hey!/Let the Sunshine in My Heart	1956	7.50	15.00	30.00
☐ 122	The Midnite Creeper (Part 1)/The Midnite Creeper (Part 2)	1956	7.50	15.00	30.00
☐ 132	My Eyes Are Full of Tears/Turtle Dove	1957	7.50	15.00	30.00
☐ 134	Wa Wa (Part 1)/Wa Wa (Part 2)	1957	7.50	15.00	30.00
☐ 139	Stop, Look and Love Me/The Night Is Young	1957	7.50	15.00	30.00

Eldo

Number	Title (A Side/B Side)	Year	VG	VG+	NM
☐ 106	The New Bo Diddley/The Jelly Roll	1960	3.75	7.50	15.00
☐ 152	Keep the Faith (Part 1)/Keep the Faith (Part 2)	1968	2.00	4.00	8.00
☐ 153	Long Distance/Banana Peels	1968	2.00	4.00	8.00

Epic

Number	Title (A Side/B Side)	Year	VG	VG+	NM
☐ 10606	You Can Depend on Me/The Watts Breakaway	1970		3.00	6.00
☐ 10757	Willie and the Hand Jive/Goin' Back to L.A.	1971		3.00	6.00

With Delmar Evans

Kent

Number	Title (A Side/B Side)	Year	VG	VG+	NM
☐ 4521	Shuggie's Blues/Cool Ade	1969	2.00	4.00	8.00
☐ 506	Country Girl/Bye Bye Baby	1969	2.00	4.00	8.00

King

Number	Title (A Side/B Side)	Year	VG	VG+	NM
☐ 5581	Hand Jive One More Time/Baby I Got News for You	1961	3.75	7.50	15.00
☐ 5606	She's All Right/It Must Be Love	1962	3.75	7.50	15.00
☐ 5634	Queen of the Twist/I Know My Love Is True	1962	3.75	7.50	15.00
☐ 5690	The Hey Hey Hey Song/Early in the Morning Blues	1962	3.75	7.50	15.00
☐ 5707	Somebody Call the Station/Yes	1963	3.00	6.00	12.00
☐ 5790	Bye, Bye Baby/The Hash	1963	3.00	6.00	12.00

Mercury

Number	Title (A Side/B Side)	Year	VG	VG+	NM
☐ 8263	Oopy Doo/Stardust	1952	12.50	25.00	50.00

Number	Title (A Side/B Side)		Year	VG	VG+	NM
❑ 8273	One-Nighter Blues/Goomp Blues		1952	12.50	25.00	50.00
❑ 8289	Call Operator 210/Baby Baby Blues		1952	12.50	25.00	50.00
❑ 8295	Gypsy Blues/The Candle's Burning Low		1952	12.50	25.00	50.00
❑ 70038	Why Don't You Believe Me/Wishing Well		1953	12.50	25.00	50.00
❑ 70050	Love Bug Boogie/Brown Skin Butterball		1953	12.50	25.00	50.00

Okeh

❑ 7332	Watts Breakaway/You Can Depend On Me		1969		3.00	6.00

Peacock

❑ 1625	Young Girl/Rock Me Baby		1953	20.00	40.00	80.00
❑ 1636	Shake It/I Won't Be Your Fool No More		1954	12.50	25.00	50.00
❑ 1648	Sittin' Here Drinkin'/You Got Me Crying		1955	12.50	25.00	50.00
❑ 1675	Butter Ball/Dandy's Boogie		1957	12.50	25.00	50.00

Savoy

❑ 731	Double Crossing Blues/(B-side unknown)		1950	30.00	60.00	120.00
❑ 750	Cupid Boogie/Just Can't Get Free		1950	15.00	30.00	60.00
❑ 764	Wedding Blues/Far Away Blues (Xmas Blues)		1950	15.00	30.00	60.00
❑ 766	Rockin' Blues/My Heart Tells Me		1950	15.00	30.00	60.00
❑ 777	Gee Baby/Mambo Boogie		1951	12.50	25.00	50.00
❑ 780	Doggin' Blues/Living and Loving You		1951	12.50	25.00	50.00
❑ 787	I Dream/Hangover Blues		1951	12.50	25.00	50.00
❑ 788	All Nite Long/New Love		1951	12.50	25.00	50.00
❑ 812	Warning Blues/I'll Ask My Heart		1951	12.50	25.00	50.00
❑ 815	Harlem Nocturne/Midnight in the Barrelhouse		1951	12.50	25.00	50.00
❑ 824	Get Together Blues/Chittlin' Switch		1951	12.50	25.00	50.00
❑ 855	It Ain't the Beauty/Gonna Take a Train		1952	12.50	25.00	50.00

Our Gang
Br'er Bird

❑ 001	Summertime Summertime/Theme from Leon's Garage		1966	50.00	100.00	200.00

Outlaws, The
(At least two different groups)
Crusade

❑ 92765	Chains/(B-side unknown)		1965	7.50	15.00	30.00

Dot

❑ 16512	Hold-Up/Somethin' Else		1963	10.00	20.00	40.00

Smash

❑ 2025	Don't Cry/Only for You		1966	3.00	6.00	12.00

Outsiders, The
Bell

❑ 904	Changes/Lost in My World		1970		3.00	6.00

Capitol

❑ 2055	Little Bit of Lovin'/I Will Love You		1967	2.00	4.00	8.00
❑ 2216	Oh How It Hurts/We Ain't Gonna Make It		1968	2.00	4.00	8.00
❑ 5573	Time Won't Let Me/Was It Really Real		1966	3.00	6.00	12.00
❑ 5646	Girl in Love/What Makes You So Bad		1966	2.50	5.00	10.00
❑ 5646	Girl in Love/What Makes You So Bad	PS	1966	5.00	10.00	20.00
❑ 5701	Respectable/Lost in My World		1966	2.50	5.00	10.00
❑ 5759	Help Me Girl/You Gotta Look		1966	2.50	5.00	10.00
❑ 5759	Help Me Girl/You Gotta Look	PS	1966	5.00	10.00	20.00
❑ 5843	Give Me Time/I'm Not Trying to Hurt You		1967	2.00	4.00	8.00
❑ 5892	I Just Can't See You Anymore/Gotta Leave Us Alone		1967	2.00	4.00	8.00
❑ 5955	I'll See You in Summertime/ And Now You Want My Sympathy		1967	2.00	4.00	8.00

Ellen

❑ 503	Rickity-Boom-Bal-Aye/The Bird Rattle		196?	3.75	7.50	15.00

Kapp

❑ 2104	Tinker, Tailor/Oh You're Not So Pretty		1970		3.00	6.00

Karate

❑ 505	The Guy with the Long Liverpool Hair/Outsider		1964	5.00	10.00	20.00

Owen, Mack
Sun

❑ 336	Walkin' and Talkin'/Somebody Like You		1960	5.00	10.00	20.00

Owens Brothers, The
ABC-Paramount

❑ 9775	Night Train/Don't Cry		1956	10.00	20.00	40.00

Also released on Sheraton by the Four Chaps.

Oxford Circle, The
World United

❑ 002	Mind Destruction/Foolsih Woman		196?	12.50	25.00	50.00

Oxford Circus, The
Zig Zag

❑ 101	Tracy/(B-side unknown)		1967	10.00	20.00	40.00

Number		Title (A Side/B Side)	Year	VG	VG+	NM

P

P. Funk All Stars
(Also see "Funkadelic"; "Parliament")
CBS Associated

❏ 04032		Generator Pop/Hydraulic Pump	1983		2.00	4.00

Hump

❏ 1		Hydraulic Pump (Part 1)/Hydraulic Pump (Part 2)	1981		2.50	5.00
❏ 3		One of Those Summers/(B-side unknown)	1982		2.50	5.00

Uncle Jam

❏ 04408		Pumpin' It Up/Pumpin' It Up (Special Mix)	1984		2.00	4.00

Pablo Cruise
A&M

❏ 1695		Island Woman/Denny	1975		2.50	5.00
❏ 1742		What Does It Take/In My Own Quiet Way	1975		2.50	5.00
❏ 1815		(I Think) It's Finally Over/Look to the Sky	1976		2.50	5.00
❏ 1834		Don't Believe It/Look to the Sky	1976		2.50	5.00
❏ 1876		Crystal/Look to the Sky	1976		2.50	5.00
❏ 1910		A Place in the Sun/El Verano	1977		2.50	5.00
❏ 1920		Whatcha Gonna Do?/Atlanta June	1977		2.00	4.00
❏ 1920	PS	Whatcha Gonna Do?/Atlanta June	1977		3.00	6.00
❏ 1976		A Place in the Sun/El Verano	1977		2.00	4.00
❏ 1999		Atlanta June/Never Had a Love	1977		2.00	4.00
❏ 2048		Love Will Find a Way/Always Be Together	1978		2.00	4.00
❏ 2048	PS	Love Will Find a Way/Always Be Together	1978		2.50	5.00
❏ 2076		Don't Want to Live Without It/Raging Fire	1978		2.00	4.00
❏ 2112		I Go to Rio/Raging Fire	1979		2.00	4.00
❏ 2195		I Want You Tonight/Family Man	1979		2.00	4.00
❏ 2217	DJ	Part of the Game (mono/stereo)	1980		2.50	5.00
		No stock copies known				
❏ 2349		Cool Love/Jenny	1981		2.00	4.00
❏ 2373		Slip Away/That's When	1981		2.00	4.00
❏ 2570		Another World/Will You, Won't You	1983			3.00

Pacers, The
(Probably more than one group)
Calico

❏ 101/2		I Found a Dream/I Wanna Dance with You	1958	7.50	15.00	30.00

Coral

❏ 62398		Sassy Sue/You Got Me Bugged	1964	2.50	5.00	10.00

Guyden

❏ 2064		How Sweet/No Wonder	1962	125.00	250.00	500.00

Razorback

❏ 103		Fright Street/Sooie	1958	6.25	12.50	25.00
❏ 108		Confound It/Skeeter Dape	1960	6.25	12.50	25.00
❏ 112		Don't Get Around Much/Sad Sad	1962	6.25	12.50	25.00
❏ 115		West Memphis/Dollar, Two Ninety-Eight	1963	6.25	12.50	25.00
❏ 118		Tennessee Stud/Beautiful Debbie	1964	5.00	10.00	20.00
❏ 123		The Pit/Pace Setter	1965	5.00	10.00	20.00
❏ 125		Batman/Gotham City	1966	5.00	10.00	20.00
❏ 137		Short Squashed Texan/Sock It To 'Em Soobey	1967	5.00	10.00	20.00

Pacific Gas & Electric
Columbia

❏ 45009		Redneck/Bluebuster	1969		3.00	6.00
❏ 45158		Are You Ready?/Staggolee	1970		3.00	6.00
		Available with at least three different label variations, all equal in value				
❏ 45221		Elvira/Father Come On Home	1970		2.50	5.00
❏ 45304		The Time Has Come/Death Row No. 172	1971		2.50	5.00
❏ 45444		One More River to Cross/Rocky Roller's Lament	1971		2.50	5.00
❏ 45519		Thank God for You Baby/See the Monkey Run	1971		2.50	5.00
❏ 45621		Heat Wave/We Did What We Could	1972		2.50	5.00

Power

❏ 1701		Wade in the Water/Live Love	1969	2.50	5.00	10.00

Page, Jimmy
(Of Led Zeppelin and The Firm)
Geffen

❏ 27821		Wasting My Time/Fires of Winter	1988		2.00	4.00

Pagents, The
Bamboo

❏ 525		Pa-Cha/Sad and Lonely	1963	12.50	25.00	50.00

Era

❏ 3119		Enchanted/The Big Daddy	1963	7.50	15.00	30.00
❏ 3124		Glenda/Shake	1964	7.50	15.00	30.00
❏ 3134		Pa-Cha/Sad and Lonely	1964	6.25	12.50	25.00

Ike

❏ 631		Enchanted Surf/The Big Daddy	1963	25.00	50.00	100.00

Number		Title (A Side/B Side)	Year	VG	VG+	NM

Paige, Hal
Atlantic

Number		Title (A Side/B Side)	Year	VG	VG+	NM
❑ 1032		Big Foot May/Please Say You Do	1954	37.50	75.00	150.00
❑ 996		Drive It Home/Break of Day Blues	1953	37.50	75.00	150.00

Checker

❑ 873		Don't Have to Cry No More/Pour the Corn	1957	5.00	10.00	20.00

Fury

❑ 1002		Don't Have to Cry No More/Pour the Corn	1957	20.00	40.00	80.00
❑ 1024		After Hours Blues/Going Back to My Home Town	1959	5.00	10.00	20.00

J&S

❑ 1601		Thunderbird/Sugar Bare	1957	7.50	15.00	30.00

Palace Guard, The
Orange Empire

❑ 331		All Night Long/Playgirl	1965	3.75	7.50	15.00
❑ 332		A Girl You Can Depend On/If You Need Me	1965	3.75	7.50	15.00
❑ 400		Falling Sugar/Oh Blue	1965	3.75	7.50	15.00

Parkway

❑ 111		Saturday's Child/Party Lights	1966	3.00	6.00	12.00
❑ 124		Calliope/Creed	1966	3.00	6.00	12.00

Verve

❑ 10410		Falling Sugar/Oh Blue	1966	2.50	5.00	10.00

Palisades, The
Calico

❑ 113		Close Your Eyes/I Can't Quit	1960	5.00	10.00	20.00

Chairman

❑ 4401		Heaven Is Being with You/Make the Night a Little Longer *With Carole King*	1963	6.25	12.50	25.00

Debra

❑ 1003		Chapel Bells/She Can't Stop Dancing *Also released credited to "The Magics"*	1963	37.50	75.00	150.00

Dore

❑ 609		Hometown Girl/Oh My Love	1961	3.75	7.50	15.00

Leader

❑ 806		Dear John/The Shrine	1960	5.00	10.00	20.00

Medieval

❑ 205		This Is the Night/Relic Rock	1962	5.00	10.00	20.00

Palmer, Robert
(Also see "Power Station, The")
EMI

Number		Title (A Side/B Side)	Year	VG	VG+	NM
❑ 7PRO-04???	DJ	Tell Me I'm Not Dreaming (same on both sides) *Vinyl is promo only*	1989		2.50	5.00
❑ S7-18129		Know By Now/In the Stars	1994			3.00
❑ 50183		She Makes My Day/Casting a Spell	1989			3.00

EMI Manhattan

❑ 50133		Simply Irresistible/Nova	1988			3.00
❑ 50133	PS	Simply Irresistible/Nova	1988			3.00
❑ 50157		Early in the Morning/Disturbing Behavior	1988			3.00
❑ 50157	PS	Early in the Morning/Disturbing Behavior	1988			3.00

Island

❑ 006		Sneakin' Sally Through the Alley/Epidemic	1974		2.50	5.00
❑ 015		Get Ta Steppin'/Get Right On Down	1975		2.50	5.00
❑ 042		Which One of Us Is the Fool/Get Outside	1975		2.50	5.00
❑ 049		Pressure Drop/Give Me an Inch Girl	1976		2.50	5.00
❑ 075		Man Smart, Woman Smarter/Keep in Touch	1976		2.50	5.00
❑ 081		One Last Look/Some People Can Do What They Want	1977		2.50	5.00
❑ 100		Every Kinda People/How Much Fun	1978		2.00	4.00
❑ 105		You Overwhelm Me/Come Over	1978		2.00	4.00
❑ 8697		Where Can It Go/You're Gonna Get What's Coming	1978		2.00	4.00
❑ 49016		Bad Case of Loving You (Doctor, Doctor)/Love Can Run Faster	1979		2.00	4.00
❑ 49094		In Walks Love Again/Jealous	1979		2.00	4.00
❑ 49137		Can We Still Be Friends/Remember to Remember	1979		2.00	4.00
❑ 49554		Style Kills/Johnny and Mary	1980		2.00	4.00
❑ 49620		Looking for Clues/Woke Up Laughing	1980		2.00	4.00
❑ 50042		Some Guys Have All the Luck/Too Good to Be True	1982		2.00	4.00
❑ 99139		Bad Case of Loving You/Sweet Lies	1989			3.00
❑ 99377		Sweet Lies/Want You More	1988			3.00
❑ 99377	PS	Sweet Lies/Want You More	1988			3.00
❑ 99537		I Didn't Mean to Turn You On/Get It Through Your Heart	1986			3.00
❑ 99537	PS	I Didn't Mean to Turn You On/Get It Through Your Heart	1986			3.00
❑ 99545		Hyperactive/Woke Up Laughing	1986			3.00
❑ 99570		Addicted to Love/Let's Fall in Love Tonight	1986			3.00
❑ 99570	PS	Addicted to Love/Let's Fall in Love Tonight *First version: Close-up photo of Robert Palmer*	1986		2.00	4.00
❑ 99570	PS	Addicted to Love/Let's Fall in Love Tonight *Second version: Photo of "models" band from video*	1986		2.00	4.00

Number		Title (A Side/B Side)	Year	VG	VG+	NM
❏ 99597		Discipline of Love (Why Did You Do It)/Dance for Me	1985			3.00
❏ 99597	PS	Discipline of Love (Why Did You Do It)/Dance for Me	1985			3.00
❏ 99835		Pride/(B-side unknown)	1983			3.00
❏ 99866		You Are In My System/Deadline	1983			3.00
❏ 99866	PS	You Are In My System/Deadline	1983			3.00

MCA
❏ 52643		All Around the World/It's Not Difficult	1985			3.00

Pals, The
Guyden
❏ 2019		My Baby Likes to Rock/Summer Is Here	1959	5.00	10.00	20.00

Turf
❏ 1000		My Baby Likes to Rock/Summer Is Here	1958	10.00	20.00	40.00

Papa Doo Run Run
(With Bruce Johnston)
Equinox
❏ PB-10404		Disney Girls/Be True to Your School	1975	2.50	5.00	10.00

Pappalardi, Felix
Columbia
❏ 43773		Love Someday/You Lie to Me	1966	5.00	10.00	20.00

Parade, The
A&M
❏ 841		Sunshine Girl/This Old Melody	1967	2.50	5.00	10.00
❏ 867		She's Got the Magic/Welcome, You're in Love	1967		3.00	6.00
❏ 887		Frog Prince/Hallelujah Rocket	1967		3.00	6.00
❏ 904		I Can See Love/Radio Song	1968		3.00	6.00
❏ 950		A.C.-D.C./She Sleeps Alone	1968		3.00	6.00
❏ 970		Laughing Lady/Hallelujah Rocket	1968		3.00	6.00

Paradons, The
Milestone
❏ 2003		Diamonds and Pearls/I Want Love	1960	3.00	6.00	12.00
		Green label				
❏ 2003		Diamonds and Pearls/I Want Love	1960	5.00	10.00	20.00
		Red label				
❏ 2003		Diamonds and Pearls/I Want Love	1960	7.50	15.00	30.00
		Maroon label				
❏ 2005		Bells Ring/Please Tell Me	1960	7.50	15.00	30.00
❏ 2015		I Had a Dream/Never, Never	1962	10.00	20.00	40.00

Tuffest
❏ 102		Never Again/This Is Love	1961	37.50	75.00	150.00

Warner Bros.
❏ 5186		Take All of Me/So Fine, So Fine, So Fine	1960	5.00	10.00	20.00

Paragons, The
Buddah
❏ 478		Oh Lovin' You/Con Me	1975		3.00	6.00

Century Custom
❏ 19317		Surf Drums/Sunday Morning	196?	15.00	30.00	60.00
		B-side by the Samohi Serenaders; this Paragons is not the same group as the others				

Music Clef
❏ 3001/2		Time After Time/Baby, Take My Hand	1963	5.00	10.00	20.00

Musicraft
❏ 1102		Wedding Bells/Blue Velvet	1960	6.25	12.50	25.00

Tap
❏ 500		If/Hey Baby	1961	12.50	25.00	50.00
❏ 503		In the Midst of the Night/Begin the Beguine	1961	10.00	20.00	40.00
❏ 504		These Are the Things I Love/If You Love Me	1961	10.00	20.00	40.00

Times Square
❏ 9		So You Will Know/Don't Cry Baby	1963	5.00	10.00	20.00

Winley
❏ 215		Hey Little School Girl/Florence	1957	10.00	20.00	40.00
❏ 220		Let's Start All Over Again/Stick With Me Baby	1957	10.00	20.00	40.00
❏ 223		Two Hearts Are Better Than One/Give Me Love	1958	12.50	25.00	50.00
❏ 227		The Wows of Love/Twilight	1958	25.00	50.00	100.00
		With misspelled A-side title				
❏ 227		The Vows of Love/Twilight	1958	10.00	20.00	40.00
❏ 228		Don't Cry Baby/So You Will Know	1958	10.00	20.00	40.00
❏ 236		Darling, I Love You/Doll Baby	1959	10.00	20.00	40.00
❏ 240		So You Will Know/Doll Baby	1959	7.50	15.00	30.00
❏ 250		Kneel and Pray/Just a Moment	1961	7.50	15.00	30.00

Parakeets, The
(More than one group)
Big Top
❏ 3130		I Love You Like I Do/I Want You Right Now	1962	5.00	10.00	20.00

Gem
❏ 218		Give Me Time/I'm Losing My Mind Over You	1954	100.00	200.00	400.00

Number		Title (A Side/B Side)	Year	VG	VG+	NM
Jubilee						
☐ 5407		Come Back/Shangri-La	1961	6.25	12.50	25.00
Paramounts, The						
(Several different groups)						
Carlton						
☐ 524		Girl Friend/Trying	1960	6.25	12.50	25.00
Centaur						
☐ 103		When I Dream/Where's Carolyn Tonight	1963	12.50	25.00	50.00
Combo						
☐ 156		Take My Heart/Thunderbird Baby	1960	25.00	50.00	100.00
Dot						
☐ 16175		Why Do You Have to Go/Congratulations	1961	6.25	12.50	25.00
☐ 16201		When You Dance/Year 17	1961	6.25	12.50	25.00
Fleetwood						
☐ 1014		I Know You'll Be My Love/Christopher Columbus	1960	6.25	12.50	25.00
Laurie						
☐ 3201		Just to Be with You/One More for the Road	1963	7.50	15.00	30.00
Liverpool Sound						
☐ 903		Poison Ivy/I Feel Good All Over	1964	12.50	25.00	50.00
		Early incarnation of Procol Harum				
Magnum						
☐ 722		Time Will Bring a Change/Under Your Spell	1964	5.00	10.00	20.00
Mercury						
☐ 72429		Girl with the Big Black Boots/I Won't Share Your Love	1965	3.00	6.00	12.00
Paramours, The						
(Bill Medley and Bobby Hatfield, later The Righteous Brothers)						
Moonglow						
☐ 214		That's All I Want Tonight/There She Goes	1962	10.00	20.00	40.00
		Red vinyl				
☐ 214		That's All I Want Tonight/There She Goes	1962	5.00	10.00	20.00
Smash						
☐ 1701		That's the Way We Love/Prison Break	1961	5.00	10.00	20.00
☐ 1718		Cutie Cutie/Miss Social Climber	1961	5.00	10.00	20.00
Parfays, The						
Fontana						
☐ 1526		You've Got a Good Thing Goin' Boy/In the Beginning	1965	7.50	15.00	30.00
Paris						
(With Bob Welch, ex-Fleetwood Mac)						
Capitol						
☐ 4356		Blue Robin/Big Towne, 2061	1976		2.50	5.00
Paris Sisters, The						
Capitol						
☐ 2081		Golden Days/Greener Days	1968	2.00	4.00	8.00
Decca						
☐ 29372		Ooh La La/Whose Arms Are You Missing	1954	6.25	12.50	25.00
☐ 29488		Baby, Honey, Baby/Huckleberry Pie	1955	6.25	12.50	25.00
☐ 29527		His and Hers/Truly Do	1955	6.25	12.50	25.00
		With Gary Crosby				
☐ 29574		The Know How/I Wanna	1955	6.25	12.50	25.00
☐ 29744		Lover Boy/Oh Yes You Do	1955	6.25	12.50	25.00
☐ 29891		I Love You Dear/Mistaken	1956	6.25	12.50	25.00
☐ 29970		Daughter! Daughter!/So Much -- So Very Much	1956	6.25	12.50	25.00
☐ 30554		Don't Tell Anybody/Mind Reader	1958	5.00	10.00	20.00
GNP Crescendo						
☐ 410		Stand Naked Clown/Ugliest Girl in Town	1968	2.00	4.00	8.00
Gregmark						
☐ 2		Be My Boy/I'll Be Crying Tomorrow	1961	5.00	10.00	20.00
☐ 6		I Love How You Love Me/All Through the Night	1961	6.25	12.50	25.00
☐ 10		He Knows I Love Him Too Much/Lonely Girl's Prayer	1962	5.00	10.00	20.00
☐ 12		Let Me Be the One/What Am I to Do	1962	5.00	10.00	20.00
☐ 13		Yes I Love You/Once Upon a While Ago	1962	5.00	10.00	20.00
		All the Gregmark records were Phil Spector productions				
Imperial						
☐ 5465		Old Enough to Cry/Tell Me More	1957	5.00	10.00	20.00
☐ 5487		Some Day/My Original Love	1958	5.00	10.00	20.00
Mercury						
☐ 72320		Once Upon a Time/When I Fall in Love	1964	2.50	5.00	10.00
☐ 72320	PS	Once Upon a Time/When I Fall in Love	1964	5.00	10.00	20.00
☐ 72468		Always Waitin'/Why Do I Take It from You	1965	2.50	5.00	10.00
☐ 72468	PS	Always Waitin'/Why Do I Take It from You	1965	5.00	10.00	20.00
MGM						
☐ 13236		Dream Lover/Lonely Girl	1964	3.75	7.50	15.00
☐ 13236	PS	Dream Lover/Lonely Girl	1964	6.25	12.50	25.00
Reprise						
☐ 0440		Sincerely/Too Good to Be True	1965	2.50	5.00	10.00

Number		Title (A Side/B Side)	Year	VG	VG+	NM
❑ 0472		I'm Me/You	1966	2.50	5.00	10.00
❑ 0511		It's My Party/My Good Friend	1966	2.50	5.00	10.00
❑ 0548		Some of Your Lovin'/Long After Tonight Is All Over	1967	2.50	5.00	10.00

Parker, Graham
Arista

❑ 0420		Local Girls/I Want You Back	1979		2.00	4.00
❑ 0420	PS	Local Girls/I Want You Back	1979		2.00	4.00
❑ 0439		Mercury Poisoning/I Want You Back (Alive)	1979		2.00	4.00
❑ 0523		Stupefaction/Women in Charge	1980		2.00	4.00
❑ 0523	PS	Stupefaction/Women in Charge	1980		2.00	4.00
❑ 0549		Endless Nights/No Holding Back	1980		2.00	4.00
		A-side: Guest vocals by Bruce Springsteen				
❑ 0652		Temporary Beauty/No More Excuses	1981		2.00	4.00
❑ 0687		You Hit the Spot/Habit Worth Forming	1982			3.00
❑ 9065		Life Gets Better/Beyond a Joke	1983			3.00

Elektra

❑ 69654		Wake Up (Next to You)/Bricks and Mortar	1985		2.00	4.00

Mercury

❑ DJ-491	DJ	Hold Back the Night (same on both sides)	1977	3.00	6.00	12.00
❑ DJ-531	DJ	Stick to Me (same on both sides)	1977	3.00	6.00	12.00
❑ 73834		Soul Shoes/You've Got to Be Kidding	1976	2.00	4.00	8.00
❑ 73876		Heat Treatment/Back Door Love	1976	2.00	4.00	8.00
❑ 73970		Stick to Me/The Heat in Harlem	1977	2.00	4.00	8.00
❑ 74000		Hold Back the Night/(Let Me Get) Sweet on You// White Honey/Soul Shoes	1977		2.50	5.00
		Pink vinyl				
❑ 74000		Hold Back the Night/(Let Me Get) Sweet on You// White Honey/Soul Shoes	1977		3.50	7.00
		Also on black vinyl; scarcer than pink version				
❑ 74000	PS	"The Pink Parker": Hold Back the Night/ (Let Me Get) Sweet on You//White Honey/Soul Shoes	1977		2.50	5.00

RCA

❑ 8639-7-R		(Get Started) Start a Fire/Ordinary Girl	1988			3.00

Parker, Junior
(Many of these were as "Little Junior Parker")
Blue Rock

❑ 4064		I Got Money/Lover to Friend	1968	2.00	4.00	8.00
❑ 4067		Reconsider Baby/Lovin' Man on Your Hands	1968	2.00	4.00	8.00
❑ 4080		Ain't Gon' Be No Cuttin' Loose/I'm So Satisfied	1969	2.00	4.00	8.00
❑ 4088		Easy Lovin'/You Can't Keep a Good Woman Down	1969	2.00	4.00	8.00

Capitol

❑ 2857		The Outside Man/Darling, Depend on Me	1970		3.00	6.00
❑ 2997		Drownin' on Dry Land/River's Invitation	1970		3.00	6.00

Duke

❑ 120		Dirty Friend Blues/Can't Understand	1954	15.00	30.00	60.00
❑ 127		Please Baby Please/Sittin', Drinkin' and Thinkin'	1954	15.00	30.00	60.00
❑ 137		Backtracking/I Wanna Ramble	1954	15.00	30.00	60.00
❑ 147		Driving Me/There Better Not Be No Feel	1956	12.50	25.00	50.00
❑ 157		Mother-in-Law Blues/That's My Baby	1956	12.50	25.00	50.00
❑ 164		Next Time You See Me/My Dolly Bee	1957	7.50	15.00	30.00
❑ 168		That's Alright/Pretty Baby	1957	7.50	15.00	30.00
❑ 177		Peaches/Pretty Little Doll	1957	7.50	15.00	30.00
❑ 184		Wondering/Sitting and Thinking	1958	6.25	12.50	25.00
❑ 193		Barefoot Rock/What Did I Do	1958	6.25	12.50	25.00
❑ 301		Sweet Home Chicago/Sometimes	1959	5.00	10.00	20.00
❑ 306		Five Long Years/I'm Holding On	1959	5.00	10.00	20.00
❑ 309		Stranded/Blue Letter	1959	5.00	10.00	20.00
❑ 315		Dangerous Woman/Belinda Marie	1960	3.75	7.50	15.00
❑ 317		The Next Time/You're On My Mind	1960	3.75	7.50	15.00
❑ 326		I'll Learn to Love Again/That's Just Alright	1960	3.75	7.50	15.00
❑ 330		Stand By Me/I'll Forget About You	1960	3.75	7.50	15.00
❑ 335		Driving Wheel/Seven Days	1961	3.75	7.50	15.00
❑ 341		In the Dark/How Long Can This Go On	1961	3.00	6.00	12.00
❑ 345		Annie Get Your Yo-Yo/Mary Jo	1961	3.00	6.00	12.00
❑ 351		I Feel Alright Again/Sweeter As the Days Go By	1962	3.00	6.00	12.00
❑ 357		Foxy Devil/Someone Somewhere	1962	3.00	6.00	12.00
❑ 362		It's a Pity/Last Night	1963	3.00	6.00	12.00
❑ 364		If You Don't Love Me/I Can't Forget About You	1963	3.00	6.00	12.00
❑ 367		The Tables Have Turned/Yonders Wall	1963	3.00	6.00	12.00
❑ 371		Strange Things Happening/I'm Gonna Stop	1964	3.00	6.00	12.00
❑ 376		Things I Used to Do/That's Why I'm Always Crying	1964	3.00	6.00	12.00
❑ 384		I'm in Love/Jivin' Woman	1964	3.00	6.00	12.00
❑ 389		Crying for My Baby/ Guess You Don't Know (The Golden Rule)	1965	3.00	6.00	12.00
❑ 394		These Kind of Blues (Part 1)/ These Kind of Blues (Part 2)	1966	3.00	6.00	12.00
❑ 398		Walking the Floor Over You/Goodbye Little Girl	1966	3.00	6.00	12.00
❑ 406		Get Away Blues/Why Do You Make Me Cry	1966	3.00	6.00	12.00
❑ 413		Man or Mouse/Wait for Another Day	1966	3.00	6.00	12.00

Mercury

❑ 72620		Baby Please/Just Like a Fish	1966	2.50	5.00	10.00
❑ 72651		You Can Make It If You Care/ Ooh Wee Baby, That's the Way You Make Me Feel	1967	2.50	5.00	10.00
❑ 72672		Country Girl/Sometimes I Wonder	1967	2.50	5.00	10.00

Number		Title (A Side/B Side)	Year	VG	VG+	NM
❑ 72699		I Can't Put My Finger On It/If I Had Your Love	1967	2.50	5.00	10.00
❑ 72733		Hurtin' Inside/What a Fool I Was	1967	2.50	5.00	10.00
❑ 72793		It Must Be Love/Your Love's All Over	1968	2.00	4.00	8.00

Minit

❑ 32080		Worried Life Blues/Let the Good Times Roll	1969		3.00	6.00

Sun

❑ 187		Feelin' Good/Fussin' and Fightin' Blues	1953	100.00	200.00	400.00
		As "Little Junior's Blue Flames"				
❑ 192		Mystery Train/Love My Baby	1954	50.00	100.00	200.00
		As "Little Junior's Blue Flames"				

Parker, Ray, Jr.
Arista

0283 through 0441 as "Raydio"

❑ 0283		Jack and Jill/Get Down	1977		2.50	5.00
❑ 0283	PS	Jack and Jill/Get Down	1977		3.00	6.00
❑ 0328		Is This a Love Thing/Let's Go All the Way	1978		2.50	5.00
❑ 0353		Honey I'm Rich/Betcha You Can't Love Me Just Once	1978		2.50	5.00
❑ 0399		You Can't Change That/Rock On	1979		2.50	5.00
❑ 0441		More Than One Way to Love a Woman/Hot Stuff	1979		2.50	5.00

0494 through 0641 as "Ray Parker Jr. and Raydio"

❑ 0494		Two Places at the Same Time/ Everybody Makes Mistakes	1980		2.00	4.00
❑ 0522		For Those Who Like to Groove/Can't Keep from Cryin'	1980		2.00	4.00
❑ 0554		Can't Keep from Cryin'/It's Time to Party Now	1980		2.00	4.00
❑ 0575		Little Bit of You/It's Time to Party Now	1980		2.00	4.00
❑ 0592		A Woman Needs Love (Just Like You Do)/So Into You	1981		2.00	4.00
❑ 0616		That Old Song/Old Pro	1981		2.00	4.00
❑ 0616	PS	That Old Song/Old Pro	1981		2.00	4.00
❑ 0641		It's Your Night/Old Pro	1981		2.00	4.00
❑ 0669		The Other Woman/Stay the Night	1982		2.00	4.00
❑ 0695		Let Me Go/Stop, Look Before You Love	1982		2.00	4.00
❑ 1014		It's Our Own Affair/Just Havin' Fun	1982		2.00	4.00
❑ 1030		Bad Boy/Let's Get Off	1982		2.00	4.00
❑ 1035		Christmas Time Is Here/(Instrumental)	1982		2.50	5.00
❑ 1035	PS	Christmas Time Is Here/(Instrumental)	1982		3.00	6.00
❑ 1051		The People Next Door/Streetlove	1983		2.00	4.00
❑ 9048		Woman Out of Control/(B-side unknown)	1983		2.00	4.00
❑ 9116		I Still Can't Get Over Losing You/ She Still Feels the Need	1983		2.00	4.00
❑ 9198		In the Heat of the Night/N2 U2	1984		2.00	4.00
❑ 9212		Ghostbusters/(Instrumental)	1984			3.00
❑ 9293		Jamie/Christmas Time Is Here	1984			3.00
❑ 9352		Girls Are More Fun/(B-side unknown)	1985			3.00
❑ 9352	PS	Girls Are More Fun/(B-side unknown)	1985			3.00
❑ 9451		One Sided Love Affair/(B-side unknown)	1985			3.00

Geffen

❑ 28152		Over You/After Midnite	1987			3.00
❑ 28152	PS	Over You/After Midnite	1987			3.00
		With Natalie Cole				
❑ 28417		I Don't Think That Man Should Sleep Alone/ After Midnight	1987			3.00
❑ 28417	PS	I Don't Think That Man Should Sleep Alone/ After Midnight	1987			3.00

Parks, Gino
Crazy Horse

❑ 1303		Nerves of Steel/Help Me Somebody	1968	7.50	15.00	30.00

Fortune

❑ 528		Last Night I Cried/Just Go	1957	20.00	40.00	80.00

Golden World

❑ 32		My Sophisticated Lady/Talkin' About My Baby	1966	5.00	10.00	20.00

Miracle

❑ 3		Don't Say Bye Bye/(B-side unknown)	1960	200.00	400.00	800.00

Tamla

❑ 54042		That's No Lie/Same Thing	1961	15.00	30.00	60.00
❑ 54066		For This I Thank You/Fire	1962	15.00	30.00	60.00

Parks, Ray
Capitol

❑ F3580		You're Gonna Have to Bawl, That's All/ Just a-Hangin' Around	1956	17.50	35.00	70.00

Parks, Van Dyke
(Also see "Brown, George Washington")

MGM

❑ 13441		Do What You Wanta/Number Nine	1966	3.00	6.00	12.00
❑ 13570		Come to the Sunshine/Farther Along	1966	3.00	6.00	12.00

Warner Bros.

❑ 7409		On the Rolling Sea When Jesus Speaks to Me/ The Eagle and Me	1970	2.50	5.00	10.00
❑ 7609		Occapella/Ode to Tobago	1972		3.00	6.00
❑ 7632		Riverboat/John Jones	1972		3.00	6.00

Number	Title (A Side/B Side)	Year	VG	VG+	NM

Parlet

(Female offshoot from Parliament/Funkadelic)

Casablanca

☐ 919	Pleasure Principle/(Instrumental)	1978		2.50	5.00
☐ 932	Cookie Jar/Are You Dreaming	1978		2.50	5.00
☐ 975	Ridin' High (Part 1)/Ridin' High (Part 2)	1979		2.50	5.00
☐ 995	Don't Ever Stop/Huff-N-Puff	1979		2.50	5.00
☐ 2260	Wolf Tickets/(Instrumental)	1980		2.50	5.00
☐ 2293	Help from My Friends/Watch Me Do My Thang	1980		2.50	5.00

Parliament

(Also see "Funkadelic"; "Parlet"; "Parliaments, The")

Casablanca

☐ 0003	The Goose (Part 1)/The Goose (Part 2)	1974		3.00	6.00
☐ 0013	Up for the Down Stroke/Presence of a Brain	1974		3.00	6.00
☐ 0104	Up for the Down Stroke/Presence of a Brain	1974		2.50	5.00
☐ 803	Up for the Down Stroke/Presence of a Brain	1974		2.50	5.00
☐ 811	Testify/I Can Move You	1974		2.50	5.00
☐ 831	Chocolate City/Chocolate City (Part 2)	1975		2.50	5.00
☐ 843	Ride On/Big Footin'	1975		2.50	5.00
☐ 852	P. Funk (Wants to Get Funked Up)/ Night of the Tempasaurus Peoples	1976		2.50	5.00
☐ 856	Tear the Roof Off the Sucker (Give Up the Funk)/ P-Funk	1976		2.50	5.00
	Blue label				
☐ 856	Tear the Roof Off the Sucker (Give Up the Funk)/ P-Funk	1976		2.00	4.00
	Tan label				
☐ 864	Star Child (Mothership Connection)/Supergroovealistic	1976		2.50	5.00
☐ 871	Do That Stuff/Handcuffs	1976		2.50	5.00
☐ 875	Dr. Funkenstein/Children of Production	1977		2.50	5.00
☐ 892	Fantasy Is Reality/(B-side unknown)	1977		2.50	5.00
☐ 900	Bop Gun (Endangered Species)/ I've Been Watchin' You	1977		2.50	5.00
☐ 909	Flash Light/Swing Down, Sweet Chariot	1978		2.50	5.00
☐ 921	Funkentelechy/Funkentelechy (Part 2)	1978		2.50	5.00
☐ 950	Aqua Boogie (A Psychoalphadiscobetabioaquadoloop)/ (You're a Fish and I'm a) Water Sign	1978		2.50	5.00
☐ 950 PS	Aqua Boogie (A Psychoalphadiscobetabioaquadoloop)/ (You're a Fish and I'm a) Water Sign	1978	2.50	5.00	10.00
☐ 976	Rumpofsteelskin/Liquid Sunshine	1979		2.50	5.00
☐ 2222	Party People/Party People (Part 2)	1979		2.50	5.00
☐ 2235	Theme from The Black Hole/ (You're a Fish and I'm a) Water Sign	1980		2.50	5.00
☐ 2250	The Big Bang Theory/The Big Bang Theory (Part 2)	1980		2.50	5.00
☐ 2317	Agony of DeFeet/The Freeze	1980		2.50	5.00
☐ 2330	Crush It/Body Language	1981		2.50	5.00

Invictus

☐ 9077	I Call My Baby Pussy Cat/Little Ole Country Boy	1970	2.50	5.00	10.00
☐ 9091	Red Hot Mama/Little Ole Country Boy	1971	2.50	5.00	10.00
☐ 9095	Breakdown/Little Ole Country Boy	1971	2.50	5.00	10.00
☐ 9123	Come In Out of the Rain/Little Ole Country Boy	1972	2.00	4.00	8.00

Parliaments, The

(George Clinton's first group. All of these are probably the same. Also see "Funkadelic"; "Parliament")

Apt

| ☐ 25036 | Poor Willie/Party Boys | 1959 | 10.00 | 20.00 | 40.00 |

Atco

| ☐ 6675 | A New Day Begins/I'll Wait | 1969 | 5.00 | 10.00 | 20.00 |

Flipp

☐ 100/1	Lonely Island/You Make Me Wanna Cry	1960	10.00	20.00	40.00
	Red label				
☐ 100/1	Lonely Island/You Make Me Wanna Cry	1960	7.50	15.00	30.00
	Yellow label				

Golden World

| ☐ 46 | Heart Trouble/That Was My Girl | 1966 | 12.50 | 25.00 | 50.00 |

Len

| ☐ 101 | Don't Need You Anymore/ Honey, Take Me Home with You | 1958 | 20.00 | 40.00 | 80.00 |

Revilot

☐ 207	(I Wanna) Testify/I Can Feel the Ice Melting	1967	3.75	7.50	15.00
☐ 211	All Your Goodies Are Gone (The Loser's Seat)/ Don't Be Sore at Me	1967	3.75	7.50	15.00
☐ 214	Little Man/The Goose (That Laid the Golden Egg)	1968	3.75	7.50	15.00
☐ 217	Look at What I Almost Missed/What You Been Growing	1968	3.75	7.50	15.00
☐ 223	Good Old Music/Time	1968	3.75	7.50	15.00
☐ 228	A New Day Begins/I'll Wait	1968	7.50	15.00	30.00

Symbol

| ☐ 917 | You're Cute/I'll Get You Yet | 1962 | 6.25 | 12.50 | 25.00 |

U.S.A.

| ☐ 719 | My Only Love/To Be Alone | 1961 | 5.00 | 10.00 | 20.00 |

Number	Title (A Side/B Side)	Year	VG	VG+	NM

Parris, Fred
(Of the Five Satins)
Atco
| ❑ 6439 | Land of the Broken Hearts/Bring It Home to Daddy | 1966 | 2.50 | 5.00 | 10.00 |

Birth
| ❑ 101 | Dark at the Top of My Heart/Benediction | 196? | 2.00 | 4.00 | 8.00 |

Checker
| ❑ 1108 | No Use in Crying/Walk a Little Faster | 1965 | 2.50 | 5.00 | 10.00 |

Green Sea
| ❑ 106 | Blushing Bride/Giving My Love to You | 1966 | 2.50 | 5.00 | 10.00 |
| ❑ 107 | I'll Be Hangin' On/I Can Really Satisfy | 1966 | 2.50 | 5.00 | 10.00 |

Mama Sadie
| ❑ 1001 | In the Still of the Nite "67"/Heck No | 1967 | 2.50 | 5.00 | 10.00 |

Parrots, The
Checker
| ❑ 772 | Don't Leave Me/Weep, Weep, Weep | 1953 | 125.00 | 250.00 | 500.00 |

Parsons, Alan, Project
Arista
❑ 0260	I Wouldn't Want to Be Like You/Nucleus	1977		2.00	4.00
❑ 0288	I Robot/Don't Let It Show	1977		2.00	4.00
❑ 0310	Day After Day/Breakdown	1978		2.00	4.00
❑ 0352	What Goes Up/In the Lap of the Gods	1978		2.00	4.00
❑ 0454	Damned if I Do/If I Could Change Your Mind	1979		2.00	4.00
❑ 0491	You Won't Be There/Secret Garden	1980		2.00	4.00
❑ 0502	You Lie Down with Dogs/Lucifer	1980		2.00	4.00
❑ 0573	Games People Play/Ace of Swords	1980		2.00	4.00
❑ 0598	Time/The Gold Bug	1981		2.00	4.00
❑ 0635	Snake Eyes/I Don't Wanna Go Home	1981		2.00	4.00
❑ 0696	Eye in the Sky/Gemini	1982		2.00	4.00
❑ 1029	Psychobabble/Children of the Moon	1982		2.00	4.00
❑ 1048	Old and Wise/You're Gonna Get Your Fingers Burned	1983		2.00	4.00
❑ 9108	You Don't Believe/Lucifer	1983		2.00	4.00
❑ 9160	Don't Answer Me/Don't Let It Show	1984			3.00
❑ 9160 PS	Don't Answer Me/Don't Let It Show	1984			3.00
❑ 9208	Prime Time/Gold Bug	1984			3.00
❑ 9282	Let's Talk About Me/Hawkeye	1984			3.00
❑ 9282 PS	Let's Talk About Me/Hawkeye	1984			3.00
❑ 9349	Days Are Numbers (The Traveller)/Somebody Out There	1985			3.00
❑ 9443	Stereotomy/Urbania	1985			3.00
❑ 9576	Standing on Higher Ground/Inside Looking Out	1987			3.00

20th Century
❑ 2297	(The System of) Doctor Tarr and Professor Fether/Dream Within a Dream	1976		2.50	5.00
❑ 2308	The Raven/Prelude to Fall of the House of Usher	1976		2.50	5.00
❑ 2333	To One in Paradise/The Cask of Amontillado	1977		3.00	6.00

Parsons, Bill
Fraternity
❑ 835	The All American Boy/Rubber Dolly	1959	10.00	20.00	40.00
	This record is actually by Bobby Bare miscredited				
❑ 838	Educated Rock and Roll/Carefree Wanderer	1959	7.50	15.00	30.00

Starday
| ❑ 526 | Hod Rod Volkswagen/Guitar Blues | 1960 | 7.50 | 15.00 | 30.00 |
| ❑ 544 | The Price We Pay for Livin'/A-Waitin' | 1960 | 5.00 | 10.00 | 20.00 |

Parsons, Gram
(Also see "Byrds, The"; "International Submarine Band, The")
Reprise
| ❑ 1139 | That's All It Took/She | 1972 | | 3.00 | 6.00 |
| ❑ 1192 | Love Hurts/In My Hour of Darkness | 1974 | | 3.00 | 6.00 |

Sierra
❑ 104	Medley (Bony Moronie/40 Days/Almost Grown)//Conversations/Hot Burrito #1	1982		2.50	5.00
	Second song on side 2 by Gene Parsons				
❑ 103	Love Hurts/The New Soft Shoe	1982		2.50	5.00
❑ 104 PS	Medley (Bony Moronie/40 Days/Almost Grown)//Conversations/Hot Burrito #1	1982		2.50	5.00

Warner Bros.
| ❑ 50013 | Return of the Grievous Angel/Hearts on Fire | 1982 | | 2.50 | 5.00 |

Parton, Dolly
(Also see next entry; "Rogers, Kenny, and Dolly Parton"; "Wagoner, Porter, and Dolly Parton")
Columbia
❑ 07727	I Know You by Heart/Could I Have Your Autograph	1988			3.00
	With Smokey Robinson				
❑ 07995	Make Love Mine/Two Lovers	1988			3.00
❑ 68760	Why'd You Come In Here Lookin' Like That/Wait Til I Get You Home	1989			3.00
❑ 69040	Yellow Roses/Wait Til I Get You Home	1989			3.00
❑ 73200	He's Alive/What Is It We Love	1990			3.00

Number	Title (A Side/B Side)	Year	VG	VG+	NM
☐ 73226	Time for Me to Fly/The Moon, the Stars, and Me	1990			3.00
☐ 73341	White Limozeen/The Moon, the Stars, and Me	1990			3.00
☐ 73498	Slow Healin' Heart/Take Me Back to the Country	1990			3.00
☐ 73711	Rockin' Years/What a Heartache	1991			3.00
	A-side with Ricky Van Shelton				
☐ 73826	Silver and Gold/Runaway Feelin'	1991			3.00
☐ 74011	Eagle When She Flies/Wildest Dreams	1991			3.00
☐ 74183	The Best Woman Wins/Country Road	1992			3.00
	A-side with Lorrie Morgan				
☐ 74876	Romeo/The High and the Mighty	1993			3.00
	A-side: "Dolly Parton and Friends"				
☐ 74954	More Where That Came From/I'll Make Your Bed	1993			3.00
☐ 77083	Full Circle/What Will Baby Be	1993			3.00
☐ 77294	Silver Threads and Golden Needles/Let Her Fly	1993			3.00
	Dolly Parton/Tammy Wynette/Loretta Lynn				
☐ 77723	To Daddy/PMS Blues	1994			3.00
☐ 78079	I Will Always Love You/Speakin' of the Devil	1995			3.00
	A-side: "With Special Guest Vince Gill"				

Gold Band

☐ 1086	Puppy Love/Girl Left Alone	1959	250.00	500.00	1,000

Mercury

☐ 71982	It's Sure Gonna Hurt/The Love You Gave	1962	12.50	25.00	50.00

Monument

☐ 869	I Wasted My Tears/What Do You Think About Lovin'	1965	3.75	7.50	15.00
☐ 897	Old Enough to Know Better (Too Young to Resist)/ Happy, Happy Birthday Baby	1965	3.75	7.50	15.00
☐ 913	Busy Signal/I Took Him for Granted	1965	3.75	7.50	15.00
☐ 922	Control Yourself/Don't Drop Out	1966	3.75	7.50	15.00
☐ 948	Little Things/I'll Put It Off Until Tomorrow	1966	3.75	7.50	15.00
☐ 982	Dumb Blonde/The Giving and the Taking	1967	2.50	5.00	10.00
☐ 1007	Something Fishy/I've Lived My Life	1967	2.50	5.00	10.00
☐ 1032	Why, Why, Why/I Couldn't Wait Forever	1967	2.50	5.00	10.00
☐ 1047	I'm Not Worth the Tears/Ping Pong	1968	2.00	4.00	8.00
☐ 03408	Everything Is Beautiful (In Its Own Way)/ Put It Off Until Tomorrow	1982		2.00	4.00
	A-side with Willie Nelson; B-side with Kris Kristofferson				
☐ 03781	What Do You Think About Lovin'/ You're Gonna Love Yourself (In the Morning)	1983		2.00	4.00
	A-side: Dolly Parton and Brenda Lee; B-side: Willie Nelson and Brenda Lee				

RCA

☐ 5001-7-R	Do I Ever Cross Your Mind/We Had It All	1986			3.00
☐ PB-10935	Light of a Clear Blue Morning/There	1977		2.00	4.00
☐ PB-11123	Here You Come Again/Me and Little Andy	1977		2.00	4.00
☐ PB-11241	Two Doors Down/It's All Wrong, But It's All Right	1978		2.00	4.00
☐ PB-11296	Heartbreaker/Sure Thing	1978		2.00	4.00
☐ PB-11420	Baby I'm Burning/I Really Got the Feeling	1978		2.00	4.00
☐ GB-11505	Here You Come Again/Two Doors Down	1979			3.00
	Gold Standard Series				
☐ PB-11577	You're the Only One/Down	1979		2.00	4.00
☐ PB-11705	Sweet Summer Lovin'/Great Balls of Fire	1979		2.00	4.00
☐ PB-11926	Starting Over Again/Sweet Agony	1980		2.00	4.00
☐ GB-11993	Baby I'm Burnin'/Heartbreaker	1980			3.00
	Gold Standard Series				
☐ PB-12040	Old Flames Can't Hold a Candle to You/ I Knew You When	1980		2.00	4.00
☐ PB-12133	9 to 5/Odd Jobs	1980		2.00	4.00
☐ PB-12133	PS 9 to 5/Odd Jobs	1980		2.50	5.00
☐ PB-12200	But You Know I Love You/Poor Folks' Town	1981		2.00	4.00
☐ PB-12282	The House of the Rising Sun/Working Girl	1981		2.00	4.00
☐ GB-12316	9 to 5/Old Flames Can't Hold a Candle to You	1981			3.00
	Gold Standard Series				
☐ PB-13057	Single Women/Barbara on Your Mind	1982		2.00	4.00
☐ PB-13234	Heartbreak Express/Act Like a Fool	1982		2.00	4.00
☐ PB-13260	I Will Always Love You/Do I Ever Cross Your Mind	1982		2.00	4.00
	A-side is the same song, but a different recording than that on RCA Victor APBO-0234				
☐ PB-13260	PS I Will Always Love You/Do I Ever Cross Your Mind	1982		2.50	5.00
☐ PB-13361	Hard Candy Christmas/Me and Little Andy	1982		2.00	4.00
☐ PB-13514	Potential New Boyfriend/One of Those Days	1983			3.00
☐ PB-13619	Tennessee Homesick Blues/Butterflies	1984			3.00
☐ PB-13703	Save the Last Dance for Me/Elusive Butterfly	1983			3.00
☐ PB-13756	The Great Pretender/Downtown	1984			3.00
☐ PB-13856	Sweet Lovin' Friends/Too Much Water	1984			Unreleased
☐ PB-13883	Sweet Lovin' Friends/God Won't Get You	1984			3.00
	With Sylvester Stallone				
☐ PB-13944	Medley: Winter Wonderland-Sleigh Ride/ The Christmas Song	1984			3.00
	B-side by Kenny Rogers				
☐ PB-13987	Don't Call It Love/We Got Too Much	1985			3.00
☐ GB-14070	Tennessee Homesick Blues/Hard Candy Christmas	1985			3.00
	Gold Standard Series				
☐ PB-14218	Think About Love/Come Back to Me	1985			3.00
☐ PB-14297	Tie Our Love (In a Double Knot)/ I Hope You're Never Happy	1986			3.00
☐ GB-14346	Don't Call It Love/Real Love	1986			3.00
	Gold Standard Series				

Number		Title (A Side/B Side)	Year	VG	VG+	NM
RCA Victor						
❑ 47-9548		Just Because I'm a Woman/ I Wish I Felt This Way at Home	1968	2.00	4.00	8.00
❑ 47-9657		In the Good Old Days (When Times Were Bad)/ Try Being Lonely	1968	2.00	4.00	8.00
❑ 47-9784		Daddy Come and Get Me/Chas	1969		3.00	6.00
❑ 47-9863		Mule Skinner Blues/More Than Their Share	1970		3.00	6.00
❑ 47-9928		Joshua/I'm Doing This for Your Sake	1970		3.00	6.00
❑ 47-9971		Comin' For to Carry Me Home/Golden Streets of Glory	1971		3.00	6.00
❑ 47-9999		My Blue Tears/The Mystery of the Mystery	1971		3.00	6.00
❑ 74-0132		Daddy/He's a Go-Getter	1969		3.00	6.00
❑ 74-0192		In the Ghetto/Bridge	1969		3.00	6.00
❑ 74-0243		My Blue Ridge Mountain Boy/'Til Death Do Us Part	1969		3.00	6.00
❑ 74-0538		Coat of Many Colors/Here I Am	1971		3.00	6.00
❑ 74-0662		Touch Your Woman/Mission Chapel Memories	1972		2.50	5.00
❑ 74-0757		Washday Blues/Just As Good As Gone	1972		2.50	5.00
❑ 74-0797		Lord, Hold My Hand/When I Sing for Him	1972		2.50	5.00
❑ 74-0868		My Tennessee Mountain Home/Better Part of Life	1973		2.50	5.00
❑ 74-0950		Traveling Man/I Remember	1973		2.50	5.00
❑ APBO-0145		Jolene/Love, You're So Beautiful Tonight	1973		2.50	5.00
❑ APBO-0234		I Will Always Love You/Lonely Comin' Down	1974		2.50	5.00
❑ PB-10031		Love Is Like a Butterfly/Sacred Memories	1974		2.00	4.00
❑ PB-10164		The Bargain Store/I'll Never Forget	1975		2.00	4.00
❑ GB-10165		Jolene/My Tennessee Mountain Home	1975			3.00
	Gold Standard Series					
❑ PB-10310		The Seeker/Love with Feeling	1975		2.00	4.00
❑ PB-10396		We Used To/My Heart Started Breaking	1975		2.00	4.00
❑ GB-10504		Love Is Like a Butterfly/Sacred Memories	1975			3.00
	Gold Standard Series					
❑ GB-10505		I Will Always Love You/Lovely Comin' Down	1975			3.00
	Gold Standard Series					
❑ PB-10564		Hey, Lucky Lady/Most of All, Why	1976		2.00	4.00
❑ GB-10676		The Bargain Store/The Seeker	1976			3.00
	Gold Standard Series					
❑ PB-10730		All I Can Do/Falling Out of Love with Me	1976		2.00	4.00
Rising Tide						
❑ 56041		Just When I Needed You Most/For the Good Times	1996			3.00

Parton, Dolly/Linda Ronstadt/Emmylou Harris

(Also see individual listings)

Number		Title (A Side/B Side)	Year	VG	VG+	NM
Warner Bros.						
❑ 27970		Wildflowers/Hobo's Meditation	1988			3.00
❑ 28248		Those Memories of You/My Dear Companion	1987			3.00
❑ 28371		Telling Me Lies/Rosewood Casket	1987			3.00
❑ 28492		To Know Him Is to Love Him/Farther Along	1987			3.00
❑ 28492	PS	To Know Him Is to Love Him/Farther Along	1987		2.00	4.00

Partridge Family, The

Number		Title (A Side/B Side)	Year	VG	VG+	NM
Bell						
❑ 910		I Think I Love You/Somebody Wants to Love You	1970		2.50	5.00
❑ 910	PS	I Think I Love You/Somebody Wants to Love You	1970		3.00	6.00
❑ 963		Doesn't Somebody Want to Be Wanted/ You Are Always on My Mind	1971		2.50	5.00
❑ 963	PS	Doesn't Somebody Want to Be Wanted/ You Are Always on My Mind	1971		3.00	6.00
❑ 996		I'll Meet You Halfway/Morning Rider on the Road	1971		2.50	5.00
❑ 45,130		I Woke Up in Love This Morning/ Twenty-Four Hours a Day	1971		2.50	5.00
❑ 45,160		It's One of Those Nights (Yes Love)/One Night Stand	1971		2.50	5.00
❑ 45,200		Am I Losing You/If You Ever Go	1972		2.00	4.00
❑ 45,235		Breaking Up Is Hard to Do/I'm Here, You're Here	1972		2.00	4.00
❑ 45,301		Looking Through the Eyes of Love/Storybook Love	1972		2.00	4.00
❑ 45,336		Friend and a Lover/Something's Wrong	1973		2.00	4.00
❑ 45,414		Lookin' for a Good Time/(B-side unknown)	1973		2.00	4.00

Passions, The

(Several different groups)

Number		Title (A Side/B Side)	Year	VG	VG+	NM
ABC-Paramount						
❑ 10436		The Bully/The Empty Seat	1963	6.25	12.50	25.00
Audicon						
❑ 102		Just to Be with You/Oh Melancholy Me	1959	7.50	15.00	30.00
❑ 105		I Only Want You/This Is My Love	1960	7.50	15.00	30.00
❑ 106		Gloria/Jungle Drums	1960	5.00	10.00	20.00
❑ 108		Beautiful Dreamer/One Look Is All It Took	1960	5.00	10.00	20.00
❑ 112		Made for Lovers/You Don't Have Me Anymore	1961	10.00	20.00	40.00
Back Beat						
❑ 573		Baby I Do/Man About Town	1966	2.50	5.00	10.00
Capitol						
❑ F3963		Jackie Brown/My Aching Heart	1958	7.50	15.00	30.00
Diamond						
❑ 146		Sixteen Candles/The Third Floor	1963	7.50	15.00	30.00
Dore						
❑ 505		Nervous About Sally/Tango of Love	1958	7.50	15.00	30.00
Era						
❑ 1063		Jackie Brown/My Aching Heart	1957	10.00	20.00	40.00

Number		Title (A Side/B Side)	Year	VG	VG+	NM
Jubilee						
☐ 5406		Lonely Road/One Look Is All It Took	1961	3.75	7.50	15.00
Octavia						
☐ 8005		Aphrodite/I've Gotta Know	1962	75.00	150.00	300.00
Topaz						
☐ 1317		It Ain't Fair/I'm So Afraid	196?	2.50	5.00	10.00
Tower						
☐ 424		Without a Warning/Just Like a Rolling Seal	1968	2.00	4.00	8.00
☐ 443		I Can See My Way Through/Just Another Reason	1968	2.00	4.00	8.00
☐ 443		I Can See My Way Through/Without a Warning	1968	2.00	4.00	8.00
☐ 474		Just Like a Rolling Stone/Just Another	1969	2.00	4.00	8.00
☐ 485		Hijacked/Hijacked	1969	2.00	4.00	8.00

Pastel Six, The
Chattahoochie

☐ 696		I Can't Dance/Red River Quetzal	1966	2.50	5.00	10.00
Downey						
☐ 101		Twitchin'/Wino Stomp	1962	7.50	15.00	30.00
☐ 101		Twitchin'/Open House at the Cinder	1962	7.50	15.00	30.00
☐ 102		Braum's Nightmare/Open House at the Cinder	1962	6.25	12.50	25.00
Zen						
☐ 102		The Cinnamon Cinder (It's a Very Nice Dance)/Bandido	1962	6.25	12.50	25.00
☐ 105		Sing Along Song/Strange Ghosts	1963	6.25	12.50	25.00
☐ 108		The Milkshake/Parchman Farm	1963	6.25	12.50	25.00
☐ 111		Miss Sue/Baby Please Don't Go	1963	6.25	12.50	25.00

Pastels, The
Argo

☐ 5287		Been So Long/My One and Only Dream	1958	6.25	12.50	25.00
☐ 5297		You Don't Love Me Anymore/Let's Go to the Rock 'N' Roll Ball	1958	7.50	15.00	30.00
☐ 5314		So Far Away/Don't Knock	1958	6.25	12.50	25.00
Ark						
☐ 298		Jungle Run/K-Nif	196?	12.50	25.00	50.00
Jubilee						
☐ 5495		First Star/Tokyo Melody	1965	3.00	6.00	12.00
Mascot						
☐ 123		Been So Long/My One and Only Dream	1957	75.00	150.00	300.00
United						
☐ 196		Put Your Arms Around Me/Boom De De Boom	1957	20.00	40.00	80.00

Patience and Prudence
Chatathoochie

☐ 665		Tonight You Belong to Me (New Version)/How Can I Tell Him	1965	2.50	5.00	10.00
Liberty						
☐ 55022		Tonight You Belong to Me/A Smile and a Ribbon	1956	7.50	15.00	30.00
☐ 55040		Gonna Get Along Without Ya Now/The Money Tree	1956	6.25	12.50	25.00
☐ 55058		Dreamer's Bay/We Can't Sing Rhythm and Blues	1957	6.25	12.50	25.00
☐ 55084		You Tattletale/Very Nice in Bali Bali	1957	6.25	12.50	25.00
☐ 55084	PS	You Tattletale/Very Nice in Bali Bali	1957	12.50	25.00	50.00
☐ 55107		Witchcraft/Over Here	1957	6.25	12.50	25.00
☐ 55125		Heavenly Angel/Little Wheel	1958	6.25	12.50	25.00
☐ 55154		All I Do Is Dream of You/Your Careless Love	1958	6.25	12.50	25.00
☐ 55169		Golly Oh Gee/Tom Thumb's Tune	1958	6.25	12.50	25.00
☐ 55207		Should I/Whisper Whisper	1959	3.75	7.50	15.00
		With Mike Clifford				
United Artists						
☐ 0012		Tonight You Belong to Me/Gonna Get Along Without You Now	1973		2.50	5.00
		"Silver Spotlight Series" reissue				

Patton, Jimmy
Sage and Sand

☐ 261		Call Me/Forty-Nine Women	1958	30.00	60.00	120.00
☐ 282		Ocean Full of Tears/Twinklin' Teardrops	1959	10.00	20.00	40.00
Sims						
☐ 103		Careful/Guilty	1955	12.50	25.00	50.00
		With Ann Jones				
☐ 104		Teenage Heart/Jalopy	1955	12.50	25.00	50.00
☐ 105		Ocean of Tears/I Don't Want It	1955	12.50	25.00	50.00
☐ 117		Okie's in the Pokie/Lonely Nights	1960	50.00	100.00	200.00
☐ 256		Can't Shake the Blues/(B-side unknown)	1965	3.00	6.00	12.00

Patty and the Emblems
Congress

☐ 263		Easy Come, Easy Go/It's the Little Things	1966	5.00	10.00	20.00
Herald						
☐ 590		Mixed-Up, Shook-Up, Girl/Ordinary Guy	1964	5.00	10.00	20.00
☐ 593		The Sound of Music Makes Me Want to Dance/You Took Advantage of a Good Thing	1964	3.75	7.50	15.00
☐ 595		And We Danced/You Can't Get Away from Me	1964	3.75	7.50	15.00

Number		Title (A Side/B Side)	Year	VG	VG+	NM
Kapp						
❑ 791		Let Him Go Little Heart/Try It, You Won't Forget It	1966	5.00	10.00	20.00
❑ 850		Please Don't Ever Leave Me/	1967	5.00	10.00	20.00
		All My Tomorrows Are Gone				
❑ 870		I'll Cry Later/One Man Woman	1967	5.00	10.00	20.00
❑ 897		I'm Gonna Love You a Long, Long Time/	1968	3.75	7.50	15.00
		My Heart's So Full of You				

Paul – See "Hildebrand, Ray"

Paul and Paula

(Also see "Hildebrand, Ray"; "Jackson, Jill")

Le Cam						
❑ 305		From the Top of the World/All I Want Is You	197?		2.00	4.00
		As "Jill and Ray"				
❑ 315		Hey Paula ('77 Disco)/(Instrumental)	1977		2.00	4.00
❑ 321		Hey Paula/Paula (My Love)	1978		2.00	4.00
		Reissued in 1982 with the same catalog number				
❑ 354		Hey Paula/Elmer's Tune	198?		2.00	4.00
❑ 979		Hey Paula/Bobbie Is the One	1962	12.50	25.00	50.00
		As "Jill and Ray"				
❑ 99		The Beginning of Love/All I Want Is You	1963	5.00	10.00	20.00
Philips						
❑ 40084		Hey Paula/Bobby Is the One	1962	3.75	7.50	15.00
❑ 40096		Young Lovers/Ba-Hey-Be	1963	3.00	6.00	12.00
❑ 40096	PS	Young Lovers/Ba-Hey-Be	1963	5.00	10.00	20.00
❑ 40114		First Quarrel/School Is Thru	1963	3.00	6.00	12.00
❑ 40114	PS	First Quarrel/School Is Thru	1963	5.00	10.00	20.00
❑ 40130		Something Old, Something New/Flipped Over You	1963	3.00	6.00	12.00
❑ 40142		First Day Back at School/A Perfect Pair	1963	3.00	6.00	12.00
❑ 40158		Holiday for Teens/Holiday Hootenanny	1963	3.00	6.00	12.00
❑ 40168		We'll Never Break Up for Good/Crazy Little Things	1964	2.50	5.00	10.00
❑ 40209		The Young Years/Darlin'	1964	2.50	5.00	10.00
❑ 40234		No Other Baby/Too Dark to See	1964	2.50	5.00	10.00
❑ 40268		True Love/Any Way You Want Me	1965	2.00	4.00	8.00
❑ 40296		Dear Paula/All the Love	1965	2.00	4.00	8.00
❑ 40352		All I Want Is You/The Beginning of Love	1966	2.50	5.00	10.00
Uni						
❑ 55052		All These Things/Wedding	1968	2.00	4.00	8.00
United Artists						
❑ 50712		Moments Like These/Mrs. Bean	1970		3.00	6.00

Paul, Billy

Gamble						
❑ 232		Somewhere/Bluesette	1968	3.00	6.00	12.00
Jubilee						
❑ 5081		That's Why I Dream/Why Am I	1952	7.50	15.00	30.00
❑ 5086		You Didn't Know/The Stars Are Mine	1952	7.50	15.00	30.00
Neptune						
❑ 30		Mrs. Robinson/Let's Fall in Love All Over	1970	2.50	5.00	10.00
Philadelphia Int'l.						
❑ 3120		Jesus Boy (You Only Look Like a Man)/Love Buddies	1980		2.50	5.00
❑ 3509		Love Buddies/Magic Carpet Ride	1971		3.00	6.00
❑ 3515		This Is Your Life/I Wish It Were Yesterday	1972		3.00	6.00
❑ 3521		Me and Mrs. Jones/Your Song	1972		2.50	5.00
❑ 3526		Am I Black Enough for You/	1973		2.50	5.00
		I'm Gonna Make It This Time				
❑ 3538		Thanks for Saving My Life/I Was Married	1974		2.50	5.00
❑ 3551		Be Truthful to Me/I Wish It Was Yesterday	1974		2.50	5.00
❑ 3563		Billy's Back Home/I've Got So Much to Live For	1975		2.50	5.00
❑ 3572		When It's Your Turn to Go/July, July, July, July	1975		2.50	5.00
❑ 3584		Let's Make a Baby/My Head's On Straight	1976		2.50	5.00
❑ 3593		People Power/I Want Cha Baby	1976		2.50	5.00
❑ 3613		How Good Is Your Game/I Think I'll Stay Home Today	1977		2.50	5.00
❑ 3621		Let 'Em In/We All Got a Mission	1977		2.50	5.00
❑ 3630		I Trust You/Love Won't Come Easy	1977		2.50	5.00
❑ 3635		Only the Strong Survive/Where I Belong	1977		2.50	5.00
❑ 3639		Everybody's Breakin' Up/Sooner or Later	1978		2.50	5.00
❑ 3645		One Man's Junk/Don't Give Up on Love	1978		2.50	5.00
❑ 3676		Bring the Family Back/It's Critical	1979		2.50	5.00
❑ 3699		False Faces/I Gotta Put This Life Down	1979		2.50	5.00
❑ 3736		You're My Sweetness/(B-side unknown)	1979		2.50	5.00

Paula, Marlena

Regent						
❑ 7506		I Wanna Spend Christmas with Elvis/	1956	12.50	25.00	50.00
		Once More It's Christmas				

Paulson, Butch

Virgelle						
❑ 708		Man from Mars/My Own Brother	195?	25.00	50.00	100.00
❑ 718		Candy Lou/Today Was Blue Tomorrow	195?	12.50	25.00	50.00

Number	Title (A Side/B Side)	Year	VG	VG+	NM

Paxton, Gary
(Also see "Hollywood Argyles, The"; "Skip and Flip")
Capitol

❏ 5467	My Heart Won't Let My Lips Say Goodbye/ It's My Way (Of Lovin' You)	1965	3.75	7.50	15.00
❏ 5707	Goin' Through the Motions/ You Got to Do the Best You Can	1966	3.75	7.50	15.00
❏ 5975	Mother-in-Law/Miles and Cities	1967	3.75	7.50	15.00

Felsted

❏ 8691	Sweet Senorita from Santa Fe/Kansas City	1964	5.00	10.00	20.00

Garpax

❏ 44172	It Had to Be You/Going Back Together	1963	5.00	10.00	20.00
❏ 44177	The Scavenger/ How to Be a Fool (In Six Easy Lessons)	1963	5.00	10.00	20.00
❏ 44180	Two Duel Bump Camel Named Robert E. Lee/ Your Past Is Back Again	1964	5.00	10.00	20.00

Liberty

❏ 55407	Teen Age Crush/It's So Funny I Could Cry	1962	5.00	10.00	20.00
❏ 55485	Stop Twistin' Baby/Alley Oop Was a Two Dab Man	1962	5.00	10.00	20.00
❏ 55584	Spooky Movies (Part 1)/Spooky Movies (Part 2)	1963	5.00	10.00	20.00

London

❏ 5208	Super Torque/Cute Little Coly	1964	5.00	10.00	20.00

Lute

❏ 5801	You're Ruinin' My Gladness/The Way I See It	1960	5.00	10.00	20.00

MGM

❏ 14306	Carin' for Karen/Out on a Limb	1971		3.00	6.00
❏ 14362	Rocky Top/Parchman Farm	1972		3.00	6.00

Private Stock

❏ 45,007	The Clone Affair/(B-side unknown)	1975		2.50	5.00

RCA Victor

❏ 74-0916	Shadow of Your Memory/This Little Light of Mine	1973		2.50	5.00
❏ APBO-0081	It's Hard to Be a Rock and Roll Star When You're Old and Fat/White Tornado Alias Gary S. Paxton	1973		2.50	5.00
❏ PB-10449	Too Far Gone (To Care What You Do to Me)/ Freedom Lives in a Country Song	1975		2.50	5.00

Payne, Freda
ABC

❏ 12079	Shadows on the Wall/I Get Carried Away	1975		2.50	5.00
❏ 12139	Lost in Love/You	1975		2.50	5.00

ABC Dunhill

❏ 15018	It's Yours to Have/Run for Life	1974		2.50	5.00

ABC-Paramount

❏ 10366	Desafinado/He Who Laughs Last	1962	5.00	10.00	20.00
❏ 10437	Pretty Baby/Grin and Bear It	1963	5.00	10.00	20.00

Capitol

❏ 4383	I Can't Live on a Memory/I Get High (On Your Memory)	1976		2.50	5.00
❏ 4431	Baby, You've Got What It Takes/Bring Back the Joy	1977		2.50	5.00
❏ 4494	Love Magnet/Loving You Means So Much to Me	1977		2.50	5.00
❏ 4537	Feed Me Your Love/Stares and Whispers	1978		2.50	5.00
❏ 4631	Happy Days Are Here Again-Happy Music (Dance the Night Away)/Falling in Love	1978		2.50	5.00
❏ 4695	I'll Do Anything for You (Part 1)/ I'll Do Anything for You (Part 2)	1979		2.50	5.00
❏ 4775	Red Hot/Longest Night	1979		2.50	5.00
❏ 4805	Can't Wait/Longest Night	1979		2.50	5.00

Impulse

❏ 221	It's Time/Sweet September	1963	5.00	10.00	20.00

Invictus

❏ 1255	Two Wrongs Don't Make a Right/ We've Gotta Find a Way Back to Love	1973		3.00	6.00
❏ 1257	For No Reason/Mother Misery's Favorite Child	1973		3.00	6.00
❏ 9073	The Unhooked Generation/Easiest Way to Fall	1969		3.00	6.00
❏ 9075	Band of Gold/Easiest Way to Fall	1970		3.00	6.00
❏ 9080	Deeper and Deeper/The Unhooked Generation	1970		3.00	6.00
❏ 9085	Cherish What Is Dear to You (While It Is Near to You)/ They Don't Owe Me a Thing	1971		3.00	6.00
❏ 9085 PS	Cherish What Is Dear to You (While It Is Near to You)/ They Don't Owe Me a Thing	1971	2.50	5.00	10.00
❏ 9092	Bring the Boys Home/I Shall Not Be Moved	1971		3.00	6.00
❏ 9100	You Brought the Joy/Suddenly It's Yesterday	1971		3.00	6.00
❏ 9109	I'm Not Getting Any Better/The Road We Didn't Take	1972		3.00	6.00
❏ 9128	She's in My Life/Through the Memory of My Mind	1972		3.00	6.00

MGM

❏ 13509	You've Lost That Lovin' Feelin'/Sad Sad September	1966	5.00	10.00	20.00

Sutra

❏ 117	In Motion/(Instrumental)	1982		2.50	5.00

Peacheroos, The
Excello

❏ 2044	Be-Bop Baby/Everyday My Love Is True	1954	100.00	200.00	400.00

Number		Title (A Side/B Side)	Year	VG	VG+	NM

Peaches and Herb
Columbia
☐ 03872		Remember/Come to Me	1983		2.00	4.00
☐ 04081		In My World/Keep On Smiling	1983		2.00	4.00
☐ 45386		The Sound of Silence/The Two of Us	1971		2.50	5.00
☐ 45554		God Save This World/I Can't Forget the One I Love	1972		2.50	5.00

Date
☐ 1523		Let's Fall in Love/We're In This Thing Together	1966	2.50	5.00	10.00
☐ 1549		Close Your Eyes/I Will Watch Over You	1967	2.50	5.00	10.00
☐ 1549	PS	Close Your Eyes/I Will Watch Over You	1967	3.75	7.50	15.00
☐ 1555		Cupid-Venus/Darling, How Long	1967	3.75	7.50	15.00
☐ 1563		For Your Love/I Need Your Love So Desperately	1967	2.50	5.00	10.00
☐ 1563	PS	For Your Love/I Need Your Love So Desperately	1967	3.75	7.50	15.00
☐ 1574		Love Is Strange/It's True I Love You	1967	2.50	5.00	10.00
☐ 1574	PS	Love Is Strange/It's True I Love You	1967	3.75	7.50	15.00
☐ 1586		Two Little Kids/We've Got to Love One Another	1967	2.00	4.00	8.00
☐ 1592		The Ten Commandments of Love/ What a Lovely Way (To Say Goodnight)	1968	2.00	4.00	8.00
☐ 1603		United/Thank You	1968	2.00	4.00	8.00
☐ 1603	PS	United/Thank You	1968	3.75	7.50	15.00
☐ 1623		Let's Make a Promise/Me and You	1968	2.00	4.00	8.00
☐ 1623	PS	Let's Make a Promise/Me and You	1968	3.75	7.50	15.00
☐ 1633		We've Got to Love One Another/So True	1968	2.50	5.00	10.00
☐ 1637		When He Touches Me (Nothing Else Matters)/ Thank You	1969	2.00	4.00	8.00
☐ 1649		Let Me Be the One/I Need Your Love So Desperately	1969	2.00	4.00	8.00
☐ 1655		Cupid/Darling, How Long	1969	2.00	4.00	8.00
☐ 1669		It's Just a Game, Love/Satisfy My Hunger	1970	2.00	4.00	8.00
☐ 1676		Soothe Me with Your Love/We're So Much in Love	1970	2.00	4.00	8.00

MCA
☐ 40701		We're Still Together/Love Is Here Beside Us	1977		2.50	5.00
☐ 40782		It Will Never Be the Same Again/I'm Counting on You	1977		2.50	5.00

Mercury
☐ 73350		Keep It Coming/I'm a-Hurtin' Inside	1973		2.50	5.00
☐ 73388		Can't It Wait/Thank Heaven for You	1973		2.50	5.00

Polydor
☐ 2031		Roller-Skatin' Mate (Part 1)/Roller-Skatin' Mate (Part 2)	1979		2.00	4.00
☐ 2053		I Pledge My Love/(I Want Us) Back Together	1980		2.00	4.00
☐ 2115		Funtime (Part 1)/Funtime (Part 2)	1980		2.00	4.00
☐ 2140		One Child of Love/Hearsay	1980		2.00	4.00
☐ 2157		Surrender/Love Stealers	1981		2.00	4.00
☐ 2178		Freeway/Pickin' Up the Pieces	1981		2.00	4.00
☐ 2187		Bluer Than Blue/Go with the Flow	1981		2.00	4.00
☐ 14514		Shake Your Groove Thing/All Your Love (Get It Here)	1978		2.00	4.00
☐ 14547		Reunited/Easy as Pie	1979		2.00	4.00
☐ 14577		We've Got Love/Four's a Traffic Jam	1979		2.00	4.00

Peanut Butter Conspiracy, The
Challenge
☐ 500		Back in L.A./Have a Little Faith	1969	2.00	4.00	8.00

Columbia
☐ 43985		It's a Happening Thing/Twice Is Life	1967	2.50	5.00	10.00
☐ 44063		Then Came Love/Dark on You Now	1967	2.00	4.00	8.00
☐ 44356		Turn On a Friend (To the Good Life)/Captain Sandwich	1967	2.00	4.00	8.00
☐ 44667		I'm a Fool/It's So Hard	1968	2.00	4.00	8.00

Vault
☐ 933		Time Is After You/Floating Dream	1966	3.75	7.50	15.00

Pearl Jam
Epic
☐ ZS7 4906	DJ	Sonic Reducer/Ramblings Continued	1992	5.00	10.00	20.00
☐ ZS7 4906	PS	Sonic Reducer/Ramblings Continued	1992	5.00	10.00	20.00
		Picture sleeve front states "Who Killed Rudolph?"				
☐ ZS7 5610	DJ	Angel/Ramblings	1993	3.75	7.50	15.00
☐ ZS7 5610	PS	Angel/Ramblings	1993	3.75	7.50	15.00
☐ 77771		Spin the Black Circle/Tremor Christ	1994			3.00
☐ 77771	PS	Spin the Black Circle/Tremor Christ	1994			3.00
☐ 77772		Not for You/Out of My Mind	1995			3.00
☐ 77772	PS	Not for You/Out of My Mind	1995			3.00
☐ 77873		Immortality/Rearviewmirror	1995			3.00
		B-side by The Frogs				
☐ 77873	PS	Immortality/Rearviewmirror	1995			3.00
☐ 78199		I Got I.D./Long Road	1995			2.00
		With Neil Young				
☐ 78199	PS	I Got I.D./Long Road	1995			2.00
☐ 78389		Who You Are/Habit	1996			2.00
☐ 78389	PS	Who You Are/Habit	1996			2.00

Epic Associated
☐ ZS7 4354	DJ	Let Me Sleep (Christmas Time)/Ramblings	1991	5.00	10.00	20.00
		Small hole, plays at 33 1-3 RPM				
☐ ZS7 4354	PS	Let Me Sleep (Christmas Time)/Ramblings	1991	5.00	10.00	20.00
☐ 74745		Jeremy/Alive	1992	5.00	10.00	20.00

Number		Title (A Side/B Side)	Year	VG	VG+	NM

Pearls Before Swine
ESP-Disk
| ☐ 4554 | | Morning Song/(B-side unknown) | 1967 | 10.00 | 20.00 | 40.00 |
| ☐ 4576 | | I Saw the World/(B-side unknown) | 1968 | 10.00 | 20.00 | 40.00 |

Reprise
☐ 0873		If You Don't Want To/These Things Too	1969	3.00	6.00	12.00
☐ 0916		God Save the Child/Rocket Man	1970	3.00	6.00	12.00
☐ 0949		The Jeweler/Rocket Man	1970	3.00	6.00	12.00

Pearls, The
(More than one group)
Amber
| ☐ 2003 | | I Cried/It Must Be Love | 1961 | 75.00 | 150.00 | 300.00 |

Originals have matrix number stamped into trail-off wax

Atco
| ☐ 6057 | | Shadows of Love/Yum Yummy | 1956 | 7.50 | 15.00 | 30.00 |
| ☐ 6066 | | Bells of Love/Come On Home | 1956 | 10.00 | 20.00 | 40.00 |

Bell
| ☐ 45,342 | | You Came, You Saw, You Conquered/ | 1973 | | 2.50 | 5.00 |
| | | (B-side unknown) | | | | |

On the Square
| ☐ 320 | | Band of Angels/Ugly Face | 1959 | 3.75 | 7.50 | 15.00 |

Onyx
☐ 503		Let's You and I Go Steady/Zippidy Zippidy Zoom	1956	15.00	30.00	60.00
☐ 506		My Oh My/Tree in the Meadow	1956	37.50	75.00	150.00
☐ 510		Your Cheatin' Heart/I Sure Need You	1957	15.00	30.00	60.00
☐ 511		Ice Cream Baby/Yuz-a-Ma-Tuz	1957	15.00	30.00	60.00
☐ 516		The Wheel of Love/It's Love, Love, Love	1957	30.00	60.00	120.00

Warner Bros.
| ☐ 5300 | | Happy Over You/If I Had a Choice | 1962 | 5.00 | 10.00 | 20.00 |

Pebbles and Bamm Bamm
Hanna-Barbera
☐ 449		Open Up Your Heart/The Lord Is Counting on You	1965	6.25	12.50	25.00
☐ 449	PS	Open Up Your Heart/The Lord Is Counting on You	1965	12.50	25.00	50.00
☐ 484		The World Is Full of Toys/Daddy	1966	6.25	12.50	25.00

Pedicin, Mike
ABC-Paramount
| ☐ 10303 | | Gotta Twist/When the Cats Come Twistin' In | 1962 | 3.00 | 6.00 | 12.00 |

Apollo
| ☐ 534 | | Hey Pop, Give Me the Keys/St. James Infirmary | 1959 | 10.00 | 20.00 | 40.00 |

Cameo
| ☐ 125 | | Shake a Hand/The Dickie Doo | 1957 | 6.25 | 12.50 | 25.00 |

Federal
| ☐ 12417 | | Burnt Toast/You Gotta Go, You Gotta Go | 1961 | 3.75 | 7.50 | 15.00 |

Malvern
| ☐ 101 | | The Dickie Doo/(B-side unknown) | 1957 | 7.50 | 15.00 | 30.00 |

RCA Victor
☐ 47-6043		I'm Hip/I Wanna Hug You, Kiss You, Squeeze You	1955	6.25	12.50	25.00
☐ 47-6051		Mambo Rock/D-E-V-I-L	1955	6.25	12.50	25.00
☐ 47-6150		Fe-Fi-Fo-Fum/The Hot Barcarolle	1955	6.25	12.50	25.00
☐ 47-6235		You Gotta Go/The Banjo Rock	1955	6.25	12.50	25.00
☐ 47-6285		Jackpot/When the Cats Come Marching In	1955	6.25	12.50	25.00
☐ 47-6369		The Large, Large House/Hotter Than a Pistol	1955	6.25	12.50	25.00
☐ 47-6546		The Beat/Save Us, Preacher Davis	1956	6.25	12.50	25.00
☐ 47-6676		Teenage Fairy Tales/Close All the Doors	1956	6.25	12.50	25.00
☐ 47-6847		The Hucklebuck/Calypso Rock	1957	6.25	12.50	25.00

20th Century
☐ 5006		My Heart Is Breaking/I'll Always Love You Some	195?	7.50	15.00	30.00
☐ 5009		Kiss, Kiss, Kiss/Love Every Moment	195?	7.50	15.00	30.00
☐ 5012		Never Mind/M-m-Boy	195?	7.50	15.00	30.00
☐ 5019		I've Got a Feeling It's Love/Is That What You Call Love	195?	7.50	15.00	30.00
☐ 5021		Disc Jockey's Boogie/Tiger Rag	195?	7.50	15.00	30.00
☐ 5023		It's My Heart to Give/Kiss Me Before You Say Goodbye	195?	7.50	15.00	30.00
☐ 5027		Shake a Hand/When We Meet	195?	10.00	20.00	40.00
☐ 5029		Not Somebody Else Just Me/Sweet Georgia Brown	195?	7.50	15.00	30.00

Peel, David
Apple
| ☐ PRO-6498/9 | DJ | F Is Not a Dirty Word/The Ballad of New York City | 1972 | 30.00 | 60.00 | 120.00 |
| ☐ PRO-6545/6 | DJ | Hippie from New York City/The Ballad of New York City | 1972 | 30.00 | 60.00 | 120.00 |

Orange
| ☐ 1001 | | Bring Back the Beatles/Imagine | 1977 | 2.50 | 5.00 | 10.00 |

Pejoe, Morris
Checker
☐ 766		Tired of Crying Over You/Gonna Buy Me a Telephone	1953	125.00	250.00	500.00
☐ 766		Tired of Crying Over You/Gonna Buy Me a Telephone	1953	1,500	2,250	3,000
		Red vinyl				

Number		Title (A Side/B Side)	Year	VG	VG+	NM
❑ 781		Can't Get Along/It'll Plumb Get It	1953	100.00	200.00	400.00
❑ 781		Can't Get Along/It'll Plumb Get It	1953	250.00	500.00	1,000
		Red vinyl				

Vee Jay

❑ 148		You're Gonna Need Me/Hurt My Feelings	1955	15.00	30.00	60.00

Pelicans, The
Imperial

❑ 5307		Chimes/Ain't Gonna Do It	1954	250.00	500.00	1,000

Parrot

❑ 793		White Cliffs of Dover/Aurelia	1954	250.00	500.00	1,000
❑ 793		White Cliffs of Dover/Aurelia	1954	1,000	1,500	2,000
		Red vinyl				

Pendarvis, Tracy
Sun

❑ 335		A Thousand Guitars/Is It Too Late	1960	5.00	10.00	20.00
❑ 345		Is It Me/South Bound Line	1960	6.25	12.50	25.00
❑ 359		Eternally/Belle of the Swanee	1961	5.00	10.00	20.00

Pendergrass, Teddy
(Formerly of Harold Melvin and the Blue Notes)
Asylum

❑ 69401		Joy/Let Me Be Closer	1988			3.00
❑ 69422		2 A.M./(Instrumental)	1988		2.00	4.00
❑ 69538		Let Me Be Closer/Love Emergency	1986		2.00	4.00
❑ 69568		Love 4/2//One of Us Feels in Love	1986		2.00	4.00
❑ 69595		Never Felt Like Dancin'/Love Emergency	1985		2.00	4.00
❑ 69628		Somewhere I Belong/Hot Love	1985		2.00	4.00
❑ 69628	PS	Somewhere I Belong/Hot Love	1985		2.00	4.00
❑ 69669		In My Time/Stay with Me	1985		2.00	4.00
❑ 69696		You're My Choice Tonight (Choose Me)/ So Sad the Song	1984		2.00	4.00
❑ 69720		Hold Me/Love	1984		2.00	4.00
		With Whitney Houston				
❑ 69720	PS	Hold Me/Love	1984		2.00	4.00

Elektra

❑ 69312		The Last Time/(B-side unknown)	1989			3.00
❑ 69358		Love Is the Power/I'm Ready	1988			3.00
❑ 69358	PS	Love Is the Power/I'm Ready	1988			3.00
❑ 69422		2 A.M./(Instrumental)	1988			3.00

Philadelphia Int'l.

❑ 02095		Can't You Try/Love T.K.O.	1981		2.00	4.00
❑ 02462		I Can't Live Without Your Love/You Must Live On	1981		2.00	4.00
❑ 02619		You're My Latest, Greatest Inspiration/ Keep On Lovin' Me	1981		2.00	4.00
❑ 02856		Nine Times Out of Ten/This Gift of Life	1982		2.00	4.00
❑ 03116		Love T.K.O./I Just Called to Say	1982			3.00
		Reissue				
❑ 03284		I Can't Win for Losing/ Don't Lead Me Out Along the Road	1982		2.00	4.00
❑ 03325		I Can't Win for Losing	1982		3.00	6.00
		One-sided budget release				
❑ 04302		Life Is for the Living/I Want My Baby Back	1984		2.00	4.00
❑ 3107		Can't We Try/Plenty Good Lovin'	1980		2.50	5.00
❑ 3116		Love T.K.O./I Just Called to Say	1980		2.50	5.00
❑ 3622		I Don't Love You Anymore/Somebody Told Me	1977		2.50	5.00
❑ 3633		The Whole Town's Laughing at Me/ The More I Get, The More I Want	1977		2.50	5.00
❑ 3648		Close the Door/ Get Up, Get Down, Get Funky, Get Loose	1978		2.50	5.00
❑ 3657		Only You/It Don't Hurt Now	1978		2.50	5.00
❑ 3669		Life Is a Song Worth Singing/Cold, Cold World	1978		2.50	5.00
❑ 3696		Turn Off the Lights/If You Know Like I Know	1979		2.50	5.00
❑ 3717		Come Go with Me/(B-side unknown)	1979		2.50	5.00
❑ 3733		Shout and Scream/Close the Door	1979		2.50	5.00
❑ 3742		It's You I Love/Where Did All the Lovin' Go	1980		2.50	5.00
❑ 70062		Is It Still Good to You/Girl You Know	1981		2.00	4.00

Pendletons, The
Dot

❑ 16511		Board Party/Barefoot Adventure	1963	25.00	50.00	100.00

Rendezvous

❑ 194		The Waddle/Itchy Bon Mash	1962	10.00	20.00	40.00

Penetrations, The
Icon

❑ 1002		Bring 'Em In/Fackin' Out	196?	15.00	30.00	60.00
		Blue vinyl				
❑ 1002		Bring 'Em Back Alive/Fackin' Out	196?	7.50	15.00	30.00
		Black vinyl; note slightly different A-side title				

Penguins, The
Atlantic

❑ 1132		Pledge of Love/I Knew I'd Fall in Love	1957	7.50	15.00	30.00

Number	Title (A Side/B Side)	Year	VG	VG+	NM

Dooto

❏ 348	Earth Angel/Hey Senorita	1962	5.00	10.00	20.00
	Reissue on altered label name and yellow label				
❏ 428	That's How Much I Need You/Be My Lovin' Baby	1957	10.00	20.00	40.00
❏ 432	Sweet Love/Let Me Make Up Your Mind	1958	7.50	15.00	30.00
❏ 435	Do Not Pretend/If You're Mine	1958	7.50	15.00	30.00

Dootone

❏ 345	No There Ain't No News Today/When I Am Gone	1954	75.00	150.00	300.00
	B-side by Dootsie Williams Orchestra				
❏ 348	Earth Angel/Hey Senorita	1954	37.50	75.00	150.00
	First pressings on glossy red labels				
❏ 348	Earth Angel/Hey Senorita	1955	12.50	25.00	50.00
	Maroon label				
❏ 348	Earth Angel/Hey Senorita	1955	10.00	20.00	40.00
	Blue label				
❏ 348	Earth Angel/Hey Senorita	1955	7.50	15.00	30.00
	Black label				
❏ 353	Love Will Make Your Mind Go Wild/Ookey Ook	1954	25.00	50.00	100.00
	First pressings on glossy red label				
❏ 353	Love Will Make Your Mind Go Wild/Ookey Ook	1955	12.50	25.00	50.00
	Maroon label				
❏ 353	Love Will Make Your Mind Go Wild/Ookey Ook	1955	10.00	20.00	40.00
	Blue label				
❏ 353	Love Will Make Your Mind Go Wild/Ookey Ook	1955	7.50	15.00	30.00
	Black label				
❏ 362	Baby, Let's Make Some Love/Kiss a Fool Goodbye	1955	12.50	25.00	50.00

Mercury

❏ 70610	Don't Do It/Be Mine or Be a Fool	1955	12.50	25.00	50.00
❏ 70654	Walkin' Down Broadway/It Only Happens with You	1955	12.50	25.00	50.00
❏ 70703	Promises, Promises, Promises/The Devil That I See	1955	12.50	25.00	50.00
❏ 70762	A Christmas Prayer/Jingle Jangle	1955	20.00	40.00	80.00
❏ 70799	My Troubles Are Not At an End/She's Gone, Gone	1956	6.25	12.50	25.00
	Black label				
❏ 70799	My Troubles Are Not At an End/She's Gone, Gone	1956	12.50	25.00	50.00
	Maroon label				
❏ 70943	Earth Angel/Ice	1956	10.00	20.00	40.00
	Not the same recording as the hit on Dootone				
❏ 71033	Cool Baby Cool/Will You Be Mine	1957	10.00	20.00	40.00

Original Sound

❏ 27	Memories of El Monte/Be Mine	1963	20.00	40.00	80.00
	Black and red label				
❏ 27	Memories of El Monte/Be Mine	1963	12.50	25.00	50.00
	Black and silver label; A-side written by Frank Zappa				
❏ 54	Heavenly Angel/Big Bobo's Party Train	1965	6.25	12.50	25.00

Sun State

❏ 001	Believe Me/The Pony Rock	1962	6.25	12.50	25.00

Wing

❏ 90076	Dealer of Dreams/Peace of Mind	1956	7.50	15.00	30.00

Penn, Little "Lambsie"

Atco

❏ 6082	I Wanna Spend Christmas With Elvis/Painted Lips and Pigtails	1956	12.50	25.00	50.00

Penn, William, and the Quakers

Duane

❏ 104	Coming Up My Way/Care Free	196?	10.00	20.00	40.00

Hush

❏ 230	Little Girl/Somebody's Dum Dum	196?	12.50	25.00	50.00

Melron

❏ 5013	California Sun/No More Love	1966	12.50	25.00	50.00
❏ 5024	Santa Needs Ear Muffs on His Nose/Philly	1966	15.00	30.00	60.00
❏ 5024	Santa Needs Ear Muffs on His Nose/Sweet Caroline	1966	15.00	30.00	60.00

Thunderbird

❏ 502	Blow My Mind/Swami	1966	10.00	20.00	40.00
	As the "William Penn Fyve"				

Twilight

❏ 410	Ghost of the Monks/Goodbye My Love	1967	7.50	15.00	30.00

Uptown

❏ 745	Chrome Dome Wheeler Dealer/Scrapped	1967	10.00	20.00	40.00

Pennants, The

World

❏ 102	Don't Go/Workin' Man	1961	25.00	50.00	100.00

Penner, Dick

Sun

❏ 282	Cindy Lou/Your Honey Love	1958	12.50	25.00	50.00

Number		Title (A Side/B Side)	Year	VG	VG+	NM

Pennsylvania Players, The
(Actually Dickie Goodman)
Oron
❏ 101		Washington Uptight/The Cat	1967	6.25	12.50	25.00

Pentangle, The
Reprise
| ❏ 0784 | | Let No Man Steal Your Throne/Way Behind the Sun | 1968 | 2.00 | 4.00 | 8.00 |
| ❏ 0843 | | I Saw an Angel/Once I Had a Sweetheart | 1969 | 2.00 | 4.00 | 8.00 |

People
Capitol
❏ 2078		I Love You/Somebody Tell Me My Name	1968	3.00	6.00	12.00
❏ 2251		Apple Cider/Ashes of Me	1968	2.50	5.00	10.00
❏ 2499		Turnin' Me In/Ulla	1969	2.50	5.00	10.00
❏ 5920		Organ Grinder/Riding High	1967	2.50	5.00	10.00
Paramount
❏ 0005		Love Will Take Us Higher and Higher/Livin' It Up	1969		3.00	6.00
❏ 0011		Sunshine Lady/Crosstown Bus	1969		3.00	6.00
❏ 0019		For What It's Worth/Maple Street	1970		3.00	6.00
❏ 0028		One Chain Don't Make No Prison/Keep It Alive	1970		3.00	6.00
Polydor
| ❏ 14087 | | Chant for Peace/I Don't Carry No Guns | 1971 | | 3.00 | 6.00 |
Zebra
| ❏ 102 | | Come Back Beatles (same on both sides) | 1978 | 2.50 | 5.00 | 10.00 |

Pepe and the Astros
Swami
| ❏ 553/4 | | Judy My Love/Now, Ain't That a Shame | 1961 | 12.50 | 25.00 | 50.00 |

Peppermint Rainbow, The
Decca
❏ 32316		Pink Lemonade/Walking in Different Circles	1968	2.00	4.00	8.00
❏ 32410		Will You Be Staying After Sunday/And I'll Be There	1968	2.50	5.00	10.00
❏ 32498		Don't Wake Me Up in the Morning, Michael/Rosemary	1969	2.00	4.00	8.00
❏ 32498	PS	Don't Wake Me Up in the Morning, Michael/Rosemary	1969	3.00	6.00	12.00
❏ 32562		You're the Sound of Love/Jamais	1969	2.00	4.00	8.00
❏ 32601		Good Morning Means Goodbye/ Don't Love Me Unless It's Forever	1969	2.00	4.00	8.00

Perennials, The
Ball
| ❏ 1016 | | My Big Mistake/I'm Yours 'Til the End | 1963 | 100.00 | 200.00 | 400.00 |

Perfidians, The
Husky
❏ 1		La Paz/Whiplash	1962	20.00	40.00	80.00
	Red vinyl					
❏ 1		La Paz/Whiplash	1962	10.00	20.00	40.00

Perkins, Carl
Columbia
❏ 41131		Pink Pedal Pushers/Jive After Five	1958	7.50	15.00	30.00
❏ 41131	PS	Pink Pedal Pushers/Jive After Five	1958	20.00	40.00	80.00
❏ 41207		Levi Jacket/Pop, Let Me Have the Car	1958	6.25	12.50	25.00
❏ 41296		Y-O-U/This Life I Live	1958	6.25	12.50	25.00
❏ 41379		Pointed Toe Shoes/Highway of Love	1959	6.25	12.50	25.00
❏ 41449		One Ticket to Loneliness/ I Don't See Me in Your Eyes Anymore	1959	6.25	12.50	25.00
❏ 41651		L-O-V-E-V-I-L-L-E/Too Much for a Man to Understand	1960	6.25	12.50	25.00
❏ 41825		Honey, 'Cause I Love You/Just for You	1960	6.25	12.50	25.00
❏ 42061		Anyway the Wind Blows/The Unhappy Girls	1961	6.25	12.50	25.00
❏ 42403		Hollywood City/Forget Me Next Time Around	1962			Unreleased?
❏ 42403	PS	Hollywood City/The Fool I Used to Be	1962	20.00	40.00	80.00
❏ 42405		Hollywood City/The Fool I Used to Be	1962	6.25	12.50	25.00
❏ 42514		Sister Twister/Hambone	1962	6.25	12.50	25.00
❏ 42514	PS	Sister Twister/Hambone	1962	50.00	100.00	200.00
❏ 42753		I Just Got Back from There/ Forget Me Next Time Around	1963	6.25	12.50	25.00
❏ 44723		Restless/1143	1968	2.00	4.00	8.00
❏ 44883		For Your Love/Four Letter Word	1969	2.00	4.00	8.00
❏ 44993		C.C. Rider/Soul Beat	1969	2.00	4.00	8.00
❏ 45107		All Mama's Children/Step Aside	1970	2.00	4.00	8.00
	With NRBQ					
❏ 45132		State of Confusion/My Son, My Son	1970		3.00	6.00
❏ 45253		What Every Little Boy Ought to Know/Just As Long	1970		2.50	5.00
❏ 45347		Me Without You/Red Headed Woman	1971		2.50	5.00
❏ 45466		Cotton Top/About All I Can Give You Is My Love	1971		2.50	5.00
❏ 45582		High on Love/Take Me Back to Memphis	1972		2.50	5.00
❏ 45694		Someday/The Trip	1972		2.50	5.00
Decca
❏ 31548		Help Me Find My Baby/For a Little While	1963	3.75	7.50	15.00
❏ 31591		After Sundown/I Wouldn't Have Told You	1964	3.75	7.50	15.00
❏ 31709		The Monkeyshine/Let My Baby Be	1964	3.75	7.50	15.00
❏ 31786		One of These Days/Mama of My Song	1965	3.75	7.50	15.00

Number		Title (A Side/B Side)	Year	VG	VG+	NM

Dollie

Number		Title (A Side/B Side)	Year	VG	VG+	NM
❑ 505		Country Boy's Dream/If I Could Come Back	1966	3.00	6.00	12.00
❑ 508		Shine, Shine, Shine/Almost Love	1967	3.00	6.00	12.00
❑ 512		Without You/You Can Take the Boy Out of the Country	1967	3.00	6.00	12.00
❑ 514		My Old Home Town/Back to Tennessee	1967	3.00	6.00	12.00
❑ 516		It's You/Lake County Cotton Country	1968	3.00	6.00	12.00

Flip

❑ 501		Movie Magg/Turn Around	1955	150.00	300.00	600.00

Jet

❑ 5054		Blue Suede Shoes/Rock Around the World	1979		2.00	4.00

Mercury

❑ 55009		The E.P. Express/Big Bad Blues	1977		2.00	4.00
❑ 73425		(Let's Get) Dixiefried/One More Loser Goin' Home	1973		3.00	6.00
❑ 73489		Ruby, Don't Take Your Love to Town/Sing My Song	1974		2.50	5.00
❑ 73653		You'll Always Be a Lady to Me/Low Class	1974		2.50	5.00
❑ 73690		The E.P. Express/Big Bad Blues	1975		2.50	5.00
❑ 73993		Help Me Dream/You Tore My Heaven All to Hell	1973		3.00	6.00

MMI

❑ 1016		Don't Get Off Gettin' It On/Georgia Court Room	1977		2.00	4.00
❑ 1019		Standing in the Need of Love/Georgia Court Room	1977		2.00	4.00

Music Mill

❑ 1007		Born to Boogie/Take Me Back	1976		2.00	4.00

Smash

❑ 884 760-7		Birth of Rock and Roll/Rock and Roll (Fais-Do-Do)	1986		2.00	
		B-side with Jerry Lee Lewis, Roy Orbison and Johnny Cash				
❑ 884 934-7		Sixteen Candles/Rock & Roll (Fais-Do-Do)	1986		2.00	
		B-side with Jerry Lee Lewis, Roy Orbison and Johnny Cash; A-side by Jerry Lee Lewis				
❑ 888 142-7		Class of '55/We Remember the King	1987		2.00	4.00
		B-side with Jerry Lee Lewis, Roy Orbison and Johnny Cash				

Suede

❑ 101		I Don't Want to Fall in Love Again/We Did It in '54	1978		2.00	4.00
❑ 102		Rock-a-Billy Fever/Till You Get Through with Me	1978		2.00	4.00
❑ 6777		Little Teardrops/Green Grass of Home	1977		2.00	4.00

Sun

❑ 224		Gone, Gone, Gone/Let the Jukebox Keep On Playing	1955	25.00	50.00	100.00
❑ 234		Blue Suede Shoes/Honey Don't	1956	15.00	30.00	60.00
❑ 235		Sure to Fall/Tennessee	1956			Unreleased
❑ 243		Boppin' the Blues/All Mama's Children	1956	7.50	15.00	30.00
❑ 249		Dixie Fried/I'm Sorry, I'm Not Sorry	1956	7.50	15.00	30.00
❑ 261		Matchbox/Your True Love	1957	7.50	15.00	30.00
❑ 274		That's Right/Forever Yours	1957	7.50	15.00	30.00
❑ 287		Glad All Over/Lend Me Your Comb	1958	7.50	15.00	30.00

Universal

❑ 66002		Charlene/Love Makes Dreams Come True	1989		2.00	4.00
❑ 66019		Hambone/Love Makes Dreams Come True	1989		2.00	4.00

Perkins, Laura Lee

Imperial

❑ 5493		Kiss Me Baby/I Just Don't Like This Kind of Lovin'	1958	10.00	20.00	40.00
❑ 5507		Don't Wait Up/Oh La Baby	1958	10.00	20.00	40.00

Perkins, Roy

Meladee

❑ 111		Bye Bye Baby/You're on My Mind	1958	25.00	50.00	100.00
❑ 112		You're Gone/Here Am I	1958	150.00	300.00	600.00

Mercury

❑ 71278		Drop Top/That's What the Mailman Had to Say	1958	10.00	20.00	40.00

Perry, Joe, Project

(Member of Aerosmith who went solo in the early 1980s)

Columbia

❑ 02497		Buzz Buzz/East Coast, West Coast	1981		2.00	4.00
❑ 11250		Let the Music Do the Talking/Bone to Bone	1980		2.00	4.00

Perry, Steve

(Of Journey)

Columbia

❑ 04391		Oh Sherrie/Don't Tell Me Why You're Leaving	1984			3.00
❑ 04391	PS	Oh Sherrie/Don't Tell Me Why You're Leaving	1984			3.00
❑ 04496		She's Mine/You Should Be Happy	1984			3.00
❑ 04496	PS	She's Mine/You Should Be Happy	1984			3.00
❑ 04598		Strung Out/Captured by the Moment	1984			3.00
❑ 04683		Foolish Heart/It's Only Love	1984			3.00

Personalities, The

Safari

❑ 1002		Woe Woe Baby/Yours to Command	1957	50.00	100.00	200.00
		With giraffe on label				
❑ 1002		Woe Woe Baby/Yours to Command	1957	12.50	25.00	50.00
		No giraffe on label				

Number		Title (A Side/B Side)	Year	VG	VG+	NM
Pet Shop Boys						
EMI						
❑ S7-17492		Can You Forgive Her/I Want to Wake Up	1993		2.00	4.00
❑ S7-17708		Go West/Yesterday, When I Was Mad	1994		2.00	4.00
❑ S7-18736		Paninaro '95/Girls & Boys (Live in Rio)	1995		2.00	4.00
❑ S7-57696		Was It Worth It/Miserabilism	1992		2.00	4.00
		A-side is dub version, perhaps released in error				
EMI America						
❑ 8307		West End Girls/A Man Could Get Arrested	1986		2.00	4.00
❑ 8307	PS	West End Girls/A Man Could Get Arrested	1986		2.00	4.00
❑ 8321		Opportunities (Let's Make Lots of Money)/In the Night	1986	2.50	5.00	10.00
❑ 8321	PS	Opportunities (Let's Make Lots of Money)/In the Night	1986	2.50	5.00	10.00
		EMI 8321 was withdrawn shortly after release				
❑ 8330		Opportunities (Let's Make Lots of Money)/ Was That What It Was	1986		2.00	4.00
❑ 8330	PS	Opportunities (Let's Make Lots of Money)/ Was That What It Was	1986		2.00	4.00
❑ 8338		Love Comes Quickly/That's My Impression	1986		2.00	4.00
❑ 8338	PS	Love Comes Quickly/That's My Impression	1986		2.00	4.00
❑ 8355		Suburbia/Jack the Lad	1986		2.00	4.00
❑ 8355	PS	Suburbia/Jack the Lad	1986		2.00	4.00
❑ 43027		It's a Sin/You Know Where You Went Wrong	1987		2.00	4.00
❑ 43027	PS	It's a Sin/You Know Where You Went Wrong	1987		2.00	4.00
EMI Manhattan						
❑ 50107		What Have I Done to Deserve This?/A New Life	1987		2.00	4.00
		Vocal guest: Dusty Springfield				
❑ 50107	PS	What Have I Done to Deserve This?/A New Life	1987		2.00	4.00
❑ 50123		Always on My Mind/Do I Have To?	1988		2.00	4.00
❑ 50161		Domino Dancing/Don Juan	1988		2.00	4.00
❑ 50161	PS	Domino Dancing/Don Juan	1988		2.00	4.00
❑ 50171		Left to My Own Devices/ The Sound of the Atom Splitting	1988		2.00	4.00
❑ 50171	PS	Left to My Own Devices/ The Sound of the Atom Splitting	1988	2.00	4.00	8.00
Peter and Gordon						
Capitol						
❑ CP-51	DJ	Wrong from the Start/You've Lost That Lovin' Feelin'	1966	3.00	6.00	12.00
		B-side by the Lettermen				
❑ 2071		Greener Days/Never Ever	1968	2.50	5.00	10.00
❑ 2214		You've Had Better Times/Sipping My Wine	1968	2.50	5.00	10.00
❑ 2544		I Can Remember (But Not Too Long Ago)/ Hard Time, Rainy Day	1969	2.50	5.00	10.00
❑ 5175		A World Without Love/If I Were You	1964	3.00	6.00	12.00
❑ 5211		Nobody I Know/You Don't Have to Tell Me	1964	3.00	6.00	12.00
❑ 5211	PS	Nobody I Know/You Don't Have to Tell Me	1964	4.00	8.00	16.00
❑ 5272		I Don't Want to See You Again/ I Would Buy You Presents	1964	3.00	6.00	12.00
❑ 5272	PS	I Don't Want to See You Again/ I Would Buy You Presents	1964	4.00	8.00	16.00
❑ 5335		I Go to Pieces/Love Me, Baby	1965	3.00	6.00	12.00
❑ 5335	PS	I Go to Pieces/Love Me, Baby	1965	4.00	8.00	16.00
❑ 5406		True Love Ways/If You Wish	1965	3.00	6.00	12.00
❑ 5406	PS	True Love Ways/If You Wish	1965	4.00	8.00	16.00
❑ 5460		To Know You Is to Love You/I Told You So	1965	2.50	5.00	10.00
❑ 5460	PS	To Know You Is to Love You/I Told You So	1965	3.75	7.50	15.00
❑ 5532		Don't Pity Me/Crying in the Rain	1965	2.50	5.00	10.00
❑ 5579		Woman/Wrong from the Start	1966	3.00	6.00	12.00
		A-side composer listed as "Bernard Webb"				
❑ 5579		Woman/Wrong from the Start	1966	2.50	5.00	10.00
		A-side composer listed as "A. Smith"				
❑ 5650		There's No Living Without Your Loving/ Stranger with a Black Dove	1966	2.50	5.00	10.00
❑ 5650	PS	There's No Living Without Your Loving/ Stranger with a Black Dove	1966	3.75	7.50	15.00
❑ 5684		To Show I Love You/Start Trying Someone Else	1966	2.50	5.00	10.00
❑ 5684	PS	To Show I Love You/Start Trying Someone Else	1966	3.75	7.50	15.00
❑ 5740		Lady Godiva/Morning's Calling	1966	2.50	5.00	10.00
❑ 5740		Lady Godiva/The House I Live In	1966	3.75	7.50	15.00
❑ 5808		Knight in Rusty Armour/Flower Lady	1966	2.50	5.00	10.00
❑ 5808	PS	Knight in Rusty Armour/Flower Lady	1966	3.75	7.50	15.00
❑ 5864		Sunday for Tea/Hurtin' Is Lovin'	1967	2.50	5.00	10.00
❑ 5864	PS	Sunday for Tea/Hurtin' Is Lovin'	1967	3.75	7.50	15.00
❑ 5919		The Jokers/Red Cream and Velvet	1967	2.50	5.00	10.00
Peter, Paul and Mary						
(Also see "Stookey, Paul"; "Travers, Mary"; "Yarrow, Peter")						
(No label)						
❑ (no #)	DJ	Eugene McCarthy for President	1968	6.25	12.50	25.00
Warner Bros.						
❑ (no #)		A-Soalin' (mono/stereo)	196?	3.00	6.00	12.00
		Custom label				
❑ (no #)	PS	A-Soalin' (mono/stereo)	196?	5.00	10.00	20.00
		Illustrated book with lyrics				
❑ 5274		Lemon Tree/Early in the Morning	1962	2.50	5.00	10.00

Number		Title (A Side/B Side)	Year	VG	VG+	NM
❑ 5296		If I Had a Hammer/Gone the Rainbow	1962	2.50	5.00	10.00
❑ 5325		Big Boat/Tiny Sparrow	1962	2.50	5.00	10.00
❑ 5325	PS	Big Boat/Tiny Sparrow	1962	5.00	10.00	20.00
❑ 5334		Settle Down (Goin' Down That Highway)/500 Miles	1963	2.50	5.00	10.00
❑ 5348		Puff/Pretty Mary	1963	3.00	6.00	12.00
		First pressings have no subtitle on A-side				
❑ 5348		Puff (The Magic Dragon)/Pretty Mary	1963	2.50	5.00	10.00
		Later pressings add subtitle				
❑ 5368		Blowin' in the Wind/Flora	1963	2.50	5.00	10.00
❑ 5385		Don't Think Twice, It's All Right/Autumn to May	1963	2.50	5.00	10.00
❑ 5399		Stewball/The Cruel War	1963	2.50	5.00	10.00
❑ 5402		A-Soalin'/High-A-Bye	1963	3.00	6.00	12.00
❑ 5402	PS	A-Soalin'/High-A-Bye	1963	5.00	10.00	20.00
❑ 5418		Tell It on the Mountain/Old Goat	1964	2.50	5.00	10.00
❑ 5442		Oh, Rock My Soul (Part 1)/Oh, Rock My Soul (Part 2)	1964	2.50	5.00	10.00
❑ 5496		For Lovin' Me/Monday Morning	1965	2.00	4.00	8.00
❑ 5625		When the Ship Comes In/	1965	2.00	4.00	8.00
		The Times They Are a-Changin'				
❑ 5659		Early Morning Rain/The Rising of the Moon	1965	2.00	4.00	8.00
❑ 5809		The Cruel War/Mon Vrai Destin	1966	2.00	4.00	8.00
❑ 5842		Hurry Sundown/Sometime Lover	1966			*Unreleased?*
❑ 5849		The Other Side of This Life/Sometime Lover	1966	2.00	4.00	8.00
❑ 5883		For Baby (For Bobbie)/Hurry Sundown	1967	2.00	4.00	8.00
❑ 7067		I Dig Rock and Roll Music/	1967	2.50	5.00	10.00
		The Great Mandella (The Wheel of Life)				
❑ 7092		Too Much of Nothing/The House Song	1967	2.00	4.00	8.00
❑ 7232		Yesterday's Tomorrow/Love City (Postcards to Duluth)	1968	2.00	4.00	8.00
❑ 7279		Day Is Done/Make Believe Town	1969	2.00	4.00	8.00
❑ 7340		Leaving on a Jet Plane/The House Song	1969	2.50	5.00	10.00
❑ 7359		Christmas Dinner/The Marvelous Toy	1969	2.50	5.00	10.00
❑ 8684		For the First Time/Best of Friends	1978		2.00	4.00
❑ 8728		Forever Young/Best of Friends	1978		2.00	4.00

Peterik, Jim

(Solo records made between his time in the Ides of March and Survivor)

Epic

❑ 50272		Don't Fight the Feeling/Hard Day at the World	1976		2.50	5.00
❑ 50311		Last Tango/Lay Back	1976		2.50	5.00
❑ 50406		The Closest Thing to My Mind/Don't Fight the Feeling	1977		2.50	5.00

Petersen, Paul

Colpix

❑ 620		She Can't Find Her Keys/Very Likely	1962	3.75	7.50	15.00
❑ 620	PS	She Can't Find Her Keys/Very Likely	1962	7.50	15.00	30.00
❑ 631		What Did They Do Before Rock and Roll/Very Unlikely	1962	5.00	10.00	20.00
		With Shelly Fabares				
❑ 631	PS	What Did They Do Before Rock and Roll/Very Unlikely	1962	20.00	40.00	80.00
❑ 632		Keep Your Love Locked (Deep in Your Heart)/	1962	3.00	6.00	12.00
		Be Everything to Anyone You Love				
❑ 632	PS	Keep Your Love Locked (Deep in Your Heart)/	1962	7.50	15.00	30.00
		Be Everything to Anyone You Love				
❑ 649		Lollipops and Roses/Please Mr. Sun	1962	3.00	6.00	12.00
❑ 663		My Dad/Little Boy Sad	1962	3.75	7.50	15.00
❑ 663	PS	My Dad/Little Boy Sad	1962	7.50	15.00	30.00
❑ 676		Amy/Goody Goody	1963	3.00	6.00	12.00
❑ 676		Amy/I Only Have Eyes for You	1963	3.00	6.00	12.00
❑ 697		Girls in the Summertime/Mama, Your Little Boy Fell	1963	3.00	6.00	12.00
❑ 707		The Cheer Leader/Polka Dots and Moonbeams	1963	3.00	6.00	12.00
❑ 720		She Rides with Me/Poorest Boy in Town	1964	20.00	40.00	80.00
		A-side produced by Brian Wilson				
❑ 730		Where Is She/Hey There Beautiful	1964	3.00	6.00	12.00
❑ 763		Happy/Little Dreamer	1965	3.00	6.00	12.00
❑ 785		The Ring/You Don't Need Money	1965	3.00	6.00	12.00

Motown

❑ 1108		Chained/Don't Let It Happen	1967	5.00	10.00	20.00
❑ 1129		A Little Bit for Sandy/Your Love's Got Me Runnin'	1968	5.00	10.00	20.00

Peterson, Earl

Sun

❑ 197		Boogie Blues/In the Dark	1954	125.00	250.00	500.00

Peterson, Ray

Cloud 9

❑ 134		Nobody But Me/(B-side unknown)	1975		2.50	5.00

Decca

❑ 32861		Stamp Out Loneliness/There's a Better Way	1971		2.50	5.00

Dunes

❑ 2002		Corrina, Corrina/Be My Girl	1960	6.25	12.50	25.00
		Produced by Phil Spector				
❑ 2002	PS	Corrina, Corrina/Be My Girl	1960	12.50	25.00	50.00
❑ 2004		Sweet Little Kathy/You Didn't Care	1961	3.75	7.50	15.00
❑ 2006		Missing You/You Thrill Me	1961	3.75	7.50	15.00
❑ 2009		I Could Have Loved You So Well/	1961	5.00	10.00	20.00
		Why Don't You Write Me				
		Produced by Phil Spector				
❑ 2013		You Know Me Much Too Well/You Didn't Care	1962	3.75	7.50	15.00

Number		Title (A Side/B Side)	Year	VG	VG+	NM
☐ 2018		If Only Tomorrow/You Didn't Care	1962	3.75	7.50	15.00
☐ 2019		Is It Wrong/Slowly	1963	3.75	7.50	15.00
☐ 2022		A Love to Remember/I'm Not Jimmy	1963	3.75	7.50	15.00
☐ 2024		Where Are You/Deep Are the Roots	1963	3.75	7.50	15.00
☐ 2025		Give Us Your Blessing/Without Love (There Is Nothing)	1963	3.75	7.50	15.00
☐ 2027		I Forgot What It Was Like/Be My Girl	1963	3.75	7.50	15.00
☐ 2030		Promises/Sweet Little Kathy	1963	3.75	7.50	15.00

MGM

Number		Title (A Side/B Side)	Year	VG	VG+	NM
☐ 13269		If You Were Here/Oh No	1964	2.50	5.00	10.00
☐ 13299		Across the Street (Is a Million Miles Away)/ When I Stop Dreaming	1964	2.50	5.00	10.00
☐ 13330		Unchained Melody/That's All	1965	2.00	4.00	8.00
☐ 13336		A House Without WIndows/ Wish I Could Say No to You	1965	2.00	4.00	8.00
☐ 13388		I'm Only Human/One Lonesome Rose	1965	2.00	4.00	8.00
☐ 13436		Love Hurts/Everybody	1966	2.00	4.00	8.00
☐ 13508		Amanda/I'm Gonna Change Everything	1966	2.00	4.00	8.00
☐ 13564		Just One Smile/The Whole World's Goin' Crazy	1966	2.00	4.00	8.00

RCA

Number		Title (A Side/B Side)	Year	VG	VG+	NM
☐ GB-11758		Tell Laura I Love Her/The Wonder of You	1979			3.00
	Gold Standard Series					

RCA Victor

Number		Title (A Side/B Side)	Year	VG	VG+	NM
☐ 47-7087		Fever/We're Old Enough to Cry	1957	6.25	12.50	25.00
☐ 47-7165		Let's Try Romance/Shirley Purley	1958	5.00	10.00	20.00
☐ 47-7255		Suddenly/Tall Light	1958	5.00	10.00	20.00
☐ 47-7303		Patricia/The Blue-Eyed Baby	1958	5.00	10.00	20.00
☐ 47-7336		Dream Way/I'll Always Want You Near	1958	5.00	10.00	20.00
☐ 47-7404		Richer Than I/Love Is a Woman	1958	5.00	10.00	20.00
☐ 47-7513		The Wonder of You/I'm Gone	1959	6.25	12.50	25.00
☐ 47-7578		My Blue Angel/Come and Get It	1959	5.00	10.00	20.00
☐ 47-7635		Goodnight My Love (Pleasant Dreams)/Till Then	1959	5.00	10.00	20.00
☐ 47-7635	PS	Goodnight My Love (Pleasant Dreams)/Till Then	1959	7.50	15.00	30.00
☐ 47-7703		Answer Me, My Love/ What Do You Want to Make Those Eyes At Me For	1960	5.00	10.00	20.00
☐ 47-7745		Tell Laura I Love Her/Wedding Days	1960	6.25	12.50	25.00
☐ 47-7779		Teenage Heartache/I'll Always Want You Near	1960	5.00	10.00	20.00
☐ 47-7843		My Blue Angel/I'm Tired	1961	5.00	10.00	20.00
☐ 47-8333		The Wonder of You/Goodnight My Love	1964	2.50	5.00	10.00
☐ 61-7578		My Blue Angel/Come and Get It	1959	20.00	40.00	80.00
	"Living Stereo" (large hole, plays at 45 rpm)					
☐ 61-7745		Tell Laura I Love Her/Wedding Days	1960	25.00	50.00	100.00
	"Living Stereo" (large hole, plays at 45 rpm)					

Reprise

Number		Title (A Side/B Side)	Year	VG	VG+	NM
☐ 0811		Love Rules the World/Together	1969	2.00	4.00	8.00

Uni

Number		Title (A Side/B Side)	Year	VG	VG+	NM
☐ 55249		Love the Understanding Way/Oklahoma City Rimes	1970	2.00	4.00	8.00
☐ 55268		Tell Laura I Love Her/To Wait for Love	1971		3.00	6.00
☐ 55275		Fever/Changes	1971		3.00	6.00

Petticoats, The

Challenge

Number		Title (A Side/B Side)	Year	VG	VG+	NM
☐ 9211		Surfin' Sally/Why Does Billy Play in Your Yard	1963	6.25	12.50	25.00

Dot

Number		Title (A Side/B Side)	Year	VG	VG+	NM
☐ 16052		By the Light of the Silvery Moon/Troubadour	1960	5.00	10.00	20.00
☐ 16155		For Sentimental Reasons/Cincinnati	1960	5.00	10.00	20.00

Unique

Number		Title (A Side/B Side)	Year	VG	VG+	NM
☐ 344		The Motorboat Song/The First One	1956	5.00	10.00	20.00
☐ 363		High Heels/I'll Go Along with You	1956	5.00	10.00	20.00

Petty, Norman, Trio

"X"

Number		Title (A Side/B Side)	Year	VG	VG+	NM
☐ 0040		Mood Indigo/Petty's Little Polka	1954	3.00	6.00	12.00
☐ 0071		On the Alamo/Echo Polka	1954	3.00	6.00	12.00
☐ 0104		I Wonder Why/Three Little Kisses	1955	3.00	6.00	12.00
☐ 0130		Oh! You Pretty Woman/Hey! Good Lookin'	1955	3.00	6.00	12.00
☐ 0167		Solitude/When It's Darkness on the Delta	1955	3.00	6.00	12.00

ABC-Paramount

Number		Title (A Side/B Side)	Year	VG	VG+	NM
☐ 9787		Almost Paradise/It's Been a Long, Long Time	1957	3.00	6.00	12.00

Columbia

Number		Title (A Side/B Side)	Year	VG	VG+	NM
☐ 40929		The First Kiss/(Instrumental)	1957	3.00	6.00	12.00
☐ 41039		Moondreams/Toy Boy	1957	25.00	50.00	100.00
	With Buddy Holly on guitar					

Petty, Tom, and the Heartbreakers

(Includes Tom Petty solo. Also see "Traveling Wilburys")

Backstreet

Number		Title (A Side/B Side)	Year	VG	VG+	NM
☐ 41138		Don't Do Me Like That/Casa Dega	1979		2.00	4.00
☐ 41138	PS	Don't Do Me Like That/Casa Dega	1979		2.50	5.00
☐ 41169		Refugee/It's Rainin' Again	1980		2.00	4.00
☐ 41169	PS	Refugee/It's Rainin' Again	1980		2.50	5.00
☐ 41227		Here Comes My Girl/Louisiana Rain	1980		2.00	4.00
☐ 41227	PS	Here Comes My Girl/Louisiana Rain	1980		2.50	5.00
☐ 51100		The Waiting/Nightwatchman	1981		2.00	4.00
☐ 51100	PS	The Waiting/Nightwatchman	1981		2.00	4.00
☐ 51136		A Woman in Love (It's Not Me)/Gator on the Lawn	1981		2.00	4.00

Number		Title (A Side/B Side)	Year	VG	VG+	NM
❑ 51136	PS	A Woman in Love (It's Not Me)/Gator on the Lawn	1981		2.00	4.00
❑ 52144		You Got Lucky/Between Two Worlds	1982		2.00	4.00
❑ 52144	PS	You Got Lucky/Between Two Worlds	1982		2.00	4.00
❑ 52181		Change of Heart/Heartbreakers Beach Party	1983	2.00	4.00	8.00
		Red vinyl in clear plastic sleeve with sticker				
❑ 52181		Change of Heart/Heartbreakers Beach Party	1983			3.00
❑ 52181	PS	Change of Heart/Heartbreakers Beach Party	1983		2.00	4.00
		Only issued with black-vinyl versions				

MCA

Number		Title (A Side/B Side)	Year	VG	VG+	NM
❑ 52496		Don't Come Around Here No More/Trailer	1985			4.00
		Original copies have a 4:19 version of the A-side				
❑ 52496		Don't Come Around Here No More/Trailer	1985		2.00	4.00
		Second pressings feature a 5-plus-minute version of the A-side				
❑ 52496	PS	Don't Come Around Here No More/Trailer	1985		2.00	4.00
❑ 52605		Make It Better (Forget About Me)/Crackin' Up	1985			3.00
❑ 52605	PS	Make It Better (Forget About Me)/Crackin' Up	1985			3.00
❑ 52658		Rebels/Southern Accents	1985			3.00
❑ 52658	PS	Rebels/Southern Accents	1985			3.00
❑ 52772		Needles and Pins/Spike	1985			3.00
		A-side: With Stevie Nicks				
❑ 52772	PS	Needles and Pins/Spike	1985			3.00
❑ 53065		Jammin' Me/Make That Connection	1987			3.00
❑ 53065	PS	Jammin' Me/Make That Connection	1987			3.00
❑ 53153		All Mixed Up/Let Me Up (I've Had Enough)	1987			3.00
❑ 53153	PS	All Mixed Up/Let Me Up (I've Had Enough)	1987			3.00
❑ 53669		I Won't Back Down/The Apartment Song	1989		2.00	4.00
❑ 53682		Runnin' Down a Dream/Alright for Now	1989		2.00	4.00
❑ 53748		Free Fallin'/Down the Line	1989		2.50	5.00
❑ 53781		A Face in the Crowd/A Mind with a Heart of Its Own	1990		2.00	4.00
❑ 54124		Learning to Fly/Too Good to Be True	1991		2.00	4.00
❑ 54131		Into the Great Wide Open/Makin' Some Noise	1991		2.00	4.00
❑ 54387		King's Highway/All or Nothin'	1992		2.00	4.00
❑ 54732		Mary Jane's Last Dance/The Waiting	1993		2.00	4.00
❑ 79030		Yer So Bad/Love Is a Long Road	1990		2.00	4.00

Shelter

Number		Title (A Side/B Side)	Year	VG	VG+	NM
❑ 62006		Breakdown/The Wild One, Forever	1976			Unreleased?
❑ 62006	DJ	Breakdown (Mono)/Breakdown (Stereo)	1976	2.50	5.00	10.00
❑ 62007		American Girl/Luna	1977		3.00	6.00
❑ 62008		Breakdown/Fooled Again (I Can't Take It)	1977		3.00	6.00
❑ 62010		I Need to Know/No Second Thoughts	1978		2.50	5.00
❑ 62011		Listen to Her Heart/I Don't Know What to Say to You	1978		2.50	5.00
❑ 62011	PS	Listen to Her Heart/I Don't Know What to Say to You	1978		2.50	5.00

Warner Bros.

Number		Title (A Side/B Side)	Year	VG	VG+	NM
❑ 17593		Walls (Circus)/Walls (No. 3)	1996			3.00
❑ 17925		It's Good to Be King/Cabin Down Below	1995			3.00
❑ 18026		A Higher Place/Only a Broken Heart	1995			3.00
❑ 18030		You Don't Know How It Feels/Girl on LSD	1994			3.00

Phaetons, The
(More than one group)
Hi-Q

Number		Title (A Side/B Side)	Year	VG	VG+	NM
❑ 5012		Fling/Homemade	1959	5.00	10.00	20.00

Sahara

Number		Title (A Side/B Side)	Year	VG	VG+	NM
❑ 102		I'm So Lonely/Road of Blues	1963	5.00	10.00	20.00
❑ 103		The Beatle Walk/Frantic	1964	12.50	25.00	50.00
		B-side by the Premiers				

Vin

Number		Title (A Side/B Side)	Year	VG	VG+	NM
❑ 1015		I Love My Baby/As You Know	1959	15.00	30.00	60.00

Warner Bros.

Number		Title (A Side/B Side)	Year	VG	VG+	NM
❑ 7082		She Came Like the Rain/Three Weeks, Four Days and Fifteen Hours	1967	2.50	5.00	10.00
❑ 7205		Leave It to Me/You'd Better Come Home	1968	2.50	5.00	10.00

Phantom, The
(More than one group)
Capitol

Number		Title (A Side/B Side)	Year	VG	VG+	NM
❑ 3857		Calm Before the Storm/Black Magic, White Magic	1974	3.00	6.00	12.00

Dot

Number		Title (A Side/B Side)	Year	VG	VG+	NM
❑ 16056		Love Me/Whisper Your Love	1960	37.50	75.00	150.00
❑ 16056	PS	Love Me/Whisper Your Love	1960	75.00	150.00	300.00

Hideout

Number		Title (A Side/B Side)	Year	VG	VG+	NM
❑ 1080		Calm Before the Storm/Black Magic, White Magic	1974	5.00	10.00	20.00

Philips, Terry
United Artists

Number		Title (A Side/B Side)	Year	VG	VG+	NM
❑ 351		My Foolish Ways/Hands of a Fool	1961	20.00	40.00	80.00

Phillips, John
(Of The Mamas and the Papas)
ABC Dunhill

Number		Title (A Side/B Side)	Year	VG	VG+	NM
❑ 4236		Mississippi/April Anne	1970		3.00	6.00

Atco

Number		Title (A Side/B Side)	Year	VG	VG+	NM
❑ 6960		Green-Eyed Lady/Lion	1974		3.00	6.00

Number		Title (A Side/B Side)	Year	VG	VG+	NM
Columbia						
❏ 45737		Cup of Tea/Revolution on Vacation	1972		2.50	5.00
Phillips, Michelle						
(Of the Mamas and the Papas)						
A&M						
❏ 1740		There She Goes/Aloha Louie	1975		2.50	5.00
❏ 1824		No Love Today/Aloha Louie	1976		2.00	4.00
❏ 1824	PS	No Love Today/Aloha Louie	1976		3.00	6.00
❏ 1996		The Aching Kind/Lady of Fantasy	1977		2.50	5.00
❏ 2021		There She Goes/Victim of Romance	1978		2.50	5.00
Phillips, Phil						
Khoury's						
❏ 11		Sea of Love/Juella	1959	50.00	100.00	200.00
Mercury						
❏ 10021	S	Take This Heart/Verdie Mae	1959	12.50	25.00	50.00
❏ 71465		Sea of Love/Juella	1959	6.25	12.50	25.00
❏ 71531	M	Take This Heart/Verdie Mae	1959	5.00	10.00	20.00
❏ 71611		What Will I Tell My Heart/Your True Love Once More	1960	5.00	10.00	20.00
❏ 71649		Stormy Weather/Don't Cry Baby	1960	5.00	10.00	20.00
❏ 71657		Come Back My Darling/Nobody Knows-Nobody Cares	1960	5.00	10.00	20.00
Piano Red						
Checker						
❏ 911		Get Up Mare/So Worried	1958	7.50	15.00	30.00
Groove						
❏ 0023		Decatur Street Blues/Big Rock Joe from Kokomo	1954	7.50	15.00	30.00
❏ 0101		Pay It No Mind/Jump, Man, Jump	1955	7.50	15.00	30.00
❏ 0118		Six O'Clock Bounce/Goodbye	1955	7.50	15.00	30.00
❏ 0126		Red's Blues/Gordy's Rock	1955	7.50	15.00	30.00
❏ 0136		Jumpin' with Daddy/She Knocks Me Out	1956	7.50	15.00	30.00
❏ 0145		I'm Nobody's Fool/That's My Desire	1956	7.50	15.00	30.00
❏ 0169		Woo-Ee/You Were Mine for Awhile	1956	7.50	15.00	30.00
Jax						
❏ 1000		This Old World/I Feel Good	1959	3.75	7.50	15.00
❏ 1006		Guitar Walk/I've Been Walkin'	1959	3.75	7.50	15.00
King						
❏ 6330		I Want a Bowlegged Woman/Underground Atlanta	1970		2.50	5.00
RCA Victor						
❏ 47-4265		Diggin' the Boogie/Let's Have a Good Time Tonight	1951	15.00	30.00	60.00
❏ 47-4380		Hey Good Lookin'/It Makes No Difference Now	1951	15.00	30.00	60.00
❏ 47-4524		Bouncin' with Red/Count the Days I'm Gone	1952	15.00	30.00	60.00
❏ 47-4766		She Walks Right In/Sales Tax Boogie	1952	15.00	30.00	60.00
❏ 47-4957		Yoo Doopee Doo/Daybreak	1952	15.00	30.00	60.00
❏ 47-5101		I'm Gonna Rock Some More/Everybody's Boogie	1952	10.00	20.00	40.00
❏ 47-5224		She's Dynamite/I'm Gonna Tell Everybody	1953	10.00	20.00	40.00
❏ 47-5337		Decatur Street Boogie/Your Mouth's Got a Hole In It	1953	10.00	20.00	40.00
❏ 47-5544		Right and Read, Taxi, Taxi 6963	1953	10.00	20.00	40.00
❏ 47-6856		Wild Fire/Rock Baby	1957	5.00	10.00	20.00
❏ 47-6953		Peachtree Parade/Please Don't Talk About Me	1957	5.00	10.00	20.00
❏ 47-7065		South/Coo Cha	1957	5.00	10.00	20.00
❏ 47-7217		Comin' On/One Glimpse of Heaven	1958	5.00	10.00	20.00
❏ 50-0099		Rockin' with Red/Red's Boogie	1950	25.00	50.00	100.00
		Gray label, orange vinyl				
❏ 50-0106		The Wrong Yo-Yo/My Gal Jo	1951	20.00	40.00	80.00
		Gray label, orange vinyl				
❏ 50-0118		Jumpin' the Boogie/Just Right Bounce	1951	20.00	40.00	80.00
		Gray label, orange vinyl				
❏ 50-0130		Layin' the Boogie/Baby What's Wrong	1951	20.00	40.00	80.00
		Gray label, orange vinyl				
Pickett, Bobby "Boris"						
Anthem						
❏ 205		Monster Concert/(B-side unknown)	1973		3.00	6.00
Capitol						
❏ 5063		Simon the Sensible Surfer/Simon Says So What	1963	6.25	12.50	25.00
Garpax						
❏ 724		I'm Down to My Last Heartbreak/I Can't Stop	1962	6.25	12.50	25.00
❏ 44167		Monster Mash/Monster's Mash Party	1962	7.50	15.00	30.00
❏ 44167	PS	Monster Mash/Monster's Mash Party	1962	12.50	25.00	50.00
❏ 44171		Monster's Holiday/Monster's Motion	1962	6.25	12.50	25.00
❏ 44171	PS	Monster's Holiday/Monster's Motion	1962	10.00	20.00	40.00
❏ 44175		Graduation Day/The Humpty Dumpty	1963	6.25	12.50	25.00
❏ 44175	PS	Graduation Day/The Humpty Dumpty	1963	10.00	20.00	40.00
❏ 44185		Blood Bank Blues/Me and My Mummy	1965	6.25	12.50	25.00
Metromedia						
❏ BMBO-0089		Me and My Mummy/It's Not the Same Without You	1973	2.50	5.00	10.00
		B-side by Pickett and Payne				
Parrot						
❏ 348		Monster Mash/Monster's Mash Party	1970	2.50	5.00	10.00
		Reissued in 1973 with the same number and label design				
❏ 366		Monster's Holiday/Moneter Minuet	1971	2.50	5.00	10.00

Number	Title (A Side/B Side)	Year	VG	VG+	NM

Pizzeria

| □ 1 | Star Drek/Mangy Old Sidewinder | 1977 | 2.00 | 5.00 | 10.00 |

With Peter Ferrara; originals are autographed on the label by both

Polydor

| □ 14361 | King Kong (Your Song)/Disco Kong | 1976 | | 2.50 | 5.00 |

With Peter Ferrara

RCA Victor

| □ 47-8312 | Smoke! Smoke! Smoke! (That Cigarette)/Gotta Leave This Town | 1964 | 3.75 | 7.50 | 15.00 |
| □ 47-8459 | The Werewolf Watusi/Monster Swim | 1964 | 3.75 | 7.50 | 15.00 |

White Whale

| □ 363 | Monster Man Jam/(B-side unknown) | 1970 | 6.25 | 12.50 | 25.00 |
| □ 365 | Monster Concert/(B-side unknown) | 1970 | 6.25 | 12.50 | 25.00 |

Pickett, Wilson

Atlantic

□ 2233	I'm Gonna Cry/For Better or Worse	1964	2.50	5.00	10.00
□ 2271	Come Home Baby/Take a Little Love	1965	2.50	5.00	10.00
□ 2289	In the Midnight Hour/I'm Not Tired	1965	2.50	5.00	10.00
□ 2306	Don't Fight It/It's All Over	1965	2.50	5.00	10.00
□ 2320	634-5789 (Soulsville, U.S.A.)/That's a Man's Way	1966	2.50	5.00	10.00
□ 2334	Ninety-Nine and a Half (Won't Do)/Danger Zone	1966	2.50	5.00	10.00
□ 2348	Land of 1000 Dances/You're So Fine	1966	2.50	5.00	10.00
□ 2365	Mustang Sally/Three Time Loser	1966	2.50	5.00	10.00
□ 2381	Eveybody Needs Somebody to Love/Nothing You Can Do	1967	2.50	5.00	10.00
□ 2394	I Found a Love -- Part I/I Found a Love -- Part II	1967	2.50	5.00	10.00
□ 2412	Soul Dance Number Three/You Can't Stand Alone	1967	2.50	5.00	10.00
□ 2430	Funky Broadway/I'm Sorry About That	1967	2.50	5.00	10.00
□ 2448	Stag-O-Lee/I'm In Love	1967	2.50	5.00	10.00
□ 2484	Jealous Love/I've Come a Long Way	1968	2.50	5.00	10.00
□ 2504	She's Lookin' Good/We've Got to Have Love	1968	2.00	4.00	8.00
□ 2528	I'm a Midnight Mover/Deborah	1968	2.00	4.00	8.00
□ 2558	I Found a True Love/For Better or Worse	1968	2.00	4.00	8.00
□ 2575	A Man and a Half/People Make the World (What It Is)	1968	2.00	4.00	8.00
□ 2591	Hey Jude/Search Your Heart	1968	2.00	4.00	8.00
□ 2611	Mini-Skirt Minnie/Back in Your Arms	1969	2.00	4.00	8.00
□ 2631	Born to Be Wild/Toe Hold	1969	2.00	4.00	8.00
□ 2648	Hey Joe/Night Owl	1969	2.00	4.00	8.00
□ 2682	You Keep Me Hangin' On/Now You See Me, Now You Don't	1969	2.00	4.00	8.00
□ 2722	Sugar, Sugar/Cole, Cooke, and Redding	1970	2.00	4.00	8.00
□ 2753	She Said Yes/It's Still Good	1970		3.00	6.00
□ 2765	Engine Number Nine/International Playboy	1970		3.00	6.00
□ 2781	Don't Let the Green Grass Fool You/Ain't No Doubt About It	1971		3.00	6.00
□ 2797	Don't Knock My Love (Part 1)/Don't Knock My Love (Part 2)	1971		3.00	6.00
□ 2824	Call My Name, I'll Be There/Woman Let Me Down Home	1971		3.00	6.00
□ 2852	Fire and Water/Pledging My Love	1971		3.00	6.00
□ 2878	Funk Factory/One Step Away	1972		3.00	6.00
□ 2909	Mama Told Me Not to Come/Covering the Same Old Ground	1972		3.00	6.00
□ 2961	Come Right Here/International Playboy	1973		3.00	6.00

Big Tree

| □ 16121 | Who Turned You On/Dance You Down | 1978 | | 2.50 | 5.00 |
| □ 16129 | Groovin'/Time to Let the Sun Shine In | 1978 | | 2.50 | 5.00 |

Correc-Tone

| □ 501 | Let Me Be Your Boy/My Heart Belongs to You | 1962 | 15.00 | 30.00 | 60.00 |

Cub

| □ 9113 | Let Me Be Your Boy/My Heart Belongs to You | 1962 | 7.50 | 15.00 | 30.00 |

Double L

□ 713	If You Need Me/Baby Call on Me	1963	3.00	6.00	12.00
□ 717	It's Too Late/I'm Gonna Love You	1963	3.00	6.00	12.00
□ 724	I'm Down to My Last Heartbreak/I Can't Stop	1963	3.00	6.00	12.00

EMI America

□ 8027	I Want You/Love of My Life	1979		2.50	5.00
□ 8034	Live with Me/Granny	1980		2.50	5.00
□ 8070	Ain't Gonna Give You No More/Don't Underestimate the Power of Love	1981		2.50	5.00
□ 8082	Back on the Right Track/It's You	1981		2.50	5.00

Motown

□ 1898	Don't Turn Away/Can't Stop Now	1987		2.00	4.00
□ 1916	In the Midnight Hour/Just Let Her Know	1987		2.00	4.00
□ 1938	Love Never Let Me Down/Just Let Her Know	1988		2.00	4.00
□ 53407	Love Never Let Me Down/Just Let Her Know	1988		2.00	4.00

RCA Victor

□ 74-0908	Mr. Magic Man/I Sho' Love You	1973		3.00	6.00
□ APBO-0049	Take a Closer Look at the Woman You're With/Two Women and a Wife	1973		3.00	6.00
□ APBO-0174	Soft Soul Boogie Woogie/Take That Pollution Out of Your Throat	1973		3.00	6.00

Number		Title (A Side/B Side)	Year	VG	VG+	NM
❑ APBO-0309		Take Your Pleasure Where You Find It/ What Good Is a Lie	1974		3.00	6.00
❑ PB-10067		I Was Too Nice/Isn't That So	1974		3.00	6.00

Verve

| ❑ 10378 | | Let Me Be Your Boy/My Heart Belongs to You | 1966 | 5.00 | 10.00 | 20.00 |

Wicked

| ❑ 8101 | | The Best Part of a Man/How Will I Ever Know | 1975 | | 3.00 | 6.00 |
| ❑ 8102 | | Love Will Keep Us Together/It's Gonna Be Good | 1976 | | 3.00 | 6.00 |

Picks, The
Columbia

| ❑ 41096 | | Moondreams/Look to the Future | 1958 | 12.50 | 25.00 | 50.00 |

Pilot
Arista

| ❑ 0259 | | One Good Reason Why/Get Up and Go | 1977 | | 2.00 | 4.00 |

EMI

❑ 3992		Magic/Just Let Me Be	1974		2.50	5.00
❑ 4135		Don't Speak Loudly/Just a Smile	1975		2.00	4.00
❑ 4202		January/Do Me Good	1975		2.00	4.00
❑ 4305		Canada/Mover	1976		2.00	4.00

RCA Victor

| ❑ 74-0770 | | Rider/Miss Sandy | 1972 | | 3.00 | 6.00 |

Pink Floyd
Columbia

❑ 02165		Run Like Hell/Comfortably Numb	1981			3.00
		Reissue				
❑ 03118		Another Brick in the Wall, Part 2/One of My Turns	1982			3.00
		Reissue				
❑ 03142		When the Tigers Broke Free/ Bring the Boys Back Home	1982		2.00	4.00
❑ 03142	PS	When the Tigers Broke Free/ Bring the Boys Back Home	1982		2.50	5.00
		Fold-open cardboard sleeve				
❑ X18-03176		When the Tigers Broke Free/ Bring the Boys Back Home	1982	2.50	5.00	10.00
❑ X18-03176	PS	When the Tigers Broke Free/ Bring the Boys Back Home	1982	2.50	5.00	10.00
		Fold-open cardboard sleeve				
❑ 03905		Not Now John (Obscured Version)/ The Heroes Return	1983		2.00	4.00
❑ 03905	PS	Not Now John (Obscured Version)/ The Heroes Return	1983		2.50	5.00
❑ 07363		Learning to Fly/Terminal Frost	1987		2.00	4.00
❑ 07363	PS	Learning to Fly/Terminal Frost	1987		2.00	4.00
❑ 07660		On the Turning Away/Run Like Hell	1987		2.00	4.00
❑ 07660	PS	On the Turning Away/Run Like Hell	1987		2.00	4.00
❑ 10248		Have a Cigar/Welcome to the Machine	1975	3.00	6.00	12.00
❑ 11187		Another Brick in the Wall (Part 2)/One of My Turns	1980		2.50	5.00
		Custom "wall" label				
❑ 11187		Another Brick in the Wall (Part 2)/One of My Turns	1980		2.00	4.00
		Regular Columbia orange label				
❑ 11187	PS	Another Brick in the Wall (Part 2)/One of My Turns	1980	2.00	4.00	8.00
❑ 11265		Run Like Hell/Don't Leave Me Now	1980		2.00	4.00
❑ 11311		Comfortably Numb/Hey You	1980		2.00	4.00
❑ 77493		Take It Back/Astronomy Domine (Live)	1994		2.00	4.00

Harvest

❑ 3240		Fearless/One of These Days	1971	5.00	10.00	20.00
❑ 3391		Stay/Free Four	1972	5.00	10.00	20.00
❑ 3609		Money/Any Colour You Like	1973	3.75	7.50	15.00
❑ P-3609	DJ	Money (Edited Mono)/Money (Edited Stereo)	1973	5.00	10.00	20.00
❑ 3832		Time/Us and Them	1974	5.00	10.00	20.00
❑ SPRO-6669	DJ	Money (Censored Edited Mono)/ Money (Censored Edited Stereo)	1973	3.75	7.50	15.00
		This promo was sent to radio stations with a frantic note telling them to disregard the first promo				

Tower

❑ 333		Arnold Layne/Candy and a Currant Bun	1967	50.00	100.00	200.00
❑ 333	PS	Arnold Layne/Candy and a Currant Bun	1967	200.00	400.00	800.00
		Only issued with promotional copies				
❑ 356		See Emily Play/Scarecrow	1967	50.00	100.00	200.00
❑ 356	PS	See Emily Play/Scarecrow	1967	150.00	300.00	600.00
		Photo sleeve; only issued with some promotional copies				
❑ 356	PS	See Emily Play/Scarecrow	1967	100.00	200.00	400.00
		Title sleeve; only issued with some promotional copies				
❑ 376		Midnight Sun (Part 1)/Midnight Sun (Part 2)	1967	50.00	100.00	200.00
❑ 378		The Gnome/Flaming	1967	37.50	75.00	150.00
❑ 426		It Would Be So Nice/Julia Dream	1968	62.50	125.00	250.00
❑ 440		Let There Be More Light/Remember a Day	1968	75.00	150.00	300.00

Pinkney, Bill
(Formerly with the original version of the Drifters)
Fontana

| ❑ 1956 | | Don't Call Me/I Do the Jerk | 1964 | 3.00 | 6.00 | 12.00 |

Number	Title (A Side/B Side)	Year	VG	VG+	NM

Game

☐ 394 — Ol' Man River/Millionaire — 196? — 12.50 — 25.00 — 50.00

Phillips Int'l.

☐ 3524 — After the Hop/Sally's Got a Sister — 1958 — 5.00 — 10.00 — 20.00
As "Bill Pinky"

Veep

☐ 1264 — I Found Some Lovin'/The Masquerade Is Over — 1967 — 2.50 — 5.00 — 10.00

Pipes, The

Dootone

☐ 388 — Be Fair/Let Me Give You Money — 1956 — 62.50 — 125.00 — 250.00
☐ 401 — You Are An Angel/I Love the Life I Live — 1956 — 62.50 — 125.00 — 250.00

Pipkins, The

Capitol

☐ 2819 — Gimme Dat Ding/To Love You — 1970 — — 3.00 — 6.00
☐ 2874 — Sugar and Spice-Are You Cookin' Goose/Yakety Yak — 1970 — — 2.50 — 5.00

Pips, The – See "Knight, Gladys, and the Pips"

Pirates, The

(Later recorded as The Temptations)

Mel-O-Dy

☐ 105 — Mind Over Matter (I'm Gonna Make You Mine)/I'll Love You Till I Die — 1962 — 25.00 — 50.00 — 100.00

Pistilli, Gene

Atco

☐ 6850 — Been Down So Long It Looks Like Up to Me/Lettin' Down an Old Friend — 1971 — — 2.50 — 5.00

Capitol

☐ 2627 — Mr. Bojangles/Ruby Tuesday — 1969 — — 2.50 — 5.00
☐ 2968 — Care for Me/Rosianna — 1970 — — 2.50 — 5.00
☐ 3036 — Maybe Mexico/Winterlude — 1971 — — 2.50 — 5.00
☐ 3108 — Java Jive/Chicken Bone Bone — 1971 — — 2.50 — 5.00

Pitney, Gene

Blaze

☐ 351 — Going Back to My Love/Cradle of My Arms — 1958 — 7.50 — 15.00 — 30.00
As "Billy Bryan"

Epic

☐ 50332 — Dedication AKA This Song I Want to Dedicate to You/Sandman — 1977 — — 2.50 — 5.00
☐ 50461 — It's Over, It's Over/Walkin' in the Sun — 1977 — — 2.50 — 5.00

Festival

☐ 25002 — Please Come Back/I'll Find You — 1960 — 7.50 — 15.00 — 30.00

Musicor

☐ 1002 — (I Wanna) Love My Life Away/I Laughed So Hard I Cried — 1960 — 3.75 — 7.50 — 15.00
☐ 1002 — PS — (I Wanna) Love My Life Away/I Laughed So Hard I Cried — 1960 — 6.25 — 12.50 — 25.00
☐ 1006 — Louisiana Mama/Take Me Tonight — 1961 — 3.75 — 7.50 — 15.00
☐ 1006 — PS — Louisiana Mama/Take Me Tonight — 1961 — 6.25 — 12.50 — 25.00
☐ 1009 — Town Without Pity/Air Mail Special Delivery — 1961 — 3.75 — 7.50 — 15.00
☐ 1011 — Every Breath I Take/Mr. Moon, Mr. Cupid and I — 1961 — 5.00 — 10.00 — 20.00
Produced by Phil Spector
☐ 1011 — PS — Every Breath I Take/Mr. Moon, Mr. Cupid and I — 1961 — 6.25 — 12.50 — 25.00
☐ 1020 — (The Man Who Shot) Liberty Valance/Take It Like a Man — 1962 — 3.75 — 7.50 — 15.00
☐ 1022 — Only Love Can Break a Heart/If I Didn't Have a Dime — 1962 — 3.75 — 7.50 — 15.00
☐ 1026 — Half Heaven-Half Heartache/Tower Tall — 1962 — 3.75 — 7.50 — 15.00
☐ 1028 — Mecca/Teardrop by Teardrop — 1963 — 3.75 — 7.50 — 15.00
☐ 1028 — PS — Mecca/Teardrop by Teardrop — 1963 — 5.00 — 10.00 — 20.00
☐ 1032 — True Love Never Runs Smooth/Donna Means Heartbreak — 1963 — 3.75 — 7.50 — 15.00
☐ 1034 — Twenty-Four Hours from Tulsa/Lonely Night Dream — 1963 — 3.75 — 7.50 — 15.00
☐ 1034 — PS — Twenty-Four Hours from Tulsa/Lonely Night Dream — 1963 — 5.00 — 10.00 — 20.00
☐ 1036 — That Girl Belongs to Yesterday/Who Needs It — 1964 — 5.00 — 10.00 — 20.00
A-side written by Mick Jagger and Keith Richards and produced by Andrew Oldham
☐ 1036 — PS — That Girl Belongs to Yesterday/Who Needs It — 1964 — 6.25 — 12.50 — 25.00
☐ 1038 — Yesterday's Hero/Cornflower Blue — 1964 — 3.75 — 7.50 — 15.00
☐ 1039 — I'm Gonna Find Myself a Girl/Lips Are Redder — 1964 — — *Unreleased?*
☐ 1040 — It Hurts to Be in Love/Hawaii — 1964 — 3.75 — 7.50 — 15.00
☐ 1040 — PS — It Hurts to Be in Love/Hawaii — 1964 — 5.00 — 10.00 — 20.00
☐ 1045 — I'm Gonna Be Strong/Aladdin's Lamp — 1964 — 5.00 — 10.00 — 20.00
☐ 1045 — I'm Gonna Be Strong/E Se Domani — 1964 — 3.75 — 7.50 — 15.00
☐ 1045 — PS — I'm Gonna Be Strong/E Se Domani — 1964 — 5.00 — 10.00 — 20.00
☐ 1065 — Amici Miri/I Tuoi Anni Piu Belli — 1965 — — *Unreleased?*
☐ 1070 — I Must Be Seeing Things/Marianne — 1965 — 3.00 — 6.00 — 12.00
☐ 1070 — PS — I Must Be Seeing Things/Marianne — 1965 — 3.75 — 7.50 — 15.00
☐ 1093 — Last Chance to Turn Around/Save Your Love — 1965 — 3.00 — 6.00 — 12.00
☐ 1103 — Looking Through the Eyes of Love/There's No Living Without Your Loving — 1965 — 3.00 — 6.00 — 12.00
☐ 1130 — Princess in Rags/Amore Mio — 1965 — 3.00 — 6.00 — 12.00

Number		Title (A Side/B Side)	Year	VG	VG+	NM
❏ 1135		Baby, Ain't That Fine/	1965	3.00	6.00	12.00
		Everybody Knows But You and Me				
		With Melba Montgomery				
❏ 1150		Me Voy Para El Compo/Hojas Muertas	1966			Unreleased?
❏ 1155		Lei Mi Aspetta/Nessuno Mi Puo' Guidcare	1966	3.75	7.50	15.00
❏ 1171		Backstage/Blue Color	1966	2.50	5.00	10.00
❏ 1171	PS	Backstage/Blue Color	1966	3.75	7.50	15.00
❏ 1173		King and Queen/Being Together	1966	2.50	5.00	10.00
		With Melba Montgomery				
❏ 1200		(In the) Cold Light of Day/The Boss' Daughter	1966	2.50	5.00	10.00
❏ 1200	PS	(In the) Cold Light of Day/The Boss' Daughter	1966	3.75	7.50	15.00
❏ 1219		Just One Smile/Innamorato	1966	2.50	5.00	10.00
❏ 1233		For Me, This Is Happy/I'm Gonna Listen to Me	1967	2.50	5.00	10.00
❏ 1235		Don't Mean to Be a Preacher/	1967	2.50	5.00	10.00
		Animal Crackers (In Cellophane Boxes)				
❏ 1245		Tremblin'/Where Did the Magic Go	1967	2.50	5.00	10.00
❏ 1252		Somethin' Gotten Hold of My Heart/	1967	2.50	5.00	10.00
		Building Up My Dream World				
❏ 1299		The More I Saw of Her/Won't Take Long	1968	2.00	4.00	8.00
❏ 1306		She's a Heartbreaker/Conquistador	1968	2.50	5.00	10.00
❏ 1308		Somewhere in the Country/Lonely Drifter	1968	2.00	4.00	8.00
❏ 1331		Billy, You're My Friend/She Believes in Me	1968	2.00	4.00	8.00
❏ 1331		Billy, You're My Friend/Lonely Drifter	1968	2.00	4.00	8.00
❏ 1331	PS	Billy, You're My Friend/Lonely Drifter	1968	3.00	6.00	12.00
❏ 1348		Baby, You're My Kind of Woman/Hate	1969	2.00	4.00	8.00
❏ 1358		Maria Elena/The French Horn	1969	2.00	4.00	8.00
❏ 1361		Playing Games of Love/California	1969	2.00	4.00	8.00
❏ 1384		She Lets Her Hair Down (Early in the Morning)/	1969	2.00	4.00	8.00
		I Remember				
❏ 1394		All the Young Women/I Remember	1970		3.00	6.00
❏ 1405		A Street Called Hope/Think of Us	1970		3.00	6.00
❏ 1419		Shady Lady/Billy, You're My Friend	1970		3.00	6.00
❏ 1439		Higher and Higher/Beautiful Sounds	1971		3.00	6.00
❏ 1442		A Thousand Arms (Five Hundred Hearts)/	1971		3.00	6.00
		Gene, Are You There?				
❏ 1453		I Just Can't Help Myself/Beautiful Sounds	1972		3.00	6.00
❏ 1461		Summertime Dreaming/	1972		3.00	6.00
		A Thousand Arms (Five Hundred Hearts)				
❏ 1474		Shady Lady/Run, Run Roadrunner	1973		3.00	6.00

Pitney, Gene, and George Jones
(Also see "Pitney, Gene")
Musicor

❏ 1066		I've Got Five Dollars and It's Saturday Night/	1965	3.00	6.00	12.00
		Wreck on the Highway				
❏ 1071		I've Got a New Heartache/	1965			Unreleased?
		My Shoes Keep Walking Back to You				
❏ 1097		I'm a Fool to Care/Louisiana Man	1965	3.00	6.00	12.00
❏ 1097	PS	I'm a Fool to Care/Louisiana Man	1965	3.75	7.50	15.00
❏ 1115		Your Old Standby/Big Job	1965	3.00	6.00	12.00
❏ 1115	PS	Your Old Standby/Big Job	1965	3.75	7.50	15.00
❏ 1165		Y'All Come/That's All It Took	1966	2.50	5.00	10.00

Pittman, Barbara
Phillips Int'l.

❏ 3518		Two Young Fools in Love/	1957	10.00	20.00	40.00
		I'm Getting Better All the Time				
❏ 3527		Cold, Cold Heart/Everlasting Love	1958	10.00	20.00	40.00
❏ 3553		Handsome Man/The Eleventh Commandment	1960	5.00	10.00	20.00

Sun

❏ 253		I Need a Man/No Matter Who's to Blame	1956	37.50	75.00	150.00

Pitts, Gloria Jean
Imperial

❏ 5406		I Don't Stand No Quittin'/Things You Should Know	1956	12.50	25.00	50.00

Pixies Three, The
Mercury

❏ 72130		Birthday Party/Our Love	1963	3.75	7.50	15.00
❏ 72130	PS	Birthday Party/Our Love	1963	6.25	12.50	25.00
❏ 72208		Cold, Cold Winter/442 Glenwood Avenue	1963	3.75	7.50	15.00
❏ 72208	PS	Cold, Cold Winter/442 Glenwood Avenue	1963	6.25	12.50	25.00
❏ 72250		Gee/After the Party	1964	3.75	7.50	15.00
❏ 72288		It's Summertime U.S.A./The Hootch	1964	3.75	7.50	15.00
❏ 72288	PS	It's Summertime U.S.A./The Hootch	1964	6.25	12.50	25.00
❏ 72331		Love Walked In/Orphan Boy	1964	3.75	7.50	15.00
❏ 72357		Love Me, Love Me/Your Way	1964	3.75	7.50	15.00

Plaids, The
Era

❏ 3002		Around the Corner/He Stole Flo	1959	5.00	10.00	20.00

Liberty

❏ 55167		Hungry for Your Love/Chit-Chat	1958	100.00	200.00	400.00

Nasco

❏ 6011		Till the End of the Dance/My Pretty Baby	1958	5.00	10.00	20.00

Number		Title (A Side/B Side)	Year	VG	VG+	NM

Planets, The
(Probably three different groups)
Aljon

| ❏ 1244 | | Be Sure/Once Upon a Lifetime | 1962 | 75.00 | 150.00 | 300.00 |

Era

| ❏ 1038 | | Never Again/Stand There Mountain | 1957 | 6.25 | 12.50 | 25.00 |
| ❏ 1049 | | Be Sure/Wild Leaves | 1957 | 6.25 | 12.50 | 25.00 |

Motown

| ❏ 1485 | | Break It To Me Gently/Secret | 1980 | | 2.00 | 4.00 |

Nu-Clear

| ❏ 7422 | | I Need You So/Sharin' Lockers | 1959 | 5.00 | 10.00 | 20.00 |

Roulette

| ❏ 4551 | | You Are My Sunshine/Mr. Moon | 1964 | 3.75 | 7.50 | 15.00 |

Plant, Robert
(Former lead singer of Led Zeppelin)
Es Paranza

❏ 99333		Ship of Fools/Billy's Revenge	1988			3.00
❏ 99333	PS	Ship of Fools/Billy's Revenge	1988			3.00
❏ 99348		Tall Cool One/White, Clean and Neat	1988			3.00
❏ 99348	PS	Tall Cool One/White, Clean and Neat	1988	2.50	5.00	10.00
❏ 99373		Heaven Knows/Walking Towards Paradise	1988			3.00
❏ 99373	PS	Heaven Knows/Walking Towards Paradise	1988			3.00
❏ 99622		Too Loud/Kallalou Kallalou	1985			3.00
❏ 99644		Little by Little/Trouble Your Money	1985			3.00
❏ 99644	PS	Little by Little/Trouble Your Money	1985			3.00
❏ 99820		In the Mood/Horizontal Departure	1983			3.00
❏ 99820	PS	In the Mood/Horizontal Departure	1983			3.00
❏ 99844		Big Log/Far Post	1983			3.00
❏ 99844	PS	Big Log/Far Post	1983			3.00

Swan Song

❏ 99952		Pledge Pin/Fat Lip	1982		2.00	4.00
❏ 99952	PS	Pledge Pin/Fat Lip	1982	7.50	15.00	30.00
❏ 99979		Burning Down One Side/Moonlight in Samosa	1982		2.00	4.00
❏ 99979	PS	Burning Down One Side/Moonlight in Samosa	1982		3.00	6.00

Plastic Ono Band – See "Lennon, John"; "Ono, Yoko"

Platters, The
(Also see "Williams, Tony")
Antler

| ❏ 3000/1 | | I Do It All the Time/Shake What Your Mama Gave You | 1982 | | 3.00 | 6.00 |

Avalanche

| ❏ XW224 | | Sunday with You/If the World Loved | 1973 | 2.00 | 4.00 | 8.00 |
| | | *As "The Buck Ram Platters"* | | | | |

Entree

| ❏ 107 | | Won't You Be My Friend/Run While It's Dark | 1965 | 2.00 | 4.00 | 8.00 |
| | | *As "The Platters 1965"* | | | | |

Federal

❏ 12153		Give Thanks/Hey Now	1953	75.00	150.00	300.00
		As "Tony Williams and the Platters"				
❏ 12164		I'll Cry When You're Gone/I Need You All the Time	1954	75.00	150.00	300.00
❏ 12181		Roses of Picardy/Beer Barrel Polka	1954	75.00	150.00	300.00
❏ 12188		Tell the World/Love All Night	1954	25.00	50.00	100.00
❏ 12198		Voo-Vee-Ah-Bee/Shake It Up Mambo	1954	12.50	25.00	50.00
❏ 12204		Maggie Doesn't Work Here Anymore/Take Me Back, Take Me Back	1955	15.00	30.00	60.00
❏ 12244		Only You (And You Alone)/You Made Me Cry	1955	62.50	125.00	250.00
❏ 12250		Tell the World/I Need You All the Time	1956	12.50	25.00	50.00
❏ 12271		Give Thanks/I Need You All the Time	1956	12.50	25.00	50.00

Mercury

❏ 70633		Only You (And You Alone)/Bark, Battle and Ball	1955	12.50	25.00	50.00
		Earliest pressings have pink labels				
❏ 70633		Only You (And You Alone)/Bark, Battle and Ball	1955	10.00	20.00	40.00
		Black label				
❏ 70753		The Great Pretender/I'm Just a Dancing Partner	1955	10.00	20.00	40.00
		Maroon label				
❏ 70753		The Great Pretender/I'm Just a Dancing Partner	1955	5.00	10.00	20.00
		Black label				
❏ 70819		(You've Got) The Magic Touch/Winner Take All	1956	10.00	20.00	40.00
		Maroon label				
❏ 70819		(You've Got) The Magic Touch/Winner Take All	1956	5.00	10.00	20.00
		Black label				
❏ 70893		My Prayer/Heaven on Earth	1956	10.00	20.00	40.00
		Maroon label				
❏ 70893		My Prayer/Heaven on Earth	1956	5.00	10.00	20.00
		Black label				
❏ 70948		You'll Never Never Know/It Isn't Right	1956	7.50	15.00	30.00
		Maroon label				
❏ 70948		You'll Never Never Know/It Isn't Right	1956	5.00	10.00	20.00
		Black label				
❏ 71011		One in a Million/On My Word of Honor	1956	7.50	15.00	30.00

Number		Title (A Side/B Side)	Year	VG	VG+	NM
❏ 71032		I'm Sorry/He's Mine Maroon label	1957	7.50	15.00	30.00
❏ 71032		I'm Sorry/He's Mine Black label	1957	5.00	10.00	20.00
❏ 71093		My Dream/I Wanna Maroon label	1957	7.50	15.00	30.00
❏ 71093		My Dream/I Wanna Black label	1957	5.00	10.00	20.00
❏ 71184		Only Because/The Mystery of You	1957	6.25	12.50	25.00
❏ 71246		Helpless/Indifferent	1957	6.25	12.50	25.00
❏ 71289		Twilight Time/Out of My Mind	1958	6.25	12.50	25.00
❏ 71320		You're Making a Mistake/My Old Flame	1958	6.25	12.50	25.00
❏ 71353		I Wish/It's Raining Outside Black label	1958	6.25	12.50	25.00
❏ 71353		I Wish/It's Raining Outside Blue label	1958	7.50	15.00	30.00
❏ 71383		Smoke Gets In Your Eyes/No Matter What You Are Black label	1958	6.25	12.50	25.00
❏ 71383		Smoke Gets In Your Eyes/No Matter What You Are Blue label	1958	7.50	15.00	30.00
❏ 71427		Enchanted/The Sound and the Fury	1959	5.00	10.00	20.00
❏ 71467		Remember When/Love of a Lifetime	1959	5.00	10.00	20.00
❏ 71502		Where/Wish It Were Me	1959	5.00	10.00	20.00
❏ 71538		My Secret/What Does It Matter	1959	5.00	10.00	20.00
❏ 71563		Harbor Lights/Sleepy Lagoon	1960	5.00	10.00	20.00
❏ 71563	PS	Harbor Lights/Sleepy Lagoon	1960	7.50	15.00	30.00
❏ 71624		Ebb Tide/(I'll Be With You) In Apple Blossom Time	1960	5.00	10.00	20.00
❏ 71656		Red Sails in the Sunset/Sad River	1960	5.00	10.00	20.00
❏ 71656	PS	Red Sails in the Sunset/Sad River	1960	7.50	15.00	30.00
❏ 71697		To Each His Own/Down the River of Golden Dreams	1960	5.00	10.00	20.00
❏ 71697	PS	To Each His Own/Down the River of Golden Dreams	1960	7.50	15.00	30.00
❏ 71749		If I Didn't Care/True Lover	1961	3.75	7.50	15.00
❏ 71749	PS	If I Didn't Care/True Lover	1961	7.50	15.00	30.00
❏ 71791		Trees/A Mortal Lover	1961	3.75	7.50	15.00
❏ 71791	PS	Trees/A Mortal Lover	1961	7.50	15.00	30.00
❏ 71847		I'll Never Smile Again/You Don't Say	1961	3.75	7.50	15.00
❏ 71847	PS	I'll Never Smile Again/You Don't Say	1961	7.50	15.00	30.00
❏ 71904		Song for the Lonely/You'll Never Know	1961	3.75	7.50	15.00
❏ 71921		It's Magic/Reaching for a Star	1962	3.75	7.50	15.00
❏ 71921	PS	It's Magic/Reaching for a Star	1962	7.50	15.00	30.00
❏ 71986		More Than You Know/Every Little Moment	1962	3.00	6.00	12.00
❏ 72060		Memories/Heartbreak	1962	3.00	6.00	12.00
❏ 72107		Once in a While/I'll See You in My Dreams	1963	2.50	5.00	10.00
❏ 72129		Strangers/Here Comes Heaven Again	1963	2.50	5.00	10.00
❏ 72194		Viva Ju Joy/Quando Caliente El Sol	1963	2.50	5.00	10.00
❏ 72242		Java Jive/Michael Row the Boat Ashore	1964	2.50	5.00	10.00
❏ 72305		Sincerely/P.S. I Love You	1964	2.50	5.00	10.00
❏ 72359		Love Me Tender/Little Things Mean a Lot	1964	2.50	5.00	10.00
❏ 76160		Platterama Medley/Red Sails in the Sunset	1982	3.00	6.00	

Musicor

Number		Title (A Side/B Side)	Year	VG	VG+	NM
❏ 1166		I Love You 1000 Times/Don't Hear, Speak, See No Evil	1966	2.00	4.00	8.00
❏ 1195		Alone in the Light (Without You)/Devri	1966	2.00	4.00	8.00
❏ 1211		I'll Be Home/(You've Got) The Magic Touch	1966	2.00	4.00	8.00
❏ 1229		With This Ring/If I Had a Love	1967	2.50	5.00	10.00
❏ 1251		Washed Ashore (On a Lonely Island in the Sea)/ One in a Million	1967	2.00	4.00	8.00
❏ 1251		Washed Ashore (On a Lonely Island in the Sea)/ What Name Shall I Give You, My Love	1967	2.00	4.00	8.00
❏ 1262		On Top of My Mind/Shing-a-Ling-a-Loo	1967	2.00	4.00	8.00
❏ 1275		Sweet, Sweet Lovin'/Sonata	1967	2.00	4.00	8.00
❏ 1288		Love Must Go On/How Beautiful Our Love Is	1968	2.00	4.00	8.00
❏ 1302		So Many Tears/Think Before You Walk Away	1968	2.00	4.00	8.00
❏ 1322		Hard to Get a Thing Called Love/Why	1968	2.00	4.00	8.00
❏ 1341		Fear of Loving You/Sonata	1968	2.00	4.00	8.00
❏ 1443		Be My Love/Sweet Sweet Lovin'	1971	2.00	4.00	8.00

Owl

Number		Title (A Side/B Side)	Year	VG	VG+	NM
❏ 320		Sixteen Tons/Are You Sincere	1973	2.00	4.00	8.00

Ram

Number		Title (A Side/B Side)	Year	VG	VG+	NM
❏ 1004/5		My Ship Is Coming In/Guilty	1977	2.00	4.00	8.00
❏ 4852		Personality/Who's Sorry Now	1978	2.00	4.00	8.00

Playboys, The

(Numerous different groups, none of which have anything to do with Gary Lewis or John Fred)

ABC-Paramount

Number		Title (A Side/B Side)	Year	VG	VG+	NM
❏ 10070		You're All I See/Memories	1959	5.00	10.00	20.00

Ace

| ❏ 670 | | Gotta Feelin'/How Could You Forget | 1963 | 3.00 | 6.00 | 12.00 |

Cameo

| ❏ 142 | | Over the Weekend/Double Talk | 1958 | 5.00 | 10.00 | 20.00 |

Cat

| ❏ 108 | | Tell Me/Rock, Moan and Cry | 1954 | 12.50 | 25.00 | 50.00 |
| ❏ 115 | | Good Golly Miss Molly/Honey Run | 1955 | 12.50 | 25.00 | 50.00 |

Catalina

| ❏ 1069 | | Shortnin' Bread/Cheater Stomp | 1964 | 7.50 | 15.00 | 30.00 |

Number	Title (A Side/B Side)	Year	VG	VG+	NM
Chancellor					
❏ 1074	Boston Hop/What'd I Say	1961	3.75	7.50	15.00
	B-side by the Cousins				
❏ 1106	Duck Walk/If I Had My Way	1962	3.75	7.50	15.00
Cotton					
❏ 1008	Careful with My Heart/Girl of My Dreams	1962	6.25	12.50	25.00
Dolton					
❏ 8	Party Ice/Icy Fingers	1959	5.00	10.00	20.00
Heartbeat					
❏ 60	Harlem Nocturne/Blue Moon	1963	5.00	10.00	20.00
Imperial					
❏ 5586	Sweet Talk/Crazy Daisy	1959	5.00	10.00	20.00
Legato					
❏ 101	Mope De Mope/The Night Before Christmas	1963	5.00	10.00	20.00
Martinique					
❏ 101	Over the Weekend/Double Talk	1958	7.50	15.00	30.00
❏ 400	Please Forgive Me/Sing Along	1959	7.50	15.00	30.00
Mercury					
❏ 71228	Why Do I Love You, Why Do I Care/ Don't Do Me Wrong	1957	6.25	12.50	25.00
Rik					
❏ 572	Jungle Fever/Shotgun	1959	6.25	12.50	25.00
Souvenir					
❏ 1001	Believe It or Not/Hawaiian War Chant	1959	3.75	7.50	15.00
Tetra					
❏ 4447	One Question/So Good	1956	37.50	75.00	150.00
Titan					
❏ 1732	The Scramble/Cat Walk	1963	5.00	10.00	20.00
Zipp					
❏ 101	Sweet Talk/Crazy Daisy	1959	10.00	20.00	40.00

Player

Number	Title (A Side/B Side)	Year	VG	VG+	NM
Casablanca					
❏ 2265	It's for You/Tip of the Iceberg	1980		2.00	4.00
❏ 2295	Givin' It All/Tip of the Iceberg	1980		2.00	4.00
RCA					
❏ PB-13006	If Looks Could Kill/Born to Be with You	1981		2.00	4.00
❏ PB-13089	My Mind's Made Up/ Thank You for the Use of Your Love	1982		2.00	4.00
RSO					
❏ 879	Baby Come Back/Love Is Where You Find It	1977		2.50	5.00
❏ 890	This Time I'm In It for Love/Every Which Way	1978		2.00	4.00
❏ 908	Prisoner of Your Love/Join In the Dance	1978		2.00	4.00
❏ 914	Silver Lining/Forever	1978		2.00	4.00
❏ 920	I Just Wanna Be with You/Let Me Down Easy	1979		2.00	4.00

Playmates, The

Number	Title (A Side/B Side)	Year	VG	VG+	NM
ABC-Paramount					
❏ 10422	"A" My Name Is Alice/Just a Little Bit	1963	2.50	5.00	10.00
❏ 10468	She Never Looked Better/But Not Through Tears	1963	2.50	5.00	10.00
❏ 10492	I Cross My Fingers/I'll Never Get Over You	1963	2.50	5.00	10.00
❏ 10522	Guy Behind the Wheel/One Guy Left on the Corner	1964	2.50	5.00	10.00
Bell					
❏ 45,149	Foundation of Love/Davenu	1971		3.00	6.00
Colpix					
❏ 760	Fiddler on the Roof/Piece of the Sky	1964	2.00	4.00	8.00
❏ 769	One by One the Roses Died/Spanish Perfume	1965	2.00	4.00	8.00
Congress					
❏ 245	Ballad of Stanley the Lifeguard/ Should I Ask Someone Else to Tell Her	1965	2.00	4.00	8.00
Rainbow					
❏ 360	Nickelodeon Rag/I Have Only Myself to Blame	1956	7.50	15.00	30.00
Roulette					
❏ 4003	Barefoot Girl/Pretty Woman	1957	3.75	7.50	15.00
❏ 4022	Darling It's Wonderful/Magic Shoes	1957	3.75	7.50	15.00
❏ 4022	Darling It's Wonderful/Island Girl	1957	3.75	7.50	15.00
❏ 4037	Jo-Ann/You Can't Stop Me from Dreaming	1957	6.25	12.50	25.00
❏ 4056	Let's Be Lovers/Give Me Another Chance	1958	3.75	7.50	15.00
❏ 4072	Don't Go Home/Can't You Get It Through Your Head	1958	3.75	7.50	15.00
❏ 4100	The Day I Died/While the Record Goes Around	1958	3.75	7.50	15.00
❏ 4115	Beep Beep/Your Love	1958	6.25	12.50	25.00
❏ 4136	Star Love/The Thing-A-Ma-Jig	1959	3.00	6.00	12.00
❏ 4180	What Is Love/I Am	1959	3.00	6.00	12.00
❏ 4200	First Love/A-Ciu-E	1959	3.00	6.00	12.00
❏ 4211	On the Beach/The Song Everybody's Singing	1959	3.00	6.00	12.00
❏ 4227	Second Chance/These Things I Offer You	1960	3.00	6.00	12.00
❏ 4252	Parade of Pretty Girls/Our Wedding Day	1960	3.00	6.00	12.00
❏ 4276	Wait for Me/Eyes of Angel	1960	3.00	6.00	12.00
❏ 4322	Little Mis Stuck-Up/Real Life	1961	3.00	6.00	12.00
❏ 4370	Tell Me What She Said/Cowboys Never Cry	1961	3.00	6.00	12.00
❏ 4393	Wimoweh/One Little Kiss	1961	3.00	6.00	12.00

Number		Title (A Side/B Side)	Year	VG	VG+	NM
❑ 4417		A Rose and a Star/Bachelor Flat	1962	2.50	5.00	10.00
❑ 4432		Keep Your Hands in Your Pocket/The Cop on the Beat	1962	2.50	5.00	10.00
❑ 4464		What a Funny Way to Show It/Petticoats Fly	1962	2.50	5.00	10.00

Pleasure Fair, The
(With Robb Royer, later of Bread)
Uni

❑ 55016		Morning Glory Days/Fade In, Fade Out	1967	2.00	4.00	8.00
❑ 55078		Today/I'm Gonna Hafta Let You Go	1968	2.00	4.00	8.00

Pleasure Seekers
(Suzi Quatro was in this group)
Capitol

❑ 2050		(Theme from) Valley of the Dolls/If You Climb on the Tiger's Back	1967	5.00	10.00	20.00

Hideout

❑ 1006		Never Thought You'd Leave Me/What a Way to Die	1967	25.00	50.00	100.00

Mercury

❑ 72800		Good Kind of Hurt/Light of Love	1968	6.25	12.50	25.00

Pledges, The
(Actually Clyde Battin and Gary Paxton, who recorded as "Skip and Flip")
Rev

❑ 3517		Betty Jean/Her Bermuda Shorts	1958	6.25	12.50	25.00

Plumb, Eve
(Jan Brady of The Brady Bunch)
RCA Victor

❑ 74-0409		How Will It Be/Fortune Cookie Song	1970	3.75	7.50	15.00

Plummer, Dave, and the Plungers
Maybrook

❑ 320		Surfin' Monster/King of the Road	196?	10.00	20.00	40.00

Poco
(Also see "Meisner, Randy"; "Schmit, Timothy B.")
ABC

❑ 12126		Keep On Tryin'/Georgia, Bind My Ties	1975		2.50	5.00
❑ 12159		Makin' Love/Flyin' Solo	1976		2.50	5.00
❑ 12204		Rose of Cimarron/Tulsa Turnaround	1976		2.50	5.00
❑ 12295		Indian Summer/Me and You	1977		2.50	5.00
❑ 12439		Crazy Love/Barbados	1978		2.50	5.00

Atlantic

❑ 89629	DJ	Save a Corner of Your Heart (same on both sides)	1984			3.00
		May be promo only				
❑ 89650		This Old Flame/The Storm	1984			3.00
❑ 89674		Days Gone By/Daylight	1984			3.00
❑ 89851	DJ	Break of Hearts (same on both sides)	1983			3.00
		May be promo only				
❑ 89919		Shoot for the Moon/The Midnight Rodeo	1982			3.00
❑ 89970		Crosstown/High Sierra	1982			3.00

Epic

❑ 10501		Pickin' Up the Pieces/First Love	1969	2.50	5.00	10.00
❑ 10543		My Kind of Love/Hard Luck	1969	2.50	5.00	10.00
❑ 10636		You Better Think Twice/Anyway, Bye Bye	1970	2.00	4.00	8.00
❑ 10714		C'Mon/I Guess You Made It	1971	2.00	4.00	8.00
❑ 10804		Just for Me and You/Ol' Forgiver	1971	2.00	4.00	8.00
❑ 10816		You Are the One/Railroad Days	1971	2.00	4.00	8.00
❑ 10890		Good Feeling to Know/Early Times	1972		3.00	6.00
❑ 10958		I Can See Everything/Go and Say Goodbye	1973		3.00	6.00
❑ 11055		Here We Go Again/Fools Gold	1973		3.00	6.00
❑ 11092		Magnolia/Blue Water	1974		3.00	6.00
❑ 11141		Rocky Mountain Breakdown/Faith in the Families	1974		3.00	6.00
❑ 50076		Bitter Blue/High and Dry	1975		3.00	6.00

MCA

❑ 41023		Heart of the Night/Last Goodbye	1979		2.00	4.00
❑ 41103		Legend/Indian Summer	1979		2.00	4.00
❑ 41269		Under the Gun/Reputation	1980		2.00	4.00
❑ 41326		Midnight Rain/Fool's Paradise	1980		2.00	4.00
❑ 51034		Everlasting Kind/Friends in the Distance	1980		2.00	4.00
❑ 51172		Down on the River Again/Widowmaker	1981		2.00	4.00
❑ 52001		Seas of Heartbreaks/Feudin'	1982		2.00	4.00

RCA

❑ 9038-7-R		Call It Love/Lovin' You Every Minute	1989			3.00
❑ 9038-7-R	PS	Call It Love/Lovin' You Every Minute	1989			3.00
❑ 9131-7-R		Nothin' to Hide/If It Wasn't for You	1989			3.00
❑ 9131-7-R	PS	Nothin' to Hide/If It Wasn't for You	1989			3.00

Poindexter, Buster
(Actually David Johansen, ex-New York Dolls member)
RCA

❑ 2572-7-R		Under the Sea/Debourge Yourself	1990			3.00
❑ 5357-7-R		Hot Hot Hot/Cannibal	1987			3.00
❑ 5357-7-R	PS	Hot Hot Hot/Cannibal	1987			3.00

Number		Title (A Side/B Side)	Year	VG	VG+	NM
❏ 6893-7	DJ	Zat You Santa Claus/Hot Hot Hot	1987			3.00
❏ 7638-7-R		Oh Me Oh My (I'm a Fool for You Baby)/Cannibal	1988			3.00
❏ 8914-7-R		Hit the Road Jack/Heart of Gold	1989			3.00
❏ 9007-7-R		All Night Party (Hot Mix)/All Night Party (Power Mix)	1989			3.00
❏ 9195-7-R		Under the Sea/Debourge Yourself	1990			3.00

Poindexter, Don, and the Starlite Wranglers

Sun

Number		Title	Year	VG	VG+	NM
❏ 202		Now She Cares No More for Me/My Kind of Love	1954	500.00	1,000	2,000

Pointer Sisters, The
(Also see "Pointer, Anita"; "Pointer, Bonnie"; "Pointer, June"; "Pointer, Ruth")

Atlantic

Number		Title	Year	VG	VG+	NM
❏ 2845		Don't Try to Take the Fifth/Tulsa County	1971	5.00	10.00	20.00
❏ 2893		Destination No More Heartaches/Send Him Back	1972	5.00	10.00	20.00

Blue Thumb

Number		Title	Year	VG	VG+	NM
❏ 229		Yes We Can Can/Jada	1973		3.00	6.00
❏ 243		Wang Dang Doodle/Cloudburst	1973		3.00	6.00
❏ 248		Steam Heat/Shaky Flat Blues	1974		3.00	6.00
❏ 254		Fairytale/Love In Them Thar Hills	1974	2.50	5.00	10.00
		First pressing has a gray to white label and no reference to ABC				
❏ 254		Fairytale/Love In Them Thar Hills	1974		2.50	5.00
		Second pressing has a multicolor label with ABC logo				
❏ 262		Live Your Life Before You Die/Shaky Flat Blues	1975		2.50	5.00
❏ 265		How Long (Betcha' Got a Chick on the Side)/Easy Days	1975		2.50	5.00
❏ 268		Going Down Slowly/Sleeping Alone	1975		2.50	5.00
❏ 271		You Gotta Believe/Shaky Flat Blues	1976		2.50	5.00
❏ 275		Having a Party/Lonely Gal	1977		2.50	5.00
❏ 277		I Need a Man/I'll Get By Without You	1978		2.50	5.00

Columbia

Number		Title	Year	VG	VG+	NM
❏ 08015		Power of Persuasion/(Instrumental)	1988			3.00

MCA

Number		Title	Year	VG	VG+	NM
❏ 53120		Be There/(Instrumental)	1987			3.00

Motown

Number		Title	Year	VG	VG+	NM
❏ 902		Friends' Advice (Don't Take It)/Friends' Advice (Don't Take It) (Dub)	1990		2.00	4.00

Planet

Number		Title	Year	VG	VG+	NM
❏ YB-13254		American Music/I Want to Do It with You	1982		2.00	4.00
❏ YB-13327		I'm So Excited/Nothing But a Heartache (Live)	1982		2.00	4.00
❏ YB-13430		If You Wanna Get Back Your Lady/I'm So Excited	1983		2.00	4.00
❏ GB-13485		American Music/I'm So Excited	1983			3.00
		Gold Standard Series				
❏ YB-13639		I Need You/If You Wanna Get Back Your Lady	1983		2.00	4.00
❏ YB-13730		Automatic/Nightline	1984		2.00	4.00
❏ YB-13781		Jump (For My Love)/Heart Beat	1984		2.00	4.00
❏ GB-13795		I Need You/If You Wanna Get Back Your Lady	1984			3.00
		Gold Standard Series				
❏ YB-13857		I'm So Excited/Dance Electric	1984		2.00	4.00
❏ YB-13951		Neutron Dance/Telegraph Your Love	1984		2.00	4.00
❏ YB-14041		Baby Come and Get It/Operator	1985		2.00	4.00
❏ YB-14041	PS	Baby Come and Get It/Operator	1985		2.00	4.00
❏ GB-14072		Jump (For My Love)/Automatic	1985			3.00
		Gold Standard Series				
❏ GB-14076		Fire/He's So Shy	1985			3.00
		Gold Standard Series				
❏ GB-14077		Slow Hand/Should I Do It	1985			3.00
		Gold Standard Series				
❏ 45901		Fire/Love Is Like a Rolling Stone	1978		2.00	4.00
❏ 45901	PS	Fire/Love Is Like a Rolling Stone	1978		3.00	6.00
❏ 45902		Happiness/Too Late	1979		2.00	4.00
❏ 45906		Blind Faith/The Shape I'm In	1979		2.00	4.00
❏ 47916		He's So Shy/Movin' On	1980		2.00	4.00
❏ 47918		Es Tan Timido/Cosas Especiales	1980		3.00	6.00
❏ 47920		Could I Be Dreaming/Evil	1980		2.00	4.00
❏ 47925		Where Did the Time Go/Special Things	1981		2.00	4.00
❏ 47929		Slow Hand/Holdin' Out for Love	1981		2.00	4.00
❏ 47937		What a Surprise/Fall in Love Again	1981		2.00	4.00
❏ 47945		Sweet Lover Man/Got to Find Love	1981		2.00	4.00
❏ 47960		Should I Do It/We're Gonna Make It	1982		2.00	4.00

RCA

Number		Title	Year	VG	VG+	NM
❏ 5062-7-R		Goldmine/Sexual Power	1986			3.00
❏ 5062-7-R	PS	Goldmine/Sexual Power	1986			3.00
❏ 5112-7-R		All I Know Is the Way I Feel/Translation	1987			3.00
❏ 5230-7-R		Mercury Rising/Say the Word	1987			3.00
❏ 6865-7-R		He Turned Me Out/Translation	1988			3.00
❏ 6865-7-R	PS	He Turned Me Out/Translation	1988			3.00
❏ 8378-7-R		I'm in Love/Uh-Oh	1988			3.00
❏ GB-14354		Neutron Dance/Baby Come and Get It	1986			3.00
		Gold Standard Series				
❏ PB-14126		Dare Me/I'll Be There	1985			3.00
❏ PB-14126	PS	Dare Me/I'll Be There	1985			3.00
❏ PB-14224		Freedom/Telegraph Your Love	1985			3.00
❏ PB-14224	PS	Freedom/Telegraph Your Love	1985			3.00

Number		Title (A Side/B Side)	Year	VG	VG+	NM
SBK						
☐ S7-17637		Don't Walk Away/Tell It to My Heart	1993		2.00	4.00

Pointer, Anita
(One of the Pointer Sisters)

RCA						
☐ 5291-7-R		Overnight Success/Love Me Like You Do	1987			3.00
☐ 6847-7-R		More Than a Memory/Have a Little Faith in Love	1987			3.00

Pointer, Bonnie
(One of the Pointer Sisters)

Motown						
☐ 1451		Free Me from My Freedom-Tie Me to a Tree (Handcuff Me)/(Instrumental)	1978		2.00	4.00
☐ 1451	PS	Free Me from My Freedom-Tie Me to a Tree (Handcuff Me)/(Instrumental)	1978		3.00	6.00
☐ 1459		Heaven Must Have Sent You/ Heaven Must Have Sent You (LP Version)	1979		2.00	4.00
☐ 1478		I Can't Help Myself (Sugar Pie, Honey Bunch)/ I Wanna Make It (In Your World)	1979		2.00	4.00
☐ 1484		Deep Inside My Soul/I Love to Sing to You	1980		2.00	4.00
Private I						
☐ 04449		Your Touch/There's Nobody Quite Like You	1984			3.00
☐ 04658		Premonition/Tight Blue Jeans	1984			3.00
☐ 04819		The Beast in Me/There's Nobody Quite Like You	1985			3.00
☐ 04819	PS	The Beast in Me/There's Nobody Quite Like You	1985			3.00

Pointer, June
(One of the Pointer Sisters)

Columbia						
☐ 68748		Tight on Time (I'll Fit U In)/Fool for Love	1989			3.00
Planet						
☐ YB-13522		Ready for Some Action/Always	1983		2.00	4.00
☐ YB-13592		Don't Mess With Bill/I Understand	1983		2.00	4.00

Pointer, Ruth
(One of the Pointer Sisters)

Epic						
☐ 08115		Enemies Like You and Me/I Need You *With Billy Vera*	1988			3.00

Poison

Capitol						
☐ B-5686		Talk Dirty to Me/Want Some, Need Some *Originals have Capitol logo at top with colorband*	1987			3.00
☐ B-5686	PS	Talk Dirty to Me/Want Some, Need Some	1987		2.00	4.00
☐ S7-56969		Stand/Until You Suffer Some (Fire and Ice) *Blue vinyl*	1993		3.00	6.00
☐ S7-56969		Stand/Until You Suffer Some (Fire and Ice) *Black vinyl*	1993		2.00	4.00
Enigma						
☐ B-44004		I Want Action/Play Dirty	1987			3.00
☐ B-44004	PS	I Want Action/Play Dirty	1987			3.00
☐ B-44038		I Won't Forget You/Blame It on You	1987			3.00
☐ B-44038	PS	I Won't Forget You/Blame It on You	1987			3.00
☐ B-44145		Nothin' But a Good Time/Look But You Can't Touch	1988			3.00
☐ B-44145	PS	Nothin' But a Good Time/Look But You Can't Touch	1988			3.00
☐ B-44191		Fallen Angel/Bad to Be Good	1988			3.00
☐ B-44191	PS	Fallen Angel/Bad to Be Good	1988			3.00
☐ B-44203		Every Rose Has Its Thorn/Livin' for the Minute	1988			3.00
☐ B-44203	PS	Every Rose Has Its Thorn/Livin' for the Minute	1988			3.00
☐ B-44293		Your Mama Don't Dance/(B-side unknown)	1989			3.00
☐ B-44293	PS	Your Mama Don't Dance/(B-side unknown)	1989			3.00
☐ NR-44584		Swamp Juice (Soul-O)-Unskinny Bop/ Valley of Lost Souls	1990		2.00	4.00

Police, The
(Also see "Sting")

A&M						
☐ (# unknown)	PD	Roxanne/Can't Stand Losing You *Badge-shaped picture disc*	1979	2.50	5.00	10.00
☐ (no #)	(5)	The Police File	1985	12.50	25.00	50.00
Boxed set of five "A&M Memories" singles released to radio. Price is mostly for the box.						
☐ 2096		Roxanne/Dead End Job	1978		3.00	6.00
☐ 2147		Can't Stand Losing You/No Time This Time	1979		2.50	5.00
☐ 2147	PS	Can't Stand Losing You/No Time This Time	1979	2.50	5.00	10.00
☐ 2190		Message in a Bottle/Landlord	1979		2.50	5.00
☐ 2190	PS	Message in a Bottle/Landlord *Fold-out poster sleeve*	1979	2.50	5.00	10.00
☐ 2218		Bring On the Night/Visions of the Night	1980		2.50	5.00
☐ 2275		De Do Do Do, De Da Da Da/Friends *Standard A&M late-1970s label*	1980		2.00	4.00
☐ 2275		De Do Do Do, De Da Da Da/Friends *Yellowish custom label with blueish triangle (most common version)*	1980			3.00

Number		Title (A Side/B Side)	Year	VG	VG+	NM
❏ 2275		De Do Do Do, De Da Da Da/Friends	1980		2.00	4.00
		Red custom label with silver triangle				
❏ 2275	PS	De Do Do Do, De Da Da Da/Friends	1980		3.00	6.00
		Actually a title sleeve with large center hole				
❏ 2301		Don't Stand So Close to Me/A Sermon	1981			3.00
❏ 2301	PS	Don't Stand So Close to Me/A Sermon	1981			3.00
❏ 2371		Every Little Thing She Does Is Magic/Shambelle	1981			3.00
❏ 2371	PS	Every Little Thing She Does Is Magic/Shambelle	1981			3.00
❏ 2390		Spirits in the Material World/Flexible Strategies	1982			3.00
❏ 2390	PS	Spirits in the Material World/Flexible Strategies	1982			3.00
❏ 2408		Secret Journey/Darkness	1982			3.00
❏ 2408	PS	Secret Journey/Darkness	1982			3.00
❏ 2542		Every Breath You Take/Murder by Numbers	1983			3.00
❏ 2542	PS	Every Breath You Take/Murder by Numbers	1983			3.00
❏ 2569		King of Pain/Someone to Talk To	1983			3.00
❏ 2569	PS	King of Pain/Someone to Talk To	1983			3.00
❏ 2571		Synchronicity II/Once Upon a Daydream	1983			3.00
❏ 2571	PS	Synchronicity II/Once Upon a Daydream	1983			3.00
❏ 2614		Wrapped Around Your Finger/Tea in the Sahara (Live)	1984			3.00
❏ 2614	PS	Wrapped Around Your Finger/Tea in the Sahara (Live)	1984			3.00
❏ 2879		Don't Stand So Close to Me '86/ Don't Stand So Close to Me (Live)	1986			3.00
❏ 2879	PS	Don't Stand So Close to Me '86/ Don't Stand So Close to Me (Live)	1986			3.00
❏ 2908		Walking on the Moon/Message in a Bottle	1986		2.50	5.00
❏ 2908	PS	Walking on the Moon/Message in a Bottle	1986		2.50	5.00
❏ PR-4400	DJ	Message in a Bottle/Message in a Bottle (Live)	1980	2.50	5.00	10.00
		Star-shaped badge picture disc in folder; promo only				
❏ PR-4401	DJ	Don't Stand So Close to Me/ De Do Do Do, De Da Da Da	1981	2.50	5.00	10.00
		Star-shaped badge picture disc in folder; promo only				
❏ 8622		Roxanne/Can't Stand Losing You	198?			3.00
❏ 8631		De Do Do Do, De Da Da Da/ Don't Stand So Close to Me	198?			3.00
❏ 8633		Every Little Thing She Does Is Magic/ Spirits in the Material World	198?			3.00
❏ 8640		Every Breath You Take/Wrapped Around Your Finger	198?			3.00
❏ 8649		King of Pain/Synchronicity II	198?			3.00
❏ 25000		De Do Do Do, De Da Da Da (Japanese)/ De Do Do Do, De Da Da Da (Spanish)	1981		2.50	5.00
❏ 25000	PS	De Do Do Do, De Da Da Da (Japanese)/ De Do Do Do, De Da Da Da (Spanish)	1981		2.50	5.00
❏ 75021 8738 7		Canary in a Coal Mine/Message in a Bottle	1996			3.00
		Oldies reissue; first appearance of A-side on U.S. 45				

Poni-Tails, The
ABC-Paramount

Number		Title (A Side/B Side)	Year	VG	VG+	NM
❏ 9846		Wild Eyes and Tender Lips/ It's Just My Luck to Be Fifteen	1957	5.00	10.00	20.00
❏ 9934		Born Too Late/Come On, Just Dance With Me	1958	6.25	12.50	25.00
❏ 9969		Close Friends/Seven Minutes in Heaven	1958	5.00	10.00	20.00
❏ 9995		Early to Bed/Father Time	1959	5.00	10.00	20.00
❏ 10027		Moody/Ooh-Pah Polka	1959	5.00	10.00	20.00
❏ 10047		I'll Be Seeing You/I'll Keep Tryin'	1959	5.00	10.00	20.00
❏ 10077		Before We Say Goodnight/Come Be My Love	1960	5.00	10.00	20.00
❏ 10114		Who, When and Why/Oh My, You	1960	5.00	10.00	20.00

Marc

Number	Title (A Side/B Side)	Year	VG	VG+	NM
❏ 1001	Can I Be Sure/Still in Your Teens	1957	6.25	12.50	25.00

Point

Number	Title (A Side/B Side)	Year	VG	VG+	NM
❏ 8	Your Wild Heart/Que La Bozena	1957	6.25	12.50	25.00

Poole, Brian, and the Tremeloes
(Also see "Tremeloes, The")
Audio Fidelity

Number	Title (A Side/B Side)	Year	VG	VG+	NM
❏ 112	I Go Crazy/Love Me Baby	1965	2.50	5.00	10.00
❏ 121	Good Lovin'/Could It Be You	1966	2.50	5.00	10.00

Date

Number	Title (A Side/B Side)	Year	VG	VG+	NM
❏ 539	Everything I Touch Turns to Tears/I Need Her Tonight	1966	2.50	5.00	10.00
	Brian Poole solo				

London

Number	Title (A Side/B Side)	Year	VG	VG+	NM
❏ 9600	Keep On Dancing/Blue	1963	3.75	7.50	15.00
❏ 9625	Do You Love Me/Why Can't You Love Me	1964	3.75	7.50	15.00

Monument

Number	Title (A Side/B Side)	Year	VG	VG+	NM
❏ 840	Candy Man/I Can Dream	1964	3.00	6.00	12.00
❏ 846	Someone, Someone/ (Meet Me) Where We Used to Meet	1964	3.00	6.00	12.00
❏ 882	After a While/Don't Cry	1965	3.00	6.00	12.00

Popcorn and the Mohawks
Motown

Number	Title (A Side/B Side)	Year	VG	VG+	NM
❏ 1002	Custer's Last Man/Shimmy Gully	1960	15.00	30.00	60.00

Pope, Raymond, and the Lovetones
Squalor

Number	Title (A Side/B Side)	Year	VG	VG+	NM
❏ 1313	I Love Nadine/Star	1962	37.50	75.00	150.00

Number	Title (A Side/B Side)	Year	VG	VG+	NM

Poppy Family, The
London

☐ 129	Which Way You Goin' Billy/Endless Sleep	1970		3.00	6.00
☐ 139	That's When I Went Wrong/Shadows on My Wall	1970		2.50	5.00
☐ 148	I Was Wondering/Where Evil Grows	1971		2.50	5.00
☐ 164	No Good to Cry/I'll See You There	1971		2.50	5.00
☐ 172	Good Friends/Tryin'	1972		2.50	5.00

Popsicles, The
GNP Crescendo

| ☐ 336 | I Don't Want to Be Your Baby Anymore/Baby I Miss You | 1965 | 2.50 | 5.00 | 10.00 |

Knight

| ☐ 2002 | Thumb Print/This Is the End | 1958 | 10.00 | 20.00 | 40.00 |

Populaires, The
Marvello

| ☐ 5001 | Island of Paradise/I Lost My Heart | 1957 | 50.00 | 100.00 | 200.00 |

Porter, Royce
D

| ☐ 1026 | Lookin'/I Still Belong to You | 1958 | 25.00 | 50.00 | 100.00 |

Look

| ☐ 1001 | Yes I Do/(B-side unknown) | 1957 | 62.50 | 125.00 | 250.00 |

Mercury

| ☐ 71314 | Good Time/Beach of Love | 1958 | 25.00 | 50.00 | 100.00 |

Portraits, The
(More than one group)
Capitol

| ☐ F4181 | Close to You/Easy Cash | 1959 | 7.50 | 15.00 | 30.00 |

RCA Victor

| ☐ 47-7900 | Yo-Yo Girl/My Big Brother's Friend | 1961 | 3.75 | 7.50 | 15.00 |

Sidewalk

| ☐ 928 | A Million to One/Let's Tell the World | 1967 | 3.75 | 7.50 | 15.00 |
| ☐ 935 | Over the Rainbow/Runaround Girl | 1968 | 3.75 | 7.50 | 15.00 |

Tri-Disc

| ☐ 109 | We're Gonna Party/Three Blind Mice | 1963 | 3.75 | 7.50 | 15.00 |

Positively 13 O'Clock
Hanna-Barbera

| ☐ 500 | Psychotic Reaction/13 O'Clock Theme for Psychotics | 1966 | 10.00 | 20.00 | 40.00 |

Possessions, The
Britton

| ☐ 1003 | No More Love/You and Your Lies | 1964 | 10.00 | 20.00 | 40.00 |
| ☐ 1003 | No More Love/You and Your Lies — *Blue vinyl* | 1964 | 17.50 | 35.00 | 70.00 |

Parkway

| ☐ 930 | No More Love/You and Your Lies | 1964 | 5.00 | 10.00 | 20.00 |

Possum
Highland

| ☐ 10 | The Cockroach That Ate Cincinnati/Chula Vista | 1966 | 3.75 | 7.50 | 15.00 |

Powder Puffs, The
Imperial

| ☐ 66014 | (You Can't Take) My Boyfriend's Woody/Woody Wagon | 1964 | 6.25 | 12.50 | 25.00 |

Powell, Austin
Atlantic

| ☐ 968 | Wrong Again/What More Can I Ask | 1952 | 50.00 | 100.00 | 200.00 |

Decca

| ☐ 48206 | All This Can't Be True/Some Other Spring | 1951 | 20.00 | 40.00 | 80.00 |

Powell, Sandy
Herald

| ☐ 557 | Bon Bon/Pistol-Packin' Mama | 1961 | 25.00 | 50.00 | 100.00 |

Impala

| ☐ 211 | Bon Bon/Pistol-Packin' Mama | 1961 | 75.00 | 150.00 | 300.00 |

Singular

| ☐ 714 | My Jimmie/(B-side unknown) | 1958 | 6.25 | 12.50 | 25.00 |

Power Station, The
(Also see "Palmer, Robert")
Capitol

☐ 5444	Some Like It Hot/The Heat Is On	1985			3.00
☐ 5444 PS	Some Like It Hot/The Heat Is On	1985			3.00
☐ 5479	Get It On/Go To Zero	1985			3.00
☐ 5479 PS	Get It On/Go To Zero	1985			3.00
☐ 5511	Communication/Murderess	1985			3.00
☐ 5511 PS	Communication/Murderess	1985			3.00

Number	Title (A Side/B Side)	Year	VG	VG+	NM
Powers, Joey					
Amy					
❑ 892	Midnight Mary/ Where Do You Want the World Delivered	1963	3.00	6.00	12.00
❑ 898	Billy Old Buddy/In the Morning Gloria	1964	2.50	5.00	10.00
❑ 903	Love Is a Season/You Comb Her Hair	1964	2.50	5.00	10.00
❑ 914	Tears Keep Falling/Where Did the Summer Go	1964	2.50	5.00	10.00
❑ 986	Gimmie Gimmie/Baila Maria	1967	2.00	4.00	8.00
MGM					
❑ 13421	I Love You/Leave Me Alone	1965	2.00	4.00	8.00
RCA Victor					
❑ 47-8039	Two Tickets and a Candy Heart/ Jenny, Won't You Walk Up?	1962	2.50	5.00	10.00
❑ 47-8119	Don't Envy Me/Me, Myself and I	1962	2.50	5.00	10.00
❑ 47-9790	Hard to Be Without You/You're in a Bad Way	1969		2.50	5.00
	As "Joey Powers' Flower"				
❑ 74-0326	Land of the Midnight Sun/ So Sing the Children on the Avenue	1970		2.50	5.00
	As "Joey Powers' Flower"				
Powers, Johnny					
Fortune					
❑ 199	Honey Let's Go (To a Rock and Roll Show)/ Your Love	1955	50.00	100.00	200.00
Fox					
❑ 916	Rock Rock/Long Blonde Hair, Red Rose Lips	1957	125.00	250.00	500.00
Hi-Q					
❑ 5044	Rock the Universe/ Honey Let's Go (To a Rock and Roll Show)	1958	25.00	50.00	100.00
Sun					
❑ 327	With Your Love, With Your Kiss/Be Mine, All Mine	1959	12.50	25.00	50.00
Triodex					
❑ 103	A Teenage Prayer/A Young Boy's Heart	1960	6.25	12.50	25.00
Powersource					
Powervision					
❑ 8603	Dear Mr. Jesus/(B-side unknown)	1987	3.00	6.00	12.00
Precisions, The					
Atco					
❑ 6643	Don't Double (With Trouble)/Into My Life	1969	3.00	6.00	12.00
❑ 6669	New York City/You're the Best (That Ever Did It)	1969	3.00	6.00	12.00
D-Town					
❑ 1033	My Lover Come Back/I Wanna Tell My Baby	1965	62.50	125.00	250.00
❑ 1055	Mexican Love Song/You're Sweet	1965	6.25	12.50	25.00
Drew					
❑ 1001	Such Misery/Lover's Plea	1967	6.25	12.50	25.00
❑ 1002	Why Girl/What I Want	1967	3.75	7.50	15.00
❑ 1003	If This Is Love (I'd Rather Be Lonely)/ You'll Soon Be Gone	1967	6.25	12.50	25.00
❑ 1004	Instant Heartbreak/Dream Girl	1968	3.75	7.50	15.00
❑ 1005	A Place/Never Let Her Go	1968	3.75	7.50	15.00
Preludes, The					
(More than one group)					
Arliss					
❑ 1004	Lorraine/Oh Please, Genie	1961	20.00	40.00	80.00
Cub					
❑ 9005	Kingdom of Love/Vanishing Angel	1958	37.50	75.00	150.00
Empire					
❑ 103	Don't Fall in Love Too Soon/ I Want Your Arms Around Me (All the Time)	1956	25.00	50.00	100.00
Octavia					
❑ 8008	A Place for You (In My Heart)/That Would Be So Good	1962	10.00	20.00	40.00
Premeers, The					
Herald					
❑ 577	Diary of Our Love/Gee Oh Gee	1963	7.50	15.00	30.00
Premiers, The					
(Several different groups)					
Alert					
❑ 706	Jolene/Oh, Theresa	1959	20.00	40.00	80.00
Bond					
❑ 5803/4	Hop and Skip/Uh-Huh	1958	5.00	10.00	20.00
Cindy					
❑ 3008	China Doll/Life Is Grand	1958	15.00	30.00	60.00
Dig					
❑ 106	New Moon/Baby	1956	37.50	75.00	150.00
❑ 113	My Darling/Have a Heart	1956	62.50	125.00	250.00

Number	Title (A Side/B Side)	Year	VG	VG+	NM
Faro					
❏ 615	Farmer John/Duffy's Blues	1964	6.25	12.50	25.00
❏ 621	Get Your Baby/Little Ways	1965	3.00	6.00	12.00
❏ 624	Come On and Dance/Get On the Plane	1966	3.00	6.00	12.00
❏ 627	Ring Around My Rosie (Part 1)/	1967	3.00	6.00	12.00
	Ring Around My Rosie (Part 2)				
Fortune					
❏ 527	When You Are in Love/The Trap of Love	1956	12.50	25.00	50.00
Fury					
❏ 1029	I Pray/Pigtails, Eyes Are Blue	1960	7.50	15.00	30.00
Gone					
❏ 5009	Is It a Dream/Valerie	1957	75.00	150.00	300.00
	With "Let Me Share Your Dream" by The Deltas (Gone 5010) on Side 1 by mistake				
❏ 5009	Is It a Dream/Valerie	1957	15.00	30.00	60.00
	With correct track on side 1				
King					
❏ 6061	She's Always There/I'm Better Off Now	1966	5.00	10.00	20.00
Mink					
❏ 21	Tonight/I Think I Love You	1959	12.50	25.00	50.00
Nu-Phi					
❏ 367/8	Cruisin'/(B-side unknown)	1959	7.50	15.00	30.00
❏ 701	Firewater/Younger Than You	1960	7.50	15.00	30.00
Parkway					
❏ 807	Tonight/I Think I Love You	1959	5.00	10.00	20.00
RCA Victor					
❏ 47-6958	Run Along Baby/Hey Miss Fancy	1957	7.50	15.00	30.00
Rust					
❏ 5032	Falling Star/She Gives Me Fever	1961	12.50	25.00	50.00
Stax					
❏ 177	Make It Me/You Make a Strong Girl Weak	1965	7.50	15.00	30.00
Warner Bros.					
❏ 5443	Farmer John/Duffy's Blues	1964	3.75	7.50	15.00
❏ 5464	Annie Oakley/Blues for Arlene	1964	3.00	6.00	12.00

Presley, Elvis

(Even this extensive list is not complete; for example, most promos aren't listed. But it's a good start)

RCA

Note: All RCA (not RCA Victor) releases with a "447" prefix are from the Gold Standard Series and are "dog near top" reissues

Number	Title (A Side/B Side)	Year	VG	VG+	NM
❏ 447-0600	I Forgot to Remember to Forget/Mystery Train	1977		2.00	4.00
❏ 447-0601	That's All Right/Blue Moon of Kentucky	1977		2.00	4.00
❏ 447-0602	Good Rockin' Tonight/	1977		2.00	4.00
	I Don't Care If the Sun Don't Shine				
❏ 447-0603	Milkcow Blues Boogie/You're a Heartbreaker	1977		2.00	4.00
❏ 447-0604	Baby Let's Play House/	1977		2.00	4.00
	I'm Left, You're Right, She's Gone				
❏ 447-0605	Heartbreak Hotel/I Was the One	1977		2.00	4.00
❏ 447-0607	I Want You, I Need You, I Love You/My Baby Left Me	1977		2.00	4.00
❏ 447-0608	Hound Dog/Don't Be Cruel	1977		2.00	4.00
❏ 447-0609	Blue Suede Shoes/Tutti Frutti	1977		2.00	4.00
❏ 447-0613	Blue Moon/Just Because	1977		2.00	4.00
❏ 447-0614	Money Honey/One-Sided Love Affair	1977		2.00	4.00
❏ 447-0615	Lawdy Miss Clawdy/Shake, Rattle, and Roll	1977		2.00	4.00
❏ 447-0616	Love Me Tender/	1977		2.00	4.00
	Anyway You Want Me (That's How I Will Be)				
❏ 447-0617	Too Much/Playing for Keeps	1977		2.00	4.00
❏ 447-0618	All Shook Up/That's When Your Heartaches Begin	1977		2.00	4.00
❏ 447-0619	Jailhouse Rock/Treat Me Nice	1977		2.00	4.00
❏ 447-0620	(Let Me Be Your) Teddy Bear/Loving You	1977		2.00	4.00
❏ 447-0621	Don't/I Beg of You	1977		2.00	4.00
❏ 447-0622	Wear My Ring Around Your Neck/	1977		2.00	4.00
	Don'tcha Think It's Time				
❏ 447-0623	Hard Headed Woman/Don't Ask Me Why	1977		2.00	4.00
❏ 447-0624	One Night/I Got Stung	1977		2.00	4.00
❏ 447-0625	(Now and Then There's) A Fool Such As I/	1977		2.00	4.00
	I Need Your Love Tonight				
❏ 447-0626	A Big Hunk o'Love/My Wish Came True	1977		2.00	4.00
❏ 447-0627	Stuck on You/Fame and Fortune	1977		2.00	4.00
❏ 447-0628	It's Now or Never/A Mess of Blues	1977		2.00	4.00
❏ 447-0629	Are You Lonesome To-Night?/I Gotta Know	1977		2.00	4.00
❏ 447-0630	Surrender/Lonely Man	1977		2.00	4.00
❏ 447-0631	I Feel So Bad/Wild in the Country	1977		2.00	4.00
❏ 447-0634	(Marie's the Name) His Latest Flame/Little Sister	1977		2.00	4.00
❏ 447-0635	Can't Help Falling in Love/Rock-a-Hula Baby	1977		2.00	4.00
❏ 447-0636	Good Luck Charm/Anything That's Part of You	1977		2.00	4.00
❏ 447-0637	She's Not You/Just Tell Her Jim Said Hello	1977		2.00	4.00
❏ 447-0638	Return to Sender/Where Do You Come From	1977		2.00	4.00
❏ 447-0639	Kiss Me Quick/Suspicion	1977		2.00	4.00
❏ 447-0640	One Broken Heart for Sale/	1977		2.00	4.00
	They Remind Me Too Much of You				
❏ 447-0641	(You're the) Devil in Disguise/	1977		2.00	4.00
	Please Don't Drag That String Around				
❏ 447-0642	Bossa Nova Baby/Witchcraft	1977		2.00	4.00
❏ 447-0643	Crying in the Chapel/I Believe in the Man in the Sky	1977		2.00	4.00
❏ 447-0644	Kissin' Cousins/It Hurts Me	1977		2.00	4.00

Number		Title (A Side/B Side)	Year	VG	VG+	NM
❑ 447-0645		Such a Night/Never Ending	1977		2.00	4.00
❑ 447-0646		Viva Las Vegas/What'd I Say	1977		2.00	4.00
❑ 447-0647		Blue Christmas/Santa Claus Is Back in Town	1977		2.00	4.00
❑ 447-0647	PS	Blue Christmas/Santa Claus Is Back in Town	1977	2.50	5.00	10.00
		Does not mention "Gold Standard Series" on sleeve (see RCA Victor 447-0647)				
❑ 447-0648		Do the Clam/You'll Be Gone	1977		2.00	4.00
❑ 447-0649		Ain't That Loving You Baby/Ask Me	1977		2.00	4.00
❑ 447-0650		Puppet on a String/Wooden Heart	1977		2.00	4.00
❑ 447-0651		Joshua Fit the Battle/Known Only to Him	1977		2.00	4.00
❑ 447-0653		(Such An) Easy Question/It Feels So Right	1977		2.00	4.00
❑ 447-0654		I'm Yours/(It's a) Long, Lonely Highway	1977		2.00	4.00
❑ 447-0655		Tell Me Why/Blue River	1977		2.00	4.00
❑ 447-0656		Frankie and Johnny/Please Don't Stop Loving Me	1977		2.00	4.00
❑ 447-0657		Love Letters/Come What May	1977		2.00	4.00
❑ 447-0658		Spinout/All That I Do	1977		2.00	4.00
❑ 447-0659		Indescribably Blue/Fools Fall in Love	1977		2.00	4.00
❑ 447-0661		There's Always Me/Judy	1977		2.00	4.00
❑ 447-0662		Big Boss Man/You Don't Know Me	1977		2.00	4.00
❑ 447-0663		Guitar Man/High Heel Sneakers	1977		2.00	4.00
❑ 447-0664		U.S. Male/Stay Away	1977		2.50	5.00
❑ 447-0665		You'll Never Walk Alone/We Call on Him	1977		2.00	4.00
❑ 447-0666		Let Yourself Go/Your Time Hasn't Come Yet, Baby	1977		2.00	4.00
❑ 447-0667		A Little Less Conversation/Almost in Love	1977		2.00	4.00
❑ 447-0668		If I Can Dream/Edge of Reality	1977		2.00	4.00
❑ 447-0669		Memories/Charro	1977		2.00	4.00
❑ 447-0670		How Great Thou Art/His Hand in Mine	1977		2.00	4.00
❑ 447-0671		In the Ghetto/Any Day Now	1977		2.00	4.00
❑ 447-0672		Clean Up Your Own Back Yard/The Fair Is Moving On	1977		2.00	4.00
❑ 447-0673		Suspicious Minds/You'll Think of Me	1977		2.00	4.00
❑ 447-0674		Don't Cry Daddy/Rubberneckin'	1977		2.00	4.00
❑ 447-0675		Kentucky Rain/My Little Friend	1977		2.00	4.00
❑ 447-0676		The Wonder of You/Mama Liked the Roses	1977		2.00	4.00
❑ 447-0677		I've Lost You/The Next Step Is Love	1977		2.00	4.00
❑ 447-0678		You Don't Have to Say You Love Me/Patch It Up	1977		2.00	4.00
❑ 447-0679		I Really Don't Want to Know/There Goes My Everything	1977		2.00	4.00
❑ 447-0680		Where Did They Go, Lord/Rags to Riches	1977		2.00	4.00
❑ 447-0681		If Every Day Was Like Christmas/ How Would You Like to Be	1977		2.00	4.00
❑ 447-0682		Life/Only Believe	1977		2.00	4.00
❑ 447-0683		I'm Leavin'/Heart of Rome	1977		2.00	4.00
❑ 447-0684		It's Only Love/The Sound of Your Cry	1977		2.00	4.00
❑ 447-0685		An American Trilogy/Until It's Time for You to Go	1977		2.00	4.00
❑ 8760-7-R		Heartbreak Hotel/Heartbreak Hotel	1988		2.50	5.00
		B-side by David Keith				
❑ 8760-7-R	PS	Heartbreak Hotel/Heartbreak Hotel	1988		3.00	6.00
		"Pink Cadillac" sleeve				
❑ 8760-7-R	PS	Heartbreak Hotel/Heartbreak Hotel	1988	20.00	40.00	80.00
		Promo-only sleeve of RCA executive Butch Waugh dressed as Elvis				

Note: 10156 through 10489 are Gold Standard Series originally on the RCA Victor red label, reissued on the RCA "dog near top" label

Number		Title (A Side/B Side)	Year	VG	VG+	NM
❑ GB-10156		Burning Love/Steamroller Blues	1977		2.00	4.00
❑ GB-10157		Raised on Rock/If You Talk in Your Sleep	1977		2.00	4.00
❑ GB-10485		Take Good Care of Her/ I've Got a Thing About You, Baby	1977		2.00	4.00
❑ GB-10486		Separate Ways/Always on My Mind	1977		2.00	4.00
❑ GB-10487		T-R-O-U-B-L-E/Mr. Songman	1977		2.00	4.00
❑ GB-10488		Promised Land/It's Midnight	1977		2.00	4.00
❑ GB-10489		My Boy/Thinking About You	1977		2.00	4.00
❑ PB-10601		Hurt/For the Heart	1976	25.00	50.00	100.00
		Second pressings (very rare) on the 1976-88 "dog near top" black label				
❑ JB-10857	DJ	Moody Blue/She Thinks I Still Care	1976	250.00	500.00	1,000
		Colored vinyl pressings exist in five different colors -- red, white, gold, blue, green. Value is for any of them.				
❑ PB-10857		Moody Blue/She Thinks I Still Care	1976		2.50	5.00
❑ PB-10857	PS	Moody Blue/She Thinks I Still Care	1976	2.50	5.00	10.00
❑ JH-10951	DJ	Let Me Be There (mono/stereo)	1977	50.00	100.00	200.00
		Promo only				
❑ PB-10998		Way Down/Pledging My Love	1977		2.50	5.00
❑ PB-10998	PS	Way Down/Pledging My Love	1977	2.50	5.00	10.00
❑ PB-11099		Hound Dog/Don't Be Cruel	1977		2.00	4.00
❑ PB-11099	PS	Hound Dog/Don't Be Cruel	1977		2.00	4.00
		From boxes "15 Golden Records, 30 Golden Hits" and "20 Golden Hits in Full Color Sleeves"				
❑ PB-11100		In the Ghetto/Any Day Now	1977		2.00	4.00
❑ PB-11100	PS	In the Ghetto/Any Day Now	1977		2.00	4.00
		From boxes "15 Golden Records, 30 Golden Hits" and "20 Golden Hits in Full Color Sleeves"				
❑ PB-11101		Jailhouse Rock/Treat Me Nice	1977		2.00	4.00
❑ PB-11101	PS	Jailhouse Rock/Treat Me Nice	1977		2.00	4.00
		From box "15 Golden Records, 30 Golden Hits"				
❑ PB-11102		Can't Help Falling in Love/Rock-a-Hula Baby	1977		2.00	4.00
❑ PB-11102	PS	Can't Help Falling in Love/Rock-a-Hula Baby	1977		2.00	4.00
		From boxes "15 Golden Records, 30 Golden Hits" and "20 Golden Hits in Full Color Sleeves"				
❑ PB-11103		Suspicious Minds/You'll Think of Me	1977		2.00	4.00
❑ PB-11103	PS	Suspicious Minds/You'll Think of Me	1977		2.00	4.00
		From box "15 Golden Records, 30 Golden Hits"				
❑ PB-11104		Are You Lonesome To-Night?/I Gotta Know	1977		2.00	4.00
❑ PB-11104	PS	Are You Lonesome To-Night?/I Gotta Know	1977		2.00	4.00
		From boxes "15 Golden Records, 30 Golden Hits" and "20 Golden Hits in Full Color Sleeves"				
❑ PB-11105		Heartbreak Hotel/I Was the One	1977		2.00	4.00

Number		Title (A Side/B Side)	Year	VG	VG+	NM
❏ PB-11105	PS	Heartbreak Hotel/I Was the One	1977		2.00	4.00
		From boxes "15 Golden Records, 30 Golden Hits" and "20 Golden Hits in Full Color Sleeves"				
❏ PB-11106		All Shook Up/That's When Your Heartaches Begin	1977		2.00	4.00
❏ PB-11106	PS	All Shook Up/That's When Your Heartaches Begin	1977		2.00	4.00
		From boxes "15 Golden Records, 30 Golden Hits" and "20 Golden Hits in Full Color Sleeves"				
❏ PB-11107		Blue Suede Shoes/Tutti Frutti	1977		2.00	4.00
❏ PB-11107	PS	Blue Suede Shoes/Tutti Frutti	1977		2.00	4.00
		From boxes "15 Golden Records, 30 Golden Hits" and "20 Golden Hits in Full Color Sleeves"				
❏ PB-11108		Love Me Tender/ Any Way You Want Me (That's How I Will Be)	1977		2.00	4.00
❏ PB-11108	PS	Love Me Tender/ Any Way You Want Me (That's How I Will Be)	1977		2.00	4.00
		From boxes "15 Golden Records, 30 Golden Hits" and "20 Golden Hits in Full Color Sleeves"				
❏ PB-11109		(Let Me Be Your) Teddy Bear/Loving You	1977		2.00	4.00
❏ PB-11109	PS	(Let Me Be Your) Teddy Bear/Loving You	1977		2.00	4.00
		From boxes "15 Golden Records, 30 Golden Hits" and "20 Golden Hits in Full Color Sleeves"				
❏ PB-11110		It's Now or Never/A Mess of Blues	1977		2.00	4.00
❏ PB-11110	PS	It's Now or Never/A Mess of Blues	1977		2.00	4.00
		From box "15 Golden Records, 30 Golden Hits"				
❏ PB-11111		Return to Sender/Where Do You Come From	1977		2.00	4.00
❏ PB-11111	PS	Return to Sender/Where Do You Come From	1977		2.00	4.00
		From boxes "15 Golden Records, 30 Golden Hits" and "20 Golden Hits in Full Color Sleeves"				
❏ PB-11112		One Night/I Got Stung	1977		2.00	4.00
❏ PB-11112	PS	One Night/I Got Stung	1977		2.00	4.00
		From box "15 Golden Records, 30 Golden Hits"				
❏ PB-11113		Crying in the Chapel/I Believe in the Man in the Sky	1977		2.00	4.00
❏ PB-11113	PS	Crying in the Chapel/I Believe in the Man in the Sky	1977		2.00	4.00
		From box "15 Golden Records, 30 Golden Hits"				
❏ PB-11165		My Way/America	1977		2.50	5.00
❏ PB-11165	PS	My Way/America	1977	2.50	5.00	10.00
❏ PB-11165		My Way/America the Beautiful	1977	5.00	10.00	20.00
❏ PB-11165	PS	My Way/America the Beautiful	1977	6.25	12.50	25.00
❏ PB-11212		Unchained Melody/Softly, As I Leave You	1978	2.50	5.00	10.00
		Erroneously states "Vocal Accompaniment by Sherrill Nielsen" on "Unchained Melody" side				
❏ PB-11212		Unchained Melody/Softly, As I Leave You	1978		2.50	5.00
		No credit to Sherrill Nielsen on the "Unchained Melody" side				
❏ PB-11212	PS	Unchained Melody/Softly, As I Leave You	1978	2.50	5.00	10.00
❏ PP-11301		15 Golden Records, 30 Golden Hits	1977	15.00	30.00	60.00
		Includes 15 records (11099-11113) and outer box				
❏ PB-11320		(Let Me Be Your) Teddy Bear/Puppet on a String	1978		2.50	5.00
❏ PB-11320	PS	(Let Me Be Your) Teddy Bear/Puppet on a String	1978	2.50	5.00	10.00
❏ GB-11326		Moody Blue/For the Heart	1978		2.00	4.00
		Gold Standard Series				
❏ PP-11340		20 Golden Hits in Full Color Sleeves	1977	20.00	40.00	80.00
		Includes 10 records (11099, 11100, 11102, 11104-11109, 11111) and outer box				
❏ GB-11504		Way Down/My Way	1979		2.00	4.00
		Gold Standard Series				
❏ PB-11533		Are You Sincere/Solitaire	1979		2.50	5.00
❏ PB-11533	PS	Are You Sincere/Solitaire	1979	2.50	5.00	10.00
❏ PB-11679		There's a Honky Tonk Angel (Who Will Take Me Back In)/I Got a Feelin' in My Body	1979	3.75	7.50	15.00
		Has full production credits (background vocals, strings) listed in error on both sides				
❏ PB-11679		There's a Honky Tonk Angel (Who Will Take Me Back In)/I Got a Feelin' in My Body	1979		2.50	5.00
		Has production credits removed; only producers are listed				
❏ PB-11679	PS	There's a Honky Tonk Angel (Who Will Take Me Back In)/I Got a Feelin' in My Body	1979	2.50	5.00	10.00
❏ GB-11988		Unchained Melody/Are You Sincere	1980		2.00	4.00
		Gold Standard Series				
❏ JH-12158	DJ	Guitar Man (mono/stereo)	1981	75.00	150.00	300.00
		Promo only on red vinyl				
❏ PB-12158		Guitar Man/Faded Love	1981		2.50	5.00
❏ PB-12158	PS	Guitar Man/Faded Love	1981	2.50	5.00	10.00
❏ JB-12205	DJ	Lovin' Arms/You Asked Me To	1981	75.00	150.00	300.00
		Promo only on green vinyl				
❏ PB-12205		Lovin' Arms/You Asked Me To	1981		3.00	6.00
		Not issued with picture sleeve (bootlegs exist)				
❏ PB-13058		There Goes My Everything/You'll Never Walk Alone	1982		2.50	5.00
❏ PB-13058	PS	There Goes My Everything/You'll Never Walk Alone	1982	2.50	5.00	10.00
❏ GB-13275		Suspicious Minds/You'll Think of Me	1982		2.00	4.00
		Gold Standard Series				
❏ JH-13302		The Impossible Dream (The Quest)/ An American Trilogy	1982	25.00	50.00	100.00
❏ JH-13302	PS	The Impossible Dream (The Quest)/ An American Trilogy	1982	25.00	50.00	100.00
		Promo only, distributed to visitors to Elvis' birthplace in Tupelo, Mississippi, in 1982.				
❏ JB-13351	DJ	The Elvis Medley (Long Version)/ The Elvis Medley (Short Version)	1982	75.00	150.00	300.00
		Promo only on gold vinyl				
❏ PB-13351		The Elvis Medley/Always on My Mind	1982		2.50	5.00
❏ PB-13351	PS	The Elvis Medley/Always on My Mind	1982	2.50	5.00	10.00
❏ JB-13500	DJ	I Was the One/Wear My Ring Around Your Neck	1983	75.00	150.00	300.00
		Promo only on gold vinyl				
❏ PB-13500		I Was the One/Wear My Ring Around Your Neck	1983		2.50	5.00

Number		Title (A Side/B Side)	Year	VG	VG+	NM
❏ PB-13500	PS	I Was the One/Wear My Ring Around Your Neck	1983	2.50	5.00	10.00
❏ JB-13547	DJ	Little Sister/Paralyzed	1983	75.00	150.00	300.00
		Promo only on blue vinyl				
❏ PB-13547		Little Sister/Paralyzed	1983		2.50	5.00
❏ PB-13547	PS	Little Sister/Paralyzed	1983	2.50	5.00	10.00
❏ JB-13875	DJ	Baby Let's Play House/Hound Dog	1984	50.00	100.00	200.00
		Gold vinyl, custom label				
❏ PB-13875		Baby Let's Play House/Hound Dog	1984	10.00	20.00	40.00
		Gold vinyl, custom label				
❏ PB-13875	PS	Baby Let's Play House/Hound Dog	1984	10.00	20.00	40.00
❏ PB-13885		Blue Suede Shoes/Tutti Frutti	1984		2.00	4.00
		From box "Elvis' Greatest Hits, Golden Singles, Volume 1"; gold vinyl				
❏ PB-13885	PS	Blue Suede Shoes/Tutti Frutti	1984		2.00	4.00
❏ PB-13886		Don't Be Cruel/Hound Dog	1984		2.00	4.00
		From box "Elvis' Greatest Hits, Golden Singles, Volume 1"; gold vinyl				
❏ PB-13886	PS	Don't Be Cruel/Hound Dog	1984		2.00	4.00
❏ PB-13887		I Want You, I Need You, I Love You/Love Me	1984		2.00	4.00
		From box "Elvis' Greatest Hits, Golden Singles, Volume 1"; gold vinyl				
❏ PB-13887	PS	I Want You, I Need You, I Love You/Love Me	1984		2.00	4.00
❏ PB-13888		All Shook Up/(Let Me Be Your) Teddy Bear	1984		2.00	4.00
		From box "Elvis' Greatest Hits, Golden Singles, Volume 1"; gold vinyl				
❏ PB-13888	PS	All Shook Up/(Let Me Be Your) Teddy Bear	1984		2.00	4.00
❏ PB-13889		It's Now or Never/Surrender	1984		2.00	4.00
		From box "Elvis' Greatest Hits, Golden Singles, Volume 1"; gold vinyl				
❏ PB-13889	PS	It's Now or Never/Surrender	1984		2.00	4.00
❏ PB-13890		In the Ghetto/If I Can Dream	1984		2.00	4.00
		From box "Elvis' Greatest Hits, Golden Singles, Volume 1"; gold vinyl				
❏ PB-13890	PS	In the Ghetto/If I Can Dream	1984		2.00	4.00
❏ PB-13891		That's All Right/Blue Moon of Kentucky	1984		2.00	4.00
		From box "Elvis' Greatest Hits, Golden Singles, Volume 2"; gold vinyl				
❏ PB-13891	PS	That's All Right/Blue Moon of Kentucky	1984		2.00	4.00
❏ PB-13892		Heartbreak Hotel/Jailhouse Rock	1984		2.00	4.00
		From box "Elvis' Greatest Hits, Golden Singles, Volume 2"; gold vinyl				
❏ PB-13892	PS	Heartbreak Hotel/Jailhouse Rock	1984		2.00	4.00
❏ PB-13893		Love Me Tender/Loving You	1984		2.00	4.00
		From box "Elvis' Greatest Hits, Golden Singles, Volume 2"; gold vinyl				
❏ PB-13893	PS	Love Me Tender/Loving You	1984		2.00	4.00
❏ PB-13894		(Marie's the Name) His Latest Flame/Little Sister	1984		2.00	4.00
		From box "Elvis' Greatest Hits, Golden Singles, Volume 2"; gold vinyl				
❏ PB-13894	PS	(Marie's the Name) His Latest Flame/Little Sister	1984		2.00	4.00
❏ PB-13895		Are You Lonesome Tonight/Can't Help Falling in Love	1984		2.00	4.00
		From box "Elvis' Greatest Hits, Golden Singles, Volume 2"; gold vinyl				
❏ PB-13895	PS	Are You Lonesome Tonight/Can't Help Falling in Love	1984		2.00	4.00
❏ PB-13896		Suspicious Minds/Burning Love	1984		2.00	4.00
		From box "Elvis' Greatest Hits, Golden Singles, Volume 2"; gold vinyl				
❏ PB-13896	PS	Suspicious Minds/Burning Love	1984		2.00	4.00
❏ PB-13897		Elvis' Greatest Hits, Golden Singles, Volume 1	1984	3.75	7.50	15.00
		Box set of six 45s with sleeves (13885-13890) with box				
❏ PB-13898		Elvis' Greatest Hits, Golden Singles, Volume 2	1984	3.75	7.50	15.00
		Box set of six 45s with sleeves (13891-13896) with box				
❏ PB-13929		Blue Suede Shoes/Promised Land	1984	3.75	7.50	15.00
		Blue vinyl; incorrect label -- "Blue Suede Shoes" side says "Stereo" and "Promised Land" side says "Mono"				
❏ PB-13929		Blue Suede Shoes/Promised Land	1984	3.00	6.00	12.00
		Blue vinyl; correct label -- "Blue Suede Shoes" side says "Mono" and "Promised Land" side says "Stereo"				
❏ PB-13929	PS	Blue Suede Shoes/Promised Land	1984	2.50	5.00	10.00
❏ PB-14090		Always on My Mind/My Boy	1985	2.50	5.00	10.00
		Purple vinyl				
❏ PB-14090	PS	Always on My Mind/My Boy	1985	2.50	5.00	10.00
❏ PB-14237		Merry Christmas Baby/Santa Claus Is Back in Town	1985	3.75	7.50	15.00
		Green vinyl				
❏ PB-14237		Merry Christmas Baby/Santa Claus Is Back in Town	1985	3.75	7.50	15.00
		"Elvis 50th Anniversary" label				
❏ PB-14237		Merry Christmas Baby/Santa Claus Is Back in Town	1985		2.50	5.00
		Normal black RCA label				
❏ PB-14237	PS	Merry Christmas Baby/Santa Claus Is Back in Town	1985	3.00	6.00	12.00
❏ 62402		Don't Be Cruel/	1992		2.50	5.00
		Ain't That Lovin' You Baby (Fast Version)				
❏ 62402	PS	Don't Be Cruel/	1992		2.50	5.00
		Ain't That Lovin' You Baby (Fast Version)				
		Generic white sleeve with "Elvis -- The King of Rock 'n' Roll" sticker				
❏ 62403		Blue Christmas/Love Me Tender	1992		2.50	5.00
❏ 62403	PS	Blue Christmas/Love Me Tender	1992		2.50	5.00
		Generic white sleeve with "Elvis -- The King of Rock 'n' Roll" sticker				
❏ 62411		Silver Bells (Unreleased Version)/Silver Bells	1993		2.50	5.00
❏ 62449		Heartbreak Hotel/Hound Dog	1992		2.50	5.00
❏ 64476		Heartbreak Hotel/I Was the One//	1996			3.00
		Heartbreak Hotel (Alternate Take 5)/I Was the One (Alternate Take 2)				
❏ 64476	PS	Heartbreak Hotel/I Was the One//	1996			3.00
		Heartbreak Hotel (Alternate Take 5)/I Was the One (Alternate Take 2)				

RCA Victor

(Numerical prefiixes listed first in order of prefix, followed by letter prefixes listed in numerical, not alphabetical, order)

Number		Title (A Side/B Side)	Year	VG	VG+	NM
❏ 4-834-115	DJ	I'll Be Back	1966	4,000	6,000	8,000
		One-sided promo with designation "For Special Academy Consideration Only"				

Number	Title (A Side/B Side)	Year	VG	VG+	NM
❑ 37-7850	Surrender/Lonely Man *"Compact Single 33" (small hole, plays at LP speed)*	1961	150.00	300.00	600.00
❑ 37-7850	PS Surrender/Lonely Man *Special picture sleeve for above record*	1961	250.00	500.00	1,000
❑ 37-7880	I Feel So Bad/Wild in the Country *"Compact Single 33" (small hole, plays at LP speed)*	1961	250.00	500.00	1,000
❑ 37-7880	PS I Feel So Bad/Wild in the Country *Special picture sleeve for above record*	1961	300.00	600.00	1,200
❑ 37-7908	(Marie's the Name) His Latest Flame/Little Sister *"Compact Single 33" (small hole, plays at LP speed)*	1961	375.00	750.00	1,500
❑ 37-7908	PS (Marie's the Name) His Latest Flame/Little Sister *Special picture sleeve for above record*	1961	1,000	1,500	2,000
❑ 37-7908	PS (Marie's the Name) His Latest Flame/Little Sister *Special picture sleeve for above record; says "Stereo-Orthophonic" on sleeve in error*	1961	1,125	1,687	2,250
❑ 37-7968	Can't Help Falling in Love/Rock-a-Hula Baby *"Compact Single 33" (small hole, plays at LP speed)*	1961	1,000	1,500	2,000
❑ 37-7968	PS Can't Help Falling in Love/Rock-a-Hula Baby *Special picture sleeve for above record*	1961	2,000	3,000	4,000
❑ 37-7992	Good Luck Charm/Anything That's Part of You *"Compact Single 33" (small hole, plays at LP speed)*	1962	1,250	1,875	2,500
❑ 37-7992	PS Good Luck Charm/Anything That's Part of You *Special picture sleeve for above record*	1962	2,500	3,750	5,000

(A note on the 47- series and the horizontal line found on many 1956-57 releases: Research has shown that the "line" versions actually are later pressings than the unlined versions. Thus the value difference between the lined and unlined versions has disappeared.)

Number	Title (A Side/B Side)	Year	VG	VG+	NM
❑ 47-6357	I Forgot to Remember to Forget/Mystery Train *With horizontal line on label*	1955	15.00	30.00	60.00
❑ 47-6357	I Forgot to Remember to Forget/Mystery Train *No horizontal line on label*	1955	15.00	30.00	60.00
❑ 47-6380	That's All Right/Blue Moon of Kentucky *With horizontal line on label*	1955	15.00	30.00	60.00
❑ 47-6380	That's All Right/Blue Moon of Kentucky *No horizontal line on label*	1955	15.00	30.00	60.00
❑ 47-6381	Good Rockin' Tonight/ I Don't Care If the Sun Don't Shine *With horizontal line on label*	1955	15.00	30.00	60.00
❑ 47-6381	Good Rockin' Tonight/ I Don't Care If the Sun Don't Shine *No horizontal line on label*	1955	15.00	30.00	60.00
❑ 47-6382	Milkcow Blues Boogie/You're a Heartbreaker *With horizontal line on label*	1955	15.00	30.00	60.00
❑ 47-6382	Milkcow Blues Boogie/You're a Heartbreaker *No horizontal line on label*	1955	15.00	30.00	60.00
❑ 47-6383	Baby Let's Play House/ I'm Left, You're Right, She's Gone *With horizontal line on label*	1955	15.00	30.00	60.00
❑ 47-6383	Baby Let's Play House/ I'm Left, You're Right, She's Gone *No horizontal line on label*	1955	15.00	30.00	60.00
❑ 47-6420	Heartbreak Hotel/I Was the One *With horizontal line on label*	1956	7.50	15.00	30.00
❑ 47-6420	Heartbreak Hotel/I Was the One *No horizontal line on label*	1956	7.50	15.00	30.00
❑ 47-6540	I Want You, I Need You, I Love You/My Baby Left Me *With horizontal line on label*	1956	7.50	15.00	30.00
❑ 47-6540	I Want You, I Need You, I Love You/My Baby Left Me *No horizontal line on label*	1956	7.50	15.00	30.00
❑ 47-6540	PS This Is His Life: Elvis Presley *Promo-only sleeve issued with above single; no stock picture sleeve was issued*	1956	300.00	600.00	1,200
❑ 47-6604	Don't Be Cruel/Hound Dog *With horizontal line on label*	1956	7.50	15.00	30.00
❑ 47-6604	Don't Be Cruel/Hound Dog *No horizontal line on label*	1956	7.50	15.00	30.00
❑ 47-6604	PS Don't Be Cruel/Hound Dog *"Don't Be Cruel" listed on top of "Hound Dog!"*	1956	50.00	100.00	200.00
❑ 47-6604	PS Don't Be Cruel/Hound Dog *"Hound Dog!" listed on top of "Don't Be Cruel"*	1956	25.00	50.00	100.00

(Note: 47-6636 through 47-6642 were not issued with picture sleeves. Those that exist are bootlegs.)

Number	Title (A Side/B Side)	Year	VG	VG+	NM
❑ 47-6636	Blue Suede Shoes/Tutti Frutti *With horizontal line on label*	1956	15.00	30.00	60.00
❑ 47-6636	Blue Suede Shoes/Tutti Frutti *No horizontal line on label*	1956	15.00	30.00	60.00
❑ 47-6637	I Got a Woman/I'm Countin' On You *With horizontal line on label*	1956	12.50	25.00	50.00
❑ 47-6637	I Got a Woman/I'm Countin' On You *No horizontal line on label*	1956	12.50	25.00	50.00
❑ 47-6638	I'm Gonna Sit Right Down and Cry (Over You)/ I'll Never Let You Go (Little Darlin') *With horizontal line on label*	1956	12.50	25.00	50.00
❑ 47-6638	I'm Gonna Sit Right Down and Cry (Over You)/ I'll Never Let You Go (Little Darlin') *No horizontal line on label*	1956	12.50	25.00	50.00

Number	Title (A Side/B Side)	Year	VG	VG+	NM
❑ 47-6639	Tryin' to Get to You/I Love You Because *With horizontal line on label*	1956	12.50	25.00	50.00
❑ 47-6639	Tryin' to Get to You/I Love You Because *No horizontal line on label*	1956	12.50	25.00	50.00
❑ 47-6640	Blue Moon/Just Because *With horizontal line on label*	1956	12.50	25.00	50.00
❑ 47-6640	Blue Moon/Just Because *No horizontal line on label*	1956	12.50	25.00	50.00
❑ 47-6641	Money Honey/One-Sided Love Affair *With horizontal line on label*	1956	12.50	25.00	50.00
❑ 47-6641	Money Honey/One-Sided Love Affair *No horizontal line on label*	1956	12.50	25.00	50.00
❑ 47-6642	Lawdy Miss Clawdy/Shake, Rattle, and Roll *With horizontal line on label, but with no dog*	1956	50.00	100.00	200.00
❑ 47-6642	Lawdy Miss Clawdy/Shake, Rattle, and Roll *No horizontal line on label*	1956	12.50	25.00	50.00
❑ 47-6642	Lawdy Miss Clawdy/Shake, Rattle, and Roll *With horizontal line on label, dog on label as usual*	1956	12.50	25.00	50.00
❑ 47-6643	Love Me Tender/ Anyway You Want Me (That's How I Will Be) *With horizontal line on label*	1956	7.50	15.00	30.00
❑ 47-6643	Love Me Tender/ Anyway You Want Me (That's How I Will Be) *No horizontal line on label*	1956	7.50	15.00	30.00
❑ 47-6643	Love Me Tender/ Anyway You Want Me (That's How I Will Be) *No reference to the movie "Love Me Tender" on label*	1956	10.00	20.00	40.00
❑ 47-6643	PS Love Me Tender/ Anyway You Want Me (That's How I Will Be) *Black and white sleeve*	1956	37.50	75.00	150.00
❑ 47-6643	PS Love Me Tender/ Anyway You Want Me (That's How I Will Be) *Black and green sleeve*	1956	18.75	37.50	75.00
❑ 47-6643	PS Love Me Tender/ Anyway You Want Me (That's How I Will Be) *Black and dark pink sleeve*	1956	10.00	20.00	40.00
❑ 47-6643	PS Love Me Tender/ Anyway You Want Me (That's How I Will Be) *Black and light pink sleeve*	1956	7.50	15.00	30.00
❑ 47-6800	Too Much/Playing for Keeps *With horizontal line on label, dog on label as normal*	1957	7.50	15.00	30.00
❑ 47-6800	Too Much/Playing for Keeps *With horizontal line on label, but with no dog*	1957	50.00	100.00	200.00
❑ 47-6800	Too Much/Playing for Keeps *No horizontal line on label*	1957	7.50	15.00	30.00
❑ 47-6800	PS Too Much/Playing for Keeps	1957	15.00	30.00	60.00
❑ 47-6870	All Shook Up/That's When Your Heartaches Begin *With horizontal line on label*	1957	7.50	15.00	30.00
❑ 47-6870	All Shook Up/That's When Your Heartaches Begin *No horizontal line on label*	1957	7.50	15.00	30.00
❑ 47-6870	PS All Shook Up/That's When Your Heartaches Begin	1957	15.00	30.00	60.00
❑ 47-7000	(Let Me Be Your) Teddy Bear/Loving You *Label says "Let Me Be Your TEDDY BEAR" (no parentheses)*	1957	10.00	20.00	40.00
❑ 47-7000	(Let Me Be Your) Teddy Bear/Loving You *Parentheses around "Let Me Be Your", with horizontal line on label*	1957	7.50	15.00	30.00
❑ 47-7000	(Let Me Be Your) Teddy Bear/Loving You *Parentheses around "Let Me Be Your", no horizontal line on label*	1957	7.50	15.00	30.00
❑ 47-7000	PS (Let Me Be Your) Teddy Bear/Loving You	1957	15.00	30.00	60.00
❑ 47-7035	Jailhouse Rock/Treat Me Nice *With horizontal line on label*	1957	7.50	15.00	30.00
❑ 47-7035	Jailhouse Rock/Treat Me Nice *No horizontal line on label*	1957	7.50	15.00	30.00
❑ 47-7035	PS Jailhouse Rock/Treat Me Nice	1957	15.00	30.00	60.00
❑ 47-7150	Don't/I Beg of You *With horizontal line on label*	1958	5.00	10.00	20.00
❑ 47-7150	Don't/I Beg of You *No horizontal line on label*	1958	5.00	10.00	20.00
❑ 47-7150	PS Don't/I Beg of You	1958	12.50	25.00	50.00
❑ 47-7240	Wear My Ring Around Your Neck/ Don'tcha Think It's Time	1958	5.00	10.00	20.00
❑ 47-7240	PS Wear My Ring Around Your Neck/ Don'tcha Think It's Time	1958	12.50	25.00	50.00
❑ 47-7280	Hard Headed Woman/Don't Ask Me Why	1958	5.00	10.00	20.00
❑ 47-7280	PS Hard Headed Woman/Don't Ask Me Why	1958	12.50	25.00	50.00
❑ 47-7410	One Night/I Got Stung	1958	5.00	10.00	20.00
❑ 47-7410	PS One Night/I Got Stung	1958	12.50	25.00	50.00
❑ 47-7506	(Now and Then There's) A Fool Such As I/ I Need Your Love Tonight	1959	5.00	10.00	20.00

Number		Title (A Side/B Side)	Year	VG	VG+	NM
❏ 47-7506	PS	(Now and Then There's) A Fool Such As I/	1959	250.00	500.00	1,000.
		I Need Your Love Tonight				
		Sleeve promotes the "Elvis Sails" EP				
❏ 47-7506	PS	(Now and Then There's) A Fool Such As I/	1959	12.50	25.00	50.00
		I Need Your Love Tonight				
		Sleeve lists Elvis' EPs and Gold Standard singles				
❏ 47-7600		A Big Hunk o'Love/My Wish Came True	1959	5.00	10.00	20.00
❏ 47-7600	PS	A Big Hunk o'Love/My Wish Came True	1959	10.00	20.00	40.00
❏ 47-7740		Stuck on You/Fame and Fortune	1960	3.75	7.50	15.00
❏ 47-7740	PS	Stuck on You/Fame and Fortune	1960	7.50	15.00	30.00
❏ 47-7777		It's Now or Never/A Mess of Blues	1960	250.00	500.00	1,000.
		An early mispress is missing the piano part on the A-side. Has "L2WW-0100-3S" or "L2WW-0100-4S" in trail-off area.				
❏ 47-7777		It's Now or Never/A Mess of Blues	1960	3.75	7.50	15.00
		All other pressings with overdubbed piano				
❏ 47-7777	PS	It's Now or Never/A Mess of Blues	1960	7.50	15.00	30.00
❏ 47-7810		Are You Lonesome To-Night?/I Gotta Know	1960	3.75	7.50	15.00
❏ 47-7810	PS	Are You Lonesome To-Night?/I Gotta Know	1960	7.50	15.00	30.00
❏ 47-7850		Surrender/Lonely Man	1961	3.75	7.50	15.00
❏ 47-7850	PS	Surrender/Lonely Man	1961	7.50	15.00	30.00
❏ 47-7880		I Feel So Bad/Wild in the Country	1961	3.75	7.50	15.00
❏ 47-7880	PS	I Feel So Bad/Wild in the Country	1961	7.50	15.00	30.00
❏ 47-7908		(Marie's the Name) His Latest Flame/Little Sister	1961	3.75	7.50	15.00
		All copies of this record actually read "Marie's the Name HIS LATEST FLAME" (no parentheses)				
❏ 47-7908	PS	(Marie's the Name) His Latest Flame/Little Sister	1961	7.50	15.00	30.00
❏ 47-7968		Can't Help Falling in Love/Rock-a-Hula Baby	1961	3.75	7.50	15.00
❏ 47-7968	PS	Can't Help Falling in Love/Rock-a-Hula Baby	1961	7.50	15.00	30.00
❏ 47-7992		Good Luck Charm/Anything That's Part of You	1962	3.75	7.50	15.00
❏ 47-7992	PS	Good Luck Charm/Anything That's Part of You	1962	7.50	15.00	30.00
		Titles in blue and pink letters				
❏ 47-7992	PS	Good Luck Charm/Anything That's Part of You	1962	7.50	15.00	30.00
		Titles in rust and lavender letters				
❏ 47-8041		She's Not You/Just Tell Her Jim Said Hello	1962	3.75	7.50	15.00
❏ 47-8041	PS	She's Not You/Just Tell Her Jim Said Hello	1962	7.50	15.00	30.00
❏ 47-8100		Return to Sender/Where Do You Come From	1962	3.75	7.50	15.00
❏ 47-8100	PS	Return to Sender/Where Do You Come From	1962	7.50	15.00	30.00
❏ 47-8134		One Broken Heart for Sale/	1963	3.00	6.00	12.00
		They Remind Me Too Much of You				
❏ 47-8134	PS	One Broken Heart for Sale/	1963	6.25	12.50	25.00
		They Remind Me Too Much of You				
❏ 47-8188		(You're the) Devil in Disguise/	1963	50.00	100.00	200.00
		Please Don't Drag That String Along				
		First pressing with incorrect B-side title				
▆ 47-8188		(You're the) Devil in Disguise/	1963	3.00	6.00	12.00
		Please Don't Drag That String Around				
		Second pressing with correct B-side title				
❏ 47-8188	PS	(You're the) Devil in Disguise/	1963	6.25	12.50	25.00
		Please Don't Drag That String Around				
		All sleeves have correct B-side title				
❏ 47-8243		Bossa Nova Baby/Witchcraft	1963	3.00	6.00	12.00
❏ 47-8243	PS	Bossa Nova Baby/Witchcraft	1963	6.25	12.50	25.00
		"Coming Soon" on sleeve				
❏ 47-8243	PS	Bossa Nova Baby/Witchcraft	1963	6.25	12.50	25.00
		"Ask For" on sleeve				
❏ 47-8243	PS	Bossa Nova Baby/Witchcraft	1963	6.25	12.50	25.00
		No reference to another album on sleeve				
❏ 47-8307		Kissin' Cousins/It Hurts Me	1964	3.00	6.00	12.00
❏ 47-8307	PS	Kissin' Cousins/It Hurts Me	1964	6.25	12.50	25.00
❏ 47-8360		Viva Las Vegas/What'd I Say	1964	3.00	6.00	12.00
❏ 47-8360	PS	Viva Las Vegas/What'd I Say	1964	6.25	12.50	25.00
		"Coming Soon" on sleeve				
❏ 47-8360	PS	Viva Las Vegas/What'd I Say	1964	12.50	25.00	50.00
		"Ask For" on sleeve				
❏ 47-8400		Such a Night/Never Ending	1964	3.00	6.00	12.00
❏ 47-8400	DJ	Such a Night/Never Ending	1964	2,500	3,750	5,000
		An inexplicably rare regular white label promo				
❏ 47-8400	PS	Such a Night/Never Ending	1964	6.25	12.50	25.00
❏ 47-8440		Ain't That Loving You Baby/Ask Me	1964	2.50	5.00	10.00
❏ 47-8440	PS	Ain't That Loving You Baby/Ask Me	1964	6.25	12.50	25.00
		"Coming Soon" on sleeve				
❏ 47-8440	PS	Ain't That Loving You Baby/Ask Me	1964	6.25	12.50	25.00
		"Ask For" on sleeve				
❏ 47-8500		Do the Clam/You'll Be Gone	1965	2.50	5.00	10.00
❏ 47-8500	PS	Do the Clam/You'll Be Gone	1965	6.25	12.50	25.00
❏ 47-8585		(Such An) Easy Question/It Feels So Right	1965	2.50	5.00	10.00
❏ 47-8585	PS	(Such An) Easy Question/It Feels So Right	1965	6.25	12.50	25.00
		"Coming Soon" on sleeve				
❏ 47-8585	PS	(Such An) Easy Question/It Feels So Right	1965	6.25	12.50	25.00
		"Ask For" on sleeve				
❏ 47-8657		I'm Yours/(It's a) Long, Lonely Highway	1965	2.50	5.00	10.00
❏ 47-8657	PS	I'm Yours/(It's a) Long, Lonely Highway	1965	6.25	12.50	25.00
❏ 47-8740		Tell Me Why/Blue River	1965	2.50	5.00	10.00
❏ 47-8740	PS	Tell Me Why/Blue River	1965	6.25	12.50	25.00
❏ 47-8780		Frankie and Johnny/Please Don't Stop Loving Me	1966	2.50	5.00	10.00
❏ 47-8780	PS	Frankie and Johnny/Please Don't Stop Loving Me	1966	6.25	12.50	25.00

Number		Title (A Side/B Side)	Year	VG	VG+	NM
❏ 47-8870		Love Letters/Come What May	1966	2.50	5.00	10.00
❏ 47-8870	PS	Love Letters/Come What May	1966	6.25	12.50	25.00
		"Coming Soon" on sleeve				
❏ 47-8870	PS	Love Letters/Come What May	1966	6.25	12.50	25.00
		"Ask For" on sleeve				
❏ 47-8941		Spinout/All That I Do	1966	2.50	5.00	10.00
❏ 47-8941	PS	Spinout/All That I Do	1966	6.25	12.50	25.00
		"Watch For" on sleeve				
❏ 47-8941	PS	Spinout/All That I Do	1966	6.25	12.50	25.00
		"Ask For" on sleeve				
❏ 47-8950		If Every Day Was Like Christmas/ How Would You Like to Be	1966	5.00	10.00	20.00
❏ 47-8950	PS	If Every Day Was Like Christmas/ How Would You Like to Be	1966	10.00	20.00	40.00
❏ 47-9056		Indescribably Blue/Fools Fall in Love	1966	2.50	5.00	10.00
❏ 47-9056	PS	Indescribably Blue/Fools Fall in Love	1966	6.25	12.50	25.00
❏ 47-9115		Long Legged Girl (With the Short Dress On)/ That's Someone You Never Forget	1967	2.50	5.00	10.00
❏ 47-9115	PS	Long Legged Girl (With the Short Dress On)/ That's Someone You Never Forget	1967	6.25	12.50	25.00
		"Coming Soon" on sleeve				
❏ 47-9115	PS	Long Legged Girl (With the Short Dress On)/ That's Someone You Never Forget	1967	6.25	12.50	25.00
		"Ask For" on sleeve				
❏ 47-9287		There's Always Me/Judy	1967	2.50	5.00	10.00
❏ 47-9287	PS	There's Always Me/Judy	1967	6.25	12.50	25.00
❏ 47-9341		Big Boss Man/You Don't Know Me	1967	2.50	5.00	10.00
❏ 47-9341	PS	Big Boss Man/You Don't Know Me	1967	6.25	12.50	25.00
❏ 47-9425		Guitar Man/High Heel Sneakers	1968	2.50	5.00	10.00
❏ 47-9425	PS	Guitar Man/High Heel Sneakers	1968	6.25	12.50	25.00
		"Coming Soon" on sleeve				
❏ 47-9425	PS	Guitar Man/High Heel Sneakers	1968	6.25	12.50	25.00
		"Ask For" on sleeve				
❏ 47-9465		U.S. Male/Stay Away	1968	2.50	5.00	10.00
❏ 47-9465	PS	U.S. Male/Stay Away	1968	6.25	12.50	25.00
❏ 47-9547		Let Yourself Go/Your Time Hasn't Come Yet, Baby	1968	2.50	5.00	10.00
❏ 47-9547	PS	Let Yourself Go/Your Time Hasn't Come Yet, Baby	1968	6.25	12.50	25.00
		"Coming Soon" on sleeve				
❏ 47-9547	PS	Let Yourself Go/Your Time Hasn't Come Yet, Baby	1968	6.25	12.50	25.00
		"Ask For" on sleeve				
❏ 47-9600		You'll Never Walk Alone/We Call on Him	1968	3.00	6.00	12.00
❏ 47-9600	PS	You'll Never Walk Alone/We Call on Him	1968	25.00	50.00	100.00
❏ 47-9610		A Little Less Conversation/Almost in Love	1968	2.50	5.00	10.00
❏ 47-9610	PS	A Little Less Conversation/Almost in Love	1968	6.25	12.50	25.00
❏ 47-9670		If I Can Dream/Edge of Reality	1968	2.00	4.00	8.00
		First Elvis single on orange label				
❏ 47-9670	PS	If I Can Dream/Edge of Reality	1968	5.00	10.00	20.00
		Mentions his NBC-TV special on sleeve				
❏ 47-9670	PS	If I Can Dream/Edge of Reality	1968	5.00	10.00	20.00
		Does not mention his NBC-TV special on sleeve				
❏ 47-9731		Memories/Charro	1969	2.00	4.00	8.00
❏ 47-9731	PS	Memories/Charro	1969	5.00	10.00	20.00
❏ 47-9741		In the Ghetto/Any Day Now	1969	2.00	4.00	8.00
❏ 47-9741	PS	In the Ghetto/Any Day Now	1969	5.00	10.00	20.00
		"Coming Soon" on sleeve				
❏ 47-9741	PS	In the Ghetto/Any Day Now	1969	5.00	10.00	20.00
		"Ask For" on sleeve				
❏ 47-9747		Clean Up Your Own Back Yard/The Fair Is Moving On	1969	2.00	4.00	8.00
❏ 47-9747	PS	Clean Up Your Own Back Yard/The Fair Is Moving On	1969	5.00	10.00	20.00
❏ 47-9764		Suspicious Minds/You'll Think of Me	1969	2.00	4.00	8.00
❏ 47-9764	PS	Suspicious Minds/You'll Think of Me	1969	5.00	10.00	20.00
❏ 47-9768		Don't Cry Daddy/Rubberneckin'	1969	2.00	4.00	8.00
❏ 47-9768	PS	Don't Cry Daddy/Rubberneckin'	1969	3.75	7.50	15.00
❏ 47-9791		Kentucky Rain/My Little Friend	1969	2.00	4.00	8.00
❏ 47-9791	PS	Kentucky Rain/My Little Friend	1969	3.75	7.50	15.00
❏ 47-9835		The Wonder of You/Mama Liked the Roses	1970	2.00	4.00	8.00
❏ 47-9835	PS	The Wonder of You/Mama Liked the Roses	1970	3.75	7.50	15.00
❏ 47-9873		I've Lost You/The Next Step Is Love	1970	3.00	6.00	
❏ 47-9873	PS	I've Lost You/The Next Step Is Love	1970	3.75	7.50	15.00
❏ 47-9916		You Don't Have to Say You Love Me/Patch It Up	1970	3.00	6.00	
❏ 47-9916	PS	You Don't Have to Say You Love Me/Patch It Up	1970	3.75	7.50	15.00
❏ 47-9960		I Really Don't Want to Know/There Goes My Everything	1971	3.00	6.00	
❏ 47-9960	PS	I Really Don't Want to Know/There Goes My Everything	1971	3.75	7.50	15.00
		"Coming Soon" on sleeve				
❏ 47-9960	PS	I Really Don't Want to Know/There Goes My Everything	1971	3.75	7.50	15.00
		"Ask For" on sleeve				
❏ 47-9980		Where Did They Go, Lord/Rags to Riches	1971		3.00	6.00
❏ 47-9980	PS	Where Did They Go, Lord/Rags to Riches	1971	5.00	10.00	20.00
❏ 47-9985		Life/Only Believe	1971		3.00	6.00
❏ 47-9985	PS	Life/Only Believe	1971	7.50	15.00	30.00
❏ 47-9998		I'm Leavin'/Heart of Rome	1971		3.00	6.00
❏ 47-9998	PS	I'm Leavin'/Heart of Rome	1971	5.00	10.00	20.00
❏ 48-1017		It's Only Love/The Sound of Your Cry	1971		3.00	6.00
❏ 48-1017	PS	It's Only Love/The Sound of Your Cry	1971	3.75	7.50	15.00
❏ 61-7740	S	Stuck on You/Fame and Fortune	1960	100.00	200.00	400.00
		"Living Stereo" (large hole, plays at 45 rpm)				

Number		Title (A Side/B Side)	Year	VG	VG+	NM
❑ 61-7777	S	It's Now or Never/A Mess of Blues	1960	150.00	300.00	600.00
		"Living Stereo" (large hole, plays at 45 rpm)				
❑ 61-7810	S	Are You Lonesome To-Night?/I Gotta Know	1960	150.00	300.00	600.00
		"Living Stereo" (large hole, plays at 45 rpm)				
❑ 61-7850	S	Surrender/Lonely Man	1961	200.00	400.00	800.00
		"Living Stereo" (large hole, plays at 45 rpm)				
❑ 68-7850	S	Surrender/Lonely Man	1961	1,000	1,500	2,000
		"Compact Stereo 33" in "Living Stereo"				
❑ 74-0130		How Great Thou Art/His Hand in Mine	1969	6.25	12.50	25.00
❑ 74-0130	PS	How Great Thou Art/His Hand in Mine	1969	37.50	75.00	150.00
❑ 74-0572		Merry Christmas Baby/O Come All Ye Faithful	1971	3.75	7.50	15.00
❑ 74-0572	PS	Merry Christmas Baby/O Come All Ye Faithful	1971	10.00	20.00	40.00
❑ 74-0619		Until It's Time for You to Go/We Can Make the Morning	1971		3.00	6.00
❑ 74-0619	PS	Until It's Time for You to Go/We Can Make the Morning	1971	3.75	7.50	15.00
❑ 74-0651		He Touched Me/The Bosom of Abraham	1972	37.50	75.00	150.00
		"He Touched Me" actually plays at about 35 rpm in error. A-side has "AWKS-1277" stamped in trail-off wax.				
❑ 74-0651		He Touched Me/The Bosom of Abraham	1972	2.00	4.00	8.00
		"He Touched Me" plays correctly. A-side has "APKS-1277" stamped in trail-off wax.				
❑ 74-0651	PS	He Touched Me/The Bosom of Abraham	1972	30.00	60.00	120.00
❑ 74-0672		An American Trilogy/	1972	5.00	10.00	20.00
		The First Time Ever I Saw Your Face				
❑ 74-0672	PS	An American Trilogy/	1972	10.00	20.00	40.00
		The First Time Ever I Saw Your Face				
❑ 74-0769		Burning Love/It's a Matter of Time	1972		3.00	6.00
		Originals have orange labels				
❑ 74-0769		Burning Love/It's a Matter of Time	1974	37.50	75.00	150.00
		Very rare reissues have gray labels				
❑ 74-0769	PS	Burning Love/It's a Matter of Time	1972	3.75	7.50	15.00
❑ 74-0815		Separate Ways/Always on My Mind	1972		3.00	6.00
❑ 74-0815	PS	Separate Ways/Always on My Mind	1972	3.75	7.50	15.00
❑ 74-0910		Steamroller Blues/Fool	1973		3.00	6.00
❑ 74-0910	PS	Steamroller Blues/Fool	1973	3.75	7.50	15.00
Note: All RCA Victor releases with a "447" prefix are from the Gold Standard Series, though some were actually new singles						
❑ 447-0600		I Forgot to Remember to Forget/Mystery Train	1959	3.75	7.50	15.00
		Black label, dog on top				
❑ 447-0600		I Forgot to Remember to Forget/Mystery Train	1965	2.50	5.00	10.00
		Black label, dog on left				
❑ 447-0600		I Forgot to Remember to Forget/Mystery Train	1969	6.25	12.50	25.00
		Orange label				
❑ 447-0600		I Forgot to Remember to Forget/Mystery Train	1970	2.00	4.00	8.00
		Red label				
❑ 447-0601		That's All Right/Blue Moon of Kentucky	1959	3.75	7.50	15.00
		Black label, dog on top				
❑ 447-0601	DJ	That's All Right/Blue Moon of Kentucky	1964	25.00	50.00	100.00
❑ 447-0601	PS	That's All Right/Blue Moon of Kentucky	1964	50.00	100.00	200.00
❑ 447-0601		That's All Right/Blue Moon of Kentucky	1965	2.50	5.00	10.00
		Black label, dog on left				
❑ 447-0601		That's All Right/Blue Moon of Kentucky	1969	2.00	4.00	8.00
		Red label; B-side artist credit is misspelled "Elvis Presely"				
❑ 447-0602		Good Rockin' Tonight/	1959	3.75	7.50	15.00
		I Don't Care If the Sun Don't Shine				
		Black label, dog on top				
❑ 447-0602	DJ	Good Rockin' Tonight/	1964	25.00	50.00	100.00
		I Don't Care If the Sun Don't Shine				
❑ 447-0602	PS	Good Rockin' Tonight/	1964	50.00	100.00	200.00
		I Don't Care If the Sun Don't Shine				
❑ 447-0602		Good Rockin' Tonight/	1965	2.50	5.00	10.00
		I Don't Care If the Sun Don't Shine				
		Black label, dog on left				
❑ 447-0602		Good Rockin' Tonight/	1970	2.00	4.00	8.00
		I Don't Care If the Sun Don't Shine				
		Red label				
❑ 447-0603		Milkcow Blues Boogie/You're a Heartbreaker	1959	3.75	7.50	15.00
		Black label, dog on top				
❑ 447-0603		Milkcow Blues Boogie/You're a Heartbreaker	1965	2.50	5.00	10.00
		Black label, dog on left				
❑ 447-0603		Milkcow Blues Boogie/You're a Heartbreaker	1969	6.25	12.50	25.00
		Orange label				
❑ 447-0603		Milkcow Blues Boogie/You're a Heartbreaker	1970	2.00	4.00	8.00
		Red label				
❑ 447-0604		Baby Let's Play House/	1959	3.75	7.50	15.00
		I'm Left, You're Right, She's Gone				
		Black label, dog on top				
❑ 447-0604		Baby Let's Play House/	1965	2.50	5.00	10.00
		I'm Left, You're Right, She's Gone				
		Black label, dog on left				
❑ 447-0604		Baby Let's Play House/	1970	2.00	4.00	8.00
		I'm Left, You're Right, She's Gone				
		Red label				
❑ 447-0605		Heartbreak Hotel/I Was the One	1959	3.75	7.50	15.00
		Black label, dog on top				
❑ 447-0605	DJ	Heartbreak Hotel/I Was the One	1964	25.00	50.00	100.00
❑ 447-0605	PS	Heartbreak Hotel/I Was the One	1964	50.00	100.00	200.00

Number	Title (A Side/B Side)	Year	VG	VG+	NM
❑ 447-0605	Heartbreak Hotel/I Was the One *Black label, dog on left*	1965	2.50	5.00	10.00
❑ 447-0605	Heartbreak Hotel/I Was the One *Orange label*	1969	6.25	12.50	25.00
❑ 447-0605	Heartbreak Hotel/I Was the One *Red label*	1970	2.00	4.00	8.00
❑ 447-0607	I Want You, I Need You, I Love You/My Baby Left Me *Black label, dog on top*	1959	3.75	7.50	15.00
❑ 447-0607	I Want You, I Need You, I Love You/My Baby Left Me *Black label, dog on left*	1965	2.50	5.00	10.00
❑ 447-0607	I Want You, I Need You, I Love You/My Baby Left Me *Orange label*	1969	6.25	12.50	25.00
❑ 447-0607	I Want You, I Need You, I Love You/My Baby Left Me *Red label*	1970	2.00	4.00	8.00
❑ 447-0608	Hound Dog/Don't Be Cruel *Black label, dog on top*	1959	3.75	7.50	15.00
❑ 447-0608	DJ Hound Dog/Don't Be Cruel	1964	25.00	50.00	100.00
❑ 447-0608	PS Hound Dog/Don't Be Cruel	1964	50.00	100.00	200.00
❑ 447-0608	Hound Dog/Don't Be Cruel *Black label, dog on left*	1965	2.50	5.00	10.00
❑ 447-0608	Hound Dog/Don't Be Cruel *Orange label*	1969	6.25	12.50	25.00
❑ 447-0608	Hound Dog/Don't Be Cruel *Red label*	1970	2.00	4.00	8.00
❑ 447-0609	Blue Suede Shoes/Tutti Frutti *Black label, dog on top*	1959	3.75	7.50	15.00
❑ 447-0609	Blue Suede Shoes/Tutti Frutti *Black label, dog on left*	1965	2.50	5.00	10.00
❑ 447-0609	Blue Suede Shoes/Tutti Frutti *Orange label*	1969	6.25	12.50	25.00
❑ 447-0609	Blue Suede Shoes/Tutti Frutti *Red label*	1970	2.00	4.00	8.00
❑ 447-0610	I Got a Woman/I'm Countin' On You *Black label, dog on top*	1959	3.75	7.50	15.00
❑ 447-0611	I'm Gonna Sit Right Down and Cry (Over You)/ I'll Never Let You Go (Little Darlin') *Black label, dog on top*	1959	3.75	7.50	15.00
❑ 447-0612	Tryin' to Get to You/I Love You Because *Black label, dog on top*	1959	3.75	7.50	15.00
❑ 447-0613	Blue Moon/Just Because *Black label, dog on top*	1959	3.75	7.50	15.00
❑ 447-0613	Blue Moon/Just Because *Black label, dog on left*	1965	2.50	5.00	10.00
❑ 447-0613	Blue Moon/Just Because *Orange label*	1969	6.25	12.50	25.00
❑ 447-0613	Blue Moon/Just Because *Red label*	1970	2.00	4.00	8.00
❑ 447-0614	Money Honey/One-Sided Love Affair *Black label, dog on top*	1959	3.75	7.50	15.00
❑ 447-0614	Money Honey/One-Sided Love Affair *Black label, dog on left*	1965	2.50	5.00	10.00
❑ 447-0614	Money Honey/One-Sided Love Affair *Orange label*	1969	6.25	12.50	25.00
❑ 447-0614	Money Honey/One-Sided Love Affair *Red label*	1970	2.00	4.00	8.00
❑ 447-0615	Lawdy Miss Clawdy/Shake, Rattle, and Roll *Black label, dog on top*	1959	3.75	7.50	15.00
❑ 447-0615	Lawdy Miss Clawdy/Shake, Rattle, and Roll *Black label, dog on left*	1965	2.50	5.00	10.00
❑ 447-0615	Lawdy Miss Clawdy/Shake, Rattle, and Roll *Orange label*	1969	6.25	12.50	25.00
❑ 447-0615	Lawdy Miss Clawdy/Shake, Rattle, and Roll *Red label*	1970	2.00	4.00	8.00
❑ 447-0616	Love Me Tender/ Anyway You Want Me (That's How I Will Be) *Black label, dog on top*	1959	3.75	7.50	15.00
❑ 447-0616	Love Me Tender/ Anyway You Want Me (That's How I Will Be) *Black label, dog on left*	1965	2.50	5.00	10.00
❑ 447-0616	Love Me Tender/ Anyway You Want Me (That's How I Will Be) *Orange label*	1969	6.25	12.50	25.00
❑ 447-0616	Love Me Tender/ Anyway You Want Me (That's How I Will Be) *Red label*	1970	2.00	4.00	8.00
❑ 447-0617	Too Much/Playing for Keeps *Black label, dog on top*	1959	3.75	7.50	15.00
❑ 447-0617	Too Much/Playing for Keeps *Black label, dog on left*	1965	2.50	5.00	10.00
❑ 447-0617	Too Much/Playing for Keeps *Orange label*	1969	6.25	12.50	25.00

Number	Title (A Side/B Side)	Year	VG	VG+	NM
❏ 447-0617	Too Much/Playing for Keeps *Red label*	1970	2.00	4.00	8.00
❏ 447-0618	All Shook Up/That's When Your Heartaches Begin *Black label, dog on top*	1959	3.75	7.50	15.00
❏ 447-0618 DJ	All Shook Up/That's When Your Heartaches Begin	1964	25.00	50.00	100.00
❏ 447-0618 PS	All Shook Up/That's When Your Heartaches Begin	1964	50.00	100.00	200.00
❏ 447-0618	All Shook Up/That's When Your Heartaches Begin *Black label, dog on left*	1965	2.50	5.00	10.00
❏ 447-0618	All Shook Up/That's When Your Heartaches Begin *Orange label*	1969	6.25	12.50	25.00
❏ 447-0618	All Shook Up/That's When Your Heartaches Begin *Red label*	1970	2.00	4.00	8.00
❏ 447-0619	Jailhouse Rock/Treat Me Nice *Black label, dog on top*	1959	3.75	7.50	15.00
❏ 447-0619	Jailhouse Rock/Treat Me Nice *Black label, dog on left*	1965	2.50	5.00	10.00
❏ 447-0619	Jailhouse Rock/Treat Me Nice *Orange label*	1969	6.25	12.50	25.00
❏ 447-0619	Jailhouse Rock/Treat Me Nice *Red label*	1970	2.00	4.00	8.00
❏ 447-0620	(Let Me Be Your) Teddy Bear/Loving You *Black label, dog on top*	1959	3.75	7.50	15.00
❏ 447-0620	(Let Me Be Your) Teddy Bear/Loving You *Black label, dog on left*	1965	2.50	5.00	10.00
❏ 447-0620	(Let Me Be Your) Teddy Bear/Loving You *Orange label*	1969	6.25	12.50	25.00
❏ 447-0620	(Let Me Be Your) Teddy Bear/Loving You *Red label*	1970	2.00	4.00	8.00
❏ 447-0620	Don't/I Beg of You *Red label*	1970	2.00	4.00	8.00
❏ 447-0621	Don't/I Beg of You *Black label, dog on top*	1961	3.00	6.00	12.00
❏ 447-0621	Don't/I Beg of You *Black label, dog on left*	1965	2.50	5.00	10.00
❏ 447-0621	Don't/I Beg of You *Orange label*	1969	6.25	12.50	25.00
❏ 447-0622	Wear My Ring Around Your Neck/ Don'tcha Think It's Time *Black label, dog on top*	1961	3.00	6.00	12.00
❏ 447-0622	Wear My Ring Around Your Neck/ Don'tcha Think It's Time *Black label, dog on left*	1965	2.50	5.00	10.00
❏ 447-0622	Wear My Ring Around Your Neck/ Don'tcha Think It's Time *Orange label*	1969	6.25	12.50	25.00
❏ 447-0622	Wear My Ring Around Your Neck/ Don'tcha Think It's Time *Red label*	1970	2.00	4.00	8.00
❏ 447-0623	Hard Headed Woman/Don't Ask Me Why *Black label, dog on top*	1961	3.75	7.50	15.00
❏ 447-0623	Hard Headed Woman/Don't Ask Me Why *Black label, dog on left*	1965	2.50	5.00	10.00
❏ 447-0623	Hard Headed Woman/Don't Ask Me Why *Orange label*	1969	6.25	12.50	25.00
❏ 447-0623	Hard Headed Woman/Don't Ask Me Why *Red label*	1970	2.00	4.00	8.00
❏ 447-0624	One Night/I Got Stung *Black label, dog on top*	1961	3.00	6.00	12.00
❏ 447-0624	One Night/I Got Stung *Black label, dog on left*	1965	2.50	5.00	10.00
❏ 447-0624	One Night/I Got Stung *Orange label*	1969	6.25	12.50	25.00
❏ 447-0624	One Night/I Got Stung *Red label*	1970	2.00	4.00	8.00
❏ 447-0625	(Now and Then There's) A Fool Such As I/ I Need Your Love Tonight *Black label, dog on top*	1961	3.75	7.50	15.00
❏ 447-0625	(Now and Then There's) A Fool Such As I/ I Need Your Love Tonight *Black label, dog on left*	1965	2.50	5.00	10.00
❏ 447-0625	(Now and Then There's) A Fool Such As I/ I Need Your Love Tonight *Orange label*	1969	6.25	12.50	25.00
❏ 447-0625	(Now and Then There's) A Fool Such As I/ I Need Your Love Tonight *Red label*	1970	2.00	4.00	8.00
❏ 447-0626	A Big Hunk o'Love/My Wish Came True *Black label, dog on top*	1962	3.75	7.50	15.00
❏ 447-0626	A Big Hunk o'Love/My Wish Came True *Black label, dog on left*	1965	2.50	5.00	10.00
❏ 447-0626	A Big Hunk o'Love/My Wish Came True *Orange label*	1969	6.25	12.50	25.00

Number	Title (A Side/B Side)	Year	VG	VG+	NM
❏ 447-0626	A Big Hunk o'Love/My Wish Came True *Red label*	1970	2.00	4.00	8.00
❏ 447-0627	Stuck on You/Fame and Fortune *Black label, dog on top*	1962	3.00	6.00	12.00
❏ 447-0627	Stuck on You/Fame and Fortune *Black label, dog on left*	1965	2.50	5.00	10.00
❏ 447-0627	Stuck on You/Fame and Fortune *Orange label*	1969	6.25	12.50	25.00
❏ 447-0627	Stuck on You/Fame and Fortune *Red label*	1970	2.00	4.00	8.00
❏ 447-0628	It's Now or Never/A Mess of Blues *Black label, dog on top*	1962	3.00	6.00	12.00
❏ 447-0628	It's Now or Never/A Mess of Blues *Black label, dog on left*	1965	2.50	5.00	10.00
❏ 447-0628	It's Now or Never/A Mess of Blues *Orange label*	1969	6.25	12.50	25.00
❏ 447-0628	It's Now or Never/A Mess of Blues *Red label*	1970	2.00	4.00	8.00
❏ 447-0629	Are You Lonesome To-Night?/I Gotta Know *Black label, dog on top*	1962	3.75	7.50	15.00
❏ 447-0629	Are You Lonesome To-Night?/I Gotta Know *Black label, dog on left*	1965	2.50	5.00	10.00
❏ 447-0629	Are You Lonesome To-Night?/I Gotta Know *Orange label*	1969	6.25	12.50	25.00
❏ 447-0629	Are You Lonesome To-Night?/I Gotta Know *Red label*	1970	2.00	4.00	8.00
❏ 447-0630	Surrender/Lonely Man *Black label, dog on top*	1962	6.25	12.50	25.00
❏ 447-0630	Surrender/Lonely Man *Black label, dog on left*	1965	2.50	5.00	10.00
❏ 447-0630	Surrender/Lonely Man *Orange label*	1969	6.25	12.50	25.00
❏ 447-0630	Surrender/Lonely Man *Red label*	1970	2.00	4.00	8.00
❏ 447-0631	I Feel So Bad/Wild in the Country *Black label, dog on top*	1962	3.00	6.00	12.00
❏ 447-0631	I Feel So Bad/Wild in the Country *Black label, dog on left*	1965	2.50	5.00	10.00
❏ 447-0631	I Feel So Bad/Wild in the Country *Red label*	1970	2.00	4.00	8.00
❏ 447-0634	(Marie's the Name) His Latest Flame/Little Sister *Black label, dog on top*	1962	3.00	6.00	12.00
❏ 447-0634	(Marie's the Name) His Latest Flame/Little Sister *Black label, dog on left*	1965	2.50	5.00	10.00
❏ 447-0634	(Marie's the Name) His Latest Flame/Little Sister *Orange label*	1969	6.25	12.50	25.00
❏ 447-0634	(Marie's the Name) His Latest Flame/Little Sister *Red label*	1970	2.00	4.00	8.00
❏ 447-0635	Can't Help Falling in Love/Rock-a-Hula Baby *Black label, dog on top*	1962	3.00	6.00	12.00
❏ 447-0635	Can't Help Falling in Love/Rock-a-Hula Baby *Black label, dog on left*	1965	2.50	5.00	10.00
❏ 447-0635	Can't Help Falling in Love/Rock-a-Hula Baby *Orange label*	1969	6.25	12.50	25.00
❏ 447-0635	Can't Help Falling in Love/Rock-a-Hula Baby *Red label*	1970	2.00	4.00	8.00
❏ 447-0636	Good Luck Charm/Anything That's Part of You *Black label, dog on top*	1962	3.00	6.00	12.00
❏ 447-0636	Good Luck Charm/Anything That's Part of You *Black label, dog on left*	1965	2.50	5.00	10.00
❏ 447-0636	Good Luck Charm/Anything That's Part of You *Orange label*	1969	6.25	12.50	25.00
❏ 447-0636	Good Luck Charm/Anything That's Part of You *Red label*	1970	2.00	4.00	8.00
❏ 447-0637	She's Not You/Just Tell Her Jim Said Hello *Black label, dog on top*	1963	3.00	6.00	12.00
❏ 447-0637	She's Not You/Just Tell Her Jim Said Hello *Black label, dog on left*	1965	2.50	5.00	10.00
❏ 447-0637	She's Not You/Just Tell Her Jim Said Hello *Orange label*	1969	6.25	12.50	25.00
❏ 447-0637	She's Not You/Just Tell Her Jim Said Hello *Red label*	1970	2.00	4.00	8.00
❏ 447-0638	Return to Sender/Where Do You Come From *Black label, dog on top*	1963	3.00	6.00	12.00
❏ 447-0638	Return to Sender/Where Do You Come From *Black label, dog on left*	1965	2.50	5.00	10.00
❏ 447-0638	Return to Sender/Where Do You Come From *Orange label*	1969	6.25	12.50	25.00
❏ 447-0638	Return to Sender/Where Do You Come From *Red label*	1970	2.00	4.00	8.00

Number	Title (A Side/B Side)	Year	VG	VG+	NM
❏ 447-0639	Kiss Me Quick/Suspicion	1964	2.50	5.00	10.00
	Black label, dog on top				
❏ 447-0639	PS Kiss Me Quick/Suspicion	1964	10.00	20.00	40.00
❏ 447-0639	Kiss Me Quick/Suspicion	1969	6.25	12.50	25.00
	Orange label				
❏ 447-0639	Kiss Me Quick/Suspicion	1970	2.00	4.00	8.00
	Red label				
❏ 447-0640	One Broken Heart for Sale/ They Remind Me Too Much of You	1964	6.25	12.50	25.00
	Black label, dog on top				
❏ 447-0640	One Broken Heart for Sale/ They Remind Me Too Much of You	1965	2.50	5.00	10.00
	Black label, dog on left				
❏ 447-0640	One Broken Heart for Sale/ They Remind Me Too Much of You	1969	6.25	12.50	25.00
	Orange label				
❏ 447-0640	One Broken Heart for Sale/ They Remind Me Too Much of You	1970	2.00	4.00	8.00
	Red label				
❏ 447-0641	(You're the) Devil in Disguise/ Please Don't Drag That String Around	1964	6.25	12.50	25.00
	Black label, dog on top				
❏ 447-0641	(You're the) Devil in Disguise/ Please Don't Drag That String Around	1965	2.50	5.00	10.00
	Black label, dog on left				
❏ 447-0641	(You're the) Devil in Disguise/ Please Don't Drag That String Around	1970	2.00	4.00	8.00
	Red label				
❏ 447-0642	Bossa Nova Baby/Witchcraft	1964	6.25	12.50	25.00
	Black label, dog on top				
❏ 447-0642	Bossa Nova Baby/Witchcraft	1965	2.50	5.00	10.00
	Black label, dog on left				
❏ 447-0642	Bossa Nova Baby/Witchcraft	1969	6.25	12.50	25.00
	Orange label				
❏ 447-0642	Bossa Nova Baby/Witchcraft	1970	2.00	4.00	8.00
	Red label				
❏ 447-0643	Crying in the Chapel/I Believe in the Man in the Sky	1965	2.50	5.00	10.00
	Black label, dog on left				
❏ 447-0643	PS Crying in the Chapel/I Believe in the Man in the Sky	1965	7.50	15.00	30.00
❏ 447-0643	Crying in the Chapel/I Believe in the Man in the Sky	1970	2.00	4.00	8.00
	Red label				
❏ 447-0644	Kissin' Cousins/It Hurts Me	1965	2.50	5.00	10.00
	Black label, dog on left				
❏ 447-0644	Kissin' Cousins/It Hurts Me	1969	6.25	12.50	25.00
	Orange label				
❏ 447-0644	Kissin' Cousins/It Hurts Me	1970	2.00	4.00	8.00
	Red label				
❏ 447-0645	Such a Night/Never Ending	1965	10.00	20.00	40.00
	Black label, dog on top				
❏ 447-0645	Such a Night/Never Ending	1965	2.50	5.00	10.00
	Black label, dog on left				
❏ 447-0645	Such a Night/Never Ending	1969	6.25	12.50	25.00
	Orange label				
❏ 447-0645	Such a Night/Never Ending	1970	2.00	4.00	8.00
	Red label				
❏ 447-0646	Viva Las Vegas/What'd I Say	1965	6.25	12.50	25.00
	Black label, dog on top				
❏ 447-0646	Viva Las Vegas/What'd I Say	1965	2.50	5.00	10.00
	Black label, dog on left				
❏ 447-0646	Viva Las Vegas/What'd I Say	1969	6.25	12.50	25.00
	Orange label				
❏ 447-0646	Viva Las Vegas/What'd I Say	1970	2.00	4.00	8.00
	Red label				
❏ 447-0647	Blue Christmas/Santa Claus Is Back in Town	1965	3.00	6.00	12.00
	Black label, dog on left				
❏ 447-0647	PS Blue Christmas/Santa Claus Is Back in Town Has "Gold Standard Series" on sleeve (see RCA 447-0647)	1965	7.50	15.00	30.00
❏ 447-0647	Blue Christmas/Santa Claus Is Back in Town	1969	6.25	12.50	25.00
	Orange label				
❏ 447-0647	Blue Christmas/Santa Claus Is Back in Town	1970	2.00	4.00	8.00
	Red label				
❏ 447-0648	Do the Clam/You'll Be Gone	1965	2.50	5.00	10.00
	Black label, dog on left				
❏ 447-0648	Do the Clam/You'll Be Gone	1970	2.50	5.00	10.00
	Red label				
❏ 447-0649	Ain't That Loving You Baby/Ask Me	1965	2.50	5.00	10.00
	Black label, dog on left				
❏ 447-0649	Ain't That Loving You Baby/Ask Me	1970	2.00	4.00	8.00
	Red label				
❏ 447-0650	Puppet on a String/Wooden Heart	1965	2.50	5.00	10.00
	Black label, dog on left				
❏ 447-0650	PS Puppet on a String/Wooden Heart	1965	7.50	15.00	30.00

Number			Title (A Side/B Side)	Year	VG	VG+	NM
❑ 447-0650			Puppet on a String/Wooden Heart	1970	2.00	4.00	8.00
			Red label				
❑ 447-0651			Joshua Fit the Battle/Known Only to Him	1966	3.75	7.50	15.00
			Black label, dog on left				
❑ 447-0651	PS		Joshua Fit the Battle/Known Only to Him	1966	50.00	100.00	200.00
❑ 447-0651			Joshua Fit the Battle/Known Only to Him	1970	2.00	4.00	8.00
			Red label				
❑ 447-0652			Milky White Way/Swing Down Sweet Chariot	1966	3.75	7.50	15.00
			Black label, dog on left				
❑ 447-0652	PS		Milky White Way/Swing Down Sweet Chariot	1966	50.00	100.00	200.00
❑ 447-0652			Milky White Way/Swing Down Sweet Chariot	1970	2.00	4.00	8.00
			Red label				
❑ 447-0653			(Such An) Easy Question/It Feels So Right	1966	2.50	5.00	10.00
			Black label, dog on left				
❑ 447-0653			(Such An) Easy Question/It Feels So Right	1970	2.00	4.00	8.00
			Red label				
❑ 447-0654			I'm Yours/(It's a) Long, Lonely Highway	1966	2.50	5.00	10.00
			Black label, dog on left				
❑ 447-0654			I'm Yours/(It's a) Long, Lonely Highway	1970	2.00	4.00	8.00
			Red label				
❑ 447-0655			Tell Me Why/Blue River	1968	2.50	5.00	10.00
			Black label, dog on left				
❑ 447-0655			Tell Me Why/Blue River	1970	2.00	4.00	8.00
			Red label				
❑ 447-0656			Frankie and Johnny/Please Don't Stop Loving Me	1968	2.50	5.00	10.00
			Black label, dog on left				
❑ 447-0656			Frankie and Johnny/Please Don't Stop Loving Me	1969	6.25	12.50	25.00
			Orange label				
❑ 447-0656			Frankie and Johnny/Please Don't Stop Loving Me	1970	2.00	4.00	8.00
			Red label				
❑ 447-0657			Love Letters/Come What May	1968	2.50	5.00	10.00
			Black label, dog on left				
❑ 447-0657			Love Letters/Come What May	1970	2.00	4.00	8.00
			Red label				
❑ 447-0658			Spinout/All That I Do	1968	2.50	5.00	10.00
			Black label, dog on left				
❑ 447-0658			Spinout/All That I Do	1970	2.00	4.00	8.00
			Red label				
❑ 447-0659			Indescribably Blue/Fools Fall in Love	1969	6.25	12.50	25.00
			Orange label				
❑ 447-0659			Indescribably Blue/Fools Fall in Love	1970	2.00	4.00	8.00
			Red label (as are originals of all the below 447- series except 0720)				
❑ 447-0660			Long Legged Girl (With the Short Dress On)/ There's Always Me/Judy	1970	10.00	20.00	40.00
❑ 447-0661			There's Always Me/Judy	1970	3.75	7.50	15.00
❑ 447-0662			Big Boss Man/You Don't Know Me	1970	2.50	5.00	10.00
❑ 447-0663			Guitar Man/High Heel Sneakers	1970	2.00	4.00	8.00
❑ 447-0664			U.S. Male/Stay Away	1970	2.00	4.00	8.00
❑ 447-0665			You'll Never Walk Alone/We Call on Him	1970	2.50	5.00	10.00
❑ 447-0666			Let Yourself Go/Your Time Hasn't Come Yet, Baby	1970	2.00	4.00	8.00
❑ 447-0667			A Little Less Conversation/Almost in Love	1970	2.00	4.00	8.00
❑ 447-0668			If I Can Dream/Edge of Reality	1970	2.00	4.00	8.00
❑ 447-0669			Memories/Charro	1970	2.00	4.00	8.00
❑ 447-0670			How Great Thou Art/His Hand in Mine	1970	2.50	5.00	10.00
❑ 447-0671			In the Ghetto/Any Day Now	1970	2.00	4.00	8.00
❑ 447-0672			Clean Up Your Own Back Yard/The Fair Is Moving On	1970	2.00	4.00	8.00
❑ 447-0673			Suspicious Minds/You'll Think of Me	1970	2.00	4.00	8.00
❑ 447-0674			Don't Cry Daddy/Rubberneckin'	1970	2.00	4.00	8.00
❑ 447-0675			Kentucky Rain/My Little Friend	1971	2.00	4.00	8.00
❑ 447-0676			The Wonder of You/Mama Liked the Roses	1971	2.00	4.00	8.00
❑ 447-0677			I've Lost You/The Next Step Is Love	1971	2.00	4.00	8.00
❑ 447-0678			You Don't Have to Say You Love Me/Patch It Up	1972	2.00	4.00	8.00
❑ 447-0679			I Really Don't Want to Know/ There Goes My Everything	1972	2.00	4.00	8.00
❑ 447-0680			Where Did They Go, Lord/Rags to Riches	1972	2.00	4.00	8.00
❑ 447-0681			If Every Day Was Like Christmas/ How Would You Like to Be	1972	2.00	4.00	8.00
❑ 447-0682			Life/Only Believe	1972	2.50	5.00	8.00
❑ 447-0683			I'm Leavin'/Heart of Rome	1972	2.00	4.00	8.00
❑ 447-0684			It's Only Love/The Sound of Your Cry	1972	2.00	4.00	8.00
❑ 447-0685			An American Trilogy/Until It's Time for You to Go	1973	2.00	4.00	8.00
❑ 447-0720			Blue Christmas/Wooden Heart	1964	3.75	7.50	15.00
❑ 447-0720	PS		Blue Christmas/Wooden Heart	1964	15.00	30.00	60.00
❑ CR-15	DJ		Old Shep	1956	250.00	500.00	1,000
			One-sided promo				
❑ APBO-0088			Raised on Rock/For Ol' Times Sake	1973	3.00		6.00
❑ APBO-0088	PS		Raised on Rock/For Ol' Times Sake	1973	3.75	7.50	15.00
❑ APBO-0196			Take Good Care of Her/ I've Got a Thing About You, Baby	1973		3.00	6.00
❑ APBO-0196	PS		Take Good Care of Her/ I've Got a Thing About You, Baby	1973	3.75	7.50	15.00
❑ APBO-0280			If You Talk in Your Sleep/Help Me	1974	3.00	6.00	12.00
			On the label, the title "If You Talk in Your Sleep" is all on one line				
❑ APBO-0280			If You Talk in Your Sleep/Help Me	1974		3.00	6.00
			On the label, the title "If You Talk" is on one line and "In Your Sleep" is on another line				

Number		Title (A Side/B Side)	Year	VG	VG+	NM
❑ APBO-0280	PS	If You Talk in Your Sleep/Help Me	1974	3.75	7.50	15.00
❑ HO7W-0808	DJ	Blue Christmas (same on both sides)	1957	375.00	750.00	1,500
❑ PB-10074		Promised Land/It's Midnight	1974		2.50	5.00
		Gray label (available at the same time as orange label)				
❑ PB-10074		Promised Land/It's Midnight	1974		2.50	5.00
		Orange label (available at the same time as gray label)				
❑ PB-10074		Promised Land/It's Midnight	1975	6.25	12.50	25.00
		Tan label (reissue)				
❑ PB-10074	PS	Promised Land/It's Midnight	1975	2.50	5.00	10.00
❑ GB-10156		Burning Love/Steamroller Blues	1975	2.00	4.00	8.00
		Gold Standard Series; red label				
❑ GB-10157		Raised on Rock/If You Talk in Your Sleep	1975	2.00	4.00	8.00
		Gold Standard Series; red label				
❑ PB-10191		My Boy/Thinking About You	1975		2.50	5.00
		Orange label				
❑ PB-10191		My Boy/Thinking About You	1975		2.50	5.00
		Tan label				
❑ PB-10191	PS	My Boy/Thinking About You	1975	2.50	5.00	10.00
❑ PB-10278		T-R-O-U-B-L-E/Mr. Songman	1975	2.50	5.00	10.00
		Tan label				
❑ PB-10278		T-R-O-U-B-L-E/Mr. Songman	1975	25.00	50.00	100.00
		Gray label				
❑ PB-10278		T-R-O-U-B-L-E/Mr. Songman	1975		2.50	5.00
		Orange label				
❑ PB-10278	PS	T-R-O-U-B-L-E/Mr. Songman	1975	2.50	5.00	10.00
❑ PB-10401		Bringing It Back/Pieces of My Life	1975		2.50	5.00
		Tan label				
❑ PB-10401		Bringing It Back/Pieces of My Life	1975	50.00	100.00	200.00
		Orange label				
❑ PB-10401	PS	Bringing It Back/Pieces of My Life	1975	2.50	5.00	10.00
		Tan label				
❑ GB-10485		Take Good Care of Her/ I've Got a Thing About You, Baby	1975	2.00	4.00	8.00
		Gold Standard Series; red label				
❑ GB-10486		Separate Ways/Always on My Mind	1975	2.00	4.00	8.00
		Gold Standard Series; red label				
❑ GB-10487		T-R-O-U-B-L-E/Mr. Songman	1975	2.00	4.00	8.00
		Gold Standard Series; red label				
❑ GB-10488		Promised Land/It's Midnight	1975	2.00	4.00	8.00
		Gold Standard Series; red label				
❑ GB-10489		My Boy/Thinking About You	1975	2.00	4.00	8.00
		Gold Standard Series; red label				
❑ PB-10601		Hurt/For the Heart	1976		2.50	5.00
		Originals on tan labels				
❑ PB-10601	PS	Hurt/For the Heart	1976	2.50	5.00	10.00
❑ SP-45-76	DJ	Don't Wear My Ring Around Your Neck	1960	200.00	400.00	800.00
❑ SP-45-76	PS	Don't Wear My Ring Around Your Neck	1960	1,000	1,500	2,000
❑ SP-45-118	DJ	King of the Whole Wide World/ Home Is Where the Heart Is	1962	50.00	100.00	200.00
❑ SP-45-118	PS	King of the Whole Wide World/ Home Is Where the Heart Is	1962	75.00	150.00	300.00
❑ SP-45-139	DJ	Roustabout/One Track Heart	1964	75.00	150.00	300.00
❑ SP-45-162	DJ	How Great Thou Art/So High	1967	37.50	75.00	150.00
❑ SP-45-162	PS	How Great Thou Art/So High	1967	50.00	100.00	200.00
Sun						
❑ 209		That's All Right/Blue Moon of Kentucky	1954	500.00	1,000	2,000
❑ 210		Good Rockin' Tonight/ I Don't Care If the Sun Don't Shine	1954	500.00	1,000	2,000
❑ 215		Milkcow Blues Boogie/You're a Heartbreaker	1955	625.00	1,250	2,500
❑ 217		Baby Let's Play House/ I'm Left, You're Right, She's Gone	1955	375.00	750.00	1,500
❑ 223		I Forgot to Remember to Forget/Mystery Train	1955	250.00	500.00	1,000

EPs

(As many of the records do not list the titles of the EPs on the label, we have, in most cases, listed the contents of the records. The name of the EP is listed in the picture sleeve lines.)

RCA Victor

Number		Title (A Side/B Side)	Year	VG	VG+	NM
❑ SPD-22	(2)	Elvis Presley	1956	150.00	300.00	600.00
		Value is for both discs together				
❑ SPD-22	PS	Elvis Presley	1956	150.00	300.00	600.00
		Bonus given to buyers of a Victrola				
❑ SPD-23	(3)	Elvis Presley	1956	1,000	1,500	2,000
		Value is for all three discs together				
❑ SPD-23	PS	Elvis Presley	1956	1,000	1,500	2,000
		Bonus given to buyers of a more expensive Victrola				
❑ SPA-7-37	DJ	Perfect for Parties	1956	15.00	30.00	60.00
		With horizontal line on label				
❑ SPA-7-37	DJ	Perfect for Parties	1956	15.00	30.00	60.00
		No horizontal line on label				
❑ SPA-7-37	PS	Perfect for Parties	1956	15.00	30.00	60.00
❑ LPC-126		Flaming Star/Summer Kisses, Winter Tears// Are You Lonesome To-Night?/It's Now or Never	1961	10.00	20.00	40.00
❑ LPC-126	PS	Elvis By Request	1961	10.00	20.00	40.00

Two of the five Elvis Presley Sun 45s, which are currently the hottest records in the entire field of record collecting. These can bring three figures in almost any condition, and all have hit or surpassed the $1,000 mark in Near Mint condition. At top is the Sun record considered the scarcest, "Milkcow Blues Boogie," teamed with the one considered the most common, the last one, "Mystery Train." Even though "Mystery Train" gets all the (deserved) attention today, the B-side, "I Forgot to Remember to Forget," was actually the bigger hit at the time, as it hit No. 1 on the country charts.

Number	Title (A Side/B Side)	Year	VG	VG+	NM
❑ EPA-747	Blue Suede Shoes/Tutti Frutti//I Got a Woman/ Just Because	1956	12.50	25.00	50.00
	With horizontal line on label				
❑ EPA-747	Blue Suede Shoes/Tutti Frutti//I Got a Woman/ Just Because	1956	50.00	100.00	200.00
	With horizontal line on label, but with no dog				
❑ EPA-747	Blue Suede Shoes/Tutti Frutti//I Got a Woman/ Just Because	1956	12.50	25.00	50.00
	No horizontal line on label				
❑ EPA-747	Blue Suede Shoes/Tutti Frutti//I Got a Woman/ Just Because	1965	7.50	15.00	30.00
	Black label, dog on left				
❑ EPA-747	Blue Suede Shoes/Tutti Frutti//I Got a Woman/ Just Because	1969	20.00	40.00	80.00
	Orange label				
❑ EPA-747	PS Elvis Presley	1956	150.00	300.00	600.00
	Temporary envelope sleeve with black print, "Blue Suede Shoes by Elvis Presley" in big letters				
❑ EPA-747	PS Elvis Presley	1956	250.00	500.00	1,000
	Temporary envelope sleeve with dark blue print, "Blue Suede Shoes by Elvis Presley" in big letters				
❑ EPA-747	PS Elvis Presley	1956	12.50	25.00	50.00
	Five different back covers exist, all with titles on front cover; any are of equal value				
❑ EPA-747	PS Elvis Presley	1965	7.50	15.00	30.00
	No titles at top of front cover				
❑ EPA-821	Heartbreak Hotel/I Was the One// Mystery Train/I Forgot to Remember to Forget	1956	12.50	25.00	50.00
	With horizontal line on label				
❑ EPA-821	Heartbreak Hotel/I Was the One//Mystery Train/I Forgot to Remember to Forget	1956	50.00	100.00	200.00
	With horizontal line on label, but with no dog				
❑ EPA-821	Heartbreak Hotel/I Was the One// Mystery Train/I Forgot to Remember to Forget	1956	12.50	25.00	50.00
	No horizontal line on label				
❑ EPA-821	Heartbreak Hotel/I Was the One// Mystery Train/I Forgot to Remember to Forget	1965	7.50	15.00	30.00
	Black label, dog on left				
❑ EPA-821	Heartbreak Hotel/I Was the One// Mystery Train/I Forgot to Remember to Forget	1969	20.00	40.00	80.00
	Orange label				
❑ EPA-821	PS Heartbreak Hotel	1956	12.50	25.00	50.00
❑ EPA-830	Shake, Rattle and Roll/I Love You Because// Blue Moon/Lawdy, Miss Clawdy	1956	12.50	25.00	50.00
	With horizontal line on label				
❑ EPA-830	Shake, Rattle and Roll/I Love You Because// Blue Moon/Lawdy, Miss Clawdy	1956	50.00	100.00	200.00
	With horizontal line on label, but with no dog				
❑ EPA-830	Shake, Rattle and Roll/I Love You Because// Blue Moon/Lawdy, Miss Clawdy	1956	12.50	25.00	50.00
	No horizontal line on label				
❑ EPA-830	Shake, Rattle and Roll/I Love You Because// Blue Moon/Lawdy, Miss Clawdy	1965	7.50	15.00	30.00
	Black label, dog on left				
❑ EPA-830	Shake, Rattle and Roll/I Love You Because// Blue Moon/Lawdy, Miss Clawdy	1969	20.00	40.00	80.00
	Orange label				
❑ EPA-830	PS Elvis Presley	1956	12.50	25.00	50.00
❑ EPA-940	Don't Be Cruel/I Want You, I Need You, I Love You// Hound Dog/My Baby Left Me	1956	10.00	20.00	40.00
	With horizontal line on label				
❑ EPA-940	Don't Be Cruel/I Want You, I Need You, I Love You// Hound Dog/My Baby Left Me	1956	50.00	100.00	200.00
	With horizontal line on label, but with no dog				
❑ EPA-940	Don't Be Cruel/I Want You, I Need You, I Love You//Hound Dog/My Baby Left Me	1956	10.00	20.00	40.00
	No horizontal line on label				
❑ EPA-940	PS The Real Elvis	1956	10.00	20.00	40.00
❑ EPA-965	Anyway You Want Me (That's How I Will Be)/ I'm Left, You're Right, She's Gone//I Don't Care If the Sun Don't Shine/Mystery Train	1956	10.00	20.00	40.00
	With horizontal line on label				
❑ EPA-965	Anyway You Want Me (That's How I Will Be)/ I'm Left, You're Right, She's Gone//I Don't Care If the Sun Don't Shine/Mystery Train	1956	50.00	100.00	200.00
	With horizontal line on label, but with no dog				
❑ EPA-965	Anyway You Want Me (That's How I Will Be)/ I'm Left, You're Right, She's Gone//I Don't Care If the Sun Don't Shine/Mystery Train	1956	10.00	20.00	40.00
	No horizontal line on label				
❑ EPA-965	Anyway You Want Me (That's How I Will Be)/ I'm Left, You're Right, She's Gone//I Don't Care If the Sun Don't Shine/Mystery Train	1965	7.50	15.00	30.00
	Black label, dog on left				
❑ EPA-965	Anyway You Want Me (That's How I Will Be)/ I'm Left, You're Right, She's Gone//I Don't Care If the Sun Don't Shine/Mystery Train	1969	20.00	40.00	80.00
	Orange label				
❑ EPA-965	PS Anyway You Want Me	1956	12.50	25.00	50.00
	With song titles and catalog number on front				
❑ EPA-965	PS Anyway You Want Me	196?	10.00	20.00	40.00
	Without song titles and catalog number on front				

Number	Title (A Side/B Side)	Year	VG	VG+	NM
❏ EPA-992	Rip It Up/Love Me// When My Blue Moon Turns to Gold Again/Paralyzed *With horizontal line on label*	1956	10.00	20.00	40.00
❏ EPA-992	Rip It Up/Love Me// When My Blue Moon Turns to Gold Again/Paralyzed *With horizontal line on label; but with no dog*	1956	50.00	100.00	200.00
❏ EPA-992	Rip It Up/Love Me// When My Blue Moon Turns to Gold Again/Paralyzed *No horizontal line on label*	1956	10.00	20.00	40.00
❏ EPA-992	Rip It Up/Love Me// When My Blue Moon Turns to Gold Again/Paralyzed *Black label, dog on left*	1965	7.50	15.00	30.00
❏ EPA-992	Rip It Up/Love Me// When My Blue Moon Turns to Gold Again/Paralyzed *Orange label*	1969	20.00	40.00	80.00
❏ EPA-992	PS Elvis (Volume 1)	1956	12.50	25.00	50.00
❏ EPA-993	So Glad You're Mine/Old Shep//Ready Teddy/ Anyplace Is Paradise *With horizontal line on label*	1956	10.00	20.00	40.00
❏ EPA-993	So Glad You're Mine/Old Shep//Ready Teddy/ Anyplace Is Paradise *With horizontal line on label, but with no dog*	1956	50.00	100.00	200.00
❏ EPA-993	So Glad You're Mine/Old Shep//Ready Teddy/ Anyplace Is Paradise *No horizontal line on label*	1956	10.00	20.00	40.00
❏ EPA-993	So Glad You're Mine/Old Shep//Ready Teddy/ Anyplace Is Paradise *Black label, dog on left*	1965	7.50	15.00	30.00
❏ EPA-993	So Glad You're Mine/Old Shep//Ready Teddy/ Anyplace Is Paradise *Orange label*	1969	20.00	40.00	80.00
❏ EPA-993	PS Elvis (Volume 2) *Titles at top of front cover*	1956	12.50	25.00	50.00
❏ EPA-993	PS Elvis (Volume 2) *No titles at top of front cover*	1965	7.50	15.00	30.00
❏ EPA-994	Long Tall Sally/First in Line// How Do You Think I Feel/How's the World Treating You *With horizontal line on label*	1956	12.50	25.00	50.00
❏ EPA-994	Long Tall Sally/First in Line// How Do You Think I Feel/How's the World Treating You *With horizontal line on label, but with no dog*	1956	50.00	100.00	200.00
❏ EPA-994	Long Tall Sally/First in Line// How Do You Think I Feel/How's the World Treating You *No horizontal line on label*	1956	12.50	25.00	50.00
❏ EPA-994	Long Tall Sally/First in Line// How Do You Think I Feel/How's the World Treating You *Black label, dog on left*	1965	7.50	15.00	30.00
❏ EPA-994	Long Tall Sally/First in Line// How Do You Think I Feel/How's the World Treating You *Orange label*	1969	20.00	40.00	80.00
❏ EPA-994	PS Strictly Elvis (Elvis, Vol. 3) *With titles listed on front cover*	1956	12.50	25.00	50.00
❏ EPA-994	PS Strictly Elvis (Elvis, Vol. 3) *No titles listed on front cover*	1965	7.50	15.00	30.00
❏ EPB-1254	(2) Elvis Presley *With horizontal line on label; eight songs on two discs; value is for both discs together*	1956	50.00	100.00	200.00
❏ EPB-1254	(2) Elvis Presley *No horizontal line on label; eight songs on two discs; value is for both discs together*	1956	50.00	100.00	200.00
❏ EPB-1254	PS Elvis Presley *Three different back covers exist hyping other non-Elvis RCA Victor releases; any are of equal value*	1956	50.00	100.00	200.00
❏ EPB-1254	PS Elvis Presley *With no hype of other non-Elvis releases on back*	1956	37.50	75.00	150.00
❏ EPB-1254	(2) Elvis Presley *Two records have three songs on each side (12 total), as opposed to the two on each side of the standard release*	1956	375.00	750.00	1,500
❏ EPB-1254	PS Elvis Presley... the most talked-about new personality in the last ten years of recorded music	1956	375.00	750.00	1,500
❏ EPA-1-1515	Loving You/Party//(Let Me Be Your) Teddy Bear/ True Love *With horizontal line on label*	1957	10.00	20.00	40.00
❏ EPA-1-1515	Loving You/Party//(Let Me Be Your) Teddy Bear/ True Love *No horizontal line on label*	1957	10.00	20.00	40.00
❏ EPA-1-1515	Loving You/Party//(Let Me Be Your) Teddy Bear/ True Love *Black label, dog on left*	1965	7.50	15.00	30.00
❏ EPA-1-1515	Loving You/Party//(Let Me Be Your) Teddy Bear/ True Love *Orange label*	1969	20.00	40.00	80.00
❏ EPA-1-1515	PS Loving You, Vol. I	1957	10.00	20.00	40.00
❏ EPA-2-1515	Lonesome Cowboy/Hot Dog// Mean Woman Blues/Got a Lot of Livin' to Do *With horizontal line on label*	1957	10.00	20.00	40.00

Number	Title (A Side/B Side)	Year	VG	VG+	NM
❏ EPA-2-1515	Lonesome Cowboy/Hot Dog// Mean Woman Blues/Got a Lot of Livin' to Do *No horizontal line on label*	1957	10.00	20.00	40.00
❏ EPA-2-1515	Lonesome Cowboy/Hot Dog// Mean Woman Blues/Got a Lot of Livin' to Do *Black label, dog on left*	1965	7.50	15.00	30.00
❏ EPA-2-1515	Lonesome Cowboy/Hot Dog// Mean Woman Blues/Got a Lot of Livin' to Do *Orange label*	1969	20.00	40.00	80.00
❏ EPA-2-1515	PS Loving You, Vol. II *With song titles on top of front cover*	1957	10.00	20.00	40.00
❏ EPA-2-1515	PS Loving You, Vol. II *No song titles on top of front cover*	1965	7.50	15.00	30.00
❏ EPA-4006	Love Me Tender/Let Me//Poor Boy/We're Gonna Move *With horizontal line on label*	1956	12.50	25.00	50.00
❏ EPA-4006	Love Me Tender/Let Me//Poor Boy/We're Gonna Move *With horizontal line on label, but with no dog*	1956	50.00	100.00	200.00
❏ EPA-4006	Love Me Tender/Let Me//Poor Boy/We're Gonna Move *No horizontal line on label*	1956	12.50	25.00	50.00
❏ EPA-4006	Love Me Tender/Let Me//Poor Boy/We're Gonna Move *Black label, dog on left*	1965	7.50	15.00	30.00
❏ EPA-4006	Love Me Tender/Let Me//Poor Boy/We're Gonna Move *Orange label*	1969	20.00	40.00	80.00
❏ EPA-4006	PS Love Me Tender *With song titles on top of front cover*	1956	12.50	25.00	50.00
❏ EPA-4006	PS Love Me Tender *No song titles on top of front cover*	1965	7.50	15.00	30.00
❏ EPA-4041	I Need You So/Have I Told You Lately//Blueberry Hill/ Is It So Strange *With horizontal line on label, but with no dog*	1957	50.00	100.00	200.00
❏ EPA-4041	I Need You So/Have I Told You Lately//Blueberry Hill/ Is It So Strange *With horizontal line on label*	1957	10.00	20.00	40.00
❏ EPA-4041	I Need You So/Have I Told You Lately//Blueberry Hill/ Is It So Strange *No horizontal line on label*	1957	10.00	20.00	40.00
❏ EPA-4041	I Need You So/Have I Told You Lately//Blueberry Hill/ Is It So Strange *Black label, dog on left*	1965	7.50	15.00	30.00
❏ EPA-4041	I Need You So/Have I Told You Lately//Blueberry Hill/ Is It So Strange *Orange label*	1969	20.00	40.00	80.00
❏ EPA-4041	PS Just for You (Elvis Presley)	1957	10.00	20.00	40.00
❏ EPA-4054	(There'll Be) Peace in the Valley (For Me)/ It Is No Secret (What God Can Do)//I Believe/Take My Hand, Precious Lord *With horizontal line on label*	1957	10.00	20.00	40.00
❏ EPA-4054	(There'll Be) Peace in the Valley (For Me)/ It Is No Secret (What God Can Do)//I Believe/Take My Hand, Precious Lord *No horizontal line on label*	1957	10.00	20.00	40.00
❏ EPA-4054	PS Peace in the Valley	1957	10.00	20.00	40.00
❏ EPA-4108	Santa Bring My Baby Back (To Me)/Blue Christmas// Santa Claus Is Back in Town/I'll Be Home for Christmas *Black label, dog on top*	1957	10.00	20.00	40.00
❏ EPA-4108	Santa Bring My Baby Back (To Me)/Blue Christmas// Santa Claus Is Back in Town/I'll Be Home for Christmas *Black label, dog on left*	1965	7.50	15.00	30.00
❏ EPA-4108	Santa Bring My Baby Back (To Me)/Blue Christmas// Santa Claus Is Back in Town/I'll Be Home for Christmas *Orange label*	1969	20.00	40.00	80.00
❏ EPA-4108	PS Elvis Sings Christmas Songs	1957	10.00	20.00	40.00
❏ EPA-4114	Jailhouse Rock/Young and Beautiful// I Want to Be Free/Don't Leave Me Now/(You're So Square) Baby I Don't Care *Black label, dog on top*	1957	10.00	20.00	40.00
❏ EPA-4114	Jailhouse Rock/Young and Beautiful// I Want to Be Free/Don't Leave Me Now/(You're So Square) Baby I Don't Care *Black label, dog on left*	1965	7.50	15.00	30.00
❏ EPA-4114	Jailhouse Rock/Young and Beautiful// I Want to Be Free/Don't Leave Me Now/(You're So Square) Baby I Don't Care *Orange label*	1969	20.00	40.00	80.00
❏ EPA-4114	PS Jailhouse Rock	1957	7.50	15.00	30.00
❏ EPA-4319	King Creole/New Orleans//As Long As I Have You/ Lover Doll	1958	10.00	20.00	40.00
❏ EPA-4319	PS King Creole *With copyright notice on front cover*	1958	12.50	25.00	50.00
❏ EPA-4319	PS King Creole *Without copyright notice on front cover*	1958	10.00	20.00	40.00
❏ EPA-4321	Trouble/Young Dreams//Crawfish/Dixieland Rock *Black label, dog on top*	1958	10.00	20.00	40.00
❏ EPA-4321	Trouble/Young Dreams//Crawfish/Dixieland Rock *Black label, dog on left*	1965	7.50	15.00	30.00
❏ EPA-4321	Trouble/Young Dreams//Crawfish/Dixieland Rock *Orange label*	1969	20.00	40.00	80.00
❏ EPA-4321	PS King Creole, Vol. 2	1958	10.00	20.00	40.00

Number		Title (A Side/B Side)	Year	VG	VG+	NM
❏ EPA-4325		Press Interview with Elvis Presley//	1958	12.50	25.00	50.00
		Elvis Presley's Newsreel Interview/Pat Hernon Interviews Elvis...				
❏ EPA-4325	PS	Elvis Sails	1958	15.00	30.00	60.00
		With 1959 calendar and a hole to make it suitable for hanging				
❏ EPA-4340		White Christmas/Here Comes Santa Claus//	1958	17.50	35.00	70.00
		Oh Little Town of Bethlehem/Silent Night				
		Black label, dog on top				
❏ EPA-4340		White Christmas/Here Comes Santa Claus//	1965	10.00	20.00	40.00
		Oh Little Town of Bethlehem/Silent Night				
		Black label, dog on left				
❏ EPA-4340		White Christmas/Here Comes Santa Claus//	1969	20.00	40.00	80.00
		Oh Little Town of Bethlehem/Silent Night				
		Orange label				
❏ EPA-4340	PS	Christmas with Elvis	1958	20.00	40.00	80.00
		With copyright notice and "Printed in U.S.A." at lower right				
❏ EPA-4340	PS	Christmas with Elvis	1965	10.00	20.00	40.00
		Without copyright notice and "Printed in U.S.A." at lower right				
❏ EPA-4368		Follow That Dream/Angel//	1962	10.00	20.00	40.00
		What a Wonderful Life/I'm Not the Marrying Kind				
		Black label, dog on top, with playing times on label				
❏ EPA-4368		Follow That Dream/Angel//	1962	7.50	15.00	30.0
		What a Wonderful Life/I'm Not the Marrying Kind				
		Black label, dog on top, no playing times on label				
❏ EPA-4368		Follow That Dream/Angel//	1965	6.25	12.50	25.00
		What a Wonderful Life/I'm Not the Marrying Kind				
		Black label, dog on left				
❏ EPA-4368		Follow That Dream/Angel//	1969	20.00	40.00	80.00
		What a Wonderful Life/I'm Not the Marrying Kind				
		Orange label				
❏ EPA-4368	PS	Follow That Dream	1962	37.50	75.00	150.00
		Paper sleeve with "Coin Operator -- DJ Prevue" at top; print is in red				
❏ EPA-4368	PS	Follow That Dream	1962	10.00	20.00	40.00
		Incorrect playing times on back cover; "Follow That Dream" is listed as 1:35 but is actually 1:38, and two others are wrong also				
❏ EPA-4368	PS	Follow That Dream	1965	6.25	12.50	25.00
		Correct playing times on back cover				
❏ EPA-4371		King of the Whole Wide World/This Is Living/	1962	10.00	20.00	40.00
		Riding the Rainbow//Home Is Where the Heart Is/I Got Lucky/A Whistling Tune				
		Black label, dog on top				
❏ EPA-4371		King of the Whole Wide World/This Is Living/	1965	7.50	15.00	30.00
		Riding the Rainbow//Home Is Where the Heart Is/I Got Lucky/A Whistling Tune				
		Black label, dog on left				
❏ EPA-4371		King of the Whole Wide World/This Is Living/	1969	20.00	40.00	80.00
		Riding the Rainbow//Home Is Where the Heart Is/I Got Lucky/A Whistling Tune				
		Orange label				
❏ EPA-4371	PS	Kid Galahad	1962	10.00	20.00	40.00
❏ EPA-4382		If You Think I Don't Need You/	1964	10.00	20.00	40.00
		I Need Somebody to Lean On//C'mon Everybody/Today, Tomorrow and Forever				
		Black label, dog on top				
❏ EPA-4382		If You Think I Don't Need You/	1965	7.50	15.00	30.00
		I Need Somebody to Lean On//C'mon Everybody/Today, Tomorrow and Forever				
		Black label, dog on left				
❏ EPA-4382		If You Think I Don't Need You/	1969	20.00	40.00	80.00
		I Need Somebody to Lean On//C'mon Everybody/Today, Tomorrow and Forever				
		Orange label				
❏ EPA-4382	PS	Viva Las Vegas	1964	10.00	20.00	40.00
❏ EPA-4383		I Feel That I've Known You Forever/Slowly But Surely//	1965	7.50	15.00	30.00
		Night Rider/Dirty Feeling				
		Black label, dog on left				
❏ EPA-4383		I Feel That I've Known You Forever/Slowly But Surely//	1969	20.00	40.00	80.00
		Night Rider/Dirty Feeling				
		Orange label				
❏ EPA-4383	PS	Tickle Me	1965	7.50	15.00	30.00
		"Coming Soon" on front cover				
❏ EPA-4383	PS	Tickle Me	1965	7.50	15.00	30.00
		"Ask For" on front cover				
❏ EPA-4383	PS	Tickle Me	1969	8.75	17.50	35.00
		No blurb for new album on front cover				
❏ EPA-4387		Easy Come, Easy Go/The Love Machine/	1967	7.50	15.00	30.00
		Yoga Is As Yoga Does//You Gotta Shop/Sing You Children/I'll Take Love				
		All copies appear to be black label, dog on left				
❏ EPA-4387	PS	Easy Come, Easy Go	1967	7.50	15.00	30.00
❏ EPA-5088		Hard Headed Woman/Good Rockin' Tonight//	1959	100.00	200.00	400.00
		Don't/I Beg of You				
		Maroon label				
❏ EPA-5088		Hard Headed Woman/Good Rockin' Tonight//	1959	10.00	20.00	40.00
		Don't/I Beg of You				
		Black label, dog on top				
❏ EPA-5088		Hard Headed Woman/Good Rockin' Tonight//	1965	7.50	15.00	30.00
		Don't/I Beg of You				
		Black label, dog on left				
❏ EPA-5088		Hard Headed Woman/Good Rockin' Tonight//	1969	20.00	40.00	80.00
		Don't/I Beg of You				
		Orange label				

Number		Title (A Side/B Side)	Year	VG	VG+	NM
❑ EPA-5088	PS	A Touch of Gold	1959	10.00	20.00	40.00
❑ EPA-5101		Wear My Ring Around Your Neck/Treat Me Nice// One Night/That's All Right	1959	100.00	200.00	400.00
		Maroon label				
❑ EPA-5101		Wear My Ring Around Your Neck/Treat Me Nice// One Night/That's All Right	1959	10.00	20.00	40.00
		Black label, dog on top				
❑ EPA-5101		Wear My Ring Around Your Neck/Treat Me Nice// One Night/That's All Right	1965	7.50	15.00	30.00
		Black label, dog on left				
❑ EPA-5101		Wear My Ring Around Your Neck/Treat Me Nice// One Night/That's All Right	1969	20.00	40.00	80.00
		Orange label				
❑ EPA-5101	PS	A Touch of Gold, Volume II	1959	10.00	20.00	40.00
❑ EPA-5120		Don't Be Cruel/I Want You, I Need You, I Love You// Hound Dog/My Baby Left Me	1959	7.50	15.00	30.00
		Black label, dog on top				
❑ EPA-5120		Don't Be Cruel/I Want You, I Need You, I Love You// Hound Dog/My Baby Left Me	1959	150.00	300.00	600.00
		Maroon label				
❑ EPA-5120		Don't Be Cruel/I Want You, I Need You, I Love You// Hound Dog/My Baby Left Me	1965	6.25	12.50	25.00
		Black label, dog on left				
❑ EPA-5120		Don't Be Cruel/I Want You, I Need You, I Love You// Hound Dog/My Baby Left Me	1969	20.00	40.00	80.00
		Orange label				
❑ EPA-5120	PS	The Real Elvis	1959	7.50	15.00	30.00
❑ EPA-5121		(There'll Be) Peace in the Valley (For Me)/ It Is No Secret (What God Can Do)//I Believe/Take My Hand, Precious Lord	1959	100.00	200.00	400.00
		Maroon label				
❑ EPA-5121		(There'll Be) Peace in the Valley (For Me)/ It Is No Secret (What God Can Do)//I Believe/Take My Hand, Precious Lord	1959	7.50	15.00	30.00
		Black label, dog on top				
❑ EPA-5121		(There'll Be) Peace in the Valley (For Me)/ It Is No Secret (What God Can Do)//I Believe/Take My Hand, Precious Lord	1965	6.25	12.50	25.00
		Black label, dog on left				
❑ EPA-5121		(There'll Be) Peace in the Valley (For Me)/ It Is No Secret (What God Can Do)//I Believe/Take My Hand, Precious Lord	1969	20.00	40.00	80.00
		Orange label				
❑ EPA-5121	PS	Peace in the Valley	1959	10.00	20.00	40.00
		Three slightly different cover variations with no difference in value				
❑ EPA-5122		King Creole/New Orleans//As Long As I Have You/ Lover Doll	1959	1,000	1,500	2,000
		Maroon label				
❑ EPA-5122		King Creole/New Orleans//As Long As I Have You/ Lover Doll	1959	7.50	15.00	30.00
		Black label, dog on top				
❑ EPA-5122		King Creole/New Orleans//As Long As I Have You/ Lover Doll	1965	6.25	12.50	25.00
		Black label, dog on left				
❑ EPA-5122		King Creole/New Orleans//As Long As I Have You/ Lover Doll	1969	20.00	40.00	80.00
		Orange label				
❑ EPA-5122	PS	King Creole	1959	10.00	20.00	40.00
		With "Gold Standard Series" on front cover				
❑ EPA-5122	PS	King Creole	1965	7.50	15.00	30.00
		Without "Gold Standard Series" on front cover				
❑ EPA-5141		All Shook Up/Don't Ask Me Why//Too Much/ Blue Moon of Kentucky	1959	100.00	200.00	400.00
		Maroon label				
❑ EPA-5141		All Shook Up/Don't Ask Me Why//Too Much/ Blue Moon of Kentucky	1959	10.00	20.00	40.00
		Black label, dog on top				
❑ EPA-5141		All Shook Up/Don't Ask Me Why//Too Much/ Blue Moon of Kentucky	1965	7.50	15.00	30.00
		Black label, dog on left				
❑ EPA-5141		All Shook Up/Don't Ask Me Why//Too Much/ Blue Moon of Kentucky	1969	20.00	40.00	80.00
		Orange label				
❑ EPA-5141	PS	A Touch of Gold, Volume 3	1959	10.00	20.00	40.00
❑ EPA-5157		Press Interview with Elvis Presley// Elvis Presley's Newsreel Interview/Pat Hernon Interviews Elvis...	1965	7.50	15.00	30.00
		Black label, dog on top				
❑ EPA-5157		Press Interview with Elvis Presley// Elvis Presley's Newsreel Interview/Pat Hernon Interviews Elvis...	1969	20.00	40.00	80.00
		Orange label				
❑ EPA-5157	PS	Elvis Sails	1965	7.50	15.00	30.00
❑ G8-MW-8705	DJ	TV Guide Presents Elvis Presley	1956	300.00	600.00	1,200
		Blue label, locked grooves (needle has to be lifted to play each of the four excerpts)				

Preston, Billy
A&M

❑ 1320		Outa-Space/I Wrote a Simple Song	1972		2.50	5.00
❑ 1340		Should Have Known Better/The Bus	1972		2.50	5.00

Number		Title (A Side/B Side)	Year	VG	VG+	NM
☐ 1380		Slaughter/God Loves You	1972		2.50	5.00
☐ 1380	PS	Slaughter/God Loves You	1972		3.00	6.00
☐ 1411		Will It Go Round in Circles/Blackbird	1973		2.00	4.00
☐ 1463		Space Race/We're Gonna Make It	1973		2.00	4.00
☐ 1463	PS	Space Race/We're Gonna Make It	1973		3.00	6.00
☐ 1492		You're So Unique/How Long Has the Train Been Gone	1973		2.00	4.00
☐ 1536		Creature Feature/My Soul Is a Witness	1974		2.00	4.00
☐ 1544		Nothing from Nothing/My Soul Is a Witness	1974		2.00	4.00
☐ 1544	PS	Nothing from Nothing/My Soul Is a Witness	1974		3.00	6.00
☐ 1644		Struttin'/You Are So Beautiful	1974		2.00	4.00
☐ 1735		Fancy Lady/Song of Joy	1975		2.00	4.00
☐ 1768		Do It While You Can/Song of Joy	1975		2.00	4.00
☐ 1892		Do What You Want/I've Got the Spirit	1976		2.00	4.00
☐ 1925		Girl/Ecstasy	1977		2.00	4.00
☐ 1954		Wide Stride/When You Are Mine	1977		2.00	4.00
☐ 1980		A Whole New Thing/Wide Stride	1977		2.00	4.00
☐ 2012		I Really Miss You/Attitudes	1978		2.00	4.00
☐ 2071		Get Back/Space Race	1978		2.00	4.00

Apple

☐ 1808		That's the Way God Planned It/What About You	1969	2.00	4.00	8.00
☐ 1808	PS	That's the Way God Planned It/What About You	1969	2.50	5.00	10.00
☐ 1808		That's the Way God Planned It/What About You	1972	2.00	4.00	8.00

With "Mono" on both sides of record and reference to LP

☐ 1814		Everything's All Right/I Want to Thank You	1969	2.00	4.00	8.00
☐ 1817		All That I've Got (I'm Gonna Give It to You)/ As I Get Older	1970	2.00	4.00	8.00
☐ 1817	PS	All That I've Got (I'm Gonna Give It to You)/ As I Get Older	1970	3.75	7.50	15.00
☐ 1826		My Sweet Lord/Little Girl	1970	3.00	6.00	12.00

With star on A-side label

☐ 1826		My Sweet Lord/Little Girl	1970	2.00	4.00	8.00
☐ PRO-6555	DJ	That's the Way God Planned It (Parts 1 & 2) (mono/stereo)	1969	15.00	30.00	60.00

Apple/Americom

☐ 1808P/M-433		That's the Way God Planned It (Edit)/What About You	1969	100.00	200.00	400.00

Four-inch flexi-disc sold from vending machines

Capitol

☐ 2309		Hey Brother (Part 1)/Hey Brother (Part 2)	1968	2.00	4.00	8.00
☐ 5611		The Girl's Got "It"/The Night	1966	2.00	4.00	8.00
☐ 5660		In the Midnight Hour/Advice	1966	2.00	4.00	8.00
☐ 5730		Sunny/Let the Music Play	1966	2.00	4.00	8.00
☐ 5797		Phony Friends/Can't She Tell	1966	2.00	4.00	8.00

MGM

☐ 14001		The Split/It's Just a Love Game	1968	2.00	4.00	8.00

Motown

☐ 1470		It Will Come In Time/All I Wanted Was You	1979		2.00	4.00
☐ 1505		Sock-It Rocket/Hope	1981		2.00	4.00
☐ 1511		A Change Is Gonna Come/You	1981		2.00	4.00
☐ 1625		I'm Never Gonna Say Goodbye/Love You So	1982		2.00	4.00

Vee Jay

☐ 646		Don't Let the Sun Catch You Cryin'/(B-side unknown)	1965			Cancelled?
☐ 653		Don't Let the Sun Catch You Cryin'/Billy's Bag	1965	2.50	5.00	10.00
☐ 692		Log Cabin/Drown in My Own Tears	1965	2.50	5.00	10.00

Preston, Billy, and Syreeta

Motown

☐ 1460		With You I'm Born Again/Go For It	1979		2.50	5.00
☐ 1477		With You I'm Born Again/All I Wanted Was You	1979		2.00	4.00
☐ 1520		Searchin'/Hey You	1981		2.00	4.00
☐ 1522		Just for You (Put the Boogie in Your Body)/Hey You	1981		2.00	4.00

Tamla

☐ 54312		Dance For Me Children/One More Time for Love	1980		2.00	4.00
☐ 54319		Please Stay/Signed, Sealed, Delivered (I'm Yours)	1980		2.00	4.00

Preston, Johnny

ABC

☐ 11085		I'm Only Human/There's No One Like You	1968	2.50	5.00	10.00
☐ 11187		Kick the Can/I've Just Been Wasting My Time	1969	2.50	5.00	10.00

Hallway

☐ 1201		All Around the World/Just Plain Hurt	1964	3.75	7.50	15.00
☐ 1204		Willie and the Hand Jive/I've Got My Eyes on You	1964	3.75	7.50	15.00
☐ 1927		Running Bear '65/Dedicated to the One I Love	1965	3.75	7.50	15.00

Imperial

☐ 5924		This Little Bitty Tear/The Day the World Stood Still	1963	2.50	5.00	10.00
☐ 5947		I've Got My Eyes on You/I Couldn't Take It Again	1963	2.50	5.00	10.00

Mercury

☐ 10027	S	Cradle of Love/City of Tears	1960	12.50	25.00	50.00
☐ 10036	S	Feel So Fine/I'm Starting to Go Steady	1960	15.00	30.00	60.00
☐ 71474		Running Bear/My Heart Knows	1959	6.25	12.50	25.00
☐ 71598	M	Cradle of Love/City of Tears	1960	5.00	10.00	20.00
☐ 71598	PS	Cradle of Love/City of Tears	1960	7.50	15.00	30.00
☐ 71651	M	Feel So Fine/I'm Starting to Go Steady	1960	5.00	10.00	20.00
☐ 71651	PS	Feel So Fine/I'm Starting to Go Steady	1960	7.50	15.00	30.00
☐ 71691		Charming Billy/Up in the Air	1960	5.00	10.00	20.00

Number		Title (A Side/B Side)	Year	VG	VG+	NM
❑ 71728		New Baby for Christmas/ (I Want a) Rock and Roll Guitar	1960	5.00	10.00	20.00
❑ 71761		Leave My Kitten Alone/Token of Love	1961	5.00	10.00	20.00
❑ 71761	PS	Leave My Kitten Alone/Token of Love	1961	7.50	15.00	30.00
❑ 71803		I Feel Good/Willy Walk	1961	5.00	10.00	20.00
❑ 71865		Let Them Talk/She Once Belonged to Me	1961	5.00	10.00	20.00
❑ 71908		Free Me/Kissin' Tree	1961	5.00	10.00	20.00
❑ 71908	PS	Free Me/Kissin' Tree	1961	7.50	15.00	30.00
❑ 71951		Let's Leave It That Way/Broken Hearts Anonymous	1962	3.75	7.50	15.00
❑ 72049		Let the Big Boss Man (Pull You Through)/ The Day After Forever	1962	3.75	7.50	15.00

TCF Hall

Number		Title (A Side/B Side)	Year	VG	VG+	NM
❑ 101		Running Bear '65/Dedicated to the One I Love	1965	2.50	5.00	10.00
❑ 110		Sounds Like Trouble/You Can Make It If You Try	1965	3.75	7.50	15.00
❑ 120		I'm Askin' Forgiveness/Good Good Lovin'	1965	2.50	5.00	10.00

Pretenders
American Pie

Number		Title (A Side/B Side)	Year	VG	VG+	NM
❑ 9014		Stop Your Sobbing/Talk of the Town	198?			3.00
		Reissue label; first appearance of B-side on U.S. stock 45				

MCA

Number		Title (A Side/B Side)	Year	VG	VG+	NM
❑ 54615		I'm Not in Love/I'm Not in Love (instrumental)	1993			3.00

Polydor

Number		Title (A Side/B Side)	Year	VG	VG+	NM
❑ 887 816-7		Window of the World/1969	1988			3.00
❑ 887 816-7	PS	Window of the World/1969	1988			3.00

Sire

Number		Title (A Side/B Side)	Year	VG	VG+	NM
❑ GSRE 0448		Back on the Chain Gang/My City Was Gone	198?			3.00
		"Back to Back Hits" reissue				
❑ GSRE 0474		Brass in Pocket/Middle of the Road	198?			3.00
		"Back to Back Hits" reissue				
❑ GSRE 0496		Show Me/Thin Line Between Love and Hate	198?			3.00
		"Back to Back Hits" reissue				
❑ PRO-S-942	DJ	Message of Love/Talk of the Town	1981	2.50	5.00	10.00
❑ 18160		I'll Stand By You/Rebel Rock Me	1994			3.00
❑ 18163		Night in My Veins/Angel of the Morning	1994			3.00
❑ 28354		Hymn to Her (She Will Always Carry On)/ Tradition of Love	1987			3.00
❑ 28354	PS	Hymn to Her (She Will Always Carry On)/ Tradition of Love	1987			3.00
❑ 28496		My Baby/Room Full of Mirrors	1987			3.00
❑ 28496	PS	My Baby/Room Full of Mirrors	1987			3.00
❑ 28630		Don't Get Me Wrong/Dance!	1986			3.00
❑ 28630	PS	Don't Get Me Wrong/Dance!	1986			3.00
❑ 29249		Thin Line Between Love and Hate/Time the Avenger	1984			3.00
❑ 29249	PS	Thin Line Between Love and Hate/Time the Avenger	1984			3.00
❑ 29317		Show Me/Fast or Slow (The Law Is The Law)	1984			3.00
❑ 29317	PS	Show Me/Fast or Slow (The Law Is The Law)	1984			3.00
❑ 29444		Middle of the Road/2000 Miles	1983			3.00
❑ 29444	PS	Middle of the Road/2000 Miles	1983			3.00
❑ 29840		Back on the Chain Gang/My City Was Gone	1982			3.00
❑ 29840	PS	Back on the Chain Gang/My City Was Gone	1982			3.00
❑ 49181		Brass in Pocket (I'm Special)/Space Invader	1980		2.00	4.00
❑ 49506		Stop Your Sobbing/Phone Call	1980	2.00	4.00	8.00
❑ 49506	PS	Stop Your Sobbing/Phone Call	1980		2.00	4.00
❑ 49533		Kid/Tattooed Love Boys	1980		2.00	4.00
❑ 49819		Louie Louie/In the Sticks	1981		2.00	4.00
❑ 49819	PS	Louie Louie/In the Sticks	1981		2.00	4.00
❑ 49861		I Go to Sleep/Waste Not Want Not	1981		2.00	4.00

Warner Bros.

Number		Title (A Side/B Side)	Year	VG	VG+	NM
❑ 28259		If There Was a Man/Into Vienna	1987			3.00
		B-side by John Barry				
❑ 28259	PS	If There Was a Man/Into Vienna	1987			3.00
		B-side by John Barry				

Pretenders, The
(Includes all groups with this name except the Chrissie Hynde-led band)

Apt

Number		Title (A Side/B Side)	Year	VG	VG+	NM
❑ 25026		Blue and Lonely/Daddy Needs Baby	1959	75.00	150.00	300.00

Bethlehem

Number		Title (A Side/B Side)	Year	VG	VG+	NM
❑ 3050		The Day You Are Mine/Ding Dong Bells	1962	50.00	100.00	200.00

Central

Number		Title (A Side/B Side)	Year	VG	VG+	NM
❑ 2605		Blue and Lonely/Daddy Needs Baby	1958	250.00	500.00	1,000

Chattahoochie

Number		Title (A Side/B Side)	Year	VG	VG+	NM
❑ 685		Pepita's Theme/Tijuana Taxi	1965	5.00	10.00	20.00

Power-Martin

Number		Title (A Side/B Side)	Year	VG	VG+	NM
❑ 1001		Smile/I'm So Happy	1961	25.00	50.00	100.00

Rama

Number		Title (A Side/B Side)	Year	VG	VG+	NM
❑ 198		Possessive Love/I've Got to Have You Baby	1956	25.00	50.00	100.00

Whirlin' Disc

Number		Title (A Side/B Side)	Year	VG	VG+	NM
❑ 106		Close Your Eyes/Part-Time Sweetheart	1957	30.00	60.00	120.00

Number		Title (A Side/B Side)	Year	VG	VG+	NM

Pretty Boy – See "Covay, Don"

Pretty Things, The
Fontana

❏ 1508		I Can Never Say/Honey, I Need	1965	3.75	7.50	15.00
❏ 1518		Cry to Me/Judgment Day	1965	3.75	7.50	15.00
❏ 1518		Cry to Me/I Can Never Say	1965	3.75	7.50	15.00
❏ 1540		Midnight to Six Man/Can't Stand Pain	1966	3.75	7.50	15.00
❏ 1550		Come See Me/Progress	1966	3.75	7.50	15.00
❏ 1550		Come See Me/Judgment Day	1966	3.75	7.50	15.00
❏ 1916		Big Boss Man/Rosalyn	1964	3.75	7.50	15.00
❏ 1941		Don't Bring Me Down/We'll Be Together	1964	3.75	7.50	15.00

Laurie

❏ 3458		Talkin' About the Good Times/ Walking Through My Dreams	1968	7.50	15.00	30.00

Rare Earth

❏ 5005		Private Sorrow/Balloon Burning	1969	3.75	7.50	15.00

Swan Song

❏ 70104		Come Home Momma/Joey	1975		2.50	5.00
❏ 70107		It Isn't Rock & Roll/Remember That Boy	1975		2.50	5.00

Price, Alan
(Formerly of the Animals)
Cotillion

❏ 44044		Falling in Love Again/Sly Sadie	1969		3.00	6.00

Epic

❏ 04319		I Don't Feel No Pain No More (Time and Tide)/ Rowf and Snitter Run to Sea	1984		2.00	4.00

Jet

❏ XW1119		I Wanna Dance/Just for You	1978		2.00	4.00
❏ 5056		This Is Your Lucky Day/Mama Don't Go Home	1979		2.00	4.00

Parrot

❏ 3001		I Put a Spell on You/Iechyd-Da	1966	2.50	5.00	10.00
❏ 3007		Hi-Lili, Hi-Lo/Take Me Home	1966	2.50	5.00	10.00
❏ 3009		Tickle Me/ Simon Smith and His Amazing Dancing Bears	1966	2.50	5.00	10.00
❏ 3013		Who Cares/The House That Jack Built	1967	2.00	4.00	8.00
❏ 3014		Shame/Don't Do That Again	1967	2.00	4.00	8.00
❏ 3019		Not Born to Follow/To Ramona	1968	2.00	4.00	8.00

Warner Bros.

❏ 7717		Poor People/O Lucky Man	1973		2.50	5.00

Price, Lloyd
ABC

❏ 1237		Stagger Lee/Personality	1969		3.00	6.00

"Golden Treasure Chest" reissue; contains the "sanitized" version of "Stagger Lee" with Mr. Lee and Billy arguing over a woman

❏ 11016		Personality/Just Because	1967	2.00	4.00	8.00

ABC-Paramount

❏ 9792		Just Because/Why	1957	5.00	10.00	20.00
❏ 9972	M	Stagger Lee/You Need Love	1958	5.00	10.00	20.00

Most, if not all, copies contain the "raunchy" version of "Stagger Lee" with Mr. Lee and Billy playing cards

❏ S-9972	S	Stagger Lee/You Need Love	1958	10.00	20.00	40.00
❏ 9997	M	Where Were You (On Our Wedding Day)?/ Is It Really Love	1959	5.00	10.00	20.00
❏ S-9997	S	Where Were You (On Our Wedding Day)?/ Is It Really Love	1959	10.00	20.00	40.00
❏ 10018	M	Personality/Have You Ever Had the Blues	1959	5.00	10.00	20.00
❏ S-10018	S	Personality/Have You Ever Had the Blues	1959	12.50	25.00	50.00
❏ 10018	M	(You've Got) Personality/Have You Ever Had the Blues	1959	5.00	10.00	20.00

Note longer title

❏ 10032	M	I'm Gonna Get Married/Three Little Pigs	1959	5.00	10.00	20.00
❏ S-10032	S	I'm Gonna Get Married/Three Little Pigs	1959	12.50	25.00	50.00
❏ 10062		Come Into My Heart/Won't Cha Come Home	1959	3.75	7.50	15.00
❏ 10075		Lady Luck/Never Let Me Go	1960	3.75	7.50	15.00
❏ 10102		No If's -- No And's/For Love	1960	3.75	7.50	15.00
❏ 10123		Question/If I Look a Little Blue	1960	3.75	7.50	15.00
❏ 10139		Just Call Me (And I'll Understand)/ Who Could've Told You	1960	3.75	7.50	15.00
❏ 10162		(You Better) Know What You're Doin'/ That's Why Tears Come and Go	1960	3.75	7.50	15.00
❏ 10177		Boo Hoo/I Made You Cry	1961	3.75	7.50	15.00
❏ 10197		One Hundred Percent/Say I'm the One	1961	3.75	7.50	15.00
❏ 10206		String of Pearls/Chantilly Lace	1961	3.75	7.50	15.00
❏ 10221		Mary and Man-O/I Ain't Givin' Up Nothin'	1961	3.75	7.50	15.00
❏ 10229		Talk to Me/I Cover the Waterfront	1961	3.75	7.50	15.00
❏ 10288		Be a Leader/'Nother Fairy Tale	1962	3.75	7.50	15.00
❏ 10299		Twistin' the Blues/Pop Eye's Irresistible You	1962	3.75	7.50	15.00
❏ 10342		Counterfeit Friends/Your Picture	1962	3.75	7.50	15.00
❏ 10372		Under Your Spell Again/Happy Birthday Mama	1962	3.75	7.50	15.00
❏ 10412		Who's Sorry Now/Hello Bill	1963	3.75	7.50	15.00

Double-L

❏ 714		Pistol Packin' Mama/Tennessee Waltz	1963	2.50	5.00	10.00
❏ 722		Misty/Cry On	1963	2.50	5.00	10.00

Number		Title (A Side/B Side)	Year	VG	VG+	NM
☐ 728		Merry Christmas Mama/Auld Lang Syne	1963	3.00	6.00	12.00
☐ 729		Billie Baby/Try a Little Bit of Tenderness	1964	2.50	5.00	10.00
☐ 729	PS	Billie Baby/Try a Little Bit of Tenderness	1964	6.25	12.50	25.00
☐ 730		I'll Be a Fool for You/	1964	2.50	5.00	10.00
		You're Nobody Till Somebody Loves You				
☐ 736		Go On Little Girl/You're Reading Me	1965	2.50	5.00	10.00
☐ 739		Every Night/Peeping and Hiding	1966	2.50	5.00	10.00
☐ 740		Send Me Some Loving/Somewhere Along	1966	2.50	5.00	10.00

GSF

☐ 6882		Sing a Song/(B-side unknown)	1972		3.00	6.00
☐ 6894		Love Music/Just for Baby	1973		3.00	6.00
☐ 6904		Trying to Slip (Away)/They Get Down	1973		3.00	6.00

Hurd

☐ 82		Misty '66/Saturday Night	1966	2.00	4.00	8.00

Jad

☐ 208		Luv, Luv, Luv/Take All	1968	2.00	4.00	8.00
☐ 212		Don't Stop Now/The Truth	1968	2.00	4.00	8.00

KRC

☐ 301		Lonely Chair/The Chicken and the Bop	1957	12.50	25.00	50.00
☐ 303		Hello Little Girl/Georgianna	1957	6.25	12.50	25.00
☐ 305		How Many Times/To Love and Be Loved	1957	6.25	12.50	25.00
☐ 587		Just Because/Why	1957	20.00	40.00	80.00
☐ 5000		No Limit to Love/Such a Mess	195?	6.25	12.50	25.00
☐ 5002		Gonna Let You Come Back Home/Down by the River	195?	6.25	12.50	25.00

LPG

☐ 111		What Did You Do with My Love/Love Music	1976		3.00	6.00

Ludix

☐ 4747		Feelin' Good/Cupid's Bandwagon	197?		3.00	6.00

Monument

☐ 856		Don't Cry/I Love You, I Just Love You	1964	2.50	5.00	10.00
☐ 865		Amen/I'd Fight the World	1964	2.50	5.00	10.00
☐ 877		Oh, Lady Luck/Woman	1965	2.50	5.00	10.00
☐ 887		If I Had My Life to Live Over/Two for Love	1965	2.50	5.00	10.00

Paramount

☐ 0168		In the Eyes of God/The Legend of Nigger Charley	1972		3.00	6.00

Reprise

☐ 0499		I Won't Cry Anymore/The Man Who Took the Valise	1966	2.00	4.00	8.00
☐		Off the Floor at Grand Central Station at Noon				

Scepter

☐ 12310		Hooked on a Feeling/If You Really Love Him	1971		3.00	6.00
☐ 12327		Mr. and Mrs. Untrue/Natural SInner	1971		3.00	6.00

Specialty

☐ 428		Lawdy Miss Clawdy/Mailman Blues	1952	25.00	50.00	100.00
☐ 428		Lawdy Miss Clawdy/Mailman Blues	1952	150.00	300.00	600.00
		Red vinyl				
☐ 440		Oooh-Oooh-Oooh/Restless Heart	1952	12.50	25.00	50.00
☐ 452		Ain't It a Shame?/Tell Me Pretty Baby	1953	12.50	25.00	50.00
☐ 452		Ain't It a Shame?/Tell Me Pretty Baby	1953	37.50	75.00	150.00
		Red vinyl				
☐ 457		What's the Matter Now/So Long	1953	12.50	25.00	50.00
☐ 457		What's the Matter Now/So Long	1953	37.50	75.00	150.00
		Red vinyl				
☐ 463		Where You At?/Baby Don't Turn Your Back on Me	1953	12.50	25.00	50.00
☐ 463		Where You At?/Baby Don't Turn Your Back on Me	1953	37.50	75.00	150.00
		Red vinyl				
☐ 471		I Wish Your Picture Was You/Frog Legs	1953	12.50	25.00	50.00
☐ 483		Let Me Come Home, Baby/Too Late for Tears	1954	12.50	25.00	50.00
☐ 483		Let Me Come Home, Baby/Too Late for Tears	1954	37.50	75.00	150.00
		Red vinyl				
☐ 494		Walkin' the Track/Jimmie Lee	1954	12.50	25.00	50.00
☐ 535		Oo-Ee Baby/Chee-Koo Baby	1954	7.50	15.00	30.00
☐ 540		Trying to Find Someone to Love/Lord, Lord, Amen!	1955	7.50	15.00	30.00
☐ 571		Woe Ho Ho/I Yi Yi Gomen-a-Sai (I'm Sorry)	1956	7.50	15.00	30.00
☐ 578		Country Boy Rock/Rock 'N' Dance	1956	10.00	20.00	40.00
☐ 582		Forgive Me, Clawdy/I'm Glad	1956	7.50	15.00	30.00
☐ 602		Baby Please Come Home/	1957	7.50	15.00	30.00
		Breaking My Heart (All Over Again)				
☐ 661		Lawdy Miss Clawdy/Mailman Blues	1959	5.00	10.00	20.00

Turntable

☐ 501		I Understand/The Grass Will Sing (For You)	1969	2.00	4.00	8.00
☐ 502		I Heard It Through the Grapevine/It's Your Thing	1969	2.00	4.00	8.00
☐ 506		Bad Conditions/The Truth	1969	2.00	4.00	8.00
☐ 509		Lawdy Miss Clawdy/Little Volcano	1969	2.00	4.00	8.00

Priesman, Magel

Sun

☐ 294		Memories of You/I Feel So Blue	1958	6.25	12.50	25.00

Primettes, The

(Early version of the Supremes)

LuPine

☐ 120		Tears of Sorrow/Pretty	1962	75.00	150.00	300.00

Number		Title (A Side/B Side)	Year	VG	VG+	NM

Primitives, The
Parkway
| ❏ 940 | | Help Me/Let Them Fall | 1965 | 5.00 | 10.00 | 20.00 |

Pickwick
| ❏ 1001 | | The Ostrich/Sneaky Pete | 1964 | 75.00 | 150.00 | 300.00 |

Lou Reed was in this group

Prince
(Includes Prince and the Revolution; Prince and the New Power Generation [N.P.G.])

Paisley Park
❏ GWB 0528		Purple Rain/Raspberry Beret	1986			3.00
		"Back to Back Hits" reissue				
❏ GWB 0529		Pop Life/America	1986			3.00
		"Back to Back Hits" reissue				
❏ PRO-S-3371		I Wish U Heaven (Radio Edit of Remix)/	1988	3.75	7.50	15.00
		I Wish U Heaven (Single Edit of Remix)				
❏ 18583		The Morning Papers/Live 4 Love	1993			3.00
❏ 18700		Damn U/2 Whom It May Concern	1993			3.00
❏ 18707		My Name Is Prince/Sexy Mutha	1992			3.00
❏ 18817		Sexy M.F./Strollin'	1992			3.00
❏ 18824		7/7 (Acoustic Version)	1992			3.00
❏ 19020		Money Don't Matter 2 Night/Call the Law	1992			3.00
❏ 19083		Diamonds and Pearls/X-Cerpts	1991			3.00
❏ 19090		Insatiable/I Love U in Me	1991			3.00
❏ 19175		Cream/Horny Pony	1991			3.00
❏ 19225		Gett Off/Horny Pony	1991			3.00
❏ 19525		New Power Generation/New Power Generation	1990			3.00
❏ 19751		Thieves in the Temple/Thieves in the Temple	1990			3.00
❏ 27745		I Wish U Heaven/Scarlet Pussy	1988			3.00
❏ 27745	PS	I Wish U Heaven/Scarlet Pussy	1988			3.00
❏ 27806		Glam Slam/Escape	1988			3.00
❏ 27806	PS	Glam Slam/Escape	1988			3.00
		Heavy plastic sleeve with title sticker				
❏ 27900		Alphabet St./Alphabet St. Part 2	1988			3.00
❏ 27900	PS	Alphabet St./Alphabet St. Part 2	1988			3.00
		Heavy plastic sleeve with title sticker				
❏ 28288		I Could Never Take the Place of Your Man/Hot Thing	1987			3.00
❏ 28288	PS	I Could Never Take the Place of Your Man/Hot Thing	1987			3.00
❏ 28289		U Got the Look/Housequake	1987			3.00
❏ 28289	PS	U Got the Look/Housequake	1987			3.00
❏ 28334		If I Was Your Girlfriend/Shockadelica	1987			3.00
❏ 28334	PS	If I Was Your Girlfriend/Shockadelica	1987			3.00
❏ 28399		Sign "O" the Times/La, La, La, Hee, Hee, Hee	1987			3.00
❏ 28399	PS	Sign "O" the Times/La, La, La, Hee, Hee, Hee	1987			3.00
❏ 28620		Anotherloverholenyohead/Girls and Boys	1986			3.00
❏ 28620	PS	Anotherloverholenyohead/Girls and Boys	1986			3.00
❏ 28711		Mountains/Alexa de Paris	1986			3.00
❏ 28711	PS	Mountains/Alexa de Paris	1986			3.00
❏ 28751		Kiss/Love or $	1986			3.00
❏ 28751	PS	Kiss/Love or $	1986			3.00
❏ 28972		Raspberry Beret/She's Always In My Hair	1985			3.00
❏ 28972	PS	Raspberry Beret/She's Always In My Hair	1985			3.00
❏ 28998		Pop Life/Hello	1985			3.00
❏ 28998	PS	Pop Life/Hello	1985			3.00
❏ 28999		America/Girl	1985			3.00
❏ 28999	PS	America/Girl	1985			3.00
❏ 29052		Paisley Park/She's Always In My Hair	1985			Unreleased
❏ 29052	PS	Paisley Park/She's Always In My Hair	1985	125.00	250.00	500.00

Warner Bros.
❏ GWB 0392		I Wanna Be Your Lover/	1982		2.00	4.00
		Why You Wanna Treat Me So Bad?				
		"Back to Back Hits" reissue				
❏ GWB 0468		1999/Little Red Corvette	1984			3.00
		"Back to Back Hits" reissue				
❏ GWB 0476		Delirious/Let's Pretend We're Married	1984			3.00
		"Back to Back Hits" reissue				
❏ GWB 0516		When Doves Cry/Let's Go Crazy	1985			3.00
		"Back to Back Hits" reissue				
❏ GWB 0517		I Would Die 4 U/Take Me With U	1985			3.00
		"Back to Back Hits" reissue				
❏ 8619		Soft and Wet/So Blue	1978	7.50	15.00	30.00
❏ 8619	DJ	Soft and Wet (mono/stereo)	1978	3.75	7.50	15.00
❏ 8713		Just As Long As We're Together/In Love	1978	7.50	15.00	30.00
❏ 8713	DJ	Just As Long As We're Together (mono/stereo)	1978	3.75	7.50	15.00
❏ 17715		Gold/Rock 'N' Roll Is Alive! (and it lives in Minneapolis)	1995			3.00
❏ 17811		I Hate U/I Hate U	1995			3.00
❏ 17903		Purple Medley/Kirk J's B Sides Remix	1995			3.00
❏ 18012		Space (Radio Remix)/Space (Album Version)	1994			3.00
❏ 18074		Letitgo/Solo	1994			3.00
❏ 18371		Pink Cashmere/Soft and Wet	1993			3.00
❏ 18372		Peach/Nothing Compares 2 U (Live)	1993			3.00

Note: Warner Bros. 21000 series are "Back to Back Hits" reissues.

❏ 21858		I Could Never Take the Place of Your Man/Alphabet St.	1989			3.00
❏ 21859		Batdance/Partyman	1989			3.00
❏ 21938		Sign "O" the Times/U Got the Look	1988			3.00
❏ 21980		Anotherloverholenyohead/Mountains	1987			3.00

Number		Title (A Side/B Side)	Year	VG	VG+	NM
❑ 21981		Uptown/Controversy	1987			3.00
❑ 21982		Kiss/Soft and Wet	1987			3.00
❑ 22757		The Arms of Orion/I Love U in Me	1989			3.00
❑ 22757	PS	The Arms of Orion/I Love U in Me	1989			3.00

With Sheena Easton

Number		Title (A Side/B Side)	Year	VG	VG+	NM
❑ 22814		Partyman/Feel U Up	1989			3.00
❑ 22814	PS	Partyman/Feel U Up	1989			3.00
❑ 22824		Scandalous/When 2 R In Love	1989			3.00
❑ 22824	PS	Scandalous/When 2 R In Love	1989			3.00
❑ 22924		Batdance/200 Balloons	1989			3.00
❑ 22924	PS	Batdance/200 Balloons	1989			3.00
❑ 29079		Take Me With U/Baby I'm a Star	1985		2.00	4.00
❑ 29079	PS	Take Me With U/Baby I'm a Star	1985		2.00	4.00
❑ 29121		I Would Die 4 U/Another Lonely Christmas	1984		2.00	4.00
❑ 29121	PS	I Would Die 4 U/Another Lonely Christmas	1984		2.00	4.00
❑ 29174		Purple Rain/God	1984		2.00	4.00

Purple vinyl

Number		Title (A Side/B Side)	Year	VG	VG+	NM
❑ 29174		Purple Rain/God	1984	2.00	4.00	8.00

Black vinyl

Number		Title (A Side/B Side)	Year	VG	VG+	NM
❑ 29174	PS	Purple Rain/God	1984	2.00	4.00	8.00

Plastic semi-transparent sleeve

Number		Title (A Side/B Side)	Year	VG	VG+	NM
❑ 29216		Let's Go Crazy/Erotic City	1984		2.00	4.00
❑ 29216	PS	Let's Go Crazy/Erotic City	1984	2.00	4.00	8.00
❑ 29286		When Doves Cry/17 Days	1984			3.00

Black vinyl

Number		Title (A Side/B Side)	Year	VG	VG+	NM
❑ 29286	DJ	When Doves Cry/17 Days	1984	2.50	5.00	10.00

Purple vinyl

Number		Title (A Side/B Side)	Year	VG	VG+	NM
❑ 29286	PS	When Doves Cry/17 Days	1984			3.00
❑ 29503		Delirious/Horny Toad	1983		3.00	6.00

Label erroneously lists A-side time at 3:56

Number		Title (A Side/B Side)	Year	VG	VG+	NM
❑ 29503		Delirious/Horny Toad	1983			5.00

Label lists correct A-side time of 2:37

Number		Title (A Side/B Side)	Year	VG	VG+	NM
❑ 29503	PS	Delirious/Horny Toad	1983	12.50	25.00	50.00

Fold-out poster sleeve

Number		Title (A Side/B Side)	Year	VG	VG+	NM
❑ 29548		Let's Pretend We're Married/Irresistible Bitch	1983		2.50	5.00
❑ 29548	PS	Let's Pretend We're Married/Irresistible Bitch	1983	2.50	5.00	10.00
❑ 29746		Little Red Corvette/All the Critics Love U in New York	1983		2.50	5.00
❑ 29896		1999/How Come U Don't Call Me Anymore?	1982		2.50	5.00
❑ 29896	PS	1999/How Come U Don't Call Me Anymore?	1982	2.50	5.00	10.00
❑ 29942		Do Me, Baby/Private Joy	1982	3.75	7.50	15.00
❑ 29942	DJ	Do Me, Baby (same on both sides)	1982	3.75	7.50	
❑ 49050	DJ	My Love Is Forever (mono/stereo)	1979	3.75	7.50	15.00
❑ 49050	PS	My Love Is Forever	1979	18.75	37.50	75.00

Promo-only sleeve; withdrawn when "I Wanna Be Your Lover" was pushed as the A-side

Number		Title (A Side/B Side)	Year	VG	VG+	NM
❑ 49050		I Wanna Be Your Lover/My Love Is Forever	1979	2.50	5.00	10.00
❑ 49050	DJ	I Wanna Be Your Lover (mono/stereo)	1979	3.75	7.50	15.00
❑ 49178		Why You Wanna Treat Me So Bad/Baby	1980	7.50	15.00	30.00
❑ 49178	DJ	Why You Wanna Treat Me So Bad (mono/stereo)	1980	3.75	7.50	15.00
❑ 49226		Still Waiting/Bambi	1980	3.75	7.50	15.00
❑ 49226	DJ	Still Waiting (mono/stereo)	1980		3.75	7.50
❑ 49559		Uptown/Crazy You	1980	3.75	7.50	15.00
❑ 49559	DJ	Uptown (mono/stereo)	1980		3.75	7.50
❑ 49559	PS	Uptown/Crazy You	1980	3.75	7.50	15.00
❑ 49638		Dirty Mind/When We're Dancing Close and Slow	1980	3.75	7.50	15.00
❑ 49638	DJ	Dirty Mind (same on both sides)	1980		3.75	7.50
❑ 49808		Controversy/When You Were Mine	1981	3.75	7.50	15.00
❑ 49808	DJ	Controversy (same on both sides)	1981		3.75	7.50
❑ 50002		Let's Work/Ronnie Talk to Russia	1982	3.75	7.50	15.00
❑ 50002	DJ	Let's Work (same on both sides)	1982		3.75	7.50

Prisonaires, The

Sun

Number		Title (A Side/B Side)	Year	VG	VG+	NM
❑ 186		Just Walking in the Rain/Baby Please	1953	200.00	400.00	600.00
❑ 189		Softly and Tenderly/My God Is Real	1953	150.00	325.00	500.00
❑ 191		A Prisoner's Prayer/I Know	1953	100.00	200.00	400.00
❑ 207		There Is Love in You/What'll You Do Next	1954	5,000	7,500	10,000

One of record collecting's legendary rarities, this could bring much more at open auction.

Proby, P.J.

Imperial

Number		Title (A Side/B Side)	Year	VG	VG+	NM
❑ 66079		Rocking Pneumonia/Just Call, I'll Be There	1964	3.75	7.50	15.00
❑ 66084		Somewhere/Just Like Him	1965			Unreleased

Liberty

Number		Title (A Side/B Side)	Year	VG	VG+	NM
❑ 55367		There Stands the One/Try to Forget Her	1961	3.75	7.50	15.00
❑ 55505		The Other Side of Town/Watch Me Walk Away	1962	3.75	7.50	15.00
❑ 55588		So Do I/I Can't Take It Like You Can	1963	3.75	7.50	15.00
❑ 55757		Somewhere/Just Like Him	1964	3.00	6.00	12.00
❑ 55777		Rocking Pneumonia/I Apologize	1965	3.00	6.00	12.00
❑ 55791		Stagger Lee/Mission Bell	1965	3.00	6.00	12.00
❑ 55806		That Means a Lot/Let the Water Run Down	1965	3.75	7.50	15.00

The A-side is a Lennon-McCartney song; the Beatles' own version was not released until 1996

Number		Title (A Side/B Side)	Year	VG	VG+	NM
❑ 55850		Good Things Are Coming My Way/Maria	1965	3.00	6.00	12.00
❑ 55875		My Prayer/Wicked Woman	1966	3.00	6.00	12.00
❑ 55915		If I Ruled the World/I Can't Make It Alone	1966	3.00	6.00	12.00
❑ 55936		Niki-Hoeky/Good Things Are Coming My Way	1966	2.50	5.00	10.00

Number		Title (A Side/B Side)	Year	VG	VG+	NM
❏ 55974		Work with Me Annie/You Can't Come Home Again (If You Leave Me Now)	1967	2.50	5.00	10.00
❏ 55989		Butterfly High/Just Holding On	1967	2.50	5.00	10.00
❏ 56031		It's Your Day Today/I Apologize	1968	2.00	4.00	8.00
❏ 56051		What's Wrong with My World/Turn Her Away	1968	2.00	4.00	8.00

London

❏ 9648		Hold Me/The Tip of My Fingers	1964	3.75	7.50	15.00
❏ 9688		Hold Me/The Tip of My Fingers	1964	3.75	7.50	15.00
❏ 9705		Sweet and Tender Romance/Together	1964	3.75	7.50	15.00

Surfside

❏ 714		You Got Me Crying/I Need Love	1965	5.00	10.00	20.00

United Artists

❏ 0070		Niki-Hoeky/Let the Water Run Down	1973		2.00	4.00

"Silver Spotlight Series" reissue

Procol Harum

A&M

❏ 885		Homburg/Good Captain Clack	1967	3.00	6.00	12.00
❏ 927		In the Wee Small Hours of Sixpence/Quite Rightly So	1968	3.00	6.00	12.00
❏ 1069		A Salty Dog/Long Gone Geek	1969	2.00	4.00	8.00
❏ 1111		The Devil Came from Kansas/Boredom	1969	2.00	4.00	8.00
❏ 1218		Whiskey Train/About to Die	1970		3.00	6.00
❏ 1264		Power Failure/Broken Barricades	1971		3.00	6.00
❏ 1287		Song for a Dreamer/Simple Sister	1971		3.00	6.00
❏ 1347		Conquistador/A Salty Dog	1972		2.50	5.00
❏ 1347	PS	Conquistador/A Salty Dog	1972	2.00	4.00	8.00
❏ 1389		A Whiter Shade of Pale/Lime Street Blues	1972		2.50	5.00
❏ 1389	PS	A Whiter Shade of Pale/Lime Street Blues	1972		2.50	5.00

Chrysalis

❏ 2013		Grand Hotel/Fires	1973		2.50	5.00
❏ 2032		Nothing But the Truth/Drunk Again	1973		2.50	5.00
❏ 2109		Pandora's Box/Piper's Tune	1975		2.50	5.00

Deram

❏ 7507		A Whiter Shade of Pale/Lime Street Blues	1967	3.75	7.50	15.00

Professor Morrison's Lollipop

White Whale

❏ 275		Gypsy Lady/You Got the Love	1968	2.50	5.00	10.00
❏ 288		Angela/Duba Duba Doo	1968	2.50	5.00	10.00
❏ 293		Oo Poo Pah Susie/You Can Take It	1969	2.50	5.00	10.00

Proffitt, Randy, and the Beachcombers

Bett-Coe

❏ 103		Check That Baby Out One Time/Young Love in Spring	196?	12.50	25.00	50.00

Profiles, The

Gait

❏ 1444		Never/Right By Her Side	1962	50.00	100.00	200.00

Puckett, Gary, and the Union Gap

Columbia

❏ 44297		Woman, Woman/Don't Make Promises	1967	2.00	4.00	8.00
❏ 44297	PS	Woman, Woman/Don't Make Promises	1967	3.00	6.00	12.00

As "The Union Gap"

❏ 44450		Young Girl/I'm Losing You	1968	2.00	4.00	8.00
❏ 44450	PS	Young Girl/I'm Losing You	1968	3.00	6.00	12.00

As "The Union Gap"

❏ 44547		Lady Willpower/Daylight Strangers	1968	2.00	4.00	8.00
❏ 44547	PS	Lady Willpower/Daylight Strangers	1968	3.00	6.00	12.00

As "The Union Gap"

❏ 44644		Over You/If the Day Would Come	1968		3.00	6.00
❏ 44788		Don't Give In to Him/Could I	1969		3.00	6.00
❏ 44967		This Girl Is a Woman Now/His Other Woman	1969		3.00	6.00
❏ 45097		Let's Give Adam and Eve Another Chance/The Beggar	1970		3.00	6.00
❏ 45097	PS	Let's Give Adam and Eve Another Chance/The Beggar	1970	2.00	4.00	8.00
❏ 45249		I Just Don't Know What to Do With Myself/All That Matters	1970		2.50	5.00
❏ 45303		Keep the Customer Satisfied/No One Really Knows	1971		2.50	5.00
❏ 45358		Life Has Its Little Ups and Downs/Shimmering Eyes	1971		2.50	5.00
❏ 45438		Hello Morning/Gentle Woman	1971		2.50	5.00
❏ 45509		Hello Morning/I Can't Hold On	1971		2.50	5.00
❏ 45678		Bless the Child/Leavin' in the Morning	1972		2.50	5.00

Pufnstuf

Decca

❏ 32702		Pufnstuf/Nonsense	1970	3.75	7.50	15.00

Pullen, Dwight

Carlton

❏ 455		Sunglasses After Dark/Teenage Bug	1958	75.00	150.00	300.00

Sage and Sand

❏ 279		By You, By the Bayou/It's Over With	1959	7.50	15.00	30.00
❏ 283		I Lived a Lifetime Last Night/You'll Get Yours Some Day	1959	7.50	15.00	30.00

Number	Title (A Side/B Side)	Year	VG	VG+	NM

Purify, James and Bobby
Bell

☐ 648	I'm Your Puppet/So Many Reasons	1966	2.50	5.00	10.00
☐ 660	Wish You Didn't Have to Go/ You Can't Keep a Good Man Down	1967	2.00	4.00	8.00
☐ 669	Shake a Tail Feather/Goodness Gracious	1967	2.00	4.00	8.00
☐ 680	I Take What I Want/Sixteen Tons	1967	2.00	4.00	8.00
☐ 685	Let Love Come Between Us/ I Don't Want to Have to Go	1967	2.00	4.00	8.00
☐ 700	Do Unto Me/Everybody Needs Somebody	1967	2.00	4.00	8.00
☐ 721	I Can Remember/I Was Born to Lose Out	1968	2.00	4.00	8.00
☐ 735	Help Yourself (To All of My Lovin')/Last Piece of Love	1968	2.00	4.00	8.00
☐ 751	Untie Me/We're Finally Gonna Make It	1968	2.00	4.00	8.00
☐ 774	I Don't Know What It Is You Got/Section C	1969	2.00	4.00	8.00

Casablanca

☐ 812	Do Your Thing/Why Love	1974		2.50	5.00
☐ 827	Man Can't Be a Man Without a Woman/ You and Me Together Forever	1975		2.50	5.00
☐ 830	All the Love I Got/(B-side unknown)	1975		2.50	5.00

Mercury

☐ 73767	I'm Your Puppet/Lay Me Down Easy	1976		2.50	5.00
☐ 73806	Morning Glory/Turning Back the Pages	1976		2.50	5.00
☐ 73884	I Ain't Got to Love Nobody Else/ What's Better Than Love	1977		2.50	5.00
☐ 73893	Get Closer/What's Better Than Love	1977		2.50	5.00

Pyramids, The
(Several different groups)
Best

☐ 1	Pyramid's Stomp/Paul	1963	7.50	15.00	30.00
☐ 102	Penetration/Here Comes Marsha	1963	10.00	20.00	40.00
☐ 13001	Pyramid's Stomp/Paul	1963	5.00	10.00	20.00
☐ 13002	Penetration/Here Comes Marsha *No mention of London Records on label*	1964	5.00	10.00	20.00
☐ 13002	Penetration/Here Comes Marsha *With "Dist. by London" or similar wording on label*	1964	3.75	7.50	15.00
☐ 13002	PS Penetration/Here Comes Marsha *Black sleeve*	1964	10.00	20.00	40.00
☐ 13002	PS Penetration/Here Comes Marsha *Red sleeve*	1964	10.00	20.00	40.00

Cedwicke

☐ 13005	Midnight Run/Custom Caravan	1964	10.00	20.00	40.00
☐ 13006	Contact/Pressure	1964	10.00	20.00	40.00

Cub

☐ 9112	I'm the Playboy/Cryin'	1962	5.00	10.00	20.00

Davis

☐ 453	At Any Cost/Okay, Baby!	1956	12.50	25.00	50.00
☐ 457	Why Did You Go/Before It's Too Late	1957	12.50	25.00	50.00

Federal

☐ 12233	Deep in My Heart for You/And I Need You	1955	100.00	200.00	400.00

Hollywood

☐ 1047	Someday/Bow Wow	1955	125.00	250.00	500.00

RCA Victor

☐ 47-7556	Long Long Time/Oh No You Won't (Oh Yes You Will)	1959	3.75	7.50	15.00

Shell

☐ 304	Ankle Bracelet/Hot Dog Dooly Wah *As "The Original Pyramids"*	1961	6.25	12.50	25.00
☐ 711	Ankle Bracelet/Hot Dog Dooly Wah	1958	12.50	25.00	50.00

Sonbert

☐ 82861	I'm the Playboy/Cryin'	1962	10.00	20.00	40.00

Vee Jay

☐ 489	What Is Love/Shakin' Fit	1963	6.25	12.50	25.00

Python Lee Jackson
(With Rod Stewart on vocals)
GNP Crescendo

☐ 449	In a Broken Dream/Doin' Fine	1972		3.00	6.00
☐ 449	In a Broken Dream/Turn the Music Down	1972		3.00	6.00
☐ 462	Cloud Nine/Rod's Blues	1973		3.00	6.00

Q

Quarter Notes, The
Bison

☐ 757	Frantic Flip/Canadian Sunset	1960	7.50	15.00	30.00

Boom

☐ 60018	Hey Little Girl/I've Been Loved	1966	3.75	7.50	15.00

DeLuxe

☐ 6116	Loneliness/Come De Nite	1957	6.25	12.50	25.00
☐ 6129	My Fantasy/Ten Minutes to Midnight	1957	6.25	12.50	25.00

Number		Title (A Side/B Side)	Year	VG	VG+	NM
Dot						
❏ 15685		Please Come Home/Like You Bug Me	1958	6.25	12.50	25.00
Guyden						
❏ 2083		Pretty Pretty Eyes/I Don't Wanna Go Home	1963	5.00	10.00	20.00
Imperial						
❏ 5647		Frantic Flip/Canadian Sunset	1960	3.75	7.50	15.00
RCA Victor						
❏ 47-7327		The Interview/Punkanilla	1958	3.75	7.50	15.00
Wizz						
❏ 715		Record Hop Blues/Suki-Yaki-Rocki	1959	6.25	12.50	25.00

Quarterflash
(Also see "Seafood Mama")

Number		Title (A Side/B Side)	Year	VG	VG+	NM
Geffen						
❏ 28894		Walking on Ice/Talk to Me	1985			3.00
❏ 28908		Talk to Me/Grace Under Fire	1985			3.00
❏ 28908	PS	Talk to Me/Grace Under Fire	1985			3.00
❏ 29523		Take Another Picture/One More Round to Go	1983		2.00	4.00
❏ 29523	PS	Take Another Picture/One More Round to Go	1983		2.00	4.00
❏ 29603		Take Me to Heart/Nowhere Left to Hide	1983		2.00	4.00
❏ 29603	PS	Take Me to Heart/Nowhere Left to Hide	1983		2.00	4.00
❏ 29882		Try to Make It True/Critical Times	1982		2.00	4.00
❏ 29994		Right Kind of Love/You're Holdin' Me Back	1982		2.00	4.00
❏ 29994	PS	Right Kind of Love/You're Holdin' Me Back	1982		2.00	4.00
❏ 49824		Harden My Heart/Don't Be Lonely	1981		2.00	4.00
❏ 50006		Find Another Fool/Cruisin' with the Deuce	1982		2.00	4.00
❏ 50006	PS	Find Another Fool/Cruisin' with the Deuce	1982		2.00	4.00
Warner Bros.						
❏ 29932		Night Shift/Love Could Be So Kind	1982		2.00	4.00

Quatro, Suzi
(Also see "Pleasure Seekers, The")

Number		Title (A Side/B Side)	Year	VG	VG+	NM
Arista						
❏ 0106		Your Mama Won't Like Me/Peter Peter	1975		2.50	5.00
Bell						
❏ 45,401		48 Crash/Little Bitch Blue	1973		2.50	5.00
❏ 45,416		Can the Can/48 Crash	1973		2.50	5.00
❏ 45,477		All Shook Up/Glycerine Queen	1974		2.50	5.00
❏ 45,609		Devil Gate Drive/In the Morning	1974		2.50	5.00
❏ 45,615		Keep a-Knockin'/Cat Size	1974		2.50	5.00
Big Tree						
❏ 16053		Can the Can/Don't Mess Around	1975		2.50	5.00
Dreamland						
❏ 104		Rock Hard/State of Mind	1980		2.00	4.00
❏ 104	PS	Rock Hard/State of Mind	1980		2.00	4.00
❏ 107		Lipstick/Woman Cry	1980		2.00	4.00
Rak						
❏ 4512		Brain Confusion (For All the Lonely People)/ Rolling Stone	1972	2.50	5.00	10.00
RSO						
❏ 917		Stumblin' In/A Stranger to Paradise	1979		2.00	4.00
		With Chris Norman (lead singer of Smokie)				
❏ 929		If You Can't Give Me Love/Non-Citizen	1979		2.00	4.00
❏ 1001		I've Never Been in Love/Space Cadets	1979		2.00	4.00
❏ 1014		Starlight Lady/She's in Love with You	1979		2.00	4.00

Queen
(Also see "Mercury, Freddie"; "Taylor, Roger")

Number		Title (A Side/B Side)	Year	VG	VG+	NM
Capitol						
❏ B-5317		Radio Ga Ga/I Go Crazy	1984		2.00	4.00
❏ B-5317	PS	Radio Ga Ga/I Go Crazy	1984		2.00	4.00
❏ B-5350		I Want to Break Free/Machines (Or Back to Humans)	1984		2.00	4.00
❏ B-5350	PS	I Want to Break Free/Machines (Or Back to Humans)	1984		2.50	5.00
		With John Deacon in center				
❏ B-5350	PS	I Want to Break Free/Machines (Or Back to Humans)	1984		2.50	5.00
		With Brian May in center				
❏ B-5350	PS	I Want to Break Free/Machines (Or Back to Humans)	1984		2.50	5.00
		With Freddie Mercury in center				
❏ B-5350	PS	I Want to Break Free/Machines (Or Back to Humans)	1984		2.50	5.00
		With Roger Taylor in center				
❏ B-5372		It's a Hard Life/Is This the World We Created?	1984		2.50	5.00
❏ B-5372	PS	It's a Hard Life/Is This the World We Created?	1984		2.50	5.00
❏ B-5424		Hammer to Fall/Tear It Up	1984		2.50	5.00
❏ B-5424	PS	Hammer to Fall/Tear It Up	1984		2.50	5.00
❏ B-5530		One Vision/Blurred Vision	1985		2.00	4.00
❏ B-5530	PS	One Vision/Blurred Vision	1985		2.00	4.00
❏ B-5568		Princes of the Universe/ A Dozen Red Roses for My Darling	1985		2.00	4.00
❏ B-5590		A Kind of Magic/A Dozen Red Roses for My Darling	1986		2.00	4.00
❏ B-5590	PS	A Kind of Magic/A Dozen Red Roses for My Darling	1986		2.00	4.00
❏ B-5633		Pain Is So Close to Pleasure/Don't Lose Your Head	1986		2.00	4.00
❏ B-5633	PS	Pain Is So Close to Pleasure/Don't Lose Your Head	1986		2.00	4.00

Two very early and highly collectible records by highly collectible British artists. First is a promo copy of Pink Floyd's second single, "See Emily Play." Any Floyd single on Tower is sought-after, with stock copies even more desirable than the almost impossible promos. Below that is "I Can Hear Music" by Larry Lurex, who was actually Queen's Freddy Mercury in disguise! This record actually was added to WFIL in Philadelphia's playlist in 1973, but very few other stations did. There are actually two variations of this disc; the more common, with the "A0009-REMIX" on the lower right, is pictured. Stock copies also exist with "A0009" without the remix.

Number		Title (A Side/B Side)	Year	VG	VG+	NM
❏ 7PRO-9114	DJ	I Want to Break Free	1984	3.00	6.00	12.00
		No song title or name of group on label				
❏ 7PRO-9546/7	DJ	One Vision (4:00)/One Vision (3:46)	1985	3.00	6.00	12.00
❏ B-44372		I Want It All/Hang On In There	1989		2.50	5.00
❏ B-44372	PS	I Want It All/Hang On In There	1989		2.50	5.00
❏ 7PRO-79685	DJ	Breakthru (same on both sides)	1989	3.00	6.00	12.00
		Vinyl is promo only				

Elektra

❏ 45226		Killer Queen/Flick of the Wrist	1975	2.00	4.00	8.00
❏ 45268		Keep Yourself Alive//Lily of the Valley/	1975	2.00	4.00	8.00
		God Save the Queen				
❏ 45297		Bohemian Rhapsody/I'm in Love with My Car	1975	2.00	4.00	8.00
❏ 45362		You're My Best Friend/'39	1976		3.00	6.00
❏ 45385		Somebody to Love/White Man	1976		3.00	6.00
❏ 45385		Tie Your Mother Down/Drowse	1977		3.00	6.00
❏ 45412		Long Way/You and I	1977	2.00	4.00	8.00
❏ 45441		We Are the Champions/We Will Rock You	1977		3.00	6.00
❏ 45441	PS	We Are the Champions/We Will Rock You	1977	2.50	5.00	10.00
❏ 45478		It's Late/Sheer Heart Attack	1978		3.00	6.00
❏ 45478	PS	It's Late/Sheer Heart Attack	1978	2.50	5.00	10.00
❏ 45541		Bicycle Race/Fat Bottomed Girls	1978		3.00	6.00
❏ 45541	PS	Bicycle Race/Fat Bottomed Girls	1978	3.00	6.00	12.00
❏ 45863		Keep Yourself Alive/Son and Daughter	1973	3.75	7.50	15.00
❏ 45884		Liar/Doing All Right	1974	3.00	6.00	12.00
❏ 45891		Seven Seas of Rhye/See What a Fool I've Been	1974	3.00	6.00	12.00
❏ 46008		Don't Stop Me Now/More of That Jazz	1979		3.00	6.00
❏ 46039		Jealousy/Fun It	1979		3.00	6.00
❏ 46532		We Will Rock You (Live)/Let Me Entertain You	1979	2.00	4.00	8.00
❏ 46579		Crazy Little Thing Called Love/Spread Your Wings	1979		2.00	4.00
❏ 46652		Play the Game/A Human Body	1980		2.00	4.00
❏ 46652	PS	Play the Game/A Human Body	1980		2.50	5.00
❏ 47031		Another One Bites the Dust/Don't Try Suicide	1980		2.00	4.00
❏ 47086		Need Your Loving Tonight/Rock It (prime jive)	1980		2.00	4.00
❏ 47092		Flash's Theme AKA Flash/Football Fight	1980		2.00	4.00
❏ 47092	PS	Flash's Theme AKA Flash/Football Fight	1980		2.50	5.00
❏ 47230		Under Pressure/Soul Brother	1981		2.00	4.00
		A-side with David Bowie				
❏ 47230	PS	Under Pressure/Soul Brother	1981		3.00	6.00
❏ 47452		Body Language/Life Is Real (Song for Lennon)	1981		2.00	4.00
		Most copies of this did not come with picture sleeves				
❏ 47452	PS	Body Language/Life Is Real (Song for Lennon)	1981	3.75	7.50	15.00
		Nude bodies sleeve				
❏ 47452	PS	Body Language/Life Is Real (Song for Lennon)	1981	2.50	5.00	10.00
		All-white sleeve				
❏ 69941		Back Chat/Staying Power	1982		2.00	4.00
❏ 69941	PS	Back Chat/Staying Power	1982		2.50	5.00
❏ 69981		Calling All Girls/Put Out the Fire	1981		2.00	4.00
❏ 69981	PS	Calling All Girls/Put Out the Fire	1981		2.50	5.00

Hollywood

❏ 64725		We Are the Champions/	1992		2.00	4.00
		These Are the Days of Our Lives				
❏ 64794		Bohemian Rhapsody/The Show Must Go On	1992		2.00	4.00

Queensryche

EMI

❏ S7-18305		Bridge/I Am I	1995		2.00	4.00
❏ S7-18553		Disconnected/Bridge	1995		2.00	4.00
❏ 50201		Eyes of a Stranger/(B-side unknown)	1989	2.50	5.00	10.00
❏ 50214		I Don't Believe/(B-side unknown)	1989	2.50	5.00	10.00
❏ S7-57752		Anybody Listening?/Silent Lucidity	1992	2.50	5.00	10.00

? (Question Mark) and the Mysterians

Abkco

❏ 4020		96 Tears/Can't Get Enough of You, Baby	1973	3.00	6.00	12.00
		Reissue; contains full-length version of A-side (Cameo single is edited)				
❏ 4033		I Need Somebody/Girl (You Captivate Me)	1973	3.00	6.00	12.00
		Reissue				

Cameo

❏ 428		96 Tears/Midnight Hour	1966	5.00	10.00	20.00
❏ 441		I Need Somebody/"8" Teen	1966	3.75	7.50	15.00
❏ 467		Can't Get Enough of You, Baby/Smokes	1967	3.75	7.50	15.00
❏ 479		Girl (You Captivate Me)/Got To	1967	3.75	7.50	15.00
❏ 496		Do Something to Me/Love Me, Baby	1967	3.75	7.50	15.00

Capitol

❏ 2162		Make You Mine/	1968	5.00	10.00	20.00
		I Love You, Baby (Like Nobody's Business)				

Chicory

❏ 410		Talk Is Cheap/She Goes to Church on Sunday	1968	7.50	15.00	30.00

Luv

❏ 159		Funky Lady/Hot N' Groovin'	1975	3.75	7.50	15.00

Pa-Go-Go

❏ 102		96 Tears/Midnight Hour	1965	150.00	300.00	600.00

Super K

❏ 102		Hang In/Sha La La	1969	3.75	7.50	15.00

Number	Title (A Side/B Side)	Year	VG	VG+	NM

Tangerine

| ❏ 989 | Ain't It a Shame/
Turn Around Baby (Don't Ever Look Back) | 1970 | 3.75 | 7.50 | 15.00 |

Quick, The
(Featuring Eric Carmen)
Epic

| ❏ 10516 | Ain't Nothing Gonna Stop Me/Southern Comfort | 1969 | 6.25 | 12.50 | 25.00 |

Quickly, Tommy
Liberty

| ❏ 55732 | It's As Simple As That/You Might As Well Forget Him | 1964 | 2.50 | 5.00 | 10.00 |
| ❏ 55753 | Wild Side of Life/Forget the Other Guy | 1964 | 2.50 | 5.00 | 10.00 |

Quicksilver Messenger Service
Capitol

❏ 2194	Pride of Man/Dino's Song	1968	3.00	6.00	12.00
❏ 2320	Stand By Me/Bears	1968	3.00	6.00	12.00
❏ 2557	Who Do You Love/Which Do You Love	1969	3.00	6.00	12.00
❏ 2670	Words Can't Say/Holy Holy	1969	3.00	6.00	12.00
❏ 2800	Shady Grove/Three or Four Feet from Home	1970	2.50	5.00	10.00
❏ 2920	Fresh Air/Freeway Flyer	1970	2.50	5.00	10.00
❏ 3046	Good Old Rock and Roll/What About Me	1971	2.00	4.00	8.00
❏ 3233	Hope/I Found Love	1971	2.00	4.00	8.00
❏ 3349	Doin' Time in the U.S.A./Changes	1972	2.00	4.00	8.00
❏ 3417	Fresh Air/Freeway Flyer	1972	2.00	4.00	8.00
❏ 4206	Gypsy Lights/Witches' Moon	1976		3.00	6.00

Quin-Tones, The
Hunt

| ❏ 321 | Down the Aisle of Love/Please Dear | 1958 | 6.25 | 12.50 | 25.00 |
| ❏ 322 | There'll Be No Sorrow/What Am I to Do | 1958 | 5.00 | 10.00 | 20.00 |

Red Top

| ❏ 108 | Down the Aisle of Love/Please Dear | 1958 | 15.00 | 30.00 | 60.00 |

Quinteros. Eddie
Brent

❏ 7009	Come Dance with Me/Vivian	1960	7.50	15.00	30.00
❏ 7012	Please Don't Go/Lookin' for My Baby	1960	8.75	17.50	35.00
❏ 7014	Slow Down Sandy/Lindy Lou	1960	12.50	25.00	50.00

Quintones, The
(More than one group)
Chess

| ❏ 1685 | I Try So Hard/Ding Dong | 1957 | 10.00 | 20.00 | 40.00 |

Gee

| ❏ 1009 | I'm Willing/Strange As It Seems | 1956 | 15.00 | 30.00 | 60.00 |

Jordan

| ❏ 1601 | The Lonely Telephone/Just a Little Loving | 196? | 75.00 | 150.00 | 300.00 |

Park

| ❏ 111/2 | South Sea Island/More Than a Notion | 1957 | 100.00 | 200.00 | 400.00 |

Phillips Int'l.

| ❏ 3586 | Times Sho' Gettin' Ruff/Softie | 1963 | 5.00 | 10.00 | 20.00 |

Quotations, The
(More than one group; the records on DeVenus, Downstairs and Imperial feature Linda Evans)
Admiral

| ❏ 753 | In the Night/Oh No, I Still Love Her | 1964 | 5.00 | 10.00 | 20.00 |

DeVenus

| ❏ 107 | It Can Happen to You/You Don't Have to Worry | 1968 | 3.00 | 6.00 | 12.00 |

Downstairs

| ❏ 1003 | Night/Why Do You Do Me Like You Do | 1970 | 2.00 | 4.00 | 8.00 |

Imperial

| ❏ 66338 | Havin' a Good Time/Can I Have Someone | 1968 | 2.50 | 5.00 | 10.00 |
| ❏ 66368 | Havin' a Good Time (With My Baby)/
Can I Have Someone (For Once) | 1969 | 2.50 | 5.00 | 10.00 |

Liberty

| ❏ 55527 | Listen, My Children, And You Shall Hear/
Speak Softly and Carry a Big Horn | 1962 | 6.25 | 12.50 | 25.00 |
| ❏ | | | | | |

Verve

❏ 10245	Imagination/Ala-Men-Say	1961	7.50	15.00	30.00
❏ 10252	This Love of Mine/We'll Reach Heaven Together	1962	7.50	15.00	30.00
❏ 10261	See You in September/Sumemrtime Goodbye	1962	12.50	25.00	50.00

R

R.E.M.
Evatone

| ❏ 105900-15 | Dark Globe (one-sided) | 1989 | | 3.00 | 6.00 |

5-inch black flexi-disc included in issue of Sassy magazine (double value if record is still attached to magazine)

Number	Title (A Side/B Side)	Year	VG	VG+	NM

Fan Club

☐ REM 92	Where's Captain Kirk?/Toyland	1992	3.75	7.50	15.00
☐ REM 92	PS Where's Captain Kirk?/Toyland	1992	3.75	7.50	15.00
	White sleeve				
☐ REM 92	PS Where's Captain Kirk?/Toyland	1992	3.75	7.50	15.00
	Any of three variations of a gray sleeve				
☐ REM 94	Sex Bomb/Christmas in Tunisia	1994	2.50	5.00	10.00
☐ REM 94	PS Sex Bomb/Christmas in Tunisia	1994	3.75	7.50	15.00
	Picture sleeve also included a magnet, stamps and sticker				
☐ REM 95	Wicked Game/Java	1995	2.50	5.00	10.00
☐ REM 95	PS Wicked Game/Java	1995	2.50	5.00	10.00
☐ REM 1993	Silver Bells/Christmas Time Is Here	1993	3.75	7.50	15.00
☐ REM 1993	PS Silver Bells/Christmas Time Is Here	1993	3.75	7.50	15.00
☐ U-23518M	Parade of the Wooden Soldiers/See No Evil	1988	12.50	25.00	50.00
	Green vinyl				
☐ U-23518M	PS Parade of the Wooden Soldiers/See No Evil	1988	12.50	25.00	50.00
☐ 122589	Good King Wenceslas/Academy Fight Song	1989	12.50	25.00	50.00
☐ 122589	PS Good King Wenceslas/Academy Fight Song	1989	12.50	25.00	50.00
	Fold-out poster sleeve				
☐ 122590	Ghost Reindeer in the Sky/Summertime	1990	7.50	15.00	30.00
☐ 122590	PS Ghost Reindeer in the Sky/Summertime	1990	7.50	15.00	30.00
☐ 122591	Baby Baby/Christmas Griping	1991	7.50	15.00	30.00
☐ 122591	PS Baby Baby/Christmas Griping	1991	7.50	15.00	30.00

Hib-Tone

☐ HT-0001	Radio Free Europe/Sitting Still	1981	18.75	37.50	75.00
	First pressing, with no address for Hib-Tone Records on label				
☐ HT-0001	Radio Free Europe/Sitting Still	1981	12.50	25.00	50.00
☐ HT-0001	PS Radio Free Europe/Sitting Still	1981	18.75	37.50	75.00

I.R.S.

☐ 9916	Radio Free Europe/There She Goes Again	1983	2.50	5.00	10.00
☐ 9916	PS Radio Free Europe/There She Goes Again	1983	7.50	15.00	30.00
☐ 9927	So. Central Rain (I'm Sorry)/King of the Road	1984	2.00	4.00	
☐ 9927	PS So. Central Rain (I'm Sorry)/King of the Road	1984	2.50	5.00	10.00
☐ 9931	(Don't Go Back to) Rockville/Catapult (Live)	1984	2.50	5.00	10.00
☐ 9931	PS (Don't Go Back to) Rockville/Catapult (Live)	1984	2.50	5.00	10.00
☐ 52642	Can't Get There from Here/Bandwagon	1985		3.00	6.00
☐ 52642	PS Can't Get There from Here/Bandwagon	1985		3.00	6.00
☐ 52678	Driver 8/Crazy	1985		3.00	6.00
☐ 52678	PS Driver 8/Crazy	1985		3.00	6.00
☐ 52883	Fall on Me/Rotary Ten	1986		2.50	5.00
☐ 52883	PS Fall on Me/Rotary Ten	1986		2.50	5.00
☐ 52971	Superman/White Tornado	1986		2.50	5.00
☐ 52971	PS Superman/White Tornado	1986		2.50	5.00
☐ 53171	The One I Love/Maps and Legends	1987			3.00
☐ 53171	PS The One I Love/Maps and Legends	1987			3.00
☐ 53220	It's the End of the World As We Know It (And I Feel Fine)/Last Date	1987			3.00
☐ 53220	PS It's the End of the World As We Know It (And I Feel Fine)/Last Date	1987			3.00

The Bob

☐ 5	Tighten Up (one-sided)	198?	4.50	9.00	18.00
☐ 20	Femme Fatale (one-sided)	1986	3.75	7.50	15.00
	Flexi-disc included with The Bob magazine; red				
☐ 20	Femme Fatale (one-sided)	1986	3.75	7.50	15.00
	Flexi-disc included with The Bob magazine; black				
☐ 20	PS Femme Fatale (one-sided)	1986	10.00	20.00	40.00
	Picture sleeve sent to The Bob subscribers only				

Warner Bros.

☐ 17529	E-Bow the Letter/Tricycle	1996			3.00
☐ 17737	Tongue/Tongue (Live)	1995			3.00
☐ 17900	Strange Currencies/(Instrumental)	1995			3.00
☐ 17994	Bang and Blame/(Instrumental)	1995			3.00
☐ 18050	What's the Frequency, Kenneth?/(Instrumental)	1994			3.00
☐ 18523	The Sidewinder Sleeps Tonite/The Lion Sleeps Tonight	1993			3.00
☐ 18638	Everybody Hurts/Mandolin Strum	1993			3.00
☐ 18642	Man on the Moon/New Orleans Instrumental #2	1992			3.00
☐ 18729	Drive/Winged Mammal Theme	1992			3.00
☐ 19242	Shiny Happy People/Forty Second Song	1991			3.00
☐ 19246	Radio Song/Love Is All Around	1991			3.00
☐ 19392	Losing My Religion/Rotary Eleven	1991			3.00
☐ 21864	Stand/Pop Song 89	1989			3.00
	"Back to Back Hits" series				
☐ 22780	Singleactiongreen	1989	6.25	12.50	25.00
	Box set of 4 7-inch 45s (WB 27688, 927 652, 27640 and 22791), each with picture sleeve, plus poster. Sticker on box claims the set contains "Orange Crush" b/w "Ghost Rider" but it actually contains "Orange Crush" b/w "Memphis Train Blues."				
☐ 22791	Get Up/Funtime	1989			3.00
☐ 22791	PS Get Up/Funtime	1989			3.00
☐ 27640	Pop Song 89/Pop Song 89 (Acoustic Version)	1989			3.00
☐ 27640	PS Pop Song 89/Pop Song 89 (Acoustic Version)	1989			
	Only issued as part of Warner Bros. 22780; not available otherwise				
☐ 27688	Stand/Memphis Train Blues	1988			3.00
☐ 27688	PS Stand/Memphis Train Blues	1988			3.00
☐ 927 652	Orange Crush/Memphis Train Blues	1989			
	Import with large hole, issued in U.S. as part of Warner Bros. 22780				

Number		Title (A Side/B Side)	Year	VG	VG+	NM
❑ 927 652	PS	Orange Crush/Memphis Train Blues	1989			
		Import, issued in U.S. as part of Warner Bros. 22780				

Rabbitt, Eddie
Capitol
❑ NR-44527		On Second Thought/Only One Love in My Life	1990		2.00	4.00
		This may exist only as cassette, but we've put it in just in case				
❑ NR-44538		Runnin' with the Wind/Feel Like a Stranger	1990			3.00

Date
❑ 1599		The Bed/Holding On	1968	3.00	6.00	12.00

Elektra
❑ 45237		Forgive and Forget/Pure Love	1975		2.50	5.00
❑ 45269		I Should Have Married You/Sweet Janine	1975		2.50	5.00
❑ 45301		Drinkin' My Baby (Off My Mind)/When I Was Young	1976		2.50	5.00
❑ 45315		Rocky Mountain Music/Do You Right Tonight	1976		2.50	5.00
❑ 45357		Two Dollars in the Jukebox/Don't Wanna Make Love	1976		2.50	5.00
❑ 45381		Could You Love a Poor Boy, Dolly/There's Someone She Lies To (To Lie Here with Me)	1977		3.00	6.00
❑ 45390		I Can't Help Myself/She Loves Me Like She Means It	1977		2.00	4.00
❑ 45418		We Can't Go On Living Like This/We Made Love Beautiful	1977		2.00	4.00
❑ 45461		Hearts on Fire/Girl on My Mind	1978		2.00	4.00
❑ 45488		You Don't Love Me Anymore/Caroline	1978		2.00	4.00
❑ 45531		I Just Want to Love You/Crossin' the Mississippi	1978		2.00	4.00
❑ 45554		Every Which Way But Loose/Under the Double Eagle	1978		2.00	4.00
❑ 45895		You Get to Me/Que Pasa	1974		2.50	5.00
❑ 46053		Suspicions/I Don't Want to Make Love (With Anyone But You)	1979		2.00	4.00
❑ 46558		Pour Me Another Tequila/I Will Never Let You Go	1979		2.00	4.00
❑ 46613		Gone Too Far/Loveline	1980		2.00	4.00
❑ 46656		Drivin' My Life Away/Pretty Lady	1980		2.00	4.00
❑ 47066		I Love a Rainy Night/Short Road to Love	1980		2.00	4.00
❑ 47174		Step By Step/My Only Wish	1981		2.00	4.00
❑ 47174	PS	Step By Step/My Only Wish	1981		3.00	6.00
❑ 47239		Someone Could Lose a Heart Tonight/Nobody Loves Me Like My Baby	1981		2.00	4.00
❑ 47435		I Don't Know Where to Start/Skip-A-Beat	1982		2.00	4.00
❑ 69936		You and I/All My Life, All My Love	1982		2.00	4.00
		A-side: With Crystal Gayle				

RCA
❑ 5012-7-R		Gotta Have You/Singing in the Subway	1986			3.00
❑ 5093-7-R		When We Make Love/(B-side unknown)	1987			3.00
❑ 5238-7-R		Wanna Dance with You/Gotta Have You	1987			3.00
❑ 8306-7-R		The Wanderer/Workin' Out	1988			3.00
❑ 8716-7-R		We Must Be Doing Something Right/He's a Cheater	1988			3.00
❑ 8819-7-R		That's Why I Fell in Love with You/She's An Old Cadillac	1988			3.00
❑ PB-14192		A World Without Love/1-2-3, You Really Got a Hold on Me (The Wrestling Song)	1985			3.00
❑ PB-14317		Repetitive Love/Letter from Home	1986			3.00
❑ PB-14377		Both to Each Other (Friends and Lovers)/A World Without Love	1986			3.00
		With Juice Newton				
❑ PB-14377	PS	Both to Each Other (Friends and Lovers)/A World Without Love	1986		2.50	5.00

20th Fox
❑ 474		Six Nights and Seven Days/Next to the Note	1964	5.00	10.00	20.00

Universal
❑ 66025		On Second Thought/Only One Love in My Life	1989		2.00	4.00

Warner Bros.
❑ 28976		She's Comin' Back to Say Goodbye/Dial That Telephone	1985		2.00	4.00
❑ 29089		Warning Sign/Go to Sleep, Big Bertha	1985		2.00	4.00
❑ 29279		B-B-B-Burnin' Up with Love/747	1984		2.00	4.00
❑ 29431		Nothing Like Falling in Love/Gone Too Far	1983		2.00	4.00
❑ 29512		Our Love Will Survive/You Put the Beat in My Heart	1983		2.00	4.00
❑ 29712		You Can't Run from Love/You Got Me Now	1983		2.00	4.00

Rachel and the Revolvers
Dot
❑ 16392		The Revo-Lution/Number One	1962	125.00	250.00	500.00
		Produced by Brian Wilson				

Radha Krishna Temple
Apple
❑ 1810		Hare Krishna Mantra/Prayer to the Spiritual Masters	1969	2.00	4.00	8.00
❑ 1821		Govinda/Govinda Jai Jai	1970	2.50	5.00	10.00
		With Capitol logo on B-side label bottom				
❑ 1821		Govinda/Govinda Jai Jai	1970	2.00	4.00	8.00
❑ 1821	PS	Govinda/Govinda Jai Jai	1970	2.50	5.00	10.00
❑ PRO-5013/4	DJ	Govinda/Govinda Jai Jai	1970	6.25	12.50	25.00
		With an edit of the A-side				
❑ SPRO-5067/8	DJ	Govinda (Edit)/Govinda	1970	10.00	20.00	40.00

Number	Title (A Side/B Side)	Year	VG	VG+	NM

Radiants, The
ABC
❑ 12394	I Need a Vacation/Just Like You	1978		2.50	5.00

Chess
❑ 1832	Father Knows Best/One Day I'll Show You	1962	3.75	7.50	15.00
❑ 1849	Please Don't Leave Me/Heartbreak Society	1963	3.75	7.50	15.00
❑ 1872	I'm in Love/Shy Guy	1963	3.75	7.50	15.00
❑ 1887	Noble the Bargain Man/ I Got to Dance to Keep My Baby	1964	3.75	7.50	15.00
❑ 1904	Voice Your Choice/If I Only Had You	1964	3.00	6.00	12.00
❑ 1925	It Ain't No Big Thing/I Got a Girl	1965	3.00	6.00	12.00
❑ 1939	Whole Lot of Love/Tomorrow	1965	3.00	6.00	12.00
❑ 1986	(Don't It Make You) Feel Kind of Bad/ Anything You Do Is Alright	1967	3.00	6.00	12.00
❑ 2021	Don't Take Your Love/The Clown Is Clever	1967	3.00	6.00	12.00
❑ 2037	Hold On/I'm Glad I'm the Loser	1968	3.00	6.00	12.00
❑ 2057	Tears of a Clown/I'm Just a Man	1968	3.00	6.00	12.00
❑ 2066	Choo Choo/Ida Mae Foster	1969	2.50	5.00	10.00
❑ 2078	Book of Love/Another Mule Is Kicking In Your Stall	1969	2.50	5.00	10.00
❑ 2083	I'm So Glad I'm the Loser/Shadow of a Doubt	1970	2.50	5.00	10.00

Twinight
❑ 153	My Sunshine Girl/Don't Wanna Face the Truth	1971	2.00	4.00	8.00

Rafferty, Gerry
(Also see "Stealers Wheel")
Blue Thumb
❑ 231	Can I Have My Money Back/Sign on the Dotted Line	1973	2.00	4.00	8.00

Liberty
❑ 1482	Good Intentions/Standing at the Gates	1982		2.00	4.00

Signpost
❑ 70001	Make You, Break You/Mary Skeffington	1972	2.50	5.00	10.00

United Artists
❑ XW1098	Mattie's Rag/City to City	1977		2.50	5.00
❑ XW1192	Baker Street/Big Change in the Weather	1978	2.00	4.00	8.00
	Mispress with the full-length album version of "Baker Street" on A-side There is no "E" in the trail-off wax.				
❑ XW1192	Baker Street/Big Change in the Weather	1978		2.00	4.00
	Regular press with the edited, slightly sped-up version of "Baker Street" on A-side				
❑ XW1233	Right Down the Line/Waiting for the Day	1978		2.00	4.00
❑ XW1233 PS	Right Down the Line/Waiting for the Day	1978		2.50	5.00
❑ XW1266	Home and Dry/Mattie's Rag	1978		2.00	4.00
❑ XW1298	Days Gone Down (Still Got That Light in Your Eyes)/ Why Won't You Talk to Me	1979		2.00	4.00
❑ 1316	Get It Right Next Time/It's Gonna Be a Long Night	1979		2.00	4.00
❑ 1366	The Royal Mile/In Transit	1980		2.00	4.00

Ragland, Lou
Amy
❑ 988	Travel Alone/Big Wheel	1967	50.00	100.00	200.00

Raiders, The
(More than one group. Also see "Revere, Paul, and the Raiders" for all their releases as "Raiders")
Andex
❑ 4015	Yoo Hoo/Hocus Pocus	1958	30.00	60.00	120.00

Atco
❑ 6125	Raiders from Outer Space/The Castle of Love	1958	15.00	30.00	60.00

Brunswick
❑ 55090	Walking Through the Jungle/My Steady Girl	1958	10.00	20.00	40.00

Liberty
❑ 55393	Dardanella/What Time Is It	1961	7.50	15.00	30.00

Spring-Dale
❑ 102	Raiders' Rhythm/Tall Texas Women	1964	12.50	25.00	50.00

Van
❑ 00262	Stick Shift/Skipping Around	1962	12.50	25.00	50.00
❑ 00663	On a Straight Away/It's Motivation	1963	5.00	10.00	20.00
❑ 00763	Supercharger/Cruisin' Low	1963	5.00	10.00	20.00
❑ 01064	Raisin' Cain/Repetition	1964	5.00	10.00	20.00

Vee Jay
❑ 504	Stick Shift/Skipping Around	1963	5.00	10.00	20.00

Rain
A.P.I.
❑ 336	Outta My Life/E.S.P.	1967	10.00	20.00	40.00
❑ 337	Substitute/Hear You Cry	1967	10.00	20.00	40.00

London
❑ 107	Outta My Life/E.S.P.	1967	6.25	12.50	25.00
❑ 111	Substitute/Hear You Cry	1967	7.50	15.00	30.00

MGM
❑ 13622	Take It Away/City Lovin'	1966	6.25	12.50	25.00

Paramount
❑ 0087	Show Me the Road Home/Funky Junky Blues	1971	5.00	10.00	20.00

Number	Title (A Side/B Side)	Year	VG	VG+	NM

Rainbo
(Sissy Spacek is on this record)
Roulette

❏ 7030	John You Went Too Far This Time/ C'mon Teach Me to Live	1969	5.00	10.00	20.00

Rainbows, The
(More than one group)
Argyle

❏ 1012	Shirley/Stay	1962	6.25	12.50	25.00

Dave

❏ 908	I Know/Only a Picture	1963	7.50	15.00	30.00
❏ 909	I Wouldn't Be Right/Family Monkey	1963	7.50	15.00	30.00

Dot

❏ 16612	My Ringo/He's Hooked on J's	1964	3.75	7.50	15.00
❏ 16920	Color of Love/Down the Block	1966	2.50	5.00	10.00

Epic

❏ 9900	Balla Balla/Ju Ju Hand	1966	2.50	5.00	10.00

Fury

❏ 1012	Mary Lee/Evening	1960	5.00	10.00	20.00

Gramo

❏ 5508	Till Tomorrow/Mama, Take Your Daughter Back	196?	5.00	10.00	20.00

Jamie

❏ 1339	Balla Balla/Ju Ju Hand	1967	2.00	4.00	8.00

MGM

❏ 13058	Old Man's Twist/Straight Ahead	1962	5.00	10.00	20.00

Pilgrim

❏ 703	Mary Lee/Evening	1956	12.50	25.00	50.00
❏ 711	Shirley/Stay	1956	50.00	100.00	200.00

Rama

❏ 209	Minnie/They Say	1956	100.00	200.00	400.00

Red Robin

❏ 134	Mary Lee/Evening	1955	125.00	250.00	500.00

Note: Red Robin 141 is a bootleg

Raindrops, The
(More than one group)
Capitol

❏ F4136	Rockababy Rock/Rain	1959	5.00	10.00	20.00

Corsair

❏ 104	Maybe/Love Is Like a Mountain	1960	15.00	30.00	60.00

Dore

❏ 561	Maybe/Love Is Like a Mountain	1960	6.25	12.50	25.00

Hamilton

❏ 50021	Oh Why/Without Love, Love, Love	1960	5.00	10.00	20.00

Imperial

❏ 5785	I Remember in the Still of the Night/Sweet Song	1961	7.50	15.00	30.00

Jubilee

❏ 5444	What a Guy/It's So Wonderful	1963	3.75	7.50	15.00
❏ 5455	The Kind of Boy You Can't Forget/ Even Though You Can't Dance	1963	5.00	10.00	20.00
❏ 5466	That Boy John/Hanky Panky	1963	5.00	10.00	20.00
❏ 5469	Book of Love/I Won't Cry	1964	3.75	7.50	15.00
❏ 5475	Let's Go Together/You Got What I Like	1964	3.75	7.50	15.00
❏ 5487	One More Tear/Another Boy Like Mine	1964	3.75	7.50	15.00
❏ 5497	Don't Let Go/My Mama Don't Like Him	1965	3.75	7.50	15.00

Spin-It

❏ 104	(I Found) Heaven in Love/I Prayed for Gold	195?	50.00	100.00	200.00
❏ 106	Little One/Rockin' on the Farm	195?	50.00	100.00	200.00

Rainy Daze, The
Chicory

❏ 404	That Acapulco Gold/In My Mind Lives a Forest	1967	3.75	7.50	15.00

Uni

❏ 55002	That Acapulco Gold/In My Mind Lives a Forest	1967	2.50	5.00	10.00
❏ 55011	Discount City/Good Morning, Mr. Smith	1967	2.50	5.00	10.00
❏ 55026	Stop Sign/Blood of Oblivion	1967	2.50	5.00	10.00

White Whale

❏ 279	My Door Is Always Open/Make Me Laugh	1968	2.50	5.00	10.00

Raitt, Bonnie
A&M

❏ 1249	Baby Mine/Mickey Mouse March	1988		2.00	4.00

A-side with Was (Not Was); B-side by Aaron Neville

Arista

❏ 12795	You Got It/Feeling of Falling	1995			3.00

Capitol

❏ S7-17818	Love Sneakin' Up on You/Hell to Pay	1994			3.00
❏ S7-18039	You/Feeling of Falling	1994		2.00	4.00

Red vinyl

Number	Title (A Side/B Side)	Year	VG	VG+	NM
☐ S7-18299	Storm Warning/Longing in Their Hearts	1995		3.00	
☐ B-44364	Nick of Time/The Road's My Middle Name	1989		2.00	4.00
☐ B-44365	Thing Called Love/The Road's My Middle Name	1989		2.00	4.00
☐ NR-44729	I Can't Make You Love Me/Come to Me	1991		2.00	4.00
	White label, but not a promo				
☐ S7-56799	All at Once/Come to Me	1992		2.00	4.00
☐ S7-57698	Not the Only One/All at Once	1992		2.00	4.00
☐ S7-57741	I Can't Make You Love Me/Something to Talk About	1992		2.00	4.00
☐ S7-57879	Good Man, Good Woman/Nick of Time	1992		2.00	4.00
	A-side: Duet with Delbert McClinton				
☐ 7PRO-79940	DJ Have a Heart (same on both sides)	1990		2.50	5.00
	Vinyl is promo only				
Full Moon					
☐ 49612	Once in a Lifetime/You're Only Lonely	1980		2.00	4.00
	B-side by J.D. Souther				
Full Moon/Asylum					
☐ 47033	Don't It Make You Wanna Dance/ Orange Blossom Special	1980		2.50	5.00
	B-side by Gilley's Urban Cowboy Band				
☐ 47033	PS Don't It Make You Wanna Dance/ Orange Blossom Special	1980		3.00	6.00
Reprise					
☐ 1370	When You Touch Me This Way/ Since I've Been With You Babe	1976		2.50	5.00
	By Geoff Muldaur and Bonnie Raitt				
Warner Bros.					
☐ 7554	Bluebird/Women Be Wise	1972	2.00	4.00	8.00
☐ 7645	Too Long at the Fair/Under the Falling Sky	1972	2.00	4.00	8.00
☐ 7758	Everybody's Cryin' Mercy/ You've Been in Love Too Long	1973		3.00	6.00
☐ 8044	I Got Plenty/You Got to Be Ready for Love	1974		3.00	6.00
☐ 8166	Good Enough/My First Night Alone Without You	1975		3.00	6.00
☐ 8189	Run Like a Thief/Walk Out the Front Door	1976		2.50	5.00
☐ 8382	Runaway/Louise	1977		2.50	5.00
☐ 8430	Two Lives/Three Time Loser	1977		2.50	5.00
☐ 8485	Gamblin' Man/About to Make Me Leave Home	1977		2.50	5.00
☐ 28450	Crimes of Passion/Stand Up to the Night	1987		2.00	4.00
☐ 28615	No Way to Treat a Lady/Stand Up to the Night	1986		2.00	4.00
☐ 29992	River of Tears/Me and the Boys	1982		2.00	4.00
☐ 49116	You're Gonna Get What's Comin'/The Glow	1979		2.00	4.00
☐ 49185	Wild for You Baby/ (I Could Have Been Your) Best Old Friend	1980		2.00	4.00
☐ 50022	Can't Get Enough/Keep This Heart in Mind	1982		2.00	4.00

Rajahs, The
Klik
☐ 7805	I Fell in Love/Shifting Sands	1957	75.00	150.00	300.00

Rally Packs, The
(Steve Barri and P.F. Sloan [with Jan and Dean])
Imperial
☐ 66036	Move Out Little Mustang/Bucket Seats	1964	15.00	30.00	60.00

Ramblers, The
(More than one group)
Addit
☐ 1257	Rambling/Devil Train	1960	7.50	15.00	30.00

Almont
☐ 311	Barbara (I Loved You)/Father Sebastian	1964	5.00	10.00	20.00
☐ 315	Surfin' Santa/Silly Little Boy	1964	6.25	12.50	25.00

Federal
☐ 12286	Don't You Know?/The Heaven and Earth	1957	25.00	50.00	100.00

Impact
☐ 10	Yaba Daba Ah Doo/Funny Papers	1961	6.25	12.50	25.00

Jax
☐ 319	Search My Heart/50-50 Love	1953	100.00	200.00	400.00

MGM
☐ 11850	Vadunt-Un-Va-Da Song (Oui Oui Baby)/ Please Bring Yourself Back Home	1954	75.00	150.00	300.00
☐ 55006	Bad Girl/Rickey-Do, Rickey-Do	1955	37.50	75.00	150.00

RCA Victor
☐ 47-5240	Mama He Treats Your Daughter Mean/ And the Bull Walked Around Olay	1953	100.00	200.00	400.00

Sidewinder
☐ 101	Ticonderoga/Mozart Stomp	1964	10.00	20.00	40.00

Ramistella, Johnny – See "Rivers, Johnny"

Ramrods
Amy
☐ 813	(Ghost) Riders in the Sky/Zig Zag	1961	6.25	12.50	25.00

Number		Title (A Side/B Side)	Year	VG	VG+	NM
❑ 817		Loch Lomond Rock/ Take Me Back to My Boots and Saddle	1961	5.00	10.00	20.00
❑ 846		War Cry/Boing!	1962	5.00	10.00	20.00
Queen						
❑ 240145		Slee-Zee/Slouchee	1962	5.00	10.00	20.00
R&H						
❑ 1001		Moonlight Surf/Night Ride	1963	12.50	25.00	50.00

Rams, The
Flair

Number		Title (A Side/B Side)	Year	VG	VG+	NM
❑ 1066		Sweet Thing/Rock Bottom	1955	37.50	75.00	150.00

Ran-Dells, The
Chairman

Number		Title (A Side/B Side)	Year	VG	VG+	NM
❑ 4403		Martian Hop/Forgive Me, Darling (I Have Lied)	1963	5.00	10.00	20.00
❑ 4403	PS	Martian Hop/Forgive Me, Darling (I Have Lied)	1963	12.50	25.00	50.00
❑ 4407		Sound of the Sun/Come On and Love Me	1964	3.75	7.50	15.00
R.S.V.P.						
❑ 1104		Beyond the Stars/Wintertime	1964	3.75	7.50	15.00

Rancheros, The
Dot

Number		Title (A Side/B Side)	Year	VG	VG+	NM
❑ 16572		Linda's Tune/Little Linda	1964	6.25	12.50	25.00
Lonnie						
❑ 5005		Linda's Tune/Little Linda	1963	12.50	25.00	50.00

Randell, Lynne
ABC

Number		Title (A Side/B Side)	Year	VG	VG+	NM
❑ 11112		Open Letter/Right to Cry	1968	5.00	10.00	20.00
Epic						
❑ 10147		Stranger in My Arms/Ciao Baby	1967	7.50	15.00	30.00
❑ 10197		I Need You Boy/That's a Hoe-Down	1967	7.50	15.00	30.00

Randolph, Barbara
Soul

Number		Title (A Side/B Side)	Year	VG	VG+	NM
❑ 35038		I Got a Feeling/You Got Me Hurtin' All Over	1967	5.00	10.00	20.00
❑ 35050		Can I Get a Witness/You Got Me Hurtin' All Over	1968	5.00	10.00	20.00

Randy and the Radiants
Sun

Number		Title (A Side/B Side)	Year	VG	VG+	NM
❑ 395		The Mountain's High/Peek-a-Boo	1965	6.25	12.50	25.00
❑ 398		My Way of Thinking/Truth from My Eyes	1966	6.25	12.50	25.00

Randy and the Rainbows
Ambient Sound

Number		Title (A Side/B Side)	Year	VG	VG+	NM
❑ 02872		Debbie/Try the Impossible	1982		2.50	5.00
B.T. Puppy						
❑ 535		I'll Be Seeing You/Oh to Get Away	1967	2.50	5.00	10.00
Mike						
❑ 4001		Lovely Lies/I'll Forget Her Tomorrow	1966	3.00	6.00	12.00
❑ 4004		Quarter to Three/He's a Fugitive	1966	3.00	6.00	12.00
❑ 4008		Bonnie's Part of Town/Can It Be	1966	3.00	6.00	12.00
Rust						
❑ 5059		Denise/Come Back *Blue label*	1963	7.50	15.00	30.00
❑ 5059		Denise/Come Back *Mostly white label*	1963	5.00	10.00	20.00
❑ 5073		She's My Angel/Why Do Kids Grow Up	1964	3.75	7.50	15.00
❑ 5080		Happy Teenager/Dry Your Eyes	1964	3.75	7.50	15.00
❑ 5091		Little Star/Sharin'	1964	3.75	7.50	15.00
❑ 5101		Joy Ride/Little Hot Rod Suzie	1965	3.75	7.50	15.00

Rangers, The
Challenge

Number		Title (A Side/B Side)	Year	VG	VG+	NM
❑ 59229		Snow Skiing/Mogul Monster	1964	5.00	10.00	20.00
❑ 59239		Justine/Reputation	1964	5.00	10.00	20.00
FTP						
❑ 404		Four on the Floor/Riders in the Sky	1961	7.50	15.00	30.00

Ranglin, Ernest
Studio

Number		Title (A Side/B Side)	Year	VG	VG+	NM
❑ 1		Surfing (Part 1)/Surfing (Part 2)	196?	12.50	25.00	50.00

Rank, Ken
Fenton

Number		Title (A Side/B Side)	Year	VG	VG+	NM
❑ 2194		Twin City Saucer/Ken's Thing	1968	7.50	15.00	30.00

Rare Breed, The
(Later known as the Ohio Express)
Attack

Number		Title (A Side/B Side)	Year	VG	VG+	NM
❑ 1401		Beg, Borrow and Steal/Jeri's Theme	1966	7.50	15.00	30.00
❑ 1403		Come and Take a Ride in My Boat/ Take Me to This World of Yours	1966	5.00	10.00	20.00

Number		Title (A Side/B Side)	Year	VG	VG+	NM

Rare Earth

Prodigal

☐ 0637		Crazy Love/Is Your Teacher Cool	1977		2.50	5.00
☐ 0640		Warm Ride/Would You Like to Come Along	1978		2.50	5.00
☐ 0643		I Can Feel My Love Risin'/S.O.S. (Stop Her On Sight)	1978		2.50	5.00

Rare Earth

☐ 5010		Generation (Light of the Sky)/Magic Key	1969	3.00	6.00	12.00
☐ 5012		Get Ready/Magic Key	1970		3.00	6.00
☐ 5017		(I Know) I'm Losing You/When Joanie Smiles	1970		3.00	6.00
☐ 5021		Born to Wander/Here Comes the Night	1970		3.00	6.00
☐ 5031		I Just Want to Celebrate/The Seed	1971		3.00	6.00
☐ 5031	PS	I Just Want to Celebrate/The Seed	1971	2.50	5.00	10.00
☐ 5038		Hey Big Brother/Under God's Light	1971		3.00	6.00
☐ 5043		What'd I Say/Nice to Be with You	1972		3.00	6.00
☐ 5048		Good Time Sally/Love Shines Down	1972		3.00	6.00
☐ 5052		We're Gonna Have a Good Time/ Would You Like to Come Along	1973		3.00	6.00
☐ 5053		Ma/(Instrumental)	1973		3.00	6.00
☐ 5054		Hum Along and Dance/Come with Me	1973		3.00	6.00
☐ 5056		Big John Is My Name/Ma	1974		3.00	6.00
☐ 5057		Chained/Fresh from the Can	1974		3.00	6.00
☐ 5058		It Makes You Happy (But It Ain't Gonna Last Too Long)/Boogie with Me Children	1975		3.00	6.00
☐ 5059		Let Me Be Your Sunshine/Keep Me Out of the Storm	1976		3.00	6.00
☐ 5060		Midnight Lady/Walking Shtick	1976		3.00	6.00

RCA

☐ PB-13076		Howzabout Some Love/Let Me Take You Out	1982			Unreleased

Verve

☐ 10622		Stop-Where Did Our Love Go/Mother's Oats	1968	3.00	6.00	12.00

Rascals, The

(Also see "Brigati"; "Cavaliere, Felix"; "Cornish, Gene")

Atlantic

From here through Atlantic 2463, as "The Young Rascals"

☐ 2312		I Ain't Gonna Eat Out My Heart Anymore/Slow Down	1965	2.50	5.00	10.00
☐ 2321		Good Lovin'/Mustang Sally	1966	2.50	5.00	10.00
☐ 2338		You Better Run/Love Is a Beautiful Thing	1966	2.00	4.00	8.00
☐ 2338	PS	You Better Run/Love Is a Beautiful Thing	1966	5.00	10.00	20.00
☐ 2353		Come On Up/What Is the Reason	1966	2.00	4.00	8.00
☐ 2377		I've Been Lonely Too Long/If You Knew	1967	2.00	4.00	8.00
☐ 2377	PS	I've Been Lonely Too Long/If You Knew	1967	5.00	10.00	20.00
☐ 2401		Groovin'/Sueno	1967	2.00	4.00	8.00
☐ 2401	PS	Groovin'/Sueno	1967	5.00	10.00	20.00
☐ 2424		A Girl Like You/It's Love	1967	2.00	4.00	8.00
☐ 2424	PS	A Girl Like You/It's Love	1967	5.00	10.00	20.00
☐ 2428		Groovin' (Spanish)/Groovin' (Italian)	1967	5.00	10.00	20.00
☐ 2438		How Can I Be Sure/I'm So Happy Now	1967	2.00	4.00	8.00
☐ 2463		It's Wonderful/Of Course	1967	2.00	4.00	8.00
☐ 2493		A Beautiful Morning/Rainy Day	1968		3.00	6.00
		First record to credit "The Rascals"				
☐ 2493	PS	A Beautiful Morning/Rainy Day	1968	5.00	10.00	20.00
☐ 2537		People Got to Be Free/My World	1968		3.00	6.00
☐ 2537	PS	People Got to Be Free/My World	1968	3.00	6.00	12.00
☐ 2584		A Ray of Hope/Any Dance'll Do	1968		3.00	6.00
☐ 2584	PS	A Ray of Hope/Any Dance'll Do	1968	3.00	6.00	12.00
☐ 2599		Heaven/Baby I'm Blue	1969		3.00	6.00
☐ 2634		See/Away Away	1969		3.00	6.00
☐ 2634	PS	See/Away Away	1969	3.00	6.00	12.00
☐ 2664		Carry Me Back/Real Thing	1969		3.00	6.00
☐ 2664	PS	Carry Me Back/Real Thing	1969	3.00	6.00	12.00
☐ 2695		Hold On/I Believe	1969		3.00	6.00
☐ 2695	PS	Hold On/I Believe	1969	3.00	6.00	12.00
☐ 2743		Glory Glory/You Don't Know	1970		3.00	6.00
☐ 2743	PS	Glory Glory/You Don't Know	1970	3.00	6.00	12.00
☐ 2773		Right On/Almost Home	1970		3.00	6.00

Columbia

☐ 45400		Love Me/Happy Song	1971		3.00	6.00
☐ 45491		Lucky Day/Love Letter	1971		3.00	6.00
☐ 45568		Brother Tree/Saga of New York	1972		3.00	6.00
☐ 45600		Echoes/Hummin' Song	1972		3.00	6.00
☐ 45649		Jungle Walk/Saga of New York	1972	2.50	5.00	10.00

Philco

☐ HP-18		A Girl Like You/I've Been Lonely Too Long	1967	3.00	6.00	12.00
		4-inch flexi-disc in "Philco Hip-Pocket Record" series (price includes sleeve)				

Raspberries

Capitol

☐ 3280		Don't Want to Say Goodbye/Rock and Roll Mama	1972	2.00	4.00	8.00
☐ 3280	PS	Don't Want to Say Goodbye/Rock and Roll Mama	1972	6.25	12.50	25.00
☐ 3348		Go All the Way/With You in My Life	1972		3.00	6.00
☐ 3473		I Wanna Be with You/Goin' Nowhere Tonight	1972		3.00	6.00
☐ 3546		Let's Pretend/Every Way I Can	1973		3.00	6.00
☐ 3546	PS	Let's Pretend/Every Way I Can	1973	3.00	6.00	12.00
☐ 3610		Tonight/Had to Get Over a Heartbreak	1973		3.00	6.00
☐ 3765		I'm a Rocker/Money Down	1973		3.00	6.00
☐ 3826		Don't Want to Say Goodbye/Ecstasy	1974		3.00	6.00

Number		Title (A Side/B Side)	Year	VG	VG+	NM
❏ 3885		Drivin' Around/Might As Well	1974		3.00	6.00
❏ 3946		Overnight Sensation (Hit Record)/Hands on You	1974		3.00	6.00
❏ 4001		The Party's Over/Cruisin' Music	1974		3.00	6.00

Rationals, The
A-Square

❏ 101		Look What You're Doin'/Gave My Love	1966	6.25	12.50	25.00
❏ 103		Feelin' Lost/Little Girls Cry	1966	5.00	10.00	20.00
❏ 103/4	DJ	Feelin' Lost/Respect	1966	7.50	15.00	30.00
❏ 104		Respect/Leavin' Here	1966	5.00	10.00	20.00
❏ 107		I Need You/Out in the Streets	1968	5.00	10.00	20.00

Cameo

❏ 437		Respect/Feelin' Lost	1966	3.00	6.00	12.00
❏ 455		Hold On Baby/Sing	1967	3.75	7.50	15.00
❏ 481		Leavin' Here/Not Like It Is	1967	3.75	7.50	15.00

Capitol

❏ 2124		I Need You/Out in the Streets	1968	3.00	6.00	12.00

Crewe

❏ 360		Handbags and Gladrags/Guitar Army	1969	2.50	5.00	10.00

Raven, Paul – See "Glitter, Gary"

Ravenairs, The
Algonquin

❏ 718		A Night to Remember/Together Forever	1958	25.00	50.00	100.00
		Originally released as "The Rivieras"				

Ravens, The
Argo

❏ 5255		Kneel and Pray/I Can't Believe	1956	10.00	20.00	40.00
❏ 5261		A Simple Prayer/Water Boy	1956	20.00	40.00	80.00
❏ 5276		That'll Be the Day/Dear One	1957	7.50	15.00	30.00
❏ 5284		Here Is My Heart/Lazy Mule	1957	7.50	15.00	30.00

Checker

❏ 871		That'll Be the Day/Dear One	1957	5.00	10.00	20.00

Columbia

❏ 1-903		Don't Look Now/Time Takes Care of Everything	1950	225.00	450.00	900.00
		Microgroove 33 1/3 single				
❏ 1-925		My Baby's Gone/I'm So Crazy for Love	1950	187.50	375.00	750.00
		Microgroove 33 1/3 single				
❏ 6-903		Don't Look Now/Time Takes Care of Everything	1950	187.50	375.00	750.00
❏ 6-925		My Baby's Gone/I'm So Crazy for Love	1950	150.00	300.00	600.00
❏ 39112		You Don't Have to Drop a Heart/Midnight Blues	1950	150.00	300.00	600.00
❏ 39194		You're Always in My Dreams/Gotta Find My Baby	1951	150.00	300.00	600.00
❏ 39408		You Foolish Thing/Honey I Don't Want You	1951	250.00	500.00	1,000

Jubilee

❏ 5184		Bye Bye Baby Blues/Happy Go Lucky Baby	1955	7.50	15.00	30.00
❏ 5217		On Chapel Hill/We'll Raise a Ruckus Tonight	1955	7.50	15.00	30.00
❏ 5237		I'll Always Be in Love with You/	1956	7.50	15.00	30.00
		(Take Me Back To My) Boots and Saddles				
		As "Jimmy Ricks and the Ravens"				

Mercury

❏ 5764		There's No Use Pretending/Wagon Wheels	1951	75.00	150.00	300.00
❏ 5800		Begin the Beguine/Looking for My Baby	1952	62.50	125.00	250.00
❏ 5853		Why Did You Leave Me/Chloe	1952	62.50	125.00	250.00
❏ 70060		I'll Be Back/Don't Mention My Name	1953	50.00	100.00	200.00
❏ 70119		Come a Little Bit Closer/She's Got to Go	1953	37.50	75.00	150.00
❏ 70213		Who'll Be the Fool/Rough Ridin'	1953	37.50	75.00	150.00
❏ 70240		Without a Song/Walkin' My Blues Away	1953	37.50	75.00	150.00
❏ 70307		September Song/Escortin' Or Courtin'	1954	37.50	75.00	150.00
❏ 70330		Going Home/Lonesome Road	1954	37.50	75.00	150.00
❏ 70413		I've Got You Under My Skin/Love Is No Dream	1954	62.50	125.00	250.00
		Pink label				
❏ 70413		I've Got You Under My Skin/Love Is No Dream	1954	25.00	50.00	100.00
		Black label				
❏ 70505		White Christmas/Silent Night	1954	50.00	100.00	200.00
		Pink label				
❏ 70505		White Christmas/Silent Night	1954	25.00	50.00	100.00
		Black label				
❏ 70554		Ol' Man River/Write Me a Letter	1955	50.00	100.00	200.00
		Pink label				
❏ 70554		Ol' Man River/Write Me a Letter	1955	25.00	50.00	100.00
		Black label				
❏ 8291		Rock Me All Night Long/One Sweet Letter	1952	37.50	75.00	150.00

National

❏ 9111		Count Every Star/	1950	1,500	2,250	3,000
		I'm Gonna Paper All My Walls with Your Love				
		The only known Ravens single on a National 45; 20 other Ravens singles exist on National 78s				

Okeh

❏ 6825		The Whiffenpoof Song/	1951	125.00	250.00	500.00
		I Get All My Lovin' on a Saturday Night				
❏ 6843		That Old Gang of Mine/Everything But You	1951	125.00	250.00	500.00
❏ 6888		Mam'selle/Calypso Song	1952	100.00	200.00	400.00

Number		Title (A Side/B Side)	Year	VG	VG+	NM
Savoy						
❑ 1540		White Christmas/Silent Night	1958	5.00	10.00	20.00
Top Rank						
❑ 2003		Into the Shadows/The Rising Sun	1959	6.25	12.50	25.00
❑ 2016		Solitude/Hole in the Middle of the Moon	1959	6.25	12.50	25.00
Rawls, Lou						
Arista						
❑ 0103		Baby You Don't Know How Good You Are/Hour Glass	1975		3.00	6.00
Bell						
❑ 45,608		She's Gone/Hour Glass	1974		3.00	6.00
❑ 45,616		Who Can Tell Us Why?/ Now You're Coming Back Michelle	1974		3.00	6.00
Candix						
❑ 305		In My Little Black Book/ Just Thought You'd Like to Know	1960	5.00	10.00	20.00
❑ 312		When We Get Old/Eighty Ways	1961	5.00	10.00	20.00
Capitol						
❑ 2026		Little Drummer Boy/A Child with a Toy	1967	2.00	4.00	8.00
❑ 2084		Evil Woman/My Ancestors	1968	2.00	4.00	8.00
❑ 2172		Soul Serenade/You're Good for Me	1968	2.00	4.00	8.00
❑ 2252		Down Here on the Ground/ I'm Satisfied (The Duffy Theme)	1968	2.00	4.00	8.00
❑ 2348		The Split/Why Can't I Speak	1968	2.00	4.00	8.00
❑ 2408		It's You/Sweet Charity	1969	2.00	4.00	8.00
❑ 2550		Your Good Thing (Is About to End)/ Season of the Witch	1969	2.00	4.00	8.00
❑ 2668		I Can't Make It Alone/Make the World Go Away	1969	2.00	4.00	8.00
❑ 2734		You've Made Me So Very Happy/ Let's Burn Down the Cornfield	1970	2.00	4.00	8.00
❑ 2856		Bring It On Home/ Can You Dig It-Take Me for What I Am	1970	2.00	4.00	8.00
❑ 2942		Win Your Love for Me/Coppin' a Plea	1970	2.00	4.00	8.00
❑ 4622		That Lucky Old Sun/In My Heart	1961	3.75	7.50	15.00
❑ 4669		Nine-Pound Hammer/Above My Head	1961	3.75	7.50	15.00
❑ 4695		The Wedding (The Bride)/The Biggest Lover in Town	1962	3.00	6.00	12.00
❑ 4743		Trust Me/Please Let Me Be the First to Know	1962	3.00	6.00	12.00
❑ 4761		Save Your Love for Me/Trust Me	1962	3.00	6.00	12.00
❑ 4803		Stormy Monday/Sweet Lover	1962	3.00	6.00	12.00
	With Les McCann					
❑ 5049		Tobacco Road/Blues for Four-String Guitar	1963	3.00	6.00	12.00
❑ 5160		The House Next Door/Come On In, Mr. Blues	1964	3.00	6.00	12.00
❑ 5227		Love Is Blind/I Fell in Love	1964	3.00	6.00	12.00
❑ 5424		Three O'Clock in the Morning/ Nothing Really Feels the Same	1965	3.00	6.00	12.00
❑ 5505		What'll I Do/Can I Please	1965	3.00	6.00	12.00
❑ 5655		The Shadow of Your Smile/Southside Blues	1966	2.50	5.00	10.00
❑ 5709		Love Is a Hurtin' Thing/Memory Lane	1966	2.50	5.00	10.00
❑ 5790		You Can Bring Me All Your Heartaches/ A Woman Who's a Woman	1966	2.50	5.00	10.00
❑ 5824		Trouble Down Here Below/The Life That I Lead	1967	2.50	5.00	10.00
❑ 5824	PS	Trouble Down Here Below/The Life That I Lead	1967	2.50	5.00	10.00
❑ 5869		Dead End Street/Yes It Hurts, Doesn't It	1967	2.50	5.00	10.00
❑ 5941		Show Business/When Love Goes Wrong	1967	2.50	5.00	10.00
❑ S7-18908		What Are You Doing New Year's Eve?/ Have Yourself a Merry Little Christmas	1995	3.00		
Epic						
❑ 02999		Now Is the Time for Love/ Will You Kiss Me One More Time	1982		2.00	4.00
❑ 03299		Together Again/Here Comes Garfield	1982		2.00	4.00
	Lou Rawls and Desiree Goyette					
❑ 03357		Let Me Show You How/Watch Your Back	1982		2.00	4.00
❑ 03758		Wind Beneath My Wings/Midnight Sun	1983		2.00	4.00
❑ 03944		Couple More Years/Upside Down	1983		2.00	4.00
❑ 04079		The One I Sing My Love Songs To/ You Can't Take It With You	1983		2.00	4.00
❑ 04550		All-Time Lover/When We Were Young	1984		2.00	4.00
❑ 04677		Close Company/The Lady in My Life	1984		2.00	4.00
❑ 04773		Close Company/Forever I Do	1985		2.00	4.00
❑ 05714		Learn to Love Again/Ready or Not	1985		2.00	4.00
❑ 05831		Are You With Me/(Instrumental)	1986		2.00	4.00
❑ 06145		Stop Me from Starting This Feeling/ Never Entered My Mind	1986		2.00	4.00
Gamble & Huff						
❑ 310		I Wish You Belonged to Me/(B-side unknown)	1987		2.50	5.00
MGM						
❑ 14262		A Natural Man/You Can't Hold On	1971		3.00	6.00
❑ 14349		His Song Shall Be Sung/I'm Waiting	1972		3.00	6.00
❑ 14428		Politician/Walk On In	1972		3.00	6.00
❑ 14489		Man of Value/Learning Cup	1973		3.00	6.00
❑ 14527		Star Spangled Banner/Just a Closer Walk with Thee	1973		3.00	6.00
❑ 14574		Send for Me/Morning Comes Around	1973		3.00	6.00
❑ 14652		Dead End Street/Love Is a Hurtin' Thing	1973		3.00	6.00
Philadelphia Int'l.						
❑ 3102		Ain't That Loving You (For More Reasons Than One)/ (B-side unknown)	1980		2.50	5.00

Number		Title (A Side/B Side)	Year	VG	VG+	NM
❑ 3114		I Go Crazy/Be Anything (But Be Mine)	1980		2.50	5.00
❑ 3592		You'll Never Find Another Love Like Mine/ Let's Fall in Love All Over Again	1976		2.50	5.00
❑ 3604		Groovy People/This Song Will Last Forever	1976		2.50	5.00
❑ 3623		See You When I Git There/Spring Again	1977		2.50	5.00
❑ 3634		Lady Love/Not the Staying Kind	1977		2.50	5.00
❑ 3643		One Life to Live/If I Coulda, Woulda, Shoulda	1978		2.50	5.00
❑ 3653		There Will Be Love/Unforgettable	1978		2.50	5.00
❑ 3672		Send In the Clowns/This Song Will Last Forever	1978		2.50	5.00
❑ 3684		Let Me Be Good to You/Lover's Holiday	1979		2.50	5.00
❑ 3738		Sit Down and Talk to Me/(B-side unknown)	1979		2.50	5.00
❑ 70051		Hoochie Coochie Man/You've Lost That Lovin' Feelin'	1981		2.50	5.00

Ray and the Darchaes
Aljon

Number		Title (A Side/B Side)	Year	VG	VG+	NM
❑ 1249		Carol/Little Girl So Fine	1962	20.00	40.00	80.00

Buzzy

Number		Title (A Side/B Side)	Year	VG	VG+	NM
❑ 202		Darling Forever/There Will Always Be	1962	25.00	50.00	100.00

Ray, Danny
Vin

Number		Title (A Side/B Side)	Year	VG	VG+	NM
❑ 1025		Love Me/Gone	1960	25.00	50.00	100.00

Ray, Diane
Mercury

Number		Title (A Side/B Side)	Year	VG	VG+	NM
❑ 72117		Please Don't Talk to the Lifeguard/ That's All I Want from You	1963	3.75	7.50	15.00
❑ 72117	PS	Please Don't Talk to the Lifeguard/ That's All I Want from You	1963	10.00	20.00	40.00
❑ 72195		My Summer Love/Where Is the Boy	1963	3.75	7.50	15.00
❑ 72195	PS	My Summer Love/Where Is the Boy	1963	10.00	20.00	40.00
❑ 72223		Snow Man/Just So Bobby Can See	1963	3.75	7.50	15.00
❑ 72223	PS	Snow Man/Just So Bobby Can See	1963	7.50	15.00	30.00
❑ 72248		No Arms Can Ever Hold You/Tied Up with Mary	1964	3.75	7.50	15.00
❑ 72276		Happy Happy Birthday Baby/ That Boy's Gonna Be Mine	1964	3.75	7.50	15.00

Ray, James
Caprice

Number		Title (A Side/B Side)	Year	VG	VG+	NM
❑ 110		If You Gotta Make a Fool of Somebody/ It's Been a Drag	1961	7.50	15.00	30.00
❑ 114		Itty Bitty Pieces/You Remember the Face	1962	6.25	12.50	25.00
❑ 117		Things Are Gonna Be Different/A Miracle	1962	6.25	12.50	25.00

Congress

Number		Title (A Side/B Side)	Year	VG	VG+	NM
❑ 109		Marie/The Old Man and the Mule	1963	5.00	10.00	20.00
❑ 201		Do the Monkey/Put Me in Your Diary	1963	5.00	10.00	20.00
❑ 203		The Masquerade Is Over/One by One	1963	5.00	10.00	20.00
❑ 218		We Got a Thing Goin' On/On That Day	1964	5.00	10.00	20.00

Ray-Vons, The
Laurie

Number		Title (A Side/B Side)	Year	VG	VG+	NM
❑ 3248		Judy/Regina	1964	20.00	40.00	80.00

Raydio – See "Parker, Ray, Jr."

Rays, The
Amy

Number		Title (A Side/B Side)	Year	VG	VG+	NM
❑ 900		Love Another Girl/Sad Saturday	1964	2.00	4.00	8.00

Cameo

Number		Title (A Side/B Side)	Year	VG	VG+	NM
❑ 117		Silhouettes/Daddy Cool	1957	6.25	12.50	25.00
❑ 128		Rendezvous/Triangle	1958	7.50	15.00	30.00
❑ 133		Rags to Riches/The Man Above	1958	7.50	15.00	30.00

Chess

Number		Title (A Side/B Side)	Year	VG	VG+	NM
❑ 1613		Tippity Top/Moo-Goo-Gai-Pan	1956	6.25	12.50	25.00
❑ 1678		How Long Must I Wait/Second Fiddle	1957	6.25	12.50	25.00

Perri

Number		Title (A Side/B Side)	Year	VG	VG+	NM
❑ 1004		Are You Happy Now/Bright Brown Eyes	1962	7.50	15.00	30.00
		Frankie Valli performed on this record				

Unart

Number		Title (A Side/B Side)	Year	VG	VG+	NM
❑ 2001		Souvenirs of Summertime/Elevator Operator	1958	10.00	20.00	40.00

XYZ

Number		Title (A Side/B Side)	Year	VG	VG+	NM
❑ 100		My Steady Girl/No One Loves You Like I Do	1957	15.00	30.00	60.00
❑ 102		Silhouettes/Daddy Cool *Gray label*	1957	37.50	75.00	150.00
❑ 102		Silhouettes/Daddy Cool *Blue label*	1957	15.00	30.00	60.00
❑ 106		Souvenirs of Summertime/Elevator Operator	1958	12.50	25.00	50.00
❑ 600		Why Do You Look the Other Way/Zimbo Lula	1959	12.50	25.00	50.00
❑ 605		It's a Cryin' Shame/Mediterranean Moon	1959	10.00	20.00	40.00
❑ 607		Magic Moon/Louie Hoo Hoo *Blue label*	1960	10.00	20.00	40.00
❑ 607		Magic Moon/Louie Hoo Hoo *Red label*	1960	6.25	12.50	25.00
❑ 608		Old Devil Moon/Silver Starlight	1960	6.25	12.50	25.00

Number	Title (A Side/B Side)	Year	VG	VG+	NM
Re'vells, The					
Roman Press					
❏ 201	Let It Please Be You/Love Walked In	1962	25.00	50.00	100.00
❏ 201	Let It Please Be You/Love Walked In	1962	20.00	40.00	80.00
Re-Vels, The					
Atlas					
❏ 1035	My Lost Love/Love Me, Baby	1954	100.00	200.00	400.00
	As "The Re-Vels Quartette"				
Chess					
❏ 1708	False Alarm/When You Come Back to Me	1958	37.50	75.00	150.00
Sound					
❏ 129	You Lied to Me/Later, Later Baby	1956	37.50	75.00	150.00
❏ 135	Dream, My Darlin', Dream/Cha Cha Toni	1956	37.50	75.00	150.00
Teen					
❏ 122	So in Love/It Happened to Me	1955	200.00	400.00	600.00
Real Original Beatles, The					
(Yeah, right.)					
Dot					
❏ 16655	The Beatle Story (Part 1)/The Beatle Story (Part 2)	1964	5.00	10.00	20.00
Rebels, The					
(Also see "Rockin' Rebels")					
King's X					
❏ 3362	In the Park/In My Heart	1959	50.00	100.00	200.00
Peacock					
❏ 1909	The Donkey Step/Just Give Me Your Heart	1962	5.00	10.00	20.00
Rebenack, Mac					
(Later recorded as "Dr. John")					
A.F.O.					
❏ 309	The Point/One Naughty Flat	1962	6.25	12.50	25.00
Ace					
❏ 611	Good Times/Sahara	1961	6.25	12.50	25.00
Rex					
❏ 1008	Storm Warning/Foolish Little Girl	1959	12.50	25.00	50.00
Rebounds, The					
(Later became the Stampeders)					
Tower					
❏ 288	Since I Fell for You/I'm Not Your Steppin' Stone	1966	3.75	7.50	15.00
Recalls, The					
Arrow					
❏ 2002	No Reason/Nobody's Guy	196?	20.00	40.00	80.00
Record, Eugene					
(Of the Chi-Lites)					
Warner Bros.					
❏ 8386	Mother of Love/Overdose of Joy	1977		2.50	5.00
❏ 8570	You Are the Star of My Show/Trying to Get to You	1978		2.00	4.00
❏ 8836	I Don't Mind/Take Everything	1979		2.00	4.00
❏ 8890	Sweet Insanity/Where Are You	1979		2.00	4.00
❏ 49060	Sweet Insanity/Where Are You	1979		2.00	4.00
❏ 49126	Help Yourself to Love/Fan the Fire	1979		2.00	4.00
Redbone					
(Pat and Lolly Vegas)					
Epic					
❏ 10597	Crazy Cajun Cade Walk Band/Night Come Down	1970		3.00	6.00
❏ 10670	Maggie/New Blue Sermonette	1970		3.00	6.00
❏ 10712	Who Can Say/Light as a Feather	1971		3.00	6.00
❏ 10749	The Witch Queen of New Orleans/Chant: 13th Hour	1971		3.00	6.00
❏ 10839	When You Got Trouble/(B-side unknown)	1972		2.50	5.00
❏ 10866	One Monkey (Don't Stop No Show)/Message from a Drum	1972		2.50	5.00
❏ 10910	Already Here/Fais-Do	1972		2.50	5.00
❏ 10946	Poison Ivy/Condition Your Condition	1973		2.50	5.00
❏ 10979	We Were All Wounded at Wounded Knee/Speakeasy	1973		2.50	5.00
❏ 11035	Come and Get Your Love/Day to Day Life	1973		2.50	5.00
❏ 11035	Come and Get Your Love/Your Miserable Face	1973		2.50	5.00
❏ 11131	Wovoka/Clouds in My Sunshine	1974		2.00	4.00
❏ 50015	Suzie Girl/Interstate Highway 101	1974		2.00	4.00
❏ 50043	One More Time/Blood, Sweat and Tears	1974		2.00	4.00
❏ 50074	Only You and Rock and Roll/Interstate Highway 101	1975		2.00	4.00
❏ 50107	Physical Attraction/I've Got to Find the Right Woman	1975		2.00	4.00
RCA					
❏ PB-11096	Give Our Love Another Try/Funny Silk	1977		2.00	4.00
❏ PB-11182	Checkin' It Out/Funky Silk	1977		2.00	4.00

Number	Title (A Side/B Side)	Year	VG	VG+	NM

Redding, Otis
(Also see "Otis and Carla")
Atco

❑ 6592	Hard to Handle/Amen	1968	2.50	5.00	10.00
❑ 6612	I've Got Dreams to Remember/ Nobody's Fault But Mine	1968	2.50	5.00	10.00
❑ 6631	White Christmas/Merry Christmas, Baby	1968	2.50	5.00	10.00
❑ 6636	Papa's Got a Brand New Bag/Direct Me	1968	2.50	5.00	10.00
❑ 6654	A Lover's Question/You Made a Man Out of Me	1969	2.50	5.00	10.00
❑ 6677	Love Man/I Can't Turn You Loose	1969	2.50	5.00	10.00
❑ 6700	Free Me/Higher and Higher	1969	2.50	5.00	10.00
❑ 6723	Look at the Girl/That's a Good Idea	1969	2.50	5.00	10.00
❑ 6742	Demonstration/Johnny's Heartbreak	1970	2.00	4.00	8.00
❑ 6766	Giving Away None of My Love/Snatch a Little Piece	1970	2.00	4.00	8.00
❑ 6802	Try a Little Tenderness/ I've Been Loving You Too Long (To Stop Now)	1971		3.00	6.00
❑ 6907	My Girl/Good to Me	1972		2.50	5.00
❑ 7069	White Christmas/Merry Christmas, Baby	1976		2.50	5.00
❑ 7321	White Christmas/Merry Christmas, Baby	1980		2.00	4.00
❑ 99955	White Christmas/Merry Christmas, Baby	1982		2.00	4.00

Bethlehem

❑ 3083	Shout Bamalama/Fat Girl	1964	5.00	10.00	20.00

Confederate

❑ 135	Shout Bamalama/Fat Girl	1962	12.50	25.00	50.00

Finer Arts

❑ 2016	She's Alright/Tough Enuff	1961	12.50	25.00	50.00
	Originally released on Trans World by "The Shooters"				

King

❑ 6149	Shout Bamalama/Fat Girl	1968	2.50	5.00	10.00

Orbit

❑ 135	Shout Bamalama/Fat Girl	1961	75.00	150.00	300.00

Stone

❑ 209	You Left the Water Running/The Otis Jam	1976	3.00	6.00	12.00
	B-side by the Memphis Studio Band				

Volt

❑ 103	These Arms of Mine/Hey, Hey Baby	1962	5.00	10.00	20.00
❑ 109	That's What My Heart Needs/Mary's Little Lamb	1963	5.00	10.00	20.00
❑ 112	Pain in My Heart/Something Is Worrying Me	1963	5.00	10.00	20.00
❑ 116	Come to Me/Don't Leave Me This Way	1964	3.75	7.50	15.00
❑ 117	Security/I Want to Thank You	1964	3.75	7.50	15.00
❑ 121	Chained and Bound/Your One and Only Man	1964	3.75	7.50	15.00
❑ 124	Mr. Pitiful/That's How Strong My Love Is	1965	3.00	6.00	12.00
❑ 126	I've Been Loving You Too Long (To Stop Now)/ I'm Depending on You	1965	3.00	6.00	12.00
❑ 128	Respect/Ole Man Trouble	1965	3.00	6.00	12.00
❑ 130	I Can't Turn You Loose/Just One More Day	1965	3.00	6.00	12.00
❑ 132	Satisfaction/Any Ole Way	1966	3.00	6.00	12.00
❑ 136	My Lover's Prayer/Don't Mess with Cupid	1966	3.00	6.00	12.00
❑ 138	Fa-Fa-Fa-Fa-Fa (Sad Song)/Good to Me	1966	3.00	6.00	12.00
❑ 141	Try a Little Tenderness/I'm Sick Y'All	1966	3.00	6.00	12.00
❑ 146	I Love You More Than Words Can Say/ Let Me Come On Home	1967	3.00	6.00	12.00
❑ 149	Shake/You Don't Miss Your Water	1967	3.00	6.00	12.00
❑ 152	Glory of Love/I'm Coming Home	1967	3.00	6.00	12.00
❑ 157	(Sittin' On) The Dock of the Bay/Sweet Lorene	1968	3.00	6.00	12.00
	Black and red label				
❑ 157	(Sittin' On) The Dock of the Bay/Sweet Lorene	1968	2.50	5.00	10.00
	Multicolor (mostly brown) label				
❑ 163	The Happy Song (Dum-Dum)/Open That Door	1968	2.50	5.00	10.00

Redell, Teddy
Atco

❑ 6162	Judy/Can't You See	1960	5.00	10.00	20.00

Hi

❑ 2024	Pipeliner/I Want to Hold You	1960	5.00	10.00	20.00

Vaden

❑ 110	Knockin' on the Backside/Before It Began	1960	30.00	60.00	120.00
❑ 115	Goldust/Corrine, Corrina	1960	30.00	60.00	120.00
❑ 116	Judy/Can't You See	1960	30.00	60.00	120.00
❑ 117	Pipeliner/I Want to Hold You	1960	30.00	60.00	120.00
❑ 301	Pipeliner/I Want to Hold You	1961	20.00	40.00	80.00
❑ 305	I'll Sail My Ship Alone/Don't Grow Old Alone	1961	20.00	40.00	80.00

Redjacks, The
Apt

❑ 25006	Big Brown Eyes/To Make You Mine	1958	5.00	10.00	20.00

Oklahoma

❑ 5005	Big Brown Eyes/To Make You Mine	1958	12.50	25.00	50.00

Number	Title (A Side/B Side)	Year	VG	VG+	NM

Rednow, Eivets – See "Wonder, Stevie"

Redwoods, The
Epic

❑ 9447	Shake, Shake Sherry/The Memory Lingers On	1961	7.50	15.00	30.00
	Originally issued as "The Flairs"				
❑ 9473	Never Take It Away/Unemployment Insurance	1961	7.50	15.00	30.00
❑ 9505	Please, Mr. Scientist/Where You Need to Be	1962	10.00	20.00	40.00

Reed, Jimmy
ABC

❑ 10887	Got Nowhere to Go/Two Ways to Skin (A Cat)	1966	2.00	4.00	8.00

Bluesway

❑ 61003	I Wanna Know/Two Heads Are Better Than One	1967	2.00	4.00	8.00
❑ 61006	Don't Press Your Luck Woman/	1967	2.00	4.00	8.00
	Feel Like I Want to Ramble				
❑ 61013	Buy Me a Hound Dog/Crazy About Oklahoma	1968	2.00	4.00	8.00
❑ 61020	Peepin' and Hidin'/My Baby Told Me	1968	2.00	4.00	8.00
❑ 61025	Don't Light My Fire/The Judge Should Know	1969	2.00	4.00	8.00

Canyon

❑ 38	Hard Walkin' Hannah (Part 1)/	196?	2.00	4.00	8.00
	Hard Walkin' Hannah (Part 2)				

Chance

❑ 1142	High and Lonesome/Roll and Rhumba	1953	500.00	1,000	1,500

Exodus

❑ 2005	Knockin' At Your Door/(B-side unknown)	1966	2.50	5.00	10.00

Vee Jay

❑ 100	High and Lonesome/Roll and Rumba	1953	75.00	150.00	300.00
❑ 100	High and Lonesome/Roll and Rumba	1953	150.00	300.00	600.00
	Red vinyl				
❑ 105	I Found My Baby/Jimmy's Boogie	1953	25.00	50.00	100.00
❑ 105	I Found My Baby/Jimmy's Boogie	1953	100.00	200.00	400.00
	Red vinyl				
❑ 119	You Don't Have to Go/Boogie in the Dark	1954	25.00	50.00	100.00
❑ 119	You Don't Have to Go/Boogie in the Dark	1954	100.00	200.00	400.00
	Red vinyl				
❑ 132	Pretty Thing/I'm Gonna Ruin You	1955	25.00	50.00	100.00
❑ 153	I Don't Go for That/She Don't Want Me No More	1955	12.50	25.00	50.00
❑ 168	Ain't That Lovin' You Baby/	1956	10.00	20.00	40.00
	Baby, Don't Say That No More				
❑ 186	Can't Stand to See You Go/Rockin' with Reed	1956	10.00	20.00	40.00
❑ 203	I Love You Baby/My First Plea	1956	7.50	15.00	30.00
❑ 226	You've Got Me Dizzy/Honey, Don't Let Me Go	1956	7.50	15.00	30.00
❑ 237	Honey, Where You Going/Little Rain	1957	7.50	15.00	30.00
❑ 248	The Sun Is Shining/Baby, What's On Your Mind	1957	7.50	15.00	30.00
❑ 253	Honest I Do/Signals of Love	1957	7.50	15.00	30.00
❑ 270	You're Something Else/A String to My Heart	1958	7.50	15.00	30.00
❑ 275	You Got Me Crying/Go On to School	1958	7.50	15.00	30.00
❑ 287	I Know It's a Sin/Down in Virginia	1958	7.50	15.00	30.00
❑ 298	I'm Gonna Get My Baby/Odds and Ends	1958	7.50	15.00	30.00
❑ 304	I Told You Baby/Ends and Odds (Instrumental)	1958	7.50	15.00	30.00
❑ 314	Take Out Some Insurance/You Know I Love You	1959	6.25	12.50	25.00
❑ 326	I Wanna Be Loved/Going to New York	1959	6.25	12.50	25.00
❑ 333	Baby What You Want Me to Do/Caress Me, Baby	1959	6.25	12.50	25.00
❑ 347	Found Love/Where Can You Be	1960	5.00	10.00	20.00
❑ 357	Hush Hush/Going to the River, Part 2	1960	5.00	10.00	20.00
❑ 373	Laughing at the Blues/Close Together	1961	3.75	7.50	15.00
❑ 380	Big Boss Man/I'm a Love Man	1961	3.75	7.50	15.00
❑ 398	Bright Lights, Big City/I'm Mr. Luck	1961	3.75	7.50	15.00
❑ 425	Aw, Shucks, Hush Your Mouth/Baby, What's Wrong	1962	3.75	7.50	15.00
❑ 449	Tell Me You Love Me/Good Lover	1962	3.75	7.50	15.00
❑ 459	I'll Change My Style/Too Much	1962	3.75	7.50	15.00
❑ 473	Let's Get Together/Oh, John	1962	3.75	7.50	15.00
❑ 509	There'll Be a Day/Shame, Shame, Shame	1963	3.00	6.00	12.00
❑ 552	Mary Mary/I'm Gonna Help You	1963	3.00	6.00	12.00
❑ 570	Outskirts of Town/St. Louis Blues	1963	3.00	6.00	12.00
❑ 584	See See Rider/Wee Wee Baby Blues	1964	3.00	6.00	12.00
❑ 593	Help Yourself/Heading for a Fall	1964	3.00	6.00	12.00
❑ 616	Oh John/Down in Mississippi	1964	3.00	6.00	12.00
❑ 622	I'm Going Upside Your Head/The Devil's Shoestring	1964	3.00	6.00	12.00
❑ 642	I Wanna Be Loved/A New Leaf	1965	3.00	6.00	12.00
❑ 702	I'm the Man Down There/Left Handed Woman	1965	3.00	6.00	12.00
❑ 709	Don't Think I'm Through/When Girls Do It	1966	3.00	6.00	12.00

Reed, Lou
(Formerly of The Velvet Underground)
A&M

❑ 2781	September Song/Oh Heavenly Salvation	1985		2.00	4.00
	B-side by Mark Bingham/Johnny Adams/Aaron Neville				
❑ 2883	Soul Man/Sweet Sarah	1986			3.00
	With Sam Moore				

Arista

❑ 0215	I Believe in Love/Senselessly Cruel	1976		2.00	4.00
❑ 0431	City Lights/I Want to Boogie with You	1979		2.00	4.00
❑ 0535	Growing Up in Public/The Power of Positive Drinking	1980		2.00	4.00

Number		Title (A Side/B Side)	Year	VG	VG+	NM
Atlantic						
❑ 89468		My Love Is Chemical/(B-side unknown)	1985			3.00
❑ 89468	PS	My Love Is Chemical/(B-side unknown)	1985			3.00
RCA						
❑ JB-13558		Martial Law/Don't Talk to Me About Work	1983			3.00
❑ PB-13841		I Love You Suzanne/My Friend George	1984			3.00
❑ PB-14368		No Money Down/Don't Hurt a Woman	1986			3.00
RCA Victor						
❑ 74-0727		I Can't Stand It/Going Down	1972		3.00	6.00
❑ 74-0784		Walk and Talk It/Wild Child	1972		3.00	6.00
❑ 74-0887		Walk on the Wild Side/Perfect Day	1973		3.00	6.00
❑ 74-0964		Satellite of Love/Walk and Talk It	1973		3.00	6.00
❑ APBO-0054		Vicious/Good Night Ladies	1973		2.50	5.00
❑ APBO-0172		Lady Day/How Do You Think It Feels	1973		2.50	5.00
❑ APBO-0238		Sweet Jane/Lady Day	1974	7.50	15.00	30.00
		Part of U.S. numbering system, but pressed for export.				
❑ PB-10053		Sally Can't Dance/Vicious	1974		2.00	4.00
❑ PB-10081		Sally Can't Dance/Ennui	1974		2.00	4.00
❑ GB-10162		Walk on the Wild Side/Vicious	1975			3.00
		Gold Standard Series reissue				
❑ PB-10573		Charley's Girl/Nowhere At All	1976		2.00	4.00
❑ PB-10648		Crazy Feeling/Nowhere At All	1976		2.00	4.00
Sire						
❑ 22876		Romeo Had Juliette/Busload of Faith	1989			3.00
❑ 22876	PS	Romeo Had Juliette/Busload of Faith	1989			3.00

Reed, Tawney

Number	Title (A Side/B Side)	Year	VG	VG+	NM
Congress					
❑ 270	My Heart Cried/Can't Take It Away	1966	3.00	6.00	12.00
Red Bird					
❑ 10-044	Needle in a Haystack/I Got a Feeling	1965	10.00	20.00	40.00

Reed, Ursula

Number	Title (A Side/B Side)	Year	VG	VG+	NM
Old Town					
❑ 1001	You're Laffin' "Cause I'm Cryin'/Ursula's Blues	1954	100.00	200.00	400.00

Reeder, Bill

Number	Title (A Side/B Side)	Year	VG	VG+	NM
Fernwood					
❑ 121	You're My Baby/Where Were You Last Night	1960	20.00	40.00	80.00
Hi					
❑ 2037	Till I Waltz Again with You/There Was a Time	1961	20.00	40.00	80.00
❑ 2041	Secret Love/Judy	1961	5.00	10.00	20.00
Voll					
❑ 100	Till I Waltz Again with You/There Was a Time	1961	50.00	100.00	200.00

Reekers, The

Number	Title (A Side/B Side)	Year	VG	VG+	NM
Ry-Jac					
❑ 13	Grindin'/Don't Call Me Flyface	1964	12.50	25.00	50.00

Reeves, Martha

(Also see "Martha and the Vandellas")

Number	Title (A Side/B Side)	Year	VG	VG+	NM
Arista					
❑ 0124	Love Blind/This Time I'll Be Sweeter	1975		2.50	5.00
❑ 0160	Now That We Found Love/Higher and Higher	1975		2.00	4.00
❑ 0211	The Rest of My Life/Thank You	1976		2.00	4.00
❑ 0228	You've Lost That Lovin' Feelin'/Now That We Found Love	1977		2.00	4.00
Fantasy					
❑ 825	Love Don't Come No Stronger/You're Like Sunshine	1978		2.00	4.00
❑ 868	Dancin' in the Streets (Skatin' in the Streets)/When You Came	1979		2.00	4.00
❑ 887	Really Like Your Rap/That's What I Want	1979		2.00	4.00
MCA					
❑ 40194	Power of Love/Stand By Me	1974		2.50	5.00
❑ 40274	Stand By Me/Wild Night	1974		2.50	5.00
❑ 40329	My Man/Facsimile	1974		2.50	5.00

Reflections, The

Number	Title (A Side/B Side)	Year	VG	VG+	NM
ABC					
❑ 10794	Like Adam and Eve/Vito's House	1966	6.25	12.50	25.00
❑ 10822	You're Gonna Find Out (You Love Me)/Long Cigarette	1966	7.50	15.00	30.00
Capitol					
❑ 4078	Three Steps from True Love/How Could We Let the Love Get Away	1975		2.50	5.00
❑ 4137	Love on Delivery/One Into One	1975		2.50	5.00
❑ 4222	Are You Ready (Here I Am)/Day After Day (Night After Night)	1976		2.50	5.00
❑ 4358	Gift Wrap My Love/She's My Summer Breeze	1976		2.50	5.00
Crossroads					
❑ 401	I Really Must Know/Maybe Tomorrow	1961	15.00	30.00	60.00
❑ 402	Rocket to the Moon/Because of You	1962	15.00	30.00	60.00

Number	Title (A Side/B Side)	Year	VG	VG+	NM
Golden World					
❏ 9	(Just Like) Romeo and Juliet/ Can't You Tell By the Look in His Eyes	1964	5.00	10.00	20.00
❏ 12	Like Columbus Did/Lonely Girl	1964	3.75	7.50	15.00
❏ 15	Oowee Now/Talkin' Bout My Girl	1964	3.75	7.50	15.00
❏ 16	Henpecked Guy/Don't Do That to Me	1964	3.75	7.50	15.00
❏ 19	You're My Baby/Shabby Little Hut	1964	3.75	7.50	15.00
❏ 20	Poor Man's Son/Comin' At You	1965	3.75	7.50	15.00
❏ 22	Wheelin' and Dealin'/Deborah Ann	1965	3.75	7.50	15.00
❏ 24	June Bride/Out of the Picture	1965	3.75	7.50	15.00
❏ 29	Girl in the Candy Store/Your Kind of Love	1965	3.75	7.50	15.00
Kay-Ko					
❏ 1003	Helpless/You Said Goodbye	1963	50.00	100.00	200.00
RCA					
❏ PB-11408	Boogie City/I'm Gonna Let You Go This Time	1978		2.50	5.00
Tigre					
❏ 602	In the Still of the Night/Tic Toc	1962	10.00	20.00	40.00
Regals, The					
(Two different groups)					
Aladdin					
❏ 3266	Run Pretty Baby/ May the Good Lord Bless and Keep You	1954	30.00	60.00	120.00
Atlantic					
❏ 1062	I'm So Lonely/Got the Water Boiling	1955	15.00	30.00	60.00
Last Chance					
❏ 109	See You in the Morning/Yes My Love	1961	2.50	5.00	10.00
Lavender					
❏ 1452	See You in the Morning/Yes My Love	1960	7.50	15.00	30.00
United Artists					
❏ 380	Icy Fingers/Tiger Tears	1961	7.50	15.00	30.00
Regan, Eddie					
ABC					
❏ 10795	Playin' Hide and Seek/Talk About Heartaches	1966	7.50	15.00	30.00
Regan, Tommy					
Colpix					
❏ 725	I'll Never Stop Loving You/This Time I'm Losing You	1964	25.00	50.00	100.00
World Artists					
❏ 1049	I Adore You/9 to 5	1965	3.75	7.50	15.00
Regents, The					
(More than one group)					
Argo					
❏ 5268	Isle of Trinidad/Bamboo Tree	1957	6.25	12.50	25.00
Blue Cat					
❏ 110	Playmates/Me and You	1965	2.50	5.00	10.00
Cousins					
❏ 1002	Barbara-Ann/I'm So Lonely	1961	100.00	200.00	400.00
Dot					
❏ 16970	The Russian Spy and I/Bald Headed Woman	1966	2.50	5.00	10.00
Gee					
❏ 1065	Barbara-Ann/I'm So Lonely	1961	6.25	12.50	25.00
❏ 1071	Runaround/Laura My Darling	1961	6.25	12.50	25.00
❏ 1073	Don't Be a Fool/Liar	1961	6.25	12.50	25.00
❏ 1075	Lonesome Boy/Oh Baby	1961	6.25	12.50	25.00
Kayo					
❏ 101	(That's What I Call) A Real Good Time/ No Hard Feelings	1960	6.25	12.50	25.00
Peoria					
❏ 8	Summertime Blues/(B-side unknown)	196?	3.75	7.50	15.00
Reprise					
❏ 0430	She's Got Her Own Way of Lovin'/ When I Die, Don't You Cry	1965	7.50	15.00	30.00
	Michael McDonald, later of the Doobie Brothers, was in this group				
Reid, Matthew					
ABC-Paramount					
❏ 10259	Jane/Why Start	1961	6.25	12.50	25.00
❏ 10305	Tarzan Twist (Bwana Ungava)/Through My Tears	1962	6.25	12.50	25.00
Decca					
❏ 31662	One More Minute/Hurt Me	1964	3.00	6.00	12.00
Philips					
❏ 40634	Outward Bound/Hey There Sweet Sue	1969	2.50	5.00	10.00
Scepter					
❏ 1238	Faded Roses/Tomorrow	1962	6.25	12.50	25.00
Topix					
❏ 6006	Cry Myself to Sleep/Lollipops Went Out of Style	1961	10.00	20.00	40.00

Number		Title (A Side/B Side)	Year	VG	VG+	NM

Relf, Keith
(Lead singer of The Yardbirds)
Epic

❑ 10044		Mr. Zero/Knowing	1966	12.50	25.00	50.00
❑ 10044	DJ	Mr. Zero/Knowing	1966	37.50	75.00	150.00
		Promo on red vinyl				
❑ 10110		Shapes in My Mind/Blue Sands	1966	12.50	25.00	50.00
❑ 10110	DJ	Shapes in My Mind/Blue Sands	1966	37.50	75.00	150.00
		Promo on red vinyl				
❑ 10110	PS	Shapes in My Mind/Blue Sands	1966	25.00	50.00	100.00

Remains, The
Epic

❑ 9777		You Say You're Sorry/I'm Talking About You	1965	10.00	20.00	40.00
❑ 9783		My Babe/Why Do I Cry	1965	10.00	20.00	40.00
❑ 9872		But I Ain't Got You/I Can't Get Away from You	1965	10.00	20.00	40.00
❑ 10001		Diddy Wah Diddy/Once Before	1966	10.00	20.00	40.00
❑ 10001	DJ	Diddy Wah Diddy/Once Before	1966	27.50	75.00	150.00
		Promo on red vinyl				
❑ 10001	PS	To Be Seen and Heard: Diddy Wah Diddy	1966	25.00	50.00	100.00
		Promo-only sleeve				
❑ 10060		Don't Look Back/Me Right Now	1966	10.00	20.00	40.00

Reminiscents, The
Day

❑ 1000		Zoom Zoom Zoom/Oh Let Me Dream	1963	12.50	25.00	50.00
		Blue vinyl				

Marcel

❑ 1000		Cards of Love/Flames	1962	30.00	60.00	120.00

Remus, Eugene
Motown

❑ 1001		You Never Miss a Good Thing/Hold Me Tight	1960	150.00	300.00	600.00
❑ 1001		You Never Miss a Good Thing/Gotta Have Your Lovin'	1960	125.00	250.00	500.00

Renaissance
Capitol

❑ 3487		Prologue/Spare Some Love	1972	2.00	4.00	8.00
❑ 3715		Carpet of the Sun/Bound for Infinity	1973	2.00	4.00	8.00

I.R.S.

❑ 9904		Remember/Bon Jour Swan Song	1982		2.50	5.00
❑ 9914		Richard IX/(B-side unknown)	1982		2.50	5.00

Sire

❑ 714		Mother Russia/I Think of You	1974		3.00	6.00
❑ 728		Carpet of the Sun/Kiev	1976		3.00	6.00
❑ 740		Midas Man/Captive Heart	1977		3.00	6.00
❑ 1022		Northern Lights/Opening Out	1978		2.50	5.00
❑ 1041		Northern Lights/Opening Out	1979		2.50	5.00
❑ 49041		Forever Changing/Jekyll and Hyde	1979		2.50	5.00

Renay, Diane
Atco

❑ 6240		Falling Star/Little White Lies	1962	3.00	6.00	12.00
❑ 6262		Dime a Dozen/Tender	1963	3.00	6.00	12.00

Fontana

❑ 1679		Hold Me, Thrill Me, Kiss Me/Yesterday	1969	2.50	5.00	10.00

MGM

❑ 13296		Billy Blue Eyes/Watch Out Sally	1964	2.50	5.00	10.00
❑ 13335		I Had a Dream/Troublemaker	1965	5.00	10.00	20.00

New Voice

❑ 800		Words/The Company You Keep	1965	2.50	5.00	10.00
❑ 803		Cross My Heart, Hope to Die/	1965	2.50	5.00	10.00
		Happy Birthday, Broken Heart				

20th Fox

❑ 456		Navy Blue/Unbelievable Boy	1964	3.00	6.00	12.00
❑ 477		Kiss Me Sailor/Soft Spoken Guy	1964	2.50	5.00	10.00
❑ 514		Growin' Up Too Fast/Waitin' for Joey	1964	2.50	5.00	10.00
❑ 533		It's In Your Tears/Present from Eddie	1964	2.50	5.00	10.00

United Artists

❑ 50048		Dynamite/Please Gypsy	1966	3.75	7.50	15.00

Rendezvous
Reprise

❑ 20,089		Congratulations Baby/Faithfully	1962	7.50	15.00	30.00

Rust

❑ 5041		It Breaks My Heart/Take a Break	1961	10.00	20.00	40.00

Renegades, The
American Int'l.

❑ 537		Charge/Geronimo	1959	12.50	25.00	50.00

Congress

❑ 241		Cadillac/Matelot (Sailor Boy)	1965	7.50	15.00	30.00

Number		Title (A Side/B Side)	Year	VG	VG+	NM
Dorset						
❏ 5007		Stolen Angel/Keep Laughin'	1961	12.50	25.00	50.00
Garland						
❏ 2036		I'm a Loner/Travelin' Through This Countryside	196?	2.50	5.00	10.00
Karate						
❏ 519		Take a Heart/If It Gets Lonesome	1966	3.75	7.50	15.00

Reno, Al
Kapp

❏ 432		Cheryl/Congratulations	1961	10.00	20.00	40.00

Reno, Mike, and Ann Wilson
(Of Loverboy and Heart, respectively)
Columbia

❏ 04418		Almost Paradise...Love Theme from Footloose/ Strike Zone	1984			3.00
❏ 04418	PS	Almost Paradise...Love Theme from Footloose/ Strike Zone	1984		2.00	4.00

REO Speedwagon
Epic

❏ 01054		Take It on the Run/Someone Tonight	1981		2.00	4.00
❏ 02127		Don't Let Him Go/I Wish You Were There	1981		2.00	4.00
❏ 02127	PS	Don't Let Him Go/I Wish You Were There	1981		2.50	5.00
❏ 02153		Keep On Loving You/Time for Me to Fly	1981			3.00
		Reissue				
❏ 02457		In Your Letter/Shakin' It Loose	1981		2.00	4.00
❏ 02967		Keep the Fire Burnin'/I'll Follow You	1982		2.00	4.00
❏ 03175		Sweet Time/Stillness of the Night	1982		2.00	4.00
❏ 03175	PS	Sweet Time/Stillness of the Night	1982		2.50	5.00
❏ 03264		Sweet Time	1982		2.50	5.00
		One-sided budget release				
❏ 03400		Let's Be-Bop/The Key	1982		2.00	4.00
❏ 03846		Keep the Fire Burnin'/Take It on the Run	1983			3.00
		Reissue				
❏ 03847		In Your Letter/Don't Let Him Go	1983			3.00
		Reissue				
❏ 04659		I Do'Wanna Know/Rock 'N Roll Star	1984			3.00
❏ 04659	PS	I Do'Wanna Know/Rock 'N Roll Star	1984		2.00	4.00
❏ 04713		Can't Fight This Feeling/Break His Spell	1984			3.00
❏ 04713	PS	Can't Fight This Feeling/Break His Spell	1984		3.00	6.00
❏ 04848		One Lonely Night/Wheels Are Turnin'	1985			3.00
❏ 04848	PS	One Lonely Night/Wheels Are Turnin'	1985		2.00	4.00
❏ 05412		Live Every Moment/Gotta Feel More	1985			3.00
❏ 06656		That Ain't Love/Accidents Can Happen	1987			3.00
❏ 06656	PS	That Ain't Love/Accidents Can Happen	1987			3.00
❏ 07055		Variety Tonight/Tired of Gettin' Nowhere	1987			3.00
❏ 07055	PS	Variety Tonight/Tired of Gettin' Nowhere	1987			3.00
❏ 07255		In My Dreams/Over the Edge	1987			3.00
❏ 07255	PS	In My Dreams/Over the Edge	1987			3.00
❏ 07901		Here with Me/Wherever You're Goin' (It's Alright)	1988			3.00
❏ 07901	PS	Here with Me/Wherever You're Goin' (It's Alright)	1988			3.00
❏ 08030		I Don't Want to Lose You/On the Road Again	1988			3.00
❏ 10827		Sophisticated Lady/Prison Women	1972	3.00	6.00	12.00
❏ 10847		157 Riverside Avenue/Five Men Were Killed Today	1972	3.00	6.00	12.00
❏ 10892		Lay Me Down/Gypsy Woman's Passion	1972	3.00	6.00	12.00
❏ 10975		Golden Country/Little Queenie	1973	3.00	6.00	12.00
❏ 11078		Ridin' the Storm Out/Whiskey Night	1974	3.00	6.00	12.00
❏ 11132		Start a New Life/Open Up	1974	2.50	5.00	10.00
❏ 50059		Sky Blues/Throw the Chains Away	1975	2.00	4.00	8.00
❏ 50120		Out of Control/Running Blind	1975	2.00	4.00	8.00
❏ 50180		Reelin'/Headed for a Fall	1975	2.00	4.00	8.00
❏ 50254		Tonight/Keep Pushin'	1976		3.00	6.00
❏ 50288		Flying Turkey Trot/Keep Pushin'	1976		3.00	6.00
❏ 50367		Ridin' the Storm Out/Being Kind	1977		3.00	6.00
❏ 50459		Flying Turkey Trot/Keep Pushin'	1977		3.00	6.00
❏ 50545		Roll with the Changes/Unidentified Flying Tuna Trot	1978		2.50	5.00
❏ 50582		Time for Me to Fly/Runnin' Blind	1978		2.50	5.00
❏ 50764		I Need You Tonight/Easy Money	1979		2.50	5.00
❏ 50790		Only the Strong Survive/Drop It (An Old Disguise)	1979		2.50	5.00
❏ 50858		Time for Me to Fly/Lightning	1980		2.00	4.00
❏ 50953		Keep On Loving You/Follow My Heart	1980		2.00	4.00
❏ 51006		Take It on the Run/Someone Tonight	1981			*Unreleased?*
❏ 73499		Live It Up/All Heaven Broke Loose	1990			3.00
❏ 73540		Love Is a Rock/Go for Broke	1990			3.00

Reparata and the Delrons
Big Tree

❏ 114		Just You/There's So Little Time	1971		2.50	5.00
Kapp						
❏ 989		(That's What Sends Men to) The Bowery/ I've Got an Awful Lot of Losing to Do	1969		3.00	6.00
❏ 2010		San Juan/We're Gonna Hold the Night	1969		3.00	6.00
❏ 2050		Waking in the Rain/Got Fear of Losing You	1969		3.00	6.00

Number	Title (A Side/B Side)	Year	VG	VG+	NM
Laurie					
❏ 3252	Your Big Mistake/Leave Us Alone	1964	7.50	15.00	30.00
	As "The Delrons"				
❏ 3589	Octopus' Garden/Your Life Is Gone	1972		2.50	5.00
	As "Reparata"				
Mala					
❏ 589	Captain of Your Ship/Toom Toom Is a Little Boy	1968		3.00	6.00
❏ 12000	Saturday Night Didn't Happen/Panic	1968		3.00	6.00
❏ 12016	You Can't Change a Young Boy's Mind/ Weather Forecast	1968		3.00	6.00
❏ 12026	Heaven Only Knows/Summer Laughter	1968		3.00	6.00
Polydor					
❏ 14271	Shoes/Song for All	1975		2.00	4.00
	As "Reparata"				
❏ 14298	Jezebee Lancer the Belly Dancer/We Need You	1975			*Unreleased*
RCA Victor					
❏ 47-8721	I Can Tell/Take a Look Around You	1965	2.50	5.00	10.00
❏ 47-8820	I'm Nobody's Baby Now/The Loneliest Girl in Town	1966	2.50	5.00	10.00
❏ 47-8921	Mama's Little Girl/He Don't Want You	1966	2.50	5.00	10.00
❏ 47-9123	Boys and Girls/That Kind of Trouble That I Love	1967	2.50	5.00	10.00
❏ 47-9185	I Can Hear the Rain/Always Waitin'	1967	2.50	5.00	10.00
World Artists					
❏ 1036	Whenever a Teenager Cries/He's My Guy	1964	2.50	5.00	10.00
❏ 1051	Tommy/Mama Don't Allow	1965	2.50	5.00	10.00
❏ 1057	He's the Greatest/A Summer Thought	1965	2.50	5.00	10.00
❏ 1062	The Boy I Love/I Found My Place	1965	2.50	5.00	10.00
Reunion					
A&M					
❏ 1308	City Song/No Good Alone	1971		2.00	4.00
Bell					
❏ 45,222	Smile (Theme from Modern Times)/ Turn Back the Hands of Time (Gotta Have You Back)	1972		2.00	4.00
❏ 45,287	Living Together, Growing Together/Just Say Goodbye	1974		2.00	4.00
RCA Victor					
❏ PB-10056	Life Is a Rock (But the Radio Rolled Me)/ Are You Ready to Believe	1974		2.50	5.00
❏ PB-10150	Disco-Tekin/Goodstuff	1975		2.00	4.00
❏ PB-10252	They Don't Make 'Em Like That Anymore/Goodstuff	1975		2.00	4.00
❏ GB-10491	Life Is a Rock (But the Radio Rolled Me)/ Are You Ready to Believe	1975			3.00
	Gold Standard Series				
Revalons, The					
Pet					
❏ 802	Dreams Are for Fools/This Is the Moment	1958	20.00	40.00	80.00
Revels, The					
(More than one group)					
Andie					
❏ 5077	Please/Two Little Monkeys (In a Banana Tree)	1960	5.00	10.00	20.00
CT					
❏ 1	Church Key/Vesuvius	1960	25.00	50.00	100.00
Diamond					
❏ 143	Lots of Luck/Gonna Have Some Fun	1963	3.75	7.50	15.00
Downey					
❏ 123	Intoxica/Comanche	1964	6.25	12.50	25.00
Impact					
❏ 1	Church Key/Vesuvius	1960	6.25	12.50	25.00
❏ 1	Church Key/Vesuvius	1960	12.50	25.00	50.00
	Red vinyl				
❏ 3	Intoxica/Tequila	1961	6.25	12.50	25.00
❏ 7	Comanche/Rampage	1961	6.25	12.50	25.00
❏ 7	Comanche/Rampage	1961	12.50	25.00	50.00
	Yellow vinyl				
❏ 13	Party Time/Soft Top	1961	6.25	12.50	25.00
❏ 22	Conga Twist/Revellion	1962	12.50	25.00	50.00
	Yellow vinyl; Both A-sides of Impact 22 are the same song				
❏ 22	The Monkey Bird/Revellion	1962	6.25	12.50	25.00
❏ 22	The Monkey Bird/Revellion	1962	12.50	25.00	50.00
	Yellow vinyl				
❏ 22	Conga Twist/Revellion	1962	6.25	12.50	25.00
Jamie					
❏ 1318	True Love/Everybody Can Do the New Dog But Me	1966	2.50	5.00	10.00
Kapp					
❏ 621	Downtown/Dollar Sign	1964	7.50	15.00	30.00
Lynn					
❏ 1302	Six Pak/Good Grief	1960	15.00	30.00	60.00
Norgolde					
❏ 103	Dead Man's Stroll/Talking to My Heart	1959	30.00	60.00	120.00

Number	Title (A Side/B Side)	Year	VG	VG+	NM
❑ 103	Midnight Stroll/Talking to My Heart	1959	6.25	12.50	25.00
	Same A-side as above, but with revised title				
❑ 104	Tweedlee Dee/Foo Man Choo	1959	5.00	10.00	20.00
Palette					
❑ 5074	O How I Love You/I Met My Lost Love	1961	5.00	10.00	20.00
Swingin'					
❑ 620	Six Pak/Good Grief	1960	10.00	20.00	40.00
Westco					
❑ 3/4	Party Time/Soft Top	1963	12.50	25.00	50.00
	Red and yellow vinyl				

Revere, Paul, and the Raiders

Columbia

Number		Title (A Side/B Side)	Year	VG	VG+	NM
❑ CSP-262		SS 396/Corvair Baby	1965	6.25	12.50	25.00
❑ CSM-466		SS 396/Camaro	1967	6.25	12.50	25.00
		B-side by The Cyrcle				
❑ CSM-466	PS	SS 396/Camaro	1967	12.50	25.00	50.00
		B-side by The Cyrcle				
❑ 10126		Gonna Have a Good Time/ Your Love (Is the Only Love)	1975	2.50	5.00	10.00
❑ 42814		Louie Louie/Night Train	1963	10.00	20.00	40.00
❑ 43008		Louie Go Home/Have Love Will Travel	1964	3.75	7.50	15.00
❑ 43114		Over You/Swim	1964	3.75	7.50	15.00
❑ 43273		Ooh Poo Pah Doo/Sometimes	1965	3.75	7.50	15.00
❑ 43375		Steppin' Out/Blue Fox	1965	2.50	5.00	10.00
❑ 43375	DJ	Steppin' Out (same on both sides)	1965	12.50	25.00	50.00
		Red vinyl promo				
❑ 43461		Just Like Me/B.F.R.D.F. Blues	1965	2.50	5.00	10.00
❑ 43461	DJ	Just Like Me (same on both sides)	1965	12.50	25.00	50.00
		Red vinyl promo				
❑ 43556		Kicks/Shake It Up	1966	2.50	5.00	10.00
❑ 43556	DJ	Kicks (same on both sides)	1966	12.50	25.00	50.00
		Red vinyl promo				
❑ 43678		Hungry/There She Goes	1966	2.50	5.00	10.00
❑ 43678	DJ	Hungry (same on both sides)	1966	12.50	25.00	50.00
		Red vinyl promo				
❑ 43678	PS	Hungry/There She Goes	1966	5.00	10.00	20.00
❑ 43810		The Great Airplane Strike/In My Community	1966	2.50	5.00	10.00
❑ 43810	DJ	The Great Airplane Strike (same on both sides)	1966	12.50	25.00	50.00
		Red vinyl promo				
❑ 43810	PS	The Great Airplane Strike/In My Community	1966	3.75	7.50	15.00
❑ 43907		Good Thing/Undecided Man	1966	2.50	5.00	10.00
❑ 43907	PS	Good Thing/Undecided Man	1966	5.00	10.00	20.00
❑ 44026		Ups and Downs/Leslie	1967	2.50	5.00	10.00
❑ 44026	PS	Ups and Downs/Leslie	1967	3.75	7.50	15.00
❑ 44094		Him or Me -- What's It Gonna Be?/ Legend of Paul Revere	1967	2.50	5.00	10.00
❑ 44094	PS	Him or Me -- What's It Gonna Be?/ Legend of Paul Revere	1967	3.75	7.50	15.00
❑ 44227		I Had a Dream/Upon Your Leaving	1967	2.00	4.00	8.00
❑ 44227	PS	I Had a Dream/Upon Your Leaving	1967	2.50	5.00	10.00
❑ 44335		Peace of Mind/Do Unto Others	1967	2.00	4.00	8.00
❑ 44335	PS	Peace of Mind/Do Unto Others	1967	2.50	5.00	10.00
❑ 44444		Too Much Talk/Happening '68	1968	2.00	4.00	8.00
❑ 44444	PS	Too Much Talk/Happening '68	1968	2.50	5.00	10.00
❑ 44553		Don't Take It Too Hard/ Observation from Flight 285 (In 3/4 Time)	1968		3.00	6.00
❑ 44553	PS	Don't Take It Too Hard/ Observation from Flight 285 (In 3/4 Time)	1968	2.50	5.00	10.00
❑ 44655		Cinderella Sunshine/It's Happening	1968	2.00	4.00	8.00
❑ 44744		Mr. Sun, Mr. Moon/Without You	1969		3.00	6.00
❑ 44744	PS	Mr. Sun, Mr. Moon/Without You	1969	2.50	5.00	10.00
❑ 44854		Let Me/I Don't Know	1969		3.00	6.00
❑ 44970		We Gotta All Get Together/Frankfort Side Street	1969		3.00	6.00
❑ 45082		Just Seventeen/Sorceress with Blue Eyes	1970		3.00	6.00
		As "Raiders"				
❑ 45150		Gone Movin' On/Interlude (To Be Forgotten)	1970		3.00	6.00
		As "Raiders"				
❑ 45332		Indian Reservation (The Lament of the Cherokee Reservation Indian)/Terry's Tune	1971	2.00	4.00	8.00
		As "Raiders"; red label, black print				
❑ 45332		Indian Reservation (The Lament of the Cherokee Reservation Indian)/Terry's Tune	1971		3.00	6.00
		As "Raiders"; orange label with "Columbia" background print				
❑ 45453		Birds of a Feather/The Turkey	1971		3.00	6.00
		As "Raiders"				
❑ 45535		Country Wine/It's So Hard Getting Up Today	1972		3.00	6.00
		As "Raiders"				
❑ 45601		Powder Blue Mercedes Queen/ Golden Girls Sometimes	1972	2.00	4.00	8.00
		As "Raiders"				
❑ 45688		Song Seller/A Simple Song	1972	2.00	4.00	8.00
		As "Raiders"				
❑ 45759		Love Music/Goodbye, No. 9	1973	2.00	4.00	8.00
		As "Raiders"				

Number	Title (A Side/B Side)	Year	VG	VG+	NM
❑ 45898	All Over You/Seaboard Line Boogie	1973	2.00	4.00	8.00
	As "Raiders"				
Drive					
❑ 6248	Ain't Nothing Wrong/You're Really Saying Something	1976		2.50	5.00
Gardena					
❑ 106	Beatnik Sticks/Orbit (The Spy)	1960	7.50	15.00	30.00
❑ 115	Paul Revere's Ride/Unfinished Fifth	1960	10.00	20.00	40.00
❑ 116	Like, Long Hair/Sharon	1961	7.50	15.00	30.00
❑ 118	Like, Charleston/Midnite Ride	1961	6.25	12.50	25.00
❑ 124	All Night Long/Groovey	1962	10.00	20.00	40.00
❑ 127	Like, Bluegrass/Leatherneck	1962	10.00	20.00	40.00
❑ 131	Shake It Up (Part 1)/Shake It Up (Part 2)	1962	10.00	20.00	40.00
❑ 137	Tall Cool One/Road Runner	1963	12.50	25.00	50.00
Jerden					
❑ 807	So Fine/Blues Stay Away	1966	6.25	12.50	25.00
Sande					
❑ 101	Louie Louie/Night Train	1963	50.00	100.00	200.00
20th Century					
❑ 2283	The British Are Coming/Surrender at Appomattox	1976		2.50	5.00
	B-side by Susie Allanson				

Reveres, The
(More than one group)

Glory

❑ 272	Leonore/Honeystroller	1958	5.00	10.00	20.00
	B-side by the Honeystrollers				
Jubilee					
❑ 5463	Beyond the Sea/The Show Must Go On	1963	6.25	12.50	25.00
Valiant					
❑ 6041	Big "T"/Me and My Spider	1964	12.50	25.00	50.00
	Bruce Johnston appears on this record				

Revlons, The
(Probably more than one group)

Capitol

❑ 4739	Dry Your Eyes/She'll Come to Me	1962	7.50	15.00	30.00
Parkway					
❑ 107	Ya Ya/It Could Happen to You	1966	3.00	6.00	12.00
Rae Cox					
❑ 105	This Restless Heart/I Promise Love	1961	7.50	15.00	30.00
Times Square					
❑ 15	Ride Away/Betty	1963	6.25	12.50	25.00
	B-side by the Centuries				
Toy					
❑ 101	What a Love This Is/Did I Make a Mistake	1962	5.00	10.00	20.00

Reynolds, Jody

Brent

❑ 7042	Raggedy Ann/The Girl from King Marie	1963	2.50	5.00	10.00
Demon					
❑ 1507	Endless Sleep/Tight Capris	1958	7.50	15.00	30.00
❑ 1509	Fire of Love/Daisy Mae	1958	6.25	12.50	25.00
❑ 1511	Closin' In/Elope with Me	1958	6.25	12.50	25.00
❑ 1515	Golden Idol/Beulah Lee	1959	6.25	12.50	25.00
❑ 1519	The Storm/Please Remember	1959	6.25	12.50	25.00
❑ 1523	Whipping Post/I Wanna Be with You Tonight	1960	6.25	12.50	25.00
❑ 1524	Stone Cold/(The Girl with) The Raven Hair	1960	6.25	12.50	25.00
Indigo					
❑ 127	Tarantula/Thunder	1961	12.50	25.00	50.00
Pulsar					
❑ 2419	Endless Sleep/My Baby's Eyes	1969		3.00	6.00
Smash					
❑ 1810	Don't Jump/Stormy	1963	3.00	6.00	12.00
Titan					
❑ 1734	Devil Girl/A Tear for Hesse	1963	3.75	7.50	15.00
❑ 1736	Requiem for Love/Stranger in the Mirror	1963	3.75	7.50	15.00
	With Bobbie Gentry				

Rhodes, Slim

Sun

❑ 216	Don't Believe/Uncertain Blues	1955	25.00	50.00	100.00
❑ 225	Are You Ashamed of Me/The House of Sin	1955	75.00	150.00	300.00
❑ 238	Bad Girl/Gonna Romp and Stomp	1956	25.00	50.00	100.00
❑ 256	Do What I Do/Take and Give	1956	12.50	25.00	50.00

Rhythm Aces, The

Ace

❑ 518	Rock and Roll March/Look What You've Done	1956	10.00	20.00	40.00
	B-side by Bob Douglas				
Mark-X					
❑ 8004	Boppin' Sloppin' Baby/Crazy Jealousy	1960	7.50	15.00	30.00

Number		Title (A Side/B Side)	Year	VG	VG+	NM
Roulette						
❏ 4268		Mohawk Rock/It'll Do	1960	3.75	7.50	15.00
❏ 4426		Raunchy Twist/Mockin' Bird Twist	1962	3.75	7.50	15.00
Sioux						
❏ 82260		Allan's Rock/Go Get It	1960	7.50	15.00	30.00
❏ 102261		Yahma/What'd I Say Twist	1961	7.50	15.00	30.00
Universal Artists						
❏ 3160		Mohawk Rock/It'll Do	1960	7.50	15.00	30.00
Vee Jay						
❏ 124		I Wonder Why/Get Lost	1954	50.00	100.00	200.00
❏ 124		I Wonder Why/Get Lost	1954	125.00	250.00	500.00
	Red vinyl					
❏ 138		Whisper to Me/Olly, Olly, Oxsen Free	1955	50.00	100.00	200.00
❏ 138		Whisper to Me/Olly, Olly, Oxsen Free	1955	100.00	200.00	400.00
	Red vinyl					
❏ 160		That's My Sugar/Flippety Flop	1955	30.00	60.00	120.00

Rhythm Cadets, The

Vesta						
❏ 501/2		Dearest Doryce/Rocking Jimmy	1957	200.00	400.00	800.00

Rhythm Masters, The

Flip						
❏ 314		Baby We Two/Patricia	1956	75.00	150.00	300.00

Rhythm Rockers

Challenge						
❏ 9196		Rendezvous Stomp/The Slide	1963	6.25	12.50	25.00
Fenton						
❏ 944		Surf Around/Three Strikes	1962	12.50	25.00	50.00
Satin						
❏ 921		Oh Boy/We Belong Together	1960	15.00	30.00	60.00
❏ 921	PS	Oh Boy/We Belong Together	1960	25.00	50.00	100.00
Sun						
❏ 248		Fiddle Bop/Juke Box, Help Me Find My Baby	1956	15.00	30.00	60.00
Wipe Out						
❏ 1001		Foot Cruising/Get It On	1962	10.00	20.00	40.00

Rhythm, Johnny

MGM						
❏ 13043		This Is It/Wouldn't It Be Nice	1961	10.00	20.00	40.00

Ria and the Reasons

Amy						
❏ 888		Memories Linger On/Sorry I Lied	1963	6.25	12.50	25.00
❏ 888		Memories Linger On/Sorry I Lied	1963	20.00	40.00	80.00
	Blue vinyl					
RSVP						
❏ 1110		He's Not There/She Fell in Love	1965	5.00	10.00	20.00
	As "Ria and the Revellons"					

Rialtos, The

CB						
❏ 5009		Let Me In/It Hurts	1962	50.00	100.00	200.00

Ric-A-Shays, The

(Harry Nilsson was in this group)

Lola						
❏ 002		Groovy/Turn On	1964	6.25	12.50	25.00

Ricardos, The

Star-X						
❏ 512		Mary's Little Lamb/I Mean Really	1958	40.00	80.00	160.00

Rice, Tony

Action						
❏ 100		My Darling Y-O-U/I Thank You Baby	1961	7.50	15.00	30.00
Princeton						
❏ 101		Summer's Love/Please Don't	1960	15.00	30.00	60.00
Rae Cox						
❏ 106		Little School Girl/Blue Bird of Happiness	1961	5.00	10.00	20.00

Rich, Charlie

Elektra						
❏ 45553		I'll Wake You Up When I Get Home/Salty Dog Blues	1978		2.00	4.00
❏ 47047		A Man Just Doesn't Know	1980		2.00	4.00
		What a Woman Goes Through/Marie				
❏ 47104		Are We Dreamin' the Same Dream/Angelina	1981		2.00	4.00
Epic						
❏ 02058		You Made It Beautiful/How Good It Used to Be	1981		2.00	4.00
❏ 03165		Try a Little Tenderness/As Time Goes By	1982		2.00	4.00
❏ 10287		I'll Just Go Away/Set Me Free	1968		3.00	6.00

Number		Title (A Side/B Side)	Year	VG	VG+	NM
☐ 10358		Raggedy Ann/Nothing in the World	1968		3.00	6.00
☐ 10492		Life's Little Ups and Downs/It Takes Time	1969		3.00	6.00
☐ 10585		July 12, 1939/I'm Flying to Nashville Tonight	1970		3.00	6.00
☐ 10662		I Can't Even Drink It Away/Nice 'N' Easy	1970		3.00	6.00
☐ 10745		Have a Heart/Woman Left Lonely	1971		2.50	5.00
☐ 10809		A Sunday Kind of Woman/Part of Your Life	1971		2.50	5.00
☐ 10867		I Take It On Home/Peace on You	1972		2.50	5.00
☐ 10950		Behind Closed Doors/A Sunday Kind of Woman	1973		2.50	5.00
		Originals have yellow labels				
☐ 10950		Behind Closed Doors/A Sunday Kind of Woman	1973		2.00	4.00
		Repressings have orange labels				
☐ 11040		The Most Beautiful Girl/I Feel Like Going Home	1973		2.00	4.00
☐ 11091		A Very Special Love Song/I Can't Even Drink It Away	1974		2.00	4.00
☐ 20006		I Love My Friend/Why Oh Why	1974		2.00	4.00
☐ 50064		My Elusive Dreams/Whatever Happened	1975		2.00	4.00
☐ 50103		Every Time You Touch Me (I Get High)/Pass On By	1975		2.00	4.00
☐ 50142		You & I/All Over Me	1975		2.00	4.00
☐ 50182		She/Since I Fell for You	1975		2.00	4.00
☐ 50222		America the Beautiful (1976)/Down By the Riverside	1976		2.00	4.00
☐ 50268		The Grass Is Always Greener/The Road Song	1976		2.00	4.00
☐ 50328		My Lady/Easy Look	1976		2.00	4.00
☐ 50392		Rollin' with the Flow/To Sing a Love Song	1977		2.00	4.00
☐ 50562		Everybody Wrote That Song for Me/Beautiful Woman	1978		2.00	4.00
☐ 50616		On My Knees/Mellow Melody	1978		2.00	4.00
☐ 50701		I Do My Swingin' at Home/Spanish Eyes	1979		2.00	4.00
☐ 50869		Even a Fool Would Let Go/Pretty People	1980		2.00	4.00

Groove

Number		Title (A Side/B Side)	Year	VG	VG+	NM
☐ 58-0020		The Grass Is Always Greener/ She Loved Everybody But Me	1963	3.75	7.50	15.00
☐ 58-0020	PS	The Grass Is Always Greener/ She Loved Everybody But Me	1963	7.50	15.00	30.00
☐ 58-0025		Big Boss Man/Let Me Go My Merry Way	1963	3.75	7.50	15.00
☐ 58-0032		Lady Love/Why, Oh Why	1964	3.75	7.50	15.00
☐ 58-0035		The Ways of a Woman in Love/My Mountain Dew	1964	3.75	7.50	15.00
☐ 58-0041		Nice 'N' Easy/Turn Around and Face Me	1964	3.75	7.50	15.00

Hi

Number		Title (A Side/B Side)	Year	VG	VG+	NM
☐ 2116		Love Is After Me/Pass On By	1966	2.50	5.00	10.00
☐ 2123		My Heart Would Know/Nobody's Lonesome for Me	1967	2.50	5.00	10.00
☐ 2134		Hurry Up Freight Train/Only Me	1967	2.50	5.00	10.00

Mercury

Number		Title (A Side/B Side)	Year	VG	VG+	NM
☐ 73466		I Washed My Hands in Muddy Water/No Home	1974		2.50	5.00
☐ 73498		A Field of Yellow Daisies/Party Girl	1974		2.50	5.00
☐ 73646		Something Just Came Over Me/Best Years	1974		2.50	5.00

Phillips Int'l.

Number		Title (A Side/B Side)	Year	VG	VG+	NM
☐ 3532		Whirlwind/Philadelphia Baby	1959	6.25	12.50	25.00
☐ 3542		Rebound/Big Man	1959	6.25	12.50	25.00
☐ 3552		Lonely Weekends/Everything I Do Is Wrong	1960	6.25	12.50	25.00
☐ 3560		School Days/Gonna Be Waiting	1960	5.00	10.00	20.00
☐ 3562		On My Knees/Stay	1960	5.00	10.00	20.00
☐ 3566		Who Will the Next Fool Be/Caught in the Middle	1961	5.00	10.00	20.00
☐ 3572		Just a Little Sweet/It's Too Late	1962	5.00	10.00	20.00
☐ 3576		Easy Money/Midnight Blues	1962	5.00	10.00	20.00
☐ 3582		Sittin' and Thinkin'/Finally Found Out	1962	5.00	10.00	20.00
☐ 3584		There's Another Place I Can't Go/I Need Your Love	1963	5.00	10.00	20.00

RCA

Number		Title (A Side/B Side)	Year	VG	VG+	NM
☐ PB-10859		My Mountain Dew/Nice 'N Easy	1976		2.00	4.00
☐ PB-10966		Nice 'N Easy/It's All Over Now	1977		2.00	4.00

RCA Victor

Number		Title (A Side/B Side)	Year	VG	VG+	NM
☐ 47-8468		It's All Over Now/Too Many Teardrops	1964	3.75	7.50	15.00
☐ 47-8536		There Won't Be Anymore/Gentleman Jim	1965	5.00	10.00	20.00
☐ 47-8817		Nice 'N' Easy/Ol' Man River	1966	3.00	6.00	12.00
☐ 74-0983		Tomorrow Night/The Ways of a Woman in Love	1973		2.00	4.00
☐ APBO-0195		There Won't Be Anymore/It's All Over Now	1973		2.50	5.00
☐ APBO-0260		I Don't See Me in Your Eyes Anymore/ No Room to Dance	1974		2.00	4.00
☐ PB-10062		She Called Me Baby/$10 and a Clean White Shirt	1974		2.00	4.00
☐ GB-10159		There Won't Be Anymore/Tomorrow Night	1975			3.00
		Gold Standard Series				
☐ PB-10256		It's All Over Now/Big Jack	1975		2.00	4.00
☐ PB-10458		Not Everybody Knows/I've Got You Under My Skin	1975		2.00	4.00
☐ GB-10512		She Called Me Baby/$10 And a Clean White Shirt	1975			3.00
		Gold Standard Series				

Smash

Number		Title (A Side/B Side)	Year	VG	VG+	NM
☐ 1993		Mohair Sam/I Washed My Hands in Muddy Water	1965	2.50	5.00	10.00
☐ 2012		Dance of Love/I Can't Go On	1965	2.50	5.00	10.00
☐ 2022		Hawg Jaw/Something Just Came Over Me	1966	2.50	5.00	10.00
☐ 2038		No Home/Tears a-Go-Go	1966	2.50	5.00	10.00
☐ 2060		That's the Way/When My Baby Comes Home	1966	2.50	5.00	10.00

Sun

Number		Title (A Side/B Side)	Year	VG	VG+	NM
☐ 1110		Who Will the Next Fool Be/Stay	1970		2.50	5.00
☐ 1151		The Breakup/Be-Bop-a-Lula	1980		2.00	4.00
		B-side by Jerry Lee Lewis; both sides are duets with Orion				

United Artists

Number		Title (A Side/B Side)	Year	VG	VG+	NM
☐ XW1193		Ghost of Another Man/Puttin' In Overtime at Home	1978		2.00	4.00
☐ XW1223		I Still Believe in Love/Wishful Thinking	1978		2.00	4.00

Number		Title (A Side/B Side)	Year	VG	VG+	NM
❑ XW1269		I Loved You All the Way/The Fool Strikes Again	1978		2.00	4.00
❑ XW1280		I Lost My Head/She Knows Just How to Touch Me	1979		2.00	4.00
❑ XW1307		Life Goes On/Standing Tall	1979		2.00	4.00
❑ 1325		You're Gonna Love Yourself in the Morning/	1979		2.00	4.00
		Top of the Stairs				
❑ 1340		All You Ever Have to Do Is Touch Me/I'd Build a Bridge	1980		2.00	4.00

Richard, Cliff

(Also see "Shadows, The")

ABC-Paramount

❑ 10042		Living Doll/Apron Strings	1959	6.25	12.50	25.00
❑ 10066		Dynamite/Travellin' Light	1959	5.00	10.00	20.00
❑ 10093		Voice in the Wilderness/Don't Be Mad at Me	1960	5.00	10.00	20.00
❑ 10109		Fall in Love with You/Choppin' 'N' Changin'	1960	5.00	10.00	20.00
❑ 10136		Where Is My Heart/Please Don't Tease	1960	5.00	10.00	20.00
❑ 10175		Catch Me, I'm Falling/"D" in Love	1961	5.00	10.00	20.00
❑ 10195		Mumblin' Mosie/Theme for a Dream	1961	10.00	20.00	40.00

Big Top

❑ 3101		Young Ones/We Say Yeah	1962	5.00	10.00	20.00

Capitol

❑ F4096		Move It/High Class Baby	1958	10.00	20.00	40.00
❑ F4154		Livin' Lovin' Doll/Steady with You	1959	10.00	20.00	40.00

Dot

❑ 16399		Wonderful to Be Young/Got a Funny Feeling	1962	5.00	10.00	20.00

EMI America

❑ 8025		We Don't Talk Anymore/Count Me Out	1979		2.00	4.00
❑ 8035		Carrie/Language of Love	1980		2.00	4.00
❑ 8057		Dreaming/Dynamite	1980		2.50	5.00
		Green label				
❑ 8057		Dreaming/Dynamite	1980		2.00	4.00
		Gray label				
❑ 8068		A Little in Love/Everyman	1980		2.00	4.00
❑ 8076		Give a Little Bit More/Keep Lookin'	1981		2.00	4.00
❑ 8076	PS	Give a Little Bit More/Keep Lookin'	1981		2.50	5.00
❑ 8095		Wired for Sound/Hold On	1981		2.00	4.00
❑ 8103		Daddy's Home/Summer Rain	1982		2.00	4.00
❑ 8135		The Only Way Out/Be in My Heart	1982		2.00	4.00
❑ 8149		Little Town/Be in My Heart	1982		2.00	4.00
❑ 8180		Never Say Die (Give a Little Bit More)/Front Page	1983		2.00	4.00
❑ 8193		Donna/Ocean Deep	1984		2.00	4.00

Epic

❑ 9597		Lucky Lips/Next Time	1963	5.00	10.00	20.00
❑ 9597	PS	Lucky Lips/Next Time	1963	6.25	12.50	25.00
❑ 9633		It's All in the Game/I'm Looking Out the Window	1963	5.00	10.00	20.00
❑ 9633	PS	It's All in the Game/I'm Looking Out the Window	1963	6.25	12.50	25.00
❑ 9670		I'm the Lonely One/I Only Have Eyes for You	1964	5.00	10.00	20.00
❑ 9670	PS	I'm the Lonely One/I Only Have Eyes for You	1964	6.25	12.50	25.00
❑ 9691		Bachelor Boy/True, True Lovin'	1964	5.00	10.00	20.00
❑ 9737		I Don't Wanna Love You/Look in My Eyes Maria	1964	3.75	7.50	15.00
❑ 9757		Again/The Minute You're Gone	1965	3.75	7.50	15.00
❑ 9810		I Could Easily Fall (In Love with You)/On My Word	1965	3.75	7.50	15.00
❑ 9839		The Twelfth of Never/Paradise Lost	1965	3.75	7.50	15.00
❑ 9866		Wind Me Up (and Let Me Go)/Eye of a Needle	1965	3.75	7.50	15.00
❑ 10018		Blue Turns to Grey/I'll Walk Alone	1966	3.75	7.50	15.00
❑ 10070		Visions/Quando, Quando, Quando	1966	3.75	7.50	15.00
❑ 10101		Time Drags By/The La La La Song	1966	3.75	7.50	15.00
❑ 10178		Heartbeat/It's All Over	1967	3.75	7.50	15.00

Monument

❑ 1211		You Never Can Tell/Goodbye Sam, Hello Samantha	1970		3.00	6.00
❑ 1229		I Ain't Got Time Anymore/Morning Comes Too Soon	1970		3.00	6.00

Polydor

❑ 885 336-7		All I Ask of You/Phantom of the Opera Overture, Act 2	1987		2.00	4.00
		With Sarah Brightman				

Rocket

❑ RB-11463		Green Light/Needing a Friend	1979		2.00	4.00
❑ 40531		Miss You Nights/Love Enough	1976		2.00	4.00
❑ 40574		Devil Woman/Love On (Shine On)	1976		2.50	5.00
❑ 40652		Junior Cowboy/I Can't Ask for Anymore Than You	1976		2.00	4.00
❑ 40724		Don't Turn the Light Out/Nothing Left for Me to Say	1977		2.00	4.00
❑ 40771		You've Got Me Wondering/Try a Smile	1977		2.00	4.00

Sire

❑ 703		Living in Harmony/Jesus	1973		2.50	5.00
❑ 707		Power to All Our Friends/Come Back Billie Joe	1973		2.50	5.00

Uni

❑ 55061		All My Love/Our Story Book	1968	2.50	5.00	10.00
❑ 55069		Congratulations/High 'N' Dry	1968	2.50	5.00	10.00
❑ 55145		One Day I Met Marie/Sweet Little Jesus Boy	1969	3.00	6.00	12.00

Warner Bros.

❑ 7344		Reflections/Throw Down a Line	1969	2.00	4.00	8.00
		B-side by Cliff and Hank				

Number		Title (A Side/B Side)	Year	VG	VG+	NM

Richards, Keith
(Of the Rolling Stones)
Rolling Stones
| ☐ 19311 | | Run Rudolph Run/The Harder They Come | 1978 | 5.00 | 10.00 | 20.00 |

Virgin
☐ S7-56955		Eileen/Wicked As It Seems	1993		2.00	4.00
☐ 99240		Make No Mistake/It Means a Lot	1988			3.00
☐ 99240	PS	Make No Mistake/It Means a Lot	1988			3.00
☐ 99297		Take It So Hard/I Could Have Stood You Up	1988			3.00
☐ 99297	PS	Take It So Hard/I Could Have Stood You Up	1988			3.00

Richardson, Jape
(Also recorded as "The Big Bopper")
Mercury
| ☐ 71219 | | Beggar to a King/Crazy Blue | 1957 | 15.00 | 30.00 | 60.00 |
| ☐ 71312 | | A Teenage Mom/Monkey Song | 1958 | 15.00 | 30.00 | 60.00 |

Richardson, Rudi
Sun
| ☐ 271 | | Fools Hall of Fame/Why Should I Cry | 1957 | 7.50 | 15.00 | 30.00 |

Richie and the Royals
Golden Crest
| ☐ 573 | | Be My Girl/We're Strollin' | 1962 | 12.50 | 25.00 | 50.00 |
Rello
| ☐ 1 | | And When I'm Near You/Goody Goody | 1961 | 20.00 | 40.00 | 80.00 |
| ☐ 3 | | Be My Girl/We're Strollin' | 1962 | 50.00 | 100.00 | 200.00 |

Richie and the Saxons
Tip
| ☐ 1020 | | Bottom of the Barrel/Easy Now | 196? | 12.50 | 25.00 | 50.00 |

Richie, Lionel
(Formerly of the Commodores)
Mercury
| ☐ 852 856-7 | | Don't Wanna Lose You (Radio Version)/Don't Wanna Lose You (Album Version) | 1996 | | | 3.00 |

Motown
☐ 1519		Endless Love/(Instrumental)	1981		2.00	4.00
		With Diana Ross				
☐ 1644		Truly/Just Put Some Love in Your Heart	1982		2.00	4.00
☐ 1657		You Are/You Mean More to Me	1983		2.00	4.00
☐ 1657	PS	You Are/You Mean More to Me	1983		2.50	5.00
☐ 1677		My Love/Round and Round	1983		2.00	4.00
☐ 1677	PS	My Love/Round and Round	1983		2.50	5.00
☐ 1698		All Night Long (All Night)/Wandering Stranger	1983		2.00	4.00
☐ 1710		Running with the Night/(B-side unknown)	1983		2.00	4.00
☐ 1722		Hello/You Mean More to Me	1984		2.00	4.00
☐ 1746		Stuck on You/Round and Round	1984		2.00	4.00
☐ 1746	PS	Stuck on You/Round and Round	1984		2.00	4.00
☐ 1762		Penny Lover/Tell Me	1984		2.00	4.00
☐ 1762	PS	Penny Lover/Tell Me	1984		2.50	5.00
☐ 1819		Say You, Say Me/Can't Slow Down	1985			3.00
☐ 1819	PS	Say You, Say Me/Can't Slow Down	1985		2.00	4.00
		Two different sleeves were released, each of equal value				
☐ 1843		Dancing on the Ceiling/Love Will Find a Way	1986			3.00
☐ 1843	PS	Dancing on the Ceiling/Love Will Find a Way	1986			3.00
☐ 1866		Love Will Conquer All/The Only One	1986			3.00
☐ 1866	PS	Love Will Conquer All/The Only One	1986			3.00
☐ 1873		Ballerina Girl/Deep River Woman	1986			3.00
		B-side with Alabama				
☐ 1873	PS	Ballerina Girl/Deep River Woman	1986		2.00	4.00
☐ 1883		Se La/Serves You Right	1987			3.00
☐ 1883	PS	Se La/Serves You Right	1987			3.00
☐ 2160		Do It To Me (Edit)/Do It To Me (LP Version)	1992		2.00	4.00

Richy, Paul
Sun
| ☐ 338 | | The Legend of the Big Steeple/Broken Hearted Willie | 1960 | 5.00 | 10.00 | 20.00 |

Rick and the Keens
Austin
| ☐ 303 | | Peanuts/I'll Be Home | 1961 | 12.50 | 25.00 | 50.00 |
Jamie
| ☐ 1219 | | Your Turn to Cry/Tender Years | 1962 | 5.00 | 10.00 | 20.00 |
Le Cam
| ☐ 133 | | Darla/Someone New | 1964 | 7.50 | 15.00 | 30.00 |
| ☐ 721 | | Peanuts/I'll Be Home | 1961 | 12.50 | 25.00 | 50.00 |
Smash
| ☐ 1705 | | Peanuts/I'll Be Home | 1961 | 5.00 | 10.00 | 20.00 |
| ☐ 1722 | | Maybe/Popcorn | 1961 | 5.00 | 10.00 | 20.00 |
Tollie
| ☐ 9016 | | Darla/Someone New | 1964 | 5.00 | 10.00 | 20.00 |

Number		Title (A Side/B Side)	Year	VG	VG+	NM

Rick and the Masters

Cameo

❏ 226		Flame of Love/Here Comes Nancy	1962	12.50	25.00	50.00
❏ 247		Let It Please Be You/I Don't Want Your Love	1963	12.50	25.00	50.00

Haral

❏ 776		Bewitched, Bothered and Bewildered/A Kissin' Friend	1962	15.00	30.00	60.00

Taba

❏ 101		Flame of Love/Here Comes Nancy	1962	37.50	75.00	150.00

Rick and the Randells

ABC-Paramount

❏ 10055		Let It Be You/Honey Doll	1959	10.00	20.00	40.00

Rick and the Ravens

(With Ray Manzarek, later of the Doors)

Aura

❏ 4506		Henrietta/Just for Me	1965	15.00	30.00	60.00
❏ 4511		Soul Train/Geraldine	1965	12.50	25.00	50.00

Posae

❏ 101		Big Bucket "T"/Rampage	196?	20.00	40.00	80.00

Rickie and the Hallmarks

Amy

❏ 877		Wherever You Are/Joanie Don't You Cry	1963	10.00	20.00	40.00

Ricky and the Vacels

Express

❏ 711		Lorraine/Bubble Gum	1962	7.50	15.00	30.00

Fargo

❏ 1050		His Girl/Don't Want Your Love No More	1963	7.50	15.00	30.00
❏ 1050		His Girl/Don't Want Your Love No More	1963	20.00	40.00	80.00
		Blue vinyl				

Rico and the Ravens

Autumn

❏ 6		Don't You Know/In My Heart	1965	3.75	7.50	15.00

Rally

❏ 1601		Don't You Know/In My Heart	1965	10.00	20.00	40.00

Riffs, The

Jamie

❏ 1296		Tell Her/I Been Thinkin'	1965	3.00	6.00	12.00

Old Town

❏ 1179		Tell Tale Friends/Why Are the Nights So Cold	1965	12.50	25.00	50.00

Sunny

❏ 22		Little Girl/Why Are the Nights So Cold	1964	20.00	40.00	80.00

Righteous Brothers, The

(Also see "Hatfield, Bobby"; "Paramours, The")

Haven

❏ 800		Hold On to What You Got/Let Me Make the Music	1976		2.00	4.00
❏ 7002		Rock and Roll Heaven/I Just Wanna Be Me	1974		2.50	5.00
❏ 7004		Give It to the People/Love Is Not a Dirty Word	1974		2.00	4.00
❏ 7006		Dream On/Dr. Rock and Roll	1974		2.00	4.00
❏ 7011		High Blood Pressure/Never Say I Love You	1975		2.00	4.00
❏ 7014		Young Blood/Substitute	1975		2.00	4.00

Moonglow

❏ 215		Little Latin Lupe Lu/I'm So Lonely	1963	5.00	10.00	20.00
❏ 215	DJ	Little Latin Lupe Lu (same on both sides)	1963	12.50	25.00	50.00
		Red vinyl promo				
❏ 221		Gotta Tell You How I Feel/I	1963	5.00	10.00	20.00
		If You're Lying, You'll Be Crying				
❏ 223		My Babe/Fee-Fi-Fidily-I-Oh	1963	5.00	10.00	20.00
❏ 224		Ko Ko Joe/B-Flat Blues	1963	5.00	10.00	20.00
❏ 231		Try to Find Another Man/I Still Love You	1964	5.00	10.00	20.00
❏ 234		Bring Your Love to Me/	1964	5.00	10.00	20.00
		If You're Lying, You'll Be Crying				
❏ 235		This Little Girl of Mine/	1964	3.75	7.50	15.00
		If You're Lying, You'll Be Crying				
❏ 238		Bring Your Love to Me/Fannie Mae	1965	3.75	7.50	15.00
❏ 239		You Can Have Her/Love or Magic	1965	3.75	7.50	15.00
❏ 242		Justine/In That Great Gettin' Up Morning	1965	3.75	7.50	15.00
❏ 243		For Your Love/Gotta Tell You How I Feel	1965	3.75	7.50	15.00
❏ 244		Georgia on My Mind/My Tears Will Go Away	1966	3.75	7.50	15.00
❏ 245		I Need a Girl/Bring Your Love to Me	1966	3.75	7.50	15.00

Philles

❏ 124		You've Lost That Lovin' Feelin'/There's a Woman	1964	3.00	6.00	12.00
❏ 127		Just Once in My Life/The Blues	1965	3.00	6.00	12.00
❏ 127	PS	Just Once in My Life/The Blues	1965	6.25	12.50	25.00
❏ 129		Unchained Melody/Hung on You	1965	3.75	7.50	15.00
❏ 130		Ebb Tide/(I Love You) For Sentimental Reasons	1965	3.00	6.00	12.00
❏ 130	PS	Ebb Tide/(I Love You) For Sentimental Reasons	1965	6.25	12.50	25.00
❏ 132		The White Cliffs of Dover/She's Mine, All Mine	1966	3.75	7.50	15.00

Number		Title (A Side/B Side)	Year	VG	VG+	NM
Verve						
❑ 10383		(You're My) Soul and Inspiration/B Side Blues	1966	3.00	6.00	12.00
❑ 10383	PS	(You're My) Soul and Inspiration/B Side Blues	1966	5.00	10.00	20.00
❑ 10403		Rat Race/Green Onions	1966	3.75	7.50	15.00
❑ 10406		He/He Will Break Your Heart	1966	2.50	5.00	10.00
❑ 10406	PS	He/He Will Break Your Heart	1966	3.75	7.50	15.00
❑ 10430		Go Ahead and Cry/Things Didn't Go Your Way	1966	2.50	5.00	10.00
❑ 10449		On This Side of Goodbye/A Man Without a Dream	1966	2.50	5.00	10.00
❑ 10479		Along Came Jones/Jimmy's Blues	1967	2.00	4.00	8.00
❑ 10507		Melancholy Music Man/Don't Give Up on Me	1967	2.00	4.00	8.00
❑ CS8-5		Celebrity Scene: The Righteous Brothers	1967	15.00	30.00	60.00

Box set of five singles. Price includes box, all 5 singles, jukebox title strips, bio. Records are sometimes found by themselves, so they are listed separately below.

❑ 10520		(You're My) Soul and Inspiration/Go Ahead and Cry	1967	2.50	5.00	10.00
❑ 10521		Hold On, I'm Coming/He Will Break Your Heart	1967	2.50	5.00	10.00
❑ 10522		Melancholy Music Man/I Believe	1967	2.50	5.00	10.00
❑ 10523		I (Who Have Nothing)/Island in the Sun	1967	2.50	5.00	10.00
❑ 10524		My Girl/Something You Got	1967	2.50	5.00	10.00
❑ 10551		Stranded in the Middle of No Place/Been So Nice	1967	2.00	4.00	8.00
❑ 10551	PS	Stranded in the Middle of No Place/Been So Nice	1967	3.75	7.50	15.00
❑ 10577		Here I Am/So Many Lonely Nights Ahead	1968	2.00	4.00	8.00
❑ 10637		Let the Good Times Roll/You've Lost That Lovin' Feelin'	1968	2.00	4.00	8.00
❑ 10648		And the Party Goes On/Woman, Man Needs Ya	1968	2.00	4.00	8.00
❑ 10649		Good N' Nuff/Po' Folks	1968	2.00	4.00	8.00
❑ 871 882-7		Unchained Melody/Hung on You	1989	2.00	4.00	

Riley, Billy Lee
Atlantic

❑ 2525		Sittin' and a Waitin'/Happy Man	1968	2.00	4.00	8.00

Brunswick

❑ 55085		Rockin' on the Moon/Is That All to the Ball	1958	50.00	100.00	200.00

Entrance

❑ 7508		I Got a Thing About You Baby/You Don't Love Me	1972		2.50	5.00

GNP Crescendo

❑ 371		Gonna Find a Cave/That's the Bag I'm In	1966	2.50	5.00	10.00
❑ 377		The Way I Feel/St. James Infirmary	1966	2.50	5.00	10.00

Hip

❑ 8006		Family Portrait/Going Back to Memphis	1968	2.00	4.00	8.00
❑ 8011		Show Me Your Soul/Midnight Hour	1968	2.00	4.00	8.00

Home of the Blues

❑ 233		Flip, Flop, and Fly/Teenage Letter	1961	7.50	15.00	30.00

Mercury

❑ 72314		Bo Diddley/Memphis	1964	3.75	7.50	15.00
❑ 72385		Mojo Workout/Charlene	1965	3.00	6.00	12.00

Mojo

❑ 1933		Southern Soul/Midnight Hour	1967	2.50	5.00	10.00

Sun

❑ 245		Trouble Bound/Rock with Me, Baby	1956	25.00	50.00	100.00
❑ 260		Flying Saucers Rock and Roll/I Want You Baby	1957	15.00	30.00	60.00
❑ 277		Red Hot/Pearly Lee	1957	7.50	15.00	30.00
❑ 289		Baby Please Don't Go/Wouldn't You Know	1958	12.50	25.00	50.00
❑ 313		Down by the Riverside/No Name Girl	1959	6.25	12.50	25.00
❑ 322		One More Time/Got the Water Boilin'	1959	12.50	25.00	50.00
❑ 1100		Kay/Looking for Her Heart	1969		3.00	6.00
❑ 1105		Pilot Town L.A./Workin' on the River	1969		3.00	6.00
❑ 1116		Tallahassee/Old Home Place	1970		2.50	5.00

Rinky Dinks, The – See "Darin, Bobby"

Rio, Chuck
(Of the Champs)
Challenge

❑ 59019		Bad Boy/Denise	1958	5.00	10.00	20.00
❑ 59073		Ramblin' Through Dixie/Akiko	1960	5.00	10.00	20.00

Flair

❑ 103		You Don't Have to Be a Baby to Cry/Big Boy	1962	10.00	20.00	40.00

Jackpot

❑ 48016		Margarita/C'est La Vie	1960	7.50	15.00	30.00

Kent

❑ 308		Bye Bye Baby/No Matter What You Do	1958	5.00	10.00	20.00

Saturn

❑ 402		Kreschendo Stomp/Rock-A-Nova	1962	12.50	25.00	50.00

Tequila

❑ 100		Caravan/El Bracero	1961	5.00	10.00	20.00
❑ 103		La Cha Cha Twist/	1961	5.00	10.00	20.00
		If You Were the Only Girl in the World				

Rios, Augie
Metro

❑ 20010		Donde Esta Santa Claus?/Ol' Fatso	1958	10.00	20.00	40.00
❑ 20016		Run Rattler Run/Hop, Skip and Jump	1959	7.50	15.00	30.00
❑ 20027		Trip to the Island/Teacher Walked Out of the Room	1959	7.50	15.00	30.00

Number		Title (A Side/B Side)	Year	VG	VG+	NM
MGM						
❏ 12966		Feliz Navidades/Gypsy Boy	1960	5.00	10.00	20.00
❏ 13292		Donde Esta Santa Claus?/Ol' Fatso	1964	2.50	5.00	10.00
Shelley						
❏ 181		I've Got a Girl/There's a Girl Down the Way	1963	10.00	20.00	40.00
❏ 186		When You Dance/No One	1963	7.50	15.00	30.00
❏ 192		Teach Me Tonight/Linda Lou	1964	5.00	10.00	20.00

Rip Chords, The
Columbia

Number		Title (A Side/B Side)	Year	VG	VG+	NM
❏ 42687		Here I Stand/Karen	1963	3.75	7.50	15.00
❏ 42687	DJ	Here I Stand (same on both sides)	1963	12.50	25.00	50.00
		Green vinyl promo				
❏ 42687	PS	Here I Stand (same on both sides)	1963	12.50	25.00	50.00
		Sleeve is promo only				
❏ 42812		Gone/She Thinks I Still Care	1963	3.75	7.50	15.00
❏ 42812	DJ	Gone (same on both sides)	1963	12.50	25.00	50.00
		Blue vinyl promo				
❏ 42812	PS	Gone (same on both sides)	1963	12.50	25.00	50.00
		Sleeve is promo only				
❏ 42921		Hey, Little Cobra/The Queen	1963	5.00	10.00	20.00
❏ 42921	DJ	Hey, Little Cobra (same on both sides)	1963	12.50	25.00	50.00
		Yellow vinyl promo				
❏ 43035		Three Window Coupe/Hot Rod U.S.A.	1964	3.75	7.50	15.00
❏ 43035	DJ	Three Window Coupe (same on both sides)	1964	12.50	25.00	50.00
		Red vinyl promo				
❏ 43093		One Piece Topless Bathing Suit/Wah-Wahini	1964	3.75	7.50	15.00
❏ 43221		Don't Be Scared/Bunny Hill	1965	3.75	7.50	15.00

Rip-Chords, The
Abco

Number		Title (A Side/B Side)	Year	VG	VG+	NM
❏ 105		I Love You the Most/Let's Do the Razzle Dazzle	1956	100.00	200.00	400.00
❏ 105		I Love You the Most/Let's Do the Razzle Dazzle	1956	200.00	400.00	800.00
		Red vinyl				

Riperton, Minnie
(Also see "Rotary Connection")
Capitol

Number	Title (A Side/B Side)	Year	VG	VG+	NM
❏ 4706	Memory Lane/I'm a Woman	1979		2.00	4.00
❏ 4761	Lover and Friend/Return to Forever	1979		2.00	4.00
❏ 4902	Here We Go/Return to Forever	1980		2.00	4.00
❏ 4955	Give Me Time/Island in the Sun	1980		2.00	4.00

Chess

Number	Title (A Side/B Side)	Year	VG	VG+	NM
❏ 1980	Lonely Girl/You Gave Me Soul	1966	2.50	5.00	10.00
	As "Andrea Davis"				

Epic

Number	Title (A Side/B Side)	Year	VG	VG+	NM
❏ 11139	Every Time He Comes Around/Reasons	1974		2.50	5.00
❏ 50020	Edge of a Dream/Seeing You This Way	1974		2.50	5.00
❏ 50057	Lovin' You/Edge of a Dream	1974		2.50	5.00
❏ 50128	Don't Let Anyone Bring You Down/Inside My Love	1975		2.50	5.00
❏ 50155	When It Comes Down To It/Minnie's Lament	1975		2.50	5.00
❏ 50166	Simple Things/Minnie's Lament	1975		2.50	5.00
❏ 50190	Adventures in Paradise/When It Comes Down To It	1976		2.50	5.00
❏ 50337	Stick Together (Part One)/Stick Together (Part Two)	1977		2.50	5.00
❏ 50351	Young, Willing and Able/Stick Together	1977		2.50	5.00
❏ 50394	Wouldn't Matter Where You Are	1977		2.50	5.00
❏ 50427	How Could I Love You More/Young, Willing and Able	1977		2.50	5.00

GRT

Number	Title (A Side/B Side)	Year	VG	VG+	NM
❏ 42	Oh! By the Way/Le Fleur	1972		3.00	6.00

Ripley Cotton Choppers
Sun

Number	Title (A Side/B Side)	Year	VG	VG+	NM
❏ 190	Silver Bells/Blues Waltz	1953			
	Unknown on 45 rpm, though nine Suns with lower numbers do exist on 45s.				

Ripples and Waves plus Michael, The – See "Jacksons, The"

Rita Marie
Sun

Number	Title (A Side/B Side)	Year	VG	VG+	NM
❏ 1106	Lottie's Lament/Trouble	1969		2.50	5.00

Rites of Spring, The
Parkway

Number	Title (A Side/B Side)	Year	VG	VG+	NM
❏ 109	Why/Comin' On to Me	1966	7.50	15.00	30.00

Rites, The
Decca

Number	Title (A Side/B Side)	Year	VG	VG+	NM
❏ 32218	Things/Hour Glass	1967	6.25	12.50	25.00

Rituals, The
(Featuring Arnie Ginsburg, formerly of Jan and Arnie)
Arwin

Number	Title (A Side/B Side)	Year	VG	VG+	NM
❏ 120	Girl in Zanzibar/Guitarro	1963	7.50	15.00	30.00
❏ 127	This Is Paradise/Gone	1964	7.50	15.00	30.00
❏ 128	Surfers Rule/Gone	1964	10.00	20.00	40.00

Number		Title (A Side/B Side)	Year	VG	VG+	NM
Rivers, Johnny						
Atlantic						
❑ 3011		Sitting in Limbo/Artists and Poets	1974		2.50	5.00
❑ 3028		Six Days on the Road/Artists and Poets	1974		2.50	5.00
❑ 3230		John Lee Hooker '74/Get It Up for Love	1974		2.50	5.00
Big Tree						
❑ 16094		Swayin' to the Music (Slow Dancin')/Outside Help	1977		2.00	4.00
❑ 16106		Curious Mind (Um, Um, Um, Um, Um, Um)/ Ashes and Sand	1977		2.00	4.00
Capitol						
❑ 4850		Long Black Veil/This Could Be the One	1962	3.75	7.50	15.00
❑ 4913		If You Want It, I've Got It/My Heart Is In Your Hands	1963	3.75	7.50	15.00
❑ 5232		Long Black Veil/Don't Look Now	1964	3.75	7.50	15.00
Chancellor						
❑ 1070		I Get So Doggone Lonesome/Knock Three Times	1961	5.00	10.00	20.00
❑ 1108		To Be Loved/Too Good to Last	1962	5.00	10.00	20.00
Coral						
❑ 62425		That's My Baby/Your First and Last Love	1964	3.75	7.50	15.00
Cub						
❑ 9047		Everyday/Darling Talk to Me	1959	6.25	12.50	25.00
❑ 9058		Answer Me My Love/The Customary Thing	1960	5.00	10.00	20.00
Dee Dee						
❑ 239		The White Cliffs of Dover/Your First and Last Love	1959	5.00	10.00	20.00
Epic						
❑ 50121		Help Me Rhonda/New Lovers and Old Friends	1975		2.50	5.00
		A-side features Brian Wilson on backing vocals				
❑ 50150		Can I Change My Mind/John Lee Hooker	1975		2.00	4.00
❑ 50208		Welcome Home/Outside Help	1976		2.00	4.00
❑ 50248		Linda Lue/Outside Help	1976		2.00	4.00
Era						
❑ 3037		Call Me/Andersonville	1961	5.00	10.00	20.00
Gone						
❑ 5026		Baby Come Back/Long Long Walk	1958	10.00	20.00	40.00
Guyden						
❑ 2003		You're the One/A Hole in the Ground	1958	6.25	12.50	25.00
❑ 2110		You're the One/A Hole in the Ground	1964	3.75	7.50	15.00
Imperial						
❑ 66032		Memphis/It Wouldn't Happen with Me	1964	3.00	6.00	12.00
❑ 66056		Maybelline/Walk Myself On Home	1964	2.50	5.00	10.00
❑ 66056	PS	Maybelline/Walk Myself On Home	1964	3.75	7.50	15.00
❑ 66075		Mountain of Love/Moody River	1964	2.50	5.00	10.00
❑ 66087		Midnight Special/Cupid	1965	2.50	5.00	10.00
❑ 66112		Seventh Son/Unsquare Dance	1965	2.50	5.00	10.00
❑ 66112	PS	Seventh Son/Unsquare Dance	1965	3.75	7.50	15.00
❑ 66133		Where Have All the Flowers Gone/ Love Me While You Can	1965	2.50	5.00	10.00
❑ 66144		Under Your Spell Again/Long Time Man	1965	2.50	5.00	10.00
❑ 66144	PS	Under Your Spell Again/Long Time Man	1965	3.75	7.50	15.00
❑ 66159		Secret Agent Man/You Dig	1966	3.00	6.00	12.00
❑ 66159	PS	Secret Agent Man/You Dig	1966	3.75	7.50	15.00
❑ 66175		(I Washed My Hands In) Muddy Water/Roogalator	1966	2.50	5.00	10.00
❑ 66205		Poor Side of Town/A Man Can Cry	1966	3.00	6.00	12.00
❑ 66205	PS	Poor Side of Town/A Man Can Cry	1966	3.75	7.50	15.00
❑ 66227		Baby I Need Your Lovin'/Gettin' Ready for Tomorrow	1967	2.50	5.00	10.00
❑ 66227	PS	Baby I Need Your Lovin'/Gettin' Ready for Tomorrow	1967	3.75	7.50	15.00
❑ 66244		The Tracks of My Tears/Rewind Medley	1967	2.50	5.00	10.00
❑ 66244	PS	The Tracks of My Tears/Rewind Medley	1967	3.75	7.50	15.00
❑ 66267		Summer Rain/Memory of the Coming Good	1967	2.50	5.00	10.00
❑ 66286		Look To Your Soul/Something's Strange	1968	2.00	4.00	8.00
❑ 66286	PS	Look To Your Soul/Something's Strange	1968	3.00	6.00	12.00
❑ 66314		Everybody's Talkin'/The Way We Live	1968			*Unreleased*
❑ 66335		Right Relations/Better Life	1968	2.00	4.00	8.00
❑ 66335	PS	Right Relations/Better Life	1968	3.00	6.00	12.00
❑ 66360		These Are Not My People/Going Back to Big Sur	1969	2.00	4.00	8.00
❑ 66386		Muddy River/Resurrection	1969	2.00	4.00	8.00
❑ 66386	PS	Muddy River/Resurrection	1969	3.00	6.00	12.00
❑ 66418		One Woman/Ode to John Lee	1969	2.00	4.00	8.00
❑ 66448		Into the Mystic/Jesus Is a Soul Man	1970	2.00	4.00	8.00
❑ 66453		Fire and Rain/Apple Tree	1970	2.00	4.00	8.00
MCA						
❑ 52502		Heartbreak Love/Why Can't We Communicate	1984		2.00	4.00
MGM						
❑ 13266		Answer Me, My Love/Customary Thing	1964	3.75	7.50	15.00
Riveraire						
❑ 1001		Don't Bug Me Baby/Haunting Black Eyes	1959	7.50	15.00	30.00
Roulette						
❑ 4565		Baby Come Back/Long Long Walk	1964	5.00	10.00	20.00
RSO						
❑ 1030		Romance (Give Me a Chance)/ Don't Need No Other Now	1980		2.00	4.00
❑ 1045		China/The Price	1980		2.00	4.00

Number	Title (A Side/B Side)	Year	VG	VG+	NM
Soul City					
❏ 007	Ashes and Sand/Outside Help	1977		2.50	5.00
❏ 008	Swayin' to the Music (Slow Dancin')/Outside Help	1977	2.00	4.00	8.00
❏ 010	Little White Lie/Be My Baby	1980		2.50	5.00
❏ 014	RSVP/The Price	1982		2.50	5.00
Suede					
❏ 1401	Little Girl/Two by Two	1957	25.00	50.00	100.00
	As "Johnny Ramistella"				
United Artists					
0101 through 0105 are "Silver Spotlight Series" reissues					
❏ 0101	Memphis/Secret Agent Man	1973		2.00	4.00
❏ 0102	Mountain of Love/Maybellene	1973		2.00	4.00
❏ 0103	Seventh Son/Midnight Special	1973		2.00	4.00
❏ 0104	Poor Side of Town/Baby I Need Your Lovin'	1973		2.00	4.00
❏ 0105	Summer Rain/The Tracks of My Tears	1973		2.00	4.00
❏ XW198	Blue Suede Shoes/Stories to a Child	1973		2.50	5.00
❏ XW226	Searchin'-So Fine/New York City Dues	1973		2.50	5.00
❏ XW310	I'll Feel a Whole Lot Better/Over the Line	1973		2.50	5.00
❏ XW522	Rockin' Pneumonia-Boogie Woogie Flu/ Blue Suede Shoes	1974		2.00	4.00
	Reissue				
❏ XW523	Where Have All the Flowers Gone/ (I Washed My Hands in) Muddy Water	1974		2.00	4.00
	Reissue				
❏ 741	Oh What a Kiss/Knock Three Times	1964	3.00	6.00	12.00
❏ 769	Dream Doll/To Be Loved	1964	3.00	6.00	12.00
❏ 50778	Sea Cruise/Our Lady of the Well	1971		3.00	6.00
❏ 50822	Think His Name/Permanent Change	1971		3.00	6.00
❏ 50948	On the Borderline/Come Home America	1972		2.50	5.00
❏ 50960	Rockin' Pneumonia-Boogie Woogie Flu/ Come Home America	1972		3.00	6.00
	On most pressings, the intro of the A-side lasts about 35 seconds				
❏ 50960	Rockin' Pneumonia-Boogie Woogie Flu/ Come Home America	1972		3.00	6.00
	On some pressings, the intro of the A-side is not repeated (lasts about 20 seconds)				
Rivieras, The					
(More than one group)					
Algonquin					
❏ 718	Together Forever/A Night to Remember	1958	50.00	100.00	200.00
	Reissued as "The Ravenairs"				
Coed					
❏ 503	Count Every Star/True Love Is Hard to Find	1958	12.50	25.00	50.00
❏ 508	Moonlight Serenade/Neither Rain Nor Snow	1959	10.00	20.00	40.00
❏ 513	Our Love/True Love Is Hard to Find	1959	7.50	15.00	30.00
❏ 513	Our Love/Midnight Flyer	1959	7.50	15.00	30.00
❏ 522	Since I Made You Cry/11th Hour Melody	1959	7.50	15.00	30.00
❏ 529	Blessing of Love/Moonlight Cocktails	1960	6.25	12.50	25.00
❏ 538	My Friend/Great Big Eyes	1960	6.25	12.50	25.00
❏ 542	Easy to Remember/Stay in My Heart	1960	6.25	12.50	25.00
❏ 551	El Doraado/Refrigerator	1961	6.25	12.50	25.00
❏ 592	Moonlight Cocktails/Midnight Flyer	1964	3.75	7.50	15.00
Riviera					
❏ 1401	California Sun/H.B. Goose Step	1964	5.00	10.00	20.00
❏ 1401	California Sun/Played On	1964	10.00	20.00	40.00
	Possibly as few as 1,000 were pressed with this B-side				
❏ 1402	Little Donna/Let's Have a Party	1964	3.75	7.50	15.00
❏ 1403	Rockin' Robin/Battle Line	1964	3.75	7.50	15.00
❏ 1405	Whole Lotta Shakin'/Rip It Up	1965	3.75	7.50	15.00
❏ 1405	Whole Lotta Shakin'/Lakeview Lane	1965	5.00	10.00	20.00
❏ 1406	Let's Go to Hawaii/Lakeview Lane	1965	3.75	7.50	15.00
❏ 1407	Somebody Asked Me/Somebody New	1965	3.75	7.50	15.00
	Credited to the Rivieras, but actually by Bobby Whiteside				
❏ 1409	Bug Juice/Never Feel the Pain	1965	5.00	10.00	20.00
Rivileers, The					
Baton					
❏ 200	A Thousand Stars/Hey Chiquita	1953	30.00	60.00	120.00
❏ 201	Forever/Darling Farewell	1954	30.00	60.00	120.00
❏ 205	Carolyn/Eternal Love	1954	30.00	60.00	120.00
❏ 207	(I Love You) For Sentimental Reasons/ I Want to See My Baby	1955	15.00	30.00	60.00
❏ 209	Little Girl/Don't Ever Leave Me	1955	15.00	30.00	60.00
❏ 241	A Thousand Stars/Who Is the Girl	1957	10.00	20.00	40.00
Rivingtons, The					
A.R.E. American					
❏ 100	All That Glitters/You Move Me Baby	1964	3.75	7.50	15.00
AGC					
❏ 5	I Lost the Love/Mind Your Man	1968		2.00	4.00	8.00
Baton Master					
❏ 202	Teach Me Tonight/Reach Our Goal	1967		2.00	4.00	8.00

Number	Title (A Side/B Side)	Year	VG	VG+	NM

Columbia

☐ 43581	A Rose Growing in the Ruins/Tend to Business	1966	3.00	6.00	12.00
☐ 43772	Yadi Yadi Yum Yum/Yadi Yadi Revisited	1966	3.00	6.00	12.00

J.D.

☐ 122	Don't Hate Your Father (Part 1)/ Don't Hate Your Father (Part 2)	1976		2.50	5.00

Liberty

☐ 1484	DJ Papa-Oom-Mow-Mow (same on both sides) *Reissue; promo only*	1982		3.00	6.00
☐ 55427	Papa-Oom-Mow-Mow/Deep Water	1962	5.00	10.00	20.00
☐ 55513	Kickapoo Joy Juice/My Reward	1962	3.75	7.50	15.00
☐ 55528	Mama-Oom-Mow-Mow/Waiting	1962	3.75	7.50	15.00
☐ 55553	The Bird's the Word/I'm Losing My Grip	1963	3.75	7.50	15.00
☐ 55585	The Shaky Bird (Part 1)/The Shaky Bird (Part 2)	1963	3.75	7.50	15.00
☐ 55610	Little Sally Walker/Cherry	1963	7.50	15.00	30.00
☐ 55671	Fairy Tales/Wee Jee Walk	1964	3.75	7.50	15.00

Quan

☐ 1379	I Don't Want a New Baby/You're Gonna Pay	1967	2.50	5.00	10.00

RCA Victor

☐ 74-0301	Pop Your Corn (Part 1)/Pop Your Corn (Part 2)	1969	2.00	4.00	8.00

Reprise

☐ 0293	I Tried/One Monkey Don't Stop No Show	1964	3.00	6.00	12.00

United Artists

☐ 0096	Papa-Oom-Mow-Mow/The Bird's the Word *"Silver Spotlight Series" reissue*	1973		2.00	4.00

Vee Jay

☐ 634	All That Glitters/You Move Me Baby	1964	3.00	6.00	12.00
☐ 649	I Love You Always/Years of Tears	1965	3.00	6.00	12.00
☐ 677	The Willy/Just Got to Be Mine	1965	3.00	6.00	12.00

Wand

☐ 11253	Papa-Oom-Mow-Mow/I Don't Want a New Baby	1973		2.50	5.00

Road Runners, The

Challenge

☐ 9197	Dead Man/Pretty Girls	1963	5.00	10.00	20.00

Felsted

☐ 8692	Quasimoto/Road Runnah	1964	10.00	20.00	40.00

Miramar

☐ 116	Take Me/I'll Make It Up to You	1965	3.75	7.50	15.00

Morocco

☐ 001	Goodbye/Tell Her You Love Her	1966	5.00	10.00	20.00

Reprise

☐ 0418	Take Me/I'll Make It Up to You	1965	3.75	7.50	15.00

Robbins, Eddie

David

☐ 1001	Janice/It Was Fun	196?	6.25	12.50	25.00

Dot

☐ 15702	A Girl Like You/Dear Parents	1958	10.00	20.00	40.00

Power

☐ 214	A Girl Like You/Dear Parents	1958	30.00	60.00	120.00

Robbins, Marty

Audiograph

☐ 454	Love Me/Safely in the Arms of Jesus *With Jeanne Pruett; Pruett solo on B-side*	1983		2.50	5.00

Columbia

☐ 02444	Jumper Cable Man/Good Hearted Woman	1981		2.00	4.00
☐ 02575	Teardrops on My Heart/Honeycomb	1981		2.00	4.00
☐ 02854	Lover, Lover/Some Memories Just Won't Die	1982		2.00	4.00
☐ 03236	Tie Your Dream to Mine/That's All She Wrote	1982		2.00	4.00
☐ 03789	Change of Heart/Devil in a Cowboy Hat	1983		2.00	4.00
☐ 03927	Baby That's Love/What If I Said I Love You	1983		2.00	4.00
☐ 10305	El Paso City/When I'm Gone	1976		2.50	5.00
☐ 10396	Among My Souvenirs/She's Just a Drifter	1976		2.50	5.00
☐ 10472	Adios Amigo/Helen	1977		2.50	5.00
☐ 10536	I Don't Know Why (I Just Do)/Inspiration for a Song	1977		2.50	5.00
☐ 10629	Don't Let Me Touch You/ Tomorrow, Tomorrow, Tomorrow	1977		2.50	5.00
☐ 10673	Return to Me/More Than Anything, I Miss You	1978		2.50	5.00
☐ 10821	Please Don't Play a Love Song/Jenny	1978		2.50	5.00
☐ 10905	Touch Me with Magic/Confused and Lonely	1979		2.50	5.00
☐ 11016	All Around Cowboy/The Dreamer	1979		2.50	5.00
☐ 11102	Buenos Dias Argentina/Ballad of a Small Man	1979		2.50	5.00
☐ 11240	She's Made of Faith/Misery in My Soul	1980		2.00	4.00
☐ 11291	One Man's Trash (Is Another Man's Treasure)/ I Can't Wait Until Tomorrow	1980		2.00	4.00
☐ 11372	An Occasional Rose/Holding On to You	1980		2.00	4.00
☐ 11425	Completely Out of Love/Another Cup of Coffee	1981		2.00	4.00
☐ 20925	Tomorrow You'll Be Gone/Love Me or Leave Me Alone	1952	7.50	15.00	30.00
☐ 20965	Crying 'Cause I Love You/I Wish Somebody Loved Me	1952	7.50	15.00	30.00
☐ 21022	I'll Go On Alone/You're Breaking My Heart	1952	7.50	15.00	30.00

Number		Title (A Side/B Side)	Year	VG	VG+	NM
❑ 21032		My Isle of Golden Dreams/Sweet Hawaiian Dream	1952			Unreleased
❑ 21075		I Couldn't Keep from Crying/After You Leave	1953	7.50	15.00	30.00
❑ 21111		A Castle in the Sky/A Half-Way Chance with You	1953	7.50	15.00	30.00
❑ 21145		Sing Me Something Sentimental/ At the End of Long, Lonely Days	1953	7.50	15.00	30.00
❑ 21172		Blessed Jesus Should I Fall Don't Let Me Lay/ Kneel and Let the Lord Take Your Load	1953	7.50	15.00	30.00
❑ 21176		Don't Make Me Ashamed/It's a Long, Long Ride	1953	7.50	15.00	30.00
❑ 21213		My Isle of Golden Dreams/Aloha Oe	1954	7.50	15.00	30.00
❑ 21246		Pretty Words/Your Heart's Turn to Break	1954	7.50	15.00	30.00
❑ 21291		Call Me Up (And I'll Come Calling on You)/ I'm Too Big to Cry	1954	7.50	15.00	30.00
❑ 21324		Time Goes By/It's a Pity What Money Can Do	1954	7.50	15.00	30.00
❑ 21351		That's All Right/Gossip	1955	12.50	25.00	50.00
❑ 21352		God Understands/Have Thine Own Way, Lord	1955	6.25	12.50	25.00
❑ 21388		Daddy Loves You/Pray for Me, Mother of Mine	1955	6.25	12.50	25.00
❑ 21414		It Looks Like I'm Just in the Way/ I'll Love You Till the Day I Die	1955	6.25	12.50	25.00
❑ 21446		Maybellene/This Broken Heart of Mine	1955	12.50	25.00	50.00
❑ 21461		Pretty Mama/Don't Let Me Hang Around	1955	12.50	25.00	50.00
❑ 21477		Tennessee Toddy/Mean Mama Blues	1955	12.50	25.00	50.00
❑ 21508		Singing the Blues/I Can't Quit (I've Gone Too Far)	1956	10.00	20.00	40.00
❑ 21525		I'll Know You're Gone/How Long Will It Be	1956	6.25	12.50	25.00
	With Lee Emerson					
❑ 21545		Singing the Blues/I Can't Quit (I've Gone Too Far)	1956	7.50	15.00	30.00
❑ 31124	S	titles unknown	1961	5.00	10.00	20.00
❑ 31125	S	titles unknown	1961	5.00	10.00	20.00
❑ 31126	S	titles unknown	1961	5.00	10.00	20.00
❑ 31127	S	titles unknown	1961	5.00	10.00	20.00
❑ 31128	S	titles unknown	1961	5.00	10.00	20.00
	Anyone who can fill in these gaps -- the above five all are Columbia "Stereo 7" singles -- please let us know.					
❑ 40679		Long Tall Sally/Mr. Teardrop	1956	12.50	25.00	50.00
❑ 40706		Respectfully Miss Brooks/You Don't Owe Me a Thing	1956	12.50	25.00	50.00
❑ 40815		Knee Deep in the Blues/The Same Two Lips	1957	6.25	12.50	25.00
❑ 40864		A White Sport Coat (And a Pink Carnation)/ Grown Up Tears	1957	6.25	12.50	25.00
❑ 40864	PS	A White Sport Coat (And a Pink Carnation)/ Grown Up Tears	1957	10.00	20.00	40.00
❑ 40868		I Cried Like a Baby/Where D'Ja Go	1957	6.25	12.50	25.00
	With Lee Emerson					
❑ 40969		Please Don't Blame Me/Teen-Age Dream	1957	6.25	12.50	25.00
❑ 41013		The Story of My Life/Once-a-Week Date	1957	6.25	12.50	25.00
❑ 41013	PS	The Story of My Life/Once-a-Week Date	1957	10.00	20.00	40.00
❑ 41143		Just Married/Stairway of Love	1958	5.00	10.00	20.00
❑ 41208		She Was Only Seventeen (He Was One Year More)/ Sittin' in a Tree House	1958	5.00	10.00	20.00
❑ 41208	PS	She Was Only Seventeen (He Was One Year More)/ Sittin' in a Tree House	1958	10.00	20.00	40.00
❑ 41282		Ain't I the Lucky One/The Last Time I Saw My Heart	1958	5.00	10.00	20.00
❑ 41325		The Hanging Tree/The Blues, Country Style	1959	5.00	10.00	20.00
❑ 41325	PS	The Hanging Tree/The Blues, Country Style	1959	10.00	20.00	40.00
❑ 41408		Cap and Gown/Last Night About This Time	1959	5.00	10.00	20.00
❑ 41511		El Paso/Running Gun	1959	5.00	10.00	20.00
❑ 41511	PS	El Paso/Running Gun	1959	7.50	15.00	30.00
❑ 41589		Big Iron/Saddle Tramp	1960	3.75	7.50	15.00
❑ 41686		Is There Any Chance/I Told My Heart	1960	3.75	7.50	15.00
❑ 41766		Don't Worry/A Time and a Place for Everything	1960			Unreleased
❑ 41771		Five Brothers/Ride, Cowboy, Ride	1960	3.75	7.50	15.00
❑ 41809		Ballad of the Alamo/A Time and a Place for Everything	1960	3.75	7.50	15.00
❑ 41809	PS	Ballad of the Alamo/A Time and a Place for Everything	1960	7.50	15.00	30.00
❑ 41922		Don't Worry/Like All the Other Times	1961	3.75	7.50	15.00
❑ 41922	PS	Don't Worry/Like All the Other Times	1961	6.25	12.50	25.00
❑ 42008		Jimmy Martinez/Ghost Train	1961	3.75	7.50	15.00
❑ 42008	PS	Jimmy Martinez/Ghost Train	1961	6.25	12.50	25.00
❑ 42065		It's Your World/You Told Me So	1961	3.75	7.50	15.00
❑ 42065	PS	It's Your World/You Told Me So	1961	6.25	12.50	25.00
❑ 42246		I Told the Brook/Sometimes I'm Tempted	1961	3.75	7.50	15.00
❑ 42246	PS	I Told the Brook/Sometimes I'm Tempted	1961	6.25	12.50	25.00
❑ 42375		Love Can't Wait/Too Far Gone	1962	3.75	7.50	15.00
❑ 42375	PS	Love Can't Wait/Too Far Gone	1962	6.25	12.50	25.00
❑ 42486		Devil Woman/April Fool's Day	1962	3.75	7.50	15.00
❑ 42486	PS	Devil Woman/April Fool's Day	1962	6.25	12.50	25.00
❑ 42614		Ruby Ann/Won't You Forgive	1962	3.75	7.50	15.00
❑ 42614	PS	Ruby Ann/Won't You Forgive	1962	6.25	12.50	25.00
❑ 42672		Hawaii's Calling Me/Ka-Lu-A	1963	3.00	6.00	12.00
❑ 42702		Cigarettes and Coffee Blues/Teenager's Dad	1963	3.00	6.00	12.00
❑ 42702	PS	Cigarettes and Coffee Blues/Teenager's Dad	1963	6.25	12.50	25.00
❑ 42747		titles unknown	1963	5.00	10.00	20.00
❑ 42748		titles unknown	1963	5.00	10.00	20.00
❑ 42749		titles unknown	1963	5.00	10.00	20.00
❑ 42750		titles unknown	1963	5.00	10.00	20.00
❑ 42751		titles unknown	1963	5.00	10.00	20.00
	The above five are two songs each of selections from the "Devil Woman" LP. We don't know which titles go with which single.					
❑ 42781		No Sign of Loneliness Here/I'm Not Ready Yet	1963	3.00	6.00	12.00
❑ 42831		Not So Long Ago/I Hope You Learn a Lot	1963	3.00	6.00	12.00
❑ 42890		Begging to You/Over High Mountain	1963	3.00	6.00	12.00
❑ 42968		Girl from Spanish Town/Kingston Girl	1964	2.50	5.00	10.00

Number	Title (A Side/B Side)	Year	VG	VG+	NM
❏ 43049	The Cowboy in the Continental Suit/ Man Walks Among Us	1964	2.50	5.00	10.00
❏ 43134	One of These Days/Up in the Air	1964	2.50	5.00	10.00
❏ 43196	I Eish-Tay-Mah-Su (I Love You)/A Whole Lot Easier	1964	2.50	5.00	10.00
❏ 43258	Ribbon of Darkness/Little Robin	1965	2.50	5.00	10.00
❏ 43377	Old Red/Matilda	1965	2.00	4.00	8.00
❏ 43428	While You're Dancing/Lonely Too Long	1965	2.00	4.00	8.00
❏ 43500	Count Me Out/Private Wilson White	1965	2.00	4.00	8.00
❏ 43651	Ain't I Right/My Own Native Land	1966			Unreleased
❏ 43680	The Shoe Goes On the Other Foot Tonight/ It Kind of Reminds Me of You	1966	2.00	4.00	8.00
❏ 43845	No Tears Milady/Fly Butterfly Fly	1966	2.00	4.00	8.00
❏ 43870	Mr. Shorty/Tall Handsome Strangers	1966	2.00	4.00	8.00
❏ 44128	Tonight Carmen/Waiting in Reno	1967		3.00	6.00
❏ 44271	Gardenias in Her Hair/In the Valley of the Rio Grande	1967		3.00	6.00
❏ 44509	Love Is In the Air/I've Been Leaving Everyday	1968		3.00	6.00
❏ 44633	I Walk Alone/Lily of the Valley	1968		3.00	6.00
❏ 44641	It Finally Happened/Big Mouthin' Around	1968		3.00	6.00
	By "Marty Robbins Jr. and Sr."				
❏ 44739	It's a Sin/I Feel Another Heartache Coming On	1969		2.50	5.00
❏ 44895	I Can't Say Goodbye/Hello Daily News	1969		2.50	5.00
❏ 45024	Camelia/Virginia	1969		2.50	5.00
❏ 45091	My Woman, My Woman, My Wife/Martha Ellen Jenkins	1970		2.50	5.00
❏ 45215	Jolie Girl/The City	1970		2.50	5.00
❏ 45273	Padre/At Times	1970		3.00	6.00
❏ 45346	Little Spot in Heaven/ Wait a Little Longer Please, Jesus	1971		3.00	6.00
❏ 45377	The Chair/Seventeen Years	1971		2.50	5.00
❏ 45442	Early Morning Sunshine/Another Day Has Gone By	1971		2.50	5.00
❏ 45520	The Best Part of Living/Gone with the Wind	1971		2.50	5.00
❏ 45668	I've Got a Woman's Love/A Little Spot in Heaven	1972		2.50	5.00
❏ 45775	Laura (What's He Got That I Ain't Got)/ It Kind of Reminds Me of You	1973		2.50	5.00

Decca

❏ 33006	This Much a Man/Guess I'll Stand Here Looking Dumb	1972		2.50	5.00

MCA

❏ 40012	Franklin, Tennessee/Walking Piece of Heaven	1973		2.50	5.00
❏ 40067	A Man and a Train/Las Vegas, Nevada	1973		2.50	5.00
❏ 40134	Love Me/Crawling on My Knees	1973		2.50	5.00
❏ 40172	I'm Wanting To/Twentieth Century Drifter	1973		2.50	5.00
❏ 40236	Don't You Think/I Couldn't Believe It Was True	1974		2.50	5.00
❏ 40296	Two-Gun Daddy/Queen of the Big Rodeo	1974		2.50	5.00
❏ 40342	Life/It Takes Faith	1974		2.50	5.00
❏ 40425	These Are My Souvenirs/Shotgun Rider	1975		2.50	5.00
❏ 52197	Two Gun Daddy/Life	1983		2.50	5.00

Warner Bros.

❏ 29847	Honkytonk Man/Shotgun Rag	1982		2.00	4.00
	B-side by Johnny Gimble and the Texas Swing Band				

Robbins, Mel
Argo

❏ 5340	Save It/To Know You	1959	25.00	50.00	100.00

Robby and the Robbins
Todd

❏ 1089	Surfer's Life/She Cried	1963	10.00	20.00	40.00

Robert and Johnny
Old Town

❏ 1021	I Believe You/Train to Paradise	1956	12.50	25.00	50.00
❏ 1029	You're Mine/Million Dollar Bills	1956	10.00	20.00	40.00
❏ 1038	Don't Do It/Baby Come Home	1957	10.00	20.00	40.00
❏ 1043	Broken Hearted Man/Indian Marriage	1957	10.00	20.00	40.00
❏ 1047	We Belong Together/In the Rain	1958	7.50	15.00	30.00
❏ 1052	I Believe in You/Marry Me	1958	7.50	15.00	30.00
❏ 1052	I Know/Marry Me	1958	10.00	20.00	40.00
❏ 1058	Eternity with You/I'm Truly, Truly Yours	1958	7.50	15.00	30.00
❏ 1065	Give Me the Key to Your Heart/Truly in Love	1959	7.50	15.00	30.00
❏ 1068	Dream Girl/Oh My Love	1959	7.50	15.00	30.00
❏ 1072	Wear This Ring/Bad Dan	1959	7.50	15.00	30.00
❏ 1078	Hear My Heartbeat/Try Me Pretty Baby	1960	6.25	12.50	25.00
❏ 1086	We Belong Together/In the Rain	1960	6.25	12.50	25.00
❏ 1100	You're Mine/Please Me Please	1961	5.00	10.00	20.00
❏ 1108	Togetherness/I Got You	1961	5.00	10.00	20.00
❏ 1117	Wear This Ring/Broken Hearted Man	1962	5.00	10.00	20.00

Sue

❏ 792	A Perfect Wife/Brown, Pretty Brown Eyes	1963	6.25	12.50	25.00

Roberts, Austin
ABC

❏ 11289	Life Is for Living/I Can Make It Better	1971		3.00	6.00

Arista

❏ 0335	Don't Stop Me Baby/Question of Love	1978		2.00	4.00

Chelsea

❏ 78-0101	Something's Wrong with Me/My Song	1972		2.50	5.00
❏ 78-0110	Keep On Singing/Take Away the Sunshine	1973		2.50	5.00

Number	Title (A Side/B Side)	Year	VG	VG+	NM
❑ 78-0123	The Last Thing on My Mind/ Losing You Is More Than I Can Stand	1973		2.50	5.00
❑ BCBO-0053	Baby Don't You Walk Out on Me/One Word	1973		2.00	4.00
❑ AMBO-0129	Something's Wrong with Me/Keep On Singing	1973		2.00	4.00
	Gold Standard Series reissue				
❑ BCBO-0219	Somethin' to Believe In/ Nothing Seems the Same When You're Not Here	1974		2.00	4.00

Philips

❑ 40560	I'll Smile/Mary and Me	1968		3.00	6.00
❑ 40586	Ricky Ticky Ta Ta Ta/No Last Goodbyes	1969		3.00	6.00
❑ 40638	Runaway-Just a Little (Medley)/Sarah	1969		3.00	6.00
❑ 40649	Baltimore/Sarah	1969		3.00	6.00
❑ 40660	One Night Ann/The Other Side	1970		3.00	6.00

Private Stock

❑ 45,020	Rocky/You Got the Power	1975		2.00	4.00
❑ 45,051	Fool/Children of the Rain	1975		2.00	4.00
❑ 45,061	Is There Somethin' Goin' On/Just to Make You Mine	1975		2.00	4.00
❑ 45,080	This Time I'm In It for Love/Susannah	1976		2.00	4.00

Roberts, Lance
Sun

❑ 348	The Good Guy Always Wins/The Time Is Right	1960	5.00	10.00	20.00

Roberts, Wayne
(Actually Neil Bogart, later owner of the Buddah, Casablanca and Boardwalk record labels)
20th Fox

❑ 6644	Little Girl/One Piece Bathing Suit	1966	6.25	12.50	25.00

Robertson, Robbie
(Formerly of The Band)
Geffen

❑ 28111	Somewhere Down the Crazy River/Hell's Half Acre	1988		2.00	4.00
❑ 28175	Showdown at Big Sky/Hell's Half Acre	1987		2.00	4.00

Robins, The
(More than one group)
Ardent

❑ 106	Batman/Batarang	1966	7.50	15.00	30.00

Arvee

❑ 5001	Just Like That/Whole Lot of Imagination	1960	5.00	10.00	20.00
❑ 5013	Live Wire Suzie/Oh No	1960	5.00	10.00	20.00

Atco

❑ 6059	Smokey Joe's Cafe/Just Like a Fool	1956	12.50	25.00	50.00

Crown

❑ 106	I Made a Vow/Double Crossing Baby	1954	100.00	200.00	400.00
❑ 120	Key to My Heart/All I Do Is Rock	1954	75.00	150.00	300.00

Dot

❑ 16519	Blue Grass Blues/Top 40 Blues	1963	3.00	6.00	12.00

Gone

❑ 5101	Baby Love/We Loved	1961	8.75	17.50	35.00

Knight

❑ 2001	Quarter to Twelve/Pretty Little Dolly	1958	8.75	17.50	35.00
❑ 2008	It's Never Too Late/A Little Bird Told Me	1958	18.75	37.50	75.00

Lavender

❑ 001	The White Cliffs of Dover/How Many More Times	1961	5.00	10.00	20.00
❑ 002	Magic of a Dream/ Mary Lou Loves to Hootchy Kootchy Koo	1961	5.00	10.00	20.00

Musicor

❑ 1050	Cry Over You/Lucy Watusi	1964	3.75	7.50	15.00

New Hit

❑ 3010	Johnny/Doing the Popeye	1963	3.75	7.50	15.00

RCA Victor

❑ 47-5175	(Now and Then There's) A Fool Such As I/ My Heart's the Biggest Fool	1953	125.00	250.00	500.00
❑ 47-5271	Oh Why/All Night Baby	1953	75.00	150.00	300.00
❑ 47-5434	How Would You Know/Let's Go to the Dance	1953	75.00	150.00	300.00
❑ 47-5486	My Baby Done Told Me/I'll Do It	1953	50.00	100.00	200.00
❑ 47-5489	Ten Days in Jail/Empty Bottles	1953	30.00	60.00	120.00
❑ 47-5564	Get It Off Your Mind/Don't Stop Now	1953	30.00	60.00	120.00

Spark

❑ 103	Riot in Cell Block #9/Wrap It Up	1954	25.00	50.00	100.00
❑ 107	Loop De Loop Mambo/Framed	1954	37.50	75.00	150.00
	Silver top label				
❑ 107	Loop De Loop Mambo/Framed	1954	25.00	50.00	100.00
	Red label				
❑ 110	If Teardrops Were Kisses/Whadaya Want	1955	50.00	100.00	200.00
	Blue label				
❑ 110	If Teardrops Were Kisses/Whadaya Want	1955	25.00	50.00	100.00
	Red label				
❑ 113	One Kiss/I Love Paris	1955	50.00	100.00	200.00
❑ 116	I Must Be Dreamin'/The Hatchet Man	1955	37.50	75.00	150.00
	Red label				

Number		Title (A Side/B Side)	Year	VG	VG+	NM
❑ 116		I Must Be Dreamin'/The Hatchet Man	1955	25.00	50.00	100.00
		Yellow label				
❑ 122		Smokey Joe's Cafe/Just Like a Fool	1955	75.00	150.00	300.00
Sweet Taffy						
❑ 400		Johnny/Doing the Popeye	1963	6.25	12.50	25.00
Whippet						
❑ 200		Cherry Lips/Out of the Picture	1956	10.00	20.00	40.00
❑ 201		Hurt Me/Merry-Go-Rock	1956	10.00	20.00	40.00
❑ 203		That Old Black Magic/Since I First Met You	1956	10.00	20.00	40.00
❑ 206		A Fool in Love/All of a Sudden My Heart Sings	1957	10.00	20.00	40.00
❑ 208		Every Night/Where's the Fire	1957	10.00	20.00	40.00
❑ 211		In My Dreams/Keep Your Mind on Me	1957	10.00	20.00	40.00
❑ 212		Snowball/You Wanted Fun	1958	10.00	20.00	40.00

Robinson, Smokey

(Of The Miracles)

Columbia

Number		Title (A Side/B Side)	Year	VG	VG+	NM
❑ 07727		I Know You by Heart/Could I Have Your Autograph	1988			3.00
		With Dolly Parton				
Motown						
❑ 914		(It's the) Same Old Love/(Instrumental)	1990		2.00	4.00
❑ 1877		Just to See Her/	1987			3.00
		I'm Gonna Love You Like There's No Tomorrow				
❑ 1877	PS	Just to See Her/	1987	2.00	4.00	8.00
		I'm Gonna Love You Like There's No Tomorrow				
❑ 1897		One Heartbeat/	1987			3.00
		Love Will Set You Free (Theme from Solarbabies)				
❑ 1897	PS	One Heartbeat/	1987		3.00	6.00
		Love Will Set You Free (Theme from Solarbabies)				
❑ 1911		What's Too Much/	1987			3.00
		I've Made Love to You a Thousand Times				
❑ 1911	PS	What's Too Much/	1987		2.50	5.00
		I've Made Love to You a Thousand Times				
❑ 1925		Love Don't Give No Reason/Hanging On by a Thread	1988			3.00
❑ 1925	PS	Love Don't Give No Reason/Hanging On by a Thread	1988		2.50	5.00
SBK						
❑ 07379		Double Good Everything/Guess What I Got for You	1991		2.00	4.00
Tamla						
❑ 1601		Tell Me Tomorrow (Part 1)/Tell Me Tomorrow (Part 2)	1982		2.00	4.00
❑ 1615		Old Fashioned Love/Destiny	1982		2.00	4.00
❑ 1630		Are You Still Here/Yes It's You Lady	1982		2.00	4.00
❑ 1655		I've Made Love to You a Thousand Times/	1983		2.00	4.00
		Into Each Rain Some Life Must Fall				
❑ 1678		Touch the Sky/All My Life's a Lie	1983		2.00	4.00
❑ 1684		Blame It on Love/Even Tho'	1983		2.00	4.00
		With Barbara Mitchell				
❑ 1700		Don't Play Another Love Song/	1983		2.00	4.00
		Wouldn't You Like to Know				
❑ 1735		And I Don't Love You/Dynamite	1984		2.00	4.00
❑ 1756		I Can't Find/Gimme What You Want	1984		2.00	4.00
❑ 1786		First Time on a Ferris Wheel/Train of Thought	1985		2.00	4.00
❑ 1828		Hold On to Your Love/Train of Thought	1985		2.00	4.00
❑ 1828	PS	Hold On to Your Love/Train of Thought	1985		3.00	6.00
❑ 1839		Sleepless Nights/Close Encounters of the First Kind	1986		2.00	4.00
❑ 1855		Girl I'm Standing There/	1986		2.00	4.00
		Because of You (It's the Best It's Ever Been)				
❑ 1868		Love Will Set You Free (Theme from Solarbabies)	1986		2.00	4.00
		(Parts 1 & 2)				
❑ 54233		Sweet Harmony/Want to Know My Mind	1973		2.50	5.00
❑ 54239		Baby Come Close/	1973		2.50	5.00
		A Silent Partner in a Three-Way Love Affair				
❑ 54246		It's Her Turn to Live/Just My Soul Responding	1974		2.50	5.00
❑ 54250		Virgin Man/Fulfill Your Need	1974		2.50	5.00
❑ 54251		I Am, I Am/The Family Song	1974		2.50	5.00
❑ 54258		Baby That's Backatcha/Just Passing Through	1975		2.50	5.00
❑ 54261		The Agony and the Ecstasy/Wedding Song	1975		2.50	5.00
❑ 54265		Quiet Storm/Asleep on My Love	1975		2.50	5.00
❑ 54267		Open/Coincidentally	1976		2.50	5.00
❑ 54269		When You Came/Coincidentally	1976	3.00	6.00	12.00
		Released only in Canada				
❑ 54272		An Old Fashioned Man/(B-side unassigned)	1976			Unreleased
❑ 54276		An Old Fashioned Man/Just Passing Through	1976		2.50	5.00
❑ 54279		There Will Come a Day (I'm Gonna Happen to You)/	1977		2.50	5.00
		Humming Song				
❑ 54284		Vitamin U/Holly	1977		2.50	5.00
❑ 54288		Theme from Big Time (Part 1)/	1977		2.50	5.00
		Theme from Big Time (Part 2)				
❑ 54293		Daylight and Darkness/	1978		2.50	5.00
		Why You Wanna See My Bad Side				
❑ 54296		I'm Loving You Softly/Shoe Soul	1978		2.50	5.00
❑ 54301		Get Ready/Ever Had a Dream	1979		2.00	4.00
❑ 54306		Cruisin'/Ever Had a Dream	1979		2.00	4.00
❑ 54311		Let Me Be the Clock/Travelin' Through	1980		2.00	4.00
❑ 54313		Heavy on Pride/I Love the Nearness of You	1980		2.00	4.00
❑ 54318		I Want to Be Your Love/Wine, Women and Song	1980		2.00	4.00
❑ 54321		Being with You/What's In Your Life for Me	1981		2.00	4.00
❑ 54325		Aquicontigo/Being with You (Aquicontigo)	1981		2.00	4.00

Number		Title (A Side/B Side)	Year	VG	VG+	NM
☐ 54327		You Are Forever/I Hear the Children Singing	1981		2.00	4.00
☐ 54332		Who's Sad/Food for Thought	1981		2.00	4.00

Robinson, Smokey, and the Miracles – See "Miracles, The"

Rocco, Lenny
Delsey

| ☐ 301 | | Sugar Girl/Rochelle | 1961 | 75.00 | 150.00 | 300.00 |

Rochell and the Candles
Challenge

☐ 9158	:	Turn Her Down/Each Night	1962	10.00	20.00	40.00
☐ 9191		Annie's Not an Orphan Anymore/	1963	5.00	10.00	20.00
		Let's Run Away and Get Married				

Swingin'

☐ 623		Once Upon a Time/When My Baby Is Gone	1960	5.00	10.00	20.00
☐ 634		So Far Away/Hey, Pretty Baby	1961	5.00	10.00	20.00
☐ 640		Peg of My Heart/Squat with Me, Baby	1962	5.00	10.00	20.00
☐ 652		Big Boy Pete/A Long Time Ago	1963	5.00	10.00	20.00

Rock Brothers, The
King

| ☐ 4851 | | Dungaree Doll/Livin' It Up | 1955 | 7.50 | 15.00 | 30.00 |
| ☐ 4882 | | Oh, Didn't I Ramble/I Gotta Get Back | 1956 | 6.25 | 12.50 | 25.00 |

Rock-A-Teens, The
Doran

| ☐ 3515 | | Woo Hoo/Untrue | 1959 | 37.50 | 75.00 | 150.00 |

Roulette

| ☐ 4192 | | Woo Hoo/Untrue | 1959 | 7.50 | 15.00 | 30.00 |
| ☐ 4217 | | Twangy/Doggone It, Baby | 1959 | 6.25 | 12.50 | 25.00 |

Rockaways, The
Red Bird

| ☐ 10-005 | | Top Down Time/Don't Cry | 1964 | 6.25 | 12.50 | 25.00 |

Rockers, The
Carter

| ☐ 3029 | | Tell Me Why/Count Every Star | 1955 | 200.00 | 400.00 | 800.00 |

Federal

| ☐ 12267 | | What Am I to Do/I'll Die in Love with You | 1956 | 50.00 | 100.00 | 200.00 |
| ☐ 12273 | | Down in the Bottom/Why Don't You Believe Me | 1956 | 25.00 | 50.00 | 100.00 |

Rocketeers, The
(More than one group)
Glad Hamp

| ☐ 2017 | | Drag Strip/Summertime | 1963 | 10.00 | 20.00 | 40.00 |

Herald

☐ 415		Foolish One/Gonna Feed My Baby Poison	1953	75.00	150.00	300.00
☐ 415		Foolish One/Gonna Feed My Baby Poison	1953	150.00	300.00	600.00
	Red vinyl					

M.J.C.

| ☐ 501 | | My Reckless Heart/ | 1958 | 150.00 | 300.00 | 600.00 |
| | | They Turned the Party Out Down at Bessie's House | | | | |

Modern

| ☐ 999 | | Talk It Over Baby/Hey Rube | 1956 | 10.00 | 20.00 | 40.00 |

Val-ue

| ☐ 102 | | Rippin' and Rockin'/Downtown | 1960 | 7.50 | 15.00 | 30.00 |

Rocketones, The
Melba

| ☐ 113 | | Mexico/I Do | 1957 | 15.00 | 30.00 | 60.00 |

Rockets, The
(More than one group)
Atlantic

| ☐ 988 | | Open the Door/Big Leg Mama | 1953 | 25.00 | 50.00 | 100.00 |

Capitol

| ☐ 5262 | | Turn Up the Radio/Can't Sleep | 1983 | | | 3.00 |
| ☐ 5262 | PS | Turn Up the Radio/Can't Sleep | 1983 | | | 3.00 |

Columbia

| ☐ 41512 | | Gibraltar Rock/Walkin' Home | 1959 | 6.25 | 12.50 | 25.00 |

Elektra

| ☐ 47212 | | Lift You Up/Tired of Wearing Black | 1981 | | | 3.00 |
| ☐ 69985 | | Rollin' By the Record Machine | 1982 | | | 3.00 |

Modern

| ☐ 992 | | You Are the First One/Be Lovey Dovey | 1956 | 10.00 | 20.00 | 40.00 |

RSO

☐ 926		Can't Sleep/Something Ain't Right	1979		2.00	4.00
☐ 935		Oh Well/Love Me Once More	1979		2.00	4.00
☐ 1022		Desire/Troublemaker	1980		2.00	4.00
☐ 1028		Sad Song/Takin' It Back	1980		2.00	4.00

Number	Title (A Side/B Side)	Year	VG	VG+	NM

Tortoise Int'l.

☐ TB-11207 She's a Pretty One/I've Got to Move — 1978 — — 2.00 — 4.00

White Whale

☐ 270 Hole in My Pocket/Let Me Go — 1968 — 3.75 — 7.50 — 15.00
Features three future members of Crazy Horse

Rockettes, The

Parrot

☐ 789 I Can't Forget/Love Nobody — 1954 — 375.00 — 750.00 — 1,500

Rockin' Chairs, The

Recorte

☐ 402 Rockin' Chair Boogie/A Kiss Is a Kiss — 1958 — 25.00 — 50.00 — 100.00
☐ 404 Please Mary/Come On Baby — 1958 — 12.50 — 25.00 — 50.00

Rockin' Dukes, The

O.J.

☐ 1007 Angel and a Rose/My Baby Left Me — 1957 — 75.00 — 150.00 — 300.00

Rockin' Kids, The

Dot

☐ 15749 Black Stockings/Yea Yea (I'm in the Mood) — 1958 — 7.50 — 15.00 — 30.00

Rockin' R's, The

Stepheny

☐ 1842 Walkin' You to School/ — 1960 — 6.25 — 12.50 — 25.00
Bewitched (Bothered and Bewildered)

Tempus

☐ 1507 Nameless/Heat — 1959 — 7.50 — 15.00 — 30.00
☐ 1515 Mustang/I'm Still in Love with You — 1959 — 7.50 — 15.00 — 30.00
☐ 7541 Crazy Baby/The Beat — 1959 — 10.00 — 20.00 — 40.00

Vee Jay

☐ 334 Mustang/I'm Still in Love with You — 1959 — 5.00 — 10.00 — 20.00
☐ 346 Hum Bug/The Mix — 1960 — 5.00 — 10.00 — 20.00

Rockin' Ramrods, The

Bon-Bon

☐ 1315 She Lies/The Girl Can't Help It — 1964 — 10.00 — 20.00 — 40.00

Claridge

☐ 301 Don't Fool with Fu Manchu/Tears — 1965 — 5.00 — 10.00 — 20.00
☐ 317 Play It/Got My Mojo Workin' — 1966 — 7.50 — 15.00 — 30.00

Plymouth

☐ 2961 I Wanna Be Your Man/I'll Be On My Way — 1964 — 7.50 — 15.00 — 30.00
☐ 2963 Mister Wind/Bright Lit Blue Skies — 1966 — 6.25 — 12.50 — 25.00
As "The Ramrods"

☐ 2965 Flowers in My Mind/Mary, Mary — 1967 — 7.50 — 15.00 — 30.00
As "The Ramrods"

Rockin' Rebels, The

Itzy

☐ 8 Wild Weekend/Wild Weekend Cha Cha — 1963 — 5.00 — 10.00 — 20.00

Mar-Lee

☐ 0094 Wild Weekend/Wild Weekend Cha Cha — 1960 — 12.50 — 25.00 — 50.00
As "The Rebels"

☐ 0095 Buffalo Blues/Donkey Walk — 1961 — 7.50 — 15.00 — 30.00
As "The Buffalo Rebels"

☐ 0096 Theme from Rebel/Any Way You Want Me — 1961 — 7.50 — 15.00 — 30.00
As "The Buffalo Rebels"

Stork

☐ 3 Bongo Blue Beat/Burn Baby Burn — 1964 — 6.25 — 12.50 — 25.00

Swan

☐ 4125 Wild Weekend/Wild Weekend Cha Cha — 1962 — 10.00 — 20.00 — 40.00
First pressings credit "The Rebels"

☐ 4125 Wild Weekend/Wild Weekend Cha Cha — 1962 — 7.50 — 15.00 — 30.00
Second pressings credit "Rockin' Rebels" and do not have "Don't Drop Out" on the label

☐ 4125 Wild Weekend/Wild Weekend Cha Cha — 1963 — 5.00 — 10.00 — 20.00
Later pressings credit "Rockin' Rebels" and have "Don't Drop Out" on the label

☐ 4140 Rockin' Crickets/Hully Gully Rock — 1963 — 6.25 — 12.50 — 25.00
☐ 4150 Another Wild Weekend/Happy Popcorn — 1963 — 6.25 — 12.50 — 25.00
☐ 4161 Monday Morning/Flibbity Jibbit — 1963 — 6.25 — 12.50 — 25.00
☐ 4248 Wild Weekend/Dockey Twine — 1966 — 5.00 — 10.00 — 20.00

Rockin' Saints, The

Decca

☐ 30990 Saints Rock/Alright Baby — 1959 — 7.50 — 15.00 — 30.00
☐ 31144 Cheat on Me, Baby/Half and Half — 1960 — 20.00 — 40.00 — 80.00

Rockin' Stockins

Sun

☐ 350 Yulesville U.S.A./Rockin' Lang Syne — 1960 — 7.50 — 15.00 — 30.00

Number		Title (A Side/B Side)	Year	VG	VG+	NM

Rocky Fellers, The
Donna

| ❏ 1383 | | Don't Sit Down/The Beachcomber Song | 1963 | 3.00 | 6.00 | 12.00 |

Parkway

| ❏ 836 | | Long Tall Sally/South Pacific Twist | 1962 | 3.00 | 6.00 | 12.00 |

Scepter

| ❏ 1245 | | Santa Santa/Great Big World | 1962 | 5.00 | 10.00 | 20.00 |

A-side is a very early Neil Diamond composition

❏ 1246		Killer Joe/Lonely Teardrops	1963	3.75	7.50	15.00
❏ 1254		Like the Big Guys Do/Great Big World	1963	3.00	6.00	12.00
❏ 1254	PS	Like the Big Guys Do/Great Big World	1963	5.00	10.00	20.00
❏ 1258		Ching-a-Ling Baby/Hey Little Donkey	1963	3.00	6.00	12.00
❏ 1263		Bye Bye Baby/She Makes Me Wanna Dance	1963	3.00	6.00	12.00
❏ 1271		My Prayer/Two Guys from Trinidad	1964	3.00	6.00	12.00

Valmor

| ❏ 2004 | | Opus/Orange Peel | 1962 | 3.75 | 7.50 | 15.00 |

Warner Bros.

❏ 5440		(Everybody Wants to Be a) Tiger/Jeannie Memsoh	1964	2.50	5.00	10.00
❏ 5459		Better Let Her Go/Nina	1964	2.50	5.00	10.00
❏ 5497		Man with the Blue Guitar/Don't Throw My Toys Away	1965	2.50	5.00	10.00
❏ 5613		Rented Tuxedo/ Two Steps Downstairs in the Basement	1965	2.50	5.00	10.00

Rodgers, Jimmie
A&M

❏ 842		I'll Say Goodbye/Shadows	1967		3.00	6.00
❏ 871		Child of Clay/Turnaround	1967		3.00	6.00
❏ 898		If I Were the Man/What a Strange Town	1967		3.00	6.00
❏ 902		I Believe It All/You Pass Me By	1968		3.00	6.00
❏ 976		Today/The Lovers	1968		3.00	6.00
❏ 1055		The Windmills of Your Mind/ L.A. Break Down (And Take Me Back In)	1969		3.00	6.00
❏ 1120		Father Paul/Me About You	1969		3.00	6.00
❏ 1152		Cycles/Tomorrow My Friends	1969		3.00	6.00
❏ 1213		Troubled Times/The Dum Dum Song	1970		2.50	5.00

Dot

❏ 16378		No One Will Ever Know/Because	1962	2.50	5.00	10.00
❏ 16378	PS	No One Will Ever Know/Because	1962	3.75	7.50	15.00
❏ 16407		Rainbow at Midnight/Rhumba Boogie	1962	2.50	5.00	10.00
❏ 16428		I'll Never Stand in Your Way/Afraid	1963	2.50	5.00	10.00
❏ 16450		Lonely Tears/A Face in the Crowd	1963	2.50	5.00	10.00
❏ 16467		(I Don't Know Why) I Just Do/ Load 'Em Up (And Keep a Steppin')	1963	2.50	5.00	10.00
❏ 16490		Poor Little Raggedy Ann/I'm Gonna Be the Winner	1963	2.50	5.00	10.00
❏ 16527		Two-Ten Six-Eighteen	1963	2.50	5.00	10.00
		Doesn't Anybody Know My Name)/The Banana Boat Song				
❏ 16561		Together/Mama Was a Cotton Picker	1963	2.50	5.00	10.00
❏ 16595		The World I Used to Know/ I Forgot More Than You'll Ever Know	1964	2.50	5.00	10.00
❏ 16653		Water Boy/Someplace Green	1964	2.50	5.00	10.00
❏ 16673		Two Tickets/I Forgot More Than You'll Ever Know	1964	2.50	5.00	10.00
❏ 16694		(All My Friends Are Gonna Be) Strangers/ Bon Soir Mademoiselle	1965	2.00	4.00	8.00
❏ 16720		Careless Love/When I'm Right You Don't Remember	1965	2.00	4.00	8.00
❏ 16749		Are You Going My Way (Little Beachcomber)/ Little Schoolgirl	1965	2.00	4.00	8.00
❏ 16781		Bye Bye Love/Hollow Words	1965	2.00	4.00	8.00
❏ 16795		The Chipmunk Song (Christmas Don't Be Late)/ In the Snow	1965	2.00	4.00	8.00
❏ 16826		A Fallen Star/Brother, Where Are You	1966	2.00	4.00	8.00
❏ 16861		It's Over/Anita, You're Dreaming	1966	2.50	5.00	10.00
❏ 16916		Morning Means Tomorrow/New Ideas	1966	2.00	4.00	8.00
❏ 16973		Love Me, Please Love Me/Wonderful You	1966	2.00	4.00	8.00
❏ 17040		Time/Yours and Mine	1967	2.00	4.00	8.00

Epic

| ❏ 10828 | | Froggy's Fable/Daylight Lights the Dawning | 1972 | | 2.50 | 5.00 |
| ❏ 10857 | | Kick the Can/Go On By | 1972 | | 2.50 | 5.00 |

MGM

| ❏ 11732 | | Mama, Don't Cry at My Wedding/
You Don't Live Here No More | 1954 | 6.25 | 12.50 | 25.00 |

Roulette

❏ 4015		Honeycomb/Their Hearts Were Full of Spring	1957	5.00	10.00	20.00
❏ 4031		Kisses Sweeter Than Wine/ Better Loved You'll Never Be	1957	5.00	10.00	20.00
❏ 4045		Oh-Oh, I'm Falling in Love Again/ The Long Hot Summer	1958	5.00	10.00	20.00

Red label

| ❏ 4045 | | Oh-Oh, I'm Falling in Love Again/
The Long Hot Summer | 1958 | 3.75 | 7.50 | 15.00 |

White label with colored spokes

❏ 4070		Secretly/Make Me a Miracle	1958	5.00	10.00	20.00
❏ 4070	PS	Secretly/Make Me a Miracle	1958	10.00	20.00	40.00
❏ 4090		Are You Really Mine/The Wizard	1958	3.75	7.50	15.00
❏ 4116		Bimbombey/You Understand Me	1958	3.75	7.50	15.00
❏ 4129		I'm Never Gonna Tell/Because You're Young	1959	3.75	7.50	15.00

Number		Title (A Side/B Side)	Year	VG	VG+	NM
☐ 4158	M	Ring-a-Ling-a-Lario/Wonderful You	1959	3.75	7.50	15.00
☐ 4158	PS	Ring-a-Ling-a-Lario/Wonderful You	1959	6.25	12.50	25.00
☐ SSR-4158	S	Ring-a-Ling-a-Lario/Wonderful You	1959	7.50	15.00	30.00
☐ 4191		Tucumcari/That Night You Became Seventeen	1959	3.75	7.50	15.00
☐ 4205		It's Christmas Once Again/Wistful Willie	1959	5.00	10.00	20.00
☐ 4218	M	T.L.C. Tender Love and Care/Waltzing Matilda	1960	3.00	6.00	12.00
☐ SSR-4218	S	T.L.C. Tender Love and Care/Waltzing Matilda	1960	7.50	15.00	30.00
☐ 4234		Just a Closer Walk with Thee/ Joshua Fit the Battle of Jericho	1960	3.00	6.00	12.00
☐ 4260		The Wreck of the John B/Four Little Girls in Motion	1960	3.00	6.00	12.00
☐ 4293		Woman from Liberia/Come Along Julie	1960	3.00	6.00	12.00
☐ 4293	PS	Woman from Liberia/Come Along Julie	1960	5.00	10.00	20.00
☐ 4318		When Love Is Young/ The Little Shepherd of Kingdom Come	1960	3.00	6.00	12.00
☐ 4349		Everytime My Heart Sings/I'm On My Way	1961	3.00	6.00	12.00
☐ 4371		John Brown's Baby/I'm Going Home	1961	3.00	6.00	12.00
☐ 4384		A Little Dog Cried/English Country Garden	1961	3.00	6.00	12.00
☐ 4439		You Are Everything to Me/Wanderin' Eyes	1962	3.00	6.00	12.00
☐ SSR-8001	S	Bo Diddley/Soldier Won't You Marry Me	1959	7.50	15.00	30.00
☐ SSR-8007	S	Froggy Went a-Courtin'/Lisa	1959	7.50	15.00	30.00
☐ SSR-8010	S	St. James Infirmary/Just a Wearyin' for You	1959	7.50	15.00	30.00

ScrimShaw

☐ 1313		A Good Woman Likes to Drink with the Boys/ Dancing on the Moon	1977		2.00	4.00
☐ 1314		Everytime I Sing a Love Song/Just a Little Time	1978		2.00	4.00
☐ 1316		When Our Love Began (Cowboys and Indians)/ (B-side unknown)	1978		2.00	4.00
☐ 1318		Secretly/Shovelin' Coal	1978		2.00	4.00
☐ 1319/20		Easy to Love/Easy	1979		2.00	4.00
		With Michele				

Rodgers, Paul
(Of Free, Bad Company, The Firm)

Atlantic

☐ 89709		The Morning After the Night Before/Northwinds	1984		2.00	4.00
☐ 89749		Cut Loose/Talking Guitar Blues	1983		2.00	4.00

Roe, Tommy

ABC

☐ 10762		Sweet Pea/Much More Love	1966	2.50	5.00	10.00
		Reissue; this was the common version when this song was a hit				
☐ 10852		Hooray for Hazel/Need Your Love	1966	2.50	5.00	10.00
☐ 10888		It's Now Winters Day/Kick Me Charlie	1966	2.00	4.00	8.00
☐ 10888	PS	It's Now Winters Day/Kick Me Charlie	1966	3.75	7.50	15.00
☐ 10908		Sing Along with Me/Night Time	1967	2.00	4.00	8.00
☐ 10933		Moon Talk/Sweet Sounds	1967	2.00	4.00	8.00
☐ 10945		Little Miss Sunshine/You I Need	1967	2.00	4.00	8.00
☐ 10989		Melancholy Mood/Paisley Dreams	1967	2.00	4.00	8.00
☐ 11039		Dottie I Like It/Soft Words	1968	2.00	4.00	8.00
☐ 11076		An Oldie But a Goodie/Sugar Cane	1968	2.00	4.00	8.00
☐ 11140		It's Gonna Hurt Me/Gotta Keep Rolling Along	1968	2.00	4.00	8.00
☐ 11164		Dizzy/The You I Need	1969	2.50	5.00	10.00
☐ 11211		Heather Honey/Money Is My Pay	1969		3.00	6.00
☐ 11229		Jack and Jill/Tip Toe Tina	1969		3.00	6.00
☐ 11247		Jam Up Jelly Tight/Moontalk	1969	2.00	4.00	8.00
☐ 11247	PS	Jam Up Jelly Tight/Moontalk	1969	3.00	6.00	12.00
☐ 11258		Stir It Up and Serve It/Fire Fly	1970		3.00	6.00
☐ 11266		Pearl/A Dollar's Worth of Pennies	1970		3.00	6.00
☐ 11273		We Can Make Music/Gotta Keep Rolling Along	1970		3.00	6.00
☐ 11273	PS	We Can Make Music/Gotta Keep Rolling Along	1970		3.00	6.00
☐ 11281		King of Fools/Brush a Little Sunshine	1970		3.00	6.00
☐ 11287		Little Miss Goodie Two Shoes/Traffic Jam	1971		3.00	6.00
☐ 11293		King of Fools/Pistol-Legged Mama	1971		3.00	6.00
☐ 11307		Stagger Lee/Back Streets and Alleys	1971		3.00	6.00

ABC-Paramount

☐ 10329		Sheila/Save Your Kisses	1962	3.75	7.50	15.00
☐ 10362		Susie Darlin'/Piddle De Pat	1962	3.00	6.00	12.00
☐ 10362	PS	Susie Darlin'/Piddle De Pat	1962	6.25	12.50	25.00
☐ 10379		Town Crier/Rainbow	1962	3.00	6.00	12.00
☐ 10389		Don't Cry Donna/Gonna Take a Chance	1962	3.00	6.00	12.00
☐ 10423		The Folk Singer/Count on Me	1963	2.50	5.00	10.00
☐ 10454		Kiss and Run/What Makes the Blues	1963	2.50	5.00	10.00
☐ 10478		Everybody/Sorry I'm Late, Lisa	1963	3.75	7.50	15.00
☐ 10515		Come On/There Will Be Better Years	1964	2.50	5.00	10.00
☐ 10543		Carol/Be a Good Little Girl	1964	2.50	5.00	10.00
☐ 10555		Dance with Me, Henry/Wild Water Skiing Weekend	1964	5.00	10.00	20.00
☐ 10579		Oh So Right/I Think I Love You	1964	3.00	6.00	12.00
☐ 10604		Party Girl/Oh How I Could Love You	1964	2.50	5.00	10.00
☐ 10623		Love Me, Love Me/Diane from Manchester Square	1965	3.00	6.00	12.00
☐ 10665		Fourteen Pair of Shoes/Combo Music	1965	2.50	5.00	10.00
☐ 10696		The Gunfighter/I'm a Rambler, I'm a Gambler	1965	5.00	10.00	20.00
☐ 10706		I Keep Remembering (Things I Forgot)/ Wish You Didn't Have to Go	1965	2.50	5.00	10.00
☐ 10738		Doesn't Anybody Know My Name/ Everytime a Bluebird Cries	1965	2.50	5.00	10.00
☐ 10762		Sweet Pea/Much More Love	1966	6.25	12.50	25.00

BGO

☐ 1003		She Do Run Run/(B-side unknown)	1982	2.50	5.00	10.00

Number	Title (A Side/B Side)	Year	VG	VG+	NM
Judd					
❏ 1018	Caveman/I Gotta Girl	1960	12.50	25.00	50.00
❏ 1022	Sheila/Pretty Girl	1960	20.00	40.00	80.00
Mark IV					
❏ 001	Caveman/I Gotta Girl	1960	25.00	50.00	100.00
MCA Curb					
❏ 52711	Some Such Foolishness/Barbara Lou	1985		2.00	4.00
❏ 52778	Radio Romance/Barbara Lou	1986		2.00	4.00
Mercury					
❏ 888 206-7	Let's Be Fools Like That Again/Barbara Lou	1986			3.00
❏ 888 497-7	Back When It Really Mattered/Radio Romance	1987			3.00
MGM South					
❏ 7001	Mean Little Woman, Rosalie/Skyline	1972		2.50	5.00
❏ 7008	Sarah My Love/Chewing on Sugar Cane	1972		2.50	5.00
❏ 7013	Working Class Hero/Sun in My Eyes	1973		2.50	5.00
❏ 7025	Silver Eyes/Memphis Me	1973		3.00	6.00
Monument					
❏ 8644	Glitter and Gleam/Bad News	1975		2.50	5.00
❏ 8662	Snowing Me Under/Rita and Her Band	1975		2.50	5.00
❏ 8684	Slow Dancing/Burn On Love Light	1976		2.50	5.00
❏ 8705	Everybody/Energy	1976		2.50	5.00
❏ 45205	Early in the Morning/Bad News	1976		2.50	5.00
❏ 45228	Your Love Will See Me Through/Working Class Hero	1977		2.50	5.00
Trumpet					
❏ 1401	Caveman/I Gotta Girl	1960	50.00	100.00	200.00
Warner Bros.					
❏ 8660	Dreamin' Again/Love the Way You Love Me Up	1978		2.00	4.00
❏ 8720	Just Look at Me/Love the Way You Love Me Up	1978		2.50	5.00
❏ 8800	Massachusetts/Just Look at Me	1979		2.50	5.00
❏ 49085	You Better Move On/Just Look at Me	1979		2.00	4.00
❏ 49235	There Is No Sun on Sunset Boulevard/ Charlie, I Love Your Wife	1980		2.00	4.00

Roemans, The
(Tommy Roe's backup group)

ABC					
❏ 10814	When the Sun Shines in the Mornin'/ Love (That's All I Want)	1966	3.75	7.50	15.00
❏ 10871	All the Good Things/Pleasing You Pleases Me	1966	3.75	7.50	15.00
ABC-Paramount					
❏ 10583	Give Me a Chance/Your Friend	1964	5.00	10.00	20.00
❏ 10671	Miserlou/Don't	1965	5.00	10.00	20.00
❏ 10723	Universal Soldier/Lost Little Girl	1965	5.00	10.00	20.00
❏ 10757	Listen to Me/You Make Me Feel Good	1965	5.00	10.00	20.00

Roger and the Travelers

Ember					
❏ 1079	You're Daddy's Little Girl/Just Gonna Be That Way	1961	25.00	50.00	100.00

Rogers, Kenny
(Also see "First Edition, The" and duet partners following)

Carlton					
❏ 454	That Crazy Feeling/We'll Always Have Each Other	1958	12.50	25.00	50.00
	Carlton titles as "Kenneth Rogers"				
❏ 468	For You Alone/I've Got a Lot to Learn	1958	12.50	25.00	50.00
Jolly Rogers					
❏ 1001	Lady, Play Your Symphony/ There's An Old Man in Our Town	1973		2.50	5.00
❏ 1003	(Do You Remember) The First Time/Indian Joe	1973		2.50	5.00
❏ 1004	Today I Started Loving You Again/ She Thinks I Still Care	1973		2.50	5.00
❏ 1006	Whatcha Gonna Do/Something About Your Song	1973		2.50	5.00
❏ 1007	A Stranger in My Place/Makin' Music for Money	1974		2.50	5.00
Ken-Lee					
❏ 102	Jole Blon/Lonely	195?	25.00	50.00	100.00
Liberty					
❏ 1380	Lady/Sweet Music Man	1980		2.00	4.00
❏ 1380 PS	Lady/Sweet Music Man	1980		2.50	5.00
❏ 1391	Long Arm of the Law/You Have a Good Friend	1980		2.00	4.00
❏ 1415	I Don't Need You/Without You in Your Life	1981			3.00
❏ 1415 PS	I Don't Need You/Without You in My Life	1981		2.00	4.00
❏ 1430	Share Your Love with Me/Greybeard	1981			3.00
❏ 1430 PS	Share Your Love with Me/Greybeard	1981		2.00	4.00
❏ 1438	Kentucky Homemade Christmas/Carol of the Bells	1981		2.50	5.00
❏ 1441	Blaze of Glory/The Good Life	1981			3.00
❏ 1444	Through the Years/So In Love with You	1981			3.00
❏ 1471	Love Will Turn You Around/I Want a Son	1982			3.00
❏ 1471 PS	Love Will Turn You Around/I Want a Son	1982		2.50	5.00
❏ 1485	A Love Song/Fool in Me	1982			3.00
❏ 1492	We've Got Tonight/You Are So Beautiful	1983			3.00
	A-side: With Sheena Easton				
❏ 1492 PS	We've Got Tonight/You Are So Beautiful	1983		2.00	4.00
❏ 1495	All My Life/The Farther I Go	1983			3.00

Number		Title (A Side/B Side)	Year	VG	VG+	NM
❑ 1503		Scarlet Fever/What I Learned from Loving You	1983			3.00
❑ 1511		Sweet Music Man/You Were a Good Friend	1983			3.00
❑ 1524		A Stranger in My Place/Love Is What We Make It	1985			3.00
❑ 1525		Twentieth Century Fool/It Turns Me Inside Out	1985			3.00
❑ 1526		Abraham, Martin and John/Goodbye Marie	1985			3.00

Mercury

❑ 72545		Here's That Rainy Day/Take Life in Stride	1966	6.25	12.50	25.00

RCA

❑ 5016-7-R		They Don't Make Them Like They Used To/ Just the Thought of Losing You	1986			3.00
❑ 5209-7-R		Make No Mistake, She's Mine/You're My Love	1987			3.00
		With Ronnie Milsap				
❑ 5258-7-R		I Prefer the Moonlight/We're Doin' Alright	1987			3.00
❑ 6832-7-R		The Factory/One More Day	1987			3.00
❑ 8381-7-R		I Prefer the Moonlight/Make No Mistake, She's Mine	1988			3.00
		Gold Standard Series; B-side with Ronnie Milsap				
❑ 8390-7-R		I Don't Call Him Daddy/We're Doin' Alright	1988			3.00
❑ PB-13710		This Woman/Buried Treasure	1984			3.00
❑ PB-13710	PS	This Woman/Buried Treasure	1984		2.00	4.00
❑ PB-13774		Eyes That See in the Dark/Hold Me	1984			3.00
❑ PB-13832		Evening Star/Midsummer Nights	1984			3.00
❑ PB-13899		What About Me/The Rest of Last Night	1984			3.00
		With Kim Carnes and James Ingram				
❑ PB-13899	PS	What About Me/The Rest of Last Night	1984		2.00	4.00
❑ PB-13944		The Christmas Song/ Medley: Winter Wonderland-Sleigh Ride	1984		2.00	4.00
		B-side by Dolly Parton				
❑ PB-13975		Crazy/The Stranger	1984			3.00
❑ GB-14074		This Woman/What About Me	1985			3.00
		Gold Standard Series; B-side by Kenny Rogers, Kim Carnes and James Ingram				
❑ PB-14194		Morning Desire/People in Love	1985			3.00
❑ PB-14194	PS	Morning Desire/People in Love	1985		2.00	4.00
❑ PB-14298		Tomb of the Unknown Love/Our Perfect Song	1986			3.00
❑ GB-14353		Crazy/Morning Desire	1986			3.00
		Gold Standard Series				
❑ PB-14384		The Pride Is Back/Didn't We?	1986		2.00	4.00
		A-side: With Nickie Ryder				
❑ PB-14384	PS	The Pride Is Back/Didn't We?	1986		2.00	4.00

Reprise

❑ 18835		Bed of Roses/I'll Be There for You	1992			3.00
❑ 18967		Someone Must Feel Like a Fool Tonight/Sunshine	1992			3.00
❑ 19080		If You Want to Find Love/Sunshine	1991			3.00
❑ 19324		Walk Away/What I Did for Love	1991			3.00
❑ 19504		Lay My Body Down/Crazy in Love	1991			3.00
❑ 19972		Maybe/If I Knew Then What I Know Now	1990			3.00
		A-side: With Holly Dunn; B-side: With Gladys Knight				
❑ 22750		Christmas in America/Joy to the World	1989			3.00
❑ 22750	PS	Christmas in America/Joy to the World	1989			3.00
❑ 22828		The Vows Go Unbroken (Always True to You)/ One Night	1989			3.00
❑ 22853		(Something Inside) So Strong/ When You Put Your Heart In It	1989			3.00
❑ 27690		Planet Texas/When You Put Your Heart in It	1988			3.00
❑ 27812		When You Put Your Heart In It/(Instrumental)	1988			3.00

United Artists

❑ XW746		Love Lifted Me/Home-Made Love	1975		2.00	4.00
❑ XW798		There's an Old Man in Our Town/Home-Made Love	1976		2.00	4.00
❑ XW812		I Would Like to See You Again/ While the Feeling's Good	1976		2.00	4.00
❑ XW868		Laura (What's He Got That I Ain't Got)/ I Wasn't Mad Enough	1976		2.00	4.00
❑ XW929		Lucille/Till I Get It Right	1976		2.00	4.00
❑ XW1027		Daytime Friends/We Don't Make Love Anymore	1977		2.00	4.00
❑ XW1095		Sweet Music Man/Lying Again	1977		2.00	4.00
❑ XW1151		Love Lifted Me/Reuben James	1978		2.00	4.00
❑ XW1152		Today I Started Loving You Again/ Just Dropped In (To See What Condition My Condition Was In)	1978		2.00	4.00
❑ XW1153		Daytime Friends/But You Know I Love You	1978		2.00	4.00
❑ XW1154		Lucille/Something's Burning	1978		2.00	4.00
❑ XW1155		Sweet Music Man/Ruby, Don't Take Your Love to Town	1978		2.00	4.00
		B-sides of the above five singles are re-recordings of First Edition hits paired with early United Artists country hits				
❑ XW1210		Love Or Something Like It/Starting Again	1978		2.00	4.00
❑ XW1250		The Gambler/Momma's Waiting	1978		2.00	4.00
❑ XW1273		She Believes in Me/Morgana Jones	1979		2.00	4.00
❑ XW1273	PS	She Believes in Me/Morgana Jones	1979		2.50	5.00
❑ 1315		You Decorated My Life/One Man's Woman	1979		2.00	4.00
❑ 1315	PS	You Decorated My Life/One Man's Woman	1979		2.50	5.00
❑ 1327		Coward of the County/I Wanna Make You Smile	1979		2.00	4.00
❑ 1345		Don't Fall in Love with a Dreamer/ Intro: Goin' Home to the Rock-Gideon Tanner	1980		2.00	4.00
		A-side: With Kim Carnes				
❑ 1345	PS	Don't Fall in Love with a Dreamer/ Intro: Goin' Home to the Rock-Gideon Tanner	1980		2.50	5.00
❑ 1359		Love the World Away/Sayin' Goodbye-Requiem	1980		2.00	4.00

Number		Title (A Side/B Side)	Year	VG	VG+	NM

Rogers, Kenny, and Dolly Parton
RCA
❏ 5352-7-R		Christmas Without You/I Believe in Santa Claus	1987			3.00
		B-side by Dolly Parton				
❏ 9070-7-R		Christmas Without You/	1989			3.00
		Medley: Winter Wonderland-Sleigh Ride				
		B-side by Dolly Parton				
❏ PB-13615		Islands in the Stream/I Will Always Love You	1983			3.00
❏ PB-13615	PS	Islands in the Stream/I Will Always Love You	1983		2.50	5.00
		Version 1: With "(Duet with Dolly Parton)" in small letters				
❏ PB-13615	PS	Islands in the Stream/I Will Always Love You	1983		2.00	4.00
		Version 2: With Dolly Parton's name the same size as Kenny Rogers'				
❏ PB-13945		The Greatest Gift of All/White Christmas	1984		2.00	4.00
❏ PB-14058		Real Love/I Can't Be True	1985			3.00
❏ GB-14073		Islands in the Stream/Eyes That See in the Dark	1985			3.00
		Gold Standard Series; B-side by Kenny Rogers				
❏ PB-14261		Christmas Without You/A Christmas to Remember	1985			3.00
❏ PB-14261	PS	Christmas Without You/A Christmas to Remember	1985		2.00	4.00
Reprise						
❏ 19760		Love Is Strange/Walk Away	1990			3.00

Rogers, Kenny, and Dottie West
Liberty
❏ 1516		Baby I'm-a Want You/Together Again	1984			3.00
United Artists						
❏ XW1137		Every Time Two Fools Collide/We Love Each Other	1978		2.00	4.00
❏ XW1234		Anyone Who Isn't Me Tonight/You and Me	1978		2.00	4.00
❏ XW1276		All I Ever Need Is You/	1979		2.00	4.00
		Another Somebody Done Somebody Wrong Song				
❏ XW1299		Till I Can Make It on My Own/Midnight Flyer	1979		2.00	4.00

Rogers, Kenny, and the First Edition – See "First Edition, The"

Rogers, Morris, and the Continentals
Delta
| ❏ 601/2 | | The Leg/Wonders of Love | 1963 | 50.00 | 100.00 | 200.00 |

Rogers, Timmie
Cadet
❏ 5685		Super Soul Brothers/It Rolls Through Everything	1971		2.50	5.00
Cameo						
❏ 116		Back to School Again/I've Got a Dog Who Loves Me	1957	7.50	15.00	30.00
❏ 131		Take Me to Your Leader/Fla-Ga-La-Pa	1958	6.25	12.50	25.00
Capitol						
❏ F2406		Saturday Night/If I Were You, Baby	1953	6.25	12.50	25.00
❏ F2509		Oh Yeah/Nothin' Wrong with Nothin'	1953	6.25	12.50	25.00
Epic						
❏ 9813		If You Can't Smile and Say Yes	1965	2.00	4.00	8.00
		(Please Don't Cry and Say No)/Chum Goy Tum Toy Fricasee (Soy Soy Soo)				
❏ 9899		Everybody Wants to Go to Heaven,	1966	2.00	4.00	8.00
		But Nobody Wants to Die/Too Young to Go Steady				
Mercury						
❏ 70451		If I Give My Heart to You/Teedle-Dee Teedle-Dum	1954	10.00	20.00	40.00
Par-Tee						
❏ 1303		Watergate/Snake Hips	1973		2.50	5.00
Parkway						
❏ 814		I Love Ya, I Love Ya, I Love Ya/Tee-Hee	1960	3.75	7.50	15.00
Philips						
❏ 40074		Oh Yeah/Fla-Ga-La-Pa	1962	2.50	5.00	10.00
Signature						
❏ 12037		First Proposal/Underwater Cha Cha Cha	1960	3.75	7.50	15.00

Rogers, Weldon
Imperial
❏ 5451		So Long, Good Luck and Goodbye/Trying to Get to You	1957	50.00	100.00	200.00
		B-side is actually The Teen Kings' version rather than Rogers'; by mistake, the wrong recording left Norman Petty's studio..				
Je-Wel						
❏ 103		Everybody Wants You/This Song's Just for You	1956	250.00	500.00	1,000

Rolie, Gregg
(Formerly of Santana and Journey)
Columbia
| ❏ 05581 | | Young Love/Deep Blue Sea | 1985 | | | 3.00 |
| ❏ 07351 | | The Hands of Time/I Will Get to You | 1987 | | | 3.00 |

Rollers, The
Liberty
❏ 55303		Bonneville/Got My Eye on You	1961	5.00	10.00	20.00
❏ 55320		The Continental Walk/I Want You So	1961	5.00	10.00	20.00
❏ 55357		The Bounce/Teenager's Waltz	1961	5.00	10.00	20.00

Number		Title (A Side/B Side)	Year	VG	VG+	NM

Rolling Stones, The
(Also see "Jagger, Mick"; "Richards, Keith"; "Wood, Ron"; "Wyman, Bill")

Abkco

Number		Title (A Side/B Side)	Year	VG	VG+	NM
❏ 4701		I Don't Know Why/Try a Little Harder	1975	2.50	5.00	10.00
		With A-side writing credits of "Jagger, Richards, Taylor"				
❏ 4701		I Don't Know Why/Try a Little Harder	1975		2.50	5.00
		With A-side writing credits of "Wonder, Riser, Hunter, Hardaway"				
❏ 4702		Out of Time/Jiving Sister Fanny	1975		3.00	6.00

London

Number		Title (A Side/B Side)	Year	VG	VG+	NM
▧ 901		Paint It, Black/Stupid Girl	1966	2.50	5.00	10.00
▧ 901	PS	Paint It, Black/Stupid Girl	1966	7.50	15.00	30.00
❏ 902		Mothers Little Helper/Lady Jane	1966	2.50	5.00	10.00
▧ 902	PS	Mothers Little Helper/Lady Jane	1966	7.50	15.00	30.00
❏ 903		Have You Seen Your Mother, Baby, Standing in the Shadow?/Who's Driving My Plane	1966	2.50	5.00	10.00
▧ 903	PS	Have You Seen Your Mother, Baby, Standing in the Shadow?/Who's Driving My Plane	1966	10.00	20.00	40.00
❏ 904		Ruby Tuesday/Let's Spend the Night Together	1967	2.50	5.00	10.00
❏ 904	PS	Let's Spend the Night Together/Ruby Tuesday	1967	7.50	15.00	30.00
❏ 905		Dandelion/We Love You	1967	3.75	7.50	15.00
❏ 905	PS	We Love You/Dandelion	1967	100.00	200.00	400.00
❏ 906		She's a Rainbow/2000 Light Years from Home	1967	3.75	7.50	15.00
❏ 906	PS	She's a Rainbow/2000 Light Years from Home	1967	12.50	25.00	50.00
❏ 907		In Another Land/The Lantern	1967	5.00	10.00	20.00
		A-side credited to Bill Wyman, though taken from "Their Satanic Majesties Request"				
❏ 907	PS	In Another Land/The Lantern	1967	12.50	25.00	50.00
❏ 908		Jumpin' Jack Flash/Child of the Moon	1968	2.50	5.00	10.00
❏ 908	PS	Jumpin' Jack Flash/Child of the Moon	1968	6.25	12.50	25.00
❏ 909		Street Fighting Man/No Expectations	1968	3.00	6.00	12.00
❏ 909	PS	Street Fighting Man/No Expectations	1968	4,000	6,000	8,000
❏ 910		Honky Tonk Women/ You Can't Always Get What You Want	1969	2.50	5.00	10.00
❏ 910	PS	Honky Tonk Women/ You Can't Always Get What You Want	1969	5.00	10.00	20.00
❏ 9641		I Wanna Be Your Man/Stoned	1964	2,000	3,000	4,000
❏ 9641	DJ	I Wanna Be Your Man/Stoned	1964	125.00	250.00	500.00
❏ 9657		Not Fade Away/I Wanna Be Your Man	1964	5.00	10.00	20.00
		White, purple and blue label				
❏ 9657		Not Fade Away/I Wanna Be Your Man	1964	2.00	4.00	8.00
		Blue swirl label				
❏ 9657	PS	Not Fade Away/I Wanna Be Your Man	1964	62.50	125.00	250.00
❏ 9682		Tell Me (You're Coming Back)/ I Just Want to Make Love to You	1964	5.00	10.00	20.00
		White, purple and blue label				
❏ 9682		Tell Me (You're Coming Back)/ I Just Want to Make Love to You	1964	2.00	4.00	8.00
		Blue swirl label				
❏ 9682	PS	Tell Me (You're Coming Back)/ I Just Want to Make Love to You	1964	25.00	50.00	100.00
❏ 9687		It's All Over Now/Good Times, Bad Times	1964	5.00	10.00	20.00
		White, purple and blue label				
▧ 9687		It's All Over Now/Good Times Bad Times	1964	2.00	4.00	8.00
		Blue swirl label				
❏ 9687	PS	It's All Over Now/Good Times, Bad Times	1964	25.00	50.00	100.00
❏ 9708		Time Is On My Side/Congratulations	1964	5.00	10.00	20.00
		White, purple and blue label				
❏ 9708		Time Is On My Side/Congratulations	1964	2.00	4.00	8.00
		Blue swirl label				
❏ 9708	PS	Time Is On My Side/Congratulations	1964	20.00	40.00	80.00
❏ 9725		Heart of Stone/What a Shame	1964	5.00	10.00	20.00
		White, purple and blue label				
❏ 9725		Heart of Stone/What a Shame	1964	2.00	4.00	8.00
		Blue swirl label				
❏ 9725	PS	Heart of Stone/What a Shame	1964	125.00	250.00	500.00
❏ 9741		The Last Time/Play with Fire	1965	7.50	15.00	30.00
		White, purple and blue label				
▧ 9741		The Last Time/Play with Fire	1965	3.75	7.50	15.00
		Blue swirl label, "London" in white letters				
❏ 9741		The Last Time/Play with Fire	1965	2.00	4.00	8.00
		Blue swirl label, "London" in black letters				
❏ 9741	PS	The Last Time/Play with Fire	1965	15.00	30.00	60.00
❏ 9766		(I Can't Get No) Satisfaction/ The Under Assistant West Coast Promotion Man	1965	2.50	5.00	10.00
❏ 9766	PS	(I Can't Get No) Satisfaction/ The Under Assistant West Coast Promotion Man	1965	50.00	100.00	200.00
▧ 9792		Get Off of My Cloud/I'm Free	1965	2.50	5.00	10.00
❏ 9792	PS	Get Off of My Cloud/I'm Free	1965	7.50	15.00	30.00
▧ 9808		As Tears Go By/Gotta Get Away	1965	2.50	5.00	10.00
▧ 9808	PS	As Tears Go By/Gotta Get Away	1965	7.50	15.00	30.00
▧ 9823		19th Nervous Breakdown/Sad Day	1966	2.50	5.00	10.00
▧ 9823	PS	19th Nervous Breakdown/Sad Day	1966	10.00	20.00	40.00

Rolling Stones

Number		Title (A Side/B Side)	Year	VG	VG+	NM
❏ PR 228	DJ	Time Waits for No One (mono/stereo)	1974	7.50	15.00	30.00
❏ PR 228	PS	Time Waits for No One (mono/stereo)	1974	10.00	20.00	40.00

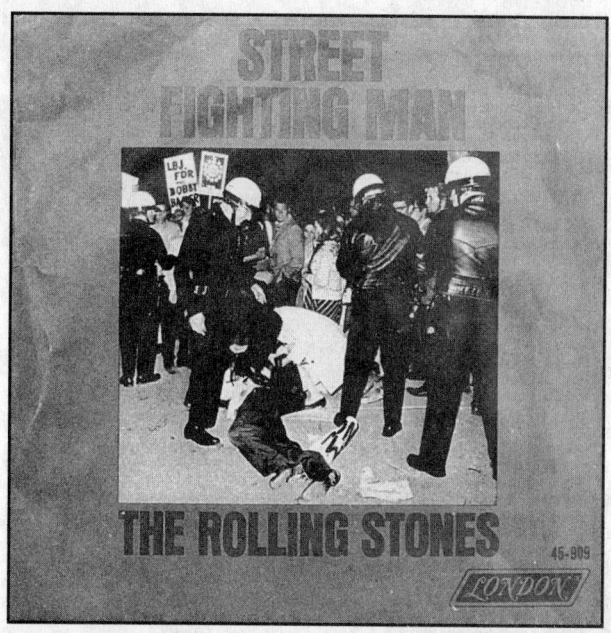

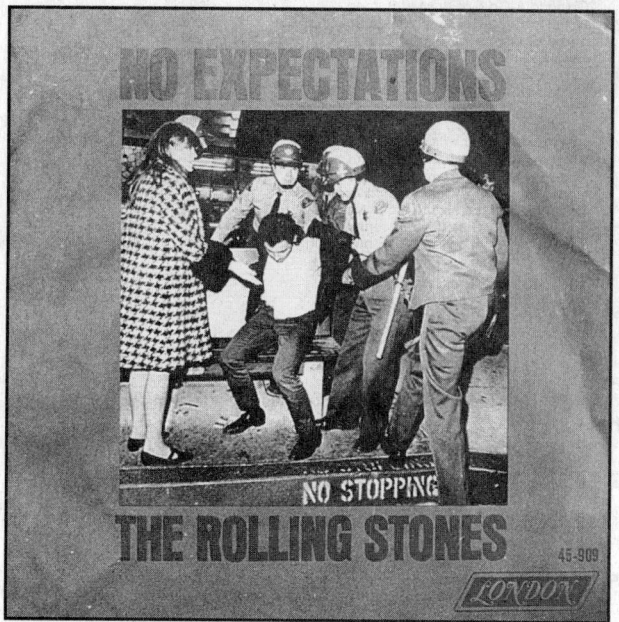

Here it is, possibly for the first time anywhere: Both sides of the world's most valuable picture sleeve. The A-side, "Street Fighting Man," has been often seen in photographs, but the B-side, "No Expectations," is rarely seen. About a dozen copies of this sleeve are known to exist, compared to the hundreds of thousands of copies of the record that were pressed.

Number		Title (A Side/B Side)	Year	VG	VG+	NM
❏ PR 316	DJ	Before They Make Me Run (mono/stereo)	1978	6.25	12.50	25.00
❏ PR 316	PS	Before They Make Me Run (mono/stereo)	1978	7.50	15.00	30.00
❏ 05802		Harlem Shuffle/Had It with You	1986			3.00
❏ 05802	PS	Harlem Shuffle/Had It with You	1986			3.00
❏ 05906		One Hit (To the Body)/Fight	1986			3.00
❏ 05906	PS	One Hit (To the Body)/Fight	1986			3.00
❏ 19100		Brown Sugar/Bitch	1971		2.50	5.00
❏ 19101		Wild Horses/Sway	1971		2.50	5.00
❏ 19103		Tumbling Dice/Sweet Black Angel	1972		2.50	5.00
❏ 19104		Happy/All Down the Line	1972		2.50	5.00
❏ 19105		Silver Train/Angie	1973	3.00	6.00	12.00

With "Silver Train" listed as "Side One" and "Angie" as "Side Two"

Number		Title (A Side/B Side)	Year	VG	VG+	NM
❏ 19105		Angie/Silver Train	1973		2.50	5.00

With "Angie" listed as "Side One" and "Silver Train" as "Side Two", or with no reference at all to "Side One" and "Side Two"

Number		Title (A Side/B Side)	Year	VG	VG+	NM
❏ 19109		Doo Doo Doo Doo Doo (Heartbreaker)/ Dancing with Mr. D.	1973		2.50	5.00
❏ 19301		It's Only Rock 'N' Roll (But I Like It)/ Through the Lonely Nights	1974		2.50	5.00
❏ 19302		Ain't Too Proud to Beg/Dance Little Sister	1974		2.50	5.00
❏ 19304		Fool to Cry/Hot Stuff	1976		2.00	4.00
❏ 19304		Fool to Cry/Crazy Mama	1976			

Promotional 12-inch singles exist with this coupling, but do U.S. 45s? Please advise.

Number		Title (A Side/B Side)	Year	VG	VG+	NM
❏ 19307		Miss You/Far Away Eyes	1978		2.00	4.00
❏ 19307	PS	Miss You/Far Away Eyes	1978		2.00	4.00
❏ 19309		Beast of Burden/Before They Make Me Run	1978		2.00	4.00
❏ 19309	PS	Beast of Burden/Before They Make Me Run	1978	400.00	800.00	1,200
❏ 19310		Shattered/Everything Is Turning to Gold	1978		2.00	4.00
❏ 19310	PS	Shattered/Everything Is Turning to Gold	1978		3.00	6.00
❏ 20001		Emotional Rescue/Down in the Hole	1980		2.00	4.00
❏ 20001	PS	Emotional Rescue/Down in the Hole	1980		2.00	4.00
❏ 21001		She's So Cold/Send It to Me	1980		2.00	4.00
❏ 21001	PS	She's So Cold/Send It to Me	1980		3.00	6.00
❏ 21003		Start Me Up/No Use in Crying	1981		2.00	4.00
❏ 21003	PS	Start Me Up/No Use in Crying	1981		2.00	4.00
❏ 21004		Waiting on a Friend/Little T & A	1981		2.00	4.00
❏ 21004	PS	Waiting on a Friend/Little T & A	1981		2.00	4.00
❏ 21300		Hang Fire/Neighbours	1982		2.00	4.00
❏ 21301		Going to A-Go-Go/Beast of Burden	1982		2.00	4.00
❏ 21301	PS	Going to A-Go-Go/Beast of Burden	1982		2.00	4.00
❏ 69008		Mixed Emotions/Fancy Man Blues	1989			3.00
❏ 73057		Rock and a Hard Place/Cook Cook Blues	1989			3.00
❏ 73093		Almost Hear You Sigh/Break the Spell	1989			3.00
❏ 73742		Highwire/2000 Light Years from Home	1991		2.50	5.00
❏ 73789		Sexdrive/Undercover of the Night	1991	2.00	4.00	8.00
❏ 99724		Too Tough/Miss You	1984	10.00	20.00	40.00

Value is for stock copy, which does exist. Promos are worth about 25% of this price.

Number		Title (A Side/B Side)	Year	VG	VG+	NM
❏ 99788		She Was Hot/Think I'm Going Mad	1984			3.00
❏ 99788	PS	She Was Hot/Think I'm Going Mad	1984			3.00
❏ 99813		Undercover of the Night/All the Way Down	1983			3.00
❏ 99813	PS	Undercover of the Night/All the Way Down	1983			3.00
❏ 99978		Time Is On My Side (Live)/Twenty Flight Rock	1982		2.50	5.00
❏ 99978	PS	Time Is On My Side (Live)/Twenty Flight Rock	1982		2.50	5.00

Virgin

Number		Title (A Side/B Side)	Year	VG	VG+	NM
❏ 38446		Love Is Strong//The Storm/ Love Is Strong (Teddy Riley Remix)	1994		2.50	5.00
❏ 38446	PS	Love Is Strong//The Storm/ Love Is Strong (Teddy Riley Remix)	1994		2.50	5.00
❏ 38459		Out of Tears// Out of Tears (Bob Clearmountain Remix Edit)/I'm Gonna Drive	1994		2.50	5.00
❏ 38459	PS	Out of Tears// Out of Tears (Bob Clearmountain Remix Edit)/I'm Gonna Drive	1994		2.50	5.00

Romantics, The

Bomp!

Number		Title (A Side/B Side)	Year	VG	VG+	NM
❏ 120		Tell It to Carrie/First in Line	1978			3.00
❏ 120	PS	Tell It to Carrie/First in Line	1978			3.00

Columbia

Number		Title (A Side/B Side)	Year	VG	VG+	NM
❏ 06445		Talking in Your Sleep/Mystified	198?			3.00

Reissue

Number		Title (A Side/B Side)	Year	VG	VG+	NM
❏ 07527		What I Like About You/First in Line	198?			3.00

Reissue

Nemperor

Number		Title (A Side/B Side)	Year	VG	VG+	NM
❏ 02581		No One Like You/She's Hot	1981		2.00	4.00
❏ 04135		Talking in Your Sleep/I'm Hip	1983			3.00
❏ 04373		One in a Million/Do Me Anyway You Wanna	1984			3.00
❏ 04373	PS	One in a Million/Do Me Anyway You Wanna	1984			3.00
❏ 05587		Test of Time/Better Make a Move	1985			3.00
❏ 05587	PS	Test of Time/Better Make a Move	1985			3.00
❏ 05587	PS	Test of Time	1985		2.50	5.00

"Demonstration -- Not for Sale" on back

Number		Title (A Side/B Side)	Year	VG	VG+	NM
❏ 05684		Mystified/Make It Last	1985			3.00
❏ 7527		What I Like About You/First in Line	1979		2.50	5.00
❏ 7527	PS	What I Like About You/First in Line	1979	2.50	5.00	10.00
❏ 7530		When I Look in Your Eyes/Little White Lies	1980			3.00
❏ 7531		Tell It to Carrie/Hung on You	1980			3.00

Number		Title (A Side/B Side)	Year	VG	VG+	NM
❑ 7537		Forever Yours/New Cover Story	1981		2.00	4.00
❑ 70063		A Night Like This/I Ain't Got You	1981		2.00	4.00
Spider						
❑ SPDR-101		Little White Lies/I Can't Tell You Anything	1977		2.00	4.00
❑ SPDR-101	PS	Little White Lies/I Can't Tell You Anything	1977		2.00	4.00

Romeos, The
(Several different groups)

Amy

Number	Title (A Side/B Side)	Year	VG	VG+	NM
❑ 840	The Tiger's Wide Awake (The Lion Sleeps Tonight)/ Hitch-Hikin'	1962	3.75	7.50	15.00

Apollo

❑ 461	Love Me/I Beg You Please	1954	75.00	150.00	300.00

Atco

❑ 6107	Moments to Remember You By/Fine, Fine Baby	1958	12.50	25.00	50.00

Felsted

❑ 8528	Two Innocent Loves/Love-Mobile	1958	7.50	15.00	30.00
❑ 8672	Julie/I'm Gonna Rebuild This World	1963	5.00	10.00	20.00

Fox

❑ 749	Gone, Gone, Get Away/Let's Be Partners *Cream label*	1957	75.00	150.00	300.00
❑ 749	Gone, Gone, Get Away/Let's Be Partners *Yellow label*	1957	30.00	60.00	120.00
❑ 846	Moments to Remember You By/Fine, Fine Baby *Cream label*	1957	75.00	150.00	300.00
❑ 846	Moments to Remember You By/Fine, Fine Baby *Yellow label*	1957	30.00	60.00	120.00

Loma

❑ 2028	Mucho Soul/Are You Ready for That	1966	3.00	6.00	12.00
❑ 2041	Calypso Chili/Mon Petite Chow	1966	3.00	6.00	12.00

Mark II

❑ 101	Precious Memories/Juicy Lucy	1967	3.75	7.50	15.00
❑ 103	A Tear and a Smile/Seaching	1967	3.75	7.50	15.00

The Mark II group features Philly Soul producers Kenny Gamble and Leon Huff

Romero, Chan

Challenge

❑ 59285	The Funniest Things/It's Not Fine	1965	2.50	5.00	10.00

Del-Fi

❑ 4119	The Hippy Hippy Shake/If I Had My Way	1959	10.00	20.00	40.00
❑ 4126	I Don't Care Now/My Little Rudy	1959	7.50	15.00	30.00

Philips

❑ 40391	Humpy Bumpy/Man Can't Dog a Woman	1966	2.50	5.00	10.00

Ron and Bill
(Ron White and Bill "Smokey" Robinson)

Argo

❑ 5350	It/Don't Say Bye Bye	1959	12.50	25.00	50.00

Tamla

❑ 54025	It/Don't Say Bye Bye	1960	30.00	60.00	120.00

Ronettes, The
(Also see "Spector, Ronnie")

A&M

❑ 1040	You Came, You Saw, You Conquered/Oh, I Love You	1969	4.00	8.00	16.00

Buddah

❑ 384	Go Out and Get It/Lover, Lover As "Ronnie Spector and the Ronettes"	1973	5.00	10.00	20.00
❑ 408	I Wish I Never Saw the Sunshine/ I Wonder What He's Doing	1974	5.00	10.00	20.00

Colpix

❑ 601	I Want a Boy/Sweet Sixteen As "Ronnie and the Relatives"	1961	12.50	25.00	50.00
❑ 646	I'm Gonna Quit While I'm Ahead/I'm On the Wagon	1962	15.00	30.00	60.00

Dimension

❑ 1046	He Did It/Recipe for Love	1965	12.50	25.00	50.00

May

❑ 111	My Darling Angel/I'm Gonna Quit While I'm Ahead As "Ronnie and the Relatives"	1961	20.00	40.00	80.00
❑ 114	Silhouettes/You Bet I Would	1962	12.50	25.00	50.00
❑ 138	Memory/Good Girls	1963	12.50	25.00	50.00

Pavillion

❑ 03333	I Saw Mommy Kissing Santa Claus/ Rudolph the Red-Nosed Reindeer *B-side by The Crystals*	1982		2.50	5.00

Philles

❑ 116	Be My Baby/Tedesco and Pittman	1963	5.00	10.00	20.00
❑ 118	Baby I Love You/Miss Joan and Mr. Sam	1963	5.00	10.00	20.00
❑ 120	(The Best Part of) Breakin' Up/Big Red	1964	6.25	12.50	25.00
❑ 121	Do I Love You?/Bebe and Susu	1964	6.25	12.50	25.00

Number		Title (A Side/B Side)	Year	VG	VG+	NM
☐ 123		Walkin' in the Rain/How Does It Feel	1964	5.00	10.00	20.00
☐ 123	PS	Walkin' in the Rain/How Does It Feel	1964	20.00	40.00	80.00
☐ 126		Born to Be Together/Blues for Baby	1965	5.00	10.00	20.00
☐ 126	PS	Born to Be Together/Blues for Baby	1965	20.00	40.00	80.00
☐ 128		Is This What I Get for Loving You?/Oh, I Love You	1965	5.00	10.00	20.00
☐ 128	PS	Is This What I Get for Loving You?/Oh, I Love You	1965	25.00	50.00	100.00
☐ 133		I Can Hear Music/When I Saw You	1966	6.25	12.50	25.00

Ronnie and the Del-Aires – See "Del-Aires, The"

Ronnie and the Hi-Lites
ABC-Paramount

☐ 10685		High School Romance/Too Young	1965	5.00	10.00	20.00

Joy

☐ 260		I Wish That We Were Married/Twistin' and Kissin'	1962	6.25	12.50	25.00
☐ 265		Be Kind/Send My Love (Special Delivery)	1962	5.00	10.00	20.00

Raven

☐ 8000		Valerie/The Fact of the Matter	1963	5.00	10.00	20.00

Win

☐ 250		A Slow Dance/What the Next Day May Bring	1963	5.00	10.00	20.00
☐ 251		The Fact of the Matter/You Keep Me Guessin'	1963	5.00	10.00	20.00
☐ 252		High School Romance/Uptown-Downtown	1963	6.25	12.50	25.00

Ronnie and the Relatives – See "Ronettes, The"

Ronnie and the Rockin' Kings
RCA Victor

☐ 47-7248		Rock and Roll Sal/You Know	1958	10.00	20.00	40.00

Ronny and the Daytonas
Mala

☐ 481		G.T.O./Hot Rod Baby	1964	6.25	12.50	25.00
☐ 490		California Bound/Hey Little Girl	1964	5.00	10.00	20.00
☐ 492		Bucket "T"/Little Rail Job	1964	5.00	10.00	20.00
☐ 497		Little Scrambler/Teenage Years	1965	5.00	10.00	20.00
☐ 503		Beach Boy/No Wheels	1965	6.25	12.50	25.00
☐ 513		Sandy/(Instrumental)	1965	5.00	10.00	20.00
☐ 525		Goodbye Baby/Somebody to Love Me	1966	5.00	10.00	20.00
☐ 531		Antique '32 Studebaker Dictator Coupe/ Then the Rains Came	1966	5.00	10.00	20.00
☐ 542		I'll Think of Summer/Little Scrambler	1966	3.75	7.50	15.00

RCA Victor

☐ 47-8896		All American Girl/Dianne, Dianne	1966	3.00	6.00	12.00
☐ 47-9022		Winter Weather/Young	1966	3.00	6.00	12.00
☐ 47-9107		Walk with the Sun/The Last Letter	1967	3.00	6.00	12.00
☐ 47-9435		The Girls and the Boys/Alfie	1968	3.00	6.00	12.00

Show Biz

☐ 21207	DJ	4-Cast She'll Love Me Again One-sided promo	1968	5.00	10.00	20.00

Ronson, Mick
RCA Victor

☐ APBO-0212		Love Me Tender/Only After Dark	1974		3.00	6.00
☐ APBO-0291		Slaughter on Tenth Avenue/Leave My Heart Alone	1974		3.00	6.00
☐ PB-10237		Easy Days/Billy Porter	1975		3.00	6.00

EPs
RCA Victor

☐ DJEO-0259	DJ	Slaughter on 10th Avenue/Growing Up and I'm Fine// All Cut Up on You/Andy Warhol Promo-only EP with B-side by Dana Gillespie	1974	3.00	6.00	12.00

Ronstadt, Linda
(Also see "Christmas Spirit"; "Stone Poneys")
Asylum

☐ 11026		Love Has No Pride/I Can Almost See It	1973		2.50	5.00
☐ 11032		Silver Threads and Golden Needles/Don't Cry Now	1974		2.50	5.00
☐ 11039		Desperado/Colorado	1974		2.50	5.00
☐ 45271		Love Is a Rose/Silver Blue May only exist as a double-sided promo of "Love Is a Rose"	1975	2.00	4.00	8.00
☐ 45282		Heat Wave/Love Is a Rose	1975		2.00	4.00
☐ 45295		Tracks of My Tears/The Sweetest Gift	1975		2.00	4.00
☐ 45340		That'll Be the Day/Try Me Again Clouds label	1976		2.00	4.00
☐ 45340		That'll Be the Day/Try Me Again All-blue label	1976		2.50	5.00
☐ 45361		Someone to Lay Down Beside Me/Crazy	1976		2.00	4.00
☐ 45402		Lose Again/Lo Siento Mi Vida	1977	2.00	4.00	8.00
☐ 45431		Blue Bayou/Old Paint	1977		2.00	4.00
☐ 45438		It's So Easy/Lo Siento Mi Vida	1977		2.00	4.00
☐ 45462		Poor Poor Pitiful Me/Simple Man, Simple Dream	1978		2.00	4.00
☐ 45464		Lago Azul/Lo Siento Mi Vida	1978	2.00	4.00	8.00
☐ 45479		Tumbling Dice/I Never Will Marry	1978		2.00	4.00
☐ 45519		Back in the U.S.A./White Rhythm and Blues	1978		2.00	4.00
☐ 45519	PS	Back in the U.S.A./White Rhythm and Blues	1978		3.00	6.00

Number		Title (A Side/B Side)	Year	VG	VG+	NM
❏ 45546		Ooh Baby Baby/Blowing Away	1978		2.00	4.00
❏ 46011		Just One Look/Love Me Tender	1979		2.00	4.00
❏ 46034		Alison/Mohammed's Radio	1979		2.00	4.00
❏ 46602		How Do I Make You/Rambler Gambler	1980		2.00	4.00
❏ 46602	PS	How Do I Make You/Rambler Gambler	1980		2.50	5.00
❏ 46624		Hurt So Bad/Justine	1980		2.00	4.00
❏ 46654		I Can't Let Go/Look Out for My Love	1980		2.00	4.00
❏ 69476		(I Love You) For Sentimental Reasons/ Straighten Up and Fly Right	1987		2.00	4.00
❏ 69507		When You Wish Upon a Star/Little Girl Blue	1986		2.00	4.00
❏ 69653		When I Fall in Love/It Never Entered My Mind	1985		2.00	4.00
❏ 69671		Lush Life/Skylark	1985		2.00	4.00
❏ 69725		Someone to Watch Over Me/What'll I Do	1984		2.00	4.00
❏ 69752		I've Got a Crush on You/Lover Man	1984		2.00	4.00
❏ 69780		What's New/Crazy He Calls Me	1983		2.00	4.00
❏ 69838		Easy for You to Say/Mr. Radio	1983		2.00	4.00
❏ 69853		I Knew You When/Talk to Me of Mendocino	1982		2.00	4.00
❏ 69853	PS	I Knew You When/Talk to Me of Mendocino	1982		2.50	5.00
❏ 69948		Get Closer/Sometimes You Just Can't Win	1982		2.00	4.00
❏ 69948	PS	Get Closer/Sometimes You Just Can't Win	1982		2.50	5.00

Capitol

❏ 2438		Dolphins/The Long Way Around	1969	3.00	6.00	12.00
❏ 2767		Lovesick Blues/Will You Love Me Tomorrow	1970	2.00	4.00	8.00
❏ 2846		Long Long Time/Nobody's	1970	2.00	4.00	8.00
❏ 3021		The Long Way Around/(She's a) Very Lovely Woman	1971		3.00	6.00
❏ 3210		I Fall to Pieces/Can It Be True	1971		3.00	6.00
❏ 3273		Rock Me on the Water/Crazy Arms	1972		3.00	6.00
❏ 3990		You're No Good/I Can't Help It (If I'm Still in Love with You)	1974		2.00	4.00
❏ 4050		When Will I Be Loved/It Doesn't Matter Anymore	1975		2.00	4.00

Elektra

❏ 64427		The Waiting/Walk On	1995			3.00
❏ 64987		All My Life/Shattered	1990			3.00
		With Aaron Neville				
❏ 69261		Don't Know Much/Cry Like a Rainstorm	1989			3.00
		With Aaron Neville				

MCA

❏ 52973		Somewhere Out There/(Instrumental)	1986			3.00
		With James Ingram				
❏ 52973	PS	Somewhere Out There/(Instrumental)	1986		2.00	4.00

Roomates, The

(Also see "Cathy Jean and the Roomates")

Ban

❏ 691		A Place Called Love/Knowing You	1985		2.50	5.00

Cameo

❏ 233		Sunday Kind of Love/ A Lovely Way to Spend An Evening	1962	7.50	15.00	30.00

Canadian American

❏ 166		My Heart/Just for Tonight	1964	10.00	20.00	40.00

Philips

❏ 40105		Gee/Answer Me, My Love	1963	6.25	12.50	25.00
❏ 40153		The Nearness of You/Don't Cheat on Me	1963	6.25	12.50	25.00

Promo

❏ 2211		I Want a Little Girl/Making Believe	196?	5.00	10.00	20.00
		Sources conflict as to date (1960 or 1964)				

Valmor

❏ 008		Glory of Love/Never Know	1961	5.00	10.00	20.00
❏ 010		Band of Gold/O Baby Love	1961	5.00	10.00	20.00
❏ 013		My Foolish Heart/My Kisses for Your Thoughts	1962	5.00	10.00	20.00

Rooney, Teddy

Imperial

❏ 5644		Bite Your Tongue/After the Dance	1960	10.00	20.00	40.00

Rose Garden, The

Atco

❏ 6510		Next Plane to London/Flower Town	1967	3.00	6.00	12.00
❏ 6564		Here's Today/If My World Falls Through	1968	2.50	5.00	10.00

Rose Royce

Atlantic

❏ 88942		Perfect Lover/You Get Right Down To It	1989			3.00

C&R

❏ 7684		Magic Touch/(B-side unknown)	1984		2.50	5.00

Epic

❏ 02818		Best Love/Dance with Me	1982		2.00	4.00
❏ 02996		Fire in the Funk/Still in Love	1982		2.00	4.00
❏ 03319		Somehow We Made It Through the Rain/You Blew It	1982		2.00	4.00

Number	Title (A Side/B Side)	Year	VG	VG+	NM

MCA
❏ 40615	Car Wash/Water	1976		2.50	5.00
❏ 40662	I Wanna Get Next to You/Sunrise	1976		2.50	5.00
❏ 40721	I'm Going Down/Yo Yo	1977		2.50	5.00
❏ 40814	Ooh Boy/Put Your Money Where Your Mouth Is	1977		2.50	5.00

Omni
| ❏ 99476 | Lonely Road/I Found Someone | 1987 | | | 3.00 |
| ❏ 99488 | Doesn't Have to Be That Way/You're My Peace of Mind | 1986 | | | 3.00 |

Whitfield
❏ 8440	Do Your Dance -- Part 1/Do Your Dance -- Part 2	1977		2.50	5.00
❏ 8491	Ooh Boy/You Can't Please Everybody	1977		2.50	5.00
❏ 8531	Wishing on a Star/Love, More Love	1978		2.50	5.00
❏ 8629	I'm in Love (And I Love the Feeling)/ Get Up Off Your Fat	1978		2.50	5.00
❏ 8712	Love Don't Live Here Anymore/ That's What's Wrong with Me	1978		2.50	5.00
❏ 8789	First Come, First Serve/Let Me Be the First to Know	1979		2.50	5.00
❏ 49049	Is It Love You're After/You Can't Run from Yourself	1979		2.50	5.00
❏ 49127	What You Waitin' For/Shine Your Light	1979		2.50	5.00
❏ 49274	Pop Your Fingers/I Wonder Where You Are Tonight	1980		2.50	5.00
❏ 49583	You're a Winner/Pazazz	1980		2.50	5.00
❏ 49624	Funkin' Around/Help Yourself	1980		2.50	5.00
❏ 49681	Golden Touch/Love Is In the Air	1981		2.50	5.00
❏ 49735	I Wanna Make It with You/Love Is in the Air	1981		2.50	5.00
❏ 49830	Fight It/R.R. Express	1981		2.50	5.00

Rosella, Carmela
Nancy
| ❏ 1004 | Oh, It Was Elvis/Where? | 1961 | 10.00 | 20.00 | 40.00 |

Rosie
RCA
| ❏ PB-11090 | Mississippi Baby/Words Don't Matter | 1977 | | 2.00 | 4.00 |

RCA Victor
| ❏ PB-10610 | Roll Me Through the Rushes/Denny's Ditty | 1976 | | 2.00 | 4.00 |

Rosie and the Originals
Brunswick
| ❏ 55205 | Lonely Blue Nights/We'll Have a Chance
By "Rosie, formerly with the Originals" | 1961 | 6.25 | 12.50 | 25.00 |
| ❏ 55212 | My Darling Forever/The Time Is Near
By "Rosie, formerly with the Originals" | 1961 | 6.25 | 12.50 | 25.00 |

Highland
| ❏ 1011 | Angel Baby/Give Me Love | 1960 | 7.50 | 15.00 | 30.00 |

Ross, Diana
(Also see "Supremes, The" and duet partner below)
Columbia
| ❏ 04507 | All of You/The Last Time
A-side: Diana Ross and Julio Iglesias; B-side: Iglesias solo | 1984 | | | 3.00 |
| ❏ 04507 | PS All of You/The Last Time | 1984 | | | 3.00 |

MCA
❏ 40947	Ease On Down the Road/Poppy Girls With Michael Jackson	1978		2.50	5.00
❏ 40947	PS Ease On Down the Road/Poppy Girls With Michael Jackson	1978		2.50	5.00
❏ 53448	If We Hold On Together/(Instrumental)	1988			3.00

Motown
❏ 1165	Reach Out and Touch (Somebody's Hand)/ Dark Side of the World	1970		2.50	5.00
❏ 1165	PS Reach Out and Touch (Somebody's Hand)/ Dark Side of the World	1970	3.00	6.00	12.00
❏ 1169	Ain't No Mountain High Enough/ Can't It Wait Until Tomorrow	1970		2.50	5.00
❏ 1169	PS Ain't No Mountain High Enough/ Can't It Wait Until Tomorrow	1970	3.00	6.00	12.00
❏ 1176	Remember Me/What About You	1971		2.50	5.00
❏ 1176	PS Remember Me/What About You	1971	3.00	6.00	12.00
❏ 1184	Reach Out I'll Be There/Close to You	1971		2.50	5.00
❏ 1188	Surrender/I'm a Winner	1971		2.50	5.00
❏ 1192	I'm Still Waiting/A Simple Thing Like Cry	1971		2.50	5.00
❏ 1211	Good Morning Heartache/God Bless the Child	1972		2.50	5.00
❏ 1211	PS Good Morning Heartache/God Bless the Child	1972	2.50	5.00	10.00
❏ 1239	Touch Me in the Morning/ I Won't Last a Day Without You	1973		2.50	5.00
❏ 1278	Last Time I Saw Him/Save the Children	1973		2.50	5.00
❏ 1295	Sleepin'/You	1974		2.50	5.00
❏ 1335	Sorry Doesn't Always Make It Right/Together	1975		2.50	5.00
❏ 1377	Do You Know Where You're Going To/ No One's Gonna Be a Fool Forever Possibly Canadian release only, with different A-side title	1975	3.00	6.00	12.00
❏ 1377	Theme from Mahogany (Do You Know Where You're Going To)/ No One's Gonna Be a Fool Forever	1975		2.50	5.00

Number		Title (A Side/B Side)	Year	VG	VG+	NM
❏ 1377	PS	Theme from Mahogany (Do You Know Where You're Going To)/ No One's Gonna Be a Fool Forever	1975	5.00	10.00	20.00
❏ 1387		I Thought It Took a Little Time (But Today I Fell in Love)/After You	1976		2.50	5.00
❏ 1392		Love Hangover/Kiss Me Now	1976		2.50	5.00
❏ 1398		One Love in My Lifetime/Smile	1976		2.50	5.00
❏ 1427		Gettin' Ready for Love/Confide in Me	1977		2.50	5.00
❏ 1436		Your Love Is So Good for Me/Baby It's Me	1978		2.50	5.00
❏ 1442		You Got It/Too Shy to Say	1978		2.50	5.00
❏ 1450		Lovin' Livin' and Givin'/Baby It's Me	1978			Unreleased
❏ 1456		What You Gave Me/Together	1979		2.00	4.00
❏ 1462		The Boss/I'm in the World	1979		2.00	4.00
❏ 1471		It's My House/Sparkle	1979		2.00	4.00
❏ 1491		I'm Coming Out/Friend to Friend	1980		2.00	4.00
❏ 1494		Upside Down/Friend to Friend	1980		2.00	4.00
❏ 1496		It's My Turn/Together	1980		2.00	4.00
❏ 1496	PS	It's My Turn/Together	1980	3.00	6.00	12.00
❏ 1508		One More Chance/After You	1981		2.00	4.00
❏ 1513		Crying My Heart Out for You/To Love Again	1981		2.00	4.00
❏ 1519		Endless Love/(Instrumental)	1981		2.00	4.00
		With Lionel Richie				
❏ 1531		My Old Piano/Now That You're Gone	1981		2.00	4.00
❏ 1626		We Can Never Light That Old Flame Again/ Old Funky Rolls	1982		2.00	4.00
❏ 1924		Workin' Overtime/(Instrumental)	1989			3.00
❏ 1924	PS	Workin' Overtime/(Instrumental)	1989			3.00
❏ 1998		This House/Paradise	1989			3.00
❏ 2003		Bottom Line/(Instrumental)	1989			3.00
❏ 2139		When You Tell Me That You Love Me/You and I	1991		2.00	4.00
RCA						
❏ 5172-7-R		Dirty Looks/So Close	1987			3.00
❏ 5172-7-R	PS	Dirty Looks/So Close	1987			3.00
❏ 5297-7-R		Tell Me Again/I Am Me	1987			3.00
❏ PB-12349		Why Do Fools Fall in Love/Think I'm in Love	1981		2.00	4.00
❏ JB-13013	DJ	Endless Love (Long)/Endless Love (Short)	1981	2.50	5.00	10.00
		Promo only				
❏ PB-13021		Mirror, Mirror/Sweet Nothings	1981		2.00	4.00
❏ PB-13201		Work That Body/You Can Make It	1982		2.00	4.00
❏ PB-13348		Muscles/I Am Me	1982		2.00	4.00
❏ PB-13348	PS	Muscles/I Am Me	1982		2.00	4.00
❏ PB-13424		So Close/Fool for Your Love	1983		2.00	4.00
❏ GB-13479		Why Do Fools Fall in Love/Mirror, Mirror	1983			3.00
		Gold Standard Series				
❏ PB-13549		Pieces of Ice/Still in Love	1983		2.00	4.00
❏ PB-13549	PS	Pieces of Ice/Still in Love	1983		2.00	4.00
❏ PB-13624		Up Front/Love or Loneliness	1983		2.00	4.00
❏ PB-13671		Let's Go Up/Girls	1983		2.00	4.00
❏ GB-13798		Muscles/Pieces of Ice	1984			3.00
		Gold Standard Series				
❏ PB-13864		Swept Away/Fight for It	1984			3.00
❏ PB-13864	PS	Swept Away/Fight for It	1984			3.00
❏ PB-13966		Missing You/We Are the Children of the World	1984			3.00
❏ PB-13966	PS	Missing You/We Are the Children of the World	1984			3.00
❏ PB-14032		Telephone/Fool for Your Love	1985			3.00
❏ PB-14032	PS	Telephone/Fool for Your Love	1985			3.00
❏ PB-14181		Eaten Alive/(Instrumental)	1985			3.00
❏ PB-14181	PS	Eaten Alive/(Instrumental)	1985			3.00
❏ PB-14244		Chain Reaction/More and More	1985		2.00	4.00
❏ PB-14244	PS	Chain Reaction/More and More	1985			3.00
❏ PB-14244		Chain Reaction (Remix)/More and More	1986			3.00
❏ GB-14342		Missing You/Swept Away	1986			3.00
		Gold Standard Series				

Ross, Diana, and Marvin Gaye

Motown

❏ 1269		My Mistake (Was to Love You)/Include Me in Your Life	1973		2.50	5.00
❏ 1280		You're a Special Part of Me/I'm Falling in Love with You	1973		2.50	5.00
❏ 1296		Don't Knock My Love/Just Say Just Say	1974		2.50	5.00

Ross, Diana, and the Supremes – See "Supremes, The"

Ross, Diana; Marvin Gaye; Smokey Robinson; and Stevie Wonder

Motown

❏ 1455		Pops, We Love You/(Instrumental)	1979		2.00	4.00

Rossington

(Also see "Lynyrd Skynyrd")

Atlantic

❏ 89364		Turn It Up/The Path Less Chosen	1986			3.00

Number		Title (A Side/B Side)	Year	VG	VG+	NM

Rossington-Collins Band
(Surviving members of Lynyrd Skynyrd [Gary Rossington, Allen Collins] with lead singer Dale Krantz)
MCA

❑ 41284		Don't Misunderstand Me/Winners and Losers	1980		2.00	4.00
❑ 51023		Getaway/Sometimes You Can Put It Out	1980		2.00	4.00
❑ 51218		Don't Stop Me Now/Gotta Get It Straight	1981		2.00	4.00

Rossini, Toni
Sun

❑ 349		I Gotta Know/Is It Too Late	1960	5.00	10.00	20.00
❑ 366		Well I Ask Ya/Darlena	1961	5.00	10.00	20.00
❑ 378		Meet Me After School/Just Around the Corner	1962	5.00	10.00	20.00
❑ 380		New Girl in Town/You Made It Sound So Easy	1962	5.00	10.00	20.00
❑ 387		Nobody/Moved to Kansas City	1964	5.00	10.00	20.00

Rotary Connection
(With Minnie Riperton)
Cadet Concept

❑ 7000		Like a Rollin' Stone/Turn Me On	1967	2.50	5.00	10.00
❑ 7002		Ruby Tuesday/Soul Man	1968	2.50	5.00	10.00
❑ 7007		Paper Castle/Teach Me How to Fly	1968	2.50	5.00	10.00
❑ 7008		Aladdin/Magical World	1968	2.50	5.00	10.00
❑ 7009		Silent Night Chant/Peace At Last	1968	2.50	5.00	10.00
❑ 7014		The Weight/Respect	1969	2.50	5.00	10.00
❑ 7018		Want You to Know/Memory Band	1969	2.50	5.00	10.00
❑ 7021		Love Me Now/May Our Amens Be True	1970	2.50	5.00	10.00
❑ 7027		Stormy Monday Blues/Teach Me How to Fly	1970	2.50	5.00	10.00
❑ 7028		Hey Love/If I Sing My Song	1971	2.50	5.00	10.00
		As "New Rotary Connection"				

Janus

❑ 249		Living Alone/Magical World	1975		2.50	5.00
		As "Minnie Riperton and Rotary Connection"				

Rotations, The
(More than one group)
Frantic

❑ 200		Put a Nickel on D-9/(B-side unknown)	1965	37.50	75.00	150.00
❑ 202		Changed Man/(B-side unknown)	1967	25.00	50.00	100.00

Mala

❑ 576		Misty Roses/Trying to Make You My Own	1967	7.50	15.00	30.00

Original Sound

❑ 41		The Crusher/Heavies	1964	25.00	50.00	100.00
		Produced by Frank Zappa				

Roth, David Lee
(Formerly of Van Halen)
Warner Bros.

❑ 27825		Skyscraper/Damn Good	1988			3.00
❑ 28108		Stand Up/Knucklebones	1988			3.00
❑ 28108	PS	Stand Up/Knucklebones	1988			3.00
❑ 28119		Just Like Paradise/Bottom Line	1988			3.00
❑ 28119	PS	Just Like Paradise/Bottom Line	1988			3.00
❑ 28511		That's Life/Bump and Grind	1986			3.00
❑ 28511	PS	That's Life/Bump and Grind	1986			3.00
❑ 28584		Goin' Crazy!/Occo Deo Calor!	1986			3.00
❑ 28584	PS	Goin' Crazy!/Occo Deo Calor!	1986			3.00
❑ 28656		Yankee Rose/Shyboy	1986			3.00
❑ 28656	PS	Yankee Rose/Shyboy	1986			3.00
❑ 29040		Just a Gigolo-I Ain't Got Nobody/Just a Gigolo-I Ain't Got Nobody	1985			3.00
❑ 29040	PS	Just a Gigolo-I Ain't Got Nobody/Just a Gigolo-I Ain't Got Nobody	1985			3.00
❑ 29102		California Girls/California Girls (Remix)	1985			3.00
❑ 29102	PS	California Girls/California Girls (Remix)	1985			3.00

Roulettes, The
(More than one group)
Angle

❑ 1001		Surfer's Charge/Archibald II (Duke of Nothing)	1963	12.50	25.00	50.00

Champ

❑ 102		I See a Star/Come On, Baby	1958	12.50	25.00	50.00

Ebb

❑ 124		The Way You Carry On/You Don't Care Anymore	1957	7.50	15.00	30.00

Scepter

❑ 1204		Hasten Jason/Wouldn't It Be Goin' Steady	1959	100.00	200.00	400.00

United Artists

❑ 718		Can You Go/Soon You'll Be Leaving Me	1964	2.50	5.00	10.00
❑ 990		Long Cigarette/Junk	1966	2.50	5.00	10.00

Routers, The
Mercury

❑ 73418		Superbird/Sack of Woe	1973		3.00	6.00

Number		Title (A Side/B Side)	Year	VG	VG+	NM
Warner Bros.						
❑ 5283		Let's Go (pony)/Mashy	1962	3.75	7.50	15.00
❑ 5332		Half Time/Make It Snappy	1963	3.00	6.00	12.00
❑ 5349		Sting Ray/Snap Happy	1963	3.00	6.00	12.00
❑ 5379		A-Ooga/Big Band	1963	3.00	6.00	12.00
❑ 5403		Snap, Crackle and Pop/Amoeba	1963	3.00	6.00	12.00
❑ 5444		Crack Up/Let's Dance	1964	3.00	6.00	12.00
❑ 5467		Stamp and Shake/Ah-Ya	1964	3.00	6.00	12.00
❑ 7117		Let's Go (pony)/Mashy	1967	2.50	5.00	10.00

Rovers, The
(Also see "Irish Rovers, The" – the Cleveland and Epic records are by that group renamed)

Capitol						
❑ F3078		Why Oh-h/Ichi-Bon Tami Dachi	1955	10.00	20.00	40.00
Cleveland Int'l.						
❑ 02148		Mexican Girl/Pheasant Pluckers Son	1981		2.00	4.00
❑ 02728		Daddys/Pain in My Past	1982		2.00	4.00
❑ 02911		People Who Read People Magazine/Roly Poly Ladies	1982		2.00	4.00
❑ 51007		Wasn't That a Party/	1981		2.50	5.00
		Match Stalk Men and Match Stalk Cats & Dogs				
Epic						
❑ 03089		Wasn't That a Party/Pain in My Past	1982			3.00
		Reissue				
Music City						
❑ 750		Why Oh-h/Ichi-Bon Tami Dachi	1954	12.50	25.00	50.00
❑ 750		Why Oh-h/Ichi-Bon Tami Dachi	1954	50.00	100.00	200.00
		Red vinyl				
❑ 780		Salute to Johnny Ace/Jadda	1955	12.50	25.00	50.00
❑ 780		Salute to Johnny Ace/Jadda	1955	50.00	100.00	200.00
		Red vinyl				

Roxette

Capitol						
❑ B-5380		Teaser Japanese/Can You Touch Me	1984		3.00	6.00
❑ S7-17400		Almost Unreal/The Heart Shaped Sea	1993		2.00	4.00
EMI						
❑ 7PRO-04409	DJ	Listen to Your Heart (same on both sides)	1989	2.00	4.00	8.00
		Vinyl originally was promo only				
❑ S7-18044		Sleeping in My Car/The Look (Unplugged)	1994		2.00	4.00
		Yellow vinyl				
❑ S7-18128		Crash! Boom! Bang!/Joyride (Unplugged)	1994		2.00	4.00
		Yellow vinyl				
❑ 50190		The Look/Silver Blue	1989		2.00	4.00
❑ 50204		Dressed for Success/The Look	1989		2.00	4.00
❑ 50223		Listen to Your Heart/Half a Woman, Half a Shadow	1990	2.50	5.00	10.00
❑ 50233		Dangerous/Dangerous (12" Version)	1990	2.50	5.00	10.00
❑ 50283		It Must Have Been Love/Chances	1990	2.50	5.00	10.00
❑ S7-57697		Church of Your Heart/I Call Your Name	1992		2.00	4.00
❑ S7-57991		How Do You Do!/Fading Like a Flower (Live)	1992		2.00	4.00

Roxy Music

Atco						
❑ 7018		The Thrill of It All/The Application Failed	1975		2.00	4.00
❑ 7042		Love Is the Drug/Both Ends Burning	1975		2.00	4.00
❑ 7100		Dance Away/Trash 2	1979		2.00	4.00
❑ 7204		Angel Eyes/My Little Girl	1979		2.00	4.00
❑ 7301		Over You/My Only Love	1980		2.00	4.00
❑ 7310		Oh Yeah (On the Radio)/Rain, Rain, Rain	1980		2.00	4.00
❑ 7315		In the Midnight Hour/(B-side unknown)	1980		2.00	4.00
❑ 7329		Jealous Guy/To Turn You On	1981		2.00	4.00
❑ 7329	PS	Jealous Guy/To Turn You On	1981		2.00	4.00
Atlantic						
❑ 13269		Love Is the Drug/Dance Away	198?			3.00
		Oldies Series reissue				
Reprise						
❑ 1124		Virginia Plan/The Numberer	1972		2.50	5.00
Warner Bros.						
❑ GWB 0316		Do the Strand/Virginia Plain	197?			3.00
		"Back to Back Hits" series				
❑ 7719		Do the Strand/Editions of You	1973		2.50	5.00
❑ 29912		More Than This/Always Unknowing	1982			3.00
❑ 29978		Take a Chance with Me/India	1982			3.00
❑ 29978	PS	Take a Chance with Me/India	1982			3.00

Royal Drifters, The

Teen						
❑ 506		S'Why Hard/Little Linda	1959	25.00	50.00	100.00
❑ 508		To Each His Own/Da Kind	1959	37.50	75.00	150.00

Royal Guardsmen, The

Laurie						
❑ 3359		Baby Let's Wait/Leaving Me	1966	2.50	5.00	10.00
❑ 3366		Snoopy vs. the Red Baron/I Needed You	1966	3.00	6.00	12.00
❑ 3379		The Return of the Red Baron/Sweetmeats Slide	1967	2.50	5.00	10.00

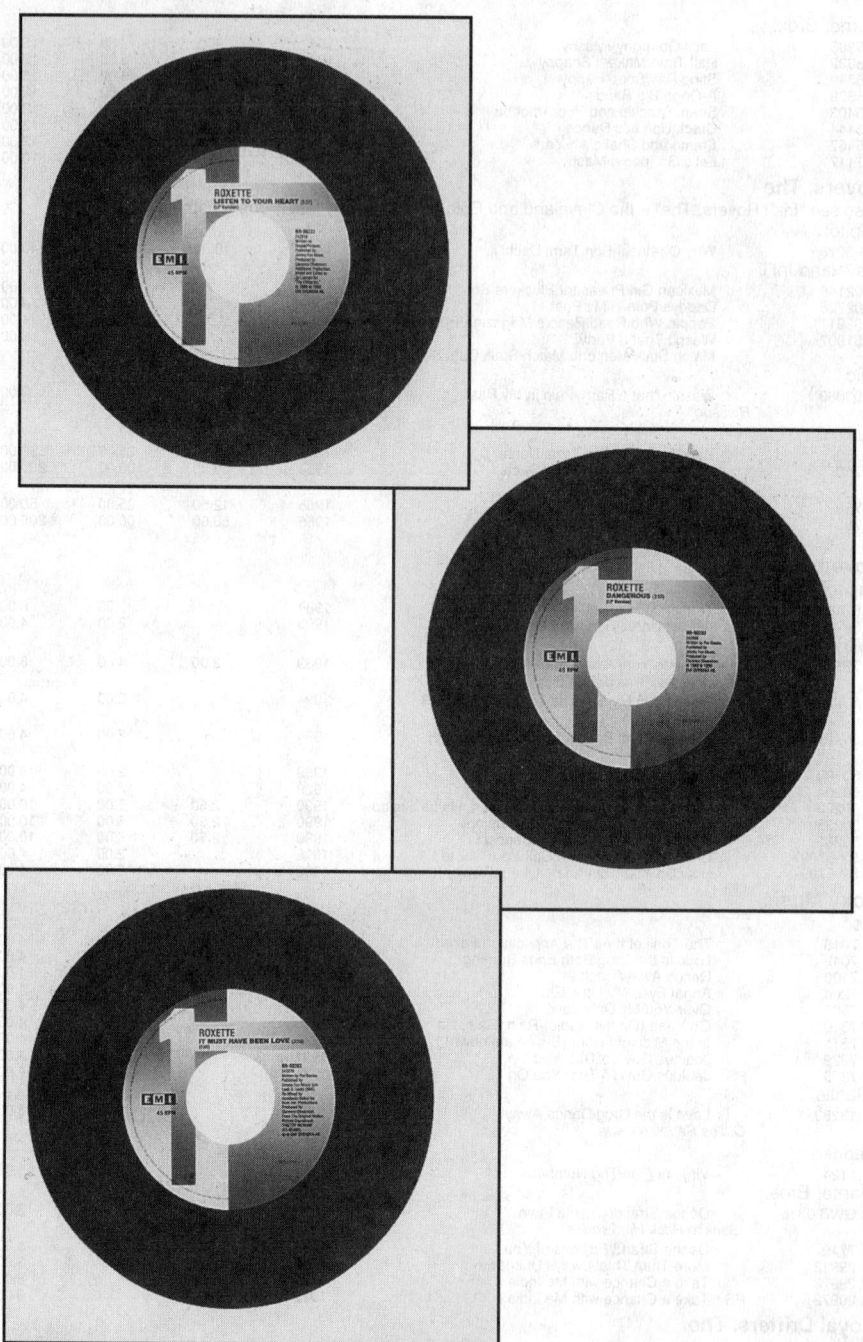

These records don't exist, if you believe trade publications and most other sources. But here are three singles by the Swedish group Roxette, done on EMI labels by Capitol here in America in 1990 because of demand for the three titles. From the top: "Listen to Your Heart"; "Dangerous"; and "It Must Have Been Love." All three were pressed in small quantities with limited distribution. They are pictured for the first time.

Number	Title (A Side/B Side)	Year	VG	VG+	NM
❏ 3391	Airplane Song (My Airplane)/Om	1967	2.00	4.00	8.00
❏ 3397	Wednesday/So Right (To Be in Love)	1967	2.00	4.00	8.00
❏ 3416	Snoopy's Christmas/It Kinda Looks Like Christmas	1967	2.50	5.00	10.00
❏ 3428	I Say Love/I'm Not Gonna Stay	1968	2.00	4.00	8.00
❏ 3451	Snoopy for President/Down Behind the Lines	1968	2.00	4.00	8.00
❏ 3461	Baby Let's Wait/Biplane "Evermore"	1968	2.00	4.00	8.00
❏ 3461	Baby Let's Wait/So Right (To Be in Love)	1968	2.00	4.00	8.00
❏ 3494	Magic Window/Mother, Where's Your Daughter	1969	2.50	5.00	10.00
❏ 3590	Snoopy for President/Down Behind the Lines	1972		3.00	6.00
❏ 3646	Snoopy for President/Sweetmeats Slide	1976		2.50	5.00

Royal Halos, The
Aladdin

❏ 3460	My Love Is True/Nobody But Me and My Girl	1959	10.00	20.00	40.00

Royal Holidays, The
Carlton

❏ 472	Margaret/I'm Sorry	1958	6.25	12.50	25.00

Herald

❏ 536	Rockin' at the Bandstand/Down in Cuba	1959	37.50	75.00	150.00

Most, and perhaps all, copies were labeled "Chip Chip"/"Running to You" by the Mello-Kings

Penthouse

❏ 9357	Margaret/I'm Sorry	1958	37.50	75.00	150.00

Royal Teens, The
ABC-Paramount

❏ 9882	Short Shorts/Planet Rock	1958	7.50	15.00	30.00
❏ 9918	Big Name Button/Sham Rock	1958	6.25	12.50	25.00
❏ 9945	Harvey's Got a Girl Friend/Hangin' Around	1958	6.25	12.50	25.00
❏ 9955	Open the Door/My Kind of Dream	1958	6.25	12.50	25.00

Allnew

❏ 1415	Short Short Twist/Royal Twist	1962	5.00	10.00	20.00

Astra

❏ 1012	Mad Gass/Sittin' with My Baby	196?	3.75	7.50	15.00

Capitol

❏ 4335	The Moon's Not Meant for Lovers/Was It a Dream	1960	7.50	15.00	30.00
❏ 4402	With You/It's the Talk of the Town	1960	7.50	15.00	30.00
❏ F4261	Believe Me/Little Cricket	1959	7.50	15.00	30.00

Jubilee

❏ 5418	Short Short Twist/Royal Twist	1962	3.75	7.50	15.00

Mighty

❏ 111	Leotards/Royal Blues	1959	6.25	12.50	25.00
❏ 112	Cave Man/Wounded Heart	1959	7.50	15.00	30.00
❏ 200	My Memories of You/Little Trixie	1961	10.00	20.00	40.00

Musicor

❏ 1398	Smile a Little Smile for Me/Hey Jude	1969	2.50	5.00	10.00

Power

❏ 113	Mad Gass/Sittin' with My Baby	1959	10.00	20.00	40.00
❏ 215	Short Shorts/Planet Rock	1957	25.00	50.00	100.00

Swan

❏ 4200	I'll Love You ('Til the End of Time)/(Instrumental)	1965	25.00	50.00	100.00

TCF Hall

❏ 117	Bad Girl/Do the Montoona	1965	3.75	7.50	15.00

Royal Tones, The
Titanic

❏ 5014	Black Lightnin'/Surfer's Junction	1964	15.00	30.00	60.00

Royal, Billy Joe
All Wood

❏ 401	Wait for Me Baby/If It Wasn't for a Woman	1962	5.00	10.00	20.00

Atlantic

❏ 2328	Never in a Hundred Years/ We Haven't a Moment to Lose	1966	2.50	5.00	10.00
❏ 87770	If the Jukebox Took Teardrops/How Could You	1991		2.00	4.00
❏ 87867	Ring Where a Ring Used to Be/We Need to Walk	1990		2.00	4.00
❏ 87933	Searchin' for Some Kind of Clue/This Too Shall Pass	1990		2.00	4.00
❏ 88815	Till I Can't Take It Anymore/He Don't Know	1990		2.00	4.00

Atlantic America

❏ 99217	Love Has No Right/Cross My Heart and Hope to Try	1989			3.00
❏ 99242	Tell It Like It Is/Losing You	1989			3.00
❏ 99295	It Keeps Right On Hurtin'/Let It Rain	1988			3.00
❏ 99364	Out of Sight and On My Mind/ She Don't Cry Like She Used To	1988			3.00
❏ 99404	I'll Pin a Note on Your Pillow/A Place for a Heartache	1987			3.00
❏ 99519	I Miss You Already/Another Endless Night	1986			3.00
❏ 99555	Boardwalk Angel/Out of Sight and On My Mind	1986			3.00
❏ 99599	Burned Like a Rocket/Lonely Loving You	1985			3.00

Number		Title (A Side/B Side)	Year	VG	VG+	NM
Columbia						
❏ 43305		Down in the Boondocks/Oh, What a Night	1965	2.50	5.00	10.00
❏ 43305	DJ	Down in the Boondocks (same on both sides)	1965	10.00	20.00	40.00
		Red vinyl promo				
❏ 43390		I Knew You When/Steal Away	1965	2.50	5.00	10.00
❏ 43465		I've Got to Be Somebody/	1965	2.00	4.00	8.00
		You Make Me Feel Like a Man				
❏ 43538		It's a Good Time/Don't Wait Up for Me Mama	1966	2.00	4.00	8.00
❏ 43622		Heart's Desire/Keep Inside Me	1966	2.00	4.00	8.00
❏ 43740		Campfire Girls/Should I Come Back	1966	2.00	4.00	8.00
❏ 43883		Yo-Yo/We Tried	1966	2.00	4.00	8.00
❏ 44003		Wisdom of a Fool/Everything Turned Blue	1967	2.00	4.00	8.00
❏ 44103		These Are Not My People/The Greatest Love	1967	2.00	4.00	8.00
❏ 44277		Hush/Watching from the Bandstand	1967	2.00	4.00	8.00
❏ 44468		Don't You Be Ashamed (To Call My Name)/	1968	2.00	4.00	8.00
		Don't You Think It's Time				
❏ 44574		Storybook Children/Just Between You and Me	1968	2.00	4.00	8.00
❏ 44677		Movies in My Mind/Gabriel	1968		3.00	6.00
❏ 44743		Bed of Roses/The Greatest Love	1969		3.00	6.00
❏ 44814		Nobody Loves You But Me/Baby I'm Thinking of You	1969		2.50	5.00
❏ 44902		Cherry Hill Park/Helping Hand	1969	2.00	4.00	8.00
❏ 45085		Mama's Song/Me Without You	1970		2.50	5.00
❏ 45220		Burning a Hole/Every Night	1970		2.50	5.00
❏ 45289		Tulsa/Pick Up the Pieces	1970		2.50	5.00
❏ 45406		Poor Little Pearl/Lady Lives to Love	1971		2.50	5.00
❏ 45495		Colorado Rain/We Go Back	1971		2.50	5.00
❏ 45557		Later/The Family	1972		3.00	6.00
❏ 45620		Child of Mine/Natchez Trace	1972		3.00	6.00
Fairlane						
❏ 21009		Never in a Hundred Years/	1961	7.50	15.00	30.00
		We Haven't a Moment to Lose				
❏ 21013		Dark Glasses/Perhaps	1962	7.50	15.00	30.00
Kat Family						
❏ 01044		(Who is Like You) Sweet America/	1981		2.00	4.00
		No Love Like a First Love				
❏ 02074		You Really Got a Hold on Me/No Love Like a First Love	1981		2.00	4.00
❏ 02297		Wasted Time/Outrun the Sun	1981		2.00	4.00
Mercury						
❏ 76069		Mr. Kool/Let's Talk It Over	1980		2.00	4.00
❏ 888 680-7		Members Only/Funny Face	1987			3.00
		A-side with Donna Fargo; B-side by Fargo solo				
MGM South						
❏ 7011		This Magic Moment/Mountain Woman	1973		2.50	5.00
❏ 7018		Summertime Skies/Look What I Found	1973		2.50	5.00
❏ 7022		If This Is the Last Time/Perfect Harmony	1973		2.50	5.00
❏ 7032		Star Again/Sugar Blue	1974		2.50	5.00
Player's						
❏ 1		I'm Specialized/Really You	1965	5.00	10.00	20.00
Private Stock						
❏ 45,192		Under the Boardwalk/Precious Time	1978		2.50	5.00
❏ 45,212	DJ	Anchors Aweigh (mono/stereo)	1979		2.50	5.00
Scepter						
❏ 12419		All Night Rain/Time Don't Pass By Here	1976		2.00	4.00
Tollie						
❏ 9011		Mama Didn't Raise No Fools/Get Behind Me, Devil	1964	3.75	7.50	15.00

Royalettes, The

Number		Title (A Side/B Side)	Year	VG	VG+	NM
Chancellor						
❏ 1133		No Big Thing/Yesterday's Lovers	1963	5.00	10.00	20.00
❏ 1140		Willie the Wolf/Blue Summer	1963	3.75	7.50	15.00
MGM						
❏ 13283		He's Gone/Don't You Cry	1964	3.00	6.00	12.00
❏ 13327		Poor Boy/Watch What Happens	1965	3.00	6.00	12.00
❏ 13366		It's Gonna Take a Miracle/Out of Sight, Out of Mind	1965	3.75	7.50	15.00
❏ 13405		I Want to Meet Him/Never Again	1965	3.00	6.00	12.00
❏ 13451		You Bring Me Down/Only When You're Lonely	1966	3.00	6.00	12.00
❏ 13507		It's a Big Mistake/It's Better Not to Know	1966	3.00	6.00	12.00
❏ 13544		I Don't Want to Be the One/An Affair to Remember	1966	3.00	6.00	12.00
❏ 13588		Love Without An End/When Summer's Gone	1966	3.00	6.00	12.00
❏ 13627		My Man/Take My Love	1966	3.00	6.00	12.00
Roulette						
❏ 4768		River of Ters/Something Wonderful	1967	2.50	5.00	10.00
Warner Bros.						
❏ 5439		There He Goes/Come to Me	1964	3.75	7.50	15.00

Royals, The

(More than one group)

Number		Title (A Side/B Side)	Year	VG	VG+	NM
Federal						
❏ 12064		Every Beat of My Heart/All Night Long	1952	200.00	400.00	800.00
❏ 12064AA		Every Beat of My Heart/All Night Long	1952	1,000	1,500	2,000
		Blue vinyl				

Number		Title (A Side/B Side)	Year	VG	VG+	NM
❏ 12077		I Know I Love You So/Starting From Tonight	1952	250.00	500.00	1,000
❏ 12088		Moonrise/Fifth Street Blues	1952	250.00	500.00	1,000
❏ 12088		Moonrise/Fifth Street Blues	1952	1,000	1,500	2,000
		Blue vinyl				
❏ 12098		A Love in My Heart/I'll Never Let You Go	1952	175.00	350.00	700.00
❏ 12113		Are You Forgetting?/What Did I Do	1952	175.00	350.00	700.00
❏ 12121		The Shrine of St. Cecelia/I Feel So Blue	1953	175.00	350.00	700.00
❏ 12133		Get It/No It Ain't	1953	50.00	100.00	200.00
❏ 12150		Hello Miss Fine/I Feel That-A-Way	1953	37.50	75.00	150.00
❏ 12160		That's It/Someone Like You	1953	37.50	75.00	150.00
❏ 12169		Work With Me Annie/Until I Die	1954	25.00	50.00	100.00
		Original pressing; for reissues, see "Midnighters, The"				
❏ 12177	DJ	Give It Up/That Woman	1954	25.00	50.00	100.00
		Evidently, some promos exist crediting The Royals. For stock copies, see "Midnighters, The"				

Okeh
❏ 6832		If You Love Me/Dreams of You	1951	150.00	300.00	600.00
		This Royals features Chuck Willis				

Penguin
❏ 1008		Thunder Wagon/Teen Beat	1959	7.50	15.00	30.00

Vagabond
❏ 134		Surfin' Lagoon/Wild Safari	1962	12.50	25.00	50.00
❏ 444		Christmas Party/White Christmas	1963	12.50	25.00	50.00
❏ 444		Christmas Party/White Christmas	1963	25.00	50.00	100.00
		Red vinyl				

Venus
❏ 103		Someday We'll Meet Again/ I Want You to Be My Mambo Baby	1954	100.00	200.00	400.00
		This Royals later became The Scooters				

Rozzi, Little Sammy
Pelham
❏ 722		Christine/Over the Rainbow	1961	50.00	100.00	200.00

Ruben and the Jets – See "Zappa, Frank"

Rubin
Kapp
❏ 869		You've Been Away/Baby, You're My Everything	1967	15.00	30.00	60.00

Ruby and the Romantics
A&M
❏ 1042		Hurting Each Other/ Baby, I Could Be So Good at Loving You	1969	2.00	4.00	8.00

ABC
❏ 10911		Twilight Time/Una Bella Brazilian Melody	1967	2.50	5.00	10.00
❏ 10941		Only Heaven Knows/This Is No Laughing Matter	1967	2.50	5.00	10.00
❏ 11065		On a Clear Day You Can See Forever/ More Than Yesterday, Less Than Tomorrow	1968	2.50	5.00	10.00

Kapp
❏ 501		Our Day Will Come/Moonlight and Music	1963	3.75	7.50	15.00
❏ 525		My Summer Love/Sweet Love and Sweet Forgiveness	1963	3.00	6.00	12.00
❏ 544		Hey There Lonely Boy/Not a Moment Too Soon	1963	3.00	6.00	12.00
❏ 544	PS	Hey There Lonely Boy/Not a Moment Too Soon	1963	3.75	7.50	15.00
❏ 557		Young Wings Can Fly (Higher Than You Know)/ Day Dreaming	1963	3.00	6.00	12.00
❏ 557	PS	Young Wings Can Fly (Higher Than You Know)/ Day Dreaming	1963	3.75	7.50	15.00
❏ 578		Our Everlasting Love/ Much Better Off Than I've Ever Been	1964	3.00	6.00	12.00
❏ 601		Baby Come Home/Every Day's a Holiday	1964	3.00	6.00	12.00
❏ 615		When You're Young and In Love/I Cry Alone	1964	3.00	6.00	12.00
❏ 646		Does He Really Care for Me/ Nevertheless (I'm in Love with You)	1965	3.00	6.00	12.00
❏ 665		We'll Meet Again/ Your Baby Doesn't Love You Anymore	1965	3.00	6.00	12.00
❏ 702		Nobody But My Baby/Imagination	1965	3.00	6.00	12.00
❏ 759		We Can Make It/Remember Me	1966	2.50	5.00	10.00
❏ 773		Hey There Lonely Boy/Think	1966	2.50	5.00	10.00
❏ 839		I Know/We'll Love Again	1967	2.50	5.00	10.00

Ruffin Brothers, The
Soul
❏ 35076		Stand By Me/Your Love Was Worth Waiting For	1970		2.50	5.00
❏ 35082		When My Love Hand Comes Do Down/ Steppin' On a Dream	1971		2.50	5.00
❏ 35086		Lo and Behold/The Things We Have to Do	1971		2.50	5.00
		As "David & Jimmy Ruffin"				

Ruffin, David
(Also see "Temptations, The")
Anna
❏ 1127		I'm in Love/One of These Days	1961	15.00	30.00	60.00

Number	Title (A Side/B Side)	Year	VG	VG+	NM
Check Mate					
❑ 1003	You Can Get What I Got/ Action Speaks Louder Than Words	1961	15.00	30.00	60.00
❑ 1010	Mr. Bus Driver -- Hurry!/Knock You Out (With Love)	1962	15.00	30.00	60.00
Motown					
❑ 1140	My Whole World Ended (The Moment You Left Me)/ I've Got to Find Myself a Brand New Baby	1968		3.00	6.00
❑ 1149	I've Lost Everything I've Ever Loved/ We'll Have a Good Thing Going On	1969		3.00	6.00
❑ 1158	I'm So Glad I Fell for You/ I Pray Every Day You Won't Regret Loving Me	1969		3.00	6.00
❑ 1178	Each Day Is a Lifetime/Don't Stop Loving Me	1971		3.00	6.00
❑ 1187	You Can Come Right Back to Me/Dinah	1971		3.00	6.00
❑ 1204	A Day in the Life of a Working Man/A Little More Trust	1972		3.00	6.00
❑ 1223	Blood Donors Needed/Go On with Your Bad Self	1973		3.00	6.00
❑ 1259	Common Man/I'm Just a Mortal Man	1973		3.00	6.00
❑ 1327	Me and Rock and Roll (Are Here to Stay)/ Smiling Faces Sometimes	1974		3.00	6.00
❑ 1332	Take Me Clear from Here/I Just Want to Celebrate	1975			Unreleased
❑ 1336	Superstar/No Matter Where	1975		2.50	5.00
❑ 1376	Walk Away from Love/ Love Can Be Hazardous to Your Health	1975		2.50	5.00
❑ 1388	Heavy Love/Love Can Be Hazardous To Your Health	1976		2.50	5.00
❑ 1393	Everything's Coming Up Love/No Matter Where	1976		2.50	5.00
❑ 1405	On and Off/Statue of a Fool	1976		2.50	5.00
❑ 1420	Just Let Me Hold You for a Night/ Rode by the Place (Where We Used to Stay)	1977		2.50	5.00
❑ 1435	You're My Peace of Mind/ Rode By the Place (Where We Used to Stay)	1978		2.50	5.00
Warner Bros.					
❑ 49030	Sexy Dancer/Break My Heart	1979		2.00	4.00
❑ 49123	I Get Excited/Chain on the Brain	1979		2.00	4.00
❑ 49277	Slow Dance/Don't You Go Home	1980		2.00	4.00
❑ 49577	Still in Love with You/I Wanna Be with You	1980		2.00	4.00

Ruffin, David, and Eddie Kendrick

(Also see individual listings and "Temptations, The")

RCA

| ❑ 5313-7-R | I Couldn't Believe It/Don't Know Why You're Dreamin' | 1987 | | | 3.00 |
| ❑ 6925-7-R | One More for the Lonely Hearts Club/ Don't Know Why You're Dreaming | 1988 | | | 3.00 |

Ruffin, Jimmy

(Also see "Ruffin Brothers, The")

Chess

| ❑ 2160 | Tell Me What You Want/Do You Know Me | 1974 | | 2.50 | 5.00 |
| ❑ 2168 | What You See (Ain't Always What You Get)/ Boy from Mississippi | 1975 | | 2.50 | 5.00 |

Epic

| ❑ 50339 | Fallin' in Love with You/Fallin' in Love with You | 1977 | | 2.50 | 5.00 |
| ❑ 50384 | Fallin' in Love with You/Fallin' in Love with You | 1977 | | 2.50 | 5.00 |

Miracle

| ❑ 1 | Don't Feel Sorry for Me/Heart | 1961 | 50.00 | 100.00 | 200.00 |

RSO

| ❑ 1021 | Hold On to My Love/(Instrumental) | 1980 | | 2.50 | 5.00 |
| ❑ 1042 | Night of Love/Searchin' | 1980 | | 2.50 | 5.00 |

Soul

❑ 35002	Since I've Lost You/I Want Her Love	1964	10.00	20.00	40.00
❑ 35016	As Long As There Is L-O-V-E/How Can I Say I'm Sorry	1965	2.50	5.00	10.00
❑ 35022	What Becomes of the Brokenhearted/Baby I've Got It	1966	2.00	4.00	8.00
❑ 35027	I've Passed This Way Before/Tomorrow's Tears	1966	2.00	4.00	8.00
❑ 35032	Gonna Give Her All the Love I've Got/ World So Wide (Nowhere to Hide from Your Heart)	1967	2.00	4.00	8.00
❑ 35035	Don't You Miss Me A Little Bit Baby/I Want Her Love	1967	2.00	4.00	8.00
❑ 35043	I'll Say Forever My Love/Everybody Needs Love	1968	2.00	4.00	8.00
❑ 35046	Don't Let Him Take Your Love from Me/ Lonely, Lonely Man Am I	1968	2.00	4.00	8.00
❑ 35053	Sad and Lonesome Feeling/ Gonna Keep On Trying Till I Win Your Love	1968	2.00	4.00	8.00
❑ 35060	Farewell Is a Lonely Sound/ If You Will Let Me, I Know I Can	1969	2.00	4.00	8.00
❑ 35077	Maria (You Were the Only One)/ Living in a World I Created For Myself	1970	2.00	4.00	8.00
❑ 35092	Our Favorite Melody/You Gave Me Love	1972		3.00	6.00

Rufus

(Many listed as "Rufus Featuring Chaka Khan" or as "Rufus And Chaka". Also see "Khan, Chaka")

ABC

❑ 11356	Slip 'N Slide/I Finally Found You	1973	2.00	4.00	8.00
❑ 11376	Whoever's Thrilling You (Is Killing Me)/ I Finally Found You	1973		3.00	6.00
❑ 11394	Feel Good/Keep It Coming	1973		3.00	6.00

Number		Title (A Side/B Side)	Year	VG	VG+	NM
☐ 11427		Tell Me Something Good/Smokin' Room	1974		3.00	6.00
☐ 12010		Tell Me Something Good/Smokin' Room	1974		2.50	5.00
☐ 12032		You Got the Love/Rags to Rufus	1974		2.50	5.00
☐ 12066		Once You Get Started/Rufusized	1975		2.50	5.00
☐ 12099		Please Pardon Me (You Remind Me of a Friend)/ Somebody's Watching You	1975		2.50	5.00
☐ 12149		Sweet Thing/Circles	1975		2.50	5.00
☐ 12179		Dance Wit' Me/Everybody's Got an Aura	1976		2.50	5.00
☐ 12197		Jive Talkin'/On Time	1976		2.50	5.00
☐ 12239		At Midnight (My Love Will Lift You Up)/Better Days	1976		2.50	5.00
☐ 12269		Hollywood/Earth Song	1977		2.50	5.00
☐ 12296		Everlasting Love/Close the Door	1977		2.50	5.00
☐ 12349		Stay/My Ship Will Sail	1978		2.50	5.00
☐ 12390		Blue Love/Turn	1978		2.50	5.00
☐ 12444		Keep It Together (Declaration of Love)/Red Hot Poker	1979		2.50	5.00

Epic

Number		Title (A Side/B Side)	Year	VG	VG+	NM
☐ 10691		Read All About It/Brand New Day	1971	3.00	6.00	12.00
☐ 10726		Follow the Lamb/Fire One, Fire Two, Fire Three	1971	3.00	6.00	12.00

MCA

Number		Title (A Side/B Side)	Year	VG	VG+	NM
☐ 41025		Ain't Nobody Like You/You're to Blame	1979		2.00	4.00
☐ 41131		Do You Love What You Feel/Dancin' Mood	1979		2.00	4.00
☐ 41191		What Am I Missing/Any Love	1980		2.00	4.00
☐ 41230		I'm Dancing for Your Love/Walk the Rockway	1980		2.00	4.00
☐ 51070		Tonight We Love/Afterwards	1981		2.00	4.00
☐ 51125		Party 'Til You're Broke/Hold On to a Friend	1981		2.00	4.00
☐ 51203		Sharing the Love/We Got the Way	1981		2.00	4.00
☐ 52002		True Love/Better Together	1982		2.00	4.00

Warner Bros.

Number		Title (A Side/B Side)	Year	VG	VG+	NM
☐ 29406		One Million Kisses/Stay	1983		2.00	4.00
☐ 29555		Ain't Nobody/Sweet Thing	1983		2.00	4.00
☐ 29675		Blinded by the Boogie/You're Really Out of Line	1983		2.00	4.00
☐ 29790		Take It to the Hop/Distant Lover	1983		2.00	4.00

Rufus and Carla

(Rufus and Carla Thomas, father and daughter. Also see individual entries)

Atco

Number		Title (A Side/B Side)	Year	VG	VG+	NM
☐ 6177		Cause I Love You/Deep Down Inside	1960	6.25	12.50	25.00
		As "Carla and Rufus"				
☐ 6199		I Didn't Believe/Yeah, Yea-Ah	1961	6.25	12.50	25.00
		As "Rufus and Friend"				

Satellite

Number		Title (A Side/B Side)	Year	VG	VG+	NM
☐ 102		Cause I Love You/Deep Down Inside	1960	10.00	20.00	40.00

Stax

Number		Title (A Side/B Side)	Year	VG	VG+	NM
☐ 151		That's Really Some Good/Night Time Is the Right Time	1964	3.00	6.00	12.00
☐ 176		When You Move You Lose/We're Tight	1965	3.00	6.00	12.00
☐ 184		Birds and Bees/Never Let You Go	1966	3.00	6.00	12.00

Rumblers, The

Dot

Number		Title (A Side/B Side)	Year	VG	VG+	NM
☐ 16421		Boss/I Don't Need You No More	1963	3.75	7.50	15.00
☐ 16455		Boss Strikes Back/Sorry	1963	3.75	7.50	15.00
☐ 16480		Angry Sea (Walmea)/Bugged	1963	3.75	7.50	15.00
☐ 16521		It's a Gas/Tootananny	1963	3.75	7.50	15.00

Downey

Number		Title (A Side/B Side)	Year	VG	VG+	NM
☐ 103		Boss/I Don't Need You No More	1962	7.50	15.00	30.00
☐ 106		Boss Strikes Back/Sorry	1963	7.50	15.00	30.00
☐ 107		Angry Sea (Walmea)/Bugged	1963	7.50	15.00	30.00
☐ 111		It's a Gas/Tootananny	1963	7.50	15.00	30.00
☐ 114		High Octane/Night Scene	1964	6.25	12.50	25.00
☐ 119		The Hustler/Riot in Cell Block #9	1964	6.25	12.50	25.00
☐ 127		Soulful Jerk/Hey-Did-a-Da-Do	1964	6.25	12.50	25.00
☐ 133		Boss Soul/Till Always	1965	6.25	12.50	25.00

Highland

Number		Title (A Side/B Side)	Year	VG	VG+	NM
☐ 1026		Intersection/Stomping Theme	1962	12.50	25.00	50.00

Run-D.M.C.

MCA

Number		Title (A Side/B Side)	Year	VG	VG+	NM
☐ 53680		Ghost Busters/Ghost Busters (Ghost Power Instrumental)	1989		3.50	7.00

Profile

Number		Title (A Side/B Side)	Year	VG	VG+	NM
☐ 5019		It's Like That/(instrumental)	1983		2.50	5.00
☐ 5036		Hard Times-Jam Master Jay/(instrumental)	1983		2.50	5.00
☐ 5045		Rock Box/Rock Box (Dub Version)	1984		2.50	5.00
☐ 5051		30 Days/30 Days (instrumental)	1984		2.50	5.00
☐ 5058		Hollis Crew/Hollis Crew (instrumental)	1984		2.50	5.00
☐ 5064		King of Rock/King of Rock (instrumental)	1985		2.50	5.00
☐ 5069		You Talk Too Much/Daryll and Joe (Krush Groove)	1985		2.50	5.00
☐ 5080		Jam-Master Jammin'/(instrumental)	1985		2.50	5.00
☐ 5088		Can You Rock Like This/Together Forever	1986		2.50	5.00
☐ 5102		My Adidas/Peter Piper	1986		2.00	4.00
☐ 5102	PS	My Adidas/Peter Piper	1986		2.00	4.00

Number		Title (A Side/B Side)	Year	VG	VG+	NM
❏ 5112		Walk This Way/King of Rock	1986		2.00	4.00
		A-side: With Steven Tyler and Joe Perry of Aerosmith				
❏ 5112	PS	Walk This Way/King of Rock	1986		2.00	4.00
❏ 5119		You Be Illin'/Hit It Run	1986		2.00	4.00
❏ 5119	PS	You Be Illin'/Hit It Run	1986		2.00	4.00
❏ 5131		It's Tricky/Proud to Be Black	1987		2.00	4.00
❏ 5131	PS	It's Tricky/Proud to Be Black	1987		2.00	4.00
❏ 5202		Run's House/Beats to the Rhyme	1988		2.00	4.00
❏ 5202	PS	Run's House/Beats to the Rhyme	1988		2.00	4.00
❏ 5211		Mary, Mary/Rock Box	1988		2.00	4.00
❏ 5211	PS	Mary, Mary/Rock Box	1988		2.00	4.00
❏ 5224		I'm Not Going Out Like That/How'd Ya Do It Dee	1988		2.00	4.00
❏ 5224	PS	I'm Not Going Out Like That/How'd Ya Do It Dee	1988		2.00	4.00

Runarounds, The
Capitol

❏ 5644		Perfect Woman/You're a Drag	1966	6.25	12.50	25.00

Cousins

❏ 1004		Mashed Potato Mary/I'm All Alone	1964	5.00	10.00	20.00

Felsted

❏ 8704		Send Her Back/Carrie, You're An Angel	1964	7.50	15.00	30.00

KC

❏ 116		Unbelievable/Hurray for Love	1963	6.25	12.50	25.00
❏ 116		Unbelievable/Hurray for Love	1963	10.00	20.00	40.00
		Brown vinyl				

MGM

❏ 13763		My Little Girl/You Lied	1967	3.75	7.50	15.00

Pio

❏ 107		The Nearest Thing to Heaven/Lover's Lane	1961	37.50	75.00	150.00

Tarheel

❏ 065		Are You Looking for a Sweetheart/Let Them Talk	1963	5.00	10.00	20.00

Rundgren, Todd
(Also see "Nazz"; "Utopia")
Ampex

❏ 31001		We Gotta Get You a Woman/Medley	1970	2.50	5.00	10.00
		As "Runt"				

Bearsville

❏ 0003		I Saw the Light/Marlene	1972	3.00	6.00	12.00
		Blue vinyl				
❏ 0003		I Saw the Light/Marlene	1972	3.00	6.00	12.00
❏ 0007		Couldn't I Just Tell You/Wolfman Jack	1972		3.00	6.00
❏ 0009		Hello It's Me/Cold Morning Light	1973		3.00	6.00
❏ 0020		A Dream Goes On Forever/Heavy Metal Kids	1974		3.00	6.00
❏ 0030		We Gotta Get You a Woman/I Saw the Light	1973		2.00	4.00
		"Back to Back Hits" series				
❏ 0301		Breathless/Wolfman Jack	1974		3.00	6.00
❏ 0304		Real Man/Prana	1975		2.50	5.00
❏ 0309		Good Vibrations/When I Pray	1976		2.50	5.00
❏ 0310		Love of the Common Man/Black and White	1976		2.50	5.00
❏ 0326		Can We Still Be Friends/Determination	1978		2.50	5.00
❏ 0326		Can We Still Be Friends/Out of Control	1978		2.50	5.00
❏ 0330		You Cried Wolf/Onomatopoeia	1978		2.50	5.00
❏ 0335		It Wouldn't Have Made Any Difference/	1979		2.50	5.00
		Did You Ever Learn				
❏ 29686		Bang the Drum All Day/Chant	1983		3.00	6.00
❏ 29759		Emperor of the Highway/Hideaway	1983		2.00	4.00
❏ 31002		Be Nice to Me/Broke Down and Busted	1971	2.00	4.00	8.00
		As "Runt-Todd Rundgren"				
❏ 31004		A Long Time, A Long Way to Go/Parole	1971	2.00	4.00	8.00
		As "Runt-Todd Rundgren"				
❏ 49696		Time Heals/Tiny Demon	1981		2.00	4.00
❏ 49771		Compassion/Pulse	1981		2.50	5.00

Columbia

❏ 06151		Loving You's a Dirty Job (But Somebody's Gotta Do It)/	1986		2.00	4.00
		(B-side unknown)				
		With Bonnie Tyler				

Rhino

❏ 74426		Bang the Drum All Day/Can We Still Be Friends	1987		2.00	4.00

Warner Bros.

❏ 22868		I Love My Life/Parallel Lines	1989			3.00
❏ 28821		Something to Fall Back On/Lockjaw	1986		2.00	4.00

Rush
Mercury

❏ 73623	DJ	Finding My Way (mono/stereo)	1974	10.00	20.00	40.00
		May be promo only				
❏ 73647		In the Mood/What You're Doing	1974	6.25	12.50	25.00
❏ 73681		Anthem/Fly by Night	1975	2.50	5.00	10.00
❏ 73737		Bastille Day/Lakeside Park	1975	2.50	5.00	10.00

Number		Title (A Side/B Side)	Year	VG	VG+	NM
❑ 73803		Lessons/Twilight Zone	1976	2.50	5.00	10.00
❑ 73873		Fly by Night-In the Mood/Something for Nothing	1976	2.50	5.00	10.00
❑ 73912		Making Memories/Temples of Syrinx	1977	2.50	5.00	10.00
❑ 73958		Closer to the Heart/Madrigal	1977	2.50	5.00	10.00
❑ 73990		Anthem/Fly by Night	1978	2.50	5.00	10.00
❑ 74051		The Trees/Circumstances	1979	2.50	5.00	10.00
❑ 76044		The Spirit of Radio/Circumstances	1980	2.50	5.00	10.00
❑ 76060		Entre Nous/Different Strings	1980	2.50	5.00	10.00
❑ 76095		Limelight/XYZ	1981	2.50	5.00	10.00
❑ 76109		Tom Sawyer/Witch Hunt	1981	2.50	5.00	10.00
❑ 76109	PS	Tom Sawyer/Witch Hunt	1981	6.25	12.50	25.00
❑ 76124		Closer to the Heart/Freewill	1981	2.00	4.00	8.00
❑ 76179		New World Man/Vital Signs	1982	2.00	4.00	8.00
❑ 76179	PS	New World Man/Vital Signs	1982	3.75	7.50	15.00
❑ 76196		Countdown/Subdivision	1982	2.50	5.00	10.00
❑ 880 050-7		Body Electric/Between the Wheels	1984	2.00	4.00	8.00
❑ 884 191-7		The Big Money/Red Sector A	1985	2.00	4.00	8.00
❑ 884 191-7	PS	The Big Money/Red Sector A	1985	3.75	7.50	15.00
❑ 888 891-7		Time Stand Still/High Water	1987	3.00	6.00	
❑ 888 891-7	PS	Time Stand Still/High Water	1987	2.50	5.00	10.00

Moon

❑ 001		Not Fade Away/You Can't Fight It	1973	125.00	250.00	500.00
		Canada-only release				

Russell, Lee – See "Russell, Leon"

Russell, Leon

A&M

❑ 734		Cindy/Misty	1964	5.00	10.00	20.00

Columbia

❑ 11023		Heartbreak Hotel/Sioux City Sue	1979		2.00	4.00
		With Willie Nelson				
❑ 11119		Trouble in Mind/	1979		2.00	4.00
		One for My Baby (And One More for the Road)				
		With Willie Nelson				

Dot

❑ 16771		Everybody's Talkin' 'Bout the Young/It's Alright with Me	1965	3.75	7.50	15.00

Paradise

❑ 628		Good Time Charlie's Got the Blues/(B-side unknown)	1984		2.00	4.00
❑ 629		Wabash Cannonball/Tennessee Waltz	1984		2.00	4.00
		As "Hank Wilson"; A-side with Willie Nelson				
❑ 8208		Rainbow in Your Eyes/	1976		2.00	4.00
		Love's Supposed to Be That Way				
		As "Leon and Mary Russell"				
❑ 8274		Satisfy You/Windsong	1976		2.00	4.00
		As "Leon and Mary Russell"				
❑ 8369		Love Crazy/Say You Will	1977		2.00	4.00
		As "Leon and Mary Russell"				
❑ 8438		Easy Love/Hold On to This Feeling	1977		2.00	4.00
		As "Leon and Mary Russell"				
❑ 8667		Elvis and Marilyn/Anita Bryant	1978		2.50	5.00
❑ 8667	PS	Elvis and Marilyn/Anita Bryant	1978		2.50	5.00
❑ 8719		Midnight Lover/From Maine to Mexico	1978		2.50	5.00
❑ 49662		Over the Rainbow/I've Just Seen a Face	1981		2.00	4.00

RCA Victor

❑ 47-6884		(I Tasted) Tears on Your Lips/A Catchy Tune	1957	7.50	15.00	30.00
		As "Lee Russell"				

Roulette

❑ 4049		Honky Tonk Woman/Rainbow at Midnight	1958	6.25	12.50	25.00
		As "Lee Russell"				

Shelter

❑ 301		Roll Away the Stone/Hummingbird	1970		3.00	6.00
❑ 7302		It Takes a Lot to Laugh, It Takes a Train to Cry/	1970		3.00	6.00
		Home Sweet Oklahoma				
❑ 7305		A Hard Rain's A-Gonna Fall/Me and Baby Jane	1971		3.00	6.00
❑ 7316		A Song for You/A Hard Rain's A-Gonna Fall	1971		3.00	6.00
❑ 7325		Tight Rope/This Masquerade	1972		2.50	5.00
❑ 7328		Slippin' Into Christmas/Christmas in Chicago	1972		2.50	5.00
❑ 7336		Roll in My Sweet Baby's Arms/	1973		2.50	5.00
		I'm So Lonesome I Could Cry				
		As "Hank Wilson"				
❑ 7337		Queen of the Roller Derby/Roll Away the Stone	1973		2.50	5.00
❑ 7338		Six Pack to Go/Uncle Pen	1973		2.50	5.00
		As "Hank Wilson"				
❑ 40210		If I Were a Carpenter/Wild Horses	1974		2.00	4.00
❑ 40277		Time for Love/Leaving Whipporwhill	1974		2.00	4.00
❑ 40378		Lady Blue/Laying Right Here in Heaven	1975		2.00	4.00
❑ 40483		Back to the Island/Little Hideaway	1975		2.00	4.00
❑ 62004		Bluebird/Back to the Island	1976		2.00	4.00

Number		Title (A Side/B Side)	Year	VG	VG+	NM

Rutherford, Mike
(Of Genesis and Mike + The Mechanics)
Atlantic

Number		Title (A Side/B Side)	Year	VG	VG+	NM
❑ 89976		Halfway There/A Day to Remember	1982		2.00	4.00
❑ 89981		Maxine/A Day to Remember	1982		2.00	4.00

Passport

❑ 7919		Moonshine/Working in Line	1980		2.50	5.00

Rutles, The
Warner Bros.

❑ 8560		I Must Be in Love/Doubleback Alley	1978	3.00	6.00	12.00

Rydell, Bobby
Cameo

❑ (no #)	DJ	Steel Pier	1963	6.25	12.50	25.00
		One-sided "Steel Pier Promotion"				
❑ 160		Please Don't Be Mad/Kissin' Time	1959	12.50	25.00	50.00
❑ 164		All I Want Is You/For You, For You	1959	5.00	10.00	20.00
❑ 167		Kissin' Time/You'll Never Tame Me	1959	3.75	7.50	15.00
❑ 167	PS	Kissin' Time/You'll Never Tame Me	1959	6.25	12.50	25.00
❑ 169		We Got Love/I Dig Girls	1959	3.75	7.50	15.00
❑ 169	PS	We Got Love/I Dig Girls	1959	6.25	12.50	25.00
❑ 171		Wild One/Little Bitty Girl	1960	3.75	7.50	15.00
❑ 171	PS	Wild One/Little Bitty Girl	1960	6.25	12.50	25.00
❑ 175		Swingin' School/Ding-a-Ling	1960	3.75	7.50	15.00
❑ 175	PS	Swingin' School/Ding-a-Ling	1960	6.25	12.50	25.00
❑ 179		Volare/I'd Do It Again	1960	3.75	7.50	15.00
❑ 179	PS	Volare/I'd Do It Again	1960	6.25	12.50	25.00
❑ 186		Good Time Baby/Cherie	1961	3.75	7.50	15.00
❑ 186	PS	Good Time Baby/Cherie	1961	6.25	12.50	25.00
❑ 190		That Old Black Magic/Don't Be Afraid (To Fall in Love)	1961	3.75	7.50	15.00
❑ 190	PS	That Old Black Magic/Don't Be Afraid (To Fall in Love)	1961	6.25	12.50	25.00
❑ 192		The Fish/The Third House	1961	3.75	7.50	15.00
❑ 192	PS	The Fish/The Third House	1961	6.25	12.50	25.00
❑ 201		I Wanna Thank You/The Door to Paradise	1961	3.75	7.50	15.00
❑ 201	PS	I Wanna Thank You/The Door to Paradise	1961	6.25	12.50	25.00
❑ 209		I've Got Bonnie/Lose Her	1962	3.00	6.00	12.00
❑ 209	PS	I've Got Bonnie/Lose Her	1962	5.00	10.00	20.00
❑ 217		I'll Never Dance Again/Gee It's Wonderful	1962	3.00	6.00	12.00
❑ 217	PS	I'll Never Dance Again/Gee It's Wonderful	1962	5.00	10.00	20.00
❑ 228		The Cha-Cha-Cha/The Best Man Cried	1962	3.75	7.50	15.00
❑ 228	PS	The Cha-Cha-Cha/The Best Man Cried	1962	6.25	12.50	25.00
❑ 242		Butterfly Baby/Love Is Blind	1963	3.75	7.50	15.00
❑ 242	PS	Butterfly Baby/Love Is Blind	1963	6.25	12.50	25.00
❑ 252		Wildwood Days/Will You Be My Baby	1963	3.00	6.00	12.00
❑ 252	PS	Wildwood Days/Will You Be My Baby	1963	5.00	10.00	20.00
❑ 265		Little Queenie/The Woodpecker Song	1963	3.75	7.50	15.00
❑ 265	PS	Little Queenie/The Woodpecker Song	1963	6.25	12.50	25.00
❑ 272		Let's Make Love Tonight/Childhood Sweetheart	1963	3.00	6.00	12.00
❑ 272	PS	Let's Make Love Tonight/Childhood Sweetheart	1963	5.00	10.00	20.00
❑ 280		Forget Him/Love, Love Go Away	1963	3.00	6.00	12.00
❑ 280	PS	Forget Him/Love, Love Go Away	1963	5.00	10.00	20.00
❑ 309		Make Me Forget/Little Girl, You've Had a Busy Day	1964	3.00	6.00	12.00
❑ 309	PS	Make Me Forget/Little Girl, You've Had a Busy Day	1964	5.00	10.00	20.00
❑ 320		A World Without Love/Our Faded Love	1964	3.75	7.50	15.00
❑ 320	PS	A World Without Love/Our Faded Love	1964	6.25	12.50	25.00
❑ 361		Ciao, Ciao Bambino/Voce de la Notte	1965	3.75	7.50	15.00
❑ 1070		Forget Him/A Message from Bobby	1963	5.00	10.00	20.00
		Bonus single with Cameo LP C-1070, "Top Hits of 1963"				

Capitol

❑ 5305		I Just Can't Say Goodbye/Two Is the Loneliest Number	1964	2.50	5.00	10.00
❑ 5305	PS	I Just Can't Say Goodbye/Two Is the Loneliest Number	1964	3.75	7.50	15.00
❑ 5352		Diana/Stranger in the World	1965	2.50	5.00	10.00
❑ 5436		The Joker/Side Show	1965	2.50	5.00	10.00
❑ 5513		When I See That Girl of Mine/It Takes Two	1965	2.50	5.00	10.00
❑ 5556		Roses in the Snow/A Word for Today	1965	2.50	5.00	10.00
❑ 5696		She Was the Girl/Not You	1966	2.50	5.00	10.00
❑ 5780		Open for Business As Usual/You Gotta Enjoy Joy	1966	2.50	5.00	10.00

P.I.P.

❑ 6515		Sway/Feels Good	1976		2.50	5.00
❑ 6521		You're Not the Only Girl for Me/Give Me Your Answer	1976		2.00	4.00
❑ 6531		It's Getting Better/The Singles Scene	1976		2.00	4.00

Perception

❑ 519		California Sunshine/Honey Buns	1973		2.50	5.00
❑ 552		Everything Seemed Better (When I Was Younger)/ Sunday Son	1974		2.50	5.00

RCA Victor

❑ 47-9892		Chapel on the Hill/It Must Be Love	1970		3.00	6.00

Reprise

❑ 0656		The Lovin' Thing/It's Getting Better	1968	2.00	4.00	8.00
❑ 0684		The River Is Wide/ Absence Makes the Heart Grow Fonder	1968	2.00	4.00	8.00
❑ 0751		Every Little Bit Hurts/Time and Changes	1968	2.00	4.00	8.00

Number		Title (A Side/B Side)	Year	VG	VG+	NM

Veko
| ❑ 731 | | Fatty Fatty/Dream Age | 1958 | 12.50 | 25.00 | 50.00 |

Venise
| ❑ 201 | | Fatty Fatty/Happy Happy | 1958 | 7.50 | 15.00 | 30.00 |

Rydell, Bobby/Chubby Checker
(Also see individual listings)

Cameo
❑ 205		Jingle Bell Rock/Jingle Bell Imitations	1961	3.75	7.50	15.00
❑ 205	PS	Jingle Bell Rock/Jingle Bell Imitations	1961	6.25	12.50	25.00
❑ 214		Teach Me to Twist/Swingin' Together	1962	3.75	7.50	15.00
❑ 214	PS	Teach Me to Twist/Swingin' Together	1962	6.25	12.50	25.00

Ryder, Mitch
(Formerly of the Detroit Wheels)

Avco Embassy
| ❑ 4550 | | Jenny Take a Ride/I Never Had It Better | 1970 | 2.50 | 5.00 | 10.00 |

Dot
| ❑ 17290 | | I Believe (There Must Be Someone)/ Sugar Bee (We Three) | 1970 | | 3.00 | 6.00 |
| ❑ 17325 | | It's Been a Long, Long, Long Time/Direct Me | 1970 | | 3.00 | 6.00 |

DynoVoice
❑ 901		What Now My Love/Blessing in Disguise	1967	2.00	4.00	8.00
❑ 905		Personality-Chantilly Lace/I Make a Fool of Myself	1968	2.00	4.00	8.00
❑ 916		Lights of the Night/I Need Loving You	1968	2.00	4.00	8.00
❑ 934		Baby I Need Your Loving/Ring Your Bell	1969	2.00	4.00	8.00

New Voice
❑ 824		Joy/I'd Rather Go to Jail	1967	2.00	4.00	8.00
❑ 826		You Are My Sunshine/Wild Child	1967	2.00	4.00	8.00
❑ 828		Come See About Me/A Face in the Crowd	1968	2.00	4.00	8.00
❑ 830		Ruby Baby/You Get Your Kicks	1968	2.00	4.00	8.00

Riva
| ❑ 213 | | When You Were Mine/Stand | 1983 | | 2.50 | 5.00 |

Ryder, Mitch, and the Detroit Wheels
(Also see "Ryder, Mitch")

New Voice
❑ 801		I Need Help/I Hope	1965	2.50	5.00	10.00
❑ 806		Jenny Take a Ride!/Baby Jane (Mo-Mo Jane)	1965	3.00	6.00	12.00
		Actual A-side title				
❑ 806		Jenny Takes a Ride!/Baby Jane (Mo-Mo Jane)	1965	6.25	12.50	25.00
		Note slightly different A-side title				
❑ 808		Little Latin Lupe Lu/I Hope	1966	2.50	5.00	10.00
❑ 811		Break Out/I Need Help	1966	2.50	5.00	10.00
❑ 814		Takin' All I Can Get/You Get Your Kicks	1966	2.50	5.00	10.00
❑ 817		Devil with a Blue Dress On & Good Golly Miss Molly/ I Had It Made	1966	3.00	6.00	12.00
❑ 820		Sock It To Me -- Baby!/I Never Had It Better	1967	6.25	12.50	25.00
		Version 1: With lyric "Feels like a punch," mumbled to the point that it sounds obscene				
❑ 820		Sock It To Me -- Baby!/I Never Had It Better	1967	2.50	5.00	10.00
		Version 2: With lyric "Hits me like a PUNCH!" with no doubt about the last word. We don't know how, or if it's indeed possible, to tell them apart without playing the record				
❑ 820	PS	Sock It To Me -- Baby!/I Never Had It Better	1967	5.00	10.00	20.00
❑ 822		Too Many Fish in the Sea & Three Little Fishes/ One Grain of Sand	1967	2.50	5.00	10.00
❑ 822	PS	Too Many Fish in the Sea & Three Little Fishes/ One Grain of Sand	1967	5.00	10.00	20.00

S

Sabre, Johnny, and the Passions
Adonis
| ❑ 103 | | Wish It Could Be Me/Dolly in a Toy Shop | 1959 | 50.00 | 100.00 | 200.00 |

Sacco
(Actually Lou Christie)

Lifesong
| ❑ 1775 | | Theme from "People" (Part 1)/ Theme from "People" (Part 2) | 1978 | 12.50 | 25.00 | 50.00 |

Safaris, The
Eldo
❑ 101		Image of a Girl/Four Steps to Love	1960	6.25	12.50	25.00
❑ 105		The Girl with the Story in Her Eyes/Summer Nights	1960	6.25	12.50	25.00
❑ 110		In the Still of the Night/Shadows	1960	7.50	15.00	30.00
❑ 113		Garden of Love/Soldier of Fortune	1961	7.50	15.00	30.00

Valiant
| ❑ 6036 | | Kick Out/Lonely Surf Guitar | 1963 | 7.50 | 15.00 | 30.00 |

Number		Title (A Side/B Side)	Year	VG	VG+	NM

Sahm, Doug
(Also see "Sir Douglas Quintet")
ABC/Dot

❑ 17656		Cowboy Peyton Place/ I Love the Way You Love (The Way I Love You)	1976		3.00	6.00
❑ 17674		Crying Inside Sometimes/I'm Missing You	1976		3.00	6.00

Atlantic

❑ 2946		Is Anybody Going to San Antone/Don't Turn Around	1973	2.00	4.00	8.00

Cobra

❑ 116		Just a Moment/Sapphire	1961	12.50	25.00	50.00

Crazy Cajun

❑ 2004		If You Really Want/Not Tomato Man	1974		2.50	5.00

Harlem

❑ 108		Baby Tell Me/Sapphire	1960	12.50	25.00	50.00
❑ 108	DJ	Baby Tell Me/Sapphire	1960	25.00	50.00	100.00
		Gold vinyl promo				
❑ 113		More and More/Slow Down	1960	12.50	25.00	50.00

Mercury

❑ 73098		Be Real/I Don't Want to Go Home	1970	5.00	10.00	20.00
		As "Wayne Douglas"				

Personality

❑ 260		Baby, What's On Your Mind/Crazy, Crazy Feeling	1962	12.50	25.00	50.00

Renner

❑ 212		Big Hat/Makes No Difference	1961	10.00	20.00	40.00
❑ 212	DJ	Big Hat/Makes No Difference	1961	25.00	50.00	100.00
		Red vinyl promo				
❑ 215		Baby, What's On Your Mind/Crazy, Crazy Feeling	1961	10.00	20.00	40.00
❑ 215	DJ	Baby, What's On Your Mind/Crazy, Crazy Feeling	1961	25.00	50.00	100.00
		Red vinyl promo				
❑ 226		Two Hearts in Love/Just Because	1962	10.00	20.00	40.00
❑ 232		Little Angel/Cry	1963	10.00	20.00	40.00
❑ 240		Lucky Me/A Year Ago Tonight	1963	10.00	20.00	40.00
❑ 247		Mr. Kool/Bill Beatty	1964	12.50	25.00	50.00

Sarg

❑ 113		A Real American Joe/Rolling Rolling	1958	25.00	50.00	100.00
		As "Little Doug"				

Satin

❑ 100		Crazy Daisy/I Can't Believe You Wanna Leave	1959	12.50	25.00	50.00

Soft

❑ 1031		Cry/Down the Pike	1965	7.50	15.00	30.00

Swingin'

❑ 625		Why, Why, Why/If You Ever Need Me	1960	6.25	12.50	25.00

Tear Drop

❑ 3074		It's a Man Down There/4 A.M.	1966	6.25	12.50	25.00
		As "Him"				

Teardrop

❑ 3479		Who Were You Thinking Of/Velma	1982		2.00	4.00
		With Augie Myers				
❑ 3481		I'm Not a Fool Anymore/Don't Fight It	1982		2.00	4.00
		With Augie Myers				

Warner Bros.

❑ 7819		Girls Today/Groover's Paradise	1974		2.50	5.00

Warrior

❑ 507		Crazy Daisy/If I Ever Need You	1958	20.00	40.00	80.00

Saigons, The
Dootone

❑ 375		You're Heavenly/Honey Gee	1955	100.00	200.00	400.00

St. James, Holly
ABC

❑ 10996		That's Not Love/Two Good Reasons	1967	15.00	30.00	60.00
❑ 11042		Waiting for My Friend/Magic Moments	1968	5.00	10.00	20.00

St. John, Dick
(Of Dick and Deedee)
Dot

❑ 17080		Childhood/Lady of the Burning Green-Jade	1968	2.00	4.00	8.00
❑ 17140		Leaving on a Jet Plane/Brand New Season	1968	2.00	4.00	8.00

Liberty

❑ 55380		Gonna Stick By You/Sha-Ta	1961	3.00	6.00	12.00

Philips

❑ 40256		Love's a Funny Little Game/Believe Me Baby	1965	2.50	5.00	10.00
❑ 40325		Swanee River/You Know What I Mean	1965	2.50	5.00	10.00

Pom Pom

❑ 4156		Gonna Stick By You/Sha-Ta	1961	6.25	12.50	25.00

Roma

❑ 1001		Hey, Little Gal/Boogie Man (I Ain't Afraid of You)	1961	3.75	7.50	15.00

Number	Title (A Side/B Side)	Year	VG	VG+	NM

St. Peters, Crispian
Jamie
❑ 1309	At This Moment/No No No	1966	2.50	5.00	10.00
❑ 1310	You Were On My Mind/What I'm Gonna Be	1966	2.50	5.00	10.00
❑ 1320	The Pied Piper/Sweet Dawn My True Love	1966	3.00	6.00	12.00
❑ 1324	Changes/My Little Brown Eyes	1966	2.50	5.00	10.00
❑ 1334	Almost Persuaded/You Are Gone	1967	2.50	5.00	10.00
❑ 1344	Free Spirit/I'm Always Crying	1967	2.50	5.00	10.00
❑ 1359	Please Take Me Back/Look Into My Teardrops	1968	2.00	4.00	8.00

Sales, Soupy
ABC-Paramount
❑ 10646	The Mouse/Pachalafaka	1965	3.00	6.00	12.00
❑ 10681	Speedy Gonzales/Hey, Pearl	1965	2.50	5.00	10.00
❑ 10747	I'm a Bird Watching Man/Where the Blue Folks Go	1965	2.50	5.00	10.00

Brunswick
❑ 55472	Break Your Back/Tom Jones (Push and Pull)	1972	2.50		10.00

Capitol
❑ 5752	Spanish Flea/That Wasn't No Girl	1966	2.50	5.00	10.00
❑ 5766	Backwards Alphabet/Use Your Noggin	1966	2.50	5.00	10.00

Motown
❑ 1141	Muck-Arty Park/Green Grow the Lilacs	1968	10.00	20.00	40.00

Reprise
❑ 0244	Santa Claus Is Surfin' to Town/ Santa Claus Is Comin' to Town	1963	3.75	7.50	15.00
❑ 0368	Pie in the Face/Soupy Sez	1965	3.75	7.50	15.00
❑ 20,041	Hippy's Cha Cha Hips/White Fang	1961	3.75	7.50	15.00
❑ 20,064	Because of Black Tooth/Soupy's Theme	1962	3.75	7.50	15.00
❑ 20,108	My Baby's Got a Crush on Frankenstein/ Doggone Doggie	1962	3.75	7.50	15.00
❑ 20,189	And That's a Shame/Hilly Billy Ding Dong Choo Choo	1963	3.75	7.50	15.00

Sam and Dave
Atlantic
❑ 2517	You Don't Know What You Mean to Me/ This Is Your World	1968		3.00	6.00
❑ 2540	Can't You Find Another Way (Of Doing It)/ Still Is the Night	1968		3.00	6.00
❑ 2568	Everybody Got to Believe in Somebody/ If I Didn't Have a Girl Like You	1968		3.00	6.00
❑ 2590	Soul Sister, Brown Sugar/Come On In	1968		3.00	6.00
❑ 2608	Born Again/Get It	1969		3.00	6.00
❑ 2668	Holdin' On/Ooh Ooh Ooh	1969		3.00	6.00
❑ 2714	I'm Not an Indian Giver/Baby-Baby Don't Stop Now	1970		3.00	6.00
❑ 2728	One Part Love, Two Parts Pain/ When You Steal from Me	1970		3.00	6.00
❑ 2733	When You Steal from Me (You're Only Hurting Yourself)/You Easily Excite Me	1970		3.00	6.00
❑ 2839	Don't Pull Your Love/Jody Ryder Got Killed	1971		3.00	6.00

Roulette
❑ 4419	I Need Love/Keep a-Walkin'	1962	3.00	6.00	12.00
❑ 4445	No More Pain/My Love Belongs to You	1962	3.00	6.00	12.00
❑ 4461	She's Alright/It Feels So Nice	1962	3.00	6.00	12.00
❑ 4480	It Was So Nice While It Lasted/ You Ain't No Big Thing, Baby	1963	3.00	6.00	12.00
❑ 4508	If She'll Still Have Me/Listening for My Name	1963	3.00	6.00	12.00
❑ 4533	I Found Out/I Got a Thing Going On	1963	3.00	6.00	12.00
❑ 4671	It Feels So Nice/It Was So Nice While It Lasted	1966	2.00	4.00	8.00

Stax
❑ 168	Goodnight Baby/A Place Nobody Can Find	1965	3.75	7.50	15.00
❑ 175	I Take What I Want/Sweet Home	1965	3.00	6.00	12.00
❑ 180	You Don't Know Like I Know/ Blame Me (Don't Blame My Heart)	1965	2.50	5.00	10.00
❑ 189	Hold On! I'm a-Comin'/I Got Everything I Need	1966	2.50	5.00	10.00
❑ 198	Said I Wasn't Gonna Tell Nobody/If You Got the Loving	1966	2.50	5.00	10.00
❑ 204	You Got Me Hummin'/Sleep Good Tonight	1967	2.50	5.00	10.00
❑ 210	When Something Is Wrong with My Baby/ Small Portion of Your Love	1967	2.50	5.00	10.00
❑ 218	Soothe Me/I Can't Stand Up for Falling Down	1967	2.50	5.00	10.00
❑ 231	Soul Man/May I Baby	1967	3.00	6.00	12.00
❑ 242	I Thank You/Wrap It Up	1968	3.00	6.00	12.00

United Artists
❑ XW438	A Little Bit of Good (Cures a Whole Lot of Bad)/ Blinded by Love	1974		3.00	6.00
❑ XW531	Under the Boardwalk/Give It What You Can	1974		3.00	6.00

Sam the Sham and the Pharaohs
Atlantic
❑ 2767	Me and Bobby McGee/Key to the Highway As "Sam Samudio"	1970		2.50	5.00

Dingo
❑ 001	Haunted House/How Does a Cheating Woman Feel	1964	50.00	100.00	200.00

Number		Title (A Side/B Side)	Year	VG	VG+	NM
Fretone						
❏ 048		Wookie (Part 1)/Wookie (Part 2)	1977	2.50	5.00	10.00
		As "Sam the Sham"				
❏ 049		Ain't No Lie/Baby You Got It	1977	2.50	5.00	10.00
		As "Sam the Sham"				
MGM						
❏ 13322		Wooly Bully/Ain't Gonna Move	1965	3.75	7.50	15.00
❏ 13364		Ju Ju Hand/Big City Lights	1965	3.00	6.00	12.00
❏ 13364	PS	Ju Ju Hand/Big City Lights	1965	5.00	10.00	20.00
❏ 13397		Ring Dang Doo/Don't Try It Again	1965	3.00	6.00	12.00
❏ 13397	PS	Ring Dang Doo/Don't Try It Again	1965	5.00	10.00	20.00
❏ 13452		Red Hot/Long Long Way	1966	3.00	6.00	12.00
❏ 13506		Lil' Red Riding Hood/Love Me Like Before	1966	3.75	7.50	15.00
❏ 13581		The Hair on My Chinny Chin Chin/ (I'm In with the) Out Crowd	1966	3.00	6.00	12.00
❏ 13581	PS	The Hair on My Chinny Chin Chin/ (I'm In with the) Out Crowd	1966	5.00	10.00	20.00
❏ 13649		How Do You Catch a Girl/Love You Left Behind	1966	3.00	6.00	12.00
❏ 13649	PS	How Do You Catch a Girl/Love You Left Behind	1966	5.00	10.00	20.00
❏ 13713		Oh That's Good, No That's Bad/ Take What You Can Get	1967	2.50	5.00	10.00
❏ 13747		Black Sheep/My Day's Gonna Come	1967	2.50	5.00	10.00
❏ 13803		Banned in Boston/Money's My Problem	1967	2.50	5.00	10.00
		As "The Sam the Sham Revue"				
❏ 13863		Yakety Yak/Let Our Love Light Shine	1967	2.50	5.00	10.00
		As "The Sam the Sham Revue"				
❏ 13920		Old Mac Donald Has a Boogaloo Farm/ I Never Was No One	1968	2.50	5.00	10.00
❏ 13972		I Couldn't Spell !!@!/Down Home Strut	1968	3.75	7.50	15.00
❏ 14021		Wolly Bully/Ain't Gonna Move	1968	2.50	5.00	10.00
❏ 14642		Fate/Oh Lo	1973	2.50	5.00	10.00
Tupelo						
❏ 2982		Betty and Dupree/Manchild	1963	15.00	30.00	60.00
XL						
❏ 905		The Signifyin' Monkey/Juimonos	1964	12.50	25.00	50.00
❏ 906		Wooly Bully/Ain't Gonna Move	1965	37.50	75.00	150.00

Sammy and the Del-Larks

Number		Title (A Side/B Side)	Year	VG	VG+	NM
Ea-Jay						
❏ 100		Baby Come On/I Never Will Forget	1961	50.00	100.00	200.00

Samudio, Sam – See "Sam the Sham and the Pharaohs"

Sanders, Bobby

Number		Title (A Side/B Side)	Year	VG	VG+	NM
Kaybo						
❏ 618		It Was You/I'm On My Way	1961	25.00	50.00	100.00
Kent						
❏ 382		Maybe I'm Wrong/You've Forgotten Me	1962	75.00	150.00	300.00
Pick-A-Hit						
❏ 100		Lover/The Way I Feel	196?	2.50	5.00	10.00

Sandmen, The

(Brook Benton was in this group)

Number		Title (A Side/B Side)	Year	VG	VG+	NM
Okeh						
❏ 7052		When I Grow Too Old to Dream/Somebody to Love	1955	12.50	25.00	50.00

Sands, Jodie

Number		Title (A Side/B Side)	Year	VG	VG+	NM
ABC-Paramount						
❏ 10337		We Had Words/Uno Momento	1962	3.00	6.00	12.00
❏ 10376		Hello, Heartache/This Little Fool	1962	3.00	6.00	12.00
❏ 10451		Time to Love/Charming Little Barefoot	1963	3.00	6.00	12.00
Bernlo						
❏ 1003		Love Me Always/Everybody Needs Somebody	1957	6.25	12.50	25.00
Chancellor						
❏ 1003		With All My Heart/More Than Only Friends	1957	6.25	12.50	25.00
❏ 1005		If You're Not Completely Satisfied/Sayonara	1957	5.00	10.00	20.00
❏ 1009		The Way I Love You/Tantalizin' Love	1957	5.00	10.00	20.00
❏ 1015		Love Me Again/All I Ask of You	1958	5.00	10.00	20.00
❏ 1023		Someday/Always in My Heart	1958	5.00	10.00	20.00
Paris						
❏ 543		I'd Cry No Tears/Kiss By Kiss	1960	3.75	7.50	15.00
❏ 551		Love Me Forever/Give Me a Break	1960	3.75	7.50	15.00
Signature						
❏ 12015		Turnabout Heart/Solo A Te Mio Amor	1959	3.75	7.50	15.00
Teen						
❏ 109		Love Me Always/Everybody Needs Somebody	1955	10.00	20.00	40.00
Thor						
❏ 101		Hold Me/What Does It Mean	1959	5.00	10.00	20.00

Sands, Tommy

Number		Title (A Side/B Side)	Year	VG	VG+	NM
ABC-Paramount						
❏ 10466		Connie/Young Man's Fancy	1963	2.50	5.00	10.00
❏ 10480		Cinderella/Only 'Cause I'm Lonely	1963	2.50	5.00	10.00

Number		Title (A Side/B Side)	Year	VG	VG+	NM
❏ 10539		Won't You Be My Girl/	1964	2.50	5.00	10.00
		Ten Dollars and a Clean White Shirt				
❏ 10591		Something More/Kisses (Love Theme)	1964	2.50	5.00	10.00

Capitol

Number		Title (A Side/B Side)	Year	VG	VG+	NM
❏ F3639		Teen-Age Crush/Hep Dee Hootie	1957	6.25	12.50	25.00
❏ F3690		Ring-A-Ding-A-Ding/My Love Song	1957	6.25	12.50	25.00
❏ F3723		Goin' Steady/Ring My Phone	1957	6.25	12.50	25.00
❏ F3743		Let Me Be Loved/Fantastically Foolish	1957	5.00	10.00	20.00
❏ F3810		A Swingin' Romance/Man, Like Wow!	1957	5.00	10.00	20.00
❏ F3867		Sing, Boy, Sing/Crazy 'Cause I Love You	1957	5.00	10.00	20.00
❏ F3953		Teenage Doll/Hawaiian Rock	1958	5.00	10.00	20.00
❏ F3985		Big Date/After the Senior Prom	1958	5.00	10.00	20.00
❏ F4036		Blue Ribbon Baby/I Love You Because	1958	5.00	10.00	20.00
❏ F4082		Bigger Than Texas/The Worryin' Kind	1958	5.00	10.00	20.00
❏ F4160		Is It Ever Gonna Happen/I Ain't Gittin' Rid of You	1959	3.75	7.50	15.00
❏ F4231		Sinner Man/Bring Me Your Love	1959	3.75	7.50	15.00
❏ F4259		I'll Be Seeing You/That's the Way I Am	1959	3.75	7.50	15.00
❏ F4259	PS	I'll Be Seeing You/That's the Way I Am	1959	7.50	15.00	30.00
❏ 4316		You Hold the Future/I Gotta Have You	1959	3.75	7.50	15.00
❏ 4366		That's Love/Crossroads	1960	3.75	7.50	15.00
❏ 4405		The Old Oaken Bucket/These Are the Things You Are	1960	3.75	7.50	15.00
❏ 4470		Doctor Heartache/On and On	1960	3.75	7.50	15.00
❏ 4580		Love in a Goldfish Bowl/I Love My Baby	1961	3.00	6.00	12.00
❏ 4611		Rainbow/Remember Me to Jennie	1961	3.00	6.00	12.00
❏ 4660		Wrong Side of Love/Jimmy's Song	1961	3.00	6.00	12.00

Imperial

Number		Title (A Side/B Side)	Year	VG	VG+	NM
❏ 66174		As Long As I'm Travelin'/It's the Only One I've Got	1966	2.00	4.00	8.00
❏ 66229		Second Star to the Left/Candy Store Prophet	1967	2.00	4.00	8.00

Liberty

Number		Title (A Side/B Side)	Year	VG	VG+	NM
❏ 55807		Love's Funny/One Rose Today, One Rose Tomorrow	1965	2.00	4.00	8.00
❏ 55842		The Statue/Little Rosita	1965	2.00	4.00	8.00
❏ 55864		Waitin' in Your Welfare Line/Don't Do It Darlin'	1966			Unreleased

RCA Victor

Number		Title (A Side/B Side)	Year	VG	VG+	NM
❏ 47-5435		Love Pains/Transfer	1953	7.50	15.00	30.00
❏ 47-5510		Roses Speak Louder Than Words/Spanish Coquita	1953	7.50	15.00	30.00
❏ 47-5628		A Dime and a Dollar/Life Is So Lonesome	1954	7.50	15.00	30.00
❏ 47-5697		Never Let Me Go/I Know About the Bees	1954	7.50	15.00	30.00
❏ 47-5800		Don't Drop It/A Place for Girls Like You	1954	7.50	15.00	30.00
❏ 47-6007		Kissin' Ain't No Fun/Something's Bound to Go Wrong	1955	7.50	15.00	30.00
❏ 47-6868		Don't Drop It/Love Pains	1957	5.00	10.00	20.00

Sandy and Dick
(With Dick St. John)

Congress

Number		Title (A Side/B Side)	Year	VG	VG+	NM
❏ 6015		Groove With What You Got/	1970	2.00	4.00	8.00
		Sing Along with Groove With What You Got				
❏ 6021		Sweet Sweet Lovin'/Quick Like a Bunny	1970	2.00	4.00	8.00

Sandy, Frank

Mark

Number		Title (A Side/B Side)	Year	VG	VG+	NM
❏ 138		Shamrock/Here She Comes	1959	10.00	20.00	40.00

MGM

Number		Title (A Side/B Side)	Year	VG	VG+	NM
❏ 12626		Somebody Loves Me/Tarantella Rock	1958	12.50	25.00	50.00
❏ 12678		Let's Go Rock 'N' Roll/Midnight Stomp	1958	25.00	50.00	100.00

Santana

Columbia

Number	Title (A Side/B Side)	Year	VG	VG+	NM
❏ 01050	Winning/The Brightest Star	1981		2.00	4.00
❏ 02178	The Sensitive Kind/American Gypsy	1981		2.00	4.00
❏ 02519	Searchin'/Tales of Kilimanjaro	1981		2.00	4.00
❏ 03160	Hold On/Oxun	1982		2.00	4.00
❏ 03268	Hold On	1982		3.00	6.00
	One-sided budget release				
❏ 03376	Nowhere to Run/Nueva York	1982		2.00	4.00
❏ 03925	Tales of Kilimanjaro/Watch Your Step	1983		2.00	4.00
❏ 04034	Havana Moon/Lightnin'	1983		2.00	4.00
❏ 04758	Say It Again/Touchdown Raiders	1985			3.00
❏ 04912	I'm the One Who Loves You/Right Now	1985			3.00
❏ 05677	They All Went to Mexico/Slow Movin' Outlaw	1985			3.00
	A-side: Willie Nelson and Carlos Santana; B-side: Willie and Lacy J. Dalton				
❏ 06654	Vera Cruz/Manuela	1987		2.00	4.00
❏ 07038	Vera Cruz (Remix)/Manuela	1987			3.00
❏ 07140	Praise/Love Is You	1987			3.00
❏ 10073	Mirage/Flor de Canela	1974		2.50	5.00
❏ 10088	Give and Take/Love Is Anew	1975		2.50	5.00
❏ 10336	Let It Shine/Tell Me Are You Tired	1976		2.50	5.00
❏ 10353	Dance Sister Dance (Baila Mi Hermana)/Let Me	1976		2.50	5.00
❏ 10421	Take Me with You/	1976		2.50	5.00
	Europa (Earth's Cry Heaven's Smile)				
❏ 10481	Let the Children Play/Carnival	1977		2.50	5.00
❏ 10524	Give Me Love/Revelations	1977		2.50	5.00
❏ 10616	She's Not There/Zulu	1977		2.50	5.00
❏ 10677	Black Magic Woman/I'll Be Waiting	1978		2.50	5.00
❏ 10839	Well, All Right/Jericho	1978		2.50	5.00
❏ 10873	Stormy/Move On	1978		2.50	5.00

Number		Title (A Side/B Side)	Year	VG	VG+	NM
❏ 10938		One Chain (Don't Make a Prison)/	1979		2.00	4.00
		Life Is a Lady-Holiday				
❏ 11144		You Know That I Love You/Aqua Marine	1979		2.00	4.00
❏ 11218		All I Ever Wanted/Lightning in the Sky	1980		2.00	4.00
❏ 45010		Jingo/Persuasion	1969		3.00	6.00
❏ 45010		Jin-Go-Lo-Ba/Persuasion	1969		3.00	6.00
		Same song, different A-side title				
❏ 45069		Evil Ways/Waiting	1970		3.00	6.00
❏ 45270		Black Magic Woman/Hope You're Feeling Better	1970		3.00	6.00
❏ 45330		Oye Como Va/Samba Pa Ti	1971		2.50	5.00
❏ 45330	PS	Oye Como Va/Samba Pa Ti	1971	2.00	4.00	8.00
❏ 45472		Everybody's Everything/Guajira	1971		2.50	5.00
❏ 45552		No One to Depend On/Taboo	1972		2.50	5.00
❏ 45552	PS	No One to Depend On/Taboo	1972	2.00	4.00	8.00
❏ 45666		Them Changes/Evil Ways	1972		2.50	5.00
		With Buddy Miles				
❏ 45753		Look Up/All the Love of the Universe	1973		2.50	5.00
❏ 45999		When I Look Into Your Eyes/Samba De Sausalito	1974		2.50	5.00
❏ 46067		Incident at Neshabur/Samba Pa Ti	1974		2.50	5.00

Santo and Johnny
Canadian American

Number		Title (A Side/B Side)	Year	VG	VG+	NM
❏ 103		Sleep Walk/All Night Diner	1959	5.00	10.00	20.00
❏ 107		Tear Drop/The Long Walk Home	1959	3.75	7.50	15.00
❏ 111		Caravan/Summertime	1960	3.75	7.50	15.00
❏ 115		The Breeze and I/Lazy Day	1960	3.75	7.50	15.00
❏ 118		Love Lost/Annie	1960	3.75	7.50	15.00
❏ 120		Twistin' Bells/Bulls Eye	1960	4.00	8.00	16.00
❏ 120	PS	Twistin' Bells/Bulls Eye	1960	10.00	20.00	40.00
❏ 124		Hop Scotch/Sea Shells	1961	3.75	7.50	15.00
❏ 128		Theme from Come September/The Long Walk Home	1961	3.75	7.50	15.00
❏ 131		The Mouse/Birmingham	1961	3.75	7.50	15.00
❏ 132		Twistin' Bells/Christmas Day	1961	5.00	10.00	20.00
		B-side by Linda Scott				
❏ 137		Spanish Harlem/Stage to Cimarron	1962	3.00	6.00	12.00
❏ 141		Three Caballeros/Step Aside	1962	3.00	6.00	12.00
❏ 144		Misirlou/Tokyo Twilight	1962	3.00	6.00	12.00
❏ 148		Twistin' Bells/Manhattan	1962	3.00	6.00	12.00
❏ 151		On Your Mark/Manhattan	1963	3.00	6.00	12.00
❏ 155		The Wandering Sea/Manhattan Spiritual	1963	3.00	6.00	12.00
❏ 161		Love Letters in the Sand/Lido Beach	1963	3.00	6.00	12.00
❏ 164		I'll Remember (In the Still of the Night)/	1964	3.00	6.00	12.00
		Song for Rosemary				
❏ 164	PS	I'll Remember (In the Still of the Night)/	1964	6.25	12.50	25.00
		Song for Rosemary				
❏ 167		A Thousand Miles Away/Road Block	1964	3.00	6.00	12.00
❏ 167	PS	A Thousand Miles Away/Road Block	1964	6.25	12.50	25.00
❏ 174		Sugar Stroll/Rattler	1964	3.00	6.00	12.00
❏ 177		A Hard Day's Night/And I Love Her	1964	3.75	7.50	15.00
❏ 182		Goldfinger/Sleep Walk	1964	3.00	6.00	12.00
❏ 182	PS	Goldfinger/Sleep Walk	1964	6.25	12.50	25.00
❏ 189		Brazilian Summer/Off Tempo	1965	3.00	6.00	12.00
❏ 194		Watermelon Man/Return to Naples	1965	3.00	6.00	12.00
❏ 204		Come with Me/The Young World	1967	2.50	5.00	10.00

Imperial

Number		Title (A Side/B Side)	Year	VG	VG+	NM
❏ 66269		Live for Life/See You in September	1968	2.50	5.00	10.00
❏ 66292		Sleep Walk '68/It Must Be Him	1968	2.50	5.00	10.00

Pausa

Number		Title (A Side/B Side)	Year	VG	VG+	NM
❏ 703		Come Back Soldier/Flamingo	1976		2.50	5.00

United Artists

Number		Title (A Side/B Side)	Year	VG	VG+	NM
❏ 970		Thunderball/Mister Kiss Kiss Bang Bang	1966	2.50	5.00	10.00

Santos, Larry
Atlantic

Number		Title (A Side/B Side)	Year	VG	VG+	NM
❏ 2250		Someday (When I'm Gone)/True	1964	5.00	10.00	20.00
		With the Four Seasons on backup				

Casablanca

Number		Title (A Side/B Side)	Year	VG	VG+	NM
❏ 844		Can't Get You Off My Mind/We Can't Hide It Anymore	1975		3.00	6.00
		With "Can't Get You Off My Mind" listed as "Side A"				
❏ 844		We Can't Hide It Anymore/Can't Get You Off My Mind	1976		2.00	4.00
		With "We Can't Hide It Anymore" listed as "Side A"				
❏ 869		You Are Everything I Need/Long, Long Time	1976		2.00	4.00
❏ 881		Magic Mountain/Don't Let the Music Stop	1977		2.00	4.00

Evolution

Number		Title (A Side/B Side)	Year	VG	VG+	NM
❏ 1007		Tomorrow Without Love/	1969		3.00	6.00
		You Got Me Where You Want Me				
❏ 1010		Subway Man/Woman-Child	1969		3.00	6.00
❏ 1018		Great Divide/Paper Chase	1970		3.00	6.00
❏ 1024		Mornin' Sun/Wandering Man	1970		3.00	6.00
❏ 1029		Now That I Have Found You/Wandering Man	1970		3.00	6.00
❏ 1039		Let It End/Little Bit of You	1971		3.00	6.00
❏ 1043		I Love You More Than Everything/Let It End	1971		3.00	6.00

Number	Title (A Side/B Side)	Year	VG	VG+	NM

Sapphires, The
ABC-Paramount

❏ 10559	Hearts Are Made to Be Broken/Let's Break Up for Awhile	1964	3.75	7.50	15.00
❏ 10590	Thank You for Loving Me/Our Love Is Everywhere	1964	3.75	7.50	15.00
❏ 10639	Gee I'm Sorry, Baby/Gotta Have Your Love	1965	3.75	7.50	15.00
❏ 10693	Evil One/How Could I Say Goodbye	1965	3.75	7.50	15.00
❏ 10753	You'll Never Stop Me from Loving You/Gonna Be a Big Thing	1965	3.75	7.50	15.00
❏ 10778	Our Love Is Everywhere/Slow Fizz	1966	3.75	7.50	15.00

Itzy

| ❏ 8 | Who Do You Love/Oh So Soon | 1963 | 10.00 | 20.00 | 40.00 |

RCA Victor

| ❏ 47-7357 | Everyone Knows/So Glad | 1958 | 5.00 | 10.00 | 20.00 |

Swan

❏ 4143	Your True Love/Where Is Johnny Now	1963	3.75	7.50	15.00
❏ 4162	Who Do You Love/Oh So Soon	1963	3.75	7.50	15.00
❏ 4177	I Found Out Too Late/I've Got Mine, You Better Get Yours	1964	3.75	7.50	15.00
❏ 4184	Gotta Be More Than Friends/Moulin Rouge	1964	3.75	7.50	15.00

Sardo, Frankie
ABC-Paramount

| ❏ 10003 | No Love Like Mine/Oh Linda | 1959 | 5.00 | 10.00 | 20.00 |
| ❏ 9963 | Class Room/Fake Out | 1958 | 5.00 | 10.00 | 20.00 |

Lido

| ❏ 602 | Kiss and Make Up/The Girl I'm Gonna Dream About | 1959 | 5.00 | 10.00 | 20.00 |

MGM

| ❏ 12621 | May I/My Story of Love | 1958 | 5.00 | 10.00 | 20.00 |

Newtown

| ❏ 5005 | I Got You Where I Want You/Mr. Make Believe | 1962 | 6.25 | 12.50 | 25.00 |

Rayna

| ❏ 5005 | Ring of Love/She Taught Me How to Cry | 1962 | 3.75 | 7.50 | 15.00 |

Studio

| ❏ 9910 | Just You Watch Me/I'm Sittin' at Home | 1961 | 12.50 | 25.00 | 50.00 |

20th Fox

| ❏ 208 | I Know Why and So Do You/When the Bells Stop Ringing | 1960 | 5.00 | 10.00 | 20.00 |
| ❏ 221 | Dream Lover/Bonnie, Bonnie | 1960 | 6.25 | 12.50 | 25.00 |

Sardo, Johnny
Chock Full-O-Hits

| ❏ 104 | (Hip Hop) Take a Ride with Me/Hollywood Sign | 1958 | 25.00 | 50.00 | 100.00 |

Warner Bros.

| ❏ 5044 | Late, Late, Late to School/New Kid in Town | 1959 | 6.25 | 12.50 | 25.00 |

Satan and the Disciples
(Allegedly, this is Freddy Fender)
Goldband

| ❏ 1188 | Mummies Curse/Cat's Meow | 1969 | 6.25 | 12.50 | 25.00 |

Satellites, The
(More than one group)
ABC-Paramount

| ❏ 10038 | Linda Jean/Rockateen | 1959 | 10.00 | 20.00 | 40.00 |

Class

| ❏ 234 | Heavenly Angel/You Ain't Sayin' Nothin' | 1958 | 7.50 | 15.00 | 30.00 |

D-M-G

| ❏ 4001 | Each Night/Darktown Strutters Ball | 1960 | 7.50 | 15.00 | 30.00 |

Malynn

| ❏ 231 | Heavenly Angel/You Ain't Sayin' Nothin' | 1958 | 6.25 | 12.50 | 25.00 |

Palace

| ❏ 102 | Buzz Buzz/We Like Birdland | 1960 | 5.00 | 10.00 | 20.00 |

Parrot

| ❏ 313 | Bodacious/El San Juan | 1966 | 6.25 | 12.50 | 25.00 |

United Artists

| ❏ 141 | I Found a Girl/My Piggie's Gotta Dance | 1958 | 10.00 | 20.00 | 40.00 |

Satintones, The
Motown

| ❏ 1000 | Sugar Daddy/My Beloved | 1960 | 100.00 | 200.00 | 400.00 |

With strings. Matrix number of A-side is "1000 G-3"

| ❏ 1000 | Sugar Daddy/My Beloved | 1960 | 100.00 | 200.00 | 400.00 |

Without strings. Matrix number of A-side is "MNT 12345"

| ❏ 1006 | Angel/A Love That Can Never Be | 1961 | 375.00 | 750.00 | 1,500 |
| ❏ 1006 | Tomorrow and Always/A Love That Can Never Be | 1961 | 62.50 | 125.00 | 250.00 |

With strings

| ❏ 1006 | Tomorrow and Always/A Love That Can Never Be | 1961 | 62.50 | 125.00 | 250.00 |

Without strings

| ❏ 1010 | I Know How It Feels/My Kind of Love | 1961 | 50.00 | 100.00 | 200.00 |
| ❏ 1020 | Zing Went the Strings of My Heart/Faded Letter | 1962 | 50.00 | 100.00 | 200.00 |

Number		Title (A Side/B Side)	Year	VG	VG+	NM
Tamla						
❏ 54026		Motor City/Going to the Hop	1960	200.00	400.00	800.00

Saturday Knights, The
Nocturne

❏ 1030		Sea Mist/Queen of the Nile	1963	12.50	25.00	50.00
Swan						
❏ 4075		Ticonderoga/Tiger Lily	1961	5.00	10.00	20.00
❏ 4081		Hawaiian Tears/Texas Tommy	1961	5.00	10.00	20.00

Saturday, Patty
Swan

| ❏ 4022 | | Ladies Choice/Love Is a Beautiful Thing | 1959 | 6.25 | 12.50 | 25.00 |

Saunders, Little Butchie
Herald

| ❏ 485 | | Lindy Lou/Rock 'N' Roll Indian Dance | 1956 | 12.50 | 25.00 | 50.00 |
| ❏ 491 | | Great Big Heart/I Wanna Holler | 1956 | 12.50 | 25.00 | 50.00 |

Savage, Duke, and the Arribins
Argo

| ❏ 5346 | | Your Love/Hey Baby | 1959 | 10.00 | 20.00 | 40.00 |

Sawyer, Ray
(Of Dr. Hook [and the Medicine Show])
Capitol

❏ 4344		(One More Year of) Daddy's Little Girl/ I Need That High (But I Can't Stand the Taste)	1976		2.00	4.00
❏ 4386		Red-Winged Blackbird/The One I'm Holding Now	1977		2.00	4.00
❏ 4416		Walls and Doors/ I Need That HIgh (But I Can't Stand the Taste)	1977		2.00	4.00
❏ 4592		Dancing Fool/Rhythm Guitar	1978		2.00	4.00
❏ 4747		What I'm Holding/I Want Johnny's Job	1979		2.00	4.00
❏ 4820		Drinking Wine Alone/I Don't Feel Like Smilin'	1980		2.00	4.00
Sandy						
❏ 1030		Rockin' Satellite/Bells in My Heart	1961	10.00	20.00	40.00
❏ 1037		I'm Gonna Leave/You Gave Me the Right	1961	6.25	12.50	25.00

Saxon, Eddie, and the Paramounts
Empress

| ❏ 106 | | Blues No More/If It's Meant to Be | 1962 | 37.50 | 75.00 | 150.00 |
| ❏ 106 | DJ | Blues No More
Single-sided promo | 1962 | 50.00 | 100.00 | 200.00 |

Saxon, Sky
(Later recorded with The Seeds; also see "March, Ritchie")
Conquest

| ❏ 777 | | They Say/Go Ahead and Cry | 1964 | 7.50 | 15.00 | 30.00 |

Sayer, Leo
Warner Bros.

❏ 7768		The Show Must Go On/Innocent Bystander	1974	2.00	4.00	8.00
❏ 7824		One Man Band/Drop Back	1974		3.00	6.00
❏ 8043		Long Tall Glasses/In My Life	1974		3.00	6.00
		First pressings have no A-side subtitle				
❏ 8043		Long Tall Glasses (I Can Dance)/In My Life	1975		2.50	5.00
		Later pressings add subtitle to A-side				
❏ 8097		One Man Band/Telepath	1975		2.50	5.00
❏ 8153		Moonlighting/Streets of Your Town	1975		2.50	5.00
❏ 8283		You Make Me Feel Like Dancing/Magdalena	1976		2.50	5.00
❏ 8319		How Much Love/I Hear the Laughter	1977		2.50	5.00
❏ 8332		When I Need You/I Think We Fell in Love Too Fast	1977		2.50	5.00
❏ 8419		Do You Believe in Love at First Sight/Do I Have to Cry	1977		2.50	5.00
❏ 8465		Thunder in My Heart/Get the Girl	1977		2.50	5.00
❏ 8502		Easy to Love/Haunting Me	1977		2.50	5.00
❏ 8682		Raining in My Heart/No Looking Back	1978		2.00	4.00
❏ 8738		Don't Look Back/No Looking Back	1979		2.00	4.00
❏ 29904		Paris Dies in the Morning/We've Got Ourselves in Love	1982		2.00	4.00
❏ 29960		End of the Game/Heart	1982		2.00	4.00
❏ 49134		Oh Girl/Englishman in the U.S.A.	1979		2.00	4.00
❏ 49565		More Than I Can Say/Millionaire	1980		2.00	4.00
❏ 49657		Living in a Fantasy/Only Foolin'	1981		2.00	4.00
❏ 49714		Where Did We Go Wrong/She's Not Coming Back	1981		2.00	4.00
❏ 50060		Have You Ever Been in Love/ I Don't Need Dreaming Anymore	1982		2.00	4.00

Scaffold, The
(With Mike McGear, Paul McCartney's brother)
Bell

❏ 701		Thank U Very Much/Ide B the First	1968	4.00	8.00	16.00
❏ 724		Do You Remember/Carry On Krow	1968	4.00	8.00	16.00
❏ 747		Lily the Pink/Buttons of Your Mind	1968	4.00	8.00	16.00
❏ 821		Charity Bubbles/Goose	1969	4.00	8.00	16.00
❏ 849		Jelly Covered Cloud/Liver Birds	1969	3.00	6.00	12.00

Number		Title (A Side/B Side)	Year	VG	VG+	NM
Warner Bros.						
❑ 8001		Liverpool Lou/Ten Years After on Strawberry Jam	1974		3.00	6.00

Scaggs, Boz
(Early member of the Steve Miller Band)
Atlantic

❑ 2692		I'm Easy/I'll Be Long Gone	1969	2.50	5.00	10.00

Columbia

❑ 01023		You Can Have Me Anytime/Georgia	1981		2.00	4.00
❑ 02423		Jojo/Miss Sun	1981			3.00
	Reissue					
❑ 02424		Breakdown Dead Ahead/Look What You've Done to Me	1981			3.00
	Reissue					
❑ 07780		Heart of Mine/You'll Never Know	1988			3.00
❑ 07780	PS	Heart of Mine/You'll Never Know	1988		2.00	4.00
❑ 07981		Cool Running/You'll Never Know	1988			3.00
❑ 08068		What's Number 1/Claudia	1988			3.00
❑ 10027		Slow Dancer/Pain of Love	1974		3.00	6.00
❑ 10124		You Make It So Hard (To Say Goodbye)/There Is Something Else	1975		2.50	5.00
❑ 10319		It's Over/Harbor Lights	1976		2.50	5.00
❑ 10367		Lowdown/Harbor Lights	1976		2.50	5.00
❑ 10440		What Can I Say/We're All Alone	1976		2.50	5.00
❑ 10491		Lido Shuffle/We're All Alone	1977		2.50	5.00
❑ 10606		Hard Times/We're Waiting	1977		2.50	5.00
❑ 10606	PS	Hard Times/We're Waiting	1977	2.50	5.00	10.00
❑ 10679		Hollywood/A Clue	1978		2.50	5.00
❑ 11241		Breakdown Dead Ahead/Isn't It Time	1980		2.00	4.00
❑ 11281		Jojo/Do Like You Do in New York	1980		2.00	4.00
❑ 11349		Look What You've Done to Me/Simone	1980		2.00	4.00
❑ 11406		Miss Sun/Dinah Flo	1980		2.00	4.00
❑ 45353		We Were Always Sweethearts/Painted Bells	1971		3.00	6.00
❑ 45408		Near You/Downright Woman	1971		3.00	6.00
❑ 45540		Here to Stay/Runnin' Blue	1972		3.00	6.00
❑ 45670		Dinah Flo/He's a Fool for You	1972		3.00	6.00
❑ 46025		You Make It So Hard (To Say Goodbye)/There Is Someone Else	1974		3.00	6.00

Full Moon

❑ 49676		You Make It So Hard (To Say Goodbye)/Something's Missing in My Life	1981		2.00	4.00
	B-side by Lady Sylvia					

Virgin

❑ S7-18048		I'll Be the One/Time Change	1994		2.00	4.00

Scarlets, The
(More than one group)
Dot

❑ 16004		Stampede/Park Avenue	1959	6.25	12.50	25.00

Event

❑ 4287		Dear One/I've Lost	1958	6.25	12.50	25.00

Fury

❑ 1036		Truly Yours/East of the Sun	1960	7.50	15.00	30.00

Prince

❑ 1207		Stampede/Park Avenue	1959	12.50	25.00	50.00

Red Robin

❑ 128		Dear One/I've Lost	1954	50.00	100.00	200.00
❑ 133		Darling, I'm Yours/Love Doll	1954	50.00	100.00	200.00
❑ 135		True Love/Cry Baby	1955	50.00	100.00	200.00
❑ 138		Kiss Me/Indian Fever	1955	100.00	200.00	400.00

Tower

❑ 144		I've Had It/You Don't Love Me	1965	2.50	5.00	10.00

Scavengers, The
Fenton

❑ 987		Curfew/Oasis	1964	12.50	25.00	50.00

Mobile Fidelity

❑ 1005		The Angels Listened In/My Love Waits for Me	1963	7.50	15.00	30.00
❑ 1212		Devil's Reef/Little Annie	1963	7.50	15.00	30.00

Stars of Hollywood

❑ 1210		Shot Gun/Cream Puff	1963	12.50	25.00	50.00
❑ 1211		Shot Gun/Zip Code	1963	12.50	25.00	50.00
	"Cream Puff" and "Zip Code" are different titles for the same recording					
❑ 1212		Devil's Reef/Little Annie	1963	12.50	25.00	50.00

Suemi

❑ 4552		Bogus/Ghost Riders '65	1965	6.25	12.50	25.00

Schiling, Johnny, and the Sherwoods
C&A

❑ 507		King of the World/Marcelle	1963	25.00	50.00	100.00

Number		Title (A Side/B Side)	Year	VG	VG+	NM

Schmit, Timothy B.
(Of the Eagles and Poco)
Asylum
❏ 69600		Playin' It Cool/Wrong Number	1984			3.00
❏ 69939		So Much in Love/	1982		2.00	4.00
		She's My Baby and She's Outta Control				
		B-side by Palmer/Jost				
❏ 69939	PS	So Much in Love/	1982		2.50	5.00
		She's My Baby and She's Outta Control				

MCA
❏ 53137		Boys Night Out/Into the Night	1987			3.00
❏ 53137	PS	Boys Night Out/Into the Night	1987			3.00
❏ 53233		Don't Give Up/Jazz Street	1987			3.00
❏ 53284		Everybody Needs a Lover/Into the Night	1988			3.00

Schumacher, Christine, Sings with the Supremes
Motown
❏ L294-MO5	DJ	Mother You, Smother You (same on both sides)	1968	75.00	150.00	300.00
		Schumacher won a "Record a Record with the Supremes" contest on WKNR of Detroit. This is the rare result.				

Scott, Jack
ABC
❏ 10843		Before the Bird Flies/Insane	1966	5.00	10.00	20.00

ABC-Paramount
❏ 9818		Baby She's Mine/You Can Bet Your Bottom Dollar	1957	37.50	75.00	150.00
❏ 9860		Two Timin' Woman/I Need Your Love	1957	37.50	75.00	150.00

Capitol
❏ 4554		A Little Feeling (Called Love)/Now That I	1961	6.25	12.50	25.00
❏ 4554	PS	A Little Feeling (Called Love)/Now That I	1961	12.50	25.00	50.00
❏ 4597		My Dream Came True/Strange Desire	1961	5.00	10.00	20.00
❏ 4597	PS	My Dream Came True/Strange Desire	1961	12.50	25.00	50.00
❏ 4637		Steps 1 and 2/One of These Days	1961	5.00	10.00	20.00
❏ 4637	PS	Steps 1 and 2/One of These Days	1961	12.50	25.00	50.00
❏ 4689		Cry, Cry, Cry/Grizzly Bear	1962	5.00	10.00	20.00
❏ 4738		The Part Where I Cry/	1962	5.00	10.00	20.00
		You Only See What You Wanna See				
❏ 4796		Sad Story/I Can't Hold Your Letters	1962	5.00	10.00	20.00
❏ 4855		If Only/Green, Green Valley	1962	5.00	10.00	20.00
❏ 4903		Strangers/Laugh and the World Laughs With You	1963	5.00	10.00	20.00
❏ 4955		All I See Is Blue/Meo Myo	1963	5.00	10.00	20.00

Carlton
❏ 462		My True Love/Leroy	1958	7.50	15.00	30.00
❏ 483		With Your Love/Geraldine	1958	7.50	15.00	30.00
❏ 483	PS	With Your Love/Geraldine	1958	12.50	25.00	50.00
❏ 493		Goodbye Baby/Save My Soul	1959	7.50	15.00	30.00
❏ 493	PS	Goodbye Baby/Save My Soul	1959	12.50	25.00	50.00
❏ 504		I Never Felt Like This/Bella	1959	7.50	15.00	30.00
❏ 514		The Way I Walk/Midgie	1959	7.50	15.00	30.00
❏ 519	M	There Comes a Time/Baby Marie	1959	5.00	10.00	20.00
❏ ST-519	S	There Comes a Time/Baby Marie	1959	10.00	20.00	40.00

Dot
❏ 17475		May You Never Be Alone/Face to the Wall	1973		2.50	5.00
❏ 17504		You're Just Getting Better/Walk Through My Mind	1974		2.50	5.00

Groove
❏ 58-0027		There's Trouble Brewin'/Jingle Bell Slide	1963	5.00	10.00	20.00
❏ 58-0031		Blue Skies (Moving In on Me)/I Knew You First	1964	3.75	7.50	15.00
❏ 58-0037		Wiggle On Out/What a Wonderful Night Out	1964	5.00	10.00	20.00
❏ 58-0042		Thou Shalt Not Steal/I Prayed for an Angel	1964	3.75	7.50	15.00
❏ 58-0049		Flakey John/Tall Tales	1964	5.00	10.00	20.00

GRT
❏ 35		Billy Jack/Mary, Marry Me	1971		2.50	5.00

Guaranteed
❏ 209		What Am I Living For/Indiana Waltz	1960	7.50	15.00	30.00
❏ 211		No One Will Ever Know/Go Wild Little Sadie	1960	7.50	15.00	30.00

Jubilee
❏ 5606		My Special Angel/I Keep Changin' My Mind	1967	5.00	10.00	20.00

Ponie
❏ 4104-30		Spirit of '76/(Instrumental)	1976		2.00	4.00
❏ 5121-15		Baby She's Gone/Two Timin' Woman	197?		2.00	4.00
❏ 6063-20		Leroy/Go Wild Little Sadie	197?		2.00	4.00
❏ 6083-20		Country Witch/Blues, Stay Away from Me-Stones	197?		2.00	4.00
❏ 7021-10		Geraldine/Midgie	197?		2.00	4.00
❏ 7021-11		There's Trouble Brewin'/Jingle Bell Slide	197?		2.00	4.00
❏ 7021-12		Flakey John/Wiggle On Out	197?		2.00	4.00

RCA Victor
❏ 47-8505		Separation's Now Granted/	1965	3.75	7.50	15.00
		I Don't Believe in Tea Leaves				
❏ 47-8685		Looking for Linda/I Hope I Think I Wish	1965	3.75	7.50	15.00
❏ 47-8724		Don't Hush the Laughter/Let's Learn to Live	1965	3.75	7.50	15.00

Top Rank
❏ 2028	M	What in the World's Come Over You/Baby Baby	1959	5.00	10.00	20.00
❏ 2028	S	What in the World's Come Over You/Baby Baby	1959	10.00	20.00	40.00
❏ 2041	M	Burning Bridges/Oh Little One	1960	5.00	10.00	20.00

Number		Title (A Side/B Side)	Year	VG	VG+	NM
❑ 2041	PS	Burning Bridges/Oh Little One	1960	12.50	25.00	50.00
❑ 2041	S	Burning Bridges/Oh Little One	1960	10.00	20.00	40.00
❑ 2055		It Only Happened Yesterday/Cool Water	1960	5.00	10.00	20.00
❑ 2075		Patsy/Old Time Religion	1960	5.00	10.00	20.00
❑ 2093		Is There Something on Your Mind/Found a Woman	1960	5.00	10.00	20.00
❑ 2093	PS	Is There Something on Your Mind/Found a Woman	1960	12.50	25.00	50.00

Scott, Joel
Philles

❑ 101		Here I Stand/You're My Only Love	1962	6.25	12.50	25.00

Scott, Linda
Canadian American

❑ 123		I've Told Every Little Star/Three Guesses	1961	5.00	10.00	20.00
❑ 127		Don't Bet Money Honey/Starlight, Starbright	1961	5.00	10.00	20.00
❑ 129		I Don't Know Why/It's All Because	1961	5.00	10.00	20.00
❑ 132		Christmas Day/Twistin' Bells	1961	5.00	10.00	20.00
		B-side by Santo and Johnny				
❑ 133		Count Every Star/Land of Stars	1962	3.75	7.50	15.00
❑ 134		Bermuda/Lonely for You	1962	3.75	7.50	15.00

Congress

❑ 101		Yessiree/Town Crier	1962	3.75	7.50	15.00
❑ 103		Never in a Million Years/Through the Summer	1962	3.75	7.50	15.00
❑ 106		I Left My Heart in the Balcony/Lopsided Love Affair	1962	3.75	7.50	15.00
❑ 108		I'm So Afraid of Losing You/The Loneliest Girl in Town	1962	3.75	7.50	15.00
❑ 110		I'm Gonna Sit Right Down and Write Myself a Letter/Ain't That Fun	1963	3.75	7.50	15.00
❑ 200		Let's Fall in Love/I Know It, You Know It	1963	3.75	7.50	15.00
❑ 204		Who's Been Sleeping in My Bed/My Baby	1963	3.75	7.50	15.00
❑ 206		Let's Fall in Love/I Know It, You Know It	1964	3.75	7.50	15.00
❑ 209		I Envy You/Everybody Stopped Laughing at Jane	1964	3.75	7.50	15.00

Kapp

❑ 610		That Old Feeling/This Is My Prayer	1964	2.50	5.00	10.00
❑ 641		If I Love Again/Patch It Up	1965	2.50	5.00	10.00
❑ 677		Don't Lose Your Head/I'll See You in My Dreams	1965	2.50	5.00	10.00
❑ 713		You Baby/I Can't Get Through to You	1965	2.50	5.00	10.00
❑ 762		Toys/Take a Walk Bobby	1966	2.50	5.00	10.00

RCA Victor

❑ 47-9424		They Don't Know You/Three Miles High	1967	2.50	5.00	10.00

Scott, Ricky
Cub

❑ 9079		I Didn't Mean It/Darlin' Darlin'	1960	5.00	10.00	20.00

X-Clusive

❑ 1001		I Didn't Mean It/Darlin' Darlin'	1960	20.00	40.00	80.00

Scott, Rodney
Canon

❑ 225		Granny Went Rockin'/Bitter Tears	1961	50.00	100.00	200.00
❑ 231		You're So Square (Baby I Don't Care)/He'll Be There	1961	50.00	100.00	200.00

Mr. Peeke

❑ 119		You're So Square (Baby I Don't Care)/He'll Be There	1962	20.00	40.00	80.00
❑ 126		That's the Way It Goes/Bitter Tears	1963	7.50	15.00	30.00

Scott, Sherree
Robbins

❑ 1036		Fascinating Baby/You and I	1957	37.50	75.00	150.00

Rocket

❑ 101		Whole Lotta Shakin' Goin' On/Unhappy Birthday	1958	37.50	75.00	150.00
❑ 101	PS	Whole Lotta Shakin' Goin' On/Unhappy Birthday	1958	50.00	100.00	200.00

Scott, Walter
(Of Bob Kuban and the In-Men)
Musicland U.S.A.

❑ 20,009		Watch Out/My Shadow Is Gone	1966	3.75	7.50	15.00
❑ 20,014		It's Been a Long Time/Proud	1966	3.75	7.50	15.00

Pzazz

❑ 026		Soul Stew Recipe/Feeling Something New Inside	1969	2.50	5.00	10.00

White Whale

❑ 259		Just You Wait/Silly Girl	1967	5.00	10.00	20.00

Sea Shells, The
Goliath

❑ 1357		Love Those Beach Boys/Close to Jimmy	1964	10.00	20.00	40.00

Jubilee

❑ 5587		Hit the Surf/Barefoot in the Sand	1967	5.00	10.00	20.00

Seafood Mama
(Early incarnation of Quarterflash)
Whitefire

❑ (no #)		Harden My Heart/(B-side unknown)	1980	6.25	12.50	25.00
❑ (no #)	PS	Harden My Heart/(B-side unknown)	1980	6.25	12.50	25.00

Number		Title (A Side/B Side)	Year	VG	VG+	NM

Seals and Crofts
(Latter-day members of The Champs. Also see "Seals, Jimmy")
T-A

Number		Title (A Side/B Side)	Year	VG	VG+	NM
☐ 188		In Tune/Seldom's Sister	1969	2.00	4.00	8.00
☐ 191		See My Life/(B-side unknown)	1969	2.00	4.00	8.00
☐ 206		See My Life/In Tune//Hollow Reed/Leave	1970	2.50	5.00	10.00
☐ 208		Ridin' Thumb/Leave	1970	2.00	4.00	8.00
☐ 210		Gabriel Go On Home/Robin	1971	2.00	4.00	8.00

Warner Bros.

Number		Title (A Side/B Side)	Year	VG	VG+	NM
☐ 7536		When You Meet Them/Irish Linen	1971		3.00	6.00
☐ 7565		Sudan Village/High on a Mountain	1972		3.00	6.00
☐ 7606		Summer Breeze/East of Ginger Trees	1972		2.50	5.00
☐ 7671		Hummingbird/Say	1972		2.50	5.00
☐ 7697		We May Never Pass This Way (Again)/ Intone My Servant	1973		Unreleased?	
☐ 7708		Diamond Girl/Wisdom	1973		2.50	5.00
☐ 7740		We May Never Pass This Way (Again)/Jessica	1973		2.50	5.00
☐ 7771		Unborn Child/Ledges	1974		2.00	4.00
☐ 7810		King of Nothing/Follow Me	1974		2.00	4.00
☐ 8075		I'll Play for You/Truth Is But a Woman	1975		2.00	4.00
☐ 8130		Castles in the Sand/Golden Rainbow	1975		2.00	4.00
☐ 8190		Get Closer/Don't Fail	1976		2.00	4.00
☐ 8277		Baby, I'll Give It to You/Advance Guards	1976		2.00	4.00
☐ 8405		My Fair Share/East of Ginger Trees	1977		2.00	4.00
☐ 8405	PS	My Fair Share/East of Ginger Trees	1977		3.00	6.00
☐ 8551		You're the Love/Midnight Blue	1978		2.00	4.00
☐ 8639		Magnolia Moon/Takin' It Easy	1978		2.00	4.00
☐ 49522		First Love/Kite Dreams	1980		2.00	4.00

Seals, Jimmy
(Also see "Champs, The"; "Seals and Crofts")
Carlton

Number		Title (A Side/B Side)	Year	VG	VG+	NM
☐ 470		Sneaky Pete/Benguela	1958	7.50	15.00	30.00

Challenge

Number		Title (A Side/B Side)	Year	VG	VG+	NM
☐ 59270		Everybody's Doing the Jerk/Wa-Hoo	1965	5.00	10.00	20.00
☐ 59299		She's Not a Bad Girl/The Yesterday of Our Love	1965	5.00	10.00	20.00
☐ 9153		Wish for You, Want for You, Wait for You/ Runaway Heart	1962	7.50	15.00	30.00
☐ 9200		Lady Heartbreak/Grounded	1963	7.50	15.00	30.00

Winston

Number		Title (A Side/B Side)	Year	VG	VG+	NM
☐ 1021		Sneaky Pete/Benguela	1958	10.00	20.00	50.00
☐ 1027		Biscayne Bay/Juarez	1958	10.00	20.00	50.00

Sean and the Brandywines
Decca

Number		Title (A Side/B Side)	Year	VG	VG+	NM
☐ 31910		She Ain't No Good/Cod'ine	1966	5.00	10.00	20.00

Searchers, The
Kapp

Number		Title (A Side/B Side)	Year	VG	VG+	NM
☐ KCS-27		Love Potion Number Nine/Hi-Heel Sneakers	1964	2.50	5.00	10.00
		Orange label "Winners Circle Series"; no black label counterpart				
☐ KCS-29		Bumble Bee/Everything You Do	1964	2.50	5.00	10.00
		Orange label "Winners Circle Series"; no black label counterpart				
☐ KCS-49		Bumble Bee/A Tear Fell	1965	2.50	5.00	10.00
		Orange label "Winners Circle Series"; no black label counterpart				
☐ 577		Needles and Pins/Ain't That Just Like Me	1964	2.50	5.00	10.00
☐ 577	PS	Needles and Pins/Ain't That Just Like Me	1964	7.50	15.00	30.00
☐ 577	PS	Needles and Pins (promo-only version)	1964	12.50	25.00	50.00
☐ 584		Ain't That Just Like Me/Ain't Gonna Kiss You	1964	2.50	5.00	10.00
☐ 584	PS	Ain't That Just Like Me (special promo sleeve)	1964	12.50	25.00	50.00
☐ 593		Don't Throw Your Love Away/I'll Pretend I'm with You	1964	2.50	5.00	10.00
☐ 609		Someday We're Gonna Love Again/ No One Else Could Love Me	1964	2.50	5.00	10.00
☐ 609	PS	Someday We're Gonna Love Again/ No One Else Could Love Me	1964	7.50	15.00	30.00
☐ 618		When You Walk in the Room/I'll Be Missing You	1964	2.50	5.00	10.00
☐ 644		What Have They Done to the Rain/This Feeling Inside	1965	2.50	5.00	10.00
☐ 658		Goodbye My Lover Goodbye/'Til I Met You	1965	2.50	5.00	10.00
☐ 686		He's Got No Love/So Far Away	1965	2.50	5.00	10.00
☐ 706		Don't You Know Why/You Can't Lie to a Liar	1965	2.50	5.00	10.00
☐ 729		Take Me for What I'm Worth/Too Many Miles	1966	2.50	5.00	10.00
☐ 783		Have You Ever Loved Somebody/It's Just the Way	1966	2.50	5.00	10.00
☐ 811		Lovers/Popcorn Double Feature	1966	2.50	5.00	10.00

Liberty

Number		Title (A Side/B Side)	Year	VG	VG+	NM
☐ 55646		Sugar and Spice/Saints and Sinners	1963	6.25	12.50	25.00
☐ 55689		Sugar and Spice/Saints and Sinners	1964	3.75	7.50	15.00

Mercury

Number		Title (A Side/B Side)	Year	VG	VG+	NM
☐ 72172		Sweets for My Sweet/It's All Been a Dream	1963	6.25	12.50	25.00
☐ 72390		(Ain't That) Just Like Me/I Can Tell	1964	3.75	7.50	15.00

RCA Victor

Number		Title (A Side/B Side)	Year	VG	VG+	NM
☐ 74-0484		Desdemona/The World Is Waiting for Tomorrow	1971		3.00	6.00
☐ 74-0652		Love Is Everywhere/And the Button	1972		3.00	6.00

Number		Title (A Side/B Side)	Year	VG	VG+	NM
Sire						
❑ 49175		It's Too Late/Don't Hang On	1980		2.00	4.00
❑ 49665		Love's Melody/Little Bit of Heaven	1981		2.00	4.00
World Pacific						
❑ 77908		Umbrella Man/Over the Weekend	1969	2.00	4.00	8.00

Sebastian, John
(Of the Lovin' Spoonful)

Number		Title (A Side/B Side)	Year	VG	VG+	NM
Kama Sutra						
❑ 254		She's a Lady/The Room Nobody Lives In	1968	2.50	5.00	10.00
❑ 254	PS	She's a Lady/The Room Nobody Lives In	1968	3.75	7.50	15.00
❑ 505		Younger Generation/Boredom	1970	2.00	4.00	8.00
MGM						
❑ 14122		Rainbows All Over Your Blues/You're a Big Boy Now	1970		3.00	6.00
Reprise						
❑ 0902		Fa-Fana-Fa/Magical Connection	1970		3.00	6.00
❑ 0918		What She Thinks About/Red-Eye Express	1970		3.00	6.00
❑ 1026		I Don't Want Nobody Else/Sweet Muse	1971		3.00	6.00
❑ 1050		We'll See/Well, Well, Well	1971		3.00	6.00
❑ 1074		Give Us a Break/	1972		3.00	6.00
		Music for People Who Don't Speak English				
❑ 1349		Welcome Back Kotter/Warm Baby	1976	2.00	4.00	8.00
		Original A-side title				
❑ 1349		Welcome Back/Warm Baby	1976		2.00	4.00
		Revised A-side title				
❑ 1355		Hideaway/One Step Forward, Two Steps Back	1976		2.00	4.00

Secrets, The

Number		Title (A Side/B Side)	Year	VG	VG+	NM
Omen						
❑ 15		Here I Am/I Feel a Thrill Coming On	1966	2.50	5.00	10.00
Philips						
❑ 40146		The Boy Next Door/Learnin' to Forget	1963	3.75	7.50	15.00
❑ 40173		Hey Big Boy/The Other Side of Town	1964	3.00	6.00	12.00
❑ 40173	PS	Hey Big Boy/The Other Side of Town	1964	5.00	10.00	20.00
❑ 40196		Here He Comes/Oh Donnie	1964	3.00	6.00	12.00
❑ 40222		He's the Boy/He Doesn't Want You	1964	3.00	6.00	12.00
Red Bird						
❑ 10-076		Every Day/A Smile Upside Down	1966	2.50	5.00	10.00
Swan						
❑ 4097		Hot Toddy/Twin Exhaust	1962	6.25	12.50	25.00
❑ 4097	PS	Hot Toddy/Twin Exhaust	1962	12.50	25.00	50.00

Sedaka, Neil

Number		Title (A Side/B Side)	Year	VG	VG+	NM
Decca						
❑ 30520		Laura Lee/Showtime	1957	15.00	30.00	60.00
Elektra						
❑ 45406		Amarillo/The Leaving Game	1977		2.00	4.00
❑ 45421		Alone at Last/Sleazy Love	1977		2.00	4.00
❑ 45525		Candy Kisses/All You Need Is the Music	1978		2.00	4.00
❑ 46017		Sad, Sad Story/Tillie the Twirler	1979		2.00	4.00
❑ 46615		Should've Never Let You Go/You're So Good for Me	1980		2.00	4.00
		With Dara Sedaka				
❑ 47017		Letting Go/It's Good to Be Alive Again	1980		2.00	4.00
❑ 47184		My World Keeps Slipping Away/	1981		2.00	4.00
		Love Is Spreading Over the World				
Guyden						
❑ 2004		Ring-a-Rockin'/Fly, Don't Fly on Me	1958	12.50	25.00	50.00
Kirshner						
❑ 63-5017		I'm a Song (Sing Me)/Silent Movies	1971		2.50	5.00
❑ 63-5020		Superbird/Rosemary Blue	1972		2.50	5.00
❑ 63-5024		Beautiful You (Long)/Beautiful You (Short)	1972		2.50	5.00
Legion						
❑ 133		Ring-a-Rockin'/Fly, Don't Fly on Me	1958	25.00	50.00	100.00
MCA Curb						
❑ 52307		Your Precious Love/Searchin'	1983		2.00	4.00
		With Dara Sedaka				
❑ 52400		New Orleans/Rhythm of the Rain	1984		2.00	4.00
		With Gary U.S. Bonds				
MGM						
❑ 14564		Standing on the Inside/Let Daddy Know	1973		2.50	5.00
❑ 14661		Alone in New York in the Rain/Suspicions	1973		2.50	5.00
Pyramid						
❑ 623		Oh Delilah/Neil's Twist	1962	7.50	15.00	30.00
RCA Victor						
❑ 37-7829		Calendar Girl/The Same Old Fool	1960	12.50	25.00	50.00
		"Compact Single 33" (small hole, plays at LP speed)				
❑ 37-7874		Little Devil/I Must Be Dreaming	1961	12.50	25.00	50.00
		"Compact Single 33" (small hole, plays at LP speed)				
❑ 37-7922		Sweet Little You/I Found My World in You	1961	12.50	25.00	50.00
		"Compact Single 33" (small hole, plays at LP speed)				

Number		Title (A Side/B Side)	Year	VG	VG+	NM
❏ 37-7957		Happy Birthday Sweet Sixteen/Don't Lead Me On	1961	12.50	25.00	50.00
		"Compact Single 33" (small hole, plays at LP speed)				
❏ 47-7408		The Diary/No Vacancy	1958	5.00	10.00	20.00
❏ 47-7473		I Go Ape/Moon of Gold	1959	5.00	10.00	20.00
❏ 47-7530		You Gotta Learn Your Rhythm and Blues/	1959	6.25	12.50	25.00
		Crying My Heart Out for You				
❏ 47-7595		Oh! Carol/One Way Ticket (To the Blues)	1959	5.00	10.00	20.00
❏ 47-7709		Stairway to Heaven/Forty Winks Away	1960	3.75	7.50	15.00
❏ 47-7781		You Mean Everything to Me/Run Samson Run	1960	3.75	7.50	15.00
❏ 47-7781	PS	You Mean Everything to Me/Run Samson Run	1960	6.25	12.50	25.00
❏ 47-7829		Calendar Girl/The Same Old Fool	1960	3.75	7.50	15.00
❏ 47-7829	PS	Calendar Girl/The Same Old Fool	1960	6.25	12.50	25.00
❏ 47-7874		Little Devil/I Must Be Dreaming	1961	3.75	7.50	15.00
❏ 47-7874	PS	Little Devil/I Must Be Dreaming	1961	6.25	12.50	25.00
❏ 47-7922		Sweet Little You/I Found My World in You	1961	3.75	7.50	15.00
❏ 47-7922	PS	Sweet Little You/I Found My World in You	1961	6.25	12.50	25.00
❏ 47-7957		Happy Birthday Sweet Sixteen/Don't Lead Me On	1961	3.75	7.50	15.00
❏ 47-8007		King of Clowns/Walk with Me	1962	3.75	7.50	15.00
❏ 47-8007	PS	King of Clowns/Walk with Me	1962	6.25	12.50	25.00
❏ 47-8046		Breaking Up Is Hard to Do/As Long As I Live	1962	3.75	7.50	15.00
❏ 47-8046	PS	Breaking Up Is Hard to Do/As Long As I Live	1962	6.25	12.50	25.00
❏ 47-8086		Next Door to An Angel/I Belong to You	1962	3.75	7.50	15.00
❏ 47-8086	PS	Next Door to An Angel/I Belong to You	1962	6.25	12.50	25.00
❏ 47-8137		Alice in Wonderland/Circulate	1963	3.00	6.00	12.00
❏ 47-8137	PS	Alice in Wonderland/Circulate	1963	6.25	12.50	25.00
❏ 47-8169		Let's Go Steady Again/Waiting for Never	1963	3.00	6.00	12.00
❏ 47-8169	PS	Let's Go Steady Again/Waiting for Never	1963	6.25	12.50	25.00
❏ 47-8209		The Dreamer/Look Inside Your Heart	1963	3.00	6.00	12.00
❏ 47-8209	PS	The Dreamer/Look Inside Your Heart	1963	6.25	12.50	25.00
❏ 47-8254		Bad Girl/Wait 'Til You See My Baby	1963	3.00	6.00	12.00
❏ 47-8341		The Closest Thing to Heaven/Without a Song	1964	2.50	5.00	10.00
❏ 47-8382		Sunny/She'll Never Be You	1964	2.50	5.00	10.00
❏ 47-8453		I Hope He Breaks Your Heart/Too Late	1964	2.50	5.00	10.00
❏ 47-8511		Let the People Talk/In the Chapel with You	1965	2.50	5.00	10.00
❏ 47-8637		The World Through a Tear/High On a Mountain	1965	2.50	5.00	10.00
❏ 47-8637	PS	The World Through a Tear/High On a Mountain	1965	5.00	10.00	20.00
❏ 47-8737		The Answer to My Prayer/Blue Boy	1965	2.50	5.00	10.00
❏ 47-8844		The Answer Lies Within/Grown-Up Games	1966	2.50	5.00	10.00
❏ 47-9004		We Can Make It If We Try/Too Late	1966	2.50	5.00	10.00
❏ 61-7595		Oh! Carol/One Way Ticket (To the Blues)	1959	12.50	25.00	50.00
		"Living Stereo" (large hole, plays at 45 rpm)				
❏ 61-7709		Stairway to Heaven/Forty Winks Away	1960	12.50	25.00	50.00
		"Living Stereo" (large hole, plays at 45 rpm)				
❏ 61-7781		You Mean Everything to Me/Run Samson Run	1960	12.50	25.00	50.00
		"Living Stereo" (large hole, plays at 45 rpm)				
❏ 61-7829		Calendar Girl/The Same Old Fool	1960	12.50	25.00	50.00
		"Living Stereo" (large hole, plays at 45 rpm)				

Rocket

Number	Title (A Side/B Side)	Year	VG	VG+	NM
❏ 40313	Laughter in the Rain/Endlessly	1974		2.00	4.00
❏ 40370	The Immigrant/Hey Mister Sunshine	1975		2.00	4.00
❏ 40426	That's When the Music Takes Me/	1975		2.00	4.00
	Standing on the Inside				
❏ 40460	Bad Blood/Your Favorite Entertainer	1975		2.00	4.00
❏ 40500	Breaking Up Is Hard to Do/Nana's Song	1975		2.00	4.00
❏ 40543	Love in the Shadows/Baby Don't Let It Mess Your Mind	1976		2.00	4.00
❏ 40582	Steppin' Out/I Let You Walk Away	1976		2.00	4.00
❏ 40614	You Gotta Make Your Own Sunshine/Perfect Strangers	1976		2.00	4.00

SGC

Number	Title (A Side/B Side)	Year	VG	VG+	NM
❏ 005	Star-Crossed Lovers/We Had a Good Thing Going	1969		3.00	6.00
❏ 008	Rainy Jane/Jeannine	1970		3.00	6.00

Seeds, The

(Also see "Saxon, Sky")

GNP Crescendo

Number		Title (A Side/B Side)	Year	VG	VG+	NM
❏ 354		Can't Seem to Make You Mine/Daisy Mae	1965	3.75	7.50	15.00
❏ 354		Can't Seem to Make You Mine/I'll Tell Myself	1967	2.50	5.00	10.00
❏ 354	PS	Can't Seem to Make You Mine/I'll Tell Myself	1967	5.00	10.00	20.00
❏ 364		You're Pushing Too Hard/Out of the Question	1965	3.75	7.50	15.00
❏ 370		The Other Place/Try to Understand	1966	3.75	7.50	15.00
❏ 372		Pushin' Too Hard/Try to Understand	1966	3.00	6.00	12.00
❏ 383		Mr. Farmer/No Escape	1967	2.00	4.00	8.00
❏ 383		Mr. Farmer/Up in Her Room	1967	2.00	4.00	8.00
❏ 383	PS	Mr. Farmer/Up in Her Room	1967	7.50	15.00	30.00
❏ 394		A Thousand Shadows/March of the Flower Children	1967	2.00	4.00	8.00
❏ 394	PS	A Thousand Shadows/March of the Flower Children	1967	5.00	10.00	20.00
❏ 398		The Wind Blows Your Hair/Six Dreams	1967	2.00	4.00	8.00
❏ 408		Satisfy You/900 Million People Daily	1968	2.00	4.00	8.00
❏ 422		Fallin' Off the Edge of My Mind/Wild Blood	1969	2.50	5.00	10.00

MGM

Number	Title (A Side/B Side)	Year	VG	VG+	NM
❏ 14163	Wish Me Up/Bad Part of Town	1970	5.00	10.00	20.00
❏ 14190	Did He Die/Love in a Summer Blanket	1970	5.00	10.00	20.00

Philco

Number	Title (A Side/B Side)	Year	VG	VG+	NM
❏ HP-26	Pushin' Too Hard/Can't Seem to Make You Mine	1968	3.75	7.50	15.00
	4-inch flexi-disc in "Philco Hip-Pocket Record" series (price includes sleeve)				

Number		Title (A Side/B Side)	Year	VG	VG+	NM
Seekers, The						
Capitol						
☐ 2013		When the Good Apples Fall/Myra (Shake Up the Party)	1967	2.50	5.00	10.00
☐ 2122		Love Is Kind, Love Is Wine/All I Can Remember	1968	2.50	5.00	10.00
☐ 5383		I'll Never Find Another You/ Open Up Them Pearly Gates	1965	3.00	6.00	12.00
☐ 5430		A World of Our Own/Sinner Man	1965	3.00	6.00	12.00
☐ 5430	PS	A World of Our Own/Sinner Man	1965	5.00	10.00	20.00
☐ 5531		The Carnival Is Over/We Shall Not Be Moved	1965	2.50	5.00	10.00
☐ 5622		Some Day, One Day/ Nobody Knows the Trouble I've Seen	1966	2.50	5.00	10.00
☐ 5756		Georgy Girl/When the Stars Begin to Fall	1966	3.00	6.00	12.00
▶ 5787		Morningtown Ride/Walk with Me	1967	2.50	5.00	10.00
☐ 5974		I Wish You Could Be Here/On the Other Side	1967	2.50	5.00	10.00
Seger, Bob						
Abkco						
☐ 4015		East Side Story/East Side Sound	1973			*Unreleased?*
☐ 4016		Chain Smokin'/Persecution Smith	1973			*Unreleased?*
☐ 4017		Heavy Music/Heavy Music (Part 2)	1973			*Unreleased?*
☐ 4031		Heavy Music/Heavy Music (Part 2)	1973		2.50	5.00
Cameo						
☐ 438		East Side Story/East Side Sound	1966	6.25	12.50	25.00
☐ 444		Sock It To Me, Santa/Florida Time	1966	7.50	15.00	30.00
☐ 465		Chain Smokin'/Persecution Smith	1967	6.25	12.50	25.00
☐ 473		Vagrant Winter/Very Few	1967	6.25	12.50	25.00
☐ 494		Heavy Music/Heavy Music (Part 2)	1967	5.00	10.00	20.00
Capitol						
☐ 2143		2 + 2 = ?/Death Row	1968	3.75	7.50	15.00
☐ 2297		Ramblin' Gamblin' Man/Tales of Lucy Blue	1968	3.00	6.00	12.00
☐ 2480		Ivory/The Lost Song (Love Needs to Be Loved)	1969	2.00	4.00	8.00
☐ 2576		Noah/Lennie Johnson	1969	2.00	4.00	8.00
☐ 2640		Lonely Man/Innervenus Eyes	1970	2.00	4.00	8.00
☐ 2748		Lucifer/Big River	1970	2.00	4.00	8.00
☐ 3187		Lookin' Back/Highway Child	1971	2.00	4.00	8.00
☐ 4062		Beautiful Loser/Fine Memory	1975		2.50	5.00
☐ 4116		Katmandu/Black Night	1975		2.50	5.00
☐ 4183		Nutbush City Limits/Travelin' Man	1975		2.50	5.00
☐ 4269		Nutbush City Limits/Lookin' Back	1976		2.50	5.00
☐ 4300		Beautiful Loser/Travelin' Man	1976		2.50	5.00
☐ 4369		Night Moves/Ship of Fools	1976		2.00	4.00
☐ 4422		Mainstreet/Jody Girl	1977		2.00	4.00
☐ 4449		Rock and Roll Never Forgets/Fire Down Below	1977		2.00	4.00
☐ 4581		Still the Same/Feel Like a Number	1978		2.00	4.00
☐ 4618		Hollywood Nights/Brave Strangers	1978		2.00	4.00
☐ 4663		We've Got Tonite/Ain't Got No Money	1978		2.00	4.00
☐ 4663	DJ	We've Got Tonite (mono/stereo) *Silver vinyl*	1978	2.50	5.00	10.00
☐ 4663	PS	We've Got Tonite/Ain't Got No Money	1978		3.00	6.00
☐ 4702		Old Time Rock and Roll/Sunspot Baby	1979		2.00	4.00
☐ 4702	PS	Old Time Rock and Roll/Sunspot Baby	1979		3.00	6.00
☐ 4836		Fire Lake/Long Twin Silver Line	1980		2.00	4.00
☐ 4836	PS	Fire Lake/Long Twin Silver Line	1980		3.00	6.00
☐ 4863		Against the Wind/No Man's Land	1980		2.00	4.00
☐ 4863	PS	Against the Wind/No Man's Land	1980		3.00	6.00
☐ 4904		You'll Accomp'ny Me/Betty Lou's Gettin' Out Tonight	1980		2.50	5.00
☐ 4904	PS	You'll Accomp'ny Me/Betty Lou's Gettin' Out Tonight	1980		3.00	6.00
☐ 4951		The Horizontal Bop/Her Strut	1980		2.50	5.00
☐ 4951	PS	The Horizontal Bop/Her Strut	1980	25.00	50.00	100.00
☐ A-5042		Tryin' to Live My Life Without You/Brave Strangers	1981			3.00
☐ A-5042	PS	Tryin' to Live My Life Without You/Brave Strangers	1981		2.00	4.00
☐ A-5077		Feel Like a Number/Hollywood Nights	1981		2.00	4.00
☐ A-5077	PS	Feel Like a Number/Hollywood Nights	1981		2.50	5.00
☐ B-5187		Shame on the Moon/House Behind a House	1982			3.00
☐ B-5187	PS	Shame on the Moon/House Behind a House	1982		2.00	4.00
☐ B-5213		Even Now/Little Victories	1983			3.00
☐ B-5213	PS	Even Now/Little Victories	1983		2.00	4.00
☐ B-5235		Roll Me Away/Boomtown Blues	1983			3.00
☐ B-5235	PS	Roll Me Away/Boomtown Blues	1983		2.00	4.00
☐ B-5276		Old Time Rock and Roll/Till It Shines	1983			3.00
☐ B-5276	PS	Old Time Rock and Roll/Till It Shines	1983		2.50	5.00
☐ B-5413		Understanding/East L.A.	1984			3.00
☐ B-5413	PS	Understanding/East L.A.	1984		2.00	4.00
☐ B-5532		American Storm/Fortunate Son	1986			3.00
☐ B-5532	PS	American Storm/Fortunate Son	1986			3.00
☐ B-5592		Like a Rock/Livin' Inside My Heart	1986			3.00
☐ B-5592	PS	Like a Rock/Livin' Inside My Heart	1986			3.00
☐ B-5623		It's You/The Aftermath (12" Remix)	1986			3.00
☐ B-5623	PS	It's You/The Aftermath (12" Remix)	1986			3.00
☐ B-5658		Miami/Somewhere Tonight	1986			3.00
☐ SPRO 8433	DJ	Travelin' Man/Beautiful Loser	1976	2.50	5.00	10.00
☐ S7-18298		C'est La Vie/Night Moves	1995		2.00	4.00
☐ NR-44761		The Real Love/Roll Me Away	1991		2.00	4.00
☐ NR-44793		The Fire Inside/New Coat of Paint	1991		2.00	4.00
☐ S7-56784		Like a Rock/Sunspot Baby	1992		2.00	4.00
☐ S7-57732		New Coat of Paint/Blind Love	1992		2.00	4.00
☐ S7-57742		Night Moves/Her Strut	1992		2.00	4.00
☐ S7-57797		Old Time Rock and Roll/Turn the Page	1992		2.00	4.00

Number		Title (A Side/B Side)	Year	VG	VG+	NM
Hideout						
❑ 1013		East Side Story/East Side Sound	1966	12.50	25.00	50.00
❑ 1014		Chain Smokin'/Persecution Smith	1966	12.50	25.00	50.00
MCA						
❑ 53094		Shakedown/The Aftermath	1987			3.00
❑ 53094	PS	Shakedown/The Aftermath	1987		3.00	6.00
		Picture of Eddie Murphy as Axel Foley on cover				
❑ 53094	PS	Shakedown/The Aftermath	1987		2.00	4.00
		Picture of Bob Seger on cover				
Palladium						
❑ 1079		If I Were a Carpenter/Jesse James	1972	2.50	5.00	10.00
❑ 1117		Turn On Your Love Light/Who Do You Love?	1972	2.50	5.00	10.00
❑ 1143		Rosalie/Neon Sky	1972	2.50	5.00	10.00
❑ 1171		Need Ya/Seen a Lot of Floors	1973	2.50	5.00	10.00
❑ 1205		Get Out of Denver/Long Song Comin'	1974	2.50	5.00	10.00
❑ 1316		This Ole House/U.M.C.	1974	3.75	7.50	15.00
Reprise						
❑ PRO 571	DJ	Midnight Rider (same on both sides)	1972	3.75	7.50	15.00

Selections, The

Number		Title (A Side/B Side)	Year	VG	VG+	NM
Antone						
❑ 101		Guardian Angel/Soft and Sweet	1958	50.00	100.00	200.00
Mona Lee						
❑ 129		Guardian Angel/Soft and Sweet	1959	12.50	25.00	50.00

Self, Mack

Number		Title (A Side/B Side)	Year	VG	VG+	NM
Phillips Int'l.						
❑ 3548		Mad at You/Willie Brown	1959	6.25	12.50	25.00
Sun						
❑ 273		Easy to Love/Every Day	1957	7.50	15.00	30.00

Self, Ronnie

Number		Title (A Side/B Side)	Year	VG	VG+	NM
ABC-Paramount						
❑ 9714		Pretty Bad Blues/Three Hearts Later	1956	25.00	50.00	100.00
❑ 9768		Alone/Sweet Love	1956	25.00	50.00	100.00
Amy						
❑ 11009		High on Life/The Road Keeps Winding	1968	2.50	5.00	10.00
Columbia						
❑ 40989		Ain't I'm a Dog/Rocky Road Blues	1957	10.00	20.00	40.00
❑ 41101		Bop-A-Lena/I Ain't Going Nowhere	1958	7.50	15.00	30.00
❑ 41166		Big Blon' Baby/Date Bait	1958	7.50	15.00	30.00
❑ 41241		Petrified/You're So Right for Me	1958	20.00	40.00	80.00
Decca						
❑ 30958		Big Town/This Must Be the Place	1959	6.25	12.50	25.00
❑ 31131		I've Been There/So High	1960	6.25	12.50	25.00
❑ 31351		Instant Man/Some Things You Can't Change	1962	6.25	12.50	25.00
❑ 31431		Oh Me, Oh My/Past, Present and Future	1962	6.25	12.50	25.00
Kapp						
❑ 546		Houdini/Bless My Broken Heart	1963	5.00	10.00	20.00

Senators, The
(More than one group)

Number		Title (A Side/B Side)	Year	VG	VG+	NM
ABC-Paramount						
❑ 10178		There's a New Man in the White House/ A Sing-Along Song	1961	3.75	7.50	15.00
Abner						
❑ 1031		Julie/It Doesn't Matter	1959	18.75	37.50	75.00
Bristol						
❑ 1916		Scheming/Tafu	1959	37.50	75.00	150.00
Golden Crest						
❑ 514		Loretta/Poor Little Puppet	1958	37.50	75.00	150.00
Winn						
❑ 1917		Wedding Bells/I Shouldn't Care	1962	62.50	125.00	250.00

Seniors, The
(More than one group)

Number		Title (A Side/B Side)	Year	VG	VG+	NM
ABC-Paramount						
❑ 10736		No Surfin' 'Round Here/Cindy	1965	7.50	15.00	30.00
Decca						
❑ 31112		I've Lived Before/Hello Mr. Robin	1960	5.00	10.00	20.00
❑ 31244		When I Fall in Love/Baby, Say the Word	1961	5.00	10.00	20.00
ESV						
❑ 1016		Ah Sweet Mystery of Love/Rock and Rolly	1960	6.25	12.50	25.00
Excello						
❑ 2130		Why Did You Leave Me/Sloo Foot Soo	1958	10.00	20.00	40.00
Kent						
❑ 342		Hully Gully Fever/Pitter Patter Heart	1960	5.00	10.00	20.00
Tampa						
❑ 163		Who's Gonna Know/It's Been a Long Time	1959	10.00	20.00	40.00

Number	Title (A Side/B Side)	Year	VG	VG+	NM
Tetra					
❑ 4446	Evening Shadows Falling (I Think of You)/ I've Got Plenty of Love	1956	40.00	80.00	160.00

Senors, The
(Allegedly the Isley Brothers in disguise)

Sue					
❑ 756	May I Have This Dance/Searching for Olive Oil	1962	12.50	25.00	50.00

Sentinals, The

Admiral					
❑ 900	Roughshod/Copy Cat Walk	1961	12.50	25.00	50.00
Del-Fi					
❑ 4197	Big Surf/Sunset Beach	1963	7.50	15.00	30.00
Era					
❑ 3082	Torchula/Latin'ia	1962	7.50	15.00	30.00
❑ 3097	Christmas Eve/Latin Soul	1962	7.50	15.00	30.00
❑ 3117	Infinity/Encinada	1963	7.50	15.00	30.00
	As "The Sentinel Six"				
Point					
❑ 5100	The Bee/Over You	1963	12.50	25.00	50.00
❑ 5101	Blue Booze/Bony Moronie	1962	12.50	25.00	50.00
WCEB					
❑ 23	Torchula/Latin'ia	1962	12.50	25.00	50.00
Westco					
❑ 12	I've Been Blue/Hit the Road	1964	7.50	15.00	30.00
❑ 14	Tell Me/Hit the Road	1964	7.50	15.00	30.00

Sequins, The
(More than one group)

A&M					
❑ 761	I'll Be Satisfied/ Who Says You Can't Jerk to the Old Time Music	1965	3.00	6.00	12.00
Ascot					
❑ 2140	You Can't Sit Still/Mr. Leader of the Band	1963	3.75	7.50	15.00
Cameo					
❑ 161	To Be Young/The Mountains	1959	5.00	10.00	20.00
Red Robin					
❑ 140	Why Can't You Treat Me Right/Don't Fall in Love	1956	100.00	200.00	400.00
Terrace					
❑ 7511	Love Me Forever/You're Dancing Now	1962	3.75	7.50	15.00
❑ 7515	Hideaway/I Ain't Gonna Cry (No More)	1963	3.75	7.50	15.00

Serenaders, The
(More than one group)

Chock Full O' Hits					
❑ 101	I Wrote a Letter/Never Let Me Go	1957	75.00	150.00	300.00
❑ 102	Dance Darling, Dance/Give Me a Girl	1957	50.00	100.00	200.00
Coral					
❑ 60720	It's Funny/Confession Is Good for the Soul	1952	75.00	150.00	300.00
❑ 65093	Misery/But I Forgive You	1952	75.00	150.00	300.00
DeLuxe					
❑ 6022	Please, Please Forgive Me/Baby	1953	62.50	125.00	250.00
Hanover					
❑ 4507	Honolulu/Summer Job	1959	3.75	7.50	15.00
❑ 4514	Alaska/Where Did You Go	1959	3.75	7.50	15.00
JVB					
❑ 2001	Tomorrow Night/Why Don't You Do Right	1952	100.00	200.00	400.00
MGM					
❑ 12623	I Wrote a Letter/Never Let Me Go	1958	20.00	40.00	80.00
❑ 12666	Dance Darling, Dance/Give Me a Girl	1958	30.00	60.00	120.00
Motown					
❑ 1046	If Your Heart Says Yes/I'll Cry Tomorrow	1963	1,000	1,500	2,000
Rae Cox					
❑ 101	Gotta Go to School/My Girl Flip-Flop	1959	15.00	30.00	60.00
Red Robin					
❑ 115	Will She Know?/I Want to Love You Baby	1953	62.50	125.00	250.00
Riverside					
❑ 4549	Adios, My Love/Two Lovers Make One Fool	1963	25.00	50.00	100.00
Starfire					
❑ 115	Nite Owl/I'm Gonna Love You	1980		2.50	5.00
Swing Time					
❑ 347	M-A-Y-B-E-L-L/Ain't Gonna Cry No More	1954	200.00	400.00	800.00
Teen Life					
❑ 9	Love Me Now/Gates of Gold	1958	125.00	250.00	500.00
V.I.P.					
❑ 25002	If Your Heart Says Yes/I'll Cry Tomorrow	1964	25.00	50.00	100.00

Number		Title (A Side/B Side)	Year	VG	VG+	NM

Serratt, Howard
Sun
☐ 198 — I Must Be Saved/Troublesome Waters — 1954 — 500.00 — 1,000 — 2,000

7th Avenue Aviators, The
Congress
☐ 255 — You Should 'A Held On/The Boy Next Door — 1965 — 30.00 — 60.00 — 120.00

Seville, David
(Also see "Bagdasarian, Ross"; "Chipmunks, The, David Seville and")
Liberty

Number		Title (A Side/B Side)	Year	VG	VG+	NM
☐ 55041		Armen's Theme/Carousel in Rome	1956	6.25	12.50	25.00
☐ 55055		The Donkey and the Schoolboy/The Gift	1957	6.25	12.50	25.00
☐ 55079		Camel Rock/Gotta Get to Your House	1957	6.25	12.50	25.00
☐ 55079	PS	Camel Rock/Gotta Get to Your House	1957	12.50	25.00	50.00
☐ 55105		Pretty Dark Eyes/Cecelia	1957	6.25	12.50	25.00
☐ 55113		Bagdad Express/Starlight, Starbright	1957	6.25	12.50	25.00
☐ 55124		Bonjour Tristesse/Dance from Bonjour Tristesse	1958	6.25	12.50	25.00
☐ 55132		Witch Doctor/Don't Whistle at Me Baby	1958	7.50	15.00	30.00
☐ 55140		The Bird on My Head/Hey There Moon	1958	6.25	12.50	25.00
☐ 55153		Little Brass Band/Take Five	1958	6.25	12.50	25.00
☐ 55163		The Mountain/Mr. Grape	1958	6.25	12.50	25.00
☐ 55272		Witch Doctor/Swanee River	1960	5.00	10.00	20.00
☐ 55314		Oh Judge, Your Honor, Dear Sir, Sweetheart/ Freddy, Freddy	1961	6.25	12.50	25.00

United Artists
☐ 0063 — Witch Doctor/The Bird on My Head — 1973 — — 2.00 — 4.00
"Silver Spotlight Series" reissue

Seymour, Phil
(Of the Dwight Twilley Band)
Boardwalk

Number		Title (A Side/B Side)	Year	VG	VG+	NM
☐ NB7-11-116		I Really Love You/(B-side unknown)	1981		2.50	5.00
☐ NB7-11-145		Better to Me Than You/Surrender	1982		2.50	5.00
☐ NB7-11-154		Talk to Me/(B-side unknown)	1982		2.50	5.00
☐ 02056		Let Her Dance/We Don't Get Along	1981		2.50	5.00
☐ 5703		Precious to Me/Baby It's You	1981		2.50	5.00

Sh-Booms, The – See "Chords, The"

Sha Na Na
Kama Sutra

Number		Title (A Side/B Side)	Year	VG	VG+	NM
☐ 503		Lovers Never Say Goodbye/Remember Then	1970		3.00	6.00
☐ 507		Pay Day/Rock and Roll Is Here to Stay	1970		3.00	6.00
☐ 522		Only One Song/Yakety Yak	1971		3.00	6.00
☐ 528		Top Forty of the Lord/I Wonder Why	1971		3.00	6.00
☐ 555		Bounce in Your Buggy/Bless My Soul	1972		3.00	6.00
☐ 560		In the Still of the Night/Sea Cruise	1972		2.50	5.00
☐ 578	DJ	In the Still of the Night (mono/stereo)	1973	3.75	7.50	15.00

As "Eddie and the Evergreens"; may be promo only

Number		Title (A Side/B Side)	Year	VG	VG+	NM
☐ 592		Maybe I'm Old Fashioned/Stroll All Night	1974		2.50	5.00
☐ 596		Too Chubby to Boogie/(B-side unknown)	1974		2.50	5.00
☐ 602		Just Like Romeo and Juliet/Circles of Love	1975		2.50	5.00
☐ 603		You're the Only Light on My Horizon Now	1975		2.50	5.00
☐ 604		Shanghied/Chills in My Spine	1975		2.50	5.00

RSO
☐ 909 — Rock and Roll Is Here to Stay/Greased Lightnin' — 1978 — — 2.00 — 4.00
B-side by John Travolta
☐ 930 — Blue Moon/Sandy — 1979 — — 2.00 — 4.00
B-side by John Travolta

Sha-Wees, The
Aladdin
☐ 3170 — No One to Love Me/Early Sunday Morning — 1953 — 1,000 — 1,500 — 2,000

Shades of Blue
Impact

Number		Title (A Side/B Side)	Year	VG	VG+	NM
☐ 1007		Oh, How Happy/Little Orphan Boy	1966	5.00	10.00	20.00
☐ 1014		Lonely Summer/With This Ring	1966	5.00	10.00	20.00
☐ 1015		Happiness/The Night	1966	5.00	10.00	20.00
☐ 1026		All I Want Is Love/How Do You Save a Dying Love	1967	5.00	10.00	20.00
☐ 1028		Penny Arcade/Funny Kind of Love	1967	5.00	10.00	20.00

Shadows of Knight, The
Atco

Number		Title (A Side/B Side)	Year	VG	VG+	NM
☐ 6634		Gloria '69/A Spaniard at My Door	1968	4.00	8.00	16.00
☐ 6776		I Am the Hunter/Warwick County Affair	1970	4.00	8.00	16.00

Dunwich

Number		Title (A Side/B Side)	Year	VG	VG+	NM
☐ 116		Gloria/Dark Side	1966	6.25	12.50	25.00

Yellow label, no mention of Atco Records

| ☐ 116 | | Gloria/Dark Side | 1966 | 5.00 | 10.00 | 20.00 |

Yellow label, mentions Atco Records

| ☐ 116 | | Gloria/Dark Side | 1966 | 3.75 | 7.50 | 15.00 |

Pink label; other label variations may exist

| ☐ 122 | | Oh Yeah/Light Bulb Blues | 1966 | 5.00 | 10.00 | 20.00 |
| ☐ 122 | PS | Oh Yeah/Light Bulb Blues | 1966 | 7.50 | 15.00 | 30.00 |

Number		Title (A Side/B Side)	Year	VG	VG+	NM
❑ 128		Bad Little Woman/Gospel Zone	1966	3.75	7.50	15.00
❑ 128	PS	Bad Little Woman/Gospel Zone	1966	12.50	25.00	50.00
❑ 141		I'm Gonna Make You Mine/I'll Make You Sorry	1966	6.25	12.50	25.00
❑ 151		The Behemoth/Willie Jean	1967	5.00	10.00	20.00
❑ 167		Someone Like Me/There for Love	1967	5.00	10.00	20.00

Super K

❑ 108		Taurus/My Fire Department Needs a Fireman	1969	2.50	5.00	10.00
❑ 110		Run, Run, Billy Porter/	1969	2.50	5.00	10.00
		My Fire Department Needs a Fireman				

Team

❑ 520		Shake/From Way Out to Way In	1968	4.00	8.00	16.00

Shadows, The

(More than one group)

ABC-Paramount

❑ 10073		Saturday Dance/Lonesome Fella	1960	7.50	15.00	30.00
❑ 10138		Apache/Quartermaster's Stories	1960	7.50	15.00	30.00

Atlantic

❑ 2111		FBI/The Frightened City	1961	5.00	10.00	20.00
❑ 2135		Kon-Tiki/Man of Mystery	1962	5.00	10.00	20.00
❑ 2146		Stars Fell on Stockton/Wonderful Land	1962	5.00	10.00	20.00
❑ 2166		Guitar Tango/What a Lovely Thing	1962	5.00	10.00	20.00
❑ 2177		Dance On/The Rumble	1963	5.00	10.00	20.00
❑ 2235		Theme for Young Lovers/	1964	5.00	10.00	20.00
		The Rise and Fall of Flingel Bunt				
❑ 2257		Rhythm and Greens/The Miracle	1964	5.00	10.00	20.00

Capitol

❑ F4220		Feelin' Fine/Don't Be a Fool	1959	10.00	20.00	40.00
		As "The Drifters"				
❑ F4270		Driftin'/Jet Black	1959	10.00	20.00	40.00
		As "The Four Jets"				

Decca

❑ 28765		No Use/Stay	1953	62.50	125.00	250.00
❑ 48307		Tell Her/Don't Be Bashful	1954	75.00	150.00	300.00
❑ 48322		Big Mouth Mama/Better Than Gold	1954	75.00	150.00	300.00

Del-Fi

❑ 4109		Under the Stars of Love/Jungle Fever	1958	10.00	20.00	40.00

Delta

❑ 1509		Bop-A-Lena/There Stands the Glass	1958	30.00	60.00	120.00

Dottie

❑ 1006		I Wonder Why/Tell This Lonely Heart Goodbye	1961	3.75	7.50	15.00

Epic

❑ 9793		Mary Anne/Chu Chi	1965	5.00	10.00	20.00
❑ 9826		Alice in Sunderland/Stingray	1965	5.00	10.00	20.00
❑ 9848		My Grandfather's Clock/Don't Make My Baby Blue	1965	5.00	10.00	20.00
❑ 10020		I Met a Girl/Last Night Set	1966	5.00	10.00	20.00

Shalamar

(Also see "Watley, Jody")

Columbia

❑ 04372		Dancing in the Sheets/(Instrumental)	1984		2.00	4.00
❑ 04372	PS	Dancing in the Sheets/(Instrumental)	1984		2.00	4.00
❑ 08421		Dancing in the Sheets/(Instrumental)	1988			3.00
		Reissue				

MCA

❑ 52335		Deadline U.S.A./	1984		2.00	4.00
		One More Time Around the Block Ophelia				
		B-side by Gary U.S. Bonds				
❑ 52345		Deadline U.S.A./Knock Me On My Feet	1984		2.00	4.00
❑ 52594		Don't Get Stopped in Beverly Hills/The Discovery	1985			3.00
		B-side by Harold Faltermeyer				
❑ 52594	PS	Don't Get Stopped in Beverly Hills/The Discovery	1985			3.00

Solar

❑ YB-11379		Take That to the Bank/Shalamar Disco Gardens	1978		2.00	4.00
❑ YB-11542		Stay Close to Love/Cindy, Cindy	1979		2.00	4.00
❑ YB-11709		The Second Time Around/Leave It All Up to Love	1979		2.00	4.00
❑ YB-11929		Right in the Socket/Girl	1980		2.00	4.00
❑ GB-11979		Uptown Festival (Part 1)/Take That to the Bank	1980			3.00
		Gold Standard Series				
❑ YB-12049		I Owe You One/Right Time for Us	1980		2.00	4.00
❑ YB-12152		Full of Fire/Let's Find the Time for Love	1981		2.00	4.00
❑ GB-12231		The Second Time Around/Right in the Socket	1981			3.00
		Gold Standard Series				
❑ YB-12250		This Is For the Lover in You/	1981		2.00	4.00
		Some Things Never Change				
❑ YB-12329		Sweeter As the Days Go By/The Final Analysis	1981		2.00	4.00
❑ YB-13033		Talk to Me/Appeal	1981		2.00	4.00
❑ YB-13262		Attention to My Baby/Somewhere There's a Love	1982			Unreleased
❑ GB-13486		Make That Move/It's a Love Thing	1983			3.00
		Gold Standard Series; B-side by the Whispers				
❑ 48005		A Night to Remember/On Top of the World	1982		2.00	4.00
❑ 48013		I Can Make You Feel Good/	1982		2.00	4.00
		I Just Stopped By Because I Had To				

Number		Title (A Side/B Side)	Year	VG	VG+	NM
❏ 69635		Just One of the Guys/Hard Way	1985		2.00	4.00
❏ 69660		My Girl Loves Me/Right Here	1985		2.00	4.00
❏ 69765		You Can Count on Me/The Look	1984		2.00	4.00
❏ 69787		Over and Over/You Won't Miss Love (Until It's Gone)	1983		2.00	4.00
❏ 69819		Dead Giveaway/I Don't Wanna Be the Last to Know	1983		2.00	4.00
❏ 69819	PS	Dead Giveaway/I Don't Wanna Be the Last to Know	1983		2.50	5.00
❏ 69958		There It Is/(B-side unknown)	1982		2.00	4.00
❏ 70008		Circumstantial Evidence/(Instrumental)	1987			3.00
❏ 70013		Games/(Instrumental)	1987			3.00
❏ 70021		I Want You (To Be My Playthang)/(Instrumental)	1988			3.00

Soul Train

Number		Title (A Side/B Side)	Year	VG	VG+	NM
❏ SB-10885		Uptown Festival (Part 1)/Uptown Festival (Part 2)	1977		2.50	5.00
❏ SB-11045		Ooh, Baby, Baby/You Know	1977		2.50	5.00

Shane, Bob

(Of the Kingston Trio)

Decca

Number	Title (A Side/B Side)	Year	VG	VG+	NM
❏ 32239	Simple Gifts/Weeping Annaleah	1967	2.50	5.00	10.00
❏ 32275	Honey/I Don't Think of You Anymore	1968	2.50	5.00	10.00

Shangri-Las, The

Mercury

Number	Title (A Side/B Side)	Year	VG	VG+	NM
❏ 72645	I'll Never Learn/Sweet Sounds of Summer	1966	5.00	10.00	20.00
❏ 72670	Footsteps on the Roof/Take the Time	1967	5.00	10.00	20.00

Red Bird

Number	Title (A Side/B Side)	Year	VG	VG+	NM
❏ 10-008	Remember (Walkin' in the Sand)/It's Easier to Cry	1964	5.00	10.00	20.00
❏ 10-014	Leader of the Pack/What Is Love	1964	5.00	10.00	20.00
❏ 10-018	Give Him a Great Big Kiss/Twist and Shout	1964	5.00	10.00	20.00
❏ 10-019	Maybe/Shout	1964	5.00	10.00	20.00
❏ 10-025	Out in the Streets/The Boy	1965	5.00	10.00	20.00
❏ 10-030	Give Us Your Blessings/Heaven Only Knows	1965	5.00	10.00	20.00
❏ 10-036	Right Now and Not Later/The Train from Kansas City	1965	5.00	10.00	20.00
❏ 10-043	I Can Never Go Home Anymore/Sophisticated Boom Boom	1965	6.25	12.50	25.00
❏ 10-043	I Can Never Go Home Anymore/Bull Dog	1965	5.00	10.00	20.00
❏ 10-048	Long Live Our Love/Bull Dog	1966	5.00	10.00	20.00
❏ 10-048	Long Live Our Love/Sophisticated Boom Boom	1966	5.00	10.00	20.00
❏ 10-053	He Cried/Dressed in Black	1966	5.00	10.00	20.00
❏ 10-068	Past, Present and Future/Love You More Than Yesterday	1966	5.00	10.00	20.00

Scepter

Number	Title (A Side/B Side)	Year	VG	VG+	NM
❏ 1291	Wishing Well/Hate to Say I Told You So	1964	5.00	10.00	20.00

Smash

Number	Title (A Side/B Side)	Year	VG	VG+	NM
❏ 1866	Simon Says/Simon Speaks	1963	10.00	20.00	40.00

Spokane

Number	Title (A Side/B Side)	Year	VG	VG+	NM
❏ 4006	Wishing Well/Hate to Say I Told You So	1964	7.50	15.00	30.00

Shankar, Ravi

Apple

Number		Title (A Side/B Side)	Year	VG	VG+	NM
❏ 1838		Joi Bangla-Oh Bhaugowan/Raga Mishra-Jhinjhoti	1971	2.00	4.00	8.00
		By Ravi Shankar & Ali Akbar with Alla Rakah				
❏ 1838	PS	Joi Bangla-Oh Bhaugowan/Raga Mishra-Jhinjhoti	1971	5.00	10.00	20.00

Dark Horse

Number	Title (A Side/B Side)	Year	VG	VG+	NM
❏ 10001	I Am Missing You/Lost	1974		2.50	5.00

World Pacific

Number	Title (A Side/B Side)	Year	VG	VG+	NM
❏ 77871	Pather Panchali/Gat Kirawani	1967	2.00	4.00	8.00
❏ 77898	Charly Theme/Love Montage	1968	2.00	4.00	8.00

Shannon, Del

ABC Dunhill

Number	Title (A Side/B Side)	Year	VG	VG+	NM
❏ 4193	Sweet Mary Lou/Comin' Back to Me	1969	3.75	7.50	15.00
❏ 4224	Sister Isabelle/Colorado Rain	1970	3.75	7.50	15.00

Amy

Number	Title (A Side/B Side)	Year	VG	VG+	NM
❏ 897	Mary Jane/Stains on My Letter	1964	6.25	12.50	25.00
❏ 905	Handy Man/Give Me Lots of Lovin'	1964	3.75	7.50	15.00
❏ 911	Do You Want to Dance/This Is All I Have to Give	1964	3.75	7.50	15.00
❏ 915	Keep Searchin' (We'll Follow the Sun)/Broken Promises	1964	4.00	8.00	16.00
❏ 919	Stranger in Town/Over You	1965	4.00	8.00	16.00
❏ 925	Why Don't You Tell Him/Break Up	1965	3.75	7.50	15.00
❏ 937	Move It On Over/She Still Remembers Tony	1965	3.75	7.50	15.00
❏ 947	I Can't Believe My Ears/I Wish I Wasn't Me Tonight	1966	10.00	20.00	40.00
	Withdrawn shortly after release; promos worth about half these values				

Berlee

Number	Title (A Side/B Side)	Year	VG	VG+	NM
❏ 501	Sue's Gotta Be Mine/Now She's Gone	1963	3.75	7.50	15.00
❏ 502	That's the Way Love Is/Time of the Day	1964	3.75	7.50	15.00

Big Top

Number	Title (A Side/B Side)	Year	VG	VG+	NM
❏ 3067	Runaway/Jody	1961	6.25	12.50	25.00
❏ 3075	Hats Off to Larry/Don't Gild the Lily, Lily	1961	5.00	10.00	20.00
❏ 3083	So Long Baby/The Answer to Everything	1961	5.00	10.00	20.00
❏ 3091	Hey! Little Girl/I Don't Care Anymore	1961	5.00	10.00	20.00
❏ 3098	Ginny in the Mirror/I Won't Be There	1962	5.00	10.00	20.00
❏ 3112	Cry Myself to Sleep/I'm Gonna Move On	1962	5.00	10.00	20.00
❏ 3117	The Swiss Maid/You Never Talked About Me	1962	5.00	10.00	20.00

Number		Title (A Side/B Side)	Year	VG	VG+	NM
❑ 3131		Little Town Flirt/The Wamboo	1962	5.00	10.00	20.00
❑ 3143		Two Kinds of Teardrops/Kelly	1963	5.00	10.00	20.00
❑ 3152		From Me to You/Two Silhouettes	1963	12.50	25.00	50.00
		A-side is the first American version of a Beatles song				

Eric
❑ 189	S	Runaway/Hats Off to Larry	1972		3.00	6.00
		Both sides of this reissue are the original recordings in true stereo!				

Island
❑ 021		Tell Her No/Restless	1975	3.75	7.50	15.00
❑ 038		Cry Baby Cry/In My Arms Again	1975	3.75	7.50	15.00

Liberty
❑ 55866		The Big Hurt/I Got It Bad	1966	3.00	6.00	12.00
❑ 55889		Hey Little Star/For a Little While	1966	3.00	6.00	12.00
❑ 55894		Show Me/Never Thought I Could	1966	3.00	6.00	12.00
❑ 55904		Under My Thumb/She Was Mine	1966	3.00	6.00	12.00
❑ 55939		She/What Makes You Run	1967	3.00	6.00	12.00
❑ 55961		Led Along/I Can't Be True	1967	3.00	6.00	12.00
❑ 55993		Runaway '67/He Cheated	1967	3.75	7.50	15.00
❑ 56018		Runnin' On Back/Thinkin' It Over	1968	2.50	5.00	10.00
❑ 56018	PS	Runnin' On Back/Thinkin' It Over	1968	7.50	15.00	30.00
❑ 56036		Magical Musical Box/Gemini	1968	2.50	5.00	10.00
❑ 56070		Raindrops/You Don't Love Me	1968	2.50	5.00	10.00

Network
❑ 47951		Sea of Love/Midnight Train	1981		2.50	5.00
❑ 48006		To Love Someone/Liar	1982		2.50	5.00

Twirl
❑ 4001		Runaway/Hey Little Girl	196?		3.00	6.00
❑ 4002		Hats Off to Larry/Little Town Flirt	196?		3.00	6.00

Warner Bros.
❑ 28853		Stranger on the Run/What You Gonna Do with That	1985		2.50	5.00
❑ 29098		In My Arms Again/You Can't Forgive Me	1985		2.50	5.00

Shannon, Jackie – See "DeShannon, Jackie"

Sharon Marie

Capitol
❑ 5064		Run-Around Lover/Summertime	1963	62.50	125.00	250.00
❑ 5195		The Story of My Life/Thinkin' 'Bout You Baby	1964	50.00	100.00	200.00
		Both these records were produced by Brian Wilson				

Sharp, Dee Dee

(Includes Dee Dee Sharp Gamble)

Atco
❑ 6445		Bye Bye Baby/My Best Friend's Man	1966	2.50	5.00	10.00
❑ 6502		Baby I Love You/What Am I Gonna Do	1967	2.00	4.00	8.00
❑ 6557		We Got a Thing Goin' On/ What 'Cha Gonna Do About It	1968	2.00	4.00	8.00
		With Ben E. King				
❑ 6576		Woman Will Do Wrong/You're Just a Fool in Love	1968	2.00	4.00	8.00
❑ 6587		This Love Won't Run Out/Help Me Find My Glove	1968	2.00	4.00	8.00

Cameo
❑ 212		Mashed Potato Time/Set My Heart at Ease	1962	5.00	10.00	20.00
❑ 219		Gravy (For My Mashed Potatoes)/Baby Cakes	1962	3.75	7.50	15.00
❑ 219	PS	Gravy (For My Mashed Potatoes)/Baby Cakes	1962	6.25	12.50	25.00
❑ 230		Ride!/The Night	1962	3.75	7.50	15.00
❑ 230	PS	Ride!/The Night	1962	6.25	12.50	25.00
❑ 244		Do the Bird/Lover Boy	1963	3.75	7.50	15.00
❑ 244	PS	Do the Bird/Lover Boy	1963	6.25	12.50	25.00
❑ 260		Rock Me in the Cradle of Love/You'll Never Be Mine	1963	3.75	7.50	15.00
❑ 260	PS	Rock Me in the Cradle of Love/You'll Never Be Mine	1963	6.25	12.50	25.00
❑ 274		Wild!/Why Doncha Ask Me	1963	3.75	7.50	15.00
❑ 274	PS	Wild!/Why Doncha Ask Me	1963	6.25	12.50	25.00
❑ 296		Where Did I Go Wrong/Willyam, Willyam	1964	3.00	6.00	12.00
❑ 296	PS	Where Did I Go Wrong/Willyam, Willyam	1964	5.00	10.00	20.00
❑ 329		Never Pick a Pretty Boy/He's No Ordinary Guy	1964	3.00	6.00	12.00
❑ 335		Deep Dark Secret/Good	1964	3.00	6.00	12.00
❑ 347		To Know Him Is to Love Him/ There Ain't Nothin' I Wouldn't Do for You	1965	2.50	5.00	10.00
❑ 357		Let's Twine/That's What My Mama Said	1965	2.50	5.00	10.00
❑ 375		I Really Love You/Standing in the Need of Love	1965	2.50	5.00	10.00
❑ 375	PS	I Really Love You/Standing in the Need of Love	1965	3.75	7.50	15.00
❑ 382		It's a Funny Situation/ There Ain't Nothin' I Wouldn't Do for You	1965	2.50	5.00	10.00

Fairmount
❑ 1004		(It's Wonderful) The Love I Feel for You/ Willyam, Wilyam	1966	2.50	5.00	10.00

Gamble
❑ 219		What Kind of Lady/ You're Gonna Miss Me (When I'm Gone)	1968	5.00	10.00	20.00
❑ 4005		The Bottle or Me/ You're Gonna Miss Me (When I'm Gone)	1969	3.75	7.50	15.00

Philadelphia Int'l.
Note: Philadelphia International records as "Dee Dee Sharp Gamble"
❑ 02041		Breaking and Entering/I Love You Anyway	1981		2.00	4.00
❑ 3625		Flashback/Nobody Can Take Your Place	1977		2.50	5.00

Number		Title (A Side/B Side)	Year	VG	VG+	NM
❑ 3636		I'd Really Love to See You Tonight/What Color Is Love	1977		2.50	5.00
❑ 3638		I Believe in Love/Just As Long As I Know You're Mine	1978		2.50	5.00
❑ 3644		Tryin' to Get the Feeling Again/ I Wanna Be Your Woman	1978		2.50	5.00
❑ 70058		I Love You Anyway/Easy Money	1981		2.00	4.00

TSOP

❑ 4776		Happy 'Bout the Whole Thing/Touch My Life	1976		2.50	5.00
❑ 4778		I'm Not in Love/Make It Till Tomorrow	1976		2.50	5.00

Sharps, The
(More than one group)

Aladdin

❑ 3401		What Will I Gain/Shufflin'	1957	12.50	25.00	50.00
❑ 3401		What Will I Gain/Shufflin'	1957	100.00	200.00	400.00
		Purple vinyl				

Chess

❑ 1690		6 Months, 3 Weeks, 2 Days/Cha-Cho Bop	1958	7.50	15.00	30.00
		B-side by Jack McVea				

Combo

❑ 146		All My Love/Look What You've Done to Me	1958	12.50	25.00	50.00

Dot

❑ 15806		All My Love/Look What You've Done to Me	1958	3.75	7.50	15.00

Jamie

❑ 1040		Sweet Sweetheart/Come On	1957	10.00	20.00	40.00
❑ 1108		Have Love, Will Travel/Look at Me	1958	12.50	25.00	50.00
❑ 1114		Here's My Heart/Gig-A-Lene	1958	7.50	15.00	30.00

Lamp

❑ 2007		Our Love Is Here to Stay/Lock My Heart	1957	7.50	15.00	30.00

Star-Hi

❑ 10406		Double Clutch/If Love Is What You Want	1960	7.50	15.00	30.00

Tag

❑ 2200		6 Months, 3 Weeks, 2 Days/Cha-Cho Bop	1957	25.00	50.00	100.00
		B-side by Jack McVea				

Vik

❑ 0264		Sweet Sweetheart/Come On	1957	6.25	12.50	25.00

Win

❑ 702		Teenage Girl/We Three	1958	12.50	25.00	50.00

Shaw, John, and the Dell-Os

U-C

❑ 5002		Why Did You Leave Me/Why Does It Have to Be Her	1957	2,000	3,000	4,000

Shaw, Sandie

Mercury

❑ 72315		Ya, Ya, Da, Da/As Long As You're Happy	1964	3.75	7.50	15.00

RCA Victor

❑ 47-9594		Together/One More Lie	1968	2.00	4.00	8.00
❑ 74-0118		Voice in the Crowd/Monsieur Dupont	1969	2.00	4.00	8.00
❑ 74-0370		Love Is For the Two of Us/Wight Is Wight	1970	2.00	4.00	8.00

Reprise

❑ 0320		(There's) Always Something There to Remind Me/ Don't You Know	1964	3.00	6.00	12.00
❑ 0342		Girl Don't Come/I'd Be Far Better Off Without You	1965	2.50	5.00	10.00
❑ 0365		I'll Stop at Nothing/You Can't Blame Him	1965	2.50	5.00	10.00
❑ 0375		Long Live Love/I've Heard About Him	1965	2.50	5.00	10.00
❑ 0394		Stop Feeling Sorry for Yourself/I'll Stop at Nothing	1965	2.50	5.00	10.00
❑ 0427		If Ever You Need Me/How Can You Tell	1965	2.50	5.00	10.00
❑ 0449		Tomorrow/Hurting You	1966	2.50	5.00	10.00
❑ 0488		Nothing Comes Easy/Stop Before You Start	1966	2.50	5.00	10.00
❑ 0546		Think Sometime About Me/Hide All Emotion	1967	2.50	5.00	10.00
❑ 0575		Puppet on a String/I Had a Dream Last Night	1967	2.50	5.00	10.00
❑ 20,191		Me/Now	1963	3.75	7.50	15.00
		B-side by Bob Candee				

Shaw, Tommy
(Member of Styx)

A&M

❑ 2676		Girls with Guns/Heads Up	1984			3.00
❑ 2676	PS	Girls with Guns/Heads Up	1984		2.00	4.00
❑ 2696		Lonely School/Come In and Explain	1984			3.00
❑ 2715		Free to Love You/Come In and Explain	1985			3.00
❑ 2773		Remo's Theme (What If)/Kiss Me Hello	1985			3.00
❑ 2773	PS	Remo's Theme (What If)/Kiss Me Hello	1985			3.00
❑ 2800		Jealousy/This Is Not a Test	1985			3.00

Atlantic

❑ 89138		Ever Since the World Began/The Outsider	1988			3.00
❑ 89138	PS	Ever Since the World Began/The Outsider	1988			3.00
❑ 89183		No Such Thing/The Outsider	1987			3.00

Shean and Jenkyns

GNP Crescendo

❑ 198		Goofy-Footer Ho-Dad/Do the Commercial	1963	6.25	12.50	25.00

Number	Title (A Side/B Side)	Year	VG	VG+	NM

Sheep, The
(By the same people who gave us The Strangeloves)
Boom

| ☐ 60,000 | Hide and Seek/Twelve Months Later | 1966 | 5.00 | 10.00 | 20.00 |
| ☐ 60,007 | Dynamite/I Feel Good | 1966 | 5.00 | 10.00 | 20.00 |

Sheiks, The
(Several different groups; some of these may have been spelled "The Shieks")
Amy

| ☐ 807 | Come On Back/Please Don't Take Away the Girl I Love | 1960 | 50.00 | 100.00 | 200.00 |

Cat

| ☐ 116 | Walk That Walk/The Kissing Song (Sweetie Lover) | 1955 | 10.00 | 20.00 | 40.00 |

Ef-N-De

| ☐ 1000 | Give Me Another Chance/Baby Don't You Cry | 1955 | 200.00 | 400.00 | 600.00 |

Federal

| ☐ 12237 | So Fine/Sentimental Heart | 1955 | 37.50 | 75.00 | 150.00 |

Jamie

| ☐ 1147 | Candlelight Cafe/The Song of Old Paree | 1959 | 5.00 | 10.00 | 20.00 |

LeGrand

| ☐ 1013 | What I'd Do for Your Love/Why Should I Dance | 1961 | 25.00 | 50.00 | 100.00 |
| ☐ 1016 | Cocoanut Woman/Twist That Twist | 1962 | 6.25 | 12.50 | 25.00 |

MGM

| ☐ 12876 | Baghdad Rock (Part 1)/Baghdad Rock (Part 2) | 1960 | 5.00 | 10.00 | 20.00 |

Shells, The
End

| ☐ 1022 | Pretty Little Girl/Sippin' Soda | 1958 | 37.50 | 75.00 | 150.00 |
| ☐ 1050 | Whispering Wings/Shooma Dom Dom | 1959 | 12.50 | 25.00 | 50.00 |

Gone

| ☐ 5103 | Pretty Little Girl/Sippin' Soda | 1961 | 6.25 | 12.50 | 25.00 |

Johnson

☐ 099	My Cherie/Explain It to Me	1972	3.00	6.00	
☐ 104	Baby Oh Baby/Angel Eyes	1957	10.00	20.00	40.00
☐ 104	Baby Oh Baby/What's in An Angel Eyes	1960	3.75	7.50	15.00
	Note lengthened B-side title				
☐ 106	Don't Say Goodbye/Pleading	1958	25.00	50.00	100.00
☐ 107	Explain It to Me/An Island Unknown	1961	6.25	12.50	25.00
☐ 109	Better Forget Him/Can't Take It	1961	6.25	12.50	25.00
☐ 110	In the Dim Light of the Dark/O-Mi Yum-Mi Yum-Mi	1961	6.25	12.50	25.00
☐ 112	Sweetest One/Baby Walk On In	1961	7.50	15.00	30.00
☐ 119	Deep in My Heart/(It's a) Happy Holiday	1962	7.50	15.00	30.00
☐ 120	The Drive/A Toast to Your Birthday	1962	7.50	15.00	30.00
☐ 127	On My Honor/My Royal Love	1963	12.50	25.00	50.00
☐ 332	Explain It to Me/An Island Unknown	1961	3.75	7.50	15.00

Josie

| ☐ 912 | Deep in My Heart/Our Wedding Day | 1963 | 5.00 | 10.00 | 20.00 |

Roulette

| ☐ 4156 | The Thief/She Wasn't Meant for Me | 1959 | 7.50 | 15.00 | 30.00 |

Shelton, Gary
Alpine

| ☐ 56 | Honey Bee/Till the End of the Line | 1960 | 7.50 | 15.00 | 30.00 |

Mark

| ☐ 145 | Goodbye, Little Darlin', Goodbye/Stop the World | 1960 | 50.00 | 100.00 | 200.00 |

Mercury

| ☐ 71310 | Kissin' at the Drive-In/Yours Till I Die | 1958 | 7.50 | 15.00 | 30.00 |

Shep and the Limelites
(Lead singer: James "Shep" Sheppard, formerly of The Heartbeats)
Hull

☐ 740	Daddy's Home/This I Know	1961	6.25	12.50	25.00
	Pink label				
☐ 740	Daddy's Home/This I Know	1961	5.00	10.00	20.00
	Red label				
☐ 740	Daddy's Home/This I Know	1961	4.00	8.00	16.00
	Tan label. Note: Any colored vinyl version is a counterfeit.				
☐ 742	Ready for Your Love/You'll Be Sorry	1961	5.00	10.00	20.00
☐ 747	Three Steps from the Altar/Oh What a Feeling	1961	5.00	10.00	20.00
☐ 748	Our Anniversary/Who Told the Sandman	1962	5.00	10.00	20.00
☐ 751	What Did Daddy Do/ Teach Me, Teach Me How to Twist	1962	5.00	10.00	20.00
☐ 753	Gee Baby, What About You/ Everything Is Going to Be Alright	1962		10.00	20.00
☐ 756	Remember Baby/The Monkey	1963	5.00	10.00	20.00
☐ 757	Stick By Me (And I'll Stick By You)/It's All Over Now	1963	5.00	10.00	20.00
☐ 759	Steal Away (With Your Baby)/For All My Love	1963	5.00	10.00	20.00
☐ 761	Easy to Remember (When You Want to Forget)/ Why, Why Won't You Believe Me	1964	5.00	10.00	20.00
☐ 767	I'm All Alone/Why Did You Fall for Me	1964	5.00	10.00	20.00
☐ 770	Party for Two/You Better Believe	1965	7.50	15.00	30.00
☐ 772	In Case I Forget/I'm a-Hurting Inside	1965	5.00	10.00	20.00

Number	Title (A Side/B Side)	Year	VG	VG+	NM

Shepards, The
ABC-Paramount

| ☐ 10758 | Little Girl Lost/Let Yourself Go | 1965 | 6.25 | 12.50 | 25.00 |

Shepherd Sisters
(Some of these are spelled "Shepard" or "Sheppard", but all appear to be the same group)
Atlantic

| ☐ 2176 | What Makes Little Girls Cry/Don't Mention My Name | 1963 | 2.50 | 5.00 | 10.00 |
| ☐ 2195 | Talk Is Cheap/The Greatest Lover | 1963 | 2.50 | 5.00 | 10.00 |

Big Top

| ☐ 3066 | Hapsburg Serenade/Schoen-A, Schoen-A | 1961 | 3.75 | 7.50 | 15.00 |

Lance

| ☐ 125 | Alone (Why Must I Be Alone)/Congratulations to Someone | 1957 | 6.25 | 12.50 | 25.00 |

Melba

| ☐ 100 | Gone with the Wind/Rock and Roll, Cha Cha | 1956 | 6.25 | 12.50 | 25.00 |
| ☐ 108 | Remember That Crazy Rock and Roll Turf/I Walked Beside the Sea | 1957 | 6.25 | 12.50 | 25.00 |

Mercury

| ☐ 71244 | Gettin' Ready for Freddie/The Best Thing There Is | 1957 | 6.25 | 12.50 | 25.00 |

MGM

| ☐ 12766 | Heart and Soul/(It's No) Sin | 1959 | 5.00 | 10.00 | 20.00 |

Private Stock

| ☐ 45,063 | Our Town/(B-side unknown) | 1975 | | 3.00 | 6.00 |

20th Fox

| ☐ 468 | I've Got a Secret/Finders Keepers | 1964 | 2.50 | 5.00 | 10.00 |

United Artists

| ☐ 350 | Deeply/I'm Still Dancin' | 1961 | 3.00 | 6.00 | 12.00 |
| ☐ 456 | Lolita Ya Ya/Marvin | 1962 | 3.00 | 6.00 | 12.00 |

Warwick

☐ 511	Here Comes Heaven Again/I Think It's Time	1959	3.75	7.50	15.00
☐ 530	Alone/Rocky	1960	3.75	7.50	15.00
☐ 548	Yea Yea Dixie/How Softly a Heart Breaks	1960	3.75	7.50	15.00

York

| ☐ 50002 | Alone (New Version)/Alone (Original Version) | 1965 | 2.50 | 5.00 | 10.00 |

Sheppard, Buddy, and the Holidays
(The Belmonts in disguise)
Sabina

| ☐ 506 | My Love Is Real/Brahms' Lullaby (Time to Dream) | 1962 | 12.50 | 25.00 | 50.00 |
| ☐ 510 | Now It's All Over/That Background Sound | 1963 | 12.50 | 25.00 | 50.00 |

Sheppard, Neil
Almont

| ☐ 314 | You Can't Go Far Without a Guitar (Unless You're Ringo Starr)/Betty Is the Girl for You | 1964 | 7.50 | 15.00 | 30.00 |

Sheppard, Shane
(Also see "Shep and the Limelites")
Apt

| ☐ 25039 | Too Young to Wed/Two Loving Hearts | 1960 | 12.50 | 25.00 | 50.00 |
| ☐ 25046 | One Week from Today/I'm So Lonely (What Can I Do) | 1960 | 10.00 | 20.00 | 40.00 |

Sheridan, Bobby
Sun

| ☐ 354 | Red Man/Sad News | 1961 | 7.50 | 15.00 | 30.00 |

Sheridan, Mike, and the Nightriders
Liverpool Sound

| ☐ 902 | Please Mr. Postman/In Love | 1964 | 30.00 | 60.00 | 120.00 |

Sheridan, Tony
(The guy who made some records with four Liverpool lads in 1961)
London Int'l.

| ☐ 10616 | Dance with Me/A Million Drums | 1964 | 3.75 | 7.50 | 15.00 |

Sheridan, Tony, and the Beat Brothers – See "Beatles, The"

Sheriff and the Ravels
Vee Jay

| ☐ 306 | Shombalor/Lonely One | 1959 | 10.00 | 20.00 | 40.00 |

Sherman, Bobby
Cameo

☐ 403		Happiness Is/Can't Get Used to Loving You	1966	2.50	5.00	10.00
☐ 403	DJ	Happiness Is	1966	5.00	10.00	20.00
		One-sided promo				

Condor

| ☐ 1002 | I'll Never Tell You/Telegram | 1969 | 2.50 | 5.00 | 10.00 |

Decca

| ☐ 31672 | Man Overboard/You Make Me Happy | 1964 | 3.75 | 7.50 | 15.00 |

Number		Title (A Side/B Side)	Year	VG	VG+	NM
❑ 31741		It Hurts Me/Give Me Your Word	1965	3.75	7.50	15.00
❑ 31741	PS	It Hurts Me/Give Me Your Word	1965	12.50	25.00	50.00
❑ 31779		Hey Little Girl/Well All Right	1965	3.75	7.50	15.00

Dot

❑ 16566		I Want to Hear It From Her/Nobody's Sweetheart	1963	3.75	7.50	15.00

Epic

❑ 10181		Cold Girl/Think of Rain	1967	2.50		10.00
❑ 10181	PS	Cold Girl/Think of Rain	1967	5.00	10.00	20.00

Janus

❑ 246		Runaway/Mr. Success	1975		2.00	4.00
❑ 254		Our Last Song Together/Sunshine Rose	1975		2.00	4.00

Metromedia

❑ 121		Little Woman/One Too Many Mornings	1969		2.50	5.00
❑ 121	PS	Little Woman/One Too Many Mornings	1969		2.50	5.00
❑ 150		La La La (If I Had You)/Time	1969		2.50	5.00
❑ 150	PS	La La La (If I Had You)/Time	1969		2.50	5.00
❑ 177		Easy Come, Easy Go/July Seventeen	1970		2.50	5.00
❑ 177		Easy Come, Easy Go/Sounds Along the Way	1970		2.50	5.00
❑ 177	PS	Easy Come, Easy Go/July Seventeen	1970		2.50	5.00
❑ 188		Hey, Mister Sun/Two Blind Mice	1970		2.50	5.00
❑ 188	PS	Hey, Mister Sun/Two Blind Mice	1970		2.50	5.00
❑ 194		Julie, Do Ya Love Me/Spend Some Time Lovin' Me	1970		2.50	5.00
❑ 194	PS	Julie, Do Ya Love Me/Spend Some Time Lovin' Me	1970		2.50	5.00
❑ 204		Goin' Home (Sing a Song of Christmas Cheer)/ Love's What You're Gettin' for Christmas	1970		3.00	6.00
❑ 204	PS	Goin' Home (Sing a Song of Christmas Cheer)/ Love's What You're Gettin' for Christmas	1970		3.00	6.00
❑ 206		Cried Like a Baby/Is Anybody There	1971		2.50	5.00
❑ 206	PS	Cried Like a Baby/Is Anybody There	1971		2.50	5.00
❑ 217		The Drum/Free Now to Roam	1971		2.50	5.00
❑ 217	PS	The Drum/Free Now to Roam	1971		2.50	5.00
❑ 222		Waiting at the Bus Stop/Run Away	1971		2.50	5.00
❑ 222	PS	Waiting at the Bus Stop/Run Away	1971		2.50	5.00
❑ 227		Jennifer/Getting Together	1971		2.50	5.00
❑ 227	PS	Jennifer/Getting Together	1971		2.50	5.00
❑ 240		Together Again/Picture a Little Girl	1972		2.50	5.00
❑ 240	PS	Together Again/Picture a Little Girl	1972		2.50	5.00
❑ 249		I Don't Believe in Magic/Just a Little While Longer	1972		2.50	5.00
❑ 68-0100		Early in the Morning/Unborn Lullaby	1973		2.50	5.00

Parkway

❑ 967		Goody Galumshus/Anything Your Little Heart Desires	1966	2.50	5.00	10.00

Starcrest

❑ 100		Judy, You'll Never Know/Telegram	1962	5.00	10.00	20.00

Shieks, The – See "Sheiks, The"

Shields, Billy
(Pseudonym of Tony Orlando)

Harbour

❑ 304		I Was a Boy/Moments from Now	1969	6.25	12.50	25.00

Shields, Bobby

Melba

❑ 105		Land of Rock and Roll/ I Wouldn't Change You for the World	1956	15.00	30.00	60.00

Shields, The

Atco

❑ 7071		The Way I Feel Tonight/All Right by Me	1977		2.50	5.00

Continental

❑ 4072		You Told Another Lie/Barnyard Dance	1961	100.00	200.00	400.00

Dot

❑ 15805		You Cheated/That's the Way It's Gonna Be	1958	5.00	10.00	20.00
❑ 15856		I'm Sorry Now/Nature Boy	1958	7.50	15.00	30.00
❑ 15940		Fare Thee Well/Play the Game Fair	1959	5.00	10.00	20.00

Tender

❑ 513		You Cheated/That's the Way It's Gonna Be *No reference to Dot Records on label*	1958	25.00	50.00	100.00
❑ 513		You Cheated/That's the Way It's Gonna Be	1958	10.00	20.00	40.00
❑ 518		I'm Sorry Now/Nature Boy	1958	15.00	30.00	60.00
❑ 521		Fare Thee Well/Play the Game Fair	1959	15.00	30.00	60.00

Transcontinental

❑ 1013		The Girl Around the Corner/Fare Thee Well, My Love	1960	25.00	50.00	100.00

Shindigs, The
(Also known as the Bobby Fuller Four)

Mustang

❑ 3003		Thunder Reef/Wolfman	1965	10.00	20.00	40.00

Shirelles, The

Bell

❑ 760		A Most Unusual Boy/ Look What You've Done to My Heart	1969	2.50	5.00	10.00
❑ 787		Looking Glass/Playthings	1969	2.50	5.00	10.00

Number		Title (A Side/B Side)	Year	VG	VG+	NM
☐ 815		Never Give You Up/Go Away and Find Yourself	1969	2.50	5.00	10.00
Blue Rock						
☐ 4051		Don't Mess with Cupid/Sweet Sweet Lovin'	1968	2.50	5.00	10.00
☐ 4066		Call Me/There's a Storm Goin' Home in My Heart	1968	2.50	5.00	10.00
Decca						
☐ 30588		I Met Him on a Sunday/I Want You to Be My Boyfriend	1958	6.25	12.50	25.00
☐ 30669		My Love Is a Charm/Slop Time	1958	10.00	20.00	40.00
☐ 30761		Stop Me/I Got the Message	1958	10.00	20.00	40.00
RCA Victor						
☐ 47-0902		Let's Give Each Other Love/Deep in the Night	1973	2.00	4.00	8.00
☐ 48-1019		No Sugar Tonight/Strange, I Still Love You	1971	2.50	5.00	10.00
☐ 48-1032		Brother, Brother/Sunday Dreaming	1972	2.50	5.00	10.00
☐ APBO-0192		Touch the Wind (Eres Tu)/Do What You've a Mind To	1973	2.00	4.00	8.00
Scepter						
☐ 1203		Dedicated to the One I Love/Look A Here Baby *White label*	1958	7.50	15.00	30.00
☐ 1203		Dedicated to the One I Love/Look A Here Baby *Red label*	1958	5.00	10.00	20.00
☐ 1205		A Teardrop and a Lollipop/Doin' the Ronde *White label*	1959	7.50	15.00	30.00
☐ 1205		A Teardrop and a Lollipop/Doin' the Ronde *Red label*	1959	5.00	10.00	20.00
☐ 1207		Please Be My Boyfriend/I Saw a Tear *White label*	1960	7.50	15.00	30.00
☐ 1207		Please Be My Boyfriend/I Saw a Tear *Red label*	1960	5.00	10.00	20.00
☐ 1208		Tonight's the Night/The Dance Is Over *White label*	1960	7.50	15.00	30.00
☐ 1208		Tonight's the Night/The Dance Is Over *Red label*	1960	5.00	10.00	20.00
☐ 1211		Tomorrow/Boys *Original A-side title*	1960	7.50	15.00	30.00
☐ 1211		Will You Love Me Tomorrow/Boys *Revised A-side title*	1960	5.00	10.00	20.00
☐ 1217		Mama Said/Blue Holiday	1961	3.75	7.50	15.00
☐ 1220		A Thing of the Past/What a Sweet Thing That Was	1961	3.75	7.50	15.00
☐ 1223		Big John/Twenty-One	1961	3.75	7.50	15.00
☐ 1227		Baby It's You/Things I Want to Hear (Pretty Words)	1961	3.75	7.50	15.00
☐ 1228		Soldier Boy/Love Is a Swingin' Thing	1962	3.75	7.50	15.00
☐ 1234		Welcome Home Baby/Mama, Here Comes the Bride	1962	3.75	7.50	15.00
☐ 1237		Stop the Music/It's Love That Really Counts	1962	3.75	7.50	15.00
☐ 1243		Everybody Loves a Lover/I Don't Think So	1962	3.75	7.50	15.00
☐ 1248		Foolish Little Girl/Not for All the Money in the World	1963	3.75	7.50	15.00
☐ 1248	PS	Foolish Little Girl/Not for All the Money in the World	1963	10.00	20.00	40.00
☐ 1255		Don't Say Goodnight and Mean Goodbye/ I Didn't Mean to Hurt You	1963	3.00	6.00	12.00
☐ 1255	PS	Don't Say Goodnight and Mean Goodbye/ I Didn't Mean to Hurt You	1963	10.00	20.00	40.00
☐ 1259		What Does a Girl Do?/Don't Let It Happen to You	1963	3.00	6.00	12.00
☐ 1260		It's a Mad, Mad, Mad World/31 Flavors	1963	3.00	6.00	12.00
☐ 1264		Tonight You're Gonna Fall in Love with Me/ 20th Century Rock and Roll	1963	3.00	6.00	12.00
☐ 1267		Sha-La-La/His Lips Get In the Way	1964	3.00	6.00	12.00
☐ 1278		Thank You Baby/Doomsday	1964	3.00	6.00	12.00
☐ 1284		Maybe Tonight/Lost Love	1964	3.00	6.00	12.00
☐ 1292		Are You Still My Baby/I Saw a Tear	1964	3.00	6.00	12.00
☐ 1296		Shh, I'm Watching the Movies/A Plus B	1965	3.00	6.00	12.00
☐ 12101		March (You'll Be Sorry)/Everybody's Goin' Mad	1965	2.50	5.00	10.00
☐ 12114		My Heart Belongs to You/Love That Man	1965	2.50	5.00	10.00
☐ 12123		(Mama) My Soldier Boy Is Coming Home/Soldier Boy	1965	2.50	5.00	10.00
☐ 12132		I Met Him on a Sunday -- '66/Love That Man	1966	2.50	5.00	10.00
☐ 12150		Till My Baby Comes Home/Que Sera, Sera	1966	2.50	5.00	10.00
☐ 12162		Shades of Blue/After Midnight	1966	2.50	5.00	10.00
☐ 12162		Shades of Blue/Looking Around	1966	2.50	5.00	10.00
☐ 12178		Teasin' Me/Love Away	1966	2.50	5.00	10.00
☐ 12185		Don't Go Home (My Little Baby)/ Nobody Baby After You	1967	2.50	5.00	10.00
☐ 12192		Too Much of a Good Thing/Bright Shiny Colors	1967	2.50	5.00	10.00
☐ 12198		Last Minute Miracle/No Doubt About It	1967	2.50	5.00	10.00
☐ 12209		Wild and Sweet/Wait Till I Give the Signal	1968	2.50	5.00	10.00
☐ 12217		Hippie Walk (Part 1)/Hippie Walk (Part 2)	1968	2.50	5.00	10.00
Tiara						
☐ 6112		I Met Him on a Sunday/I Want You to Be My Boyfriend	1958	100.00	200.00	400.00
United Artists						
☐ 50648		There Goes My Baby-Be My Baby/ Strange, I Still Love You	1970	2.00	4.00	8.00
☐ 50693		It's Gonna Take a Miracle/Lost	1970	2.00	4.00	8.00
☐ 50740		Take Me for a Little While/Dedicated to the One I Love	1971	2.00	4.00	8.00

Shirley (and Company)
(Shirley Goodman, also of Shirley and Lee)

Number	Title (A Side/B Side)	Year	VG	VG+	NM
Vibration					
☐ 532	Shame, Shame, Shame/(Instrumental)	1974		2.50	5.00
☐ 535	Cry, Cry, Cry/(Instrumental)	1975		2.50	5.00
☐ 539	Disco Shirley/Keep On Rolling On	1975		2.50	5.00

Number		Title (A Side/B Side)	Year	VG	VG+	NM
☐ 542		I Like to Dance/Jim Doc C'ain	1976		2.50	5.00
☐ 579		Revelations True/(Instrumental)	1978		2.50	5.00

Shirley and Lee
(Also see "Goodman, Shirley"; "Shirley [and Company]")
Aladdin

☐ 3153		I'm Gone/Sweethearts	1952	25.00	50.00	100.00
☐ 3173		Baby/Shirley Come Back to Me	1953	30.00	60.00	120.00
☐ 3192		Shirley's Back/So In Love	1953	15.00	30.00	60.00
☐ 3205		Two Happy People/The Proposal	1953	12.50	25.00	50.00
☐ 3222		Why Did I/Lee Goofed	1954	12.50	25.00	50.00
☐ 3244		Confessin'/Keep On	1954	12.50	25.00	50.00
☐ 3258		Comin' Over/Takes Money	1954	12.50	25.00	50.00
☐ 3289		Feel So Good/You'd Be Thinking of Me	1955	10.00	20.00	40.00
☐ 3302		Let's Dream/I'll Do It	1955	7.50	15.00	30.00
☐ 3325		Let the Good Times Roll/Do You Mean to Hurt Me So	1956	7.50	15.00	30.00
☐ 3338		I Feel Good/Now That It's Over	1956	6.25	12.50	25.00
☐ 3362		When I Saw You/That's What I Want to Do	1957	5.00	10.00	20.00
☐ 3369		I Want to Dance/Marry Me	1957	5.00	10.00	20.00
☐ 3380		Rock All Night/Don't You Know I Love You	1957	5.00	10.00	20.00
☐ 3390		Rockin' with the Clock/The Flirt	1957	5.00	10.00	20.00
☐ 3405		Love No One But You (I Love You So)/I'll Thrill You	1958	5.00	10.00	20.00
☐ 3418		Everybody's Rocking/Don't Leave Me Here to Cry	1958	5.00	10.00	20.00
☐ 3432		Come On and Have Your Fun/All I Want to Do Is Cry	1958	5.00	10.00	20.00
☐ 3455		True Love/When Day Is Done	1959	5.00	10.00	20.00

Imperial

☐ 5818		Together We Stand (Divided We Fall)/The Joker	1962	2.50	5.00	10.00
☐ 5854		My Last Letter/I'm Early Enough	1962	2.50	5.00	10.00
☐ 5868		Don't Stop Now/A Little Thing	1962	2.50	5.00	10.00
☐ 5922		The Golden Rule/Hey Little Boy	1963	2.50	5.00	10.00
☐ 5970		Dancing World/I'm Gone	1963	2.50	5.00	10.00
☐ 5979		Paper Doll/The Brink of Disaster	1963	2.50	5.00	10.00
☐ 66000		Somebody Put a Jukebox in the Study Hall/Never Let Me Go	1963	2.50	5.00	10.00

United Artists

☐ 0087		Let the Good Times Roll/Feel So Good	1973		2.00	4.00
		"Silver Spotlight Series" reissue				
☐ XW274		Let the Good Times Roll/That's What I Wanna Do	1973		2.50	5.00

Warwick

☐ 581		Let the Good Times Roll/Keep Loving Me	1960	3.00	6.00	12.00
☐ 609		Two Peas in a Pod/Your Love Makes the Difference	1961	3.00	6.00	12.00
☐ 664		Well-a, Well-a/Our Kids	1961	3.00	6.00	12.00
☐ 679		Let's Live It Up/Girl, You're Married Now	1962	3.00	6.00	12.00

Shocking Blue, The
Buddah

☐ 258		Sleepless at Midnight/Serenade	1971		3.00	6.00

Colossus

☐ 108		Venus/Hot Sand	1969		5.00	10.00
☐ 108	PS	Venus/Hot Sand	1969	3.75	7.50	15.00
☐ 111		Mighty Joe/I'm a Woman	1970	2.00	4.00	8.00
☐ 111	PS	Mighty Joe/I'm a Woman	1970	3.00	6.00	12.00
☐ 116		Long and Lonesome Road/Ackaragh	1970	2.00	4.00	8.00
☐ 123		Never Love a Railroad Man/Never Marry	1970	2.00	4.00	8.00
☐ 141		Boll Weevil/Long and Lonesome Road	1971		3.00	6.00

MGM

☐ 14481		When I Was a Girl/Eve and the Apple	1973		3.00	6.00
☐ 14543		Oh Love/Inkpot	1973		3.00	6.00

21 Records

☐ 99517		Venus/Mighty Joe	1986		2.00	4.00

Shondell, Troy
AVM

☐ 14		(I'm Looking for Some) New Blue Jeans/(B-side unknown)	1988		2.00	4.00

Decca

☐ 31712		You Can't Catch Me/Walkin' in a Memory	1964	2.50	5.00	10.00

Everest

☐ 2015		Gone/Some People Never Learn	1963	2.50	5.00	10.00
☐ 2018		I've Got a Woman/No Fool Like an Old Fool	1963	2.50	5.00	10.00
☐ 2041		Trouble/Little Miss Tease	1964	2.50	5.00	10.00

Gaye

☐ 2010		This Time/I Catch Myself Crying	1961	10.00	20.00	40.00

Goldcrest

☐ 161		This Time/Girl After Girl	1961	7.50	15.00	30.00
☐ 161-A		This Time/Girl After Girl	1961	6.25	12.50	25.00

Liberty

☐ 55353		This Time/Girl After Girl	1961	5.00	10.00	20.00
☐ 55398		Tears from an Angel/Island in the Sky	1961	4.00	8.00	16.00
☐ 55445		Just Because/Na-No-No	1962	4.00	8.00	16.00

Ric

☐ 174		Just a Dream/Just Like Me	1965	2.50	5.00	10.00
☐ 184		Big Windy City/I Thought That You Were Mine	1966	2.50	5.00	10.00

Number		Title (A Side/B Side)	Year	VG	VG+	NM
Star-Fox						
❑ 77		Still Loving You/(B-side unknown)	1979		2.50	5.00
TeleSonic						
❑ 804		(Sittin' Here) Lovin' You/(B-side unknown)	1980		2.50	5.00
TRX						
❑ 5001		A Rose and a Baby Ruth/Here It Comes Again	1967	2.00	4.00	8.00
❑ 5003		Head Man/She's Got Everything She Needs	1967	2.00	4.00	8.00
❑ 5015		Let's Go All the Way/Let Me Love You	1968	2.00	4.00	8.00
❑ 5019		Something's Wrong in Indiana/	1969	2.00	4.00	8.00
		A Rose and a Baby Ruth				

Shooters, The
(With Otis Redding)
Trans World

❑ 6908		Tuff Enuff/She's All Right	1960	25.00	50.00	100.00

Shotgun Express
(With Rod Stewart)
Uptown

❑ 747		I Could Feel the Whole World Turn/Curtains	1967	7.50	15.00	30.00

Showmen, The
Amy

❑ 11036		Action/What Would It Take	1968	2.00	4.00	8.00
Imperial						
❑ 66033		It Will Stand/Country Fool	1964	3.00	6.00	12.00
❑ 66071		Country Fool/Somebody Help Me	1964	3.00	6.00	12.00
Liberty						
❑ 56166		It Will Stand/Country Fool	1970		2.50	5.00
Minit						
❑ 632		It Will Stand/Country Fool	1961	7.50	15.00	30.00
	Orange label					
❑ 632		It Will Stand/Country Fool	1961	3.75	7.50	15.00
	Black label					
❑ 643		The Wrong Girl/Fate Planned It This Way	1962	12.50	25.00	50.00
❑ 647		Com'n Home/I Love You, Can't You See	1962	6.25	12.50	25.00
❑ 654		True Fine Mama/The Owl Sees You	1962	6.25	12.50	25.00
❑ 662		39-21-46/Swish Fish	1963	6.25	12.50	25.00
Swan						
❑ 4213		In Paradise/Take It Baby	1965	2.50	5.00	10.00
❑ 4219		Our Love Will Grow/You're Everything	1965	2.50	5.00	10.00
❑ 4241		Please Try and Understand/Honey House	1966	2.50	5.00	10.00
United Artists						
❑ 0100		It Will Stand/I'm a Happy Man	1973		2.50	5.00
	"Silver Spotlight Series" reissue; B-side by the Jive Five					

Shuffles, The
Rayco

❑ 508		Do You Remember My Darling/Dancin' Little Girl	1963	50.00	100.00	200.00

Shut Downs, The
Dimension

❑ 1016		Four on the Floor/Beach Buggy	1963	6.25	12.50	25.00
Karsong						
❑ 501		Four on the Floor/Straightaway	1963	12.50	25.00	50.00

Sicknicks, The
Amy

❑ 824		The Presidential Press Conference (Part 1)/	1961	3.75	7.50	15.00
❑		The Presidential Press Conference (Part 2)				
❑ 824	PS	The Presidential Press Conference (Part 1)/	1961	6.25	12.50	25.00
❑		The Presidential Press Conference (Part 2)				
❑ 831		Wadja Say Mr. K (Part 1)/Wadja Say Mr. K (Part 2)	1961	3.75	7.50	15.00

Sidewalk Surfers, The
Jubilee

❑ 5496		Skate Board/Fun Last Summer	1965	12.50	25.00	50.00

Sierras, The
Knox

❑ 102		So Many Sleepless Nights/Nearer My Heart	1962	25.00	50.00	100.00
Mail Call						
❑ 2333/4		Stormy Weather/Chance	1963	50.00	100.00	200.00

Signatures, The
Norman

❑ 210		Julie Is Her Name/Someone in Love	1957	75.00	150.00	300.00
Whippet						
❑ 210		Julie Is Her Name/Someone in Love	1957	12.50	25.00	50.00

Number	Title (A Side/B Side)	Year	VG	VG+	NM

Silhouettes, The
Ace
❑ 552	I Sold My Heart to the Junkman/What Would You Do	1958	5.00	10.00	20.00
❑ 562	Evelyn/Never Will Part	1959	5.00	10.00	20.00

As "Bill Horton and the Silhouettes"

Ember
☑ 1029	Get a Job/I Am Lonely	1958	6.25	12.50	25.00

Red label

❑ 1029	Get a Job/I Am Lonely	1960	3.00	6.00	12.00

Black label

❑ 1032	Headin' for the Poorhouse/Miss Thing	1958	5.00	10.00	20.00
❑ 1037	Bing Bong/Voodoo Eyes	1958	5.00	10.00	20.00

Goodway
❑ 101	Not Me Baby/(B-side unknown)	1966	50.00	100.00	200.00

Grand
❑ 142	Wish I Could Be There/Move On Over	1956	50.00	100.00	200.00

Imperial
❑ 5899	The Push/Which Way Did She Go	1962	3.00	6.00	12.00

Junior
❑ 391	Get a Job/I Am Lonely	1957	100.00	200.00	400.00

Brown label (first press)

❑ 391	Get a Job/I Am Lonely	1957	100.00	200.00	400.00

Blue label (second press)

❑ 396	I Sold My Heart to the Junkman/What Would You Do	1958	15.00	30.00	60.00
❑ 400	Evelyn/Never Will Part	1959	50.00	100.00	200.00
❑ 993	Your Love/Rent Man	1963	7.50	15.00	30.00

United Artists
❑ 147	I Sold My Heart to the Junkman/What Would You Do	1958			Unreleased

Silkie, The
Fontana
❑ 1525	You've Got to Hide Your Love Away/City Winds	1965	3.75	7.50	15.00

A-side was produced by John Lennon and Paul McCartney, with the two and George Harrison playing along

❑ 1536	The Keys to My Soul/Leave Me to Cry	1965	2.50	5.00	10.00
❑ 1551	Born to Be With You/I'm So Sorry	1966	2.50	5.00	10.00

Silva Tones, The
Argo
❑ 5281	That's All I Want from You/Roses Are Blooming	1957	7.50	15.00	30.00
❑ 5281	That's All I Want from You/Chi-Wa-Wa	1957	7.50	15.00	30.00

Monarch
❑ 615	That's All I Want from You/Roses Are Blooming	1957	12.50	25.00	50.00

Yellow label

❑ 615	That's All I Want from You/Roses Are Blooming	1957	7.50	15.00	30.00

Black label

Silver
(With Brent Mydland, later of the Grateful Dead)
Arista
❑ 0189	Wham Bam Shang-a-Lang/Right on Time	1976		2.50	5.00

Originals on white labels with pale blue logo

❑ 0189	Wham Bam Shang-a-Lang/Right on Time	1976		2.50	5.00

Second pressings on pale blue labels with white logo

❑ 0189	Wham Bam/Right on Time	1976		2.00	4.00

Third pressings: Same label as second pressings with altered title

❑ 0210	Memory/So Much for the Past	1976		2.00	4.00
❑ 0227	Musician (It's Not An Easy Life)/Goodbye, So Long	1977		2.00	4.00

Silver Dust
Sun
❑ 1124	Father and Son/Castle in the Sun	1971		2.50	5.00

Silver Fleet
(A precursor to 10CC)
Uni
❑ 55271	Look Out World/C'mon Plane	1971	6.25	12.50	25.00

Simmons, "Jumpin'" Gene
(Some were released as Gene Simmons)
AGP
❑ 119	Back Home Again/Don't Worry About Me	1969	2.00	4.00	8.00

Checker
❑ 948	Bad Boy Willie/Goin' Back to Memphis	1960	3.00	6.00	12.00

Epic
❑ 10601	She's There When I Come Home/Magnolia Street	1970		3.00	6.00

Hi
❑ 2034	Teddy Bear/Your True Love	1961	2.50	5.00	10.00
❑ 2050	Caldonia/Be Her Number One	1962	2.50	5.00	10.00
❑ 2076	Haunted House/Hey, Hey Little Girl	1964	3.75	7.50	15.00

As "Gene Simmons"

Number		Title (A Side/B Side)	Year	VG	VG+	NM
❑ 2076		Haunted House/Hey, Hey Little Girl	1964	3.75	7.50	15.00
		As "Jumpin' Gene Simmons"				
❑ 2080		The Dodo/The Jump	1964	2.50	5.00	10.00
❑ 2086		Skinnie Minnie/I'm a Ramblin' Man	1965	2.50	5.00	10.00
❑ 2092		Mattie Rae/Folsom Prison Blues	1965	2.50	5.00	10.00
❑ 2102		The Batman/Bossy Boss	1966	3.75	7.50	15.00
❑ 2113		Go On Shoes/Keep That Meat in the Pan	1966	2.50	5.00	10.00

Mala

Number		Title (A Side/B Side)	Year	VG	VG+	NM
❑ 12012		I'm Just a Loser/Lila	1968	2.50	5.00	10.00

Sandy

Number		Title (A Side/B Side)	Year	VG	VG+	NM
❑ 1027		The Waiting Game/Shenandoah Waltz	1959	5.00	10.00	20.00
		As "Morris Gene Simmons"				

Sun

Number		Title (A Side/B Side)	Year	VG	VG+	NM
❑ 299		Drinkin' Wine/I Done Told You	1958	37.50	75.00	150.00

Simmons, Gene
(Of Kiss)
Casablanca

Number		Title (A Side/B Side)	Year	VG	VG+	NM
❑ 951		Radioactive/See You in Your Dreams	1978		3.00	6.00

Simmons, Patrick
(Of the Doobie Brothers)
Elektra

Number		Title (A Side/B Side)	Year	VG	VG+	NM
❑ 69817		Don't Make Me Do It/Sue Sad	1983		2.00	4.00
❑ 69839		So Wrong/If You Want a Little Love	1983		2.00	4.00

Simon and Garfunkel
(Also see "Garfunkel, Art"; "Simon, Paul"; "Tom and Jerry")
ABC-Paramount

Number		Title (A Side/B Side)	Year	VG	VG+	NM
❑ 10788		That's My Story/Tia-Juana Blues	1966	5.00	10.00	20.00
		Outtakes from Tom and Jerry days				

Columbia

Number		Title (A Side/B Side)	Year	VG	VG+	NM
❑ AS 43	DJ	America/Keep the Customer Satisfied	1972	3.00	6.00	12.00
❑ 10230		My Little Town//Art Garfunkel: Rag Doll/ Paul Simon: You're Kind	1975		2.50	5.00
❑ 10230	PS	My Little Town//Art Garfunkel: Rag Doll/ Paul Simon: You're Kind	1975		2.50	5.00
❑ 43396		The Sounds of Silence/ We've Got a Groovy Thing Goin'	1965	2.50	5.00	10.00
❑ 43396	DJ	The Sounds of Silence (same on both sides)	1965	12.50	25.00	50.00
		Red vinyl promo				
❑ 43511		Homeward Bound/Leaves That Are Green	1966	2.50	5.00	10.00
❑ 43511	DJ	Homeward Bound (same on both sides)	1966	12.50	25.00	50.00
		Red vinyl promo				
❑ 43617		I Am a Rock/Flowers Never Bend with the Rainfall	1966	2.50	5.00	10.00
❑ 43617	DJ	I Am a Rock (same on both sides)	1966	12.50	25.00	50.00
		Red vinyl promo				
❑ 43728		The Dangling Conversation/ The Big Bright Green Pleasure Machine	1966	2.50	5.00	10.00
❑ 43728	PS	The Dangling Conversation/ The Big Bright Green Pleasure Machine	1966	5.00	10.00	20.00
❑ 43873		A Hazy Shade of Winter/ For Emily, Wherever I May Find Her	1966	2.50	5.00	10.00
❑ 44046		At the Zoo/ The 59th Street Bridge Song (Feelin' Groovy)	1967	2.50	5.00	10.00
❑ 44046	PS	At the Zoo/ The 59th Street Bridge Song (Feelin' Groovy)	1967	10.00	20.00	40.00
🔖 44232		Fakin' It/You Don't Know Where Your Interest Lies	1967	3.75	7.50	15.00
		The B-side still has never appeared on a legitimate U.S. album or CD release				
❑ 44465		Scarborough Fair (/Canticle)/April Come She Will	1968	2.50	5.00	10.00
❑ 44511		Mrs. Robinson/Old Friends-Bookends	1968	2.50	5.00	10.00
		Label says "From the Motion Picture 'The Graduate'"				
❑ 44511		Mrs. Robinson/Old Friends-Bookends	1968	2.00	4.00	8.00
		Label says "From the Columbia Lp BOOKENDS," etc. with no reference to "The Graduate"				
❑ 44785		The Boxer/Baby Driver	1969	3.00	6.00	
		B-side mix (mono) is different than stereo LP version, especially near the end of the song				
❑ 44785	PS	The Boxer/Baby Driver	1969	2.00	4.00	8.00
❑ 45079		Bridge Over Troubled Water/ Keep the Customer Satisfied	1970	3.00	6.00	
❑ 45079	PS	Bridge Over Troubled Water/ Keep the Customer Satisfied	1970	2.00	4.00	8.00
❑ 45133		Cecelia/The Only Living Boy in New York	1970	3.00	6.00	
❑ 45133	PS	Cecelia/The Only Living Boy in New York	1970	2.00	4.00	8.00
❑ 45237		El Condor Pasa/Why Don't You Write Me	1970	3.00	6.00	
❑ 45663		America/For Emily, Wherever I May Find Her	1972	3.00	6.00	
❑ JZSP 116469	DJ	7 O'Clock News–Silent Night (same on both sides)	1967	6.25	12.50	25.00
		Promo-only Christmas release for radio stations				

Warner Bros.

Number		Title (A Side/B Side)	Year	VG	VG+	NM
❑ 50053		Wake Up Little Susie/ Me and Julio Down by the Schoolyard	1982		2.00	4.00

Number		Title (A Side/B Side)	Year	VG	VG+	NM

Simon Sisters, The
(Carly and Lucy Simon)
Children's Records of America

| ☐ 100 | | My Love Is Like a Red, Red Rose/The Lamb | 1968 | 5.00 | 10.00 | 20.00 |

Kapp

| ☐ 586 | | Winkin', Blinkin' and Nod/So Glad I'm Here | 1964 | 3.75 | 7.50 | 15.00 |
| ☐ 624 | | Cuddlebug/No One to Talk My Troubles To | 1964 | 3.75 | 7.50 | 15.00 |

Simon, Carly
(Also see "Simon Sisters, The")
Arista

☐ 2083		Better Not Tell Her/Happy Birthday	1990			3.00
☐ 2164		Life Is Eternal/We Just Got Here	1990			3.00
☐ 9525		Coming Around Again/Itsy Bitsy Spider	1986			3.00
☐ 9525	PS	Coming Around Again/Itsy Bitsy Spider	1986		2.50	5.00
		With "Heartburn" movie scenes				
☐ 9525	PS	Coming Around Again/Itsy Bitsy Spider	1986		2.00	4.00
		Black and white photo of Carly Simon				
☐ 9525	PS	Coming Around Again/Itsy Bitsy Spider	1986		2.00	4.00
		Color photo of Carly Simon				
☐ 9587		Give Me All Night/Sleight of Hand	1987			3.00
☐ 9587	PS	Give Me All Night/Sleight of Hand	1987			3.00
☐ 9619		The Stuff That Dreams Are Made Of/As Time Goes By	1987			3.00
☐ 9653		All I Want Is You/On a Hot Summer Night	1987			3.00
☐ 9653	PS	All I Want Is You/On a Hot Summer Night	1987			3.00
☐ 9754		You're So Vain/Do the Walls Come Down	1988			3.00
☐ 9793		Let the River Run/The Turn of the Tide	1988			3.00
☐ 9793	PS	Let the River Run/The Turn of the Tide	1988			3.00

Columbia

☐ 02675		Maryanne/(B-side unknown)	1982		2.00	4.00
		With Lucy Simon				
☐ 45840		Red, Red Rose/Lobster Quadrille	1973		3.00	6.00
		With Lucy Simon				

Elektra

☐ 45246		Attitude Dancing/Are You Ticklish	1975		2.50	5.00
☐ 45248		Slave/Look Me in the Eyes	1975			*Unreleased?*
☐ 45263		Waterfall/After the Storm	1975		2.50	5.00
☐ 45278		More and More/Love Out in the Street	1975		2.50	5.00
☐ 45325		It Keeps You Runnin'/Look Me in the Eyes	1976		2.00	4.00
☐ 45341		Half a Chance/Libby	1976		2.00	4.00
☐ 45413		Nobody Does It Better/After the Storm	1977		2.00	4.00
☐ 45477		You Belong to Me/In a Small Moment	1978		2.00	4.00
☐ 45477	PS	You Belong to Me/In a Small Moment	1978		3.00	6.00
☐ 45506		Devoted to You/Boys in the Trees	1978		2.00	4.00
		A-side with James Taylor				
☐ 45544		Tranquillo (Melt My Heart)/Back Down to Earth	1978		2.00	4.00
☐ 45724		That's the Way I've Always Heard It Should Be/Alone	1971		3.00	6.00
☐ 45748		Our First Day Together/Share the Land	1971			*Unreleased*
☐ 45759		Anticipation/The Garden	1971		3.00	6.00
☐ 45774		Legend in Your Own Time/Julie Through the Glass	1972		3.00	6.00
☐ 45796		The Girl You Think You Are/Share the Land	1972		3.00	6.00
☐ 45824		You're So Vain/	1972		3.00	6.00
		His Friends Are More Than Fond of Robin				
☐ 45843		The Right Thing to Do/We Have No Secrets	1973		2.50	5.00
☐ 45880		Mockingbird/Grownup	1974		2.50	5.00
		A-side with James Taylor				
☐ 45887		Haven't Got Time for the Pain/Mind on My Man	1974		2.50	5.00
☐ 46051		Vengeance/Love You by Heart	1979		2.00	4.00
☐ 46051	PS	Vengeance/Love You by Heart	1979		2.50	5.00
☐ 46514		Spy/Pure Sin	1979		2.00	4.00
☐ 69953		Hidin' Away/Fight for It	1982		2.00	4.00
		With Jesse Colin Young				

Epic

☐ 05419		Tired of Being Blonde/Black Honeymoon	1985			3.00
☐ 05419	PS	Tired of Being Blonde/Black Honeymoon	1985		2.00	4.00
☐ 05596		My New Boyfriend/The Wives Are in Connecticut	1985			3.00

Mirage

☐ 4051		Why/Why	1982		2.00	4.00
		B-side by Chic				
☐ 99963		Why/(Instrumental)	1982		2.00	4.00

Planet

| ☐ YB-13779 | | Someone Waits for You/(B-side unknown) | 1984 | | 2.00 | 4.00 |

Warner Bros.

☐ 29428		Hello Big Man/Dawn You Get to Me	1983		2.00	4.00
☐ 29484		You Know What to Do/Orpheus	1983		2.00	4.00
☐ 29484	PS	You Know What to Do/Orpheus	1983		2.50	5.00
☐ 49518		Jesse/Stardust	1980		2.00	4.00
☐ 49518	PS	Jesse/Stardust	1980		2.50	5.00
☐ 49630		Take Me As I Am/James	1980		2.00	4.00
☐ 49689		Come Upstairs/Them	1981		2.00	4.00
☐ 49880		From the Heart/Hurt	1981		2.00	4.00
☐ 50027		Body and Soul/Get Along Without You Very Well	1982		2.00	4.00

Number	Title (A Side/B Side)	Year	VG	VG+	NM

Simon, Paul *
(Includes his pre-fame solo records under aliases. Also see "Simon and Garfunkel"; "Tico and the Triumphs")

Amy

❑ 875	The Lone Teen Ranger/Lisa	1962	15.00	30.00	60.00
	As "Jerry Landis"				

Big

❑ 614	True or False/Teenage Fool	1958	25.00	50.00	100.00
	As "True Taylor"				

Canadian American

❑ 130	I'm Lonely/I Wish I Weren't in Love	1961	25.00	50.00	100.00
	As "Jerry Landis"; the rarest of his pre-Columbia solo singles				

Columbia

❑ 10197	Gone at Last/Take Me to the Mardi Gras	1975		2.50	5.00
	A-side: With Phoebe Snow and the Jesse Dixon Singers				
❑ 10270	50 Ways to Leave Your Lover/ Some Folks Lives Roll Easy	1975		2.50	5.00
❑ 10332	Still Crazy After All These Years/ I Do It for Your Love (Live)	1976		2.50	5.00
❑ 10630	Slip Slidin' Away/Something So Right	1977		3.00	6.00
	First pressings claim the A-side came from the LP "Blatant Greatest Hits." The Oak Ridge Boys are not mentioned.				
❑ 10630	Slip Slidin' Away/Something So Right	1977		2.50	5.00
	Later pressings correct the LP title to "Greatest Hits, Etc." The Oak Ridge Boys are credited in the fine print.				
❑ 10711	Stranded in a Limousine/Have a Good Time	1978		3.00	6.00
❑ 45547	Mother and Child Reunion/Paranoia Blues	1972		2.50	5.00
❑ 45585	Me and Julio Down by the Schoolyard/Congratulations	1972		2.50	5.00
❑ 45638	Duncan/Run That Body Down	1972		2.50	5.00
❑ 45859	Kodachrome/Tenderness	1973		3.00	6.00
	With no trademark disclaimer on label				
❑ 45859	Kodachrome/Tenderness	1973		3.00	6.00
	With sticker on label: "Kodachrome is a registered trademark for color film."				
❑ 45859	Kodachrome/Tenderness	1973		2.50	5.00
	With printing on label: "Kodachrome is a registered trademark for color film."				
❑ 45900	American Tune/ One Man's Ceiling Is Another Man's Floor	1973		2.50	5.00
❑ 45900 PS	American Tune/ One Man's Ceiling Is Another Man's Floor	1973	2.50	5.00	10.00
❑ 45907	Loves Me Like a Rock/Learn How to Fall	1973		2.50	5.00
	With the Dixie Hummingbirds				
❑ 46038	The Sound of Silence/Mother and Child Reunion	1974	2.00	4.00	8.00

MGM

❑ 12822	Anna Belle/Loneliness	1959	12.50	25.00	50.00
	As "Jerry Landis"				

Tribute

❑ 128	Carlos Dominguez/He Was My Brother	1963	15.00	30.00	60.00
	As "Paul Kane"; authentic copies make no mention of Paul Simon on the label				

Warner Bros.

❑ 19464	Proof/The Coast	1991			3.00
❑ 27903	Graceland/Hearts and Bones	1988		2.50	5.00
❑ 28221	Under African Skies/I Know What I Know	1987			3.00
	A-side with Linda Ronstadt				
❑ 28389	Diamonds on the Soles of Her Shoes/ All Around the World Or the Myth of Fingerprints	1987			3.00
❑ 28460	The Boy in the Bubble/Crazy Love, Part 2	1987			3.00
❑ 28460 PS	The Boy in the Bubble/Crazy Love, Part 2	1987			3.00
❑ 28522	Graceland/Hearts and Bones	1986			3.00
❑ 28522 PS	Graceland/Hearts and Bones	1986			3.00
❑ 28667	You Can Call Me Al/Gumboots	1986			3.00
❑ 28667 PS	You Can Call Me Al/Gumboots	1986			3.00
❑ 29333	Think Too Much/Song About the Moon	1984		2.00	4.00
❑ 29453	Allergies/Think Too Much (ii)	1983		2.00	4.00
❑ 29453 PS	Allergies/Think Too Much (ii)	1983		2.00	4.00
❑ 49511	Late in the Evening/ How the Heart Approaches What It Yearns	1980		2.00	4.00
❑ 49511 PS	Late in the Evening/ How the Heart Approaches What It Yearns	1980		2.50	5.00
❑ 49601	One-Trick Pony/Long, Long Day	1980		2.00	4.00
❑ 49675	Oh, Marion/God Bless the Absentee	1981		2.00	4.00

Warwick

❑ 522	Swanee/Toot, Toot, Tootsie Goodbye	1960	12.50	25.00	50.00
	As "Jerry Landis"				
❑ 552	Shy/Just a Boy	1960	12.50	25.00	50.00
	As "Jerry Landis"				
❑ 588	I'd Like to Be/Just a Boy	1960	12.50	25.00	50.00
	As "Jerry Landis"				
❑ 619	Play Me a Sad Song/It Means a Lot to Them	1961	12.50	25.00	50.00
	As "Jerry Landis"				

Simpson, Valerie
(Of Ashford and Simpson)

Tamla

❑ 54204	Back to Nowhere/Can't It Wait Until Tomorrow	1971		2.50	5.00

Number		Title (A Side/B Side)	Year	VG	VG+	NM
☐ 54224		Silly Wasn't I/I Believe I'm Gonna Take This Ride	1972		2.50	5.00
☐ 54231		Genius/One More Baby Child Born	1973		2.50	5.00

Sinatra, Frank

(No label)

☐ KB-2077/8		High Hopes with Jack Kennedy/	1960	75.00	150.00	300.00
		Jack Kennedy All the Way				

No artist or label shown, but Sinatra does sing the A-side

Capitol

☐ F2450		I'm Walking Behind You/Lean Baby	1953	6.25	12.50	25.00
☐ F2505		My One and Only Love/I've Got the World on a String	1953	5.00	10.00	20.00
☐ F2560		Anytime, Anywhere/From Here to Eternity	1953	5.00	10.00	20.00
☐ F2638		I Love You/South of the Border	1953	5.00	10.00	20.00
☐ F2703		Young at Heart/Take a Chance	1953	5.00	10.00	20.00
☐ F2787		Don't Worry 'Bout Me/I Could Have Told You	1954	5.00	10.00	20.00
☐ F2816		Three Coins in the Fountain/Rain	1954	5.00	10.00	20.00
☐ F2864		The Girl That Got Away/Half as Lovely	1954	5.00	10.00	20.00
☐ F2922		It Worries Me/When I Stop Loving You	1954	5.00	10.00	20.00
☐ F2954		White Christmas/The Christmas Waltz	1954	5.00	10.00	20.00
☐ 2954		White Christmas/The Christmas Waltz	1962	2.50	5.00	10.00

Also known to exist without the "F" prefix on orange and yellow swirl label

☐ F2993		You My Love/Someone to Watch Over Me	1954	5.00	10.00	20.00
☐ F3018		Melody of Love/I'm Gonna Live Till I Die	1954	5.00	10.00	20.00
☐ F3050		Why Should I Cry Over You?/	1954	5.00	10.00	20.00
		Don't Change Your Mind About Me				
☐ F3084		Two Hearts, Two Kisses/From the Bottom to the Top	1955	3.75	7.50	15.00
☐ F3102		Learnin' the Blues/If I Had Three Wishes	1955	3.75	7.50	15.00
☐ F3130		Not as a Stranger/	1955	3.75	7.50	15.00
		How Could You Do a Thing Like That to Me?				
☐ F3218		Same Old Saturday Night/Fairy Tale	1955	3.75	7.50	15.00
☐ F3260		Love and Marriage/The Impatient Years	1955	5.00	10.00	20.00
☐ F3290		(Love Is) The Tender Trap/Weep They Will	1955	3.75	7.50	15.00
☐ F3350		Flowers Mean Forgiveness/You'll Get Yours	1956	3.75	7.50	15.00
☐ F3423		(How Little It Matters) How Little We Know/	1956	3.75	7.50	15.00
		Five Hundred Guys				
☐ F3469		You're Sensational/	1956	3.75	7.50	15.00
		Johnny Concho Theme (Wait for Me)				
☐ F3507		Well, Did You Evah?/True Love	1956	3.75	7.50	15.00

A-side by Bing Crosby and Frank Sinatra; B-side by Bing Crosby and Grace Kelly

☐ F3508		Who Wants to Be a Millionaire/	1956	3.75	7.50	15.00
		Mind If I Make Love to You?				
☐ F3552		Jealous Lover/You Forgot All the Words	1956	6.25	12.50	25.00

Original pressings contain this title

☐ F3552		Hey! Jealous Lover/You Forgot All the Words	1956	3.75	7.50	15.00
☐ F3608		Can I Steal a Little Love/Your Love for Me	1956	3.75	7.50	15.00
☐ F3703		Crazy Love/So Long, My Love	1957	3.00	6.00	12.00
☐ F3744		You're Cheatin' Yourself (If You're Cheatin' On Me)/	1957	3.00	6.00	12.00
		Something Wonderful Happens in Summer				
☐ F3793		All the Way/Chicago	1957	3.00	6.00	12.00
☐ F3859		Witchcraft/Tell Her You Love Her	1957	3.00	6.00	12.00
☐ F3900		Mistletoe and Holly/The Christmas Waltz	1957	3.75	7.50	15.00

"The Christmas Waltz" here is a different version than that on Capitol 2954.

☐ F3952		How Are Ya' Fixed for Love?/Nothin' in Common	1958	3.00	6.00	12.00

By Frank Sinatra and Keely Smith

☐ F4003		Same Old Song and Dance/	1958	3.00	6.00	12.00
		Monique (Song from Kings Go Forth)				
☐ F4070		Mr. Success/Sleep Warm	1958	3.00	6.00	12.00
☐ F4103		No One Ever Tells You/To Love and Be Loved	1958	3.00	6.00	12.00
☐ F4155		French Foreign Legion/Time After Time	1959	3.00	6.00	12.00
☐ F4214		High Hopes/All My Tomorrows	1959	3.75	7.50	15.00
☐ F4214	PS	High Hopes/All My Tomorrows	1959	50.00	100.00	200.00
☐ F4284		Talk to Me/They Came to Cordura	1959	3.00	6.00	12.00
☐ 4376		River, Stay 'Way from My Door/	1960	3.00	6.00	12.00
		It's Over, It's Over				
☐ 4408		Nice 'N' Easy/This Was My Love	1960	3.00	6.00	12.00
☐ 4466		Ol' MacDonald/You'll Always Be the One I Love	1960	3.00	6.00	12.00
☐ 4546		My Blue Heaven/Sentimental Baby	1960	3.00	6.00	12.00
☐ 4615		American Beauty Rose/Sentimental Journey	1961	3.00	6.00	12.00
☐ 4677		The Moon Was Yellow/I Gotta Right to Sing the Blues	1962	3.00	6.00	12.00
☐ 4677		I've Heard That Song Before/	1962	3.00	6.00	12.00
		I Gotta Right to Sing the Blues				
☐ 4729		Five Minutes More/I'll Remember April	1962	3.00	6.00	12.00
☐ 4815		I Love Paris/Hidden Persuasion	1962	3.00	6.00	12.00
☐ 6019		Young at Heart/Learnin' the Blues	196?	3.00	6.00	

Starline reissue label

☐ 6027		All the Way/High Hopes	196?		3.00	6.00

Starline reissue label

☐ 6078		Witchcraft/Chicago	1966		3.00	6.00

Starline reissue label

☐ S7-17704		I've Got You Under My Skin/Come Rain or Come Shine	1994			Unreleased

A-side with Bono, B-side with Gloria Estefan

☐ S7-18204		Jingle Bells/I'll Be Home for Christmas	1994		2.50	5.00

Red vinyl

Columbia

Note: All records with a "1-" prefix before three-digit numbers are Microgroove 33 1/3 rpm 7-inch singles; the "6-" prefix are 45s

☐ 1-106		Sunflower/Once in Love with Amy	1948	15.00	30.00	60.00

Number	Title (A Side/B Side)	Year	VG	VG+	NM
☐ 1-112	Why Can't You Behave/No Orchids for My Lady	1948	15.00	30.00	60.00
☐ 1-130	Comme Ci, Comme Ca/ While the Angelus Was Ringing	1948	15.00	30.00	60.00
☐ 1-144	When Is Sometime/If You Stub Your Toe on the Moon	1949	15.00	30.00	60.00
☐ 1-154	Where Is the One/Bop Goes My Heart	1949	15.00	30.00	60.00
☐ 1-174	Bali Ha'i/Some Enchanted Evening	1949	15.00	30.00	60.00
☐ 1-191	The Right Girl for Me/Night After Night	1949	15.00	30.00	60.00
☐ 1-222	It Happens Every Spring/The Hucklebuck	1949	15.00	30.00	60.00
☐ 1-260	Let's Take an Old-Fashioned Walk/ Just One Way to Say I Love You	1949	15.00	30.00	60.00
	With Doris Day				
☐ 1-307	I Only Have Eyes for You/It All Depends on You	1949	15.00	30.00	60.00
☐ 1-315	Don't Cry Joe/The Wedding of Lili Marlene	1949	15.00	30.00	60.00
☐ 1-316	Just a Kiss Apart/Bye Bye Baby	1949	15.00	30.00	60.00
☐ 1-326	If I Ever Love Again/Every Man Should Marry	1949	15.00	30.00	60.00
☐ 1-372	Could'ja/That Lucky Old Sun	1949	15.00	30.00	60.00
☐ 1-380	On the Island of Stromboli/Mad About You	1949	15.00	30.00	60.00
☐ 1-427	The Old Master Painter/Lost in the Stars	1949	15.00	30.00	60.00
☐ 1-440	Sorry/Why Remind Me	1949	15.00	30.00	60.00
☐ 1-491	Sunshine Cake/We've Got a Sure Thing	1949	15.00	30.00	60.00
☐ 1-496	Chattanoogie Shoe Shine Boy/God's Country	1950	15.00	30.00	60.00
☐ 1-508	You'll Never Walk Alone/Begin the Beguine	1950	15.00	30.00	60.00
☐ 1-511	Among My Souvenirs/September Song	1950	15.00	30.00	60.00
☐ 1-611	Kisses and Tears/When the Sun Goes Down	1950	15.00	30.00	60.00
☐ 1-624	American Beauty Rose/Just An Old Stone House	1950	15.00	30.00	60.00
☐ 1-650	Poinciana/There's No Business Like Show Business	1950	15.00	30.00	60.00
☐ 1-669	Peachtree Street/This Is the Night	1950	15.00	30.00	60.00
☐ 1-718	Goodnight Irene/My Blue Heaven	1950	15.00	30.00	60.00
☐ 6-718	Goodnight Irene/My Blue Heaven	1950	7.50	15.00	30.00
☐ 1-780	Life Is So Peculiar/Dear Little Boy of Mine	1950	15.00	30.00	60.00
☐ 1-845	One Finger Melody/Accidents Will Happen	1950	15.00	30.00	60.00
☐ 1-888	Nevertheless/I Guess I'll Have to Dream the Rest	1950	15.00	30.00	60.00
☐ 6-888	Nevertheless/I Guess I'll Have to Dream the Rest	1950	7.50	15.00	30.00
☐ 1-924	Remember Me in Your Dreams/ Let It Snow, Let It Snow, Let It Snow	1950	15.00	30.00	60.00
☐ 6-924	Remember Me in Your Dreams/ Let It Snow, Let It Snow, Let It Snow	1950	7.50	15.00	30.00
☐ 1-936	I Am Loved/You Don't Remind Me	1950	15.00	30.00	60.00
☐ 6-936	I Am Loved/You Don't Remind Me	1950	7.50	15.00	30.00
	Note: Many Columbia singles below are reissues of titles that first appeared on 78s				
☐ 3-33011	Nancy/Ol' Man River	1961	12.50	25.00	50.00
	Hall of Fame series; Compact Single 33				
☐ 4-33011	Nancy/Ol' Man River	1960	2.50	5.00	10.00
☐ 13-33011	Nancy/Ol' Man River	1975		3.00	6.00
	Hall of Fame series; new prefix				
☐ 33306	I've Got a Crush on You/The Birth of the Blues	1977		3.00	6.00
	Hall of Fame series				
☐ 33319	Among My Souvenirs/September Song	1977		3.00	6.00
	Hall of Fame series				
☐ 36814	If You Are But a Dream/Put Your Dreams Away	1950	5.00	10.00	20.00
☐ 36825	You'll Never Walk Alone/If I Loved You	1950	5.00	10.00	20.00
☐ 36918	You Go to My Head/I Don't Know Why	1950	5.00	10.00	20.00
☐ 36919	These Foolish Things/A Ghost of a Chance	1950	5.00	10.00	20.00
☐ 36920	Why Shouldn't I?/Try a Little Tenderness	1950	5.00	10.00	20.00
☐ 36921	Paradise/Someone to Watch Over Me	1950	5.00	10.00	20.00
☐ 37161	Among My Souvenirs/September Song	1950	5.00	10.00	20.00
☐ 37257	That Old Black Magic/How Deep Is the Ocean?	1950	5.00	10.00	20.00
☐ 37259	She's Funny That Way/Embraceable You	1950	5.00	10.00	20.00
☐ 38151	I've Got a Crush on You/Ever Homeward	1950	5.00	10.00	20.00
☐ 38163	All of Me/I Went Down to Virginia	1950	5.00	10.00	20.00
☐ 38256	Silent Night/Adeste Fideles	1950	5.00	10.00	20.00
☐ 38257	Jingle Bells/White Christmas	1950	5.00	10.00	20.00
☐ 38258	O Little Town of Bethlehem/ It Came Upon a Midnight Clear	1950	5.00	10.00	20.00
☐ 38259	Have Yourself a Merry Little Christmas/ Santa Claus Is Comin' to Town	1950	5.00	10.00	20.00
☐ 38446	Bali Ha'i/Some Enchanted Evening	1950	5.00	10.00	20.00
☐ 38650	Lost in the Stars/Old Master Painter	1950	5.00	10.00	20.00
☐ 38662	Sorry/Why Remind Me?	1950	5.00	10.00	20.00
☐ 38683	The Moon Was Yellow/The Music Stopped	1950	5.00	10.00	20.00
☐ 38684	Strange Music/I Love You	1950	5.00	10.00	20.00
☐ 38685	Where or When/None But the Lonely Heart	1950	5.00	10.00	20.00
☐ 38686	Always/Why Was I Born?	1950	5.00	10.00	20.00
☐ 38705	Sunshine Cake/Sure Thing	1950	5.00	10.00	20.00
☐ 38790	Kisses and Tears/When the Sun Goes Down	1950	6.25	12.50	25.00
☐ 38809	American Beauty Rose/Just an Old Stone House	1950	6.25	12.50	25.00
☐ 38829	Poinciana/There's No Business Like Show Business	1950	5.00	10.00	20.00
☐ 38853	Peachtree Street/This Is the Night	1950	5.00	10.00	20.00
☐ 38892	Goodnight Irene/My Blue Heaven	1950	3.75	7.50	15.00
	Reissue of Columbia 6-718				
☐ 38960	Life Is So Peculiar/Dear Little Boy of Mine	1950	5.00	10.00	20.00
☐ 38996	Lover/When You're Smiling	1950	5.00	10.00	20.00
☐ 38997	The Continental/It's Only a Paper Moon	1950	5.00	10.00	20.00
☐ 38998	Should I?/My Blue Heaven	1950	5.00	10.00	20.00
☐ 38999	It All Depends on You/You Do Something to Me	1950	5.00	10.00	20.00
☐ 39014	Accidents Will Happen/One Finger Melody	1950	5.00	10.00	20.00
☐ 39044	Nevertheless/I Guess I'll Have to Dream the Rest	1950	3.75	7.50	15.00
	Reissue of Columbia 6-888				

Number		Title (A Side/B Side)	Year	VG	VG+	NM
❑ 39069		Remember Me in Your Dreams/	1950	3.75	7.50	15.00
		Let It Snow, Let It Snow, Let It Snow				
		Reissue of Columbia 6-924				
❑ 39079		I Am Loved/You Don't Remind Me	1950	3.75	7.50	15.00
		Reissue of Columbia 6-936				
❑ 3-39118		Take My Love/Come Back to Sorrento	1950	12.50	25.00	50.00
		Microgroove 33 1/3 rpm, 7-inch single				
❑ 39118		Take My Love/Come Back to Sorrento	1950	3.75	7.50	15.00
❑ 3-39141		Love Means Love/Cherry Pies Ought to Be You	1951	12.50	25.00	50.00
		Microgroove 33 1/3 rpm, 7-inch single				
❑ 39141		Love Means Love/Cherry Pies Ought to Be You	1951	6.25	12.50	25.00
❑ 3-39213		Faithful/You're the One	1951	12.50	25.00	50.00
		Microgroove 33 1/3 rpm, 7-inch single				
❑ 39213		Faithful/You're the One	1951	5.00	10.00	20.00
❑ 39294		Hello, Young Lovers/We Kissed in a Shadow	1951	3.75	7.50	15.00
❑ 39346		I Whistle a Happy Tune/Love Me	1951	3.75	7.50	15.00
❑ 39425		Mama Will Bark/I'm a Fool to Want You	1951	10.00	20.00	40.00
		"Frank Sinatra & Dagmar"; the record Ol' Blue Eyes calls his worst				
❑ 39493		I Fall in Love with You Everyday/	1951	5.00	10.00	20.00
		It's a Long Way from Your House				
❑ 39498		It Never Entered My Mind/Try a Little Tenderness	1951	3.75	7.50	15.00
❑ 39527		Castle Rock/Deep Night	1951	5.00	10.00	20.00
❑ 39592		April in Paris/London by Night	1951	3.75	7.50	15.00
❑ 39652		I Hear a Rhapsody/I Could Write a Book	1952	3.75	7.50	15.00
❑ 39687		Feet of Clay/Don't Ever Be Afraid to Go Home	1952	5.00	10.00	20.00
❑ 39726		My Girl/Walkin' in the Sunshine	1952	5.00	10.00	20.00
❑ 39787		Luna Rosa/Tennessee Newsboy	1952	5.00	10.00	20.00
❑ 39819		Azure-Te/Bim Bam Baby	1952	3.75	7.50	15.00
❑ 39882		The Birth of the Blues/Why Try to Change Me Now?	1952	3.75	7.50	15.00
❑ 40229		I'm Glad There Is You/	1953	5.00	10.00	20.00
		You Can Take My Word For It Baby				
❑ 40522		Dream/American Beauty Rose	1953	3.75	7.50	15.00
❑ 40565		Sheila/Day by Day	1953	7.50	15.00	30.00
❑ 41133		I'm a Fool to Want You/If I Forget You	1953	3.75	7.50	15.00
Note: 50003-50079 are from the Hall of Fame series						
❑ 50003		Among My Souvenirs/September Song	1954	2.50	5.00	10.00
❑ 50028		I've Got a Crush on You/The Birth of the Blues	1954	2.50	5.00	10.00
❑ 50053		Nancy/The Girl That I Marry	1954	2.50	5.00	10.00
❑ 50066		You'll Never Walk Alone/If I Loved You	1954	2.50	5.00	10.00
❑ 50069		Saturday Night/Five Minutes More	1954	2.50	5.00	10.00
❑ 50079		Silent Night/Adeste Fideles	1954	2.50	5.00	10.00

Island/Capitol

Number		Title (A Side/B Side)	Year	VG	VG+	NM
❑ 858 076-7		I've Got You Under My Skin/Stay (Faraway, So Close!)	1994		2.00	4.00
❑ 858 076-7	PS	I've Got You Under My Skin/Stay (Faraway, So Close!)	1994		2.00	4.00
		A-side: Frank Sinatra and Bono; B-side: U2				

MCA

Number		Title (A Side/B Side)	Year	VG	VG+	NM
❑ 55127		Fly Me to the Moon/Check Yes or No	1995			3.00
		A-side with George Strait; B-side is George Strait solo				

Qwest

Number		Title (A Side/B Side)	Year	VG	VG+	NM
❑ 28844		The Best of Everything/Teach Me Tonight	1985		2.00	4.00
❑ 29139		Mack the Knife/It's All Right with Me	1984		2.50	5.00
❑ 29223		L.A. Is My Lady/Until the Real Thing Comes Along	1984		2.50	5.00
❑ 29223	PS	L.A. Is My Lady/Until the Real Thing Comes Along	1984	3.75	7.50	15.00

RCA Victor

Note: All RCA 45s are reissues of material first issued on 78s.

Number		Title (A Side/B Side)	Year	VG	VG+	NM
❑ 27-0012		Night and Day/The Lamplighter's Serenade	1948	3.75	7.50	15.00
❑ 27-0015		Daybreak/There Are Such Things	1948	3.75	7.50	15.00
❑ 447-0116		I'll Never Smile Again/I'll Be Seeing You	1950	3.00	6.00	12.00
❑ 447-0123		Stardust/There Are Such Things	1950	3.00	6.00	12.00
❑ 447-0408		Night and Day/The Lamplighter's Serenade	1952	3.00	6.00	12.00
❑ 447-0445		Street of Dreams/East of the Sun	1952	3.00	6.00	12.00
❑ 447-0928		Night and Day/The Night We Called It a Day	1972		3.00	6.00
❑ 447-0929		The Song Is You/The Lamplighter's Serenade	1972		3.00	6.00
❑ DTA-03001		Street of Dreams/Whispering	1955	3.00	6.00	12.00
❑ DTA-03012		The One I Love/(B-side unknown)	1955	3.00	6.00	12.00

Reprise

Number		Title (A Side/B Side)	Year	VG	VG+	NM
❑ GRE 0113		Bad, Bad Leroy Brown/Let Me Try Again	1975		2.00	4.00
		"Back to Back Hits" series				
❑ GRE 0122		Theme from New York, New York/	1981		2.00	4.00
		You and Me (We Wanted It All)				
		"Back to Back Hits" series				
❑ 0243		Have Yourself a Merry Little Christmas/	1963	5.00	10.00	20.00
		How Shall I Send Thee?				
		B-side by Les Baxter				
❑ 0249		Stay with Me/Talk to Me Baby	1963	2.50	5.00	10.00
❑ 0279		My Kind of Town/I Like to Lead When I Dance	1964	2.50	5.00	10.00
❑ 0279	PS	My Kind of Town/I Like to Lead When I Dance	1964	37.50	75.00	150.00
		Sleeve issued with promo copies only				
❑ 0301		Softly, As I Leave You/Then Suddenly Love	1964	2.50	5.00	10.00
❑ 0314		I Heard the Bells on Christmas Day/	1964	5.00	10.00	20.00
		The Little Drummer Boy				
❑ 0314	PS	I Heard the Bells on Christmas Day/	1964	12.50	25.00	50.00
		The Little Drummer Boy				
❑ 0317		We Wish You the Merriest/Go Tell It on the Mountain	1964	5.00	10.00	20.00

Number		Title (A Side/B Side)	Year	VG	VG+	NM
❏ 0317	PS	We Wish You the Merriest/Go Tell It on the Mountain	1964	12.50	25.00	50.00
		By Frank Sinatra/Bing Crosby/Fred Waring				
❏ 0332		Somewhere in Your Heart/Emily	1964	2.00	4.00	8.00
❏ 0350		Anytime at All/Available	1964	2.00	4.00	8.00
❏ 0373		Tell Her (You Love Her Each Day)/Here's to the Losers	1965	2.00	4.00	8.00
❏ 0380		Forget Domani/I Can't Believe I'm Losing You	1965	2.00	4.00	8.00
❏ 0398		When Somebody Loves You/	1965	2.00	4.00	8.00
		When I'm Not Near the Girl I Love				
❏ 0410		Everybody Has the Right to Be Wrong/	1965	2.00	4.00	8.00
		I'll Only Miss Her When I Think of Her				
❏ 0429		It Was a Very Good Year/Moment to Moment	1965	2.00	4.00	8.00
❏ 0429	PS	It Was a Very Good Year/Moment to Moment	1965	6.25	12.50	25.00
❏ 0470		Strangers in the Night/Oh, You Crazy Moon	1966	2.50	5.00	10.00
❏ 0493	DJ	Frank Sinatra Reads from Gunga Din	1966	125.00	250.00	500.00
		300 pressed and given away to friends; no stock copies				
❏ 0509		Summer Wind/You Make Me Feel So Young	1966	2.50	5.00	10.00
❏ 0531		That's Life/The September of My Years	1966	2.50	5.00	10.00
❏ 0531	PS	That's Life/The September of My Years	1966	6.25	12.50	25.00
❏ 0561		Somethin' Stupid/I Will Wait for You	1967	2.00	4.00	8.00
		A-side: Nancy Sinatra and Frank Sinatra				
❏ 0561		Somethin' Stupid/Give Her Love	1967	2.50	5.00	10.00
		A-side: Nancy Sinatra and Frank Sinatra				
❏ 0610		The World We Knew (Over and Over)/You Are There	1967	2.00	4.00	8.00
❏ 0631		This Town/This Is My Love	1967	2.00	4.00	8.00
❏ 0677		I Can't Believe I'm Losing You/How Old Am I?	1967	2.00	4.00	8.00
❏ 0702		My Kind of Town/That's Life	1968		2.50	5.00
		"Back to Back Hits" series				
❏ 0706		September of My Years/Softly, As I Leave You	1968		2.50	5.00
		"Back to Back Hits" series				
❏ 0710		Strangers in the Night/Summer Wind	1968		2.50	5.00
		"Back to Back Hits" series				
❏ 0713		It Was a Very Good Year/Stay with Me	1968		2.50	5.00
		"Back to Back Hits" series				
❏ 0727		Somethin' Stupid/The World We Knew (Over and Over)	1968		2.50	5.00
		"Back to Back Hits" series; A-side with Nancy Sinatra				
❏ 0734		My Way/Cycles	1970		2.50	5.00
		"Back to Back Hits" series				
❏ 0764		Cycles/My Way of Life	1968		3.00	6.00
		From here though 0865, yellow label with "W7/:r" logo				
❏ 0790		Whatever Happened to Christmas?/I	1968	3.00	6.00	12.00
		Wouldn't Trade Christmas				
		B-side by The Sinatra Family				
❏ 0798		Rain in My Heart/Star	1968		3.00	6.00
❏ 0817		My Way/Blue Lace	1969	2.50	5.00	10.00
❏ 0852		Love's Been Good to Me/A Man Alone	1969	2.00	4.00	8.00
❏ 0865		Goin' Out of My Head/Forget to Remember	1969	2.00	4.00	8.00
❏ 0895		I Would Be in Love (Anyway)/Watertown	1970	2.00	4.00	8.00
❏ 0980		Feelin' Kinda Sunday/Kids	1970	2.00	4.00	8.00
		A-side by Nancy Sinatra and Frank Sinatra; B-side by Nancy Sinatra				
❏ 0981		Something/Bein' Green	1970	2.00	4.00	8.00
❏ 1010		Witchcraft/Young at Heart	1971	2.00	4.00	8.00
❏ 1011		Life's a Trippy Thing/I'm Not Afraid	1971	2.00	4.00	8.00
		A-side by Nancy Sinatra and Frank Sinatra				
❏ 1181		Let Me Try Again/Send In the Clowns	1973	2.00	4.00	8.00
❏ 1190		You Will Be My Music/Winners	1973	2.00	4.00	8.00
❏ 1196		Bad, Bad Leroy Brown/I'm Gonna Make It All the Way	1974	2.00	4.00	8.00
❏ 1208		You Turned My World Around/	1974	2.00	4.00	8.00
		Satisfy Me One More Time				
❏ 1327		Anytime (I'll Be There)/The Hurt Doesn't Go Away	1975	2.00	4.00	8.00
❏ 1335		I Believe I'm Gonna Love You/	1975	2.00	4.00	8.00
		The Only Couple on the Floor				
❏ 1335	PS	I Believe I'm Gonna Love You	1975	10.00	20.00	40.00
		Issued with promo copies only				
❏ 1342		A Baby Just Like You/Christmas Mem'ries	1975	2.50	5.00	10.00
❏ 1342	PS	A Baby Just Like You/Christmas Mem'ries	1975	5.00	10.00	20.00
		Red and black printing, released with stock copies				
❏ 1342	PS	A Baby Just Like You/Christmas Mem'ries	1975	10.00	20.00	40.00
		Blue printing, released with promo copies only				
❏ 1343		Empty Tables/The Saddest Thing of All	1976	2.00	4.00	8.00
❏ 1347		I Sing the Songs (I Write the Songs)/Empty Tables	1976	2.50	5.00	10.00
❏ 1364		Stargazer/The Best I Ever Had	1976	2.00	4.00	8.00
❏ 1364	PS	Stargazer/The Best I Ever Had	1976	3.75	7.50	15.00
		Special sleeve: "New Sinatra Single"				
❏ 1377		Dry Your Eyes/Like a Sad Song	1976	2.00	4.00	8.00
❏ 1382		I Love My Wife/Send In the Clowns	1976	2.50	5.00	10.00
❏ 1386		Night and Day/Everybody Ought to Be in Love	1977	2.00	4.00	8.00
❏ 19355		Fly Me to the Moon/The Last Dance	1991		2.00	4.00
❏ 20,001		The Second Time Around/Tina	1960	6.25	12.50	25.00
		Originals on light blue label				
❏ 20,010		Granada/The Curse of an Aching Heart	1961	3.75	7.50	15.00
❏ 20,010	PS	Granada/The Curse of an Aching Heart	1961	6.25	12.50	25.00
❏ 20,023		I'll Be Seeing You/The One I Love	1961	3.75	7.50	15.00
❏ 20,024		Imagination/It's Always You	1961		Unreleased?	
❏ 20,025		East of the Sun/I'm Getting Sentimental Over You	1961		Unreleased?	
❏ 20,026		There Are Such Things/Polkadots and Moonbeams	1961	3.75	7.50	15.00
❏ 20,027		Without a Song/It Started All Over Again	1961	3.75	7.50	15.00

Number		Title (A Side/B Side)	Year	VG	VG+	NM
☐ 20,028		Take Me/Daybreak	1961	3.75	7.50	15.00
☐ 20,040		Pocketful of Miracles/Name It and It's Yours	1961	3.75	7.50	15.00
☐ 20,040	PS	Pocketful of Miracles/Name It and It's Yours	1961	7.50	15.00	30.00
☐ 20,053		I'll Be Seeing You/Without a Song	1962			Unreleased
☐ 20,059		Stardust/Come Rain or Come Shine	1962	3.75	7.50	15.00
☐ 20,063		Everybody's Twistin'/Nothin' But the Best	1962	3.75	7.50	15.00
☐ 20,063	PS	Everybody's Twistin'/Nothin' But the Best	1962	7.50	15.00	30.00
☐ 20,092		Goody, Goody/Love Is Just Around the Corner	1962	3.00	6.00	12.00
☐ 20,107		The Look of Love/Indiscreet	1962	3.00	6.00	12.00
☐ 20,107		The Look of Love/I Left My Heart in San Francisco	1962	12.50	25.00	50.00
☐ 20,128		Me and My Shadow/Sam's Song	1962	3.75	7.50	15.00
☐ 20,128	PS	Me and My Shadow/Sam's Song	1962	12.50	25.00	50.00
		A-side by Frank Sinatra and Sammy Davis, Jr.; B-side by Sammy Davis, Jr. and Dean Martin				
☐ 20,151	DJ	Call Me Irresponsible/Come Blow Your Horn	1963	25.00	50.00	100.00
☐ 20,151	PS	Call Me Irresponsible/Come Blow Your Horn	1963	50.00	100.00	200.00
		Sleeve accompanies promo copies only.				
☐ 20,151		Call Me Irresponsible/Tina	1963	2.50	5.00	10.00
		B-side changed for commercial release				
☐ 20,157	DJ	California/America the Beautiful	1963	62.50	125.00	250.00
		No stock copies isssued				
☐ 20,157	PS	California/America the Beautiful	1963	187.50	375.00	750.00
		No stock copies isssued				
☐ 20,184		I Have Dreamed/Come Blow Your Horn	1963	2.50	5.00	10.00
☐ 20,209		Love Isn't Just for the Young/	1963	3.00	6.00	12.00
		You Brought a New Kind of Love to Me				
☐ 20,209	PS	Love Isn't Just for the Young/	1963	12.50	25.00	50.00
		You Brought a New Kind of Love to Me				
☐ 20,217		Fugue for Tinhorns/	1963	3.75	7.50	15.00
		The Oldest Established (Permanent Floating Crap Game in New York)				
☐ 20,217	PS	Fugue for Tinhorns/	1963	18.75	37.50	75.00
		The Oldest Established (Permanent Floating Crap Game in New York)				
		By Frank Sinatra/Bing Crosby/Dean Martin				
☐ 20,235		Tangerine/A New Kind of Love	1963			Unreleased?
☐ 29677		Here's to the Band/It's Sunday	1983	2.00	4.00	8.00
☐ 29903		To Love a Child/That's What God Looks Like to Me	1982	2.00	4.00	8.00
☐ 29903	PS	To Love a Child/That's What God Looks Like to Me	1982	3.75	7.50	15.00
☐ RP8-29903		To Love a Child (mono/stereo)	1982	75.00	150.00	300.00
		Special pressing of 500 with small hole, given to Nancy Reagan for distribuuion at a White House function.				
☐ 49233		Theme from New York, New York/	1980	2.50	5.00	10.00
		That's What God Looks Like to Me				
☐ 49233	PS	Theme from New York, New York/	1980	3.75	7.50	15.00
		That's What God Looks Like to Me				
☐ 49517		You and Me (We Wanted It All)/I've Been There	1980	2.00	4.00	8.00
☐ 49827		Say Hello/Good Thing Going	1981	2.00	4.00	8.00

Sinatra, Nancy

Elektra

Number		Title (A Side/B Side)	Year	VG	VG+	NM
☐ 46659		Let's Keep It That Way/One Jump Ahead of the Storm	1979		2.50	5.00
☐ 47157		Texas Cowboy Night/After the Lovin'	1981		2.00	4.00
		With Mel Tillis				
☐ 47247		Where Would I Be/Play Me or Trade Me	1981		2.00	4.00
		With Mel Tillis				

Private Stock

Number		Title (A Side/B Side)	Year	VG	VG+	NM
☐ 45,022		Annabel of Mobile/(B-side unknown)	1975		2.50	5.00
☐ 45,075		Kinky Love/	1976		2.50	5.00
		She Played the Piano and He Beat the Drum				
☐ 45,108		Indian Summer/Holly and Hawkeye	1976		2.50	5.00
		With Lee Hazelwood				
☐ 45,158		It's For My Dad/A Gentle Man Like You	1977		2.50	5.00

RCA Victor

Number		Title (A Side/B Side)	Year	VG	VG+	NM
☐ 74-0614		Paris Summer/Down from Dover	1971	2.00	4.00	8.00
		With Lee Hazelwood				
☐ 74-0864		It's the Love/Kind of a Woman	1973	2.00	4.00	8.00
☐ APBO-0029		Ain't No Sunshine/Sugar Me	1973		2.50	5.00

Reprise

Number		Title (A Side/B Side)	Year	VG	VG+	NM
☐ 0238		Tammy/Thanks to You	1963	5.00	10.00	20.00
☐ 0263		Where Do the Lonely Go/	1964	5.00	10.00	20.00
		Just Think About the Good Times				
☐ 0292		This Love of Mine/There Goes the Bride	1964	5.00	10.00	20.00
☐ 0335		The Answer to Everything/True Love	1965	3.75	7.50	15.00
☐ 0407		So Long Babe/If He'd Love Me	1965	3.75	7.50	15.00
☐ 0432		These Boots Are Made for Walkin'/	1965	3.00	6.00	12.00
		The City Never Sleeps at Night				
☐ 0461		How Does That Grab You, Darlin'?/	1966	2.50	5.00	10.00
		The Last of the Secret Agents				
☐ 0491		Friday's Child/Hutchinson Jail	1966	2.50	5.00	10.00
☐ 0514		In Our Time/Leave My Dog Alone	1966	2.50	5.00	10.00
☐ 0527		Sugar Town/Summer Wine	1966	3.00	6.00	12.00
☐ 0559		Love Eyes/Coastin'	1967	2.50	5.00	10.00
☐ 0561		Somethin' Stupid/Give Her Love	1967	2.50	5.00	10.00
		A-side: Nancy Sinatra and Frank Sinatra; B-side: Frank Sinatra				
☐ 0561		Somethin' Stupid/I Will Wait for You	1967	2.00	4.00	8.00
		A-side: Nancy Sinatra and Frank Sinatra; B-side: Frank Sinatra				
☐ 0595		Jackson/You Only Live Twice	1967	2.50	5.00	10.00
		A-side with Lee Hazelwood				

Number		Title (A Side/B Side)	Year	VG	VG+	NM
❏ 0620		Lightning's Girl/Until It's Time for You to Go	1967	2.50	5.00	10.00
❏ 0620	PS	Lightning's Girl/Until It's Time for You to Go	1967	5.00	10.00	20.00
❏ 0629		Lady Bird/Sand	1967	2.00	4.00	8.00
		With Lee Hazlewood				
❏ 0636		Tony Rome/This Town	1967	2.00	4.00	8.00
❏ 0651		Some Velvet Morning/Oh Lonesome Me	1967	2.00	4.00	8.00
		With Lee Hazlewood				
❏ 0670		100 Years/See the Little Children	1968	2.00	4.00	8.00
❏ 0701		These Boots Are Made for Walkin'/Love Eyes	1968		2.50	5.00
		"Back to Back Hits" series				
❏ 0721		Sugar Town/Summer Wine	1968		2.50	5.00
		"Back to Back Hits" series				
❏ 0726		Jackson/Summer Wine	1968		2.50	5.00
		With Lee Hazlewood; "Back to Back Hits" series				
❏ 0729		Lightning's Girl/One Velvet Morning	1968		2.50	5.00
		B-side with Lee Hazlewood; "Back to Back Hits" series				
❏ 0756		Happy/Nice 'N' Easy	1968	2.00	4.00	8.00
❏ 0789		Good Time Girl/Old Devil Moon	1968	2.00	4.00	8.00
❏ 0813		God Knows I Love You/Just Plain Old Me	1969	2.00	4.00	8.00
❏ 0821		Here We Go Again/Memories	1969	2.00	4.00	8.00
❏ 0851		Drummer Man/Home	1969	2.00	4.00	8.00
❏ 0869		Highway Song/(B-side unknown)	1969	5.00	10.00	20.00
		Released only in England				
❏ 0880		It's Such a Lonely Time of Year/Kids	1969	2.50	5.00	10.00
❏ 0890		I Love Them All/Home	1970	2.00	4.00	8.00
❏ 0932		Hello L.A., Bye Bye Birmingham/White Tattoo	1970	2.00	4.00	8.00
❏ 0968		I'm Not a Girl Anymore/How Are Things in California	1970	2.00	4.00	8.00
❏ 0980		Feelin' Kinda Sunday/Kids	1970	2.00	4.00	8.00
		A-side by Nancy Sinatra and Frank Sinatra				
❏ 0991		Is Anybody Goin' to San Antone/Hook and Ladder	1971	2.00	4.00	8.00
❏ 0991	PS	Is Anybody Goin' to San Antone/Hook and Ladder	1971	3.75	7.50	15.00
❏ 1011		Life's a Trippy Thing/I'm Not Afraid	1971	2.00	4.00	8.00
		A-side by Nancy Sinatra and Frank Sinatra; B-side by Frank Sinatra solo				
❏ 1021		Did You Ever/Back on the Road	1971	2.00	4.00	8.00
		As "Nancy and Lee" (Hazlewood)				
❏ 1034		Glory Road/Is Anybody Goin' to San Antone	1971	2.00	4.00	8.00
❏ 20,017		Not Just Your Friend/Cuff Links and a Tie Clip	1961	5.00	10.00	20.00
❏ 20,045		To Know Him Is to Love Him/Like I Do	1962	5.00	10.00	20.00
❏ 20,097		June, July and August/Think of Me	1962	5.00	10.00	20.00
❏ 20,127		Tonight You Belong to Me/You Can Have Any Boy	1962	5.00	10.00	20.00
❏ 20,144		Put Your Head on My Shoulder/I See the Moon	1963	5.00	10.00	20.00
❏ 20,188		The Cruel War/One Way	1963	5.00	10.00	20.00

Sinceres, The

Columbia

❏ 43110		Sincerely/Snap Your Fingers	1964	3.75	7.50	15.00

Epic

❏ 9583		Kookie Ookie/Our Winter Love	1963	3.75	7.50	15.00

Jordan

❏ 117		You're Too Young/Forbidden Love	1960	62.50	125.00	250.00

Richie

❏ 545		Please Don't Cheat on Me/If You Should Leave Me	1961	75.00	150.00	300.00
		No mention of Roulette Records on label				
❏ 545		Please Don't Cheat on Me/If You Should Leave Me	1961	15.00	30.00	60.00
		With Roulette Records distribution mentioned on label				

Sigma

❏ 1003/4		Darling/Do You Remember	1960	100.00	200.00	400.00

Taurus

❏ 377		The Magic of Love/Tell Her	1966	7.50	15.00	30.00

Singleton, Shana Stacey

Sun

❏ 1177		Listen to Daddy (I'll Sing You What to Dream)/Remember Bethlehem	1982		2.00	4.00

Sir Douglas Quintet

(Also see "Sahm, Doug")

Atlantic

❏ 2965		The Nitty Gritty/I'm Just Tired of Getting Burned	1973	2.00	4.00	8.00
❏ 2985		Texas Tornado/Blue Horizon	1973	2.00	4.00	8.00
		As "Sir Douglas Band"				

Casablanca

❏ 828		Roll With the Punches/I'm Not That Kat Anymore	1975	6.25	12.50	25.00

Mercury

❏ 73257		Michoacan/Westside Blues Again	1971		3.00	6.00

Pacemaker

❏ 280		Sugar Bee/Blue Norther	1964	5.00	10.00	20.00

Philips

❏ 40676		What About Tomorrow/A Nice Song	1970	2.00	4.00	8.00
❏ 40676	PS	What About Tomorrow/A Nice Song	1970	3.75	7.50	15.00
❏ 40687		Pretty Flower/Catch the Man on the Fly	1970	2.00	4.00	8.00
❏ 40708		Wasted Days, Wasted Nights/Me and My Destiny	1971	2.00	4.00	8.00

Number	Title (A Side/B Side)	Year	VG	VG+	NM

Smash
❏ 2169	Are Inlaws Really Outlaws/Sell a Song	1968	2.00	4.00	8.00
❏ 2191	Mendocino/I Wanna Be Your Mama Again	1968	2.00	4.00	8.00
❏ 2222	Lawd, I'm Just a Country Boy in This Great Big Freaky City/It Didn't Even Bring Me Down	1969	2.00	4.00	8.00
❏ 2233	Dynamite Woman/Too Many Dociled Minds	1969	2.00	4.00	8.00
❏ 2253	At the Crossroads/Texas Me	1969	2.00	4.00	8.00
❏ 2259	Nuevo Laredo/I Don't Wanna Go Home	1970	2.00	4.00	8.00

Tribe
❏ 8308	She's About a Mover/We'll Take Our Last Walk Tonight	1965	3.00	6.00	12.00
❏ 8310	The Tracker/Blue Brother	1965	2.50	5.00	10.00
❏ 8312	In Time/The Story of John Hardy	1965	2.50	5.00	10.00
❏ 8314	The Rains Came/Bacon Fat	1966	2.50	5.00	10.00
❏ 8317	She's Gotta Be Boss/Quarter to Three	1966	2.50	5.00	10.00
❏ 8318	Beginning of the End/Love Don't Treat Me Fair	1966	2.50	5.00	10.00
❏ 8321	She Digs My Love/When I Sing the Blues	1966	2.50	5.00	10.00
❏ 8323	Hang Loose/I'm Sorry	1967	2.50	5.00	10.00

Sisk, Shirley
Sun
| ❏ 365 | I Forgot to Remember to Forget/The Other Side | 1961 | 6.25 | 12.50 | 25.00 |

Six Pentz, The
Brent
| ❏ 7062 | Imitation Situation/Please Come Home | 1967 | 5.00 | 10.00 | 20.00 |
| ❏ 7064 | Don't Say You're Sorry/Tinkle Talk | 1967 | 5.00 | 10.00 | 20.00 |

Sixpence, The
All American
❏ 313	Fortune Teller/My Flash on You	1966	10.00	20.00	40.00
❏ 333	Hey Joe/(B-side unknown)	1967	7.50	15.00	30.00
❏ 353	Fortune Teller/My Flash on You	1967	7.50	15.00	30.00

Dot
| ❏ 16959 | Fortune Teller/My Flash on You | 1966 | 6.25 | 12.50 | 25.00 |

Impact
| ❏ 1025 | What to Do/You're the Love | 1967 | 6.25 | 12.50 | 25.00 |

Skelton, Eddie
Dixie
| ❏ 2011 | Keep It Swinging/Without You | 1958 | 500.00 | 1,000 | 1,500 |

Starday
| ❏ 294 | My Heart Gets Lonely/Let Me Be With You Forever | 1957 | 37.50 | 75.00 | 150.00 |

Skip and Flip
(Also see "Paxton, Gary")

Brent
❏ 7002	It Was I/Lunch Hour	1959	6.25	12.50	25.00
❏ 7005	Fancy Nancy/It Could Be	1959	6.25	12.50	25.00
❏ 7010	Cherry Pie/I'll Quit Cryin' Over You	1960	6.25	12.50	25.00
❏ 7013	Teenage Honeymoon/Hully Gully Cha Cha Cha	1960	5.00	10.00	20.00
❏ 7017	The Green Door/Willow Tree	1960	5.00	10.00	20.00
❏ 7028	Over the Mountain/One More Drink for Julie	1962	5.00	10.00	20.00

California
| ❏ 2325 | Tossin' and Turnin'/Everyday I Have to Cry | 1963 | 3.75 | 7.50 | 15.00 |

Rev
| ❏ 3523 | Why Not Confess/Johnny Risk *As "Gary and Clyde"* | 1959 | 6.25 | 12.50 | 25.00 |

Time
| ❏ 1007 | Why Not Confess/Johnny Risk *As "Gary and Clyde"* | 1959 | 5.00 | 10.00 | 20.00 |
| ❏ 1031 | Betty Jean/Doubt | 1961 | 5.00 | 10.00 | 20.00 |

Skylarks, The
(More than one group)

Admiral
| ❏ 500 | I'll Surf Around the World/How Many Times | 1963 | 7.50 | 15.00 | 30.00 |

Decca
| ❏ 48241 | The Glory of Love/You and I | 1951 | 125.00 | 250.00 | 500.00 |

Everlast
| ❏ 5022 | Everybody's Got Somebody/Jeannie | 1963 | 5.00 | 10.00 | 20.00 |

RCA Victor
| ❏ 47-5257 | Home in Pasadena/I Had the Craziest Dream | 1953 | 6.25 | 12.50 | 25.00 |

Verve
| ❏ 10082 | Ol' Man River/There's a Boat Dat's Leavin' for New York | 1957 | 5.00 | 10.00 | 20.00 |

Skyliners, The
Atco
| ❏ 6270 | Since I Fell for You/I'd Die | 1963 | 10.00 | 20.00 | 40.00 |

Calico
| ❏ 103/4 | Since I Don't Have You/One Night, One Night | 1959 | 6.25 | 12.50 | 25.00 |
| ❏ 106 | This I Swear/Tomorrow | 1959 | 6.25 | 12.50 | 25.00 |

Number		Title (A Side/B Side)	Year	VG	VG+	NM
❏ 109		It Happened Today/Lonely Way	1959	6.25	12.50	25.00
❏ 114		How Much/Lorraine from Spain	1960	6.25	12.50	25.00
❏ 117		Pennies from Heaven/I'll Be Seeing You	1960	6.25	12.50	25.00
❏ 120		Believe Me/Happy Time	1960	6.25	12.50	25.00

Cameo

| ❏ 215 | | Three Coins in the Fountain/Everyone But You | 1962 | 10.00 | 20.00 | 40.00 |

Capitol

| ❏ 3979 | | Where Have They Gone/
I Could Have Loved You So Well | 1974 | 6.25 | 12.50 | 25.00 |
| | | *As "Jimmy Beaumont and the Skyliners"* | | | | |

Colpix

| ❏ 188 | | I'll Close My Eyes/The Door Is Still Open | 1961 | 10.00 | 20.00 | 40.00 |
| ❏ 613 | | Close Your Eyes/Our Love Will Last | 1961 | 10.00 | 20.00 | 40.00 |

Drive

| ❏ 6250 | | Our Day Is Here/The Day the Clown Died | 1976 | 2.00 | 4.00 | 8.00 |

Jubilee

❏ 5506		The Loser/Everything Is Fine	1965	3.75	7.50	15.00
❏ 5512		Who Do You Love/Get Yourself a Baby	1965	3.75	7.50	15.00
❏ 5520		I Run to You/Don't Hurt Me Baby	1965	3.75	7.50	15.00

Motown

| ❏ 1046 | DJ | Since I Fell for You/I'd Die | 1963 | 1,000 | 1,500 | 2,000 |
| | | *Record never got beyond the test pressing stage (2 known copies)* | | | | |

Original Sound

❏ 35		Since I Don't Have You/One Night, One Night	1963	3.75	7.50	15.00
❏ 36		Pennies from Heaven/I'll Be Seeing You	1963	3.75	7.50	15.00
❏ 37		This I Swear/It Happened Today	1963	3.75	7.50	15.00

Tortoise Int'l.

| ❏ PB-11243 | | Oh How Happy/We've Got Love on Our Side | 1978 | 2.00 | 4.00 | 8.00 |
| ❏ PB-11312 | | Smile On Me/Love Bug (Done Bit Me Again) | 1978 | 2.00 | 4.00 | 8.00 |

Viscount

| ❏ 104 | | Comes Love/Tell Me | 1962 | 5.00 | 10.00 | 20.00 |

Slade

CBS Associated

❏ 04398		Run Runaway/Don't Take a Hurricane	1984		2.00	4.00
❏ 04528		My Oh My/High and Dry	1984		2.00	4.00
❏ 04865		Little Sheila/Lock Up Your Daughters	1985		2.00	4.00

Cotillion

❏ 44128		Get Down and Get With It/ The Gospel According to Rasputin	1971	6.25	12.50	25.00
❏ 44139		Cos I Love You/Gotta Keep a-Rockin'	1971	6.25	12.50	25.00
❏ 44150		Look Wot You Dun/Candidate	1972	6.25	12.50	25.00

Polydor

❏ 15041		Look Wot You Dun/Candidate	1972	2.50	5.00	10.00
❏ 15044		Cuz I Love You/My Life Is Natural	1972	2.50	5.00	10.00
❏ 15046		Take Me Back 'Ome/Wondering Why	1972	2.50	5.00	10.00
❏ 15053		Mama Weer All Crazee Now/Man Who Speeks Evil	1972	2.50	5.00	10.00
❏ 15060		Gudbuy T' Jane/I Won't Let It 'Appen Again	1973	2.50	5.00	10.00
❏ 15069		Cum On Feel the Noize/ I'm Mee, I'm Now, An' That's Orl	1973	3.75	7.50	15.00
❏ 15080		Let the Good Times Roll/Feel So Fine-I Don' Mind	1973	2.50	5.00	10.00

Reprise

| ❏ 1182 | | Skweeze Me Pleeze Me/My Town | 1973 | 2.00 | 4.00 | 8.00 |

Warner Bros.

❏ 7759		Merry Christmas Everybody/Don't Blame Me	1973	2.50	5.00	10.00
❏ 7777		Good Time Gals/We're Really Gonna Raise the Roof	1974	2.00	4.00	8.00
❏ 7808		How Can It Be/When the Lights Are Out	1974	2.00	4.00	8.00
❏ 8134		How Does It Feel/OK, Yesterday Was Yesterday	1975	2.00	4.00	8.00
❏ 8185		Nobody's Fool/When the Chips Are Down	1976	2.00	4.00	8.00

Slades, The

Domino

❏ 500		You Cheated/The Waddle	1958	10.00	20.00	40.00
❏ 800		You Gambled/No Time	1959	10.00	20.00	40.00
❏ 901		Just You/It's Better to Love	1959	7.50	15.00	30.00
❏ 906		It's Your Turn/Take My Heart	1961	10.00	20.00	40.00
❏ 1000		Summertime/You Must Try	1961	7.50	15.00	30.00

Liberty

❏ 55118		Baby/You Mean Everything to Me	1957	12.50	25.00	50.00
		As "The Spades," in error				
❏ 55118		Baby/You Mean Everything to Me	1957	6.25	12.50	25.00

Sled, Bob, and the Toboggans

Cameo

| ❏ 400 | | Here We Go (Surfer Boys Are Going Skiing)/
Sea and Ski | 1966 | 12.50 | 25.00 | 50.00 |

Sledge, Percy

Atlantic

❏ 2326		When a Man Loves a Woman/ Love Me Like You Mean It	1966	3.75	7.50	15.00
❏ 2343		Warm and Tender Love/Sugar Puddin'	1966	2.50	5.00	10.00
❏ 2358		It Tears Me Up/Heart of a Child	1966	2.50	5.00	10.00

Number		Title (A Side/B Side)	Year	VG	VG+	NM
❑ 2383		Baby, Help Me/You Got That Something Wonderful	1967	2.50	5.00	10.00
❑ 2396		Out of Left Field/It Can't Be Stopped	1967	2.50	5.00	10.00
❑ 2414		Love Me Tender/What Am I Living For	1967	2.50	5.00	10.00
❑ 2434		Just Out of Reach (Of My Two Empty Arms)/ Hard to Believe	1967	2.50	5.00	10.00
❑ 2453		Cover Me/Behind Every Great Man There Is a Woman	1967	2.50	5.00	10.00
❑ 2490		Take Time to Know Her/It's All Wrong But It's Alright	1968	3.00	6.00	12.00
❑ 2539		Sudden Stop/Between These Arms	1968	2.50	5.00	10.00
❑ 2563		You're All Around Me/Self-Preservation	1968	2.50	5.00	10.00
❑ 2594		My Special Prayer/Bless Your Little Sweet Soul	1969	2.00	4.00	8.00
❑ 2616		Any Day Now/The Angels Listened In	1969	2.50	5.00	10.00
❑ 2646		Woman of the Night/Kind Woman	1969	2.00	4.00	8.00
❑ 2679		Faithful and True/True Love Travels on a Gravel Road	1969	2.00	4.00	8.00
❑ 2719		Too Many Rivers to Cross/Push Mr. Pride Aside	1970	2.00	4.00	8.00
❑ 2754		Help Me Make It Through the Night/Thief in the Night	1970	2.00	4.00	8.00
❑ 2826		Stop the World Tonight/That's the Way I Want to Live	1971		3.00	6.00
❑ 2848		Rainbow Road/Standing on the Mountain	1971		3.00	6.00
❑ 2886		Sunday Brother/Everything You'll Ever Need	1972		3.00	6.00
❑ 2963		Sunshine/Unchanging Love	1973		3.00	6.00
❑ 89262		When a Man Loves a Woman/Cover Me	1987			3.00
❑ 89262	PS	When a Man Loves a Woman/Cover Me	1987		2.00	4.00

Capricorn

❑ 0209		I'll Be Your Everything/Blue Water	1974		2.50	5.00
❑ 0220		If This Is the Last Time/Behind Closed Doors	1975		2.50	5.00
❑ 0273		When a Boy Becomes a Man/When She Touches Me	1977		2.50	5.00

Monument

❑ 03612		You Had to Be There/Hard Lovin' Woman	1983		2.00	4.00
❑ 03878		She's Too Pretty to Cry/Home Type Thing	1983		2.00	4.00

Slick, Grace

(Of Jefferson Airplane/Jefferson Starship/Starship. Also see "Great Society, The")

Grunt

❑ BFBO-0183		Theme from "Manhole"/Come Again, Toucan	1973		3.00	6.00

RCA

❑ PB-11939		Seasons/Angel of Night	1980		2.00	4.00
❑ PB-12041		Dreams/Do It the Hard Way	1980		2.00	4.00
❑ PB-12171		Sea of Love/Full Moon Man	1981		2.00	4.00
❑ PB-12172		Mistreater/Full Moon Man	1981			Unreleased
❑ PB-12186		Round and Round/Full Moon Man	1981			Unreleased
❑ PB-13764		Through the Window/Habits	1984		2.00	4.00

Sllednats, The – See "Standells, The"

Sloan, P.F.

Aladdin

❑ 3461		All I Want Is Lovin'/Little Girl in the Cabin	1959	6.25	12.50	25.00
		As "Flip Sloan"				

Atco

❑ 6663		Star Gazin'/New Design	1969	5.00	10.00	20.00

Dunhill

❑ 4007		Sins of the Family/This Mornin'	1965	3.75	7.50	15.00
❑ 4016		Halloween Mary/I'd Have to Be Out of My Mind	1965	3.75	7.50	15.00
❑ 4016	PS	Halloween Mary/I'd Have to Be Out of My Mind	1965	6.25	12.50	25.00
		Sleeve is promo only				
❑ 4024		From a Distance/Patterns	1966	6.25	12.50	25.00
❑ 4037		City Women/Top of a Fence	1966	3.75	7.50	15.00
❑ 4054		I Found a Girl/A Melody for You	1966	3.75	7.50	15.00
❑ 4064		Sunflower, Sunflower/The Man Behind the Red Balloon	1967	6.25	12.50	25.00
❑ 4064	PS	Sunflower, Sunflower/The Man Behind the Red Balloon	1967	7.50	15.00	30.00
❑ 4106		Karma (Study of Divination)/ I Can't Help But Wonder, Elizabeth	1967	6.25	12.50	25.00
		As "Philip Sloan"				

Mart

❑ 802		She's My Girl/If You Believe in Me	1960	20.00	40.00	80.00

Mums

❑ 6010		Let Me Be/Springtime	1972	5.00	10.00	20.00

Sly and the Family Stone

(Also see "Stewart, Sly")

Epic

❑ 10229		Higher/Underdog	1967	2.50	5.00	10.00
❑ 10256		Dance to the Music/Let Me Hear It from You	1967	2.50	5.00	10.00
❑ 10353		Life/M'Lady	1968	2.00	4.00	8.00
❑ 10407		Everyday People/Sing a Simple Song	1968	2.50	5.00	10.00
❑ 10407	PS	Everyday People/Sing a Simple Song	1968	3.00	6.00	12.00
❑ 10450		Stand!/I Want to Take You Higher	1969	2.50	5.00	10.00
❑ 10450	PS	Stand!/I Want to Take You Higher	1969	3.00	6.00	12.00
❑ 10497		Hot Fun in the Summertime/Fun	1969	2.50	5.00	10.00
❑ 10555		Thank You Falettinme Be Mice Elf Agin/ Everybody Is a Star	1969		3.00	6.00
❑ 10555	PS	Thank You Falettinme Be Mice Elf Agin/ Everybody Is a Star	1969	2.50	5.00	10.00
❑ 10805		Family Affair/Luv N' Haight	1971		3.00	6.00
❑ 10829		Runnin' Away/Brave & Strong	1972		3.00	6.00
❑ 10850		Smilin'/Luv N' Haight	1972		3.00	6.00

Number		Title (A Side/B Side)	Year	VG	VG+	NM
❑ 11017		If You Want Me to Stay/Thankful N' Thoughtful	1973		3.00	6.00
❑ 11017		If You Want Me to Stay/Babies Makin' Babies	1973		3.00	6.00
❑ 11060		Frisky/If It Were Left Up to Me	1973		3.00	6.00
❑ 11140		Time for Livin'/Small Talk	1974		3.00	6.00
❑ 50035		Loose Booty/Can't Strain My Brain	1974		3.00	6.00
❑ 50119		Hot Fun in the Summertime/Fun	1975	2.00	4.00	8.00
❑ 50135		I Get High on You/That's Lovin' You	1975		2.50	5.00
❑ 50175		Li Lo Li/Who Do You Love	1975		2.50	5.00
❑ 50201		Greed/Crossword Puzzle	1976		2.50	5.00
❑ 50331		Again/Nothing Less Than Happiness	1977		2.50	5.00

Warner Bros.

❑ 29682		High Y'All/Ha Ha He He	1983		2.00	4.00
❑ 49062		Sheer Energy/Remember Who You Are	1979		2.00	4.00
❑ 49132		Who's to Say/Same Thing	1979		2.00	4.00

Small Faces
(Includes Faces. Also see "Stewart, Rod"; "Wood, Ron")

Immediate

❑ 501		Itchykoo Park/I'm Only Dreaming	1967	3.00	6.00	12.00
❑ 1902		Here Come the Nice/Talk to You	1967	2.50	5.00	10.00
❑ 5003		Tin Soldier/I Feel Much Better	1968	2.50	5.00	10.00
❑ 5003	PS	Tin Soldier/I Feel Much Better	1968	6.25	12.50	25.00
❑ 5007		Last Sunday/Rollin' Over	1968	2.50	5.00	10.00
❑ 5009		The Universal/Donkey Rides A Penny A Glass	1968	3.75	7.50	15.00
❑ 5012		Mad John/The Journey	1969	3.75	7.50	15.00
❑ 5014		Afterglow of Your Love/Wham, Bam, Thank You Ma'am	1969	3.75	7.50	15.00

Press

❑ 5007		Almost Grown/Hey Girl	1969	5.00	10.00	20.00
❑ 9794		What 'Cha Gonna Do About It/What's a Matter	1965	6.25	12.50	25.00
❑ 9826		Sha-La-La-La-Lee/Grow Your Own	1966	3.75	7.50	15.00

Pride

❑ 1006		Runaway/Shake	1972	3.00	6.00	12.00

RCA Victor

❑ 47-8949		Understanding/All or Nothing	1966	5.00	10.00	20.00
❑ 47-9055		My Mind's Eye/I Can't Dance with You	1966	5.00	10.00	20.00

Warner Bros.

❑ 7393		Around the Phynth/Wicked Messenger	1970	2.50	5.00	10.00
❑ 7442		Had Me a Real Good Time/Real Wheel Skid	1970	2.50	5.00	10.00

Note: From 7483 on, as "Faces"

❑ 7483		Maybe I'm Amazed/Oh Lord I'm Browned Off	1971	2.00	4.00	8.00
❑ 7545		Stay with Me/You're So Rude	1971		3.00	6.00
❑ 7681		Cindy Incidentally/Skewiff (Mend the Fuse)	1973		2.50	5.00
❑ 7681	PS	Cindy Incidentally/Skewiff (Mend the Fuse)	1973		3.00	6.00
❑ 7711		Ooh-La-La/Borstal Boys	1973		2.50	5.00

Smart Tones, The
Herald

❑ 529		Bob-O-Link/Ginny	1958	25.00	50.00	100.00

Smile
Mercury

Brian May and Roger Taylor, later of Queen, were in this group

❑ 72977		Earth/Step on Me	1968	50.00	100.00	200.00

Uni

Probably not the same Smile that evolved into Queen

❑ 55313		A Year Every Night/Southbound	1972		3.00	6.00
❑ 55336		Tonight/One Night Stand	1972		3.00	6.00

Smith, Arlene
(Of the Chantels)

Big Top

❑ 3073		Love, Love, Love/He Knows I Love Him Too Much	1961	7.50	15.00	30.00

Spectorious

❑ 150		Good Girls/Everything	196?	25.00	50.00	100.00

Smith, Bobbie, and the Dream Girls – See "Dream Girls, The"

Smith, Huey "Piano"
Ace

❑ 521		Everybody's Wailin'/Little Liza Jane	1956	6.25	12.50	25.00
❑ 530		Rockin' Pneumonia and the Boogie Woogie Flu (Part 1/Part 2)	1957	6.25	12.50	25.00
❑ 538		Free, Single and Disengaged/Just a Lonely Clown	1957	6.25	12.50	25.00
❑ 545		Don't You Just Know It/High Blood Pressure	1958	6.25	12.50	25.00
❑ 548		Havin' a Good Time/We Like Birdland	1958	5.00	10.00	20.00
❑ 553		Don't You Know Yockomo/Well, I'll Be John Brown	1958	5.00	10.00	20.00
❑ 562		Would You Believe It (I Have a Cold)/Genevieve	1959	5.00	10.00	20.00
❑ 571		Tu-Ber-Cu-Lucas and the Sinus Blues/Dearest Darling	1959	5.00	10.00	20.00
❑ 584		Beatnik Blues/For Cryin' Out Loud	1960	3.75	7.50	15.00
❑ 638		She Got Low Down/Mean, Mean, Mean	1961	3.75	7.50	15.00
❑ 639		She Got Low Down/Mean, Mean, Mean// Little Liza Jane/Rockin' Pnuemonia	1961	6.25	12.50	25.00
❑ 649		Pop-Eye/Scald Dog	1962	3.75	7.50	15.00
❑ 672		Every Once in a While/Somebody Told It	1962	3.00	6.00	12.00

Number		Title (A Side/B Side)	Year	VG	VG+	NM
☐ 8002		Talk to Me Baby/If It Ain't One Thing, It's Another	1962	3.00	6.00	12.00
☐ 8008		Let's Bring 'Em Back Again/Quiet as It's Kept	1963	3.75	7.50	15.00

Constellation

☐ 102		He's Back Again/Quiet As It's Kept	1963	2.50	5.00	10.00

Cotillion

☐ 44142		Rockin' Pneumonia and the Boogie Woogie Flu (Part 1/Part 2)	1971		3.00	6.00

Imperial

☐ 5721		The Little Moron/Someone to Love	1961	3.00	6.00	12.00
☐ 5747		Behind the Wheel -- Part 1/Behind the Wheel -- Part 2	1961	3.00	6.00	12.00
☐ 5772		More Girls/Sassy Sara	1961	3.00	6.00	12.00
☐ 5789		Don't Knock It/Shag-a-Tooth	1961	3.00	6.00	12.00

Instant

☐ 3287		I'll Never Forget/Bury Me Dead	1967	2.00	4.00	8.00
☐ 3297		Two Way Pockaway (Part 1)/Two Way Pockaway (Part 2)	1969	2.00	4.00	8.00
☐ 3301		Epitaph of Uncle Tom/Eight Bars of Amen	1969	2.00	4.00	8.00
☐ 3303		You Got Too (Part 1)/You Got Too (Part 2)	1969	2.00	4.00	8.00
☐ 3305		Ballad of a Black Man/The Whatcha Call 'Em	1970	2.00	4.00	8.00

Savoy

☐ 1113		You Made Me Cry/You're Down with Me	1953	25.00	50.00	100.00

Vin

☐ 1024		I Didn't Do It/They Kept On	1960	3.75	7.50	15.00

Smith, Hurricane

Capitol

☐ 3148		Don't Let It Die/The Writer Sings His Song	1971		2.50	5.00
☐ 3383		Oh Babe, What Would You Say?/Getting to Know You	1972		3.00	6.00
		Red and orange "target" label				
☐ 3383		Oh Babe, What Would You Say?/Getting to Know You	1972		2.00	4.00
		Orange label with "Capitol" at bottom				
☐ 3455		Who Was It?/Take Suki Home	1972		2.00	4.00

EMI

☐ 3809		Beautiful Day-Beautiful Night/Sam	1973		2.00	4.00

Smith, Lendon, and the Jesters

Meteor

☐ 5030		Women/Lost Love	1956	37.50	75.00	150.00

Smith, Leon

Epic

☐ 9326		Little 40 Ford/Cry All the Time	1959	10.00	20.00	40.00

Lavender

☐ 1851		Basic Surf/Jailer, Bring Me Water	196?	7.50	15.00	30.00

Williamette

☐ 101		Little 40 Ford/Once I Had a Heart	1959	30.00	60.00	120.00
☐ 105		Honey Honey/That's the Way	1959	7.50	15.00	30.00
☐ 109		Flip, Flop and Fly/Sweet Love	1960	7.50	15.00	30.00

Smith, Patti, Group

Arista

☐ SP-2	DJ	Pissing in the River (mono/stereo)	1976	6.25	12.50	25.00
☐ SP-4	DJ	Ask the Angels (mono/stereo)	1977	6.25	12.50	25.00
		With lyric insert (deduct 20% if missing)				
☐ 0171		Gloria/My Generation	1976	2.50	5.00	10.00
☐ 0171	PS	Gloria/My Generation	1976	2.50	5.00	10.00
☐ 0318		Because the Night/God Speed	1978		2.00	4.00
		A-side co-written by Bruce Springsteen				
☐ 0318	PS	Because the Night/God Speed	1978	2.00	4.00	8.00
☐ 0427		Frederick/Frederick (Live)	1979		2.00	4.00
☐ 0427	PS	Frederick/Frederick (Live)	1979	2.00	4.00	8.00
☐ 0453		So You Want to Be a Rock and Roll Star// 5-4-3-2-1/A Fire of Unknown Origin	1979		2.00	4.00
☐ 0453	PS	So You Want to Be a Rock and Roll Star// 5-4-3-2-1/A Fire of Unknown Origin	1979	5.00	10.00	20.00
☐ 9173		Because the Night/ So You Want to Be a Rock 'n' Roll Star	198?			3.00
		"Flashback" reissue				
☐ 9689		People Have the Power/Wild Leaves	1988			3.00
☐ 9689	PS	People Have the Power/Wild Leaves	1988			3.00
☐ 9762		I Was (Looking for You)/Up There Down There	1988			3.00

Mer

☐ 601		Hey Joe/Piss Factory	1974	20.00	40.00	80.00

Sire

☐ 1009		Hey Joe/Piss Factory	1977	2.00	4.00	8.00
☐ 1009	PS	Hey Joe/Piss Factory	1977	2.00	4.00	8.00

Smith, Ray

Celebrity Circle

☐ 6901		I Walk the Line/Fool #1	1964	3.75	7.50	15.00

Cinnamon

☐ 755		Tilted Cup of Love/I'd Traded Better for Worse	1973		2.50	5.00
☐ 760		It Wasn't Easy/It's Just Not the Same	1973		2.50	5.00

Number	Title (A Side/B Side)	Year	VG	VG+	NM
☐ 773	The First Lonely Weekend/A Handful of Friends	1973		2.50	5.00
☐ 795	Ten Steps Out in Front/Because of Losing You	1974		2.50	5.00

Diamond
☐ 193	Everybody's Goin' Somewhere/Au-Go-Go-Go	1965	3.75	7.50	15.00

Heart
☐ 250	Gone, Baby, Gone/(B-side unknown)	195?	1,000	1,500	2,000

Infinity
☐ 003	After This Night Is Through/Turn On the Moonlight	1961	3.75	7.50	15.00
☐ 007	Let Yourself Go/Johnny the Hummer	1961	3.75	7.50	15.00

Judd
☐ 1016	Rockin' Little Angel/That's All Right	1959	7.50	15.00	30.00
☐ 1017	Maria Elena/Put Your Arms Around Me Honey	1960	7.50	15.00	30.00
☐ 1019	One Wonderful Love/Makes Me Feel Good	1960	7.50	15.00	30.00
☐ 1021	Blonde Hair, Blue Eyes/You Don't Want Me	1960	7.50	15.00	30.00

Nu-Tone
☐ 1182	Deep in My Heart/She's Mine	1964	3.75	7.50	15.00

Smash
☐ 1787	Room 503/These Four Precious Years	1962	3.75	7.50	15.00

Sun
☐ 298	So Right/Right Behind You Baby	1958	7.50	15.00	30.00
☐ 308	Why, Why, Why/You Made a Hit	1958	7.50	15.00	30.00
☐ 319	Rockin' Bandit/Sail Away	1959	7.50	15.00	30.00
☐ 372	Travelin' Salesman/I Won't Miss You ('Til You're Gone)	1961	7.50	15.00	30.00
☐ 375	Hey Boss Man/Candy Doll	1962	7.50	15.00	30.00

Tollie
☐ 9029	There Comes My Baby Back Again/Did We Have a Party	1964	5.00	10.00	20.00

Toppa
☐ 1071	Almost Alone/A Place Within My Heart	1962	5.00	10.00	20.00

Vee Jay
☐ 579	Rockin' Robin/Robbin' the Cradle	1964	3.75	7.50	15.00

Warner Bros.
☐ 5371	I'm Snowed/Turn Over a New Leaf	1963	3.75	7.50	15.00

Zirkon
☐ 1055	After This Night Is Through/Turn On the Moonlight	1961	5.00	10.00	20.00

Smith, Shelby

Rebel
☐ 728	Rockin' Mama/Since My Baby Said Goodbye	1962	100.00	200.00	400.00

Smith, Warren

Liberty
☐ 55248	I Don't Believe I'll Fall in Love Today/Cave-In	1960	5.00	10.00	20.00
☐ 55302	Odds and Ends (Bits and Pieces)/A Whole Lot of Nothin'	1961	5.00	10.00	20.00
☐ 55336	Call of the Wild/Old Lonesome Feeling	1961	5.00	10.00	20.00
☐ 55361	Why Baby Why/Why I'm Walking	1961	5.00	10.00	20.00
	With Shirley Collie				
☐ 55409	Bad News Gets Around/Five Minutes of the Latest Blues	1962	5.00	10.00	20.00
☐ 55475	Book of Broken Hearts/160 Pounds of Hurt	1962	5.00	10.00	20.00
☐ 55615	Big City Ways/That's Why I Sing in a Honky Tonk	1963	3.75	7.50	15.00
☐ 55699	Blue Smoke/Judge and Jury	1964	3.75	7.50	15.00

Mercury
☐ 72825	Lie to Me/When the Heartaches Get to Me	1968	2.50	5.00	10.00

Sun
☐ 239	Rock and Roll Ruby/I'd Rather Be Safe Than Sorry	1956	25.00	50.00	100.00
☐ 250	Ubangi Stomp/Black Jack David	1956	12.50	25.00	50.00
☐ 268	Miss Froggie/So Long, I'm Gone	1957	10.00	20.00	40.00
☐ 286	I Fell in Love/I've Got Love If You Want It	1958	7.50	15.00	30.00
☐ 314	Goodbye Mr. Love/Sweet Sweet Girl	1959	10.00	20.00	40.00

Warner Bros.
☐ 5125	Dear Santa/The Meaning of Christmas	1959	6.25	12.50	25.00

Smokey Joe

Flip
☐ 228	The Signifying Monkey/Listen to Me Baby	1955	125.00	250.00	500.00

Sun
☐ 228	The Signifying Monkey/Listen to Me Baby	1956	75.00	150.00	300.00
☐ 393	The Signifying Monkey/Listen to Me Baby	1964	50.00	100.00	200.00

Smoothies, The
(With John Phillips and Scott McKenzie)

Decca
☐ 31105	Softly/Joanie	1960	5.00	10.00	20.00
☐ 31159	Ride, Ride, Ride/Lonely Boy and Pretty Girl	1960	5.00	10.00	20.00

Snow Men, The
(Later known as the Sunrays)

Challenge
☐ 59227	Ski Storm (Part 1)/Ski Storm (Part 2)	1964	7.50	15.00	30.00

Number	Title (A Side/B Side)	Year	VG	VG+	NM

Snow, Eddie
Sun

| ❏ 226 | Ain't That Right/Bring Your Love Back Home | 1955 | 50.00 | 100.00 | 200.00 |

Snow, Phoebe
Columbia

❏ 10315	Two Fisted Love/Inspired Insanity	1976		2.50	5.00
❏ 10351	All Over/No Regrets	1976		2.50	5.00
❏ 10463	Shakey Ground/Don't Sleep with Your Eyes Closed	1976		2.50	5.00
❏ 10504	Teach Me Tonight/Autobiography (Shine, Shine, Shine)	1977		2.50	5.00
❏ 10626	Never Letting Go/The Middle of the Night	1977		2.50	5.00
❏ 10654	Love Makes a Woman/Electra	1977		2.50	5.00
❏ 10856	Every Night/Random Time	1978		2.50	5.00

Elektra

| ❏ 69290 | Something Real/Best of My Love | 1989 | | | 3.00 |
| ❏ 69305 | If I Can Just Get Through the Night/Soothin' | 1989 | | | 3.00 |

Mirage

❏ 3800	Games/Down in the Basement	1981		2.00	4.00
❏ 3818	Mercy, Mercy, Mercy/Something Good	1981		2.00	4.00
❏ 3843	Rock Away/Baby Please	1981		2.00	4.00

Shelter

❏ 40278	Harpo's Blues/Let the Good Times Roll	1974		2.50	5.00
❏ 40353	Poetry Man/Either or Both	1974		3.00	6.00
❏ 40400	Easy Street/Harpo's Blues	1975		2.50	5.00

Society's Children
Atco

❏ 6538	White Christmas/I'll Let You Know	1967	2.50	5.00	10.00
❏ 6553	Count the Ways/Golden Child	1968	2.50	5.00	10.00
❏ 6597	Live for Today/I'll Let You Know	1968	2.50	5.00	10.00
❏ 6618	A Tribute to the Four Seasons/Golden Child	1968	5.00	10.00	20.00

Sof-Tones, The
Cee Bee

| ❏ 1062 | Oh Why/(B-side unknown) | 195? | 4,000 | 6,000 | 8,000 |

Soldier Boys, The
(With Don Covay)
Scepter

| ❏ 1230 | I'm Your Soldier Boy/You Picked Me | 1962 | 15.00 | 30.00 | 60.00 |

Solitaires, The
Argo

| ❏ 5316 | Walking Along/Please Kiss This Letter | 1958 | 7.50 | 15.00 | 30.00 |

MGM

| ❏ 13221 | Fool That I Am/Fair Weather Lover | 1964 | 7.50 | 15.00 | 30.00 |

Old Town

❏ 1000	Blue Valentine/Wonder Boy	1954	125.00	250.00	500.00
❏ 1000	Blue Valentine/Wonder Boy	1954	200.00	400.00	800.00
	Red vinyl				
❏ 1003	Chapel of St. Clair/If I Loved You	1954			Unreleased?
❏ 1006/7	Please Remember My Heart/South of the Border	1954	150.00	300.00	600.00
	Red vinyl				
❏ 1006/7	Please Remember My Heart/South of the Border	1954	100.00	200.00	400.00
❏ 1006/8	Please Remember My Heart/Chances I've Taken	1954	37.50	75.00	150.00
❏ 1008	Please Remember My Heart/Chances I've Taken	196?	6.25	12.50	25.00
	Blue label				
❏ 1008	Chances I've Taken/Lonely	1954	125.00	250.00	500.00
❏ 1010	I Don't Stand a Ghost of a Chance/Girl of Mine	1955	125.00	250.00	500.00
❏ 1012	My Dear/What Did She Say	1955	100.00	200.00	400.00
	Logo in Old English style				
❏ 1012	My Dear/What Did She Say	1956	18.75	37.50	75.00
	Logo in block letters				
❏ 1014	The Wedding/Don't Fall in Love	1955	25.00	50.00	100.00
❏ 1015	Magic Rose/Later for You Baby	1955	25.00	50.00	100.00
❏ 1019	The Honeymoon/Fine Little Girl	1956	25.00	50.00	100.00
❏ 1026	You've Sinned/The Angels Sang	1956	25.00	50.00	100.00
❏ 1026	You've Sinned/You're Back with Me	1956	75.00	150.00	300.00
❏ 1032	Give Me One More Chance/Nothing Like a Little Love	1956	50.00	100.00	200.00
❏ 1034	Walking Along/Please Kiss This Letter	1957	18.75	37.50	75.00
	Yellow label				
❏ 1034	Walking Along/Please Kiss This Letter	196?	6.25	12.50	25.00
	Blue label				
❏ 1044	I Really Love You So/Thrill of Love	1957	100.00	200.00	400.00
❏ 1049	Walkin' and Talkin'/No More Sorrows	1958	25.00	50.00	100.00
❏ 1059	Please Remember My Heart/Big Mary's House	1958	10.00	20.00	40.00
❏ 1066	Embraceable You/Round Goes My Heart	1959	10.00	20.00	40.00
❏ 1071	Light a Candle in the Chapel/Helpless	1959	10.00	20.00	40.00
❏ 1096	Lonesome Lover/Pretty Thing	1961	10.00	20.00	40.00
❏ 1139	The Time Is Here/Honey Babe	1963	7.50	15.00	30.00

Something Wild
Psychedelic

| ❏ 1691 | Trippin' Out/She's Kinda Weird | 1966 | 12.50 | 25.00 | 50.00 |

Number	Title (A Side/B Side)	Year	VG	VG+	NM

Sommers, Ronny – See "Sonny"

Sonics, The
(More than one group)
Amco
| ❏ 001 | It's You/Preacher Man | 1962 | 30.00 | 60.00 | 120.00 |

Armonia
| ❏ 102 | Funny/I Get That Feeling | 1962 | 25.00 | 50.00 | 100.00 |

Burdette
| ❏ 106 | Dirty Old Man/Bama Lama Bama Loo | 1975 | | 2.50 | 5.00 |

Checker
| ❏ 922 | This Broken Heart/You Made Me Cry | 1959 | 6.25 | 12.50 | 25.00 |

Etiquette
❏ 11	Keep a-Knockin'/The Witch	1965	7.50	15.00	30.00
❏ 16	The Hustler/Boss Hoss	1965	7.50	15.00	30.00
❏ 18	Don't Be Afraid of the Dark/Shot Down	1965	7.50	15.00	30.00
❏ 22	Don't Believe in Christmas/Christmas Spirit	1965	7.50	15.00	30.00
	B-side by the Wailers				
❏ 23	Louie Louie/Cinderella	1966	7.50	15.00	30.00

Gaiety
| ❏ 114 | Marlene/(B-side unknown) | 1959 | 1,000 | 1,500 | 2,000 |

Great Northwest
| ❏ 702 | The Witch/Bama Lama Bama Loo | 1979 | | 2.50 | 5.00 |

Groove
| ❏ 0112 | Bumble Bee/As I Live On | 1955 | 50.00 | 100.00 | 200.00 |

Harvard
| ❏ 801 | This Broken Heart/You Made Me Cry | 1959 | 62.50 | 125.00 | 250.00 |
| ❏ 922 | This Broken Heart/You Made Me Cry | 1959 | 12.50 | 25.00 | 50.00 |

Jamie
| ❏ 1235 | Sugaree/Beautiful Brown Eyes | 1962 | 5.00 | 10.00 | 20.00 |

Jerden
❏ 809	Love Lights/You Got Your Head On Backwards	1966	3.75	7.50	15.00
❏ 810	The Witch/Like No Other	1966	3.75	7.50	15.00
❏ 811	Psycho/Maintaining My Cool	1966	3.75	7.50	15.00

Nocturne
| ❏ 110 | Triangle Love/Evil Eye | 1959 | 10.00 | 20.00 | 40.00 |

Piccadilly
| ❏ 244 | Anyway the Wind Blows/Lost Love | 1967 | 5.00 | 10.00 | 20.00 |
| | *A-side written by Frank Zappa* | | | | |

RKO Unique
| ❏ 411 | Triangle Love/Evil Eye | 1957 | 15.00 | 30.00 | 60.00 |

Uni
| ❏ 55039 | Anyway the Wind Blows/Lost Love | 1967 | 3.75 | 7.50 | 15.00 |
| | *A-side written by Frank Zappa* | | | | |

X-Tra
| ❏ 107 | Once in a Lifetime/It Ain't True | 1958 | 125.00 | 250.00 | 500.00 |

Sonny
(Of Sonny and Cher)
Atco
❏ 6369	Laugh at Me/Gip Pony	1965	3.00	6.00	12.00
❏ 6386	The Revolution Kind/Georgia and John Quetzal	1965	3.00	6.00	12.00
❏ 6505	Misty Roses/I Told My Girl to Go Away	1967	2.50	5.00	10.00
❏ 6531	Pammie's on a Bummer/	1967	2.50	5.00	10.00
	My Best Friend's Girl Is Out of Sight				

Fidelity
| ❏ 3020 | Wearing Black/Don't Have to Tell Me | 1960 | 6.25 | 12.50 | 25.00 |
| | *As "Don Christy"* | | | | |

Go
| ❏ 1001 | As Long As You Love Me/I'll Always Be Grateful | 1960 | 6.25 | 12.50 | 25.00 |
| | *As "Don Christy"* | | | | |

Highland
| ❏ 1160 | I'll Change/Try It Out on Me | 1963 | 7.50 | 15.00 | 30.00 |
| | *As "Sonny Bono"* | | | | |

MCA
❏ 40139	Laugh at Me/Rub Your Nose	1973		2.00	4.00
	As "Sonny Bono"				
❏ 40271	Classified 1A/Our Last Show	1974		2.00	4.00
	As "Sonny Bono"				

Name
| ❏ 3 | As Long As You Love Me/I'll Always Be Grateful | 1960 | 6.25 | 12.50 | 25.00 |
| | *As "Don Christy"* | | | | |

Specialty
❏ 672	Wearing Black/One Little Answer	1959	6.25	12.50	25.00
	As "Don Christy"				
❏ 733	One Little Answer/Comin' Down the Chimney	1974		3.00	6.00
	As "Sonny Bono and Little Tootsie"				

Number	Title (A Side/B Side)	Year	VG	VG+	NM
Swami					
☐ 1001	Don't Shake My Tree/	1961	6.25	12.50	25.00
	(Mama) Come Get Your Baby Boy				
	As "Ronny Sommers"				
Vee Jay					
☐ 710	Midnight Surf/Ride the Wild Quetzal	1966	6.25	12.50	25.00
	As "Sonny Bono"				

Sonny and Cher
(Also see "Cher"; "Sonny")

Number	Title (A Side/B Side)	Year	VG	VG+	NM
Atco					
☐ 6345	Just You/Sing C'est La Vie	1965	2.50	5.00	10.00
☐ 6359	I Got You Babe/It's Gonna Rain	1965	3.00	6.00	12.00
☐ 6381	But You're Mine/Hello	1965	3.00	6.00	12.00
☐ 6395	What Now My Love/I Look for You	1965	3.00	6.00	12.00
☐ 6420	Have I Stayed Too Long/Leave Me Be	1966	2.50	5.00	10.00
☐ 6440	Little Man/Monday	1966	2.50	5.00	10.00
☐ 6449	Living for You/Love Don't Come	1966	2.50	5.00	10.00
☐ 6461	The Beat Goes On/Love Don't Come	1967	3.00	6.00	12.00
☐ 6480	A Beautiful Story/Podunk	1967	2.50	5.00	10.00
☐ 6486	Plastic Man/It's the Little Things	1967	2.50	5.00	10.00
☐ 6507	It's the Little Things/Don't Talk to Strangers	1967	2.50	5.00	10.00
☐ 6541	Good Combination/You and Me	1968	2.50	5.00	10.00
☐ 6555	Circus/I Would Marry Today	1968	2.50	5.00	10.00
☐ 6605	You Gotta Have a Thing of Your Own/I Got You Babe	1968	2.50	5.00	10.00
☐ 6684	You're a Friend of Mine/I Would Marry You Today	1969	2.50	5.00	10.00
☐ 6758	Get It Together/Hold Me Tighter	1970	2.00	4.00	8.00
Kapp					
☐ 2141	Real People/Somebody	1971		2.00	4.00
☐ 2151	All I Ever Need Is You/I Got You Babe	1971		2.50	5.00
☐ 2163	A Cowboy's Work Is Never Done/Somebody	1972		2.50	5.00
☐ 2176	When You Say Love/Crystal Clear and Muddy Waters	1972		2.00	4.00
MCA					
☐ 40026	Mama Was a Rock and Roll Singer,	1973		2.00	4.00
	Papa Used to Write All Her Songs/(B-side unknown)				
☐ 40083	The Greatest Show on Earth/You Know Darn Well	1973		2.00	4.00
Reprise					
☐ 0308	Love Is Strange/Do You Want to Dance	1964	5.00	10.00	20.00
	As "Caesar and Cleo"				
☐ 0309	Baby Don't Go/Walkin' the Quetzal	1964	5.00	10.00	20.00
☐ 0392	Baby Don't Go/Walkin' the Quetzal	1965	3.75	7.50	15.00
☐ 0419	Love Is Strange/Let the Good Times Roll	1965	5.00	10.00	20.00
	As "Caesar and Cleo"				
☐ 0419	PS Love Is Strange/Let the Good Times Roll	1965	10.00	20.00	40.00
	As "Caesar and Cleo"				
☐ 0723	Baby Don't Go/Love Is Strange	1968		2.50	5.00
	"Back to Back Hits" series -- originals have both "r:" and "W7" logos				
Vault					
☐ 909	The Letter/Spring Fever	1964	7.50	15.00	30.00
	As "Caesar and Cleo"				
☐ 916	The Letter/Spring Fever	1965	3.00	6.00	12.00
☐ 916	PS The Letter/Spring Fever	1965	12.50	25.00	50.00
Warner Bros.					
☐ 8341	You're Not Right for Me/Wrong Number	1977		2.50	5.00

Sons of Champlin, The
(With Bill Champlin, later of Chicago)

Number	Title (A Side/B Side)	Year	VG	VG+	NM
Ariola America					
☐ 7606	Look Out/Queen of the Rain	1975		2.00	4.00
☐ 7627	Hold On/Still in Love with You	1976		2.00	4.00
☐ 7633	You/Imagination's Sake	1976		2.00	4.00
☐ 7653	Follow Your Heart/Here Is Where Your Love Belongs	1976		2.00	4.00
☐ 7664	Saved by the Grace of Your Love/West End	1977		2.00	4.00
Capitol					
☐ 2437	1982-A/Black and Blue Rainbow	1969	2.00	4.00	8.00
☐ 2534	Freedom/Hello Sunlight	1969	2.00	4.00	8.00
☐ 2663	It's Time/Why Do People Run	1969	2.00	4.00	8.00
☐ 2786	You Can Fly/Terry's Tune	1970		3.00	6.00
Columbia					
☐ 45872	Welcome to the Dance/Swim	1973		2.50	5.00
Goldmine					
☐ 101	Look Out/Queen of the Rain	1975		2.50	5.00
Verve					
☐ 10500	Sing Me a Lullaby/Fat City	1967	2.50	5.00	10.00

Sootz, Manny

Number	Title (A Side/B Side)	Year	VG	VG+	NM
Pirate					
☐ 841	Cape Canaveral (Part 1)/Cape Canaveral (Part 2)	1957	6.25	12.50	25.00

Sophisticates, The

Number	Title (A Side/B Side)	Year	VG	VG+	NM
Viva					
☐ 61	When Elvis Comes Marching Home/Woody's Place	1960	12.50	25.00	50.00

Number		Title (A Side/B Side)	Year	VG	VG+	NM

Sorenson Brothers, The
Marlinda
| ❑ 7507/8 | | They've Landed/Stowaway | 196? | 12.50 | 25.00 | 50.00 |

Soul Brothers Six
Atlantic
❑ 2406		Some Kind of Wonderful/I'll Be Loving You	1967	3.75	7.50	15.00
❑ 2456		You Better Check Yourself/ What Can You Do When You Ain't Got Nobody	1967	3.00	6.00	12.00
❑ 2535		Your Love Is Such a Wonderful Love/ I Can't Live Without You	1968	3.00	6.00	12.00
❑ 2592		Somebody Else Is Loving My Baby/ Thank You Baby for Loving Me	1969	3.00	6.00	12.00
❑ 2645		What You Got (Is So Good for Me)/Drive	1969	3.00	6.00	12.00

Phil-L.A. of Soul
❑ 355		Funky Funky Way of Making Love/Let Me Be the One	1972		3.00	6.00
❑ 360		You're My World/You Gotta Come a Little Closer	1973		3.00	6.00
❑ 365		Let Me Do What We Ain't Doin'/Lost the Will to Live	1974		3.00	6.00

Soul Clan, The
(Solomon Burke, Arthur Conley, Don Covay, Ben E. King and Joe Tex)
Atlantic
| ❑ 2530 | | Soul Meeting/That's How It Feels | 1968 | 2.50 | 5.00 | 10.00 |
| ❑ 2530 | PS | Soul Meeting/That's How It Feels | 1968 | 3.75 | 7.50 | 15.00 |

Soul Surfers, The
Challenge
❑ 59249		Cannonball/In the Misty Moonlight	1964	3.75	7.50	15.00
		B-side by Jerry Wallace				
❑ 9209		Cannonball/Home from Camp	1963	10.00	20.00	40.00

Soul Survivors
(More than one group)
Atco
❑ 6627		Turn Out the Fire/Go Out Walking	1968	2.00	4.00	8.00
❑ 6650		Tell Daddy/Mama Soul	1969	2.00	4.00	8.00
❑ 6735		Still Got My Head/Tempting 'Bout to Get Me	1970	2.00	4.00	8.00

Crimson
❑ 1010		Expressway to Your Heart/Hey Gyp	1967	3.00	6.00	12.00
❑ 1012		Explosion (In Your Soul)/Dathon's Theme	1967	2.50	5.00	10.00
❑ 1016		Poor Man's Dream/Impossible Mission	1968	2.50	5.00	10.00

Decca
| ❑ 32080 | | Devil with a Blue Dress On/Shakin' with Linda | 1967 | 3.75 | 7.50 | 15.00 |

Dot
| ❑ 16793 | | Look at Me/Can't Stand to Be in Love with You | 1965 | 5.00 | 10.00 | 20.00 |
| ❑ 16830 | | Hung Up on Losin'/Snow Man | 1966 | 3.00 | 6.00 | 12.00 |

Philadelphia Int'l.
| ❑ 3595 | | Happy Birthday America (Part 1)/
Happy Birthday America (Part 2) | 1976 | | 2.50 | 5.00 |

TSOP
❑ 4756		City of Brotherly Love/ The Best Time Was the Last Time	1974		3.00	6.00
❑ 4760		What It Takes/Virgin Girl	1974		3.00	6.00
❑ 4768		Your Love/Lover to Me	1975		3.00	6.00

Soul, Jimmy
SPQR
❑ 3221		My Little Room/Ella Is Yella	1964	2.50	5.00	10.00
❑ 3300		Twistin' Matilda/I Can't Hold Out Any Longer	1962	3.00	6.00	12.00
❑ 3302		When Matilda Comes Back/Some Kinda Nut	1962	3.00	6.00	12.00
❑ 3304		Guess Things Happen That Way/ My Baby Loves to Bowl	1963	3.00	6.00	12.00
❑ 3305		If You Wanna Be Happy/Don't Release Me	1963	3.75	7.50	15.00
❑ 3305	PS	If You Wanna Be Happy/Don't Release Me	1963	6.25	12.50	25.00
❑ 3310		Treat 'Em Tough/Church Street in the Summertime	1963	3.00	6.00	12.00
❑ 3312		Go 'Way Christina/Everybody's Gone Ape	1963	3.00	6.00	12.00
❑ 3314		Change Partners/I Hate You Baby	1963	3.00	6.00	12.00
❑ 3315		My Girl-She Sure Can Cook/ A Woman Is Smarter in Every Kinda Way	1964	2.50	5.00	10.00
❑ 3318		You Can't Have Your Cake/Take Me to Los Angeles	1964	2.50	5.00	10.00
❑ 3319		Twistin' Matilda/Treat 'Em Tough	1964	2.50	5.00	10.00

20th Fox
| ❑ 413 | | Respectable/I Wish I Could Dance | 1963 | 2.50 | 5.00 | 10.00 |

Sounds Like Us
Fontana
| ❑ 1570 | | Outside Chance/Clock on the Wall | 1967 | 6.25 | 12.50 | 25.00 |

Jill Ann
| ❑ 101 | | Outside Chance/Clock on the Wall | 1966 | 12.50 | 25.00 | 50.00 |

Soma
| ❑ 8108 | | It Was a Very Good Year/The Other Side of the Record | 1967 | 5.00 | 10.00 | 20.00 |

Number	Title (A Side/B Side)	Year	VG	VG+	NM
South, Joe					
Allwood					
❑ 402	Just Remember You're Mine/Silly Me	1962	3.00	6.00	12.00
Apt					
❑ 25084	Deep Inside Me/I Want to Be Somebody	1965	2.50	5.00	10.00
Capitol					
❑ 2060	Birds of a Feather/It Got Away	1967	2.00	4.00	8.00
❑ 2169	How Can I Unlove You/She's Almost You	1968	2.00	4.00	8.00
❑ 2248	Games People Play/Mirror of Your Mind	1968	2.00	4.00	8.00
❑ 2284	Redneck/Don't Throw Your Love to the Wind	1968	2.00	4.00	8.00
❑ 2491	Leanin' On You/Don't You Be Ashamed	1969		3.00	6.00
❑ 2532	Birds of a Feather/These Are Not My People	1969		3.00	6.00
❑ 2592	Don't It Make You Want to Go Home/Heart's Desire	1969		3.00	6.00
❑ 2704	Walk a Mile in My Shoes/Sheltered	1969		3.00	6.00
❑ 2755	Children/The Clock Up On the Wall	1970		2.50	5.00
❑ 2916	Why Does a Man Do What He Has to Do/Be a Believer	1970		2.50	5.00
❑ 3008	Rose Garden/Mirror of Your Mind	1971		3.00	6.00
❑ 3053	United We Stand/So the Seeds Are Growing	1971		2.50	5.00
❑ 3204	Fool Me/Devil May Care	1971		2.50	5.00
❑ 3450	One Man Band/Coming Down All Alone	1972		2.50	5.00
❑ 3487	I'm a Star/Misunderstanding	1972		2.50	5.00
❑ 3554	Real Thing/Save Your Best	1973		2.50	5.00
❑ 3717	Riverdog/It Hurts Me Too	1973		2.50	5.00
Columbia					
❑ 43983	Backfield in Motion/I'll Come Back to You	1967	3.00	6.00	12.00
❑ 44218	A Fool in Love/Great Day	1967	3.00	6.00	12.00
Fairlane					
❑ 21006	You're the Reason/Jukebox	1961	3.00	6.00	12.00
❑ 21010	Masquerade/I'm Sorry for You	1961	3.00	6.00	12.00
❑ 21015	Slippin' Around/Just to Be with You Again	1962	3.00	6.00	12.00
Island					
❑ 034	To Have, to Hold and Let Go/Midnight Rainbows	1975		2.00	4.00
MGM					
❑ 13145	Same Old Song/Standing Invitation	1963	2.50	5.00	10.00
❑ 13196	Concrete Jungle/The Last One to Know	1963	2.50	5.00	10.00
❑ 13276	Naughty Claudie/Little Queenie	1964	2.50	5.00	10.00
NRC					
❑ 002	I'm Snowed/It's Only You	1958	10.00	20.00	40.00
❑ 022	Chills/What a Night	1959	3.75	7.50	15.00
❑ 041	Little Bluebird/Play It Cool	1959	3.75	7.50	15.00
❑ 053	Tell the Truth/If You Only Knew Her	1960	3.75	7.50	15.00
❑ 065	Let's Talk It Over/Formality	1961	3.75	7.50	15.00
❑ 5000	The Purple People Eater Meets the Witch Doctor/ My Fondest Memories	1958	3.75	7.50	15.00
❑ 5001	One Fool to Another/Texas Ain't the Biggest Anymore	1958	3.75	7.50	15.00
Souvenirs, The					
Dooto					
❑ 412	So Long Daddy/Arlene, Sweet Little Texas Queen	1957	12.50	25.00	50.00
Inferno					
❑ 2001	I Could Have Danced All Night/It's Too Bad	1967	12.50	25.00	50.00
Reprise					
❑ 20,065	The Worm/The Bump	1962	3.75	7.50	15.00
❑ 20,066	The Real McCoy/The Watusi	1962	3.75	7.50	15.00
Spades, The					
Liberty					
See "Slades, The"					
Major					
❑ 1007	Close to You/I'm on Fire	1959	15.00	30.00	60.00
Zero					
This Spades was later known as The Thirteenth Floor Elevators					
❑ 10001	I Need a Girl/(B-side unknown)	1966	125.00	250.00	500.00
❑ 10002	You're Gonna Miss Me/We Sell Soul	1966	75.00	150.00	300.00
Spaniels, The					
Buddah					
❑ 153	Goodnight Sweetheart/Maybe	1969	2.00	4.00	8.00
Calla					
❑ 172	Fairy Tales/Jealous Heart	1970		3.00	6.00
Canterbury					
❑ 101	Peace of Mind/She Sang to Me/Danny Boy	1974		2.50	5.00
Chance					
❑ 1141	Baby It's You/Bounce	1953	125.00	250.00	500.00
❑ 1141	Baby It's You/Bounce	1953	200.00	400.00	800.00
	Red vinyl				
North American					
❑ 001	Fairy Tales/Jealous Heart	1970		2.50	5.00
❑ 002	Stand in Line/Lonely Man	1970		2.50	5.00
❑ 1114	Come Back to These Arms/Money Blues	1970		2.50	5.00

Number		Title (A Side/B Side)	Year	VG	VG+	NM
Owl						
❏ 328		Little Joe/The Posse	1973		2.50	5.00
Vee Jay						
❏ 101		Baby It's You/Bounce	1953	250.00	500.00	1,000
		Red vinyl				
❏ 101		Baby It's You/Bounce	1953	150.00	300.00	600.00
		Black vinyl, maroon label				
❏ 101		Baby It's You/Bounce	1961	10.00	20.00	40.00
		Black vinyl, black label				
❏ 103		The Bells Ring Out/House Cleaning	1953	150.00	300.00	600.00
		Red vinyl				
❏ 103		The Bells Ring Out/House Cleaning	1953	75.00	150.00	300.00
❏ 107		Goodnite, Sweetheart, Goodnite/You Don't Move Me	1953	75.00	150.00	300.00
		Black vinyl; as "Spanials"				
❏ 107		Goodnite, Sweetheart, Goodnite/You Don't Move Me	1953	50.00	100.00	200.00
		Black vinyl, correct spelling				
❏ 107		Goodnite, Sweetheart, Goodnite/You Don't Move Me	1953	200.00	400.00	800.00
		Red vinyl; no "Trade Mark Reg" on label				
❏ 107		Goodnite, Sweetheart, Goodnite/You Don't Move Me	1993	2.00	4.00	8.00
		Red vinyl; "Trade Mark Reg" on label; included in Vee-Jay CD box set				
❏ 116		Play It Cool/Let's Make Up	1954	125.00	250.00	500.00
		Red vinyl				
❏ 116		Play It Cool/Let's Make Up	1954	25.00	50.00	100.00
❏ 131		Do-Wah/Don'cha Go	1955	125.00	250.00	500.00
		Red vinyl				
❏ 131		Do-Wah/Don'cha Go	1955	20.00	40.00	80.00
❏ 154		You Painted Pictures/Hey, Sister Lizzie	1955	12.50	25.00	50.00
		As "Spanials"				
❏ 154		You Painted Pictures/Hey, SIster Lizzie	1955	15.00	30.00	60.00
❏ 178		False Love/Do You Really	1956	37.50	75.00	150.00
❏ 189		Dear Heart/Why Won't You Dance	1956	37.50	75.00	150.00
❏ 202		Since I Fell for You/Baby Come Along with Me	1956	37.50	75.00	150.00
❏ 229		Please Don't Tease/You Gave Me Peace of Mind	1956	15.00	30.00	60.00
❏ 246		Everyone's Laughing/I.O.U.	1957	15.00	30.00	60.00
❏ 257		You're Gonna Cry/I Need Your Kisses	1957	15.00	30.00	60.00
❏ 264		I Love You/Crazee Babee	1958	15.00	30.00	60.00
❏ 278		Tina/Great Googly Moo	1958	15.00	30.00	60.00
❏ 290		Stormy Weather/Here Is Why I Love You	1958	15.00	30.00	60.00
❏ 301		Baby It's You/Heart and Soul	1958	15.00	30.00	60.00
❏ 310		Trees/I Like It Like That	1959	15.00	30.00	60.00
❏ 328		These Three Words/100 Years from Today	1959	15.00	30.00	60.00
❏ 342		People Will Say We're in Love/The Bells Ring Out	1960	25.00	50.00	100.00
❏ 350		I Know/Bus Fare Home	1960	10.00	20.00	40.00

Spanky and Our Gang

Number		Title (A Side/B Side)	Year	VG	VG+	NM
Epic						
❏ 50170		When I Wanna/I Won't Brand You	1975		2.50	5.00
❏ 50206		L.A. Freeway/Standing Room Only	1976		2.50	5.00
Mercury						
❏ 72598		And Your Bird Can Sing/Sealed with a Kiss	1966	5.00	10.00	20.00
❏ 72679		Sunday Will Never Be the Same/Distance	1967	2.00	4.00	8.00
❏ 72714		Making Every Minute Count/If You Could Only Be Me	1967	2.00	4.00	8.00
❏ 72714	PS	Making Every Minute Count/If You Could Only Be Me	1967	2.50	5.00	10.00
❏ 72732		Lazy Day/(It Ain't Necessarily) Byrd Avenue	1967	2.00	4.00	8.00
❏ 72732	PS	Lazy Day/(It Ain't Necessarily) Byrd Avenue	1967	2.50	5.00	10.00
❏ 72765		Sunday Morning/Echoes	1968	2.00	4.00	8.00
❏ 72765	PS	Sunday Morning/Echoes	1968	2.50	5.00	10.00
❏ 72795		Like to Get to Know You/Three Ways from Tomorrow	1968	2.00	4.00	8.00
❏ 72795	PS	Like to Get to Know You/Three Ways from Tomorrow	1968	2.50	5.00	10.00
❏ 72831		Give a Damn/Swinging Gate	1968	2.00	4.00	8.00
❏ 72871		Yesterday's Rain/Without Rhyme or Reason	1968	2.00	4.00	8.00
❏ 72890		Anything You Choose/Mecca Flat Blues	1969	2.00	4.00	8.00
❏ 72926		And She's Mine/Leopard Skinned Phones	1969	2.00	4.00	8.00
❏ 72982		Everybody's Talkin'/(B-side unknown)	1969	2.00	4.00	8.00

Sparkletones, The

(Also see "Bennett, Joe, and the Sparkletones")

Number	Title (A Side/B Side)	Year	VG	VG+	NM
ABC-Paramount					
❏ 10659	Run Rabbit Run/Well Dressed Man	1965	3.75	7.50	15.00

Sparks of Rhythm, The

Number	Title (A Side/B Side)	Year	VG	VG+	NM
Apollo					
❏ 479	Women, Women, Women/Don't Love You Anymore	1955	75.00	150.00	300.00
❏ 481	Hurry Home/Stars Are in the Sky	1955	75.00	150.00	300.00
❏ 541	Handy Man/Everybody Rock and Roll	1959	12.50	25.00	50.00

Sparrow, The

(Evolved into Steppenwolf)

Number	Title (A Side/B Side)	Year	VG	VG+	NM
Columbia					
❏ 10234	Eli's Coming/Oh Doctor	1975	2.50	5.00	10.00
❏ 43755	Tomorrow's Ship/Isn't It Strange	1966	6.25	12.50	25.00
	As "The Sparrows"				
❏ 43960	Green Bottle Lover/Down Goes Your Love Life	1967	6.25	12.50	25.00
	As "The Sparrows"				

Number		Title (A Side/B Side)	Year	VG	VG+	NM

Sparrows, The
Davis

| ❏ 456 | | Love Me Tender/Come Back to Me | 1957 | 75.00 | 150.00 | 300.00 |

Jay Dee

| ❏ 783 | | Tell Me Baby/Why Did You Leave Me | 1953 | 125.00 | 250.00 | 500.00 |
| ❏ 790 | | I'll Be Loving You/Hey! | 1954 | 125.00 | 250.00 | 500.00 |

Spector, Phil
(Also see "Harvey, Phil"; "Spectors Three, The"; "Teddy Bears, The")
Pavillion

| ❏ AE7 1354 | DJ | Phil Spector's Christmas Medley (same on both sides) | 1981 | 3.75 | 7.50 | 15.00 |

Promo-only sampler from the Pavillion reissue of Phil Spector's Christmas Album

Philles

| ❏ (no #) | DJ | Thanks for Giving Me the Right Time! (same on both sides) | 1965 | 125.00 | 250.00 | 500.00 |

Spector, Ronnie
(Also see "Ronettes, The"; "Veronica")
Alston

| ❏ 3738 | | It's a Heartache/I Wanna Come Over | 1978 | 2.00 | 4.00 | 8.00 |

Apple

| ❏ 1832 | | Try Some, Buy Some/Tandoori Chicken | 1971 | 2.00 | 4.00 | 8.00 |

With star on A-side label

| ❏ 1832 | | Try Some, Buy Some/Tandoori Chicken | 1971 | 3.50 | 7.00 | |
| ❏ 1832 | PS | Try Some, Buy Some/Tandoori Chicken | 1971 | 2.50 | 5.00 | 10.00 |

Columbia

❏ 07082		Who Can Sleep/When We Danced	1987		2.00	4.00
❏ 07082	PS	Who Can Sleep/When We Danced	1987		2.00	4.00
❏ 07300		Love on a Rooftop/Good Love Is Hard to Find	1987		2.00	4.00

Epic

| ❏ 50374 | | Say Goodbye to Hollywood/Baby Please Don't Go | 1977 | 2.50 | 5.00 | 10.00 |
| ❏ 50374 | PS | Say Goodbye to Hollywood/Baby Please Don't Go | 1977 | 6.25 | 12.50 | 25.00 |

Polish

| ❏ 202 | | Darlin'/Tonight | 1980 | | 2.50 | 5.00 |

Tom Cat

| ❏ JB-10380 | DJ | You'd Be Good for Me/Something Tells Me | 1975 | 2.50 | 5.00 | 10.00 |

Promo only on blue vinyl

| ❏ PB-10380 | | You'd Be Good for Me/Something Tells Me | 1975 | | 2.50 | 5.00 |

Warner/Spector

| ❏ 0409 | | Paradise/When I Saw You | 1976 | 2.50 | 5.00 | 10.00 |

Spectors Three, The
(With Phil Spector)
Troy

| ❏ 3001 | | I Really Do/I Know Why | 1959 | 6.25 | 12.50 | 25.00 |
| ❏ 3005 | | My Heart Stood Still/Mr. Robin | 1960 | 6.25 | 12.50 | 25.00 |

Speedy and the Reverbs
Reverb

| ❏ 51 | | 100 Proof/Gas Chamber | 196? | 12.50 | 25.00 | 50.00 |

Spencer and Spencer
(Dickie Goodman and Mickey Shorr)
Argo

| ❏ 5331 | | Russian Bandstand/Brass Wail | 1959 | 6.25 | 12.50 | 25.00 |

Gone

| ❏ 5053 | | Stagger Lawrence/Strogonoff Cha Cha | 1959 | 6.25 | 12.50 | 25.00 |

Spencer, Jeremy
(Ex-Fleetwood Mac)
Atlantic

❏ 3588		Cool Breeze/You Got the Right	1979		2.50	5.00
❏ 3601		Cool Breeze/You Got the Right	1979		2.50	5.00
❏ 3624	DJ	Travelin' (same on both sides)	1979		2.50	5.00

May be promo-only

Columbia

| ❏ 45854 | | Can You Hear the Song/The World in Her Heart | 1973 | | 2.50 | 5.00 |

Spices, The
Carlton

| ❏ 480 | | Tell Me Little Girl/Money, Fortune and Fame | 1958 | 75.00 | 150.00 | 300.00 |

Spidells, The
Coral

| ❏ 62508 | | Pushed Out of the Picture/With You in Mind | 1966 | 12.50 | 25.00 | 50.00 |
| ❏ 62531 | | Don't You Forget That You're My Baby/ If It Ain't One Thing (It's Another) | 1967 | 5.00 | 10.00 | 20.00 |

Number	Title (A Side/B Side)	Year	VG	VG+	NM

Spiders
(Early Alice Cooper)
Mascot
| ❑ 112 | Why Don't You Love Me/Hitch Hike | 1965 | 1,000 | 1,500 | 2,000 |

Santa Cruz
| ❑ 003 | Don't Blow Your Mind/No Price Tag | 1966 | 500.00 | 1,000 | 1,500 |

Spiders, The
Imperial
❑ 5265	I Didn't Want to Do It/You're the One	1954	25.00	50.00	100.00
❑ 5280	Tears Begin to Flow/I'll Stop Cryin'	1954	20.00	40.00	80.00
❑ 5291	I'm Searching/I'm Slippin' In	1954	25.00	50.00	100.00
❑ 5305	The Real Thing/Mm Mm Baby	1954	25.00	50.00	100.00
❑ 5318	She Keeps Me Wondering/(3 x 7) = "21"	1954	25.00	50.00	100.00
❑ 5331	That's Enough/Lost and Bewildered	1955	18.75	37.50	75.00
❑ 5344	Am I the One/Sukey, Sukey, Sukey	1955	18.75	37.50	75.00
❑ 5354	Bells in My Heart/For a Thrill	1955	25.00	50.00	100.00
	Red label				
❑ 5354	Bells in My Heart/For a Thrill	1957	7.50	15.00	30.00
	Black label				
❑ 5366	Is It True/Witchcraft	1955	18.75	37.50	75.00
	Blue label				
❑ 5366	Is It True/Witchcraft	1955	10.00	20.00	40.00
	Red label				
❑ 5376	Don't Pity Me/How I Feel	1956	10.00	20.00	40.00
	Featuring Chuck Carbo				
❑ 5618	I Didn't Want to Do It/You're the One	1959	7.50	15.00	30.00
❑ 5714	You're the One/Tennessee Slim	1960	7.50	15.00	30.00
❑ 5739	Witchcraft/(True) You Don't Love Me	1961	7.50	15.00	30.00

Lawn
| ❑ 234 | Run Boy Run/Baby Doll | 1964 | 3.00 | 6.00 | 12.00 |

Philips
| ❑ 40363 | No No Boy/How Could I Fall in Love | 1966 | 2.00 | 4.00 | 8.00 |

Spike Drivers, The
Om 1000
| ❑ 1676 | High Time/
Baby Won't You Let Me Tell You How I Lost My Mind | 1966 | 7.50 | 15.00 | 30.00 |

Reprise
| ❑ 0535 | High Time/
Baby Won't You Let Me Tell You How I Lost My Mind | 1966 | 5.00 | 10.00 | 20.00 |
| ❑ 0558 | Strange Mysterious Sounds/Break Out the Wine | 1967 | 5.00 | 10.00 | 20.00 |

Spindles, The
ABC
| ❑ 10802 | To Make You Mine/And the Band Played On | 1966 | 5.00 | 10.00 | 20.00 |
| ❑ 10850 | No One Loves You (The Way I Do)/Ten Shades of Blue | 1966 | 6.25 | 12.50 | 25.00 |

Spinners
Atlantic
❑ 2904	I'll Be Around/How Could I Let You Get Away	1972		2.50	5.00
❑ 2927	Could It Be I'm Falling in Love/Just You and Me Baby	1972		2.50	5.00
❑ 2962	One of a Kind (Love Affair)/ Don't Let the Green Grass Fool You	1973		2.50	5.00
❑ 2973	Ghetto Child/We Belong Together	1973		2.50	5.00
❑ 3006	Mighty Love -- Pt. 1/Mighty Love -- Pt. 2	1974		2.50	5.00
❑ 3027	I'm Coming Home/He'll Never Love You Like I Do	1974		2.50	5.00
❑ 3029	Then Came You/Just As Long As We Have Love	1974		3.00	6.00
	With Dionne Warwicke (sic)				
❑ 3202	Then Came You/Just As Long As We Have Love	1974		2.50	5.00
	With Dionne Warwicke (sic)				
❑ 3206	Love Don't Love Nobody (Part 1)/ Love Don't Love Nobody (Part 2)	1974		2.50	5.00
❑ 3252	Living a Little, Loving a Little/ Smile, We Have Each Other	1975		2.50	5.00
❑ 3268	Sadie/Lazy Susan	1975		2.50	5.00
❑ 3284	Games People Play/I Don't Want to Lose You	1975	2.50	5.00	10.00
❑ 3284	They Just Can't Stop It the (Games People Play)/ I Don't Want to Lose You	1975		2.50	5.00
	Same A-side, altered title				
❑ 3309	Love Or Leave/You Made a Promise to Me	1975		2.50	5.00
❑ 3341	Wake Up Susan/If You Can't Be in Love	1976		2.50	5.00
❑ 3355	The Rubberband Man/Now That We're Together	1976		2.50	5.00
❑ 3382	You're Throwing a Good Love Away/ You're All I Need in Life	1977		2.50	5.00
❑ 3400	Me and My Music/I'm Riding Your Shadow	1977		2.50	5.00
❑ 3425	Heaven on Earth (So Fine)/I'm Tired of Giving	1977		2.50	5.00
❑ 3462	Easy Come, Easy Go/Love Is One Step Away	1978		2.50	5.00
❑ 3483	If You Wanna Do a Dance/One in a Life Proposal	1978		2.50	5.00
❑ 3546	Are You Ready for Love/Once You Fall in Love	1978		2.50	5.00
❑ 3590	Don't Let the Man Get You/I Love the Music	1979		2.50	5.00
❑ 3619	Body Language/With My Eyes	1979		2.50	5.00
❑ 3637	Working My Way Back to You/Disco Ride	1979	2.00	4.00	8.00
	Original pressings mention only one song on the A-side				

Number	Title (A Side/B Side)	Year	VG	VG+	NM
❏ 3637	Working My Way Back to You-Forgive Me, Girl/ Disco Ride	1979		2.00	4.00
❏ 3664	Cupid-I've Loved You for a Long Time/Pipedreams	1980		2.00	4.00
❏ 3757	Love Trippin'/Now That You're Mine Again	1980		2.00	4.00
❏ 3765	I Just Want to Fall in Love/Heavy on the Sunshine	1980		2.00	4.00
❏ 3798	Yesterday Once More-Nothing Remains the Same/ Be My Love	1981		2.00	4.00
❏ 3814	Long Live Soul Music/Give Your Lady What She Wants	1981		2.00	4.00
❏ 3827	Winter of Our Love/The Deacon	1981		2.00	4.00
❏ 3848	What You Feel Is Real/Street Talk	1981		2.00	4.00
	With Gino Soccio				
❏ 3865	You Go Your Way (I'll Go Mine)/Got to Be Love	1981		2.00	4.00
❏ 3882 DJ	Love Connection (same on both sides)	1981		2.50	5.00
	May be promo only				
❏ 4007	Never Thought I'd Fall in Love/Send a Little Love	1982		2.00	4.00
❏ 89226	Spaceballs/Spaceballs (Dub Version)	1987			3.00
❏ 89648	(We Have Come Into) Our Time for All/All Your Love	1984		2.00	4.00
❏ 89689	Right or Wrong/Love Is In Season	1984		2.00	4.00
❏ 89862	City Full of Memories/No Other Love	1983		2.00	4.00
❏ 89922	Funny How Time Slips Away//I'm Calling You Now	1982		2.00	4.00
❏ 89962	Magic in the Moonlight/So Far Away	1982		2.00	4.00

Mirage

Number	Title (A Side/B Side)	Year	VG	VG+	NM
❏ 99580	She Does/(B-side unknown)	1986			3.00
❏ 99604	Put Us Together Again/Show Us Your Magic	1985			3.00

Motown

Number	Title (A Side/B Side)	Year	VG	VG+	NM
❏ 1067	Sweet Thing/How Can I	1964	3.75	7.50	15.00
❏ 1078	I'll Always Love You/Tomorrow May Never Come	1965	3.75	7.50	15.00
❏ 1093	Truly Yours/Where Is That Girl	1966	3.75	7.50	15.00
❏ 1109	For All We Know/Cross My Heart	1967	3.75	7.50	15.00
❏ 1136	I Just Can't Help But Feel the Pain/Bad, Bad Weather	1968	3.75	7.50	15.00
❏ 1155	In My Diary/(She's Gonna Love Me) At Sundown	1969	375.00	750.00	1,500
❏ 1235	Together We Can Make Such Sweet Music/ Bad, Bad Weather	1973	2.00	4.00	8.00

Tri-Phi

Number	Title (A Side/B Side)	Year	VG	VG+	NM
❏ 1001	That's What Girls Are Made For/Heebie-Jeebies	1961	6.25	12.50	25.00
❏ 1004	Love (I Am So Glad I Found You)/Sudbuster	1961	6.25	12.50	25.00
❏ 1007	What Did She Use/ Itching for My Baby, I Know Where to Scratch	1962	6.25	12.50	25.00
❏ 1010	She Loves Me So/Whistling About You	1962	6.25	12.50	25.00
❏ 1013	I've Been Hurt/ I Got Your Water Boiling Baby (I'm Gonna Cook Your Goose)	1962	6.25	12.50	25.00
❏ 1018	She Don't Love Me/Too Young, Too Much, Too Soon	1962	7.50	15.00	30.00

V.I.P.

Number	Title (A Side/B Side)	Year	VG	VG+	NM
❏ 25050	In My Diary/(She's Gonna Love Me) At Sundown	1969	6.25	12.50	25.00
❏ 25054	Message from a Black Man/ (She's Gonna Love Me) At Sundown	1970	3.00	6.00	12.00
❏ 25057	It's a Shame/ Together We Can Make Such Sweet Music	1970	3.00	6.00	12.00
❏ 25060	We'll Have It Made/ My Whole World Ended (The Moment You Left Me)	1971	3.00	6.00	12.00

Spinners, The

(Several different groups, none of which were the popular soul group)

Capitol

Number	Title (A Side/B Side)	Year	VG	VG+	NM
❏ F3955	Love's Prayer/Goofin'	1958	10.00	20.00	40.00

Crystalette

Number	Title (A Side/B Side)	Year	VG	VG+	NM
❏ 736	Boomerang/Slave Chain	1960	12.50	25.00	50.00
	Reissued under different titles and on different labels credited to the Crestriders and Duke Mitchell				

End

Number	Title (A Side/B Side)	Year	VG	VG+	NM
❏ 1045	Bird Watcher/Richard Pry, Private Eye	1959	25.00	50.00	100.00
	Gray label				
❏ 1045	Bird Watcher/Richard Pry, Private Eye	1959	10.00	20.00	40.00
	Multicolor label				

Lawson

Number	Title (A Side/B Side)	Year	VG	VG+	NM
❏ 324	Surfing Monkey/Beatle Mania	1964	7.50	15.00	30.00

Liberty

Number	Title (A Side/B Side)	Year	VG	VG+	NM
❏ 55339	Till the End of Time/Dream	1961	2.50	5.00	10.00

RCA Victor

Number	Title (A Side/B Side)	Year	VG	VG+	NM
❏ 47-8427	All I Want/It Must Be Love	1964	2.50	5.00	10.00

Rhythm

Number	Title (A Side/B Side)	Year	VG	VG+	NM
❏ 125	Marvella/My Love and Your Love	1958	100.00	200.00	400.00

Smash

Number	Title (A Side/B Side)	Year	VG	VG+	NM
❏ 1845	Happy Hootenanny/Nothin'	1963	2.50	5.00	10.00

Warner Bros.

Number	Title (A Side/B Side)	Year	VG	VG+	NM
❏ 5084	Little Otis/Rag Mop	1959	3.00	6.00	12.00

Spirals, The

Capitol

Number	Title (A Side/B Side)	Year	VG	VG+	NM
❏ F4084	Rockin' Cow/Everybody Knows	1958	12.50	25.00	50.00

Smash

Number	Title (A Side/B Side)	Year	VG	VG+	NM
❏ 1719	Please Be My Love/Forever and a Day	1961	25.00	50.00	100.00

Number		Title (A Side/B Side)	Year	VG	VG+	NM

Spirit
Epic
❑ 10648		Animal Zoo/Red Light Roll On	1970		3.00	6.00
❑ 10685		Soldier/Mr. Skin	1970		3.00	6.00
❑ 10701		Mr. Skin/Nature's Way	1971		2.50	5.00
❑ 10849		Darkness/Cadillac Cowboys	1972		2.50	5.00
❑ 11020		Mr. Skin/Nature's Way	1973		2.00	4.00

Mercury
❑ 73697		America the Beautiful-The Times They Are a-Changin'/ Lady of the Lakes	1975		2.50	5.00
❑ 73722		Holy Man/Looking Into Darkness	1975		2.50	5.00
❑ 73837		Atomic Boogie/Farther Along	1976		2.00	4.00

Ode
❑ 108		Mechanical World/Uncle Jack	1967	2.50	5.00	10.00
❑ 115		I Got a Line on You/She Smiles	1968	2.50	5.00	10.00
❑ 122		Dark Eyed Woman/New Dope in Town	1969	2.00	4.00	8.00
❑ 128		1984/Sweet Stella Baby	1969	2.00	4.00	8.00

Splinter
Dark Horse
❑ 8439		Round and Round/I'll Bend for You	1977		2.00	4.00
❑ 8523		I Need Your Love/Motions of Love	1978		2.00	4.00
❑ 10002		Costafine Town/Elly-Mae	1974		3.00	6.00
❑ 10003		China Light/Haven't Got Time	1975		3.00	6.00
❑ 10007		Which Way Will I Get Home/ What Is It (If You Never Tried It Yourself)	1975		3.00	6.00
❑ 10010		After Five Years/Halfway There	1976		2.50	5.00

Spokesmen, The
Decca
❑ 31844		The Dawn of Correction/For You Babe	1965	3.00	6.00	12.00
❑ 31874		It Ain't Fair/Have Courage, Be Careful	1965	2.50	5.00	10.00
❑ 31895		Michelle/Better Days Are Yet to Come	1966	2.50	5.00	10.00
❑ 31948		Today's the Day/Enchante	1966	2.50	5.00	10.00
❑ 32049		I Love How You Love Me/Beautiful Girl	1966	2.50	5.00	10.00

Winchester
❑ 1001		Mary Jane/Flashback	1967	3.00	6.00	12.00

Sportones, The
Munich
❑ 101		In My Dreams/So Sincere	1959	125.00	250.00	500.00

Spotlighters, The
Aladdin
❑ 3436		Please Be My Girlfriend/Whisper	1958	25.00	50.00	100.00
❑ 3441		This Is My Story/Preaching	1959	25.00	50.00	100.00

Imperial
❑ 5342		It's Cold/Bam Jingle Jingle	1955	31.25	62.50	125.00
❑ 5342		It's Cold/Bam Jingle Jingle	1955	62.50	125.00	250.00
	Red vinyl					

Spring
(Also see "American Spring")
United Artists
❑ 50848		Now Everything's Been Said/Awake	1971	7.50	15.00	30.00
❑ 50907		Good Times/Sweet Mountain	1972	20.00	40.00	80.00

Springfield, Dusty
(Also see "Springfields, The")
ABC Dunhill
❑ 4341		Who Gets Your Love/Of All the Things	1973		3.00	6.00
❑ 4344		Mama's Little Girl/Learn to Say Goodbye	1973		3.00	6.00
❑ 4357		Mama's Little Girl/Learn to Say Goodbye	1973	2.00	4.00	8.00

Atlantic
❑ 2580		Son-of-a-Preacher-Man/Just a Little Lovin'	1968	2.50	5.00	10.00
❑ 2580	PS	Son-of-a-Preacher-Man/Just a Little Lovin'	1968	3.75	7.50	15.00
❑ 2606		Breakfast in Bed/Don't Forget About Me	1969	2.00	4.00	8.00
❑ 2623		The Windmills of Your Mind/ I Don't Want to Hear It Anymore	1969	2.00	4.00	8.00
❑ 2647		Willie & Laura May Jones/That Old Sweet Roll	1969		3.00	6.00
❑ 2673		In the Land of Make Believe/So Much Love	1969		3.00	6.00
❑ 2685		A Brand New Me/Bad Case of the Blues	1969		3.00	6.00
❑ 2705		Silly, Silly, Fool/Joe	1970		3.00	6.00
❑ 2729		I Wanna Be a Free Girl/Let Me In Your Way	1970		3.00	6.00
❑ 2739		Never Love Again/Lost	1970		3.00	6.00
❑ 2771		What Good Is I Love You/ What Do You Do When Love Dies	1970		3.00	6.00
❑ 2825		Nothing Is Forever/Haunted	1971		3.00	6.00
❑ 2841		I Believe in You/Someone Who Cared	1971		3.00	6.00

Casablanca
❑ 2356		I Am Curious/Donnez-Moi	1981		2.00	4.00

Enigma
❑ 75042		Nothing Has Been Proved/(Instrumental)	1989		2.50	5.00

Number		Title (A Side/B Side)	Year	VG	VG+	NM
Philips						
❏ 40162		I Only Want to Be with You/Once Upon a Time	1963	3.00	6.00	12.00
❏ 40180		Stay Awhile/Something Special	1964	2.50	5.00	10.00
❏ 40180	PS	Stay Awhile/Something Special	1964	5.00	10.00	20.00
❏ 40207		Wishin' and Hopin'/ Do Re Mi (Forget About the Do and Think About Me)	1964	3.00	6.00	12.00
❏ 40229		All Cried Out/I Wish I'd Never Loved You	1964	2.50	5.00	10.00
❏ 40229	PS	All Cried Out/I Wish I'd Never Loved You	1964	5.00	10.00	20.00
❏ 40245		Guess Who/Live It Up	1964	2.50	5.00	10.00
❏ 40245	PS	Guess Who/Live It Up	1964	5.00	10.00	20.00
❏ 40270		Losing You/Here She Comes	1965	2.50	5.00	10.00
❏ 40270	PS	Losing You/Here She Comes	1965	5.00	10.00	20.00
❏ 40303		In the Middle of Nowhere/Baby, Don't You Know	1965	2.50	5.00	10.00
❏ 40303	PS	In the Middle of Nowhere/Baby, Don't You Know	1965	5.00	10.00	20.00
❏ 40319		I Just Don't Know What to Do with Myself/ Some of Your Lovin'	1965	2.50	5.00	10.00
❏ 40319	PS	I Just Don't Know What to Do with Myself/ Some of Your Lovin'	1965	5.00	10.00	20.00
❏ 40371		You Don't Have to Say You Love Me/Little by Little	1966	2.50	5.00	10.00
❏ 40371	PS	You Don't Have to Say You Love Me/Little by Little	1966	5.00	10.00	20.00
❏ 40396		All I See Is You/I'm Gonna Leave You	1966	2.50	5.00	10.00
❏ 40396	PS	All I See Is You/I'm Gonna Leave You	1966	5.00	10.00	20.00
❏ 40439		I'll Try Anything/The Corrupt Ones	1967	2.50	5.00	10.00
❏ 40439	PS	I'll Try Anything/The Corrupt Ones	1967	5.00	10.00	20.00
❏ 40465		The Look of Love/Give Me Time	1967	2.50	5.00	10.00
❏ 40498		What's It Gonna Be/Small Town Girl	1967	2.50	5.00	10.00
❏ 40498	PS	What's It Gonna Be/Small Town Girl	1967	4.00	8.00	16.00
❏ 40547		Sweet Ride/No Stranger Am I	1968	2.50	5.00	10.00
❏ 40553		La Bamba/I Close My Eyes and Count to Ten	1968	2.50	5.00	10.00
20th Century						
❏ 2457		It Goes Like It Goes/I Wish That Love Would Last	1980		2.50	5.00
United Artists						
❏ XW1006		Let Me Love You Once Before You Go/I'm Your Child	1977		2.50	5.00
❏ XW1205		Checkmate/Sandra	1978		2.50	5.00
❏ XW1225		Give Me the Night/Checkmate	1978		2.50	5.00
❏ XW1255		Living Without Your Love/Get Yourself to Love	1978		2.50	5.00
Springfield, Rick						
Capitol						
❏ 3340		Speak to the Sky/Why	1972	2.00	4.00	8.00
❏ 3340	PS	Speak to the Sky/Why	1972	3.75	7.50	15.00
❏ 3466		What Would the Children Think/Come On Everybody	1972	2.00	4.00	8.00
❏ 3637		I'm Your Superman/Why Are You Waiting	1973	2.00	4.00	8.00
❏ 3713		Believe in Me/The Liar	1973	3.00	6.00	12.00
Chelsea						
❏ 3051		Take a Hand/Archangel	1976		2.50	5.00
❏ 3055		Million Dollar Face/(B-side unknown)	1976		2.50	5.00
❏ 3056		Jessica/(B-side unknown)	1976		2.50	5.00
Columbia						
❏ 45935		Believe in Me/The Liar	1973		3.00	6.00
❏ 46032		Streakin' Across the U.S.A./Music to Streak By	1974		3.00	6.00
❏ 46057		American Girls/Weep No More	1974		2.50	5.00
Mercury						
❏ 880 405-7		Bruce/Guenevere	1984		2.00	4.00
❏ 880 405-7	PS	Bruce/Guenevere	1984		2.50	5.00
RCA						
❏ 6853-7-R		Rock of Life/The Language of Love	1988			3.00
❏ 6853-7-R	PS	Rock of Life/The Language of Love	1988			3.00
❏ 8391-7-R		Honeymoon in Beirut/My Brother's Chair	1988			3.00
❏ PB-12166		I've Done Everything for You/Red Hot and Blue Love	1981		2.00	4.00
❏ PB-12166	PS	I've Done Everything for You/Red Hot and Blue Love	1981		2.00	4.00
❏ PB-12201		Jessie's Girl/Carry Me Away	1981		2.00	4.00
❏ PB-12201	PS	Jessie's Girl/Carry Me Away	1981		2.50	5.00
❏ PB-13008		Love Is Alright Tonite/Everybody's Girl	1981		2.00	4.00
❏ PB-13008	PS	Love Is Alright Tonite/Everybody's Girl	1981		2.00	4.00
❏ PB-13070		Don't Talk to Strangers/Tonight	1982		2.00	4.00
❏ PB-13070	PS	Don't Talk to Strangers/Tonight	1982		2.00	4.00
❏ PB-13245		What Kind of Fool Am I/How Do You Talk to Girls	1982		2.00	4.00
❏ PB-13303		I Get Excited/Kristina	1982		2.00	4.00
❏ PB-13303	PS	I Get Excited/Kristina	1982		2.00	4.00
❏ GB-13482		Jessie's Girl/I've Done Everything for You *Gold Standard Series*	1983			3.00
❏ GB-13483		Don't Talk to Strangers/What Kind of Fool Am I *Gold Standard Series*	1983			3.00
❏ PB-13497		Affair of the Heart/Like Father, Like Son	1983			3.00
❏ PB-13497	PS	Affair of the Heart/Like Father, Like Son	1983		2.00	4.00
❏ PB-13577		Human Touch/Alison	1983			3.00
❏ PB-13650		Souls/Souls (Live)	1983			3.00
❏ PB-13650	PS	Souls/Souls (Live)	1983		2.00	4.00
❏ PB-13738		Love Somebody/The Great Lost Art of Conversation	1984			3.00
❏ PB-13738	PS	Love Somebody/The Great Lost Art of Conversation	1984			3.00
❏ GB-13794		Affair of the Heart/Human Touch *Gold Standard Series*	1984			3.00
❏ PB-13813		Don't Walk Away/S.F.O.	1984			3.00
❏ PB-13813	PS	Don't Walk Away/S.F.O.	1984			3.00

Number		Title (A Side/B Side)	Year	VG	VG+	NM
❏ PB-13861		Bop 'Til You Drop/Taxi Dancing	1984			3.00
		B-side with Randy Crawford				
❏ PB-13861	PS	Bop 'Til You Drop/Taxi Dancing	1984			3.00
❏ PB-14047		Celebrate Youth/Stranger in the House	1985			3.00
❏ PB-14047	PS	Celebrate Youth/Stranger in the House	1985			3.00
❏ PB-14120		State of the Heart/The Power of Love (The Tao of Love)	1985			3.00
❏ PB-14120	PS	State of the Heart/The Power of Love (The Tao of Love)	1985			3.00

Springfields, The
(Also see "Springfield, Dusty")
Philips

Number		Title (A Side/B Side)	Year	VG	VG+	NM
❏ 40038		Silver Threads and Golden Needles/Aunt Rhody	1962	3.75	7.50	15.00
❏ 40072		Dear Hearts and Gentle People/Gotta Travel On	1962	3.00	6.00	12.00
❏ 40092		Little By Little/Waf-Woof	1963	3.00	6.00	12.00
❏ 40099		Foggy Mountain Top/Island of Dreams	1963	3.00	6.00	12.00
❏ 40121		Say I Won't Be There/Little Boat	1963	3.00	6.00	12.00

Springsteen, Bruce
Columbia

Number		Title (A Side/B Side)	Year	VG	VG+	NM
❏ AE7 1088	DJ	Rosalita (Come Out Tonight)//Spirit in the Night/Growin' Up	1974	75.00	150.00	300.00
		Small hole, plays at 33 1/3 RPM				
❏ AE7 1332	DJ	Santa Claus Is Coming to Town (same on both sides)	1981	5.00	10.00	20.00
❏ AE7 1332	PS	Santa Claus Is Coming to Town (same on both sides)	1981	6.25	12.50	25.00
❏ 03243		Hungry Heart/Fade Away	1983		2.00	4.00
		"Columbia Hall of Fame" series; red label				
❏ 03243		Hungry Heart/Fade Away	198?			3.00
		"Columbia Hall of Fame" series; gray label				
❏ 04463		Dancing in the Dark/Pink Cadillac	1984		2.00	4.00
❏ 04463	PS	Dancing in the Dark/Pink Cadillac	1984		2.50	5.00
❏ 04561		Cover Me/Jersey Girl	1984	2.50	5.00	10.00
		First pressings have a spoken intro to "Jersey Girl." Dead wax has matrix number followed by "-1" and a letter.				
❏ 04561		Cover Me/Jersey Girl	1984			4.00
		Spoken intro to "Jersey Girl" is deleted. Dead wax has matrix number followed by "-2" and a letter.				
❏ 04561	PS	Cover Me/Jersey Girl	1984		2.50	5.00
❏ 04680		Born in the U.S.A./Shut Out the Light	1984		2.00	4.00
❏ 04680	PS	Born in the U.S.A./Shut Out the Light	1984		2.50	5.00
❏ 04772		I'm on Fire/Johnny Bye Bye	1985		2.00	4.00
❏ 04772	PS	I'm on Fire/Johnny Bye Bye	1985		2.50	5.00
❏ 04924		Glory Days/Stand On It	1985		2.00	4.00
❏ 04924	PS	Glory Days/Stand On It	1985		2.50	5.00
❏ 05603		I'm Goin' Down/Janey, Don't You Lose Heart	1985		2.00	4.00
❏ 05603	PS	I'm Goin' Down/Janey, Don't You Lose Heart	1985		2.50	5.00
❏ 05728		My Hometown/Santa Claus Is Coming to Town	1985		2.00	4.00
❏ 05728	PS	My Hometown/Santa Claus Is Coming to Town	1985		2.00	4.00
❏ 06432		War/Merry Christmas Baby	1986		2.00	4.00
❏ 06432	PS	War/Merry Christmas Baby	1986		2.00	4.00
❏ 06657		Fire/Incident on 57th Street	1987		2.50	5.00
❏ 06657	PS	Fire/Incident on 57th Street	1987		2.50	5.00
❏ 07595		Brilliant Disguise/Lucky Man	1987		2.00	4.00
❏ 07595	PS	Brilliant Disguise/Lucky Man	1987		2.00	4.00
❏ 07663		Tunnel of Love/Two for the Road	1987		2.00	4.00
❏ 07663	PS	Tunnel of Love/Two for the Road	1987		2.00	4.00
❏ 07726		One Step Up/Roulette	1988		2.00	4.00
❏ 07726	PS	One Step Up/Roulette	1988		2.00	4.00
❏ 08408		Dancing in the Dark/Pink Cadillac	1984			3.00
		Gray label reissue				
❏ 08409		Cover Me/Jersey Girl	1984			3.00
		Gray label reissue				
❏ 08410		Born in the U.S.A./Shut Out the Light	1984			3.00
		Gray label reissue				
❏ 08411		I'm on Fire/Johnny Bye Bye	1985			3.00
		Gray label reissue				
❏ 08412		Glory Days/Stand On It	1985			3.00
		Gray label reissue				
❏ 08413		I'm Goin' Down/Janey, Don't You Lose Heart	1985			3.00
		Gray label reissue				
❏ 08414		My Hometown/Santa Claus Is Coming to Town	1985			3.00
		Gray label reissue; many copies of this were issued with Columbia 05728 picture sleeves				
❏ 10209		Born to Run/Meeting Across the River	1975	5.00	10.00	20.00
❏ 10274		Tenth Avenue Freeze-Out/She's the One	1976	3.75	7.50	15.00
❏ 10763		Prove It All Night/Factory	1978	3.00	6.00	12.00
❏ 10801		Badlands/Streets of Fire	1978	3.00	6.00	12.00
❏ 11391		Hungry Heart/Held Up Without a Gun	1980		2.00	4.00
❏ 11391	PS	Hungry Heart/Held Up Without a Gun	1980		3.00	6.00
❏ 11431		Fade Away/To Be True	1981	6.25	12.50	25.00
		Erroneous first pressing				
❏ 11431		Fade Away/Be True	1981		2.00	4.00
		Corrected second pressing				
❏ 11431	PS	Fade Away/Be True	1981		3.00	6.00
❏ 33323		Born to Run/Spirit in the Night	1976		2.00	4.00
		"Columbia Hall of Fame" series; red label				
❏ 33323		Born to Run/Spirit in the Night	198?			3.00
		"Columbia Hall of Fame" series; gray label				
❏ 45805		Blinded by the Light/The Angel	1972	125.00	250.00	500.00
❏ 45805	DJ	Blinded by the Light (mono/stereo)	1972	15.00	30.00	60.00

Number		Title (A Side/B Side)	Year	VG	VG+	NM
☐ 45805	PS	Blinded by the Light/The Angel	1972	125.00	250.00	500.00
☐ 45864		Spirit in the Night/For You	1973	400.00	800.00	1,200
☐ 45864	DJ	Spirit in the Night (mono/stereo)	1973	12.50	25.00	50.00
☐ 73796		Tunnel of Love/Two for the Road	1991			3.00
		Reissue				
☐ 73943		One Step Up/Roulette	1991			3.00
		Reissue				
☐ 74273		Human Touch/Better Days	1992		2.00	4.00
☐ 74354		57 Channels (And Nothin' On)/Part Man Part Monkey	1992		2.00	4.00
☐ 77384		Streets of Philadelphia/If I Should Fall Behind	1994		2.00	4.00
☐ 77847		Secret Garden/Thunder Road (Live)	1995			3.00
☐ 77847	PS	Secret Garden/Thunder Road (Live)	1995			3.00

Sputniks, The
Class
☐ 217		My Love Is Gone/Hey Maryann	1958	12.50	25.00	50.00
☐ 222		Wait a Little While/Johnny's Little Lamb	1958	10.00	20.00	40.00

Pam Mar
☐ 601		My Love Is Gone/Hey Maryann	1957	62.50	125.00	250.00

Squier, Billy
Capitol
☐ 4877		Like I'm Lovin' You/You Should Be High Love	1980		2.50	5.00
☐ 4901		Music's Alright/Big Beat	1980		2.50	5.00
☐ A-5005		The Stroke/Too Daze Gone	1981		2.00	4.00
☐ A-5005	PS	The Stroke/Too Daze Gone	1981		2.50	5.00
☐ A-5037		My Kinda Lover/ Christmas Is the Time to Say "I Love You"	1981		2.00	4.00
☐ A-5037	PS	My Kinda Lover/ Christmas Is the Time to Say "I Love You"	1981		2.50	5.00
☐ A-5040		In the Dark/Whadda You Want from Me	1981		2.00	4.00
☐ A-5040	PS	In the Dark/Whadda You Want from Me	1981		2.50	5.00
☐ B-5135		Emotions in Motion/It Keeps You Rockin'	1982		2.00	4.00
☐ B-5135	PS	Emotions in Motion/It Keeps You Rockin'	1982		2.50	5.00
☐ B-5163		Everybody Wants You/Keep Me Satisfied	1982		2.00	4.00
☐ B-5163	PS	Everybody Wants You/Keep Me Satisfied	1982		2.50	5.00
☐ B-5202		She's a Runner/In Your Eyes	1983		2.00	4.00
☐ B-5202	PS	She's a Runner/In Your Eyes	1983		2.50	5.00
☐ B-5303		Christmas Is the Time to Say "I Love You"/ White Christmas	1983		2.50	5.00
☐ B-5303	PS	Christmas Is the Time to Say "I Love You"/ White Christmas	1983		3.00	6.00
☐ B-5370		Rock Me Tonite/Can't Get Next to You	1984			3.00
☐ B-5370	PS	Rock Me Tonite/Can't Get Next to You	1984		2.00	4.00
☐ B-5416		Eye on You/Calley Oh	1984			3.00
☐ B-5416	PS	Eye on You/Calley Oh	1984		2.00	4.00
☐ B-5422		All Night Long/Calley Oh	1984			3.00
☐ B-5422	PS	All Night Long/Calley Oh	1984		2.00	4.00
☐ B-5619		Love Is the Hero/Learn How to Live (Live)	1986			3.00
☐ B-5619	PS	Love Is the Hero/Learn How to Live (Live)	1986			3.00
☐ B-5657		Shot O' Love/One Good Woman	1986			3.00
☐ S7-17395		Rhythm (A Bridge So Far)/Lovin' You Ain't So Hard	1993		2.00	4.00
☐ S7-18207		Christmas Is the Time to Say "I Love You"/ Everybody Wants You	1994		2.00	4.00
		Green vinyl				
☐ S7-57890		Christmas Is the Time to Say "I Love You"/ Christmas Blues	1992		2.50	5.00
		B-side by Canned Heat				
☐ 7PRO-79694	DJ	Don't Say You Love Me (same on both sides)	1989	2.50	5.00	10.00
		Vinyl is promo only				

Squire, Chris
(Member of Yes)
Atlantic
☐ 3317		Lucky Seven/Silently Falling	1976		2.50	5.00

Squire, Chris, and Alan White
(Members of Yes)
Atlantic
☐ 3886		Run with the Fox/Return of the Fox	1982		2.50	5.00

Squires, The
(More than one group)
Aladdin
☐ 3360		Dreamy Eyes/Danglin' with My Heart	1957	18.75	37.50	75.00

Atco
☐ 6442		Go Ahead/Going All the Way	1966	10.00	20.00	40.00

Chan
☐ 102		Movin' Out/Our Theme	1961	7.50	15.00	30.00
☐ 105		Mean Misery/Chattanooga Choo Choo	1962	7.50	15.00	30.00

Combo
☐ 35		Let's Give Love a Try/Whop	1952	125.00	250.00	500.00
☐ 42		Oh Darling/My Little Girl	1953	150.00	300.00	600.00

Congress
☐ 223		Joyce/Can't Believe That You've Grown Up	1964	15.00	30.00	60.00

Number	Title (A Side/B Side)	Year	VG	VG+	NM
Flair					
❑ 1030	Sayonara/Mia Bella Donna	1954	7.50	15.00	30.00
Gee					
❑ 1082	Don't Accuse Me/So Many Tears Ago	1962	12.50	25.00	50.00
Herald					
❑ 580	Why Should I Suffer/Walkin'	1963	7.50	15.00	30.00
Kicks					
❑ 1	Dream Come True/Lucy Lou	1954	125.00	250.00	500.00
Mambo					
❑ 105	Sindy/Do-Be-Do-Be-Wop-Wop	1955	30.00	60.00	120.00
MGM					
❑ 13044	Movin' Out/Our Theme	1961	3.75	7.50	15.00
Starlite					
❑ 1/2	Movin'/Night Road	1964	12.50	25.00	50.00
V					
❑ 109	The Sultan/Aurora	1961	250.00	500.00	1,000
	Canadian release only; with a very early Neil Young				
Vita					
❑ 105	Sindy/Do-Be-Do-Be-Wop-Wop	1960	15.00	30.00	60.00
❑ 113	Sweet Girl/Me and My Deal	1955	15.00	30.00	60.00
❑ 116	Heavenly Angel/Sweet Girl	1955	25.00	50.00	100.00

Stafford, Terry

A&M					
❑ 707	Heartaches on the Way/You Left Me Here to Cry	1963	3.00	6.00	12.00
Atlantic					
❑ 4006	Say, Has Anybody Seen My Sweet Gypsy Rose/ Amarillo by Morning	1973		2.50	5.00
❑ 4015	Captured/It Sure Is Bad to Love Her	1974		2.00	4.00
❑ 4026	We've Grown Close/Stop If You Love Me	1976		2.00	4.00
Casino					
❑ 113	It Sure Is Bad to Love Her/(B-side unknown)	1977		2.00	4.00
Crusader					
❑ 101	Suspicion/Judy	1964	3.75	7.50	15.00
❑ 105	I'll Touch a Star/Playing with Fire	1964	3.00	6.00	12.00
❑ 109	Follow the Rainbow/Are You a Fool Like Me	1964	3.00	6.00	12.00
❑ 110	A Little Bit Better/Hoping	1964	3.00	6.00	12.00
Melodyland					
❑ 6009	Darling, Think It Over/I Can't Find It	1975		2.00	4.00
Mercury					
❑ 72538	Out of the Picture/Forbidden	1966	2.50	5.00	10.00
MGM					
❑ 14232	Mean Woman Blues-Candy Man/Chilly Chicago	1971		2.50	5.00
❑ 14271	California Dancer/The Walk	1971		2.50	5.00
Player					
❑ 134	Lonestar Lonesome/(B-side unknown)	1989		2.00	4.00
Sidewalk					
❑ 902	Soldier Boy/When Sin Stops, Love Begins	1966	2.50	5.00	10.00
❑ 914	A Step or Two Behind You/The Joke's on Me	1967	2.50	5.00	10.00
Warner Bros.					
❑ 7286	Big in Dallas/Will a Man Ever Learn	1969		3.00	6.00

Stairsteps, The – See "Five Stairsteps, The"

Stalk-Forrest Group, The

(Early version of Blue Oyster Cult)

Elektra					
❑ 45693	What Is Quicksand/Arthur Comics	1970	12.50	25.00	50.00

Stampeders

Bell					
❑ 45,120	Sweet City Woman/Gator Road	1971		3.00	6.00
❑ 45,154	Devil You/Giant in the Streets	1971		2.50	5.00
❑ 45,188	Monday Morning Choo-Choo/ Then Came the White Man	1972		3.00	6.00
❑ 45,226	Wild Eyes/Carryin' On	1972		3.00	6.00
❑ 45,331	Oh My Lady/No Destination	1973		3.00	6.00
Capitol					
❑ 3868	Goodbye Goodbye/Me and My Stone	1974		2.00	4.00
❑ 3964	Running Out of Time/Ramona	1974		2.00	4.00
MGM					
❑ 13970	Be a Woman/I Don't Believe	1968	3.00	6.00	12.00
Polydor					
❑ 14060	Carry Me/I Didn't Need You Anyhow	1970	2.50	5.00	10.00
Quality					
❑ 501	Hard Lovin' Woman/Hit the Road Jack	1976		2.00	4.00
❑ 505	Sweet Love Bandit/Let It Begin	1976		2.00	4.00

Number		Title (A Side/B Side)	Year	VG	VG+	NM

Standards, The
Amos
| ☐ 134 | | When You Wish Upon a Star/(Instrumental) | 1969 | 2.50 | 5.00 | 10.00 |

Chess
| ☐ 1869 | | My Heart Belongs to You/Hello Love | 1963 | 10.00 | 20.00 | 40.00 |

Debro
| ☐ 3178 | | Tears Bring Heartaches/No, No, No | 1963 | 50.00 | 100.00 | 200.00 |

Glenden
| ☐ 1315 | | It Isn't Fair/Everybody Knows | 1964 | 5.00 | 10.00 | 20.00 |

Magna
| ☐ 1314 | | My Heart Belongs to You/Hello Love | 1963 | 20.00 | 40.00 | 80.00 |
| ☐ 1315 | | It Isn't Fair/Everybody Knows | 1963 | 12.50 | 25.00 | 50.00 |

Roulette
| ☐ 4487 | | Tears Bring Heartaches/No, No, No | 1963 | 7.50 | 15.00 | 30.00 |

Standells, The
Liberty
☐ 55680		The Peppermint Beatle/The Shake	1964	6.25	12.50	25.00
☐ 55722		Help Yourself/I'll Go Crazy	1964	5.00	10.00	20.00
☐ 55743		So Fine/Linda Lou	1964	5.00	10.00	20.00

MGM
| ☐ 13350 | | Someday You'll Cry/Zebra in the Kitchen | 1965 | 7.50 | 15.00 | 30.00 |

Sunset
| ☐ 61000 | | Ooh Poo Pah Doo/Help Yourself | 1966 | 5.00 | 10.00 | 20.00 |

Tower
☐ 185		Dirty Water/Rari	1966	5.00	10.00	20.00
☐ 257		Sometimes Good Guys Don't Wear White/ Why Did You Hurt Me	1966	3.75	7.50	15.00
☐ 282		Why Pick on Me/Mr. Nobody	1966	3.75	7.50	15.00
☐ 310		Try It/Poor Shell of a Man	1967	3.75	7.50	15.00
☐ 310	PS	Try It/Poor Shell of a Man	1967	7.50	15.00	30.00
☐ 312		Don't Tell Me What to Do/When I Was a Cowboy By "The Sllednats" (Standells backwards)	1967	5.00	10.00	20.00
☐ 314		Riot on Sunset Strip/Black Hearted Woman	1967	3.75	7.50	15.00
☐ 348		Can't Help But Love You/Ninety-Nine and One Half	1967	3.75	7.50	15.00
☐ 398		Animal Girl/Soul Drippin'	1968	3.75	7.50	15.00

Vee Jay
| ☐ 643 | | The Boy Next Door/B.J. Quetzal | 1965 | 5.00 | 10.00 | 20.00 |
| ☐ 679 | | Big Boss Man/Don't Say Goodbye | 1965 | 5.00 | 10.00 | 20.00 |

Stanley, Paul
(Member of Kiss)
Casablanca
| ☐ 940 | | Goodbye/Hold Me, Touch Me | 1978 | | 3.00 | 6.00 |

Staple Singers, The
Curtom
| ☐ 0109 | | Let's Do It Again/After Sex | 1975 | | 2.00 | 4.00 |
| ☐ 0113 | | New Orleans/A Whole Lot of Love | 1976 | | 2.00 | 4.00 |

Epic
☐ 9748		Be Careful of Stones That You Throw/ More Than a Hammer and Nail	1964	2.50	5.00	10.00
☐ 9776		Do Something for Yourself/Samson and Delilah	1965	2.50	5.00	10.00
☐ 9825		Freedom Highway/The Funeral	1965	2.50	5.00	10.00
☐ 9880		Why/What Are They Doing	1965	2.50	5.00	10.00
☐ 10054		King of Kings/Step Aside	1966	2.50	5.00	10.00
☐ 10104		Pray On/It's Been a Change	1966	2.50	5.00	10.00
☐ 10158		Why (Am I Treated So Bad)/ What Are They Doing (In Heaven Today)	1967	2.00	4.00	8.00
☐ 10220		For What It's Worth/Are You Sure	1967	2.00	4.00	8.00
☐ 10264		Deliver Me/He	1967	2.00	4.00	8.00
☐ 10294		Let's Get Together/Power of Love	1968	2.00	4.00	8.00
☐ 10339		Crying in the Chapel/Nothing Lasts Forever	1968	2.00	4.00	8.00
☐ 10742		For What It's Worth/Why	1971		3.00	6.00

Private I
☐ 04384		H-A-T-E (Don't Live Here Anymore)/Can You Hang	1984		2.00	4.00
☐ 04583		Slippery People/On My Own Again	1984		2.00	4.00
☐ 04711		This Is Our Night/Turning Point	1984		2.00	4.00
☐ 05565		Are You Ready/Love Works in Strange Ways	1985		2.00	4.00
☐ 05565	PS	Are You Ready/Love Works in Strange Ways	1985		3.00	6.00
☐ 05727		Nobody Can Make It on Their Own/Reasons to Love	1985		2.00	4.00

Riverside
☐ 4518		Gloryland/Hammer and Nails	1962	3.00	6.00	12.00
☐ 4531		Gambling Man/Use What You Got	1962	3.00	6.00	12.00
☐ 4540		There Was a Star/The Virgin Mary Had One Son	1962	3.00	6.00	12.00
☐ 4553		I Can't Help from Cryin'/Let That Liar Again	1963	3.00	6.00	12.00
☐ 4563		Cotton Fields/This Land	1963	3.00	6.00	12.00
☐ 4568		Blowing in the Wind/Wish I Had Answered	1963	3.00	6.00	12.00

Sharp
| ☐ 603 | | This May Be the Last Time/This Same Jesus | 1960 | 3.75 | 7.50 | 15.00 |

Stax
| ☐ 0007 | | Long Walk to D.C./Stay with Us | 1968 | | 3.00 | 6.00 |

Number	Title (A Side/B Side)	Year	VG	VG+	NM
❑ 0019	The Ghetto/Got to Be Some Changes Made	1968		3.00	6.00
❑ 0031	(Sittin' On) The Dock of the Bay/Top of the Mountain	1969		3.00	6.00
❑ 0039	The Gardener/The Challenge	1969		3.00	6.00
❑ 0052	When Will We Be Paid/Tend to Your Own Business	1969		3.00	6.00
❑ 0066	Give a Damn/God Bless the Children	1970		3.00	6.00
❑ 0074	Brand New Day/God Bless the Children	1970		3.00	6.00
❑ 0083	Heavy Makes You Happy (Sha-Na-Boom-Boom)/ Love Is Plentiful	1970		3.00	6.00
❑ 0084	Who Took the Merry Out of Christmas/(Instrumental)	1970		3.00	6.00
❑ 0093	You've Got to Earn It/I'm a Lover	1971		2.50	5.00
❑ 0104	Respect Yourself/You're Gonna Make Me Cry	1971		2.50	5.00
❑ 0125	I'll Take You There/I'm Just Another Soldier	1972		2.50	5.00
❑ 0137	This World/Are You Sure	1972		2.50	5.00
❑ 0156	Oh La De Da/We the People	1973		2.50	5.00
❑ 0164	Be What You Are/I Like the Things About Me	1973		2.50	5.00
	B-side by Cal Starr				
❑ 0179	If You're Ready (Come Go with Me)/ Love Comes in All Colors	1973		2.50	5.00
❑ 0196	Touch a Hand, Make a Friend/Tellin' Lies	1974		2.50	5.00
❑ 0213	What's Your Thing/Whicha Way Did It Go	1974		2.50	5.00
	B-side by Pops Staples				
❑ 0215	City in the Sky/That's What Friends Are For	1974		2.50	5.00
❑ 0227	My Main Man/Who Made the Man	1974		2.50	5.00
❑ 0248	Back Road Into Town/My Main Man	1975		2.50	5.00

20th Century

❑ 2508	Hold On to Your Dreams/Cold and Windy Night	1981		2.00	4.00

United

❑ 165	It Rained Children/Won't You Sit Down	1955	100.00	200.00	400.00

Vee Jay

❑ 169	God's Wonderful Love/If I Could Hear My Mother	1956	5.00	10.00	20.00
❑ 224	Uncloudy Day/I Know I Got Religion	1956	5.00	10.00	20.00
❑ 846	Let Me Ride/I'm Coming Home	1957	5.00	10.00	20.00
❑ 856	I Had a Dream/Help Me Jesus	1958	3.75	7.50	15.00
❑ 866	Love Is the Way/On My Way to Heaven	1959	3.75	7.50	15.00
❑ 870	I'm Leaving/Going Away	1959	3.75	7.50	15.00
❑ 881	Downward Road/So Soon	1959	3.75	7.50	15.00
❑ 893	Pray On/Too Close	1960	3.00	6.00	12.00
❑ 902	I've Been Scorned/Don't Knock	1961	3.00	6.00	12.00
❑ 912	Sit Down Servant/Swing Low	1962	3.00	6.00	12.00
❑ 930	Swing Low Sweet Chariot/I'm So Glad	1963	3.00	6.00	12.00

Warner Bros.

Warner Bros. titles as "The Staples"

❑ 8279	Love Me, Love Me, Love Me/Pass It On	1976		2.00	4.00
❑ 8317	Sweeter Than the Sweet/Making Love	1977		2.00	4.00
❑ 8460	See a Little Further (Than My Bed)/ Let's Go to the Disco	1977		2.00	4.00
❑ 8510	I Honestly Love You/Family Tree	1978		2.00	4.00
❑ 8669	Unlock Your Mind/Mystery Train	1978		2.00	4.00
❑ 8748	Chica Boom/Handwriting on the Wall	1979		2.00	4.00
❑ 49598	God Can/Unlock Your Mind	1980		2.00	4.00

Staples, Gordon, and the Motown Strings

Motown

❑ 1180	Strung Out/Sounds of the Zodiac	1971	7.50	15.00	30.00

Star Fires, The

Haral

❑ 777	Each Night at Nine/What Good Is Money	1962	25.00	50.00	100.00

Laurie

❑ 3332	You Done Me Wrong/Like Socks and Shoes	1966	5.00	10.00	20.00

Starfires, The

(Several different groups)

Apt

❑ 25030	Fender Bender/Camel Walk	1959		10.00	20.00

Bargain

❑ 5001	You're the One/So Much	1961	5.00	10.00	20.00
❑ 5003	Love Will Break Your Heart/The Dances	1961	5.00	10.00	20.00

Bernice

❑ 201	Yearning for You/Do-Ko-Icki-No	1958	37.50	75.00	150.00

D&H

❑ 200	These Foolish Things/Let's Do the Pony	1961	20.00	40.00	80.00

Decca

❑ 30730	Three Roses/I Have Someone	1958	10.00	20.00	40.00
❑ 30916	Love Is Here to Stay/Tomorrow	1959	12.50	25.00	50.00

Duel

❑ 518	Fools Fall in Love/Under the Stars	1962	12.50	25.00	50.00

Pace

❑ 101	Fender Bender/Camel Walk	1959	10.00	20.00	40.00

Pama

❑ 115	Ring of Love/Cheating Game	196?	10.00	20.00	40.00
❑ 117	Chartreuse Caboose/Billy's Blues	196?	10.00	20.00	40.00
	Early version of the Outsiders				

Number		Title (A Side/B Side)	Year	VG	VG+	NM
Round						
❑ 1016		Space Needle/The Jordan Stomp	1962	10.00	20.00	40.00
❑ 1016	PS	Space Needle/The Jordan Stomp	1962	15.00	30.00	60.00
Sonic						
❑ 7163		Re-Entry/Hand Full of Blood	1963	7.50	15.00	30.00
Triumph						
❑ 61		Fink/Work Out Fine	1965	5.00	10.00	20.00

Starlets, The
(More than one group)

Number		Title (A Side/B Side)	Year	VG	VG+	NM
Astro						
❑ 202/3	P.S.	I Love You/Where Is My Love Tonight	1960	5.00	10.00	20.00
❑ 204		Romeo and Juliet/Listen for a Lonely Tambourine	1960	6.25	12.50	25.00

This Starlets later recorded as the Angels

Number		Title (A Side/B Side)	Year	VG	VG+	NM
Chess						
❑ 1997		My Baby's Real/Loving You Is Something New	1967	5.00	10.00	20.00
❑ 2038		I Wanna Be Good to You/Watered Down	1968	5.00	10.00	20.00
Lute						
❑ 5909		I'm So Young/He's Got It	1960	6.25	12.50	25.00
Pam						
❑ 1003		Better Tell Him No/You Are the One	1961	5.00	10.00	20.00
❑ 1004		My Last Cry/Money Hungry	1961	5.00	10.00	20.00

This is the same group that, as the Blue-Belles, recorded "I Sold My Heart to the Junkman"

Starlighters, The

Number	Title (A Side/B Side)	Year	VG	VG+	NM
End					
❑ 1031	It's Twelve O'Clock/The Birdland	1958	125.00	250.00	500.00
❑ 1049	I Cried/You're the One to Blame	1959	20.00	40.00	80.00
❑ 1072	A Story of Love/Let's Take a Stroll	1960	30.00	60.00	120.00
Irma					
❑ 101	Love Cry/Last Night	1956	100.00	200.00	400.00
Lamp					
❑ 2014	Slipping Out/Rocking Too Much	1958	12.50	25.00	50.00
Sun Coast					
❑ 1001	Until You Return/Whomp, Whomp	1956	62.50	125.00	250.00
Wheel					
❑ 1004	Hot Licks/Creepin'	1960	3.75	7.50	15.00

Starlings, The

Number	Title (A Side/B Side)	Year	VG	VG+	NM
Dawn					
❑ 212	I'm Just a Crying Fool/Hokey-Smokey Mama	1955	150.00	300.00	600.00
❑ 213	A-Loo, A-Loo/I Gotta Go Now	1955	100.00	200.00	400.00
Josie					
❑ 760	My Plea for Love/Music, Maestro, Please	1954	125.00	250.00	500.00
World Pacific					
❑ 809	All I Want/That's Me	1959	10.00	20.00	40.00

Starr, Andy

Number	Title (A Side/B Side)	Year	VG	VG+	NM
Kapp					
❑ 190	Do It Right Now/I Waited for You to Remember	1957	6.25	12.50	25.00
MGM					
❑ 12263	Rockin' Rollin' Stone/I Wanna Go South	1956	37.50	75.00	150.00
❑ 12315	She's a-Going, Jessie/Old Deacon Jones	1956	37.50	75.00	150.00
❑ 12364	Round and Round/Give Me a Woman	1957	37.50	75.00	150.00
❑ 12421	No Room for Your Kind/One More Time	1957	37.50	75.00	150.00

Starr, Edwin

Number		Title (A Side/B Side)	Year	VG	VG+	NM
Gordy						
❑ 7066		Gonna Keep On Tryin' Til I Win Your Love/ I Want My Baby Back	1967		3.00	6.00
❑ 7071		I Am the Man for You Baby/My Weakness Is You	1968		3.00	6.00
❑ 7078		Way Over There/If My Heart Could Tell the Story	1968		3.00	6.00
❑ 7083		Twenty-Five Miles/Love Is the Destination	1969		3.00	6.00
❑ 7087		I'm Still a Struggling Man/Pretty Little Angel	1969		3.00	6.00
❑ 7090		Oh How Happy/Ooh Baby Baby	1969		3.00	6.00
	With Blinky					
❑ 7097		Time/Running Back and Forth	1970		3.00	6.00
❑ 7101		War/He Who Picks a Rose	1970		3.00	6.00
❑ 7104		Stop the War Now/ Gonna Keep On Tryin' Til I Win Your Love	1970		3.00	6.00
❑ 7107		Funky Music Sho Nuff Turns Me On/Cloud Nine	1971		3.00	6.00
Granite						
❑ 522		Pain/I'll Never Forget You	1975		2.50	5.00
❑ 528		Stay with Me/Party	1975		2.50	5.00
❑ 532		Abyssinia Jones/Beginning	1975		2.50	5.00
Montage						
❑ 1216		Tired of It/(B-side unknown)	1982		2.00	4.00
Motown						
❑ 1276		You've Got My Soul on Fire/ Love (The Lonely People's Prayer)	1973		2.50	5.00
❑ 1284		Ain't It Hell Up in Harlem/Don't It Feel Good to Be Free	1973		2.50	5.00

Number		Title (A Side/B Side)	Year	VG	VG+	NM
☐ 1300		Big Papa/Like We Used to Do	1974		2.50	5.00
☐ 1326		Who's Right or Wrong/Lonely Rainy Days in San Diego	1974		2.50	5.00

Ric-Tic

Number		Title (A Side/B Side)	Year	VG	VG+	NM
☐ 103		Agent Double-O-Soul/(Instrumental)	1965	3.75	7.50	15.00
☐ 107		Back Street/(Instrumental)	1965	3.75	7.50	15.00
☐ 109		Stop Her on Sight (S.O.S.)/I Have Faith in You	1966	3.75	7.50	15.00
☐ 109X	DJ	Scott's On Swingers (S.O.S.)/I Have Faith in You	1966	12.50	25.00	50.00
☐ 114		Headline News/Harlem	1966	3.75	7.50	15.00
☐ 118		It's My Turn Now/Girls Are Getting Prettier	1967	3.75	7.50	15.00
☐ 120		You're My Mellow/My Kind of Woman	1967	15.00	30.00	60.00

Soul

Number		Title (A Side/B Side)	Year	VG	VG+	NM
☐ 35096		Take Me Clear from Here/Ball of Confusion	1972		3.00	6.00
☐ 35100		Who Is the Leader of the People/Don't Tell Me I'm Crazy	1972		3.00	6.00
☐ 35103		There You Go/(Instrumental)	1973		3.00	6.00

20th Century

Number		Title (A Side/B Side)	Year	VG	VG+	NM
☐ 2338		I Just Wanna Do My Thing/Mr. Davenport and Mr. James	1977		2.00	4.00
☐ 2389		I'm So Into You/Don't Waste Your Time	1978		2.00	4.00
☐ 2396		Contact/Don't Waste Your Time	1978		2.00	4.00
☐ 2408		H.A.P.P.Y. Radio/My Friend	1979		2.00	4.00
☐ 2420		It's Called the Rock/Patiently	1979		2.00	4.00
☐ 2423		It's Called the Rock/H.A.P.P.Y. Radio	1979		2.00	4.00
☐ 2441		It's Called the Rock/H.A.P.P.Y. Radio	1980		2.00	4.00
☐ 2445		Stronger Than You Think I Am/(Instrumental)	1980		2.00	4.00
☐ 2450		Tell-A-Star/Boop Boop Song	1980		2.00	4.00
☐ 2455		Get Up-Whirlpool/Better and Better	1980		2.00	4.00
☐ 2477		Twenty-Five Miles/Never Turn My Back on You	1980		2.00	4.00
☐ 2496		Real Live #10/Sweat	1981		2.00	4.00

Starr, Ringo

(Also see "Beatles, The")

Apple

Number		Title (A Side/B Side)	Year	VG	VG+	NM
☐ 1826	PS	Beaucoups of Blues/Coochy-Coochy *Sleeve with wrong catalog number (actually 2969)*	1970	10.00	20.00	40.00
☐ 1831		It Don't Come Easy/Early 1970 *With star on A-side label*	1971	3.00	6.00	12.00
☐ 1831		It Don't Come Easy/Early 1970	1971	2.00	4.00	8.00
☐ 1831	PS	It Don't Come Easy/Early 1970	1971	7.50	15.00	30.00
☐ 1831		It Don't Come Easy/Early 1970 *With "All rights reserved" on label*	1975	7.50	15.00	30.00
☐ 1849		Back Off Boogaloo/Blindman *Blue-background label*	1972	18.75	37.50	75.00
☐ 1849		Back Off Boogaloo/Blindman *Green-background label*	1972	2.00	4.00	8.00
☐ 1849	DJ	Back Off Boogaloo/Blindman *White label*	1972	37.50	75.00	150.00
☐ 1849	PS	Back Off Boogaloo/Blindman *Glossy black on one side, gray on the other*	1972	10.00	20.00	40.00
☐ 1849	PS	Back Off Boogaloo/Blindman *Glossy black paper on both sides*	1972	10.00	20.00	40.00
☐ 1849	PS	Back Off Boogaloo/Blindman *Black paper with flat finish*	1972	3.75	7.50	15.00
☐ 1865		Photograph/Down and Out *Custom star label*	1973		3.00	6.00
☐ 1865	PS	Photograph/Down and Out	1973	5.00	10.00	20.00
☐ P-1865	DJ	Photograph (mono/stereo)	1973	12.50	25.00	50.00
☐ 1870		You're Sixteen/Devil Woman *Custom star label*	1973		3.00	6.00
☐ 1870		You're Sixteen/Devil Woman *Regular Apple label*	1973	6.25	12.50	25.00
☐ 1870	PS	You're Sixteen/Devil Woman	1973	6.25	12.50	25.00
☐ P-1870	DJ	You're Sixteen (mono/stereo)	1973	12.50	25.00	50.00
☐ 1871		Oh My My/Step Lightly *Custom star label*	1974		3.00	6.00
☐ 1871		Oh My My/Step Lightly *Regular Apple label*	1974	2.00	4.00	8.00
☐ P-1871	DJ	Oh My My (Edited Mono)/Oh My My (Long Stereo)	1974	12.50	25.00	50.00
☐ 1876		Only You/Call Me *Custom nebula label*	1974		3.00	6.00
☐ 1876X		Only You/Call Me *Regular Apple label*	1974	2.00	4.00	8.00
☐ 1876	PS	Only You/Call Me	1974	5.00	10.00	20.00
☐ P-1876	DJ	Only You (mono/stereo)	1974	10.00	20.00	40.00
☐ 1880		No No Song/Snookeroo *Custom nebula label*	1975		3.00	6.00
☐ P-1880	DJ	No No Song/Snookeroo (both stereo)	1975	10.00	20.00	40.00
☐ P-1880	DJ	No No Song/Snookeroo (both mono)	1975	10.00	20.00	40.00
☐ 1882		It's All Down to Goodnight Vienna/Oo-Wee *Custom nebula label*	1975		3.00	6.00
☐ 1882	PS	It's All Down to Goodnight Vienna/Oo-Wee	1975	5.00	10.00	20.00
☐ P-1882	DJ	It's All Down to Goodnight Vienna (mono/stereo)	1975	10.00	20.00	40.00
☐ P-1882	DJ	Oo-Wee (mono/stereo)	1975	17.50	35.00	70.00

Number		Title (A Side/B Side)	Year	VG	VG+	NM
❏ 2969		Beaucoups of Blues/Coochy-Coochy	1970	6.25	12.50	25.00
		With small Capitol logo on bottom of B-side label and star on A-side label				
❏ 2969		Beaucoups of Blues/Coochy-Coochy	1970	10.00	20.00	40.00
		With "Mfd. by Apple" on label and star on A-side label				
❏ 2969		Beaucoups of Blues/Coochy-Coochy	1970	2.00	4.00	8.00
		With "Mfd. by Apple" on label and no star on A-side label				
❏ 2969	PS	Beaucoups of Blues/Coochy-Coochy	1970	12.50	25.00	50.00
		Sleeve with correct catalog number				

Atlantic

Number		Title (A Side/B Side)	Year	VG	VG+	NM
❏ 3361		A Dose of Rock 'N' Roll/Cryin'	1976	2.50	5.00	10.00
❏ 3371		Hey Baby/Lady Gaye	1976	7.50	15.00	30.00
❏ 3412		Drowning in the Sea of Love/Just a Dream	1977	30.00	60.00	120.00
❏ 3429		Wings/Just a Dream	1977	7.50	15.00	30.00

Boardwalk

Number		Title (A Side/B Side)	Year	VG	VG+	NM
❏ NB7-11-130		Wrack My Brain/Drumming Is My Madness	1981		2.50	5.00
❏ NB7-11-130	PS	Wrack My Brain/Drumming Is My Madness	1981		2.50	5.00
❏ NB7-11-134		Private Property/	1982	3.00	6.00	12.00
		Stop and Take the Time to Smell the Roses				

Capitol

Number		Title (A Side/B Side)	Year	VG	VG+	NM
❏ 1831		It Don't Come Easy/Early 1970	1976	6.25	12.50	25.00
		Orange label				
❏ 1831		It Don't Come Easy/Early 1970	1978		3.00	6.00
		Purple late-1970s label				
❏ 1831		It Don't Come Easy/Early 1970	1983		3.00	6.00
		Black colorband label				
❏ 1831		It Don't Come Easy/Early 1970	1988		2.50	5.00
		Purple late-1980s label (wider)				
❏ 1849		Back Off Boogaloo/Blindman	1976	7.50	15.00	30.00
		Orange label				
❏ 1849		Back Off Boogaloo/Blindman	1978	2.00	4.00	8.00
		Purple late-1970s label				
❏ 1865		Photograph/Down and Out	1978	2.00	4.00	8.00
		Purple late-1970s label				
❏ 1865		Photograph/Down and Out	1983	2.00	4.00	8.00
		Black colorband label				
❏ 1865		Photograph/Down and Out	1988		3.00	6.00
		Purple late-1980s label (wider)				
❏ 1870		You're Sixteen/Devil Woman	1976	15.00	30.00	60.00
		Orange label				
❏ 1870		You're Sixteen/Devil Woman	1978	2.00	4.00	8.00
		Purple late-1970s label				
❏ 1870		You're Sixteen/Devil Woman	1983	2.00	4.00	8.00
		Black colorband label				
❏ 1870		You're Sixteen/Devil Woman	1988		2.50	5.00
		Purple late-1980s label (wider)				
❏ 1876		Only You/Call Me	1978	2.00	4.00	8.00
		Purple late-1970s label				
❏ 1876		Only You/Call Me	1983	25.00	50.00	100.00
		Black colorband label				
❏ 1880		No No Song/Snookeroo	1978	2.00	4.00	8.00
		Purple late-1970s label				
❏ 1880		No No Song/Snookeroo	1983	2.00	4.00	8.00
		Black colorband label				
❏ 1880		No No Song/Snookeroo	1988	7.50	15.00	30.00
		Purple late-1980s label (wider)				
❏ 1882		It's All Down to Goodnight Vienna/Oo-Wee	1978	2.00	4.00	8.00
		Purple late-1970s label				
❏ 2969		Beaucoups of Blues/Coochy-Coochy	1976	10.00	20.00	40.00
		Orange label				
❏ B-44409		Act Naturally/Key's in the Mailbox	1989	3.75	7.50	15.00
		A-side with Buck Owens; B-side is Owens solo				

Portrait

Number		Title (A Side/B Side)	Year	VG	VG+	NM
❏ 70015		Lipstick Traces (On a Cigarette)/Old Time Relovin'	1978	3.75	7.50	15.00
❏ 70018		Heart on My Sleeve/Who Needs a Heart	1978	3.75	7.50	15.00

The Right Stuff

Number		Title (A Side/B Side)	Year	VG	VG+	NM
❏ S7-18178		In My Car/She's About a Mover	1994		3.00	6.00
		Gold/orange vinyl				
❏ S7-18179		Wrack My Brain/Private Property	1994		3.00	6.00
		Red vinyl				

Starr, Sally

(With Bill Haley and the Comets helping out)

Arcade

Number	Title (A Side/B Side)	Year	VG	VG+	NM
❏ 157	Rocky the Rockin' Rabbit/Sing a Song of Happiness	1960	7.50	15.00	30.00

Clymax

Number	Title (A Side/B Side)	Year	VG	VG+	NM
❏ 301	Rockin' in the Nursery/(B-side unknown)	1959	10.00	20.00	40.00

Starship

(Jefferson Starship without Paul Kantner)

Elektra

Number	Title (A Side/B Side)	Year	VG	VG+	NM
❏ 69349	Wild Again/Laying It on the Line	1988			3.00

Number		Title (A Side/B Side)	Year	VG	VG+	NM
Grunt						
❏ 5109-7-R		Nothing's Gonna Stop Us Now/Layin' It on the Line	1987			3.00
❏ 5109-7-R	PS	Nothing's Gonna Stop Us Now/Layin' It on the Line	1987			3.00
❏ 5225-7-R		It's Not Over ('Til It's Over)/Babylon	1987			3.00
❏ 5225-7-R	PS	It's Not Over ('Til It's Over)/Babylon	1987			3.00
❏ 5308-7-R		Beat Patrol/Girls Like You	1987			3.00
❏ 5308-7-R	PS	Beat Patrol/Girls Like You	1987			3.00
❏ JK-14170	DJ	We Built This City (Short)/We Built This City (Long)	1985	2.00	4.00	8.00
❏ PB-14170		We Built This City/Private Room	1985			3.00
❏ PB-14170	PS	We Built This City/Private Room	1985		2.50	5.00
❏ JB-14200	DJ	We Built This City (Special Non-DJ Rock Radio Version)/We Built This City	1985	2.50	5.00	10.00
❏ PB-14253		Sara/Hearts of the World (Will Understand)	1985			3.00
❏ PB-14253		Sara/Hearts of the World (Will Understand)	1985	2.00	4.00	8.00
		Originals on blue vinyl				
❏ PB-14253	PS	Sara/Hearts of the World (Will Understand)	1985		2.50	5.00
❏ PB-14332		Tomorrow Doesn't Matter Tonight/Love Rusts	1986			3.00
❏ PB-14332	PS	Tomorrow Doesn't Matter Tonight/Love Rusts	1986	12.50	25.00	50.00
❏ PB-14393		Before I Go/Cut You Down to Size	1986			3.00
❏ PB-14393	PS	Before I Go/Cut You Down to Size	1986		2.50	5.00
Lion						
❏ 132		Johnny B. Goode/It's Amazing to Me	1973	6.25	12.50	25.00
		No relation to the other Starship, this features Micky Dolenz, ex-Monkees				
RCA						
❏ 6964-7-R		Set the Night to Music/I Don't Know Why	1988		2.00	4.00
❏ 8377-7-R		Nothing's Gonna Stop Us Now/Beat Patrol	1988			3.00
Gold Standard Series						
❏ 9032-7-R		It's Not Enough/Love Among the Cannibals	1989			3.00
❏ 9032-7-R	PS	It's Not Enough/Love Among the Cannibals	1989			3.00
Starz						
Capitol						
❏ 4343		Monkey Business/(She's Just A) Fallen Angel	1976		2.50	5.00
❏ 4343	PS	Monkey Business/(She's Just A) Fallen Angel	1976		3.50	7.00
❏ 4399		Cherry Baby/Rock Six Times	1977	3.00	6.00	12.00
		Originals on yellow vinyl				
❏ 4399		Cherry Baby/Rock Six Times	1977		2.00	4.00
❏ 4399	PS	Cherry Baby/Rock Six Times	1977		3.00	6.00
❏ 4434		Sing It, Shout It/Subway Terror	1977	3.00	6.00	12.00
		Originals on yellow vinyl				
❏ 4434		Sing It, Shout It/Subway Terror	1977		2.00	4.00
❏ 4434	PS	Sing It, Shout It/Subway Terror	1977		3.00	6.00
❏ 4546		(Any Way That You Want It) I'll Be There/Texas	1978		2.00	4.00
❏ 4546	PS	(Any Way That You Want It) I'll Be There/Texas	1978		2.50	5.00
❏ 4566		Hold On to the Night/Texas	1978		2.00	4.00
❏ 4637		So Young, So Bad/Coliseum Rock	1978		2.00	4.00
❏ 4637	PS	So Young, So Bad/Coliseum Rock	1978		2.50	5.00
❏ 4671		Last Night I Wrote a Letter/Coliseum Rock	1979		2.00	4.00
Statens, The						
Mark-X						
❏ 8011		Summertime Is the Time for Love/That Certain Kind	1961	20.00	40.00	80.00
Statlers, The						
Little Star						
❏ 108		Vicky/Gone	1962	37.50	75.00	150.00
Statues, The						
Liberty						
❏ 55245		Blue Velvet/Keep the Hall Light Burning	1959	5.00	10.00	20.00
❏ 55292		White Christmas/Jeannie with the Light Brown Hair	1960	6.25	12.50	25.00
❏ 55363		Ten Commandments of Love/Love at First Sight	1961	5.00	10.00	20.00
Status Quo						
A&M						
❏ 1425		Don't Waste My Time/All the Reasons	1973		2.50	5.00
❏ 1445		Paper Plane/All the Reasons	1973		2.50	5.00
❏ 1510		Carolina/Softer Ride	1974		2.50	5.00
Bell						
❏ 45,417		Gerdundula/(B-side unknown)	1973		2.50	5.00
Cadet Concept						
❏ 7001		Pictures of Matchstick Men/ Gentleman Jim's Sidewalk Cafe	1968	2.50	5.00	10.00
❏ 7006		Ice in the Sun/When My Mind Is Not Live	1968	2.00	4.00	8.00
❏ 7010		Technicolor Dreams/Spicks and Specks	1969	2.00	4.00	8.00
❏ 7015		Black Veils of Melancholy/To Be Free	1969	2.00	4.00	8.00
❏ 7017		The Price of Love/Little Miss Nothing	1969	2.00	4.00	8.00
Capitol						
❏ 4039		Nightride/Down Down	1975		2.00	4.00
❏ 4125		Bye Bye Johnny/Down Down	1975		2.00	4.00
❏ 4407		Wild Side of Life/All Through the Night	1977		2.00	4.00
Janus						
❏ 127		Down the Dustpipe/Face Without a Soul	1970		3.00	6.00
❏ 141		Gerdundula/In My Chair	1970		3.00	6.00

Number		Title (A Side/B Side)	Year	VG	VG+	NM
Pye						
☐ 65000		Good Thinking/Tuned to the Music	1971		3.00	6.00
☐ 65017		Mean Girl/Everything	1971		3.00	6.00
Riva						
☐ 206		Living on an Island/(B-side unknown)	1980		2.50	5.00
Stealers Wheel						
(With Gerry Rafferty)						
A&M						
☐ 1416		Stuck in the Middle with You/Jose	1973		2.50	5.00
☐ 1450		Everyone's Agreed That Everything Will Turn Out Fine/Next to Me	1973		2.00	4.00
☐ 1483		Star/What More Could You Want	1973		2.00	4.00
☐ 1483	PS	Star/What More Could You Want	1973		3.00	6.00
☐ 1529		You Put Something Better Inside of Me/Wheelin'	1974		2.00	4.00
☐ 1675		This Morning/Found My Way to You	1975		2.00	4.00
☐ 2075		(Everyone's Agreed That) Everything Will Turn Out Fine/Who Cares	1978		2.50	5.00
Steam						
Fontana						
☐ 1667		Na Na Hey Hey Kiss Him Goodbye/ It's the Magic in You Girl	1969	2.00	4.00	8.00
Mercury						
☐ 30160		Na Na Hey Hey Kiss Him Goodbye/ Don't Stop Lovin' Me	1976		2.00	4.00
		Reissue				
☐ 30160	PS	Na Na Hey Hey Kiss Him Goodbye/ Don't Stop Lovin' Me	1976	5.00	10.00	20.00
		Special Chicago White Sox sleeve, available only in that area				
☐ 73020		I've Gotta Make You Love Me/One Good Woman	1970		3.00	6.00
☐ 73053		What I'm Saying Is True/I'm the One Who Loves You	1970		3.00	6.00
☐ 73117		Don't Stop Lovin' Me/Do Unto Others	1970		3.00	6.00
Steely Dan						
ABC						
☐ 11323		Dallas/Sail the Waterway	1972	6.25	12.50	25.00
		Neither of these songs has appeared on a U.S. Steely Dan album				
☐ 11338		Do It Again/Fire in the Hole	1972		2.00	4.00
☐ 11352		Reeling In the Years/Only a Fool Would Say That	1973		2.00	4.00
☐ 11382		Show Biz Kids/Razor Boy	1973		2.00	4.00
☐ 11396		My Old School/Pearl of the Quarter	1973		2.00	4.00
☐ 11439		Rikki Don't Lose That Number/ Any Major Dude Will Tell You	1974		2.00	4.00
☐ 12014		Rikki Don't Lose That Number/ Any Major Dude Will Tell You	1974		3.00	6.00
☐ 12033		Pretzel Logic/Through with Buzz	1974		2.00	4.00
☐ 12101		Black Friday/Throw Back the Little Ones	1975		2.00	4.00
☐ 12128		Chain Lightning/Bad Sneakers	1975		2.00	4.00
☐ 12195		Kid Charlemagne/Green Earrings	1976		2.00	4.00
☐ 12222		The Fez/Sign In Stranger	1976		2.00	4.00
☐ 12320		Peg/I Got the News	1977		2.00	4.00
☐ 12355		Deacon Blues/Home at Last	1978		2.00	4.00
☐ 12404		Josie/Black Cow	1978		2.00	4.00
MCA						
☐ 40894		FM (No Static at All)/(Instrumental)	1978		2.00	4.00
☐ 51036		Hey Nineteen/Bodhisattva	1980		2.00	4.00
☐ 51082		Time Out of Mind/Bodhisattva	1981		2.00	4.00
Stein, Frank N., and the Tombstones						
Marco						
☐ 003		Mess Around/Graveyard Giggle	1962	10.00	20.00	40.00
Stein, Frankie, and the Ghouls						
King						
☐ 6414		Franken Boogie/All She Wants to Do Is Boogie	1972	2.50	5.00	10.00
Power						
☐ 338		Goon River/Weerdo the Wolf	1964	6.25	12.50	25.00
☐ 338	PS	Goon River/Weerdo the Wolf	1964	7.50	15.00	30.00
Steppenwolf						
(Also see "Sparrow, The")						
ABC						
☐ 1436		The Pusher/Born to Be Wild	1970		2.00	4.00
		"Goldies 45" series				
☐ 1436	PS	The Pusher/Born to Be Wild	1970		3.00	6.00
ABC Dunhill						
☐ 4138		Born to Be Wild/Everybody's Next One	1968	2.00	4.00	8.00
☐ 4161		Magic Carpet Ride/Sookie Sookie	1968	2.00	4.00	8.00
☐ 4182		Rock Me/Jupiter Child	1969	2.00	4.00	8.00
☐ 4192		It's Never Too Late/Happy Birthday	1969		3.00	6.00
☐ 4205		Move Over/Power Play	1969		3.00	6.00
☐ 4221		Monster/Berry Rides Again	1969		3.00	6.00
☐ 4234		Hey Lawdy Mama/Twisted	1970		3.00	6.00
☐ 4248		Screaming Night Hog/Spiritual Fantasy	1970		3.00	6.00

Number		Title (A Side/B Side)	Year	VG	VG+	NM
☐ 4261		Who Needs Ya/Earschplittenloudenboomer	1970		3.00	6.00
☐ 4269		Snow Blind Friend/Hippo Stomp	1971		2.50	5.00
☐ 4283		Ride with Me/Black Pit	1971		2.50	5.00
☐ 4283		Ride with Me/For Madmen Only	1971		2.50	5.00
☐ 4283	PS	Ride with Me/For Madmen Only	1971		3.00	6.00
☐ 4292		For Ladies Only/Sparkle Eyes	1971		2.50	5.00

Dunhill

Number		Title (A Side/B Side)	Year	VG	VG+	NM
☐ 4109		The Ostrich/A Girl I Know	1967	2.50	5.00	10.00
☐ 4123		Sookie Sookie/Take What You Need	1968	2.50	5.00	10.00

Mums

Number		Title (A Side/B Side)	Year	VG	VG+	NM
☐ 6031		Straight Shootin' Woman/Justice, Don't Be Slow	1974		2.00	4.00
☐ 6031	PS	Straight Shootin' Woman/Justice, Don't Be Slow	1974		3.00	6.00
☐ 6034		Get Into the Wind/Morning Blue	1974		2.00	4.00
☐ 6036		Fool's Fantasy/Smokey Factory Blues	1975		2.00	4.00
☐ 6040		Caroline (Are You Ready for the Outlaw)/Angel Drawers	1975		2.00	4.00

Stevens, Cat

A&M

Number		Title (A Side/B Side)	Year	VG	VG+	NM
☐ 1211		Lady D'Arbanville/Time -- Fill My Eyes	1970		2.50	5.00
☐ 1231		Wild World/Miles from Nowhere	1970		2.50	5.00
☐ 1265		Moon Shadow/I Think I See the Light	1971		2.00	4.00
☐ 1265	PS	Moon Shadow/I Think I See the Light	1971		3.00	6.00
☐ 1291		Peace Train/Where Do the Children Play	1971		2.00	4.00
☐ 1291	PS	Peace Train/Where Do the Children Play	1971		3.00	6.00
☐ 1335		Morning Has Broken/I Want to Live in a Wigwam	1972		2.00	4.00
☐ 1335	PS	Morning Has Broken/I Want to Live in a Wigwam	1972		3.00	6.00
☐ 1396		Sitting/Crab Dance	1972		2.00	4.00
☐ 1396	PS	Sitting/Crab Dance	1972		3.00	6.00
☐ 1418		The Hurt/Silent Sunlight	1973		2.00	4.00
☐ 1418	PS	The Hurt/Silent Sunlight	1973		3.00	6.00
☐ 1503		Oh Very Young/100 I Dream	1974		2.00	4.00
☐ 1503	PS	Oh Very Young/100 I Dream	1974		3.00	6.00
☐ 1549		Another Saturday Night/Home in the Sky	1974			Unreleased?
☐ 1602		Another Saturday Night/Home in the Sky	1974		2.00	4.00
☐ 1602	PS	Another Saturday Night/Home in the Sky	1974		3.00	6.00
☐ 1645		Ready/I Think I See the Light	1974		2.00	4.00
☐ 1700		Two Fine People/Bad Penny	1975		2.00	4.00
☐ 1785		Banapple Gas/Ghost Town	1976		2.00	4.00
☐ 1924		(I Never Wanted) To Be a Star/Land O' Freelove and Goodbye	1977		2.00	4.00
☐ 1948		(Remember the Days of the) Old School Yard/Land O' Freelove and Goodbye	1977		2.00	4.00
☐ 1948	PS	(Remember the Days of the) Old School Yard/Land O' Freelove and Goodbye	1977		3.00	6.00
☐ 1971		Was Dog a Doughnut/Sweet Jamaica	1977		2.00	4.00
☐ 2109		Bad Brakes/Nascimento	1979		2.00	4.00
☐ 2126		Randy/Nascimento	1979		2.00	4.00
☐ 2683		If You Want to Sing Out, Sing Out/I Want to Live in a Wigwam	1984		2.00	4.00
☐ 2711	DJ	Father and Son (same on both sides)	1985	2.50	5.00	10.00
		No stock copies issued				

Deram

Number		Title (A Side/B Side)	Year	VG	VG+	NM
☐ 7501		I Love My Dog/Portobello Road	1966	2.50	5.00	10.00
☐ 7505		Matthew and Son/Granny	1967	2.50	5.00	10.00
☐ 7518		Kitty/The Blackness of the Night	1968	2.00	4.00	8.00
☐ 85006		I'm Gonna Get Me a Gun/School Is Out	1967	2.50	5.00	10.00
☐ 85015		Laughing Apple/Bad Night	1967	2.50	5.00	10.00
☐ 85079		Kitty/Where Are You	1972		3.00	6.00

Stevens, Dodie

Crystalette

Number		Title (A Side/B Side)	Year	VG	VG+	NM
☐ 724		Pink Shoe Laces/Coming of Age	1959	5.00	10.00	20.00
☐ 724	PS	Pink Shoe Laces/Coming of Age	1959	10.00	20.00	40.00
☐ 728		Yes-Sir-Ee/The Five Pennies	1959	5.00	10.00	20.00

Dolton

Number		Title (A Side/B Side)	Year	VG	VG+	NM
☐ 83		You Don't Have to Prove a Thing to Me/I Wore Out Our Record	1963	3.00	6.00	12.00
☐ 88		Sailor Boy/Does Goodnight Mean Goodbye	1964	3.00	6.00	12.00

Dot

Number		Title (A Side/B Side)	Year	VG	VG+	NM
☐ 15975		Miss Lonely Heart/Poor Butterfly	1959	5.00	10.00	20.00
☐ 16002		Steady Date/Mairzy Doats	1959	5.00	10.00	20.00
☐ 16067		Candy Store Blues/Gringo's Guitar	1960	3.75	7.50	15.00
☐ 16103		No/A Tisket, A Tasket	1960	3.75	7.50	15.00
☐ 16139		Am I Too Young/So Let's Dance	1960	5.00	10.00	20.00
☐ 16166		Merry Christmas Baby/Jingle Bells	1960	5.00	10.00	20.00
☐ 16167		Yes, I'm Lonesome Tonight/Too Young	1960	5.00	10.00	20.00
☐ 16200		I Fall to Pieces/Turn Around	1961	3.75	7.50	15.00
☐ 16259		Let Me Tell You About Johnny/You Are the Only One	1961	3.75	7.50	15.00
☐ 16279		The In-Between Years/Trade Winds	1961	3.75	7.50	15.00
☐ 16339		I Cried/Dancing on My Ceiling	1962	3.75	7.50	15.00
☐ 16389		Pink Shoelaces/Yes-Sir-Ee	1962	3.75	7.50	15.00

Imperial

Number		Title (A Side/B Side)	Year	VG	VG+	NM
☐ 5908		Don't Send Me No Roses/Daddy Could Get Me One of These	1963	3.75	7.50	15.00
☐ 5930		Hello Stranger/For a Little While	1963	3.75	7.50	15.00

Number		Title (A Side/B Side)	Year	VG	VG+	NM

Stevens, Mark, and the Charmers
Allison

Number		Title (A Side/B Side)	Year	VG	VG+	NM
❑ 921		Magic Rose/Come Back to My Heart	1962	15.00	30.00	60.00

Stevens, Neil
Brunswick

| ❑ 55095 | | More and More/What Could Be Better | 1958 | 7.50 | 15.00 | 30.00 |
| | | With the Dee-Vines | | | | |

Goldisc

| ❑ 3019 | | Ballad of Love/Tonight My Heart She Is Crying | 1961 | 5.00 | 10.00 | 20.00 |
| | | With the Temptations | | | | |

Gone

| ❑ 5067 | | Ballad of Love/Gambler's Game | 1959 | 12.50 | 25.00 | 50.00 |

Stevens, Ray
Barnaby

Number		Title (A Side/B Side)	Year	VG	VG+	NM
❑ 600		The Streak/You've Got the Music Inside	1974		2.50	5.00
		White label (not a promo)				
❑ 600		The Streak/You've Got the Music Inside	1974		2.00	4.00
		Multicolor label				
❑ 605		Moonlight Special/Just So Proud to Be Here	1974		2.00	4.00
❑ 610		Everybody Needs a Rainbow/Inside	1974		2.00	4.00
❑ 614		Misty/Sunshine	1975		2.00	4.00
❑ 616		Indian Love Call/Piece of Paradise	1975		2.00	4.00
❑ 618		Young Love/Deep Purple	1975		2.00	4.00
❑ 619		Lady of Spain/Mockingbird Hill	1976		2.00	4.00
❑ 2011		Everything Is Beautiful/A Brighter Day	1970		3.00	6.00
❑ 2016		America, Communicate with Me/ Monkey See, Monkey Do	1970		2.50	5.00
❑ 2021		Sunset Strip/Islands	1970		2.50	5.00
❑ 2024		Bridget the Midget (The Queen of the Blues)/ Night People	1970		2.50	5.00
❑ 2024	PS	Bridget the Midget (The Queen of the Blues)/ Night People	1970	2.50	5.00	10.00
❑ 2029		A Mama and a Papa/Melt	1971		2.50	5.00
❑ 2039		All My Trials/Have a Little Talk with Myself	1971		2.50	5.00
❑ 2048		Turn Your Radio On/Loving You on Paper	1971		2.50	5.00
❑ 2058		Love Lifted Me/Glory Special	1972		2.50	5.00
❑ 2058		Love Lifted Me/Monkey See, Monkey Do	1972		2.50	5.00
❑ 2065		Losing Streak/Inside	1972		2.50	5.00
❑ 5020		Golden Age/Nashville	1973		2.00	4.00
❑ 5028		Love Me Longer/Float	1973		2.00	4.00

Capitol

❑ F3967		Chickie Chickie Wah Wah/Crying Goodbye	1958	6.25	12.50	25.00
❑ F4030		Cat Pants/Love Goes On Forever	1958	7.50	15.00	30.00
❑ F4101		The School/The Clown	1958	6.25	12.50	25.00
❑ 7PRO-79430	DJ	Help Me Make It Through the Night (same on both sides)	1991		2.50	5.00
		Vinyl is promo only				

MCA

❑ 52451		Joggin'/I'm Kissin' You Goodbye	1984		2.00	4.00
❑ 52492		Mississippi Squirrel Revival/Red Nostril	1984		2.00	4.00
❑ 52548		It's Me Again, Margaret/Joggin'	1985			3.00
❑ 52657		The Haircut Song/Punk Country Love	1985			3.00
❑ 52738		Santa Claus Is Watchin' You/Armchair Quarterback	1985		2.00	4.00
❑ 52771		Vacation Bible School/The Ballad of the Blue Cyclone	1986			3.00
❑ 52906		The Camping Trip/Southern Air	1986			3.00
❑ 52924		People's Court/Dudley Doright (Of the Highway Patrol)	1986			3.00
❑ 53007		Can He Love You Half As Much As I Do/ Dudley Doright (Of the Highway Patrol)	1987			3.00
❑ 53101		Would Jesus Wear a Rolex?/Cool Down Willard	1987		2.00	4.00
❑ 53178		Three-Legged Man/Doctor, Doctor (Have Mercy on Me)	1987			3.00
❑ 53232		Sex Symbols/The Ballad of Cactus Pete and Lefty	1987			3.00
❑ 53372		Surfin' U.S.S.R./Language, Nudity, Violence & Sex	1988			3.00
❑ 53423		The Day I Tried to Teach Charlene MacKenzie How to Drive/I Don't Need None of That	1988			3.00
❑ 53661		I Saw Elvis in a U.F.O./I Used to Be Crazy	1989	2.50	5.00	10.00

Mercury

❑ 71843		Jeremiah Peabody's Poly Unsaturated Quick Dissolving Fast Acting Pleasant Tasting Green and Purple Pills/Teen Years	1961	3.75	7.50	15.00
❑ 71843	PS	Jeremiah Peabody's Poly Unsaturated Quick Dissolving Fast Acting Pleasant Tasting Green and Purple Pills/Teen Years	1961	6.25	12.50	25.00
❑ 71888		Scratch My Back/When You Wish Upon a Star	1961	3.75	7.50	15.00
❑ 71966		Ahab, the Arab/It's Been So Long	1962	3.75	7.50	15.00
❑ 71966	PS	Ahab, the Arab/It's Been So Long	1962	7.50	15.00	30.00
❑ 72039		Further More/Saturday Night at the Movies	1962	3.75	7.50	15.00
❑ 72058		Santa Claus Is Watching You/Loved and Lost	1962	3.75	7.50	15.00
❑ 72058	PS	Santa Claus Is Watching You/Loved and Lost	1962	6.25	12.50	25.00
❑ 72098		Funny Man/Just One of Life's Little Tragedies	1963	3.75	7.50	15.00
❑ 72125		Harry the Hairy Ape/Little Stone Statue	1963	3.75	7.50	15.00
❑ 72125	PS	Harry the Hairy Ape/Little Stone Statue	1963	6.25	12.50	25.00
❑ 72189		Speed Ball/It's Party Time	1963	3.75	7.50	15.00
❑ 72255		Butch Barbarian (Sure Footed Mountain Climber World Famous Yodeling Champion)/Don't Say Anything	1963	3.75	7.50	15.00

Number		Title (A Side/B Side)	Year	VG	VG+	NM
☐ 72307		Bubble Gum the Bubble Dancer/	1964	3.75	7.50	15.00
		Laughing Over My Grave				
☐ 72382		Rockin' Teenage Mummies/It Only Hurts When I Love	1965	5.00	10.00	20.00
☐ 72430		Mr. Baker the Undertaker/Old English Surfer	1965	5.00	10.00	20.00
☐ 72816		Funny Man/Just One of Life's Little Tragedies	1968	3.00	6.00	12.00
☐ 812 496-7		Piece of Paradise Called Tennessee/Mary Lou Nights	1983		2.00	4.00
☐ 812 906-7		My Dad/Game Show Love	1983		2.50	5.00
☐ 814196-7		Love Will Beat Your Brains Out/Game Show Love	1983		2.00	4.00
☐ 818 057-7		My Dad/Me	1984		2.00	4.00
Monument						
☐ 911		A-B-C/Party People	1966	2.50	5.00	10.00
☐ 927		Devil-May-Care/Make a Few Memories	1966	2.50	5.00	10.00
☐ 946		Freddy Feelgood (And His Funky Little	1966	2.50	5.00	10.00
		Five Piece Band)/There's One in Every Crowd				
☐ 1001		Mary, My Secretary/Answer Me, My Love	1967	2.00	4.00	8.00
☐ 1048		Unwind/For He's a Jolly Good Fellow	1968	2.00	4.00	8.00
☐ 1083		Mr. Businessman/Face the Music	1968	2.00	4.00	8.00
☐ 1099		Isn't It Lonely Together/The Great Escape	1968	2.00	4.00	8.00
☐ 1131		Gitarzan/Bagpipes-That's My Bag	1969	2.00	4.00	8.00
☐ 1150		Along Came Jones/Yakety Yak	1969	2.00	4.00	8.00
☐ 1163		Sunday Mornin' Comin' Down/The Minority	1969		3.00	6.00
☐ 1171		Have a Little Talk with Myself/Little Woman	1969		3.00	6.00
☐ 1187		I'll Be Your Baby Tonight/Fool on the Hill	1970		3.00	6.00
NRC						
☐ 031		High School Yearbook (Deck of Cards)/Truly True	1959	6.25	12.50	25.00
☐ 042		What Would I Do Without You/My Heart Cries for You	1959	6.25	12.50	25.00
☐ 057		Sergeant Preston of the Yukon/Who Do You Love	1960	6.25	12.50	25.00
☐ 063		Happy Blue Year/White Christmas	1960	6.25	12.50	25.00
Prep						
☐ 108		Rang Tang Ding Dong (I'm the Japanese Sandman)/	1957	6.25	12.50	25.00
		Silver Bracelet				
☐ 122		Five More Steps/Tingle	1957	6.25	12.50	25.00
RCA						
☐ GB-12368		Everything Is Beautiful/Gitarzan	1981			3.00
	Gold Standard Series					
☐ GB-12370		Shriner's Convention/	1981			3.00
		You're Never Goin' to Tampa with Me				
	Gold Standard Series					
☐ PB-11911		Shriner's Convention/	1980			
		You're Never Goin' to Tampa With Me				
☐ PB-12069		Night Games/Let's Do It Right This Time	1980			
☐ PB-12170		One More Last Chance/I Believe You Love Me	1981			
☐ PB-12185		The Streak/Misty	1981			
☐						
☐ PB-13038		Written Down in My Heart/	1981			
		Country Boy, Country Club Girl				
☐ PB-13207		Where the Sun Don't Shine/	1982			
		Why Don't We Go Somewhere and Love				
Warner Bros.						
☐ 8198		You Are So Beautiful/One Man Band	1976		2.00	4.00
☐ 8237		Honky Tonk Waltz/Om	1976		2.00	4.00
☐ 8301		In the Mood/Classical Cluck	1976		3.00	6.00
	As "Henhouse Five Plus Too"					
☐ 8318		Get Crazy with Me/Dixie Hummingbird	1977		2.00	4.00
☐ 8393		Dixie Hummingbird/Feel the Music	1977		2.00	4.00
☐ 8603		Be Your Own Best Friend/With a Smile	1978		2.00	4.00
☐ 8785		I Need Your Help Barry Manilow/Daydream Romance	1979		2.00	4.00
☐ 8785	PS	I Need Your Help Barry Manilow/Daydream Romance	1979		3.00	6.00
☐ 8849		The Feeling's Not Right Again/Get Crazy with Me	1979		2.00	4.00

Stewart Brothers, The
(With Sylvester Stewart, later of Sly and the Family Stone)

Number		Title (A Side/B Side)	Year	VG	VG+	NM
Ensign						
☐ 4032		The Rat/Ra Ra Roo	1959	25.00	50.00	100.00
Keen						
☐ 2113		Sleep on the Porch/Yum Yum	1960	25.00	50.00	100.00

Stewart, Billy

Number		Title (A Side/B Side)	Year	VG	VG+	NM
Argo						
☐ 5256		Billy's Blues (Part 1)/Billy's Blues (Part 2)	1956	10.00	20.00	40.00
Chess						
☐ 1625		Billy's Blues (Part 1)/Billy's Blues (Part 2)	1956	15.00	30.00	60.00
☐ 1820		Reap What You Sow/Fat Boy	1962	3.00	6.00	12.00
☐ 1835		True Fine Lovin'/Wedding Bells	1962	3.00	6.00	12.00
☐ 1852		Scramble/Oh What Can the Matter Be	1963	3.00	6.00	12.00
☐ 1868		Strange Feeling/Sugar and Spice	1963	3.00	6.00	12.00
☐ 1888		Count Me Out/A Fat Boy Can Cry	1964	2.50	5.00	10.00
☐ 1905		Tell It Like It Is/My Sweet Senorita	1964	2.50	5.00	10.00
☐ 1922		I Do Love You/Keep Loving	1965	2.50	5.00	10.00
☐ 1932		Sitting in the Park/Once Again	1965	2.50	5.00	10.00
☐ 1941		How Nice It Is/No Girl	1965	2.50	5.00	10.00
☐ 1948		Because I Love You/Mountain of Love	1965	2.50	5.00	10.00
☐ 1960		Love Me/Why Am I Lonely	1966	2.50	5.00	10.00
☐ 1966		Summertime/To Love, To Love	1966	3.75	7.50	15.00
	Black label					

Number	Title (A Side/B Side)	Year	VG	VG+	NM
❑ 1966	Summertime/To Love, To Love	1966	3.00	6.00	12.00
	Blueish label				
❑ 1978	Secret Love/Look Back and Smile	1966	2.50	5.00	10.00
❑ 1991	Every Day I Have the Blues/Ol' Man River	1967	2.50	5.00	10.00
❑ 2002	Cross My Heart/Why (Do I Love You So)	1967	2.50	5.00	10.00
❑ 2053	Tell Me the Truth/What Have I Done	1968	2.50	5.00	10.00
❑ 2063	I'm in Love (Oh Yes I Am)/Crazy 'Bout You Baby	1969	2.50	5.00	10.00
❑ 2080	By the Time I Get to Phoenix/We'll Always Be Together	1969	2.50	5.00	10.00
Okeh					
❑ 7095	Baby, You're My Only Love/Billy's Heartache	1957	75.00	150.00	300.00
United Artists					
❑ 340	This Is a Fine Time/Young in Years	1961	3.75	7.50	15.00

Stewart, Danny

(Later known as Sylvester Stewart [Sly Stone])

Luke

Number	Title (A Side/B Side)	Year	VG	VG+	NM
❑ 1008	A Long Time Alone/I'm Just a Fool	1961	62.50	125.00	250.00

Stewart, John

(Ex-Kingston Trio)

Capitol

Number	Title (A Side/B Side)	Year	VG	VG+	NM
❑ 2469	Mother Country/Shackles and Chains	1969		3.00	6.00
❑ 2538	July, You're a Woman/She Believes in Me	1969		3.00	6.00
❑ 2605	Armstrong/Anna on a Memory	1969		3.00	6.00
❑ 2711	Earth Rider/The Lady and the Outlaw	1969		3.00	6.00
❑ 2712	World of No Return/Wild Is Love	1969		3.00	6.00
	B-side by Patti Drew				
❑ 2842	Clack Clack/Marshall Wind	1970		3.00	6.00
RCA Victor					
❑ 74-0970	Chilly Winds/Durango	1973		2.50	5.00
❑ APBO-0109	Anna on a Memory/Wheatfield	1973		2.50	5.00
❑ PB-10003	July, You're a Woman/Runaway Fool of Love	1974		2.50	5.00
❑ PB-10227	Survivors/Josie	1975		2.50	5.00
❑ PB-10268	Survivors/Josie	1975		2.50	5.00
RSO					
❑ 894	Promise the Wind/Morning Thunder	1978		2.00	4.00
❑ 931	Gold/Comin' Out of Nowhere	1979		2.00	4.00
❑ 1000	Midnight Wind/Somewhere Down the Line	1979		2.00	4.00
❑ 1016	Lost Her in the Sun/Heart of the Dream	1979		2.00	4.00
❑ 1031	(Odin) Spirit of the Water/Love Has Tied My Wings	1980		2.00	4.00
Vita					
❑ 169	Rockin' Anna/Lorraine	1958	62.50	125.00	250.00
	As "Johnny Stewart"				
Warner Bros.					
❑ 7525	Daydream Believer/Sweet Lizard	1971		2.50	5.00
❑ 7552	Light Come Shine/A Little Road and a Stone to Roll	1972		2.50	5.00
❑ 7592	An Accent of Halley's Comet/Arkansas Breakout	1972		2.50	5.00

Stewart, Rod

(Also see "Beck, Jeff, Group"; "Python Lee Jackson"; "Small Faces")

Geffen

Number		Title (A Side/B Side)	Year	VG	VG+	NM
❑ 28303		Twistin' the Night Away/Let's Get Small	1987		2.00	4.00
		B-side by Steve Martin				
❑ 28303	PS	Twistin' the Night Away/Let's Get Small	1987		2.00	4.00
Mercury						
❑ 73009		Handbags and Gladrags/ An Old Raincoat Won't Ever Let You Down	1970	2.50	5.00	10.00
❑ 73031		Handbags and Gladrags/Man of Constant Sorrow	1970	2.00	4.00	8.00
❑ 73095		It's All Over Now/Joe's Lament	1970	2.50	5.00	10.00
❑ 73115		Only a Hero/Gasoline Alley	1970		5.00	10.00
❑ 73156		Cut Across Shorty/Gasoline Alley	1970	2.50	5.00	10.00
❑ 73175		My Way of Giving/Lady Day	1971		3.00	6.00
❑ 73196		Country Comfort/Gasoline Alley	1971		3.00	6.00
❑ 73224		Maggie May/Reason to Believe	1971		3.00	6.00
❑ 73244		(I Know) I'm Losing You/Mandolin Wind	1971		2.50	5.00
❑ 73330		You Wear It Well/True Blue	1972		2.50	5.00
❑ 73330	PS	You Wear It Well/True Blue	1972	3.75	7.50	15.00
❑ 73344		Angel/Lost Paraguayos	1972		2.50	5.00
❑ 73412		Twistin' the Night Away//True Blue-Lady Day	1973		2.50	5.00
❑ 73412	PS	Twistin' the Night Away//True Blue-Lady Day	1973		3.00	6.00
❑ 73426		Oh No Not My Baby/Jodie	1973		2.50	5.00
❑ 73426	PS	Oh No Not My Baby/Jodie	1973		3.00	6.00
❑ 73636		Mine for Me/Farewell	1974		2.50	5.00
❑ 73660		Sailing/Let Me Be Your Car	1974		3.00	6.00
❑ 73802		Every Picture Tells a Story/ What's Made Milwaukee Famous (Has Made a Loser Out of Me)	1976		2.50	5.00
Private Stock						
❑ 45,130		Shake/Bright Lights, Big City	1976		3.00	6.00
Warner Bros.						
❑ 8066		As Long As You Tell Him/ You Can Make Me Dance, Sing or Anything	1975		2.50	5.00
		As "Rod Stewart and Faces"				

Number		Title (A Side/B Side)	Year	VG	VG+	NM
❏ 8102		As Long As You Tell Him/	1975		2.00	4.00
		You Can Make Me Dance, Sing or Anything				
		As "Rod Stewart and Faces"				
❏ 8146		Sailing/All in the Name of Rock and Roll	1975		2.00	4.00
❏ 8262		Tonight's the Night (Gonna Be Alright)/Fool for You	1976		2.00	4.00
❏ 8321		The First Cut Is the Deepest/Ball Trap	1977		2.00	4.00
❏ 8396		The Killing of Georgie (Part 1 and 2)/Rosie	1977		2.00	4.00
❏ 8475		You're In My Heart (The Final Acclaim)/	1977		2.00	4.00
		You Got a Nerve				
❏ 8535		Hot Legs/You're Insane	1978		2.00	4.00
❏ 8535	PS	Hot Legs/You're Insane	1978		2.50	5.00
❏ 8568		I Was Only Joking/Born Loose	1978		2.00	4.00
❏ 8568	PS	I Was Only Joking/Born Loose	1978		2.50	5.00
❏ 8724		Da Ya Think I'm Sexy?/Scarred and Scared	1978		2.00	4.00
❏ 8724	PS	Da Ya Think I'm Sexy?/Scarred and Scared	1978		2.50	5.00
❏ 8810		Ain't Love a Bitch/Last Summer	1979		2.00	4.00
❏ 8810	PS	Ain't Love a Bitch/Last Summer	1979		2.50	5.00
❏ 17459		If We Fall in Love Tonight/	1996			3.00
		Tom Traubert's Blues (Waltzing Matilda)				
❏ 17847		Leave Virginia Alone/Shock to the System	1995			3.00
❏ 17854		This/The Groom's Still Waiting at the Altar	1995			3.00
❏ 18424		Having a Party/Sweet Little Rock and Roller	1993			3.00
❏ 18427		Reason to Believe/It's All Over Now	1993		2.00	4.00
❏ 18511		Have I Told You Lately/Gasoline Alley	1993			3.00
Note: Warner Bros. 19274 does not exist on 45						
❏ 19322		The Motown Song/Sweet Soul Marie	1991			3.00
❏ 19366		Rhythm of My Heart/Moment of Glory	1991			3.00
❏ 19983		This Old Heart of Mine/You're In My Heart	1990			3.00
❏ 22685		Downtown Train/The Killing of Georgie (Part 1 and 2)	1989		3.00	6.00
❏ 22685	PS	Downtown Train/The Killing of Georgie (Part 1 and 2)	1989			3.00
❏ 27657		Crazy About Her/Dynamite	1989			3.00
❏ 27729		My Heart Can't Tell You No/The Wild Horse	1988			3.00
❏ 27729	PS	My Heart Can't Tell You No/The Wild Horse	1988			3.00
❏ 27796		Forever Young/Days of Rage	1988			3.00
❏ 27796	PS	Forever Young/Days of Rage	1988			3.00
❏ 27927		Lost in You/Almost Illegal	1988			3.00
❏ 27927	PS	Lost in You/Almost Illegal	1988			3.00
❏ 28625		Every Beat of My Heart/Trouble	1986			3.00
❏ 28625	PS	Every Beat of My Heart/Trouble	1986			3.00
❏ 28631		Another Heartache/	1986			3.00
		You're In My Heart (The Final Acclaim)				
❏ 28631	PS	Another Heartache/	1986			3.00
		You're In My Heart (The Final Acclaim)				
❏ 28668		Love Touch (Love Theme from Legal Eagles)/	1986			3.00
		Heart Is on the Line				
❏ 28668	PS	Love Touch (Love Theme from Legal Eagles)/	1986			3.00
		Heart Is on the Line				
❏ 29122		All Right Now/Dancin' Alone	1984		2.00	4.00
❏ 29215		Some Guys Have All the Luck/I Was Only Joking	1984		2.00	4.00
❏ 29215	PS	Some Guys Have All the Luck/I Was Only Joking	1984		2.00	4.00
❏ 29256		Infatuation/She Won't Dance with Me	1984		2.00	4.00
❏ 29256	PS	Infatuation/She Won't Dance with Me	1984		2.00	4.00
❏ 29564		What Am I Gonna Do (I'm So in Love with You)/	1983			
		Dancin' Alone			2.00	4.00
❏ 29564	PS	What Am I Gonna Do (I'm So in Love with You)/	1983			
		Dancin' Alone			2.00	4.00
❏ 29608		Baby Jane/Ready Now	1983		2.00	4.00
❏ 29874		Guess I'll Always Love You/Rock My Plimsoul	1982		2.00	4.00
❏ 49138		I Don't Want to Talk About It/Best Days of My Life	1979		2.50	5.00
❏ 49138	PS	I Don't Want to Talk About It/Best Days of My Life	1979		2.00	4.00
❏ 49617		Passion/Better Off Dead	1980		2.50	5.00
❏ 49617	PS	Passion/Better Off Dead	1980		2.00	4.00
❏ 49686		Somebody Special/She Won't Dance with Me	1981		2.00	4.00
❏ 49843		Young Turks/Sonny	1981		2.50	5.00
❏ 49843	PS	Young Turks/Sonny	1981		2.00	4.00
❏ 49886		Tonight I'm Yours (Don't Hurt Me)/Tora, Tora, Tora	1981		2.50	5.00
❏ 49886	PS	Tonight I'm Yours (Don't Hurt Me)/Tora, Tora, Tora	1981		2.00	4.00
❏ 50051		How Long/Jealous	1982		2.50	5.00
❏ 50051	PS	How Long/Jealous	1982		2.50	5.00

Stewart, Sly
(Sylvester Stewart, later "Sly" of The Family Stone)
Autumn

Number		Title (A Side/B Side)	Year	VG	VG+	NM
❏ 3		I Just Learned How to Swim/Scat Swim	1964	5.00	10.00	20.00
❏ 14		Buttermilk/Buttermilk -- Part 2	1965	5.00	10.00	20.00
❏ 26		Temptation Walk/Temptation Walk -- Part 2	1966	5.00	10.00	20.00

G&P

Number		Title (A Side/B Side)	Year	VG	VG+	NM
❏ 901		Help Me With My Heart/A Long Time Away	1962	62.50	125.00	250.00
		As "Sylvester Stewart"				

Stillroven, The
August

Number		Title (A Side/B Side)	Year	VG	VG+	NM
❏ 101		Little Picture Playhouse/	1968	6.25	12.50	25.00
		Cast Thy Burden Upon the Stone				
❏ 102		Necessary Person/Have You Ever Seen Me	1968	6.25	12.50	25.00
❏ 102		Necessary Person/Come in the Morning	1968	25.00	50.00	100.00

Number		Title (A Side/B Side)	Year	VG	VG+	NM
Falcon						
❑ 69		Hey Joe/Sunny Day	1967	12.50	25.00	50.00
❑ 7296		She's Your Woman/I'm Not Your Steppin' Stone	1966	50.00	100.00	200.00
Roulette						
❑ 4748		Hey Joe/Sunny Day	1967	3.75	7.50	15.00

Stills, Stephen
(Of the Buffalo Springfield and Crosby, Stills and Nash [and Young])

Number		Title (A Side/B Side)	Year	VG	VG+	NM
Atlantic						
❑ 2778		Love the One You're With/To a Flame	1970		3.00	6.00
❑ 2790		Sit Yourself Down/We Are Not Helpless	1971		2.50	5.00
❑ 2806		Change Partners/Relaxing Town	1971		2.50	5.00
❑ 2806	PS	Change Partners/Relaxing Town	1971		3.00	6.00
❑ 2820		Marianne/Nothin' to Do But Today	1971		2.50	5.00
❑ 2876		It Doesn't Matter/Rock & Roll's Crazy Medley	1972		2.50	5.00
❑ 2888		Rock and Roll Crazies/Colorado	1972		2.50	5.00
		With Manassas				
❑ 2917		Down the Road/Guaguanco De Vero	1972		2.50	5.00
		With Manassas				
❑ 2959		So Many Times/Isn't It About Time	1973		2.50	5.00
❑ 89597		Only Love Can Break Your Heart/Love Again	1984		2.00	4.00
❑ 89611		Can't Let Go/Grey to Green	1984		2.00	4.00
		With Walter Finnegan				
❑ 89633		Stranger/No Hiding Place	1984		2.00	4.00
Columbia						
❑ 10179		Turn Back the Pages/Shuffle Just as Bad	1975		2.50	5.00
❑ 10369		Buyin' Time/Soldier	1976		2.50	5.00
❑ 10804		Lowdown/Can't Get No Booty	1978		2.50	5.00
❑ 10872		Thoroughfare Gap/Lowdown	1978		2.50	5.00

Stills-Young Band, The
(Stephen Stills and Neil Young)

Number		Title (A Side/B Side)	Year	VG	VG+	NM
Reprise						
❑ 1365		Long May You Run//12/8 Blues (All the Same)	1976		3.00	6.00
❑ 1378		Midnight on the Bay/Black Coral	1976		2.50	5.00

Sting
(Of the Police)

Number		Title (A Side/B Side)	Year	VG	VG+	NM
A&M						
❑ 1200		Englishman in New York/If You're There	1988			3.00
❑ 1200	PS	Englishman in New York/If You're There	1988			3.00
❑ 1211		Fragile/Gragilidad	1988			3.00
❑ 1242		They Dance Alone (Gueca Solo)/ They Dance Alone (Gueca Solo)	1988			3.00
❑ 1541		All This Time/I Miss You Kate	1991		2.00	4.00
❑ 2501		Spread a Little Happiness/Only You	1982		2.00	4.00
❑ 2738		If You Love Somebody Set Them Free/Another Day	1985			3.00
		Normal red and black label				
❑ 2738		If You Love Somebody Set Them Free/Another Day	1985		2.00	4.00
		Blue custom label				
❑ 2738	PS	If You Love Somebody Set Them Free/Another Day	1985			3.00
❑ 2765		If You Love Somebody Set Them Free/Another Day	1985		2.50	5.00
❑ 2765	PS	If You Love Somebody Set Them Free/Another Day	1985		2.50	5.00
❑ 2767		Fortress Around Your Heart/Consider Me Gone	1985			3.00
❑ 2767	PS	Fortress Around Your Heart/Consider Me Gone	1985			3.00
❑ 2787		Love Is the Seventh Wave/ The Dream of the Blue Turtles	1985			3.00
❑ 2787	PS	Love Is the Seventh Wave/ The Dream of the Blue Turtles	1985			3.00
❑ 2799		Russians/Gabriel's Message	1985			3.00
❑ 2799	PS	Russians/Gabriel's Message	1985			3.00
❑ 2983		We'll Be Together/Conversation with a Dog	1987			3.00
❑ 2983	PS	We'll Be Together/Conversation with a Dog	1987			3.00
❑ 2992		Be Still My Beating Heart/Ghost in the Strand	1987			3.00
❑ 2992	PS	Be Still My Beating Heart/Ghost in the Strand	1987			3.00
❑ 31458 0530 7		Shape of My Heart/If I Ever Lose My Faith in You	1994			3.00
❑ 31458 0838 7		When We Dance/Fields of Gold	1994			3.00
❑ 31458 1582 7		You Still Touch Me/Let Your Soul Be Your Pilot	1996			3.00
❑ 31458 1582 7	PS	You Still Touch Me/Let Your Soul Be Your Pilot	1996			2.00
❑ 31458 1982 7		I'm So Happy I Can't Stop Crying/ This Was Never Meant to Be	1996			3.00
❑ 8655		If You Love Somebody Set Them Free/ Fortress Around Your Heart	198?			3.00
		Reissue				
❑ 8656		Love Is the Seventh Wave/Russians	198?			3.00
		Reissue				
❑ 8722		All This Time/Be Still My Beating Heart	199?			3.00
		Reissue				
❑ 8723		The Soul Cages/Why Should I Cry for You?	199?			3.00
		Reissue series; first appearance on U.S. 45 for both sides				
❑ 8740		Shape of My Heart/If I Ever Lose My Faith in You	1996			3.00
		Reissue				

Number	Title (A Side/B Side)	Year	VG	VG+	NM

Stinit, Dane
Sun
| ❏ 402 | Always on the Go/
Don't Knock What You Don't Understand | 1966 | 3.75 | 7.50 | 15.00 |
| ❏ 405 | Sweet Country Girl/That Muddy Ole River | 1967 | 3.75 | 7.50 | 15.00 |

Stites, Gary
Carlton
❏ 508	Lonely for You/Shine That Ring	1959	5.00	10.00	20.00
❏ 516	A Girl Like You/Hey Little Girl	1959	5.00	10.00	20.00
❏ 521	Starry Eyed/Without Your Love	1959	5.00	10.00	20.00
❏ 525	Lawdy Miss Clawdy/Don't Wanna Say Goodbye	1960	5.00	10.00	20.00
❏ 529	Gloria Lee/Hey, Hey	1960	5.00	10.00	20.00
Epic
❏ 10064	Hurting/Thinking of You	1966	3.00	6.00	12.00
Madison
❏ 138	Young Love/Little Tear	1960	3.75	7.50	15.00
❏ 155	Honey Girl/Little Lonely One	1961	3.75	7.50	15.00
Mr. Peeke
❏ 122	You Doubted Me/Only a Fool Would Say	1962	3.75	7.50	15.00

Stompers, The
Gone
| ❏ 5120 | Stompin' Round the Christmas Tree/Forgive Me | 1961 | 37.50 | 75.00 | 150.00 |
Landa
| ❏ 684 | Foolish One/Surf Stompin' | 1962 | 6.25 | 12.50 | 25.00 |
| ❏ 684 | Foolish One/Quarter to Four Stomp | 1962 | 6.25 | 12.50 | 25.00 |
Mercury
| ❏ 72111 | Frump/Blacksmith Blues | 1963 | 3.75 | 7.50 | 15.00 |
| | *As "The Ski Stompers"* | | | | |
Souvenir
| ❏ 1003 | I Miss You So/Blue Moon of Kentucky | 1960 | 25.00 | 50.00 | 100.00 |

Stone Poneys
(With Linda Ronstadt)
Capitol
❏ 2004	Different Drum/I've Got to Know	1967	3.75	7.50	15.00
❏ 2110	Up to My Neck in High Muddy Water/Carnival Bear	1968	2.50	5.00	10.00
❏ 2110	PS Up to My Neck in High Muddy Water/Carnival Bear	1968	10.00	20.00	40.00
	By "Linda Ronstadt and the Stone Poneys"				
❏ 2195	Hobo (Mornin' Glory)/Some of Shelly's Blues	1968	2.50	5.00	10.00
❏ 5838	All the Beautiful Things/Sweet Summer Blue and Gold	1967	2.50	5.00	10.00
❏ 5910	One for One/Evergreen	1967	2.50	5.00	10.00
Sidewalk
❏ 937	So Fine/Everyone Has Their Own Ideas	1968	50.00	100.00	200.00

Stone, Jimmy
Cross Country
| ❏ 523 | Found/Mine | 1956 | 75.00 | 150.00 | 300.00 |
Gone
| ❏ 5001 | Found/Mine | 1957 | 50.00 | 100.00 | 200.00 |

Stone, Sly
(Of Sly and the Family Stone. Also see "Stewart, Sly")
A&M
❏ 2890	Eek-Ah-Bo-Static Automatic/Black Girls	1986			3.00
	B-side by Rae Dawn Chong				
❏ 2896	Love and Affection/Black Girls	1986			3.00
	A-side with Martha Davis; B-side by Rae Dawn Chong				
Epic
❏ 50794	Dance to the Music/Sing a Simple Song	1979		2.50	5.00

Stones, The
Solly
| ❏ 928 | She Said Yeah/Watch Me | 1966 | 6.25 | 12.50 | 25.00 |
| | *Reissued with group renamed "The Tracers"* | | | | |

Stoney and Meatloaf
Rare Earth
| ❏ 5027 | What You See Is What You Get/Lady Be Mine | 1971 | | 3.00 | 6.00 |
| ❏ 5033 | The Way You Do the Things You Do/
It Takes All Kinds of People | 1971 | | 3.00 | 6.00 |

Stooges, The – See "Iggy and the Stooges"

Stookey, Paul
(Of Peter, Paul and Mary)
Warner Bros.
❏ 7511	Wedding Song (There Is Love)/Give a Damn	1971		3.00	6.00
❏ 7602	Hey, Sad Sack/Sebastian	1972		2.50	5.00
❏ 7683	Funky Monkey (Part 1)/Blessed	1973		2.50	5.00
	As "Noel Paul Stookey"				

Number	Title (A Side/B Side)	Year	VG	VG+	NM

Stories
(With Michael Brown, ex-Left Banke)
Kama Sutra

☐ 545	I'm Coming Home/You Told Me	1972		2.00	4.00
☐ 558	Top of the City/Stepback	1972		2.00	4.00
☐ 566	Darling/Take Cover	1972		2.00	4.00
☐ 574	Love in Motion/Changes Have Begun	1973		2.00	4.00
☐ 577	Brother Louie/Changes Have Begun	1973		3.00	6.00
☐ 577	Brother Louie/What Comes After	1973		2.50	5.00
☐ 584	Mammy Blue/Travelling Underground	1973		2.00	4.00
☐ 588	Circles/If It Feels Good	1974		2.00	4.00
☐ 594	Another Love/Love Is In Motion	1974		2.00	4.00

Storm, Rory, and the Hurricanes
(The group that Ringo Starr drummed for before joining the Beatles)
Columbia

☐ 43018	I Can Tell/Next Stop	1964	6.25	12.50	25.00
	B-side by Faron's Flamingos				

Storm, Tom, and the Peps
Ge Ge

☐ 501	I Love You/That's the Way Love Is	1965	7.50	15.00	30.00

Storms, The
(Also see "Reynolds, Jody")
Sundown

☐ 114	Thunder/Tarantula	1959	12.50	25.00	50.00
	This was re-recorded on Indigo 127				

Storytellers, The
Capitol

☐ 5042	I Don't Want an Angel/Down in the Valley	1964	6.25	12.50	25.00

Dimension

☐ 1014	When Two People/Time Will Tell	1963	5.00	10.00	20.00

Ramarca

☐ 501	When Two People/Time Will Tell	1963	7.50	15.00	30.00

Stack

☐ 500	Hey Baby/You Played Me for a Fool	1959	50.00	100.00	200.00

Strangeloves, The
(Also see "Sheep, The")
Bang

☐ 501	I Want Candy/It's About My Baby	1965	3.75	7.50	15.00
☐ 508	Cara-Lin/(Roll On) Mississippi	1965	3.00	6.00	12.00
☐ 514	Night Time/Rhythm of Love	1965	3.00	6.00	12.00
☐ 524	Hand Jive/I Gotta Dance	1966	3.00	6.00	12.00
☐ 544	Just the Way You Are/Quarter to Three	1967	3.00	6.00	12.00

Sire

☐ 4102	I Wanna Do It/Honey Do	1968	2.50	5.00	10.00

Swan

☐ 4192	Love Love (That's All I Want from You)/I'm on Fire	1964	5.00	10.00	20.00

Strangers, The
(Several different groups)
Chattahoochie

☐ 710	Like a Stranger/Can't Get the Water from My Eye	1966	3.00	6.00	12.00

Checker

☐ 1010	Darlin'/Pa and Billie	1962	3.75	7.50	15.00

Choice

☐ 5	"Bart" Maverick/"Bret" Maverick	1960	5.00	10.00	20.00

Christy

☐ 107	We're in Love, We're in Love, We're in Love/Crab Louie	1959	7.50	15.00	30.00
☐ 108	J-U-D-Y/The Lord Will Welcome You	1959	6.25	12.50	25.00

Cuca

☐ 1172	Runaway/John Henry	1960	50.00	100.00	200.00

Jubilee

☐ 5514	Plan On Someone New/What's the Matter Baby	1965	3.00	6.00	12.00

King

☐ 4697	My Friends/I've Got Eyes	1954	75.00	150.00	300.00
☐ 4709	Blue Flowers/Beg and Steal	1954	100.00	200.00	400.00
☐ 4728	Hoping You'll Understand/Just Don't Care	1954	75.00	150.00	300.00
☐ 4745	Drop Down to My Place/Get It One More Time	1954	75.00	150.00	300.00
☐ 4766	How Long Must I Wait/Dreams Came True	1955	62.50	125.00	250.00
☐ 4821	Without a Friend/Think Again	1955	62.50	125.00	250.00
	Without "High Fidelity" on label (original)				
☐ 4821	Without a Friend/Think Again	1955	10.00	20.00	40.00
	With "High Fidelity" on label				

Liberty

☐ 55481	Toy Soldier/Loco	1962	5.00	10.00	20.00
☐ 55550	Card Shark/Mindreader	1963	5.00	10.00	20.00

Number		Title (A Side/B Side)	Year	VG	VG+	NM

Linda
| ❑ 118 | | Easy Livin'/Tell Me | 1965 | 7.50 | 15.00 | 30.00 |

MGM
| ❑ 11980 | | Strange Lady in Town/North Dakota | 1955 | 10.00 | 20.00 | 40.00 |

Titan
❑ 1701		The Caterpillar Crawl/Rockin' Rebel	1959	7.50	15.00	30.00
❑ 1702		Hill Stomp/A Lost Soul	1959	6.25	12.50	25.00
❑ 1704		Boogie Man/Young Maggie	1960	6.25	12.50	25.00
❑ 1711		Navajo/Dance of the Ants	1960	6.25	12.50	25.00

Warner Bros.
| ❑ 5438 | | Night Winds/These Are the Things I Love | 1964 | 5.00 | 10.00 | 20.00 |

Strawberry Alarm Clock

All American
| ❑ 373 | | Incense and Peppermints/The Birdman of Alcatrash | 1967 | 50.00 | 100.00 | 200.00 |

Uni
❑ 55018		Incense and Peppermints/The Birdman of Alcatrash	1967	3.00	6.00	12.00
❑ 55046		Tomorrow/Birds in My Tree	1967	2.50	5.00	10.00
❑ 55055		Pretty Song from Psych-Out/Sit with the Guru	1968	2.50	5.00	10.00
❑ 55076		Barefoot in Baltimore/Angry Young Man	1968	2.50	5.00	10.00
❑ 55093		Paxton's Back Street Carnival/Sea Shell	1968	2.50	5.00	10.00
❑ 55113		Stand By/Miss Attraction	1969	2.00	4.00	8.00
❑ 55125		Good Morning Starshine/Me and the Township	1969	2.00	4.00	8.00
❑ 55158		Desiree/Changes	1969	2.00	4.00	8.00
❑ 55185		Small Package/Starting Out the Day	1969	2.00	4.00	8.00
❑ 55190		I Climbed the Mountain/Three	1969	2.00	4.00	8.00
❑ 55218		California Day/Three	1970	5.00	10.00	20.00
❑ 55241		Girl from the City/Three	1970	5.00	10.00	20.00

Strawbs, The

A&M
❑ 944		Oh How She Changed/Or Am I Dreaming	1968		2.50	5.00
❑ 998		Poor Jimmy Wilson/The Man Who Called Himself Jesus	1968		2.50	5.00
❑ 1242	DJ	Where Is This Dream of Your Youth (mono/stereo)	1971		3.00	6.00
		No stock copies known				
❑ 1364		Heavy Disguise/Benedictus	1972		2.50	5.00
❑ 1419		Part of the Union/Tomorrow	1973		2.50	5.00
❑ 1451		Lay Down/The Winter and the Summer	1973		2.50	5.00
❑ 1476		Shine On Silver Sun/And Wherefore	1973		2.50	5.00
❑ 1519		Round and Round/The Heroine's Theme	1974		2.50	5.00
❑ 1687		Where Do You Go/Lemon Pie	1975		2.00	4.00
❑ 1747		Little Sleepy/Golden Salamander	1975		2.00	4.00

Arista
| ❑ 0327 | | I Don't Want to Talk About It/Words of Wisdom | 1978 | | 2.00 | 4.00 |

Oyster
❑ 702		I Only Want My Love to Grow on You/ (Wasting My Time) Thinking of You	1976		2.00	4.00
❑ 704		So Close and Yet So Far Away/(B-side unknown)	1977		2.00	4.00
❑ 705		Burning for Me/Heartbreaker	1977		2.00	4.00

Stray Cats

EMI America
❑ 8122		Stray Cat Strut/You Don't Believe Me	1982			3.00
❑ 8122	PS	Stray Cat Strut/You Don't Believe Me	1982		3.00	6.00
❑ 8132		Rock This Town/You Can't Hurry Love	1982			3.00
❑ 8132	PS	Rock This Town/You Can't Hurry Love	1982			3.00
❑ 8168		(She's) Sexy + 17/Lookin' Better Every Beer	1983			3.00
❑ 8168	PS	(She's) Sexy + 17/Lookin' Better Every Beer	1983			3.00
❑ 8169-1		(She's) Sexy + 17/Lookin' Better Every Beer	1983		2.50	5.00
		Paired with 8169-2				
❑ 8169-2		Cruisin'/Lucky Charm	1983		2.50	5.00
		Paired with 8169-1				
❑ 8169-1/2	PS	(She's) Sexy + 17/Lookin' Better Every Beer/Cruisin'/ Lucky Charm	1983		2.50	5.00
		Gatefold sleeve for two-record set				
❑ 8185		I Won't Stand In Your Way/ I Won't Stand In Your Way (Acapella Version)	1983			3.00
❑ 8194		Look at That Cadillac/Lucky Charm	1984			3.00
❑ 8194	PS	Look at That Cadillac/Lucky Charm	1984			3.00

Streamers, The

Dot
| ❑ 16648 | | Slip-Stream/Blue Mountain | 1964 | 7.50 | 15.00 | 30.00 |

Street Cleaners, The
(Yet another incarnation of P.F. Sloan and Steve Barri)

Amy
| ❑ 914 | | Garbage City/That's Cool, That's Trash | 1964 | 7.50 | 15.00 | 30.00 |

Streisand, Barbra
(Also see "Barbra and Neil")

Arista
| ❑ 0123 | | How Lucky Can You Get/More Than You Know | 1975 | | 3.00 | 6.00 |

Number		Title (A Side/B Side)	Year	VG	VG+	NM
Columbia						
❏ 02065		Promises/Make It Like a Memory	1981		2.00	4.00
❏ 02621		Comin' In and Out of Your Life/Lost Inside of You	1981		2.00	4.00
❏ 02717		Memory/Love Theme from "A Star Is Born"	1982		2.00	4.00
❏ 04177		The Way He Makes Me Feel (Studio)/ The Way He Makes Me Feel (Film Version)	1983			3.00
❏ 04177	PS	The Way He Makes Me Feel (Studio)/ The Way He Makes Me Feel (Film Version)	1983		2.00	4.00
❏ 04357		Will Someone Ever Look at Me That Way/ Papa Can You Hear Me?	1984			3.00
❏ 04605		Left in the Dark/Here We Are at Last	1984			3.00
❏ 04605	PS	Left in the Dark/Here We Are at Last	1984		2.00	4.00
❏ 04695		Make No Mistake, He's Mine/Clear Sailing	1984			3.00
		A-side with Kim Carnes				
❏ 04695	PS	Make No Mistake, He's Mine/Clear Sailing	1984		2.00	4.00
❏ 04707		Emotion/Here We Are at Last	1984			3.00
❏ 04707	PS	Emotion/Here We Are at Last	1984		2.00	4.00
❏ 05680		Somewhere/Not While I'm Around	1985			3.00
❏ 05680	PS	Somewhere/Not While I'm Around	1985		2.00	4.00
❏ 05837		Send In the Clowns/Being Alive	1986			3.00
❏ 08026		All I Ask of You/On My Way to You	1988		2.00	4.00
❏ 08026	PS	All I Ask of You/On My Way to You	1988		2.00	4.00
❏ 08062		Till I Loved You/Two People	1988			3.00
		A-side with Don Johnson				
❏ 08062	PS	Till I Loved You/Two People	1988		2.00	4.00
❏ 10075		Love in the Afternoon/Guava Jelly	1974		2.50	5.00
❏ 10130		Let the Good Times Roll/Jubilation	1975		2.50	5.00
❏ 10198		My Father's Song/By the Way	1975		2.50	5.00
❏ 10272		Shake Me, Wake Me, When It's Over/Widescreen	1975		2.50	5.00
❏ 10450		Love Theme from "A Star Is Born" (Evergreen)/ I Believe in Love	1976		2.50	5.00
❏ 10450	PS	Love Theme from "A Star Is Born" (Evergreen)/ I Believe in Love	1976		3.00	6.00
❏ 10555		My Heart Belongs to Me/Answer Me	1977		2.50	5.00
❏ 10756		Songbird/Honey Can I Put On Your Clothes	1978		2.00	4.00
❏ 10777		Love Theme from "Eyes of Laura Mars" (Prisoner)/ Laura and Nevil	1978		2.00	4.00
❏ 10931		Superman/A Man I Loved	1979		2.00	4.00
❏ 11008		The Main Event/Fight//(Instrumental)	1979		2.00	4.00
❏ 11125		No More Tears (Enough Is Enough)/Wet	1979		2.00	4.00
		A-side with Donna Summer				
❏ 11125	PS	No More Tears (Enough Is Enough)/Wet	1979		2.50	5.00
❏ 11179		Kiss Me in the Rain/I Ain't Gonna Cry Tonight	1980		2.00	4.00
❏ 11364		Woman in Love/Run Wild	1980		2.00	4.00
❏ 11390		Guilty/Life Story	1980		2.00	4.00
		A-side with Barry Gibb				
❏ 11430		What Kind of Fool/The Lovin' Side	1981		2.00	4.00
		A-side with Barry Gibb				
❏ 42631		Happy Days Are Here Again/When the Sun Comes Out	1962	5.00	10.00	20.00
❏ 42648		My Coloring Book/Lover Come Back to Me	1962	3.75	7.50	15.00
❏ 42937		Gotta Move/Make Believe	1964	3.75	7.50	15.00
❏ 42965		People/I Am Woman	1964	2.50	5.00	10.00
❏ 43127		Funny Girl/Absent Minded Me	1964	2.50	5.00	10.00
❏ 43248		Why Did I Choose You/My Love	1965	2.00	4.00	8.00
❏ 43323		My Man/Where Is the Wonder	1965	2.00	4.00	8.00
❏ 43403		He Touched Me/I Like Him	1965	2.00	4.00	8.00
❏ 43469		Second Hand Rose/The Kind of Man a Woman Needs	1965	2.00	4.00	8.00
❏ 43518		Where Am I Going?/You Wanna Bet	1966		3.00	6.00
❏ 43612		Sam, You Made the Pants Too Long/The Minute Waltz	1966		3.00	6.00
❏ 43739		La Mer/C'est Rien	1966	2.00	4.00	8.00
❏ 43808		Free Again/I've Been There	1966		3.00	6.00
❏ 43896		Sleep in Heavenly Peace (Silent Night)/Ave Maria	1966		3.00	6.00
❏ 43896	PS	Sleep in Heavenly Peace (Silent Night)/Ave Maria	1966	3.00	6.00	12.00
❏ 44225		Stout-Hearted Men/Look	1967		3.00	6.00
❏ 44331		Lover Man (Oh, Where Can You Be)/ My Funny Valentine	1967		3.00	6.00
❏ 44350		Jingle Bells?/White Christmas	1967		3.00	6.00
❏ 44350	PS	Jingle Bells?/White Christmas	1967	2.50	5.00	10.00
❏ 44351		Have Yourself a Merry Little Christmas/The Best Gifts	1967		3.00	6.00
❏ 44351	PS	Have Yourself a Merry Little Christmas/The Best Gifts	1967	2.50	5.00	10.00
❏ 44352		My Favorite Things/The Christmas Song	1967		3.00	6.00
❏ 44352	PS	My Favorite Things/The Christmas Song	1967	2.50	5.00	10.00
❏ 44354		I Wonder As I Wander/The Lord's Prayer	1967		3.00	6.00
❏ 44476		Our Corner of the Night/He Could Show Me	1968		2.50	5.00
❏ 44532		Morning After/Where Is the Wonder	1968		2.50	5.00
❏ 44622		Funny Girl/I'd Rather Be Blue Over You	1968		2.50	5.00
❏ 44704		Don't Rain on My Parade/My Man	1968		3.00	6.00
❏ 44775		Punky's Dilemma/Frank Mills	1969		2.50	5.00
❏ 44921		Honey Pie/Little Tin Soldier	1969		2.50	5.00
❏ 45040		What About Today/ What Are You Doing the Rest of Your Life	1969		2.50	5.00
❏ 45072		Love Is Only Love/Before the Parade Passes By	1970		2.50	5.00
❏ 45147		The Best Thing You've Ever Done/ Summer Me, Winter Me	1970		2.50	5.00
❏ 45236		Stoney End/I'll Be Home	1970		2.50	5.00
❏ 45341		Time and Love/No Easy Way Down	1971		2.50	5.00
❏ 45384		Flim Flam Man/Maybe	1971		2.50	5.00
❏ 45414		Where You Lead/Since I Fell for You	1971		2.50	5.00

Number	Title (A Side/B Side)	Year	VG	VG+	NM
❏ 45471	Mother/The Summer Knows	1971		2.50	5.00
❏ 45511	One Less Bell to Answer-A House Is Not a Home/ Space Captain	1971		2.50	5.00
❏ 45626	Sweet Inspiration-Where You Lead/Didn't We	1972		2.50	5.00
❏ 45686	Sing a Song-Make Your Own Kind of Music/ Starting Here-Starting Now	1972		2.50	5.00
❏ 45739	Didn't We/On a Clear Day	1972		2.50	5.00
❏ 45780	If I Close My Eyes/(Instrumental)	1973		2.50	5.00
❏ 45944	The Way We Were/ What Are You Doing the Rest of Your Life	1973		2.50	5.00
	A-side contains a different vocal than most of the album versions				
❏ 46024	All in Love Is Fair/My Buddy-How About Me	1974		2.50	5.00
❏ 68691	What Were We Thinking Of/Why Let It Go	1989			3.00
❏ 73016	We're Not Makin' Love Anymore/Here We Are at Last	1989			3.00
❏ 73794	Till I Loved You/Two People	1991			3.00
	Reissue				
❏ 73944	All I Ask of You/On My Way to You	1991			3.00
	Reissue				
❏ 77533	Ordinary Miracles/Ordinary Miracles (Live)	1994		2.00	4.00

Strength, Bill

Sun
❏ 346	Guess I'd Better Go/Senorita	1960	6.25	12.50	25.00

Striders, The

Apollo
❏ 480	I Wonder/Hesitating Fool	1955	75.00	150.00	300.00

Columbia
❏ 43738	Sorrow/Say You Love Me	1966	5.00	10.00	20.00
❏ 43948	Am I On Your Mind/There's a Storm Comin'	1966	5.00	10.00	20.00
❏ 44143	When You Walk In the Room/Do It Now	1967	3.75	7.50	15.00

Derby
❏ 857	Come Back to Me Tomorrow/Rollin'	1954	50.00	100.00	200.00

Strikes, The

Imperial
❏ 5433	Baby I'm Sorry/If You Can't Rock Me	1957	12.50	25.00	50.00
❏ 5446	Rockin'/I Don't Want to Cry Over You	1957	12.50	25.00	50.00

Lin
❏ 5006	Baby I'm Sorry/If You Can't Rock Me	1957	18.75	37.50	75.00

String-A-Longs, The

Atco
❏ 6694	Popi/Places I Remember	1969	2.00	4.00	8.00

Dot
❏ 16331	Twistwatch/Sunday	1962	2.50	5.00	10.00
❏ 16379	Spinnin' My Wheels/My Blue Heaven	1962	2.50	5.00	10.00
❏ 16393	Matilda/Replica	1962	2.50	5.00	10.00
❏ 16448	Heartaches/Happy Melody	1963	2.50	5.00	10.00
❏ 16575	Myna Bird/My Babe	1964	2.50	5.00	10.00
❏ 16708	Caravan/Matilda	1965	2.50	5.00	10.00

Warwick
❏ 603	Wheels/Tell the World	1960	6.25	12.50	25.00
	White label (not marked as a promo)				
❏ 603	Wheels/Tell the World	1960	5.00	10.00	20.00
	Red label				
❏ 603	Wheels/Am I Asking Too Much	1960	3.75	7.50	15.00
❏ 606	Tell the World/For an Angel	1960	3.75	7.50	15.00
❏ 625	Brass Buttons/Panic Button	1961	3.75	7.50	15.00
❏ 654	Take a Minute/Should I	1961	3.75	7.50	15.00
❏ 668	Myna Bird/Scottie	1961	3.75	7.50	15.00
❏ 675	Theme for Twisters/Nearly Sunrise	1962	3.75	7.50	15.00

Strong, Barrett

Anna
❏ 1111	Money (That's What I Want)/Oh I Apologize	1960	6.25	12.50	25.00
❏ 1116	You Know What to Do/Yes, No, Maybe So	1960	6.25	12.50	25.00

Atco
❏ 6225	Seven Sins/What Went Wrong	1962	10.00	20.00	40.00

Capitol
❏ 4052	Is It True/Anywhere	1975		2.50	5.00
❏ 4120	Surrender/There's Something About You	1975		2.50	5.00
❏ 4223	Gonna Make It Right/The Man Up in the Sky	1976		2.50	5.00

Epic
❏ 11011	Stand Up and Cheer for the Preacher (Part 1)/ Stand Up and Cheer for the Preacher (Part 2)	1973		2.50	5.00

Phase II
❏ 02048	Rock It Easy/Love Will Make It Right	1981		2.00	4.00

Tamla
❏ 54022	Let's Rock/(B-side unknown)	1960	1,000	1,500	2,000
❏ 54027	Money (That's What I Want)/Oh I Apologize	1960	25.00	50.00	100.00
	Horizontal lines label				

Number		Title (A Side/B Side)	Year	VG	VG+	NM
❏ 54027		Money (That's What I Want)/Oh I Apologize	1960	12.50	25.00	50.00
		Globe label				
❏ 54029		You Know What to Do/Yes, No, Maybe So	1960	12.50	25.00	50.00
❏ 54033		I'm Gonna Cry/Whirl Wind	1960	12.50	25.00	50.00
❏ 54035		You Got What It Takes/Money and Me	1961	12.50	25.00	50.00
❏ 54043		Two Wrongs Don't Make a Right/Misery	1961	12.50	25.00	50.00

Stuart, Chad
(Of Chad and Jeremy)
Sidewalk

Number		Title (A Side/B Side)	Year	VG	VG+	NM
❏ 944		Good Morning Sunrise/Paxton's Song	1968	2.00	4.00	8.00
❏ 944	PS	Good Morning Sunrise/Paxton's Song	1968	3.75	7.50	15.00

Stuart, Chad and Jill
Columbia

Number		Title (A Side/B Side)	Year	VG	VG+	NM
❏ 43467		The Cruel War/I Can't Talk to You	1965	2.00	4.00	8.00
❏ 43467	PS	The Cruel War/I Can't Talk to You	1965	3.75	7.50	15.00

Stuart, Chad, and Jeremy Clyde – See "Chad and Jeremy"

Stubbs, Joe
Lu-Pine

Number	Title (A Side/B Side)	Year	VG	VG+	NM
❏ 120	Keep On Loving Me/What's My Destiny	1964	50.00	100.00	200.00

Students, The
Argo

Number	Title (A Side/B Side)	Year	VG	VG+	NM
❏ 5386	I'm So Young/Every Day of the Week	1961	5.00	10.00	20.00

Checker

Number	Title (A Side/B Side)	Year	VG	VG+	NM
❏ 902	I'm So Young/Every Day of the Week	1958	10.00	20.00	40.00
❏ 1004	My Vow to You/That's How I Feel	1962	3.75	7.50	15.00

Note

Number	Title (A Side/B Side)	Year	VG	VG+	NM
❏ 10012	I'm So Young/Every Day of the Week	1958	100.00	200.00	400.00
❏ 10019	My Vow to You/That's How I Feel	1959	100.00	200.00	400.00

Red Top

Number	Title (A Side/B Side)	Year	VG	VG+	NM
❏ 100	My Heart Is an Open Door/Mommy and Daddy	1958	50.00	100.00	200.00
	Blue label				
❏ 100	My Heart Is an Open Door/Mommy and Daddy	1958	10.00	20.00	40.00
	Red label				

Stylers, The
Golden Crest

Number	Title (A Side/B Side)	Year	VG	VG+	NM
❏ 118	You Tell Me/Blues in the Night	1957	10.00	20.00	40.00
❏ 129	Kiss and Run Lover/Girlie, Girlie, Girlie	1957	10.00	20.00	40.00

Gordy

Number	Title (A Side/B Side)	Year	VG	VG+	NM
❏ 7018	Going Steady Anniversary/Pushing Up Daisies	1963	15.00	30.00	60.00

Jubilee

Number	Title (A Side/B Side)	Year	VG	VG+	NM
❏ 5168	Believe It or Not/The World Is Yours	1954	10.00	20.00	40.00
❏ 5188	Shoo Shoo Sha La La/I Love Ya Like Crazy	1955	10.00	20.00	40.00
❏ 5246	Lost John/Huffin' and Puffin'	1956	10.00	20.00	40.00
❏ 5253	Confession of a Sinner/Gonna Tell 'Em	1956	10.00	20.00	40.00
❏ 5279	Breaker of Hearts/Miracle in Milan	1957	7.50	15.00	30.00

Kicks

Number	Title (A Side/B Side)	Year	VG	VG+	NM
❏ 2	Gentle as a Teardrop/There Were Others	1954	125.00	250.00	500.00

Styles, The
Josie

Number	Title (A Side/B Side)	Year	VG	VG+	NM
❏ 920	I Love You for Sentimental Reasons/ School Bells to Chapel Bells	1964	15.00	30.00	60.00

Modern

Number	Title (A Side/B Side)	Year	VG	VG+	NM
❏ 1048	I Know You Know That I Know/Baby You're Alive	1967	3.00	6.00	12.00

Serene

Number	Title (A Side/B Side)	Year	VG	VG+	NM
❏ 1501	Scarlet Angel/Gotta Go, Go, Go	1961	37.50	75.00	150.00

Swan

Number	Title (A Side/B Side)	Year	VG	VG+	NM
❏ 4258	I Do Love You/Hush Little Girl	1966	3.00	6.00	12.00

Stylistics, The
Amherst

Number	Title (A Side/B Side)	Year	VG	VG+	NM
❏ 301	Because I Love You Girl/My Love, Come Live With Me	1985		2.00	4.00

Avco

Number	Title (A Side/B Side)	Year	VG	VG+	NM
❏ 4581	You Are Everything/Country Living	1971		2.50	5.00
❏ 4591	Betcha by Golly, Wow/Ebony Eyes	1972		2.50	5.00
❏ 4595	People Make the World Go Round/Point of No Return	1972		2.50	5.00
❏ 4603	I'm Stone in Love with You/Make It Last	1972		2.50	5.00
❏ 4611	Break Up to Make Up/You and Me	1973		2.50	5.00
❏ 4618	You'll Never Get to Heaven (If You Break My Heart)/ If You Don't Watch Out	1973		2.50	5.00
❏ 4625	Rockin' Roll Baby/Pieces	1973		2.50	5.00
❏ 4634	You Make Me Feel Brand New/Only for the Children	1974		2.50	5.00
❏ 4640	Let's Put It All Together/I Take It Out on You	1974		2.50	5.00
❏ 4647	Heavy Fallin' Out/Go Now	1974		2.50	5.00
❏ 4649	Star on a TV Show/Hey Girl, Come and Get It	1975		2.50	5.00
❏ 4652	Thank You Baby/Sing, Baby, Sing	1975		2.50	5.00
❏ 4656	Can't Give You Anything (But My Love)/ I'd Rather Be Hurt by You	1975		2.50	5.00

Number		Title (A Side/B Side)	Year	VG	VG+	NM
❑ 4661		Funky Weekend/If You Are There	1975		2.50	5.00
❑ 4664		You Are Beautiful/Michael and Me	1976		2.50	5.00
❑ 4664	PS	You Are Beautiful/Michael and Me	1976	2.50	5.00	10.00

Avco Embassy

❑ 4555		You're a Big Girl Now/Let the Junkie Beat the Pusher	1970		3.00	6.00
❑ 4572		Stop, Look, Listen (To Your Heart)/If I Love You	1971		3.00	6.00

H&L

❑ 4669		Can't Help Falling in Love/Jenny	1976		2.00	4.00
❑ 4674		Because I Love You, Girl/You Are	1976		2.00	4.00
❑ 4676		Only You/What Goes Around Comes Around	1976		2.00	4.00
❑ 4678		I Got a Letter/Satin Doll	1977		2.00	4.00
❑ 4681		Shame and Scandal in the Family/That Don't Shake Me	1977		2.00	4.00
❑ 4686		I'm Coming Home/I Run to You	1977		2.00	4.00
❑ 4695		Fool of the Year/Good Thing Goin'	1978		2.00	4.00

Mercury

❑ 74005	First Impressions/ Your Love's Too Good to Be Forgotten	1978		2.00	4.00
❑ 74022	I Can't Stop Livin'/You're the Best Thing in My Life	1978		2.00	4.00
❑ 74042	Love at First Sight/Broken Wing	1979		2.00	4.00
❑ 74057	Don't Know Where I'm Going/ You Make Me Feel So Doggone Good	1979		2.00	4.00

Philadelphia Int'l.

❑ 02901	Callin' You/Don't Come Telling Me Lies	1982		2.00	4.00
❑ 03085	Lighten Up/We Should Be Lovers	1982		2.00	4.00

Sebring

❑ 8370	You're a Big Girl Now/Let the Junkie Beat the Pusher	1970	7.50	15.00	30.00

Streetwise

❑ 1136	Give a Little Love/ Give a Little Love (Sing Along Version)	1984		2.00	4.00
❑ 1137	Some Things Never Change/Row Your Love	1985		2.00	4.00
❑ 1138	Special/(B-side unknown)	1985		2.00	4.00

TSOP

❑ 02195	What's Your Name/Almost There	1981			
❑ 02588	Mine All Mine/Closer Than Close	1981			
❑ 02702	Habit/I've Got This Feeling	1982			
❑ 4789	Hurry Up This Way Again/It Started Out	1980		2.00	4.00
❑ 4798	And I'll See You No More/Driving Me Wild	1980		2.00	4.00

Styx
(Also see "Shaw, Tommy")

A&M

❑ 1786		Lorelei/Midnight Ride	1976		2.00	4.00
❑ 1818		Born for Adventure/Light Up	1976		2.50	5.00
❑ 1877		Mademoiselle/Light Up	1976		2.50	5.00
❑ 1900		Jennifer/Shooz	1976		2.50	5.00
❑ 1931		Crystal Ball/Put Me On	1977		2.50	5.00
❑ 1977		Come Sail Away/Put Me On	1977		2.00	4.00
❑ 1977	PS	Come Sail Away/Put Me On	1977		3.00	6.00
❑ 2007		Fooling Yourself (The Angry Young Man)/ The Grand Finale	1978		2.00	4.00
❑ 2007	PS	Fooling Yourself (The Angry Young Man)/ The Grand Finale	1978		3.00	6.00
❑ 2087		Blue Collar Man (Long Nights)/Superstars	1978		2.00	4.00
❑ 2087	PS	Blue Collar Man (Long Nights)/Superstars	1978		3.00	6.00
❑ 2110		Sing for the Day/Queen of Spades	1979		2.50	5.00
❑ 2110		Renegade/Sing for the Day	1979		2.00	4.00
❑ 2110	PS	Renegade/Sing for the Day	1979		2.50	5.00
❑ 2188		Babe/I'm O.K.	1979		2.00	4.00
❑ 2206		Why Me/Lights	1979		2.00	4.00
❑ 2228		Borrowed Time/Eddie	1980		2.00	4.00
❑ 2294		The Best of Times/Lights	1980			Unreleased?
❑ 2300		The Best of Times/Lights	1981		2.00	4.00
❑ 2300	PS	The Best of Times/Lights	1981		2.00	4.00
❑ 2323		Too Much Time on My Hands/Queen of Spades	1981		2.00	4.00
❑ 2348		Nothing Ever Goes As Planned/Never Say Never	1981		2.00	4.00
❑ 2525		Mr. Roboto/Snowblind	1983			3.00
❑ 2525	PS	Mr. Roboto/Snowblind	1983			3.00
❑ 2543		Don't Let It End/Rockin' the Paradise	1983			3.00
❑ 2543	PS	Don't Let It End/Rockin' the Paradise	1983			3.00
❑ 2560		Double Life/Haven't We Been Here Before	1983			3.00
❑ 2568		High Time/Double Life	1983			3.00
❑ 2625		Music Time/Heavy Metal Poisoning	1984			3.00
❑ 2625	PS	Music Time/Heavy Metal Poisoning	1984			3.00
❑ 8696		Show Me the Way/Love at First Sight	1993		2.00	4.00

Reissue series; both songs were unreleased on 45 until this record

ABC

❑ 10848	Don't Bring Me Down/MacDougal Street	1966	3.00	6.00	12.00

Not the 1970s-era Styx.

Paramount

❑ 0104	Promised Land/Soul Flow	1971		3.00	6.00

Wooden Nickel

❑ 65-0106	Best Thing/What Has Come Between	1972		2.50	5.00
❑ 65-0111	I'm Gonna Make You Feel It/ Quick Is the Beat of My Heart	1972		2.50	5.00
❑ 65-0116	Lady/You Better Ask	1973	2.50	5.00	10.00

Number	Title (A Side/B Side)	Year	VG	VG+	NM
❑ BWBO-0065	You Need Love/Winner Take All	1973		2.50	5.00
❑ BWBO-0252	Young Man/Unfinished Song	1974		2.50	5.00
❑ PB-10027	Lies/22 Years	1974		2.50	5.00
❑ PB-10102	Lady/Children of the Land	1974		2.50	5.00
❑ PB-10272	You Need Love/You Better Ask	1975		2.50	5.00
❑ PB-10329	Best Thing/Havin' a Ball	1975		2.50	5.00
❑ GB-10492	Lady/Children of the Land	1975		2.00	4.00
	Gold Standard Series				
❑ PB-11205	Winner Take All/Best Thing	1978		2.50	5.00

Suddens, The
(Also recorded as "The Safaris")
Sudden

❑ 103	Garden of Love/Childish Ways	1961	25.00	50.00	100.00

Sugarloaf
(Also includes "Sugarloaf/Jerry Corbetta")
Brut

❑ 805	Round and Round/Colorado Jones	1973		2.50	5.00
❑ 815	I Got a Song/Myra, Myra	1973		2.50	5.00
❑ 815 PS	I Got a Song/Myra, Myra	1973		3.00	6.00

Claridge

❑ 402	Don't Call Us, We'll Call You/Texas Two-Lane	1974		2.50	5.00
❑ 405	Stars in My Eyes/Myra, Myra	1975		2.50	5.00
❑ 408	Boogie Man/I Got a Song	1975		2.50	5.00
❑ 415	Have a Good Time/You Set My Dreams to Music	1976		2.50	5.00
❑ 422	Last Dance, Take a Chance/Satisfaction Guaranteed	1976		2.50	5.00

Liberty

❑ 56183	Green-Eyed Lady/West of Tomorrow	1970		3.00	6.00
❑ 56218	Tongue in Cheek/Woman	1970		2.50	5.00
❑ 56218 PS	Tongue in Cheek/Woman	1970	2.50	5.00	10.00

United Artists

❑ 0062	Green-Eyed Lady/Tongue in Cheek	1973		2.00	4.00
	"Silver Spotlight Series" reissue				
❑ 50757	Woman/Tongue in Cheek	1971			*Unreleased*
❑ 50784	Chest Fever/Mother Nature's Wine	1971		2.50	5.00

Suggs, Brad
Meteor

❑ 5034	Charcoal Suit/Bop Baby Bop	1956	100.00	200.00	400.00

Phillips Int'l.

❑ 3545	Low Outside/706 Union	1959	6.25	12.50	25.00
❑ 3549	I Walk the Line/Ooh-Wee	1959	6.25	12.50	25.00
❑ 3554	Cloudy/Partly Cloudy	1960	6.25	12.50	25.00
❑ 3563	My Gypsy/Sam's Tune	1960	6.25	12.50	25.00
❑ 3571	Elephant Walk/Catching Up	1961	6.25	12.50	25.00

Sullivan, Niki
(Former member of The Crickets)
Dot

❑ 15751	Three Steps to Heaven/It's All Over	1958	18.75	37.50	75.00

Joli

❑ 073	Do the Dive/My Lost Dream	196?	15.00	30.00	60.00
❑ 075	It Really Doesn't Matter/You Better Get a Move On	196?	18.75	37.50	75.00

Sultans, The
(More than one group)
Ascot

❑ 2228	I Wanna Know/Gloria	1967	5.00	10.00	20.00

Duke

❑ 125	Good Thing Baby/How Deep Is the Ocean	1954	25.00	50.00	100.00
❑ 133	I Cried My Heart Out/Baby Don't Put Me Down	1954	25.00	50.00	100.00
❑ 135	Boppin' with the Mambo/What Makes Me Feel This Way	1954	25.00	50.00	100.00
❑ 178	My Love Is So High/If I Could Tell	1957	12.50	25.00	50.00

Guyden

❑ 2079	Someone You Can Trust/Christina	1963	3.75	7.50	15.00

Jam

❑ 103	Toss in My Sleep/I Feel Your Love Growing Cold	1962	6.25	12.50	25.00
❑ 107	Mary, Mary/How Far Does a Friendship Go	1963	6.25	12.50	25.00
❑ 113	Poor Boy/Don't Tie Me Down	1964	6.25	12.50	25.00

Jubilee

❑ 5054	Lemon Squeezing Daddy/You Captured My Heart	1951	62.50	125.00	250.00
❑ 5077	Blues at Dawn/Don't Be Angry	1952	100.00	200.00	400.00

Tilt

❑ 782	It'll Be Easy/You Got Me Goin'	1961	25.00	50.00	100.00
	Yellow label				
❑ 782	It'll Be Easy/You Got Me Goin'	1961	7.50	15.00	30.00
	Black label				

Number		Title (A Side/B Side)	Year	VG	VG+	NM

Summer, Donna

Atlantic

❏ 88840		Love's About to Change My Heart/ Love's About to Change My Heart	1989			3.00
❏ 88899		This Time I Know It's for Real/ If It Makes You Feel Good	1989			3.00
❏ 88899	PS	This Time I Know It's for Real/ If It Makes You Feel Good	1989		2.00	4.00

Casablanca

❏ 872		Spring Affair/The Landing	1976		2.50	5.00
❏ 874		Winter Melody/Spring Affair	1977		2.50	5.00
❏ 884		Can't We Just Sit Down (And Talk It Over)/I Feel Love	1977		3.00	6.00
Original copies have "I Feel Love" listed as "Side B"						
❏ 884		I Feel Love/Can't We Just Sit Down (And Talk It Over)	1977		2.50	5.00
Second pressings have "I Feel Love" listed as "Side A"						
❏ 907		I Love You/Once Upon a Time	1977		2.50	5.00
❏ 916		Rumour Has It/Once Upon a Time	1978		2.50	5.00
❏ 926		Last Dance/With Your Love	1978		2.00	4.00
❏ 939		Mac Arthur Park/Once Upon a Time	1978		2.00	4.00
❏ 959		Heaven Knows/Only One Love	1979		2.00	4.00
A-side with Brooklyn Dreams						
❏ 978		Hot Stuff/Journey to the Center of Your Heart	1979		2.00	4.00
❏ 988		Bad Girls/On My Honor	1979		2.00	4.00
❏ 2201		Dim All the Lights/There Will Always Be a You	1979		2.00	4.00
❏ 2236		On the Radio/There Will Always Be a You	1980		2.00	4.00
❏ 2273		Our Love/Sunset People	1980		2.50	5.00
❏ 2300		Walk Away/Could It Be Magic	1980		2.00	4.00
❏ 858 366-7		Melody of Love/The Christmas Song	1994			3.00
❏ 858 366-7	PS	Melody of Love/The Christmas Song	1994			3.00

Geffen

❏ 27939		Fascination/All Systems Go	1988		2.00	4.00
❏ 28165		Only the Fool Survives/Love Shock	1987		2.00	4.00
A-side with Mickey Thomas						
❏ 28418		Dinner with Gershwin/(Instrumental)	1987		2.00	4.00
❏ 28418	PS	Dinner with Gershwin/(Instrumental)	1987		2.00	4.00
❏ 29142		Supernatural Love/Face the Music	1984		2.00	4.00
❏ 29142	PS	Supernatural Love/Face the Music	1984		2.00	4.00
❏ 29291		There Goes My Baby/Maybe It's Over	1984		2.00	4.00
❏ 29291	PS	There Goes My Baby/Maybe It's Over	1984		2.00	4.00
❏ 29805		The Woman in Me/Livin' in America	1982		2.00	4.00
❏ 29805	PS	The Woman in Me/Livin' in America	1982		2.00	4.00
❏ 29895		State of Independence/Love Is Just a Breath Away	1982		2.00	4.00
❏ 29895	PS	State of Independence/Love Is Just a Breath Away	1982		2.00	4.00
❏ 29982		Love Is In Control (Finger on the Trigger)/ Sometimes Like Butterflies	1982			
❏ 29982	PS	Love Is In Control (Finger on the Trigger)/ Sometimes Like Butterflies	1982		2.50	5.00
❏ 49563		The Wanderer/Stop Me	1980		2.00	4.00
Second pressings have WB logo replaced by Geffen logo; also see "Warner Bros./Geffen" listing						
❏ 49563	PS	The Wanderer/Stop Me	1980		2.50	5.00
❏ 49634		Cold Love/Grand Illusion	1980		2.00	4.00
❏ 49634	PS	Cold Love/Grand Illusion	1980		2.50	5.00
❏ 49664		Who Do You Think You're Foolin'/Runnin' for Cover	1981		2.00	4.00

Mercury

❏ 812 370-7		She Works Hard for the Money/ I Do Fall in Love	1983		2.00	4.00
❏ 812 370-7	PS	She Works Hard for the Money /I Do Fall in Love	1983		2.50	5.00
❏ 814 088-7		Unconditional Love/People, People	1983		2.00	4.00
❏ 814 088-7	PS	Unconditional Love/People, People	1983		2.50	5.00
❏ 814 922-7		Love Has a Mind of Its Own/Stop, Look and Listen	1983		2.00	4.00

Oasis

❏ 401 A/B		Love to Love You Baby/Need-A-Man Blues	1975	3.00	6.00	12.00
"Love to Love You Baby" has a radically different mix on the above first pressing						
❏ 401 AA/BB		Love to Love You Baby (4:55)/ Love to Love You Baby (3:24)	1975		3.00	6.00
❏ 405		Could It Be Magic/Whispering Waves	1976		3.00	6.00
❏ 406		Try Me, I Know We Can Make It/Wasted	1976		3.00	6.00
❏ 406	PS	Try Me, I Know We Can Make It/Wasted	1976	2.00	4.00	8.00

Warner Bros./Geffen

❏ 49563		The Wanderer/Stop Me	1980		3.00	6.00
Original pressings have a WB logo on the left side and "Geffen Records" in a box at the top of the label						

Summers, Andy

(Of the Police)

A&M

❏ 2513	DJ	I Advance Masked (same on both sides)	1982		2.00	4.00
With Robert Fripp; no stock copy was issued						
❏ 2699		Parade/Train	1984			3.00
With Robert Fripp						
❏ 2704		2010/To Hal and Back	1984			3.00
❏ 2704	PS	2010/To Hal and Back	1984			3.00

MCA

❏ 53112		Love Is the Strangest Way/XYZ	1987			3.00

Number		Title (A Side/B Side)	Year	VG	VG+	NM

Summers, Gene
Capri
❏ 502		Blue Diamond/You Said You Loved Me	196?	5.00	10.00	20.00
❏ 507		Alabama Shake/Just Because	196?	10.00	20.00	40.00

Jamie
❏ 1273		Blue Diamond/You Said You Loved Me	1964	3.75	7.50	15.00

Jan
❏ 100		School of Rock 'N' Roll/Straight Skirt	1958	12.50	25.00	50.00
❏ 102		Nervous/Gotta Love That	1959	10.00	20.00	40.00
❏ 106		Twisteen/(B-side unknown)	1959	10.00	20.00	40.00

Mercury
❏ 72606		Green-Eyed Monster/The Clown	1966	3.75	7.50	15.00

Teardrop
❏ 3405	DJ	Goodbye Priscilla (Bye Bye Blue Baby) *Single-sided promo copies have erroneous subtitle*	1977	3.00	6.00	12.00
❏ 3405		Goodbye Priscilla (Bye Bye Baby Blue)/ Down on the Farm	1977	2.00	4.00	8.00

Sun-Rays, The
Sun
❏ 293		Love Is a Stranger/The Lonely Hours	1958	10.00	20.00	40.00

Sunbeams, The
Dot
❏ 1271		I'm Gonna Go Home to Mama/Blue Mountain Waltz	1955	7.50	15.00	30.00
❏ 1280		How About It/Wrap It Up and Save It	1956	7.50	15.00	30.00

Herald
❏ 451		Tell Me Why/Come Back Baby	1955	75.00	150.00	300.00

Sundials, The
Guyden
❏ 2065		Chapel of Love/Whether to Resist	1962	50.00	100.00	200.00

Sundown Playboys, The
Apple
❏ 1852		Saturday Night Special/Valse De Soleil Coucher	1972	3.75	7.50	15.00

Sunny and the Horizons
Luxor
❏ 1013		Nature's Creation/Because They Tell Me *Yellow label*	1962	50.00	100.00	200.00
❏ 1013		Nature's Creation/Because They Tell Me *Red label*	1962	18.75	37.50	75.00

Sunrays, The
Tower
❏ 101		Outta Gas/Car Party	1964	5.00	10.00	20.00
❏ 148		I Live for the Sun/Bye Baby Bye	1965	3.00	6.00	12.00
❏ 191		Andrea/You Don't Phase Me	1966	3.00	6.00	12.00
❏ 224		Still/When You're Not There	1966	3.00	6.00	12.00
❏ 256		Don't Take Yourself Too Seriously/ I Look Baby, I Can't See	1966	3.00	6.00	12.00
❏ 256	PS	Don't Take Yourself Too Seriously/ I Look Baby, I Can't See	1966	6.25	12.50	25.00
❏ 290		Hi, How Are You/Just 'Round the River Bend	1966	3.75	7.50	15.00
❏ 340		Loaded with Love/Time (A Special Thing)	1967	3.75	7.50	15.00

Warner Bros.
❏ 5253		Talk to Him/Gideon	1962	3.75	7.50	15.00

Sunsets, The
Challenge
❏ 9186		C.C. Rider/The Chug-a-Lug	1963	10.00	20.00	40.00
❏ 9198		Lonely Surfer Boy/Playmate of the Year	1963	10.00	20.00	40.00
❏ 9208		My Little Beach Bunny/My Little Surfin' Woody	1963	12.50	25.00	50.00

Petal
❏ 1040		Lydia/Only You, Only Me	1963	12.50	25.00	50.00

Rae Cox
❏ 102		How Will I Remember/Sittin' and Cryin'	1959	10.00	20.00	40.00

Sunshine Company, The
Imperial
❏ 66241		Up Up and Away/Blue May	1967			*Unreleased*
❏ 66247		Happy/Blue May	1967	2.50	5.00	10.00
❏ 66260		Back on the Street Again/I Just Want to Be Your Friend	1967	2.50	5.00	10.00
❏ 66278		Reflections on an Angel/It's Sunday	1968			*Unreleased*
❏ 66290		Look, Here Comes the Sun/It's Sunday	1968	2.50	5.00	10.00
❏ 66298		Let's Get Together/Sunday Brought the Rain	1968	2.50	5.00	10.00
❏ 66308		On a Beautiful Day/Darcy Farrow	1968	2.50	5.00	10.00
❏ 66324		Love Poem/Willie Jean	1968	2.50	5.00	10.00
❏ 66399		The Only Thing That Matters/Bolaro	1969	2.50	5.00	10.00

United Artists
❏ 0132		Happy/Back on the Street Again *"Silver Spotlight Series" reissue*	1973		2.00	4.00

Number	Title (A Side/B Side)	Year	VG	VG+	NM

Superiors, The
(More than one group)

Atco
❑ 6106	Lost Love/Don't Say Goodbye	1957	10.00	20.00	40.00

Fal
❑ 301	What Is Love/Flee the Scene	1961	7.50	15.00	30.00

Federal
❑ 12436	I'm Sorry Baby (I Didn't Mean to Do You Wrong)/ Dance of Love	1961	6.25	12.50	25.00

Main Line
❑ 104	Lost Love/Don't Say Goodbye *With Philadelphia address on label*	1958	75.00	150.00	300.00
❑ 104	Lost Love/Don't Say Goodbye *No address on label*	1962	7.50	15.00	30.00

MGM
❑ 13503	Can't Make It Without You/Let Me Make You Happy	1966	3.00	6.00	12.00

Sue
❑ 12	Heavenly Angel/I'd Rather Die	1969	2.00	4.00	8.00

Verve
❑ 10370	Tell Me to Go/What Would I Do	1965	5.00	10.00	20.00

Supertramp

A&M
Number	Title (A Side/B Side)	Year	VG	VG+	NM
❑ 1305	Forever/Your Poppa Don't Mind	1971		3.00	6.00
❑ 1660	Bloody Well Right/Dreamer	1975		2.50	5.00
❑ 1766	Lady/ You Started Laughing When I Held You in My Arms	1975			Unreleased?
❑ 1793	Lady/ You Started Laughing When I Held You in My Arms	1976		2.50	5.00
❑ 1814	Sister Moonshine/Ain't Nobody But Me	1976		2.50	5.00
❑ 1938	Give a Little Bit/Downstream	1977		2.00	4.00
❑ 1938	PS Give a Little Bit/Downstream	1977		3.00	6.00
❑ 1981	Dreamer/From Now On	1977		2.50	5.00
❑ 1981	PS Dreamer/From Now On	1977		3.00	6.00
❑ 2128	The Logical Song/Just Another Nervous Wreck	1979		2.00	4.00
❑ 2128	PS The Logical Song/Just Another Nervous Wreck	1979		2.50	5.00
❑ 2162	Goodbye Stranger/Even in the Quietest Moments	1979		2.00	4.00
❑ 2162	PS Goodbye Stranger/Even in the Quietest Moments	1979		2.50	5.00
❑ 2193	Take the Long Way Home/Ruby	1979		2.00	4.00
❑ 2193	PS Take the Long Way Home/Ruby *With yellow maze*	1979		2.00	4.00
❑ 2193	PS Take the Long Way Home/Ruby *With green maze*	1979		2.50	5.00
❑ 2193	PS Take the Long Way Home/Ruby *With red maze. Other colors may exist, too; please let us know.*	1979		2.50	5.00
❑ 2269	Dreamer/From Now On	1980		2.00	4.00
❑ 2269	PS Dreamer/From Now On	1980		2.50	5.00
❑ 2292	Breakfast in America/You Started Laughing	1980		2.00	4.00
❑ 2502	It's Raining Again/Monnie	1982		2.00	4.00
❑ 2502	PS It's Raining Again/Monnie	1982		2.00	4.00
❑ 2517	My Kind of Lady/Know Who You Are	1983		2.00	4.00
❑ 2517	PS My Kind of Lady/Know Who You Are	1983		2.00	4.00
❑ 2720	DJ Still in Love with You (same on both sides)	1985			Unreleased?
❑ 2731	Cannonball/Every Open Door	1985			3.00
❑ 2731	PS Cannonball/Every Open Door	1985			3.00
❑ 2760	Better Days/No In-Between	1985			3.00
❑ 2985	I'm Beggin' You/No In-Between	1987			3.00
❑ 2996	Free as a Bird/Thing for You	1987			3.00

Supremes, The
(All the groups that are not the Motown group)

Ace
❑ 534	Just for You and I/Don't Leave Me Here to Cry	1957	10.00	20.00	40.00

Apt
❑ 25055	Another Chance to Love/Fidgety	1961	10.00	20.00	40.00

Kitten
❑ 6969	Could This Be You/Margie	1956	125.00	250.00	500.00

Mark
❑ 129	Nobody Can Love You/Snap, Crackle and Pop	1958	150.00	300.00	600.00

Mascot
❑ 126	Little Sally Walker/Just Yell	1960	25.00	50.00	100.00

Old Town
❑ 1024	Tonight/My Babe	1956	20.00	40.00	80.00
❑ 1024	Tonight/She Don't Want Me No More	1956	30.00	60.00	120.00

Supremes, The
(Also see "Ballard, Florence"; "Ross, Diana"; "Schumacher, Christine"; and the duet listings that follow)

EEOC
❑ (# unknown)	DJ Things Are Changing (same on both sides)	1965	37.50	75.00	150.00
❑ (# unknown)	PS Things Are Changing (same on both sides) *Promotional item for the Equal Employment Opportunity Commission*	1965	37.50	75.00	150.00

Number		Title (A Side/B Side)	Year	VG	VG+	NM

George Alexander Inc.

| ❑ 1079 | DJ | The Only Time I'm Happy/Supremes Interview | 1965 | 15.00 | 30.00 | 60.00 |

Motown

❑ 1008		I Want a Guy/Never Again	1961	375.00	750.00	1,500
❑ 1027		Your Heart Belongs to Me/(He's) Seventeen	1962	6.25	12.50	25.00
❑ 1027	PS	Your Heart Belongs to Me/(He's) Seventeen	1962	25.00	50.00	100.00
❑ 1034		Let Me Go the Right Way/Time Changes Things	1962	12.50	25.00	50.00
❑ 1040		My Heart Can't Take It No More/ You Bring Back Memories	1963	10.00	20.00	40.00
❑ 1044		A Breath Taking, First Sight Soul Shaking, One Night Love Making,Next Day Heart Breaking Guy/Rock and Roll Banjo Man	1963	25.00	50.00	100.00

Original pressing with long title. This does exist on stock copies as well as on promos.

❑ 1044		A Breath Taking Guy/Rock and Roll Banjo Man	1963	6.25	12.50	25.00
❑ 1051		When the Lovelight Starts Shining Through His Eyes/ Standing at the Crossroads of Love	1963	3.75	7.50	15.00
❑ 1054		Run, Run, Run/I'm Giving You Your Freedom	1964	6.25	12.50	25.00
❑ 1060		Where Did Our Love Go/He Means the World to Me	1964	2.50	5.00	10.00
❑ 1060	PS	Where Did Our Love Go/He Means the World to Me	1964	6.25	12.50	25.00
❑ 1066		Baby Love/Ask Any Girl	1964	2.50	5.00	10.00
❑ 1066	PS	Baby Love/Ask Any Girl	1964	6.25	12.50	25.00
❑ 1068		Come See About Me/Always in My Heart	1964	2.50	5.00	10.00
❑ 1074		Stop! In the Name of Love/I'm in Love Again	1965	2.50	5.00	10.00
❑ 1074	PS	Stop! In the Name of Love/I'm in Love Again	1965	6.25	12.50	25.00
❑ 1075		Back in My Arms Again/Whisper You Love Me Boy	1965	2.50	5.00	10.00
❑ 1075	PS	Back in My Arms Again/Whisper You Love Me Boy	1965	6.25	12.50	25.00
❑ 1080		Nothing But Heartaches/He Holds His Own	1965	2.50	5.00	10.00
❑ 1080	PS	Nothing But Heartaches/He Holds His Own	1965	6.25	12.50	25.00
❑ 1083		I Hear a Symphony/Who Could Ever Doubt My Love	1965	2.50	5.00	10.00
❑ 1085		Children's Christmas Song/Twinkle, Twinkle Little Me	1965	3.75	7.50	15.00
❑ 1089		My World Is Empty Without You/ Everything Is Good About You	1966	2.00	4.00	8.00
❑ 1094		Love Is Like an Itching in My Heart/He's All I Got	1966	2.00	4.00	8.00
❑ 1097		You Can't Hurry Love/Put Yourself in My Place	1966	2.00	4.00	8.00
❑ 1097	PS	You Can't Hurry Love/Put Yourself in My Place	1966	6.25	12.50	25.00
❑ 1101		You Keep Me Hangin' On/Remove This Doubt	1966	2.00	4.00	8.00
❑ 1101	PS	You Keep Me Hangin' On/Remove This Doubt	1966	6.25	12.50	25.00
❑ 1103		Love Is Here and Now You're Gone/ There's No Stopping Us Now	1967	2.00	4.00	8.00
❑ 1107		The Happening/All I Know About You	1967	2.00	4.00	8.00
❑ 1111		Reflections/Going Down for the Third Time	1967	2.00	4.00	8.00

Starting with 1111, through 1156, as "Diana Ross and the Supremes"

❑ 1116		In and Out of Love/I Guess I'll Always Love You	1967		3.50	7.00
❑ 1122		Forever Came Today/Time Changes Things	1968		3.50	7.00
❑ 1125		What the World Needs Now/Your Kiss of Fire	1968			Unreleased
❑ 1126		Some Things You Never Get Used To/ You've Been So Wonderful to Me	1968		3.50	7.00
❑ 1135		Love Child/Will This Be the Day	1968		3.50	7.00
❑ 1139		I'm Livin' in Shame/I'm So Glad I Got Somebody	1969		3.50	7.00
❑ 1146		The Composer/The Beginning of the End	1969		3.50	7.00
❑ 1148		No Matter What Sign You Are/The Young Folks	1969		3.50	7.00
❑ 1156		Someday We'll Be Together/He's My Sunny Boy	1969		3.50	7.00
❑ 1162		Up the Ladder to the Roof/ Bill, When Are You Coming Home	1970		3.00	6.00

Starting with 1162, name reverts to "The Supremes" (unless noted)

❑ 1167		Everybody's Got the Right to Love/But I Love You More	1970		3.00	6.00
❑ 1172		Stoned Love/Shine on Me	1970		3.00	6.00
❑ 1182		Nathan Jones/Happy (Is a Bumpy Road)	1971		3.00	6.00
❑ 1190		Touch/It's So Hard for Me to Say Goodbye	1971		3.00	6.00
❑ 1195		Floy Joy/This Is the Story	1972		2.50	5.00
❑ 1200		Automatically Sunshine/Precious Little Things	1972		2.50	5.00
❑ 1206		Your Wonderful, Sweet Sweet Love/ The Wisdom of Time	1972		2.50	5.00
❑ 1213		I Guess I'll Miss the Man/Over and Over	1972		2.50	5.00
❑ 1225		Bad Weather/Oh Be My Love	1973		2.50	5.00
❑ 1350		It's All Been Said Before/(B-side unassigned)	1975			Unreleased
❑ 1357		He's My Man/Give Out But Don't Give Up	1975		2.50	5.00
❑ 1374		Where Do I Go from Here/Give Out But Don't Give Up	1975		2.50	5.00
❑ 1391		I'm Gonna Let My Heart Do the Walking/ Early Morning Love	1976		2.50	5.00
❑ 1407		You're My Driving Wheel/ You're What's Missing in My Life	1976		2.50	5.00
❑ 1415		Let Yourself Go/You Are the Heart of Me	1977		2.50	5.00
❑ 1488		Medley of Hits/Where Did We Go Wrong	1980		2.00	4.00

As "Diana Ross and the Supremes"

| ❑ 1523 | | Medley of Hits/Where Did We Go Wrong | 1981 | | 2.00 | 4.00 |

As "Diana Ross and the Supremes"

Tamla

| ❑ 54038 | | I Want a Guy/Never Again | 1961 | 31.25 | 62.50 | 125.00 |

Lines label

| ❑ 54038 | | I Want a Guy/Never Again | 1961 | 15.00 | 30.00 | 60.00 |

Globes label

| ❑ 54045 | | Buttered Popcorn/Who's Lovin' You | 1961 | 31.25 | 62.50 | 125.00 |

Lines label

| ❑ 54045 | | Buttered Popcorn/Who's Lovin' You | 1961 | 15.00 | 30.00 | 60.00 |

Globes label

Number		Title (A Side/B Side)	Year	VG	VG+	NM
Topps/Motown						
❑ 1		Baby Love	1967	18.75	37.50	75.00
		Cardboard record				
❑ 2		Stop in the Name of Love	1967	18.75	37.50	75.00
		Cardboard record				
❑ 3		Where Did Our Love Go	1967	18.75	37.50	75.00
		Cardboard record				
❑ 15		Come See About Me	1967	18.75	37.50	75.00
		Cardboard record				
❑ 16		My World Is Empty Without You	1967	18.75	37.50	75.00
		Cardboard record				

Supremes, The, and the Four Tops
(Also see individual listings)

Number		Title (A Side/B Side)	Year	VG	VG+	NM
Motown						
❑ 1173		River Deep-Mountain High/	1970		3.00	6.00
		Together We Can Make Such Sweet Music				
❑ 1181		You Gotta Have Love in Your Heart/I'm Glad About It	1971		3.00	6.00

Supremes, The, Diana Ross and, and the Temptations
(Also see individual listings)

Number		Title (A Side/B Side)	Year	VG	VG+	NM
Motown						
❑ 1137		I'm Gonna Make You Love Me/A Place in the Sun	1968		3.50	7.00
❑ 1137	PS	I'm Gonna Make You Love Me/A Place in the Sun	1968	5.00	10.00	20.00
❑ 1142		I'll Try Something New/	1969		3.50	7.00
		The Way You Do the Things You Do				
❑ 1150		Stubborn Kind of Fellow/Try It Baby	1969		3.50	7.00
❑ 1153		The Weight/For Better or Worse	1969		3.50	7.00

Supremes Four, The

Number		Title (A Side/B Side)	Year	VG	VG+	NM
Sara						
❑ 1032		I Lost My Job/I Love You Patricia	1958	100.00	200.00	400.00

Surf Boys, The

Number		Title (A Side/B Side)	Year	VG	VG+	NM
Karate						
❑ 526		Da Doo Ron Ron/Hurt	1966	6.25	12.50	25.00
Scepter						
❑ 12180		Stuck in the Chimney/I Told Santa Claus I Want You	1966	6.25	12.50	25.00

Surf Breakers, The

Number		Title (A Side/B Side)	Year	VG	VG+	NM
Mercury						
❑ 72174		Hang Ten/Ridin' In #9	1963	12.50	25.00	50.00

Surf Bunnies, The

Number		Title (A Side/B Side)	Year	VG	VG+	NM
Dot						
❑ 16523		Our Surfer Boys/Surf Bunny Beach	1963	7.50	15.00	30.00
Goliath						
❑ 1352		Our Surfer Boys/Surf Bunny Beach	1963	12.50	25.00	50.00
❑ 1353		Surf City High/Met the Boy I Adore	1963	12.50	25.00	50.00

Surf Riders, The

Number		Title (A Side/B Side)	Year	VG	VG+	NM
Decca						
❑ 31477		The Birds/Blues for the Birds	1963	7.50	15.00	30.00
Nasco						
❑ 6008		I'm Out/Rocko Socko	1958	15.00	30.00	60.00

Surfaris, The
(Two different groups)

Number		Title (A Side/B Side)	Year	VG	VG+	NM
Chancellor						
❑ 1142		The Midnight Surf/Psyche-Out	1963	12.50	25.00	50.00
Decca						
❑ 31538		Point Panic/Waikiki Run	1963	3.75	7.50	15.00
❑ 31561		Surfer's Christmas List/Santa's Speed Shop	1963	7.50	15.00	30.00
❑ 31581		I Wanna Take a Trip to the Islands/Scatter Shield	1964	5.00	10.00	20.00
❑ 31605		Murphy the Surfie/Go Go Go For Louie's Place	1964	3.75	7.50	15.00
❑ 31641		Bossa Barracuda/Dune Buggy	1964	3.75	7.50	15.00
❑ 31682		Hot Rod High/Karen	1964	3.75	7.50	15.00
❑ 31731		Beat '65/Black Denim	1965	5.00	10.00	20.00
❑ 31784		Theme of the Battle Maiden/Somethin' Else	1965	5.00	10.00	20.00
❑ 31835		Catch a Little Ride with Me/Don't Hurt My Little Sister	1965	5.00	10.00	20.00
❑ 31954		Hey Joe Where Are You Going/So Get Out	1966	5.00	10.00	20.00
❑ 32003		Wipe Out/I'm a Hog for You	1966	2.50	5.00	10.00
Del-Fi						
❑ 4219		Surfari/Bombora	1963	25.00	50.00	100.00
DFS						
❑ 11/12		Wipe Out/Surfer Joe	1963	1,500	2,250	3,000
Dot						
❑ 144		Wipe Out/Surfer Joe	1966	2.50	5.00	10.00
❑ 144	DJ	Wipe Out (same on both sides)	1966	25.00	50.00	100.00
		Red vinyl				

The world's most valuable surf record is "Wipe Out" by the Surfaris on this very, very rare original pressing on the DFS label. Even as worn as this record is, it fetched $1,375 at auction in 1996. Think what a near-mint copy would sell for if one became available! Also sought after are "Wipe Out" pressings on the Princess label, and also a red-vinyl promo reissue on Dot from 1966.

Number		Title (A Side/B Side)	Year	VG	VG+	NM
❑ 144	DJ	Wipe Out (same on both sides)	1966	37.50	75.00	150.00
		Red vinyl; error pressing with "Surfer Joe" on both sides				
❑ 16479		Wipe Out/Surfer Joe	1963	3.75	7.50	15.00
❑ 16757		Surfer Joe/Can't Sit Down	1965	7.50	15.00	30.00
		B-side by the Challengers, but credited to the Surfaris				
❑ 16757		Surfer Joe/Can't Sit Down	1965	12.50	25.00	50.00
		B-side by the Challengers, and credited correctly				
❑ 16966		Show Biz/Chicago Green	1966	2.50	5.00	10.00
❑ 17008		Shake/The Search	1967	2.50	5.00	10.00

Felsted

❑ 8688		Tor-Chula/Psyche-Out	1964	12.50	25.00	50.00

Northridge

❑ 1001		Moment of Truth/Church Key	1963	15.00	30.00	60.00
		B-side by the Biscaynes				

Princess

❑ 50		Wipe Out/Surfer Joe	1963	100.00	200.00	400.00
		With long versions of both songs. No "RE-1" is in the trail-off area.				
❑ 50		Wipe Out/Surfer Joe	1963	25.00	50.00	100.00
		With short versions of both songs. "RE-1" is in the trail-off area.				

Regano

❑ 1062		Surfin' '63/Boss Beat	1963	12.50	25.00	50.00
		As "The Original Surfaris"				

Reprise

❑ 20,180		Moment of Truth/Church Key	1963	7.50	15.00	30.00
		B-side by the Biscaynes				

Surfari

❑ 301		Gum Dipped Slicks/High Time	1964	25.00	50.00	100.00
		As "The Original Surfaris"				

Survivor

(With Jim Peterik, ex-Ides of March)

Casablanca

❑ 880 053-7		Moment of Truth/It Doesn't Have to Be That Way	1984		2.00	4.00

Scotti Bros.

❑ 511		Somwhere in America/Freelance	1980		2.50	5.00
❑ 517		Rebel Girl/Freelance	1980		2.50	5.00
❑ 02434		Memphis/Love Isn't Easy	1981		2.00	4.00
❑ 02560		Poor Man's Son/Love Is On My Side	1981		2.00	4.00
❑ 02700		Summer Nights/Take You on a Saturday	1982		2.00	4.00
❑ 02912		Eye of the Tiger/Take You on a Saturday	1982		2.00	4.00
❑ 02912	PS	Eye of the Tiger/Take You on a Saturday	1982		3.00	6.00
❑ 03213		American Heartbeat/Silver Girl	1982		2.00	4.00
❑ 03213	PS	American Heartbeat/Silver Girl	1982		2.50	5.00
❑ 03485		The One That Really Matters/Hesitation Dance	1983		2.00	4.00
❑ 04074		Caught in the Game/Slander	1983		2.00	4.00
❑ 04074	PS	Caught in the Game/Slander	1983		2.50	5.00
❑ 04347		I Never Stopped Loving You/Ready for the Real Thing	1984		2.00	4.00
❑ 04603		I Can't Hold Back/I See You in Everyone	1984			3.00
❑ 04603	PS	I Can't Hold Back/I See You in Everyone	1984		2.00	4.00
❑ 04685		High on You/Broken Promises	1984			3.00
❑ 04685	PS	High on You/Broken Promises	1984		2.00	4.00
❑ 04871		The Search Is Over/It's the Singer, Not the Song	1985			3.00
❑ 04871	PS	The Search Is Over/It's the Singer, Not the Song	1985		2.00	4.00
❑ 05579		First Night/Feels Like Love	1985			3.00
❑ 05579	PS	First Night/Feels Like Love	1985		2.00	4.00
❑ 05663		Burning Heart/Feels Like Love	1985			3.00
❑ 05663	PS	Burning Heart/Feels Like Love	1985		2.00	4.00
❑ 06381		Is This Love/Can't Let You Go	1986			3.00
❑ 06381	PS	Is This Love/Can't Let You Go	1986		2.00	4.00
❑ 06705		How Much Love/Backstreet Love Affair	1987			3.00
❑ 07070		Man Against the World/Oceans	1987			3.00
❑ 07070	PS	Man Against the World/Oceans	1987		2.00	4.00
❑ 08067		Didn't Know It Was Love/Rhythm of the City	1988			3.00
❑ 68526		Across the Miles/Burning Bridges	1989			3.00

Survivors, The

(Not the Beach Boys, but Dave Nowlen, Bob Norberg and friends with help from Brian Wilson)

Capitol

❑ 5102		Pamela Jean/After the Game	1963	250.00	500.00	1,000

Susie and the Four Trumpets

United Artists

❑ 471		Starry Eyes/Blue Little Girl	1962	15.00	30.00	60.00

Suzy and the Red Stripes

(Linda McCartney and Wings; also see "McCartney, Paul")

Capitol

❑ B-5608		Seaside Woman/B-Side to Seaside	1986	7.50	15.00	30.00

Epic

❑ 50403		Seaside Woman/B-Side to Seaside	1977	2.50	5.00	10.00
❑ 50403	DJ	Seaside Woman (mono/stereo)	1977	25.00	50.00	100.00
		"Advance Promotion" label, black vinyl				

Number	Title (A Side/B Side)	Year	VG	VG+	NM
❑ 50403	DJ Seaside Woman (mono/stereo)	1977	6.25	12.50	25.00
	Red vinyl, orange label on one side, white on the other				
❑ 50403	DJ Seaside Woman (mono/stereo)	1977	25.00	50.00	100.00
	Black vinyl, orange label on one side, white on the other				

Swallows, The
(More than one group)
After Hours
❑ 104	My Baby/Good Time Girls	1954	200.00	400.00	800.00

Federal
❑ 12319	Oh Lonesome Me/Angel Baby	1958	10.00	20.00	40.00
❑ 12328	We Want to Rock/Rock-a-Bye-Baby Rock	1958	10.00	20.00	40.00
❑ 12329	Beside You/Laughing Boy	1958	10.00	20.00	40.00
❑ 12333	Itchy Twitchy Feeling/Who Knows, Do You?	1958	10.00	20.00	40.00

Guyden
❑ 2023	How Long Must a Fool Go On/You Must Try	1959	12.50	25.00	50.00
	This record was reissued credited to "The Guides"				

King
❑ 4458	Will You Be Mine/Dearest	1951	500.00	1,000	1,500
❑ 4466	Since You've Been Away/Wishing for You	1951		Unconfirmed on 45 rpm	
❑ 4501	Eternally/It Ain't the Heat	1952	1,000	1,500	2,000
	Red vinyl				
❑ 4501	Eternally/It Ain't the Heat	1952	250.00	500.00	1,000
❑ 4515	Tell Me Why/Roll, Roll, Pretty Baby	1952	1,000	1,500	2,000
❑ 4525	Beside You/You Left Me	1952	100.00	200.00	400.00
❑ 4533	You Walked In/I Only Have Eyes for You	1952	200.00	400.00	800.00
❑ 4579	Where Do I Go from Here/Please, Baby, Please	1952	200.00	400.00	800.00
❑ 4612	Laugh (Though You Want to Cry)/Our Love Is Dying	1953	125.00	250.00	500.00
❑ 4632	Nobody's Lovin' Me/Bicycle Tillie	1953	125.00	250.00	500.00
❑ 4656	Trust Me/Pleading Blues	1953	100.00	200.00	400.00
❑ 4676	I'll Be Waiting/It Feels So Good	1953	100.00	200.00	400.00

Swamp Rats, The
Co & Ce
❑ 245	In the Midnight Hour/It's Not Easy	1967	5.00	10.00	20.00

St. Clair
❑ 69	Louie Louie/Hey Joe	1966	12.50	25.00	50.00
❑ 2222	Psycho/Here, There and Everywhere	1966	50.00	100.00	200.00
❑ 3333	Two Tymes Two/(B-side unknown)	1966	12.50	25.00	50.00
❑ 711,711	It's Not Easy/No Friend of Mine	1966	12.50	25.00	50.00

Swans, The
(More than one group)
Ballad
❑ 1003/6	It's a Must/Night Train	1954	150.00	300.00	600.00
❑ 1007	Happy/The Santa Claus Boogie	1955	150.00	300.00	600.00

Cameo
❑ 302	The Boy with the Beatle Hair/Please Hurry Home	1964	10.00	20.00	40.00

Fortune
❑ 822	I'll Forever Love You/Mister Cool Breeze	1955	100.00	200.00	400.00

Parkway
❑ 881	Daydreamin' of You/The Promise	1963	7.50	15.00	30.00

Rainbow
❑ 233	No More/My True Love	1954	500.00	1,000	1,500
	Red vinyl				

Roulette
❑ 4213	He Wasn't On the Air Again Today/ If I Could Stop Every Clock	1959	6.25	12.50	25.00

Steamboat
❑ 101	Believe in Me/In the Morning	1956	75.00	150.00	300.00

Swan
❑ 4151	He's Mine/You Better Be a Good Girl Now	1963	7.50	15.00	30.00

Swanson, Bobby
Donna
❑ 1326	Tom and Susie/China Doll	1960	6.25	12.50	25.00
❑ 1336	Janie's Face/Peggy's Last Birthday	1961	6.25	12.50	25.00
❑ 1356	Twisting at the Top/Hello There Lover Doll	1962	6.25	12.50	25.00

Igloo
❑ 1003	Rockin' Little Eskimo/Ballad of an Angel	1959	100.00	200.00	400.00

Sweet Inspirations, The
(Also see "Houston, Cissy")
Atlantic
❑ 2410	Why (Am I Treated So Bad)/I Don't Want to Go On Without You	1967	2.00	4.00	8.00
❑ 2418	Let It Be Me/When Something Is Wrong with My Baby	1967	2.00	4.00	8.00
❑ 2436	I've Been Loving You Too Long (To Stop Now)/ That's How Strong My Love Is	1967	2.00	4.00	8.00
❑ 2449	O' What a Fool I've Been/Don't Fight It	1967	2.00	4.00	8.00
❑ 2465	Reach Out for Me/Do Right Woman -- Do Right Man	1967	2.00	4.00	8.00
❑ 2476	Sweet Inspiration/I'm Blue	1968	2.00	4.00	8.00

Number	Title (A Side/B Side)	Year	VG	VG+	NM
❏ 2529	To Love Somebody/Where Did It Go	1968	2.00	4.00	8.00
❏ 2551	Unchained Melody/	1968	2.00	4.00	8.00
	Am I Ever Gonna See My Baby Again				
❏ 2571	What the World Needs Now Is Love/	1968	2.00	4.00	8.00
	You Really Didn't Mean It				
❏ 2620	Crying in the Rain/Everyday WIll Be Like a Holiday	1969	2.00	4.00	8.00
❏ 2638	Sweets for My Sweet/Get a Little Order	1969	2.00	4.00	8.00
❏ 2653	Don't Go/Chained	1969	2.00	4.00	8.00
❏ 2686	(Gotta Find) A Brand New Lover -- Part I/	1969	2.00	4.00	8.00
	(Gotta Find) A Brand New Lover -- Part II				
❏ 2720	At Last I Found a Love/That's the Way My Baby Is	1970		3.00	6.00
❏ 2732	Them Boys/Flash in the Pan	1970		3.00	6.00
❏ 2750	This World/A Light Sings	1970		3.00	6.00
❏ 2779	Evidence/Change Me Not	1970		3.00	6.00

Caribou

❏ 9022	Black Sunday/(Instrumental)	1977		2.00	4.00

RSO

❏ 932	Love Is On the Way/(Instrumental)	1979		2.50	5.00
❏ 1013	Love Is On the Way/(Instrumental)	1979		2.00	4.00

Stax

❏ 0178	Emercury/Slipped and Tripped	1973		2.50	5.00
❏ 0203	Try a Little Tenderness/Dirty Tricks	1974		2.50	5.00

Sweet Marquees, The

Apache

❏ 1516	You Lied/I Love My Baby	1961	75.00	150.00	300.00

Sweet Sick Teens, The

RCA Victor

❏ 37-7940	The Pretzel/Agnes, the Teenage Russian Spy	1961	20.00	40.00	80.00
	"Compact Single 33" (small hole, plays at LP speed)				
❏ 47-7940	The Pretzel/Agnes, the Teenage Russian Spy	1961	10.00	20.00	40.00

Sweet, The

Bell

❏ 45,106	Funny, Funny/You're Not Wrong for Loving Me	1971		3.00	6.00
❏ 45,126	Co-Co/You're Not Wrong for Loving Me	1971		3.00	6.00
❏ 45,184	Poppa Joe/Jeanie	1972		3.00	6.00
❏ 45,251	Little Willy/Man from Mecca	1972		2.50	5.00
❏ 45,361	Blockbuster/Need a Lot of Lovin'	1973		2.50	5.00
❏ 45,408	Wig-Wam Bam/New York Connection	1973		2.50	5.00

Capitol

❏ 4055	Ballroom Blitz/Restless	1975		2.00	4.00
❏ 4157	Fox on the Run/Burn On the Flame	1975		2.00	4.00
❏ 4220	Action/Medussa	1976		2.00	4.00
❏ 4429	Fever of Love/Heartbreak Today	1977		2.00	4.00
❏ 4454	Funk It Up (David's Song)/Stairway to the Stars	1977		2.00	4.00
❏ 4549	Love Is Like Oxygen/Cover Girl	1978		2.00	4.00
❏ 4610	California Nights/Dream On	1978		2.00	4.00
❏ 4730	Mother Earth/Why Don't You	1979		2.00	4.00
❏ 4908	Sixties Man/Water's Edge	1980		2.00	4.00

Paramount

❏ 0044	The Juicer/All You'll Ever Get from Me	1970	3.75	7.50	15.00

Smash

❏ 2116	Got to Have More Love/You Can't Win at Love	1967	3.75	7.50	15.00
❏ 2136	Broken Heart Attack/Don't Do It	1967	3.75	7.50	15.00

20th Century

❏ 2033	It's Lonely Out There/I'm On My Way	1973	2.50	5.00	10.00

Swift, Basil, and the Seegrams

(Danny Hutton is The Seegrams)

Mercury

❏ 72386	Farmer's Daughter/Shambles	1965	50.00	100.00	200.00

Swingin' Medallions

Capitol

❏ 2338	Sun, Sand and Sea/Hey, Hey Baby	1968	2.00	4.00	8.00

Dot

❏ 16721	Bye Bye, Silly Girl/I Want to Be Your Guy	1965	3.00	6.00	12.00

4 Sale

❏ 002	Double Shot (Of My Baby's Love)/Here It Comes Again	1966	10.00	20.00	40.00

1-2-3

❏ 1723	We're Gonna Hate Ourselves in the Morning/It's Alright	1970	2.00	4.00	8.00
❏ 1732	Rollin' Rovin' River/	1971	2.00	4.00	8.00
	Don't Let Your Feet Touch the Ground				

Smash

❏ 2033	Double Shot (Of My Baby's Love)/Here It Comes Again	1966	3.75	7.50	15.00
❏ 2050	She Drives Me Out of My Mind/You Gotta Have Faith	1966	3.00	6.00	12.00
❏ 2075	I Don't Want to Lose It for You Baby/Night Owl	1966	3.00	6.00	12.00
❏ 2084	Don't Cry No More/I Found a Rainbow	1967	2.50	5.00	10.00
❏ 2107	Turn On the Music/Summer's Not the Same This Year	1967	2.50	5.00	10.00
❏ 2129	Bow and Arrow/Where Can I Go to Get Soul	1967	2.50	5.00	10.00

Number	Title (A Side/B Side)	Year	VG	VG+	NM

Swinging Blue Jeans, The
Imperial

☐ 66021	Hippy Hippy Shake/Now I Must Go	1964	3.75	7.50	15.00
☐ 66030	Good Golly Miss Molly/Shaking Feeling	1964	3.00	6.00	12.00
☐ 66049	Shake, Rattle and Roll/You're No Good	1964	3.00	6.00	12.00
☐ 66059	Tutti Frutti/Promise You'll Tell Her	1964	3.00	6.00	12.00
☐ 66090	It Isn't There/One of These Days	1965	3.00	6.00	12.00
☐ 66154	Don't Make Me Over/What Can I Do Today	1966	3.00	6.00	12.00
☐ 66225	Now the Summer's Gone/ Rumors, Gossip, Words Untrue	1967	2.50	5.00	10.00
☐ 66255	Something's Coming Along/Tremblin'	1967	2.50	5.00	10.00

Swinging Tigers
Tamla

☐ 54024	Snake Walk (Part 1)/Snake Walk (Part 2)	1960	75.00	150.00	300.00

Sycamores, The
Groove

☐ 0121	I'll Be Waiting/Darling, Is It True	1955	50.00	100.00	200.00

Sylvester, Terry
(Member of The Hollies)
Epic

☐ 20002	It's Better Off This Way/For the Peace of All Mankind	1974		2.00	4.00
☐ 50017	It's Better Off This Way/For the Peace of All Mankind	1974		2.00	4.00
☐ 50532	Silver and Gold/Realistic Situation	1978		2.00	4.00

Sylvia
(Of Mickey and Sylvia, not the country singer)
All Platinum

☐ 2303	I Can't Help It/It's a Good Life	1969	2.00	4.00	8.00
☐ 2350	Sho Nuff Boogie (Part 1)/Sho Nuff Boogie (Part 2) *With the Moments*	1974		2.50	5.00

Jubilee

☐ 5093	Drive, Daddy, Drive/I Found Somebody to Love *As "Little Sylvia"*	1952	12.50	25.00	50.00

Stang

☐ 5015	Have You Had Any Lately/Anytime	1970		3.00	6.00

Sugar Hill

☐ 781	It's Good to Be the Queen/(B-side unknown)	1982		2.00	4.00

Vibration

☐ 512	Next Time I See You/Gimme a Little Action	1972		3.00	6.00
☐ 521	Pillow Talk/My Thing	1973		2.50	5.00
☐ 524	Didn't I/Had Any Lately	1973		2.50	5.00
☐ 525	Soul Je T'Aime/(B-side unknown) *With Ralfi Pagan*	1973		2.50	5.00
☐ 527	Alfredo/Lay It On Me	1973		2.50	5.00
☐ 528	Private Performance/If You Get the Notion	1974		2.50	5.00
☐ 529	Sweet Stuff/Had Any Lately	1974		2.50	5.00
☐ 530	Easy Evil/Give It Up in Vain	1974		2.50	5.00
☐ 536	Pussy Cat (Part 1)/Pussy Cat (Part 2)	1975		2.50	5.00
☐ 567	L.A. Sunshine/Taxi	1976		2.50	5.00
☐ 572	Lay It On Me/Lollipop Man	1977		2.50	5.00
☐ 576	Automatic Lover/Stop Boy	1978		2.50	5.00

Syndicate, The
Dore

☐ 743	My Baby Is Barefoot/Love Will Take Away	1965	10.00	20.00	40.00

Dot

☐ 16807	Egyptian Thing/She Haunts You	1965	10.00	20.00	40.00

Syndicate of Sound
Bell

☐ 640	Little Girl/You	1966	5.00	10.00	20.00
☐ 646	Rumors/Upper Hand	1966	3.75	7.50	15.00
☐ 655	Goodtime Music/Keep It Up	1966	3.75	7.50	15.00
☐ 666	Mary/That Kind of Man	1967	3.75	7.50	15.00

Buddah

☐ 156	Brown Paper Bag/Reverb Beat	1970	2.50	5.00	10.00
☐ 183	Mexico/First to Love You	1970	2.50	5.00	10.00

Capitol

☐ 2426	You're Looking Fine/Change the World	1969	2.50	5.00	10.00

Del-Fi

☐ 4304	Prepare for Love/Tell the World	1965	5.00	10.00	20.00

Hush

☐ 228	Little Girl/You	1966	12.50	25.00	50.00

Scarlet

☐ 503	Prepare for Love/Tell the World	1965	7.50	15.00	30.00

Number	Title (A Side/B Side)	Year	VG	VG+	NM

T

T-Birds, The
(Jesse Belvin and Jimmy Norman)
Chess
❑ 1778	Green Stamps/Come On Dance with Me	1961	6.25	12.50	25.00
❑ 1792	Hog Wild/Taco Harry	1961	6.25	12.50	25.00

Gone
❑ 5141	Wild Stomp/Soft Smoke	1962	5.00	10.00	20.00

Vegas
❑ 720	Nobody But You/(B-side unknown)	196?	15.00	30.00	60.00

T-Bones, The
(Evolved into "Hamilton, Joe Frank and Reynolds")
Liberty
❑ 55677	Draggin'/Rail-Vette	1964	5.00	10.00	20.00
❑ 55814	That's Where It's At/Pearlin'	1965	3.75	7.50	15.00
❑ 55836	No Matter What Shape (Your Stomach's In)/ Feelin' Fine	1965	3.00	6.00	12.00
❑ 55867	Sippin' & Chippin'/Moment of Softness	1966	2.50	5.00	10.00
❑ 55885	Underwater/Wherever You Look, Wherever You Go	1966	2.50	5.00	10.00
❑ 55906	Let's Go Get Stoned/Fare Thee Well	1966	2.50	5.00	10.00
❑ 55925	Balboa Blues/Walkin' My Cat Named Dog	1966	2.50	5.00	10.00
❑ 55951	Tee Hee Hee (My Life Seems Different Now)/ Proper Thing to Do	1967	2.50	5.00	10.00

United Artists
❑ 0068	No Matter What Shape (Your Stomach's In)/ Sippin' N Chippin' "Silver Spotlight Series" reissue	1973		2.50	5.00

T. Rex
A&M
❑ 955	Child Star/Debora As "Tyrannosaurus Rex"	1968	3.00	6.00	12.00

Blue Thumb
❑ 212	By the Light of the Magical Moon/Find a Little Wood	1971		3.00	6.00
❑ SP-6115	DJ Ride a White Swan/Is It Love As "Tyrannosaurus Rex"	1970	3.00	6.00	12.00
❑ 7121	Ride a White Swan/Summertime Blues As "Tyrannosaurus Rex"	1970	2.00	4.00	8.00

Casablanca
❑ 810	Precious Star/(B-side unknown)	1974		3.00	6.00

Reprise
❑ 1006	Hot Love//One Inch Rock/Seagull Woman	1971		3.00	6.00
❑ 1032	Bang a Gong (Get It On)/Raw Ramp	1971	2.00	4.00	8.00
❑ 1056	Jeepster/Rip Off	1971		3.00	6.00
❑ 1078	Telegram Sam/Cadillac	1972		3.00	6.00
❑ 1095	Metal Guru/Lady	1972		3.00	6.00
❑ 1122	The Slider/Rock On	1972		3.00	6.00
❑ 1150	Bang a Gong (Get It On)/Telegram Sam "Back to Back Hits" series	1972		2.00	4.00
❑ 1151	Jeepster/Metal Guru "Back to Back Hits" series	1972		2.00	4.00
❑ 1161	Born to Boogie/The Groover	1973		2.50	5.00
❑ 1161	PS Born to Boogie/The Groover	1973	6.25	12.50	25.00
❑ 1170	Hot Love/Rip Off	1973		2.50	5.00

T.C. Atlantic
Aesop's Label
❑ 6044	Once Upon a Melody/I Love You So, Little Girl	1965	10.00	20.00	40.00

B. Sharp
❑ 272	Mona/My Babe	1966	7.50	15.00	30.00

Candy Floss
❑ 101	I'm So Glad/Twenty Years Ago	1968	10.00	20.00	40.00

Paramount
❑ 0098	Judgment Train/Shine the Light	1971	3.75	7.50	15.00

Parrot
❑ 330	I'm So Glad/Twenty Years Ago	1968	5.00	10.00	20.00
❑ 338	Love Is Just/Faces	1969	5.00	10.00	20.00

Turtle
❑ 1103	Faces/Baby, Please Don't Go	1966	25.00	50.00	100.00
❑ 1105	Shake/Spanish Harlem	1967	10.00	20.00	40.00

T.I.M.E.
Liberty
❑ 56020	Take Me Along/Make It Right	1968	2.50	5.00	10.00
❑ 56020	PS Take Me Along/Make It Right	1968	3.75	7.50	15.00
❑ 56060	Tripping Into Sunshine/ What Would Life Be Without You	1968	2.50	5.00	10.00

Number	Title (A Side/B Side)	Year	VG	VG+	NM

Tabbys, The
Time
| ☐ 1008 | Yes I Do/My Darling
Red label | 1959 | 6.25 | 12.50 | 25.00 |
| ☐ 1008 | Yes I Do/My Darling
Blue label | 1959 | 12.50 | 25.00 | 50.00 |

Tabs, The
Dot
| ☐ 15887 | Avenue of Tears/The First Star | 1959 | 7.50 | 15.00 | 30.00 |
Gardena
| ☐ 110 | Never Forget/Rock and Roll Holiday | 1960 | 12.50 | 25.00 | 50.00 |
Nasco
| ☐ 6016 | Will We Meet Again/Still Love You Baby | 1958 | 7.50 | 15.00 | 30.00 |
Noble
| ☐ 719 | Never Forget/Rock and Roll Holiday | 1959 | 37.50 | 75.00 | 150.00 |
| ☐ 720 | Oops/My Girl Is Gone | 1959 | 100.00 | 200.00 | 400.00 |
Vee Jay
| ☐ 418 | Dance All By Myself/Dance Party | 1961 | 5.00 | 10.00 | 20.00 |
| ☐ 446 | Mash Dem Taters/But You're My Baby | 1962 | 5.00 | 10.00 | 20.00 |
Wand
| ☐ 130 | Two Stupid Feet/Footsteps | 1962 | 3.75 | 7.50 | 15.00 |
| ☐ 139 | I'm with You/Take My Love Along with You | 1963 | 3.75 | 7.50 | 15.00 |

Tads, The
Dot
| ☐ 15518 | Your Reason/The Pink Panther | 1956 | 6.25 | 12.50 | 25.00 |
Liberty Bell
| ☐ 9010 | Your Reason/The Pink Panther | 1956 | 12.50 | 25.00 | 50.00 |
Rev
| ☐ 3513 | Wolf Call/She Is My Dream | 1958 | 12.50 | 25.00 | 50.00 |

Tages, The
(With Peter Frampton)
Verve
| ☐ 10626 | Halcyon Days/I Read You Like an Open Book | 1968 | 5.00 | 10.00 | 20.00 |

Talking Heads
Sire
☐ GSRE 0452	Take Me to the River/Life During Wartime "Back to Back Hits" reissue	198?			3.00
☐ GSRE 0479	Burning Down the House/This Must Be the Place "Back to Back Hits" reissue	198?			3.00
☐ 737	Love Goes to Building on Fire/New Feeling	1977	2.00	4.00	8.00
☐ 737 PS	Love Goes to Building on Fire/New Feeling	1977	2.00	4.00	8.00
☐ 1002	Uh-Oh, Love Comes to Town/ I Wish You Wouldn't Say That	1977		3.00	6.00
☐ 1002 PS	Uh-Oh, Love Comes to Town/ I Wish You Wouldn't Say That	1977		3.00	6.00
☐ 1013	Psycho Killer/Psycho Killer (Acoustic)	1978	2.00	4.00	8.00
☐ 1013 PS	Psycho Killer/Psycho Killer (Acoustic)	1978	2.00	4.00	8.00
☐ 1032	Take Me to the River/ Thank You for Sending Me an Angel (Version)	1978		2.00	4.00
☐ 1032 PS	Take Me to the River/ Thank You for Sending Me an Angel (Version)	1978		2.00	4.00
☐ 21975	Wild, Wild Life/And She Was "Back to Back Hits" reissue	198?			3.00
☐ 27948	Blind/Still	1988			2.00
☐ 27948 PS	Blind/Still	1988			2.00
☐ 27992	(Nothing But) Flowers/Ruby Dear	1988			2.00
☐ 27992 PS	(Nothing But) Flowers/Ruby Dear	1988			2.00
☐ 28497	Love for Sale/Hey Now	1987			2.00
☐ 28497 PS	Love for Sale/Hey Now	1987			2.00
☐ 28629	Wild Wild Life/People Like Us (Movie Version)	1986			2.00
☐ 28629 PS	Wild Wild Life/People Like Us (Movie Version)	1986			2.00
☐ 28917	And She Was/And She Was (Dub)	1985			2.00
☐ 28917 PS	And She Was/And She Was (Dub)	1985			2.00
☐ 28987	Road to Nowhere/Give Me Back My Name	1985			3.00
☐ 28987 PS	Road to Nowhere/Give Me Back My Name	1985			3.00
☐ 29080	Stop Making Sense (Girlfriend Is Better)/Heaven	1985			3.00
☐ 29163	Once in a Lifetime/ This Must Be the Place (Naive Melody)	1984			3.00
☐ 29163 PS	Once in a Lifetime/ This Must Be the Place (Naive Melody)	1984			3.00
☐ 29451	This Must Be the Place (Naive Melody)/Moon Rocks	1983			3.00
☐ 29451 PS	This Must Be the Place (Naive Melody)/Moon Rocks	1983			3.00
☐ 29565	Burning Down the House/I Get Wild-Wild Gravity	1983			3.00
☐ 29565 PS	Burning Down the House/I Get Wild-Wild Gravity	1983			3.00
☐ 49075	Life During Wartime (This Ain't No Party... This Ain't No Disco...This Ain't No Foolin' Around)/Electric Guitar	1979		2.00	4.00
☐ 49649	Once in a Lifetime/Seen and Not Seen	1981		2.00	4.00
☐ 49734	Houses in Motion/The Overload	1981		2.00	4.00

Number	Title (A Side/B Side)	Year	VG	VG+	NM

Tallysmen, The
Tally

❏ 200,688	Little By Little/You Don't Care About Me	1966	15.00	30.00	60.00

Tamaneers, The
Bramley

❏ 102	Searching/Be Anything (But Be Mine)	1960	100.00	200.00	400.00

Tamblyn, Larry
Faro

❏ 601	Patty Ann/Dearest	1960	5.00	10.00	20.00
❏ 603	The Lie/My Bride-to-Be	1960	5.00	10.00	20.00
❏ 612	This Is the Night/Destiny	1961	6.25	12.50	25.00

Linda

❏ 112	You'll Be Mine Someday/The Girl in My Heart	1963	5.00	10.00	20.00
	With the Standells				

Tams, The
(More than one group)
ABC

❏ 10825	Holding On/Is It Better to Have Loved a Little	1966	2.00	4.00	8.00
❏ 10885	Shelter/Get Away (Leave Me Alone)	1966	2.00	4.00	8.00
❏ 10929	Breaking Up/How 'Bout It	1967	2.00	4.00	8.00
❏ 10956	Everything Else Is Gone/Mary, Mary, Row Your Boat	1967	2.00	4.00	8.00
❏ 11019	All My Heard Times/A Little More Soul	1967	2.00	4.00	8.00
❏ 11066	Be Young, Be Foolish, Be Happy/That Same Old Song	1968	2.00	4.00	8.00
❏ 11128	Laugh at the World/Trouble Maker	1968	2.00	4.00	8.00
❏ 11183	Sunshine, Rainbow, Blue Sky, Brown Eyed Girl/	1969	2.00	4.00	8.00
	There's a Great Big Change in Me				
❏ 11228	Be Young, Be Foolish, Be Happy/Love, Love, Love	1969	2.00	4.00	8.00
❏ 11358	Don't You Just Know It/Making Music	1973		2.50	5.00

ABC Dunhill

❏ 4290	Hey Girl Don't Bother Me/Weep Little Girl	1971		3.00	6.00

ABC-Paramount

❏ 10502	What Kind of Fool (Do You Think I Am)/Laugh It Off	1963	3.75	7.50	15.00
❏ 10533	It's All Right (You're Just in Love)/	1964	3.00	6.00	12.00
	You Lied to Your Daddy				
❏ 10573	Hey Girl Don't Bother Me/Take Away	1964	3.00	6.00	12.00
❏ 10601	Silly Little Girl/Weep Little Girl	1964	3.00	6.00	12.00
❏ 10614	The Truth Hurts/Why Did My Little Girl Cry	1965	2.50	5.00	10.00
❏ 10635	What Do You Do/Unlove You	1965	2.50	5.00	10.00
❏ 10702	Concrete Jungle/Till the End of Time	1965	2.50	5.00	10.00
❏ 10741	Carryin' On/I've Been Hurt	1965	2.50	5.00	10.00
❏ 10779	Got to Get Used to a Broken Heart/Riding for a Fall	1966	2.50	5.00	10.00

Apt

❏ 26010	Long Distance Operator/Numbers	1970		3.00	6.00

Arlen

❏ 711	Untie Me/Disillusioned	1962	3.00	6.00	12.00
❏ 717	Deep Inside Me/	1962	3.00	6.00	12.00
	If You're So Smart (Why Do You Have a Broken Heart)				
❏ 720	You'll Never Know/Blue Shadows	1963	3.00	6.00	12.00
❏ 729	Don't Ever Go/Find Another Love	1963	3.00	6.00	12.00

Capitol

❏ 3050	The Tams Medley/Wire Help	1971		3.00	6.00

Compleat

❏ 109	My Baby Sure Can Shag/Making True Love	1983		2.00	4.00

General American

❏ 714	My Baby Loves Me/Find Another Love	1962	3.75	7.50	15.00

King

❏ 6012	Untie Me/Find Another Love	1965	2.50	5.00	10.00

Mink

❏ 22	Memory Lane/Teenage Kids	1959	10.00	20.00	40.00
	Originally issued as "The Stereos"				

1-2-3

❏ 1726	How Long Love/Too Much Foolin' Around	1970		3.00	6.00

Parkway

❏ 863	Memory Lane/A Lovely Piano	1963	5.00	10.00	20.00
	The same record was reissued as "The Hippies"				

Swan

❏ 4055	Sorry/Valley of Love	1960	3.75	7.50	15.00

Tangeers, The
Okeh

❏ 7319	Let My Heart and Soul Be Free/	1968	10.00	20.00	40.00
	What's the Use of Me Trying				

Tangiers, The
(Also known as "The Hollywood Flames")
A-J

❏ 905	The Plea/The Waddle	1962	6.25	12.50	25.00

Number		Title (A Side/B Side)	Year	VG	VG+	NM
Class						
❏ 224		School Days Will Be Over/Don't Try	1958	7.50	15.00	30.00
Decca						
❏ 29603		I Won't Be Around/Tabarin	1955	37.50	75.00	150.00
❏ 29971		Remember Me/Oh, Baby!	1956	37.50	75.00	150.00
Strand						
❏ 25039		Ping Pong/Don't Stop the Music	1961	7.50	15.00	30.00
Tantones, The						
Lamp						
❏ 2002		No Matter/I Love You, Really I Do	1957	37.50	75.00	150.00
❏ 2008		So Afraid/Tell Me	1957	37.50	75.00	150.00
Targets, The						
King						
❏ 5538		It Doesn't Matter/Girls, Girls, Girls	1961	10.00	20.00	40.00
Tarriers, The						
Decca						
❏ 31387		Last Night I Had the Strangest Dream/ Lonesome Traveler	1962	2.50	5.00	10.00
❏ 31470		Casey Jones/Mary Ann	1963	2.50	5.00	10.00
❏ 31524		Lonesome Traveller/Seven Daffodils	1963	2.50	5.00	10.00
❏ 31631		San Francisco Bay Blues/Guantanamera	1964	2.50	5.00	10.00
Glory						
❏ 246		Wishing Well Song/East Virginia	1956	3.75	7.50	15.00
❏ 249		The Banana Boat Song/No Hidin' Place	1956	5.00	10.00	20.00
❏ 254		Those Brown Eyes/Chaucon	1957	3.75	7.50	15.00
❏ 255		I Know Where I'm Going/Pretty Boy	1957	3.75	7.50	15.00
❏ 264		Dunya/Quinto	1957	3.75	7.50	15.00
❏ 271		Lonesome Traveler/East Virginia	1958	3.75	7.50	15.00
❏ 286		Tom Dooley/Everybody Loves Saturday Night	1958	3.75	7.50	15.00
United Artists						
❏ 168		Hard Travelin'/Times Are Getting Hard	1959	3.00	6.00	12.00
Tarrytons, The						
Dot						
❏ 16537		Rough Surfin'/Mansion on the Hill	1963	6.25	12.50	25.00
Exclusive						
❏ 2270		Rough Surfin'/Mansion on the Hill	1963	10.00	20.00	40.00
Tassels, The						
Amy						
❏ 946		To a Soldier Boy/The Boy for Me	1966	2.50	5.00	10.00
Madison						
❏ 117		To a Soldier Boy/The Boy for Me	1959	6.25	12.50	25.00
❏ 121		To a Young Lover/My Guy and I	1959	5.00	10.00	20.00
Taste of Honey, A						
Capitol						
❏ 4565		Boogie Oogie Oogie/World Spin	1978		2.00	4.00
❏ 4565	PS	Boogie Oogie Oogie/World Spin	1978		2.50	5.00
❏ 4655		Distant/You're in Good Hands	1978		2.00	4.00
❏ 4668		Disco Dancin'/Sky High	1978		2.00	4.00
❏ 4744		Do It Good/I Love You	1979		2.00	4.00
❏ 4776		Let's Begin/Race	1979		2.00	4.00
❏ 4888		Rescue Me/Say That You'll Stay	1980		2.00	4.00
❏ 4932		I'm Talkin' 'Bout You/Don't You Lead Me On	1980		2.00	4.00
❏ 4953		Sukiyaki/Don't You Lead Me On	1980		2.00	4.00
❏ 4953	PS	Sukiyaki/Don't You Lead Me On	1980		2.50	5.00
❏ B-5099		I'll Try Something New/Good-Bye Baby	1982		2.00	4.00
❏ B-5099	PS	I'll Try Something New/Good-Bye Baby	1982		2.50	5.00
❏ B-5132		We've Got the Groove/This Love of Ours	1982		2.00	4.00
Tate, Billy						
Imperial						
❏ 5337		Single Life/You Told Me	1955	50.00	100.00	200.00
		Script logo				
Peacock						
❏ 1671		Don't Call My Name/Right from Wrong	1957	7.50	15.00	30.00
Tate, Laurie						
Atlantic						
❏ 965		Rock Me Daddy/You Can't Stop My Crying	1952	25.00	50.00	100.00
Taupin, Bernie						
(Elton John's songwriting partner)						
RCA						
❏ 5162-7-R		Friend of the Flag/Backbone	1987			3.00
❏ 5216-7-R		Citizen Jane/White Boys in Chains	1987			3.00
Tavares						
Capitol						
❏ 3674		Check It Out/The Judgment Day	1973		2.50	5.00

Number	Title (A Side/B Side)	Year	VG	VG+	NM
❑ 3794	That's the Sound That Lonely Makes/Little Girl	1973		2.50	5.00
❑ 3882	Too Late/Leave It Up to the Lady	1974		2.50	5.00
❑ 3957	She's Gone/To Love You	1974		2.50	5.00
❑ 4010	Remember What I Told You to Forget/My Ship	1974		2.50	5.00
❑ 4111	It Only Takes a Minute/I Hope She Chooses Me	1975		2.50	5.00
❑ 4184	Free Ride/In the Eyes of Love	1975		2.50	5.00
❑ 4221	The Love I Never Had/In the City	1976		2.50	5.00
❑ 4270	Heaven Must Be Missing An Angel (Part 1)/Heaven Must Be Missing An Angel (Part 2)	1976		2.50	5.00
❑ 4348	Don't Take Away the Music/Guiding Star	1976		2.50	5.00
❑ 4398	Whodunit/Fool of the Year	1977		2.50	5.00
❑ 4453	Goodnight My Love/Watchin' the Woman's Movement	1977		2.50	5.00
❑ 4500	More Than a Woman/Keep in Touch	1977		2.00	4.00
❑ 4544	The Ghost of Love (Part 1)/The Ghost of Love (Part 2)	1978		2.00	4.00
❑ 4583	Timber/Feel So Good	1978		2.00	4.00
❑ 4658	Never Had a Love Like This Before/Positive Forces	1978		2.00	4.00
❑ 4703	Straight from the Heart/I'm Back for Me	1979		2.00	4.00
❑ 4738	One Telephone Call Away/Let Me Heal the Bruises	1979		2.00	4.00
❑ 4781	Hard Core Poetry/Stabilize	1979		2.00	4.00
❑ 4811	Bad Times/Got to Have Your Love	1979		2.00	4.00
❑ 4846	I Can't Go On Living Without You/Why Can't We Fall in Love	1980		2.00	4.00
❑ 4880	I Don't Want You Anymore/Paradise	1980		2.00	4.00
❑ 4933	Love Uprising/Not Love	1980		2.00	4.00
❑ 4969	Loneliness/Break Down for Love	1981		2.00	4.00
❑ A-5019	Turn Out the Nightlight/House of Music	1981		2.00	4.00
❑ A-5043	Loveline/Right On Time	1981		2.00	4.00

RCA

Number	Title (A Side/B Side)	Year	VG	VG+	NM
❑ PB-13292	A Penny for Your Thoughts/The Skin You're In	1982		2.00	4.00
❑ PB-13433	Got to Find My Way Back to You/I Hope You Will Be Very Unhappy Without Me	1983		2.00	4.00
❑ PB-13530	Abra-Ca-Dabra Love You Too/Mystery Lady	1983		2.00	4.00
❑ PB-13611	Deeper in Love/I Really Miss You Baby	1983		2.00	4.00
❑ PB-13684	Words and Music/I'll Send Love (We Go Together)	1983		2.00	4.00
❑ GB-13799	A Penny for Your Thoughts/Got to Find My Way Back to You	1984			3.00

Gold Standard Series

Taylor, Andrew
Gone

Number	Title (A Side/B Side)	Year	VG	VG+	NM
❑ 5109	That's How I Feel About You/Never Bite Off More Than You Could Chew	1961	50.00	100.00	200.00

Taylor, Andy
(Member of Duran Duran)
Atlantic

Number	Title (A Side/B Side)	Year	VG	VG+	NM
❑ 89414	Take It Easy/Angel Eyes	1986			3.00
❑ 89414 PS	Take It Easy/Angel Eyes	1986			3.00

MCA

Number	Title (A Side/B Side)	Year	VG	VG+	NM
❑ 52946	When the Rain Comes Down/Broken Windows	1986			3.00
❑ 52946 PS	When the Rain Comes Down/Broken Windows	1986			3.00
❑ 52999	Life Goes On/Broken Window	1987			3.00
❑ 53085	Don't Let Me Die Young/Broken Window	1987			3.00

Taylor, Bill, and Smokey Jo
Flip

Number	Title (A Side/B Side)	Year	VG	VG+	NM
❑ 502	Split Personality/Lonely Sweetheart	1955	375.00	750.00	1,500

Taylor, Billy
Citation

Number	Title (A Side/B Side)	Year	VG	VG+	NM
❑ 5002	Income Taxes and You/Lullaby to Carolyn	1962	3.75	7.50	15.00

Fame

Number	Title (A Side/B Side)	Year	VG	VG+	NM
❑ 502	Little Jewel/Study Hall Romance	196?	75.00	150.00	300.00

Felco

Number	Title (A Side/B Side)	Year	VG	VG+	NM
❑ 101	Wombie Zombie/I'm Young	1959	5.00	10.00	20.00

Felsted

Number	Title (A Side/B Side)	Year	VG	VG+	NM
❑ 8564	Bandstand Baby/Cat with No Future	1959	5.00	10.00	20.00

Tower

Number	Title (A Side/B Side)	Year	VG	VG+	NM
❑ 421	Sunny/I Wish I Knew How I Would Feel to Be Free	1968	2.00	4.00	8.00

Taylor, Bobby, and the Vancouvers
Gordy

Number	Title (A Side/B Side)	Year	VG	VG+	NM
❑ 7069	Does Your Mama Know About Me/Fading Away	1968	5.00	10.00	20.00
❑ 7073	I Am Your Man/If You Love Her	1968	5.00	10.00	20.00
❑ 7079	Malinda/It's Growing	1968	5.00	10.00	20.00
❑ 7088	Oh I've Been Blessed/It Should Have Been Me Loving Her	1969	150.00	300.00	600.00
❑ 7092	My Girl Is Gone/It Should Have Been Me Loving Her	1969	5.00	10.00	20.00

Integra

Number	Title (A Side/B Side)	Year	VG	VG+	NM
❑ 103	This Is My Woman/(B-side unknown)	1968	25.00	50.00	100.00

Mowest

Number	Title (A Side/B Side)	Year	VG	VG+	NM
❑ 5006	Hey Lordy/Just a Little Bit Closer	1971	3.75	7.50	15.00

Playboy

Number	Title (A Side/B Side)	Year	VG	VG+	NM
❑ 6046	Why Play Games/Don't Wonder Why	1975		2.50	5.00

Number		Title (A Side/B Side)	Year	VG	VG+	NM

Sunflower

| ❑ 126 | | There Are Roses Somewhere in the World/ It Was a Good Time | 1972 | 6.25 | 12.50 | 25.00 |

V.I.P.

| ❑ 25053 | | Oh I've Been Blessed/Blackmail | 1969 | 6.25 | 12.50 | 25.00 |

Taylor, Carmen

Apollo

| ❑ 489 | | Oh Please/Teen Age Ball | 1956 | 15.00 | 30.00 | 60.00 |

Atlantic

❑ 1002		Lovin' Daddy/Ding Dong	1953	12.50	25.00	50.00
❑ 1015		Big Mamou Daddy/Mamma Me and Johnny Free	1953	12.50	25.00	50.00
❑ 1041		Freddie/Ooh I	1954	30.00	60.00	120.00

Guyden

| ❑ 100 | | Let Me Go Lover/No More, No Less | 1954 | 10.00 | 20.00 | 40.00 |

Kama Sutra

| ❑ 206 | | My Son/You're Puttin' Me On | 1966 | 3.00 | 6.00 | 12.00 |

King

| ❑ 5085 | | So What/Why Did You Leave Me Alone | 1957 | 12.50 | 25.00 | 50.00 |

Taylor, James

Apple

❑ 1805		Carolina in My Mind/Taking It In	1969	75.00	150.00	300.00
❑ 1805		Carolina in My Mind/Something's Wrong	1970	2.50	5.00	10.00
		With star on A-side label				
❑ 1805		Carolina in My Mind/Something's Wrong	1970	2.00	4.00	8.00
		Without star on A-side label				
❑ 1805	DJ	Carolina on My Mind/Something's Wrong	1970	7.50	15.00	30.00
		Promo with error in title on A-side				

Columbia

❑ 02093		Hard Times/Summer's Here	1981			3.00
❑ 02093	PS	Hard Times/Summer's Here	1981		2.00	4.00
❑ 05681		Everyday/Limousine Driver	1985			3.00
❑ 05681	PS	Everyday/Limousine Driver	1985		2.00	4.00
❑ 05785		Only One/Mona	1986			3.00
❑ 05884		That's Why I'm Here/Going Around One More Time	1986			3.00
❑ 06278		Only a Dream in Rio/Turn Away	1986			3.00
❑ 07616		Never Die Young/Valentine's Day	1987			3.00
❑ 07616	PS	Never Die Young/Valentine's Day	1987		2.00	4.00
❑ 07948		Baby Boom Baby/Letter in the Mail	1988			3.00
❑ 08493		Sweet Potato Pie/First of May	1988			3.00
❑ 10557		Handy Man/Bartender's Blues	1977		2.00	4.00
❑ 10622		Your Smiling Face/If I Keep My Heart Out of Sight	1977		2.00	4.00
❑ 10676		(What a) Wonderful World/Wooden Planes	1978		3.00	6.00
		By Art Garfunkel with Paul Simon and James Taylor; B-side is Garfunkel solo				
❑ 10689		Honey Don't Leave L.A./Another Grey Morning	1978		2.00	4.00
❑ 11005		Up on the Roof/Chanson Francaise	1979		2.00	4.00
❑ 60514		Her Town Too/Believe It or Not	1981		2.00	4.00
		A-side: James Taylor and J.D. Souther				

Warner Bros.

❑ 7387		Sweet Baby James/Suite for 20G	1970	2.00	4.00	8.00
❑ 7423		Fire and Rain/Anywhere Like Heaven	1970	2.00	4.00	8.00
❑ 7460		Country Road/Sunny Skies	1970		3.00	6.00
❑ 7498		You've Got a Friend/You Can Close Your Eyes	1971		3.00	6.00
❑ 7521		Long Ago and Far Away/Let Me Ride	1971		2.50	5.00
❑ 7655		Don't Let Me Be Lonely Tonight/Wow, Don't You Know	1972		2.50	5.00
❑ 7682		One Man Parade/Nobody But You	1973		2.50	5.00
❑ 7695		Hymn/Fanfare	1973		2.50	5.00
❑ 8015		Let It All Fall Down/Daddy's Baby	1974		2.50	5.00
❑ 8028		Walking Man/Daddy's Baby	1974		2.50	5.00
❑ 8109		How Sweet It Is (To Be Loved By You)/Sarah Maria	1975		2.50	5.00
❑ 8137		Mexico/Gorilla	1975		2.50	5.00
❑ 8222		Shower the People/I Can Dream of You	1976		2.50	5.00
❑ 8278		Woman's Gotta Have It/You Make It Easy	1976		2.50	5.00

Taylor, John

(Member of Duran Duran)

Capitol

| ❑ 5551 | | I Do What I Do...(Theme for 9 1/2 Weeks)/Jazz | 1986 | | | 3.00 |
| ❑ 5551 | PS | I Do What I Do...(Theme for 9 1/2 Weeks)/Jazz | 1986 | | | 3.00 |

Taylor, Johnnie

Beverly Glen

❑ 2003		What About My Love/Reaganomics	1982		2.00	4.00
❑ 2004		I'm So Proud/I Need a Freak	1982		2.00	4.00
❑ 2007		Just Ain't Good Enough/Don't Wait	1983		2.00	4.00
❑ 2016		Seconds of Your Love/Shoot for the Stars	1983		2.00	4.00

Columbia

❑ 10281		Disco Lady/You're the Best in the World	1976		2.50	5.00
❑ 10334		Somebody's Gettin' It/ Please Don't Stop (That Song from Playing)	1976		2.50	5.00
❑ 10478		Love Is Better in the A.M. (Part 1)/ Love Is Better in the A.M. (Part 2)	1977		2.50	5.00

Number	Title (A Side/B Side)	Year	VG	VG+	NM
❑ 10541	Your Love Is Rated X/	1977		2.50	5.00
	Here I Go (Through These Chains Again)				
❑ 10610	Disco 9000/Right Now	1977		2.00	4.00
❑ 10709	Keep On Dancing/	1978		2.00	4.00
	I Love to Make Love When It's Raining				
❑ 10776	Give Me My Baby/Ever Ready	1978		2.00	4.00
❑ 11084	(Ooh-Wee) She's Killing Me/Play Something Pretty	1979		2.00	4.00
❑ 11315	I Got This Thing for Your Love/Signing Off with Love	1980		2.00	4.00
❑ 11373	I Wanna Get Into You/Baby Don't Hesitate	1980		2.00	4.00

Derby

Number	Title (A Side/B Side)	Year	VG	VG+	NM
❑ 101	Shine, Shine, Shine/Dance What You Wanna	1963	3.75	7.50	15.00
❑ 1006	Baby, We've Got Love/In Love with You	1963	3.75	7.50	15.00
❑ 1010	I Need Lots of Love/Getting Married Soon	1964	3.75	7.50	15.00

Malaco

Number	Title (A Side/B Side)	Year	VG	VG+	NM
❑ 2107	Lady, My Whole World Is You/L-O-V-E	1984			3.00
❑ 2111	Good with My Hips/This Is Your Night	1985			3.00
❑ 2118	Still Called the Blues/She's Cheatin' on Me	1985			3.00
❑ 2125	Wall to Wall/(B-side unknown)	1986			3.00
❑ 2128	Can I Love You/There's Nothing I Wouldn't Do	1986			3.00
❑ 2132	Just Because/When She Stops Asking	1987			3.00
❑ 2135	Don't Make Me Late/Happy Time	1987			3.00
❑ 2140	If I Lose Your Love/Something Is Going Wrong	1987			3.00
❑ 2143	Everything's Out in the Open/	1988			3.00
	Got to Leave This Woman				
❑ 2153	In Control/I Found a Love	1989			3.00
❑ 2159	Still Crazy for You/(B-side unknown)	1989			3.00

RCA

Number	Title (A Side/B Side)	Year	VG	VG+	NM
❑ PB-11137	I Want You Back Again/Heaven Bless This Home	1977		2.50	5.00

Sar

Number	Title (A Side/B Side)	Year	VG	VG+	NM
❑ 114	A Whole Lotta Woman/Why Oh Why	1961	5.00	10.00	20.00
❑ 131	Never Never/Rome (Wasn't Built in a Day)	1962	10.00	20.00	40.00
❑ 156	Oh, How I Love You/Run, But You Can't Hide	1964	3.75	7.50	15.00

Stax

Number	Title (A Side/B Side)	Year	VG	VG+	NM
❑ 0009	Who's Making Love/I'm Trying	1968	2.00	4.00	8.00
❑ 0023	Take Care of Your Homework/Hold On This Time	1969	2.00	4.00	8.00
❑ 0033	Testify (I Wanna)/I Had a Fight with Love	1969	2.00	4.00	8.00
❑ 0042	Just Keep On Loving Me/My Life	1969	2.00	4.00	8.00
	With Carla Thomas				
❑ 0046	I Could Never Be President/It's Amazing	1969	2.00	4.00	8.00
❑ 0055	Love Bones/Mr. Nobody Is Somebody	1969	2.00	4.00	8.00
❑ 0068	Steal Away/Friday Night	1970		3.00	6.00
❑ 0078	I Am Somebody (Part 1)/I Am Somebody (Part 2)	1970		3.00	6.00
❑ 0085	Jody's Got Your Girl and Gone/A Fool Like Me	1970		3.00	6.00
❑ 0089	I Don't Wanna Lose You/Party Life	1971		3.00	6.00
❑ 0096	Hijackin' Love/Love in the Streets	1971		3.00	6.00
❑ 0114	Standing In for Jody/Shackin' Up	1972		3.00	6.00
❑ 0122	Doing My Own Thing (Part 1)/	1972		3.00	6.00
	Doing My Own Thing (Part 2)				
❑ 0142	Stop Doggin' Me/Stop Teasin' Me	1972		3.00	6.00
❑ 0155	Don't You Fool with My Soul (Part 1)/	1973		3.00	6.00
	Don't You Fool with My Soul (Part 2)				
❑ 0161	I Believe in You (You Believe in Me)/Love Depression	1973		3.00	6.00
❑ 0176	Cheaper to Keep Her/I Can Read Between the Lines	1973		3.00	6.00
❑ 0193	We're Getting Careless with Our Love/	1974		3.00	6.00
	Poor Make Believer				
❑ 0208	I've Been Born Again/At Night Time	1974		3.00	6.00
❑ 0226	It's September/Just One Moment	1974		3.00	6.00
❑ 0241	Try Me Tonight/Free	1975		3.00	6.00
❑ 186	I Had a Dream/Changes	1966	2.50	5.00	10.00
❑ 193	I Got to Love Somebody's Baby/	1966	2.50	5.00	10.00
	Just the One I've Been Looking For				
❑ 202	Little Bluebird/Toe Hold	1967	2.50	5.00	10.00
❑ 209	Ain't That Loving You/Outside Love	1967	2.50	5.00	10.00
❑ 226	If I Had It to Do Over/You Can't Get Away from It	1967	2.50	5.00	10.00
❑ 235	Somebody's Sleeping in My Bed/Strange Thing	1967	2.50	5.00	10.00
❑ 247	Next Time/Sundown	1968	2.50	5.00	10.00
❑ 253	I Ain't Particular/Where There's Smoke There's Fire	1968	2.50	5.00	10.00
❑ 3201	It Don't Pay to Get Up in the Mornin'/	1977		2.50	5.00
	Just Keep On Loving Me				

Taylor, Mad Man

EastWest

Number	Title (A Side/B Side)	Year	VG	VG+	NM
❑ 117	Rumble Tumble/Rock and Roll Espanola	1958	18.75	37.50	75.00

Taylor, Mick
(Ex-Rolling Stones)

Columbia

Number	Title (A Side/B Side)	Year	VG	VG+	NM
❑ 11065	Leather Jacket/Show Blues	1979		2.50	5.00

Taylor, R. Dean

Audio Master

Number	Title (A Side/B Side)	Year	VG	VG+	NM
❑ 1	At the High School Dance/(B-side unknown)	1960	50.00	100.00	200.00

Farr

Number	Title (A Side/B Side)	Year	VG	VG+	NM
❑ 001	We'll Show Them All/Magdalena	1976		2.50	5.00

Mala

Number	Title (A Side/B Side)	Year	VG	VG+	NM
❑ 444	I'll Remember/It's a Long Way to St. Louis	1962	25.00	50.00	100.00

Number		Title (A Side/B Side)	Year	VG	VG+	NM

Rare Earth

❑ 5013		Indiana Wants Me/Love's Your Name	1970		3.00	6.00
❑ 5023		Ain't It a Sad Thing/Back Street	1970		2.50	5.00
❑ 5023	PS	Ain't It a Sad Thing/Back Street	1970	2.50	5.00	10.00
❑ 5026		Gotta See Jane/Back Street	1971		2.50	5.00
❑ 5030		Candy Apple Red/Woman Alive	1971		2.50	5.00
❑ 5041		Taos New Mexico/Shadow	1972		2.50	5.00

20th Century

❑ 2510		Let's Talk It Over/Add Up the Score	1981		2.00	4.00

V.I.P.

❑ 25027		Let's Go Somewhere/Poor Girl	1965	6.25	12.50	25.00
❑ 25042		Don't Fool Around/There's a Ghost in My House	1966	6.25	12.50	25.00
❑ 25045		Gotta See Jane/Don't Fool Around	1967	6.25	12.50	25.00

Taylor, Roger
(Of Queen)
Capitol

❑ B-5364		Man on Fire/Killing Time	1984		2.00	4.00
❑ B-5420		Strange Frontier/ I Cry for You (Love, Hope and Confusion)	1984		2.00	4.00

Elektra

❑ 47151		Let's Get Crazy/Laugh Or Cry	1981		2.50	5.00

Taylor, Sherri
Gloreco

❑ 1002		I've Got a Crush/(B-side unknown)	196?	15.00	30.00	60.00

Motown

❑ 1004		Lover/That's Why I Love You So Much	1960	10.00	20.00	40.00
		With Singin' Sammy Ward				

Taylor, True – See "Simon, Paul"

Taylor, Vernon
Dot

❑ 15632		I've Got the Blues/The Losing Game	1957	25.00	50.00	100.00
❑ 15697		Satisfaction Guaranteed/Why Must You Leave Me	1958	12.50	25.00	50.00

Sun

❑ 310		Breeze/Today Is a Blue Day	1958	6.25	12.50	25.00
❑ 325		Sweet and Easy to Love/Mystery Train	1959	8.75	17.50	35.00

Taylor, Zola
RPM

❑ 405		Make Love to Me/Oh My Dear	1954	75.00	150.00	300.00

Teardrops, The
(More than one group)
Dore

❑ 679		Little Orphan Boy/(Instrumental)	1963	3.00	6.00	12.00

Dot

❑ 15669		Bridge of Love/Jellyfish	1957	6.25	12.50	25.00

Josie

❑ 766		The Stars Are Out Tonight/Oh Stop It	1954	50.00	100.00	200.00
❑ 771		My Heart/Ooh Baby	1954	125.00	250.00	500.00
❑ 856		We Won't Tell/Al Chiar Di Luna (Porto Fortuna)	1959	6.25	12.50	25.00
❑ 862		Cry No More/You're My Hollywood Star	1959	6.25	12.50	25.00
❑ 873		Daddy's Little Girl/Always You	1960	6.25	12.50	25.00

King

❑ 5004		My Inspiration/I Prayed for Love	1956	6.25	12.50	25.00
❑ 5037		After School/Don't Be Afraid to Love	1957	6.25	12.50	25.00

Laurie

❑ 3642		Welcome Back Kotter/Champagne Lady	1976	2.00	4.00	8.00
❑ 3660		Goodnight Elvis/Hey Gingerbread	1977	2.00	4.00	8.00

Musicor

❑ 1139		Tears Come Tumbling/You Won't Be There	1965	2.50	5.00	10.00

Rendezvous

❑ 102		Catch Me, I'm Falling Again/Sugar Baby	1958	7.50	15.00	30.00

Sampson

❑ 634		Come Back to Me/Sweet Lovin' Daddy-O	1952	100.00	200.00	400.00

Saxony

❑ 1007		Tonight I'm Gonna Fall in Love Again/ That's Why I'll Get By	1964	2.50	5.00	10.00
❑ 1008		I'm Gonna Steal Your Boyfriend/ Call Me and I'll Be Happy	1965	2.50	5.00	10.00
❑ 1009		Tears Come Tumbling/You Won't Be There	1965	2.50	5.00	10.00

Tears For Fears
Fontana

❑ 874 710-7		Sowing the Seeds of Love/Tears Roll Down	1989			3.00
❑ 874 710-7	PS	Sowing the Seeds of Love/Tears Roll Down	1989			3.00
❑ 876 248-7		Woman in Chains/Always in the Past	1990			3.00
❑ 876 248-7	PS	Woman in Chains/Always in the Past	1990			3.00

Number		Title (A Side/B Side)	Year	VG	VG+	NM
Mercury						
❏ 812 677-7		Change/The Conflict	1983		2.00	4.00
❏ 862 240-7		Break It Down Again/Bloodletting Go	1993			3.00
❏ 862 804-7		Goodnight Song/New Star	1993			3.00
❏ 880 294-7		Shout/The Big Chair	1985			3.00
❏ 880 294-7	PS	Shout/The Big Chair	1985			3.00
❏ 880 659-7		Everybody Wants to Rule the World/Pharaohs	1985			3.00
❏ 880 899-7		Head Over Heels/When in Love with a Blind Man	1985			3.00
❏ 880 899-7	PS	Head Over Heels/When in Love with a Blind Man	1985			3.00
❏ 884 636-7		Mothers Talk/(B-side unknown)	1986			3.00
❏ 884 636-7	PS	Mothers Talk/(B-side unknown)	1986			3.00
❏ PRO 392-7	DJ	Head Over Heels (Live) (same on both sides)	1985	2.50	5.00	10.00
Teasers, The						
Checker						
❏ 800		I Was a Fool to Love You/How Could You Hurt One So	1954	150.00	300.00	600.00
❏ 800		I Was a Fool to Love You/How Could You Hurt One So	1954	300.00	600.00	1,200
		Red vinyl				
Technics, The						
Chex						
❏ 1010		Has He Told You/Workout With a Pretty Girl	1963	7.50	15.00	30.00
		As "Tony and the Technics"				
❏ 1012		Because I Really Love You/A Man's Confusion	1963	7.50	15.00	30.00
❏ 1013		Hey Girl Don't Leave Me/	1963	10.00	20.00	40.00
		I Met Her on the First of September				
Techniques, The						
Roulette						
❏ 4030		Hey Little Girl/In a Round-About Way	1957	6.25	12.50	25.00
❏ 4048		(Why Did I Ever) Let Her Go/Marindy	1958	6.25	12.50	25.00
❏ 4097		The Wisest Man You Know/Moon Tan	1958	6.25	12.50	25.00
Stars						
❏ 551		Hey Little Girl/In a Round-About Way	1957	10.00	20.00	40.00
Teddy and His Patches						
Chance						
❏ 100		Suzy Creamcheese/From Day to Day	1967	25.00	50.00	100.00
❏ 668		Suzy Creamcheese/It Ain't Nothin'	1967	25.00	50.00	100.00
❏ 669		Haight Ashbury/It Ain't Nothin'	1967	25.00	50.00	100.00
Teddy and the Continentals						
Pik						
❏ 235		Tick Tick Tock/Everybody Pony	1961	6.25	12.50	25.00
Rago						
❏ 201		Tick Tick Tock/Wild Christening Party	1962	6.25	12.50	25.00
		B-side by the Teen Kings				
Richie						
❏ 445		Do You/Tighten Up	1961	10.00	20.00	40.00
		With Roulette Records distribution mentioned on label				
❏ 445		Do You/Tighten Up	1961	25.00	50.00	100.00
		With no mention of Roulette distribution on label				
❏ 453		Crying Over You/Crossfire With Me Baby	1963	12.50	25.00	50.00
❏ 1001		Tick Tick Tock/Everybody Pony	1961	15.00	30.00	60.00
Teddy Bears, The						
(With Phil Spector and Annette Kleinbard [a.k.a. Carol Connors])						
Dore						
❏ 503		To Know Him, Is to Love Him/	1958	6.25	12.50	25.00
		Don't You Worry My Little Pet				
❏ 520		Wonderful Loveable You/Till You'll Be Mine	1959	5.00	10.00	20.00
Imperial						
❏ 5562		Oh Why/I Don't Need You Anymore	1959	7.50	15.00	30.00
❏ 5581		You Said Goodbye/If You Only Knew	1959	7.50	15.00	30.00
❏ 5594		Seven Lonely Days/Don't Go Away	1959	7.50	15.00	30.00
Tee Set, The						
Colossus						
❏ 107		Ma Belle Amie/Angels Coming in the Holy Night	1969		2.50	5.00
❏ 107	PS	Ma Belle Amie/Angels Coming in the Holy Night	1969		3.00	6.00
❏ 114		If You Do Believe in Love/Charmaine	1970		2.00	4.00
❏ 139		She Likes Weeds/(B-side unknown)	1971		2.00	4.00
Teen Angels, The						
Sun						
❏ 388		Ain't Gonna Let You (Break My Heart)/Tell Me My Love	1964	7.50	15.00	30.00
Teen Kings, The – See "Orbison, Roy"						
Teen Queens, The						
Antler						
❏ 4014		There's Nothing on My Mind (Part 1)/	1959	3.75	7.50	15.00
		There's Nothing on My Mind (Part 2)				
❏ 4015		Politician/I'm a Fool	1959	3.75	7.50	15.00

Number		Title (A Side/B Side)	Year	VG	VG+	NM
❑ 4016		Donny (Part 1)/Donny (Part 2)	1960	3.75	7.50	15.00
❑ 4017		I Hear Violins/Magoo Can See	1960	3.75	7.50	15.00

Kent

| ❑ 359 | | Eddie My Love/Just Goofed | 1961 | 3.00 | 6.00 | 12.00 |

RCA Victor

| ❑ 47-7206 | | Dear Tommy/You Good Boy-You Get Cookie | 1958 | 4.00 | 8.00 | 16.00 |
| ❑ 47-7396 | | Movie Star/First Crush | 1958 | 4.00 | 8.00 | 16.00 |

RPM

❑ 453		Eddie My Love/Just Goofed	1956	7.50	15.00	30.00
❑ 460		So All Alone/Baby Mine	1956	6.25	12.50	25.00
❑ 464		Billy Boy/Until the Day I Die	1956	6.25	12.50	25.00
❑ 470		Red Top/Love Sweet Love	1956	6.25	12.50	25.00
❑ 480		My First Love/(B-side unknown)	1956	6.25	12.50	25.00
❑ 484		Rock Everybody/My Heart's Desire	1957	5.00	10.00	20.00
❑ 500		I Miss You/Two Loves and Two Lives	1957	5.00	10.00	20.00

Teen-Kings, The
Bee

| ❑ 1114/5 | | That's a Teen-Age Love/Tell Me If You Know | 1959 | 500.00 | 1,000 | 1,500 |

Willett

| ❑ 118 | | Don't Just Stand There/My Greatest Wish | 1959 | 50.00 | 100.00 | 200.00 |

Teen-Tones, The
Dandy Dan

| ❑ 2 | | Darling I Love You/My Sweet | 1958 | 20.00 | 40.00 | 80.00 |

Teena Marie
Epic

❑ 04124		Fix It/(Instrumental)	1983			3.00
❑ 04271		Midnight Magnet/(Instrumental)	1983			3.00
❑ 04415		Dear Lover/Playboy	1984			3.00
❑ 04619		Lovergirl/(Instrumental)	1984			3.00
❑ 04619	PS	Lovergirl/(Instrumental)	1984		3.00	6.00
❑ 04738		Jammin'/(Instrumental)	1985			3.00
❑ 04738	PS	Jammin'/(Instrumental)	1985		2.00	4.00
❑ 04943		Out on a Limb/Starchild	1985			3.00
❑ 04943	PS	Out on a Limb/Starchild	1985			3.00
❑ 05599		14K/(Instrumental)	1985			3.00
❑ 05599	PS	14K/(Instrumental)	1985			3.00
❑ 05872		Lips to Find You/(Instrumental)	1986			3.00
❑ 05872	PS	Lips to Find You/(Instrumental)	1986			3.00
❑ 06292		Love Me Down Easy/(Instrumental)	1986			3.00
❑ 06292	PS	Love Me Down Easy/(Instrumental)	1986			3.00
❑ 06535		Lead Me On/(Instrumental)	1986			3.00
❑ 07708		Ooh La La La/Sing One to Your Love	1988			3.00
❑ 07708	PS	Ooh La La La/Sing One to Your Love	1988			3.00
❑ 07902		Work It/(Instrumental)	1988			3.00
❑ 07902	PS	Work It/(Instrumental)	1988			3.00
❑ 08040		Surrealistic Pillow/(Instrumental)	1988			3.00
❑ 08444		Lovergirl/Out on a Limb	1988			3.00
	Reissue					
❑ 68591		Bad Boy/Trick Bag	1989			3.00

Gordy

❑ 7169		I'm a Sucker for Your Love/ Deja Vu (I've Been There Before)	1979		2.00	4.00
❑ 7173		Don't Look Back/ I'm Gonna Have My Cake (And Eat It Too)	1979		2.00	4.00
❑ 7180		Can It Be Love/Too Many Colors	1980		2.00	4.00
❑ 7184		Behind the Groove/You're All the Boogie I Need	1980		2.00	4.00
❑ 7189		I Need Your Lovin'/Irons in the Fire	1980		2.00	4.00
❑ 7194		First Class Love/Young Love	1981		2.00	4.00
❑ 7202		Square Biz/Opus III (Does Anybody Care)	1981		2.00	4.00
❑ 7212		It Must Be Magic/Yes I Need	1981		2.00	4.00
❑ 7216		Portuguese Love/The Ballad of Cradle Rob and Me	1981		2.00	4.00

Teenage Moonlighters
Mark

| ❑ 134 | | Sorry Sorry/I Want to Cry | 1960 | 1,000 | 1,500 | 2,000 |

Teenagers, The
(Without Frankie Lymon; also see "Lymon, Frankie, and the Teenagers")
End

| ❑ 1071 | | Crying/Tonight's the Night | 1960 | 15.00 | 30.00 | 60.00 |
| ❑ 1076 | | Can You Tell Me/A Little Wiser Now | 1960 | 10.00 | 20.00 | 40.00 |

Gee

| ❑ 1046 | | Flip Flop/Everything to Me | 1957 | 7.50 | 15.00 | 30.00 |

Roulette

| ❑ 4086 | | My Broken Heart/Momma Wanna Rock | 1958 | 20.00 | 40.00 | 80.00 |

Teenbeats, The
Teenbeat

| ❑ (No #) | | Surfbound/Mr. Moto | 1963 | 20.00 | 40.00 | 80.00 |

Number	Title (A Side/B Side)	Year	VG	VG+	NM

Telstars, The
Imperial

❏ 5903	Continental Mash/Stomp Happy	1962	6.25	12.50	25.00

Teen

❏ 510	Continental Mash/Stomp Happy	1962	10.00	20.00	40.00
❏ 513	Pow Wow/Lovina	1963	8.75	17.50	35.00
❏ 516	Topless/Spaghetti Strap	1964	8.75	17.50	35.00
❏ 517	Tough George/'Cause I Really Do	1964	8.75	17.50	35.00

Tempo-Tones, The
Acme

❏ 713	Get Yourself Another Fool/Ride Along	1957	37.50	75.00	150.00
❏ 715	In My Dreams/My Boy Sleep Pete	1957	125.00	250.00	500.00
❏ 718	Come Into My Heart/Somewhere There Is Sunshine	1957	125.00	250.00	500.00
❏ 722	The Day I Met You/Wishing All the Time	1957	100.00	200.00	400.00

Tempos, The
(More than one group)
Ascot

❏ 2167	When You Loved Me/My Barbara Ann	1965	6.25	12.50	25.00
❏ 2173	I Wish It Were Summer/My Barbara Ann	1965	6.25	12.50	25.00

Canterbury

❏ 504	Here I Come (Countdown) Part 1/ Here I Come (Countdown) Part 2	1967	3.75	7.50	15.00

Climax

❏ 102	See You in September/Bless You My Love	1959	5.00	10.00	20.00
❏ 105	The Crossroads of Love/Whatever Happens	1959	5.00	10.00	20.00

Fairmount

❏ 611	Oh Play That Thing/Monkey Doo	1963	3.00	6.00	12.00

Hi-Q

❏ 100	It's Tough/Sham-Rock	1959	10.00	20.00	40.00

Kapp

❏ 178	Kingdom of Love/That's What You Do to Me	1957	6.25	12.50	25.00
❏ 199	Prettiest Girl in School/Never You Mind	1957	6.25	12.50	25.00
❏ 213	I Got a Job/Strollin' with My Baby	1958	6.25	12.50	25.00

Montel

❏ 955	I Gotta Make a Move/It Was You	1966	3.75	7.50	15.00

Paris

❏ 550	Look Homeward, Angel/Under Ten Flags	1960	5.00	10.00	20.00

Rhythm

❏ 121	Promise Me/Never Let Me Go	1958	125.00	250.00	500.00

Riley's

❏ 8781	Don't Leave Me/I Need You	1966	7.50	15.00	30.00

U.S.A.

❏ 810	Why Don't You Write Me/A Thief in the Night	1965	6.25	12.50	25.00

Temptations
(Includes any group that is not the Motown group)
Goldisc

❏ 3001	Barbara/Someday *All-black label*	1960	7.50	15.00	30.00
❏ 3001	Barbara/Someday *Multicolor (black, red, gold) label*	1960	5.00	10.00	20.00
❏ 3007	Letter of Devotion/Fickle Little Girl	1960	6.25	12.50	25.00

King

❏ 5118	Standing Alone/Roaches Rock	1958	75.00	150.00	300.00

P&L

❏ 1001	Blue Surf/Egyptian Surf	1963	15.00	30.00	60.00

Parkway

❏ 803	Temptations/Birds N' Bees	1959	7.50	15.00	30.00

Savoy

❏ 1532	Mister Juke Box/Mad at Love	1958	5.00	10.00	20.00
❏ 1550	I Love You/Don't You Know	1958	5.00	10.00	20.00

Temptations, The
(Also see "Kendricks, Eddie"; "Pirates, The"; "Ruffin, David")
Atlantic

❏ 3436	In a Lifetime/I Could Never Stop Loving You	1977		2.00	4.00
❏ 3461	Think for Yourself/Let's Live in Place	1978		2.00	4.00
❏ 3517	Bare Back/I See My Child	1978		2.00	4.00
❏ 3538	Ever Ready Love/Touch Me Again	1978		2.00	4.00
❏ 3567	Mystic Woman/I Just Don't Know How to Let You Go	1979		2.00	4.00

Gordy

❏ 1616	Standing on the Top-Part 1/Standing on the Top-Part 2 *With Rick James*	1982		2.00	4.00
❏ 1631	More on the Inside/Money's Hard to Get	1982		2.00	4.00
❏ 1654	Silent Night/Everything for Christmas	1982		3.00	6.00
❏ 1666	Love on My Mind Tonight/Bring Your Body Here	1983		2.00	4.00
❏ 1683	Made in America/Surface Thrills	1983		2.00	4.00
❏ 1707	Miss Busy Body (Get Your Body Busy)/(Instrumental)	1983		2.00	4.00

Number		Title (A Side/B Side)	Year	VG	VG+	NM
❏ 1713		Silent Night/Everything for Christmas	1983		2.50	5.00
❏ 1720		Sail Away/Isn't the Night Fantastic	1984		2.00	4.00
❏ 1765		Treat Her Like a Lady/Isn't the Night Fantastic	1984		2.00	4.00
❏ 1781		My Love Is True (Truly for You)/Set Your Love Right	1985		2.00	4.00
❏ 1789		How Can You Say That It's Over/ I'll Keep My Light in My Window	1985		2.00	4.00
❏ 1818		Do You Really Love Your Baby/ I'll Keep My Light in My Window	1985		2.00	4.00
❏ 1834		Touch Me/Set Your Love Right	1986		2.00	4.00
❏ 1856		Lady Soul/Put Us Together Again	1986		2.00	4.00
❏ 1871		To Be Continued/You're the One	1986		2.00	4.00
❏ 1871	PS	To Be Continued/You're the One	1986		3.00	6.00
❏ 1881		Someone/Love Me Right	1987		2.00	4.00
❏ 7001		Dream Come True/Isn't She Pretty	1962	10.00	20.00	40.00
❏ 7010		Paradise/Slow Down Heart	1962	7.50	15.00	30.00
❏ 7015		I Want a Love I Can See/ The Further You Look, The Less You See	1963	6.25	12.50	25.00
❏ 7020		May I Have This Dance?/Farewell, My Love	1963	6.25	12.50	25.00
❏ 7028		The Way You Do the Things You Do/Just Let Me Know	1964	3.00	6.00	12.00
❏ 7032		I'll Be in Trouble/The Girl's Alright with Me	1964	3.00	6.00	12.00
❏ 7035		Girl (Why You Wanna Make Me Blue)/ Baby, Baby I Need You	1964	3.00	6.00	12.00
❏ 7038		My Girl/Nobody But My Baby	1965	2.50	5.00	10.00
❏ 7038	PS	My Girl/Nobody But My Baby	1965	25.00	50.00	100.00
❏ 7040		It's Growing/What Love Has Joined Together	1965	2.50	5.00	10.00
❏ 7043		Since I Lost My Baby/You've Got to Earn It	1965	2.50	5.00	10.00
❏ 7047		My Baby/Don't Look Back	1965	2.50	5.00	10.00
❏ 7049		Get Ready/Fading Away	1966	2.50	5.00	10.00
❏ 7054		Ain't Too Proud to Beg/You'll Lose a Precious Love	1966	2.50	5.00	10.00
❏ 7055		Beauty Is Only Skin Deep/You're Not an Ordinary Girl	1966	2.00	4.00	8.00
❏ 7055	PS	Beauty Is Only Skin Deep/You're Not an Ordinary Girl	1966	10.00	20.00	40.00
❏ 7057		(I Know) I'm Losing You/I Couldn't Cry If I Wanted To	1966	2.00	4.00	8.00
❏ 7061		All I Need/Sorry Is a Sorry Word	1967	2.00	4.00	8.00
❏ 7063		You're My Everything/I've Been Good to You	1967	2.00	4.00	8.00
❏ 7065		(Loneliness Made Me Realize) It's You That I Need/ Don't Send Me Away	1967	2.00	4.00	8.00
❏ 7068		I Wish It Would Rain/I Truly, Truly Believe	1967	2.00	4.00	8.00
❏ 7072		I Could Never Love Another (After Loving You)/ Gonna Give Her All the Love I've Got	1968	2.00	4.00	8.00
❏ 7074		Please Return Your Love to Me/How Can I Forget	1968	2.00	4.00	8.00
❏ 7081		Cloud Nine/Why Did She Have to Leave Me	1968		3.50	7.00
❏ 7082		Silent Night/Rudolph, the Red-Nosed Reindeer	1968	2.50	5.00	10.00
❏ 7084		Run Away Child, Running Wild/I Need Your Love	1969		3.50	7.00
❏ 7086		Don't Let the Joneses Get You Down/ Since I've Lost You	1969		3.50	7.00
❏ 7093		I Can't Get Next to You/ Running Away (Ain't Gonna Help You)	1969		3.50	7.00
❏ 7096		Psychedelic Shack/That's the Way Love Is	1970		3.00	6.00
❏ 7099		Ball of Confusion (That's What the World Is Today)/ It's Summer	1970		3.00	6.00
❏ 7099	PS	Ball of Confusion (That's What the World Is Today)/ It's Summer	1970	5.00	10.00	20.00
❏ 7102		Ungena Za Ulimwengu (Unite the World)/ Hum Along and Dance	1970		3.00	6.00
❏ 7105		Just My Imagination (Running Away with Me)/ You Make Your Own Heaven and Hell Right Here on Earth	1971		3.00	6.00
❏ 7109		It's Summer/I'm the Exception to the Rule	1971		3.00	6.00
❏ 7111		Superstar (Remember How You Got Where You Are)/ Gonna Keep On Tryin' Till I Win Your Love	1971		3.00	6.00
❏ 7115		Take a Look Around/Smooth Sailing (From Now On)	1972		3.00	6.00
❏ 7119		Mother Nature/Funky Music Sho Nuff Turns Me On	1972		3.00	6.00
❏ 7121		Papa Was a Rollin' Stone/(Instrumental)	1972		3.00	6.00
❏ 7126		Masterpiece/(Instrumental)	1973		3.00	6.00
❏ 7129		Plastic Man/Hurry Tomorrow	1973		3.00	6.00
❏ 7131		Hey Girl (I Like Your Style)/Ma	1973		3.00	6.00
❏ 7133		Let Your Hair Down/Ain't No Justice	1973		3.00	6.00
❏ 7135		Heavenly/Zoom	1974		3.00	6.00
❏ 7136		You've Got My Soul on Fire/I Need You	1974		3.00	6.00
❏ 7138		Happy People/(Instrumental)	1974		3.00	6.00
❏ 7142		Shakey Ground/I'm a Bachelor	1975		3.00	6.00
❏ 7144		Glasshouse/The Prophet	1975		3.00	6.00
❏ 7146		Keep Holding On/ What You Need Most (I Do Best of All)	1975		3.00	6.00
❏ 7150		Up the Creek (Without a Paddle)/ Darling Stand By Me (Song for a Woman)	1976		3.00	6.00
❏ 7151		Who Are You (And What Are You Doing the Rest of Your Life)/Darling Stand By Me (Song for a Woman)	1976			Unreleased
❏ 7152		Let Me Count the Ways (I Love You)/ Who Are You (And What Are You Doing the Rest of Your Life)	1976		3.00	6.00
❏ 7183		Power/Power (Part 2)	1980		2.00	4.00
❏ 7188		Struck by Lightning Twice/I'm Coming Home	1980		2.00	4.00
❏ 7208		Aiming at Your Heart/Life of a Cowboy	1981		2.00	4.00
❏ 7213		Oh What a Night/Isn't the Night Fantastic	1981		2.00	4.00

Miracle

Number		Title (A Side/B Side)	Year	VG	VG+	NM
❏ 5		Oh, Mother of Mine/Romance Without Finance	1961	25.00	50.00	100.00
❏ 12		Check Yourself/Your Wonderful Love	1961	25.00	50.00	100.00

Motown

Number		Title (A Side/B Side)	Year	VG	VG+	NM
❏ 903		One Step at a Time/(Instrumental)	1990			3.00
❏ 1501		Take Me Away/There's More Where That Came From	1980		2.00	4.00

Number		Title (A Side/B Side)	Year	VG	VG+	NM
❏ 1837		A Fine Mess/Wishful Thinking	1986		2.00	4.00
❏ 1837	PS	A Fine Mess/Wishful Thinking	1986		3.00	6.00
❏ 1908		I Wonder Who She's Seeing Now/Girls (They Like It)	1987			3.00
❏ 1908	PS	I Wonder Who She's Seeing Now/Girls (They Like It)	1987		2.00	4.00
❏ 1920		Look What You Started/More Love, Your Love	1987			3.00
❏ 1933		Do You Wanna Go with Me/Put Your Foot Down	1988			3.00
❏ 1974		All I Want from You/(Instrumental)	1989			3.00

Topps/Motown

❏ 4		My Girl	1967	18.75	37.50	75.00
		Cardboard record				
❏ 13		The Way You Do the Things You Do	1967	18.75	37.50	75.00
		Cardboard record				

Temptones, The
(Daryl Hall was in this group)
Arctic

❏ 130		Girl, I Love You/Good-Bye	1967	10.00	20.00	40.00
❏ 136		Say These Words of Love/	1967	10.00	20.00	40.00
		This Could Be the Start of Something Good				

Ten Broken Hearts
(Allegedly, Neil Diamond appears on this record)
Diamond

❏ 123		Ten Lonely Guys/Shining Star	1962	10.00	20.00	40.00

10CC
Mercury

❏ 73678		I'm Not in Love/Channel Swimmer	1975		2.50	5.00
❏ 73725		Art for Art's Sake/Get It While You Can	1975		2.50	5.00
❏ 73725	PS	Art for Art's Sake/Get It While You Can	1975	2.00	4.00	8.00
❏ 73779		I'm Mandy Fly Me/How Dare You	1976		2.50	5.00
❏ 73875		The Things We Do for Love/Hot to Trot	1976		2.50	5.00
❏ 73917		People in Love/Don't Squeeze Me Like Toothpaste	1977		2.50	5.00
❏ 73943		Good Morning Judge/I'm So Laid Back I'm Laid Out	1977		2.50	5.00
❏ 73980		You've Got a Cold/The Wall Street Shuffle	1977		2.50	5.00

Polydor

❏ 14511		Dreadlock Holiday/Nothing Can Move Me	1978		2.50	5.00
❏ 14528		For You and I/Take These Chains	1978		2.50	5.00

UK

❏ 49005		Donna/Hot Sun Rock	1972		3.00	6.00
❏ 49015		Ruber Bullets/Waterfall	1973		3.00	6.00
❏ 49019		Headline Hustler/Speed Kills	1973		3.00	6.00
❏ 49023		The Wall Street Shuffle/Gismo My Way	1974		3.00	6.00

Warner Bros.

❏ 29973		Power of Love/Action Man in Motown Suit	1982		2.50	5.00
❏ 49266		It Doesn't Matter Anymore/Strange Lover	1980		2.50	5.00

10,000 Maniacs
Elektra

❏ 64595		Because the Night/Eat for Two	1993			3.00
❏ 65962		Like the Weather/Peace Train	198?			3.00
		"Spun Gold" reissue				
❏ 69253		You Happy Puppet/Gunshy	1989		2.00	4.00
❏ 69298		Trouble Me/The Lion's Share	1989		2.00	4.00
❏ 69298	PS	Trouble Me/The Lion's Share	1989		2.00	4.00
❏ 69388		What's the Matter Here?/Cherry Tree	1988		2.00	4.00
❏ 69388	PS	What's the Matter Here?/Cherry Tree	1988		2.00	4.00
❏ 69418		Like the Weather/A Campfire Song	1988		2.00	4.00
❏ 69418	PS	Like the Weather/A Campfire Song	1988		2.00	4.00
❏ 69439		Don't Talk/City of Angels	1987		2.00	4.00
❏ 69439	PS	Don't Talk/City of Angels	1987		2.00	4.00
❏ 69457		Peace Train/Painted Desert	1987		2.00	4.00
❏ 69457	PS	Peace Train/Painted Desert	1987		2.00	4.00

Ten Years After
Columbia

❏ 45457		I'd Love to Change the World/Let the Sky Fall	1971		2.50	5.00
❏ 45530		Baby Won't You Let Me Rock 'N' Roll/	1972		2.50	5.00
		Once There Was a Time				
❏ 45736		You Can't Win Them All/Choo Choo Mama	1972		2.50	5.00
❏ 45787		Tomorrow, I'll Be Out of Town/Convention Prevention	1973		2.50	5.00
❏ 45915		I'm Going Home/You Give Me Loving	1973		2.50	5.00
❏ 46061		It's Getting Harder/I Wanted to Boogie	1974		2.50	5.00

Deram

❏ 7529		If You Should Love Me/Love Like a Man	1970	2.00	4.00	8.00
❏ 85027		Portable People/The Sounds	1968	2.00	4.00	8.00
❏ 85035		Hear Me Calling/I'm Coming Home	1968	2.00	4.00	8.00

Tender Tones, The
Ducky

❏ 713		I Love You So/Just for a Little While	1959	200.00	400.00	800.00

Tenderfoots, The
Federal

❏ 12214		Kissing Bug/Watussi Wussi Wo	1955	15.00	30.00	60.00

Number	Title (A Side/B Side)	Year	VG	VG+	NM
❏ 12219	My Confession/Save Me Some Kisses	1955	15.00	30.00	60.00
❏ 12225	Those Golden Bells/I'm Yours Anyhow	1955	20.00	40.00	80.00
❏ 12228	Sindy/Sugar Ways	1955	30.00	60.00	120.00

Tennessee Guitars, The
Sun

❏ 1102	Tennessee Toddy/Trophy Run	1969		3.00	6.00

Tennille, Toni
(Of the Captain and Tennille)
Mirage

❏ 99733	More Than You Know/Let's Do It	1984			3.00

Termites, The
Bee

❏ 1825	Give Me Your Heart/Carrie Lou	1964	12.50	25.00	50.00

Terracetones, The
Apt

❏ 25016	Words of Wisdom/Ride of Paul Revere	1958	25.00	50.00	100.00

Terrell, Tammi
(Also see "Gaye, Marvin, and Tammi Terrell"; "Montgomery, Tammi")
Motown

❏ 1086	I Can't Believe You Love Me/Hold Me Oh My Darling	1965	2.50	5.00	10.00
❏ 1095	Come On and See Me/Baby Don'tcha Worry	1966	2.50	5.00	10.00
❏ 1115	What a Good Man He Is/There Are Things	1967	2.50	5.00	10.00
❏ 1138	This Old Heart of Mine (Is Weak for You)/Just Too Much to Hope For	1968	2.50	5.00	10.00

Terri and the Velveteens
Kerwood

❏ 711	Bells of Love/You've Broken My Heart	1962	10.00	20.00	40.00

Terri-Tones, The
Cortland

❏ 105	Go/The Sinner	1962	12.50	25.00	50.00

Regency

❏ 929	Go/The Sinner	1962	7.50	15.00	30.00

Terry and the Pirates
Chess

❏ 1696	Talk About the Girl/What Did He Say	1958	10.00	20.00	40.00

Terry and the Tags
Sylvester

❏ 100	Rampage/The Twomp	1962	12.50	25.00	50.00

Terry, Don
Lin

❏ 5018	Knees Shakin'/She Giggles	1959	37.50	75.00	150.00

Terry, Gene
Goldband

❏ 1066	Cindy Lou/Teardrops in My Eyes	1958	30.00	60.00	120.00
❏ 1081	Never Let Her Go/No Mail Today	1958	10.00	20.00	40.00
❏ 1088	Cinderella, Cinderella/Guy with a Million Dreams	1959	7.50	15.00	30.00

Savoy

❏ 1559	This Should Go On Forever/Fine, Fine, Fine	1959	5.00	10.00	20.00

Terry, Larry
Testa

❏ 006	Hep Cat/(B-side unknown)	1960	300.00	600.00	1,200

Terry, Nat
Imperial

❏ 5150	Take It Easy/I Don't Know Why	1951	25.00	50.00	100.00

Tex and the Chex
Atlantic

❏ 2116	I Do Love You/My Love	1961	15.00	30.00	60.00

Newtown

❏ 5010	Watching Willie Wobble/Be on the Lookout for My Girl	1963	5.00	10.00	20.00

20th Fox

❏ 411	Beach Party/Now (Love Me)	1963	7.50	15.00	30.00

Tex, Joe
Ace

❏ 544	Cut It Out/Just for You and Me	1958	15.00	30.00	60.00
❏ 550	Mother's Advice/You Little Baby Face Thing	1958	20.00	40.00	80.00
❏ 559	Charlie Brown Got Expelled/Blessed Are These Tears	1959	15.00	30.00	60.00
❏ 572	Don't Hold It Against Me/Yum, Yum, Yum	1959	15.00	30.00	60.00
❏ 591	Boys Will Be Boys/Grannie Stole the Show	1960	10.00	20.00	40.00
❏ 674	Boys Will Be Boys/Baby You're Right	1963	3.75	7.50	15.00

Number		Title (A Side/B Side)	Year	VG	VG+	NM
Anna						
❏ 1119		All I Could Do Was Cry (Part 1)/	1960	10.00	20.00	40.00
		All I Could Do Was Cry (Part 2)				
❏ 1124		I'll Never Break Your Heart (Part 1)/	1960	10.00	20.00	40.00
		I'll Never Break Your Heart (Part 2)				
❏ 1128		Baby, You're Right/Ain't It a Mess	1961	10.00	20.00	40.00
Atlantic						
❏ 2874		I'll Never Fall in Love Again (Part 1)/	1972		3.00	6.00
		I'll Never Fall in Love Again (Part 2)				
Checker						
❏ 1104		Baby, You're Right/All I Could Do Was Cry (Part 2)	1965	3.00	6.00	12.00
Dial						
❏ 1001		Bad Feet/I Know Him	1971		3.00	6.00
❏ 1003		Papa's Dream/I'm Comin' Home	1971		3.00	6.00
❏ 1006	DJ	King Thaddeus (mono/stereo)	1971		3.50	7.00
		May be promo only				
❏ 1008		Give the Baby Anything the Baby Wants/	1971		3.00	6.00
		Takin' a Chance				
❏ 1010		I Gotcha/A Mother's Prayer	1972		3.00	6.00
❏ 1012		You Said a Bad Word/It Ain't Gonna Work Baby	1972		3.00	6.00
❏ 1018		Rain Go Away/King Thaddeus	1973		3.00	6.00
❏ 1020		Woman Stealer/Cat's Got Her Tongue	1973		3.00	6.00
❏ 1020	PS	Woman Stealer/Cat's Got Her Tongue	1973	2.00	4.00	8.00
❏ 1021		All the Heaven a Man Really Needs/	1973		3.00	6.00
		Let's Go Somewhere and Talk				
❏ 1024		Trying to Win Your Love/I've Seen Enough	1973		3.00	6.00
❏ 1154		Sassy Sexy Wiggle/Under Your Powerful Love	1975		3.00	6.00
❏ 1155		I'm Goin' Back Again/My Body Wants You	1975		3.00	6.00
❏ 1156		Baby, It's Rainin'/Have You Ever	1975		3.00	6.00
❏ 1157		Mama Red/Love Shortage	1975		3.00	6.00
❏ 2800		Loose Caboose/Music Ain't Got No Color	1979		2.50	5.00
❏ 2801		Who Gave Birth to the Funk/If You Don't Want the Man	1979		2.50	5.00
❏ 2802		Discomania/Fat People	1979		2.50	5.00
❏ 3000		What Should I Do/The Only Girl I've Ever Loved	1961	3.00	6.00	12.00
❏ 3002		One Giant Step/The Rib	1961	3.00	6.00	12.00
❏ 3003		Popeye Johnny/	1962	3.00	6.00	12.00
		Hand Shakin', Love Makin', Girl Talkin', Son-of-a-Gun From Next Door				
❏ 3007		Meet Me in Church/Be Your Own Judge	1962	3.00	6.00	12.00
❏ 3009		I Let Her Get Away/The Peck	1963	3.00	6.00	12.00
❏ 3013		Someone to Take Your Place/	1963	3.00	6.00	12.00
		I Should Have Kissed You More				
❏ 3016		I Wanna Be Free/Blood's Thicker Than Water	1963	3.00	6.00	12.00
❏ 3019		Looking for My Pig/Say Thank You	1964	3.00	6.00	12.00
❏ 3020		I'd Rather Have You/Old Time Lover	1964	3.00	6.00	12.00
❏ 3023		I Had a Good Thing But I Left (Part 1)/	1964	3.00	6.00	12.00
		I Had a Good Thing But I Left (Part 2)				
❏ 4001		Hold What You've Got/Fresh Out of Tears	1964	2.50	5.00	10.00
❏ 4003		You Better Get It/You Got What It Takes	1965	2.00	4.00	8.00
❏ 4006		A Woman Can Change a Man/	1965	2.00	4.00	8.00
		Don't Let Your Left Hand Know				
❏ 4011		One Monkey Don't Stop No Show/	1965	2.00	4.00	8.00
		Build Your Love on a Solid Foundation				
❏ 4016		I Want To (Do Everything For You)/Funny Bone	1965	2.00	4.00	8.00
❏ 4022		A Sweet Woman Like You/Close the Door	1965	2.00	4.00	8.00
❏ 4026		The Love You Save (May Be Your Own)/	1966	2.00	4.00	8.00
		If Sugar Was As Sweet As You				
❏ 4028		S.Y.S.L.J.F.M. (Letter Song)/I'm a Man	1966	2.00	4.00	8.00
❏ 4032		I Believe I'm Gonna Make It/Better Believe It, Baby	1966	2.00	4.00	8.00
❏ 4045		I've Got to Do a Little Bit Better/What in the World	1966	2.00	4.00	8.00
❏ 4051		Papa Was Too/Truest Woman in the World	1966	2.00	4.00	8.00
❏ 4055		Show Me/	1967	2.00	4.00	8.00
		A Woman Sees a Hard Time (When Her Man Is Gone)				
❏ 4059		Woman Like That, Yeah/I'm Going and Get It	1967	2.00	4.00	8.00
❏ 4061		A Woman's Hands/See See Rider	1967	2.00	4.00	8.00
❏ 4063		Skinny Legs and All/Watch the One	1967	2.00	4.00	8.00
❏ 4068		I'll Make Everyday Christmas/Don't Give Up	1967	2.00	4.00	8.00
❏ 4069		Men Are Gettin' Scarce/	1968	2.00	4.00	8.00
		You're Gonna Thank Me, Woman				
❏ 4076		I'll Never Do You Wrong/Wooden Spoon	1968	2.00	4.00	8.00
❏ 4079		Chocolate Cherry/Betwixt and Between	1968	2.00	4.00	8.00
❏ 4083		Keep the One You Got/Go Home and Do It	1968	2.00	4.00	8.00
❏ 4086		You Need Me, Baby/Baby, Be Good	1968	2.00	4.00	8.00
❏ 4089		That's Your Baby/Sweet, Sweet Woman	1968	2.00	4.00	8.00
❏ 4090		Buying a Book/Chicken Crazy	1969	2.00	4.00	8.00
❏ 4093		That's the Way/Anything You Wanna Know	1969	2.00	4.00	8.00
❏ 4094		We Can't Sit Down Now/It Ain't Sanitary	1969	2.00	4.00	8.00
❏ 4095		I Can't See You No More /	1969	2.00	4.00	8.00
		(When Johnny Comes Marching Home Again) Sure Is Good				
❏ 4096		Everything Happens on Time/	1970	2.00	4.00	8.00
		You're Right, Ray Charles				
❏ 4098		I'll Never Fall in Love Again/	1970	2.00	4.00	8.00
		The Only Way I Know to Love You				
Epic						
❏ 50313		Ain't Gonna Bump No More (With No Big Fat Woman)/	1976		2.50	5.00
		I Mess Up Everything I Get My Hands On				
❏ 50426		Hungry for Your Love/I Almost Got to Heaven Once	1977		2.50	5.00
❏ 50494		Rub Down/Be Kind to Old People	1977		2.50	5.00
❏ 50530		Get Back, Leroy/You Can Be My Star	1978		2.50	5.00

Number	Title (A Side/B Side)	Year	VG	VG+	NM

Handshake
| ❑ 02565 | Don't Do Da Do/ Here Comes No. 34 (Do the Earl Campbell) | 1981 | | 2.00 | 4.00 |

King
❑ 4840	Come In This House/Baby, You Upset My Home	1955	15.00	30.00	60.00
❑ 4884	My Biggest Mistake/Right Back to My Arms	1956	12.50	25.00	50.00
❑ 4911	She's Mine/I Had to Come Back to You	1956	12.50	25.00	50.00
❑ 4980	Get Way Back/Pneumonia	1956	12.50	25.00	50.00
❑ 5064	I Want to Have a Talk with You/ Ain't Nobody's Business	1957	12.50	25.00	50.00
❑ 5981	Come In This House/I Want to Have a Talk with You	1965	2.50	5.00	10.00

Texans, The
(Johnny and Dorsey Burnette)
Gothic
| ❑ 001 | Old Reb/Rockin' Johnny Home | 1961 | 7.50 | 15.00 | 30.00 |

Infinity
| ❑ 001 | Green Grass of Texas/Bloody River | 1961 | 7.50 | 15.00 | 30.00 |

Jox
| ❑ 001 | Old Reb/Rockin' Johnny Home | 1965 | 7.50 | 15.00 | 30.00 |

Vee Jay
| ❑ 658 | Green Grass of Texas/Bloody River | 1965 | 5.00 | 10.00 | 20.00 |

Tharp, Chuck, and the Fireballs – See "Fireballs, The"

Thee Midnighters
Chattahoochie
❑ 666	Land of a Thousand Dances (Part 1)/ Land of a Thousand Dances (Part 2)	1965	3.75	7.50	15.00
❑ 666-2	Land of a Thousand Dances (Part 1)/Ball O' Twine	1965	3.75	7.50	15.00
❑ 674	Sad Girl/Heat Wave	1965	4.00	8.00	16.00
❑ 675	Sad Girl/Heat Wave	1965	3.75	7.50	15.00
❑ 684	Whittier Blvd./Evil Love	1965	3.75	7.50	15.00
❑ 693	I Need Someone/Empty Heart	1965	5.00	10.00	20.00
❑ 695	Brother, Where Are You/Heat Wave	1966	3.75	7.50	15.00
❑ 706	Are You Angry/I Found a Peanut	1966	3.75	7.50	15.00

Uni
| ❑ 55170 | She Only Wants What She Can't Get/I've Come Alive | 1969 | 2.50 | 5.00 | 10.00 |

Whittier
❑ 201	That's All/To Be with You	196?	3.00	6.00	12.00
❑ 500	Love, Special Delivery/Don't Go Away	1966	5.00	10.00	20.00
❑ 501	The Midnite Feeling/It'll Never Be Over for Me	1966	5.00	10.00	20.00
❑ 503	Dragon Fly/The Big Ranch	1966	5.00	10.00	20.00
❑ 504	Never Knew I Had It So Bad/ Everybody Needs Somebody	1967	7.50	15.00	30.00
❑ 504	Never Knew I Had It So Bad/The Walking Song	1967	5.00	10.00	20.00
❑ 507	Jump Five and Harmonize/Looking Out a Window	1967	5.00	10.00	20.00
❑ 508	Chile Con Soul/Tu Despedida	1967	5.00	10.00	20.00
❑ 509	Breakfast on the Grass/Dreaming Casually	1967	5.00	10.00	20.00
❑ 511	You're Gonna Make Me Cry/Make Ends Meet	1968	50.00	100.00	200.00
❑ 512	The Ballad of Cesar Chavez/ The Ballad of Cesar Chavez (Spanish)	1968	5.00	10.00	20.00
❑ 513	Chicano Power/Never Goin' to Give You Up	1968	5.00	10.00	20.00
❑ 674	Sad Girl/Heat Wave	1968	3.00	6.00	12.00
❑ 694	It's Not Unusual/It's Not Unusual	1969	3.00	6.00	12.00

Them
(More than one group. Also see "Morrison, Van"; he only appears on the A&M and Parrot sides)
A&M
| ❑ 1201 | Baby Please Don't Go/Danger Heartbreak Dead Ahead B-side by the Marvelettes | 1988 | | 2.00 | 4.00 |
| ❑ 1201 | PS Danger Heartbreak Dead Ahead/Baby Please Don't Go "Good Morning Vietnam" sleeve | 1988 | | 2.00 | 4.00 |

Happy Tiger
| ❑ 525 | Lonely Weekends/I Am Waiting | 1969 | 3.75 | 7.50 | 15.00 |
| ❑ 534 | Memphis Lady/Nobody Cares | 1970 | 3.00 | 6.00 | 12.00 |

King
| ❑ 5967 | Don't Look Now/A Girl Like You Different group | 1964 | 3.75 | 7.50 | 15.00 |

Parrot
❑ 365	Gloria/Bring 'Em On In	1971	2.50	5.00	10.00
❑ 3003	Richard Cory/Don't You Know	1966	3.75	7.50	15.00
❑ 3006	Don't Start Crying Now/ I Can Only Give You Everything	1966	3.75	7.50	15.00
❑ 9702	Don't Start Crying Now/One, Two Brown Eyes	1964	5.00	10.00	20.00
❑ 9727	Gloria/Baby, Please Don't Go	1965	4.00	8.00	16.00
❑ 9749	Here Comes the Night/All By Myself	1965	3.75	7.50	15.00
❑ 9784	Gonna Dress in Black/Half As Much	1965	3.75	7.50	15.00
❑ 9796	Mystic Eyes/If You and I Could Be As Two	1965	3.75	7.50	15.00
❑ 9819	Call My Name/Bring 'Em On In	1966	3.75	7.50	15.00

Ruff
| ❑ 1088 | Walking in the Queen's Garden/I Happen to Love You | 1967 | 6.25 | 12.50 | 25.00 |

Number	Title (A Side/B Side)	Year	VG	VG+	NM

Tower

❏ 384	Walking in the Queen's Garden/I Happen to Love You	1967	3.00	6.00	12.00
❏ 407	But It's Alright/Square Room	1968	3.00	6.00	12.00
❏ 461	Waltz of the Flies/We All Agreed to Help	1969	3.00	6.00	12.00
❏ 493	Corina/Dark Are the Shadows	1969	3.00	6.00	12.00

Themes, Inc.
(P.F. Sloan and Steve Barri, again)

Vee Jay

❏ 635	Theme from Petyon Place/Paula's Percussion	1964	3.75	7.50	15.00

Thin Lizzy

London

❏ 20076	Whiskey in the Jar/Black Boys on the Corner	1972	2.00	4.00	8.00
❏ 20078	Broken Dreams/Randolph's Tango	1973	2.00	4.00	8.00
❏ 20082	Little Darling/The Rocket	1973	2.00	4.00	8.00

Mercury

❏ 73786	The Boys Are Back in Town/Jailbreak	1976		2.50	5.00
❏ 73841	Cowboy Song/Angel from the Coast	1976		2.50	5.00
❏ 73867	Rocky/Half-Caste	1976		2.50	5.00
❏ 73882	Old Flame/Johnny the Fox Meets Jimmy the Weed	1977		2.50	5.00
❏ 73892	Don't Believe a Word/Boogie Woogie Dance	1977		2.50	5.00
❏ 73945	Bad Reputation/ Dancing in the Moonlight (It's Caught Me in the Spotlight)	1977		2.50	5.00

Vertigo

❏ 202	Night Life/Showdown	1974		3.00	6.00
❏ 205	Wild One/Freedom Song	1975		3.00	6.00

Warner Bros.

❏ 49019	S & M/Do Anything You Want To	1979		2.50	5.00
❏ 49078	Got to Give It Up/With Love	1979		2.50	5.00
❏ 49643	Killer on the Loose/Sugar Blues	1980		2.00	4.00
❏ 49679	We Will Be Strong/Sweetheart	1981		2.00	4.00
❏ 50056	Hollywood/Pressure Will Blow	1982		2.00	4.00
❏ 8648	Cowboy Song/Johnny the Fox Meets Jimmy the Weed	1978		2.50	5.00

Things to Come

Dunwich

❏ 124	I'm Not Talkin'/'Til the End	1966	12.50	25.00	50.00

Starfire

❏ 103	Sweet Gina/(B-side unknown)	1966	10.00	20.00	40.00

Warner Bros.

❏ 7164	Come Alive/Dancer	1968	3.75	7.50	15.00
❏ 7228	Cool Day/Hello	1968	3.75	7.50	15.00

Think

Big Tree

❏ 15000	Once You Understand/Gather	1974		2.00	4.00

Columbia

❏ 44627	Faster Faster/Stop Runnin' Away	1968		3.00	6.00
❏ 44848	California (Is Getting So Heavy)/It's a Good Thing	1969		3.00	6.00

Laurie

❏ 3583	Once You Understand/Gather	1972		2.50	5.00
❏ 3594	It's Not the World -- It's the People/ Who Are You to Tell Me What to Do?	1972		2.50	5.00

Thirteenth Floor Elevators, The

Contact

❏ 5269	You're Gonna Miss Me/Tried to Hide	1966	25.00	50.00	100.00

Hanna-Barbera

❏ 492	You're Gonna Miss Me/Tried to Hide	1966	50.00	100.00	200.00

International Artists

❏ 107	You're Gonna Miss Me/Tried to Hide *Blue label*	1967	7.50	15.00	30.00
❏ 107	You're Gonna Miss Me/Tried to Hide *Yellow label*	1967	5.00	10.00	20.00
❏ 111	Reverberation (Doubt)/Fire Engine	1967	5.00	10.00	20.00
❏ 113	Before You Accuse Me/Levitation	1968	5.00	10.00	20.00
❏ 121	Baby Blue/She Lives	1968	5.00	10.00	20.00
❏ 122	Slip Inside This House/Splash 1	1968	5.00	10.00	20.00
❏ 126	May the Circle Remain Unbroken/ I'm Gonna Love You Too	1968	5.00	10.00	20.00
❏ 130	Livin' On/Scarlet and Gold	1969	10.00	20.00	40.00

.38 Special

A&M

❏ 1246		Rock and Roll Strategy/Love Strikes	1988			3.00
❏ 1246	PS	Rock and Roll Strategy/Love Strikes	1988			3.00
❏ 1273		Second Chance/Comin' Down Tonight	1989			3.00
❏ 1424		Comin' Down Tonight/Chauahoocie	1989			3.00
❏ 1946		Long Time Gone/Four Wheels	1977		2.00	4.00
❏ 1964		Tell Everybody/Play a Simple Song	1977		2.00	4.00
❏ 2051		I'm a Fool for You/Travelin' Man	1978		2.00	4.00
❏ 2205		Rockin' Into the Night/Robin Hood	1979		2.00	4.00
❏ 2242		Stone Cold Believer/Stone Cold Believer (Part 2)	1980		2.00	4.00

Number		Title (A Side/B Side)	Year	VG	VG+	NM
❑ 2316		Hold On Loosely/Throw Out the Line	1981			4.00
❑ 2330		Fantasy Girl/Honky Tonk Dancer	1981		2.00	4.00
❑ 2330	PS	Fantasy Girl/Honky Tonk Dancer	1981		2.00	4.00
❑ 2412		Caught Up in You/Firestarter	1982		2.00	4.00
❑ 2412	PS	Caught Up in You/Firestarter	1982		2.00	4.00
❑ 2431		You Keep Runnin' Away/Prisoners of Rock and Roll	1982		2.00	4.00
❑ 2431	PS	You Keep Runnin' Away/Prisoners of Rock and Roll	1982		2.00	4.00
❑ 2505		Chain Lightnin'/Back on the Track	1982		2.00	4.00
❑ 2594		If I'd Been the One/Twentieth Century Fox	1983			3.00
❑ 2594	PS	If I'd Been the One/Twentieth Century Fox	1983			3.00
❑ 2615		Back Where You Belong/Undercover Lover	1984			3.00
❑ 2615	PS	Back Where You Belong/Undercover Lover	1984			3.00
❑ 2633		Long Distance Affair/One Time for Old Times	1984			3.00
❑ 2831		Like No Other Night/Hearts on Fire	1986			3.00
❑ 2831	PS	Like No Other Night/Hearts on Fire	1986			3.00
❑ 2854		Somebody Like You/Against the Night	1986			3.00
❑ 2854	PS	Somebody Like You/Against the Night	1986			3.00
❑ 2873		One in a Million/Last Time	1986			3.00
❑ 2955		Back to Paradise/(B-side unknown)	1987			3.00
❑ 2955	PS	Back to Paradise/(B-side unknown)	1987			3.00

Capitol

Number		Title (A Side/B Side)	Year	VG	VG+	NM
❑ B-5405		Teacher Teacher/Twentieth Century Fox	1984			3.00
❑ B-5405	PS	Teacher Teacher/Twentieth Century Fox	1984			3.00

Thomas, B.J.

ABC

Number	Title (A Side/B Side)	Year	VG	VG+	NM
❑ 12054	(Hey, Won't You Play) Another Somebody Done Somebody Wrong Song/City Blues	1974		2.00	4.00
❑ 12123	We Are Happy Together/ Help Me Make It (To My Rockin' Chair)	1975		2.00	4.00

Bragg

Number	Title (A Side/B Side)	Year	VG	VG+	NM
❑ 103	Billy and Sue/Never Tell	1964	5.00	10.00	20.00

Cleveland Int'l.

Number	Title (A Side/B Side)	Year	VG	VG+	NM
❑ 03492	Whatever Happened to Old Fashioned Love/I Just Sing	1983		2.00	4.00
❑ 04608	From This Moment On/The Girl Most Likely To	1984		2.00	4.00

Columbia

Number	Title (A Side/B Side)	Year	VG	VG+	NM
❑ 03985	New Looks from an Old Lover/ You Keep the Man in Me Happy	1983		2.00	4.00
❑ 04237	Two Car Garage/Beautiful World	1983		2.00	4.00
❑ 04431	The Whole World's in Love When You're Lonely/ We're Here to Love	1984			3.00
❑ 04531	Rock and Roll Shoes/Then I'll Be Over You	1984			3.00
	Ray Charles and B.J. Thomas				
❑ 05647	A Part of Me That Needs You Most/Northern Lights	1985			3.00
❑ 05771	America Is/Broken Toys	1986			3.00
❑ 06314	Night Life/Make the World Go Away	1986			3.00

Hickory

Number	Title (A Side/B Side)	Year	VG	VG+	NM
❑ 1395	Billy and Sue/Never Tell	1966	2.50	5.00	10.00

Lori

Number	Title (A Side/B Side)	Year	VG	VG+	NM
❑ 9547	I've Got a Feeling/Hey Judy	1963	6.25	12.50	25.00
❑ 9561	For Your Precious Love/Here I Am Again	1964	6.25	12.50	25.00

MCA

Number	Title (A Side/B Side)	Year	VG	VG+	NM
❑ 40735	Don't Worry Baby/My Love	1977		2.00	4.00
❑ 40812	Still the Lovin' Is Fun/Play Me a Little Traveling Music	1977		2.00	4.00
❑ 40854	Everybody Loves a Rain Song/Dusty Roads	1978		2.00	4.00
❑ 40914	Sweet Young America/Aloha	1978		2.00	4.00
❑ 40986	We Could Have Been the Closest of Friends/ In My Heart	1979		2.00	4.00
❑ 41134	On This Christmas Night/God Bless the Children	1979		2.00	4.00
❑ 41207	Nothin' Could Be Better/Walkin' on a Cloud	1980		2.00	4.00
❑ 41281	Everything Always Works Out for the Best/No Limit	1980		2.00	4.00
❑ 51087	Some Love Songs Never Die/There Ain't No Love	1981		2.00	4.00
❑ 51151	The Lovin' Kind/I Recall a Gypsy Woman	1981		2.00	4.00
❑ 52053	I Really Got the Feeling/But Love Me	1982		2.00	4.00

Myrrh

Number	Title (A Side/B Side)	Year	VG	VG+	NM
❑ 166	Home Where I Belong/Hallelujah	1977		2.50	5.00
❑ 176	Without a Doubt/(B-side unknown)	1977		2.50	5.00
❑ 234	Uncloudy Day/(B-side unknown)	1981		2.50	5.00

Pacemaker

Number	Title (A Side/B Side)	Year	VG	VG+	NM
❑ 227	I'm So Lonesome I Could Cry/Candy Baby	1964	5.00	10.00	20.00
❑ 231	Mama/Wendy	1965	3.75	7.50	15.00
❑ 234	Bring Back the Time/I Don't Have a Mind of My Own	1965	3.75	7.50	15.00
❑ 239	Tomorrow Never Comes/Your Tears Leave Me Cold	1965	3.75	7.50	15.00
❑ 247	Plain Jane/My Home Town	1965	3.75	7.50	15.00
❑ 253	I'm Not a Fool Anymore/Baby Cried	1965	3.75	7.50	15.00
❑ 256	I Can't Help It (If I'm Still in Love with You)/Baby Cried	1965	3.75	7.50	15.00
❑ 259	Pretty Country Girl/Houston Town	1965	3.75	7.50	15.00

Paramount

Number	Title (A Side/B Side)	Year	VG	VG+	NM
❑ 0218	Goodbye's a Long, Long Time/Songs	1973		2.50	5.00
❑ 0239	Sunday Sunrise/Talkin' Confidentially	1973		2.50	5.00
❑ 0239	Sunday Sunrise/Early Morning Rush	1973		2.50	5.00
❑ 0277	Play Something Sweet (Brickyard Blues)/ Talkin' Confidentially	1974		2.50	5.00

Reprise

Number	Title (A Side/B Side)	Year	VG	VG+	NM
❑ 22837	Don't Leave Love (Out There All Alone)/One Woman	1989			3.00

Number	Title (A Side/B Side)	Year	VG	VG+	NM

Scepter

Number	Title (A Side/B Side)	Year	VG	VG+	NM
❏ 12129	I'm So Lonesome I Could Cry/Candy Baby	1966	2.50	5.00	10.00
❏ 12139	Mama/Wendy	1966	2.00	4.00	8.00
❏ 12154	Bring Back the Time/I Don't Have a Mind of My Own	1966	2.00	4.00	8.00
❏ 12165	Tomorrow Never Comes/Your Tears Leave Me Cold	1966	2.00	4.00	8.00
❏ 12179	Plain Jane/My Home Town	1966	2.00	4.00	8.00
❏ 12194	I Can't Help It (If I'm Still in Love with You)/Baby Cried	1967	2.00	4.00	8.00
❏ 12200	Just the Wisdom of a Fool/Treasure of Love	1967	2.00	4.00	8.00
❏ 12201	Wisdom of a Fool/Human	1967	2.00	4.00	8.00
❏ 12205	The Girl Can't Help It/Walkin' Back	1967	2.00	4.00	8.00
❏ 12219	The Eyes of a New York Woman/ I May Never Get to Heaven	1968	2.00	4.00	8.00
❏ 12230	Hooked on a Feeling/ I've Been Down This Road Before	1968	2.00	4.00	8.00
❏ 12244	It's Only Love/You Don't Love Me Anymore	1969		3.00	6.00
❏ 12255	Pass the Apple Eve/Fairy Tale of Time	1969		3.00	6.00
❏ 12259	You Don't Love Me Anymore/Skip a Rope	1969		3.00	6.00
❏ 12265	Raindrops Keep Fallin' on My Head/ Never Had It So Good	1969		3.50	7.00
❏ 12277	Everybody's Out of Town/Living Again	1970		3.00	6.00
❏ 12283	I Just Can't Help Believing/ Send My Picture to Scranton, Pa.	1970		3.00	6.00
❏ 12299	Most of All/The Mask	1970		2.50	5.00
❏ 12307	No Love at All/Have a Heart	1971		2.50	5.00
❏ 12320	Mighty Clouds of Joy/Life	1971		2.50	5.00
❏ 12335	Long Ago Tomorrow/Burnin' a Hole in My Mind	1971		2.50	5.00
❏ 12344	Rock and Roll Lullaby/Are We Losing Touch	1972		3.00	6.00
❏ 12354	That's What Friends Are For/I Get Enthused	1972		2.50	5.00
❏ 12364	Happier Than the Morning Sun/ We Have Got to Get Our Ship Together	1972		2.50	5.00
❏ 12379	Sweet Cherry Wine/Roads	1973		2.50	5.00

Valerie

Number	Title (A Side/B Side)	Year	VG	VG+	NM
❏ 226	I've Got a Feeling/Hey Judy	1963	5.00	10.00	20.00

Warner Bros.

Number	Title (A Side/B Side)	Year	VG	VG+	NM
❏ 5491	Billy and Sue/Never Tell	1964	5.00	10.00	20.00

Thomas, Carla

(Also see "Otis and Carla"; "Rufus and Carla")

Atlantic

Number	Title (A Side/B Side)	Year	VG	VG+	NM
❏ 2086	Gee Whiz (Look at His Eyes)/For You	1960	3.75	7.50	15.00
❏ 2101	A Love of My Own/Promises	1961	3.00	6.00	12.00
❏ 2113	Wish Me Good Luck/In Your Spare Time	1961	3.00	6.00	12.00
❏ 2132	The Masquerade Is Over/I Kinda Think He Does	1962	3.00	6.00	12.00
❏ 2163	I'll Bring It On Home to You/I Can't Take It	1962	3.00	6.00	12.00
❏ 2189	What a Fool I've Been/The Life I Live	1963	3.00	6.00	12.00
❏ 2212	Gee Whiz, It's Christmas/ All I Want for Christmas Is You	1963	3.00	6.00	12.00
❏ 2238	I've Got No Time to Love/A Boy Named Tom	1964	2.50	5.00	10.00
❏ 2258	A Woman's Love/Don't Let the Love Light Leave	1964	2.50	5.00	10.00
❏ 2272	How Do You Quit (Someone You Love)/The Puppet	1965	2.50	5.00	10.00

Satellite

Number	Title (A Side/B Side)	Year	VG	VG+	NM
❏ 104	Gee Whiz (Look at His Eyes)/For You	1960	50.00	100.00	200.00

Stax

Number	Title (A Side/B Side)	Year	VG	VG+	NM
❏ 0011	I've Fallen in Love/Where Do I Go	1968	2.00	4.00	8.00
❏ 0024	I Like What You're Doing (To Me)/Strong Guy	1969	2.00	4.00	8.00
❏ 0042	Just Keep On Loving Me/My Love	1969	2.00	4.00	8.00
	With Johnnie Taylor				
❏ 0044	I Can't Stop/I Need You Woman	1969		2.50	5.00
	With William Bell				
❏ 0056	Guide Me Well/ Some Other Man (Is Beating Your Time)	1970	2.00	4.00	8.00
❏ 0061	The Time for Love Is Anytime/Living in the City	1970		3.00	6.00
❏ 0067	All I Have to Do Is Dream/Leave the Girl Alone	1970		2.50	5.00
	With William Bell				
❏ 0080	Hi De Ho (That Old Sweet Roll)/ I Loved You Like I Love My Very Life	1970		3.00	6.00
❏ 0113	You've Got a Cushion to Fall On/ Love Means (You Never Have to Say You're Sorry)	1972		3.00	6.00
❏ 0133	Sugar/You've Got a Cushion to Fall On	1972		3.00	6.00
❏ 0149	I May Not Be All You Want/Sugar	1972		3.00	6.00
❏ 0173	I Have a God Who Loves/Love Among People	1973		3.00	6.00
❏ 172	Stop! Look What You're Doing/ Every Ounce of Strength	1965	2.50	5.00	10.00
❏ 183	Comfort Me/I'm for You	1966	2.50	5.00	10.00
❏ 188	Let Me Be Good to You/Another Night Without My Man	1966	2.50	5.00	10.00
❏ 195	B-A-B-Y/What Have You Got to Offer Me	1966	2.50	5.00	10.00
❏ 206	All I Want for Christmas Is You/Winter Snow	1966	3.00	6.00	12.00
❏ 207	Something Good (Is Going to Happen to You)/ It's Starting to Grow	1967	2.50	5.00	10.00
❏ 214	Unchanging Love/When Tomorrow Comes	1967	2.50	5.00	10.00
❏ 222	I'll Always Have Faith in You/Stop Thief	1967	2.50	5.00	10.00
❏ 239	Pick Up the Pieces/Separation	1967	2.50	5.00	10.00
❏ 251	A Dime a Dozen/I Want You Back	1968	2.50	5.00	10.00

Number		Title (A Side/B Side)	Year	VG	VG+	NM

Thomas, Mickey
(Lead singer for Elvin Bishop; later with Jefferson Starship and Starship)

MCA

❏ 40732		Can You Fool/Where Are We	1977		2.00	4.00
❏ 40767		Somebody to Love/Where Are We	1977		2.00	4.00

RCA

❏ PB-11244		The Theme from Skateboard/(Instrumental)	1978		2.00	4.00
❏ PB-14273		Stand in the Fire/Opening Score	1986			3.00

Thomas, Rufus
(Also see "Rufus and Carla")

Artists of America

❏ 126		If There Were No Music/Blues in the Basement	1976		2.50	5.00

AVI

❏ 149		Who's Makin' Love to Your Old Lady/Hot Grits	1977		2.00	4.00
❏ 178		I Ain't Gettin' Older, I'm Gettin' Better (Part 1)/I Ain't Gettin' Older, I'm Gettin' Better (Part 2)	1977		2.00	4.00

Hi

❏ 78520		Fried Chicken/I Ain't Got Time	1978		2.00	4.00

Meteor

❏ 5039		I'm Steady Holdin' On/The Easy Livin' Plan	1956	37.50	75.00	150.00

Stax

❏ 0010		Funky Mississippi/So Hard to Get Along With	1968		3.00	6.00
❏ 0022		Funky Way/I Want to Hold You	1969		3.00	6.00
❏ 0059		Do the Funky Chicken/Turn Your Damper Down	1969		3.00	6.00
❏ 0071		Sixty Minute Man/The Preacher and the Bear	1970		3.00	6.00
❏ 0079		(Do the) Push and Pull Part I/(Do the) Push and Pull Part II	1970		3.00	6.00
❏ 0090		The World Is Round/(I Love You) For Sentimental Reasons	1971		3.00	6.00
❏ 0098		The Breakdown (Part 1)/The Breakdown (Part 2)	1971		3.00	6.00
❏ 0112		Do the Funky Penguin (Part 1)/Do the Funky Penguin (Part 2)	1971		3.00	6.00
❏ 0129		Love Trap/6-3-8	1972		3.00	6.00
❏ 0140		Itch and Scratch (Part 1)/Itch and Scratch (Part 2)	1972		3.00	6.00
❏ 0153		Funky Robot (Part 1)/Funky Robot (Part 2)	1973		3.00	6.00
❏ 0177		I Know You Don't Want Me No More/I'm Still in Love with You	1973		3.00	6.00
❏ 0187		That Makes Christmas Baby/I'll Be Your Baby	1973		3.00	6.00
❏ 0192		The Funky Bird/Steal a Little	1974		3.00	6.00
❏ 0219		Boogie Ain't Nothin' (But Gettin' Down) (Part 1)/Boogie Ain't Nothin' (But Gettin' Down) (Part 2)	1974		3.00	6.00
❏ 0236		Do the Double Bump/Do the Double Bump	1975		3.00	6.00
❏ 0254		Jump Back '75 (Part 1)/Jump Back '75 (Part 2)	1975		3.00	6.00
❏ 126		It's Aw-Rite/Can't Ever Let You Go	1962	3.75	7.50	15.00
❏ 130		The Dog/Did You Ever Love a Woman	1963	2.50	5.00	10.00
❏ 140		Walking the Dog/You Said	1963	2.50	5.00	10.00
❏ 140		Walking the Dog/Fine and Mellow	1963	2.50	5.00	10.00
❏ 144		Can Your Monkey Do the Dog/I Want to Get Married	1964	2.50	5.00	10.00
❏ 149		Somebody Stole My Dog/I Want to Be Loved	1964	2.50	5.00	10.00
❏ 157		Jump Back/All Night Worker	1964	2.00	4.00	8.00
❏ 167		Baby Walk/Little Sally Walker	1965	2.00	4.00	8.00
❏ 173		Willy Nilly/Sho' Gonna Mess Him Up	1965	2.00	4.00	8.00
❏ 200		Talkin' 'Bout True Love/Sister's Got a Boyfriend	1967	2.00	4.00	8.00
❏ 221		Sophisticated Sissy/Greasy Spoon	1967	2.00	4.00	8.00
❏ 240		Down Ta My House/Steady Holding On	1968	2.00	4.00	8.00
❏ 250		The Memphis Train/I Think I Made a Boo-Boo	1968	2.00	4.00	8.00

Sun

❏ 181		Bear Cat (The Answer to Hound Dog)/Walking in the Rain	1953	50.00	100.00	200.00
❏ 181		Bear Cat/Walking in the Rain	1953	30.00	60.00	120.00
❏ 188		Tiger Man (King of the Jungle)/Save Your Money	1953	75.00	150.00	300.00

Thomas, Vic

Philips

❏ 40183		Napoleon Bonaparte/Marianne	1964	18.75	37.50	75.00
❏ 40228		Village of Love/There Stands An Empty Man	1964	18.75	37.50	75.00

Thompson Twins

Arista

❏ 0671		In the Name of Love/Coastline	1982		2.00	4.00
❏ 1024		Lies/Beach Culture	1982		2.00	4.00
❏ 1056		Love On Your Side/Love On Your Back	1983		2.00	4.00
❏ 1056	PS	Love On Your Side/Love On Your Back	1983		2.00	4.00
❏ 9013		Love On Your Side/Love On Your Back	1983			3.00
❏ 9013	PS	Love On Your Side/Love On Your Back	1983			3.00
❏ 9164		Hold Me Now/Let Loving Start	1984			3.00
❏ 9164	PS	Hold Me Now/Let Loving Start	1984			3.00
❏ 9209		Doctor! Doctor!/Nurse Shark	1984			3.00
❏ 9209	PS	Doctor! Doctor!/Nurse Shark	1984			3.00
❏ 9237		Lies/Love on Your Side	1984			3.00
		"Flashback" reissue				
❏ 9238		In the Name of Love/Coastline	1984			3.00
		"Flashback" reissue				
❏ 9244		You Take Me Up/Passion Planet	1984			3.00

Number		Title (A Side/B Side)	Year	VG	VG+	NM
❏ 9244	PS	You Take Me Up/Passion Planet	1984			3.00
❏ 9290		The Gap/Out of the Gap	1984			3.00
❏ 9347		Hold Me Now/Doctor! Doctor!	1985			3.00
		Reissue				
❏ 9396		Lay Your Hands on Me/ The Lewis Carroll (Adventures in Wonderland)	1985			3.00
❏ 9396	PS	Lay Your Hands on Me/ The Lewis Carroll (Adventures in Wonderland)	1985			3.00
❏ 9450		King for a Day/Rollunder	1985			3.00
❏ 9450	PS	King for a Day/Rollunder	1985			3.00
❏ 9485		Lay Your Hands on Me/King for a Day	1986			3.00
		Reissue				
❏ 9511		Nothing in Common/Nothing to Lose	1986			3.00
❏ 9511	PS	Nothing in Common/Nothing to Lose	1986			3.00
❏ 9577		Get That Love/Perfect Day	1987			3.00
❏ 9577	PS	Get That Love/Perfect Day	1987			3.00
❏ 9609		Long Goodbye/Dancin' in Your Shoes	1987			3.00
❏ 9622		Follow Your Heart/Bush Baby	1987			3.00
Warner Bros.						
❏ 22819		Sugar Daddy/Monkey Man	1989			3.00
❏ 22819	PS	Sugar Daddy/Monkey Man	1989			3.00

Thompson, Billy

Columbus

Number		Title (A Side/B Side)	Year	VG	VG+	NM
❏ 1043		Black Eyed Girl/Kiss Tomorrow Goodbye	1965	50.00	100.00	200.00
Wand						
❏ 1108		Black Eyed Girl/Kiss Tomorrow Goodbye	1966	15.00	30.00	60.00

Thompson, Chris

(Lead singer with Manfred Mann's Earth Band 1976-on, and also with Night)

Planet

Number	Title (A Side/B Side)	Year	VG	VG+	NM
❏ 45904	If You Remember Me/Theme from "The Champ"	1979		3.00	6.00
❏ 45909	If You Remember Me/You Ain't Pretty Enough	1979		2.00	4.00
	As "Chris Thompson and Night"				

Thompson, Junior

Atco

Number	Title (A Side/B Side)	Year	VG	VG+	NM
❏ 6500	You're the One/Jungle Girl	1967	3.00	6.00	12.00
Meteor					
❏ 5029	Mama's Little Baby/Raw Deal	1956	100.00	200.00	400.00

Thompson, Loretta

Skoop

Number	Title (A Side/B Side)	Year	VG	VG+	NM
❏ 1050	Buddy-Big Bopper-Ritchie/Square from Nowhere	1959	12.50	25.00	50.00
United					
❏ 214	He Do Ho Rock 'N' Roll/Let's Change the Alphabet	1958	10.00	20.00	40.00

Thompson, Sue

Decca

Number	Title (A Side/B Side)	Year	VG	VG+	NM
❏ 29314	Walkin' in the Snow/Come a Little Bit Closer	1954	6.25	12.50	25.00
	With Hank Penny				
❏ 29545	Day Dreaming/Your Mommie and Your Daddy	1955	6.25	12.50	25.00
❏ 30435	Walkin' to Missouri/Red Hot Honey Brown	1957	6.25	12.50	25.00
Hickory					
❏ 303	Warm Love/Fly the Friendly Skies with Jesus	1973		2.50	5.00
	With Don Gibson				
❏ 308	Just Plain Country/Oh Johnny, Oh Johnny, Oh	1973		2.50	5.00
❏ 313	Find Out/Stay Another Day	1974		2.50	5.00
❏ 320	Making Love to You Is Just Like Eating Peanuts/ Sweet Memories	1974		2.50	5.00
❏ 324	Good Old Fashioned Country Love/Ages and Ages Ago	1974		2.50	5.00
	With Don Gibson				
❏ 330	Trains/And Love Me	1974		2.50	5.00
❏ 339	The Thought of Losing You/Tennessee Waltz	1975		2.00	4.00
❏ 342	No One Will Ever Know/Put It Off Till Tomorrow	1975		2.00	4.00
	With Don Gibson				
❏ 346	I Can't Stop Loving You/Any Other Morning	1975		2.00	4.00
❏ 350	Oh, How Love Changes/Sweet and Tender Times	1975		2.00	4.00
	With Don Gibson				
❏ 354	Big Mabel Murphy/Big Daddy	1975		2.00	4.00
❏ 360	Maybe Tomorrow/I Can't Tell My Heart That	1975		2.00	4.00
	With Don Gibson				
❏ 364	Never Naughty Rosie/He Cheats on Me	1976		2.00	4.00
❏ 367	Get Ready, Here I Come/Once More	1976		2.00	4.00
	With Don Gibson				
❏ 370	Baby's Not Home/I Want It All	1976		2.00	4.00
❏ 373	You've Still Got a Place in My Heart/Let's Get Together	1976		2.00	4.00
	With Don Gibson				
❏ 1153	Sad Movies (Make Me Cry)/Nine Little Teardrops	1961	5.00	10.00	20.00
❏ 1159	Norman/Never Love Again	1961	5.00	10.00	20.00
❏ 1166	Two of a Kind/It Has to Be	1962	3.75	7.50	15.00
❏ 1174	Have a Good Time/If the Boy Only Knew	1962	3.75	7.50	15.00
❏ 1183	James (Hold the Ladder Steady)/My Hero	1962	3.75	7.50	15.00
❏ 1196	Willie Can/Too Much in Love	1962	3.75	7.50	15.00

Number	Title (A Side/B Side)	Year	VG	VG+	NM
❑ 1204	What's Wrong Bill/I Need a Harbor	1963	3.75	7.50	15.00
❑ 1217	True Confession/Suzie	1963	3.75	7.50	15.00
❑ 1221	Too Hot to Dance/I Like Your Kind of Love	1963	3.00	6.00	12.00
	With Bob Luman				
❑ 1234	'Cause I Ask You To/It's 12:35	1963	3.00	6.00	12.00
❑ 1240	Big Daddy/I'd Like to Know You Better	1964	3.00	6.00	12.00
❑ 1255	Bad Boy/Toys	1964	3.00	6.00	12.00
❑ 1270	Big Hearted Me/Looking for a Good Boy	1964	3.00	6.00	12.00
❑ 1284	Paper Tiger/Mama, Don't Cry at My Wedding	1964	3.00	6.00	12.00
❑ 1308	Stop Th' Music/What I'm Needin' Is You	1965	3.75	7.50	15.00
❑ 1328	Afraid/It's Break-Up Time	1965	3.00	6.00	12.00
❑ 1340	Just Kiss Me/Sweet Hunk of Misery	1965	3.00	6.00	12.00
❑ 1359	Walkin' My Baby/I'm Lookin' (For a World)	1965	3.00	6.00	12.00
❑ 1381	What Should I Do/After the Heartache	1966	3.00	6.00	12.00
❑ 1403	I Can't Help It/Put It Back	1966	2.50	5.00	10.00
❑ 1423	Someone/From My Balcony	1966	2.50	5.00	10.00
❑ 1431	Language of Love/Let Me Down Hard	1967	2.50	5.00	10.00
❑ 1457	Don't Forget to Cry/Ferris Wheel	1967	2.50	5.00	10.00
❑ 1469	That's Just Too Much/Straight to Helen	1967	2.50	5.00	10.00
❑ 1488	Dear Boy/Love Has Come My Way	1967	2.50	5.00	10.00
❑ 1493	How Do You Start Over/Why Not	1968	2.00	4.00	8.00
❑ 1512	You Deserve Each Other/Doin' Nothing	1968	2.00	4.00	8.00
❑ 1524	Don't Try to Change Me/The Real Me	1968	2.00	4.00	8.00
❑ 1534	Tennessee Waltz/Who's Gonna Mow Your Grass	1969	2.00	4.00	8.00
❑ 1547	Pair of Broken Hearts/You Two-Timed Me One Time Too Often	1969	2.00	4.00	8.00
❑ 1558	Talk Back Trembling Lips/Till I Can't Take It Anymore	1970		3.00	6.00
	With Roy Acuff, Jr.				
❑ 1560	I Just Keep Hangin' On/Lost Highway	1970		3.00	6.00
❑ 1573	Don't Let the Stars Get In Your Eyes/Why You Been Gone	1970		3.00	6.00
	With Roy Acuff, Jr.				
❑ 1577	Whole Lot of Walkin'/Guess Who's Coming to Dinner Tonight	1970		3.00	6.00
❑ 1587	Because You Love Me/Take a Little Time	1971		3.00	6.00
❑ 1596	Here's To Forever/What You See Is What You Get	1971		3.00	6.00
❑ 1607	The Two of Us Together/Oh Yes, I Love You	1971		3.00	6.00
	With Don Gibson				
❑ 1612	Swiss Cottage Place/Thanks to Rumors	1971		3.00	6.00
❑ 1622	Let Your Thoughts Be Sweet/What a Woman in Love Won't Do	1972		3.00	6.00
❑ 1629	Did You Ever Think/Love Garden	1972		3.00	6.00
	With Don Gibson				
❑ 1641	Sweet Memories/Take Me As I Am	1972		3.00	6.00
❑ 1646	I Think They Call It Love/Over There's the Door	1972		3.00	6.00
	With Don Gibson				
❑ 1652	Candy and Roses/Full Time Job	1972		3.00	6.00
❑ 1654	Cause I Love You/My Tears Don't Show	1972		3.00	6.00
	With Don Gibson				
❑ 1665	Go with Me/Two of Us Together	1973		2.50	5.00
	With Don Gibson				
❑ 1669	How I Love Them Old Songs/Just Two Young People	1973		2.50	5.00

Mercury

❑ 6325	You're Getting a Good Girl (When You Get Me)/What've You Got (That Makes Me Love You So)	1951	10.00	20.00	40.00
❑ 6377	Just Walking Out the Door/I'll Hate Myself in the Morning	1952	7.50	15.00	30.00
❑ 6390	Junior's a Big Boy Now/Tadpole	1952	7.50	15.00	30.00
❑ 6407	You Belong to Me/You're an Angel on the Outside	1952	7.50	15.00	30.00
❑ 6416	Red Hot Henrietta Brown/Last Night I Heard Somebody Cry	1952	7.50	15.00	30.00
❑ 70066	How Many Tears/If You Should Change	1953	6.25	12.50	25.00
❑ 70084	Take Care My Love/Things I Might Have Been	1953	6.25	12.50	25.00
❑ 70089	You and Me/Say It with Your Heart	1953	6.25	12.50	25.00
❑ 70152	I'm Not That Kind of Girl/I Long to Tell You	1953	6.25	12.50	25.00
❑ 70309	Donna Wanna/Gee But I Hate to Go Home Alone	1954	6.25	12.50	25.00

Thor-Ables, The

Titanic

❑ 1001	Our Love Song/Get That Bread	1962	75.00	150.00	300.00
❑ 1002	My Reckless Heart/Batman and Robin	1962	75.00	150.00	300.00

Thornton, Fradkin and Unger

ESP-Disk

❑ 63019	God Bless California/Sometimes	1972	3.75	7.50	15.00
	Paul McCartney appears on this record				

Three Blonde Mice

Atco

❑ 6324	Ringo Bells/12 Days of Christmas	1964	7.50	15.00	30.00
❑ 6353	Alley Cat/What Did I Say	1965	2.50	5.00	10.00

Three Chuckles, The

"X"

❑ 0066	Runaround/At Last You Understand	1954	6.25	12.50	25.00
❑ 0095	Foolishly/If I Should Love Again	1955	6.25	12.50	25.00
❑ 0134	So Long/You Should Have Told Me	1955	6.25	12.50	25.00

Number	Title (A Side/B Side)	Year	VG	VG+	NM
❏ 0150	Blue Lover/Realize	1955	6.25	12.50	25.00
❏ 0162	Times Two, I Love You/Still Thinking of You	1955	6.25	12.50	25.00
❏ 0186	Anyway/The Funny Little Things We Used to Do	1956	6.25	12.50	25.00
❏ 0194	Tell Me/And the Angels Sing	1956	6.25	12.50	25.00
❏ 0216	Gypsy in My Soul/We're Still Holding Hands	1956	6.25	12.50	25.00

Boulevard

❏ 100	Runaround/At Last You Understand	1954	20.00	40.00	80.00

Vik

❏ 0186	Anyway/The Funny Little Things We Used to Do	1956	5.00	10.00	20.00
❏ 0194	Tell Me/And the Angels Sing	1956	5.00	10.00	20.00
❏ 0216	Gypsy in My Soul/We're Still Holding Hands	1956	5.00	10.00	20.00
❏ 0232	Fallen Out of Love/Midnight 'Til Dawn	1956	5.00	10.00	20.00
❏ 0244	Won't You Give Me a Chance/ We're Gonna Rock Tonight	1956	5.00	10.00	20.00

Three D's, The

Brunswick

❏ 55152	Nothing to Wear/The Happiest Boy and Girl	1959	6.25	12.50	25.00

Dean

❏ 521	Broken Hearted/I Love You So	1961	5.00	10.00	20.00

Paris

❏ 503	Little Billy Boy/Let Me Know	1957	5.00	10.00	20.00
❏ 508	Never Let You Go/Birth of An Angel	1957	5.00	10.00	20.00
❏ 511	Baby Doll/Crazy Little Woman	1958	5.00	10.00	20.00
❏ 514	Jumpin' Jack/I Never Saw My Pretty Little Baby Alone	1958	5.00	10.00	20.00

Pilgrim

❏ 719	Broken Dreams/Tell Me That You Love Me	1956	6.25	12.50	25.00

Square

❏ 502	Squeeze/Graveyard Cha-Cha	1959	15.00	30.00	60.00

Three Degrees, The

Ariola America

❏ 801	Simple Heart/(B-side unknown)	1980		2.00	4.00
❏ 7721	Giving Up, Giving In/Woman in Love	1978		2.00	4.00
❏ 7742	Woman in Love/Out of Love Again	1979		2.00	4.00
❏ 7746	The Runner/Out of Love Again	1979		2.00	4.00

Epic

❏ 50283	What I Did for Love/Macaroni Man	1976		2.00	4.00
❏ 50330	In Love We Grow/Standing Up for Love	1977		2.00	4.00

Metromedia

❏ 109	Down in the Boondocks/Warm Weather Music	1969	2.00	4.00	8.00
❏ 128	Feeling of Love/Warm Weather Music	1969	2.00	4.00	8.00

Neptune

❏ 23	Reflections of Yesterday/What I See	1970		3.00	6.00

Philadelphia Int'l.

❏ 3534	Dirty Ol Man/Can't You See What You're Doing to Me	1973		3.00	6.00
❏ 3539	Year of Decision/A Woman Needs a Good Man	1974		2.50	5.00
❏ 3550	When Will I See You Again/Year of Decision	1974		2.50	5.00
❏ 3561	I Didn't Know/Dirty Ol Man	1975		2.50	5.00
❏ 3568	Take Good Care of Yourself/Here I Am	1975		2.50	5.00
❏ 3585	Free Ride/Loving Cup	1976		2.50	5.00

Roulette

❏ 7072	Melting Pot/The Grass Will Sing for You	1970		3.00	6.00
❏ 7079	Maybe/Collage	1970		3.00	6.00
❏ 7088	I Do Take You/You're the Fool	1970		3.00	6.00
❏ 7097	You're the One/Stardust	1971		3.00	6.00
❏ 7102	There's So Much Love All Around/Yours	1971		3.00	6.00
❏ 7105	Ebb Tide/Low Down	1971		3.00	6.00
❏ 7117	Trade Winds/I Turn to You	1972		3.00	6.00
❏ 7125	Find My Way/I Wanna Be Your Baby	1972		3.00	6.00
❏ 7137	I Won't Let You Go/Through Misty Eyes	1972		3.00	6.00

Swan

❏ 4197	Gee Baby (I'm Sorry)/Do What You're Supposed to Do	1965	3.00	6.00	12.00
❏ 4214	I'm Gonna Need You/Just Right for Love	1965	3.00	6.00	12.00
❏ 4224	Close Your Eyes/Gotta Draw the Line	1965	3.00	6.00	12.00
❏ 4235	Look in My Eyes/Drivin' Me Mad	1965	3.00	6.00	12.00
❏ 4245	Maybe/Yours	1966	3.00	6.00	12.00
❏ 4253	I Wanna Be Your Baby/Tales Are True	1966	3.00	6.00	12.00
❏ 4267	Love of My Life/Are You Satisfied	1967	3.00	6.00	12.00

Warner Bros.

❏ 7198	Contact/Oh No Not Again	1968	2.50	5.00	10.00

Three Dog Night

(Also see "Hutton, Danny")

ABC

❏ 12114	'Til the World Ends/ Yo Te Quiero Hablo (Take You Down)	1975		2.00	4.00
❏ 12192	Everybody Is a Masterpiece/Drive On, Ride On	1976		2.00	4.00

ABC Dunhill

❏ 4168	Nobody/It's for You	1968	3.00	6.00	12.00
❏ 4168 PS	Nobody/It's for You	1968	7.50	15.00	30.00
	Sleeve is promo only				
❏ 4177	Try a Little Tenderness/That No One Ever Hurt So Bad	1969	2.00	4.00	8.00

Number		Title (A Side/B Side)	Year	VG	VG+	NM
❏ 4191		One/Chest Fever	1969	2.00	4.00	8.00
❏ 4203		Easy to Be Hard/Dreaming Isn't Good for You	1969	2.00	4.00	8.00
❏ 4229		Celebrate/Feeling Alright	1970		3.00	6.00
❏ 4235		Eli's Coming/Circle for a Landing	1969	2.00	4.00	8.00
❏ 4239		Mama Told Me (Not to Come)/Rock and Roll Widow	1970		3.00	6.00
❏ 4239	PS	Mama Told Me (Not to Come)/Rock and Roll Widow	1970	3.00	6.00	12.00
❏ 4250		Out in the Country/Good Time Living	1970		3.00	6.00
❏ 4262		One Man Band/It Ain't Easy	1970		3.00	6.00
❏ 4272		Joy to the World/I Can Hear You Calling	1971		2.50	5.00
❏ 4282		Liar/Can't Get Enough of It	1971		2.50	5.00
❏ 4294		An Old Fashioned Love Song/Jam	1971		2.50	5.00
❏ 4299		Never Been to Spain/Peace of Mind	1972		2.50	5.00
❏ 4306		The Family of Man/Going in Circles	1972		2.50	5.00
❏ 4317		Black and White/Freedom for the Stallion	1972		2.50	5.00
❏ 4331		Pieces of April/The Writings on the Wall	1972		2.50	5.00
❏ 4352		Shambala/Our "B" Side	1973		2.50	5.00

First pressings have "Dunhill" spelled out in children's blocks

| ❏ 4352 | | Shambala/Our "B" Side | 1973 | | 2.50 | 5.00 |

Transitional pressings have "Dunhill" in children's blocks on one label and "Dunhill" in a box on the other label

| ❏ 4352 | | Shambala/Our "B" Side | 1973 | | 2.00 | 4.00 |

Later pressings have "Dunhill" in a box on both labels (1968-72 style)

❏ 4370		Let Me Serenade You/Storybook Feeling	1973		2.00	4.00
❏ 4382		The Show Must Go On/On the Way Back Home	1974		2.00	4.00
❏ 15001		Sure As I'm Sittin' Here/Anytime Babe	1974		2.00	4.00
❏ 15010		The Show Must Go On/On the Way Back Home	1974	2.00	4.00	8.00
❏ 15013		Play Something Sweet (Brickyard Blues)/I'd Be So Happy	1974		2.00	4.00

Passport

| ❏ 7921 | | It's a Jungle Out There/Somebody's Gonna Get Hurt | 1983 | | 2.50 | 5.00 |

Three Dots and a Dash
(With Jesse Belvin)
Imperial

| ❏ 5164 | | I'll Never Love Again/Let's Do It | 1951 | 125.00 | 250.00 | 500.00 |

Three Friends, The
(Probably more than one group)
Brunswick

| ❏ 55032 | | Jinx/Chinese Tearoom | 1957 | 6.25 | 12.50 | 25.00 |

Cal-Gold

| ❏ 169 | | Walkin' Shoes/Blue Ribbon Baby | 1961 | 50.00 | 100.00 | 200.00 |

Imperial

| ❏ 5763 | | Dedicated (To the Songs I Love)/Happy as a Man Can Be | 1961 | 5.00 | 10.00 | 20.00 |
| ❏ 5773 | | You're a Square/Go On to School | 1961 | 5.00 | 10.00 | 20.00 |

Lido

❏ 500		Baby I'll Cry/Blanche *Gray label*	1956	7.50	15.00	30.00
❏ 500		Baby I'll Cry/Blanche *Blue label*	1956	5.00	10.00	20.00
❏ 502		I'm Only a Boy/Jinx	1957	5.00	10.00	20.00
❏ 504		Now That You've Gone/Chinese Tea Room	1957	5.00	10.00	20.00

Three Vales, The
Cindy

| ❏ 3007 | | Blue Lights/Ay, Ay, Ay | 1957 | 30.00 | 60.00 | 120.00 |

Threeteens, The
Rev

| ❏ 3516 | | Dear 53310761/Doowaddie | 1958 | 10.00 | 20.00 | 40.00 |
| ❏ 3522 | | X + Y = Z/For the Love of Mike | 1959 | 6.25 | 12.50 | 25.00 |

Todd

| ❏ 1021 | | X + Y = Z/For the Love of Mike | 1959 | 5.00 | 10.00 | 20.00 |

Thrillers, The
(More than one group)
Big Town

| ❏ 109 | | The Drunkard/Mattie, Leave Me Alone | 1953 | 100.00 | 200.00 | 400.00 |

Herald

| ❏ 432 | | Lizabeth/Please Talk to Me | 1954 | 100.00 | 200.00 | 400.00 |

Thriller

| ❏ 3530 | | Lessie Mae/I'm Going to Live My Life Alone | 1953 | 250.00 | 500.00 | 1,000 |

Uptown

| ❏ 715 | | Come What May/This I Know Little Girl | 1965 | 3.00 | 6.00 | 12.00 |

Thrills, The
Capitol

❏ 5631		What Can Go Wrong/No One	1966	5.00	10.00	20.00
❏ 5719		Here's a Heart/Bring It On Home to Me	1966	5.00	10.00	20.00
❏ 5871		Show the World Where It's At/Underneath My Make-Up	1967	5.00	10.00	20.00

Number		Title (A Side/B Side)	Year	VG	VG+	NM

Thudpucker, Jimmy
(Fictional singing star from Garry Trudeau's "Doonesbury" comic strip)
Warner Bros.

Number		Title (A Side/B Side)	Year	VG	VG+	NM
❑ 8245		Ginny's Song (Part 1)/Ginny's Song (Part 2)	1976		3.00	6.00
❑ 8245	PS	Ginny's Song (Part 1)/Ginny's Song (Part 2)	1976		3.00	6.00

Windsong

Number		Title (A Side/B Side)	Year	VG	VG+	NM
❑ CB-11230		You Can't Fight It/Take Your Life	1978		2.50	5.00
❑ CB-11230	PS	You Can't Fight It/Take Your Life	1978		2.50	5.00

Thunder Bolts, The
Rondack

Number	Title (A Side/B Side)	Year	VG	VG+	NM
❑ 7546	Thunder Head/Blending	196?	12.50	25.00	50.00

Thunder Heads, The
Cartwheel

Number	Title (A Side/B Side)	Year	VG	VG+	NM
❑ 100	Thunder Head/Unemployment	1966	7.50	15.00	30.00

Thunderclap Newman
(Jimmy McCulloch, later of Wings, was in this group)
Track

Number	Title (A Side/B Side)	Year	VG	VG+	NM
❑ 2656	Something in the Air/Wilhelmina	1969	2.50	5.00	10.00
❑ 2769	Something in the Air/Wilhelmina	1970		3.00	6.00

Thursday's Children
International Artists

Number	Title (A Side/B Side)	Year	VG	VG+	NM
❑ 110	Air Conditioned Man/Sominoes	1967	37.50	75.00	150.00
❑ 115	Help, Murder, Police/You Can't Forget About That	1967	37.50	75.00	150.00

N-Joy

Number	Title (A Side/B Side)	Year	VG	VG+	NM
❑ 1019	Running Around on Me/I Don't Need Your Love	1967	3.75	7.50	15.00

Thyme
A-Square

Number	Title (A Side/B Side)	Year	VG	VG+	NM
❑ 201	Somehow/Shame, Shame	1969	10.00	20.00	40.00
❑ 202	Time of the Season/I Found a Love	1969	10.00	20.00	40.00

Bang

Number	Title (A Side/B Side)	Year	VG	VG+	NM
❑ 546	Love to Love/Very Last Day	1967	5.00	10.00	20.00

Tiatt, Lynn, and the Comets
Pussycat

Number	Title (A Side/B Side)	Year	VG	VG+	NM
❑ 1	Dad Is Home/Vilma's Jump-Up	195?	75.00	150.00	300.00

Tico and the Triumphs
(Paul Simon was a member)
Amy

Number	Title (A Side/B Side)	Year	VG	VG+	NM
❑ 835	Motorcycle/I Don't Believe Them	1961	25.00	50.00	100.00
❑ 845	Wildflower/Express Train	1962	25.00	50.00	100.00
❑ 860	Cry, Lil' Boy, Cry/Get Up and Do the Wobble	1962	25.00	50.00	100.00
❑ 876	Cards of Love/Noise	1963	50.00	100.00	200.00

Madison

Number	Title (A Side/B Side)	Year	VG	VG+	NM
❑ 169	Motorcycle/I Don't Believe Them	1961	50.00	100.00	200.00

"Tico" is Paul Simon

Tiffanys, The
(More than one group)
Arctic

Number	Title (A Side/B Side)	Year	VG	VG+	NM
❑ 101	Love Me/Happiest Girl in the World	1964	5.00	10.00	20.00

Atlantic

Number	Title (A Side/B Side)	Year	VG	VG+	NM
❑ 2240	Gossip/Please Tell Me	1964	3.75	7.50	15.00

Josie

Number	Title (A Side/B Side)	Year	VG	VG+	NM
❑ 942	I Feel the Same Way Too/I Just Wanna Be a Girl	1965	3.00	6.00	12.00
❑ 952	Heaven on Earth/Take Another Look at Me	1966	3.00	6.00	12.00

KR

Number	Title (A Side/B Side)	Year	VG	VG+	NM
❑ 120	He's Good for Me/It's Got to Be a Great Song	1967	5.00	10.00	20.00

As "The Tiffanies"

RKO

Number	Title (A Side/B Side)	Year	VG	VG+	NM
❑ 120	He's Good for Me/It's Got to Be a Great Song	1967	2.50	5.00	10.00

Are the KR and RKO releases one and the same? We don't know

Rockin' Robin

Number	Title (A Side/B Side)	Year	VG	VG+	NM
❑ 1	I've Got a Girl/I Don't Dig Western Movies	1963	75.00	150.00	300.00

Swan

Number	Title (A Side/B Side)	Year	VG	VG+	NM
❑ 4104	Atlanta/The Pleasure of Love	1962	5.00	10.00	20.00

Tigers, The
Colpix

Number		Title (A Side/B Side)	Year	VG	VG+	NM
❑ 773		GeeTO Tiger/The Prowl	1965	12.50	25.00	50.00
❑ 773	PS	GeeTO Tiger/The Prowl	1965	50.00	100.00	200.00

Number		Title (A Side/B Side)	Year	VG	VG+	NM

'Til Tuesday
Epic

❑ 04795		Voices Carry/Are You Serious	1985			3.00
❑ 04795	PS	Voices Carry	1985		2.50	5.00
		"Demonstration -- Not for Sale" on back				
❑ 04795	PS	Voices Carry/Are You Serious	1985			3.00
❑ 04935		Looking Over My Shoulder (Single Mix)/	1985			3.00
		Don't Watch Me Bleed				
❑ 04935	PS	Looking Over My Shoulder (Single Mix)/	1985			3.00
		Don't Watch Me Bleed				
❑ 05673		Love in a Vacuum/No More Crying	1985			3.00
❑ 06289		What About Love/Will She Just Fall Down	1986			3.00
❑ 06289	PS	What About Love/Will She Just Fall Down	1986			3.00
❑ 06450		Voices Carry/Love in a Vacuum	1986			3.00
		Reissue				
❑ 06571		Coming Up Close/Angels Never Call	1986			3.00
❑ 06571	PS	Coming Up Close/Angels Never Call	1986		3.00	6.00
❑ 08059		(Believed You Were) Lucky/Limits to Love	1988			3.00
❑ 08059	PS	(Believed You Were) Lucky/Limits to Love	1988			3.00
❑ 68622		Rip in Heaven/How Can You Give Up	1989			3.00

Til, Sonny
(Of the Orioles)
Jubilee

❑ 5060		I Never Knew (I Could Love Anybody)/My Prayer	1951	75.00	150.00	300.00
❑ 5066		Fool's World/For All We Know	1951	75.00	150.00	300.00
❑ 5066		Fool's World/For All We Know	1951	200.00	400.00	800.00
		Red vinyl				
❑ 5090		Once in Awhile/I Only Have Eyes for You	1952	12.50	25.00	50.00
		With Edna McGriff				
❑ 5099		Good/Picadilly	1952	12.50	25.00	50.00
		With Edna McGriff				
❑ 5112		Have You Heard/Lonely Wine	1953	25.00	50.00	100.00
❑ 5118		(Danger) Soft Shoulders/Congratulations to Someone	1953	25.00	50.00	100.00
❑ 5394		Night and Day/Shimmy Time	1960	5.00	10.00	20.00

RCA Victor

❑ 47-9733		You're All I Need/After You	1969	2.00	4.00	8.00
❑ 47-9759		Tears and Misery/I Better Leave Love Alone	1969	2.00	4.00	8.00
❑ 74-0390		Don't Feel No Pain/One Big Happy Family	1970	2.00	4.00	8.00
❑ 74-0432		Colours/Love Is What It's All About	1971	2.00	4.00	8.00
❑ 74-0529		'Til Then/Love or Desire	1971	2.00	4.00	8.00
❑ 74-0606		Crying in the Chapel/	1971	2.00	4.00	8.00
		What Are You Doing New Year's Eve				

Roulette

❑ 4079		Shy/First Blush	1958	5.00	10.00	20.00

Tillotson, Johnny
Amos

❑ 117		Tears on My Pillow/Remember When	1969		3.00	6.00
❑ 125		What Am I Living For/Joy to the World	1969		3.00	6.00
❑ 128		Raining in My Heart/Today I Started Loving You Again	1969		3.00	6.00
❑ 136		Susan/Love Waits for Me	1970		3.00	6.00
❑ 146		I Don't Believe In It Anymore/Kansas City, Kansas	1970		3.00	6.00

Atlantic

❑ 87978		Bim Bam Boom/(B-side unknown)	1990		2.00	4.00

Buddah

❑ 232		Star Spangled Bus/Apple Bend	1971		2.50	5.00
❑ 256		Welfare Hero/	1971		2.50	5.00
		The Flower Kissed the Shoes That Jesus Wore				
❑ 279		Make Me Believe/	1972		2.50	5.00
		The Flower Kissed the Shoes That Jesus Wore				
❑ 311		Your Love's Been a Long Time Comin'/Apple Bend	1972		2.50	5.00

Cadence

❑ 1353		Dreamy Eyes/Well, I'm Your Man	1958	5.00	10.00	20.00
❑ 1354		I'm Never Gonna Kiss You/Cherie, Cherie	1958	6.25	12.50	25.00
		With Genevieve				
❑ 1365		True True Happiness/Love Is Blind	1959	5.00	10.00	20.00
❑ 1372		Why Do I Love You So/Never Let Me Go	1959	5.00	10.00	20.00
❑ 1377		Earth Angel/Pledging My Love	1960	5.00	10.00	20.00
❑ 1377	PS	Earth Angel/Pledging My Love	1960	7.50	15.00	30.00
❑ 1384		Poetry in Motion/Princess, Princess	1960	5.00	10.00	20.00
❑ 1391		Jimmy's Girl/His True Love Said Godbye	1960	3.75	7.50	15.00
❑ 1391	PS	Jimmy's Girl/His True Love Said Godbye	1960	7.50	15.00	30.00
❑ 1404		Without You/Cutie Pie	1961	3.75	7.50	15.00
❑ 1409		Dreamy Eyes/Well, I'm Your Man	1961	3.75	7.50	15.00
❑ 1418		It Keeps Right On a-Hurtin'/	1962	3.75	7.50	15.00
		She Gave Sweet Love to Me				
❑ 1424		Send Me the Pillow You Dream On/What'll I Do	1962	3.75	7.50	15.00
❑ 1432		I Can't Help It (If I'm Still in Love with You)/	1962	3.75	7.50	15.00
		I'm So Lonesome I Could Cry				
❑ 1434		Out of My Mind/Empty Feelin'	1963	3.75	7.50	15.00
❑ 1437		You Can Never Stop Me Loving You/Judy, Judy, Judy	1963	3.75	7.50	15.00
❑ 1441		Funny How Time Slips Away/	1963	3.75	7.50	15.00
		A Very Good Year for Girls				

Number		Title (A Side/B Side)	Year	VG	VG+	NM
Columbia						
❑ 10125		Big Ole Jean/Mississippi Lady	1975		2.50	5.00
❑ 10199		Right Here in Your Arms/Willow County Request Live	1975		2.50	5.00
❑ 45842		Sunshine of My Life/If You Wouldn't Be My Lady	1973		2.50	5.00
❑ 45984		So Much of My Life/I Love How She Needs Me	1973		2.50	5.00
❑ 46065		Till I Can't Take It Anymore/Sunday Kind of Woman	1974		2.50	5.00
MGM						
❑ 13181		Talk Back Trembling Lips/Another You	1963	3.00	6.00	12.00
❑ 13181	PS	Talk Back Trembling Lips/Another You	1963	5.00	10.00	20.00
❑ 13193		Worried Guy/Please Don't Go Away	1963	2.50	5.00	10.00
❑ 13193	PS	Worried Guy/Please Don't Go Away	1963	5.00	10.00	20.00
❑ 13232		I Rise, I Fall/I'm Watching My Watch	1964	2.50	5.00	10.00
❑ 13232	PS	I Rise, I Fall/I'm Watching My Watch	1964	5.00	10.00	20.00
❑ 13255		Worry/Suff'rin' from a Heartache	1964	2.50	5.00	10.00
❑ 13255	PS	Worry/Suff'rin' from a Heartache	1964	5.00	10.00	20.00
❑ 13284		She Understands Me/Tomorrow	1964	2.50	5.00	10.00
❑ 13284	PS	She Understands Me/Tomorrow	1964	5.00	10.00	20.00
❑ 13316		Angel/Little Boy	1965	2.50	5.00	10.00
❑ 13316	PS	Angel/Little Boy	1965	5.00	10.00	20.00
❑ 13344		Then I'll Count Again/One's Yours, One's Mine	1965	2.50	5.00	10.00
❑ 13344	PS	Then I'll Count Again/One's Yours, One's Mine	1965	5.00	10.00	20.00
❑ 13376		Heartaches by the Number/Your Mem'ry Comes Along	1965	2.50	5.00	10.00
❑ 13376	PS	Heartaches by the Number/Your Mem'ry Comes Along	1965	5.00	10.00	20.00
❑ 13408		Our World/(Wait 'Till You See) My Gidget	1965	2.50	5.00	10.00
❑ 13445		Hello Enemy/I Never Loved You Anyway	1966	2.50	5.00	10.00
❑ 13499		Me, Myself and I/Country Boy, Country Boy	1966	2.50	5.00	10.00
❑ 13519		No Love at All/What Am I Gonna Do	1966	2.50	5.00	10.00
❑ 13598		More Than Before/Baby's Gone	1966	2.50	5.00	10.00
❑ 13598		More Than Before/Open Up Your Heart	1966	2.50	5.00	10.00
❑ 13633		Christmas Country Style/Christmas Is the Best of All	1966	2.50	5.00	10.00
❑ 13684		Strange Things Happen/Tommy Jones	1967	2.50	5.00	10.00
❑ 13738		Don't Tell Me It's Raining/Takin' It Easy	1967	2.50	5.00	10.00
❑ 13829		You're the Reason/Countin' My Teardrops	1967	2.50	5.00	10.00
❑ 13888		I Can Spot a Cheater/It Keeps Right On a-Hurtin'	1968	2.00	4.00	8.00
❑ 13924		I Haven't Begun to Love You Yet/Why So Lonely	1968	2.00	4.00	8.00
❑ 13977		Letter to Emily/Your Mem'ry Comes Along	1968	2.00	4.00	8.00
Reward						
❑ 03327		Baby You Do It for Me (And I'll Do It for You)/ She's Not As Married As She Used to Be	1982		2.00	4.00
❑ 03901		Crying/You're a Beautiful Place to Be	1983		2.00	4.00
❑ 04123		Burnin'/What's Another Year	1983		2.00	4.00
❑ 04346		Lay Back (In the Arms of Somebody)/ What's Another Year	1984		2.00	4.00
Scepter						
❑ 12389		Song for Hank Williams (mono/stereo)	1973	2.00	4.00	8.00
		With John Edward Beland; may be promo-only				
United Artists						
❑ XW860		It Could've Been Nashville/Summertime Lovin'	1976		2.50	5.00
❑ XW986		Toy Hearts/Just An Ordinary Man	1977		2.50	5.00

Tim Tam and the Turn-Ons

Number	Title (A Side/B Side)	Year	VG	VG+	NM
Palmer					
❑ 5002	Wait a Minute/Ophelia	1965	6.25	12.50	25.00
❑ 5003	Cheryl Ann/Sealed with a Kiss	1966	7.50	15.00	30.00
❑ 5006	Kimberly/I Leave You in Tears	1966	10.00	20.00	40.00
❑ 5014	Don't Say Hi/(Instrumental)	1967	6.25	12.50	25.00

Timers, The
(With Gary Usher and Brian Wilson)

Number	Title (A Side/B Side)	Year	VG	VG+	NM
Reprise					
❑ 20,231	No-Go Showboat/Competition Coupe	1963	25.00	50.00	100.00

Tin Tin

Number	Title (A Side/B Side)	Year	VG	VG+	NM
Atco					
❑ 6794	Toast and Marmalade for Tea/Manhattan Woman	1971	2.00	4.00	8.00
❑ 6821	Is That the Way/Swans on the Canal	1971		3.00	6.00
❑ 6853	Set Sail for England/The Cavalry Is Coming	1971		3.00	6.00
Sire					
❑ 29750	Kiss Me/Kiss Me	1983		2.50	5.00

Titans, The
(More than one group)

Number	Title (A Side/B Side)	Year	VG	VG+	NM
Bangar					
❑ 00611	Surfer's Lullaby/Motivation	1964	6.25	12.50	25.00
Class					
❑ 244	No Time/The Tootin' Tutor	1959	6.25	12.50	25.00
Fidelity					
❑ 3016	What Have I Done/Everybody Happy?	1960	7.50	15.00	30.00
MGM					
❑ 13207	Yojimbo/Midnight in Tokyo	1964	3.00	6.00	12.00
	B-side by the Tokyo Boys				
Nolta					
❑ 351	A-Rab/Marquette	1961	6.25	12.50	25.00

Number		Title (A Side/B Side)	Year	VG	VG+	NM
Soma						
❑ 1402		A Summer Place/Tchaikovsky Rides Again	1963	5.00	10.00	20.00
❑ 1411		The No Place Special/Reveille Rock	1964	5.00	10.00	20.00
Specialty						
❑ 614		Sweet Peach/Free and Easy	1957	6.25	12.50	25.00
❑ 625		Don't You Just Know It/Can It Be	1958	6.25	12.50	25.00
❑ 632		Arlene/Love Is a Wonderful Thing	1958	6.25	12.50	25.00
Studio City						
❑ 1008		The No Place Special/Reveille Rock	1964	10.00	20.00	40.00
Vita						
❑ 148		Rhythm and Blues/So Hard to Laugh, So Easy to Cry	1957	18.75	37.50	75.00
❑ 158		G'Wan Home Calypso/Look What You're Doing Baby	1957	15.00	30.00	60.00
Titones, The						
Scepter						
❑ 1206		Symbol of Love/The Movies *White label*	1960	12.50	25.00	50.00
❑ 1206		Symbol of Love/The Movies *Red label*	1960	6.25	12.50	25.00
Wand						
❑ 105		Symbol of Love/My Movie Queen	1960	5.00	10.00	20.00
Toby Beau						
RCA						
❑ PB-11250		My Angel Baby/California	1978		2.50	5.00
❑ PB-11388		Into the Night/Wink of an Eye	1978		2.00	4.00
❑ PB-11670		Then You Can Tell Me Goodbye/Boogie Woogie Melody	1979		2.00	4.00
❑ PB-11964		If I Were You/If You Believe	1980		2.00	4.00
❑ PB-12098		Ships in the Night/Little Miss American Dream	1980		2.00	4.00
Today and Tomorrow						
Noose						
❑ 812		Dooley Swings (Part 1)/Dooley Swings (Part 2)	1959	10.00	20.00	40.00
Todd, Dylan						
RCA Victor						
❑ 47-6463		The Ballad of James Dean/More Precious Than Gold	1956	7.50	15.00	30.00
❑ 47-6463	PS	The Ballad of James Dean/More Precious Than Gold	1956	12.50	25.00	50.00
❑ 47-6711		Timber/Golden Spurs and a Silver Saddle	1956	5.00	10.00	20.00
Todd, Johnny						
Modern						
❑ 1003		Pink Cadillac/What's Up	1956	30.00	60.00	120.00
Todd, Nick						
Dot						
❑ 15643		Plaything/The Honey Song	1957	5.00	10.00	20.00
❑ 15675		At the Hop/I Do	1957	5.00	10.00	20.00
❑ 15688		Teen-Age Cutie/Ever Since I Met Lucy	1958	5.00	10.00	20.00
❑ 15772		Forever and a Day/Too Much Rosita	1958	5.00	10.00	20.00
❑ 15860		My Little Girl/Does Your Heart Beat for Me?	1958	5.00	10.00	20.00
❑ 15893		Red Roses for a Blue Lady/Little Rosey Red	1959	3.75	7.50	15.00
❑ 15951		Tiger/Twice As Nice	1959	3.75	7.50	15.00
❑ 15981		Invisible Man/Sayin' Something	1959	3.75	7.50	15.00
❑ 16109		Each Moment/Your Love's Gotta Grip on Me	1960	3.75	7.50	15.00
Tokays, The						
Bonnie						
❑ 102		Lost and Found/Fatty-Boom Bi Laddy	1962	25.00	50.00	100.00
Brute						
❑ 001		Hey Senorita/Baby Baby Baby	1967	30.00	60.00	120.00
Scorpio						
❑ 403		Now/Ask Me No Questions	1966	5.00	10.00	20.00
Tokens, The						
(The Date and Gary records are by a different group than the others.)						
Atco						
❑ 7009		The Lord Can't Sing a Solo/Penny Whistle Band	1974		3.00	6.00
B.T. Puppy						
❑ 500		A Girl Named Arlene/Swing	1964	3.00	6.00	12.00
❑ 502		He's in Town/Oh Cathy	1964	3.00	6.00	12.00
❑ 504		You're My Girl/Havin' Fun	1964	3.00	6.00	12.00
❑ 505		Nobody But You/Mr. Cupid	1965	2.50	5.00	10.00
❑ 507		A Message to the World/Sylvie Sleepin'	1965	2.50	5.00	10.00
❑ 512		Only My Friend/Cattle Call	1965	2.50	5.00	10.00
❑ 513		The Bells of St. Mary/Just One Smile	1966	2.50	5.00	10.00
❑ 515		The Three Bells/Message to the World	1966	2.50	5.00	10.00
❑ 518		I Hear Trumpets Blow/Don't Cry, Sing Along with the Music	1966	2.50	5.00	10.00
❑ 519		Breezy/Greatest Moments of a Girl's Life	1966	2.50	5.00	10.00
❑ 525		Green Plant/Saloogy	1967	2.50	5.00	10.00
❑ 552		Please Say You Want Me/Get a Job	1969	2.50	5.00	10.00

Number	Title (A Side/B Side)	Year	VG	VG+	NM
Bell					
❏ 45,190	You and Me/I Like to Throw My Head Back and Sing	1972		3.00	6.00
Buddah					
❏ 151	She Lets Her Hair Down (Early in the Morning)/ Oh to Get Away	1970		3.00	6.00
❏ 159	If the Shoe Fits Ya Baby/Don't Worry Baby	1970		2.50	5.00
❏ 174	Both Sides Now/I Could See Me (Dancin' with You)	1970		2.50	5.00
❏ 187	Listen to the Words (Listen to the Music)/ Groovin' On the Sunshine	1970		2.50	5.00
Date					
❏ 2737	Oh What a Night/(Hey Hey) Juanita	1961	12.50	25.00	50.00
Gary					
❏ 1006	Doom-Lang/Come Dance with Me	1961	12.50	25.00	50.00
Laurie					
❏ 3180	I'll Always Love You/Please Write	1963	5.00	10.00	20.00
Melba					
❏ 104	While I Dream/I Love My Baby	1956	12.50	25.00	50.00
RCA					
❏ 8749-7-R	Re-Doo-Wopp/I'm Through with You	1988		2.00	4.00
❏ 8836-7-R	Re-Doo-Wopp (Edit)/I'm Through with You	1988		2.00	4.00
RCA Victor					
❏ 37-7896	When I Go to Sleep at Night/Dry Your Eyes *"Compact Single 33" (small hole, plays at LP speed)*	1961	10.00	20.00	40.00
❏ 37-7925	Sincerely/When the Summer Is Through *"Compact Single 33" (small hole, plays at LP speed)*	1961	10.00	20.00	40.00
❏ 37-7954	The Lion Sleeps Tonight/Tina *"Compact Single 33" (small hole, plays at LP speed)*	1961	12.50	25.00	50.00
❏ 37-7991	B'wa Nina/Weeping River *"Compact Single 33" (small hole, plays at LP speed)*	1962	10.00	20.00	40.00
❏ 37-8018	The Riddle/Big Boat *"Compact Single 33" (small hole, plays at LP speed)*	1962	10.00	20.00	40.00
❏ 47-7896	When I Go to Sleep at Night/Dry Your Eyes	1961	5.00	10.00	20.00
❏ 47-7896	PS When I Go to Sleep at Night/Dry Your Eyes	1961	10.00	20.00	40.00
❏ 47-7925	Sincerely/When the Summer Is Through	1961	5.00	10.00	20.00
❏ 47-7954	The Lion Sleeps Tonight/Tina	1961	6.25	12.50	25.00
❏ 47-7991	B'wa Nina/Weeping River	1962	5.00	10.00	20.00
❏ 47-7991	PS B'wa Nina/Weeping River *No mention of "The Lion Sleeps Tonight" LP on sleeve*	1962	12.50	25.00	50.00
❏ 47-7991	PS B'wa Nina/Weeping River *"The Lion Sleeps Tonight" LP mentioned on sleeve*	1962	7.50	15.00	30.00
❏ 47-8018	The Riddle/Big Boat	1962	5.00	10.00	20.00
❏ 47-8018	PS The Riddle/Big Boat	1962	10.00	20.00	40.00
❏ 47-8052	La Bomba/A Token of Love	1962	5.00	10.00	20.00
❏ 47-8052	PS La Bomba/A Token of Love	1962	10.00	20.00	40.00
❏ 47-8089	I'll Do My Crying Tomorrow/Dream Angel Goodnight	1962	5.00	10.00	20.00
❏ 47-8089	PS I'll Do My Crying Tomorrow/Dream Angel Goodnight	1962	10.00	20.00	40.00
❏ 47-8114	A Bird Flies Out of Sight/Wishing	1962	5.00	10.00	20.00
❏ 47-8114	PS A Bird Flies Out of Sight/Wishing	1962	10.00	20.00	40.00
❏ 47-8148	Tonight I Met An Angel/Hindi Lullabye	1963	3.75	7.50	15.00
❏ 47-8210	Hear the Bells/ABC 1-2-3	1963	3.75	7.50	15.00
❏ 47-8309	Two Cars/Let's Go to the Drag Strip	1963	3.75	7.50	15.00
Roulette					
❏ 4174	Roses Are Red/Pictures in My Wallet *As "Darrell and the Oxfords"*	1959	7.50	15.00	30.00
❏ 4230	Can't You Tell/Your Mother Said So *As "Darrell and the Oxfords"*	1960	7.50	15.00	30.00
Rust					
❏ 5094	Arlene/Rumble in the Park	1965	2.50	5.00	10.00
Warner Bros.					
❏ 5900	Portrait of My Love/She Comes and Goes	1967	2.00	4.00	8.00
❏ 5900	PS Portrait of My Love/She Comes and Goes	1967	5.00	10.00	20.00
❏ 7056	It's a Happening World/How Nice	1967		3.00	6.00
❏ 7099	Ain't That Peculiar/Bye, Bye, Bye	1967		3.00	6.00
❏ 7118	Portrait of My Love/It's a Happening World *"Back to Back Hits" series -- originals have green labels with "W7" logo*	1968		2.50	5.00
❏ 7169	Till/Poor Man	1968		3.00	6.00
❏ 7183	Mister Swail/Needles of Evergreen *As "Margo, Margo, Medress and Siegel"*	1968	2.50	5.00	10.00
❏ 7202	Animal/Bathroom Wall	1968		3.00	6.00
❏ 7233	Grandfather/The Banana Boat Song	1968		3.00	6.00
❏ 7255	The World Is Full of Wonderful Things/ Some People Sleep	1968		3.00	6.00
❏ 7280	Go Away Little Girl-Young Girl/I Want to Make Love to You	1969		3.00	6.00
❏ 7323	I Could Be/End of the World	1969		3.00	6.00
Warwick					
❏ 615	Tonight I Fell in Love/I'll Always Love You	1961	7.50	15.00	30.00

Tolliver, Mickey, and the Capitols

Number	Title (A Side/B Side)	Year	VG	VG+	NM
Cindy					
❏ 3002	Rose Marie/Millie	1957	50.00	100.00	200.00

Dispelling a myth, here is the Bell record by Tom and Jerry, "Baby Talk." Because of its number, 120, it often was listed as a 1971 issue. But Bell 120 in 1971 was "Sweet City Woman" by the Stampeders. Anyway, this doesn't look like the 1970s Bell label (check a Partridge Family, Dawn or other Bell record of the era for proof). Bell Records was a budget label in the 1950s, releasing sound-alike cover versions of the hits at a fraction of what the "real" hits cost. And during one of the low points of their career, two years after "Hey Schoolgirl," Tom and Jerry (the future Simon and Garfunkel) covered Jan and Dean's hit for the low-budget label in 1959. Other cover versions of 1958-59 hits have been discovered on Bell as well, though not by any other name artists.

Number	Title (A Side/B Side)	Year	VG	VG+	NM

Tom & Jerry
(Country instrumental duo; listed to avoid confusion with the future Simon and Garfunkel)
Mercury

☐ 71753	Golden Wildwood Flower/South	1961	5.00	10.00	20.00
☐ 71827	Swing Low/Sugarfoot Rag	1961	5.00	10.00	20.00
☐ 71930	I'll Drown in My Tears/French Twist	1961	5.00	10.00	20.00

Tom and Jerry
(Tom [Graph] and Jerry [Landis] are Art Garfunkel and Paul Simon)
ABC-Paramount

| ☐ 10363 | Surrender, Please Surrender/Fightin' Mad | 1962 | 10.00 | 20.00 | 40.00 |
| ☐ 10788 | That's My Story/Tia-Juana Blues | 1966 | 5.00 | 10.00 | 20.00 |

As "Simon and Garfunkel" (may have been reissued as "Tom and Jerry", but we don't know)

Bell

| ☐ 120 | Baby Talk/I'm Gonna Get Married | 1959 | 12.50 | 25.00 | 50.00 |

B-side by Ronnie Lawrence

Big

| ☐ 613 | Hey, Schoolgirl/Dancin' Wild | 1957 | 12.50 | 25.00 | 50.00 |

With songwriting credits as "Paul Simon-Art Garfunkel"

| ☐ 613 | Hey, Schoolgirl/Dancin' Wild | 1957 | 12.50 | 25.00 | 50.00 |

With songwriting credits as "Tommy Graph-Jerry Landis"

☐ 616	Our Song/Two Teen Agers	1958	12.50	25.00	50.00
☐ 618	That's My Story/Don't Say Goodbye	1958	12.50	25.00	50.00
621	Baby Talk/Two Teen Agers 1959 Unreleased?				

Ember

| ☐ 1094 | I'm Lonesome/Looking at You | 1959 | 12.50 | 25.00 | 50.00 |

Hunt

| ☐ 319 | That's My Story/Don't Say Goodbye | 1959 | 12.50 | 25.00 | 50.00 |

King

| ☐ 5167 | Hey, Schoolgirl/Dancin' Wild | 1958 | 20.00 | 40.00 | 80.00 |

Tommy and the Hustlers
Fantasy

| ☐ 573 | Diggin' Out/The Right Size | 1963 | 6.25 | 12.50 | 25.00 |
| ☐ 573 | Diggin' Out/The Right Size | 1963 | 10.00 | 20.00 | 40.00 |

Green vinyl

Tonettes, The
ABC-Paramount

| ☐ 9905 | Oh What a Baby/Howie | 1958 | 5.00 | 10.00 | 20.00 |

Doe

| ☐ 101 | Oh What a Baby/Howie | 1958 | 15.00 | 30.00 | 60.00 |
| ☐ 103 | Uh Oh/He Loves Me, He Loves Me Not | 1958 | 10.00 | 20.00 | 40.00 |

Modern

| ☐ 997 | Tonight You Belong to Me/Don't Fall in Love Too Soon | 1956 | 6.25 | 12.50 | 25.00 |

Volt

| ☐ 101 | Please Don't Go/No Tears | 1962 | 5.00 | 10.00 | 20.00 |
| ☐ 104 | Stolen Angel/Teardrop Sea | 1963 | 5.00 | 10.00 | 20.00 |

Tony and the Daydreams
Planet

| ☐ 1008 | Why Don't You Be Nice/I'll Never Tell | 1958 | 25.00 | 50.00 | 100.00 |
| ☐ 1054 | Christmas Lullaby/Handin' Hand | 1961 | 50.00 | 100.00 | 200.00 |

Tony and the Holidays
ABC-Paramount

| ☐ 10295 | There Goes My Heart Again/My Love Is Real | 1962 | 50.00 | 100.00 | 200.00 |

Tony and the Masquins
Ruthie

| ☐ 1000 | My Angel Eyes/Fugi Womma | 1961 | 25.00 | 50.00 | 100.00 |

Tony and the Raindrops
Chesapeke

| ☐ 609 | While Walking/Our Love Is Over | 1961 | 15.00 | 30.00 | 60.00 |

Crosley

| ☐ 340 | Tina/My Heart Cried | 1962 | 50.00 | 100.00 | 200.00 |

Tony and the Technics – See "Technics, The"

Tony and the Twilighters
(Later known as "Anthony and the Sophomores")
Jalynne

| ☐ 106 | Be My Girl/Did You Make Up Your Mind | 1960 | 20.00 | 40.00 | 80.00 |

Red Top

| ☐ 127 | Key to My Heart/Yes or No | 1960 | 50.00 | 100.00 | 200.00 |

Toomorrow
(Olivia Newton-John was in this group)
Kirshner

| ☐ 63-5005 | Goin' Back/You're My Baby Now | 1970 | 15.00 | 30.00 | 60.00 |

Number	Title (A Side/B Side)	Year	VG	VG+	NM

Top Hits, The

Norman

| ❏ 504 | Love No One/Thum-A-Lum-A | 1961 | 50.00 | 100.00 | 200.00 |

Topics, The

(Also see "Four Seasons, The")

Perri

| ❏ 1007 | The Girl in My Dreams | 1961 | 37.50 | 75.00 | 150.00 |
| | *One-sided record* | | | | |

Toppers, The

(More than one group)

ABC-Paramount

❏ 9667	George Washington/Honey, Honey	1956	5.00	10.00	20.00
❏ 9699	God Bless Kids and Little Animals/Tornado	1956	5.00	10.00	20.00
❏ 9759	Three Roads/Lonely	1956	5.00	10.00	20.00

Avalon

| ❏ 63707 | I Love You, I Love You/Bow-Legged Boy | 1954 | 10.00 | 20.00 | 40.00 |

Decca

❏ 30209	The Purple Hills/Stashu Pandowski	1957	3.75	7.50	15.00
❏ 30297	Pots and Pans/	1957	3.75	7.50	15.00
	It Was Twice As Big As I Thought It Was				

Jubilee

| ❏ 5136 | Let Me Bang Your Box/ | 1954 | 30.00 | 60.00 | 120.00 |
| | You're Laughing 'Cause I'm Crying | | | | |

Stacy

| ❏ 927 | Tell Me Why/All Around | 1962 | 3.00 | 6.00 | 12.00 |

Topps, The

Red Robin

| ❏ 126 | What Do You Do (To Make Me Love You So)/Tippin' | 1954 | 75.00 | 150.00 | 300.00 |
| ❏ 131 | I've Got a Feeling/Won't You Come Home Baby | 1954 | 75.00 | 150.00 | 300.00 |

Tops, The

Singular

| ❏ 712 | An Innocent Kiss/Walkin' with My Baby | 1957 | 30.00 | 60.00 | 120.00 |

Tornadoes, The

(At least two different groups)

ABC-Paramount

| ❏ 10174 | Cora/Like a Frog | 1960 | 5.00 | 10.00 | 20.00 |

Aertaun

❏ 100	Bustin' Surfboards/Beyond the Surf	1962	7.50	15.00	30.00
❏ 101	The Gremmie (Part 1)/The Gremmie (Part 2)	1963	6.25	12.50	25.00
	As "The Hollywood Tornadoes"				
❏ 102	Inebriated Surfer/Moon Dawg	1963	7.50	15.00	30.00
	As "The Hollywood Tornadoes"				
❏ 103	Phantom Surfer/Shootin' Beavers	1963	7.50	15.00	30.00
❏ 103	Phantom Surfer/Lightnin'	1964	6.25	12.50	25.00
	B-side is same recording as "Shootin' Beavers" but retitled				

Cuca

❏ 1092	Scalping Party/7-0-7	1962	10.00	20.00	40.00
❏ 1099	Loneliest Guy in the World/It Always Makes Me Cry	1962	7.50	15.00	30.00
❏ 1104	Hey There/Standing Watch	1963	7.50	15.00	30.00

London

❏ 9561	Telstar/Jungle Fever	1962	6.25	12.50	25.00
❏ 9579	Globetrottin'/Like Locomotion	1963	5.00	10.00	20.00
❏ 9581	The Breeze and I/Ridin' the Wind	1963	5.00	10.00	20.00
❏ 9599	Life on Venus (Telstar II)/Robot	1963	5.00	10.00	20.00
❏ 9614	Theme from "The Scales of Justice"/	1963	5.00	10.00	20.00
	The Ice Cream Man				
❏ 11003	Telstar/Jungle Fever	1964	5.00	10.00	20.00
	Gold label "Demand Performance" with misspelled A-side				

Tower

| ❏ 152 | Stompin' Through the Rye/Early Bird | 1965 | 3.75 | 7.50 | 15.00 |
| ❏ 171 | Stingray/Aqua Marina | 1965 | 3.75 | 7.50 | 15.00 |

Torquays, The

Aertaun

| ❏ 1020 | Turmoil/Crying in the Chapel | 1964 | 7.50 | 15.00 | 30.00 |

Colpix

| ❏ 782 | Image of a Girl/Stolen Moments | 1965 | 5.00 | 10.00 | 20.00 |

Gee Cee

| ❏ 8163 | Escondido/Surfer's City | 1963 | 12.50 | 25.00 | 50.00 |

Gypsy

| ❏ 265 | Busting Point/The Other Side | 1965 | 12.50 | 25.00 | 50.00 |

Original Sound

| ❏ 66 | Harmonica Man/Our Teenage Love | 1967 | 5.00 | 10.00 | 20.00 |

Punch

| ❏ 1007 | Shake a Tail Feather/Temptation | 196? | 5.00 | 10.00 | 20.00 |

Number		Title (A Side/B Side)	Year	VG	VG+	NM

Rock-It
| ❑ 1004 | | Image of a Girl/Stolen Moments | 1965 | 7.50 | 15.00 | 30.00 |
| ❑ 1005 | | Hooked on Her/Harmonica Man | 1965 | 7.50 | 15.00 | 30.00 |

Torquetts, The
Santa Cruz
| ❑ 10002 | | Any More/(Who's Got The) Tortillas | 196? | 12.50 | 25.00 | 50.00 |

Torquett
| ❑ 005/6 | | Feedback/Bacardi | 196? | 12.50 | 25.00 | 50.00 |
| ❑ 007/8 | | Side Swiped/Blue Corral | 196? | 6.25 | 12.50 | 25.00 |

Torrence, Johnny
Imperial
| ❑ 5230 | | Sad Day/Bad Habit | 1953 | 30.00 | 60.00 | 120.00 |
| ❑ 5897 | | Rat Race/Your Lover Man | 1962 | 3.75 | 7.50 | 15.00 |

R&B
| ❑ 1306 | | Rosalie/Living from Day to Day | 1954 | 50.00 | 100.00 | 200.00 |
| | | *With the Jewels* | | | | |

Toto
Columbia
❑ 01056		It's the Last Night/Turn Back	1981		2.00	4.00
❑ 02811		Rosanna/It's a Feeling	1982		2.00	4.00
❑ 03143		Make Believe/We Made It	1982		2.00	4.00
❑ 03143	PS	Make Believe/We Made It	1982		2.50	5.00
❑ 03267		Make Believe	1982		3.00	6.00
		One-sided budget release				
❑ 03335		Africa/Good for You	1982		2.00	4.00
❑ 03399		Africa	1982		3.00	6.00
		One-sided budget release				
❑ 03597		I Won't Hold You Back/Afraid of Love	1983			3.00
❑ 03597	PS	I Won't Hold You Back/Afraid of Love	1983		2.00	4.00
❑ 03981		Waiting for Your Love/Lovers in the Night	1983			3.00
❑ 04672		Stranger in Town/Change of Heart	1984			3.00
❑ 04672	PS	Stranger in Town/Change of Heart	1984		2.00	4.00
❑ 04752		Holyanna/Mr. Friendly	1985			3.00
❑ 04752	PS	Holyanna/Mr. Friendly	1985		2.00	4.00
❑ 04844		How Does It Feel/Mr. Friendly	1985			3.00
❑ 06280		I'll Be Over You/In a Word	1986			3.00
❑ 06280	PS	I'll Be Over You/In a Word	1986			3.00
❑ 06570		Without Your Love/Can't Stand It Any Longer	1987			3.00
❑ 06570	PS	Without Your Love/Can't Stand It Any Longer	1987			3.00
❑ 07030		Till the End/Don't Stop Me Now	1987			3.00
❑ 07715		Pamela/The Seventh One	1988			3.00
❑ 07715	PS	Pamela/The Seventh One	1988			3.00
❑ 07945		Straight for the Heart/The Seventh One	1988			3.00
❑ 08010		Anna/The Seventh One	1988			3.00
❑ 10830		Hold the Line/Takin' It Back	1978		2.50	5.00
❑ 10898		I'll Supply the Love/You Are the Flower	1979		2.00	4.00
❑ 10944		Georgy Porgy/Child's Anthem	1979		2.50	5.00
❑ 11040		Georgy Porgy/Child's Anthem	1979		2.00	4.00
❑ 11173		99/Hydra	1980		2.00	4.00
❑ 11238		All Us Boys/Hydra	1980		2.00	4.00
❑ 11437		Goodbye Eleanore/Turn Back	1981		2.00	4.00

Polydor
| ❑ 881 628-7 | | Dune (Desert Theme)/Theme from Dune | 1985 | | 2.00 | 4.00 |

Townsend, Sherrell
Gone
| ❑ 5135 | | He Thinks I Still Care/Glass of Tears | 1962 | 5.00 | 10.00 | 20.00 |

Little Star
| ❑ 115 | | I Love You Alone/Summer Days Are Here | 1962 | 10.00 | 20.00 | 40.00 |

Lute
| ❑ 6015 | | I Love You Alone/Summer Days Are Here | 1961 | 7.50 | 15.00 | 30.00 |

Townshend, Pete
(Of The Who)
Atco
❑ 7217		Let My Love Open the Door/And I Moved	1980		2.00	4.00
❑ 7312		A Little Is Enough/Cat's in a Cupboard	1980		2.00	4.00
❑ 7318		Rough Boys/Jools and Jim	1980		2.00	4.00
❑ 99499		Barefootin'/Behind Blue Eyes	1986			3.00
❑ 99553		Secondhand Love/White City Fighting	1986			3.00
❑ 99577		Give Blood/Magic Bus	1986			3.00
❑ 99590		Face the Face/Hiding Out	1985			3.00
❑ 99590	PS	Face the Face/Hiding Out	1985			3.00
❑ 99884		Bargain/Dirty Water	1983		2.00	4.00
❑ 99973		Slit Skirts/Uniforms	1982		2.00	4.00
❑ 99989		Face Dances Part Two/Man Watching	1982		2.00	4.00

Atlantic
| ❑ 88875 | | A Friend Is a Friend/Man Machines | 1989 | | | 3.00 |
| ❑ 88875 | PS | A Friend Is a Friend/Man Machines | 1989 | | | 3.00 |

Number	Title (A Side/B Side)	Year	VG	VG+	NM
MCA					
❑ 40818	My Baby Gives It Away/April Fool	1977		2.00	4.00
	With Ronnie Lane				
❑ 40878	Nowhere to Run/Keep Me Turning	1978		2.00	4.00
	With Ronnie Lane				
Townsmen, The					
(More than one group)					
Columbia					
❑ 43207	Please Don't Say Goodbye/Gotta Get Moving	1965	2.50	5.00	10.00
Herald					
❑ 585	Is It All Over/Just a Little Bit	1963	3.75	7.50	15.00
Joey					
❑ 6202	Moonlight Was Made for Lovers/	1963	6.25	12.50	25.00
	I'm in the Mood for Love				
PJ					
❑ 1341	That's All I'll Ever Need/I Can't Let Go	1963	50.00	100.00	200.00
Vanity					
❑ 579/80	It's Time/Little Jeanie	1960	5.00	10.00	20.00
Warner Bros.					
❑ 5190	You're Having the Last Dance with Me/	1960	3.00	6.00	12.00
	Gloria's Theme from "Butterfield-8"				
Toys, The					
Dyno Voice					
❑ 209	A Lover's Concerto/This Night	1965	3.00	6.00	12.00
❑ 214	Attack/See How They Run	1965	2.50	5.00	10.00
❑ 218	My My Heart Be Cast Into Stone/On Backstreet	1966	2.50	5.00	10.00
❑ 219	Can't Get Enough of You Baby/Silver Spoon	1966	2.50	5.00	10.00
❑ 222	Baby Toys/Happy Birthday Broken Heart	1966	2.50	5.00	10.00
Musicor					
❑ 1300	You Got It Baby/You've Got to Give Her Love	1968	2.00	4.00	8.00
❑ 1319	Sealed with a Kiss/I Got My Heart Set on You	1968	2.00	4.00	8.00
Philips					
❑ 40432	Ciao Baby/I Got Carried Away	1967	2.50	5.00	10.00
❑ 40456	My Love Sonata/I Close My Eyes	1967	2.50	5.00	10.00
Tracers, The					
Sully					
❑ 928	She Said Yeah/Watch Me	1966	6.25	12.50	25.00
	Originally released under the name "The Stones"				
Trade Winds, The					
Kama Sutra					
❑ 212	Mind Excursion/Little Susan's Dreamin'	1966	3.00	6.00	12.00
❑ 218	I Believe in Her/Catch Me in the Meadow	1966	3.00	6.00	12.00
❑ 234	Mind Excursion/Only When I'm Dreamin'	1967	3.00	6.00	12.00
Red Bird					
❑ 10-020	New York's a Lonely Town/Club Seventeen	1965	6.25	12.50	25.00
❑ 10-028	Girl from Greenwich Village/	1965	6.25	12.50	25.00
	There's a Rock and Roll Show in Town				
❑ 10-033	Summertime Girl/The Party Starts at Nine	1965	10.00	20.00	40.00
Tradewinds, The					
Dawn Cory					
❑ 1005	Surfin' Thunder/Gotcha	196?	20.00	40.00	80.00
RCA Victor					
❑ 47-7511	Toni/Twins	1959	5.00	10.00	20.00
❑ 47-7553	Crossroads/Furry Murry	1959	5.00	10.00	20.00
Traffic					
(Also see "Winwood, Steve")					
Asylum					
❑ 45207	Walking in the Wind/(Instrumental)	1974		2.50	5.00
Island					
❑ 1201	Rock and Roll Stew (Part 1)/	1972		2.50	5.00
	Rock and Roll Stew (Part 2)				
United Artists					
❑ 0129	Paper Sun/Empty Pages	1973		2.00	4.00
	"Silver Spotlight Series" reissue				
❑ 50195	Paper Sun/Giving to You	1967	2.50	5.00	10.00
❑ 50218	Hole in My Shoe/Smiling Phases	1967	2.50	5.00	10.00
❑ 50232	Here We Go 'Round the Mulberry Bush/Coloured Rain	1967	2.50	5.00	10.00
❑ 50261	Heaven Is In Your Mind/	1968	2.00	4.00	8.00
	No Face, No Name and No Number				
❑ 50460	Feelin' Alright?/Withering Tree	1968	2.00	4.00	8.00
❑ 50500	Medicated Goo/Pearly Queen	1969		3.00	6.00
❑ 50692	Empty Pages/Stranger to Himself	1970		3.00	6.00
❑ 50841	Gimme Some Lovin' (Part 1)/	1971		3.00	6.00
	Gimme Some Lovin' (Part 2)				
	By "Traffic, Etc."				
❑ 50883	Glad (Part 1)/Glad (Part 2)	1972		3.00	6.00

Number	Title (A Side/B Side)	Year	VG	VG+	NM
Virgin					
❏ S7-17971	Here Comes a Man (Rock Mix)/Glad (Live)	1994		2.00	4.00
❏ S7-18134	Some Kinda Woman/Forty Thousand Headmen (Live)	1994		2.00	4.00

Trammell, Bobby Lee

Number	Title (A Side/B Side)	Year	VG	VG+	NM
ABC-Paramount					
❏ 9890	Shirley Lee/I Sure Do Love You Baby	1958	20.00	40.00	80.00
Alley					
❏ 1001	It's All Your Fault/Arkansas Twist	1962	6.25	12.50	25.00
❏ 1004	Come On Baby/I Tried Not to Cry	1963	6.25	12.50	25.00
Atlantic					
❏ 2332	Shimmy Loo/You Make Me Feel So Fine	1966	3.00	6.00	12.00
Capitol					
❏ 3718	Love Don't Let Me Down/I Couldn't Believe My Eyes	1973	2.00	4.00	8.00
❏ 3801	You Mostest Girl/ You Stand a Chance of Losing What You've Got	1973	2.00	4.00	8.00
Fabor					
❏ 127	You Mostest Girl/Uh Oh	1964	3.00	6.00	12.00
❏ 4038	Shirley Lee/I Sure Do Love You Baby	1957	37.50	75.00	150.00
Radio					
❏ 102	You Mostest Girl/Uh Oh	1958	12.50	25.00	50.00
❏ 114	My Susie Jane/Should I Make Amends	1958	10.00	20.00	40.00
Santo					
❏ 9052	Hi-O Silver/Don't You Know I Love You	196?	5.00	10.00	20.00
Sims					
❏ 183	Good Lovin'/New Dance in France	1964	3.00	6.00	12.00
❏ 195	Come On and Love Me/ If You Don't Wanna, You Don't Have To	1964	3.00	6.00	12.00
❏ 225	Twenty-Four Hours/ Just Let Me Move You One More Time	1965	3.00	6.00	12.00
Skyla					
❏ 1307	You Mostest Girl/Uh Oh	1961	3.75	7.50	15.00
Souncot					
❏ 1100	I Dare America to Be Great/A Gift from God	1970		3.00	6.00
❏ 1104	24 Hours a Day/I Lost the Girl I Love Tonight	1970		3.00	6.00
❏ 1113	You Mostest Girl/Whole Lotta Shakin' Goin' On	1971		3.00	6.00
❏ 1119	My Shoes Keep Walkin' Back to You/ Let's Wash the World and Make It Clean	1971		3.00	6.00
❏ 1128	Don't Let the Stars Get In Your Eyes/Sheila	1971		3.00	6.00
❏ 1130	You Were Worth the Wait/Wadin' in the Water	1972		3.00	6.00
❏ 1135	Love Isn't Love (Till You Give It Away)/ Tell Me That You Want Me	1972		3.00	6.00
❏ 1143	I Believe in You/My Love Keeps Growing	1972		3.00	6.00
❏ 1145	You Put Love Back in My Heart/ I Lost the Girl I Love Tonight	1972		3.00	6.00
Sun					
❏ 1135	Jenny Lee/It's All Your Fault	1977		3.00	6.00

Trammps, The

Number	Title (A Side/B Side)	Year	VG	VG+	NM
Atlantic					
❏ 3286	Hooked for Life/I'm Alright	1975		2.50	5.00
❏ 3306	That's Where the Happy People Go (Short)/ That's Where the Happy People Go (Long)	1975		2.50	5.00
❏ 3345	Soul Searchin' Time/Love Is a Funky Thing	1976		2.50	5.00
❏ 3365	Ninety-Nine and a Half (Won't Do)/ Can We Come Together	1976		2.50	5.00
❏ 3389	Disco Inferno/You Touch My Hot Line	1977		3.00	6.00
❏ 3389	Disco Inferno/That's Where the Happy People Go	1978		2.50	5.00
	Reissue in conjunction with the success of "Saturday Night Fever"				
❏ 3403	I Feel Like I've Been Livin' (On the Dark Side of the Moon)/Don't Burn Bridges	1977		2.50	5.00
❏ 3442	The Night the Lights Went Out/ I'm So Glad You Came Along	1977		2.50	5.00
❏ 3460	Seasons for Girls/Love Ain't Been Easy	1978		2.50	5.00
❏ 3537	Soul Bones/Love Magnet	1978		2.50	5.00
❏ 3573	More Good Times to Remember/Teaser	1979		2.50	5.00
❏ 3654	Dance Contest/Hard Rock and Disco	1980		2.00	4.00
❏ 3669	Music Freek/V.I.P.	1980		2.00	4.00
❏ 3777	Mellow Out/Looking for You	1980		2.00	4.00
❏ 3797	I Don't Want to Ever Lose Your Love/ Breathtaking View	1981		2.00	4.00
Buddah					
❏ 306	Zing Went the Strings of My Heart/ Penguin at the Big Apple	1972	2.50	5.00	10.00
	As "Tramps"				
❏ 306	Zing Went the Strings of My Heart/ Penguin at the Big Apple	1972		3.00	6.00
	As "Trammps"				
❏ 321	Sixty Minute Man/Scrub Board	1972		3.00	6.00
❏ 339	Rubber Band/Pray All You Sinners	1973		3.00	6.00
❏ 507	Hold Back the Night/Tom's Song	1975		2.50	5.00

Number		Title (A Side/B Side)	Year	VG	VG+	NM

Golden Fleece
❑ 3251		Love Epidemic/(B-side unknown)	1973		3.00	6.00
❑ 3253		Where Do We Go from Here/(B-side unknown)	1974		3.00	6.00
❑ 3255		Trusting Heart/(B-side unknown)	1974		3.00	6.00

Trash
Apple
❑ 1804		Road to Nowhere/Illusions	1969	25.00	50.00	100.00
With star on A-side label						
❑ 1804		Road to Nowhere/Illusions	1969	12.50	25.00	50.00
Without star on A-side label						
❑ 1811		Golden Slumbers-Carry That Weight/Trash Can	1969	3.75	7.50	15.00
A-side listed as "Golden Slumbers/Carry That Weight"						
❑ 1811		Golden Slumbers-Carry That Weight/Trash Can	1969	5.00	10.00	20.00
A-side listed as "Golden Slumbers Carry That Weight"						
❑ 1811		Golden Slumbers-Carry That Weight/Trash Can	1969	5.00	10.00	20.00
A-side listed as "Golden Slumbers and Carry That Weight"						
❑ PRO-4671/2		Road to Nowhere (Edit)/Road to Nowhere	1969	20.00	40.00	80.00

Trashmen, The
Argo
| ❑ 5516 | | Bird '65/Ubangi Stomp | 1965 | 12.50 | 25.00 | 50.00 |

Bear
| ❑ 1966 | | Keep Your Hands Off My Baby/Lost Angel | 1965 | 5.00 | 10.00 | 20.00 |

Garrett
❑ 4002		Surfin' Bird/King of the Surf	1963	6.25	12.50	25.00
❑ 4003		Bird Dance Beat/A-Bone	1964	5.00	10.00	20.00
❑ 4005		Bad News/On the Move	1964	5.00	10.00	20.00
❑ 4010		Peppermint Man/New Generation	1964	5.00	10.00	20.00
❑ 4012		Whoa Dad/Walkin' My Baby	1964	5.00	10.00	20.00
❑ 4012	PS	Whoa Dad/Walkin' My Baby	1964	25.00	50.00	100.00
❑ 4013		Dancing with Santa/Real Live Doll	1964	6.25	12.50	25.00
❑ 4013	PS	Dancing with Santa/Real Live Doll	1964	37.50	75.00	150.00

Metrobeat
| ❑ 7927 | | Green, Green Backs of Home/Address Enclosed | 1968 | 3.75 | 7.50 | 15.00 |

Soma
| ❑ 1469 | | Surfin' Bird/Liar, Liar | 1966 | 3.00 | 6.00 | 12.00 |
| *B-side by the Castaways* | | | | | | |

Sundazed
❑ 102		Henrietta/Rumble	1995			2.00
❑ 102	PS	Henrietta/Rumble	1995			2.00
❑ 103		Lucille/Green Onions	1995			2.00
❑ 103	PS	Lucille/Green Onions	1995			2.00
❑ 104		Roll Over Beethoven/Betty Jean	1995			2.00
❑ 104	PS	Roll Over Beethoven/Betty Jean	1995			2.00
❑ 112		Dancing with Santa/Real Live Doll	1996			2.00
❑ 112	PS	Dancing with Santa/Real Live Doll	1996			2.00

Tribe
| ❑ 8315 | | Hanging On Me/Some Lies | 1966 | 6.25 | 12.50 | 25.00 |

Travelers, The
(More than one group)
ABC-Paramount
| ❑ 10119 | | June, July, August and September/What a Weekend | 1960 | 5.00 | 10.00 | 20.00 |

Andex
❑ 2011		I'll Be Home for Christmas/Katie the Kangaroo	1958	7.50	15.00	30.00
❑ 4033		I Go for You/I'll Always Be in Love with You	1959	7.50	15.00	30.00
❑ 34006		Why/Teenage Machine Age	1957	7.50	15.00	30.00
❑ 34012		He's Got the Whole World in His Hands/ Green Town Girl	1957	7.50	15.00	30.00

Decca
| ❑ 31215 | | Ivy on the Old School Wall/Cadwallader 0002 | 1961 | 10.00 | 20.00 | 40.00 |
| ❑ 31282 | | White Rose/Oh My Love (Love Me) | 1961 | 10.00 | 20.00 | 40.00 |

Don Ray
| ❑ 5965 | | Traveler/Seven Minutes Till Four | 1963 | 12.50 | 25.00 | 50.00 |

Magic Lamp
| ❑ 516 | | Big House/Goin' Home | 1964 | 3.00 | 6.00 | 12.00 |

Vault
| ❑ 911 | | Spanish Moon/She's Got the Blues | 1964 | 3.75 | 7.50 | 15.00 |

Yellow Sand
❑ 2		Windy and Warm/Last Date	1963	12.50	25.00	50.00
❑ 451		Groovy/(B-side unknown)	1965	7.50	15.00	30.00
❑ 452		Malibu Sunset/Hang On	1965	7.50	15.00	30.00

Traveling Wilburys
(Bob Dylan, George Harrison, Jeff Lynne and Tom Petty, with Roy Orbison on the Wilbury releases only)
Warner Bros.
❑ 19443		Wilbury Twist/New Blue Moon	1991	2.50	5.00	10.00
Issued only in Europe						
❑ 19443	PS	Wilbury Twist/New Blue Moon	1991	2.50	5.00	10.00

Number		Title (A Side/B Side)	Year	VG	VG+	NM
❏ 19523		She's My Baby/New Blue Moon	1990	2.50	5.00	10.00
		"Wilbury" logo on label; issued only in Europe				
❏ 19523	PS	She's My Baby/New Blue Moon	1990	2.50	5.00	10.00
❏ 19773		Nobody's Child/Lumiere	1990	2.50	5.00	10.00
		B-side by Dave Stewart and the Spiritual Cowboys; "Wilbury" logo on label; issued only in Europe				
❏ 19773	PS	Nobody's Child/Lumiere	1989	2.50	5.00	10.00

Wilbury

❏ 21867		Handle with Care/End of the Line	1990	3.75	7.50	15.00
		"Back to Back Hits" series				
❏ 27637		End of the Line/Congratulations	1989	3.75	7.50	15.00
❏ 27637	PS	End of the Line/Congratulations	1989	5.00	10.00	20.00
❏ 27637	DJ	End of the Line (same on both sides)	1989	5.00	10.00	20.00
❏ 27732		Handle with Care/Margarita	1988	2.00	4.00	8.00
❏ 27732	PS	Handle with Care/Margarita	1988	2.00	4.00	8.00
❏ 27732	DJ	Handle with Care (same on both sides)	1988	3.75	7.50	15.00

Travellers, The
Gass

❏ 1000		Tie Me Surfer Board Down, Sport/In the Pines	1963	10.00	20.00	40.00

Travers, Mary
(Of Peter, Paul and Mary)
Chrysalis

❏ 2202		The Air That I Breathe/You Turn Me Around	1977		2.50	5.00
❏ 2367		Freedom/(B-side unknown)	1979		2.00	4.00

Warner Bros.

❏ 7481		Follow Me/I Guess He'd Rather Be in Colorado	1971		2.50	5.00
❏ 7517		The Song Is Love/Ericka with the Windy Yellow Hair	1971		2.50	5.00
❏ 7588		Morning Glory/That's Enough for Me	1972		2.50	5.00
❏ 7675		Too Many Mondays/That Year There Was No Winter	1972		2.50	5.00
❏ 7731		Five Hundred Miles/Oh, What a Feeling	1973		2.50	5.00
❏ 7790		Circles/I'll Have to Say I Love You in a Song	1974		2.50	5.00

Travis and Bob
Big Top

❏ 3054		Pocahontas/Day Dreams	1960	3.75	7.50	15.00

Mercury

❏ 71797		Give Your Love to Me/Stay Close to Me	1961	3.75	7.50	15.00
❏ 71866		The Spider and the Fly/What a Change	1961	3.75	7.50	15.00

Sandy

❏ 1017		Tell Him No/We're Too Young	1959	6.25	12.50	25.00
		With no mention of Dot Records on label				
❏ 1017		Tell Him No/We're Too Young	1959	5.00	10.00	20.00
		With Dot Records distribution mentioned on label				
❏ 1019		Teenage Vision/Little Bitty Johnny	1959	5.00	10.00	20.00
❏ 1024		Lover's Rendezvous/Oh Yeah	1959	5.00	10.00	20.00
❏ 1029		That's How Long/Wake Up and Cry	1960	5.00	10.00	20.00

Travolta, John
(Also see next entry)
Midland Int'l.

❏ MB-10623		Let Her In/Big Trouble	1976		2.50	5.00
❏ MB-10623	PS	Let Her In/Big Trouble	1976	2.00	4.00	8.00
❏ MB-10780		Whenever I'm Away from You/Razzamatazz	1976		2.50	5.00
❏ MB-10780	PS	Whenever I'm Away from You/Razzamatazz	1976		3.00	6.00
❏ MB-10907		All Strung Out on You/Easy Evil	1977		2.50	5.00
❏ MB-10907	PS	All Strung Out on You/Easy Evil	1977		3.00	6.00
❏ MB-10977		Slow Dancin'/Moonlight	1977		2.50	5.00
❏ MB-11206		What Would They Say/Razzamatazz	1978		2.50	5.00

Midsong Int'l.

❏ 1000		Big Trouble/Can't Let You Go	1978		2.50	5.00
❏ 72007		You Set My Dreams to Music/It Had to Be You	1980		2.50	5.00

RCA

❏ GB-10945		Let Her In/Whenever I'm Away from You	1977		2.00	4.00
		Gold Standard Series				

RSO

❏ 909		Greased Lightnin'/Rock and Roll Is Here to Stay	1978		2.00	4.00
		B-side by Sha Na Na				
❏ 909	PS	Greased Lightnin'/Rock and Roll Is Here to Stay	1978		2.50	5.00
❏ 930		Sandy/Blue Moon	1979		2.00	4.00
		B-side by Sha Na Na				

Travolta, John, and Olivia Newton-John
(Also see individual entries)
RSO

❏ 891		You're the One That I Want/Alone at a Drive-In Movie	1978		2.00	4.00
❏ 891	PS	You're the One That I Want/Alone at a Drive-In Movie	1978		2.50	5.00
❏ 906		Summer Nights/Rock 'N' Roll Party Queen	1978		2.00	4.00
		B-side by Louis St. Louis				

Number		Title (A Side/B Side)	Year	VG	VG+	NM

Traynor, Jay
(The original "Jay" of Jay and the Americans)
ABC

❏ 10809		Come On/The Merry-Go-Round Is Slowing You Down	1966	3.75	7.50	15.00
❏ 10845		Up and Over/Don't Let the End Begin	1966	7.50	15.00	30.00

Coral

❏ 62396		How Sweet It Is/I Rise, I Fall	1964	3.00	6.00	12.00
❏ 62420		I've Known You All My Life/Little Sister	1964	3.00	6.00	12.00

Treasurers, The
Crown

❏ 005		Story of Love/I Walk with An Angel	1961	75.00	150.00	300.00

Treasures, The
Valor

❏ (# unknown)		Minor Chaos/Valley of the Broken Hearts	1964	100.00	200.00	400.00
		Marbled vinyl				
❏ (# unknown)		Minor Chaos/Valley of the Broken Hearts	1964	50.00	100.00	200.00
		Green vinyl				
❏ (# unknown)		Minor Chaos/Valley of the Broken Hearts	1964	25.00	50.00	100.00
		Sources differ as to what the number of this record is, and we've never seen a copy, so we haven't listed a number				

Treble Chords, The
Decca

❏ 31015		Teresa/My Little Girl	1959	25.00	50.00	100.00

Tremaines, The
Cash

❏ 100/1		Jingle, Jingle/Moon Shining Bright	1958	100.00	200.00	400.00

Kane

❏ 008		Heavenly/Wonderful, Marvelous	1959	12.50	25.00	50.00

Old Town

❏ 1051		Jingle, Jingle/Moon Shining Bright	1958	12.50	25.00	50.00

V-Tone

❏ 507		Heavenly/Wonderful, Marvelous	1959	6.25	12.50	25.00

Val

❏ 100/1		Jingle, Jingle/Moon Shining Bright	1958	20.00	40.00	80.00

Tremeloes, The
(Also see "Poole, Brian, and the Tremeloes")
DJM

❏ 1008		Hard Woman/My Friend Delaney	1976		2.50	5.00
❏ 1016		September, November, December/(B-side unknown)	1976		2.50	5.00

Epic

❏ 10075		Good Day Sunshine/What a State I'm In	1966	3.00	6.00	12.00
❏ 10139		Here Comes My Baby/Gentlemen of Pleasure	1967	2.50	5.00	10.00
❏ 10184		Silence Is Golden/Let Your Hair Hang Down	1967	2.50	5.00	10.00
❏ 10184	PS	Silence Is Golden/Let Your Hair Hang Down	1967	3.75	7.50	15.00
❏ 10233		Even the Bad Times Are Good/Jenny's All Right	1967	2.00	4.00	8.00
❏ 10233	PS	Even the Bad Times Are Good/Jenny's All Right	1967	3.75	7.50	15.00
❏ 10293		Suddenly You Love Me/Suddenly Winter	1968	2.00	4.00	8.00
❏ 10328		Girl from Nowhere/Helule, Helule	1968	2.00	4.00	8.00
❏ 10376		My Little Lady/All the World to Me	1968	2.00	4.00	8.00
❏ 10437		I Shall Be Released/I Miss My Baby	1969	2.00	4.00	8.00
❏ 10467		Up, Down, All Around/Hello World	1969	2.00	4.00	8.00
❏ 10548		(Call Me) Number One/Instant Whip	1969	2.00	4.00	8.00
❏ 10621		Breakheart Motel/By the Way	1970	2.50	5.00	10.00
❏ 10682		Try Me/Me and My Life	1970	2.00	4.00	8.00
❏ 10807		My Woman/Hello Buddy	1971		3.00	6.00
❏ 10996		Yodelay/Blue Suede Tie	1973		3.00	6.00

Tremelos, The
Rockland

❏ 102		Jaguar/Fly	196?	12.50	25.00	50.00

Tremonts, The
Brunswick

❏ 55217		Believe My Heart/Legend of Love	1961	7.50	15.00	30.00

Pat Riccio

❏ 101		Believe My Heart/Legend of Love	1961	25.00	50.00	100.00

Tren-Teens, The
Carnival

❏ 501		My Baby's Gone/Your Yah Yah Is Gone	1964	25.00	50.00	100.00

Trends, The
(More than one group)
ABC

❏ 10817		A Night for Love/Gonna Have to Show You	1966	5.00	10.00	20.00
❏ 10881		No One There/That's How I Like It	1966	6.25	12.50	25.00
❏ 10944		Check My Tears/Don't Drop Out of School	1967	5.00	10.00	20.00

Number	Title (A Side/B Side)	Year	VG	VG+	NM
❑ 10993	Thanks for a Little Lovin'/ I Never Knew How Good I Had It	1967	5.00	10.00	20.00
❑ 11091	Soul Clap/Big Parade	1968	5.00	10.00	20.00
❑ 11150	Not Another Day/You Sure Know How to Hurt a Guy	1968	10.00	20.00	40.00

ABC-Paramount

❑ 10731	Not Too Old to Cry/If You Don't Dig the Blues	1965	10.00	20.00	40.00

Argo

❑ 5341	I'll Be True/Class Ring	1959	5.00	10.00	20.00

RCA Victor

❑ 47-7733	The Beard/Chug-a-Lug	1960	3.75	7.50	15.00

Scope

❑ 102	Gone Again/Silly Grin	1959	12.50	25.00	50.00

Smash

❑ 1914	Dance with My Baby/To Be Happy Enough	1964	6.25	12.50	25.00
❑ 1933	Get Something Going/That's the Way the Story Goes	1964	6.25	12.50	25.00

Trentons, The

Shepherd

❑ 2204	All Alone/Star Bright	1962	20.00	40.00	80.00

Triangles, The

(More than one group?)

Fargo

❑ 1023	Dance the Magoo/Step-Up-and-Go	1962	3.75	7.50	15.00

Fifo

❑ 107	My Oh My/Really I Do	1964	50.00	100.00	200.00

Herald

❑ 549	Savin' My Love/'Tis a Pity	1960	10.00	20.00	40.00

Trickels, The

Gone

❑ 5078	With Each Step a Tear/Outside the Chapel Door	1959	25.00	50.00	100.00

Power

❑ 250	With Each Step a Tear/When I Fall in Love	1958	50.00	100.00	200.00

Tridels, The

San-Dee

❑ 1009	Land of Love/Image of My Love	1963	12.50	25.00	50.00

Trinidads, The

Formal

❑ 1005	Don't Say Goodbye/On My Happy Way	1959	50.00	100.00	200.00
❑ 1006	One Lonely Night/When We're Together	1959	50.00	100.00	200.00

Troggs, The

Atco

❑ 6415	Wild Thing/With a Girl Like You *"Wild Thing" writer is incorrectly credited as "Presley."*	1966	5.00	10.00	20.00
❑ 6415	Wild Thing/With a Girl Like You *"Wild Thing" writer is correctly credited as "Taylor."*	1966	4.00	8.00	16.00
❑ 6415	Wild Thing/I Want You	1966	4.00	8.00	16.00
❑ 6444	I Can't Control Myself/Gonna Make You	1966	3.00	6.00	12.00

Bell

❑ 45,405	Listen to the Man/Queen of Sorrow	1973	2.00	4.00	8.00
❑ 45,426	Strange Movies/I'm on Fire	1973	2.00	4.00	8.00

Fontana

❑ 1548	Wild Thing/From Home	1966	2.50	5.00	10.00
❑ 1552	With a Girl Like You/I Want You	1966	2.50	5.00	10.00
❑ 1557	I Can't Control Myself/Gonna Make You	1966	2.50	5.00	10.00
❑ 1576	You're Lying/Give It To Me	1967	2.00	4.00	8.00
❑ 1585	6-5-4-3-2-1/Anyway That You Want Me	1967	2.00	4.00	8.00
❑ 1593	Night of the Long Grass/Girl in Black	1967	2.00	4.00	8.00
❑ 1607	Love Is All Around/When Will the Rain Come	1967	2.50	5.00	10.00
❑ 1622	You Can Cry If You Want To/ There's Something About You	1968	2.00	4.00	8.00
❑ 1630	Surprise, Surprise/Cousin Jane	1968	2.00	4.00	8.00
❑ 1634	Hip Hip Hooray/Say Darlin'	1968	2.00	4.00	8.00

Page One

❑ 21026	Evil Woman/Heads Or Tails	1969		3.00	6.00
❑ 21030	Easy Lovin'/Give Me Something	1970		3.00	6.00
❑ 21032	Come Now/Lover	1970		3.00	6.00
❑ 21035	The Raver/You	1970		3.00	6.00

Private Stock

❑ 45,102	Rolling Stone/(B-side unknown)	1976		2.50	5.00

Pye

❑ 65011	Feels Like a Woman/Everything's Funny	1972	2.00	4.00	8.00
❑ 71015	Good Vibrations/Push It Up to Me	1975		2.50	5.00
❑ 71035	Summertime/Jerry Come Down	1975		2.50	5.00
❑ 71054	Satisfaction/(B-side unknown)	1975		2.50	5.00

Number		Title (A Side/B Side)	Year	VG	VG+	NM

Trophies, The
(More than one group)
Challenge
❑ 9133		Desire/Doggone It	1962	15.00	30.00	60.00
❑ 9149		Peg O' My Heart/I Laughed So Hard I Cried	1962	3.75	7.50	15.00
❑ 9170		That's All I Want from You/Felicia	1962	3.75	7.50	15.00

Kapp
| ❑ 714 | | Everywhere I Go/Baby Don't Live Here Anymore | 1965 | 3.75 | 7.50 | 15.00 |
| ❑ 750 | | Leave My Girl Alone/You're the Queen | 1966 | 3.75 | 7.50 | 15.00 |

Nork
| ❑ 79907 | | Walkin' the Dog/Somethin' Blue | 196? | 5.00 | 10.00 | 20.00 |

Troy, Doris
Apple
| ❑ 1820 | | Ain't That Cute/Vaya Con Dios | 1970 | 2.00 | 4.00 | 8.00 |
| ❑ 1824 | | Jacob's Ladder/Get Back | 1970 | 2.00 | 4.00 | 8.00 |

Atlantic
❑ 2188		Just One Look/Bossa Nova Blues	1963	3.00	6.00	12.00
❑ 2206		Tomorrow Is Another Day/What'cha Gonna Do About It	1963	2.50	5.00	10.00
❑ 2222		One More Chance/Please Little Angel	1964	2.50	5.00	10.00
❑ 2269		Hurry/He Don't Belong to Me	1965	2.50	5.00	10.00

Calla
| ❑ 114 | | Heartaches/I'll Do Anything | 1966 | 5.00 | 10.00 | 20.00 |

Capitol
| ❑ 2043 | | Face Up to the Truth/He's Qualified | 1967 | 2.00 | 4.00 | 8.00 |

Midland Int'l.
| ❑ MB-10806 | | Lyin' Eyes/Give God Glory | 1976 | | 2.50 | 5.00 |
| ❑ MB-11082 | | Can't Hold On/Another Look | 1977 | | 2.50 | 5.00 |

Tru-Tones, The
Chart
| ❑ 634 | | Tears in My Eyes/Magic | 1957 | 200.00 | 400.00 | 800.00 |

Tubes, The
A&M
❑ 1733		White Punks on Dope/White Punks on Dope	1975		2.50	5.00
❑ 1755		What Do You Want from Life/Space Baby	1975		2.50	5.00
❑ 1826		Don't Touch Me There/Proud to Be an American	1976		2.50	5.00
❑ 1956		This Town/I'm Just a Mess	1977		2.50	5.00
❑ 2037		Show Me a Reason/I Saw Her Standing There	1978		2.50	5.00
❑ 2120		Prime Time/No Way Out	1979		2.50	5.00
❑ 2149		Love's a Mystery (I Don't Understand)/Telecide	1979		2.50	5.00
❑ 8591		White Punks on Dope/What Do You Want from Life?	198?			3.00
		Reissue				

Capitol
❑ 5007		Don't Want to Wait Anymore/Think About Me	1981			3.00
❑ 5007	PS	Don't Want to Wait Anymore/Think About Me	1981			3.00
❑ 5016		Talk To Ya Later/Power Tools	1981		2.00	4.00
❑ 5091		Gonna Get It Next Time/Sports Fans	1982		2.00	4.00
❑ 5217		She's a Beauty/When You're Ready to Come	1983		2.00	4.00
		First pressing: Purple label				
❑ 5217		She's a Beauty/When You're Ready to Come	1983			3.00
		Second pressing: Black label with multi-colored ring				
❑ 5217	PS	She's a Beauty/When You're Ready to Come	1983		2.00	4.00
		Sleeve only came with first pressing, and then not with all of them				
❑ 5254		The Monkey Time/Sports Fans	1983			3.00
❑ 5254	PS	The Monkey Time/Sports Fans	1983			3.00
❑ 5258		Tip of My Tongue/Keyboard Kids	1983			3.00
❑ 5443		Piece by Piece/The Right People	1985			3.00
❑ SPRO-9740	DJ	Sports Fans (same on both sides)	1982		2.50	5.00

Tucker, Billy Joe
Dot
| ❑ 16240 | | Boogie Woogie Bill/Mail Train | 1961 | 25.00 | 50.00 | 100.00 |

Maha
| ❑ 103 | | Boogie Woogie Bill/Mail Train | 1961 | 75.00 | 150.00 | 300.00 |

Tully, Lee, and Milt Moss
Flair-X
| ❑ 3007 | | Around the World with Elwood Pretzel (Part 1)/Around the World with Elwood Pretzel (Part 2) | 1956 | 12.50 | 25.00 | 50.00 |

Tune Weavers, The
Casa Grande
❑ 101		Little Boy/Look Down That Lonesome Road	1959	10.00	20.00	40.00
❑ 3038		My Congratulations Baby/This Can't Be Love	1960	7.50	15.00	30.00
❑ 4037		Happy, Happy Birthday Baby/Ol' Man River	1957	15.00	30.00	60.00
❑ 4038		I Remember Dear/Pamela Jean	1957	7.50	15.00	30.00
❑ 4040		There Stands My Love/I'm Cold	1958	10.00	20.00	40.00

Checker
❑ 872		Happy, Happy Birthday Baby/Ol' Man River	1957	6.25	12.50	25.00
❑ 872		Happy, Happy Birthday Baby/Yo Yo Walk	1957	6.25	12.50	25.00
		B-side by Paul Gayten				

Number	Title (A Side/B Side)	Year	VG	VG+	NM
❏ 880	Ol' Man River/Tough Enough	1957	6.25	12.50	25.00
	B-side by Paul Gayten				
❏ 1007	Congratulations on Your Wedding/Your Skies of Blue	1962	6.25	12.50	25.00

Classic Artists

Number	Title (A Side/B Side)	Year	VG	VG+	NM
❏ 104	Come Back to Me/I've Tried	1988		2.00	4.00
	As "Margo Sylvia and Tune Weavers"				
❏ 107	Merry, Merry Christmas Baby/ What Are You Doing New Year's Eve	1988		2.00	4.00
	As "Margo Sylvia and Tune Weavers"				

Tunedrops, The
Gone

Number	Title (A Side/B Side)	Year	VG	VG+	NM
❏ 5003	Rosie Lee/Speak for Yourself	1957	10.00	20.00	40.00
❏ 5072	Smoothie/Jumpin' Jellybeans	1959	6.25	12.50	25.00

Metro

Number	Title (A Side/B Side)	Year	VG	VG+	NM
❏ 20028	Smoothie/Jumpin' Jelly Beans	1959	10.00	20.00	40.00

Tunemasters, The
Mark

Number	Title (A Side/B Side)	Year	VG	VG+	NM
❏ 7002	Sending This Letter/It's All Over	1957	75.00	150.00	300.00

Turbans, The
Herald

Number	Title (A Side/B Side)	Year	VG	VG+	NM
❏ 458	When You Dance/Let Me Show You (Around My Heart)	1955	12.50	25.00	50.00
	Yellow label, script print inside flag				
❏ 458	When You Dance/Let Me Show You (Around My Heart)	195?	5.00	10.00	20.00
	Yellow label, block print inside flag				
❏ 469	Sister Sookey/I'll Always Watch Over You	1956	7.50	15.00	30.00
❏ 478	B-I-N-G-O (Bingo)/I'm Nobody's	1956	7.50	15.00	30.00
❏ 486	It Was a Nite Like This/All of My Love	1956	7.50	15.00	30.00
❏ 495	Valley of Love/Bye and Bye	1957	7.50	15.00	30.00
❏ 510	Congratulations/The Wadda-Do	1957	6.25	12.50	25.00

Imperial

Number	Title (A Side/B Side)	Year	VG	VG+	NM
❏ 5807	Six Questions/The Lament of Silver Gulch	1962	10.00	20.00	40.00
❏ 5828	This Is My Story/Clicky Clicky Clack	1962	6.25	12.50	25.00
❏ 5847	I Wonder (I Wanna Know)/The Damage Is Done	1962	5.00	10.00	20.00

Money

Number	Title (A Side/B Side)	Year	VG	VG+	NM
❏ 209	Tick Tock Awoo/No No Cherry	1955	50.00	100.00	200.00
❏ 209	Tick Tock Awoo/Nest Is Warm	1955	50.00	100.00	200.00

Parkway

Number	Title (A Side/B Side)	Year	VG	VG+	NM
❏ 820	When You Dance/Golden Rings	1961	6.25	12.50	25.00

Red Top

Number	Title (A Side/B Side)	Year	VG	VG+	NM
❏ 115	I Promise You Love/Curfew Time	1959	12.50	25.00	50.00

Roulette

Number	Title (A Side/B Side)	Year	VG	VG+	NM
❏ 4281	Diamonds and Pearls/Bad Man	1960	5.00	10.00	20.00
❏ 4326	Three Friends (Two Lovers)/ I'm Not Your Fool Anymore	1961	5.00	10.00	20.00

Turley, Richard
Dot

Number	Title (A Side/B Side)	Year	VG	VG+	NM
❏ 16231	I Wanna Dance/Since I Met You	1961	10.00	20.00	40.00

Fraternity

Number	Title (A Side/B Side)	Year	VG	VG+	NM
❏ 845	Makin' Love with My Baby/All About Ann	1959	10.00	20.00	40.00

Turner, Ike
(Also see "Turner, Ike and Tina")
Artistic

Number	Title (A Side/B Side)	Year	VG	VG+	NM
❏ 1504	(I Know) You Don't Love Me/Down and Out	1958	7.50	15.00	30.00

Cobra

Number	Title (A Side/B Side)	Year	VG	VG+	NM
❏ 5033	Box Top/Walking Down the Aisle	1959	7.50	15.00	30.00

Federal

Number	Title (A Side/B Side)	Year	VG	VG+	NM
❏ 12297	Do You Mean It/She Made My Blood Run Cold	1957	25.00	50.00	100.00
❏ 12304	Rock a Bucket/The Big Question	1957	12.50	25.00	50.00
❏ 12307	You've Changed My Love/Trail Blazer	1957	10.00	20.00	40.00

Flair

Number	Title (A Side/B Side)	Year	VG	VG+	NM
❏ 1040	Cubano Jump/Loosely	1954	15.00	30.00	60.00
❏ 1059	Cuban Getaway/Go To It	1955	15.00	30.00	60.00

King

Number	Title (A Side/B Side)	Year	VG	VG+	NM
❏ 5553	The Big Question/She Made My Blood Run Cold	1961	3.75	7.50	15.00

Liberty

Number	Title (A Side/B Side)	Year	VG	VG+	NM
❏ 56194	Takin' Back My Name/Love Is a Game	1970		2.50	5.00

RPM

Number	Title (A Side/B Side)	Year	VG	VG+	NM
❏ 356	You're Driving Me Insane/Trouble and Heartaches	1952	25.00	50.00	100.00
❏ 362	My Heart Belongs to You/Lookin' for My Baby	1952	15.00	30.00	60.00
	As "Bonnie and Ike Turner"				
❏ 446	As Long As I Have You/I Wanna Make Love to You	1955	10.00	20.00	40.00

Sue

Number	Title (A Side/B Side)	Year	VG	VG+	NM
❏ 722	My Love/That's All I Need	1959	5.00	10.00	20.00

United Artists

Number	Title (A Side/B Side)	Year	VG	VG+	NM
❏ XW460	Take My Hand, Precious Lord/Father Alone	1974		2.50	5.00
❏ 50865	River Deep Mountain High/Na Na	1971		2.50	5.00

Number	Title (A Side/B Side)	Year	VG	VG+	NM
❑ 50900	Right On/Tacks in My Shoes	1972		2.50	5.00
❑ 50930	Lawdy Miss Clawdy/Tacks in My Shoes	1972		2.50	5.00
❑ 51102	Dust My Broom/You Won't Let Me Go	1973		2.50	5.00

Turner, Ike and Tina
(Also see individual listings)

A&M
❑ 1118	River Deep, Mountain High/I'll Keep You Happy	1969	2.50	5.00	10.00
❑ 1170	A Love Like Yours/Save the Last Dance for Me	1970	2.50	5.00	10.00

Blue Thumb
❑ 101	I've Been Loving You Too Long/Grumbling	1969		3.00	6.00
❑ 102	The Hunter/Crazy 'Bout You Baby	1969		3.00	6.00
❑ 104	Bold Soul Sister/I Know	1969		3.00	6.00
❑ 202	I've Been Loving You Too Long/Crazy 'Bout You Baby	1971		2.50	5.00

Cenco
❑ 112	Get It-Get It/You Weren't Ready (For My Love)	1967	3.75	7.50	15.00

Innis
❑ 6667	So Fine/So Blue Over You	1968	2.50	5.00	10.00

Kent
❑ 402	I Can't Believe What You Say (For Seeing What You Do)/My Baby Now	1964	2.50	5.00	10.00
❑ 409	Am I a Fool in Love/Please, Please, Please	1964	2.50	5.00	10.00
❑ 418	Chicken Shack/He's the One	1965	2.50	5.00	10.00
❑ 4514	Please, Please, Please (Part 1)/ Please, Please, Please (Part 2)	1970		3.00	6.00

Liberty
❑ 56177	I Want to Take You Higher/Contact High	1970		3.00	6.00
❑ 56207	Workin' Together/The Way You Love Me	1970		3.00	6.00
❑ 56216	Proud Mary/Funkier Than a Mosquito's Tweeter	1970		3.00	6.00

Loma
❑ 2011	I'm Thru with Love/Tell Her I'm Not Home	1965	2.50	5.00	10.00
❑ 2015	Somebody Needs You/Just to Be with You	1965	2.50	5.00	10.00

Minit
❑ 32060	I'm Gonna Do All I Can (To Do Right By My Man)/ You've Got Too Many Ties That Bind	1969		3.00	6.00
❑ 32068	I Wish It Would Rain/With a Little Help from My Friends	1969		3.00	6.00
❑ 32077	I Wanna Jump/Treating Us Funky	1969		3.00	6.00
❑ 32087	Come Together/Honky Tonk Women	1970		3.00	6.00

Modern
❑ 1007	Good Bye, So Long/Hurt Is All You Gave Me	1965	2.50	5.00	10.00
❑ 1012	I Don't Need/Gonna Have Fun	1965	2.50	5.00	10.00

Philles
❑ 131	River Deep -- Mountain High/I'll Keep You Happy	1966	3.75	7.50	15.00
❑ 134	Two to Tango/A Man Is a Man Is a Man	1966	3.75	7.50	15.00
❑ 135	I'll Never Need More Love Than This/ The Cash Box Blues Or (Oops We Printed the Wrong Story Again)	1967	3.75	7.50	15.00
❑ 136	I Idolize You/A Love Like Yours	1967	3.75	7.50	15.00

Pompeii
❑ 7003	Betcha Can't Kiss Me/Cussin', Cryin', and Carryin' On	1969	2.00	4.00	8.00
❑ 66675	It Sho' Ain't Me/We Need An Understanding	1968	2.00	4.00	8.00
❑ 66700	Shake a Tail Feather/Cussin', Cryin', and Carryin' On	1969	2.00	4.00	8.00

Sue
❑ 135	Two Is a Couple/Tin Top House	1965	3.75	7.50	15.00
❑ 138	The New Breed (Part 1)/The New Breed (Part 2)	1965	3.75	7.50	15.00
❑ 139	Stagger Lee and Billy/Can't Chance a Breakup	1965	3.75	7.50	15.00
❑ 146	Dear John/I Made a Promise Up Above	1966	3.00	6.00	12.00
❑ 730	A Fool in Love/The Way You Love Me	1960	5.00	10.00	20.00
❑ 734	You're My Baby/A Fool Too Long	1960	6.25	12.50	25.00
❑ 735	I Idolize You/Letter from Tina	1960	5.00	10.00	20.00
❑ 740	I'm Jealous/You're My Baby	1961	5.00	10.00	20.00
❑ 749	It's Gonna Work Out Fine/Won't You Forgive Me	1961	5.00	10.00	20.00
❑ 753	Poor Fool/Can You Blame Me	1961	5.00	10.00	20.00
❑ 757	Tra La La La/Puppy Love	1962	3.75	7.50	15.00
❑ 760	Prancing/It's Gonna Work Out Fine	1962	3.75	7.50	15.00
❑ 765	You Shoulda Treated Me Right/Sleepless	1962	3.75	7.50	15.00
❑ 768	Tina's Dilemma/I Idolize You	1962	3.75	7.50	15.00
❑ 772	The Argument/Mind in a Whirl	1962	3.75	7.50	15.00
❑ 774	Please Don't Hurt Me/Worried and Hurtin' Inside	1962	3.75	7.50	15.00
❑ 784	Don't Play Me Cheap/Wake Up	1963	3.75	7.50	15.00

Tangerine
❑ 963	Beauty Is Only Skin Deep/ Anything You Wasn't Born With	1966	2.50	5.00	10.00
❑ 967	Dust My Broom/I'm Hooked	1966	2.50	5.00	10.00

United Artists
0119 through 0122 are "Silver Spotlight Series" reissues

❑ 0119	A Fool in Love/I Idolize You	1973		2.00	4.00
❑ 0120	It's Gonna Work Out Fine/Poor Fool	1973		2.00	4.00
❑ 0121	I Want to Take You Higher/Come Together	1973		2.00	4.00
❑ 0122	Proud Mary/Tra La La La La	1973		2.00	4.00
❑ XW174	With a Little Help from My Friends/Early One Morning	1973		2.50	5.00
❑ XW257	Work On Me/Born Free	1973		2.50	5.00
❑ XW298	Nutbush City Limits/Help Him	1973		3.00	6.00
❑ XW409	Get it Out of Your Mind/Sweet Rhode Island Red	1974		2.50	5.00

Number		Title (A Side/B Side)	Year	VG	VG+	NM
❑ XW524		Nutbush City Limits/Ooh Poo Pah Doo	1974		2.00	4.00
	Reissue					
❑ XW528		Sexy Ida (Part 1)/Sexy Ida (Part 2)	1974		2.50	5.00
❑ XW598		Help Me Make It Through the Night/Baby, Get It On	1975		2.50	5.00
❑ 50782		Ooh Poo Pah Doo/I Wanna Jump	1971		2.50	5.00
❑ 50837		I'm Yours/Doin' It	1971		2.50	5.00
❑ 50881		Do Wah Ditty (Got to Get Ya)/Up in Heah	1972		2.50	5.00
❑ 50913		Outrageous/Feel Good	1972		2.50	5.00
❑ 50939		Games People Play/Pick Me Up	1972		2.50	5.00
❑ 50955		Let Me Touch Your Mind/Chopper	1972		2.50	5.00

Warner Bros.

❑ 5433		A Fool for a Fool/No Tears to Cry	1964	3.00	6.00	12.00
❑ 5433	PS	A Fool for a Fool/No Tears to Cry	1964	10.00	20.00	40.00
❑ 5461		It's All Over/Finger Poppin'	1964	3.00	6.00	12.00
❑ 5493		Ooh Poop A Doo/Merry Christmas Baby	1964	3.00	6.00	12.00

Turner, Jesse Lee
Carlton

❑ 496		The Little Space Girl/Shake, Baby, Shake	1959	5.00	10.00	20.00
❑ 509		Baby Please Don't Tease/Thinkin'	1959	5.00	10.00	20.00
❑ 509	PS	Baby Please Don't Tease/Thinkin'	1959	10.00	20.00	40.00

Fraternity

❑ 855		Teen-Age Misery/That's My Girl	1959	5.00	10.00	20.00
❑ 855	PS	Teen-Age Misery/That's My Girl	1959	10.00	20.00	40.00

GNP Crescendo

❑ 184		All You Gotta Do (Is Ask Me To)/Voice Changing Song	1962	3.00	6.00	12.00
❑ 188		Shotgun Boogie/Ballad of Billy Sol Estes	1962	15.00	30.00	60.00

Imperial

❑ 5635		Slippin' Around/Early in the Morning	1960			
❑ 5649		I'm the Little Space Girl's Father/Valley of Lost Soldiers	1960			

Top Rank

❑ 2064		Do I Worry/All Right, Be That Way	1960	5.00	10.00	20.00

Turner, Joe
Atlantic

❑ 939		Chains of Love/After My Laughter Came Tears	1951	50.00	100.00	200.00
❑ 949		The Chill Is On/Bump Miss Suzie	1951	50.00	100.00	200.00
❑ 960		Sweet Sixteen/I'll Never Stop Loving You	1952	37.50	75.00	150.00
❑ 970		Don't You Cry/Poor Lover's Blues	1952	25.00	50.00	100.00
❑ 982		Still in Love/Baby I Still Want You	1953	25.00	50.00	100.00
❑ 1001		Honey Hush/Crawdad Hole	1953	20.00	40.00	80.00
❑ 1016		TV Mama/Oke-She-Moke-She-Pop	1954	25.00	50.00	100.00
❑ 1026		Shake, Rattle, and Roll/You Know I Love You	1954	10.00	20.00	40.00
❑ 1040		Well All Right/Married Woman	1954	7.50	15.00	30.00
❑ 1053		Flip, Flop, and Fly/Ti-Ri-Lee	1955	7.50	15.00	30.00
❑ 1069		Hide and Seek/Midnight Cannonball	1955	7.50	15.00	30.00
❑ 1080		Morning, Noon and Night/The Chicken and the Hawk	1956	7.50	15.00	30.00
❑ 1088		Corinne, Corinna/Boogie Woogie Country Girl	1956	7.50	15.00	30.00
❑ 1100		Rock a While/Lipstick, Powder, and Paint	1956	7.50	15.00	30.00
❑ 1122		Midnight Special Train/Feeling Happy	1957	7.50	15.00	30.00
❑ 1131		Red Sails in the Sunset/After a While	1957	7.50	15.00	30.00
❑ 1146		Love Roller Coaster/A World of Trouble	1957	7.50	15.00	30.00
❑ 1155		I Need a Girl/Trouble in Mind	1957	7.50	15.00	30.00
❑ 1167		Teen-Age Letter/Wee Baby Blues	1957	7.50	15.00	30.00
❑ 1184		Blues in the Night/Jump for Joy	1958	7.50	15.00	30.00
❑ 2034		Got You On My Mind/Love, Oh Careless Love	1959	5.00	10.00	20.00
❑ 2044		Tomorrow Night/Honey Hush	1959	5.00	10.00	20.00
❑ 2054		Chains of Love/My Little Honey Dripper	1960	5.00	10.00	20.00
❑ 2072		My Reason for Living/Sweet Sue	1960	5.00	10.00	20.00

Bayou

❑ 015		The Blues Jumped the Rabbit/The Sun Is Shining	1951	75.00	150.00	300.00

Bluestime

❑ 45001		Two Loves Have I/(B-side unknown)	195?	10.00	20.00	40.00

Bluesway

❑ 61009		Big Wheel/Bluer Than Blue	1967	2.00	4.00	8.00

Coral

❑ 62408		I Walk a Lonely Mile/I'm Packin' Up	1964	3.75	7.50	15.00
❑ 62429		Shake, Rattle and Roll/There'll Be Some Tears Falling	1964	3.75	7.50	15.00

Decca

❑ 29711		Piney Brown Blues/ I Got a Gal for Every Day of the Week	1955	10.00	20.00	40.00
❑ 29924		Corrine, Corrina/It's the Same Old Story	1956	10.00	20.00	40.00

Kent

❑ 512		Love Ain't Nothin'/10-20-25-30	1969		3.00	6.00
❑ 4561		Chains of Love/Battle Hymn of the Republic	1971		3.00	6.00
❑ 4569		One Hour in Your Garden/ You've Been Squeezin' My Lemons	1972		3.00	6.00

MGM

❑ 10719		Moody Baby/Feeling So Sad	1951	75.00	150.00	300.00

Ronn

❑ 28		Up on the Mountain/I Love You Baby	1969		3.00	6.00
❑ 35		Morning Glory/Night-Time Is the Right Time	1969		3.00	6.00

Number		Title (A Side/B Side)	Year	VG	VG+	NM

RPM

| ❑ 345 | | Riding Blues/Playful Baby | 1952 | 50.00 | 100.00 | 200.00 |
| | | *With Pete Johnson* | | | | |

Turner, Odelle

Atlantic

| ❑ 964 | | Alarm Clock Boogie/Draggin' Hours | 1952 | 37.50 | 75.00 | 150.00 |

Turner, Sammy

Big Top

❑ 3007		Thunderbolt/Sweet Annie Laurie	1959	6.25	12.50	25.00
❑ 3016		Lavender Blue/Wrapped Up in a Dream	1959	5.00	10.00	20.00
❑ 3029	M	Always/Symphony	1959	5.00	10.00	20.00
❑ 3029	S	Always/Symphony	1959	12.50	25.00	50.00
❑ 3032		Paradise/I'd Be a Fool Again	1960	5.00	10.00	20.00
❑ 3038		Goodnight Irene/I Want to Be Loved	1960	5.00	10.00	20.00
❑ 3049		Fools Fall in Love/Stay My Love	1960	5.00	10.00	20.00
❑ 3061		Falling/The Things I Do	1961	3.75	7.50	15.00
❑ 3065		Little Sir Echo/Love Keeps Calling	1961	3.75	7.50	15.00
❑ 3070		Starlight, Starbright/Let's Donkey On Down	1961	3.75	7.50	15.00
❑ 3082		Pour It On/The Fool of the Year	1961	3.75	7.50	15.00
❑ 3089		Falling/Raincoat in the River	1961	6.25	12.50	25.00

Millennium

| ❑ 616 | | Do You Know (What Life Is All About)/ | 1978 | | 2.50 | 5.00 |
| | | Nothing Can Separate Me (From Your Love) | | | | |

Motown

| ❑ 1055 | | Only You/Right Now | 1964 | 7.50 | 15.00 | 30.00 |

20th Fox

| ❑ 6610 | | For Your Love I'll Die/The House I Live In | 1965 | 2.50 | 5.00 | 10.00 |

Verve

| ❑ 10465 | | A Child Was Born/Come to Me Comf'tably | 1966 | 7.50 | 15.00 | 30.00 |

Turner, Tina

(Also see "Turner, Ike and Tina")

Capitol

❑ B-5322		Let's Stay Together/I Wrote a Letter	1984			3.00
❑ B-5322	PS	Let's Stay Together/I Wrote a Letter	1984		2.50	5.00
❑ B-5354		What's Love Got to Do with It/Rock 'N' Roll Widow	1984			3.00
❑ B-5354	PS	What's Love Got to Do with It/Rock 'N' Roll Widow	1984		2.00	4.00
❑ B-5387		Better Be Good to Me/When I Was Young	1984			3.00
❑ B-5387	PS	Better Be Good to Me/When I Was Young	1984		2.00	4.00
❑ B-5433		Private Dancer/Nutbush City Limits	1984			3.00
❑ B-5433	PS	Private Dancer/Nutbush City Limits	1984		2.00	4.00
❑ B-5461		Show Some Respect/Let's Pretend We're Married	1985			3.00
❑ B-5461	PS	Show Some Respect/Let's Pretend We're Married	1985		2.00	4.00
❑ B-5491		We Don't Need Another Hero (Thunderdome)/	1985			3.00
		(Instrumental)				
❑ B-5491	PS	We Don't Need Another Hero (Thunderdome)/	1985		2.00	4.00
		(Instrumental)				
❑ B-5518		One of the Living/One of the Living (Dub)	1985			3.00
❑ B-5518	PS	One of the Living/One of the Living (Dub)	1985		2.00	4.00
❑ B-5615		Typical Male/Don't Turn Around	1986			3.00
❑ B-5615	PS	Typical Male/Don't Turn Around	1986			3.00
❑ B-5644		Two People/Havin' a Party	1986			3.00
❑ B-5644	PS	Two People/Havin' a Party	1986			3.00
❑ B-5668		What You Get Is What You See/	1987			3.00
		What You Get Is What You See (Live)				
❑ B-5668	PS	What You Get Is What You See/	1987			3.00
		What You Get Is What You See (Live)				
❑ B-44003		Break Every Rule/Take Me to the River	1987			3.00
❑ B-44003	PS	Break Every Rule/Take Me to the River	1987			3.00
❑ B-44111		Afterglow/Afterglow	1987			3.00
❑ B-44442		The Best/Undercover Agent for the Blues	1989			3.00
❑ B-44442	PS	The Best/Undercover Agent for the Blues	1989			3.00
❑ B-44473		Steamy Windows/The Best	1989			3.00
❑ B-44473	PS	Steamy Windows/The Best	1989			3.00
❑ NR-44510		Look Me in the Heart/Stronger Than the Wind	1990			3.00
❑ S7-57702		Way of the World/You Know Who	1992			3.00

Fantasy

| ❑ 948 | | Lean On Me/Shame, Shame, Shame | 1984 | | 2.00 | 4.00 |

Polydor

| ❑ PRO-002 | DJ | Acid Queen/Pinball Wizard | 1975 | 10.00 | 20.00 | 40.00 |
| | | *B-side by Elton John; promo-only* | | | | |

Pompeii

| ❑ 66682 | | Too Hot to Hold/You Got What You Wanted | 1968 | 2.50 | 5.00 | 10.00 |

United Artists

❑ XW 724		Whole Lotta Love/Rockin' 'N' Rollin'	1975		3.00	6.00
❑ XW 730		Delilah's Power/That's My Power	1975		3.00	6.00
❑ XW 920		Come Together/I Want to Take You Higher	1977		3.00	6.00
❑ XW 1265		Fire Down Below/Viva La Money	1979		2.50	5.00

Virgin

| ❑ S7-17401 | | I Don't Wanna Fight/Tina's Wish | 1993 | | | 3.00 |

Number		Title (A Side/B Side)	Year	VG	VG+	NM
❑ S7-17498		Why Must We Wait Until Tomorrow/	1993			3.00
		Shake a Tail Feather				
❑ S7-18047		Proud Mary (Edit Live Version)/The Best (Live)	1994			3.00
❑ S7-19217		Missing You/Do Something	1996			3.00

Turnpikes, The
Capitol

| ❑ 2234 | | Cast a Spell/Nothing But Promises | 1968 | 6.25 | 12.50 | 25.00 |

Turtles, The
RCA Victor

| ❑ 47-6356 | | Mystery Train/Say You Care | 1955 | 6.25 | 12.50 | 25.00 |
| | | *Not the same Turtles as the 1960s hitmakers* | | | | |

White Whale

❑ 222		It Ain't Me, Babe/Almost There	1965	3.00	6.00	12.00
◹ 224		Let Me Be/Your Maw Said You Cried	1965	2.50	5.00	10.00
❑ 227		You Baby/Wanderin' Kind	1966	2.50	5.00	10.00
❑ 231		Grim Reaper of Love/Come Back	1966	5.00	10.00	20.00
❑ 234		We'll Meet Again/Outside Chance	1966	3.75	7.50	15.00
❑ 237		Outside Chance/Making My Mind Up	1966	2.50	5.00	10.00
❑ 238		Can I Get to Know You Better?/Like the Seasons	1966	2.50	5.00	10.00
❑ 244		Happy Together/Like the Seasons	1967	2.00	4.00	8.00
❑ 244	PS	Happy Together/Like the Seasons	1967	5.00	10.00	20.00
◹ 249		She'd Rather Be with Me/The Walking Song	1967	2.00	4.00	8.00
❑ 249	PS	She'd Rather Be with Me/The Walking Song	1967	6.25	12.50	25.00
❑ 251		Guide for the Married Man/Think I'll Run Away	1967	10.00	20.00	40.00
		Withdrawn shortly after release				
❑ 254		You Know What I Mean/Rugs of Woods and Flowers	1967	2.00	4.00	8.00
❑ 254	PS	You Know What I Mean/Rugs of Woods and Flowers	1967	3.75	7.50	15.00
❑ 260		She's My Girl/Chicken Little Was Right	1967	2.00	4.00	8.00
❑ 260	PS	She's My Girl/Chicken Little Was Right	1967	5.00	10.00	20.00
◹ 264		Sound Asleep/Umbassa the Dragon	1968	2.00	4.00	8.00
❑ 264	PS	Sound Asleep/Umbassa the Dragon	1968	3.75	7.50	15.00
❑ 273		The Story of Rock and Roll/Can't You Hear the Cows	1968	2.00	4.00	8.00
❑ 273	PS	The Story of Rock and Roll/Can't You Hear the Cows	1968	7.50	15.00	30.00
❑ 276		Elenore/Surfer Dan	1968	2.00	4.00	8.00
❑ 276	PS	Elenore/Surfer Dan	1968	3.00	6.00	12.00
❑ 292		You Showed Me/Buzz Saw	1969	2.00	4.00	8.00
❑ 292	PS	You Showed Me/Buzz Saw	1969	3.00	6.00	12.00
❑ 306		House on the Hill/Come Over	1969	5.00	10.00	20.00
❑ 308		You Don't Have to Walk in the Rain/Come Over	1969	2.00	4.00	8.00
❑ 308	PS	You Don't Have to Walk in the Rain/Come Over	1969	2.50	5.00	10.00
❑ 326		Love in the City/Bachelor Mother	1969	2.00	4.00	8.00
❑ 326	PS	Love in the City/Bachelor Mother	1969	2.50	5.00	10.00
❑ 334		Lady-O/Somewhere Friday Nite	1969	2.00	4.00	8.00
❑ 341		Who Would Ever Think That I Would Marry Margaret?/	1970	3.75	7.50	15.00
		We Ain't Gonna Party No More				
❑ 350		Is It Any Wonder?/Wanderin' Kind	1970	2.00	4.00	8.00
❑ 355		Eve of Destruction/Wanderin' Kind	1970	2.00	4.00	8.00
❑ 364		Me About You/Think I'll Run Away	1970	2.00	4.00	8.00

Tweeters, The
Decca

| ❑ 30725 | | Mascara Mama/The Campus Rock | 1958 | 7.50 | 15.00 | 30.00 |

Twice As Much
MGM

❑ 13530		Sittin' on a Fence/Baby I Want You	1966	3.75	7.50	15.00
		A-side is a Mick Jagger-Keith Richards song that only later was released by the Rolling Stones.				
❑ 13530	PS	Sittin' on a Fence/Baby I Want You	1966	7.50	15.00	30.00
❑ 13600		Step Out of Line/Simplified	1966	2.50	5.00	10.00

Twilighters, The
(Several different groups)
Bell

| ❑ 624 | | Be Faithful/Thumper | 1965 | 5.00 | 10.00 | 20.00 |

Bubble

| ❑ 1334 | | My Silent Prayer/Little Bitty Bed Bug | 1962 | 5.00 | 10.00 | 20.00 |

Caddy

| ❑ 103 | | Eternally/I Believe | 1955 | 50.00 | 100.00 | 200.00 |

Chess

| ❑ 1803 | | Scratchin'/Tears | 1961 | 5.00 | 10.00 | 20.00 |

Cholly

| ❑ 712 | | Let There Be Love/Eternally | 1957 | 125.00 | 250.00 | 500.00 |

Dot

| ❑ 15526 | | Eternally/I Believe | 1957 | 10.00 | 20.00 | 40.00 |

Ebb

| ❑ 117 | | Pride and Joy/Live Like a King | 1957 | 10.00 | 20.00 | 40.00 |

Eldo

| ❑ 115 | | Nothin'/Do You Believe | 1961 | 5.00 | 10.00 | 20.00 |

Fraternity

| ❑ 889 | | To Love in Vain/The Beginning of Love | 1961 | 5.00 | 10.00 | 20.00 |
| | | *As "The Twi-Lighters"* | | | | |

Number	Title (A Side/B Side)		Year	VG	VG+	NM
Groove						
❑ 0154	Sittin' in a Corner/It's a Cold, Cold, Rainy Day		1956	15.00	30.00	60.00
	As "The Twi-Lighters"					
Imperial						
❑ 66201	Shake a Tail Feather/Road to Fortune		1966	3.00	6.00	12.00
❑ 66238	I Still Love You/Meat Ball		1967	3.00	6.00	12.00
JVB						
❑ 83	How Many Times/Water-Water		1957	75.00	150.00	300.00
Marshall						
❑ 702	Please Tell Me You're Mine/Wondering		1953	30.00	60.00	120.00
❑ 702	Please Tell Me You're Mine/Wondering		1953	150.00	300.00	600.00
	Red vinyl					
MGM						
❑ 55011	Little Did I Dream/Gotta Get On the Train		1955	50.00	100.00	200.00
❑ 55014	Lovely Lady/Half Angel		1955	75.00	150.00	300.00
Ricki						
❑ 907	Help Me/Rockin' Mule		1961	10.00	20.00	40.00
Sara						
❑ 1048	Restless Love/Can't You Stay a Little Longer		1961	15.00	30.00	60.00
Specialty						
❑ 548	It's True/Wha-Bop-Sh-Wah		1955	15.00	30.00	60.00
Spin						
❑ 0001	Yes You Are/A Possibility		1960	30.00	60.00	120.00
Vanco						
❑ 204	Out of My Mind/I Need Your Lovin'		1968	2.50	5.00	10.00

Twilley, Dwight
(Also includes The Dwight Twilley Band)

Number	Title (A Side/B Side)		Year	VG	VG+	NM
Arista						
❑ 0278	Rock and Roll 47/Twilley Don't Mind		1977		2.50	5.00
❑ 0299	Trying to Find My Baby/Here She Comes		1977		2.50	5.00
❑ 0311	Looking for the Magic/Invasion		1978		2.50	5.00
❑ 0415	Out of My Hands/ Nothing's Ever Gonna Change So Fast		1979		2.00	4.00
❑ 0433	Runaway/Burnin' Sand		1979		2.00	4.00
❑ 0478	Somebody to Love/Money (That's What I Want)		1979		2.00	4.00
CBS Associated						
❑ 06050	Sexual/Wild Dogs		1986			3.00
EMI America						
❑ 8109	Later That Night/Somebody to Love		1982		2.00	4.00
❑ 8115	I Found the Magic/I'm Back Again		1982		2.00	4.00
❑ 8196	Girls/To Get to You		1984			3.00
❑ 8196	PS Girls/To Get to You		1984		2.00	4.00
❑ 8206	Little Bit of Love/Mad Dog		1984			3.00
❑ 8206	PS Little Bit of Love/Mad Dog		1984		2.00	4.00
❑ 8235	Why You Wanna Break My Heart/Chilly D's Theme		1984			3.00
Private I						
❑ 04820	Keep On Working/(Instrumental)		1985			3.00
Shelter						
❑ 40380	I'm on Fire/Did You See What Happened		1975		2.50	5.00
❑ 40380	PS I'm on Fire/Did You See What Happened		1975	2.50	5.00	10.00
❑ 40450	Sincerely/You Were So Warm		1975		2.50	5.00
❑ 62003	Could Be Love/Feeling in the Dark		1976		2.50	5.00

Twisters, The
(More than one group)

Number	Title (A Side/B Side)	Year	VG	VG+	NM
Apt					
❑ 25045	Come Go with Me/Pretty Little Girl Next Door	1960	5.00	10.00	20.00
Campus					
❑ 125	Elvis Leaves Sorrento/Street Dance	1961	7.50	15.00	30.00
Capitol					
❑ 4451	Turn the Page/Dancing Little Clown	1960	5.00	10.00	20.00
Felco					
❑ 103	Count Down 1-2-3/Speed Limit	1959	6.25	12.50	25.00
Sun-Set					
❑ 501	Please Come Back/This Is the End	1961	150.00	300.00	600.00

Twistin' Kings

Number	Title (A Side/B Side)	Year	VG	VG+	NM
Motown					
❑ 1022	Xmas Twist/White House Twist	1961	10.00	20.00	40.00
❑ 1023	Congo (Part 1)/Congo (Part 2)	1962	10.00	20.00	40.00

Twitty, Conway
(Also see next entry)

Number	Title (A Side/B Side)	Year	VG	VG+	NM
ABC-Paramount					
❑ 10507	Go On and Cry/She Loves Me	1963	3.75	7.50	15.00
❑ 10550	Such a Night/My Baby Left Me	1964	6.25	12.50	25.00

Number		Title (A Side/B Side)	Year	VG	VG+	NM
Decca						
☐ 31833		Together Forever/That Kind of Girl	1965	2.00	4.00	8.00
☐ 31897		Guess My Eyes Were Bigger Than Her Heart/ Honky Tonk Man	1966	2.00	4.00	8.00
☐ 31983		Look Into My Teardrops/If You Were Mine to Lose	1966	2.00	4.00	8.00
☐ 32081		I Don't Want to Be with Me/Before I'll Set Her Free	1967	2.00	4.00	8.00
☐ 32147		Don't Put Your Hurt in My Heart/Walk Me to the Door	1967	2.00	4.00	8.00
☐ 32208		Funny (But I'm Not Laughing)/Working Girl	1967	2.00	4.00	8.00
☐ 32272		The Image of Me/D im Lights, Truck Smoke (And Loud, Loud Music)	1968	2.00	4.00	8.00
☐ 32361		Next in Line/I'm Checking Out	1968	2.00	4.00	8.00
☐ 32424		Darling, You Know I Wouldn't Lie/Table in the Corner	1968	2.00	4.00	8.00
☐ 32481		I Love You More Today/Bad Girl	1969	2.00	4.00	8.00
☐ 32546		To See My Angel Cry/I Did the Best I Could	1969	2.00	4.00	8.00
☐ 32599		That's When She Started to Stop Loving You/ I'll Get Over Losing You	1969	2.00	4.00	8.00
☐ 32661		Hello Darlin'/Girl at the Bar	1970		3.00	6.00
☐ 32742		Fifteen Years Ago/Up Comes the Bottle	1970		3.00	6.00
☐ 32801		How Much More Can She Stand/Just Like a Stranger	1971		3.00	6.00
☐ 32842		I Wonder What She'll Think About Me Leaving/ A Heartache Just Walked In	1971		3.00	6.00
☐ 32895		I Can't See Me Without You/I Didn't Lose Her	1971		3.00	6.00
☐ 32945		(Lost Her Love) On Our Last Date/ I'll Never Make It Home Tonight	1972		3.00	6.00
☐ 32988		I Can't Stop Loving You/ Since She's Not with the One She Loves	1972		3.00	6.00
☐ 32988		I Can't Stop Loving You/ She Needs Someone to Hold Her (When She Cries)	1972		3.00	6.00
☐ 33033		She Needs Someone to Hold Her (When She Cries)/ This Road That I Walk	1972		3.00	6.00
Elektra						
☐ 47302		The Clown/The Boy Next Door	1982		2.00	4.00
☐ 47443		Slow Hand/When Love Was Something Else	1982		2.00	4.00
☐ 69854		The Rose/It's Only Make Believe	1982		2.00	4.00
☐ 69854	PS	The Rose/It's Only Make Believe	1982		2.50	5.00
☐ 69964		We Did But Now You Don't/(B-side unknown)	1982		2.00	4.00
MCA						
☐ 40027		Baby's Gone/Dim Lovely Places	1973		2.50	5.00
☐ 40094		You've Never Been This Far Before/You Make It Hard	1973		2.50	5.00
☐ 40173		There's a Honky Tonk Angel (Who'll Take Me Back In)/ Don't Let It Go to Your Heart	1973		2.50	5.00
☐ 40224		I'm Not Through Loving You Yet/Before Your Time	1974		2.50	5.00
☐ 40282		I See the Want To in Your Eyes/Girl from Tupelo	1974		2.50	5.00
☐ 40339		Linda on My Mind/She's Just Not Over You Yet	1974		2.50	5.00
☐ 40407		Touch the Hand/Don't Cry Joni	1975		2.50	5.00
☐ 40495		This Time I've Hurt Her More Than She Loves Me/ She Did, It Did, I Didn't	1975		2.50	5.00
☐ 40534		After All the Good Is Gone/I Got a Good Thing Going	1976		2.50	5.00
☐ 40601		The Games That Daddies Play/ There's More Love in the Arms You're Leaving	1976		2.50	5.00
☐ 40649		I Can't Believe She Gives It All to Me/ I Can't Help It If She Can't Stop Loving Me	1976		2.50	5.00
☐ 40682		Play, Guitar, Play/One in a Million	1977		2.50	5.00
☐ 40754		I've Already Loved You in My Mind/I Changed My Mind	1977		2.50	5.00
☐ 40805		Talkin' 'Bout You/Georgia Keeps Pulling on My Ring	1977		2.50	5.00
☐ 40857		I'm Used to Losing You/The Grandest Lady of Them All	1978		2.50	5.00
☐ 40929		That's All She Wrote/Boogie Grass Band	1978		2.50	5.00
☐ 40963		Your Love Had Taken Me That High/My Woman Knows	1978		2.50	5.00
☐ 41002		Don't Take It Away/Draggin' Chains	1979		2.00	4.00
☐ 41059		I May Never Get to Heaven/Grand Ole Blues	1979		2.00	4.00
☐ 41135		Happy Birthday Darlin'/Heavy Tears	1979		2.00	4.00
☐ 41174		I'd Love to Lay You Down/She Thinks I Still Care	1980		2.50	5.00
		Note slightly different A-side title				
☐ 41174		I'd Just Love to Lay You Down/She Thinks I Still Care	1980		2.00	4.00
☐ 41271		I've Never Seen the Likes of You/Soulful Woman	1980		2.00	4.00
☐ 51011		A Bridge That Just Won't Burn/You'll Be Back	1980		2.00	4.00
☐ 51059		Rest Your Love on Me/ I Am the Dreamer (You Are the Dream)	1981		2.00	4.00
☐ 51137		Tight Fittin' Jeans/I Made You a Woman	1981		2.00	4.00
☐ 51199		Red Neckin' Love Makin' Night/Hearts	1981		2.00	4.00
☐ 52032		Over Thirty (Not Over the Hill)/Love Salvation	1982		2.00	4.00
☐ 52154		We Had It All/Cheatin' Fire	1983		2.00	4.00
☐ 53034		Julia/Everybody Needs a Hero	1987		2.00	4.00
☐ 53134		I Want to Know You Before We Make Love/ Snake Boots	1987		2.00	4.00
☐ 53200		That's My Job/Lonely Town	1987		2.00	4.00
☐ 53276		Goodbye Time/Your Loving Side	1988		2.00	4.00
☐ 53373		Saturday Night Special/If You Were Mine to Lose	1988		2.00	4.00
☐ 53456		I Wish I Was Still in Your Dreams/ If You Were Mine to Lose	1988		2.00	4.00
☐ 53633		She's Got a Single Thing in Mind/ Too White to Sing the Blues	1989		2.00	4.00
☐ 53688		The House on Old Lonesome Road/ Nobody Can Fill Your Shoes	1989		2.00	4.00
☐ 53759		Who's Gonna Know/Private Part of My Heart	1989		2.00	4.00
☐ 53983		I Couldn't See You Leavin'/ Just the Thought of Losing You	1991		2.00	4.00
☐ 54077		One Bridge I Didn't Burn/I'm Tired of Being Something	1991		2.00	4.00

Number		Title (A Side/B Side)	Year	VG	VG+	NM
❑ 54186		She's Got a Man on Her Mind/You Put It There	1991		2.00	4.00
❑ 54281		Who Did They Think He Was/	1991		2.00	4.00
		Let the Pretty Lady Dance				
❑ 54717		I'm the Only Thing (I'll Hold Against You)/Final Touches	1993		2.00	4.00
❑ 54766		Don't It Make You Lonely/I Don't Love You	1993		2.00	4.00
❑ 79000		Fit to Be Tied Down/	1990		2.00	4.00
		When You're Cool (The Sun Shines All the Time)				
❑ 79067		Crazy in Love/Hearts Breakin' All Over Town	1990		2.00	4.00

Mercury

Number		Title (A Side/B Side)	Year	VG	VG+	NM
❑ 71086		I Need Your Lovin'/Born to Sing the Blues	1957	10.00	20.00	40.00
❑ 71148		Maybe Baby/Shake It Up	1957	10.00	20.00	40.00
❑ 71384		Why Can't I Get Through to You/Double Talk Baby	1958	10.00	20.00	40.00

MGM

Number		Title (A Side/B Side)	Year	VG	VG+	NM
❑ 12677	M	It's Only Make Believe/I'll Try	1958	6.25	12.50	25.00
❑ 12748		The Story of My Love/Make Me Know You're Mine	1959	6.25	12.50	25.00
❑ 12785		Hey Little Lucy! (Don'tcha Put No Lipstick On)/	1959	6.25	12.50	25.00
		When I'm Not with You				
❑ 12804		Mona Lisa/Heavenly	1959	6.25	12.50	25.00
❑ 12826	M	Danny Boy/Halfway to Heaven	1959	6.25	12.50	25.00
		First pressings on yellow labels				
❑ 12826	M	Danny Boy/Halfway to Heaven	1959	5.00	10.00	20.00
		Second pressings on black labels				
❑ 12857		Lonely Blue Boy/Star Spangled Heaven	1959	5.00	10.00	20.00
❑ 12886		What Am I Living For/The Hurt in My Heart	1960	5.00	10.00	20.00
❑ 12886	PS	What Am I Living For/The Hurt in My Heart	1960	12.50	25.00	50.00
❑ 12911		Is a Blue Bird Blue/She's Mine	1960	5.00	10.00	20.00
❑ 12911	PS	Is a Blue Bird Blue/She's Mine	1960	12.50	25.00	50.00
❑ 12918		What a Dream/Tell Me One More Time	1960	3.75	7.50	15.00
❑ 12943		Teasin'/I Need You So	1960	3.75	7.50	15.00
❑ 12962		Whole Lot of Shakin' Going On/The Flame	1960	3.75	7.50	15.00
❑ 12969		C'est Si Bon (It's So Good)/	1960	3.75	7.50	15.00
		Don't You Dare Let Me Down				
❑ 12969	PS	C'est Si Bon (It's So Good)/	1960	12.50	25.00	50.00
		Don't You Dare Let Me Down				
❑ 12998		The Next Kiss (Is the Last Goodbye)/A Man Alone	1961	3.75	7.50	15.00
❑ 12998	PS	The Next Kiss (Is the Last Goodbye)/A Man Alone	1961	12.50	25.00	50.00
❑ 13011		I'm in a Blue, Blue Mood/A Million Teardrops	1961	3.75	7.50	15.00
❑ 13034		It's Drivin' Me Wild/Sweet Sorrow	1961	3.75	7.50	15.00
❑ 13050		Portrait of a Fool/Tower of Tears	1961	3.75	7.50	15.00
❑ 13072		Little Piece of My Heart/Comfy N' Cozy	1962	3.75	7.50	15.00
❑ 13089		There's Something on Your Mind/Unchained Melody	1962	3.75	7.50	15.00
❑ 13112		I Hope, I Think, I Wish/The Pickup	1962	3.75	7.50	15.00
❑ 13149		I Got My Mojo Working/She Ain't No Angel	1963	3.75	7.50	15.00
❑ 14172		It's Only Make Believe/Lonely Blue Boy	1970		2.50	5.00
❑ 14205		What Am I Living For/I'll Try	1970		2.50	5.00
❑ 14274		What a Dream/Long Black Train	1971		2.50	5.00
❑ 14355		It's Too Late/I Hope, I Think, I Wish	1972		2.50	5.00
❑ 14408		Walk On By/Hey Miss Ruby	1972		2.50	5.00
❑ 14447		Boss Man/Fever	1972		2.50	5.00
❑ 14582		Danny Boy/The Pickup	1973		2.50	5.00
❑ SK-50107	S	It's Only Make Believe/I'll Try	1958	25.00	50.00	100.00
❑ SK-50130	S	Danny Boy/Halfway to Heaven	1959	25.00	50.00	100.00

Warner Bros.

Number		Title (A Side/B Side)	Year	VG	VG+	NM
❑ 28577		Fallin' for You for Years/I'll Try	1986		2.00	4.00
❑ 28692		Desperado Love/I Can't See Me Without You	1986		2.00	4.00
❑ 28772		You'll Never Know How Much I Needed You Today/	1986		2.00	4.00
		Fifteen Years Ago				
❑ 28866		The Legend and the Man/	1985		2.00	4.00
		(I Can't Believe) She Gives It All to Me				
❑ 28966		Between Blue Eyes and Jeans/Baby's Gone	1985		2.00	4.00
❑ 29057		Don't Call Him a Cowboy/After All the Good Is Gone	1985		2.00	4.00
❑ 29137		White Christmas/Happy the Christmas Clown	1984		2.50	5.00
❑ 29137		Ain't She Somethin' Else/	1984		2.00	4.00
		The Games That Daddies Play				
❑ 29227		I Don't Know a Thing About Love (The Moon Song)/	1984		2.00	4.00
		Don't Cry Joni				
❑ 29308		Somebody's Needin' Somebody/	1984		2.00	4.00
		(Lying Here with) Linda on My Mind				
❑ 29395		Three Times a Lady/I Think I'm in Love	1983		2.00	4.00
❑ 29505		Heartache Tonight/Hello Darlin'	1983		2.00	4.00
❑ 29636		Lost in the Feeling/You've Never Been This Far Before	1983		2.00	4.00

Twitty, Conway, and Loretta Lynn

Decca

Number	Title (A Side/B Side)	Year	VG	VG+	NM
❑ 32776	After the Fire Is Gone/The One I Can't Live Without	1971		3.00	6.00
❑ 32873	Lead Me On/Four Glass Walls	1971		3.00	6.00

MCA

Number	Title (A Side/B Side)	Year	VG	VG+	NM
❑ 40079	Louisiana Woman, Mississippi Man/	1973		2.50	5.00
	Living Together Alone				
❑ 40251	As Soon As I Hang Up the Phone/A Lifetime Before	1974		2.50	5.00
❑ 40283	Trouble in Paradise/We've Already Tasted Love	1974		2.50	5.00
❑ 40420	Feelin's/You Done Lost Your Baby	1975		2.50	5.00
❑ 40572	The Letter/God Bless America Again	1976		2.50	5.00
❑ 40728	The Bed I'm Dreaming On/I Can't Love You Enough	1977		2.50	5.00
❑ 40920	You're the Reason Our Kids Are Ugly/	1978		2.50	5.00
	From Seven Until Ten				
❑ 41141	The Sadness of It All/You Know Just What I'd Do	1979		2.50	5.00
❑ 41232	Hit the Road Jack/It's True Love	1980		2.00	4.00

Number		Title (A Side/B Side)	Year	VG	VG+	NM
❑ 51050		Lovin' What Your Lovin' Does to Me/Silent Partners	1981		2.00	4.00
❑ 51114		I Still Believe in Waltzes/Oh Honey	1981		2.00	4.00
❑ 53417		Making Believe/	1988		2.00	4.00
		As Soon As I Hang Up the Phone (The Telephone Song)				

Two Chaps, The
(With Jay Black, later of Jay and the Americans)
Atlantic

❑ 1195		Forgive Me/No More	1958	7.50	15.00	30.00

Tyler, Bonnie
Chrysalis

❑ 2130		Lost in France/(B-side unknown)	1976		3.00	6.00

Columbia

❑ 03906		Total Eclipse of the Heart/Straight from the Heart	1983		2.00	4.00
❑ 04246		Take Me Back/Gettin' So Excited	1983		2.00	4.00
❑ 04246	PS	Take Me Back/Gettin' So Excited	1983		2.50	5.00
❑ 04370		Holding Out for a Hero/Faster Than the Speed of Night	1984			3.00
❑ 04370	PS	Holding Out for a Hero/Faster Than the Speed of Night	1984		2.00	4.00
❑ 04548		Here She Comes/Obsession	1984			3.00
❑ 04548	PS	Here She Comes/Obsession	1984		2.00	4.00
❑ 05839		If You Were a Woman (And I Was a Man)/	1986			3.00
		Under Suspicion				
❑ 05839	PS	If You Were a Woman (And I Was a Man)/	1986		2.00	4.00
		Under Suspicion				
❑ 06151		Loving You's a Dirty Job (But Somebody's Gotta Do It)/	1986		2.00	4.00
		(B-side unknown)				
		With Todd Rundgren				
❑ 06527		Band of Gold/Tears	1986			3.00
❑ 07758		Hide Your Heart/Fire Below	1988			3.00
❑ 08497		Save Up All Your Tears/It's Not Enough	1988			3.00

RCA

❑ PB-11249		It's a Heartache/It's About Time	1978		2.50	5.00
❑ PB-11349		If I Sing You a Love Song/Heaven	1978		2.00	4.00
❑ PB-11468		My Guns Are Loaded/Baby I Just Love You	1979		2.00	4.00
❑ PB-11630		Married Man/If You Ever Need Me Again	1979		2.00	4.00
❑ PB-11763		I Believe in Your Sweet Love/	1979		2.00	4.00
		Come On, Give Me Loving				

Tyler, Frankie
(Actually Frankie Valli)
Okeh

❑ 7103		I Go Ape/If You Care	1958	75.00	150.00	300.00

Tyler, Kip
Challenge

❑ 1014		She Got Eyes/Shadow Street	1957	7.50	15.00	30.00
❑ 59008		Jungle Hop/Ooh Yeah Baby	1958	10.00	20.00	40.00

Ebb

❑ 154		She's My Witch/Rumble Rock	1959	12.50	25.00	50.00
❑ 156		Oh Linda/Kali Lou	1959	12.50	25.00	50.00

Gyro Disc

❑ 711		Surfer's Lament (Eternity)/Toledo	1963	12.50	25.00	50.00

Imperial

❑ 5641		Rocket 'Round the Universe/The Goblin Trot	1960	7.50	15.00	30.00

Tymes, The
Capitol

❑ 3440		When I Look Around Me/Smile a Tender Smile	1972		3.00	6.00

Columbia

❑ 44630		People/For Love of Ivy	1968	2.00	4.00	8.00
❑ 44799		God Bless the Child/The Love That You're Looking For	1969		3.00	6.00
❑ 44917		Find My Way/If You Love Me Baby	1969		3.00	6.00
❑ 45078		Love Child/Most Beautiful Married Lady	1970		3.00	6.00
❑ 45336		She's Gone/Someone to Watch Over Me	1971		3.00	6.00

MGM

❑ 13536		Pretend/Street Talk	1966	5.00	10.00	20.00
❑ 13631		(Touch of) Baby/What Would I Do	1966	5.00	10.00	20.00

Parkway

❑ 871		So in Love/Roscoe James McClain	1963	6.25	12.50	25.00
		Original title of A-side				
❑ 871		So Much in Love/Roscoe James McClain	1963	3.75	7.50	15.00
❑ 871	PS	So Much in Love/Roscoe James McClain	1963	6.25	12.50	25.00
❑ 884		Wonderful! Wonderful!/Come with Me to the Sea	1963	3.75	7.50	15.00
❑ 884	PS	Wonderful! Wonderful!/Come with Me to the Sea	1963	6.25	12.50	25.00
❑ 891		Somewhere/View from My Window	1963	3.75	7.50	15.00
❑ 891	PS	Somewhere/View from My Window	1963	6.25	12.50	25.00
❑ 908		To Each His Own/Wonderland By Night	1964	3.75	7.50	15.00
❑ 908	PS	To Each His Own/Wonderland By Night	1964	6.25	12.50	25.00
❑ 919		The Magic of Our Summer Love/With All My Heart	1964	3.75	7.50	15.00
❑ 919	PS	The Magic of Our Summer Love/With All My Heart	1964	6.25	12.50	25.00
❑ 924		Here She Comes/Malibu	1964	3.75	7.50	15.00
❑ 924	PS	Here She Comes/Malibu	1964	6.25	12.50	25.00
❑ 933		The Twelfth of Never/Here She Comes	1964	3.75	7.50	15.00

Number	Title (A Side/B Side)	Year	VG	VG+	NM
RCA					
☐ PB-10862	Love's Illusion/Savannah Sunny Sunday	1976		2.00	4.00
☐ PB-11136	I'll Take You There/	1977		2.00	4.00
	How Am I to Know (The Things a Girl in Love Should Know)				
☐ GB-12082	You Little Trustmaker/Ms. Grace	1980			Unreleased?
RCA Victor					
☐ PB-10022	You Little Trustmaker/The North Hills	1974		2.50	5.00
☐ PB-10128	Ms. Grace/The Crutch	1974		2.00	4.00
☐ PB-10244	Interloop/Someday, Somehow I'm Keeping You	1975		2.00	4.00
☐ PB-10422	God's Gonna Punish You/If I Can't Make You Smile	1975		2.00	4.00
☐ GB-10493	You Little Trustmaker/The North Hills	1975		2.00	4.00
Gold Standard Series					
☐ PB-10561	Good Morning Dear Lord/It's Cool	1976		2.00	4.00
☐ PB-10713	Goin' Through the Motions/Only Your Love	1976		2.00	4.00
Winchester					
☐ 1002	These Foolish Things (Remind Me of You)/	1967	2.50	5.00	10.00
	This Time It's Love				

Tyrannosaurus Rex – See "T. Rex"

Tyrell, Danny, and the Cleeshays

Eastman					
☐ 784	You're Only Seventeen/Let's Walk, Let's Talk	1958	10.00	20.00	40.00

U

U2

Number		Title (A Side/B Side)	Year	VG	VG+	NM
Island						
☐ PR 564	DJ	I Will Follow (Mini LP Version)/	1983	7.50	15.00	30.00
		I Will Follow (Radio Remix)				
☐ 49716		I Will Follow/Out of Control (Live)	1980	2.50	5.00	10.00
☐ 49716	PS	I Will Follow/Out of Control (Live)	1980	2.50	5.00	10.00
☐ 49716	PS	I Will Follow/Out of Control (Live)	1980	6.25	12.50	25.00
		Promo-only poster sleeve with tour dates				
☐ 94961		With or Without You/In God's Country	1988		2.00	4.00
		Gold label "Revival of the Fittest" series				
☐ 94974		Gloria/Sunday Bloody Sunday	1987		2.50	5.00
		Gold label "Revival of the Fittest" series; first U.S. 45 release for either				
☐ 94975		New Year's Day/Two Hearts Beat As One	1987		2.00	4.00
		Gold label "Revival of the Fittest" series				
☐ 94976		I Will Follow/Pride (In the Name of Love)	1987		2.00	4.00
		Gold label "Revival of the Fittest" series				
☐ 99199		All I Want Is You/Unchained Melody	1989			3.00
☐ 99199	PS	All I Want Is You/Unchained Melody	1989			3.00
☐ 99225		When Love Comes to Town/Dancing Barefoot	1989			3.00
		A-side with B.B. King				
☐ 99225	PS	When Love Comes to Town/Dancing Barefoot	1989			3.00
☐ 99250		Desire/Hallelujah Here She Comes	1988			3.00
☐ 99250	PS	Desire/Hallelujah Here She Comes	1988		3.00	6.00
		Cardboard gatefold sleeve				
☐ 99250	PS	Desire/Hallelujah Here She Comes	1988			3.00
		Standard paper sleeve				
☐ 99254		Angel of Harlem/A Room at the Heartbreak Hotel	1988			3.00
☐ 99254	PS	Angel of Harlem/A Room at the Heartbreak Hotel	1988			3.00
☐ 99384		In God's Country/Bullet the Blue Sky	1988			3.00
		Black label jukebox pressing; both sides play at 45 rpm				
☐ 99385		In God's Country//Bullet the Blue Sky/	1988		2.00	4.00
		Running to Stand Still				
☐ 99385	PS	In God's Country//Bullet the Blue Sky/	1988		2.00	4.00
		Running to Stand Still				
		Cardboard sleeve				
☐ 99385	PS	In God's Country//Bullet the Blue Sky/	1988		2.00	4.00
		Running to Stand Still				
		Paper sleeve				
☐ 99407		Where the Streets Have No Name/Silver and Gold	1987		2.00	4.00
		Black label jukebox pressing; both sides play at 45 rpm				
☐ 99408		Where the Streets Have No Name//Silver and Gold/	1987			3.00
		Sweetest Thing				
☐ 99408	PS	Where the Streets Have No Name//Silver and Gold/	1987		2.00	4.00
		Sweetest Thing				
		Cardboard sleeve				
☐ 99408	PS	Where the Streets Have No Name//Silver and Gold/	1987			3.00
		Sweetest Thing				
		Paper sleeve				
☐ 99430		I Still Haven't Found What I'm Looking For//	1987			3.00
		Spanish Eyes/Deep in the Heart				
☐ 99430	PS	I Still Haven't Found What I'm Looking For//	1987		2.00	4.00
		Spanish Eyes/Deep in the Heart				
		Cardboard sleeve				
☐ 99430	PS	I Still Haven't Found What I'm Looking For//	1987			3.00
		Spanish Eyes/Deep in the Heart				
		Paper sleeve				

Number		Title (A Side/B Side)	Year	VG	VG+	NM
❏ 99431		I Still Haven't Found What I'm Looking For/	1987	2.50	5.00	10.00
		Spanish Eyes				
		Black label jukebox pressing; both sides play at 45 rpm				
❏ 99453		With or Without You/Walk on the Water	1987	2.50	5.00	10.00
		White label jukebox pressing, both sides play at 45 rpm				
❏ 99469		With or Without You//	1987			3.00
		Luminous Times (Hold On to Love)/Walk on the Water				
❏ 99469	PS	With or Without You//	1987		2.00	4.00
		Luminous Times (Hold On to Love)/Walk on the Water				
		Cardboard sleeve				
❏ 99469	PS	With or Without You//	1987			3.00
		Luminous Times (Hold On to Love)/Walk on the Water				
		Paper sleeve				
❏ 99704		Pride (In the Name of Love)/Boomerang	1984		2.00	4.00
❏ 99704	PS	Pride (In the Name of Love)/Boomerang	1984		2.00	4.00
❏ 99789		I Will Follow (Live)/Two Hearts Beat as One (Live)	1983		2.50	5.00
❏ 99861		Two Hearts Beat as One/Endless Deep	1983		2.50	5.00
❏ 99861	PS	Two Hearts Beat as One/Endless Deep	1983		2.50	5.00
❏ 99915		New Year's Day/	1983		2.50	5.00
		Treasure (Whatever Happened to Pete the Chop?)				

Island/Capitol

❏ 858 076-7		Stay (Faraway, So Close!)/I've Got You Under My Skin	1994		2.00	4.00
❏ 858 076-7	PS	Stay (Faraway, So Close!)/I've Got You Under My Skin	1994		2.00	4.00
		B-side: Frank Sinatra and Bono				

Ullman, Tracey
MCA

❏ 52347		They Don't Know/You Broke My Heart in 17 Places	1984		2.00	4.00
❏ 52347	PS	They Don't Know/You Broke My Heart in 17 Places	1984		2.00	4.00
❏ 52385		Break-A-Way/Long Live Love	1984		2.00	4.00
❏ 52385	PS	Break-A-Way/Long Live Love	1984		2.00	4.00
❏ 52441		Bobby's Girl/Oh, What a Night	1984		2.00	4.00

Ultimate Spinach
MGM

❏ 14023		(Just Like) Romeo and Juliet/	1969	3.00	6.00	12.00
		Some Days You Just Can't Win				

Unbeatables, The
Dawn

❏ 552		I Love Paris/What I Say	1964	10.00	20.00	40.00

Underbeats, The
Bangar

❏ 00632		Annie Do the Dog/Sweet Words of Love	1964	15.00	30.00	60.00
❏ 00657		Broken Arrow/Little Romance	1964	15.00	30.00	60.00

Garrett

❏ 4004		Foot Stompin'/Route 66	1964	6.25	12.50	25.00

Metrobeat

❏ 4449		Sweetest Girl in the World/It's Gonna Rain Today	1967	6.25	12.50	25.00

Soma

❏ 1449		Book of Love/Darling Lorraine	1966	6.25	12.50	25.00
❏ 1458		I Can't Stand It/Shake It for Me	1966	5.00	10.00	20.00

Twin-Town

❏ 706		Jo Jo Gunne/Our Love	1965	7.50	15.00	30.00

Underdogs, The
Hideout

❏ 1001		The Man in the Glass/	1965	7.50	15.00	30.00
		Friday at the Hideout (Judy Be Mine)				
❏ 1004		Little Girl/Don't Pretend	1965	7.50	15.00	30.00
❏ 1011		Surprise Surprise/Get Down on Your Knees	1966	10.00	20.00	40.00

Reprise

❏ 0422		The Man in the Glass/	1965	3.75	7.50	15.00
		Friday at the Hideout (Judy Be Mine)				
❏ 0446		Little Girl/Don't Pretend	1966	3.75	7.50	15.00

V.I.P.

❏ 25040		Love's Gone Bad/Mo Jo Hanna	1966	6.25	12.50	25.00

Underground Sunshine
Intrepid

❏ 75002		Birthday/All I Want Is You	1969	3.00	6.00	12.00
❏ 75012		Don't Shut Me Out/Take Me, Break Me	1969	2.50	5.00	10.00
❏ 75019		Nine to Five (Ain't My Bag)/Rotten Woman Blues	1969	2.50	5.00	10.00
❏ 75029		Jesus Is Just Alright/Six O'Clock	1970	2.50	5.00	10.00

Undisputed Truth, The
Gordy

❏ 7106		Save My Love for a Rainy Day/Since I've Lost You	1971	2.00	4.00	8.00
❏ 7108		Smiling Faces Sometimes/You Got the Love I Need	1971		3.00	6.00
❏ 7112		You Make Your Own Heaven and Hell Right	1971		3.00	6.00
		Here on Earth/Ball of Confusion (That's What the World Is Today)				
❏ 7114		What It Is/California Soul	1972		3.00	6.00
❏ 7117		Papa Was a Rollin' Stone/Friendship Train	1972		3.00	6.00

Number	Title (A Side/B Side)	Year	VG	VG+	NM
❑ 7122	With a Little Help from My Friends/Girl You're Alright	1972		3.00	6.00
❑ 7124	Mama I Got a Brand New Thing (Don't Say No)/Gonna Keep On Tryin' Till I Win Your Love	1973		3.00	6.00
❑ 7130	Law of the Land/Just My Imagination (Running Away with Me)	1973		3.00	6.00
❑ 7134	Help Yourself/What's Going On	1974		3.00	6.00
❑ 7139	I'm a Fool for You/Girl's Alright with Me	1974		3.00	6.00
❑ 7140	Big John Is My Name/L'il Red Ridin' Hood	1974		3.00	6.00
❑ 7141	Earthquake Shake/Spaced Out	1975			Unreleased
❑ 7143	UFO's/Got to Get My Hands on Some Lovin'	1975		3.00	6.00
❑ 7145	Higher Than High/Spaced Out	1975		3.00	6.00
❑ 7147	Boogie Bump Boogie/I Saw Her When You Met Her	1975		3.00	6.00

Whitfield

Number	Title	Year	VG	VG+	NM
❑ 8231	You + Me = Love/You + Me = Love (Disco Version)	1976		2.50	5.00
❑ 8295	Let's Get Down to the Disco/Loose	1977		2.50	5.00
❑ 8362	Hole in the Wall/Sunshine	1977		2.50	5.00
❑ 8783	Showtime/Misunderstood	1979		2.00	4.00
❑ 8873	I Can't Get Enough of Your Love/Misunderstood	1979		2.00	4.00

Unforgettables, The

Colpix

Number	Title	Year	VG	VG+	NM
❑ 192	It Hurts/Was It All Right	1961	5.00	10.00	20.00

Pamela

| ❑ 204 | Oh Wishing Well/Daddy Must Be a Man | 1961 | 75.00 | 150.00 | 300.00 |
| ❑ 204 | Oh Wishing Well/Daddy Must Be a Man *Blue vinyl* | 1961 | 125.00 | 250.00 | 500.00 |

Titanic

| ❑ 5012 | He'll Be Sorry/Oh There He Goes | 1963 | 10.00 | 20.00 | 40.00 |

Union Gap, The – See "Puckett, Gary, and the Union Gap"

Unique Echoes, The

Southern Sound

| ❑ 108 | Zoom/Italian Twist | 1962 | 12.50 | 25.00 | 50.00 |

Unique Teens, The

Dynamic

| ❑ 110 | Whatcha Know Now/Run Fast | 1959 | 7.50 | 15.00 | 30.00 |

Hanover

| ❑ 4510 | Jeannie/At the Ball | 1959 | 10.00 | 20.00 | 40.00 |

Ivy

| ❑ 112 | Jeannie/At the Ball | 1958 | 10.00 | 20.00 | 40.00 |

Uniques, The

(Several different groups)

Amber

| ❑ 2004 | Taboo/Ghost Riders in the Sky | 1961 | 12.50 | 25.00 | 50.00 |

Bangar

| ❑ 00609 | Baby Don't Cry/Little Angel | 196? | 3.75 | 7.50 | 15.00 |

Bliss

| ❑ 1004 | I'm So Unhappy/I'm Confessin' | 1961 | 125.00 | 250.00 | 500.00 |

Capitol

| ❑ 4949 | Loving You/Blue Skies | 1963 | | | |

Demand

| ❑ 2490 | Times Change/Alright, OK, You Win | 1964 | 12.50 | 25.00 | 50.00 |
| ❑ 2936 | Merry Christmas Darling/Rockin' Rudolph | 1963 | 12.50 | 25.00 | 50.00 |

Dot

| ❑ 16533 | Merry Christmas Darling/Times Change | 1963 | 6.25 | 12.50 | 25.00 |

End

| ❑ 1012 | Tell the Angels/Hey, Little Cupid | 1958 | 62.50 | 125.00 | 250.00 |

Flippin'

| ❑ 202 | Come Marry Me/Do You Remember | 1959 | 12.50 | 25.00 | 50.00 |

Gone

| ❑ 5113 | I'm So Unhappy/It's Got to Come | 1961 | 12.50 | 25.00 | 50.00 |
| ❑ 5113 | I'm So Unhappy/I'm Confessin' | 1961 | 50.00 | 100.00 | 200.00 |

Lucky Four

| ❑ 1024 | Silvery Moon/Chocolate Bar | 1962 | 50.00 | 100.00 | 200.00 |

Mr. Cee

| ❑ 100 | Look at Me/Bossa Nova Cha Cha | 1960 | 75.00 | 150.00 | 300.00 |

Paramount

❑ 0017	Eunice/No One But You	1970		2.50	5.00
❑ 0058	Shadow of Love/Lazy Afternoon	1970		2.50	5.00
❑ 0116	Lucille/One Night with You	1971		2.50	5.00
❑ 0172	Will You Love Me Tomorrow/I Am a Gemini	1972		2.50	5.00

Paula

❑ 219	Not Too Long Ago/Fast Way of Living	1965	2.50	5.00	10.00
❑ 222	Too Good to Be True/Never Been in Love	1965	2.00	4.00	8.00
❑ 227	Lady's Man/Bolivar	1965	2.00	4.00	8.00
❑ 231	Strange/You Ain't Tuff	1966	2.00	4.00	8.00
❑ 238	All These Things/Tell Me What to Do	1966	2.00	4.00	8.00
❑ 245	Goodbye, So Long/Run and Hide	1966	2.00	4.00	8.00

Number	Title (A Side/B Side)	Year	VG	VG+	NM
❑ 255	Please Come Home for Christmas/ Please Come Home for Christmas	1966	2.00	4.00	8.00
❑ 264	Groovin' Out/Areba	1967	2.00	4.00	8.00
❑ 275	Every Now and Then (I Cry)/Love Is a Precious Thing	1967	2.00	4.00	8.00
❑ 289	Go On and Leave/I'll Do Anything	1967	2.00	4.00	8.00
	B-side by University of Utah Chamber Choir				
❑ 299	It's All Over Now/All I Took Was Love	1968		3.00	6.00
❑ 307	It Hurts Me to Remember/ I Sure Feel More (Like I Do Then I Did When I Got Here)	1968		3.00	6.00
❑ 313	How Lucky Can One Man Be/ You Don't Miss Your Water	1968		3.00	6.00
❑ 320	Sha-La Love/You Know (That I Love You)	1970		2.50	5.00
❑ 324	My Babe/Toys Are Made for Children	1970		2.50	5.00
❑ 332	All These Things/You Know That I Love You	1970		2.50	5.00

Peacock

❑ 1677	Right Now/Somewhere	1957	6.25	12.50	25.00
❑ 1695	Mysterious/Picture of My Baby	1960	6.25	12.50	25.00

Pride

❑ 1018	I'm So Unhappy/It's Got to Come	1960	25.00	50.00	100.00

Roulette

❑ 4528	Send Him to Me/This Little Boy of Mine	1963	5.00	10.00	20.00

Tee Kay

❑ 112	One Million Miles Away/All at Once	1962	10.00	20.00	40.00

United Southern

❑ 104	Renegade/Malaguena	1961	75.00	15.00	30.00

Unit Four Plus Two

London

❑ 1009	I Was Only Playing Games/I Won't Let You Down	1966	3.00	6.00	12.00
❑ 9732	Sorrow and Pain/Woman from Liberia	1965	3.00	6.00	12.00
❑ 9751	Concrete and Clay/Wild Is the Wind	1965	4.00	8.00	16.00
❑ 9751	Concrete and Clay/When I Fall in Love	1965	3.00	6.00	12.00
❑ 9790	Stop Wasting Your Time/Hark	1965	3.00	6.00	12.00

United States Double Quartet

(The Tokens and The Happenings)

B.T. Puppy

❑ 524	Life Is Groovy/Split	1966	2.50	5.00	10.00
❑ 547	Walking Along-Happy Wanderer/When I Lock My Door	1968	2.50	5.00	10.00
❑ 551	Do Re Mi/When I Lock My Door	1969	2.50	5.00	10.00

Universals, The

Ascot

❑ 2124	Dear Ruth/Gotta Little Girl	1963	15.00	30.00	60.00

Cora-Lee

❑ 501	The Picture/He's So Right	1958	10.00	20.00	40.00

Festival

❑ 1601	Dreaming/Love Bound	1961	15.00	30.00	60.00
	No subtitle on A-side				
❑ 25001	(I'll Just Have to Go On) Dreaming/Love Bound	1961	6.25	12.50	25.00

Mark-X

❑ 7004	Teenage Love/Again	1957	37.50	75.00	150.00

Modern

❑ 1057	New Lease on Life/Without Friends	1968	2.50	5.00	10.00

Shepherd

❑ 2200	A Love Only You Can Give/I'm in Love	1962	12.50	25.00	50.00

Southern

❑ 102	Dear Ruth/Prayer of Love	1963	12.50	25.00	50.00

Unknown, The

Autograph

❑ 206	I Have Returned/Keep Talking, Baby	1960	10.00	20.00	40.00

Unknowns, The

Marlin

❑ 16008	Tighter/Young Enough to Cry	1966	6.25	12.50	25.00

Parrot

❑ 307	Melody for an Unknown Girl/Keith's Song	1966	6.25	12.50	25.00

Shield

❑ 7101	One More Chance/You and Me	196?	6.25	12.50	25.00

X-Tra

❑ 102	One More Chance/You and Me	1957	150.00	300.00	600.00

Unrelated Segments, The

Hanna-Barbera

❑ 514	It's Unfair/Story of My Life	1967	5.00	10.00	20.00

Liberty

❑ 55992	It's Gonna Rain/Where You Gonna Go	1967	6.25	12.50	25.00
❑ 56052	Cry, Cry, Cry/It's Not Fair	1968	10.00	20.00	40.00

Number	Title (A Side/B Side)	Year	VG	VG+	NM

Untouchables, The
(More than one group)
Alan K
| ❏ 6901 | Little Mary/Funny What a Little Kiss Can Do | 1962 | 50.00 | 100.00 | 200.00 |

Dot
| ❏ 16306 | Blues in the Night/Bondaru | 1962 | 3.75 | 7.50 | 15.00 |

Liberty
| ❏ 55335 | You're on Top/Lovely Dee | 1961 | 5.00 | 10.00 | 20.00 |
| ❏ 55423 | Papa/Medicine Man | 1962 | 5.00 | 10.00 | 20.00 |

Madison
❏ 128	Poor Boy Need a Preacher/New Fad	1960	6.25	12.50	25.00
❏ 134	Goodnight Sweetheart Goodnight/Vickie Lee	1960	6.25	12.50	25.00
❏ 139	Sixty Minute Man/Everybody's Laughin'	1960	6.25	12.50	25.00
❏ 147	Do Your Best/Raisin' Cain	1961	6.25	12.50	25.00

Nau Voo
| ❏ 809 | Blue Chip Bounce (Part 1)/Blue Chip Bounce (Part 2) | 1960 | 3.75 | 7.50 | 15.00 |

Wasp
| ❏ 105 | Don't Go, I'm Beggin'/Baby, Let's Wait | 1967 | 6.25 | 12.50 | 25.00 |

Upfronts, The
Lummtone
❏ 103	It Took Time/Betty Lou and the Lions	1960	12.50	25.00	50.00
❏ 104	Too Far to Turn Around/Married Jive	1960	10.00	20.00	40.00
❏ 106	Why You Kiss Me/Little Girl	1961	12.50	25.00	50.00
❏ 107	Send Me Someone to Love Who Will Love Me/Baby For Your Love *Black label*	1961	7.50	15.00	30.00
❏ 107	Send Me Someone to Love Who Will Love Me/Baby For Your Love *White label*	1961	12.50	25.00	50.00
❏ 108	It Took Time/Baby For Your Love	1962	6.25	12.50	25.00
❏ 114	Do the Beetle/Most of the Pretty Girls	1964	15.00	30.00	60.00

Upsetters, The
(More than one group)
ABC
| ❏ 11081 | Tossin' and Turnin'/Always in the Wrong Place at the Wrong Time | 1968 | 2.50 | 5.00 | 10.00 |
| ❏ 11120 | Don't Be Cruel/Down Home | 1968 | 2.50 | 5.00 | 10.00 |

Autumn
| ❏ 4 | Autumn's Here/Draggin' the Main | 1964 | 6.25 | 12.50 | 25.00 |

Falcon
| ❏ 1010 | The Upsetter/The Strip | 1958 | 5.00 | 10.00 | 20.00 |

Fire
| ❏ 1029 | Jaywalking/Steppin' Out | 1960 | 5.00 | 10.00 | 20.00 |

Gee
| ❏ 1055 | The Blues/Rollin' On | 1960 | 5.00 | 10.00 | 20.00 |

Little Star
| ❏ 123 | Yes, It's Me/Every Night About This Time
With Little Richard | 1962 | 12.50 | 25.00 | 50.00 |

Uptones, The
Lute
❏ 6225	No More/I'll Be There *Black label*	1962	7.50	15.00	30.00
❏ 6225	No More/I'll Be There *Multicolor label*	1962	5.00	10.00	20.00
❏ 6229	Be Mine/Dreamin'	1962	10.00	20.00	40.00

Magnum
| ❏ 714 | Dreaming/Wear My Ring | 1963 | 5.00 | 10.00 | 20.00 |

Watts
| ❏ 1080 | Dreaming/Wear My Ring | 1963 | 7.50 | 15.00 | 30.00 |

Uriah Heep
Chrysalis
| ❏ 2274 | Come Back to Me/Love or Nothing | 1978 | | 2.00 | 4.00 |

Mercury
❏ 73103	Gypsy/Real Turned On	1970	2.00	4.00	8.00
❏ 73145	Come Away Melinda/Wake Up	1970	2.00	4.00	8.00
❏ 73154	I Wanna Be Free/What Should Be Done	1971	2.00	4.00	8.00
❏ 73174	High Priestess/(B-side unknown)	1970	2.50	5.00	10.00
❏ 73243	Look at Yourself/Love Machine	1971	2.00	4.00	8.00
❏ 73271	Why/The Wizard	1971	2.00	4.00	8.00
❏ 73307	Easy Livin'/All My Life	1972	2.00	4.00	8.00
❏ 73349	Sweet Lorraine/Blind Eye	1972		3.00	6.00
❏ 73406	Tears in My Eyes/July Morning	1973		3.00	6.00

Warner Bros.
| ❏ 7738 | Stealin'/Sunshine | 1973 | | 2.50 | 5.00 |
| ❏ 7836 | Something or Nothing/What Can I Do | 1974 | | | *Unreleased?* |

Number	Title (A Side/B Side)	Year	VG	VG+	NM
❑ 8013	Something or Nothing/What Can I Do	1974		2.50	5.00
❑ 8132	Prima Dance/Stealin'	1975		2.50	5.00
❑ 8581	Masquerade/Free Me	1978		2.50	5.00

US3
Blue Note
❑ S7-17707	Cantaloop (Flip Fantasia)/It's Like That	1994			3.00
❑ S7-17967	Tukka Yoot's Riddim/I Go to Work	1994			3.00

USA For Africa
Columbia
❑ US7-04839	We Are the World/Grace	1985		2.00	4.00
	B-side by Quincy Jones				
❑ US7-04839 PS	We Are the World/Grace	1985		2.00	4.00

Usher, Gary
Capitol
❑ 5128	The Beetle/Jody	1964	12.50	25.00	50.00
❑ 5193	Sacramento/That's the Way I Feel	1964	20.00	40.00	80.00
	Produced by Brian Wilson				
❑ 5403	It's a Lie/Jody	1965	12.50	25.00	50.00
Dot
| ❑ 16518 | Three Surfer Boys/Milky Way | 1963 | 100.00 | 200.00 | 400.00 |
Lan-Cet
| ❑ 144 | Tomorrow/Lies | 1961 | 15.00 | 30.00 | 60.00 |
Titan
| ❑ 1716 | Driven Insane/You're the Girl | 1961 | 37.50 | 75.00 | 150.00 |

Utmosts, The
Pan-Or
❑ 1123	I Need You/Big Man	1962	30.00	60.00	120.00

Utopia
(Also see "Rundgren, Todd")
Bearsville
❑ 0317	Sunburst Finish/Communion with the Sun	1977		2.00	4.00
❑ 0321	Love Is the Answer/Marriage of Heaven and Hell	1977		2.00	4.00
❑ 29947	Junk Rock/Lysistrata	1982		2.50	5.00
❑ 49180	Set Me Free/Umbrella Man	1980		2.50	5.00
❑ 49247	Love Alone/Very Last Time	1980		2.00	4.00
❑ 49545	Second Nature/You Make Me Crazy	1980		2.00	4.00
❑ 49579	Always Late/I Just Want to Touch You	1980		2.00	4.00
❑ 50062	One World/Special Interest	1982		2.50	5.00
Network
| ❑ 69830 | Hammer in My Heart/
I'm Looking at You But I'm Talking to Myself | 1983 | | 2.00 | 4.00 |
| ❑ 69859 | Feet Don't Fail Me Now/There Goes My Inspiration | 1982 | | 2.00 | 4.00 |
Passport
❑ 7923	Cry Baby/Winston Smith Takes It on the Jaw	1984		2.00	4.00
❑ 7923 PS	Cry Baby/Winston Smith Takes It on the Jaw	1984		2.50	5.00
❑ 7927	Stand for Something/Mated	1985		2.00	4.00

Utopians, The
Imperial
❑ 5861	Dutch Treat/Ain't No Such Thing	1962	7.50	15.00	30.00
❑ 5876	Along My Lonely Way/Hurry to Your Date	1962	100.00	200.00	400.00
❑ 5921	Let Love Come Later/Opera vs. the Blues	1963	6.25	12.50	25.00

V

V-Eights, The
ABC-Paramount
❑ 10201	Papa's Yellow Tie/My Heart	1961	5.00	10.00	20.00
Most
| ❑ 711/3 | Pretty Girl/Please Come Back | 1959 | 25.00 | 50.00 | 100.00 |
Vibro
| ❑ 4005 | Papa's Yellow Tie/My Heart | 1960 | 7.50 | 15.00 | 30.00 |
| ❑ 4007 | Let's Take a Chance/Hot Water | 1961 | 7.50 | 15.00 | 30.00 |

Vagrants, The
Atco
❑ 6473	Respect/I Love You Yes I Do	1967	2.50	5.00	10.00
❑ 6513	Beside the Sea/Sunny Summer Rain	1967	2.50	5.00	10.00
❑ 6552	And When It's Over/I Don't Need Your Lovin'	1968	2.50	5.00	10.00
Southern Sound
| ❑ 204 | Oh, Those Eyes/You're Too Young | 1966 | 6.25 | 12.50 | 25.00 |
Vanguard
| ❑ 35038 | I Can't Make a Friend/Young Blues | 1966 | 3.75 | 7.50 | 15.00 |
| ❑ 35042 | Final Hour/Your Hasty Heart | 1966 | 5.00 | 10.00 | 20.00 |

Number		Title (A Side/B Side)	Year	VG	VG+	NM

Val-Aires, The
(Later known as the Vogues)
Coral

| ❏ 62177 | | Laurie My Love/Which One Will It Be | 1960 | 20.00 | 40.00 | 80.00 |

Willette

| ❏ 114 | | Laurie My Love/Which One Will It Be | 1959 | 100.00 | 200.00 | 400.00 |

Val-Chords, The
Game Time

❏ 104		Candy Store Love/You're Laughing at Me	1957	50.00	100.00	200.00
		With no sword logo				
❏ 104		Candy Store Love/You're Laughing at Me	1957	10.00	20.00	40.00
		With sword logo				

Val-Tones, The
DeLuxe

| ❏ 6084 | | Tender Darling/Siam Sam | 1955 | 37.50 | 75.00 | 150.00 |

Valadiers, The
Gordy

| ❏ 7003 | | While I'm Away/Because I Love Her | 1962 | 15.00 | 30.00 | 60.00 |
| ❏ 7013 | | I Found a Girl/You'll Be Sorry Someday | 1963 | 15.00 | 30.00 | 60.00 |

Miracle

❏ 6		Greetings/Take a Chance	1961	20.00	40.00	80.00
		With no subtitle on A-side and 2:23 version of B-side				
❏ 6		Greeting (This Is Uncle Sam)/Take a Chance	1961	12.50	25.00	50.00
		With subtitle on A-side and 2:15 version of B-side				

Valaquons, The
Laguna

| ❏ 102 | | Teardrops/Madeleine | 1964 | 50.00 | 100.00 | 200.00 |

Rayco

| ❏ 516 | | Jolly Green Giant/Diddy Bop | 1965 | 7.50 | 15.00 | 30.00 |

Tangerine

| ❏ 951 | | I Wanna Woman/Window Shopping on Girl's Avenue | 1965 | 6.25 | 12.50 | 25.00 |

Valens, Ritchie
Del-Fi

❏ 4106		Come On, Let's Go/Framed	1958	12.50	25.00	50.00
❏ 4110		Donna/La Bamba	1958	6.25	12.50	25.00
		Light blue label				
❏ 4110		Donna/La Bamba	1958	7.50	15.00	30.00
		Green label				
❏ 4110		Donna/La Bamba	1958	7.50	15.00	30.00
		Blue/black label with circles				
❏ 4111		Fast Freight/Big Baby Blues	1959	10.00	20.00	40.00
		As "Arvee Allens"				
❏ 4114		That's My Little Susie/In a Turkish Town	1959	7.50	15.00	30.00
❏ 4114	PS	That's My Little Susie/In a Turkish Town	1959	25.00	50.00	100.00
❏ 4117		Little Girl/We Belong Together	1959	7.50	15.00	30.00
❏ 4117	PS	Little Girl/We Belong Together	1959	25.00	50.00	100.00
❏ 4128		Stay Beside Me/Big Baby Blues	1959	6.25	12.50	25.00
❏ 4133		The Paddiwack Song/Cry, Cry, Cry	1960	6.25	12.50	25.00

Valentine, Penny
Liberty

| ❏ 55774 | | I Want to Kiss Ringo Goodbye/ Show Me the Way to Love You | 1964 | 7.50 | 15.00 | 30.00 |

Valentines, The
Bethlehem

| ❏ 3055 | | I'll Forget You/Yes, You Made It That Way | 1962 | 6.25 | 12.50 | 25.00 |

Iona

| ❏ 1003 | | The Sock/Sixteen Senoritas | 196? | 3.75 | 7.50 | 15.00 |

King

❏ 5338		Please Don't Leave, Please Don't Go/That's It Man	1960	5.00	10.00	20.00
❏ 5433		That's How I Feel/Hey Ruby	1960	5.00	10.00	20.00
❏ 5830		I Have Two Loves/Camping Out	1963	3.75	7.50	15.00

Ludix

| ❏ 102 | | Johnny One Heart/Mama I Have Come Home | 1962 | 5.00 | 10.00 | 20.00 |

Old Town

| ❏ 1009 | | Tonight Kathleen/Summer Love | 1954 | 200.00 | 400.00 | 800.00 |

Rama

❏ 171		Lily Maebelle/Falling for You	1955	37.50	75.00	150.00
		Blue label				
❏ 171		Lily Maebelle/Falling for You	1955	10.00	20.00	40.00
		Red label				
❏ 181		I Love You Darling/Hand Me Down Love	1955	37.50	75.00	150.00
❏ 186		Christmas Prayer/K-I-S-S Me	1955	100.00	200.00	400.00
		Blue label				
❏ 186		Christmas Prayer/K-I-S-S Me	1955	10.00	20.00	40.00
		Red label				

Number	Title (A Side/B Side)	Year	VG	VG+	NM
❏ 196	Why/The Woo Woo Train	1956	25.00	50.00	100.00
	Blue label				
❏ 196	Why/The Woo Woo Train	1956	10.00	20.00	40.00
	Red label				
❏ 201	Twenty Minutes (Before the Hour)/I'll Never Let You Go	1956	25.00	50.00	100.00
❏ 208	Nature's Creation/My Story of Love	1956	25.00	50.00	100.00
❏ 228	Don't Say Goodnight/I Cried Oh, Oh	1957	37.50	75.00	150.00

Sound Stage 7
❏ 2646	I'm Alright Now/Gotta Get Yourself Together	1969	3.75	7.50	15.00
❏ 2663	If You Love Me/Breakaway	1970	3.00	6.00	12.00

United Artists
❏ 764	Alone in the Night/Mink Coats and Sneakers	1964	3.75	7.50	15.00

Valentino and the Lovers

Donna
❏ 1345	One Teardrop Too Late/I'm Gonna Love	1961	10.00	20.00	40.00

Valentino, Sal
(Of the Beau Brummels)

Falco
❏ 306	Lisa Marie/I Wanna Twist	1962	10.00	20.00	40.00

Warner Bros.
❏ 7268	An Added Attraction (Come and See Me)/Alligator Man	1969	2.50	5.00	10.00
❏ 7289	Friends and Lovers/Alligator Man	1969	2.50	5.00	10.00
❏ 7368	Silkie/Going for Rochelle	1970	2.50	5.00	10.00

Valery, Dana

ABC
❏ 11138	The Lamplighter's Psalm/Didn't I	1968	3.00	6.00	12.00
❏ 11161	A Girl Without Love/Happy Birthday to Me	1968	3.00	6.00	12.00
❏ 11214	Surround Yourself with Sorrow/Breakfast in Bed	1969	3.00	6.00	12.00

Columbia
❏ 44004	Having You Around/ You Don't Know Where Your Interest Lies	1967	6.25	12.50	25.00
	With Paul Simon				

Liberty
❏ 56156	Clinging Vine/Get In Line Girl	1970	2.00	4.00	8.00
❏ 56209	Point of No Return/Put Your Hand in the Hand	1970	2.00	4.00	8.00

Phantom
❏ HB-10566	Will You Love Me Tomorrow/I Never Had It So Good	1975		2.50	5.00

Scotti Bros.
❏ 509	I Don't Want to Be Lonely/Rainbow Connection	1979		2.00	4.00
❏ 612	I Gave You My Love/Roses and Rainbows	1980		2.00	4.00

Valets, The

Jon
❏ 4025	I Need Someone/When I Met You	1958	25.00	50.00	100.00
❏ 4219	Sherry/You and You Alone	1959	7.50	15.00	30.00

Vulcan
❏ 135	Sherry/You and You Alone	1959	50.00	100.00	200.00

Valiants, The

Dot
❏ 16884	I'll Return to You/Don't Make the Same Mistake	1966	3.00	6.00	12.00

Fairlane
❏ 21007	Blue Jeans and a Pony Tail/See Saw	1961	3.75	7.50	15.00

Imperial
❏ 5843	Love Comes in Many Ways/ You Are Sweeter Than Wine	1962	3.75	7.50	15.00
❏ 5915	Living in Paradise/I'm in a World of My Own	1963	3.75	7.50	15.00

Joy
❏ 235	Let Me Go Lover/Let Me Ride	1960	3.75	7.50	15.00

KC
❏ 108	Frankie's Angel/Are You Ready	1962	3.75	7.50	15.00

Keen
❏ 34004	This Is the Nite/Good Golly Miss Molly	1957	7.50	15.00	30.00
❏ 34007	Lover Lover/Walkin' Girl	1958	7.50	15.00	30.00
❏ 4008	Temptation of My Heart/Freida, Freida	1958	10.00	20.00	40.00
❏ 4026	Please Wait My Love/Freida, Freida	1958	12.50	25.00	50.00
❏ 82120	This Is the Nite/Walkin' Girl	1960	5.00	10.00	20.00

Roulette
❏ 4510	Johnny Lonely/Eternal Triangle	1963	5.00	10.00	20.00

Shar-Dee
❏ 703	Dear Cindy/Surprise	1959	15.00	30.00	60.00
	No mention of London distribution on label				
❏ 703	Dear Cindy/Surprise	1959	7.50	15.00	30.00
	With London distribution credit on label				

Speck
❏ 1001	Wedding Bells/Velma	1958	200.00	400.00	800.00

Number		Title (A Side/B Side)	Year	VG	VG+	NM

Valli
Scepter
| ☐ 1233 | | Hurry Home to Me (Soldier Boy)/Jimmy's in a Hurry | 1962 | 3.75 | 7.50 | 15.00 |

With the Shirelles backing up

Valli, Frankie
(Of the Four Seasons)
Atlantic
| ☐ 89720 | | American Pop/Why | 1983 | | 2.00 | 4.00 |

With Manhattan Transfer

Capitol
| ☐ B-5115 | | Can't Say No to You/You Make It Beautiful | 1982 | | 2.00 | 4.00 |

With Cheryl Ladd

| ☐ B-5115 | PS | Can't Say No to You/You Make It Beautiful | 1982 | | 2.50 | 5.00 |

Cindy
| ☐ 3012 | | Come Si Bella/Real (This Is Real) | 1958 | 50.00 | 100.00 | 200.00 |

As "Franke Valli and the Romans"

Corona
| ☐ 1234 | | My Mother's Eyes/The Laugh's on Me | 1953 | 500.00 | 1,000 | 1,500 |

As "Frank Valley"

Decca
| ☐ 30994 | | It May Be Wrong/Please Take a Chance | 1959 | 50.00 | 100.00 | 200.00 |

As "Frankie Vally"

MCA
| ☐ 41253 | | Doctor Dance/Where Did We Go Wrong | 1980 | | 2.50 | 5.00 |

With Chris Forde

Mercury
| ☐ 70381 | | Forgive and Forget/Somebody Else Took Her Home | 1954 | 75.00 | 150.00 | 300.00 |

As "Frankie Valley"; maroon label

| ☐ 70381 | | Forgive and Forget/Somebody Else Took Her Home | 1954 | 50.00 | 100.00 | 200.00 |

As "Frankie Valley"; black label

Motown
| ☐ 1251 | | You've Got Your Troubles/Listen to Yesterday | 1973 | 3.00 | 6.00 | 12.00 |
| ☐ 1279 | | The Scalawag Song (And I Will Love You)/Listen to Yesterday | 1973 | 3.00 | 6.00 | 12.00 |

Mowest
| ☐ 5025 | | The Night (mono/stereo) | 1972 | 2.50 | 5.00 | 10.00 |

Evidently, stock copies do not exist

Philips
☐ 40407		The Proud One/Ivy	1966	2.50	5.00	10.00
☐ 40407	PS	The Proud One/Ivy	1966	3.75	7.50	15.00
☐ 40446		Can't Take My Eyes Off You/The Trouble with Me	1967	2.50	5.00	10.00
☐ 40446	PS	Can't Take My Eyes Off You/The Trouble with Me	1967	3.75	7.50	15.00
☐ 40484		I Make a Fool of Myself/September Rain (Here Comes the Rain)	1967	2.50	5.00	10.00
☐ 40484	PS	I Make a Fool of Myself/September Rain (Here Comes the Rain)	1967	3.75	7.50	15.00
☐ 40510		To Give (The Reason I Live)/Watch Where You Walk	1967	2.50	5.00	10.00
☐ 40510	PS	To Give (The Reason I Live)/Watch Where You Walk	1967	3.75	7.50	15.00
☐ 40622		The Girl I'll Never Know (Angels Never Fly This Low)/A Face Without a Name	1969	2.50	5.00	10.00
☐ 40622	PS	The Girl I'll Never Know (Angels Never Fly This Low)/A Face Without a Name	1969	3.75	7.50	15.00
☐ 40661		You've Got Your Troubles/A Dream of Kings	1970	3.00	6.00	12.00
☐ 40680		Circles in the Sand/My Mother's Eyes	1970	2.50	5.00	10.00

Private Stock
☐ 45,003		My Eyes Adored You/Watch Where You Walk	1974		2.50	5.00
☐ 45,021		Swearin' to God/Why	1975		2.50	5.00
☐ 45,043		Our Day Will Come/You Can Bet	1975		2.50	5.00
☐ 45,074		Fallen Angel/Carrie (I Would Marry You)	1976		2.50	5.00
☐ 45,098		We're All Alone/You to Me Are Everything	1976		2.50	5.00
☐ 45,109		Boomerang/Look at the World, It's Changing	1976		2.50	5.00
☐ 45,140		Easily/What Good Am I Without You	1977		2.50	5.00
☐ 45,154		Second Thoughts/So She Says	1977		2.50	5.00
☐ 45,169		I Need You/I'm Gonna Love You	1977		2.50	5.00
☐ 45,180		I Could Have Loved You/Rainstorm	1978		2.50	5.00

RSO
| ☐ 897 | | Grease/Grease (Instrumental) | 1978 | | 3.00 | 6.00 |

Smash
| ☐ 1995 | | The Sun Ain't Gonna Shine (Anymore)/This Is Goodbye | 1965 | 2.50 | 5.00 | 10.00 |
| ☐ 2015 | | (You're Gonna) Hurt Yourself/Night Hawk | 1965 | 3.75 | 7.50 | 15.00 |

B-side by the Valli Boys

| ☐ 2037 | | You're Ready Now/Cry for Me | 1966 | 2.50 | 5.00 | 10.00 |

Warner Bros.
| ☐ 8670 | | No Love at All/Save Me, Save Me | 1978 | | 2.50 | 5.00 |
| ☐ 8734 | | Fancy Dancer/Needing You | 1979 | | 2.50 | 5.00 |

Valor, Tony
Musictone
| ☐ 1119 | | There's a Story in My Heart/So Tenderly | 1963 | 37.50 | 75.00 | 150.00 |

Number	Title (A Side/B Side)	Year	VG	VG+	NM
Valquins, The					
Gaity					
❑ 161/2	My Dear/Falling Star	1959	200.00	400.00	800.00
❑ 161/2	My Dear/Falling Star	1959	500.00	1,000	1,500
	Red vinyl				
Valrays, The					
Parkway					
❑ 880	Get A Board/Pee Wee	1963	7.50	15.00	30.00
❑ 904	Yo Me Pregunto/Tonky	1964	5.00	10.00	20.00
Vals, The					
Ascot					
❑ 2163	Too Late/I'm Stepping Out with My Memories	1964	7.50	15.00	30.00
Unique Laboratories					
❑ (no #)	The Song of a Lover/Compensation Blues	1962	250.00	500.00	1,000
Valtones, The					
Gee					
❑ 1004	You Belong to My Heart/Have You Ever Met an Angel	1956	75.00	150.00	300.00
Valumes, The – See "Volumes, The"					
Vampires, The					
Carroll					
❑ 104	Why Didn't I Listen to Mother?/ Did Anybody Lose a Tear	1962	37.50	75.00	150.00
Van Dyke, Earl, and the Soul Brothers					
Renaissance					
❑ 5000	September Song/(B-side unknown)	196?	18.75	37.50	75.00
Soul					
❑ 35006	Soul Stomp/Hot 'N' Tot	1964	5.00	10.00	20.00
❑ 35009	All for You/Too Many Fish in the Sea	1965	200.00	400.00	800.00
❑ 35014	I Can't Help Myself/ How Sweet It Is To Be Loved By You	1965	5.00	10.00	20.00
❑ 35018	The Flick (Part 1)/The Flick (Part 2)	1966	5.00	10.00	20.00
❑ 35028	6 x 6/There Is No Greater Love	1967	5.00	10.00	20.00
	By Earl Van Dyke and the Motown Brass				
❑ 35059	Runaway Child, Running Wild/ Gonna Give Her All the Love I've Got	1969	5.00	10.00	20.00
Van Dyke, Leroy					
(See the Goldmine Country Western Price Guide for more listings)					
Sun					
❑ 1146	Save Me a Seat by the Fire/Rev. Edmond Giles	1979		2.00	4.00
Van Dykes, The					
(More than one group)					
Atlantic					
❑ 2161	King of Fools/Stupidity	1962	3.75	7.50	15.00
Co-Op					
❑ 515	Rich Girl/Miracle After Miracle	1967	5.00	10.00	20.00
❑ 516	Rock-a-Bye Girl/I'll Be By	1967	5.00	10.00	20.00
Decca					
❑ 30654	The Fixer/Run Betty, Run	1958	10.00	20.00	40.00
❑ 30762	Come On Baby/Lambie Baby	1958	10.00	20.00	40.00
❑ 31036	Better Come Back to Me/I Don't Know What to Do	1959	15.00	30.00	60.00
DeLuxe					
❑ 6193	The Bells Are Ringing/The Meaning of Love	1960	5.00	10.00	20.00
Donna					
❑ 1333	Gift of Love/Guardian Angel	1961	10.00	20.00	40.00
Felsted					
❑ 8565	Once Upon a Dream/Dame Tu Corazon	1959	6.25	12.50	25.00
Green Sea					
❑ 101	Rich Girl/Again and Again	1965	10.00	20.00	40.00
❑ 105	Rock-a-Bye Girl/I'll Be By	1966	12.50	25.00	50.00
❑ 108	Miracle After Miracle/How Can I Forget Her	1966	10.00	20.00	40.00
Hue					
❑ 6501	No Man Is an Island/I Won't Hold It Against You	1965	7.50	15.00	30.00
King					
❑ 5158	The Bells Are Ringing/The Meaning of Love	1958	12.50	25.00	50.00
Mala					
❑ 520	No Man Is an Island/I Won't Hold It Against You	1965	3.00	6.00	12.00
❑ 530	I've Got to Go On Without You/ What Will I Do If I Lose You	1966	3.00	6.00	12.00
❑ 539	Never Let Me Go/I've Got to Find a Love	1966	3.00	6.00	12.00
❑ 549	You Need Confidence/You're Shakin' Me Up	1966	3.00	6.00	12.00
❑ 566	A Sunday Kind of Love/I'm So Happy	1967	5.00	10.00	20.00
❑ 584	Tears of Joy/Save My Love for a Rainy Day	1967	10.00	20.00	40.00
Spring					
❑ 1113	Gift of Love/Guardian Angel	1961	25.00	50.00	100.00

Number		Title (A Side/B Side)	Year	VG	VG+	NM

Van Eaten, Lon and Derrek
A&M
All A&M records as "Lon and Derrek"

☐ 1643		Wildfire/Music Lover	1974		2.50	5.00
☐ 1662		Who Do You Outdo/All You're Hungry For Is Love	1975		2.50	5.00
☐ 1696		The Harder You Pull... The Tighter It Gets/ Dancing in the Dark	1975		2.50	5.00
☐ 1845		Loving You/Baby It's You	1976		2.00	4.00

Apple

| ☐ 1845 | | Sweet Music/Song of Songs | 1972 | 2.00 | 4.00 | 8.00 |
| ☐ 1845 | PS | Sweet Music/Song of Songs | 1972 | 2.50 | 5.00 | 10.00 |

Van Halen
(Also see "Roth, David Lee")
Warner Bros.

☐ 8515		You Really Got Me/Atomic Punk	1978		2.50	5.00
☐ 8556		Runnin' with the Devil/Eruption	1978		2.00	4.00
☐ 8556	PS	Runnin' with the Devil/Eruption	1978	7.50	15.00	30.00
☐ 8631		Jamie's Cryin'/I'm the One	1978		2.00	4.00
☐ 8707		Feel Your Love Tonight/Ain't Talkin' 'Bout Love	1978		2.00	4.00
☐ 8823		Dance the Night Away/Outta Love Again	1979		2.00	4.00
☐ 8823	PS	Dance the Night Away/Outta Love Again	1979	3.00	6.00	12.00
☐ 17810		Not Enough/Amsterdam	1995			3.00
☐ 17909		Can't Stop Lovin' You/Crossing Over	1995			3.00
☐ 18592		Judgment Day/Dreams	1993			3.00
☐ 19151		Top of the World/Poundcake	1992			3.00
☐ 27565		Feels So Good/Sucker in a 3-Piece	1989			3.00
☐ 27746		Finish What Ya Started/Sucker in a 3-Piece	1988			3.00
☐ 27746	PS	Finish What Ya Started/Sucker in a 3-Piece	1988			3.00
☐ 27827		When It's Love/Cabo Wabo	1988			3.00
☐ 27827	PS	When It's Love/Cabo Wabo	1988			3.00
☐ 27891		Black and Blue/Apolitical Blues	1988			3.00
☐ 27891	PS	Black and Blue/Apolitical Blues	1988			3.00
☐ 28505		Best of Both Worlds/Best of Both Worlds (Live)	1986			3.00
☐ 28626		Love Walks In/Summer Nights	1986			3.00
☐ 28626	PS	Love Walks In/Summer Nights	1986			3.00
☐ 28702		Dreams/Inside	1986			3.00
☐ 28740		Why Can't This Be Love/Get Up	1986			3.00
☐ 28740	PS	Why Can't This Be Love/Get Up	1986			3.00
☐ 29199		Hot for Teacher/Little Dreamer	1984			3.00
☐ 29199	PS	Hot for Teacher/Little Dreamer	1984	2.00	4.00	8.00
		Special plastic sleeve with inserts				
☐ 29199	PS	Hot for Teacher/Little Dreamer	1984		2.00	4.00
		Regular picture sleeve				
☐ 29307		I'll Wait/Girl Gone Bad	1984			3.00
☐ 29307	PS	I'll Wait/Girl Gone Bad	1984			3.00
☐ 29384		Jump/House of Pain	1984			3.00
☐ 29384	PS	Jump/House of Pain	1984			3.00
☐ 29929		Secrets/Big Bad Bill	1982		2.00	4.00
☐ 29986		Dancing in the Street/Full Bug	1982		2.00	4.00
☐ 49035		Beautiful Girls/D.O.A.	1979		2.00	4.00
☐ 49501		And the Cradle Will Rock.../Could This Be Magic	1980		2.00	4.00
☐ 49751		So This Is Love/Read About It Later	1981		2.00	4.00
☐ 50003		Pretty Woman/Happy Trails	1982		2.50	5.00
☐ 50003	PS	Pretty Woman/Happy Trails	1982		2.50	5.00
		Original copies of both record and sleeve have no subtitles				
☐ 50003		(Oh) Pretty Woman/Happy Trails	1982		2.00	4.00
☐ 50003	PS	(Oh) Pretty Woman/Happy Trails	1982		2.00	4.00

Vanguards, The
(More than one group)
Derby

| ☐ 854 | | Don't Let It Happen Again/So Live | 1954 | 100.00 | 200.00 | 400.00 |

Dot

| ☐ 15791 | | Baby Doll/My Friend Mary Ann | 1958 | 6.25 | 12.50 | 25.00 |

Ivy

☐ 103		Moonlight/I'm Movin'	1958	25.00	50.00	100.00
		With mention of "Billy Butler's Orchestra"				
☐ 103		Moonlight/I'm Movin'	1958	7.50	15.00	30.00
		No mention of "Billy Butler's Orchestra"				

Lamp

☐ 652		It's To Late for Love/(B-side unknown)	1970	3.00	6.00	12.00
		Yes, the label misspelled the A-side				
☐ 653		Girl Go Away/(B-side unknown)	1970	3.00	6.00	12.00

Warner Bros.

| ☐ 5800 | | Girl/A Stranger in Your Town | 1966 | 3.00 | 6.00 | 12.00 |

Whiz

| ☐ 612 | | Somebody Please/(B-side unknown) | 1969 | 2.50 | 5.00 | 10.00 |

Vanilla Fudge
Atco

| ☐ 6495 | | You Keep Me Hangin' On/Take Me for a Little While | 1967 | 3.00 | 6.00 | 12.00 |
| ☐ 6554 | | The Look of Love/Where Is My Mind | 1968 | 2.00 | 4.00 | 8.00 |

Number		Title (A Side/B Side)	Year	VG	VG+	NM
6590		You Keep Me Hangin' On/	1968	2.50	5.00	10.00
		Come by Day, Come by Night				
6616		Take Me for a Little While/Thoughts	1968	2.00	4.00	8.00
6632		Season of the Witch (Part 1)/	1968	2.00	4.00	8.00
		Season of the Witch (Part 2)				
6655		Good Good Lovin'/Shot Gun	1969	2.00	4.00	8.00
6679		People/Some Velvet Morning	1969	2.00	4.00	8.00
6703		Need Love/I Can't Make It Alone	1969	2.00	4.00	8.00
6728		Windmills of Your Mind/Lord in the Country	1970		3.00	6.00
99729		Mystery/The Stranger	1984		2.00	4.00

Vanity Fare
Brent
7067		Peter Who (Peter Pan)/Salt Water Babies	1967	2.00	4.00	8.00

DJM
70024		Where Did All the Good Times Go/Stand	1971		2.50	5.00
70029		Big Parade/Nowhere to Go	1971		2.50	5.00

Page One
21,007		I Live for the Sun/On the Other Side of Life	1969		3.00	6.00
21,020		Highway of Dreams/Waiting for the Nightfall	1969		3.00	6.00
21,027		Early in the Morning/You Made Me Love You	1969	2.00	4.00	8.00
21,029		Hitchin' a Ride/Man Child	1970	2.00	4.00	8.00
21,033		(I Remember) Summer Morning/	1970		3.00	6.00
		Megowd (Something Tells Me)				
21,036		Where Did All the Good Times Go/Stand	1970		3.50	7.00

20th Century
2012		Rock and Roll Is Back/Making for the Sun	1973		2.50	5.00
2036		Down Home/Take It, Shake It, Break My Heart	1973		2.50	5.00

Vaqueros, The
Audition
6102		Desert Wind/Echo	1964	12.50	25.00	50.00

Bangar
00647		Birds and Bees/80-Foot Wave	1964	10.00	20.00	40.00

Vare, Ronnie, and the Inspirations
Dell
5203		Let's Rock, Little Girl/Love Is Just for Two	1959	12.50	25.00	50.00

Varner, Don
Quincy
8002		Tear Stained Face/Meet Me in the Church	1969	62.50	125.00	250.00

Veep
1296		Tear Stained Face/Meet Me in the Church	1969	50.00	100.00	200.00

Vaughan Brothers, The
(Stevie Ray and Jimmie Vaughan)
CBS Associated
73576		Tick Tock/Brothers	1990		2.00	4.00
73673		Good Texan/Mama Said	1991		2.00	4.00

Vaughan, Stevie Ray
(Also see "Cobras, The")
Epic
04031		Pride and Joy/Rude Mood	1983		2.50	5.00
05731		Change It/Look at Little Sister	1985		2.00	4.00
06601		Superstition/Pride and Joy	1987		2.00	4.00
06696		Willie the Wimp/Superstition	1987		2.00	4.00
07340		Pipeline/Love Struck Baby	1987		2.00	4.00
	With Dick Dale					
69025		Double Crossfire/Travis Walk	1989		2.00	4.00
73212		This House Is Rockin'/Tightrope	1990		2.00	4.00
74142		The Sky Is Crying/Chitlins Con Carne	1991		2.00	4.00
74198		Empty Arms/Wham	1992		2.00	4.00
78205		Taxman/The House Is Rockin'	1995			3.00

Vaughn, Yvonne
Dot
16751		Lonely Little Girl/When You Gonna Tell Her About Me	1965	37.50	75.00	150.00

Vee, Bobby
Cognito
010		Tremble On/Always Be Each Other's Best Friend	1981		2.50	5.00

Liberty
55208		Suzie Baby/Flyin' High	1959	6.25	12.50	25.00
55234		What Do You Want/My Love Loves Me	1959	5.00	10.00	20.00
55251		Laurie/One Last Kiss	1960	3.75	7.50	15.00
55270		Devil or Angel/Since I Met You Baby	1960	5.00	10.00	20.00
55270	PS	Devil or Angel/Since I Met You Baby	1960	7.50	15.00	30.00
55287		Rubber Ball/Everyday	1960	5.00	10.00	20.00
55287	PS	Rubber Ball/Everyday	1960	7.50	15.00	30.00
55296		More Than I Can Say/Stayin' In	1961	3.75	7.50	15.00
55296	PS	More Than I Can Say/Stayin' In	1961	7.50	15.00	30.00
55325		How Many Tears/Baby Face	1961	3.75	7.50	15.00
55331	PS	How Many Tears/Baby Face	1961	7.50	15.00	30.00

Number		Title (A Side/B Side)	Year	VG	VG+	NM
❏ 55354		Take Good Care of My Baby/Bashful Bob	1961	3.75	7.50	15.00
❏ 55388		Run to Him/Walkin' with My Angel	1961	5.00	10.00	20.00
❏ 55419		Please Don't Ask About Barbara/I Can't Say Goodbye	1962	3.75	7.50	15.00
❏ 55419	PS	Please Don't Ask About Barbara/I Can't Say Goodbye	1962	6.25	12.50	25.00
❏ 55451		Sharing You/In My Baby's Eyes	1962	3.75	7.50	15.00
❏ 55479		Punish Her/Someday (When I'm Gone from You)	1962	5.00	10.00	20.00
❏ 55479	PS	Punish Her/Someday (When I'm Gone from You)	1962	7.50	15.00	30.00
		With the Crickets				
❏ 55517		A Not-So-Merry Christmas/Christmas Vacation	1962	7.50	15.00	30.00
		This record's existence has been questioned				
❏ 55521		The Night Has a Thousand Eyes/ Anonymous Phone Call	1962	3.00	6.00	12.00
❏ 55530		Charms/Bobby Tomorrow	1963	3.00	6.00	12.00
❏ 55530	PS	Charms/Bobby Tomorrow	1963	5.00	10.00	20.00
❏ 55581		Be True to Yourself/A Letter from Betty	1963	2.50	5.00	10.00
❏ 55581	PS	Be True to Yourself/A Letter from Betty	1963	5.00	10.00	20.00
❏ 55636		Yesterday and You (Armen's Theme)/ Never Love a Robin	1963	2.50	5.00	10.00
❏ 55654		Stranger in Your Arms/1963	1963	2.50	5.00	10.00
❏ 55654	PS	Stranger in Your Arms/1963	1963	5.00	10.00	20.00
❏ 55670		I'll Make You Mine/She's Sorry	1964	2.50	5.00	10.00
❏ 55700		Hickory, Dick and Doc/I Wish You Were Mine Again	1964	2.50	5.00	10.00
❏ 55726		Where Is She/How to Make a Farewell	1964	2.50	5.00	10.00
❏ 55751		(There'll Come a Day When) Ev'ry Little Bit Hurts/ Pretend You Don't See Her	1964	2.50	5.00	10.00
❏ 55761		Cross My Heart/This Is the End	1965	2.00	4.00	8.00
❏ 55790		Keep On Trying/You Won't Forget Me	1965	2.00	4.00	8.00
❏ 55828		Run with the Devil/Take a Look Around Us	1965	2.00	4.00	8.00
❏ 55843		The Story of My Life/High Coin	1965	2.00	4.00	8.00
❏ 55854		A Girl I Used to Know/Gone	1965	2.00	4.00	8.00
❏ 55877		Look at Me Girl/Butterfly	1966	2.00	4.00	8.00
❏ 55877		Look at Me Girl/Save a Love	1966	2.00	4.00	8.00
❏ 55921		Before You Go/Here Today	1966	2.00	4.00	8.00
❏ 55964		Come Back When You Grow Up/Swahili Serenade	1967	2.00	4.00	8.00
❏ 55964		Come Back When You Grow Up/ That's All There Is to That	1967	2.00	4.00	8.00
❏ 56009		Beautiful People/I May Be Gone	1967	2.00	4.00	8.00
❏ 56014		Maybe Just Today/You're a Big Girl Now	1968		3.00	6.00
❏ 56014	PS	Maybe Just Today/You're a Big Girl Now	1968	3.00	6.00	12.00
❏ 56033		Medley: My Girl-Hey Girl/Just Keep It Up	1968		3.00	6.00
❏ 56057		Do What You Gotta Do/Thank You	1968		3.00	6.00
❏ 56080		I'm Into Lookin' for Someone to Love Me/Thank You	1968		3.00	6.00
❏ 56096		Jenny Come to Me/Santa Cruz	1969		3.00	6.00
❏ 56124		Let's Call It a Day Girl/I'm Gonna Make It Up to You	1969		3.00	6.00
❏ 56149		Electric Trains and You/In and Out of Love	1969		3.00	6.00
❏ 56178		The Woman in My Life/No Obligations	1970		3.00	6.00
❏ 56208		Sweet Sweetheart/Rock and Roll Music and You	1970		3.00	6.00

Shadybrook

Number		Title (A Side/B Side)	Year	VG	VG+	NM
❏ 45013		Saying Goodbye/(I'm) Lovin' You	1975		2.50	5.00
❏ 45026		You're Never Gonna Find Someone Like Me	1976		2.50	5.00
		(Long Version)/You're Never Gonna Find Someone Like Me (Short Version)				
❏ 45030		It's Good to Be Here/If I Needed You	1976		2.50	5.00

Soma

Number		Title (A Side/B Side)	Year	VG	VG+	NM
❏ 1110		Suzie Baby/Flyin' High	1959	15.00	30.00	60.00

United Artists

0020 through 0025 are "Silver Spotlight Series" reissues

Number		Title (A Side/B Side)	Year	VG	VG+	NM
❏ 0020		Devil or Angel/Stayin' In	1973		2.00	4.00
❏ 0021		Rubber Ball/Punish Her	1973		2.00	4.00
❏ 0022		Take Good Care of My Baby/ Please Don't Ask About Barbara	1973		2.00	4.00
❏ 0023		Run to Him/Sharing You	1973		2.00	4.00
❏ 0024		The Night Has a Thousand Eyes/Charms	1973		2.00	4.00
❏ 0025		Come Back When You Grow Up/Beautiful People	1973		2.00	4.00
❏ XW199		Take Good Care of My Baby/Every Opportunity	1973		2.50	5.00
		As "Robert Thomas Velline"				
❏ XW1142		Well All Right/Something Has Come Between Us	1978		2.50	5.00
❏ 50755		Signs/Something to Say	1971		2.50	5.00
❏ 50875		Sweet Sweetheart/Electric Trains and You	1972		2.50	5.00

Veers, Russ

Trend

Number		Title (A Side/B Side)	Year	VG	VG+	NM
❏ 30010		Warm As Toast/The Answer	1958	125.00	250.00	500.00

Vega, Suzanne

A&M

Number		Title (A Side/B Side)	Year	VG	VG+	NM
❏ 2759		Neighborhood Girls/Marlene on the Wall	1985			3.00
❏ 2834		Left of Center/Small Blue Thing	1986			3.00
❏ 2937		Luka/Night Vision	1987			3.00
❏ 2937	PS	Luka/Night Vision	1987		2.00	4.00
❏ 2960		Solitude Standing/Tom's Diner	1987			3.00
❏ 2960	PS	Solitude Standing/Tom's Diner	1987		2.00	4.00
❏ 2988		Gypsy/Left of Center	1987			3.00
❏ 2988	PS	Gypsy/Left of Center	1987	12.50	25.00	50.00

Number	Title (A Side/B Side)	Year	VG	VG+	NM

Vel-Tones, The
(Probably more than one group; some may be listed as "Veltones")
Coy

❑ 101	Cal's Tune/Playboy	1959	1,000	1,500	2,000

Goldwax

| ❑ 301 | Darling/I Do | 1966 | 3.75 | 7.50 | 15.00 |

Jin

| ❑ 107 | Lover Blues/Take a Ride | 1959 | 10.00 | 20.00 | 40.00 |
| ❑ 115 | Jailbird/I'm Yours Now | 1959 | 10.00 | 20.00 | 40.00 |

Kapp

| ❑ 268 | Cal's Tune/Playboy | 1959 | 25.00 | 50.00 | 100.00 |

Lost-Nite

| ❑ 103 | Now/I Need You So | 1961 | 6.25 | 12.50 | 25.00 |

Mercury

| ❑ 71526 | Fool in Love/Someday | 1959 | 7.50 | 15.00 | 30.00 |

Satellite

| ❑ 100 | Fool in Love/Someday | 1959 | 25.00 | 50.00 | 100.00 |

Vel

| ❑ 9178 | Broken Heart/Please Say You'll Be True | 1960 | 125.00 | 250.00 | 500.00 |

Wedge

| ❑ 1013 | My Dear/I Want to Know | 1964 | 50.00 | 100.00 | 200.00 |

Zara

| ❑ 901 | Now/I Need You So | 1960 | 20.00 | 40.00 | 80.00 |

Vells, The
(Later recorded as [Martha and] the Vandellas)
Mel-O-Dy

| ❑ 103 | There He Is At My Door/
You'll Never Cherish a Love So True | 1962 | 25.00 | 50.00 | 100.00 |

Velons, The
BJM

| ❑ 6568 | Summer Love/Why Don't You Write | 1965 | 5.00 | 10.00 | 20.00 |
| ❑ 6569 | That's What Love Can Do/That's All Right | 1965 | 5.00 | 10.00 | 20.00 |

Blast

| ❑ 216 | Shelly/From the Chapel | 1964 | 25.00 | 50.00 | 100.00 |

Velours, The
(More than one group)
Cub

| ❑ 9014 | Crazy Love/I'll Never Smile Again | 1958 | 6.25 | 12.50 | 25.00 |
| ❑ 9029 | Blue Velvet/Tired of Your Rock and Rollin' | 1959 | 6.25 | 12.50 | 25.00 |

End

| ❑ 1090 | Lover Come Back/The Lonely One | 1961 | 5.00 | 10.00 | 20.00 |

Goldisc

| ❑ 3012 | Daddy Warbucks/Sweet Sixteen | 1960 | 6.25 | 12.50 | 25.00 |

Gone

| ❑ 5092 | Can I Come Over Tonight/Where There's a Way | 1960 | 5.00 | 10.00 | 20.00 |

MGM

| ❑ 13780 | Don't Pity Me/I'm Gonna Change | 1967 | 7.50 | 15.00 | 30.00 |

Onyx

❑ 501	My Love Come Back/Honey Drop	1956	50.00	100.00	200.00
❑ 508	What You Do to Me/Romeo	1957	75.00	150.00	300.00
❑ 512	Can I Come Over Tonight/ Where There's a Will (There's a Way)	1957	37.50	75.00	150.00
❑ 515	This Could Be the Night/Hands Across the Table	1957	30.00	60.00	120.00
❑ 520	Remember/Can I Walk You Home	1958	15.00	30.00	60.00

Orbit

| ❑ 9001 | Remember/Can I Walk You Home | 1958 | 12.50 | 25.00 | 50.00 |

Rona

| ❑ 010 | Woman for Me/(B-side unknown) | 1966 | 6.25 | 12.50 | 25.00 |

Studo

| ❑ 9902 | I Promise/Little Sweetheart | 1959 | 12.50 | 25.00 | 50.00 |

Velvatones, The
Meteor

| ❑ 5042 | Real Gone Baby/Feeling Kinda Lonely | 1957 | 50.00 | 100.00 | 200.00 |

Nu Kat

| ❑ 110 | Impossible/I'm Leaving Home | 1959 | 12.50 | 25.00 | 50.00 |

Velvelettes, The
I.P.G.

| ❑ 1002 | There He Goes/That's the Reason Why | 1963 | 25.00 | 50.00 | 100.00 |

Soul

| ❑ 35025 | These Things Will Keep Me Loving You/
Since You've Been Loving Me | 1966 | 5.00 | 10.00 | 20.00 |

V.I.P.

| ❑ 25007 | Needle in a Haystack/Should I Tell Them | 1964 | 6.25 | 12.50 | 25.00 |
| ❑ 25013 | He Was Really Sayin' Somethin'/Throw a Farewell Kiss | 1965 | 6.25 | 12.50 | 25.00 |

Number		Title (A Side/B Side)	Year	VG	VG+	NM
❑ 25017		I'm the Exception to the Rule/Lonely, Lonely Girl Am I	1965	5.00	10.00	20.00
❑ 25021		A Bird in the Hand (Is Worth Two in the Bush)/ (B-side unknown)	1965	200.00	400.00	800.00
❑ 25030		A Bird in the Hand (Is Worth Two in the Bush)/ Since You've Been Loving Me	1965	5.00	10.00	20.00
❑ 25034		These Things Will Keep Me Loving You/ Since You've Been Loving Me	1966	7.50	15.00	30.00

Velvet Keys, The
King
| ❑ 5090 | | My Baby's Gone/Let's Stay After School | 1957 | 20.00 | 40.00 | 80.00 |
| ❑ 5109 | | Don't Take My Picture, Take Me/ The Truth About Youth | 1958 | 20.00 | 40.00 | 80.00 |

Velvet Underground, The
(Also see "Reed, Lou")
Cotillion
| ❑ 44107 | | Who Loves the Sun/Oh, Sweet Nothin' | 1971 | 75.00 | 150.00 | 300.00 |
| ❑ 44107 | DJ | Who Loves the Sun (mono/stereo) | 1971 | 25.00 | 50.00 | 100.00 |
MGM
❑ 14057		What Goes On/Jesus	1969	75.00	150.00	300.00
		Existence of a stock copy of this record has been questioned.				
❑ 14057	DJ	What Goes On/Jesus	1969	50.00	100.00	200.00
Verve
❑ 10427		All Tomorrow's Parties/I'll Be Your Mirror	1966	100.00	200.00	400.00
❑ 10427	DJ	All Tomorrow's Parties/I'll Be Your Mirror	1966	75.00	150.00	300.00
❑ 10427	PS	All Tomorrow's Parties/I'll Be Your Mirror	1966	2,500	3,750	5,000
❑ 10466		Femme Fatale/Sunday Morning	1966	75.00	150.00	300.00
❑ 10466	DJ	Femme Fatale/Sunday Morning	1966	50.00	100.00	200.00
❑ 10560		White Light/White Heat//Here She Comes Now	1967	75.00	150.00	300.00
❑ 10560	DJ	White Light/White Heat//I Heard Her Call My Name	1967	75.00	150.00	300.00

Velveteens, The
Golden Artists
| ❑ 614 | | I Feel Sorry for You Baby/Ching Bam Bah | 1965 | 2.50 | 5.00 | 10.00 |
Laurie
| ❑ 3126 | | I Thank You/Meant to Be | 1962 | 3.75 | 7.50 | 15.00 |
Stark
❑ 101		Please Holy Father/Baby Baby	1961	12.50	25.00	50.00
		Original title of A-side				
❑ 101		The Teen Prayer/Baby Baby	1961	7.50	15.00	30.00
		New A-side title				
❑ 101		Teen Prayer/Baby Baby	1961	5.00	10.00	20.00
		Slightly altered A-side title				
❑ 105		I Thank You/Meant to Be	1962	6.25	12.50	25.00

Velveteers, The
Spitfire
| ❑ 15 | | Tell Me You're Mine/Boo Wacka Boo | 1956 | 2,000 | 3,000 | 4,000 |

Velvetiers, The
Ric
| ❑ 958 | | Oh Baby/Feelin' Right Saturday Night | 1958 | 75.00 | 150.00 | 300.00 |

Velvetones, The
(More than one group)
Aladdin
❑ 3372		Glory of Love/I Love Her So	1957	50.00	100.00	200.00
❑ 3391		I Found My Love/Melody of Love	1957	50.00	100.00	200.00
❑ 3463		My Every Thought/Little Girl I Love You So	1960	50.00	100.00	200.00
Ascot
| ❑ 2117 | | I Want Him So Bad/Yes I Will | 1962 | 3.75 | 7.50 | 15.00 |
| ❑ 2126 | | Starry Eyed/I'm Ashamed | 1963 | 3.75 | 7.50 | 15.00 |
D
| ❑ 1049 | | Come Back/Penalty of Love | 1959 | 25.00 | 50.00 | 100.00 |
| ❑ 1072 | | Worried Over You/Space Man | 1959 | 20.00 | 40.00 | 80.00 |
Deb
| ❑ 1008 | | Stars of Wonder/Who Took My Girl | 1959 | 20.00 | 40.00 | 80.00 |
GARP
❑ 102		Mister X/(B-side unknown)	1965	15.00	30.00	60.00
❑ 102		Mister X/(B-side unknown)	1965	30.00	60.00	120.00
		Red vinyl				
Glenn
| ❑ 309 | | Doheny Run/Static | 1965 | 7.50 | 15.00 | 30.00 |
Imperial
| ❑ 5878 | | The Glory of Love/I Love Her So | 1962 | 6.25 | 12.50 | 25.00 |
| ❑ 66020 | | The Glory of Love/I Found My Love | 1964 | 3.75 | 7.50 | 15.00 |
Velvet
| ❑ 101 | | Doheny Run/Static | 1965 | 18.75 | 37.50 | 75.00 |
Verve
| ❑ 10514 | | What Can the Matter Be/Hairy Lumpty Bump | 1967 | 3.00 | 6.00 | 12.00 |

Number	Title (A Side/B Side)	Year	VG	VG+	NM

Velvets, The
(More than one group)

Fury
❑ 1012	I-I-I (Love You So-So-So)/Dance Honey Dance	1958	10.00	20.00	40.00

Monument
❑ 435	That Lucky Old Sun/Time and Again	1961	6.25	12.50	25.00
❑ 441	Tonight (Could be the Night)/Spring Fever	1961	7.50	15.00	30.00
❑ 448	Lana/Laugh	1961	6.25	12.50	25.00
❑ 458	The Love Express/Don't Let Him Take My Baby	1962	6.25	12.50	25.00
❑ 464	Let the Good Times Roll/	1962	6.25	12.50	25.00
	The Lights Go On, The Lights Go Off				
❑ 810	Crying in the Chapel/Dawn	1963	5.00	10.00	20.00
❑ 836	Nightmare/Here Comes That Song Again	1964	5.00	10.00	20.00
❑ 861	If/Let the Fool Kiss You	1964	5.00	10.00	20.00
❑ 961	Baby the Magic Is Gone/Let the Fool Kiss You	1966	3.75	7.50	15.00

Pilgrim
❑ 706	I/At Last	1956	12.50	25.00	50.00
❑ 710	Tell Her/I Cried	1956	12.50	25.00	50.00

Plaid
❑ 101	Everybody Knows/Hand Jivin' Baby	1959	6.25	12.50	25.00

Red Robin
❑ 120	They Tried/She's Gotta Grin	1953	50.00	100.00	200.00
❑ 122	I/At Last	1953	37.50	75.00	150.00
❑ 127	Tell Her/I Cried	1954	37.50	75.00	150.00

20th Fox
❑ 165	Happy Days Are Here Again/If I Could Be with You	1959	5.00	10.00	20.00

Ventures, The

Blue Horizon
❑ 100	The Real McCoy/Cookies and Coke	1960	150.00	300.00	600.00
❑ 101	Walk-Don't Run/Home	1960	300.00	600.00	1,200
❑ 102	Hold Me, Thrill Me, Kiss Me/No Next Time	1960	50.00	100.00	200.00
	As "Scott Douglas and the Venture Quintet"				

Dolton
❑ 25		Walk -- Don't Run/Home	1960	6.25	12.50	25.00
❑ 25X		Walk -- Don't Run/The McCoy	1960	5.00	10.00	20.00
❑ 28		Perfidia/No Trespassing	1960	5.00	10.00	20.00
❑ 28	PS	Perfidia/No Trespassing	1960	12.50	25.00	50.00
❑ 32		Ram-Bunk-Shush/Lonely Heart	1961	5.00	10.00	20.00
❑ 41		Lullaby of the Leaves/Ginchy	1961	5.00	10.00	20.00
❑ 44		(Theme from) Silver City/Bluer Than Blue	1961	5.00	10.00	20.00
❑ 47		Blue Moon/Lady of Spain	1961	5.00	10.00	20.00
❑ 50		Yellow Jacket/Genesis	1962	5.00	10.00	20.00
❑ 55		Instant Mashed/My Bonnie	1962	5.00	10.00	20.00
❑ 60		Lolita Ya-Ya/Lucille	1962	5.00	10.00	20.00
❑ 67		The 2,000 Pound Bee (Part 1)/	1962	5.00	10.00	20.00
		The 2,000 Pound Bee (Part 2)				
❑ 68		El Cumbanchero/Skip To M'Limbo	1963	3.75	7.50	15.00
❑ 78		The Ninth Wave/Damaged Goods	1963	3.75	7.50	15.00
❑ 85		The Savage/The Chase	1963	3.75	7.50	15.00
❑ 91		Journey to the Stars/Walkin' with Pluto	1964	3.75	7.50	15.00
❑ 94		Fugitive/Scratchin'	1964	3.75	7.50	15.00
❑ 96		Walk... Don't Run '64/The Cruel Sea	1964	3.75	7.50	15.00
❑ 96	PS	Walk... Don't Run '64/The Cruel Sea	1964	7.50	15.00	30.00
❑ 300		Slaughter on Tenth Avenue/Rap City	1964		6.00	12.00
❑ 300	PS	Slaughter on Tenth Avenue/Rap City	1964	6.25	12.50	25.00
❑ 303		Diamond Head/Lonely Girl	1965	3.00	6.00	12.00
❑ 306		Pedal Pusher/The Swingin' Creeper	1965	3.00	6.00	12.00
❑ 308		Ten Seconds to Heaven/Bird Rockers	1965	3.00	6.00	12.00
❑ 311		La Bomba/Gemini	1965	3.00	6.00	12.00
❑ 312		Sleigh Ride/Snow Flakes	1965	3.75	7.50	15.00
❑ 316		Secret Agent Man/00-711	1966	3.00	6.00	12.00
❑ 320		Blue Star/Comin' Home Baby	1966	3.00	6.00	12.00
❑ 320	PS	Blue Star/Comin' Home Baby	1966	6.25	12.50	25.00
❑ 321		Arabesque/Ginza Lights	1966	3.00	6.00	12.00
❑ 323		Green Hornet Theme/Fuzzy and Wild	1966	3.00	6.00	12.00
❑ 323	PS	Green Hornet Theme/Fuzzy and Wild	1966	7.50	15.00	30.00
❑ 325		Penetration/Wild Thing	1966	3.00	6.00	12.00
❑ 325	PS	Penetration/Wild Thing	1966	6.25	12.50	25.00
❑ 327		Theme from "The Wild Angels"/Kickstand	1967	3.00	6.00	12.00

EMI
❑ S7-18212	Jingle Bell Rock/Jingle Bells	1994		2.00	4.00
	Red vinyl				

Liberty
❑ 55967	Strawberry Fields Forever/Endless Dream	1967	2.00	4.00	8.00
❑ 55977	Theme from "Endless Summer"/	1967	2.00	4.00	8.00
	Strawberry Fields Forever				
❑ 56007	On the Road/Mirrors and Shadows	1967	2.00	4.00	8.00
❑ 56019	Flights of Fantasy/Vibrations	1968		3.00	6.00
❑ 56044	Walk Don't Run-Land of 1000 Dances/	1968		3.00	6.00
	Too Young to Know My Mind				
❑ 56068	Hawaii Five-O/Soul Breeze	1968	2.00	4.00	8.00
❑ 56115	Theme from A Summer Place/A Summer Love	1969		3.00	6.00

Number	Title (A Side/B Side)	Year	VG	VG+	NM
☐ 56153	Expo '70/Swan Lake	1970		3.00	6.00
☐ 56169	The Wanderer/The Mercenary	1970		3.00	6.00
☐ 56189	Storefront Lawyers (Theme)/Kern County Line	1970		3.00	6.00

Tridex

☐ 501	Surfin' and Spyin'/Rumble at Newport	1981		2.50	5.00

A-side with Charlotte Caffey and Jane Wiedlin of the Go-Go's, who did their own version on an early single

☐ 501 PS	Surfin' and Spyin'/Rumble at Newport	1981		2.50	5.00

United Artists

☐ 0050	Walk--Don't Run/Ram-Bunk-Shush	1973		2.00	4.00
☐ 0051	Perfidia/Telstar	1973		2.00	4.00
☐ 0052	Hawaii Five-O/Walk--Don't Run '64	1973		2.00	4.00

0050, 0051 and 0052 are "Silver Spotlight Series" reissues

☐ XW207	Last Tango in Paris/Prima Vera	1973		3.00	6.00
☐ XW277	Skylab/The Little People	1973		3.00	6.00
☐ XW333	Also Sprach Zarathustra (2001)/The Cisco Kid	1973		3.00	6.00
☐ XW369	The Young and the Restless/Eloise	1973		3.00	6.00
☐ XW392	The Young and the Restless/Eloise	1974		3.00	6.00
☐ XW578	Theme from "Airport 1975"/The Man with the Golden Gun	1974		3.00	6.00
☐ XW687	Superstar Revue (Part 1)/Superstar Revue (Part 2)	1975		3.00	6.00
☐ XW784	Moonlight Serenade (Part 1)/Moonlight Serenade (Part 2)	1976	2.00	4.00	8.00

As "The New Ventures"

☐ XW942	Theme from "Charlie's Angels"/Theme from "Starsky and Hutch"	1977	2.00	4.00	8.00
☐ XW1100	Walk Don't Run '77/Amanda's Theme	1977		3.00	6.00
☐ XW1161	Wipe Out/Nadia's Theme	1978		2.00	4.00

Reissue

☐ 50800	Indian Sun/Squaw Man	1971		3.00	6.00
☐ 50851	Theme from "Shaft"/Tight Fit	1971		3.00	6.00
☐ 50872	Joy/Cherries Jubilee	1972		3.00	6.00
☐ 50903	Beethoven's Sonata in G Minor/Peter and the Wolf	1972		3.00	6.00
☐ 50925	Honky Tonk (Part 1)/Honky Tonk (Part 2)	1972		3.00	6.00
☐ 50989	Last Night/Ram-Bunk-Shush	1972		3.00	6.00

Vernon Girls, The
Challenge

☐ 59234	We Love the Beatles/Hey Lover Boy	1964	7.50	15.00	30.00
☐ 59261	Only You Can Do It/Stupid Little Girl	1964	2.50	5.00	10.00

Veronica
(Ronnie Spector of The Ronettes)
Phil Spector

☐ 1	So Young/Larry L	1964	50.00	100.00	200.00
☐ 2	Why Can't They Let Us Fall in Love/Chubby Danny D	1964	150.00	300.00	600.00

Note slightly different A-side title

☐ 2	Why Don't They Let Us Fall in Love/Chubby Danny D	1964	50.00	100.00	200.00

Versatiles, The
(More than one group)
Atlantic

☐ 2004	Passing By/Crying	1958	10.00	20.00	40.00

Peacock

☐ 1910	White Cliffs of Dover/Just Words	1963	7.50	15.00	30.00

Ramco

☐ 3717	Blue Feeling/Just Pretending	1962	50.00	100.00	200.00

Ro-Cal

☐ 1002	I'll Whisper in Your Ear/Lundee Dundee	1960	25.00	50.00	100.00

Sea Crest

☐ 6001	Lonely Boy/Moon Dawg	1964	6.25	12.50	25.00

Versatones, The
(More than one group)
All Star

☐ 501	Tight Skirt and Sweater/Bila	1958	10.00	20.00	40.00

Atlantic

☐ 2211	Tight Skirt and Sweater/Bila	1963	5.00	10.00	20.00

Fenway

☐ 7001	Tight Skirt and Sweater/Bila	1960	6.25	12.50	25.00

RCA Victor

☐ 47-6917	Wait for Me/De Obeah Man	1957	3.75	7.50	15.00
☐ 47-6976	Lovely Teenage Girl/Bikini Baby	1957	3.75	7.50	15.00

Vertues Four, The
Sea Seven

☐ 22	Angel Baby/Uphill, Downhill	1963	10.00	20.00	40.00

Vespers, The
Swan

☐ 4156	Cupid/When I Walk with My Angel	1963	10.00	20.00	40.00

Number	Title (A Side/B Side)	Year	VG	VG+	NM

Vettes, The
MGM

❏ 13186	Little Ford Ragtop/	1963	12.50	25.00	50.00
	Happy Hodaddy (With Ragtop Caddy)				
	With Bruce Johnston				

Vibes, The
ABC-Paramount

❏ 9810	Darling/Come Back Baby	1957	12.50	25.00	50.00

After Hours

❏ 105	Stop Torturing Me/Stop Jibing, Baby	1954	250.00	500.00	1,000

Allied

❏ 10006	What's Her Name/You Are	1958	15.00	30.00	60.00
❏ 10007	Misunderstood/Let the Old Folks Talk	1959	10.00	20.00	40.00

Chariot

❏ 105	Stop Torturing Me/Stop Jibing, Baby	1954	250.00	500.00	1,000

Rayna

❏ 103	You Got Me Crying/A Killer Came to Town	196?	6.25	12.50	25.00

Vibra-Sonics, The
Ideal

❏ 94874	Thunder Storm/Drag Race	1964	12.50	25.00	50.00

Vibranaires, The
After Hours

❏ 103	Doll Face/Ooh,I Feel So Good	1954	250.00	500.00	1,000

Chariot

❏ 103	Doll Face/Ooh,I Feel So Good	1954	250.00	500.00	1,000

Vibrations, The
Atlantic

❏ 2204	Between Hello and Goodbye/	1963	3.00	6.00	12.00
	Lonesome Little Lonely Girl				
❏ 2221	My Girl Sloopy/Daddy Woo-Woo	1964	3.00	6.00	12.00

Bet

❏ 1	So Blue/Love Me Like You Should	1960	25.00	50.00	100.00

Checker

❏ 954	So Blue/Love Me Like You Should	1960	7.50	15.00	30.00
❏ 961	Feel So Bad/Cave Man	1960	5.00	10.00	20.00
❏ 967	Doing the Slop/So Little Time	1961	5.00	10.00	20.00
❏ 969	The Watusi/Wallflower	1961	5.00	10.00	20.00
❏ 974	The Continental/The Junkeroo	1961	5.00	10.00	20.00
❏ 982	Don't Say Goodbye/Stranded in the Jungle	1961	5.00	10.00	20.00
❏ 987	All My Love Belongs to You/Stop Right Now	1961	10.00	20.00	40.00
❏ 990	Let's Pony Again/What Made You Change Your Mind	1961	5.00	10.00	20.00
❏ 1002	Over the Rainbow/Oh, Cindy	1962	3.75	7.50	15.00
❏ 1011	The New Hully Gully/Anytime	1962	3.75	7.50	15.00
❏ 1022	Hamburgers on a Bun/If He Don't	1962	3.75	7.50	15.00
❏ 1038	Since I Fell for You/May the Best Man Win	1963	3.75	7.50	15.00
❏ 1061	Dancing Danny/(Instrumental)	1963	3.75	7.50	15.00

Chess

❏ 2151	Shake It Up/Make It Last	1974		3.00	6.00

Epic

❏ 10418	I Took an Overdose/Because You're Mine	1968	5.00	10.00	20.00

Mandala

❏ 2511	Ain't No Greens in Harlem/Wind-Up Toy	1972		3.00	6.00
❏ 2514	Man Overboard/(B-side unknown)	1972		3.00	6.00

Neptune

❏ 19	Expressway to Your Heart/Who's Gonna Help Me Now	1969	2.00	4.00	8.00
❏ 21	Smoke Signals/Who's Gonna Help Me Now	1970	2.00	4.00	8.00
❏ 28	Right On Brothers, Right On/Surprise Party for Baby	1970	2.00	4.00	8.00

Okeh

❏ 7205	Sloop Dance/Watusi Time	1964	3.00	6.00	12.00
❏ 7212	Hello Happiness/Keep On Keeping On	1965	3.00	6.00	12.00
❏ 7220	End Up Crying/Ain't Love That Way	1965	3.00	6.00	12.00
❏ 7228	Talkin' 'Bout Love/If You Only Knew	1965	3.00	6.00	12.00
❏ 7230	Misty/Finding Out the Hard Way	1965	3.00	6.00	12.00
❏ 7238	Gina/The Story of a Starry Night	1966			*Unreleased*
❏ 7241	Canadian Sunset/The Story of a Starry Night	1966	2.50	5.00	10.00
❏ 7249	Forgive and Forget/Gonna Get Along Without You Now	1966	2.50	5.00	10.00
❏ 7257	And I Love Her/Soul a-Go-Go	1966	2.50	5.00	10.00
❏ 7276	Pick Me/You Better Beware	1967	2.50	5.00	10.00
❏ 7297	Together/Come To Yourself	1967	2.50	5.00	10.00
❏ 7311	Love in Them There Hills/Remember the Rain	1968	2.50	5.00	10.00

Vic, Paul and Bruce – See "Canadian Beadles, The"

Viceroys, The
(Several different groups; some may be listed as "Vice-Roys")
Aladdin

❏ 3273	Please, Baby, Please/I'm Yours As Long As I Live	1955	100.00	200.00	400.00

Number	Title (A Side/B Side)	Year	VG	VG+	NM
Bethlehem					
❏ 3045	Seagrams/Moasin'	1962	6.25	12.50	25.00
	Original A-side title				
❏ 3045	Sea Green/Moasin'	1962	5.00	10.00	20.00
❏ 3070	The Fox/Buzz Bomb	1963	6.25	12.50	25.00
	Original A-side title				
❏ 3070	Joshin'/Buzz Bomb	1963	5.00	10.00	20.00
❏ 3088	Not Too Much Twist/Tears on My Pillow	1965	5.00	10.00	20.00
Bolo					
❏ 736	Granny's Pad/Blues Bouquet	1962	3.00	6.00	12.00
❏ 739	Goin' Back to Granny's/Get Set	1963	3.00	6.00	12.00
❏ 743	Granny's Medley/Dartell Stomp	1964	2.50	5.00	10.00
❏ 749	Tiger Shark/Please, Please, Please	1964	2.50	5.00	10.00
❏ 750	Bacon Fat/Until	1965	2.50	5.00	10.00
❏ 754	That Sound/Tired of Waiting for You	1965	2.50	5.00	10.00
Dot					
❏ 16456	Granny's Pad/Blues Bouquet	1963	2.00	4.00	8.00
E'den					
❏ 9001	Don't Let Go/Down Beat Blues	1962	3.00	6.00	12.00
Imperial					
❏ 66058	Death of an Angel/Earth Angel	1964	3.00	6.00	12.00
Little Star					
❏ 107	I'm So Sorry (It's Ending with You)/Uncle Sam Needs You	1961	37.50	75.00	150.00
Original Sound					
❏ 15	Dreamy Eyes/Ball 'N' Chain	1961	10.00	20.00	40.00
Ramco					
❏ 3715	My Heart/I Need Your Love So Bad	1962	2,000	3,000	4,000
Smash					
❏ 1716	I'm So Sorry (It's Ending with You)/Uncle Sam Needs You	1961	5.00	10.00	20.00

Victorials, The
Imperial

❏ 5398	I Get That Feeling/The Prettiest Girl in the World	1956	12.50	25.00	50.00

Victorians, The
(More than one group)
Arnold

❏ 571	Move In a Little Closer/Lovin'	1963	5.00	10.00	20.00
Bang					
❏ 550	Merry-Go-Round/Wasn't the Summer Short	1967	3.75	7.50	15.00
Liberty					
❏ 55574	Climb Every Mountain/What Makes Little Girls Cry	1963	3.75	7.50	15.00
❏ 55656	The Monkey Stroll/You're Invited to a Party	1964	3.75	7.50	15.00
❏ 55693	Happy Birthday Blues/Oh What a Night for Love	1964	3.75	7.50	15.00
❏ 55728	If I Loved You/The Monkey Stroll	1964	3.75	7.50	15.00
Reprise					
❏ 0434	I Saw My Girl/Baby Toys	1965	3.75	7.50	15.00
Saxony					
❏ 103	Heartbreaking Moon/I'm Rollin'	1956	125.00	250.00	500.00
Selma					
❏ 1002	Wedding Bells/Please Say You Do	1956	75.00	150.00	300.00

Victory Five, The
Terp

❏ 101	I Never Knew/Swing Low	1958	150.00	300.00	600.00
	All copies on colored vinyl				

Vidaltones, The
Josie

❏ 900	Forever/Someone to Love	1962	10.00	20.00	40.00

Videls, The
Early

❏ 702	I Wish/Blow, Winds, Blow	1960	100.00	200.00	400.00
JDS					
❏ 5004	Mr. Lonely/I'll Forget You	1960	7.50	15.00	30.00
	Gray label				
❏ 5004	Mr. Lonely/I'll Forget You	1960	5.00	10.00	20.00
	Multicolor label				
❏ 5005	She's Not Coming Home/Now That Summer Is Here	1960	7.50	15.00	30.00
	Gray label				
❏ 5005	She's Not Coming Home/Now That Summer Is Here	1960	5.00	10.00	20.00
	Multicolor label				
Kapp					
❏ 361	Streets of Love/I'll Keep On Waiting	1960	5.00	10.00	20.00
❏ 405	A Letter from Ann/This Year's Mister New	1961	10.00	20.00	40.00
Medieval					
❏ 203	Be My Girl/A Place in Your Heart	1961	3.75	7.50	15.00

Number	Title (A Side/B Side)	Year	VG	VG+	NM

Musicnote
| ❏ 117 | We Belong Together/It's All Over | 1963 | 12.50 | 25.00 | 50.00 |

Rhody
| ❏ 2000 | Be My Girl/A Place in Your Heart | 1959 | 12.50 | 25.00 | 50.00 |

Tic Tac Toe
| ❏ 5005 | She's Not Coming Home/Now That Summer Is Here | 1962 | 12.50 | 25.00 | 50.00 |

Vigrass and Osborne
(With Gary Osborne, later a collaborator with Elton John)

Epic
| ❏ 50044 | Gypsy Woman/Haystacks | 1974 | | 2.50 | 5.00 |

Uni
❏ 55330	Forever Autumn/Men of Learning	1972		3.00	6.00
❏ 55344	Virginia/Ballerina	1972		2.50	5.00
❏ 55355	Remember Pearl Harbor/Mister Deadline	1972		2.50	5.00

Village People

Casablanca
❏ 896	San Francisco (You've Got Me)/Village People	1977		3.00	6.00
❏ 922	Macho Man/Key West	1978		2.50	5.00
❏ 945	Y.M.C.A./I'm a Cruiser	1978		2.50	5.00
❏ 973	In the Navy/Manhattan Woman	1979		2.50	5.00
	A picture sleeve is said to exist for this record, but has not been confirmed				
❏ 984	Go West/Citizens of the World	1979		2.50	5.00
❏ 2213	Sleazy/Save Me (Uptempo)	1979		2.00	4.00
❏ 2220	Ready for the 80's/Sleazy	1979		2.00	4.00
❏ 2261	Stop the Music/Milkshake	1980		2.00	4.00
❏ 2291	Magic Night/I Love You to Death	1980		2.00	4.00

RCA
| ❏ PB-12258 | 5 O'Clock in the Morning/Food Fight | 1981 | | 2.00 | 4.00 |
| ❏ PB-12331 | Jungle City/Action Man | 1981 | | 2.00 | 4.00 |

Village Voices, The – See "Four Seasons, The"

Vince and the Waikiki Rumblers

Big Ben
| ❏ 1003 | Waikiki Rumble/Pacifica | 1965 | 12.50 | 25.00 | 50.00 |

Zodiac
| ❏ 1004 | Waikiki Rumble/Pacifica | 1965 | 20.00 | 40.00 | 80.00 |

Vincent, Gene

Capitol
❏ F3450	Be-Bop-a-Lula/Woman Love	1956	12.50	25.00	50.00
	With large Capitol logo				
❏ F3450	Be-Bop-a-Lula/Woman Love	1956	7.50	15.00	30.00
	With small Capitol logo				
❏ F3530	Race with the Devil/Gonna Back Up, Baby	1956	7.50	15.00	30.00
❏ F3558	Bluejean Bop/Who Slapped John	1956	7.50	15.00	30.00
❏ F3617	Crazy Legs/Important Words	1956	10.00	20.00	40.00
❏ F3678	B-I-Bickey-Bi-Bo-Bo-Go/Five Days, Five Days	1957	10.00	20.00	40.00
❏ F3763	Lotta Lovin'/Wear My Ring	1957	7.50	15.00	30.00
❏ F3839	Dance to the Bop/I Got It	1957	7.50	15.00	30.00
❏ 3871	Be-Bop-a-Lula/Lotta Lovin'	1974	3.75	7.50	15.00
❏ F3874	Walkin' Home from School/I Gotta Baby	1958	10.00	20.00	40.00
❏ F3959	Baby Blue/True to You	1958	12.50	25.00	50.00
❏ F4010	Yes I Love You Baby/Rocky Road Blues	1958	10.00	20.00	40.00
❏ F4051	Little Lover/Git It	1958	10.00	20.00	40.00
❏ F4105	Say Mama/Be-Bop Boogie Boy	1958	12.50	25.00	50.00
❏ F4153	Over the Rainbow/Who's Pushin' Your Swing	1959	12.50	25.00	50.00
❏ F4237	The Night Is So Lonely/Right Now	1959	12.50	25.00	50.00
❏ F4237 PS	The Night Is So Lonely/Right Now	1959	500.00	1,000	1,500
❏ 4313	Wild Cat/Right Here on Earth	1959	12.50	25.00	50.00
❏ 4442	Pistol Packin' Mama/Anna Annabella	1960	10.00	20.00	40.00
❏ 4525	Mister Loneliness/If You Want My Lovin'	1961	6.25	12.50	25.00
❏ 4665	Lucy Star/Baby Don't Believe Him	1961	6.25	12.50	25.00

Challenge
❏ 59337	Bird Doggin'/Ain't That Too Much	1966	5.00	10.00	20.00
❏ 59347	Lonely Street/I've Got My Eyes on You	1966	5.00	10.00	20.00
❏ 59365	Born to Be a Rolling Stone/Pickin' Poppies	1967	5.00	10.00	20.00

Forever
| ❏ 6001 | Story of the Rockers/Pickin' Poppies | 1969 | 12.50 | 25.00 | 50.00 |

Kama Sutra
| ❏ 514 | Sunshine/Geese | 1970 | 3.00 | 6.00 | 12.00 |
| ❏ 518 | High On Life/The Day the World Turned Blue | 1971 | 3.00 | 6.00 | 12.00 |

Playground
| ❏ 100 | Story of the Rockers/Pickin' Poppies | 1968 | 50.00 | 100.00 | 200.00 |

Vinton, Bobby

ABC
❏ 12022	My Melody of Love/I'll Be Loving You	1974		2.50	5.00
	Black label				
❏ 12022	My Melody of Love/I'll Be Loving You	1974		2.00	4.00
	Multi-colored label				

Number		Title (A Side/B Side)	Year	VG	VG+	NM
❏ 12056		Beer Barrel Polka/Dick and Jane	1974		2.00	4.00
❏ 12100		Wooden Heart/Polka Pose	1975		2.00	4.00
❏ 12131		My Gypsy Love/Midnight Show	1975		2.00	4.00
❏ 12178		Moonight Serenade/Why Can't I Get Over You	1976		2.00	4.00
❏ 12186		Save Your Kisses for Me/Love Shine	1976		2.00	4.00
❏ 12229		Love Is the Reason/Nobody But Me	1976		2.00	4.00
❏ 12265		Only Love Can Break a Heart/Once More with Feeling	1977		2.00	4.00
❏ 12293		Hold Me, Thrill Me, Kiss Me/Her Name Is Love	1977		2.00	4.00
❏ 12308		All My Todays/Strike Up the Band for Love	1977		2.00	4.00

Alpine

Number		Title (A Side/B Side)	Year	VG	VG+	NM
❏ 50		First Impression/You'll Never Forget	1959	7.50	15.00	30.00
❏ 59		The Sheik/A Freshman and a Sophomore	1960	6.25	12.50	25.00

Curb

Number		Title (A Side/B Side)	Year	VG	VG+	NM
❏ 10512		The Last Rose/Sealed with a Kiss	1988			3.00
❏ 10541		Please Tell Her That I Said Hello/	1989			3.00
		Getting Used to Being Loved Again				
❏ 10560		It's Been One of Those Days/	1989			3.00
		(Now and Then There's) A Fool Such As I				

Diamond

Number		Title (A Side/B Side)	Year	VG	VG+	NM
❏ 121		I Love You the Way You Are/You're My Girl	1962	5.00	10.00	20.00
		B-side by Chuck and Johnny				

Elektra

Number		Title (A Side/B Side)	Year	VG	VG+	NM
❏ 45503		My First, My Only Love/Summerlove Sensation	1978		2.00	4.00

Epic

Number		Title (A Side/B Side)	Year	VG	VG+	NM
❏ 06537		Blue Velvet/Blue on Blue	1986		2.50	5.00
❏ 9417		Posin'/Tornado	1960	3.75	7.50	15.00
❏ 9440		Corrina, Corrina/Little Lonely One	1961	3.75	7.50	15.00
❏ 9469		Hip-Swinging, High-Stepping, Drum Majorette/	1961	3.75	7.50	15.00
		Will I Ask Ya				
■ 9509		Roses Are Red (My Love)/You and I	1962	3.00	6.00	12.00
❏ 9509	PS	Roses Are Red (My Love)/You and I	1962	3.75	7.50	15.00
		Bobby Vinton looks straight ahead, chin in hand				
❏ 9509	PS	Roses Are Red (My Love)/You and I	1962	3.75	7.50	15.00
		Bobby Vinton looks toward the lower right corner				
❏ 9532		Rain, Rain Go Away/Over and Over	1962	3.00	6.00	12.00
❏ 9532	PS	Rain, Rain Go Away/Over and Over	1962	3.75	7.50	15.00
❏ 9550		Excerpts from "Roses Are Red"	1962	3.00	6.00	12.00
❏ 9551		Excerpts from "Roses Are Red"	1962	3.00	6.00	12.00
❏ 9552		Excerpts from "Roses Are Red"	1962	3.00	6.00	12.00
❏ 9553		Excerpts from "Roses Are Red"	1962	3.00	6.00	12.00
❏ 9554		Excerpts from "Roses Are Red"	1962	3.00	6.00	12.00
❏ 9561		Trouble Is My Middle Name/Let's Kiss and Make Up	1962	2.50	5.00	10.00
❏ 9561	PS	Trouble Is My Middle Name/Let's Kiss and Make Up	1962	3.75	7.50	15.00
❏ 9577		Over the Mountain (Across the Sea)/Faded Pictures	1963	2.50	5.00	10.00
❏ 9577	PS	Over the Mountain (Across the Sea)/Faded Pictures	1963	3.75	7.50	15.00
❏ 9593		Blue on Blue/Those Little Things	1963	3.00	6.00	12.00
❏ 9593	PS	Blue on Blue/Those Little Things	1963	3.75	7.50	15.00
■ 9614		Blue Velvet/Is There a Place (Where I Can Go)	1963	3.00	6.00	12.00
❏ 9614	PS	Blue Velvet/Is There a Place (Where I Can Go)	1963	3.75	7.50	15.00
❏ 9638		There! I've Said It Again/	1963	3.00	6.00	12.00
		The Girl with the Bow in Her Hair				
❏ 9638	PS	There! I've Said It Again/	1963	3.75	7.50	15.00
		The Girl with the Bow in Her Hair				
❏ 9662		My Heart Belongs to Only You/Warm and Tender	1964	2.50	5.00	10.00
❏ 9662	PS	My Heart Belongs to Only You/Warm and Tender	1964	3.75	7.50	15.00
❏ 9687		Tell Me Why/Remembering	1964	2.00	4.00	8.00
❏ 9687	PS	Tell Me Why/Remembering	1964	3.75	7.50	15.00
❏ 9705		Clinging Vine/Imagination Is a Magic Dream	1964	2.00	4.00	8.00
❏ 9705	PS	Clinging Vine/Imagination Is a Magic Dream	1964	3.00	6.00	12.00
❏ 9730		Mr. Lonely/It's Better to Have Loved	1964	2.50	5.00	10.00
❏ 9730	PS	Mr. Lonely/It's Better to Have Loved	1964	3.00	6.00	12.00
❏ 9741		The Bell That Couldn't Jingle/Dearest Santa	1964	2.50	5.00	10.00
❏ 9768		Long Lonely Nights/Satin	1965	2.00	4.00	8.00
❏ 9768	PS	Long Lonely Nights/Satin	1965	3.00	6.00	12.00
❏ 9791		L-O-N-E-L-Y/Graduation Tears	1965	2.00	4.00	8.00
❏ 9791	PS	L-O-N-E-L-Y/Graduation Tears	1965	3.00	6.00	12.00
❏ 9814		Theme from "Harlow" (Lonely Girl)/	1965	2.00	4.00	8.00
		If I Should Lose Your Love				
❏ 9814	PS	Theme from "Harlow" (Lonely Girl)/	1965	3.00	6.00	12.00
		If I Should Lose Your Love				
❏ 9846		What Color (Is a Man)/Love or Infatuation	1965	2.00	4.00	8.00
❏ 9869		Satin Pillows/Careless	1965	2.00	4.00	8.00
❏ 9869	PS	Satin Pillows/Careless	1965	3.00	6.00	12.00
❏ 9894		Tears/Go Away Pain	1966		3.00	6.00
❏ 10014		Dum-De-Da/Blue Clarinet	1966		3.00	6.00
❏ 10014	PS	Dum-De-Da/Blue Clarinet	1966	2.50	5.00	10.00
❏ 10048		Petticoat White (Summer Sky Blue)/	1966		3.00	6.00
		All the King's Horses				
❏ 10048	PS	Petticoat White (Summer Sky Blue)/	1966	2.50	5.00	10.00
		All the King's Horses				
❏ 10090		Coming Home Soldier/Don't Let My Mary Go Around	1966		3.00	6.00
❏ 10090	PS	Coming Home Soldier/Don't Let My Mary Go Around	1966	2.50	5.00	10.00
❏ 10136		For He's a Jolly Good Fellow/Sweet Maria	1967		3.00	6.00
❏ 10136	PS	For He's a Jolly Good Fellow/Sweet Maria	1967	2.50	5.00	10.00
❏ 10168		Red Roses for Mom/College Town	1967		3.00	6.00
❏ 10228		Please Love Me Forever/Miss America	1967	2.00	4.00	8.00
❏ 10228	PS	Please Love Me Forever/Miss America	1967	2.50	5.00	10.00

Number		Title (A Side/B Side)	Year	VG	VG+	NM
❑ 10266		Just As Much As Ever/Another Memory	1967		3.00	6.00
❑ 10266	PS	Just As Much As Ever/Another Memory	1967	2.50	5.00	10.00
❑ 10305		Take Good Care of My Baby/Strange Sensations	1968		3.00	6.00
❑ 10305	PS	Take Good Care of My Baby/Strange Sensations	1968	2.50	5.00	10.00
❑ 10350		Halfway to Paradise/(My Little) Christie	1968		3.00	6.00
❑ 10350	PS	Halfway to Paradise/(My Little) Christie	1968	2.50	5.00	10.00
❑ 10397		I Love How You Love Me/Little Barefoot Boy	1968		3.00	6.00
❑ 10397	PS	I Love How You Love Me/Little Barefoot Boy	1968	2.50	5.00	10.00
❑ 10461		To Know You Is to Love You/The Beat of My Heart	1969		2.50	5.00
❑ 10461	PS	To Know You Is to Love You/The Beat of My Heart	1969	2.50	5.00	10.00
❑ 10485		The Days of Sand and Shovels/So Many Lonely Girls	1969		2.50	5.00
❑ 10485	PS	The Days of Sand and Shovels/So Many Lonely Girls	1969	2.50	5.00	10.00
❑ 10554		Where Is Love/For All We Know	1969		2.50	5.00
❑ 10576		My Elusive Dreams/Over and Over	1970		2.50	5.00
❑ 10576	PS	My Elusive Dreams/Over and Over	1970	2.50	5.00	10.00
❑ 10629		No Arms Can Ever Hold You/ I've Got That Lovin' Feelin'	1970		2.50	5.00
❑ 10629	PS	No Arms Can Ever Hold You/ I've Got That Lovin' Feelin'	1970	2.00	4.00	8.00
❑ 10651		Why Don't They Understand/Where Is Love	1970		2.50	5.00
❑ 10689		Christmas Eve in My Hometown/The Christmas Angel	1970		3.00	6.00
❑ 10711		She Loves Me/I'll Make You My Baby	1971		2.50	5.00
❑ 10736		And I Love You So/She Loves Me	1971		2.50	5.00
❑ 10790		A Little Bit of You/God Bless America	1971		2.50	5.00
❑ 10822		Every Day of My Life/You Can Do It to Me Anytime	1972		2.50	5.00
❑ 10822	PS	Every Day of My Life/You Can Do It to Me Anytime	1972	2.00	4.00	8.00
❑ 10861		Sealed with a Kiss/All My Life	1972		2.50	5.00
❑ 10861	PS	Sealed with a Kiss/All My Life	1972	2.00	4.00	8.00
❑ 10936		But I Do/When You Love	1972		2.50	5.00
❑ 10936	PS	But I Do/When You Love	1972	2.00	4.00	8.00
❑ 10980		I Love You the Way You Are/Hurt	1973		2.50	5.00
❑ 11038		Where Are the Children/ I Can't Believe That It's All Over	1973		2.50	5.00
❑ 50080		Clinging Vine/I Can't Believe That It's All Over	1975		2.50	5.00
❑ 50169		Christmas Eve in My Home Town/The Christmas Angel	1975		2.50	5.00

Larc

❑ 81019		You Are Love/Ghost of Another Man	1983		2.00	4.00

Melody

❑ 5001/2		Always in My Heart/Harlem Nocturne	1960	6.25	12.50	25.00

Tapestry

❑ 001		Disco Polka (Pennsylvania Polka)/ I Could Have Danced All Night	1979		2.00	4.00
❑ 002		Make Believe It's Your First Time/ I Remember Loving You	1979		2.00	4.00
❑ 003		He/My First and Only Love	1980		2.00	4.00
❑ 005		It Was Nice to Know You John/Ain't That Lovin' You	1981		2.50	5.00
❑ 006		Let Me Love You, Goodbye/You Are Love	1981		2.00	4.00
❑ 007		Forever and Ever/(B-side unknown)	1982		2.00	4.00
❑ 008		She Will Survive (Poland)/Love Is the Reason	1982		2.00	4.00
❑ 010		It Hurts to Be in Love/Love Makes Everything Better	1985		2.00	4.00
❑ 013		What Did You Do with Your Old 45s/(B-side unknown)	1986		2.00	4.00
❑ 100		Santa Must Be Polish/Santa Claus Is Coming to Town	1987			3.00
❑ 100	PS	Santa Must Be Polish/Santa Claus Is Coming to Town	1987			3.00
❑ 1986		Sweet Lady of Liberty (same on both sides)	1986		2.00	4.00
❑ 4009		Bed of Roses/I Know a Goodbye	1984		2.00	4.00

Virtues, The

ABC-Paramount

❑ 10071		Blues in the Cellar/Vaya Con Dios	1959	3.75	7.50	15.00

Arcade

❑ 135		Ooh You Gotta/I Make a Mistake *As "Frank Virtue"*	1955	7.50	15.00	30.00

Fayette

❑ 1626		Guitar Boogie Shuffle '65/Moon Maid	1965	3.75	7.50	15.00

Highland

❑ 2505		Bye Bye Blues/Happy Guitar	1960	6.25	12.50	25.00
❑ 2505X		Bye Bye Blues/Strollin' Again	1960	6.25	12.50	25.00

Hunt

❑ 324	M	Guitar Boogie Shuffle/Guitar in Orbit	1959	6.25	12.50	25.00
❑ S-324	S	Guitar Boogie Shuffle/Guitar in Orbit	1959	12.50	25.00	50.00
❑ 327		Flippin' In/Shufflin' Along	1959	5.00	10.00	20.00
❑ 328		Pickin' the Stroll/Virtue's Boogie Woogie	1959	5.00	10.00	20.00
❑ 329		Pony Walk/Virtue's Boogie Woogie	1959	5.00	10.00	20.00
❑ 331		Blues in the Cellar/Vaya Con Dios	1960	5.00	10.00	20.00

Liberty

❑ 55706		Dream World/Move On *As "Frank Virtuoso"*	1964	3.00	6.00	12.00

Sure

❑ 501		Guitar Boogie Shuffle/Guitar in Orbit	1959	12.50	25.00	50.00
❑ 1733		Guitar Boogie Shuffle Twist/Guitar Boogie Stomp	1962	3.75	7.50	15.00
❑ 1779		Tel-Star Guitar/Jersey Bounce	1962	3.75	7.50	15.00

Virnon

❑ 603		Guitar Boogie Twist/Guitar Shimmy	1960	3.75	7.50	15.00

Number	Title (A Side/B Side)	Year	VG	VG+	NM
Virtue					
❑ 190	Cotton Candy/Love You	1966	2.50	5.00	10.00
❑ 2503	Guitar on the Wild Side/Meditation of the Soul	1970		3.00	6.00
Wynne					
❑ 123	Highland Guitar/Pickin' Plankin' Boogie	1960	3.75	7.50	15.00

Viscaynes, The
(Sylvester Stewart [Sly Stone] was a member)

Number	Title (A Side/B Side)	Year	VG	VG+	NM
Tropo					
❑ 101	I Guess I'll Be/Stop What You're Doing	1958	37.50	75.00	150.00
VPM					
❑ 1006	Yellow Moon/Heavenly Angel	1961	10.00	20.00	40.00

Vistas, The

Number	Title (A Side/B Side)	Year	VG	VG+	NM
Rebel					
❑ 77755	Ghost Wave/Surfer's Minuet	1963	12.50	25.00	50.00
Venpro					
❑ 1000	Ghost Wave/Surfer's Minuet	1963	20.00	40.00	80.00

Visuals, The

Number	Title (A Side/B Side)	Year	VG	VG+	NM
Poplar					
❑ 115	The Submarine Race/Maybe You	1962	10.00	20.00	40.00
❑ 117	My Juanita/A Boy, a Girl, and a Dream	1963	12.50	25.00	50.00
❑ 121	Please Don't Be Mad at Me/Blue Enough to Cry	1963	75.00	150.00	300.00

Vitells, The

Number	Title (A Side/B Side)	Year	VG	VG+	NM
Decca					
❑ 31362	Shirley/The Dip	1962	7.50	15.00	30.00

Vito and the Salutations

Number	Title (A Side/B Side)	Year	VG	VG+	NM
Apt					
❑ 25079	High Noon/Walkin'	1965	12.50	25.00	50.00
Boom					
❑ 60020	Bring Back Yesterday/I Want You to Be My Baby	1966	5.00	10.00	20.00
Crystal Ball					
❑ 105	Unchained Melody/So Much	1978		2.50	5.00
Herald					
❑ 583	Unchained Melody/Hey Hey Baby	1963	7.50	15.00	30.00
❑ 586	Eenie Meenie/Extraordinary Girl	1964	6.25	12.50	25.00
Kram					
❑ 5002	Your Way/Hey, Hey Baby	1962	12.50	25.00	50.00
Rayna					
❑ 5009	Gloria/Let's Untwist the Twist	1962	12.50	25.00	50.00
Red Boy					
❑ 1001	So Wonderful (My Love)/I'd Best Be Going	1966	6.25	12.50	25.00
❑ 5009	Gloria/Let's Untwist the Twist	1962	7.50	15.00	30.00
Regina					
❑ 1320	Get a Job/Girls I Know	1964	7.50	15.00	30.00
Rust					
❑ 5106	Can I Depend on You/Hello Dolly	1966	5.00	10.00	20.00
Sandbag					
❑ 103	So Wonderful (My Love)/I'd Best Be Going	1966	5.00	10.00	20.00
Wells					
❑ 1008	Can I Depend on You/Liverpool Bound	1964	12.50	25.00	50.00
	Yellow vinyl				
❑ 1008	Can I Depend on You/Liverpool Bound	1964	6.25	12.50	25.00
❑ 1010	The Banana Boat Song (Day-O)/Don't Count on Me	1964	6.25	12.50	25.00

Vocaleers, The

Number	Title (A Side/B Side)	Year	VG	VG+	NM
Old Town					
❑ 1089	This Is the Night/Love and Devotion	1960	6.25	12.50	25.00
Paradise					
❑ 113	I Need Your Love So Bad/ Have You Ever Loved Someone	1959	10.00	20.00	40.00
Red Robin					
❑ 113	Be True/Oh! Where	1953	75.00	150.00	300.00
❑ 114	Is It a Dream/Hurry Home	1953	50.00	100.00	200.00
❑ 119	I Walk Alone/How Soon	1953	75.00	150.00	300.00
❑ 125	Will You Be True/Love You	1954	75.00	150.00	300.00
❑ 132	Angel Face/Lovin' Baby	1954	50.00	100.00	200.00
Twistime					
❑ 11	Cootie Snap/A Golden Tear	1962	7.50	15.00	30.00
Vest					
❑ 832	Hear My Plea/The Night Is Quiet	1960	20.00	40.00	80.00

Vogues, The
(The Dot and Cascade records are by a different group than the others. Also see "Val-Aires, The")

Number	Title (A Side/B Side)	Year	VG	VG+	NM
ABC-Paramount					
❑ 10672	Big Man/Golden Locket	1965	5.00	10.00	20.00

Number		Title (A Side/B Side)	Year	VG	VG+	NM
Astra						
❏ 1029		You're the One/Goodnight My Love	1973		2.50	5.00
❏ 1030		Five O'Clock World/Land of Milk and Honey	1973		2.50	5.00
Bell						
❏ 991		Love Song/We're On Our Way	1971		2.50	5.00
❏ 45,127		Take Time to Tell Her/I'll Be with You	1971		2.50	5.00
❏ 45,158		An American Family/Gotta Have You Back	1971		2.50	5.00
Blue Star						
❏ 229		You're the One/Some Words	1965	6.25	12.50	25.00
Cascade						
❏ 5908		Ev'ry Day, Ev'ry Night/Now I Lay Me Down to Cry	1959	5.00	10.00	20.00
Co & Ce						
❏ 229		You're the One/Some Words	1965	3.00	6.00	12.00
❏ 232		Five O'Clock World/Nothing to Offer You	1965	3.00	6.00	12.00
❏ 234		Magic Town/Humpty Dumpty	1966	2.50	5.00	10.00
❏ 238		The Land of Milk and Honey/True Lovers	1966	2.50	5.00	10.00
❏ 240		Please Mr. Sun/Don't Blame the Rain	1966	2.50	5.00	10.00
❏ 242		That's the Tune/Midnight Dreams	1966	2.50	5.00	10.00
❏ 244		Take a Chance on My Heart/Summer Afternoon	1967	2.50	5.00	10.00
❏ 246		Brighter Days/Lovers of the World Unite	1967	2.50	5.00	10.00
Dot						
❏ 15798		Love Is a Funny Little Game/Which Witch Doctor	1958	6.25	12.50	25.00
❏ 15859		Try, Baby, Try/Falling Star	1958	6.25	12.50	25.00
Mainstream						
❏ 5524		Need You/(B-side unknown)	1972		2.50	5.00
MGM						
❏ 13813		Brighter Days/Lovers of the World Unite	1967	2.00	4.00	8.00
Reprise						
❏ 0663		I've Got You on My Mind/Just What I've Been Looking For	1968	2.50	5.00	10.00
❏ 0686		Turn Around, Look at Me/Then	1968	2.00	4.00	8.00
❏ 0731		Turn Around, Look at Me/My Special Angel	1969		2.50	5.00
		"Back to Back Hits" series				
❏ 0736		No, Not Much/Earth Angel (Will You Be Mine)	1970		2.50	5.00
		"Back to Back Hits" series				
❏ 0766		My Special Angel/I Keep It Hid	1968	2.00	4.00	8.00
❏ 0788		Till/I Will	1968	2.00	4.00	8.00
❏ 0803		Woman Helping Man/I'll Know My Love	1969	2.00	4.00	8.00
❏ 0803		Woman Helping Man/No, Not Much	1969		3.00	6.00
❏ 0820		Earth Angel (Will You Be Mine)/P.S. I Love You	1969		3.00	6.00
❏ 0831		Moments to Remember/Once in a While	1969		3.00	6.00
❏ 0844		Green Fields/Easy to Say	1969		3.00	6.00
❏ 0856		See That Girl/If We Only Have Love	1969		3.00	6.00
❏ 0887		God Only Knows/Moody	1970		3.00	6.00
❏ 0909		Over the Rainbow/Hey, That's No Way to Say Goodbye	1970		3.00	6.00
❏ 0931		50's Medley/Come Into My Arms	1970		3.00	6.00
❏ 0969		Since I Don't Have You/I Know You as a Woman	1970		3.00	6.00
20th Century						
❏ 2041		My Prayer/I've Got to Learn to Live Without You	1973		2.50	5.00
❏ 2060		Wonderful Summer/Guess Who	1973		2.50	5.00
❏ 2085		As Time Goes By/Prisoner of Love	1974		2.50	5.00

Voice Masters, The

(Lamont Dozier and David Ruffin were originally in this group, though not on the 1968-70 releases)

Number		Title (A Side/B Side)	Year	VG	VG+	NM
Anna						
❏ 101		Hope and Pray/Oop's I'm Sorry	1959	50.00	100.00	200.00
❏ 102		Needed/Needed (For Lovers Only)	1959	50.00	100.00	200.00
Bamboo						
❏ 103		You've Hurt Me Baby/If a Woman Catches a Fool	1968	6.25	12.50	25.00
❏ 105		Never Gonna Leave You/If a Woman Catches a Fool	1969	3.75	7.50	15.00
❏ 113		Dance Right Into My Heart/If a Woman Catches a Fool	1970	3.75	7.50	15.00
Frisco						
❏ 15235		In Love in Vain/Two Lovers	196?	25.00	50.00	100.00

Voices That Care

(Among the many singers on this record is, believe it or not, Frank Sinatra!)

Number		Title (A Side/B Side)	Year	VG	VG+	NM
Giant						
❏ 19350		Voices That Care/Messages of Care	1991			3.00

Voight, Wes

Number		Title (A Side/B Side)	Year	VG	VG+	NM
DeLuxe						
❏ 6176		Midnight Blues/Another Guy's Line	1958	25.00	50.00	100.00
❏ 6180		I Want a Lover/Little Joan	1958	10.00	20.00	40.00
King						
❏ 5211	M	I'm Loving It/Everything's the Same	1959	15.00	30.00	60.00
❏ S-5211	S	I'm Loving It/Everything's the Same	1959	50.00	100.00	200.00
❏ 5231	M	I'm Ready to Go Steady/The Wind and the Cold Black Night	1959	10.00	20.00	40.00
❏ S-5231	S	I'm Ready to Go Steady/The Wind and the Cold Black Night	1959	25.00	50.00	100.00

Number	Title (A Side/B Side)	Year	VG	VG+	NM

Volk, Val, and the Matched Aces
Rocket

❑ 1050	A Rockin' Party Tonight/Spring Time Rock	195?	50.00	100.00	200.00

Volumes, The
American Arts

❑ 6	Gotta Give Her Love/I Can't Live Without You	1964	7.50	15.00	30.00
❑ 18	I Just Can't Help Myself/One Way Lover	1965	7.50	15.00	30.00

Chex

❑ 1000.2	I Love You/Dreams	1962	75.00	150.00	300.00
	With typographical error crediting "The Valumes"				
❑ 1002	I Love You/Dreams	1962	7.50	15.00	30.00
❑ 1005	Come Back Into My Heart/The Bell	1962	10.00	20.00	40.00

Impact

❑ 1017	That Same Old Feeling/The Trouble I've Seen	1966	12.50	25.00	50.00

Inferno

❑ 2001	A Way to Love You/You Got It Baby	1967	5.00	10.00	20.00
❑ 2004	My Road Is the Right Road/My Kind of Girl	1967	5.00	10.00	20.00
❑ 5001	Ain't That Lovin' You/I Love You Baby	1968	5.00	10.00	20.00

Jubilee

❑ 5446	Sandra/Teenage Paradise	1963	5.00	10.00	20.00
❑ 5454	Our Song/Oh My Mother-in-Law	1963	5.00	10.00	20.00

Karen

❑ 1551	Am I Losing You/Ain't Gonna Give You Up	1970	2.00	4.00	8.00

Old Town

❑ 1154	Why/Monkey Hop	1964	6.25	12.50	25.00

Vows, The
Markay

❑ 103	I Wanna Chance/Have You Heard	1962	10.00	20.00	40.00
	Black label				
❑ 103	I Wanna Chance/Have You Heard	1962	100.00	200.00	400.00
	Orange label				

Ran-Dee

❑ 112	Girl in Red/(B-side unknown)	196?	15.00	30.00	60.00

Sta-Set

❑ 402	Say You'll Be Mine/When a Boy Loves a Girl	1963	15.00	30.00	60.00

Tamara

❑ 506	The Things You Do to Me/Dottie	1963	10.00	20.00	40.00
❑ 760	Say You'll Be Mine/When a Boy Loves a Girl	1964	6.25	12.50	25.00

V.I.P.

❑ 25016	Buttered Popcorn/Tell Me	1965	10.00	20.00	40.00

Voxpoppers, The
Amp 3

❑ 1004	Wishing for Your Love/The Last Drag	1958	7.50	15.00	30.00

Mercury

❑ 71282	Wishing for Your Love/The Last Drag	1958	5.00	10.00	20.00
❑ 71315	Pony Tail/Ping Pong Baby	1958	5.00	10.00	20.00

Poplar

❑ 107	Come Back Little Girl/A Love to Last a Lifetime	1959	5.00	10.00	20.00

Versailles

❑ 200	Can't Understand It/A Blessing After All	1959	7.50	15.00	30.00

Warwick

❑ 589	Lonely for You/Helen Isn't Tellin'	1960	3.00	6.00	12.00
	As "Freddie and the Voxpoppers"				

Vy-Dells, The
Garnet

❑ 101	What I'm Gonna Do/Unknown	196?	25.00	50.00	100.00

W

Wade and Dick
Sun

❑ 269	Bop Bop Baby/Don't Need Your Lovin' Baby	1957	7.50	15.00	30.00

Wade, Don
San

❑ 206	Gone, Gone, Gone/(B-side unknown)	1958	75.00	150.00	300.00
❑ 207	Forever Yours/Oh Love	1958	7.50	15.00	30.00

Wade, Ronny
King

❑ 5061	Gotta Make Her Mine/Let Me Cry	1957	20.00	40.00	80.00
❑ 5078	I Know But I'll Never Tell/I'll Never Fall in Love Again	1957	12.50	25.00	50.00
❑ 5099	Annie Don't Work/I'll Sail My Ship Alone	1958	12.50	25.00	50.00
❑ 5112	All I Want/A King and a Vow	1958	12.50	25.00	50.00

Number	Title (A Side/B Side)	Year	VG	VG+	NM

Wagner, Danny, and Kindred Soul
Imperial

❏ 66305	I Lost a True Love/My Buddy	1968	7.50	15.00	30.00
❏ 66327	Harlem Shuffle/When Johnny Comes Marching Home	1968	5.00	10.00	20.00

Wagoner, Porter, and Dolly Parton
(Also see "Parton, Dolly")
RCA

❏ PB-11983	Making Plans/Beneath the Sweet Magnolia Trees	1980		2.00	4.00
❏ PB-12119	If You Go, I'll Follow You/Hide Me Away	1980		2.00	4.00

RCA Victor

❏ 47-9369	The Last Thing on My Mind/Love Is Worth Living	1967	2.00	4.00	8.00
❏ 47-9490	Holding On to Nothing/Just Between You and Me	1968	2.00	4.00	8.00
❏ 47-9577	We'll Get Ahead Someday/Jeannie's Afraid of the Dark	1968	2.00	4.00	8.00
❏ 47-9799	Tomorrow Is Forever/Mandy Never Sleeps	1969		3.00	6.00
❏ 47-9875	Daddy Was An Old Time Preacher Man/Good Understanding	1970		3.00	6.00
❏ 47-9958	Better Move It On Home/Two of a Kind	1971		3.00	6.00
❏ 47-9994	The Right Combination/The Part of Loving You	1971		3.00	6.00
❏ 74-0104	Malena/Yours, Love	1969		3.00	6.00
❏ 74-0172	Always, Always/No Need to Hurry Home	1969		3.00	6.00
❏ 74-0247	Just Someone I Used to Know/My Hands Are Tied	1969		3.00	6.00
❏ 74-0565	Burning the Midnight Oil/More Than Words Can Tell	1971		3.00	6.00
❏ 74-0675	Lost Forever in Your Kiss/The Fog Has Lifted	1972		2.50	5.00
❏ 74-0773	Together Always/Love's All Over	1972		2.50	5.00
❏ 74-0893	We Found It/Lord Have Mercy on Us	1973		2.50	5.00
❏ 74-0981	If Teardrops Were Pennies/Come to Me	1973		2.50	5.00
❏ PB-10010	Please Don't Stop Loving Me/Sounds of Nature	1974		2.00	4.00
❏ PB-10328	Say Forever You'll Be Mine/How Can I Help You Forgive Me	1975		2.00	4.00
❏ GB-10506	Please Don't Stop Loving Me/Sounds of Nature	1975		2.00	4.00
	Gold Standard Series				
❏ GB-10675	Say Forever You'll Be Mine/How Can I Help You Forgive Me	1976		2.00	4.00
	Gold Standard Series				
❏ PB-10652	Is Forever Longer Than Always/If You Say I Can	1976		2.00	4.00

Wailers, The
(More than one group)
Bell

❏ 694	Thinking Out Loud/You Can't Fly	1967	2.50	5.00	10.00

Columbia

❏ 40288	Hot Love/Stop the Clock	1954	30.00	60.00	120.00

Etiquette

❏ 2	Mashi/Velva	1962	3.75	7.50	15.00
❏ 4	Stompin' Willie/Doin' the Seaside	1963	3.75	7.50	15.00
❏ 6	We're Goin' Surfin'/Shakedown	1963	3.75	7.50	15.00
❏ 7	Seattle/Party Time U.S.A.	1963	3.75	7.50	15.00
❏ 9	Tall Cool One/Frenzy	1964	3.75	7.50	15.00
❏ 12	You Better Believe It/Don't Take It So Hard	1965	3.75	7.50	15.00
❏ 15	You Weren't Using Your Head/Back to You	1965	3.75	7.50	15.00
❏ 19	Hang Up/Dirty Robber	1965	3.75	7.50	15.00
❏ 21	Out of Our Tree/I Got Me	1966	3.75	7.50	15.00
❏ 22	Christmas Spirit/Don't Believe in Christmas	1965	7.50	15.00	30.00
	B-side by the Sonics				
❏ 24	It's You Alone/Tears	1966	6.25	12.50	25.00

Golden Crest

❏ 375	Beat Guitar/Driftwood	19??	2.50	5.00	10.00
❏ 518	Tall Cool One/Roadrunner	1959	7.50	15.00	30.00
	Photo of group on label				
❏ 518	Tall Cool One/Roadrunner	1964	3.75	7.50	15.00
	No photo on label				
❏ 526	Mau-Mau/Dirty Robber	1959	6.25	12.50	25.00
	Photo of group on label				
❏ 526	Mau-Mau/Dirty Robber	1964	3.00	6.00	12.00
	No photo on label				
❏ 532	Wailin'/Shanghai'd	1960	6.25	12.50	25.00
	Photo of group on label				
❏ 532	Wailin'/Shanghai'd	1964	3.00	6.00	12.00
	No photo on label				
❏ 545	Lucille/Scratchin'	1960	6.25	12.50	25.00
	Photo of group on label				
❏ 545	Lucille/Scratchin'	1964	3.00	6.00	12.00
	No photo of group				
❏ 591	Mau-Mau/Beat Guitar	1964	2.50	5.00	10.00

Imperial

❏ 66028	Tall Cool One/Frenzy	1964		*Unreleased*	
❏ 66045	Mashi/On the Rocks	1964	3.75	7.50	15.00

United Artists

❏ 50026	Tears/It's You Alone	1966	2.50	5.00	10.00
❏ 50065	End of the Summer/Think Kindly Baby	1966	2.50	5.00	10.00
❏ 50110	Tears (Don't Have to Fall)/You Won't Lead Me On	1967	2.50	5.00	10.00

Number	Title (A Side/B Side)	Year	VG	VG+	NM
Viva					
❏ 614	I'm Determined/I Don't Want to Follow You	1967	2.50	5.00	10.00

Wakeman, Rick
(Of Yes)
A&M

Number	Title (A Side/B Side)	Year	VG	VG+	NM
❏ 1430	Catherine/Anne	1973		2.50	5.00
❏ 1627	The Journey/The Return	1974		2.50	5.00
❏ 1708	Merlin the Magician/Sir Galahad	1975		2.50	5.00
❏ 1937	White Rock/After the Ball	1977		2.50	5.00
❏ 2010	The Birdman of Alcatraz/And Now a Word from Our Sponsor	1978		2.50	5.00

Walcos, The
Drum

Number	Title (A Side/B Side)	Year	VG	VG+	NM
❏ 011	Tell Me Why/Moonlight Rock	1959	25.00	50.00	100.00

Wales, Howard, and Jerry Garcia
(Also see "Garcia, Jerry")
Douglas

Number	Title (A Side/B Side)	Year	VG	VG+	NM
❏ 76501	South Side Strut/Uncle Martin's	1971	3.75	7.50	15.00

Walker Brothers, The
(The Kay-Y record is by a different group than the others)
Kay-Y

Number	Title (A Side/B Side)	Year	VG	VG+	NM
❏ 66785	Beautiful Brown Eyes/Ninety-Seven	1960	12.50	25.00	50.00

Smash

Number		Title (A Side/B Side)	Year	VG	VG+	NM
❏ 1952		Doin' the Jerk/Pretty Girls Everywhere	1964	3.00	6.00	12.00
❏ 1976		Love Her/Seventh Dawn	1965	3.00	6.00	12.00
❏ 2000		Make It Easy on Yourself/But I Do	1965	3.75	7.50	15.00
❏ 2009		Make It Easy on Yourself/Doin' the Jerk	1965	3.00	6.00	12.00
❏ 2009	PS	Make It Easy on Yourself/Doin' the Jerk	1965	5.00	10.00	20.00
❏ 2016		My Ship Is Comin' In/You're All Around Me	1966	3.00	6.00	12.00
❏ 2016	PS	My Ship Is Comin' In/You're All Around Me	1966	5.00	10.00	20.00
❏ 2032		The Sun Ain't Gonna Shine (Anymore)/After the Lights Go Out	1966	3.00	6.00	12.00
❏ 2048		(Baby) You Don't Have to Tell Me/Young Man Cried	1966	3.00	6.00	12.00
❏ 2063		Another Tear Falls/Saddest Night in the World	1966	3.00	6.00	12.00

Tower

Number	Title (A Side/B Side)	Year	VG	VG+	NM
❏ 218	I Only Came to Dance with You/Greens	1966	3.00	6.00	12.00

Walker, Jr., and the All Stars
Harvey

Number	Title (A Side/B Side)	Year	VG	VG+	NM
❏ 113	Willie's Blues/Twist Lackawanna	1962	6.25	12.50	25.00
❏ 117	Cleo's Mood/Brain Washer	1963	5.00	10.00	20.00
❏ 119	Good Rockin'/Brain Washer	1963	5.00	10.00	20.00

Motown

Number	Title (A Side/B Side)	Year	VG	VG+	NM
❏ 1352	Country Boy/What Does It Take (To Win Your Love)	1975		2.50	5.00
❏ 1380	I'm So Glad/Hot Shot	1976			*Unreleased*
❏ 1689	Blow the House Down/Ball Baby	1983		2.00	4.00

Soul

Number		Title (A Side/B Side)	Year	VG	VG+	NM
❏ 35003		Monkey Jump/Satan's Blues	1964	3.75	7.50	15.00
❏ 35008		Shotgun/Hot Cha	1965	2.50	5.00	10.00
❏ 35008	PS	Shotgun/Hot Cha	1965	6.25	12.50	25.00
❏ 35012		Do the Boomerang/Tune Up	1965	2.00	4.00	8.00
❏ 35013		Shake and Fingerpop/Cleo's Back	1965	2.00	4.00	8.00
❏ 35015		(I'm a) Road Runner/Shoot Your Shot	1965	2.00	4.00	8.00
❏ 35017		Cleo's Mood/Baby You Know It Ain't Right	1966	2.00	4.00	8.00
❏ 35024		How Sweet It Is (To Be Loved By You)/Nothing But Soul	1966	2.00	4.00	8.00
❏ 35024	PS	How Sweet It Is (To Be Loved By You)/Nothing But Soul	1966	5.00	10.00	20.00
❏ 35026		Money (That's What I Want) Part I/Money (That's What I Want) Part II	1966	2.00	4.00	8.00
❏ 35030		Pucker Up Buttercup/Anyway You Wanna	1967	2.00	4.00	8.00
❏ 35036		Shoot Your Shot/Ain't That the Truth	1967	2.00	4.00	8.00
❏ 35041		Come See About Me/Sweet Soul	1967	2.00	4.00	8.00
❏ 35048		Hip City -- Part 1/Hip City -- Part 2	1968	2.00	4.00	8.00
❏ 35055		Home Cookin'/Mutiny	1969	2.00	4.00	8.00
❏ 35062		What Does It Take (To Win Your Love)/Brainwasher -- Part 1	1969	2.00	4.00	8.00
❏ 35067		These Eyes/Got to Find a Way to Win Maria Back	1969		3.00	6.00
❏ 35070		Gotta Hold On to This Feeling/Clinging to the Theory That She's Coming Back	1970		3.00	6.00
❏ 35073		Do You See My Love (For You Growing)/Groove and More	1970		3.00	6.00
❏ 35081		Holly Holy/Carry Your Own Load	1970		3.00	6.00
❏ 35084		Take Me Girl, I'm Ready/Right On Brothers and Sisters	1971		3.00	6.00
❏ 35090		Way Back Home/(Instrumental)	1971		3.00	6.00
❏ 35095		Walk in the Night/I Don't Want to Do Wrong	1972		3.00	6.00
❏ 35097		Groove Thang/Me and My Family	1972		3.00	6.00
❏ 35104		Gimme That Beat (Part 1)/Gimme That Beat (Part 2)	1973		3.00	6.00
❏ 35106		I Don't Need No Reason/Country Boy	1973		3.00	6.00
❏ 35108		Peace and Understanding (Is Hard to Find)/Soul Clappin'	1973		3.00	6.00

Number	Title (A Side/B Side)	Year	VG	VG+	NM
❑ 35110	Dancing Like They Do on Soul Train/ I Ain't That Easy to Love	1973		3.00	6.00
❑ 35114	You Are the Sunshine of My Life/ Until You Come Back to Me	1974			*Unreleased*
❑ 35116	I'm So Glad/Soul Clappin'	1975		2.50	5.00
❑ 35118	Hot Shot/You're No Ordinary Woman	1976		2.50	5.00
❑ 35122	Whopper Bopper Show Stopper/Hard Love	1977		2.50	5.00

Whitfield

Number	Title	Year	VG	VG+	NM
❑ 8861	Back Street Boogie/Don't Let Me Go Away	1979		2.00	4.00
❑ 49052	Wishing on a Star/Hole in the Wall	1979		2.00	4.00

Walker, T-Bone

Atlantic

Number	Title	Year	VG	VG+	NM
❑ 1045	Papa Ain't Salty/T-Bone Shuffle	1955	7.50	15.00	30.00
❑ 1074	Why Not/Play On Little Girl	1955	7.50	15.00	30.00

Bluesway

Number	Title	Year	VG	VG+	NM
❑ 61008	Confusion Blues/Every Night I Have to Cry	1967	2.00	4.00	8.00

Capitol

Number	Title	Year	VG	VG+	NM
❑ F799	Go Back to the One You Love/On Your Way Blues	1950	37.50	75.00	150.00
❑ F944	Too Much Trouble Blues/ She's My Old Time Used to Be	1950	37.50	75.00	150.00

Imperial

Note: T-Bone Walker records on Imperial before 5202 are unconfirmed on 45 rpm.

Number	Title	Year	VG	VG+	NM
❑ 5202	Street Walkin' Woman/The Blues Is a Woman	1952	20.00	40.00	80.00
❑ 5216	Blue Mood/Got No Use for You	1953	15.00	30.00	60.00
❑ 5228	Railroad Station Blues/Long Distance Blues	1953	15.00	30.00	60.00
❑ 5239	Party Girl/You're Here in the Dark	1953	15.00	30.00	60.00
❑ 5247	Everytime/Tell Me What's the Reason	1953	15.00	30.00	60.00
❑ 5261	I'm About to Lose My Mind/I Miss You Baby	1954	15.00	30.00	60.00
❑ 5264	Pony Tail/When the Sun Goes Down	1954	15.00	30.00	60.00
❑ 5274	Vida Lee/My Baby Is Now on My Mind	1954	15.00	30.00	60.00
❑ 5284	Bye Bye Baby/Wanderin' Heart	1954	15.00	30.00	60.00
❑ 5299	Teenage Baby/Strugglin' Blues	1954	15.00	30.00	60.00
❑ 5311	Love Is Just a Gamble/High Society	1954	15.00	30.00	60.00
❑ 5330	I'll Understand/The Hard Way	1955	12.50	25.00	50.00
❑ 5384	You Don't Understand/Say! Pretty Baby	1956	12.50	25.00	50.00
❑ 5695	Travelin' Blues/Strollin' with Bones	1960	3.75	7.50	15.00
❑ 5832	Evil Hearted Woman/Life Is Too Short	1962	3.75	7.50	15.00
❑ 5962	Doin' Time/Cold, Cold Water	1963	3.00	6.00	12.00

Jetstream

Number	Title	Year	VG	VG+	NM
❑ 726	Reconsider Baby/I'm Not Your Fool Anymore	1966	2.50	5.00	10.00
❑ 730	T-Bone's Back/She's a Hit	1967	2.50	5.00	10.00

Modern

Number	Title	Year	VG	VG+	NM
❑ 1004	Should I Let Her Go/Hey Hey Baby	1965	2.50	5.00	10.00

Post

Number	Title	Year	VG	VG+	NM
❑ 2002	I Get So Weary/Tell Me What's the Reason	1955	15.00	30.00	60.00

Walker, Wayne

ABC-Paramount

Number	Title	Year	VG	VG+	NM
❑ 9735	It's My Way/All I Can Do Is Cry	1956	15.00	30.00	60.00

Brunswick

Number	Title	Year	VG	VG+	NM
❑ 55133	Little Ole You/What Kind of God Do You Think You Are	1959	10.00	20.00	40.00

Columbia

Number	Title	Year	VG	VG+	NM
❑ 40905	A Teenage Love Affair/Whatever You Desire	1957	6.25	12.50	25.00
❑ 40979	Just a-Walkin' Around/Sands of Gold	1957	6.25	12.50	25.00
❑ 41042	Bo-Bo Sha Diddle Diddle/Come Away from His Arms	1957	6.25	12.50	25.00
❑ 41130	I'm Finally Free/It's Written in Your Arms	1958	6.25	12.50	25.00

Coral

Number	Title	Year	VG	VG+	NM
❑ 62328	Battle of the Bulge/Reaching for the Impossible	1962	3.75	7.50	15.00

Everest

Number	Title	Year	VG	VG+	NM
❑ 19380	Love, Love, Love/Sweet Chains of Love	1960	3.75	7.50	15.00

Wallace, Jerry

Allied

Number	Title	Year	VG	VG+	NM
❑ 5015	Little Miss One/Petrillo	1954	12.50	25.00	50.00
	B-side by Eddie Oliver and the Oliver Twisters				
❑ 5019	That's What a Woman Can Do/ I Hate to Go Home Alone	1954	10.00	20.00	40.00
❑ 5023	Runnin' After Love/Dixie Anna	1954	10.00	20.00	40.00

BMA

Number	Title	Year	VG	VG+	NM
❑ 7-002	I Miss You Already/At the End of a Rainbow	1977		2.00	4.00
❑ 7-005	I'll Promise You Tomorrow/You're on the Run	1977		2.00	4.00
❑ 8-006	At the End of a Rainbow/Looking for a Memory	1978		2.00	4.00
❑ 8-008	My Last Sad Song/Wickenburg Way	1978		2.00	4.00

Challenge

Number	Title	Year	VG	VG+	NM
❑ 1003	Blue Jean Baby/Fool's Hall of Fame	1957	5.00	10.00	20.00
❑ 9107	Life's a Holiday/I Can See an Angel Walking	1961	3.00	6.00	12.00
❑ 9117	Eyes (Don't Give My Secrets Away)/Lonesome	1961	3.00	6.00	12.00
❑ 9130	Rollin' River/I Hang My Head and Cry	1961	3.00	6.00	12.00
❑ 9139	Little Miss Tease/Mr. Lonely	1962	3.00	6.00	12.00
❑ 9152	Here I Go/You'll Never Know	1962	3.00	6.00	12.00
❑ 9171	Shutters and Boards/Am I That Easy to Forget	1962	3.00	6.00	12.00
❑ 9185	Move Over/On a Merry-Go-Round	1963	3.00	6.00	12.00
❑ 9195	Just Walking in the Rain/San Francisco Mama	1963	3.00	6.00	12.00

Number		Title (A Side/B Side)	Year	VG	VG+	NM
❏ 9205		Empty Arms Again/Bambola (My Darling One)	1963	3.00	6.00	12.00
❏ 59000		The Other Me/Good and Bad	1958	5.00	10.00	20.00
❏ 59013		How the Time Flies/With This Ring	1958	5.00	10.00	20.00
❏ 59027		Diamond Ring/All My Love Belongs to You	1958	5.00	10.00	20.00
❏ 59040		A Touch of Pink/Off Stage	1959	3.75	7.50	15.00
❏ 59047		Primrose Lane/By Your Side	1959	4.50	9.00	18.00
❏ 59060		Little Coco Palm/Mission Bell Blues	1959	3.75	7.50	15.00
❏ 59060	PS	Little Coco Palm/Mission Bell Blues	1959	10.00	20.00	40.00
❏ 59072		King of the Mountain/ You're Singing Our Love Song to Somebody Else	1960	3.75	7.50	15.00
❏ 59082		Swingin' Down the Lane/Teardrops in the Rain	1960	3.75	7.50	15.00
❏ 59098		There She Goes/Angel on My Shoulder	1960	3.75	7.50	15.00
❏ 59223		Auf Wiedesehn/If I Make It Through Today	1963	2.50	5.00	10.00
❏ 59246		In the Misty Moonlight/Even the Bad Times Are Good	1964	2.50	5.00	10.00
❏ 59249		In the Misty Moonlight/Cannon Ball	1964	3.75	7.50	15.00
		B-side by the Soul Surfers				
❏ 59265		Even the Bad Times Are Good/Spanish Guitars	1964	2.50	5.00	10.00
❏ 59278		You're Driving You Out of My Mind/Helpless	1965	2.50	5.00	10.00

Class

❏ 502		Taj Mahal/Autumn Has Come and Gone	1955	6.25	12.50	25.00

Decca

❏ 32777		After You/She'll Remember	1971		3.00	6.00
❏ 32859		The Morning After/I Can't Take It Anymore	1971		3.00	6.00
❏ 32914		To Get to You/Time	1972		3.00	6.00
❏ 32989		If You Leave Me Tonight I'll Cry/ What's He Doin' in My World	1972		3.00	6.00
❏ 33036		Do You Know What It's Like to Be Lonesome/ Where Did He Come From	1972		3.00	6.00

Door Knob

❏ 116		You've Still Got Me/Now That Sandy's Gone	1979		2.00	4.00
❏ 127		Cling to Me/Paper Madonna	1980		2.00	4.00
❏ 134		If I Could Set My Love to Music/Cling to Me	1980		2.00	4.00

4-Star

❏ 1035		I Wanna Go to Heaven/After You	1978		2.00	4.00
❏ 1036		Yours Love/(B-side unknown)	1979		2.00	4.00

Glenolden

❏ 159		Are You Ready/That's the Fool in Me	1968		3.00	6.00

Liberty

❏ 55957		Runaway Bay/Dispossessed	1967	2.00	4.00	8.00
❏ 56001		This One's on the House/A New Sun Risin'	1967	2.00	4.00	8.00
❏ 56027		The Closest I Ever Came/That's What Fools Are For	1968			Unreleased
❏ 56028		Another Time, Another Place, Another World/ That's What Fools Are For	1968		3.00	6.00
❏ 56059		Sweet Child of Sunshine/Our House on Paper	1968		3.00	6.00
❏ 56095		Temptation/Son	1969		3.00	6.00
❏ 56105		Venus/Soon We'll Be There	1969		3.00	6.00
❏ 56130		Swiss Cottage Place/With Aging	1969		3.00	6.00
❏ 56147		Honey Eyed Girl/Glory of My Girl	1969		3.00	6.00
❏ 56155		Even the Bad Times Are Good/For All We Know	1970		3.00	6.00

MCA

❏ 40037		A Song Nobody Sings/Sound of Goodbye	1973		2.50	5.00
❏ 40111		Don't Give Up on Me/You Look Like Forever	1973		2.50	5.00
❏ 40183		Guess Who/All I Ever Want from You	1974		2.50	5.00
❏ 40248		My Wife's House/A Better Way to Say I Love You	1974		2.50	5.00
❏ 40321		Make Hay While the Sun Shines/ I Wonder Whose Baby	1974		2.50	5.00

Mercury

❏ 70684		Taj Mahal/Autumn Has Come and Gone	1955	5.00	10.00	20.00
❏ 70758		The Greatest Magic of All/Walking in the Rain	1955	5.00	10.00	20.00
❏ 70812		One Night When Flowers Were Dancing/Gloria	1956	5.00	10.00	20.00
❏ 72246		In the Misty Moonlight/Even the Bad Times Are Good	1964	3.00	6.00	12.00
❏ 72258		Butterfly/Let the Tears Begin	1964	2.50	5.00	10.00
❏ 72292		It's a Cotton Candy World/Keep a Lamp Burning	1964	2.50	5.00	10.00
❏ 72356		Careless Hands/San Francisco d'Assisi	1964	2.50	5.00	10.00
❏ 72406		Rainbow/Time	1965	2.50	5.00	10.00
❏ 72461		Life's Gone and Slipped Away/Twelve Little Roses	1965	2.50	5.00	10.00
❏ 72529		Diamonds and Horseshoes/Will the Pain Fade Away	1966	2.50	5.00	10.00
❏ 72589		Wallpaper Roses/Son of a Green Beret	1966	2.50	5.00	10.00
❏ 72619		Not That I Care/Release Me	1966	2.50	5.00	10.00

MGM

❏ 14788		Comin' Home to You/The River St. Marie	1975		2.50	5.00
❏ 14809		Wanted Man/Your Love	1975		2.50	5.00
❏ 14832		Georgia Rain/In the Garden	1975		2.50	5.00

Polydor

❏ 14322		The Fool I've Been Today/Jenny Angel	1976		2.00	4.00

Tops

❏ 369		P.S. I Love You/ Vaya Con Dios (May God Be With You)	1953	10.00	20.00	40.00
		B-side by Betty Ford				

United Artists

❏ XW239		Take Me As I Am/Touch Me	1973		2.50	5.00
❏ XW618		With Pen in Hand/All I Want Is You	1975		2.50	5.00
❏ 50971		Funny How Time Slips Away/ Thanks to You for Loving Me	1972		2.50	5.00

Number	Title (A Side/B Side)	Year	VG	VG+	NM
Wing					
❏ 90065	Eyes of Fire, Lips of Wine/Monkey See, Monkey Do	1956	5.00	10.00	20.00
Wallace, Sonny					
Yucca					
❏ 127	Black Cadillac/If a Man Could See	1961	25.00	50.00	100.00
Waller, Gordon					
(Of Peter and Gordon)					
Bell					
❏ 794	The Lady in the Window/	1969	2.00	4.00	8.00
	I Was a Boy When You Needed a Man				
❏ 882	Sunshine/You Gonna Hurt Yourself	1970		3.00	6.00
Capitol					
❏ 2346	Everyday/Because of a Woman	1968	2.00	4.00	8.00
❏ 5886	Speak for Me/Little Nonie	1967	2.00	4.00	8.00
Walls, Van					
Atlantic					
❏ 980	After Midnight/Blue Sender	1952	25.00	50.00	100.00
Walsh, Joe					
(Also see "James Gang, The"; "Eagles")					
ABC					
❏ 12115	Time Out/Help Me Through the Night	1975		2.50	5.00
❏ 12187	Walk Away/Help Me Through the Night	1976		2.50	5.00
❏ 12426	Rocky Mountain Way/Turn to Stone	1978		2.00	4.00
ABC Dunhill					
❏ 4327	I'll Tell the World About You/Mother Says	1972		2.50	5.00
❏ 4361	Rocky Mountain Way/Prayer	1973		2.50	5.00
❏ 4373	Meadows/Bookends	1973		2.50	5.00
❏ 15026	Turn to Stone/All Night Laundromat Blues	1974		2.50	5.00
Asylum					
❏ 45493	Life's Been Good/Theme from Boat Weirdos	1978		2.00	4.00
❏ 45536	At the Station/Over and Over	1978		2.00	4.00
❏ 47144	A Life of Illusion/Rockets	1981		2.00	4.00
❏ 47197	Made Your Mind Up/Things	1981		2.00	4.00
Epic					
❏ 73843	Ordinary Average Guy/Alphabetical Order	1991			3.00
Full Moon					
❏ 69951	Waffle Stomp/Things	1982		2.00	4.00
Full Moon/Asylum					
❏ 46639	All Night Long/Orange Blossom Special	1980		2.00	4.00
	B-side by Gilley's Urban Cowboy Band				
❏ 46639 PS	All Night Long/Orange Blossom Special	1980		2.50	5.00
Warner Bros.					
❏ 28225	In My Car/How Ya Doin'?	1987			3.00
❏ 28304	The Radio Song/How Ya Doin'?	1987			3.00
❏ 28910	Good Man Down/I Broke My Leg	1985		2.00	4.00
❏ 29454	I.L.B.T.'s/Love Letters	1983		2.00	4.00
❏ 29519	Here We Are Now/I Can Play That Rock and Roll	1983		2.00	4.00
❏ 29611	Space Age Whiz Kids/Theme from Island Weirdos	1983		2.00	4.00
❏ 29611 PS	Space Age Whiz Kids/Theme from Island Weirdos	1983		2.50	5.00
Wanderers, The					
(More than one group?)					
Cub					
❏ 9003	A Teenage Quarrel/My Shining Hour	1958	7.50	15.00	30.00
❏ 9019	Collecting Hearts/Two Hearts on a Window Pane	1958	10.00	20.00	40.00
❏ 9023	Please/Shadrack, Meshack, and Abednego	1959	7.50	15.00	30.00
❏ 9035	Only When You're Lonely/I'm Not Ashamed	1959	7.50	15.00	30.00
❏ 9054	I Walked Through a Forest/	1959	7.50	15.00	30.00
	I'm Waiting for Green Pastures				
❏ 9075	I Need You More/I Could Make You Mine	1960	7.50	15.00	30.00
❏ 9089	For Your Love/Sally Goodheart	1961	7.50	15.00	30.00
❏ 9094	I'll Never Smile Again/A Little Too Long	1961	7.50	15.00	30.00
❏ 9099	She Wears My Ring/Somebody Else's Sweetheart	1961	12.50	25.00	50.00
❏ 9109	There Is No Greater Love/As Time Goes By	1962	7.50	15.00	30.00
Gone					
❏ 5005	Mask Off/My Lady Chocaonine	1957	7.50	15.00	30.00
MGM					
❏ 13082	There Is No Greater Love/As Time Goes By	1962	5.00	10.00	20.00
Onyx					
❏ 518	Thinking of You/Great Jumpin' Catfish	1957	15.00	30.00	60.00
Orbit					
❏ 9003	A Teenage Quarrel/My Shining Hour	1958	10.00	20.00	40.00
Panama					
❏ 3900	Quiet Night/One Look	1960	3.75	7.50	15.00
Savoy					
❏ 1109	We Could Find Happiness/Holy Mae Ethel	1953	100.00	200.00	400.00

Number		Title (A Side/B Side)	Year	VG	VG+	NM
United Artists						
❑ 570		After He Breaks Your Heart/Run, Run Senorita	1963	3.75	7.50	15.00
❑ 648		I'll Know/You Can't Run Away from Me	1963	7.50	15.00	30.00

Wang Chung

Number		Title (A Side/B Side)	Year	VG	VG+	NM
A&M						
❑ 2728		Fire in the Twilight/The Reggae (Instrumental)	1985		2.50	5.00
Arista						
❑ 1012	DJ	Hold Back the Tears (same on both sides)	1983	2.00	4.00	8.00
		As "Huang Chung"; stock copy appears not to exist				
Geffen						
❑ 22969		Praying to a New God/Tall Trees in a Blue Sky	1989			2.00
❑ 22969	PS	Praying to a New God/Tall Trees in a Blue Sky	1989			2.00
❑ 28359		Hypnotise Me/Lullabye	1987			2.00
❑ 28359	PS	Hypnotise Me/Lullabye	1987			2.00
❑ 28531		Let's Go!/The World In Which You Live	1986			2.00
❑ 28531	PS	Let's Go!/The World In Which You Live	1986			2.00
❑ 28562		Everybody Have Fun Tonight/Fun Tonight: The Early Years	1986			2.00
❑ 28562	PS	Everybody Have Fun Tonight/Fun Tonight: The Early Years	1986			2.00
❑ 28891		To Live and Die in L.A./Black-Blue-White	1985			2.00
❑ 28891	PS	To Live and Die in L.A./Black-Blue-White	1985			2.00
❑ 29193		Don't Be My Enemy/Wait	1984			3.00
❑ 29310		Dance Hall Days/Ornamental Elephant	1984			3.00
❑ 29310	PS	Dance Hall Days/Ornamental Elephant	1984			3.00
❑ 29377		Don't Let Go/There Is a Nation	1984			3.00
❑ 29377	PS	Don't Let Go/There Is a Nation	1984			3.00

War

(Also see "Burdon, Eric, and War")

Number		Title (A Side/B Side)	Year	VG	VG+	NM
Blue Note						
❑ 1009		L.A. Sunshine/Slowly We Walk Together	1977		2.50	5.00
Coco Plum						
❑ 2002		Groovin'/(B-side unknown)	1985		2.00	4.00
LAX						
❑ 02120		Cinco de Mayo/Don't Let No One Get You Down	1981		2.50	5.00
MCA						
❑ 40820		Galaxy (Part 1)/Galaxy (Part 2)	1977		2.50	5.00
❑ 40820	PS	Galaxy (Part 1)/Galaxy (Part 2)	1977		3.00	6.00
❑ 40883		Hey Senorita/Sweet Fighting Lady	1978		2.50	5.00
❑ 40995		Good, Good Feelin'/Baby Face (She Said Do Do Do Do)	1979		2.50	5.00
❑ 41061		I'm the One Who Understands/Corns & Callouses	1979		2.50	5.00
❑ 41158		Don't Take It Away/The Music Band 2 (We Are the Music Band)	1979		2.50	5.00
❑ 41209		I'll Be Around/The Music Band 2 (We Are the Music Band)	1980		2.50	5.00
RCA						
❑ PB-13061		You Got the Power/Cinco de Mayo	1982		2.00	4.00
❑ PB-13239		Outlaw/I'm About Somebody	1982		2.00	4.00
❑ PB-13322		Just Because/The Jungle (Medley)	1982		2.00	4.00
❑ JH-13426	DJ	Baby, It's Cold Outside (same on both sides)	1982		2.50	5.00
❑ PB-13544		Life (Is So Strange)/W.W. III	1983		2.00	4.00
United Artists						
❑ XW163		The Cisco Kid/Beetles in the Bog	1973		2.50	5.00
❑ XW281		Gypsy Man/Deliver the Word	1973		2.50	5.00
❑ XW350		Me and Baby Brother/In Your Eyes	1973		2.50	5.00
❑ XW432		Ballero/Slippin' Into Darkness	1974		2.50	5.00
❑ XW629		Why Can't We Be Friends?/In Mazatlin	1975		2.50	5.00
❑ XW629	PS	Why Can't We Be Friends?/In Mazatlin	1975		3.00	6.00
❑ XW706		Low Rider/So	1975		2.50	5.00
❑ XW706	PS	Low Rider/So	1975		3.00	6.00
❑ XW834		Summer/All Day Music	1976		2.50	5.00
❑ XW1213		Youngblood/(Instrumental)	1978		2.50	5.00
❑ XW1247		Sing a Happy Song/This Funky Music Makes You Feel Good	1978		2.50	5.00
❑ 50746		Lonely Feelin'/Sun Oh Sun	1971	2.00	4.00	8.00
❑ 50746	PS	Lonely Feelin'/Sun Oh Sun	1971	3.00	6.00	12.00
❑ 50815		All Day Music/Get Down	1971	2.00	4.00	8.00
❑ 50867		Slippin' Into Darkness/Happy Head	1971		3.00	6.00
❑ 50975		The World Is a Ghetto/Four Cornered Room	1972		3.00	6.00

Ward, Billy, and the Dominoes

(Includes "The Dominoes" also)

Number		Title (A Side/B Side)	Year	VG	VG+	NM
ABC-Paramount						
❑ 10128		You're Mine/The World Is Waiting for the Sunrise	1960	5.00	10.00	20.00
❑ 10156		You/Gypsy	1960	5.00	10.00	20.00
Decca						
❑ 29933		St. Therese of the Roses/Home Is Where You Hang Your Hat	1956	7.50	15.00	30.00
❑ 30043		Come On, Shake, Let's Crawl/Will You Remember	1956	7.50	15.00	30.00
❑ 30149		Half a Love (Is Better Than None)/Evermore	1956	7.50	15.00	30.00

Number	Title (A Side/B Side)	Year	VG	VG+	NM
❏ 30199	Rock, Plymouth Rock/Till Kingdom Come	1957	7.50	15.00	30.00
❏ 30420	To Each His Own/I Don't Stand a Ghost of a Chance	1957	7.50	15.00	30.00
❏ 30514	September Song/When the Saints Go Marching In	1957	7.50	15.00	30.00

Federal

❏ 12001	Do Something For Me/Chicken Blues	1951	150.00	300.00	600.00

Note: Federal 12010 and 12016 were issued only on 78s

❏ 12022AA	Sixty Minute Man/I Can't Escape from You	1951	75.00	150.00	300.00
❏ 12036	Heart to Heart/Looking for a Man to Satisfy My Soul	1951	125.00	250.00	500.00

With Little Esther

❏ 12039	I Am with You/Weeping Willow Blues	1951	100.00	200.00	400.00
❏ 12059	That's What You're Doing to Me/ When the Swallows Come Back to Capistrano	1952	100.00	200.00	400.00
❏ 12068AA	Have Mercy Baby/Deep Sea Blues	1952	50.00	100.00	200.00
❏ 12072	Love, Love, Love/That's What You're Doing to Me	1952	50.00	100.00	200.00
❏ 12105	I'd Be Satisfied/No Room	1952	45.00	90.00	180.00
❏ 12106	I'm Lonely/Yours Forever	1952	45.00	90.00	180.00
❏ 12114	The Bells/Pedal Pushin' Papa	1952	50.00	100.00	200.00
❏ 12129	These Foolish Things Remind Me of You/ Don't Leave Me This Way	1953	75.00	150.00	300.00

Green label, gold top

❏ 12129	These Foolish Things Remind Me of You/ Don't Leave Me This Way	1954	25.00	50.00	100.00

Green label, silver top

❏ 12129	These Foolish Things Remind Me of You/ Don't Leave Me This Way	1955	7.50	15.00	30.00

All green label

❏ 12139	You Can't Keep a Good Man Down/ Where Now Little Heart	1953	25.00	50.00	100.00
❏ 12162	Until the Real Thing Comes Along/My Baby's 3 D	1954	25.00	50.00	100.00
❏ 12178	Tootsie Roll/Move to the Outskirts of Town	1954	25.00	50.00	100.00
❏ 12184	Handwriting on the Wall/One Moment with You	1954	50.00	100.00	200.00
❏ 12193	Above Jacob's Ladder/Little Black Train	1954	12.50	25.00	50.00
❏ 12209	Can't Do Sixty No More/If I Never Get to Heaven	1955	25.00	50.00	100.00
❏ 12218	Love Me Now or Let Me Go/Cave Man	1955	12.50	25.00	50.00
❏ 12263	Bobby Sox Baby/How Long, How Long Blues	1956	12.50	25.00	50.00
❏ 12301	St. Louis Blues/One Moment with You	1957	12.50	25.00	50.00
❏ 12308	Have Mercy Baby/Love, Love, Love	1957	10.00	20.00	40.00

Jubilee

❏ 5163	Gimme, Gimme, Gimme/Come to Me, Baby	1954	7.50	15.00	30.00
❏ 5213	Sweethearts on Parade/Take Me Back to Heaven	1955	7.50	15.00	30.00

King

❏ 1280	Rags to Riches/Don't Ask Me	1953	12.50	25.00	50.00
❏ 1281	Christmas in Heaven/Ringing In	1953	25.00	50.00	100.00
❏ 1342	Tenderly/Little Lie	1954	12.50	25.00	50.00
❏ 1364	Three Coins in the Fountain/Lonesome Road	1954	12.50	25.00	50.00
❏ 1368	Little Things Mean a Lot/I Really Don't Want to Know	1954	10.00	20.00	40.00
❏ 1492	Learnin' the Blues/May I Never Love	1955	10.00	20.00	40.00
❏ 1502	Over the Rainbow/Give Me You	1955	10.00	20.00	40.00
❏ 5322	Sixty Minute Man/Have Mercy Baby	1960	5.00	10.00	20.00
❏ 5463	Lay It on the Line/ That's How You Know You're Growing Old	1961	5.00	10.00	20.00
❏ 6002	I'm Walking Behind You/This Love of Mine	1965	5.00	10.00	20.00
❏ 6016	O Holy Night/What Are You Doin' New Year's Eve	1965	5.00	10.00	20.00
❏ 6106	O Holy Night/What Are You Doin' New Year's Eve	1967	3.75	7.50	15.00

Liberty

❏ 55071	Star Dust/Lucinda	1957	6.25	12.50	25.00
❏ 55099	Deep Purple/Do It Again	1957	6.25	12.50	25.00
❏ 55111	My Proudest Possession/Someone Greater Than I	1957	6.25	12.50	25.00
❏ 55126	Solitude/You Grow Sweeter As the Years Go By	1958	6.25	12.50	25.00
❏ 55136	Jennie Lee/Music, Maestro, Please	1958	6.25	12.50	25.00
❏ 55181	Please Don't Say No/Behave, Hula Girl	1959	6.25	12.50	25.00

Ro-Zan

❏ 10001	Man in the Stain Glass Window/ My Fair Weather Friend	1961	5.00	10.00	20.00

United Artists

❏ 0017	Stardust/These Foolish Things	1973		2.50	5.00

"Silver Spotlight Series" reissue

Ward, Burt

MGM

❏ 13632	Boy Wonder I Love You/Orange Colored Sky	1966	50.00	100.00	200.00

Written and produced by Frank Zappa

Ward, Herb

Argo

❏ 5510	Strange Change/Why Do You Want to Leave	1965	20.00	40.00	80.00

RCA Victor

❏ 47-9688	Honest to Goodness/If You Got to Leave Me	1968	15.00	30.00	60.00

Ward, Singin' Sammy

Motown

❏ 1004	Lover/That's Why I Love You So Much	1960	10.00	20.00	40.00

With Sherri Taylor

Number	Title (A Side/B Side)	Year	VG	VG+	NM

Soul

| ❏ 35004 | Bread Winner/You've Got to Change | 1964 | 12.50 | 25.00 | 50.00 |

Tamla

❏ 54030	What Makes You Love Him/The Child Is Really Wild	1960	50.00	100.00	200.00
	With lines label				
❏ 54030	What Makes You Love Him/The Child Is Really Wild	1960	18.75	37.50	75.00
	With globe label				
❏ 54049	What Makes You Love Him/Don't Take It Away	1961	12.50	25.00	50.00
❏ 54057	Everybody Knew It/Big Joe Moe	1962	12.50	25.00	50.00
❏ 54071	Part Time Love/Someday Pretty Baby	1962	12.50	25.00	50.00

Ward, Walter, and the Challengers

(Later recorded as The Olympics)

Melatone

| ❏ 1002 | I Can Tell/The Mambo Beat | 1957 | 100.00 | 200.00 | 400.00 |

Ware, Curtis, and the Four Do-Matics

Kaybee

| ❏ 101 | Flame in My Heart/Am I in Love | 1961 | 125.00 | 250.00 | 500.00 |

Ware, Eddie

States

| ❏ 130 | That's the Stuff I Like/Lonely Broken Heart | 1954 | 30.00 | 60.00 | 120.00 |

Warlocks, The

(More than one group)

Ara

| ❏ 1017 | If You Really Want Me to Stay/Good Time Trippin' | 1968 | 30.00 | 60.00 | 120.00 |
| | Members later joined ZZ Top | | | | |

Decca

| ❏ 31806 | I'll Go Crazy/Temper Tantrum | 1965 | 5.00 | 10.00 | 20.00 |

Washington Square

| ❏ 2023 | Hey Joe/Girl | 1966 | 5.00 | 10.00 | 20.00 |

Warren, Bobby, Five

Jordan

| ❏ 119 | Nite-Beat/Medicine Man | 1960 | 10.00 | 20.00 | 40.00 |

Warwick, Dee Dee

Atco

❏ 6754	Make Love to Me/	1970		3.00	6.00
	She Didn't Know (She Kept On Talkin')				
❏ 6769	I'm Only Human/If This Was the Last Song	1970		3.00	6.00
❏ 6796	Cold Night in Georgia/Searchin'	1971		3.00	6.00
❏ 6810	Suspicious Minds/I'm Glad I'm a Woman	1971		3.00	6.00
❏ 6840	Everybody's Got to Believe in Somebody/	1971		3.00	6.00
	Signed, Dee Dee				

Blue Rock

❏ 4008	Do It with All Your Heart/Happiness	1965	2.50	5.00	10.00
❏ 4027	We're Doing Fine/I Want to Be with You	1965	2.50	5.00	10.00
❏ 4032	Baby I'm Yours/Gotta Get a Hold of Myself	1965	2.50	5.00	10.00

Jubilee

| ❏ 5459 | You're No Good/Don't Call Me | 1963 | 3.00 | 6.00 | 12.00 |

Mercury

❏ 72584	I Want to Be with You/Lover's Chant	1966	2.00	4.00	8.00
❏ 72638	I'm Gonna Make You Love Me/Yours Until Tomorrow	1966	2.00	4.00	8.00
❏ 72667	When Love Slips Away/House of Gold	1967	2.00	4.00	8.00
❏ 72710	Locked in Your Love/Alfie	1967	2.00	4.00	8.00
❏ 72738	Don't You Ever Give Up on Me/	1967	2.00	4.00	8.00
	We've Got Everything Going for Us				
❏ 72788	Girls Need Love/It's Not Fair	1968	2.00	4.00	8.00
❏ 72834	I'll Be Better Off (Without You)/Monday, Monday	1968	2.00	4.00	8.00
❏ 72880	Foolish Fool/Thank You Girl	1969	2.00	4.00	8.00
❏ 72927	That's Not Love/It's Not Fair	1969	2.00	4.00	8.00
❏ 72940	Next Time (You Fall in Love)/Ring of White Water	1969	2.00	4.00	8.00
❏ 72966	I (Who Have Nothing)/Where Is That Rainbow	1969	2.00	4.00	8.00

Private Stock

❏ 45,011	Get Out of My Life/Funny How We Change Places	1975		2.50	5.00
❏ 45,033	This Time May Be My Last/	1975		2.50	5.00
	Funny How We Change Places				

Sutra

| ❏ 134 | Move with the World/(B-side unknown) | 1984 | | 2.00 | 4.00 |

Warwick, Dionne

(Some of these spell her last name "Warwicke." Also see "Dionne and Friends")

Arista

❏ 0419	I'll Never Love This Way Again/In Your Eyes	1979		2.00	4.00
❏ 0459	Deja Vu/All the Time	1979		2.00	4.00
❏ 0498	After You/Out of My Hands	1980		2.00	4.00
❏ 0527	No Night So Long/Reaching for the Sky	1980		2.00	4.00
❏ 0572	Easy Love/You Never Said Goodbye	1980		2.00	4.00
❏ 0602	Some Changes Are For Good/This Time Is Ours	1981		2.00	4.00

Number		Title (A Side/B Side)	Year	VG	VG+	NM
❑ 0630		There's a Long Road Ahead of Me/Medley of Hits	1981		2.00	4.00
❑ 0673		Friends in Love/What Is This	1982		2.00	4.00
		A-side with Johnny Mathis				
❑ 0701		For You/What Is This	1982		2.00	4.00
❑ 1015		Heartbreaker/I Can't See Anything But You	1982		2.00	4.00
❑ 1040		Take the Short Way Home/Just One More Night	1983		2.00	4.00
❑ 1067		All the Love in the World/You Are My Love	1983			*Unreleased?*
❑ 9032		All the Love in the World/You Are My Love	1983		2.00	4.00
❑ 9073		How Many Times Can We Say Goodbye/ What Can a Miracle Do	1983		2.00	4.00
		With Luther Vandross				
❑ 9145		Got a Date/Two Ships Passing in the Night	1984		2.00	4.00
❑ 9281		Finder of Lost Loves/It's Love	1984		2.00	4.00
		A-side with Glen Jones				
❑ 9341		Run to Me/No Love in Sight	1985			3.00
		A-side with Barry Manilow				
❑ 9460		Whisper in the Dark/Extravagant Gestures	1986			3.00
❑ 9460	PS	Whisper in the Dark/Extravagant Gestures	1986			3.00
❑ 9567		Love Power/In a World Such As This	1987			3.00
		A-side with Jeffrey Osborne				
❑ 9567	PS	Love Power/In a World Such As This	1987			3.00
❑ 9638		Reservations for Two/For Everything You Are	1987			3.00
		A-side with Kashif				
❑ 9638	PS	Reservations for Two/For Everything You Are	1987			3.00
❑ 9652		Another Chance for Love/Cry on Me	1987			3.00
		A-side with Howard Hewett				
❑ 9652	PS	Another Chance for Love/Cry on Me	1987			3.00
❑ 9901		Take Good Care of You and Me/Heartbreak of Love	1989			3.00
		A-side with Jeffrey Osborne; B-side with June Pointer				
❑ 9940		I Don't Need Another Love/Heartbreaker	1990			3.00
		A-side with the Spinners				
❑ 9940	PS	I Don't Need Another Love/Heartbreaker	1990			3.00

Atlantic

Number		Title (A Side/B Side)	Year	VG	VG+	NM
❑ 3029		Then Came You/Just As Long As We Have Love	1974		3.00	6.00
		With the Spinners				
❑ 3202		Then Came You/Just As Long As We Have Love	1974		2.50	5.00
		With the Spinners				

Musicor

Number		Title (A Side/B Side)	Year	VG	VG+	NM
❑ 6303		If I Ruled the World/Only Love Can Break a Heart	1977		2.50	5.00

Scepter

Number		Title (A Side/B Side)	Year	VG	VG+	NM
❑ 1239		Don't Make Me Over/I Smiled Yesterday	1962	3.00	6.00	12.00
❑ 1247		This Empty Place/Wishin' and Hopin'	1963	3.00	6.00	12.00
❑ 1247	PS	This Empty Place/Wishin' and Hopin'	1963	5.00	10.00	20.00
❑ 1253		Make the Music Play/Please Make Him Love Me	1963	3.00	6.00	12.00
❑ 1262		Anyone Who Had a Heart/The Love of a Boy	1963	3.00	6.00	12.00
❑ 1274		Walk On By/Any Old Time of Day	1964	3.00	6.00	12.00
❑ 1282		You'll Never Get to Heaven (If You Break My Heart)/ A House Is Not a Home	1964	2.50	5.00	10.00
❑ 1285		Reach Out for Me/How Many Days of Sadness	1964	2.50	5.00	10.00
❑ 1294		You Can Have Him/Is There Another Way to Love Him	1965	2.50	5.00	10.00
❑ 1298		Who Can I Turn To/ Don't Say I Didn't Tell You Something	1965	2.50	5.00	10.00
❑ 12104		Here I Am/They Long to Be Close to You	1965	2.50	5.00	10.00
❑ 12111		Looking with My Eyes/Only the Strong, Only the Brave	1965	2.50	5.00	10.00
❑ 12122		Are You There (With Another Girl)/ If I Ever Make You Cry	1965	2.50	5.00	10.00
❑ 12133		Message to Michael/Here Where There Is Love	1966	2.00	4.00	8.00
❑ 12153		Trains and Boats and Planes/ Don't Go Breaking My Heart	1966	2.00	4.00	8.00
❑ 12167		I Just Don't Know What to Do with Myself/ In Between the Heartaches	1966	2.00	4.00	8.00
❑ 12181		Another Night/Go with Love	1966	2.00	4.00	8.00
❑ 12187		Alfie/The Beginning of Loneliness	1967	2.00	4.00	8.00
❑ 12196		The Windows of the World/Walk Little Dolly	1967	2.00	4.00	8.00
❑ 12203		I Say a Little Prayer/(Theme from) Valley of the Dolls	1967	2.00	4.00	8.00
❑ 12216		Do You Know the Way to San Jose?/Let Me Be Lonely	1968	2.00	4.00	8.00
❑ 12226		Who Is Gonna Love Me?/ (There's) Always Something There to Remind Me	1968	2.00	4.00	8.00
❑ 12231		Promises, Promises/Whoever You Are, I Love You	1968		3.50	7.00
❑ 12241		This Girl's In Love with You/Dream Sweet Dreamer	1969		3.50	7.00
❑ 12249		The April Fools/Slaves	1969		3.50	7.00
❑ 12256		Odds and Ends/As Long As There's an Apple Tree	1969		3.50	7.00
❑ 12262		You've Lost That Lovin' Feeling/Window Wishing	1969		3.50	7.00
❑ 12273		I'll Never Fall in Love Again/ What the World Needs Now Is Love	1970		3.50	7.00
❑ 12276		Let Me Go to Him/ Loneliness Remembers What Happiness Forgets	1970		3.00	6.00
❑ 12285		Paper Mache/The Wine Is Young	1970		3.00	6.00
❑ 12294		Make It Easy on Yourself/Knowing When to Leave	1970		3.00	6.00
❑ 12300		The Green Grass Starts to Grow/ They Don't Give Medals to Yesterday's Heroes	1970		3.00	6.00
❑ 12309		Who Gets the Guy/Walk the Way You Talk	1971		3.00	6.00
❑ 12326		Amanda/He's Moving On	1971		3.00	6.00
❑ 12336		The Love of My Man/Hurts So Bad	1971		3.00	6.00
❑ 12346		Raindrops Keep Falling on My Head/ Is There Another Way to Love You	1972		3.00	6.00

Number		Title (A Side/B Side)	Year	VG	VG+	NM
❏ 12352		I'm Your Puppet/Don't Make Me Over	1972		3.00	6.00
❏ 12383		Medley: Reach Out and Touch (Somebody's Hand)- All Kinds of People/The Good Life	1973		3.00	6.00

Warner Bros.

Number		Title (A Side/B Side)	Year	VG	VG+	NM
❏ 7669		Don't Let My Teardrops Bother You/ I Think You Need Love	1973		2.50	5.00
❏ 7693		(I'm) Just Being Myself/You're Gonna Need Me	1973		2.50	5.00
❏ 8026		Sure Thing/Who Knows	1974		2.50	5.00
❏ 8088		Take it from Me/It's Magic	1975		2.50	5.00
❏ 8154		Once You Hit the Road/World of My Dreams	1975		2.50	5.00
❏ 8183		His House and Me/Ronnie Lee	1976		2.50	5.00
❏ 8280		I Didn't Mean to Love You/He's Not for You	1976		2.50	5.00
❏ 8501		Keepin' My Head Above Water/ Livin' It Up Is Startin' to Get Me Down	1977		2.50	5.00
❏ 8530		Don't Ever Take Your Love Away/Do I Have to Cry	1978		2.00	4.00

Washington, Dinah, and Brook Benton

(Also see "Benton, Brook")

Mercury

Number		Title (A Side/B Side)	Year	VG	VG+	NM
❏ 71565		Baby (You Got What It Takes)/I Do	1960	3.75	7.50	15.00
❏ 71629		A Rockin' Good Way (To Mess Around and Fall in Love)/I Believe	1960	3.75	7.50	15.00
❏ 71629	PS	A Rockin' Good Way (To Mess Around and Fall in Love)/I Believe	1960	6.25	12.50	25.00

Waters, Muddy

Chess

Note: Muddy Waters records on Chess before 1509 are unconfirmed on 45 rpm

Number		Title (A Side/B Side)	Year	VG	VG+	NM
❏ 1509		All Night Long/Country Boy	1952	200.00	400.00	800.00
❏ 1514		Please Have Mercy/Looking for My Baby	1952	200.00	400.00	800.00
❏ 1526		Standing Around Crying/Gone to Main St.	1952	125.00	250.00	500.00
❏ 1537		She's All Right/Sad, Sad Day	1953	62.50	125.00	250.00
❏ 1542		Who's Gonna Be Your Sweet Man/ Turn the Lamp Down Low	1953	62.50	125.00	250.00
❏ 1550		Mad Love/Blow, Wind, Blow	1953	30.00	60.00	120.00
❏ 1560		I'm Your Hoochie Coochie Man/You're So Pretty	1954	20.00	40.00	80.00
❏ 1571		Just Make Love to Me/Oh Yeh!	1954	12.50	25.00	50.00
❏ 1579		I'm Ready/I Don't Know Why	1954	12.50	25.00	50.00
❏ 1585		Lovin' Man/I'm a Natural Born Lover	1955	12.50	25.00	50.00
❏ 1596		I Want to Be Loved/My Eyes Keep Me in Trouble	1955	12.50	25.00	50.00
❏ 1602		Manish Boy/Young Fashion Ways	1955	10.00	20.00	40.00
❏ 1612		Trouble, No More/Sugar Sweet	1955	7.50	15.00	30.00
❏ 1620		Forty Days and Forty Nights/All Aboard	1956	7.50	15.00	30.00
❏ 1630		Don't Go No Farther/Diamonds at Your Feet	1956	7.50	15.00	30.00
❏ 1644		I Got to Find My Baby/Just to Be with You	1956	7.50	15.00	30.00
❏ 1652		Got My Mojo Working/Rock Me	1957	7.50	15.00	30.00
❏ 1667		Good News/Come Home Baby	1957	7.50	15.00	30.00
❏ 1680		I Live the Life I Love/Evil	1958	6.25	12.50	25.00
❏ 1692		I Won't Go/She's Got It	1958	6.25	12.50	25.00
❏ 1704		Close to You/She's Nineteen Years Old	1958	6.25	12.50	25.00
❏ 1718		Mean Mistreater/Walking Thru the Park	1959	6.25	12.50	25.00
❏ 1724		Ooh Wee/Clouds in My Heart	1959	6.25	12.50	25.00
❏ 1733		Take the Bitter with the Sweet/She's Into Somethin'	1959	6.25	12.50	25.00
❏ 1739		Recipe for Love/Tell Me Baby	1959	6.25	12.50	25.00
❏ 1748		I Feel So Good/When I Get to Thinking	1960	6.25	12.50	25.00
❏ 1752		I'm Your Doctor/Ready Way Back	1960	5.00	10.00	20.00
❏ 1758		Love Affair/Look What You've Done	1960	5.00	10.00	20.00
❏ 1765		Tiger in Your Tank/Meanest Woman	1960	5.00	10.00	20.00
❏ 1774		Got My Mojo Working/Woman Wanted	1960	5.00	10.00	20.00
❏ 1796		Messin' with the Man/Lonesome Room Blues	1961	3.75	7.50	15.00
❏ 1819		Going Home/Tough Times	1962	3.75	7.50	15.00
❏ 1827		Muddy Waters Twist/You Shook Me	1962	3.75	7.50	15.00
❏ 1839		You Need Love/Little Brown Bird	1962	3.75	7.50	15.00
❏ 1862		Five Long Years/Twenty-Four Hours	1963	3.75	7.50	15.00
❏ 1895		The Same Thing/You Can't Lose What You Never Had	1964	3.75	7.50	15.00
❏ 1914		Short Dress Woman/My John the Conqueror	1964	3.75	7.50	15.00
❏ 1921		Put Me in Your Lay-A-Way/Still a Fool	1965	3.00	6.00	12.00
❏ 1937		My Dog Can't Bark/I Got a Rich Man's Woman	1965	3.00	6.00	12.00
❏ 1973		I'm Your Hoochie Coochie Man/Corrina, Corrina	1966	3.00	6.00	12.00
❏ 2018		When the Eagle Flies/Birdnest on the Ground	1967	2.50	5.00	10.00
❏ 2085		Going Home/I Feel So Good	1970	2.00	4.00	8.00
❏ 2107		Making Friends/Two Steps Forward	1971	2.00	4.00	8.00
❏ 2143		Garbage Man/Can't Get No Grindin'	1973		3.00	6.00

Waters, Roger

(Ex-Pink Floyd)

Columbia

Number		Title (A Side/B Side)	Year	VG	VG+	NM
❏ 04455		5:01 A.M. (The Pros and Cons of Hitch Hiking)/ 4:30 A.M. (Apparently They Were Travelling Abroad)	1984			3.00
❏ 07180		Radio Waves/Going to Live in L.A.	1987			3.00
❏ 07364		Sunset Strip/Money	1987			3.00
❏ 07617		Who Needs Information/Molly's Song	1987			3.00
❏ 74363		What God Wants, Part 1 (Long)/ What God Wants, Part 1 (Short)	1992			3.00

Number		Title (A Side/B Side)	Year	VG	VG+	NM

Watley, Jody
(Ex-Shalamar)
MCA

☐ 52956		Looking for a New Love/ Looking for a New Love (Acapella)	1987			3.00
☐ 52956	PS	Looking for a New Love/ Looking for a New Love (Acapella)	1987			3.00
☐ 53081		Still a Thrill/Looking for a New Love	1987			3.00
☐ 53081	PS	Still a Thrill/Looking for a New Love	1987			3.00
☐ 53162		Don't You Want Me/(Instrumental)	1987			3.00
☐ 53162	PS	Don't You Want Me/(Instrumental)	1987			3.00
☐ 53235		Some Kind of Lover/(Instrumental)	1988			3.00
☐ 53235	PS	Some Kind of Lover/(Instrumental)	1988			3.00
☐ 53258		Most of All/(Instrumental)	1988			3.00
☐ 53258	PS	Most of All/(Instrumental)	1988			3.00
☐ 53484		Real Love/(Instrumental)	1988			3.00
☐ 53484	PS	Real Love/(Instrumental)	1988			3.00
☐ 53660		Friends/Private Life	1989			3.00
☐ 53714		Everything/(Instrumental)	1989			3.00
☐ 53790		Precious Love/(Instrumental)	1990			3.00

Watson, Clayton
Lavender

| ☐ 2454 | | Everybody's Boppin'/Tall Skinny Annie | 1958 | 100.00 | 200.00 | 400.00 |

Waylon and Willie
(Also see "Nelson, Willie")
RCA

☐ PB-10529		Good Hearted Woman/Heaven or Hell	1975		2.50	5.00
☐ PB-11198		Mammas Don't Let Your Babies Grow Up to Be Cowboys/I Can Get Off on You	1978		2.00	4.00
☐ GB-11499		Mammas Don't Let Your Babies Grow Up to Be Cowboys/Luckenbach, Texas (Back to the Basics of Love) *Gold Standard Series*	1979		2.00	4.00
☐ GB-11996		Mammas Don't Let Your Babies Grow Up to Be Cowboys/I Can Get Off on You *Gold Standard Series*	1980		2.00	4.00
☐ PB-13073		Just to Satisfy You/Get Naked With You	1982		2.00	4.00
☐ PB-13319		(Sittin' On) The Dock of the Bay/Luckenbach, Texas	1982		2.00	4.00

Wayne, Thomas
Capehart

| ☐ 5009 | | Tragedy/No More, No More | 1961 | 7.50 | 15.00 | 30.00 |

Chalet

| ☐ 1054 | | No One/You're Tearin' Down My Mind | 1969 | | 3.00 | 6.00 |

Fernwood

☐ 106		You're the One That Done It/This Time	1958	75.00	150.00	300.00
☐ 109		Tragedy/Saturday Date	1959	7.50	15.00	30.00
☐ 111		Eternally/Scandalizing My Name	1959	7.50	15.00	30.00
☐ 113		Gonna Be Waitin'/Just Beyond	1959	7.50	15.00	30.00
☐ 120		Guilty of Love/Pancho Villa	1960	7.50	15.00	30.00
☐ 128		Tragedy/No More, No More	1961	7.50	15.00	30.00

Mercury

| ☐ 71287 | | You're the One That Done It/This Time | 1958 | 20.00 | 40.00 | 80.00 |
| ☐ 71454 | | You're the One That Done It/This Time | 1959 | 10.00 | 20.00 | 40.00 |

Phillips Int'l.

| ☐ 3577 | | I've Got It Made/The Quiet Look | 1962 | 6.25 | 12.50 | 25.00 |

Santo

| ☐ 9053 | | Stop the River/Eighth Wonder of the World | 1962 | 6.25 | 12.50 | 25.00 |
| ☐ 9057 | | Tragedy/Gonna Be Waiting | 1962 | 6.25 | 12.50 | 25.00 |

We Five
A&M

☐ 770		You Were On My Mind/Small World	1965	3.00	6.00	12.00
☐ 784		Let's Get Together/Cast Your Fate to the Wind	1965	2.00	4.00	8.00
☐ 793		You Let a Love Burn Out/Somewhere Beyond the Sea	1966	2.00	4.00	8.00
☐ 800		Somewhere/There Stands the Door	1966	2.00	4.00	8.00
☐ 820		What's Goin' On/The First Time	1966	2.00	4.00	8.00
☐ 894		High Flying Bird/What Do I Do	1967		3.00	6.00
☐ 1072		Walk On By/It Really Doesn't Matter	1969		3.00	6.00

MGM

| ☐ 14618 | | Seven Day Change/Natural Way | 1973 | | 2.50 | 5.00 |

Vault

| ☐ 964 | | Never Goin' Back/Here Comes the Sun | 1970 | | 3.00 | 6.00 |
| ☐ 969 | | Catch the Wind/Oh, Lonesome Me | 1970 | | 3.00 | 6.00 |

Verve

| ☐ 10716 | | Bandstand Dancer/Rejoice | 1973 | | 2.50 | 5.00 |

Webb, Boogie Bill
Imperial

| ☐ 5257 | | Bad Dog/I Ain't For It | 1953 | 62.50 | 125.00 | 250.00 |

Number		Title (A Side/B Side)	Year	VG	VG+	NM

Webs, The
(Bobby Goldsboro was in this group)
Heart

Number		Title (A Side/B Side)	Year	VG	VG+	NM
❑ 333		Blue Skies/Lost (Cricket in My Ear)	1962	10.00	20.00	40.00

Lite

| ❑ 9004 | | Blue Skies/Lost (Cricket in My Ear) | 1962 | 5.00 | 10.00 | 20.00 |

Weir, Bob
(Of the Grateful Dead)
Arista

| ❑ 0315 | | Bombs Away/Easy to Slip | 1978 | | 3.00 | 6.00 |
| ❑ 0336 | | I'll Be Doggone/Shade of Grey | 1978 | | 3.00 | 6.00 |

Warner Bros.

| ❑ 7611 | | One More Saturday Night/Cassidy | 1972 | 2.50 | 5.00 | 10.00 |

Welch, Bob
(Ex-Fleetwood Mac, ex-Paris)
Capitol

❑ 4479		Sentimental Lady/Hot Love, Cold World	1977		2.00	4.00
❑ 4543		Ebony Eyes/Outskirts	1978		2.00	4.00
❑ 4588		Hot Love, Cold World/Danchiva	1978		2.00	4.00
❑ 4588	PS	Hot Love, Cold World/Danchiva	1978		3.00	6.00
❑ 4685		Precious Love/Something Strong	1979		2.00	4.00
❑ 4719		Church/Here Comes the Night	1979		2.00	4.00
❑ 4719	PS	Church/Here Comes the Night	1979		2.50	5.00
❑ 4745		Oh Jenny/Three Hearts	1979		2.00	4.00
❑ 4790		Rebel Rouser/Spanish Dancers	1979		2.00	4.00
❑ 4833		Oneonone/Don't Let Me Fall	1980		2.00	4.00
❑ 4926		Don't Rush the Good Things/Reason	1980		2.00	4.00
❑ 4954		Girl Can't Stop/Those Days Are Gone	1980		2.00	4.00

RCA

❑ PB-12356		Imaginary Fool/Two to Do	1981		2.00	4.00
❑ PB-13074		Remember/You Can't Do That	1982		2.00	4.00
❑ PB-13569		Fever/Can't Hold Your Love Back	1983		2.00	4.00
❑ PB-13669		I'll Dance Alone/Stay	1983		2.00	4.00

Wellington, Rusty
Arcade

❑ 116		Dog-Gone It Baby, I'm in Love/Every Precious Memory	1953	10.00	20.00	40.00
❑ 124		I Want a Little Lovin'/Slowly But Surely	1954	10.00	20.00	40.00
❑ 140		Blues from Tennessee/Jump Jump Honey	1955	10.00	20.00	40.00
❑ 144		The Convict and the Rose/I Ain't A-Movin' On No More	1957	10.00	20.00	40.00

MGM

| ❑ 12581 | | Rocking Chair on the Moon/I Lost My Someone | 1957 | 75.00 | 150.00 | 300.00 |

Wells, Billy, and the Crescents
Reserve

| ❑ 105 | | I Love Only You/Julie | 1956 | 150.00 | 300.00 | 600.00 |

Wells, Cory
(Ex-Three Dog Night)
A&M

❑ 2013		Starlight/I Know You're Willin' Darlin'	1978		2.00	4.00
❑ 2035		Midnight Lady (Riding in the Shadows)/I Know You're Willin' Darlin'	1978		2.00	4.00
❑ 2060		Let Tomorrow Be/You Can Count on Me	1978		2.00	4.00

Wells, Mary
Atco

❑ 6392		Dear Lover/Can't You See	1965	3.00	6.00	12.00
❑ 6423		Keep Me in Suspense/Such a Sweet Thing	1966	3.00	6.00	12.00
❑ 6436		Fancy Free/Me and My Baby	1966	3.00	6.00	12.00
❑ 6469		Coming Home/Hey You Set My Soul on Fire	1967	3.00	6.00	12.00

Epic

| ❑ 02664 | | Gigolo/I'm Changing My Ways | 1982 | | 2.00 | 4.00 |
| ❑ 02855 | | These Arms/Spend the Night With Me | 1982 | | 2.00 | 4.00 |

Jubilee

❑ 5621		The Doctor/Two Lovers' History	1968	3.75	7.50	15.00
❑ 5629		Can't Get Away From Your Love/A Woman in Love	1968	3.75	7.50	15.00
❑ 5639		Don't Look Back/500 Miles	1968	3.75	7.50	15.00
❑ 5676		Mind Reader/Never Give a Man the World	1969	3.00	6.00	12.00
❑ 5684		Dig the Way I Feel/Love Shooting Bandit	1969	3.00	6.00	12.00
❑ 5695		Sweet Love/It Must Be	1970	3.00	6.00	12.00
❑ 5718		Mr. Tough/Never Give a Man the World	1971	3.00	6.00	12.00

Motown

❑ 1003		Bye Bye Baby/Please Forgive Me	1960	6.25	12.50	25.00
❑ 1011		I Don't Want to Take a Chance/I'm Sorry	1961	6.25	12.50	25.00
		Pink "lines" label				
❑ 1011		I Don't Want to Take a Chance/I'm Sorry	1961	3.75	7.50	15.00
		Blue "map" label				
❑ 1011	PS	I Don't Want to Take a Chance/I'm Sorry	1961	12.50	25.00	50.00
❑ 1016		Strange Love/Come to Me	1961	3.75	7.50	15.00
❑ 1016	PS	Strange Love/Come to Me	1961	12.50	25.00	50.00

Number		Title (A Side/B Side)	Year	VG	VG+	NM
☐ 1024		The One Who Really Loves You/I'm Gonna Stay	1962	3.75	7.50	15.00
☐ 1024	PS	The One Who Really Loves You/I'm Gonna Stay	1962	12.50	25.00	50.00
☐ 1032		You Beat Me to the Punch/Old Love (Let's Try It Again)	1962	3.75	7.50	15.00
☐ 1032	PS	You Beat Me to the Punch/Old Love (Let's Try It Again)	1962	12.50	25.00	50.00
☐ 1035		Two Lovers/Operator	1962	3.75	7.50	15.00
☐ 1039		Laughing Boy/Two Wrongs Don't Make a Right	1963	3.75	7.50	15.00
☐ 1042		Your Old Stand By/What Love Has Joined Together	1963	3.75	7.50	15.00
☐ 1048		You Lost the Sweetest Boy/ What's Easy for Two Is So Hard for One	1963	3.75	7.50	15.00
☐ 1056		My Guy/Oh Little Boy (What Did You Do to Me)	1964	3.75	7.50	15.00
☐ 1061		When I'm Gone/Guarantee for a Lifetime	1964	150.00	300.00	600.00
☐ 1065		Whisper You Love Me/I'll Be Available	1964			Unreleased?

Reprise

Number		Title (A Side/B Side)	Year	VG	VG+	NM
☐ 1031		I Found What I Wanted/I See a Future in You	1971	2.50	5.00	10.00
☐ 1308		If You Can't Give Her Love (Give Her Up)/ Cancel My Subscription	1974	2.50	5.00	10.00

20th Fox

Number		Title (A Side/B Side)	Year	VG	VG+	NM
☐ 544		Ain't It the Truth/Stop Takin' Me for Granted	1964	3.75	7.50	15.00
☐ 555		Use Your Head/Everlovin' Boy	1965	3.75	7.50	15.00
☐ 570		Never, Never Leave Me/ Why Don't You Let Yourself Go	1965	3.75	7.50	15.00
☐ 590		He's a Lover/I'm Learnin'	1965	3.75	7.50	15.00
☐ 590	PS	He's a Lover/I'm Learnin'	1965	7.50	15.00	30.00
☐ 6606		Me Without You/I'm Sorry	1965	3.75	7.50	15.00
☐ 6619		I Should Have Known Better/Please Please Me	1965	5.00	10.00	20.00

Wendy and Lisa

(Former members of Prince and the Revolution.)

Columbia

Number		Title (A Side/B Side)	Year	VG	VG+	NM
☐ 07243		Waterfall/The Life	1987			3.00
☐ 07243	PS	Waterfall/The Life	1987			3.00
☐ 07661		Honeymoon Express	1987			3.00
☐ 68557		Are You My Baby/Happy Birthday	1989			3.00

Wesley, Fred

(Includes Fred Wesley and the J.B.'s. Also see "Brown, James")

Atlantic

Number		Title (A Side/B Side)	Year	VG	VG+	NM
☐ 3408		Up for the Down Stroke/When In Doubt	1977		2.50	5.00

People

Number		Title (A Side/B Side)	Year	VG	VG+	NM
☐ 602		Gimme Some More/The Rabbit Got the Gun	1972		3.00	6.00
		As "The J.B.'s"				
☐ 607		Pass the Peas/Hot Pants Road	1972		3.00	6.00
		As "The J.B.'s"				
☐ 610		Givin' Up Food for Funk (Part 1)/ Givin' Up Food for Funk (Part 2)	1972		3.00	6.00
		As "The J.B.'s"				
☐ 614		Backstabbers/J.B. Shout	1972		3.00	6.00
☐ 616		If You Don't Get It the First Time/ You Can Have Her Boogie	1973		3.00	6.00
☐ 617		Alone Again (Naturally)/Watermelon Man	1973		3.00	6.00
☐ 619		Sportin' Life/Dirty Harri	1973		3.00	6.00
☐ 621		Doing It to Death/Everybody Got Soul	1973		3.00	6.00
☐ 627		If You Don't Get It the First Time, Back Up and Try It Again, Party/You Can Have Watergate, Just Give Me Some Bucks and I'll Be Straight	1973		3.00	6.00
☐ 632		Same Beat - Part 1/Same Beat - Part 2	1974		3.00	6.00
☐ 638		Damn Right I Am Somebody-Part 1/ Damn Right I Am Somebody-Part 2	1974		3.00	6.00
☐ 643		Rockin' Funky Watergate (Part 1)/ Rockin' Funky Watergate (Part 2)	1974		3.00	6.00
☐ 646		Little Boy Black/Rockin' Funky Watergate (Part 2)	1974		3.00	6.00
☐ 648		Breakin' Bread/Funky Music Is My Style	1974		2.50	5.00
☐ 651		Makin' Love/Rice and Ribs	1975		2.50	5.00
☐ 654		Thank You for Lettin' Me Be Myself and Be Yours (Part 1)/Thank You for Lettin' Me Be Myself and Be Yours (Part 2)	1975		2.50	5.00
☐ 655		(It's Not the Express) It's the J.B.'s Monaurail, Part 1/ (It's Not the Express) It's the J.B.'s Monaurail, Part 2	1975		2.50	5.00
☐ 660		Thank You for Lettin' Me Be Myself (Part 1)/ Thank You for Lettin' Me Be Myself (Part 2)	1975		2.50	5.00
☐ 663		All Aboard the Funky Soul Train/ Thank You for Lettin' Me Be Myself and You Be Yourself	1976		2.50	5.00
☐ 2502		My Brother (Part 1)/My Brother (Part 2)	1971		3.00	6.00
		As "The J.B.'s"				

RSO/Curtom

Number		Title (A Side/B Side)	Year	VG	VG+	NM
☐ 1037		House Party/I Make Music	1980		2.00	4.00

Wesley, Gate

Atlantic

Number		Title (A Side/B Side)	Year	VG	VG+	NM
☐ 2319		Do the Batman/Do the Thing	1966	6.25	12.50	25.00

West Coast Pop Art Experimental Band, The

Amos

Number		Title (A Side/B Side)	Year	VG	VG+	NM
☐ 119		Free As a Bird/Where's My Daddy	1969	3.75	7.50	15.00

Reprise

Number		Title (A Side/B Side)	Year	VG	VG+	NM
☐ 0552		Shifting Sands/1906	1967	6.25	12.50	25.00
☐ 0582		Help, I'm a Rock/Transparent Day	1967	6.25	12.50	25.00
☐ 0776		The Smell of Incense/Unfree Child	1968	6.25	12.50	25.00

Number		Title (A Side/B Side)	Year	VG	VG+	NM

West, Sonny
Atlantic

| ❏ 1174 | | Rave On!/Call On Cupid | 1958 | 10.00 | 20.00 | 40.00 |

Nor Va Jak

| ❏ 1956 | | Rock-Ola Baby/(B-side unknown) | 195? | 25.00 | 50.00 | 100.00 |

Weston, Kim
(Also see "Gaye, Marvin, and Kim Weston")
Enterprise

| ❏ 9101 | | Beautiful People/Goodness Gracious | 1974 | | 2.50 | 5.00 |

Gordy

❏ 7041		I'll Never See My Love Again/A Thrill a Moment	1965	5.00	10.00	20.00
❏ 7046		Take Me in Your Arms (Rock Me a Little While)/Don't Compare Me to Her	1965	5.00	10.00	20.00
❏ 7050		Helpless/A Love Like Yours (Don't Come Knocking Every Day)	1966	5.00	10.00	20.00

MGM

❏ 13720		I Got What You Need/Someone Like You	1967	5.00	10.00	20.00
❏ 13804		That's Groovy/Land of Tomorrow	1967	5.00	10.00	20.00
❏ 13881		Nobody/You're Just the Kind of Guy	1967	5.00	10.00	20.00
❏ 13927		Lift Every Voice and Sing/This Is America	1968	5.00	10.00	20.00
❏ 13928		The Impossible Dream/When Johnny Comes Marching Home	1968	3.75	7.50	15.00
❏ 13992		I Will Understand/Thankful	1968	3.75	7.50	15.00

People

| ❏ 1001 | | Danger, Heartbreak Ahead/I'll Be Thinkin' | 1970 | 2.50 | 5.00 | 10.00 |

Pride

| ❏ 1 | | Lift Every Voice and Sing/This Is America | 1970 | 2.50 | 5.00 | 10.00 |

Tamla

❏ 54076		It Should Have Been Me/Love Me All the Way	1963	12.50	25.00	50.00
❏ 54085		Just Loving You/Another Train Coming	1963	12.50	25.00	50.00
❏ 54100		Looking for the Right Guy/Feel Alright Tonight	1964	12.50	25.00	50.00
❏ 54106		A Little More Love/Go Ahead and Laugh	1964	25.00	50.00	100.00
❏ 54110		I'm Still Loving You/Go Ahead and Laugh	1964	15.00	30.00	60.00

Volt

| ❏ 1503 | | Little By Little, Bit By Bit/(B-side unknown) | 1971 | 3.75 | 7.50 | 15.00 |

Wham!
Columbia

| ❏ CS7 2591 | DJ | Last Christmas (6:43)/Last Christmas (4:24) | 1986 | 2.50 | 5.00 | 10.00 |
| ❏ 03611 | | Young Guns (Go For It)/Going For It | 1983 | 2.50 | 5.00 | |

As "Wham! U.K."

| ❏ 03611 | PS | Young Guns (Go For It) | 1983 | 2.00 | 4.00 | 8.00 |

As "Wham! U.K."; "Demonstration -- Not for Sale" on rear

| ❏ 03611 | PS | Young Guns (Go For It)/Going For It | 1983 | | 2.50 | 5.00 |

As "Wham! U.K."

| ❏ 03932 | | Bad Boys/Bad Boys (Instrumental) | 1983 | | 2.50 | 5.00 |

As "Wham! U.K."

❏ 04552		Wake Me Up Before You Go-Go/(Instrumental)	1984			3.00
❏ 04552	PS	Wake Me Up Before You Go-Go/(Instrumental)	1984	2.00	4.00	8.00
❏ 04691		Careless Whisper/(Instrumental)	1984			3.00

As "Wham! featuring George Michael"

| ❏ 04691 | PS | Careless Whisper/(Instrumental) | 1984 | 2.00 | 4.00 | 8.00 |

As "Wham! featuring George Michael"; color sleeve

| ❏ 04691 | PS | Careless Whisper/(Instrumental) | 1984 | | 2.50 | 5.00 |

As "Wham! featuring George Michael"; black & white sleeve

| ❏ 04691 | PS | Careless Whisper | 1984 | 2.50 | 5.00 | 10.00 |

As "Wham! featuring George Michael"; color sleeve; "Demonstration -- Not for Sale" on rear

❏ 04840		Everything She Wants/Like a Baby	1985			3.00
❏ 04840	PS	Everything She Wants/Like a Baby	1985			3.00
❏ 05409		Freedom/Heartbeat	1985			3.00
❏ 05409	PS	Freedom/Heartbeat	1985			3.00
❏ 05721		I'm Your Man/Do It Right	1985			3.00
❏ 05721	PS	I'm Your Man/Do It Right	1985			3.00
❏ 06182		The Edge of Heaven/Blue (Live in China)	1986			3.00
❏ 06182	PS	The Edge of Heaven/Blue (Live in China)	1986			3.00
❏ 06294		Where Did Your Heart Go?/Wham! Rap '86	1986			3.00
❏ 06294	PS	Where Did Your Heart Go?/Wham! Rap '86	1986			3.00
❏ 68712		Wake Me Up Before You Go-Go/(Instrumental)	1988			3.00

Reissue

| ❏ 68713 | | Careless Whisper/(Instrumental) | 1988 | | | 3.00 |

Reissue

| ❏ 68715 | | Everything She Wants/Like a Baby | 1988 | | | 3.00 |

Reissue

Wheel Men, The
(Gary Usher was in this group)
Warner Bros.

| ❏ 5480 | | Hon-Da Beach/School Is a Gas | 1964 | 12.50 | 25.00 | 50.00 |

Wheeler, Mary, and the Knights
Atom

| ❏ 701 | | A Falling Tear/I Feel in My Heart | 196? | 10.00 | 20.00 | 40.00 |

Number	Title (A Side/B Side)	Year	VG	VG+	NM

Wheeler, Onie

Sun
❏ 315	Jump Right Out of This Jukebox/Tell 'Em Off	1959	7.50	15.00	30.00

Wheelers, The

Cenco
❏ 107	Once I Had a Girl/Shine 'Em On	196?	15.00	30.00	60.00

Whippoorwills, The

Josie
❏ 892	Deep Within/Going to a Party	1961	15.00	30.00	60.00

Whips, The

Dore
❏ 502	Yes, Master/Rosie's Blues	1958	5.00	10.00	20.00

Flair
❏ 1025	Pleadin' Heart/She Done Me Wrong	1954	200.00	400.00	800.00

Whirlwinds, The

Philips
❏ 40139	Heartbeat/At the Party	1963	31.25	62.50	125.00

Whispers, The
(The Gotham records are one group; the Laurie is another; the others all are by a third)

Capitol
❏ S7-18394	Make Sweet Love to Me/My Funny Valentine	1995			3.00
❏ S7-18727	Come On Home/Better Watch Your Heart	1995			3.00

Dore
❏ 724	It Only Hurts for a Little While/The Happy One	1964	6.25	12.50	25.00
❏ 729	Slow Jerk/Never Again	1965	5.00	10.00	20.00
❏ 735	The Dip/Weirdo	1965	5.00	10.00	20.00
❏ 740	As I Sit Here/Shake It, Shake It	1965	5.00	10.00	20.00
❏ 751	Doctor Love/Lonely Avenue	1966	5.00	10.00	20.00
❏ 758	Walkin' the Fat Man/I Was Born When You Kissed Me	1966	5.00	10.00	20.00
❏ 768	Take a Lesson from the Teacher/Claire De Looney	1966	5.00	10.00	20.00
❏ 792	You Got a Man on Your Hands/You Can't Fight What's Right	1967	3.75	7.50	15.00
❏ 794	Needle in a Haystack/Waltz for You	1967	3.75	7.50	15.00
❏ 833	Never Again/I Was Born When You Kissed Me	1969	3.00	6.00	12.00
❏ 842	The Dip/It Only Hurts for a Little While	1970	2.50	5.00	10.00

Fontana
❏ 1564	My Long and Sleepless Night/Knowin'	1966	5.00	10.00	20.00

Gotham
❏ 309	Fool Heart/Don't Fool with Lizzie	1953	30.00	60.00	120.00
❏ 312	Are You Sorry/We're Getting Married	1953	62.50	125.00	250.00

Janus
❏ 140	There's a Love for Everyone/It Sure Ain't Pretty	1970		3.00	6.00
❏ 150	Your Love Is So Doggone Good/Cracker Jack	1971		3.00	6.00
❏ 174	Can't Help But Love You/A Hopeless Situation	1971		3.00	6.00
❏ 184	I Only Meant to Wet My Feet/You Fill My Life with Music	1972		3.00	6.00
❏ 200	Somebody Loves You/Can We Love Forever	1972		3.00	6.00
❏ 212	POW-MIA/Does She Care	1973		3.00	6.00
❏ 222	Feel Like Comin' Home/I Love the Way You Make Me Feel	1973		3.00	6.00
❏ 231	A Mother for My Children/What More Can a Girl Ask For	1973		3.00	6.00
❏ 238	Bingo/Once More with Feeling	1974		3.00	6.00
❏ 244	What More Can a Girl Ask For/Broken Home	1974		3.00	6.00
❏ 247	All I Ever Do (Is Dream of You)/Here Comes Tomorrow	1975		3.00	6.00
❏ 253	You're What's Been Missing in My Life/Given a Little Love	1975		3.00	6.00

Laurie
❏ 3344	Here Comes Summer/If You Don't Care	1966	5.00	10.00	20.00

Solar
❏ YB-11246	(Let's Go) All the Way/Chocolate Girl	1978		2.00	4.00
❏ GB-11328	Living Together (In Sin)/One for the Money	1978			3.00
	Gold Standard Series				
❏ YB-11353	(Olivia) Lost and Turned Out/Try and Make It Better	1978		2.00	4.00
❏ YB-11449	Happy Holidays to You/Try and Make It Better	1978		2.50	5.00
❏ YB-11590	Can't Do Without Love/Headlights	1979		2.00	4.00
❏ YB-11685	Homemade Lovin'/You'll Never Get Away	1979		2.00	4.00
❏ YB-11739	A Song for Donny/(Instrumental)	1979		3.00	6.00
❏ YB-11739 PS	A Song for Donny/(Instrumental)	1979		2.00	4.00
❏ YB-11894	And the Beat Goes On/Can You Do the Boogie	1980		2.00	4.00
❏ YB-11928	Lady/I Love You	1980			3.00
❏ GB-11977	(Let's Go) All the Way/Lost and Turned Out	1980			3.00
	Gold Standard Series				
❏ YB-12050	Welcome Into My Dream/Out the Box	1980		2.00	4.00
❏ YB-12154	It's a Love Thing/Girl I Need You	1981		2.00	4.00
❏ GB-12230	And the Beat Goes On/Lady	1981			3.00
	Gold Standard Series				
❏ YB-12232	I Can Make It Better/Say You (Would Love for Me Too)	1981		2.00	4.00
❏ YB-12295	This Kind of Lovin'/What Will I Do	1981		2.00	4.00

Number		Title (A Side/B Side)	Year	VG	VG+	NM
❏ YB-13005		I'm the One for You/I'm Gonna Love You More	1981		2.00	4.00
❏ GB-13486		It's a Love Thing/Make That Move	1983			3.00
		Gold Standard Series; B-side by Shalamar				
❏ 47961		In the Raw/Small Talkin'	1982		2.00	4.00
❏ 48008		Emergency/Only You	1982		2.00	4.00
❏ 48008	PS	Emergency/Only You	1982		3.00	6.00
❏ 69639		Don't Keep Me Waiting/Suddenly	1985		2.00	4.00
❏ 69658		Some Kinda Lover/Never Too Late	1985		2.00	4.00
❏ 69683		Contagious/(B-side unknown)	1984		2.00	4.00
❏ 69809		This Time/Love for Real	1983		2.00	4.00
❏ 69827		Keep On Lovin' Me/Try It Again	1983		2.00	4.00
❏ 69842		Tonight/Small Talkin'	1983		2.00	4.00
❏ 69965		Love Is Where You Find It/Say Yes	1982		2.00	4.00
❏ 70006		Rock Steady/Are You Going My Way	1987			3.00
❏ 70012		Just Gets Better with Time/Say Yes	1987			3.00
❏ 70017		In the Mood/(Instrumental)	1987			3.00
❏ 70020		No Pain, No Gain/(Instrumental)	1988			3.00
Soul Clock						
❏ 104		Great Day/I Can't See Myself Leaving	1969	2.50	5.00	10.00
❏ 107		The Time Will Come/Flying High	1969	2.50	5.00	10.00
❏ 109		What Will I Do/Remember	1969	2.50	5.00	10.00
❏ 1001		I Can Remember/Planets of Life	1970	2.00	4.00	8.00
❏ 1004		Seems Like I Gotta Do Wrong/Needle in a Haystack	1970	2.00	4.00	8.00
❏ 1005		I'm the One/You Must Be Doing All Right	1970	2.00	4.00	8.00
Soul Train						
❏ SB-10430		In Love Forever/Fairytale	1975		2.50	5.00
❏ SB-10628		(You're a) Special Part of My Life/Grove Street	1976		2.50	5.00
❏ SB-10700		One for the Money (Part 1)/One for the Money (Part 2)	1976		2.50	5.00
❏ SB-10773		Living Together (In Sin)/I've Got a Feeling	1976		2.50	5.00
❏ SB-10878		You're Only As Good As You Think You Are/ Sounds Like a Love Song	1977		2.50	5.00
❏ SB-10996		Make It With You/You Are Number One	1977		2.50	5.00
❏ SB-11139		I'm Gonna Make You My Wife/ You Never Miss Your Water	1977		2.50	5.00

Whitcomb, Ian

Jerden

Number		Title (A Side/B Side)	Year	VG	VG+	NM
❏ 735		Soho/Bony Moronie	1964	3.75	7.50	15.00
❏ 747		This Sporting Life/Soho	1964	3.75	7.50	15.00
Tower						
❏ 120		This Sporting Life/Fizz	1965	2.50	5.00	10.00
❏ 134		You Turn Me On (Turn On Song)/Poor But Honest	1965	3.75	7.50	15.00
❏ 155		N-N-Nervous/The End	1965	2.50	5.00	10.00
❏ 170		18 Whitcomb St./Fizz	1965	2.50	5.00	10.00
❏ 189		No Tears for Johnny/Be My Baby	1966	2.50	5.00	10.00
❏ 192		High Blood Pressure/Good Hard Rock	1966	2.50	5.00	10.00
❏ 212		Lover's Prayer/ Your Baby Has Gone Down the Plug Hole	1966	2.50	5.00	10.00
❏ 251		You Won't See Me/Please Don't Put Me on the Shelf	1966	2.50	5.00	10.00
❏ 274		Where Did Robinson Crusoe Go (With Friday on Saturday Night)/Poor Little Bird	1966	3.00	6.00	12.00
❏ 336		You Really Bent Me Out of Shape/ Rolling Home Georgeanne	1967	2.50	5.00	10.00
❏ 355		You Really Bent Me Out of Shape/ Rolling Home Georgeanne	1967	2.50	5.00	10.00
❏ 385		Groovy Day/Sally Sails the Sky	1967	2.50	5.00	10.00
United Artists						
❏ XW162		They Go Wild, Simply Wild Over Me/ Yaaka Hula Hickey Dula	1973		3.00	6.00

White Plains

Deram

Number		Title (A Side/B Side)	Year	VG	VG+	NM
❏ 85058		My Baby Loves Lovin'/Show Me Your Hand	1970	2.00	4.00	8.00
❏ 85066		Show Me Your Hand/Noises	1970		3.00	6.00
❏ 85072		Carolina's Coming Home/Every Little Move She Makes	1971		3.00	6.00
❏ 85076		When You Are a King/The World Gets Better with Love	1971		3.00	6.00
❏ 85080		I Can't Stop/Julie Anne	1972		3.00	6.00
❏ 85086		Step Into a Dream/Look to See	1973		3.00	6.00
❏ 85089		Does Anybody Know Where My Baby Is/ Just for a Change	1973		3.00	6.00

White, Alan

(Member of Yes)

Atlantic

Number		Title (A Side/B Side)	Year	VG	VG+	NM
❏ 3340		Ooh Baby (Goin' to Pieces)/One Way Rag	1976		2.50	5.00

White, Barry

A&M

Number		Title (A Side/B Side)	Year	VG	VG+	NM
❏ 1203		Right Night/There's a Place (Where Love Never Ends)	1988			3.00
❏ 1459		Super Lover/I Wanna Do It Good to Ya	1989			3.00
❏ 2943		Sho' You Right/You're What's On My Mind	1987			3.00
❏ 2943	PS	Sho' You Right/You're What's On My Mind	1987			3.00
❏ 3000		For Your Love (I'd Do Most Anything)/ I'm Ready for Love	1987			3.00
❏ 3000	PS	For Your Love (I'd Do Most Anything)/ I'm Ready for Love	1987			3.00

Number	Title (A Side/B Side)	Year	VG	VG+	NM
❏ 31458 0924 7	Practice What You Preach/Come On	1995		2.50	5.00

First pressing actually contains Lo-Key?'s "I Got a Thang 4 Ya!"/"Sweet On U," which are otherwise unavailable on 45. Can be identified without playing by checking the trail-off vinyl for a different number than that on the record.

Number	Title	Year	VG	VG+	NM
❏ 31458 0924 7	Practice What You Preach/Come On	1995			3.00

Second pressing indeed contains these two songs

Number	Title	Year	VG	VG+	NM
❏ 75021 1511 7	When Will I See You Again/Goodnight My Love	1990			3.00

20th Century

Number	Title	Year	VG	VG+	NM
❏ 2018	I'm Gonna Love You Just a Little More Baby/ Just a Little More Baby	1973		2.50	5.00
❏ 2042	I've Got So Much to Give/I've Got So Much to Give	1973		2.50	5.00
❏ 2058	Never Never Gonna Give Ya Up/ No, I'm Never Gonna Give Ya Up	1973		2.50	5.00
❏ 2077	Honey Please Can't You See/ Honey Please Can't You See	1974		2.50	5.00
❏ 2120	Can't Get Enough of Your Love, Babe/Just Not Enough	1974		2.50	5.00
❏ 2133	You're the First, the Last, My Everything/ More Than Anything, You're My Everything	1974		2.50	5.00
❏ 2177	What Am I Gonna Do with You/ What Am I Gonna Do with You, Baby	1975		2.50	5.00
❏ 2208	I'll Do for You Anything You Want Me To/ Anything You Want Me To	1975		2.50	5.00
❏ 2265	Let the Music Play/(Instrumental)	1975		2.50	5.00
❏ 2277	You See the Trouble with Me/ I'm So Blue When You Are Too	1976		2.50	5.00
❏ 2298	Baby, We Better Try to Get It Together/ If You Know, Won't You Tell Me	1976		2.50	5.00
❏ 2309	Don't Make Me Wait Too Long/ Can't You See It's Only You I Want	1976		2.50	5.00
❏ 2328	I'm Qualified to Satisfy You/(Instrumental)	1977		2.50	5.00
❏ 2350	It's Ecstasy When You Lay Down Next to Me/ I Never Thought I'd Fall in Love with You	1977		2.50	5.00
❏ 2361	Playing Your Game, Baby/Of All the Guys in the World	1977		2.50	5.00
❏ 2365	Oh What a Night for Dancing/ You're So Good You're Bad	1978		2.50	5.00
❏ 2380	Your Sweetness Is My Weakness/ It's Only Love Doing Its Thing	1978		2.50	5.00
❏ 2395	Just the Way You Are/ Now I'm Gonna Make Love to You	1979		2.50	5.00
❏ 2416	I Love to Sing the Songs I Sing/Oh Me Oh My	1979		2.50	5.00
❏ 2433	How Did You Know It Was Me?/Oh Me Oh My	1979		2.50	5.00

Unlimited Gold

Number	Title	Year	VG	VG+	NM
❏ 1401	Any Fool Could See (You Were Meant for Me)/ You're the One I Need	1979		2.00	4.00
❏ 1404	It Ain't Love, Babe (Until You Give It)/ Hung Up in Your Love	1979		2.00	4.00
❏ 1411	Love Ain't Easy/I Found Love	1980		2.00	4.00
❏ 1415	Sheet Music/(Instrumental)	1980		2.00	4.00
❏ 1418	Love Makin' Music/ Ella Es Todo Mi (She's Everything to Me)	1980		2.00	4.00
❏ 1420	I Believe in Love/You're the One I Need	1980		2.00	4.00
❏ 02087	I Want You/Our Theme (Part 1)	1981		2.00	4.00

By "Barry and Glodean White"

Number	Title	Year	VG	VG+	NM
❏ 02425	Louie Louie/Ghetto Letto	1981		2.00	4.00
❏ 02580	Beware/Tell Me Who Do You Love	1981		2.00	4.00
❏ 02956	Change/I Like You, You Like Me	1982		2.00	4.00
❏ 03379	Passion/It's All About Love	1982		2.00	4.00
❏ 03957	America/Life	1983		2.00	4.00
❏ 04098	Don't Let 'Em Blow Your Mind/Dreams	1983		2.00	4.00
❏ 70064	Didn't We Make It Happen, Baby/Our Theme (Part 2)	1981		2.00	4.00

By "Barry and Glodean White"

White, Ben, and the Darchaes

Aljon

Number	Title	Year	VG	VG+	NM
❏ 1247/8	Jocko Sent Me/Nationwide Stamps	1962	100.00	200.00	400.00

White, Tony Joe

Arista

Number	Title	Year	VG	VG+	NM
❏ 0376	We'll Live on Love/You and Me Baby	1978		2.00	4.00
❏ 0395	It Must Be Love/(B-side unknown)	1979		2.00	4.00

Casablanca

Number	Title	Year	VG	VG+	NM
❏ 2279	I Get Off on It/Feelin' Loose	1980		2.00	4.00
❏ 2304	Mamas Don't Let Your Cowboys Grow Up to Be Babies/Disco Blues	1980		2.00	4.00

Columbia

Number	Title	Year	VG	VG+	NM
❏ 03967	Swamp Rap/Living in the River City	1983		2.00	4.00
❏ 04134	The Lady in My Life/We Belong Together	1983		2.00	4.00
❏ 04356	We Belong Together/Naughty Lady	1984		2.00	4.00
❏ 04476	You Just Get Better All the Time/ Do You Have a Garter Belt	1984		2.00	4.00
❏ 04683	Nobody's Baby Tonight/Down by the Border	1984		2.00	4.00

Monument

Number	Title	Year	VG	VG+	NM
❏ 1003	Georgia Pines/Ten More Miles to Louisiana	1967	2.00	4.00	8.00
❏ 1053	Watching the Trains Go By/Old Man Willie	1968	2.00	4.00	8.00
❏ 1070	I Protest/Man Can Only Stand So Much Pain	1968	2.00	4.00	8.00
❏ 1086	Soul Francisco/Whompt Out on You	1968	2.00	4.00	8.00
❏ 1104	Polk Salad Annie/Aspen Colorado	1968	2.50	5.00	10.00

There weren't many picture sleeves released with American singles by The Who. And except for the later Warner Bros. duo, "You Better You Bet" and "Athena," they are all scarce. Sometimes, they were only released with promotional copies. This sleeve for the 1976 hit "Squeeze Box," an adaptation of the LP cover of *The Who By Numbers,* never got past the promo stage. A shame, because it's a cool sleeve.

Number		Title (A Side/B Side)	Year	VG	VG+	NM
❏ 1169		Roosevelt and Ira Lee (Night of the Moccasin)/	1969		3.00	6.00
		The Migrant				
❏ 1193		High Sheriff/Groupy Girl	1970		3.00	6.00
❏ 1206		Save Your Sugar for Me/My Friend	1970		3.00	6.00
❏ 1227		Old Man Willie/Scratch My Back	1970		3.00	6.00

20th Century

❏ 2276		It Must Be Love/Susie-Q	1976		2.00	4.00
❏ 2322		Texas Woman/Hold On to Your Hiney	1976		2.00	4.00

Warner Bros.

❏ 7468		The Daddy/Voodoo Village	1971		2.50	5.00
❏ 7477		My Kind of Woman/I Just Walked Away	1971		2.50	5.00
❏ 7505		Lustful Earl and the Married Woman/	1971		2.50	5.00
		I Just Walked Away				
❏ 7523		Delta Love/That On the Road Look	1971		2.50	5.00
❏ 7591		Even Trolls Love Rock and Roll/	1972		2.50	5.00
		If I Ever Saw a Good Thing				
❏ 7607		I've Got a Thing About You, Baby/Gospel Singer	1972		2.50	5.00
❏ 7712		Backwoods Preacher Man/	1973		2.50	5.00
		Saturday Night in Oak Grove, La.				
❏ 7780		Love 'Tween You and Me/Sign of the Lion	1974		2.50	5.00
❏ 8042		Wishful Thinking/Don't Let the Door	1974		2.50	5.00

Whitesnake

Geffen

❏ 19951		The Deeper the Love/Slip of the Tongue	1990			3.00
❏ 28103		Give Me All Your Love/Straight for the Heart	1988			3.00
❏ 28103	PS	Give Me All Your Love/Straight for the Heart	1988			3.00
❏ 28233		Is This Love/Bad Boys	1987			3.00
❏ 28233	PS	Is This Love/Bad Boys	1987			3.00
❏ 28331		Still of the Night/Don't Turn Away	1987		2.00	4.00
❏ 28339		Here I Go Again/Children of the Night	1987		2.00	4.00
		A radically different version than that on the LP				
❏ 28339	PS	Here I Go Again/Children of the Night	1987		2.00	4.00
❏ 29171		Love Ain't No Stranger/Guilty of Love	1984		2.00	4.00

Mirage

❏ 3672		Fool for Your Love/Black and Blue	1980		2.50	5.00
❏ 3766		Ain't Gonna Cry No More/Sweet Talker	1980		2.50	5.00
❏ 3794	DJ	Ain't No Love in the Heart of the City	1981		2.50	5.00
		(same on both sides)				
		May be promo only				
❏ 3844		Don't Break My Heart Again/	1981		2.50	5.00
		Lonely Days, Lonely Nights				

United Artists

❏ XW1291		The Time Is Right for Love/Belgian Tom's Hot Trick	1979		2.50	5.00
❏ 1323		Long Way from Home/We Wish You Well	1979		2.50	5.00

Whitford-St. Holmes Band

(Splinter group from Aerosmith)

Columbia

❏ 02555		Shy Away/Mystery Girl	1981		2.50	5.00

Who, The

(Also see "Entwistle, John"; "Moon, Keith"; "Townshend, Pete")

Atco

❏ 6409		Substitute/Waltz for a Pig	1966	12.50	25.00	50.00
❏ 6509		Substitute/Waltz for a Pig	1967	5.00	10.00	20.00

Decca

❏ 31725		I Can't Explain/Bald Headed Woman	1965	7.50	15.00	30.00
❏ 31801		Anyway, Anyhow, Anywhere/Anytime You Want Me	1965	15.00	30.00	60.00
❏ 31877		My Generation/	1965	7.50	15.00	30.00
		Out in the Street (You're Going to Know Me)				
❏ 31988		The Kids Are Alright/A Legal Matter	1966	7.50	15.00	30.00
❏ 32058		I'm a Boy/In the City	1966	7.50	15.00	30.00
❏ 32114		Happy Jack/Whiskey Man	1967	3.00	6.00	12.00
❏ 32114	PS	Happy Jack/Whiskey Man	1967	7.50	15.00	30.00
❏ 32156		Pictures of Lily/Doctor, Doctor	1967	3.00	6.00	12.00
❏ 32206		I Can See for Miles/Mary-Anne with the Shaky Hands	1967	3.00	6.00	12.00
❏ 32288		Call Me Lightning/Dr. Jeckyll & Mr. Hyde	1968	3.75	7.50	15.00
❏ 32362		Magic Bus/Someone's Coming	1968	3.00	6.00	12.00
❏ 32465		Pinball Wizard/Dogs Part Two	1969	2.50	5.00	10.00
❏ 32465	PS	Pinball Wizard/Dogs Part Two	1969	5.00	10.00	20.00
❏ 32519		I'm Free/We're Not Gonna Take It	1969	2.50	5.00	10.00
❏ 32670		The Seeker/Here for More	1970	3.00	6.00	12.00
❏ 32708		Summertime Blues/Heaven and Hell	1970	3.00	6.00	12.00
❏ 32729		See Me, Feel Me/Overture from Tommy	1970	3.00	6.00	12.00
		With custom gold label				
❏ 32729	PS	See Me, Feel Me/Overture from Tommy	1970	5.00	10.00	20.00
❏ 32737	DJ	Young Man Blues/Substitute	1970	30.00	60.00	120.00
		Only promos are known to exist				
❏ 32737	PS	Young Man Blues/Substitute	1970	75.00	150.00	300.00
❏ 32846		Won't Get Fooled Again/I Don't Even Know Myself	1971	2.50	5.00	10.00
❏ 32888		Behind Blue Eyes/My Wife	1971	2.50	5.00	10.00
❏ 32983		Join Together/Baby, Don't You Do It	1972	2.50	5.00	10.00

MCA

❏ L45-1809	DJ	Had Enough (same on both sides)	1978	2.50	5.00	10.00
❏ 40475		Squeeze Box/Success Story	1975	2.50	5.00	

Number			Title (A Side/B Side)	Year	VG	VG+	NM
❑ 40475	PS		Squeeze Box/Success Story	1975	7.50	15.00	30.00
			Sleeve is promo only				
❑ 40603			Slip Kid/Dreaming from the Waist	1976		2.50	5.00
❑ 40949			Who Are You/Had Enough	1978		2.50	5.00
❑ 40978			Trick of the Light/9:05	1978		2.50	5.00
❑ 41053			Long Live Rock/My Wife	1979		2.50	5.00

Polydor

Number			Title (A Side/B Side)	Year	VG	VG+	NM
❑ DJ-570	DJ		I'm the Face/Zoot Suit	1980		2.50	5.00
❑ DJ-570	PS		I'm the Face/Zoot Suit	1980		2.50	5.00
			As "The High Numbers"				
❑ 2022			5:15/I'm One	1979		2.00	4.00
❑ 2022	PS		5:15/I'm One	1979		2.50	5.00

Track

Number			Title (A Side/B Side)	Year	VG	VG+	NM
❑ 33041			The Relay/Waspman	1972	2.50	5.00	10.00
❑ 40152			Love, Reign O'er Me/Water	1973	2.00	4.00	8.00
❑ 40182			The Real Me/I'm One	1974	2.00	4.00	8.00
❑ 40330			Postcard/Put the Money Down	1974	10.00	20.00	40.00

Warner Bros.

Number			Title (A Side/B Side)	Year	VG	VG+	NM
❑ 29731			It's Hard/Dangerous	1983		2.50	5.00
❑ 29814			Eminence Front/One at a Time	1983		2.50	5.00
❑ 29905			Athena/It's Your Turn	1982		2.00	4.00
❑ 29905	PS		Athena/It's Your Turn	1982		2.50	5.00
❑ 49698			You Better You Bet/Quiet One	1981		2.00	4.00
❑ 49698	PS		You Better You Bet/Quiet One	1981		2.50	5.00
❑ 49743			Don't Let Go the Coat/You	1981		2.00	4.00

Whyte Boots, The

Philips

Number		Title (A Side/B Side)	Year	VG	VG+	NM
❑ 40422		Nightmare/Let No One Come Between Us	1967	20.00	40.00	80.00

Wichita Train Whistle, The

Dot

Number		Title (A Side/B Side)	Year	VG	VG+	NM
❑ 17152		Tapioca Tundra/Don't Cry Now	1968	3.75	7.50	15.00
		Produced by Michael Nesmith				

Wiedlin, Jane

(Of the Go-Go's)

EMI Manhattan

Number			Title (A Side/B Side)	Year	VG	VG+	NM
❑ 50118			Rush Hour/The End of Love	1988			2.00
❑ 50118	PS		Rush Hour/The End of Love	1988		2.00	4.00
❑ 50145			Inside a Dream/Song of the Factory	1988			2.00
❑ 50145	PS		Inside a Dream/Song of the Factory	1988			2.00

I.R.S.

Number			Title (A Side/B Side)	Year	VG	VG+	NM
❑ 52674			Blue Kiss/My Traveling Heart	1985			3.00
❑ 52674	PS		Blue Kiss/My Traveling Heart	1985			3.00

Wild Bees, The

RCA Victor

Number		Title (A Side/B Side)	Year	VG	VG+	NM
❑ 47-7275		Doctor Rock/Bamboozled	1958	7.50	15.00	30.00

Wild Cherry

A&M

Number		Title (A Side/B Side)	Year	VG	VG+	NM
❑ 1656		Voodoo Doll/Because Your Love Is Mine	1974		2.50	5.00

Epic

Number		Title (A Side/B Side)	Year	VG	VG+	NM
❑ 50225		Play That Funky Music/The Lady Wants Your Money	1976		2.50	5.00
❑ 50306		Get It Up/Baby Don't You Know	1976		2.00	4.00
❑ 50362		Hot to Trot/Put Yourself in My Shoes	1977		2.00	4.00
❑ 50401		Are You Boogieing Around on Your Daddy/Hold On (With Strings)	1977		2.00	4.00
❑ 50500		Don't Stop, Get Off/I Love My Music	1978		2.00	4.00
❑ 50551		1-2-3 Kind of Love/Fools Fall in Love	1978		2.00	4.00
❑ 50619		This Old Heart of Mine (Is Weak for You)/Lana	1978		2.00	4.00
❑ 50702		Try a Piece of My Love/Take Me Back	1979		2.00	4.00

United Artists

Number		Title (A Side/B Side)	Year	VG	VG+	NM
❑ XW217	DJ	Get Down (mono/stereo)	1973		2.50	5.00
		Stock copy not known to exist				

Wildcats, The

(More than one group)

RCA Victor

Number		Title (A Side/B Side)	Year	VG	VG+	NM
❑ 47-6386		Keep Talkin'/Beatin' on a Rug	1956	10.00	20.00	40.00

Reprise

Number		Title (A Side/B Side)	Year	VG	VG+	NM
❑ 0253		3625 Groovy Street/What Are We Gonna Do in '64	1964	5.00	10.00	20.00
		Actually the Blossoms				

United Artists

Number		Title (A Side/B Side)	Year	VG	VG+	NM
❑ 154		Gazachstahagen/Billy's Cha Cha	1958	6.25	12.50	25.00
❑ 169		Dancing Elephants/King Size Guitar	1959	6.25	12.50	25.00

Wilde, Kim

EMI America

Number			Title (A Side/B Side)	Year	VG	VG+	NM
❑ 8110			Kids in America/You'll Never Be So Wrong	1982		2.00	4.00
❑ 8110	PS		Kids in America/You'll Never Be So Wrong	1982		2.00	4.00
❑ 8139			Chequered Love/Everything We Know	1982		2.00	4.00

Number		Title (A Side/B Side)	Year	VG	VG+	NM
MCA						
❑ 52513		Go For It/Lovers on a Beach	1984			3.00
❑ 52513	PS	Go For It/Lovers on a Beach	1984		3.00	6.00
		Fold-out poster sleeve				
❑ 52925		Say You Really Want Me/(Instrumental)	1986		2.00	4.00
❑ 52952		Say You Really Want Me/	1986			3.00
		Say You Really Want Me (Radio Edit)				
❑ 53024		You Keep Me Hangin' On/Loving You	1987			3.00
❑ 53024	PS	You Keep Me Hangin' On/Loving You	1987			3.00
❑ 53130		Say You Really Want Me/She Hasn't Got Time for You	1987			3.00
❑ 53130	PS	Say You Really Want Me/She Hasn't Got Time for You	1987			3.00
❑ 53192		Another Step (Closer to You)/Hold Back	1987			3.00
❑ 53370		You Came/Tell Me Where You Are	1988			3.00
❑ 53370	PS	You Came/Tell Me Where You Are	1988			3.00
❑ 53480		Four Letter Word/She Hasn't Got Time for You	1988			3.00
Wilder, Matthew						
Arista						
❑ 0703		Work So Hard/(B-side unknown)	1982		2.00	4.00
Private I						
❑ 04113		Break My Stride/(Instrumental)	1983		2.00	4.00
❑ 04363		The Kid's American/Ladders of Love	1984		2.00	4.00
❑ 04617		Bouncin' Off the Walls/Love of an Amazon	1984		2.00	4.00
❑ 04617	PS	Bouncin' Off the Walls/Love of an Amazon	1984		2.00	4.00
Wilding, Bobby						
ABC-Paramount						
❑ 10275		Mama/You Give Me No Choice	1961	3.00	6.00	12.00
DCP						
❑ 1009		I Want to Be a Beatle/	1964	5.00	10.00	20.00
		Since I've Been Wearing My Hair Like a Beatle				
❑ 1106		I Want You/Too Young to Fall in Love	1964	3.00	6.00	12.00
May						
❑ 125		Slide (Part 1)/Slide (Part 2)	1962	3.00	6.00	12.00
Wildwoods, The						
(Actually the Five Satins)						
Caprice						
❑ 101		When the Swallows Come Back to Capistrano/	1961	37.50	75.00	150.00
		Heart of Mine				
May						
❑ 106		Golden Sunset/Here Comes Big Ed	1961	7.50	15.00	30.00
Wiley, Chuck						
Jax						
❑ 1004		I Love You So Much/I Begin to Miss You	1959	25.00	50.00	100.00
United Artists						
❑ 113		Tear It Up/Shake Up the Dance	1958	18.75	37.50	75.00
❑ 120		By My Side/Door to Door	1958			*Unreleased*
Wilkens, Artie, and the Palms						
States						
❑ 157		Darling Patricia/Please Come Back	1956	150.00	300.00	600.00
Williams, Barry						
(Greg Brady of The Brady Bunch)						
Paramount						
❑ 0122		Sweet Sweetheart/Sunny	1971	3.75	7.50	15.00
❑ 0122	PS	Sweet Sweetheart/Sunny	1971	5.00	10.00	20.00
Williams, Bernie						
Bell						
❑ 768		Ever Again/Next to You	1969	50.00	100.00	200.00
Williams, Cora/Shirley Haven and the Four Jacks						
Federal						
❑ 12079		I Ain't Coming Back Anymore/Sure Cure for the Blues	1952	150.00	300.00	600.00
Williams, Danny						
United Artists						
❑ 348		Lonely/We Will Never Be As Young As This Again	1961	3.00	6.00	12.00
❑ 411		Jeannie/Weaver of Dreams	1962	3.00	6.00	12.00
❑ 480		Something's Gotta Give/Miracle of You	1962	3.00	6.00	12.00
❑ 493		Tears/Miracle of You	1962	3.00	6.00	12.00
❑ 601		More (Theme from Mondo Cane)/Rhapsody	1963	3.00	6.00	12.00
❑ 685		White on White/The Comedy Is Ended	1964	3.75	7.50	15.00
❑ 729		The Truth Hurts/Little Toy Balloon	1964	2.50	5.00	10.00
❑ 762		I Watched a Flower Grow/Forget Her, Forget Her	1964	2.50	5.00	10.00
❑ 825		How Soon/The Seventh Dawn	1965	2.50	5.00	10.00
❑ 860		All's Fair in Love and War/Masquerade	1965	2.50	5.00	10.00
❑ 959		The Stranger/I Can't Believe I'm Losing You	1965	2.50	5.00	10.00
❑ 50020		Blue on White/It's Not for Me to Say	1966	2.00	4.00	8.00

Number		Title (A Side/B Side)	Year	VG	VG+	NM

Williams, Jim
Sun
| ❑ 270 | | Please Don't Cry Over Me/That Depends on You | 1957 | 7.50 | 15.00 | 30.00 |

Williams, Jimmy
ABC-Paramount
| ❑ 10471 | | I Gave My Love a Cherry/Half Man | 1963 | 3.00 | 6.00 | 12.00 |
| ❑ 10523 | | Green Pastures (23rd Psalm)/
I'm Strung Out Over You, Baby | 1964 | 3.00 | 6.00 | 12.00 |
Atlantic
| ❑ 2296 | | Walking on Air/I'm So Lost | 1965 | 2.50 | 5.00 | 10.00 |
Cub
| ❑ 9031 | | My Pledge and My Promise/Keep Me with You | 1959 | 3.75 | 7.50 | 15.00 |
| ❑ 9039 | | C'mon Baby (What's Your Name)/
Don't Put It Off (Do It Now) | 1959 | 3.75 | 7.50 | 15.00 |
Dub
| ❑ 2842 | | You're Always Late/I Belong to You | 1958 | 25.00 | 50.00 | 100.00 |
Dyno Voice
| ❑ 931 | | Mushroom City/Standing There | 1969 | 2.00 | 4.00 | 8.00 |
Hull
| ❑ 765 | | I Can't Help Falling in Love/Smile | 1964 | 2.50 | 5.00 | 10.00 |
Limelight
| ❑ 3038 | | Mrs. Cherry/Keoto'To | 1964 | 2.50 | 5.00 | 10.00 |
MGM
❑ 11938		No One Knows/These Blues Are Over You	1955	5.00	10.00	20.00
❑ 12262		Alpha and Omega/Where Will I Shelter My Sheep	1956	5.00	10.00	20.00
❑ 12362		Throwing My Life Away/We're Drifting Further Apart	1956	5.00	10.00	20.00
❑ 12596		You're the One/I'll Only Give My Love	1957	6.25	12.50	25.00
Orbit
| ❑ 9002 | | You're the One/I'll Only Give My Love | 1958 | 3.75 | 7.50 | 15.00 |
Roulette
| ❑ 4303 | | There Is No Doubt/What a Change | 1960 | 3.75 | 7.50 | 15.00 |

Williams, Larry
Bell
| ❑ 813 | | I Could Love You Baby/Can
't Find No Substitute for Love
With Johnny Watson | 1969 | 2.50 | 5.00 | 10.00 |
Chess
❑ 1736		My Baby's Got Soul/Every Day I Wonder	1959	5.00	10.00	20.00
❑ 1745		Get Ready/Baby, Baby	1959	5.00	10.00	20.00
❑ 1761		I Wanna Know/Like a Gentle Man	1960	5.00	10.00	20.00
❑ 1764		Oh Baby/I Hear My Baby	1960	5.00	10.00	20.00
❑ 1805		Lawdy Mama/Fresh Out of Tears	1961	5.00	10.00	20.00
Fantasy
❑ 806		Doing the Best I Can (With What I Got)/Gimme Some	1977		2.50	5.00
❑ 810		One Thing or the Other (Part 1)/ One Thing or the Other (Part 2)	1977		2.50	5.00
❑ 841		The Resurrection of Funk/(B-side unknown)	1978		2.50	5.00
Mercury
| ❑ 72147 | | Woman/Can't Help Myself | 1963 | 3.75 | 7.50 | 15.00 |
Okeh
❑ 7259		This Old Heart (Is So Lonely)/ I'd Rather Fight Than Switch	1966	2.50	5.00	10.00
❑ 7274		Mercy, Mercy, Mercy/A Quitter Never Wins *With Johnny Watson*	1967	2.50	5.00	10.00
❑ 7280		I Am the One/You Ask for One Good Reason	1967	2.50	5.00	10.00
❑ 7281		Too Late/Two for the Price of One *With Johnny Watson*	1967	2.50	5.00	10.00
❑ 7294		Just Because/Boss Lovin'	1967	2.50	5.00	10.00
❑ 7300		Find Yourself Someone to Love/Nobody *With Johnny Watson; backed by Kaleidoscope*	1967	6.25	12.50	25.00
Smash
| ❑ 2035 | | Call on Me/Boss Lovin' | 1966 | 3.00 | 6.00 | 12.00 |
Specialty
❑ 597		Just Because/Let Me Tell You Baby	1957	7.50	15.00	30.00
❑ 608		Short Fat Fannie/High School Dance	1957	7.50	15.00	30.00
❑ 615		Bony Moronie/You Bug Me, Baby	1957	7.50	15.00	30.00
❑ 626		Dizzy, Miss Lizzy/Slow Down	1958	7.50	15.00	30.00
❑ 626	PS	Dizzy, Miss Lizzy/Slow Down	1958	37.50	75.00	150.00
❑ 634		Hootchy-Koo/The Dummy	1958	6.25	12.50	25.00
❑ 647		I Was a Fool/Peaches and Cream	1958	6.25	12.50	25.00
❑ 658		Bad Boy/She Said "Yeah"	1959	6.25	12.50	25.00
❑ 665		Steal a Little Kiss/I Can't Stop Loving You	1959	6.25	12.50	25.00
❑ 677		Give Me Your Love/Teardrops	1959	6.25	12.50	25.00
❑ 682		Ting-a-Ling/Little Schoolgirl	1960	6.25	12.50	25.00
Venture
| ❑ 622 | | Shake Your Body Girl/Love I Can't Seem to Find It | 1968 | 2.50 | 5.00 | 10.00 |
| ❑ 627 | | Wake Up (Nothing Comes to a Sleeper But a Dream)/
Love I Can't Seem to Find It | 1968 | 2.50 | 5.00 | 10.00 |

Number	Title (A Side/B Side)	Year	VG	VG+	NM

Williams, Lew
Imperial

☐ 5394	Cat Talk/Gone Ape Man	1956	30.00	60.00	120.00
☐ 5411	Bop Bop Ba Doo Bop/Something I Said	1956	30.00	60.00	120.00
☐ 5429	Centipede/Abra Cadabra	1957	30.00	60.00	120.00
☐ 8306	Don't Mention My Name/I'll Play Your Game	1956			

Williams, Maurice, and the Zodiacs
(Maurice Williams also was in The Gladiolas)
Atlantic

☐ 2199	Funny/Loneliness	1963	3.75	7.50	15.00
	As "The Zodiacs"				
☐ 2741	Sweetness/Whirlpool	1970		2.50	5.00

Cole

| ☐ 100 | Golly Gee/"I" Town | 1959 | 12.50 | 25.00 | 50.00 |
| ☐ 101 | Lover (Where Are You)/She's Mine | 1959 | 10.00 | 20.00 | 40.00 |

Deesu

☐ 302	Baby Baby/Being Without You	1967	5.00	10.00	20.00
☐ 304	May I/This Feeling	1967	5.00	10.00	20.00
☐ 307	Ooh Poo Pa Doo (Part 1)/Ooh Poo Pa Doo (Part 2)	1967	5.00	10.00	20.00
☐ 309	Don't Ever Leave Me/Surely	1967	5.00	10.00	20.00
☐ 311	Don't Be Half Safe/How to Pick a Winner	1967	5.00	10.00	20.00
☐ 318	Stay '68 (Live Version)/Dance, Dance, Dance	1968	3.75	7.50	15.00

Herald

☐ 552	Stay/Do You Believe	1960	5.00	10.00	20.00
☐ 556	Always/I Remember	1961	3.75	7.50	15.00
☐ 559	Do I/Come Along	1961	3.75	7.50	15.00
☐ 563	Someday/Come and Get It	1961	3.75	7.50	15.00
☐ 565	Please/High Blood Pressure	1961	3.75	7.50	15.00
☐ 572	It's Alright/Here I Stand	1962	3.75	7.50	15.00

RCA

| ☐ 5363-7-R | Stay/She's Like the Wind | 1987 | | | 3.00 |
| | *B-side by Patrick Swayze* | | | | |

Scepter

| ☐ 12113 | Nobody Knows/I Know | 1965 | 3.75 | 7.50 | 15.00 |

Sea Horn

| ☐ 503 | My Baby's Gone/Return | 1964 | 3.75 | 7.50 | 15.00 |

Selwyn

| ☐ 5121 | Say Yeah/College Girl | 1959 | 12.50 | 25.00 | 50.00 |

Sphere Sound

| ☐ 707 | So Fine/The Winds | 1965 | 3.00 | 6.00 | 12.00 |

Vee Jay

| ☐ 678 | May I/Lollipop | 1965 | 5.00 | 10.00 | 20.00 |

Veep

| ☐ 1294 | My Reason for Living/The Four Corners | 1969 | 2.00 | 4.00 | 8.00 |

Williams, Otis, and His Charms
(Also see "Charms, The." The members, other than Williams, are totally different in the two entries.)
DeLuxe

☐ 6088	Miss the Love/Tell Me Now	1955	7.50	15.00	30.00
	As "Otis Williams and His New Group"				
☐ 6090	Gum Drop/Save Me, Save Me	1955	7.50	15.00	30.00
	As "Otis Williams and His New Group"				
☐ 6091	That's Your Mistake/Too Late I Learned	1955	7.50	15.00	30.00
☐ 6092	Rolling Home/Do Be You	1956	7.50	15.00	30.00
☐ 6093	Ivory Tower/In Paradise	1956	7.50	15.00	30.00
☐ 6095	One Night Only/It's All Over	1956	7.50	15.00	30.00
☐ 6097	I'd Like to Thank You Mr. D.J./Whirlwind	1956	7.50	15.00	30.00
☐ 6098	Gypsy Lady/I'll Remember You	1956	7.50	15.00	30.00
☐ 6105	Blues Stay Away from Me/Pardon Me	1957	6.25	12.50	25.00
☐ 6115	Walkin' After Midnight/I'm Waiting Just for You	1957	6.25	12.50	25.00
☐ 6130	Nowhere on Earth/No Got De Woman	1957	6.25	12.50	25.00
☐ 6137	Talking to Myself/One Kind Word from You	1957	6.25	12.50	25.00
☐ 6138	United/Don't Deny Me	1957	6.25	12.50	25.00
☐ 6149	Dynamite Darling/Well Oh Well	1957	6.25	12.50	25.00
☐ 6158	Could This Be Magic/Oh Julie	1958	6.25	12.50	25.00
☐ 6160	Let Some Love in Your Heart/Baby-O	1958	6.25	12.50	25.00
☐ 6165	Burnin' Lips/Red Hot Love (Do This Love)	1958	6.25	12.50	25.00
☐ 6174	Don't Wake Up the Kids/You'll Remain Forever	1958	6.25	12.50	25.00
☐ 6178	My Friends/The Secret	1958	6.25	12.50	25.00
☐ 6181	Pretty Little Things Called Girls/Welcome Home	1959	6.25	12.50	25.00
☐ 6183	My Prayer Tonight/Watch Dog	1959	6.25	12.50	25.00
☐ 6185	I Knew It All the Time/Tears of Happiness	1959	6.25	12.50	25.00
☐ 6186	In Paradise/Who Knows	1959	6.25	12.50	25.00
☐ 6187	Blues Stay Away from Me/ Funny What True Love Can Do	1959	6.25	12.50	25.00

King

☐ 5323	Chief Um (Take It Easy)/It's a Treat	1960	5.00	10.00	20.00
☐ 5332	Silver Star/Rickety Rickshaw Man	1960	5.00	10.00	20.00
☐ 5372	Image of a Girl/Wait a Minute Baby	1960	12.50	25.00	50.00
☐ 5389	The First Sign of Love/So Be It	1960	5.00	10.00	20.00
☐ 5421	Wait/And Take My Love	1960	5.00	10.00	20.00
☐ 5455	Little Turtle Dove/So Can I	1961	5.00	10.00	20.00

Number		Title (A Side/B Side)	Year	VG	VG+	NM
❑ 5497		Just Forget About Me/You Know How Much I Care	1961	5.00	10.00	20.00
❑ 5527		Pardon Me/Panic	1961	5.00	10.00	20.00
❑ 5558		Two Hearts/The Secret	1961	5.00	10.00	20.00
❑ 5682		When We Get Together/Only Young Once	1962	3.75	7.50	15.00
❑ 5816		It Just Ain't Right/It'll Never Happen Again	1963	3.75	7.50	15.00
❑ 5880		Unchain My Heart/Friends Call Me a Fool	1964	3.75	7.50	15.00
❑ 6034		Bye Bye Baby/Please Believe in Me	1966	3.75	7.50	15.00
Okeh						
❑ 7225		Baby, You Turn Me On/Love Don't Grow on Trees	1965	3.75	7.50	15.00
❑ 7235		I Fall to Pieces/Gotta Get Myself Together	1965	3.75	7.50	15.00
❑ 7248		I Got Loving/Welcome Home	1966	3.75	7.50	15.00
❑ 7261		Ain't Gonna Walk Your Dog No More/	1966	3.75	7.50	15.00
❑		Your Sweet Love (Rained Over Me)				
Scepter						
❑ 12376		Here Lie the Bones of Nellie Jones/	1973	2.00	4.00	8.00
		When You Turn On the Love				
Stop						
❑ 301		Begging to You/(B-side unknown)	1968	2.50	5.00	10.00
❑ 306		Begging to You/Everybody's Got a Song But Me	1968	2.50	5.00	10.00
❑ 346		Jesus Is a Soul Man/	1969	2.50	5.00	10.00
		Make a Woman Feel Like a Woman				
❑ 360		Ling, Ting, Tong/For the Love	1970	2.50	5.00	10.00
❑ 388		I Wanna Go Country/Rocky Top	1971	2.00	4.00	8.00
		As "Otis Williams and the Midnight Cowboys"				

Williams, Paul
(Of the Temptations)
Gordy

Number	Title (A Side/B Side)	Year	VG	VG+	NM
❑ 7125	Feel Like Givin' Up/Once I Had a Heart	1973			*Unreleased*

Williams, Timmy
Mala

Number	Title (A Side/B Side)	Year	VG	VG+	NM
❑ 515	Competition/Wipe Away Your Tears	1965	75.00	150.00	300.00

Williams, Tony
(Of the Platters)
Dot

Number	Title (A Side/B Side)	Year	VG	VG+	NM
❑ 16806	Endless Street/Smoke, Drink, Play 21	1965	2.00	4.00	8.00
Mercury					
❑ 71158	Let's Start All Over Again/When You Return	1957	5.00	10.00	20.00
❑ 71532	Charmaine/Peg o' My Heart	1959	5.00	10.00	20.00
Philips					
❑ 40069	Chloe/Second Best	1962	2.50	5.00	10.00
❑ 40123	Twenty-Four Lonely Hours/Save Me	1963	2.50	5.00	10.00
❑ 40141	How Come/When I Had You	1963	2.50	5.00	10.00
Reprise					
❑ 20,019	Sleepless Nights/Movin' In	1961	3.75	7.50	15.00
❑ 20,030	Miracle/My Prayer	1961	3.75	7.50	15.00
❑ 20,056	It's So Easy to Surrender/That's More Like It	1962	10.00	20.00	40.00
	Released only in Italy				
❑ 20,067	Come Along Now/That's More Like It	1962	3.75	7.50	15.00
❑ 20,073	Sing, Lover, Sing/Mandalino	1962	10.00	20.00	40.00
	Released only in Hong Kong				
❑ 20,136	Dream/Loving You	1963	10.00	20.00	40.00
	Released only in Italy				

Willie and the Poor Boys
(All-star group including Charlie Watts, Bill Wyman, Jimmy Page and Paul Rodgers, etc.)
Passport

Number		Title (A Side/B Side)	Year	VG	VG+	NM
❑ 7928		Baby Please Don't Go/Poor Boy Boogie	1985		2.50	5.00
❑ 7928	PS	Baby Please Don't Go/Poor Boy Boogie	1985		3.00	6.00
❑ 7929		These Arms of Mine/Let's Talk It Over	1985		2.50	5.00

Willie and the Wheels
(Still another P.F. Sloan-Steve Barri creation)
Dunhill

Number	Title (A Side/B Side)	Year	VG	VG+	NM
❑ 4002	Skateboard Craze/Do What You Do	1965	10.00	20.00	40.00

Willis, Chuck
Atlantic

Number	Title (A Side/B Side)	Year	VG	VG+	NM
❑ 1098	It's Too Late/Kansas City Woman	1956	6.25	12.50	25.00
❑ 1112	Juanita/	1956	6.25	12.50	25.00
	Whatcha' Gonna Do When Your Baby Leaves You				
❑ 1130	C.C. Rider/Ease the Pain	1957	6.25	12.50	25.00
❑ 1148	Love Me, Cherry/That Train Has Gone	1957	6.25	12.50	25.00
❑ 1168	Betty and Dupree/My Crying Eyes	1958	6.25	12.50	25.00
❑ 1179	What Am I Living For/	1958	7.50	15.00	30.00
	Hang Up My Rock And Roll Shoes				
❑ 1192	Thunder and Lightning/My Life	1958	5.00	10.00	20.00
❑ 2005	You'll Be My Love/Keep a-Driving	1958	5.00	10.00	20.00
❑ 2029	My Baby/Just One Kiss	1959	5.00	10.00	20.00
Okeh					
❑ 6810	I Tried/I Rule My House	1951	25.00	50.00	100.00
❑ 6841	Let's Jump Tonight/It's Too Late Baby	1951	20.00	40.00	80.00

Number		Title (A Side/B Side)	Year	VG	VG+	NM
❑ 6873		Loud Mouth Lucy/Here I Come	1952	20.00	40.00	80.00
❑ 6905		My Story/Caldonia	1952	12.50	25.00	50.00
❑ 6930		Salty Tears/Wrong Lake to Catch a Fish	1953	12.50	25.00	50.00
❑ 6952		Going to the River/Baby Has Left Me Again	1953	12.50	25.00	50.00
❑ 6985		Don't Deceive Me/I've Been Treated Wrong Too Long	1953	12.50	25.00	50.00
❑ 7004		My Baby's Coming Home/When My Day Is Over	1953	12.50	25.00	50.00
❑ 7015		You're Still My Baby/What's Your Name	1954	12.50	25.00	50.00
❑ 7029		I Feel So Bad/Need One More Chance	1954	15.00	30.00	60.00
❑ 7041		Change My Mind/My Heart's Been Broke Again	1954	10.00	20.00	40.00
❑ 7048		Give and Take/I've Been Away Too Long	1954	10.00	20.00	40.00
❑ 7051		Lawdy Miss Mary/Love-Struck	1955	10.00	20.00	40.00
❑ 7055		I Can Tell/One More Break	1955	10.00	20.00	40.00
❑ 7062		Search My Heart/Ring-Ding-Doo	1955	10.00	20.00	40.00
❑ 7067		Come On Home/It Were You	1956	10.00	20.00	40.00
❑ 7070		Two Spoons of Tears/Charged with Cheating	1956	10.00	20.00	40.00

Willis, Hal
Atlantic

Number		Title (A Side/B Side)	Year	VG	VG+	NM
❑ 1114		Bop-A-Dee, Bop-A-Doo/My Pink Cadillac	1956	50.00	100.00	200.00

Willows, The
4-Star

Number		Title (A Side/B Side)	Year	VG	VG+	NM
❑ 1753		There's a Dance Goin' On/Now That I Have You	1961	75.00	150.00	300.00

Heidi

Number		Title (A Side/B Side)	Year	VG	VG+	NM
❑ 103		It's Such a Shame/Tears in Your Eyes	1964	3.75	7.50	15.00
❑ 107		Sit by the Fire/Such a Night	1965	3.75	7.50	15.00

Melba

Number		Title (A Side/B Side)	Year	VG	VG+	NM
❑ 102		Church Bells Are Ringing/Baby Tell Me	1956	75.00	150.00	300.00
		Original A-side title				
❑ 102		Church Bells May Ring/Baby Tell Me	1956	15.00	30.00	60.00
❑ 106		Do You Love Me/My Angel	1956	15.00	30.00	60.00
❑ 115		Little Darlin'/My Angel	1957	20.00	40.00	80.00

MGM

Number		Title (A Side/B Side)	Year	VG	VG+	NM
❑ 13484		Hurtin' All Over/My Kinda Guy	1966	3.00	6.00	12.00
❑ 13714		Snow Song/Outside the City	1967	3.00	6.00	12.00

Wilson, Ann
(Of Heart)
Capitol

Number		Title (A Side/B Side)	Year	VG	VG+	NM
❑ B-5654		The Best Man in the World/(Instrumental)	1986			3.00
❑ B-5654	PS	The Best Man in the World/(Instrumental)	1986		2.00	4.00
❑ B-44288		Surrender to Me/Tequila Dreams	1988			3.00
		A-side with Robin Zander; B-side by Dave Grusin				
❑ B-44288	PS	Surrender to Me/Tequila Dreams	1988		2.00	4.00

Topaz

Number		Title (A Side/B Side)	Year	VG	VG+	NM
❑ 1311		Standin' Watchin' You/Wonder How I Managed	1967	30.00	60.00	120.00
❑ 1312		Through Eyes and Glass/ I'm Gonna Drink My Hurt Away	1967	30.00	60.00	120.00
		Topaz records as "Ann Wilson and the Daybreaks"				

Wilson, Brian
(Also see "Beach Boys, The")
Capitol

Number		Title (A Side/B Side)	Year	VG	VG+	NM
❑ 5610		Caroline, No/Summer Means New Love	1966	6.25	12.50	25.00
		Actually a Beach Boys recording released as a solo Brian record				

Sire

Number		Title (A Side/B Side)	Year	VG	VG+	NM
❑ 27694		Melt Away/Being with the One You Love	1988	5.00	10.00	20.00
❑ 27787	DJ	Night Time (same on both sides)	1988	7.50	15.00	30.00
		Stock copies not known to exist				
❑ 27787	PS	Night Time	1988	15.00	30.00	60.00
❑ 27814		Love and Mercy/ He Couldn't Get His Poor Old Body to Move	1988	2.50	5.00	10.00
		Promo copies go for 50% of this price				
❑ 27814	PS	Love and Mercy/ He Couldn't Get His Poor Old Body to Move	1988		2.50	5.00
		Accompanied both stock and promo copies				
❑ 28350		Let's Go to Heaven in My Car/Too Much Sugar	1987	2.50	5.00	10.00
		Promo copies go for 50% of this price				
❑ 28350	PS	Let's Go to Heaven in My Car/Too Much Sugar	1987		2.50	5.00
		Accompanied both stock and promo copies				

Wilson, Brian, and Mike Love
(Beach Boys recordings released under these two names)
Brother

Number		Title (A Side/B Side)	Year	VG	VG+	NM
❑ 1002		Gettin' Hungry/Devoted to You	1967	7.50	15.00	30.00

Wilson, Carl
(Of the Beach Boys)
Caribou

Number		Title (A Side/B Side)	Year	VG	VG+	NM
❑ 01049		Hold Me/Hurry Love	1981		2.50	5.00
❑ 02136		Heaven/Hurry Love	1981		2.50	5.00
❑ 03590		What You Do to Me/Time	1983		2.50	5.00
❑ 04020		Givin' You Up/Too Early to Tell	1983		2.50	5.00

Number		Title (A Side/B Side)	Year	VG	VG+	NM

Wilson, Dennis
(Of the Beach Boys)
Caribou

❑ 9023		You and I/Friday Night	1978	3.75	7.50	15.00

Wilson, Frank
Soul

❑ 35019		Sweeter As the Days Go By/Do I Love You	1966	6,000	9,000	12,000

Wilson, Hank – See "Russell, Leon"

Wilson, J. Frank, and the Cavaliers
Charay

❑ 13		Last Kiss '69/Black Car	1969		3.00	6.00

Josie

❑ 923		Last Kiss/That's How Much I Love You	1964	3.00	6.00	12.00
❑ 924		Tears of Happiness/Summertime	1964	2.50	5.00	10.00
		As "The Cavaliers"				
❑ 926		Hey Little One/Speak to Me	1964	2.50	5.00	10.00
❑ 929		Say It Now/Six Boys	1965	2.50	5.00	10.00
❑ 931		Dreams of a Fool/Open Your Eyes	1965	2.50	5.00	10.00
❑ 938		Forget Me Not/ A White Sport Coat (And a Pink Carnation)	1965	2.50	5.00	10.00

Le Cam

❑ 722		Last Kiss/Carla	1964	7.50	15.00	30.00

Solly

❑ 927		Me and My Teardrops/ Unmarked and Uncovered with Sand	1966	2.50	5.00	10.00

Tamara

❑ 761		Last Kiss/That's How Much I Love You	1964	6.25	12.50	25.00

Virgo

❑ 506		Last Kiss/(B-side unknown)	1973		2.50	5.00

Wilson, Jackie
Brunswick

❑ 55024		Reet Petite (The Finest Girl You Ever Want to Meet)/ By the Light of the Silvery Moon	1957	7.50	15.00	30.00
❑ 55052		To Be Loved/Come Back to Me	1958	6.25	12.50	25.00
❑ 55070		As Long As I Live/I'm Wanderin'	1958	6.25	12.50	25.00
❑ 55086		We Have Love/Singing a Song	1958	6.25	12.50	25.00
❑ 55105		Lonely Teardrops/In the Blue of the Evening	1958	6.25	12.50	25.00
❑ 55121		That's Why (I Love You So)/Love Is All	1959	6.25	12.50	25.00
❑ 55121	PS	That's Why (I Love You So)/Love Is All	1959	15.00	30.00	60.00
❑ 55136		I'll Be Satisfied/Ask	1959	6.25	12.50	25.00
❑ 55149		You Better Know It/Never Go Away	1959	5.00	10.00	20.00
❑ 55165		Talk That Talk/Only You and Only Me	1959	5.00	10.00	20.00
❑ 55165	PS	Talk That Talk/Only You and Only Me	1959	12.50	25.00	50.00
❑ 55166		Night/Doggin' Around	1960	10.00	20.00	40.00
		Maroon label (scarce original)				
❑ 55166		Night/Doggin' Around	1960	3.75	7.50	15.00
		Orange label				
❑ 55166	PS	Night/Doggin' Around	1960	12.50	25.00	50.00
❑ 55167		(You Were Made for) All My Love/ A Woman, A Lover, A Friend	1960	5.00	10.00	20.00
❑ 55170		Alone at Last/Am I the Man	1960	5.00	10.00	20.00
❑ 55170	PS	Alone at Last/Am I the Man	1960	12.50	25.00	50.00
❑ 55201		My Empty Arms/The Tear of the Year	1961	3.75	7.50	15.00
❑ 55201	PS	My Empty Arms/The Tear of the Year	1961	10.00	20.00	40.00
❑ 55208		Please Tell Me Why/Your One and Only Love	1961	3.75	7.50	15.00
❑ 55216		I'm Comin' On Back to You/Lonely Life	1961	3.75	7.50	15.00
❑ 55219		Years from Now/You Don't Know What It Means	1961	3.75	7.50	15.00
❑ 55220		The Way I Am/My Heart Belongs to Only You	1961	3.75	7.50	15.00
❑ 55221		The Greatest Hurt/There'll Be No Next Time	1962	3.75	7.50	15.00
❑ 55224		I Found Love/There's Nothing Like Love	1962	3.00	6.00	12.00
		With Linda Hopkins				
❑ 55225		Hearts/Sing (And Tell the Blues So Long)	1962	3.75	7.50	15.00
❑ 55229		I Just Can't Help It/My Tale of Woe	1962	3.75	7.50	15.00
❑ 55233		Forever and a Day/Baby That's All	1962	3.00	6.00	12.00
❑ 55236		How Good Am I Without You/A Girl Named Tamiko	1962	3.00	6.00	12.00
❑ 55239		Baby Workout/I'm Going Crazy	1963	3.00	6.00	12.00
❑ 55243		Shake a Hand/Say I Do	1963	2.50	5.00	10.00
		With Linda Hopkins				
❑ 55246		Shake! Shake! Shake!/He's a Fool	1963	2.50	5.00	10.00
❑ 55250		Baby Get It (And Don't Quit It)/The New Breed	1963	2.50	5.00	10.00
❑ 55254		Silent Night/Oh Holy Night	1963	3.00	6.00	12.00
❑ 55260		Haunted House/I'm Travelin' On	1964	2.50	5.00	10.00
❑ 55263		Call Her Up/The Kickapoo	1964	2.50	5.00	10.00
❑ 55266		Big Boss Line/Be My Girl	1964	2.50	5.00	10.00
❑ 55269		Squeeze Her-Tease Her (But Love Her)/ Give Me Back My Heart	1964	2.50	5.00	10.00
❑ 55273		Watch Out/She's All Right	1964	2.50	5.00	10.00
❑ 55277		Danny Boy/Soul Time	1965	2.00	4.00	8.00
❑ 55278		Yes Indeed/When the Saints Go Marching In	1965	2.00	4.00	8.00
		With Linda Hopkins				
❑ 55280		No Pity (In the Naked City)/I'm So Lonely	1965	2.00	4.00	8.00

Number		Title (A Side/B Side)	Year	VG	VG+	NM
❏ 55283		I Believe I'll Love On/Lonely Teardrops	1965	2.00	4.00	8.00
❏ 55287		Think Twice/Please Don't Hurt Me	1965	2.00	4.00	8.00
	With LaVern Baker					
❏ 55289		I've Got to Get Back/3 Days, 1 Hour, 30 Minutes	1966	2.00	4.00	8.00
❏ 55290		Soul Galore/Brand New Things	1966	2.00	4.00	8.00
❏ 55294		I Believe/Be My Love	1966	2.00	4.00	8.00
❏ 55300		Whispers (Gettin' Louder)/The Fairest of Them All	1966	2.00	4.00	8.00
❏ 55309		I Don't Want to Lose You/Just Be Sincere	1967	2.00	4.00	8.00
❏ 55321		I've Lost You/Those Heartaches	1967	2.00	4.00	8.00
❏ 55336		(Your Love Keeps Lifting Me) Higher and Higher/ I'm the One to Do It	1967	2.50	5.00	10.00
❏ 55354		Since You Showed Me How to Be Happy/ The Who Who Song	1967	2.00	4.00	8.00
❏ 55365		For Your Precious Love/Uptight	1968	2.00	4.00	8.00
❏ 55373		Chain Gang/Funky Broadway	1968	2.00	4.00	8.00
❏ 55381		I Get the Sweetest Feeling/Nothing But Heartaches	1968	2.00	4.00	8.00
❏ 55392		For Once in My Life/You Brought About a Change in Me	1968	2.00	4.00	8.00
❏ 55402		I Still Love You/Hum De Dum De Do	1969	2.00	4.00	8.00
❏ 55418		Helpless/Do It the Right Way	1969	2.00	4.00	8.00
❏ 55423		With These Hands/Why Don't You (Do Your Thing)	1969	2.00	4.00	8.00
❏ 55435		Let This Be a Letter (To My Baby)/Didn't I	1970		3.00	6.00
❏ 55435	PS	Let This Be a Letter (To My Baby)/Didn't I	1970	3.00	6.00	12.00
❏ 55443		(I Can Feel Those Vibrations) This Love Is Real/ Love Uprising	1970		3.00	6.00
❏ 55449		This Guy's in Love with You/Say You Will	1971		3.00	6.00
❏ 55454		Say You Will/(B-side unknown)	1971		3.00	6.00
❏ 55461		Love Is Funny That Way/Try It Again	1971		3.00	6.00
❏ 55467		You Got Me Walking/The Mountain	1972		3.00	6.00
❏ 55475		The Girl Turned Me On/Forever and a Day	1972		3.00	6.00
❏ 55480		What a Lovely Way/You Left the Fire Burning	1972		3.00	6.00
❏ 55490		Beautiful Day/What 'Cha Gonna Do About Love	1973		3.00	6.00
❏ 55495		Because of You/Go Away	1973		3.00	6.00
❏ 55499		Sing a Little Song/No More Goodbyes	1973		3.00	6.00
❏ 55504		It's All Over/Shake a Leg	1973		3.00	6.00
❏ 55522		Don't Burn No Bridges/(Instrumental)	1975		3.00	6.00
	With the Chi-Lites					
❏ 55536		Nobody But You/I've Learned About Life	1977		3.00	6.00

Columbia

❏ 07329		Reet Petite/You Better Know It	1987		2.50	5.00
❏ 07329	PS	Reet Petite/You Better Know It	1987		2.50	5.00

Wilson, Mary
(Of the Supremes)
Motown

❏ 1467		Midnight Dancer/Red Hot	1979		2.50	5.00

Wilson, Murry
(Father of Brian, Carl and Dennis Wilson of the Beach Boys)
Capitol

❏ 2063		Leaves/Plumber's Tune	1967	3.00	6.00	12.00

Wilson, Nancy (of Heart)
WTG

❏ 68678		All for Love/Taste the Rain	1989	2.50	5.00	10.00
	B-side by Red Hot Chili Peppers					

Wilson, Peanuts
Brunswick

❏ 55039		Cast Iron Arm/You've Got Love	1957	37.50	75.00	150.00

Wilson, Sonny
Sun

❏ 341		The Great Pretender/I'm Gonna Take a Walk	1960	5.00	10.00	20.00

Wilson, Wally
Sabre

❏ 106		If You Don't Love Me/The Hunt	1954	150.00	300.00	600.00

Wimberley, Maggie Sue
Sun

❏ 229		Daydreams Come True/How Long	1956	15.00	30.00	60.00

Winchell, Danny
Recorte

❏ 406		Jeannie/Beware You've Fallen in Love	1959	10.00	20.00	40.00
❏ 410		We're Gonna Have a Rockin' Party/ Don't Say You're Sorry	1959	12.50	25.00	50.00
❏ 415		Come Back Baby/I've Chosen You	1959	10.00	20.00	40.00

Wind
(Tony Orlando was in this group)
Forward

❏ 152		Groovin' with Mr. Bloe/Are You Nuts?	1970		2.50	5.00
	As "Cool Heat"					

Number		Title (A Side/B Side)	Year	VG	VG+	NM

Life
☐ 200		Make Believe/Groovin' with Mr. Bloe	1969		2.50	5.00
☐ 202		Teeny Bopper/I'll Hold Out My Hand	1969		2.50	5.00
☐ 203		Groovin' with Mr. Bloe/Are You Nuts?	1970		3.00	6.00
		As "Cool Heat"				

Wind in the Willows
(With Debbie Harry, later of Blondie)
Capitol
| ☐ 2274 | | Uptown Girl/Moments Spent | 1968 | 2.50 | 5.00 | 10.00 |

Windsors, The
(More than one group)
ABC-Paramount
| ☐ 10563 | | Keep Away/Fingers and Thumbs | 1964 | 3.75 | 7.50 | 15.00 |

Back Beat
| ☐ 506 | | My Gloria/Cool Seabreeze | 1958 | 4,000 | 6,000 | 8,000 |

United Artists
| ☐ 128 | | Saki Rock/Caramba | 1958 | 5.00 | 10.00 | 20.00 |

Wig Wag
| ☐ 203 | | Carol Ann/Keep Me from Crying | 1959 | 50.00 | 100.00 | 200.00 |

Wings – See "McCartney, Paul"

Winkley and Nutley
MK
| ☐ 101 | | Report to the Nation (Part 1)/
Report to the Nation (Part 2) | 1960 | 5.00 | 10.00 | 20.00 |

Winwood, Steve
(Of the Spencer Davis Group, Blind Faith and Traffic)
Island
☐ 091		Time Is Running Out/Hold On	1977		2.50	5.00
☐ 28122		Talking Back to the Night/There's a River	1988		2.00	4.00
☐ 28122	PS	Talking Back to the Night/There's a River	1988		2.00	4.00
☐ 28231		Valerie/Talking Back to the Night (Instrumental)	1987			3.00
☐ 28231	PS	Valerie/Talking Back to the Night (Instrumental)	1987			3.00
☐ 28472		Back in the High Life Again/Night Train	1987			3.00
☐ 28472	PS	Back in the High Life Again/Night Train	1987			3.00
☐ 28498		The Finer Things/Night Train	1987			3.00
☐ 28498	PS	The Finer Things/Night Train	1987			3.00
☐ 28595		Freedom Overspill/Help Me Angel	1986			3.00
☐ 28595	PS	Freedom Overspill/Help Me Angel	1986			3.00
☐ 28710		Higher Love/And I Go	1986			3.00
☐ 28710	PS	Higher Love/And I Go	1986			3.00
☐ 29879		Valerie/Slowdown	1982		2.50	5.00
☐ 29940		Still in the Game/Dust	1982		2.00	4.00
☐ 49656		While You See a Chance/Vacant Chair	1981		2.00	4.00
☐ 49656	PS	While You See a Chance/Vacant Chair	1981		2.50	5.00
☐ 49726		Arc of a Diver/Dust	1981		2.00	4.00
☐ 49726	PS	Arc of a Diver/Dust	1981		2.50	5.00
☐ 49773		Night Train (Part 1)/Night Train (Part 2)	1981		2.00	4.00

Virgin
☐ 98892		One and Only Man/(Instrumental)	1990			3.00
☐ 99234		Hearts On Fire (7" Remix)/(Instrumental)	1989			3.00
☐ 99234	PS	Hearts On Fire (7" Remix)/(Instrumental)	1989			3.00
☐ 99261		Holding On/(Instrumental)	1988			3.00
☐ 99261	PS	Holding On/(Instrumental)	1988			3.00
☐ 99290		Don't You Know What the Night Can Do/(Instrumental)	1988			3.00
☐ 99290	PS	Don't You Know What the Night Can Do/(Instrumental)	1988			3.00
☐ 99326		Roll With It/The Morning Side	1988			3.00
☐ 99326	PS	Roll With It/The Morning Side	1988			3.00

Wisdoms, The
Gaity
| ☐ 169 | | Two Hearts Make One Love/Lost in Dreams | 1959 | 150.00 | 300.00 | 600.00 |

Withers, Bill
Columbia
☐ 02071		I Want to Spend the Night/Memories Are That Way	1981		2.00	4.00
☐ 02651		USA/Paint Your Pretty Picture	1981		2.00	4.00
☐ 02651	PS	USA/Paint Your Pretty Picture	1981		2.50	5.00
☐ 04841		Oh Yeah!/Just Like the First Time	1985		2.00	4.00
☐ 05424		Something That Turns You On/ You Tried to Find a Love	1985		2.00	4.00
☐ 05424	PS	Something That Turns You On/ You Tried to Find a Love	1985		2.00	4.00
☐ 05675		We Could Be Sweet Lovers/ You Just Can't Smile It Away	1985		2.00	4.00
☐ 10255		Make Love to Your Mind/I Love You Dawn	1975		2.50	5.00
☐ 10308		I Wish You Well/She's Lonely	1976		2.50	5.00
☐ 10357		Family Table/Hello Like Before	1976		2.50	5.00
☐ 10420		If I Didn't Mean You Well/My Imagination	1976		2.50	5.00
☐ 10459		Close to Me/I'll Be with You	1976		2.50	5.00
☐ 10627		Lovely Day/It Ain't Because of Me Baby	1977		2.50	5.00
☐ 10702		Lovely Night for Dancing/I Want to Spend the Night	1978		2.50	5.00

Number		Title (A Side/B Side)	Year	VG	VG+	NM
❑ 10892		Don't It Make It Better/Love Is	1979		2.00	4.00
❑ 10958		You Got the Stuff/Look to Each Other for Love	1979		2.00	4.00

Sussex

Number		Title (A Side/B Side)	Year	VG	VG+	NM
❑ 219		Ain't No Sunshine/Harlem	1971		3.00	6.00
❑ 227		Grandma's Hands/Sweet Wanomi	1971		2.50	5.00
❑ 235		Lean On Me/Better Off Dead	1972		3.00	6.00
❑ 241		Use Me/Let Me In Your Life	1972		2.50	5.00
❑ 247		Let Us Love/The Gift of Giving	1972		2.50	5.00
❑ 247	PS	Let Us Love/The Gift of Giving	1972	2.00	4.00	8.00
❑ 250		Kissing My Love/I Don't Know	1973		2.50	5.00
❑ 257		Friend of Mine/Lonely Town, Lonely Street	1973		2.50	5.00
❑ 513		The Same Love That Made Me Laugh/ Make a Smile for Me	1974		2.50	5.00
❑ 518		You/Stories	1974		2.50	5.00
❑ 629		Heartbreak Road/Ruby Lee	1974		2.50	5.00
❑ 638		Who Is He (And What Is He to You)/Harlem	1975		2.50	5.00

Wolfe, Danny

Dot

Number		Title (A Side/B Side)	Year	VG	VG+	NM
❑ 15591		Pretty Blue Jean Baby/Once with You	1957	10.00	20.00	40.00
❑ 15667		Let's Flat Get It/I'm Glad I Waited	1957	15.00	30.00	60.00
❑ 15715		I'd Rather Be Lucky/Pucker Paint	1958	10.00	20.00	40.00

Womack, Bobby

Arista

Number		Title (A Side/B Side)	Year	VG	VG+	NM
❑ 0421		How Could You Break My Heart/I Honestly Love You	1979		2.00	4.00
❑ 0446		The Roads of Life/Give It Up	1979		2.00	4.00

Atlantic

Number		Title (A Side/B Side)	Year	VG	VG+	NM
❑ 2388		Night Train/It's Karate Time	1967	2.50	5.00	10.00

Beverly Glen

Number		Title (A Side/B Side)	Year	VG	VG+	NM
❑ 2000		If You Think You're Lonely Now/Secrets	1981		2.00	4.00
❑ 2001		Where Do We Go from Here/Just My Imagination	1982		2.00	4.00
❑ 2012		Love Has Finally Come at Last/American Dream With Patti LaBelle	1984		2.00	4.00
❑ 2014		Tell Me Why/(B-side unknown)	1984		2.00	4.00
❑ 2018		It Takes a Lot of Strength to Say Goodbye/ Who's Foolin' Who A-side with Patti LaBelle	1984		2.00	4.00
❑ 2021		Someday We'll All Be Free/ I Wish I Had Someone to Go Home To	1985		2.00	4.00
❑ 2023		I'm So Proud/Searching for My Love	1985		2.00	4.00

Checker

Number		Title (A Side/B Side)	Year	VG	VG+	NM
❑ 1122		Lonesome Man/I Found a True Love	1965	3.75	7.50	15.00

Columbia

Number		Title (A Side/B Side)	Year	VG	VG+	NM
❑ 10437		Home Is Where the Heart Is/We've Only Just Begun	1976		2.50	5.00
❑ 10493		Standing in the Safety Zone/A Change Is Gonna Come	1977		2.50	5.00
❑ 10672		Trust Your Heart/When Love Begins, Friendship Ends	1978		2.50	5.00
❑ 10732		Wind It Up/Stop Before We Start	1978		2.50	5.00

Liberty

Number		Title (A Side/B Side)	Year	VG	VG+	NM
❑ 56186		I'm Gonna Forget About You/Don't Look Back	1970	2.00	4.00	8.00
❑ 56207		Something/Everybody's Talkin'	1970	2.00	4.00	8.00

MCA

Number		Title (A Side/B Side)	Year	VG	VG+	NM
❑ 52624		I Wish He Didn't Trust Me So Much/ Got to Be with You Tonight	1985		2.00	4.00
❑ 52624	PS	I Wish He Didn't Trust Me So Much/ Got to Be with You Tonight	1985		2.00	4.00
❑ 52709		Let Me Kiss It Where It Hurts/Check It Out	1985		2.00	4.00
❑ 52793		Gypsy Woman/What Ever Happened to the Times	1986			3.00
❑ 52955		(I Wanna) Make Love to You/The Launch	1986			3.00
❑ 52955	PS	(I Wanna) Make Love to You/The Launch	1986			3.00
❑ 53190		Living in a Box/I Can't Stay Mad	1987			3.00
❑ 53263		Outside Myself/A Woman Likes to Hear That	1988			3.00

Minit

Number		Title (A Side/B Side)	Year	VG	VG+	NM
❑ 32024		Baby, I Can't Stand It/Trust Me	1967	2.50	5.00	10.00
❑ 32030		Somebody Special/Broadway Walk	1967	2.50	5.00	10.00
❑ 32037		What Is This/ What You Gonna Do (When Your Love Is Gone)	1968	2.50	5.00	10.00
❑ 32048		Fly Me to the Moon/Take Me	1968	2.50	5.00	10.00
❑ 32055		California Dreamin'/Baby, You Oughta Think It Over	1968	2.50	5.00	10.00
❑ 32059		I Left My Heart in San Francisco/ Love, The Time Is Now	1969	2.00	4.00	8.00
❑ 32071		It's Gonna Rain/Thank You	1969	2.00	4.00	8.00
❑ 32081		How I Miss You Baby/Tried and Convicted	1969	2.00	4.00	8.00
❑ 32093		More Than I Can Stand/Arkansas State Prison	1970	2.00	4.00	8.00

Solar

Number		Title (A Side/B Side)	Year	VG	VG+	NM
❑ 74006		Save the Children/(Instrumental)	1989			3.00

United Artists

Number		Title (A Side/B Side)	Year	VG	VG+	NM
❑ 0123		That's the Way I Feel About Cha/ Woman's Gotta Have It "Silver Spotlight Series" reissue	1973		2.00	4.00
❑ XW196		Across 110th Street/Hang On In There	1973		2.50	5.00
❑ XW255		Nobody Wants You When You're Down and Out/ I'm Thru Trying to Prove My Love	1973		2.50	5.00
❑ XW375		Lookin' for a Love/Let It Hang Out	1973		2.50	5.00
❑ XW439		You're Welcome, Stop On By/I Don't Want to Be Hurt	1974		2.50	5.00

Number	Title (A Side/B Side)	Year	VG	VG+	NM
☐ XW525	Lookin' for a Love/	1974		2.00	4.00
	Nobody Wants You When You're Down and Out				
	Reissue				
☐ XW526	Harry Hippie/Sweet Caroline	1974		2.00	4.00
	Reissue				
☐ XW527	California Dreamin'/Fly Me to the Moon	1974		2.50	5.00
☐ XW561	I Don't Know/Yes, Jesus Loves Me	1974		2.50	5.00
☐ XW621	Check It Out/Interlude No. 2	1975		2.50	5.00
☐ XW674	It's All Over Now/Git It	1975		2.50	5.00
☐ XW735	Where There's a Will, There's a Way/	1975		2.50	5.00
	Everything's Gonna Be Alright				
☐ XW763	Daylight/Trust Me	1976		2.50	5.00
☐ XW804	I Feel a Groove Comin' On/Trust Me	1976		2.50	5.00
☐ 50773	The Preacher/More Than I Can Stand	1971		3.00	6.00
☐ 50816	Communication/Fire and Rain	1971		3.00	6.00
☐ 50847	That's the Way I Feel About 'Cha/Come L'Amore	1971		3.00	6.00
☐ 50902	Woman's Gotta Have It/Give It Back	1972		3.00	6.00
☐ 50946	Harry Hippie/	1972		3.00	6.00
	Sweet Caroline (Good Times Never Seemed So Good)				
☐ 50988	DJ Harry Hippie (mono/stereo)	1972	2.00	4.00	8.00
	Apparently, no stock copy exists				

Wonder Who?, The – See "Four Seasons, The"

Wonder, Stevie
Columbia

Number	Title (A Side/B Side)	Year	VG	VG+	NM
☐ 02860	Ebony and Ivory/Rainclouds	1982		2.00	4.00
	A-side with Paul McCartney; B-side is McCartney solo				
☐ 02860	PS Ebony and Ivory/Rainclouds	1982		2.00	4.00

Gordy

Number	Title (A Side/B Side)	Year	VG	VG+	NM
☐ 7076	Alfie/More Than a Dream	1968	6.25	12.50	25.00
	As "Eivets Rednow" (read it backwards)				

Motown

Number	Title (A Side/B Side)	Year	VG	VG+	NM
☐ 1650	Used to Be/I Want to Come Back As A Song	1982			3.00
	A-side with Charlene; B-side is Charlene solo				
☐ 1650	PS Used to Be/I Want to Come Back As A Song	1982			3.00
☐ 1745	I Just Called to Say I Love You/(Instrumental)	1984			3.00
☐ 1745	PS I Just Called to Say I Love You/(Instrumental)	1984	12.50	25.00	50.00
☐ 1769	Love Light in Flight/It's More Than You	1984			3.00
☐ 1769	PS Love Light in Flight/It's More Than You	1984		2.00	4.00
☐ 1907	Skeletons/(Instrumental)	1987			3.00
☐ 1907	PS Skeletons/(Instrumental)	1987		2.00	4.00
☐ 1919	You Will Know/(Instrumental)	1988			3.00
☐ 1919	PS You Will Know/(Instrumental)	1988		2.00	4.00
☐ 1930	Get It/(Instrumental)	1988			3.00
	A-side with Michael Jackson				
☐ 1930	PS Get It/(Instrumental)	1988			3.00
☐ 1946	My Eyes Don't Cry/(Instrumental)	1988			3.00
☐ 1953	With Each Beat of My Heart/(Instrumental)	1989			3.00
☐ 2081	Gotta Have You/Feeding Off the Love of the Land	1991		2.00	4.00
☐ 2127	Fun Day/(Instrumental)	1991		2.00	4.00
☐ 2143	These Three Words (same on both sides)	1991		2.00	4.00
☐ 860 310-7	For Your Love/(Instrumental)	1995			3.00
☐ 860 418-7	Tomorrow Robins Will Sing/For Your Love	1995			3.00

Tamla

Number	Title (A Side/B Side)	Year	VG	VG+	NM
☐ 1602	That Girl/All I Do	1982		2.00	4.00
☐ 1612	Do I Do/Rocket Love	1982		2.00	4.00
☐ 1639	Ribbon in the Sky/Black Orchid	1982		2.00	4.00
☐ 1639	PS Ribbon in the Sky/Black Orchid	1982		2.00	4.00
☐ 1808	Part-Time Lover/(Instrumental)	1985			3.00
☐ 1808	PS Part-Time Lover/(Instrumental)	1985		2.00	4.00
☐ 1817	Go Home/(Instrumental)	1985			3.00
☐ 1817	PS Go Home/(Instrumental)	1985		2.00	4.00
☐ 1832	Overjoyed/(Instrumental)	1986			3.00
☐ 1832	PS Overjoyed/(Instrumental)	1986		2.00	4.00
☐ 1846	Land of La La/(Instrumental)	1986			3.00
☐ 1846	PS Land of La La/(Instrumental)	1986		2.00	4.00
☐ 54061	I Call It Pretty Music But The Old People	1962	6.25	12.50	25.00
	Call It the Blues (Part 1)/I Call It Pretty Music But The Old People Call It the Blues (Part 2)				
☐ 54061	PS I Call It Pretty Music But The Old People	1962	15.00	30.00	60.00
	Call It the Blues (Part 1)/I Call It Pretty Music But The Old People Call It the Blues (Part 2)				
☐ 54070	Little Water Boy/La La La La La	1962	6.25	12.50	25.00
☐ 54074	Contract on Love/Sunset	1963	6.25	12.50	25.00
☐ 54080	Fingertips -- Pt. 2/Fingertips -- Pt. 1	1963	3.00	6.00	12.00
☐ 54080	PS Fingertips -- Pt. 2/Fingertips -- Pt. 1	1963	15.00	30.00	60.00
☐ 54086	Workout Stevie, Workout/Monkey Talk	1963	3.00	6.00	12.00
☐ 54090	Castles in the Sand/	1964	3.75	7.50	15.00
	Thank You (For Loving Me All the Way)				
	Up to and including the above, as "Little Stevie Wonder"				
☐ 54096	Hey Harmonica Man/This Little Girl	1964	3.75	7.50	15.00
☐ 54096	PS Hey Harmonica Man/This Little Girl	1964	10.00	20.00	40.00
☐ 54103	Sad Boy/Happy Street	1964	5.00	10.00	20.00
☐ 54108	Pretty Little Angel/Tears in Vain	1964			Unreleased
☐ 54114	Kiss Me Baby/Tears in Vain	1965	2.50	5.00	10.00
☐ 54119	High Heel Sneakers/Music Talk	1965	2.50	5.00	10.00
☐ 54119	High Heel Sneakers/Funny How Time Slips Away	1965	3.75	7.50	15.00
☐ 54124	Uptight (Everything's Alright)/Purple Rain Drops	1965	2.50	5.00	10.00

Number		Title (A Side/B Side)	Year	VG	VG+	NM
❑ 54130		Nothing's Too Good for My Baby/With a Child's Heart	1966	2.50	5.00	10.00
❑ 54136		Blowin' in the Wind/Ain't That Asking for Trouble	1966	2.50	5.00	10.00
❑ 54136	PS	Blowin' in the Wind/Ain't That Asking for Trouble	1966	6.25	12.50	25.00
❑ 54139		A Place in the Sun/Sylvia	1966	2.50	5.00	10.00
❑ 54139	PS	A Place in the Sun/Sylvia	1966	6.25	12.50	25.00
❑ 54142		Some Day at Christmas/Miracles of Christmas	1966	3.75	7.50	15.00
❑ 54147		Travlin' Man/Hey Love	1967	2.50	5.00	10.00
❑ 54151		I Was Made to Love Her/Hold Me	1967	2.00	4.00	8.00
❑ 54157		I'm Wondering/Every Time I See You I Go Wild	1967	2.00	4.00	8.00
❑ 54165		Shoo-Be-Doo-Be-Doo-Da-Day/ Why Don't You Lead Me to Love	1968	2.00	4.00	8.00
❑ 54168		You Met Your Match/My Girl	1968	2.00	4.00	8.00
❑ 54174		For Once in My Life/Angie Girl	1968	2.00	4.00	8.00
❑ 54180		I Don't Know Why/My Cherie Amour	1969	2.50	5.00	10.00
❑ 54180		My Cherie Amour/Don't Know Why I Love You	1969	2.00	4.00	8.00
		Re-release with A and B side switched and new title on B-side				
❑ 54188		Yester-Me, Yester-You, Yesterday/ I'd Be a Fool Right Now	1969	2.00		4.00	8.00
❑ 54191		Never Had a Dream Come True/ Somebody Knows, Somebody Cares	1970		3.00	6.00
❑ 54196		Signed, Sealed, Delivered, I'm Yours/ I'm More Than Happy	1970		3.00	6.00
❑ 54200		Heaven Help Us All/I Gotta Have a Song	1970		3.00	6.00
❑ 54202		We Can Work It Out/ Never Dreamed You'd Leave in Summer	1971		3.00	6.00
❑ 54208		If You Really Love Me/Think of Me As Your Soldier	1971		3.00	6.00
❑ 54214		What Christmas Means to Me/Bedtime for Toys	1971		3.00	6.00
❑ 54216		Superwoman (Where Were You When I Needed You)/ I Love Every Little Thing About You	1972		3.00	6.00
❑ 54223		Keep On Running/Evil	1972		3.00	6.00
❑ 54226		Superstition/You've Got It Bad Girl	1972		2.50	5.00
❑ 54232		You Are the Sunshine of My Life/Tuesday Heartbreak	1973		2.50	5.00
❑ 54235		Higher Ground/Too High	1973		2.50	5.00
❑ 54242		Living for the City/Visions	1973		2.50	5.00
❑ 54245		Don't You Worry 'Bout a Thing/Blame It on the Sun	1974		2.50	5.00
❑ 54252		You Haven't Done Nothin'/Big Brother	1974		2.50	5.00
❑ 54254		Boogie On Reggae Woman/Seems So Long	1974		2.50	5.00
❑ 54274		I Wish/You and I	1976		2.50	5.00
❑ 54281		Sir Duke/He's Misstra Know-It-All	1977		2.50	5.00
❑ 54281	PS	Sir Duke/He's Misstra Know-It-All	1977	2.50	5.00	10.00
❑ 54286		Another Star/Creepin'	1977		2.50	5.00
❑ 54291		As/Contusion	1977		2.50	5.00
❑ 54303		Send One Your Love/(Instrumental)	1979		2.00	4.00
❑ 54303	PS	Send One Your Love/(Instrumental)	1979		3.00	6.00
❑ 54308		Outside My Window/Same Old Story	1980		2.00	4.00
❑ 54308	PS	Outside My Window/Same Old Story	1980		3.00	6.00
❑ 54317		Master Blaster (Jammin')/(Instrumental)	1980		2.00	4.00
❑ 54317	PS	Master Blaster (Jammin')/(Instrumental)	1980		3.00	6.00
❑ 54320		I Ain't Gonna Stand For It/Knocks Me Off My Feet	1980		2.00	4.00
❑ 54323		Lately/If It's Magic	1981		2.00	4.00
❑ 54328		Did I Hear You Say You Love Me/ As If You Read My Mind	1981		2.00	4.00
❑ 54331		Happy Birthday/(Instrumental)	1981			*Unreleased*

Topps/Motown

❑ 8		Fingertips (Part 2)	1967	18.75	37.50	75.00
		Cardboard record				
❑ 10		Uptight (Everything's Alright)	1967	18.75	37.50	75.00
		Cardboard record				

Wood, Anita
Sun

❑ 361		I'll Wait Forever/I Can't Show How I Feel	1961	7.50	15.00	30.00

Wood, Bobby
Sun

❑ 369	DJ	Everybody's Searchin'/Human Emotions	1961	200.00	400.00	600.00
		No stock copies known; should one be discovered, it would be worth much more				

Wood, Brenton
Brent

❑ 7052		Good Lovin'/I Want to Love	1966	3.75	7.50	15.00
❑ 7057		Cross the Bridge/Sweet Molly Malone	1966	6.25	12.50	25.00
❑ 7068		I Want Love/Sweet Molly Malone	1967	2.50	5.00	10.00

Cream

❑ 7602		All That Jazz/Bless Your Little Heart	1976		2.00	4.00
❑ 7716		Come Softly to Me/You're Everything I Need	1977		2.00	4.00
❑ 7720		Number One/(B-side unknown)	1977		2.00	4.00
❑ 7833		Let's Get Crazy Together/Love Is Free	1978		2.00	4.00

Double Shot

❑ 111		The Oogum Boogum Song/ I Like the Way You Love Me	1967	2.50	5.00	10.00
❑ 116		Gimme Little Sign/ I Think You've Got Your Fools Mixed Up	1967	2.50	5.00	10.00
❑ 121		Baby You Got It/Catch You on the Rebound	1967	2.00	4.00	8.00
❑ 126		Lovey Dovey Kinda Lovin'/Two-Time Loser	1968	2.00	4.00	8.00
❑ 130		Some Got It, Some Don't/Me and You	1968	2.00	4.00	8.00
❑ 135		Trouble/It's Just a Game, Love	1968	2.00	4.00	8.00

Number	Title (A Side/B Side)	Year	VG	VG+	NM
❑ 137	Where Are You/A Change Is Gonna Come	1969	2.00	4.00	8.00
❑ 142	Whoop It On Me/Take a Chance	1969	2.00	4.00	8.00
❑ 147	Can You Dig It/Great Big Bubble of Love	1970		3.00	6.00
❑ 150	Bogaloosa, Lousiana/I Need Your Love So Bad	1970		3.00	6.00
❑ 156	Sad Little Song/Who But a Fool	1971		3.00	6.00

Prophesy

❑ 3002	Sticky Boom Boom Too Cold (Part 1)/ Sticky Boom Boom Too Cold (Part 2)	1973		2.50	5.00
❑ 3003	Another Saturday Night/(B-side unknown)	1973		2.50	5.00

Wand

❑ 145	Mr. Schemer/Hide-A-Way	1963	10.00	20.00	40.00

Warner Bros.

❑ 8079	All That Jazz/Rainin' Love	1975		2.50	5.00
❑ 8144	Better Believe It/It Only Makes Me Want It More	1975		2.50	5.00

Wood, Ron

(Of Faces and the Rolling Stones)

Columbia

❑ 11014	Seven Days/Breakin' My Heart	1979		3.00	6.00

Warner Bros.

❑ 8036	Breathe on Me/I Can Feel the Fire	1974		3.00	6.00
❑ 8131	I Got a Feeling/If You Don't Want My Love	1975		3.00	6.00

Wood, Roy

(Formerly of the Move and the first Electric Light Orchestra album)

United Artists

❑ XW160	Ball Park Incident/Carlsberg Special	1973		2.50	5.00
	As "Wizzard/Roy Wood"				
❑ XW272	See My Baby Jive/Bend Over Beethoven	1973		2.50	5.00
❑ XW320	Dear Elaine/Song of Praise	1973		2.50	5.00
❑ XW394	Forever/Woodbe	1974		2.50	5.00
❑ XW792	Any Old Time Will Do/ Why Does Such a Pretty Girl Sing Those Sad Songs	1976		2.00	4.00

Woods, Bennie

Atlas

❑ 1040	I Cross My Fingers/Wheel Baby Wheel	1955	200.00	400.00	800.00
	As "Bennie Woods and the Five Dukes"				
❑ 1040	I Cross My Fingers/Wheel Baby Wheel	1955	125.00	250.00	500.00
	As "Bennie Woods and Rockin' Townies"				

Woods, Mickey

Tamla

❑ 54039	They Rode Through the Valley/Poor Sam Jones	1961	12.50	25.00	50.00
❑ 54052	Please Mr. Kennedy/(They Call Me) Cupid	1962	10.00	20.00	40.00

Woody, Don

Decca

❑ 30277	You're Barking Up the Wrong Tree/Bird-Dog	1957	25.00	50.00	100.00

Wray, Link

Cadence

❑ 1347	Rumble/The Swag	1958	7.50	15.00	30.00

Epic

❑ 9300	Raw-Hide/Dixie-Doodle	1958	6.25	12.50	25.00
❑ 9321	Comanche/Lillian	1959	6.25	12.50	25.00
❑ 9343	Rendezvous/Slinky	1959	6.25	12.50	25.00
❑ 9361	Trail of the Lonesome Pine/Golden Strings	1960	6.25	12.50	25.00
❑ 9419	Mary Ann/Ain't That Lovin' You Baby	1960	6.25	12.50	25.00
❑ 9454	El Toro/Tijuana	1961	6.25	12.50	25.00

Heavy

❑ 101	Rumble '68/Blow Your Mind	1968	3.75	7.50	15.00

Kay

❑ 3690	I Sez Baby/(B-side unknown)	1958	25.00	50.00	100.00

Mala

❑ 458	There's a Hole in the Middle of the Moon/Dancing Party	1963	5.00	10.00	20.00

Mr, G.

❑ 820	Rumble '69/Mind Blower	1969	2.50	5.00	10.00

Okeh

❑ 7166	Rumble Mambo/Ham Bone	1963	5.00	10.00	20.00
	B-side by Red Saunders				
❑ 7282	Rumble Mambo/Ham Bone	1967	3.75	7.50	15.00
	B-side by Red Saunders				

Polydor

❑ 14084	Fire and Brimstone/Juke Box Mama	1970	2.00	4.00	8.00
❑ 14096	Fallin' Rain/Juke Box Mama	1971	2.00	4.00	8.00
❑ 14188	Shine the Light/Lawdy Miss Clawdy	1973		3.00	6.00
❑ 14256	I Got to Ramble/She's That Kind of Woman	1974		3.00	6.00

Rumble

❑ 1000	Jack the Ripper/The Stranger	1961	10.00	20.00	40.00

Number		Title (A Side/B Side)	Year	VG	VG+	NM

Swan

	Number	Title (A Side/B Side)	Year	VG	VG+	NM
❏	4137	Jack the Ripper/The Black Widow	1963	5.00	10.00	20.00
❏	4154	Weekend/Turnpike U.S.A.	1963	5.00	10.00	20.00
❏	4163	Run Chicken Run/The Sweeper	1963	5.00	10.00	20.00
❏	4171	The Shadow Knows/My Alberta	1964	5.00	10.00	20.00
❏	4187	Deuces Wild/Summer Dream	1964	5.00	10.00	20.00
❏	4201	Good Rockin' Tonight/I'll Do Anything for You	1965	6.25	12.50	25.00
❏	4211	Branded/Hang On	1965	5.00	10.00	20.00
❏	4232	Girl from the North Country/You Hurt Me So	1965	5.00	10.00	20.00
❏	4239	The Fuzz/Ace of Spades	1966	5.00	10.00	20.00
❏	4244	Batman Theme/Alone	1966	6.25	12.50	25.00
❏	4261	Ace of Spades/Hidden Charms	1966	6.25	12.50	25.00
❏	4284	Jack the Ripper/I'll Do Anything for You	1967	3.75	7.50	15.00

Trans Atlas

	Number	Title (A Side/B Side)	Year	VG	VG+	NM
❏	687	Big City Stomp/Poppin' Popeye	1962	5.00	10.00	20.00

Wrens, The

Rama

	Number	Title (A Side/B Side)	Year	VG	VG+	NM
❏	53	Love's Something That's Made for Two/Beggin' for Love	1955	100.00	200.00	400.00
❏	65	Come Back My Love/Beggin' for Love	1955	37.50	75.00	150.00
❏	65	Come Back My Love/Eleven Roses	1955	100.00	200.00	400.00
❏	110	Love's Something That's Made for Two/Eleven Roses	1955	75.00	150.00	300.00
❏	174	Hey Girl/Serenade of the Bells	1955	100.00	200.00	400.00
❏	184	I Won't Come to Your Wedding/What Makes You Do the Things That You Do	1956	100.00	200.00	400.00
❏	194	C'est La Vie/C'est La Vie	1956	100.00	200.00	400.00
		B-side by Jimmy Wright and His Orchestra				

Wyman, Bill

(Of the Rolling Stones)

A&M

	Number		Title (A Side/B Side)	Year	VG	VG+	NM
❏	2367		(Si Si) Je Suis Un Rock Star/Rio De Janeiro	1981		2.50	5.00
❏	2367	PS	(Si Si) Je Suis Un Rock Star/Rio De Janeiro	1981	2.50	5.00	10.00

Rolling Stones

	Number	Title (A Side/B Side)	Year	VG	VG+	NM
❏	19111	White Lightning/I Wanna Get Me a Gun	1974		2.50	5.00
❏	19119	A Quarter to Three/Soul Satisfying	1975		2.50	5.00
❏	19303	Apache Woman/Soul Satisfying	1975		2.50	5.00

X

X-Tremes, The

Star Trek

	Number	Title (A Side/B Side)	Year	VG	VG+	NM
❏	1221	Substitute/Facts of Life	1966	6.25	12.50	25.00

XTC

Epic

	Number	Title (A Side/B Side)	Year	VG	VG+	NM
❏	02875	Senses Working Overtime/English Roundabout	1982		2.50	5.00

Geffen

	Number		Title (A Side/B Side)	Year	VG	VG+	NM
❏	22953		King for a Day/Toys	1989			2.00
❏	22953	PS	King for a Day/Toys	1989			2.00
❏	27552		The Mayor of Simpleton/One of the Millions	1989			2.00
❏	27552	PS	The Mayor of Simpleton/One of the Millions	1989			2.00
❏	28394		Dear God/Mermaid Smiled	1987			3.00
❏	29351		Wonderland/Jump	1984		2.00	4.00

Virgin

	Number		Title (A Side/B Side)	Year	VG	VG+	NM
❏	PR 344	DJ	Limelight//Day In Day Out/Chain of Command	1979		3.00	6.00
			7-inch 33 1/3 record with small center hole; included in first 15,000 copies of album 13134				
❏	67004		Ten Feet Tall//Helicopter/Somnabulist	1980		3.50	7.00
❏	67004	DJ	Ten Feet Tall (mono/stereo)	1980			3.00
❏	67004	PS	Ten Feet Tall//Helicopter/Somnabulist	1980			3.00
❏	67009		Making Plans for Nigel//This Is Pop/Meccanik Dancing	1980		3.50	7.00
❏	67009	PS	Making Plans for Nigel//This Is Pop/Meccanik Dancing	1980			3.00
❏	67009	DJ	Making Plans for Nigel (mono/stereo)	1980			3.00

Virgin/RSO

	Number	Title (A Side/B Side)	Year	VG	VG+	NM
❏	300	Generals and Majors/Living Through Another Cuba	1981		2.50	5.00
❏	301	Love at First Sight/Rocket from a Bottle	1981		2.50	5.00

Y

Yanovsky, Zalman

(Ex-Lovin' Spoonful)

Buddah

	Number	Title (A Side/B Side)	Year	VG	VG+	NM
❏	12	As Long As You're Here/Ereh Er'uoy Sa Gnol Sa	1967	2.50	5.00	10.00

Yardbirds, The

(Also see "Page, Jimmy"; "Relf, Keith")

Epic

	Number		Title (A Side/B Side)	Year	VG	VG+	NM
❏	9709		I Wish You Could/I Ain't Got You	1964			*Unreleased?*
❏	9709		I Wish You Could/A Certain Girl	1964	10.00	20.00	40.00
❏	9709	PS	I Wish You Could	1964	200.00	400.00	800.00
			Promo-only picture sleeve				

Number		Title (A Side/B Side)	Year	VG	VG+	NM
❑ 9709		I Wish You Would/A Certain Girl	1964	12.50	25.00	50.00
❑ 9790		For Your Love/Got to Hurry	1965	3.75	7.50	15.00
❑ 9823		Heart Full of Soul/Steeled Blues	1965	3.75	7.50	15.00
❑ 9823	PS	Heart Full of Soul/Steeled Blues	1965	12.50	25.00	50.00
❑ 9857		I'm a Man/Still I'm Sad	1965	3.75	7.50	15.00
❑ 9881		Shapes of Things/I'm Not Talking	1966	3.75	7.50	15.00
❑ 10006		New York City Blues/You're a Better Man Than I	1966			Unreleased
❑ 10006		Shapes of Things/New York City Blues	1966	5.00	10.00	20.00
❑ 10035		Over Under Sideways Down/Jeff's Boogie	1966	3.75	7.50	15.00
❑ 10035	PS	Over Under Sideways Down/Jeff's Boogie	1966	10.00	20.00	40.00
❑ 10094		Happenings Ten Years Time Ago/Psycho Daisies	1966			Unreleased
❑ 10094		Happenings Ten Years Time Ago/The Nazz Are Blue	1966	3.75	7.50	15.00
❑ 10094	PS	Happenings Ten Years Time Ago/The Nazz Are Blue	1966	10.00	20.00	40.00
❑ 10156		Little Games/Puzzles	1967	5.00	10.00	20.00
❑ 10204		Ha Ha Said the Clown/Tinker, Tailor, Soldier, Sailor	1967	5.00	10.00	20.00
❑ 10248		Ten Little Indians/Drinking Muddy Water	1967	5.00	10.00	20.00
❑ 10303		Goodnight Sweet Josephine/Think About It	1968	12.50	25.00	50.00

Yarrow, Peter
(Of Peter, Paul and Mary)
Warner Bros.

❑ 7236		Don't Remind Me Now of Time/Teenage Fair	1968	2.00	4.00	8.00
		B-side by Rosko				
❑ 7567		Don't Ever Take Away My Freedom/Greenwood	1972		2.50	5.00
❑ 7587		Weave Me the Sunshine/Wings of Time	1972		2.50	5.00
❑ 7761		Old Father Time/Isn't That So	1973		2.00	4.00
❑ 8114		Wanderin'/Another Chain Unbound	1975		2.00	4.00

Yates, Bill
Sun

❑ 390		Stop, Wait and Listen/Don't Step on My Dog	1964	3.75	7.50	15.00
❑ 397		Carleen/Too Late to Right My Wrong	1965	3.75	7.50	15.00
❑ 399		Big Big World/I Dropped My M & M's	1966	3.75	7.50	15.00

Yellow Balloon, The
Canterbury

❑ 508		Yellow Balloon/Noollab Wolley	1967	3.00	6.00	12.00
❑ 513		Good Feeling Time/I've Got a Feeling for Love	1967	2.50	5.00	10.00
❑ 516		Stained Glass Window/Can't Get Enough of Your Love	1967	2.50	5.00	10.00

Yellow Payges, The
Showplace

❑ 216		Sleeping Minds/(B-side unknown)	1967	7.50	15.00	30.00
❑ 217		Love in the Making/Jezebel	1967	5.00	10.00	20.00

Uni

❑ 55043		Our Time Is Running Out/Sweet Sunrise	1967	3.75	7.50	15.00
❑ 55072		Judge Carter/Childhood Friends	1968	3.75	7.50	15.00
❑ 55089		You're Just What I Was Looking For Today/Crowd Pleaser	1968	3.75	7.50	15.00
❑ 55107		The Two of Us/Never Put Away My Love for You	1969	3.75	7.50	15.00
❑ 55153		Would You Mind If I Loved You/Vanilla on My Mind	1969	3.75	7.50	15.00
❑ 55176		Slow Down/Fresco Annie	1969	3.75	7.50	15.00
❑ 55192		Little Women/Follow the Bouncing Ball	1970	3.75	7.50	15.00
❑ 55225		I'm a Man/Home Again	1970	3.75	7.50	15.00

Yelvington, Malcolm
Sun

❑ 211		Drinkin' Wine Spo-Dee-O-Dee/Just Rolling Along	1954	25.00	50.00	100.00
❑ 246		Rockin' with My Baby/It's Me Baby	1956	25.00	50.00	100.00

Yes
(Also see "Howe, Steve")
Arista

❑ 2218		Lift Me Up/Give and Take	1991		2.00	4.00

Atco

❑ 99419		Rhythm of Love/City of Love	1987			3.00
❑ 99419	PS	Rhythm of Love/City of Love	1987			3.00
❑ 99449		Love Will Find a Way/Holy Lamb	1987			3.00
❑ 99449	PS	Love Will Find a Way/Holy Lamb	1987			3.00
❑ 99745		It Can Happen/It Can Happen (Live)	1984			3.00
❑ 99745	PS	It Can Happen/It Can Happen (Live)	1984			3.00
❑ 99787		Leave It/Leave It (Acapella)	1984			3.00
❑ 99787	PS	Leave It/Leave It (Acapella)	1984			3.00
❑ 99817		Owner of a Lonely Heart/Our Song	1983			3.00
❑ 99817	PS	Owner of a Lonely Heart/Our Song	1983			3.00

Atlantic

❑ 2709		Every Little Thing/Sweetness	1970		3.00	6.00
❑ 2819		Your Move/Clap	1971		2.50	5.00
❑ 2854		Roundabout/Long Distance Runaround	1972		2.50	5.00
❑ 2854	DJ	Roundabout (mono/stereo)	1972	25.00	50.00	100.00
		Promo only on yellow vinyl				
❑ 2899		America/Total Mass Retain	1972		2.50	5.00
❑ 2920		And You And I (Part 1)/And You And I (Part 2)	1972		2.50	5.00
❑ 3242		Sound Chaser/Soon	1975		2.50	5.00
❑ 3416		Awaken (Part 1)/Wonderful Stories	1977		2.50	5.00
❑ 3534		Don't Kill the Whale/Release, Release	1978		2.50	5.00

Number	Title (A Side/B Side)	Year	VG	VG+	NM
❑ 3767	Into the Lens/Does It Really Happen	1980		2.50	5.00
❑ 3801	Run Through the Light/White Car	1981		2.50	5.00

York, Rusty
Capitol
| ❑ 4663 | That's What I Need/Just Like You | 1961 | 3.75 | 7.50 | 15.00 |

Chess
| ❑ 1730 | Sugaree/Red Rooster | 1959 | 5.00 | 10.00 | 20.00 |

Gaylord
| ❑ 6428 | Sally Was a Good Old Girl/
I Might Just Walk Right Back Again | 1962 | 3.75 | 7.50 | 15.00 |

King
❑ 5103	Peggy Sue/Shake 'Em Up Baby	1958	6.25	12.50	25.00
❑ 5511	Love Struck/ Goodnight Cincinnati, Good Morning Tennessee	1961	3.75	7.50	15.00
❑ 5587	Tramblin'/Tore Up Over You	1961	3.75	7.50	15.00

Note
| ❑ 10021 | Sugaree/Red Rooster | 1959 | 6.25 | 12.50 | 25.00 |

P.J.
| ❑ 100 | Sugaree/Red Rooster | 1959 | 7.50 | 15.00 | 30.00 |

Sage and Sand
| ❑ 266 | Sadie May/Margaret Ann | 1960 | 5.00 | 10.00 | 20.00 |

Young Generation, The
(With Janis Siegel, pre-Manhattan Transfer)
Red Bird
| ❑ 10-065 | Hideaway/Hymn of Love | 1966 | 3.75 | 7.50 | 15.00 |

Young Lads, The
Felice
| ❑ 712 | Graduation Kiss/Night After Night | 1963 | 25.00 | 50.00 | 100.00 |

Neil
| ❑ 100 | Moonlight/I'm in Love | 1956 | 17.50 | 35.00 | 70.00 |

Young Lions, The
Dot
| ❑ 16172 | Little Girl/It Would Be | 1960 | 12.50 | 25.00 | 50.00 |

Young Rascals, The – See "Rascals, The"

Young World Singers, The
Decca
| ❑ 31660 | Ringo for President/Like That | 1964 | 3.00 | 6.00 | 12.00 |

Young, Bobby
Guyden
| ❑ 2087 | To Each His Own/The Only Girl for Me | 1963 | 62.50 | 125.00 | 250.00 |

Young, Colin
(Formerly of the Foundations)
Uni
| ❑ 55286 | You're No Good/Any Time at All | 1971 | | 3.00 | 6.00 |

Young, Georgie
Cameo
| ❑ 150 | Nine More Miles/The Sneak | 1958 | 6.25 | 12.50 | 25.00 |
| ❑ 168 | Georgie Porgie/Where Is Your Heart | 1959 | 5.00 | 10.00 | 20.00 |

Chancellor
| ❑ 1066 | Autumn Lovers/Indian Summer | 1960 | 3.75 | 7.50 | 15.00 |
| ❑ 1069 | Birdland Hully Gully/Marie | 1961 | 3.75 | 7.50 | 15.00 |

Columbia
| ❑ 42773 | Supercar/Chicken Scratch | 1963 | 7.50 | 15.00 | 30.00 |

Fortune
| ❑ 524 | Shakin' Shelley/Buggin' Baby | 1957 | 6.25 | 12.50 | 25.00 |

Mercury
| ❑ 71259 | Can't Stop Me/Come Back to Me | 1958 | 20.00 | 40.00 | 80.00 |

Parkway
| ❑ 809 | Gold Rush/That's Tough | 1960 | 5.00 | 10.00 | 20.00 |

Swan
| ❑ 4059 | Yogi/By George | 1960 | 3.75 | 7.50 | 15.00 |

Young, Kathy, and the Innocents
(Some of these are credited to Kathy Young solo. Also see "Innocents, The")
Indigo
❑ 108		A Thousand Stars/Eddie My Darling	1960	6.25	12.50	25.00
❑ 115		Happy Birthday Blues/Someone to Love	1961	5.00	10.00	20.00
❑ 115	PS	Happy Birthday Blues/Someone to Love	1961	12.50	25.00	50.00
❑ 121		Our Parents Talked It Over/ Just As Though You Were Here	1961	5.00	10.00	20.00
❑ 125		Magic Is the Night/Du Du'nt Du	1961	5.00	10.00	20.00
❑ 125	PS	Magic Is the Night/Du Du'nt Du	1961	12.50	25.00	50.00
❑ 137		Baby, Oh Baby/The Great Pretender	1961	5.00	10.00	20.00

Number		Title (A Side/B Side)	Year	VG	VG+	NM
❏ 141		Time/Dee Dee Di Oh	1962	5.00	10.00	20.00
❏ 146		Lonely Blue Nights/I'll Hang My Letters Out to Dry	1962	5.00	10.00	20.00
❏ 147		Send Her Away/Dream Awhile	1962	5.00	10.00	20.00

Monogram

❏ 506		Dreamboy/I'll Love That Man	1962	5.00	10.00	20.00

Port

❏ 3025		A Thousand Stars/Eddie My Darling	196?		2.50	5.00

Starfire

❏ 112		Sparkle and Shine/Please Love Me Forever	1979		2.50	5.00

Young, Leon

Atco

❏ 6274		Sea Winds/Spinning Jenny	1963	2.00	4.00	8.00
❏ 6301		John, Paul, George and Ringo/Westward Ho	1964	3.00	6.00	12.00

Young, Neil

(Also see "Buffalo Springfield"; Squires, The"; "Stills-Young Band, The")

Columbia

❏ 05566		Are There Any More Real Cowboys/I'm a Memory	1985			3.00
		A-side: Willie Nelson and Neil Young. B-side: Willie Nelson				

Geffen

❏ 28196		Mideast Vacation/Long Walk Home	1987			3.00
❏ 28623		Weight of the World/Pressure	1986			3.00
❏ 28623	PS	Weight of the World/Pressure	1986			3.00
❏ 28753		Old Ways/Once an Angel	1986			3.00
❏ 28883		Get Back to the Country/Misfits	1985			3.00
❏ 29433		Cry, Cry, Cry/Payola Blues	1983		2.00	4.00
❏ 29574		Wonderin'/Payola Blues	1983		2.00	4.00
❏ 29574	PS	Wonderin'/Payola Blues	1983		2.00	4.00
❏ 29707		Mr. Soul/Mr. Soul	1983		2.00	4.00
❏ 29887		Little Thing Called Love/We Are In Control	1982		2.00	4.00
❏ 29887	PS	Little Thing Called Love/We Are In Control	1982		2.00	4.00

Reprise

❏ 0746		Only Love Can Break Your Heart/Cinnamon Girl	1971			3.00
		"Back to Back Hits" release				
❏ 0785		The Loner/Sugar Mountain	1968	12.50	25.00	50.00
❏ 0819		Everyone Knows This Is Nowhere/	1969	12.50	25.00	50.00
		The Emperor of Wyoming				
❏ 0819	DJ	Everyone Knows This Is Nowhere/	1969	75.00	150.00	300.00
		The Emperor of Wyoming				
		Alternate acoustic version of A-side				
❏ 0819	DJ	Everyone Knows This Is Nowhere/	1969	5.00	10.00	20.00
		The Emperor of Wyoming				
		Standard version of A-side, with "RE-1" in trail-off wax				
❏ 0836		Down By the River/(When You're On the) Losing End	1969	12.50	25.00	50.00
❏ 0861		Oh, Lonesome Me/Sugar Mountain	1969	12.50	25.00	50.00
❏ 0898		I've Been Waiting for You/Oh, Lonesome Me	1970	12.50	25.00	50.00
❏ 0911		Cinnamon Girl/Sugar Mountain	1970		2.50	5.00
❏ 0958		Only Love Can Break Your Heart/Birds	1970		2.50	5.00
❏ 0996		When You Dance I Can Really Love/Sugar Mountain	1971		2.50	5.00
❏ 1023		Brave Belt/Rock and Roll Band	1971		2.50	5.00
		With Graham Nash				
❏ 1065		Heart of Gold/Sugar Mountain	1971		2.00	4.00
		Without reference to "Harvest" LP on label				
❏ 1065		Heart of Gold/Sugar Mountain	1971		2.50	5.00
		With reference to "Harvest" LP on label				
❏ 1084		Old Man/The Needle and the Damage Done	1972		2.00	4.00
❏ 1099		War Song/The Needle and the Damage Done	1972		2.00	4.00
		With Graham Nash				
❏ 1152		Heart of Gold/Old Man	1972			3.00
		"Back to Back Hits" release				
❏ 1184		Time Fades Away/The Last Train to Tulsa (Live)	1973	2.50	5.00	10.00
❏ 1209		Walk On/For the Turnstiles	1974	2.00	4.00	
❏ 1209	DJ	Walk On (same on both sides)	1974	3.75	7.50	15.00
		Small hole				
❏ 1209	DJ	Walk On (same on both sides)	1974	2.50	5.00	10.00
		Large hole				
❏ 1344		Lookin' for a Love/Sugar Mountain	1976		2.00	4.00
❏ 1350		Drive Back/Stupid Girl	1976		2.00	4.00
❏ 1390		Hey Baby/Homegrown	1977		2.00	4.00
❏ 1391		Like a Hurricane/Hold Back the Tears	1978		2.00	4.00
❏ 1393		Sugar Mountain/The Needle and the Damage Done	1978		2.00	4.00
❏ 1395		Comes a Time/Motorcycle Mama	1978		2.00	4.00
❏ 1395	PS	Comes a Time/Motorcycle Mama	1978		2.00	4.00
❏ 1396		Four Strong Winds/Human Highway	1979		2.00	4.00
❏ 18685		Harvest Moon/Old King	1992		2.00	4.00
❏ 22776		Rockin' in the Free World/	1989		2.00	4.00
		Rockin' in the Free World (Live)				
❏ 22776	DJ	Rockin' in the Free World (same on both sides)	1989	2.50	5.00	10.00
❏ 22776	PS	Rockin' in the Free World/	1989		2.00	4.00
		Rockin' in the Free World (Live)				
❏ 27848		This Note's For You (LP Version)/	1988		2.00	4.00
		This Note's For You (Edited Live Version)				
❏ 27848	PS	This Note's For You (LP Version)/	1988		2.00	4.00
		This Note's For You (Edited Live Version)				

Number		Title (A Side/B Side)	Year	VG	VG+	NM
☐ 27908		Ten Men Workin'/I'm Goin'	1988			3.00
☐ 27908	PS	Ten Men Workin'/I'm Goin'	1988	2.00	4.00	8.00
☐ 49031		Rust Never Sleeps (Hey Hey, My My [Into the Black])/	1979		2.00	4.00
		Rust Never Sleeps (My My, Hey Hey [Out of the Blue])				
☐ 49031	PS	Rust Never Sleeps (Hey Hey, My My [Into the Black])/	1979	2.50	5.00	10.00
		Rust Never Sleeps (My My, Hey Hey [Out of the Blue])				
☐ 49189		The Loner/Cinnamon Girl	1980		2.00	4.00
☐ 49555		Hawks and Doves/Union Man	1980			3.00
☐ 49555	PS	Hawks and Doves/Union Man	1980			3.00
☐ 49641		Stayin' Power/Captain America	1980			3.00
☐ 49870		Southern Pacific/Motor City	1981			3.00
☐ 50014		Opera Star/Surfer Joe and Moe the Sleaze	1982			3.00

Young, Paul
Collectables

☐ 4685		Oh Girl/Don't Dream It's Over	1996			3.00

First release of these tracks on U.S. 45

Columbia

☐ 04071		Wherever I Lay My Hat (That's My Home)/	1983		2.00	4.00
		The Tender Trap				
☐ 04071	PS	Wherever I Lay My Hat (That's My Home)/	1983		2.00	4.00
		The Tender Trap				
☐ 04313		Come Back and Stay/Yours	1984			3.00
☐ 04313	PS	Come Back and Stay/Yours	1984		2.00	4.00
☐ 04453		Love of the Common People/Behind Your Smile	1984			3.00
☐ 04453	PS	Love of the Common People/Behind Your Smile	1984		2.00	4.00
☐ 04867		Everytime You Go Away/This Means Anything	1985			3.00
☐ 04867	PS	Everytime You Go Away/This Means Anything	1985		2.50	5.00
☐ 05577		I'm Gonna Tear Your Playhouse Down/Broken Man	1985			3.00
☐ 05577	PS	I'm Gonna Tear Your Playhouse Down/Broken Man	1985		2.00	4.00
☐ 05712		Everything Must Change/Give Me My Freedom	1985			3.00
☐ 05712	PS	Everything Must Change/Give Me My Freedom	1985		2.00	4.00
☐ 06423		Some People/Steps to Go	1986			3.00
☐ 06423	PS	Some People/Steps to Go	1986			3.00
☐ 06630		Why Does a Man Have to Be Strong/Matter of Fact	1987			3.00
☐ 06630	PS	Why Does a Man Have to Be Strong/Matter of Fact	1987			3.00

MCA

☐ 54331		What Becomes of the Brokenhearted/Ghost Train	1992		2.00	4.00

Young-Holt Unlimited
Brunswick

☐ 55305	Wack Wack/This Little Light of Mine	1966	2.00	4.00	8.00
As "The Young-Holt Trio"					
☐ 55317	Ain't There Something Money Can't Buy/Mellow Yellow	1967	2.00	4.00	8.00
As "The Young-Holt Trio"					
☐ 55338	The Beat Goes On/Doin' the Thing	1967	2.00	4.00	8.00
As "The Young-Holt Trio"					
☐ 55356	Dig Her Walk/You Gimmie Thum	1967	2.00	4.00	8.00
☐ 55374	Soul Sister/Give It Up	1968	2.00	4.00	8.00
☐ 55391	Soulful Strut/Country Slicker Joe	1968	2.00	4.00	8.00
☐ 55400	Who's Making Love/Just Ain't No Love	1969		3.00	6.00
☐ 55410	Just a Melody/Young and Holtful	1969		3.00	6.00
☐ 55417	Straight Ahead/California Montage	1969		3.00	6.00
☐ 55420	Soulful Samba/Horoscope	1969		3.00	6.00

Cotillion

☐ 44092	Mellow Dreaming/Got to Get My Baby Back Home	1970		2.50	5.00
☐ 44111	Luv Bugg/Wah Wah Man	1971		2.50	5.00
☐ 44120	Hot Pants/I'll Be There	1971		2.50	5.00

Paula

☐ 380	Superfly/Give Me Your Love	1973		2.50	5.00
☐ 382	Could It Be I'm Falling in Love/HeyPancho	1973		2.50	5.00

Youngbloods, The
Mercury

☐ 72583	Sometimes/Rider	1966	5.00	10.00	20.00
As "Jesse Colin and the Youngbloods"					
☐ 73068	Sometimes/Rider	1969	2.50	5.00	10.00

RCA Victor

☐ 47-9015	Grizzly Bear/Tears Are Falling	1966	2.50	5.00	10.00
☐ 47-9142	Merry-Go-Round/Foolin' Around (The Waltz)	1967	2.50	5.00	10.00
☐ 47-9222	The Wine Song/Euphoria	1967	2.50	5.00	10.00
☐ 47-9264	Get Together/All My Dreams Blue	1967	3.75	7.50	15.00
☐ 47-9360	Fool Me/I Can Tell	1967	2.50	5.00	10.00
☐ 47-9422	Dreamer's Dream/Quicksand	1967	2.50	5.00	10.00
☐ 47-9752	Get Together/Beautiful	1969	2.00	4.00	8.00
☐ 74-0129	On Sir Francis Drake/Darkness, Darkness	1969	2.00	4.00	8.00
☐ 74-0270	Sunlight/Trillium	1969	2.00	4.00	8.00
☐ 74-0342	On Sir Francis Drake/Darkness, Darkness	1970		3.50	7.00
☐ 74-0380	On Sir Francis Drake/Darkness, Darkness	1970		3.00	6.00
☐ 74-0465	Reason to Believe/Sunlight	1971		3.00	6.00

Warner Bros.

☐ 7445	Hippie from Leomi/Misty Roses	1970		2.50	5.00
☐ 7499	It's a Lovely Day/Ice Bag	1971		2.50	5.00
☐ 7563	Will the Circle Be Unbroken/Light Shine	1972		2.50	5.00

Number	Title (A Side/B Side)	Year	VG	VG+	NM
☐ 7639	Dreamboat/Kind Hearted Woman	1972		2.50	5.00
☐ 7660	Running Bear/Kind Hearted Woman	1972		2.50	5.00

Youngtones, The
Brunswick

☐ 55089	Come On Baby/Oh Tell Me	1958	15.00	30.00	60.00

Yum Yums, The
ABC-Paramount

☐ 10697	Looky, Looky (What I Got)/Gonna Be a Big Thing	1965	5.00	10.00	20.00

Yuro, Timi
Liberty

☐ 55343	Hurt/I Apologize	1961	3.75	7.50	15.00
☐ 55375	Smile/She Really Loves You	1961	3.00	6.00	12.00
☐ 55400	I Believe/A Mother's Love	1961	2.50	5.00	10.00
	With Johnnie Ray				
☐ 55410	Let Me Call You Sweetheart/Satan Never Sleeps	1962	2.50	5.00	10.00
☐ 55432	I Know (I Love You)/Count Everything	1962	2.50	5.00	10.00
☐ 55469	What's a Matter Baby (Is It Hurting You)/ Thirteenth Hour	1962	3.00	6.00	12.00
☐ 55519	The Love of a Boy/I Ain't Gonna Cry No More	1962	2.50	5.00	10.00
☐ 55551	Insult to Injury/Talkin' About Hurt	1963			*Unreleased*
☐ 55552	Insult to Injury/Just About the Time	1963	2.50	5.00	10.00
☐ 55587	Make the World Go Away/Look Down	1963	2.50	5.00	10.00
☐ 55634	Gotta Travel On/Down in the Valley	1963	2.50	5.00	10.00
☐ 55665	Call Me/Permanently Lonely	1964	2.00	4.00	8.00
☐ 55701	A Legend in My Time/Should I Ever Love Again	1964	2.00	4.00	8.00
☐ 55747	I'm Movin' On (Part 1)/I'm Movin' On (Part 2)	1964	2.00	4.00	8.00
☐ 56049	Wrong/Something Bad on My Mind	1968		3.00	6.00
☐ 56061	I Must Have Been Out of My Head/Interlude	1968		3.00	6.00

Mercury

☐ 72316	If/The Masquerade Is Over	1964	2.00	4.00	8.00
☐ 72355	I Got It Bad and That Ain't Good/Johnny	1964	2.00	4.00	8.00
☐ 72391	Could This Be Magic/You Can Have Him	1965	2.00	4.00	8.00
☐ 72431	Can't Stop Running Away/Get Out of My Life	1965	2.00	4.00	8.00
☐ 72478	Big Mistake/Teardrops Till Dawn	1965	2.00	4.00	8.00
☐ 72515	Once a Day/Pretend	1966	2.00	4.00	8.00
☐ 72601	Don't Keep Me Lonely Too Long/ You Took My Happy Away	1966	2.00	4.00	8.00
☐ 72628	Turn the World Around the Other Way/Just a Ribbon	1966	2.00	4.00	8.00
☐ 72674	Why Not Now/Cuttin' In	1967	2.00	4.00	8.00

Playboy

☐ 6050	Southern Lady/Lovin' You Is All I Ever Had	1975		2.50	5.00

United Artists

☐ 0042	Hurt/What's a Matter Baby (Is It Hurting You)	1973		2.00	4.00
	"Silver Spotlight Series" reissue				

Z

Zacharias and the Tree People
Viking

☐ 1004	We're All Paul Bearers (Part 1)/ We're All Paul Bearers (Part 2)	1969	5.00	10.00	20.00

Zacherle, John
Cameo

☐ 130	Igor/Dinner with Drac	1958	10.00	20.00	40.00
☐ 130	Dinner with Drac (Part 1)/Dinner with Drac (Part 2)	1958	7.50	15.00	30.00
	Orange label				
☐ 130	Dinner with Drac (Part 1)/Dinner with Drac (Part 2)	1960	5.00	10.00	20.00
	Red and black label				
☐ 139	Lunch with Mother Goose/82 Tombstones	1958	7.50	15.00	30.00
☐ 145	I Was a Teenage Caveman/Dummy Doll	1958	7.50	15.00	30.00

Colpix

☐ 743	Monsters Have Problems Too/Hello Dolly	1964	6.25	12.50	25.00

Parkway

☐ 853	Dinner with Drac/Hurry Bury Baby	1962	6.25	12.50	25.00
☐ 885	Clementine/Surfboard 109	1963	6.25	12.50	25.00
	As "Zacherley"				
☐ 888	Scarey Tales from Mother Goose/Monster Monkey	1963	6.25	12.50	25.00
	As "Zacherley"				

Zack, Eddie, and Cousin Richie
Columbia

☐ 21387	Rocky Road Blues/Lover, Lover	1955	37.50	75.00	150.00
☐ 21441	I'm Gonna Rock and Roll/Foolish Me	1955	37.50	75.00	150.00

Zager and Evans
RCA Victor

☐ 47-9816	Help One Man Today/Year 32	1969		2.50	5.00
☐ 74-0174	In the Year 2525 (Exordium & Terminus)/Little Kids	1969		3.00	6.00

Number	Title (A Side/B Side)	Year	VG	VG+	NM
☐ 74-0246	Mr. Turnkey/Cary Lynn Jones	1969		2.50	5.00
☐ 74-0299	Listen to the People/She Never Sleeps Beside Me	1969		2.50	5.00
☐ 74-0359	Plastic Park/Crutches	1970		2.50	5.00

Truth

☐ (# unknown)	In the Year 2525 (Exordium & Terminus)/Little Kids	1967	5.00	10.00	20.00

Vanguard

☐ 35125	Hydra 15,000/I Am	1971		2.50	5.00

Zanies, The

Dore

☐ 509	The Blob/Do You Dig Me, Mr. Pygmy	1958	6.25	12.50	25.00
☐ 515	The Mad Scientist/She's a Winner	1958	6.25	12.50	25.00
☐ 597	It's Lovely/Saxophone Safari	1961	5.00	10.00	20.00
☐ 632	Rockin' Chopin/Frustration	1962	5.00	10.00	20.00
☐ 638	London Rock/Stalled	1962	5.00	10.00	20.00
☐ 647	Sleepwalker/Alexander's Ragtime Band	1962	5.00	10.00	20.00
☐ 655	Comin' Down the Track/Hello Jackie	1962	5.00	10.00	20.00
☐ 658	Russian Roulette/Caught in a Ringer	1963	5.00	10.00	20.00
☐ 683	Chicken Surfer/London Rick	1963	5.00	10.00	20.00
☐ 705	Slinky/Camel Walk	1964	3.75	7.50	15.00
☐ 734	Bless 'Em All/Last Dance at the Prom	1965	3.75	7.50	15.00
☐ 853	Will the Real Dr. Frankenstein Please Stand Up/Frankenstein's Laboratory	1971	3.75	7.50	15.00
☐ 875	Do the 1-2-3/Mr. President-to-Be	1972	2.50	5.00	10.00
☐ 889	Let Out a Scream (Part 1)/Let Out a Scream (Part 2)	1973	2.00	4.00	8.00
☐ 893	Flakey/(Instrumental)	1974		3.00	6.00
☐ 900	Los Angeles, Los Angeles/Let Out a Scream	1974		3.00	6.00
☐ 912	Frustration/Roller Coaster	1975		2.50	5.00
☐ 920	Old Man River/Los Angeles, Los Angeles	1976		2.50	5.00
☐ 957	Janie for President/Los Angeles, Los Angeles	1980		2.00	4.00
☐ 959	The Song of the Masochist/Special	1980		2.00	4.00
☐ 959	The Song of the Masochist/What Is a One	1980		2.00	4.00
☐ 959	What Is a One/Louie's Market	1980		2.00	4.00
☐ 962	Curvacious Cora and Carlos Condo/Percolator	1980		2.00	4.00
☐ 963	I Love Life, Men, Candy and Paree/I Love Life, Men, Candy and Paree (X-Rated Adult Version)	1981		2.00	4.00
☐ 968	From Peanuts to Jelly Beans/For He's a Jolly Good Fellow	1981		2.00	4.00
☐ 974	I Hate Baseball/Dancing with Ronnie Cey	1982		2.50	5.00
	With "A. Player"				
☐ 975	Just Another Day in L.A./I'll Be Waiting	1983		2.00	4.00
☐ 978	Is There An Echo in the Joint/Doin' the Head	1983		2.00	4.00
☐ 979	Gesundheit/Darlin' Come Back	1983		2.00	4.00
☐ 980	The Raiders, the Steelers, the Cowboys and Bills (same on both sides)	1984		2.00	4.00
☐ 1015	Politics, Religion, and Sin (Part 1)/Politics, Religion, and Sin (Part 2)	198?		2.00	4.00

Zappa, Frank

(Includes The Mothers of Invention; label credit is mentioned if not "Frank Zappa")

Barking Pumpkin

☐ 02972	Valley Girl/You Are What You Is	1982			3.00
	A-side: Frank and Moon Zappa				
☐ 02972	PS Valley Girl/You Are What You Is	1982		3.50	7.00
	A-side: Frank and Moon Zappa				

Bizarre

☐ 0840	My Guitar/Dog Breath	1969	12.50	25.00	50.00
	The Mothers of Invention				
☐ 0889	Peaches En Regalia/Little Umbrellas	1970	12.50	25.00	50.00
☐ 0892	WPLJ/My Guitar	1970	12.50	25.00	50.00
	The Mothers of Invention				
☐ 0967	Tell Me You Love Me/Would You Go All the Way for the U.S.A.?	1970	12.50	25.00	50.00
☐ 1027	Tears Began to Fall/Junior Mintz Boogie	1971	12.50	25.00	50.00
	Junior Mintz				
☐ 1052	Tears Began to Fall/Junior Mintz Boogie	1971	12.50	25.00	50.00
	Frank Zappa and The Mothers of Invention				
☐ 1127	Cletus Awreetus-Awrightus/Eat That Question	1972	8.75	17.50	35.00
	The Mothers of Invention				

DiscReet

☐ 1180	I'm the Slime/Montana	1973	6.25	12.50	25.00
	The Mothers				
☐ 1312	Don't Eat the Yellow Snow/Cosmic Debris	1974	3.75	7.50	15.00

United Artists

☐ 50857	Magic Fingers/Daddy, Daddy, Daddy	1971	12.50	25.00	50.00

Verve

☐ 10418	How Could I Be Such a Fool/Help I'm a Rock (3rd Movement: It Can't Happen Here)	1966	50.00	100.00	200.00
	The Mothers of Invention				
☐ 10418	DJ How Could I Be Such a Fool/Help I'm a Rock (3rd Movement: It Can't Happen Here)	1966	25.00	50.00	100.00
	The Mothers of Invention				
☐ 10458	Who Are the Brain Police/Trouble Comin' Every Day	1966	50.00	100.00	200.00
	The Mothers of Invention; the existence of this stock copy has been questioned				

Number	Title (A Side/B Side)	Year	VG	VG+	NM
❑ 10458	DJ Who Are the Brain Police/Trouble Comin' Every Day *The Mothers of Invention*	1966	25.00	50.00	100.00
❑ 10513	Why Don't You Do Me Right/Big Leg Emma *The Mothers of Invention*	1967	50.00	100.00	200.00
❑ 10513	DJ Why Don't You Do Me Right/Big Leg Emma *The Mothers of Invention*	1967	25.00	50.00	100.00
❑ 10570	Mother People/Lonely Little Girl *The Mothers of Invention*	1967	50.00	100.00	200.00
❑ 10570	DJ Mother People/Lonely Little Girl *The Mothers of Invention*	1967	25.00	50.00	100.00
❑ 10632	Jelly Roll Gum Drop/Any Way the Wind Blows *Ruben & The Jets*	1968	37.50	75.00	150.00
❑ 10632	Jelly Roll Gum Drop/Deseri *Ruben & The Jets*	1968	37.50	75.00	150.00
❑ 10632	DJ Jelly Roll Gum Drop/Any Way the Wind Blows *Ruben & The Jets*	1968	18.75	37.50	75.00
❑ 10632	DJ Jelly Roll Gum Drop/Deseri *Ruben & The Jets*	1968	18.75	37.50	75.00

Warner Bros.

Number	Title (A Side/B Side)	Year	VG	VG+	NM
❑ 8296	Find Her Finer/Zoot Allures	1976	6.25	12.50	25.00
❑ 8342	Disco Boy/Miss Pinky	1977	6.25	12.50	25.00

Zappa

Number	Title (A Side/B Side)	Year	VG	VG+	NM
❑ Z-10	Dancin' Fool/Baby Snakes	1979	2.50	5.00	10.00
❑ ZR 1001	I Don't Wanna Get Drafted/Ancient Armaments (Live)	1980	2.00	4.00	

Zebulons, The
Cub

Number	Title (A Side/B Side)	Year	VG	VG+	NM
❑ 9069	Falling Water/Wo-Ho-La-Tee-Da	1960	15.00	30.00	60.00

Zee, Tommy
Amy

Number	Title (A Side/B Side)	Year	VG	VG+	NM
❑ 815	Rebecca, Remember/Worlds Apart	1961	10.00	20.00	40.00

Zekley, Gary
Ava

Number	Title (A Side/B Side)	Year	VG	VG+	NM
❑ 151	Vagabond/When I Go to Sleep *With Dean Torrence on backing vocals*	1963	10.00	20.00	40.00

Zella, Danny
Dial

Number	Title (A Side/B Side)	Year	VG	VG+	NM
❑ 100	Sapphire/You Made Me Blue	1959	50.00	100.00	200.00

Fox

Number	Title (A Side/B Side)	Year	VG	VG+	NM
❑ 10057	Wicked Ruby//(B-side unknown)	1959	7.50	15.00	30.00

Zeroes, The
Ty-Tex

Number	Title (A Side/B Side)	Year	VG	VG+	NM
❑ 105	Flossie Mae/Twisting with Crazee Babee	1963	50.00	100.00	200.00

Zevon, Warren
Asylum

Number	Title (A Side/B Side)	Year	VG	VG+	NM
❑ 45356	Mohammad's Radio/Hasten Down the Wind	1976		2.50	5.00
❑ 45472	Werewolves of London/ Roland the Headless Thompson Gunner	1978		2.50	5.00
❑ 45498	Lawyers, Guns and Money/Vera Cruz	1978		2.50	5.00
❑ 45526	Johnny Strikes Up the Band/ Night Time in the Switching Yard	1978		2.50	5.00
❑ 46610	A Certain Girl/Empty-Handed Heart	1980		2.00	4.00
❑ 46641	Gorilla, You're a Desperado/Jungle Work	1980		2.00	4.00
❑ 47118	Lawyers, Guns and Money/Down on My Luck	1981		2.00	4.00
❑ 69946	Let Nothing Come Between You/The Hula Hula Boys	1982		2.00	4.00
❑ 69966	Looking for the Next Best Thing/The Hula Hula Boys	1982		2.00	4.00

Elektra

Number	Title (A Side/B Side)	Year	VG	VG+	NM
❑ 69509	Jesus Mentioned/Werewolves of London	1986			3.00

Virgin

Number	Title (A Side/B Side)	Year	VG	VG+	NM
❑ 99370	Factory/Reconsider Me	1988			3.00
❑ 99440	Leave My Monkey Alone/ Leave My Monkey Alone (Latin Rascals Dub)	1987			3.00

Zimmerman, George, and the Thrills
Jab

Number	Title (A Side/B Side)	Year	VG	VG+	NM
❑ 103	Whose Baby Are You/ I Ain't Got the Money to Pay for This Drink	1956	100.00	200.00	400.00

Zine, Ben
Parkway

Number	Title (A Side/B Side)	Year	VG	VG+	NM
❑ 994	Village of Tears/What the Heck's the Hanky Panky	1966	20.00	40.00	80.00

Zip Codes, The
Liberty

Number	Title (A Side/B Side)	Year	VG	VG+	NM
❑ 55703	Run, Little Mustang/Fancy Filly from Detroit City	1964	7.50	15.00	30.00

Number		Title (A Side/B Side)	Year	VG	VG+	NM

Zombies, The

Columbia
❏ 44363		Care of Cell 44/Maybe After He's Gone	1967			Unreleased?

Date
❏ 1604		Time of the Season/I'll Call You Mine	1968	5.00	10.00	20.00
❏ 1612		Butcher's Tale (Western Front 1914)/	1968	2.50	5.00	10.00
		This Will Be Our Year				
❏ 1628		Time of the Season/Friends of Mine	1968	3.00	6.00	12.00
❏ 1644		Imagine the Swan/Conversation of Floral Street	1969	2.50	5.00	10.00
❏ 1648		If It Don't Work Out/Don't Cry for Me	1969	2.50	5.00	10.00

Epic
❏ 11145		Time of the Season/Imagine the Swan	1974		2.50	5.00

Parrot
❏ 3004		Indication/How We Were Before	1966	2.50	5.00	10.00
❏ 9695		She's Not There/You Make Me Feel So Good	1964	3.00	6.00	12.00
❏ 9723		Tell Her No/Leave Me Be	1965	3.00	6.00	12.00
❏ 9723	PS	Tell Her No/Leave Me Be	1965	6.25	12.50	25.00
❏ 9747		She's Coming Home/I Must Move	1965	2.50	5.00	10.00
❏ 9747	PS	She's Coming Home/I Must Move	1965	6.25	12.50	25.00
❏ 9769		I Want You Back Again/Once Upon a Time	1965	2.50	5.00	10.00
❏ 9786		I Love You/Whenever You're Ready	1965	2.50	5.00	10.00
❏ 9797		Just Out of Reach/Remember You	1965	2.50	5.00	10.00
❏ 9821		Don't Go Away/Is This the Dream	1966	2.50	5.00	10.00

ZZ Top

London
❏ 131		Salt Lick/Miller's Farm	1970		3.00	6.00
❏ 138		(Somebody Else Been) Shakin' Your Tree/	1970		3.00	6.00
		Neighbor, Neighbor				
❏ 179		Francene/Francene (Spanish)	1972		3.00	6.00
❏ 203		La Grange/Just Got Paid	1973		3.00	6.00
❏ 220		Tush/Blue Jean Blues	1975		2.50	5.00
❏ 220	PS	Tush/Blue Jean Blues	1975	2.00	4.00	8.00
❏ 241		It's Only Love/Asleep in the Desert	1976		2.00	4.00
❏ 241	PS	It's Only Love/Asleep in the Desert	1976		3.00	6.00
❏ 251		Arrested for Driving While Blind/It's Only Love	1977		2.00	4.00
❏ 252		Enjoy and Get It On/El Diablo	1977		2.00	4.00

RCA
❏ 62812		Breakaway/Pincushion	1994		2.00	4.00
❏ 62928		Fuzzbox Voodoo/Girl in a T-Shirt	1994		2.00	4.00

Scat
❏ 500		Salt Lick/Miller's Farm	1969	50.00	100.00	200.00

Warner Bros.
❏ 18979		Viva Las Vegas/2000 Blues	1992			3.00
❏ 19812		Doubleback/Planet of Women	1990			3.00
❏ 19812	PS	Doubleback/Planet of Women	1990		3.00	6.00
❏ 28650		Velcro Fly/Woke Up with Wood	1986			3.00
❏ 28733		Rough Boy/Delicious	1986			3.00
❏ 28733	PS	Rough Boy/Delicious	1986			3.00
❏ 28810		Stages/Can't Stop Rockin'	1986			3.00
❏ 28810	PS	Stages/Can't Stop Rockin'	1986			3.00
❏ 28884		Sleeping Bag/Party on the Patio	1985			3.00
❏ 28884	PS	Sleeping Bag/Party on the Patio	1985			3.00
❏ 29272		Legs/Bad Girl	1984		2.00	4.00
❏ 29272	PS	Legs/Bad Girl	1984		2.00	4.00
❏ 29576		Sharp Dressed Man/I Got the Six	1983		2.00	4.00
❏ 29693		Gimme All Your Lovin/If I Could Only Flag Her Down	1983		2.00	4.00
❏ 29693	PS	Gimme All Your Lovin/If I Could Only Flag Her Down	1983		2.50	5.00
❏ 49163		I Thank You/Fool for Your Stockings	1980		2.00	4.00
❏ 49220		Cheap Sunglasses/Esther Be the One	1980		2.00	4.00
❏ 49782		Don't Tease Me/Leila	1981		2.00	4.00
❏ 49865		Tube Snake Boogie/Heaven, Hell or Houston	1981		2.00	4.00